This
Bible
Belongs To

____

____

____

____

TIME LINE OF THE OLD TESTAMENT

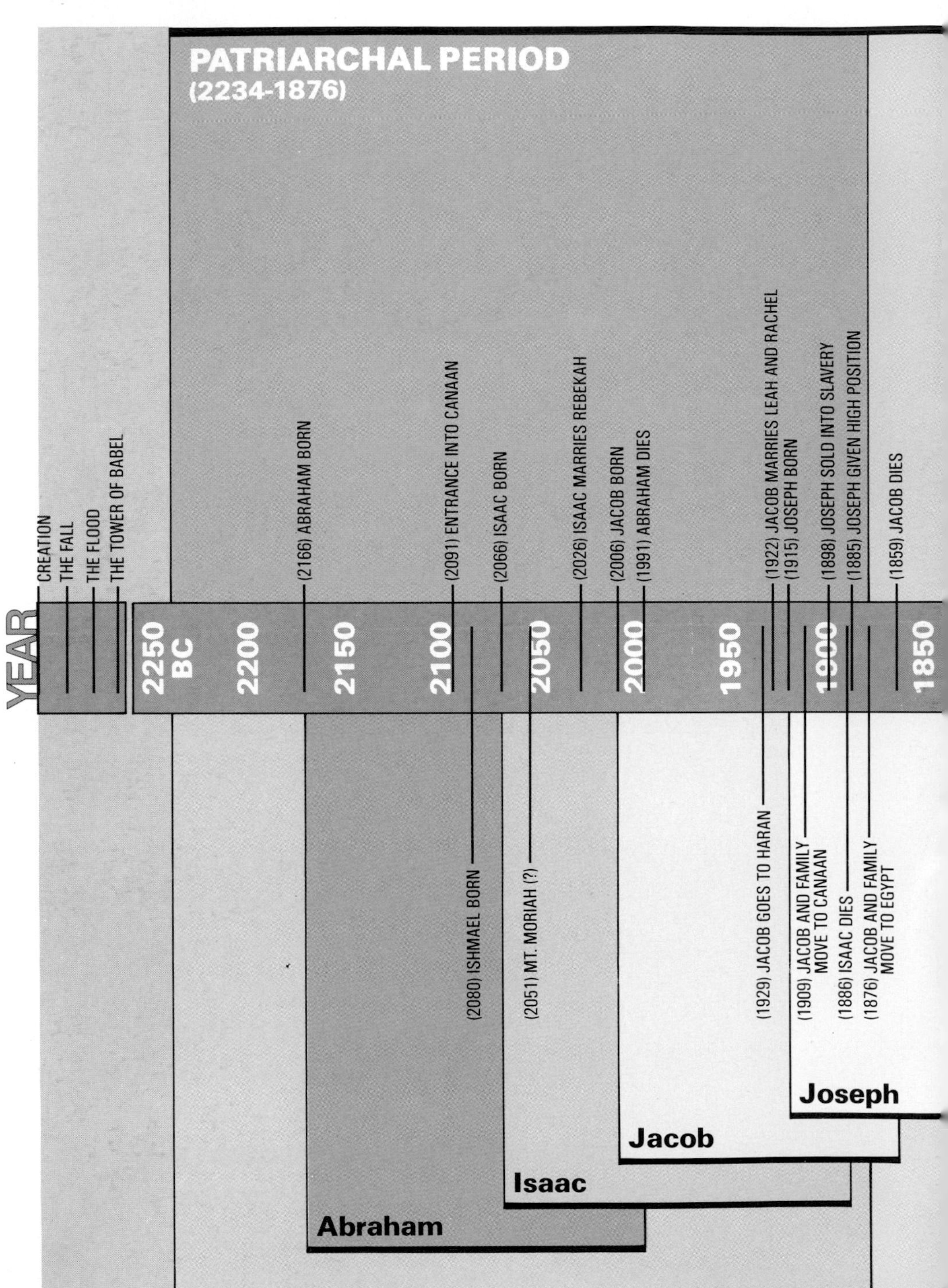

PATRIARCHAL PERIOD
(2234-1876)
YEAR
CREATION
THE FALL
THE FLOOD
THE TOWER OF BABEL
2250 BC
2200
2150
2100
2050
2000
1950
1900
1850
(2166) ABRAHAM BORN
(2091) ENTRANCE INTO CANAAN
(2066) ISAAC BORN
(2026) ISAAC MARRIES REBEKAH
(2006) JACOB BORN
(1991) ABRAHAM DIES
(1922) JACOB MARRIES LEAH AND RACHEL
(1915) JOSEPH BORN
(1898) JOSEPH SOLD INTO SLAVERY
(1885) JOSEPH GIVEN HIGH POSITION
(1859) JACOB DIES
(2080) ISHMAEL BORN
(2051) MT. MORIAH (?)
(1929) JACOB GOES TO HARAN
(1909) JACOB AND FAMILY MOVE TO CANAAN
(1886) ISAAC DIES
(1876) JACOB AND FAMILY MOVE TO EGYPT
Joseph
Jacob
Isaac
Abraham

EGYPTIAN PERIOD
(1875-1449)

(1805) JOSEPH DIES

1800 · 1750 · 1700 · 1650 · 1600 · 1550 · 1500

FROM EGYPT TO CANAAN
(1450-1297)

(1450) BIRTH OF MOSES

1450 · 1400

(1370) THE EXODUS

1350

(1311) JOSHUA APPOINTED LEADER

(1310-1297) CONQUEST OF CANAAN

1300

TIME LINE OF THE OLD TESTAMENT — CONTINUED

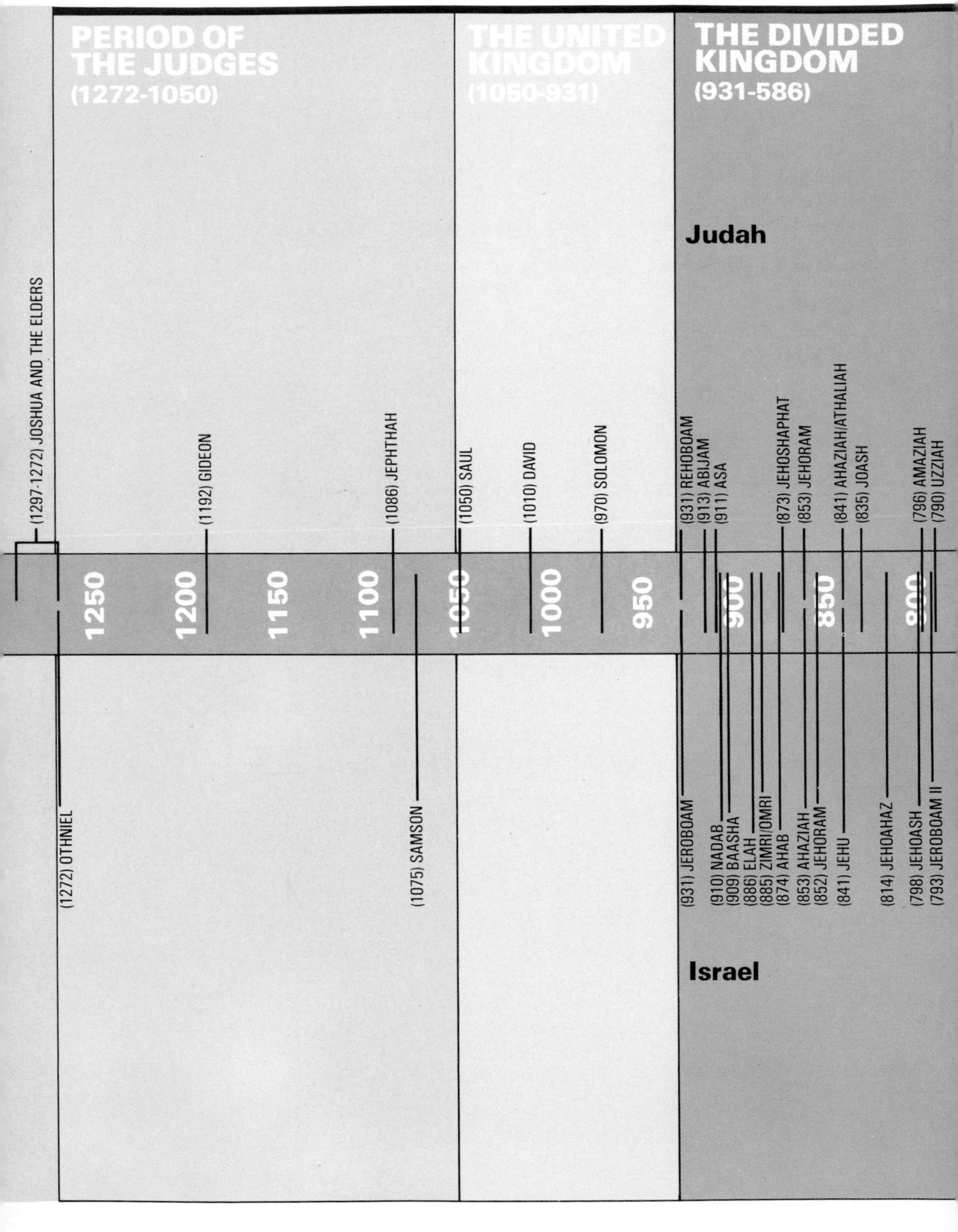

PERIOD OF THE JUDGES (1272-1050)

(1297-1272) JOSHUA AND THE ELDERS
(1272) OTHNIEL
(1192) GIDEON
(1086) JEPHTHAH
(1075) SAMSON

1250 · 1200 · 1150 · 1100

THE UNITED KINGDOM (1050-931)

(1050) SAUL
(1010) DAVID
(970) SOLOMON

1050 · 1000 · 950

THE DIVIDED KINGDOM (931-586)

Judah

(931) REHOBOAM
(913) ABIJAM
(911) ASA
(873) JEHOSHAPHAT
(853) JEHORAM
(841) AHAZIAH/ATHALIAH
(835) JOASH
(796) AMAZIAH
(790) UZZIAH

900 · 850 · 800

Israel

(931) JEROBOAM
(910) NADAB
(909) BAASHA
(886) ELAH
(885) ZIMRI/OMRI
(874) AHAB
(853) AHAZIAH
(852) JEHORAM
(841) JEHU
(814) JEHOAHAZ
(798) JEHOASH
(793) JEROBOAM II

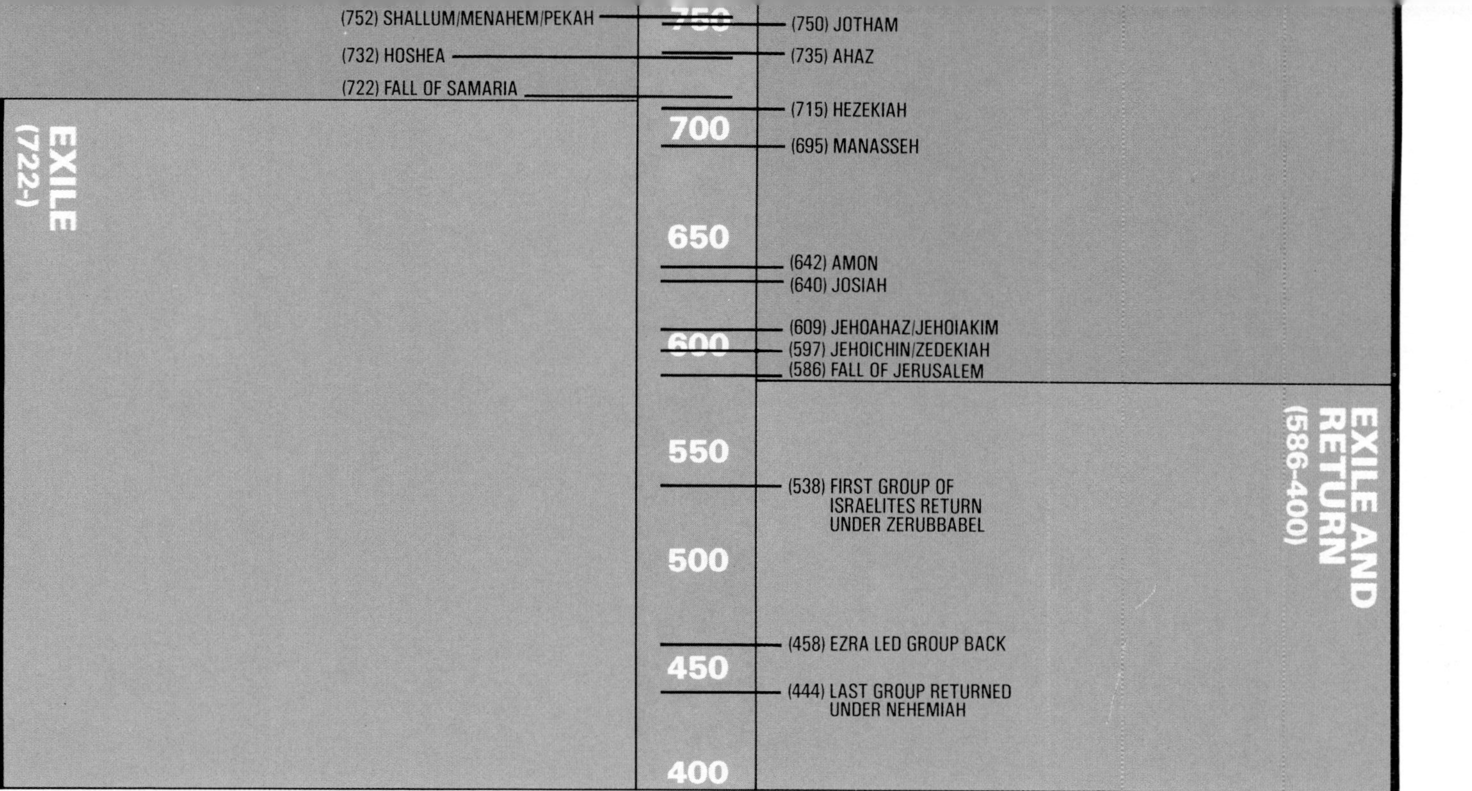

750
(752) SHALLUM/MENAHEM/PEKAH
(750) JOTHAM
(732) HOSHEA
(735) AHAZ
(722) FALL OF SAMARIA
(715) HEZEKIAH
700
(695) MANASSEH
EXILE
(722-)
650
(642) AMON
(640) JOSIAH
(609) JEHOAHAZ/JEHOIAKIM
600
(597) JEHOICHIN/ZEDEKIAH
(586) FALL OF JERUSALEM
EXILE AND RETURN
(586-400)
550
(538) FIRST GROUP OF ISRAELITES RETURN UNDER ZERUBBABEL
500
(458) EZRA LED GROUP BACK
450
(444) LAST GROUP RETURNED UNDER NEHEMIAH
400

KINGS AND PROPHETS OF ISRAEL AND JUDAH

THE UNITED KINGDOM

- (1050) SAUL
- (1010) DAVID
- (970) SOLOMON

THE DIVIDED KINGDOM

Judah

PROPHETS OF JUDAH

- *Obadiah*
- *Joel*

KINGS OF JUDAH

- (931) REHOBOAM
- (913) ABIJAM
- (911) ASA
- (873) JEHOSHAPHAT
- (853) JEHORAM
- (841) AHAZIAH/ATHALIAH
- (835) JOASH
- (796) AMAZIAH
- (790) UZZIAH
- (750) JOTHAM
- (735) AHAZ

YEAR

1050 BC · 1000 · 950 · 900 · 850 · 800 · 750

KINGS OF ISRAEL

- (931) JEROBOAM
- (910) NADAB
- (909) BAASHA
- (886) ELAH
- (885) ZIMRI/OMRI
- (874) AHAB
- (853) AHAZIAH
- (852) JEHORAM
- (841) JEHU
- (814) JEHOAHAZ
- (798) JEHOASH
- (793) JEROBOAM II
- (753) ZECHARIAH
- (752) SHALLUM/MENAHEM/PEKAH
- (732) HOSHEA

PROPHETS OF ISRAEL

- *Elijah*
- *Elisha*
- *Jonah*
- *Amos*
- *Hosea*

Israel

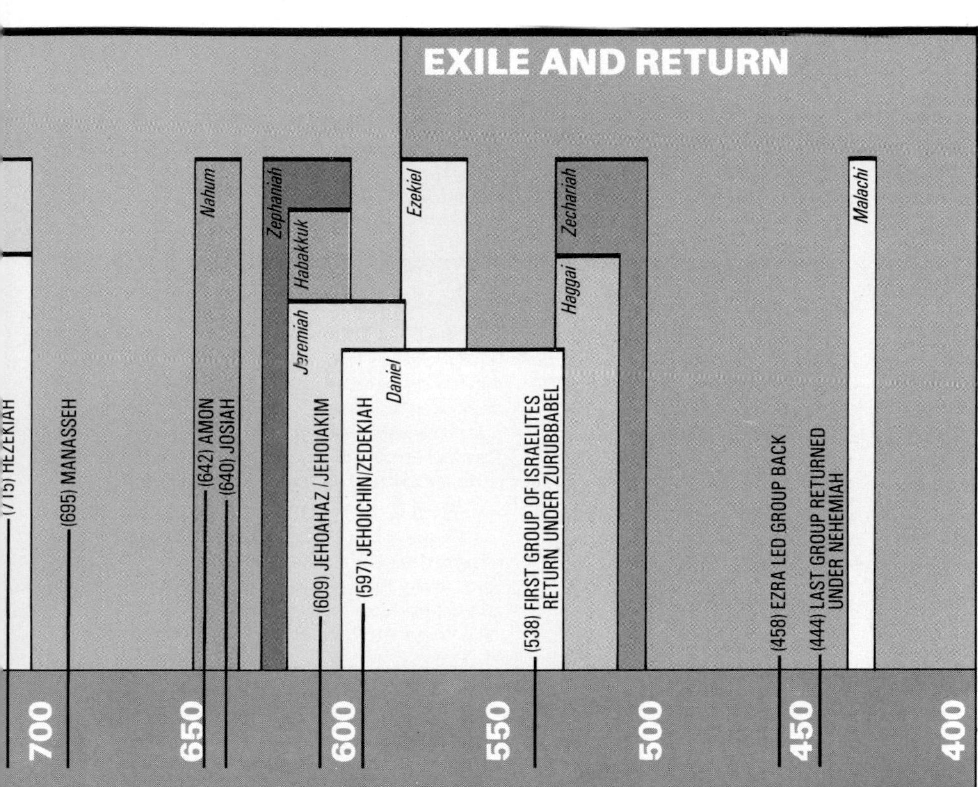

EXILE AND RETURN
Nahum
Zephaniah
Habakkuk
Jeremiah
Ezekiel
Daniel
Zechariah
Haggai
Malachi
(695) MANASSEH
(642) AMON
(640) JOSIAH
(609) JEHOAHAZ / JEHOIAKIM
(597) JEHOICHIN/ZEDEKIAH
(538) FIRST GROUP OF ISRAELITES RETURN UNDER ZURUBBABEL
(458) EZRA LED GROUP BACK
(444) LAST GROUP RETURNED UNDER NEHEMIAH
700
650
600
550
500
450
400

EXILE

CAPTIVITY AND RETURN

ASSYRIAN CAPTIVITY OF ISRAEL

1 734 B.C. **2 Kings 15:29**
Tiglath-pileser III, king of Assyria from 745-727 B.C., marched against King Pekah of Israel and King Rezin of Syria because they made war against his vassal, King Ahaz of Judah. He punished Israel by carrying some of their people into exile (2 Kings 16:7-9).

2 722 B.C. **2 Kings 17:1-6**
Israel was destroyed and taken after a three-year siege by Shalmaneser V, king of Assyria from 727-722 B.C. Assyrian inscriptions say that 27,290 people were taken captive and deported, some to Gozan in Mesopotamia and others to Media.

BABYLONIAN CAPTIVITY OF JUDAH

1 608 B.C. **Daniel 1:1-7**
After the battle of Carchemish, Nebuchadnezzar, as crown prince of Babylon, advanced to Jerusalem. He spared King Jehoiakim, who had rebelled against him, but carried off several of the princes of Judah, among them Daniel, Shadrach, Meshach, and Abednego.

2 597 B.C. **2 Kings 24:1-16**
Nebuchadnezzar was now king of Babylon (608-562 B.C.) and again conquered Jerusalem. Among the captives taken in this battle was the prophet Ezekiel.

3 586 B.C. **2 Kings 24:20-25:21; Jer. 39:1-10**
King Zedekiah took an oath of allegiance to the Babylonian monarch but soon became disloyal. So Nebuchadnezzar besieged the city from 10 January 587 to 9 July 586 B.C. Approximately eighty distinguished leaders of the community were executed. The royal palace and the city were set on fire, and the survivors (except the poorest of the land) were taken into captivity.

4 581 B.C. **2 Kings 25:22-26; Jer. 40-44**
This part of the captivity was caused by the rebellion of the remaining Hebrews of strong anti-Babylonian feeling. They fled to Egypt, forcing Jeremiah, who had been given special consideration by Nebuchadnezzar, to accompany them.

It is thought that 70,000 Jews were taken into captivity.

JUDAH'S RETURN FROM EXILE TO JERUSALEM

1 538 B.C. **Ezra 1-6**
Cyrus, the Persian king, destroyed the Babylonian Empire and in the same year issued a decree permitting the Jews to return to their native land. As many as wished to could return, and the temple could be rebuilt partially financed by the royal treasury. The temple vessels also were returned. The number of those returning was 49,697, and were led by Zerubbabel.

2 458 B.C. **Ezra 7-10**
This return took place under Artaxerxes I, king of Persia from 464-424 B.C., and was led by Ezra. Finances for the journey were provided by the royal treasury and the people were allowed to have their own judges. The group numbered about 5500 men and women, besides 38 Levites and 220 servants of the temple.

3 444 B.C. **Nehemiah 1-2**
This group was led by Nehemiah, cupbearer to Artaxerxes and later governor of Judea. Ezra and Nehemiah, furnished with royal power, were able in spite of difficulties to establish the Jewish community. They were allowed to rebuild the wall, and the wall was rebuilt in 52 days, despite opposition from Sanballat, Tobiah and Geshem. Nehemiah 7:66 tells us the whole Jewish community numbered 42,360 men, or possibly 125,000 people.

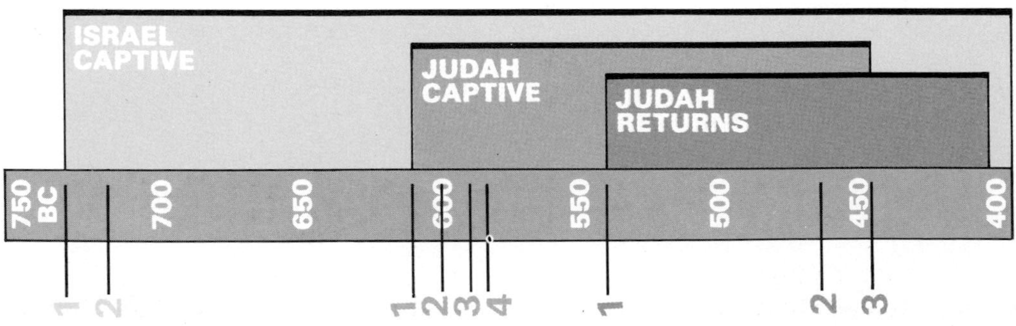

BETWEEN THE TESTAMENTS

THE PERSIAN PERIOD (400-330 B.C.)

For about 150 years after Nehemiah's time the Persians controlled Judea, but the Jews were allowed to carry on their religious observances and were not interferred with. During this time Judea was ruled by high priests who were responsible to the Jewish government.

THE GREEK PERIOD (330-166 B.C.)

In 333 B.C. the Persian armies stationed in Macedonia were defeated by Alexander the Great. He was convinced that Greek culture was the one force that could unify the world. Alexander permitted the Jews to observe their laws and even granted them exemption from tribute or tax during their sabbatical years. When he built Alexandria in Egypt, he encouraged Jews to live there and gave them some of the same privileges he gave his Greek subjects. The Greek conquest prepared the way for the translation of the Old Testament into Greek (Septuagint version) about 250 B.C.

THE HASMONEAN PERIOD (166-63 B.C.)

When this historical period began, the Jews were being greatly oppressed. The Ptolemies had been tolerant of the Jews and their religious practices but the Seleucid rulers were determined to force Hellenism on them. Copies of the Scriptures were ordered destroyed and laws were enforced with extreme cruelty. The oppressed Jews revolted, led by Judas the Maccabee. The Syrians were defeated in a series of battles, which secured the independence of the province of Judea, and was the foundation of the Hasmonean dynasty. This time period was filled with many political struggles and posed many problems to the religiously oriented Jews.

THE ROMAN PERIOD (63 B.C.-A.D. 37)

In the year 63 B.C. Pompey, the Roman general, captured Jerusalem, and the provinces of Palestine became subject to Rome. The local government was entrusted part of the time to princes and the rest of the time to procurators who were appointed by the emperors. Herod the Great was ruler of all Palestine at the time of Christ's birth.

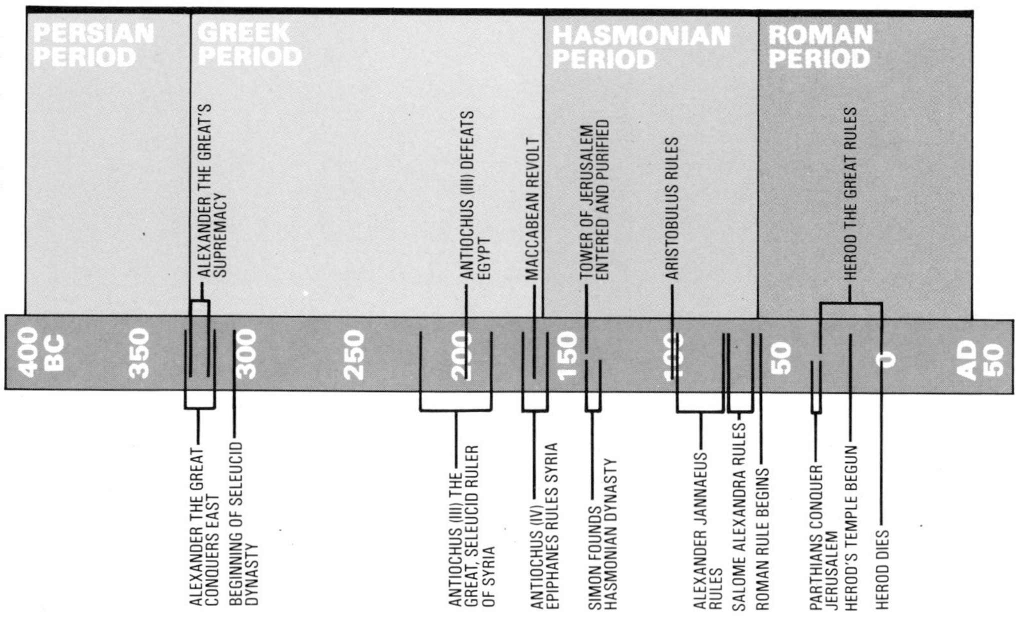

TIME LINE OF THE NEW TESTAMENT

YEAR

CHRIST'S EARLY LIFE

4 BC — (4 B.C.) CHRIST'S BIRTH
(4 B.C.) HEROD THE GREAT'S DEATH

0

AD 5

10 — (A.D. 9) CHRIST AT TEMPLE WHEN 12

15

20 — (18) CAIAPHAS BECAME HIGH PRIEST

25 — (26) PILATE ARRIVED IN JUDEA

(29) BEGINNING OF JOHN THE BAPTIST'S MINISTRY

THE EARLY CHURCH

(33) PENTECOST
(34) THE STONING OF STEPHEN
(34) PAUL'S CONVERSION TO CHRISTIANITY

35

40 — (35-43) PAUL'S SILENT YEARS

(44) MARTYRDOM OF JAMES/IMPRISONMENT OF PETER

45 — (44) DEATH OF HEROD AGRIPPA I
(46-49) PAUL'S FIRST MISSIONARY JOURNEY

CHRIST'S MINISTRY

29 — (29) BEGINNING OF CHRIST'S MINISTRY
(29) JESUS BAPTISM

30 — (30) CHRIST'S FIRST PASSOVER (JOHN 2:13)
(30/31) JOHN THE BAPTIST IMPRISONED

31 — (31) CHRIST'S SECOND PASSOVER

32 — (31/32) JOHN THE BAPTIST'S DEATH
(32) CHRIST'S THIRD PASSOVER

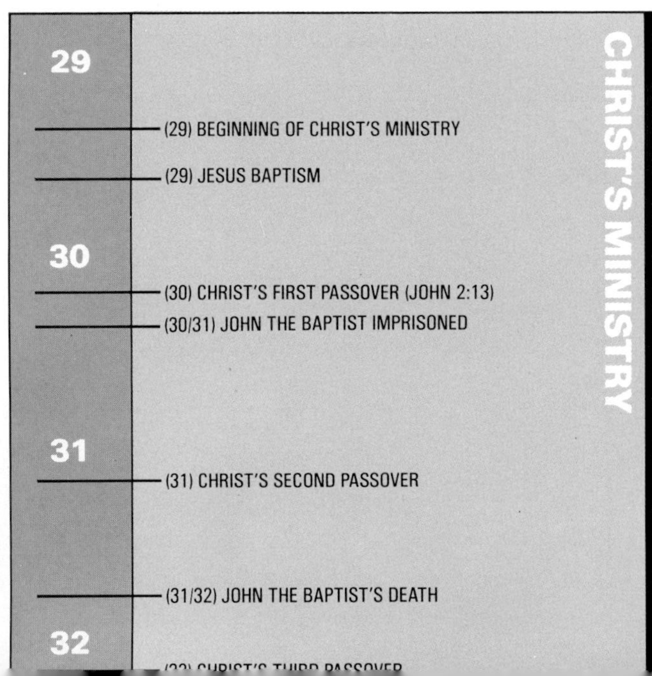

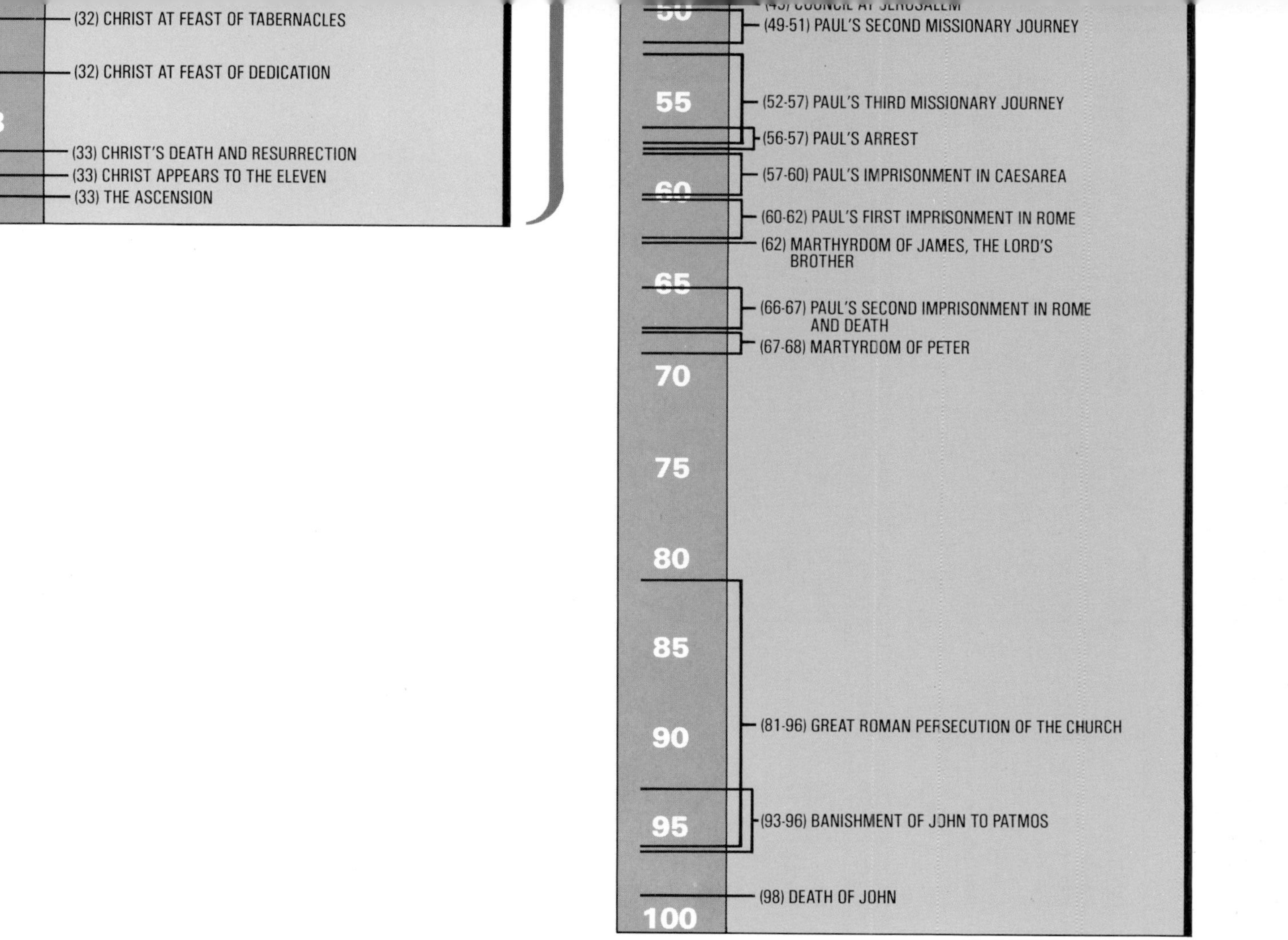
(32) CHRIST AT FEAST OF TABERNACLES
(32) CHRIST AT FEAST OF DEDICATION
33
(33) CHRIST'S DEATH AND RESURRECTION
(33) CHRIST APPEARS TO THE ELEVEN
(33) THE ASCENSION
(49-51) PAUL'S SECOND MISSIONARY JOURNEY
55
(52-57) PAUL'S THIRD MISSIONARY JOURNEY
(56-57) PAUL'S ARREST
(57-60) PAUL'S IMPRISONMENT IN CAESAREA
(60-62) PAUL'S FIRST IMPRISONMENT IN ROME
(62) MARTHYRDOM OF JAMES, THE LORD'S BROTHER
65
(66-67) PAUL'S SECOND IMPRISONMENT IN ROME AND DEATH
(67-68) MARTYRDOM OF PETER
70
75
80
85
(81-96) GREAT ROMAN PERSECUTION OF THE CHURCH
90
(93-96) BANISHMENT OF JOHN TO PATMOS
95
(98) DEATH OF JOHN
100

THE MINISTRY OF JESUS

THE YEAR OF INAUGURATION

Event	Place	Date	Matthew	Mark	Luke	John
Jesus baptized	Jordan River	about	3:13-17	1:9-11	3:21-23	1:29-39
Jesus tempted by Satan	Wilderness	A.D. 26	4:1-11	1:12,13	4:1-13	
Jesus' first miracle	Cana					2:1-11
Jesus and Nicodemus	Judea	A.D. 27				3:1-21
Jesus talks to the Samaritan woman	Samaria					4:5-42
Jesus heals a nobleman's son	Cana					4:46-54
The people of Jesus' home town try to kill him	Nazareth				4:16-31	

THE YEAR OF POPULARITY

Event	Place	Date	Matthew	Mark	Luke	John
4 fishermen become Jesus' followers	Sea of Galilee		4:18-22	1:16-20	5:1-11	
Jesus heals Peter's mother-in-law	Capernaum		8:14-17	1:29-34	4:38-41	
Jesus begins his first preaching trip through Galilee	Galilee		4:23-25	1:35-39	4:42-44	
Matthew decides to follow Jesus	Capernaum		9:9-13	2:13-17	5:27-32	
Jesus chooses the 12 disciples		A.D. 28		3:13-19	6:12-15	
Jesus preaches the "Sermon on the Mount"			5:1-7:29		6:20-49	
A sinful woman anoints Jesus	Capernaum				7:36-50	
Jesus travels again through Galilee					8:1-3	
Jesus tells parables about the kingdom			13:1-52	4:1-34	8:4-18	
Jesus quiets the storm	Sea of Galilee		8:23-27	4:35-41	8:22-25	
Jairus' daughter is brought back to life by Jesus	Capernaum		9:18-26	5:21-43	8:40-56	
Jesus sends his 12 followers out to preach and heal			9:35-11:1	6:6-13	9:1-6	

THE YEAR OF OPPOSITION

Event	Place	Date	Matthew	Mark	Luke	John
John the Baptist is killed by Herod	Machaerus		14:1-12	6:14-29	9:7-9	
Jesus feeds 5,000 people	Near Bethsaida	Spring A.D. 29	14:13-21	6:30-44	9:10-17	6:1-14
Jesus walks on water			14:22,23	6:45-52		6:16-21
Jesus feeds 4,000 people		Later in the year	15:32-39	8:1-9		
Peter says that Jesus is the Son of God			16:13-20	8:27-30	9:18-21	
Jesus tells his disciples he is going to die soon	Caesarea Philippi		16:21-26	8:31-37	9:22-25	
Jesus is transfigured			17:1-13	9:2-13	9:28-36	
Jesus pays his temple taxes	Capernaum		17:24-27			
Jesus attends the Feast of Tabernacles	Jerusalem	October A.D. 29				7:11-52
Jesus heals a man who was born blind	Jerusalem	Later in				9:1-41
Jesus visits Mary and Martha	Bethany	the year			10:38-42	
Jesus raises Lazarus from the dead	Bethany	Winter A.D. 29				11:1-44
Jesus begins his last trip to Jerusalem		A.D. 30			17:11	
Jesus blesses the little children	Across the Jordan		19:13-15	10:13-16	18:15-17	

Event	Place	Date	Matthew	Mark	Luke	John
Jesus talks to the rich young man	Across the Jordan		19:16-30	10:17-31	18:18-30	
Jesus again tells about his death and resurrection	Near the Jordan		20:17-19	10:32-34	18:31-34	
Jesus heals blind Bartimaeus	Jericho		20:29-34	10:46-52	18:35-43	
Jesus talks to Zacchaeus	Jericho				19:1-10	
Jesus returns to Bethany to visit Mary and Martha	Bethany					11:55-12:1

THE LAST WEEK

Event	Place	Date	Matthew	Mark	Luke	John .
The triumphal entry	Jerusalem	Sunday	21:1-11	11:1-10	19:29-44	12:12-19
Jesus curses the fig tree	Jerusalem	Monday	21:18,19	11:12-14		
Jesus cleanses the temple	Jerusalem	Monday	21:12,13	11:15-18	19:45-48	
The authority of Jesus questioned	Jerusalem	Tuesday	21:23-27	11:27-33	20:1-8	
Jesus teaches in the temple	Jerusalem	Tuesday	21:28-23:29	12:1-44	20:9-21:4	
Jesus annointed	Bethany	Tuesday	26:6-13	14:3-9		12:2-11
The plot against Jesus	Jerusalem	Wednesday	26:14-16	14:10,11	22:3-6	
The Last Supper	Jerusalem	Thursday	26:17-29	14:12-25	22:7-20	13:1-38
Jesus comforts the disciples	Jerusalem	Thursday				14:1-16:33
Gethsemane	Jerusalem	Thursday	26:36-46	14:32-42	22:40-46	
Jesus' arrest and trial	Jerusalem	Friday	26:47-27:26	14:43-15:15	22:47-23:25	18:2-19:16
Jesus' crucifixion and death	Golgotha	Friday	27:27-56	15:16-41	23:26-49	19:17-30
The burial of Jesus	Garden Tomb	Friday	27:57-66	15:42-47	23:50-56	19:31-42

AFTER THE RESURRECTION

Event	Place	Date	Matthew	Mark	Luke	John
The empty tomb	Jerusalem	Sunday	28:1-10	16:1-8	24:1-12	20:1-10
Mary Magdalene sees Jesus in the garden	Jerusalem			16:9-11		20:11-18
Jesus appears to the two going to Emmaus				16:12,13	24:13-35	
Jesus appears to 10 disciples	Jerusalem			16:14	24:36-43	20:19-25
Jesus appears to the 11 disciples	Jerusalem	One week				20:26-31
Jesus talks with some of his disciples	Sea of Galilee	later				21:1-25
Jesus returns to his Father in heaven	Mt. of Olives	40 days Later	28:16-20	16:19,20	24:44-53	

PARABLES

OLD TESTAMENT

Parable	References	Parable	References
Of Balaam	Num. 23:7, 18; 24:3, 15, 20-23	Potter and the clay	Jer. 18:1-10
The trees	Judges 9:7-15	Two baskets of figs	Jer. 24:1-10
Ewe lamb	2 Sam. 12:1-4	Cup of God's wrath	Jer. 25:15-38
Two sons	2 Sam. 14:1-24	Useless vine	Ezek. 15:1-8
Wounded prophet	1 Kings 20:35-43	Cooking pot	Ezek. 24:1-4
Thistle and the cedar	2 Kings 14:8-14	Valley of dry bones	Ezek. 37:1-14
The vineyard	Isa. 5:1-7	Rising waters	Ezek. 47:1-12
Almond rod and boiling pot	Jer. 1:11-19	Measuring line	Zech. 2:1-13
Linen belt	Jer. 13:1-11	Golden lampstand and two olive trees	Zech. 4:1-14
Wineskins	Jer. 13:12-14	Flying scroll	Zech. 5:1-4

NEW TESTAMENT

Parable	References	Parable	References
Wise and foolish builders	Matt. 7:24-27 Luke 6:47, 49	Fig tree	Matt. 24:32-35; Mark 13:28; Luke 21:29
New wine in old wineskins	Matt. 9:16-17; Mark 2:21-22; Luke 5:36	Wise and wicked servants	Matt. 24:45-51; Luke 12:42-48
Sower and the seed	Matt. 13:1-8, 18-23; Mark 4:3-8, 14-20; Luke 8:5-8, 11-15	Ten virgins	Matt. 25:1-13
		Talents	Matt. 25:14-30
		Sheep and goats	Matt. 25:31-46
Weeds	Matt. 13:24-30, 36-43	Growing seed	Mark 4:26-29
Mustard seed	Matt. 13:31-32; Mark 4:30-32; Luke 13:18-19	Watchful porter	Mark 13:34-37
		Two debtors	Luke 7:41-43
		Good Samaritan	Luke 10:30-37
Yeast (leaven)	Matt. 13:33; Luke 13:20-21	Friend at midnight	Luke 11:5-8
Hidden treasure	Matt. 13:44	The rich fool	Luke 12:16-21
		Watchful servants	Luke 12:35-48
Pearl of great price (hidden treasure)	Matt. 13:45-46	Barren fig tree	Luke 13:6-9
Dragnet (net)	Matt. 13:47-50	Lowest seat at the feast	Luke 14:7-11
Householder	Matt. 13:52	The great supper	Luke 14:15-24
The lost sheep	Matt. 18:12-14; Luke 15:3-7	The lost coin	Luke 15:8-10
		The lost son (Prodigal)	Luke 15:11-32
Unmerciful servant	Matt. 18:23-25	Shrewd manager (unjust steward)	Luke 16:1-10
Workers in the vineyard	Matt. 20:1-6	Rich man and Lazarus	Luke 16:19-31
Two sons	Matt. 21:28-32	Unworthy servants	Luke 17:7-10
Tenants (wicked husbandman)	Matt. 21:33-46; Mark 12:1-12; Luke 20:9-18	Persistant widow (unjust judge)	Luke 18:1-8
		Pharisee and tax collector (publican)	Luke 18:9-14
Wedding banquet	Matt. 22:1-4	Ten minnas (pounds)	Luke 19:11-27

MIRACLES

OLD TESTAMENT

Miracle	References	Miracle	References
Burning bush	Exod. 3:1-14	Widow's son raised from dead	1 Kings 17:17-24
Rod becoming a snake	Exod. 4:1-5; 7:8-13	Sacrifice consumed by fire	1 Kings 18:16-39
Leprous hand	Exod. 4:6-12	Rain in answer to prayer	1 Kings 18:41-45
Ten plagues	Exod. 8:14-12: 30	Jordan divided	2 Kings 2:1-8
Dividing of the Red sea	Exod. 14:21-31	Waters sweetened	2 Kings 2:19-22
Water from the rock	Exod. 17:1-9	Widow's oil multiplied	2 Kings 4:1-7
Destruction of Korah	Num. 16:31-35	Shunammite's son restored to life	2 Kings 4:8-37
Aaron's staff budding	Num. 17:1-19	Poison stew rendered harmless	2 Kings 4:38-41
Water from the rock in Kadesh	Num. 20:9-11	Feeding of 100 men	2 Kings 4:42-44
Bronze snake	Num. 21:4-9	Naaman healed of leprosy	2 Kings 5:1-19
Balaam's donkey	Num. 22:20-35	Floating axhead	2 Kings 6:1-7
Jordan divided	Josh. 3:7-17	Blinded eyes	2 Kings 6:8-23
Fall of Jericho	Josh. 6:1-20	Dead man restored to life	2 Kings 13:21
Sun standing still	Josh. 10:1-14	Hezekiah healed	2 Kings 20:1-7
Slain lion	Judg. 14:5-10	Daniel and friends delivered from blazing furnace	Dan. 3:23-27
Dagon's temple pulled down	Judg. 16:23-30	Daniel delivered from den of lions	Dan. 6:10-23
Thunder and rain	1 Sam. 12:16-18	Sea stilled when Jonah cast in	Jonah 1:15
Jeroboam's hand withered and restored	1 Kings 13:1-16	Jonah delivered from fish's stomach	Jonah 2:10
Elijah fed by ravens	1 Kings 17:1-6	Withering of the vine	Jonah 4:6, 7
Widow's flour and oil	1 Kings 17:8-16		

NEW TESTAMENT

NATURE MIRACLES

Miracle	References	Miracle	References
Turning of water into wine	John 2:1-11	Walking on the sea	Matt. 14:22-33 Mark 6:45-52 John 6:16-21
First catch of fish	Luke 5:1-11	Feeding of the 4000	Matt. 15:32-39 Mark 8:1-9
Calming of the storm	Matt. 8:22-27 Mark 4:35-41 Luke 8:22-25	Tax money in the fish's mouth	Matt. 17:24-27
Feeding of the 5000	Matt. 14:15-21 Mark 6:35-44 Luke 9:12-17 John 6:5-15	Withering of the fig tree	Matt. 21:17-22 Mark 11:12-14, 20-25
		Second catch of fish	John 21:1-14

HEALING MIRACLES

Miracle	References	Miracle	References
Healing of the nobleman's son	John 4:46-54	Healing of a paralytic	Matt. 9:1-8 Mark 2:1-12 Luke 5:17-26
Restoring of demon-possessed man	Mark 1:23-27 Luke 4:33-36	Healing of an invalid at Bethesda	John 5:1-18
Healing of Peter's mother-in-law	Matt. 8:14-17 Mark 1:29-31 Luke 4:38-39	Restoration of a withered hand	Matt. 12:9-14 Mark 3:1-6 Luke 6:6-11
Curing of a man with leprosy	Matt. 8:1-4 Mark 1:40-45 Luke 5:12-15	Healing of a centurion's servant	Matt. 8:5-13 Luke 7:1-10

NEW TESTAMENT

Miracle	References	Miracle	References
Raising of the son of the widow of Nain	Luke 7:11-16	Restoring of sight to blind man at Bethsaida	Mark 8:22-26
Restoring of the blind and mute demoniac	Matt. 12:22 Luke 11:14,15	Healing of the child with a demon	Matt. 17:14-20 Mark 9:14-29 Luke 9:37-43
Curing of the demon-possessed man (men)	Matt. 8:28-34 Mark 5:1-20 Luke 8:26-39	Healing of ten men with leprosy	Luke 17:11-19
Raising of Jairus' daughter	Matt. 9:18-26 Mark 5:22-24, 35-43 Luke 8:41-42, 49-56	Restoring of sight to man born blind	John 9:1-41
		Raising of Lazarus	John 11:1-45
Curing of the woman with the flow of blood	Matt. 9:20-22 Mark 5:25-34 Luke 8:43-48	Restoring of woman crippled for 18 years	Luke 13:10-17
		Healing of man with dropsy	Luke 14:1-6
Giving of sight to two blind men	Matt. 9:27-31	Restoring of sight to blind Bartimaeus	Matt. 20:29-34 Mark 10:46-52 Luke 18:35-43
Healing of the mute demoniac	Matt. 9:32-34		
Healing of the Syrophoenician girl	Matt. 15:21-28 Mark 7:24-30	Restoring of Malchus' ear	Luke 22:49-51 John 18:10-11
Healing of the deaf mute	Mark 7:31-37		

ZONDERVAN

The HOLY BIBLE

NEW INTERNATIONAL VERSION

Containing The Old Testament

and The New Testament

ZONDERVAN BIBLE PUBLISHERS
GRAND RAPIDS, MICHIGAN

Library of Congress Catalog Card Number 78-69799
Published by The Zondervan Corporation
Grand Rapids, Michigan 49506, U.S.A.
Printed in Great Britain

Fourth Printing — 230,000 copies in print
RC—4-89

You will be pleased to know that a portion of the purchase price of your new NIV Bible has been provided to the International Bible Society to help spread the Gospel of Jesus Christ around the world!

Contents

Alphabetical Order of The Books of the Bible

Preface

Preface

THE NEW INTERNATIONAL VERSION is a completely new translation of the Holy Bible made by over a hundred scholars working directly from the best available Hebrew, Aramaic and Greek texts. It had its beginning in 1965 when, after several years of exploratory study by committees from the Christian Reformed Church and the National Association of Evangelicals, a group of scholars met at Palos Heights, Illinois, and concurred in the need for a new translation of the Bible in contemporary English. This group, though not made up of official church representatives, was transdenominational. Its conclusion was endorsed by a large number of leaders from many denominations who met in Chicago in 1966.

Responsibility for the new version was delegated by the Palos Heights group to a self-governing body of fifteen, the Committee on Bible Translation, composed for the most part of biblical scholars from colleges, universities and seminaries. In 1967 the New York Bible Society (now the International Bible Society) generously undertook the financial sponsorship of the project—a sponsorship that made it possible to enlist the help of many distinguished scholars. The fact that participants from the United States, Great Britain, Canada, Australia and New Zealand worked together gave the project its international scope. That they were from many denominations—including Anglican, Assemblies of God, Baptist, Brethren, Christian Reformed, Church of Christ, Evangelical Free, Lutheran, Mennonite, Methodist, Nazarene, Presbyterian, Wesleyan and other churches—helped to safeguard the translation from sectarian bias.

How it was made helps to give the New International Version its distinctiveness. The translation of each book was assigned to a team of scholars. Next, one of the Intermediate Editorial Committees revised the initial translation, with constant reference to the Hebrew, Aramaic or Greek. Their work then went to one of the General Editorial Committees, which checked it in detail and made another thorough revision. This revision in turn was carefully reviewed by the Committee on Bible Translation, which made further changes and then released the final version for publication. In this way the entire Bible underwent three revisions, during each of which the translation was examined for its faithfulness to the original languages and for its English style.

All this involved many thousands of hours of research and discussion regarding the meaning of the texts and the precise way of putting them into English. It may well be that no other translation has been made by a more thorough process of review and revision from committee to committee than this one.

From the beginning of the project, the Committee on Bible Translation held to certain goals for the New International Version: that it would be an accurate translation and one that would have clarity and literary quality and so prove suitable for public and private reading, teaching, preaching, memorizing and liturgical use. The Committee also sought to preserve some measure of continuity with the long tradition of translating the Scriptures into English.

In working toward these goals, the translators were united in their commitment to the authority and infallibility of the Bible as God's Word in written form. They believe that it contains the divine answer to the deepest needs of humanity, that it sheds unique light on our path in a dark world, and that it sets forth the way to our eternal well-being.

The first concern of the translators has been the accuracy of the translation and its fidelity to the thought of the biblical writers. They have weighed the significance of the lexical and grammatical details of the Hebrew, Aramaic and Greek texts. At the same time, they have striven for more than a word-for-word translation. Because thought patterns and syntax differ from language to language, faithful communication of the meaning of the writers of the Bible demands frequent modifications in sentence structure and constant regard for the contextual meanings of words.

A sensitive feeling for style does not always accompany scholarship. Accordingly the Committee on Bible Translation submitted the developing version to a number of stylistic consultants. Two of them read every book of both Old and New Testaments twice—once before and once after the last major revision—and made invaluable suggestions. Samples of the translation were tested for clarity and ease of reading by various kinds of people—young and old, highly educated and less well educated, ministers and laymen.

Concern for clear and natural English—that the New International Version should be idiomatic but not idiosyncratic, contemporary but not dated—motivated the translators and consultants. At the same time, they tried to reflect the differing styles of the biblical writers. In view of the international use of English, the translators sought to avoid obvious Americanisms on the one hand and obvious Anglicisms on the other. A British edition reflects the comparatively few differences of significant idiom and of spelling.

As for the traditional pronouns "thou," "thee" and "thine" in reference to the Deity, the translators judged that to use these archaisms (along with the old verb forms such as "doest," "wouldest" and "hadst") would violate accuracy in translation. Neither Hebrew, Aramaic nor Greek uses special pronouns for the persons of the Godhead. A present-day translation is not enhanced by forms that in the time of the King James Version were used in everyday speech, whether referring to God or man.

For the Old Testament the standard Hebrew text, the Masoretic Text as published in the latest editions of *Biblia Hebraica,* was used throughout. The Dead Sea Scrolls contain material bearing on an earlier stage of the Hebrew text. They were consulted, as were the Samaritan Pentateuch and the ancient scribal traditions relating to textual changes. Sometimes a variant Hebrew reading in the margin of the Masoretic Text was followed instead of the text itself. Such instances, being variants within the Masoretic tradition, are not specified by footnotes. In rare cases, words in the consonantal text were divided differently from the way they appear in the Masoretic Text. Footnotes indicate this. The translators also consulted the more important early versions—the Septuagint; Symmachus and Theodotion; the Vulgate; the Syriac Peshitta; the Targums; and for the Psalms the *Juxta Hebraica* of Jerome. Readings from these versions were occasionally followed where the Masoretic Text seemed doubtful and where accepted principles of textual criticism showed that one or more of these textual witnesses appeared to provide the correct reading. Such instances are footnoted. Sometimes vowel letters and vowel signs did not, in the judgment of the translators, represent the correct vowels for the original consonantal text. Accordingly some words were read with a different set of vowels. These instances are usually not indicated by footnotes.

The Greek text used in translating the New Testament was an eclectic one. No other piece of ancient literature has such an abundance of manuscript witnesses as does the New Testament. Where existing manuscripts differ, the translators made their choice of readings according to accepted principles of New Testament textual criticism. Footnotes call attention to places where there was uncertainty about what the original text was. The best current printed texts of the Greek New Testament were used.

There is a sense in which the work of translation is never wholly finished. This applies to all great literature and uniquely so to the Bible. In 1973 the New Testament in the New International Version was published. Since then, suggestions for corrections and revisions have been received from various sources. The Committee on Bible Translation carefully considered the suggestions and adopted a number of them. These are incorporated in the first printing of the entire Bible. Additional revisions were made by the Committee on Bible Translation in 1983 and appear in printings after that date.

As in other ancient documents, the precise meaning of the biblical texts is sometimes uncertain. This is more often the case with the Hebrew and Aramaic texts than with the Greek text. Although archaeological and linguistic discoveries in this century aid in understanding difficult passages, some uncertainties remain. The more significant of these have been called to the reader's attention in the footnotes.

In regard to the divine name *YHWH,* commonly referred to as the *Tetragrammaton,* the translators adopted the device used in most English versions of rendering that name as "LORD" in capital letters to distinguish it from *Adonai,* another Hebrew word rendered "Lord," for which small letters are used. Wherever the two names stand together in the Old Testament as a compound name of God, they are rendered "Sovereign LORD."

Because for most readers today the phrases "the LORD of hosts" and "God of hosts" have little meaning, this version renders them "the LORD Almighty" and "God Almighty." These renderings convey the sense of the Hebrew, namely, "he who is sovereign over all the 'hosts' (powers) in heaven and on earth, especially over the 'hosts' (armies) of Israel." For readers unacquainted with Hebrew this does not make clear the distinction between *Sabaoth* ("hosts" or "Almighty") and *Shaddai* (which can also be translated "Almighty"), but the latter occurs infrequently and is always footnoted. When *Adonai* and *YHWH Sabaoth* occur together, they are rendered "the Lord, the LORD Almighty."

As for other proper nouns, the familiar spellings of the King James Version are generally retained. Names traditionally spelled with "ch," except where it is final, are usually spelled in this translation with "k" or "c," since the biblical languages do not have the sound that "ch" frequently indicates in English—for example, in *chant.* For well-known names such as Zechariah, however, the traditional spelling has been retained. Variation in the spelling of names in the original languages has usually not been indicated. Where a person or place has two or more different names in the Hebrew, Aramaic or Greek texts, the more familiar one has generally been used, with footnotes where needed.

To achieve clarity the translators sometimes supplied words not in the original texts but required by the context. If there was uncertainty about such material, it is enclosed in brackets. Also for the sake of clarity or style, nouns, including some proper nouns, are sometimes substituted for pronouns, and vice versa. And though the Hebrew writers often shifted back and forth between first, second and third personal pronouns without change of antecedent, this translation often makes them uniform, in accordance with English style and without the use of footnotes.

Poetical passages are printed as poetry, that is, with indentation of lines and with separate stanzas. These are generally designed to reflect the structure of Hebrew poetry. This poetry is normally characterized by parallelism in balanced lines. Most of the poetry in the Bible is in the Old Testament, and scholars differ regarding the scansion of Hebrew lines. The translators determined the stanza divisions for the most part by analysis of the subject matter. The stanzas therefore serve as poetic paragraphs.

As an aid to the reader, italicized sectional headings are inserted in most of the books. They are not to be regarded as part of the NIV text, are not for oral reading, and are not intended to dictate the interpretation of the sections they head.

The footnotes in this version are of several kinds, most of which need no explanation. Those giving alternative translations begin with "Or" and generally introduce the alternative with the last word preceding it in the text, except when it is a single-word alternative; in poetry quoted in a footnote a slant mark indicates a line division. Footnotes introduced by "Or" do not have uniform significance. In some cases two possible translations were considered to have about equal validity. In other cases, though the translators were convinced that the translation in the text was correct, they judged that another interpretation was possible and of sufficient importance to be represented in a footnote.

In the New Testament, footnotes that refer to uncertainty regarding the original text are introduced by "Some manuscripts" or similar expressions. In the Old Testament, evidence for the reading chosen is given first and evidence for the alternative is added after a semicolon (for example: Septuagint; Hebrew *father*). In such notes the term "Hebrew" refers to the Masoretic Text.

It should be noted that minerals, flora and fauna, architectural details, articles of clothing and jewelry, musical instruments and other articles cannot always be identified with precision. Also measures of capacity in the biblical period are particularly uncertain (see the table of weights and measures following the text).

Like all translations of the Bible, made as they are by imperfect man, this one undoubtedly falls short of its goals. Yet we are grateful to God for the extent to which he has enabled us to realize these goals and for the strength he has given us and our colleagues to complete our task. We offer this version of the Bible to him in whose name and for whose glory it has been made. We pray that it will lead many into a better understanding of the Holy Scriptures and a fuller knowledge of Jesus Christ the incarnate Word, of whom the Scriptures so faithfully testify.

The Committee on Bible Translation

June 1978
(Revised August 1983)

Names of the translators and editors may be secured
from the International Bible Society,
translation sponsors of the New International Version,
P.O. Box 62970, Colorado Springs, Colorado 80962-2970

The Old Testament

Genesis

Introduction:

The word Genesis means "beginnings." The book of Genesis is about many beginnings—the beginning of the universe, the beginning of man and woman, the beginning of human sin, the beginning of God's promises and plans for salvation, and the beginning of a special relationship between Abraham and God. Genesis tells us about God's special people and his plan for their lives. Some of these people are: Adam and Eve, Noah, Abraham, Isaac, Jacob, and Joseph and his brothers.

Genesis is the first book in what is called the Pentateuch—a word that means five books, and includes the first five books of the Bible. These books are also known as the books of the law because they contain God's instructions and laws for the people of Israel. Genesis is included because it tells the history of how Israel became God's special people. These five books were most likely written by Moses, except for the last chapter of Deuteronomy which tells about Moses' death.

Outline of contents:

The universe, the earth, and man (1:1–2:25)
Man's fall and the results of sin (3:1–5:32)
The story of Noah (6:1–9:29)
The scattering of the human race (10:1–11:32)
The life of Abraham (12:1–25:18)
Isaac and his family (25:19–26:35)
Jacob and his sons (27:1–37:1)
The life of Joseph (37:2–50:26)

The Beginning

1 In the beginning God created the
heavens and the earth. 2Now the earth
was[a] formless and empty, darkness
was over the surface of the deep, and
the Spirit of God was hovering over the
waters.
3And God said, "Let there be light," and
there was light. 4God saw that the light
was good, and he separated the light
from the darkness. 5God called the
light "day," and the darkness he called
"night." And there was evening, and
there was morning—the first day.
6And God said, "Let there be an expanse
between the waters to separate water
from water." 7So God made the
expanse and separated the water
under the expanse from the water
above it. And it was so. 8God called the
expanse "sky." And there was
evening, and there was morning—the
second day.
9And God said, "Let the water under the sky
be gathered to one place, and let dry
ground appear." And it was so. 10God
called the dry ground "land," and the
gathered waters he called "seas." And
God saw that it was good.
11Then God said, "Let the land
produce vegetation: seed-bearing
plants and trees on the land that bear
fruit with seed in it, according to their
various kinds." And it was so. 12The
land produced vegetation: plants
bearing seed according to their kinds
and trees bearing fruit with seed in it
according to their kinds. And God saw
that it was good. 13And there was

a2 Or possibly *became*

evening, and there was morning—the
third day.
14And God said, "Let there be lights in the
expanse of the sky to separate the day
from the night, and let them serve as
signs to mark seasons and days and
years, 15and let them be lights in the
expanse of the sky to give light on the
earth." And it was so. 16God made two
great lights—the greater light to govern
the day and the lesser light to govern
the night. He also made the stars.
17God set them in the expanse of the
sky to give light on the earth, 18to
govern the day and the night, and to
separate light from darkness. And God
saw that it was good. 19And there was
evening, and there was morning—the
fourth day.
20And God said, "Let the water teem with
living creatures, and let birds fly above
the earth across the expanse of the
sky." 21So God created the great
creatures of the sea and every living
and moving thing with which the water
teems, according to their kinds, and
every winged bird according to its kind.
And God saw that it was good. 22God
blessed them and said, "Be fruitful and
increase in number and fill the water in
the seas, and let the birds increase on
the earth." 23And there was evening,
and there was morning—the fifth day.
24And God said, "Let the land produce living
creatures according to their kinds:
livestock, creatures that move along
the ground, and wild animals, each
according to its kind." And it was so.
25God made the wild animals
according to their kinds, the livestock
according to their kinds, and all the
creatures that move along the ground
according to their kinds. And God saw
that it was good.
26Then God said, "Let us make man
in our image, in our likeness, and let
them rule over the fish of the sea and
the birds of the air, over the livestock,
over all the earth,[a] and over all the
creatures that move along the ground."
27So God created man in his own image,
in the image of God he created him;
male and female he created them.
28God blessed them and said to
them, "Be fruitful and increase in
number; fill the earth and subdue it.
Rule over the fish of the sea and the
birds of the air and over every living
creature that moves on the ground."
29Then God said, "I give you every
seed-bearing plant on the face of the
whole earth and every tree that has
fruit with seed in it. They will be yours
for food. 30And to all the beasts of the
earth and all the birds of the air and all
the creatures that move on the
ground—everything that has the
breath of life in it—I give every green
plant for food." And it was so.
31God saw all that he had made, and
it was very good. And there was
evening, and there was morning—the
sixth day.

2 Thus the heavens and the earth
were completed in all their vast array.
2By the seventh day God had finished the
work he had been doing; so on the
seventh day he rested[b] from all his
work. 3And God blessed the seventh
day and made it holy, because on it he
rested from all the work of creating that
he had done.

Adam and Eve

4This is the account of the heavens and
the earth when they were created.

When the LORD God made the earth and
the heavens— 5and no shrub of the field had
yet appeared on the earth[c] and no plant of
the field had yet sprung up, for the LORD God
had not sent rain on the earth[c] and there was
no man to work the ground, 6but streams[d]
came up from the earth and watered the
whole surface of the ground— 7the LORD God
formed the man[e] from the dust of the ground
and breathed into his nostrils the breath of
life, and the man became a living being.
8Now the LORD God had planted a garden
in the east, in Eden; and there he put the
man he had formed. 9And the LORD God
made all kinds of trees grow out of the
ground—trees that were pleasing to the eye
and good for food. In the middle of the garden were the tree of life and the tree of the
knowledge of good and evil.

[a]26 Hebrew; Syriac *all the wild animals* [b]2 Or *ceased*; also in verse 3 [c]5 Or *land*; also in verse 6 [d]6 Or *mist* [e]7 The Hebrew for *man (adam)* sounds like and may be related to the Hebrew for *ground (adamah)*; it is also the name *Adam* (see Gen. 2:20).

10A river watering the garden flowed from
Eden; from there it was separated into four
headwaters. 11The name of the first is the
Pishon; it winds through the entire land of
Havilah, where there is gold. 12(The gold of
that land is good; aromatic resin[a] and onyx
are also there.) 13The name of the second
river is the Gihon; it winds through the entire
land of Cush.[b] 14The name of the third river is
the Tigris; it runs along the east side of
Asshur. And the fourth river is the Euphrates.

15The LORD God took the man and put him
in the Garden of Eden to work it and take
care of it. 16And the LORD God commanded
the man, "You are free to eat from any tree in
the garden; 17but you must not eat from the
tree of the knowledge of good and evil, for
when you eat of it you will surely die."

18The LORD God said, "It is not good for the
man to be alone. I will make a helper suitable
for him."

19Now the LORD God had formed out of the
ground all the beasts of the field and all the
birds of the air. He brought them to the man
to see what he would name them; and whatever the man called each living creature, that
was its name. 20So the man gave names to
all the livestock, the birds of the air and all the
beasts of the field.

But for Adam[c] no suitable helper was
found. 21So the LORD God caused the man to
fall into a deep sleep; and while he was
sleeping, he took one of the man's ribs[d] and
closed up the place with flesh. 22Then the
LORD God made a woman from the rib[e] he
had taken out of the man, and he brought her
to the man.

23The man said,

"This is now bone of my bones
  and flesh of my flesh;
she shall be called 'woman,[f]'
  for she was taken out of man."

24For this reason a man will leave his father
and mother and be united to his wife, and
they will become one flesh.

25The man and his wife were both naked,
and they felt no shame.

The Fall of Man

3 Now the serpent was more crafty than
any of the wild animals the LORD God had
made. He said to the woman, "Did God really
say, 'You must not eat from any tree in the
garden'?"

2The woman said to the serpent, "We may
eat fruit from the trees in the garden, 3but
God did say, 'You must not eat fruit from the
tree that is in the middle of the garden, and
you must not touch it, or you will die.' "

4"You will not surely die," the serpent said
to the woman. 5"For God knows that when
you eat of it your eyes will be opened, and
you will be like God, knowing good and evil."

6When the woman saw that the fruit of the
tree was good for food and pleasing to the
eye, and also desirable for gaining wisdom,
she took some and ate it. She also gave
some to her husband, who was with her, and
he ate it. 7Then the eyes of both of them were
opened, and they realized they were naked;
so they sewed fig leaves together and made
coverings for themselves.

8Then the man and his wife heard the
sound of the LORD God as he was walking in
the garden in the cool of the day, and they
hid from the LORD God among the trees of the
garden. 9But the LORD God called to the man,
"Where are you?"

10He answered, "I heard you in the garden,
and I was afraid because I was naked; so I
hid."

11And he said, "Who told you that you were
naked? Have you eaten from the tree that I
commanded you not to eat from?"

12The man said, "The woman you put here
with me—she gave me some fruit from the
tree, and I ate it."

13Then the LORD God said to the woman,
"What is this you have done?"

The woman said, "The serpent deceived
me, and I ate."

14So the LORD God said to the serpent,
"Because you have done this,

"Cursed are you above all the livestock
  and all the wild animals!
You will crawl on your belly
  and you will eat dust
  all the days of your life.
15And I will put enmity
  between you and the woman,
  and between your offspring[g] and hers;
he will crush[h] your head,
  and you will strike his heel."

16To the woman he said,

[a] 12 Or *good; pearls* [b] 13 Possibly southeast Mesopotamia [c] 20 Or *the man* [d] 21 Or *took part of the man's side* [e] 22 Or *part* [f] 23 The Hebrew for *woman* sounds like the Hebrew for *man.* [g] 15 Or *seed* [h] 15 Or *strike*

"I will greatly increase your pains in
childbearing;
with pain you will give birth to children.
Your desire will be for your husband,
and he will rule over you."

17To Adam he said, "Because you listened
to your wife and ate from the tree about
which I commanded you, 'You must not eat
of it,'

"Cursed is the ground because of you;
through painful toil you will eat of it
all the days of your life.
18It will produce thorns and thistles for you,
and you will eat the plants of the field.
19By the sweat of your brow
you will eat your food
until you return to the ground,
since from it you were taken;
for dust you are
and to dust you will return."

20Adam[a] named his wife Eve,[b] because
she would become the mother of all the living.
21The LORD God made garments of skin for
Adam and his wife and clothed them. 22And
the LORD God said, "The man has now
become like one of us, knowing good and
evil. He must not be allowed to reach out his
hand and take also from the tree of life and
eat, and live forever." 23So the LORD God
banished him from the Garden of Eden to
work the ground from which he had been
taken. 24After he drove the man out, he
placed on the east side[c] of the Garden of
Eden cherubim and a flaming sword flashing
back and forth to guard the way to the tree of
life.

Cain and Abel

4 Adam[a] lay with his wife Eve, and she
became pregnant and gave birth to
Cain.[d] She said, "With the help of the LORD I
have brought forth[e] a man." 2Later she gave
birth to his brother Abel.

Now Abel kept flocks, and Cain worked
the soil. 3In the course of time Cain brought
some of the fruits of the soil as an offering to
the LORD. 4But Abel brought fat portions from
some of the firstborn of his flock. The LORD
looked with favor on Abel and his offering,
5but on Cain and his offering he did not look
with favor. So Cain was very angry, and his
face was downcast.

6Then the LORD said to Cain, "Why are you
angry? Why is your face downcast? 7If you
do what is right, will you not be accepted?
But if you do not do what is right, sin is
crouching at your door; it desires to have
you, but you must master it."

8Now Cain said to his brother Abel, "Let's
go out to the field."[f] And while they were in
the field, Cain attacked his brother Abel and
killed him.

9Then the LORD said to Cain, "Where is
your brother Abel?"

"I don't know," he replied. "Am I my brother's keeper?"

10The LORD said, "What have you done?
Listen! Your brother's blood cries out to me
from the ground. 11Now you are under a
curse and driven from the ground, which
opened its mouth to receive your brother's
blood from your hand. 12When you work the
ground, it will no longer yield its crops for
you. You will be a restless wanderer on the
earth."

13Cain said to the LORD, "My punishment is
more than I can bear. 14Today you are driving me from the land, and I will be hidden
from your presence; I will be a restless wanderer on the earth, and whoever finds me will
kill me."

15But the LORD said to him, "Not so[g]; if
anyone kills Cain, he will suffer vengeance
seven times over." Then the LORD put a mark
on Cain so that no one who found him would
kill him. 16So Cain went out from the LORD's
presence and lived in the land of Nod,[h] east
of Eden.

17Cain lay with his wife, and she became
pregnant and gave birth to Enoch. Cain was
then building a city, and he named it after his
son Enoch. 18To Enoch was born Irad, and
Irad was the father of Mehujael, and Mehujael was the father of Methushael, and Methushael was the father of Lamech.

19Lamech married two women, one named
Adah and the other Zillah. 20Adah gave birth
to Jabal; he was the father of those who live
in tents and raise livestock. 21His brother's
name was Jubal; he was the father of all who
play the harp and flute. 22Zillah also had a
son, Tubal-Cain, who forged all kinds of tools

[a]20,1 Or *The man* [b]20 *Eve* probably means *living.* [c]24 Or *placed in front* [d]1 *Cain* sounds like the Hebrew for *brought forth* or *acquired.* [e]1 Or *have acquired* [f]8 Samaritan Pentateuch, Septuagint, Vulgate and Syriac; Masoretic Text does not have *"Let's go out to the field."* [g]15 Septuagint, Vulgate and Syriac; Hebrew *Very well* [h]16 *Nod* means *wandering* (see verses 12 and 14).

out of[a] bronze and iron. Tubal-Cain's sister
was Naamah.
23Lamech said to his wives,

"Adah and Zillah, listen to me;
wives of Lamech, hear my words.
I have killed[b] a man for wounding me,
a young man for injuring me.
24If Cain is avenged seven times,
then Lamech seventy-seven times."

25Adam lay with his wife again, and she
gave birth to a son and named him Seth,[c]
saying, "God has granted me another child
in place of Abel, since Cain killed him."
26Seth also had a son, and he named him
Enosh.

At that time men began to call on[d] the
name of the LORD.

From Adam to Noah

5 This is the written account of Adam's
line.

When God created man, he made him in
the likeness of God. 2He created them male
and female and blessed them. And when
they were created, he called them "man.[e]"
3When Adam had lived 130 years, he had
a son in his own likeness, in his own image;
and he named him Seth. 4After Seth was
born, Adam lived 800 years and had other
sons and daughters. 5Altogether, Adam lived
930 years, and then he died.
6When Seth had lived 105 years, he
became the father[f] of Enosh. 7And after he
became the father of Enosh, Seth lived 807
years and had other sons and daughters.
8Altogether, Seth lived 912 years, and then
he died.
9When Enosh had lived 90 years, he
became the father of Kenan. 10And after he
became the father of Kenan, Enosh lived
815 years and had other sons and daughters. 11Altogether, Enosh lived 905 years,
and then he died.
12When Kenan had lived 70 years, he
became the father of Mahalalel. 13And after
he became the father of Mahalalel, Kenan
lived 840 years and had other sons and
daughters. 14Altogether, Kenan lived 910
years, and then he died.
15When Mahalalel had lived 65 years, he
became the father of Jared. 16And after he
became the father of Jared, Mahalalel lived
830 years and had other sons and daughters. 17Altogether, Mahalalel lived 895 years,
and then he died.
18When Jared had lived 162 years, he
became the father of Enoch. 19And after he
became the father of Enoch, Jared lived 800
years and had other sons and daughters.
20Altogether, Jared lived 962 years, and then
he died.
21When Enoch had lived 65 years, he
became the father of Methuselah. 22And after he became the father of Methuselah,
Enoch walked with God 300 years and had
other sons and daughters. 23Altogether,
Enoch lived 365 years. 24Enoch walked with
God; then he was no more, because God
took him away.
25When Methuselah had lived 187 years,
he became the father of Lamech. 26And after
he became the father of Lamech, Methuselah lived 782 years and had other sons
and daughters. 27Altogether, Methuselah
lived 969 years, and then he died.
28When Lamech had lived 182 years, he
had a son. 29He named him Noah[g] and said,
"He will comfort us in the labor and painful
toil of our hands caused by the ground the
LORD has cursed." 30After Noah was born,
Lamech lived 595 years and had other sons
and daughters. 31Altogether, Lamech lived
777 years, and then he died.
32After Noah was 500 years old, he
became the father of Shem, Ham and
Japheth.

The Flood

6 When men began to increase in number
on the earth and daughters were born to
them, 2the sons of God saw that the daughters of men were beautiful, and they married
any of them they chose. 3Then the LORD said,
"My Spirit will not contend with[h] man forever,
for he is mortal[i]; his days will be a hundred
and twenty years."
4The Nephilim were on the earth in those
days—and also afterward—when the sons
of God went to the daughters of men and had
children by them. They were the heroes of
old, men of renown.
5The LORD saw how great man's wickedness on the earth had become, and that
every inclination of the thoughts of his heart
was only evil all the time. 6The LORD was

[a]22 Or *who instructed all who work in* [b]23 Or *I will kill* [c]25 *Seth* probably means *granted.* [d]26 Or *to proclaim* [e]2 Hebrew *adam* [f]6 *Father* may mean *ancestor;* also in verses 7-26. [g]29 *Noah* sounds like the Hebrew for *comfort.* [h]3 Or *My spirit will not remain in* [i]3 Or *corrupt*

grieved that he had made man on the earth, and his heart was filled with pain. 7So the LORD said, "I will wipe mankind, whom I have created, from the face of the earth—men and animals, and creatures that move along the ground, and birds of the air—for I am grieved that I have made them." 8But Noah found favor in the eyes of the LORD.

9This is the account of Noah.

Noah was a righteous man, blameless among the people of his time, and he walked with God. 10Noah had three sons: Shem, Ham and Japheth.

11Now the earth was corrupt in God's sight and was full of violence. 12God saw how corrupt the earth had become, for all the people on earth had corrupted their ways. 13So God said to Noah, "I am going to put an end to all people, for the earth is filled with violence because of them. I am surely going to destroy both them and the earth. 14So make yourself an ark of cypress[a] wood; make rooms in it and coat it with pitch inside and out. 15This is how you are to build it: The ark is to be 450 feet long, 75 feet wide and 45 feet high.[b] 16Make a roof for it and finish[c] the ark to within 18 inches[d] of the top. Put a door in the side of the ark and make lower, middle and upper decks. 17I am going to bring floodwaters on the earth to destroy all life under the heavens, every creature that has the breath of life in it. Everything on earth will perish. 18But I will establish my covenant with you, and you will enter the ark—you and your sons and your wife and your sons' wives with you. 19You are to bring into the ark two of all living creatures, male and female, to keep them alive with you. 20Two of every kind of bird, of every kind of animal and of every kind of creature that moves along the ground will come to you to be kept alive. 21You are to take every kind of food that is to be eaten and store it away as food for you and for them."

22Noah did everything just as God commanded him.

7 The LORD then said to Noah, "Go into the ark, you and your whole family, because I have found you righteous in this generation. 2Take with you seven[e] of every kind of clean animal, a male and its mate, and two of every kind of unclean animal, a male and its mate, 3and also seven of every kind of bird, male and female, to keep their various kinds alive throughout the earth. 4Seven days from now I will send rain on the earth for forty days and forty nights, and I will wipe from the face of the earth every living creature I have made."

5And Noah did all that the LORD commanded him.

6Noah was six hundred years old when the floodwaters came on the earth. 7And Noah and his sons and his wife and his sons' wives entered the ark to escape the waters of the flood. 8Pairs of clean and unclean animals, of birds and of all creatures that move along the ground, 9male and female, came to Noah and entered the ark, as God had commanded Noah. 10And after the seven days the floodwaters came on the earth.

11In the six hundredth year of Noah's life, on the seventeenth day of the second month—on that day all the springs of the great deep burst forth, and the floodgates of the heavens were opened. 12And rain fell on the earth forty days and forty nights.

13On that very day Noah and his sons, Shem, Ham and Japheth, together with his wife and the wives of his three sons, entered the ark. 14They had with them every wild animal according to its kind, all livestock according to their kinds, every creature that moves along the ground according to its kind and every bird according to its kind, everything with wings. 15Pairs of all creatures that have the breath of life in them came to Noah and entered the ark. 16The animals going in were male and female of every living thing, as God had commanded Noah. Then the LORD shut him in.

17For forty days the flood kept coming on the earth, and as the waters increased they lifted the ark high above the earth. 18The waters rose and increased greatly on the earth, and the ark floated on the surface of the water. 19They rose greatly on the earth, and all the high mountains under the entire heavens were covered. 20The waters rose and covered the mountains to a depth of more than twenty feet.[f,g] 21Every living thing that moved on the earth perished—birds, livestock, wild animals, all the creatures that swarm over the earth, and all mankind. 22Everything on dry land that had the breath of life in its nostrils died. 23Every living thing on the face of the earth was wiped out; men

[a]14 The meaning of the Hebrew for this word is uncertain. [b]15 Hebrew *300 cubits long, 50 cubits wide and 30 cubits high* (about 140 meters long, 23 meters wide and 13.5 meters high) [c]16 Or *Make an opening for light by finishing* [d]16 Hebrew *a cubit* (about 0.5 meter) [e]2 Or *seven pairs*; also in verse 3 [f]20 Hebrew *fifteen cubits* (about 6.9 meters) [g]20 Or *rose more than twenty feet, and the mountains were covered*

and animals and the creatures that move
along the ground and the birds of the air were
wiped from the earth. Only Noah was left,
and those with him in the ark.
24The waters flooded the earth for a hundred and fifty days.

8 But God remembered Noah and all the
wild animals and the livestock that were
with him in the ark, and he sent a wind over
the earth, and the waters receded. 2Now the
springs of the deep and the floodgates of the
heavens had been closed, and the rain had
stopped falling from the sky. 3The water
receded steadily from the earth. At the end of
the hundred and fifty days the water had
gone down, 4and on the seventeenth day of
the seventh month the ark came to rest on
the mountains of Ararat. 5The waters continued to recede until the tenth month, and
on the first day of the tenth month the tops of
the mountains became visible.
6After forty days Noah opened the window
he had made in the ark 7and sent out a raven,
and it kept flying back and forth until the
water had dried up from the earth. 8Then he
sent out a dove to see if the water had receded from the surface of the ground. 9But the
dove could find no place to set its feet because there was water over all the surface of
the earth; so it returned to Noah in the ark.
He reached out his hand and took the dove
and brought it back to himself in the ark. 10He
waited seven more days and again sent out
the dove from the ark. 11When the dove returned to him in the evening, there in its beak
was a freshly plucked olive leaf! Then Noah
knew that the water had receded from the
earth. 12He waited seven more days and
sent the dove out again, but this time it did
not return to him.
13By the first day of the first month of
Noah's six hundred and first year, the water
had dried up from the earth. Noah then removed the covering from the ark and saw
that the surface of the ground was dry. 14By
the twenty-seventh day of the second month
the earth was completely dry.
15Then God said to Noah, 16"Come out of
the ark, you and your wife and your sons and
their wives. 17Bring out every kind of living
creature that is with you—the birds, the animals, and all the creatures that move along
the ground—so they can multiply on the
earth and be fruitful and increase in number
upon it."
18So Noah came out, together with his
sons and his wife and his sons' wives. 19All
the animals and all the creatures that move
along the ground and all the birds—everything that moves on the earth—came out of
the ark, one kind after another.
20Then Noah built an altar to the LORD and,
taking some of all the clean animals and
clean birds, he sacrificed burnt offerings on
it. 21The LORD smelled the pleasing aroma
and said in his heart: "Never again will I
curse the ground because of man, even
though[a] every inclination of his heart is evil
from childhood. And never again will I destroy all living creatures, as I have done.

22"As long as the earth endures,
seedtime and harvest,
cold and heat,
summer and winter,
day and night
will never cease."

God's Covenant With Noah

9 Then God blessed Noah and his sons,
saying to them, "Be fruitful and increase
in number and fill the earth. 2The fear and
dread of you will fall upon all the beasts of the
earth and all the birds of the air, upon every
creature that moves along the ground, and
upon all the fish of the sea; they are given
into your hands. 3Everything that lives and
moves will be food for you. Just as I gave you
the green plants, I now give you everything.
4"But you must not eat meat that has its
lifeblood still in it. 5And for your lifeblood I will
surely demand an accounting. I will demand
an accounting from every animal. And from
each man, too, I will demand an accounting
for the life of his fellow man.

6"Whoever sheds the blood of man,
by man shall his blood be shed;
for in the image of God
has God made man.

7As for you, be fruitful and increase in number; multiply on the earth and increase upon
it."
8Then God said to Noah and to his sons
with him: 9"I now establish my covenant with
you and with your descendants after you
10and with every living creature that was with
you—the birds, the livestock and all the wild
animals, all those that came out of the ark
with you—every living creature on earth. 11I

[a] 21 Or *man, for*

establish my covenant with you: Never again
will all life be cut off by the waters of a flood;
never again will there be a flood to destroy
the earth."
12And God said, "This is the sign of the
covenant I am making between me and you
and every living creature with you, a covenant for all generations to come: 13I have
set my rainbow in the clouds, and it will be
the sign of the covenant between me and the
earth. 14Whenever I bring clouds over the
earth and the rainbow appears in the clouds,
15I will remember my covenant between me
and you and all living creatures of every kind.
Never again will the waters become a flood
to destroy all life. 16Whenever the rainbow
appears in the clouds, I will see it and
remember the everlasting covenant between God and all living creatures of every
kind on the earth."
17So God said to Noah, "This is the sign of
the covenant I have established between me
and all life on the earth."

The Sons of Noah

18The sons of Noah who came out of the
ark were Shem, Ham and Japheth. (Ham
was the father of Canaan.) 19These were the
three sons of Noah, and from them came the
people who were scattered over the earth.
20Noah, a man of the soil, proceeded[a] to
plant a vineyard. 21When he drank some of
its wine, he became drunk and lay uncovered inside his tent. 22Ham, the father of Canaan, saw his father's nakedness and told
his two brothers outside. 23But Shem and
Japheth took a garment and laid it across
their shoulders; then they walked in backward and covered their father's nakedness.
Their faces were turned the other way so that
they would not see their father's nakedness.
24When Noah awoke from his wine and
found out what his youngest son had done to
him, 25he said,

"Cursed be Canaan!
The lowest of slaves
will he be to his brothers."

26He also said,

"Blessed be the LORD, the God of Shem!
May Canaan be the slave of Shem.[b]
27May God extend the territory of Japheth[c];
may Japheth live in the tents of Shem,
and may Canaan be his[d] slave."

28After the flood Noah lived 350 years.
29Altogether, Noah lived 950 years, and then
he died.

The Table of Nations

10 This is the account of Shem, Ham
and Japheth, Noah's sons, who
themselves had sons after the flood.

The Japhethites

2The sons[e] of Japheth:
Gomer, Magog, Madai, Javan, Tubal, Meshech and Tiras.
3The sons of Gomer:
Ashkenaz, Riphath and Togarmah.
4The sons of Javan:
Elishah, Tarshish, the Kittim and the
Rodanim.[f] 5(From these the mari-
time peoples spread out into their
territories by their clans within their
nations, each with its own language.)

The Hamites

6The sons of Ham:
Cush, Mizraim,[g] Put and Canaan.
7The sons of Cush:
Seba, Havilah, Sabtah, Raamah and
Sabteca.
The sons of Raamah:
Sheba and Dedan.

8Cush was the father[h] of Nimrod, who
grew to be a mighty warrior on the earth. 9He
was a mighty hunter before the LORD; that is
why it is said, "Like Nimrod, a mighty hunter
before the LORD." 10The first centers of his
kingdom were Babylon, Erech, Akkad and
Calneh, in[i] Shinar.[j] 11From that land he
went to Assyria, where he built Nineveh,
Rehoboth Ir,[k] Calah 12and Resen, which is
between Nineveh and Calah; that is the
great city.

13Mizraim was the father of
the Ludites, Anamites, Lehabites,
Naphtuhites, 14Pathrusites, Caslu-
hites (from whom the Philistines
came) and Caphtorites.

[a]20 Or *soil, was the first* [b]26 Or *be his slave* [c]27 *Japheth* sounds like the Hebrew for *extend.*
[d]27 Or *their* [e]2 *Sons* may mean *descendants* or *successors* or *nations;* also in verses 3, 4, 6, 7, 20-23, 29 and 31. [f]4 Some manuscripts of the Masoretic Text and Samaritan Pentateuch (see also Septuagint and 1 Chron. 1:7); most manuscripts of the Masoretic Text *Dodanim* [g]6 That is, Egypt; also in verse 13
[h]8 *Father* may mean *ancestor* or *predecessor* or *founder;* also in verses 13, 15, 24 and 26. [i]10 Or *Erech and* Akkad—all of them in [j]10 That is, Babylonia [k]11 Or *Nineveh with its city squares*

15Canaan was the father of
Sidon his firstborn,[a] and of the Hittites, 16Jebusites, Amorites, Girgashites, 17Hivites, Arkites, Sinites,
18Arvadites, Zemarites and Hamathites.

Later the Canaanite clans scattered 19and
the borders of Canaan reached from Sidon
toward Gerar as far as Gaza, and then
toward Sodom, Gomorrah, Admah and Zeboiim, as far as Lasha.
20These are the sons of Ham by their clans
and languages, in their territories and nations.

The Semites

21Sons were also born to Shem, whose
older brother was[b] Japheth; Shem was the
ancestor of all the sons of Eber.

22The sons of Shem:
Elam, Asshur, Arphaxad, Lud and
Aram.
23The sons of Aram:
Uz, Hul, Gether and Meshech.[c]
24Arphaxad was the father of[d] Shelah,
and Shelah the father of Eber.
25Two sons were born to Eber:
One was named Peleg,[e] because in
his time the earth was divided; his
brother was named Joktan.
26Joktan was the father of
Almodad, Sheleph, Hazarmaveth,
Jerah, 27Hadoram, Uzal, Diklah,
28Obal, Abimael, Sheba, 29Ophir,
Havilah and Jobab. All these were
sons of Joktan.

30The region where they lived stretched from
Mesha toward Sephar, in the eastern hill
country.
31These are the sons of Shem by their
clans and languages, in their territories and
nations.

32These are the clans of Noah's sons, according to their lines of descent, within their
nations. From these the nations spread out
over the earth after the flood.

The Tower of Babel

11 Now the whole world had one language and a common speech. 2As
men moved eastward,[f] they found a plain in
Shinar[g] and settled there.
3They said to each other, "Come, let's
make bricks and bake them thoroughly."
They used brick instead of stone, and tar for
mortar. 4Then they said, "Come, let us build
ourselves a city, with a tower that reaches to
the heavens, so that we may make a name
for ourselves and not be scattered over the
face of the whole earth."
5But the LORD came down to see the city
and the tower that the men were building.
6The LORD said, "If as one people speaking
the same language they have begun to do
this, then nothing they plan to do will be impossible for them. 7Come, let us go down
and confuse their language so they will not
understand each other."
8So the LORD scattered them from there
over all the earth, and they stopped building
the city. 9That is why it was called Babel[h]—because there the LORD confused the
language of the whole world. From there the
LORD scattered them over the face of the
whole earth.

From Shem to Abram

10This is the account of Shem.

Two years after the flood, when Shem was
100 years old, he became the father[i] of Arphaxad. 11And after he became the father of
Arphaxad, Shem lived 500 years and had
other sons and daughters.
12When Arphaxad had lived 35 years, he
became the father of Shelah. 13And after he
became the father of Shelah, Arphaxad lived
403 years and had other sons and daughters.[j]
14When Shelah had lived 30 years, he
became the father of Eber. 15And after he
became the father of Eber, Shelah lived 403
years and had other sons and daughters.
16When Eber had lived 34 years, he
became the father of Peleg. 17And after he

[a]*15* Or *of the Sidonians, the foremost* [b]*21* Or *Shem, the older brother of* [c]*23* See Septuagint and 1 Chron. 1:17; Hebrew *Mash* [d]*24* Hebrew; Septuagint *father of Cainan, and Cainan was the father of* [e]*25 Peleg* means *division.* [f]*2* Or *from the east;* or *in the east* [g]*2* That is, Babylonia [h]*9* That is, Babylon; *Babel* sounds like the Hebrew for *confused.* [i]*10 Father* may mean *ancestor,* also in verses 11-25. [j]*12,13* Hebrew; Septuagint (see also Luke 3:35, 36 and note at Gen. 10:24) *35 years, he became the father of Cainan. 13And after he became the father of Cainan, Arphaxad lived 430 years and had other sons and daughters, and then he died. When Cainan had lived 130 years, he became the father of Shelah. And after he became the father of Shelah, Cainan lived 330 years and had other sons and daughters*

became the father of Peleg, Eber lived 430
years and had other sons and daughters.
18When Peleg had lived 30 years, he
became the father of Reu. 19And after he
became the father of Reu, Peleg lived 209
years and had other sons and daughters.
20When Reu had lived 32 years, he
became the father of Serug. 21And after he
became the father of Serug, Reu lived 207
years and had other sons and daughters.
22When Serug had lived 30 years, he
became the father of Nahor. 23And after he
became the father of Nahor, Serug lived 200
years and had other sons and daughters.
24When Nahor had lived 29 years, he
became the father of Terah. 25And after he
became the father of Terah, Nahor lived 119
years and had other sons and daughters.
26After Terah had lived 70 years, he
became the father of Abram, Nahor and Haran.

27This is the account of Terah.

Terah became the father of Abram, Nahor
and Haran. And Haran became the father of
Lot. 28While his father Terah was still alive,
Haran died in Ur of the Chaldeans, in the
land of his birth. 29Abram and Nahor both
married. The name of Abram's wife was
Sarai, and the name of Nahor's wife was
Milcah; she was the daughter of Haran, the
father of both Milcah and Iscah. 30Now Sarai
was barren; she had no children.
31Terah took his son Abram, his grandson
Lot son of Haran, and his daughter-in-law
Sarai, the wife of his son Abram, and together they set out from Ur of the Chaldeans
to go to Canaan. But when they came to
Haran, they settled there.
32Terah lived 205 years, and he died in
Haran.

The Call of Abram

12 The LORD had said to Abram, "Leave
your country, your people and your
father's household and go to the land I will
show you.

2"I will make you into a great nation
  and I will bless you;
I will make your name great,
  and you will be a blessing.
3I will bless those who bless you,
  and whoever curses you I will curse;
and all peoples on earth
  will be blessed through you."

4So Abram left, as the LORD had told him;
and Lot went with him. Abram was seventy-
five years old when he set out from Haran.
5He took his wife Sarai, his nephew Lot, all
the possessions they had accumulated and
the people they had acquired in Haran, and
they set out for the land of Canaan, and they
arrived there.
6Abram traveled through the land as far as
the site of the great tree of Moreh at Shechem. At that time the Canaanites were in
the land. 7The LORD appeared to Abram and
said, "To your offspring[a] I will give this land."
So he built an altar there to the LORD, who
had appeared to him.
8From there he went on toward the hills
east of Bethel and pitched his tent, with Bethel on the west and Ai on the east. There he
built an altar to the LORD and called on the
name of the LORD. 9Then Abram set out and
continued toward the Negev.

Abram in Egypt

10Now there was a famine in the land, and
Abram went down to Egypt to live there for a
while because the famine was severe. 11As
he was about to enter Egypt, he said to his
wife Sarai, "I know what a beautiful woman
you are. 12When the Egyptians see you, they
will say, 'This is his wife.' Then they will kill
me but will let you live. 13Say you are my
sister, so that I will be treated well for your
sake and my life will be spared because of
you."
14When Abram came to Egypt, the Egyptians saw that she was a very beautiful
woman. 15And when Pharaoh's officials saw
her, they praised her to Pharaoh, and she
was taken into his palace. 16He treated
Abram well for her sake, and Abram acquired sheep and cattle, male and female
donkeys, menservants and maidservants,
and camels.
17But the LORD inflicted serious diseases
on Pharaoh and his household because of
Abram's wife Sarai. 18So Pharaoh summoned Abram. "What have you done to
me?" he said. "Why didn't you tell me she
was your wife? 19Why did you say, 'She is my
sister,' so that I took her to be my wife? Now
then, here is your wife. Take her and go!"
20Then Pharaoh gave orders about Abram to
his men, and they sent him on his way, with
his wife and everything he had.

[a]7 Or *seed*

Abram and Lot Separate

13 So Abram went up from Egypt to the Negev, with his wife and everything he had, and Lot went with him. 2Abram had become very wealthy in livestock and in silver and gold.

3From the Negev he went from place to place until he came to Bethel, to the place between Bethel and Ai where his tent had been earlier 4and where he had first built an altar. There Abram called on the name of the LORD.

5Now Lot, who was moving about with Abram, also had flocks and herds and tents. 6But the land could not support them while they stayed together, for their possessions were so great that they were not able to stay together. 7And quarreling arose between Abram's herdsmen and the herdsmen of Lot. The Canaanites and Perizzites were also living in the land at that time.

8So Abram said to Lot, "Let's not have any quarreling between you and me, or between your herdsmen and mine, for we are brothers. 9Is not the whole land before you? Let's part company. If you go to the left, I'll go to the right; if you go to the right, I'll go to the left."

10Lot looked up and saw that the whole plain of the Jordan was well watered, like the garden of the LORD, like the land of Egypt, toward Zoar. (This was before the LORD destroyed Sodom and Gomorrah.) 11So Lot chose for himself the whole plain of the Jordan and set out toward the east. The two men parted company: 12Abram lived in the land of Canaan, while Lot lived among the cities of the plain and pitched his tents near Sodom. 13Now the men of Sodom were wicked and were sinning greatly against the LORD.

14The LORD said to Abram after Lot had parted from him, "Lift up your eyes from where you are and look north and south, east and west. 15All the land that you see I will give to you and your offspring[a] forever. 16I will make your offspring like the dust of the earth, so that if anyone could count the dust, then your offspring could be counted. 17Go, walk through the length and breadth of the land, for I am giving it to you."

18So Abram moved his tents and went to live near the great trees of Mamre at Hebron, where he built an altar to the LORD.

Abram Rescues Lot

14 At this time Amraphel king of Shinar,[b] Arioch king of Ellasar, Kedorlaomer king of Elam and Tidal king of Goiim 2went to war against Bera king of Sodom, Birsha king of Gomorrah, Shinab king of Admah, Shemeber king of Zeboiim, and the king of Bela (that is, Zoar). 3All these latter kings joined forces in the Valley of Siddim (the Salt Sea[c]). 4For twelve years they had been subject to Kedorlaomer, but in the thirteenth year they rebelled.

5In the fourteenth year, Kedorlaomer and the kings allied with him went out and defeated the Rephaites in Ashteroth Karnaim, the Zuzites in Ham, the Emites in Shaveh Kiriathaim 6and the Horites in the hill country of Seir, as far as El Paran near the desert. 7Then they turned back and went to En Mishpat (that is, Kadesh), and they conquered the whole territory of the Amalekites, as well as the Amorites who were living in Hazazon Tamar.

8Then the king of Sodom, the king of Gomorrah, the king of Admah, the king of Zeboiim and the king of Bela (that is, Zoar) marched out and drew up their battle lines in the Valley of Siddim 9against Kedorlaomer king of Elam, Tidal king of Goiim, Amraphel king of Shinar and Arioch king of Ellasar—four kings against five. 10Now the Valley of Siddim was full of tar pits, and when the kings of Sodom and Gomorrah fled, some of the men fell into them and the rest fled to the hills. 11The four kings seized all the goods of Sodom and Gomorrah and all their food; then they went away. 12They also carried off Abram's nephew Lot and his possessions, since he was living in Sodom.

13One who had escaped came and reported this to Abram the Hebrew. Now Abram was living near the great trees of Mamre the Amorite, a brother[d] of Eshcol and Aner, all of whom were allied with Abram. 14When Abram heard that his relative had been taken captive, he called out the 318 trained men born in his household and went in pursuit as far as Dan. 15During the night Abram divided his men to attack them and he routed them, pursuing them as far as Hobah, north of Damascus. 16He recovered all the goods and brought back his relative Lot and his possessions, together with the women and the other people.

[a] *15* Or *seed;* also in verse 16 [b] *1* That is, Babylonia; also in verse 9 [c] *3* That is, the Dead Sea
[d] *13* Or *a relative;* or *an ally*

17After Abram returned from defeating Kedorlaomer and the kings allied with him, the king of Sodom came out to meet him in the Valley of Shaveh (that is, the King's Valley).

18Then Melchizedek king of Salem[a] brought out bread and wine. He was priest of God Most High, 19and he blessed Abram, saying,

"Blessed be Abram by God Most High,
  Creator[b] of heaven and earth.
20And blessed be[c] God Most High,
  who delivered your enemies into your
    hand."

Then Abram gave him a tenth of everything.

21The king of Sodom said to Abram, "Give me the people and keep the goods for yourself."

22But Abram said to the king of Sodom, "I have raised my hand to the LORD, God Most High, Creator of heaven and earth, and have taken an oath 23that I will accept nothing belonging to you, not even a thread or the thong of a sandal, so that you will never be able to say, 'I made Abram rich.' 24I will accept nothing but what my men have eaten and the share that belongs to the men who went with me—to Aner, Eshcol and Mamre. Let them have their share."

God's Covenant With Abram

15 After this, the word of the LORD came to Abram in a vision:

"Do not be afraid, Abram.
  I am your shield,[d]
  your very great reward.[e]"

2But Abram said, "O Sovereign LORD, what can you give me since I remain childless and the one who will inherit[f] my estate is Eliezer of Damascus?" 3And Abram said, "You have given me no children; so a servant in my household will be my heir."

4Then the word of the LORD came to him: "This man will not be your heir, but a son coming from your own body will be your heir." 5He took him outside and said, "Look up at the heavens and count the stars—if indeed you can count them." Then he said to him, "So shall your offspring be."

6Abram believed the LORD, and he credited it to him as righteousness.

7He also said to him, "I am the LORD, who brought you out of Ur of the Chaldeans to give you this land to take possession of it."

8But Abram said, "O Sovereign LORD, how can I know that I will gain possession of it?"

9So the LORD said to him, "Bring me a heifer, a goat and a ram, each three years old, along with a dove and a young pigeon."

10Abram brought all these to him, cut them in two and arranged the halves opposite each other; the birds, however, he did not cut in half. 11Then birds of prey came down on the carcasses, but Abram drove them away.

12As the sun was setting, Abram fell into a deep sleep, and a thick and dreadful darkness came over him. 13Then the LORD said to him, "Know for certain that your descendants will be strangers in a country not their own, and they will be enslaved and mistreated four hundred years. 14But I will punish the nation they serve as slaves, and afterward they will come out with great possessions. 15You, however, will go to your fathers in peace and be buried at a good old age. 16In the fourth generation your descendants will come back here, for the sin of the Amorites has not yet reached its full measure."

17When the sun had set and darkness had fallen, a smoking firepot with a blazing torch appeared and passed between the pieces. 18On that day the LORD made a covenant with Abram and said, "To your descendants I give this land, from the river[g] of Egypt to the great river, the Euphrates— 19the land of the Kenites, Kenizzites, Kadmonites, 20Hittites, Perizzites, Rephaites, 21Amorites, Canaanites, Girgashites and Jebusites."

Hagar and Ishmael

16 Now Sarai, Abram's wife, had borne him no children. But she had an Egyptian maidservant named Hagar; 2so she said to Abram, "The LORD has kept me from having children. Go, sleep with my maidservant; perhaps I can build a family through her."

Abram agreed to what Sarai said. 3So after Abram had been living in Canaan ten years, Sarai his wife took her Egyptian maidservant Hagar and gave her to her husband to be his wife. 4He slept with Hagar, and she conceived.

When she knew she was pregnant, she began to despise her mistress. 5Then Sarai said to Abram, "You are responsible for the

[a] *18* That is, Jerusalem [b] *19* Or *Possessor;* also in verse 22 [c] *20* Or *And praise be to* [d] *1* Or *sovereign* [e] *1* Or *shield; / your reward will be very great* [f] *2* The meaning of the Hebrew for this phrase is uncertain. [g] *18* Or *Wadi*

wrong I am suffering. I put my servant in your arms, and now that she knows she is pregnant, she despises me. May the LORD judge between you and me."

6"Your servant is in your hands," Abram said. "Do with her whatever you think best." Then Sarai mistreated Hagar; so she fled from her.

7The angel of the LORD found Hagar near a spring in the desert; it was the spring that is beside the road to Shur. 8And he said, "Hagar, servant of Sarai, where have you come from, and where are you going?"

"I'm running away from my mistress Sarai," she answered.

9Then the angel of the LORD told her, "Go back to your mistress and submit to her." 10The angel added, "I will so increase your descendants that they will be too numerous to count."

11The angel of the LORD also said to her:

"You are now with child
  and you will have a son.
You shall name him Ishmael,[a]
  for the LORD has heard of your misery.
12He will be a wild donkey of a man;
  his hand will be against everyone
  and everyone's hand against him,
and he will live in hostility
  toward[b] all his brothers."

13She gave this name to the LORD who spoke to her: "You are the God who sees me," for she said, "I have now seen[c] the One who sees me." 14That is why the well was called Beer Lahai Roi[d]; it is still there, between Kadesh and Bered.

15So Hagar bore Abram a son, and Abram gave the name Ishmael to the son she had borne. 16Abram was eighty-six years old when Hagar bore him Ishmael.

The Covenant of Circumcision

17 When Abram was ninety-nine years old, the LORD appeared to him and said, "I am God Almighty[e]; walk before me and be blameless. 2I will confirm my covenant between me and you and will greatly increase your numbers."

3Abram fell facedown, and God said to him, 4"As for me, this is my covenant with you: You will be the father of many nations. 5No longer will you be called Abram[f]; your name will be Abraham,[g] for I have made you a father of many nations. 6I will make you very fruitful; I will make nations of you, and kings will come from you. 7I will establish my covenant as an everlasting covenant between me and you and your descendants after you for the generations to come, to be your God and the God of your descendants after you. 8The whole land of Canaan, where you are now an alien, I will give as an everlasting possession to you and your descendants after you; and I will be their God."

9Then God said to Abraham, "As for you, you must keep my covenant, you and your descendants after you for the generations to come. 10This is my covenant with you and your descendants after you, the covenant you are to keep: Every male among you shall be circumcised. 11You are to undergo circumcision, and it will be the sign of the covenant between me and you. 12For the generations to come every male among you who is eight days old must be circumcised, including those born in your household or bought with money from a foreigner—those who are not your offspring. 13Whether born in your household or bought with your money, they must be circumcised. My covenant in your flesh is to be an everlasting covenant. 14Any uncircumcised male, who has not been circumcised in the flesh, will be cut off from his people; he has broken my covenant."

15God also said to Abraham, "As for Sarai your wife, you are no longer to call her Sarai; her name will be Sarah. 16I will bless her and will surely give you a son by her. I will bless her so that she will be the mother of nations; kings of peoples will come from her."

17Abraham fell facedown; he laughed and said to himself, "Will a son be born to a man a hundred years old? Will Sarah bear a child at the age of ninety?" 18And Abraham said to God, "If only Ishmael might live under your blessing!"

19Then God said, "Yes, but your wife Sarah will bear you a son, and you will call him Isaac.[h] I will establish my covenant with him as an everlasting covenant for his descendants after him. 20And as for Ishmael, I have heard you: I will surely bless him; I will make him fruitful and will greatly increase his numbers. He will be the father of twelve rulers, and I will make him into a great nation. 21But my covenant I will establish with Isaac, whom Sarah will bear to you by this time next

[a] 11 *Ishmael* means *God hears.* [b] 12 Or *live to the east / of* [c] 13 Or *seen the back of* [d] 14 *Beer Lahai Roi* means *well of the Living One who sees me.* [e] 1 Hebrew *El-Shaddai* [f] 5 *Abram* means *exalted father.* [g] 5 *Abraham* means *father of many.* [h] 19 *Isaac* means *he laughs.*

year." 22When he had finished speaking with
Abraham, God went up from him.
23On that very day Abraham took his son
Ishmael and all those born in his household
or bought with his money, every male in his
household, and circumcised them, as God
told him. 24Abraham was ninety-nine years
old when he was circumcised, 25and his son
Ishmael was thirteen; 26Abraham and his
son Ishmael were both circumcised on that
same day. 27And every male in Abraham's
household, including those born in his
household or bought from a foreigner, was
circumcised with him.

The Three Visitors

18 The LORD appeared to Abraham near
the great trees of Mamre while he
was sitting at the entrance to his tent in the
heat of the day. 2Abraham looked up and
saw three men standing nearby. When he
saw them, he hurried from the entrance of
his tent to meet them and bowed low to the
ground.
3He said, "If I have found favor in your
eyes, my lord,[a] do not pass your servant by.
4Let a little water be brought, and then you
may all wash your feet and rest under this
tree. 5Let me get you something to eat, so
you can be refreshed and then go on your
way—now that you have come to your servant."
"Very well," they answered, "do as you
say."
6So Abraham hurried into the tent to Sarah. "Quick," he said, "get three seahs[b] of
fine flour and knead it and bake some
bread."
7Then he ran to the herd and selected a
choice, tender calf and gave it to a servant,
who hurried to prepare it. 8He then brought
some curds and milk and the calf that had
been prepared, and set these before them.
While they ate, he stood near them under a
tree.
9"Where is your wife Sarah?" they asked
him.
"There, in the tent," he said.
10Then the LORD[c] said, "I will surely return
to you about this time next year, and Sarah
your wife will have a son."
Now Sarah was listening at the entrance
to the tent, which was behind him. 11Abra-
ham and Sarah were already old and well
advanced in years, and Sarah was past the
age of childbearing. 12So Sarah laughed to
herself as she thought, "After I am worn out
and my master[d] is old, will I now have this
pleasure?"
13Then the LORD said to Abraham, "Why
did Sarah laugh and say, 'Will I really have a
child, now that I am old?' 14Is anything too
hard for the LORD? I will return to you at the
appointed time next year and Sarah will have
a son."
15Sarah was afraid, so she lied and said, "I
did not laugh."
But he said, "Yes, you did laugh."

Abraham Pleads for Sodom

16When the men got up to leave, they
looked down toward Sodom, and Abraham
walked along with them to see them on their
way. 17Then the LORD said, "Shall I hide from
Abraham what I am about to do? 18Abraham
will surely become a great and powerful nation, and all nations on earth will be blessed
through him. 19For I have chosen him, so that
he will direct his children and his household
after him to keep the way of the LORD by
doing what is right and just, so that the LORD
will bring about for Abraham what he has
promised him."
20Then the LORD said, "The outcry against
Sodom and Gomorrah is so great and their
sin so grievous 21that I will go down and see
if what they have done is as bad as the outcry that has reached me. If not, I will know."
22The men turned away and went toward
Sodom, but Abraham remained standing before the LORD.[e] 23Then Abraham approached
him and said: "Will you sweep away the
righteous with the wicked? 24What if there
are fifty righteous people in the city? Will you
really sweep it away and not spare[f] the
place for the sake of the fifty righteous
people in it? 25Far be it from you to do such a
thing—to kill the righteous with the wicked,
treating the righteous and the wicked alike.
Far be it from you! Will not the Judge[g] of all
the earth do right?"
26The LORD said, "If I find fifty righteous
people in the city of Sodom, I will spare the
whole place for their sake."
27Then Abraham spoke up again: "Now
that I have been so bold as to speak to the
Lord, though I am nothing but dust and
ashes, 28what if the number of the righteous

[a] 3 Or *O Lord* [b] 6 That is, probably about 20 quarts (about 22 liters) [c] 10 Hebrew *Then he* [d] 12 Or *husband* [e] 22 Masoretic Text; an ancient Hebrew scribal tradition *but the LORD remained standing before Abraham* [f] 24 Or *forgive*; also in verse 26 [g] 25 Or *Ruler*

is five less than fifty? Will you destroy the whole city because of five people?"

"If I find forty-five there," he said, "I will not destroy it."

29 Once again he spoke to him, "What if only forty are found there?"

He said, "For the sake of forty, I will not do it."

30 Then he said, "May the Lord not be angry, but let me speak. What if only thirty can be found there?"

He answered, "I will not do it if I find thirty there."

31 Abraham said, "Now that I have been so bold as to speak to the Lord, what if only twenty can be found there?"

He said, "For the sake of twenty, I will not destroy it."

32 Then he said, "May the Lord not be angry, but let me speak just once more. What if only ten can be found there?"

He answered, "For the sake of ten, I will not destroy it."

33 When the LORD had finished speaking with Abraham, he left, and Abraham returned home.

Sodom and Gomorrah Destroyed

19 The two angels arrived at Sodom in the evening, and Lot was sitting in the gateway of the city. When he saw them, he got up to meet them and bowed down with his face to the ground. 2 "My lords," he said, "please turn aside to your servant's house. You can wash your feet and spend the night and then go on your way early in the morning."

"No," they answered, "we will spend the night in the square."

3 But he insisted so strongly that they did go with him and entered his house. He prepared a meal for them, baking bread without yeast, and they ate. 4 Before they had gone to bed, all the men from every part of the city of Sodom—both young and old—surrounded the house. 5 They called to Lot, "Where are the men who came to you tonight? Bring them out to us so that we can have sex with them."

6 Lot went outside to meet them and shut the door behind him 7 and said, "No, my friends. Don't do this wicked thing. 8 Look, I have two daughters who have never slept with a man. Let me bring them out to you, and you can do what you like with them. But don't do anything to these men, for they have come under the protection of my roof."

9 "Get out of our way," they replied. And they said, "This fellow came here as an alien, and now he wants to play the judge! We'll treat you worse than them." They kept bringing pressure on Lot and moved forward to break down the door.

10 But the men inside reached out and pulled Lot back into the house and shut the door. 11 Then they struck the men who were at the door of the house, young and old, with blindness so that they could not find the door.

12 The two men said to Lot, "Do you have anyone else here—sons-in-law, sons or daughters, or anyone else in the city who belongs to you? Get them out of here, 13 because we are going to destroy this place. The outcry to the LORD against its people is so great that he has sent us to destroy it."

14 So Lot went out and spoke to his sons-in-law, who were pledged to marry[a] his daughters. He said, "Hurry and get out of this place, because the LORD is about to destroy the city!" But his sons-in-law thought he was joking.

15 With the coming of dawn, the angels urged Lot, saying, "Hurry! Take your wife and your two daughters who are here, or you will be swept away when the city is punished."

16 When he hesitated, the men grasped his hand and the hands of his wife and of his two daughters and led them safely out of the city, for the LORD was merciful to them. 17 As soon as they had brought them out, one of them said, "Flee for your lives! Don't look back, and don't stop anywhere in the plain! Flee to the mountains or you will be swept away!"

18 But Lot said to them, "No, my lords,[b] please! 19 Your[c] servant has found favor in your[c] eyes, and you[c] have shown great kindness to me in sparing my life. But I can't flee to the mountains; this disaster will overtake me, and I'll die. 20 Look, here is a town near enough to run to, and it is small. Let me flee to it—it is very small, isn't it? Then my life will be spared."

21 He said to him, "Very well, I will grant this request too; I will not overthrow the town you speak of. 22 But flee there quickly, because I

[a] *14* Or *were married to* [b] *18* Or *No, Lord;* or *No, my lord* [c] *19* The Hebrew is singular.

cannot do anything until you reach it." (That
is why the town was called Zoar.[a])
23By the time Lot reached Zoar, the sun
had risen over the land. 24Then the LORD
rained down burning sulfur on Sodom and
Gomorrah—from the LORD out of the heavens. 25Thus he overthrew those cities and
the entire plain, including all those living in
the cities—and also the vegetation in the
land. 26But Lot's wife looked back, and she
became a pillar of salt.
27Early the next morning Abraham got up
and returned to the place where he had
stood before the LORD. 28He looked down
toward Sodom and Gomorrah, toward all the
land of the plain, and he saw dense smoke
rising from the land, like smoke from a furnace.
29So when God destroyed the cities of the
plain, he remembered Abraham, and he
brought Lot out of the catastrophe that overthrew the cities where Lot had lived.

Lot and His Daughters

30Lot and his two daughters left Zoar and
settled in the mountains, for he was afraid to
stay in Zoar. He and his two daughters lived
in a cave. 31One day the older daughter said
to the younger, "Our father is old, and there
is no man around here to lie with us, as is the
custom all over the earth. 32Let's get our father to drink wine and then lie with him and
preserve our family line through our father."
33That night they got their father to drink
wine, and the older daughter went in and lay
with him. He was not aware of it when she lay
down or when she got up.
34The next day the older daughter said to
the younger, "Last night I lay with my father.
Let's get him to drink wine again tonight, and
you go in and lie with him so we can preserve
our family line through our father." 35So they
got their father to drink wine that night also,
and the younger daughter went and lay with
him. Again he was not aware of it when she
lay down or when she got up.
36So both of Lot's daughters became pregnant by their father. 37The older daughter
had a son, and she named him Moab[b]; he is
the father of the Moabites of today. 38The
younger daughter also had a son, and she
named him Ben-Ammi[c]; he is the father of
the Ammonites of today.

Abraham and Abimelech

20 Now Abraham moved on from there
into the region of the Negev and lived
between Kadesh and Shur. For a while he
stayed in Gerar, 2and there Abraham said of
his wife Sarah, "She is my sister." Then
Abimelech king of Gerar sent for Sarah and
took her.
3But God came to Abimelech in a dream
one night and said to him, "You are as good
as dead because of the woman you have
taken; she is a married woman."
4Now Abimelech had not gone near her, so
he said, "Lord, will you destroy an innocent
nation? 5Did he not say to me, 'She is my
sister,' and didn't she also say, 'He is my
brother'? I have done this with a clear conscience and clean hands."
6Then God said to him in the dream, "Yes,
I know you did this with a clear conscience,
and so I have kept you from sinning against
me. That is why I did not let you touch her.
7Now return the man's wife, for he is a
prophet, and he will pray for you and you will
live. But if you do not return her, you may be
sure that you and all yours will die."
8Early the next morning Abimelech summoned all his officials, and when he told
them all that had happened, they were very
much afraid. 9Then Abimelech called Abraham in and said, "What have you done to
us? How have I wronged you that you have
brought such great guilt upon me and my
kingdom? You have done things to me that
should not be done." 10And Abimelech
asked Abraham, "What was your reason for
doing this?"
11Abraham replied, "I said to myself,
'There is surely no fear of God in this place,
and they will kill me because of my wife.'
12Besides, she really is my sister, the daughter of my father though not of my mother; and
she became my wife. 13And when God had
me wander from my father's household, I
said to her, 'This is how you can show your
love to me: Everywhere we go, say of me,
"He is my brother." ' "
14Then Abimelech brought sheep and cattle and male and female slaves and gave
them to Abraham, and he returned Sarah his
wife to him. 15And Abimelech said, "My land
is before you; live wherever you like."
16To Sarah he said, "I am giving your

[a]22 *Zoar* means *small.* [b]37 *Moab* sounds like the Hebrew for *from father.* [c]38 *Ben-Ammi* means *son of my people.*

brother a thousand shekels[a] of silver. This is
to cover the offense against you before all
who are with you; you are completely vindicated."
17Then Abraham prayed to God, and God
healed Abimelech, his wife and his slave
girls so they could have children again, 18for
the LORD had closed up every womb in
Abimelech's household because of Abraham's wife Sarah.

The Birth of Isaac

21 Now the LORD was gracious to Sarah
as he had said, and the LORD did for
Sarah what he had promised. 2Sarah
became pregnant and bore a son to Abraham in his old age, at the very time God had
promised him. 3Abraham gave the name
Isaac[b] to the son Sarah bore him. 4When his
son Isaac was eight days old, Abraham circumcised him, as God commanded him.
5Abraham was a hundred years old when his
son Isaac was born to him.
6Sarah said, "God has brought me laughter, and everyone who hears about this will
laugh with me." 7And she added, "Who
would have said to Abraham that Sarah
would nurse children? Yet I have borne him a
son in his old age."

Hagar and Ishmael Sent Away

8The child grew and was weaned, and on
the day Isaac was weaned Abraham held a
great feast. 9But Sarah saw that the son
whom Hagar the Egyptian had borne to
Abraham was mocking, 10and she said to
Abraham, "Get rid of that slave woman and
her son, for that slave woman's son will never share in the inheritance with my son
Isaac."
11The matter distressed Abraham greatly
because it concerned his son. 12But God
said to him, "Do not be so distressed about
the boy and your maidservant. Listen to
whatever Sarah tells you, because it is
through Isaac that your offspring[c] will be
reckoned. 13I will make the son of the maidservant into a nation also, because he is your
offspring."
14Early the next morning Abraham took
some food and a skin of water and gave
them to Hagar. He set them on her shoulders
and then sent her off with the boy. She went
on her way and wandered in the desert of
Beersheba.
15When the water in the skin was gone,
she put the boy under one of the bushes.
16Then she went off and sat down nearby,
about a bowshot away, for she thought, "I
cannot watch the boy die." And as she sat
there nearby, she[d] began to sob.
17God heard the boy crying, and the angel
of God called to Hagar from heaven and said
to her, "What is the matter, Hagar? Do not be
afraid; God has heard the boy crying as he
lies there. 18Lift the boy up and take him by
the hand, for I will make him into a great
nation."
19Then God opened her eyes and she saw
a well of water. So she went and filled the
skin with water and gave the boy a drink.
20God was with the boy as he grew up. He
lived in the desert and became an archer.
21While he was living in the Desert of Paran,
his mother got a wife for him from Egypt.

The Treaty at Beersheba

22At that time Abimelech and Phicol the
commander of his forces said to Abraham,
"God is with you in everything you do. 23Now
swear to me here before God that you will not
deal falsely with me or my children or my
descendants. Show to me and the country
where you are living as an alien the same
kindness I have shown to you."
24Abraham said, "I swear it."
25Then Abraham complained to Abimelech about a well of water that Abimelech's
servants had seized. 26But Abimelech said,
"I don't know who has done this. You did not
tell me, and I heard about it only today."
27So Abraham brought sheep and cattle
and gave them to Abimelech, and the two
men made a treaty. 28Abraham set apart
seven ewe lambs from the flock, 29and
Abimelech asked Abraham, "What is the
meaning of these seven ewe lambs you
have set apart by themselves?"
30He replied, "Accept these seven lambs
from my hand as a witness that I dug this
well."
31So that place was called Beersheba,[e]
because the two men swore an oath there.
32After the treaty had been made at Beersheba, Abimelech and Phicol the commander of his forces returned to the land of
the Philistines. 33Abraham planted a tama-

[a]*16* That is, about 25 pounds (about 11.5 kilograms) [b]*3* *Isaac* means *he laughs.* [c]*12* Or *seed*
[d]*16* Hebrew; Septuagint *the child* [e]*31* *Beersheba* can mean *well of seven* or *well of the oath.*

risk tree in Beersheba, and there he called upon the name of the LORD, the Eternal God. 34And Abraham stayed in the land of the Philistines for a long time.

Abraham Tested

22 Some time later God tested Abraham. He said to him, "Abraham!"

"Here I am," he replied.

2Then God said, "Take your son, your only son, Isaac, whom you love, and go to the region of Moriah. Sacrifice him there as a burnt offering on one of the mountains I will tell you about."

3Early the next morning Abraham got up and saddled his donkey. He took with him two of his servants and his son Isaac. When he had cut enough wood for the burnt offering, he set out for the place God had told him about. 4On the third day Abraham looked up and saw the place in the distance. 5He said to his servants, "Stay here with the donkey while I and the boy go over there. We will worship and then we will come back to you."

6Abraham took the wood for the burnt offering and placed it on his son Isaac, and he himself carried the fire and the knife. As the two of them went on together, 7Isaac spoke up and said to his father Abraham, "Father?"

"Yes, my son?" Abraham replied.

"The fire and wood are here," Isaac said, "but where is the lamb for the burnt offering?"

8Abraham answered, "God himself will provide the lamb for the burnt offering, my son." And the two of them went on together.

9When they reached the place God had told him about, Abraham built an altar there and arranged the wood on it. He bound his son Isaac and laid him on the altar, on top of the wood. 10Then he reached out his hand and took the knife to slay his son. 11But the angel of the LORD called out to him from heaven, "Abraham! Abraham!"

"Here I am," he replied.

12"Do not lay a hand on the boy," he said. "Do not do anything to him. Now I know that you fear God, because you have not withheld from me your son, your only son."

13Abraham looked up and there in a thicket he saw a ram[a] caught by its horns. He went over and took the ram and sacrificed it as a burnt offering instead of his son. 14So Abraham called that place The LORD Will Provide. And to this day it is said, "On the mountain of the LORD it will be provided."

15The angel of the LORD called to Abraham from heaven a second time 16and said, "I swear by myself, declares the LORD, that because you have done this and have not withheld your son, your only son, 17I will surely bless you and make your descendants as numerous as the stars in the sky and as the sand on the seashore. Your descendants will take possession of the cities of their enemies, 18and through your offspring[b] all nations on earth will be blessed, because you have obeyed me."

19Then Abraham returned to his servants, and they set off together for Beersheba. And Abraham stayed in Beersheba.

Nahor's Sons

20Some time later Abraham was told, "Milcah is also a mother; she has borne sons to your brother Nahor: 21Uz the firstborn, Buz his brother, Kemuel (the father of Aram), 22Kesed, Hazo, Pildash, Jidlaph and Bethuel." 23Bethuel became the father of Rebekah. Milcah bore these eight sons to Abraham's brother Nahor. 24His concubine, whose name was Reumah, also had sons: Tebah, Gaham, Tahash and Maacah.

The Death of Sarah

23 Sarah lived to be a hundred and twenty-seven years old. 2She died at Kiriath Arba (that is, Hebron) in the land of Canaan, and Abraham went to mourn for Sarah and to weep over her.

3Then Abraham rose from beside his dead wife and spoke to the Hittites.[c] He said, 4"I am an alien and a stranger among you. Sell me some property for a burial site here so I can bury my dead."

5The Hittites replied to Abraham, 6"Sir, listen to us. You are a mighty prince among us. Bury your dead in the choicest of our tombs. None of us will refuse you his tomb for burying your dead."

7Then Abraham rose and bowed down before the people of the land, the Hittites. 8He said to them, "If you are willing to let me bury my dead, then listen to me and intercede with Ephron son of Zohar on my behalf 9so he will sell me the cave of Machpelah, which belongs to him and is at the end of his field.

[a] *13* Many manuscripts of the Masoretic Text, Samaritan Pentateuch, Septuagint and Syriac; most manuscripts of the Masoretic Text *a ram behind* ⌊*him*⌋ [b] *18* Or *seed* [c] *3* Or *the sons of Heth;* also in verses 5, 7, 10, 16, 18 and 20

Ask him to sell it to me for the full price as a burial site among you."

10Ephron the Hittite was sitting among his people and he replied to Abraham in the hearing of all the Hittites who had come to the gate of his city. 11"No, my lord," he said. "Listen to me; I give[a] you the field, and I give[a] you the cave that is in it. I give[a] it to you in the presence of my people. Bury your dead."

12Again Abraham bowed down before the people of the land 13and he said to Ephron in their hearing, "Listen to me, if you will. I will pay the price of the field. Accept it from me so I can bury my dead there."

14Ephron answered Abraham, 15"Listen to me, my lord; the land is worth four hundred shekels[b] of silver, but what is that between me and you? Bury your dead."

16Abraham agreed to Ephron's terms and weighed out for him the price he had named in the hearing of the Hittites: four hundred shekels of silver, according to the weight current among the merchants.

17So Ephron's field in Machpelah near Mamre—both the field and the cave in it, and all the trees within the borders of the field—was deeded 18to Abraham as his property in the presence of all the Hittites who had come to the gate of the city. 19Afterward Abraham buried his wife Sarah in the cave in the field of Machpelah near Mamre (which is at Hebron) in the land of Canaan. 20So the field and the cave in it were deeded to Abraham by the Hittites as a burial site.

Isaac and Rebekah

24 Abraham was now old and well advanced in years, and the LORD had blessed him in every way. 2He said to the chief[c] servant in his household, the one in charge of all that he had, "Put your hand under my thigh. 3I want you to swear by the LORD, the God of heaven and the God of earth, that you will not get a wife for my son from the daughters of the Canaanites, among whom I am living, 4but will go to my country and my own relatives and get a wife for my son Isaac."

5The servant asked him, "What if the woman is unwilling to come back with me to this land? Shall I then take your son back to the country you came from?"

6"Make sure that you do not take my son back there," Abraham said. 7"The LORD, the God of heaven, who brought me out of my father's household and my native land and who spoke to me and promised me on oath, saying, 'To your offspring[d] I will give this land'—he will send his angel before you so that you can get a wife for my son from there. 8If the woman is unwilling to come back with you, then you will be released from this oath of mine. Only do not take my son back there." 9So the servant put his hand under the thigh of his master Abraham and swore an oath to him concerning this matter.

10Then the servant took ten of his master's camels and left, taking with him all kinds of good things from his master. He set out for Aram Naharaim[e] and made his way to the town of Nahor. 11He had the camels kneel down near the well outside the town; it was toward evening, the time the women go out to draw water.

12Then he prayed, "O LORD, God of my master Abraham, give me success today, and show kindness to my master Abraham. 13See, I am standing beside this spring, and the daughters of the townspeople are coming out to draw water. 14May it be that when I say to a girl, 'Please let down your jar that I may have a drink,' and she says, 'Drink, and I'll water your camels too'—let her be the one you have chosen for your servant Isaac. By this I will know that you have shown kindness to my master."

15Before he had finished praying, Rebekah came out with her jar on her shoulder. She was the daughter of Bethuel son of Milcah, who was the wife of Abraham's brother Nahor. 16The girl was very beautiful, a virgin; no man had ever lain with her. She went down to the spring, filled her jar and came up again.

17The servant hurried to meet her and said, "Please give me a little water from your jar."

18"Drink, my lord," she said, and quickly lowered the jar to her hands and gave him a drink.

19After she had given him a drink, she said, "I'll draw water for your camels too, until they have finished drinking." 20So she quickly emptied her jar into the trough, ran back to the well to draw more water, and drew enough for all his camels. 21Without saying a word, the man watched her closely to learn

[a] *11* Or *sell* [b] *15* That is, about 10 pounds (about 4.5 kilograms) [c] *2* Or *oldest* [d] *7* Or *seed*
[e] *10* That is, Northwest Mesopotamia

whether or not the LORD had made his journey successful.

22When the camels had finished drinking, the man took out a gold nose ring weighing a beka[a] and two gold bracelets weighing ten shekels.[b] 23Then he asked, "Whose daughter are you? Please tell me, is there room in your father's house for us to spend the night?"

24She answered him, "I am the daughter of Bethuel, the son that Milcah bore to Nahor." 25And she added, "We have plenty of straw and fodder, as well as room for you to spend the night."

26Then the man bowed down and worshiped the LORD, 27saying, "Praise be to the LORD, the God of my master Abraham, who has not abandoned his kindness and faithfulness to my master. As for me, the LORD has led me on the journey to the house of my master's relatives."

28The girl ran and told her mother's household about these things. 29Now Rebekah had a brother named Laban, and he hurried out to the man at the spring. 30As soon as he had seen the nose ring, and the bracelets on his sister's arms, and had heard Rebekah tell what the man said to her, he went out to the man and found him standing by the camels near the spring. 31"Come, you who are blessed by the LORD," he said. "Why are you standing out here? I have prepared the house and a place for the camels."

32So the man went to the house, and the camels were unloaded. Straw and fodder were brought for the camels, and water for him and his men to wash their feet. 33Then food was set before him, but he said, "I will not eat until I have told you what I have to say."

"Then tell us," ⌊Laban⌋ said.

34So he said, "I am Abraham's servant. 35The LORD has blessed my master abundantly, and he has become wealthy. He has given him sheep and cattle, silver and gold, menservants and maidservants, and camels and donkeys. 36My master's wife Sarah has borne him a son in her[c] old age, and he has given him everything he owns. 37And my master made me swear an oath, and said, 'You must not get a wife for my son from the daughters of the Canaanites, in whose land I live, 38but go to my father's family and to my own clan, and get a wife for my son.'

39"Then I asked my master, 'What if the woman will not come back with me?'

40"He replied, 'The LORD, before whom I have walked, will send his angel with you and make your journey a success, so that you can get a wife for my son from my own clan and from my father's family. 41Then, when you go to my clan, you will be released from my oath even if they refuse to give her to you—you will be released from my oath.'

42"When I came to the spring today, I said, 'O LORD, God of my master Abraham, if you will, please grant success to the journey on which I have come. 43See, I am standing beside this spring; if a maiden comes out to draw water and I say to her, "Please let me drink a little water from your jar," 44and if she says to me, "Drink, and I'll draw water for your camels too," let her be the one the LORD has chosen for my master's son.'

45"Before I finished praying in my heart, Rebekah came out, with her jar on her shoulder. She went down to the spring and drew water, and I said to her, 'Please give me a drink.'

46"She quickly lowered her jar from her shoulder and said, 'Drink, and I'll water your camels too.' So I drank, and she watered the camels also.

47"I asked her, 'Whose daughter are you?'

"She said, 'The daughter of Bethuel son of Nahor, whom Milcah bore to him.'

"Then I put the ring in her nose and the bracelets on her arms, 48and I bowed down and worshiped the LORD. I praised the LORD, the God of my master Abraham, who had led me on the right road to get the granddaughter of my master's brother for his son. 49Now if you will show kindness and faithfulness to my master, tell me; and if not, tell me, so I may know which way to turn."

50Laban and Bethuel answered, "This is from the LORD; we can say nothing to you one way or the other. 51Here is Rebekah; take her and go, and let her become the wife of your master's son, as the LORD has directed."

52When Abraham's servant heard what they said, he bowed down to the ground before the LORD. 53Then the servant brought out gold and silver jewelry and articles of clothing and gave them to Rebekah; he also gave costly gifts to her brother and to her mother. 54Then he and the men who were with him ate and drank and spent the night there.

[a] *22* That is, about 1/5 ounce (about 5.5 grams) [b] *22* That is, about 4 ounces (about 110 grams) [c] *36* Or *his*

When they got up the next morning, he said, "Send me on my way to my master."

55But her brother and her mother replied, "Let the girl remain with us ten days or so; then you[a] may go."

56But he said to them, "Do not detain me, now that the LORD has granted success to my journey. Send me on my way so I may go to my master."

57Then they said, "Let's call the girl and ask her about it." 58So they called Rebekah and asked her, "Will you go with this man?"

"I will go," she said.

59So they sent their sister Rebekah on her way, along with her nurse and Abraham's servant and his men. 60And they blessed Rebekah and said to her,

"Our sister, may you increase
to thousands upon thousands;
may your offspring possess
the gates of their enemies."

61Then Rebekah and her maids got ready and mounted their camels and went back with the man. So the servant took Rebekah and left.

62Now Isaac had come from Beer Lahai Roi, for he was living in the Negev. 63He went out to the field one evening to meditate,[b] and as he looked up, he saw camels approaching. 64Rebekah also looked up and saw Isaac. She got down from her camel 65and asked the servant, "Who is that man in the field coming to meet us?"

"He is my master," the servant answered. So she took her veil and covered herself.

66Then the servant told Isaac all he had done. 67Isaac brought her into the tent of his mother Sarah, and he married Rebekah. So she became his wife, and he loved her; and Isaac was comforted after his mother's death.

The Death of Abraham

25 Abraham took[c] another wife, whose name was Keturah. 2She bore him Zimran, Jokshan, Medan, Midian, Ishbak and Shuah. 3Jokshan was the father of Sheba and Dedan; the descendants of Dedan were the Asshurites, the Letushites and the Leummites. 4The sons of Midian were Ephah, Epher, Hanoch, Abida and Eldaah. All these were descendants of Keturah.

5Abraham left everything he owned to Isaac. 6But while he was still living, he gave gifts to the sons of his concubines and sent them away from his son Isaac to the land of the east.

7Altogether, Abraham lived a hundred and seventy-five years. 8Then Abraham breathed his last and died at a good old age, an old man and full of years; and he was gathered to his people. 9His sons Isaac and Ishmael buried him in the cave of Machpelah near Mamre, in the field of Ephron son of Zohar the Hittite, 10the field Abraham had bought from the Hittites.[d] There Abraham was buried with his wife Sarah. 11After Abraham's death, God blessed his son Isaac, who then lived near Beer Lahai Roi.

Ishmael's Sons

12This is the account of Abraham's son Ishmael, whom Sarah's maidservant, Hagar the Egyptian, bore to Abraham.

13These are the names of the sons of Ishmael, listed in the order of their birth: Nebaioth the firstborn of Ishmael, Kedar, Adbeel, Mibsam, 14Mishma, Dumah, Massa, 15Hadad, Tema, Jetur, Naphish and Kedemah. 16These were the sons of Ishmael, and these are the names of the twelve tribal rulers according to their settlements and camps. 17Altogether, Ishmael lived a hundred and thirty-seven years. He breathed his last and died, and he was gathered to his people. 18His descendants settled in the area from Havilah to Shur, near the border of Egypt, as you go toward Asshur. And they lived in hostility toward[e] all their brothers.

Jacob and Esau

19This is the account of Abraham's son Isaac.

Abraham became the father of Isaac, 20and Isaac was forty years old when he married Rebekah daughter of Bethuel the Aramean from Paddan Aram[f] and sister of Laban the Aramean.

21Isaac prayed to the LORD on behalf of his wife, because she was barren. The LORD answered his prayer, and his wife Rebekah became pregnant. 22The babies jostled each other within her, and she said, "Why is this happening to me?" So she went to inquire of the LORD.

23The LORD said to her,

[a] 55 Or *she* [b] 63 The meaning of the Hebrew for this word is uncertain. [c] 1 Or *had taken* [d] 10 Or *the sons of Heth* [e] 18 Or *lived to the east of* [f] 20 That is, Northwest Mesopotamia

"Two nations are in your womb,
and two peoples from within you will be separated;
one people will be stronger than the other,
and the older will serve the younger."

24When the time came for her to give birth, there were twin boys in her womb. 25The first to come out was red, and his whole body was like a hairy garment; so they named him Esau.[a] 26After this, his brother came out, with his hand grasping Esau's heel; so he was named Jacob.[b] Isaac was sixty years old when Rebekah gave birth to them.

27The boys grew up, and Esau became a skillful hunter, a man of the open country, while Jacob was a quiet man, staying among the tents. 28Isaac, who had a taste for wild game, loved Esau, but Rebekah loved Jacob.

29Once when Jacob was cooking some stew, Esau came in from the open country, famished. 30He said to Jacob, "Quick, let me have some of that red stew! I'm famished!" (That is why he was also called Edom.[c])

31Jacob replied, "First sell me your birthright."

32"Look, I am about to die," Esau said. "What good is the birthright to me?"

33But Jacob said, "Swear to me first." So he swore an oath to him, selling his birthright to Jacob.

34Then Jacob gave Esau some bread and some lentil stew. He ate and drank, and then got up and left.

So Esau despised his birthright.

Isaac and Abimelech

26 Now there was a famine in the land—besides the earlier famine of Abraham's time—and Isaac went to Abimelech king of the Philistines in Gerar. 2The LORD appeared to Isaac and said, "Do not go down to Egypt; live in the land where I tell you to live. 3Stay in this land for a while, and I will be with you and will bless you. For to you and your descendants I will give all these lands and will confirm the oath I swore to your father Abraham. 4I will make your descendants as numerous as the stars in the sky and will give them all these lands, and through your offspring[d] all nations on earth will be blessed, 5because Abraham obeyed me and kept my requirements, my commands, my decrees and my laws." 6So Isaac stayed in Gerar.

7When the men of that place asked him about his wife, he said, "She is my sister," because he was afraid to say, "She is my wife." He thought, "The men of this place might kill me on account of Rebekah, because she is beautiful."

8When Isaac had been there a long time, Abimelech king of the Philistines looked down from a window and saw Isaac caressing his wife Rebekah. 9So Abimelech summoned Isaac and said, "She is really your wife! Why did you say, 'She is my sister'?"

Isaac answered him, "Because I thought I might lose my life on account of her."

10Then Abimelech said, "What is this you have done to us? One of the men might well have slept with your wife, and you would have brought guilt upon us."

11So Abimelech gave orders to all the people: "Anyone who molests this man or his wife shall surely be put to death."

12Isaac planted crops in that land and the same year reaped a hundredfold, because the LORD blessed him. 13The man became rich, and his wealth continued to grow until he became very wealthy. 14He had so many flocks and herds and servants that the Philistines envied him. 15So all the wells that his father's servants had dug in the time of his father Abraham, the Philistines stopped up, filling them with earth.

16Then Abimelech said to Isaac, "Move away from us; you have become too powerful for us."

17So Isaac moved away from there and encamped in the Valley of Gerar and settled there. 18Isaac reopened the wells that had been dug in the time of his father Abraham, which the Philistines had stopped up after Abraham died, and he gave them the same names his father had given them.

19Isaac's servants dug in the valley and discovered a well of fresh water there. 20But the herdsmen of Gerar quarreled with Isaac's herdsmen and said, "The water is ours!" So he named the well Esek,[e] because they disputed with him. 21Then they dug another well, but they quarreled over that one also; so he named it Sitnah.[f] 22He moved on from there and dug another well, and no one

[a]25 *Esau* may mean *hairy*; he was also called Edom, which means *red*. [b]26 *Jacob* means *he grasps the heel* (figuratively, *he deceives*). [c]30 *Edom* means *red*. [d]4 Or *seed* [e]20 *Esek* means *dispute*. [f]21 *Sitnah* means *opposition*.

quarreled over it. He named it Rehoboth,[a]
saying, "Now the LORD has given us room
and we will flourish in the land."
23From there he went up to Beersheba.
24That night the LORD appeared to him and
said, "I am the God of your father Abraham.
Do not be afraid, for I am with you; I will bless
you and will increase the number of your
descendants for the sake of my servant
Abraham."
25Isaac built an altar there and called on
the name of the LORD. There he pitched his
tent, and there his servants dug a well.
26Meanwhile, Abimelech had come to him
from Gerar, with Ahuzzath his personal adviser and Phicol the commander of his
forces. 27Isaac asked them, "Why have you
come to me, since you were hostile to me
and sent me away?"
28They answered, "We saw clearly that the
LORD was with you; so we said, 'There ought
to be a sworn agreement between
us'—between us and you. Let us make a
treaty with you 29that you will do us no harm,
just as we did not molest you but always
treated you well and sent you away in peace.
And now you are blessed by the LORD."
30Isaac then made a feast for them, and
they ate and drank. 31Early the next morning
the men swore an oath to each other. Then
Isaac sent them on their way, and they left
him in peace.
32That day Isaac's servants came and told
him about the well they had dug. They said,
"We've found water!" 33He called it Shibah,[b]
and to this day the name of the town has
been Beersheba.[c]
34When Esau was forty years old, he married Judith daughter of Beeri the Hittite, and
also Basemath daughter of Elon the Hittite.
35They were a source of grief to Isaac and
Rebekah.

Jacob Gets Isaac's Blessing

27 When Isaac was old and his eyes
were so weak that he could no longer
see, he called for Esau his older son and said
to him, "My son."
"Here I am," he answered.
2Isaac said, "I am now an old man and
don't know the day of my death. 3Now then,
get your weapons—your quiver and bow—
and go out to the open country to hunt some
wild game for me. 4Prepare me the kind of
tasty food I like and bring it to me to eat, so
that I may give you my blessing before I die."
5Now Rebekah was listening as Isaac
spoke to his son Esau. When Esau left for
the open country to hunt game and bring it
back, 6Rebekah said to her son Jacob,
"Look, I overheard your father say to your
brother Esau, 7'Bring me some game and
prepare me some tasty food to eat, so that I
may give you my blessing in the presence of
the LORD before I die.' 8Now, my son, listen
carefully and do what I tell you: 9Go out to the
flock and bring me two choice young goats,
so I can prepare some tasty food for your
father, just the way he likes it. 10Then take it
to your father to eat, so that he may give you
his blessing before he dies."
11Jacob said to Rebekah his mother, "But
my brother Esau is a hairy man, and I'm a
man with smooth skin. 12What if my father
touches me? I would appear to be tricking
him and would bring down a curse on myself
rather than a blessing."
13His mother said to him, "My son, let the
curse fall on me. Just do what I say; go and
get them for me."
14So he went and got them and brought
them to his mother, and she prepared some
tasty food, just the way his father liked it.
15Then Rebekah took the best clothes of
Esau her older son, which she had in the
house, and put them on her younger son
Jacob. 16She also covered his hands and the
smooth part of his neck with the goatskins.
17Then she handed to her son Jacob the
tasty food and the bread she had made.
18He went to his father and said, "My father."
"Yes, my son," he answered. "Who is it?"
19Jacob said to his father, "I am Esau your
firstborn. I have done as you told me. Please
sit up and eat some of my game so that you
may give me your blessing."
20Isaac asked his son, "How did you find it
so quickly, my son?"
"The LORD your God gave me success," he
replied.
21Then Isaac said to Jacob, "Come near
so I can touch you, my son, to know whether
you really are my son Esau or not."
22Jacob went close to his father Isaac, who
touched him and said, "The voice is the
voice of Jacob, but the hands are the hands
of Esau." 23He did not recognize him, for his

[a]22 *Rehoboth* means *room.* [b]33 *Shibah* can mean *oath* or *seven.* [c]33 *Beersheba* can mean *well of the oath* or *well of seven.*

hands were hairy like those of his brother
Esau; so he blessed him. 24"Are you really
my son Esau?" he asked.
"I am," he replied.
25Then he said, "My son, bring me some of
your game to eat, so that I may give you my
blessing."
Jacob brought it to him and he ate; and he
brought some wine and he drank. 26Then his
father Isaac said to him, "Come here, my
son, and kiss me."
27So he went to him and kissed him. When
Isaac caught the smell of his clothes, he
blessed him and said,

"Ah, the smell of my son
is like the smell of a field
that the LORD has blessed.
28May God give you of heaven's dew
and of earth's richness—
an abundance of grain and new wine.
29May nations serve you
and peoples bow down to you.
Be lord over your brothers,
and may the sons of your mother bow
down to you.
May those who curse you be cursed
and those who bless you be blessed."

30After Isaac finished blessing him and
Jacob had scarcely left his father's presence, his brother Esau came in from hunting.
31He too prepared some tasty food and
brought it to his father. Then he said to him,
"My father, sit up and eat some of my game,
so that you may give me your blessing."
32His father Isaac asked him, "Who are
you?"
"I am your son," he answered, "your firstborn, Esau."
33Isaac trembled violently and said, "Who
was it, then, that hunted game and brought it
to me? I ate it just before you came and I
blessed him—and indeed he will be
blessed!"
34When Esau heard his father's words, he
burst out with a loud and bitter cry and said to
his father, "Bless me—me too, my father!"
35But he said, "Your brother came deceitfully and took your blessing."
36Esau said, "Isn't he rightly named
Jacob[a]? He has deceived me these two
times: He took my birthright, and now he's
taken my blessing!" Then he asked,
"Haven't you reserved any blessing for me?"
37Isaac answered Esau, "I have made him
lord over you and have made all his relatives
his servants, and I have sustained him with
grain and new wine. So what can I possibly
do for you, my son?"
38Esau said to his father, "Do you have
only one blessing, my father? Bless me too,
my father!" Then Esau wept aloud.
39His father Isaac answered him,

"Your dwelling will be
away from the earth's richness,
away from the dew of heaven above.
40You will live by the sword
and you will serve your brother.
But when you grow restless,
you will throw his yoke
from off your neck."

Jacob Flees to Laban

41Esau held a grudge against Jacob because of the blessing his father had given
him. He said to himself, "The days of mourning for my father are near; then I will kill my
brother Jacob."
42When Rebekah was told what her older
son Esau had said, she sent for her younger
son Jacob and said to him, "Your brother
Esau is consoling himself with the thought of
killing you. 43Now then, my son, do what I
say: Flee at once to my brother Laban in
Haran. 44Stay with him for a while until your
brother's fury subsides. 45When your brother
is no longer angry with you and forgets what
you did to him, I'll send word for you to come
back from there. Why should I lose both of
you in one day?"
46Then Rebekah said to Isaac, "I'm dis-
gusted with living because of these Hittite
women. If Jacob takes a wife from among
the women of this land, from Hittite women
like these, my life will not be worth living."

28 So Isaac called for Jacob and
blessed[b] him and commanded him:
"Do not marry a Canaanite woman. 2Go at
once to Paddan Aram,[c] to the house of your
mother's father Bethuel. Take a wife for
yourself there, from among the daughters of
Laban, your mother's brother. 3May God Almighty[d] bless you and make you fruitful and
increase your numbers until you become a
community of peoples. 4May he give you and
your descendants the blessing given to
Abraham, so that you may take possession

[a]36 *Jacob* means *he grasps the heel* (figuratively, *he deceives*). [b]1 Or *greeted* [c]2 That is, Northwest Mesopotamia; also in verses 5, 6 and 7 [d]3 Hebrew *El-Shaddai*

of the land where you now live as an alien,
the land God gave to Abraham." 5Then Isaac
sent Jacob on his way, and he went to Paddan Aram, to Laban son of Bethuel the Aramean, the brother of Rebekah, who was the
mother of Jacob and Esau.

6Now Esau learned that Isaac had blessed
Jacob and had sent him to Paddan Aram to
take a wife from there, and that when he
blessed him he commanded him, "Do not
marry a Canaanite woman," 7and that Jacob
had obeyed his father and mother and had
gone to Paddan Aram. 8Esau then realized
how displeasing the Canaanite women were
to his father Isaac; 9so he went to Ishmael
and married Mahalath, the sister of Nebaioth
and daughter of Ishmael son of Abraham, in
addition to the wives he already had.

Jacob's Dream at Bethel

10Jacob left Beersheba and set out for Haran. 11When he reached a certain place, he
stopped for the night because the sun had
set. Taking one of the stones there, he put it
under his head and lay down to sleep. 12He
had a dream in which he saw a stairway[a]
resting on the earth, with its top reaching to
heaven, and the angels of God were ascending and descending on it. 13There above it[b]
stood the LORD, and he said: "I am the LORD,
the God of your father Abraham and the God
of Isaac. I will give you and your descendants the land on which you are lying. 14Your
descendants will be like the dust of the earth,
and you will spread out to the west and to the
east, to the north and to the south. All peoples on earth will be blessed through you and
your offspring. 15I am with you and will watch
over you wherever you go, and I will bring
you back to this land. I will not leave you until
I have done what I have promised you."

16When Jacob awoke from his sleep, he
thought, "Surely the LORD is in this place, and
I was not aware of it." 17He was afraid and
said, "How awesome is this place! This is
none other than the house of God; this is the
gate of heaven."

18Early the next morning Jacob took the
stone he had placed under his head and set
it up as a pillar and poured oil on top of it.
19He called that place Bethel,[c] though the
city used to be called Luz.

20Then Jacob made a vow, saying, "If God
will be with me and will watch over me on this
journey I am taking and will give me food to
eat and clothes to wear 21so that I return
safely to my father's house, then the LORD[d]
will be my God 22and[e] this stone that I have
set up as a pillar will be God's house, and of
all that you give me I will give you a tenth."

Jacob Arrives in Paddan Aram

29 Then Jacob continued on his journey
and came to the land of the eastern
peoples. 2There he saw a well in the field,
with three flocks of sheep lying near it because the flocks were watered from that well.
The stone over the mouth of the well was
large. 3When all the flocks were gathered
there, the shepherds would roll the stone
away from the well's mouth and water the
sheep. Then they would return the stone to
its place over the mouth of the well.

4Jacob asked the shepherds, "My brothers, where are you from?"

"We're from Haran," they replied.

5He said to them, "Do you know Laban,
Nahor's grandson?"

"Yes, we know him," they answered.

6Then Jacob asked them, "Is he well?"

"Yes, he is," they said, "and here comes
his daughter Rachel with the sheep."

7"Look," he said, "the sun is still high; it is
not time for the flocks to be gathered. Water
the sheep and take them back to pasture."

8"We can't," they replied, "until all the
flocks are gathered and the stone has been
rolled away from the mouth of the well. Then
we will water the sheep."

9While he was still talking with them, Rachel came with her father's sheep, for she
was a shepherdess. 10When Jacob saw Rachel daughter of Laban, his mother's brother,
and Laban's sheep, he went over and rolled
the stone away from the mouth of the well
and watered his uncle's sheep. 11Then
Jacob kissed Rachel and began to weep
aloud. 12He had told Rachel that he was a
relative of her father and a son of Rebekah.
So she ran and told her father.

13As soon as Laban heard the news about
Jacob, his sister's son, he hurried to meet
him. He embraced him and kissed him and
brought him to his home, and there Jacob
told him all these things. 14Then Laban said
to him, "You are my own flesh and blood."

[a]12 Or *ladder* [b]13 Or *There beside him* [c]19 *Bethel* means *house of God.* [d]20,21 Or *Since God . . . father's house, the LORD* [e]21,22 Or *house, and the LORD will be my God,* [22]*then*

Jacob Marries Leah and Rachel

After Jacob had stayed with him for a whole month, 15 Laban said to him, "Just because you are a relative of mine, should you work for me for nothing? Tell me what your wages should be."

16 Now Laban had two daughters; the name of the older was Leah, and the name of the younger was Rachel. 17 Leah had weak[a] eyes, but Rachel was lovely in form, and beautiful. 18 Jacob was in love with Rachel and said, "I'll work for you seven years in return for your younger daughter Rachel."

19 Laban said, "It's better that I give her to you than to some other man. Stay here with me." 20 So Jacob served seven years to get Rachel, but they seemed like only a few days to him because of his love for her.

21 Then Jacob said to Laban, "Give me my wife. My time is completed, and I want to lie with her."

22 So Laban brought together all the people of the place and gave a feast. 23 But when evening came, he took his daughter Leah and gave her to Jacob, and Jacob lay with her. 24 And Laban gave his servant girl Zilpah to his daughter as her maidservant.

25 When morning came, there was Leah! So Jacob said to Laban, "What is this you have done to me? I served you for Rachel, didn't I? Why have you deceived me?"

26 Laban replied, "It is not our custom here to give the younger daughter in marriage before the older one. 27 Finish this daughter's bridal week; then we will give you the younger one also, in return for another seven years of work."

28 And Jacob did so. He finished the week with Leah, and then Laban gave him his daughter Rachel to be his wife. 29 Laban gave his servant girl Bilhah to his daughter Rachel as her maidservant. 30 Jacob lay with Rachel also, and he loved Rachel more than Leah. And he worked for Laban another seven years.

Jacob's Children

31 When the LORD saw that Leah was not loved, he opened her womb, but Rachel was barren. 32 Leah became pregnant and gave birth to a son. She named him Reuben,[b] for she said, "It is because the LORD has seen my misery. Surely my husband will love me now."

33 She conceived again, and when she gave birth to a son she said, "Because the LORD heard that I am not loved, he gave me this one too." So she named him Simeon.[c]

34 Again she conceived, and when she gave birth to a son she said, "Now at last my husband will become attached to me, because I have borne him three sons." So he was named Levi.[d]

35 She conceived again, and when she gave birth to a son she said, "This time I will praise the LORD." So she named him Judah.[e] Then she stopped having children.

30 When Rachel saw that she was not bearing Jacob any children, she became jealous of her sister. So she said to Jacob, "Give me children, or I'll die!"

2 Jacob became angry with her and said, "Am I in the place of God, who has kept you from having children?"

3 Then she said, "Here is Bilhah, my maidservant. Sleep with her so that she can bear children for me and that through her I too can build a family."

4 So she gave him her servant Bilhah as a wife. Jacob slept with her, 5 and she became pregnant and bore him a son. 6 Then Rachel said, "God has vindicated me; he has listened to my plea and given me a son." Because of this she named him Dan.[f]

7 Rachel's servant Bilhah conceived again and bore Jacob a second son. 8 Then Rachel said, "I have had a great struggle with my sister, and I have won." So she named him Naphtali.[g]

9 When Leah saw that she had stopped having children, she took her maidservant Zilpah and gave her to Jacob as a wife. 10 Leah's servant Zilpah bore Jacob a son. 11 Then Leah said, "What good fortune!"[h] So she named him Gad.[i]

12 Leah's servant Zilpah bore Jacob a second son. 13 Then Leah said, "How happy I am! The women will call me happy." So she named him Asher.[j]

14 During wheat harvest, Reuben went out into the fields and found some mandrake plants, which he brought to his mother Leah. Rachel said to Leah, "Please give me some of your son's mandrakes."

[a] 17 Or *delicate* [b] 32 *Reuben* sounds like the Hebrew for *he has seen my misery;* the name means *see, a son.* [c] 33 *Simeon* probably means *one who hears.* [d] 34 *Levi* sounds like and may be derived from the Hebrew for *attached.* [e] 35 *Judah* sounds like and may be derived from the Hebrew for *praise.* [f] 6 *Dan* here means *he has vindicated.* [g] 8 *Naphtali* means *my struggle.* [h] 11 Or *"A troop is coming!"* [i] 11 *Gad* can mean *good fortune* or *a troop.* [j] 13 *Asher* means *happy.*

15But she said to her, "Wasn't it enough
that you took away my husband? Will you
take my son's mandrakes too?"

"Very well," Rachel said, "he can sleep
with you tonight in return for your son's mandrakes."

16So when Jacob came in from the fields
that evening, Leah went out to meet him.
"You must sleep with me," she said. "I have
hired you with my son's mandrakes." So he
slept with her that night.

17God listened to Leah, and she became
pregnant and bore Jacob a fifth son. 18Then
Leah said, "God has rewarded me for giving
my maidservant to my husband." So she
named him Issachar.[a]

19Leah conceived again and bore Jacob a
sixth son. 20Then Leah said, "God has
presented me with a precious gift. This time
my husband will treat me with honor, because I have borne him six sons." So she
named him Zebulun.[b]

21Some time later she gave birth to a
daughter and named her Dinah.

22Then God remembered Rachel; he listened to her and opened her womb. 23She
became pregnant and gave birth to a son
and said, "God has taken away my disgrace." 24She named him Joseph,[c] and said,
"May the LORD add to me another son."

Jacob's Flocks Increase

25After Rachel gave birth to Joseph, Jacob
said to Laban, "Send me on my way so I can
go back to my own homeland. 26Give me my
wives and children, for whom I have served
you, and I will be on my way. You know how
much work I've done for you."

27But Laban said to him, "If I have found
favor in your eyes, please stay. I have
learned by divination that[d] the LORD has
blessed me because of you." 28He added,
"Name your wages, and I will pay them."

29Jacob said to him, "You know how I have
worked for you and how your livestock has
fared under my care. 30The little you had
before I came has increased greatly, and the
LORD has blessed you wherever I have been.
But now, when may I do something for my
own household?"

31"What shall I give you?" he asked.

"Don't give me anything," Jacob replied.
"But if you will do this one thing for me, I will
go on tending your flocks and watching over
them: 32Let me go through all your flocks
today and remove from them every speckled
or spotted sheep, every dark-colored lamb
and every spotted or speckled goat. They
will be my wages. 33And my honesty will testify for me in the future, whenever you check
on the wages you have paid me. Any goat in
my possession that is not speckled or spotted, or any lamb that is not dark-colored, will
be considered stolen."

34"Agreed," said Laban. "Let it be as you
have said." 35That same day he removed all
the male goats that were streaked or spotted, and all the speckled or spotted female
goats (all that had white on them) and all the
dark-colored lambs, and he placed them in
the care of his sons. 36Then he put a three-
day journey between himself and Jacob,
while Jacob continued to tend the rest of
Laban's flocks.

37Jacob, however, took fresh-cut branches
from poplar, almond and plane trees and
made white stripes on them by peeling the
bark and exposing the white inner wood of
the branches. 38Then he placed the peeled
branches in all the watering troughs, so that
they would be directly in front of the flocks
when they came to drink. When the flocks
were in heat and came to drink, 39they mated
in front of the branches. And they bore young
that were streaked or speckled or spotted.
40Jacob set apart the young of the flock by
themselves, but made the rest face the
streaked and dark-colored animals that belonged to Laban. Thus he made separate
flocks for himself and did not put them with
Laban's animals. 41Whenever the stronger
females were in heat, Jacob would place the
branches in the troughs in front of the animals so they would mate near the branches,
42but if the animals were weak, he would not
place them there. So the weak animals went
to Laban and the strong ones to Jacob. 43In
this way the man grew exceedingly prosperous and came to own large flocks, and maidservants and menservants, and camels and
donkeys.

Jacob Flees From Laban

31 1Jacob heard that Laban's sons were
saying, "Jacob has taken everything
our father owned and has gained all this
wealth from what belonged to our father."

[a]18 *Issachar* sounds like the Hebrew for *reward.* [b]20 *Zebulun* probably means *honor.* [c]24 *Joseph* means *may he add.* [d]27 Or possibly *have become rich and*

2And Jacob noticed that Laban's attitude
toward him was not what it had been.
3Then the LORD said to Jacob, "Go back to
the land of your fathers and to your relatives,
and I will be with you."
4So Jacob sent word to Rachel and Leah
to come out to the fields where his flocks
were. 5He said to them, "I see that your father's attitude toward me is not what it was
before, but the God of my father has been
with me. 6You know that I've worked for your
father with all my strength, 7yet your father
has cheated me by changing my wages ten
times. However, God has not allowed him to
harm me. 8If he said, 'The speckled ones will
be your wages,' then all the flocks gave birth
to speckled young; and if he said, 'The
streaked ones will be your wages,' then all
the flocks bore streaked young. 9So God has
taken away your father's livestock and has
given them to me.
10"In breeding season I once had a dream
in which I looked up and saw that the male
goats mating with the flock were streaked,
speckled or spotted. 11The angel of God said
to me in the dream, 'Jacob.' I answered,
'Here I am.' 12And he said, 'Look up and see
that all the male goats mating with the flock
are streaked, speckled or spotted, for I have
seen all that Laban has been doing to you. 13I
am the God of Bethel, where you anointed a
pillar and where you made a vow to me. Now
leave this land at once and go back to your
native land.' "
14Then Rachel and Leah replied, "Do we
still have any share in the inheritance of our
father's estate? 15Does he not regard us as
foreigners? Not only has he sold us, but he
has used up what was paid for us. 16Surely
all the wealth that God took away from our
father belongs to us and our children. So do
whatever God has told you."
17Then Jacob put his children and his
wives on camels, 18and he drove all his livestock ahead of him, along with all the goods
he had accumulated in Paddan Aram,[a] to go
to his father Isaac in the land of Canaan.
19When Laban had gone to shear his
sheep, Rachel stole her father's household
gods. 20Moreover, Jacob deceived Laban
the Aramean by not telling him he was running away. 21So he fled with all he had, and
crossing the River,[b] he headed for the hill
country of Gilead.

Laban Pursues Jacob

22On the third day Laban was told that
Jacob had fled. 23Taking his relatives with
him, he pursued Jacob for seven days and
caught up with him in the hill country of Gilead. 24Then God came to Laban the Aramean in a dream at night and said to him,
"Be careful not to say anything to Jacob,
either good or bad."
25Jacob had pitched his tent in the hill
country of Gilead when Laban overtook him,
and Laban and his relatives camped there
too. 26Then Laban said to Jacob, "What have
you done? You've deceived me, and you've
carried off my daughters like captives in war.
27Why did you run off secretly and deceive
me? Why didn't you tell me, so I could send
you away with joy and singing to the music of
tambourines and harps? 28You didn't even
let me kiss my grandchildren and my daughters good-by. You have done a foolish thing.
29I have the power to harm you; but last night
the God of your father said to me, 'Be careful
not to say anything to Jacob, either good or
bad.' 30Now you have gone off because you
longed to return to your father's house. But
why did you steal my gods?"
31Jacob answered Laban, "I was afraid,
because I thought you would take your
daughters away from me by force. 32But if
you find anyone who has your gods, he shall
not live. In the presence of our relatives, see
for yourself whether there is anything of
yours here with me; and if so, take it." Now
Jacob did not know that Rachel had stolen
the gods.
33So Laban went into Jacob's tent and into
Leah's tent and into the tent of the two maidservants, but he found nothing. After he
came out of Leah's tent, he entered Rachel's
tent. 34Now Rachel had taken the household
gods and put them inside her camel's saddle
and was sitting on them. Laban searched
through everything in the tent but found nothing.
35Rachel said to her father, "Don't be angry, my lord, that I cannot stand up in your
presence; I'm having my period." So he
searched but could not find the household
gods.
36Jacob was angry and took Laban to task.
"What is my crime?" he asked Laban. "What
sin have I committed that you hunt me

[a] *18* That is, Northwest Mesopotamia [b] *21* That is, the Euphrates

down? 37Now that you have searched through all my goods, what have you found that belongs to your household? Put it here in front of your relatives and mine, and let them judge between the two of us.

38"I have been with you for twenty years now. Your sheep and goats have not miscarried, nor have I eaten rams from your flocks. 39I did not bring you animals torn by wild beasts; I bore the loss myself. And you demanded payment from me for whatever was stolen by day or night. 40This was my situation: The heat consumed me in the daytime and the cold at night, and sleep fled from my eyes. 41It was like this for the twenty years I was in your household. I worked for you fourteen years for your two daughters and six years for your flocks, and you changed my wages ten times. 42If the God of my father, the God of Abraham and the Fear of Isaac, had not been with me, you would surely have sent me away empty-handed. But God has seen my hardship and the toil of my hands, and last night he rebuked you."

43Laban answered Jacob, "The women are my daughters, the children are my children, and the flocks are my flocks. All you see is mine. Yet what can I do today about these daughters of mine, or about the children they have borne? 44Come now, let's make a covenant, you and I, and let it serve as a witness between us."

45So Jacob took a stone and set it up as a pillar. 46He said to his relatives, "Gather some stones." So they took stones and piled them in a heap, and they ate there by the heap. 47Laban called it Jegar Sahadutha,[a] and Jacob called it Galeed.[b]

48Laban said, "This heap is a witness between you and me today." That is why it was called Galeed. 49It was also called Mizpah,[c] because he said, "May the LORD keep watch between you and me when we are away from each other. 50If you mistreat my daughters or if you take any wives besides my daughters, even though no one is with us, remember that God is a witness between you and me."

51Laban also said to Jacob, "Here is this heap, and here is this pillar I have set up between you and me. 52This heap is a witness, and this pillar is a witness, that I will not go past this heap to your side to harm you and that you will not go past this heap and pillar to my side to harm me. 53May the God of Abraham and the God of Nahor, the God of their father, judge between us."

So Jacob took an oath in the name of the Fear of his father Isaac. 54He offered a sacrifice there in the hill country and invited his relatives to a meal. After they had eaten, they spent the night there.

55Early the next morning Laban kissed his grandchildren and his daughters and blessed them. Then he left and returned home.

Jacob Prepares to Meet Esau

32 Jacob also went on his way, and the angels of God met him. 2When Jacob saw them, he said, "This is the camp of God!" So he named that place Mahanaim.[d]

3Jacob sent messengers ahead of him to his brother Esau in the land of Seir, the country of Edom. 4He instructed them: "This is what you are to say to my master Esau: 'Your servant Jacob says, I have been staying with Laban and have remained there till now. 5I have cattle and donkeys, sheep and goats, menservants and maidservants. Now I am sending this message to my lord, that I may find favor in your eyes.' "

6When the messengers returned to Jacob, they said, "We went to your brother Esau, and now he is coming to meet you, and four hundred men are with him."

7In great fear and distress Jacob divided the people who were with him into two groups,[e] and the flocks and herds and camels as well. 8He thought, "If Esau comes and attacks one group,[f] the group[f] that is left may escape."

9Then Jacob prayed, "O God of my father Abraham, God of my father Isaac, O LORD, who said to me, 'Go back to your country and your relatives, and I will make you prosper,' 10I am unworthy of all the kindness and faithfulness you have shown your servant. I had only my staff when I crossed this Jordan, but now I have become two groups. 11Save me, I pray, from the hand of my brother Esau, for I am afraid he will come and attack me, and also the mothers with their children. 12But you have said, 'I will surely make you prosper and will make your descendants like the sand of the sea, which cannot be counted.' "

13He spent the night there, and from what he had with him he selected a gift for his

[a]47 The Aramaic *Jegar Sahadutha* means *witness heap.* [b]47 The Hebrew *Galeed* means *witness heap.*
[c]49 *Mizpah* means *watchtower.* [d]2 *Mahanaim* means *two camps.* [e]7 Or *camps*; also in verse 10
[f]8 Or *camp*

brother Esau: 14two hundred female goats
and twenty male goats, two hundred ewes
and twenty rams, 15thirty female camels with
their young, forty cows and ten bulls, and
twenty female donkeys and ten male donkeys. 16He put them in the care of his servants, each herd by itself, and said to his
servants, "Go ahead of me, and keep some
space between the herds."

17He instructed the one in the lead: "When
my brother Esau meets you and asks, 'To
whom do you belong, and where are you
going, and who owns all these animals in
front of you?' 18then you are to say, 'They
belong to your servant Jacob. They are a gift
sent to my lord Esau, and he is coming behind us.' "

19He also instructed the second, the third
and all the others who followed the herds:
"You are to say the same thing to Esau when
you meet him. 20And be sure to say, 'Your
servant Jacob is coming behind us.' " For he
thought, "I will pacify him with these gifts I am
sending on ahead; later, when I see him,
perhaps he will receive me." 21So Jacob's
gifts went on ahead of him, but he himself
spent the night in the camp.

Jacob Wrestles With God

22That night Jacob got up and took his two
wives, his two maidservants and his eleven
sons and crossed the ford of the Jabbok.
23After he had sent them across the stream,
he sent over all his possessions. 24So Jacob
was left alone, and a man wrestled with him
till daybreak. 25When the man saw that he
could not overpower him, he touched the
socket of Jacob's hip so that his hip was
wrenched as he wrestled with the man.
26Then the man said, "Let me go, for it is
daybreak."

But Jacob replied, "I will not let you go
unless you bless me."

27The man asked him, "What is your
name?"

"Jacob," he answered.

28Then the man said, "Your name will no
longer be Jacob, but Israel,[a] because you
have struggled with God and with men and
have overcome."

29Jacob said, "Please tell me your name."

But he replied, "Why do you ask my
name?" Then he blessed him there.

30So Jacob called the place Peniel,[b] saying, "It is because I saw God face to face,
and yet my life was spared."

31The sun rose above him as he passed
Peniel,[c] and he was limping because of his
hip. 32Therefore to this day the Israelites do
not eat the tendon attached to the socket of
the hip, because the socket of Jacob's hip
was touched near the tendon.

Jacob Meets Esau

33 Jacob looked up and there was
Esau, coming with his four hundred
men; so he divided the children among Leah,
Rachel and the two maidservants. 2He put
the maidservants and their children in front,
Leah and her children next, and Rachel and
Joseph in the rear. 3He himself went on
ahead and bowed down to the ground seven
times as he approached his brother.

4But Esau ran to meet Jacob and embraced him; he threw his arms around his
neck and kissed him. And they wept. 5Then
Esau looked up and saw the women and
children. "Who are these with you?" he
asked.

Jacob answered, "They are the children
God has graciously given your servant."

6Then the maidservants and their children
approached and bowed down. 7Next, Leah
and her children came and bowed down.
Last of all came Joseph and Rachel, and
they too bowed down.

8Esau asked, "What do you mean by all
these droves I met?"

"To find favor in your eyes, my lord," he
said.

9But Esau said, "I already have plenty, my
brother. Keep what you have for yourself."

10"No, please!" said Jacob. "If I have
found favor in your eyes, accept this gift from
me. For to see your face is like seeing the
face of God, now that you have received me
favorably. 11Please accept the present that
was brought to you, for God has been gracious to me and I have all I need." And because Jacob insisted, Esau accepted it.

12Then Esau said, "Let us be on our way;
I'll accompany you."

13But Jacob said to him, "My lord knows
that the children are tender and that I must
care for the ewes and cows that are nursing
their young. If they are driven hard just one
day, all the animals will die. 14So let my lord
go on ahead of his servant, while I move

[a]28 *Israel* means *he struggles with God.* [b]30 *Peniel* means *face of God.* [c]31 Hebrew *Penuel,* a variant of *Peniel*

along slowly at the pace of the droves before
me and that of the children, until I come to my
lord in Seir."
15 Esau said, "Then let me leave some of
my men with you."
"But why do that?" Jacob asked. "Just let
me find favor in the eyes of my lord."
16 So that day Esau started on his way back
to Seir. 17 Jacob, however, went to Succoth,
where he built a place for himself and made
shelters for his livestock. That is why the
place is called Succoth.[a]
18 After Jacob came from Paddan Aram,[b]
he arrived safely at the[c] city of Shechem in
Canaan and camped within sight of the city.
19 For a hundred pieces of silver,[d] he bought
from the sons of Hamor, the father of Shechem, the plot of ground where he pitched
his tent. 20 There he set up an altar and called
it El Elohe Israel.[e]

Dinah and the Shechemites

34 Now Dinah, the daughter Leah had
borne to Jacob, went out to visit the
women of the land. 2 When Shechem son of
Hamor the Hivite, the ruler of that area, saw
her, he took her and violated her. 3 His heart
was drawn to Dinah daughter of Jacob, and
he loved the girl and spoke tenderly to her.
4 And Shechem said to his father Hamor,
"Get me this girl as my wife."
5 When Jacob heard that his daughter
Dinah had been defiled, his sons were in the
fields with his livestock; so he kept quiet
about it until they came home.
6 Then Shechem's father Hamor went out
to talk with Jacob. 7 Now Jacob's sons had
come in from the fields as soon as they heard
what had happened. They were filled with
grief and fury, because Shechem had done a
disgraceful thing in[f] Israel by lying with
Jacob's daughter—a thing that should not be
done.
8 But Hamor said to them, "My son Shechem has his heart set on your daughter.
Please give her to him as his wife. 9 Intermarry with us; give us your daughters and take
our daughters for yourselves. 10 You can settle among us; the land is open to you. Live in
it, trade[g] in it, and acquire property in it."
11 Then Shechem said to Dinah's father
and brothers, "Let me find favor in your eyes,
and I will give you whatever you ask. 12 Make
the price for the bride and the gift I am to
bring as great as you like, and I'll pay whatever you ask me. Only give me the girl as my
wife."
13 Because their sister Dinah had been
defiled, Jacob's sons replied deceitfully as
they spoke to Shechem and his father Hamor. 14 They said to them, "We can't do such
a thing; we can't give our sister to a man who
is not circumcised. That would be a disgrace
to us. 15 We will give our consent to you on
one condition only: that you become like us
by circumcising all your males. 16 Then we
will give you our daughters and take your
daughters for ourselves. We'll settle among
you and become one people with you. 17 But
if you will not agree to be circumcised, we'll
take our sister[h] and go."
18 Their proposal seemed good to Hamor
and his son Shechem. 19 The young man,
who was the most honored of all his father's
household, lost no time in doing what they
said, because he was delighted with Jacob's
daughter. 20 So Hamor and his son Shechem
went to the gate of their city to speak to their
fellow townsmen. 21 "These men are friendly
toward us," they said. "Let them live in our
land and trade in it; the land has plenty of
room for them. We can marry their daughters
and they can marry ours. 22 But the men will
consent to live with us as one people only on
the condition that our males be circumcised,
as they themselves are. 23 Won't their livestock, their property and all their other animals become ours? So let us give our consent to them, and they will settle among us."
24 All the men who went out of the city gate
agreed with Hamor and his son Shechem,
and every male in the city was circumcised.
25 Three days later, while all of them were
still in pain, two of Jacob's sons, Simeon and
Levi, Dinah's brothers, took their swords and
attacked the unsuspecting city, killing every
male. 26 They put Hamor and his son Shechem to the sword and took Dinah from Shechem's house and left. 27 The sons of Jacob
came upon the dead bodies and looted the
city where[i] their sister had been defiled.
28 They seized their flocks and herds and
donkeys and everything else of theirs in the
city and out in the fields. 29 They carried off all
their wealth and all their women and chil-

[a]17 *Succoth* means *shelters.* [b]18 That is, Northwest Mesopotamia [c]18 Or *arrived at Shalem, a* [d]19 Hebrew *hundred kesitahs*; a kesitah was a unit of money of unknown weight and value. [e]20 *El Elohe Israel* can mean *God, the God of Israel* or *mighty is the God of Israel.* [f]7 Or *against* [g]10 Or *move about freely;* also in verse 21 [h]17 Hebrew *daughter* [i]27 Or *because*

dren, taking as plunder everything in the
houses.
30Then Jacob said to Simeon and Levi,
"You have brought trouble on me by making
me a stench to the Canaanites and Perizzites, the people living in this land. We are
few in number, and if they join forces against
me and attack me, I and my household will
be destroyed."
31But they replied, "Should he have treated our sister like a prostitute?"

Jacob Returns to Bethel

35 Then God said to Jacob, "Go up to
Bethel and settle there, and build an
altar there to God, who appeared to you
when you were fleeing from your brother
Esau."
2So Jacob said to his household and to all
who were with him, "Get rid of the foreign
gods you have with you, and purify yourselves and change your clothes. 3Then
come, let us go up to Bethel, where I will
build an altar to God, who answered me in
the day of my distress and who has been
with me wherever I have gone." 4So they
gave Jacob all the foreign gods they had and
the rings in their ears, and Jacob buried them
under the oak at Shechem. 5Then they set
out, and the terror of God fell upon the towns
all around them so that no one pursued
them.
6Jacob and all the people with him came to
Luz (that is, Bethel) in the land of Canaan.
7There he built an altar, and he called the
place El Bethel,[a] because it was there that
God revealed himself to him when he was
fleeing from his brother.
8Now Deborah, Rebekah's nurse, died
and was buried under the oak below Bethel.
So it was named Allon Bacuth.[b]
9After Jacob returned from Paddan
Aram,[c] God appeared to him again and
blessed him. 10God said to him, "Your name
is Jacob,[d] but you will no longer be called
Jacob; your name will be Israel.[e]" So he
named him Israel.
11And God said to him, "I am God Almighty[f]; be fruitful and increase in number.
A nation and a community of nations will
come from you, and kings will come from
your body. 12The land I gave to Abraham and
Isaac I also give to you, and I will give this
land to your descendants after you." 13Then
God went up from him at the place where he
had talked with him.
14Jacob set up a stone pillar at the place
where God had talked with him, and he
poured out a drink offering on it; he also
poured oil on it. 15Jacob called the place
where God had talked with him Bethel.[g]

The Deaths of Rachel and Isaac

16Then they moved on from Bethel. While
they were still some distance from Ephrath,
Rachel began to give birth and had great
difficulty. 17And as she was having great difficulty in childbirth, the midwife said to her,
"Don't be afraid, for you have another son."
18As she breathed her last—for she was dying—she named her son Ben-Oni.[h] But his
father named him Benjamin.[i]
19So Rachel died and was buried on the
way to Ephrath (that is, Bethlehem). 20Over
her tomb Jacob set up a pillar, and to this day
that pillar marks Rachel's tomb.
21Israel moved on again and pitched his
tent beyond Migdal Eder. 22While Israel was
living in that region, Reuben went in and
slept with his father's concubine Bilhah, and
Israel heard of it.

Jacob had twelve sons:
23The sons of Leah:
Reuben the firstborn of Jacob,
Simeon, Levi, Judah, Issachar and
Zebulun.
24The sons of Rachel:
Joseph and Benjamin.
25The sons of Rachel's maidservant Bil-
hah:
Dan and Naphtali.
26The sons of Leah's maidservant Zilpah:
Gad and Asher.
These were the sons of Jacob, who were
born to him in Paddan Aram.

27Jacob came home to his father Isaac in
Mamre, near Kiriath Arba (that is, Hebron),
where Abraham and Isaac had stayed.
28Isaac lived a hundred and eighty years.
29Then he breathed his last and died and
was gathered to his people, old and full of
years. And his sons Esau and Jacob buried
him.

[a]7 *El Bethel* means *God of Bethel.* [b]8 *Allon Bacuth* means *oak of weeping.* [c]9 That is, Northwest Mesopotamia; also in verse 26 [d]10 *Jacob* means *he grasps the heel* (figuratively, *he deceives*). [e]10 *Israel* means *he struggles with God.* [f]11 Hebrew *El-Shaddai* [g]15 *Bethel* means *house of God.* [h]18 *Ben-Oni* means *son of my trouble.* [i]18 *Benjamin* means *son of my right hand.*

Esau's Descendants

36 This is the account of Esau (that is, Edom).

[2]Esau took his wives from the women
of Canaan: Adah daughter of Elon the
Hittite, and Oholibamah daughter of
Anah and granddaughter of Zibeon the
Hivite— [3]also Basemath daughter of
Ishmael and sister of Nebaioth.

[4]Adah bore Eliphaz to Esau, Basemath bore Reuel, [5]and Oholibamah
bore Jeush, Jalam and Korah. These
were the sons of Esau, who were born
to him in Canaan.

[6]Esau took his wives and sons and
daughters and all the members of his
household, as well as his livestock and
all his other animals and all the goods
he had acquired in Canaan, and moved
to a land some distance from his brother
Jacob. [7]Their possessions were too
great for them to remain together; the
land where they were staying could not
support them both because of their livestock. [8]So Esau (that is, Edom) settled
in the hill country of Seir.

[9]This is the account of Esau the father of
the Edomites in the hill country of Seir.

[10]These are the names of Esau's sons:
Eliphaz, the son of Esau's wife Adah,
and Reuel, the son of Esau's wife
Basemath.

[11]The sons of Eliphaz:
Teman, Omar, Zepho, Gatam and
Kenaz.
[12]Esau's son Eliphaz also had a con-
cubine named Timna, who bore him
Amalek. These were grandsons of
Esau's wife Adah.

[13]The sons of Reuel:
Nahath, Zerah, Shammah and Miz-
zah. These were grandsons of
Esau's wife Basemath.

[14]The sons of Esau's wife Oholibamah
daughter of Anah and granddaughter
of Zibeon, whom she bore to Esau:
Jeush, Jalam and Korah.

[15]These were the chiefs among Esau's descendants:
The sons of Eliphaz the firstborn of
Esau:
Chiefs Teman, Omar, Zepho,
Kenaz, [16]Korah,[a] Gatam and Amalek. These were the chiefs descended from Eliphaz in Edom; they were
grandsons of Adah.

[17]The sons of Esau's son Reuel:
Chiefs Nahath, Zerah, Shammah
and Mizzah. These were the chiefs
descended from Reuel in Edom;
they were grandsons of Esau's wife
Basemath.

[18]The sons of Esau's wife Oholibamah:
Chiefs Jeush, Jalam and Korah.
These were the chiefs descended
from Esau's wife Oholibamah
daughter of Anah.

[19]These were the sons of Esau (that is,
Edom), and these were their chiefs.

[20]These were the sons of Seir the Horite,
who were living in the region:
Lotan, Shobal, Zibeon, Anah, [21]Di-
shon, Ezer and Dishan. These
sons of Seir in Edom were Horite
chiefs.

[22]The sons of Lotan:
Hori and Homam.[b] Timna was Lotan's sister.

[23]The sons of Shobal:
Alvan, Manahath, Ebal, Shepho and
Onam.

[24]The sons of Zibeon:
Aiah and Anah. This is the Anah who
discovered the hot springs[c] in the
desert while he was grazing the donkeys of his father Zibeon.

[25]The children of Anah:
Dishon and Oholibamah daughter of
Anah.

[26]The sons of Dishon[d]:
Hemdan, Eshban, Ithran and Keran.

[27]The sons of Ezer:
Bilhan, Zaavan and Akan.

[28]The sons of Dishan:
Uz and Aran.

[29]These were the Horite chiefs:
Lotan, Shobal, Zibeon, Anah, [30]Di-
shon, Ezer and Dishan. These were
the Horite chiefs, according to their
divisions, in the land of Seir.

[a]16 Masoretic Text; Samaritan Pentateuch (see also Gen. 36:11 and 1 Chron. 1:36) does not have *Korah.*
[b]22 Hebrew *Hemam,* a variant of *Homam* (see 1 Chron. 1:39) [c]24 Vulgate; Syriac *discovered water;* the meaning of the Hebrew for this word is uncertain. [d]26 Hebrew *Dishan,* a variant of *Dishon*

The Rulers of Edom

31These were the kings who reigned in
Edom before any Israelite king reigned[a]:

32Bela son of Beor became king of
Edom. His city was named Dinhabah.

33When Bela died, Jobab son of Zerah
from Bozrah succeeded him as king.

34When Jobab died, Husham from the
land of the Temanites succeeded
him as king.

35When Husham died, Hadad son of
Bedad, who defeated Midian in the
country of Moab, succeeded him as
king. His city was named Avith.

36When Hadad died, Samlah from Masrekah succeeded him as king.

37When Samlah died, Shaul from Rehoboth on the river[b] succeeded him as
king.

38When Shaul died, Baal-Hanan son of
Acbor succeeded him as king.

39When Baal-Hanan son of Acbor died,
Hadad[c] succeeded him as king. His
city was named Pau, and his wife's
name was Mehetabel daughter of
Matred, the daughter of Me-Zahab.

40These were the chiefs descended from
Esau, by name, according to their clans and
regions:

Timna, Alvah, Jetheth, 41Oholibamah, Elah, Pinon, 42Kenaz, Teman,
Mibzar, 43Magdiel and Iram. These
were the chiefs of Edom, according
to their settlements in the land they
occupied.

This was Esau the father of the Edomites.

Joseph's Dreams

37 Jacob lived in the land where his father had stayed, the land of Canaan.

2This is the account of Jacob.

Joseph, a young man of seventeen, was
tending the flocks with his brothers, the sons
of Bilhah and the sons of Zilpah, his father's
wives, and he brought their father a bad report about them.

3Now Israel loved Joseph more than any of
his other sons, because he had been born to
him in his old age; and he made a richly
ornamented[d] robe for him. 4When his brothers saw that their father loved him more than
any of them, they hated him and could not
speak a kind word to him.

5Joseph had a dream, and when he told it
to his brothers, they hated him all the more.
6He said to them, "Listen to this dream I had:
7We were binding sheaves of grain out in the
field when suddenly my sheaf rose and
stood upright, while your sheaves gathered
around mine and bowed down to it."

8His brothers said to him, "Do you intend
to reign over us? Will you actually rule us?"
And they hated him all the more because of
his dream and what he had said.

9Then he had another dream, and he told it
to his brothers. "Listen," he said, "I had another dream, and this time the sun and moon
and eleven stars were bowing down to me."

10When he told his father as well as his
brothers, his father rebuked him and said,
"What is this dream you had? Will your
mother and I and your brothers actually
come and bow down to the ground before
you?" 11His brothers were jealous of him, but
his father kept the matter in mind.

Joseph Sold by His Brothers

12Now his brothers had gone to graze their
father's flocks near Shechem, 13and Israel
said to Joseph, "As you know, your brothers
are grazing the flocks near Shechem. Come,
I am going to send you to them."

"Very well," he replied.

14So he said to him, "Go and see if all is
well with your brothers and with the flocks,
and bring word back to me." Then he sent
him off from the Valley of Hebron.

When Joseph arrived at Shechem, 15a
man found him wandering around in the
fields and asked him, "What are you looking
for?"

16He replied, "I'm looking for my brothers.
Can you tell me where they are grazing their
flocks?"

17"They have moved on from here," the
man answered. "I heard them say, 'Let's go
to Dothan.' "

So Joseph went after his brothers and
found them near Dothan. 18But they saw him
in the distance, and before he reached them,
they plotted to kill him.

19"Here comes that dreamer!" they said to
each other. 20"Come now, let's kill him and

[a]31 Or *before an Israelite king reigned over them* [b]37 Possibly the Euphrates [c]39 Many manuscripts of the Masoretic Text, Samaritan Pentateuch and Syriac (see also 1 Chron. 1:50); most manuscripts of the Masoretic Text *Hadar* [d]3 The meaning of the Hebrew for *richly ornamented* is uncertain; also in verses 23 and 32.

throw him into one of these cisterns and say that a ferocious animal devoured him. Then we'll see what comes of his dreams."

[21]When Reuben heard this, he tried to rescue him from their hands. "Let's not take his life," he said. [22]"Don't shed any blood. Throw him into this cistern here in the desert, but don't lay a hand on him." Reuben said this to rescue him from them and take him back to his father.

[23]So when Joseph came to his brothers, they stripped him of his robe—the richly ornamented robe he was wearing— [24]and they took him and threw him into the cistern. Now the cistern was empty; there was no water in it.

[25]As they sat down to eat their meal, they looked up and saw a caravan of Ishmaelites coming from Gilead. Their camels were loaded with spices, balm and myrrh, and they were on their way to take them down to Egypt.

[26]Judah said to his brothers, "What will we gain if we kill our brother and cover up his blood? [27]Come, let's sell him to the Ishmaelites and not lay our hands on him; after all, he is our brother, our own flesh and blood." His brothers agreed.

[28]So when the Midianite merchants came by, his brothers pulled Joseph up out of the cistern and sold him for twenty shekels[a] of silver to the Ishmaelites, who took him to Egypt.

[29]When Reuben returned to the cistern and saw that Joseph was not there, he tore his clothes. [30]He went back to his brothers and said, "The boy isn't there! Where can I turn now?"

[31]Then they got Joseph's robe, slaughtered a goat and dipped the robe in the blood. [32]They took the ornamented robe back to their father and said, "We found this. Examine it to see whether it is your son's robe."

[33]He recognized it and said, "It is my son's robe! Some ferocious animal has devoured him. Joseph has surely been torn to pieces."

[34]Then Jacob tore his clothes, put on sackcloth and mourned for his son many days. [35]All his sons and daughters came to comfort him, but he refused to be comforted. "No," he said, "in mourning will I go down to the grave[b] to my son." So his father wept for him.

[36]Meanwhile, the Midianites[c] sold Joseph in Egypt to Potiphar, one of Pharaoh's officials, the captain of the guard.

Judah and Tamar

38 At that time, Judah left his brothers and went down to stay with a man of Adullam named Hirah. [2]There Judah met the daughter of a Canaanite man named Shua. He married her and lay with her; [3]she became pregnant and gave birth to a son, who was named Er. [4]She conceived again and gave birth to a son and named him Onan. [5]She gave birth to still another son and named him Shelah. It was at Kezib that she gave birth to him.

[6]Judah got a wife for Er, his firstborn, and her name was Tamar. [7]But Er, Judah's firstborn, was wicked in the LORD's sight; so the LORD put him to death.

[8]Then Judah said to Onan, "Lie with your brother's wife and fulfill your duty to her as a brother-in-law to produce offspring for your brother." [9]But Onan knew that the offspring would not be his; so whenever he lay with his brother's wife, he spilled his semen on the ground to keep from producing offspring for his brother. [10]What he did was wicked in the LORD's sight; so he put him to death also.

[11]Judah then said to his daughter-in-law Tamar, "Live as a widow in your father's house until my son Shelah grows up." For he thought, "He may die too, just like his brothers." So Tamar went to live in her father's house.

[12]After a long time Judah's wife, the daughter of Shua, died. When Judah had recovered from his grief, he went up to Timnah, to the men who were shearing his sheep, and his friend Hirah the Adullamite went with him.

[13]When Tamar was told, "Your father-in-law is on his way to Timnah to shear his sheep," [14]she took off her widow's clothes, covered herself with a veil to disguise herself, and then sat down at the entrance to Enaim, which is on the road to Timnah. For she saw that, though Shelah had now grown up, she had not been given to him as his wife.

[15]When Judah saw her, he thought she was a prostitute, for she had covered her face. [16]Not realizing that she was his daughter-in-law, he went over to her by the road-

[a]*28* That is, about 8 ounces (about 0.2 kilogram) [b]*35* Hebrew *Sheol* [c]*36* Samaritan Pentateuch, Septuagint, Vulgate and Syriac (see also verse 28); Masoretic Text *Medanites*

side and said, "Come now, let me sleep with
you."
"And what will you give me to sleep with
you?" she asked.
17"I'll send you a young goat from my
flock," he said.
"Will you give me something as a pledge
until you send it?" she asked.
18He said, "What pledge should I give
you?"
"Your seal and its cord, and the staff in
your hand," she answered. So he gave them
to her and slept with her, and she became
pregnant by him. 19After she left, she took off
her veil and put on her widow's clothes
again.
20Meanwhile Judah sent the young goat by
his friend the Adullamite in order to get his
pledge back from the woman, but he did not
find her. 21He asked the men who lived there,
"Where is the shrine prostitute who was beside the road at Enaim?"
"There hasn't been any shrine prostitute
here," they said.
22So he went back to Judah and said, "I
didn't find her. Besides, the men who lived
there said, 'There hasn't been any shrine
prostitute here.' "
23Then Judah said, "Let her keep what she
has, or we will become a laughingstock. After all, I did send her this young goat, but you
didn't find her."
24About three months later Judah was told,
"Your daughter-in-law Tamar is guilty of
prostitution, and as a result she is now pregnant."
Judah said, "Bring her out and have her
burned to death!"
25As she was being brought out, she sent a
message to her father-in-law. "I am pregnant
by the man who owns these," she said. And
she added, "See if you recognize whose
seal and cord and staff these are."
26Judah recognized them and said, "She
is more righteous than I, since I wouldn't give
her to my son Shelah." And he did not sleep
with her again.
27When the time came for her to give birth,
there were twin boys in her womb. 28As she
was giving birth, one of them put out his
hand; so the midwife took a scarlet thread
and tied it on his wrist and said, "This one
came out first." 29But when he drew back his
hand, his brother came out, and she said,
"So this is how you have broken out!" And he
was named Perez.[a] 30Then his brother, who
had the scarlet thread on his wrist, came out
and he was given the name Zerah.[b]

Joseph and Potiphar's Wife

39 Now Joseph had been taken down to
Egypt. Potiphar, an Egyptian who
was one of Pharaoh's officials, the captain of
the guard, bought him from the Ishmaelites
who had taken him there.
2The LORD was with Joseph and he prospered, and he lived in the house of his Egyptian master. 3When his master saw that the
LORD was with him and that the LORD gave
him success in everything he did, 4Joseph
found favor in his eyes and became his attendant. Potiphar put him in charge of his
household, and he entrusted to his care
everything he owned. 5From the time he put
him in charge of his household and of all that
he owned, the LORD blessed the household of
the Egyptian because of Joseph. The
blessing of the LORD was on everything Potiphar had, both in the house and in the field.
6So he left in Joseph's care everything he
had; with Joseph in charge, he did not concern himself with anything except the food
he ate.
Now Joseph was well-built and handsome, 7and after a while his master's wife
took notice of Joseph and said, "Come to
bed with me!"
8But he refused. "With me in charge," he
told her, "my master does not concern himself with anything in the house; everything he
owns he has entrusted to my care. 9No one is
greater in this house than I am. My master
has withheld nothing from me except you,
because you are his wife. How then could I
do such a wicked thing and sin against
God?" 10And though she spoke to Joseph
day after day, he refused to go to bed with
her or even be with her.
11One day he went into the house to attend
to his duties, and none of the household servants was inside. 12She caught him by his
cloak and said, "Come to bed with me!" But
he left his cloak in her hand and ran out of the
house.
13When she saw that he had left his cloak
in her hand and had run out of the house,
14she called her household servants. "Look,"
she said to them, "this Hebrew has been
brought to us to make sport of us! He came in
here to sleep with me, but I screamed.

[a]29 *Perez* means *breaking out.* [b]30 *Zerah* can mean *scarlet* or *brightness.*

15When he heard me scream for help, he left his cloak beside me and ran out of the house."

16She kept his cloak beside her until his master came home. 17Then she told him this story: "That Hebrew slave you brought us came to me to make sport of me. 18But as soon as I screamed for help, he left his cloak beside me and ran out of the house."

19When his master heard the story his wife told him, saying, "This is how your slave treated me," he burned with anger. 20Joseph's master took him and put him in prison, the place where the king's prisoners were confined.

But while Joseph was there in the prison, 21the LORD was with him; he showed him kindness and granted him favor in the eyes of the prison warden. 22So the warden put Joseph in charge of all those held in the prison, and he was made responsible for all that was done there. 23The warden paid no attention to anything under Joseph's care, because the LORD was with Joseph and gave him success in whatever he did.

The Cupbearer and the Baker

40 Some time later, the cupbearer and the baker of the king of Egypt offended their master, the king of Egypt. 2Pharaoh was angry with his two officials, the chief cupbearer and the chief baker, 3and put them in custody in the house of the captain of the guard, in the same prison where Joseph was confined. 4The captain of the guard assigned them to Joseph, and he attended them.

After they had been in custody for some time, 5each of the two men—the cupbearer and the baker of the king of Egypt, who were being held in prison—had a dream the same night, and each dream had a meaning of its own.

6When Joseph came to them the next morning, he saw that they were dejected. 7So he asked Pharaoh's officials who were in custody with him in his master's house, "Why are your faces so sad today?"

8"We both had dreams," they answered, "but there is no one to interpret them."

Then Joseph said to them, "Do not interpretations belong to God? Tell me your dreams."

9So the chief cupbearer told Joseph his dream. He said to him, "In my dream I saw a vine in front of me, 10and on the vine were three branches. As soon as it budded, it blossomed, and its clusters ripened into grapes. 11Pharaoh's cup was in my hand, and I took the grapes, squeezed them into Pharaoh's cup and put the cup in his hand."

12"This is what it means," Joseph said to him. "The three branches are three days. 13Within three days Pharaoh will lift up your head and restore you to your position, and you will put Pharaoh's cup in his hand, just as you used to do when you were his cupbearer. 14But when all goes well with you, remember me and show me kindness; mention me to Pharaoh and get me out of this prison. 15For I was forcibly carried off from the land of the Hebrews, and even here I have done nothing to deserve being put in a dungeon."

16When the chief baker saw that Joseph had given a favorable interpretation, he said to Joseph, "I too had a dream: On my head were three baskets of bread.[a] 17In the top basket were all kinds of baked goods for Pharaoh, but the birds were eating them out of the basket on my head."

18"This is what it means," Joseph said. "The three baskets are three days. 19Within three days Pharaoh will lift off your head and hang you on a tree.[b] And the birds will eat away your flesh."

20Now the third day was Pharaoh's birthday, and he gave a feast for all his officials. He lifted up the heads of the chief cupbearer and the chief baker in the presence of his officials: 21He restored the chief cupbearer to his position, so that he once again put the cup into Pharaoh's hand, 22but he hanged[c] the chief baker, just as Joseph had said to them in his interpretation.

23The chief cupbearer, however, did not remember Joseph; he forgot him.

Pharaoh's Dreams

41 When two full years had passed, Pharaoh had a dream: He was standing by the Nile, 2when out of the river there came up seven cows, sleek and fat, and they grazed among the reeds. 3After them, seven other cows, ugly and gaunt, came up out of the Nile and stood beside those on the riverbank. 4And the cows that were ugly and gaunt ate up the seven sleek, fat cows. Then Pharaoh woke up.

5He fell asleep again and had a second dream: Seven heads of grain, healthy and

[a] 16 Or *three wicker baskets* [b] 19 Or *and impale you on a pole* [c] 22 Or *impaled*

good, were growing on a single stalk. 6After
them, seven other heads of grain sprouted—
thin and scorched by the east wind. 7The thin
heads of grain swallowed up the seven
healthy, full heads. Then Pharaoh woke up;
it had been a dream.
8In the morning his mind was troubled, so
he sent for all the magicians and wise men of
Egypt. Pharaoh told them his dreams, but no
one could interpret them for him.
9Then the chief cupbearer said to Pharaoh, "Today I am reminded of my shortcom-
ings. 10Pharaoh was once angry with his servants, and he imprisoned me and the chief
baker in the house of the captain of the
guard. 11Each of us had a dream the same
night, and each dream had a meaning of its
own. 12Now a young Hebrew was there with
us, a servant of the captain of the guard. We
told him our dreams, and he interpreted
them for us, giving each man the interpretation of his dream. 13And things turned out
exactly as he interpreted them to us: I was
restored to my position, and the other man
was hanged.[a]"
14So Pharaoh sent for Joseph, and he was
quickly brought from the dungeon. When he
had shaved and changed his clothes, he
came before Pharaoh.
15Pharaoh said to Joseph, "I had a dream,
and no one can interpret it. But I have heard
it said of you that when you hear a dream you
can interpret it."
16"I cannot do it," Joseph replied to Pharaoh, "but God will give Pharaoh the answer
he desires."
17Then Pharaoh said to Joseph, "In my
dream I was standing on the bank of the Nile,
18when out of the river there came up seven
cows, fat and sleek, and they grazed among
the reeds. 19After them, seven other cows
came up—scrawny and very ugly and lean. I
had never seen such ugly cows in all the land
of Egypt. 20The lean, ugly cows ate up the
seven fat cows that came up first. 21But even
after they ate them, no one could tell that
they had done so; they looked just as ugly as
before. Then I woke up.
22"In my dreams I also saw seven heads of
grain, full and good, growing on a single
stalk. 23After them, seven other heads
sprouted—withered and thin and scorched
by the east wind. 24The thin heads of grain
swallowed up the seven good heads. I told
this to the magicians, but none could explain
it to me."
25Then Joseph said to Pharaoh, "The
dreams of Pharaoh are one and the same.
God has revealed to Pharaoh what he is
about to do. 26The seven good cows are
seven years, and the seven good heads of
grain are seven years; it is one and the same
dream. 27The seven lean, ugly cows that
came up afterward are seven years, and so
are the seven worthless heads of grain
scorched by the east wind: They are seven
years of famine.
28"It is just as I said to Pharaoh: God has
shown Pharaoh what he is about to do.
29Seven years of great abundance are coming throughout the land of Egypt, 30but seven
years of famine will follow them. Then all the
abundance in Egypt will be forgotten, and
the famine will ravage the land. 31The abundance in the land will not be remembered,
because the famine that follows it will be so
severe. 32The reason the dream was given to
Pharaoh in two forms is that the matter has
been firmly decided by God, and God will do
it soon.
33"And now let Pharaoh look for a discerning and wise man and put him in charge of
the land of Egypt. 34Let Pharaoh appoint
commissioners over the land to take a fifth of
the harvest of Egypt during the seven years
of abundance. 35They should collect all the
food of these good years that are coming
and store up the grain under the authority of
Pharaoh, to be kept in the cities for food.
36This food should be held in reserve for the
country, to be used during the seven years of
famine that will come upon Egypt, so that the
country may not be ruined by the famine."
37The plan seemed good to Pharaoh and
to all his officials. 38So Pharaoh asked them,
"Can we find anyone like this man, one in
whom is the spirit of God[b]?"
39Then Pharaoh said to Joseph, "Since
God has made all this known to you, there is
no one so discerning and wise as you. 40You
shall be in charge of my palace, and all my
people are to submit to your orders. Only
with respect to the throne will I be greater
than you."

Joseph in Charge of Egypt

41So Pharaoh said to Joseph, "I hereby put
you in charge of the whole land of Egypt."

[a] *13* Or *impaled* [b] *38* Or *of the gods*

42Then Pharaoh took his signet ring from his
finger and put it on Joseph's finger. He
dressed him in robes of fine linen and put a
gold chain around his neck. 43He had him
ride in a chariot as his second-in-command,[a]
and men shouted before him, "Make way[b]!"
Thus he put him in charge of the whole land
of Egypt.

44Then Pharaoh said to Joseph, "I am
Pharaoh, but without your word no one will
lift hand or foot in all Egypt." 45Pharaoh gave
Joseph the name Zaphenath-Paneah and
gave him Asenath daughter of Potiphera,
priest of On,[c] to be his wife. And Joseph
went throughout the land of Egypt.

46Joseph was thirty years old when he entered the service of Pharaoh king of Egypt.
And Joseph went out from Pharaoh's presence and traveled throughout Egypt. 47Dur-
ing the seven years of abundance the land
produced plentifully. 48Joseph collected all
the food produced in those seven years of
abundance in Egypt and stored it in the cities. In each city he put the food grown in the
fields surrounding it. 49Joseph stored up
huge quantities of grain, like the sand of the
sea; it was so much that he stopped keeping
records because it was beyond measure.

50Before the years of famine came, two
sons were born to Joseph by Asenath
daughter of Potiphera, priest of On. 51Joseph
named his firstborn Manasseh[d] and said, "It
is because God has made me forget all my
trouble and all my father's household." 52The
second son he named Ephraim[e] and said, "It
is because God has made me fruitful in the
land of my suffering."

53The seven years of abundance in Egypt
came to an end, 54and the seven years of
famine began, just as Joseph had said.
There was famine in all the other lands, but in
the whole land of Egypt there was food.
55When all Egypt began to feel the famine,
the people cried to Pharaoh for food. Then
Pharaoh told all the Egyptians, "Go to Joseph and do what he tells you."

56When the famine had spread over the
whole country, Joseph opened the storehouses and sold grain to the Egyptians, for
the famine was severe throughout Egypt.
57And all the countries came to Egypt to buy
grain from Joseph, because the famine was
severe in all the world.

Joseph's Brothers Go to Egypt

42 When Jacob learned that there was
grain in Egypt, he said to his sons,
"Why do you just keep looking at each
other?" 2He continued, "I have heard that
there is grain in Egypt. Go down there and
buy some for us, so that we may live and not
die."

3Then ten of Joseph's brothers went down
to buy grain from Egypt. 4But Jacob did not
send Benjamin, Joseph's brother, with the
others, because he was afraid that harm
might come to him. 5So Israel's sons were
among those who went to buy grain, for the
famine was in the land of Canaan also.

6Now Joseph was the governor of the land,
the one who sold grain to all its people. So
when Joseph's brothers arrived, they bowed
down to him with their faces to the ground.
7As soon as Joseph saw his brothers, he
recognized them, but he pretended to be a
stranger and spoke harshly to them. "Where
do you come from?" he asked.

"From the land of Canaan," they replied,
"to buy food."

8Although Joseph recognized his brothers,
they did not recognize him. 9Then he remembered his dreams about them and said to
them, "You are spies! You have come to see
where our land is unprotected."

10"No, my lord," they answered. "Your servants have come to buy food. 11We are all
the sons of one man. Your servants are honest men, not spies."

12"No!" he said to them. "You have come
to see where our land is unprotected."

13But they replied, "Your servants were
twelve brothers, the sons of one man, who
lives in the land of Canaan. The youngest is
now with our father, and one is no more."

14Joseph said to them, "It is just as I told
you: You are spies! 15And this is how you will
be tested: As surely as Pharaoh lives, you
will not leave this place unless your youngest
brother comes here. 16Send one of your
number to get your brother; the rest of you
will be kept in prison, so that your words may
be tested to see if you are telling the truth. If
you are not, then as surely as Pharaoh lives,
you are spies!" 17And he put them all in custody for three days.

18On the third day, Joseph said to them,

[a]43 Or *in the chariot of his second-in-command;* or *in his second chariot* [b]43 Or *Bow down* [c]45 That is, Heliopolis; also in verse 50 [d]51 *Manasseh* sounds like and may be derived from the Hebrew for *forget.* [e]52 *Ephraim* sounds like the Hebrew for *twice fruitful.*

"Do this and you will live, for I fear God: 19If
you are honest men, let one of your brothers
stay here in prison, while the rest of you go
and take grain back for your starving
households. 20But you must bring your youngest brother to me, so that your words may
be verified and that you may not die." This
they proceeded to do.
21They said to one another, "Surely we are
being punished because of our brother. We
saw how distressed he was when he pleaded with us for his life, but we would not listen;
that's why this distress has come upon
us."
22Reuben replied, "Didn't I tell you not to
sin against the boy? But you wouldn't listen!
Now we must give an accounting for his
blood." 23They did not realize that Joseph
could understand them, since he was using
an interpreter.
24He turned away from them and began to
weep, but then turned back and spoke to
them again. He had Simeon taken from them
and bound before their eyes.
25Joseph gave orders to fill their bags with
grain, to put each man's silver back in his
sack, and to give them provisions for their
journey. After this was done for them, 26they
loaded their grain on their donkeys and left.
27At the place where they stopped for the
night one of them opened his sack to get
feed for his donkey, and he saw his silver in
the mouth of his sack. 28"My silver has been
returned," he said to his brothers. "Here it is
in my sack."
Their hearts sank and they turned to each
other trembling and said, "What is this that
God has done to us?"
29When they came to their father Jacob in
the land of Canaan, they told him all that had
happened to them. They said, 30"The man
who is lord over the land spoke harshly to us
and treated us as though we were spying on
the land. 31But we said to him, 'We are honest men; we are not spies. 32We were twelve
brothers, sons of one father. One is no more,
and the youngest is now with our father in
Canaan.'
33"Then the man who is lord over the land
said to us, 'This is how I will know whether
you are honest men: Leave one of your
brothers here with me, and take food for your
starving households and go. 34But bring your
youngest brother to me so I will know that
you are not spies but honest men. Then I will
give your brother back to you, and you can
trade[a] in the land.' "
35As they were emptying their sacks, there
in each man's sack was his pouch of silver!
When they and their father saw the money
pouches, they were frightened. 36Their father
Jacob said to them, "You have deprived me
of my children. Joseph is no more and Simeon is no more, and now you want to take
Benjamin. Everything is against me!"
37Then Reuben said to his father, "You
may put both of my sons to death if I do not
bring him back to you. Entrust him to my
care, and I will bring him back."
38But Jacob said, "My son will not go down
there with you; his brother is dead and he is
the only one left. If harm comes to him on the
journey you are taking, you will bring my gray
head down to the grave[b] in sorrow."

The Second Journey to Egypt

43 Now the famine was still severe in
the land. 2So when they had eaten all
the grain they had brought from Egypt, their
father said to them, "Go back and buy us a
little more food."
3But Judah said to him, "The man warned
us solemnly, 'You will not see my face again
unless your brother is with you.' 4If you will
send our brother along with us, we will go
down and buy food for you. 5But if you will not
send him, we will not go down, because the
man said to us, 'You will not see my face
again unless your brother is with you.' "
6Israel asked, "Why did you bring this trouble on me by telling the man you had another
brother?"
7They replied, "The man questioned us
closely about ourselves and our family. 'Is
your father still living?' he asked us. 'Do you
have another brother?' We simply answered
his questions. How were we to know he
would say, 'Bring your brother down here'?"
8Then Judah said to Israel his father,
"Send the boy along with me and we will go
at once, so that we and you and our children
may live and not die. 9I myself will guarantee
his safety; you can hold me personally responsible for him. If I do not bring him back to
you and set him here before you, I will bear
the blame before you all my life. 10As it is, if
we had not delayed, we could have gone and
returned twice."
11Then their father Israel said to them, "If it

[a]*34* Or *move about freely* [b]*38* Hebrew *Sheol*

must be, then do this: Put some of the best
products of the land in your bags and take
them down to the man as a gift—a little balm
and a little honey, some spices and myrrh,
some pistachio nuts and almonds. 12Take
double the amount of silver with you, for you
must return the silver that was put back into
the mouths of your sacks. Perhaps it was a
mistake. 13Take your brother also and go
back to the man at once. 14And may God
Almighty[a] grant you mercy before the man
so that he will let your other brother and
Benjamin come back with you. As for me, if I
am bereaved, I am bereaved."

15So the men took the gifts and double the
amount of silver, and Benjamin also. They
hurried down to Egypt and presented themselves to Joseph. 16When Joseph saw Benjamin with them, he said to the steward of his
house, "Take these men to my house,
slaughter an animal and prepare dinner; they
are to eat with me at noon."

17The man did as Joseph told him and took
the men to Joseph's house. 18Now the men
were frightened when they were taken to his
house. They thought, "We were brought
here because of the silver that was put back
into our sacks the first time. He wants to
attack us and overpower us and seize us as
slaves and take our donkeys."

19So they went up to Joseph's steward and
spoke to him at the entrance to the house.
20"Please, sir," they said, "we came down
here the first time to buy food. 21But at the
place where we stopped for the night we
opened our sacks and each of us found his
silver—the exact weight—in the mouth of his
sack. So we have brought it back with us.
22We have also brought additional silver with
us to buy food. We don't know who put our
silver in our sacks."

23"It's all right," he said. "Don't be afraid.
Your God, the God of your father, has given
you treasure in your sacks; I received your
silver." Then he brought Simeon out to them.

24The steward took the men into Joseph's
house, gave them water to wash their feet
and provided fodder for their donkeys.
25They prepared their gifts for Joseph's arrival at noon, because they had heard that they
were to eat there.

26When Joseph came home, they
presented to him the gifts they had brought
into the house, and they bowed down before
him to the ground. 27He asked them how they
were, and then he said, "How is your aged
father you told me about? Is he still living?"

28They replied, "Your servant our father is
still alive and well." And they bowed low to
pay him honor.

29As he looked about and saw his brother
Benjamin, his own mother's son, he asked,
"Is this your youngest brother, the one you
told me about?" And he said, "God be gracious to you, my son." 30Deeply moved at the
sight of his brother, Joseph hurried out and
looked for a place to weep. He went into his
private room and wept there.

31After he had washed his face, he came
out and, controlling himself, said, "Serve the
food."

32They served him by himself, the brothers
by themselves, and the Egyptians who ate
with him by themselves, because Egyptians
could not eat with Hebrews, for that is detestable to Egyptians. 33The men had been seated before him in the order of their ages, from
the firstborn to the youngest; and they
looked at each other in astonishment.
34When portions were served to them from
Joseph's table, Benjamin's portion was five
times as much as anyone else's. So they
feasted and drank freely with him.

A Silver Cup in a Sack

44 Now Joseph gave these instructions
to the steward of his house: "Fill the
men's sacks with as much food as they can
carry, and put each man's silver in the mouth
of his sack. 2Then put my cup, the silver one,
in the mouth of the youngest one's sack,
along with the silver for his grain." And he did
as Joseph said.

3As morning dawned, the men were sent
on their way with their donkeys. 4They had
not gone far from the city when Joseph said
to his steward, "Go after those men at once,
and when you catch up with them, say to
them, 'Why have you repaid good with evil?
5Isn't this the cup my master drinks from and
also uses for divination? This is a wicked
thing you have done.' "

6When he caught up with them, he repeated these words to them. 7But they said
to him, "Why does my lord say such things?
Far be it from your servants to do anything
like that! 8We even brought back to you from
the land of Canaan the silver we found inside
the mouths of our sacks. So why would we
steal silver or gold from your master's

[a] 14 Hebrew *El-Shaddai*

house? 9If any of your servants is found to
have it, he will die; and the rest of us will
become my lord's slaves."

10"Very well, then," he said, "let it be as
you say. Whoever is found to have it will
become my slave; the rest of you will be free
from blame."

11Each of them quickly lowered his sack to
the ground and opened it. 12Then the steward proceeded to search, beginning with the
oldest and ending with the youngest. And the
cup was found in Benjamin's sack. 13At this,
they tore their clothes. Then they all loaded
their donkeys and returned to the city.

14Joseph was still in the house when
Judah and his brothers came in, and they
threw themselves to the ground before him.
15Joseph said to them, "What is this you
have done? Don't you know that a man like
me can find things out by divination?"

16"What can we say to my lord?" Judah
replied. "What can we say? How can we
prove our innocence? God has uncovered
your servants' guilt. We are now my lord's
slaves—we ourselves and the one who was
found to have the cup."

17But Joseph said, "Far be it from me to do
such a thing! Only the man who was found to
have the cup will become my slave. The rest
of you, go back to your father in peace."

18Then Judah went up to him and said:
"Please, my lord, let your servant speak a
word to my lord. Do not be angry with your
servant, though you are equal to Pharaoh
himself. 19My lord asked his servants, 'Do
you have a father or a brother?' 20And we
answered, 'We have an aged father, and
there is a young son born to him in his old
age. His brother is dead, and he is the only
one of his mother's sons left, and his father
loves him.'

21"Then you said to your servants, 'Bring
him down to me so I can see him for myself.'
22And we said to my lord, 'The boy cannot
leave his father; if he leaves him, his father
will die.' 23But you told your servants, 'Unless
your youngest brother comes down with you,
you will not see my face again.' 24When we
went back to your servant my father, we told
him what my lord had said.

25"Then our father said, 'Go back and buy
a little more food.' 26But we said, 'We cannot
go down. Only if our youngest brother is with
us will we go. We cannot see the man's face
unless our youngest brother is with us.'

27"Your servant my father said to us, 'You
know that my wife bore me two sons. 28One
of them went away from me, and I said, "He
has surely been torn to pieces." And I have
not seen him since. 29If you take this one
from me too and harm comes to him, you will
bring my gray head down to the grave[a] in
misery.'

30"So now, if the boy is not with us when I
go back to your servant my father and if my
father, whose life is closely bound up with the
boy's life, 31sees that the boy isn't there, he
will die. Your servants will bring the gray
head of our father down to the grave in sorrow. 32Your servant guaranteed the boy's
safety to my father. I said, 'If I do not bring
him back to you, I will bear the blame before
you, my father, all my life!'

33"Now then, please let your servant remain here as my lord's slave in place of the
boy, and let the boy return with his brothers.
34How can I go back to my father if the boy is
not with me? No! Do not let me see the misery that would come upon my father."

Joseph Makes Himself Known

45 Then Joseph could no longer control
himself before all his attendants, and
he cried out, "Have everyone leave my presence!" So there was no one with Joseph
when he made himself known to his brothers. 2And he wept so loudly that the Egyptians heard him, and Pharaoh's household
heard about it.

3Joseph said to his brothers, "I am Joseph!
Is my father still living?" But his brothers
were not able to answer him, because they
were terrified at his presence.

4Then Joseph said to his brothers, "Come
close to me." When they had done so, he
said, "I am your brother Joseph, the one you
sold into Egypt! 5And now, do not be distressed and do not be angry with yourselves
for selling me here, because it was to save
lives that God sent me ahead of you. 6For
two years now there has been famine in the
land, and for the next five years there will not
be plowing and reaping. 7But God sent me
ahead of you to preserve for you a remnant
on earth and to save your lives by a great
deliverance.[b]

8"So then, it was not you who sent me
here, but God. He made me father to Pharaoh, lord of his entire household and ruler of
all Egypt. 9Now hurry back to my father and

[a] *29* Hebrew *Sheol;* also in verse 31
[b] *7* Or *save you as a great band of survivors*

say to him, 'This is what your son Joseph
says: God has made me lord of all Egypt.
Come down to me; don't delay. 10You shall
live in the region of Goshen and be near
me—you, your children and grandchildren,
your flocks and herds, and all you have. 11I
will provide for you there, because five years
of famine are still to come. Otherwise you
and your household and all who belong to
you will become destitute.'
12"You can see for yourselves, and so can
my brother Benjamin, that it is really I who
am speaking to you. 13Tell my father about all
the honor accorded me in Egypt and about
everything you have seen. And bring my father down here quickly."
14Then he threw his arms around his brother Benjamin and wept, and Benjamin embraced him, weeping. 15And he kissed all his
brothers and wept over them. Afterward his
brothers talked with him.
16When the news reached Pharaoh's palace that Joseph's brothers had come, Pharaoh and all his officials were pleased.
17Pharaoh said to Joseph, "Tell your brothers, 'Do this: Load your animals and return to
the land of Canaan, 18and bring your father
and your families back to me. I will give you
the best of the land of Egypt and you can
enjoy the fat of the land.'
19"You are also directed to tell them, 'Do
this: Take some carts from Egypt for your
children and your wives, and get your father
and come. 20Never mind about your belongings, because the best of all Egypt will be
yours.'"
21So the sons of Israel did this. Joseph
gave them carts, as Pharaoh had commanded, and he also gave them provisions
for their journey. 22To each of them he gave
new clothing, but to Benjamin he gave three
hundred shekels[a] of silver and five sets of
clothes. 23And this is what he sent to his
father: ten donkeys loaded with the best
things of Egypt, and ten female donkeys
loaded with grain and bread and other provisions for his journey. 24Then he sent his
brothers away, and as they were leaving he
said to them, "Don't quarrel on the way!"
25So they went up out of Egypt and came
to their father Jacob in the land of Canaan.
26They told him, "Joseph is still alive! In fact,
he is ruler of all Egypt." Jacob was stunned;
he did not believe them. 27But when they told
him everything Joseph had said to them, and
when he saw the carts Joseph had sent to
carry him back, the spirit of their father Jacob
revived. 28And Israel said, "I'm convinced!
My son Joseph is still alive. I will go and see
him before I die."

Jacob Goes to Egypt

46 So Israel set out with all that was his,
and when he reached Beersheba, he
offered sacrifices to the God of his father
Isaac.
2And God spoke to Israel in a vision at
night and said, "Jacob! Jacob!"
"Here I am," he replied.
3"I am God, the God of your father," he
said. "Do not be afraid to go down to Egypt,
for I will make you into a great nation there. 4I
will go down to Egypt with you, and I will
surely bring you back again. And Joseph's
own hand will close your eyes."
5Then Jacob left Beersheba, and Israel's
sons took their father Jacob and their children and their wives in the carts that Pharaoh had sent to transport him. 6They also
took with them their livestock and the
possessions they had acquired in Canaan,
and Jacob and all his offspring went to
Egypt. 7He took with him to Egypt his sons
and grandsons and his daughters and
granddaughters—all his offspring.

8These are the names of the sons of Israel
(Jacob and his descendants) who went to
Egypt:

Reuben the firstborn of Jacob.
9The sons of Reuben:
Hanoch, Pallu, Hezron and Carmi.
10The sons of Simeon:
Jemuel, Jamin, Ohad, Jakin, Zohar
and Shaul the son of a Canaanite
woman.
11The sons of Levi:
Gershon, Kohath and Merari.
12The sons of Judah:
Er, Onan, Shelah, Perez and Zerah
(but Er and Onan had died in the
land of Canaan).
The sons of Perez:
Hezron and Hamul.
13The sons of Issachar:
Tola, Puah,[b] Jashub[c] and Shimron.
14The sons of Zebulun:
Sered, Elon and Jahleel.

[a]22 That is, about 7 1/2 pounds (about 3.5 kilograms) [b]13 Samaritan Pentateuch and Syriac (see also I Chron. 7:1); Masoretic Text *Puvah* [c]13 Samaritan Pentateuch and some Septuagint manuscripts (see also Num. 26:24 and I Chron. 7:1); Masoretic Text *Iob*

15These were the sons Leah bore to Jacob in Paddan Aram,[a] besides his daughter Dinah. These sons and daughters of his were thirty-three in all.

16The sons of Gad:
 Zephon,[b] Haggi, Shuni, Ezbon, Eri, Arodi and Areli.
17The sons of Asher:
 Imnah, Ishvah, Ishvi and Beriah.
 Their sister was Serah.
 The sons of Beriah:
  Heber and Malkiel.

18These were the children born to Jacob by Zilpah, whom Laban had given to his daughter Leah—sixteen in all.

19The sons of Jacob's wife Rachel:
 Joseph and Benjamin. 20In Egypt, Manasseh and Ephraim were born to Joseph by Asenath daughter of Potiphera, priest of On.[c]
21The sons of Benjamin:
 Bela, Beker, Ashbel, Gera, Naaman, Ehi, Rosh, Muppim, Huppim and Ard.

22These were the sons of Rachel who were born to Jacob—fourteen in all.

23The son of Dan:
 Hushim.
24The sons of Naphtali:
 Jahziel, Guni, Jezer and Shillem.

25These were the sons born to Jacob by Bilhah, whom Laban had given to his daughter Rachel—seven in all.

26All those who went to Egypt with Jacob—those who were his direct descendants, not counting his sons' wives—numbered sixty-six persons. 27With the two sons[d] who had been born to Joseph in Egypt, the members of Jacob's family, which went to Egypt, were seventy[e] in all.

28Now Jacob sent Judah ahead of him to Joseph to get directions to Goshen. When they arrived in the region of Goshen, 29Joseph had his chariot made ready and went to Goshen to meet his father Israel. As soon as Joseph appeared before him, he threw his arms around his father[f] and wept for a long time.

30Israel said to Joseph, "Now I am ready to die, since I have seen for myself that you are still alive."

31Then Joseph said to his brothers and to his father's household, "I will go up and speak to Pharaoh and will say to him, 'My brothers and my father's household, who were living in the land of Canaan, have come to me. 32The men are shepherds; they tend livestock, and they have brought along their flocks and herds and everything they own.' 33When Pharaoh calls you in and asks, 'What is your occupation?' 34you should answer, 'Your servants have tended livestock from our boyhood on, just as our fathers did.' Then you will be allowed to settle in the region of Goshen, for all shepherds are detestable to the Egyptians."

47

Joseph went and told Pharaoh, "My father and brothers, with their flocks and herds and everything they own, have come from the land of Canaan and are now in Goshen." 2He chose five of his brothers and presented them before Pharaoh.

3Pharaoh asked the brothers, "What is your occupation?"

"Your servants are shepherds," they replied to Pharaoh, "just as our fathers were." 4They also said to him, "We have come to live here awhile, because the famine is severe in Canaan and your servants' flocks have no pasture. So now, please let your servants settle in Goshen."

5Pharaoh said to Joseph, "Your father and your brothers have come to you, 6and the land of Egypt is before you; settle your father and your brothers in the best part of the land. Let them live in Goshen. And if you know of any among them with special ability, put them in charge of my own livestock."

7Then Joseph brought his father Jacob in and presented him before Pharaoh. After Jacob blessed[g] Pharaoh, 8Pharaoh asked him, "How old are you?"

9And Jacob said to Pharaoh, "The years of my pilgrimage are a hundred and thirty. My years have been few and difficult, and they do not equal the years of the pilgrimage of my fathers." 10Then Jacob blessed[h] Pharaoh and went out from his presence.

11So Joseph settled his father and his brothers in Egypt and gave them property in the best part of the land, the district of Rame-

[a] 15 That is, Northwest Mesopotamia [b] 16 Samaritan Pentateuch and Septuagint (see also Num. 26:15); Masoretic Text *Ziphion* [c] 20 That is, Heliopolis [d] 27 Hebrew; Septuagint *the nine children* [e] 27 Hebrew (see also Exodus 1:5 and footnote); Septuagint (see also Acts 7:14) *seventy-five* [f] 29 Hebrew *around him* [g] 7 Or *greeted* [h] 10 Or *said farewell to*

ses, as Pharaoh directed. 12Joseph also provided his father and his brothers and all his
father's household with food, according to
the number of their children.

Joseph and the Famine

13There was no food, however, in the
whole region because the famine was
severe; both Egypt and Canaan wasted
away because of the famine. 14Joseph collected all the money that was to be found in
Egypt and Canaan in payment for the grain
they were buying, and he brought it to Pharaoh's palace. 15When the money of the
people of Egypt and Canaan was gone, all
Egypt came to Joseph and said, "Give us
food. Why should we die before your eyes?
Our money is used up."

16"Then bring your livestock," said Joseph. "I will sell you food in exchange for
your livestock, since your money is gone."
17So they brought their livestock to Joseph,
and he gave them food in exchange for their
horses, their sheep and goats, their cattle
and donkeys. And he brought them through
that year with food in exchange for all their
livestock.

18When that year was over, they came to
him the following year and said, "We cannot
hide from our lord the fact that since our
money is gone and our livestock belongs to
you, there is nothing left for our lord except
our bodies and our land. 19Why should we
perish before your eyes—we and our land as
well? Buy us and our land in exchange for
food, and we with our land will be in bondage
to Pharaoh. Give us seed so that we may live
and not die, and that the land may not
become desolate."

20So Joseph bought all the land in Egypt
for Pharaoh. The Egyptians, one and all,
sold their fields, because the famine was too
severe for them. The land became Pharaoh's, 21and Joseph reduced the people to
servitude,[a] from one end of Egypt to the
other. 22However, he did not buy the land of
the priests, because they received a regular
allotment from Pharaoh and had food
enough from the allotment Pharaoh gave
them. That is why they did not sell their
land.

23Joseph said to the people, "Now that I
have bought you and your land today for
Pharaoh, here is seed for you so you can
plant the ground. 24But when the crop comes
in, give a fifth of it to Pharaoh. The other
four-fifths you may keep as seed for the
fields and as food for yourselves and your
households and your children."

25"You have saved our lives," they said.
"May we find favor in the eyes of our lord; we
will be in bondage to Pharaoh."

26So Joseph established it as a law concerning land in Egypt—still in force today—
that a fifth of the produce belongs to Pharaoh. It was only the land of the priests that
did not become Pharaoh's.

27Now the Israelites settled in Egypt in the
region of Goshen. They acquired property
there and were fruitful and increased greatly
in number.

28Jacob lived in Egypt seventeen years,
and the years of his life were a hundred and
forty-seven. 29When the time drew near for
Israel to die, he called for his son Joseph and
said to him, "If I have found favor in your
eyes, put your hand under my thigh and
promise that you will show me kindness and
faithfulness. Do not bury me in Egypt, 30but
when I rest with my fathers, carry me out of
Egypt and bury me where they are buried."

"I will do as you say," he said.

31"Swear to me," he said. Then Joseph
swore to him, and Israel worshiped as he
leaned on the top of his staff.[b]

Manasseh and Ephraim

48 Some time later Joseph was told,
"Your father is ill." So he took his two
sons Manasseh and Ephraim along with him.
2When Jacob was told, "Your son Joseph
has come to you," Israel rallied his strength
and sat up on the bed.

3Jacob said to Joseph, "God Almighty[c]
appeared to me at Luz in the land of Canaan,
and there he blessed me 4and said to me, 'I
am going to make you fruitful and will increase your numbers. I will make you a community of peoples, and I will give this land as
an everlasting possession to your descendants after you.'

5"Now then, your two sons born to you in
Egypt before I came to you here will be reckoned as mine; Ephraim and Manasseh will
be mine, just as Reuben and Simeon are
mine. 6Any children born to you after them
will be yours; in the territory they inherit they
will be reckoned under the names of their

[a]21 Samaritan Pentateuch and Septuagint (see also Vulgate); Masoretic Text *and he moved the people into the cities* [b]31 Or *Israel bowed down at the head of his bed* [c]3 Hebrew *El-Shaddai*

brothers. 7As I was returning from Paddan,[a]
to my sorrow Rachel died in the land of Canaan while we were still on the way, a little
distance from Ephrath. So I buried her there
beside the road to Ephrath" (that is, Bethlehem).
8When Israel saw the sons of Joseph, he
asked, "Who are these?"
9"They are the sons God has given me
here," Joseph said to his father.
Then Israel said, "Bring them to me so I
may bless them."
10Now Israel's eyes were failing because
of old age, and he could hardly see. So Joseph brought his sons close to him, and his
father kissed them and embraced them.
11Israel said to Joseph, "I never expected
to see your face again, and now God has
allowed me to see your children too."
12Then Joseph removed them from Israel's knees and bowed down with his face to
the ground. 13And Joseph took both of them,
Ephraim on his right toward Israel's left hand
and Manasseh on his left toward Israel's
right hand, and brought them close to him.
14But Israel reached out his right hand and
put it on Ephraim's head, though he was the
younger, and crossing his arms, he put his
left hand on Manasseh's head, even though
Manasseh was the firstborn.
15Then he blessed Joseph and said,

"May the God before whom my fathers
Abraham and Isaac walked,
the God who has been my shepherd
all my life to this day,
16the Angel who has delivered me from all
harm
—may he bless these boys.
May they be called by my name
and the names of my fathers Abraham
and Isaac,
and may they increase greatly
upon the earth."

17When Joseph saw his father placing his
right hand on Ephraim's head he was displeased; so he took hold of his father's hand
to move it from Ephraim's head to Manasseh's head. 18Joseph said to him, "No,
my father, this one is the firstborn; put your
right hand on his head."
19But his father refused and said, "I know,
my son, I know. He too will become a people,
and he too will become great. Nevertheless,
his younger brother will be greater than he,
and his descendants will become a group of
nations." 20He blessed them that day and
said,

"In your[b] name will Israel pronounce this
blessing:
'May God make you like Ephraim and
Manasseh.' "

So he put Ephraim ahead of Manasseh.
21Then Israel said to Joseph, "I am about
to die, but God will be with you[c] and take
you[c] back to the land of your[c] fathers. 22And
to you, as one who is over your brothers, I
give the ridge of land[d] I took from the Amorites with my sword and my bow."

Jacob Blesses His Sons

49 Then Jacob called for his sons and
said: "Gather around so I can tell you
what will happen to you in days to come.

2"Assemble and listen, sons of Jacob;
listen to your father Israel.

3"Reuben, you are my firstborn,
my might, the first sign of my strength,
excelling in honor, excelling in power.
4Turbulent as the waters, you will no
longer excel,
for you went up onto your father's bed,
onto my couch and defiled it.

5"Simeon and Levi are brothers—
their swords[e] are weapons of violence.
6Let me not enter their council,
let me not join their assembly,
for they have killed men in their anger
and hamstrung oxen as they pleased.
7Cursed be their anger, so fierce,
and their fury, so cruel!
I will scatter them in Jacob
and disperse them in Israel.

8"Judah,[f] your brothers will praise you;
your hand will be on the neck of your
enemies;
your father's sons will bow down to
you.
9You are a lion's cub, O Judah;
you return from the prey, my son.
Like a lion he crouches and lies down,
like a lioness—who dares to rouse
him?
10The scepter will not depart from Judah,

[a]7 That is, Northwest Mesopotamia [b]20 The Hebrew is singular. [c]21 The Hebrew is plural. [d]22 Or *And to you I give one portion more than to your brothers—the portion* [e]5 The meaning of the Hebrew for this word is uncertain. [f]8 *Judah* sounds like and may be derived from the Hebrew for *praise.*

nor the ruler's staff from between his
feet,
until he comes to whom it belongs[a]
and the obedience of the nations is his.
11He will tether his donkey to a vine,
his colt to the choicest branch;
he will wash his garments in wine,
his robes in the blood of grapes.
12His eyes will be darker than wine,
his teeth whiter than milk.[b]

13"Zebulun will live by the seashore
and become a haven for ships;
his border will extend toward Sidon.

14"Issachar is a rawboned[c] donkey
lying down between two saddlebags.[d]
15When he sees how good is his resting
place
and how pleasant is his land,
he will bend his shoulder to the burden
and submit to forced labor.

16"Dan[e] will provide justice for his people
as one of the tribes of Israel.
17Dan will be a serpent by the roadside,
a viper along the path,
that bites the horse's heels
so that its rider tumbles backward.

18"I look for your deliverance, O LORD.

19"Gad[f] will be attacked by a band of
raiders,
but he will attack them at their heels.

20"Asher's food will be rich;
he will provide delicacies fit for a king.

21"Naphtali is a doe set free
that bears beautiful fawns.[g]

22"Joseph is a fruitful vine,
a fruitful vine near a spring,
whose branches climb over a wall.[h]
23With bitterness archers attacked him;
they shot at him with hostility.
24But his bow remained steady,
his strong arms stayed[i] limber,
because of the hand of the Mighty One of
Jacob,
because of the Shepherd, the Rock of
Israel,
25because of your father's God, who helps
you,
because of the Almighty,[j] who blesses
you
with blessings of the heavens above,
blessings of the deep that lies below,
blessings of the breast and womb.
26Your father's blessings are greater
than the blessings of the ancient
mountains,
than[k] the bounty of the age-old hills.
Let all these rest on the head of Joseph,
on the brow of the prince among[l] his
brothers.

27"Benjamin is a ravenous wolf;
in the morning he devours the prey,
in the evening he divides the plunder."

28All these are the twelve tribes of Israel,
and this is what their father said to them
when he blessed them, giving each the
blessing appropriate to him.

The Death of Jacob

29Then he gave them these instructions: "I
am about to be gathered to my people. Bury
me with my fathers in the cave in the field of
Ephron the Hittite, 30the cave in the field of
Machpelah, near Mamre in Canaan, which
Abraham bought as a burial place from
Ephron the Hittite, along with the field.
31There Abraham and his wife Sarah were
buried, there Isaac and his wife Rebekah
were buried, and there I buried Leah. 32The
field and the cave in it were bought from the
Hittites.[m]"
33When Jacob had finished giving instructions to his sons, he drew his feet up into the
bed, breathed his last and was gathered to
his people.

50 Joseph threw himself upon his father
and wept over him and kissed him.
2Then Joseph directed the physicians in his
service to embalm his father Israel. So the
physicians embalmed him, 3taking a full forty
days, for that was the time required for em-
balming. And the Egyptians mourned for him
seventy days.
4When the days of mourning had passed,
Joseph said to Pharaoh's court, "If I have
found favor in your eyes, speak to Pharaoh
for me. Tell him, 5'My father made me swear
an oath and said, "I am about to die; bury me

[a] *10 Or until Shiloh comes;* or *until he comes to whom tribute belongs* [b] *12 Or will be dull from wine, / his teeth white from milk* [c] *14 Or strong* [d] *14 Or campfires* [e] *16 Dan* here means *he provides justice.* [f] *19 Gad* can mean *attack* and *band of raiders.* [g] *21 Or free; / he utters beautiful words* [h] *22 Or Joseph is a wild colt, / a wild colt near a spring, / a wild donkey on a terraced hill* [i] *23,24 Or archers will attack . . . will shoot . . . will remain . . . will stay* [j] *25* Hebrew *Shaddai* [k] *26 Or of my progenitors, / as great as* [l] *26 Or the one separated from* [m] *32 Or the sons of Heth*

in the tomb I dug for myself in the land of
Canaan." Now let me go up and bury my
father; then I will return.' "
6Pharaoh said, "Go up and bury your father, as he made you swear to do."
7So Joseph went up to bury his father. All
Pharaoh's officials accompanied him—the
dignitaries of his court and all the dignitaries
of Egypt— 8besides all the members of Joseph's household and his brothers and those
belonging to his father's household. Only
their children and their flocks and herds were
left in Goshen. 9Chariots and horsemen[a]
also went up with him. It was a very large
company.
10When they reached the threshing floor of
Atad, near the Jordan, they lamented loudly
and bitterly; and there Joseph observed a
seven-day period of mourning for his father.
11When the Canaanites who lived there saw
the mourning at the threshing floor of Atad,
they said, "The Egyptians are holding a solemn ceremony of mourning." That is why
that place near the Jordan is called Abel
Mizraim.[b]
12So Jacob's sons did as he had commanded them: 13They carried him to the land
of Canaan and buried him in the cave in the
field of Machpelah, near Mamre, which Abraham had bought as a burial place from
Ephron the Hittite, along with the field. 14After
burying his father, Joseph returned to Egypt,
together with his brothers and all the others
who had gone with him to bury his father.

Joseph Reassures His Brothers

15When Joseph's brothers saw that their
father was dead, they said, "What if Joseph
holds a grudge against us and pays us back
for all the wrongs we did to him?" 16So they
sent word to Joseph, saying, "Your father left
these instructions before he died: 17'This is
what you are to say to Joseph: I ask you to
forgive your brothers the sins and the
wrongs they committed in treating you so
badly.' Now please forgive the sins of the
servants of the God of your father." When
their message came to him, Joseph wept.
18His brothers then came and threw themselves down before him. "We are your
slaves," they said.
19But Joseph said to them, "Don't be
afraid. Am I in the place of God? 20You intended to harm me, but God intended it for
good to accomplish what is now being done,
the saving of many lives. 21So then, don't be
afraid. I will provide for you and your children." And he reassured them and spoke
kindly to them.

The Death of Joseph

22Joseph stayed in Egypt, along with all his
father's family. He lived a hundred and ten
years 23and saw the third generation of
Ephraim's children. Also the children of
Makir son of Manasseh were placed at birth
on Joseph's knees.[c]
24Then Joseph said to his brothers, "I am
about to die. But God will surely come to your
aid and take you up out of this land to the
land he promised on oath to Abraham, Isaac
and Jacob." 25And Joseph made the sons of
Israel swear an oath and said, "God will
surely come to your aid, and then you must
carry my bones up from this place."
26So Joseph died at the age of a hundred
and ten. And after they embalmed him, he
was placed in a coffin in Egypt.

a9 Or *charioteers*

b11 *Abel Mizraim* means *mourning of the Egyptians.*

c23 That is, were counted as his

Exodus

Introduction:

Exodus means "exit" or "departure." The title of this book comes from one of the greatest miracles of God's care for his people in the Old Testament—the Israelites being freed from slavery and leaving Egypt.

The book of Exodus continues the story of God's people, now called Israelites. The story of the Israelites, began with Abraham in the book of Genesis.

From Moses' birth, God chose him for a special task—to lead the Israelites out of Egypt and to the land God had promised them, Canaan. Moses is the main character and author of this book. Although he was weak in his own strength, God made him strong with his power and encouragement (7:6–11). God showed his power to the Israelites and the Egyptians in the ten plagues (7:14–11:10); the last plague made it possible for the Israelites to leave Egypt. Before leaving Egypt they celebrated the Passover (12).

The Israelites began their journey protected and guided by God in a pillar of cloud by day and a pillar of fire by night. With Moses leading them they crossed the Red Sea (Sea of Reeds) and settled in the desert at the foot of Mount Sinai for about one year. Here God set up his covenant with the Israelites by giving them the laws for living and worshiping.

The covenant between God and Israel began a relationship in which Israel was identified as God's holy nation. God gave his people the Ten Commandments, priests, and a tabernacle to help them live lives that showed they were truly God's people.

Outline of contents:

Moses, God's leader (1:1–4:31)
The contest with Pharaoh (5:1–13:19)
From Egypt to Mount Sinai (13:20–19:2)
God's covenant and laws (19:3–24:8)
The tabernacle for worship (24:9–40:38)

The Israelites Oppressed

1 These are the names of the sons of Israel who went to Egypt with Jacob, each
with his family: 2Reuben, Simeon, Levi and
Judah; 3Issachar, Zebulun and Benjamin;
4Dan and Naphtali; Gad and Asher. 5The
descendants of Jacob numbered seventy[a] in
all; Joseph was already in Egypt.
6Now Joseph and all his brothers and all
that generation died, 7but the Israelites were
fruitful and multiplied greatly and became
exceedingly numerous, so that the land was
filled with them.
8Then a new king, who did not know about
Joseph, came to power in Egypt. 9"Look," he
said to his people, "the Israelites have
become much too numerous for us. 10Come,
we must deal shrewdly with them or they will
become even more numerous and, if war
breaks out, will join our enemies, fight
against us and leave the country."
11So they put slave masters over them to
oppress them with forced labor, and they
built Pithom and Rameses as store cities for
Pharaoh. 12But the more they were oppressed, the more they multiplied and
spread; so the Egyptians came to dread the
Israelites 13and worked them ruthlessly.
14They made their lives bitter with hard labor
in brick and mortar and with all kinds of work
in the fields; in all their hard labor the Egyptians used them ruthlessly.

[a]5 Masoretic Text (see also Gen. 46:27); Dead Sea Scrolls and Septuagint (see also Acts 7:14 and note at Gen. 46:27) *seventy-five*

15The king of Egypt said to the Hebrew
midwives, whose names were Shiphrah and
Puah, 16"When you help the Hebrew women
in childbirth and observe them on the delivery stool, if it is a boy, kill him; but if it is a girl,
let her live." 17The midwives, however,
feared God and did not do what the king of
Egypt had told them to do; they let the boys
live. 18Then the king of Egypt summoned the
midwives and asked them, "Why have you
done this? Why have you let the boys live?"
19The midwives answered Pharaoh, "Hebrew women are not like Egyptian women;
they are vigorous and give birth before the
midwives arrive."
20So God was kind to the midwives and the
people increased and became even more
numerous. 21And because the midwives
feared God, he gave them families of their
own.
22Then Pharaoh gave this order to all his
people: "Every boy that is born[a] you must
throw into the Nile, but let every girl live."

The Birth of Moses

2 Now a man of the house of Levi married
a Levite woman, 2and she became pregnant and gave birth to a son. When she saw
that he was a fine child, she hid him for three
months. 3But when she could hide him no
longer, she got a papyrus basket for him and
coated it with tar and pitch. Then she placed
the child in it and put it among the reeds
along the bank of the Nile. 4His sister stood
at a distance to see what would happen to
him.
5Then Pharaoh's daughter went down to
the Nile to bathe, and her attendants were
walking along the river bank. She saw the
basket among the reeds and sent her slave
girl to get it. 6She opened it and saw the
baby. He was crying, and she felt sorry for
him. "This is one of the Hebrew babies," she
said.
7Then his sister asked Pharaoh's daughter, "Shall I go and get one of the Hebrew
women to nurse the baby for you?"
8"Yes, go," she answered. And the girl
went and got the baby's mother. 9Pharaoh's
daughter said to her, "Take this baby and
nurse him for me, and I will pay you." So the
woman took the baby and nursed him.
10When the child grew older, she took him to
Pharaoh's daughter and he became her son.
She named him Moses,[b] saying, "I drew him
out of the water."

Moses Flees to Midian

11One day, after Moses had grown up, he
went out to where his own people were and
watched them at their hard labor. He saw an
Egyptian beating a Hebrew, one of his own
people. 12Glancing this way and that and
seeing no one, he killed the Egyptian and hid
him in the sand. 13The next day he went out
and saw two Hebrews fighting. He asked the
one in the wrong, "Why are you hitting your
fellow Hebrew?"
14The man said, "Who made you ruler and
judge over us? Are you thinking of killing me
as you killed the Egyptian?" Then Moses
was afraid and thought, "What I did must
have become known."
15When Pharaoh heard of this, he tried to
kill Moses, but Moses fled from Pharaoh and
went to live in Midian, where he sat down by
a well. 16Now a priest of Midian had seven
daughters, and they came to draw water and
fill the troughs to water their father's flock.
17Some shepherds came along and drove
them away, but Moses got up and came to
their rescue and watered their flock.
18When the girls returned to Reuel their
father, he asked them, "Why have you returned so early today?"
19They answered, "An Egyptian rescued
us from the shepherds. He even drew water
for us and watered the flock."
20"And where is he?" he asked his daughters. "Why did you leave him? Invite him to
have something to eat."
21Moses agreed to stay with the man, who
gave his daughter Zipporah to Moses in marriage. 22Zipporah gave birth to a son, and
Moses named him Gershom,[c] saying, "I
have become an alien in a foreign land."
23During that long period, the king of Egypt
died. The Israelites groaned in their slavery
and cried out, and their cry for help because
of their slavery went up to God. 24God heard
their groaning and he remembered his covenant with Abraham, with Isaac and with
Jacob. 25So God looked on the Israelites and
was concerned about them.

Moses and the Burning Bush

3 Now Moses was tending the flock of
Jethro his father-in-law, the priest of

[a]22 Masoretic Text; Samaritan Pentateuch, Septuagint and Targums *born to the Hebrews* [b]10 *Moses* sounds like the Hebrew for *draw out.* [c]22 *Gershom* sounds like the Hebrew for *an alien there.*

Midian, and he led the flock to the far side of the desert and came to Horeb, the mountain of God. 2There the angel of the LORD appeared to him in flames of fire from within a bush. Moses saw that though the bush was on fire it did not burn up. 3So Moses thought, "I will go over and see this strange sight—why the bush does not burn up."

4When the LORD saw that he had gone over to look, God called to him from within the bush, "Moses! Moses!"

And Moses said, "Here I am."

5"Do not come any closer," God said. "Take off your sandals, for the place where you are standing is holy ground." 6Then he said, "I am the God of your father, the God of Abraham, the God of Isaac and the God of Jacob." At this, Moses hid his face, because he was afraid to look at God.

7The LORD said, "I have indeed seen the misery of my people in Egypt. I have heard them crying out because of their slave drivers, and I am concerned about their suffering. 8So I have come down to rescue them from the hand of the Egyptians and to bring them up out of that land into a good and spacious land, a land flowing with milk and honey—the home of the Canaanites, Hittites, Amorites, Perizzites, Hivites and Jebusites. 9And now the cry of the Israelites has reached me, and I have seen the way the Egyptians are oppressing them. 10So now, go. I am sending you to Pharaoh to bring my people the Israelites out of Egypt."

11But Moses said to God, "Who am I, that I should go to Pharaoh and bring the Israelites out of Egypt?"

12And God said, "I will be with you. And this will be the sign to you that it is I who have sent you: When you have brought the people out of Egypt, you[a] will worship God on this mountain."

13Moses said to God, "Suppose I go to the Israelites and say to them, 'The God of your fathers has sent me to you,' and they ask me, 'What is his name?' Then what shall I tell them?"

14God said to Moses, "I AM WHO I AM.[b] This is what you are to say to the Israelites: 'I AM has sent me to you.' "

15God also said to Moses, "Say to the Israelites, 'The LORD,[c] the God of your fathers—the God of Abraham, the God of Isaac and the God of Jacob—has sent me to you.' This is my name forever, the name by which I am to be remembered from generation to generation.

16"Go, assemble the elders of Israel and say to them, 'The LORD, the God of your fathers—the God of Abraham, Isaac and Jacob— appeared to me and said: I have watched over you and have seen what has been done to you in Egypt. 17And I have promised to bring you up out of your misery in Egypt into the land of the Canaanites, Hittites, Amorites, Perizzites, Hivites and Jebusites—a land flowing with milk and honey.'

18"The elders of Israel will listen to you. Then you and the elders are to go to the king of Egypt and say to him, 'The LORD, the God of the Hebrews, has met with us. Let us take a three-day journey into the desert to offer sacrifices to the LORD our God.' 19But I know that the king of Egypt will not let you go unless a mighty hand compels him. 20So I will stretch out my hand and strike the Egyptians with all the wonders that I will perform among them. After that, he will let you go.

21"And I will make the Egyptians favorably disposed toward this people, so that when you leave you will not go empty-handed. 22Every woman is to ask her neighbor and any woman living in her house for articles of silver and gold and for clothing, which you will put on your sons and daughters. And so you will plunder the Egyptians."

Signs for Moses

4 Moses answered, "What if they do not believe me or listen to me and say, 'The LORD did not appear to you'?"

2Then the LORD said to him, "What is that in your hand?"

"A staff," he replied.

3The LORD said, "Throw it on the ground."

Moses threw it on the ground and it became a snake, and he ran from it. 4Then the LORD said to him, "Reach out your hand and take it by the tail." So Moses reached out and took hold of the snake and it turned back into a staff in his hand. 5"This," said the LORD, "is so that they may believe that the LORD, the God of their fathers—the God of Abraham, the God of Isaac and the God of Jacob—has appeared to you."

6Then the LORD said, "Put your hand inside your cloak." So Moses put his hand into his

[a] *12* The Hebrew is plural. [b] *14* Or *I WILL BE WHAT I WILL BE* [c] *15* The Hebrew for *LORD* sounds like and may be derived from the Hebrew for *I AM* in verse 14.

cloak, and when he took it out, it was leprous,[a] like snow.

7“Now put it back into your cloak,” he said. So Moses put his hand back into his cloak, and when he took it out, it was restored, like the rest of his flesh.

8Then the LORD said, “If they do not believe you or pay attention to the first miraculous sign, they may believe the second. 9But if they do not believe these two signs or listen to you, take some water from the Nile and pour it on the dry ground. The water you take from the river will become blood on the ground.”

10Moses said to the LORD, “O Lord, I have never been eloquent, neither in the past nor since you have spoken to your servant. I am slow of speech and tongue.”

11The LORD said to him, “Who gave man his mouth? Who makes him deaf or mute? Who gives him sight or makes him blind? Is it not I, the LORD? 12Now go; I will help you speak and will teach you what to say.”

13But Moses said, “O Lord, please send someone else to do it.”

14Then the LORD's anger burned against Moses and he said, “What about your brother, Aaron the Levite? I know he can speak well. He is already on his way to meet you, and his heart will be glad when he sees you. 15You shall speak to him and put words in his mouth; I will help both of you speak and will teach you what to do. 16He will speak to the people for you, and it will be as if he were your mouth and as if you were God to him. 17But take this staff in your hand so you can perform miraculous signs with it.”

Moses Returns to Egypt

18Then Moses went back to Jethro his father-in-law and said to him, “Let me go back to my own people in Egypt to see if any of them are still alive.”

Jethro said, “Go, and I wish you well.”

19Now the LORD had said to Moses in Midian, “Go back to Egypt, for all the men who wanted to kill you are dead.” 20So Moses took his wife and sons, put them on a donkey and started back to Egypt. And he took the staff of God in his hand.

21The LORD said to Moses, “When you return to Egypt, see that you perform before Pharaoh all the wonders I have given you the power to do. But I will harden his heart so that he will not let the people go. 22Then say to Pharaoh, ‘This is what the LORD says: Israel is my firstborn son, 23and I told you, “Let my son go, so he may worship me.” But you refused to let him go; so I will kill your firstborn son.’ ”

24At a lodging place on the way, the LORD met ⌊Moses⌋[b] and was about to kill him. 25But Zipporah took a flint knife, cut off her son's foreskin and touched ⌊Moses'⌋ feet with it.[c] “Surely you are a bridegroom of blood to me,” she said. 26So the LORD let him alone. (At that time she said “bridegroom of blood,” referring to circumcision.)

27The LORD said to Aaron, “Go into the desert to meet Moses.” So he met Moses at the mountain of God and kissed him. 28Then Moses told Aaron everything the LORD had sent him to say, and also about all the miraculous signs he had commanded him to perform.

29Moses and Aaron brought together all the elders of the Israelites, 30and Aaron told them everything the LORD had said to Moses. He also performed the signs before the people, 31and they believed. And when they heard that the LORD was concerned about them and had seen their misery, they bowed down and worshiped.

Bricks Without Straw

5 Afterward Moses and Aaron went to Pharaoh and said, “This is what the LORD, the God of Israel, says: ‘Let my people go, so that they may hold a festival to me in the desert.’ ”

2Pharaoh said, “Who is the LORD, that I should obey him and let Israel go? I do not know the LORD and I will not let Israel go.”

3Then they said, “The God of the Hebrews has met with us. Now let us take a three-day journey into the desert to offer sacrifices to the LORD our God, or he may strike us with plagues or with the sword.”

4But the king of Egypt said, “Moses and Aaron, why are you taking the people away from their labor? Get back to your work!” 5Then Pharaoh said, “Look, the people of the land are now numerous, and you are stopping them from working.”

6That same day Pharaoh gave this order to the slave drivers and foremen in charge of the people: 7“You are no longer to supply the people with straw for making bricks; let them

[a]6 The Hebrew word was used for various diseases affecting the skin—not necessarily leprosy. [b]24 Or ⌊*Moses' son*⌋; Hebrew *him* [c]25 Or *and drew near* ⌊*Moses'*⌋ *feet*

go and gather their own straw. 8But require
them to make the same number of bricks as
before; don't reduce the quota. They are
lazy; that is why they are crying out, 'Let us
go and sacrifice to our God.' 9Make the work
harder for the men so that they keep working
and pay no attention to lies."

10Then the slave drivers and the foremen
went out and said to the people, "This is what
Pharaoh says: 'I will not give you any more
straw. 11Go and get your own straw
wherever you can find it, but your work will
not be reduced at all.' " 12So the people scattered all over Egypt to gather stubble to use
for straw. 13The slave drivers kept pressing
them, saying, "Complete the work required
of you for each day, just as when you had
straw." 14The Israelite foremen appointed by
Pharaoh's slave drivers were beaten and
were asked, "Why didn't you meet your
quota of bricks yesterday or today, as before?"

15Then the Israelite foremen went and appealed to Pharaoh: "Why have you treated
your servants this way? 16Your servants are
given no straw, yet we are told, 'Make
bricks!' Your servants are being beaten, but
the fault is with your own people."

17Pharaoh said, "Lazy, that's what you
are—lazy! That is why you keep saying, 'Let
us go and sacrifice to the LORD.' 18Now get to
work. You will not be given any straw, yet you
must produce your full quota of bricks."

19The Israelite foremen realized they were
in trouble when they were told, "You are not
to reduce the number of bricks required of
you for each day." 20When they left Pharaoh,
they found Moses and Aaron waiting to meet
them, 21and they said, "May the LORD look
upon you and judge you! You have made us
a stench to Pharaoh and his officials and
have put a sword in their hand to kill us."

God Promises Deliverance

22Moses returned to the LORD and said, "O
Lord, why have you brought trouble upon
this people? Is this why you sent me? 23Ever
since I went to Pharaoh to speak in your
name, he has brought trouble upon this
people, and you have not rescued your
people at all."

6 Then the LORD said to Moses, "Now you
will see what I will do to Pharaoh: Because of my mighty hand he will let them go;
because of my mighty hand he will drive
them out of his country."

2God also said to Moses, "I am the LORD. 3I
appeared to Abraham, to Isaac and to Jacob
as God Almighty,[a] but by my name the LORD[b]
I did not make myself known to them.[c] 4I also
established my covenant with them to give
them the land of Canaan, where they lived as
aliens. 5Moreover, I have heard the groaning
of the Israelites, whom the Egyptians are
enslaving, and I have remembered my covenant.

6"Therefore, say to the Israelites: 'I am the
LORD, and I will bring you out from under the
yoke of the Egyptians. I will free you from
being slaves to them, and I will redeem you
with an outstretched arm and with mighty
acts of judgment. 7I will take you as my own
people, and I will be your God. Then you will
know that I am the LORD your God, who
brought you out from under the yoke of the
Egyptians. 8And I will bring you to the land I
swore with uplifted hand to give to Abraham,
to Isaac and to Jacob. I will give it to you as a
possession. I am the LORD.' "

9Moses reported this to the Israelites, but
they did not listen to him because of their
discouragement and cruel bondage.

10Then the LORD said to Moses, 11"Go, tell
Pharaoh king of Egypt to let the Israelites go
out of his country."

12But Moses said to the LORD, "If the Israelites will not listen to me, why would Pharaoh
listen to me, since I speak with faltering
lips[d]?"

Family Record of Moses and Aaron

13Now the LORD spoke to Moses and Aaron
about the Israelites and Pharaoh king of
Egypt, and he commanded them to bring the
Israelites out of Egypt.

14These were the heads of their families[e]:

The sons of Reuben the firstborn son
of Israel were Hanoch and Pallu, Hezron and Carmi. These were the clans of
Reuben.

15The sons of Simeon were Jemuel,
Jamin, Ohad, Jakin, Zohar and Shaul
the son of a Canaanite woman. These
were the clans of Simeon.

16These were the names of the sons
of Levi according to their records: Ger-

[a]3 Hebrew *El-Shaddai* [b]3 See note at Exodus 3:15. [c]3 Or *Almighty, and by my name the LORD did I not let myself be known to them?* [d]12 Hebrew *I am uncircumcised of lips*; also in verse 30 [e]14 The Hebrew for *families* here and in verse 25 refers to units larger than clans.

shon, Kohath and Merari. Levi lived 137
years.
17The sons of Gershon, by clans,
were Libni and Shimei.
18The sons of Kohath were Amram,
Izhar, Hebron and Uzziel. Kohath lived
133 years.
19The sons of Merari were Mahli and
Mushi.
These were the clans of Levi according to their records.
20Amram married his father's sister
Jochebed, who bore him Aaron and
Moses. Amram lived 137 years.
21The sons of Izhar were Korah, Nepheg and Zicri.
22The sons of Uzziel were Mishael,
Elzaphan and Sithri.
23Aaron married Elisheba, daughter
of Amminadab and sister of Nahshon,
and she bore him Nadab and Abihu,
Eleazar and Ithamar.
24The sons of Korah were Assir, Elkanah and Abiasaph. These were the Korahite clans.
25Eleazar son of Aaron married one of
the daughters of Putiel, and she bore
him Phinehas.

These were the heads of the Levite
families, clan by clan.

26It was this same Aaron and Moses to
whom the LORD said, "Bring the Israelites out
of Egypt by their divisions." 27They were the
ones who spoke to Pharaoh king of Egypt
about bringing the Israelites out of Egypt. It
was the same Moses and Aaron.

Aaron to Speak for Moses

28Now when the LORD spoke to Moses in
Egypt, 29he said to him, "I am the LORD. Tell
Pharaoh king of Egypt everything I tell you."
30But Moses said to the LORD, "Since I
speak with faltering lips, why would Pharaoh
listen to me?"

7 Then the LORD said to Moses, "See, I
have made you like God to Pharaoh, and
your brother Aaron will be your prophet. 2You
are to say everything I command you, and
your brother Aaron is to tell Pharaoh to let the
Israelites go out of his country. 3But I will
harden Pharaoh's heart, and though I multiply my miraculous signs and wonders in
Egypt, 4he will not listen to you. Then I will lay
my hand on Egypt and with mighty acts of
judgment I will bring out my divisions, my
people the Israelites. 5And the Egyptians will
know that I am the LORD when I stretch out my
hand against Egypt and bring the Israelites
out of it."
6Moses and Aaron did just as the LORD
commanded them. 7Moses was eighty years
old and Aaron eighty-three when they spoke
to Pharaoh.

Aaron's Staff Becomes a Snake

8The LORD said to Moses and Aaron,
9"When Pharaoh says to you, 'Perform a
miracle,' then say to Aaron, 'Take your staff
and throw it down before Pharaoh,' and it will
become a snake."
10So Moses and Aaron went to Pharaoh
and did just as the LORD commanded. Aaron
threw his staff down in front of Pharaoh and
his officials, and it became a snake. 11Pharaoh then summoned wise men and sorcerers, and the Egyptian magicians also did the
same things by their secret arts: 12Each one
threw down his staff and it became a snake.
But Aaron's staff swallowed up their staffs.
13Yet Pharaoh's heart became hard and he
would not listen to them, just as the LORD had
said.

The Plague of Blood

14Then the LORD said to Moses, "Pharaoh's
heart is unyielding; he refuses to let the
people go. 15Go to Pharaoh in the morning
as he goes out to the water. Wait on the bank
of the Nile to meet him, and take in your hand
the staff that was changed into a snake.
16Then say to him, 'The LORD, the God of the
Hebrews, has sent me to say to you: Let my
people go, so that they may worship me in
the desert. But until now you have not listened. 17This is what the LORD says: By this
you will know that I am the LORD: With the
staff that is in my hand I will strike the water
of the Nile, and it will be changed into blood.
18The fish in the Nile will die, and the river will
stink; the Egyptians will not be able to drink
its water.' "
19The LORD said to Moses, "Tell Aaron,
'Take your staff and stretch out your hand
over the waters of Egypt—over the streams
and canals, over the ponds and all the reservoirs'—and they will turn to blood. Blood will
be everywhere in Egypt, even in the wooden
buckets and stone jars."
20Moses and Aaron did just as the LORD
had commanded. He raised his staff in the
presence of Pharaoh and his officials and
struck the water of the Nile, and all the water
was changed into blood. 21The fish in the Nile

died, and the river smelled so bad that the
Egyptians could not drink its water. Blood
was everywhere in Egypt.
22But the Egyptian magicians did the same
things by their secret arts, and Pharaoh's
heart became hard; he would not listen to
Moses and Aaron, just as the LORD had said.
23Instead, he turned and went into his palace, and did not take even this to heart.
24And all the Egyptians dug along the Nile to
get drinking water, because they could not
drink the water of the river.

The Plague of Frogs

25Seven days passed after the LORD struck
8 the Nile. 1Then the LORD said to Moses,
"Go to Pharaoh and say to him, 'This is
what the LORD says: Let my people go, so
that they may worship me. 2If you refuse to
let them go, I will plague your whole country
with frogs. 3The Nile will teem with frogs.
They will come up into your palace and your
bedroom and onto your bed, into the houses
of your officials and on your people, and into
your ovens and kneading troughs. 4The
frogs will go up on you and your people and
all your officials.' "
5Then the LORD said to Moses, "Tell Aaron,
'Stretch out your hand with your staff over
the streams and canals and ponds, and
make frogs come up on the land of Egypt.' "
6So Aaron stretched out his hand over the
waters of Egypt, and the frogs came up and
covered the land. 7But the magicians did the
same things by their secret arts; they also
made frogs come up on the land of Egypt.
8Pharaoh summoned Moses and Aaron
and said, "Pray to the LORD to take the frogs
away from me and my people, and I will let
your people go to offer sacrifices to the
LORD."
9Moses said to Pharaoh, "I leave to you
the honor of setting the time for me to pray
for you and your officials and your people
that you and your houses may be rid of the
frogs, except for those that remain in the
Nile."
10"Tomorrow," Pharaoh said.
Moses replied, "It will be as you say, so
that you may know there is no one like the
LORD our God. 11The frogs will leave you and
your houses, your officials and your people;
they will remain only in the Nile."
12After Moses and Aaron left Pharaoh,
Moses cried out to the LORD about the frogs
he had brought on Pharaoh. 13And the LORD
did what Moses asked. The frogs died in the
houses, in the courtyards and in the fields.
14They were piled into heaps, and the land
reeked of them. 15But when Pharaoh saw
that there was relief, he hardened his heart
and would not listen to Moses and Aaron,
just as the LORD had said.

The Plague of Gnats

16Then the LORD said to Moses, "Tell
Aaron, 'Stretch out your staff and strike the
dust of the ground,' and throughout the land
of Egypt the dust will become gnats." 17They
did this, and when Aaron stretched out his
hand with the staff and struck the dust of the
ground, gnats came upon men and animals.
All the dust throughout the land of Egypt
became gnats. 18But when the magicians
tried to produce gnats by their secret arts,
they could not. And the gnats were on men
and animals.
19The magicians said to Pharaoh, "This is
the finger of God." But Pharaoh's heart was
hard and he would not listen, just as the LORD
had said.

The Plague of Flies

20Then the LORD said to Moses, "Get up
early in the morning and confront Pharaoh
as he goes to the water and say to him, 'This
is what the LORD says: Let my people go, so
that they may worship me. 21If you do not let
my people go, I will send swarms of flies on
you and your officials, on your people and
into your houses. The houses of the Egyptians will be full of flies, and even the ground
where they are.
22" 'But on that day I will deal differently
with the land of Goshen, where my people
live; no swarms of flies will be there, so that
you will know that I, the LORD, am in this land.
23I will make a distinction[a] between my
people and your people. This miraculous
sign will occur tomorrow.' "
24And the LORD did this. Dense swarms of
flies poured into Pharaoh's palace and into
the houses of his officials, and throughout
Egypt the land was ruined by the flies.
25Then Pharaoh summoned Moses and
Aaron and said, "Go, sacrifice to your God
here in the land."
26But Moses said, "That would not be right.
The sacrifices we offer the LORD our God

[a]23 Septuagint and Vulgate; Hebrew *will put a deliverance*

would be detestable to the Egyptians. And if we offer sacrifices that are detestable in their eyes, will they not stone us? 27We must take a three-day journey into the desert to offer sacrifices to the LORD our God, as he commands us."

28Pharaoh said, "I will let you go to offer sacrifices to the LORD your God in the desert, but you must not go very far. Now pray for me."

29Moses answered, "As soon as I leave you, I will pray to the LORD, and tomorrow the flies will leave Pharaoh and his officials and his people. Only be sure that Pharaoh does not act deceitfully again by not letting the people go to offer sacrifices to the LORD."

30Then Moses left Pharaoh and prayed to the LORD, 31and the LORD did what Moses asked: The flies left Pharaoh and his officials and his people; not a fly remained. 32But this time also Pharaoh hardened his heart and would not let the people go.

The Plague on Livestock

9 Then the LORD said to Moses, "Go to Pharaoh and say to him, 'This is what the LORD, the God of the Hebrews, says: "Let my people go, so that they may worship me." 2If you refuse to let them go and continue to hold them back, 3the hand of the LORD will bring a terrible plague on your livestock in the field—on your horses and donkeys and camels and on your cattle and sheep and goats. 4But the LORD will make a distinction between the livestock of Israel and that of Egypt, so that no animal belonging to the Israelites will die.' "

5The LORD set a time and said, "Tomorrow the LORD will do this in the land." 6And the next day the LORD did it: All the livestock of the Egyptians died, but not one animal belonging to the Israelites died. 7Pharaoh sent men to investigate and found that not even one of the animals of the Israelites had died. Yet his heart was unyielding and he would not let the people go.

The Plague of Boils

8Then the LORD said to Moses and Aaron, "Take handfuls of soot from a furnace and have Moses toss it into the air in the presence of Pharaoh. 9It will become fine dust over the whole land of Egypt, and festering boils will break out on men and animals throughout the land."

10So they took soot from a furnace and stood before Pharaoh. Moses tossed it into the air, and festering boils broke out on men and animals. 11The magicians could not stand before Moses because of the boils that were on them and on all the Egyptians. 12But the LORD hardened Pharaoh's heart and he would not listen to Moses and Aaron, just as the LORD had said to Moses.

The Plague of Hail

13Then the LORD said to Moses, "Get up early in the morning, confront Pharaoh and say to him, 'This is what the LORD, the God of the Hebrews, says: Let my people go, so that they may worship me, 14or this time I will send the full force of my plagues against you and against your officials and your people, so you may know that there is no one like me in all the earth. 15For by now I could have stretched out my hand and struck you and your people with a plague that would have wiped you off the earth. 16But I have raised you up[a] for this very purpose, that I might show you my power and that my name might be proclaimed in all the earth. 17You still set yourself against my people and will not let them go. 18Therefore, at this time tomorrow I will send the worst hailstorm that has ever fallen on Egypt, from the day it was founded till now. 19Give an order now to bring your livestock and everything you have in the field to a place of shelter, because the hail will fall on every man and animal that has not been brought in and is still out in the field, and they will die.' "

20Those officials of Pharaoh who feared the word of the LORD hurried to bring their slaves and their livestock inside. 21But those who ignored the word of the LORD left their slaves and livestock in the field.

22Then the LORD said to Moses, "Stretch out your hand toward the sky so that hail will fall all over Egypt—on men and animals and on everything growing in the fields of Egypt." 23When Moses stretched out his staff toward the sky, the LORD sent thunder and hail, and lightning flashed down to the ground. So the LORD rained hail on the land of Egypt; 24hail fell and lightning flashed back and forth. It was the worst storm in all the land of Egypt since it had become a nation. 25Throughout Egypt hail struck everything in the fields—both men and animals; it beat down everything growing in the fields and stripped every

[a]16 Or *have spared you*

tree. 26The only place it did not hail was the land of Goshen, where the Israelites were.

27Then Pharaoh summoned Moses and Aaron. "This time I have sinned," he said to them. "The LORD is in the right, and I and my people are in the wrong. 28Pray to the LORD, for we have had enough thunder and hail. I will let you go; you don't have to stay any longer."

29Moses replied, "When I have gone out of the city, I will spread out my hands in prayer to the LORD. The thunder will stop and there will be no more hail, so you may know that the earth is the LORD's. 30But I know that you and your officials still do not fear the LORD God."

31(The flax and barley were destroyed, since the barley had headed and the flax was in bloom. 32The wheat and spelt, however, were not destroyed, because they ripen later.)

33Then Moses left Pharaoh and went out of the city. He spread out his hands toward the LORD; the thunder and hail stopped, and the rain no longer poured down on the land. 34When Pharaoh saw that the rain and hail and thunder had stopped, he sinned again: He and his officials hardened their hearts. 35So Pharaoh's heart was hard and he would not let the Israelites go, just as the LORD had said through Moses.

The Plague of Locusts

10 Then the LORD said to Moses, "Go to Pharaoh, for I have hardened his heart and the hearts of his officials so that I may perform these miraculous signs of mine among them 2that you may tell your children and grandchildren how I dealt harshly with the Egyptians and how I performed my signs among them, and that you may know that I am the LORD."

3So Moses and Aaron went to Pharaoh and said to him, "This is what the LORD, the God of the Hebrews, says: 'How long will you refuse to humble yourself before me? Let my people go, so that they may worship me. 4If you refuse to let them go, I will bring locusts into your country tomorrow. 5They will cover the face of the ground so that it cannot be seen. They will devour what little you have left after the hail, including every tree that is growing in your fields. 6They will fill your houses and those of all your officials and all the Egyptians—something neither your fathers nor your forefathers have ever seen from the day they settled in this land till now.' " Then Moses turned and left Pharaoh.

7Pharaoh's officials said to him, "How long will this man be a snare to us? Let the people go, so that they may worship the LORD their God. Do you not yet realize that Egypt is ruined?"

8Then Moses and Aaron were brought back to Pharaoh. "Go, worship the LORD your God," he said. "But just who will be going?"

9Moses answered, "We will go with our young and old, with our sons and daughters, and with our flocks and herds, because we are to celebrate a festival to the LORD."

10Pharaoh said, "The LORD be with you—if I let you go, along with your women and children! Clearly you are bent on evil.[a] 11No! Have only the men go; and worship the LORD, since that's what you have been asking for." Then Moses and Aaron were driven out of Pharaoh's presence.

12And the LORD said to Moses, "Stretch out your hand over Egypt so that locusts will swarm over the land and devour everything growing in the fields, everything left by the hail."

13So Moses stretched out his staff over Egypt, and the LORD made an east wind blow across the land all that day and all that night. By morning the wind had brought the locusts; 14they invaded all Egypt and settled down in every area of the country in great numbers. Never before had there been such a plague of locusts, nor will there ever be again. 15They covered all the ground until it was black. They devoured all that was left after the hail—everything growing in the fields and the fruit on the trees. Nothing green remained on tree or plant in all the land of Egypt.

16Pharaoh quickly summoned Moses and Aaron and said, "I have sinned against the LORD your God and against you. 17Now forgive my sin once more and pray to the LORD your God to take this deadly plague away from me."

18Moses then left Pharaoh and prayed to the LORD. 19And the LORD changed the wind to a very strong west wind, which caught up the locusts and carried them into the Red Sea.[b] Not a locust was left anywhere in Egypt. 20But the LORD hardened Pharaoh's heart, and he would not let the Israelites go.

[a] *10* Or *Be careful, trouble is in store for you!*
[b] *19* Hebrew *Yam Suph;* that is, Sea of Reeds

The Plague of Darkness

21Then the Lord said to Moses, "Stretch out your hand toward the sky so that darkness will spread over Egypt—darkness that can be felt." 22So Moses stretched out his hand toward the sky, and total darkness covered all Egypt for three days. 23No one could see anyone else or leave his place for three days. Yet all the Israelites had light in the places where they lived.

24Then Pharaoh summoned Moses and said, "Go, worship the Lord. Even your women and children may go with you; only leave your flocks and herds behind."

25But Moses said, "You must allow us to have sacrifices and burnt offerings to present to the Lord our God. 26Our livestock too must go with us; not a hoof is to be left behind. We have to use some of them in worshiping the Lord our God, and until we get there we will not know what we are to use to worship the Lord."

27But the Lord hardened Pharaoh's heart, and he was not willing to let them go. 28Pharaoh said to Moses, "Get out of my sight! Make sure you do not appear before me again! The day you see my face you will die."

29"Just as you say," Moses replied, "I will never appear before you again."

The Plague on the Firstborn

11 Now the Lord had said to Moses, "I will bring one more plague on Pharaoh and on Egypt. After that, he will let you go from here, and when he does, he will drive you out completely. 2Tell the people that men and women alike are to ask their neighbors for articles of silver and gold." 3(The Lord made the Egyptians favorably disposed toward the people, and Moses himself was highly regarded in Egypt by Pharaoh's officials and by the people.)

4So Moses said, "This is what the Lord says: 'About midnight I will go throughout Egypt. 5Every firstborn son in Egypt will die, from the firstborn son of Pharaoh, who sits on the throne, to the firstborn son of the slave girl, who is at her hand mill, and all the firstborn of the cattle as well. 6There will be loud wailing throughout Egypt—worse than there has ever been or ever will be again. 7But among the Israelites not a dog will bark at any man or animal.' Then you will know that the Lord makes a distinction between Egypt and Israel. 8All these officials of yours will come to me, bowing down before me and saying, 'Go, you and all the people who follow you!' After that I will leave." Then Moses, hot with anger, left Pharaoh.

9The Lord had said to Moses, "Pharaoh will refuse to listen to you—so that my wonders may be multiplied in Egypt." 10Moses and Aaron performed all these wonders before Pharaoh, but the Lord hardened Pharaoh's heart, and he would not let the Israelites go out of his country.

The Passover

12 The Lord said to Moses and Aaron in Egypt, 2"This month is to be for you the first month, the first month of your year. 3Tell the whole community of Israel that on the tenth day of this month each man is to take a lamb[a] for his family, one for each household. 4If any household is too small for a whole lamb, they must share one with their nearest neighbor, having taken into account the number of people there are. You are to determine the amount of lamb needed in accordance with what each person will eat. 5The animals you choose must be year-old males without defect, and you may take them from the sheep or the goats. 6Take care of them until the fourteenth day of the month, when all the people of the community of Israel must slaughter them at twilight. 7Then they are to take some of the blood and put it on the sides and tops of the doorframes of the houses where they eat the lambs. 8That same night they are to eat the meat roasted over the fire, along with bitter herbs, and bread made without yeast. 9Do not eat the meat raw or cooked in water, but roast it over the fire—head, legs and inner parts. 10Do not leave any of it till morning; if some is left till morning, you must burn it. 11This is how you are to eat it: with your cloak tucked into your belt, your sandals on your feet and your staff in your hand. Eat it in haste; it is the Lord's Passover.

12"On that same night I will pass through Egypt and strike down every firstborn—both men and animals—and I will bring judgment on all the gods of Egypt. I am the Lord. 13The blood will be a sign for you on the houses where you are; and when I see the blood, I will pass over you. No destructive plague will touch you when I strike Egypt.

14"This is a day you are to commemorate; for the generations to come you shall cele-

[a]3 The Hebrew word can mean *lamb* or *kid*; also in verse 4.

brate it as a festival to the LORD—a lasting
ordinance. 15For seven days you are to eat
bread made without yeast. On the first day
remove the yeast from your houses, for whoever eats anything with yeast in it from the
first day through the seventh must be cut off
from Israel. 16On the first day hold a sacred
assembly, and another one on the seventh
day. Do no work at all on these days, except
to prepare food for everyone to eat—that is
all you may do.

17"Celebrate the Feast of Unleavened
Bread, because it was on this very day that I
brought your divisions out of Egypt. Celebrate this day as a lasting ordinance for the
generations to come. 18In the first month you
are to eat bread made without yeast, from
the evening of the fourteenth day until the
evening of the twenty-first day. 19For seven
days no yeast is to be found in your houses.
And whoever eats anything with yeast in it
must be cut off from the community of Israel,
whether he is an alien or native-born. 20Eat
nothing made with yeast. Wherever you live,
you must eat unleavened bread."

21Then Moses summoned all the elders of
Israel and said to them, "Go at once and
select the animals for your families and
slaughter the Passover lamb. 22Take a
bunch of hyssop, dip it into the blood in the
basin and put some of the blood on the top
and on both sides of the doorframe. Not one
of you shall go out the door of his house until
morning. 23When the LORD goes through the
land to strike down the Egyptians, he will see
the blood on the top and sides of the doorframe and will pass over that doorway, and
he will not permit the destroyer to enter your
houses and strike you down.

24"Obey these instructions as a lasting ordinance for you and your descendants.
25When you enter the land that the LORD will
give you as he promised, observe this
ceremony. 26And when your children ask
you, 'What does this ceremony mean to
you?' 27then tell them, 'It is the Passover
sacrifice to the LORD, who passed over the
houses of the Israelites in Egypt and spared
our homes when he struck down the Egyptians.' " Then the people bowed down and
worshiped. 28The Israelites did just what the
LORD commanded Moses and Aaron.

29At midnight the LORD struck down all the
firstborn in Egypt, from the firstborn of Pharaoh, who sat on the throne, to the firstborn of
the prisoner, who was in the dungeon, and
the firstborn of all the livestock as well.
30Pharaoh and all his officials and all the
Egyptians got up during the night, and there
was loud wailing in Egypt, for there was not a
house without someone dead.

The Exodus

31During the night Pharaoh summoned
Moses and Aaron and said, "Up! Leave my
people, you and the Israelites! Go, worship
the LORD as you have requested. 32Take your
flocks and herds, as you have said, and go.
And also bless me."

33The Egyptians urged the people to hurry
and leave the country. "For otherwise," they
said, "we will all die!" 34So the people took
their dough before the yeast was added, and
carried it on their shoulders in kneading
troughs wrapped in clothing. 35The Israelites
did as Moses instructed and asked the Egyptians for articles of silver and gold and for
clothing. 36The LORD had made the Egyptians
favorably disposed toward the people, and
they gave them what they asked for; so they
plundered the Egyptians.

37The Israelites journeyed from Rameses
to Succoth. There were about six hundred
thousand men on foot, besides women and
children. 38Many other people went up with
them, as well as large droves of livestock,
both flocks and herds. 39With the dough they
had brought from Egypt, they baked cakes of
unleavened bread. The dough was without
yeast because they had been driven out of
Egypt and did not have time to prepare food
for themselves.

40Now the length of time the Israelite
people lived in Egypt[a] was 430 years. 41At
the end of the 430 years, to the very day, all
the LORD's divisions left Egypt. 42Because the
LORD kept vigil that night to bring them out of
Egypt, on this night all the Israelites are to
keep vigil to honor the LORD for the generations to come.

Passover Restrictions

43The LORD said to Moses and Aaron,
"These are the regulations for the Passover:

"No foreigner is to eat of it. 44Any slave you
have bought may eat of it after you have
circumcised him, 45but a temporary resident
and a hired worker may not eat of it.

46"It must be eaten inside one house; take
none of the meat outside the house. Do not

[a]40 Masoretic Text; Samaritan Pentateuch and Septuagint *Egypt and Canaan*

break any of the bones. 47The whole community of Israel must celebrate it.

48"An alien living among you who wants to celebrate the LORD's Passover must have all the males in his household circumcised; then he may take part like one born in the land. No uncircumcised male may eat of it. 49The same law applies to the native-born and to the alien living among you."

50All the Israelites did just what the LORD had commanded Moses and Aaron. 51And on that very day the LORD brought the Israelites out of Egypt by their divisions.

Consecration of the Firstborn

13 The LORD said to Moses, 2"Consecrate to me every firstborn male. The first offspring of every womb among the Israelites belongs to me, whether man or animal."

3Then Moses said to the people, "Commemorate this day, the day you came out of Egypt, out of the land of slavery, because the LORD brought you out of it with a mighty hand. Eat nothing containing yeast. 4Today, in the month of Abib, you are leaving. 5When the LORD brings you into the land of the Canaanites, Hittites, Amorites, Hivites and Jebusites—the land he swore to your forefathers to give you, a land flowing with milk and honey—you are to observe this ceremony in this month: 6For seven days eat bread made without yeast and on the seventh day hold a festival to the LORD. 7Eat unleavened bread during those seven days; nothing with yeast in it is to be seen among you, nor shall any yeast be seen anywhere within your borders. 8On that day tell your son, 'I do this because of what the LORD did for me when I came out of Egypt.' 9This observance will be for you like a sign on your hand and a reminder on your forehead that the law of the LORD is to be on your lips. For the LORD brought you out of Egypt with his mighty hand. 10You must keep this ordinance at the appointed time year after year.

11"After the LORD brings you into the land of the Canaanites and gives it to you, as he promised on oath to you and your forefathers, 12you are to give over to the LORD the first offspring of every womb. All the firstborn males of your livestock belong to the LORD. 13Redeem with a lamb every firstborn donkey, but if you do not redeem it, break its neck. Redeem every firstborn among your sons.

14"In days to come, when your son asks you, 'What does this mean?' say to him, 'With a mighty hand the LORD brought us out of Egypt, out of the land of slavery. 15When Pharaoh stubbornly refused to let us go, the LORD killed every firstborn in Egypt, both man and animal. This is why I sacrifice to the LORD the first male offspring of every womb and redeem each of my firstborn sons.' 16And it will be like a sign on your hand and a symbol on your forehead that the LORD brought us out of Egypt with his mighty hand."

Crossing the Sea

17When Pharaoh let the people go, God did not lead them on the road through the Philistine country, though that was shorter. For God said, "If they face war, they might change their minds and return to Egypt." 18So God led the people around by the desert road toward the Red Sea.[a] The Israelites went up out of Egypt armed for battle.

19Moses took the bones of Joseph with him because Joseph had made the sons of Israel swear an oath. He had said, "God will surely come to your aid, and then you must carry my bones up with you from this place."[b]

20After leaving Succoth they camped at Etham on the edge of the desert. 21By day the LORD went ahead of them in a pillar of cloud to guide them on their way and by night in a pillar of fire to give them light, so that they could travel by day or night. 22Neither the pillar of cloud by day nor the pillar of fire by night left its place in front of the people.

14 Then the LORD said to Moses, 2"Tell the Israelites to turn back and encamp near Pi Hahiroth, between Migdol and the sea. They are to encamp by the sea, directly opposite Baal Zephon. 3Pharaoh will think, 'The Israelites are wandering around the land in confusion, hemmed in by the desert.' 4And I will harden Pharaoh's heart, and he will pursue them. But I will gain glory for myself through Pharaoh and all his army, and the Egyptians will know that I am the LORD." So the Israelites did this.

5When the king of Egypt was told that the people had fled, Pharaoh and his officials changed their minds about them and said, "What have we done? We have let the Isra-

[a] *18* Hebrew *Yam Suph;* that is, Sea of Reeds   [b] *19* See Gen. 50:25.

elites go and have lost their services!" 6So he had his chariot made ready and took his army with him. 7He took six hundred of the best chariots, along with all the other chariots of Egypt, with officers over all of them. 8The LORD hardened the heart of Pharaoh king of Egypt, so that he pursued the Israelites, who were marching out boldly. 9The Egyptians—all Pharaoh's horses and chariots, horsemen[a] and troops—pursued the Israelites and overtook them as they camped by the sea near Pi Hahiroth, opposite Baal Zephon.

10As Pharaoh approached, the Israelites looked up, and there were the Egyptians, marching after them. They were terrified and cried out to the LORD. 11They said to Moses, "Was it because there were no graves in Egypt that you brought us to the desert to die? What have you done to us by bringing us out of Egypt? 12Didn't we say to you in Egypt, 'Leave us alone; let us serve the Egyptians'? It would have been better for us to serve the Egyptians than to die in the desert!"

13Moses answered the people, "Do not be afraid. Stand firm and you will see the deliverance the LORD will bring you today. The Egyptians you see today you will never see again. 14The LORD will fight for you; you need only to be still."

15Then the LORD said to Moses, "Why are you crying out to me? Tell the Israelites to move on. 16Raise your staff and stretch out your hand over the sea to divide the water so that the Israelites can go through the sea on dry ground. 17I will harden the hearts of the Egyptians so that they will go in after them. And I will gain glory through Pharaoh and all his army, through his chariots and his horsemen. 18The Egyptians will know that I am the LORD when I gain glory through Pharaoh, his chariots and his horsemen."

19Then the angel of God, who had been traveling in front of Israel's army, withdrew and went behind them. The pillar of cloud also moved from in front and stood behind them, 20coming between the armies of Egypt and Israel. Throughout the night the cloud brought darkness to the one side and light to the other side; so neither went near the other all night long.

21Then Moses stretched out his hand over the sea, and all that night the LORD drove the sea back with a strong east wind and turned it into dry land. The waters were divided, 22and the Israelites went through the sea on dry ground, with a wall of water on their right and on their left.

23The Egyptians pursued them, and all Pharaoh's horses and chariots and horsemen followed them into the sea. 24During the last watch of the night the LORD looked down from the pillar of fire and cloud at the Egyptian army and threw it into confusion. 25He made the wheels of their chariots come off[b] so that they had difficulty driving. And the Egyptians said, "Let's get away from the Israelites! The LORD is fighting for them against Egypt."

26Then the LORD said to Moses, "Stretch out your hand over the sea so that the waters may flow back over the Egyptians and their chariots and horsemen." 27Moses stretched out his hand over the sea, and at daybreak the sea went back to its place. The Egyptians were fleeing toward[c] it, and the LORD swept them into the sea. 28The water flowed back and covered the chariots and horsemen—the entire army of Pharaoh that had followed the Israelites into the sea. Not one of them survived.

29But the Israelites went through the sea on dry ground, with a wall of water on their right and on their left. 30That day the LORD saved Israel from the hands of the Egyptians, and Israel saw the Egyptians lying dead on the shore. 31And when the Israelites saw the great power the LORD displayed against the Egyptians, the people feared the LORD and put their trust in him and in Moses his servant.

The Song of Moses and Miriam

15 Then Moses and the Israelites sang this song to the LORD:

"I will sing to the LORD,
for he is highly exalted.
The horse and its rider
he has hurled into the sea.
2The LORD is my strength and my song;
he has become my salvation.
He is my God, and I will praise him,
my father's God, and I will exalt him.
3The LORD is a warrior;
the LORD is his name.
4Pharaoh's chariots and his army

[a] 9 Or *charioteers;* also in verses 17, 18, 23, 26 and 28 [b] 25 Or *He jammed the wheels of their chariots* (see Samaritan Pentateuch, Septuagint and Syriac) [c] 27 Or *from*

he has hurled into the sea.
The best of Pharaoh's officers
are drowned in the Red Sea.[a]
5The deep waters have covered them;
they sank to the depths like a stone.

6"Your right hand, O LORD,
was majestic in power.
Your right hand, O LORD,
shattered the enemy.
7In the greatness of your majesty
you threw down those who opposed you.
You unleashed your burning anger;
it consumed them like stubble.
8By the blast of your nostrils
the waters piled up.
The surging waters stood firm like a wall;
the deep waters congealed in the heart of the sea.

9"The enemy boasted,
'I will pursue, I will overtake them.
I will divide the spoils;
I will gorge myself on them.
I will draw my sword
and my hand will destroy them.'
10But you blew with your breath,
and the sea covered them.
They sank like lead
in the mighty waters.

11"Who among the gods is like you,
O LORD?
Who is like you—
majestic in holiness,
awesome in glory,
working wonders?
12You stretched out your right hand
and the earth swallowed them.

13"In your unfailing love you will lead
the people you have redeemed.
In your strength you will guide them
to your holy dwelling.
14The nations will hear and tremble;
anguish will grip the people of Philistia.
15The chiefs of Edom will be terrified,
the leaders of Moab will be seized with trembling,
the people[b] of Canaan will melt away;
16 terror and dread will fall upon them.
By the power of your arm
they will be as still as a stone—
until your people pass by, O LORD,
until the people you bought[c] pass by.
17You will bring them in and plant them
on the mountain of your inheritance—
the place, O LORD, you made for your dwelling,
the sanctuary, O Lord, your hands established.
18The LORD will reign
for ever and ever."

19When Pharaoh's horses, chariots and
horsemen[d] went into the sea, the LORD
brought the waters of the sea back over
them, but the Israelites walked through the
sea on dry ground. 20Then Miriam the prophetess, Aaron's sister, took a tambourine in
her hand, and all the women followed her,
with tambourines and dancing. 21Miriam
sang to them:

"Sing to the LORD,
for he is highly exalted.
The horse and its rider
he has hurled into the sea."

The Waters of Marah and Elim

22Then Moses led Israel from the Red Sea
and they went into the Desert of Shur. For
three days they traveled in the desert without
finding water. 23When they came to Marah,
they could not drink its water because it was
bitter. (That is why the place is called Marah.[e]) 24So the people grumbled against
Moses, saying, "What are we to drink?"

25Then Moses cried out to the LORD, and
the LORD showed him a piece of wood. He
threw it into the water, and the water became
sweet.

There the LORD made a decree and a law
for them, and there he tested them. 26He
said, "If you listen carefully to the voice of the
LORD your God and do what is right in his
eyes, if you pay attention to his commands
and keep all his decrees, I will not bring on
you any of the diseases I brought on the
Egyptians, for I am the LORD, who heals you."

27Then they came to Elim, where there
were twelve springs and seventy palm trees,
and they camped there near the water.

Manna and Quail

16 The whole Israelite community set
out from Elim and came to the Desert
of Sin, which is between Elim and Sinai, on
the fifteenth day of the second month after
they had come out of Egypt. 2In the desert

[a]4 Hebrew *Yam Suph;* that is, Sea of Reeds; also in verse 22 [b]15 Or *rulers* [c]16 Or *created* [d]19 Or *charioteers* [e]23 *Marah* means *bitter.*

the whole community grumbled against Moses and Aaron. [3]The Israelites said to them, "If only we had died by the LORD's hand in Egypt! There we sat around pots of meat and ate all the food we wanted, but you have brought us out into this desert to starve this entire assembly to death."

[4]Then the LORD said to Moses, "I will rain down bread from heaven for you. The people are to go out each day and gather enough for that day. In this way I will test them and see whether they will follow my instructions. [5]On the sixth day they are to prepare what they bring in, and that is to be twice as much as they gather on the other days."

[6]So Moses and Aaron said to all the Israelites, "In the evening you will know that it was the LORD who brought you out of Egypt, [7]and in the morning you will see the glory of the LORD, because he has heard your grumbling against him. Who are we, that you should grumble against us?" [8]Moses also said, "You will know that it was the LORD when he gives you meat to eat in the evening and all the bread you want in the morning, because he has heard your grumbling against him. Who are we? You are not grumbling against us, but against the LORD."

[9]Then Moses told Aaron, "Say to the entire Israelite community, 'Come before the LORD, for he has heard your grumbling.' "

[10]While Aaron was speaking to the whole Israelite community, they looked toward the desert, and there was the glory of the LORD appearing in the cloud.

[11]The LORD said to Moses, [12]"I have heard the grumbling of the Israelites. Tell them, 'At twilight you will eat meat, and in the morning you will be filled with bread. Then you will know that I am the LORD your God.' "

[13]That evening quail came and covered the camp, and in the morning there was a layer of dew around the camp. [14]When the dew was gone, thin flakes like frost on the ground appeared on the desert floor. [15]When the Israelites saw it, they said to each other, "What is it?" For they did not know what it was.

Moses said to them, "It is the bread the LORD has given you to eat. [16]This is what the LORD has commanded: 'Each one is to gather as much as he needs. Take an omer[a] for each person you have in your tent.' "

[17]The Israelites did as they were told; some gathered much, some little. [18]And when they measured it by the omer, he who gathered much did not have too much, and he who gathered little did not have too little. Each one gathered as much as he needed.

[19]Then Moses said to them, "No one is to keep any of it until morning."

[20]However, some of them paid no attention to Moses; they kept part of it until morning, but it was full of maggots and began to smell. So Moses was angry with them.

[21]Each morning everyone gathered as much as he needed, and when the sun grew hot, it melted away. [22]On the sixth day, they gathered twice as much—two omers[b] for each person—and the leaders of the community came and reported this to Moses. [23]He said to them, "This is what the LORD commanded: 'Tomorrow is to be a day of rest, a holy Sabbath to the LORD. So bake what you want to bake and boil what you want to boil. Save whatever is left and keep it until morning.' "

[24]So they saved it until morning, as Moses commanded, and it did not stink or get maggots in it. [25]"Eat it today," Moses said, "because today is a Sabbath to the LORD. You will not find any of it on the ground today. [26]Six days you are to gather it, but on the seventh day, the Sabbath, there will not be any."

[27]Nevertheless, some of the people went out on the seventh day to gather it, but they found none. [28]Then the LORD said to Moses, "How long will you[c] refuse to keep my commands and my instructions? [29]Bear in mind that the LORD has given you the Sabbath; that is why on the sixth day he gives you bread for two days. Everyone is to stay where he is on the seventh day; no one is to go out." [30]So the people rested on the seventh day.

[31]The people of Israel called the bread manna.[d] It was white like coriander seed and tasted like wafers made with honey. [32]Moses said, "This is what the LORD has commanded: 'Take an omer of manna and keep it for the generations to come, so they can see the bread I gave you to eat in the desert when I brought you out of Egypt.' "

[33]So Moses said to Aaron, "Take a jar and put an omer of manna in it. Then place it before the LORD to be kept for the generations to come."

[34]As the LORD commanded Moses, Aaron

[a] *16* That is, probably about 2 quarts (about 2 liters); also in verses 18, 32, 33 and 36 [b] *22* That is, probably about 4 quarts (about 4.5 liters) [c] *28* The Hebrew is plural. [d] *31* *Manna* means *What is it?* (see verse 15).

put the manna in front of the Testimony, that it might be kept. 35The Israelites ate manna forty years, until they came to a land that was settled; they ate manna until they reached the border of Canaan.

36(An omer is one tenth of an ephah.)

Water From the Rock

17 The whole Israelite community set out from the Desert of Sin, traveling from place to place as the LORD commanded. They camped at Rephidim, but there was no water for the people to drink. 2So they quarreled with Moses and said, "Give us water to drink."

Moses replied, "Why do you quarrel with me? Why do you put the LORD to the test?"

3But the people were thirsty for water there, and they grumbled against Moses. They said, "Why did you bring us up out of Egypt to make us and our children and livestock die of thirst?"

4Then Moses cried out to the LORD, "What am I to do with these people? They are almost ready to stone me."

5The LORD answered Moses, "Walk on ahead of the people. Take with you some of the elders of Israel and take in your hand the staff with which you struck the Nile, and go. 6I will stand there before you by the rock at Horeb. Strike the rock, and water will come out of it for the people to drink." So Moses did this in the sight of the elders of Israel. 7And he called the place Massah[a] and Meribah[b] because the Israelites quarreled and because they tested the LORD saying, "Is the LORD among us or not?"

The Amalekites Defeated

8The Amalekites came and attacked the Israelites at Rephidim. 9Moses said to Joshua, "Choose some of our men and go out to fight the Amalekites. Tomorrow I will stand on top of the hill with the staff of God in my hands."

10So Joshua fought the Amalekites as Moses had ordered, and Moses, Aaron and Hur went to the top of the hill. 11As long as Moses held up his hands, the Israelites were winning, but whenever he lowered his hands, the Amalekites were winning. 12When Moses' hands grew tired, they took a stone and put it under him and he sat on it. Aaron and Hur held his hands up—one on one side, one on the other—so that his hands remained steady till sunset. 13So Joshua overcame the Amalekite army with the sword.

14Then the LORD said to Moses, "Write this on a scroll as something to be remembered and make sure that Joshua hears it, because I will completely blot out the memory of Amalek from under heaven."

15Moses built an altar and called it The LORD is my Banner. 16He said, "For hands were lifted up to the throne of the LORD. The[c] LORD will be at war against the Amalekites from generation to generation."

Jethro Visits Moses

18 Now Jethro, the priest of Midian and father-in-law of Moses, heard of everything God had done for Moses and for his people Israel, and how the LORD had brought Israel out of Egypt.

2After Moses had sent away his wife Zipporah, his father-in-law Jethro received her 3and her two sons. One son was named Gershom,[d] for Moses said, "I have become an alien in a foreign land"; 4and the other was named Eliezer,[e] for he said, "My father's God was my helper; he saved me from the sword of Pharaoh."

5Jethro, Moses' father-in-law, together with Moses' sons and wife, came to him in the desert, where he was camped near the mountain of God. 6Jethro had sent word to him, "I, your father-in-law Jethro, am coming to you with your wife and her two sons."

7So Moses went out to meet his father-in-law and bowed down and kissed him. They greeted each other and then went into the tent. 8Moses told his father-in-law about everything the LORD had done to Pharaoh and the Egyptians for Israel's sake and about all the hardships they had met along the way and how the LORD had saved them.

9Jethro was delighted to hear about all the good things the LORD had done for Israel in rescuing them from the hand of the Egyptians. 10He said, "Praise be to the LORD, who rescued you from the hand of the Egyptians and of Pharaoh, and who rescued the people from the hand of the Egyptians. 11Now I know that the LORD is greater than all other gods, for he did this to those who had treated Israel arrogantly." 12Then Jethro, Moses' father-in-law, brought a burnt offering and other sacri-

[a]7 *Massah* means *testing.* [b]7 *Meribah* means *quarreling.* [c]16 Or *"Because a hand was against the throne of the LORD, the* [d]3 *Gershom* sounds like the Hebrew for *an alien there.* [e]4 *Eliezer* means *my God is helper.*

fices to God, and Aaron came with all the
elders of Israel to eat bread with Moses' father-in-law in the presence of God.
13The next day Moses took his seat to
serve as judge for the people, and they stood
around him from morning till evening.
14When his father-in-law saw all that Moses
was doing for the people, he said, "What is
this you are doing for the people? Why do
you alone sit as judge, while all these people
stand around you from morning till evening?"
15Moses answered him, "Because the
people come to me to seek God's will.
16Whenever they have a dispute, it is brought
to me, and I decide between the parties and
inform them of God's decrees and laws."
17Moses' father-in-law replied, "What you
are doing is not good. 18You and these
people who come to you will only wear yourselves out. The work is too heavy for you;
you cannot handle it alone. 19Listen now to
me and I will give you some advice, and may
God be with you. You must be the people's
representative before God and bring their
disputes to him. 20Teach them the decrees
and laws, and show them the way to live and
the duties they are to perform. 21But select
capable men from all the people—men who
fear God, trustworthy men who hate dishonest gain—and appoint them as officials over
thousands, hundreds, fifties and tens.
22Have them serve as judges for the people
at all times, but have them bring every difficult case to you; the simple cases they can
decide themselves. That will make your load
lighter, because they will share it with you.
23If you do this and God so commands, you
will be able to stand the strain, and all these
people will go home satisfied."
24Moses listened to his father-in-law and
did everything he said. 25He chose capable
men from all Israel and made them leaders
of the people, officials over thousands, hundreds, fifties and tens. 26They served as
judges for the people at all times. The difficult
cases they brought to Moses, but the simple
ones they decided themselves.
27Then Moses sent his father-in-law on his
way, and Jethro returned to his own country.

At Mount Sinai

19 In the third month after the Israelites
left Egypt—on the very day—they
came to the Desert of Sinai. 2After they set
out from Rephidim, they entered the Desert
of Sinai, and Israel camped there in the
desert in front of the mountain.
3Then Moses went up to God, and the LORD
called to him from the mountain and said,
"This is what you are to say to the house of
Jacob and what you are to tell the people of
Israel: 4'You yourselves have seen what I did
to Egypt, and how I carried you on eagles'
wings and brought you to myself. 5Now if you
obey me fully and keep my covenant, then
out of all nations you will be my treasured
possession. Although the whole earth is
mine, 6you[a] will be for me a kingdom of
priests and a holy nation.' These are the
words you are to speak to the Israelites."
7So Moses went back and summoned the
elders of the people and set before them all
the words the LORD had commanded him to
speak. 8The people all responded together,
"We will do everything the LORD has said."
So Moses brought their answer back to the
LORD.
9The LORD said to Moses, "I am going to
come to you in a dense cloud, so that the
people will hear me speaking with you and
will always put their trust in you." Then
Moses told the LORD what the people had
said.
10And the LORD said to Moses, "Go to the
people and consecrate them today and tomorrow. Have them wash their clothes 11and
be ready by the third day, because on that
day the LORD will come down on Mount Sinai
in the sight of all the people. 12Put limits for
the people around the mountain and tell
them, 'Be careful that you do not go up the
mountain or touch the foot of it. Whoever
touches the mountain shall surely be put to
death. 13He shall surely be stoned or shot
with arrows; not a hand is to be laid on him.
Whether man or animal, he shall not be permitted to live.' Only when the ram's horn
sounds a long blast may they go up to the
mountain."
14After Moses had gone down the mountain to the people, he consecrated them, and
they washed their clothes. 15Then he said to
the people, "Prepare yourselves for the third
day. Abstain from sexual relations."
16On the morning of the third day there was
thunder and lightning, with a thick cloud over
the mountain, and a very loud trumpet blast.
Everyone in the camp trembled. 17Then
Moses led the people out of the camp to
meet with God, and they stood at the foot of

[a]5,6 Or *possession, for the whole earth is mine.* 6*You*

the mountain. 18Mount Sinai was covered
with smoke, because the LORD descended on
it in fire. The smoke billowed up from it like
smoke from a furnace, the whole mountain[a]
trembled violently, 19and the sound of the
trumpet grew louder and louder. Then
Moses spoke and the voice of God answered him.[b]

20The LORD descended to the top of Mount
Sinai and called Moses to the top of the
mountain. So Moses went up 21and the LORD
said to him, "Go down and warn the people
so they do not force their way through to see
the LORD and many of them perish. 22Even
the priests, who approach the LORD, must
consecrate themselves, or the LORD will
break out against them."

23Moses said to the LORD, "The people
cannot come up Mount Sinai, because you
yourself warned us, 'Put limits around the
mountain and set it apart as holy.' "

24The LORD replied, "Go down and bring
Aaron up with you. But the priests and the
people must not force their way through to
come up to the LORD, or he will break out
against them."

25So Moses went down to the people and
told them.

The Ten Commandments

20 And God spoke all these words:
2"I am the LORD your God, who
brought you out of Egypt, out of
the land of slavery.
3"You shall have no other gods before[c]
me.
4"You shall not make for yourself an idol
in the form of anything in heaven
above or on the earth beneath or
in the waters below. 5You shall
not bow down to them or worship
them; for I, the LORD your God, am
a jealous God, punishing the children for the sin of the fathers to
the third and fourth generation of
those who hate me, 6but showing
love to a thousand ⌊generations⌋
of those who love me and keep
my commandments.
7"You shall not misuse the name of the
LORD your God, for the LORD will
not hold anyone guiltless who
misuses his name.
8"Remember the Sabbath day by keeping it holy. 9Six days you shall labor and do all your work, 10but the
seventh day is a Sabbath to the
LORD your God. On it you shall not
do any work, neither you, nor your
son or daughter, nor your manservant or maidservant, nor your
animals, nor the alien within your
gates. 11For in six days the LORD
made the heavens and the earth,
the sea, and all that is in them, but
he rested on the seventh day.
Therefore the LORD blessed the
Sabbath day and made it holy.
12"Honor your father and your mother, so
that you may live long in the land
the LORD your God is giving you.
13"You shall not murder.
14"You shall not commit adultery.
15"You shall not steal.
16"You shall not give false testimony
against your neighbor.
17"You shall not covet your neighbor's
house. You shall not covet your
neighbor's wife, or his manservant or maidservant, his ox or
donkey, or anything that belongs
to your neighbor."

18When the people saw the thunder and
lightning and heard the trumpet and saw the
mountain in smoke, they trembled with fear.
They stayed at a distance 19and said to
Moses, "Speak to us yourself and we will
listen. But do not have God speak to us or we
will die."

20Moses said to the people, "Do not be
afraid. God has come to test you, so that the
fear of God will be with you to keep you from
sinning."

21The people remained at a distance,
while Moses approached the thick darkness
where God was.

Idols and Altars

22Then the LORD said to Moses, "Tell the
Israelites this: 'You have seen for yourselves
that I have spoken to you from heaven: 23Do
not make any gods to be alongside me; do
not make for yourselves gods of silver or
gods of gold.

24" 'Make an altar of earth for me and sacrifice on it your burnt offerings and fellowship
offerings,[d] your sheep and goats and your
cattle. Wherever I cause my name to be hon-

[a] 18 Most Hebrew manuscripts; a few Hebrew manuscripts and Septuagint *all the people* [b] 19 Or *and God answered him with thunder* [c] 3 Or *besides* [d] 24 Traditionally *peace offerings*

ored, I will come to you and bless you. 25If
you make an altar of stones for me, do not
build it with dressed stones, for you will defile
it if you use a tool on it. 26And do not go up to
my altar on steps, lest your nakedness be
exposed on it.'

21 "These are the laws you are to set
before them:

Hebrew Servants

2"If you buy a Hebrew servant, he is to
serve you for six years. But in the seventh
year, he shall go free, without paying anything. 3If he comes alone, he is to go free
alone; but if he has a wife when he comes,
she is to go with him. 4If his master gives him
a wife and she bears him sons or daughters,
the woman and her children shall belong to
her master, and only the man shall go free.
5"But if the servant declares, 'I love my
master and my wife and children and do not
want to go free,' 6then his master must take
him before the judges.[a] He shall take him to
the door or the doorpost and pierce his ear
with an awl. Then he will be his servant for
life.
7"If a man sells his daughter as a servant,
she is not to go free as menservants do. 8If
she does not please the master who has
selected her for himself,[b] he must let her be
redeemed. He has no right to sell her to
foreigners, because he has broken faith with
her. 9If he selects her for his son, he must
grant her the rights of a daughter. 10If he
marries another woman, he must not deprive
the first one of her food, clothing and marital
rights. 11If he does not provide her with these
three things, she is to go free, without any
payment of money.

Personal Injuries

12"Anyone who strikes a man and kills him
shall surely be put to death. 13However, if he
does not do it intentionally, but God lets it
happen, he is to flee to a place I will designate. 14But if a man schemes and kills another man deliberately, take him away from
my altar and put him to death.
15"Anyone who attacks[c] his father or his
mother must be put to death.
16"Anyone who kidnaps another and either
sells him or still has him when he is caught
must be put to death.
17"Anyone who curses his father or mother
must be put to death.
18"If men quarrel and one hits the other
with a stone or with his fist[d] and he does not
die but is confined to bed, 19the one who
struck the blow will not be held responsible if
the other gets up and walks around outside
with his staff; however, he must pay the injured man for the loss of his time and see that
he is completely healed.
20"If a man beats his male or female slave
with a rod and the slave dies as a direct
result, he must be punished, 21but he is not to
be punished if the slave gets up after a day or
two, since the slave is his property.
22"If men who are fighting hit a pregnant
woman and she gives birth prematurely[e] but
there is no serious injury, the offender must
be fined whatever the woman's husband demands and the court allows. 23But if there is
serious injury, you are to take life for life,
24eye for eye, tooth for tooth, hand for hand,
foot for foot, 25burn for burn, wound for
wound, bruise for bruise.
26"If a man hits a manservant or maidservant in the eye and destroys it, he must let
the servant go free to compensate for the
eye. 27And if he knocks out the tooth of a
manservant or maidservant, he must let the
servant go free to compensate for the tooth.
28"If a bull gores a man or a woman to
death, the bull must be stoned to death, and
its meat must not be eaten. But the owner of
the bull will not be held responsible. 29If, however, the bull has had the habit of goring and
the owner has been warned but has not kept
it penned up and it kills a man or woman, the
bull must be stoned and the owner also must
be put to death. 30However, if payment is
demanded of him, he may redeem his life by
paying whatever is demanded. 31This law
also applies if the bull gores a son or daughter. 32If the bull gores a male or female slave,
the owner must pay thirty shekels[f] of silver
to the master of the slave, and the bull must
be stoned.
33"If a man uncovers a pit or digs one and
fails to cover it and an ox or a donkey falls
into it, 34the owner of the pit must pay for the
loss; he must pay its owner, and the dead
animal will be his.
35"If a man's bull injures the bull of another
and it dies, they are to sell the live one and
divide both the money and the dead animal

[a] 6 Or *before God* [b] 8 Or *master so that he does not choose her* [c] 15 Or *kills* [d] 18 Or *with a tool*
[e] 22 Or *she has a miscarriage* [f] 32 That is, about 12 ounces (about 0.3 kilogram)

equally. 36However, if it was known that the bull had the habit of goring, yet the owner did not keep it penned up, the owner must pay, animal for animal, and the dead animal will be his.

Protection of Property

22 "If a man steals an ox or a sheep and slaughters it or sells it, he must pay back five head of cattle for the ox and four sheep for the sheep.

2"If a thief is caught breaking in and is struck so that he dies, the defender is not guilty of bloodshed; 3but if it happens[a] after sunrise, he is guilty of bloodshed.

"A thief must certainly make restitution, but if he has nothing, he must be sold to pay for his theft.

4"If the stolen animal is found alive in his possession—whether ox or donkey or sheep—he must pay back double.

5"If a man grazes his livestock in a field or vineyard and lets them stray and they graze in another man's field, he must make restitution from the best of his own field or vineyard.

6"If a fire breaks out and spreads into thornbushes so that it burns shocks of grain or standing grain or the whole field, the one who started the fire must make restitution.

7"If a man gives his neighbor silver or goods for safekeeping and they are stolen from the neighbor's house, the thief, if he is caught, must pay back double. 8But if the thief is not found, the owner of the house must appear before the judges[b] to determine whether he has laid his hands on the other man's property. 9In all cases of illegal possession of an ox, a donkey, a sheep, a garment, or any other lost property about which somebody says, 'This is mine,' both parties are to bring their cases before the judges. The one whom the judges declare[c] guilty must pay back double to his neighbor.

10"If a man gives a donkey, an ox, a sheep or any other animal to his neighbor for safekeeping and it dies or is injured or is taken away while no one is looking, 11the issue between them will be settled by the taking of an oath before the LORD that the neighbor did not lay hands on the other person's property. The owner is to accept this, and no restitution is required. 12But if the animal was stolen from the neighbor, he must make restitution to the owner. 13If it was torn to pieces by a wild animal, he shall bring in the remains as evidence and he will not be required to pay for the torn animal.

14"If a man borrows an animal from his neighbor and it is injured or dies while the owner is not present, he must make restitution. 15But if the owner is with the animal, the borrower will not have to pay. If the animal was hired, the money paid for the hire covers the loss.

Social Responsibility

16"If a man seduces a virgin who is not pledged to be married and sleeps with her, he must pay the bride-price, and she shall be his wife. 17If her father absolutely refuses to give her to him, he must still pay the bride-price for virgins.

18"Do not allow a sorceress to live.

19"Anyone who has sexual relations with an animal must be put to death.

20"Whoever sacrifices to any god other than the LORD must be destroyed.[d]

21"Do not mistreat an alien or oppress him, for you were aliens in Egypt.

22"Do not take advantage of a widow or an orphan. 23If you do and they cry out to me, I will certainly hear their cry. 24My anger will be aroused, and I will kill you with the sword; your wives will become widows and your children fatherless.

25"If you lend money to one of my people among you who is needy, do not be like a moneylender; charge him no interest.[e] 26If you take your neighbor's cloak as a pledge, return it to him by sunset, 27because his cloak is the only covering he has for his body. What else will he sleep in? When he cries out to me, I will hear, for I am compassionate.

28"Do not blaspheme God[f] or curse the ruler of your people.

29"Do not hold back offerings from your granaries or your vats.[g]

"You must give me the firstborn of your sons. 30Do the same with your cattle and your sheep. Let them stay with their mothers for seven days, but give them to me on the eighth day.

31"You are to be my holy people. So do not eat the meat of an animal torn by wild beasts; throw it to the dogs.

[a]3 Or *if he strikes him* [b]8 Or *before God;* also in verse 9 [c]9 Or *whom God declares* [d]20 The Hebrew term refers to the irrevocable giving over of things or persons to the LORD, often by totally destroying them. [e]25 Or *excessive interest* [f]28 Or *Do not revile the judges* [g]29 The meaning of the Hebrew for this phrase is uncertain.

Laws of Justice and Mercy

23 "Do not spread false reports. Do not
help a wicked man by being a malicious witness.
2"Do not follow the crowd in doing wrong.
When you give testimony in a lawsuit, do not
pervert justice by siding with the crowd, 3and
do not show favoritism to a poor man in his
lawsuit.
4"If you come across your enemy's ox or
donkey wandering off, be sure to take it back
to him. 5If you see the donkey of someone
who hates you fallen down under its load, do
not leave it there; be sure you help him
with it.
6"Do not deny justice to your poor people
in their lawsuits. 7Have nothing to do with a
false charge and do not put an innocent or
honest person to death, for I will not acquit
the guilty.
8"Do not accept a bribe, for a bribe blinds
those who see and twists the words of the
righteous.
9"Do not oppress an alien; you yourselves
know how it feels to be aliens, because you
were aliens in Egypt.

Sabbath Laws

10"For six years you are to sow your fields
and harvest the crops, 11but during the seventh year let the land lie unplowed and
unused. Then the poor among your people
may get food from it, and the wild animals
may eat what they leave. Do the same with
your vineyard and your olive grove.
12"Six days do your work, but on the seventh day do not work, so that your ox and
your donkey may rest and the slave born in
your household, and the alien as well, may
be refreshed.
13"Be careful to do everything I have said
to you. Do not invoke the names of other
gods; do not let them be heard on your lips.

The Three Annual Festivals

14"Three times a year you are to celebrate
a festival to me.
15"Celebrate the Feast of Unleavened
Bread; for seven days eat bread made without yeast, as I commanded you. Do this at
the appointed time in the month of Abib, for in
that month you came out of Egypt.
"No one is to appear before me empty-
handed.
16"Celebrate the Feast of Harvest with the
firstfruits of the crops you sow in your field.
"Celebrate the Feast of Ingathering at the
end of the year, when you gather in your
crops from the field.
17"Three times a year all the men are to
appear before the Sovereign LORD.
18"Do not offer the blood of a sacrifice to
me along with anything containing yeast.
"The fat of my festival offerings must not
be kept until morning.
19"Bring the best of the firstfruits of your
soil to the house of the LORD your God.
"Do not cook a young goat in its mother's
milk.

God's Angel to Prepare the Way

20"See, I am sending an angel ahead of
you to guard you along the way and to bring
you to the place I have prepared. 21Pay attention to him and listen to what he says. Do
not rebel against him; he will not forgive your
rebellion, since my Name is in him. 22If you
listen carefully to what he says and do all that
I say, I will be an enemy to your enemies and
will oppose those who oppose you. 23My angel will go ahead of you and bring you into
the land of the Amorites, Hittites, Perizzites,
Canaanites, Hivites and Jebusites, and I will
wipe them out. 24Do not bow down before
their gods or worship them or follow their
practices. You must demolish them and
break their sacred stones to pieces. 25Wor-
ship the LORD your God, and his blessing will
be on your food and water. I will take away
sickness from among you, 26and none will
miscarry or be barren in your land. I will give
you a full life span.
27"I will send my terror ahead of you and
throw into confusion every nation you encounter. I will make all your enemies turn
their backs and run. 28I will send the hornet
ahead of you to drive the Hivites, Canaanites
and Hittites out of your way. 29But I will not
drive them out in a single year, because the
land would become desolate and the wild
animals too numerous for you. 30Little by little
I will drive them out before you, until you
have increased enough to take possession
of the land.
31"I will establish your borders from the
Red Sea[a] to the Sea of the Philistines,[b] and
from the desert to the River.[c] I will hand over
to you the people who live in the land and
you will drive them out before you. 32Do not
make a covenant with them or with their

[a]31 Hebrew *Yam Suph;* that is, Sea of Reeds [b]31 That is, the Mediterranean [c]31 That is, the Euphrates

gods. 33Do not let them live in your land, or they will cause you to sin against me, because the worship of their gods will certainly be a snare to you."

The Covenant Confirmed

24 Then he said to Moses, "Come up to the LORD, you and Aaron, Nadab and Abihu, and seventy of the elders of Israel. You are to worship at a distance, 2but Moses alone is to approach the LORD; the others must not come near. And the people may not come up with him."

3When Moses went and told the people all the LORD's words and laws, they responded with one voice, "Everything the LORD has said we will do." 4Moses then wrote down everything the LORD had said.

He got up early the next morning and built an altar at the foot of the mountain and set up twelve stone pillars representing the twelve tribes of Israel. 5Then he sent young Israelite men, and they offered burnt offerings and sacrificed young bulls as fellowship offerings[a] to the LORD. 6Moses took half of the blood and put it in bowls, and the other half he sprinkled on the altar. 7Then he took the Book of the Covenant and read it to the people. They responded, "We will do everything the LORD has said; we will obey."

8Moses then took the blood, sprinkled it on the people and said, "This is the blood of the covenant that the LORD has made with you in accordance with all these words."

9Moses and Aaron, Nadab and Abihu, and the seventy elders of Israel went up 10and saw the God of Israel. Under his feet was something like a pavement made of sapphire,[b] clear as the sky itself. 11But God did not raise his hand against these leaders of the Israelites; they saw God, and they ate and drank.

12The LORD said to Moses, "Come up to me on the mountain and stay here, and I will give you the tablets of stone, with the law and commands I have written for their instruction."

13Then Moses set out with Joshua his aide, and Moses went up on the mountain of God. 14He said to the elders, "Wait here for us until we come back to you. Aaron and Hur are with you, and anyone involved in a dispute can go to them."

15When Moses went up on the mountain, the cloud covered it, 16and the glory of the LORD settled on Mount Sinai. For six days the cloud covered the mountain, and on the seventh day the LORD called to Moses from within the cloud. 17To the Israelites the glory of the LORD looked like a consuming fire on top of the mountain. 18Then Moses entered the cloud as he went on up the mountain. And he stayed on the mountain forty days and forty nights.

Offerings for the Tabernacle

25 The LORD said to Moses, 2"Tell the Israelites to bring me an offering. You are to receive the offering for me from each man whose heart prompts him to give. 3These are the offerings you are to receive from them: gold, silver and bronze; 4blue, purple and scarlet yarn and fine linen; goat hair; 5ram skins dyed red and hides of sea cows[c]; acacia wood; 6olive oil for the light; spices for the anointing oil and for the fragrant incense; 7and onyx stones and other gems to be mounted on the ephod and breastpiece.

8"Then have them make a sanctuary for me, and I will dwell among them. 9Make this tabernacle and all its furnishings exactly like the pattern I will show you.

The Ark

10"Have them make a chest of acacia wood—two and a half cubits long, a cubit and a half wide, and a cubit and a half high.[d] 11Overlay it with pure gold, both inside and out, and make a gold molding around it. 12Cast four gold rings for it and fasten them to its four feet, with two rings on one side and two rings on the other. 13Then make poles of acacia wood and overlay them with gold. 14Insert the poles into the rings on the sides of the chest to carry it. 15The poles are to remain in the rings of this ark; they are not to be removed. 16Then put in the ark the Testimony, which I will give you.

17"Make an atonement cover[e] of pure gold—two and a half cubits long and a cubit and a half wide.[f] 18And make two cherubim out of hammered gold at the ends of the cover. 19Make one cherub on one end and the second cherub on the other; make the cherubim of one piece with the cover, at the two ends. 20The cherubim are to have their wings spread upward, overshadowing the

[a] 5 Traditionally *peace offerings* [b] 10 Or *lapis lazuli* [c] 5 That is, dugongs [d] 10 That is, about 3 3/4 feet (about 1.1 meters) long and 2 1/4 feet (about 0.7 meter) wide and high [e] 17 Traditionally *a mercy seat* [f] 17 That is, about 3 3/4 feet (about 1.1 meters) long and 2 1/4 feet (about 0.7 meter) wide

cover with them. The cherubim are to face each other, looking toward the cover. 21Place the cover on top of the ark and put in the ark the Testimony, which I will give you. 22There, above the cover between the two cherubim that are over the ark of the Testimony, I will meet with you and give you all my commands for the Israelites.

The Table

23"Make a table of acacia wood—two cubits long, a cubit wide and a cubit and a half high.[a] 24Overlay it with pure gold and make a gold molding around it. 25Also make around it a rim a handbreadth[b] wide and put a gold molding on the rim. 26Make four gold rings for the table and fasten them to the four corners, where the four legs are. 27The rings are to be close to the rim to hold the poles used in carrying the table. 28Make the poles of acacia wood, overlay them with gold and carry the table with them. 29And make its plates and dishes of pure gold, as well as its pitchers and bowls for the pouring out of offerings. 30Put the bread of the Presence on this table to be before me at all times.

The Lampstand

31"Make a lampstand of pure gold and hammer it out, base and shaft; its flowerlike cups, buds and blossoms shall be of one piece with it. 32Six branches are to extend from the sides of the lampstand—three on one side and three on the other. 33Three cups shaped like almond flowers with buds and blossoms are to be on one branch, three on the next branch, and the same for all six branches extending from the lampstand. 34And on the lampstand there are to be four cups shaped like almond flowers with buds and blossoms. 35One bud shall be under the first pair of branches extending from the lampstand, a second bud under the second pair, and a third bud under the third pair—six branches in all. 36The buds and branches shall all be of one piece with the lampstand, hammered out of pure gold.

37"Then make its seven lamps and set them up on it so that they light the space in front of it. 38Its wick trimmers and trays are to be of pure gold. 39A talent[c] of pure gold is to be used for the lampstand and all these accessories. 40See that you make them according to the pattern shown you on the mountain.

The Tabernacle

26 "Make the tabernacle with ten curtains of finely twisted linen and blue, purple and scarlet yarn, with cherubim worked into them by a skilled craftsman. 2All the curtains are to be the same size—twenty-eight cubits long and four cubits wide.[d] 3Join five of the curtains together, and do the same with the other five. 4Make loops of blue material along the edge of the end curtain in one set, and do the same with the end curtain in the other set. 5Make fifty loops on one curtain and fifty loops on the end curtain of the other set, with the loops opposite each other. 6Then make fifty gold clasps and use them to fasten the curtains together so that the tabernacle is a unit.

7"Make curtains of goat hair for the tent over the tabernacle—eleven altogether. 8All eleven curtains are to be the same size—thirty cubits long and four cubits wide.[e] 9Join five of the curtains together into one set and the other six into another set. Fold the sixth curtain double at the front of the tent. 10Make fifty loops along the edge of the end curtain in one set and also along the edge of the end curtain in the other set. 11Then make fifty bronze clasps and put them in the loops to fasten the tent together as a unit. 12As for the additional length of the tent curtains, the half curtain that is left over is to hang down at the rear of the tabernacle. 13The tent curtains will be a cubit[f] longer on both sides; what is left will hang over the sides of the tabernacle so as to cover it. 14Make for the tent a covering of ram skins dyed red, and over that a covering of hides of sea cows.[g]

15"Make upright frames of acacia wood for the tabernacle. 16Each frame is to be ten cubits long and a cubit and a half wide,[h] 17with two projections set parallel to each other. Make all the frames of the tabernacle in this way. 18Make twenty frames for the south side of the tabernacle 19and make forty silver bases to go under them—two bases for each frame, one under each projection.

[a] *23* That is, about 3 feet (about 0.9 meter) long and 1 1/2 feet (about 0.5 meter) wide and 2 1/4 feet (about 0.7 meter) high [b] *25* That is, about 3 inches (about 8 centimeters) [c] *39* That is, about 75 pounds (about 34 kilograms) [d] *2* That is, about 42 feet (about 12.5 meters) long and 6 feet (about 1.8 meters) wide [e] *8* That is, about 45 feet (about 13.5 meters) long and 6 feet (about 1.8 meters) wide [f] *13* That is, about 1 1/2 feet (about 0.5 meter) [g] *14* That is, dugongs [h] *16* That is, about 15 feet (about 4.5 meters) long and 2 1/4 feet (about 0.7 meter) wide

20For the other side, the north side of the
tabernacle, make twenty frames 21and forty
silver bases—two under each frame. 22Make
six frames for the far end, that is, the west
end of the tabernacle, 23and make two
frames for the corners at the far end. 24At
these two corners they must be double from
the bottom all the way to the top, and fitted
into a single ring; both shall be like that. 25So
there will be eight frames and sixteen silver
bases—two under each frame.

26"Also make crossbars of acacia wood:
five for the frames on one side of the tabernacle, 27five for those on the other side, and
five for the frames on the west, at the far end
of the tabernacle. 28The center crossbar is to
extend from end to end at the middle of the
frames. 29Overlay the frames with gold and
make gold rings to hold the crossbars. Also
overlay the crossbars with gold.

30"Set up the tabernacle according to the
plan shown you on the mountain.

31"Make a curtain of blue, purple and scarlet yarn and finely twisted linen, with cherubim worked into it by a skilled craftsman.
32Hang it with gold hooks on four posts of
acacia wood overlaid with gold and standing
on four silver bases. 33Hang the curtain from
the clasps and place the ark of the Testimony behind the curtain. The curtain will
separate the Holy Place from the Most Holy
Place. 34Put the atonement cover on the ark
of the Testimony in the Most Holy Place.
35Place the table outside the curtain on the
north side of the tabernacle and put the
lampstand opposite it on the south side.

36"For the entrance to the tent make a curtain of blue, purple and scarlet yarn and finely twisted linen—the work of an embroiderer.
37Make gold hooks for this curtain and five
posts of acacia wood overlaid with gold. And
cast five bronze bases for them.

The Altar of Burnt Offering

27 "Build an altar of acacia wood, three
cubits[a] high; it is to be square, five
cubits long and five cubits wide.[b] 2Make a
horn at each of the four corners, so that the
horns and the altar are of one piece, and
overlay the altar with bronze. 3Make all its
utensils of bronze—its pots to remove the
ashes, and its shovels, sprinkling bowls,
meat forks and firepans. 4Make a grating for
it, a bronze network, and make a bronze ring
at each of the four corners of the network.
5Put it under the ledge of the altar so that it is
halfway up the altar. 6Make poles of acacia
wood for the altar and overlay them with
bronze. 7The poles are to be inserted into the
rings so they will be on two sides of the altar
when it is carried. 8Make the altar hollow, out
of boards. It is to be made just as you were
shown on the mountain.

The Courtyard

9"Make a courtyard for the tabernacle. The
south side shall be a hundred cubits[c] long
and is to have curtains of finely twisted linen,
10with twenty posts and twenty bronze bases
and with silver hooks and bands on the
posts. 11The north side shall also be a hundred cubits long and is to have curtains, with
twenty posts and twenty bronze bases and
with silver hooks and bands on the posts.

12"The west end of the courtyard shall be
fifty cubits[d] wide and have curtains, with ten
posts and ten bases. 13On the east end,
toward the sunrise, the courtyard shall also
be fifty cubits wide. 14Curtains fifteen cubits[e]
long are to be on one side of the entrance,
with three posts and three bases, 15and curtains fifteen cubits long are to be on the other
side, with three posts and three bases.

16"For the entrance to the courtyard, provide a curtain twenty cubits[f] long, of blue,
purple and scarlet yarn and finely twisted
linen—the work of an embroiderer—with
four posts and four bases. 17All the posts
around the courtyard are to have silver
bands and hooks, and bronze bases. 18The
courtyard shall be a hundred cubits long and
fifty cubits wide,[g] with curtains of finely twisted linen five cubits[h] high, and with bronze
bases. 19All the other articles used in the
service of the tabernacle, whatever their
function, including all the tent pegs for it and
those for the courtyard, are to be of bronze.

Oil for the Lampstand

20"Command the Israelites to bring you
clear oil of pressed olives for the light so that
the lamps may be kept burning. 21In the Tent
of Meeting, outside the curtain that is in front
of the Testimony, Aaron and his sons are to

[a] *1* That is, about 4 1/2 feet (about 1.3 meters) [b] *1* That is, about 7 1/2 feet (about 2.3 meters) long and wide
[c] *9* That is, about 150 feet (about 46 meters); also in verse 11 [d] *12* That is, about 75 feet (about 23 meters); also in verse 13 [e] *14* That is, about 22 1/2 feet (about 6.9 meters); also in verse 15 [f] *16* That is, about 30 feet (about 9 meters) [g] *18* That is, about 150 feet (about 46 meters) long and 75 feet (about 23 meters) wide
[h] *18* That is, about 7 1/2 feet (about 2.3 meters)

keep the lamps burning before the LORD from evening till morning. This is to be a lasting ordinance among the Israelites for the generations to come.

The Priestly Garments

28 "Have Aaron your brother brought to you from among the Israelites, along with his sons Nadab and Abihu, Eleazar and Ithamar, so they may serve me as priests. 2Make sacred garments for your brother Aaron, to give him dignity and honor. 3Tell all the skilled men to whom I have given wisdom in such matters that they are to make garments for Aaron, for his consecration, so he may serve me as priest. 4These are the garments they are to make: a breastpiece, an ephod, a robe, a woven tunic, a turban and a sash. They are to make these sacred garments for your brother Aaron and his sons, so they may serve me as priests. 5Have them use gold, and blue, purple and scarlet yarn, and fine linen.

The Ephod

6"Make the ephod of gold, and of blue, purple and scarlet yarn, and of finely twisted linen—the work of a skilled craftsman. 7It is to have two shoulder pieces attached to two of its corners, so it can be fastened. 8Its skillfully woven waistband is to be like it—of one piece with the ephod and made with gold, and with blue, purple and scarlet yarn, and with finely twisted linen.

9"Take two onyx stones and engrave on them the names of the sons of Israel 10in the order of their birth—six names on one stone and the remaining six on the other. 11Engrave the names of the sons of Israel on the two stones the way a gem cutter engraves a seal. Then mount the stones in gold filigree settings 12and fasten them on the shoulder pieces of the ephod as memorial stones for the sons of Israel. Aaron is to bear the names on his shoulders as a memorial before the LORD. 13Make gold filigree settings 14and two braided chains of pure gold, like a rope, and attach the chains to the settings.

The Breastpiece

15"Fashion a breastpiece for making decisions—the work of a skilled craftsman. Make it like the ephod: of gold, and of blue, purple and scarlet yarn, and of finely twisted linen. 16It is to be square—a span[a] long and a span wide—and folded double. 17Then mount four rows of precious stones on it. In the first row there shall be a ruby, a topaz and a beryl; 18in the second row a turquoise, a sapphire[b] and an emerald; 19in the third row a jacinth, an agate and an amethyst; 20in the fourth row a chrysolite, an onyx and a jasper.[c] Mount them in gold filigree settings. 21There are to be twelve stones, one for each of the names of the sons of Israel, each engraved like a seal with the name of one of the twelve tribes.

22"For the breastpiece make braided chains of pure gold, like a rope. 23Make two gold rings for it and fasten them to two corners of the breastpiece. 24Fasten the two gold chains to the rings at the corners of the breastpiece, 25and the other ends of the chains to the two settings, attaching them to the shoulder pieces of the ephod at the front. 26Make two gold rings and attach them to the other two corners of the breastpiece on the inside edge next to the ephod. 27Make two more gold rings and attach them to the bottom of the shoulder pieces on the front of the ephod, close to the seam just above the waistband of the ephod. 28The rings of the breastpiece are to be tied to the rings of the ephod with blue cord, connecting it to the waistband, so that the breastpiece will not swing out from the ephod.

29"Whenever Aaron enters the Holy Place, he will bear the names of the sons of Israel over his heart on the breastpiece of decision as a continuing memorial before the LORD. 30Also put the Urim and the Thummim in the breastpiece, so they may be over Aaron's heart whenever he enters the presence of the LORD. Thus Aaron will always bear the means of making decisions for the Israelites over his heart before the LORD.

Other Priestly Garments

31"Make the robe of the ephod entirely of blue cloth, 32with an opening for the head in its center. There shall be a woven edge like a collar[d] around this opening, so that it will not tear. 33Make pomegranates of blue, purple and scarlet yarn around the hem of the robe, with gold bells between them. 34The gold bells and the pomegranates are to alternate around the hem of the robe. 35Aaron must wear it when he ministers. The sound of the

[a] *16* That is, about 9 inches (about 22 centimeters) [b] *18* Or *lapis lazuli* [c] *20* The precise identification of some of these precious stones is uncertain. [d] *32* The meaning of the Hebrew for this word is uncertain.

bells will be heard when he enters the Holy Place before the LORD and when he comes out, so that he will not die.

36"Make a plate of pure gold and engrave on it as on a seal: HOLY TO THE LORD. 37Fasten a blue cord to it to attach it to the turban; it is to be on the front of the turban. 38It will be on Aaron's forehead, and he will bear the guilt involved in the sacred gifts the Israelites consecrate, whatever their gifts may be. It will be on Aaron's forehead continually so that they will be acceptable to the LORD.

39"Weave the tunic of fine linen and make the turban of fine linen. The sash is to be the work of an embroiderer. 40Make tunics, sashes and headbands for Aaron's sons, to give them dignity and honor. 41After you put these clothes on your brother Aaron and his sons, anoint and ordain them. Consecrate them so they may serve me as priests.

42"Make linen undergarments as a covering for the body, reaching from the waist to the thigh. 43Aaron and his sons must wear them whenever they enter the Tent of Meeting or approach the altar to minister in the Holy Place, so that they will not incur guilt and die.

"This is to be a lasting ordinance for Aaron and his descendants.

Consecration of the Priests

29 "This is what you are to do to consecrate them, so they may serve me as priests: Take a young bull and two rams without defect. 2And from fine wheat flour, without yeast, make bread, and cakes mixed with oil, and wafers spread with oil. 3Put them in a basket and present them in it—along with the bull and the two rams. 4Then bring Aaron and his sons to the entrance to the Tent of Meeting and wash them with water. 5Take the garments and dress Aaron with the tunic, the robe of the ephod, the ephod itself and the breastpiece. Fasten the ephod on him by its skillfully woven waistband. 6Put the turban on his head and attach the sacred diadem to the turban. 7Take the anointing oil and anoint him by pouring it on his head. 8Bring his sons and dress them in tunics 9and put headbands on them. Then tie sashes on Aaron and his sons.[a] The priesthood is theirs by a lasting ordinance. In this way you shall ordain Aaron and his sons.

10"Bring the bull to the front of the Tent of Meeting, and Aaron and his sons shall lay their hands on its head. 11Slaughter it in the LORD's presence at the entrance to the Tent of Meeting. 12Take some of the bull's blood and put it on the horns of the altar with your finger, and pour out the rest of it at the base of the altar. 13Then take all the fat around the inner parts, the covering of the liver, and both kidneys with the fat on them, and burn them on the altar. 14But burn the bull's flesh and its hide and its offal outside the camp. It is a sin offering.

15"Take one of the rams, and Aaron and his sons shall lay their hands on its head. 16Slaughter it and take the blood and sprinkle it against the altar on all sides. 17Cut the ram into pieces and wash the inner parts and the legs, putting them with the head and the other pieces. 18Then burn the entire ram on the altar. It is a burnt offering to the LORD, a pleasing aroma, an offering made to the LORD by fire.

19"Take the other ram, and Aaron and his sons shall lay their hands on its head. 20Slaughter it, take some of its blood and put it on the lobes of the right ears of Aaron and his sons, on the thumbs of their right hands, and on the big toes of their right feet. Then sprinkle blood against the altar on all sides. 21And take some of the blood on the altar and some of the anointing oil and sprinkle it on Aaron and his garments and on his sons and their garments. Then he and his sons and their garments will be consecrated.

22"Take from this ram the fat, the fat tail, the fat around the inner parts, the covering of the liver, both kidneys with the fat on them, and the right thigh. (This is the ram for the ordination.) 23From the basket of bread made without yeast, which is before the LORD, take a loaf, and a cake made with oil, and a wafer. 24Put all these in the hands of Aaron and his sons and wave them before the LORD as a wave offering. 25Then take them from their hands and burn them on the altar along with the burnt offering for a pleasing aroma to the LORD an offering made to the LORD by fire. 26After you take the breast of the ram for Aaron's ordination; wave it before the LORD as a wave offering, and it will be your share.

27"Consecrate those parts of the ordination ram that belong to Aaron and his sons: the breast that was waved and the thigh that was presented. 28This is always to be the regular share from the Israelites for Aaron

[a]9 Hebrew; Septuagint *on them*

and his sons. It is the contribution the Israelites are to make to the LORD from their fellowship offerings.[a]
29"Aaron's sacred garments will belong to
his descendants so that they can be anointed and ordained in them. 30The son who
succeeds him as priest and comes to the
Tent of Meeting to minister in the Holy Place
is to wear them seven days.
31"Take the ram for the ordination and
cook the meat in a sacred place. 32At the
entrance to the Tent of Meeting, Aaron and
his sons are to eat the meat of the ram and
the bread that is in the basket. 33They are to
eat these offerings by which atonement was
made for their ordination and consecration.
But no one else may eat them, because they
are sacred. 34And if any of the meat of the
ordination ram or any bread is left over till
morning, burn it up. It must not be eaten,
because it is sacred.
35"Do for Aaron and his sons everything I
have commanded you, taking seven days to
ordain them. 36Sacrifice a bull each day as a
sin offering to make atonement. Purify the
altar by making atonement for it, and anoint it
to consecrate it. 37For seven days make
atonement for the altar and consecrate it.
Then the altar will be most holy, and whatever touches it will be holy.
38"This is what you are to offer on the altar
regularly each day: two lambs a year old.
39Offer one in the morning and the other at
twilight. 40With the first lamb offer a tenth of
an ephah[b] of fine flour mixed with a quarter
of a hin[c] of oil from pressed olives, and a
quarter of a hin of wine as a drink offering.
41Sacrifice the other lamb at twilight with the
same grain offering and its drink offering as
in the morning—a pleasing aroma, an offering made to the LORD by fire.
42"For the generations to come this burnt
offering is to be made regularly at the entrance to the Tent of Meeting before the
LORD. There I will meet you and speak to you;
43there also I will meet with the Israelites, and
the place will be consecrated by my glory.
44"So I will consecrate the Tent of Meeting
and the altar and will consecrate Aaron and
his sons to serve me as priests. 45Then I will
dwell among the Israelites and be their God.
46They will know that I am the LORD their God,
who brought them out of Egypt so that I might
dwell among them. I am the LORD their God.

The Altar of Incense

30 "Make an altar of acacia wood for
burning incense. 2It is to be square, a
cubit long and a cubit wide, and two cubits
high[d]—its horns of one piece with it. 3Over-
lay the top and all the sides and the horns
with pure gold, and make a gold molding
around it. 4Make two gold rings for the altar
below the molding—two on opposite sides—
to hold the poles used to carry it. 5Make the
poles of acacia wood and overlay them with
gold. 6Put the altar in front of the curtain that
is before the ark of the Testimony—before
the atonement cover that is over the Testimony—where I will meet with you.
7"Aaron must burn fragrant incense on the
altar every morning when he tends the
lamps. 8He must burn incense again when
he lights the lamps at twilight so incense will
burn regularly before the LORD for the generations to come. 9Do not offer on this altar any
other incense or any burnt offering or grain
offering, and do not pour a drink offering on
it. 10Once a year Aaron shall make atonement on its horns. This annual atonement
must be made with the blood of the atoning
sin offering for the generations to come. It is
most holy to the LORD."

Atonement Money

11Then the LORD said to Moses, 12"When
you take a census of the Israelites to count
them, each one must pay the LORD a ransom
for his life at the time he is counted. Then no
plague will come on them when you number
them. 13Each one who crosses over to those
already counted is to give a half shekel,[e]
according to the sanctuary shekel, which
weighs twenty gerahs. This half shekel is an
offering to the LORD. 14All who cross over,
those twenty years old or more, are to give
an offering to the LORD. 15The rich are not to
give more than a half shekel and the poor are
not to give less when you make the offering
to the LORD to atone for your lives. 16Receive
the atonement money from the Israelites and
use it for the service of the Tent of Meeting. It
will be a memorial for the Israelites before
the LORD, making atonement for your lives."

Basin for Washing

17Then the LORD said to Moses, 18"Make a
bronze basin, with its bronze stand, for

[a]28 Traditionally *peace offerings* [b]40 That is, probably about 2 quarts (about 2 liters) [c]40 That is, probably about 1 quart (about 1 liter) [d]2 That is, about 1 1/2 feet (about 0.5 meter) long and wide and about 3 feet (about 0.9 meter) high [e]13 That is, about 1/5 ounce (about 6 grams); also in verse 15

washing. Place it between the Tent of Meeting and the altar, and put water in it. [19]Aaron and his sons are to wash their hands and feet with water from it. [20]Whenever they enter the Tent of Meeting, they shall wash with water so that they will not die. Also, when they approach the altar to minister by presenting an offering made to the LORD by fire, [21]they shall wash their hands and feet so that they will not die. This is to be a lasting ordinance for Aaron and his descendants for the generations to come."

Anointing Oil

[22]Then the LORD said to Moses, [23]"Take the following fine spices: 500 shekels[a] of liquid myrrh, half as much (that is, 250 shekels) of fragrant cinnamon, 250 shekels of fragrant cane, [24]500 shekels of cassia—all according to the sanctuary shekel—and a hin[b] of olive oil. [25]Make these into a sacred anointing oil, a fragrant blend, the work of a perfumer. It will be the sacred anointing oil. [26]Then use it to anoint the Tent of Meeting, the ark of the Testimony, [27]the table and all its articles, the lampstand and its accessories, the altar of incense, [28]the altar of burnt offering and all its utensils, and the basin with its stand. [29]You shall consecrate them so they will be most holy, and whatever touches them will be holy.

[30]"Anoint Aaron and his sons and consecrate them so they may serve me as priests. [31]Say to the Israelites, 'This is to be my sacred anointing oil for the generations to come. [32]Do not pour it on men's bodies and do not make any oil with the same formula. It is sacred, and you are to consider it sacred. [33]Whoever makes perfume like it and whoever puts it on anyone other than a priest must be cut off from his people.' "

Incense

[34]Then the LORD said to Moses, "Take fragrant spices—gum resin, onycha and galbanum—and pure frankincense, all in equal amounts, [35]and make a fragrant blend of incense, the work of a perfumer. It is to be salted and pure and sacred. [36]Grind some of it to powder and place it in front of the Testimony in the Tent of Meeting, where I will meet with you. It shall be most holy to you. [37]Do not make any incense with this formula for yourselves; consider it holy to the LORD. [38]Whoever makes any like it to enjoy its fragrance must be cut off from his people."

Bezalel and Oholiab

31 Then the LORD said to Moses, [2]"See, I have chosen Bezalel son of Uri, the son of Hur, of the tribe of Judah, [3]and I have filled him with the Spirit of God, with skill, ability and knowledge in all kinds of crafts—[4]to make artistic designs for work in gold, silver and bronze, [5]to cut and set stones, to work in wood, and to engage in all kinds of craftsmanship. [6]Moreover, I have appointed Oholiab son of Ahisamach, of the tribe of Dan, to help him. Also I have given skill to all the craftsmen to make everything I have commanded you: [7]the Tent of Meeting, the ark of the Testimony with the atonement cover on it, and all the other furnishings of the tent— [8]the table and its articles, the pure gold lampstand and all its accessories, the altar of incense, [9]the altar of burnt offering and all its utensils, the basin with its stand—[10]and also the woven garments, both the sacred garments for Aaron the priest and the garments for his sons when they serve as priests, [11]and the anointing oil and fragrant incense for the Holy Place. They are to make them just as I commanded you."

The Sabbath

[12]Then the LORD said to Moses, [13]"Say to the Israelites, 'You must observe my Sabbaths. This will be a sign between me and you for the generations to come, so you may know that I am the LORD, who makes you holy.[c]

[14]" 'Observe the Sabbath, because it is holy to you. Anyone who desecrates it must be put to death; whoever does any work on that day must be cut off from his people. [15]For six days, work is to be done, but the seventh day is a Sabbath of rest, holy to the LORD. Whoever does any work on the Sabbath day must be put to death. [16]The Israelites are to observe the Sabbath, celebrating it for the generations to come as a lasting covenant. [17]It will be a sign between me and the Israelites forever, for in six days the LORD made the heavens and the earth, and on the seventh day he abstained from work and rested.' "

[18]When the LORD finished speaking to Moses on Mount Sinai, he gave him the two

[a]*23* That is, about 12 1/2 pounds (about 6 kilograms) [b]*24* That is, probably about 4 quarts (about 4 liters)
[c]*13* Or *who sanctifies you;* or *who sets you apart as holy*

tablets of the Testimony, the tablets of stone inscribed by the finger of God.

The Golden Calf

32 When the people saw that Moses was so long in coming down from the mountain, they gathered around Aaron and said, "Come, make us gods[a] who will go before us. As for this fellow Moses who brought us up out of Egypt, we don't know what has happened to him."

2Aaron answered them, "Take off the gold earrings that your wives, your sons and your daughters are wearing, and bring them to me." 3So all the people took off their earrings and brought them to Aaron. 4He took what they handed him and made it into an idol cast in the shape of a calf, fashioning it with a tool. Then they said, "These are your gods,[b] O Israel, who brought you up out of Egypt."

5When Aaron saw this, he built an altar in front of the calf and announced, "Tomorrow there will be a festival to the LORD." 6So the next day the people rose early and sacrificed burnt offerings and presented fellowship offerings.[c] Afterward they sat down to eat and drink and got up to indulge in revelry.

7Then the LORD said to Moses, "Go down, because your people, whom you brought up out of Egypt, have become corrupt. 8They have been quick to turn away from what I commanded them and have made themselves an idol cast in the shape of a calf. They have bowed down to it and sacrificed to it and have said, 'These are your gods, O Israel, who brought you up out of Egypt.'

9"I have seen these people," the LORD said to Moses, "and they are a stiff-necked people. 10Now leave me alone so that my anger may burn against them and that I may destroy them. Then I will make you into a great nation."

11But Moses sought the favor of the LORD his God. "O LORD," he said, "why should your anger burn against your people, whom you brought out of Egypt with great power and a mighty hand? 12Why should the Egyptians say, 'It was with evil intent that he brought them out, to kill them in the mountains and to wipe them off the face of the earth'? Turn from your fierce anger; relent and do not bring disaster on your people. 13Remember your servants Abraham, Isaac and Israel, to whom you swore by your own self: 'I will make your descendants as numerous as the stars in the sky and I will give your descendants all this land I promised them, and it will be their inheritance forever.' " 14Then the LORD relented and did not bring on his people the disaster he had threatened.

15Moses turned and went down the mountain with the two tablets of the Testimony in his hands. They were inscribed on both sides, front and back. 16The tablets were the work of God; the writing was the writing of God, engraved on the tablets.

17When Joshua heard the noise of the people shouting, he said to Moses, "There is the sound of war in the camp."

18Moses replied:

"It is not the sound of victory,
  it is not the sound of defeat;
  it is the sound of singing that I hear."

19When Moses approached the camp and saw the calf and the dancing, his anger burned and he threw the tablets out of his hands, breaking them to pieces at the foot of the mountain. 20And he took the calf they had made and burned it in the fire; then he ground it to powder, scattered it on the water and made the Israelites drink it.

21He said to Aaron, "What did these people do to you, that you led them into such great sin?"

22"Do not be angry, my lord," Aaron answered. "You know how prone these people are to evil. 23They said to me, 'Make us gods who will go before us. As for this fellow Moses who brought us up out of Egypt, we don't know what has happened to him.' 24So I told them, 'Whoever has any gold jewelry, take it off.' Then they gave me the gold, and I threw it into the fire, and out came this calf!"

25Moses saw that the people were running wild and that Aaron had let them get out of control and so become a laughingstock to their enemies. 26So he stood at the entrance to the camp and said, "Whoever is for the LORD, come to me." And all the Levites rallied to him.

27Then he said to them, "This is what the LORD, the God of Israel, says: 'Each man strap a sword to his side. Go back and forth through the camp from one end to the other, each killing his brother and friend and neighbor.' " 28The Levites did as Moses commanded, and that day about three thousand

[a]1 Or *a god*; also in verses 23 and 31 [b]4 Or *This is your god;* also in verse 8 [c]6 Traditionally *peace offerings*

of the people died. 29Then Moses said, "You have been set apart to the LORD today, for you were against your own sons and brothers, and he has blessed you this day."

30The next day Moses said to the people, "You have committed a great sin. But now I will go up to the LORD; perhaps I can make atonement for your sin."

31So Moses went back to the LORD and said, "Oh, what a great sin these people have committed! They have made themselves gods of gold. 32But now, please forgive their sin—but if not, then blot me out of the book you have written."

33The LORD replied to Moses, "Whoever has sinned against me I will blot out of my book. 34Now go, lead the people to the place I spoke of, and my angel will go before you. However, when the time comes for me to punish, I will punish them for their sin."

35And the LORD struck the people with a plague because of what they did with the calf Aaron had made.

33 Then the LORD said to Moses, "Leave this place, you and the people you brought up out of Egypt, and go up to the land I promised on oath to Abraham, Isaac and Jacob, saying, 'I will give it to your descendants.' 2I will send an angel before you and drive out the Canaanites, Amorites, Hittites, Perizzites, Hivites and Jebusites. 3Go up to the land flowing with milk and honey. But I will not go with you, because you are a stiff-necked people and I might destroy you on the way."

4When the people heard these distressing words, they began to mourn and no one put on any ornaments. 5For the LORD had said to Moses, "Tell the Israelites, 'You are a stiff-necked people. If I were to go with you even for a moment, I might destroy you. Now take off your ornaments and I will decide what to do with you.' " 6So the Israelites stripped off their ornaments at Mount Horeb.

The Tent of Meeting

7Now Moses used to take a tent and pitch it outside the camp some distance away, calling it the "tent of meeting." Anyone inquiring of the LORD would go to the tent of meeting outside the camp. 8And whenever Moses went out to the tent, all the people rose and stood at the entrances to their tents, watching Moses until he entered the tent. 9As Moses went into the tent, the pillar of cloud would come down and stay at the entrance, while the LORD spoke with Moses. 10Whenever the people saw the pillar of cloud standing at the entrance to the tent, they all stood and worshiped, each at the entrance to his tent. 11The LORD would speak to Moses face to face, as a man speaks with his friend. Then Moses would return to the camp, but his young aide Joshua son of Nun did not leave the tent.

Moses and the Glory of the LORD

12Moses said to the LORD, "You have been telling me, 'Lead these people,' but you have not let me know whom you will send with me. You have said, 'I know you by name and you have found favor with me.' 13If you are pleased with me, teach me your ways so I may know you and continue to find favor with you. Remember that this nation is your people."

14The LORD replied, "My Presence will go with you, and I will give you rest."

15Then Moses said to him, "If your Presence does not go with us, do not send us up from here. 16How will anyone know that you are pleased with me and with your people unless you go with us? What else will distinguish me and your people from all the other people on the face of the earth?"

17And the LORD said to Moses, "I will do the very thing you have asked, because I am pleased with you and I know you by name."

18Then Moses said, "Now show me your glory."

19And the LORD said, "I will cause all my goodness to pass in front of you, and I will proclaim my name, the LORD, in your presence. I will have mercy on whom I will have mercy, and I will have compassion on whom I will have compassion. 20But," he said, "you cannot see my face, for no one may see me and live."

21Then the LORD said, "There is a place near me where you may stand on a rock. 22When my glory passes by, I will put you in a cleft in the rock and cover you with my hand until I have passed by. 23Then I will remove my hand and you will see my back; but my face must not be seen."

The New Stone Tablets

34 The LORD said to Moses, "Chisel out two stone tablets like the first ones, and I will write on them the words that were on the first tablets, which you broke. 2Be ready in the morning, and then come up on Mount Sinai. Present yourself to me there on top of the mountain. 3No one is to come with

you or be seen anywhere on the mountain;
not even the flocks and herds may graze in
front of the mountain."
4So Moses chiseled out two stone tablets
like the first ones and went up Mount Sinai
early in the morning, as the LORD had commanded him; and he carried the two stone
tablets in his hands. 5Then the LORD came
down in the cloud and stood there with him
and proclaimed his name, the LORD. 6And he
passed in front of Moses, proclaiming, "The
LORD, the LORD, the compassionate and gracious God, slow to anger, abounding in love
and faithfulness, 7maintaining love to thousands, and forgiving wickedness, rebellion
and sin. Yet he does not leave the guilty
unpunished; he punishes the children and
their children for the sin of the fathers to the
third and fourth generation."
8Moses bowed to the ground at once and
worshiped. 9"O Lord, if I have found favor in
your eyes," he said, "then let the Lord go
with us. Although this is a stiff-necked
people, forgive our wickedness and our sin,
and take us as your inheritance."
10Then the LORD said: "I am making a covenant with you. Before all your people I will
do wonders never before done in any nation
in all the world. The people you live among
will see how awesome is the work that I, the
LORD, will do for you. 11Obey what I command
you today. I will drive out before you the
Amorites, Canaanites, Hittites, Perizzites,
Hivites and Jebusites. 12Be careful not to
make a treaty with those who live in the land
where you are going, or they will be a snare
among you. 13Break down their altars,
smash their sacred stones and cut down
their Asherah poles.[a] 14Do not worship any
other god, for the LORD, whose name is Jealous, is a jealous God.
15"Be careful not to make a treaty with
those who live in the land; for when they
prostitute themselves to their gods and sacrifice to them, they will invite you and you will
eat their sacrifices. 16And when you choose
some of their daughters as wives for your
sons and those daughters prostitute themselves to their gods, they will lead your sons
to do the same.
17"Do not make cast idols.
18"Celebrate the Feast of Unleavened
Bread. For seven days eat bread made without yeast, as I commanded you. Do this at
the appointed time in the month of Abib, for in
that month you came out of Egypt.
19"The first offspring of every womb belongs to me, including all the firstborn males
of your livestock, whether from herd or flock.
20Redeem the firstborn donkey with a lamb,
but if you do not redeem it, break its neck.
Redeem all your firstborn sons.
"No one is to appear before me empty-
handed.
21"Six days you shall labor, but on the seventh day you shall rest; even during the
plowing season and harvest you must rest.
22"Celebrate the Feast of Weeks with the
firstfruits of the wheat harvest, and the Feast
of Ingathering at the turn of the year.[b]
23Three times a year all your men are to
appear before the Sovereign LORD, the God
of Israel. 24I will drive out nations before you
and enlarge your territory, and no one will
covet your land when you go up three times
each year to appear before the LORD your
God.
25"Do not offer the blood of a sacrifice to
me along with anything containing yeast,
and do not let any of the sacrifice from the
Passover Feast remain until morning.
26"Bring the best of the firstfruits of your
soil to the house of the LORD your God.
"Do not cook a young goat in its mother's
milk."
27Then the LORD said to Moses, "Write
down these words, for in accordance with
these words I have made a covenant with
you and with Israel." 28Moses was there with
the LORD forty days and forty nights without
eating bread or drinking water. And he wrote
on the tablets the words of the covenant—
the Ten Commandments.

The Radiant Face of Moses

29When Moses came down from Mount
Sinai with the two tablets of the Testimony in
his hands, he was not aware that his face
was radiant because he had spoken with the
LORD. 30When Aaron and all the Israelites
saw Moses, his face was radiant, and they
were afraid to come near him. 31But Moses
called to them; so Aaron and all the leaders
of the community came back to him, and he
spoke to them. 32Afterward all the Israelites
came near him, and he gave them all the
commands the LORD had given him on Mount
Sinai.

[a]*13* That is, symbols of the goddess Asherah
[b]*22* That is, in the fall

33When Moses finished speaking to them, he put a veil over his face. 34But whenever he entered the LORD's presence to speak with him, he removed the veil until he came out. And when he came out and told the Israelites what he had been commanded, 35they saw that his face was radiant. Then Moses would put the veil back over his face until he went in to speak with the LORD.

Sabbath Regulations

35 Moses assembled the whole Israelite community and said to them, "These are the things the LORD has commanded you to do: 2For six days, work is to be done, but the seventh day shall be your holy day, a Sabbath of rest to the LORD. Whoever does any work on it must be put to death. 3Do not light a fire in any of your dwellings on the Sabbath day."

Materials for the Tabernacle

4Moses said to the whole Israelite community, "This is what the LORD has commanded: 5From what you have, take an offering for the LORD. Everyone who is willing is to bring to the LORD an offering of gold, silver and bronze; 6blue, purple and scarlet yarn and fine linen; goat hair; 7ram skins dyed red and hides of sea cows[a]; acacia wood; 8olive oil for the light; spices for the anointing oil and for the fragrant incense; 9and onyx stones and other gems to be mounted on the ephod and breastpiece.

10"All who are skilled among you are to come and make everything the LORD has commanded: 11the tabernacle with its tent and its covering, clasps, frames, crossbars, posts and bases; 12the ark with its poles and the atonement cover and the curtain that shields it; 13the table with its poles and all its articles and the bread of the Presence; 14the lampstand that is for light with its accessories, lamps and oil for the light; 15the altar of incense with its poles, the anointing oil and the fragrant incense; the curtain for the doorway at the entrance to the tabernacle; 16the altar of burnt offering with its bronze grating, its poles and all its utensils; the bronze basin with its stand; 17the curtains of the courtyard with its posts and bases, and the curtain for the entrance to the courtyard; 18the tent pegs for the tabernacle and for the courtyard, and their ropes; 19the woven garments worn for ministering in the sanctuary—both the sacred garments for Aaron the priest and the garments for his sons when they serve as priests."

20Then the whole Israelite community withdrew from Moses' presence, 21and everyone who was willing and whose heart moved him came and brought an offering to the LORD for the work on the Tent of Meeting, for all its service, and for the sacred garments. 22All who were willing, men and women alike, came and brought gold jewelry of all kinds: brooches, earrings, rings and ornaments. They all presented their gold as a wave offering to the LORD. 23Everyone who had blue, purple or scarlet yarn or fine linen, or goat hair, ram skins dyed red or hides of sea cows brought them. 24Those presenting an offering of silver or bronze brought it as an offering to the LORD, and everyone who had acacia wood for any part of the work brought it. 25Every skilled woman spun with her hands and brought what she had spun—blue, purple or scarlet yarn or fine linen. 26And all the women who were willing and had the skill spun the goat hair. 27The leaders brought onyx stones and other gems to be mounted on the ephod and breastpiece. 28They also brought spices and olive oil for the light and for the anointing oil and for the fragrant incense. 29All the Israelite men and women who were willing brought to the LORD freewill offerings for all the work the LORD through Moses had commanded them to do.

Bezalel and Oholiab

30Then Moses said to the Israelites, "See, the LORD has chosen Bezalel son of Uri, the son of Hur, of the tribe of Judah, 31and he has filled him with the Spirit of God, with skill, ability and knowledge in all kinds of crafts—32to make artistic designs for work in gold, silver and bronze, 33to cut and set stones, to work in wood and to engage in all kinds of artistic craftsmanship. 34And he has given both him and Oholiab son of Ahisamach, of the tribe of Dan, the ability to teach others. 35He has filled them with skill to do all kinds of work as craftsmen, designers, embroiderers in blue, purple and scarlet yarn and fine linen, and weavers—all of them master craftsmen and designers.

36 1So Bezalel, Oholiab and every skilled person to whom the LORD has given skill and ability to know how to carry out all the work of con-

[a]7 That is, dugongs; also in verse 23

structing the sanctuary are to do the work just as the Lord has commanded."

2Then Moses summoned Bezalel and Oholiab and every skilled person to whom the LORD had given ability and who was willing to come and do the work. 3They received from Moses all the offerings the Israelites had brought to carry out the work of constructing the sanctuary. And the people continued to bring freewill offerings morning after morning. 4So all the skilled craftsmen who were doing all the work on the sanctuary left their work 5and said to Moses, "The people are bringing more than enough for doing the work the LORD commanded to be done."

6Then Moses gave an order and they sent this word throughout the camp: "No man or woman is to make anything else as an offering for the sanctuary." And so the people were restrained from bringing more, 7because what they already had was more than enough to do all the work.

The Tabernacle

8All the skilled men among the workmen made the tabernacle with ten curtains of finely twisted linen and blue, purple and scarlet yarn, with cherubim worked into them by a skilled craftsman. 9All the curtains were the same size—twenty-eight cubits long and four cubits wide.[a] 10They joined five of the curtains together and did the same with the other five. 11Then they made loops of blue material along the edge of the end curtain in one set, and the same was done with the end curtain in the other set. 12They also made fifty loops on one curtain and fifty loops on the end curtain of the other set, with the loops opposite each other. 13Then they made fifty gold clasps and used them to fasten the two sets of curtains together so that the tabernacle was a unit.

14They made curtains of goat hair for the tent over the tabernacle—eleven altogether. 15All eleven curtains were the same size—thirty cubits long and four cubits wide.[b] 16They joined five of the curtains into one set and the other six into another set. 17Then they made fifty loops along the edge of the end curtain in one set and also along the edge of the end curtain in the other set. 18They made fifty bronze clasps to fasten the tent together as a unit. 19Then they made for the tent a covering of ram skins dyed red, and over that a covering of hides of sea cows.[c]

20They made upright frames of acacia wood for the tabernacle. 21Each frame was ten cubits long and a cubit and a half wide,[d] 22with two projections set parallel to each other. They made all the frames of the tabernacle in this way. 23They made twenty frames for the south side of the tabernacle 24and made forty silver bases to go under them—two bases for each frame, one under each projection. 25For the other side, the north side of the tabernacle, they made twenty frames 26and forty silver bases—two under each frame. 27They made six frames for the far end, that is, the west end of the tabernacle, 28and two frames were made for the corners of the tabernacle at the far end. 29At these two corners the frames were double from the bottom all the way to the top and fitted into a single ring; both were made alike. 30So there were eight frames and sixteen silver bases—two under each frame.

31They also made crossbars of acacia wood: five for the frames on one side of the tabernacle, 32five for those on the other side, and five for the frames on the west, at the far end of the tabernacle. 33They made the center crossbar so that it extended from end to end at the middle of the frames. 34They overlaid the frames with gold and made gold rings to hold the crossbars. They also overlaid the crossbars with gold.

35They made the curtain of blue, purple and scarlet yarn and finely twisted linen, with cherubim worked into it by a skilled craftsman. 36They made four posts of acacia wood for it and overlaid them with gold. They made gold hooks for them and cast their four silver bases. 37For the entrance to the tent they made a curtain of blue, purple and scarlet yarn and finely twisted linen—the work of an embroiderer; 38and they made five posts with hooks for them. They overlaid the tops of the posts and their bands with gold and made their five bases of bronze.

The Ark

37 Bezalel made the ark of acacia wood—two and a half cubits long, a cubit and a half wide, and a cubit and a half high.[e] 2He overlaid it with pure gold, both

[a] *9* That is, about 42 feet (about 12.5 meters) long and 6 feet (about 1.8 meters) wide [b] *15* That is, about 45 feet (about 13.5 meters) long and 6 feet (about 1.8 meters) wide [c] *19* That is, dugongs [d] *21* That is, about 15 feet (about 4.5 meters) long and 2 1/4 feet (about 0.7 meter) wide [e] *1* That is, about 3 3/4 feet (about 1.1 meters) long and 2 1/4 feet (about 0.7 meter) wide and high

inside and out, and made a gold molding
around it. 3He cast four gold rings for it and
fastened them to its four feet, with two rings
on one side and two rings on the other.
4Then he made poles of acacia wood and
overlaid them with gold. 5And he inserted the
poles into the rings on the sides of the ark to
carry it.

6He made the atonement cover of pure
gold—two and a half cubits long and a cubit
and a half wide.[a] 7Then he made two cherubim out of hammered gold at the ends of the
cover. 8He made one cherub on one end and
the second cherub on the other; at the two
ends he made them of one piece with the
cover. 9The cherubim had their wings spread
upward, overshadowing the cover with them.
The cherubim faced each other, looking
toward the cover.

The Table

10They[b] made the table of acacia wood—
two cubits long, a cubit wide, and a cubit and
a half high.[c] 11Then they overlaid it with pure
gold and made a gold molding around it.
12They also made around it a rim a handbreadth[d] wide and put a gold molding on the
rim. 13They cast four gold rings for the table
and fastened them to the four corners, where
the four legs were. 14The rings were put
close to the rim to hold the poles used in
carrying the table. 15The poles for carrying
the table were made of acacia wood and
were overlaid with gold. 16And they made
from pure gold the articles for the table—its
plates and dishes and bowls and its pitchers
for the pouring out of drink offerings.

The Lampstand

17They made the lampstand of pure gold
and hammered it out, base and shaft; its
flowerlike cups, buds and blossoms were of
one piece with it. 18Six branches extended
from the sides of the lampstand—three on
one side and three on the other. 19Three
cups shaped like almond flowers with buds
and blossoms were on one branch, three on
the next branch and the same for all six
branches extending from the lampstand.
20And on the lampstand were four cups
shaped like almond flowers with buds and
blossoms. 21One bud was under the first pair
of branches extending from the lampstand, a
second bud under the second pair, and a
third bud under the third pair—six branches
in all. 22The buds and the branches were all
of one piece with the lampstand, hammered
out of pure gold.

23They made its seven lamps, as well as its
wick trimmers and trays, of pure gold. 24They
made the lampstand and all its accessories
from one talent[e] of pure gold.

The Altar of Incense

25They made the altar of incense out of
acacia wood. It was square, a cubit long and
a cubit wide, and two cubits high[f]—its horns
of one piece with it. 26They overlaid the top
and all the sides and the horns with pure
gold, and made a gold molding around it.
27They made two gold rings below the molding—two on opposite sides—to hold the
poles used to carry it. 28They made the poles
of acacia wood and overlaid them with gold.

29They also made the sacred anointing oil
and the pure, fragrant incense—the work of
a perfumer.

The Altar of Burnt Offering

38 They[g] built the altar of burnt offering
of acacia wood, three cubits[h] high; it
was square, five cubits long and five cubits
wide.[i] 2They made a horn at each of the four
corners, so that the horns and the altar were
of one piece, and they overlaid the altar with
bronze. 3They made all its utensils of
bronze—its pots, shovels, sprinkling bowls,
meat forks and firepans. 4They made a grating for the altar, a bronze network, to be
under its ledge, halfway up the altar. 5They
cast bronze rings to hold the poles for the
four corners of the bronze grating. 6They
made the poles of acacia wood and overlaid
them with bronze. 7They inserted the poles
into the rings so they would be on the sides
of the altar for carrying it. They made it hollow, out of boards.

Basin for Washing

8They made the bronze basin and its
bronze stand from the mirrors of the women

[a]6 That is, about 3 3/4 feet (about 1.1 meters) long and 2 1/4 feet (about 0.7 meter) wide [b]10 Or *He;* also in verses 11-29 [c]10 That is, about 3 feet (about 0.9 meter) long, 1 1/2 feet (about 0.5 meter) wide, and 2 1/4 feet (about 0.7 meter) high [d]12 That is, about 3 inches (about 8 centimeters) [e]24 That is, about 75 pounds (about 34 kilograms) [f]25 That is, about 1 1/2 feet (about 0.5 meter) long and wide, and about 3 feet (about 0.9 meter) high [g]1 Or *He;* also in verses 2-9 [h]1 That is, about 4 1/2 feet (about 1.3 meters) [i]1 That is, about 7 1/2 feet (about 2.3 meters) long and wide

who served at the entrance to the Tent of Meeting.

The Courtyard

9Next they made the courtyard. The south side was a hundred cubits[a] long and had curtains of finely twisted linen, 10with twenty posts and twenty bronze bases, and with silver hooks and bands on the posts. 11The north side was also a hundred cubits long and had twenty posts and twenty bronze bases, with silver hooks and bands on the posts.

12The west end was fifty cubits[b] wide and had curtains, with ten posts and ten bases, with silver hooks and bands on the posts. 13The east end, toward the sunrise, was also fifty cubits wide. 14Curtains fifteen cubits[c] long were on one side of the entrance, with three posts and three bases, 15and curtains fifteen cubits long were on the other side of the entrance to the courtyard, with three posts and three bases. 16All the curtains around the courtyard were of finely twisted linen. 17The bases for the posts were bronze. The hooks and bands on the posts were silver, and their tops were overlaid with silver; so all the posts of the courtyard had silver bands.

18The curtain for the entrance to the courtyard was of blue, purple and scarlet yarn and finely twisted linen—the work of an embroiderer. It was twenty cubits[d] long and, like the curtains of the courtyard, five cubits[e] high, 19with four posts and four bronze bases. Their hooks and bands were silver, and their tops were overlaid with silver. 20All the tent pegs of the tabernacle and of the surrounding courtyard were bronze.

The Materials Used

21These are the amounts of the materials used for the tabernacle, the tabernacle of the Testimony, which were recorded at Moses' command by the Levites under the direction of Ithamar son of Aaron, the priest. 22(Bezalel son of Uri, the son of Hur, of the tribe of Judah, made everything the LORD commanded Moses; 23with him was Oholiab son of Ahisamach, of the tribe of Dan—a craftsman and designer, and an embroiderer in blue, purple and scarlet yarn and fine linen.) 24The total amount of the gold from the wave offering used for all the work on the sanctuary was 29 talents and 730 shekels,[f] according to the sanctuary shekel.

25The silver obtained from those of the community who were counted in the census was 100 talents and 1,775 shekels,[g] according to the sanctuary shekel— 26one beka per person, that is, half a shekel,[h] according to the sanctuary shekel, from everyone who had crossed over to those counted, twenty years old or more, a total of 603,550 men. 27The 100 talents[i] of silver were used to cast the bases for the sanctuary and for the curtain—100 bases from the 100 talents, one talent for each base. 28They used the 1,775 shekels[j] to make the hooks for the posts, to overlay the tops of the posts, and to make their bands.

29The bronze from the wave offering was 70 talents and 2,400 shekels.[k] 30They used it to make the bases for the entrance to the Tent of Meeting, the bronze altar with its bronze grating and all its utensils, 31the bases for the surrounding courtyard and those for its entrance and all the tent pegs for the tabernacle and those for the surrounding courtyard.

The Priestly Garments

39 From the blue, purple and scarlet yarn they made woven garments for ministering in the sanctuary. They also made sacred garments for Aaron, as the LORD commanded Moses.

The Ephod

2They[l] made the ephod of gold, and of blue, purple and scarlet yarn, and of finely twisted linen. 3They hammered out thin sheets of gold and cut strands to be worked into the blue, purple and scarlet yarn and fine linen—the work of a skilled craftsman. 4They made shoulder pieces for the ephod, which were attached to two of its corners, so it could be fastened. 5Its skillfully woven waistband was like it—of one piece with the ephod and made with gold, and with blue, purple

a9 That is, about 150 feet (about 46 meters) *b12* That is, about 75 feet (about 23 meters) *c14* That is, about 22 1/2 feet (about 6.9 meters) *d18* That is, about 30 feet (about 9 meters) *e18* That is, about 7 1/2 feet (about 2.3 meters) *f24* The weight of the gold was a little over one ton (about 1 metric ton). *g25* The weight of the silver was a little over 3 3/4 tons (about 3.4 metric tons). *h26* That is, about 1/5 ounce (about 5.5 grams) *i27* That is, about 3 3/4 tons (about 3.4 metric tons) *j28* That is, about 45 pounds (about 20 kilograms) *k29* The weight of the bronze was about 2 1/2 tons (about 2.4 metric tons). *l2* Or *He;* also in verses 7, 8 and 22 and scarlet yarn, and with finely twisted linen, as the LORD commanded Moses.

6They mounted the onyx stones in gold filigree settings and engraved them like a seal with the names of the sons of Israel. 7Then they fastened them on the shoulder pieces of the ephod as memorial stones for the sons of Israel, as the LORD commanded Moses.

The Breastpiece

8They fashioned the breastpiece—the work of a skilled craftsman. They made it like the ephod: of gold, and of blue, purple and scarlet yarn, and of finely twisted linen. 9It was square—a span[a] long and a span wide—and folded double. 10Then they mounted four rows of precious stones on it. In the first row there was a ruby, a topaz and a beryl; 11in the second row a turquoise, a sapphire[b] and an emerald; 12in the third row a jacinth, an agate and an amethyst; 13in the fourth row a chrysolite, an onyx and a jasper.[c] They were mounted in gold filigree settings. 14There were twelve stones, one for each of the names of the sons of Israel, each engraved like a seal with the name of one of the twelve tribes.

15For the breastpiece they made braided chains of pure gold, like a rope. 16They made two gold filigree settings and two gold rings, and fastened the rings to two of the corners of the breastpiece. 17They fastened the two gold chains to the rings at the corners of the breastpiece, 18and the other ends of the chains to the two settings, attaching them to the shoulder pieces of the ephod at the front. 19They made two gold rings and attached them to the other two corners of the breastpiece on the inside edge next to the ephod. 20Then they made two more gold rings and attached them to the bottom of the shoulder pieces on the front of the ephod, close to the seam just above the waistband of the ephod. 21They tied the rings of the breastpiece to the rings of the ephod with blue cord, connecting it to the waistband so that the breastpiece would not swing out from the ephod—as the LORD commanded Moses.

Other Priestly Garments

22They made the robe of the ephod entirely of blue cloth—the work of a weaver— 23with an opening in the center of the robe like the opening of a collar,[d] and a band around this opening, so that it would not tear. 24They made pomegranates of blue, purple and scarlet yarn and finely twisted linen around the hem of the robe. 25And they made bells of pure gold and attached them around the hem between the pomegranates. 26The bells and pomegranates alternated around the hem of the robe to be worn for ministering, as the LORD commanded Moses.

27For Aaron and his sons, they made tunics of fine linen—the work of a weaver— 28and the turban of fine linen, the linen headbands and the undergarments of finely twisted linen. 29The sash was of finely twisted linen and blue, purple and scarlet yarn—the work of an embroiderer—as the LORD commanded Moses.

30They made the plate, the sacred diadem, out of pure gold and engraved on it, like an inscription on a seal: HOLY TO THE LORD. 31Then they fastened a blue cord to it to attach it to the turban, as the LORD commanded Moses.

Moses Inspects the Tabernacle

32So all the work on the tabernacle, the Tent of Meeting, was completed. The Israelites did everything just as the LORD commanded Moses. 33Then they brought the tabernacle to Moses: the tent and all its furnishings, its clasps, frames, crossbars, posts and bases; 34the covering of ram skins dyed red, the covering of hides of sea cows[e] and the shielding curtain; 35the ark of the Testimony with its poles and the atonement cover; 36the table with all its articles and the bread of the Presence; 37the pure gold lampstand with its row of lamps and all its accessories, and the oil for the light; 38the gold altar, the anointing oil, the fragrant incense, and the curtain for the entrance to the tent; 39the bronze altar with its bronze grating, its poles and all its utensils; the basin with its stand; 40the curtains of the courtyard with its posts and bases, and the curtain for the entrance to the courtyard; the ropes and tent pegs for the courtyard; all the furnishings for the tabernacle, the Tent of Meeting; 41and the woven garments worn for ministering in the sanctuary, both the sacred garments for Aaron the priest and the garments for his sons when serving as priests.

42The Israelites had done all the work just as the LORD had commanded Moses.

[a]9 That is, about 9 inches (about 22 centimeters)
[b]11 Or *lapis lazuli*
[c]13 The precise identification of some of these precious stones is uncertain.
[d]23 The meaning of the Hebrew for this word is uncertain.
[e]34 That is, dugongs

43Moses inspected the work and saw that they had done it just as the LORD had commanded. So Moses blessed them.

Setting Up the Tabernacle

40 Then the LORD said to Moses: 2"Set up the tabernacle, the Tent of Meeting, on the first day of the first month. 3Place the ark of the Testimony in it and shield the ark with the curtain. 4Bring in the table and set out what belongs on it. Then bring in the lampstand and set up its lamps. 5Place the gold altar of incense in front of the ark of the Testimony and put the curtain at the entrance to the tabernacle.

6"Place the altar of burnt offering in front of the entrance to the tabernacle, the Tent of Meeting; 7place the basin between the Tent of Meeting and the altar and put water in it. 8Set up the courtyard around it and put the curtain at the entrance to the courtyard.

9"Take the anointing oil and anoint the tabernacle and everything in it; consecrate it and all its furnishings, and it will be holy. 10Then anoint the altar of burnt offering and all its utensils; consecrate the altar, and it will be most holy. 11Anoint the basin and its stand and consecrate them.

12"Bring Aaron and his sons to the entrance to the Tent of Meeting and wash them with water. 13Then dress Aaron in the sacred garments, anoint him and consecrate him so he may serve me as priest. 14Bring his sons and dress them in tunics. 15Anoint them just as you anointed their father, so they may serve me as priests. Their anointing will be to a priesthood that will continue for all generations to come." 16Moses did everything just as the LORD commanded him.

17So the tabernacle was set up on the first day of the first month in the second year. 18When Moses set up the tabernacle, he put the bases in place, erected the frames, inserted the crossbars and set up the posts. 19Then he spread the tent over the tabernacle and put the covering over the tent, as the LORD commanded him.

20He took the Testimony and placed it in the ark, attached the poles to the ark and put the atonement cover over it. 21Then he brought the ark into the tabernacle and hung the shielding curtain and shielded the ark of the Testimony, as the LORD commanded him.

22Moses placed the table in the Tent of Meeting on the north side of the tabernacle outside the curtain 23and set out the bread on it before the LORD, as the LORD commanded him.

24He placed the lampstand in the Tent of Meeting opposite the table on the south side of the tabernacle 25and set up the lamps before the LORD, as the LORD commanded him.

26Moses placed the gold altar in the Tent of Meeting in front of the curtain 27and burned fragrant incense on it, as the LORD commanded him. 28Then he put up the curtain at the entrance to the tabernacle.

29He set the altar of burnt offering near the entrance to the tabernacle, the Tent of Meeting, and offered on it burnt offerings and grain offerings, as the LORD commanded him.

30He placed the basin between the Tent of Meeting and the altar and put water in it for washing, 31and Moses and Aaron and his sons used it to wash their hands and feet. 32They washed whenever they entered the Tent of Meeting or approached the altar, as the LORD commanded Moses.

33Then Moses set up the courtyard around the tabernacle and altar and put up the curtain at the entrance to the courtyard. And so Moses finished the work.

The Glory of the LORD

34Then the cloud covered the Tent of Meeting, and the glory of the LORD filled the tabernacle. 35Moses could not enter the Tent of Meeting because the cloud had settled upon it, and the glory of the LORD filled the tabernacle.

36In all the travels of the Israelites, whenever the cloud lifted from above the tabernacle, they would set out; 37but if the cloud did not lift, they did not set out—until the day it lifted. 38So the cloud of the LORD was over the tabernacle by day, and fire was in the cloud by night, in the sight of all the house of Israel during all their travels.

Leviticus

Introduction:

Leviticus means "about the Levites." The Levites were God's priests, and the book of Leviticus contains many of the rules they needed to do their work—rules for worshiping God, making sacrifices, and handling everyday problems concerning cleanliness. Although many of the rules were given only for the Levites, the purpose of all the laws that were given was to help the Israelites worship and live as God's holy people. A key statement for the entire book is "Be holy, because I am holy." (11:44,45)

Outline of contents:

The laws and instructions for offerings (1:1–7:38)
The appointment of Aaron and his sons as God's priests (8:1–10:20)
Rules for holy living (11:1–15:33)
The Day of Atonement (16:1–34)
Practical holiness (17:1–22:33)
The Sabbath, feasts and seasons (23:1–25:55)
Conditions for God's blessings (26:1–27:34)

The Burnt Offering

1 The LORD called to Moses and spoke to
him from the Tent of Meeting. He said,
2"Speak to the Israelites and say to them:
'When any of you brings an offering to the
LORD, bring as your offering an animal from
either the herd or the flock.
3" 'If the offering is a burnt offering from the
herd, he is to offer a male without defect. He
must present it at the entrance to the Tent of
Meeting so that it[a] will be acceptable to the
LORD. 4He is to lay his hand on the head of the
burnt offering, and it will be accepted on his
behalf to make atonement for him. 5He is to
slaughter the young bull before the LORD, and
then Aaron's sons the priests shall bring the
blood and sprinkle it against the altar on all
sides at the entrance to the Tent of Meeting.
6He is to skin the burnt offering and cut it into
pieces. 7The sons of Aaron the priest are to
put fire on the altar and arrange wood on the
fire. 8Then Aaron's sons the priests shall arrange the pieces, including the head and the
fat, on the burning wood that is on the altar.
9He is to wash the inner parts and the legs
with water, and the priest is to burn all of it on
the altar. It is a burnt offering, an offering
made by fire, an aroma pleasing to the LORD.
10" 'If the offering is a burnt offering from
the flock, from either the sheep or the goats,
he is to offer a male without defect. 11He is to
slaughter it at the north side of the altar before the LORD, and Aaron's sons the priests
shall sprinkle its blood against the altar on all
sides. 12He is to cut it into pieces, and the
priest shall arrange them, including the head
and the fat, on the burning wood that is on
the altar. 13He is to wash the inner parts and
the legs with water, and the priest is to bring
all of it and burn it on the altar. It is a burnt
offering, an offering made by fire, an aroma
pleasing to the LORD.
14" 'If the offering to the LORD is a burnt
offering of birds, he is to offer a dove or a
young pigeon. 15The priest shall bring it to
the altar, wring off the head and burn it on the
altar; its blood shall be drained out on the
side of the altar. 16He is to remove the crop
with its contents[b] and throw it to the east side
of the altar, where the ashes are. 17He shall
tear it open by the wings, not severing it
completely, and then the priest shall burn it
on the wood that is on the fire on the altar. It
is a burnt offering, an offering made by fire,
an aroma pleasing to the LORD.

[a]3 Or *he* [b]16 Or *crop and the feathers;* the meaning of the Hebrew for this word is uncertain.

The Grain Offering

2 " 'When someone brings a grain offering
to the LORD, his offering is to be of fine
flour. He is to pour oil on it, put incense on it
2and take it to Aaron's sons the priests. The
priest shall take a handful of the fine flour and
oil, together with all the incense, and burn
this as a memorial portion on the altar, an
offering made by fire, an aroma pleasing to
the LORD. 3The rest of the grain offering belongs to Aaron and his sons; it is a most holy
part of the offerings made to the LORD by
fire.

4" 'If you bring a grain offering baked in an
oven, it is to consist of fine flour: cakes made
without yeast and mixed with oil, or[a] wafers
made without yeast and spread with oil. 5If
your grain offering is prepared on a griddle, it
is to be made of fine flour mixed with oil, and
without yeast. 6Crumble it and pour oil on it; it
is a grain offering. 7If your grain offering is
cooked in a pan, it is to be made of fine flour
and oil. 8Bring the grain offering made of
these things to the LORD; present it to the
priest, who shall take it to the altar. 9He shall
take out the memorial portion from the grain
offering and burn it on the altar as an offering
made by fire, an aroma pleasing to the LORD.
10The rest of the grain offering belongs to
Aaron and his sons; it is a most holy part of
the offerings made to the LORD by fire.

11" 'Every grain offering you bring to the
LORD must be made without yeast, for you
are not to burn any yeast or honey in an
offering made to the LORD by fire. 12You may
bring them to the LORD as an offering of the
firstfruits, but they are not to be offered on
the altar as a pleasing aroma. 13Season all
your grain offerings with salt. Do not leave
the salt of the covenant of your God out of
your grain offerings; add salt to all your offerings.

14" 'If you bring a grain offering of firstfruits
to the LORD, offer crushed heads of new grain
roasted in the fire. 15Put oil and incense on it;
it is a grain offering. 16The priest shall burn
the memorial portion of the crushed grain
and the oil, together with all the incense, as
an offering made to the LORD by fire.

The Fellowship Offering

3 " 'If someone's offering is a fellowship
offering,[b] and he offers an animal from
the herd, whether male or female, he is to
present before the LORD an animal without
defect. 2He is to lay his hand on the head of
his offering and slaughter it at the entrance to
the Tent of Meeting. Then Aaron's sons the
priests shall sprinkle the blood against the
altar on all sides. 3From the fellowship offering he is to bring a sacrifice made to the LORD
by fire: all the fat that covers the inner parts
or is connected to them, 4both kidneys with
the fat on them near the loins, and the covering of the liver, which he will remove with the
kidneys. 5Then Aaron's sons are to burn it on
the altar on top of the burnt offering that is on
the burning wood, as an offering made by
fire, an aroma pleasing to the LORD.

6" 'If he offers an animal from the flock as a
fellowship offering to the LORD, he is to offer a
male or female without defect. 7If he offers a
lamb, he is to present it before the LORD. 8He
is to lay his hand on the head of his offering
and slaughter it in front of the Tent of Meeting. Then Aaron's sons shall sprinkle its
blood against the altar on all sides. 9From the
fellowship offering he is to bring a sacrifice
made to the LORD by fire: its fat, the entire fat
tail cut off close to the backbone, all the fat
that covers the inner parts or is connected to
them, 10both kidneys with the fat on them
near the loins, and the covering of the liver,
which he will remove with the kidneys. 11The
priest shall burn them on the altar as food, an
offering made to the LORD by fire.

12" 'If his offering is a goat, he is to present
it before the LORD. 13He is to lay his hand on
its head and slaughter it in front of the Tent of
Meeting. Then Aaron's sons shall sprinkle its
blood against the altar on all sides. 14From
what he offers he is to make this offering to
the LORD by fire: all the fat that covers the
inner parts or is connected to them, 15both
kidneys with the fat on them near the loins,
and the covering of the liver, which he will
remove with the kidneys. 16The priest shall
burn them on the altar as food, an offering
made by fire, a pleasing aroma. All the fat is
the LORD's.

17" 'This is a lasting ordinance for the generations to come, wherever you live: You
must not eat any fat or any blood.' "

The Sin Offering

4 The LORD said to Moses, 2"Say to the
Israelites: 'When anyone sins uninten-

[a]4 Or *and* [b]1 Traditionally *peace offering*; also in verses 3, 6 and 9

tionally and does what is forbidden in any of
the LORD's commands—

3" 'If the anointed priest sins, bringing guilt
on the people, he must bring to the LORD a
young bull without defect as a sin offering for
the sin he has committed. 4He is to present
the bull at the entrance to the Tent of Meeting
before the LORD. He is to lay his hand on its
head and slaughter it before the LORD. 5Then
the anointed priest shall take some of the
bull's blood and carry it into the Tent of Meeting. 6He is to dip his finger into the blood and
sprinkle some of it seven times before the
LORD, in front of the curtain of the sanctuary.
7The priest shall then put some of the blood
on the horns of the altar of fragrant incense
that is before the LORD in the Tent of Meeting.
The rest of the bull's blood he shall pour out
at the base of the altar of burnt offering at the
entrance to the Tent of Meeting. 8He shall
remove all the fat from the bull of the sin
offering—the fat that covers the inner parts
or is connected to them, 9both kidneys with
the fat on them near the loins, and the covering of the liver, which he will remove with the
kidneys— 10just as the fat is removed from
the ox[a] sacrificed as a fellowship offering.[b]
Then the priest shall burn them on the altar of
burnt offering. 11But the hide of the bull and
all its flesh, as well as the head and legs, the
inner parts and offal— 12that is, all the rest of
the bull—he must take outside the camp to a
place ceremonially clean, where the ashes
are thrown, and burn it in a wood fire on the
ash heap.

13" 'If the whole Israelite community sins
unintentionally and does what is forbidden in
any of the LORD's commands, even though
the community is unaware of the matter, they
are guilty. 14When they become aware of the
sin they committed, the assembly must bring
a young bull as a sin offering and present it
before the Tent of Meeting. 15The elders of
the community are to lay their hands on the
bull's head before the LORD, and the bull shall
be slaughtered before the LORD. 16Then the
anointed priest is to take some of the bull's
blood into the Tent of Meeting. 17He shall dip
his finger into the blood and sprinkle it before
the LORD seven times in front of the curtain.
18He is to put some of the blood on the horns
of the altar that is before the LORD in the Tent
of Meeting. The rest of the blood he shall
pour out at the base of the altar of burnt
offering at the entrance to the Tent of Meeting. 19He shall remove all the fat from it and
burn it on the altar, 20and do with this bull just
as he did with the bull for the sin offering. In
this way the priest will make atonement for
them, and they will be forgiven. 21Then he
shall take the bull outside the camp and burn
it as he burned the first bull. This is the sin
offering for the community.

22" 'When a leader sins unintentionally and
does what is forbidden in any of the commands of the LORD his God, he is guilty.
23When he is made aware of the sin he committed, he must bring as his offering a male
goat without defect. 24He is to lay his hand on
the goat's head and slaughter it at the place
where the burnt offering is slaughtered before the LORD. It is a sin offering. 25Then the
priest shall take some of the blood of the sin
offering with his finger and put it on the horns
of the altar of burnt offering and pour out the
rest of the blood at the base of the altar. 26He
shall burn all the fat on the altar as he burned
the fat of the fellowship offering. In this way
the priest will make atonement for the man's
sin, and he will be forgiven.

27" 'If a member of the community sins
unintentionally and does what is forbidden in
any of the LORD's commands, he is guilty.
28When he is made aware of the sin he committed, he must bring as his offering for the
sin he committed a female goat without defect. 29He is to lay his hand on the head of the
sin offering and slaughter it at the place of
the burnt offering. 30Then the priest is to take
some of the blood with his finger and put it on
the horns of the altar of burnt offering and
pour out the rest of the blood at the base of
the altar. 31He shall remove all the fat, just as
the fat is removed from the fellowship offering, and the priest shall burn it on the altar as
an aroma pleasing to the LORD. In this way
the priest will make atonement for him, and
he will be forgiven.

32" 'If he brings a lamb as his sin offering,
he is to bring a female without defect. 33He is
to lay his hand on its head and slaughter it for
a sin offering at the place where the burnt
offering is slaughtered. 34Then the priest
shall take some of the blood of the sin offering with his finger and put it on the horns of
the altar of burnt offering and pour out the

[a]*10* The Hebrew word can include both male and female. [b]*10* Traditionally *peace offering;* also in verses 26, 31 and 35

rest of the blood at the base of the altar. [35]He shall remove all the fat, just as the fat is removed from the lamb of the fellowship offering, and the priest shall burn it on the altar on top of the offerings made to the LORD by fire. In this way the priest will make atonement for him for the sin he has committed, and he will be forgiven.

5 " 'If a person sins because he does not speak up when he hears a public charge to testify regarding something he has seen or learned about, he will be held responsible.

[2]" 'Or if a person touches anything ceremonially unclean—whether the carcasses of unclean wild animals or of unclean livestock or of unclean creatures that move along the ground—even though he is unaware of it, he has become unclean and is guilty.

[3]" 'Or if he touches human uncleanness—anything that would make him unclean—even though he is unaware of it, when he learns of it he will be guilty.

[4]" 'Or if a person thoughtlessly takes an oath to do anything, whether good or evil—in any matter one might carelessly swear about—even though he is unaware of it, in any case when he learns of it he will be guilty.

[5]" 'When anyone is guilty in any of these ways, he must confess in what way he has sinned [6]and, as a penalty for the sin he has committed, he must bring to the LORD a female lamb or goat from the flock as a sin offering; and the priest shall make atonement for him for his sin.

[7]" 'If he cannot afford a lamb, he is to bring two doves or two young pigeons to the LORD as a penalty for his sin—one for a sin offering and the other for a burnt offering. [8]He is to bring them to the priest, who shall first offer the one for the sin offering. He is to wring its head from its neck, not severing it completely, [9]and is to sprinkle some of the blood of the sin offering against the side of the altar; the rest of the blood must be drained out at the base of the altar. It is a sin offering. [10]The priest shall then offer the other as a burnt offering in the prescribed way and make atonement for him for the sin he has committed, and he will be forgiven.

[11]" 'If, however, he cannot afford two doves or two young pigeons, he is to bring as an offering for his sin a tenth of an ephah[a] of fine flour for a sin offering. He must not put oil or incense on it, because it is a sin offering. [12]He is to bring it to the priest, who shall take a handful of it as a memorial portion and burn it on the altar on top of the offerings made to the LORD by fire. It is a sin offering. [13]In this way the priest will make atonement for him for any of these sins he has committed, and he will be forgiven. The rest of the offering will belong to the priest, as in the case of the grain offering.' "

The Guilt Offering

[14]The LORD said to Moses: [15]"When a person commits a violation and sins unintentionally in regard to any of the LORD's holy things, he is to bring to the LORD as a penalty a ram from the flock, one without defect and of the proper value in silver, according to the sanctuary shekel.[b] It is a guilt offering. [16]He must make restitution for what he has failed to do in regard to the holy things, add a fifth of the value to that and give it all to the priest, who will make atonement for him with the ram as a guilt offering, and he will be forgiven.

[17]"If a person sins and does what is forbidden in any of the LORD's commands, even though he does not know it, he is guilty and will be held responsible. [18]He is to bring to the priest as a guilt offering a ram from the flock, one without defect and of the proper value. In this way the priest will make atonement for him for the wrong he has committed unintentionally, and he will be forgiven. [19]It is a guilt offering; he has been guilty of[c] wrongdoing against the LORD."

6 The LORD said to Moses: [2]"If anyone sins and is unfaithful to the LORD by deceiving his neighbor about something entrusted to him or left in his care or stolen, or if he cheats him, [3]or if he finds lost property and lies about it, or if he swears falsely, or if he commits any such sin that people may do—[4]when he thus sins and becomes guilty, he must return what he has stolen or taken by extortion, or what was entrusted to him, or the lost property he found, [5]or whatever it was he swore falsely about. He must make restitution in full, add a fifth of the value to it and give it all to the owner on the day he presents his guilt offering. [6]And as a penalty he must bring to the priest, that is, to the LORD, his guilt offering, a ram from the flock, one without defect and of the proper value. [7]In this way the priest will make atonement

[a] *11* That is, probably about 2 quarts (about 2 liters)
[b] *15* That is, about 2/5 ounce (about 11.5 grams)
[c] *19* Or *has made full expiation for his*

for him before the LORD, and he will be forgiven for any of these things he did that
made him guilty."

The Burnt Offering

8The LORD said to Moses: 9"Give Aaron
and his sons this command: 'These are the
regulations for the burnt offering: The burnt
offering is to remain on the altar hearth
throughout the night, till morning, and the fire
must be kept burning on the altar. 10The
priest shall then put on his linen clothes, with
linen undergarments next to his body, and
shall remove the ashes of the burnt offering
that the fire has consumed on the altar and
place them beside the altar. 11Then he is to
take off these clothes and put on others, and
carry the ashes outside the camp to a place
that is ceremonially clean. 12The fire on the
altar must be kept burning; it must not go out.
Every morning the priest is to add firewood
and arrange the burnt offering on the fire and
burn the fat of the fellowship offerings[a] on it.
13The fire must be kept burning on the altar
continuously; it must not go out.

The Grain Offering

14" 'These are the regulations for the grain
offering: Aaron's sons are to bring it before
the LORD, in front of the altar. 15The priest is to
take a handful of fine flour and oil, together
with all the incense on the grain offering, and
burn the memorial portion on the altar as an
aroma pleasing to the LORD. 16Aaron and his
sons shall eat the rest of it, but it is to be
eaten without yeast in a holy place; they are
to eat it in the courtyard of the Tent of Meeting. 17It must not be baked with yeast; I have
given it as their share of the offerings made
to me by fire. Like the sin offering and the
guilt offering, it is most holy. 18Any male descendant of Aaron may eat it. It is his regular
share of the offerings made to the LORD by
fire for the generations to come. Whatever
touches them will become holy.[b]' "

19The LORD also said to Moses, 20"This is
the offering Aaron and his sons are to bring
to the LORD on the day he[c] is anointed: a
tenth of an ephah[d] of fine flour as a regular
grain offering, half of it in the morning and
half in the evening. 21Prepare it with oil on a
griddle; bring it well-mixed and present the
grain offering broken[e] in pieces as an aroma
pleasing to the LORD. 22The son who is to
succeed him as anointed priest shall prepare
it. It is the LORD's regular share and is to be
burned completely. 23Every grain offering of
a priest shall be burned completely; it must
not be eaten."

The Sin Offering

24The LORD said to Moses, 25"Say to Aaron
and his sons: 'These are the regulations for
the sin offering: The sin offering is to be
slaughtered before the LORD in the place the
burnt offering is slaughtered; it is most holy.
26The priest who offers it shall eat it; it is to be
eaten in a holy place, in the courtyard of the
Tent of Meeting. 27Whatever touches any of
the flesh will become holy, and if any of the
blood is spattered on a garment, you must
wash it in a holy place. 28The clay pot the
meat is cooked in must be broken; but if it is
cooked in a bronze pot, the pot is to be
scoured and rinsed with water. 29Any male in
a priest's family may eat it; it is most holy.
30But any sin offering whose blood is brought
into the Tent of Meeting to make atonement
in the Holy Place must not be eaten; it must
be burned.

The Guilt Offering

7 " 'These are the regulations for the guilt
offering, which is most holy: 2The guilt
offering is to be slaughtered in the place
where the burnt offering is slaughtered, and
its blood is to be sprinkled against the altar
on all sides. 3All its fat shall be offered: the fat
tail and the fat that covers the inner parts,
4both kidneys with the fat on them near the
loins, and the covering of the liver, which is to
be removed with the kidneys. 5The priest
shall burn them on the altar as an offering
made to the LORD by fire. It is a guilt offering.
6Any male in a priest's family may eat it, but it
must be eaten in a holy place; it is most holy.

7" 'The same law applies to both the sin
offering and the guilt offering: They belong to
the priest who makes atonement with them.
8The priest who offers a burnt offering for
anyone may keep its hide for himself. 9Every
grain offering baked in an oven or cooked in
a pan or on a griddle belongs to the priest
who offers it, 10and every grain offering,
whether mixed with oil or dry, belongs equally to all the sons of Aaron.

[a] *12* Traditionally *peace offerings* [b] *18* Or *Whoever touches them must be holy*; similarly in verse 27
[c] *20* Or *each* [d] *20* That is, probably about 2 quarts (about 2 liters) [e] *21* The meaning of the Hebrew for this word is uncertain.

The Fellowship Offering

11" 'These are the regulations for the fellowship offering[a] a person may present to the LORD:

12" 'If he offers it as an expression of thankfulness, then along with this thank offering he is to offer cakes of bread made without yeast and mixed with oil, wafers made without yeast and spread with oil, and cakes of fine flour well-kneaded and mixed with oil. 13Along with his fellowship offering of thanksgiving he is to present an offering with cakes of bread made with yeast. 14He is to bring one of each kind as an offering, a contribution to the LORD; it belongs to the priest who sprinkles the blood of the fellowship offerings. 15The meat of his fellowship offering of thanksgiving must be eaten on the day it is offered; he must leave none of it till morning.

16" 'If, however, his offering is the result of a vow or is a freewill offering, the sacrifice shall be eaten on the day he offers it, but anything left over may be eaten on the next day. 17Any meat of the sacrifice left over till the third day must be burned up. 18If any meat of the fellowship offering is eaten on the third day, it will not be accepted. It will not be credited to the one who offered it, for it is impure; the person who eats any of it will be held responsible.

19" 'Meat that touches anything ceremonially unclean must not be eaten; it must be burned up. As for other meat, anyone ceremonially clean may eat it. 20But if anyone who is unclean eats any meat of the fellowship offering belonging to the LORD, that person must be cut off from his people. 21If anyone touches something unclean—whether human uncleanness or an unclean animal or any unclean, detestable thing—and then eats any of the meat of the fellowship offering belonging to the LORD, that person must be cut off from his people.' "

Eating Fat and Blood Forbidden

22The LORD said to Moses, 23"Say to the Israelites: 'Do not eat any of the fat of cattle, sheep or goats. 24The fat of an animal found dead or torn by wild animals may be used for any other purpose, but you must not eat it. 25Anyone who eats the fat of an animal from which an offering by fire may be[b] made to the LORD must be cut off from his people. 26And wherever you live, you must not eat the blood of any bird or animal. 27If anyone eats blood, that person must be cut off from his people.' "

The Priests' Share

28The LORD said to Moses, 29"Say to the Israelites: 'Anyone who brings a fellowship offering to the LORD is to bring part of it as his sacrifice to the LORD. 30With his own hands he is to bring the offering made to the LORD by fire; he is to bring the fat, together with the breast, and wave the breast before the LORD as a wave offering. 31The priest shall burn the fat on the altar, but the breast belongs to Aaron and his sons. 32You are to give the right thigh of your fellowship offerings to the priest as a contribution. 33The son of Aaron who offers the blood and the fat of the fellowship offering shall have the right thigh as his share. 34From the fellowship offerings of the Israelites, I have taken the breast that is waved and the thigh that is presented and have given them to Aaron the priest and his sons as their regular share from the Israelites.' "

35This is the portion of the offerings made to the LORD by fire that were allotted to Aaron and his sons on the day they were presented to serve the LORD as priests. 36On the day they were anointed, the LORD commanded that the Israelites give this to them as their regular share for the generations to come.

37These, then, are the regulations for the burnt offering, the grain offering, the sin offering, the guilt offering, the ordination offering and the fellowship offering, 38which the LORD gave Moses on Mount Sinai on the day he commanded the Israelites to bring their offerings to the LORD, in the Desert of Sinai.

The Ordination of Aaron and His Sons

8 The LORD said to Moses, 2"Bring Aaron and his sons, their garments, the anointing oil, the bull for the sin offering, the two rams and the basket containing bread made without yeast, 3and gather the entire assembly at the entrance to the Tent of Meeting." 4Moses did as the LORD commanded him, and the assembly gathered at the entrance to the Tent of Meeting.

5Moses said to the assembly, "This is what the LORD has commanded to be done." 6Then Moses brought Aaron and his sons forward and washed them with water. 7He put the tunic on Aaron, tied the sash around

[a]11 Traditionally *peace offering*; also in verses 13-37

[b]25 Or *fire is*

him, clothed him with the robe and put the ephod on him. He also tied the ephod to him by its skillfully woven waistband; so it was fastened on him. [8]He placed the breastpiece on him and put the Urim and Thummim in the breastpiece. [9]Then he placed the turban on Aaron's head and set the gold plate, the sacred diadem, on the front of it, as the LORD commanded Moses.

[10]Then Moses took the anointing oil and anointed the tabernacle and everything in it, and so consecrated them. [11]He sprinkled some of the oil on the altar seven times, anointing the altar and all its utensils and the basin with its stand, to consecrate them. [12]He poured some of the anointing oil on Aaron's head and anointed him to consecrate him. [13]Then he brought Aaron's sons forward, put tunics on them, tied sashes around them and put headbands on them, as the LORD commanded Moses.

[14]He then presented the bull for the sin offering, and Aaron and his sons laid their hands on its head. [15]Moses slaughtered the bull and took some of the blood, and with his finger he put it on all the horns of the altar to purify the altar. He poured out the rest of the blood at the base of the altar. So he consecrated it to make atonement for it. [16]Moses also took all the fat around the inner parts, the covering of the liver, and both kidneys and their fat, and burned it on the altar. [17]But the bull with its hide and its flesh and its offal he burned up outside the camp, as the LORD commanded Moses.

[18]He then presented the ram for the burnt offering, and Aaron and his sons laid their hands on its head. [19]Then Moses slaughtered the ram and sprinkled the blood against the altar on all sides. [20]He cut the ram into pieces and burned the head, the pieces and the fat. [21]He washed the inner parts and the legs with water and burned the whole ram on the altar as a burnt offering, a pleasing aroma, an offering made to the LORD by fire, as the LORD commanded Moses.

[22]He then presented the other ram, the ram for the ordination, and Aaron and his sons laid their hands on its head. [23]Moses slaughtered the ram and took some of its blood and put it on the lobe of Aaron's right ear, on the thumb of his right hand and on the big toe of his right foot. [24]Moses also brought Aaron's sons forward and put some of the blood on the lobes of their right ears, on the thumbs of their right hands and on the big toes of their right feet. Then he sprinkled blood against the altar on all sides. [25]He took the fat, the fat tail, all the fat around the inner parts, the covering of the liver, both kidneys and their fat and the right thigh. [26]Then from the basket of bread made without yeast, which was before the LORD, he took a cake of bread, and one made with oil, and a wafer; he put these on the fat portions and on the right thigh. [27]He put all these in the hands of Aaron and his sons and waved them before the LORD as a wave offering. [28]Then Moses took them from their hands and burned them on the altar on top of the burnt offering as an ordination offering, a pleasing aroma, an offering made to the LORD by fire. [29]He also took the breast—Moses' share of the ordination ram—and waved it before the LORD as a wave offering, as the LORD commanded Moses.

[30]Then Moses took some of the anointing oil and some of the blood from the altar and sprinkled them on Aaron and his garments and on his sons and their garments. So he consecrated Aaron and his garments and his sons and their garments.

[31]Moses then said to Aaron and his sons, "Cook the meat at the entrance to the Tent of Meeting and eat it there with the bread from the basket of ordination offerings, as I commanded, saying,[a] 'Aaron and his sons are to eat it.' [32]Then burn up the rest of the meat and the bread. [33]Do not leave the entrance to the Tent of Meeting for seven days, until the days of your ordination are completed, for your ordination will last seven days. [34]What has been done today was commanded by the LORD to make atonement for you. [35]You must stay at the entrance to the Tent of Meeting day and night for seven days and do what the LORD requires, so you will not die; for that is what I have been commanded." [36]So Aaron and his sons did everything the LORD commanded through Moses.

The Priests Begin Their Ministry

9 On the eighth day Moses summoned Aaron and his sons and the elders of Israel. [2]He said to Aaron, "Take a bull calf for your sin offering and a ram for your burnt offering, both without defect, and present them before the LORD. [3]Then say to the Israelites: 'Take a male goat for a sin offering, a calf and a lamb—both a year old and without

[a]31 Or *I was commanded:*

defect—for a burnt offering, 4and an ox[a] and a ram for a fellowship offering[b] to sacrifice before the LORD, together with a grain offering mixed with oil. For today the LORD will appear to you.' "

5They took the things Moses commanded to the front of the Tent of Meeting, and the entire assembly came near and stood before the LORD. 6Then Moses said, "This is what the LORD has commanded you to do, so that the glory of the LORD may appear to you."

7Moses said to Aaron, "Come to the altar and sacrifice your sin offering and your burnt offering and make atonement for yourself and the people; sacrifice the offering that is for the people and make atonement for them, as the LORD has commanded."

8So Aaron came to the altar and slaughtered the calf as a sin offering for himself. 9His sons brought the blood to him, and he dipped his finger into the blood and put it on the horns of the altar; the rest of the blood he poured out at the base of the altar. 10On the altar he burned the fat, the kidneys and the covering of the liver from the sin offering, as the LORD commanded Moses; 11the flesh and the hide he burned up outside the camp.

12Then he slaughtered the burnt offering. His sons handed him the blood, and he sprinkled it against the altar on all sides. 13They handed him the burnt offering piece by piece, including the head, and he burned them on the altar. 14He washed the inner parts and the legs and burned them on top of the burnt offering on the altar.

15Aaron then brought the offering that was for the people. He took the goat for the people's sin offering and slaughtered it and offered it for a sin offering as he did with the first one.

16He brought the burnt offering and offered it in the prescribed way. 17He also brought the grain offering, took a handful of it and burned it on the altar in addition to the morning's burnt offering.

18He slaughtered the ox and the ram as the fellowship offering for the people. His sons handed him the blood, and he sprinkled it against the altar on all sides. 19But the fat portions of the ox and the ram—the fat tail, the layer of fat, the kidneys and the covering of the liver— 20these they laid on the breasts, and then Aaron burned the fat on the altar. 21Aaron waved the breasts and the right thigh before the LORD as a wave offering, as Moses commanded.

22Then Aaron lifted his hands toward the people and blessed them. And having sacrificed the sin offering, the burnt offering and the fellowship offering, he stepped down.

23Moses and Aaron then went into the Tent of Meeting. When they came out, they blessed the people; and the glory of the LORD appeared to all the people. 24Fire came out from the presence of the LORD and consumed the burnt offering and the fat portions on the altar. And when all the people saw it, they shouted for joy and fell facedown.

The Death of Nadab and Abihu

10 Aaron's sons Nadab and Abihu took their censers, put fire in them and added incense; and they offered unauthorized fire before the LORD, contrary to his command. 2So fire came out from the presence of the LORD and consumed them, and they died before the LORD. 3Moses then said to Aaron, "This is what the LORD spoke of when he said:

" 'Among those who approach me
  I will show myself holy;
in the sight of all the people
  I will be honored.' "

Aaron remained silent.

4Moses summoned Mishael and Elzaphan, sons of Aaron's uncle Uzziel, and said to them, "Come here; carry your cousins outside the camp, away from the front of the sanctuary." 5So they came and carried them, still in their tunics, outside the camp, as Moses ordered.

6Then Moses said to Aaron and his sons Eleazar and Ithamar, "Do not let your hair become unkempt,[c] and do not tear your clothes, or you will die and the LORD will be angry with the whole community. But your relatives, all the house of Israel, may mourn for those the LORD has destroyed by fire. 7Do not leave the entrance to the Tent of Meeting or you will die, because the LORD's anointing oil is on you." So they did as Moses said.

8Then the LORD said to Aaron, 9"You and your sons are not to drink wine or other fermented drink whenever you go into the Tent of Meeting, or you will die. This is a lasting ordinance for the generations to come. 10You must distinguish between the holy and

[a]4 The Hebrew word can include both male and female; also in verses 18 and 19. [b]4 Traditionally *peace offering*; also in verses 18 and 22 [c]6 Or *Do not uncover your heads*

the common, between the unclean and the
clean, 11and you must teach the Israelites all
the decrees the LORD has given them through
Moses."

12Moses said to Aaron and his remaining
sons, Eleazar and Ithamar, "Take the grain
offering left over from the offerings made to
the LORD by fire and eat it prepared without
yeast beside the altar, for it is most holy.
13Eat it in a holy place, because it is your
share and your sons' share of the offerings
made to the LORD by fire; for so I have been
commanded. 14But you and your sons and
your daughters may eat the breast that was
waved and the thigh that was presented. Eat
them in a ceremonially clean place; they
have been given to you and your children as
your share of the Israelites' fellowship offerings.[a] 15The thigh that was presented and
the breast that was waved must be brought
with the fat portions of the offerings made by
fire, to be waved before the LORD as a wave
offering. This will be the regular share for you
and your children, as the LORD has commanded."

16When Moses inquired about the goat of
the sin offering and found that it had been
burned up, he was angry with Eleazar and
Ithamar, Aaron's remaining sons, and
asked, 17"Why didn't you eat the sin offering
in the sanctuary area? It is most holy; it was
given to you to take away the guilt of the
community by making atonement for them
before the LORD. 18Since its blood was not
taken into the Holy Place, you should have
eaten the goat in the sanctuary area, as I
commanded."

19Aaron replied to Moses, "Today they
sacrificed their sin offering and their burnt
offering before the LORD, but such things as
this have happened to me. Would the LORD
have been pleased if I had eaten the sin
offering today?" 20When Moses heard this,
he was satisfied.

Clean and Unclean Food

11 The LORD said to Moses and Aaron,
2"Say to the Israelites: 'Of all the animals that live on land, these are the ones you
may eat: 3You may eat any animal that has a
split hoof completely divided and that chews
the cud.

4" 'There are some that only chew the cud
or only have a split hoof, but you must not eat
them. The camel, though it chews the cud,
does not have a split hoof; it is ceremonially
unclean for you. 5The coney,[b] though it
chews the cud, does not have a split hoof; it
is unclean for you. 6The rabbit, though it
chews the cud, does not have a split hoof; it
is unclean for you. 7And the pig, though it has
a split hoof completely divided, does not
chew the cud; it is unclean for you. 8You
must not eat their meat or touch their carcasses; they are unclean for you.

9" 'Of all the creatures living in the water of
the seas and the streams, you may eat any
that have fins and scales. 10But all creatures
in the seas or streams that do not have fins
and scales—whether among all the swarm-
ing things or among all the other living creatures in the water—you are to detest. 11And
since you are to detest them, you must not
eat their meat and you must detest their carcasses. 12Anything living in the water that
does not have fins and scales is to be detestable to you.

13" 'These are the birds you are to detest
and not eat because they are detestable: the
eagle, the vulture, the black vulture, 14the red
kite, any kind of black kite, 15any kind of raven, 16the horned owl, the screech owl, the
gull, any kind of hawk, 17the little owl, the
cormorant, the great owl, 18the white owl, the
desert owl, the osprey, 19the stork, any kind
of heron, the hoopoe and the bat.[c]

20" 'All flying insects that walk on all fours
are to be detestable to you. 21There are,
however, some winged creatures that walk
on all fours that you may eat: those that have
jointed legs for hopping on the ground. 22Of
these you may eat any kind of locust, katy-
did, cricket or grasshopper. 23But all other
winged creatures that have four legs you are
to detest.

24" 'You will make yourselves unclean by
these; whoever touches their carcasses will
be unclean till evening. 25Whoever picks up
one of their carcasses must wash his
clothes, and he will be unclean till evening.

26" 'Every animal that has a split hoof not
completely divided or that does not chew the
cud is unclean for you; whoever touches ⌞the
carcass of⌟ any of them will be unclean. 27Of
all the animals that walk on all fours, those
that walk on their paws are unclean for you;
whoever touches their carcasses will be unclean till evening. 28Anyone who picks up

[a]14 Traditionally *peace offerings* [b]5 That is, the hyrax or rock badger [c]19 The precise identification of some of the birds, insects and animals in this chapter is uncertain.

their carcasses must wash his clothes, and
he will be unclean till evening. They are unclean for you.
29" 'Of the animals that move about on the
ground, these are unclean for you: the wea-
sel, the rat, any kind of great lizard, 30the
gecko, the monitor lizard, the wall lizard, the
skink and the chameleon. 31Of all those that
move along the ground, these are unclean
for you. Whoever touches them when they
are dead will be unclean till evening. 32When
one of them dies and falls on something, that
article, whatever its use, will be unclean,
whether it is made of wood, cloth, hide or
sackcloth. Put it in water; it will be unclean till
evening, and then it will be clean. 33If one of
them falls into a clay pot, everything in it will
be unclean, and you must break the pot.
34Any food that could be eaten but has water
on it from such a pot is unclean, and any
liquid that could be drunk from it is unclean.
35Anything that one of their carcasses falls
on becomes unclean; an oven or cooking pot
must be broken up. They are unclean, and
you are to regard them as unclean. 36A
spring, however, or a cistern for collecting
water remains clean, but anyone who
touches one of these carcasses is unclean.
37If a carcass falls on any seeds that are to
be planted, they remain clean. 38But if water
has been put on the seed and a carcass falls
on it, it is unclean for you.
39" 'If an animal that you are allowed to eat
dies, anyone who touches the carcass will
be unclean till evening. 40Anyone who eats
some of the carcass must wash his clothes,
and he will be unclean till evening. Anyone
who picks up the carcass must wash his
clothes, and he will be unclean till evening.
41" 'Every creature that moves about on
the ground is detestable; it is not to be eaten.
42You are not to eat any creature that moves
about on the ground, whether it moves on its
belly or walks on all fours or on many feet; it
is detestable. 43Do not defile yourselves by
any of these creatures. Do not make yourselves unclean by means of them or be
made unclean by them. 44I am the LORD your
God; consecrate yourselves and be holy, because I am holy. Do not make yourselves
unclean by any creature that moves about
on the ground. 45I am the LORD who brought
you up out of Egypt to be your God; therefore
be holy, because I am holy.
46" 'These are the regulations concerning
animals, birds, every living thing that moves
in the water and every creature that moves
about on the ground. 47You must distinguish
between the unclean and the clean, between
living creatures that may be eaten and those
that may not be eaten.' "

Purification After Childbirth

12 The LORD said to Moses, 2"Say to the
Israelites: 'A woman who becomes
pregnant and gives birth to a son will be
ceremonially unclean for seven days, just as
she is unclean during her monthly period.
3On the eighth day the boy is to be circumcised. 4Then the woman must wait thirty-
three days to be purified from her bleeding.
She must not touch anything sacred or go to
the sanctuary until the days of her purification are over. 5If she gives birth to a daughter, for two weeks the woman will be unclean, as during her period. Then she must
wait sixty-six days to be purified from her
bleeding.
6" 'When the days of her purification for a
son or daughter are over, she is to bring to
the priest at the entrance to the Tent of Meeting a year-old lamb for a burnt offering and a
young pigeon or a dove for a sin offering. 7He
shall offer them before the LORD to make
atonement for her, and then she will be ceremonially clean from her flow of blood.
" 'These are the regulations for the woman
who gives birth to a boy or a girl. 8If she
cannot afford a lamb, she is to bring two
doves or two young pigeons, one for a burnt
offering and the other for a sin offering. In this
way the priest will make atonement for her,
and she will be clean.' "

Regulations About Infectious Skin Diseases

13 The LORD said to Moses and Aaron,
2"When anyone has a swelling or a
rash or a bright spot on his skin that may
become an infectious skin disease,[a] he must
be brought to Aaron the priest or to one of his
sons[b] who is a priest. 3The priest is to examine the sore on his skin, and if the hair in the
sore has turned white and the sore appears
to be more than skin deep,[c] it is an infectious
skin disease. When the priest examines him,

[a]2 Traditionally *leprosy;* the Hebrew word was used for various diseases affecting the skin—not necessarily leprosy; also elsewhere in this chapter. [b]2 Or *descendants* [c]3 Or *be lower than the rest of the skin;* also elsewhere in this chapter

he shall pronounce him ceremonially unclean. 4If the spot on his skin is white but does not appear to be more than skin deep and the hair in it has not turned white, the priest is to put the infected person in isolation for seven days. 5On the seventh day the priest is to examine him, and if he sees that the sore is unchanged and has not spread in the skin, he is to keep him in isolation another seven days. 6On the seventh day the priest is to examine him again, and if the sore has faded and has not spread in the skin, the priest shall pronounce him clean; it is only a rash. The man must wash his clothes, and he will be clean. 7But if the rash does spread in his skin after he has shown himself to the priest to be pronounced clean, he must appear before the priest again. 8The priest is to examine him, and if the rash has spread in the skin, he shall pronounce him unclean; it is an infectious disease.

9"When anyone has an infectious skin disease, he must be brought to the priest. 10The priest is to examine him, and if there is a white swelling in the skin that has turned the hair white and if there is raw flesh in the swelling, 11it is a chronic skin disease and the priest shall pronounce him unclean. He is not to put him in isolation, because he is already unclean.

12"If the disease breaks out all over his skin and, so far as the priest can see, it covers all the skin of the infected person from head to foot, 13the priest is to examine him, and if the disease has covered his whole body, he shall pronounce that person clean. Since it has all turned white, he is clean. 14But whenever raw flesh appears on him, he will be unclean. 15When the priest sees the raw flesh, he shall pronounce him unclean. The raw flesh is unclean; he has an infectious disease. 16Should the raw flesh change and turn white, he must go to the priest. 17The priest is to examine him, and if the sores have turned white, the priest shall pronounce the infected person clean; then he will be clean.

18"When someone has a boil on his skin and it heals, 19and in the place where the boil was, a white swelling or reddish-white spot appears, he must present himself to the priest. 20The priest is to examine it, and if it appears to be more than skin deep and the hair in it has turned white, the priest shall pronounce him unclean. It is an infectious skin disease that has broken out where the boil was. 21But if, when the priest examines it, there is no white hair in it and it is not more than skin deep and has faded, then the priest is to put him in isolation for seven days. 22If it is spreading in the skin, the priest shall pronounce him unclean; it is infectious. 23But if the spot is unchanged and has not spread, it is only a scar from the boil, and the priest shall pronounce him clean.

24"When someone has a burn on his skin and a reddish-white or white spot appears in the raw flesh of the burn, 25the priest is to examine the spot, and if the hair in it has turned white, and it appears to be more than skin deep, it is an infectious disease that has broken out in the burn. The priest shall pronounce him unclean; it is an infectious skin disease. 26But if the priest examines it and there is no white hair in the spot and if it is not more than skin deep and has faded, then the priest is to put him in isolation for seven days. 27On the seventh day the priest is to examine him, and if it is spreading in the skin, the priest shall pronounce him unclean; it is an infectious skin disease. 28If, however, the spot is unchanged and has not spread in the skin but has faded, it is a swelling from the burn, and the priest shall pronounce him clean; it is only a scar from the burn.

29"If a man or woman has a sore on the head or on the chin, 30the priest is to examine the sore, and if it appears to be more than skin deep and the hair in it is yellow and thin, the priest shall pronounce that person unclean; it is an itch, an infectious disease of the head or chin. 31But if, when the priest examines this kind of sore, it does not seem to be more than skin deep and there is no black hair in it, then the priest is to put the infected person in isolation for seven days. 32On the seventh day the priest is to examine the sore, and if the itch has not spread and there is no yellow hair in it and it does not appear to be more than skin deep, 33he must be shaved except for the diseased area, and the priest is to keep him in isolation another seven days. 34On the seventh day the priest is to examine the itch, and if it has not spread in the skin and appears to be no more than skin deep, the priest shall pronounce him clean. He must wash his clothes, and he will be clean. 35But if the itch does spread in the skin after he is pronounced clean, 36the priest is to examine him, and if the itch has spread in the skin, the priest does not need to look for yellow hair; the person is unclean. 37If, however, in his judgment it is unchanged and black hair has grown in it, the itch is healed. He is clean, and the priest shall pronounce him clean.

38"When a man or woman has white spots on the skin, 39the priest is to examine them, and if the spots are dull white, it is a harmless rash that has broken out on the skin; that person is clean.

40"When a man has lost his hair and is bald, he is clean. 41If he has lost his hair from the front of his scalp and has a bald forehead, he is clean. 42But if he has a reddish-white sore on his bald head or forehead, it is an infectious disease breaking out on his head or forehead. 43The priest is to examine him, and if the swollen sore on his head or forehead is reddish-white like an infectious skin disease, 44the man is diseased and is unclean. The priest shall pronounce him unclean because of the sore on his head.

45"The person with such an infectious disease must wear torn clothes, let his hair be unkempt,[a] cover the lower part of his face and cry out, 'Unclean! Unclean!' 46As long as he has the infection he remains unclean. He must live alone; he must live outside the camp.

Regulations About Mildew

47"If any clothing is contaminated with mildew—any woolen or linen clothing, 48any woven or knitted material of linen or wool, any leather or anything made of leather—49and if the contamination in the clothing, or leather, or woven or knitted material, or any leather article, is greenish or reddish, it is a spreading mildew and must be shown to the priest. 50The priest is to examine the mildew and isolate the affected article for seven days. 51On the seventh day he is to examine it, and if the mildew has spread in the clothing, or the woven or knitted material, or the leather, whatever its use, it is a destructive mildew; the article is unclean. 52He must burn up the clothing, or the woven or knitted material of wool or linen, or any leather article that has the contamination in it, because the mildew is destructive; the article must be burned up.

53"But if, when the priest examines it, the mildew has not spread in the clothing, or the woven or knitted material, or the leather article, 54he shall order that the contaminated article be washed. Then he is to isolate it for another seven days. 55After the affected article has been washed, the priest is to examine it, and if the mildew has not changed its appearance, even though it has not spread, it is unclean. Burn it with fire, whether the mildew has affected one side or the other. 56If, when the priest examines it, the mildew has faded after the article has been washed, he is to tear the contaminated part out of the clothing, or the leather, or the woven or knitted material. 57But if it reappears in the clothing, or in the woven or knitted material, or in the leather article, it is spreading, and whatever has the mildew must be burned with fire. 58The clothing, or the woven or knitted material, or any leather article that has been washed and is rid of the mildew, must be washed again, and it will be clean."

59These are the regulations concerning contamination by mildew in woolen or linen clothing, woven or knitted material, or any leather article, for pronouncing them clean or unclean.

Cleansing From Infectious Skin Diseases

14 The LORD said to Moses, 2"These are the regulations for the diseased person at the time of his ceremonial cleansing, when he is brought to the priest: 3The priest is to go outside the camp and examine him. If the person has been healed of his infectious skin disease,[b] 4the priest shall order that two live clean birds and some cedar wood, scarlet yarn and hyssop be brought for the one to be cleansed. 5Then the priest shall order that one of the birds be killed over fresh water in a clay pot. 6He is then to take the live bird and dip it, together with the cedar wood, the scarlet yarn and the hyssop, into the blood of the bird that was killed over the fresh water. 7Seven times he shall sprinkle the one to be cleansed of the infectious disease and pronounce him clean. Then he is to release the live bird in the open fields.

8"The person to be cleansed must wash his clothes, shave off all his hair and bathe with water; then he will be ceremonially clean. After this he may come into the camp, but he must stay outside his tent for seven days. 9On the seventh day he must shave off all his hair; he must shave his head, his beard, his eyebrows and the rest of his hair.

[a]45 Or *clothes, uncover his head* [b]3 Traditionally *leprosy;* the Hebrew word was used for various diseases affecting the skin—not necessarily leprosy; also elsewhere in this chapter.

He must wash his clothes and bathe himself with water, and he will be clean.

10“On the eighth day he must bring two male lambs and one ewe lamb a year old, each without defect, along with three-tenths of an ephah[a] of fine flour mixed with oil for a grain offering, and one log[b] of oil. 11The priest who pronounces him clean shall present both the one to be cleansed and his offerings before the LORD at the entrance to the Tent of Meeting.

12“Then the priest is to take one of the male lambs and offer it as a guilt offering, along with the log of oil; he shall wave them before the LORD as a wave offering. 13He is to slaughter the lamb in the holy place where the sin offering and the burnt offering are slaughtered. Like the sin offering, the guilt offering belongs to the priest; it is most holy. 14The priest is to take some of the blood of the guilt offering and put it on the lobe of the right ear of the one to be cleansed, on the thumb of his right hand and on the big toe of his right foot. 15The priest shall then take some of the log of oil, pour it in the palm of his own left hand, 16dip his right forefinger into the oil in his palm, and with his finger sprinkle some of it before the LORD seven times. 17The priest is to put some of the oil remaining in his palm on the lobe of the right ear of the one to be cleansed, on the thumb of his right hand and on the big toe of his right foot, on top of the blood of the guilt offering. 18The rest of the oil in his palm the priest shall put on the head of the one to be cleansed and make atonement for him before the LORD.

19“Then the priest is to sacrifice the sin offering and make atonement for the one to be cleansed from his uncleanness. After that, the priest shall slaughter the burnt offering 20and offer it on the altar, together with the grain offering, and make atonement for him, and he will be clean.

21“If, however, he is poor and cannot afford these, he must take one male lamb as a guilt offering to be waved to make atonement for him, together with a tenth of an ephah[c] of fine flour mixed with oil for a grain offering, a log of oil, 22and two doves or two young pigeons, which he can afford, one for a sin offering and the other for a burnt offering.

23“On the eighth day he must bring them for his cleansing to the priest at the entrance to the Tent of Meeting, before the LORD. 24The priest is to take the lamb for the guilt offering, together with the log of oil, and wave them before the LORD as a wave offering. 25He shall slaughter the lamb for the guilt offering and take some of its blood and put it on the lobe of the right ear of the one to be cleansed, on the thumb of his right hand and on the big toe of his right foot. 26The priest is to pour some of the oil into the palm of his own left hand, 27and with his right forefinger sprinkle some of the oil from his palm seven times before the LORD. 28Some of the oil in his palm he is to put on the same places he put the blood of the guilt offering—on the lobe of the right ear of the one to be cleansed, on the thumb of his right hand and on the big toe of his right foot. 29The rest of the oil in his palm the priest shall put on the head of the one to be cleansed, to make atonement for him before the LORD. 30Then he shall sacrifice the doves or the young pigeons, which the person can afford, 31one[d] as a sin offering and the other as a burnt offering, together with the grain offering. In this way the priest will make atonement before the LORD on behalf of the one to be cleansed.”

32These are the regulations for anyone who has an infectious skin disease and who cannot afford the regular offerings for his cleansing.

Cleansing From Mildew

33The LORD said to Moses and Aaron, 34“When you enter the land of Canaan, which I am giving you as your possession, and I put a spreading mildew in a house in that land, 35the owner of the house must go and tell the priest, ‘I have seen something that looks like mildew in my house.’ 36The priest is to order the house to be emptied before he goes in to examine the mildew, so that nothing in the house will be pronounced unclean. After this the priest is to go in and inspect the house. 37He is to examine the mildew on the walls, and if it has greenish or reddish depressions that appear to be deeper than the surface of the wall, 38the priest shall go out the doorway of the house and close it up for seven days. 39On the seventh day the priest shall return to inspect the house. If the mildew has spread on the walls, 40he is to order that the contaminated stones be torn out and thrown into an unclean place outside the town. 41He must have all the in-

[a] *10* That is, probably about 6 quarts (about 6.5 liters) [b] *10* That is, probably about 2/3 pint (about 0.3 liter); also in verses 12, 15, 21 and 24 [c] *21* That is, probably about 2 quarts (about 2 liters) [d] *31* Septuagint and Syriac; Hebrew *31such as the person can afford, one*

side walls of the house scraped and the
material that is scraped off dumped into an
unclean place outside the town. 42Then they
are to take other stones to replace these and
take new clay and plaster the house.

43"If the mildew reappears in the house
after the stones have been torn out and the
house scraped and plastered, 44the priest is
to go and examine it and, if the mildew has
spread in the house, it is a destructive mildew; the house is unclean. 45It must be torn
down—its stones, timbers and all the plaster—and taken out of the town to an unclean
place.

46"Anyone who goes into the house while it
is closed up will be unclean till evening.
47Anyone who sleeps or eats in the house
must wash his clothes.

48"But if the priest comes to examine it and
the mildew has not spread after the house
has been plastered, he shall pronounce the
house clean, because the mildew is gone.
49To purify the house he is to take two birds
and some cedar wood, scarlet yarn and hyssop. 50He shall kill one of the birds over fresh
water in a clay pot. 51Then he is to take the
cedar wood, the hyssop, the scarlet yarn and
the live bird, dip them into the blood of the
dead bird and the fresh water, and sprinkle
the house seven times. 52He shall purify the
house with the bird's blood, the fresh water,
the live bird, the cedar wood, the hyssop and
the scarlet yarn. 53Then he is to release the
live bird in the open fields outside the town.
In this way he will make atonement for the
house, and it will be clean."

54These are the regulations for any infectious skin disease, for an itch, 55for mildew in
clothing or in a house, 56and for a swelling, a
rash or a bright spot, 57to determine when
something is clean or unclean.

These are the regulations for infectious
skin diseases and mildew.

Discharges Causing Uncleanness

15 The Lord said to Moses and Aaron,
2"Speak to the Israelites and say to
them: 'When any man has a bodily discharge, the discharge is unclean. 3Whether it
continues flowing from his body or is
blocked, it will make him unclean. This is
how his discharge will bring about uncleanness:

4" 'Any bed the man with a discharge lies
on will be unclean, and anything he sits on
will be unclean. 5Anyone who touches his
bed must wash his clothes and bathe with
water, and he will be unclean till evening.
6Whoever sits on anything that the man with
a discharge sat on must wash his clothes
and bathe with water, and he will be unclean
till evening.

7" 'Whoever touches the man who has a
discharge must wash his clothes and bathe
with water, and he will be unclean till evening.

8" 'If the man with the discharge spits on
someone who is clean, that person must
wash his clothes and bathe with water, and
he will be unclean till evening.

9" 'Everything the man sits on when riding
will be unclean, 10and whoever touches any
of the things that were under him will be
unclean till evening; whoever picks up those
things must wash his clothes and bathe with
water, and he will be unclean till evening.

11" 'Anyone the man with a discharge
touches without rinsing his hands with water
must wash his clothes and bathe with water,
and he will be unclean till evening.

12" 'A clay pot that the man touches must
be broken, and any wooden article is to be
rinsed with water.

13" 'When a man is cleansed from his discharge, he is to count off seven days for his
ceremonial cleansing; he must wash his
clothes and bathe himself with fresh water,
and he will be clean. 14On the eighth day he
must take two doves or two young pigeons
and come before the Lord to the entrance to
the Tent of Meeting and give them to the
priest. 15The priest is to sacrifice them, the
one for a sin offering and the other for a burnt
offering. In this way he will make atonement
before the Lord for the man because of his
discharge.

16" 'When a man has an emission of semen, he must bathe his whole body with
water, and he will be unclean till evening.
17Any clothing or leather that has semen on it
must be washed with water, and it will be
unclean till evening. 18When a man lies with
a woman and there is an emission of semen,
both must bathe with water, and they will be
unclean till evening.

19" 'When a woman has her regular flow of
blood, the impurity of her monthly period will
last seven days, and anyone who touches
her will be unclean till evening.

20" 'Anything she lies on during her period
will be unclean, and anything she sits on will
be unclean. 21Whoever touches her bed
must wash his clothes and bathe with water,
and he will be unclean till evening. 22Who-

ever touches anything she sits on must wash his clothes and bathe with water, and he will be unclean till evening. 23Whether it is the bed or anything she was sitting on, when anyone touches it, he will be unclean till evening.

24" 'If a man lies with her and her monthly flow touches him, he will be unclean for seven days; any bed he lies on will be unclean.

25" 'When a woman has a discharge of blood for many days at a time other than her monthly period or has a discharge that continues beyond her period, she will be unclean as long as she has the discharge, just as in the days of her period. 26Any bed she lies on while her discharge continues will be unclean, as is her bed during her monthly period, and anything she sits on will be unclean, as during her period. 27Whoever touches them will be unclean; he must wash his clothes and bathe with water, and he will be unclean till evening.

28" 'When she is cleansed from her discharge, she must count off seven days, and after that she will be ceremonially clean. 29On the eighth day she must take two doves or two young pigeons and bring them to the priest at the entrance to the Tent of Meeting. 30The priest is to sacrifice one for a sin offering and the other for a burnt offering. In this way he will make atonement for her before the LORD for the uncleanness of her discharge.

31" 'You must keep the Israelites separate from things that make them unclean, so they will not die in their uncleanness for defiling my dwelling place,[a] which is among them.' "

32These are the regulations for a man with a discharge, for anyone made unclean by an emission of semen, 33for a woman in her monthly period, for a man or a woman with a discharge, and for a man who lies with a woman who is ceremonially unclean.

The Day of Atonement

16 The LORD spoke to Moses after the death of the two sons of Aaron who died when they approached the LORD. 2The LORD said to Moses: "Tell your brother Aaron not to come whenever he chooses into the Most Holy Place behind the curtain in front of the atonement cover on the ark, or else he will die, because I appear in the cloud over the atonement cover.

3"This is how Aaron is to enter the sanctuary area: with a young bull for a sin offering and a ram for a burnt offering. 4He is to put on the sacred linen tunic, with linen undergarments next to his body; he is to tie the linen sash around him and put on the linen turban. These are sacred garments; so he must bathe himself with water before he puts them on. 5From the Israelite community he is to take two male goats for a sin offering and a ram for a burnt offering.

6"Aaron is to offer the bull for his own sin offering to make atonement for himself and his household. 7Then he is to take the two goats and present them before the LORD at the entrance to the Tent of Meeting. 8He is to cast lots for the two goats—one lot for the LORD and the other for the scapegoat.[b] 9Aaron shall bring the goat whose lot falls to the LORD and sacrifice it for a sin offering. 10But the goat chosen by lot as the scapegoat shall be presented alive before the LORD to be used for making atonement by sending it into the desert as a scapegoat.

11"Aaron shall bring the bull for his own sin offering to make atonement for himself and his household, and he is to slaughter the bull for his own sin offering. 12He is to take a censer full of burning coals from the altar before the LORD and two handfuls of finely ground fragrant incense and take them behind the curtain. 13He is to put the incense on the fire before the LORD, and the smoke of the incense will conceal the atonement cover above the Testimony, so that he will not die. 14He is to take some of the bull's blood and with his finger sprinkle it on the front of the atonement cover; then he shall sprinkle some of it with his finger seven times before the atonement cover.

15"He shall then slaughter the goat for the sin offering for the people and take its blood behind the curtain and do with it as he did with the bull's blood: He shall sprinkle it on the atonement cover and in front of it. 16In this way he will make atonement for the Most Holy Place because of the uncleanness and rebellion of the Israelites, whatever their sins have been. He is to do the same for the Tent of Meeting, which is among them in the midst of their uncleanness. 17No one is to be in the Tent of Meeting from the time Aaron goes in to make atonement in the Most Holy Place until he comes out, having made atonement

[a]31 Or *my tabernacle* [b]8 That is, the goat of removal; Hebrew *azazel;* also in verses 10 and 26

for himself, his household and the whole
community of Israel.
18“Then he shall come out to the altar that
is before the LORD and make atonement for it.
He shall take some of the bull’s blood and
some of the goat’s blood and put it on all the
horns of the altar. 19He shall sprinkle some of
the blood on it with his finger seven times to
cleanse it and to consecrate it from the uncleanness of the Israelites.
20“When Aaron has finished making
atonement for the Most Holy Place, the Tent
of Meeting and the altar, he shall bring forward the live goat. 21He is to lay both hands
on the head of the live goat and confess over
it all the wickedness and rebellion of the Israelites—all their sins—and put them on the
goat’s head. He shall send the goat away
into the desert in the care of a man appointed
for the task. 22The goat will carry on itself all
their sins to a solitary place; and the man
shall release it in the desert.
23“Then Aaron is to go into the Tent of
Meeting and take off the linen garments he
put on before he entered the Most Holy
Place, and he is to leave them there. 24He
shall bathe himself with water in a holy place
and put on his regular garments. Then he
shall come out and sacrifice the burnt offering for himself and the burnt offering for the
people, to make atonement for himself and
for the people. 25He shall also burn the fat of
the sin offering on the altar.
26“The man who releases the goat as a
scapegoat must wash his clothes and bathe
himself with water; afterward he may come
into the camp. 27The bull and the goat for the
sin offerings, whose blood was brought into
the Most Holy Place to make atonement,
must be taken outside the camp; their hides,
flesh and offal are to be burned up. 28The
man who burns them must wash his clothes
and bathe himself with water; afterward he
may come into the camp.
29“This is to be a lasting ordinance for you:
On the tenth day of the seventh month you
must deny yourselves[a] and not do any
work—whether native-born or an alien living
among you— 30because on this day atonement will be made for you, to cleanse you.
Then, before the LORD, you will be clean from
all your sins. 31It is a sabbath of rest, and you
must deny yourselves; it is a lasting ordinance. 32The priest who is anointed and ordained to succeed his father as high priest is
to make atonement. He is to put on the sacred linen garments 33and make atonement
for the Most Holy Place, for the Tent of Meeting and the altar, and for the priests and all
the people of the community.
34“This is to be a lasting ordinance for you:
Atonement is to be made once a year for all
the sins of the Israelites.”
And it was done, as the LORD commanded
Moses.

Eating Blood Forbidden

17 The LORD said to Moses, 2“Speak to
Aaron and his sons and to all the
Israelites and say to them: ‘This is what the
LORD has commanded: 3Any Israelite who
sacrifices an ox,[b] a lamb or a goat in the
camp or outside of it 4instead of bringing it to
the entrance to the Tent of Meeting to
present it as an offering to the LORD in front of
the tabernacle of the LORD—that man shall
be considered guilty of bloodshed; he has
shed blood and must be cut off from his
people. 5This is so the Israelites will bring to
the LORD the sacrifices they are now making
in the open fields. They must bring them to
the priest, that is, to the LORD, at the entrance
to the Tent of Meeting and sacrifice them as
fellowship offerings.[c] 6The priest is to sprinkle the blood against the altar of the LORD at
the entrance to the Tent of Meeting and burn
the fat as an aroma pleasing to the LORD.
7They must no longer offer any of their sacrifices to the goat idols[d] to whom they prostitute themselves. This is to be a lasting ordinance for them and for the generations to
come.’
8“Say to them: ‘Any Israelite or any alien
living among them who offers a burnt offering or sacrifice 9and does not bring it to the
entrance to the Tent of Meeting to sacrifice it
to the LORD—that man must be cut off from
his people.
10“ ‘Any Israelite or any alien living among
them who eats any blood—I will set my face
against that person who eats blood and will
cut him off from his people. 11For the life of a
creature is in the blood, and I have given it to
you to make atonement for yourselves on
the altar; it is the blood that makes atonement for one’s life. 12Therefore I say to the
Israelites, “None of you may eat blood, nor
may an alien living among you eat blood.”

[a]29 Or *must fast;* also in verse 31
[b]3 The Hebrew word can include both male and female.
[c]5 Traditionally *peace offerings*
[d]7 Or *demons*

13“ ‘Any Israelite or any alien living among you who hunts any animal or bird that may be eaten must drain out the blood and cover it with earth, 14because the life of every creature is its blood. That is why I have said to the Israelites, “You must not eat the blood of any creature, because the life of every creature is its blood; anyone who eats it must be cut off.”

15“ ‘Anyone, whether native-born or alien, who eats anything found dead or torn by wild animals must wash his clothes and bathe with water, and he will be ceremonially unclean till evening; then he will be clean. 16But if he does not wash his clothes and bathe himself, he will be held responsible.’ ”

Unlawful Sexual Relations

18 The LORD said to Moses, 2“Speak to the Israelites and say to them: ‘I am the LORD your God. 3You must not do as they do in Egypt, where you used to live, and you must not do as they do in the land of Canaan, where I am bringing you. Do not follow their practices. 4You must obey my laws and be careful to follow my decrees. I am the LORD your God. 5Keep my decrees and laws, for the man who obeys them will live by them. I am the LORD.

6“ ‘No one is to approach any close relative to have sexual relations. I am the LORD.

7“ ‘Do not dishonor your father by having sexual relations with your mother. She is your mother; do not have relations with her.

8“ ‘Do not have sexual relations with your father’s wife; that would dishonor your father.

9“ ‘Do not have sexual relations with your sister, either your father’s daughter or your mother’s daughter, whether she was born in the same home or elsewhere.

10“ ‘Do not have sexual relations with your son’s daughter or your daughter’s daughter; that would dishonor you.

11“ ‘Do not have sexual relations with the daughter of your father’s wife, born to your father; she is your sister.

12“ ‘Do not have sexual relations with your father’s sister; she is your father’s close relative.

13“ ‘Do not have sexual relations with your mother’s sister, because she is your mother’s close relative.

14“ ‘Do not dishonor your father’s brother by approaching his wife to have sexual relations; she is your aunt.

15“ ‘Do not have sexual relations with your daughter-in-law. She is your son’s wife; do not have relations with her.

16“ ‘Do not have sexual relations with your brother’s wife; that would dishonor your brother.

17“ ‘Do not have sexual relations with both a woman and her daughter. Do not have sexual relations with either her son’s daughter or her daughter’s daughter; they are her close relatives. That is wickedness.

18“ ‘Do not take your wife’s sister as a rival wife and have sexual relations with her while your wife is living.

19“ ‘Do not approach a woman to have sexual relations during the uncleanness of her monthly period.

20“ ‘Do not have sexual relations with your neighbor’s wife and defile yourself with her.

21“ ‘Do not give any of your children to be sacrificed[a] to Molech, for you must not profane the name of your God. I am the LORD.

22“ ‘Do not lie with a man as one lies with a woman; that is detestable.

23“ ‘Do not have sexual relations with an animal and defile yourself with it. A woman must not present herself to an animal to have sexual relations with it; that is a perversion.

24“ ‘Do not defile yourselves in any of these ways, because this is how the nations that I am going to drive out before you became defiled. 25Even the land was defiled; so I punished it for its sin, and the land vomited out its inhabitants. 26But you must keep my decrees and my laws. The native-born and the aliens living among you must not do any of these detestable things, 27for all these things were done by the people who lived in the land before you, and the land became defiled. 28And if you defile the land, it will vomit you out as it vomited out the nations that were before you.

29“ ‘Everyone who does any of these detestable things—such persons must be cut off from their people. 30Keep my requirements and do not follow any of the detestable customs that were practiced before you came and do not defile yourselves with them. I am the LORD your God.’ ”

Various Laws

19 The LORD said to Moses, 2“Speak to the entire assembly of Israel and say to them: ‘Be holy because I, the LORD your God, am holy.

a21 Or *to be passed through* ⌊*the fire*⌋

3" 'Each of you must respect his mother
and father, and you must observe my Sabbaths. I am the LORD your God.
4" 'Do not turn to idols or make gods of cast
metal for yourselves. I am the LORD your
God.
5" 'When you sacrifice a fellowship offering[a] to the LORD, sacrifice it in such a way that
it will be accepted on your behalf. 6It shall be
eaten on the day you sacrifice it or on the
next day; anything left over until the third day
must be burned up. 7If any of it is eaten on
the third day, it is impure and will not be
accepted. 8Whoever eats it will be held responsible because he has desecrated what
is holy to the LORD; that person must be cut
off from his people.
9" 'When you reap the harvest of your
land, do not reap to the very edges of your
field or gather the gleanings of your harvest.
10Do not go over your vineyard a second time
or pick up the grapes that have fallen. Leave
them for the poor and the alien. I am the LORD
your God.
11" 'Do not steal.
" 'Do not lie.
" 'Do not deceive one another.
12" 'Do not swear falsely by my name and
so profane the name of your God. I am the
LORD.
13" 'Do not defraud your neighbor or rob
him.
" 'Do not hold back the wages of a hired
man overnight.
14" 'Do not curse the deaf or put a stumbling block in front of the blind, but fear your
God. I am the LORD.
15" 'Do not pervert justice; do not show
partiality to the poor or favoritism to the
great, but judge your neighbor fairly.
16" 'Do not go about spreading slander
among your people.
" 'Do not do anything that endangers your
neighbor's life. I am the LORD.
17" 'Do not hate your brother in your heart.
Rebuke your neighbor frankly so you will not
share in his guilt.
18" 'Do not seek revenge or bear a grudge
against one of your people, but love your
neighbor as yourself. I am the LORD.
19" 'Keep my decrees.
" 'Do not mate different kinds of animals.
" 'Do not plant your field with two kinds of
seed.
" 'Do not wear clothing woven of two kinds
of material.
20" 'If a man sleeps with a woman who is a
slave girl promised to another man but who
has not been ransomed or given her freedom, there must be due punishment. Yet
they are not to be put to death, because she
had not been freed. 21The man, however,
must bring a ram to the entrance to the Tent
of Meeting for a guilt offering to the LORD.
22With the ram of the guilt offering the priest
is to make atonement for him before the LORD
for the sin he has committed, and his sin will
be forgiven.
23" 'When you enter the land and plant any
kind of fruit tree, regard its fruit as forbidden.[b] For three years you are to consider
it forbidden[b]; it must not be eaten. 24In the
fourth year all its fruit will be holy, an offering
of praise to the LORD. 25But in the fifth year
you may eat its fruit. In this way your harvest will be increased. I am the LORD your
God.
26" 'Do not eat any meat with the blood still
in it.
" 'Do not practice divination or sorcery.
27" 'Do not cut the hair at the sides of your
head or clip off the edges of your beard.
28" 'Do not cut your bodies for the dead or
put tattoo marks on yourselves. I am the
LORD.
29" 'Do not degrade your daughter by making her a prostitute, or the land will turn to
prostitution and be filled with wickedness.
30" 'Observe my Sabbaths and have reverence for my sanctuary. I am the LORD.
31" 'Do not turn to mediums or seek out
spiritists, for you will be defiled by them. I am
the LORD your God.
32" 'Rise in the presence of the aged, show
respect for the elderly and revere your God. I
am the LORD.
33" 'When an alien lives with you in your
land, do not mistreat him. 34The alien living
with you must be treated as one of your native-born. Love him as yourself, for you were
aliens in Egypt. I am the LORD your God.
35" 'Do not use dishonest standards when
measuring length, weight or quantity. 36Use
honest scales and honest weights, an honest ephah[c] and an honest hin.[d] I am the LORD
your God, who brought you out of Egypt.
37" 'Keep all my decrees and all my laws
and follow them. I am the LORD.' "

[a]5 Traditionally *peace offering* [b]23 Hebrew *uncircumcised* [c]36 An ephah was a dry measure.
[d]36 A hin was a liquid measure.

Punishments for Sin

20 The LORD said to Moses, 2"Say to the Israelites: 'Any Israelite or any alien living in Israel who gives[a] any of his children to Molech must be put to death. The people of the community are to stone him. 3I will set my face against that man and I will cut him off from his people; for by giving his children to Molech, he has defiled my sanctuary and profaned my holy name. 4If the people of the community close their eyes when that man gives one of his children to Molech and they fail to put him to death, 5I will set my face against that man and his family and will cut off from their people both him and all who follow him in prostituting themselves to Molech.

6" 'I will set my face against the person who turns to mediums and spiritists to prostitute himself by following them, and I will cut him off from his people.

7" 'Consecrate yourselves and be holy, because I am the LORD your God. 8Keep my decrees and follow them. I am the LORD, who makes you holy.[b]

9" 'If anyone curses his father or mother, he must be put to death. He has cursed his father or his mother, and his blood will be on his own head.

10" 'If a man commits adultery with another man's wife—with the wife of his neighbor—both the adulterer and the adulteress must be put to death.

11" 'If a man sleeps with his father's wife, he has dishonored his father. Both the man and the woman must be put to death; their blood will be on their own heads.

12" 'If a man sleeps with his daughter-in-law, both of them must be put to death. What they have done is a perversion; their blood will be on their own heads.

13" 'If a man lies with a man as one lies with a woman, both of them have done what is detestable. They must be put to death; their blood will be on their own heads.

14" 'If a man marries both a woman and her mother, it is wicked. Both he and they must be burned in the fire, so that no wickedness will be among you.

15" 'If a man has sexual relations with an animal, he must be put to death, and you must kill the animal.

16" 'If a woman approaches an animal to have sexual relations with it, kill both the woman and the animal. They must be put to death; their blood will be on their own heads.

17" 'If a man marries his sister, the daughter of either his father or his mother, and they have sexual relations, it is a disgrace. They must be cut off before the eyes of their people. He has dishonored his sister and will be held responsible.

18" 'If a man lies with a woman during her monthly period and has sexual relations with her, he has exposed the source of her flow, and she has also uncovered it. Both of them must be cut off from their people.

19" 'Do not have sexual relations with the sister of either your mother or your father, for that would dishonor a close relative; both of you would be held responsible.

20" 'If a man sleeps with his aunt, he has dishonored his uncle. They will be held responsible; they will die childless.

21" 'If a man marries his brother's wife, it is an act of impurity; he has dishonored his brother. They will be childless.

22" 'Keep all my decrees and laws and follow them, so that the land where I am bringing you to live may not vomit you out. 23You must not live according to the customs of the nations I am going to drive out before you. Because they did all these things, I abhorred them. 24But I said to you, "You will possess their land; I will give it to you as an inheritance, a land flowing with milk and honey." I am the LORD your God, who has set you apart from the nations.

25" 'You must therefore make a distinction between clean and unclean animals and between unclean and clean birds. Do not defile yourselves by any animal or bird or anything that moves along the ground—those which I have set apart as unclean for you. 26You are to be holy to me[c] because I, the LORD, am holy, and I have set you apart from the nations to be my own.

27" 'A man or woman who is a medium or spiritist among you must be put to death. You are to stone them; their blood will be on their own heads.' "

Rules for Priests

21 The LORD said to Moses, "Speak to the priests, the sons of Aaron, and say to them: 'A priest must not make himself ceremonially unclean for any of his people who die, 2except for a close relative, such as

[a]2 Or *sacrifices;* also in verses 3 and 4 [b]8 Or *who sanctifies you;* or *who sets you apart as holy* [c]26 Or *be my holy ones*

his mother or father, his son or daughter, his brother, 3or an unmarried sister who is dependent on him since she has no husband—for her he may make himself unclean. 4He must not make himself unclean for people related to him by marriage,[a] and so defile himself.

5" 'Priests must not shave their heads or shave off the edges of their beards or cut their bodies. 6They must be holy to their God and must not profane the name of their God. Because they present the offerings made to the LORD by fire, the food of their God, they are to be holy.

7" 'They must not marry women defiled by prostitution or divorced from their husbands, because priests are holy to their God. 8Regard them as holy, because they offer up the food of your God. Consider them holy, because I the LORD am holy—I who make you holy.[b]

9" 'If a priest's daughter defiles herself by becoming a prostitute, she disgraces her father; she must be burned in the fire.

10" 'The high priest, the one among his brothers who has had the anointing oil poured on his head and who has been ordained to wear the priestly garments, must not let his hair become unkempt[c] or tear his clothes. 11He must not enter a place where there is a dead body. He must not make himself unclean, even for his father or mother, 12nor leave the sanctuary of his God or desecrate it, because he has been dedicated by the anointing oil of his God. I am the LORD.

13" 'The woman he marries must be a virgin. 14He must not marry a widow, a divorced woman, or a woman defiled by prostitution, but only a virgin from his own people, 15so he will not defile his offspring among his people. I am the LORD, who makes him holy.[d] ' "

16The LORD said to Moses, 17"Say to Aaron: 'For the generations to come none of your descendants who has a defect may come near to offer the food of his God. 18No man who has any defect may come near: no man who is blind or lame, disfigured or deformed; 19no man with a crippled foot or hand, 20or who is hunchbacked or dwarfed, or who has any eye defect, or who has festering or running sores or damaged testicles. 21No descendant of Aaron the priest who has any defect is to come near to present the offerings made to the LORD by fire. He has a defect; he must not come near to offer the food of his God. 22He may eat the most holy food of his God, as well as the holy food; 23yet because of his defect, he must not go near the curtain or approach the altar, and so desecrate my sanctuary. I am the LORD, who makes them holy.[e] ' "

24So Moses told this to Aaron and his sons and to all the Israelites.

22 The LORD said to Moses, 2"Tell Aaron and his sons to treat with respect the sacred offerings the Israelites consecrate to me, so they will not profane my holy name. I am the LORD.

3"Say to them: 'For the generations to come, if any of your descendants is ceremonially unclean and yet comes near the sacred offerings that the Israelites consecrate to the LORD, that person must be cut off from my presence. I am the LORD.

4" 'If a descendant of Aaron has an infectious skin disease[f] or a bodily discharge, he may not eat the sacred offerings until he is cleansed. He will also be unclean if he touches something defiled by a corpse or by anyone who has an emission of semen, 5or if he touches any crawling thing that makes him unclean, or any person who makes him unclean, whatever the uncleanness may be. 6The one who touches any such thing will be unclean till evening. He must not eat any of the sacred offerings unless he has bathed himself with water. 7When the sun goes down, he will be clean, and after that he may eat the sacred offerings, for they are his food. 8He must not eat anything found dead or torn by wild animals, and so become unclean through it. I am the LORD.

9" 'The priests are to keep my requirements so that they do not become guilty and die for treating them with contempt. I am the LORD, who makes them holy.[g]

10" 'No one outside a priest's family may eat the sacred offering, nor may the guest of a priest or his hired worker eat it. 11But if a priest buys a slave with money, or if a slave is born in his household, that slave may eat his food. 12If a priest's daughter marries anyone other than a priest, she may not eat any

[a]4 Or *unclean as a leader among his people* [b]8 Or *who sanctify you;* or *who set you apart as holy* [c]10 Or *not uncover his head* [d]15 Or *who sanctifies him;* or *who sets him apart as holy* [e]23 Or *who sanctifies them;* or *who sets them apart as holy* [f]4 Traditionally *leprosy;* the Hebrew word was used for various diseases affecting the skin—not necessarily leprosy. [g]9 Or *who sanctifies them;* or *who sets them apart as holy;* also in verse 16

of the sacred contributions. 13But if a priest's daughter becomes a widow or is divorced, yet has no children, and she returns to live in her father's house as in her youth, she may eat of her father's food. No unauthorized person, however, may eat any of it.

14" 'If anyone eats a sacred offering by mistake, he must make restitution to the priest for the offering and add a fifth of the value to it. 15The priests must not desecrate the sacred offerings the Israelites present to the LORD 16by allowing them to eat the sacred offerings and so bring upon them guilt requiring payment. I am the LORD, who makes them holy.' "

Unacceptable Sacrifices

17The LORD said to Moses, 18"Speak to Aaron and his sons and to all the Israelites and say to them: 'If any of you—either an Israelite or an alien living in Israel—presents a gift for a burnt offering to the LORD, either to fulfill a vow or as a freewill offering, 19you must present a male without defect from the cattle, sheep or goats in order that it may be accepted on your behalf. 20Do not bring anything with a defect, because it will not be accepted on your behalf. 21When anyone brings from the herd or flock a fellowship offering[a] to the LORD to fulfill a special vow or as a freewill offering, it must be without defect or blemish to be acceptable. 22Do not offer to the LORD the blind, the injured or the maimed, or anything with warts or festering or running sores. Do not place any of these on the altar as an offering made to the LORD by fire. 23You may, however, present as a freewill offering an ox[b] or a sheep that is deformed or stunted, but it will not be accepted in fulfillment of a vow. 24You must not offer to the LORD an animal whose testicles are bruised, crushed, torn or cut. You must not do this in your own land, 25and you must not accept such animals from the hand of a foreigner and offer them as the food of your God. They will not be accepted on your behalf, because they are deformed and have defects.' "

26The LORD said to Moses, 27"When a calf, a lamb or a goat is born, it is to remain with its mother for seven days. From the eighth day on, it will be acceptable as an offering made to the LORD by fire. 28Do not slaughter a cow or a sheep and its young on the same day.

29"When you sacrifice a thank offering to the LORD, sacrifice it in such a way that it will be accepted on your behalf. 30It must be eaten that same day; leave none of it till morning. I am the LORD.

31"Keep my commands and follow them. I am the LORD. 32Do not profane my holy name. I must be acknowledged as holy by the Israelites. I am the LORD, who makes[c] you holy[d] 33and who brought you out of Egypt to be your God. I am the LORD."

23

The LORD said to Moses, 2"Speak to the Israelites and say to them: 'These are my appointed feasts, the appointed feasts of the LORD, which you are to proclaim as sacred assemblies.

The Sabbath

3" 'There are six days when you may work, but the seventh day is a Sabbath of rest, a day of sacred assembly. You are not to do any work; wherever you live, it is a Sabbath to the LORD.

The Passover and Unleavened Bread

4" 'These are the LORD's appointed feasts, the sacred assemblies you are to proclaim at their appointed times: 5The LORD's Passover begins at twilight on the fourteenth day of the first month. 6On the fifteenth day of that month the LORD's Feast of Unleavened Bread begins; for seven days you must eat bread made without yeast. 7On the first day hold a sacred assembly and do no regular work. 8For seven days present an offering made to the LORD by fire. And on the seventh day hold a sacred assembly and do no regular work.' "

Firstfruits

9The LORD said to Moses, 10"Speak to the Israelites and say to them: 'When you enter the land I am going to give you and you reap its harvest, bring to the priest a sheaf of the first grain you harvest. 11He is to wave the sheaf before the LORD so it will be accepted on your behalf; the priest is to wave it on the day after the Sabbath. 12On the day you wave the sheaf, you must sacrifice as a burnt offering to the LORD a lamb a year old without defect, 13together with its grain offering of two-tenths of an ephah[e] of fine flour mixed with oil—an offering made to the LORD by fire,

[a]21 Traditionally *peace offering* [b]23 The Hebrew word can include both male and female. [c]32 Or *made* [d]32 Or *who sanctifies you;* or *who sets you apart as holy* [e]13 That is, probably about 4 quarts (about 4.5 liters); also in verse 17

a pleasing aroma—and its drink offering of a quarter of a hin[a] of wine. 14You must not eat any bread, or roasted or new grain, until the very day you bring this offering to your God. This is to be a lasting ordinance for the generations to come, wherever you live.

Feast of Weeks

15" 'From the day after the Sabbath, the day you brought the sheaf of the wave offering, count off seven full weeks. 16Count off fifty days up to the day after the seventh Sabbath, and then present an offering of new grain to the LORD. 17From wherever you live, bring two loaves made of two-tenths of an ephah of fine flour, baked with yeast, as a wave offering of firstfruits to the LORD. 18Present with this bread seven male lambs, each a year old and without defect, one young bull and two rams. They will be a burnt offering to the LORD, together with their grain offerings and drink offerings—an offering made by fire, an aroma pleasing to the LORD. 19Then sacrifice one male goat for a sin offering and two lambs, each a year old, for a fellowship offering.[b] 20The priest is to wave the two lambs before the LORD as a wave offering, together with the bread of the firstfruits. They are a sacred offering to the LORD for the priest. 21On that same day you are to proclaim a sacred assembly and do no regular work. This is to be a lasting ordinance for the generations to come, wherever you live.

22" 'When you reap the harvest of your land, do not reap to the very edges of your field or gather the gleanings of your harvest. Leave them for the poor and the alien. I am the LORD your God.' "

Feast of Trumpets

23The LORD said to Moses, 24"Say to the Israelites: 'On the first day of the seventh month you are to have a day of rest, a sacred assembly commemorated with trumpet blasts. 25Do no regular work, but present an offering made to the LORD by fire.' "

Day of Atonement

26The LORD said to Moses, 27"The tenth day of this seventh month is the Day of Atonement. Hold a sacred assembly and deny yourselves,[c] and present an offering made to the LORD by fire. 28Do no work on that day, because it is the Day of Atonement, when atonement is made for you before the LORD your God. 29Anyone who does not deny himself on that day must be cut off from his people. 30I will destroy from among his people anyone who does any work on that day. 31You shall do no work at all. This is to be a lasting ordinance for the generations to come, wherever you live. 32It is a sabbath of rest for you, and you must deny yourselves. From the evening of the ninth day of the month until the following evening you are to observe your sabbath."

Feast of Tabernacles

33The LORD said to Moses, 34"Say to the Israelites: 'On the fifteenth day of the seventh month the LORD's Feast of Tabernacles begins, and it lasts for seven days. 35The first day is a sacred assembly; do no regular work. 36For seven days present offerings made to the LORD by fire, and on the eighth day hold a sacred assembly and present an offering made to the LORD by fire. It is the closing assembly; do no regular work.

37(" 'These are the LORD's appointed feasts, which you are to proclaim as sacred assemblies for bringing offerings made to the LORD by fire—the burnt offerings and grain offerings, sacrifices and drink offerings required for each day. 38These offerings are in addition to those for the LORD's Sabbaths and[d] in addition to your gifts and whatever you have vowed and all the freewill offerings you give to the LORD.)

39" 'So beginning with the fifteenth day of the seventh month, after you have gathered the crops of the land, celebrate the festival to the LORD for seven days; the first day is a day of rest, and the eighth day also is a day of rest. 40On the first day you are to take choice fruit from the trees, and palm fronds, leafy branches and poplars, and rejoice before the LORD your God for seven days. 41Celebrate this as a festival to the LORD for seven days each year. This is to be a lasting ordinance for the generations to come; celebrate it in the seventh month. 42Live in booths for seven days: All native-born Israelites are to live in booths 43so your descendants will know that I had the Israelites live in booths when I brought them out of Egypt. I am the LORD your God.' "

44So Moses announced to the Israelites the appointed feasts of the LORD.

[a]13 That is, probably about 1 quart (about 1 liter) [b]19 Traditionally *peace offering* [c]27 Or *and fast;* also in verses 29 and 32 [d]38 Or *These feasts are in addition to the LORD's Sabbaths, and these offerings are*

Oil and Bread Set Before the LORD

24 The LORD said to Moses, 2"Command the Israelites to bring you clear oil of pressed olives for the light so that the lamps may be kept burning continually. 3Outside the curtain of the Testimony in the Tent of Meeting, Aaron is to tend the lamps before the LORD from evening till morning, continually. This is to be a lasting ordinance for the generations to come. 4The lamps on the pure gold lampstand before the LORD must be tended continually.

5"Take fine flour and bake twelve loaves of bread, using two-tenths of an ephah[a] for each loaf. 6Set them in two rows, six in each row, on the table of pure gold before the LORD. 7Along each row put some pure incense as a memorial portion to represent the bread and to be an offering made to the LORD by fire. 8This bread is to be set out before the LORD regularly, Sabbath after Sabbath, on behalf of the Israelites, as a lasting covenant. 9It belongs to Aaron and his sons, who are to eat it in a holy place, because it is a most holy part of their regular share of the offerings made to the LORD by fire."

A Blasphemer Stoned

10Now the son of an Israelite mother and an Egyptian father went out among the Israelites, and a fight broke out in the camp between him and an Israelite. 11The son of the Israelite woman blasphemed the Name with a curse; so they brought him to Moses. (His mother's name was Shelomith, the daughter of Dibri the Danite.) 12They put him in custody until the will of the LORD should be made clear to them.

13Then the LORD said to Moses: 14"Take the blasphemer outside the camp. All those who heard him are to lay their hands on his head, and the entire assembly is to stone him. 15Say to the Israelites: 'If anyone curses his God, he will be held responsible; 16anyone who blasphemes the name of the LORD must be put to death. The entire assembly must stone him. Whether an alien or native-born, when he blasphemes the Name, he must be put to death.

17" 'If anyone takes the life of a human being, he must be put to death. 18Anyone who takes the life of someone's animal must make restitution—life for life. 19If anyone injures his neighbor, whatever he has done must be done to him: 20fracture for fracture, eye for eye, tooth for tooth. As he has injured the other, so he is to be injured. 21Whoever kills an animal must make restitution, but whoever kills a man must be put to death. 22You are to have the same law for the alien and the native-born. I am the LORD your God.' "

23Then Moses spoke to the Israelites, and they took the blasphemer outside the camp and stoned him. The Israelites did as the LORD commanded Moses.

The Sabbath Year

25 The LORD said to Moses on Mount Sinai, 2"Speak to the Israelites and say to them: 'When you enter the land I am going to give you, the land itself must observe a sabbath to the LORD. 3For six years sow your fields, and for six years prune your vineyards and gather their crops. 4But in the seventh year the land is to have a sabbath of rest, a sabbath to the LORD. Do not sow your fields or prune your vineyards. 5Do not reap what grows of itself or harvest the grapes of your untended vines. The land is to have a year of rest. 6Whatever the land yields during the sabbath year will be food for you—for yourself, your manservant and maidservant, and the hired worker and temporary resident who live among you, 7as well as for your livestock and the wild animals in your land. Whatever the land produces may be eaten.

The Year of Jubilee

8" 'Count off seven sabbaths of years—seven times seven years—so that the seven sabbaths of years amount to a period of forty-nine years. 9Then have the trumpet sounded everywhere on the tenth day of the seventh month; on the Day of Atonement sound the trumpet throughout your land. 10Consecrate the fiftieth year and proclaim liberty throughout the land to all its inhabitants. It shall be a jubilee for you; each one of you is to return to his family property and each to his own clan. 11The fiftieth year shall be a jubilee for you; do not sow and do not reap what grows of itself or harvest the untended vines. 12For it is a jubilee and is to be holy for you; eat only what is taken directly from the fields.

13" 'In this Year of Jubilee everyone is to return to his own property.

14" 'If you sell land to one of your countrymen or buy any from him, do not take advan-

[a]5 That is, probably about 4 quarts (about 4.5 liters)

tage of each other. 15 You are to buy from
your countryman on the basis of the number
of years since the Jubilee. And he is to sell to
you on the basis of the number of years left
for harvesting crops. 16 When the years are
many, you are to increase the price, and
when the years are few, you are to decrease
the price, because what he is really selling
you is the number of crops. 17 Do not take
advantage of each other, but fear your God.
I am the LORD your God.

18 " 'Follow my decrees and be careful to
obey my laws, and you will live safely in the
land. 19 Then the land will yield its fruit, and
you will eat your fill and live there in safety.
20 You may ask, "What will we eat in the seventh year if we do not plant or harvest our
crops?" 21 I will send you such a blessing in
the sixth year that the land will yield enough
for three years. 22 While you plant during the
eighth year, you will eat from the old crop and
will continue to eat from it until the harvest of
the ninth year comes in.

23 " 'The land must not be sold permanently, because the land is mine and you are but
aliens and my tenants. 24 Throughout the
country that you hold as a possession, you
must provide for the redemption of the land.

25 " 'If one of your countrymen becomes
poor and sells some of his property, his nearest relative is to come and redeem what his
countryman has sold. 26 If, however, a man
has no one to redeem it for him but he himself prospers and acquires sufficient means
to redeem it, 27 he is to determine the value
for the years since he sold it and refund the
balance to the man to whom he sold it; he
can then go back to his own property. 28 But if
he does not acquire the means to repay him,
what he sold will remain in the possession of
the buyer until the Year of Jubilee. It will be
returned in the Jubilee, and he can then go
back to his property.

29 " 'If a man sells a house in a walled city,
he retains the right of redemption a full year
after its sale. During that time he may redeem it. 30 If it is not redeemed before a full
year has passed, the house in the walled city
shall belong permanently to the buyer and
his descendants. It is not to be returned in
the Jubilee. 31 But houses in villages without
walls around them are to be considered as
open country. They can be redeemed, and
they are to be returned in the Jubilee.

32 " 'The Levites always have the right to
redeem their houses in the Levitical towns,
which they possess. 33 So the property of the
Levites is redeemable—that is, a house sold
in any town they hold—and is to be returned
in the Jubilee, because the houses in the
towns of the Levites are their property
among the Israelites. 34 But the pastureland
belonging to their towns must not be sold; it
is their permanent possession.

35 " 'If one of your countrymen becomes
poor and is unable to support himself among
you, help him as you would an alien or a
temporary resident, so he can continue to
live among you. 36 Do not take interest of any
kind[a] from him, but fear your God, so that
your countryman may continue to live among
you. 37 You must not lend him money at interest or sell him food at a profit. 38 I am the LORD
your God, who brought you out of Egypt to
give you the land of Canaan and to be your
God.

39 " 'If one of your countrymen becomes
poor among you and sells himself to you, do
not make him work as a slave. 40 He is to be
treated as a hired worker or a temporary
resident among you; he is to work for you
until the Year of Jubilee. 41 Then he and his
children are to be released, and he will go
back to his own clan and to the property of
his forefathers. 42 Because the Israelites are
my servants, whom I brought out of Egypt,
they must not be sold as slaves. 43 Do not rule
over them ruthlessly, but fear your God.

44 " 'Your male and female slaves are to
come from the nations around you; from
them you may buy slaves. 45 You may also
buy some of the temporary residents living
among you and members of their clans born
in your country, and they will become your
property. 46 You can will them to your children
as inherited property and can make them
slaves for life, but you must not rule over your
fellow Israelites ruthlessly.

47 " 'If an alien or a temporary resident
among you becomes rich and one of your
countrymen becomes poor and sells himself
to the alien living among you or to a member
of the alien's clan, 48 he retains the right of
redemption after he has sold himself. One of
his relatives may redeem him: 49 An uncle or
a cousin or any blood relative in his clan may
redeem him. Or if he prospers, he may redeem himself. 50 He and his buyer are to
count the time from the year he sold himself
up to the Year of Jubilee. The price for his

[a] *36* Or *take excessive interest*; similarly in verse 37

release is to be based on the rate paid to a
hired man for that number of years. 51If many
years remain, he must pay for his redemption a larger share of the price paid for him.
52If only a few years remain until the Year of
Jubilee, he is to compute that and pay for his
redemption accordingly. 53He is to be treated
as a man hired from year to year; you must
see to it that his owner does not rule over him
ruthlessly.

54" 'Even if he is not redeemed in any of
these ways, he and his children are to be
released in the Year of Jubilee, 55for the Israelites belong to me as servants. They are my
servants, whom I brought out of Egypt. I am
the LORD your God.

Reward for Obedience

26 " 'Do not make idols or set up an image or a sacred stone for yourselves,
and do not place a carved stone in your land
to bow down before it. I am the LORD your
God.

2" 'Observe my Sabbaths and have reverence for my sanctuary. I am the LORD.

3" 'If you follow my decrees and are careful
to obey my commands, 4I will send you rain
in its season, and the ground will yield its
crops and the trees of the field their fruit.
5Your threshing will continue until grape harvest and the grape harvest will continue until
planting, and you will eat all the food you
want and live in safety in your land.

6" 'I will grant peace in the land, and you
will lie down and no one will make you afraid.
I will remove savage beasts from the land,
and the sword will not pass through your
country. 7You will pursue your enemies, and
they will fall by the sword before you. 8Five of
you will chase a hundred, and a hundred of
you will chase ten thousand, and your enemies will fall by the sword before you.

9" 'I will look on you with favor and make
you fruitful and increase your numbers, and I
will keep my covenant with you. 10You will
still be eating last year's harvest when you
will have to move it out to make room for the
new. 11I will put my dwelling place[a] among
you, and I will not abhor you. 12I will walk
among you and be your God, and you will be
my people. 13I am the LORD your God, who
brought you out of Egypt so that you would
no longer be slaves to the Egyptians; I broke
the bars of your yoke and enabled you to
walk with heads held high.

Punishment for Disobedience

14" 'But if you will not listen to me and carry
out all these commands, 15and if you reject
my decrees and abhor my laws and fail to
carry out all my commands and so violate my
covenant, 16then I will do this to you: I will
bring upon you sudden terror, wasting diseases and fever that will destroy your sight
and drain away your life. You will plant seed
in vain, because your enemies will eat it. 17I
will set my face against you so that you will
be defeated by your enemies; those who
hate you will rule over you, and you will flee
even when no one is pursuing you.

18" 'If after all this you will not listen to me,
I will punish you for your sins seven times
over. 19I will break down your stubborn pride
and make the sky above you like iron and the
ground beneath you like bronze. 20Your
strength will be spent in vain, because your
soil will not yield its crops, nor will the trees of
the land yield their fruit.

21" 'If you remain hostile toward me and
refuse to listen to me, I will multiply your
afflictions seven times over, as your sins deserve. 22I will send wild animals against you,
and they will rob you of your children, destroy
your cattle and make you so few in number
that your roads will be deserted.

23" 'If in spite of these things you do not
accept my correction but continue to be hostile toward me, 24I myself will be hostile
toward you and will afflict you for your sins
seven times over. 25And I will bring the sword
upon you to avenge the breaking of the covenant. When you withdraw into your cities, I
will send a plague among you, and you will
be given into enemy hands. 26When I cut off
your supply of bread, ten women will be able
to bake your bread in one oven, and they will
dole out the bread by weight. You will eat, but
you will not be satisfied.

27" 'If in spite of this you still do not listen to
me but continue to be hostile toward me,
28then in my anger I will be hostile toward
you, and I myself will punish you for your sins
seven times over. 29You will eat the flesh of
your sons and the flesh of your daughters. 30I
will destroy your high places, cut down your
incense altars and pile your dead bodies on
the lifeless forms of your idols, and I will
abhor you. 31I will turn your cities into ruins
and lay waste your sanctuaries, and I will
take no delight in the pleasing aroma of your

[a]11 Or *my tabernacle*

offerings. 32I will lay waste the land, so that your enemies who live there will be appalled. 33I will scatter you among the nations and will draw out my sword and pursue you. Your land will be laid waste, and your cities will lie in ruins. 34Then the land will enjoy its sabbath years all the time that it lies desolate and you are in the country of your enemies; then the land will rest and enjoy its sabbaths. 35All the time that it lies desolate, the land will have the rest it did not have during the sabbaths you lived in it.

36" 'As for those of you who are left, I will make their hearts so fearful in the lands of their enemies that the sound of a windblown leaf will put them to flight. They will run as though fleeing from the sword, and they will fall, even though no one is pursuing them. 37They will stumble over one another as though fleeing from the sword, even though no one is pursuing them. So you will not be able to stand before your enemies. 38You will perish among the nations; the land of your enemies will devour you. 39Those of you who are left will waste away in the lands of their enemies because of their sins; also because of their fathers' sins they will waste away.

40" 'But if they will confess their sins and the sins of their fathers—their treachery against me and their hostility toward me, 41which made me hostile toward them so that I sent them into the land of their enemies—then when their uncircumcised hearts are humbled and they pay for their sin, 42I will remember my covenant with Jacob and my covenant with Isaac and my covenant with Abraham, and I will remember the land. 43For the land will be deserted by them and will enjoy its sabbaths while it lies desolate without them. They will pay for their sins because they rejected my laws and abhorred my decrees. 44Yet in spite of this, when they are in the land of their enemies, I will not reject them or abhor them so as to destroy them completely, breaking my covenant with them. I am the LORD their God. 45But for their sake I will remember the covenant with their ancestors whom I brought out of Egypt in the sight of the nations to be their God. I am the LORD.' "

46These are the decrees, the laws and the regulations that the LORD established on Mount Sinai between himself and the Israelites through Moses.

Redeeming What Is the LORD's

27 The LORD said to Moses, 2"Speak to the Israelites and say to them: 'If anyone makes a special vow to dedicate persons to the LORD by giving equivalent values, 3set the value of a male between the ages of twenty and sixty at fifty shekels[a] of silver, according to the sanctuary shekel[b]; 4and if it is a female, set her value at thirty shekels.[c] 5If it is a person between the ages of five and twenty, set the value of a male at twenty shekels[d] and of a female at ten shekels.[e] 6If it is a person between one month and five years, set the value of a male at five shekels[f] of silver and that of a female at three shekels[g] of silver. 7If it is a person sixty years old or more, set the value of a male at fifteen shekels[h] and of a female at ten shekels. 8If anyone making the vow is too poor to pay the specified amount, he is to present the person to the priest, who will set the value for him according to what the man making the vow can afford.

9" 'If what he vowed is an animal that is acceptable as an offering to the LORD, such an animal given to the LORD becomes holy. 10He must not exchange it or substitute a good one for a bad one, or a bad one for a good one; if he should substitute one animal for another, both it and the substitute become holy. 11If what he vowed is a ceremonially unclean animal—one that is not acceptable as an offering to the LORD—the animal must be presented to the priest, 12who will judge its quality as good or bad. Whatever value the priest then sets, that is what it will be. 13If the owner wishes to redeem the animal, he must add a fifth to its value.

14" 'If a man dedicates his house as something holy to the LORD, the priest will judge its quality as good or bad. Whatever value the priest then sets, so it will remain. 15If the man who dedicates his house redeems it, he must add a fifth to its value, and the house will again become his.

16" 'If a man dedicates to the LORD part of his family land, its value is to be set according to the amount of seed required for it—fifty shekels of silver to a homer[i] of barley seed.

[a]3 That is, about 1 1/4 pounds (about 0.6 kilogram); also in verse 16 [b]3 That is, about 2/5 ounce (about 11.5 grams); also in verse 25 [c]4 That is, about 12 ounces (about 0.3 kilogram) [d]5 That is, about 8 ounces (about 0.2 kilogram) [e]5 That is, about 4 ounces (about 110 grams); also in verse 7 [f]6 That is, about 2 ounces (about 55 grams) [g]6 That is, about 1 1/4 ounces (about 35 grams) [h]7 That is, about 6 ounces (about 170 grams) [i]16 That is, probably about 6 bushels (about 220 liters)

17If he dedicates his field during the Year of
Jubilee, the value that has been set remains.
18But if he dedicates his field after the Jubilee, the priest will determine the value according to the number of years that remain
until the next Year of Jubilee, and its set
value will be reduced. 19If the man who dedicates the field wishes to redeem it, he must
add a fifth to its value, and the field will again
become his. 20If, however, he does not redeem the field, or if he has sold it to someone
else, it can never be redeemed. 21When the
field is released in the Jubilee, it will become
holy, like a field devoted to the LORD; it will
become the property of the priests.[a]

22" 'If a man dedicates to the LORD a field
he has bought, which is not part of his family
land, 23the priest will determine its value up
to the Year of Jubilee, and the man must pay
its value on that day as something holy to the
LORD. 24In the Year of Jubilee the field will
revert to the person from whom he bought it,
the one whose land it was. 25Every value is to
be set according to the sanctuary shekel,
twenty gerahs to the shekel.

26" 'No one, however, may dedicate the
firstborn of an animal, since the firstborn already belongs to the LORD; whether an ox[b] or
a sheep, it is the LORD's. 27If it is one of the
unclean animals, he may buy it back at its set
value, adding a fifth of the value to it. If he
does not redeem it, it is to be sold at its set
value.

28" 'But nothing that a man owns and
devotes[c] to the LORD—whether man or animal or family land—may be sold or redeemed; everything so devoted is most holy
to the LORD.

29" 'No person devoted to destruction[d]
may be ransomed; he must be put to
death.

30" 'A tithe of everything from the land,
whether grain from the soil or fruit from the
trees, belongs to the LORD; it is holy to the
LORD. 31If a man redeems any of his tithe, he
must add a fifth of the value to it. 32The entire
tithe of the herd and flock—every tenth animal that passes under the shepherd's rod—
will be holy to the LORD. 33He must not pick
out the good from the bad or make any substitution. If he does make a substitution, both
the animal and its substitute become holy
and cannot be redeemed.' "

34These are the commands the LORD gave
Moses on Mount Sinai for the Israelites.

[a]21 Or *priest* [b]26 The Hebrew word can include both male and female. [c]28 The Hebrew term refers to the irrevocable giving over of things or persons to the LORD. [d]29 The Hebrew term refers to the irrevocable giving over of things or persons to the LORD, often by totally destroying them.

Numbers

Introduction:

Numbers gets its name from the two accounts in chapters 1 and 26 of the numberings or countings of the people of Israel. Moses is the author of this book as well as the leader of the Israelites.

The first part of the book tells about Israel's year while camped at the foot of Mount Sinai. The second part of the book tells of the journey of Israel from Mount Sinai to the east side of the Dead Sea. The third part of the book tells of the preparations for entering and conquering Canaan.

Throughout the thirty-eight years of wandering in the desert, one thing became clear to Israel—God's constant care for them. He miraculously supplied the Israelites with manna, water and quails for their forty years in the desert. God loved and forgave his people continually even though they rebelled against him and their leaders.

Outline of contents:

Instructions for camping and march (1:1–10:10)
From Sinai to the plains of Moab (10:11–21:35)
Balaam, Balak, and Israel (22:1–25:18)
Instructions for conquest and possession of the land of Canaan (26:1–36:13)

The Census

1 The Lord spoke to Moses in the Tent of
Meeting in the Desert of Sinai on the first
day of the second month of the second year
after the Israelites came out of Egypt. He
said: 2"Take a census of the whole Israelite
community by their clans and families, listing
every man by name, one by one. 3You and
Aaron are to number by their divisions all the
men in Israel twenty years old or more who
are able to serve in the army. 4One man from
each tribe, each the head of his family, is to
help you. 5These are the names of the men
who are to assist you:

from Reuben, Elizur son of Shedeur;
6from Simeon, Shelumiel son of Zurishaddai;
7from Judah, Nahshon son of Amminadab;
8from Issachar, Nethanel son of Zuar;
9from Zebulun, Eliab son of Helon;
10from the sons of Joseph:
from Ephraim, Elishama son of Ammihud;
from Manasseh, Gamaliel son of Pedahzur;
11from Benjamin, Abidan son of Gideoni;
12from Dan, Ahiezer son of Ammishaddai;
13from Asher, Pagiel son of Ocran;
14from Gad, Eliasaph son of Deuel;
15from Naphtali, Ahira son of Enan."

16These were the men appointed from the
community, the leaders of their ancestral
tribes. They were the heads of the clans of
Israel.
17Moses and Aaron took these men whose
names had been given, 18and they called the
whole community together on the first day of
the second month. The people indicated
their ancestry by their clans and families,
and the men twenty years old or more were
listed by name, one by one, 19as the Lord
commanded Moses. And so he counted
them in the Desert of Sinai:

20From the descendants of Reuben the firstborn son of Israel:

All the men twenty years old or more who were able to serve in the army were listed by name, one by one, according to the records of their

clans and families. [21]The number
from the tribe of Reuben was 46,500.

[22]From the descendants of Simeon:
All the men twenty years old or more
who were able to serve in the army
were counted and listed by name,
one by one, according to the records
of their clans and families. [23]The
number from the tribe of Simeon was
59,300.

[24]From the descendants of Gad:
All the men twenty years old or more
who were able to serve in the army
were listed by name, according to
the records of their clans and families. [25]The number from the tribe of
Gad was 45,650.

[26]From the descendants of Judah:
All the men twenty years old or more
who were able to serve in the army
were listed by name, according to
the records of their clans and families. [27]The number from the tribe of
Judah was 74,600.

[28]From the descendants of Issachar:
All the men twenty years old or more
who were able to serve in the army
were listed by name, according to
the records of their clans and families. [29]The number from the tribe of
Issachar was 54,400.

[30]From the descendants of Zebulun:
All the men twenty years old or more
who were able to serve in the army
were listed by name, according to
the records of their clans and families. [31]The number from the tribe of
Zebulun was 57,400.

[32]From the sons of Joseph:
From the descendants of Ephraim:
All the men twenty years old or more
who were able to serve in the army
were listed by name, according to
the records of their clans and families. [33]The number from the tribe of
Ephraim was 40,500.

[34]From the descendants of Manasseh:
All the men twenty years old or more
who were able to serve in the army
were listed by name, according to
the records of their clans and families. [35]The number from the tribe of
Manasseh was 32,200.

[36]From the descendants of Benjamin:
All the men twenty years old or more
who were able to serve in the army
were listed by name, according to
the records of their clans and families. [37]The number from the tribe of
Benjamin was 35,400.

[38]From the descendants of Dan:
All the men twenty years old or more
who were able to serve in the army
were listed by name, according to
the records of their clans and families. [39]The number from the tribe of
Dan was 62,700.

[40]From the descendants of Asher:
All the men twenty years old or more
who were able to serve in the army
were listed by name, according to
the records of their clans and families. [41]The number from the tribe of
Asher was 41,500.

[42]From the descendants of Naphtali:
All the men twenty years old or more
who were able to serve in the army
were listed by name, according to
the records of their clans and families. [43]The number from the tribe of
Naphtali was 53,400.

[44]These were the men counted by Moses
and Aaron and the twelve leaders of Israel,
each one representing his family. [45]All the
Israelites twenty years old or more who were
able to serve in Israel's army were counted
according to their families. [46]The total number was 603,550.

[47]The families of the tribe of Levi, however,
were not counted along with the others.
[48]The LORD had said to Moses: [49]"You must
not count the tribe of Levi or include them in
the census of the other Israelites. [50]Instead,
appoint the Levites to be in charge of the
tabernacle of the Testimony—over all its furnishings and everything belonging to it. They
are to carry the tabernacle and all its furnishings; they are to take care of it and encamp around it. [51]Whenever the tabernacle
is to move, the Levites are to take it down,
and whenever the tabernacle is to be set up,
the Levites shall do it. Anyone else who goes
near it shall be put to death. [52]The Israelites
are to set up their tents by divisions, each
man in his own camp under his own standard. [53]The Levites, however, are to set up
their tents around the tabernacle of the Testi-

mony so that wrath will not fall on the Israelite
community. The Levites are to be responsible for the care of the tabernacle of the Testimony."
[54]The Israelites did all this just as the LORD
commanded Moses.

The Arrangement of the Tribal Camps

2 The LORD said to Moses and Aaron:
[2]"The Israelites are to camp around the
Tent of Meeting some distance from it, each
man under his standard with the banners of
his family."

[3]On the east, toward the sunrise, the
divisions of the camp of Judah are to
encamp under their standard. The leader of the people of Judah is Nahshon
son of Amminadab. [4]His division numbers 74,600.
[5]The tribe of Issachar will camp next
to them. The leader of the people of
Issachar is Nethanel son of Zuar. [6]His
division numbers 54,400.
[7]The tribe of Zebulun will be next. The
leader of the people of Zebulun is Eliab
son of Helon. [8]His division numbers
57,400.
[9]All the men assigned to the camp of
Judah, according to their divisions,
number 186,400. They will set out first.

[10]On the south will be the divisions of
the camp of Reuben under their standard. The leader of the people of Reuben is Elizur son of Shedeur. [11]His division numbers 46,500.
[12]The tribe of Simeon will camp next
to them. The leader of the people of
Simeon is Shelumiel son of Zurishaddai. [13]His division numbers 59,300.
[14]The tribe of Gad will be next. The
leader of the people of Gad is Eliasaph
son of Deuel.[a] [15]His division numbers
45,650.
[16]All the men assigned to the camp of
Reuben, according to their divisions,
number 151,450. They will set out second.

[17]Then the Tent of Meeting and the
camp of the Levites will set out in the
middle of the camps. They will set out in
the same order as they encamp, each in
his own place under his standard.

[18]On the west will be the divisions of
the camp of Ephraim under their standard. The leader of the people of
Ephraim is Elishama son of Ammihud.
[19]His division numbers 40,500.
[20]The tribe of Manasseh will be next to
them. The leader of the people of Manasseh is Gamaliel son of Pedahzur.
[21]His division numbers 32,200.
[22]The tribe of Benjamin will be next.
The leader of the people of Benjamin is
Abidan son of Gideoni. [23]His division
numbers 35,400.
[24]All the men assigned to the camp of
Ephraim, according to their divisions,
number 108,100. They will set out third.

[25]On the north will be the divisions of
the camp of Dan, under their standard.
The leader of the people of Dan is Ahiezer son of Ammishaddai. [26]His division
numbers 62,700.
[27]The tribe of Asher will camp next to
them. The leader of the people of Asher
is Pagiel son of Ocran. [28]His division
numbers 41,500.
[29]The tribe of Naphtali will be next.
The leader of the people of Naphtali is
Ahira son of Enan. [30]His division numbers 53,400.
[31]All the men assigned to the camp of
Dan number 157,600. They will set out
last, under their standards.

[32]These are the Israelites, counted
according to their families. All those in
the camps, by their divisions, number
603,550. [33]The Levites, however, were
not counted along with the other Israelites, as the LORD commanded Moses.

[34]So the Israelites did everything the LORD
commanded Moses; that is the way they encamped under their standards, and that is
the way they set out, each with his clan and
family.

The Levites

3 This is the account of the family of Aaron
and Moses at the time the LORD talked
with Moses on Mount Sinai.
[2]The names of the sons of Aaron were
Nadab the firstborn and Abihu, Eleazar and
Ithamar. [3]Those were the names of Aaron's
sons, the anointed priests, who were or-

[a]14 Many manuscripts of the Masoretic Text, Samaritan Pentateuch and Vulgate (see also Num. 1:14); most manuscripts of the Masoretic Text *Reuel*

dained to serve as priests. 4Nadab and Abihu, however, fell dead before the LORD when they made an offering with unauthorized fire before him in the Desert of Sinai. They had no sons; so only Eleazar and Ithamar served as priests during the lifetime of their father Aaron.

5The LORD said to Moses, 6"Bring the tribe of Levi and present them to Aaron the priest to assist him. 7They are to perform duties for him and for the whole community at the Tent of Meeting by doing the work of the tabernacle. 8They are to take care of all the furnishings of the Tent of Meeting, fulfilling the obligations of the Israelites by doing the work of the tabernacle. 9Give the Levites to Aaron and his sons; they are the Israelites who are to be given wholly to him.[a] 10Appoint Aaron and his sons to serve as priests; anyone else who approaches the sanctuary must be put to death."

11The LORD also said to Moses, 12"I have taken the Levites from among the Israelites in place of the first male offspring of every Israelite woman. The Levites are mine, 13for all the firstborn are mine. When I struck down all the firstborn in Egypt, I set apart for myself every firstborn in Israel, whether man or animal. They are to be mine. I am the LORD."

14The LORD said to Moses in the Desert of Sinai, 15"Count the Levites by their families and clans. Count every male a month old or more." 16So Moses counted them, as he was commanded by the word of the LORD.

17These were the names of the sons of
Levi:
Gershon, Kohath and Merari.

18These were the names of the Gershonite clans:
Libni and Shimei.

19The Kohathite clans:
Amram, Izhar, Hebron and Uzziel.

20The Merarite clans:
Mahli and Mushi.

These were the Levite clans, according to their families.

21To Gershon belonged the clans of the Libnites and Shimeites; these were the Gershonite clans. 22The number of all the males a month old or more who were counted was 7,500. 23The Gershonite clans were to camp on the west, behind the tabernacle. 24The leader of the families of the Gershonites was Eliasaph son of Lael. 25At the Tent of Meeting the Gershonites were responsible for the care of the tabernacle and tent, its coverings, the curtain at the entrance to the Tent of Meeting, 26the curtains of the courtyard, the curtain at the entrance to the courtyard surrounding the tabernacle and altar, and the ropes—and everything related to their use.

27To Kohath belonged the clans of the Amramites, Izharites, Hebronites and Uzzielites; these were the Kohathite clans. 28The number of all the males a month old or more was 8,600.[b] The Kohathites were responsible for the care of the sanctuary. 29The Kohathite clans were to camp on the south side of the tabernacle. 30The leader of the families of the Kohathite clans was Elizaphan son of Uzziel. 31They were responsible for the care of the ark, the table, the lampstand, the altars, the articles of the sanctuary used in ministering, the curtain, and everything related to their use. 32The chief leader of the Levites was Eleazar son of Aaron, the priest. He was appointed over those who were responsible for the care of the sanctuary.

33To Merari belonged the clans of the Mahlites and the Mushites; these were the Merarite clans. 34The number of all the males a month old or more who were counted was 6,200. 35The leader of the families of the Merarite clans was Zuriel son of Abihail; they were to camp on the north side of the tabernacle. 36The Merarites were appointed to take care of the frames of the tabernacle, its crossbars, posts, bases, all its equipment, and everything related to their use, 37as well as the posts of the surrounding courtyard with their bases, tent pegs and ropes.

38Moses and Aaron and his sons were to camp to the east of the tabernacle, toward the sunrise, in front of the Tent of Meeting. They were responsible for the care of the sanctuary on behalf of the Israelites. Anyone else who approached the sanctuary was to be put to death.

39The total number of Levites counted at the LORD's command by Moses and Aaron according to their clans, including every male a month old or more, was 22,000.

[a]9 Most manuscripts of the Masoretic Text; some manuscripts of the Masoretic Text, Samaritan Pentateuch and Septuagint (see also Num. 8:16) *to me* [b]28 Hebrew; some Septuagint manuscripts *8,300*

40The LORD said to Moses, "Count all the
firstborn Israelite males who are a month old
or more and make a list of their names.
41Take the Levites for me in place of all the
firstborn of the Israelites, and the livestock
of the Levites in place of all the firstborn
of the livestock of the Israelites. I am the
LORD."

42So Moses counted all the firstborn of the
Israelites, as the LORD commanded him.
43The total number of firstborn males a
month old or more, listed by name, was
22,273.

44The LORD also said to Moses, 45"Take the
Levites in place of all the firstborn of Israel,
and the livestock of the Levites in place of
their livestock. The Levites are to be mine. I
am the LORD. 46To redeem the 273 firstborn
Israelites who exceed the number of the Levites, 47collect five shekels[a] for each one,
according to the sanctuary shekel, which
weighs twenty gerahs. 48Give the money for
the redemption of the additional Israelites to
Aaron and his sons."

49So Moses collected the redemption
money from those who exceeded the number redeemed by the Levites. 50From the
firstborn of the Israelites he collected silver
weighing 1,365 shekels,[b] according to the
sanctuary shekel. 51Moses gave the redemption money to Aaron and his sons, as
he was commanded by the word of the LORD.

The Kohathites

4 The LORD said to Moses and Aaron:
2"Take a census of the Kohathite branch
of the Levites by their clans and families.
3Count all the men from thirty to fifty years of
age who come to serve in the work in the
Tent of Meeting.

4"This is the work of the Kohathites in the
Tent of Meeting: the care of the most holy
things. 5When the camp is to move, Aaron
and his sons are to go in and take down the
shielding curtain and cover the ark of the
Testimony with it. 6Then they are to cover
this with hides of sea cows,[c] spread a cloth
of solid blue over that and put the poles in
place.

7"Over the table of the Presence they are
to spread a blue cloth and put on it the plates,
dishes and bowls, and the jars for drink offerings; the bread that is continually there is to
remain on it. 8Over these they are to spread
a scarlet cloth, cover that with hides of sea
cows and put its poles in place.

9"They are to take a blue cloth and cover
the lampstand that is for light, together with
its lamps, its wick trimmers and trays, and all
its jars for the oil used to supply it. 10Then
they are to wrap it and all its accessories in a
covering of hides of sea cows and put it on a
carrying frame.

11"Over the gold altar they are to spread a
blue cloth and cover that with hides of sea
cows and put its poles in place.

12"They are to take all the articles used for
ministering in the sanctuary, wrap them in a
blue cloth, cover that with hides of sea cows
and put them on a carrying frame.

13"They are to remove the ashes from the
bronze altar and spread a purple cloth over
it. 14Then they are to place on it all the utensils used for ministering at the altar, including
the firepans, meat forks, shovels and sprinkling bowls. Over it they are to spread a
covering of hides of sea cows and put its
poles in place.

15"After Aaron and his sons have finished
covering the holy furnishings and all the holy
articles, and when the camp is ready to
move, the Kohathites are to come to do the
carrying. But they must not touch the holy
things or they will die. The Kohathites are to
carry those things that are in the Tent of
Meeting.

16"Eleazar son of Aaron, the priest, is to
have charge of the oil for the light, the fragrant incense, the regular grain offering and
the anointing oil. He is to be in charge of the
entire tabernacle and everything in it, including its holy furnishings and articles."

17The LORD said to Moses and Aaron,
18"See that the Kohathite tribal clans are not
cut off from the Levites. 19So that they may
live and not die when they come near the
most holy things, do this for them: Aaron and
his sons are to go into the sanctuary and
assign to each man his work and what he is
to carry. 20But the Kohathites must not go in
to look at the holy things, even for a moment,
or they will die."

The Gershonites

21The LORD said to Moses, 22"Take a census also of the Gershonites by their families
and clans. 23Count all the men from thirty to

[a]47 That is, about 2 ounces (about 55 grams) [b]50 That is, about 35 pounds (about 15.5 kilograms)
[c]6 That is, dugongs; also in verses 8, 10, 11, 12, 14 and 25

fifty years of age who come to serve in the work at the Tent of Meeting.

24"This is the service of the Gershonite clans as they work and carry burdens: 25They are to carry the curtains of the tabernacle, the Tent of Meeting, its covering and the outer covering of hides of sea cows, the curtains for the entrance to the Tent of Meeting, 26the curtains of the courtyard surrounding the tabernacle and altar, the curtain for the entrance, the ropes and all the equipment used in its service. The Gershonites are to do all that needs to be done with these things. 27All their service, whether carrying or doing other work, is to be done under the direction of Aaron and his sons. You shall assign to them as their responsibility all they are to carry. 28This is the service of the Gershonite clans at the Tent of Meeting. Their duties are to be under the direction of Ithamar son of Aaron, the priest.

The Merarites

29"Count the Merarites by their clans and families. 30Count all the men from thirty to fifty years of age who come to serve in the work at the Tent of Meeting. 31This is their duty as they perform service at the Tent of Meeting: to carry the frames of the tabernacle, its crossbars, posts and bases, 32as well as the posts of the surrounding courtyard with their bases, tent pegs, ropes, all their equipment and everything related to their use. Assign to each man the specific things he is to carry. 33This is the service of the Merarite clans as they work at the Tent of Meeting under the direction of Ithamar son of Aaron, the priest."

The Numbering of the Levite Clans

34Moses, Aaron and the leaders of the community counted the Kohathites by their clans and families. 35All the men from thirty to fifty years of age who came to serve in the work in the Tent of Meeting, 36counted by clans, were 2,750. 37This was the total of all those in the Kohathite clans who served in the Tent of Meeting. Moses and Aaron counted them according to the LORD's command through Moses.

38The Gershonites were counted by their clans and families. 39All the men from thirty to fifty years of age who came to serve in the work at the Tent of Meeting, 40counted by their clans and families, were 2,630. 41This was the total of those in the Gershonite clans who served at the Tent of Meeting. Moses and Aaron counted them according to the LORD's command.

42The Merarites were counted by their clans and families. 43All the men from thirty to fifty years of age who came to serve in the work at the Tent of Meeting, 44counted by their clans, were 3,200. 45This was the total of those in the Merarite clans. Moses and Aaron counted them according to the LORD's command through Moses.

46So Moses, Aaron and the leaders of Israel counted all the Levites by their clans and families. 47All the men from thirty to fifty years of age who came to do the work of serving and carrying the Tent of Meeting 48numbered 8,580. 49At the LORD's command through Moses, each was assigned his work and told what to carry.

Thus they were counted, as the LORD commanded Moses.

The Purity of the Camp

5 The LORD said to Moses, 2"Command the Israelites to send away from the camp anyone who has an infectious skin disease[a] or a discharge of any kind, or who is ceremonially unclean because of a dead body. 3Send away male and female alike; send them outside the camp so they will not defile their camp, where I dwell among them." 4The Israelites did this; they sent them outside the camp. They did just as the LORD had instructed Moses.

Restitution for Wrongs

5The LORD said to Moses, 6"Say to the Israelites: 'When a man or woman wrongs another in any way[b] and so is unfaithful to the LORD, that person is guilty 7and must confess the sin he has committed. He must make full restitution for his wrong, add one fifth to it and give it all to the person he has wronged. 8But if that person has no close relative to whom restitution can be made for the wrong, the restitution belongs to the LORD and must be given to the priest, along with the ram with which atonement is made for him. 9All the sacred contributions the Israelites bring to a priest will belong to him. 10Each man's sacred gifts are his own, but what he gives to the priest will belong to the priest.' "

[a]2 Traditionally *leprosy;* the Hebrew word was used for various diseases affecting the skin—not necessarily leprosy.
[b]6 Or *woman commits any wrong common to mankind*

The Test for an Unfaithful Wife

11Then the LORD said to Moses, 12"Speak
to the Israelites and say to them: 'If a man's
wife goes astray and is unfaithful to him 13by
sleeping with another man, and this is hidden from her husband and her impurity is
undetected (since there is no witness
against her and she has not been caught in
the act), 14and if feelings of jealousy come
over her husband and he suspects his wife
and she is impure—or if he is jealous and
suspects her even though she is not impure— 15then he is to take his wife to the
priest. He must also take an offering of a
tenth of an ephah[a] of barley flour on her
behalf. He must not pour oil on it or put incense on it, because it is a grain offering for
jealousy, a reminder offering to draw attention to guilt.

16" 'The priest shall bring her and have her
stand before the LORD. 17Then he shall take
some holy water in a clay jar and put some
dust from the tabernacle floor into the water.
18After the priest has had the woman stand
before the LORD, he shall loosen her hair and
place in her hands the reminder offering, the
grain offering for jealousy, while he himself
holds the bitter water that brings a curse.
19Then the priest shall put the woman under
oath and say to her, "If no other man has
slept with you and you have not gone astray
and become impure while married to your
husband, may this bitter water that brings a
curse not harm you. 20But if you have gone
astray while married to your husband and
you have defiled yourself by sleeping with a
man other than your husband"— 21here the
priest is to put the woman under this curse of
the oath—"may the LORD cause your people
to curse and denounce you when he causes
your thigh to waste away and your abdomen
to swell.[b] 22May this water that brings a curse
enter your body so that your abdomen swells
and your thigh wastes away.[c]"

" 'Then the woman is to say, "Amen. So
be it."

23" 'The priest is to write these curses on a
scroll and then wash them off into the bitter
water. 24He shall have the woman drink the
bitter water that brings a curse, and this
water will enter her and cause bitter suffering. 25The priest is to take from her hands the
grain offering for jealousy, wave it before the
LORD and bring it to the altar. 26The priest is
then to take a handful of the grain offering as
a memorial offering and burn it on the altar;
after that, he is to have the woman drink the
water. 27If she has defiled herself and been
unfaithful to her husband, then when she is
made to drink the water that brings a curse, it
will go into her and cause bitter suffering; her
abdomen will swell and her thigh waste
away,[d] and she will become accursed
among her people. 28If, however, the woman
has not defiled herself and is free from impurity, she will be cleared of guilt and will be
able to have children.

29" 'This, then, is the law of jealousy when
a woman goes astray and defiles herself
while married to her husband, 30or when feelings of jealousy come over a man because
he suspects his wife. The priest is to have
her stand before the LORD and is to apply this
entire law to her. 31The husband will be innocent of any wrongdoing, but the woman will
bear the consequences of her sin.' "

The Nazirite

6 The LORD said to Moses, 2"Speak to the
Israelites and say to them: 'If a man or
woman wants to make a special vow, a vow
of separation to the LORD as a Nazirite, 3he
must abstain from wine and other fermented
drink and must not drink vinegar made from
wine or from other fermented drink. He must
not drink grape juice or eat grapes or raisins.
4As long as he is a Nazirite, he must not eat
anything that comes from the grapevine, not
even the seeds or skins.

5" 'During the entire period of his vow of
separation no razor may be used on his
head. He must be holy until the period of his
separation to the LORD is over; he must let the
hair of his head grow long. 6Throughout the
period of his separation to the LORD he must
not go near a dead body. 7Even if his own
father or mother or brother or sister dies, he
must not make himself ceremonially unclean
on account of them, because the symbol of
his separation to God is on his head.
8Throughout the period of his separation he
is consecrated to the LORD.

9" 'If someone dies suddenly in his presence, thus defiling the hair he has dedicated,
he must shave his head on the day of his

[a] *15* That is, probably about 2 quarts (about 2 liters) [b] *21* Or *causes you to have a miscarrying womb and barrenness* [c] *22* Or *body and cause you to be barren and have a miscarrying womb* [d] *27* Or *suffering; she will have barrenness and a miscarrying womb*

cleansing—the seventh day. 10Then on the
eighth day he must bring two doves or two
young pigeons to the priest at the entrance to
the Tent of Meeting. 11The priest is to offer
one as a sin offering and the other as a burnt
offering to make atonement for him because
he sinned by being in the presence of the
dead body. That same day he is to consecrate his head. 12He must dedicate himself to
the LORD for the period of his separation and
must bring a year-old male lamb as a guilt
offering. The previous days do not count,
because he became defiled during his separation.
13" 'Now this is the law for the Nazirite
when the period of his separation is over. He
is to be brought to the entrance to the Tent of
Meeting. 14There he is to present his offerings to the LORD: a year-old male lamb without defect for a burnt offering, a year-old ewe
lamb without defect for a sin offering, a ram
without defect for a fellowship offering,[a] 15to-
gether with their grain offerings and drink
offerings, and a basket of bread made without yeast—cakes made of fine flour mixed
with oil, and wafers spread with oil.
16" 'The priest is to present them before
the LORD and make the sin offering and the
burnt offering. 17He is to present the basket
of unleavened bread and is to sacrifice the
ram as a fellowship offering to the LORD, together with its grain offering and drink offering.
18" 'Then at the entrance to the Tent of
Meeting, the Nazirite must shave off the hair
that he dedicated. He is to take the hair and
put it in the fire that is under the sacrifice of
the fellowship offering.
19" 'After the Nazirite has shaved off the
hair of his dedication, the priest is to place in
his hands a boiled shoulder of the ram, and a
cake and a wafer from the basket, both made
without yeast. 20The priest shall then wave
them before the LORD as a wave offering;
they are holy and belong to the priest, together with the breast that was waved and
the thigh that was presented. After that, the
Nazirite may drink wine.
21" 'This is the law of the Nazirite who vows
his offering to the LORD in accordance with
his separation, in addition to whatever else
he can afford. He must fulfill the vow he
has made, according to the law of the Nazirite.' "

The Priestly Blessing

22The LORD said to Moses, 23"Tell Aaron
and his sons, 'This is how you are to bless
the Israelites. Say to them:

24" ' "The LORD bless you
and keep you;
25the LORD make his face shine upon you
and be gracious to you;
26the LORD turn his face toward you
and give you peace." '

27"So they will put my name on the Israelites, and I will bless them."

Offerings at the Dedication of the Tabernacle

7 When Moses finished setting up the tabernacle, he anointed it and consecrated
it and all its furnishings. He also anointed
and consecrated the altar and all its utensils.
2Then the leaders of Israel, the heads of
families who were the tribal leaders in
charge of those who were counted, made
offerings. 3They brought as their gifts before
the LORD six covered carts and twelve oxen—
an ox from each leader and a cart from every
two. These they presented before the tabernacle.
4The LORD said to Moses, 5"Accept these
from them, that they may be used in the work
at the Tent of Meeting. Give them to the
Levites as each man's work requires."
6So Moses took the carts and oxen and
gave them to the Levites. 7He gave two carts
and four oxen to the Gershonites, as their
work required, 8and he gave four carts and
eight oxen to the Merarites, as their work
required. They were all under the direction of
Ithamar son of Aaron, the priest. 9But Moses
did not give any to the Kohathites, because
they were to carry on their shoulders the holy
things, for which they were responsible.
10When the altar was anointed, the leaders
brought their offerings for its dedication and
presented them before the altar. 11For the
LORD had said to Moses, "Each day one leader is to bring his offering for the dedication of
the altar."

12The one who brought his offering on the
first day was Nahshon son of Amminadab of
the tribe of Judah.
13His offering was one silver plate

[a]14 Traditionally *peace offering*; also in verses 17 and 18

weighing a hundred and thirty shekels,[a]
and one silver sprinkling bowl weighing
seventy shekels,[b] both according to the
sanctuary shekel, each filled with fine
flour mixed with oil as a grain offering;
14one gold dish weighing ten shekels,[c]
filled with incense; 15one young bull, one
ram and one male lamb a year old, for a
burnt offering; 16one male goat for a sin
offering; 17and two oxen, five rams, five
male goats and five male lambs a year
old, to be sacrificed as a fellowship offering.[d] This was the offering of Nahshon son of Amminadab.

18On the second day Nethanel son of Zuar,
the leader of Issachar, brought his offering.
19The offering he brought was one silver
plate weighing a hundred and thirty
shekels, and one silver sprinkling bowl
weighing seventy shekels, both according to the sanctuary shekel, each filled
with fine flour mixed with oil as a grain
offering; 20one gold dish weighing ten
shekels, filled with incense; 21one young
bull, one ram and one male lamb a year
old, for a burnt offering; 22one male goat
for a sin offering; 23and two oxen, five
rams, five male goats and five male
lambs a year old, to be sacrificed as a
fellowship offering. This was the offering
of Nethanel son of Zuar.

24On the third day, Eliab son of Helon, the
leader of the people of Zebulun, brought his
offering.
25His offering was one silver plate
weighing a hundred and thirty shekels,
and one silver sprinkling bowl weighing
seventy shekels, both according to the
sanctuary shekel, each filled with fine
flour mixed with oil as a grain offering;
26one gold dish weighing ten shekels,
filled with incense; 27one young bull, one
ram and one male lamb a year old, for a
burnt offering; 28one male goat for a sin
offering; 29and two oxen, five rams, five
male goats and five male lambs a year
old, to be sacrificed as a fellowship offering. This was the offering of Eliab son
of Helon.

30On the fourth day Elizur son of Shedeur,
the leader of the people of Reuben, brought
his offering.
31His offering was one silver plate
weighing a hundred and thirty shekels,
and one silver sprinkling bowl weighing
seventy shekels, both according to the
sanctuary shekel, each filled with fine
flour mixed with oil as a grain offering;
32one gold dish weighing ten shekels,
filled with incense; 33one young bull, one
ram and one male lamb a year old, for a
burnt offering; 34one male goat for a sin
offering; 35and two oxen, five rams, five
male goats and five male lambs a year
old, to be sacrificed as a fellowship offering. This was the offering of Elizur
son of Shedeur.

36On the fifth day Shelumiel son of Zurishaddai, the leader of the people of Simeon,
brought his offering.
37His offering was one silver plate
weighing a hundred and thirty shekels,
and one silver sprinkling bowl weighing
seventy shekels, both according to the
sanctuary shekel, each filled with fine
flour mixed with oil as a grain offering;
38one gold dish weighing ten shekels,
filled with incense; 39one young bull, one
ram and one male lamb a year old, for a
burnt offering; 40one male goat for a sin
offering; 41and two oxen, five rams, five
male goats and five male lambs a year
old, to be sacrificed as a fellowship offering. This was the offering of Shelumiel son of Zurishaddai.

42On the sixth day Eliasaph son of Deuel, the
leader of the people of Gad, brought his offering.
43His offering was one silver plate
weighing a hundred and thirty shekels,
and one silver sprinkling bowl weighing
seventy shekels, both according to the
sanctuary shekel, each filled with fine
flour mixed with oil as a grain offering;
44one gold dish weighing ten shekels,
filled with incense; 45one young bull, one
ram and one male lamb a year old, for a
burnt offering; 46one male goat for a sin
offering; 47and two oxen, five rams, five
male goats and five male lambs a year
old, to be sacrificed as a fellowship offering. This was the offering of Eliasaph
son of Deuel.

48On the seventh day Elishama son of Am-

[a] *13* That is, about 3 1/4 pounds (about 1.5 kilograms); also elsewhere in this chapter [b] *13* That is, about 1 3/4 pounds (about 0.8 kilogram); also elsewhere in this chapter [c] *14* That is, about 4 ounces (about 110 grams); also elsewhere in this chapter [d] *17* Traditionally *peace offering*; also elsewhere in this chapter

mihud, the leader of the people of Ephraim,
brought his offering.

49 His offering was one silver plate
weighing a hundred and thirty shekels,
and one silver sprinkling bowl weighing
seventy shekels, both according to the
sanctuary shekel, each filled with fine
flour mixed with oil as a grain offering;
50 one gold dish weighing ten shekels,
filled with incense; 51 one young bull, one
ram and one male lamb a year old, for a
burnt offering; 52 one male goat for a sin
offering; 53 and two oxen, five rams, five
male goats and five male lambs a year
old, to be sacrificed as a fellowship offering. This was the offering of Elishama
son of Ammihud.

54 On the eighth day Gamaliel son of Pedahzur, the leader of the people of Manasseh,
brought his offering.

55 His offering was one silver plate
weighing a hundred and thirty shekels,
and one silver sprinkling bowl weighing
seventy shekels, both according to the
sanctuary shekel, each filled with fine
flour mixed with oil as a grain offering;
56 one gold dish weighing ten shekels,
filled with incense; 57 one young bull, one
ram and one male lamb a year old, for a
burnt offering; 58 one male goat for a sin
offering; 59 and two oxen, five rams, five
male goats and five male lambs a year
old, to be sacrificed as a fellowship offering. This was the offering of Gamaliel
son of Pedahzur.

60 On the ninth day Abidan son of Gideoni,
the leader of the people of Benjamin,
brought his offering.

61 His offering was one silver plate
weighing a hundred and thirty shekels,
and one silver sprinkling bowl weighing
seventy shekels, both according to the
sanctuary shekel, each filled with fine
flour mixed with oil as a grain offering;
62 one gold dish weighing ten shekels,
filled with incense; 63 one young bull, one
ram and one male lamb a year old, for a
burnt offering; 64 one male goat for a sin
offering; 65 and two oxen, five rams, five
male goats and five male lambs a year
old, to be sacrificed as a fellowship offering. This was the offering of Abidan
son of Gideoni.

66 On the tenth day Ahiezer son of Ammishaddai, the leader of the people of Dan,
brought his offering.

67 His offering was one silver plate
weighing a hundred and thirty shekels,
and one silver sprinkling bowl weighing
seventy shekels, both according to the
sanctuary shekel, each filled with fine
flour mixed with oil as a grain offering;
68 one gold dish weighing ten shekels,
filled with incense; 69 one young bull, one
ram and one male lamb a year old, for a
burnt offering; 70 one male goat for a sin
offering; 71 and two oxen, five rams, five
male goats and five male lambs a year
old, to be sacrificed as a fellowship offering. This was the offering of Ahiezer
son of Ammishaddai.

72 On the eleventh day Pagiel son of Ocran,
the leader of the people of Asher, brought his
offering.

73 His offering was one silver plate
weighing a hundred and thirty shekels,
and one silver sprinkling bowl weighing
seventy shekels, both according to the
sanctuary shekel, each filled with fine
flour mixed with oil as a grain offering;
74 one gold dish weighing ten shekels,
filled with incense; 75 one young bull, one
ram and one male lamb a year old, for a
burnt offering; 76 one male goat for a sin
offering; 77 and two oxen, five rams, five
male goats and five male lambs a year
old, to be sacrificed as a fellowship offering. This was the offering of Pagiel
son of Ocran.

78 On the twelfth day Ahira son of Enan, the
leader of the people of Naphtali, brought his
offering.

79 His offering was one silver plate
weighing a hundred and thirty shekels,
and one silver sprinkling bowl weighing
seventy shekels, both according to the
sanctuary shekel, each filled with fine
flour mixed with oil as a grain offering;
80 one gold dish weighing ten shekels,
filled with incense; 81 one young bull, one
ram and one male lamb a year old, for a
burnt offering; 82 one male goat for a sin
offering; 83 and two oxen, five rams, five
male goats and five male lambs a year
old, to be sacrificed as a fellowship offering. This was the offering of Ahira son
of Enan.

84 These were the offerings of the Israelite

leaders for the dedication of the altar when it was anointed: twelve silver plates, twelve silver sprinkling bowls and twelve gold dishes. 85Each silver plate weighed a hundred and thirty shekels, and each sprinkling bowl seventy shekels. Altogether, the silver dishes weighed two thousand four hundred shekels,[a] according to the sanctuary shekel. 86The twelve gold dishes filled with incense weighed ten shekels each, according to the sanctuary shekel. Altogether, the gold dishes weighed a hundred and twenty shekels.[b] 87The total number of animals for the burnt offering came to twelve young bulls, twelve rams and twelve male lambs a year old, together with their grain offering. Twelve male goats were used for the sin offering. 88The total number of animals for the sacrifice of the fellowship offering came to twenty-four oxen, sixty rams, sixty male goats and sixty male lambs a year old. These were the offerings for the dedication of the altar after it was anointed.

89When Moses entered the Tent of Meeting to speak with the LORD, he heard the voice speaking to him from between the two cherubim above the atonement cover on the ark of the Testimony. And he spoke with him.

Setting Up the Lamps

8 The LORD said to Moses, 2"Speak to Aaron and say to him, 'When you set up the seven lamps, they are to light the area in front of the lampstand.' "

3Aaron did so; he set up the lamps so that they faced forward on the lampstand, just as the LORD commanded Moses. 4This is how the lampstand was made: It was made of hammered gold—from its base to its blossoms. The lampstand was made exactly like the pattern the LORD had shown Moses.

The Setting Apart of the Levites

5The LORD said to Moses: 6"Take the Levites from among the other Israelites and make them ceremonially clean. 7To purify them, do this: Sprinkle the water of cleansing on them; then have them shave their whole bodies and wash their clothes, and so purify themselves. 8Have them take a young bull with its grain offering of fine flour mixed with oil; then you are to take a second young bull for a sin offering. 9Bring the Levites to the front of the Tent of Meeting and assemble the whole Israelite community. 10You are to bring the Levites before the LORD, and the Israelites are to lay their hands on them. 11Aaron is to present the Levites before the LORD as a wave offering from the Israelites, so that they may be ready to do the work of the LORD.

12"After the Levites lay their hands on the heads of the bulls, use the one for a sin offering to the LORD and the other for a burnt offering, to make atonement for the Levites. 13Have the Levites stand in front of Aaron and his sons and then present them as a wave offering to the LORD. 14In this way you are to set the Levites apart from the other Israelites, and the Levites will be mine.

15"After you have purified the Levites and presented them as a wave offering, they are to come to do their work at the Tent of Meeting. 16They are the Israelites who are to be given wholly to me. I have taken them as my own in place of the firstborn, the first male offspring from every Israelite woman. 17Every firstborn male in Israel, whether man or animal, is mine. When I struck down all the firstborn in Egypt, I set them apart for myself. 18And I have taken the Levites in place of all the firstborn sons in Israel. 19Of all the Israelites, I have given the Levites as gifts to Aaron and his sons to do the work at the Tent of Meeting on behalf of the Israelites and to make atonement for them so that no plague will strike the Israelites when they go near the sanctuary."

20Moses, Aaron and the whole Israelite community did with the Levites just as the LORD commanded Moses. 21The Levites purified themselves and washed their clothes. Then Aaron presented them as a wave offering before the LORD and made atonement for them to purify them. 22After that, the Levites came to do their work at the Tent of Meeting under the supervision of Aaron and his sons. They did with the Levites just as the LORD commanded Moses.

23The LORD said to Moses, 24"This applies to the Levites: Men twenty-five years old or more shall come to take part in the work at the Tent of Meeting, 25but at the age of fifty, they must retire from their regular service and work no longer. 26They may assist their brothers in performing their duties at the Tent of Meeting, but they themselves must not do the work. This, then, is how you are to assign the responsibilities of the Levites."

[a]*85* That is, about 60 pounds (about 28 kilograms) [b]*86* That is, about 3 pounds (about 1.4 kilograms)

The Passover

9 The LORD spoke to Moses in the Desert of Sinai in the first month of the second year after they came out of Egypt. He said, 2"Have the Israelites celebrate the Passover at the appointed time. 3Celebrate it at the appointed time, at twilight on the fourteenth day of this month, in accordance with all its rules and regulations."

4So Moses told the Israelites to celebrate the Passover, 5and they did so in the Desert of Sinai at twilight on the fourteenth day of the first month. The Israelites did everything just as the LORD commanded Moses.

6But some of them could not celebrate the Passover on that day because they were ceremonially unclean on account of a dead body. So they came to Moses and Aaron that same day 7and said to Moses, "We have become unclean because of a dead body, but why should we be kept from presenting the LORD's offering with the other Israelites at the appointed time?"

8Moses answered them, "Wait until I find out what the LORD commands concerning you."

9Then the LORD said to Moses, 10"Tell the Israelites: 'When any of you or your descendants are unclean because of a dead body or are away on a journey, they may still celebrate the LORD's Passover. 11They are to celebrate it on the fourteenth day of the second month at twilight. They are to eat the lamb, together with unleavened bread and bitter herbs. 12They must not leave any of it till morning or break any of its bones. When they celebrate the Passover, they must follow all the regulations. 13But if a man who is ceremonially clean and not on a journey fails to celebrate the Passover, that person must be cut off from his people because he did not present the LORD's offering at the appointed time. That man will bear the consequences of his sin.

14" 'An alien living among you who wants to celebrate the LORD's Passover must do so in accordance with its rules and regulations. You must have the same regulations for the alien and the native-born.' "

The Cloud Above the Tabernacle

15On the day the tabernacle, the Tent of the Testimony, was set up, the cloud covered it. From evening till morning the cloud above the tabernacle looked like fire. 16That is how it continued to be; the cloud covered it, and at night it looked like fire. 17Whenever the cloud lifted from above the Tent, the Israelites set out; wherever the cloud settled, the Israelites encamped. 18At the LORD's command the Israelites set out, and at his command they encamped. As long as the cloud stayed over the tabernacle, they remained in camp. 19When the cloud remained over the tabernacle a long time, the Israelites obeyed the LORD's order and did not set out. 20Sometimes the cloud was over the tabernacle only a few days; at the LORD's command they would encamp, and then at his command they would set out. 21Sometimes the cloud stayed only from evening till morning, and when it lifted in the morning, they set out. Whether by day or by night, whenever the cloud lifted, they set out. 22Whether the cloud stayed over the tabernacle for two days or a month or a year, the Israelites would remain in camp and not set out; but when it lifted, they would set out. 23At the LORD's command they encamped, and at the LORD's command they set out. They obeyed the LORD's order, in accordance with his command through Moses.

The Silver Trumpets

10 The LORD said to Moses: 2"Make two trumpets of hammered silver, and use them for calling the community together and for having the camps set out. 3When both are sounded, the whole community is to assemble before you at the entrance to the Tent of Meeting. 4If only one is sounded, the leaders—the heads of the clans of Israel—are to assemble before you. 5When a trumpet blast is sounded, the tribes camping on the east are to set out. 6At the sounding of a second blast, the camps on the south are to set out. The blast will be the signal for setting out. 7To gather the assembly, blow the trumpets, but not with the same signal.

8"The sons of Aaron, the priests, are to blow the trumpets. This is to be a lasting ordinance for you and the generations to come. 9When you go into battle in your own land against an enemy who is oppressing you, sound a blast on the trumpets. Then you will be remembered by the LORD your God and rescued from your enemies. 10Also at your times of rejoicing—your appointed feasts and New Moon festivals—you are to sound the trumpets over your burnt offerings

and fellowship offerings,[a] and they will be a
memorial for you before your God. I am the
LORD your God."

The Israelites Leave Sinai

11On the twentieth day of the second
month of the second year, the cloud lifted
from above the tabernacle of the Testimony.
12Then the Israelites set out from the Desert
of Sinai and traveled from place to place until
the cloud came to rest in the Desert of Paran.
13They set out, this first time, at the LORD's
command through Moses.

14The divisions of the camp of Judah went
first, under their standard. Nahshon son of
Amminadab was in command. 15Nethanel
son of Zuar was over the division of the tribe
of Issachar, 16and Eliab son of Helon was
over the division of the tribe of Zebulun.
17Then the tabernacle was taken down, and
the Gershonites and Merarites, who carried
it, set out.

18The divisions of the camp of Reuben
went next, under their standard. Elizur son of
Shedeur was in command. 19Shelumiel son
of Zurishaddai was over the division of the
tribe of Simeon, 20and Eliasaph son of Deuel
was over the division of the tribe of Gad.
21Then the Kohathites set out, carrying the
holy things. The tabernacle was to be set up
before they arrived.

22The divisions of the camp of Ephraim
went next, under their standard. Elishama
son of Ammihud was in command. 23Gamali-
el son of Pedahzur was over the division of
the tribe of Manasseh, 24and Abidan son of
Gideoni was over the division of the tribe of
Benjamin.

25Finally, as the rear guard for all the units,
the divisions of the camp of Dan set out,
under their standard. Ahiezer son of Ammishaddai was in command. 26Pagiel son of
Ocran was over the division of the tribe of
Asher, 27and Ahira son of Enan was over the
division of the tribe of Naphtali. 28This was
the order of march for the Israelite divisions
as they set out.

29Now Moses said to Hobab son of Reuel
the Midianite, Moses' father-in-law, "We are
setting out for the place about which the LORD
said, 'I will give it to you.' Come with us and
we will treat you well, for the LORD has promised good things to Israel."

30He answered, "No, I will not go; I am
going back to my own land and my own
people."

31But Moses said, "Please do not leave us.
You know where we should camp in the
desert, and you can be our eyes. 32If you
come with us, we will share with you whatever good things the LORD gives us."

33So they set out from the mountain of the
LORD and traveled for three days. The ark of
the covenant of the LORD went before them
during those three days to find them a place
to rest. 34The cloud of the LORD was over
them by day when they set out from the
camp.

35Whenever the ark set out, Moses said,

"Rise up, O LORD!
May your enemies be scattered;
may your foes flee before you."

36Whenever it came to rest, he said,

"Return, O LORD,
to the countless thousands of Israel."

Fire From the LORD

11 Now the people complained about
their hardships in the hearing of the
LORD, and when he heard them his anger
was aroused. Then fire from the LORD burned
among them and consumed some of the outskirts of the camp. 2When the people cried
out to Moses, he prayed to the LORD and the
fire died down. 3So that place was called
Taberah,[b] because fire from the LORD had
burned among them.

Quail From the LORD

4The rabble with them began to crave
other food, and again the Israelites started
wailing and said, "If only we had meat to eat!
5We remember the fish we ate in Egypt at no
cost—also the cucumbers, melons, leeks,
onions and garlic. 6But now we have lost our
appetite; we never see anything but this
manna!"

7The manna was like coriander seed and
looked like resin. 8The people went around
gathering it, and then ground it in a handmill
or crushed it in a mortar. They cooked it in a
pot or made it into cakes. And it tasted like
something made with olive oil. 9When the
dew settled on the camp at night, the manna
also came down.

10Moses heard the people of every family

[a] *10* Traditionally *peace offerings* [b] *3* *Taberah* means *burning.*

wailing, each at the entrance to his tent. The
LORD became exceedingly angry, and Moses
was troubled. 11He asked the LORD, "Why
have you brought this trouble on your servant? What have I done to displease you that
you put the burden of all these people on
me? 12Did I conceive all these people? Did I
give them birth? Why do you tell me to carry
them in my arms, as a nurse carries an infant, to the land you promised on oath to their
forefathers? 13Where can I get meat for all
these people? They keep wailing to me,
'Give us meat to eat!' 14I cannot carry all
these people by myself; the burden is too
heavy for me. 15If this is how you are going to
treat me, put me to death right now—if I have
found favor in your eyes—and do not let me
face my own ruin."

16The LORD said to Moses: "Bring me seventy of Israel's elders who are known to you
as leaders and officials among the people.
Have them come to the Tent of Meeting, that
they may stand there with you. 17I will come
down and speak with you there, and I will
take of the Spirit that is on you and put the
Spirit on them. They will help you carry the
burden of the people so that you will not have
to carry it alone.

18"Tell the people: 'Consecrate yourselves
in preparation for tomorrow, when you will
eat meat. The LORD heard you when you
wailed, "If only we had meat to eat! We were
better off in Egypt!" Now the LORD will give
you meat, and you will eat it. 19You will not
eat it for just one day, or two days, or five, ten
or twenty days, 20but for a whole month—
until it comes out of your nostrils and you
loathe it—because you have rejected the
LORD, who is among you, and have wailed
before him, saying, "Why did we ever leave
Egypt?"'"

21But Moses said, "Here I am among six
hundred thousand men on foot, and you say,
'I will give them meat to eat for a whole
month!' 22Would they have enough if flocks
and herds were slaughtered for them?
Would they have enough if all the fish in the
sea were caught for them?"

23The LORD answered Moses, "Is the
LORD's arm too short? You will now see
whether or not what I say will come true for
you."

24So Moses went out and told the people
what the LORD had said. He brought together
seventy of their elders and had them stand
around the Tent. 25Then the LORD came
down in the cloud and spoke with him, and
he took of the Spirit that was on him and put
the Spirit on the seventy elders. When the
Spirit rested on them, they prophesied, but
they did not do so again.[a]

26However, two men, whose names were
Eldad and Medad, had remained in the
camp. They were listed among the elders,
but did not go out to the Tent. Yet the Spirit
also rested on them, and they prophesied in
the camp. 27A young man ran and told
Moses, "Eldad and Medad are prophesying
in the camp."

28Joshua son of Nun, who had been
Moses' aide since youth, spoke up and said,
"Moses, my lord, stop them!"

29But Moses replied, "Are you jealous for
my sake? I wish that all the LORD's people
were prophets and that the LORD would put
his Spirit on them!" 30Then Moses and the
elders of Israel returned to the camp.

31Now a wind went out from the LORD and
drove quail in from the sea. It brought them[b]
down all around the camp to about three
feet[c] above the ground, as far as a day's
walk in any direction. 32All that day and night
and all the next day the people went out and
gathered quail. No one gathered less than
ten homers.[d] Then they spread them out all
around the camp. 33But while the meat was
still between their teeth and before it could
be consumed, the anger of the LORD burned
against the people, and he struck them with
a severe plague. 34Therefore the place was
named Kibroth Hattaavah,[e] because there
they buried the people who had craved other
food.

35From Kibroth Hattaavah the people traveled to Hazeroth and stayed there.

Miriam and Aaron Oppose Moses

12 Miriam and Aaron began to talk
against Moses because of his Cushite wife, for he had married a Cushite. 2"Has
the LORD spoken only through Moses?" they
asked. "Hasn't he also spoken through us?"
And the LORD heard this.

3(Now Moses was a very humble man,
more humble than anyone else on the face of
the earth.)

4At once the LORD said to Moses, Aaron
and Miriam, "Come out to the Tent of Meet-

[a]25 Or *prophesied and continued to do so* [b]31 Or *They flew* [c]31 Hebrew *two cubits* (about 1 meter)
[d]32 That is, probably about 60 bushels (about 2.2 kiloliters) [e]34 *Kibroth Hattaavah* means *graves of craving.*

ing, all three of you." So the three of them
came out. 5Then the LORD came down in a
pillar of cloud; he stood at the entrance to the
Tent and summoned Aaron and Miriam.
When both of them stepped forward, 6he
said, "Listen to my words:

"When a prophet of the LORD is among
you,
I reveal myself to him in visions,
I speak to him in dreams.
7But this is not true of my servant Moses;
he is faithful in all my house.
8With him I speak face to face,
clearly and not in riddles;
he sees the form of the LORD.
Why then were you not afraid
to speak against my servant Moses?"

9The anger of the LORD burned against
them, and he left them.
10When the cloud lifted from above the
Tent, there stood Miriam—leprous,[a] like
snow. Aaron turned toward her and saw that
she had leprosy; 11and he said to Moses,
"Please, my lord, do not hold against us the
sin we have so foolishly committed. 12Do not
let her be like a stillborn infant coming from
its mother's womb with its flesh half eaten
away."
13So Moses cried out to the LORD, "O God,
please heal her!"
14The LORD replied to Moses, "If her father
had spit in her face, would she not have been
in disgrace for seven days? Confine her outside the camp for seven days; after that she
can be brought back." 15So Miriam was confined outside the camp for seven days, and
the people did not move on till she was
brought back.
16After that, the people left Hazeroth and
encamped in the Desert of Paran.

Exploring Canaan

13 The LORD said to Moses, 2"Send
some men to explore the land of Canaan, which I am giving to the Israelites.
From each ancestral tribe send one of its
leaders."
3So at the LORD's command Moses sent
them out from the Desert of Paran. All of
them were leaders of the Israelites. 4These
are their names:

from the tribe of Reuben, Shammua
son of Zaccur;
5from the tribe of Simeon, Shaphat son
of Hori;
6from the tribe of Judah, Caleb son of
Jephunneh;
7from the tribe of Issachar, Igal son of
Joseph;
8from the tribe of Ephraim, Hoshea son
of Nun;
9from the tribe of Benjamin, Palti son of
Raphu;
10from the tribe of Zebulun, Gaddiel son
of Sodi;
11from the tribe of Manasseh (a tribe of
Joseph), Gaddi son of Susi;
12from the tribe of Dan, Ammiel son of
Gemalli;
13from the tribe of Asher, Sethur son of
Michael;
14from the tribe of Naphtali, Nahbi son of
Vophsi;
15from the tribe of Gad, Geuel son of
Maki.

16These are the names of the men Moses
sent to explore the land. (Moses gave Hoshea son of Nun the name Joshua.)
17When Moses sent them to explore Canaan, he said, "Go up through the Negev
and on into the hill country. 18See what the
land is like and whether the people who live
there are strong or weak, few or many.
19What kind of land do they live in? Is it good
or bad? What kind of towns do they live in?
Are they unwalled or fortified? 20How is the
soil? Is it fertile or poor? Are there trees on it
or not? Do your best to bring back some of
the fruit of the land." (It was the season for
the first ripe grapes.)
21So they went up and explored the land
from the Desert of Zin as far as Rehob,
toward Lebo[b] Hamath. 22They went up
through the Negev and came to Hebron,
where Ahiman, Sheshai and Talmai, the descendants of Anak, lived. (Hebron had been
built seven years before Zoan in Egypt.)
23When they reached the Valley of Eshcol,[c]
they cut off a branch bearing a single cluster
of grapes. Two of them carried it on a pole
between them, along with some pomegranates and figs. 24That place was called the
Valley of Eshcol because of the cluster of
grapes the Israelites cut off there. 25At the
end of forty days they returned from exploring the land.

[a] *10* The Hebrew word was used for various diseases affecting the skin—not necessarily leprosy. [b] *21* Or *toward the entrance to* [c] *23* *Eshcol* means *cluster;* also in verse 24.

Report on the Exploration

26They came back to Moses and Aaron
and the whole Israelite community at Kadesh
in the Desert of Paran. There they reported
to them and to the whole assembly and
showed them the fruit of the land. 27They
gave Moses this account: "We went into the
land to which you sent us, and it does flow
with milk and honey! Here is its fruit. 28But
the people who live there are powerful, and
the cities are fortified and very large. We
even saw descendants of Anak there. 29The
Amalekites live in the Negev; the Hittites,
Jebusites and Amorites live in the hill country; and the Canaanites live near the sea and
along the Jordan."
30Then Caleb silenced the people before
Moses and said, "We should go up and take
possession of the land, for we can certainly
do it."
31But the men who had gone up with him
said, "We can't attack those people; they are
stronger than we are." 32And they spread
among the Israelites a bad report about the
land they had explored. They said, "The land
we explored devours those living in it. All the
people we saw there are of great size. 33We
saw the Nephilim there (the descendants of
Anak come from the Nephilim). We seemed
like grasshoppers in our own eyes, and we
looked the same to them."

The People Rebel

14 That night all the people of the community raised their voices and wept
aloud. 2All the Israelites grumbled against
Moses and Aaron, and the whole assembly
said to them, "If only we had died in Egypt!
Or in this desert! 3Why is the LORD bringing us
to this land only to let us fall by the sword?
Our wives and children will be taken as plunder. Wouldn't it be better for us to go back to
Egypt?" 4And they said to each other, "We
should choose a leader and go back to
Egypt."
5Then Moses and Aaron fell facedown in
front of the whole Israelite assembly gathered there. 6Joshua son of Nun and Caleb
son of Jephunneh, who were among those
who had explored the land, tore their clothes
7and said to the entire Israelite assembly,
"The land we passed through and explored
is exceedingly good. 8If the LORD is pleased
with us, he will lead us into that land, a land
flowing with milk and honey, and will give it to
us. 9Only do not rebel against the LORD. And
do not be afraid of the people of the land,
because we will swallow them up. Their protection is gone, but the LORD is with us. Do not
be afraid of them."
10But the whole assembly talked about
stoning them. Then the glory of the LORD appeared at the Tent of Meeting to all the Israelites. 11The LORD said to Moses, "How long
will these people treat me with contempt?
How long will they refuse to believe in me, in
spite of all the miraculous signs I have performed among them? 12I will strike them
down with a plague and destroy them, but I
will make you into a nation greater and
stronger than they."
13Moses said to the LORD, "Then the Egyptians will hear about it! By your power you
brought these people up from among them.
14And they will tell the inhabitants of this land
about it. They have already heard that you, O
LORD, are with these people and that you, O
LORD, have been seen face to face, that your
cloud stays over them, and that you go before them in a pillar of cloud by day and a
pillar of fire by night. 15If you put these people
to death all at one time, the nations who have
heard this report about you will say, 16'The
LORD was not able to bring these people into
the land he promised them on oath; so he
slaughtered them in the desert.'
17"Now may the Lord's strength be displayed, just as you have declared: 18'The
LORD is slow to anger, abounding in love and
forgiving sin and rebellion. Yet he does not
leave the guilty unpunished; he punishes the
children for the sin of the fathers to the third
and fourth generation.' 19In accordance with
your great love, forgive the sin of these
people, just as you have pardoned them
from the time they left Egypt until now."
20The LORD replied, "I have forgiven them,
as you asked. 21Nevertheless, as surely as I
live and as surely as the glory of the LORD fills
the whole earth, 22not one of the men who
saw my glory and the miraculous signs I performed in Egypt and in the desert but who
disobeyed me and tested me ten times—
23not one of them will ever see the land I
promised on oath to their forefathers. No one
who has treated me with contempt will ever
see it. 24But because my servant Caleb has a
different spirit and follows me wholeheartedly, I will bring him into the land he went to,
and his descendants will inherit it. 25Since
the Amalekites and Canaanites are living in
the valleys, turn back tomorrow and set out

toward the desert along the route to the Red
Sea.[a]"
26The LORD said to Moses and Aaron:
27"How long will this wicked community
grumble against me? I have heard the complaints of these grumbling Israelites. 28So tell
them, 'As surely as I live, declares the LORD,
I will do to you the very things I heard you
say: 29In this desert your bodies will fall—
every one of you twenty years old or more
who was counted in the census and who has
grumbled against me. 30Not one of you will
enter the land I swore with uplifted hand to
make your home, except Caleb son of Jephunneh and Joshua son of Nun. 31As for
your children that you said would be taken as
plunder, I will bring them in to enjoy the land
you have rejected. 32But you—your bodies
will fall in this desert. 33Your children will be
shepherds here for forty years, suffering for
your unfaithfulness, until the last of your bodies lies in the desert. 34For forty years—one
year for each of the forty days you explored
the land—you will suffer for your sins and
know what it is like to have me against you.'
35I, the LORD, have spoken, and I will surely
do these things to this whole wicked community, which has banded together against me.
They will meet their end in this desert; here
they will die."
36So the men Moses had sent to explore
the land, who returned and made the whole
community grumble against him by spreading a bad report about it— 37these men responsible for spreading the bad report about
the land were struck down and died of a
plague before the LORD. 38Of the men who
went to explore the land, only Joshua son of
Nun and Caleb son of Jephunneh survived.
39When Moses reported this to all the Israelites, they mourned bitterly. 40Early the next
morning they went up toward the high hill
country. "We have sinned," they said. "We
will go up to the place the LORD promised."
41But Moses said, "Why are you disobeying the LORD's command? This will not
succeed! 42Do not go up, because the LORD is
not with you. You will be defeated by your
enemies, 43for the Amalekites and Canaanites will face you there. Because you have
turned away from the LORD, he will not be with
you and you will fall by the sword."
44Nevertheless, in their presumption they
went up toward the high hill country, though
neither Moses nor the ark of the LORD's covenant moved from the camp. 45Then the
Amalekites and Canaanites who lived in that
hill country came down and attacked them
and beat them down all the way to Hormah.

Supplementary Offerings

15 The LORD said to Moses, 2"Speak to
the Israelites and say to them: 'After
you enter the land I am giving you as a home
3and you present to the LORD offerings made
by fire, from the herd or the flock, as an
aroma pleasing to the LORD—whether burnt
offerings or sacrifices, for special vows or
freewill offerings or festival offerings— 4then
the one who brings his offering shall present
to the LORD a grain offering of a tenth of an
ephah[b] of fine flour mixed with a quarter of a
hin[c] of oil. 5With each lamb for the burnt
offering or the sacrifice, prepare a quarter of
a hin of wine as a drink offering.
6" 'With a ram prepare a grain offering of
two-tenths of an ephah[d] of fine flour mixed
with a third of a hin[e] of oil, 7and a third of a hin
of wine as a drink offering. Offer it as an
aroma pleasing to the LORD.
8" 'When you prepare a young bull as a
burnt offering or sacrifice, for a special vow
or a fellowship offering[f] to the LORD, 9bring
with the bull a grain offering of three-tenths of
an ephah[g] of fine flour mixed with half a hin[h]
of oil. 10Also bring half a hin of wine as a drink
offering. It will be an offering made by fire, an
aroma pleasing to the LORD. 11Each bull or
ram, each lamb or young goat, is to be prepared in this manner. 12Do this for each one,
for as many as you prepare.
13" 'Everyone who is native-born must do
these things in this way when he brings an
offering made by fire as an aroma pleasing to
the LORD. 14For the generations to come,
whenever an alien or anyone else living
among you presents an offering made by fire
as an aroma pleasing to the LORD, he must do
exactly as you do. 15The community is to
have the same rules for you and for the alien
living among you; this is a lasting ordinance
for the generations to come. You and the
alien shall be the same before the LORD:
16The same laws and regulations will apply

[a]25 Hebrew *Yam Suph;* that is, Sea of Reeds [b]4 That is, probably about 2 quarts (about 2 liters) [c]4 That is, probably about 1 quart (about 1 liter); also in verse 5 [d]6 That is, probably about 4 quarts (about 4.5 liters) [e]6 That is, probably about 1 1/4 quarts (about 1.2 liters); also in verse 7 [f]8 Traditionally *peace offering* [g]9 That is, probably about 6 quarts (about 6.5 liters) [h]9 That is, probably about 2 quarts (about 2 liters); also in verse 10

both to you and to the alien living among
you.' "

17The LORD said to Moses, 18"Speak to the
Israelites and say to them: 'When you enter
the land to which I am taking you 19and you
eat the food of the land, present a portion as
an offering to the LORD. 20Present a cake from
the first of your ground meal and present it as
an offering from the threshing floor.
21Throughout the generations to come you
are to give this offering to the LORD from the
first of your ground meal.

Offerings for Unintentional Sins

22" 'Now if you unintentionally fail to keep
any of these commands the LORD gave
Moses— 23any of the LORD's commands to
you through him, from the day the LORD gave
them and continuing through the generations to come— 24and if this is done unintentionally without the community being aware
of it, then the whole community is to offer a
young bull for a burnt offering as an aroma
pleasing to the LORD, along with its prescribed grain offering and drink offering, and
a male goat for a sin offering. 25The priest is
to make atonement for the whole Israelite
community, and they will be forgiven, for it
was not intentional and they have brought to
the LORD for their wrong an offering made by
fire and a sin offering. 26The whole Israelite
community and the aliens living among them
will be forgiven, because all the people were
involved in the unintentional wrong.

27" 'But if just one person sins unintentionally, he must bring a year-old female goat for
a sin offering. 28The priest is to make atonement before the LORD for the one who erred
by sinning unintentionally, and when atonement has been made for him, he will be forgiven. 29One and the same law applies to
everyone who sins unintentionally, whether
he is a native-born Israelite or an alien.

30" 'But anyone who sins defiantly,
whether native-born or alien, blasphemes
the LORD, and that person must be cut off
from his people. 31Because he has despised
the LORD's word and broken his commands,
that person must surely be cut off; his guilt
remains on him.' "

The Sabbath-Breaker Put to Death

32While the Israelites were in the desert, a
man was found gathering wood on the Sabbath day. 33Those who found him gathering
wood brought him to Moses and Aaron and
the whole assembly, 34and they kept him in
custody, because it was not clear what
should be done to him. 35Then the LORD said
to Moses, "The man must die. The whole
assembly must stone him outside the camp."
36So the assembly took him outside the
camp and stoned him to death, as the LORD
commanded Moses.

Tassels on Garments

37The LORD said to Moses, 38"Speak to the
Israelites and say to them: 'Throughout the
generations to come you are to make tassels
on the corners of your garments, with a blue
cord on each tassel. 39You will have these
tassels to look at and so you will remember
all the commands of the LORD, that you may
obey them and not prostitute yourselves by
going after the lusts of your own hearts and
eyes. 40Then you will remember to obey all
my commands and will be consecrated to
your God. 41I am the LORD your God, who
brought you out of Egypt to be your God. I
am the LORD your God.' "

Korah, Dathan and Abiram

16 Korah son of Izhar, the son of
Kohath, the son of Levi, and certain
Reubenites—Dathan and Abiram, sons of
Eliab, and On son of Peleth—became insolent[a] 2and rose up against Moses. With them
were 250 Israelite men, well-known community leaders who had been appointed members of the council. 3They came as a group to
oppose Moses and Aaron and said to them,
"You have gone too far! The whole community is holy, every one of them, and the LORD
is with them. Why then do you set yourselves
above the LORD's assembly?"

4When Moses heard this, he fell facedown.
5Then he said to Korah and all his followers:
"In the morning the LORD will show who belongs to him and who is holy, and he will
have that person come near him. The man
he chooses he will cause to come near him.
6You, Korah, and all your followers are to do
this: Take censers 7and tomorrow put fire
and incense in them before the LORD. The
man the LORD chooses will be the one who is
holy. You Levites have gone too far!"

8Moses also said to Korah, "Now listen,
you Levites! 9Isn't it enough for you that the
God of Israel has separated you from the
rest of the Israelite community and brought

[a]1 Or *Peleth—took* ⌊*men*⌋

you near himself to do the work at the LORD's tabernacle and to stand before the community and minister to them? [10]He has brought you and all your fellow Levites near himself, but now you are trying to get the priesthood too. [11]It is against the LORD that you and all your followers have banded together. Who is Aaron that you should grumble against him?"

[12]Then Moses summoned Dathan and Abiram, the sons of Eliab. But they said, "We will not come! [13]Isn't it enough that you have brought us up out of a land flowing with milk and honey to kill us in the desert? And now you also want to lord it over us? [14]Moreover, you haven't brought us into a land flowing with milk and honey or given us an inheritance of fields and vineyards. Will you gouge out the eyes of[a] these men? No, we will not come!"

[15]Then Moses became very angry and said to the LORD, "Do not accept their offering. I have not taken so much as a donkey from them, nor have I wronged any of them."

[16]Moses said to Korah, "You and all your followers are to appear before the LORD tomorrow—you and they and Aaron. [17]Each man is to take his censer and put incense in it—250 censers in all—and present it before the LORD. You and Aaron are to present your censers also." [18]So each man took his censer, put fire and incense in it, and stood with Moses and Aaron at the entrance to the Tent of Meeting. [19]When Korah had gathered all his followers in opposition to them at the entrance to the Tent of Meeting, the glory of the LORD appeared to the entire assembly. [20]The LORD said to Moses and Aaron, [21]"Separate yourselves from this assembly so I can put an end to them at once."

[22]But Moses and Aaron fell facedown and cried out, "O God, God of the spirits of all mankind, will you be angry with the entire assembly when only one man sins?"

[23]Then the LORD said to Moses, [24]"Say to the assembly, 'Move away from the tents of Korah, Dathan and Abiram.'"

[25]Moses got up and went to Dathan and Abiram, and the elders of Israel followed him. [26]He warned the assembly, "Move back from the tents of these wicked men! Do not touch anything belonging to them, or you will be swept away because of all their sins." [27]So they moved away from the tents of Korah, Dathan and Abiram. Dathan and Abiram had come out and were standing with their wives, children and little ones at the entrances to their tents.

[28]Then Moses said, "This is how you will know that the LORD has sent me to do all these things and that it was not my idea: [29]If these men die a natural death and experience only what usually happens to men, then the LORD has not sent me. [30]But if the LORD brings about something totally new, and the earth opens its mouth and swallows them, with everything that belongs to them, and they go down alive into the grave,[b] then you will know that these men have treated the LORD with contempt."

[31]As soon as he finished saying all this, the ground under them split apart [32]and the earth opened its mouth and swallowed them, with their households and all Korah's men and all their possessions. [33]They went down alive into the grave, with everything they owned; the earth closed over them, and they perished and were gone from the community. [34]At their cries, all the Israelites around them fled, shouting, "The earth is going to swallow us too!"

[35]And fire came out from the LORD and consumed the 250 men who were offering the incense.

[36]The LORD said to Moses, [37]"Tell Eleazar son of Aaron, the priest, to take the censers out of the smoldering remains and scatter the coals some distance away, for the censers are holy— [38]the censers of the men who sinned at the cost of their lives. Hammer the censers into sheets to overlay the altar, for they were presented before the LORD and have become holy. Let them be a sign to the Israelites."

[39]So Eleazar the priest collected the bronze censers brought by those who had been burned up, and he had them hammered out to overlay the altar, [40]as the LORD directed him through Moses. This was to remind the Israelites that no one except a descendant of Aaron should come to burn incense before the LORD, or he would become like Korah and his followers.

[41]The next day the whole Israelite community grumbled against Moses and Aaron. "You have killed the LORD's people," they said.

[42]But when the assembly gathered in opposition to Moses and Aaron and turned toward the Tent of Meeting, suddenly the

[a]14 Or *you make slaves of;* or *you deceive* [b]30 Hebrew *Sheol*; also in verse 33

cloud covered it and the glory of the LORD appeared. 43Then Moses and Aaron went to the front of the Tent of Meeting, 44and the LORD said to Moses, 45"Get away from this assembly so I can put an end to them at once." And they fell facedown.

46Then Moses said to Aaron, "Take your censer and put incense in it, along with fire from the altar, and hurry to the assembly to make atonement for them. Wrath has come out from the LORD; the plague has started." 47So Aaron did as Moses said, and ran into the midst of the assembly. The plague had already started among the people, but Aaron offered the incense and made atonement for them. 48He stood between the living and the dead, and the plague stopped. 49But 14,700 people died from the plague, in addition to those who had died because of Korah. 50Then Aaron returned to Moses at the entrance to the Tent of Meeting, for the plague had stopped.

The Budding of Aaron's Staff

17 The LORD said to Moses, 2"Speak to the Israelites and get twelve staffs from them, one from the leader of each of their ancestral tribes. Write the name of each man on his staff. 3On the staff of Levi write Aaron's name, for there must be one staff for the head of each ancestral tribe. 4Place them in the Tent of Meeting in front of the Testimony, where I meet with you. 5The staff belonging to the man I choose will sprout, and I will rid myself of this constant grumbling against you by the Israelites."

6So Moses spoke to the Israelites, and their leaders gave him twelve staffs, one for the leader of each of their ancestral tribes, and Aaron's staff was among them. 7Moses placed the staffs before the LORD in the Tent of the Testimony.

8The next day Moses entered the Tent of the Testimony and saw that Aaron's staff, which represented the house of Levi, had not only sprouted but had budded, blossomed and produced almonds. 9Then Moses brought out all the staffs from the LORD's presence to all the Israelites. They looked at them, and each man took his own staff.

10The LORD said to Moses, "Put back Aaron's staff in front of the Testimony, to be kept as a sign to the rebellious. This will put an end to their grumbling against me, so that they will not die." 11Moses did just as the LORD commanded him.

12The Israelites said to Moses, "We will die! We are lost, we are all lost! 13Anyone who even comes near the tabernacle of the LORD will die. Are we all going to die?"

Duties of Priests and Levites

18 The LORD said to Aaron, "You, your sons and your father's family are to bear the responsibility for offenses against the sanctuary, and you and your sons alone are to bear the responsibility for offenses against the priesthood. 2Bring your fellow Levites from your ancestral tribe to join you and assist you when you and your sons minister before the Tent of the Testimony. 3They are to be responsible to you and are to perform all the duties of the Tent, but they must not go near the furnishings of the sanctuary or the altar, or both they and you will die. 4They are to join you and be responsible for the care of the Tent of Meeting—all the work at the Tent—and no one else may come near where you are.

5"You are to be responsible for the care of the sanctuary and the altar, so that wrath will not fall on the Israelites again. 6I myself have selected your fellow Levites from among the Israelites as a gift to you, dedicated to the LORD to do the work at the Tent of Meeting. 7But only you and your sons may serve as priests in connection with everything at the altar and inside the curtain. I am giving you the service of the priesthood as a gift. Anyone else who comes near the sanctuary must be put to death."

Offerings for Priests and Levites

8Then the LORD said to Aaron, "I myself have put you in charge of the offerings presented to me; all the holy offerings the Israelites give me I give to you and your sons as your portion and regular share. 9You are to have the part of the most holy offerings that is kept from the fire. From all the gifts they bring me as most holy offerings, whether grain or sin or guilt offerings, that part belongs to you and your sons. 10Eat it as something most holy; every male shall eat it. You must regard it as holy.

11"This also is yours: whatever is set aside from the gifts of all the wave offerings of the Israelites. I give this to you and your sons and daughters as your regular share. Everyone in your household who is ceremonially clean may eat it.

12"I give you all the finest olive oil and all the finest new wine and grain they give the LORD as the firstfruits of their harvest. 13All the land's firstfruits that they bring to the LORD will be yours. Everyone in your household who is ceremonially clean may eat it.

14"Everything in Israel that is devoted[a] to the LORD is yours. 15The first offspring of every womb, both man and animal, that is offered to the LORD is yours. But you must redeem every firstborn son and every firstborn male of unclean animals. 16When they are a month old, you must redeem them at the redemption price set at five shekels[b] of silver, according to the sanctuary shekel, which weighs twenty gerahs.

17"But you must not redeem the firstborn of an ox, a sheep or a goat; they are holy. Sprinkle their blood on the altar and burn their fat as an offering made by fire, an aroma pleasing to the LORD. 18Their meat is to be yours, just as the breast of the wave offering and the right thigh are yours. 19Whatever is set aside from the holy offerings the Israelites present to the LORD I give to you and your sons and daughters as your regular share. It is an everlasting covenant of salt before the LORD for both you and your offspring."

20The LORD said to Aaron, "You will have no inheritance in their land, nor will you have any share among them; I am your share and your inheritance among the Israelites.

21"I give to the Levites all the tithes in Israel as their inheritance in return for the work they do while serving at the Tent of Meeting. 22From now on the Israelites must not go near the Tent of Meeting, or they will bear the consequences of their sin and will die. 23It is the Levites who are to do the work at the Tent of Meeting and bear the responsibility for offenses against it. This is a lasting ordinance for the generations to come. They will receive no inheritance among the Israelites. 24Instead, I give to the Levites as their inheritance the tithes that the Israelites present as an offering to the LORD. That is why I said concerning them: 'They will have no inheritance among the Israelites.' "

25The LORD said to Moses, 26"Speak to the Levites and say to them: 'When you receive from the Israelites the tithe I give you as your inheritance, you must present a tenth of that tithe as the LORD's offering. 27Your offering will be reckoned to you as grain from the threshing floor or juice from the winepress. 28In this way you also will present an offering to the LORD from all the tithes you receive from the Israelites. From these tithes you must give the LORD's portion to Aaron the priest. 29You must present as the LORD's portion the best and holiest part of everything given to you.'

30"Say to the Levites: 'When you present the best part, it will be reckoned to you as the product of the threshing floor or the winepress. 31You and your households may eat the rest of it anywhere, for it is your wages for your work at the Tent of Meeting. 32By presenting the best part of it you will not be guilty in this matter; then you will not defile the holy offerings of the Israelites, and you will not die.' "

The Water of Cleansing

19 The LORD said to Moses and Aaron: 2"This is a requirement of the law that the LORD has commanded: Tell the Israelites to bring you a red heifer without defect or blemish and that has never been under a yoke. 3Give it to Eleazar the priest; it is to be taken outside the camp and slaughtered in his presence. 4Then Eleazar the priest is to take some of its blood on his finger and sprinkle it seven times toward the front of the Tent of Meeting. 5While he watches, the heifer is to be burned—its hide, flesh, blood and offal. 6The priest is to take some cedar wood, hyssop and scarlet wool and throw them onto the burning heifer. 7After that, the priest must wash his clothes and bathe himself with water. He may then come into the camp, but he will be ceremonially unclean till evening. 8The man who burns it must also wash his clothes and bathe with water, and he too will be unclean till evening.

9"A man who is clean shall gather up the ashes of the heifer and put them in a ceremonially clean place outside the camp. They shall be kept by the Israelite community for use in the water of cleansing; it is for purification from sin. 10The man who gathers up the ashes of the heifer must also wash his clothes, and he too will be unclean till evening. This will be a lasting ordinance both for the Israelites and for the aliens living among them.

11"Whoever touches the dead body of anyone will be unclean for seven days. 12He must purify himself with the water on the third day and on the seventh day; then he will be

[a] *14* The Hebrew term refers to the irrevocable giving over of things or persons to the LORD. [b] *16* That is, about 2 ounces (about 55 grams)

clean. But if he does not purify himself on the
third and seventh days, he will not be clean.
13Whoever touches the dead body of anyone
and fails to purify himself defiles the LORD's
tabernacle. That person must be cut off from
Israel. Because the water of cleansing has
not been sprinkled on him, he is unclean; his
uncleanness remains on him.

14"This is the law that applies when a person dies in a tent: Anyone who enters the
tent and anyone who is in it will be unclean
for seven days, 15and every open container
without a lid fastened on it will be unclean.

16"Anyone out in the open who touches
someone who has been killed with a sword
or someone who has died a natural death, or
anyone who touches a human bone or a
grave, will be unclean for seven days.

17"For the unclean person, put some
ashes from the burned purification offering
into a jar and pour fresh water over them.
18Then a man who is ceremonially clean is to
take some hyssop, dip it in the water and
sprinkle the tent and all the furnishings and
the people who were there. He must also
sprinkle anyone who has touched a human
bone or a grave or someone who has been
killed or someone who has died a natural
death. 19The man who is clean is to sprinkle
the unclean person on the third and seventh
days, and on the seventh day he is to purify
him. The person being cleansed must wash
his clothes and bathe with water, and that
evening he will be clean. 20But if a person
who is unclean does not purify himself, he
must be cut off from the community, because
he has defiled the sanctuary of the LORD. The
water of cleansing has not been sprinkled on
him, and he is unclean. 21This is a lasting
ordinance for them.

"The man who sprinkles the water of
cleansing must also wash his clothes, and
anyone who touches the water of cleansing
will be unclean till evening. 22Anything that
an unclean person touches becomes unclean, and anyone who touches it becomes
unclean till evening."

Water From the Rock

20 In the first month the whole Israelite
community arrived at the Desert of
Zin, and they stayed at Kadesh. There Miriam died and was buried.

2Now there was no water for the community, and the people gathered in opposition to
Moses and Aaron. 3They quarreled with
Moses and said, "If only we had died when
our brothers fell dead before the LORD! 4Why
did you bring the LORD's community into this
desert, that we and our livestock should die
here? 5Why did you bring us up out of Egypt
to this terrible place? It has no grain or figs,
grapevines or pomegranates. And there is
no water to drink!"

6Moses and Aaron went from the assembly to the entrance to the Tent of Meeting and
fell facedown, and the glory of the LORD appeared to them. 7The LORD said to Moses,
8"Take the staff, and you and your brother
Aaron gather the assembly together. Speak
to that rock before their eyes and it will pour
out its water. You will bring water out of the
rock for the community so they and their
livestock can drink."

9So Moses took the staff from the LORD's
presence, just as he commanded him. 10He
and Aaron gathered the assembly together
in front of the rock and Moses said to them,
"Listen, you rebels, must we bring you water
out of this rock?" 11Then Moses raised his
arm and struck the rock twice with his staff.
Water gushed out, and the community and
their livestock drank.

12But the LORD said to Moses and Aaron,
"Because you did not trust in me enough to
honor me as holy in the sight of the Israelites,
you will not bring this community into the
land I give them."

13These were the waters of Meribah,[a]
where the Israelites quarreled with the LORD
and where he showed himself holy among
them.

Edom Denies Israel Passage

14Moses sent messengers from Kadesh to
the king of Edom, saying:

> "This is what your brother Israel says:
> You know about all the hardships that
> have come upon us. 15Our forefathers
> went down into Egypt, and we lived
> there many years. The Egyptians mis-
> treated us and our fathers, 16but when
> we cried out to the LORD, he heard our
> cry and sent an angel and brought us
> out of Egypt.
>
> "Now we are here at Kadesh, a town
> on the edge of your territory. 17Please let
> us pass through your country. We will
> not go through any field or vineyard, or

[a] 13 *Meribah* means *quarreling.*

drink water from any well. We will travel along the king's highway and not turn to the right or to the left until we have passed through your territory."

18But Edom answered:

"You may not pass through here; if you try, we will march out and attack you with the sword."

19The Israelites replied:

"We will go along the main road, and if we or our livestock drink any of your water, we will pay for it. We only want to pass through on foot—nothing else."

20Again they answered:

"You may not pass through."

Then Edom came out against them with a large and powerful army. 21Since Edom refused to let them go through their territory, Israel turned away from them.

The Death of Aaron

22The whole Israelite community set out from Kadesh and came to Mount Hor. 23At Mount Hor, near the border of Edom, the LORD said to Moses and Aaron, 24"Aaron will be gathered to his people. He will not enter the land I give the Israelites, because both of you rebelled against my command at the waters of Meribah. 25Get Aaron and his son Eleazar and take them up Mount Hor. 26Remove Aaron's garments and put them on his son Eleazar, for Aaron will be gathered to his people; he will die there."

27Moses did as the LORD commanded: They went up Mount Hor in the sight of the whole community. 28Moses removed Aaron's garments and put them on his son Eleazar. And Aaron died there on top of the mountain. Then Moses and Eleazar came down from the mountain, 29and when the whole community learned that Aaron had died, the entire house of Israel mourned for him thirty days.

Arad Destroyed

21 When the Canaanite king of Arad, who lived in the Negev, heard that Israel was coming along the road to Atharim, he attacked the Israelites and captured some of them. 2Then Israel made this vow to the LORD: "If you will deliver these people into our hands, we will totally destroy[a] their cities." 3The LORD listened to Israel's plea and gave the Canaanites over to them. They completely destroyed them and their towns; so the place was named Hormah.[b]

The Bronze Snake

4They traveled from Mount Hor along the route to the Red Sea,[c] to go around Edom. But the people grew impatient on the way; 5they spoke against God and against Moses, and said, "Why have you brought us up out of Egypt to die in the desert? There is no bread! There is no water! And we detest this miserable food!"

6Then the LORD sent venomous snakes among them; they bit the people and many Israelites died. 7The people came to Moses and said, "We sinned when we spoke against the LORD and against you. Pray that the LORD will take the snakes away from us." So Moses prayed for the people.

8The LORD said to Moses, "Make a snake and put it up on a pole; anyone who is bitten can look at it and live." 9So Moses made a bronze snake and put it up on a pole. Then when anyone was bitten by a snake and looked at the bronze snake, he lived.

The Journey to Moab

10The Israelites moved on and camped at Oboth. 11Then they set out from Oboth and camped in Iye Abarim, in the desert that faces Moab toward the sunrise. 12From there they moved on and camped in the Zered Valley. 13They set out from there and camped alongside the Arnon, which is in the desert extending into Amorite territory. The Arnon is the border of Moab, between Moab and the Amorites. 14That is why the Book of the Wars of the LORD says:

". . . Waheb in Suphah[d] and the ravines,
the Arnon 15and[e] the slopes of the ravines
that lead to the site of Ar
and lie along the border of Moab."

16From there they continued on to Beer, the well where the LORD said to Moses, "Gather

[a]2 The Hebrew term refers to the irrevocable giving over of things or persons to the LORD, often by totally destroying them; also in verse 3. [b]3 *Hormah* means *destruction.* [c]4 Hebrew *Yam Suph;* that is, Sea of Reeds
[d]14 The meaning of the Hebrew for this phrase is uncertain. [e]14,15 Or *"I have been given from Suphah and the ravines / of the Arnon 15to*

the people together and I will give them
water."

[17]Then Israel sang this song:

"Spring up, O well!
Sing about it,
[18]about the well that the princes dug,
that the nobles of the people sank—
the nobles with scepters and staffs."

Then they went from the desert to Mattanah,
[19]from Mattanah to Nahaliel, from Nahaliel to
Bamoth, [20]and from Bamoth to the valley in
Moab where the top of Pisgah overlooks the
wasteland.

Defeat of Sihon and Og

[21]Israel sent messengers to say to Sihon
king of the Amorites:

[22]"Let us pass through your country. We will not turn aside into any field or vineyard, or drink water from any well. We will travel along the king's highway until we have passed through your territory."

[23]But Sihon would not let Israel pass
through his territory. He mustered his entire
army and marched out into the desert
against Israel. When he reached Jahaz, he
fought with Israel. [24]Israel, however, put him
to the sword and took over his land from the
Arnon to the Jabbok, but only as far as the
Ammonites, because their border was fortified. [25]Israel captured all the cities of the
Amorites and occupied them, including
Heshbon and all its surrounding settlements.
[26]Heshbon was the city of Sihon king of the
Amorites, who had fought against the former
king of Moab and had taken from him all his
land as far as the Arnon.

[27]That is why the poets say:

"Come to Heshbon and let it be rebuilt;
let Sihon's city be restored.

[28]"Fire went out from Heshbon,
a blaze from the city of Sihon.
It consumed Ar of Moab,
the citizens of Arnon's heights.
[29]Woe to you, O Moab!
You are destroyed, O people of
Chemosh!
He has given up his sons as fugitives
and his daughters as captives
to Sihon king of the Amorites.

[30]"But we have overthrown them;
Heshbon is destroyed all the way to
Dibon.
We have demolished them as far as
Nophah,
which extends to Medeba."

[31]So Israel settled in the land of the Amorites.

[32]After Moses had sent spies to Jazer, the
Israelites captured its surrounding settlements and drove out the Amorites who were
there. [33]Then they turned and went up along
the road toward Bashan, and Og king of Bashan and his whole army marched out to
meet them in battle at Edrei.

[34]The LORD said to Moses, "Do not be
afraid of him, for I have handed him over to
you, with his whole army and his land. Do to
him what you did to Sihon king of the Amorites, who reigned in Heshbon."

[35]So they struck him down, together with
his sons and his whole army, leaving them
no survivors. And they took possession of
his land.

Balak Summons Balaam

22 Then the Israelites traveled to the
plains of Moab and camped along
the Jordan across from Jericho.[a]

[2]Now Balak son of Zippor saw all that Israel had done to the Amorites, [3]and Moab
was terrified because there were so many
people. Indeed, Moab was filled with dread
because of the Israelites.

[4]The Moabites said to the elders of Midian,
"This horde is going to lick up everything
around us, as an ox licks up the grass of the
field."

So Balak son of Zippor, who was king of
Moab at that time, [5]sent messengers to summon Balaam son of Beor, who was at Pethor,
near the River,[b] in his native land. Balak
said:

"A people has come out of Egypt;
they cover the face of the land and have
settled next to me. [6]Now come and put a
curse on these people, because they
are too powerful for me. Perhaps then I
will be able to defeat them and drive
them out of the country. For I know that
those you bless are blessed, and those
you curse are cursed."

[7]The elders of Moab and Midian left, taking
with them the fee for divination. When they

[a]1 Hebrew *Jordan of Jericho*; possibly an ancient name for the Jordan River

[b]5 That is, the Euphrates

came to Balaam, they told him what Balak
had said.
8"Spend the night here," Balaam said to
them, "and I will bring you back the answer
the LORD gives me." So the Moabite princes
stayed with him.
9God came to Balaam and asked, "Who
are these men with you?"
10Balaam said to God, "Balak son of Zippor, king of Moab, sent me this message:
11'A people that has come out of Egypt
covers the face of the land. Now come and
put a curse on them for me. Perhaps then I
will be able to fight them and drive them
away.' "
12But God said to Balaam, "Do not go with
them. You must not put a curse on those
people, because they are blessed."
13The next morning Balaam got up and
said to Balak's princes, "Go back to your
own country, for the LORD has refused to let
me go with you."
14So the Moabite princes returned to Balak
and said, "Balaam refused to come with us."
15Then Balak sent other princes, more numerous and more distinguished than the
first. 16They came to Balaam and said:

> "This is what Balak son of Zippor
> says: Do not let anything keep you from
> coming to me, 17because I will reward
> you handsomely and do whatever you
> say. Come and put a curse on these
> people for me."

18But Balaam answered them, "Even if
Balak gave me his palace filled with silver
and gold, I could not do anything great or
small to go beyond the command of the LORD
my God. 19Now stay here tonight as the others did, and I will find out what else the LORD
will tell me."
20That night God came to Balaam and
said, "Since these men have come to summon you, go with them, but do only what I tell
you."

Balaam's Donkey

21Balaam got up in the morning, saddled
his donkey and went with the princes of
Moab. 22But God was very angry when he
went, and the angel of the LORD stood in the
road to oppose him. Balaam was riding on
his donkey, and his two servants were with
him. 23When the donkey saw the angel of the
LORD standing in the road with a drawn sword
in his hand, she turned off the road into a
field. Balaam beat her to get her back on the
road.
24Then the angel of the LORD stood in a
narrow path between two vineyards, with
walls on both sides. 25When the donkey saw
the angel of the LORD, she pressed close to
the wall, crushing Balaam's foot against it.
So he beat her again.
26Then the angel of the LORD moved on
ahead and stood in a narrow place where
there was no room to turn, either to the right
or to the left. 27When the donkey saw the
angel of the LORD, she lay down under Balaam, and he was angry and beat her with his
staff. 28Then the LORD opened the donkey's
mouth, and she said to Balaam, "What have
I done to you to make you beat me these
three times?"
29Balaam answered the donkey, "You
have made a fool of me! If I had a sword in
my hand, I would kill you right now."
30The donkey said to Balaam, "Am I not
your own donkey, which you have always
ridden, to this day? Have I been in the habit
of doing this to you?"
"No," he said.
31Then the LORD opened Balaam's eyes,
and he saw the angel of the LORD standing in
the road with his sword drawn. So he bowed
low and fell facedown.
32The angel of the LORD asked him, "Why
have you beaten your donkey these three
times? I have come here to oppose you because your path is a reckless one before
me.[a] 33The donkey saw me and turned away
from me these three times. If she had not
turned away, I would certainly have killed
you by now, but I would have spared her."
34Balaam said to the angel of the LORD, "I
have sinned. I did not realize you were
standing in the road to oppose me. Now if
you are displeased, I will go back."
35The angel of the LORD said to Balaam,
"Go with the men, but speak only what I tell
you." So Balaam went with the princes of
Balak.
36When Balak heard that Balaam was
coming, he went out to meet him at the Moabite town on the Arnon border, at the edge
of his territory. 37Balak said to Balaam, "Did I
not send you an urgent summons? Why
didn't you come to me? Am I really not able
to reward you?"
38"Well, I have come to you now," Balaam

[a]*32* The meaning of the Hebrew for this clause is uncertain.

replied. "But can I say just anything? I must
speak only what God puts in my mouth."
[39]Then Balaam went with Balak to Kiriath
Huzoth. [40]Balak sacrificed cattle and sheep,
and gave some to Balaam and the princes
who were with him. [41]The next morning
Balak took Balaam up to Bamoth Baal, and
from there he saw part of the people.

Balaam's First Oracle

23 Balaam said, "Build me seven altars
here, and prepare seven bulls and
seven rams for me." [2]Balak did as Balaam
said, and the two of them offered a bull and a
ram on each altar.
[3]Then Balaam said to Balak, "Stay here
beside your offering while I go aside. Perhaps the LORD will come to meet with me.
Whatever he reveals to me I will tell you."
Then he went off to a barren height.
[4]God met with him, and Balaam said, "I
have prepared seven altars, and on each
altar I have offered a bull and a ram."
[5]The LORD put a message in Balaam's
mouth and said, "Go back to Balak and give
him this message."
[6]So he went back to him and found him
standing beside his offering, with all the
princes of Moab. [7]Then Balaam uttered his
oracle:

"Balak brought me from Aram,
the king of Moab from the eastern
mountains.
'Come,' he said, 'curse Jacob for me;
come, denounce Israel.'
[8]How can I curse
those whom God has not cursed?
How can I denounce
those whom the LORD has not
denounced?
[9]From the rocky peaks I see them,
from the heights I view them.
I see a people who live apart
and do not consider themselves one of
the nations.
[10]Who can count the dust of Jacob
or number the fourth part of Israel?
Let me die the death of the righteous,
and may my end be like theirs!"

[11]Balak said to Balaam, "What have you
done to me? I brought you to curse my enemies, but you have done nothing but bless
them!"
[12]He answered, "Must I not speak what the
LORD puts in my mouth?"

Balaam's Second Oracle

[13]Then Balak said to him, "Come with me
to another place where you can see them;
you will see only a part but not all of them.
And from there, curse them for me." [14]So he
took him to the field of Zophim on the top of
Pisgah, and there he built seven altars and
offered a bull and a ram on each altar.
[15]Balaam said to Balak, "Stay here beside
your offering while I meet with him over
there."
[16]The LORD met with Balaam and put a
message in his mouth and said, "Go back to
Balak and give him this message."
[17]So he went to him and found him standing beside his offering, with the princes of
Moab. Balak asked him, "What did the LORD
say?"
[18]Then he uttered his oracle:

"Arise, Balak, and listen;
hear me, son of Zippor.
[19]God is not a man, that he should lie,
nor a son of man, that he should
change his mind.
Does he speak and then not act?
Does he promise and not fulfill?
[20]I have received a command to bless;
he has blessed, and I cannot change it.

[21]"No misfortune is seen in Jacob,
no misery observed in Israel.[a]
The LORD their God is with them;
the shout of the King is among them.
[22]God brought them out of Egypt;
they have the strength of a wild ox.
[23]There is no sorcery against Jacob,
no divination against Israel.
It will now be said of Jacob
and of Israel, 'See what God has done!'
[24]The people rise like a lioness;
they rouse themselves like a lion
that does not rest till he devours his prey
and drinks the blood of his victims."

[25]Then Balak said to Balaam, "Neither
curse them at all nor bless them at all!"
[26]Balaam answered, "Did I not tell you I
must do whatever the LORD says?"

Balaam's Third Oracle

[27]Then Balak said to Balaam, "Come, let

[a]21 Or *He has not looked on Jacob's offenses / or on the wrongs found in Israel.*

me take you to another place. Perhaps it will
please God to let you curse them for me from
there." 28And Balak took Balaam to the top of
Peor, overlooking the wasteland.
29Balaam said, "Build me seven altars
here, and prepare seven bulls and seven
rams for me." 30Balak did as Balaam had
said, and offered a bull and a ram on each
altar.

24 Now when Balaam saw that it
pleased the LORD to bless Israel, he
did not resort to sorcery as at other times, but
turned his face toward the desert. 2When
Balaam looked out and saw Israel encamped tribe by tribe, the Spirit of God came
upon him 3and he uttered his oracle:

"The oracle of Balaam son of Beor,
the oracle of one whose eye sees
clearly,
4the oracle of one who hears the words of
God,
who sees a vision from the Almighty,[a]
who falls prostrate, and whose eyes
are opened:

5"How beautiful are your tents, O Jacob,
your dwelling places, O Israel!

6"Like valleys they spread out,
like gardens beside a river,
like aloes planted by the LORD,
like cedars beside the waters.
7Water will flow from their buckets;
their seed will have abundant water.

"Their king will be greater than Agag;
their kingdom will be exalted.

8"God brought them out of Egypt;
they have the strength of a wild ox.
They devour hostile nations
and break their bones in pieces;
with their arrows they pierce them.
9Like a lion they crouch and lie down,
like a lioness—who dares to rouse
them?

"May those who bless you be blessed
and those who curse you be cursed!"

10Then Balak's anger burned against Balaam. He struck his hands together and said
to him, "I summoned you to curse my enemies, but you have blessed them these three
times. 11Now leave at once and go home! I
said I would reward you handsomely, but the
LORD has kept you from being rewarded."
12Balaam answered Balak, "Did I not tell
the messengers you sent me, 13'Even if
Balak gave me his palace filled with silver
and gold, I could not do anything of my own
accord, good or bad, to go beyond the command of the LORD—and I must say only what
the LORD says'? 14Now I am going back to my
people, but come, let me warn you of what
this people will do to your people in days to
come."

Balaam's Fourth Oracle

15Then he uttered his oracle:

"The oracle of Balaam son of Beor,
the oracle of one whose eye sees
clearly,
16the oracle of one who hears the words of
God,
who has knowledge from the Most
High,
who sees a vision from the Almighty,
who falls prostrate, and whose eyes
are opened:

17"I see him, but not now;
I behold him, but not near.
A star will come out of Jacob;
a scepter will rise out of Israel.
He will crush the foreheads of Moab,
the skulls[b] of[c] all the sons of Sheth.[d]
18Edom will be conquered;
Seir, his enemy, will be conquered,
but Israel will grow strong.
19A ruler will come out of Jacob
and destroy the survivors of the city."

Balaam's Final Oracles

20Then Balaam saw Amalek and uttered
his oracle:

"Amalek was first among the nations,
but he will come to ruin at last."

21Then he saw the Kenites and uttered his
oracle:

"Your dwelling place is secure,
your nest is set in a rock;
22yet you Kenites will be destroyed
when Asshur takes you captive."

23Then he uttered his oracle:

"Ah, who can live when God does this?[e]

[a]4 Hebrew *Shaddai*; also in verse 16 [b]17 Samaritan Pentateuch (see also Jer. 48:45); the meaning of the word in the Masoretic Text is uncertain. [c]17 Or possibly *Moab, / batter* [d]17 Or *all the noisy boasters*
[e]23 Masoretic Text; with a different word division of the Hebrew *A people will gather from the north.*

24 Ships will come from the shores of
Kittim;
they will subdue Asshur and Eber,
but they too will come to ruin."

25Then Balaam got up and returned home
and Balak went his own way.

Moab Seduces Israel

25 While Israel was staying in Shittim,
the men began to indulge in sexual
immorality with Moabite women, 2who invited them to the sacrifices to their gods. The
people ate and bowed down before these
gods. 3So Israel joined in worshiping the
Baal of Peor. And the LORD's anger burned
against them.

4The LORD said to Moses, "Take all the
leaders of these people, kill them and expose them in broad daylight before the LORD,
so that the LORD's fierce anger may turn away
from Israel."

5So Moses said to Israel's judges, "Each
of you must put to death those of your men
who have joined in worshiping the Baal of
Peor."

6Then an Israelite man brought to his
family a Midianite woman right before the
eyes of Moses and the whole assembly of
Israel while they were weeping at the entrance to the Tent of Meeting. 7When Phinehas son of Eleazar, the son of Aaron, the
priest, saw this, he left the assembly, took a
spear in his hand 8and followed the Israelite
into the tent. He drove the spear through
both of them—through the Israelite and into
the woman's body. Then the plague against
the Israelites was stopped; 9but those who
died in the plague numbered 24,000.

10The LORD said to Moses, 11"Phinehas
son of Eleazar, the son of Aaron, the priest,
has turned my anger away from the Israelites; for he was as zealous as I am for my
honor among them, so that in my zeal I did
not put an end to them. 12Therefore tell him I
am making my covenant of peace with him.
13He and his descendants will have a covenant of a lasting priesthood, because he
was zealous for the honor of his God and
made atonement for the Israelites."

14The name of the Israelite who was killed
with the Midianite woman was Zimri son of
Salu, the leader of a Simeonite family. 15And
the name of the Midianite woman who was
put to death was Cozbi daughter of Zur, a
tribal chief of a Midianite family.

16The LORD said to Moses, 17"Treat the
Midianites as enemies and kill them, 18be-
cause they treated you as enemies when
they deceived you in the affair of Peor and
their sister Cozbi, the daughter of a Midianite
leader, the woman who was killed when the
plague came as a result of Peor."

The Second Census

26 After the plague the LORD said to
Moses and Eleazar son of Aaron, the
priest, 2"Take a census of the whole Israelite
community by families—all those twenty
years old or more who are able to serve in
the army of Israel." 3So on the plains of Moab
by the Jordan across from Jericho,[a] Moses
and Eleazar the priest spoke with them and
said, 4"Take a census of the men twenty
years old or more, as the LORD commanded
Moses."

These were the Israelites who came out of
Egypt:

5The descendants of Reuben, the firstborn
son of Israel, were:
through Hanoch, the Hanochite clan;
through Pallu, the Palluite clan;
6through Hezron, the Hezronite clan;
through Carmi, the Carmite clan.
7These were the clans of Reuben; those
numbered were 43,730.

8The son of Pallu was Eliab, 9and the sons
of Eliab were Nemuel, Dathan and Abiram.
The same Dathan and Abiram were the community officials who rebelled against Moses
and Aaron and were among Korah's followers when they rebelled against the LORD.
10The earth opened its mouth and swallowed
them along with Korah, whose followers died
when the fire devoured the 250 men. And
they served as a warning sign. 11The line of
Korah, however, did not die out.

12The descendants of Simeon by their clans
were:
through Nemuel, the Nemuelite clan;
through Jamin, the Jaminite clan;
through Jakin, the Jakinite clan;
13through Zerah, the Zerahite clan;
through Shaul, the Shaulite clan.
14These were the clans of Simeon; there
were 22,200 men.

15The descendants of Gad by their clans
were:
through Zephon, the Zephonite clan;

[a]3 Hebrew *Jordan of Jericho*; possibly an ancient name for the Jordan River; also in verse 63

through Haggi, the Haggite clan;
through Shuni, the Shunite clan;
16 through Ozni, the Oznite clan;
through Eri, the Erite clan;
17 through Arodi,[a] the Arodite clan;
through Areli, the Arelite clan.
18 These were the clans of Gad; those numbered were 40,500.

19 Er and Onan were sons of Judah, but they died in Canaan.
20 The descendants of Judah by their clans were:
through Shelah, the Shelanite clan;
through Perez, the Perezite clan;
through Zerah, the Zerahite clan.
21 The descendants of Perez were:
through Hezron, the Hezronite clan;
through Hamul, the Hamulite clan.
22 These were the clans of Judah; those numbered were 76,500.

23 The descendants of Issachar by their clans were:
through Tola, the Tolaite clan;
through Puah, the Puite[b] clan;
24 through Jashub, the Jashubite clan;
through Shimron, the Shimronite clan.
25 These were the clans of Issachar; those numbered were 64,300.

26 The descendants of Zebulun by their clans were:
through Sered, the Seredite clan;
through Elon, the Elonite clan;
through Jahleel, the Jahleelite clan.
27 These were the clans of Zebulun; those numbered were 60,500.

28 The descendants of Joseph by their clans through Manasseh and Ephraim were:

29 The descendants of Manasseh:
through Makir, the Makirite clan (Makir was the father of Gilead);
through Gilead, the Gileadite clan.
30 These were the descendants of Gilead:
through Iezer, the Iezerite clan;
through Helek, the Helekite clan;
31 through Asriel, the Asrielite clan;
through Shechem, the Shechemite clan;
32 through Shemida, the Shemidaite clan;
through Hepher, the Hepherite clan.
33 (Zelophehad son of Hepher had no sons; he had only daughters, whose names were Mahlah, Noah, Hoglah, Milcah and Tirzah.)
34 These were the clans of Manasseh; those numbered were 52,700.

35 These were the descendants of Ephraim by their clans:
through Shuthelah, the Shuthelahite clan;
through Beker, the Bekerite clan;
through Tahan, the Tahanite clan.
36 These were the descendants of Shuthelah:
through Eran, the Eranite clan.
37 These were the clans of Ephraim; those numbered were 32,500.

These were the descendants of Joseph by their clans.

38 The descendants of Benjamin by their clans were:
through Bela, the Belaite clan;
through Ashbel, the Ashbelite clan;
through Ahiram, the Ahiramite clan;
39 through Shupham,[c] the Shuphamite clan;
through Hupham, the Huphamite clan.
40 The descendants of Bela through Ard and Naaman were:
through Ard,[d] the Ardite clan;
through Naaman, the Naamite clan.
41 These were the clans of Benjamin; those numbered were 45,600.

42 These were the descendants of Dan by their clans:
through Shuham, the Shuhamite clan.
These were the clans of Dan: 43 All of them were Shuhamite clans; and those numbered were 64,400.

44 The descendants of Asher by their clans were:
through Imnah, the Imnite clan;
through Ishvi, the Ishvite clan;
through Beriah, the Beriite clan;
45 and through the descendants of Beriah:
through Heber, the Heberite clan;
through Malkiel, the Malkielite clan.

[a] *17* Samaritan Pentateuch and Syriac (see also Gen. 46:16); Masoretic Text *Arod* [b] *23* Samaritan Pentateuch, Septuagint, Vulgate and Syriac (see also 1 Chron. 7:1); Masoretic Text *through Puvah, the Punite* [c] *39* A few manuscripts of the Masoretic Text, Samaritan Pentateuch, Vulgate and Syriac (see also Septuagint); most manuscripts of the Masoretic Text *Shephupham* [d] *40* Samaritan Pentateuch and Vulgate (see also Septuagint); Masoretic Text does not have *through Ard.*

46(Asher had a daughter named Serah.)
47These were the clans of Asher; those numbered were 53,400.

48The descendants of Naphtali by their clans
were:
through Jahzeel, the Jahzeelite clan;
through Guni, the Gunite clan;
49through Jezer, the Jezerite clan;
through Shillem, the Shillemite clan.
50These were the clans of Naphtali; those
numbered were 45,400.

51The total number of the men of Israel was
601,730.

52The LORD said to Moses, 53"The land is to
be allotted to them as an inheritance based
on the number of names. 54To a larger group
give a larger inheritance, and to a smaller
group a smaller one; each is to receive its
inheritance according to the number of those
listed. 55Be sure that the land is distributed by
lot. What each group inherits will be according to the names for its ancestral tribe.
56Each inheritance is to be distributed by lot
among the larger and smaller groups."

57These were the Levites who were counted
by their clans:
through Gershon, the Gershonite clan;
through Kohath, the Kohathite clan;
through Merari, the Merarite clan.
58These also were Levite clans:
the Libnite clan,
the Hebronite clan,
the Mahlite clan,
the Mushite clan,
the Korahite clan.
(Kohath was the forefather of Amram;
59the name of Amram's wife was Jochebed, a descendant of Levi, who was
born to the Levites[a] in Egypt. To Amram
she bore Aaron, Moses and their sister
Miriam. 60Aaron was the father of Nadab
and Abihu, Eleazar and Ithamar. 61But
Nadab and Abihu died when they made
an offering before the LORD with unauthorized fire.)

62All the male Levites a month old or more
numbered 23,000. They were not counted
along with the other Israelites because they
received no inheritance among them.

63These are the ones counted by Moses
and Eleazar the priest when they counted
the Israelites on the plains of Moab by the
Jordan across from Jericho. 64Not one of
them was among those counted by Moses
and Aaron the priest when they counted the
Israelites in the Desert of Sinai. 65For the
LORD had told those Israelites they would
surely die in the desert, and not one of them
was left except Caleb son of Jephunneh and
Joshua son of Nun.

Zelophehad's Daughters

27 The daughters of Zelophehad son of
Hepher, the son of Gilead, the son of
Makir, the son of Manasseh, belonged to the
clans of Manasseh son of Joseph. The
names of the daughters were Mahlah, Noah,
Hoglah, Milcah and Tirzah. They approached 2the entrance to the Tent of Meeting and stood before Moses, Eleazar the
priest, the leaders and the whole assembly,
and said, 3"Our father died in the desert. He
was not among Korah's followers, who banded together against the LORD, but he died for
his own sin and left no sons. 4Why should our
father's name disappear from his clan because he had no son? Give us property
among our father's relatives."

5So Moses brought their case before the
LORD 6and the LORD said to him, 7"What Zelophehad's daughters are saying is right. You
must certainly give them property as an inheritance among their father's relatives and
turn their father's inheritance over to them.

8"Say to the Israelites, 'If a man dies and
leaves no son, turn his inheritance over to his
daughter. 9If he has no daughter, give his
inheritance to his brothers. 10If he has no
brothers, give his inheritance to his father's
brothers. 11If his father had no brothers, give
his inheritance to the nearest relative in his
clan, that he may possess it. This is to be a
legal requirement for the Israelites, as the
LORD commanded Moses.' "

Joshua to Succeed Moses

12Then the LORD said to Moses, "Go up this
mountain in the Abarim range and see the
land I have given the Israelites. 13After you
have seen it, you too will be gathered to your
people, as your brother Aaron was, 14for
when the community rebelled at the waters
in the Desert of Zin, both of you disobeyed
my command to honor me as holy before
their eyes." (These were the waters of Meribah Kadesh, in the Desert of Zin.)

[a]59 Or *Jochebed, a daughter of Levi, who was born to Levi*

15Moses said to the LORD, 16"May the LORD,
the God of the spirits of all mankind, appoint
a man over this community 17to go out and
come in before them, one who will lead them
out and bring them in, so the LORD's people
will not be like sheep without a shepherd."
18So the LORD said to Moses, "Take
Joshua son of Nun, a man in whom is the
spirit,[a] and lay your hand on him. 19Have him
stand before Eleazar the priest and the entire assembly and commission him in their
presence. 20Give him some of your authority
so the whole Israelite community will obey
him. 21He is to stand before Eleazar the
priest, who will obtain decisions for him by
inquiring of the Urim before the LORD. At his
command he and the entire community of
the Israelites will go out, and at his command
they will come in."
22Moses did as the LORD commanded him.
He took Joshua and had him stand before
Eleazar the priest and the whole assembly.
23Then he laid his hands on him and commis-
sioned him, as the LORD instructed through
Moses.

Daily Offerings

28 The LORD said to Moses, 2"Give this
command to the Israelites and say to
them: 'See that you present to me at the
appointed time the food for my offerings
made by fire, as an aroma pleasing to me.'
3Say to them: 'This is the offering made by
fire that you are to present to the LORD: two
lambs a year old without defect, as a regular
burnt offering each day. 4Prepare one lamb
in the morning and the other at twilight, 5to-
gether with a grain offering of a tenth of an
ephah[b] of fine flour mixed with a quarter of a
hin[c] of oil from pressed olives. 6This is the
regular burnt offering instituted at Mount
Sinai as a pleasing aroma, an offering made
to the LORD by fire. 7The accompanying drink
offering is to be a quarter of a hin of fermented drink with each lamb. Pour out the drink
offering to the LORD at the sanctuary. 8Pre-
pare the second lamb at twilight, along with
the same kind of grain offering and drink
offering that you prepare in the morning. This
is an offering made by fire, an aroma pleasing to the LORD.

Sabbath Offerings

9" 'On the Sabbath day, make an offering
of two lambs a year old without defect, together with its drink offering and a grain offering of two-tenths of an ephah[d] of fine flour
mixed with oil. 10This is the burnt offering for
every Sabbath, in addition to the regular
burnt offering and its drink offering.

Monthly Offerings

11" 'On the first of every month, present to
the LORD a burnt offering of two young bulls,
one ram and seven male lambs a year old, all
without defect. 12With each bull there is to be
a grain offering of three-tenths of an ephah[e]
of fine flour mixed with oil; with the ram, a
grain offering of two-tenths of an ephah of
fine flour mixed with oil; 13and with each
lamb, a grain offering of a tenth of an ephah
of fine flour mixed with oil. This is for a burnt
offering, a pleasing aroma, an offering made
to the LORD by fire. 14With each bull there is to
be a drink offering of half a hin[f] of wine; with
the ram, a third of a hin[g]; and with each lamb,
a quarter of a hin. This is the monthly burnt
offering to be made at each new moon during the year. 15Besides the regular burnt offering with its drink offering, one male goat is
to be presented to the LORD as a sin offering.

The Passover

16" 'On the fourteenth day of the first month
the LORD's Passover is to be held. 17On the
fifteenth day of this month there is to be a
festival; for seven days eat bread made without yeast. 18On the first day hold a sacred
assembly and do no regular work. 19Present
to the LORD an offering made by fire, a burnt
offering of two young bulls, one ram and
seven male lambs a year old, all without defect. 20With each bull prepare a grain offering
of three-tenths of an ephah of fine flour
mixed with oil; with the ram, two-tenths;
21and with each of the seven lambs, one-
tenth. 22Include one male goat as a sin offering to make atonement for you. 23Prepare
these in addition to the regular morning burnt
offering. 24In this way prepare the food for the
offering made by fire every day for seven
days as an aroma pleasing to the LORD; it is to

[a] 18 Or *Spirit* [b] 5 That is, probably about 2 quarts (about 2 liters); also in verses 13, 21 and 29 [c] 5 That is, probably about 1 quart (about 1 liter); also in verses 7 and 14 [d] 9 That is, probably about 4 quarts (about 4.5 liters); also in verses 12, 20 and 28 [e] 12 That is, probably about 6 quarts (about 6.5 liters); also in verses 20 and 28 [f] 14 That is, probably about 2 quarts (about 2 liters) [g] 14 That is, probably about 1 1/4 quarts (about 1.2 liters)

be prepared in addition to the regular burnt offering and its drink offering. 25On the seventh day hold a sacred assembly and do no regular work.

Feast of Weeks

26" 'On the day of firstfruits, when you present to the LORD an offering of new grain during the Feast of Weeks, hold a sacred assembly and do no regular work. 27Present a burnt offering of two young bulls, one ram and seven male lambs a year old as an aroma pleasing to the LORD. 28With each bull there is to be a grain offering of three-tenths of an ephah of fine flour mixed with oil; with the ram, two-tenths; 29and with each of the seven lambs, one-tenth. 30Include one male goat to make atonement for you. 31Prepare these together with their drink offerings, in addition to the regular burnt offering and its grain offering. Be sure the animals are without defect.

Feast of Trumpets

29 " 'On the first day of the seventh month hold a sacred assembly and do no regular work. It is a day for you to sound the trumpets. 2As an aroma pleasing to the LORD, prepare a burnt offering of one young bull, one ram and seven male lambs a year old, all without defect. 3With the bull prepare a grain offering of three-tenths of an ephah[a] of fine flour mixed with oil; with the ram, two-tenths[b]; 4and with each of the seven lambs, one-tenth.[c] 5Include one male goat as a sin offering to make atonement for you. 6These are in addition to the monthly and daily burnt offerings with their grain offerings and drink offerings as specified. They are offerings made to the LORD by fire—a pleasing aroma.

Day of Atonement

7" 'On the tenth day of this seventh month hold a sacred assembly. You must deny yourselves[d] and do no work. 8Present as an aroma pleasing to the LORD a burnt offering of one young bull, one ram and seven male lambs a year old, all without defect. 9With the bull prepare a grain offering of three-tenths of an ephah of fine flour mixed with oil; with the ram, two-tenths; 10and with each of the seven lambs, one-tenth. 11Include one male goat as a sin offering, in addition to the sin offering for atonement and the regular burnt offering with its grain offering, and their drink offerings.

Feast of Tabernacles

12" 'On the fifteenth day of the seventh month, hold a sacred assembly and do no regular work. Celebrate a festival to the LORD for seven days. 13Present an offering made by fire as an aroma pleasing to the LORD, a burnt offering of thirteen young bulls, two rams and fourteen male lambs a year old, all without defect. 14With each of the thirteen bulls prepare a grain offering of three-tenths of an ephah of fine flour mixed with oil; with each of the two rams, two-tenths; 15and with each of the fourteen lambs, one-tenth. 16Include one male goat as a sin offering, in addition to the regular burnt offering with its grain offering and drink offering.

17" 'On the second day prepare twelve young bulls, two rams and fourteen male lambs a year old, all without defect. 18With the bulls, rams and lambs, prepare their grain offerings and drink offerings according to the number specified. 19Include one male goat as a sin offering, in addition to the regular burnt offering with its grain offering, and their drink offerings.

20" 'On the third day prepare eleven bulls, two rams and fourteen male lambs a year old, all without defect. 21With the bulls, rams and lambs, prepare their grain offerings and drink offerings according to the number specified. 22Include one male goat as a sin offering, in addition to the regular burnt offering with its grain offering and drink offering.

23" 'On the fourth day prepare ten bulls, two rams and fourteen male lambs a year old, all without defect. 24With the bulls, rams and lambs, prepare their grain offerings and drink offerings according to the number specified. 25Include one male goat as a sin offering, in addition to the regular burnt offering with its grain offering and drink offering.

26" 'On the fifth day prepare nine bulls, two rams and fourteen male lambs a year old, all without defect. 27With the bulls, rams and lambs, prepare their grain offerings and drink offerings according to the number specified. 28Include one male goat as a sin offering, in addition to the regular burnt offering with its grain offering and drink offering.

29" 'On the sixth day prepare eight bulls,

[a]3 That is, probably about 6 quarts (about 6.5 liters); also in verses 9 and 14 [b]3 That is, probably about 4 quarts (about 4.5 liters); also in verses 9 and 14 [c]4 That is, probably about 2 quarts (about 2 liters); also in verses 10 and 15 [d]7 Or *must fast*

two rams and fourteen male lambs a year old, all without defect. [30]With the bulls, rams and lambs, prepare their grain offerings and drink offerings according to the number specified. [31]Include one male goat as a sin offering, in addition to the regular burnt offering with its grain offering and drink offering.

[32]" 'On the seventh day prepare seven bulls, two rams and fourteen male lambs a year old, all without defect. [33]With the bulls, rams and lambs, prepare their grain offerings and drink offerings according to the number specified. [34]Include one male goat as a sin offering, in addition to the regular burnt offering with its grain offering and drink offering.

[35]" 'On the eighth day hold an assembly and do no regular work. [36]Present an offering made by fire as an aroma pleasing to the LORD, a burnt offering of one bull, one ram and seven male lambs a year old, all without defect. [37]With the bull, the ram and the lambs, prepare their grain offerings and drink offerings according to the number specified. [38]Include one male goat as a sin offering, in addition to the regular burnt offering with its grain offering and drink offering.

[39]" 'In addition to what you vow and your freewill offerings, prepare these for the LORD at your appointed feasts: your burnt offerings, grain offerings, drink offerings and fellowship offerings.[a]' "

[40]Moses told the Israelites all that the LORD commanded him.

Vows

30 Moses said to the heads of the tribes of Israel: "This is what the LORD commands: [2]When a man makes a vow to the LORD or takes an oath to obligate himself by a pledge, he must not break his word but must do everything he said.

[3]"When a young woman still living in her father's house makes a vow to the LORD or obligates herself by a pledge [4]and her father hears about her vow or pledge but says nothing to her, then all her vows and every pledge by which she obligated herself will stand. [5]But if her father forbids her when he hears about it, none of her vows or the pledges by which she obligated herself will stand; the LORD will release her because her father has forbidden her.

[6]"If she marries after she makes a vow or after her lips utter a rash promise by which she obligates herself [7]and her husband hears about it but says nothing to her, then her vows or the pledges by which she obligated herself will stand. [8]But if her husband forbids her when he hears about it, he nullifies the vow that obligates her or the rash promise by which she obligates herself, and the LORD will release her.

[9]"Any vow or obligation taken by a widow or divorced woman will be binding on her.

[10]"If a woman living with her husband makes a vow or obligates herself by a pledge under oath [11]and her husband hears about it but says nothing to her and does not forbid her, then all her vows or the pledges by which she obligated herself will stand. [12]But if her husband nullifies them when he hears about them, then none of the vows or pledges that came from her lips will stand. Her husband has nullified them, and the LORD will release her. [13]Her husband may confirm or nullify any vow she makes or any sworn pledge to deny herself. [14]But if her husband says nothing to her about it from day to day, then he confirms all her vows or the pledges binding on her. He confirms them by saying nothing to her when he hears about them. [15]If, however, he nullifies them some time after he hears about them, then he is responsible for her guilt."

[16]These are the regulations the LORD gave Moses concerning relationships between a man and his wife, and between a father and his young daughter still living in his house.

Vengeance on the Midianites

31 The LORD said to Moses, [2]"Take vengeance on the Midianites for the Israelites. After that, you will be gathered to your people."

[3]So Moses said to the people, "Arm some of your men to go to war against the Midianites and to carry out the LORD's vengeance on them. [4]Send into battle a thousand men from each of the tribes of Israel." [5]So twelve thousand men armed for battle, a thousand from each tribe, were supplied from the clans of Israel. [6]Moses sent them into battle, a thousand from each tribe, along with Phinehas son of Eleazar, the priest, who took with him articles from the sanctuary and the trumpets for signaling.

[7]They fought against Midian, as the LORD commanded Moses, and killed every man. [8]Among their victims were Evi, Rekem, Zur,

[a]39 Traditionally *peace offerings*

Hur and Reba—the five kings of Midian.
They also killed Balaam son of Beor with the
sword. 9The Israelites captured the Midianite
women and children and took all the Midianite herds, flocks and goods as plunder.
10They burned all the towns where the Midianites had settled, as well as all their camps.
11They took all the plunder and spoils, including the people and animals, 12and brought
the captives, spoils and plunder to Moses
and Eleazar the priest and the Israelite assembly at their camp on the plains of Moab,
by the Jordan across from Jericho.[a]

13Moses, Eleazar the priest and all the
leaders of the community went to meet them
outside the camp. 14Moses was angry with
the officers of the army—the commanders of
thousands and commanders of hundreds—
who returned from the battle.

15"Have you allowed all the women to
live?" he asked them. 16"They were the ones
who followed Balaam's advice and were the
means of turning the Israelites away from the
LORD in what happened at Peor, so that a
plague struck the LORD's people. 17Now kill all
the boys. And kill every woman who has
slept with a man, 18but save for yourselves
every girl who has never slept with a man.

19"All of you who have killed anyone or
touched anyone who was killed must stay
outside the camp seven days. On the third
and seventh days you must purify yourselves and your captives. 20Purify every garment as well as everything made of leather,
goat hair or wood."

21Then Eleazar the priest said to the soldiers who had gone into battle, "This is the
requirement of the law that the LORD gave
Moses: 22Gold, silver, bronze, iron, tin, lead
23and anything else that can withstand fire
must be put through the fire, and then it will
be clean. But it must also be purified with the
water of cleansing. And whatever cannot
withstand fire must be put through that
water. 24On the seventh day wash your
clothes and you will be clean. Then you may
come into the camp."

Dividing the Spoils

25The LORD said to Moses, 26"You and
Eleazar the priest and the family heads of the
community are to count all the people and
animals that were captured. 27Divide the
spoils between the soldiers who took part in
the battle and the rest of the community.
28From the soldiers who fought in the battle,
set apart as tribute for the LORD one out of
every five hundred, whether persons, cattle,
donkeys, sheep or goats. 29Take this tribute
from their half share and give it to Eleazar the
priest as the LORD's part. 30From the Israelites' half, select one out of every fifty,
whether persons, cattle, donkeys, sheep,
goats or other animals. Give them to the
Levites, who are responsible for the care of
the LORD's tabernacle." 31So Moses and
Eleazar the priest did as the LORD commanded Moses.

32The plunder remaining from the spoils
that the soldiers took was 675,000 sheep,
3372,000 cattle, 3461,000 donkeys 35and 32,-
000 women who had never slept with a man.

36The half share of those who fought in the
battle was:

337,500 sheep, 37of which the tribute for
the LORD was 675;

3836,000 cattle, of which the tribute for the
LORD was 72;

3930,500 donkeys, of which the tribute for
the LORD was 61;

4016,000 people, of which the tribute for
the LORD was 32.

41Moses gave the tribute to Eleazar the
priest as the LORD's part, as the LORD commanded Moses.

42The half belonging to the Israelites,
which Moses set apart from that of the fighting men— 43the community's half—was
337,500 sheep, 4436,000 cattle, 4530,500
donkeys 46and 16,000 people. 47From the
Israelites' half, Moses selected one out of
every fifty persons and animals, as the LORD
commanded him, and gave them to the Levites, who were responsible for the care of
the LORD's tabernacle.

48Then the officers who were over the units
of the army—the commanders of thousands
and commanders of hundreds—went to
Moses 49and said to him, "Your servants
have counted the soldiers under our command, and not one is missing. 50So we have
brought as an offering to the LORD the gold
articles each of us acquired—armlets,
bracelets, signet rings, earrings and necklaces—to make atonement for ourselves before the LORD."

51Moses and Eleazar the priest accepted
from them the gold—all the crafted articles.
52All the gold from the commanders of thou-

[a]12 Hebrew *Jordan of Jericho*; possibly an ancient name for the Jordan River

sands and commanders of hundreds that
Moses and Eleazar presented as a gift to the
LORD weighed 16,750 shekels.[a] 53Each soldier had taken plunder for himself. 54Moses
and Eleazar the priest accepted the gold
from the commanders of thousands and
commanders of hundreds and brought it into
the Tent of Meeting as a memorial for the
Israelites before the LORD.

The Transjordan Tribes

32 The Reubenites and Gadites, who
had very large herds and flocks, saw
that the lands of Jazer and Gilead were suitable for livestock. 2So they came to Moses
and Eleazar the priest and to the leaders of
the community, and said, 3"Ataroth, Dibon,
Jazer, Nimrah, Heshbon, Elealeh, Sebam,
Nebo and Beon— 4the land the LORD subdued before the people of Israel—are suitable for livestock, and your servants have
livestock. 5If we have found favor in your
eyes," they said, "let this land be given to
your servants as our possession. Do not
make us cross the Jordan."

6Moses said to the Gadites and Reubenites, "Shall your countrymen go to war while
you sit here? 7Why do you discourage the
Israelites from going over into the land the
LORD has given them? 8This is what your
fathers did when I sent them from Kadesh
Barnea to look over the land. 9After they
went up to the Valley of Eshcol and viewed
the land, they discouraged the Israelites
from entering the land the LORD had given
them. 10The LORD's anger was aroused that
day and he swore this oath: 11'Because they
have not followed me wholeheartedly, not
one of the men twenty years old or more who
came up out of Egypt will see the land I
promised on oath to Abraham, Isaac and
Jacob— 12not one except Caleb son of Jephunneh the Kenizzite and Joshua son of
Nun, for they followed the LORD wholeheartedly.' 13The LORD's anger burned against Israel and he made them wander in the desert
forty years, until the whole generation of
those who had done evil in his sight was
gone.

14"And here you are, a brood of sinners,
standing in the place of your fathers and
making the LORD even more angry with Israel. 15If you turn away from following him, he
will again leave all this people in the desert,
and you will be the cause of their destruction."

16Then they came up to him and said, "We
would like to build pens here for our livestock
and cities for our women and children. 17But
we are ready to arm ourselves and go ahead
of the Israelites until we have brought them
to their place. Meanwhile our women and
children will live in fortified cities, for protection from the inhabitants of the land. 18We will
not return to our homes until every Israelite
has received his inheritance. 19We will not
receive any inheritance with them on the
other side of the Jordan, because our inheritance has come to us on the east side of the
Jordan."

20Then Moses said to them, "If you will do
this—if you will arm yourselves before the
LORD for battle, 21and if all of you will go
armed over the Jordan before the LORD until
he has driven his enemies out before him—
22then when the land is subdued before the
LORD, you may return and be free from your
obligation to the LORD and to Israel. And this
land will be your possession before the
LORD.

23"But if you fail to do this, you will be
sinning against the LORD; and you may be
sure that your sin will find you out. 24Build
cities for your women and children, and pens
for your flocks, but do what you have promised."

25The Gadites and Reubenites said to
Moses, "We your servants will do as our lord
commands. 26Our children and wives, our
flocks and herds will remain here in the cities
of Gilead. 27But your servants, every man
armed for battle, will cross over to fight before the LORD, just as our lord says."

28Then Moses gave orders about them to
Eleazar the priest and Joshua son of Nun
and to the family heads of the Israelite tribes.
29He said to them, "If the Gadites and Reubenites, every man armed for battle, cross
over the Jordan with you before the LORD,
then when the land is subdued before you,
give them the land of Gilead as their possession. 30But if they do not cross over with you
armed, they must accept their possession
with you in Canaan."

31The Gadites and Reubenites answered,
"Your servants will do what the LORD has
said. 32We will cross over before the LORD
into Canaan armed, but the property we inherit will be on this side of the Jordan."

[a]52 That is, about 420 pounds (about 190 kilograms)

33Then Moses gave to the Gadites, the
Reubenites and the half-tribe of Manasseh
son of Joseph the kingdom of Sihon king of
the Amorites and the kingdom of Og king of
Bashan—the whole land with its cities and
the territory around them.
34The Gadites built up Dibon, Ataroth, Aroer, 35Atroth Shophan, Jazer, Jogbehah,
36Beth Nimrah and Beth Haran as fortified
cities, and built pens for their flocks. 37And
the Reubenites rebuilt Heshbon, Elealeh
and Kiriathaim, 38as well as Nebo and Baal
Meon (these names were changed) and Sibmah. They gave names to the cities they
rebuilt.
39The descendants of Makir son of Manasseh went to Gilead, captured it and drove
out the Amorites who were there. 40So
Moses gave Gilead to the Makirites, the descendants of Manasseh, and they settled
there. 41Jair, a descendant of Manasseh,
captured their settlements and called them
Havvoth Jair.[a] 42And Nobah captured
Kenath and its surrounding settlements and
called it Nobah after himself.

Stages in Israel's Journey

33 Here are the stages in the journey of
the Israelites when they came out of
Egypt by divisions under the leadership of
Moses and Aaron. 2At the LORD's command
Moses recorded the stages in their journey.
This is their journey by stages:

3The Israelites set out from Rameses
on the fifteenth day of the first month,
the day after the Passover. They
marched out boldly in full view of all the
Egyptians, 4who were burying all their
firstborn, whom the LORD had struck
down among them; for the LORD had
brought judgment on their gods.
5The Israelites left Rameses and
camped at Succoth.
6They left Succoth and camped at
Etham, on the edge of the desert.
7They left Etham, turned back to Pi
Hahiroth, to the east of Baal Zephon,
and camped near Migdol.
8They left Pi Hahiroth[b] and passed
through the sea into the desert, and
when they had traveled for three days in
the Desert of Etham, they camped at
Marah.
9They left Marah and went to Elim,
where there were twelve springs and
seventy palm trees, and they camped
there.
10They left Elim and camped by the
Red Sea.[c]
11They left the Red Sea and camped
in the Desert of Sin.
12They left the Desert of Sin and
camped at Dophkah.
13They left Dophkah and camped at
Alush.
14They left Alush and camped at
Rephidim, where there was no water for
the people to drink.
15They left Rephidim and camped in
the Desert of Sinai.
16They left the Desert of Sinai and
camped at Kibroth Hattaavah.
17They left Kibroth Hattaavah and
camped at Hazeroth.
18They left Hazeroth and camped at
Rithmah.
19They left Rithmah and camped at
Rimmon Perez.
20They left Rimmon Perez and
camped at Libnah.
21They left Libnah and camped at Rissah.
22They left Rissah and camped at
Kehelathah.
23They left Kehelathah and camped at
Mount Shepher.
24They left Mount Shepher and
camped at Haradah.
25They left Haradah and camped at
Makheloth.
26They left Makheloth and camped at
Tahath.
27They left Tahath and camped at
Terah.
28They left Terah and camped at Mithcah.
29They left Mithcah and camped at
Hashmonah.
30They left Hashmonah and camped
at Moseroth.
31They left Moseroth and camped at
Bene Jaakan.
32They left Bene Jaakan and camped
at Hor Haggidgad.
33They left Hor Haggidgad and
camped at Jotbathah.

[a] 41 Or *them the settlements of Jair* [b] 8 Many manuscripts of the Masoretic Text, Samaritan Pentateuch and Vulgate; most manuscripts of the Masoretic Text *left from before Hahiroth* [c] 10 Hebrew *Yam Suph;* that is, Sea of Reeds; also in verse 11

34They left Jotbathah and camped at
Abronah.
35They left Abronah and camped at
Ezion Geber.
36They left Ezion Geber and camped
at Kadesh, in the Desert of Zin.
37They left Kadesh and camped at
Mount Hor, on the border of Edom. 38At
the LORD's command Aaron the priest
went up Mount Hor, where he died on
the first day of the fifth month of the
fortieth year after the Israelites came out
of Egypt. 39Aaron was a hundred and
twenty-three years old when he died on
Mount Hor.
40The Canaanite king of Arad, who
lived in the Negev of Canaan, heard that
the Israelites were coming.
41They left Mount Hor and camped at
Zalmonah.
42They left Zalmonah and camped at
Punon.
43They left Punon and camped at
Oboth.
44They left Oboth and camped at Iye
Abarim, on the border of Moab.
45They left Iyim[a] and camped at Dibon Gad.
46They left Dibon Gad and camped at
Almon Diblathaim.
47They left Almon Diblathaim and
camped in the mountains of Abarim,
near Nebo.
48They left the mountains of Abarim
and camped on the plains of Moab by
the Jordan across from Jericho.[b]
49There on the plains of Moab they
camped along the Jordan from Beth
Jeshimoth to Abel Shittim.

50On the plains of Moab by the Jordan
across from Jericho the LORD said to Moses,
51"Speak to the Israelites and say to them:
'When you cross the Jordan into Canaan,
52drive out all the inhabitants of the land before you. Destroy all their carved images and
their cast idols, and demolish all their high
places. 53Take possession of the land and
settle in it, for I have given you the land to
possess. 54Distribute the land by lot, according to your clans. To a larger group give a
larger inheritance, and to a smaller group a
smaller one. Whatever falls to them by lot will
be theirs. Distribute it according to your
ancestral tribes.
55" 'But if you do not drive out the inhabitants of the land, those you allow to remain
will become barbs in your eyes and thorns in
your sides. They will give you trouble in the
land where you will live. 56And then I will do to
you what I plan to do to them.' "

Boundaries of Canaan

34 The LORD said to Moses, 2"Command
the Israelites and say to them: 'When
you enter Canaan, the land that will be allotted to you as an inheritance will have these
boundaries:

3" 'Your southern side will include some of
the Desert of Zin along the border of Edom.
On the east, your southern boundary will
start from the end of the Salt Sea,[c] 4cross
south of Scorpion[d] Pass, continue on to Zin
and go south of Kadesh Barnea. Then it will
go to Hazar Addar and over to Azmon,
5where it will turn, join the Wadi of Egypt and
end at the Sea.[e]
6" 'Your western boundary will be the
coast of the Great Sea. This will be your
boundary on the west.
7" 'For your northern boundary, run a line
from the Great Sea to Mount Hor 8and from
Mount Hor to Lebo[f] Hamath. Then the
boundary will go to Zedad, 9continue to Ziph-
ron and end at Hazar Enan. This will be your
boundary on the north.
10" 'For your eastern boundary, run a line
from Hazar Enan to Shepham. 11The boundary will go down from Shepham to Riblah on
the east side of Ain and continue along the
slopes east of the Sea of Kinnereth.[g] 12Then
the boundary will go down along the Jordan
and end at the Salt Sea.
" 'This will be your land, with its boundaries on every side.' "
13Moses commanded the Israelites: "Assign this land by lot as an inheritance. The
LORD has ordered that it be given to the nine
and a half tribes, 14because the families of
the tribe of Reuben, the tribe of Gad and the
half-tribe of Manasseh have received their
inheritance. 15These two and a half tribes
have received their inheritance on the east
side of the Jordan of Jericho,[h] toward the
sunrise."

[a] *45* That is, Iye Abarim [b] *48* Hebrew *Jordan of Jericho*; possibly an ancient name for the Jordan River; also in verse 50 [c] *3* That is, the Dead Sea; also in verse 12 [d] *4* Hebrew *Akrabbim* [e] *5* That is, the Mediterranean; also in verses 6 and 7 [f] *8* Or *to the entrance to* [g] *11* That is, Galilee [h] *15* *Jordan of Jericho* was possibly an ancient name for the Jordan River.

16The LORD said to Moses, 17"These are
the names of the men who are to assign the
land for you as an inheritance: Eleazar the
priest and Joshua son of Nun. 18And appoint
one leader from each tribe to help assign the
land. 19These are their names:

Caleb son of Jephunneh,
from the tribe of Judah;
20Shemuel son of Ammihud,
from the tribe of Simeon;
21Elidad son of Kislon,
from the tribe of Benjamin;
22Bukki son of Jogli,
the leader from the tribe of Dan;
23Hanniel son of Ephod,
the leader from the tribe of Manasseh son of Joseph;
24Kemuel son of Shiphtan,
the leader from the tribe of Ephraim son of Joseph;
25Elizaphan son of Parnach,
the leader from the tribe of Zebulun;
26Paltiel son of Azzan,
the leader from the tribe of Issachar;
27Ahihud son of Shelomi,
the leader from the tribe of Asher;
28Pedahel son of Ammihud,
the leader from the tribe of Naphtali."

29These are the men the LORD commanded
to assign the inheritance to the Israelites in
the land of Canaan.

Towns for the Levites

35 On the plains of Moab by the Jordan
across from Jericho,[a] the LORD said
to Moses, 2"Command the Israelites to give
the Levites towns to live in from the inheritance the Israelites will possess. And give
them pasturelands around the towns. 3Then
they will have towns to live in and pasturelands for their cattle, flocks and all their other
livestock.

4"The pasturelands around the towns that
you give the Levites will extend out fifteen
hundred feet[b] from the town wall. 5Outside
the town, measure three thousand feet[c] on
the east side, three thousand on the south
side, three thousand on the west and three
thousand on the north, with the town in the
center. They will have this area as pastureland for the towns.

Cities of Refuge

6"Six of the towns you give the Levites will
be cities of refuge, to which a person who
has killed someone may flee. In addition,
give them forty-two other towns. 7In all you
must give the Levites forty-eight towns, together with their pasturelands. 8The towns
you give the Levites from the land the Israelites possess are to be given in proportion to
the inheritance of each tribe: Take many
towns from a tribe that has many, but few
from one that has few."

9Then the LORD said to Moses: 10"Speak to
the Israelites and say to them: 'When you
cross the Jordan into Canaan, 11select some
towns to be your cities of refuge, to which a
person who has killed someone accidentally
may flee. 12They will be places of refuge from
the avenger, so that a person accused of
murder may not die before he stands trial
before the assembly. 13These six towns you
give will be your cities of refuge. 14Give three
on this side of the Jordan and three in Canaan as cities of refuge. 15These six towns
will be a place of refuge for Israelites, aliens
and any other people living among them, so
that anyone who has killed another accidentally can flee there.

16" 'If a man strikes someone with an iron
object so that he dies, he is a murderer; the
murderer shall be put to death. 17Or if anyone
has a stone in his hand that could kill, and he
strikes someone so that he dies, he is a
murderer; the murderer shall be put to death.
18Or if anyone has a wooden object in his
hand that could kill, and he hits someone so
that he dies, he is a murderer; the murderer
shall be put to death. 19The avenger of blood
shall put the murderer to death; when he
meets him, he shall put him to death. 20If
anyone with malice aforethought shoves another or throws something at him intentionally so that he dies 21or if in hostility he hits him
with his fist so that he dies, that person shall
be put to death; he is a murderer. The avenger of blood shall put the murderer to death
when he meets him.

22" 'But if without hostility someone suddenly shoves another or throws something at
him unintentionally 23or, without seeing him,
drops a stone on him that could kill him, and
he dies, then since he was not his enemy
and he did not intend to harm him, 24the
assembly must judge between him and the
avenger of blood according to these regulations. 25The assembly must protect the one

[a]1 Hebrew *Jordan of Jericho*; possibly an ancient name for the Jordan River [b]4 Hebrew *a thousand cubits* (about 450 meters) [c]5 Hebrew *two thousand cubits* (about 900 meters)

accused of murder from the avenger of blood
and send him back to the city of refuge to
which he fled. He must stay there until the
death of the high priest, who was anointed
with the holy oil.
26" 'But if the accused ever goes outside
the limits of the city of refuge to which he has
fled 27and the avenger of blood finds him
outside the city, the avenger of blood may kill
the accused without being guilty of murder.
28The accused must stay in his city of refuge
until the death of the high priest; only after
the death of the high priest may he return to
his own property.
29" 'These are to be legal requirements for
you throughout the generations to come,
wherever you live.
30" 'Anyone who kills a person is to be put
to death as a murderer only on the testimony
of witnesses. But no one is to be put to death
on the testimony of only one witness.
31" 'Do not accept a ransom for the life of a
murderer, who deserves to die. He must
surely be put to death.
32" 'Do not accept a ransom for anyone
who has fled to a city of refuge and so allow
him to go back and live on his own land
before the death of the high priest.
33" 'Do not pollute the land where you are.
Bloodshed pollutes the land, and atonement
cannot be made for the land on which blood
has been shed, except by the blood of the
one who shed it. 34Do not defile the land
where you live and where I dwell, for I, the
LORD, dwell among the Israelites.' "

Inheritance of Zelophehad's Daughters

36 The family heads of the clan of Gilead son of Makir, the son of Manasseh, who were from the clans of the descendants of Joseph, came and spoke before Moses and the leaders, the heads of the
Israelite families. 2They said, "When the
LORD commanded my lord to give the land as
an inheritance to the Israelites by lot, he ordered you to give the inheritance of our
brother Zelophehad to his daughters. 3Now
suppose they marry men from other Israelite
tribes; then their inheritance will be taken
from our ancestral inheritance and added to
that of the tribe they marry into. And so part
of the inheritance allotted to us will be taken
away. 4When the Year of Jubilee for the Israelites comes, their inheritance will be added
to that of the tribe into which they marry, and
their property will be taken from the tribal
inheritance of our forefathers."
5Then at the LORD's command Moses gave
this order to the Israelites: "What the tribe of
the descendants of Joseph is saying is right.
6This is what the LORD commands for Zelophehad's daughters: They may marry anyone they please as long as they marry within
the tribal clan of their father. 7No inheritance
in Israel is to pass from tribe to tribe, for
every Israelite shall keep the tribal land inherited from his forefathers. 8Every daughter
who inherits land in any Israelite tribe must
marry someone in her father's tribal clan, so
that every Israelite will possess the inheritance of his fathers. 9No inheritance may
pass from tribe to tribe, for each Israelite
tribe is to keep the land it inherits."
10So Zelophehad's daughters did as the
LORD commanded Moses. 11Zelophehad's
daughters—Mahlah, Tirzah, Hoglah, Milcah
and Noah—married their cousins on their
father's side. 12They married within the clans
of the descendants of Manasseh son of Joseph, and their inheritance remained in their
father's clan and tribe.
13These are the commands and regulations the LORD gave through Moses to the
Israelites on the plains of Moab by the Jordan across from Jericho.[a]

[a]13 Hebrew *Jordan of Jericho;* possibly an ancient name for the Jordan River

Deuteronomy

Introduction:

Deuteronomy means "second law." After forty years the Israelites were about to enter the Promised Land of Canaan. But before they did, Moses wanted to remind them of their history, all that God and had done for them, and the laws they had to continue to obey as God's chosen people.

His first speech reminded the people of God's goodness to them through their journey and his giving them the land of Canaan. Moses' second speech was a summary of God's laws including the Ten Commandments. Moses told the people to "love the LORD your God with all your heart and with all your soul and with all your strength" in order to continue to enjoy God's blessing. Moses also emphasized the fact that to keep their relationship right with God, the people had to teach their children to love the Lord and obey his commandments.

Deuteronomy ends with the people of Israel being reminded of the covenant God had made with them (29), Joshua's appointment to be the new leader (31), and Moses' death (34). It is generally accepted that Moses wrote Deuteronomy except for the chapter about his death.

Outline of contents:

Moses' first speech: Israel's history (1:1–4:43)
Moses' second speech: review of the law (4:44–11:32)
Rules for daily living (12:1–26:19)
The results of obedience and disobedience (27:1–28:68)
The renewal of the covenant (29:1–30:20)
Moses' blessing on Israel and his death (31:1–34:12)

The Command to Leave Horeb

1 These are the words Moses spoke to all
Israel in the desert east of the Jordan—
that is, in the Arabah—opposite Suph, between Paran and Tophel, Laban, Hazeroth
and Dizahab. 2(It takes eleven days to go
from Horeb to Kadesh Barnea by the Mount
Seir road.)
3In the fortieth year, on the first day of the
eleventh month, Moses proclaimed to the
Israelites all that the LORD had commanded
him concerning them. 4This was after he had
defeated Sihon king of the Amorites, who
reigned in Heshbon, and at Edrei had defeated Og king of Bashan, who reigned in
Ashtaroth.
5East of the Jordan in the territory of Moab,
Moses began to expound this law, saying:
6The LORD our God said to us at Horeb,
"You have stayed long enough at this mountain. 7Break camp and advance into the hill
country of the Amorites; go to all the neighboring peoples in the Arabah, in the mountains, in the western foothills, in the Negev
and along the coast, to the land of the Canaanites and to Lebanon, as far as the great
river, the Euphrates. 8See, I have given you
this land. Go in and take possession of the
land that the LORD swore he would give to
your fathers—to Abraham, Isaac and
Jacob—and to their descendants after
them."

The Appointment of Leaders

9At that time I said to you, "You are too
heavy a burden for me to carry alone. 10The
LORD your God has increased your numbers
so that today you are as many as the stars in
the sky. 11May the LORD, the God of your
fathers, increase you a thousand times and
bless you as he has promised! 12But how can
I bear your problems and your burdens and
your disputes all by myself? 13Choose some
wise, understanding and respected men

from each of your tribes, and I will set them over you."

14You answered me, "What you propose to do is good."

15So I took the leading men of your tribes, wise and respected men, and appointed them to have authority over you—as commanders of thousands, of hundreds, of fifties and of tens and as tribal officials. 16And I charged your judges at that time: Hear the disputes between your brothers and judge fairly, whether the case is between brother Israelites or between one of them and an alien. 17Do not show partiality in judging; hear both small and great alike. Do not be afraid of any man, for judgment belongs to God. Bring me any case too hard for you, and I will hear it. 18And at that time I told you everything you were to do.

Spies Sent Out

19Then, as the LORD our God commanded us, we set out from Horeb and went toward the hill country of the Amorites through all that vast and dreadful desert that you have seen, and so we reached Kadesh Barnea. 20Then I said to you, "You have reached the hill country of the Amorites, which the LORD our God is giving us. 21See, the LORD your God has given you the land. Go up and take possession of it as the LORD, the God of your fathers, told you. Do not be afraid; do not be discouraged."

22Then all of you came to me and said, "Let us send men ahead to spy out the land for us and bring back a report about the route we are to take and the towns we will come to."

23The idea seemed good to me; so I selected twelve of you, one man from each tribe. 24They left and went up into the hill country, and came to the Valley of Eshcol and explored it. 25Taking with them some of the fruit of the land, they brought it down to us and reported, "It is a good land that the LORD our God is giving us."

Rebellion Against the LORD

26But you were unwilling to go up; you rebelled against the command of the LORD your God. 27You grumbled in your tents and said, "The LORD hates us; so he brought us out of Egypt to deliver us into the hands of the Amorites to destroy us. 28Where can we go? Our brothers have made us lose heart. They say, 'The people are stronger and taller than we are; the cities are large, with walls up to the sky. We even saw the Anakites there.' "

29Then I said to you, "Do not be terrified; do not be afraid of them. 30The LORD your God, who is going before you, will fight for you, as he did for you in Egypt, before your very eyes, 31and in the desert. There you saw how the LORD your God carried you, as a father carries his son, all the way you went until you reached this place."

32In spite of this, you did not trust in the LORD your God, 33who went ahead of you on your journey, in fire by night and in a cloud by day, to search out places for you to camp and to show you the way you should go. 34When the LORD heard what you said, he was angry and solemnly swore: 35"Not a man of this evil generation shall see the good land I swore to give your forefathers, 36except Caleb son of Jephunneh. He will see it, and I will give him and his descendants the land he set his feet on, because he followed the LORD wholeheartedly."

37Because of you the LORD became angry with me also and said, "You shall not enter it, either. 38But your assistant, Joshua son of Nun, will enter it. Encourage him, because he will lead Israel to inherit it. 39And the little ones that you said would be taken captive, your children who do not yet know good from bad—they will enter the land. I will give it to them and they will take possession of it. 40But as for you, turn around and set out toward the desert along the route to the Red Sea.[a]"

41Then you replied, "We have sinned against the LORD. We will go up and fight, as the LORD our God commanded us." So every one of you put on his weapons, thinking it easy to go up into the hill country.

42But the LORD said to me, "Tell them, 'Do not go up and fight, because I will not be with you. You will be defeated by your enemies.' "

43So I told you, but you would not listen. You rebelled against the LORD's command and in your arrogance you marched up into the hill country. 44The Amorites who lived in those hills came out against you; they chased you like a swarm of bees and beat you down from Seir all the way to Hormah. 45You came back and wept before the LORD, but he paid no attention to your weeping and turned a deaf ear to you. 46And so you stayed

[a]40 Hebrew *Yam Suph;* that is, Sea of Reeds

in Kadesh many days—all the time you
spent there.

Wanderings in the Desert

2 Then we turned back and set out toward
the desert along the route to the Red
Sea,[a] as the LORD had directed me. For a
long time we made our way around the hill
country of Seir.
2Then the LORD said to me, 3"You have
made your way around this hill country long
enough; now turn north. 4Give the people
these orders: 'You are about to pass through
the territory of your brothers the descendants of Esau, who live in Seir. They will be
afraid of you, but be very careful. 5Do not
provoke them to war, for I will not give you
any of their land, not even enough to put your
foot on. I have given Esau the hill country of
Seir as his own. 6You are to pay them in
silver for the food you eat and the water you
drink.' "
7The LORD your God has blessed you in all
the work of your hands. He has watched over
your journey through this vast desert. These
forty years the LORD your God has been with
you, and you have not lacked anything.
8So we went on past our brothers the descendants of Esau, who live in Seir. We
turned from the Arabah road, which comes
up from Elath and Ezion Geber, and traveled
along the desert road of Moab.
9Then the LORD said to me, "Do not harass
the Moabites or provoke them to war, for I will
not give you any part of their land. I have
given Ar to the descendants of Lot as a
possession."
10(The Emites used to live there—a people
strong and numerous, and as tall as the Anakites. 11Like the Anakites, they too were considered Rephaites, but the Moabites called
them Emites. 12Horites used to live in Seir,
but the descendants of Esau drove them out.
They destroyed the Horites from before them
and settled in their place, just as Israel did in
the land the LORD gave them as their possession.)
13And the LORD said, "Now get up and
cross the Zered Valley." So we crossed the
valley.
14Thirty-eight years passed from the time
we left Kadesh Barnea until we crossed the
Zered Valley. By then, that entire generation
of fighting men had perished from the camp,
as the LORD had sworn to them. 15The LORD's
hand was against them until he had completely eliminated them from the camp.
16Now when the last of these fighting men
among the people had died, 17the LORD said
to me, 18"Today you are to pass by the region of Moab at Ar. 19When you come to the
Ammonites, do not harass them or provoke
them to war, for I will not give you possession
of any land belonging to the Ammonites. I
have given it as a possession to the descendants of Lot."
20(That too was considered a land of the
Rephaites, who used to live there; but the
Ammonites called them Zamzummites.
21They were a people strong and numerous,
and as tall as the Anakites. The LORD destroyed them from before the Ammonites,
who drove them out and settled in their
place. 22The LORD had done the same for the
descendants of Esau, who lived in Seir,
when he destroyed the Horites from before
them. They drove them out and have lived in
their place to this day. 23And as for the Avvites who lived in villages as far as Gaza, the
Caphtorites coming out from Caphtor[b] destroyed them and settled in their place.)

Defeat of Sihon King of Heshbon

24"Set out now and cross the Arnon Gorge.
See, I have given into your hand Sihon the
Amorite, king of Heshbon, and his country.
Begin to take possession of it and engage
him in battle. 25This very day I will begin to
put the terror and fear of you on all the nations under heaven. They will hear reports of
you and will tremble and be in anguish because of you."
26From the desert of Kedemoth I sent messengers to Sihon king of Heshbon offering
peace and saying, 27"Let us pass through
your country. We will stay on the main road;
we will not turn aside to the right or to the left.
28Sell us food to eat and water to drink for
their price in silver. Only let us pass through
on foot— 29as the descendants of Esau, who
live in Seir, and the Moabites, who live in Ar,
did for us—until we cross the Jordan into the
land the LORD our God is giving us." 30But
Sihon king of Heshbon refused to let us pass
through. For the LORD your God had made
his spirit stubborn and his heart obstinate in
order to give him into your hands, as he has
now done.
31The LORD said to me, "See, I have begun
to deliver Sihon and his country over to you.

[a] *1* Hebrew *Yam Suph;* that is, Sea of Reeds
[b] *23* That is, Crete

Now begin to conquer and possess his
land."
32When Sihon and all his army came out to
meet us in battle at Jahaz, 33the LORD our
God delivered him over to us and we struck
him down, together with his sons and his
whole army. 34At that time we took all his
towns and completely destroyed[a] them—
men, women and children. We left no survivors. 35But the livestock and the plunder from
the towns we had captured we carried off for
ourselves. 36From Aroer on the rim of the
Arnon Gorge, and from the town in the
gorge, even as far as Gilead, not one town
was too strong for us. The LORD our God
gave us all of them. 37But in accordance with
the command of the LORD our God, you did
not encroach on any of the land of the Ammonites, neither the land along the course of
the Jabbok nor that around the towns in the
hills.

Defeat of Og King of Bashan

3 Next we turned and went up along the
road toward Bashan, and Og king of Bashan with his whole army marched out to
meet us in battle at Edrei. 2The LORD said to
me, "Do not be afraid of him, for I have handed him over to you with his whole army and
his land. Do to him what you did to Sihon king
of the Amorites, who reigned in Heshbon."
3So the LORD our God also gave into our
hands Og king of Bashan and all his army.
We struck them down, leaving no survivors.
4At that time we took all his cities. There was
not one of the sixty cities that we did not take
from them—the whole region of Argob, Og's
kingdom in Bashan. 5All these cities were
fortified with high walls and with gates and
bars, and there were also a great many unwalled villages. 6We completely destroyed[a]
them, as we had done with Sihon king of
Heshbon, destroying[a] every city—men,
women and children. 7But all the livestock
and the plunder from their cities we carried
off for ourselves.
8So at that time we took from these two
kings of the Amorites the territory east of the
Jordan, from the Arnon Gorge as far as
Mount Hermon. 9(Hermon is called Sirion by
the Sidonians; the Amorites call it Senir.)
10We took all the towns on the plateau, and
all Gilead, and all Bashan as far as Salecah
and Edrei, towns of Og's kingdom in Bashan.
11(Only Og king of Bashan was left of the
remnant of the Rephaites. His bed[b] was
made of iron and was more than thirteen feet
long and six feet wide.[c] It is still in Rabbah of
the Ammonites.)

Division of the Land

12Of the land that we took over at that time,
I gave the Reubenites and the Gadites the
territory north of Aroer by the Arnon Gorge,
including half the hill country of Gilead, together with its towns. 13The rest of Gilead
and also all of Bashan, the kingdom of Og, I
gave to the half tribe of Manasseh. (The
whole region of Argob in Bashan used to be
known as a land of the Rephaites. 14Jair, a
descendant of Manasseh, took the whole region of Argob as far as the border of the
Geshurites and the Maacathites; it was
named after him, so that to this day Bashan
is called Havvoth Jair.[d]) 15And I gave Gilead
to Makir. 16But to the Reubenites and the
Gadites I gave the territory extending from
Gilead down to the Arnon Gorge (the middle
of the gorge being the border) and out to the
Jabbok River, which is the border of the Ammonites. 17Its western border was the Jordan
in the Arabah, from Kinnereth to the Sea of
the Arabah (the Salt Sea[e]), below the slopes
of Pisgah.
18I commanded you at that time: "The LORD
your God has given you this land to take
possession of it. But all your able-bodied
men, armed for battle, must cross over
ahead of your brother Israelites. 19However,
your wives, your children and your livestock
(I know you have much livestock) may stay in
the towns I have given you, 20until the LORD
gives rest to your brothers as he has to you,
and they too have taken over the land that
the LORD your God is giving them, across the
Jordan. After that, each of you may go back
to the possession I have given you."

Moses Forbidden to Cross the Jordan

21At that time I commanded Joshua: "You
have seen with your own eyes all that the
LORD your God has done to these two kings.
The LORD will do the same to all the kingdoms
over there where you are going. 22Do not be
afraid of them; the LORD your God himself will
fight for you."
23At that time I pleaded with the LORD: 24"O
Sovereign LORD, you have begun to show to

[a]34,6 The Hebrew term refers to the irrevocable giving over of things or persons to the LORD, often by totally destroying them. [b]11 Or *sarcophagus* [c]11 Hebrew *nine cubits long and four cubits wide* (about 4 meters long and 1.8 meters wide) [d]14 Or *called the settlements of Jair* [e]17 That is, the Dead Sea

your servant your greatness and your strong hand. For what god is there in heaven or on earth who can do the deeds and mighty works you do? 25Let me go over and see the good land beyond the Jordan—that fine hill country and Lebanon."

26But because of you the LORD was angry with me and would not listen to me. "That is enough," the LORD said. "Do not speak to me anymore about this matter. 27Go up to the top of Pisgah and look west and north and south and east. Look at the land with your own eyes, since you are not going to cross this Jordan. 28But commission Joshua, and encourage and strengthen him, for he will lead this people across and will cause them to inherit the land that you will see." 29So we stayed in the valley near Beth Peor.

Obedience Commanded

4 Hear now, O Israel, the decrees and laws I am about to teach you. Follow them so that you may live and may go in and take possession of the land that the LORD, the God of your fathers, is giving you. 2Do not add to what I command you and do not subtract from it, but keep the commands of the LORD your God that I give you.

3You saw with your own eyes what the LORD did at Baal Peor. The LORD your God destroyed from among you everyone who followed the Baal of Peor, 4but all of you who held fast to the LORD your God are still alive today.

5See, I have taught you decrees and laws as the LORD my God commanded me, so that you may follow them in the land you are entering to take possession of it. 6Observe them carefully, for this will show your wisdom and understanding to the nations, who will hear about all these decrees and say, "Surely this great nation is a wise and understanding people." 7What other nation is so great as to have their gods near them the way the LORD our God is near us whenever we pray to him? 8And what other nation is so great as to have such righteous decrees and laws as this body of laws I am setting before you today?

9Only be careful, and watch yourselves closely so that you do not forget the things your eyes have seen or let them slip from your heart as long as you live. Teach them to your children and to their children after them. 10Remember the day you stood before the LORD your God at Horeb, when he said to me, "Assemble the people before me to hear my words so that they may learn to revere me as long as they live in the land and may teach them to their children." 11You came near and stood at the foot of the mountain while it blazed with fire to the very heavens, with black clouds and deep darkness. 12Then the LORD spoke to you out of the fire. You heard the sound of words but saw no form; there was only a voice. 13He declared to you his covenant, the Ten Commandments, which he commanded you to follow and then wrote them on two stone tablets. 14And the LORD directed me at that time to teach you the decrees and laws you are to follow in the land that you are crossing the Jordan to possess.

Idolatry Forbidden

15You saw no form of any kind the day the LORD spoke to you at Horeb out of the fire. Therefore watch yourselves very carefully, 16so that you do not become corrupt and make for yourselves an idol, an image of any shape, whether formed like a man or a woman, 17or like any animal on earth or any bird that flies in the air, 18or like any creature that moves along the ground or any fish in the waters below. 19And when you look up to the sky and see the sun, the moon and the stars—all the heavenly array—do not be enticed into bowing down to them and worshiping things the LORD your God has apportioned to all the nations under heaven. 20But as for you, the LORD took you and brought you out of the iron-smelting furnace, out of Egypt, to be the people of his inheritance, as you now are.

21The LORD was angry with me because of you, and he solemnly swore that I would not cross the Jordan and enter the good land the LORD your God is giving you as your inheritance. 22I will die in this land; I will not cross the Jordan; but you are about to cross over and take possession of that good land. 23Be careful not to forget the covenant of the LORD your God that he made with you; do not make for yourselves an idol in the form of anything the LORD your God has forbidden. 24For the LORD your God is a consuming fire, a jealous God.

25After you have had children and grandchildren and have lived in the land a long time—if you then become corrupt and make any kind of idol, doing evil in the eyes of the LORD your God and provoking him to anger, 26I call heaven and earth as witnesses against you this day that you will quickly per-

ish from the land that you are crossing the
Jordan to possess. You will not live there
long but will certainly be destroyed. 27The
LORD will scatter you among the peoples, and
only a few of you will survive among the
nations to which the LORD will drive you.
28There you will worship man-made gods of
wood and stone, which cannot see or hear or
eat or smell. 29But if from there you seek the
LORD your God, you will find him if you look for
him with all your heart and with all your soul.
30When you are in distress and all these
things have happened to you, then in later
days you will return to the LORD your God and
obey him. 31For the LORD your God is a merciful God; he will not abandon or destroy you or
forget the covenant with your forefathers,
which he confirmed to them by oath.

The LORD Is God

32Ask now about the former days, long before your time, from the day God created
man on the earth; ask from one end of the
heavens to the other. Has anything so great
as this ever happened, or has anything like it
ever been heard of? 33Has any other people
heard the voice of God[a] speaking out of fire,
as you have, and lived? 34Has any god ever
tried to take for himself one nation out of
another nation, by testings, by miraculous
signs and wonders, by war, by a mighty hand
and an outstretched arm, or by great and
awesome deeds, like all the things the LORD
your God did for you in Egypt before your
very eyes?

35You were shown these things so that you
might know that the LORD is God; besides him
there is no other. 36From heaven he made
you hear his voice to discipline you. On earth
he showed you his great fire, and you heard
his words from out of the fire. 37Because he
loved your forefathers and chose their descendants after them, he brought you out of
Egypt by his Presence and his great
strength, 38to drive out before you nations
greater and stronger than you and to bring
you into their land to give it to you for your
inheritance, as it is today.

39Acknowledge and take to heart this day
that the LORD is God in heaven above and on
the earth below. There is no other. 40Keep
his decrees and commands, which I am giving you today, so that it may go well with you
and your children after you and that you may
live long in the land the LORD your God gives
you for all time.

Cities of Refuge

41Then Moses set aside three cities east of
the Jordan, 42to which anyone who had killed
a person could flee if he had unintentionally
killed his neighbor without malice aforethought. He could flee into one of these cities
and save his life. 43The cities were these:
Bezer in the desert plateau, for the Reubenites; Ramoth in Gilead, for the Gadites; and
Golan in Bashan, for the Manassites.

Introduction to the Law

44This is the law Moses set before the Israelites. 45These are the stipulations, decrees
and laws Moses gave them when they came
out of Egypt 46and were in the valley near
Beth Peor east of the Jordan, in the land of
Sihon king of the Amorites, who reigned in
Heshbon and was defeated by Moses and
the Israelites as they came out of Egypt.
47They took possession of his land and the
land of Og king of Bashan, the two Amorite
kings east of the Jordan. 48This land extended from Aroer on the rim of the Arnon
Gorge to Mount Siyon[b] (that is, Hermon),
49and included all the Arabah east of the
Jordan, as far as the Sea of the Arabah,[c]
below the slopes of Pisgah.

The Ten Commandments

5 Moses summoned all Israel and said:
Hear, O Israel, the decrees and laws I
declare in your hearing today. Learn them
and be sure to follow them. 2The LORD our
God made a covenant with us at Horeb. 3It
was not with our fathers that the LORD made
this covenant, but with us, with all of us who
are alive here today. 4The LORD spoke to you
face to face out of the fire on the mountain.
5(At that time I stood between the LORD and
you to declare to you the word of the LORD,
because you were afraid of the fire and did
not go up the mountain.) And he said:

6"I am the LORD your God, who brought
you out of Egypt, out of the land of
slavery.

7"You shall have no other gods before[d]
me.

8"You shall not make for yourself an idol
in the form of anything in heaven

[a]33 Or *of a god* [b]48 Hebrew; Syriac (see also Deut. 3:9) *Sirion* [c]49 That is, the Dead Sea [d]7 Or *besides*

above or on the earth beneath or
in the waters below. 9You shall
not bow down to them or worship
them; for I, the LORD your God, am
a jealous God, punishing the children for the sin of the fathers to
the third and fourth generation of
those who hate me, 10but showing love to a thousand ⌞genera-
tions⌟ of those who love me and
keep my commandments.
11"You shall not misuse the name of the
LORD your God, for the LORD will
not hold anyone guiltless who
misuses his name.
12"Observe the Sabbath day by keeping
it holy, as the LORD your God has
commanded you. 13Six days you
shall labor and do all your work,
14but the seventh day is a Sabbath to the LORD your God. On it
you shall not do any work, neither
you, nor your son or daughter, nor
your manservant or maidservant,
nor your ox, your donkey or any of
your animals, nor the alien within
your gates, so that your manservant and maidservant may rest,
as you do. 15Remember that you
were slaves in Egypt and that the
LORD your God brought you out of
there with a mighty hand and an
outstretched arm. Therefore the
LORD your God has commanded you to observe the Sabbath
day.
16"Honor your father and your mother, as
the LORD your God has com-
manded you, so that you may live
long and that it may go well with
you in the land the LORD your God
is giving you.
17"You shall not murder.
18"You shall not commit adultery.
19"You shall not steal.
20"You shall not give false testimony
against your neighbor.
21"You shall not covet your neighbor's
wife. You shall not set your desire
on your neighbor's house or land,
his manservant or maidservant,
his ox or donkey, or anything that
belongs to your neighbor."

22These are the commandments the LORD
proclaimed in a loud voice to your whole
assembly there on the mountain from out of
the fire, the cloud and the deep darkness;
and he added nothing more. Then he wrote
them on two stone tablets and gave them to
me.
23When you heard the voice out of the
darkness, while the mountain was ablaze
with fire, all the leading men of your tribes
and your elders came to me. 24And you said,
"The LORD our God has shown us his glory
and his majesty, and we have heard his
voice from the fire. Today we have seen that
a man can live even if God speaks with him.
25But now, why should we die? This great fire
will consume us, and we will die if we hear
the voice of the LORD our God any longer.
26For what mortal man has ever heard the
voice of the living God speaking out of fire, as
we have, and survived? 27Go near and listen
to all that the LORD our God says. Then tell us
whatever the LORD our God tells you. We will
listen and obey."

28The LORD heard you when you spoke to
me and the LORD said to me, "I have heard
what this people said to you. Everything they
said was good. 29Oh, that their hearts would
be inclined to fear me and keep all my commands always, so that it might go well with
them and their children forever!

30"Go, tell them to return to their tents.
31But you stay here with me so that I may
give you all the commands, decrees and
laws you are to teach them to follow in the
land I am giving them to possess."

32So be careful to do what the LORD your
God has commanded you; do not turn aside
to the right or to the left. 33Walk in all the way
that the LORD your God has commanded you,
so that you may live and prosper and prolong
your days in the land that you will possess.

Love the LORD Your God

6 These are the commands, decrees and
laws the LORD your God directed me to
teach you to observe in the land that you are
crossing the Jordan to possess, 2so that you,
your children and their children after them
may fear the LORD your God as long as you
live by keeping all his decrees and commands that I give you, and so that you may
enjoy long life. 3Hear, O Israel, and be careful to obey so that it may go well with you and
that you may increase greatly in a land flowing with milk and honey, just as the LORD, the
God of your fathers, promised you.

4Hear, O Israel: The LORD our God, the

LORD is one.[a] 5Love the LORD your God with
all your heart and with all your soul and with
all your strength. 6These commandments
that I give you today are to be upon your
hearts. 7Impress them on your children. Talk
about them when you sit at home and when
you walk along the road, when you lie down
and when you get up. 8Tie them as symbols
on your hands and bind them on your foreheads. 9Write them on the doorframes of
your houses and on your gates.

10When the LORD your God brings you into
the land he swore to your fathers, to Abraham, Isaac and Jacob, to give you—a land
with large, flourishing cities you did not build,
11houses filled with all kinds of good things
you did not provide, wells you did not dig,
and vineyards and olive groves you did not
plant—then when you eat and are satisfied,
12be careful that you do not forget the LORD,
who brought you out of Egypt, out of the land
of slavery.

13Fear the LORD your God, serve him only
and take your oaths in his name. 14Do not
follow other gods, the gods of the peoples
around you; 15for the LORD your God, who is
among you, is a jealous God and his anger
will burn against you, and he will destroy you
from the face of the land. 16Do not test the
LORD your God as you did at Massah. 17Be
sure to keep the commands of the LORD your
God and the stipulations and decrees he has
given you. 18Do what is right and good in the
LORD's sight, so that it may go well with you
and you may go in and take over the good
land that the LORD promised on oath to your
forefathers, 19thrusting out all your enemies
before you, as the LORD said.

20In the future, when your son asks you,
"What is the meaning of the stipulations, decrees and laws the LORD our God has commanded you?" 21tell him: "We were slaves of
Pharaoh in Egypt, but the LORD brought us
out of Egypt with a mighty hand. 22Before our
eyes the LORD sent miraculous signs and
wonders—great and terrible—upon Egypt
and Pharaoh and his whole household. 23But
he brought us out from there to bring us in
and give us the land that he promised on
oath to our forefathers. 24The LORD commanded us to obey all these decrees and to
fear the LORD our God, so that we might always prosper and be kept alive, as is the
case today. 25And if we are careful to obey all
this law before the LORD our God, as he has
commanded us, that will be our righteousness."

Driving Out the Nations

7 When the LORD your God brings you into
the land you are entering to possess and
drives out before you many nations—the Hittites, Girgashites, Amorites, Canaanites,
Perizzites, Hivites and Jebusites, seven nations larger and stronger than you— 2and
when the LORD your God has delivered them
over to you and you have defeated them,
then you must destroy them totally.[b] Make
no treaty with them, and show them no
mercy. 3Do not intermarry with them. Do not
give your daughters to their sons or take their
daughters for your sons, 4for they will turn
your sons away from following me to serve
other gods, and the LORD's anger will burn
against you and will quickly destroy you.
5This is what you are to do to them: Break
down their altars, smash their sacred stones,
cut down their Asherah poles[c] and burn their
idols in the fire. 6For you are a people holy to
the LORD your God. The LORD your God has
chosen you out of all the peoples on the face
of the earth to be his people, his treasured
possession.

7The LORD did not set his affection on you
and choose you because you were more
numerous than other peoples, for you were
the fewest of all peoples. 8But it was because
the LORD loved you and kept the oath he
swore to your forefathers that he brought you
out with a mighty hand and redeemed you
from the land of slavery, from the power of
Pharaoh king of Egypt. 9Know therefore that
the LORD your God is God; he is the faithful
God, keeping his covenant of love to a thousand generations of those who love him and
keep his commands. 10But

> those who hate him he will repay to their
> face by destruction;
> he will not be slow to repay to their face
> those who hate him.

11Therefore, take care to follow the commands, decrees and laws I give you today.

12If you pay attention to these laws and are
careful to follow them, then the LORD your
God will keep his covenant of love with you,

[a]4 Or *The LORD our God is one LORD;* or *The LORD is our God, the LORD is one;* or *The LORD is our God, the LORD alone* [b]2 The Hebrew term refers to the irrevocable giving over of things or persons to the LORD, often by totally destroying them; also in verse 26. [c]5 That is, symbols of the goddess Asherah; here and elsewhere in Deuteronomy

as he swore to your forefathers. 13He will
love you and bless you and increase your
numbers. He will bless the fruit of your
womb, the crops of your land—your grain,
new wine and oil—the calves of your herds
and the lambs of your flocks in the land that
he swore to your forefathers to give you.
14You will be blessed more than any other
people; none of your men or women will be
childless, nor any of your livestock without
young. 15The LORD will keep you free from
every disease. He will not inflict on you the
horrible diseases you knew in Egypt, but he
will inflict them on all who hate you. 16You
must destroy all the peoples the LORD your
God gives over to you. Do not look on them
with pity and do not serve their gods, for that
will be a snare to you.

17You may say to yourselves, "These nations are stronger than we are. How can we
drive them out?" 18But do not be afraid of
them; remember well what the LORD your
God did to Pharaoh and to all Egypt. 19You
saw with your own eyes the great trials, the
miraculous signs and wonders, the mighty
hand and outstretched arm, with which the
LORD your God brought you out. The LORD
your God will do the same to all the peoples
you now fear. 20Moreover, the LORD your God
will send the hornet among them until even
the survivors who hide from you have perished. 21Do not be terrified by them, for the
LORD your God, who is among you, is a great
and awesome God. 22The LORD your God will
drive out those nations before you, little by
little. You will not be allowed to eliminate
them all at once, or the wild animals will
multiply around you. 23But the LORD your God
will deliver them over to you, throwing them
into great confusion until they are destroyed.
24He will give their kings into your hand, and
you will wipe out their names from under
heaven. No one will be able to stand up
against you; you will destroy them. 25The
images of their gods you are to burn in the
fire. Do not covet the silver and gold on them,
and do not take it for yourselves, or you will
be ensnared by it, for it is detestable to the
LORD your God. 26Do not bring a detestable
thing into your house or you, like it, will be set
apart for destruction. Utterly abhor and detest it, for it is set apart for destruction.

Do Not Forget the LORD

8 Be careful to follow every command I am
giving you today, so that you may live
and increase and may enter and possess the
land that the LORD promised on oath to your
forefathers. 2Remember how the LORD your
God led you all the way in the desert these
forty years, to humble you and to test you in
order to know what was in your heart,
whether or not you would keep his commands. 3He humbled you, causing you to
hunger and then feeding you with manna,
which neither you nor your fathers had
known, to teach you that man does not live
on bread alone but on every word that comes
from the mouth of the LORD. 4Your clothes did
not wear out and your feet did not swell during these forty years. 5Know then in your
heart that as a man disciplines his son, so
the LORD your God disciplines you.

6Observe the commands of the LORD your
God, walking in his ways and revering him.
7For the LORD your God is bringing you into a
good land—a land with streams and pools of
water, with springs flowing in the valleys and
hills; 8a land with wheat and barley, vines
and fig trees, pomegranates, olive oil and
honey; 9a land where bread will not be
scarce and you will lack nothing; a land
where the rocks are iron and you can dig
copper out of the hills.

10When you have eaten and are satisfied,
praise the LORD your God for the good land
he has given you. 11Be careful that you do
not forget the LORD your God, failing to observe his commands, his laws and his decrees that I am giving you this day. 12Other-
wise, when you eat and are satisfied, when
you build fine houses and settle down, 13and
when your herds and flocks grow large and
your silver and gold increase and all you
have is multiplied, 14then your heart will
become proud and you will forget the LORD
your God, who brought you out of Egypt, out
of the land of slavery. 15He led you through
the vast and dreadful desert, that thirsty and
waterless land, with its venomous snakes
and scorpions. He brought you water out of
hard rock. 16He gave you manna to eat in the
desert, something your fathers had never
known, to humble and to test you so that in
the end it might go well with you. 17You may
say to yourself, "My power and the strength
of my hands have produced this wealth for
me." 18But remember the LORD your God, for
it is he who gives you the ability to produce
wealth, and so confirms his covenant, which
he swore to your forefathers, as it is today.

19If you ever forget the LORD your God and
follow other gods and worship and bow down
to them, I testify against you today that you

will surely be destroyed. 20Like the nations
the LORD destroyed before you, so you will be
destroyed for not obeying the LORD your God.

Not Because of Israel's Righteousness

9 Hear, O Israel. You are now about to
cross the Jordan to go in and dispossess
nations greater and stronger than you, with
large cities that have walls up to the sky.
2The people are strong and tall—Anakites!
You know about them and have heard it said:
"Who can stand up against the Anakites?"
3But be assured today that the LORD your
God is the one who goes across ahead of
you like a devouring fire. He will destroy
them; he will subdue them before you. And
you will drive them out and annihilate them
quickly, as the LORD has promised you.
4After the LORD your God has driven them
out before you, do not say to yourself, "The
LORD has brought me here to take possession of this land because of my righteousness." No, it is on account of the wickedness
of these nations that the LORD is going to
drive them out before you. 5It is not because
of your righteousness or your integrity that
you are going in to take possession of their
land; but on account of the wickedness of
these nations, the LORD your God will drive
them out before you, to accomplish what he
swore to your fathers, to Abraham, Isaac and
Jacob. 6Understand, then, that it is not because of your righteousness that the LORD
your God is giving you this good land to possess, for you are a stiff-necked people.

The Golden Calf

7Remember this and never forget how you
provoked the LORD your God to anger in the
desert. From the day you left Egypt until you
arrived here, you have been rebellious
against the LORD. 8At Horeb you aroused the
LORD's wrath so that he was angry enough to
destroy you. 9When I went up on the mountain to receive the tablets of stone, the tablets of the covenant that the LORD had made
with you, I stayed on the mountain forty days
and forty nights; I ate no bread and drank no
water. 10The LORD gave me two stone tablets
inscribed by the finger of God. On them were
all the commandments the LORD proclaimed
to you on the mountain out of the fire, on the
day of the assembly.
11At the end of the forty days and forty
nights, the LORD gave me the two stone tablets, the tablets of the covenant. 12Then the
LORD told me, "Go down from here at once,
because your people whom you brought out
of Egypt have become corrupt. They have
turned away quickly from what I commanded
them and have made a cast idol for themselves."
13And the LORD said to me, "I have seen
this people, and they are a stiff-necked
people indeed! 14Let me alone, so that I may
destroy them and blot out their name from
under heaven. And I will make you into a
nation stronger and more numerous than
they."
15So I turned and went down from the
mountain while it was ablaze with fire. And
the two tablets of the covenant were in my
hands.[a] 16When I looked, I saw that you had
sinned against the LORD your God; you had
made for yourselves an idol cast in the shape
of a calf. You had turned aside quickly from
the way that the LORD had commanded you.
17So I took the two tablets and threw them
out of my hands, breaking them to pieces
before your eyes.
18Then once again I fell prostrate before
the LORD for forty days and forty nights; I ate
no bread and drank no water, because of all
the sin you had committed, doing what was
evil in the LORD's sight and so provoking him
to anger. 19I feared the anger and wrath of
the LORD, for he was angry enough with you
to destroy you. But again the LORD listened to
me. 20And the LORD was angry enough with
Aaron to destroy him, but at that time I
prayed for Aaron too. 21Also I took that sinful
thing of yours, the calf you had made, and
burned it in the fire. Then I crushed it and
ground it to powder as fine as dust and threw
the dust into a stream that flowed down the
mountain.
22You also made the LORD angry at Taberah, at Massah and at Kibroth Hattaavah.
23And when the LORD sent you out from
Kadesh Barnea, he said, "Go up and take
possession of the land I have given you." But
you rebelled against the command of the
LORD your God. You did not trust him or obey
him. 24You have been rebellious against the
LORD ever since I have known you.
25I lay prostrate before the LORD those forty
days and forty nights because the LORD had
said he would destroy you. 26I prayed to the
LORD and said, "O Sovereign LORD, do not
destroy your people, your own inheritance

[a]15 Or *And I had the two tablets of the covenant with me, one in each hand*

that you redeemed by your great power and brought out of Egypt with a mighty hand. 27Remember your servants Abraham, Isaac and Jacob. Overlook the stubbornness of this people, their wickedness and their sin. 28Otherwise, the country from which you brought us will say, 'Because the LORD was not able to take them into the land he had promised them, and because he hated them, he brought them out to put them to death in the desert.' 29But they are your people, your inheritance that you brought out by your great power and your outstretched arm."

Tablets Like the First Ones

10 At that time the LORD said to me, "Chisel out two stone tablets like the first ones and come up to me on the mountain. Also make a wooden chest.[a] 2I will write on the tablets the words that were on the first tablets, which you broke. Then you are to put them in the chest."

3So I made the ark out of acacia wood and chiseled out two stone tablets like the first ones, and I went up on the mountain with the two tablets in my hands. 4The LORD wrote on these tablets what he had written before, the Ten Commandments he had proclaimed to you on the mountain, out of the fire, on the day of the assembly. And the LORD gave them to me. 5Then I came back down the mountain and put the tablets in the ark I had made, as the LORD commanded me, and they are there now.

6(The Israelites traveled from the wells of the Jaakanites to Moserah. There Aaron died and was buried, and Eleazar his son succeeded him as priest. 7From there they traveled to Gudgodah and on to Jotbathah, a land with streams of water. 8At that time the LORD set apart the tribe of Levi to carry the ark of the covenant of the LORD, to stand before the LORD to minister and to pronounce blessings in his name, as they still do today. 9That is why the Levites have no share or inheritance among their brothers; the LORD is their inheritance, as the LORD your God told them.)

10Now I had stayed on the mountain forty days and nights, as I did the first time, and the LORD listened to me at this time also. It was not his will to destroy you. 11"Go," the LORD said to me, "and lead the people on their way, so that they may enter and possess the land that I swore to their fathers to give them."

Fear the LORD

12And now, O Israel, what does the LORD your God ask of you but to fear the LORD your God, to walk in all his ways, to love him, to serve the LORD your God with all your heart and with all your soul, 13and to observe the LORD's commands and decrees that I am giving you today for your own good?

14To the LORD your God belong the heavens, even the highest heavens, the earth and everything in it. 15Yet the LORD set his affection on your forefathers and loved them, and he chose you, their descendants, above all the nations, as it is today. 16Circumcise your hearts, therefore, and do not be stiff-necked any longer. 17For the LORD your God is God of gods and Lord of lords, the great God, mighty and awesome, who shows no partiality and accepts no bribes. 18He defends the cause of the fatherless and the widow, and loves the alien, giving him food and clothing. 19And you are to love those who are aliens, for you yourselves were aliens in Egypt. 20Fear the LORD your God and serve him. Hold fast to him and take your oaths in his name. 21He is your praise; he is your God, who performed for you those great and awesome wonders you saw with your own eyes. 22Your forefathers who went down into Egypt were seventy in all, and now the LORD your God has made you as numerous as the stars in the sky.

Love and Obey the LORD

11 Love the LORD your God and keep his requirements, his decrees, his laws and his commands always. 2Remember today that your children were not the ones who saw and experienced the discipline of the LORD your God: his majesty, his mighty hand, his outstretched arm; 3the signs he performed and the things he did in the heart of Egypt, both to Pharaoh king of Egypt and to his whole country; 4what he did to the Egyptian army, to its horses and chariots, how he overwhelmed them with the waters of the Red Sea[b] as they were pursuing you, and how the LORD brought lasting ruin on them. 5It was not your children who saw what he did for you in the desert until you arrived at this place, 6and what he did to Dathan and Abiram, sons of Eliab the Reubenite, when the earth opened its mouth right in the middle of all Israel and swallowed them up with their

[a]1 That is, an ark [b]4 Hebrew *Yam Suph;* that is, Sea of Reeds

households, their tents and every living thing that belonged to them. 7But it was your own eyes that saw all these great things the LORD has done.

8Observe therefore all the commands I am giving you today, so that you may have the strength to go in and take over the land that you are crossing the Jordan to possess, 9and so that you may live long in the land that the LORD swore to your forefathers to give to them and their descendants, a land flowing with milk and honey. 10The land you are entering to take over is not like the land of Egypt, from which you have come, where you planted your seed and irrigated it by foot as in a vegetable garden. 11But the land you are crossing the Jordan to take possession of is a land of mountains and valleys that drinks rain from heaven. 12It is a land the LORD your God cares for; the eyes of the LORD your God are continually on it from the beginning of the year to its end.

13So if you faithfully obey the commands I am giving you today—to love the LORD your God and to serve him with all your heart and with all your soul— 14then I will send rain on your land in its season, both autumn and spring rains, so that you may gather in your grain, new wine and oil. 15I will provide grass in the fields for your cattle, and you will eat and be satisfied.

16Be careful, or you will be enticed to turn away and worship other gods and bow down to them. 17Then the LORD's anger will burn against you, and he will shut the heavens so that it will not rain and the ground will yield no produce, and you will soon perish from the good land the LORD is giving you. 18Fix these words of mine in your hearts and minds; tie them as symbols on your hands and bind them on your foreheads. 19Teach them to your children, talking about them when you sit at home and when you walk along the road, when you lie down and when you get up. 20Write them on the doorframes of your houses and on your gates, 21so that your days and the days of your children may be many in the land that the LORD swore to give your forefathers, as many as the days that the heavens are above the earth.

22If you carefully observe all these commands I am giving you to follow—to love the LORD your God, to walk in all his ways and to hold fast to him— 23then the LORD will drive out all these nations before you, and you will dispossess nations larger and stronger than you. 24Every place where you set your foot will be yours: Your territory will extend from the desert to Lebanon, and from the Euphrates River to the western sea.[a] 25No man will be able to stand against you. The LORD your God, as he promised you, will put the terror and fear of you on the whole land, wherever you go.

26See, I am setting before you today a blessing and a curse— 27the blessing if you obey the commands of the LORD your God that I am giving you today; 28the curse if you disobey the commands of the LORD your God and turn from the way that I command you today by following other gods, which you have not known. 29When the LORD your God has brought you into the land you are entering to possess, you are to proclaim on Mount Gerizim the blessings, and on Mount Ebal the curses. 30As you know, these mountains are across the Jordan, west of the road,[b] toward the setting sun, near the great trees of Moreh, in the territory of those Canaanites living in the Arabah in the vicinity of Gilgal. 31You are about to cross the Jordan to enter and take possession of the land the LORD your God is giving you. When you have taken it over and are living there, 32be sure that you obey all the decrees and laws I am setting before you today.

The One Place of Worship

12 These are the decrees and laws you must be careful to follow in the land that the LORD, the God of your fathers, has given you to possess—as long as you live in the land. 2Destroy completely all the places on the high mountains and on the hills and under every spreading tree where the nations you are dispossessing worship their gods. 3Break down their altars, smash their sacred stones and burn their Asherah poles in the fire; cut down the idols of their gods and wipe out their names from those places.

4You must not worship the LORD your God in their way. 5But you are to seek the place the LORD your God will choose from among all your tribes to put his Name there for his dwelling. To that place you must go; 6there bring your burnt offerings and sacrifices, your tithes and special gifts, what you have vowed to give and your freewill offerings, and the firstborn of your herds and flocks. 7There, in the presence of the LORD your

[a]24 That is, the Mediterranean [b]30 Or *Jordan, westward*

God, you and your families shall eat and
shall rejoice in everything you have put your
hand to, because the LORD your God has
blessed you.
8You are not to do as we do here today,
everyone as he sees fit, 9since you have not
yet reached the resting place and the inheritance the LORD your God is giving you. 10But
you will cross the Jordan and settle in the
land the LORD your God is giving you as an
inheritance, and he will give you rest from all
your enemies around you so that you will live
in safety. 11Then to the place the LORD your
God will choose as a dwelling for his Name—
there you are to bring everything I command
you: your burnt offerings and sacrifices, your
tithes and special gifts, and all the choice
possessions you have vowed to the LORD.
12And there rejoice before the LORD your
God, you, your sons and daughters, your
menservants and maidservants, and the Levites from your towns, who have no allotment or inheritance of their own. 13Be careful
not to sacrifice your burnt offerings anywhere you please. 14Offer them only at the
place the LORD will choose in one of your
tribes, and there observe everything I command you.
15Nevertheless, you may slaughter your
animals in any of your towns and eat as
much of the meat as you want, as if it were
gazelle or deer, according to the blessing the
LORD your God gives you. Both the ceremonially unclean and the clean may eat it. 16But
you must not eat the blood; pour it out on the
ground like water. 17You must not eat in your
own towns the tithe of your grain and new
wine and oil, or the firstborn of your herds
and flocks, or whatever you have vowed to
give, or your freewill offerings or special gifts.
18Instead, you are to eat them in the presence of the LORD your God at the place the
LORD your God will choose—you, your sons
and daughters, your menservants and maidservants, and the Levites from your towns—
and you are to rejoice before the LORD your
God in everything you put your hand to. 19Be
careful not to neglect the Levites as long as
you live in your land.
20When the LORD your God has enlarged
your territory as he promised you, and you
crave meat and say, "I would like some
meat," then you may eat as much of it as you
want. 21If the place where the LORD your God
chooses to put his Name is too far away from
you, you may slaughter animals from the
herds and flocks the LORD has given you, as I
have commanded you, and in your own
towns you may eat as much of them as you
want. 22Eat them as you would gazelle or
deer. Both the ceremonially unclean and the
clean may eat. 23But be sure you do not eat
the blood, because the blood is the life, and
you must not eat the life with the meat. 24You
must not eat the blood; pour it out on the
ground like water. 25Do not eat it, so that it
may go well with you and your children after
you, because you will be doing what is right
in the eyes of the LORD.
26But take your consecrated things and
whatever you have vowed to give, and go to
the place the LORD will choose. 27Present
your burnt offerings on the altar of the LORD
your God, both the meat and the blood. The
blood of your sacrifices must be poured beside the altar of the LORD your God, but you
may eat the meat. 28Be careful to obey all
these regulations I am giving you, so that it
may always go well with you and your children after you, because you will be doing
what is good and right in the eyes of the LORD
your God.
29The LORD your God will cut off before you
the nations you are about to invade and dispossess. But when you have driven them out
and settled in their land, 30and after they
have been destroyed before you, be careful
not to be ensnared by inquiring about their
gods, saying, "How do these nations serve
their gods? We will do the same." 31You
must not worship the LORD your God in their
way, because in worshiping their gods, they
do all kinds of detestable things the LORD
hates. They even burn their sons and daughters in the fire as sacrifices to their gods.
32See that you do all I command you; do
not add to it or take away from it.

Worshiping Other Gods

13 If a prophet, or one who foretells by
dreams, appears among you and announces to you a miraculous sign or wonder,
2and if the sign or wonder of which he has
spoken takes place, and he says, "Let us
follow other gods" (gods you have not
known) "and let us worship them," 3you must
not listen to the words of that prophet or
dreamer. The LORD your God is testing you to
find out whether you love him with all your
heart and with all your soul. 4It is the LORD
your God you must follow, and him you must
revere. Keep his commands and obey him;
serve him and hold fast to him. 5That prophet
or dreamer must be put to death, because he

preached rebellion against the LORD your
God, who brought you out of Egypt and redeemed you from the land of slavery; he has
tried to turn you from the way the LORD your
God commanded you to follow. You must
purge the evil from among you.
[6]If your very own brother, or your son or
daughter, or the wife you love, or your closest friend secretly entices you, saying, "Let
us go and worship other gods" (gods that
neither you nor your fathers have known,
[7]gods of the peoples around you, whether
near or far, from one end of the land to the
other), [8]do not yield to him or listen to him.
Show him no pity. Do not spare him or shield
him. [9]You must certainly put him to death.
Your hand must be the first in putting him to
death, and then the hands of all the people.
[10]Stone him to death, because he tried to
turn you away from the LORD your God, who
brought you out of Egypt, out of the land of
slavery. [11]Then all Israel will hear and be
afraid, and no one among you will do such an
evil thing again.
[12]If you hear it said about one of the towns
the LORD your God is giving you to live in
[13]that wicked men have arisen among you
and have led the people of their town astray,
saying, "Let us go and worship other gods"
(gods you have not known), [14]then you must
inquire, probe and investigate it thoroughly.
And if it is true and it has been proved that
this detestable thing has been done among
you, [15]you must certainly put to the sword all
who live in that town. Destroy it completely,[a]
both its people and its livestock. [16]Gather all
the plunder of the town into the middle of the
public square and completely burn the town
and all its plunder as a whole burnt offering to
the LORD your God. It is to remain a ruin
forever, never to be rebuilt. [17]None of those
condemned things[a] shall be found in your
hands, so that the LORD will turn from his
fierce anger; he will show you mercy, have
compassion on you, and increase your numbers, as he promised on oath to your forefathers, [18]because you obey the LORD your
God, keeping all his commands that I am
giving you today and doing what is right in his
eyes.

Clean and Unclean Food

14 You are the children of the LORD your
God. Do not cut yourselves or shave
the front of your heads for the dead, [2]for you
are a people holy to the LORD your God. Out
of all the peoples on the face of the earth, the
LORD has chosen you to be his treasured
possession.
[3]Do not eat any detestable thing. [4]These
are the animals you may eat: the ox, the
sheep, the goat, [5]the deer, the gazelle, the
roe deer, the wild goat, the ibex, the antelope
and the mountain sheep.[b] [6]You may eat any
animal that has a split hoof divided in two and
that chews the cud. [7]However, of those that
chew the cud or that have a split hoof completely divided you may not eat the camel,
the rabbit or the coney.[c] Although they chew
the cud, they do not have a split hoof; they
are ceremonially unclean for you. [8]The pig is
also unclean; although it has a split hoof, it
does not chew the cud. You are not to eat
their meat or touch their carcasses.
[9]Of all the creatures living in the water, you
may eat any that has fins and scales. [10]But
anything that does not have fins and scales
you may not eat; for you it is unclean.
[11]You may eat any clean bird. [12]But these
you may not eat: the eagle, the vulture, the
black vulture, [13]the red kite, the black kite,
any kind of falcon, [14]any kind of raven, [15]the
horned owl, the screech owl, the gull, any
kind of hawk, [16]the little owl, the great owl,
the white owl, [17]the desert owl, the osprey,
the cormorant, [18]the stork, any kind of heron,
the hoopoe and the bat.
[19]All flying insects that swarm are unclean
to you; do not eat them. [20]But any winged
creature that is clean you may eat.
[21]Do not eat anything you find already
dead. You may give it to an alien living in any
of your towns, and he may eat it, or you may
sell it to a foreigner. But you are a people
holy to the LORD your God.
Do not cook a young goat in its mother's
milk.

Tithes

[22]Be sure to set aside a tenth of all that
your fields produce each year. [23]Eat the tithe
of your grain, new wine and oil, and the firstborn of your herds and flocks in the presence
of the LORD your God at the place he will
choose as a dwelling for his Name, so that
you may learn to revere the LORD your God
always. [24]But if that place is too distant and
you have been blessed by the LORD your God

[a] *15,17* The Hebrew term refers to the irrevocable giving over of things or persons to the LORD, often by totally destroying them. [b] *5* The precise identification of some of the birds and animals in this chapter is uncertain. [c] *7* That is, the hyrax or rock badger

and cannot carry your tithe (because the place where the LORD will choose to put his Name is so far away), 25then exchange your tithe for silver, and take the silver with you and go to the place the LORD your God will choose. 26Use the silver to buy whatever you like: cattle, sheep, wine or other fermented drink, or anything you wish. Then you and your household shall eat there in the presence of the LORD your God and rejoice. 27And do not neglect the Levites living in your towns, for they have no allotment or inheritance of their own.

28At the end of every three years, bring all the tithes of that year's produce and store it in your towns, 29so that the Levites (who have no allotment or inheritance of their own) and the aliens, the fatherless and the widows who live in your towns may come and eat and be satisfied, and so that the LORD your God may bless you in all the work of your hands.

The Year for Canceling Debts

15 At the end of every seven years you must cancel debts. 2This is how it is to be done: Every creditor shall cancel the loan he has made to his fellow Israelite. He shall not require payment from his fellow Israelite or brother, because the LORD's time for canceling debts has been proclaimed. 3You may require payment from a foreigner, but you must cancel any debt your brother owes you. 4However, there should be no poor among you, for in the land the LORD your God is giving you to possess as your inheritance, he will richly bless you, 5if only you fully obey the LORD your God and are careful to follow all these commands I am giving you today. 6For the LORD your God will bless you as he has promised, and you will lend to many nations but will borrow from none. You will rule over many nations but none will rule over you.

7If there is a poor man among your brothers in any of the towns of the land that the LORD your God is giving you, do not be hardhearted or tightfisted toward your poor brother. 8Rather be openhanded and freely lend him whatever he needs. 9Be careful not to harbor this wicked thought: "The seventh year, the year for canceling debts, is near," so that you do not show ill will toward your needy brother and give him nothing. He may then appeal to the LORD against you, and you will be found guilty of sin. 10Give generously to him and do so without a grudging heart; then because of this the LORD your God will bless you in all your work and in everything you put your hand to. 11There will always be poor people in the land. Therefore I command you to be openhanded toward your brothers and toward the poor and needy in your land.

Freeing Servants

12If a fellow Hebrew, a man or a woman, sells himself to you and serves you six years, in the seventh year you must let him go free. 13And when you release him, do not send him away empty-handed. 14Supply him liberally from your flock, your threshing floor and your winepress. Give to him as the LORD your God has blessed you. 15Remember that you were slaves in Egypt and the LORD your God redeemed you. That is why I give you this command today.

16But if your servant says to you, "I do not want to leave you," because he loves you and your family and is well off with you, 17then take an awl and push it through his ear lobe into the door, and he will become your servant for life. Do the same for your maidservant.

18Do not consider it a hardship to set your servant free, because his service to you these six years has been worth twice as much as that of a hired hand. And the LORD your God will bless you in everything you do.

The Firstborn Animals

19Set apart for the LORD your God every firstborn male of your herds and flocks. Do not put the firstborn of your oxen to work, and do not shear the firstborn of your sheep. 20Each year you and your family are to eat them in the presence of the LORD your God at the place he will choose. 21If an animal has a defect, is lame or blind, or has any serious flaw, you must not sacrifice it to the LORD your God. 22You are to eat it in your own towns. Both the ceremonially unclean and the clean may eat it, as if it were gazelle or deer. 23But you must not eat the blood; pour it out on the ground like water.

Passover

16 Observe the month of Abib and celebrate the Passover of the LORD your God, because in the month of Abib he brought you out of Egypt by night. 2Sacrifice as the Passover to the LORD your God an animal from your flock or herd at the place the LORD will choose as a dwelling for his

Name. 3Do not eat it with bread made with yeast, but for seven days eat unleavened bread, the bread of affliction, because you left Egypt in haste—so that all the days of your life you may remember the time of your departure from Egypt. 4Let no yeast be found in your possession in all your land for seven days. Do not let any of the meat you sacrifice on the evening of the first day remain until morning.

5You must not sacrifice the Passover in any town the LORD your God gives you 6except in the place he will choose as a dwelling for his Name. There you must sacrifice the Passover in the evening, when the sun goes down, on the anniversary[a] of your departure from Egypt. 7Roast it and eat it at the place the LORD your God will choose. Then in the morning return to your tents. 8For six days eat unleavened bread and on the seventh day hold an assembly to the LORD your God and do no work.

Feast of Weeks

9Count off seven weeks from the time you begin to put the sickle to the standing grain. 10Then celebrate the Feast of Weeks to the LORD your God by giving a freewill offering in proportion to the blessings the LORD your God has given you. 11And rejoice before the LORD your God at the place he will choose as a dwelling for his Name—you, your sons and daughters, your menservants and maidservants, the Levites in your towns, and the aliens, the fatherless and the widows living among you. 12Remember that you were slaves in Egypt, and follow carefully these decrees.

Feast of Tabernacles

13Celebrate the Feast of Tabernacles for seven days after you have gathered the produce of your threshing floor and your winepress. 14Be joyful at your Feast—you, your sons and daughters, your menservants and maidservants, and the Levites, the aliens, the fatherless and the widows who live in your towns. 15For seven days celebrate the Feast to the LORD your God at the place the LORD will choose. For the LORD your God will bless you in all your harvest and in all the work of your hands, and your joy will be complete.

16Three times a year all your men must appear before the LORD your God at the place he will choose: at the Feast of Unleavened Bread, the Feast of Weeks and the Feast of Tabernacles. No man should appear before the LORD empty-handed: 17Each of you must bring a gift in proportion to the way the LORD your God has blessed you.

Judges

18Appoint judges and officials for each of your tribes in every town the LORD your God is giving you, and they shall judge the people fairly. 19Do not pervert justice or show partiality. Do not accept a bribe, for a bribe blinds the eyes of the wise and twists the words of the righteous. 20Follow justice and justice alone, so that you may live and possess the land the LORD your God is giving you.

Worshiping Other Gods

21Do not set up any wooden Asherah pole[b] beside the altar you build to the LORD your God, 22and do not erect a sacred stone, for these the LORD your God hates.

17 Do not sacrifice to the LORD your God an ox or a sheep that has any defect or flaw in it, for that would be detestable to him.

2If a man or woman living among you in one of the towns the LORD gives you is found doing evil in the eyes of the LORD your God in violation of his covenant, 3and contrary to my command has worshiped other gods, bowing down to them or to the sun or the moon or the stars of the sky, 4and this has been brought to your attention, then you must investigate it thoroughly. If it is true and it has been proved that this detestable thing has been done in Israel, 5take the man or woman who has done this evil deed to your city gate and stone that person to death. 6On the testimony of two or three witnesses a man shall be put to death, but no one shall be put to death on the testimony of only one witness. 7The hands of the witnesses must be the first in putting him to death, and then the hands of all the people. You must purge the evil from among you.

Law Courts

8If cases come before your courts that are too difficult for you to judge—whether bloodshed, lawsuits or assaults—take them to the place the LORD your God will choose. 9Go to the priests, who are Levites, and to the judge who is in office at that time. Inquire of them

[a]6 Or *down, at the time of day*
[b]21 Or *Do not plant any tree dedicated to Asherah*

and they will give you the verdict. 10You must act according to the decisions they give you at the place the LORD will choose. Be careful to do everything they direct you to do. 11Act according to the law they teach you and the decisions they give you. Do not turn aside from what they tell you, to the right or to the left. 12The man who shows contempt for the judge or for the priest who stands ministering there to the LORD your God must be put to death. You must purge the evil from Israel. 13All the people will hear and be afraid, and will not be contemptuous again.

The King

14When you enter the land the LORD your God is giving you and have taken possession of it and settled in it, and you say, "Let us set a king over us like all the nations around us," 15be sure to appoint over you the king the LORD your God chooses. He must be from among your own brothers. Do not place a foreigner over you, one who is not a brother Israelite. 16The king, moreover, must not acquire great numbers of horses for himself or make the people return to Egypt to get more of them, for the LORD has told you, "You are not to go back that way again." 17He must not take many wives, or his heart will be led astray. He must not accumulate large amounts of silver and gold.

18When he takes the throne of his kingdom, he is to write for himself on a scroll a copy of this law, taken from that of the priests, who are Levites. 19It is to be with him, and he is to read it all the days of his life so that he may learn to revere the LORD his God and follow carefully all the words of this law and these decrees 20and not consider himself better than his brothers and turn from the law to the right or to the left. Then he and his descendants will reign a long time over his kingdom in Israel.

Offerings for Priests and Levites

18 The priests, who are Levites—indeed the whole tribe of Levi—are to have no allotment or inheritance with Israel. They shall live on the offerings made to the LORD by fire, for that is their inheritance. 2They shall have no inheritance among their brothers; the LORD is their inheritance, as he promised them.

3This is the share due the priests from the people who sacrifice a bull or a sheep: the shoulder, the jowls and the inner parts. 4You are to give them the firstfruits of your grain, new wine and oil, and the first wool from the shearing of your sheep, 5for the LORD your God has chosen them and their descendants out of all your tribes to stand and minister in the LORD's name always.

6If a Levite moves from one of your towns anywhere in Israel where he is living, and comes in all earnestness to the place the LORD will choose, 7he may minister in the name of the LORD his God like all his fellow Levites who serve there in the presence of the LORD. 8He is to share equally in their benefits, even though he has received money from the sale of family possessions.

Detestable Practices

9When you enter the land the LORD your God is giving you, do not learn to imitate the detestable ways of the nations there. 10Let no one be found among you who sacrifices his son or daughter in[a] the fire, who practices divination or sorcery, interprets omens, engages in witchcraft, 11or casts spells, or who is a medium or spiritist or who consults the dead. 12Anyone who does these things is detestable to the LORD, and because of these detestable practices the LORD your God will drive out those nations before you. 13You must be blameless before the LORD your God.

The Prophet

14The nations you will dispossess listen to those who practice sorcery or divination. But as for you, the LORD your God has not permitted you to do so. 15The LORD your God will raise up for you a prophet like me from among your own brothers. You must listen to him. 16For this is what you asked of the LORD your God at Horeb on the day of the assembly when you said, "Let us not hear the voice of the LORD our God nor see this great fire anymore, or we will die."

17The LORD said to me: "What they say is good. 18I will raise up for them a prophet like you from among their brothers; I will put my words in his mouth, and he will tell them everything I command him. 19If anyone does not listen to my words that the prophet speaks in my name, I myself will call him to account. 20But a prophet who presumes to speak in my name anything I have not commanded him to say, or a prophet who speaks

[a]*10* Or *who makes his son or daughter pass through*

in the name of other gods, must be put to
death."
21You may say to yourselves, "How can
we know when a message has not been
spoken by the Lord?" 22If what a prophet
proclaims in the name of the Lord does not
take place or come true, that is a message
the Lord has not spoken. That prophet has
spoken presumptuously. Do not be afraid of
him.

Cities of Refuge

19 When the Lord your God has destroyed the nations whose land he is
giving you, and when you have driven them
out and settled in their towns and houses,
2then set aside for yourselves three cities
centrally located in the land the Lord your
God is giving you to possess. 3Build roads to
them and divide into three parts the land the
Lord your God is giving you as an inheritance, so that anyone who kills a man may
flee there.
4This is the rule concerning the man who
kills another and flees there to save his life—
one who kills his neighbor unintentionally,
without malice aforethought. 5For instance, a
man may go into the forest with his neighbor
to cut wood, and as he swings his ax to fell a
tree, the head may fly off and hit his neighbor
and kill him. That man may flee to one of
these cities and save his life. 6Otherwise, the
avenger of blood might pursue him in a rage,
overtake him if the distance is too great, and
kill him even though he is not deserving of
death, since he did it to his neighbor without
malice aforethought. 7This is why I command
you to set aside for yourselves three cities.
8If the Lord your God enlarges your territory, as he promised on oath to your forefathers, and gives you the whole land he
promised them, 9because you carefully follow all these laws I command you today—to
love the Lord your God and to walk always in
his ways—then you are to set aside three
more cities. 10Do this so that innocent blood
will not be shed in your land, which the Lord
your God is giving you as your inheritance,
and so that you will not be guilty of bloodshed.
11But if a man hates his neighbor and lies
in wait for him, assaults and kills him, and
then flees to one of these cities, 12the elders
of his town shall send for him, bring him back
from the city, and hand him over to the
avenger of blood to die. 13Show him no pity.
You must purge from Israel the guilt of shedding innocent blood, so that it may go well
with you.
14Do not move your neighbor's boundary
stone set up by your predecessors in the
inheritance you receive in the land the Lord
your God is giving you to possess.

Witnesses

15One witness is not enough to convict a
man accused of any crime or offense he may
have committed. A matter must be established by the testimony of two or three witnesses.
16If a malicious witness takes the stand to
accuse a man of a crime, 17the two men
involved in the dispute must stand in the
presence of the Lord before the priests and
the judges who are in office at the time. 18The
judges must make a thorough investigation,
and if the witness proves to be a liar, giving
false testimony against his brother, 19then do
to him as he intended to do to his brother.
You must purge the evil from among you.
20The rest of the people will hear of this and
be afraid, and never again will such an evil
thing be done among you. 21Show no pity:
life for life, eye for eye, tooth for tooth, hand
for hand, foot for foot.

Going to War

20 When you go to war against your
enemies and see horses and chariots and an army greater than yours, do not
be afraid of them, because the Lord your
God, who brought you up out of Egypt, will be
with you. 2When you are about to go into
battle, the priest shall come forward and address the army. 3He shall say: "Hear, O Israel, today you are going into battle against
your enemies. Do not be fainthearted or
afraid; do not be terrified or give way to panic
before them. 4For the Lord your God is the
one who goes with you to fight for you
against your enemies to give you victory."
5The officers shall say to the army: "Has
anyone built a new house and not dedicated
it? Let him go home, or he may die in battle
and someone else may dedicate it. 6Has
anyone planted a vineyard and not begun to
enjoy it? Let him go home, or he may die in
battle and someone else enjoy it. 7Has anyone become pledged to a woman and not
married her? Let him go home, or he may die
in battle and someone else marry her."
8Then the officers shall add, "Is any man
afraid or fainthearted? Let him go home so
that his brothers will not become disheart-

ened too." 9When the officers have finished
speaking to the army, they shall appoint
commanders over it.
10When you march up to attack a city,
make its people an offer of peace. 11If they
accept and open their gates, all the people in
it shall be subject to forced labor and shall
work for you. 12If they refuse to make peace
and they engage you in battle, lay siege to
that city. 13When the LORD your God delivers
it into your hand, put to the sword all the men
in it. 14As for the women, the children, the
livestock and everything else in the city, you
may take these as plunder for yourselves.
And you may use the plunder the LORD your
God gives you from your enemies. 15This is
how you are to treat all the cities that are at a
distance from you and do not belong to the
nations nearby.
16However, in the cities of the nations the
LORD your God is giving you as an inheritance, do not leave alive anything that
breathes. 17Completely destroy[a] them—the
Hittites, Amorites, Canaanites, Perizzites,
Hivites and Jebusites—as the LORD your God
has commanded you. 18Otherwise, they will
teach you to follow all the detestable things
they do in worshiping their gods, and you will
sin against the LORD your God.
19When you lay siege to a city for a long
time, fighting against it to capture it, do not
destroy its trees by putting an ax to them,
because you can eat their fruit. Do not cut
them down. Are the trees of the field people,
that you should besiege them?[b] 20However,
you may cut down trees that you know are
not fruit trees and use them to build siege
works until the city at war with you falls.

Atonement for an Unsolved Murder

21 If a man is found slain, lying in a field
in the land the LORD your God is giving you to possess, and it is not known who
killed him, 2your elders and judges shall go
out and measure the distance from the body
to the neighboring towns. 3Then the elders of
the town nearest the body shall take a heifer
that has never been worked and has never
worn a yoke 4and lead her down to a valley
that has not been plowed or planted and
where there is a flowing stream. There in the
valley they are to break the heifer's neck.
5The priests, the sons of Levi, shall step forward, for the LORD your God has chosen
them to minister and to pronounce blessings
in the name of the LORD and to decide all
cases of dispute and assault. 6Then all the
elders of the town nearest the body shall
wash their hands over the heifer whose neck
was broken in the valley, 7and they shall declare: "Our hands did not shed this blood,
nor did our eyes see it done. 8Accept this
atonement for your people Israel, whom you
have redeemed, O LORD, and do not hold
your people guilty of the blood of an innocent
man." And the bloodshed will be atoned for.
9So you will purge from yourselves the guilt
of shedding innocent blood, since you have
done what is right in the eyes of the LORD.

Marrying a Captive Woman

10When you go to war against your enemies and the LORD your God delivers them
into your hands and you take captives, 11if
you notice among the captives a beautiful
woman and are attracted to her, you may
take her as your wife. 12Bring her into your
home and have her shave her head, trim her
nails 13and put aside the clothes she was
wearing when captured. After she has lived
in your house and mourned her father and
mother for a full month, then you may go to
her and be her husband and she shall be
your wife. 14If you are not pleased with her,
let her go wherever she wishes. You must
not sell her or treat her as a slave, since you
have dishonored her.

The Right of the Firstborn

15If a man has two wives, and he loves one
but not the other, and both bear him sons but
the firstborn is the son of the wife he does not
love, 16when he wills his property to his sons,
he must not give the rights of the firstborn to
the son of the wife he loves in preference to
his actual firstborn, the son of the wife he
does not love. 17He must acknowledge the
son of his unloved wife as the firstborn by
giving him a double share of all he has. That
son is the first sign of his father's strength.
The right of the firstborn belongs to him.

A Rebellious Son

18If a man has a stubborn and rebellious
son who does not obey his father and mother
and will not listen to them when they discipline him, 19his father and mother shall take
hold of him and bring him to the elders at the

[a] *17* The Hebrew term refers to the irrevocable giving over of things or persons to the LORD, often by totally destroying them. [b] *19* Or *down to use in the siege, for the fruit trees are for the benefit of man.*

gate of his town. 20They shall say to the elders, "This son of ours is stubborn and rebellious. He will not obey us. He is a profligate
and a drunkard." 21Then all the men of his
town shall stone him to death. You must
purge the evil from among you. All Israel will
hear of it and be afraid.

Various Laws

22If a man guilty of a capital offense is put
to death and his body is hung on a tree, 23you
must not leave his body on the tree overnight. Be sure to bury him that same day,
because anyone who is hung on a tree is
under God's curse. You must not desecrate
the land the LORD your God is giving you as
an inheritance.

22 If you see your brother's ox or sheep
straying, do not ignore it but be sure
to take it back to him. 2If the brother does not
live near you or if you do not know who he is,
take it home with you and keep it until he
comes looking for it. Then give it back to him.
3Do the same if you find your brother's donkey or his cloak or anything he loses. Do not
ignore it.

4If you see your brother's donkey or his ox
fallen on the road, do not ignore it. Help him
get it to its feet.

5A woman must not wear men's clothing,
nor a man wear women's clothing, for the
LORD your God detests anyone who does
this.

6If you come across a bird's nest beside
the road, either in a tree or on the ground,
and the mother is sitting on the young or on
the eggs, do not take the mother with the
young. 7You may take the young, but be sure
to let the mother go, so that it may go well
with you and you may have a long life.

8When you build a new house, make a
parapet around your roof so that you may not
bring the guilt of bloodshed on your house if
someone falls from the roof.

9Do not plant two kinds of seed in your
vineyard; if you do, not only the crops you
plant but also the fruit of the vineyard will be
defiled.[a]

10Do not plow with an ox and a donkey
yoked together.

11Do not wear clothes of wool and linen
woven together.

12Make tassels on the four corners of the
cloak you wear.

Marriage Violations

13If a man takes a wife and, after lying with
her, dislikes her 14and slanders her and
gives her a bad name, saying, "I married this
woman, but when I approached her, I did not
find proof of her virginity," 15then the girl's
father and mother shall bring proof that she
was a virgin to the town elders at the gate.
16The girl's father will say to the elders, "I
gave my daughter in marriage to this man,
but he dislikes her. 17Now he has slandered
her and said, 'I did not find your daughter to
be a virgin.' But here is the proof of my
daughter's virginity." Then her parents shall
display the cloth before the elders of the
town, 18and the elders shall take the man and
punish him. 19They shall fine him a hundred
shekels of silver[b] and give them to the girl's
father, because this man has given an Israelite virgin a bad name. She shall continue to
be his wife; he must not divorce her as long
as he lives.

20If, however, the charge is true and no
proof of the girl's virginity can be found, 21she
shall be brought to the door of her father's
house and there the men of her town shall
stone her to death. She has done a disgraceful thing in Israel by being promiscuous while
still in her father's house. You must purge the
evil from among you.

22If a man is found sleeping with another
man's wife, both the man who slept with her
and the woman must die. You must purge
the evil from Israel.

23If a man happens to meet in a town a
virgin pledged to be married and he sleeps
with her, 24you shall take both of them to the
gate of that town and stone them to death—
the girl because she was in a town and did
not scream for help, and the man because
he violated another man's wife. You must
purge the evil from among you.

25But if out in the country a man happens
to meet a girl pledged to be married and
rapes her, only the man who has done this
shall die. 26Do nothing to the girl; she has
committed no sin deserving death. This case
is like that of someone who attacks and murders his neighbor, 27for the man found the girl
out in the country, and though the betrothed
girl screamed, there was no one to rescue
her.

28If a man happens to meet a virgin who is
not pledged to be married and rapes her and

[a]9 Or *be forfeited to the sanctuary* [b]19 That is, about 2 1/2 pounds (about 1 kilogram)

they are discovered, 29he shall pay the girl's
father fifty shekels of silver.[a] He must marry
the girl, for he has violated her. He can never
divorce her as long as he lives.
30A man is not to marry his father's wife; he
must not dishonor his father's bed.

Exclusion From the Assembly

23 No one who has been emasculated
by crushing or cutting may enter the
assembly of the LORD.
2No one born of a forbidden marriage[b] nor
any of his descendants may enter the assembly of the LORD, even down to the tenth
generation.
3No Ammonite or Moabite or any of his
descendants may enter the assembly of the
LORD, even down to the tenth generation.
4For they did not come to meet you with
bread and water on your way when you
came out of Egypt, and they hired Balaam
son of Beor from Pethor in Aram Naharaim[c]
to pronounce a curse on you. 5However, the
LORD your God would not listen to Balaam but
turned the curse into a blessing for you, because the LORD your God loves you. 6Do not
seek a treaty of friendship with them as long
as you live.
7Do not abhor an Edomite, for he is your
brother. Do not abhor an Egyptian, because
you lived as an alien in his country. 8The third
generation of children born to them may enter the assembly of the LORD.

Uncleanness in the Camp

9When you are encamped against your
enemies, keep away from everything impure. 10If one of your men is unclean because of a nocturnal emission, he is to go
outside the camp and stay there. 11But as
evening approaches he is to wash himself,
and at sunset he may return to the camp.
12Designate a place outside the camp
where you can go to relieve yourself. 13As
part of your equipment have something to
dig with, and when you relieve yourself, dig a
hole and cover up your excrement. 14For the
LORD your God moves about in your camp to
protect you and to deliver your enemies to
you. Your camp must be holy, so that he will
not see among you anything indecent and
turn away from you.

Miscellaneous Laws

15If a slave has taken refuge with you, do
not hand him over to his master. 16Let him
live among you wherever he likes and in
whatever town he chooses. Do not oppress
him.
17No Israelite man or woman is to become
a shrine prostitute. 18You must not bring the
earnings of a female prostitute or of a male
prostitute[d] into the house of the LORD your
God to pay any vow, because the LORD your
God detests them both.
19Do not charge your brother interest,
whether on money or food or anything else
that may earn interest. 20You may charge a
foreigner interest, but not a brother Israelite,
so that the LORD your God may bless you in
everything you put your hand to in the land
you are entering to possess.
21If you make a vow to the LORD your God,
do not be slow to pay it, for the LORD your God
will certainly demand it of you and you will be
guilty of sin. 22But if you refrain from making
a vow, you will not be guilty. 23Whatever your
lips utter you must be sure to do, because
you made your vow freely to the LORD your
God with your own mouth.
24If you enter your neighbor's vineyard,
you may eat all the grapes you want, but do
not put any in your basket. 25If you enter your
neighbor's grainfield, you may pick kernels
with your hands, but you must not put a sickle to his standing grain.

24 If a man marries a woman who
becomes displeasing to him because
he finds something indecent about her, and
he writes her a certificate of divorce, gives it
to her and sends her from his house, 2and if
after she leaves his house she becomes the
wife of another man, 3and her second husband dislikes her and writes her a certificate
of divorce, gives it to her and sends her from
his house, or if he dies, 4then her first husband, who divorced her, is not allowed to
marry her again after she has been defiled.
That would be detestable in the eyes of the
LORD. Do not bring sin upon the land the LORD
your God is giving you as an inheritance.
5If a man has recently married, he must not
be sent to war or have any other duty laid on
him. For one year he is to be free to stay at
home and bring happiness to the wife he has
married.

[a]29 That is, about 1 1/4 pounds (about 0.6 kilogram) [b]2 Or *one of illegitimate birth* [c]4 That is, Northwest Mesopotamia [d]18 Hebrew *of a dog*

6Do not take a pair of millstones—not even
the upper one—as security for a debt, because that would be taking a man's livelihood as security.

7If a man is caught kidnapping one of his
brother Israelites and treats him as a slave or
sells him, the kidnapper must die. You must
purge the evil from among you.

8In cases of leprous[a] diseases be very
careful to do exactly as the priests, who are
Levites, instruct you. You must follow carefully what I have commanded them.
9Remember what the LORD your God did to
Miriam along the way after you came out of
Egypt.

10When you make a loan of any kind to
your neighbor, do not go into his house to get
what he is offering as a pledge. 11Stay outside and let the man to whom you are making
the loan bring the pledge out to you. 12If the
man is poor, do not go to sleep with his
pledge in your possession. 13Return his
cloak to him by sunset so that he may sleep
in it. Then he will thank you, and it will be
regarded as a righteous act in the sight of the
LORD your God.

14Do not take advantage of a hired man
who is poor and needy, whether he is a
brother Israelite or an alien living in one of
your towns. 15Pay him his wages each day
before sunset, because he is poor and is
counting on it. Otherwise he may cry to the
LORD against you, and you will be guilty of sin.

16Fathers shall not be put to death for their
children, nor children put to death for their
fathers; each is to die for his own sin.

17Do not deprive the alien or the fatherless
of justice, or take the cloak of the widow as a
pledge. 18Remember that you were slaves in
Egypt and the LORD your God redeemed you
from there. That is why I command you to do
this.

19When you are harvesting in your field
and you overlook a sheaf, do not go back to
get it. Leave it for the alien, the fatherless
and the widow, so that the LORD your God
may bless you in all the work of your hands.
20When you beat the olives from your trees,
do not go over the branches a second time.
Leave what remains for the alien, the fatherless and the widow. 21When you harvest the
grapes in your vineyard, do not go over the
vines again. Leave what remains for the
alien, the fatherless and the widow.
22Remember that you were slaves in Egypt.
That is why I command you to do this.

25 When men have a dispute, they are
to take it to court and the judges will
decide the case, acquitting the innocent and
condemning the guilty. 2If the guilty man deserves to be beaten, the judge shall make
him lie down and have him flogged in his
presence with the number of lashes his
crime deserves, 3but he must not give him
more than forty lashes. If he is flogged more
than that, your brother will be degraded in
your eyes.

4Do not muzzle an ox while it is treading
out the grain.

5If brothers are living together and one of
them dies without a son, his widow must not
marry outside the family. Her husband's
brother shall take her and marry her and
fulfill the duty of a brother-in-law to her. 6The
first son she bears shall carry on the name of
the dead brother so that his name will not be
blotted out from Israel.

7However, if a man does not want to marry
his brother's wife, she shall go to the elders
at the town gate and say, "My husband's
brother refuses to carry on his brother's
name in Israel. He will not fulfill the duty of a
brother-in-law to me." 8Then the elders of his
town shall summon him and talk to him. If he
persists in saying, "I do not want to marry
her," 9his brother's widow shall go up to him
in the presence of the elders, take off one of
his sandals, spit in his face and say, "This is
what is done to the man who will not build up
his brother's family line." 10That man's line
shall be known in Israel as The Family of the
Unsandaled.

11If two men are fighting and the wife of
one of them comes to rescue her husband
from his assailant, and she reaches out and
seizes him by his private parts, 12you shall
cut off her hand. Show her no pity.

13Do not have two differing weights in your
bag—one heavy, one light. 14Do not have
two differing measures in your house—one
large, one small. 15You must have accurate
and honest weights and measures, so that
you may live long in the land the LORD your
God is giving you. 16For the LORD your God
detests anyone who does these things, anyone who deals dishonestly.

17Remember what the Amalekites did to
you along the way when you came out of

[a]8 The Hebrew word was used for various diseases affecting the skin—not necessarily leprosy.

Egypt. 18When you were weary and worn out, they met you on your journey and cut off all who were lagging behind; they had no fear of God. 19When the LORD your God gives you rest from all the enemies around you in the land he is giving you to possess as an inheritance, you shall blot out the memory of Amalek from under heaven. Do not forget!

Firstfruits and Tithes

26 When you have entered the land the LORD your God is giving you as an inheritance and have taken possession of it and settled in it, 2take some of the firstfruits of all that you produce from the soil of the land the LORD your God is giving you and put them in a basket. Then go to the place the LORD your God will choose as a dwelling for his Name 3and say to the priest in office at the time, "I declare today to the LORD your God that I have come to the land the LORD swore to our forefathers to give us." 4The priest shall take the basket from your hands and set it down in front of the altar of the LORD your God. 5Then you shall declare before the LORD your God: "My father was a wandering Aramean, and he went down into Egypt with a few people and lived there and became a great nation, powerful and numerous. 6But the Egyptians mistreated us and made us suffer, putting us to hard labor. 7Then we cried out to the LORD, the God of our fathers, and the LORD heard our voice and saw our misery, toil and oppression. 8So the LORD brought us out of Egypt with a mighty hand and an outstretched arm, with great terror and with miraculous signs and wonders. 9He brought us to this place and gave us this land, a land flowing with milk and honey; 10and now I bring the firstfruits of the soil that you, O LORD, have given me." Place the basket before the LORD your God and bow down before him. 11And you and the Levites and the aliens among you shall rejoice in all the good things the LORD your God has given to you and your household.

12When you have finished setting aside a tenth of all your produce in the third year, the year of the tithe, you shall give it to the Levite, the alien, the fatherless and the widow, so that they may eat in your towns and be satisfied. 13Then say to the LORD your God: "I have removed from my house the sacred portion and have given it to the Levite, the alien, the fatherless and the widow, according to all you commanded. I have not turned aside from your commands nor have I forgotten any of them. 14I have not eaten any of the sacred portion while I was in mourning, nor have I removed any of it while I was unclean, nor have I offered any of it to the dead. I have obeyed the LORD my God; I have done everything you commanded me. 15Look down from heaven, your holy dwelling place, and bless your people Israel and the land you have given us as you promised on oath to our forefathers, a land flowing with milk and honey."

Follow the LORD's Commands

16The LORD your God commands you this day to follow these decrees and laws; carefully observe them with all your heart and with all your soul. 17You have declared this day that the LORD is your God and that you will walk in his ways, that you will keep his decrees, commands and laws, and that you will obey him. 18And the LORD has declared this day that you are his people, his treasured possession as he promised, and that you are to keep all his commands. 19He has declared that he will set you in praise, fame and honor high above all the nations he has made and that you will be a people holy to the LORD your God, as he promised.

The Altar on Mount Ebal

27 Moses and the elders of Israel commanded the people: "Keep all these commands that I give you today. 2When you have crossed the Jordan into the land the LORD your God is giving you, set up some large stones and coat them with plaster. 3Write on them all the words of this law when you have crossed over to enter the land the LORD your God is giving you, a land flowing with milk and honey, just as the LORD, the God of your fathers, promised you. 4And when you have crossed the Jordan, set up these stones on Mount Ebal, as I command you today, and coat them with plaster. 5Build there an altar to the LORD your God, an altar of stones. Do not use any iron tool upon them. 6Build the altar of the LORD your God with fieldstones and offer burnt offerings on it to the LORD your God. 7Sacrifice fellowship offerings[a] there, eating them and rejoicing in the presence of the LORD your God. 8And you shall write very clearly all the words of this law on these stones you have set up."

[a]7 Traditionally *peace offerings*

Curses From Mount Ebal

9Then Moses and the priests, who are Levites, said to all Israel, "Be silent, O Israel, and listen! You have now become the people of the LORD your God. 10Obey the LORD your God and follow his commands and decrees that I give you today."

11On the same day Moses commanded the people:

12When you have crossed the Jordan, these tribes shall stand on Mount Gerizim to bless the people: Simeon, Levi, Judah, Issachar, Joseph and Benjamin. 13And these tribes shall stand on Mount Ebal to pronounce curses: Reuben, Gad, Asher, Zebulun, Dan and Naphtali.

14The Levites shall recite to all the people of Israel in a loud voice:

15"Cursed is the man who carves an image or casts an idol—a thing detestable to the LORD, the work of the craftsman's hands—and sets it up in secret."

Then all the people shall say, "Amen!"

16"Cursed is the man who dishonors his father or his mother."

Then all the people shall say, "Amen!"

17"Cursed is the man who moves his neighbor's boundary stone."

Then all the people shall say, "Amen!"

18"Cursed is the man who leads the blind astray on the road."

Then all the people shall say, "Amen!"

19"Cursed is the man who withholds justice from the alien, the fatherless or the widow."

Then all the people shall say, "Amen!"

20"Cursed is the man who sleeps with his father's wife, for he dishonors his father's bed."

Then all the people shall say, "Amen!"

21"Cursed is the man who has sexual relations with any animal."

Then all the people shall say, "Amen!"

22"Cursed is the man who sleeps with his sister, the daughter of his father or the daughter of his mother."

Then all the people shall say, "Amen!"

23"Cursed is the man who sleeps with his mother-in-law."

Then all the people shall say, "Amen!"

24"Cursed is the man who kills his neighbor secretly."

Then all the people shall say, "Amen!"

25"Cursed is the man who accepts a bribe to kill an innocent person."

Then all the people shall say, "Amen!"

26"Cursed is the man who does not uphold the words of this law by carrying them out."

Then all the people shall say, "Amen!"

Blessings for Obedience

28 If you fully obey the LORD your God and carefully follow all his commands I give you today, the LORD your God will set you high above all the nations on earth. 2All these blessings will come upon you and accompany you if you obey the LORD your God:

3You will be blessed in the city and blessed in the country.

4The fruit of your womb will be blessed, and the crops of your land and the young of your livestock—the calves of your herds and the lambs of your flocks.

5Your basket and your kneading trough will be blessed.

6You will be blessed when you come in and blessed when you go out.

7The LORD will grant that the enemies who rise up against you will be defeated before you. They will come at you from one direction but flee from you in seven.

8The LORD will send a blessing on your barns and on everything you put your hand to. The LORD your God will bless you in the land he is giving you.

9The LORD will establish you as his holy people, as he promised you on oath, if you keep the commands of the LORD your God and walk in his ways. 10Then all the peoples on earth will see that you are called by the name of the LORD, and they will fear you. 11The LORD will grant you abundant prosperity—in the fruit of your womb, the young of your livestock and the crops of your ground—in the land he swore to your forefathers to give you.

12The LORD will open the heavens, the storehouse of his bounty, to send rain on your land in season and to bless all the work of your hands. You will lend to many nations but will borrow from none. 13The LORD will make you the head, not the tail. If you pay attention to the commands of the LORD your God that I give you this day and carefully follow them, you will always be at the top, never at the bottom. 14Do not turn aside from any of the commands I give you today, to the right or to the left, following other gods and serving them.

Curses for Disobedience

15However, if you do not obey the LORD
your God and do not carefully follow all his
commands and decrees I am giving you today, all these curses will come upon you and
overtake you:

16You will be cursed in the city and
cursed in the country.
17Your basket and your kneading
trough will be cursed.
18The fruit of your womb will be
cursed, and the crops of your land, and
the calves of your herds and the lambs
of your flocks.
19You will be cursed when you come
in and cursed when you go out.

20The LORD will send on you curses, confusion and rebuke in everything you put your
hand to, until you are destroyed and come to
sudden ruin because of the evil you have
done in forsaking him.[a] 21The LORD will
plague you with diseases until he has destroyed you from the land you are entering to
possess. 22The LORD will strike you with wasting disease, with fever and inflammation,
with scorching heat and drought, with blight
and mildew, which will plague you until you
perish. 23The sky over your head will be
bronze, the ground beneath you iron. 24The
LORD will turn the rain of your country into
dust and powder; it will come down from the
skies until you are destroyed.

25The LORD will cause you to be defeated
before your enemies. You will come at them
from one direction but flee from them in
seven, and you will become a thing of horror
to all the kingdoms on earth. 26Your carcasses will be food for all the birds of the air
and the beasts of the earth, and there will be
no one to frighten them away. 27The LORD will
afflict you with the boils of Egypt and with
tumors, festering sores and the itch, from
which you cannot be cured. 28The LORD will
afflict you with madness, blindness and confusion of mind. 29At midday you will grope
about like a blind man in the dark. You will be
unsuccessful in everything you do; day after
day you will be oppressed and robbed, with
no one to rescue you.

30You will be pledged to be married to a
woman, but another will take her and ravish
her. You will build a house, but you will not
live in it. You will plant a vineyard, but you will
not even begin to enjoy its fruit. 31Your ox will
be slaughtered before your eyes, but you will
eat none of it. Your donkey will be forcibly
taken from you and will not be returned. Your
sheep will be given to your enemies, and no
one will rescue them. 32Your sons and
daughters will be given to another nation,
and you will wear out your eyes watching for
them day after day, powerless to lift a hand.
33A people that you do not know will eat what
your land and labor produce, and you will
have nothing but cruel oppression all your
days. 34The sights you see will drive you
mad. 35The LORD will afflict your knees and
legs with painful boils that cannot be cured,
spreading from the soles of your feet to the
top of your head.

36The LORD will drive you and the king you
set over you to a nation unknown to you or
your fathers. There you will worship other
gods, gods of wood and stone. 37You will
become a thing of horror and an object of
scorn and ridicule to all the nations where the
LORD will drive you.

38You will sow much seed in the field but
you will harvest little, because locusts will
devour it. 39You will plant vineyards and cultivate them but you will not drink the wine or
gather the grapes, because worms will eat
them. 40You will have olive trees throughout
your country but you will not use the oil, because the olives will drop off. 41You will have
sons and daughters but you will not keep
them, because they will go into captivity.
42Swarms of locusts will take over all your
trees and the crops of your land.

43The alien who lives among you will rise
above you higher and higher, but you will
sink lower and lower. 44He will lend to you,
but you will not lend to him. He will be the
head, but you will be the tail.

45All these curses will come upon you.
They will pursue you and overtake you until
you are destroyed, because you did not obey
the LORD your God and observe the commands and decrees he gave you. 46They will
be a sign and a wonder to you and your
descendants forever. 47Because you did not
serve the LORD your God joyfully and gladly in
the time of prosperity, 48therefore in hunger
and thirst, in nakedness and dire poverty,
you will serve the enemies the LORD sends
against you. He will put an iron yoke on your
neck until he has destroyed you.

49The LORD will bring a nation against you
from far away, from the ends of the earth, like

[a]20 Hebrew *me*

an eagle swooping down, a nation whose
language you will not understand, 50a fierce-
looking nation without respect for the old or
pity for the young. 51They will devour the
young of your livestock and the crops of your
land until you are destroyed. They will leave
you no grain, new wine or oil, nor any calves
of your herds or lambs of your flocks until you
are ruined. 52They will lay siege to all the
cities throughout your land until the high fortified walls in which you trust fall down. They
will besiege all the cities throughout the land
the LORD your God is giving you.

53Because of the suffering that your enemy will inflict on you during the siege, you will
eat the fruit of the womb, the flesh of the sons
and daughters the LORD your God has given
you. 54Even the most gentle and sensitive
man among you will have no compassion on
his own brother or the wife he loves or his
surviving children, 55and he will not give to
one of them any of the flesh of his children
that he is eating. It will be all he has left
because of the suffering your enemy will inflict on you during the siege of all your cities.
56The most gentle and sensitive woman
among you—so sensitive and gentle that
she would not venture to touch the ground
with the sole of her foot—will begrudge the
husband she loves and her own son or
daughter 57the afterbirth from her womb and
the children she bears. For she intends to eat
them secretly during the siege and in the
distress that your enemy will inflict on you in
your cities.

58If you do not carefully follow all the words
of this law, which are written in this book, and
do not revere this glorious and awesome
name—the LORD your God— 59the LORD will
send fearful plagues on you and your descendants, harsh and prolonged disasters,
and severe and lingering illnesses. 60He will
bring upon you all the diseases of Egypt that
you dreaded, and they will cling to you. 61The
LORD will also bring on you every kind of sickness and disaster not recorded in this Book
of the Law, until you are destroyed. 62You
who were as numerous as the stars in the
sky will be left but few in number, because
you did not obey the LORD your God. 63Just as
it pleased the LORD to make you prosper and
increase in number, so it will please him to
ruin and destroy you. You will be uprooted
from the land you are entering to possess.

64Then the LORD will scatter you among all
nations, from one end of the earth to the
other. There you will worship other gods—
gods of wood and stone, which neither you
nor your fathers have known. 65Among those
nations you will find no repose, no resting
place for the sole of your foot. There the LORD
will give you an anxious mind, eyes weary
with longing, and a despairing heart. 66You
will live in constant suspense, filled with
dread both night and day, never sure of your
life. 67In the morning you will say, "If only it
were evening!" and in the evening, "If only it
were morning!"—because of the terror that
will fill your hearts and the sights that your
eyes will see. 68The LORD will send you back
in ships to Egypt on a journey I said you
should never make again. There you will offer yourselves for sale to your enemies as
male and female slaves, but no one will buy
you.

Renewal of the Covenant

29 These are the terms of the covenant
the LORD commanded Moses to
make with the Israelites in Moab, in addition
to the covenant he had made with them at
Horeb.

2Moses summoned all the Israelites and
said to them:

Your eyes have seen all that the LORD did
in Egypt to Pharaoh, to all his officials and to
all his land. 3With your own eyes you saw
those great trials, those miraculous signs
and great wonders. 4But to this day the LORD
has not given you a mind that understands or
eyes that see or ears that hear. 5During the
forty years that I led you through the desert,
your clothes did not wear out, nor did the
sandals on your feet. 6You ate no bread and
drank no wine or other fermented drink. I did
this so that you might know that I am the LORD
your God.

7When you reached this place, Sihon king
of Heshbon and Og king of Bashan came out
to fight against us, but we defeated them.
8We took their land and gave it as an inheritance to the Reubenites, the Gadites and the
half-tribe of Manasseh.

9Carefully follow the terms of this covenant, so that you may prosper in everything
you do. 10All of you are standing today in the
presence of the LORD your God—your leaders and chief men, your elders and officials,
and all the other men of Israel, 11together
with your children and your wives, and the
aliens living in your camps who chop your
wood and carry your water. 12You are standing here in order to enter into a covenant with

the LORD your God, a covenant the LORD is
making with you this day and sealing with an
oath, 13to confirm you this day as his people,
that he may be your God as he promised you
and as he swore to your fathers, Abraham,
Isaac and Jacob. 14I am making this covenant, with its oath, not only with you 15who
are standing here with us today in the presence of the LORD our God but also with those
who are not here today.

16You yourselves know how we lived in
Egypt and how we passed through the countries on the way here. 17You saw among
them their detestable images and idols of
wood and stone, of silver and gold. 18Make
sure there is no man or woman, clan or tribe
among you today whose heart turns away
from the LORD our God to go and worship the
gods of those nations; make sure there is no
root among you that produces such bitter
poison.

19When such a person hears the words of
this oath, he invokes a blessing on himself
and therefore thinks, "I will be safe, even
though I persist in going my own way." This
will bring disaster on the watered land as well
as the dry.[a] 20The LORD will never be willing to
forgive him; his wrath and zeal will burn
against that man. All the curses written in this
book will fall upon him, and the LORD will blot
out his name from under heaven. 21The LORD
will single him out from all the tribes of Israel
for disaster, according to all the curses of the
covenant written in this Book of the Law.
22Your children who follow you in later generations and foreigners who come from distant lands will see the calamities that have
fallen on the land and the diseases with
which the LORD has afflicted it. 23The whole
land will be a burning waste of salt and sulfur—nothing planted, nothing sprouting, no
vegetation growing on it. It will be like the
destruction of Sodom and Gomorrah, Admah and Zeboiim, which the LORD overthrew
in fierce anger. 24All the nations will ask:
"Why has the LORD done this to this land?
Why this fierce, burning anger?"

25And the answer will be: "It is because
this people abandoned the covenant of the
LORD, the God of their fathers, the covenant
he made with them when he brought them
out of Egypt. 26They went off and worshiped
other gods and bowed down to them, gods
they did not know, gods he had not given
them. 27Therefore the LORD's anger burned
against this land, so that he brought on it all
the curses written in this book. 28In furious
anger and in great wrath the LORD uprooted
them from their land and thrust them into
another land, as it is now."

29The secret things belong to the LORD our
God, but the things revealed belong to us
and to our children forever, that we may follow all the words of this law.

Prosperity After Turning to the LORD

30 When all these blessings and curses
I have set before you come upon you
and you take them to heart wherever the
LORD your God disperses you among the nations, 2and when you and your children return to the LORD your God and obey him with
all your heart and with all your soul according
to everything I command you today, 3then
the LORD your God will restore your fortunes[b]
and have compassion on you and gather you
again from all the nations where he scattered
you. 4Even if you have been banished to the
most distant land under the heavens, from
there the LORD your God will gather you and
bring you back. 5He will bring you to the land
that belonged to your fathers, and you will
take possession of it. He will make you more
prosperous and numerous than your fathers.
6The LORD your God will circumcise your
hearts and the hearts of your descendants,
so that you may love him with all your heart
and with all your soul, and live. 7The LORD
your God will put all these curses on your
enemies who hate and persecute you. 8You
will again obey the LORD and follow all his
commands I am giving you today. 9Then the
LORD your God will make you most prosperous in all the work of your hands and in the
fruit of your womb, the young of your livestock and the crops of your land. The LORD
will again delight in you and make you prosperous, just as he delighted in your fathers,
10if you obey the LORD your God and keep his
commands and decrees that are written in
this Book of the Law and turn to the LORD your
God with all your heart and with all your soul.

The Offer of Life or Death

11Now what I am commanding you today is
not too difficult for you or beyond your reach.
12It is not up in heaven, so that you have to
ask, "Who will ascend into heaven to get it
and proclaim it to us so we may obey it?"
13Nor is it beyond the sea, so that you have to

[a] 19 *Or way, in order to add drunkenness to thirst."* [b] 3 *Or will bring you back from captivity*

ask, "Who will cross the sea to get it and
proclaim it to us so we may obey it?" 14No,
the word is very near you; it is in your mouth
and in your heart so you may obey it.
15See, I set before you today life and prosperity, death and destruction. 16For I command you today to love the LORD your God, to
walk in his ways, and to keep his commands,
decrees and laws; then you will live and increase, and the LORD your God will bless you
in the land you are entering to possess.
17But if your heart turns away and you are
not obedient, and if you are drawn away to
bow down to other gods and worship them,
18I declare to you this day that you will certainly be destroyed. You will not live long in
the land you are crossing the Jordan to enter
and possess.
19This day I call heaven and earth as witnesses against you that I have set before
you life and death, blessings and curses.
Now choose life, so that you and your children may live 20and that you may love the
LORD your God, listen to his voice, and hold
fast to him. For the LORD is your life, and he
will give you many years in the land he swore
to give to your fathers, Abraham, Isaac and
Jacob.

Joshua to Succeed Moses

31 Then Moses went out and spoke
these words to all Israel: 2"I am now a
hundred and twenty years old and I am no
longer able to lead you. The LORD has said to
me, 'You shall not cross the Jordan.' 3The
LORD your God himself will cross over ahead
of you. He will destroy these nations before
you, and you will take possession of their
land. Joshua also will cross over ahead of
you, as the LORD said. 4And the LORD will do to
them what he did to Sihon and Og, the kings
of the Amorites, whom he destroyed along
with their land. 5The LORD will deliver them to
you, and you must do to them all that I have
commanded you. 6Be strong and courageous. Do not be afraid or terrified because
of them, for the LORD your God goes with you;
he will never leave you nor forsake you."
7Then Moses summoned Joshua and said
to him in the presence of all Israel, "Be
strong and courageous, for you must go with
this people into the land that the LORD swore
to their forefathers to give them, and you
must divide it among them as their inheritance. 8The LORD himself goes before you
and will be with you; he will never leave you
nor forsake you. Do not be afraid; do not be
discouraged."

The Reading of the Law

9So Moses wrote down this law and gave it
to the priests, the sons of Levi, who carried
the ark of the covenant of the LORD, and to all
the elders of Israel. 10Then Moses commanded them: "At the end of every seven
years, in the year for canceling debts, during
the Feast of Tabernacles, 11when all Israel
comes to appear before the LORD your God at
the place he will choose, you shall read this
law before them in their hearing. 12Assemble
the people—men, women and children, and
the aliens living in your towns—so they can
listen and learn to fear the LORD your God
and follow carefully all the words of this law.
13Their children, who do not know this law,
must hear it and learn to fear the LORD your
God as long as you live in the land you are
crossing the Jordan to possess."

Israel's Rebellion Predicted

14The LORD said to Moses, "Now the day of
your death is near. Call Joshua and present
yourselves at the Tent of Meeting, where I
will commission him." So Moses and Joshua
came and presented themselves at the Tent
of Meeting.
15Then the LORD appeared at the Tent in a
pillar of cloud, and the cloud stood over the
entrance to the Tent. 16And the LORD said to
Moses: "You are going to rest with your fathers, and these people will soon prostitute
themselves to the foreign gods of the land
they are entering. They will forsake me and
break the covenant I made with them. 17On
that day I will become angry with them and
forsake them; I will hide my face from them,
and they will be destroyed. Many disasters
and difficulties will come upon them, and on
that day they will ask, 'Have not these disasters come upon us because our God is not
with us?' 18And I will certainly hide my face
on that day because of all their wickedness
in turning to other gods.
19"Now write down for yourselves this
song and teach it to the Israelites and have
them sing it, so that it may be a witness for
me against them. 20When I have brought
them into the land flowing with milk and
honey, the land I promised on oath to their
forefathers, and when they eat their fill and
thrive, they will turn to other gods and worship them, rejecting me and breaking my

covenant. 21 And when many disasters and
difficulties come upon them, this song will
testify against them, because it will not be
forgotten by their descendants. I know what
they are disposed to do, even before I bring
them into the land I promised them on oath."
22 So Moses wrote down this song that day
and taught it to the Israelites.

23 The LORD gave this command to Joshua son of Nun: "Be strong and courageous, for you will bring the Israelites into the land I promised them on oath, and I myself will be with you."

24 After Moses finished writing in a book the
words of this law from beginning to end, 25 he
gave this command to the Levites who carried the ark of the covenant of the LORD:
26 "Take this Book of the Law and place it
beside the ark of the covenant of the LORD
your God. There it will remain as a witness
against you. 27 For I know how rebellious and
stiff-necked you are. If you have been rebellious against the LORD while I am still alive
and with you, how much more will you rebel
after I die! 28 Assemble before me all the elders of your tribes and all your officials, so
that I can speak these words in their hearing
and call heaven and earth to testify against
them. 29 For I know that after my death you
are sure to become utterly corrupt and to turn
from the way I have commanded you. In
days to come, disaster will fall upon you because you will do evil in the sight of the LORD
and provoke him to anger by what your
hands have made."

The Song of Moses

30 And Moses recited the words of this song from beginning to end in the hearing of the whole assembly of Israel:

32 Listen, O heavens, and I will speak;
hear, O earth, the words of my mouth.
2 Let my teaching fall like rain
and my words descend like dew,
like showers on new grass,
like abundant rain on tender plants.

3 I will proclaim the name of the LORD.
Oh, praise the greatness of our God!
4 He is the Rock, his works are perfect,
and all his ways are just.
A faithful God who does no wrong,
upright and just is he.

5 They have acted corruptly toward him;
to their shame they are no longer his children,
but a warped and crooked generation.[a]
6 Is this the way you repay the LORD,
O foolish and unwise people?
Is he not your Father, your Creator,[b]
who made you and formed you?

7 Remember the days of old;
consider the generations long past.
Ask your father and he will tell you,
your elders, and they will explain to you.
8 When the Most High gave the nations their inheritance,
when he divided all mankind,
he set up boundaries for the peoples
according to the number of the sons of Israel.[c]
9 For the LORD's portion is his people,
Jacob his allotted inheritance.

10 In a desert land he found him,
in a barren and howling waste.
He shielded him and cared for him;
he guarded him as the apple of his eye,
11 like an eagle that stirs up its nest
and hovers over its young,
that spreads its wings to catch them
and carries them on its pinions.
12 The LORD alone led him;
no foreign god was with him.

13 He made him ride on the heights of the land
and fed him with the fruit of the fields.
He nourished him with honey from the rock,
and with oil from the flinty crag,
14 with curds and milk from herd and flock
and with fattened lambs and goats,
with choice rams of Bashan
and the finest kernels of wheat.
You drank the foaming blood of the grape.

15 Jeshurun[d] grew fat and kicked;
filled with food, he became heavy and sleek.
He abandoned the God who made him
and rejected the Rock his Savior.
16 They made him jealous with their foreign gods
and angered him with their detestable idols.

[a] 5 Or *Corrupt are they and not his children, / a generation warped and twisted to their shame* [b] 6 Or *Father, who bought you* [c] 8 Masoretic Text; Dead Sea Scrolls (see also Septuagint) *sons of God* [d] 15 *Jeshurun* means *the upright one,* that is, Israel.

[17]They sacrificed to demons, which are not God—
gods they had not known,
gods that recently appeared,
gods your fathers did not fear.
[18]You deserted the Rock, who fathered you;
you forgot the God who gave you birth.

[19]The LORD saw this and rejected them
because he was angered by his sons and daughters.
[20]"I will hide my face from them," he said,
"and see what their end will be;
for they are a perverse generation,
children who are unfaithful.
[21]They made me jealous by what is no god
and angered me with their worthless idols.
I will make them envious by those who are not a people;
I will make them angry by a nation that has no understanding.
[22]For a fire has been kindled by my wrath,
one that burns to the realm of death[a] below.
It will devour the earth and its harvests
and set afire the foundations of the mountains.

[23]"I will heap calamities upon them
and spend my arrows against them.
[24]I will send wasting famine against them,
consuming pestilence and deadly plague;
I will send against them the fangs of wild beasts,
the venom of vipers that glide in the dust.
[25]In the street the sword will make them childless;
in their homes terror will reign.
Young men and young women will perish,
infants and gray-haired men.
[26]I said I would scatter them
and blot out their memory from mankind,
[27]but I dreaded the taunt of the enemy,
lest the adversary misunderstand
and say, 'Our hand has triumphed;
the LORD has not done all this.' "

[28]They are a nation without sense,
there is no discernment in them.
[29]If only they were wise and would understand this
and discern what their end will be!
[30]How could one man chase a thousand,
or two put ten thousand to flight,
unless their Rock had sold them,
unless the LORD had given them up?
[31]For their rock is not like our Rock,
as even our enemies concede.
[32]Their vine comes from the vine of Sodom
and from the fields of Gomorrah.
Their grapes are filled with poison,
and their clusters with bitterness.
[33]Their wine is the venom of serpents,
the deadly poison of cobras.

[34]"Have I not kept this in reserve
and sealed it in my vaults?
[35]It is mine to avenge; I will repay.
In due time their foot will slip;
their day of disaster is near
and their doom rushes upon them."

[36]The LORD will judge his people
and have compassion on his servants
when he sees their strength is gone
and no one is left, slave or free.
[37]He will say: "Now where are their gods,
the rock they took refuge in,
[38]the gods who ate the fat of their sacrifices
and drank the wine of their drink offerings?
Let them rise up to help you!
Let them give you shelter!

[39]"See now that I myself am He!
There is no god besides me.
I put to death and I bring to life,
I have wounded and I will heal,
and no one can deliver out of my hand.
[40]I lift my hand to heaven and declare:
As surely as I live forever,
[41]when I sharpen my flashing sword
and my hand grasps it in judgment,
I will take vengeance on my adversaries
and repay those who hate me.
[42]I will make my arrows drunk with blood,
while my sword devours flesh:
the blood of the slain and the captives,
the heads of the enemy leaders."

[43]Rejoice, O nations, with his people,[b,c]
for he will avenge the blood of his servants;
he will take vengeance on his enemies
and make atonement for his land and people.

[44]Moses came with Joshua[d] son of Nun

[a]22 Hebrew *to Sheol* [b]43 Or *Make his people rejoice, O nations* [c]43 Masoretic Text; Dead Sea Scrolls (see also Septuagint) *people, / and let all the angels worship him /* [d]44 Hebrew *Hoshea,* a variant of *Joshua*

and spoke all the words of this song in the
hearing of the people. 45 When Moses finished reciting all these words to all Israel,
46 he said to them, "Take to heart all the
words I have solemnly declared to you this
day, so that you may command your children
to obey carefully all the words of this law.
47 They are not just idle words for you—they
are your life. By them you will live long in the
land you are crossing the Jordan to possess."

Moses to Die on Mount Nebo

48 On that same day the LORD told Moses,
49 "Go up into the Abarim Range to Mount
Nebo in Moab, across from Jericho, and
view Canaan, the land I am giving the Israelites as their own possession. 50 There on the
mountain that you have climbed you will die
and be gathered to your people, just as your
brother Aaron died on Mount Hor and was
gathered to his people. 51 This is because
both of you broke faith with me in the presence of the Israelites at the waters of Meribah Kadesh in the Desert of Zin and because
you did not uphold my holiness among the
Israelites. 52 Therefore, you will see the land
only from a distance; you will not enter the
land I am giving to the people of Israel."

Moses Blesses the Tribes

33 This is the blessing that Moses the
man of God pronounced on the Israelites before his death. 2 He said:

"The LORD came from Sinai
and dawned over them from Seir;
he shone forth from Mount Paran.
He came with[a] myriads of holy ones
from the south, from his mountain slopes.[b]
3 Surely it is you who love the people;
all the holy ones are in your hand.
At your feet they all bow down,
and from you receive instruction,
4 the law that Moses gave us,
the possession of the assembly of Jacob.
5 He was king over Jeshurun[c]
when the leaders of the people assembled,
along with the tribes of Israel.

6 "Let Reuben live and not die,
nor[d] his men be few."

7 And this he said about Judah:

"Hear, O LORD, the cry of Judah;
bring him to his people.
With his own hands he defends his cause.
Oh, be his help against his foes!"

8 About Levi he said:

"Your Thummim and Urim belong
to the man you favored.
You tested him at Massah;
you contended with him at the waters of Meribah.
9 He said of his father and mother,
'I have no regard for them.'
He did not recognize his brothers
or acknowledge his own children,
but he watched over your word
and guarded your covenant.
10 He teaches your precepts to Jacob
and your law to Israel.
He offers incense before you
and whole burnt offerings on your altar.
11 Bless all his skills, O LORD,
and be pleased with the work of his hands.
Smite the loins of those who rise up against him;
strike his foes till they rise no more."

12 About Benjamin he said:

"Let the beloved of the LORD rest secure in him,
for he shields him all day long,
and the one the LORD loves rests between his shoulders."

13 About Joseph he said:

"May the LORD bless his land
with the precious dew from heaven above
and with the deep waters that lie below;
14 with the best the sun brings forth
and the finest the moon can yield;
15 with the choicest gifts of the ancient mountains
and the fruitfulness of the everlasting hills;
16 with the best gifts of the earth and its fullness
and the favor of him who dwelt in the burning bush.
Let all these rest on the head of Joseph,

[a]2 Or *from* [b]2 The meaning of the Hebrew for this phrase is uncertain. [c]5 *Jeshurun* means *the upright one,* that is, Israel; also in verse 26. [d]6 Or *but let*

on the brow of the prince among[a] his
brothers.
17In majesty he is like a firstborn bull;
his horns are the horns of a wild ox.
With them he will gore the nations,
even those at the ends of the earth.
Such are the ten thousands of Ephraim;
such are the thousands of Manasseh."

18About Zebulun he said:

"Rejoice, Zebulun, in your going out,
and you, Issachar, in your tents.
19They will summon peoples to the
mountain
and there offer sacrifices of
righteousness;
they will feast on the abundance of the
seas,
on the treasures hidden in the sand."

20About Gad he said:

"Blessed is he who enlarges Gad's
domain!
Gad lives there like a lion,
tearing at arm or head.
21He chose the best land for himself;
the leader's portion was kept for him.
When the heads of the people
assembled,
he carried out the LORD's righteous will,
and his judgments concerning Israel."

22About Dan he said:

"Dan is a lion's cub,
springing out of Bashan."

23About Naphtali he said:

"Naphtali is abounding with the favor of
the LORD
and is full of his blessing;
he will inherit southward to the lake."

24About Asher he said:

"Most blessed of sons is Asher;
let him be favored by his brothers,
and let him bathe his feet in oil.
25The bolts of your gates will be iron and
bronze,
and your strength will equal your days.

26"There is no one like the God of
Jeshurun,
who rides on the heavens to help
you
and on the clouds in his majesty.
27The eternal God is your refuge,
and underneath are the everlasting
arms.
He will drive out your enemy before
you,
saying, 'Destroy him!'
28So Israel will live in safety alone;
Jacob's spring is secure
in a land of grain and new wine,
where the heavens drop dew.
29Blessed are you, O Israel!
Who is like you,
a people saved by the LORD?
He is your shield and helper
and your glorious sword.
Your enemies will cower before you,
and you will trample down their high
places.[b]"

The Death of Moses

34 Then Moses climbed Mount Nebo
from the plains of Moab to the top of
Pisgah, across from Jericho. There the LORD
showed him the whole land—from Gilead to
Dan, 2all of Naphtali, the territory of Ephraim
and Manasseh, all the land of Judah as far as
the western sea,[c] 3the Negev and the whole
region from the Valley of Jericho, the City of
Palms, as far as Zoar. 4Then the LORD said to
him, "This is the land I promised on oath to
Abraham, Isaac and Jacob when I said, 'I will
give it to your descendants.' I have let you
see it with your eyes, but you will not cross
over into it."
5And Moses the servant of the LORD died
there in Moab, as the LORD had said. 6He
buried him[d] in Moab, in the valley opposite
Beth Peor, but to this day no one knows
where his grave is. 7Moses was a hundred
and twenty years old when he died, yet his
eyes were not weak nor his strength gone.
8The Israelites grieved for Moses in the
plains of Moab thirty days, until the time of
weeping and mourning was over.
9Now Joshua son of Nun was filled with the
spirit[e] of wisdom because Moses had laid
his hands on him. So the Israelites listened
to him and did what the LORD had commanded Moses.
10Since then, no prophet has risen in Israel

[a] 16 Or *of the one separated from* [b] 29 Or *will tread upon their bodies* [c] 2 That is, the Mediterranean
[d] 6 Or *He was buried* [e] 9 Or *Spirit*

like Moses, whom the LORD knew face to
face, 11who did all those miraculous signs
and wonders the LORD sent him to do in
Egypt—to Pharaoh and to all his officials and
to his whole land. 12For no one has ever
shown the mighty power or performed the
awesome deeds that Moses did in the sight
of all Israel.

Joshua

Introduction:

This book has the name of its leading character as its title. Joshua had been chosen and appointed by God just before Moses' death.

The book of Joshua is the story of both Joshua and Israel as they, with God's help, conquered the Promised Land—Canaan. The people miraculously crossed the Jordan River and conquered the town of Jericho. Then, with God's help again, they quickly took possession of all the main areas of Canaan.

Before Joshua died, he reminded the people of God's covenant promises to them. He instructed the people to keep on loving and obeying God. Publicly, he spoke of his own willingness to serve God when he said ". . . choose for yourselves this day whom you will serve, . . . But as for me and my household, we will serve the LORD" (24:15).

Outline of contents:

Preparation for possession of Canaan (1:1–5:15)
The conquest of Canaan (6:1–12:24)
The division of land by tribes (13:1–21:45)
Farewell and death of Joshua (22:1–24:33)

The LORD Commands Joshua

1 After the death of Moses the servant of
the LORD, the LORD said to Joshua son of
Nun, Moses' aide: 2"Moses my servant is
dead. Now then, you and all these people,
get ready to cross the Jordan River into the
land I am about to give to them—to the Israelites. 3I will give you every place where you
set your foot, as I promised Moses. 4Your
territory will extend from the desert to Lebanon, and from the great river, the Euphrates—all the Hittite country—to the Great
Sea[a] on the west. 5No one will be able to
stand up against you all the days of your life.
As I was with Moses, so I will be with you; I
will never leave you nor forsake you.
6"Be strong and courageous, because you
will lead these people to inherit the land I
swore to their forefathers to give them. 7Be
strong and very courageous. Be careful to
obey all the law my servant Moses gave you;
do not turn from it to the right or to the left,
that you may be successful wherever you
go. 8Do not let this Book of the Law depart
from your mouth; meditate on it day and
night, so that you may be careful to do everything written in it. Then you will be prosperous and successful. 9Have I not commanded
you? Be strong and courageous. Do not be
terrified; do not be discouraged, for the LORD
your God will be with you wherever you go."
10So Joshua ordered the officers of the
people: 11"Go through the camp and tell the
people, 'Get your supplies ready. Three days
from now you will cross the Jordan here to go
in and take possession of the land the LORD
your God is giving you for your own.' "
12But to the Reubenites, the Gadites and
the half-tribe of Manasseh, Joshua said,
13"Remember the command that Moses the
servant of the LORD gave you: 'The LORD your
God is giving you rest and has granted you
this land.' 14Your wives, your children and
your livestock may stay in the land that
Moses gave you east of the Jordan, but all
your fighting men, fully armed, must cross
over ahead of your brothers. You are to help
your brothers 15until the LORD gives them
rest, as he has done for you, and until they
too have taken possession of the land that
the LORD your God is giving them. After that,
you may go back and occupy your own land,
which Moses the servant of the LORD gave
you east of the Jordan toward the sunrise."

[a]4 That is, the Mediterranean

[16]Then they answered Joshua, "Whatever you have commanded us we will do, and wherever you send us we will go. [17]Just as we fully obeyed Moses, so we will obey you. Only may the LORD your God be with you as he was with Moses. [18]Whoever rebels against your word and does not obey your words, whatever you may command them, will be put to death. Only be strong and courageous!"

Rahab and the Spies

2 Then Joshua son of Nun secretly sent two spies from Shittim. "Go, look over the land," he said, "especially Jericho." So they went and entered the house of a prostitute[a] named Rahab and stayed there.

[2]The king of Jericho was told, "Look! Some of the Israelites have come here tonight to spy out the land." [3]So the king of Jericho sent this message to Rahab: "Bring out the men who came to you and entered your house, because they have come to spy out the whole land."

[4]But the woman had taken the two men and hidden them. She said, "Yes, the men came to me, but I did not know where they had come from. [5]At dusk, when it was time to close the city gate, the men left. I don't know which way they went. Go after them quickly. You may catch up with them." [6](But she had taken them up to the roof and hidden them under the stalks of flax she had laid out on the roof.) [7]So the men set out in pursuit of the spies on the road that leads to the fords of the Jordan, and as soon as the pursuers had gone out, the gate was shut.

[8]Before the spies lay down for the night, she went up on the roof [9]and said to them, "I know that the LORD has given this land to you and that a great fear of you has fallen on us, so that all who live in this country are melting in fear because of you. [10]We have heard how the LORD dried up the water of the Red Sea[b] for you when you came out of Egypt, and what you did to Sihon and Og, the two kings of the Amorites east of the Jordan, whom you completely destroyed.[c] [11]When we heard of it, our hearts melted and everyone's courage failed because of you, for the LORD your God is God in heaven above and on the earth below. [12]Now then, please swear to me by the LORD that you will show kindness to my family, because I have shown kindness to you. Give me a sure sign [13]that you will spare the lives of my father and mother, my brothers and sisters, and all who belong to them, and that you will save us from death."

[14]"Our lives for your lives!" the men assured her. "If you don't tell what we are doing, we will treat you kindly and faithfully when the LORD gives us the land."

[15]So she let them down by a rope through the window, for the house she lived in was part of the city wall. [16]Now she had said to them, "Go to the hills so the pursuers will not find you. Hide yourselves there three days until they return, and then go on your way."

[17]The men said to her, "This oath you made us swear will not be binding on us [18]unless, when we enter the land, you have tied this scarlet cord in the window through which you let us down, and unless you have brought your father and mother, your brothers and all your family into your house. [19]If anyone goes outside your house into the street, his blood will be on his own head; we will not be responsible. As for anyone who is in the house with you, his blood will be on our head if a hand is laid on him. [20]But if you tell what we are doing, we will be released from the oath you made us swear."

[21]"Agreed," she replied. "Let it be as you say." So she sent them away and they departed. And she tied the scarlet cord in the window.

[22]When they left, they went into the hills and stayed there three days, until the pursuers had searched all along the road and returned without finding them. [23]Then the two men started back. They went down out of the hills, forded the river and came to Joshua son of Nun and told him everything that had happened to them. [24]They said to Joshua, "The LORD has surely given the whole land into our hands; all the people are melting in fear because of us."

Crossing the Jordan

3 Early in the morning Joshua and all the Israelites set out from Shittim and went to the Jordan, where they camped before crossing over. [2]After three days the officers went throughout the camp, [3]giving orders to the people: "When you see the ark of the covenant of the LORD your God, and the priests, who are Levites, carrying it, you are to move out from your positions and follow it.

[a]*1* Or possibly *an innkeeper* [b]*10* Hebrew *Yam Suph;* that is, Sea of Reeds [c]*10* The Hebrew term refers to the irrevocable giving over of things or persons to the LORD, often by totally destroying them.

4Then you will know which way to go, since
you have never been this way before.
But keep a distance of about a thousand
yards[a] between you and the ark; do not go
near it."

5Joshua told the people, "Consecrate
yourselves, for tomorrow the LORD will do
amazing things among you."

6Joshua said to the priests, "Take up the
ark of the covenant and pass on ahead of the
people." So they took it up and went ahead
of them.

7And the LORD said to Joshua, "Today I will
begin to exalt you in the eyes of all Israel, so
they may know that I am with you as I was
with Moses. 8Tell the priests who carry the
ark of the covenant: 'When you reach the
edge of the Jordan's waters, go and stand in
the river.'"

9Joshua said to the Israelites, "Come here
and listen to the words of the LORD your God.
10This is how you will know that the living
God is among you and that he will certainly
drive out before you the Canaanites, Hittites,
Hivites, Perizzites, Girgashites, Amorites
and Jebusites. 11See, the ark of the covenant
of the Lord of all the earth will go into the
Jordan ahead of you. 12Now then, choose
twelve men from the tribes of Israel, one from
each tribe. 13And as soon as the priests who
carry the ark of the LORD—the Lord of all the
earth—set foot in the Jordan, its waters flowing downstream will be cut off and stand up
in a heap."

14So when the people broke camp to cross
the Jordan, the priests carrying the ark of the
covenant went ahead of them. 15Now the
Jordan is at flood stage all during harvest.
Yet as soon as the priests who carried the
ark reached the Jordan and their feet
touched the water's edge, 16the water from
upstream stopped flowing. It piled up in a
heap a great distance away, at a town called
Adam in the vicinity of Zarethan, while the
water flowing down to the Sea of the Arabah
(the Salt Sea[b]) was completely cut off. So
the people crossed over opposite Jericho.
17The priests who carried the ark of the covenant of the LORD stood firm on dry ground in
the middle of the Jordan, while all Israel
passed by until the whole nation had completed the crossing on dry ground.

4 When the whole nation had finished
crossing the Jordan, the LORD said to
Joshua, 2"Choose twelve men from among
the people, one from each tribe, 3and tell
them to take up twelve stones from the middle of the Jordan from right where the priests
stood and to carry them over with you and
put them down at the place where you stay
tonight."

4So Joshua called together the twelve men
he had appointed from the Israelites, one
from each tribe, 5and said to them, "Go over
before the ark of the LORD your God into the
middle of the Jordan. Each of you is to take
up a stone on his shoulder, according to the
number of the tribes of the Israelites, 6to
serve as a sign among you. In the future,
when your children ask you, 'What do these
stones mean?' 7tell them that the flow of the
Jordan was cut off before the ark of the covenant of the LORD. When it crossed the Jordan, the waters of the Jordan were cut off.
These stones are to be a memorial to the
people of Israel forever."

8So the Israelites did as Joshua commanded them. They took twelve stones from
the middle of the Jordan, according to the
number of the tribes of the Israelites, as the
LORD had told Joshua; and they carried them
over with them to their camp, where they put
them down. 9Joshua set up the twelve
stones that had been[c] in the middle of the
Jordan at the spot where the priests who
carried the ark of the covenant had stood.
And they are there to this day.

10Now the priests who carried the ark remained standing in the middle of the Jordan
until everything the LORD had commanded
Joshua was done by the people, just as
Moses had directed Joshua. The people hurried over, 11and as soon as all of them had
crossed, the ark of the LORD and the priests
came to the other side while the people
watched. 12The men of Reuben, Gad and the
half-tribe of Manasseh crossed over, armed,
in front of the Israelites, as Moses had directed them. 13About forty thousand armed for
battle crossed over before the LORD to the
plains of Jericho for war.

14That day the LORD exalted Joshua in the
sight of all Israel; and they revered him all the
days of his life, just as they had revered
Moses.

15Then the LORD said to Joshua, 16"Command the priests carrying the ark of the Testimony to come up out of the Jordan."

[a]4 Hebrew *about two thousand cubits* (about 900 meters) [b]*16* That is, the Dead Sea [c]9 Or *Joshua also set up twelve stones*

17So Joshua commanded the priests, "Come up out of the Jordan."

18And the priests came up out of the river carrying the ark of the covenant of the LORD. No sooner had they set their feet on the dry ground than the waters of the Jordan returned to their place and ran at flood stage as before.

19On the tenth day of the first month the people went up from the Jordan and camped at Gilgal on the eastern border of Jericho. 20And Joshua set up at Gilgal the twelve stones they had taken out of the Jordan. 21He said to the Israelites, "In the future when your descendants ask their fathers, 'What do these stones mean?' 22tell them, 'Israel crossed the Jordan on dry ground.' 23For the LORD your God dried up the Jordan before you until you had crossed over. The LORD your God did to the Jordan just what he had done to the Red Sea[a] when he dried it up before us until we had crossed over. 24He did this so that all the peoples of the earth might know that the hand of the LORD is powerful and so that you might always fear the LORD your God."

Circumcision at Gilgal

5 Now when all the Amorite kings west of the Jordan and all the Canaanite kings along the coast heard how the LORD had dried up the Jordan before the Israelites until we had crossed over, their hearts melted and they no longer had the courage to face the Israelites.

2At that time the LORD said to Joshua, "Make flint knives and circumcise the Israelites again." 3So Joshua made flint knives and circumcised the Israelites at Gibeath Haaraloth.[b]

4Now this is why he did so: All those who came out of Egypt—all the men of military age—died in the desert on the way after leaving Egypt. 5All the people that came out had been circumcised, but all the people born in the desert during the journey from Egypt had not. 6The Israelites had moved about in the desert forty years until all the men who were of military age when they left Egypt had died, since they had not obeyed the LORD. For the LORD had sworn to them that they would not see the land that he had solemnly promised their fathers to give us, a land flowing with milk and honey. 7So he raised up their sons in their place, and these were the ones Joshua circumcised. They were still uncircumcised because they had not been circumcised on the way. 8And after the whole nation had been circumcised, they remained where they were in camp until they were healed.

9Then the LORD said to Joshua, "Today I have rolled away the reproach of Egypt from you." So the place has been called Gilgal[c] to this day.

10On the evening of the fourteenth day of the month, while camped at Gilgal on the plains of Jericho, the Israelites celebrated the Passover. 11The day after the Passover, that very day, they ate some of the produce of the land: unleavened bread and roasted grain. 12The manna stopped the day after[d] they ate this food from the land; there was no longer any manna for the Israelites, but that year they ate of the produce of Canaan.

The Fall of Jericho

13Now when Joshua was near Jericho, he looked up and saw a man standing in front of him with a drawn sword in his hand. Joshua went up to him and asked, "Are you for us or for our enemies?"

14"Neither," he replied, "but as commander of the army of the LORD I have now come." Then Joshua fell facedown to the ground in reverence, and asked him, "What message does my Lord[e] have for his servant?"

15The commander of the LORD's army replied, "Take off your sandals, for the place where you are standing is holy." And Joshua did so.

6 Now Jericho was tightly shut up because of the Israelites. No one went out and no one came in.

2Then the LORD said to Joshua, "See, I have delivered Jericho into your hands, along with its king and its fighting men. 3March around the city once with all the armed men. Do this for six days. 4Have seven priests carry trumpets of rams' horns in front of the ark. On the seventh day, march around the city seven times, with the priests blowing the trumpets. 5When you hear them sound a long blast on the trumpets, have all the people give a loud shout; then the wall of the city will collapse and the people will go up, every man straight in."

[a]23 Hebrew *Yam Suph;* that is, Sea of Reeds [b]3 *Gibeath Haaraloth* means *hill of foreskins.* [c]9 *Gilgal* sounds like the Hebrew for *roll.* [d]12 Or *the day* [e]14 Or *lord*

6So Joshua son of Nun called the priests
and said to them, "Take up the ark of the
covenant of the LORD and have seven priests
carry trumpets in front of it." 7And he ordered
the people, "Advance! March around the
city, with the armed guard going ahead of the
ark of the LORD."

8When Joshua had spoken to the people,
the seven priests carrying the seven trumpets before the LORD went forward, blowing
their trumpets, and the ark of the LORD's covenant followed them. 9The armed guard
marched ahead of the priests who blew the
trumpets, and the rear guard followed the
ark. All this time the trumpets were sounding.
10But Joshua had commanded the people,
"Do not give a war cry, do not raise your
voices, do not say a word until the day I tell
you to shout. Then shout!" 11So he had the
ark of the LORD carried around the city, cir-
cling it once. Then the people returned to
camp and spent the night there.

12Joshua got up early the next morning
and the priests took up the ark of the LORD.
13The seven priests carrying the seven trumpets went forward, marching before the ark
of the LORD and blowing the trumpets. The
armed men went ahead of them and the rear
guard followed the ark of the LORD, while the
trumpets kept sounding. 14So on the second
day they marched around the city once and
returned to the camp. They did this for six
days.

15On the seventh day, they got up at daybreak and marched around the city seven
times in the same manner, except that on
that day they circled the city seven times.
16The seventh time around, when the priests
sounded the trumpet blast, Joshua commanded the people, "Shout! For the LORD
has given you the city! 17The city and all that
is in it are to be devoted[a] to the LORD. Only
Rahab the prostitute[b] and all who are with
her in her house shall be spared, because
she hid the spies we sent. 18But keep away
from the devoted things, so that you will not
bring about your own destruction by taking
any of them. Otherwise you will make the
camp of Israel liable to destruction and bring
trouble on it. 19All the silver and gold and the
articles of bronze and iron are sacred to the
LORD and must go into his treasury."

20When the trumpets sounded, the people
shouted, and at the sound of the trumpet,
when the people gave a loud shout, the wall
collapsed; so every man charged straight in,
and they took the city. 21They devoted the
city to the LORD and destroyed with the sword
every living thing in it—men and women,
young and old, cattle, sheep and donkeys.

22Joshua said to the two men who had
spied out the land, "Go into the prostitute's
house and bring her out and all who belong
to her, in accordance with your oath to her."
23So the young men who had done the spying went in and brought out Rahab, her father and mother and brothers and all who
belonged to her. They brought out her entire
family and put them in a place outside the
camp of Israel.

24Then they burned the whole city and
everything in it, but they put the silver and
gold and the articles of bronze and iron into
the treasury of the LORD's house. 25But
Joshua spared Rahab the prostitute, with her
family and all who belonged to her, because
she hid the men Joshua had sent as spies to
Jericho—and she lives among the Israelites
to this day.

26At that time Joshua pronounced this solemn oath: "Cursed before the LORD is the
man who undertakes to rebuild this city, Jericho:

"At the cost of his firstborn son
  will he lay its foundations;
at the cost of his youngest
  will he set up its gates."

27So the LORD was with Joshua, and his
fame spread throughout the land.

Achan's Sin

7 But the Israelites acted unfaithfully in regard to the devoted things[c]; Achan son
of Carmi, the son of Zimri,[d] the son of Zerah,
of the tribe of Judah, took some of them. So
the LORD's anger burned against Israel.

2Now Joshua sent men from Jericho to Ai,
which is near Beth Aven to the east of Bethel,
and told them, "Go up and spy out the region." So the men went up and spied out Ai.

3When they returned to Joshua, they said,
"Not all the people will have to go up against
Ai. Send two or three thousand men to take it

[a]*17* The Hebrew term refers to the irrevocable giving over of things or persons to the LORD, often by totally destroying them; also in verses 18 and 21. [b]*17* Or possibly *innkeeper;* also in verses 22 and 25 [c]*1* The Hebrew term refers to the irrevocable giving over of things or persons to the LORD, often by totally destroying them; also in verses 11, 12, 13 and 15. [d]*1* See Septuagint and 1 Chronicles 2:6; Hebrew *Zabdi;* also in verses 17 and 18.

and do not weary all the people, for only a few men are there." 4So about three thousand men went up; but they were routed by the men of Ai, 5who killed about thirty-six of them. They chased the Israelites from the city gate as far as the stone quarries[a] and struck them down on the slopes. At this the hearts of the people melted and became like water.

6Then Joshua tore his clothes and fell facedown to the ground before the ark of the Lord, remaining there till evening. The elders of Israel did the same, and sprinkled dust on their heads. 7And Joshua said, "Ah, Sovereign Lord, why did you ever bring this people across the Jordan to deliver us into the hands of the Amorites to destroy us? If only we had been content to stay on the other side of the Jordan! 8O Lord, what can I say, now that Israel has been routed by its enemies? 9The Canaanites and the other people of the country will hear about this and they will surround us and wipe out our name from the earth. What then will you do for your own great name?"

10The Lord said to Joshua, "Stand up! What are you doing down on your face? 11Israel has sinned; they have violated my covenant, which I commanded them to keep. They have taken some of the devoted things; they have stolen, they have lied, they have put them with their own possessions. 12That is why the Israelites cannot stand against their enemies; they turn their backs and run because they have been made liable to destruction. I will not be with you anymore unless you destroy whatever among you is devoted to destruction.

13"Go, consecrate the people. Tell them, 'Consecrate yourselves in preparation for tomorrow; for this is what the Lord, the God of Israel, says: That which is devoted is among you, O Israel. You cannot stand against your enemies until you remove it.

14" 'In the morning, present yourselves tribe by tribe. The tribe that the Lord takes shall come forward clan by clan; the clan that the Lord takes shall come forward family by family; and the family that the Lord takes shall come forward man by man. 15He who is caught with the devoted things shall be destroyed by fire, along with all that belongs to him. He has violated the covenant of the Lord and has done a disgraceful thing in Israel!' "

16Early the next morning Joshua had Israel come forward by tribes, and Judah was taken. 17The clans of Judah came forward, and he took the Zerahites. He had the clan of the Zerahites come forward by families, and Zimri was taken. 18Joshua had his family come forward man by man, and Achan son of Carmi, the son of Zimri, the son of Zerah, of the tribe of Judah, was taken.

19Then Joshua said to Achan, "My son, give glory to the Lord,[b] the God of Israel, and give him the praise.[c] Tell me what you have done; do not hide it from me."

20Achan replied, "It is true! I have sinned against the Lord, the God of Israel. This is what I have done: 21When I saw in the plunder a beautiful robe from Babylonia,[d] two hundred shekels[e] of silver and a wedge of gold weighing fifty shekels,[f] I coveted them and took them. They are hidden in the ground inside my tent, with the silver underneath."

22So Joshua sent messengers, and they ran to the tent, and there it was, hidden in his tent, with the silver underneath. 23They took the things from the tent, brought them to Joshua and all the Israelites and spread them out before the Lord.

24Then Joshua, together with all Israel, took Achan son of Zerah, the silver, the robe, the gold wedge, his sons and daughters, his cattle, donkeys and sheep, his tent and all that he had, to the Valley of Achor. 25Joshua said, "Why have you brought this trouble on us? The Lord will bring trouble on you today."

Then all Israel stoned him, and after they had stoned the rest, they burned them. 26Over Achan they heaped up a large pile of rocks, which remains to this day. Then the Lord turned from his fierce anger. Therefore that place has been called the Valley of Achor[g] ever since.

Ai Destroyed

8 Then the Lord said to Joshua, "Do not be afraid; do not be discouraged. Take the whole army with you, and go up and attack Ai. For I have delivered into your hands the king of Ai, his people, his city and his land. 2You shall do to Ai and its king as

[a]5 Or *as far as Shebarim* [b]19 A solemn charge to tell the truth [c]19 Or *and confess to him*
[d]21 Hebrew *Shinar* [e]21 That is, about 5 pounds (about 2.3 kilograms) [f]21 That is, about 1 1/4 pounds (about 0.6 kilogram) [g]26 *Achor* means *trouble.*

you did to Jericho and its king, except that you may carry off their plunder and livestock for yourselves. Set an ambush behind the city."

3So Joshua and the whole army moved out to attack Ai. He chose thirty thousand of his best fighting men and sent them out at night 4with these orders: "Listen carefully. You are to set an ambush behind the city. Don't go very far from it. All of you be on the alert. 5I and all those with me will advance on the city, and when the men come out against us, as they did before, we will flee from them. 6They will pursue us until we have lured them away from the city, for they will say, 'They are running away from us as they did before.' So when we flee from them, 7you are to rise up from ambush and take the city. The LORD your God will give it into your hand. 8When you have taken the city, set it on fire. Do what the LORD has commanded. See to it; you have my orders."

9Then Joshua sent them off, and they went to the place of ambush and lay in wait between Bethel and Ai, to the west of Ai—but Joshua spent that night with the people.

10Early the next morning Joshua mustered his men, and he and the leaders of Israel marched before them to Ai. 11The entire force that was with him marched up and approached the city and arrived in front of it. They set up camp north of Ai, with the valley between them and the city. 12Joshua had taken about five thousand men and set them in ambush between Bethel and Ai, to the west of the city. 13They had the soldiers take up their positions—all those in the camp to the north of the city and the ambush to the west of it. That night Joshua went into the valley.

14When the king of Ai saw this, he and all the men of the city hurried out early in the morning to meet Israel in battle at a certain place overlooking the Arabah. But he did not know that an ambush had been set against him behind the city. 15Joshua and all Israel let themselves be driven back before them, and they fled toward the desert. 16All the men of Ai were called to pursue them, and they pursued Joshua and were lured away from the city. 17Not a man remained in Ai or Bethel who did not go after Israel. They left the city open and went in pursuit of Israel.

18Then the LORD said to Joshua, "Hold out toward Ai the javelin that is in your hand, for into your hand I will deliver the city." So Joshua held out his javelin toward Ai. 19As soon as he did this, the men in the ambush rose quickly from their position and rushed forward. They entered the city and captured it and quickly set it on fire.

20The men of Ai looked back and saw the smoke of the city rising against the sky, but they had no chance to escape in any direction, for the Israelites who had been fleeing toward the desert had turned back against their pursuers. 21For when Joshua and all Israel saw that the ambush had taken the city and that smoke was going up from the city, they turned around and attacked the men of Ai. 22The men of the ambush also came out of the city against them, so that they were caught in the middle, with Israelites on both sides. Israel cut them down, leaving them neither survivors nor fugitives. 23But they took the king of Ai alive and brought him to Joshua.

24When Israel had finished killing all the men of Ai in the fields and in the desert where they had chased them, and when every one of them had been put to the sword, all the Israelites returned to Ai and killed those who were in it. 25Twelve thousand men and women fell that day—all the people of Ai. 26For Joshua did not draw back the hand that held out his javelin until he had destroyed[a] all who lived in Ai. 27But Israel did carry off for themselves the livestock and plunder of this city, as the LORD had instructed Joshua.

28So Joshua burned Ai and made it a permanent heap of ruins, a desolate place to this day. 29He hung the king of Ai on a tree and left him there until evening. At sunset, Joshua ordered them to take his body from the tree and throw it down at the entrance of the city gate. And they raised a large pile of rocks over it, which remains to this day.

The Covenant Renewed at Mount Ebal

30Then Joshua built on Mount Ebal an altar to the LORD, the God of Israel, 31as Moses the servant of the LORD had commanded the Israelites. He built it according to what is written in the Book of the Law of Moses—an altar of uncut stones, on which no iron tool had been used. On it they offered to the LORD burnt offerings and sacrificed fellowship offerings.[b] 32There, in the presence of the Isra-

[a]*26* The Hebrew term refers to the irrevocable giving over of things or persons to the LORD, often by totally destroying them. [b]*31* Traditionally *peace offerings*

elites, Joshua copied on stones the law of
Moses, which he had written. 33All Israel,
aliens and citizens alike, with their elders,
officials and judges, were standing on both
sides of the ark of the covenant of the LORD,
facing those who carried it—the priests, who
were Levites. Half of the people stood in front
of Mount Gerizim and half of them in front of
Mount Ebal, as Moses the servant of the
LORD had formerly commanded when he
gave instructions to bless the people of Israel.
34Afterward, Joshua read all the words of
the law—the blessings and the curses—just
as it is written in the Book of the Law. 35There
was not a word of all that Moses had commanded that Joshua did not read to the
whole assembly of Israel, including the
women and children, and the aliens who
lived among them.

The Gibeonite Deception

9 Now when all the kings west of the Jordan heard about these things—those in
the hill country, in the western foothills, and
along the entire coast of the Great Sea[a] as
far as Lebanon (the kings of the Hittites, Amorites, Canaanites, Perizzites, Hivites and
Jebusites)— 2they came together to make
war against Joshua and Israel.
3However, when the people of Gibeon
heard what Joshua had done to Jericho and
Ai, 4they resorted to a ruse: They went as a
delegation whose donkeys were loaded[b]
with worn-out sacks and old wineskins,
cracked and mended. 5The men put worn
and patched sandals on their feet and wore
old clothes. All the bread of their food supply
was dry and moldy. 6Then they went to
Joshua in the camp at Gilgal and said to him
and the men of Israel, "We have come from a
distant country; make a treaty with us."
7The men of Israel said to the Hivites, "But
perhaps you live near us. How then can we
make a treaty with you?"
8"We are your servants," they said to
Joshua.
But Joshua asked, "Who are you and
where do you come from?"
9They answered: "Your servants have
come from a very distant country because of
the fame of the LORD your God. For we have
heard reports of him: all that he did in Egypt,
10and all that he did to the two kings of the
Amorites east of the Jordan—Sihon king of
Heshbon, and Og king of Bashan, who
reigned in Ashtaroth. 11And our elders and all
those living in our country said to us, 'Take
provisions for your journey; go and meet
them and say to them, "We are your servants; make a treaty with us."' 12This bread
of ours was warm when we packed it at
home on the day we left to come to you. But
now see how dry and moldy it is. 13And these
wineskins that we filled were new, but see
how cracked they are. And our clothes and
sandals are worn out by the very long journey."
14The men of Israel sampled their provisions but did not inquire of the LORD. 15Then
Joshua made a treaty of peace with them to
let them live, and the leaders of the assembly
ratified it by oath.
16Three days after they made the treaty
with the Gibeonites, the Israelites heard that
they were neighbors, living near them. 17So
the Israelites set out and on the third day
came to their cities: Gibeon, Kephirah,
Beeroth and Kiriath Jearim. 18But the Israelites did not attack them, because the leaders
of the assembly had sworn an oath to them
by the LORD, the God of Israel.
The whole assembly grumbled against the
leaders, 19but all the leaders answered, "We
have given them our oath by the LORD, the
God of Israel, and we cannot touch them
now. 20This is what we will do to them: We
will let them live, so that wrath will not fall on
us for breaking the oath we swore to them."
21They continued, "Let them live, but let
them be woodcutters and water carriers for
the entire community." So the leaders' promise to them was kept.
22Then Joshua summoned the Gibeonites
and said, "Why did you deceive us by saying, 'We live a long way from you,' while
actually you live near us? 23You are now
under a curse: You will never cease to serve
as woodcutters and water carriers for the
house of my God."
24They answered Joshua, "Your servants
were clearly told how the LORD your God had
commanded his servant Moses to give you
the whole land and to wipe out all its inhabitants from before you. So we feared for our
lives because of you, and that is why we did
this. 25We are now in your hands. Do to us
whatever seems good and right to you."

[a] *1* That is, the Mediterranean [b] *4* Most Hebrew manuscripts; some Hebrew manuscripts, Vulgate and Syriac (see also Septuagint) *They prepared provisions and loaded their donkeys*

26So Joshua saved them from the Israelites, and they did not kill them. 27That day he
made the Gibeonites woodcutters and water
carriers for the community and for the altar of
the LORD at the place the LORD would choose.
And that is what they are to this day.

The Sun Stands Still

10 Now Adoni-Zedek king of Jerusalem
heard that Joshua had taken Ai and
totally destroyed[a] it, doing to Ai and its king
as he had done to Jericho and its king, and
that the people of Gibeon had made a treaty
of peace with Israel and were living near
them. 2He and his people were very much
alarmed at this, because Gibeon was an important city, like one of the royal cities; it was
larger than Ai, and all its men were good
fighters. 3So Adoni-Zedek king of Jerusalem
appealed to Hoham king of Hebron, Piram
king of Jarmuth, Japhia king of Lachish and
Debir king of Eglon. 4"Come up and help me
attack Gibeon," he said, "because it has
made peace with Joshua and the Israelites."
5Then the five kings of the Amorites—the
kings of Jerusalem, Hebron, Jarmuth, Lachish and Eglon—joined forces. They
moved up with all their troops and took up
positions against Gibeon and attacked it.
6The Gibeonites then sent word to Joshua
in the camp at Gilgal: "Do not abandon your
servants. Come up to us quickly and save
us! Help us, because all the Amorite kings
from the hill country have joined forces
against us."
7So Joshua marched up from Gilgal with
his entire army, including all the best fighting
men. 8The LORD said to Joshua, "Do not be
afraid of them; I have given them into your
hand. Not one of them will be able to withstand you."
9After an all-night march from Gilgal,
Joshua took them by surprise. 10The LORD
threw them into confusion before Israel, who
defeated them in a great victory at Gibeon.
Israel pursued them along the road going up
to Beth Horon and cut them down all the way
to Azekah and Makkedah. 11As they fled before Israel on the road down from Beth Horon
to Azekah, the LORD hurled large hailstones
down on them from the sky, and more of
them died from the hailstones than were
killed by the swords of the Israelites.
12On the day the LORD gave the Amorites
over to Israel, Joshua said to the LORD in the
presence of Israel:

"O sun, stand still over Gibeon,
O moon, over the Valley of Aijalon."
13So the sun stood still,
and the moon stopped,
till the nation avenged itself on[b] its
enemies,
as it is written in the Book of Jashar.

The sun stopped in the middle of the sky
and delayed going down about a full day.
14There has never been a day like it before or
since, a day when the LORD listened to a man.
Surely the LORD was fighting for Israel!
15Then Joshua returned with all Israel to
the camp at Gilgal.

Five Amorite Kings Killed

16Now the five kings had fled and hidden in
the cave at Makkedah. 17When Joshua was
told that the five kings had been found hiding
in the cave at Makkedah, 18he said, "Roll
large rocks up to the mouth of the cave, and
post some men there to guard it. 19But don't
stop! Pursue your enemies, attack them from
the rear and don't let them reach their cities,
for the LORD your God has given them into
your hand."
20So Joshua and the Israelites destroyed
them completely—almost to a man—but the
few who were left reached their fortified cities. 21The whole army then returned safely to
Joshua in the camp at Makkedah, and no
one uttered a word against the Israelites.
22Joshua said, "Open the mouth of the
cave and bring those five kings out to me."
23So they brought the five kings out of the
cave—the kings of Jerusalem, Hebron, Jarmuth, Lachish and Eglon. 24When they had
brought these kings to Joshua, he summoned all the men of Israel and said to the
army commanders who had come with him,
"Come here and put your feet on the necks
of these kings." So they came forward and
placed their feet on their necks.
25Joshua said to them, "Do not be afraid;
do not be discouraged. Be strong and courageous. This is what the LORD will do to all the
enemies you are going to fight." 26Then
Joshua struck and killed the kings and hung
them on five trees, and they were left hanging on the trees until evening.
27At sunset Joshua gave the order and

[a] *1* The Hebrew term refers to the irrevocable giving over of things or persons to the LORD, often by totally destroying them; also in verses 28, 35, 37, 39 and 40. [b] *13* Or *nation triumphed over*

they took them down from the trees and threw them into the cave where they had been hiding. At the mouth of the cave they placed large rocks, which are there to this day.

28That day Joshua took Makkedah. He put the city and its king to the sword and totally destroyed everyone in it. He left no survivors. And he did to the king of Makkedah as he had done to the king of Jericho.

Southern Cities Conquered

29Then Joshua and all Israel with him moved on from Makkedah to Libnah and attacked it. 30The LORD also gave that city and its king into Israel's hand. The city and everyone in it Joshua put to the sword. He left no survivors there. And he did to its king as he had done to the king of Jericho.

31Then Joshua and all Israel with him moved on from Libnah to Lachish; he took up positions against it and attacked it. 32The LORD handed Lachish over to Israel, and Joshua took it on the second day. The city and everyone in it he put to the sword, just as he had done to Libnah. 33Meanwhile, Horam king of Gezer had come up to help Lachish, but Joshua defeated him and his army—until no survivors were left.

34Then Joshua and all Israel with him moved on from Lachish to Eglon; they took up positions against it and attacked it. 35They captured it that same day and put it to the sword and totally destroyed everyone in it, just as they had done to Lachish.

36Then Joshua and all Israel with him went up from Eglon to Hebron and attacked it. 37They took the city and put it to the sword, together with its king, its villages and everyone in it. They left no survivors. Just as at Eglon, they totally destroyed it and everyone in it.

38Then Joshua and all Israel with him turned around and attacked Debir. 39They took the city, its king and its villages, and put them to the sword. Everyone in it they totally destroyed. They left no survivors. They did to Debir and its king as they had done to Libnah and its king and to Hebron.

40So Joshua subdued the whole region, including the hill country, the Negev, the western foothills and the mountain slopes, together with all their kings. He left no survivors. He totally destroyed all who breathed, just as the LORD, the God of Israel, had commanded. 41Joshua subdued them from Kadesh Barnea to Gaza and from the whole region of Goshen to Gibeon. 42All these kings and their lands Joshua conquered in one campaign, because the LORD, the God of Israel, fought for Israel.

43Then Joshua returned with all Israel to the camp at Gilgal.

Northern Kings Defeated

11 When Jabin king of Hazor heard of this, he sent word to Jobab king of Madon, to the kings of Shimron and Acshaph, 2and to the northern kings who were in the mountains, in the Arabah south of Kinnereth, in the western foothills and in Naphoth Dor[a] on the west; 3to the Canaanites in the east and west; to the Amorites, Hittites, Perizzites and Jebusites in the hill country; and to the Hivites below Hermon in the region of Mizpah. 4They came out with all their troops and a large number of horses and chariots—a huge army, as numerous as the sand on the seashore. 5All these kings joined forces and made camp together at the Waters of Merom, to fight against Israel.

6The LORD said to Joshua, "Do not be afraid of them, because by this time tomorrow I will hand all of them over to Israel, slain. You are to hamstring their horses and burn their chariots."

7So Joshua and his whole army came against them suddenly at the Waters of Merom and attacked them, 8and the LORD gave them into the hand of Israel. They defeated them and pursued them all the way to Greater Sidon, to Misrephoth Maim, and to the Valley of Mizpah on the east, until no survivors were left. 9Joshua did to them as the LORD had directed: He hamstrung their horses and burned their chariots.

10At that time Joshua turned back and captured Hazor and put its king to the sword. (Hazor had been the head of all these kingdoms.) 11Everyone in it they put to the sword. They totally destroyed[b] them, not sparing anything that breathed, and he burned up Hazor itself.

12Joshua took all these royal cities and their kings and put them to the sword. He totally destroyed them, as Moses the servant of the LORD had commanded. 13Yet Israel did not burn any of the cities built on their

[a]2 Or *in the heights of Dor* [b]11 The Hebrew term refers to the irrevocable giving over of things or persons to the LORD, often by totally destroying them; also in verses 12, 20 and 21.

mounds—except Hazor, which Joshua
burned. 14The Israelites carried off for themselves all the plunder and livestock of these
cities, but all the people they put to the sword
until they completely destroyed them, not
sparing anyone that breathed. 15As the LORD
commanded his servant Moses, so Moses
commanded Joshua, and Joshua did it; he
left nothing undone of all that the LORD commanded Moses.

16So Joshua took this entire land: the hill
country, all the Negev, the whole region of
Goshen, the western foothills, the Arabah
and the mountains of Israel with their foothills, 17from Mount Halak, which rises toward
Seir, to Baal Gad in the Valley of Lebanon
below Mount Hermon. He captured all their
kings and struck them down, putting them to
death. 18Joshua waged war against all these
kings for a long time. 19Except for the Hivites
living in Gibeon, not one city made a treaty of
peace with the Israelites, who took them all
in battle. 20For it was the LORD himself who
hardened their hearts to wage war against
Israel, so that he might destroy them totally,
exterminating them without mercy, as the
LORD had commanded Moses.

21At that time Joshua went and destroyed
the Anakites from the hill country: from Hebron, Debir and Anab, from all the hill country
of Judah, and from all the hill country of Israel. Joshua totally destroyed them and their
towns. 22No Anakites were left in Israelite
territory; only in Gaza, Gath and Ashdod did
any survive. 23So Joshua took the entire
land, just as the LORD had directed Moses,
and he gave it as an inheritance to Israel
according to their tribal divisions.

Then the land had rest from war.

List of Defeated Kings

12 These are the kings of the land whom
the Israelites had defeated and
whose territory they took over east of the
Jordan, from the Arnon Gorge to Mount Hermon, including all the eastern side of the
Arabah:

2Sihon king of the Amorites,
who reigned in Heshbon. He ruled from
Aroer on the rim of the Arnon Gorge—
from the middle of the gorge—to the
Jabbok River, which is the border of the
Ammonites. This included half of Gilead. 3He also ruled over the eastern
Arabah from the Sea of Kinnereth[a] to
the Sea of the Arabah (the Salt Sea[b]), to
Beth Jeshimoth, and then southward
below the slopes of Pisgah.

4And the territory of Og king of Bashan,
one of the last of the Rephaites, who
reigned in Ashtaroth and Edrei. 5He
ruled over Mount Hermon, Salecah, all
of Bashan to the border of the people of
Geshur and Maacah, and half of Gilead
to the border of Sihon king of Heshbon.

6Moses, the servant of the LORD, and the
Israelites conquered them. And Moses the
servant of the LORD gave their land to the
Reubenites, the Gadites and the half-tribe of
Manasseh to be their possession.

7These are the kings of the land that
Joshua and the Israelites conquered on the
west side of the Jordan, from Baal Gad in the
Valley of Lebanon to Mount Halak, which
rises toward Seir (their lands Joshua gave as
an inheritance to the tribes of Israel according to their tribal divisions— 8the hill country,
the western foothills, the Arabah, the mountain slopes, the desert and the Negev—the
lands of the Hittites, Amorites, Canaanites,
Perizzites, Hivites and Jebusites):

9the king of Jericho	one
the king of Ai (near Bethel)	one
10the king of Jerusalem	one
the king of Hebron	one
11the king of Jarmuth	one
the king of Lachish	one
12the king of Eglon	one
the king of Gezer	one
13the king of Debir	one
the king of Geder	one
14the king of Hormah	one
the king of Arad	one
15the king of Libnah	one
the king of Adullam	one
16the king of Makkedah	one
the king of Bethel	one
17the king of Tappuah	one
the king of Hepher	one
18the king of Aphek	one
the king of Lasharon	one
19the king of Madon	one
the king of Hazor	one
20the king of Shimron Meron	one
the king of Acshaph	one
21the king of Taanach	one
the king of Megiddo	one
22the king of Kedesh	one
the king of Jokneam in Carmel	one

[a]3 That is, Galilee [b]3 That is, the Dead Sea

[23]the king of Dor (in Naphoth Dor[a]) one
the king of Goyim in Gilgal one
[24]the king of Tirzah one
thirty-one kings in all.

Land Still to Be Taken

13 When Joshua was old and well advanced in years, the LORD said to him, "You are very old, and there are still very large areas of land to be taken over.

[2]"This is the land that remains: all the regions of the Philistines and Geshurites: [3]from the Shihor River on the east of Egypt to the territory of Ekron on the north, all of it counted as Canaanite (the territory of the five Philistine rulers in Gaza, Ashdod, Ashkelon, Gath and Ekron—that of the Avvites); [4]from the south, all the land of the Canaanites, from Arah of the Sidonians as far as Aphek, the region of the Amorites, [5]the area of the Gebalites[b]; and all Lebanon to the east, from Baal Gad below Mount Hermon to Lebo[c] Hamath.

[6]"As for all the inhabitants of the mountain regions from Lebanon to Misrephoth Maim, that is, all the Sidonians, I myself will drive them out before the Israelites. Be sure to allocate this land to Israel for an inheritance, as I have instructed you, [7]and divide it as an inheritance among the nine tribes and half of the tribe of Manasseh."

Division of the Land East of the Jordan

[8]The other half of Manasseh,[d] the Reubenites and the Gadites had received the inheritance that Moses had given them east of the Jordan, as he, the servant of the LORD, had assigned it to them.

[9]It extended from Aroer on the rim of the Arnon Gorge, and from the town in the middle of the gorge, and included the whole plateau of Medeba as far as Dibon, [10]and all the towns of Sihon king of the Amorites, who ruled in Heshbon, out to the border of the Ammonites. [11]It also included Gilead, the territory of the people of Geshur and Maacah, all of Mount Hermon and all Bashan as far as Salecah— [12]that is, the whole kingdom of Og in Bashan, who had reigned in Ashtaroth and Edrei and had survived as one of the last of the Rephaites. Moses had defeated them and taken over their land. [13]But the Israelites did not drive out the people of Geshur and Maacah, so they continue to live among the Israelites to this day.

[14]But to the tribe of Levi he gave no inheritance, since the offerings made by fire to the LORD, the God of Israel, are their inheritance, as he promised them.

[15]This is what Moses had given to the tribe of Reuben, clan by clan:

[16]The territory from Aroer on the rim of the Arnon Gorge, and from the town in the middle of the gorge, and the whole plateau past Medeba [17]to Heshbon and all its towns on the plateau, including Dibon, Bamoth Baal, Beth Baal Meon, [18]Jahaz, Kedemoth, Mephaath, [19]Kiriathaim, Sibmah, Zereth Shahar on the hill in the valley, [20]Beth Peor, the slopes of Pisgah, and Beth Jeshimoth [21]—all the towns on the plateau and the entire realm of Sihon king of the Amorites, who ruled at Heshbon. Moses had defeated him and the Midianite chiefs, Evi, Rekem, Zur, Hur and Reba—princes allied with Sihon—who lived in that country. [22]In addition to those slain in battle, the Israelites had put to the sword Balaam son of Beor, who practiced divination. [23]The boundary of the Reubenites was the bank of the Jordan. These towns and their villages were the inheritance of the Reubenites, clan by clan.

[24]This is what Moses had given to the tribe of Gad, clan by clan:

[25]The territory of Jazer, all the towns of Gilead and half the Ammonite country as far as Aroer, near Rabbah; [26]and from Heshbon to Ramath Mizpah and Betonim, and from Mahanaim to the territory of Debir; [27]and in the valley, Beth Haram, Beth Nimrah, Succoth and Zaphon with the rest of the realm of Sihon king of Heshbon (the east side of the Jordan, the territory up to the end of the Sea of Kinnereth[e]). [28]These towns and their villages were the inheritance of the Gadites, clan by clan.

[29]This is what Moses had given to the half-

[a]23 Or *in the heights of Dor* [b]5 That is, the area of Byblos [c]5 Or *to the entrance to* [d]8 Hebrew *With it* (that is, with the other half of Manasseh) [e]27 That is, Galilee

tribe of Manasseh, that is, to half the family of the descendants of Manasseh, clan by clan:

> 30 The territory extending from Mahanaim and including all of Bashan, the entire realm of Og king of Bashan—all the settlements of Jair in Bashan, sixty towns, 31 half of Gilead, and Ashtaroth and Edrei (the royal cities of Og in Bashan). This was for the descendants of Makir son of Manasseh—for half of the sons of Makir, clan by clan.

32 This is the inheritance Moses had given when he was in the plains of Moab across the Jordan east of Jericho. 33 But to the tribe of Levi, Moses had given no inheritance; the LORD, the God of Israel, is their inheritance, as he promised them.

Division of the Land West of the Jordan

14 Now these are the areas the Israelites received as an inheritance in the land of Canaan, which Eleazar the priest, Joshua son of Nun and the heads of the tribal clans of Israel allotted to them. 2 Their inheritances were assigned by lot to the nine-and-a-half tribes, as the LORD had commanded through Moses. 3 Moses had granted the two-and-a-half tribes their inheritance east of the Jordan but had not granted the Levites an inheritance among the rest, 4 for the sons of Joseph had become two tribes—Manasseh and Ephraim. The Levites received no share of the land but only towns to live in, with pasturelands for their flocks and herds. 5 So the Israelites divided the land, just as the LORD had commanded Moses.

Hebron Given to Caleb

6 Now the men of Judah approached Joshua at Gilgal, and Caleb son of Jephunneh the Kenizzite said to him, "You know what the LORD said to Moses the man of God at Kadesh Barnea about you and me. 7 I was forty years old when Moses the servant of the LORD sent me from Kadesh Barnea to explore the land. And I brought him back a report according to my convictions, 8 but my brothers who went up with me made the hearts of the people melt with fear. I, however, followed the LORD my God wholeheartedly. 9 So on that day Moses swore to me, 'The land on which your feet have walked will be your inheritance and that of your children forever, because you have followed the LORD my God wholeheartedly.'[a]

10 "Now then, just as the LORD promised, he has kept me alive for forty-five years since the time he said this to Moses, while Israel moved about in the desert. So here I am today, eighty-five years old! 11 I am still as strong today as the day Moses sent me out; I'm just as vigorous to go out to battle now as I was then. 12 Now give me this hill country that the LORD promised me that day. You yourself heard then that the Anakites were there and their cities were large and fortified, but, the LORD helping me, I will drive them out just as he said."

13 Then Joshua blessed Caleb son of Jephunneh and gave him Hebron as his inheritance. 14 So Hebron has belonged to Caleb son of Jephunneh the Kenizzite ever since, because he followed the LORD, the God of Israel, wholeheartedly. 15 (Hebron used to be called Kiriath Arba after Arba, who was the greatest man among the Anakites.)

Then the land had rest from war.

Allotment for Judah

15 The allotment for the tribe of Judah, clan by clan, extended down to the territory of Edom, to the Desert of Zin in the extreme south.

> 2 Their southern boundary started from the bay at the southern end of the Salt Sea,[b] 3 crossed south of Scorpion[c] Pass, continued on to Zin and went over to the south of Kadesh Barnea. Then it ran past Hezron up to Addar and curved around to Karka. 4 It then passed along to Azmon and joined the Wadi of Egypt, ending at the sea. This is their[d] southern boundary.
>
> 5 The eastern boundary is the Salt Sea as far as the mouth of the Jordan.
>
> The northern boundary started from the bay of the sea at the mouth of the Jordan, 6 went up to Beth Hoglah and continued north of Beth Arabah to the Stone of Bohan son of Reuben. 7 The boundary then went up to Debir from the Valley of Achor and turned north to Gilgal, which faces the Pass of Adummim south of the gorge. It continued along to the waters of En Shemesh and came out at En Rogel. 8 Then it ran up the Valley of Ben Hinnom along the southern slope of the Jebusite city (that is,

[a] 9 Deut. 1:36 [b] 2 That is, the Dead Sea; also in verse 5 [c] 3 Hebrew *Akrabbim* [d] 4 Hebrew *your*

Jerusalem). From there it climbed to the top of the hill west of the Hinnom Valley at the northern end of the Valley of Rephaim. 9From the hilltop the boundary headed toward the spring of the waters of Nephtoah, came out at the towns of Mount Ephron and went down toward Baalah (that is, Kiriath Jearim). 10Then it curved westward from Baalah to Mount Seir, ran along the northern slope of Mount Jearim (that is, Kesalon), continued down to Beth Shemesh and crossed to Timnah. 11It went to the northern slope of Ekron, turned toward Shikkeron, passed along to Mount Baalah and reached Jabneel. The boundary ended at the sea.

12The western boundary is the coastline of the Great Sea.[a]

These are the boundaries around the people of Judah by their clans.

13In accordance with the LORD's command to him, Joshua gave to Caleb son of Jephunneh a portion in Judah—Kiriath Arba, that is, Hebron. (Arba was the forefather of Anak.) 14From Hebron Caleb drove out the three Anakites—Sheshai, Ahiman and Talmai—descendants of Anak. 15From there he marched against the people living in Debir (formerly called Kiriath Sepher). 16And Caleb said, "I will give my daughter Acsah in marriage to the man who attacks and captures Kiriath Sepher." 17Othniel son of Kenaz, Caleb's brother, took it; so Caleb gave his daughter Acsah to him in marriage.

18One day when she came to Othniel, she urged him[b] to ask her father for a field. When she got off her donkey, Caleb asked her, "What can I do for you?"

19She replied, "Do me a special favor. Since you have given me land in the Negev, give me also springs of water." So Caleb gave her the upper and lower springs.

20This is the inheritance of the tribe of Judah, clan by clan:

21The southernmost towns of the tribe of Judah in the Negev toward the boundary of Edom were:

Kabzeel, Eder, Jagur, 22Kinah, Dimonah, Adadah, 23Kedesh, Hazor, Ithnan, 24Ziph, Telem, Bealoth, 25Hazor Hadattah, Kerioth Hezron (that is, Hazor), 26Amam, Shema, Moladah, 27Hazar Gaddah, Heshmon, Beth Pelet, 28Hazar Shual, Beersheba, Biziothiah, 29Baalah, Iim, Ezem, 30Eltolad, Kesil, Hormah, 31Ziklag, Madmannah, Sansannah, 32Lebaoth, Shilhim, Ain and Rimmon—a total of twenty-nine towns and their villages.

33In the western foothills:

Eshtaol, Zorah, Ashnah, 34Zanoah, En Gannim, Tappuah, Enam, 35Jarmuth, Adullam, Socoh, Azekah, 36Shaaraim, Adithaim and Gederah (or Gederothaim)[c]—fourteen towns and their villages.

37Zenan, Hadashah, Migdal Gad, 38Dilean, Mizpah, Joktheel, 39Lachish, Bozkath, Eglon, 40Cabbon, Lahmas, Kitlish, 41Gederoth, Beth Dagon, Naamah and Makkedah—sixteen towns and their villages.

42Libnah, Ether, Ashan, 43Iphtah, Ashnah, Nezib, 44Keilah, Aczib and Mareshah—nine towns and their villages.

45Ekron, with its surrounding settlements and villages; 46west of Ekron, all that were in the vicinity of Ashdod, together with their villages; 47Ashdod, its surrounding settlements and villages; and Gaza, its settlements and villages, as far as the Wadi of Egypt and the coastline of the Great Sea.

48In the hill country:

Shamir, Jattir, Socoh, 49Dannah, Kiriath Sannah (that is, Debir), 50Anab, Eshtemoh, Anim, 51Goshen, Holon and Giloh—eleven towns and their villages.

52Arab, Dumah, Eshan, 53Janim, Beth Tappuah, Aphekah, 54Humtah, Kiriath Arba (that is, Hebron) and Zior—nine towns and their villages.

55Maon, Carmel, Ziph, Juttah, 56Jezreel, Jokdeam, Zanoah, 57Kain, Gibeah and Timnah—ten towns and their villages.

58Halhul, Beth Zur, Gedor, 59Maarath, Beth Anoth and Eltekon—six towns and their villages.

60Kiriath Baal (that is, Kiriath Jearim) and Rabbah—two towns and their villages.

61In the desert:

[a]*12* That is, the Mediterranean; also in verse 47 [b]*18* Hebrew and some Septuagint manuscripts; other Septuagint manuscripts (see also note at Judges 1:14) *Othniel, he urged her* [c]*36* Or *Gederah and Gederothaim*

Beth Arabah, Middin, Secacah, 62Nibshan, the City of Salt and En Gedi—six towns and their villages.

63Judah could not dislodge the Jebusites, who were living in Jerusalem; to this day the Jebusites live there with the people of Judah.

Allotment for Ephraim and Manasseh

16 The allotment for Joseph began at the Jordan of Jericho,[a] east of the waters of Jericho, and went up from there through the desert into the hill country of Bethel. 2It went on from Bethel (that is, Luz),[b] crossed over to the territory of the Arkites in Ataroth, 3descended westward to the territory of the Japhletites as far as the region of Lower Beth Horon and on to Gezer, ending at the sea.

4So Manasseh and Ephraim, the descendants of Joseph, received their inheritance.

5This was the territory of Ephraim, clan by clan:

The boundary of their inheritance went from Ataroth Addar in the east to Upper Beth Horon 6and continued to the sea. From Micmethath on the north it curved eastward to Taanath Shiloh, passing by it to Janoah on the east. 7Then it went down from Janoah to Ataroth and Naarah, touched Jericho and came out at the Jordan. 8From Tappuah the border went west to the Kanah Ravine and ended at the sea. This was the inheritance of the tribe of the Ephraimites, clan by clan. 9It also included all the towns and their villages that were set aside for the Ephraimites within the inheritance of the Manassites.

10They did not dislodge the Canaanites living in Gezer; to this day the Canaanites live among the people of Ephraim but are required to do forced labor.

17 This was the allotment for the tribe of Manasseh as Joseph's firstborn, that is, for Makir, Manasseh's firstborn. Makir was the ancestor of the Gileadites, who had received Gilead and Bashan because the Makirites were great soldiers. 2So this allotment was for the rest of the people of Manasseh—the clans of Abiezer, Helek, Asriel, Shechem, Hepher and Shemida. These are the other male descendants of Manasseh son of Joseph by their clans.

3Now Zelophehad son of Hepher, the son of Gilead, the son of Makir, the son of Manasseh, had no sons but only daughters, whose names were Mahlah, Noah, Hoglah, Milcah and Tirzah. 4They went to Eleazar the priest, Joshua son of Nun, and the leaders and said, "The Lord commanded Moses to give us an inheritance among our brothers." So Joshua gave them an inheritance along with the brothers of their father, according to the Lord's command. 5Manasseh's share consisted of ten tracts of land besides Gilead and Bashan east of the Jordan, 6because the daughters of the tribe of Manasseh received an inheritance among the sons. The land of Gilead belonged to the rest of the descendants of Manasseh.

7The territory of Manasseh extended from Asher to Micmethath east of Shechem. The boundary ran southward from there to include the people living at En Tappuah. 8(Manasseh had the land of Tappuah, but Tappuah itself, on the boundary of Manasseh, belonged to the Ephraimites.) 9Then the boundary continued south to the Kanah Ravine. There were towns belonging to Ephraim lying among the towns of Manasseh, but the boundary of Manasseh was the northern side of the ravine and ended at the sea. 10On the south the land belonged to Ephraim, on the north to Manasseh. The territory of Manasseh reached the sea and bordered Asher on the north and Issachar on the east.

11Within Issachar and Asher, Manasseh also had Beth Shan, Ibleam and the people of Dor, Endor, Taanach and Megiddo, together with their surrounding settlements (the third in the list is Naphoth[c]).

12Yet the Manassites were not able to occupy these towns, for the Canaanites were determined to live in that region. 13However, when the Israelites grew stronger, they subjected the Canaanites to forced labor but did not drive them out completely.

14The people of Joseph said to Joshua, "Why have you given us only one allotment and one portion for an inheritance? We are a numerous people and the Lord has blessed us abundantly."

15"If you are so numerous," Joshua answered, "and if the hill country of Ephraim is

[a] 1 *Jordan of Jericho* was possibly an ancient name for the Jordan River. [b] 2 Septuagint; Hebrew *Bethel to Luz*
[c] 11 That is, Naphoth Dor

too small for you, go up into the forest and clear land for yourselves there in the land of the Perizzites and Rephaites."

16The people of Joseph replied, "The hill country is not enough for us, and all the Canaanites who live in the plain have iron chariots, both those in Beth Shan and its settlements and those in the Valley of Jezreel."

17But Joshua said to the house of Joseph—to Ephraim and Manasseh—"You are numerous and very powerful. You will have not only one allotment 18but the forested hill country as well. Clear it, and its farthest limits will be yours; though the Canaanites have iron chariots and though they are strong, you can drive them out."

Division of the Rest of the Land

18 The whole assembly of the Israelites gathered at Shiloh and set up the Tent of Meeting there. The country was brought under their control, 2but there were still seven Israelite tribes who had not yet received their inheritance.

3So Joshua said to the Israelites: "How long will you wait before you begin to take possession of the land that the LORD, the God of your fathers, has given you? 4Appoint three men from each tribe. I will send them out to make a survey of the land and to write a description of it, according to the inheritance of each. Then they will return to me. 5You are to divide the land into seven parts. Judah is to remain in its territory on the south and the house of Joseph in its territory on the north. 6After you have written descriptions of the seven parts of the land, bring them here to me and I will cast lots for you in the presence of the LORD our God. 7The Levites, however, do not get a portion among you, because the priestly service of the LORD is their inheritance. And Gad, Reuben and the half-tribe of Manasseh have already received their inheritance on the east side of the Jordan. Moses the servant of the LORD gave it to them."

8As the men started on their way to map out the land, Joshua instructed them, "Go and make a survey of the land and write a description of it. Then return to me, and I will cast lots for you here at Shiloh in the presence of the LORD." 9So the men left and went through the land. They wrote its description on a scroll, town by town, in seven parts, and returned to Joshua in the camp at Shiloh. 10Joshua then cast lots for them in Shiloh in the presence of the LORD, and there he distributed the land to the Israelites according to their tribal divisions.

Allotment for Benjamin

11The lot came up for the tribe of Benjamin, clan by clan. Their allotted territory lay between the tribes of Judah and Joseph:

12On the north side their boundary began at the Jordan, passed the northern slope of Jericho and headed west into the hill country, coming out at the desert of Beth Aven. 13From there it crossed to the south slope of Luz (that is, Bethel) and went down to Ataroth Addar on the hill south of Lower Beth Horon.

14From the hill facing Beth Horon on the south the boundary turned south along the western side and came out at Kiriath Baal (that is, Kiriath Jearim), a town of the people of Judah. This was the western side.

15The southern side began at the outskirts of Kiriath Jearim on the west, and the boundary came out at the spring of the waters of Nephtoah. 16The boundary went down to the foot of the hill facing the Valley of Ben Hinnom, north of the Valley of Rephaim. It continued down the Hinnom Valley along the southern slope of the Jebusite city and so to En Rogel. 17It then curved north, went to En Shemesh, continued to Geliloth, which faces the Pass of Adummim, and ran down to the Stone of Bohan son of Reuben. 18It continued to the northern slope of Beth Arabah[a] and on down into the Arabah. 19It then went to the northern slope of Beth Hoglah and came out at the northern bay of the Salt Sea,[b] at the mouth of the Jordan in the south. This was the southern boundary.

20The Jordan formed the boundary on the eastern side.

These were the boundaries that marked out the inheritance of the clans of Benjamin on all sides.

21The tribe of Benjamin, clan by clan, had the following cities:

Jericho, Beth Hoglah, Emek Keziz, 22Beth Arabah, Zemaraim, Bethel, 23Avvim, Parah, Ophrah, 24Kephar Ammoni,

[a] *18* Septuagint; Hebrew *slope facing the Arabah* [b] *19* That is, the Dead Sea

Ophni and Geba—twelve towns and
their villages.
25Gibeon, Ramah, Beeroth, 26Mizpah,
Kephirah, Mozah, 27Rekem, Irpeel,
Taralah, 28Zelah, Haeleph, the Jebusite
city (that is, Jerusalem), Gibeah and
Kiriath—fourteen towns and their villages.
This was the inheritance of Benjamin for its
clans.

Allotment for Simeon

19 The second lot came out for the tribe
of Simeon, clan by clan. Their inheritance lay within the territory of Judah. 2It included:
Beersheba (or Sheba),[a] Moladah,
3Hazar Shual, Balah, Ezem, 4Eltolad,
Bethul, Hormah, 5Ziklag, Beth Marcaboth, Hazar Susah, 6Beth Lebaoth
and Sharuhen—thirteen towns and their
villages;
7Ain, Rimmon, Ether and Ashan—
four towns and their villages— 8and all
the villages around these towns as far
as Baalath Beer (Ramah in the Negev).
This was the inheritance of the tribe of the
Simeonites, clan by clan. 9The inheritance of
the Simeonites was taken from the share of
Judah, because Judah's portion was more
than they needed. So the Simeonites received their inheritance within the territory of
Judah.

Allotment for Zebulun

10The third lot came up for Zebulun, clan by
clan:
The boundary of their inheritance
went as far as Sarid. 11Going west it ran
to Maralah, touched Dabbesheth, and
extended to the ravine near Jokneam.
12It turned east from Sarid toward the
sunrise to the territory of Kisloth Tabor
and went on to Daberath and up to
Japhia. 13Then it continued eastward to
Gath Hepher and Eth Kazin; it came out
at Rimmon and turned toward Neah.
14There the boundary went around on
the north to Hannathon and ended at
the Valley of Iphtah El. 15Included were
Kattath, Nahalal, Shimron, Idalah and
Bethlehem. There were twelve towns
and their villages.
16These towns and their villages were the
inheritance of Zebulun, clan by clan.

Allotment for Issachar

17The fourth lot came out for Issachar, clan
by clan. 18Their territory included:
Jezreel, Kesulloth, Shunem, 19Haph-
araim, Shion, Anaharath, 20Rabbith,
Kishion, Ebez, 21Remeth, En Gannim,
En Haddah and Beth Pazzez. 22The
boundary touched Tabor, Shahazumah
and Beth Shemesh, and ended at the
Jordan. There were sixteen towns and
their villages.
23These towns and their villages were the
inheritance of the tribe of Issachar, clan by
clan.

Allotment for Asher

24The fifth lot came out for the tribe of Asher,
clan by clan. 25Their territory included:
Helkath, Hali, Beten, Acshaph, 26Al-
lammelech, Amad and Mishal. On the
west the boundary touched Carmel and
Shihor Libnath. 27It then turned east
toward Beth Dagon, touched Zebulun
and the Valley of Iphtah El, and went
north to Beth Emek and Neiel, passing
Cabul on the left. 28It went to Abdon,[b]
Rehob, Hammon and Kanah, as far as
Greater Sidon. 29The boundary then
turned back toward Ramah and went to
the fortified city of Tyre, turned toward
Hosah and came out at the sea in the
region of Aczib, 30Ummah, Aphek and
Rehob. There were twenty-two towns
and their villages.
31These towns and their villages were the
inheritance of the tribe of Asher, clan by clan.

Allotment for Naphtali

32The sixth lot came out for Naphtali, clan by
clan:
33Their boundary went from Heleph
and the large tree in Zaanannim, passing Adami Nekeb and Jabneel to Lak-
kum and ending at the Jordan. 34The
boundary ran west through Aznoth Tabor and came out at Hukkok. It touched
Zebulun on the south, Asher on the west
and the Jordan[c] on the east. 35The fortified cities were Ziddim, Zer, Hammath,
Rakkath, Kinnereth, 36Adamah, Ramah,

[a]2 Or *Beersheba, Sheba;* 1 Chron. 4:28 does not have *Sheba.* [b]28 Some Hebrew manuscripts (see also Joshua 21:30); most Hebrew manuscripts *Ebron* [c]34 Septuagint; Hebrew *west, and Judah, the Jordan,*

Hazor, [37]Kedesh, Edrei, En Hazor,
[38]Iron, Migdal El, Horem, Beth Anath
and Beth Shemesh. There were nineteen towns and their villages.

[39]These towns and their villages were the
inheritance of the tribe of Naphtali, clan by
clan.

Allotment for Dan

[40]The seventh lot came out for the tribe of
Dan, clan by clan. [41]The territory of their inheritance included:

Zorah, Eshtaol, Ir Shemesh, [42]Shaa-
labbin, Aijalon, Ithlah, [43]Elon, Timnah,
Ekron, [44]Eltekeh, Gibbethon, Baalath,
[45]Jehud, Bene Berak, Gath Rimmon,
[46]Me Jarkon and Rakkon, with the area
facing Joppa.

[47](But the Danites had difficulty taking
possession of their territory, so they went up
and attacked Leshem, took it, put it to the
sword and occupied it. They settled in Leshem and named it Dan after their forefather.)

[48]These towns and their villages were the
inheritance of the tribe of Dan, clan by clan.

Allotment for Joshua

[49]When they had finished dividing the land
into its allotted portions, the Israelites gave
Joshua son of Nun an inheritance among
them, [50]as the LORD had commanded. They
gave him the town he asked for—Timnath
Serah[a] in the hill country of Ephraim. And he
built up the town and settled there.

[51]These are the territories that Eleazar the
priest, Joshua son of Nun and the heads of
the tribal clans of Israel assigned by lot at
Shiloh in the presence of the LORD at the
entrance to the Tent of Meeting. And so they
finished dividing the land.

Cities of Refuge

20 Then the LORD said to Joshua: [2]"Tell
the Israelites to designate the cities
of refuge, as I instructed you through Moses,
[3]so that anyone who kills a person accidentally and unintentionally may flee there and
find protection from the avenger of blood.

[4]"When he flees to one of these cities, he
is to stand in the entrance of the city gate and
state his case before the elders of that city.
Then they are to admit him into their city and
give him a place to live with them. [5]If the
avenger of blood pursues him, they must not
surrender the one accused, because he
killed his neighbor unintentionally and without malice aforethought. [6]He is to stay in that
city until he has stood trial before the assembly and until the death of the high priest who
is serving at that time. Then he may go back
to his own home in the town from which he
fled."

[7]So they set apart Kedesh in Galilee in the
hill country of Naphtali, Shechem in the hill
country of Ephraim, and Kiriath Arba (that is,
Hebron) in the hill country of Judah. [8]On the
east side of the Jordan of Jericho[b] they designated Bezer in the desert on the plateau in
the tribe of Reuben, Ramoth in Gilead in the
tribe of Gad, and Golan in Bashan in the tribe
of Manasseh. [9]Any of the Israelites or any
alien living among them who killed someone
accidentally could flee to these designated
cities and not be killed by the avenger of
blood prior to standing trial before the assembly.

Towns for the Levites

21 Now the family heads of the Levites
approached Eleazar the priest,
Joshua son of Nun, and the heads of the
other tribal families of Israel [2]at Shiloh in
Canaan and said to them, "The LORD commanded through Moses that you give us
towns to live in, with pasturelands for our
livestock." [3]So, as the LORD had commanded, the Israelites gave the Levites the
following towns and pasturelands out of their
own inheritance:

[4]The first lot came out for the Kohathites,
clan by clan. The Levites who were descendants of Aaron the priest were allotted thirteen
towns from the tribes of Judah, Simeon and
Benjamin. [5]The rest of Kohath's descendants were allotted ten towns from the clans of
the tribes of Ephraim, Dan and half of Manasseh.

[6]The descendants of Gershon were allotted thirteen towns from the clans of the tribes
of Issachar, Asher, Naphtali and the half-
tribe of Manasseh in Bashan.

[7]The descendants of Merari, clan by clan,
received twelve towns from the tribes of
Reuben, Gad and Zebulun.

[8]So the Israelites allotted to the Levites
these towns and their pasturelands, as the
LORD had commanded through Moses.

[a]50 Also known as *Timnath Heres* (see Judges 2:9)

[b]8 *Jordan of Jericho* was possibly an ancient name for the Jordan River.

9From the tribes of Judah and Simeon they
allotted the following towns by name 10(these
towns were assigned to the descendants of
Aaron who were from the Kohathite clans of
the Levites, because the first lot fell to them):
11They gave them Kiriath Arba (that
is, Hebron), with its surrounding pastureland, in the hill country of Judah.
(Arba was the forefather of Anak.) 12But
the fields and villages around the city
they had given to Caleb son of Jephunneh as his possession.
13So to the descendants of Aaron the
priest they gave Hebron (a city of refuge
for one accused of murder), Libnah,
14Jattir, Eshtemoa, 15Holon, Debir,
16Ain, Juttah and Beth Shemesh, together with their pasturelands—nine
towns from these two tribes.
17And from the tribe of Benjamin they
gave them Gibeon, Geba, 18Anathoth
and Almon, together with their pasturelands—four towns.
19All the towns for the priests, the descendants of Aaron, were thirteen, together with
their pasturelands.

20The rest of the Kohathite clans of the Levites were allotted towns from the tribe of
Ephraim:
21In the hill country of Ephraim they
were given Shechem (a city of refuge for
one accused of murder) and Gezer,
22Kibzaim and Beth Horon, together
with their pasturelands—four towns.
23Also from the tribe of Dan they received Eltekeh, Gibbethon, 24Aijalon
and Gath Rimmon, together with their
pasturelands—four towns.
25From half the tribe of Manasseh
they received Taanach and Gath Rimmon, together with their pasturelands—
two towns.
26All these ten towns and their pasturelands
were given to the rest of the Kohathite clans.

27The Levite clans of the Gershonites were
given:
from the half-tribe of Manasseh,
Golan in Bashan (a city of refuge for one
accused of murder) and Be Eshtarah,
together with their pasturelands—two
towns;
28from the tribe of Issachar,
Kishion, Daberath, 29Jarmuth and En
Gannim, together with their pasturelands—four towns;
30from the tribe of Asher,
Mishal, Abdon, 31Helkath and Rehob,
together with their pasturelands—four
towns;
32from the tribe of Naphtali,
Kedesh in Galilee (a city of refuge for
one accused of murder), Hammoth Dor
and Kartan, together with their pasturelands—three towns.
33All the towns of the Gershonite clans were
thirteen, together with their pasturelands.

34The Merarite clans (the rest of the Levites)
were given:
from the tribe of Zebulun,
Jokneam, Kartah, 35Dimnah and Nahalal, together with their pasturelands—
four towns;
36from the tribe of Reuben,
Bezer, Jahaz, 37Kedemoth and Mephaath, together with their pasturelands—
four towns;
38from the tribe of Gad,
Ramoth in Gilead (a city of refuge for
one accused of murder), Mahanaim,
39Heshbon and Jazer, together with
their pasturelands—four towns in all.
40All the towns allotted to the Merarite clans,
who were the rest of the Levites, were
twelve.
41The towns of the Levites in the territory
held by the Israelites were forty-eight in all,
together with their pasturelands. 42Each of
these towns had pasturelands surrounding
it; this was true for all these towns.

43So the LORD gave Israel all the land he
had sworn to give their forefathers, and they
took possession of it and settled there. 44The
LORD gave them rest on every side, just as he
had sworn to their forefathers. Not one of
their enemies withstood them; the LORD
handed all their enemies over to them. 45Not
one of all the LORD's good promises to the
house of Israel failed; every one was fulfilled.

Eastern Tribes Return Home

22 Then Joshua summoned the Reubenites, the Gadites and the half-
tribe of Manasseh 2and said to them, "You
have done all that Moses the servant of the
LORD commanded, and you have obeyed me
in everything I commanded. 3For a long time
now—to this very day—you have not deserted your brothers but have carried out the
mission the LORD your God gave you. 4Now
that the LORD your God has given your brothers rest as he promised, return to your
homes in the land that Moses the servant of

the LORD gave you on the other side of the
Jordan. 5But be very careful to keep the commandment and the law that Moses the servant of the LORD gave you: to love the LORD
your God, to walk in all his ways, to obey his
commands, to hold fast to him and to serve
him with all your heart and all your soul."
6Then Joshua blessed them and sent
them away, and they went to their homes.
7(To the half-tribe of Manasseh Moses had
given land in Bashan, and to the other half of
the tribe Joshua gave land on the west side
of the Jordan with their brothers.) When
Joshua sent them home, he blessed them,
8saying, "Return to your homes with your
great wealth—with large herds of livestock,
with silver, gold, bronze and iron, and a great
quantity of clothing—and divide with your
brothers the plunder from your enemies."
9So the Reubenites, the Gadites and the
half-tribe of Manasseh left the Israelites at
Shiloh in Canaan to return to Gilead, their
own land, which they had acquired in accordance with the command of the LORD through
Moses.
10When they came to Geliloth near the Jordan in the land of Canaan, the Reubenites,
the Gadites and the half-tribe of Manasseh
built an imposing altar there by the Jordan.
11And when the Israelites heard that they
had built the altar on the border of Canaan at
Geliloth near the Jordan on the Israelite side,
12the whole assembly of Israel gathered at
Shiloh to go to war against them.
13So the Israelites sent Phinehas son of
Eleazar, the priest, to the land of Gilead—to
Reuben, Gad and the half-tribe of Manasseh. 14With him they sent ten of the chief
men, one for each of the tribes of Israel, each
the head of a family division among the Israelite clans.
15When they went to Gilead—to Reuben,
Gad and the half-tribe of Manasseh—they
said to them: 16"The whole assembly of the
LORD says: 'How could you break faith with
the God of Israel like this? How could you
turn away from the LORD and build yourselves
an altar in rebellion against him now? 17Was
not the sin of Peor enough for us? Up to this
very day we have not cleansed ourselves
from that sin, even though a plague fell on
the community of the LORD! 18And are you
now turning away from the LORD?
"'If you rebel against the LORD today, tomorrow he will be angry with the whole community of Israel. 19If the land you possess is
defiled, come over to the LORD's land, where
the LORD's tabernacle stands, and share the
land with us. But do not rebel against the
LORD or against us by building an altar for
yourselves, other than the altar of the LORD
our God. 20When Achan son of Zerah acted
unfaithfully regarding the devoted things,[a]
did not wrath come upon the whole community of Israel? He was not the only one who
died for his sin.'"
21Then Reuben, Gad and the half-tribe of
Manasseh replied to the heads of the clans
of Israel: 22"The Mighty One, God, the LORD!
The Mighty One, God, the LORD! He knows!
And let Israel know! If this has been in rebellion or disobedience to the LORD, do not
spare us this day. 23If we have built our own
altar to turn away from the LORD and to offer
burnt offerings and grain offerings, or to sacrifice fellowship offerings[b] on it, may the LORD
himself call us to account.
24"No! We did it for fear that some day your
descendants might say to ours, 'What do you
have to do with the LORD, the God of Israel?
25The LORD has made the Jordan a boundary
between us and you—you Reubenites and
Gadites! You have no share in the LORD.' So
your descendants might cause ours to stop
fearing the LORD.
26"That is why we said, 'Let us get ready
and build an altar—but not for burnt offerings
or sacrifices.' 27On the contrary, it is to be a
witness between us and you and the generations that follow, that we will worship the LORD
at his sanctuary with our burnt offerings, sacrifices and fellowship offerings. Then in the
future your descendants will not be able to
say to ours, 'You have no share in the LORD.'
28"And we said, 'If they ever say this to us,
or to our descendants, we will answer: Look
at the replica of the LORD's altar, which our
fathers built, not for burnt offerings and sacrifices, but as a witness between us and you.'
29"Far be it from us to rebel against the
LORD and turn away from him today by building an altar for burnt offerings, grain offerings
and sacrifices, other than the altar of the
LORD our God that stands before his tabernacle."
30When Phinehas the priest and the leaders of the community—the heads of the
clans of the Israelites—heard what Reuben,

[a]*20* The Hebrew term refers to the irrevocable giving over of things or persons to the LORD, often by totally destroying them. [b]*23* Traditionally *peace offerings;* also in verse 27

Gad and Manasseh had to say, they were
pleased. 31And Phinehas son of Eleazar, the
priest, said to Reuben, Gad and Manasseh,
"Today we know that the LORD is with us,
because you have not acted unfaithfully
toward the LORD in this matter. Now you have
rescued the Israelites from the LORD's hand."

32Then Phinehas son of Eleazar, the
priest, and the leaders returned to Canaan
from their meeting with the Reubenites and
Gadites in Gilead and reported to the Israelites. 33They were glad to hear the report and
praised God. And they talked no more about
going to war against them to devastate the
country where the Reubenites and the Gadites lived.

34And the Reubenites and the Gadites
gave the altar this name: A Witness Between
Us that the LORD is God.

Joshua's Farewell to the Leaders

23 After a long time had passed and the
LORD had given Israel rest from all
their enemies around them, Joshua, by then
old and well advanced in years, 2summoned
all Israel—their elders, leaders, judges and
officials—and said to them: "I am old and
well advanced in years. 3You yourselves
have seen everything the LORD your God has
done to all these nations for your sake; it was
the LORD your God who fought for you.
4Remember how I have allotted as an inheritance for your tribes all the land of the nations that remain—the nations I conquered—between the Jordan and the Great
Sea[a] in the west. 5The LORD your God himself will drive them out of your way. He will
push them out before you, and you will take
possession of their land, as the LORD your
God promised you.

6"Be very strong; be careful to obey all that
is written in the Book of the Law of Moses,
without turning aside to the right or to the left.
7Do not associate with these nations that
remain among you; do not invoke the names
of their gods or swear by them. You must not
serve them or bow down to them. 8But you
are to hold fast to the LORD your God, as you
have until now.

9"The LORD has driven out before you great
and powerful nations; to this day no one has
been able to withstand you. 10One of you
routs a thousand, because the LORD your
God fights for you, just as he promised. 11So
be very careful to love the LORD your God.

12"But if you turn away and ally yourselves
with the survivors of these nations that remain among you and if you intermarry with
them and associate with them, 13then you
may be sure that the LORD your God will no
longer drive out these nations before you.
Instead, they will become snares and traps
for you, whips on your backs and thorns in
your eyes, until you perish from this good
land, which the LORD your God has given
you.

14"Now I am about to go the way of all the
earth. You know with all your heart and soul
that not one of all the good promises the LORD
your God gave you has failed. Every promise
has been fulfilled; not one has failed. 15But
just as every good promise of the LORD your
God has come true, so the LORD will bring on
you all the evil he has threatened, until he
has destroyed you from this good land he
has given you. 16If you violate the covenant
of the LORD your God, which he commanded
you, and go and serve other gods and bow
down to them, the LORD's anger will burn
against you, and you will quickly perish from
the good land he has given you."

The Covenant Renewed at Shechem

24 Then Joshua assembled all the
tribes of Israel at Shechem. He summoned the elders, leaders, judges and officials of Israel, and they presented themselves before God.

2Joshua said to all the people, "This is
what the LORD, the God of Israel, says: 'Long
ago your forefathers, including Terah the father of Abraham and Nahor, lived beyond the
River[b] and worshiped other gods. 3But I took
your father Abraham from the land beyond
the River and led him throughout Canaan
and gave him many descendants. I gave him
Isaac, 4and to Isaac I gave Jacob and Esau.
I assigned the hill country of Seir to Esau, but
Jacob and his sons went down to Egypt.

5" 'Then I sent Moses and Aaron, and I
afflicted the Egyptians by what I did there,
and I brought you out. 6When I brought your
fathers out of Egypt, you came to the sea,
and the Egyptians pursued them with chariots and horsemen[c] as far as the Red Sea.[d]
7But they cried to the LORD for help, and he
put darkness between you and the Egyptians; he brought the sea over them and

[a] *4* That is, the Mediterranean [b] *2* That is, the Euphrates; also in verses 3, 14 and 15 [c] *6* Or *charioteers*
[d] *6* Hebrew *Yam Suph;* that is, Sea of Reeds

covered them. You saw with your own eyes what I did to the Egyptians. Then you lived in the desert for a long time.

8" 'I brought you to the land of the Amorites who lived east of the Jordan. They fought against you, but I gave them into your hands. I destroyed them from before you, and you took possession of their land. 9When Balak son of Zippor, the king of Moab, prepared to fight against Israel, he sent for Balaam son of Beor to put a curse on you. 10But I would not listen to Balaam, so he blessed you again and again, and I delivered you out of his hand.

11" 'Then you crossed the Jordan and came to Jericho. The citizens of Jericho fought against you, as did also the Amorites, Perizzites, Canaanites, Hittites, Girgashites, Hivites and Jebusites, but I gave them into your hands. 12I sent the hornet ahead of you, which drove them out before you—also the two Amorite kings. You did not do it with your own sword and bow. 13So I gave you a land on which you did not toil and cities you did not build; and you live in them and eat from vineyards and olive groves that you did not plant.'

14"Now fear the LORD and serve him with all faithfulness. Throw away the gods your forefathers worshiped beyond the River and in Egypt, and serve the LORD. 15But if serving the LORD seems undesirable to you, then choose for yourselves this day whom you will serve, whether the gods your forefathers served beyond the River, or the gods of the Amorites, in whose land you are living. But as for me and my household, we will serve the LORD."

16Then the people answered, "Far be it from us to forsake the LORD to serve other gods! 17It was the LORD our God himself who brought us and our fathers up out of Egypt, from that land of slavery, and performed those great signs before our eyes. He protected us on our entire journey and among all the nations through which we traveled. 18And the LORD drove out before us all the nations, including the Amorites, who lived in the land. We too will serve the LORD, because he is our God."

19Joshua said to the people, "You are not able to serve the LORD. He is a holy God; he is a jealous God. He will not forgive your rebellion and your sins. 20If you forsake the LORD and serve foreign gods, he will turn and bring disaster on you and make an end of you, after he has been good to you."

21But the people said to Joshua, "No! We will serve the LORD."

22Then Joshua said, "You are witnesses against yourselves that you have chosen to serve the LORD."

"Yes, we are witnesses," they replied.

23"Now then," said Joshua, "throw away the foreign gods that are among you and yield your hearts to the LORD, the God of Israel."

24And the people said to Joshua, "We will serve the LORD our God and obey him."

25On that day Joshua made a covenant for the people, and there at Shechem he drew up for them decrees and laws. 26And Joshua recorded these things in the Book of the Law of God. Then he took a large stone and set it up there under the oak near the holy place of the LORD.

27"See!" he said to all the people. "This stone will be a witness against us. It has heard all the words the LORD has said to us. It will be a witness against you if you are untrue to your God."

Buried in the Promised Land

28Then Joshua sent the people away, each to his own inheritance.

29After these things, Joshua son of Nun, the servant of the LORD, died at the age of a hundred and ten. 30And they buried him in the land of his inheritance, at Timnath Serah[a] in the hill country of Ephraim, north of Mount Gaash.

31Israel served the LORD throughout the lifetime of Joshua and of the elders who outlived him and who had experienced everything the LORD had done for Israel.

32And Joseph's bones, which the Israelites had brought up from Egypt, were buried at Shechem in the tract of land that Jacob bought for a hundred pieces of silver[b] from the sons of Hamor, the father of Shechem. This became the inheritance of Joseph's descendants.

33And Eleazar son of Aaron died and was buried at Gibeah, which had been allotted to his son Phinehas in the hill country of Ephraim.

a30 Also known as *Timnath Heres* (see Judges 2:9)

b32 Hebrew *hundred kesitahs;* a kesitah was a unit of money of unknown weight and value.

Judges

Introduction:

This book tells of Israel's history for the period between the death of Joshua and the ministry of Samuel. This time period was known for its heroes—called judges—who ruled the tribes of Israel.

The events in Judges followed a certain pattern:

1. The Israelites lived in peace while serving and loving God.
2. The Israelites forgot God and worshiped idols.
3. God punished his people by sending a neighboring nation to fight and rule over them.
4. The Israelites turned to God and asked for forgiveness.
5. God forgave his people and saved them by sending a judge to help conquer their enemy.

This pattern of events repeated itself many times during this time period in Israel's history.

A total of fifteen judges are listed for their leadership. The best-known judges are Deborah, Gideon and Samson.

Outline of contents:

Conditions during the time of the judges (1:1–3:6)
Conquering nations and ruling judges (3:7–16:31)
Idolatry and civil war (17:1–21:35)

Israel Fights the Remaining Canaanites

1 After the death of Joshua, the Israelites
asked the LORD, "Who will be the first to
go up and fight for us against the Canaanites?"
2The LORD answered, "Judah is to go; I
have given the land into their hands."
3Then the men of Judah said to the Simeonites their brothers, "Come up with us into
the territory allotted to us, to fight against the
Canaanites. We in turn will go with you into
yours." So the Simeonites went with them.
4When Judah attacked, the LORD gave the
Canaanites and Perizzites into their hands
and they struck down ten thousand men at
Bezek. 5It was there that they found Adoni-
Bezek and fought against him, putting to rout
the Canaanites and Perizzites. 6Adoni-
Bezek fled, but they chased him and caught
him, and cut off his thumbs and big toes.
7Then Adoni-Bezek said, "Seventy kings
with their thumbs and big toes cut off have
picked up scraps under my table. Now God
has paid me back for what I did to them."
They brought him to Jerusalem, and he died
there.
8The men of Judah attacked Jerusalem
also and took it. They put the city to the
sword and set it on fire.
9After that, the men of Judah went down to
fight against the Canaanites living in the hill
country, the Negev and the western foothills.
10They advanced against the Canaanites living in Hebron (formerly called Kiriath Arba)
and defeated Sheshai, Ahiman and Talmai.
11From there they advanced against the
people living in Debir (formerly called Kiriath
Sepher). 12And Caleb said, "I will give my
daughter Acsah in marriage to the man who
attacks and captures Kiriath Sepher." 13Oth-
niel son of Kenaz, Caleb's younger brother,
took it; so Caleb gave his daughter Acsah to
him in marriage.
14One day when she came to Othniel, she
urged him[a] to ask her father for a field. When
she got off her donkey, Caleb asked her,
"What can I do for you?"

[a] 14 Hebrew; Septuagint and Vulgate *Othniel, he urged her*

15She replied, "Do me a special favor. Since you have given me land in the Negev, give me also springs of water." Then Caleb gave her the upper and lower springs.

16The descendants of Moses' father-in-law, the Kenite, went up from the City of Palms[a] with the men of Judah to live among the people of the Desert of Judah in the Negev near Arad.

17Then the men of Judah went with the Simeonites their brothers and attacked the Canaanites living in Zephath, and they totally destroyed[b] the city. Therefore it was called Hormah.[c] 18The men of Judah also took[d] Gaza, Ashkelon and Ekron—each city with its territory.

19The LORD was with the men of Judah. They took possession of the hill country, but they were unable to drive the people from the plains, because they had iron chariots. 20As Moses had promised, Hebron was given to Caleb, who drove from it the three sons of Anak. 21The Benjamites, however, failed to dislodge the Jebusites, who were living in Jerusalem; to this day the Jebusites live there with the Benjamites.

22Now the house of Joseph attacked Bethel, and the LORD was with them. 23When they sent men to spy out Bethel (formerly called Luz), 24the spies saw a man coming out of the city and they said to him, "Show us how to get into the city and we will see that you are treated well." 25So he showed them, and they put the city to the sword but spared the man and his whole family. 26He then went to the land of the Hittites, where he built a city and called it Luz, which is its name to this day.

27But Manasseh did not drive out the people of Beth Shan or Taanach or Dor or Ibleam or Megiddo and their surrounding settlements, for the Canaanites were determined to live in that land. 28When Israel became strong, they pressed the Canaanites into forced labor but never drove them out completely. 29Nor did Ephraim drive out the Canaanites living in Gezer, but the Canaanites continued to live there among them. 30Neither did Zebulun drive out the Canaanites living in Kitron or Nahalol, who remained among them; but they did subject them to forced labor. 31Nor did Asher drive out those living in Acco or Sidon or Ahlab or Aczib or Helbah or Aphek or Rehob, 32and because of this the people of Asher lived among the Canaanite inhabitants of the land. 33Neither did Naphtali drive out those living in Beth Shemesh or Beth Anath; but the Naphtalites too lived among the Canaanite inhabitants of the land, and those living in Beth Shemesh and Beth Anath became forced laborers for them. 34The Amorites confined the Danites to the hill country, not allowing them to come down into the plain. 35And the Amorites were determined also to hold out in Mount Heres, Aijalon and Shaalbim, but when the power of the house of Joseph increased, they too were pressed into forced labor. 36The boundary of the Amorites was from Scorpion[e] Pass to Sela and beyond.

The Angel of the LORD at Bokim

2 The angel of the LORD went up from Gilgal to Bokim and said, "I brought you up out of Egypt and led you into the land that I swore to give to your forefathers. I said, 'I will never break my covenant with you, 2and you shall not make a covenant with the people of this land, but you shall break down their altars.' Yet you have disobeyed me. Why have you done this? 3Now therefore I tell you that I will not drive them out before you; they will be ⌞thorns⌟ in your sides and their gods will be a snare to you."

4When the angel of the LORD had spoken these things to all the Israelites, the people wept aloud, 5and they called that place Bokim.[f] There they offered sacrifices to the LORD.

Disobedience and Defeat

6After Joshua had dismissed the Israelites, they went to take possession of the land, each to his own inheritance. 7The people served the LORD throughout the lifetime of Joshua and of the elders who outlived him and who had seen all the great things the LORD had done for Israel.

8Joshua son of Nun, the servant of the LORD, died at the age of a hundred and ten. 9And they buried him in the land of his inheritance, at Timnath Heres[g] in the hill country of Ephraim, north of Mount Gaash.

10After that whole generation had been gathered to their fathers, another generation grew up, who knew neither the LORD nor what

[a] *16* That is, Jericho [b] *17* The Hebrew term refers to the irrevocable giving over of things or persons to the LORD, often by totally destroying them. [c] *17* *Hormah* means *destruction.* [d] *18* Hebrew; Septuagint *Judah did not take* [e] *36* Hebrew *Akrabbim* [f] *5* *Bokim* means *weepers.* [g] *9* Also known as *Timnath Serah* (see Joshua 19:50 and 24:30)

he had done for Israel. 11Then the Israelites did evil in the eyes of the LORD and served the Baals. 12They forsook the LORD, the God of their fathers, who had brought them out of Egypt. They followed and worshiped various gods of the peoples around them. They provoked the LORD to anger 13because they forsook him and served Baal and the Ashtoreths. 14In his anger against Israel the LORD handed them over to raiders who plundered them. He sold them to their enemies all around, whom they were no longer able to resist. 15Whenever Israel went out to fight, the hand of the LORD was against them to defeat them, just as he had sworn to them. They were in great distress.

16Then the LORD raised up judges,[a] who saved them out of the hands of these raiders. 17Yet they would not listen to their judges but prostituted themselves to other gods and worshiped them. Unlike their fathers, they quickly turned from the way in which their fathers had walked, the way of obedience to the LORD's commands. 18Whenever the LORD raised up a judge for them, he was with the judge and saved them out of the hands of their enemies as long as the judge lived; for the LORD had compassion on them as they groaned under those who oppressed and afflicted them. 19But when the judge died, the people returned to ways even more corrupt than those of their fathers, following other gods and serving and worshiping them. They refused to give up their evil practices and stubborn ways.

20Therefore the LORD was very angry with Israel and said, "Because this nation has violated the covenant that I laid down for their forefathers and has not listened to me, 21I will no longer drive out before them any of the nations Joshua left when he died. 22I will use them to test Israel and see whether they will keep the way of the LORD and walk in it as their forefathers did." 23The LORD had allowed those nations to remain; he did not drive them out at once by giving them into the hands of Joshua.

3 These are the nations the LORD left to test all those Israelites who had not experienced any of the wars in Canaan 2(he did this only to teach warfare to the descendants of the Israelites who had not had previous battle experience): 3the five rulers of the Philistines, all the Canaanites, the Sidonians, and the Hivites living in the Lebanon mountains from Mount Baal Hermon to Lebo[b] Hamath. 4They were left to test the Israelites to see whether they would obey the LORD's commands, which he had given their forefathers through Moses.

5The Israelites lived among the Canaanites, Hittites, Amorites, Perizzites, Hivites and Jebusites. 6They took their daughters in marriage and gave their own daughters to their sons, and served their gods.

Othniel

7The Israelites did evil in the eyes of the LORD; they forgot the LORD their God and served the Baals and the Asherahs. 8The anger of the LORD burned against Israel so that he sold them into the hands of Cushan-Rishathaim king of Aram Naharaim,[c] to whom the Israelites were subject for eight years. 9But when they cried out to the LORD, he raised up for them a deliverer, Othniel son of Kenaz, Caleb's younger brother, who saved them. 10The Spirit of the LORD came upon him, so that he became Israel's judge[d] and went to war. The LORD gave Cushan-Rishathaim king of Aram into the hands of Othniel, who overpowered him. 11So the land had peace for forty years, until Othniel son of Kenaz died.

Ehud

12Once again the Israelites did evil in the eyes of the LORD, and because they did this evil the LORD gave Eglon king of Moab power over Israel. 13Getting the Ammonites and Amalekites to join him, Eglon came and attacked Israel, and they took possession of the City of Palms.[e] 14The Israelites were subject to Eglon king of Moab for eighteen years.

15Again the Israelites cried out to the LORD, and he gave them a deliverer—Ehud, a left-handed man, the son of Gera the Benjamite. The Israelites sent him with tribute to Eglon king of Moab. 16Now Ehud had made a double-edged sword about a foot and a half[f] long, which he strapped to his right thigh under his clothing. 17He presented the tribute to Eglon king of Moab, who was a very fat man. 18After Ehud had presented the tribute, he sent on their way the men who had carried it. 19At the idols[g] near Gilgal he himself

[a]16 Or *leaders;* similarly in verses 17-19 [b]3 Or *to the entrance to* [c]8 That is, Northwest Mesopotamia [d]10 Or *leader* [e]13 That is, Jericho [f]16 Hebrew *a cubit* (about 0.5 meter) [g]19 Or *the stone quarries;* also in verse 26

turned back and said, "I have a secret message for you, O king."

The king said, "Quiet!" And all his attendants left him.

20Ehud then approached him while he was sitting alone in the upper room of his summer palace[a] and said, "I have a message from God for you." As the king rose from his seat, 21Ehud reached with his left hand, drew the sword from his right thigh and plunged it into the king's belly. 22Even the handle sank in after the blade, which came out his back. Ehud did not pull the sword out, and the fat closed in over it. 23Then Ehud went out to the porch[b]; he shut the doors of the upper room behind him and locked them.

24After he had gone, the servants came and found the doors of the upper room locked. They said, "He must be relieving himself in the inner room of the house." 25They waited to the point of embarrassment, but when he did not open the doors of the room, they took a key and unlocked them. There they saw their lord fallen to the floor, dead.

26While they waited, Ehud got away. He passed by the idols and escaped to Seirah. 27When he arrived there, he blew a trumpet in the hill country of Ephraim, and the Israelites went down with him from the hills, with him leading them.

28"Follow me," he ordered, "for the LORD has given Moab, your enemy, into your hands." So they followed him down and, taking possession of the fords of the Jordan that led to Moab, they allowed no one to cross over. 29At that time they struck down about ten thousand Moabites, all vigorous and strong; not a man escaped. 30That day Moab was made subject to Israel, and the land had peace for eighty years.

Shamgar

31After Ehud came Shamgar son of Anath, who struck down six hundred Philistines with an oxgoad. He too saved Israel.

Deborah

4 After Ehud died, the Israelites once again did evil in the eyes of the LORD. 2So the LORD sold them into the hands of Jabin, a king of Canaan, who reigned in Hazor. The commander of his army was Sisera, who lived in Harosheth Haggoyim. 3Because he had nine hundred iron chariots and had cruelly oppressed the Israelites for twenty years, they cried to the LORD for help.

4Deborah, a prophetess, the wife of Lappidoth, was leading[c] Israel at that time. 5She held court under the Palm of Deborah between Ramah and Bethel in the hill country of Ephraim, and the Israelites came to her to have their disputes decided. 6She sent for Barak son of Abinoam from Kedesh in Naphtali and said to him, "The LORD, the God of Israel, commands you: 'Go, take with you ten thousand men of Naphtali and Zebulun and lead the way to Mount Tabor. 7I will lure Sisera, the commander of Jabin's army, with his chariots and his troops to the Kishon River and give him into your hands.' "

8Barak said to her, "If you go with me, I will go; but if you don't go with me, I won't go."

9"Very well," Deborah said, "I will go with you. But because of the way you are going about this,[d] the honor will not be yours, for the LORD will hand Sisera over to a woman." So Deborah went with Barak to Kedesh, 10where he summoned Zebulun and Naphtali. Ten thousand men followed him, and Deborah also went with him.

11Now Heber the Kenite had left the other Kenites, the descendants of Hobab, Moses' brother-in-law,[e] and pitched his tent by the great tree in Zaanannim near Kedesh.

12When they told Sisera that Barak son of Abinoam had gone up to Mount Tabor, 13Sisera gathered together his nine hundred iron chariots and all the men with him, from Harosheth Haggoyim to the Kishon River.

14Then Deborah said to Barak, "Go! This is the day the LORD has given Sisera into your hands. Has not the LORD gone ahead of you?" So Barak went down Mount Tabor, followed by ten thousand men. 15At Barak's advance, the LORD routed Sisera and all his chariots and army by the sword, and Sisera abandoned his chariot and fled on foot. 16But Barak pursued the chariots and army as far as Harosheth Haggoyim. All the troops of Sisera fell by the sword; not a man was left.

17Sisera, however, fled on foot to the tent of Jael, the wife of Heber the Kenite, because there were friendly relations between Jabin king of Hazor and the clan of Heber the Kenite.

18Jael went out to meet Sisera and said to him, "Come, my lord, come right in. Don't be

[a]*20* The meaning of the Hebrew for this phrase is uncertain. [b]*23* The meaning of the Hebrew for this word is uncertain. [c]*4* Traditionally *judging* [d]*9* Or *But on the expedition you are undertaking* [e]*11* Or *father-in-law*

afraid." So he entered her tent, and she put a
covering over him.
19"I'm thirsty," he said. "Please give me
some water." She opened a skin of milk,
gave him a drink, and covered him up.
20"Stand in the doorway of the tent," he
told her. "If someone comes by and asks
you, 'Is anyone here?' say 'No.' "
21But Jael, Heber's wife, picked up a tent
peg and a hammer and went quietly to him
while he lay fast asleep, exhausted. She
drove the peg through his temple into the
ground, and he died.
22Barak came by in pursuit of Sisera, and
Jael went out to meet him. "Come," she said,
"I will show you the man you're looking for."
So he went in with her, and there lay Sisera
with the tent peg through his temple—dead.
23On that day God subdued Jabin, the Canaanite king, before the Israelites. 24And the
hand of the Israelites grew stronger and
stronger against Jabin, the Canaanite king,
until they destroyed him.

The Song of Deborah

5 On that day Deborah and Barak son of
Abinoam sang this song:

2"When the princes in Israel take the lead,
when the people willingly offer
themselves—
praise the LORD!

3"Hear this, you kings! Listen, you rulers!
I will sing to[a] the LORD, I will sing;
I will make music to[b] the LORD, the God
of Israel.

4"O LORD, when you went out from Seir,
when you marched from the land of
Edom,
the earth shook, the heavens poured,
the clouds poured down water.
5The mountains quaked before the LORD,
the One of Sinai,
before the LORD, the God of Israel.

6"In the days of Shamgar son of Anath,
in the days of Jael, the roads were
abandoned;
travelers took to winding paths.
7Village life[c] in Israel ceased,
ceased until I,[d] Deborah, arose,
arose a mother in Israel.
8When they chose new gods,
war came to the city gates,
and not a shield or spear was seen
among forty thousand in Israel.
9My heart is with Israel's princes,
with the willing volunteers among the
people.
Praise the LORD!

10"You who ride on white donkeys,
sitting on your saddle blankets,
and you who walk along the road,
consider 11the voice of the singers[e] at the
watering places.
They recite the righteous acts of the
LORD,
the righteous acts of his warriors[f] in
Israel.

"Then the people of the LORD
went down to the city gates.
12'Wake up, wake up, Deborah!
Wake up, wake up, break out in song!
Arise, O Barak!
Take captive your captives, O son of
Abinoam.'

13"Then the men who were left
came down to the nobles;
the people of the LORD
came to me with the mighty.
14Some came from Ephraim, whose roots
were in Amalek;
Benjamin was with the people who
followed you.
From Makir captains came down,
from Zebulun those who bear a
commander's staff.
15The princes of Issachar were with
Deborah;
yes, Issachar was with Barak,
rushing after him into the valley.
In the districts of Reuben
there was much searching of heart.
16Why did you stay among the campfires[g]
to hear the whistling for the flocks?
In the districts of Reuben
there was much searching of heart.
17Gilead stayed beyond the Jordan.
And Dan, why did he linger by the
ships?
Asher remained on the coast
and stayed in his coves.
18The people of Zebulun risked their very
lives;
so did Naphtali on the heights of the
field.

[a]3 Or *of* [b]3 Or / *with song I will praise* [c]7 Or *Warriors* [d]7 Or *you* [e]11 Or *archers;* the meaning of the Hebrew for this word is uncertain. [f]11 Or *villagers* [g]16 Or *saddlebags*

[19]"Kings came, they fought;
the kings of Canaan fought
at Taanach by the waters of Megiddo,
but they carried off no silver, no plunder.
[20]From the heavens the stars fought,
from their courses they fought against Sisera.
[21]The river Kishon swept them away,
the age-old river, the river Kishon.
March on, my soul; be strong!
[22]Then thundered the horses' hoofs—
galloping, galloping go his mighty steeds.
[23]'Curse Meroz,' said the angel of the LORD.
'Curse its people bitterly,
because they did not come to help the LORD,
to help the LORD against the mighty.'

[24]"Most blessed of women be Jael,
the wife of Heber the Kenite,
most blessed of tent-dwelling women.
[25]He asked for water, and she gave him milk;
in a bowl fit for nobles she brought him curdled milk.
[26]Her hand reached for the tent peg,
her right hand for the workman's hammer.
She struck Sisera, she crushed his head,
she shattered and pierced his temple.
[27]At her feet he sank,
he fell; there he lay.
At her feet he sank, he fell;
where he sank, there he fell—dead.

[28]"Through the window peered Sisera's mother;
behind the lattice she cried out,
'Why is his chariot so long in coming?
Why is the clatter of his chariots delayed?'
[29]The wisest of her ladies answer her;
indeed, she keeps saying to herself,
[30]'Are they not finding and dividing the spoils:
a girl or two for each man,
colorful garments as plunder for Sisera,
colorful garments embroidered,
highly embroidered garments for my neck—
all this as plunder?'

[31]"So may all your enemies perish, O LORD!
But may they who love you be like the sun
when it rises in its strength."

Then the land had peace forty years.

Gideon

6 Again the Israelites did evil in the eyes of
the LORD, and for seven years he gave
them into the hands of the Midianites. [2]Be-
cause the power of Midian was so oppressive, the Israelites prepared shelters for
themselves in mountain clefts, caves and
strongholds. [3]Whenever the Israelites
planted their crops, the Midianites, Amalekites and other eastern peoples invaded the
country. [4]They camped on the land and
ruined the crops all the way to Gaza and did
not spare a living thing for Israel, neither
sheep nor cattle nor donkeys. [5]They came
up with their livestock and their tents like
swarms of locusts. It was impossible to count
the men and their camels; they invaded the
land to ravage it. [6]Midian so impoverished
the Israelites that they cried out to the LORD
for help.

[7]When the Israelites cried to the LORD because of Midian, [8]he sent them a prophet,
who said, "This is what the LORD, the God of
Israel, says: I brought you up out of Egypt,
out of the land of slavery. [9]I snatched you
from the power of Egypt and from the hand of
all your oppressors. I drove them from before
you and gave you their land. [10]I said to you, 'I
am the LORD your God; do not worship the
gods of the Amorites, in whose land you live.'
But you have not listened to me."

[11]The angel of the LORD came and sat
down under the oak in Ophrah that belonged
to Joash the Abiezrite, where his son Gideon
was threshing wheat in a winepress to keep
it from the Midianites. [12]When the angel of
the LORD appeared to Gideon, he said, "The
LORD is with you, mighty warrior."

[13]"But sir," Gideon replied, "if the LORD is
with us, why has all this happened to us?
Where are all his wonders that our fathers
told us about when they said, 'Did not the
LORD bring us up out of Egypt?' But now the
LORD has abandoned us and put us into the
hand of Midian."

[14]The LORD turned to him and said, "Go in
the strength you have and save Israel out of
Midian's hand. Am I not sending you?"

[15]"But Lord,[a]" Gideon asked, "how can I

[a]15 Or *sir*

save Israel? My clan is the weakest in Manasseh, and I am the least in my family."

16The LORD answered, "I will be with you, and you will strike down all the Midianites together."

17Gideon replied, "If now I have found favor in your eyes, give me a sign that it is really you talking to me. 18Please do not go away until I come back and bring my offering and set it before you."

And the LORD said, "I will wait until you return."

19Gideon went in, prepared a young goat, and from an ephah[a] of flour he made bread without yeast. Putting the meat in a basket and its broth in a pot, he brought them out and offered them to him under the oak.

20The angel of God said to him, "Take the meat and the unleavened bread, place them on this rock, and pour out the broth." And Gideon did so. 21With the tip of the staff that was in his hand, the angel of the LORD touched the meat and the unleavened bread. Fire flared from the rock, consuming the meat and the bread. And the angel of the LORD disappeared. 22When Gideon realized that it was the angel of the LORD, he exclaimed, "Ah, Sovereign LORD! I have seen the angel of the LORD face to face!"

23But the LORD said to him, "Peace! Do not be afraid. You are not going to die."

24So Gideon built an altar to the LORD there and called it The LORD is Peace. To this day it stands in Ophrah of the Abiezrites.

25That same night the LORD said to him, "Take the second bull from your father's herd, the one seven years old.[b] Tear down your father's altar to Baal and cut down the Asherah pole[c] beside it. 26Then build a proper kind of[d] altar to the LORD your God on the top of this height. Using the wood of the Asherah pole that you cut down, offer the second[e] bull as a burnt offering."

27So Gideon took ten of his servants and did as the LORD told him. But because he was afraid of his family and the men of the town, he did it at night rather than in the daytime.

28In the morning when the men of the town got up, there was Baal's altar, demolished, with the Asherah pole beside it cut down and the second bull sacrificed on the newly built altar!

29They asked each other, "Who did this?"

When they carefully investigated, they were told, "Gideon son of Joash did it."

30The men of the town demanded of Joash, "Bring out your son. He must die, because he has broken down Baal's altar and cut down the Asherah pole beside it."

31But Joash replied to the hostile crowd around him, "Are you going to plead Baal's cause? Are you trying to save him? Whoever fights for him shall be put to death by morning! If Baal really is a god, he can defend himself when someone breaks down his altar." 32So that day they called Gideon "Jerub-Baal,[f]" saying, "Let Baal contend with him," because he broke down Baal's altar.

33Now all the Midianites, Amalekites and other eastern peoples joined forces and crossed over the Jordan and camped in the Valley of Jezreel. 34Then the Spirit of the LORD came upon Gideon, and he blew a trumpet, summoning the Abiezrites to follow him. 35He sent messengers throughout Manasseh, calling them to arms, and also into Asher, Zebulun and Naphtali, so that they too went up to meet them.

36Gideon said to God, "If you will save Israel by my hand as you have promised—37look, I will place a wool fleece on the threshing floor. If there is dew only on the fleece and all the ground is dry, then I will know that you will save Israel by my hand, as you said." 38And that is what happened. Gideon rose early the next day; he squeezed the fleece and wrung out the dew—a bowlful of water.

39Then Gideon said to God, "Do not be angry with me. Let me make just one more request. Allow me one more test with the fleece. This time make the fleece dry and the ground covered with dew." 40That night God did so. Only the fleece was dry; all the ground was covered with dew.

Gideon Defeats the Midianites

7 Early in the morning, Jerub-Baal (that is, Gideon) and all his men camped at the spring of Harod. The camp of Midian was north of them in the valley near the hill of Moreh. 2The LORD said to Gideon, "You have too many men for me to deliver Midian into their hands. In order that Israel may not boast against me that her own strength has

[a]19 That is, probably about 3/5 bushel (about 22 liters) [b]25 Or *Take a full-grown, mature bull from your father's herd* [c]25 That is, a symbol of the goddess Asherah; here and elsewhere in Judges [d]26 Or *build with layers of stone an* [e]26 Or *full-grown*; also in verse 28 [f]32 *Jerub-Baal* means *let Baal contend.*

saved her, [3]announce now to the people,
'Anyone who trembles with fear may turn
back and leave Mount Gilead.' " So twenty-
two thousand men left, while ten thousand
remained.
[4]But the LORD said to Gideon, "There are
still too many men. Take them down to the
water, and I will sift them for you there. If I
say, 'This one shall go with you,' he shall go;
but if I say, 'This one shall not go with you,'
he shall not go."
[5]So Gideon took the men down to the
water. There the LORD told him, "Separate
those who lap the water with their tongues
like a dog from those who kneel down to
drink." [6]Three hundred men lapped with their
hands to their mouths. All the rest got down
on their knees to drink.
[7]The LORD said to Gideon, "With the three
hundred men that lapped I will save you and
give the Midianites into your hands. Let all
the other men go, each to his own place."
[8]So Gideon sent the rest of the Israelites to
their tents but kept the three hundred, who
took over the provisions and trumpets of the
others.
Now the camp of Midian lay below him in
the valley. [9]During that night the LORD said to
Gideon, "Get up, go down against the camp,
because I am going to give it into your hands.
[10]If you are afraid to attack, go down to the
camp with your servant Purah [11]and listen to
what they are saying. Afterward, you will be
encouraged to attack the camp." So he and
Purah his servant went down to the outposts
of the camp. [12]The Midianites, the Amalekites and all the other eastern peoples had
settled in the valley, thick as locusts. Their
camels could no more be counted than the
sand on the seashore.
[13]Gideon arrived just as a man was telling
a friend his dream. "I had a dream," he was
saying. "A round loaf of barley bread came
tumbling into the Midianite camp. It struck
the tent with such force that the tent overturned and collapsed."
[14]His friend responded, "This can be nothing other than the sword of Gideon son of
Joash, the Israelite. God has given the Midianites and the whole camp into his hands."
[15]When Gideon heard the dream and its
interpretation, he worshiped God. He returned to the camp of Israel and called out,
"Get up! The LORD has given the Midianite
camp into your hands." [16]Dividing the three
hundred men into three companies, he
placed trumpets and empty jars in the hands
of all of them, with torches inside.
[17]"Watch me," he told them. "Follow my
lead. When I get to the edge of the camp, do
exactly as I do. [18]When I and all who are with
me blow our trumpets, then from all around
the camp blow yours and shout, 'For the
LORD and for Gideon.' "
[19]Gideon and the hundred men with him
reached the edge of the camp at the beginning of the middle watch, just after they had
changed the guard. They blew their trumpets
and broke the jars that were in their hands.
[20]The three companies blew the trumpets
and smashed the jars. Grasping the torches
in their left hands and holding in their right
hands the trumpets they were to blow, they
shouted, "A sword for the LORD and for Gideon!" [21]While each man held his position
around the camp, all the Midianites ran, crying out as they fled.
[22]When the three hundred trumpets
sounded, the LORD caused the men throughout the camp to turn on each other with their
swords. The army fled to Beth Shittah toward
Zererah as far as the border of Abel Meholah
near Tabbath. [23]Israelites from Naphtali,
Asher and all Manasseh were called out, and
they pursued the Midianites. [24]Gideon sent
messengers throughout the hill country of
Ephraim, saying, "Come down against the
Midianites and seize the waters of the Jordan ahead of them as far as Beth Barah."
So all the men of Ephraim were called out
and they took the waters of the Jordan as far
as Beth Barah. [25]They also captured two of
the Midianite leaders, Oreb and Zeeb. They
killed Oreb at the rock of Oreb, and Zeeb at
the winepress of Zeeb. They pursued the
Midianites and brought the heads of Oreb
and Zeeb to Gideon, who was by the Jordan.

Zebah and Zalmunna

8 Now the Ephraimites asked Gideon,
"Why have you treated us like this? Why
didn't you call us when you went to fight
Midian?" And they criticized him sharply.
[2]But he answered them, "What have I accomplished compared to you? Aren't the
gleanings of Ephraim's grapes better than
the full grape harvest of Abiezer? [3]God gave
Oreb and Zeeb, the Midianite leaders, into
your hands. What was I able to do compared
to you?" At this, their resentment against him
subsided.
[4]Gideon and his three hundred men, ex-

hausted yet keeping up the pursuit, came to
the Jordan and crossed it. 5He said to the
men of Succoth, "Give my troops some
bread; they are worn out, and I am still pursuing Zebah and Zalmunna, the kings of Midian."

6But the officials of Succoth said, "Do you
already have the hands of Zebah and Zalmunna in your possession? Why should we
give bread to your troops?"

7Then Gideon replied, "Just for that, when
the LORD has given Zebah and Zalmunna into
my hand, I will tear your flesh with desert
thorns and briers."

8From there he went up to Peniel[a] and
made the same request of them, but they
answered as the men of Succoth had. 9So he
said to the men of Peniel, "When I return in
triumph, I will tear down this tower."

10Now Zebah and Zalmunna were in Kar-
kor with a force of about fifteen thousand
men, all that were left of the armies of the
eastern peoples; a hundred and twenty thousand swordsmen had fallen. 11Gideon went
up by the route of the nomads east of Nobah
and Jogbehah and fell upon the unsuspecting army. 12Zebah and Zalmunna, the two
kings of Midian, fled, but he pursued them
and captured them, routing their entire army.

13Gideon son of Joash then returned from
the battle by the Pass of Heres. 14He caught
a young man of Succoth and questioned
him, and the young man wrote down for him
the names of the seventy-seven officials of
Succoth, the elders of the town. 15Then
Gideon came and said to the men of Succoth, "Here are Zebah and Zalmunna, about
whom you taunted me by saying, 'Do you
already have the hands of Zebah and Zalmunna in your possession? Why should we
give bread to your exhausted men?' " 16He
took the elders of the town and taught the
men of Succoth a lesson by punishing them
with desert thorns and briers. 17He also
pulled down the tower of Peniel and killed the
men of the town.

18Then he asked Zebah and Zalmunna,
"What kind of men did you kill at Tabor?"

"Men like you," they answered, "each one
with the bearing of a prince."

19Gideon replied, "Those were my brothers, the sons of my own mother. As surely as
the LORD lives, if you had spared their lives, I
would not kill you." 20Turning to Jether, his
oldest son, he said, "Kill them!" But Jether
did not draw his sword, because he was only
a boy and was afraid.

21Zebah and Zalmunna said, "Come, do it
yourself. 'As is the man, so is his strength.' "
So Gideon stepped forward and killed them,
and took the ornaments off their camels'
necks.

Gideon's Ephod

22The Israelites said to Gideon, "Rule over
us—you, your son and your grandson—
because you have saved us out of the hand
of Midian."

23But Gideon told them, "I will not rule over
you, nor will my son rule over you. The LORD
will rule over you." 24And he said, "I do have
one request, that each of you give me an
earring from your share of the plunder." (It
was the custom of the Ishmaelites to wear
gold earrings.)

25They answered, "We'll be glad to give
them." So they spread out a garment, and
each man threw a ring from his plunder onto
it. 26The weight of the gold rings he asked for
came to seventeen hundred shekels,[b] not
counting the ornaments, the pendants and
the purple garments worn by the kings of
Midian or the chains that were on their camels' necks. 27Gideon made the gold into an
ephod, which he placed in Ophrah, his town.
All Israel prostituted themselves by worshiping it there, and it became a snare to Gideon
and his family.

Gideon's Death

28Thus Midian was subdued before the Israelites and did not raise its head again. During Gideon's lifetime, the land enjoyed peace
forty years.

29Jerub-Baal son of Joash went back
home to live. 30He had seventy sons of his
own, for he had many wives. 31His concubine, who lived in Shechem, also bore him a
son, whom he named Abimelech. 32Gideon
son of Joash died at a good old age and was
buried in the tomb of his father Joash in
Ophrah of the Abiezrites.

33No sooner had Gideon died than the Israelites again prostituted themselves to the
Baals. They set up Baal-Berith as their god
and 34did not remember the LORD their God,
who had rescued them from the hands of all
their enemies on every side. 35They also

[a]*8* Hebrew *Penuel,* a variant of *Peniel;* also in verses 9 and 17

[b]*26* That is, about 43 pounds (about 19.5 kilograms)

failed to show kindness to the family of Jerub-Baal (that is, Gideon) for all the good things he had done for them.

Abimelech

9 Abimelech son of Jerub-Baal went to his mother's brothers in Shechem and said to them and to all his mother's clan, 2"Ask all the citizens of Shechem, 'Which is better for you: to have all seventy of Jerub-Baal's sons rule over you, or just one man?' Remember, I am your flesh and blood."

3When the brothers repeated all this to the citizens of Shechem, they were inclined to follow Abimelech, for they said, "He is our brother." 4They gave him seventy shekels[a] of silver from the temple of Baal-Berith, and Abimelech used it to hire reckless adventurers, who became his followers. 5He went to his father's home in Ophrah and on one stone murdered his seventy brothers, the sons of Jerub-Baal. But Jotham, the youngest son of Jerub-Baal, escaped by hiding. 6Then all the citizens of Shechem and Beth Millo gathered beside the great tree at the pillar in Shechem to crown Abimelech king.

7When Jotham was told about this, he climbed up on the top of Mount Gerizim and shouted to them, "Listen to me, citizens of Shechem, so that God may listen to you. 8One day the trees went out to anoint a king for themselves. They said to the olive tree, 'Be our king.'

9"But the olive tree answered, 'Should I give up my oil, by which both gods and men are honored, to hold sway over the trees?'

10"Next, the trees said to the fig tree, 'Come and be our king.'

11"But the fig tree replied, 'Should I give up my fruit, so good and sweet, to hold sway over the trees?'

12"Then the trees said to the vine, 'Come and be our king.'

13"But the vine answered, 'Should I give up my wine, which cheers both gods and men, to hold sway over the trees?'

14"Finally all the trees said to the thornbush, 'Come and be our king.'

15"The thornbush said to the trees, 'If you really want to anoint me king over you, come and take refuge in my shade; but if not, then let fire come out of the thornbush and consume the cedars of Lebanon!'

16"Now if you have acted honorably and in good faith when you made Abimelech king, and if you have been fair to Jerub-Baal and his family, and if you have treated him as he deserves— 17and to think that my father fought for you, risked his life to rescue you from the hand of Midian 18(but today you have revolted against my father's family, murdered his seventy sons on a single stone, and made Abimelech, the son of his slave girl, king over the citizens of Shechem because he is your brother)— 19if then you have acted honorably and in good faith toward Jerub-Baal and his family today, may Abimelech be your joy, and may you be his, too! 20But if you have not, let fire come out from Abimelech and consume you, citizens of Shechem and Beth Millo, and let fire come out from you, citizens of Shechem and Beth Millo, and consume Abimelech!"

21Then Jotham fled, escaping to Beer, and he lived there because he was afraid of his brother Abimelech.

22After Abimelech had governed Israel three years, 23God sent an evil spirit between Abimelech and the citizens of Shechem, who acted treacherously against Abimelech. 24God did this in order that the crime against Jerub-Baal's seventy sons, the shedding of their blood, might be avenged on their brother Abimelech and on the citizens of Shechem, who had helped him murder his brothers. 25In opposition to him these citizens of Shechem set men on the hilltops to ambush and rob everyone who passed by, and this was reported to Abimelech.

26Now Gaal son of Ebed moved with his brothers into Shechem, and its citizens put their confidence in him. 27After they had gone out into the fields and gathered the grapes and trodden them, they held a festival in the temple of their god. While they were eating and drinking, they cursed Abimelech. 28Then Gaal son of Ebed said, "Who is Abimelech, and who is Shechem, that we should be subject to him? Isn't he Jerub-Baal's son, and isn't Zebul his deputy? Serve the men of Hamor, Shechem's father! Why should we serve Abimelech? 29If only this people were under my command! Then I would get rid of him. I would say to Abimelech, 'Call out your whole army!' "[b]

30When Zebul the governor of the city heard what Gaal son of Ebed said, he was very angry. 31Under cover he sent messen-

[a]4 That is, about 1 3/4 pounds (about 0.8 kilogram)

[b]29 Septuagint; Hebrew *him." Then he said to Abimelech, "Call out your whole army!"*

gers to Abimelech, saying, "Gaal son of Ebed and his brothers have come to Shechem and are stirring up the city against you. [32]Now then, during the night you and your men should come and lie in wait in the fields. [33]In the morning at sunrise, advance against the city. When Gaal and his men come out against you, do whatever your hand finds to do."

[34]So Abimelech and all his troops set out by night and took up concealed positions near Shechem in four companies. [35]Now Gaal son of Ebed had gone out and was standing at the entrance to the city gate just as Abimelech and his soldiers came out from their hiding place.

[36]When Gaal saw them, he said to Zebul, "Look, people are coming down from the tops of the mountains!"

Zebul replied, "You mistake the shadows of the mountains for men."

[37]But Gaal spoke up again: "Look, people are coming down from the center of the land, and a company is coming from the direction of the soothsayers' tree."

[38]Then Zebul said to him, "Where is your big talk now, you who said, 'Who is Abimelech that we should be subject to him?' Aren't these the men you ridiculed? Go out and fight them!"

[39]So Gaal led out[a] the citizens of Shechem and fought Abimelech. [40]Abimelech chased him, and many fell wounded in the flight—all the way to the entrance to the gate. [41]Abimelech stayed in Arumah, and Zebul drove Gaal and his brothers out of Shechem.

[42]The next day the people of Shechem went out to the fields, and this was reported to Abimelech. [43]So he took his men, divided them into three companies and set an ambush in the fields. When he saw the people coming out of the city, he rose to attack them. [44]Abimelech and the companies with him rushed forward to a position at the entrance to the city gate. Then two companies rushed upon those in the fields and struck them down. [45]All that day Abimelech pressed his attack against the city until he had captured it and killed its people. Then he destroyed the city and scattered salt over it.

[46]On hearing this, the citizens in the tower of Shechem went into the stronghold of the temple of El-Berith. [47]When Abimelech heard that they had assembled there, [48]he and all his men went up Mount Zalmon. He took an ax and cut off some branches, which he lifted to his shoulders. He ordered the men with him, "Quick! Do what you have seen me do!" [49]So all the men cut branches and followed Abimelech. They piled them against the stronghold and set it on fire over the people inside. So all the people in the tower of Shechem, about a thousand men and women, also died.

[50]Next Abimelech went to Thebez and besieged it and captured it. [51]Inside the city, however, was a strong tower, to which all the men and women—all the people of the city—fled. They locked themselves in and climbed up on the tower roof. [52]Abimelech went to the tower and stormed it. But as he approached the entrance to the tower to set it on fire, [53]a woman dropped an upper millstone on his head and cracked his skull.

[54]Hurriedly he called to his armor-bearer, "Draw your sword and kill me, so that they can't say, 'A woman killed him.' " So his servant ran him through, and he died. [55]When the Israelites saw that Abimelech was dead, they went home.

[56]Thus God repaid the wickedness that Abimelech had done to his father by murdering his seventy brothers. [57]God also made the men of Shechem pay for all their wickedness. The curse of Jotham son of Jerub-Baal came on them.

Tola

10 After the time of Abimelech a man of Issachar, Tola son of Puah, the son of Dodo, rose to save Israel. He lived in Shamir, in the hill country of Ephraim. [2]He led[b] Israel twenty-three years; then he died, and was buried in Shamir.

Jair

[3]He was followed by Jair of Gilead, who led Israel twenty-two years. [4]He had thirty sons, who rode thirty donkeys. They controlled thirty towns in Gilead, which to this day are called Havvoth Jair.[c] [5]When Jair died, he was buried in Kamon.

Jephthah

[6]Again the Israelites did evil in the eyes of the LORD. They served the Baals and the Ashtoreths, and the gods of Aram, the gods of Sidon, the gods of Moab, the gods of the

[a]39 Or *Gaal went out in the sight of* [b]2 Traditionally *judged;* also in verse 3 [c]4 Or *called the settlements of Jair*

Ammonites and the gods of the Philistines.
And because the Israelites forsook the LORD
and no longer served him, 7he became angry
with them. He sold them into the hands of the
Philistines and the Ammonites, 8who that
year shattered and crushed them. For eighteen years they oppressed all the Israelites
on the east side of the Jordan in Gilead, the
land of the Amorites. 9The Ammonites also
crossed the Jordan to fight against Judah,
Benjamin and the house of Ephraim; and
Israel was in great distress. 10Then the Israelites cried out to the LORD, "We have sinned
against you, forsaking our God and serving
the Baals."

11The LORD replied, "When the Egyptians,
the Amorites, the Ammonites, the Philistines, 12the Sidonians, the Amalekites and
the Maonites[a] oppressed you and you cried
to me for help, did I not save you from their
hands? 13But you have forsaken me and
served other gods, so I will no longer save
you. 14Go and cry out to the gods you have
chosen. Let them save you when you are in
trouble!"

15But the Israelites said to the LORD, "We
have sinned. Do with us whatever you think
best, but please rescue us now." 16Then they
got rid of the foreign gods among them and
served the LORD. And he could bear Israel's
misery no longer.

17When the Ammonites were called to
arms and camped in Gilead, the Israelites
assembled and camped at Mizpah. 18The
leaders of the people of Gilead said to each
other, "Whoever will launch the attack
against the Ammonites will be the head of all
those living in Gilead."

11 Jephthah the Gileadite was a mighty
warrior. His father was Gilead; his
mother was a prostitute. 2Gilead's wife also
bore him sons, and when they were grown
up, they drove Jephthah away. "You are not
going to get any inheritance in our family,"
they said, "because you are the son of another woman." 3So Jephthah fled from his
brothers and settled in the land of Tob,
where a group of adventurers gathered
around him and followed him.

4Some time later, when the Ammonites
made war on Israel, 5the elders of Gilead
went to get Jephthah from the land of Tob.
6"Come," they said, "be our commander, so
we can fight the Ammonites."

7Jephthah said to them, "Didn't you hate
me and drive me from my father's house?
Why do you come to me now, when you're in
trouble?"

8The elders of Gilead said to him, "Nevertheless, we are turning to you now; come
with us to fight the Ammonites, and you will
be our head over all who live in Gilead."

9Jephthah answered, "Suppose you take
me back to fight the Ammonites and the LORD
gives them to me—will I really be your
head?"

10The elders of Gilead replied, "The LORD
is our witness; we will certainly do as you
say." 11So Jephthah went with the elders of
Gilead, and the people made him head and
commander over them. And he repeated all
his words before the LORD in Mizpah.

12Then Jephthah sent messengers to the
Ammonite king with the question: "What do
you have against us that you have attacked
our country?"

13The king of the Ammonites answered
Jephthah's messengers, "When Israel came
up out of Egypt, they took away my land from
the Arnon to the Jabbok, all the way to the
Jordan. Now give it back peaceably."

14Jephthah sent back messengers to the
Ammonite king, 15saying:

> "This is what Jephthah says: Israel did
> not take the land of Moab or the land of
> the Ammonites. 16But when they came
> up out of Egypt, Israel went through the
> desert to the Red Sea[b] and on to Ka-
> desh. 17Then Israel sent messengers to
> the king of Edom, saying, 'Give us per-
> mission to go through your country,' but
> the king of Edom would not listen. They
> sent also to the king of Moab, and he
> refused. So Israel stayed at Kadesh.
>
> 18"Next they traveled through the
> desert, skirted the lands of Edom and
> Moab, passed along the eastern side of
> the country of Moab, and camped on the
> other side of the Arnon. They did not
> enter the territory of Moab, for the Arnon
> was its border.
>
> 19"Then Israel sent messengers to Si-
> hon king of the Amorites, who ruled in
> Heshbon, and said to him, 'Let us pass
> through your country to our own place.'
> 20Sihon, however, did not trust Israel[c] to
> pass through his territory. He mustered

[a] 12 Hebrew; some Septuagint manuscripts *Midianites*
[b] 16 Hebrew *Yam Suph;* that is, Sea of Reeds
[c] 20 Or *however, would not make an agreement for Israel*

all his men and encamped at Jahaz and
fought with Israel.
21"Then the LORD, the God of Israel,
gave Sihon and all his men into Israel's
hands, and they defeated them. Israel
took over all the land of the Amorites
who lived in that country, 22capturing all
of it from the Arnon to the Jabbok and
from the desert to the Jordan.
23"Now since the LORD, the God of Israel, has driven the Amorites out before
his people Israel, what right have you to
take it over? 24Will you not take what
your god Chemosh gives you? Likewise, whatever the LORD our God has
given us, we will possess. 25Are you better than Balak son of Zippor, king of
Moab? Did he ever quarrel with Israel or
fight with them? 26For three hundred
years Israel occupied Heshbon, Aroer,
the surrounding settlements and all the
towns along the Arnon. Why didn't you
retake them during that time? 27I have
not wronged you, but you are doing me
wrong by waging war against me. Let
the LORD, the Judge,[a] decide the dispute
this day between the Israelites and the
Ammonites."

28The king of Ammon, however, paid no attention to the message Jephthah sent him.
29Then the Spirit of the LORD came upon
Jephthah. He crossed Gilead and Manasseh, passed through Mizpah of Gilead,
and from there he advanced against the Ammonites. 30And Jephthah made a vow to the
LORD: "If you give the Ammonites into my
hands, 31whatever comes out of the door of
my house to meet me when I return in triumph from the Ammonites will be the LORD's,
and I will sacrifice it as a burnt offering."
32Then Jephthah went over to fight the
Ammonites, and the LORD gave them into his
hands. 33He devastated twenty towns from
Aroer to the vicinity of Minnith, as far as Abel
Keramim. Thus Israel subdued Ammon.
34When Jephthah returned to his home in
Mizpah, who should come out to meet him
but his daughter, dancing to the sound of
tambourines! She was an only child. Except
for her he had neither son nor daughter.
35When he saw her, he tore his clothes and
cried, "Oh! My daughter! You have made me
miserable and wretched, because I have
made a vow to the LORD that I cannot break."
36"My father," she replied, "you have giv-
en your word to the LORD. Do to me just as
you promised, now that the LORD has
avenged you of your enemies, the Ammonites. 37But grant me this one request," she
said. "Give me two months to roam the hills
and weep with my friends, because I will
never marry."
38"You may go," he said. And he let her go
for two months. She and the girls went into
the hills and wept because she would never
marry. 39After the two months, she returned
to her father and he did to her as he had
vowed. And she was a virgin.
From this comes the Israelite custom
40that each year the young women of Israel
go out for four days to commemorate the
daughter of Jephthah the Gileadite.

Jephthah and Ephraim

12 The men of Ephraim called out their
forces, crossed over to Zaphon and
said to Jephthah, "Why did you go to fight the
Ammonites without calling us to go with you?
We're going to burn down your house over
your head."
2Jephthah answered, "I and my people
were engaged in a great struggle with the
Ammonites, and although I called, you didn't
save me out of their hands. 3When I saw that
you wouldn't help, I took my life in my hands
and crossed over to fight the Ammonites,
and the LORD gave me the victory over them.
Now why have you come up today to fight
me?"
4Jephthah then called together the men of
Gilead and fought against Ephraim. The Gileadites struck them down because the
Ephraimites had said, "You Gileadites are
renegades from Ephraim and Manasseh."
5The Gileadites captured the fords of the Jordan leading to Ephraim, and whenever a survivor of Ephraim said, "Let me cross over,"
the men of Gilead asked him, "Are you an
Ephraimite?" If he replied, "No," 6they said,
"All right, say 'Shibboleth.' " If he said, "Sib-
boleth," because he could not pronounce the
word correctly, they seized him and killed
him at the fords of the Jordan. Forty-two
thousand Ephraimites were killed at that
time.
7Jephthah led[b] Israel six years. Then
Jephthah the Gileadite died, and was buried
in a town in Gilead.

[a]27 Or *Ruler* [b]7 Traditionally *judged;* also in verses 8-14

Ibzan, Elon and Abdon

8After him, Ibzan of Bethlehem led Israel. 9He had thirty sons and thirty daughters. He gave his daughters away in marriage to those outside his clan, and for his sons he brought in thirty young women as wives from outside his clan. Ibzan led Israel seven years. 10Then Ibzan died, and was buried in Bethlehem.

11After him, Elon the Zebulunite led Israel ten years. 12Then Elon died, and was buried in Aijalon in the land of Zebulun.

13After him, Abdon son of Hillel, from Pirathon, led Israel. 14He had forty sons and thirty grandsons, who rode on seventy donkeys. He led Israel eight years. 15Then Abdon son of Hillel died, and was buried at Pirathon in Ephraim, in the hill country of the Amalekites.

The Birth of Samson

13 Again the Israelites did evil in the eyes of the LORD, so the LORD delivered them into the hands of the Philistines for forty years.

2A certain man of Zorah, named Manoah, from the clan of the Danites, had a wife who was sterile and remained childless. 3The angel of the LORD appeared to her and said, "You are sterile and childless, but you are going to conceive and have a son. 4Now see to it that you drink no wine or other fermented drink and that you do not eat anything unclean, 5because you will conceive and give birth to a son. No razor may be used on his head, because the boy is to be a Nazirite, set apart to God from birth, and he will begin the deliverance of Israel from the hands of the Philistines."

6Then the woman went to her husband and told him, "A man of God came to me. He looked like an angel of God, very awesome. I didn't ask him where he came from, and he didn't tell me his name. 7But he said to me, 'You will conceive and give birth to a son. Now then, drink no wine or other fermented drink and do not eat anything unclean, because the boy will be a Nazirite of God from birth until the day of his death.' "

8Then Manoah prayed to the LORD: "O Lord, I beg you, let the man of God you sent to us come again to teach us how to bring up the boy who is to be born."

9God heard Manoah, and the angel of God came again to the woman while she was out in the field; but her husband Manoah was not with her. 10The woman hurried to tell her husband, "He's here! The man who appeared to me the other day!"

11Manoah got up and followed his wife. When he came to the man, he said, "Are you the one who talked to my wife?"

"I am," he said.

12So Manoah asked him, "When your words are fulfilled, what is to be the rule for the boy's life and work?"

13The angel of the LORD answered, "Your wife must do all that I have told her. 14She must not eat anything that comes from the grapevine, nor drink any wine or other fermented drink nor eat anything unclean. She must do everything I have commanded her."

15Manoah said to the angel of the LORD, "We would like you to stay until we prepare a young goat for you."

16The angel of the LORD replied, "Even though you detain me, I will not eat any of your food. But if you prepare a burnt offering, offer it to the LORD." (Manoah did not realize that it was the angel of the LORD.)

17Then Manoah inquired of the angel of the LORD, "What is your name, so that we may honor you when your word comes true?"

18He replied, "Why do you ask my name? It is beyond understanding.[a]" 19Then Manoah took a young goat, together with the grain offering, and sacrificed it on a rock to the LORD. And the LORD did an amazing thing while Manoah and his wife watched: 20As the flame blazed up from the altar toward heaven, the angel of the LORD ascended in the flame. Seeing this, Manoah and his wife fell with their faces to the ground. 21When the angel of the LORD did not show himself again to Manoah and his wife, Manoah realized that it was the angel of the LORD.

22"We are doomed to die!" he said to his wife. "We have seen God!"

23But his wife answered, "If the LORD had meant to kill us, he would not have accepted a burnt offering and grain offering from our hands, nor shown us all these things or now told us this."

24The woman gave birth to a boy and named him Samson. He grew and the LORD blessed him, 25and the Spirit of the LORD began to stir him while he was in Mahaneh Dan, between Zorah and Eshtaol.

[a]18 Or *is wonderful*

Samson's Marriage

14 Samson went down to Timnah and
saw there a young Philistine woman.
2When he returned, he said to his father and
mother, "I have seen a Philistine woman in
Timnah; now get her for me as my wife."
3His father and mother replied, "Isn't there
an acceptable woman among your relatives
or among all our people? Must you go to the
uncircumcised Philistines to get a wife?"
But Samson said to his father, "Get her for
me. She's the right one for me." 4(His parents did not know that this was from the LORD,
who was seeking an occasion to confront the
Philistines; for at that time they were ruling
over Israel.) 5Samson went down to Timnah
together with his father and mother. As they
approached the vineyards of Timnah, suddenly a young lion came roaring toward him.
6The Spirit of the LORD came upon him in
power so that he tore the lion apart with his
bare hands as he might have torn a young
goat. But he told neither his father nor his
mother what he had done. 7Then he went
down and talked with the woman, and he
liked her.
8Some time later, when he went back to
marry her, he turned aside to look at the
lion's carcass. In it was a swarm of bees and
some honey, 9which he scooped out with his
hands and ate as he went along. When he
rejoined his parents, he gave them some,
and they too ate it. But he did not tell them
that he had taken the honey from the lion's
carcass.
10Now his father went down to see the
woman. And Samson made a feast there, as
was customary for bridegrooms. 11When he
appeared, he was given thirty companions.
12"Let me tell you a riddle," Samson said to
them. "If you can give me the answer within
the seven days of the feast, I will give you
thirty linen garments and thirty sets of
clothes. 13If you can't tell me the answer, you
must give me thirty linen garments and thirty
sets of clothes."
"Tell us your riddle," they said. "Let's hear
it."
14He replied,

"Out of the eater, something to eat;
out of the strong, something sweet."

For three days they could not give the answer.
15On the fourth[a] day, they said to Samson's wife, "Coax your husband into explaining the riddle for us, or we will burn you and
your father's household to death. Did you
invite us here to rob us?"
16Then Samson's wife threw herself on
him, sobbing, "You hate me! You don't really
love me. You've given my people a riddle,
but you haven't told me the answer."
"I haven't even explained it to my father or
mother," he replied, "so why should I explain
it to you?" 17She cried the whole seven days
of the feast. So on the seventh day he finally
told her, because she continued to press
him. She in turn explained the riddle to her
people.
18Before sunset on the seventh day the
men of the town said to him,

"What is sweeter than honey?
What is stronger than a lion?"

Samson said to them,

"If you had not plowed with my heifer,
you would not have solved my riddle."

19Then the Spirit of the LORD came upon
him in power. He went down to Ashkelon,
struck down thirty of their men, stripped them
of their belongings and gave their clothes to
those who had explained the riddle. Burning
with anger, he went up to his father's house.
20And Samson's wife was given to the friend
who had attended him at his wedding.

Samson's Vengeance on the Philistines

15 Later on, at the time of wheat harvest, Samson took a young goat and
went to visit his wife. He said, "I'm going to
my wife's room." But her father would not let
him go in.
2"I was so sure you thoroughly hated her,"
he said, "that I gave her to your friend. Isn't
her younger sister more attractive? Take her
instead."
3Samson said to them, "This time I have a
right to get even with the Philistines; I will
really harm them." 4So he went out and
caught three hundred foxes and tied them
tail to tail in pairs. He then fastened a torch to
every pair of tails, 5lit the torches and let the
foxes loose in the standing grain of the Philistines. He burned up the shocks and standing grain, together with the vineyards and
olive groves.
6When the Philistines asked, "Who did

[a] 15 Some Septuagint manuscripts and Syriac; Hebrew *seventh*

this?" they were told, "Samson, the Timnite's son-in-law, because his wife was given to his friend."

So the Philistines went up and burned her and her father to death. 7Samson said to them, "Since you've acted like this, I won't stop until I get my revenge on you." 8He attacked them viciously and slaughtered many of them. Then he went down and stayed in a cave in the rock of Etam.

9The Philistines went up and camped in Judah, spreading out near Lehi. 10The men of Judah asked, "Why have you come to fight us?"

"We have come to take Samson prisoner," they answered, "to do to him as he did to us."

11Then three thousand men from Judah went down to the cave in the rock of Etam and said to Samson, "Don't you realize that the Philistines are rulers over us? What have you done to us?"

He answered, "I merely did to them what they did to me."

12They said to him, "We've come to tie you up and hand you over to the Philistines."

Samson said, "Swear to me that you won't kill me yourselves."

13"Agreed," they answered. "We will only tie you up and hand you over to them. We will not kill you." So they bound him with two new ropes and led him up from the rock. 14As he approached Lehi, the Philistines came toward him shouting. The Spirit of the LORD came upon him in power. The ropes on his arms became like charred flax, and the bindings dropped from his hands. 15Finding a fresh jawbone of a donkey, he grabbed it and struck down a thousand men.

16Then Samson said,

"With a donkey's jawbone
  I have made donkeys of them.[a]
With a donkey's jawbone
  I have killed a thousand men."

17When he finished speaking, he threw away the jawbone; and the place was called Ramath Lehi.[b]

18Because he was very thirsty, he cried out to the LORD, "You have given your servant this great victory. Must I now die of thirst and fall into the hands of the uncircumcised?" 19Then God opened up the hollow place in Lehi, and water came out of it. When Samson drank, his strength returned and he revived. So the spring was called En Hakkore,[c] and it is still there in Lehi.

20Samson led[d] Israel for twenty years in the days of the Philistines.

Samson and Delilah

16 One day Samson went to Gaza, where he saw a prostitute. He went in to spend the night with her. 2The people of Gaza were told, "Samson is here!" So they surrounded the place and lay in wait for him all night at the city gate. They made no move during the night, saying, "At dawn we'll kill him."

3But Samson lay there only until the middle of the night. Then he got up and took hold of the doors of the city gate, together with the two posts, and tore them loose, bar and all. He lifted them to his shoulders and carried them to the top of the hill that faces Hebron.

4Some time later, he fell in love with a woman in the Valley of Sorek whose name was Delilah. 5The rulers of the Philistines went to her and said, "See if you can lure him into showing you the secret of his great strength and how we can overpower him so we may tie him up and subdue him. Each one of us will give you eleven hundred shekels[e] of silver."

6So Delilah said to Samson, "Tell me the secret of your great strength and how you can be tied up and subdued."

7Samson answered her, "If anyone ties me with seven fresh thongs[f] that have not been dried, I'll become as weak as any other man."

8Then the rulers of the Philistines brought her seven fresh thongs that had not been dried, and she tied him with them. 9With men hidden in the room, she called to him, "Samson, the Philistines are upon you!" But he snapped the thongs as easily as a piece of string snaps when it comes close to a flame. So the secret of his strength was not discovered.

10Then Delilah said to Samson, "You have made a fool of me; you lied to me. Come now, tell me how you can be tied."

11He said, "If anyone ties me securely with new ropes that have never been used, I'll become as weak as any other man."

12So Delilah took new ropes and tied him with them. Then, with men hidden in the

[a]16 Or *made a heap or two;* the Hebrew for *donkey* sounds like the Hebrew for *heap.* [b]17 *Ramath Lehi* means *jawbone hill.* [c]19 *En Hakkore* means *caller's spring.* [d]20 Traditionally *judged* [e]5 That is, about 28 pounds (about 13 kilograms) [f]7 Or *bowstrings;* also in verses 8 and 9

room, she called to him, "Samson, the Philistines are upon you!" But he snapped the
ropes off his arms as if they were threads.
13Delilah then said to Samson, "Until now,
you have been making a fool of me and lying
to me. Tell me how you can be tied."
He replied, "If you weave the seven braids
of my head into the fabric ⌞on the loom⌟ and
tighten it with the pin, I'll become as weak as
any other man." So while he was sleeping,
Delilah took the seven braids of his head,
wove them into the fabric 14and[a] tightened it
with the pin.
Again she called to him, "Samson, the
Philistines are upon you!" He awoke from his
sleep and pulled up the pin and the loom,
with the fabric.
15Then she said to him, "How can you say,
'I love you,' when you won't confide in me?
This is the third time you have made a fool of
me and haven't told me the secret of your
great strength." 16With such nagging she
prodded him day after day until he was tired
to death.
17So he told her everything. "No razor has
ever been used on my head," he said, "because I have been a Nazirite set apart to God
since birth. If my head were shaved, my
strength would leave me, and I would
become as weak as any other man."
18When Delilah saw that he had told her
everything, she sent word to the rulers of the
Philistines, "Come back once more; he has
told me everything." So the rulers of the Philistines returned with the silver in their hands.
19Having put him to sleep on her lap, she
called a man to shave off the seven braids of
his hair, and so began to subdue him.[b] And
his strength left him.
20Then she called, "Samson, the Philistines are upon you!"
He awoke from his sleep and thought, "I'll
go out as before and shake myself free." But
he did not know that the LORD had left him.
21Then the Philistines seized him, gouged
out his eyes and took him down to Gaza.
Binding him with bronze shackles, they set
him to grinding in the prison. 22But the hair on
his head began to grow again after it had
been shaved.

The Death of Samson

23Now the rulers of the Philistines assembled to offer a great sacrifice to Dagon their
god and to celebrate, saying, "Our god has
delivered Samson, our enemy, into our
hands."
24When the people saw him, they praised
their god, saying,

"Our god has delivered our enemy
  into our hands,
the one who laid waste our land
  and multiplied our slain."

25While they were in high spirits, they
shouted, "Bring out Samson to entertain us."
So they called Samson out of the prison, and
he performed for them.
When they stood him among the pillars,
26Samson said to the servant who held his
hand, "Put me where I can feel the pillars
that support the temple, so that I may lean
against them." 27Now the temple was crowded with men and women; all the rulers of the
Philistines were there, and on the roof were
about three thousand men and women
watching Samson perform. 28Then Samson
prayed to the LORD, "O Sovereign LORD,
remember me. O God, please strengthen me
just once more, and let me with one blow get
revenge on the Philistines for my two eyes."
29Then Samson reached toward the two central pillars on which the temple stood. Brac-
ing himself against them, his right hand on
the one and his left hand on the other,
30Samson said, "Let me die with the Philistines!" Then he pushed with all his might,
and down came the temple on the rulers and
all the people in it. Thus he killed many more
when he died than while he lived.
31Then his brothers and his father's whole
family went down to get him. They brought
him back and buried him between Zorah and
Eshtaol in the tomb of Manoah his father. He
had led[c] Israel twenty years.

Micah's Idols

17 Now a man named Micah from the
hill country of Ephraim 2said to his
mother, "The eleven hundred shekels[d] of
silver that were taken from you and about
which I heard you utter a curse—I have that
silver with me; I took it."
Then his mother said, "The LORD bless
you, my son!"
3When he returned the eleven hundred
shekels of silver to his mother, she said, "I
solemnly consecrate my silver to the LORD for

[a]13,14 Some Septuagint manuscripts; Hebrew *"⌞I can⌟ if you weave the seven braids of my head into the fabric ⌞on the loom⌟." 14So she*
[b]19 Hebrew; some Septuagint manuscripts *and he began to weaken*
[c]31 Traditionally *judged*
[d]2 That is, about 28 pounds (about 13 kilograms)

my son to make a carved image and a cast
idol. I will give it back to you."
4So he returned the silver to his mother,
and she took two hundred shekels[a] of silver
and gave them to a silversmith, who made
them into the image and the idol. And they
were put in Micah's house.
5Now this man Micah had a shrine, and he
made an ephod and some idols and installed
one of his sons as his priest. 6In those days
Israel had no king; everyone did as he saw
fit.
7A young Levite from Bethlehem in Judah,
who had been living within the clan of Judah,
8left that town in search of some other place
to stay. On his way[b] he came to Micah's
house in the hill country of Ephraim.
9Micah asked him, "Where are you from?"
"I'm a Levite from Bethlehem in Judah,"
he said, "and I'm looking for a place to stay."
10Then Micah said to him, "Live with me
and be my father and priest, and I'll give you
ten shekels[c] of silver a year, your clothes
and your food." 11So the Levite agreed to live
with him, and the young man was to him like
one of his sons. 12Then Micah installed the
Levite, and the young man became his priest
and lived in his house. 13And Micah said,
"Now I know that the LORD will be good to me,
since this Levite has become my priest."

Danites Settle in Laish

18 In those days Israel had no king.
And in those days the tribe of the
Danites was seeking a place of their own
where they might settle, because they had
not yet come into an inheritance among the
tribes of Israel. 2So the Danites sent five warriors from Zorah and Eshtaol to spy out the
land and explore it. These men represented
all their clans. They told them, "Go, explore
the land."
The men entered the hill country of
Ephraim and came to the house of Micah,
where they spent the night. 3When they were
near Micah's house, they recognized the
voice of the young Levite; so they turned in
there and asked him, "Who brought you
here? What are you doing in this place? Why
are you here?"
4He told them what Micah had done for
him, and said, "He has hired me and I am his
priest."
5Then they said to him, "Please inquire of
God to learn whether our journey will be successful."
6The priest answered them, "Go in peace.
Your journey has the LORD's approval."
7So the five men left and came to Laish,
where they saw that the people were living in
safety, like the Sidonians, unsuspecting and
secure. And since their land lacked nothing,
they were prosperous.[d] Also, they lived a
long way from the Sidonians and had no
relationship with anyone else.[e]
8When they returned to Zorah and Eshtaol, their brothers asked them, "How did
you find things?"
9They answered, "Come on, let's attack
them! We have seen that the land is very
good. Aren't you going to do something?
Don't hesitate to go there and take it over.
10When you get there, you will find an unsuspecting people and a spacious land that God
has put into your hands, a land that lacks
nothing whatever."
11Then six hundred men from the clan of
the Danites, armed for battle, set out from
Zorah and Eshtaol. 12On their way they set
up camp near Kiriath Jearim in Judah. This is
why the place west of Kiriath Jearim is called
Mahaneh Dan[f] to this day. 13From there they
went on to the hill country of Ephraim and
came to Micah's house.
14Then the five men who had spied out the
land of Laish said to their brothers, "Do you
know that one of these houses has an
ephod, other household gods, a carved image and a cast idol? Now you know what to
do." 15So they turned in there and went to the
house of the young Levite at Micah's place
and greeted him. 16The six hundred Danites,
armed for battle, stood at the entrance to the
gate. 17The five men who had spied out the
land went inside and took the carved image,
the ephod, the other household gods and the
cast idol while the priest and the six hundred
armed men stood at the entrance to the gate.
18When these men went into Micah's
house and took the carved image, the
ephod, the other household gods and the
cast idol, the priest said to them, "What are
you doing?"
19They answered him, "Be quiet! Don't say
a word. Come with us, and be our father and
priest. Isn't it better that you serve a tribe and
clan in Israel as priest rather than just one
man's household?" 20Then the priest was

[a]4 That is, about 5 pounds (about 2.3 kilograms) [b]8 Or *To carry on his profession* [c]10 That is, about 4 ounces (about 110 grams) [d]7 The meaning of the Hebrew for this clause is uncertain. [e]7 Hebrew; some Septuagint manuscripts *with the Arameans* [f]12 *Mahaneh Dan* means *Dan's camp.*

glad. He took the ephod, the other household gods and the carved image and went
along with the people. 21Putting their little
children, their livestock and their possessions in front of them, they turned away and
left.
22When they had gone some distance
from Micah's house, the men who lived near
Micah were called together and overtook the
Danites. 23As they shouted after them, the
Danites turned and said to Micah, "What's
the matter with you that you called out your
men to fight?"
24He replied, "You took the gods I made,
and my priest, and went away. What else do
I have? How can you ask, 'What's the matter
with you?' "
25The Danites answered, "Don't argue
with us, or some hot-tempered men will attack you, and you and your family will lose
your lives." 26So the Danites went their way,
and Micah, seeing that they were too strong
for him, turned around and went back home.
27Then they took what Micah had made,
and his priest, and went on to Laish, against
a peaceful and unsuspecting people. They
attacked them with the sword and burned
down their city. 28There was no one to rescue
them because they lived a long way from
Sidon and had no relationship with anyone
else. The city was in a valley near Beth
Rehob.
The Danites rebuilt the city and settled
there. 29They named it Dan after their forefather Dan, who was born to Israel—though
the city used to be called Laish. 30There the
Danites set up for themselves the idols, and
Jonathan son of Gershom, the son of
Moses,[a] and his sons were priests for the
tribe of Dan until the time of the captivity of
the land. 31They continued to use the idols
Micah had made, all the time the house of
God was in Shiloh.

A Levite and His Concubine

19 In those days Israel had no king.
Now a Levite who lived in a remote
area in the hill country of Ephraim took a
concubine from Bethlehem in Judah. 2But
she was unfaithful to him. She left him and
went back to her father's house in Bethlehem, Judah. After she had been there four
months, 3her husband went to her to persuade her to return. He had with him his
servant and two donkeys. She took him into
her father's house, and when her father saw
him, he gladly welcomed him. 4His father-in-
law, the girl's father, prevailed upon him to
stay; so he remained with him three days,
eating and drinking, and sleeping there.
5On the fourth day they got up early and he
prepared to leave, but the girl's father said to
his son-in-law, "Refresh yourself with something to eat; then you can go." 6So the two of
them sat down to eat and drink together.
Afterward the girl's father said, "Please stay
tonight and enjoy yourself." 7And when the
man got up to go, his father-in-law persuaded him, so he stayed there that night. 8On the
morning of the fifth day, when he rose to go,
the girl's father said, "Refresh yourself. Wait
till afternoon!" So the two of them ate together.
9Then when the man, with his concubine
and his servant, got up to leave, his father-in-
law, the girl's father, said, "Now look, it's
almost evening. Spend the night here; the
day is nearly over. Stay and enjoy yourself.
Early tomorrow morning you can get up and
be on your way home." 10But, unwilling to
stay another night, the man left and went
toward Jebus (that is, Jerusalem), with his
two saddled donkeys and his concubine.
11When they were near Jebus and the day
was almost gone, the servant said to his
master, "Come, let's stop at this city of the
Jebusites and spend the night."
12His master replied, "No. We won't go into
an alien city, whose people are not Israelites.
We will go on to Gibeah." 13He added,
"Come, let's try to reach Gibeah or Ramah
and spend the night in one of those places."
14So they went on, and the sun set as they
neared Gibeah in Benjamin. 15There they
stopped to spend the night. They went and
sat in the city square, but no one took them
into his home for the night.
16That evening an old man from the hill
country of Ephraim, who was living in Gibeah
(the men of the place were Benjamites),
came in from his work in the fields. 17When
he looked and saw the traveler in the city
square, the old man asked, "Where are you
going? Where did you come from?"
18He answered, "We are on our way from
Bethlehem in Judah to a remote area in the
hill country of Ephraim where I live. I have
been to Bethlehem in Judah and now I am
going to the house of the LORD. No one has
taken me into his house. 19We have both

[a]30 An ancient Hebrew scribal tradition, some Septuagint manuscripts and Vulgate; Masoretic Text *Manasseh*

straw and fodder for our donkeys and bread and wine for ourselves your servants—me, your maidservant, and the young man with us. We don't need anything."

20"You are welcome at my house," the old man said. "Let me supply whatever you need. Only don't spend the night in the square." 21So he took him into his house and fed his donkeys. After they had washed their feet, they had something to eat and drink.

22While they were enjoying themselves, some of the wicked men of the city surrounded the house. Pounding on the door, they shouted to the old man who owned the house, "Bring out the man who came to your house so we can have sex with him."

23The owner of the house went outside and said to them, "No, my friends, don't be so vile. Since this man is my guest, don't do this disgraceful thing. 24Look, here is my virgin daughter, and his concubine. I will bring them out to you now, and you can use them and do to them whatever you wish. But to this man, don't do such a disgraceful thing."

25But the men would not listen to him. So the man took his concubine and sent her outside to them, and they raped her and abused her throughout the night, and at dawn they let her go. 26At daybreak the woman went back to the house where her master was staying, fell down at the door and lay there until daylight.

27When her master got up in the morning and opened the door of the house and stepped out to continue on his way, there lay his concubine, fallen in the doorway of the house, with her hands on the threshold. 28He said to her, "Get up; let's go." But there was no answer. Then the man put her on his donkey and set out for home.

29When he reached home, he took a knife and cut up his concubine, limb by limb, into twelve parts and sent them into all the areas of Israel. 30Everyone who saw it said, "Such a thing has never been seen or done, not since the day the Israelites came up out of Egypt. Think about it! Consider it! Tell us what to do!"

Israelites Fight the Benjamites

20 Then all the Israelites from Dan to Beersheba and from the land of Gilead came out as one man and assembled before the LORD in Mizpah. 2The leaders of all the people of the tribes of Israel took their places in the assembly of the people of God, four hundred thousand soldiers armed with swords. 3(The Benjamites heard that the Israelites had gone up to Mizpah.) Then the Israelites said, "Tell us how this awful thing happened."

4So the Levite, the husband of the murdered woman, said, "I and my concubine came to Gibeah in Benjamin to spend the night. 5During the night the men of Gibeah came after me and surrounded the house, intending to kill me. They raped my concubine, and she died. 6I took my concubine, cut her into pieces and sent one piece to each region of Israel's inheritance, because they committed this lewd and disgraceful act in Israel. 7Now, all you Israelites, speak up and give your verdict."

8All the people rose as one man, saying,"None of us will go home. No, not one of us will return to his house. 9But now this is what we'll do to Gibeah: We'll go up against it as the lot directs. 10We'll take ten men out of every hundred from all the tribes of Israel, and a hundred from a thousand, and a thousand from ten thousand, to get provisions for the army. Then, when the army arrives at Gibeah[a] in Benjamin, it can give them what they deserve for all this vileness done in Israel." 11So all the men of Israel got together and united as one man against the city.

12The tribes of Israel sent men throughout the tribe of Benjamin, saying, "What about this awful crime that was committed among you? 13Now surrender those wicked men of Gibeah so that we may put them to death and purge the evil from Israel."

But the Benjamites would not listen to their fellow Israelites. 14From their towns they came together at Gibeah to fight against the Israelites. 15At once the Benjamites mobilized twenty-six thousand swordsmen from their towns, in addition to seven hundred chosen men from those living in Gibeah. 16Among all these soldiers there were seven hundred chosen men who were left-handed, each of whom could sling a stone at a hair and not miss.

17Israel, apart from Benjamin, mustered four hundred thousand swordsmen, all of them fighting men.

18The Israelites went up to Bethel[b] and

[a] *10* One Hebrew manuscript; most Hebrew manuscripts *Geba,* a variant of *Gibeah* [b] *18* Or *to the house of God;* also in verse 26

inquired of God. They said, "Who of us shall
go first to fight against the Benjamites?"
The LORD replied, "Judah shall go first."
19 The next morning the Israelites got up
and pitched camp near Gibeah. 20 The men
of Israel went out to fight the Benjamites and
took up battle positions against them at Gibeah. 21 The Benjamites came out of Gibeah
and cut down twenty-two thousand Israelites
on the battlefield that day. 22 But the men of
Israel encouraged one another and again
took up their positions where they had stationed themselves the first day. 23 The Israelites went up and wept before the LORD until
evening, and they inquired of the LORD. They
said, "Shall we go up again to battle against
the Benjamites, our brothers?"
The LORD answered, "Go up against
them."
24 Then the Israelites drew near to Benjamin the second day. 25 This time, when the
Benjamites came out from Gibeah to oppose
them, they cut down another eighteen thousand Israelites, all of them armed with
swords.
26 Then the Israelites, all the people, went
up to Bethel, and there they sat weeping
before the LORD. They fasted that day until
evening and presented burnt offerings and
fellowship offerings[a] to the LORD. 27 And the
Israelites inquired of the LORD. (In those days
the ark of the covenant of God was there,
28 with Phinehas son of Eleazar, the son of
Aaron, ministering before it.) They asked,
"Shall we go up again to battle with Benjamin
our brother, or not?"
The LORD responded, "Go, for tomorrow I
will give them into your hands."
29 Then Israel set an ambush around Gibeah. 30 They went up against the Benjamites
on the third day and took up positions
against Gibeah as they had done before.
31 The Benjamites came out to meet them
and were drawn away from the city. They
began to inflict casualties on the Israelites as
before, so that about thirty men fell in the
open field and on the roads—the one leading
to Bethel and the other to Gibeah.
32 While the Benjamites were saying, "We
are defeating them as before," the Israelites
were saying, "Let's retreat and draw them
away from the city to the roads."
33 All the men of Israel moved from their
places and took up positions at Baal Tamar,
and the Israelite ambush charged out of its
place on the west[b] of Gibeah.[c] 34 Then ten
thousand of Israel's finest men made a fron-
tal attack on Gibeah. The fighting was so
heavy that the Benjamites did not realize
how near disaster was. 35 The LORD defeated
Benjamin before Israel, and on that day the
Israelites struck down 25,100 Benjamites, all
armed with swords. 36 Then the Benjamites
saw that they were beaten.
Now the men of Israel had given way before Benjamin, because they relied on the
ambush they had set near Gibeah. 37 The
men who had been in ambush made a sudden dash into Gibeah, spread out and put the
whole city to the sword. 38 The men of Israel
had arranged with the ambush that they
should send up a great cloud of smoke from
the city, 39 and then the men of Israel would
turn in the battle.
The Benjamites had begun to inflict casualties on the men of Israel (about thirty), and
they said, "We are defeating them as in the
first battle." 40 But when the column of smoke
began to rise from the city, the Benjamites
turned and saw the smoke of the whole city
going up into the sky. 41 Then the men of
Israel turned on them, and the men of Benjamin were terrified, because they realized that
disaster had come upon them. 42 So they fled
before the Israelites in the direction of the
desert, but they could not escape the battle.
And the men of Israel who came out of the
towns cut them down there. 43 They surrounded the Benjamites, chased them and
easily[d] overran them in the vicinity of Gibeah
on the east. 44 Eighteen thousand Benjamites
fell, all of them valiant fighters. 45 As they
turned and fled toward the desert to the rock
of Rimmon, the Israelites cut down five thousand men along the roads. They kept pressing after the Benjamites as far as Gidom and
struck down two thousand more.
46 On that day twenty-five thousand Benjamite swordsmen fell, all of them valiant fighters. 47 But six hundred men turned and fled
into the desert to the rock of Rimmon, where
they stayed four months. 48 The men of Israel
went back to Benjamin and put all the towns
to the sword, including the animals and
everything else they found. All the towns
they came across they set on fire.

[a] *26* Traditionally *peace offerings* [b] *33* Some Septuagint manuscripts and Vulgate; the meaning of the Hebrew for this word is uncertain. [c] *33* Hebrew *Geba,* a variant of *Gibeah* [d] *43* The meaning of the Hebrew for this word is uncertain.

Wives for the Benjamites

21 The men of Israel had taken an oath at Mizpah: "Not one of us will give his daughter in marriage to a Benjamite."

2The people went to Bethel,[a] where they sat before God until evening, raising their voices and weeping bitterly. 3"O LORD, the God of Israel," they cried, "why has this happened to Israel? Why should one tribe be missing from Israel today?"

4Early the next day the people built an altar and presented burnt offerings and fellowship offerings.[b]

5Then the Israelites asked, "Who from all the tribes of Israel has failed to assemble before the LORD?" For they had taken a solemn oath that anyone who failed to assemble before the LORD at Mizpah should certainly be put to death.

6Now the Israelites grieved for their brothers, the Benjamites. "Today one tribe is cut off from Israel," they said. 7"How can we provide wives for those who are left, since we have taken an oath by the LORD not to give them any of our daughters in marriage?" 8Then they asked, "Which one of the tribes of Israel failed to assemble before the LORD at Mizpah?" They discovered that no one from Jabesh Gilead had come to the camp for the assembly. 9For when they counted the people, they found that none of the people of Jabesh Gilead were there.

10So the assembly sent twelve thousand fighting men with instructions to go to Jabesh Gilead and put to the sword those living there, including the women and children. 11"This is what you are to do," they said. "Kill every male and every woman who is not a virgin." 12They found among the people living in Jabesh Gilead four hundred young women who had never slept with a man, and they took them to the camp at Shiloh in Canaan.

13Then the whole assembly sent an offer of peace to the Benjamites at the rock of Rimmon. 14So the Benjamites returned at that time and were given the women of Jabesh Gilead who had been spared. But there were not enough for all of them.

15The people grieved for Benjamin, because the LORD had made a gap in the tribes of Israel. 16And the elders of the assembly said, "With the women of Benjamin destroyed, how shall we provide wives for the men who are left? 17The Benjamite survivors must have heirs," they said, "so that a tribe of Israel will not be wiped out. 18We can't give them our daughters as wives, since we Israelites have taken this oath: 'Cursed be anyone who gives a wife to a Benjamite.' 19But look, there is the annual festival of the LORD in Shiloh, to the north of Bethel, and east of the road that goes from Bethel to Shechem, and to the south of Lebonah."

20So they instructed the Benjamites, saying, "Go and hide in the vineyards 21and watch. When the girls of Shiloh come out to join in the dancing, then rush from the vineyards and each of you seize a wife from the girls of Shiloh and go to the land of Benjamin. 22When their fathers or brothers complain to us, we will say to them, 'Do us a kindness by helping them, because we did not get wives for them during the war, and you are innocent, since you did not give your daughters to them.' "

23So that is what the Benjamites did. While the girls were dancing, each man caught one and carried her off to be his wife. Then they returned to their inheritance and rebuilt the towns and settled in them.

24At that time the Israelites left that place and went home to their tribes and clans, each to his own inheritance.

25In those days Israel had no king; everyone did as he saw fit.

[a]2 Or *to the house of God* [b]4 Traditionally *peace offerings*

Ruth

Introduction:

This book is named after the leading character whose story is told here. It may have been written during the reign of David, whose ancestry is traced in the final verses to his great-grandfather Boaz, whose wife was Ruth.

Ruth tells the story of an Israelite couple who moved to Moab during a famine in Canaan. The husband and his two sons died, leaving the mother (Naomi) alone with her two daughters-in-law (Orpah and Ruth). Naomi decided to move back to Israel and Ruth insisted on going back with her. Back in Israel, they looked to their relative Boaz for help and Ruth finally married Boaz. From their family came the royal family of David and the Messiah, Jesus Christ.

This book teaches us much about love and devotion. It also teaches us of God's concern for our everyday needs and that he is working out his plan for salvation.

Outline of contents:

Naomi and Ruth

1 In the days when the judges ruled,[a]
there was a famine in the land, and a
man from Bethlehem in Judah, together with
his wife and two sons, went to live for a while
in the country of Moab. 2The man's name
was Elimelech, his wife's name Naomi, and
the names of his two sons were Mahlon and
Kilion. They were Ephrathites from Bethlehem,
Judah. And they went to Moab and
lived there.
3Now Elimelech, Naomi's husband, died,
and she was left with her two sons. 4They
married Moabite women, one named Orpah
and the other Ruth. After they had lived there
about ten years, 5both Mahlon and Kilion
also died, and Naomi was left without her two
sons and her husband.
6When she heard in Moab that the LORD
had come to the aid of his people by providing
food for them, Naomi and her daughters-in-law
prepared to return home from
there. 7With her two daughters-in-law she
left the place where she had been living and
set out on the road that would take them
back to the land of Judah.
8Then Naomi said to her two daughters-in-law,
"Go back, each of you, to your mother's
home. May the LORD show kindness to you,
as you have shown to your dead and to me.
9May the LORD grant that each of you will find
rest in the home of another husband."
Then she kissed them and they wept
aloud 10and said to her, "We will go back with
you to your people."
11But Naomi said, "Return home, my
daughters. Why would you come with me?
Am I going to have any more sons, who
could become your husbands? 12Return
home, my daughters; I am too old to have
another husband. Even if I thought there was
still hope for me—even if I had a husband
tonight and then gave birth to sons— 13would
you wait until they grew up? Would you remain
unmarried for them? No, my daughters.
It is more bitter for me than for you, because
the LORD's hand has gone out against
me!"
14At this they wept again. Then Orpah
kissed her mother-in-law good-by, but Ruth
clung to her.
15"Look," said Naomi, "your sister-in-law

a 1 Traditionally *judged*

is going back to her people and her gods. Go
back with her."
16 But Ruth replied, "Don't urge me to leave
you or to turn back from you. Where you go I
will go, and where you stay I will stay. Your
people will be my people and your God my
God. 17 Where you die I will die, and there I
will be buried. May the LORD deal with me, be
it ever so severely, if anything but death separates you and me." 18 When Naomi realized
that Ruth was determined to go with her, she
stopped urging her.
19 So the two women went on until they
came to Bethlehem. When they arrived in
Bethlehem, the whole town was stirred because of them, and the women exclaimed,
"Can this be Naomi?"
20 "Don't call me Naomi,[a]" she told them.
"Call me Mara,[b] because the Almighty[c] has
made my life very bitter. 21 I went away full,
but the LORD has brought me back empty.
Why call me Naomi? The LORD has afflicted[d]
me; the Almighty has brought misfortune
upon me."
22 So Naomi returned from Moab accompanied by Ruth the Moabitess, her daughter-
in-law, arriving in Bethlehem as the barley
harvest was beginning.

Ruth Meets Boaz

2 Now Naomi had a relative on her husband's side, from the clan of Elimelech,
a man of standing, whose name was Boaz.
2 And Ruth the Moabitess said to Naomi,
"Let me go to the fields and pick up the
leftover grain behind anyone in whose eyes I
find favor."
Naomi said to her, "Go ahead, my daughter." 3 So she went out and began to glean in
the fields behind the harvesters. As it turned
out, she found herself working in a field belonging to Boaz, who was from the clan of
Elimelech.
4 Just then Boaz arrived from Bethlehem
and greeted the harvesters, "The LORD be
with you!"
"The LORD bless you!" they called back.
5 Boaz asked the foreman of his harvesters, "Whose young woman is that?"
6 The foreman replied, "She is the Moabitess who came back from Moab with Naomi.
7 She said, 'Please let me glean and gather
among the sheaves behind the harvesters.'
She went into the field and has worked
steadily from morning till now, except for a
short rest in the shelter."
8 So Boaz said to Ruth, "My daughter, listen to me. Don't go and glean in another field
and don't go away from here. Stay here with
my servant girls. 9 Watch the field where the
men are harvesting, and follow along after
the girls. I have told the men not to touch you.
And whenever you are thirsty, go and get a
drink from the water jars the men have
filled."
10 At this, she bowed down with her face to
the ground. She exclaimed, "Why have I
found such favor in your eyes that you notice
me—a foreigner?"
11 Boaz replied, "I've been told all about
what you have done for your mother-in-law
since the death of your husband—how you
left your father and mother and your homeland and came to live with a people you did
not know before. 12 May the LORD repay you
for what you have done. May you be richly
rewarded by the LORD, the God of Israel, under whose wings you have come to take
refuge."
13 "May I continue to find favor in your eyes,
my lord," she said. "You have given me comfort and have spoken kindly to your servant—though I do not have the standing of
one of your servant girls."
14 At mealtime Boaz said to her, "Come
over here. Have some bread and dip it in the
wine vinegar."
When she sat down with the harvesters,
he offered her some roasted grain. She ate
all she wanted and had some left over. 15 As
she got up to glean, Boaz gave orders to his
men, "Even if she gathers among the
sheaves, don't embarrass her. 16 Rather, pull
out some stalks for her from the bundles and
leave them for her to pick up, and don't
rebuke her."
17 So Ruth gleaned in the field until evening. Then she threshed the barley she had
gathered, and it amounted to about an
ephah.[e] 18 She carried it back to town, and
her mother-in-law saw how much she had
gathered. Ruth also brought out and gave
her what she had left over after she had
eaten enough.
19 Her mother-in-law asked her, "Where
did you glean today? Where did you work?
Blessed be the man who took notice of you!"
Then Ruth told her mother-in-law about

[a] 20 *Naomi* means *pleasant,* also in verse 21. [b] 20 *Mara* means *bitter.* [c] 20 Hebrew *Shaddai;* also in verse 21 [d] 21 Or *has testified against* [e] 17 That is, probably about 3/5 bushel (about 22 liters)

the one at whose place she had been working. "The name of the man I worked with
today is Boaz," she said.
20"The LORD bless him!" Naomi said to her
daughter-in-law. "He has not stopped showing his kindness to the living and the dead."
She added, "That man is our close relative;
he is one of our kinsman-redeemers."
21Then Ruth the Moabitess said, "He even
said to me, 'Stay with my workers until they
finish harvesting all my grain.' "
22Naomi said to Ruth her daughter-in-law,
"It will be good for you, my daughter, to go
with his girls, because in someone else's
field you might be harmed."
23So Ruth stayed close to the servant girls
of Boaz to glean until the barley and wheat
harvests were finished. And she lived with
her mother-in-law.

Ruth and Boaz at the Threshing Floor

3 One day Naomi her mother-in-law said
to her, "My daughter, should I not try to
find a home[a] for you, where you will be well
provided for? 2Is not Boaz, with whose servant girls you have been, a kinsman of ours?
Tonight he will be winnowing barley on the
threshing floor. 3Wash and perfume yourself,
and put on your best clothes. Then go down
to the threshing floor, but don't let him know
you are there until he has finished eating and
drinking. 4When he lies down, note the place
where he is lying. Then go and uncover his
feet and lie down. He will tell you what to do."
5"I will do whatever you say," Ruth answered. 6So she went down to the threshing
floor and did everything her mother-in-law
told her to do.
7When Boaz had finished eating and drinking and was in good spirits, he went over to
lie down at the far end of the grain pile. Ruth
approached quietly, uncovered his feet and
lay down. 8In the middle of the night something startled the man, and he turned and
discovered a woman lying at his feet.
9"Who are you?" he asked.
"I am your servant Ruth," she said.
"Spread the corner of your garment over me,
since you are a kinsman-redeemer."
10"The LORD bless you, my daughter," he
replied. "This kindness is greater than that
which you showed earlier: You have not run
after the younger men, whether rich or poor.
11And now, my daughter, don't be afraid. I
will do for you all you ask. All my fellow
townsmen know that you are a woman of
noble character. 12Although it is true that I am
near of kin, there is a kinsman-redeemer
nearer than I. 13Stay here for the night, and in
the morning if he wants to redeem, good; let
him redeem. But if he is not willing, as surely
as the LORD lives I will do it. Lie here until
morning."
14So she lay at his feet until morning, but
got up before anyone could be recognized;
and he said, "Don't let it be known that a
woman came to the threshing floor."
15He also said, "Bring me the shawl you
are wearing and hold it out." When she did
so, he poured into it six measures of barley
and put it on her. Then he[b] went back to
town.
16When Ruth came to her mother-in-law,
Naomi asked, "How did it go, my daughter?"
Then she told her everything Boaz had
done for her 17and added, "He gave me
these six measures of barley, saying, 'Don't
go back to your mother-in-law empty-
handed.' "
18Then Naomi said, "Wait, my daughter,
until you find out what happens. For the man
will not rest until the matter is settled today."

Boaz Marries Ruth

4 Meanwhile Boaz went up to the town
gate and sat there. When the kinsman-
redeemer he had mentioned came along,
Boaz said, "Come over here, my friend, and
sit down." So he went over and sat down.
2Boaz took ten of the elders of the town
and said, "Sit here," and they did so. 3Then
he said to the kinsman-redeemer, "Naomi,
who has come back from Moab, is selling the
piece of land that belonged to our brother
Elimelech. 4I thought I should bring the matter to your attention and suggest that you buy
it in the presence of these seated here and in
the presence of the elders of my people. If
you will redeem it, do so. But if you[c] will not,
tell me, so I will know. For no one has the
right to do it except you, and I am next in
line."
"I will redeem it," he said.
5Then Boaz said, "On the day you buy the
land from Naomi and from Ruth the Moabitess, you acquire[d] the dead man's widow, in

[a] 1 Hebrew *find rest* (see Ruth 1:9) [b] 15 Most Hebrew manuscripts; many Hebrew manuscripts, Vulgate and Syriac *she* [c] 4 Many Hebrew manuscripts, Septuagint, Vulgate and Syriac; most Hebrew manuscripts *he*
[d] 5 Hebrew; Vulgate and Syriac *Naomi, you acquire Ruth the Moabitess,*

order to maintain the name of the dead with
his property."
6At this, the kinsman-redeemer said,
"Then I cannot redeem it because I might
endanger my own estate. You redeem it
yourself. I cannot do it."
7(Now in earlier times in Israel, for the redemption and transfer of property to become
final, one party took off his sandal and gave it
to the other. This was the method of legalizing transactions in Israel.)
8So the kinsman-redeemer said to Boaz,
"Buy it yourself." And he removed his sandal.
9Then Boaz announced to the elders and
all the people, "Today you are witnesses that
I have bought from Naomi all the property of
Elimelech, Kilion and Mahlon. 10I have also
acquired Ruth the Moabitess, Mahlon's
widow, as my wife, in order to maintain the
name of the dead with his property, so that
his name will not disappear from among his
family or from the town records. Today you
are witnesses!"
11Then the elders and all those at the gate
said, "We are witnesses. May the LORD make
the woman who is coming into your home
like Rachel and Leah, who together built up
the house of Israel. May you have standing
in Ephrathah and be famous in Bethlehem.
12Through the offspring the LORD gives you
by this young woman, may your family be
like that of Perez, whom Tamar bore to
Judah."

The Genealogy of David

13So Boaz took Ruth and she became his
wife. Then he went to her, and the LORD enabled her to conceive, and she gave birth to
a son. 14The women said to Naomi: "Praise
be to the LORD, who this day has not left you
without a kinsman-redeemer. May he
become famous throughout Israel! 15He will
renew your life and sustain you in your old
age. For your daughter-in-law, who loves
you and who is better to you than seven
sons, has given him birth."
16Then Naomi took the child, laid him in her
lap and cared for him. 17The women living
there said, "Naomi has a son." And they
named him Obed. He was the father of
Jesse, the father of David.
18This, then, is the family line of Perez:

Perez was the father of Hezron,
19Hezron the father of Ram,
Ram the father of Amminadab,
20Amminadab the father of Nahshon,
Nahshon the father of Salmon,[a]
21Salmon the father of Boaz,
Boaz the father of Obed,
22Obed the father of Jesse,
and Jesse the father of David.

[a]*20* A few Hebrew manuscripts, some Septuagint manuscripts and Vulgate (see also verse 21 and Septuagint of 1 Chron. 2:11); most Hebrew manuscripts *Salma*

I Samuel

Introduction:

The book of I Samuel records the lives of Samuel and Saul, and much of the life of David. First Samuel begins with the birth of Samuel and his training in the temple. It describes how he led Israel as prophet, priest and judge.

When the people of Israel demanded a king, Samuel, by God's leading, anointed Saul to be the first king of Israel. But Saul was disobedient to God and God rejected him as king. Then Samuel secretly anointed David to take Saul's place. The struggles between Saul and David make up the rest of this book. Although we learn much of these people's disobedience there is a stronger emphasis on their goodness and obedience to God.

It was during this part of Israel's history that the nation changed from judges as leaders to having a king as their neighboring nations had. Samuel, as prophet, priest and judge, had a great deal of influence throughout this time period.

Outline of contents:

Eli as priest and judge (1:1–4:22)
Samuel as leader of Israel (5:1–8:22)
Saul the first king of Israel (9:1–15:35)
David and Saul (16:1–30:31)
Death of Saul (31:1–13)

The Birth of Samuel

1 There was a certain man from Ramathaim, a Zuphite[a] from the hill country of
Ephraim, whose name was Elkanah son of
Jeroham, the son of Elihu, the son of Tohu,
the son of Zuph, an Ephraimite. [2]He had two
wives; one was called Hannah and the other
Peninnah. Peninnah had children, but Hannah had none.
[3]Year after year this man went up from his
town to worship and sacrifice to the LORD
Almighty at Shiloh, where Hophni and Phinehas, the two sons of Eli, were priests of the
LORD. [4]Whenever the day came for Elkanah
to sacrifice, he would give portions of the
meat to his wife Peninnah and to all her sons
and daughters. [5]But to Hannah he gave a
double portion because he loved her, and
the LORD had closed her womb. [6]And because the LORD had closed her womb, her
rival kept provoking her in order to irritate
her. [7]This went on year after year. Whenever
Hannah went up to the house of the LORD, her
rival provoked her till she wept and would not
eat. [8]Elkanah her husband would say to her,
"Hannah, why are you weeping? Why don't
you eat? Why are you downhearted? Don't I
mean more to you than ten sons?"
[9]Once when they had finished eating and
drinking in Shiloh, Hannah stood up. Now Eli
the priest was sitting on a chair by the doorpost of the LORD's temple.[b] [10]In bitterness of
soul Hannah wept much and prayed to the
LORD. [11]And she made a vow, saying, "O
LORD Almighty, if you will only look upon your
servant's misery and remember me, and not
forget your servant but give her a son, then I
will give him to the LORD for all the days of his
life, and no razor will ever be used on his
head."
[12]As she kept on praying to the LORD, Eli
observed her mouth. [13]Hannah was praying
in her heart, and her lips were moving but her
voice was not heard. Eli thought she was
drunk [14]and said to her, "How long will you
keep on getting drunk? Get rid of your wine."
[15]"Not so, my lord," Hannah replied, "I am
a woman who is deeply troubled. I have not

[a]*1* Or *from Ramathaim Zuphim*   [b]*9* That is, tabernacle

been drinking wine or beer; I was pouring out
my soul to the LORD. 16Do not take your servant for a wicked woman; I have been praying here out of my great anguish and grief."
17Eli answered, "Go in peace, and may the
God of Israel grant you what you have asked
of him."
18She said, "May your servant find favor in
your eyes." Then she went her way and ate
something, and her face was no longer
downcast.
19Early the next morning they arose and
worshiped before the LORD and then went
back to their home at Ramah. Elkanah lay
with Hannah his wife, and the LORD remembered her. 20So in the course of time Hannah
conceived and gave birth to a son. She
named him Samuel,[a] saying, "Because I
asked the LORD for him."

Hannah Dedicates Samuel

21When the man Elkanah went up with all
his family to offer the annual sacrifice to the
LORD and to fulfill his vow, 22Hannah did not
go. She said to her husband, "After the boy is
weaned, I will take him and present him before the LORD, and he will live there always."
23"Do what seems best to you," Elkanah
her husband told her. "Stay here until you
have weaned him; only may the LORD make
good his[b] word." So the woman stayed at
home and nursed her son until she had
weaned him.
24After he was weaned, she took the boy
with her, young as he was, along with a
three-year-old bull,[c] an ephah[d] of flour and a
skin of wine, and brought him to the house of
the LORD at Shiloh. 25When they had slaughtered the bull, they brought the boy to Eli,
26and she said to him, "As surely as you live,
my lord, I am the woman who stood here
beside you praying to the LORD. 27I prayed for
this child, and the LORD has granted me what
I asked of him. 28So now I give him to the
LORD. For his whole life he will be given over
to the LORD." And he worshiped the LORD
there.

Hannah's Prayer

2 Then Hannah prayed and said:

"My heart rejoices in the LORD;
in the LORD my horn[e] is lifted high.
My mouth boasts over my enemies,
for I delight in your deliverance.

2"There is no one holy[f] like the LORD;
there is no one besides you;
there is no Rock like our God.

3"Do not keep talking so proudly
or let your mouth speak such
arrogance,
for the LORD is a God who knows,
and by him deeds are weighed.

4"The bows of the warriors are broken,
but those who stumbled are armed with
strength.
5Those who were full hire themselves out
for food,
but those who were hungry hunger no
more.
She who was barren has borne seven
children,
but she who has had many sons pines
away.

6"The LORD brings death and makes alive;
he brings down to the grave[g] and
raises up.
7The LORD sends poverty and wealth;
he humbles and he exalts.
8He raises the poor from the dust
and lifts the needy from the ash heap;
he seats them with princes
and has them inherit a throne of honor.

"For the foundations of the earth are the
LORD's;
upon them he has set the world.
9He will guard the feet of his saints,
but the wicked will be silenced in
darkness.

"It is not by strength that one prevails;
10 those who oppose the LORD will be
shattered.
He will thunder against them from
heaven;
the LORD will judge the ends of the
earth.

"He will give strength to his king
and exalt the horn of his anointed."

11Then Elkanah went home to Ramah, but
the boy ministered before the LORD under Eli
the priest.

[a]20 *Samuel* sounds like the Hebrew for *heard of God.* [b]23 Masoretic Text; Dead Sea Scrolls, Septuagint and Syriac *your* [c]24 Dead Sea Scrolls, Septuagint and Syriac; Masoretic Text *with three bulls* [d]24 That is, probably about 3/5 bushel (about 22 liters) [e]1 *Horn* here symbolizes strength; also in verse 10. [f]2 Or *no Holy One* [g]6 Hebrew *Sheol*

Eli's Wicked Sons

[12]Eli's sons were wicked men; they had no regard for the LORD. [13]Now it was the practice of the priests with the people that whenever anyone offered a sacrifice and while the meat was being boiled, the servant of the priest would come with a three-pronged fork in his hand. [14]He would plunge it into the pan or kettle or caldron or pot, and the priest would take for himself whatever the fork brought up. This is how they treated all the Israelites who came to Shiloh. [15]But even before the fat was burned, the servant of the priest would come and say to the man who was sacrificing, "Give the priest some meat to roast; he won't accept boiled meat from you, but only raw."

[16]If the man said to him, "Let the fat be burned up first, and then take whatever you want," the servant would then answer, "No, hand it over now; if you don't, I'll take it by force."

[17]This sin of the young men was very great in the LORD's sight, for they[a] were treating the LORD's offering with contempt.

[18]But Samuel was ministering before the LORD—a boy wearing a linen ephod. [19]Each year his mother made him a little robe and took it to him when she went up with her husband to offer the annual sacrifice. [20]Eli would bless Elkanah and his wife, saying, "May the LORD give you children by this woman to take the place of the one she prayed for and gave to the LORD." Then they would go home. [21]And the LORD was gracious to Hannah; she conceived and gave birth to three sons and two daughters. Meanwhile, the boy Samuel grew up in the presence of the LORD.

[22]Now Eli, who was very old, heard about everything his sons were doing to all Israel and how they slept with the women who served at the entrance to the Tent of Meeting. [23]So he said to them, "Why do you do such things? I hear from all the people about these wicked deeds of yours. [24]No, my sons; it is not a good report that I hear spreading among the LORD's people. [25]If a man sins against another man, God[b] may mediate for him; but if a man sins against the LORD, who will intercede for him?" His sons, however, did not listen to their father's rebuke, for it was the LORD's will to put them to death.

[26]And the boy Samuel continued to grow in stature and in favor with the LORD and with men.

Prophecy Against the House of Eli

[27]Now a man of God came to Eli and said to him, "This is what the LORD says: 'Did I not clearly reveal myself to your father's house when they were in Egypt under Pharaoh? [28]I chose your father out of all the tribes of Israel to be my priest, to go up to my altar, to burn incense, and to wear an ephod in my presence. I also gave your father's house all the offerings made with fire by the Israelites. [29]Why do you[c] scorn my sacrifice and offering that I prescribed for my dwelling? Why do you honor your sons more than me by fattening yourselves on the choice parts of every offering made by my people Israel?'

[30]"Therefore the LORD, the God of Israel, declares: 'I promised that your house and your father's house would minister before me forever.' But now the LORD declares: 'Far be it from me! Those who honor me I will honor, but those who despise me will be disdained. [31]The time is coming when I will cut short your strength and the strength of your father's house, so that there will not be an old man in your family line [32]and you will see distress in my dwelling. Although good will be done to Israel, in your family line there will never be an old man. [33]Every one of you that I do not cut off from my altar will be spared only to blind your eyes with tears and to grieve your heart, and all your descendants will die in the prime of life.

[34]" 'And what happens to your two sons, Hophni and Phinehas, will be a sign to you—they will both die on the same day. [35]I will raise up for myself a faithful priest, who will do according to what is in my heart and mind. I will firmly establish his house, and he will minister before my anointed one always. [36]Then everyone left in your family line will come and bow down before him for a piece of silver and a crust of bread and plead, "Appoint me to some priestly office so I can have food to eat." ' "

The LORD Calls Samuel

3 The boy Samuel ministered before the LORD under Eli. In those days the word of the LORD was rare; there were not many visions.

[2]One night Eli, whose eyes were becom-

[a]*17* Or *men* [b]*25* Or *the judges* [c]*29* The Hebrew is plural.

ing so weak that he could barely see, was lying down in his usual place. [3]The lamp of God had not yet gone out, and Samuel was lying down in the temple[a] of the LORD, where the ark of God was. [4]Then the LORD called Samuel.

Samuel answered, "Here I am." [5]And he ran to Eli and said, "Here I am; you called me."

But Eli said, "I did not call; go back and lie down." So he went and lay down.

[6]Again the LORD called, "Samuel!" And Samuel got up and went to Eli and said, "Here I am; you called me."

"My son," Eli said, "I did not call; go back and lie down."

[7]Now Samuel did not yet know the LORD: The word of the LORD had not yet been revealed to him.

[8]The LORD called Samuel a third time, and Samuel got up and went to Eli and said, "Here I am; you called me."

Then Eli realized that the LORD was calling the boy. [9]So Eli told Samuel, "Go and lie down, and if he calls you, say, 'Speak, LORD, for your servant is listening.' " So Samuel went and lay down in his place.

[10]The LORD came and stood there, calling as at the other times, "Samuel! Samuel!"

Then Samuel said, "Speak, for your servant is listening."

[11]And the LORD said to Samuel: "See, I am about to do something in Israel that will make the ears of everyone who hears of it tingle. [12]At that time I will carry out against Eli everything I spoke against his family—from beginning to end. [13]For I told him that I would judge his family forever because of the sin he knew about; his sons made themselves contemptible,[b] and he failed to restrain them. [14]Therefore, I swore to the house of Eli, 'The guilt of Eli's house will never be atoned for by sacrifice or offering.' "

[15]Samuel lay down until morning and then opened the doors of the house of the LORD. He was afraid to tell Eli the vision, [16]but Eli called him and said, "Samuel, my son."

Samuel answered, "Here I am."

[17]"What was it he said to you?" Eli asked. "Do not hide it from me. May God deal with you, be it ever so severely, if you hide from me anything he told you." [18]So Samuel told him everything, hiding nothing from him. Then Eli said, "He is the LORD; let him do what is good in his eyes."

[19]The LORD was with Samuel as he grew up, and he let none of his words fall to the ground. [20]And all Israel from Dan to Beersheba recognized that Samuel was attested as a prophet of the LORD. [21]The LORD continued to appear at Shiloh, and there he revealed himself to Samuel through his word.

4 And Samuel's word came to all Israel.

The Philistines Capture the Ark

Now the Israelites went out to fight against the Philistines. The Israelites camped at Ebenezer, and the Philistines at Aphek. [2]The Philistines deployed their forces to meet Israel, and as the battle spread, Israel was defeated by the Philistines, who killed about four thousand of them on the battlefield. [3]When the soldiers returned to camp, the elders of Israel asked, "Why did the LORD bring defeat upon us today before the Philistines? Let us bring the ark of the LORD's covenant from Shiloh, so that it[c] may go with us and save us from the hand of our enemies."

[4]So the people sent men to Shiloh, and they brought back the ark of the covenant of the LORD Almighty, who is enthroned between the cherubim. And Eli's two sons, Hophni and Phinehas, were there with the ark of the covenant of God.

[5]When the ark of the LORD's covenant came into the camp, all Israel raised such a great shout that the ground shook. [6]Hearing the uproar, the Philistines asked, "What's all this shouting in the Hebrew camp?"

When they learned that the ark of the LORD had come into the camp, [7]the Philistines were afraid. "A god has come into the camp," they said. "We're in trouble! Nothing like this has happened before. [8]Woe to us! Who will deliver us from the hand of these mighty gods? They are the gods who struck the Egyptians with all kinds of plagues in the desert. [9]Be strong, Philistines! Be men, or you will be subject to the Hebrews, as they have been to you. Be men, and fight!"

[10]So the Philistines fought, and the Israelites were defeated and every man fled to his tent. The slaughter was very great; Israel lost thirty thousand foot soldiers. [11]The ark of God was captured, and Eli's two sons, Hophni and Phinehas, died.

[a]3 That is, tabernacle [b]13 Masoretic Text; an ancient Hebrew scribal tradition and Septuagint *sons blasphemed God* [c]3 Or *he*

Death of Eli

12That same day a Benjamite ran from the battle line and went to Shiloh, his clothes torn and dust on his head. 13When he arrived, there was Eli sitting on his chair by the side of the road, watching, because his heart feared for the ark of God. When the man entered the town and told what had happened, the whole town sent up a cry.

14Eli heard the outcry and asked, "What is the meaning of this uproar?"

The man hurried over to Eli, 15who was ninety-eight years old and whose eyes were set so that he could not see. 16He told Eli, "I have just come from the battle line; I fled from it this very day."

Eli asked, "What happened, my son?"

17The man who brought the news replied, "Israel fled before the Philistines, and the army has suffered heavy losses. Also your two sons, Hophni and Phinehas, are dead, and the ark of God has been captured."

18When he mentioned the ark of God, Eli fell backward off his chair by the side of the gate. His neck was broken and he died, for he was an old man and heavy. He had led[a] Israel forty years.

19His daughter-in-law, the wife of Phinehas, was pregnant and near the time of delivery. When she heard the news that the ark of God had been captured and that her father-in-law and her husband were dead, she went into labor and gave birth, but was overcome by her labor pains. 20As she was dying, the women attending her said, "Don't despair; you have given birth to a son." But she did not respond or pay any attention.

21She named the boy Ichabod,[b] saying, "The glory has departed from Israel"—because of the capture of the ark of God and the deaths of her father-in-law and her husband. 22She said, "The glory has departed from Israel, for the ark of God has been captured."

The Ark in Ashdod and Ekron

5 After the Philistines had captured the ark of God, they took it from Ebenezer to Ashdod. 2Then they carried the ark into Dagon's temple and set it beside Dagon. 3When the people of Ashdod rose early the next day, there was Dagon, fallen on his face on the ground before the ark of the LORD! They took Dagon and put him back in his place. 4But the following morning when they rose, there was Dagon, fallen on his face on the ground before the ark of the LORD! His head and hands had been broken off and were lying on the threshold; only his body remained. 5That is why to this day neither the priests of Dagon nor any others who enter Dagon's temple at Ashdod step on the threshold.

6The LORD's hand was heavy upon the people of Ashdod and its vicinity; he brought devastation upon them and afflicted them with tumors.[c] 7When the men of Ashdod saw what was happening, they said, "The ark of the god of Israel must not stay here with us, because his hand is heavy upon us and upon Dagon our god." 8So they called together all the rulers of the Philistines and asked them, "What shall we do with the ark of the god of Israel?"

They answered, "Have the ark of the god of Israel moved to Gath." So they moved the ark of the God of Israel.

9But after they had moved it, the LORD's hand was against that city, throwing it into a great panic. He afflicted the people of the city, both young and old, with an outbreak of tumors.[d] 10So they sent the ark of God to Ekron.

As the ark of God was entering Ekron, the people of Ekron cried out, "They have brought the ark of the god of Israel around to us to kill us and our people." 11So they called together all the rulers of the Philistines and said, "Send the ark of the god of Israel away; let it go back to its own place, or it[e] will kill us and our people." For death had filled the city with panic; God's hand was very heavy upon it. 12Those who did not die were afflicted with tumors, and the outcry of the city went up to heaven.

The Ark Returned to Israel

6 When the ark of the LORD had been in Philistine territory seven months, 2the Philistines called for the priests and the diviners and said, "What shall we do with the ark of the LORD? Tell us how we should send it back to its place."

3They answered, "If you return the ark of the god of Israel, do not send it away empty, but by all means send a guilt offering to him.

[a]18 Traditionally *judged* [b]21 *Ichabod* means *no glory.* [c]6 Hebrew; Septuagint and Vulgate *tumors. And rats appeared in their land, and death and destruction were throughout the city* [d]9 Or *with tumors in the groin* (see Septuagint) [e]11 Or *he*

Then you will be healed, and you will know
why his hand has not been lifted from you."
4The Philistines asked, "What guilt offering should we send to him?"
They replied, "Five gold tumors and five
gold rats, according to the number of the
Philistine rulers, because the same plague
has struck both you and your rulers. 5Make
models of the tumors and of the rats that are
destroying the country, and pay honor to Israel's god. Perhaps he will lift his hand from
you and your gods and your land. 6Why do
you harden your hearts as the Egyptians and
Pharaoh did? When he[a] treated them harshly, did they not send the Israelites out so they
could go on their way?
7"Now then, get a new cart ready, with two
cows that have calved and have never been
yoked. Hitch the cows to the cart, but take
their calves away and pen them up. 8Take
the ark of the LORD and put it on the cart, and
in a chest beside it put the gold objects you
are sending back to him as a guilt offering.
Send it on its way, 9but keep watching it. If it
goes up to its own territory, toward Beth Shemesh, then the LORD has brought this great
disaster on us. But if it does not, then we will
know that it was not his hand that struck us
and that it happened to us by chance."
10So they did this. They took two such
cows and hitched them to the cart and
penned up their calves. 11They placed the
ark of the LORD on the cart and along with it
the chest containing the gold rats and the
models of the tumors. 12Then the cows went
straight up toward Beth Shemesh, keeping
on the road and lowing all the way; they did
not turn to the right or to the left. The rulers of
the Philistines followed them as far as the
border of Beth Shemesh.
13Now the people of Beth Shemesh were
harvesting their wheat in the valley, and
when they looked up and saw the ark, they
rejoiced at the sight. 14The cart came to the
field of Joshua of Beth Shemesh, and there it
stopped beside a large rock. The people
chopped up the wood of the cart and sacrificed the cows as a burnt offering to the LORD.
15The Levites took down the ark of the LORD,
together with the chest containing the gold
objects, and placed them on the large rock.
On that day the people of Beth Shemesh
offered burnt offerings and made sacrifices
to the LORD. 16The five rulers of the Philistines
saw all this and then returned that same day
to Ekron.
17These are the gold tumors the Philistines
sent as a guilt offering to the LORD—one each
for Ashdod, Gaza, Ashkelon, Gath and Ekron. 18And the number of the gold rats was
according to the number of Philistine towns
belonging to the five rulers—the fortified
towns with their country villages. The large
rock, on which[b] they set the ark of the LORD,
is a witness to this day in the field of Joshua
of Beth Shemesh.
19But God struck down some of the men of
Beth Shemesh, putting seventy[c] of them to
death because they had looked into the ark
of the LORD. The people mourned because of
the heavy blow the LORD had dealt them,
20and the men of Beth Shemesh asked,
"Who can stand in the presence of the LORD,
this holy God? To whom will the ark go up
from here?"
21Then they sent messengers to the
people of Kiriath Jearim, saying, "The Philistines have returned the ark of the LORD.
Come down and take it up to your place."
7 1So the men of Kiriath Jearim came and
took up the ark of the LORD. They took it
to Abinadab's house on the hill and consecrated Eleazar his son to guard the ark of the
LORD.

Samuel Subdues the Philistines at Mizpah

2It was a long time, twenty years in all, that
the ark remained at Kiriath Jearim, and all
the people of Israel mourned and sought after the LORD. 3And Samuel said to the whole
house of Israel, "If you are returning to the
LORD with all your hearts, then rid yourselves
of the foreign gods and the Ashtoreths and
commit yourselves to the LORD and serve him
only, and he will deliver you out of the hand
of the Philistines." 4So the Israelites put
away their Baals and Ashtoreths, and served
the LORD only.
5Then Samuel said, "Assemble all Israel at
Mizpah and I will intercede with the LORD for
you." 6When they had assembled at Mizpah,
they drew water and poured it out before the
LORD. On that day they fasted and there they
confessed, "We have sinned against the
LORD." And Samuel was leader[d] of Israel at
Mizpah.
7When the Philistines heard that Israel had

[a]6 That is, God [b]18 A few Hebrew manuscripts (see also Septuagint); most Hebrew manuscripts *villages as far as Greater Abel, where* [c]19 A few Hebrew manuscripts; most Hebrew manuscripts and Septuagint *50,070*
[d]6 Traditionally *judge*

assembled at Mizpah, the rulers of the Philistines came up to attack them. And when the Israelites heard of it, they were afraid because of the Philistines. 8They said to Samuel, "Do not stop crying out to the LORD our God for us, that he may rescue us from the hand of the Philistines." 9Then Samuel took a suckling lamb and offered it up as a whole burnt offering to the LORD. He cried out to the LORD on Israel's behalf, and the LORD answered him.

10While Samuel was sacrificing the burnt offering, the Philistines drew near to engage Israel in battle. But that day the LORD thundered with loud thunder against the Philistines and threw them into such a panic that they were routed before the Israelites. 11The men of Israel rushed out of Mizpah and pursued the Philistines, slaughtering them along the way to a point below Beth Car.

12Then Samuel took a stone and set it up between Mizpah and Shen. He named it Ebenezer,[a] saying, "Thus far has the LORD helped us." 13So the Philistines were subdued and did not invade Israelite territory again.

Throughout Samuel's lifetime, the hand of the LORD was against the Philistines. 14The towns from Ekron to Gath that the Philistines had captured from Israel were restored to her, and Israel delivered the neighboring territory from the power of the Philistines. And there was peace between Israel and the Amorites.

15Samuel continued as judge over Israel all the days of his life. 16From year to year he went on a circuit from Bethel to Gilgal to Mizpah, judging Israel in all those places. 17But he always went back to Ramah, where his home was, and there he also judged Israel. And he built an altar there to the LORD.

Israel Asks for a King

8 When Samuel grew old, he appointed his sons as judges for Israel. 2The name of his firstborn was Joel and the name of his second was Abijah, and they served at Beersheba. 3But his sons did not walk in his ways. They turned aside after dishonest gain and accepted bribes and perverted justice.

4So all the elders of Israel gathered together and came to Samuel at Ramah. 5They said to him, "You are old, and your sons do not walk in your ways; now appoint a king to lead[b] us, such as all the other nations have."

6But when they said, "Give us a king to lead us," this displeased Samuel; so he prayed to the LORD. 7And the LORD told him: "Listen to all that the people are saying to you; it is not you they have rejected, but they have rejected me as their king. 8As they have done from the day I brought them up out of Egypt until this day, forsaking me and serving other gods, so they are doing to you. 9Now listen to them; but warn them solemnly and let them know what the king who will reign over them will do."

10Samuel told all the words of the LORD to the people who were asking him for a king. 11He said, "This is what the king who will reign over you will do: He will take your sons and make them serve with his chariots and horses, and they will run in front of his chariots. 12Some he will assign to be commanders of thousands and commanders of fifties, and others to plow his ground and reap his harvest, and still others to make weapons of war and equipment for his chariots. 13He will take your daughters to be perfumers and cooks and bakers. 14He will take the best of your fields and vineyards and olive groves and give them to his attendants. 15He will take a tenth of your grain and of your vintage and give it to his officials and attendants. 16Your menservants and maidservants and the best of your cattle[c] and donkeys he will take for his own use. 17He will take a tenth of your flocks, and you yourselves will become his slaves. 18When that day comes, you will cry out for relief from the king you have chosen, and the LORD will not answer you in that day."

19But the people refused to listen to Samuel. "No!" they said. "We want a king over us. 20Then we will be like all the other nations, with a king to lead us and to go out before us and fight our battles."

21When Samuel heard all that the people said, he repeated it before the LORD. 22The LORD answered, "Listen to them and give them a king."

Then Samuel said to the men of Israel, "Everyone go back to his town."

Samuel Anoints Saul

9 There was a Benjamite, a man of standing, whose name was Kish son of Abiel,

[a]12 *Ebenezer* means *stone of help.* [b]5 Traditionally *judge*; also in verses 6 and 20 [c]16 Septuagint; Hebrew *young men*

the son of Zeror, the son of Becorath, the son of Aphiah of Benjamin. 2He had a son named Saul, an impressive young man without equal among the Israelites—a head taller than any of the others.

3Now the donkeys belonging to Saul's father Kish were lost, and Kish said to his son Saul, "Take one of the servants with you and go and look for the donkeys." 4So he passed through the hill country of Ephraim and through the area around Shalisha, but they did not find them. They went on into the district of Shaalim, but the donkeys were not there. Then he passed through the territory of Benjamin, but they did not find them.

5When they reached the district of Zuph, Saul said to the servant who was with him, "Come, let's go back, or my father will stop thinking about the donkeys and start worrying about us."

6But the servant replied, "Look, in this town there is a man of God; he is highly respected, and everything he says comes true. Let's go there now. Perhaps he will tell us what way to take."

7Saul said to his servant, "If we go, what can we give the man? The food in our sacks is gone. We have no gift to take to the man of God. What do we have?"

8The servant answered him again. "Look," he said, "I have a quarter of a shekel[a] of silver. I will give it to the man of God so that he will tell us what way to take." 9(Formerly in Israel, if a man went to inquire of God, he would say, "Come, let us go to the seer," because the prophet of today used to be called a seer.)

10"Good," Saul said to his servant. "Come, let's go." So they set out for the town where the man of God was.

11As they were going up the hill to the town, they met some girls coming out to draw water, and they asked them, "Is the seer here?"

12"He is," they answered. "He's ahead of you. Hurry now; he has just come to our town today, for the people have a sacrifice at the high place. 13As soon as you enter the town, you will find him before he goes up to the high place to eat. The people will not begin eating until he comes, because he must bless the sacrifice; afterward, those who are invited will eat. Go up now; you should find him about this time."

14They went up to the town, and as they were entering it, there was Samuel, coming toward them on his way up to the high place.

15Now the day before Saul came, the LORD had revealed this to Samuel: 16"About this time tomorrow I will send you a man from the land of Benjamin. Anoint him leader over my people Israel; he will deliver my people from the hand of the Philistines. I have looked upon my people, for their cry has reached me."

17When Samuel caught sight of Saul, the LORD said to him, "This is the man I spoke to you about; he will govern my people."

18Saul approached Samuel in the gateway and asked, "Would you please tell me where the seer's house is?"

19"I am the seer," Samuel replied. "Go up ahead of me to the high place, for today you are to eat with me, and in the morning I will let you go and will tell you all that is in your heart. 20As for the donkeys you lost three days ago, do not worry about them; they have been found. And to whom is all the desire of Israel turned, if not to you and all your father's family?"

21Saul answered, "But am I not a Benjamite, from the smallest tribe of Israel, and is not my clan the least of all the clans of the tribe of Benjamin? Why do you say such a thing to me?"

22Then Samuel brought Saul and his servant into the hall and seated them at the head of those who were invited—about thirty in number. 23Samuel said to the cook, "Bring the piece of meat I gave you, the one I told you to lay aside."

24So the cook took up the leg with what was on it and set it in front of Saul. Samuel said, "Here is what has been kept for you. Eat, because it was set aside for you for this occasion, from the time I said, 'I have invited guests.'" And Saul dined with Samuel that day.

25After they came down from the high place to the town, Samuel talked with Saul on the roof of his house. 26They rose about daybreak and Samuel called to Saul on the roof, "Get ready, and I will send you on your way." When Saul got ready, he and Samuel went outside together. 27As they were going down to the edge of the town, Samuel said to Saul, "Tell the servant to go on ahead of us"—and the servant did so—"but you stay here awhile, so that I may give you a message from God."

[a]8 That is, about 1/10 ounce (about 3 grams)

10 Then Samuel took a flask of oil and poured it on Saul's head and kissed him, saying, "Has not the LORD anointed you leader over his inheritance?[a] 2When you leave me today, you will meet two men near Rachel's tomb, at Zelzah on the border of Benjamin. They will say to you, 'The donkeys you set out to look for have been found. And now your father has stopped thinking about them and is worried about you. He is asking, "What shall I do about my son?" '

3"Then you will go on from there until you reach the great tree of Tabor. Three men going up to God at Bethel will meet you there. One will be carrying three young goats, another three loaves of bread, and another a skin of wine. 4They will greet you and offer you two loaves of bread, which you will accept from them.

5"After that you will go to Gibeah of God, where there is a Philistine outpost. As you approach the town, you will meet a procession of prophets coming down from the high place with lyres, tambourines, flutes and harps being played before them, and they will be prophesying. 6The Spirit of the LORD will come upon you in power, and you will prophesy with them; and you will be changed into a different person. 7Once these signs are fulfilled, do whatever your hand finds to do, for God is with you.

8"Go down ahead of me to Gilgal. I will surely come down to you to sacrifice burnt offerings and fellowship offerings,[b] but you must wait seven days until I come to you and tell you what you are to do."

Saul Made King

9As Saul turned to leave Samuel, God changed Saul's heart, and all these signs were fulfilled that day. 10When they arrived at Gibeah, a procession of prophets met him; the Spirit of God came upon him in power, and he joined in their prophesying. 11When all those who had formerly known him saw him prophesying with the prophets, they asked each other, "What is this that has happened to the son of Kish? Is Saul also among the prophets?"

12A man who lived there answered, "And who is their father?" So it became a saying: "Is Saul also among the prophets?" 13After Saul stopped prophesying, he went to the high place.

14Now Saul's uncle asked him and his servant, "Where have you been?"

"Looking for the donkeys," he said. "But when we saw they were not to be found, we went to Samuel."

15Saul's uncle said, "Tell me what Samuel said to you."

16Saul replied, "He assured us that the donkeys had been found." But he did not tell his uncle what Samuel had said about the kingship.

17Samuel summoned the people of Israel to the LORD at Mizpah 18and said to them, "This is what the LORD, the God of Israel, says: 'I brought Israel up out of Egypt, and I delivered you from the power of Egypt and all the kingdoms that oppressed you.' 19But you have now rejected your God, who saves you out of all your calamities and distresses. And you have said, 'No, set a king over us.' So now present yourselves before the LORD by your tribes and clans."

20When Samuel brought all the tribes of Israel near, the tribe of Benjamin was chosen. 21Then he brought forward the tribe of Benjamin, clan by clan, and Matri's clan was chosen. Finally Saul son of Kish was chosen. But when they looked for him, he was not to be found. 22So they inquired further of the LORD, "Has the man come here yet?"

And the LORD said, "Yes, he has hidden himself among the baggage."

23They ran and brought him out, and as he stood among the people he was a head taller than any of the others. 24Samuel said to all the people, "Do you see the man the LORD has chosen? There is no one like him among all the people."

Then the people shouted, "Long live the king!"

25Samuel explained to the people the regulations of the kingship. He wrote them down on a scroll and deposited it before the LORD. Then Samuel dismissed the people, each to his own home.

26Saul also went to his home in Gibeah, accompanied by valiant men whose hearts God had touched. 27But some troublemakers said, "How can this fellow save us?" They despised him and brought him no gifts. But Saul kept silent.

[a] 1 Hebrew; Septuagint and Vulgate *over his people Israel? You will reign over the LORD's people and save them from the power of their enemies round about. And this will be a sign to you that the LORD has anointed you leader over his inheritance:* [b] 8 Traditionally *peace offerings*

Saul Rescues the City of Jabesh

11 Nahash the Ammonite went up and besieged Jabesh Gilead. And all the men of Jabesh said to him, "Make a treaty with us, and we will be subject to you."

2But Nahash the Ammonite replied, "I will make a treaty with you only on the condition that I gouge out the right eye of every one of you and so bring disgrace on all Israel."

3The elders of Jabesh said to him, "Give us seven days so we can send messengers throughout Israel; if no one comes to rescue us, we will surrender to you."

4When the messengers came to Gibeah of Saul and reported these terms to the people, they all wept aloud. 5Just then Saul was returning from the fields, behind his oxen, and he asked, "What is wrong with the people? Why are they weeping?" Then they repeated to him what the men of Jabesh had said.

6When Saul heard their words, the Spirit of God came upon him in power, and he burned with anger. 7He took a pair of oxen, cut them into pieces, and sent the pieces by messengers throughout Israel, proclaiming, "This is what will be done to the oxen of anyone who does not follow Saul and Samuel." Then the terror of the LORD fell on the people, and they turned out as one man. 8When Saul mustered them at Bezek, the men of Israel numbered three hundred thousand and the men of Judah thirty thousand.

9They told the messengers who had come, "Say to the men of Jabesh Gilead, 'By the time the sun is hot tomorrow, you will be delivered.'" When the messengers went and reported this to the men of Jabesh, they were elated. 10They said to the Ammonites, "Tomorrow we will surrender to you, and you can do to us whatever seems good to you."

11The next day Saul separated his men into three divisions; during the last watch of the night they broke into the camp of the Ammonites and slaughtered them until the heat of the day. Those who survived were scattered, so that no two of them were left together.

Saul Confirmed as King

12The people then said to Samuel, "Who was it that asked, 'Shall Saul reign over us?' Bring these men to us and we will put them to death."

13But Saul said, "No one shall be put to death today, for this day the LORD has rescued Israel."

14Then Samuel said to the people, "Come, let us go to Gilgal and there reaffirm the kingship." 15So all the people went to Gilgal and confirmed Saul as king in the presence of the LORD. There they sacrificed fellowship offerings[a] before the LORD, and Saul and all the Israelites held a great celebration.

Samuel's Farewell Speech

12 Samuel said to all Israel, "I have listened to everything you said to me and have set a king over you. 2Now you have a king as your leader. As for me, I am old and gray, and my sons are here with you. I have been your leader from my youth until this day. 3Here I stand. Testify against me in the presence of the LORD and his anointed. Whose ox have I taken? Whose donkey have I taken? Whom have I cheated? Whom have I oppressed? From whose hand have I accepted a bribe to make me shut my eyes? If I have done any of these, I will make it right."

4"You have not cheated or oppressed us," they replied. "You have not taken anything from anyone's hand."

5Samuel said to them, "The LORD is witness against you, and also his anointed is witness this day, that you have not found anything in my hand."

"He is witness," they said.

6Then Samuel said to the people, "It is the LORD who appointed Moses and Aaron and brought your forefathers up out of Egypt. 7Now then, stand here, because I am going to confront you with evidence before the LORD as to all the righteous acts performed by the LORD for you and your fathers.

8"After Jacob entered Egypt, they cried to the LORD for help, and the LORD sent Moses and Aaron, who brought your forefathers out of Egypt and settled them in this place.

9"But they forgot the LORD their God; so he sold them into the hand of Sisera, the commander of the army of Hazor, and into the hands of the Philistines and the king of Moab, who fought against them. 10They cried out to the LORD and said, 'We have sinned; we have forsaken the LORD and served the Baals and the Ashtoreths. But now deliver us from the hands of our ene-

a15 Traditionally *peace offerings*

mies, and we will serve you.' 11Then the LORD
sent Jerub-Baal,[a] Barak,[b] Jephthah and
Samuel,[c] and he delivered you from the
hands of your enemies on every side, so that
you lived securely.
12"But when you saw that Nahash king of
the Ammonites was moving against you, you
said to me, 'No, we want a king to rule over
us'—even though the LORD your God was
your king. 13Now here is the king you have
chosen, the one you asked for; see, the LORD
has set a king over you. 14If you fear the LORD
and serve and obey him and do not rebel
against his commands, and if both you and
the king who reigns over you follow the LORD
your God—good! 15But if you do not obey the
LORD, and if you rebel against his commands,
his hand will be against you, as it was against
your fathers.
16"Now then, stand still and see this great
thing the LORD is about to do before your
eyes! 17Is it not wheat harvest now? I will call
upon the LORD to send thunder and rain. And
you will realize what an evil thing you did in
the eyes of the LORD when you asked for a
king."
18Then Samuel called upon the LORD, and
that same day the LORD sent thunder and
rain. So all the people stood in awe of the
LORD and of Samuel.
19The people all said to Samuel, "Pray to
the LORD your God for your servants so that
we will not die, for we have added to all our
other sins the evil of asking for a king."
20"Do not be afraid," Samuel replied. "You
have done all this evil; yet do not turn away
from the LORD, but serve the LORD with all
your heart. 21Do not turn away after useless
idols. They can do you no good, nor can they
rescue you, because they are useless. 22For
the sake of his great name the LORD will not
reject his people, because the LORD was
pleased to make you his own. 23As for me,
far be it from me that I should sin against the
LORD by failing to pray for you. And I will teach
you the way that is good and right. 24But be
sure to fear the LORD and serve him faithfully
with all your heart; consider what great
things he has done for you. 25Yet if you persist in doing evil, both you and your king will
be swept away."

Samuel Rebukes Saul

13 Saul was ⌞thirty⌟[d] years old when he
became king, and he reigned over
Israel ⌞forty-⌟[e] two years.
2Saul[f] chose three thousand men from Israel; two thousand were with him at Micmash
and in the hill country of Bethel, and a thousand were with Jonathan at Gibeah in Benjamin. The rest of the men he sent back to their
homes.
3Jonathan attacked the Philistine outpost
at Geba, and the Philistines heard about it.
Then Saul had the trumpet blown throughout
the land and said, "Let the Hebrews hear!"
4So all Israel heard the news: "Saul has attacked the Philistine outpost, and now Israel
has become a stench to the Philistines." And
the people were summoned to join Saul at
Gilgal.
5The Philistines assembled to fight Israel,
with three thousand[g] chariots, six thousand
charioteers, and soldiers as numerous as
the sand on the seashore. They went up and
camped at Micmash, east of Beth Aven.
6When the men of Israel saw that their situation was critical and that their army was hard
pressed, they hid in caves and thickets,
among the rocks, and in pits and cisterns.
7Some Hebrews even crossed the Jordan to
the land of Gad and Gilead.
Saul remained at Gilgal, and all the troops
with him were quaking with fear. 8He waited
seven days, the time set by Samuel; but
Samuel did not come to Gilgal, and Saul's
men began to scatter. 9So he said, "Bring me
the burnt offering and the fellowship offerings.[h]" And Saul offered up the burnt offering. 10Just as he finished making the offering,
Samuel arrived, and Saul went out to greet
him.
11"What have you done?" asked Samuel.
Saul replied, "When I saw that the men
were scattering, and that you did not come at
the set time, and that the Philistines were
assembling at Micmash, 12I thought, 'Now
the Philistines will come down against me at
Gilgal, and I have not sought the LORD's favor.' So I felt compelled to offer the burnt
offering."
13"You acted foolishly," Samuel said. "You
have not kept the command the LORD your

[a]11 Also called *Gideon* [b]11 Some Septuagint manuscripts and Syriac; Hebrew *Bedan* [c]11 Hebrew; some Septuagint manuscripts and Syriac *Samson* [d]1 A few late manuscripts of the Septuagint; Hebrew does not have *thirty*. [e]1 See the round number in Acts 13:21; Hebrew does not have *forty-*. [f]1,2 Or *and when he had reigned over Israel two years, 2he* [g]5 Some Septuagint manuscripts and Syriac; Hebrew *thirty thousand* [h]9 Traditionally *peace offerings*

God gave you; if you had, he would have established your kingdom over Israel for all time. 14But now your kingdom will not endure; the LORD has sought out a man after his own heart and appointed him leader of his people, because you have not kept the LORD's command."

15Then Samuel left Gilgal[a] and went up to Gibeah in Benjamin, and Saul counted the men who were with him. They numbered about six hundred.

Israel Without Weapons

16Saul and his son Jonathan and the men with them were staying in Gibeah[b] in Benjamin, while the Philistines camped at Micmash. 17Raiding parties went out from the Philistine camp in three detachments. One turned toward Ophrah in the vicinity of Shual, 18another toward Beth Horon, and the third toward the borderland overlooking the Valley of Zeboim facing the desert.

19Not a blacksmith could be found in the whole land of Israel, because the Philistines had said, "Otherwise the Hebrews will make swords or spears!" 20So all Israel went down to the Philistines to have their plowshares, mattocks, axes and sickles[c] sharpened. 21The price was two thirds of a shekel[d] for sharpening plowshares and mattocks, and a third of a shekel[e] for sharpening forks and axes and for repointing goads.

22So on the day of the battle not a soldier with Saul and Jonathan had a sword or spear in his hand; only Saul and his son Jonathan had them.

Jonathan Attacks the Philistines

23Now a detachment of Philistines had gone out to the pass at Micmash.

14 1One day Jonathan son of Saul said to the young man bearing his armor, "Come, let's go over to the Philistine outpost on the other side." But he did not tell his father.

2Saul was staying on the outskirts of Gibeah under a pomegranate tree in Migron. With him were about six hundred men, 3among whom was Ahijah, who was wearing an ephod. He was a son of Ichabod's brother Ahitub son of Phinehas, the son of Eli, the LORD's priest in Shiloh. No one was aware that Jonathan had left.

4On each side of the pass that Jonathan intended to cross to reach the Philistine outpost was a cliff; one was called Bozez, and the other Seneh. 5One cliff stood to the north toward Micmash, the other to the south toward Geba.

6Jonathan said to his young armor-bearer, "Come, let's go over to the outpost of those uncircumcised fellows. Perhaps the LORD will act in our behalf. Nothing can hinder the LORD from saving, whether by many or by few."

7"Do all that you have in mind," his armor-bearer said. "Go ahead; I am with you heart and soul."

8Jonathan said, "Come, then; we will cross over toward the men and let them see us. 9If they say to us, 'Wait there until we come to you,' we will stay where we are and not go up to them. 10But if they say, 'Come up to us,' we will climb up, because that will be our sign that the LORD has given them into our hands."

11So both of them showed themselves to the Philistine outpost. "Look!" said the Philistines. "The Hebrews are crawling out of the holes they were hiding in." 12The men of the outpost shouted to Jonathan and his armor-bearer, "Come up to us and we'll teach you a lesson."

So Jonathan said to his armor-bearer, "Climb up after me; the LORD has given them into the hand of Israel."

13Jonathan climbed up, using his hands and feet, with his armor-bearer right behind him. The Philistines fell before Jonathan, and his armor-bearer followed and killed behind him. 14In that first attack Jonathan and his armor-bearer killed some twenty men in an area of about half an acre.[f]

Israel Routs the Philistines

15Then panic struck the whole army—those in the camp and field, and those in the outposts and raiding parties—and the ground shook. It was a panic sent by God.[g]

16Saul's lookouts at Gibeah of Benjamin saw the army melting away in all directions. 17Then Saul said to the men who were with him, "Muster the forces and see who has left

[a] *15* Hebrew; Septuagint *Gilgal and went his way; the rest of the people went after Saul to meet the army, and they went out of Gilgal* [b] *16* Two Hebrew manuscripts; most Hebrew manuscripts *Geba*, a variant of *Gibeah*
[c] *20* Septuagint; Hebrew *plowshares* [d] *21* Hebrew *pim*; that is, about 1/4 ounce (about 8 grams) [e] *21* That is, about 1/8 ounce (about 4 grams) [f] *14* Hebrew *half a yoke;* a "yoke" was the land plowed by a yoke of oxen in one day. [g] *15* Or *a terrible panic*

us." When they did, it was Jonathan and his armor-bearer who were not there.

18 Saul said to Ahijah, "Bring the ark of God." (At that time it was with the Israelites.)[a] 19 While Saul was talking to the priest, the tumult in the Philistine camp increased more and more. So Saul said to the priest, "Withdraw your hand."

20 Then Saul and all his men assembled and went to the battle. They found the Philistines in total confusion, striking each other with their swords. 21 Those Hebrews who had previously been with the Philistines and had gone up with them to their camp went over to the Israelites who were with Saul and Jonathan. 22 When all the Israelites who had hidden in the hill country of Ephraim heard that the Philistines were on the run, they joined the battle in hot pursuit. 23 So the LORD rescued Israel that day, and the battle moved on beyond Beth Aven.

Jonathan Eats Honey

24 Now the men of Israel were in distress that day, because Saul had bound the people under an oath, saying, "Cursed be any man who eats food before evening comes, before I have avenged myself on my enemies!" So none of the troops tasted food.

25 The entire army[b] entered the woods, and there was honey on the ground. 26 When they went into the woods, they saw the honey oozing out, yet no one put his hand to his mouth, because they feared the oath. 27 But Jonathan had not heard that his father had bound the people with the oath, so he reached out the end of the staff that was in his hand and dipped it into the honeycomb. He raised his hand to his mouth, and his eyes brightened.[c] 28 Then one of the soldiers told him, "Your father bound the army under a strict oath, saying, 'Cursed be any man who eats food today!' That is why the men are faint."

29 Jonathan said, "My father has made trouble for the country. See how my eyes brightened[d] when I tasted a little of this honey. 30 How much better it would have been if the men had eaten today some of the plunder they took from their enemies. Would not the slaughter of the Philistines have been even greater?"

31 That day, after the Israelites had struck down the Philistines from Micmash to Aijalon, they were exhausted. 32 They pounced on the plunder and, taking sheep, cattle and calves, they butchered them on the ground and ate them, together with the blood. 33 Then someone said to Saul, "Look, the men are sinning against the LORD by eating meat that has blood in it."

"You have broken faith," he said. "Roll a large stone over here at once." 34 Then he said, "Go out among the men and tell them, 'Each of you bring me your cattle and sheep, and slaughter them here and eat them. Do not sin against the LORD by eating meat with blood still in it.' "

So everyone brought his ox that night and slaughtered it there. 35 Then Saul built an altar to the LORD; it was the first time he had done this.

36 Saul said, "Let us go down after the Philistines by night and plunder them till dawn, and let us not leave one of them alive."

"Do whatever seems best to you," they replied.

But the priest said, "Let us inquire of God here."

37 So Saul asked God, "Shall I go down after the Philistines? Will you give them into Israel's hand?" But God did not answer him that day.

38 Saul therefore said, "Come here, all you who are leaders of the army, and let us find out what sin has been committed today. 39 As surely as the LORD who rescues Israel lives, even if it lies with my son Jonathan, he must die." But not one of the men said a word.

40 Saul then said to all the Israelites, "You stand over there; I and Jonathan my son will stand over here."

"Do what seems best to you," the men replied.

41 Then Saul prayed to the LORD, the God of Israel, "Give me the right answer."[e] And Jonathan and Saul were taken by lot, and the men were cleared. 42 Saul said, "Cast the lot between me and Jonathan my son." And Jonathan was taken.

43 Then Saul said to Jonathan, "Tell me what you have done."

So Jonathan told him, "I merely tasted a little honey with the end of my staff. And now must I die?"

44 Saul said, "May God deal with me, be it

[a] *18* Hebrew; Septuagint *"Bring the ephod." (At that time he wore the ephod before the Israelites.)* [b] *25* Or *Now all the people of the land* [c] *27* Or *his strength was renewed* [d] *29* Or *my strength was renewed*
[e] *41* Hebrew; Septuagint *"Why have you not answered your servant today? If the fault is in me or my son Jonathan, respond with Urim, but if the men of Israel are at fault, respond with Thummim."*

ever so severely, if you do not die, Jonathan."
45But the men said to Saul, "Should Jonathan die—he who has brought about this
great deliverance in Israel? Never! As surely
as the LORD lives, not a hair of his head will
fall to the ground, for he did this today with
God's help." So the men rescued Jonathan,
and he was not put to death.
46Then Saul stopped pursuing the Philistines, and they withdrew to their own land.
47After Saul had assumed rule over Israel,
he fought against their enemies on every
side: Moab, the Ammonites, Edom, the
kings[a] of Zobah, and the Philistines.
Wherever he turned, he inflicted punishment
on them.[b] 48He fought valiantly and defeated
the Amalekites, delivering Israel from the
hands of those who had plundered them.

Saul's Family

49Saul's sons were Jonathan, Ishvi and
Malki-Shua. The name of his older daughter
was Merab, and that of the younger was
Michal. 50His wife's name was Ahinoam
daughter of Ahimaaz. The name of the commander of Saul's army was Abner son of
Ner, and Ner was Saul's uncle. 51Saul's father Kish and Abner's father Ner were sons
of Abiel.
52All the days of Saul there was bitter war
with the Philistines, and whenever Saul saw
a mighty or brave man, he took him into his
service.

The LORD Rejects Saul as King

15 Samuel said to Saul, "I am the one
the LORD sent to anoint you king over
his people Israel; so listen now to the message from the LORD. 2This is what the LORD
Almighty says: 'I will punish the Amalekites
for what they did to Israel when they waylaid
them as they came up from Egypt. 3Now go,
attack the Amalekites and totally destroy[c]
everything that belongs to them. Do not
spare them; put to death men and women,
children and infants, cattle and sheep, camels and donkeys.' "
4So Saul summoned the men and mustered them at Telaim—two hundred thousand foot soldiers and ten thousand men
from Judah. 5Saul went to the city of Amalek
and set an ambush in the ravine. 6Then he
said to the Kenites, "Go away, leave the
Amalekites so that I do not destroy you along
with them; for you showed kindness to all the
Israelites when they came up out of Egypt."
So the Kenites moved away from the Amalekites.
7Then Saul attacked the Amalekites all the
way from Havilah to Shur, to the east of
Egypt. 8He took Agag king of the Amalekites
alive, and all his people he totally destroyed
with the sword. 9But Saul and the army
spared Agag and the best of the sheep and
cattle, the fat calves[d] and lambs—everything that was good. These they were unwilling to destroy completely, but everything that
was despised and weak they totally destroyed.
10Then the word of the LORD came to Samuel: 11"I am grieved that I have made Saul
king, because he has turned away from me
and has not carried out my instructions."
Samuel was troubled, and he cried out to the
LORD all that night.
12Early in the morning Samuel got up and
went to meet Saul, but he was told, "Saul has
gone to Carmel. There he has set up a
monument in his own honor and has turned
and gone on down to Gilgal."
13When Samuel reached him, Saul said,
"The LORD bless you! I have carried out the
LORD's instructions."
14But Samuel said, "What then is this
bleating of sheep in my ears? What is this
lowing of cattle that I hear?"
15Saul answered, "The soldiers brought
them from the Amalekites; they spared the
best of the sheep and cattle to sacrifice to the
LORD your God, but we totally destroyed the
rest."
16"Stop!" Samuel said to Saul. "Let me tell
you what the LORD said to me last night."
"Tell me," Saul replied.
17Samuel said, "Although you were once
small in your own eyes, did you not become
the head of the tribes of Israel? The LORD
anointed you king over Israel. 18And he sent
you on a mission, saying, 'Go and completely destroy those wicked people, the Amalekites; make war on them until you have wiped
them out.' 19Why did you not obey the LORD?
Why did you pounce on the plunder and do
evil in the eyes of the LORD?"
20"But I did obey the LORD," Saul said. "I

[a]47 Masoretic Text; Dead Sea Scrolls and Septuagint *king* [b]47 Hebrew; Septuagint *he was victorious*
[c]3 The Hebrew term refers to the irrevocable giving over of things or persons to the LORD, often by totally destroying them; also in verses 8, 9, 15, 18, 20 and 21. [d]9 Or *the grown bulls;* the meaning of the Hebrew for this phrase is uncertain.

went on the mission the LORD assigned me. I
completely destroyed the Amalekites and
brought back Agag their king. 21The soldiers
took sheep and cattle from the plunder, the
best of what was devoted to God, in order to
sacrifice them to the LORD your God at Gilgal."
22But Samuel replied:

"Does the LORD delight in burnt offerings
and sacrifices
as much as in obeying the voice of the
LORD?
To obey is better than sacrifice,
and to heed is better than the fat of
rams.
23For rebellion is like the sin of divination,
and arrogance like the evil of idolatry.
Because you have rejected the word of
the LORD,
he has rejected you as king."

24Then Saul said to Samuel, "I have
sinned. I violated the LORD's command and
your instructions. I was afraid of the people
and so I gave in to them. 25Now I beg you,
forgive my sin and come back with me, so
that I may worship the LORD."
26But Samuel said to him, "I will not go
back with you. You have rejected the word of
the LORD, and the LORD has rejected you as
king over Israel!"
27As Samuel turned to leave, Saul caught
hold of the hem of his robe, and it tore.
28Samuel said to him, "The LORD has torn the
kingdom of Israel from you today and has
given it to one of your neighbors—to one
better than you. 29He who is the Glory of
Israel does not lie or change his mind; for he
is not a man, that he should change his
mind."
30Saul replied, "I have sinned. But please
honor me before the elders of my people and
before Israel; come back with me, so that I
may worship the LORD your God." 31So Samuel went back with Saul, and Saul worshiped
the LORD.
32Then Samuel said, "Bring me Agag king
of the Amalekites."
Agag came to him confidently,[a] thinking,
"Surely the bitterness of death is past."
33But Samuel said,

"As your sword has made women
childless,
so will your mother be childless among
women."

And Samuel put Agag to death before the
LORD at Gilgal.
34Then Samuel left for Ramah, but Saul
went up to his home in Gibeah of Saul. 35Un-
til the day Samuel died, he did not go to see
Saul again, though Samuel mourned for him.
And the LORD was grieved that he had made
Saul king over Israel.

Samuel Anoints David

16 The LORD said to Samuel, "How long
will you mourn for Saul, since I have
rejected him as king over Israel? Fill your
horn with oil and be on your way; I am sending you to Jesse of Bethlehem. I have chosen one of his sons to be king."
2But Samuel said, "How can I go? Saul will
hear about it and kill me."
The LORD said, "Take a heifer with you and
say, 'I have come to sacrifice to the LORD.'
3Invite Jesse to the sacrifice, and I will show
you what to do. You are to anoint for me the
one I indicate."
4Samuel did what the LORD said. When he
arrived at Bethlehem, the elders of the town
trembled when they met him. They asked,
"Do you come in peace?"
5Samuel replied, "Yes, in peace; I have
come to sacrifice to the LORD. Consecrate
yourselves and come to the sacrifice with
me." Then he consecrated Jesse and his
sons and invited them to the sacrifice.
6When they arrived, Samuel saw Eliab and
thought, "Surely the LORD's anointed stands
here before the LORD."
7But the LORD said to Samuel, "Do not consider his appearance or his height, for I have
rejected him. The LORD does not look at the
things man looks at. Man looks at the outward appearance, but the LORD looks at the
heart."
8Then Jesse called Abinadab and had him
pass in front of Samuel. But Samuel said,
"The LORD has not chosen this one either."
9Jesse then had Shammah pass by, but
Samuel said, "Nor has the LORD chosen this
one." 10Jesse had seven of his sons pass
before Samuel, but Samuel said to him, "The
LORD has not chosen these." 11So he asked
Jesse, "Are these all the sons you have?"
"There is still the youngest," Jesse answered, "but he is tending the sheep."
Samuel said, "Send for him; we will not sit
down[b] until he arrives."
12So he sent and had him brought in. He

[a]32 Or *him trembling, yet* [b]11 Some Septuagint manuscripts; Hebrew *not gather around*

was ruddy, with a fine appearance and handsome features.
Then the LORD said, "Rise and anoint him;
he is the one."
13So Samuel took the horn of oil and
anointed him in the presence of his brothers,
and from that day on the Spirit of the LORD
came upon David in power. Samuel then
went to Ramah.

David in Saul's Service

14Now the Spirit of the LORD had departed
from Saul, and an evil[a] spirit from the LORD
tormented him.
15Saul's attendants said to him, "See, an
evil spirit from God is tormenting you. 16Let
our lord command his servants here to
search for someone who can play the harp.
He will play when the evil spirit from God
comes upon you, and you will feel better."
17So Saul said to his attendants, "Find
someone who plays well and bring him to
me."
18One of the servants answered, "I have
seen a son of Jesse of Bethlehem who
knows how to play the harp. He is a brave
man and a warrior. He speaks well and is a
fine-looking man. And the LORD is with him."
19Then Saul sent messengers to Jesse
and said, "Send me your son David, who is
with the sheep." 20So Jesse took a donkey
loaded with bread, a skin of wine and a
young goat and sent them with his son David
to Saul.
21David came to Saul and entered his service. Saul liked him very much, and David
became one of his armor-bearers. 22Then
Saul sent word to Jesse, saying, "Allow David to remain in my service, for I am pleased
with him."
23Whenever the spirit from God came
upon Saul, David would take his harp and
play. Then relief would come to Saul; he
would feel better, and the evil spirit would
leave him.

David and Goliath

17 Now the Philistines gathered their
forces for war and assembled at
Socoh in Judah. They pitched camp at
Ephes Dammim, between Socoh and Azekah. 2Saul and the Israelites assembled and
camped in the Valley of Elah and drew up
their battle line to meet the Philistines. 3The
Philistines occupied one hill and the Israelites another, with the valley between them.
4A champion named Goliath, who was
from Gath, came out of the Philistine camp.
He was over nine feet[b] tall. 5He had a bronze
helmet on his head and wore a coat of scale
armor of bronze weighing five thousand
shekels[c]; 6on his legs he wore bronze
greaves, and a bronze javelin was slung on
his back. 7His spear shaft was like a weaver's rod, and its iron point weighed six hundred shekels.[d] His shield bearer went ahead
of him.
8Goliath stood and shouted to the ranks of
Israel, "Why do you come out and line up for
battle? Am I not a Philistine, and are you not
the servants of Saul? Choose a man and
have him come down to me. 9If he is able to
fight and kill me, we will become your subjects; but if I overcome him and kill him, you
will become our subjects and serve us."
10Then the Philistine said, "This day I defy
the ranks of Israel! Give me a man and let us
fight each other." 11On hearing the Philistine's words, Saul and all the Israelites were
dismayed and terrified.
12Now David was the son of an Ephrathite
named Jesse, who was from Bethlehem in
Judah. Jesse had eight sons, and in Saul's
time he was old and well advanced in years.
13Jesse's three oldest sons had followed
Saul to the war: The firstborn was Eliab; the
second, Abinadab; and the third, Shammah.
14David was the youngest. The three oldest
followed Saul, 15but David went back and
forth from Saul to tend his father's sheep at
Bethlehem.
16For forty days the Philistine came forward every morning and evening and took
his stand.
17Now Jesse said to his son David, "Take
this ephah[e] of roasted grain and these ten
loaves of bread for your brothers and hurry to
their camp. 18Take along these ten cheeses
to the commander of their unit.[f] See how
your brothers are and bring back some assurance[g] from them. 19They are with Saul
and all the men of Israel in the Valley of Elah,
fighting against the Philistines."
20Early in the morning David left the flock
with a shepherd, loaded up and set out, as
Jesse had directed. He reached the camp as

[a] 14 Or *injurious;* also in verses 15, 16 and 23 [b] 4 Hebrew *was six cubits and a span* (about 3 meters)
[c] 5 That is, about 125 pounds (about 57 kilograms) [d] 7 That is, about 15 pounds (about 7 kilograms)
[e] 17 That is, probably about 3/5 bushel (about 22 liters) [f] 18 Hebrew *thousand* [g] 18 Or *some token;* or
some pledge of spoils

the army was going out to its battle positions,
shouting the war cry. 21Israel and the Philistines were drawing up their lines facing each
other. 22David left his things with the keeper
of supplies, ran to the battle lines and greeted his brothers. 23As he was talking with
them, Goliath, the Philistine champion from
Gath, stepped out from his lines and shouted
his usual defiance, and David heard it.
24When the Israelites saw the man, they all
ran from him in great fear.

25Now the Israelites had been saying, "Do
you see how this man keeps coming out? He
comes out to defy Israel. The king will give
great wealth to the man who kills him. He will
also give him his daughter in marriage and
will exempt his father's family from taxes in
Israel."

26David asked the men standing near him,
"What will be done for the man who kills this
Philistine and removes this disgrace from
Israel? Who is this uncircumcised Philistine
that he should defy the armies of the living
God?"

27They repeated to him what they had
been saying and told him, "This is what will
be done for the man who kills him."

28When Eliab, David's oldest brother,
heard him speaking with the men, he burned
with anger at him and asked, "Why have you
come down here? And with whom did you
leave those few sheep in the desert? I know
how conceited you are and how wicked your
heart is; you came down only to watch the
battle."

29"Now what have I done?" said David.
"Can't I even speak?" 30He then turned away
to someone else and brought up the same
matter, and the men answered him as before. 31What David said was overheard and
reported to Saul, and Saul sent for him.

32David said to Saul, "Let no one lose
heart on account of this Philistine; your servant will go and fight him."

33Saul replied, "You are not able to go out
against this Philistine and fight him; you are
only a boy, and he has been a fighting man
from his youth."

34But David said to Saul, "Your servant
has been keeping his father's sheep. When
a lion or a bear came and carried off a sheep
from the flock, 35I went after it, struck it and
rescued the sheep from its mouth. When it
turned on me, I seized it by its hair, struck it
and killed it. 36Your servant has killed both
the lion and the bear; this uncircumcised
Philistine will be like one of them, because
he has defied the armies of the living God.
37The LORD who delivered me from the paw of
the lion and the paw of the bear will deliver
me from the hand of this Philistine."

Saul said to David, "Go, and the LORD be
with you."

38Then Saul dressed David in his own tunic. He put a coat of armor on him and a
bronze helmet on his head. 39David fastened
on his sword over the tunic and tried walking around, because he was not used to
them.

"I cannot go in these," he said to Saul,
"because I am not used to them." So he took
them off. 40Then he took his staff in his hand,
chose five smooth stones from the stream,
put them in the pouch of his shepherd's bag
and, with his sling in his hand, approached
the Philistine.

41Meanwhile, the Philistine, with his shield
bearer in front of him, kept coming closer to
David. 42He looked David over and saw that
he was only a boy, ruddy and handsome,
and he despised him. 43He said to David,
"Am I a dog, that you come at me with
sticks?" And the Philistine cursed David by
his gods. 44"Come here," he said, "and I'll
give your flesh to the birds of the air and the
beasts of the field!"

45David said to the Philistine, "You come
against me with sword and spear and javelin,
but I come against you in the name of the
LORD Almighty, the God of the armies of Israel, whom you have defied. 46This day the
LORD will hand you over to me, and I'll strike
you down and cut off your head. Today I will
give the carcasses of the Philistine army to
the birds of the air and the beasts of the
earth, and the whole world will know that
there is a God in Israel. 47All those gathered
here will know that it is not by sword or spear
that the LORD saves; for the battle is the
LORD's, and he will give all of you into our
hands."

48As the Philistine moved closer to attack
him, David ran quickly toward the battle line
to meet him. 49Reaching into his bag and
taking out a stone, he slung it and struck the
Philistine on the forehead. The stone sank
into his forehead, and he fell facedown on
the ground.

50So David triumphed over the Philistine
with a sling and a stone; without a sword in
his hand he struck down the Philistine and
killed him.

51David ran and stood over him. He took
hold of the Philistine's sword and drew it from

the scabbard. After he killed him, he cut off
his head with the sword.

When the Philistines saw that their hero
was dead, they turned and ran. 52Then the
men of Israel and Judah surged forward with
a shout and pursued the Philistines to the
entrance of Gath[a] and to the gates of Ekron.
Their dead were strewn along the Shaaraim
road to Gath and Ekron. 53When the Israelites returned from chasing the Philistines,
they plundered their camp. 54David took the
Philistine's head and brought it to Jerusalem,
and he put the Philistine's weapons in his
own tent.

55As Saul watched David going out to meet
the Philistine, he said to Abner, commander
of the army, "Abner, whose son is that young
man?"

Abner replied, "As surely as you live, O
king, I don't know."

56The king said, "Find out whose son this
young man is."

57As soon as David returned from killing
the Philistine, Abner took him and brought
him before Saul, with David still holding the
Philistine's head.

58"Whose son are you, young man?" Saul
asked him.

David said, "I am the son of your servant
Jesse of Bethlehem."

Saul's Jealousy of David

18 After David had finished talking with
Saul, Jonathan became one in spirit
with David, and he loved him as himself.
2From that day Saul kept David with him and
did not let him return to his father's house.
3And Jonathan made a covenant with David
because he loved him as himself. 4Jonathan
took off the robe he was wearing and gave it
to David, along with his tunic, and even his
sword, his bow and his belt.

5Whatever Saul sent him to do, David did it
so successfully[b] that Saul gave him a high
rank in the army. This pleased all the people,
and Saul's officers as well.

6When the men were returning home after
David had killed the Philistine, the women
came out from all the towns of Israel to meet
King Saul with singing and dancing, with joyful songs and with tambourines and lutes.
7As they danced, they sang:

"Saul has slain his thousands,
and David his tens of thousands."

8Saul was very angry; this refrain galled
him. "They have credited David with tens of
thousands," he thought, "but me with only
thousands. What more can he get but the
kingdom?" 9And from that time on Saul kept
a jealous eye on David.

10The next day an evil[c] spirit from God
came forcefully upon Saul. He was prophesying in his house, while David was playing
the harp, as he usually did. Saul had a spear
in his hand 11and he hurled it, saying to himself, "I'll pin David to the wall." But David
eluded him twice.

12Saul was afraid of David, because the
LORD was with David but had left Saul. 13So
he sent David away from him and gave him
command over a thousand men, and David
led the troops in their campaigns. 14In everything he did he had great success,[d] because
the LORD was with him. 15When Saul saw how
successful[e] he was, he was afraid of him.
16But all Israel and Judah loved David, because he led them in their campaigns.

17Saul said to David, "Here is my older
daughter Merab. I will give her to you in marriage; only serve me bravely and fight the
battles of the LORD." For Saul said to himself,
"I will not raise a hand against him. Let the
Philistines do that!"

18But David said to Saul, "Who am I, and
what is my family or my father's clan in Israel,
that I should become the king's son-in-law?"
19So[f] when the time came for Merab, Saul's
daughter, to be given to David, she was giv-
en in marriage to Adriel of Meholah.

20Now Saul's daughter Michal was in love
with David, and when they told Saul about it,
he was pleased. 21"I will give her to him," he
thought, "so that she may be a snare to him
and so that the hand of the Philistines may
be against him." So Saul said to David, "Now
you have a second opportunity to become
my son-in-law."

22Then Saul ordered his attendants:
"Speak to David privately and say, 'Look, the
king is pleased with you, and his attendants
all like you; now become his son-in-law.' "

23They repeated these words to David. But
David said, "Do you think it is a small matter
to become the king's son-in-law? I'm only a
poor man and little known."

24When Saul's servants told him what David had said, 25Saul replied, "Say to David,
'The king wants no other price for the bride

[a]52 Some Septuagint manuscripts; Hebrew *a valley* [b]5 Or *wisely* [c]10 Or *injurious* [d]14 Or *he was very wise* [e]15 Or *wise* [f]19 Or *However,*

than a hundred Philistine foreskins, to take revenge on his enemies.' " Saul's plan was to have David fall by the hands of the Philistines.

26When the attendants told David these things, he was pleased to become the king's son-in-law. So before the allotted time elapsed, 27David and his men went out and killed two hundred Philistines. He brought their foreskins and presented the full number to the king so that he might become the king's son-in-law. Then Saul gave him his daughter Michal in marriage.

28When Saul realized that the LORD was with David and that his daughter Michal loved David, 29Saul became still more afraid of him, and he remained his enemy the rest of his days.

30The Philistine commanders continued to go out to battle, and as often as they did, David met with more success[a] than the rest of Saul's officers, and his name became well known.

Saul Tries to Kill David

19 Saul told his son Jonathan and all the attendants to kill David. But Jonathan was very fond of David 2and warned him, "My father Saul is looking for a chance to kill you. Be on your guard tomorrow morning; go into hiding and stay there. 3I will go out and stand with my father in the field where you are. I'll speak to him about you and will tell you what I find out."

4Jonathan spoke well of David to Saul his father and said to him, "Let not the king do wrong to his servant David; he has not wronged you, and what he has done has benefited you greatly. 5He took his life in his hands when he killed the Philistine. The LORD won a great victory for all Israel, and you saw it and were glad. Why then would you do wrong to an innocent man like David by killing him for no reason?"

6Saul listened to Jonathan and took this oath: "As surely as the LORD lives, David will not be put to death."

7So Jonathan called David and told him the whole conversation. He brought him to Saul, and David was with Saul as before.

8Once more war broke out, and David went out and fought the Philistines. He struck them with such force that they fled before him.

9But an evil[b] spirit from the LORD came upon Saul as he was sitting in his house with his spear in his hand. While David was playing the harp, 10Saul tried to pin him to the wall with his spear, but David eluded him as Saul drove the spear into the wall. That night David made good his escape.

11Saul sent men to David's house to watch it and to kill him in the morning. But Michal, David's wife, warned him, "If you don't run for your life tonight, tomorrow you'll be killed." 12So Michal let David down through a window, and he fled and escaped. 13Then Michal took an idol[c] and laid it on the bed, covering it with a garment and putting some goats' hair at the head.

14When Saul sent the men to capture David, Michal said, "He is ill."

15Then Saul sent the men back to see David and told them, "Bring him up to me in his bed so that I may kill him." 16But when the men entered, there was the idol in the bed, and at the head was some goats' hair.

17Saul said to Michal, "Why did you deceive me like this and send my enemy away so that he escaped?"

Michal told him, "He said to me, 'Let me get away. Why should I kill you?' "

18When David had fled and made his escape, he went to Samuel at Ramah and told him all that Saul had done to him. Then he and Samuel went to Naioth and stayed there. 19Word came to Saul: "David is in Naioth at Ramah"; 20so he sent men to capture him. But when they saw a group of prophets prophesying, with Samuel standing there as their leader, the Spirit of God came upon Saul's men and they also prophesied. 21Saul was told about it, and he sent more men, and they prophesied too. Saul sent men a third time, and they also prophesied. 22Finally, he himself left for Ramah and went to the great cistern at Secu. And he asked, "Where are Samuel and David?"

"Over in Naioth at Ramah," they said.

23So Saul went to Naioth at Ramah. But the Spirit of God came even upon him, and he walked along prophesying until he came to Naioth. 24He stripped off his robes and also prophesied in Samuel's presence. He lay that way all that day and night. This is why people say, "Is Saul also among the prophets?"

[a]*30* Or *David acted more wisely* [b]*9* Or *injurious* [c]*13* Hebrew *teraphim;* also in verse 16

David and Jonathan

20 Then David fled from Naioth at
Ramah and went to Jonathan and
asked, “What have I done? What is my
crime? How have I wronged your father, that
he is trying to take my life?”

2“Never!” Jonathan replied. “You are not
going to die! Look, my father doesn't do anything, great or small, without confiding in me.
Why would he hide this from me? It's not so!”

3But David took an oath and said, “Your
father knows very well that I have found favor
in your eyes, and he has said to himself,
‘Jonathan must not know this or he will be
grieved.’ Yet as surely as the LORD lives and
as you live, there is only a step between me
and death.”

4Jonathan said to David, “Whatever you
want me to do, I'll do for you.”

5So David said, “Look, tomorrow is the
New Moon festival, and I am supposed to
dine with the king; but let me go and hide in
the field until the evening of the day after
tomorrow. 6If your father misses me at all, tell
him, ‘David earnestly asked my permission
to hurry to Bethlehem, his hometown, because an annual sacrifice is being made
there for his whole clan.’ 7If he says, ‘Very
well,’ then your servant is safe. But if he
loses his temper, you can be sure that he is
determined to harm me. 8As for you, show
kindness to your servant, for you have
brought him into a covenant with you before
the LORD. If I am guilty, then kill me yourself!
Why hand me over to your father?”

9“Never!” Jonathan said. “If I had the least
inkling that my father was determined to
harm you, wouldn't I tell you?”

10David asked, “Who will tell me if your
father answers you harshly?”

11“Come,” Jonathan said, “let's go out into
the field.” So they went there together.

12Then Jonathan said to David: “By the
LORD, the God of Israel, I will surely sound out
my father by this time the day after tomorrow!
If he is favorably disposed toward you, will I
not send you word and let you know? 13But if
my father is inclined to harm you, may the
LORD deal with me, be it ever so severely, if I
do not let you know and send you away safely. May the LORD be with you as he has been
with my father. 14But show me unfailing kindness like that of the LORD as long as I live, so
that I may not be killed, 15and do not ever cut
off your kindness from my family—not even
when the LORD has cut off every one of David's enemies from the face of the earth.”

16So Jonathan made a covenant with the
house of David, saying, “May the LORD call
David's enemies to account.” 17And Jonathan had David reaffirm his oath out of love
for him, because he loved him as he loved
himself.

18Then Jonathan said to David: “Tomorrow is the New Moon festival. You will be
missed, because your seat will be empty.
19The day after tomorrow, toward evening,
go to the place where you hid when this
trouble began, and wait by the stone Ezel. 20I
will shoot three arrows to the side of it, as
though I were shooting at a target. 21Then I
will send a boy and say, ‘Go, find the arrows.’
If I say to him, ‘Look, the arrows are on this
side of you; bring them here,’ then come,
because, as surely as the LORD lives, you are
safe; there is no danger. 22But if I say to the
boy, ‘Look, the arrows are beyond you,’ then
you must go, because the LORD has sent you
away. 23And about the matter you and I discussed—remember, the LORD is witness between you and me forever.”

24So David hid in the field, and when the
New Moon festival came, the king sat down
to eat. 25He sat in his customary place by the
wall, opposite Jonathan,[a] and Abner sat next
to Saul, but David's place was empty. 26Saul
said nothing that day, for he thought, “Something must have happened to David to make
him ceremonially unclean—surely he is unclean.” 27But the next day, the second day of
the month, David's place was empty again.
Then Saul said to his son Jonathan, “Why
hasn't the son of Jesse come to the meal,
either yesterday or today?”

28Jonathan answered, “David earnestly
asked me for permission to go to Bethlehem.
29He said, ‘Let me go, because our family is
observing a sacrifice in the town and my
brother has ordered me to be there. If I have
found favor in your eyes, let me get away to
see my brothers.’ That is why he has not
come to the king's table.”

30Saul's anger flared up at Jonathan and
he said to him, “You son of a perverse and
rebellious woman! Don't I know that you
have sided with the son of Jesse to your own
shame and to the shame of the mother who
bore you? 31As long as the son of Jesse lives
on this earth, neither you nor your kingdom

[a]25 Septuagint; Hebrew *wall. Jonathan arose*

will be established. Now send and bring him
to me, for he must die!"
32"Why should he be put to death? What
has he done?" Jonathan asked his father.
33But Saul hurled his spear at him to kill him.
Then Jonathan knew that his father intended
to kill David.
34Jonathan got up from the table in fierce
anger; on that second day of the month he
did not eat, because he was grieved at his
father's shameful treatment of David.
35In the morning Jonathan went out to the
field for his meeting with David. He had a
small boy with him, 36and he said to the boy,
"Run and find the arrows I shoot." As the boy
ran, he shot an arrow beyond him. 37When
the boy came to the place where Jonathan's
arrow had fallen, Jonathan called out after
him, "Isn't the arrow beyond you?" 38Then
he shouted, "Hurry! Go quickly! Don't stop!"
The boy picked up the arrow and returned to
his master. 39(The boy knew nothing of all
this; only Jonathan and David knew.) 40Then
Jonathan gave his weapons to the boy and
said, "Go, carry them back to town."
41After the boy had gone, David got up
from the south side ⌊of the stone⌋ and bowed
down before Jonathan three times, with his
face to the ground. Then they kissed each
other and wept together—but David wept the
most.
42Jonathan said to David, "Go in peace, for
we have sworn friendship with each other in
the name of the LORD, saying, 'The LORD is
witness between you and me, and between
your descendants and my descendants forever.' " Then David left, and Jonathan went
back to the town.

David at Nob

21 David went to Nob, to Ahimelech the
priest. Ahimelech trembled when he
met him, and asked, "Why are you alone?
Why is no one with you?"
2David answered Ahimelech the priest,
"The king charged me with a certain matter
and said to me, 'No one is to know anything
about your mission and your instructions.' As
for my men, I have told them to meet me at a
certain place. 3Now then, what do you have
on hand? Give me five loaves of bread, or
whatever you can find."
4But the priest answered David, "I don't
have any ordinary bread on hand; however,
there is some consecrated bread here—
provided the men have kept themselves
from women."
5David replied, "Indeed women have been
kept from us, as usual whenever[a] I set out.
The men's things[b] are holy even on missions
that are not holy. How much more so today!"
6So the priest gave him the consecrated
bread, since there was no bread there except the bread of the Presence that had been
removed from before the LORD and replaced
by hot bread on the day it was taken away.
7Now one of Saul's servants was there that
day, detained before the LORD; he was Doeg
the Edomite, Saul's head shepherd.
8David asked Ahimelech, "Don't you have
a spear or a sword here? I haven't brought
my sword or any other weapon, because the
king's business was urgent."
9The priest replied, "The sword of Goliath
the Philistine, whom you killed in the Valley
of Elah, is here; it is wrapped in a cloth behind the ephod. If you want it, take it; there is
no sword here but that one."
David said, "There is none like it; give it to
me."

David at Gath

10That day David fled from Saul and went
to Achish king of Gath. 11But the servants of
Achish said to him, "Isn't this David, the king
of the land? Isn't he the one they sing about
in their dances:

" 'Saul has slain his thousands,
and David his tens of thousands'?"

12David took these words to heart and was
very much afraid of Achish king of Gath. 13So
he pretended to be insane in their presence;
and while he was in their hands he acted like
a madman, making marks on the doors of
the gate and letting saliva run down his
beard.
14Achish said to his servants, "Look at the
man! He is insane! Why bring him to me?
15Am I so short of madmen that you have to
bring this fellow here to carry on like this in
front of me? Must this man come into my
house?"

David at Adullam and Mizpah

22 David left Gath and escaped to the
cave of Adullam. When his brothers
and his father's household heard about it,
they went down to him there. 2All those who
were in distress or in debt or discontented

[a]5 Or *from us in the past few days since* [b]5 Or *bodies*

gathered around him, and he became their
leader. About four hundred men were with
him.
3From there David went to Mizpah in Moab
and said to the king of Moab, "Would you let
my father and mother come and stay with
you until I learn what God will do for me?"
4So he left them with the king of Moab, and
they stayed with him as long as David was in
the stronghold.
5But the prophet Gad said to David, "Do
not stay in the stronghold. Go into the land of
Judah." So David left and went to the forest
of Hereth.

Saul Kills the Priests of Nob

6Now Saul heard that David and his men
had been discovered. And Saul, spear in
hand, was seated under the tamarisk tree on
the hill at Gibeah, with all his officials standing around him. 7Saul said to them, "Listen,
men of Benjamin! Will the son of Jesse give
all of you fields and vineyards? Will he make
all of you commanders of thousands and
commanders of hundreds? 8Is that why you
have all conspired against me? No one tells
me when my son makes a covenant with the
son of Jesse. None of you is concerned
about me or tells me that my son has incited
my servant to lie in wait for me, as he does
today."
9But Doeg the Edomite, who was standing
with Saul's officials, said, "I saw the son of
Jesse come to Ahimelech son of Ahitub at
Nob. 10Ahimelech inquired of the LORD for
him; he also gave him provisions and the
sword of Goliath the Philistine."
11Then the king sent for the priest Ahimelech son of Ahitub and his father's whole
family, who were the priests at Nob, and they
all came to the king. 12Saul said, "Listen now,
son of Ahitub."
"Yes, my lord," he answered.
13Saul said to him, "Why have you conspired against me, you and the son of Jesse,
giving him bread and a sword and inquiring
of God for him, so that he has rebelled
against me and lies in wait for me, as he
does today?"
14Ahimelech answered the king, "Who of
all your servants is as loyal as David, the
king's son-in-law, captain of your bodyguard
and highly respected in your household?
15Was that day the first time I inquired of God
for him? Of course not! Let not the king accuse your servant or any of his father's
family, for your servant knows nothing at all
about this whole affair."
16But the king said, "You will surely die,
Ahimelech, you and your father's whole
family."
17Then the king ordered the guards at his
side: "Turn and kill the priests of the LORD,
because they too have sided with David.
They knew he was fleeing, yet they did not
tell me."
But the king's officials were not willing to
raise a hand to strike the priests of the LORD.
18The king then ordered Doeg, "You turn
and strike down the priests." So Doeg the
Edomite turned and struck them down. That
day he killed eighty-five men who wore the
linen ephod. 19He also put to the sword Nob,
the town of the priests, with its men and
women, its children and infants, and its cattle, donkeys and sheep.
20But Abiathar, a son of Ahimelech son of
Ahitub, escaped and fled to join David. 21He
told David that Saul had killed the priests of
the LORD. 22Then David said to Abiathar:
"That day, when Doeg the Edomite was
there, I knew he would be sure to tell Saul. I
am responsible for the death of your father's
whole family. 23Stay with me; don't be afraid;
the man who is seeking your life is seeking
mine also. You will be safe with me."

David Saves Keilah

23 When David was told, "Look, the
Philistines are fighting against Keilah
and are looting the threshing floors," 2he inquired of the LORD, saying, "Shall I go and
attack these Philistines?"
The LORD answered him, "Go, attack the
Philistines and save Keilah."
3But David's men said to him, "Here in
Judah we are afraid. How much more, then,
if we go to Keilah against the Philistine
forces!"
4Once again David inquired of the LORD,
and the LORD answered him, "Go down to
Keilah, for I am going to give the Philistines
into your hand." 5So David and his men went
to Keilah, fought the Philistines and carried
off their livestock. He inflicted heavy losses
on the Philistines and saved the people of
Keilah. 6(Now Abiathar son of Ahimelech
had brought the ephod down with him when
he fled to David at Keilah.)

Saul Pursues David

7Saul was told that David had gone to Keilah, and he said, "God has handed him over to me, for David has imprisoned himself by entering a town with gates and bars." 8And Saul called up all his forces for battle, to go down to Keilah to besiege David and his men.

9When David learned that Saul was plotting against him, he said to Abiathar the priest, "Bring the ephod." 10David said, "O LORD, God of Israel, your servant has heard definitely that Saul plans to come to Keilah and destroy the town on account of me. 11Will the citizens of Keilah surrender me to him? Will Saul come down, as your servant has heard? O LORD, God of Israel, tell your servant."

And the LORD said, "He will."

12Again David asked, "Will the citizens of Keilah surrender me and my men to Saul?"

And the LORD said, "They will."

13So David and his men, about six hundred in number, left Keilah and kept moving from place to place. When Saul was told that David had escaped from Keilah, he did not go there.

14David stayed in the desert strongholds and in the hills of the Desert of Ziph. Day after day Saul searched for him, but God did not give David into his hands.

15While David was at Horesh in the Desert of Ziph, he learned that Saul had come out to take his life. 16And Saul's son Jonathan went to David at Horesh and helped him find strength in God. 17"Don't be afraid," he said. "My father Saul will not lay a hand on you. You will be king over Israel, and I will be second to you. Even my father Saul knows this." 18The two of them made a covenant before the LORD. Then Jonathan went home, but David remained at Horesh.

19The Ziphites went up to Saul at Gibeah and said, "Is not David hiding among us in the strongholds at Horesh, on the hill of Hakilah, south of Jeshimon? 20Now, O king, come down whenever it pleases you to do so, and we will be responsible for handing him over to the king."

21Saul replied, "The LORD bless you for your concern for me. 22Go and make further preparation. Find out where David usually goes and who has seen him there. They tell me he is very crafty. 23Find out about all the hiding places he uses and come back to me with definite information.[a] Then I will go with you; if he is in the area, I will track him down among all the clans of Judah."

24So they set out and went to Ziph ahead of Saul. Now David and his men were in the Desert of Maon, in the Arabah south of Jeshimon. 25Saul and his men began the search, and when David was told about it, he went down to the rock and stayed in the Desert of Maon. When Saul heard this, he went into the Desert of Maon in pursuit of David.

26Saul was going along one side of the mountain, and David and his men were on the other side, hurrying to get away from Saul. As Saul and his forces were closing in on David and his men to capture them, 27a messenger came to Saul, saying, "Come quickly! The Philistines are raiding the land." 28Then Saul broke off his pursuit of David and went to meet the Philistines. That is why they call this place Sela Hammahlekoth.[b] 29And David went up from there and lived in the strongholds of En Gedi.

David Spares Saul's Life

24 After Saul returned from pursuing the Philistines, he was told, "David is in the Desert of En Gedi." 2So Saul took three thousand chosen men from all Israel and set out to look for David and his men near the Crags of the Wild Goats.

3He came to the sheep pens along the way; a cave was there, and Saul went in to relieve himself. David and his men were far back in the cave. 4The men said, "This is the day the LORD spoke of when he said[c] to you, 'I will give your enemy into your hands for you to deal with as you wish.'" Then David crept up unnoticed and cut off a corner of Saul's robe.

5Afterward, David was conscience-stricken for having cut off a corner of his robe. 6He said to his men, "The LORD forbid that I should do such a thing to my master, the LORD's anointed, or lift my hand against him; for he is the anointed of the LORD." 7With these words David rebuked his men and did not allow them to attack Saul. And Saul left the cave and went his way.

8Then David went out of the cave and called out to Saul, "My lord the king!" When Saul looked behind him, David bowed down and prostrated himself with his face to the ground. 9He said to Saul, "Why do you listen

[a]23 Or *me at Nacon* [b]28 *Sela Hammahlekoth* means *rock of parting.* [c]4 Or *"Today the LORD is saying*

when men say, 'David is bent on harming
you'? 10This day you have seen with your
own eyes how the LORD delivered you into my
hands in the cave. Some urged me to kill
you, but I spared you; I said, 'I will not lift my
hand against my master, because he is the
LORD's anointed.' 11See, my father, look at
this piece of your robe in my hand! I cut off
the corner of your robe but did not kill you.
Now understand and recognize that I am not
guilty of wrongdoing or rebellion. I have not
wronged you, but you are hunting me down
to take my life. 12May the LORD judge between you and me. And may the LORD
avenge the wrongs you have done to me, but
my hand will not touch you. 13As the old saying goes, 'From evildoers come evil deeds,'
so my hand will not touch you.

14"Against whom has the king of Israel
come out? Whom are you pursuing? A dead
dog? A flea? 15May the LORD be our judge
and decide between us. May he consider my
cause and uphold it; may he vindicate me by
delivering me from your hand."

16When David finished saying this, Saul
asked, "Is that your voice, David my son?"
And he wept aloud. 17"You are more righteous than I," he said. "You have treated me
well, but I have treated you badly. 18You
have just now told me of the good you did to
me; the LORD delivered me into your hands,
but you did not kill me. 19When a man finds
his enemy, does he let him get away unharmed? May the LORD reward you well for
the way you treated me today. 20I know that
you will surely be king and that the kingdom
of Israel will be established in your hands.
21Now swear to me by the LORD that you will
not cut off my descendants or wipe out my
name from my father's family."

22So David gave his oath to Saul. Then
Saul returned home, but David and his men
went up to the stronghold.

David, Nabal and Abigail

25 Now Samuel died, and all Israel assembled and mourned for him; and
they buried him at his home in Ramah.

Then David moved down into the Desert of
Maon.[a] 2A certain man in Maon, who had
property there at Carmel, was very wealthy.
He had a thousand goats and three thousand sheep, which he was shearing in Carmel. 3His name was Nabal and his wife's
name was Abigail. She was an intelligent
and beautiful woman, but her husband, a
Calebite, was surly and mean in his deal-
ings.

4While David was in the desert, he heard
that Nabal was shearing sheep. 5So he sent
ten young men and said to them, "Go up to
Nabal at Carmel and greet him in my name.
6Say to him: 'Long life to you! Good health to
you and your household! And good health to
all that is yours!

7" 'Now I hear that it is sheep-shearing
time. When your shepherds were with us, we
did not mistreat them, and the whole time
they were at Carmel nothing of theirs was
missing. 8Ask your own servants and they
will tell you. Therefore be favorable toward
my young men, since we come at a festive
time. Please give your servants and your son
David whatever you can find for them.' "

9When David's men arrived, they gave Nabal this message in David's name. Then they
waited.

10Nabal answered David's servants, "Who
is this David? Who is this son of Jesse?
Many servants are breaking away from their
masters these days. 11Why should I take my
bread and water, and the meat I have
slaughtered for my shearers, and give it to
men coming from who knows where?"

12David's men turned around and went
back. When they arrived, they reported
every word. 13David said to his men, "Put on
your swords!" So they put on their swords,
and David put on his. About four hundred
men went up with David, while two hundred
stayed with the supplies.

14One of the servants told Nabal's wife
Abigail: "David sent messengers from the
desert to give our master his greetings, but
he hurled insults at them. 15Yet these men
were very good to us. They did not mistreat
us, and the whole time we were out in the
fields near them nothing was missing.
16Night and day they were a wall around us
all the time we were herding our sheep near
them. 17Now think it over and see what you
can do, because disaster is hanging over our
master and his whole household. He is such
a wicked man that no one can talk to him."

18Abigail lost no time. She took two hundred loaves of bread, two skins of wine, five
dressed sheep, five seahs[b] of roasted grain,
a hundred cakes of raisins and two hundred
cakes of pressed figs, and loaded them on
donkeys. 19Then she told her servants, "Go

[a] *1* Some Septuagint manuscripts; Hebrew *Paran*

[b] *18* That is, probably about a bushel (about 37 liters)

on ahead; I'll follow you." But she did not tell her husband Nabal.

20As she came riding her donkey into a mountain ravine, there were David and his men descending toward her, and she met them. 21David had just said, "It's been useless—all my watching over this fellow's property in the desert so that nothing of his was missing. He has paid me back evil for good. 22May God deal with David,[a] be it ever so severely, if by morning I leave alive one male of all who belong to him!"

23When Abigail saw David, she quickly got off her donkey and bowed down before David with her face to the ground. 24She fell at his feet and said: "My lord, let the blame be on me alone. Please let your servant speak to you; hear what your servant has to say. 25May my lord pay no attention to that wicked man Nabal. He is just like his name—his name is Fool, and folly goes with him. But as for me, your servant, I did not see the men my master sent.

26"Now since the LORD has kept you, my master, from bloodshed and from avenging yourself with your own hands, as surely as the LORD lives and as you live, may your enemies and all who intend to harm my master be like Nabal. 27And let this gift, which your servant has brought to my master, be given to the men who follow you. 28Please forgive your servant's offense, for the LORD will certainly make a lasting dynasty for my master, because he fights the LORD's battles. Let no wrongdoing be found in you as long as you live. 29Even though someone is pursuing you to take your life, the life of my master will be bound securely in the bundle of the living by the LORD your God. But the lives of your enemies he will hurl away as from the pocket of a sling. 30When the LORD has done for my master every good thing he promised concerning him and has appointed him leader over Israel, 31my master will not have on his conscience the staggering burden of needless bloodshed or of having avenged himself. And when the LORD has brought my master success, remember your servant."

32David said to Abigail, "Praise be to the LORD, the God of Israel, who has sent you today to meet me. 33May you be blessed for your good judgment and for keeping me from bloodshed this day and from avenging myself with my own hands. 34Otherwise, as surely as the LORD, the God of Israel, lives, who has kept me from harming you, if you had not come quickly to meet me, not one male belonging to Nabal would have been left alive by daybreak."

35Then David accepted from her hand what she had brought him and said, "Go home in peace. I have heard your words and granted your request."

36When Abigail went to Nabal, he was in the house holding a banquet like that of a king. He was in high spirits and very drunk. So she told him nothing until daybreak. 37Then in the morning, when Nabal was sober, his wife told him all these things, and his heart failed him and he became like a stone. 38About ten days later, the LORD struck Nabal and he died.

39When David heard that Nabal was dead, he said, "Praise be to the LORD, who has upheld my cause against Nabal for treating me with contempt. He has kept his servant from doing wrong and has brought Nabal's wrongdoing down on his own head."

Then David sent word to Abigail, asking her to become his wife. 40His servants went to Carmel and said to Abigail, "David has sent us to you to take you to become his wife."

41She bowed down with her face to the ground and said, "Here is your maidservant, ready to serve you and wash the feet of my master's servants." 42Abigail quickly got on a donkey and, attended by her five maids, went with David's messengers and became his wife. 43David had also married Ahinoam of Jezreel, and they both were his wives. 44But Saul had given his daughter Michal, David's wife, to Paltiel[b] son of Laish, who was from Gallim.

David Again Spares Saul's Life

26 The Ziphites went to Saul at Gibeah and said, "Is not David hiding on the hill of Hakilah, which faces Jeshimon?"

2So Saul went down to the Desert of Ziph, with his three thousand chosen men of Israel, to search there for David. 3Saul made his camp beside the road on the hill of Hakilah facing Jeshimon, but David stayed in the desert. When he saw that Saul had followed him there, 4he sent out scouts and learned that Saul had definitely arrived.[c]

5Then David set out and went to the place

[a]22 Some Septuagint manuscripts; Hebrew *with David's enemies* [b]44 Hebrew *Palti*, a variant of *Paltiel*
[c]4 Or *had come to Nacon*

where Saul had camped. He saw where Saul
and Abner son of Ner, the commander of the
army, had lain down. Saul was lying inside
the camp, with the army encamped around
him.
6David then asked Ahimelech the Hittite
and Abishai son of Zeruiah, Joab's brother,
"Who will go down into the camp with me to
Saul?"
"I'll go with you," said Abishai.
7So David and Abishai went to the army by
night, and there was Saul, lying asleep inside the camp with his spear stuck in the
ground near his head. Abner and the soldiers were lying around him.
8Abishai said to David, "Today God has
delivered your enemy into your hands. Now
let me pin him to the ground with one thrust
of my spear; I won't strike him twice."
9But David said to Abishai, "Don't destroy
him! Who can lay a hand on the LORD's
anointed and be guiltless? 10As surely as the
LORD lives," he said, "the LORD himself will
strike him; either his time will come and he
will die, or he will go into battle and perish.
11But the LORD forbid that I should lay a hand
on the LORD's anointed. Now get the spear
and water jug that are near his head, and
let's go."
12So David took the spear and water jug
near Saul's head, and they left. No one saw
or knew about it, nor did anyone wake up.
They were all sleeping, because the LORD
had put them into a deep sleep.
13Then David crossed over to the other
side and stood on top of the hill some distance away; there was a wide space between them. 14He called out to the army and
to Abner son of Ner, "Aren't you going to
answer me, Abner?"
Abner replied, "Who are you who calls to
the king?"
15David said, "You're a man, aren't you?
And who is like you in Israel? Why didn't you
guard your lord the king? Someone came to
destroy your lord the king. 16What you have
done is not good. As surely as the LORD lives,
you and your men deserve to die, because
you did not guard your master, the LORD's
anointed. Look around you. Where are the
king's spear and water jug that were near his
head?"
17Saul recognized David's voice and said,
"Is that your voice, David my son?"
David replied, "Yes it is, my lord the king."
18And he added, "Why is my lord pursuing
his servant? What have I done, and what
wrong am I guilty of? 19Now let my lord the
king listen to his servant's words. If the LORD
has incited you against me, then may he
accept an offering. If, however, men have
done it, may they be cursed before the LORD!
They have now driven me from my share in
the LORD's inheritance and have said, 'Go,
serve other gods.' 20Now do not let my blood
fall to the ground far from the presence of the
LORD. The king of Israel has come out to look
for a flea—as one hunts a partridge in the
mountains."
21Then Saul said, "I have sinned. Come
back, David my son. Because you considered my life precious today, I will not try to
harm you again. Surely I have acted like a
fool and have erred greatly."
22"Here is the king's spear," David answered. "Let one of your young men come
over and get it. 23The LORD rewards every
man for his righteousness and faithfulness.
The LORD delivered you into my hands today,
but I would not lay a hand on the LORD's
anointed. 24As surely as I valued your life
today, so may the LORD value my life and
deliver me from all trouble."
25Then Saul said to David, "May you be
blessed, my son David; you will do great
things and surely triumph."
So David went on his way, and Saul returned home.

David Among the Philistines

27 But David thought to himself, "One of
these days I will be destroyed by the
hand of Saul. The best thing I can do is to
escape to the land of the Philistines. Then
Saul will give up searching for me anywhere
in Israel, and I will slip out of his hand."
2So David and the six hundred men with
him left and went over to Achish son of
Maoch king of Gath. 3David and his men
settled in Gath with Achish. Each man had
his family with him, and David had his two
wives: Ahinoam of Jezreel and Abigail of
Carmel, the widow of Nabal. 4When Saul
was told that David had fled to Gath, he no
longer searched for him.
5Then David said to Achish, "If I have
found favor in your eyes, let a place be assigned to me in one of the country towns, that
I may live there. Why should your servant
live in the royal city with you?"
6So on that day Achish gave him Ziklag,
and it has belonged to the kings of Judah
ever since. 7David lived in Philistine territory
a year and four months.

8Now David and his men went up and raided the Geshurites, the Girzites and the
Amalekites. (From ancient times these peoples had lived in the land extending to Shur
and Egypt.) 9Whenever David attacked an
area, he did not leave a man or woman alive,
but took sheep and cattle, donkeys and camels, and clothes. Then he returned to Achish.
10When Achish asked, "Where did you go
raiding today?" David would say, "Against
the Negev of Judah" or "Against the Negev
of Jerahmeel" or "Against the Negev of the
Kenites." 11He did not leave a man or woman
alive to be brought to Gath, for he thought,
"They might inform on us and say, 'This is
what David did.' " And such was his practice
as long as he lived in Philistine territory.
12Achish trusted David and said to himself,
"He has become so odious to his people, the
Israelites, that he will be my servant forever."

Saul and the Witch of Endor

28 In those days the Philistines gathered their forces to fight against Israel. Achish said to David, "You must understand that you and your men will accompany
me in the army."
2David said, "Then you will see for yourself
what your servant can do."
Achish replied, "Very well, I will make you
my bodyguard for life."
3Now Samuel was dead, and all Israel had
mourned for him and buried him in his own
town of Ramah. Saul had expelled the mediums and spiritists from the land.
4The Philistines assembled and came and
set up camp at Shunem, while Saul gathered
all the Israelites and set up camp at Gilboa.
5When Saul saw the Philistine army, he was
afraid; terror filled his heart. 6He inquired of
the LORD, but the LORD did not answer him by
dreams or Urim or prophets. 7Saul then said
to his attendants, "Find me a woman who is
a medium, so I may go and inquire of her."
"There is one in Endor," they said.
8So Saul disguised himself, putting on
other clothes, and at night he and two men
went to the woman. "Consult a spirit for me,"
he said, "and bring up for me the one I
name."
9But the woman said to him, "Surely you
know what Saul has done. He has cut off the
mediums and spiritists from the land. Why
have you set a trap for my life to bring about
my death?"
10Saul swore to her by the LORD, "As surely
as the LORD lives, you will not be punished for
this."
11Then the woman asked, "Whom shall I
bring up for you?"
"Bring up Samuel," he said.
12When the woman saw Samuel, she cried
out at the top of her voice and said to Saul,
"Why have you deceived me? You are
Saul!"
13The king said to her, "Don't be afraid.
What do you see?"
The woman said, "I see a spirit[a] coming
up out of the ground."
14"What does he look like?" he asked.
"An old man wearing a robe is coming up,"
she said.
Then Saul knew it was Samuel, and he
bowed down and prostrated himself with his
face to the ground.
15Samuel said to Saul, "Why have you disturbed me by bringing me up?"
"I am in great distress," Saul said. "The
Philistines are fighting against me, and God
has turned away from me. He no longer answers me, either by prophets or by dreams.
So I have called on you to tell me what to
do."
16Samuel said, "Why do you consult me,
now that the LORD has turned away from you
and become your enemy? 17The LORD has
done what he predicted through me. The
LORD has torn the kingdom out of your hands
and given it to one of your neighbors—to
David. 18Because you did not obey the LORD
or carry out his fierce wrath against the
Amalekites, the LORD has done this to you
today. 19The LORD will hand over both Israel
and you to the Philistines, and tomorrow you
and your sons will be with me. The LORD will
also hand over the army of Israel to the Philistines."
20Immediately Saul fell full length on the
ground, filled with fear because of Samuel's
words. His strength was gone, for he had
eaten nothing all that day and night.
21When the woman came to Saul and saw
that he was greatly shaken, she said, "Look,
your maidservant has obeyed you. I took my
life in my hands and did what you told me to
do. 22Now please listen to your servant and
let me give you some food so you may eat
and have the strength to go on your way."
23He refused and said, "I will not eat."
But his men joined the woman in urging

[a]13 Or *see spirits*; or *see gods*

him, and he listened to them. He got up from
the ground and sat on the couch.
24The woman had a fattened calf at the
house, which she butchered at once. She
took some flour, kneaded it and baked bread
without yeast. 25Then she set it before Saul
and his men, and they ate. That same night
they got up and left.

Achish Sends David Back to Ziklag

29 The Philistines gathered all their
forces at Aphek, and Israel camped
by the spring in Jezreel. 2As the Philistine
rulers marched with their units of hundreds
and thousands, David and his men were
marching at the rear with Achish. 3The commanders of the Philistines asked, "What
about these Hebrews?"
Achish replied, "Is this not David, who was
an officer of Saul king of Israel? He has already been with me for over a year, and from
the day he left Saul until now, I have found no
fault in him."
4But the Philistine commanders were angry with him and said, "Send the man back,
that he may return to the place you assigned
him. He must not go with us into battle, or he
will turn against us during the fighting. How
better could he regain his master's favor
than by taking the heads of our own men?
5Isn't this the David they sang about in their
dances:

" 'Saul has slain his thousands,
and David his tens of thousands'?"

6So Achish called David and said to him,
"As surely as the LORD lives, you have been
reliable, and I would be pleased to have you
serve with me in the army. From the day you
came to me until now, I have found no fault in
you, but the rulers don't approve of you.
7Turn back and go in peace; do nothing to
displease the Philistine rulers."
8"But what have I done?" asked David.
"What have you found against your servant
from the day I came to you until now? Why
can't I go and fight against the enemies of my
lord the king?"
9Achish answered, "I know that you have
been as pleasing in my eyes as an angel of
God; nevertheless, the Philistine commanders have said, 'He must not go up with us into
battle.' 10Now get up early, along with your
master's servants who have come with you,
and leave in the morning as soon as it is
light."
11So David and his men got up early in the
morning to go back to the land of the Philistines, and the Philistines went up to Jezreel.

David Destroys the Amalekites

30 David and his men reached Ziklag on
the third day. Now the Amalekites
had raided the Negev and Ziklag. They had
attacked Ziklag and burned it, 2and had tak-
en captive the women and all who were in it,
both young and old. They killed none of
them, but carried them off as they went on
their way.
3When David and his men came to Ziklag,
they found it destroyed by fire and their wives
and sons and daughters taken captive. 4So
David and his men wept aloud until they had
no strength left to weep. 5David's two wives
had been captured—Ahinoam of Jezreel
and Abigail, the widow of Nabal of Carmel.
6David was greatly distressed because the
men were talking of stoning him; each one
was bitter in spirit because of his sons and
daughters. But David found strength in the
LORD his God.
7Then David said to Abiathar the priest, the
son of Ahimelech, "Bring me the ephod."
Abiathar brought it to him, 8and David inquired of the LORD, "Shall I pursue this raiding party? Will I overtake them?"
"Pursue them," he answered. "You will
certainly overtake them and succeed in the
rescue."
9David and the six hundred men with him
came to the Besor Ravine, where some
stayed behind, 10for two hundred men were
too exhausted to cross the ravine. But David
and four hundred men continued the pursuit.
11They found an Egyptian in a field and
brought him to David. They gave him water
to drink and food to eat— 12part of a cake of
pressed figs and two cakes of raisins. He ate
and was revived, for he had not eaten any
food or drunk any water for three days and
three nights.
13David asked him, "To whom do you belong, and where do you come from?"
He said, "I am an Egyptian, the slave of an
Amalekite. My master abandoned me when I
became ill three days ago. 14We raided the
Negev of the Kerethites and the territory belonging to Judah and the Negev of Caleb.
And we burned Ziklag."
15David asked him, "Can you lead me
down to this raiding party?"
He answered, "Swear to me before God
that you will not kill me or hand me over to my
master, and I will take you down to them."

16He led David down, and there they were,
scattered over the countryside, eating, drinking and reveling because of the great
amount of plunder they had taken from the
land of the Philistines and from Judah. 17Da-
vid fought them from dusk until the evening
of the next day, and none of them got away,
except four hundred young men who rode off
on camels and fled. 18David recovered
everything the Amalekites had taken, including his two wives. 19Nothing was missing:
young or old, boy or girl, plunder or anything
else they had taken. David brought everything back. 20He took all the flocks and herds,
and his men drove them ahead of the
other livestock, saying, "This is David's plunder."

21Then David came to the two hundred
men who had been too exhausted to follow
him and who were left behind at the Besor
Ravine. They came out to meet David and
the people with him. As David and his men
approached, he greeted them. 22But all the
evil men and troublemakers among David's
followers said, "Because they did not go out
with us, we will not share with them the plunder we recovered. However, each man may
take his wife and children and go."

23David replied, "No, my brothers, you
must not do that with what the LORD has given
us. He has protected us and handed over to
us the forces that came against us. 24Who
will listen to what you say? The share of the
man who stayed with the supplies is to be the
same as that of him who went down to the
battle. All will share alike." 25David made this
a statute and ordinance for Israel from that
day to this.

26When David arrived in Ziklag, he sent
some of the plunder to the elders of Judah,
who were his friends, saying, "Here is a
present for you from the plunder of the LORD's
enemies."

27He sent it to those who were in Bethel,
Ramoth Negev and Jattir; 28to those in Aroer,
Siphmoth, Eshtemoa 29and Racal; to those
in the towns of the Jerahmeelites and the
Kenites; 30to those in Hormah, Bor Ashan,
Athach 31and Hebron; and to those in all the
other places where David and his men had
roamed.

Saul Takes His Life

31 Now the Philistines fought against Israel; the Israelites fled before them,
and many fell slain on Mount Gilboa. 2The
Philistines pressed hard after Saul and his
sons, and they killed his sons Jonathan,
Abinadab and Malki-Shua. 3The fighting
grew fierce around Saul, and when the archers overtook him, they wounded him criti-
cally.

4Saul said to his armor-bearer, "Draw your
sword and run me through, or these uncircumcised fellows will come and run me
through and abuse me."

But his armor-bearer was terrified and
would not do it; so Saul took his own sword
and fell on it. 5When the armor-bearer saw
that Saul was dead, he too fell on his sword
and died with him. 6So Saul and his three
sons and his armor-bearer and all his men
died together that same day.

7When the Israelites along the valley and
those across the Jordan saw that the Israelite army had fled and that Saul and his sons
had died, they abandoned their towns and
fled. And the Philistines came and occupied
them.

8The next day, when the Philistines came
to strip the dead, they found Saul and his
three sons fallen on Mount Gilboa. 9They cut
off his head and stripped off his armor, and
they sent messengers throughout the land of
the Philistines to proclaim the news in the
temple of their idols and among their people.
10They put his armor in the temple of the
Ashtoreths and fastened his body to the wall
of Beth Shan.

11When the people of Jabesh Gilead heard
of what the Philistines had done to Saul, 12all
their valiant men journeyed through the night
to Beth Shan. They took down the bodies of
Saul and his sons from the wall of Beth Shan
and went to Jabesh, where they burned
them. 13Then they took their bones and buried them under a tamarisk tree at Jabesh,
and they fasted seven days.

2 Samuel

Introduction:

Second Samuel continues the story of the beginning of Israel's kingdom. It starts with Saul's death. Then it describes David's forty-year reign. Some of the best-known stories are the capture of Jerusalem, David's sin with Bathsheba, and Absalom's rebellion.

Outline of contents:

David as king of Judah (1:1–4:12)
David unites Israel (5:1–24:25)

David Hears of Saul's Death

1 After the death of Saul, David returned
from defeating the Amalekites and
stayed in Ziklag two days. 2On the third day a
man arrived from Saul's camp, with his
clothes torn and with dust on his head. When
he came to David, he fell to the ground to pay
him honor.
3"Where have you come from?" David
asked him.
He answered, "I have escaped from the
Israelite camp."
4"What happened?" David asked. "Tell
me."
He said, "The men fled from the battle.
Many of them fell and died. And Saul and his
son Jonathan are dead."
5Then David said to the young man who
brought him the report, "How do you know
that Saul and his son Jonathan are dead?"
6"I happened to be on Mount Gilboa," the
young man said, "and there was Saul, leaning on his spear, with the chariots and riders
almost upon him. 7When he turned around
and saw me, he called out to me, and I said,
'What can I do?'
8"He asked me, 'Who are you?'
" 'An Amalekite,' I answered.
9"Then he said to me, 'Stand over me and
kill me! I am in the throes of death, but I'm still
alive.'
10"So I stood over him and killed him, because I knew that after he had fallen he could
not survive. And I took the crown that was on
his head and the band on his arm and have
brought them here to my lord."
11Then David and all the men with him took
hold of their clothes and tore them. 12They
mourned and wept and fasted till evening for
Saul and his son Jonathan, and for the army
of the LORD and the house of Israel, because
they had fallen by the sword.
13David said to the young man who
brought him the report, "Where are you
from?"
"I am the son of an alien, an Amalekite,"
he answered.
14David asked him, "Why were you not
afraid to lift your hand to destroy the LORD's
anointed?"
15Then David called one of his men and
said, "Go, strike him down!" So he struck
him down, and he died. 16For David had said
to him, "Your blood be on your own head.
Your own mouth testified against you when
you said, 'I killed the LORD's anointed.' "

David's Lament for Saul and Jonathan

17David took up this lament concerning
Saul and his son Jonathan, 18and ordered
that the men of Judah be taught this lament
of the bow (it is written in the Book of Jashar):

19"Your glory, O Israel, lies slain on your heights.
How the mighty have fallen!

20"Tell it not in Gath,
proclaim it not in the streets of Ashkelon,
lest the daughters of the Philistines be glad,
lest the daughters of the uncircumcised rejoice.

21“O mountains of Gilboa,
may you have neither dew nor rain,
nor fields that yield offerings ⌊of grain⌋.
For there the shield of the mighty was
defiled,
the shield of Saul—no longer rubbed
with oil.
22From the blood of the slain,
from the flesh of the mighty,
the bow of Jonathan did not turn back,
the sword of Saul did not return
unsatisfied.

23“Saul and Jonathan—
in life they were loved and gracious,
and in death they were not parted.
They were swifter than eagles,
they were stronger than lions.

24“O daughters of Israel,
weep for Saul,
who clothed you in scarlet and finery,
who adorned your garments with
ornaments of gold.

25“How the mighty have fallen in battle!
Jonathan lies slain on your heights.
26I grieve for you, Jonathan my brother;
you were very dear to me.
Your love for me was wonderful,
more wonderful than that of women.
27“How the mighty have fallen!
The weapons of war have perished!”

David Anointed King Over Judah

2 In the course of time, David inquired of
the LORD. “Shall I go up to one of the
towns of Judah?” he asked.
The LORD said, “Go up.”
David asked, “Where shall I go?”
“To Hebron,” the LORD answered.
2So David went up there with his two
wives, Ahinoam of Jezreel and Abigail, the
widow of Nabal of Carmel. 3David also took
the men who were with him, each with his
family, and they settled in Hebron and its
towns. 4Then the men of Judah came to Hebron and there they anointed David king over
the house of Judah.
When David was told that it was the men of
Jabesh Gilead who had buried Saul, 5he sent
messengers to the men of Jabesh Gilead to
say to them, “The LORD bless you for showing this kindness to Saul your master by
burying him. 6May the LORD now show you
kindness and faithfulness, and I too will show
you the same favor because you have done
this. 7Now then, be strong and brave, for
Saul your master is dead, and the house of
Judah has anointed me king over them.”

War Between the Houses of David and Saul

8Meanwhile, Abner son of Ner, the commander of Saul’s army, had taken Ish-
Bosheth son of Saul and brought him over to
Mahanaim. 9He made him king over Gilead,
Ashuri[a] and Jezreel, and also over Ephraim,
Benjamin and all Israel.
10Ish-Bosheth son of Saul was forty years
old when he became king over Israel, and he
reigned two years. The house of Judah,
however, followed David. 11The length of
time David was king in Hebron over the
house of Judah was seven years and six
months.
12Abner son of Ner, together with the men
of Ish-Bosheth son of Saul, left Mahanaim
and went to Gibeon. 13Joab son of Zeruiah
and David’s men went out and met them at
the pool of Gibeon. One group sat down on
one side of the pool and one group on the
other side.
14Then Abner said to Joab, “Let’s have
some of the young men get up and fight hand
to hand in front of us.”
“All right, let them do it,” Joab said.
15So they stood up and were counted off—
twelve men for Benjamin and Ish-Bosheth
son of Saul, and twelve for David. 16Then
each man grabbed his opponent by the head
and thrust his dagger into his opponent’s
side, and they fell down together. So that
place in Gibeon was called Helkath Hazzurim.[b]
17The battle that day was very fierce, and
Abner and the men of Israel were defeated
by David’s men.
18The three sons of Zeruiah were there:
Joab, Abishai and Asahel. Now Asahel was
as fleet-footed as a wild gazelle. 19He
chased Abner, turning neither to the right nor
to the left as he pursued him. 20Abner looked
behind him and asked, “Is that you, Asahel?”
“It is,” he answered.
21Then Abner said to him, “Turn aside to
the right or to the left; take on one of the
young men and strip him of his weapons.”
But Asahel would not stop chasing him.

[a]9 Or *Asher* [b]16 *Helkath Hazzurim* means *field of daggers* or *field of hostilities.*

22Again Abner warned Asahel, "Stop
chasing me! Why should I strike you down?
How could I look your brother Joab in the
face?"

23But Asahel refused to give up the pursuit;
so Abner thrust the butt of his spear into
Asahel's stomach, and the spear came out
through his back. He fell there and died on
the spot. And every man stopped when he
came to the place where Asahel had fallen
and died.

24But Joab and Abishai pursued Abner,
and as the sun was setting, they came to the
hill of Ammah, near Giah on the way to the
wasteland of Gibeon. 25Then the men of
Benjamin rallied behind Abner. They formed
themselves into a group and took their stand
on top of a hill.

26Abner called out to Joab, "Must the
sword devour forever? Don't you realize that
this will end in bitterness? How long before
you order your men to stop pursuing their
brothers?"

27Joab answered, "As surely as God lives,
if you had not spoken, the men would have
continued the pursuit of their brothers until
morning.[a]"

28So Joab blew the trumpet, and all the
men came to a halt; they no longer pursued
Israel, nor did they fight anymore.

29All that night Abner and his men
marched through the Arabah. They crossed
the Jordan, continued through the whole
Bithron[b] and came to Mahanaim.

30Then Joab returned from pursuing Abner
and assembled all his men. Besides Asahel,
nineteen of David's men were found missing.
31But David's men had killed three hundred
and sixty Benjamites who were with Abner.
32They took Asahel and buried him in his
father's tomb at Bethlehem. Then Joab and
his men marched all night and arrived at
Hebron by daybreak.

3 The war between the house of Saul and
the house of David lasted a long time.
David grew stronger and stronger, while the
house of Saul grew weaker and weaker.

2Sons were born to David in Hebron:
His firstborn was Amnon the son of
Ahinoam of Jezreel;
3his second, Kileab the son of Abigail
the widow of Nabal of Carmel;
the third, Absalom the son of Maacah daughter of Talmai king of Geshur;
4the fourth, Adonijah the son of Haggith;
the fifth, Shephatiah the son of Abital;
5and the sixth, Ithream the son of David's wife Eglah.
These were born to David in Hebron.

Abner Goes Over to David

6During the war between the house of Saul
and the house of David, Abner had been
strengthening his own position in the house
of Saul. 7Now Saul had had a concubine
named Rizpah daughter of Aiah. And Ish-
Bosheth said to Abner, "Why did you sleep
with my father's concubine?"

8Abner was very angry because of what
Ish-Bosheth said and he answered, "Am I a
dog's head—on Judah's side? This very day
I am loyal to the house of your father Saul
and to his family and friends. I haven't handed you over to David. Yet now you accuse
me of an offense involving this woman! 9May
God deal with Abner, be it ever so severely, if
I do not do for David what the LORD promised
him on oath 10and transfer the kingdom from
the house of Saul and establish David's
throne over Israel and Judah from Dan to
Beersheba." 11Ish-Bosheth did not dare to
say another word to Abner, because he was
afraid of him.

12Then Abner sent messengers on his behalf to say to David, "Whose land is it? Make
an agreement with me, and I will help you
bring all Israel over to you."

13"Good," said David. "I will make an
agreement with you. But I demand one thing
of you: Do not come into my presence unless
you bring Michal daughter of Saul when you
come to see me." 14Then David sent messengers to Ish-Bosheth son of Saul, demanding, "Give me my wife Michal, whom I
betrothed to myself for the price of a hundred
Philistine foreskins."

15So Ish-Bosheth gave orders and had her
taken away from her husband Paltiel son of
Laish. 16Her husband, however, went with
her, weeping behind her all the way to Bahurim. Then Abner said to him, "Go back
home!" So he went back.

17Abner conferred with the elders of Israel

[a]27 Or *spoken this morning, the men would not have taken up the pursuit of their brothers;* or *spoken, the men would have given up the pursuit of their brothers by morning* [b]29 Or *morning;* or *ravine;* the meaning of the Hebrew for this word is uncertain.

and said, "For some time you have wanted
to make David your king. 18Now do it! For the
LORD promised David, 'By my servant David I
will rescue my people Israel from the hand of
the Philistines and from the hand of all their
enemies.'"
19Abner also spoke to the Benjamites in
person. Then he went to Hebron to tell David
everything that Israel and the whole house of
Benjamin wanted to do. 20When Abner, who
had twenty men with him, came to David at
Hebron, David prepared a feast for him and
his men. 21Then Abner said to David, "Let
me go at once and assemble all Israel for my
lord the king, so that they may make a compact with you, and that you may rule over all
that your heart desires." So David sent Abner away, and he went in peace.

Joab Murders Abner

22Just then David's men and Joab returned from a raid and brought with them a
great deal of plunder. But Abner was no
longer with David in Hebron, because David
had sent him away, and he had gone in
peace. 23When Joab and all the soldiers with
him arrived, he was told that Abner son of
Ner had come to the king and that the king
had sent him away and that he had gone in
peace.
24So Joab went to the king and said, "What
have you done? Look, Abner came to you.
Why did you let him go? Now he is gone!
25You know Abner son of Ner; he came to
deceive you and observe your movements
and find out everything you are doing."
26Joab then left David and sent messengers after Abner, and they brought him back
from the well of Sirah. But David did not know
it. 27Now when Abner returned to Hebron,
Joab took him aside into the gateway, as
though to speak with him privately. And
there, to avenge the blood of his brother Asahel, Joab stabbed him in the stomach, and
he died.
28Later, when David heard about this, he
said, "I and my kingdom are forever innocent
before the LORD concerning the blood of Abner son of Ner. 29May his blood fall upon the
head of Joab and upon all his father's house!
May Joab's house never be without someone who has a running sore or leprosy[a] or
who leans on a crutch or who falls by the
sword or who lacks food."
30(Joab and his brother Abishai murdered
Abner because he had killed their brother
Asahel in the battle at Gibeon.)
31Then David said to Joab and all the
people with him, "Tear your clothes and put
on sackcloth and walk in mourning in front of
Abner." King David himself walked behind
the bier. 32They buried Abner in Hebron, and
the king wept aloud at Abner's tomb. All the
people wept also.
33The king sang this lament for Abner:

"Should Abner have died as the lawless
die?
34 Your hands were not bound,
your feet were not fettered.
You fell as one falls before wicked men."

And all the people wept over him again.
35Then they all came and urged David to
eat something while it was still day; but David
took an oath, saying, "May God deal with
me, be it ever so severely, if I taste bread or
anything else before the sun sets!"
36All the people took note and were
pleased; indeed, everything the king did
pleased them. 37So on that day all the people
and all Israel knew that the king had no part
in the murder of Abner son of Ner.
38Then the king said to his men, "Do you
not realize that a prince and a great man has
fallen in Israel this day? 39And today, though
I am the anointed king, I am weak, and these
sons of Zeruiah are too strong for me. May
the LORD repay the evildoer according to his
evil deeds!"

Ish-Bosheth Murdered

4 When Ish-Bosheth son of Saul heard
that Abner had died in Hebron, he lost
courage, and all Israel became alarmed.
2Now Saul's son had two men who were
leaders of raiding bands. One was named
Baanah and the other Recab; they were
sons of Rimmon the Beerothite from the tribe
of Benjamin—Beeroth is considered part of
Benjamin, 3because the people of Beeroth
fled to Gittaim and have lived there as aliens
to this day.
4(Jonathan son of Saul had a son who was
lame in both feet. He was five years old when
the news about Saul and Jonathan came
from Jezreel. His nurse picked him up and
fled, but as she hurried to leave, he fell and
became crippled. His name was Mephibosheth.)
5Now Recab and Baanah, the sons of Rim-

[a]29 The Hebrew word was used for various diseases affecting the skin—not necessarily leprosy.

mon the Beerothite, set out for the house of
Ish-Bosheth, and they arrived there in the
heat of the day while he was taking his noonday rest. 6They went into the inner part of the
house as if to get some wheat, and they
stabbed him in the stomach. Then Recab
and his brother Baanah slipped away.
7They had gone into the house while he
was lying on the bed in his bedroom. After
they stabbed and killed him, they cut off his
head. Taking it with them, they traveled all
night by way of the Arabah. 8They brought
the head of Ish-Bosheth to David at Hebron
and said to the king, "Here is the head of
Ish-Bosheth son of Saul, your enemy, who
tried to take your life. This day the LORD has
avenged my lord the king against Saul and
his offspring."
9David answered Recab and his brother
Baanah, the sons of Rimmon the Beerothite,
"As surely as the LORD lives, who has delivered me out of all trouble, 10when a man
told me, 'Saul is dead,' and thought he was
bringing good news, I seized him and put him
to death in Ziklag. That was the reward I
gave him for his news! 11How much more—
when wicked men have killed an innocent
man in his own house and on his own bed—
should I not now demand his blood from your
hand and rid the earth of you!"
12So David gave an order to his men, and
they killed them. They cut off their hands and
feet and hung the bodies by the pool in Hebron. But they took the head of Ish-Bosheth
and buried it in Abner's tomb at Hebron.

David Becomes King Over Israel

5 All the tribes of Israel came to David at
Hebron and said, "We are your own
flesh and blood. 2In the past, while Saul was
king over us, you were the one who led Israel
on their military campaigns. And the LORD
said to you, 'You will shepherd my people
Israel, and you will become their ruler.' "
3When all the elders of Israel had come to
King David at Hebron, the king made a compact with them at Hebron before the LORD,
and they anointed David king over Israel.
4David was thirty years old when he
became king, and he reigned forty years. 5In
Hebron he reigned over Judah seven years
and six months, and in Jerusalem he reigned
over all Israel and Judah thirty-three years.

David Conquers Jerusalem

6The king and his men marched to Jerusalem to attack the Jebusites, who lived there.
The Jebusites said to David, "You will not get
in here; even the blind and the lame can
ward you off." They thought, "David cannot
get in here." 7Nevertheless, David captured
the fortress of Zion, the City of David.
8On that day, David said, "Anyone who
conquers the Jebusites will have to use the
water shaft[a] to reach those 'lame and blind'
who are David's enemies.[b]" That is why they
say, "The 'blind and lame' will not enter the
palace."
9David then took up residence in the fortress and called it the City of David. He built
up the area around it, from the supporting
terraces[c] inward. 10And he became more
and more powerful, because the LORD God
Almighty was with him.
11Now Hiram king of Tyre sent messengers to David, along with cedar logs and
carpenters and stonemasons, and they built
a palace for David. 12And David knew that
the LORD had established him as king over
Israel and had exalted his kingdom for the
sake of his people Israel.
13After he left Hebron, David took more
concubines and wives in Jerusalem, and
more sons and daughters were born to him.
14These are the names of the children born
to him there: Shammua, Shobab, Nathan,
Solomon, 15Ibhar, Elishua, Nepheg, Japhia,
16Elishama, Eliada and Eliphelet.

David Defeats the Philistines

17When the Philistines heard that David
had been anointed king over Israel, they
went up in full force to search for him, but
David heard about it and went down to the
stronghold. 18Now the Philistines had come
and spread out in the Valley of Rephaim;
19so David inquired of the LORD, "Shall I go
and attack the Philistines? Will you hand
them over to me?"
The LORD answered him, "Go, for I will
surely hand the Philistines over to you."
20So David went to Baal Perazim, and
there he defeated them. He said, "As waters
break out, the LORD has broken out against
my enemies before me." So that place was
called Baal Perazim.[d] 21The Philistines

[a]8 Or *use scaling hooks* [b]8 Or *are hated by David* [c]9 Or *the Millo* [d]20 *Baal Perazim* means *the lord who breaks out.*

abandoned their idols there, and David and
his men carried them off.
22Once more the Philistines came up and
spread out in the Valley of Rephaim; 23so
David inquired of the LORD, and he answered,
"Do not go straight up, but circle around behind them and attack them in front of the
balsam trees. 24As soon as you hear the
sound of marching in the tops of the balsam
trees, move quickly, because that will mean
the LORD has gone out in front of you to strike
the Philistine army." 25So David did as the
LORD commanded him, and he struck down
the Philistines all the way from Gibeon[a] to
Gezer.

The Ark Brought to Jerusalem

6 David again brought together out of Israel chosen men, thirty thousand in all.
2He and all his men set out from Baalah of
Judah[b] to bring up from there the ark of God,
which is called by the Name,[c] the name of
the LORD Almighty, who is enthroned between the cherubim that are on the ark.
3They set the ark of God on a new cart and
brought it from the house of Abinadab, which
was on the hill. Uzzah and Ahio, sons of
Abinadab, were guiding the new cart 4with
the ark of God on it,[d] and Ahio was walking in
front of it. 5David and the whole house of
Israel were celebrating with all their might
before the LORD, with songs[e] and with harps,
lyres, tambourines, sistrums and cymbals.
6When they came to the threshing floor of
Nacon, Uzzah reached out and took hold of
the ark of God, because the oxen stumbled.
7The LORD's anger burned against Uzzah because of his irreverent act; therefore God
struck him down and he died there beside
the ark of God.
8Then David was angry because the
LORD's wrath had broken out against Uzzah,
and to this day that place is called Perez
Uzzah.[f]
9David was afraid of the LORD that day and
said, "How can the ark of the LORD ever come
to me?" 10He was not willing to take the ark of
the LORD to be with him in the City of David.
Instead, he took it aside to the house of
Obed-Edom the Gittite. 11The ark of the LORD
remained in the house of Obed-Edom the
Gittite for three months, and the LORD
blessed him and his entire household.
12Now King David was told, "The LORD has
blessed the household of Obed-Edom and
everything he has, because of the ark of
God." So David went down and brought up
the ark of God from the house of Obed-Edom
to the City of David with rejoicing. 13When
those who were carrying the ark of the LORD
had taken six steps, he sacrificed a bull and a
fattened calf. 14David, wearing a linen
ephod, danced before the LORD with all his
might, 15while he and the entire house of
Israel brought up the ark of the LORD with
shouts and the sound of trumpets.
16As the ark of the LORD was entering the
City of David, Michal daughter of Saul
watched from a window. And when she saw
King David leaping and dancing before the
LORD, she despised him in her heart.
17They brought the ark of the LORD and set
it in its place inside the tent that David had
pitched for it, and David sacrificed burnt offerings and fellowship offerings[g] before the
LORD. 18After he had finished sacrificing the
burnt offerings and fellowship offerings, he
blessed the people in the name of the LORD
Almighty. 19Then he gave a loaf of bread, a
cake of dates and a cake of raisins to each
person in the whole crowd of Israelites, both
men and women. And all the people went to
their homes.
20When David returned home to bless his
household, Michal daughter of Saul came
out to meet him and said, "How the king of
Israel has distinguished himself today, dis-
robing in the sight of the slave girls of his
servants as any vulgar fellow would!"
21David said to Michal, "It was before the
LORD, who chose me rather than your father
or anyone from his house when he appointed me ruler over the LORD's people Israel—I will celebrate before the LORD. 22I will
become even more undignified than this,
and I will be humiliated in my own eyes. But
by these slave girls you spoke of, I will be
held in honor."
23And Michal daughter of Saul had no children to the day of her death.

[a]25 Septuagint (see also 1 Chron. 14:16); Hebrew *Geba* [b]2 That is, Kiriath Jearim; Hebrew *Baale Judah*, a variant of *Baalah of Judah* [c]2 Hebrew; Septuagint and Vulgate do not have *the Name.* [d]3,4 Dead Sea Scrolls and some Septuagint manuscripts; Masoretic Text *cart* [4]*and they brought it with the ark of God from the house of Abinadab, which was on the hill* [e]5 See Dead Sea Scrolls, Septuagint and 1 Chronicles 13:8; Masoretic Text *celebrating before the LORD with all kinds of instruments made of pine.* [f]8 *Perez Uzzah* means *outbreak against Uzzah.* [g]17 Traditionally *peace offerings;* also in verse 18

God's Promise to David

7 After the king was settled in his palace and the LORD had given him rest from all his enemies around him, [2]he said to Nathan the prophet, "Here I am, living in a palace of cedar, while the ark of God remains in a tent."

[3]Nathan replied to the king, "Whatever you have in mind, go ahead and do it, for the LORD is with you."

[4]That night the word of the LORD came to Nathan, saying:

[5]"Go and tell my servant David, 'This is what the LORD says: Are you the one to build me a house to dwell in? [6]I have not dwelt in a house from the day I brought the Israelites up out of Egypt to this day. I have been moving from place to place with a tent as my dwelling. [7]Wherever I have moved with all the Israelites, did I ever say to any of their rulers whom I commanded to shepherd my people Israel, "Why have you not built me a house of cedar?"'

[8]"Now then, tell my servant David, 'This is what the LORD Almighty says: I took you from the pasture and from following the flock to be ruler over my people Israel. [9]I have been with you wherever you have gone, and I have cut off all your enemies from before you. Now I will make your name great, like the names of the greatest men of the earth. [10]And I will provide a place for my people Israel and will plant them so that they can have a home of their own and no longer be disturbed. Wicked people will not oppress them anymore, as they did at the beginning [11]and have done ever since the time I appointed leaders[a] over my people Israel. I will also give you rest from all your enemies.

"'The LORD declares to you that the LORD himself will establish a house for you: [12]When your days are over and you rest with your fathers, I will raise up your offspring to succeed you, who will come from your own body, and I will establish his kingdom. [13]He is the one who will build a house for my Name, and I will establish the throne of his kingdom forever. [14]I will be his father, and he will be my son. When he does wrong, I will punish him with the rod of men, with floggings inflicted by men. [15]But my love will never be taken away from him, as I took it away from Saul, whom I removed from before you. [16]Your house and your kingdom will endure forever before me[b]; your throne will be established forever.'"

[17]Nathan reported to David all the words of this entire revelation.

David's Prayer

[18]Then King David went in and sat before the LORD, and he said:

"Who am I, O Sovereign LORD, and what is my family, that you have brought me this far? [19]And as if this were not enough in your sight, O Sovereign LORD, you have also spoken about the future of the house of your servant. Is this your usual way of dealing with man, O Sovereign LORD?

[20]"What more can David say to you? For you know your servant, O Sovereign LORD. [21]For the sake of your word and according to your will, you have done this great thing and made it known to your servant.

[22]"How great you are, O Sovereign LORD! There is no one like you, and there is no God but you, as we have heard with our own ears. [23]And who is like your people Israel—the one nation on earth that God went out to redeem as a people for himself, and to make a name for himself, and to perform great and awesome wonders by driving out nations and their gods from before your people, whom you redeemed from Egypt?[c] [24]You have established your people Israel as your very own forever, and you, O LORD, have become their God.

[25]"And now, LORD God, keep forever the promise you have made concerning your servant and his house. Do as you promised, [26]so that your name will be great forever. Then men will say, 'The LORD Almighty is God over Israel!' And the house of your servant David will be established before you.

[27]"O LORD Almighty, God of Israel, you

[a]11 Traditionally *judges* [b]16 Some Hebrew manuscripts and Septuagint; most Hebrew manuscripts *you*
[c]23 See Septuagint and 1 Chron. 17:21; Hebrew *wonders for your land and before your people, whom you redeemed from Egypt, from the nations and their gods.*

have revealed this to your servant, saying, 'I will build a house for you.' So your servant has found courage to offer you this prayer. [28]O Sovereign LORD, you are God! Your words are trustworthy, and you have promised these good things to your servant. [29]Now be pleased to bless the house of your servant, that it may continue forever in your sight; for you, O Sovereign LORD, have spoken, and with your blessing the house of your servant will be blessed forever."

David's Victories

8 In the course of time, David defeated the Philistines and subdued them, and he took Metheg Ammah from the control of the Philistines.

[2]David also defeated the Moabites. He made them lie down on the ground and measured them off with a length of cord. Every two lengths of them were put to death, and the third length was allowed to live. So the Moabites became subject to David and brought tribute.

[3]Moreover, David fought Hadadezer son of Rehob, king of Zobah, when he went to restore his control along the Euphrates River. [4]David captured a thousand of his chariots, seven thousand charioteers[a] and twenty thousand foot soldiers. He hamstrung all but a hundred of the chariot horses.

[5]When the Arameans of Damascus came to help Hadadezer king of Zobah, David struck down twenty-two thousand of them. [6]He put garrisons in the Aramean kingdom of Damascus, and the Arameans became subject to him and brought tribute. The LORD gave David victory wherever he went.

[7]David took the gold shields that belonged to the officers of Hadadezer and brought them to Jerusalem. [8]From Tebah[b] and Berothai, towns that belonged to Hadadezer, King David took a great quantity of bronze.

[9]When Tou[c] king of Hamath heard that David had defeated the entire army of Hadadezer, [10]he sent his son Joram[d] to King David to greet him and congratulate him on his victory in battle over Hadadezer, who had been at war with Tou. Joram brought with him articles of silver and gold and bronze.

[11]King David dedicated these articles to the LORD, as he had done with the silver and gold from all the nations he had subdued: [12]Edom[e] and Moab, the Ammonites and the Philistines, and Amalek. He also dedicated the plunder taken from Hadadezer son of Rehob, king of Zobah.

[13]And David became famous after he returned from striking down eighteen thousand Edomites[f] in the Valley of Salt.

[14]He put garrisons throughout Edom, and all the Edomites became subject to David. The LORD gave David victory wherever he went.

David's Officials

[15]David reigned over all Israel, doing what was just and right for all his people. [16]Joab son of Zeruiah was over the army; Jehoshaphat son of Ahilud was recorder; [17]Zadok son of Ahitub and Ahimelech son of Abiathar were priests; Seraiah was secretary; [18]Benaiah son of Jehoiada was over the Kerethites and Pelethites; and David's sons were royal advisers.[g]

David and Mephibosheth

9 David asked, "Is there anyone still left of the house of Saul to whom I can show kindness for Jonathan's sake?"

[2]Now there was a servant of Saul's household named Ziba. They called him to appear before David, and the king said to him, "Are you Ziba?"

"Your servant," he replied.

[3]The king asked, "Is there no one still left of the house of Saul to whom I can show God's kindness?"

Ziba answered the king, "There is still a son of Jonathan; he is crippled in both feet."

[4]"Where is he?" the king asked.

Ziba answered, "He is at the house of Makir son of Ammiel in Lo Debar."

[5]So King David had him brought from Lo Debar, from the house of Makir son of Ammiel.

[6]When Mephibosheth son of Jonathan, the son of Saul, came to David, he bowed down to pay him honor.

David said, "Mephibosheth!"

"Your servant," he replied.

[a]4 Septuagint (see also Dead Sea Scrolls and 1 Chron. 18:4); Masoretic Text *captured seventeen hundred of his charioteers* [b]8 See some Septuagint manuscripts (see also 1 Chron. 18:8); Hebrew *Betah.* [c]9 Hebrew *Toi,* a variant of *Tou;* also in verse 10 [d]10 A variant of *Hadoram* [e]12 Some Hebrew manuscripts, Septuagint and Syriac (see also 1 Chron. 18:11); most Hebrew manuscripts *Aram* [f]13 A few Hebrew manuscripts, Septuagint and Syriac (see also 1 Chron. 18:12); most Hebrew manuscripts *Aram* (that is, Arameans) [g]18 Or *were priests*

7"Don't be afraid," David said to him, "for I
will surely show you kindness for the sake of
your father Jonathan. I will restore to you all
the land that belonged to your grandfather
Saul, and you will always eat at my table."
8Mephibosheth bowed down and said,
"What is your servant, that you should notice
a dead dog like me?"
9Then the king summoned Ziba, Saul's
servant, and said to him, "I have given your
master's grandson everything that belonged
to Saul and his family. 10You and your sons
and your servants are to farm the land for
him and bring in the crops, so that your master's grandson may be provided for. And Mephibosheth, grandson of your master, will
always eat at my table." (Now Ziba had fifteen sons and twenty servants.)
11Then Ziba said to the king, "Your servant
will do whatever my lord the king commands
his servant to do." So Mephibosheth ate at
David's[a] table like one of the king's sons.
12Mephibosheth had a young son named
Mica, and all the members of Ziba's household were servants of Mephibosheth. 13And
Mephibosheth lived in Jerusalem, because
he always ate at the king's table, and he was
crippled in both feet.

David Defeats the Ammonites

10 In the course of time, the king of the
Ammonites died, and his son Hanun
succeeded him as king. 2David thought, "I
will show kindness to Hanun son of Nahash,
just as his father showed kindness to me."
So David sent a delegation to express his
sympathy to Hanun concerning his father.
When David's men came to the land of the
Ammonites, 3the Ammonite nobles said to
Hanun their lord, "Do you think David is honoring your father by sending men to you to
express sympathy? Hasn't David sent them
to you to explore the city and spy it out and
overthrow it?" 4So Hanun seized David's
men, shaved off half of each man's beard,
cut off their garments in the middle at the
buttocks, and sent them away.
5When David was told about this, he sent
messengers to meet the men, for they were
greatly humiliated. The king said, "Stay at
Jericho till your beards have grown, and then
come back."
6When the Ammonites realized that they
had become a stench in David's nostrils,
they hired twenty thousand Aramean foot
soldiers from Beth Rehob and Zobah, as well
as the king of Maacah with a thousand men,
and also twelve thousand men from Tob.
7On hearing this, David sent Joab out with
the entire army of fighting men. 8The Ammonites came out and drew up in battle formation at the entrance to their city gate,
while the Arameans of Zobah and Rehob
and the men of Tob and Maacah were by
themselves in the open country.
9Joab saw that there were battle lines in
front of him and behind him; so he selected
some of the best troops in Israel and deployed them against the Arameans. 10He put
the rest of the men under the command of
Abishai his brother and deployed them
against the Ammonites. 11Joab said, "If the
Arameans are too strong for me, then you
are to come to my rescue; but if the Ammonites are too strong for you, then I will come to
rescue you. 12Be strong and let us fight
bravely for our people and the cities of our
God. The LORD will do what is good in his
sight."
13Then Joab and the troops with him advanced to fight the Arameans, and they fled
before him. 14When the Ammonites saw that
the Arameans were fleeing, they fled before
Abishai and went inside the city. So Joab
returned from fighting the Ammonites and
came to Jerusalem.
15After the Arameans saw that they had
been routed by Israel, they regrouped.
16Hadadezer had Arameans brought from
beyond the River[b]; they went to Helam, with
Shobach the commander of Hadadezer's
army leading them.
17When David was told of this, he gathered
all Israel, crossed the Jordan and went to
Helam. The Arameans formed their battle
lines to meet David and fought against him.
18But they fled before Israel, and David killed
seven hundred of their charioteers and forty
thousand of their foot soldiers.[c] He also
struck down Shobach the commander of
their army, and he died there. 19When all the
kings who were vassals of Hadadezer saw
that they had been defeated by Israel, they
made peace with the Israelites and became
subject to them.
So the Arameans were afraid to help the
Ammonites anymore.

[a]11 Septuagint; Hebrew *my* [b]16 That is, the Euphrates [c]*Some Septuagint manuscripts (see also 1 Chron. 19:18); Hebrew horsemen*

David and Bathsheba

11 In the spring, at the time when kings
go off to war, David sent Joab out
with the king's men and the whole Israelite
army. They destroyed the Ammonites and
besieged Rabbah. But David remained in
Jerusalem.
2One evening David got up from his bed
and walked around on the roof of the palace.
From the roof he saw a woman bathing. The
woman was very beautiful, 3and David sent
someone to find out about her. The man
said, "Isn't this Bathsheba, the daughter of
Eliam and the wife of Uriah the Hittite?"
4Then David sent messengers to get her.
She came to him, and he slept with her. (She
had purified herself from her uncleanness.)
Then[a] she went back home. 5The woman
conceived and sent word to David, saying, "I
am pregnant."
6So David sent this word to Joab: "Send
me Uriah the Hittite." And Joab sent him to
David. 7When Uriah came to him, David
asked him how Joab was, how the soldiers
were and how the war was going. 8Then David said to Uriah, "Go down to your house
and wash your feet." So Uriah left the palace, and a gift from the king was sent after
him. 9But Uriah slept at the entrance to the
palace with all his master's servants and did
not go down to his house.
10When David was told, "Uriah did not go
home," he asked him, "Haven't you just
come from a distance? Why didn't you go
home?"
11Uriah said to David, "The ark and Israel
and Judah are staying in tents, and my master Joab and my lord's men are camped in
the open fields. How could I go to my house
to eat and drink and lie with my wife? As
surely as you live, I will not do such a thing!"
12Then David said to him, "Stay here one
more day, and tomorrow I will send you
back." So Uriah remained in Jerusalem that
day and the next. 13At David's invitation, he
ate and drank with him, and David made him
drunk. But in the evening Uriah went out to
sleep on his mat among his master's servants; he did not go home.
14In the morning David wrote a letter to
Joab and sent it with Uriah. 15In it he wrote,
"Put Uriah in the front line where the fighting
is fiercest. Then withdraw from him so he will
be struck down and die."
16So while Joab had the city under siege,
he put Uriah at a place where he knew the
strongest defenders were. 17When the men
of the city came out and fought against Joab,
some of the men in David's army fell; moreover, Uriah the Hittite died.
18Joab sent David a full account of the
battle. 19He instructed the messenger:
"When you have finished giving the king this
account of the battle, 20the king's anger may
flare up, and he may ask you, 'Why did you
get so close to the city to fight? Didn't you
know they would shoot arrows from the wall?
21Who killed Abimelech son of Jerub-
Besheth[b]? Didn't a woman throw an upper
millstone on him from the wall, so that he
died in Thebez? Why did you get so close to
the wall?' If he asks you this, then say to him,
'Also, your servant Uriah the Hittite is
dead.' "
22The messenger set out, and when he
arrived he told David everything Joab had
sent him to say. 23The messenger said to
David, "The men overpowered us and came
out against us in the open, but we drove
them back to the entrance to the city gate.
24Then the archers shot arrows at your servants from the wall, and some of the king's
men died. Moreover, your servant Uriah the
Hittite is dead."
25David told the messenger, "Say this to
Joab: 'Don't let this upset you; the sword
devours one as well as another. Press the
attack against the city and destroy it.' Say
this to encourage Joab."
26When Uriah's wife heard that her husband was dead, she mourned for him. 27After
the time of mourning was over, David had
her brought to his house, and she became
his wife and bore him a son. But the thing
David had done displeased the LORD.

Nathan Rebukes David

12 The LORD sent Nathan to David.
When he came to him, he said,
"There were two men in a certain town, one
rich and the other poor. 2The rich man had a
very large number of sheep and cattle, 3but
the poor man had nothing except one little
ewe lamb he had bought. He raised it, and it
grew up with him and his children. It shared
his food, drank from his cup and even slept in
his arms. It was like a daughter to him.
4"Now a traveler came to the rich man, but

[a]4 Or *with her. When she purified herself from her uncleanness,* [b]21 Also known as *Jerub-Baal* (that is, Gideon)

the rich man refrained from taking one of his
own sheep or cattle to prepare a meal for the
traveler who had come to him. Instead, he
took the ewe lamb that belonged to the poor
man and prepared it for the one who had
come to him."
5David burned with anger against the man
and said to Nathan, "As surely as the LORD
lives, the man who did this deserves to die!
6He must pay for that lamb four times over,
because he did such a thing and had no
pity."
7Then Nathan said to David, "You are the
man! This is what the LORD, the God of Israel,
says: 'I anointed you king over Israel, and I
delivered you from the hand of Saul. 8I gave
your master's house to you, and your master's wives into your arms. I gave you the
house of Israel and Judah. And if all this had
been too little, I would have given you even
more. 9Why did you despise the word of the
LORD by doing what is evil in his eyes? You
struck down Uriah the Hittite with the sword
and took his wife to be your own. You killed
him with the sword of the Ammonites. 10Now,
therefore, the sword will never depart from
your house, because you despised me and
took the wife of Uriah the Hittite to be your
own.'
11"This is what the LORD says: 'Out of your
own household I am going to bring calamity
upon you. Before your very eyes I will take
your wives and give them to one who is close
to you, and he will lie with your wives in broad
daylight. 12You did it in secret, but I will do
this thing in broad daylight before all Israel.' "
13Then David said to Nathan, "I have
sinned against the LORD."
Nathan replied, "The LORD has taken away
your sin. You are not going to die. 14But because by doing this you have made the enemies of the LORD show utter contempt,[a] the
son born to you will die."
15After Nathan had gone home, the LORD
struck the child that Uriah's wife had borne to
David, and he became ill. 16David pleaded
with God for the child. He fasted and went
into his house and spent the nights lying on
the ground. 17The elders of his household
stood beside him to get him up from the
ground, but he refused, and he would not eat
any food with them.
18On the seventh day the child died. David's servants were afraid to tell him that the
child was dead, for they thought, "While the
child was still living, we spoke to David but he
would not listen to us. How can we tell him
the child is dead? He may do something
desperate."
19David noticed that his servants were
whispering among themselves and he realized the child was dead. "Is the child dead?"
he asked.
"Yes," they replied, "he is dead."
20Then David got up from the ground. After
he had washed, put on lotions and changed
his clothes, he went into the house of the
LORD and worshiped. Then he went to his
own house, and at his request they served
him food, and he ate.
21His servants asked him, "Why are you
acting this way? While the child was alive,
you fasted and wept, but now that the child is
dead, you get up and eat!"
22He answered, "While the child was still
alive, I fasted and wept. I thought, 'Who
knows? The LORD may be gracious to me and
let the child live.' 23But now that he is dead,
why should I fast? Can I bring him back
again? I will go to him, but he will not return to
me."
24Then David comforted his wife Bathsheba, and he went to her and lay with her.
She gave birth to a son, and they named him
Solomon. The LORD loved him; 25and because the LORD loved him, he sent word
through Nathan the prophet to name him
Jedidiah.[b]
26Meanwhile Joab fought against Rabbah
of the Ammonites and captured the royal
citadel. 27Joab then sent messengers to David, saying, "I have fought against Rabbah
and taken its water supply. 28Now muster the
rest of the troops and besiege the city and
capture it. Otherwise I will take the city, and it
will be named after me."
29So David mustered the entire army and
went to Rabbah, and attacked and captured
it. 30He took the crown from the head of their
king[c]—its weight was a talent[d] of gold, and it
was set with precious stones—and it was
placed on David's head. He took a great
quantity of plunder from the city 31and
brought out the people who were there, consigning them to labor with saws and with iron
picks and axes, and he made them work at
brickmaking.[e] He did this to all the Ammonite

[a]14 Masoretic Text; an ancient Hebrew scribal tradition *this you have shown utter contempt for the LORD*
[b]25 *Jedidiah* means *loved by the LORD.* [c]30 Or *of Milcom* (that is, Molech) [d]30 That is, about 75 pounds (about 34 kilograms) [e]31 The meaning of the Hebrew for this clause is uncertain.

towns. Then David and his entire army returned to Jerusalem.

Amnon and Tamar

13 In the course of time, Amnon son of
David fell in love with Tamar, the
beautiful sister of Absalom son of David.
2Amnon became frustrated to the point of
illness on account of his sister Tamar, for she
was a virgin, and it seemed impossible for
him to do anything to her.
3Now Amnon had a friend named Jonadab
son of Shimeah, David's brother. Jonadab
was a very shrewd man. 4He asked Amnon,
"Why do you, the king's son, look so haggard
morning after morning? Won't you tell me?"
Amnon said to him, "I'm in love with Tamar, my brother Absalom's sister."
5"Go to bed and pretend to be ill," Jonadab
said. "When your father comes to see you,
say to him, 'I would like my sister Tamar to
come and give me something to eat. Let her
prepare the food in my sight so I may watch
her and then eat it from her hand.' "
6So Amnon lay down and pretended to be
ill. When the king came to see him, Amnon
said to him, "I would like my sister Tamar to
come and make some special bread in my
sight, so I may eat from her hand."
7David sent word to Tamar at the palace:
"Go to the house of your brother Amnon and
prepare some food for him." 8So Tamar went
to the house of her brother Amnon, who was
lying down. She took some dough, kneaded
it, made the bread in his sight and baked it.
9Then she took the pan and served him the
bread, but he refused to eat.
"Send everyone out of here," Amnon said.
So everyone left him. 10Then Amnon said to
Tamar, "Bring the food here into my bedroom so I may eat from your hand." And
Tamar took the bread she had prepared and
brought it to her brother Amnon in his bedroom. 11But when she took it to him to eat, he
grabbed her and said, "Come to bed with
me, my sister."
12"Don't, my brother!" she said to him.
"Don't force me. Such a thing should not be
done in Israel! Don't do this wicked thing.
13What about me? Where could I get rid of
my disgrace? And what about you? You
would be like one of the wicked fools in Israel. Please speak to the king; he will not
keep me from being married to you." 14But
he refused to listen to her, and since he was
stronger than she, he raped her.
15Then Amnon hated her with intense hatred. In fact, he hated her more than he had
loved her. Amnon said to her, "Get up and
get out!"
16"No!" she said to him. "Sending me
away would be a greater wrong than what
you have already done to me."
But he refused to listen to her. 17He called
his personal servant and said, "Get this
woman out of here and bolt the door after
her." 18So his servant put her out and bolted
the door after her. She was wearing a richly
ornamented[a] robe, for this was the kind of
garment the virgin daughters of the king
wore. 19Tamar put ashes on her head and
tore the ornamented[b] robe she was wearing.
She put her hand on her head and went
away, weeping aloud as she went.
20Her brother Absalom said to her, "Has
that Amnon, your brother, been with you? Be
quiet now, my sister; he is your brother. Don't
take this thing to heart." And Tamar lived in
her brother Absalom's house, a desolate
woman.
21When King David heard all this, he was
furious. 22Absalom never said a word to Amnon, either good or bad; he hated Amnon
because he had disgraced his sister Tamar.

Absalom Kills Amnon

23Two years later, when Absalom's sheep-
shearers were at Baal Hazor near the border
of Ephraim, he invited all the king's sons to
come there. 24Absalom went to the king and
said, "Your servant has had shearers come.
Will the king and his officials please join
me?"
25"No, my son," the king replied. "All of us
should not go; we would only be a burden to
you." Although Absalom urged him, he still
refused to go, but gave him his blessing.
26Then Absalom said, "If not, please let my
brother Amnon come with us."
The king asked him, "Why should he go
with you?" 27But Absalom urged him, so he
sent with him Amnon and the rest of the
king's sons.
28Absalom ordered his men, "Listen!
When Amnon is in high spirits from drinking
wine and I say to you, 'Strike Amnon down,'
then kill him. Don't be afraid. Have not I given
you this order? Be strong and brave." 29So

[a] 18 The meaning of the Hebrew for this phrase is uncertain.
[b] 19 The meaning of the Hebrew for this word is uncertain.

Absalom's men did to Amnon what Absalom
had ordered. Then all the king's sons got up,
mounted their mules and fled.

30While they were on their way, the report
came to David: "Absalom has struck down
all the king's sons; not one of them is left."
31The king stood up, tore his clothes and lay
down on the ground; and all his servants
stood by with their clothes torn.

32But Jonadab son of Shimeah, David's
brother, said, "My lord should not think that
they killed all the princes; only Amnon is
dead. This has been Absalom's expressed
intention ever since the day Amnon raped
his sister Tamar. 33My lord the king should
not be concerned about the report that all the
king's sons are dead. Only Amnon is dead."

34Meanwhile, Absalom had fled.

Now the man standing watch looked up
and saw many people on the road west of
him, coming down the side of the hill. The
watchman went and told the king, "I see men
in the direction of Horonaim, on the side of
the hill."[a]

35Jonadab said to the king, "See, the
king's sons are here; it has happened just as
your servant said."

36As he finished speaking, the king's sons
came in, wailing loudly. The king, too, and all
his servants wept very bitterly.

37Absalom fled and went to Talmai son of
Ammihud, the king of Geshur. But King David mourned for his son every day.

38After Absalom fled and went to Geshur,
he stayed there three years. 39And the spirit
of the king[b] longed to go to Absalom, for he
was consoled concerning Amnon's death.

Absalom Returns to Jerusalem

14 Joab son of Zeruiah knew that the
king's heart longed for Absalom. 2So
Joab sent someone to Tekoa and had a wise
woman brought from there. He said to her,
"Pretend you are in mourning. Dress in
mourning clothes, and don't use any cosmet-
ic lotions. Act like a woman who has spent
many days grieving for the dead. 3Then go to
the king and speak these words to him." And
Joab put the words in her mouth.

4When the woman from Tekoa went[c] to
the king, she fell with her face to the ground
to pay him honor, and she said, "Help me, O
king!"

5The king asked her, "What is troubling
you?"

She said, "I am indeed a widow; my husband is dead. 6I your servant had two sons.
They got into a fight with each other in the
field, and no one was there to separate them.
One struck the other and killed him. 7Now the
whole clan has risen up against your servant; they say, 'Hand over the one who
struck his brother down, so that we may put
him to death for the life of his brother whom
he killed; then we will get rid of the heir as
well.' They would put out the only burning
coal I have left, leaving my husband neither
name nor descendant on the face of the
earth."

8The king said to the woman, "Go home,
and I will issue an order in your behalf."

9But the woman from Tekoa said to him,
"My lord the king, let the blame rest on me
and on my father's family, and let the king
and his throne be without guilt."

10The king replied, "If anyone says anything to you, bring him to me, and he will not
bother you again."

11She said, "Then let the king invoke the
LORD his God to prevent the avenger of blood
from adding to the destruction, so that my
son will not be destroyed."

"As surely as the LORD lives," he said, "not
one hair of your son's head will fall to the
ground."

12Then the woman said, "Let your servant
speak a word to my lord the king."

"Speak," he replied.

13The woman said, "Why then have you
devised a thing like this against the people of
God? When the king says this, does he not
convict himself, for the king has not brought
back his banished son? 14Like water spilled
on the ground, which cannot be recovered,
so we must die. But God does not take away
life; instead, he devises ways so that a banished person may not remain estranged from
him.

15"And now I have come to say this to my
lord the king because the people have made
me afraid. Your servant thought, 'I will speak
to the king; perhaps he will do what his servant asks. 16Perhaps the king will agree to
deliver his servant from the hand of the man
who is trying to cut off both me and my son
from the inheritance God gave us.'

[a] 34 Septuagint; Hebrew does not have this sentence.
[b] 39 Dead Sea Scrolls and some Septuagint manuscripts; Masoretic Text *But ⌊the spirit of⌋ David the king*
[c] 4 Many Hebrew manuscripts, Septuagint, Vulgate and Syriac; most Hebrew manuscripts *spoke*

17"And now your servant says, 'May the word of my lord the king bring me rest, for my lord the king is like an angel of God in discerning good and evil. May the LORD your God be with you.' "

18Then the king said to the woman, "Do not keep from me the answer to what I am going to ask you."

"Let my lord the king speak," the woman said.

19The king asked, "Isn't the hand of Joab with you in all this?"

The woman answered, "As surely as you live, my lord the king, no one can turn to the right or to the left from anything my lord the king says. Yes, it was your servant Joab who instructed me to do this and who put all these words into the mouth of your servant. 20Your servant Joab did this to change the present situation. My lord has wisdom like that of an angel of God—he knows everything that happens in the land."

21The king said to Joab, "Very well, I will do it. Go, bring back the young man Absalom."

22Joab fell with his face to the ground to pay him honor, and he blessed the king. Joab said, "Today your servant knows that he has found favor in your eyes, my lord the king, because the king has granted his servant's request."

23Then Joab went to Geshur and brought Absalom back to Jerusalem. 24But the king said, "He must go to his own house; he must not see my face." So Absalom went to his own house and did not see the face of the king.

25In all Israel there was not a man so highly praised for his handsome appearance as Absalom. From the top of his head to the sole of his foot there was no blemish in him. 26Whenever he cut the hair of his head—he used to cut his hair from time to time when it became too heavy for him—he would weigh it, and its weight was two hundred shekels[a] by the royal standard.

27Three sons and a daughter were born to Absalom. The daughter's name was Tamar, and she became a beautiful woman.

28Absalom lived two years in Jerusalem without seeing the king's face. 29Then Absalom sent for Joab in order to send him to the king, but Joab refused to come to him. So he sent a second time, but he refused to come. 30Then he said to his servants, "Look, Joab's field is next to mine, and he has barley there. Go and set it on fire." So Absalom's servants set the field on fire.

31Then Joab did go to Absalom's house and he said to him, "Why have your servants set my field on fire?"

32Absalom said to Joab, "Look, I sent word to you and said, 'Come here so I can send you to the king to ask, "Why have I come from Geshur? It would be better for me if I were still there!" ' Now then, I want to see the king's face, and if I am guilty of anything, let him put me to death."

33So Joab went to the king and told him this. Then the king summoned Absalom, and he came in and bowed down with his face to the ground before the king. And the king kissed Absalom.

Absalom's Conspiracy

15 In the course of time, Absalom provided himself with a chariot and horses and with fifty men to run ahead of him. 2He would get up early and stand by the side of the road leading to the city gate. Whenever anyone came with a complaint to be placed before the king for a decision, Absalom would call out to him, "What town are you from?" He would answer, "Your servant is from one of the tribes of Israel." 3Then Absalom would say to him, "Look, your claims are valid and proper, but there is no representative of the king to hear you." 4And Absalom would add, "If only I were appointed judge in the land! Then everyone who has a complaint or case could come to me and I would see that he gets justice."

5Also, whenever anyone approached him to bow down before him, Absalom would reach out his hand, take hold of him and kiss him. 6Absalom behaved in this way toward all the Israelites who came to the king asking for justice, and so he stole the hearts of the men of Israel.

7At the end of four[b] years, Absalom said to the king, "Let me go to Hebron and fulfill a vow I made to the LORD. 8While your servant was living at Geshur in Aram, I made this vow: 'If the LORD takes me back to Jerusalem, I will worship the LORD in Hebron.[c]' "

9The king said to him, "Go in peace." So he went to Hebron.

10Then Absalom sent secret messengers throughout the tribes of Israel to say, "As

[a]26 That is, about 5 pounds (about 2.3 kilograms) [b]7 Some Septuagint manuscripts, Syriac and Josephus; Hebrew *forty* [c]8 Some Septuagint manuscripts; Hebrew does not have *in Hebron.*

soon as you hear the sound of the trumpets, then say, 'Absalom is king in Hebron.'" 11Two hundred men from Jerusalem had accompanied Absalom. They had been invited as guests and went quite innocently, knowing nothing about the matter. 12While Absalom was offering sacrifices, he also sent for Ahithophel the Gilonite, David's counselor, to come from Giloh, his hometown. And so the conspiracy gained strength, and Absalom's following kept on increasing.

David Flees

13A messenger came and told David, "The hearts of the men of Israel are with Absalom."

14Then David said to all his officials who were with him in Jerusalem, "Come! We must flee, or none of us will escape from Absalom. We must leave immediately, or he will move quickly to overtake us and bring ruin upon us and put the city to the sword."

15The king's officials answered him, "Your servants are ready to do whatever our lord the king chooses."

16The king set out, with his entire household following him; but he left ten concubines to take care of the palace. 17So the king set out, with all the people following him, and they halted at a place some distance away. 18All his men marched past him, along with all the Kerethites and Pelethites; and all the six hundred Gittites who had accompanied him from Gath marched before the king.

19The king said to Ittai the Gittite, "Why should you come along with us? Go back and stay with King Absalom. You are a foreigner, an exile from your homeland. 20You came only yesterday. And today shall I make you wander about with us, when I do not know where I am going? Go back, and take your countrymen. May kindness and faithfulness be with you."

21But Ittai replied to the king, "As surely as the LORD lives, and as my lord the king lives, wherever my lord the king may be, whether it means life or death, there will your servant be."

22David said to Ittai, "Go ahead, march on." So Ittai the Gittite marched on with all his men and the families that were with him.

23The whole countryside wept aloud as all the people passed by. The king also crossed the Kidron Valley, and all the people moved on toward the desert.

24Zadok was there, too, and all the Levites who were with him were carrying the ark of the covenant of God. They set down the ark of God, and Abiathar offered sacrifices[a] until all the people had finished leaving the city.

25Then the king said to Zadok, "Take the ark of God back into the city. If I find favor in the LORD's eyes, he will bring me back and let me see it and his dwelling place again. 26But if he says, 'I am not pleased with you,' then I am ready; let him do to me whatever seems good to him."

27The king also said to Zadok the priest, "Aren't you a seer? Go back to the city in peace, with your son Ahimaaz and Jonathan son of Abiathar. You and Abiathar take your two sons with you. 28I will wait at the fords in the desert until word comes from you to inform me." 29So Zadok and Abiathar took the ark of God back to Jerusalem and stayed there.

30But David continued up the Mount of Olives, weeping as he went; his head was covered and he was barefoot. All the people with him covered their heads too and were weeping as they went up. 31Now David had been told, "Ahithophel is among the conspirators with Absalom." So David prayed, "O LORD, turn Ahithophel's counsel into foolishness."

32When David arrived at the summit, where people used to worship God, Hushai the Arkite was there to meet him, his robe torn and dust on his head. 33David said to him, "If you go with me, you will be a burden to me. 34But if you return to the city and say to Absalom, 'I will be your servant, O king; I was your father's servant in the past, but now I will be your servant,' then you can help me by frustrating Ahithophel's advice. 35Won't the priests Zadok and Abiathar be there with you? Tell them anything you hear in the king's palace. 36Their two sons, Ahimaaz son of Zadok and Jonathan son of Abiathar, are there with them. Send them to me with anything you hear."

37So David's friend Hushai arrived at Jerusalem as Absalom was entering the city.

David and Ziba

16 When David had gone a short distance beyond the summit, there was Ziba, the steward of Mephibosheth, waiting to meet him. He had a string of donkeys saddled and loaded with two hundred loaves

[a]24 Or *Abiathar went up*

of bread, a hundred cakes of raisins, a hundred cakes of figs and a skin of wine.
2The king asked Ziba, "Why have you
brought these?"
Ziba answered, "The donkeys are for the
king's household to ride on, the bread and
fruit are for the men to eat, and the wine is to
refresh those who become exhausted in the
desert."
3The king then asked, "Where is your master's grandson?"
Ziba said to him, "He is staying in Jerusalem, because he thinks, 'Today the house of
Israel will give me back my grandfather's
kingdom.' "
4Then the king said to Ziba, "All that belonged to Mephibosheth is now yours."
"I humbly bow," Ziba said. "May I find favor in your eyes, my lord the king."

Shimei Curses David

5As King David approached Bahurim, a
man from the same clan as Saul's family
came out from there. His name was Shimei
son of Gera, and he cursed as he came out.
6He pelted David and all the king's officials
with stones, though all the troops and the
special guard were on David's right and left.
7As he cursed, Shimei said, "Get out, get
out, you man of blood, you scoundrel! 8The
LORD has repaid you for all the blood you
shed in the household of Saul, in whose
place you have reigned. The LORD has handed the kingdom over to your son Absalom.
You have come to ruin because you are a
man of blood!"
9Then Abishai son of Zeruiah said to the
king, "Why should this dead dog curse my
lord the king? Let me go over and cut off his
head."
10But the king said, "What do you and I
have in common, you sons of Zeruiah? If he
is cursing because the LORD said to him,
'Curse David,' who can ask, 'Why do you do
this?' "
11David then said to Abishai and all his
officials, "My son, who is of my own flesh, is
trying to take my life. How much more, then,
this Benjamite! Leave him alone; let him
curse, for the LORD has told him to. 12It may
be that the LORD will see my distress and
repay me with good for the cursing I am
receiving today."
13So David and his men continued along
the road while Shimei was going along the
hillside opposite him, cursing as he went and
throwing stones at him and showering him
with dirt. 14The king and all the people with
him arrived at their destination exhausted.
And there he refreshed himself.

The Advice of Hushai and Ahithophel

15Meanwhile, Absalom and all the men of
Israel came to Jerusalem, and Ahithophel
was with him. 16Then Hushai the Arkite, David's friend, went to Absalom and said to him,
"Long live the king! Long live the king!"
17Absalom asked Hushai, "Is this the love
you show your friend? Why didn't you go with
your friend?"
18Hushai said to Absalom, "No, the one
chosen by the LORD, by these people, and by
all the men of Israel—his I will be, and I will
remain with him. 19Furthermore, whom
should I serve? Should I not serve the son?
Just as I served your father, so I will serve
you."
20Absalom said to Ahithophel, "Give us
your advice. What should we do?"
21Ahithophel answered, "Lie with your father's concubines whom he left to take care
of the palace. Then all Israel will hear that
you have made yourself a stench in your
father's nostrils, and the hands of everyone
with you will be strengthened." 22So they
pitched a tent for Absalom on the roof, and
he lay with his father's concubines in the
sight of all Israel.
23Now in those days the advice Ahithophel
gave was like that of one who inquires of
God. That was how both David and Absalom
regarded all of Ahithophel's advice.

17 Ahithophel said to Absalom, "I
would[a] choose twelve thousand men
and set out tonight in pursuit of David. 2I
would[b] attack him while he is weary and
weak. I would[b] strike him with terror, and
then all the people with him will flee. I would[b]
strike down only the king 3and bring all the
people back to you. The death of the man
you seek will mean the return of all; all the
people will be unharmed." 4This plan
seemed good to Absalom and to all the elders of Israel.
5But Absalom said, "Summon also Hushai
the Arkite, so we can hear what he has to
say." 6When Hushai came to him, Absalom
said, "Ahithophel has given this advice.
Should we do what he says? If not, give us
your opinion."

[a]1 Or *Let me* [b]2 Or *will*

7 Hushai replied to Absalom, "The advice Ahithophel has given is not good this time. 8 You know your father and his men; they are fighters, and as fierce as a wild bear robbed of her cubs. Besides, your father is an experienced fighter; he will not spend the night with the troops. 9 Even now, he is hidden in a cave or some other place. If he should attack your troops first,[a] whoever hears about it will say, 'There has been a slaughter among the troops who follow Absalom.' 10 Then even the bravest soldier, whose heart is like the heart of a lion, will melt with fear, for all Israel knows that your father is a fighter and that those with him are brave.

11 "So I advise you: Let all Israel, from Dan to Beersheba—as numerous as the sand on the seashore—be gathered to you, with you yourself leading them into battle. 12 Then we will attack him wherever he may be found, and we will fall on him as dew settles on the ground. Neither he nor any of his men will be left alive. 13 If he withdraws into a city, then all Israel will bring ropes to that city, and we will drag it down to the valley until not even a piece of it can be found."

14 Absalom and all the men of Israel said, "The advice of Hushai the Arkite is better than that of Ahithophel." For the LORD had determined to frustrate the good advice of Ahithophel in order to bring disaster on Absalom.

15 Hushai told Zadok and Abiathar, the priests, "Ahithophel has advised Absalom and the elders of Israel to do such and such, but I have advised them to do so and so. 16 Now send a message immediately and tell David, 'Do not spend the night at the fords in the desert; cross over without fail, or the king and all the people with him will be swallowed up.' "

17 Jonathan and Ahimaaz were staying at En Rogel. A servant girl was to go and inform them, and they were to go and tell King David, for they could not risk being seen entering the city. 18 But a young man saw them and told Absalom. So the two of them left quickly and went to the house of a man in Bahurim. He had a well in his courtyard, and they climbed down into it. 19 His wife took a covering and spread it out over the opening of the well and scattered grain over it. No one knew anything about it.

20 When Absalom's men came to the woman at the house, they asked, "Where are Ahimaaz and Jonathan?"

The woman answered them, "They crossed over the brook."[b] The men searched but found no one, so they returned to Jerusalem.

21 After the men had gone, the two climbed out of the well and went to inform King David. They said to him, "Set out and cross the river at once; Ahithophel has advised such and such against you." 22 So David and all the people with him set out and crossed the Jordan. By daybreak, no one was left who had not crossed the Jordan.

23 When Ahithophel saw that his advice had not been followed, he saddled his donkey and set out for his house in his hometown. He put his house in order and then hanged himself. So he died and was buried in his father's tomb.

24 David went to Mahanaim, and Absalom crossed the Jordan with all the men of Israel. 25 Absalom had appointed Amasa over the army in place of Joab. Amasa was the son of a man named Jether,[c] an Israelite[d] who had married Abigail,[e] the daughter of Nahash and sister of Zeruiah the mother of Joab. 26 The Israelites and Absalom camped in the land of Gilead.

27 When David came to Mahanaim, Shobi son of Nahash from Rabbah of the Ammonites, and Makir son of Ammiel from Lo Debar, and Barzillai the Gileadite from Rogelim 28 brought bedding and bowls and articles of pottery. They also brought wheat and barley, flour and roasted grain, beans and lentils,[f] 29 honey and curds, sheep, and cheese from cows' milk for David and his people to eat. For they said, "The people have become hungry and tired and thirsty in the desert."

Absalom's Death

18 David mustered the men who were with him and appointed over them commanders of thousands and commanders of hundreds. 2 David sent the troops out—a third under the command of Joab, a third under Joab's brother Abishai son of Zeruiah, and a third under Ittai the Gittite. The king

[a] 9 Or *When some of the men fall at the first attack* [b] 20 Or *"They passed by the sheep pen toward the water."* [c] 25 Hebrew *Ithra,* a variant of *Jether* [d] 25 Hebrew and some Septuagint manuscripts; other Septuagint manuscripts (see also 1 Chron. 2:17) *Ishmaelite* or *Jezreelite* [e] 25 Hebrew *Abigal,* a variant of *Abigail* [f] 28 Most Septuagint manuscripts and Syriac; Hebrew *lentils, and roasted grain*

told the troops, "I myself will surely march out with you."

3But the men said, "You must not go out; if we are forced to flee, they won't care about us. Even if half of us die, they won't care; but you are worth ten thousand of us.[a] It would be better now for you to give us support from the city."

4The king answered, "I will do whatever seems best to you."

So the king stood beside the gate while all the men marched out in units of hundreds and of thousands. 5The king commanded Joab, Abishai and Ittai, "Be gentle with the young man Absalom for my sake." And all the troops heard the king giving orders concerning Absalom to each of the commanders.

6The army marched into the field to fight Israel, and the battle took place in the forest of Ephraim. 7There the army of Israel was defeated by David's men, and the casualties that day were great—twenty thousand men. 8The battle spread out over the whole countryside, and the forest claimed more lives that day than the sword.

9Now Absalom happened to meet David's men. He was riding his mule, and as the mule went under the thick branches of a large oak, Absalom's head got caught in the tree. He was left hanging in midair, while the mule he was riding kept on going.

10When one of the men saw this, he told Joab, "I just saw Absalom hanging in an oak tree."

11Joab said to the man who had told him this, "What! You saw him? Why didn't you strike him to the ground right there? Then I would have had to give you ten shekels[b] of silver and a warrior's belt."

12But the man replied, "Even if a thousand shekels[c] were weighed out into my hands, I would not lift my hand against the king's son. In our hearing the king commanded you and Abishai and Ittai, 'Protect the young man Absalom for my sake.[d] 13And if I had put my life in jeopardy[e]—and nothing is hidden from the king—you would have kept your distance from me."

14Joab said, "I'm not going to wait like this for you." So he took three javelins in his hand and plunged them into Absalom's heart while Absalom was still alive in the oak tree. 15And ten of Joab's armor-bearers surrounded Absalom, struck him and killed him.

16Then Joab sounded the trumpet, and the troops stopped pursuing Israel, for Joab halted them. 17They took Absalom, threw him into a big pit in the forest and piled up a large heap of rocks over him. Meanwhile, all the Israelites fled to their homes.

18During his lifetime Absalom had taken a pillar and erected it in the King's Valley as a monument to himself, for he thought, "I have no son to carry on the memory of my name." He named the pillar after himself, and it is called Absalom's Monument to this day.

David Mourns

19Now Ahimaaz son of Zadok said, "Let me run and take the news to the king that the LORD has delivered him from the hand of his enemies."

20"You are not the one to take the news today," Joab told him. "You may take the news another time, but you must not do so today, because the king's son is dead."

21Then Joab said to a Cushite, "Go, tell the king what you have seen." The Cushite bowed down before Joab and ran off.

22Ahimaaz son of Zadok again said to Joab, "Come what may, please let me run behind the Cushite."

But Joab replied, "My son, why do you want to go? You don't have any news that will bring you a reward."

23He said, "Come what may, I want to run."

So Joab said, "Run!" Then Ahimaaz ran by way of the plain[f] and outran the Cushite.

24While David was sitting between the inner and outer gates, the watchman went up to the roof of the gateway by the wall. As he looked out, he saw a man running alone. 25The watchman called out to the king and reported it.

The king said, "If he is alone, he must have good news." And the man came closer and closer.

26Then the watchman saw another man running, and he called down to the gatekeeper, "Look, another man running alone!"

The king said, "He must be bringing good news, too."

[a] 3 Two Hebrew manuscripts, some Septuagint manuscripts and Vulgate; most Hebrew manuscripts *care; for now there are ten thousand like us* [b] 11 That is, about 4 ounces (about 115 grams) [c] 12 That is, about 25 pounds (about 11 kilograms) [d] 12 A few Hebrew manuscripts, Septuagint, Vulgate and Syriac; most Hebrew manuscripts may be translated *Absalom, whoever you may be.* [e] 13 Or *Otherwise, if I had acted treacherously toward him* [f] 23 That is, the plain of the Jordan

27The watchman said, "It seems to me that
the first one runs like Ahimaaz son of
Zadok."
"He's a good man," the king said. "He
comes with good news."
28Then Ahimaaz called out to the king, "All
is well!" He bowed down before the king with
his face to the ground and said, "Praise be to
the LORD your God! He has delivered up the
men who lifted their hands against my lord
the king."
29The king asked, "Is the young man Absalom safe?"
Ahimaaz answered, "I saw great confusion just as Joab was about to send the
king's servant and me, your servant, but I
don't know what it was."
30The king said, "Stand aside and wait
here." So he stepped aside and stood there.
31Then the Cushite arrived and said, "My
lord the king, hear the good news! The LORD
has delivered you today from all who rose up
against you."
32The king asked the Cushite, "Is the
young man Absalom safe?"
The Cushite replied, "May the enemies of
my lord the king and all who rise up to harm
you be like that young man."
33The king was shaken. He went up to the
room over the gateway and wept. As he
went, he said: "O my son Absalom! My son,
my son Absalom! If only I had died instead of
you—O Absalom, my son, my son!"
19 Joab was told, "The king is weeping
and mourning for Absalom." 2And for
the whole army the victory that day was
turned into mourning, because on that day
the troops heard it said, "The king is grieving
for his son." 3The men stole into the city that
day as men steal in who are ashamed when
they flee from battle. 4The king covered his
face and cried aloud, "O my son Absalom! O
Absalom, my son, my son!"
5Then Joab went into the house to the king
and said, "Today you have humiliated all
your men, who have just saved your life and
the lives of your sons and daughters and the
lives of your wives and concubines. 6You
love those who hate you and hate those who
love you. You have made it clear today that
the commanders and their men mean nothing to you. I see that you would be pleased if
Absalom were alive today and all of us were
dead. 7Now go out and encourage your men.
I swear by the LORD that if you don't go out,
not a man will be left with you by nightfall.
This will be worse for you than all the calamities that have come upon you from your
youth till now."
8So the king got up and took his seat in the
gateway. When the men were told, "The king
is sitting in the gateway," they all came before him.

David Returns to Jerusalem

Meanwhile, the Israelites had fled to their
homes. 9Throughout the tribes of Israel, the
people were all arguing with each other, saying, "The king delivered us from the hand of
our enemies; he is the one who rescued us
from the hand of the Philistines. But now he
has fled the country because of Absalom;
10and Absalom, whom we anointed to rule
over us, has died in battle. So why do
you say nothing about bringing the king
back?"
11King David sent this message to Zadok
and Abiathar, the priests: "Ask the elders of
Judah, 'Why should you be the last to bring
the king back to his palace, since what is
being said throughout Israel has reached the
king at his quarters? 12You are my brothers,
my own flesh and blood. So why should you
be the last to bring back the king?' 13And say
to Amasa, 'Are you not my own flesh and
blood? May God deal with me, be it ever so
severely, if from now on you are not the commander of my army in place of Joab.' "
14He won over the hearts of all the men of
Judah as though they were one man. They
sent word to the king, "Return, you and all
your men." 15Then the king returned and
went as far as the Jordan.
Now the men of Judah had come to Gilgal
to go out and meet the king and bring him
across the Jordan. 16Shimei son of Gera, the
Benjamite from Bahurim, hurried down with
the men of Judah to meet King David. 17With
him were a thousand Benjamites, along with
Ziba, the steward of Saul's household, and
his fifteen sons and twenty servants. They
rushed to the Jordan, where the king was.
18They crossed at the ford to take the king's
household over and to do whatever he
wished.
When Shimei son of Gera crossed the Jordan, he fell prostrate before the king 19and
said to him, "May my lord not hold me guilty.
Do not remember how your servant did
wrong on the day my lord the king left
Jerusalem. May the king put it out of his
mind. 20For I your servant know that I have
sinned, but today I have come here as the

first of the whole house of Joseph to come down and meet my lord the king."

21Then Abishai son of Zeruiah said, "Shouldn't Shimei be put to death for this? He cursed the LORD's anointed."

22David replied, "What do you and I have in common, you sons of Zeruiah? This day you have become my adversaries! Should anyone be put to death in Israel today? Do I not know that today I am king over Israel?" 23So the king said to Shimei, "You shall not die." And the king promised him on oath.

24Mephibosheth, Saul's grandson, also went down to meet the king. He had not taken care of his feet or trimmed his mustache or washed his clothes from the day the king left until the day he returned safely. 25When he came from Jerusalem to meet the king, the king asked him, "Why didn't you go with me, Mephibosheth?"

26He said, "My lord the king, since I your servant am lame, I said, 'I will have my donkey saddled and will ride on it, so I can go with the king.' But Ziba my servant betrayed me. 27And he has slandered your servant to my lord the king. My lord the king is like an angel of God; so do whatever pleases you. 28All my grandfather's descendants deserved nothing but death from my lord the king, but you gave your servant a place among those who sat at your table. So what right do I have to make any more appeals to the king?"

29The king said to him, "Why say more? I order you and Ziba to divide the fields."

30Mephibosheth said to the king, "Let him take everything, now that my lord the king has arrived home safely."

31Barzillai the Gileadite also came down from Rogelim to cross the Jordan with the king and to send him on his way from there. 32Now Barzillai was a very old man, eighty years of age. He had provided for the king during his stay in Mahanaim, for he was a very wealthy man. 33The king said to Barzillai, "Cross over with me and stay with me in Jerusalem, and I will provide for you."

34But Barzillai answered the king, "How many more years will I live, that I should go up to Jerusalem with the king? 35I am now eighty years old. Can I tell the difference between what is good and what is not? Can your servant taste what he eats and drinks? Can I still hear the voices of men and women singers? Why should your servant be an added burden to my lord the king? 36Your servant will cross over the Jordan with the king for a short distance, but why should the king reward me in this way? 37Let your servant return, that I may die in my own town near the tomb of my father and mother. But here is your servant Kimham. Let him cross over with my lord the king. Do for him whatever pleases you."

38The king said, "Kimham shall cross over with me, and I will do for him whatever pleases you. And anything you desire from me I will do for you."

39So all the people crossed the Jordan, and then the king crossed over. The king kissed Barzillai and gave him his blessing, and Barzillai returned to his home.

40When the king crossed over to Gilgal, Kimham crossed with him. All the troops of Judah and half the troops of Israel had taken the king over.

41Soon all the men of Israel were coming to the king and saying to him, "Why did our brothers, the men of Judah, steal the king away and bring him and his household across the Jordan, together with all his men?"

42All the men of Judah answered the men of Israel, "We did this because the king is closely related to us. Why are you angry about it? Have we eaten any of the king's provisions? Have we taken anything for ourselves?"

43Then the men of Israel answered the men of Judah, "We have ten shares in the king; and besides, we have a greater claim on David than you have. So why do you treat us with contempt? Were we not the first to speak of bringing back our king?"

But the men of Judah responded even more harshly than the men of Israel.

Sheba Rebels Against David

20 Now a troublemaker named Sheba son of Bicri, a Benjamite, happened to be there. He sounded the trumpet and shouted,

"We have no share in David,
no part in Jesse's son!
Every man to his tent, O Israel!"

2So all the men of Israel deserted David to follow Sheba son of Bicri. But the men of Judah stayed by their king all the way from the Jordan to Jerusalem.

3When David returned to his palace in Jerusalem, he took the ten concubines he had left to take care of the palace and put them in a house under guard. He provided for them, but did not lie with them. They were kept in confinement till the day of their death, living as widows.

4Then the king said to Amasa, "Summon the men of Judah to come to me within three days, and be here yourself." 5But when Amasa went to summon Judah, he took longer than the time the king had set for him.

6David said to Abishai, "Now Sheba son of Bicri will do us more harm than Absalom did. Take your master's men and pursue him, or he will find fortified cities and escape from us." 7So Joab's men and the Kerethites and Pelethites and all the mighty warriors went out under the command of Abishai. They marched out from Jerusalem to pursue Sheba son of Bicri.

8While they were at the great rock in Gibeon, Amasa came to meet them. Joab was wearing his military tunic, and strapped over it at his waist was a belt with a dagger in its sheath. As he stepped forward, it dropped out of its sheath.

9Joab said to Amasa, "How are you, my brother?" Then Joab took Amasa by the beard with his right hand to kiss him. 10Amasa was not on his guard against the dagger in Joab's hand, and Joab plunged it into his belly, and his intestines spilled out on the ground. Without being stabbed again, Amasa died. Then Joab and his brother Abishai pursued Sheba son of Bicri.

11One of Joab's men stood beside Amasa and said, "Whoever favors Joab, and whoever is for David, let him follow Joab!" 12Amasa lay wallowing in his blood in the middle of the road, and the man saw that all the troops came to a halt there. When he realized that everyone who came up to Amasa stopped, he dragged him from the road into a field and threw a garment over him. 13After Amasa had been removed from the road, all the men went on with Joab to pursue Sheba son of Bicri.

14Sheba passed through all the tribes of Israel to Abel Beth Maacah[a] and through the entire region of the Berites, who gathered together and followed him. 15All the troops with Joab came and besieged Sheba in Abel Beth Maacah. They built a siege ramp up to the city, and it stood against the outer fortifications. While they were battering the wall to bring it down, 16a wise woman called from the city, "Listen! Listen! Tell Joab to come here so I can speak to him." 17He went toward her, and she asked, "Are you Joab?"

"I am," he answered.

She said, "Listen to what your servant has to say."

"I'm listening," he said.

18She continued, "Long ago they used to say, 'Get your answer at Abel,' and that settled it. 19We are the peaceful and faithful in Israel. You are trying to destroy a city that is a mother in Israel. Why do you want to swallow up the LORD's inheritance?"

20"Far be it from me!" Joab replied, "Far be it from me to swallow up or destroy! 21That is not the case. A man named Sheba son of Bicri, from the hill country of Ephraim, has lifted up his hand against the king, against David. Hand over this one man, and I'll withdraw from the city."

The woman said to Joab, "His head will be thrown to you from the wall."

22Then the woman went to all the people with her wise advice, and they cut off the head of Sheba son of Bicri and threw it to Joab. So he sounded the trumpet, and his men dispersed from the city, each returning to his home. And Joab went back to the king in Jerusalem.

23Joab was over Israel's entire army; Benaiah son of Jehoiada was over the Kerethites and Pelethites; 24Adoniram[b] was in charge of forced labor; Jehoshaphat son of Ahilud was recorder; 25Sheva was secretary; Zadok and Abiathar were priests; 26and Ira the Jairite was David's priest.

The Gibeonites Avenged

21 During the reign of David, there was a famine for three successive years; so David sought the face of the LORD. The LORD said, "It is on account of Saul and his blood-stained house; it is because he put the Gibeonites to death."

2The king summoned the Gibeonites and spoke to them. (Now the Gibeonites were not a part of Israel but were survivors of the Amorites; the Israelites had sworn to ⌞spare⌟ them, but Saul in his zeal for Israel and Judah had tried to annihilate them.) 3David asked the Gibeonites, "What shall I do for you? How shall I make amends so that you will bless the LORD's inheritance?"

4The Gibeonites answered him, "We have no right to demand silver or gold from Saul or

[a]14 Or *Abel, even Beth Maacah;* also in verse 15
[b]24 Some Septuagint manuscripts (see also 1 Kings 4:6 and 5:14); Hebrew *Adoram*

his family, nor do we have the right to put
anyone in Israel to death."
"What do you want me to do for you?"
David asked.
5They answered the king, "As for the man
who destroyed us and plotted against us so
that we have been decimated and have no
place anywhere in Israel, 6let seven of his
male descendants be given to us to be killed
and exposed before the LORD at Gibeah of
Saul—the Lord's chosen one."
So the king said, "I will give them to you."
7The king spared Mephibosheth son of
Jonathan, the son of Saul, because of the
oath before the LORD between David and
Jonathan son of Saul. 8But the king took Ar-
moni and Mephibosheth, the two sons of
Aiah's daughter Rizpah, whom she had
borne to Saul, together with the five sons of
Saul's daughter Merab,[a] whom she had
borne to Adriel son of Barzillai the Mehola-
thite. 9He handed them over to the Gibeonites, who killed and exposed them on a hill
before the LORD. All seven of them fell together; they were put to death during the first
days of the harvest, just as the barley harvest was beginning.
10Rizpah daughter of Aiah took sackcloth
and spread it out for herself on a rock. From
the beginning of the harvest till the rain
poured down from the heavens on the bodies, she did not let the birds of the air touch
them by day or the wild animals by night.
11When David was told what Aiah's daughter
Rizpah, Saul's concubine, had done, 12he
went and took the bones of Saul and his son
Jonathan from the citizens of Jabesh Gilead.
(They had taken them secretly from the public square at Beth Shan, where the Philistines had hung them after they struck Saul
down on Gilboa.) 13David brought the bones
of Saul and his son Jonathan from there, and
the bones of those who had been killed and
exposed were gathered up.
14They buried the bones of Saul and his
son Jonathan in the tomb of Saul's father
Kish, at Zela in Benjamin, and did everything
the king commanded. After that, God answered prayer in behalf of the land.

Wars Against the Philistines

15Once again there was a battle between
the Philistines and Israel. David went down
with his men to fight against the Philistines,
and he became exhausted. 16And Ishbi-
Benob, one of the descendants of Rapha,
whose bronze spearhead weighed three
hundred shekels[b] and who was armed with a
new ⌊sword⌋, said he would kill David. 17But
Abishai son of Zeruiah came to David's rescue; he struck the Philistine down and killed
him. Then David's men swore to him, saying,
"Never again will you go out with us to battle,
so that the lamp of Israel will not be extinguished."
18In the course of time, there was another
battle with the Philistines, at Gob. At that
time Sibbecai the Hushathite killed Saph,
one of the descendants of Rapha.
19In another battle with the Philistines at
Gob, Elhanan son of Jaare-Oregim[c] the
Bethlehemite killed Goliath[d] the Gittite, who
had a spear with a shaft like a weaver's rod.
20In still another battle, which took place at
Gath, there was a huge man with six fingers
on each hand and six toes on each foot—
twenty-four in all. He also was descended
from Rapha. 21When he taunted Israel,
Jonathan son of Shimeah, David's brother,
killed him.
22These four were descendants of Rapha
in Gath, and they fell at the hands of David
and his men.

David's Song of Praise

22 David sang to the LORD the words of
this song when the LORD delivered
him from the hand of all his enemies and
from the hand of Saul. 2He said:

"The LORD is my rock, my fortress and my
deliverer;
3 my God is my rock, in whom I take
refuge,
my shield and the horn[e] of my
salvation.
He is my stronghold, my refuge and my
savior—
from violent men you save me.
4I call to the LORD, who is worthy of praise,
and I am saved from my enemies.

5"The waves of death swirled about me;
the torrents of destruction overwhelmed
me.
6The cords of the grave[f] coiled around
me;

[a]8 Two Hebrew manuscripts, some Septuagint manuscripts and Syriac (see also 1 Samuel 18:19); most Hebrew and Septuagint manuscripts *Michal* [b]16 That is, about 7 1/2 pounds (about 3.5 kilograms) [c]19 Or *son of Jair the weaver* [d]19 Hebrew and Septuagint; 1 Chron. 20:5 *son of Jair killed Lahmi the brother of Goliath* [e]3 *Horn* here symbolizes strength. [f]6 Hebrew *Sheol*

the snares of death confronted me.
7In my distress I called to the LORD;
I called out to my God.
From his temple he heard my voice;
my cry came to his ears.

8"The earth trembled and quaked,
the foundations of the heavens[a] shook;
they trembled because he was angry.
9Smoke rose from his nostrils;
consuming fire came from his mouth,
burning coals blazed out of it.
10He parted the heavens and came down;
dark clouds were under his feet.
11He mounted the cherubim and flew;
he soared[b] on the wings of the wind.
12He made darkness his canopy around him—
the dark[c] rain clouds of the sky.
13Out of the brightness of his presence
bolts of lightning blazed forth.
14The LORD thundered from heaven;
the voice of the Most High resounded.
15He shot arrows and scattered ⌊the enemies⌋,
bolts of lightning and routed them.
16The valleys of the sea were exposed
and the foundations of the earth laid bare
at the rebuke of the LORD,
at the blast of breath from his nostrils.

17"He reached down from on high and took hold of me;
he drew me out of deep waters.
18He rescued me from my powerful enemy,
from my foes, who were too strong for me.
19They confronted me in the day of my disaster,
but the LORD was my support.
20He brought me out into a spacious place;
he rescued me because he delighted in me.

21"The LORD has dealt with me according to my righteousness;
according to the cleanness of my hands he has rewarded me.
22For I have kept the ways of the LORD;
I have not done evil by turning from my God.
23All his laws are before me;
I have not turned away from his decrees.
24I have been blameless before him
and have kept myself from sin.
25The LORD has rewarded me according to my righteousness,
according to my cleanness[d] in his sight.

26"To the faithful you show yourself faithful,
to the blameless you show yourself blameless,
27to the pure you show yourself pure,
but to the crooked you show yourself shrewd.
28You save the humble,
but your eyes are on the haughty to bring them low.
29You are my lamp, O LORD;
the LORD turns my darkness into light.
30With your help I can advance against a troop[e];
with my God I can scale a wall.

31"As for God, his way is perfect;
the word of the LORD is flawless.
He is a shield
for all who take refuge in him.
32For who is God besides the LORD?
And who is the Rock except our God?
33It is God who arms me with strength[f]
and makes my way perfect.
34He makes my feet like the feet of a deer;
he enables me to stand on the heights.
35He trains my hands for battle;
my arms can bend a bow of bronze.
36You give me your shield of victory;
you stoop down to make me great.
37You broaden the path beneath me,
so that my ankles do not turn.

38"I pursued my enemies and crushed them;
I did not turn back till they were destroyed.
39I crushed them completely, and they could not rise;
they fell beneath my feet.
40You armed me with strength for battle;
you made my adversaries bow at my feet.
41You made my enemies turn their backs in flight,

[a]8 Hebrew; Vulgate and Syriac (see also Psalm 18:7) *mountains* [b]11 Many Hebrew manuscripts (see also Psalm 18:10); most Hebrew manuscripts *appeared* [c]12 Septuagint and Vulgate (see also Psalm 18:11); Hebrew *massed* [d]25 Hebrew; Septuagint and Vulgate (see also Psalm 18:24) *to the cleanness of my hands* [e]30 Or *can run through a barricade* [f]33 Dead Sea Scrolls, some Septuagint manuscripts, Vulgate and Syriac (see also Psalm 18:32); Masoretic Text *who is my strong refuge*

and I destroyed my foes.
42 They cried for help, but there was no one
to save them—
to the LORD, but he did not answer.
43 I beat them as fine as the dust of the
earth;
I pounded and trampled them like mud
in the streets.

44 "You have delivered me from the attacks
of my people;
you have preserved me as the head of
nations.
People I did not know are subject to me,
45 and foreigners come cringing to me;
as soon as they hear me, they obey
me.
46 They all lose heart;
they come trembling[a] from their
strongholds.

47 "The LORD lives! Praise be to my Rock!
Exalted be God, the Rock, my Savior!
48 He is the God who avenges me,
who puts the nations under me,
49 who sets me free from my enemies.
You exalted me above my foes;
from violent men you rescued me.
50 Therefore I will praise you, O LORD,
among the nations;
I will sing praises to your name.
51 He gives his king great victories;
he shows unfailing kindness to his
anointed,
to David and his descendants forever."

The Last Words of David

23 These are the last words of David:
"The oracle of David son of Jesse,
the oracle of the man exalted by the
Most High,
the man anointed by the God of Jacob,
Israel's singer of songs[b]:

2 "The Spirit of the LORD spoke through me;
his word was on my tongue.
3 The God of Israel spoke,
the Rock of Israel said to me:
'When one rules over men in
righteousness,
when he rules in the fear of God,
4 he is like the light of morning at sunrise
on a cloudless morning,
like the brightness after rain
that brings the grass from the earth.'

5 "Is not my house right with God?
Has he not made with me an
everlasting covenant,
arranged and secured in every part?
Will he not bring to fruition my salvation
and grant me my every desire?
6 But evil men are all to be cast aside like
thorns,
which are not gathered with the hand.
7 Whoever touches thorns
uses a tool of iron or the shaft of a
spear;
they are burned up where they lie."

David's Mighty Men

8 These are the names of David's mighty
men:
Josheb-Basshebeth,[c] a Tahkemonite,[d]
was chief of the Three; he raised his spear
against eight hundred men, whom he killed[e]
in one encounter.
9 Next to him was Eleazar son of Dodai the
Ahohite. As one of the three mighty men, he
was with David when they taunted the Philistines gathered ⌊at Pas Dammim⌋[f] for battle.
Then the men of Israel retreated, 10 but he
stood his ground and struck down the Philistines till his hand grew tired and froze to the
sword. The LORD brought about a great victory that day. The troops returned to Eleazar,
but only to strip the dead.
11 Next to him was Shammah son of Agee
the Hararite. When the Philistines banded
together at a place where there was a field
full of lentils, Israel's troops fled from them.
12 But Shammah took his stand in the middle
of the field. He defended it and struck the
Philistines down, and the LORD brought about
a great victory.
13 During harvest time, three of the thirty
chief men came down to David at the cave of
Adullam, while a band of Philistines was encamped in the Valley of Rephaim. 14 At that
time David was in the stronghold, and the
Philistine garrison was at Bethlehem. 15 David longed for water and said, "Oh, that
someone would get me a drink of water from
the well near the gate of Bethlehem!" 16 So
the three mighty men broke through the Phil-

[a] *46* Some Septuagint manuscripts and Vulgate (see also Psalm 18:45); Masoretic Text *they arm themselves.*
[b] *1* Or *Israel's beloved singer* [c] *8* Hebrew; some Septuagint manuscripts suggest *Ish-Bosheth,* that is, *Esh-Baal* (see also 1 Chron. 11:11 *Jashobeam*). [d] *8* Probably a variant of *Hacmonite* (see 1 Chron. 11:11)
[e] *8* Some Septuagint manuscripts (see also 1 Chron. 11:11); Hebrew and other Septuagint manuscripts *Three; it was Adino the Eznite who killed eight hundred men* [f] *9* See 1 Chron. 11:13; Hebrew *gathered there.*

istine lines, drew water from the well near the
gate of Bethlehem and carried it back to David. But he refused to drink it; instead, he
poured it out before the LORD. 17"Far be it
from me, O LORD, to do this!" he said. "Is it
not the blood of men who went at the risk of
their lives?" And David would not drink it.
Such were the exploits of the three mighty
men.

18Abishai the brother of Joab son of Zeruiah was chief of the Three.[a] He raised his
spear against three hundred men, whom he
killed, and so he became as famous as the
Three. 19Was he not held in greater honor
than the Three? He became their commander, even though he was not included
among them.

20Benaiah son of Jehoiada was a valiant
fighter from Kabzeel, who performed great
exploits. He struck down two of Moab's best
men. He also went down into a pit on a
snowy day and killed a lion. 21And he struck
down a huge Egyptian. Although the Egyptian had a spear in his hand, Benaiah went
against him with a club. He snatched the
spear from the Egyptian's hand and killed
him with his own spear. 22Such were the
exploits of Benaiah son of Jehoiada; he too
was as famous as the three mighty men.
23He was held in greater honor than any of
the Thirty, but he was not included among
the Three. And David put him in charge of his
bodyguard.

24Among the Thirty were:
Asahel the brother of Joab,
Elhanan son of Dodo from Bethlehem,
25Shammah the Harodite,
Elika the Harodite,
26Helez the Paltite,
Ira son of Ikkesh from Tekoa,
27Abiezer from Anathoth,
Mebunnai[b] the Hushathite,
28Zalmon the Ahohite,
Maharai the Netophathite,
29Heled[c] son of Baanah the Netophathite,
Ithai son of Ribai from Gibeah in Benjamin,
30Benaiah the Pirathonite,
Hiddai[d] from the ravines of Gaash,
31Abi-Albon the Arbathite,
Azmaveth the Barhumite,
32Eliahba the Shaalbonite,
the sons of Jashen,
Jonathan 33son of[e] Shammah the Hararite,
Ahiam son of Sharar[f] the Hararite,
34Eliphelet son of Ahasbai the Maacathite,
Eliam son of Ahithophel the Gilonite,
35Hezro the Carmelite,
Paarai the Arbite,
36Igal son of Nathan from Zobah,
the son of Hagri,[g]
37Zelek the Ammonite,
Naharai the Beerothite, the armor-bearer of Joab son of Zeruiah,
38Ira the Ithrite,
Gareb the Ithrite
39and Uriah the Hittite.
There were thirty-seven in all.

David Counts the Fighting Men

24 Again the anger of the LORD burned
against Israel, and he incited David
against them, saying, "Go and take a census
of Israel and Judah."

2So the king said to Joab and the army
commanders[h] with him, "Go throughout the
tribes of Israel from Dan to Beersheba and
enroll the fighting men, so that I may know
how many there are."

3But Joab replied to the king, "May the
LORD your God multiply the troops a hundred
times over, and may the eyes of my lord the
king see it. But why does my lord the king
want to do such a thing?"

4The king's word, however, overruled
Joab and the army commanders; so they left
the presence of the king to enroll the fighting
men of Israel.

5After crossing the Jordan, they camped
near Aroer, south of the town in the gorge,
and then went through Gad and on to Jazer.
6They went to Gilead and the region of Tah-
tim Hodshi, and on to Dan Jaan and around
toward Sidon. 7Then they went toward the
fortress of Tyre and all the towns of the Hi-

[a]18 Most Hebrew manuscripts (see also 1 Chron. 11:20); two Hebrew manuscripts and Syriac *Thirty*
[b]27 Hebrew; some Septuagint manuscripts (see also 1 Chron. 11:29) *Sibbecai*
[c]29 Some Hebrew manuscripts and Vulgate (see also 1 Chron. 11:30); most Hebrew manuscripts *Heleb*
[d]30 Hebrew; some Septuagint manuscripts (see also 1 Chron. 11:32) *Hurai*
[e]33 Some Septuagint manuscripts (see also 1 Chron. 11:34); Hebrew does not have *son of.*
[f]33 Hebrew; some Septuagint manuscripts (see also 1 Chron. 11:35) *Secar*
[g]36 Some Septuagint manuscripts (see also 1 Chron. 11:38); Hebrew *Haggadi*
[h]2 Septuagint (see also verse 4 and 1 Chron. 21:2); Hebrew *Joab the army commander*

vites and Canaanites. Finally, they went on
to Beersheba in the Negev of Judah.
[8]After they had gone through the entire
land, they came back to Jerusalem at the
end of nine months and twenty days.
[9]Joab reported the number of the fighting
men to the king: In Israel there were eight
hundred thousand able-bodied men who
could handle a sword, and in Judah five hundred thousand.
[10]David was conscience-stricken after he
had counted the fighting men, and he said to
the LORD, "I have sinned greatly in what I
have done. Now, O LORD, I beg you, take
away the guilt of your servant. I have done a
very foolish thing."
[11]Before David got up the next morning,
the word of the LORD had come to Gad the
prophet, David's seer: [12]"Go and tell David,
'This is what the LORD says: I am giving you
three options. Choose one of them for me to
carry out against you.'"
[13]So Gad went to David and said to him,
"Shall there come upon you three[a] years of
famine in your land? Or three months of fleeing from your enemies while they pursue
you? Or three days of plague in your land?
Now then, think it over and decide how I
should answer the one who sent me."
[14]David said to Gad, "I am in deep distress. Let us fall into the hands of the LORD,
for his mercy is great; but do not let me fall
into the hands of men."
[15]So the LORD sent a plague on Israel from
that morning until the end of the time designated, and seventy thousand of the people
from Dan to Beersheba died. [16]When the
angel stretched out his hand to destroy
Jerusalem, the LORD was grieved because of
the calamity and said to the angel who was
afflicting the people, "Enough! Withdraw
your hand." The angel of the LORD was then
at the threshing floor of Araunah the Jebusite.
[17]When David saw the angel who was
striking down the people, he said to the LORD,
"I am the one who has sinned and done
wrong. These are but sheep. What have they
done? Let your hand fall upon me and my
family."

David Builds an Altar

[18]On that day Gad went to David and said
to him, "Go up and build an altar to the LORD
on the threshing floor of Araunah the Jebusite." [19]So David went up, as the LORD had
commanded through Gad. [20]When Araunah
looked and saw the king and his men coming
toward him, he went out and bowed down
before the king with his face to the ground.
[21]Araunah said, "Why has my lord the king
come to his servant?"

"To buy your threshing floor," David answered, "so I can build an altar to the LORD, that the plague on the people may be stopped."

[22]Araunah said to David, "Let my lord the
king take whatever pleases him and offer it
up. Here are oxen for the burnt offering, and
here are threshing sledges and ox yokes for
the wood. [23]O king, Araunah gives all this to
the king." Araunah also said to him, "May the
LORD your God accept you."
[24]But the king replied to Araunah, "No, I
insist on paying you for it. I will not sacrifice to
the LORD my God burnt offerings that cost me
nothing."
So David bought the threshing floor and
the oxen and paid fifty shekels[b] of silver for
them. [25]David built an altar to the LORD there
and sacrificed burnt offerings and fellowship
offerings.[c] Then the LORD answered prayer
in behalf of the land, and the plague on Israel
was stopped.

[a] *13* Septuagint (see also 1 Chron. 21:12); Hebrew *seven*
[b] *24* That is, about 1 1/4 pounds (about 0.6 kilogram)
[c] *25* Traditionally *peace offerings*

I Kings

Introduction:

Beginning with Solomon's reign (about 971 B.C.) I Kings records the history of Israel through the divided kingdom to the death of Ahaziah, the son of Ahab. Chapters 3 through 11 describe Solomon's reign, including the building of the temple and the palace in Jerusalem.

Rehoboam, Solomon's son, took the throne after Solomon's death but lost the northern part of the kingdom to Jeroboam. After this the northern kingdom was known as Israel, and the southern kingdom was called Judah. The last chapters of I Kings tell about the evil King Ahab and God's prophet Elijah, who condemned Ahab's wickedness and Israel's disobedience.

Because the author of 1 and 2 Kings was interested in Israel's faithfulness to God and his covenant he wrote about each king showing how he/she was faithful or unfaithful to God. The author often used the phrase, "did what was right in the eyes of the LORD," or "did evil in the eyes of the LORD," to describe the goodness or wickedness of the king.

Like Judges the author records that when Israel was obedient God brought peace to the land, but when the people were disobedient and worshiped idols the land of Israel suffered wars and other disasters.

Outline of contents:

The reign of Solomon (1:1–11:43)
Rehoboam and Jeroboam (12:1–14:31)
Kings of Israel and Judah (15:1–16:34)
Elijah and Ahab (17:1–19:21)
The reign of Ahab and Jezebel (20:1–22:53)

Adonijah Sets Himself Up as King

1 When King David was old and well advanced in years, he could not keep warm
even when they put covers over him. 2So his
servants said to him, "Let us look for a young
virgin to attend the king and take care of him.
She can lie beside him so that our lord the
king may keep warm."
3Then they searched throughout Israel for
a beautiful girl and found Abishag, a Shunammite, and brought her to the king. 4The
girl was very beautiful; she took care of the
king and waited on him, but the king had no
intimate relations with her.
5Now Adonijah, whose mother was Haggith, put himself forward and said, "I will be
king." So he got chariots and horses[a] ready,
with fifty men to run ahead of him. 6(His father had never interfered with him by asking,
"Why do you behave as you do?" He was
also very handsome and was born next after
Absalom.)
7Adonijah conferred with Joab son of Zeruiah and with Abiathar the priest, and they
gave him their support. 8But Zadok the
priest, Benaiah son of Jehoiada, Nathan the
prophet, Shimei and Rei[b] and David's
special guard did not join Adonijah.
9Adonijah then sacrificed sheep, cattle
and fattened calves at the Stone of Zoheleth
near En Rogel. He invited all his brothers,
the king's sons, and all the men of Judah
who were royal officials, 10but he did not invite Nathan the prophet or Benaiah or the
special guard or his brother Solomon.
11Then Nathan asked Bathsheba, Solomon's mother, "Have you not heard that
Adonijah, the son of Haggith, has become
king without our lord David's knowing it?
12Now then, let me advise you how you can

[a]5 Or *charioteers* [b]8 Or *and his friends*

save your own life and the life of your son
Solomon. 13Go in to King David and say to
him, 'My lord the king, did you not swear to
me your servant: "Surely Solomon your son
shall be king after me, and he will sit on my
throne"? Why then has Adonijah become
king?' 14While you are still there talking to the
king, I will come in and confirm what you
have said."

15So Bathsheba went to see the aged king
in his room, where Abishag the Shunammite
was attending him. 16Bathsheba bowed low
and knelt before the king.

"What is it you want?" the king asked.

17She said to him, "My lord, you yourself
swore to me your servant by the LORD your
God: 'Solomon your son shall be king after
me, and he will sit on my throne.' 18But now
Adonijah has become king, and you, my lord
the king, do not know about it. 19He has sacrificed great numbers of cattle, fattened
calves, and sheep, and has invited all the
king's sons, Abiathar the priest and Joab the
commander of the army, but he has not invited Solomon your servant. 20My lord the
king, the eyes of all Israel are on you, to learn
from you who will sit on the throne of my lord
the king after him. 21Otherwise, as soon as
my lord the king is laid to rest with his fathers,
I and my son Solomon will be treated as
criminals."

22While she was still speaking with the
king, Nathan the prophet arrived. 23And they
told the king, "Nathan the prophet is here."
So he went before the king and bowed with
his face to the ground.

24Nathan said, "Have you, my lord the
king, declared that Adonijah shall be king
after you, and that he will sit on your throne?
25Today he has gone down and sacrificed
great numbers of cattle, fattened calves, and
sheep. He has invited all the king's sons, the
commanders of the army and Abiathar the
priest. Right now they are eating and drinking with him and saying, 'Long live King
Adonijah!' 26But me your servant, and Zadok
the priest, and Benaiah son of Jehoiada, and
your servant Solomon he did not invite. 27Is
this something my lord the king has done
without letting his servants know who should
sit on the throne of my lord the king after
him?"

David Makes Solomon King

28Then King David said, "Call in Bathsheba." So she came into the king's presence and stood before him.

29The king then took an oath: "As surely as
the LORD lives, who has delivered me out of
every trouble, 30I will surely carry out today
what I swore to you by the LORD, the God of
Israel: Solomon your son shall be king after
me, and he will sit on my throne in my place."

31Then Bathsheba bowed low with her
face to the ground and, kneeling before the
king, said, "May my lord King David live forever!"

32King David said, "Call in Zadok the
priest, Nathan the prophet and Benaiah son
of Jehoiada." When they came before the
king, 33he said to them: "Take your lord's
servants with you and set Solomon my son
on my own mule and take him down to Gihon. 34There have Zadok the priest and Nathan the prophet anoint him king over Israel.
Blow the trumpet and shout, 'Long live King
Solomon!' 35Then you are to go up with him,
and he is to come and sit on my throne and
reign in my place. I have appointed him ruler
over Israel and Judah."

36Benaiah son of Jehoiada answered the
king, "Amen! May the LORD, the God of my
lord the king, so declare it. 37As the LORD was
with my lord the king, so may he be with
Solomon to make his throne even greater
than the throne of my lord King David!"

38So Zadok the priest, Nathan the prophet,
Benaiah son of Jehoiada, the Kerethites and
the Pelethites went down and put Solomon
on King David's mule and escorted him to
Gihon. 39Zadok the priest took the horn of oil
from the sacred tent and anointed Solomon.
Then they sounded the trumpet and all the
people shouted, "Long live King Solomon!"
40And all the people went up after him, playing flutes and rejoicing greatly, so that the
ground shook with the sound.

41Adonijah and all the guests who were
with him heard it as they were finishing their
feast. On hearing the sound of the trumpet,
Joab asked, "What's the meaning of all the
noise in the city?"

42Even as he was speaking, Jonathan son
of Abiathar the priest arrived. Adonijah said,
"Come in. A worthy man like you must be
bringing good news."

43"Not at all!" Jonathan answered. "Our
lord King David has made Solomon king.
44The king has sent with him Zadok the
priest, Nathan the prophet, Benaiah son of
Jehoiada, the Kerethites and the Pelethites,
and they have put him on the king's mule,
45and Zadok the priest and Nathan the
prophet have anointed him king at Gihon.

From there they have gone up cheering, and the city resounds with it. That's the noise you hear. 46Moreover, Solomon has taken his seat on the royal throne. 47Also, the royal officials have come to congratulate our lord King David, saying, 'May your God make Solomon's name more famous than yours and his throne greater than yours!' And the king bowed in worship on his bed 48and said, 'Praise be to the LORD, the God of Israel, who has allowed my eyes to see a successor on my throne today.' "

49At this, all Adonijah's guests rose in alarm and dispersed. 50But Adonijah, in fear of Solomon, went and took hold of the horns of the altar. 51Then Solomon was told, "Adonijah is afraid of King Solomon and is clinging to the horns of the altar. He says, 'Let King Solomon swear to me today that he will not put his servant to death with the sword.' "

52Solomon replied, "If he shows himself to be a worthy man, not a hair of his head will fall to the ground; but if evil is found in him, he will die." 53Then King Solomon sent men, and they brought him down from the altar. And Adonijah came and bowed down to King Solomon, and Solomon said, "Go to your home."

David's Charge to Solomon

2 When the time drew near for David to die, he gave a charge to Solomon his son.

2"I am about to go the way of all the earth," he said. "So be strong, show yourself a man, 3and observe what the LORD your God requires: Walk in his ways, and keep his decrees and commands, his laws and requirements, as written in the Law of Moses, so that you may prosper in all you do and wherever you go, 4and that the LORD may keep his promise to me: 'If your descendants watch how they live, and if they walk faithfully before me with all their heart and soul, you will never fail to have a man on the throne of Israel.'

5"Now you yourself know what Joab son of Zeruiah did to me—what he did to the two commanders of Israel's armies, Abner son of Ner and Amasa son of Jether. He killed them, shedding their blood in peacetime as if in battle, and with that blood stained the belt around his waist and the sandals on his feet. 6Deal with him according to your wisdom, but do not let his gray head go down to the grave[a] in peace.

7"But show kindness to the sons of Barzillai of Gilead and let them be among those who eat at your table. They stood by me when I fled from your brother Absalom.

8"And remember, you have with you Shimei son of Gera, the Benjamite from Bahurim, who called down bitter curses on me the day I went to Mahanaim. When he came down to meet me at the Jordan, I swore to him by the LORD: 'I will not put you to death by the sword.' 9But now, do not consider him innocent. You are a man of wisdom; you will know what to do to him. Bring his gray head down to the grave in blood."

10Then David rested with his fathers and was buried in the City of David. 11He had reigned forty years over Israel—seven years in Hebron and thirty-three in Jerusalem. 12So Solomon sat on the throne of his father David, and his rule was firmly established.

Solomon's Throne Established

13Now Adonijah, the son of Haggith, went to Bathsheba, Solomon's mother. Bathsheba asked him, "Do you come peacefully?"

He answered, "Yes, peacefully." 14Then he added, "I have something to say to you."

"You may say it," she replied.

15"As you know," he said, "the kingdom was mine. All Israel looked to me as their king. But things changed, and the kingdom has gone to my brother; for it has come to him from the LORD. 16Now I have one request to make of you. Do not refuse me."

"You may make it," she said.

17So he continued, "Please ask King Solomon—he will not refuse you—to give me Abishag the Shunammite as my wife."

18"Very well," Bathsheba replied, "I will speak to the king for you."

19When Bathsheba went to King Solomon to speak to him for Adonijah, the king stood up to meet her, bowed down to her and sat down on his throne. He had a throne brought for the king's mother, and she sat down at his right hand.

20"I have one small request to make of you," she said. "Do not refuse me."

The king replied, "Make it, my mother; I will not refuse you."

21So she said, "Let Abishag the Shunam-

[a]6 Hebrew *Sheol;* also in verse 9

mite be given in marriage to your brother
Adonijah."
22King Solomon answered his mother,
"Why do you request Abishag the Shunammite for Adonijah? You might as well request
the kingdom for him—after all, he is my older
brother—yes, for him and for Abiathar the
priest and Joab son of Zeruiah!"
23Then King Solomon swore by the LORD:
"May God deal with me, be it ever so severely, if Adonijah does not pay with his life for
this request! 24And now, as surely as the
LORD lives—he who has established me securely on the throne of my father David and
has founded a dynasty for me as he promised—Adonijah shall be put to death today!"
25So King Solomon gave orders to Benaiah
son of Jehoiada, and he struck down Adonijah and he died.
26To Abiathar the priest the king said, "Go
back to your fields in Anathoth. You deserve
to die, but I will not put you to death now,
because you carried the ark of the Sovereign
LORD before my father David and shared all
my father's hardships." 27So Solomon removed Abiathar from the priesthood of the
LORD, fulfilling the word the LORD had spoken
at Shiloh about the house of Eli.
28When the news reached Joab, who had
conspired with Adonijah though not with Absalom, he fled to the tent of the LORD and took
hold of the horns of the altar. 29King Solomon
was told that Joab had fled to the tent of the
LORD and was beside the altar. Then Solomon ordered Benaiah son of Jehoiada, "Go,
strike him down!"
30So Benaiah entered the tent of the LORD
and said to Joab, "The king says, 'Come
out!' "
But he answered, "No, I will die here."
Benaiah reported to the king, "This is how
Joab answered me."
31Then the king commanded Benaiah, "Do
as he says. Strike him down and bury him,
and so clear me and my father's house of the
guilt of the innocent blood that Joab shed.
32The LORD will repay him for the blood he
shed, because without the knowledge of my
father David he attacked two men and killed
them with the sword. Both of them—Abner
son of Ner, commander of Israel's army, and
Amasa son of Jether, commander of Judah's
army—were better men and more upright
than he. 33May the guilt of their blood rest on
the head of Joab and his descendants forever. But on David and his descendants, his
house and his throne, may there be the
LORD's peace forever."
34So Benaiah son of Jehoiada went up and
struck down Joab and killed him, and he was
buried on his own land[a] in the desert. 35The
king put Benaiah son of Jehoiada over the
army in Joab's position and replaced Abiathar with Zadok the priest.
36Then the king sent for Shimei and said to
him, "Build yourself a house in Jerusalem
and live there, but do not go anywhere else.
37The day you leave and cross the Kidron
Valley, you can be sure you will die; your
blood will be on your own head."
38Shimei answered the king, "What you
say is good. Your servant will do as my lord
the king has said." And Shimei stayed in
Jerusalem for a long time.
39But three years later, two of Shimei's
slaves ran off to Achish son of Maacah, king
of Gath, and Shimei was told, "Your slaves
are in Gath." 40At this, he saddled his donkey
and went to Achish at Gath in search of his
slaves. So Shimei went away and brought
the slaves back from Gath.
41When Solomon was told that Shimei had
gone from Jerusalem to Gath and had returned, 42the king summoned Shimei and
said to him, "Did I not make you swear by the
LORD and warn you, 'On the day you leave to
go anywhere else, you can be sure you will
die'? At that time you said to me, 'What you
say is good. I will obey.' 43Why then did you
not keep your oath to the LORD and obey the
command I gave you?"
44The king also said to Shimei, "You know
in your heart all the wrong you did to my
father David. Now the LORD will repay you for
your wrongdoing. 45But King Solomon will be
blessed, and David's throne will remain secure before the LORD forever."
46Then the king gave the order to Benaiah
son of Jehoiada, and he went out and struck
Shimei down and killed him.
The kingdom was now firmly established
in Solomon's hands.

Solomon Asks for Wisdom

3 Solomon made an alliance with Pharaoh
king of Egypt and married his daughter.
He brought her to the City of David until he
finished building his palace and the temple of
the LORD, and the wall around Jerusalem.
2The people, however, were still sacrificing

[a]34 Or *buried in his tomb*

at the high places, because a temple had not yet been built for the Name of the LORD. 3Solomon showed his love for the LORD by walking according to the statutes of his father David, except that he offered sacrifices and burned incense on the high places.

4The king went to Gibeon to offer sacrifices, for that was the most important high place, and Solomon offered a thousand burnt offerings on that altar. 5At Gibeon the LORD appeared to Solomon during the night in a dream, and God said, "Ask for whatever you want me to give you."

6Solomon answered, "You have shown great kindness to your servant, my father David, because he was faithful to you and righteous and upright in heart. You have continued this great kindness to him and have given him a son to sit on his throne this very day.

7"Now, O LORD my God, you have made your servant king in place of my father David. But I am only a little child and do not know how to carry out my duties. 8Your servant is here among the people you have chosen, a great people, too numerous to count or number. 9So give your servant a discerning heart to govern your people and to distinguish between right and wrong. For who is able to govern this great people of yours?"

10The Lord was pleased that Solomon had asked for this. 11So God said to him, "Since you have asked for this and not for long life or wealth for yourself, nor have asked for the death of your enemies but for discernment in administering justice, 12I will do what you have asked. I will give you a wise and discerning heart, so that there will never have been anyone like you, nor will there ever be. 13Moreover, I will give you what you have not asked for—both riches and honor—so that in your lifetime you will have no equal among kings. 14And if you walk in my ways and obey my statutes and commands as David your father did, I will give you a long life." 15Then Solomon awoke—and he realized it had been a dream.

He returned to Jerusalem, stood before the ark of the Lord's covenant and sacrificed burnt offerings and fellowship offerings.[a] Then he gave a feast for all his court.

A Wise Ruling

16Now two prostitutes came to the king and stood before him. 17One of them said, "My lord, this woman and I live in the same house. I had a baby while she was there with me. 18The third day after my child was born, this woman also had a baby. We were alone; there was no one in the house but the two of us.

19"During the night this woman's son died because she lay on him. 20So she got up in the middle of the night and took my son from my side while I your servant was asleep. She put him by her breast and put her dead son by my breast. 21The next morning, I got up to nurse my son—and he was dead! But when I looked at him closely in the morning light, I saw that it wasn't the son I had borne."

22The other woman said, "No! The living one is my son; the dead one is yours."

But the first one insisted, "No! The dead one is yours; the living one is mine." And so they argued before the king.

23The king said, "This one says, 'My son is alive and your son is dead,' while that one says, 'No! Your son is dead and mine is alive.' "

24Then the king said, "Bring me a sword." So they brought a sword for the king. 25He then gave an order: "Cut the living child in two and give half to one and half to the other."

26The woman whose son was alive was filled with compassion for her son and said to the king, "Please, my lord, give her the living baby! Don't kill him!"

But the other said, "Neither I nor you shall have him. Cut him in two!"

27Then the king gave his ruling: "Give the living baby to the first woman. Do not kill him; she is his mother."

28When all Israel heard the verdict the king had given, they held the king in awe, because they saw that he had wisdom from God to administer justice.

Solomon's Officials and Governors

4 So King Solomon ruled over all Israel. 2And these were his chief officials:

Azariah son of Zadok—the priest;
3Elihoreph and Ahijah, sons of Shisha—secretaries;
Jehoshaphat son of Ahilud—recorder;
4Benaiah son of Jehoiada—commander in chief;
Zadok and Abiathar—priests;

[a]15 Traditionally *peace offerings*

5 Azariah son of Nathan—in charge of the district officers;
Zabud son of Nathan—a priest and personal adviser to the king;
6 Ahishar—in charge of the palace;
Adoniram son of Abda—in charge of forced labor.

7 Solomon also had twelve district governors over all Israel, who supplied provisions
for the king and the royal household. Each
one had to provide supplies for one month in
the year. 8 These are their names:

Ben-Hur—in the hill country of Ephraim;
9 Ben-Deker—in Makaz, Shaalbim, Beth Shemesh and Elon Bethhanan;
10 Ben-Hesed—in Arubboth (Socoh and all the land of Hepher were his);
11 Ben-Abinadab—in Naphoth Dor[a] (he was married to Taphath daughter of Solomon);
12 Baana son of Ahilud—in Taanach and Megiddo, and in all of Beth Shan next to Zarethan below Jezreel, from Beth Shan to Abel Meholah across to Jokmeam;
13 Ben-Geber—in Ramoth Gilead (the settlements of Jair son of Manasseh in Gilead were his, as well as the district of Argob in Bashan and its sixty large walled cities with bronze gate bars);
14 Ahinadab son of Iddo—in Mahanaim;
15 Ahimaaz—in Naphtali (he had married Basemath daughter of Solomon);
16 Baana son of Hushai—in Asher and in Aloth;
17 Jehoshaphat son of Paruah—in Issachar;
18 Shimei son of Ela—in Benjamin;
19 Geber son of Uri—in Gilead (the country of Sihon king of the Amorites and the country of Og king of Bashan). He was the only governor over the district.

Solomon's Daily Provisions

20 The people of Judah and Israel were as
numerous as the sand on the seashore; they
ate, they drank and they were happy. 21 And
Solomon ruled over all the kingdoms from
the River[b] to the land of the Philistines, as far
as the border of Egypt. These countries
brought tribute and were Solomon's subjects
all his life.

22 Solomon's daily provisions were thirty
cors[c] of fine flour and sixty cors[d] of meal,
23 ten head of stall-fed cattle, twenty of pas-
ture-fed cattle and a hundred sheep and
goats, as well as deer, gazelles, roebucks
and choice fowl. 24 For he ruled over all the
kingdoms west of the River, from Tiphsah to
Gaza, and had peace on all sides. 25 During
Solomon's lifetime Judah and Israel, from
Dan to Beersheba, lived in safety, each man
under his own vine and fig tree.

26 Solomon had four[e] thousand stalls for
chariot horses, and twelve thousand
horses.[f]

27 The district officers, each in his month,
supplied provisions for King Solomon and all
who came to the king's table. They saw to it
that nothing was lacking. 28 They also
brought to the proper place their quotas of
barley and straw for the chariot horses and
the other horses.

Solomon's Wisdom

29 God gave Solomon wisdom and very
great insight, and a breadth of understanding
as measureless as the sand on the seashore. 30 Solomon's wisdom was greater
than the wisdom of all the men of the East,
and greater than all the wisdom of Egypt.
31 He was wiser than any other man, including Ethan the Ezrahite—wiser than Heman,
Calcol and Darda, the sons of Mahol. And his
fame spread to all the surrounding nations.
32 He spoke three thousand proverbs and his
songs numbered a thousand and five. 33 He
described plant life, from the cedar of Lebanon to the hyssop that grows out of walls. He
also taught about animals and birds, reptiles
and fish. 34 Men of all nations came to listen
to Solomon's wisdom, sent by all the kings of
the world, who had heard of his wisdom.

Preparations for Building the Temple

5 When Hiram king of Tyre heard that
Solomon had been anointed king to succeed his father David, he sent his envoys to
Solomon, because he had always been on
friendly terms with David. 2 Solomon sent
back this message to Hiram:

3 "You know that because of the wars
waged against my father David from all

[a] *11* Or *in the heights of Dor* [b] *21* That is, the Euphrates; also in verse 24 [c] *22* That is, probably about 185 bushels (about 6.6 kiloliters) [d] *22* That is, probably about 375 bushels (about 13.2 kiloliters) [e] *26* Some Septuagint manuscripts (see also 2 Chron. 9:25); Hebrew *forty* [f] *26* Or *charioteers*

sides, he could not build a temple for the
Name of the LORD his God until the LORD
put his enemies under his feet. 4But now
the LORD my God has given me rest on
every side, and there is no adversary or
disaster. 5I intend, therefore, to build a
temple for the Name of the LORD my
God, as the LORD told my father David,
when he said, 'Your son whom I will put
on the throne in your place will build the
temple for my Name.'

6"So give orders that cedars of Lebanon be cut for me. My men will work with
yours, and I will pay you for your men
whatever wages you set. You know that
we have no one so skilled in felling timber as the Sidonians."

7When Hiram heard Solomon's message,
he was greatly pleased and said, "Praise be
to the LORD today, for he has given David a
wise son to rule over this great nation."
8So Hiram sent word to Solomon:

"I have received the message you
sent me and will do all you want in providing the cedar and pine logs. 9My men
will haul them down from Lebanon to the
sea, and I will float them in rafts by sea
to the place you specify. There I will
separate them and you can take them
away. And you are to grant my wish by
providing food for my royal household."

10In this way Hiram kept Solomon supplied
with all the cedar and pine logs he wanted,
11and Solomon gave Hiram twenty thousand
cors[a] of wheat as food for his household, in
addition to twenty thousand baths[b,c] of
pressed olive oil. Solomon continued to do
this for Hiram year after year. 12The LORD
gave Solomon wisdom, just as he had promised him. There were peaceful relations between Hiram and Solomon, and the two of
them made a treaty.

13King Solomon conscripted laborers from
all Israel—thirty thousand men. 14He sent
them off to Lebanon in shifts of ten thousand
a month, so that they spent one month in
Lebanon and two months at home. Adoniram was in charge of the forced labor.
15Solomon had seventy thousand carriers
and eighty thousand stonecutters in the hills,
16as well as thirty-three hundred[d] foremen
who supervised the project and directed the
workmen. 17At the king's command they removed from the quarry large blocks of quality
stone to provide a foundation of dressed
stone for the temple. 18The craftsmen of
Solomon and Hiram and the men of Gebal[e]
cut and prepared the timber and stone for the
building of the temple.

Solomon Builds the Temple

6 In the four hundred and eightieth[f] year
after the Israelites had come out of
Egypt, in the fourth year of Solomon's reign
over Israel, in the month of Ziv, the second
month, he began to build the temple of the
LORD.

2The temple that King Solomon built for the
LORD was sixty cubits long, twenty wide and
thirty high.[g] 3The portico at the front of the
main hall of the temple extended the width of
the temple, that is twenty cubits,[h] and pro-
jected ten cubits[i] from the front of the temple. 4He made narrow clerestory windows in
the temple. 5Against the walls of the main
hall and inner sanctuary he built a structure
around the building, in which there were side
rooms. 6The lowest floor was five cubits[j]
wide, the middle floor six cubits[k] and the
third floor seven.[l] He made offset ledges
around the outside of the temple so that
nothing would be inserted into the temple
walls.

7In building the temple, only blocks
dressed at the quarry were used, and no
hammer, chisel or any other iron tool was
heard at the temple site while it was being
built.

8The entrance to the lowest[m] floor was on
the south side of the temple; a stairway led
up to the middle level and from there to the
third. 9So he built the temple and completed
it, roofing it with beams and cedar planks.
10And he built the side rooms all along the
temple. The height of each was five cubits,
and they were attached to the temple by
beams of cedar.

[a]11 That is, probably about 125,000 bushels (about 4,400 kiloliters) [b]11 Septuagint (see also 2 Chron. 2:10); Hebrew *twenty cors* [c]11 That is, about 115,000 gallons (about 440 kiloliters) [d]16 Hebrew; some Septuagint manuscripts (see also 2 Chron. 2:2, 18) *thirty-six hundred* [e]18 That is, Byblos [f]1 Hebrew; Septuagint *four hundred and fortieth* [g]2 That is, about 90 feet (about 27 meters) long and 30 feet (about 9 meters) wide and 45 feet (about 13.5 meters) high [h]3 That is, about 30 feet (about 9 meters) [i]3 That is, about 15 feet (about 4.5 meters) [j]6 That is, about 7 1/2 feet (about 2.3 meters); also in verses 10 and 24 [k]6 That is, about 9 feet (about 2.7 meters) [l]6 That is, about 10 1/2 feet (about 3.1 meters) [m]8 Septuagint; Hebrew *middle*

11The word of the LORD came to Solomon:
12"As for this temple you are building, if you
follow my decrees, carry out my regulations
and keep all my commands and obey them, I
will fulfill through you the promise I gave to
David your father. 13And I will live among the
Israelites and will not abandon my people
Israel."

14So Solomon built the temple and completed it. 15He lined its interior walls with cedar boards, paneling them from the floor of
the temple to the ceiling, and covered the
floor of the temple with planks of pine. 16He
partitioned off twenty cubits[a] at the rear of
the temple with cedar boards from floor to
ceiling to form within the temple an inner
sanctuary, the Most Holy Place. 17The main
hall in front of this room was forty cubits[b]
long. 18The inside of the temple was cedar,
carved with gourds and open flowers. Everything was cedar; no stone was to be seen.

19He prepared the inner sanctuary within
the temple to set the ark of the covenant of
the LORD there. 20The inner sanctuary was
twenty cubits long, twenty wide and twenty
high.[c] He overlaid the inside with pure gold,
and he also overlaid the altar of cedar.
21Solomon covered the inside of the temple
with pure gold, and he extended gold chains
across the front of the inner sanctuary, which
was overlaid with gold. 22So he overlaid the
whole interior with gold. He also overlaid with
gold the altar that belonged to the inner
sanctuary.

23In the inner sanctuary he made a pair of
cherubim of olive wood, each ten cubits[d]
high. 24One wing of the first cherub was five
cubits long, and the other wing five cubits—
ten cubits from wing tip to wing tip. 25The
second cherub also measured ten cubits, for
the two cherubim were identical in size and
shape. 26The height of each cherub was ten
cubits. 27He placed the cherubim inside the
innermost room of the temple, with their
wings spread out. The wing of one cherub
touched one wall, while the wing of the other
touched the other wall, and their wings
touched each other in the middle of the
room. 28He overlaid the cherubim with gold.

29On the walls all around the temple, in
both the inner and outer rooms, he carved
cherubim, palm trees and open flowers. 30He
also covered the floors of both the inner and
outer rooms of the temple with gold.

31For the entrance of the inner sanctuary
he made doors of olive wood with five-sided
jambs. 32And on the two olive wood doors he
carved cherubim, palm trees and open flowers, and overlaid the cherubim and palm
trees with beaten gold. 33In the same way he
made four-sided jambs of olive wood for the
entrance to the main hall. 34He also made
two pine doors, each having two leaves that
turned in sockets. 35He carved cherubim,
palm trees and open flowers on them and
overlaid them with gold hammered evenly
over the carvings.

36And he built the inner courtyard of three
courses of dressed stone and one course of
trimmed cedar beams.

37The foundation of the temple of the LORD
was laid in the fourth year, in the month of
Ziv. 38In the eleventh year in the month of
Bul, the eighth month, the temple was finished in all its details according to its specifications. He had spent seven years building it.

Solomon Builds His Palace

7 It took Solomon thirteen years, however,
to complete the construction of his palace. 2He built the Palace of the Forest of
Lebanon a hundred cubits long, fifty wide
and thirty high,[e] with four rows of cedar columns supporting trimmed cedar beams. 3It
was roofed with cedar above the beams that
rested on the columns—forty-five beams, fifteen to a row. 4Its windows were placed high
in sets of three, facing each other. 5All the
doorways had rectangular frames; they were
in the front part in sets of three, facing each
other.[f]

6He made a colonnade fifty cubits long and
thirty wide.[g] In front of it was a portico, and in
front of that were pillars and an overhanging
roof.

7He built the throne hall, the Hall of Justice,
where he was to judge, and he covered it
with cedar from floor to ceiling.[h] 8And the
palace in which he was to live, set farther
back, was similar in design. Solomon also
made a palace like this hall for Pharaoh's
daughter, whom he had married.

9All these structures, from the outside to

[a] *16* That is, about 30 feet (about 9 meters) [b] *17* That is, about 60 feet (about 18 meters) [c] *20* That is, about 30 feet (about 9 meters) long, wide and high [d] *23* That is, about 15 feet (about 4.5 meters) [e] *2* That is, about 150 feet (about 46 meters) long, 75 feet (about 23 meters) wide and 45 feet (about 13.5 meters) high [f] *5* The meaning of the Hebrew for this verse is uncertain. [g] *6* That is, about 75 feet (about 23 meters) long and 45 feet (about 13.5 meters) wide [h] *7* Vulgate and Syriac; Hebrew *floor*

the great courtyard and from foundation to eaves, were made of blocks of high-grade stone cut to size and trimmed with a saw on their inner and outer faces. 10The foundations were laid with large stones of good quality, some measuring ten cubits[a] and some eight.[b] 11Above were high-grade stones, cut to size, and cedar beams. 12The great courtyard was surrounded by a wall of three courses of dressed stone and one course of trimmed cedar beams, as was the inner courtyard of the temple of the LORD with its portico.

The Temple's Furnishings

13King Solomon sent to Tyre and brought Huram,[c] 14whose mother was a widow from the tribe of Naphtali and whose father was a man of Tyre and a craftsman in bronze. Huram was highly skilled and experienced in all kinds of bronze work. He came to King Solomon and did all the work assigned to him.

15He cast two bronze pillars, each eighteen cubits high and twelve cubits around,[d] by line. 16He also made two capitals of cast bronze to set on the tops of the pillars; each capital was five cubits[e] high. 17A network of interwoven chains festooned the capitals on top of the pillars, seven for each capital. 18He made pomegranates in two rows[f] encircling each network to decorate the capitals on top of the pillars.[g] He did the same for each capital. 19The capitals on top of the pillars in the portico were in the shape of lilies, four cubits[h] high. 20On the capitals of both pillars, above the bowl-shaped part next to the network, were the two hundred pomegranates in rows all around. 21He erected the pillars at the portico of the temple. The pillar to the south he named Jakin[i] and the one to the north Boaz.[j] 22The capitals on top were in the shape of lilies. And so the work on the pillars was completed.

23He made the Sea of cast metal, circular in shape, measuring ten cubits[a] from rim to rim and five cubits high. It took a line of thirty cubits[k] to measure around it. 24Below the rim, gourds encircled it—ten to a cubit. The gourds were cast in two rows in one piece with the Sea.

25The Sea stood on twelve bulls, three facing north, three facing west, three facing south and three facing east. The Sea rested on top of them, and their hindquarters were toward the center. 26It was a handbreadth[l] in thickness, and its rim was like the rim of a cup, like a lily blossom. It held two thousand baths.[m]

27He also made ten movable stands of bronze; each was four cubits long, four wide and three high.[n] 28This is how the stands were made: They had side panels attached to uprights. 29On the panels between the uprights were lions, bulls and cherubim—and on the uprights as well. Above and below the lions and bulls were wreaths of hammered work. 30Each stand had four bronze wheels with bronze axles, and each had a basin resting on four supports, cast with wreaths on each side. 31On the inside of the stand there was an opening that had a circular frame one cubit[o] deep. This opening was round, and with its basework it measured a cubit and a half.[p] Around its opening there was engraving. The panels of the stands were square, not round. 32The four wheels were under the panels, and the axles of the wheels were attached to the stand. The diameter of each wheel was a cubit and a half. 33The wheels were made like chariot wheels; the axles, rims, spokes and hubs were all of cast metal.

34Each stand had four handles, one on each corner, projecting from the stand. 35At the top of the stand there was a circular band half a cubit[q] deep. The supports and panels were attached to the top of the stand. 36He engraved cherubim, lions and palm trees on the surfaces of the supports and on the panels, in every available space, with wreaths all around. 37This is the way he made the ten stands. They were all cast in the same molds and were identical in size and shape.

[a] *10,23* That is, about 15 feet (about 4.5 meters) [b] *10* That is, about 12 feet (about 3.6 meters) [c] *13* Hebrew *Hiram,* a variant of *Huram;* also in verses 40 and 45 [d] *15* That is, about 27 feet (about 8.1 meters) high and 18 feet (about 5.4 meters) around [e] *16* That is, about 7 1/2 feet (about 2.3 meters); also in verse 23 [f] *18* Two Hebrew manuscripts and Septuagint; most Hebrew manuscripts *made the pillars, and there were two rows* [g] *18* Many Hebrew manuscripts and Syriac; most Hebrew manuscripts *pomegranates* [h] *19* That is, about 6 feet (about 1.8 meters); also in verse 38 [i] *21* *Jakin* probably means *he establishes.* [j] *21* *Boaz* probably means *in him is strength.* [k] *23* That is, about 45 feet (about 13.5 meters) [l] *26* That is, about 3 inches (about 8 centimeters) [m] *26* That is, probably about 11,500 gallons (about 44 kiloliters); the Septuagint does not have this sentence. [n] *27* That is, about 6 feet (about 1.8 meters) long and wide and about 4 1/2 feet (about 1.3 meters) high [o] *31* That is, about 1 1/2 feet (about 0.5 meter) [p] *31* That is, about 2 1/4 feet (about 0.7 meter); also in verse 32 [q] *35* That is, about 3/4 foot (about 0.2 meter)

38He then made ten bronze basins, each holding forty baths[a] and measuring four cubits across, one basin to go on each of the ten stands. 39He placed five of the stands on the south side of the temple and five on the north. He placed the Sea on the south side, at the southeast corner of the temple. 40He also made the basins and shovels and sprinkling bowls.

So Huram finished all the work he had undertaken for King Solomon in the temple of the LORD:

41the two pillars;
the two bowl-shaped capitals on top of the pillars;
the two sets of network decorating the two bowl-shaped capitals on top of the pillars;
42the four hundred pomegranates for the two sets of network (two rows of pomegranates for each network, decorating the bowl-shaped capitals on top of the pillars);
43the ten stands with their ten basins;
44the Sea and the twelve bulls under it;
45the pots, shovels and sprinkling bowls.

All these objects that Huram made for King Solomon for the temple of the LORD were of burnished bronze. 46The king had them cast in clay molds in the plain of the Jordan between Succoth and Zarethan. 47Solomon left all these things unweighed, because there were so many; the weight of the bronze was not determined.

48Solomon also made all the furnishings that were in the LORD's temple:

the golden altar;
the golden table on which was the bread of the Presence;
49the lampstands of pure gold (five on the right and five on the left, in front of the inner sanctuary);
the gold floral work and lamps and tongs;
50the pure gold basins, wick trimmers, sprinkling bowls, dishes and censers;
and the gold sockets for the doors of the innermost room, the Most Holy Place, and also for the doors of the main hall of the temple.

51When all the work King Solomon had done for the temple of the LORD was finished, he brought in the things his father David had dedicated—the silver and gold and the furnishings—and he placed them in the treasuries of the LORD's temple.

The Ark Brought to the Temple

8 Then King Solomon summoned into his presence at Jerusalem the elders of Israel, all the heads of the tribes and the chiefs of the Israelite families, to bring up the ark of the LORD's covenant from Zion, the City of David. 2All the men of Israel came together to King Solomon at the time of the festival in the month of Ethanim, the seventh month.

3When all the elders of Israel had arrived, the priests took up the ark, 4and they brought up the ark of the LORD and the Tent of Meeting and all the sacred furnishings in it. The priests and Levites carried them up, 5and King Solomon and the entire assembly of Israel that had gathered about him were before the ark, sacrificing so many sheep and cattle that they could not be recorded or counted.

6The priests then brought the ark of the LORD's covenant to its place in the inner sanctuary of the temple, the Most Holy Place, and put it beneath the wings of the cherubim. 7The cherubim spread their wings over the place of the ark and overshadowed the ark and its carrying poles. 8These poles were so long that their ends could be seen from the Holy Place in front of the inner sanctuary, but not from outside the Holy Place; and they are still there today. 9There was nothing in the ark except the two stone tablets that Moses had placed in it at Horeb, where the LORD made a covenant with the Israelites after they came out of Egypt.

10When the priests withdrew from the Holy Place, the cloud filled the temple of the LORD. 11And the priests could not perform their service because of the cloud, for the glory of the LORD filled his temple.

12Then Solomon said, "The LORD has said that he would dwell in a dark cloud; 13I have indeed built a magnificent temple for you, a place for you to dwell forever."

14While the whole assembly of Israel was standing there, the king turned around and blessed them. 15Then he said:

"Praise be to the LORD, the God of Israel, who with his own hand has fulfilled what he promised with his own

[a]38 That is, about 230 gallons (about 880 liters)

mouth to my father David. For he said,
16'Since the day I brought my people
Israel out of Egypt, I have not chosen a
city in any tribe of Israel to have a temple
built for my Name to be there, but I have
chosen David to rule my people Israel.'

17"My father David had it in his heart
to build a temple for the Name of the
LORD, the God of Israel. 18But the LORD
said to my father David, 'Because it was
in your heart to build a temple for my
Name, you did well to have this in your
heart. 19Nevertheless, you are not the
one to build the temple, but your son,
who is your own flesh and blood—he is
the one who will build the temple for my
Name.'

20"The LORD has kept the promise he
made: I have succeeded David my father and now I sit on the throne of Israel,
just as the LORD promised, and I have
built the temple for the Name of the
LORD, the God of Israel. 21I have provided a place there for the ark, in which
is the covenant of the LORD that he made
with our fathers when he brought them
out of Egypt."

Solomon's Prayer of Dedication

22Then Solomon stood before the altar of
the LORD in front of the whole assembly of
Israel, spread out his hands toward heaven
23and said:

> "O LORD, God of Israel, there is no
> God like you in heaven above or on
> earth below—you who keep your cov-
> enant of love with your servants who
> continue wholeheartedly in your way.
> 24You have kept your promise to your
> servant David my father; with your
> mouth you have promised and with your
> hand you have fulfilled it—as it is today.
>
> 25"Now LORD, God of Israel, keep for
> your servant David my father the prom-
> ises you made to him when you said,
> 'You shall never fail to have a man to sit
> before me on the throne of Israel, if only
> your sons are careful in all they do to
> walk before me as you have done.'
> 26And now, O God of Israel, let your
> word that you promised your servant
> David my father come true.
>
> 27"But will God really dwell on earth?
> The heavens, even the highest heaven,
> cannot contain you. How much less this
> temple I have built! 28Yet give attention
> to your servant's prayer and his plea for
> mercy, O LORD my God. Hear the cry
> and the prayer that your servant is pray-
> ing in your presence this day. 29May
> your eyes be open toward this temple
> night and day, this place of which you
> said, 'My Name shall be there,' so that
> you will hear the prayer your servant
> prays toward this place. 30Hear the sup-
> plication of your servant and of your
> people Israel when they pray toward this
> place. Hear from heaven, your dwelling
> place, and when you hear, forgive.
>
> 31"When a man wrongs his neighbor
> and is required to take an oath and he
> comes and swears the oath before your
> altar in this temple, 32then hear from
> heaven and act. Judge between your
> servants, condemning the guilty and
> bringing down on his own head what he
> has done. Declare the innocent not
> guilty, and so establish his innocence.
>
> 33"When your people Israel have
> been defeated by an enemy because
> they have sinned against you, and when
> they turn back to you and confess your
> name, praying and making supplication
> to you in this temple, 34then hear from
> heaven and forgive the sin of your
> people Israel and bring them back to the
> land you gave to their fathers.
>
> 35"When the heavens are shut up and
> there is no rain because your people
> have sinned against you, and when they
> pray toward this place and confess your
> name and turn from their sin because
> you have afflicted them, 36then hear
> from heaven and forgive the sin of your
> servants, your people Israel. Teach
> them the right way to live, and send rain
> on the land you gave your people for an
> inheritance.
>
> 37"When famine or plague comes to
> the land, or blight or mildew, locusts or
> grasshoppers, or when an enemy be-
> sieges them in any of their cities, what-
> ever disaster or disease may come,
> 38and when a prayer or plea is made by
> any of your people Israel—each one
> aware of the afflictions of his own heart,
> and spreading out his hands toward this
> temple— 39then hear from heaven, your
> dwelling place. Forgive and act; deal
> with each man according to all he does,
> since you know his heart (for you alone
> know the hearts of all men), 40so that

they will fear you all the time they live in
the land you gave our fathers.
[41]"As for the foreigner who does not
belong to your people Israel but has
come from a distant land because of
your name— [42]for men will hear of your
great name and your mighty hand and
your outstretched arm—when he
comes and prays toward this temple,
[43]then hear from heaven, your dwelling
place, and do whatever the foreigner
asks of you, so that all the peoples of the
earth may know your name and fear
you, as do your own people Israel, and
may know that this house I have built
bears your Name.
[44]"When your people go to war
against their enemies, wherever you
send them, and when they pray to the
LORD toward the city you have chosen
and the temple I have built for your
Name, [45]then hear from heaven their
prayer and their plea, and uphold their
cause.
[46]"When they sin against you—for
there is no one who does not sin—and
you become angry with them and give
them over to the enemy, who takes
them captive to his own land, far away
or near; [47]and if they have a change of
heart in the land where they are held
captive, and repent and plead with you
in the land of their conquerors and say,
'We have sinned, we have done wrong,
we have acted wickedly'; [48]and if they
turn back to you with all their heart and
soul in the land of their enemies who
took them captive, and pray to you
toward the land you gave their fathers,
toward the city you have chosen and the
temple I have built for your Name; [49]then
from heaven, your dwelling place, hear
their prayer and their plea, and uphold
their cause. [50]And forgive your people,
who have sinned against you; forgive all
the offenses they have committed
against you, and cause their conquerors
to show them mercy; [51]for they are your
people and your inheritance, whom you
brought out of Egypt, out of that iron-
smelting furnace.
[52]"May your eyes be open to your servant's plea and to the plea of your
people Israel, and may you listen to
them whenever they cry out to you.
[53]For you singled them out from all the
nations of the world to be your own inheritance, just as you declared through
your servant Moses when you, O Sovereign LORD, brought our fathers out of
Egypt."

[54]When Solomon had finished all these
prayers and supplications to the LORD, he
rose from before the altar of the LORD, where
he had been kneeling with his hands spread
out toward heaven. [55]He stood and blessed
the whole assembly of Israel in a loud voice,
saying:

[56]"Praise be to the LORD, who has giv-
en rest to his people Israel just as he
promised. Not one word has failed of all
the good promises he gave through his
servant Moses. [57]May the LORD our God
be with us as he was with our fathers;
may he never leave us nor forsake us.
[58]May he turn our hearts to him, to walk
in all his ways and to keep the commands, decrees and regulations he
gave our fathers. [59]And may these
words of mine, which I have prayed before the LORD, be near to the LORD our
God day and night, that he may uphold
the cause of his servant and the cause
of his people Israel according to each
day's need, [60]so that all the peoples of
the earth may know that the LORD is God
and that there is no other. [61]But your
hearts must be fully committed to the
LORD our God, to live by his decrees and
obey his commands, as at this time."

The Dedication of the Temple

[62]Then the king and all Israel with him offered sacrifices before the LORD. [63]Solomon
offered a sacrifice of fellowship offerings[a] to
the LORD: twenty-two thousand cattle and a
hundred and twenty thousand sheep and
goats. So the king and all the Israelites dedicated the temple of the LORD.
[64]On that same day the king consecrated
the middle part of the courtyard in front of the
temple of the LORD, and there he offered
burnt offerings, grain offerings and the fat of
the fellowship offerings, because the bronze
altar before the LORD was too small to hold
the burnt offerings, the grain offerings and
the fat of the fellowship offerings.
[65]So Solomon observed the festival at that
time, and all Israel with him—a vast assem-

[a]63 Traditionally *peace offerings;* also in verse 64

bly, people from Lebo[a] Hamath to the Wadi of Egypt. They celebrated it before the LORD our God for seven days and seven days more, fourteen days in all. 66On the following day he sent the people away. They blessed the king and then went home, joyful and glad in heart for all the good things the LORD had done for his servant David and his people Israel.

The LORD *Appears to Solomon*

9 When Solomon had finished building the temple of the LORD and the royal palace, and had achieved all he had desired to do, 2the LORD appeared to him a second time, as he had appeared to him at Gibeon. 3The LORD said to him:

> "I have heard the prayer and plea you have made before me; I have consecrated this temple, which you have built, by putting my Name there forever. My eyes and my heart will always be there.
>
> 4"As for you, if you walk before me in integrity of heart and uprightness, as David your father did, and do all I command and observe my decrees and laws, 5I will establish your royal throne over Israel forever, as I promised David your father when I said, 'You shall never fail to have a man on the throne of Israel.'
>
> 6"But if you[b] or your sons turn away from me and do not observe the commands and decrees I have given you[b] and go off to serve other gods and worship them, 7then I will cut off Israel from the land I have given them and will reject this temple I have consecrated for my Name. Israel will then become a byword and an object of ridicule among all peoples. 8And though this temple is now imposing, all who pass by will be appalled and will scoff and say, 'Why has the LORD done such a thing to this land and to this temple?' 9People will answer, 'Because they have forsaken the LORD their God, who brought their fathers out of Egypt, and have embraced other gods, worshiping and serving them—that is why the LORD brought all this disaster on them.' "

Solomon's Other Activities

10At the end of twenty years, during which Solomon built these two buildings—the temple of the LORD and the royal palace— 11King Solomon gave twenty towns in Galilee to Hiram king of Tyre, because Hiram had supplied him with all the cedar and pine and gold he wanted. 12But when Hiram went from Tyre to see the towns that Solomon had given him, he was not pleased with them. 13"What kind of towns are these you have given me, my brother?" he asked. And he called them the Land of Cabul,[c] a name they have to this day. 14Now Hiram had sent to the king 120 talents[d] of gold.

15Here is the account of the forced labor King Solomon conscripted to build the LORD's temple, his own palace, the supporting terraces,[e] the wall of Jerusalem, and Hazor, Megiddo and Gezer. 16(Pharaoh king of Egypt had attacked and captured Gezer. He had set it on fire. He killed its Canaanite inhabitants and then gave it as a wedding gift to his daughter, Solomon's wife. 17And Solomon rebuilt Gezer.) He built up Lower Beth Horon, 18Baalath, and Tadmor[f] in the desert, within his land, 19as well as all his store cities and the towns for his chariots and for his horses[g]—whatever he desired to build in Jerusalem, in Lebanon and throughout all the territory he ruled.

20All the people left from the Amorites, Hittites, Perizzites, Hivites and Jebusites (these peoples were not Israelites), 21that is, their descendants remaining in the land, whom the Israelites could not exterminate[h]—these Solomon conscripted for his slave labor force, as it is to this day. 22But Solomon did not make slaves of any of the Israelites; they were his fighting men, his government officials, his officers, his captains, and the commanders of his chariots and charioteers. 23They were also the chief officials in charge of Solomon's projects—550 officials supervising the men who did the work.

24After Pharaoh's daughter had come up from the City of David to the palace Solomon had built for her, he constructed the supporting terraces.

25Three times a year Solomon sacrificed burnt offerings and fellowship offerings[i] on

[a]65 Or *from the entrance to* [b]6 The Hebrew is plural. [c]13 *Cabul* sounds like the Hebrew for *good-for-nothing.* [d]14 That is, about 4 1/2 tons (about 4 metric tons) [e]15 Or *the Millo*; also in verse 24 [f]18 The Hebrew may also be read *Tamar.* [g]19 Or *charioteers* [h]21 The Hebrew term refers to the irrevocable giving over of things or persons to the LORD, often by totally destroying them. [i]25 Traditionally *peace offerings*

the altar he had built for the LORD, burning
incense before the LORD along with them,
and so fulfilled the temple obligations.
26King Solomon also built ships at Ezion
Geber, which is near Elath in Edom, on the
shore of the Red Sea.[a] 27And Hiram sent his
men—sailors who knew the sea—to serve in
the fleet with Solomon's men. 28They sailed
to Ophir and brought back 420 talents[b] of
gold, which they delivered to King Solomon.

The Queen of Sheba Visits Solomon

10 When the queen of Sheba heard
about the fame of Solomon and his
relation to the name of the LORD, she came to
test him with hard questions. 2Arriving at
Jerusalem with a very great caravan—with
camels carrying spices, large quantities of
gold, and precious stones—she came to
Solomon and talked with him about all that
she had on her mind. 3Solomon answered all
her questions; nothing was too hard for the
king to explain to her. 4When the queen of
Sheba saw all the wisdom of Solomon and
the palace he had built, 5the food on his table, the seating of his officials, the attending
servants in their robes, his cupbearers, and
the burnt offerings he made at[c] the temple of
the LORD, she was overwhelmed.
6She said to the king, "The report I heard in
my own country about your achievements
and your wisdom is true. 7But I did not believe these things until I came and saw with
my own eyes. Indeed, not even half was told
me; in wisdom and wealth you have far exceeded the report I heard. 8How happy your
men must be! How happy your officials, who
continually stand before you and hear your
wisdom! 9Praise be to the LORD your God,
who has delighted in you and placed you on
the throne of Israel. Because of the LORD's
eternal love for Israel, he has made you king,
to maintain justice and righteousness."
10And she gave the king 120 talents[d] of
gold, large quantities of spices, and precious
stones. Never again were so many spices
brought in as those the queen of Sheba gave
to King Solomon.
11(Hiram's ships brought gold from Ophir;
and from there they brought great cargoes of
almugwood[e] and precious stones. 12The
king used the almugwood to make supports
for the temple of the LORD and for the royal
palace, and to make harps and lyres for the
musicians. So much almugwood has never
been imported or seen since that day.)
13King Solomon gave the queen of Sheba
all she desired and asked for, besides what
he had given her out of his royal bounty.
Then she left and returned with her retinue to
her own country.

Solomon's Splendor

14The weight of the gold that Solomon received yearly was 666 talents,[f] 15not including the revenues from merchants and traders and from all the Arabian kings and the
governors of the land.
16King Solomon made two hundred large
shields of hammered gold; six hundred
bekas[g] of gold went into each shield. 17He
also made three hundred small shields of
hammered gold, with three minas[h] of gold in
each shield. The king put them in the Palace
of the Forest of Lebanon.
18Then the king made a great throne inlaid
with ivory and overlaid with fine gold. 19The
throne had six steps, and its back had a
rounded top. On both sides of the seat were
armrests, with a lion standing beside each of
them. 20Twelve lions stood on the six steps,
one at either end of each step. Nothing like it
had ever been made for any other kingdom.
21All King Solomon's goblets were gold, and
all the household articles in the Palace of the
Forest of Lebanon were pure gold. Nothing
was made of silver, because silver was considered of little value in Solomon's days.
22The king had a fleet of trading ships[i] at sea
along with the ships of Hiram. Once every
three years it returned, carrying gold, silver
and ivory, and apes and baboons.
23King Solomon was greater in riches and
wisdom than all the other kings of the earth.
24The whole world sought audience with
Solomon to hear the wisdom God had put in
his heart. 25Year after year, everyone who
came brought a gift—articles of silver and
gold, robes, weapons and spices, and
horses and mules.
26Solomon accumulated chariots and
horses; he had fourteen hundred chariots
and twelve thousand horses,[j] which he kept
in the chariot cities and also with him in

[a]26 Hebrew *Yam Suph;* that is, Sea of Reeds [b]28 That is, about 16 tons (about 14.5 metric tons) [c]5 Or *the ascent by which he went up to* [d]10 That is, about 4 1/2 tons (about 4 metric tons) [e]11 Probably a variant of *algumwood*; also in verse 12 [f]14 That is, about 25 tons (about 23 metric tons) [g]16 That is, about 7 1/2 pounds (about 3.5 kilograms) [h]17 That is, about 3 3/4 pounds (about 1.7 kilograms) [i]22 Hebrew *of ships of Tarshish* [j]26 Or *charioteers*

Jerusalem. 27The king made silver as common in Jerusalem as stones, and cedar as plentiful as sycamore-fig trees in the foothills. 28Solomon's horses were imported from Egypt[a] and from Kue[b]—the royal merchants purchased them from Kue. 29They imported a chariot from Egypt for six hundred shekels[c] of silver, and a horse for a hundred and fifty.[d] They also exported them to all the kings of the Hittites and of the Arameans.

Solomon's Wives

11 King Solomon, however, loved many foreign women besides Pharaoh's daughter—Moabites, Ammonites, Edomites, Sidonians and Hittites. 2They were from nations about which the LORD had told the Israelites, "You must not intermarry with them, because they will surely turn your hearts after their gods." Nevertheless, Solomon held fast to them in love. 3He had seven hundred wives of royal birth and three hundred concubines, and his wives led him astray. 4As Solomon grew old, his wives turned his heart after other gods, and his heart was not fully devoted to the LORD his God, as the heart of David his father had been. 5He followed Ashtoreth the goddess of the Sidonians, and Molech[e] the detestable god of the Ammonites. 6So Solomon did evil in the eyes of the LORD; he did not follow the LORD completely, as David his father had done.

7On a hill east of Jerusalem, Solomon built a high place for Chemosh the detestable god of Moab, and for Molech the detestable god of the Ammonites. 8He did the same for all his foreign wives, who burned incense and offered sacrifices to their gods.

9The LORD became angry with Solomon because his heart had turned away from the LORD, the God of Israel, who had appeared to him twice. 10Although he had forbidden Solomon to follow other gods, Solomon did not keep the LORD's command. 11So the LORD said to Solomon, "Since this is your attitude and you have not kept my covenant and my decrees, which I commanded you, I will most certainly tear the kingdom away from you and give it to one of your subordinates. 12Nevertheless, for the sake of David your father, I will not do it during your lifetime. I will tear it out of the hand of your son. 13Yet I will not tear the whole kingdom from him, but will give him one tribe for the sake of David my servant and for the sake of Jerusalem, which I have chosen."

Solomon's Adversaries

14Then the LORD raised up against Solomon an adversary, Hadad the Edomite, from the royal line of Edom. 15Earlier when David was fighting with Edom, Joab the commander of the army, who had gone up to bury the dead, had struck down all the men in Edom. 16Joab and all the Israelites stayed there for six months, until they had destroyed all the men in Edom. 17But Hadad, still only a boy, fled to Egypt with some Edomite officials who had served his father. 18They set out from Midian and went to Paran. Then taking men from Paran with them, they went to Egypt, to Pharaoh king of Egypt, who gave Hadad a house and land and provided him with food.

19Pharaoh was so pleased with Hadad that he gave him a sister of his own wife, Queen Tahpenes, in marriage. 20The sister of Tahpenes bore him a son named Genubath, whom Tahpenes brought up in the royal palace. There Genubath lived with Pharaoh's own children.

21While he was in Egypt, Hadad heard that David rested with his fathers and that Joab the commander of the army was also dead. Then Hadad said to Pharaoh, "Let me go, that I may return to my own country."

22"What have you lacked here that you want to go back to your own country?" Pharaoh asked.

"Nothing," Hadad replied, "but do let me go!"

23And God raised up against Solomon another adversary, Rezon son of Eliada, who had fled from his master, Hadadezer king of Zobah. 24He gathered men around him and became the leader of a band of rebels when David destroyed the forces[f] ⌊of Zobah⌋; the rebels went to Damascus, where they settled and took control. 25Rezon was Israel's adversary as long as Solomon lived, adding to the trouble caused by Hadad. So Rezon ruled in Aram and was hostile toward Israel.

Jeroboam Rebels Against Solomon

26Also, Jeroboam son of Nebat rebelled against the king. He was one of Solomon's

[a]28 Or possibly *Muzur,* a region in Cilicia; also in verse 29 [b]28 Probably *Cilicia* [c]29 That is, about 15 pounds (about 7 kilograms) [d]29 That is, about 3 3/4 pounds (about 1.7 kilograms) [e]5 Hebrew *Milcom;* also in verse 33 [f]24 Hebrew *destroyed them*

officials, an Ephraimite from Zeredah, and
his mother was a widow named Zeruah.
27Here is the account of how he rebelled
against the king: Solomon had built the supporting terraces[a] and had filled in the gap in
the wall of the city of David his father. 28Now
Jeroboam was a man of standing, and when
Solomon saw how well the young man did
his work, he put him in charge of the whole
labor force of the house of Joseph.
29About that time Jeroboam was going out
of Jerusalem, and Ahijah the prophet of Shiloh met him on the way, wearing a new cloak.
The two of them were alone out in the country, 30and Ahijah took hold of the new cloak
he was wearing and tore it into twelve
pieces. 31Then he said to Jeroboam, "Take
ten pieces for yourself, for this is what the
LORD, the God of Israel, says: 'See, I am
going to tear the kingdom out of Solomon's
hand and give you ten tribes. 32But for the
sake of my servant David and the city of
Jerusalem, which I have chosen out of all the
tribes of Israel, he will have one tribe. 33I will
do this because they have[b] forsaken me and
worshiped Ashtoreth the goddess of the
Sidonians, Chemosh the god of the Moabites, and Molech the god of the Ammonites,
and have not walked in my ways, nor done
what is right in my eyes, nor kept my statutes
and laws as David, Solomon's father, did.
34" 'But I will not take the whole kingdom
out of Solomon's hand; I have made him
ruler all the days of his life for the sake of
David my servant, whom I chose and who
observed my commands and statutes. 35I will
take the kingdom from his son's hands and
give you ten tribes. 36I will give one tribe to
his son so that David my servant may always
have a lamp before me in Jerusalem, the city
where I chose to put my Name. 37However,
as for you, I will take you, and you will rule
over all that your heart desires; you will be
king over Israel. 38If you do whatever I command you and walk in my ways and do what
is right in my eyes by keeping my statutes
and commands, as David my servant did, I
will be with you. I will build you a dynasty as
enduring as the one I built for David and will
give Israel to you. 39I will humble David's
descendants because of this, but not forever.' "
40Solomon tried to kill Jeroboam, but Jeroboam fled to Egypt, to Shishak the king, and
stayed there until Solomon's death.

Solomon's Death

41As for the other events of Solomon's
reign—all he did and the wisdom he displayed—are they not written in the book of
the annals of Solomon? 42Solomon reigned
in Jerusalem over all Israel forty years.
43Then he rested with his fathers and was
buried in the city of David his father. And
Rehoboam his son succeeded him as king.

Israel Rebels Against Rehoboam

12 Rehoboam went to Shechem, for all
the Israelites had gone there to make
him king. 2When Jeroboam son of Nebat
heard this (he was still in Egypt, where he
had fled from King Solomon), he returned
from[c] Egypt. 3So they sent for Jeroboam,
and he and the whole assembly of Israel
went to Rehoboam and said to him: 4"Your
father put a heavy yoke on us, but now light-
en the harsh labor and the heavy yoke he put
on us, and we will serve you."
5Rehoboam answered, "Go away for three
days and then come back to me." So the
people went away.
6Then King Rehoboam consulted the elders who had served his father Solomon during his lifetime. "How would you advise me to
answer these people?" he asked.
7They replied, "If today you will be a servant to these people and serve them and
give them a favorable answer, they will always be your servants."
8But Rehoboam rejected the advice the
elders gave him and consulted the young
men who had grown up with him and were
serving him. 9He asked them, "What is your
advice? How should we answer these
people who say to me, 'Lighten the yoke your
father put on us'?"
10The young men who had grown up with
him replied, "Tell these people who have
said to you, 'Your father put a heavy yoke on
us, but make our yoke lighter'—tell them, 'My
little finger is thicker than my father's waist.
11My father laid on you a heavy yoke; I will
make it even heavier. My father scourged
you with whips; I will scourge you with scorpions.' "
12Three days later Jeroboam and all the
people returned to Rehoboam, as the king
had said, "Come back to me in three days."
13The king answered the people harshly. Rejecting the advice given him by the elders,

[a]27 Or *the Millo* [b]33 Hebrew; Septuagint, Vulgate and Syriac *because he has* [c]2 Or *he remained in*

14he followed the advice of the young men and said, "My father made your yoke heavy; I will make it even heavier. My father scourged you with whips; I will scourge you with scorpions." 15So the king did not listen to the people, for this turn of events was from the LORD, to fulfill the word the LORD had spoken to Jeroboam son of Nebat through Ahijah the Shilonite.

16When all Israel saw that the king refused to listen to them, they answered the king:

"What share do we have in David,
what part in Jesse's son?
To your tents, O Israel!
Look after your own house, O David!"

So the Israelites went home. 17But as for the Israelites who were living in the towns of Judah, Rehoboam still ruled over them.

18King Rehoboam sent out Adoniram,[a] who was in charge of forced labor, but all Israel stoned him to death. King Rehoboam, however, managed to get into his chariot and escape to Jerusalem. 19So Israel has been in rebellion against the house of David to this day.

20When all the Israelites heard that Jeroboam had returned, they sent and called him to the assembly and made him king over all Israel. Only the tribe of Judah remained loyal to the house of David.

21When Rehoboam arrived in Jerusalem, he mustered the whole house of Judah and the tribe of Benjamin—a hundred and eighty thousand fighting men—to make war against the house of Israel and to regain the kingdom for Rehoboam son of Solomon.

22But this word of God came to Shemaiah the man of God: 23"Say to Rehoboam son of Solomon king of Judah, to the whole house of Judah and Benjamin, and to the rest of the people, 24'This is what the LORD says: Do not go up to fight against your brothers, the Israelites. Go home, every one of you, for this is my doing.' " So they obeyed the word of the LORD and went home again, as the LORD had ordered.

Golden Calves at Bethel and Dan

25Then Jeroboam fortified Shechem in the hill country of Ephraim and lived there. From there he went out and built up Peniel.[b]

26Jeroboam thought to himself, "The kingdom will now likely revert to the house of David. 27If these people go up to offer sacrifices at the temple of the LORD in Jerusalem, they will again give their allegiance to their lord, Rehoboam king of Judah. They will kill me and return to King Rehoboam."

28After seeking advice, the king made two golden calves. He said to the people, "It is too much for you to go up to Jerusalem. Here are your gods, O Israel, who brought you up out of Egypt." 29One he set up in Bethel, and the other in Dan. 30And this thing became a sin; the people went even as far as Dan to worship the one there.

31Jeroboam built shrines on high places and appointed priests from all sorts of people, even though they were not Levites. 32He instituted a festival on the fifteenth day of the eighth month, like the festival held in Judah, and offered sacrifices on the altar. This he did in Bethel, sacrificing to the calves he had made. And at Bethel he also installed priests at the high places he had made. 33On the fifteenth day of the eighth month, a month of his own choosing, he offered sacrifices on the altar he had built at Bethel. So he instituted the festival for the Israelites and went up to the altar to make offerings.

The Man of God From Judah

13 By the word of the LORD a man of God came from Judah to Bethel, as Jeroboam was standing by the altar to make an offering. 2He cried out against the altar by the word of the LORD: "O altar, altar! This is what the LORD says: 'A son named Josiah will be born to the house of David. On you he will sacrifice the priests of the high places who now make offerings here, and human bones will be burned on you.' " 3That same day the man of God gave a sign: "This is the sign the LORD has declared: The altar will be split apart and the ashes on it will be poured out."

4When King Jeroboam heard what the man of God cried out against the altar at Bethel, he stretched out his hand from the altar and said, "Seize him!" But the hand he stretched out toward the man shriveled up, so that he could not pull it back. 5Also, the altar was split apart and its ashes poured out according to the sign given by the man of God by the word of the LORD.

6Then the king said to the man of God, "Intercede with the LORD your God and pray for me that my hand may be restored." So

[a] *18* Some Septuagint manuscripts and Syriac (see also 1 Kings 4:6 and 5:14); Hebrew *Adoram* [b] *25* Hebrew *Penuel,* a variant of *Peniel*

the man of God interceded with the LORD,
and the king's hand was restored and
became as it was before.
7The king said to the man of God, "Come
home with me and have something to eat,
and I will give you a gift."
8But the man of God answered the king,
"Even if you were to give me half your
possessions, I would not go with you, nor
would I eat bread or drink water here. 9For I
was commanded by the word of the LORD:
'You must not eat bread or drink water or
return by the way you came.' " 10So he took
another road and did not return by the way
he had come to Bethel.
11Now there was a certain old prophet living in Bethel, whose sons came and told him
all that the man of God had done there that
day. They also told their father what he had
said to the king. 12Their father asked them,
"Which way did he go?" And his sons
showed him which road the man of God from
Judah had taken. 13So he said to his sons,
"Saddle the donkey for me." And when they
had saddled the donkey for him, he mounted
it 14and rode after the man of God. He found
him sitting under an oak tree and asked, "Are
you the man of God who came from Judah?"
"I am," he replied.
15So the prophet said to him, "Come home
with me and eat."
16The man of God said, "I cannot turn back
and go with you, nor can I eat bread or drink
water with you in this place. 17I have been
told by the word of the LORD: 'You must not
eat bread or drink water there or return by the
way you came.' "
18The old prophet answered, "I too am a
prophet, as you are. And an angel said to me
by the word of the LORD: 'Bring him back with
you to your house so that he may eat bread
and drink water.' " (But he was lying to him.)
19So the man of God returned with him and
ate and drank in his house.
20While they were sitting at the table, the
word of the LORD came to the old prophet who
had brought him back. 21He cried out to the
man of God who had come from Judah,
"This is what the LORD says: 'You have defied
the word of the LORD and have not kept the
command the LORD your God gave you.
22You came back and ate bread and drank
water in the place where he told you not to
eat or drink. Therefore your body will not be
buried in the tomb of your fathers.' "
23When the man of God had finished eating and drinking, the prophet who had
brought him back saddled his donkey for
him. 24As he went on his way, a lion met him
on the road and killed him, and his body was
thrown down on the road, with both the donkey and the lion standing beside it. 25Some
people who passed by saw the body thrown
down there, with the lion standing beside the
body, and they went and reported it in the city
where the old prophet lived.
26When the prophet who had brought him
back from his journey heard of it, he said, "It
is the man of God who defied the word of the
LORD. The LORD has given him over to the
lion, which has mauled him and killed him, as
the word of the LORD had warned him."
27The prophet said to his sons, "Saddle
the donkey for me," and they did so. 28Then
he went out and found the body thrown down
on the road, with the donkey and the lion
standing beside it. The lion had neither eaten
the body nor mauled the donkey. 29So the
prophet picked up the body of the man of
God, laid it on the donkey, and brought it
back to his own city to mourn for him and
bury him. 30Then he laid the body in his own
tomb, and they mourned over him and said,
"Oh, my brother!"
31After burying him, he said to his sons,
"When I die, bury me in the grave where the
man of God is buried; lay my bones beside
his bones. 32For the message he declared by
the word of the LORD against the altar in Bethel and against all the shrines on the high
places in the towns of Samaria will certainly
come true."
33Even after this, Jeroboam did not
change his evil ways, but once more appointed priests for the high places from all
sorts of people. Anyone who wanted to
become a priest he consecrated for the high
places. 34This was the sin of the house of
Jeroboam that led to its downfall and to its
destruction from the face of the earth.

Ahijah's Prophecy Against Jeroboam

14 At that time Abijah son of Jeroboam
became ill, 2and Jeroboam said to his
wife, "Go, disguise yourself, so you won't be
recognized as the wife of Jeroboam. Then
go to Shiloh. Ahijah the prophet is there—the
one who told me I would be king over this
people. 3Take ten loaves of bread with you,
some cakes and a jar of honey, and go to
him. He will tell you what will happen to the
boy." 4So Jeroboam's wife did what he said
and went to Ahijah's house in Shiloh.
Now Ahijah could not see; his sight was

gone because of his age. 5But the LORD had
told Ahijah, "Jeroboam's wife is coming to
ask you about her son, for he is ill, and you
are to give her such and such an answer.
When she arrives, she will pretend to be
someone else."
6So when Ahijah heard the sound of her
footsteps at the door, he said, "Come in, wife
of Jeroboam. Why this pretense? I have
been sent to you with bad news. 7Go, tell
Jeroboam that this is what the LORD, the God
of Israel, says: 'I raised you up from among
the people and made you a leader over my
people Israel. 8I tore the kingdom away from
the house of David and gave it to you, but
you have not been like my servant David,
who kept my commands and followed me
with all his heart, doing only what was right in
my eyes. 9You have done more evil than all
who lived before you. You have made for
yourself other gods, idols made of metal; you
have provoked me to anger and thrust me
behind your back.
10" 'Because of this, I am going to bring
disaster on the house of Jeroboam. I will cut
off from Jeroboam every last male in Israel—
slave or free. I will burn up the house of
Jeroboam as one burns dung, until it is all
gone. 11Dogs will eat those belonging to
Jeroboam who die in the city, and the birds of
the air will feed on those who die in the country. The LORD has spoken!'
12"As for you, go back home. When you
set foot in your city, the boy will die. 13All
Israel will mourn for him and bury him. He is
the only one belonging to Jeroboam who will
be buried, because he is the only one in the
house of Jeroboam in whom the LORD, the
God of Israel, has found anything good.
14"The LORD will raise up for himself a king
over Israel who will cut off the family of Jeroboam. This is the day! What? Yes, even
now.[a] 15And the LORD will strike Israel, so that
it will be like a reed swaying in the water. He
will uproot Israel from this good land that he
gave to their forefathers and scatter them
beyond the River,[b] because they provoked
the LORD to anger by making Asherah poles.[c]
16And he will give Israel up because of the
sins Jeroboam has committed and has
caused Israel to commit."
17Then Jeroboam's wife got up and left
and went to Tirzah. As soon as she stepped
over the threshold of the house, the boy died.
18They buried him, and all Israel mourned for
him, as the LORD had said through his servant
the prophet Ahijah.
19The other events of Jeroboam's reign,
his wars and how he ruled, are written in the
book of the annals of the kings of Israel. 20He
reigned for twenty-two years and then rested
with his fathers. And Nadab his son succeeded him as king.

Rehoboam King of Judah

21Rehoboam son of Solomon was king in
Judah. He was forty-one years old when he
became king, and he reigned seventeen
years in Jerusalem, the city the LORD had
chosen out of all the tribes of Israel in which
to put his Name. His mother's name was
Naamah; she was an Ammonite.
22Judah did evil in the eyes of the LORD. By
the sins they committed they stirred up his
jealous anger more than their fathers had
done. 23They also set up for themselves high
places, sacred stones and Asherah poles on
every high hill and under every spreading
tree. 24There were even male shrine prostitutes in the land; the people engaged in all
the detestable practices of the nations the
LORD had driven out before the Israelites.
25In the fifth year of King Rehoboam, Shishak king of Egypt attacked Jerusalem. 26He
carried off the treasures of the temple of the
LORD and the treasures of the royal palace.
He took everything, including all the gold
shields Solomon had made. 27So King Rehoboam made bronze shields to replace them
and assigned these to the commanders of
the guard on duty at the entrance to the royal
palace. 28Whenever the king went to the
LORD's temple, the guards bore the shields,
and afterward they returned them to the
guardroom.
29As for the other events of Rehoboam's
reign, and all he did, are they not written in
the book of the annals of the kings of Judah?
30There was continual warfare between
Rehoboam and Jeroboam. 31And Rehoboam rested with his fathers and was buried
with them in the City of David. His mother's
name was Naamah; she was an Ammonite. And Abijah[d] his son succeeded him as
king.

[a] *14* The meaning of the Hebrew for this sentence is uncertain. [b] *15* That is, the Euphrates [c] *15* That is, symbols of the goddess Asherah; here and elsewhere in 1 Kings [d] *31* Some Hebrew manuscripts and Septuagint (see also 2 Chron. 12:16); most Hebrew manuscripts *Abijam*

Abijah King of Judah

15 In the eighteenth year of the reign of
Jeroboam son of Nebat, Abijah[a]
became king of Judah, 2and he reigned in
Jerusalem three years. His mother's name
was Maacah daughter of Abishalom.[b]
3He committed all the sins his father had
done before him; his heart was not fully devoted to the LORD his God, as the heart of
David his forefather had been. 4Neverthe-
less, for David's sake the LORD his God gave
him a lamp in Jerusalem by raising up a son
to succeed him and by making Jerusalem
strong. 5For David had done what was right
in the eyes of the LORD and had not failed to
keep any of the LORD's commands all the
days of his life—except in the case of Uriah
the Hittite.
6There was war between Rehoboam[c] and
Jeroboam throughout ⌊Abijah's⌋ lifetime. 7As
for the other events of Abijah's reign, and all
he did, are they not written in the book of the
annals of the kings of Judah? There was war
between Abijah and Jeroboam. 8And Abijah
rested with his fathers and was buried in the
City of David. And Asa his son succeeded
him as king.

Asa King of Judah

9In the twentieth year of Jeroboam king of
Israel, Asa became king of Judah, 10and he
reigned in Jerusalem forty-one years. His
grandmother's name was Maacah daughter
of Abishalom.
11Asa did what was right in the eyes of the
LORD, as his father David had done. 12He
expelled the male shrine prostitutes from the
land and got rid of all the idols his fathers had
made. 13He even deposed his grandmother
Maacah from her position as queen mother,
because she had made a repulsive Asherah
pole. Asa cut the pole down and burned it in
the Kidron Valley. 14Although he did not remove the high places, Asa's heart was fully
committed to the LORD all his life. 15He
brought into the temple of the LORD the silver
and gold and the articles that he and his
father had dedicated.
16There was war between Asa and Baasha king of Israel throughout their reigns.
17Baasha king of Israel went up against
Judah and fortified Ramah to prevent anyone from leaving or entering the territory of
Asa king of Judah.
18Asa then took all the silver and gold that
was left in the treasuries of the LORD's temple
and of his own palace. He entrusted it to his
officials and sent them to Ben-Hadad son of
Tabrimmon, the son of Hezion, the king of
Aram, who was ruling in Damascus. 19"Let
there be a treaty between me and you," he
said, "as there was between my father and
your father. See, I am sending you a gift of
silver and gold. Now break your treaty with
Baasha king of Israel so he will withdraw
from me."
20Ben-Hadad agreed with King Asa and
sent the commanders of his forces against
the towns of Israel. He conquered Ijon, Dan,
Abel Beth Maacah and all Kinnereth in addition to Naphtali. 21When Baasha heard this,
he stopped building Ramah and withdrew to
Tirzah. 22Then King Asa issued an order to
all Judah—no one was exempt—and they
carried away from Ramah the stones and
timber Baasha had been using there. With
them King Asa built up Geba in Benjamin,
and also Mizpah.
23As for all the other events of Asa's reign,
all his achievements, all he did and the cities
he built, are they not written in the book of the
annals of the kings of Judah? In his old age,
however, his feet became diseased. 24Then
Asa rested with his fathers and was buried
with them in the city of his father David. And
Jehoshaphat his son succeeded him as king.

Nadab King of Israel

25Nadab son of Jeroboam became king of
Israel in the second year of Asa king of
Judah, and he reigned over Israel two years.
26He did evil in the eyes of the LORD, walking
in the ways of his father and in his sin, which
he had caused Israel to commit.
27Baasha son of Ahijah of the house of
Issachar plotted against him, and he struck
him down at Gibbethon, a Philistine town,
while Nadab and all Israel were besieging it.
28Baasha killed Nadab in the third year of
Asa king of Judah and succeeded him as
king.
29As soon as he began to reign, he killed
Jeroboam's whole family. He did not leave
Jeroboam anyone that breathed, but de-

[a] 1 Some Hebrew manuscripts and Septuagint (see also 2 Chron. 12:16); most Hebrew manuscripts *Abijam*; also in verses 7 and 8 [b] 2 A variant of *Absalom*; also in verse 10 [c] 6 Most Hebrew manuscripts; some Hebrew manuscripts and Syriac *Abijam* (that is, Abijah)

stroyed them all, according to the word of the
LORD given through his servant Ahijah the
Shilonite— 30because of the sins Jeroboam
had committed and had caused Israel to
commit, and because he provoked the LORD,
the God of Israel, to anger.
31As for the other events of Nadab's reign,
and all he did, are they not written in the book
of the annals of the kings of Israel? 32There
was war between Asa and Baasha king of
Israel throughout their reigns.

Baasha King of Israel

33In the third year of Asa king of Judah,
Baasha son of Ahijah became king of all
Israel in Tirzah, and he reigned twenty-four
years. 34He did evil in the eyes of the LORD,
walking in the ways of Jeroboam and in his
sin, which he had caused Israel to commit.
16 Then the word of the LORD came to
Jehu son of Hanani against Baasha:
2"I lifted you up from the dust and made you
leader of my people Israel, but you walked in
the ways of Jeroboam and caused my
people Israel to sin and to provoke me to
anger by their sins. 3So I am about to consume Baasha and his house, and I will make
your house like that of Jeroboam son of
Nebat. 4Dogs will eat those belonging to Baasha who die in the city, and the birds of the
air will feed on those who die in the country."
5As for the other events of Baasha's reign,
what he did and his achievements, are they
not written in the book of the annals of the
kings of Israel? 6Baasha rested with his fathers and was buried in Tirzah. And Elah his
son succeeded him as king.
7Moreover, the word of the LORD came
through the prophet Jehu son of Hanani to
Baasha and his house, because of all the evil
he had done in the eyes of the LORD, provoking him to anger by the things he did, and
becoming like the house of Jeroboam—and
also because he destroyed it.

Elah King of Israel

8In the twenty-sixth year of Asa king of
Judah, Elah son of Baasha became king of
Israel, and he reigned in Tirzah two years.
9Zimri, one of his officials, who had command of half his chariots, plotted against
him. Elah was in Tirzah at the time, getting
drunk in the home of Arza, the man in charge
of the palace at Tirzah. 10Zimri came in,
struck him down and killed him in the twenty-
seventh year of Asa king of Judah. Then he
succeeded him as king.
11As soon as he began to reign and was
seated on the throne, he killed off Baasha's
whole family. He did not spare a single male,
whether relative or friend. 12So Zimri destroyed the whole family of Baasha, in accordance with the word of the LORD spoken
against Baasha through the prophet Jehu—
13because of all the sins Baasha and his son
Elah had committed and had caused Israel
to commit, so that they provoked the LORD,
the God of Israel, to anger by their worthless
idols.
14As for the other events of Elah's reign,
and all he did, are they not written in the book
of the annals of the kings of Israel?

Zimri King of Israel

15In the twenty-seventh year of Asa king of
Judah, Zimri reigned in Tirzah seven days.
The army was encamped near Gibbethon, a
Philistine town. 16When the Israelites in the
camp heard that Zimri had plotted against
the king and murdered him, they proclaimed
Omri, the commander of the army, king over
Israel that very day there in the camp. 17Then
Omri and all the Israelites with him withdrew
from Gibbethon and laid siege to Tirzah.
18When Zimri saw that the city was taken, he
went into the citadel of the royal palace and
set the palace on fire around him. So he died,
19because of the sins he had committed, doing evil in the eyes of the LORD and walking in
the ways of Jeroboam and in the sin he had
committed and had caused Israel to commit.
20As for the other events of Zimri's reign,
and the rebellion he carried out, are they not
written in the book of the annals of the kings
of Israel?

Omri King of Israel

21Then the people of Israel were split into
two factions; half supported Tibni son of
Ginath for king, and the other half supported
Omri. 22But Omri's followers proved stronger
than those of Tibni son of Ginath. So Tibni
died and Omri became king.
23In the thirty-first year of Asa king of
Judah, Omri became king of Israel, and he
reigned twelve years, six of them in Tirzah.
24He bought the hill of Samaria from Shemer
for two talents[a] of silver and built a city on the
hill, calling it Samaria, after Shemer, the
name of the former owner of the hill.

[a]24 That is, about 150 pounds (about 70 kilograms)

25But Omri did evil in the eyes of the LORD and sinned more than all those before him. 26He walked in all the ways of Jeroboam son of Nebat and in his sin, which he had caused Israel to commit, so that they provoked the LORD, the God of Israel, to anger by their worthless idols.

27As for the other events of Omri's reign, what he did and the things he achieved, are they not written in the book of the annals of the kings of Israel? 28Omri rested with his fathers and was buried in Samaria. And Ahab his son succeeded him as king.

Ahab Becomes King of Israel

29In the thirty-eighth year of Asa king of Judah, Ahab son of Omri became king of Israel, and he reigned in Samaria over Israel twenty-two years. 30Ahab son of Omri did more evil in the eyes of the LORD than any of those before him. 31He not only considered it trivial to commit the sins of Jeroboam son of Nebat, but he also married Jezebel daughter of Ethbaal king of the Sidonians, and began to serve Baal and worship him. 32He set up an altar for Baal in the temple of Baal that he built in Samaria. 33Ahab also made an Asherah pole and did more to provoke the LORD, the God of Israel, to anger than did all the kings of Israel before him.

34In Ahab's time, Hiel of Bethel rebuilt Jericho. He laid its foundations at the cost of his firstborn son Abiram, and he set up its gates at the cost of his youngest son Segub, in accordance with the word of the LORD spoken by Joshua son of Nun.

Elijah Fed by Ravens

17 Now Elijah the Tishbite, from Tishbe[a] in Gilead, said to Ahab, "As the LORD, the God of Israel, lives, whom I serve, there will be neither dew nor rain in the next few years except at my word."

2Then the word of the LORD came to Elijah: 3"Leave here, turn eastward and hide in the Kerith Ravine, east of the Jordan. 4You will drink from the brook, and I have ordered the ravens to feed you there."

5So he did what the LORD had told him. He went to the Kerith Ravine, east of the Jordan, and stayed there. 6The ravens brought him bread and meat in the morning and bread and meat in the evening, and he drank from the brook.

The Widow at Zarephath

7Some time later the brook dried up because there had been no rain in the land. 8Then the word of the LORD came to him: 9"Go at once to Zarephath of Sidon and stay there. I have commanded a widow in that place to supply you with food." 10So he went to Zarephath. When he came to the town gate, a widow was there gathering sticks. He called to her and asked, "Would you bring me a little water in a jar so I may have a drink?" 11As she was going to get it, he called, "And bring me, please, a piece of bread."

12"As surely as the LORD your God lives," she replied, "I don't have any bread—only a handful of flour in a jar and a little oil in a jug. I am gathering a few sticks to take home and make a meal for myself and my son, that we may eat it—and die."

13Elijah said to her, "Don't be afraid. Go home and do as you have said. But first make a small cake of bread for me from what you have and bring it to me, and then make something for yourself and your son. 14For this is what the LORD, the God of Israel, says: 'The jar of flour will not be used up and the jug of oil will not run dry until the day the LORD gives rain on the land.' "

15She went away and did as Elijah had told her. So there was food every day for Elijah and for the woman and her family. 16For the jar of flour was not used up and the jug of oil did not run dry, in keeping with the word of the LORD spoken by Elijah.

17Some time later the son of the woman who owned the house became ill. He grew worse and worse, and finally stopped breathing. 18She said to Elijah, "What do you have against me, man of God? Did you come to remind me of my sin and kill my son?"

19"Give me your son," Elijah replied. He took him from her arms, carried him to the upper room where he was staying, and laid him on his bed. 20Then he cried out to the LORD, "O LORD my God, have you brought tragedy also upon this widow I am staying with, by causing her son to die?" 21Then he stretched himself out on the boy three times and cried to the LORD, "O LORD my God, let this boy's life return to him!"

22The LORD heard Elijah's cry, and the boy's life returned to him, and he lived. 23Eli-

[a] 1 Or *Tishbite, of the settlers*

jah picked up the child and carried him down
from the room into the house. He gave him to
his mother and said, "Look, your son is
alive!"
24Then the woman said to Elijah, "Now I
know that you are a man of God and that the
word of the LORD from your mouth is the
truth."

Elijah and Obadiah

18 After a long time, in the third year, the
word of the LORD came to Elijah: "Go
and present yourself to Ahab, and I will send
rain on the land." 2So Elijah went to present
himself to Ahab.
Now the famine was severe in Samaria,
3and Ahab had summoned Obadiah, who
was in charge of his palace. (Obadiah was a
devout believer in the LORD. 4While Jezebel
was killing off the LORD's prophets, Obadiah
had taken a hundred prophets and hidden
them in two caves, fifty in each, and had
supplied them with food and water.) 5Ahab
had said to Obadiah, "Go through the land to
all the springs and valleys. Maybe we can
find some grass to keep the horses and
mules alive so we will not have to kill any of
our animals." 6So they divided the land they
were to cover, Ahab going in one direction
and Obadiah in another.
7As Obadiah was walking along, Elijah met
him. Obadiah recognized him, bowed down
to the ground, and said, "Is it really you, my
lord Elijah?"
8"Yes," he replied. "Go tell your master,
'Elijah is here.' "
9"What have I done wrong," asked Obadiah, "that you are handing your servant
over to Ahab to be put to death? 10As surely
as the LORD your God lives, there is not a
nation or kingdom where my master has not
sent someone to look for you. And whenever
a nation or kingdom claimed you were not
there, he made them swear they could not
find you. 11But now you tell me to go to my
master and say, 'Elijah is here.' 12I don't
know where the Spirit of the LORD may carry
you when I leave you. If I go and tell Ahab
and he doesn't find you, he will kill me. Yet I
your servant have worshiped the LORD since
my youth. 13Haven't you heard, my lord, what
I did while Jezebel was killing the prophets of
the LORD? I hid a hundred of the LORD's
prophets in two caves, fifty in each, and supplied them with food and water. 14And now
you tell me to go to my master and say,
'Elijah is here.' He will kill me!"
15Elijah said, "As the LORD Almighty lives,
whom I serve, I will surely present myself to
Ahab today."

Elijah on Mount Carmel

16So Obadiah went to meet Ahab and told
him, and Ahab went to meet Elijah. 17When
he saw Elijah, he said to him, "Is that you,
you troubler of Israel?"
18"I have not made trouble for Israel," Elijah replied. "But you and your father's family
have. You have abandoned the LORD's commands and have followed the Baals. 19Now
summon the people from all over Israel to
meet me on Mount Carmel. And bring the
four hundred and fifty prophets of Baal and
the four hundred prophets of Asherah, who
eat at Jezebel's table."
20So Ahab sent word throughout all Israel
and assembled the prophets on Mount Carmel. 21Elijah went before the people and
said, "How long will you waver between two
opinions? If the LORD is God, follow him; but if
Baal is God, follow him."
But the people said nothing.
22Then Elijah said to them, "I am the only
one of the LORD's prophets left, but Baal has
four hundred and fifty prophets. 23Get two
bulls for us. Let them choose one for themselves, and let them cut it into pieces and put
it on the wood but not set fire to it. I will
prepare the other bull and put it on the wood
but not set fire to it. 24Then you call on the
name of your god, and I will call on the name
of the LORD. The god who answers by fire—
he is God."
Then all the people said, "What you say is
good."
25Elijah said to the prophets of Baal,
"Choose one of the bulls and prepare it first,
since there are so many of you. Call on the
name of your god, but do not light the fire."
26So they took the bull given them and prepared it.
Then they called on the name of Baal from
morning till noon. "O Baal, answer us!" they
shouted. But there was no response; no one
answered. And they danced around the altar
they had made.
27At noon Elijah began to taunt them.
"Shout louder!" he said. "Surely he is a god!
Perhaps he is deep in thought, or busy, or
traveling. Maybe he is sleeping and must be
awakened." 28So they shouted louder and
slashed themselves with swords and spears,
as was their custom, until their blood flowed.
29Midday passed, and they continued their

frantic prophesying until the time for the evening sacrifice. But there was no response, no
one answered, no one paid attention.
30Then Elijah said to all the people, "Come
here to me." They came to him, and he repaired the altar of the LORD, which was in
ruins. 31Elijah took twelve stones, one for
each of the tribes descended from Jacob, to
whom the word of the LORD had come, saying, "Your name shall be Israel." 32With the
stones he built an altar in the name of the
LORD, and he dug a trench around it large
enough to hold two seahs[a] of seed. 33He
arranged the wood, cut the bull into pieces
and laid it on the wood. Then he said to them,
"Fill four large jars with water and pour it on
the offering and on the wood."
34"Do it again," he said, and they did it
again.
"Do it a third time," he ordered, and they
did it the third time. 35The water ran down
around the altar and even filled the trench.
36At the time of sacrifice, the prophet Elijah
stepped forward and prayed: "O LORD, God
of Abraham, Isaac and Israel, let it be known
today that you are God in Israel and that I am
your servant and have done all these things
at your command. 37Answer me, O LORD, answer me, so these people will know that you,
O LORD, are God, and that you are turning
their hearts back again."
38Then the fire of the LORD fell and burned
up the sacrifice, the wood, the stones and
the soil, and also licked up the water in the
trench.
39When all the people saw this, they fell
prostrate and cried, "The LORD—he is God!
The LORD—he is God!"
40Then Elijah commanded them, "Seize
the prophets of Baal. Don't let anyone get
away!" They seized them, and Elijah had
them brought down to the Kishon Valley and
slaughtered there.
41And Elijah said to Ahab, "Go, eat and
drink, for there is the sound of a heavy rain."
42So Ahab went off to eat and drink, but Elijah climbed to the top of Carmel, bent down
to the ground and put his face between his
knees.
43"Go and look toward the sea," he told his
servant. And he went up and looked.
"There is nothing there," he said.
Seven times Elijah said, "Go back."
44The seventh time the servant reported,
"A cloud as small as a man's hand is rising
from the sea."
So Elijah said, "Go and tell Ahab, 'Hitch up
your chariot and go down before the rain
stops you.' "
45Meanwhile, the sky grew black with
clouds, the wind rose, a heavy rain came on
and Ahab rode off to Jezreel. 46The power of
the LORD came upon Elijah and, tucking his
cloak into his belt, he ran ahead of Ahab all
the way to Jezreel.

Elijah Flees to Horeb

19 Now Ahab told Jezebel everything
Elijah had done and how he had
killed all the prophets with the sword. 2So
Jezebel sent a messenger to Elijah to say,
"May the gods deal with me, be it ever so
severely, if by this time tomorrow I do not
make your life like that of one of them."
3Elijah was afraid[b] and ran for his life.
When he came to Beersheba in Judah, he
left his servant there, 4while he himself went
a day's journey into the desert. He came to a
broom tree, sat down under it and prayed
that he might die. "I have had enough, LORD,"
he said. "Take my life; I am no better than my
ancestors." 5Then he lay down under the
tree and fell asleep.
All at once an angel touched him and said,
"Get up and eat." 6He looked around, and
there by his head was a cake of bread baked
over hot coals, and a jar of water. He ate and
drank and then lay down again.
7The angel of the LORD came back a second time and touched him and said, "Get up
and eat, for the journey is too much for you."
8So he got up and ate and drank. Strengthened by that food, he traveled forty days and
forty nights until he reached Horeb, the
mountain of God. 9There he went into a cave
and spent the night.

The LORD Appears to Elijah

And the word of the LORD came to him:
"What are you doing here, Elijah?"
10He replied, "I have been very zealous for
the LORD God Almighty. The Israelites have
rejected your covenant, broken down your
altars, and put your prophets to death with
the sword. I am the only one left, and now
they are trying to kill me too."
11The LORD said, "Go out and stand on the

[a]32 That is, probably about 13 quarts (about 15 liters)

[b]3 Or *Elijah saw*

mountain in the presence of the LORD, for the
LORD is about to pass by."
Then a great and powerful wind tore the
mountains apart and shattered the rocks before the LORD, but the LORD was not in the
wind. After the wind there was an earthquake, but the LORD was not in the earthquake. 12After the earthquake came a fire,
but the LORD was not in the fire. And after the
fire came a gentle whisper. 13When Elijah
heard it, he pulled his cloak over his face and
went out and stood at the mouth of the cave.
Then a voice said to him, "What are you
doing here, Elijah?"
14He replied, "I have been very zealous for
the LORD God Almighty. The Israelites have
rejected your covenant, broken down your
altars, and put your prophets to death with
the sword. I am the only one left, and now
they are trying to kill me too."
15The LORD said to him, "Go back the way
you came, and go to the Desert of Damascus. When you get there, anoint Hazael king
over Aram. 16Also, anoint Jehu son of Nimshi
king over Israel, and anoint Elisha son of
Shaphat from Abel Meholah to succeed you
as prophet. 17Jehu will put to death any who
escape the sword of Hazael, and Elisha will
put to death any who escape the sword of
Jehu. 18Yet I reserve seven thousand in Israel—all whose knees have not bowed down
to Baal and all whose mouths have not
kissed him."

The Call of Elisha

19So Elijah went from there and found Elisha son of Shaphat. He was plowing with
twelve yoke of oxen, and he himself was
driving the twelfth pair. Elijah went up to him
and threw his cloak around him. 20Elisha
then left his oxen and ran after Elijah. "Let
me kiss my father and mother good-by," he
said, "and then I will come with you."
"Go back," Elijah replied. "What have I
done to you?"
21So Elisha left him and went back. He
took his yoke of oxen and slaughtered them.
He burned the plowing equipment to cook
the meat and gave it to the people, and they
ate. Then he set out to follow Elijah and
became his attendant.

Ben-Hadad Attacks Samaria

20 Now Ben-Hadad king of Aram mustered his entire army. Accompanied
by thirty-two kings with their horses and
chariots, he went up and besieged Samaria
and attacked it. 2He sent messengers into
the city to Ahab king of Israel, saying, "This is
what Ben-Hadad says: 3'Your silver and gold
are mine, and the best of your wives and
children are mine.' "
4The king of Israel answered, "Just as you
say, my lord the king. I and all I have are
yours."
5The messengers came again and said,
"This is what Ben-Hadad says: 'I sent to demand your silver and gold, your wives and
your children. 6But about this time tomorrow
I am going to send my officials to search your
palace and the houses of your officials. They
will seize everything you value and carry it
away.' "
7The king of Israel summoned all the elders of the land and said to them, "See how
this man is looking for trouble! When he sent
for my wives and my children, my silver and
my gold, I did not refuse him."
8The elders and the people all answered,
"Don't listen to him or agree to his demands."
9So he replied to Ben-Hadad's messengers, "Tell my lord the king, 'Your servant will
do all you demanded the first time, but this
demand I cannot meet.' " They left and took
the answer back to Ben-Hadad.
10Then Ben-Hadad sent another message
to Ahab: "May the gods deal with me, be it
ever so severely, if enough dust remains in
Samaria to give each of my men a handful."
11The king of Israel answered, "Tell him:
'One who puts on his armor should not boast
like one who takes it off.' "
12Ben-Hadad heard this message while he
and the kings were drinking in their tents,[a]
and he ordered his men: "Prepare to attack."
So they prepared to attack the city.

Ahab Defeats Ben-Hadad

13Meanwhile a prophet came to Ahab king
of Israel and announced, "This is what the
LORD says: 'Do you see this vast army? I will
give it into your hand today, and then you will
know that I am the LORD.' "
14"But who will do this?" asked Ahab.
The prophet replied, "This is what the LORD
says: 'The young officers of the provincial
commanders will do it.' "

[a]12 Or *in Succoth*; also in verse 16

"And who will start the battle?" he asked.

The prophet answered, "You will."

15So Ahab summoned the young officers of the provincial commanders, 232 men. Then he assembled the rest of the Israelites, 7,000 in all. 16They set out at noon while Ben-Hadad and the 32 kings allied with him were in their tents getting drunk. 17The young officers of the provincial commanders went out first.

Now Ben-Hadad had dispatched scouts, who reported, "Men are advancing from Samaria."

18He said, "If they have come out for peace, take them alive; if they have come out for war, take them alive."

19The young officers of the provincial commanders marched out of the city with the army behind them 20and each one struck down his opponent. At that, the Arameans fled, with the Israelites in pursuit. But Ben-Hadad king of Aram escaped on horseback with some of his horsemen. 21The king of Israel advanced and overpowered the horses and chariots and inflicted heavy losses on the Arameans.

22Afterward, the prophet came to the king of Israel and said, "Strengthen your position and see what must be done, because next spring the king of Aram will attack you again."

23Meanwhile, the officials of the king of Aram advised him, "Their gods are gods of the hills. That is why they were too strong for us. But if we fight them on the plains, surely we will be stronger than they. 24Do this: Remove all the kings from their commands and replace them with other officers. 25You must also raise an army like the one you lost—horse for horse and chariot for chariot—so we can fight Israel on the plains. Then surely we will be stronger than they." He agreed with them and acted accordingly.

26The next spring Ben-Hadad mustered the Arameans and went up to Aphek to fight against Israel. 27When the Israelites were also mustered and given provisions, they marched out to meet them. The Israelites camped opposite them like two small flocks of goats, while the Arameans covered the countryside.

28The man of God came up and told the king of Israel, "This is what the LORD says: 'Because the Arameans think the LORD is a god of the hills and not a god of the valleys, I will deliver this vast army into your hands, and you will know that I am the LORD.' "

29For seven days they camped opposite each other, and on the seventh day the battle was joined. The Israelites inflicted a hundred thousand casualties on the Aramean foot soldiers in one day. 30The rest of them escaped to the city of Aphek, where the wall collapsed on twenty-seven thousand of them. And Ben-Hadad fled to the city and hid in an inner room.

31His officials said to him, "Look, we have heard that the kings of the house of Israel are merciful. Let us go to the king of Israel with sackcloth around our waists and ropes around our heads. Perhaps he will spare your life."

32Wearing sackcloth around their waists and ropes around their heads, they went to the king of Israel and said, "Your servant Ben-Hadad says: 'Please let me live.' "

The king answered, "Is he still alive? He is my brother."

33The men took this as a good sign and were quick to pick up his word. "Yes, your brother Ben-Hadad!" they said.

"Go and get him," the king said. When Ben-Hadad came out, Ahab had him come up into his chariot.

34"I will return the cities my father took from your father," Ben-Hadad offered. "You may set up your own market areas in Damascus, as my father did in Samaria."

⌞Ahab said,⌟ "On the basis of a treaty I will set you free." So he made a treaty with him, and let him go.

A Prophet Condemns Ahab

35By the word of the LORD one of the sons of the prophets said to his companion, "Strike me with your weapon," but the man refused.

36So the prophet said, "Because you have not obeyed the LORD, as soon as you leave me a lion will kill you." And after the man went away, a lion found him and killed him.

37The prophet found another man and said, "Strike me, please." So the man struck him and wounded him. 38Then the prophet went and stood by the road waiting for the king. He disguised himself with his headband down over his eyes. 39As the king passed by, the prophet called out to him, "Your servant went into the thick of the battle, and someone came to me with a captive and said, 'Guard this man. If he is missing, it will be your life for his life, or you must pay a talent[a] of silver.' 40While your servant was busy here and there, the man disappeared."

"That is your sentence," the king of Israel said. "You have pronounced it yourself."

41Then the prophet quickly removed the headband from his eyes, and the king of Israel recognized him as one of the prophets. 42He said to the king, "This is what the LORD says: 'You have set free a man I had determined should die.[b] Therefore it is your life for his life, your people for his people.'" 43Sullen and angry, the king of Israel went to his palace in Samaria.

Naboth's Vineyard

21 Some time later there was an incident involving a vineyard belonging to Naboth the Jezreelite. The vineyard was in Jezreel, close to the palace of Ahab king of Samaria. 2Ahab said to Naboth, "Let me have your vineyard to use for a vegetable garden, since it is close to my palace. In exchange I will give you a better vineyard or, if you prefer, I will pay you whatever it is worth."

3But Naboth replied, "The LORD forbid that I should give you the inheritance of my fathers."

4So Ahab went home, sullen and angry because Naboth the Jezreelite had said, "I will not give you the inheritance of my fathers." He lay on his bed sulking and refused to eat.

5His wife Jezebel came in and asked him, "Why are you so sullen? Why won't you eat?"

6He answered her, "Because I said to Naboth the Jezreelite, 'Sell me your vineyard; or if you prefer, I will give you another vineyard in its place.' But he said, 'I will not give you my vineyard.'"

7Jezebel his wife said, "Is this how you act as king over Israel? Get up and eat! Cheer up. I'll get you the vineyard of Naboth the Jezreelite."

8So she wrote letters in Ahab's name, placed his seal on them, and sent them to the elders and nobles who lived in Naboth's city with him. 9In those letters she wrote:

> "Proclaim a day of fasting and seat Naboth in a prominent place among the people. 10But seat two scoundrels opposite him and have them testify that he has cursed both God and the king. Then take him out and stone him to death."

11So the elders and nobles who lived in Naboth's city did as Jezebel directed in the letters she had written to them. 12They proclaimed a fast and seated Naboth in a prominent place among the people. 13Then two scoundrels came and sat opposite him and brought charges against Naboth before the people, saying, "Naboth has cursed both God and the king." So they took him outside the city and stoned him to death. 14Then they sent word to Jezebel: "Naboth has been stoned and is dead."

15As soon as Jezebel heard that Naboth had been stoned to death, she said to Ahab, "Get up and take possession of the vineyard of Naboth the Jezreelite that he refused to sell you. He is no longer alive, but dead." 16When Ahab heard that Naboth was dead, he got up and went down to take possession of Naboth's vineyard.

17Then the word of the LORD came to Elijah the Tishbite: 18"Go down to meet Ahab king of Israel, who rules in Samaria. He is now in Naboth's vineyard, where he has gone to take possession of it. 19Say to him, 'This is what the LORD says: Have you not murdered a man and seized his property?' Then say to him, 'This is what the LORD says: In the place where dogs licked up Naboth's blood, dogs will lick up your blood—yes, yours!'"

20Ahab said to Elijah, "So you have found me, my enemy!"

"I have found you," he answered, "because you have sold yourself to do evil in the eyes of the LORD. 21'I am going to bring disaster on you. I will consume your descendants and cut off from Ahab every last male in Israel—slave or free. 22I will make your house like that of Jeroboam son of Nebat and that of Baasha son of Ahijah, because you have provoked me to anger and have caused Israel to sin.'

23"And also concerning Jezebel the LORD says: 'Dogs will devour Jezebel by the wall of[c] Jezreel.'

24"Dogs will eat those belonging to Ahab who die in the city, and the birds of the air will feed on those who die in the country."

25(There was never a man like Ahab, who sold himself to do evil in the eyes of the LORD, urged on by Jezebel his wife. 26He behaved

[a]*39* That is, about 75 pounds (about 34 kilograms) [b]*42* The Hebrew term refers to the irrevocable giving over of things or persons to the LORD, often by totally destroying them. [c]*23* Most Hebrew manuscripts; a few Hebrew manuscripts, Vulgate and Syriac (see also 2 Kings 9:26) *the plot of ground at*

in the vilest manner by going after idols, like
the Amorites the LORD drove out before Israel.)
27When Ahab heard these words, he tore
his clothes, put on sackcloth and fasted. He
lay in sackcloth and went around meekly.
28Then the word of the LORD came to Elijah
the Tishbite: 29"Have you noticed how Ahab
has humbled himself before me? Because
he has humbled himself, I will not bring this
disaster in his day, but I will bring it on his
house in the days of his son."

Micaiah Prophesies Against Ahab

22 For three years there was no war between Aram and Israel. 2But in the
third year Jehoshaphat king of Judah went
down to see the king of Israel. 3The king of
Israel had said to his officials, "Don't you
know that Ramoth Gilead belongs to us and
yet we are doing nothing to retake it from the
king of Aram?"
4So he asked Jehoshaphat, "Will you go
with me to fight against Ramoth Gilead?"
Jehoshaphat replied to the king of Israel,
"I am as you are, my people as your people,
my horses as your horses." 5But Jehoshaphat also said to the king of Israel, "First
seek the counsel of the LORD."
6So the king of Israel brought together the
prophets—about four hundred men—and
asked them, "Shall I go to war against
Ramoth Gilead, or shall I refrain?"
"Go," they answered, "for the Lord will
give it into the king's hand."
7But Jehoshaphat asked, "Is there not a
prophet of the LORD here whom we can inquire of?"
8The king of Israel answered Jehoshaphat, "There is still one man through whom
we can inquire of the LORD, but I hate him
because he never prophesies anything good
about me, but always bad. He is Micaiah son
of Imlah."
"The king should not say that," Jehoshaphat replied.
9So the king of Israel called one of his
officials and said, "Bring Micaiah son of Imlah at once."
10Dressed in their royal robes, the king of
Israel and Jehoshaphat king of Judah were
sitting on their thrones at the threshing floor
by the entrance of the gate of Samaria, with
all the prophets prophesying before them.
11Now Zedekiah son of Kenaanah had made
iron horns and he declared, "This is what the
LORD says: 'With these you will gore the Arameans until they are destroyed.' "
12All the other prophets were prophesying
the same thing. "Attack Ramoth Gilead and
be victorious," they said, "for the LORD will
give it into the king's hand."
13The messenger who had gone to summon Micaiah said to him, "Look, as one man
the other prophets are predicting success for
the king. Let your word agree with theirs, and
speak favorably."
14But Micaiah said, "As surely as the LORD
lives, I can tell him only what the LORD tells
me."
15When he arrived, the king asked him,
"Micaiah, shall we go to war against Ramoth
Gilead, or shall I refrain?"
"Attack and be victorious," he answered,
"for the LORD will give it into the king's hand."
16The king said to him, "How many times
must I make you swear to tell me nothing but
the truth in the name of the LORD?"
17Then Micaiah answered, "I saw all Israel
scattered on the hills like sheep without a
shepherd, and the LORD said, 'These people
have no master. Let each one go home in
peace.' "
18The king of Israel said to Jehoshaphat,
"Didn't I tell you that he never prophesies
anything good about me, but only bad?"
19Micaiah continued, "Therefore hear the
word of the LORD: I saw the LORD sitting on his
throne with all the host of heaven standing
around him on his right and on his left. 20And
the LORD said, 'Who will entice Ahab into attacking Ramoth Gilead and going to his
death there?'
"One suggested this, and another that.
21Finally, a spirit came forward, stood before
the LORD and said, 'I will entice him.'
22" 'By what means?' the LORD asked.
" 'I will go out and be a lying spirit in the
mouths of all his prophets,' he said.
" 'You will succeed in enticing him,' said
the LORD. 'Go and do it.'
23"So now the LORD has put a lying spirit in
the mouths of all these prophets of yours.
The LORD has decreed disaster for you."
24Then Zedekiah son of Kenaanah went
up and slapped Micaiah in the face. "Which
way did the spirit from[a] the LORD go when he
went from me to speak to you?" he asked.
25Micaiah replied, "You will find out on the
day you go to hide in an inner room."

[a]24 Or *Spirit of*

26The king of Israel then ordered, "Take Micaiah and send him back to Amon the ruler of the city and to Joash the king's son 27and say, 'This is what the king says: Put this fellow in prison and give him nothing but bread and water until I return safely.' "

28Micaiah declared, "If you ever return safely, the LORD has not spoken through me." Then he added, "Mark my words, all you people!"

Ahab Killed at Ramoth Gilead

29So the king of Israel and Jehoshaphat king of Judah went up to Ramoth Gilead. 30The king of Israel said to Jehoshaphat, "I will enter the battle in disguise, but you wear your royal robes." So the king of Israel disguised himself and went into battle.

31Now the king of Aram had ordered his thirty-two chariot commanders, "Do not fight with anyone, small or great, except the king of Israel." 32When the chariot commanders saw Jehoshaphat, they thought, "Surely this is the king of Israel." So they turned to attack him, but when Jehoshaphat cried out, 33the chariot commanders saw that he was not the king of Israel and stopped pursuing him.

34But someone drew his bow at random and hit the king of Israel between the sections of his armor. The king told his chariot driver, "Wheel around and get me out of the fighting. I've been wounded." 35All day long the battle raged, and the king was propped up in his chariot facing the Arameans. The blood from his wound ran onto the floor of the chariot, and that evening he died. 36As the sun was setting, a cry spread through the army: "Every man to his town; everyone to his land!"

37So the king died and was brought to Samaria, and they buried him there. 38They washed the chariot at a pool in Samaria (where the prostitutes bathed),[a] and the dogs licked up his blood, as the word of the LORD had declared.

39As for the other events of Ahab's reign, including all he did, the palace he built and inlaid with ivory, and the cities he fortified, are they not written in the book of the annals of the kings of Israel? 40Ahab rested with his fathers. And Ahaziah his son succeeded him as king.

Jehoshaphat King of Judah

41Jehoshaphat son of Asa became king of Judah in the fourth year of Ahab king of Israel. 42Jehoshaphat was thirty-five years old when he became king, and he reigned in Jerusalem twenty-five years. His mother's name was Azubah daughter of Shilhi. 43In everything he walked in the ways of his father Asa and did not stray from them; he did what was right in the eyes of the LORD. The high places, however, were not removed, and the people continued to offer sacrifices and burn incense there. 44Jehoshaphat was also at peace with the king of Israel.

45As for the other events of Jehoshaphat's reign, the things he achieved and his military exploits, are they not written in the book of the annals of the kings of Judah? 46He rid the land of the rest of the male shrine prostitutes who remained there even after the reign of his father Asa. 47There was then no king in Edom; a deputy ruled.

48Now Jehoshaphat built a fleet of trading ships[b] to go to Ophir for gold, but they never set sail—they were wrecked at Ezion Geber. 49At that time Ahaziah son of Ahab said to Jehoshaphat, "Let my men sail with your men," but Jehoshaphat refused.

50Then Jehoshaphat rested with his fathers and was buried with them in the city of David his father. And Jehoram his son succeeded him.

Ahaziah King of Israel

51Ahaziah son of Ahab became king of Israel in Samaria in the seventeenth year of Jehoshaphat king of Judah, and he reigned over Israel two years. 52He did evil in the eyes of the LORD, because he walked in the ways of his father and mother and in the ways of Jeroboam son of Nebat, who caused Israel to sin. 53He served and worshiped Baal and provoked the LORD, the God of Israel, to anger, just as his father had done.

[a]38 Or *Samaria and cleaned the weapons* [b]48 Hebrew *of ships of Tarshish*

2 Kings

Introduction:

Second Kings continues the stories of the great prophets Elijah and Elisha. It also tells the history of the northern kingdom of Israel and the southern kingdom of Judah until they were both finally conquered. Israel was conquered by Assyria in 722 B.C. and Judah was conquered by the Babylonians in 586 B.C. In both kingdoms God's prophets continually warned the people that God would punish them if they did not repent from their sins.

Outline of contents:

The Lord's Judgment on Ahaziah

1 After Ahab's death, Moab rebelled
against Israel. 2Now Ahaziah had fallen
through the lattice of his upper room in Samaria and injured himself. So he sent messengers, saying to them, "Go and consult
Baal-Zebub, the god of Ekron, to see if I will
recover from this injury."
3But the angel of the Lord said to Elijah the
Tishbite, "Go up and meet the messengers
of the king of Samaria and ask them, 'Is it
because there is no God in Israel that you
are going off to consult Baal-Zebub, the god
of Ekron?' 4Therefore this is what the Lord
says: 'You will not leave the bed you are lying
on. You will certainly die!' " So Elijah went.
5When the messengers returned to the
king, he asked them, "Why have you come
back?"
6"A man came to meet us," they replied.
"And he said to us, 'Go back to the king who
sent you and tell him, "This is what the Lord
says: Is it because there is no God in Israel
that you are sending men to consult Baal-
Zebub, the god of Ekron? Therefore you will
not leave the bed you are lying on. You will
certainly die!" ' "
7The king asked them, "What kind of man
was it who came to meet you and told you
this?"
8They replied, "He was a man with a garment of hair and with a leather belt around
his waist."
The king said, "That was Elijah the Tishbite."
9Then he sent to Elijah a captain with his
company of fifty men. The captain went up to
Elijah, who was sitting on the top of a hill, and
said to him, "Man of God, the king says,
'Come down!' "
10Elijah answered the captain, "If I am a
man of God, may fire come down from
heaven and consume you and your fifty
men!" Then fire fell from heaven and consumed the captain and his men.
11At this the king sent to Elijah another
captain with his fifty men. The captain said to
him, "Man of God, this is what the king says,
'Come down at once!' "
12"If I am a man of God," Elijah replied,
"may fire come down from heaven and consume you and your fifty men!" Then the fire
of God fell from heaven and consumed him
and his fifty men.
13So the king sent a third captain with his
fifty men. This third captain went up and fell
on his knees before Elijah. "Man of God," he
begged, "please have respect for my life and
the lives of these fifty men, your servants!
14See, fire has fallen from heaven and consumed the first two captains and all their
men. But now have respect for my life!"

15 The angel of the LORD said to Elijah, "Go
down with him; do not be afraid of him." So
Elijah got up and went down with him to the
king.
16 He told the king, "This is what the LORD
says: Is it because there is no God in Israel
for you to consult that you have sent messengers to consult Baal-Zebub, the god of
Ekron? Because you have done this, you will
never leave the bed you are lying on. You will
certainly die!" 17 So he died, according to the
word of the LORD that Elijah had spoken.
Because Ahaziah had no son, Joram[a]
succeeded him as king in the second year of
Jehoram son of Jehoshaphat king of Judah.
18 As for all the other events of Ahaziah's
reign, and what he did, are they not written in
the book of the annals of the kings of Israel?

Elijah Taken Up to Heaven

2 When the LORD was about to take Elijah
up to heaven in a whirlwind, Elijah and
Elisha were on their way from Gilgal. 2 Elijah
said to Elisha, "Stay here; the LORD has sent
me to Bethel."
But Elisha said, "As surely as the LORD
lives and as you live, I will not leave you." So
they went down to Bethel.
3 The company of the prophets at Bethel
came out to Elisha and asked, "Do you know
that the LORD is going to take your master
from you today?"
"Yes, I know," Elisha replied, "but do not
speak of it."
4 Then Elijah said to him, "Stay here, Elisha; the LORD has sent me to Jericho."
And he replied, "As surely as the LORD
lives and as you live, I will not leave you." So
they went to Jericho.
5 The company of the prophets at Jericho
went up to Elisha and asked him, "Do you
know that the LORD is going to take your master from you today?"
"Yes, I know," he replied, "but do not
speak of it."
6 Then Elijah said to him, "Stay here; the
LORD has sent me to the Jordan."
And he replied, "As surely as the LORD
lives and as you live, I will not leave you." So
the two of them walked on.
7 Fifty men of the company of the prophets
went and stood at a distance, facing the
place where Elijah and Elisha had stopped at
the Jordan. 8 Elijah took his cloak, rolled it up
and struck the water with it. The water divided to the right and to the left, and the two
of them crossed over on dry ground.
9 When they had crossed, Elijah said to
Elisha, "Tell me, what can I do for you before
I am taken from you?"
"Let me inherit a double portion of your
spirit," Elisha replied.
10 "You have asked a difficult thing," Elijah
said, "yet if you see me when I am taken
from you, it will be yours—otherwise not."
11 As they were walking along and talking
together, suddenly a chariot of fire and
horses of fire appeared and separated the
two of them, and Elijah went up to heaven in
a whirlwind. 12 Elisha saw this and cried out,
"My father! My father! The chariots and
horsemen of Israel!" And Elisha saw him no
more. Then he took hold of his own clothes
and tore them apart.
13 He picked up the cloak that had fallen
from Elijah and went back and stood on the
bank of the Jordan. 14 Then he took the cloak
that had fallen from him and struck the water
with it. "Where now is the LORD, the God of
Elijah?" he asked. When he struck the water,
it divided to the right and to the left, and he
crossed over.
15 The company of the prophets from Jericho, who were watching, said, "The spirit of
Elijah is resting on Elisha." And they went to
meet him and bowed to the ground before
him. 16 "Look," they said, "we your servants
have fifty able men. Let them go and look for
your master. Perhaps the Spirit of the LORD
has picked him up and set him down on
some mountain or in some valley."
"No," Elisha replied, "do not send them."
17 But they persisted until he was too
ashamed to refuse. So he said, "Send
them." And they sent fifty men, who
searched for three days but did not find him.
18 When they returned to Elisha, who was
staying in Jericho, he said to them, "Didn't I
tell you not to go?"

Healing of the Water

19 The men of the city said to Elisha, "Look,
our lord, this town is well situated, as you can
see, but the water is bad and the land is
unproductive."
20 "Bring me a new bowl," he said, "and put
salt in it." So they brought it to him.
21 Then he went out to the spring and threw
the salt into it, saying, "This is what the LORD
says: 'I have healed this water. Never again

[a] 17 Hebrew *Jehoram,* a variant of *Joram*

will it cause death or make the land unproductive.' " 22And the water has remained
wholesome to this day, according to the
word Elisha had spoken.

Elisha Is Jeered

23From there Elisha went up to Bethel. As
he was walking along the road, some youths
came out of the town and jeered at him. "Go
on up, you baldhead!" they said. "Go on up,
you baldhead!" 24He turned around, looked
at them and called down a curse on them in
the name of the LORD. Then two bears came
out of the woods and mauled forty-two of the
youths. 25And he went on to Mount Carmel
and from there returned to Samaria.

Moab Revolts

3 Joram[a] son of Ahab became king of Israel in Samaria in the eighteenth year of
Jehoshaphat king of Judah, and he reigned
twelve years. 2He did evil in the eyes of the
LORD, but not as his father and mother had
done. He got rid of the sacred stone of Baal
that his father had made. 3Nevertheless he
clung to the sins of Jeroboam son of Nebat,
which he had caused Israel to commit; he did
not turn away from them.

4Now Mesha king of Moab raised sheep,
and he had to supply the king of Israel with a
hundred thousand lambs and with the wool
of a hundred thousand rams. 5But after Ahab
died, the king of Moab rebelled against the
king of Israel. 6So at that time King Joram set
out from Samaria and mobilized all Israel.
7He also sent this message to Jehoshaphat
king of Judah: "The king of Moab has rebelled against me. Will you go with me to
fight against Moab?"

"I will go with you," he replied. "I am as
you are, my people as your people, my
horses as your horses."

8"By what route shall we attack?" he
asked.

"Through the Desert of Edom," he answered.

9So the king of Israel set out with the king
of Judah and the king of Edom. After a
roundabout march of seven days, the army
had no more water for themselves or for the
animals with them.

10"What!" exclaimed the king of Israel.
"Has the LORD called us three kings together
only to hand us over to Moab?"

11But Jehoshaphat asked, "Is there no
prophet of the LORD here, that we may inquire
of the LORD through him?"

An officer of the king of Israel answered,
"Elisha son of Shaphat is here. He used to
pour water on the hands of Elijah.[b]"

12Jehoshaphat said, "The word of the LORD
is with him." So the king of Israel and Jehoshaphat and the king of Edom went down
to him.

13Elisha said to the king of Israel, "What do
we have to do with each other? Go to the
prophets of your father and the prophets of
your mother."

"No," the king of Israel answered, "because it was the LORD who called us three
kings together to hand us over to Moab."

14Elisha said, "As surely as the LORD Almighty lives, whom I serve, if I did not have
respect for the presence of Jehoshaphat
king of Judah, I would not look at you or even
notice you. 15But now bring me a harpist."

While the harpist was playing, the hand of
the LORD came upon Elisha 16and he said,
"This is what the LORD says: Make this valley
full of ditches. 17For this is what the LORD
says: You will see neither wind nor rain, yet
this valley will be filled with water, and you,
your cattle and your other animals will drink.
18This is an easy thing in the eyes of the
LORD; he will also hand Moab over to you.
19You will overthrow every fortified city and
every major town. You will cut down every
good tree, stop up all the springs, and ruin
every good field with stones."

20The next morning, about the time for offering the sacrifice, there it was—water flowing from the direction of Edom! And the land
was filled with water.

21Now all the Moabites had heard that the
kings had come to fight against them; so
every man, young and old, who could bear
arms was called up and stationed on the
border. 22When they got up early in the morning, the sun was shining on the water. To the
Moabites across the way, the water looked
red—like blood. 23"That's blood!" they said.
"Those kings must have fought and slaughtered each other. Now to the plunder,
Moab!"

24But when the Moabites came to the
camp of Israel, the Israelites rose up and
fought them until they fled. And the Israelites
invaded the land and slaughtered the Moabites. 25They destroyed the towns, and each
man threw a stone on every good field until it

[a] 1 Hebrew *Jehoram,* a variant of *Joram*; also in verse 6

[b] 11 That is, he was Elijah's personal servant.

was covered. They stopped up all the springs and cut down every good tree. Only Kir Hareseth was left with its stones in place, but men armed with slings surrounded it and attacked it as well.

26When the king of Moab saw that the battle had gone against him, he took with him seven hundred swordsmen to break through to the king of Edom, but they failed. 27Then he took his firstborn son, who was to succeed him as king, and offered him as a sacrifice on the city wall. The fury against Israel was great; they withdrew and returned to their own land.

The Widow's Oil

4 The wife of a man from the company of the prophets cried out to Elisha, "Your servant my husband is dead, and you know that he revered the LORD. But now his creditor is coming to take my two boys as his slaves."

2Elisha replied to her, "How can I help you? Tell me, what do you have in your house?"

"Your servant has nothing there at all," she said, "except a little oil."

3Elisha said, "Go around and ask all your neighbors for empty jars. Don't ask for just a few. 4Then go inside and shut the door behind you and your sons. Pour oil into all the jars, and as each is filled, put it to one side."

5She left him and afterward shut the door behind her and her sons. They brought the jars to her and she kept pouring. 6When all the jars were full, she said to her son, "Bring me another one."

But he replied, "There is not a jar left." Then the oil stopped flowing.

7She went and told the man of God, and he said, "Go, sell the oil and pay your debts. You and your sons can live on what is left."

The Shunammite's Son Restored to Life

8One day Elisha went to Shunem. And a well-to-do woman was there, who urged him to stay for a meal. So whenever he came by, he stopped there to eat. 9She said to her husband, "I know that this man who often comes our way is a holy man of God. 10Let's make a small room on the roof and put in it a bed and a table, a chair and a lamp for him. Then he can stay there whenever he comes to us."

11One day when Elisha came, he went up to his room and lay down there. 12He said to his servant Gehazi, "Call the Shunammite." So he called her, and she stood before him. 13Elisha said to him, "Tell her, 'You have gone to all this trouble for us. Now what can be done for you? Can we speak on your behalf to the king or the commander of the army?' "

She replied, "I have a home among my own people."

14"What can be done for her?" Elisha asked.

Gehazi said, "Well, she has no son and her husband is old."

15Then Elisha said, "Call her." So he called her, and she stood in the doorway. 16"About this time next year," Elisha said, "you will hold a son in your arms."

"No, my lord," she objected. "Don't mislead your servant, O man of God!"

17But the woman became pregnant, and the next year about that same time she gave birth to a son, just as Elisha had told her. 18The child grew, and one day he went out to his father, who was with the reapers. 19"My head! My head!" he said to his father.

His father told a servant, "Carry him to his mother." 20After the servant had lifted him up and carried him to his mother, the boy sat on her lap until noon, and then he died. 21She went up and laid him on the bed of the man of God, then shut the door and went out.

22She called her husband and said, "Please send me one of the servants and a donkey so I can go to the man of God quickly and return."

23"Why go to him today?" he asked. "It's not the New Moon or the Sabbath."

"It's all right," she said.

24She saddled the donkey and said to her servant, "Lead on; don't slow down for me unless I tell you." 25So she set out and came to the man of God at Mount Carmel.

When he saw her in the distance, the man of God said to his servant Gehazi, "Look! There's the Shunammite! 26Run to meet her and ask her, 'Are you all right? Is your husband all right? Is your child all right?' "

"Everything is all right," she said.

27When she reached the man of God at the mountain, she took hold of his feet. Gehazi came over to push her away, but the man of God said, "Leave her alone! She is in bitter distress, but the LORD has hidden it from me and has not told me why."

28"Did I ask you for a son, my lord?" she

said. "Didn't I tell you, 'Don't raise my hopes'?"

29Elisha said to Gehazi, "Tuck your cloak into your belt, take my staff in your hand and run. If you meet anyone, do not greet him, and if anyone greets you, do not answer. Lay my staff on the boy's face."

30But the child's mother said, "As surely as the LORD lives and as you live, I will not leave you." So he got up and followed her.

31Gehazi went on ahead and laid the staff on the boy's face, but there was no sound or response. So Gehazi went back to meet Elisha and told him, "The boy has not awakened."

32When Elisha reached the house, there was the boy lying dead on his couch. 33He went in, shut the door on the two of them and prayed to the LORD. 34Then he got on the bed and lay upon the boy, mouth to mouth, eyes to eyes, hands to hands. As he stretched himself out upon him, the boy's body grew warm. 35Elisha turned away and walked back and forth in the room and then got on the bed and stretched out upon him once more. The boy sneezed seven times and opened his eyes.

36Elisha summoned Gehazi and said, "Call the Shunammite." And he did. When she came, he said, "Take your son." 37She came in, fell at his feet and bowed to the ground. Then she took her son and went out.

Death in the Pot

38Elisha returned to Gilgal and there was a famine in that region. While the company of the prophets was meeting with him, he said to his servant, "Put on the large pot and cook some stew for these men."

39One of them went out into the fields to gather herbs and found a wild vine. He gathered some of its gourds and filled the fold of his cloak. When he returned, he cut them up into the pot of stew, though no one knew what they were. 40The stew was poured out for the men, but as they began to eat it, they cried out, "O man of God, there is death in the pot!" And they could not eat it.

41Elisha said, "Get some flour." He put it into the pot and said, "Serve it to the people to eat." And there was nothing harmful in the pot.

Feeding of a Hundred

42A man came from Baal Shalishah, bringing the man of God twenty loaves of barley bread baked from the first ripe grain, along with some heads of new grain. "Give it to the people to eat," Elisha said.

43"How can I set this before a hundred men?" his servant asked.

But Elisha answered, "Give it to the people to eat. For this is what the LORD says: 'They will eat and have some left over.' " 44Then he set it before them, and they ate and had some left over, according to the word of the LORD.

Naaman Healed of Leprosy

5 Now Naaman was commander of the army of the king of Aram. He was a great man in the sight of his master and highly regarded, because through him the LORD had given victory to Aram. He was a valiant soldier, but he had leprosy.[a]

2Now bands from Aram had gone out and had taken captive a young girl from Israel, and she served Naaman's wife. 3She said to her mistress, "If only my master would see the prophet who is in Samaria! He would cure him of his leprosy."

4Naaman went to his master and told him what the girl from Israel had said. 5"By all means, go," the king of Aram replied. "I will send a letter to the king of Israel." So Naaman left, taking with him ten talents[b] of silver, six thousand shekels[c] of gold and ten sets of clothing. 6The letter that he took to the king of Israel read: "With this letter I am sending my servant Naaman to you so that you may cure him of his leprosy."

7As soon as the king of Israel read the letter, he tore his robes and said, "Am I God? Can I kill and bring back to life? Why does this fellow send someone to me to be cured of his leprosy? See how he is trying to pick a quarrel with me!"

8When Elisha the man of God heard that the king of Israel had torn his robes, he sent him this message: "Why have you torn your robes? Have the man come to me and he will know that there is a prophet in Israel." 9So Naaman went with his horses and chariots and stopped at the door of Elisha's house. 10Elisha sent a messenger to say to him,

[a]*1* The Hebrew word was used for various diseases affecting the skin—not necessarily leprosy; also in verses 3, 6, 7, 11 and 27. [b]*5* That is, about 750 pounds (about 340 kilograms) [c]*5* That is, about 150 pounds (about 70 kilograms)

"Go, wash yourself seven times in the Jordan, and your flesh will be restored and you
will be cleansed."
11But Naaman went away angry and said,
"I thought that he would surely come out to
me and stand and call on the name of the
LORD his God, wave his hand over the spot
and cure me of my leprosy. 12Are not Abana
and Pharpar, the rivers of Damascus, better
than any of the waters of Israel? Couldn't I
wash in them and be cleansed?" So he
turned and went off in a rage.
13Naaman's servants went to him and
said, "My father, if the prophet had told you
to do some great thing, would you not have
done it? How much more, then, when he tells
you, 'Wash and be cleansed'!" 14So he went
down and dipped himself in the Jordan
seven times, as the man of God had told him,
and his flesh was restored and became
clean like that of a young boy.
15Then Naaman and all his attendants
went back to the man of God. He stood before him and said, "Now I know that there is
no God in all the world except in Israel.
Please accept now a gift from your servant."
16The prophet answered, "As surely as the
LORD lives, whom I serve, I will not accept a
thing." And even though Naaman urged him,
he refused.
17"If you will not," said Naaman, "please
let me, your servant, be given as much earth
as a pair of mules can carry, for your servant
will never again make burnt offerings and
sacrifices to any other god but the LORD.
18But may the LORD forgive your servant for
this one thing: When my master enters the
temple of Rimmon to bow down and he is
leaning on my arm and I bow there also—
when I bow down in the temple of Rimmon,
may the LORD forgive your servant for this."
19"Go in peace," Elisha said.
After Naaman had traveled some distance, 20Gehazi, the servant of Elisha the
man of God, said to himself, "My master was
too easy on Naaman, this Aramean, by not
accepting from him what he brought. As
surely as the LORD lives, I will run after him
and get something from him."
21So Gehazi hurried after Naaman. When
Naaman saw him running toward him, he got
down from the chariot to meet him. "Is everything all right?" he asked.
22"Everything is all right," Gehazi answered. "My master sent me to say, 'Two
young men from the company of the prophets have just come to me from the hill country
of Ephraim. Please give them a talent[a] of
silver and two sets of clothing.'"
23"By all means, take two talents," said
Naaman. He urged Gehazi to accept them,
and then tied up the two talents of silver in
two bags, with two sets of clothing. He gave
them to two of his servants, and they carried
them ahead of Gehazi. 24When Gehazi
came to the hill, he took the things from the
servants and put them away in the house. He
sent the men away and they left. 25Then he
went in and stood before his master Elisha.
"Where have you been, Gehazi?" Elisha
asked.
"Your servant didn't go anywhere," Gehazi answered.
26But Elisha said to him, "Was not my spirit
with you when the man got down from his
chariot to meet you? Is this the time to take
money, or to accept clothes, olive groves,
vineyards, flocks, herds, or menservants
and maidservants? 27Naaman's leprosy will
cling to you and to your descendants forever." Then Gehazi went from Elisha's presence and he was leprous, as white as snow.

An Axhead Floats

6 The company of the prophets said to
Elisha, "Look, the place where we meet
with you is too small for us. 2Let us go to the
Jordan, where each of us can get a pole; and
let us build a place there for us to live."
And he said, "Go."
3Then one of them said, "Won't you please
come with your servants?"
"I will," Elisha replied. 4And he went with
them.
They went to the Jordan and began to cut
down trees. 5As one of them was cutting
down a tree, the iron axhead fell into the
water. "Oh, my lord," he cried out, "it was
borrowed!"
6The man of God asked, "Where did it
fall?" When he showed him the place, Elisha
cut a stick and threw it there, and made the
iron float. 7"Lift it out," he said. Then the man
reached out his hand and took it.

Elisha Traps Blinded Arameans

8Now the king of Aram was at war with
Israel. After conferring with his officers, he

[a]22 That is, about 75 pounds (about 34 kilograms)

said, "I will set up my camp in such and such
a place."
9 The man of God sent word to the king of
Israel: "Beware of passing that place, because the Arameans are going down there."
10 So the king of Israel checked on the place
indicated by the man of God. Time and again
Elisha warned the king, so that he was on his
guard in such places.
11 This enraged the king of Aram. He summoned his officers and demanded of them,
"Will you not tell me which of us is on the side
of the king of Israel?"
12 "None of us, my lord the king," said one
of his officers, "but Elisha, the prophet who is
in Israel, tells the king of Israel the very
words you speak in your bedroom."
13 "Go, find out where he is," the king ordered, "so I can send men and capture him."
The report came back: "He is in Dothan."
14 Then he sent horses and chariots and a
strong force there. They went by night and
surrounded the city.
15 When the servant of the man of God got
up and went out early the next morning, an
army with horses and chariots had surrounded the city. "Oh, my lord, what shall we do?"
the servant asked.
16 "Don't be afraid," the prophet answered.
"Those who are with us are more than those
who are with them."
17 And Elisha prayed, "O LORD, open his
eyes so he may see." Then the LORD opened
the servant's eyes, and he looked and saw
the hills full of horses and chariots of fire all
around Elisha.
18 As the enemy came down toward him,
Elisha prayed to the LORD, "Strike these
people with blindness." So he struck them
with blindness, as Elisha had asked.
19 Elisha told them, "This is not the road
and this is not the city. Follow me, and I will
lead you to the man you are looking for." And
he led them to Samaria.
20 After they entered the city, Elisha said,
"LORD, open the eyes of these men so they
can see." Then the LORD opened their eyes
and they looked, and there they were, inside
Samaria.
21 When the king of Israel saw them, he
asked Elisha, "Shall I kill them, my father?
Shall I kill them?"
22 "Do not kill them," he answered. "Would
you kill men you have captured with your
own sword or bow? Set food and water before them so that they may eat and drink and
then go back to their master." 23 So he prepared a great feast for them, and after they
had finished eating and drinking, he sent
them away, and they returned to their master. So the bands from Aram stopped raiding
Israel's territory.

Famine in Besieged Samaria

24 Some time later, Ben-Hadad king of
Aram mobilized his entire army and marched
up and laid siege to Samaria. 25 There was a
great famine in the city; the siege lasted so
long that a donkey's head sold for eighty
shekels[a] of silver, and a quarter of a cab[b] of
seed pods[c] for five shekels.[d]
26 As the king of Israel was passing by on
the wall, a woman cried to him, "Help me, my
lord the king!"
27 The king replied, "If the LORD does not
help you, where can I get help for you? From
the threshing floor? From the winepress?"
28 Then he asked her, "What's the matter?"
She answered, "This woman said to me,
'Give up your son so we may eat him today,
and tomorrow we'll eat my son.' 29 So we
cooked my son and ate him. The next day I
said to her, 'Give up your son so we may eat
him,' but she had hidden him."
30 When the king heard the woman's
words, he tore his robes. As he went along
the wall, the people looked, and there, underneath, he had sackcloth on his body. 31 He
said, "May God deal with me, be it ever so
severely, if the head of Elisha son of Shaphat
remains on his shoulders today!"
32 Now Elisha was sitting in his house, and
the elders were sitting with him. The king
sent a messenger ahead, but before he arrived, Elisha said to the elders, "Don't you
see how this murderer is sending someone
to cut off my head? Look, when the messenger comes, shut the door and hold it shut
against him. Is not the sound of his master's
footsteps behind him?"
33 While he was still talking to them, the
messenger came down to him. And ⌊the king⌋
said, "This disaster is from the LORD. Why
should I wait for the LORD any longer?"
7 Elisha said, "Hear the word of the LORD.
This is what the LORD says: About this
time tomorrow, a seah[e] of flour will sell for a

[a] 25 That is, about 2 pounds (about 1 kilogram) [b] 25 That is, probably about 1/2 pint (about 0.3 liter)
[c] 25 Or *of dove's dung* [d] 25 That is, about 2 ounces (about 55 grams) [e] 1 That is, probably about 7 quarts
(about 7.3 liters); also in verses 16 and 18

shekel[a] and two seahs[b] of barley for a
shekel at the gate of Samaria."
2The officer on whose arm the king was
leaning said to the man of God, "Look, even
if the LORD should open the floodgates of the
heavens, could this happen?"
"You will see it with your own eyes," answered Elisha, "but you will not eat any of it!"

The Siege Lifted

3Now there were four men with leprosy[c] at
the entrance of the city gate. They said to
each other, "Why stay here until we die? 4If
we say, 'We'll go into the city'—the famine is
there, and we will die. And if we stay here, we
will die. So let's go over to the camp of the
Arameans and surrender. If they spare us,
we live; if they kill us, then we die."
5At dusk they got up and went to the camp
of the Arameans. When they reached the
edge of the camp, not a man was there, 6for
the Lord had caused the Arameans to hear
the sound of chariots and horses and a great
army, so that they said to one another,
"Look, the king of Israel has hired the Hittite
and Egyptian kings to attack us!" 7So they
got up and fled in the dusk and abandoned
their tents and their horses and donkeys.
They left the camp as it was and ran for their
lives.
8The men who had leprosy reached the
edge of the camp and entered one of the
tents. They ate and drank, and carried away
silver, gold and clothes, and went off and hid
them. They returned and entered another
tent and took some things from it and hid
them also.
9Then they said to each other, "We're not
doing right. This is a day of good news and
we are keeping it to ourselves. If we wait until
daylight, punishment will overtake us. Let's
go at once and report this to the royal palace."
10So they went and called out to the city
gatekeepers and told them, "We went into
the Aramean camp and not a man was
there—not a sound of anyone—only teth-
ered horses and donkeys, and the tents left
just as they were." 11The gatekeepers shouted the news, and it was reported within the
palace.
12The king got up in the night and said to
his officers, "I will tell you what the Arameans
have done to us. They know we are starving;
so they have left the camp to hide in the
countryside, thinking, 'They will surely come
out, and then we will take them alive and get
into the city.' "
13One of his officers answered, "Have
some men take five of the horses that are left
in the city. Their plight will be like that of all
the Israelites left here—yes, they will only be
like all these Israelites who are doomed. So
let us send them to find out what happened."
14So they selected two chariots with their
horses, and the king sent them after the Aramean army. He commanded the drivers, "Go
and find out what has happened." 15They
followed them as far as the Jordan, and they
found the whole road strewn with the clothing and equipment the Arameans had
thrown away in their headlong flight. So the
messengers returned and reported to the
king. 16Then the people went out and plundered the camp of the Arameans. So a seah
of flour sold for a shekel, and two seahs of
barley sold for a shekel, as the LORD had
said.
17Now the king had put the officer on
whose arm he leaned in charge of the gate,
and the people trampled him in the gateway,
and he died, just as the man of God had
foretold when the king came down to his
house. 18It happened as the man of God had
said to the king: "About this time tomorrow, a
seah of flour will sell for a shekel and two
seahs of barley for a shekel at the gate of
Samaria."
19The officer had said to the man of God,
"Look, even if the LORD should open the
floodgates of the heavens, could this happen?" The man of God had replied, "You will
see it with your own eyes, but you will not eat
any of it!" 20And that is exactly what happened to him, for the people trampled him in
the gateway, and he died.

The Shunammite's Land Restored

8 Now Elisha had said to the woman
whose son he had restored to life, "Go
away with your family and stay for a while
wherever you can, because the LORD has
decreed a famine in the land that will last
seven years." 2The woman proceeded to do
as the man of God said. She and her family
went away and stayed in the land of the
Philistines seven years.
3At the end of the seven years she came

[a] *1* That is, about 2/5 ounce (about 11 grams); also in verses 16 and 18 [b] *1* That is, probably about 13 quarts (about 15 liters); also in verses 16 and 18 [c] *3* The Hebrew word is used for various diseases affecting the skin—not necessarily leprosy; also in verse 8.

back from the land of the Philistines and
went to the king to beg for her house and
land. 4The king was talking to Gehazi, the
servant of the man of God, and had said,
"Tell me about all the great things Elisha has
done." 5Just as Gehazi was telling the king
how Elisha had restored the dead to life, the
woman whose son Elisha had brought back
to life came to beg the king for her house and
land.

Gehazi said, "This is the woman, my lord
the king, and this is her son whom Elisha
restored to life." 6The king asked the woman
about it, and she told him.

Then he assigned an official to her case
and said to him, "Give back everything that
belonged to her, including all the income
from her land from the day she left the country until now."

Hazael Murders Ben-Hadad

7Elisha went to Damascus, and Ben-
Hadad king of Aram was ill. When the king
was told, "The man of God has come all the
way up here," 8he said to Hazael, "Take a
gift with you and go to meet the man of God.
Consult the LORD through him; ask him, 'Will I
recover from this illness?' "

9Hazael went to meet Elisha, taking with
him as a gift forty camel-loads of all the finest
wares of Damascus. He went in and stood
before him, and said, "Your son Ben-Hadad
king of Aram has sent me to ask, 'Will I
recover from this illness?' "

10Elisha answered, "Go and say to him,
'You will certainly recover'; but[a] the LORD has
revealed to me that he will in fact die." 11He
stared at him with a fixed gaze until Hazael
felt ashamed. Then the man of God began to
weep.

12"Why is my lord weeping?" asked Hazael.

"Because I know the harm you will do to
the Israelites," he answered. "You will set
fire to their fortified places, kill their young
men with the sword, dash their little children
to the ground, and rip open their pregnant
women."

13Hazael said, "How could your servant, a
mere dog, accomplish such a feat?"

"The LORD has shown me that you will
become king of Aram," answered Elisha.

14Then Hazael left Elisha and returned to
his master. When Ben-Hadad asked, "What
did Elisha say to you?" Hazael replied, "He
told me that you would certainly recover."
15But the next day he took a thick cloth,
soaked it in water and spread it over the
king's face, so that he died. Then Hazael
succeeded him as king.

Jehoram King of Judah

16In the fifth year of Joram son of Ahab
king of Israel, when Jehoshaphat was king of
Judah, Jehoram son of Jehoshaphat began
his reign as king of Judah. 17He was thirty-
two years old when he became king, and he
reigned in Jerusalem eight years. 18He
walked in the ways of the kings of Israel, as
the house of Ahab had done, for he married a
daughter of Ahab. He did evil in the eyes of
the LORD. 19Nevertheless, for the sake of his
servant David, the LORD was not willing to
destroy Judah. He had promised to maintain
a lamp for David and his descendants forever.

20In the time of Jehoram, Edom rebelled
against Judah and set up its own king. 21So
Jehoram[b] went to Zair with all his chariots.
The Edomites surrounded him and his chariot commanders, but he rose up and broke
through by night; his army, however, fled
back home. 22To this day Edom has been in
rebellion against Judah. Libnah revolted at
the same time.

23As for the other events of Jehoram's
reign, and all he did, are they not written in
the book of the annals of the kings of Judah?
24Jehoram rested with his fathers and was
buried with them in the City of David. And
Ahaziah his son succeeded him as king.

Ahaziah King of Judah

25In the twelfth year of Joram son of Ahab
king of Israel, Ahaziah son of Jehoram king
of Judah began to reign. 26Ahaziah was
twenty-two years old when he became king,
and he reigned in Jerusalem one year. His
mother's name was Athaliah, a granddaughter of Omri king of Israel. 27He walked in the
ways of the house of Ahab and did evil in the
eyes of the LORD, as the house of Ahab had
done, for he was related by marriage to
Ahab's family.

28Ahaziah went with Joram son of Ahab to
war against Hazael king of Aram at Ramoth
Gilead. The Arameans wounded Joram; 29so
King Joram returned to Jezreel to recover

[a]*10* The Hebrew may also be read *Go and say, 'You will certainly not recover,' for.* [b]*21* Hebrew *Joram,* a variant of *Jehoram;* also in verses 23 and 24

from the wounds the Arameans had inflicted
on him at Ramoth[a] in his battle with Hazael
king of Aram.
Then Ahaziah son of Jehoram king of
Judah went down to Jezreel to see Joram son of Ahab, because he had been
wounded.

Jehu Anointed King of Israel

9 The prophet Elisha summoned a man
from the company of the prophets and
said to him, "Tuck your cloak into your belt,
take this flask of oil with you and go to
Ramoth Gilead. 2When you get there, look
for Jehu son of Jehoshaphat, the son of Nimshi. Go to him, get him away from his companions and take him into an inner room.
3Then take the flask and pour the oil on his
head and declare, 'This is what the LORD
says: I anoint you king over Israel.' Then
open the door and run; don't delay!"
4So the young man, the prophet, went to
Ramoth Gilead. 5When he arrived, he found
the army officers sitting together. "I have a
message for you, commander," he said.
"For which of us?" asked Jehu.
"For you, commander," he replied.
6Jehu got up and went into the house.
Then the prophet poured the oil on Jehu's
head and declared, "This is what the LORD,
the God of Israel, says: 'I anoint you king
over the LORD's people Israel. 7You are to
destroy the house of Ahab your master, and
I will avenge the blood of my servants the
prophets and the blood of all the LORD's servants shed by Jezebel. 8The whole house of
Ahab will perish. I will cut off from Ahab every
last male in Israel—slave or free. 9I will make
the house of Ahab like the house of Jeroboam son of Nebat and like the house of
Baasha son of Ahijah. 10As for Jezebel, dogs
will devour her on the plot of ground at Jezreel, and no one will bury her.'" Then he
opened the door and ran.
11When Jehu went out to his fellow officers, one of them asked him, "Is everything
all right? Why did this madman come to
you?"
"You know the man and the sort of things
he says," Jehu replied.
12"That's not true!" they said. "Tell us."
Jehu said, "Here is what he told me: 'This
is what the LORD says: I anoint you king over
Israel.'"
13They hurried and took their cloaks and
spread them under him on the bare steps.
Then they blew the trumpet and shouted,
"Jehu is king!"

Jehu Kills Joram and Ahaziah

14So Jehu son of Jehoshaphat, the son of
Nimshi, conspired against Joram. (Now
Joram and all Israel had been defending
Ramoth Gilead against Hazael king of Aram,
15but King Joram[b] had returned to Jezreel to
recover from the wounds the Arameans had
inflicted on him in the battle with Hazael king
of Aram.) Jehu said, "If this is the way you
feel, don't let anyone slip out of the city to go
and tell the news in Jezreel." 16Then he got
into his chariot and rode to Jezreel, because
Joram was resting there and Ahaziah king of
Judah had gone down to see him.
17When the lookout standing on the tower
in Jezreel saw Jehu's troops approaching,
he called out, "I see some troops coming."
"Get a horseman," Joram ordered. "Send
him to meet them and ask, 'Do you come in
peace?'"
18The horseman rode off to meet Jehu and
said, "This is what the king says: 'Do you
come in peace?'"
"What do you have to do with peace?"
Jehu replied. "Fall in behind me."
The lookout reported, "The messenger
has reached them, but he isn't coming
back."
19So the king sent out a second horseman.
When he came to them he said, "This is what
the king says: 'Do you come in peace?'"
Jehu replied, "What do you have to do with
peace? Fall in behind me."
20The lookout reported, "He has reached
them, but he isn't coming back either. The
driving is like that of Jehu son of Nimshi—he
drives like a madman."
21"Hitch up my chariot," Joram ordered.
And when it was hitched up, Joram king of
Israel and Ahaziah king of Judah rode out,
each in his own chariot, to meet Jehu. They
met him at the plot of ground that had belonged to Naboth the Jezreelite. 22When
Joram saw Jehu he asked, "Have you come
in peace, Jehu?"
"How can there be peace," Jehu replied,
"as long as all the idolatry and witchcraft of
your mother Jezebel abound?"

[a]29 Hebrew *Ramah,* a variant of *Ramoth* [b]15 Hebrew *Jehoram,* a variant of *Joram;* also in verses 17 and 21-24.

23Joram turned about and fled, calling out
to Ahaziah, "Treachery, Ahaziah!"
24Then Jehu drew his bow and shot Joram
between the shoulders. The arrow pierced
his heart and he slumped down in his chariot.
25Jehu said to Bidkar, his chariot officer,
"Pick him up and throw him on the field that
belonged to Naboth the Jezreelite. Remember how you and I were riding together in
chariots behind Ahab his father when the
LORD made this prophecy about him: 26'Yesterday I saw the blood of Naboth and the
blood of his sons, declares the LORD, and I
will surely make you pay for it on this plot of
ground, declares the LORD.'[a] Now then, pick
him up and throw him on that plot, in accordance with the word of the LORD."
27When Ahaziah king of Judah saw what
had happened, he fled up the road to Beth
Haggan.[b] Jehu chased him, shouting, "Kill
him too!" They wounded him in his chariot on
the way up to Gur near Ibleam, but he escaped to Megiddo and died there. 28His servants took him by chariot to Jerusalem and
buried him with his fathers in his tomb in the
City of David. 29(In the eleventh year of
Joram son of Ahab, Ahaziah had become
king of Judah.)

Jezebel Killed

30Then Jehu went to Jezreel. When Jezebel heard about it, she painted her eyes,
arranged her hair and looked out of a window. 31As Jehu entered the gate, she asked,
"Have you come in peace, Zimri, you murderer of your master?"[c]
32He looked up at the window and called
out, "Who is on my side? Who?" Two or
three eunuchs looked down at him. 33"Throw
her down!" Jehu said. So they threw her
down, and some of her blood spattered the
wall and the horses as they trampled her
underfoot.
34Jehu went in and ate and drank. "Take
care of that cursed woman," he said, "and
bury her, for she was a king's daughter."
35But when they went out to bury her, they
found nothing except her skull, her feet and
her hands. 36They went back and told Jehu,
who said, "This is the word of the LORD that
he spoke through his servant Elijah the Tishbite: On the plot of ground at Jezreel dogs
will devour Jezebel's flesh.[d] 37Jezebel's
body will be like refuse on the ground in the
plot at Jezreel, so that no one will be able to
say, 'This is Jezebel.' "

Ahab's Family Killed

10 Now there were in Samaria seventy
sons of the house of Ahab. So Jehu
wrote letters and sent them to Samaria: to
the officials of Jezreel,[e] to the elders and to
the guardians of Ahab's children. He said,
2"As soon as this letter reaches you, since
your master's sons are with you and you
have chariots and horses, a fortified city and
weapons, 3choose the best and most worthy
of your master's sons and set him on his
father's throne. Then fight for your master's
house."
4But they were terrified and said, "If two
kings could not resist him, how can we?"
5So the palace administrator, the city governor, the elders and the guardians sent this
message to Jehu: "We are your servants
and we will do anything you say. We will not
appoint anyone as king; you do whatever
you think best."
6Then Jehu wrote them a second letter,
saying, "If you are on my side and will obey
me, take the heads of your master's sons
and come to me in Jezreel by this time tomorrow."
Now the royal princes, seventy of them,
were with the leading men of the city, who
were rearing them. 7When the letter arrived,
these men took the princes and slaughtered
all seventy of them. They put their heads in
baskets and sent them to Jehu in Jezreel.
8When the messenger arrived, he told Jehu,
"They have brought the heads of the
princes."
Then Jehu ordered, "Put them in two piles
at the entrance of the city gate until morning."
9The next morning Jehu went out. He
stood before all the people and said, "You
are innocent. It was I who conspired against
my master and killed him, but who killed all
these? 10Know then, that not a word the LORD
has spoken against the house of Ahab will
fail. The LORD has done what he promised
through his servant Elijah." 11So Jehu killed
everyone in Jezreel who remained of the
house of Ahab, as well as all his chief men,
his close friends and his priests, leaving him
no survivor.
12Jehu then set out and went toward Sa-

[a]26 See 1 Kings 21:19. [b]27 Or *fled by way of the garden house* [c]31 Or *"Did Zimri have peace, who murdered his master?"* [d]36 See 1 Kings 21:23. [e]1 Hebrew; some Septuagint manuscripts and Vulgate *of the city*

maria. At Beth Eked of the Shepherds, 13he met some relatives of Ahaziah king of Judah and asked, "Who are you?"

They said, "We are relatives of Ahaziah, and we have come down to greet the families of the king and of the queen mother."

14"Take them alive!" he ordered. So they took them alive and slaughtered them by the well of Beth Eked—forty-two men. He left no survivor.

15After he left there, he came upon Jehonadab son of Recab, who was on his way to meet him. Jehu greeted him and said, "Are you in accord with me, as I am with you?"

"I am," Jehonadab answered.

"If so," said Jehu, "give me your hand." So he did, and Jehu helped him up into the chariot. 16Jehu said, "Come with me and see my zeal for the LORD." Then he had him ride along in his chariot.

17When Jehu came to Samaria, he killed all who were left there of Ahab's family; he destroyed them, according to the word of the LORD spoken to Elijah.

Ministers of Baal Killed

18Then Jehu brought all the people together and said to them, "Ahab served Baal a little; Jehu will serve him much. 19Now summon all the prophets of Baal, all his ministers and all his priests. See that no one is missing, because I am going to hold a great sacrifice for Baal. Anyone who fails to come will no longer live." But Jehu was acting deceptively in order to destroy the ministers of Baal.

20Jehu said, "Call an assembly in honor of Baal." So they proclaimed it. 21Then he sent word throughout Israel, and all the ministers of Baal came; not one stayed away. They crowded into the temple of Baal until it was full from one end to the other. 22And Jehu said to the keeper of the wardrobe, "Bring robes for all the ministers of Baal." So he brought out robes for them.

23Then Jehu and Jehonadab son of Recab went into the temple of Baal. Jehu said to the ministers of Baal, "Look around and see that no servants of the LORD are here with you—only ministers of Baal." 24So they went in to make sacrifices and burnt offerings. Now Jehu had posted eighty men outside with this warning: "If one of you lets any of the men I am placing in your hands escape, it will be your life for his life."

25As soon as Jehu had finished making the burnt offering, he ordered the guards and officers: "Go in and kill them; let no one escape." So they cut them down with the sword. The guards and officers threw the bodies out and then entered the inner shrine of the temple of Baal. 26They brought the sacred stone out of the temple of Baal and burned it. 27They demolished the sacred stone of Baal and tore down the temple of Baal, and people have used it for a latrine to this day.

28So Jehu destroyed Baal worship in Israel. 29However, he did not turn away from the sins of Jeroboam son of Nebat, which he had caused Israel to commit—the worship of the golden calves at Bethel and Dan.

30The LORD said to Jehu, "Because you have done well in accomplishing what is right in my eyes and have done to the house of Ahab all I had in mind to do, your descendants will sit on the throne of Israel to the fourth generation." 31Yet Jehu was not careful to keep the law of the LORD, the God of Israel, with all his heart. He did not turn away from the sins of Jeroboam, which he had caused Israel to commit.

32In those days the LORD began to reduce the size of Israel. Hazael overpowered the Israelites throughout their territory 33east of the Jordan in all the land of Gilead (the region of Gad, Reuben and Manasseh), from Aroer by the Arnon Gorge through Gilead to Bashan.

34As for the other events of Jehu's reign, all he did, and all his achievements, are they not written in the book of the annals of the kings of Israel?

35Jehu rested with his fathers and was buried in Samaria. And Jehoahaz his son succeeded him as king. 36The time that Jehu reigned over Israel in Samaria was twenty-eight years.

Athaliah and Joash

11 When Athaliah the mother of Ahaziah saw that her son was dead, she proceeded to destroy the whole royal family. 2But Jehosheba, the daughter of King Jehoram[a] and sister of Ahaziah, took Joash son of Ahaziah and stole him away from among the royal princes, who were about to

[a]2 Hebrew *Joram,* a variant of *Jehoram*

be murdered. She put him and his nurse in a
bedroom to hide him from Athaliah; so he
was not killed. 3He remained hidden with his
nurse at the temple of the LORD for six years
while Athaliah ruled the land.
4In the seventh year Jehoiada sent for the
commanders of units of a hundred, the Carites and the guards and had them brought to
him at the temple of the LORD. He made a
covenant with them and put them under oath
at the temple of the LORD. Then he showed
them the king's son. 5He commanded them,
saying, "This is what you are to do: You who
are in the three companies that are going on
duty on the Sabbath—a third of you guarding
the royal palace, 6a third at the Sur Gate, and
a third at the gate behind the guard, who take
turns guarding the temple— 7and you who
are in the other two companies that normally
go off Sabbath duty are all to guard the temple for the king. 8Station yourselves around
the king, each man with his weapon in his
hand. Anyone who approaches your ranks[a]
must be put to death. Stay close to the king
wherever he goes."
9The commanders of units of a hundred
did just as Jehoiada the priest ordered. Each
one took his men—those who were going on
duty on the Sabbath and those who were
going off duty—and came to Jehoiada the
priest. 10Then he gave the commanders the
spears and shields that had belonged to
King David and that were in the temple of the
LORD. 11The guards, each with his weapon in
his hand, stationed themselves around the
king—near the altar and the temple, from the
south side to the north side of the temple.
12Jehoiada brought out the king's son and
put the crown on him; he presented him with
a copy of the covenant and proclaimed him
king. They anointed him, and the people
clapped their hands and shouted, "Long live
the king!"
13When Athaliah heard the noise made by
the guards and the people, she went to the
people at the temple of the LORD. 14She
looked and there was the king, standing by
the pillar, as the custom was. The officers
and the trumpeters were beside the king,
and all the people of the land were rejoicing
and blowing trumpets. Then Athaliah tore
her robes and called out, "Treason! Treason!"
15Jehoiada the priest ordered the commanders of units of a hundred, who were in
charge of the troops: "Bring her out between
the ranks[b] and put to the sword anyone who
follows her." For the priest had said, "She
must not be put to death in the temple of the
LORD." 16So they seized her as she reached
the place where the horses enter the palace
grounds, and there she was put to death.
17Jehoiada then made a covenant between the LORD and the king and people that
they would be the LORD's people. He also
made a covenant between the king and the
people. 18All the people of the land went to
the temple of Baal and tore it down. They
smashed the altars and idols to pieces and
killed Mattan the priest of Baal in front of the
altars.
Then Jehoiada the priest posted guards at
the temple of the LORD. 19He took with him the
commanders of hundreds, the Carites, the
guards and all the people of the land, and
together they brought the king down from the
temple of the LORD and went into the palace,
entering by way of the gate of the guards.
The king then took his place on the royal
throne, 20and all the people of the land rejoiced. And the city was quiet, because
Athaliah had been slain with the sword at the
palace.
21Joash[c] was seven years old when he
began to reign.

Joash Repairs the Temple

12 In the seventh year of Jehu, Joash[d]
became king, and he reigned in
Jerusalem forty years. His mother's name
was Zibiah; she was from Beersheba.
2Joash did what was right in the eyes of the
LORD all the years Jehoiada the priest instructed him. 3The high places, however,
were not removed; the people continued to
offer sacrifices and burn incense there.
4Joash said to the priests, "Collect all the
money that is brought as sacred offerings to
the temple of the LORD—the money collected
in the census, the money received from personal vows and the money brought voluntarily to the temple. 5Let every priest receive
the money from one of the treasurers, and let
it be used to repair whatever damage is
found in the temple."
6But by the twenty-third year of King Joash
the priests still had not repaired the temple.
7Therefore King Joash summoned Jehoiada

[a]8 Or *approaches the precincts* [b]15 Or *out from the precincts* [c]21 Hebrew *Jehoash,* a variant of *Joash*
[d]1 Hebrew *Jehoash,* a variant of *Joash*; also in verses 2, 4, 6, 7 and 18

the priest and the other priests and asked them, "Why aren't you repairing the damage done to the temple? Take no more money from your treasurers, but hand it over for repairing the temple." 8 The priests agreed that they would not collect any more money from the people and that they would not repair the temple themselves.

9 Jehoiada the priest took a chest and bored a hole in its lid. He placed it beside the altar, on the right side as one enters the temple of the LORD. The priests who guarded the entrance put into the chest all the money that was brought to the temple of the LORD. 10 Whenever they saw that there was a large amount of money in the chest, the royal secretary and the high priest came, counted the money that had been brought into the temple of the LORD and put it into bags. 11 When the amount had been determined, they gave the money to the men appointed to supervise the work on the temple. With it they paid those who worked on the temple of the LORD—the carpenters and builders, 12 the masons and stonecutters. They purchased timber and dressed stone for the repair of the temple of the LORD, and met all the other expenses of restoring the temple.

13 The money brought into the temple was not spent for making silver basins, wick trimmers, sprinkling bowls, trumpets or any other articles of gold or silver for the temple of the LORD; 14 it was paid to the workmen, who used it to repair the temple. 15 They did not require an accounting from those to whom they gave the money to pay the workers, because they acted with complete honesty. 16 The money from the guilt offerings and sin offerings was not brought into the temple of the LORD; it belonged to the priests.

17 About this time Hazael king of Aram went up and attacked Gath and captured it. Then he turned to attack Jerusalem. 18 But Joash king of Judah took all the sacred objects dedicated by his fathers—Jehoshaphat, Jehoram and Ahaziah, the kings of Judah—and the gifts he himself had dedicated and all the gold found in the treasuries of the temple of the LORD and of the royal palace, and he sent them to Hazael king of Aram, who then withdrew from Jerusalem.

19 As for the other events of the reign of Joash, and all he did, are they not written in the book of the annals of the kings of Judah? 20 His officials conspired against him and assassinated him at Beth Millo, on the road down to Silla. 21 The officials who murdered him were Jozabad son of Shimeath and Jehozabad son of Shomer. He died and was buried with his fathers in the City of David. And Amaziah his son succeeded him as king.

Jehoahaz King of Israel

13 In the twenty-third year of Joash son of Ahaziah king of Judah, Jehoahaz son of Jehu became king of Israel in Samaria, and he reigned seventeen years. 2 He did evil in the eyes of the LORD by following the sins of Jeroboam son of Nebat, which he had caused Israel to commit, and he did not turn away from them. 3 So the LORD's anger burned against Israel, and for a long time he kept them under the power of Hazael king of Aram and Ben-Hadad his son.

4 Then Jehoahaz sought the LORD's favor, and the LORD listened to him, for he saw how severely the king of Aram was oppressing Israel. 5 The LORD provided a deliverer for Israel, and they escaped from the power of Aram. So the Israelites lived in their own homes as they had before. 6 But they did not turn away from the sins of the house of Jeroboam, which he had caused Israel to commit; they continued in them. Also, the Asherah pole[a] remained standing in Samaria.

7 Nothing had been left of the army of Jehoahaz except fifty horsemen, ten chariots and ten thousand foot soldiers, for the king of Aram had destroyed the rest and made them like the dust at threshing time.

8 As for the other events of the reign of Jehoahaz, all he did and his achievements, are they not written in the book of the annals of the kings of Israel? 9 Jehoahaz rested with his fathers and was buried in Samaria. And Jehoash[b] his son succeeded him as king.

Jehoasn King of Israel

10 In the thirty-seventh year of Joash king of Judah, Jehoash son of Jehoahaz became king of Israel in Samaria, and he reigned sixteen years. 11 He did evil in the eyes of the LORD and did not turn away from any of the sins of Jeroboam son of Nebat, which he had

[a]6 That is, a symbol of the goddess Asherah; here and elsewhere in 2 Kings [b]9 Hebrew *Joash,* a variant of *Jehoash*; also in verses 12-14 and 25

caused Israel to commit; he continued in
them.
12 As for the other events of the reign of
Jehoash, all he did and his achievements,
including his war against Amaziah king of
Judah, are they not written in the book of the
annals of the kings of Israel? 13 Jehoash rested with his fathers, and Jeroboam succeeded him on the throne. Jehoash was buried in Samaria with the kings of Israel.
14 Now Elisha was suffering from the illness
from which he died. Jehoash king of Israel
went down to see him and wept over him.
"My father! My father!" he cried. "The chariots and horsemen of Israel!"
15 Elisha said, "Get a bow and some arrows," and he did so. 16 "Take the bow in your
hands," he said to the king of Israel. When
he had taken it, Elisha put his hands on the
king's hands.
17 "Open the east window," he said, and he
opened it. "Shoot!" Elisha said, and he shot.
"The LORD's arrow of victory, the arrow of
victory over Aram!" Elisha declared. "You
will completely destroy the Arameans at
Aphek."
18 Then he said, "Take the arrows," and the
king took them. Elisha told him, "Strike the
ground." He struck it three times and
stopped. 19 The man of God was angry with
him and said, "You should have struck the
ground five or six times; then you would have
defeated Aram and completely destroyed
it. But now you will defeat it only three
times."
20 Elisha died and was buried.
Now Moabite raiders used to enter the
country every spring. 21 Once while some Israelites were burying a man, suddenly they
saw a band of raiders; so they threw the
man's body into Elisha's tomb. When the
body touched Elisha's bones, the man came
to life and stood up on his feet.
22 Hazael king of Aram oppressed Israel
throughout the reign of Jehoahaz. 23 But the
LORD was gracious to them and had compassion and showed concern for them because
of his covenant with Abraham, Isaac and
Jacob. To this day he has been unwilling to
destroy them or banish them from his presence.
24 Hazael king of Aram died, and Ben-
Hadad his son succeeded him as king.
25 Then Jehoash son of Jehoahaz recaptured
from Ben-Hadad son of Hazael the towns he
had taken in battle from his father Jehoahaz.
Three times Jehoash defeated him, and so
he recovered the Israelite towns.

Amaziah King of Judah

14 In the second year of Jehoash[a] son
of Jehoahaz king of Israel, Amaziah
son of Joash king of Judah began to reign.
2 He was twenty-five years old when he
became king, and he reigned in Jerusalem
twenty-nine years. His mother's name was
Jehoaddin; she was from Jerusalem. 3 He did
what was right in the eyes of the LORD, but not
as his father David had done. In everything
he followed the example of his father Joash.
4 The high places, however, were not removed; the people continued to offer sacrifices and burn incense there.
5 After the kingdom was firmly in his grasp,
he executed the officials who had murdered
his father the king. 6 Yet he did not put the
sons of the assassins to death, in accordance with what is written in the Book of the
Law of Moses where the LORD commanded:
"Fathers shall not be put to death for their
children, nor children put to death for their
fathers; each is to die for his own sins."[b]
7 He was the one who defeated ten thousand Edomites in the Valley of Salt and captured Sela in battle, calling it Joktheel, the
name it has to this day.
8 Then Amaziah sent messengers to Jehoash son of Jehoahaz, the son of Jehu,
king of Israel, with the challenge: "Come,
meet me face to face."
9 But Jehoash king of Israel replied to Amaziah king of Judah: "A thistle in Lebanon sent
a message to a cedar in Lebanon, 'Give your
daughter to my son in marriage.' Then a wild
beast in Lebanon came along and trampled
the thistle underfoot. 10 You have indeed defeated Edom and now you are arrogant.
Glory in your victory, but stay at home! Why
ask for trouble and cause your own downfall
and that of Judah also?"
11 Amaziah, however, would not listen, so
Jehoash king of Israel attacked. He and
Amaziah king of Judah faced each other at
Beth Shemesh in Judah. 12 Judah was routed
by Israel, and every man fled to his home.
13 Jehoash king of Israel captured Amaziah
king of Judah, the son of Joash, the son of
Ahaziah, at Beth Shemesh. Then Jehoash
went to Jerusalem and broke down the wall

[a] 1 Hebrew *Joash,* a variant of *Jehoash*; also in verses 13, 23 and 27 [b] 6 Deut. 24:16

of Jerusalem from the Ephraim Gate to the
Corner Gate—a section about six hundred
feet long.[a] 14He took all the gold and silver
and all the articles found in the temple of the
LORD and in the treasuries of the royal palace. He also took hostages and returned to
Samaria.

15As for the other events of the reign of
Jehoash, what he did and his achievements,
including his war against Amaziah king of
Judah, are they not written in the book of the
annals of the kings of Israel? 16Jehoash rested with his fathers and was buried in Samaria with the kings of Israel. And Jeroboam
his son succeeded him as king.

17Amaziah son of Joash king of Judah
lived for fifteen years after the death of Jehoash son of Jehoahaz king of Israel. 18As
for the other events of Amaziah's reign, are
they not written in the book of the annals of
the kings of Judah?

19They conspired against him in Jerusalem, and he fled to Lachish, but they sent
men after him to Lachish and killed him
there. 20He was brought back by horse and
was buried in Jerusalem with his fathers, in
the City of David.

21Then all the people of Judah took Azariah,[b] who was sixteen years old, and made
him king in place of his father Amaziah. 22He
was the one who rebuilt Elath and restored it
to Judah after Amaziah rested with his fathers.

Jeroboam II King of Israel

23In the fifteenth year of Amaziah son of
Joash king of Judah, Jeroboam son of Jehoash king of Israel became king in Samaria,
and he reigned forty-one years. 24He did evil
in the eyes of the LORD and did not turn away
from any of the sins of Jeroboam son of
Nebat, which he had caused Israel to commit. 25He was the one who restored the
boundaries of Israel from Lebo[c] Hamath to
the Sea of the Arabah,[d] in accordance with
the word of the LORD, the God of Israel,
spoken through his servant Jonah son of
Amittai, the prophet from Gath Hepher.

26The LORD had seen how bitterly everyone
in Israel, whether slave or free, was suffering; there was no one to help them. 27And
since the LORD had not said he would blot out
the name of Israel from under heaven, he
saved them by the hand of Jeroboam son of
Jehoash.

28As for the other events of Jeroboam's
reign, all he did, and his military achievements, including how he recovered for Israel
both Damascus and Hamath, which had belonged to Yaudi,[e] are they not written in the
book of the annals of the kings of Israel?
29Jeroboam rested with his fathers, the kings
of Israel. And Zechariah his son succeeded
him as king.

Azariah King of Judah

15 In the twenty-seventh year of Jeroboam king of Israel, Azariah son of
Amaziah king of Judah began to reign. 2He
was sixteen years old when he became king,
and he reigned in Jerusalem fifty-two years.
His mother's name was Jecoliah; she was
from Jerusalem. 3He did what was right in
the eyes of the LORD, just as his father Amaziah had done. 4The high places, however,
were not removed; the people continued to
offer sacrifices and burn incense there.

5The LORD afflicted the king with leprosy[f]
until the day he died, and he lived in a separate house.[g] Jotham the king's son had
charge of the palace and governed the
people of the land.

6As for the other events of Azariah's reign,
and all he did, are they not written in the book
of the annals of the kings of Judah? 7Azariah
rested with his fathers and was buried near
them in the City of David. And Jotham his
son succeeded him as king.

Zechariah King of Israel

8In the thirty-eighth year of Azariah king of
Judah, Zechariah son of Jeroboam became
king of Israel in Samaria, and he reigned six
months. 9He did evil in the eyes of the LORD,
as his fathers had done. He did not turn away
from the sins of Jeroboam son of Nebat,
which he had caused Israel to commit.

10Shallum son of Jabesh conspired
against Zechariah. He attacked him in front
of the people,[h] assassinated him and succeeded him as king. 11The other events of
Zechariah's reign are written in the book of
the annals of the kings of Israel. 12So the
word of the LORD spoken to Jehu was fulfilled:
"Your descendants will sit on the throne of
Israel to the fourth generation."[i]

[a]*13* Hebrew *four hundred cubits* (about 180 meters) [b]*21* Also called *Uzziah* [c]*25* Or *from the entrance to* [d]*25* That is, the Dead Sea [e]*28* Or *Judah* [f]*5* The Hebrew word was used for various diseases affecting the skin—not necessarily leprosy. [g]*5* Or *in a house where he was relieved of responsibility* [h]*10* Hebrew; some Septuagint manuscripts *in Ibleam* [i]*12* 2 Kings 10:30

Shallum King of Israel

13Shallum son of Jabesh became king in the thirty-ninth year of Uzziah king of Judah, and he reigned in Samaria one month. 14Then Menahem son of Gadi went from Tirzah up to Samaria. He attacked Shallum son of Jabesh in Samaria, assassinated him and succeeded him as king.

15The other events of Shallum's reign, and the conspiracy he led, are written in the book of the annals of the kings of Israel.

16At that time Menahem, starting out from Tirzah, attacked Tiphsah and everyone in the city and its vicinity, because they refused to open their gates. He sacked Tiphsah and ripped open all the pregnant women.

Menahem King of Israel

17In the thirty-ninth year of Azariah king of Judah, Menahem son of Gadi became king of Israel, and he reigned in Samaria ten years. 18He did evil in the eyes of the LORD. During his entire reign he did not turn away from the sins of Jeroboam son of Nebat, which he had caused Israel to commit.

19Then Pul[a] king of Assyria invaded the land, and Menahem gave him a thousand talents[b] of silver to gain his support and strengthen his own hold on the kingdom. 20Menahem exacted this money from Israel. Every wealthy man had to contribute fifty shekels[c] of silver to be given to the king of Assyria. So the king of Assyria withdrew and stayed in the land no longer.

21As for the other events of Menahem's reign, and all he did, are they not written in the book of the annals of the kings of Israel? 22Menahem rested with his fathers. And Pekahiah his son succeeded him as king.

Pekahiah King of Israel

23In the fiftieth year of Azariah king of Judah, Pekahiah son of Menahem became king of Israel in Samaria, and he reigned two years. 24Pekahiah did evil in the eyes of the LORD. He did not turn away from the sins of Jeroboam son of Nebat, which he had caused Israel to commit. 25One of his chief officers, Pekah son of Remaliah, conspired against him. Taking fifty men of Gilead with him, he assassinated Pekahiah, along with Argob and Arieh, in the citadel of the royal palace at Samaria. So Pekah killed Pekahiah and succeeded him as king.

26The other events of Pekahiah's reign, and all he did, are written in the book of the annals of the kings of Israel.

Pekah King of Israel

27In the fifty-second year of Azariah king of Judah, Pekah son of Remaliah became king of Israel in Samaria, and he reigned twenty years. 28He did evil in the eyes of the LORD. He did not turn away from the sins of Jeroboam son of Nebat, which he had caused Israel to commit.

29In the time of Pekah king of Israel, Tiglath-Pileser king of Assyria came and took Ijon, Abel Beth Maacah, Janoah, Kedesh and Hazor. He took Gilead and Galilee, including all the land of Naphtali, and deported the people to Assyria. 30Then Hoshea son of Elah conspired against Pekah son of Remaliah. He attacked and assassinated him, and then succeeded him as king in the twentieth year of Jotham son of Uzziah.

31As for the other events of Pekah's reign, and all he did, are they not written in the book of the annals of the kings of Israel?

Jotham King of Judah

32In the second year of Pekah son of Remaliah king of Israel, Jotham son of Uzziah king of Judah began to reign. 33He was twenty-five years old when he became king, and he reigned in Jerusalem sixteen years. His mother's name was Jerusha daughter of Zadok. 34He did what was right in the eyes of the LORD, just as his father Uzziah had done. 35The high places, however, were not removed; the people continued to offer sacrifices and burn incense there. Jotham rebuilt the Upper Gate of the temple of the LORD.

36As for the other events of Jotham's reign, and what he did, are they not written in the book of the annals of the kings of Judah? 37(In those days the LORD began to send Rezin king of Aram and Pekah son of Remaliah against Judah.) 38Jotham rested with his fathers and was buried with them in the City of David, the city of his father. And Ahaz his son succeeded him as king.

Ahaz King of Judah

16 In the seventeenth year of Pekah son of Remaliah, Ahaz son of Jotham king of Judah began to reign. 2Ahaz was twenty years old when he became king, and

[a]*19* Also called *Tiglath-Pileser* [b]*19* That is, about 37 tons (about 34 metric tons) [c]*20* That is, about 1 1/4 pounds (about 0.6 kilogram)

he reigned in Jerusalem sixteen years. Unlike David his father, he did not do what was
right in the eyes of the LORD his God. 3He
walked in the ways of the kings of Israel and
even sacrificed his son in[a] the fire, following
the detestable ways of the nations the LORD
had driven out before the Israelites. 4He offered sacrifices and burned incense at the
high places, on the hilltops and under every
spreading tree.

5Then Rezin king of Aram and Pekah son
of Remaliah king of Israel marched up to
fight against Jerusalem and besieged Ahaz,
but they could not overpower him. 6At that
time, Rezin king of Aram recovered Elath for
Aram by driving out the men of Judah.
Edomites then moved into Elath and have
lived there to this day.

7Ahaz sent messengers to say to Tiglath-
Pileser king of Assyria, "I am your servant
and vassal. Come up and save me out of the
hand of the king of Aram and of the king of
Israel, who are attacking me." 8And Ahaz
took the silver and gold found in the temple of
the LORD and in the treasuries of the royal
palace and sent it as a gift to the king of
Assyria. 9The king of Assyria complied by
attacking Damascus and capturing it. He deported its inhabitants to Kir and put Rezin to
death.

10Then King Ahaz went to Damascus to
meet Tiglath-Pileser king of Assyria. He saw
an altar in Damascus and sent to Uriah the
priest a sketch of the altar, with detailed
plans for its construction. 11So Uriah the
priest built an altar in accordance with all the
plans that King Ahaz had sent from Damascus and finished it before King Ahaz returned. 12When the king came back from
Damascus and saw the altar, he approached
it and presented offerings[b] on it. 13He offered
up his burnt offering and grain offering,
poured out his drink offering, and sprinkled
the blood of his fellowship offerings[c] on the
altar. 14The bronze altar that stood before the
LORD he brought from the front of the temple—from between the new altar and the
temple of the LORD—and put it on the north
side of the new altar.

15King Ahaz then gave these orders to
Uriah the priest: "On the large new altar,
offer the morning burnt offering and the evening grain offering, the king's burnt offering
and his grain offering, and the burnt offering
of all the people of the land, and their grain
offering and their drink offering. Sprinkle on
the altar all the blood of the burnt offerings
and sacrifices. But I will use the bronze altar
for seeking guidance." 16And Uriah the priest
did just as King Ahaz had ordered.

17King Ahaz took away the side panels and
removed the basins from the movable
stands. He removed the Sea from the bronze
bulls that supported it and set it on a stone
base. 18He took away the Sabbath canopy[d]
that had been built at the temple and removed the royal entryway outside the temple
of the LORD, in deference to the king of Assyria.

19As for the other events of the reign of
Ahaz, and what he did, are they not written in
the book of the annals of the kings of Judah?
20Ahaz rested with his fathers and was buried with them in the City of David. And Hezekiah his son succeeded him as king.

Hoshea Last King of Israel

17 In the twelfth year of Ahaz king of
Judah, Hoshea son of Elah became
king of Israel in Samaria, and he reigned
nine years. 2He did evil in the eyes of the
LORD, but not like the kings of Israel who
preceded him.

3Shalmaneser king of Assyria came up to
attack Hoshea, who had been Shalmaneser's vassal and had paid him tribute. 4But
the king of Assyria discovered that Hoshea
was a traitor, for he had sent envoys to So[e]
king of Egypt, and he no longer paid tribute to
the king of Assyria, as he had done year by
year. Therefore Shalmaneser seized him
and put him in prison. 5The king of Assyria
invaded the entire land, marched against Samaria and laid siege to it for three years. 6In
the ninth year of Hoshea, the king of Assyria
captured Samaria and deported the Israelites to Assyria. He settled them in Halah, in
Gozan on the Habor River and in the towns
of the Medes.

Israel Exiled Because of Sin

7All this took place because the Israelites
had sinned against the LORD their God, who
had brought them up out of Egypt from under
the power of Pharaoh king of Egypt. They
worshiped other gods 8and followed the
practices of the nations the LORD had driven
out before them, as well as the practices that

[a]3 Or *even made his son pass through* [b]12 Or *and went up* [c]13 Traditionally *peace offerings*
[d]18 Or *the dais of his throne* (see Septuagint) [e]4 Or *to Sais, to the; So* is possibly an abbreviation for
Osorkon.

the kings of Israel had introduced. 9The Israelites secretly did things against the LORD
their God that were not right. From watchtower to fortified city they built themselves
high places in all their towns. 10They set up
sacred stones and Asherah poles on every
high hill and under every spreading tree. 11At
every high place they burned incense, as the
nations whom the LORD had driven out before
them had done. They did wicked things that
provoked the LORD to anger. 12They worshiped idols, though the LORD had said, "You
shall not do this."[a] 13The LORD warned Israel
and Judah through all his prophets and
seers: "Turn from your evil ways. Observe
my commands and decrees, in accordance
with the entire Law that I commanded your
fathers to obey and that I delivered to you
through my servants the prophets."

14But they would not listen and were as
stiff-necked as their fathers, who did not trust
in the LORD their God. 15They rejected his
decrees and the covenant he had made with
their fathers and the warnings he had given
them. They followed worthless idols and
themselves became worthless. They imitat-
ed the nations around them although the
LORD had ordered them, "Do not do as they
do," and they did the things the LORD had
forbidden them to do.

16They forsook all the commands of the
LORD their God and made for themselves two
idols cast in the shape of calves, and an
Asherah pole. They bowed down to all the
starry hosts, and they worshiped Baal.
17They sacrificed their sons and daughters
in[b] the fire. They practiced divination and
sorcery and sold themselves to do evil in the
eyes of the LORD, provoking him to anger.

18So the LORD was very angry with Israel
and removed them from his presence. Only
the tribe of Judah was left, 19and even Judah
did not keep the commands of the LORD their
God. They followed the practices Israel had
introduced. 20Therefore the LORD rejected all
the people of Israel; he afflicted them and
gave them into the hands of plunderers, until
he thrust them from his presence.

21When he tore Israel away from the house
of David, they made Jeroboam son of Nebat
their king. Jeroboam enticed Israel away
from following the LORD and caused them to
commit a great sin. 22The Israelites persisted
in all the sins of Jeroboam and did not turn
away from them 23until the LORD removed
them from his presence, as he had warned
through all his servants the prophets. So the
people of Israel were taken from their homeland into exile in Assyria, and they are still
there.

Samaria Resettled

24The king of Assyria brought people from
Babylon, Cuthah, Avva, Hamath and Sepharvaim and settled them in the towns of Samaria to replace the Israelites. They took
over Samaria and lived in its towns. 25When
they first lived there, they did not worship the
LORD; so he sent lions among them and they
killed some of the people. 26It was reported to
the king of Assyria: "The people you deported and resettled in the towns of Samaria do
not know what the god of that country requires. He has sent lions among them, which
are killing them off, because the people do
not know what he requires."

27Then the king of Assyria gave this order:
"Have one of the priests you took captive
from Samaria go back to live there and teach
the people what the god of the land requires." 28So one of the priests who had
been exiled from Samaria came to live in
Bethel and taught them how to worship the
LORD.

29Nevertheless, each national group made
its own gods in the several towns where they
settled, and set them up in the shrines the
people of Samaria had made at the high
places. 30The men from Babylon made Succoth Benoth, the men from Cuthah made
Nergal, and the men from Hamath made
Ashima; 31the Avvites made Nibhaz and Tar-
tak, and the Sepharvites burned their children in the fire as sacrifices to Adrammelech
and Anammelech, the gods of Sepharvaim.
32They worshiped the LORD, but they also
appointed all sorts of their own people to
officiate for them as priests in the shrines at
the high places. 33They worshiped the LORD,
but they also served their own gods in accordance with the customs of the nations from
which they had been brought.

34To this day they persist in their former
practices. They neither worship the LORD nor
adhere to the decrees and ordinances, the
laws and commands that the LORD gave the
descendants of Jacob, whom he named Israel. 35When the LORD made a covenant with
the Israelites, he commanded them: "Do not
worship any other gods or bow down to

[a]12 Exodus 20:4, 5 [b]17 Or *They made their sons and daughters pass through*

them, serve them or sacrifice to them. 36But the LORD, who brought you up out of Egypt with mighty power and outstretched arm, is the one you must worship. To him you shall bow down and to him offer sacrifices. 37You must always be careful to keep the decrees and ordinances, the laws and commands he wrote for you. Do not worship other gods. 38Do not forget the covenant I have made with you, and do not worship other gods. 39Rather, worship the LORD your God; it is he who will deliver you from the hand of all your enemies."

40They would not listen, however, but persisted in their former practices. 41Even while these people were worshiping the LORD, they were serving their idols. To this day their children and grandchildren continue to do as their fathers did.

Hezekiah King of Judah

18 In the third year of Hoshea son of Elah king of Israel, Hezekiah son of Ahaz king of Judah began to reign. 2He was twenty-five years old when he became king, and he reigned in Jerusalem twenty-nine years. His mother's name was Abijah[a] daughter of Zechariah. 3He did what was right in the eyes of the LORD, just as his father David had done. 4He removed the high places, smashed the sacred stones and cut down the Asherah poles. He broke into pieces the bronze snake Moses had made, for up to that time the Israelites had been burning incense to it. (It was called[b] Nehushtan.[c])

5Hezekiah trusted in the LORD, the God of Israel. There was no one like him among all the kings of Judah, either before him or after him. 6He held fast to the LORD and did not cease to follow him; he kept the commands the LORD had given Moses. 7And the LORD was with him; he was successful in whatever he undertook. He rebelled against the king of Assyria and did not serve him. 8From watchtower to fortified city, he defeated the Philistines, as far as Gaza and its territory.

9In King Hezekiah's fourth year, which was the seventh year of Hoshea son of Elah king of Israel, Shalmaneser king of Assyria marched against Samaria and laid siege to it. 10At the end of three years the Assyrians took it. So Samaria was captured in Hezekiah's sixth year, which was the ninth year of Hoshea king of Israel. 11The king of Assyria deported Israel to Assyria and settled them in Halah, in Gozan on the Habor River and in towns of the Medes. 12This happened because they had not obeyed the LORD their God, but had violated his covenant—all that Moses the servant of the LORD commanded. They neither listened to the commands nor carried them out.

13In the fourteenth year of King Hezekiah's reign, Sennacherib king of Assyria attacked all the fortified cities of Judah and captured them. 14So Hezekiah king of Judah sent this message to the king of Assyria at Lachish: "I have done wrong. Withdraw from me, and I will pay whatever you demand of me." The king of Assyria exacted from Hezekiah king of Judah three hundred talents[d] of silver and thirty talents[e] of gold. 15So Hezekiah gave him all the silver that was found in the temple of the LORD and in the treasuries of the royal palace.

16At this time Hezekiah king of Judah stripped off the gold with which he had covered the doors and doorposts of the temple of the LORD, and gave it to the king of Assyria.

Sennacherib Threatens Jerusalem

17The king of Assyria sent his supreme commander, his chief officer and his field commander with a large army, from Lachish to King Hezekiah at Jerusalem. They came up to Jerusalem and stopped at the aqueduct of the Upper Pool, on the road to the Washerman's Field. 18They called for the king; and Eliakim son of Hilkiah the palace administrator, Shebna the secretary, and Joah son of Asaph the recorder went out to them.

19The field commander said to them, "Tell Hezekiah:

"'This is what the great king, the king of Assyria, says: On what are you basing this confidence of yours? 20You say you have strategy and military strength—but you speak only empty words. On whom are you depending, that you rebel against me? 21Look now, you are depending on Egypt, that splintered reed of a staff, which pierces a man's hand and wounds him if he leans on it! Such is Pharaoh king of Egypt to

[a]2 Hebrew *Abi*, a variant of *Abijah* [b]4 Or *He called it* [c]4 *Nehushtan* sounds like the Hebrew for *bronze* and *snake* and *unclean thing.* [d]14 That is, about 11 tons (about 10 metric tons) [e]14 That is, about 1 ton (about 1 metric ton)

all who depend on him. 22And if you say to me, "We are depending on the LORD our God"—isn't he the one whose high places and altars Hezekiah removed, saying to Judah and Jerusalem, "You must worship before this altar in Jerusalem"?

23" 'Come now, make a bargain with my master, the king of Assyria: I will give you two thousand horses—if you can put riders on them! 24How can you repulse one officer of the least of my master's officials, even though you are depending on Egypt for chariots and horsemen[a]? 25Furthermore, have I come to attack and destroy this place without word from the LORD? The LORD himself told me to march against this country and destroy it.' "

26Then Eliakim son of Hilkiah, and Shebna and Joah said to the field commander, "Please speak to your servants in Aramaic, since we understand it. Don't speak to us in Hebrew in the hearing of the people on the wall."

27But the commander replied, "Was it only to your master and you that my master sent me to say these things, and not to the men sitting on the wall—who, like you, will have to eat their own filth and drink their own urine?"

28Then the commander stood and called out in Hebrew: "Hear the word of the great king, the king of Assyria! 29This is what the king says: Do not let Hezekiah deceive you. He cannot deliver you from my hand. 30Do not let Hezekiah persuade you to trust in the LORD when he says, 'The LORD will surely deliver us; this city will not be given into the hand of the king of Assyria.'

31"Do not listen to Hezekiah. This is what the king of Assyria says: Make peace with me and come out to me. Then every one of you will eat from his own vine and fig tree and drink water from his own cistern, 32until I come and take you to a land like your own, a land of grain and new wine, a land of bread and vineyards, a land of olive trees and honey. Choose life and not death!

"Do not listen to Hezekiah, for he is misleading you when he says, 'The LORD will deliver us.' 33Has the god of any nation ever delivered his land from the hand of the king of Assyria? 34Where are the gods of Hamath and Arpad? Where are the gods of Sepharvaim, Hena and Ivvah? Have they rescued Samaria from my hand? 35Who of all the gods of these countries has been able to save his land from me? How then can the LORD deliver Jerusalem from my hand?"

36But the people remained silent and said nothing in reply, because the king had commanded, "Do not answer him."

37Then Eliakim son of Hilkiah the palace administrator, Shebna the secretary and Joah son of Asaph the recorder went to Hezekiah, with their clothes torn, and told him what the field commander had said.

Jerusalem's Deliverance Foretold

19 When King Hezekiah heard this, he tore his clothes and put on sackcloth and went into the temple of the LORD. 2He sent Eliakim the palace administrator, Shebna the secretary and the leading priests, all wearing sackcloth, to the prophet Isaiah son of Amoz. 3They told him, "This is what Hezekiah says: This day is a day of distress and rebuke and disgrace, as when children come to the point of birth and there is no strength to deliver them. 4It may be that the LORD your God will hear all the words of the field commander, whom his master, the king of Assyria, has sent to ridicule the living God, and that he will rebuke him for the words the LORD your God has heard. Therefore pray for the remnant that still survives."

5When King Hezekiah's officials came to Isaiah, 6Isaiah said to them, "Tell your master, 'This is what the LORD says: Do not be afraid of what you have heard—those words with which the underlings of the king of Assyria have blasphemed me. 7Listen! I am going to put such a spirit in him that when he hears a certain report, he will return to his own country, and there I will have him cut down with the sword.' "

8When the field commander heard that the king of Assyria had left Lachish, he withdrew and found the king fighting against Libnah.

9Now Sennacherib received a report that Tirhakah, the Cushite[b] king ⌞of Egypt⌟, was marching out to fight against him. So he again sent messengers to Hezekiah with this word: 10"Say to Hezekiah king of Judah: Do not let the god you depend on deceive you when he says, 'Jerusalem will not be handed over to the king of Assyria.' 11Surely you have heard what the kings of Assyria have done to all the countries, destroying them completely. And will you be delivered? 12Did

a24 Or *charioteers* b9 That is, from the upper Nile region

the gods of the nations that were destroyed
by my forefathers deliver them: the gods of
Gozan, Haran, Rezeph and the people of
Eden who were in Tel Assar? 13 Where is the
king of Hamath, the king of Arpad, the king of
the city of Sepharvaim, or of Hena or Ivvah?"

Hezekiah's Prayer

14 Hezekiah received the letter from the
messengers and read it. Then he went up to
the temple of the Lord and spread it out before the Lord. 15 And Hezekiah prayed to the
Lord: "O Lord, God of Israel, enthroned between the cherubim, you alone are God over
all the kingdoms of the earth. You have
made heaven and earth. 16 Give ear, O Lord,
and hear; open your eyes, O Lord, and see;
listen to the words Sennacherib has sent to
insult the living God.

17 "It is true, O Lord, that the Assyrian kings
have laid waste these nations and their
lands. 18 They have thrown their gods into the
fire and destroyed them, for they were not
gods but only wood and stone, fashioned by
men's hands. 19 Now, O Lord our God, deliver us from his hand, so that all kingdoms
on earth may know that you alone, O Lord,
are God."

Isaiah Prophesies Sennacherib's Fall

20 Then Isaiah son of Amoz sent a message to Hezekiah: "This is what the Lord, the
God of Israel, says: I have heard your prayer
concerning Sennacherib king of Assyria.
21 This is the word that the Lord has spoken
against him:

" 'The Virgin Daughter of Zion
despises you and mocks you.
The Daughter of Jerusalem
tosses her head as you flee.
22 Who is it you have insulted and
blasphemed?
Against whom have you raised your
voice
and lifted your eyes in pride?
Against the Holy One of Israel!
23 By your messengers
you have heaped insults on the Lord.
And you have said,
"With my many chariots
I have ascended the heights of the
mountains,
the utmost heights of Lebanon.
I have cut down its tallest cedars,
the choicest of its pines.
I have reached its remotest parts,
the finest of its forests.
24 I have dug wells in foreign lands
and drunk the water there.
With the soles of my feet
I have dried up all the streams of
Egypt."

25 " 'Have you not heard?
Long ago I ordained it.
In days of old I planned it;
now I have brought it to pass,
that you have turned fortified cities
into piles of stone.
26 Their people, drained of power,
are dismayed and put to shame.
They are like plants in the field,
like tender green shoots,
like grass sprouting on the roof,
scorched before it grows up.

27 " 'But I know where you stay
and when you come and go
and how you rage against me.
28 Because you rage against me
and your insolence has reached my
ears,
I will put my hook in your nose
and my bit in your mouth,
and I will make you return
by the way you came.'

29 "This will be the sign for you, O Hezekiah:

"This year you will eat what grows by
itself,
and the second year what springs from
that.
But in the third year sow and reap,
plant vineyards and eat their fruit.
30 Once more a remnant of the house of
Judah
will take root below and bear fruit
above.
31 For out of Jerusalem will come a
remnant,
and out of Mount Zion a band of
survivors.

The zeal of the Lord Almighty will accomplish
this.

32 "Therefore this is what the Lord says
concerning the king of Assyria:

"He will not enter this city
or shoot an arrow here.
He will not come before it with shield
or build a siege ramp against it.
33 By the way that he came he will return;

he will not enter this city,
declares the LORD.
34I will defend this city and save it,
for my sake and for the sake of David
my servant."

35That night the angel of the LORD went out
and put to death a hundred and eighty-five
thousand men in the Assyrian camp. When
the people got up the next morning—there
were all the dead bodies! 36So Sennacherib
king of Assyria broke camp and withdrew.
He returned to Nineveh and stayed there.
37One day, while he was worshiping in the
temple of his god Nisroch, his sons Adrammelech and Sharezer cut him down with the
sword, and they escaped to the land of Ararat. And Esarhaddon his son succeeded him
as king.

Hezekiah's Illness

20 In those days Hezekiah became ill
and was at the point of death. The
prophet Isaiah son of Amoz went to him and
said, "This is what the LORD says: Put your
house in order, because you are going to die;
you will not recover."
2Hezekiah turned his face to the wall and
prayed to the LORD, 3"Remember, O LORD,
how I have walked before you faithfully and
with wholehearted devotion and have done
what is good in your eyes." And Hezekiah
wept bitterly.
4Before Isaiah had left the middle court,
the word of the LORD came to him: 5"Go back
and tell Hezekiah, the leader of my people,
'This is what the LORD, the God of your father
David, says: I have heard your prayer and
seen your tears; I will heal you. On the third
day from now you will go up to the temple of
the LORD. 6I will add fifteen years to your life.
And I will deliver you and this city from the
hand of the king of Assyria. I will defend this
city for my sake and for the sake of my servant David.' "
7Then Isaiah said, "Prepare a poultice of
figs." They did so and applied it to the boil,
and he recovered.
8Hezekiah had asked Isaiah, "What will be
the sign that the LORD will heal me and that I
will go up to the temple of the LORD on the
third day from now?"
9Isaiah answered, "This is the LORD's sign
to you that the LORD will do what he has
promised: Shall the shadow go forward ten
steps, or shall it go back ten steps?"
10"It is a simple matter for the shadow to go
forward ten steps," said Hezekiah. "Rather,
have it go back ten steps."
11Then the prophet Isaiah called upon the
LORD, and the LORD made the shadow go
back the ten steps it had gone down on the
stairway of Ahaz.

Envoys From Babylon

12At that time Merodach-Baladan son of
Baladan king of Babylon sent Hezekiah letters and a gift, because he had heard of
Hezekiah's illness. 13Hezekiah received the
messengers and showed them all that was in
his storehouses—the silver, the gold, the
spices and the fine oil—his armory and
everything found among his treasures.
There was nothing in his palace or in all his
kingdom that Hezekiah did not show them.
14Then Isaiah the prophet went to King
Hezekiah and asked, "What did those men
say, and where did they come from?"
"From a distant land," Hezekiah replied.
"They came from Babylon."
15The prophet asked, "What did they see
in your palace?"
"They saw everything in my palace,"
Hezekiah said. "There is nothing among my
treasures that I did not show them."
16Then Isaiah said to Hezekiah, "Hear the
word of the LORD: 17The time will surely come
when everything in your palace, and all that
your fathers have stored up until this day, will
be carried off to Babylon. Nothing will be left,
says the LORD. 18And some of your descendants, your own flesh and blood, that will be
born to you, will be taken away, and they will
become eunuchs in the palace of the king of
Babylon."
19"The word of the LORD you have spoken
is good," Hezekiah replied. For he thought,
"Will there not be peace and security in my
lifetime?"
20As for the other events of Hezekiah's
reign, all his achievements and how he
made the pool and the tunnel by which he
brought water into the city, are they not written in the book of the annals of the kings of
Judah? 21Hezekiah rested with his fathers.
And Manasseh his son succeeded him as
king.

Manasseh King of Judah

21 Manasseh was twelve years old
when he became king, and he
reigned in Jerusalem fifty-five years. His
mother's name was Hephzibah. 2He did evil

in the eyes of the LORD, following the detestable practices of the nations the LORD had driven out before the Israelites. 3He rebuilt the high places his father Hezekiah had destroyed; he also erected altars to Baal and made an Asherah pole, as Ahab king of Israel had done. He bowed down to all the starry hosts and worshiped them. 4He built altars in the temple of the LORD, of which the LORD had said, "In Jerusalem I will put my Name." 5In both courts of the temple of the LORD, he built altars to all the starry hosts. 6He sacrificed his own son in[a] the fire, practiced sorcery and divination, and consulted mediums and spiritists. He did much evil in the eyes of the LORD, provoking him to anger.

7He took the carved Asherah pole he had made and put it in the temple, of which the LORD had said to David and to his son Solomon, "In this temple and in Jerusalem, which I have chosen out of all the tribes of Israel, I will put my Name forever. 8I will not again make the feet of the Israelites wander from the land I gave their forefathers, if only they will be careful to do everything I commanded them and will keep the whole Law that my servant Moses gave them." 9But the people did not listen. Manasseh led them astray, so that they did more evil than the nations the LORD had destroyed before the Israelites.

10The LORD said through his servants the prophets: 11"Manasseh king of Judah has committed these detestable sins. He has done more evil than the Amorites who preceded him and has led Judah into sin with his idols. 12Therefore this is what the LORD, the God of Israel, says: I am going to bring such disaster on Jerusalem and Judah that the ears of everyone who hears of it will tingle. 13I will stretch out over Jerusalem the measuring line used against Samaria and the plumb line used against the house of Ahab. I will wipe out Jerusalem as one wipes a dish, wiping it and turning it upside down. 14I will forsake the remnant of my inheritance and hand them over to their enemies. They will be looted and plundered by all their foes, 15because they have done evil in my eyes and have provoked me to anger from the day their forefathers came out of Egypt until this day."

16Moreover, Manasseh also shed so much innocent blood that he filled Jerusalem from end to end—besides the sin that he had caused Judah to commit, so that they did evil in the eyes of the LORD.

17As for the other events of Manasseh's reign, and all he did, including the sin he committed, are they not written in the book of the annals of the kings of Judah? 18Manasseh rested with his fathers and was buried in his palace garden, the garden of Uzza. And Amon his son succeeded him as king.

Amon King of Judah

19Amon was twenty-two years old when he became king, and he reigned in Jerusalem two years. His mother's name was Meshullemeth daughter of Haruz; she was from Jotbah. 20He did evil in the eyes of the LORD, as his father Manasseh had done. 21He walked in all the ways of his father; he worshiped the idols his father had worshiped, and bowed down to them. 22He forsook the LORD, the God of his fathers, and did not walk in the way of the LORD.

23Amon's officials conspired against him and assassinated the king in his palace. 24Then the people of the land killed all who had plotted against King Amon, and they made Josiah his son king in his place.

25As for the other events of Amon's reign, and what he did, are they not written in the book of the annals of the kings of Judah? 26He was buried in his grave in the garden of Uzza. And Josiah his son succeeded him as king.

The Book of the Law Found

22 Josiah was eight years old when he became king, and he reigned in Jerusalem thirty-one years. His mother's name was Jedidah daughter of Adaiah; she was from Bozkath. 2He did what was right in the eyes of the LORD and walked in all the ways of his father David, not turning aside to the right or to the left.

3In the eighteenth year of his reign, King Josiah sent the secretary, Shaphan son of Azaliah, the son of Meshullam, to the temple of the LORD. He said: 4"Go up to Hilkiah the high priest and have him get ready the money that has been brought into the temple of the LORD, which the doorkeepers have collected from the people. 5Have them entrust it to the men appointed to supervise the work on the temple. And have these men pay the workers who repair the temple of the LORD—

[a]6 Or *He made his own son pass through*

6the carpenters, the builders and the masons. Also have them purchase timber and dressed stone to repair the temple. 7But they need not account for the money entrusted to them, because they are acting faithfully."

8Hilkiah the high priest said to Shaphan the secretary, "I have found the Book of the Law in the temple of the LORD." He gave it to Shaphan, who read it. 9Then Shaphan the secretary went to the king and reported to him: "Your officials have paid out the money that was in the temple of the LORD and have entrusted it to the workers and supervisors at the temple." 10Then Shaphan the secretary informed the king, "Hilkiah the priest has given me a book." And Shaphan read from it in the presence of the king.

11When the king heard the words of the Book of the Law, he tore his robes. 12He gave these orders to Hilkiah the priest, Ahikam son of Shaphan, Acbor son of Micaiah, Shaphan the secretary and Asaiah the king's attendant: 13"Go and inquire of the LORD for me and for the people and for all Judah about what is written in this book that has been found. Great is the LORD's anger that burns against us because our fathers have not obeyed the words of this book; they have not acted in accordance with all that is written there concerning us."

14Hilkiah the priest, Ahikam, Acbor, Shaphan and Asaiah went to speak to the prophetess Huldah, who was the wife of Shallum son of Tikvah, the son of Harhas, keeper of the wardrobe. She lived in Jerusalem, in the Second District.

15She said to them, "This is what the LORD, the God of Israel, says: Tell the man who sent you to me, 16'This is what the LORD says: I am going to bring disaster on this place and its people, according to everything written in the book the king of Judah has read. 17Because they have forsaken me and burned incense to other gods and provoked me to anger by all the idols their hands have made,[a] my anger will burn against this place and will not be quenched.' 18Tell the king of Judah, who sent you to inquire of the LORD, 'This is what the LORD, the God of Israel, says concerning the words you heard: 19Because your heart was responsive and you humbled yourself before the LORD when you heard what I have spoken against this place and its people, that they would become accursed and laid waste, and because you tore your robes and wept in my presence, I have heard you, declares the LORD. 20Therefore I will gather you to your fathers, and you will be buried in peace. Your eyes will not see all the disaster I am going to bring on this place.' "

So they took her answer back to the king.

Josiah Renews the Covenant

23 Then the king called together all the elders of Judah and Jerusalem. 2He went up to the temple of the LORD with the men of Judah, the people of Jerusalem, the priests and the prophets—all the people from the least to the greatest. He read in their hearing all the words of the Book of the Covenant, which had been found in the temple of the LORD. 3The king stood by the pillar and renewed the covenant in the presence of the LORD—to follow the LORD and keep his commands, regulations and decrees with all his heart and all his soul, thus confirming the words of the covenant written in this book. Then all the people pledged themselves to the covenant.

4The king ordered Hilkiah the high priest, the priests next in rank and the doorkeepers to remove from the temple of the LORD all the articles made for Baal and Asherah and all the starry hosts. He burned them outside Jerusalem in the fields of the Kidron Valley and took the ashes to Bethel. 5He did away with the pagan priests appointed by the kings of Judah to burn incense on the high places of the towns of Judah and on those around Jerusalem—those who burned incense to Baal, to the sun and moon, to the constellations and to all the starry hosts. 6He took the Asherah pole from the temple of the LORD to the Kidron Valley outside Jerusalem and burned it there. He ground it to powder and scattered the dust over the graves of the common people. 7He also tore down the quarters of the male shrine prostitutes, which were in the temple of the LORD and where women did weaving for Asherah.

8Josiah brought all the priests from the towns of Judah and desecrated the high places, from Geba to Beersheba, where the priests had burned incense. He broke down the shrines[b] at the gates—at the entrance to the Gate of Joshua, the city governor, which is on the left of the city gate. 9Although the priests of the high places did not serve at the altar of the LORD in Jerusalem, they ate unleavened bread with their fellow priests.

[a]17 Or *by everything they have done* [b]8 Or *high places*

10 He desecrated Topheth, which was in the Valley of Ben Hinnom, so no one could use it to sacrifice his son or daughter in[a] the fire to Molech. 11 He removed from the entrance to the temple of the LORD the horses that the kings of Judah had dedicated to the sun. They were in the court near the room of an official named Nathan-Melech. Josiah then burned the chariots dedicated to the sun.

12 He pulled down the altars the kings of Judah had erected on the roof near the upper room of Ahaz, and the altars Manasseh had built in the two courts of the temple of the LORD. He removed them from there, smashed them to pieces and threw the rubble into the Kidron Valley. 13 The king also desecrated the high places that were east of Jerusalem on the south of the Hill of Corruption—the ones Solomon king of Israel had built for Ashtoreth the vile goddess of the Sidonians, for Chemosh the vile god of Moab, and for Molech[b] the detestable god of the people of Ammon. 14 Josiah smashed the sacred stones and cut down the Asherah poles and covered the sites with human bones.

15 Even the altar at Bethel, the high place made by Jeroboam son of Nebat, who had caused Israel to sin—even that altar and high place he demolished. He burned the high place and ground it to powder, and burned the Asherah pole also. 16 Then Josiah looked around, and when he saw the tombs that were there on the hillside, he had the bones removed from them and burned on the altar to defile it, in accordance with the word of the LORD proclaimed by the man of God who foretold these things.

17 The king asked, "What is that tombstone I see?"

The men of the city said, "It marks the tomb of the man of God who came from Judah and pronounced against the altar of Bethel the very things you have done to it."

18 "Leave it alone," he said. "Don't let anyone disturb his bones." So they spared his bones and those of the prophet who had come from Samaria.

19 Just as he had done at Bethel, Josiah removed and defiled all the shrines at the high places that the kings of Israel had built in the towns of Samaria that had provoked the LORD to anger. 20 Josiah slaughtered all the priests of those high places on the altars and burned human bones on them. Then he went back to Jerusalem.

21 The king gave this order to all the people: "Celebrate the Passover to the LORD your God, as it is written in this Book of the Covenant." 22 Not since the days of the judges who led Israel, nor throughout the days of the kings of Israel and the kings of Judah, had any such Passover been observed. 23 But in the eighteenth year of King Josiah, this Passover was celebrated to the LORD in Jerusalem.

24 Furthermore, Josiah got rid of the mediums and spiritists, the household gods, the idols and all the other detestable things seen in Judah and Jerusalem. This he did to fulfill the requirements of the law written in the book that Hilkiah the priest had discovered in the temple of the LORD. 25 Neither before nor after Josiah was there a king like him who turned to the LORD as he did—with all his heart and with all his soul and with all his strength, in accordance with all the Law of Moses.

26 Nevertheless, the LORD did not turn away from the heat of his fierce anger, which burned against Judah because of all that Manasseh had done to provoke him to anger. 27 So the LORD said, "I will remove Judah also from my presence as I removed Israel, and I will reject Jerusalem, the city I chose, and this temple, about which I said, 'There shall my Name be.'[c]"

28 As for the other events of Josiah's reign, and all he did, are they not written in the book of the annals of the kings of Judah?

29 While Josiah was king, Pharaoh Neco king of Egypt went up to the Euphrates River to help the king of Assyria. King Josiah marched out to meet him in battle, but Neco faced him and killed him at Megiddo. 30 Josiah's servants brought his body in a chariot from Megiddo to Jerusalem and buried him in his own tomb. And the people of the land took Jehoahaz son of Josiah and anointed him and made him king in place of his father.

Jehoahaz King of Judah

31 Jehoahaz was twenty-three years old when he became king, and he reigned in Jerusalem three months. His mother's name was Hamutal daughter of Jeremiah; she was from Libnah. 32 He did evil in the eyes of the LORD, just as his fathers had done. 33 Pharaoh Neco put him in chains at Riblah in the land

[a] *10* Or *to make his son or daughter pass through* [b] *13* Hebrew *Milcom* [c] *27* 1 Kings 8:29

of Hamath[a] so that he might not reign in Jerusalem, and he imposed on Judah a levy of a hundred talents[b] of silver and a talent[c] of gold. 34 Pharaoh Neco made Eliakim son of Josiah king in place of his father Josiah and changed Eliakim's name to Jehoiakim. But he took Jehoahaz and carried him off to Egypt, and there he died. 35 Jehoiakim paid Pharaoh Neco the silver and gold he demanded. In order to do so, he taxed the land and exacted the silver and gold from the people of the land according to their assessments.

Jehoiakim King of Judah

36 Jehoiakim was twenty-five years old when he became king, and he reigned in Jerusalem eleven years. His mother's name was Zebidah daughter of Pedaiah; she was from Rumah. 37 And he did evil in the eyes of the LORD, just as his fathers had done.

24 During Jehoiakim's reign, Nebuchadnezzar king of Babylon invaded the land, and Jehoiakim became his vassal for three years. But then he changed his mind and rebelled against Nebuchadnezzar. 2 The LORD sent Babylonian,[d] Aramean, Moabite and Ammonite raiders against him. He sent them to destroy Judah, in accordance with the word of the LORD proclaimed by his servants the prophets. 3 Surely these things happened to Judah according to the LORD's command, in order to remove them from his presence because of the sins of Manasseh and all he had done, 4 including the shedding of innocent blood. For he had filled Jerusalem with innocent blood, and the LORD was not willing to forgive.

5 As for the other events of Jehoiakim's reign, and all he did, are they not written in the book of the annals of the kings of Judah? 6 Jehoiakim rested with his fathers. And Jehoiachin his son succeeded him as king.

7 The king of Egypt did not march out from his own country again, because the king of Babylon had taken all his territory, from the Wadi of Egypt to the Euphrates River.

Jehoiachin King of Judah

8 Jehoiachin was eighteen years old when he became king, and he reigned in Jerusalem three months. His mother's name was Nehushta daughter of Elnathan; she was from Jerusalem. 9 He did evil in the eyes of the LORD, just as his father had done.

10 At that time the officers of Nebuchadnezzar king of Babylon advanced on Jerusalem and laid siege to it, 11 and Nebuchadnezzar himself came up to the city while his officers were besieging it. 12 Jehoiachin king of Judah, his mother, his attendants, his nobles and his officials all surrendered to him.

In the eighth year of the reign of the king of Babylon, he took Jehoiachin prisoner. 13 As the LORD had declared, Nebuchadnezzar removed all the treasures from the temple of the LORD and from the royal palace, and took away all the gold articles that Solomon king of Israel had made for the temple of the LORD. 14 He carried into exile all Jerusalem: all the officers and fighting men, and all the craftsmen and artisans—a total of ten thousand. Only the poorest people of the land were left.

15 Nebuchadnezzar took Jehoiachin captive to Babylon. He also took from Jerusalem to Babylon the king's mother, his wives, his officials and the leading men of the land. 16 The king of Babylon also deported to Babylon the entire force of seven thousand fighting men, strong and fit for war, and a thousand craftsmen and artisans. 17 He made Mattaniah, Jehoiachin's uncle, king in his place and changed his name to Zedekiah.

Zedekiah King of Judah

18 Zedekiah was twenty-one years old when he became king, and he reigned in Jerusalem eleven years. His mother's name was Hamutal daughter of Jeremiah; she was from Libnah. 19 He did evil in the eyes of the LORD, just as Jehoiakim had done. 20 It was because of the LORD's anger that all this happened to Jerusalem and Judah, and in the end he thrust them from his presence.

The Fall of Jerusalem

Now Zedekiah rebelled against the king of Babylon.

25 So in the ninth year of Zedekiah's reign, on the tenth day of the tenth month, Nebuchadnezzar king of Babylon marched against Jerusalem with his whole army. He encamped outside the city and built siege works all around it. 2 The city was kept under siege until the eleventh year of King Zedekiah. 3 By the ninth day of the

[a]33 Hebrew; Septuagint (see also 2 Chron. 36:3) *Neco at Riblah in Hamath removed him* [b]33 That is, about 3 3/4 tons (about 3.4 metric tons) [c]33 That is, about 75 pounds (about 35 kilograms) [d]2 Or *Chaldean*

fourth[a] month the famine in the city had become so severe that there was no food for the people to eat. 4Then the city wall was broken through, and the whole army fled at night through the gate between the two walls near the king's garden, though the Babylonians[b] were surrounding the city. They fled toward the Arabah,[c] 5but the Babylonian[d] army pursued the king and overtook him in the plains of Jericho. All his soldiers were separated from him and scattered, 6and he was captured. He was taken to the king of Babylon at Riblah, where sentence was pronounced on him. 7They killed the sons of Zedekiah before his eyes. Then they put out his eyes, bound him with bronze shackles and took him to Babylon.

8On the seventh day of the fifth month, in the nineteenth year of Nebuchadnezzar king of Babylon, Nebuzaradan commander of the imperial guard, an official of the king of Babylon, came to Jerusalem. 9He set fire to the temple of the LORD, the royal palace and all the houses of Jerusalem. Every important building he burned down. 10The whole Babylonian army, under the commander of the imperial guard, broke down the walls around Jerusalem. 11Nebuzaradan the commander of the guard carried into exile the people who remained in the city, along with the rest of the populace and those who had gone over to the king of Babylon. 12But the commander left behind some of the poorest people of the land to work the vineyards and fields.

13The Babylonians broke up the bronze pillars, the movable stands and the bronze Sea that were at the temple of the LORD and they carried the bronze to Babylon. 14They also took away the pots, shovels, wick trimmers, dishes and all the bronze articles used in the temple service. 15The commander of the imperial guard took away the censers and sprinkling bowls—all that were made of pure gold or silver.

16The bronze from the two pillars, the Sea and the movable stands, which Solomon had made for the temple of the LORD, was more than could be weighed. 17Each pillar was twenty-seven feet[e] high. The bronze capital on top of one pillar was four and a half feet[f] high and was decorated with a network and pomegranates of bronze all around. The other pillar, with its network, was similar.

18The commander of the guard took as prisoners Seraiah the chief priest, Zephaniah the priest next in rank and the three doorkeepers. 19Of those still in the city, he took the officer in charge of the fighting men and five royal advisers. He also took the secretary who was chief officer in charge of conscripting the people of the land and sixty of his men who were found in the city. 20Nebuzaradan the commander took them all and brought them to the king of Babylon at Riblah. 21There at Riblah, in the land of Hamath, the king had them executed.

So Judah went into captivity, away from her land.

22Nebuchadnezzar king of Babylon appointed Gedaliah son of Ahikam, the son of Shaphan, to be over the people he had left behind in Judah. 23When all the army officers and their men heard that the king of Babylon had appointed Gedaliah as governor, they came to Gedaliah at Mizpah—Ishmael son of Nethaniah, Johanan son of Kareah, Seraiah son of Tanhumeth the Netophathite, Jaazaniah the son of the Maacathite, and their men. 24Gedaliah took an oath to reassure them and their men. "Do not be afraid of the Babylonian officials," he said. "Settle down in the land and serve the king of Babylon, and it will go well with you."

25In the seventh month, however, Ishmael son of Nethaniah, the son of Elishama, who was of royal blood, came with ten men and assassinated Gedaliah and also the men of Judah and the Babylonians who were with him at Mizpah. 26At this, all the people from the least to the greatest, together with the army officers, fled to Egypt for fear of the Babylonians.

Jehoiachin Released

27In the thirty-seventh year of the exile of Jehoiachin king of Judah, in the year Evil-Merodach[g] became king of Babylon, he released Jehoiachin from prison on the twenty-seventh day of the twelfth month. 28He spoke kindly to him and gave him a seat of honor higher than those of the other kings who were with him in Babylon. 29So Jehoiachin put aside his prison clothes and for the rest of his life ate regularly at the king's table. 30Day by day the king gave Jehoiachin a regular allowance as long as he lived.

[a]3 See Jer. 52:6. [b]4 Or *Chaldeans;* also in verses 13, 25 and 26 [c]4 Or *the Jordan Valley* [d]5 Or *Chaldean;* also in verses 10 and 24 [e]17 Hebrew *eighteen cubits* (about 8.1 meters) [f]17 Hebrew *three cubits* (about 1.3 meters) [g]27 Also called *Amel-Marduk*

I Chronicles

Introduction:

Although the books of Chronicles seem like a repeat of Samuel and Kings they aren't. The Chronicles were written for the exiles who had returned to Israel after the Babylonian captivity to remind them they were from the royal line of David and were God's chosen people. The main theme is that God is always faithful to his covenant.

For these reasons I Chronicles begins with an outline of history from Adam through the death of King Saul. The rest of the book is about the reign of King David. These books serve as both a warning and encouragement to the Jews to be faithful to the covenant.

Outline of contents:

List of generations (1:1–9:44)
The reign of David (10:1–29:30)

Historical Records From Adam to Abraham

To Noah's Sons

1 Adam, Seth, Enosh, 2Kenan, Mahalalel,
Jared, 3Enoch, Methuselah, Lamech,
Noah.

4The sons of Noah:[a]
Shem, Ham and Japheth.

The Japhethites

5The sons[b] of Japheth:
Gomer, Magog, Madai, Javan, Tubal, Meshech and Tiras.
6The sons of Gomer:
Ashkenaz, Riphath[c] and Togarmah.
7The sons of Javan:
Elishah, Tarshish, the Kittim and the Rodanim.

The Hamites

8The sons of Ham:
Cush, Mizraim,[d] Put and Canaan.
9The sons of Cush:
Seba, Havilah, Sabta, Raamah and Sabteca.
The sons of Raamah:
Sheba and Dedan.
10Cush was the father[e] of
Nimrod, who grew to be a mighty warrior on earth.
11Mizraim was the father of
the Ludites, Anamites, Lehabites,
Naphtuhites, 12Pathrusites, Caslu-
hites (from whom the Philistines came) and Caphtorites.
13Canaan was the father of
Sidon his firstborn,[f] and of the Hittites, 14Jebusites, Amorites, Girgashites, 15Hivites, Arkites, Sinites,
16Arvadites, Zemarites and Hamathites.

The Semites

17The sons of Shem:
Elam, Asshur, Arphaxad, Lud and Aram.
The sons of Aram[g]:
Uz, Hul, Gether and Meshech.
18Arphaxad was the father of Shelah,
and Shelah the father of Eber.
19Two sons were born to Eber:
One was named Peleg,[h] because in

---

[a]4 Septuagint; Hebrew does not have *The sons of Noah:* [b]5 *Sons* may mean *descendants* or *successors* or *nations;* also in verses 6-10, 17 and 20. [c]6 Many Hebrew manuscripts and Vulgate (see also Septuagint and Gen. 10:3); most Hebrew manuscripts *Diphath* [d]8 That is, Egypt; also in verse 11 [e]10 *Father* may mean *ancestor* or *predecessor* or *founder;* also in verses 11, 13, 18 and 20. [f]13 Or *of the Sidonians, the foremost* [g]17 One Hebrew manuscript and some Septuagint manuscripts (see also Gen. 10:23); most Hebrew manuscripts do not have this line. [h]19 *Peleg* means *division.*

his time the earth was divided; his
brother was named Joktan.
20Joktan was the father of
Almodad, Sheleph, Hazarmaveth,
Jerah, 21Hadoram, Uzal, Diklah,
22Obal,[a] Abimael, Sheba, 23Ophir,
Havilah and Jobab. All these were
sons of Joktan.

24Shem, Arphaxad,[b] Shelah,
25Eber, Peleg, Reu,
26Serug, Nahor, Terah
27and Abram (that is, Abraham).

The Family of Abraham

28The sons of Abraham:
Isaac and Ishmael.

Descendants of Hagar

29These were their descendants:
Nebaioth the firstborn of Ishmael,
Kedar, Adbeel, Mibsam, 30Mishma,
Dumah, Massa, Hadad, Tema,
31Jetur, Naphish and Kedemah.
These were the sons of Ishmael.

Descendants of Keturah

32The sons born to Keturah, Abraham's concubine:
Zimran, Jokshan, Medan, Midian, Ishbak and Shuah.
The sons of Jokshan:
Sheba and Dedan.
33The sons of Midian:
Ephah, Epher, Hanoch, Abida and Eldaah.
All these were descendants of Keturah.

Descendants of Sarah

34Abraham was the father of Isaac.
The sons of Isaac:
Esau and Israel.

Esau's Sons

35The sons of Esau:
Eliphaz, Reuel, Jeush, Jalam and Korah.
36The sons of Eliphaz:
Teman, Omar, Zepho,[c] Gatam and Kenaz;
by Timna: Amalek.[d]
37The sons of Reuel:
Nahath, Zerah, Shammah and Mizzah.

The People of Seir in Edom

38The sons of Seir:
Lotan, Shobal, Zibeon, Anah, Dishon, Ezer and Dishan.
39The sons of Lotan:
Hori and Homam. Timna was Lotan's sister.
40The sons of Shobal:
Alvan,[e] Manahath, Ebal, Shepho and Onam.
The sons of Zibeon:
Aiah and Anah.
41The son of Anah:
Dishon.
The sons of Dishon:
Hemdan,[f] Eshban, Ithran and Keran.
42The sons of Ezer:
Bilhan, Zaavan and Akan.[g]
The sons of Dishan[h]:
Uz and Aran.

The Rulers of Edom

43These were the kings who reigned in Edom before any Israelite king reigned[i]:
Bela son of Beor, whose city was named Dinhabah.
44When Bela died, Jobab son of Zerah from Bozrah succeeded him as king.
45When Jobab died, Husham from the land of the Temanites succeeded him as king.
46When Husham died, Hadad son of Bedad, who defeated Midian in the country of Moab, succeeded him as king. His city was named Avith.
47When Hadad died, Samlah from Masrekah succeeded him as king.
48When Samlah died, Shaul from Reho-

[a]*22* Some Hebrew manuscripts and Syriac (see also Gen. 10:28); most Hebrew manuscripts *Ebal*
[b]*24* Hebrew; some Septuagint manuscripts *Arphaxad, Cainan* (see also note at Gen. 11:10) [c]*36* Many Hebrew manuscripts, some Septuagint manuscripts and Syriac (see also Gen. 36:11); most Hebrew manuscripts *Zephi* [d]*36* Some Septuagint manuscripts (see also Gen. 36:12); Hebrew *Gatam, Kenaz, Timna and Amalek*
[e]*40* Many Hebrew manuscripts and some Septuagint manuscripts (see also Gen. 36:23); most Hebrew manuscripts *Alian* [f]*41* Many Hebrew manuscripts and some Septuagint manuscripts (see also Gen. 36:26); most Hebrew manuscripts *Hamran* [g]*42* Many Hebrew and Septuagint manuscripts (see also Gen. 36:27); most Hebrew manuscripts *Zaavan, Jaakan* [h]*42* Hebrew *Dishon,* a variant of *Dishan* [i]*43* Or *before an Israelite king reigned over them*

both on the river[a] succeeded him as
king.
49 When Shaul died, Baal-Hanan son of
Acbor succeeded him as king.
50 When Baal-Hanan died, Hadad succeeded him as king. His city was
named Pau,[b] and his wife's name
was Mehetabel daughter of Matred,
the daughter of Me-Zahab. 51 Hadad
also died.

The chiefs of Edom were:
Timna, Alvah, Jetheth, 52 Oholibamah, Elah, Pinon, 53 Kenaz, Teman,
Mibzar, 54 Magdiel and Iram. These
were the chiefs of Edom.

Israel's Sons

2 These were the sons of Israel:
Reuben, Simeon, Levi, Judah, Is-
sachar, Zebulun, 2 Dan, Joseph,
Benjamin, Naphtali, Gad and Asher.

Judah

To Hezron's Sons

3 The sons of Judah:
Er, Onan and Shelah. These three
were born to him by a Canaanite
woman, the daughter of Shua. Er,
Judah's firstborn, was wicked in the
LORD's sight; so the LORD put him to
death. 4 Tamar, Judah's daughter-in-
law, bore him Perez and Zerah.
Judah had five sons in all.

5 The sons of Perez:
Hezron and Hamul.
6 The sons of Zerah:
Zimri, Ethan, Heman, Calcol and
Darda[c]—five in all.
7 The son of Carmi:
Achar,[d] who brought trouble on Israel by violating the ban on taking
devoted things.[e]
8 The son of Ethan:
Azariah.
9 The sons born to Hezron were:
Jerahmeel, Ram and Caleb.[f]

From Ram Son of Hezron

10 Ram was the father of
Amminadab, and Amminadab the
father of Nahshon, the leader of the
people of Judah. 11 Nahshon was the
father of Salmon,[g] Salmon the father
of Boaz, 12 Boaz the father of Obed
and Obed the father of Jesse.
13 Jesse was the father of
Eliab his firstborn; the second son
was Abinadab, the third Shimea,
14 the fourth Nethanel, the fifth Rad-
dai, 15 the sixth Ozem and the seventh David. 16 Their sisters were Zeruiah and Abigail. Zeruiah's three
sons were Abishai, Joab and Asahel. 17 Abigail was the mother of
Amasa, whose father was Jether the
Ishmaelite.

Caleb Son of Hezron

18 Caleb son of Hezron had children by
his wife Azubah (and by Jerioth).
These were her sons: Jesher, Shobab and Ardon. 19 When Azubah
died, Caleb married Ephrath, who
bore him Hur. 20 Hur was the father of
Uri, and Uri the father of Bezalel.
21 Later, Hezron lay with the daughter of
Makir the father of Gilead (he had
married her when he was sixty years
old), and she bore him Segub.
22 Segub was the father of Jair, who
controlled twenty-three towns in Gilead. 23 (But Geshur and Aram captured Havvoth Jair,[h] as well as
Kenath with its surrounding settlements—sixty towns.) All these were
descendants of Makir the father of
Gilead.

24 After Hezron died in Caleb Ephrathah,
Abijah the wife of Hezron bore him
Ashhur the father[i] of Tekoa.

Jerahmeel Son of Hezron

25 The sons of Jerahmeel the firstborn of
Hezron:
Ram his firstborn, Bunah, Oren,
Ozem and[j] Ahijah. 26 Jerahmeel had
another wife, whose name was Ata-
rah; she was the mother of Onam.

[a]48 Possibly the Euphrates [b]50 Many Hebrew manuscripts, some Septuagint manuscripts, Vulgate and Syriac (see also Gen. 36:39); most Hebrew manuscripts *Pai* [c]6 Many Hebrew manuscripts, some Septuagint manuscripts and Syriac (see also 1 Kings 4:31); most Hebrew manuscripts *Dara* [d]7 *Achar* means *trouble; Achar* is called *Achan* in Joshua. [e]7 The Hebrew term refers to the irrevocable giving over of things or persons to the LORD, often by totally destroying them. [f]9 Hebrew *Kelubai,* a variant of *Caleb* [g]11 Septuagint (see also Ruth 4:21); Hebrew *Salma* [h]23 Or *captured the settlements of Jair* [i]24 *Father* may mean *civic leader* or *military leader;* also in verses 42, 45, 49-52 and possibly elsewhere. [j]25 Or *Oren and Ozem, by*

27The sons of Ram the firstborn of Jerahmeel:
Maaz, Jamin and Eker.
28The sons of Onam:
Shammai and Jada.
The sons of Shammai:
Nadab and Abishur.
29Abishur's wife was named Abihail, who bore him Ahban and Molid.
30The sons of Nadab:
Seled and Appaim. Seled died without children.
31The son of Appaim:
Ishi, who was the father of Sheshan.
Sheshan was the father of Ahlai.
32The sons of Jada, Shammai's brother:
Jether and Jonathan. Jether died without children.
33The sons of Jonathan:
Peleth and Zaza.
These were the descendants of Jerahmeel.
34Sheshan had no sons—only daughters.
He had an Egyptian servant named
Jarha. 35Sheshan gave his daughter
in marriage to his servant Jarha, and she bore him Attai.
36Attai was the father of Nathan,
Nathan the father of Zabad,
37Zabad the father of Ephlal,
Ephlal the father of Obed,
38Obed the father of Jehu,
Jehu the father of Azariah,
39Azariah the father of Helez,
Helez the father of Eleasah,
40Eleasah the father of Sismai,
Sismai the father of Shallum,
41Shallum the father of Jekamiah,
and Jekamiah the father of Elishama.

The Clans of Caleb

42The sons of Caleb the brother of Jerahmeel:
Mesha his firstborn, who was the father of Ziph, and his son Mareshah,[a] who was the father of Hebron.
43The sons of Hebron:
Korah, Tappuah, Rekem and
Shema. 44Shema was the father of
Raham, and Raham the father of
Jorkeam. Rekem was the father of
Shammai. 45The son of Shammai
was Maon, and Maon was the father of Beth Zur.
46Caleb's concubine Ephah was the mother of Haran, Moza and Gazez.
Haran was the father of Gazez.
47The sons of Jahdai:
Regem, Jotham, Geshan, Pelet, Ephah and Shaaph.
48Caleb's concubine Maacah was the
mother of Sheber and Tirhanah.
49She also gave birth to Shaaph the
father of Madmannah and to Sheva
the father of Macbenah and Gibea.
Caleb's daughter was Acsah.
50These were the descendants of
Caleb.

The sons of Hur the firstborn of Ephrathah:
Shobal the father of Kiriath Jearim,
51Salma the father of Bethlehem, and Hareph the father of Beth Gader.
52The descendants of Shobal the father of Kiriath Jearim were:
Haroeh, half the Manahathites,
53and the clans of Kiriath Jearim: the
Ithrites, Puthites, Shumathites and Mishraites. From these descended the Zorathites and Eshtaolites.
54The descendants of Salma:
Bethlehem, the Netophathites, Atroth Beth Joab, half the Manahathites, the Zorites, 55and the clans of
scribes[b] who lived at Jabez: the Tirathites, Shimeathites and Sucathites. These are the Kenites who came from Hammath, the father of the house of Recab.[c]

The Sons of David

3 These were the sons of David born to him in Hebron:
The firstborn was Amnon the son of Ahinoam of Jezreel;
the second, Daniel the son of Abigail of Carmel;
2the third, Absalom the son of Maacah daughter of Talmai king of Geshur;
the fourth, Adonijah the son of Haggith;
3the fifth, Shephatiah the son of Abital;

[a]42 The meaning of the Hebrew for this phrase is uncertain. [b]55 Or *of the Sopherites* [c]55 Or *father of Beth Recab*

and the sixth, Ithream, by his wife Eglah.

4These six were born to David in Hebron, where he reigned seven years and six months.

David reigned in Jerusalem thirty-three years, 5and these were the children born to him there:

Shammua,[a] Shobab, Nathan and Solomon. These four were by Bathsheba[b] daughter of Ammiel. 6There were also Ibhar, Elishua,[c] Eliphelet, 7Nogah, Nepheg, Japhia, 8Elishama, Eliada and Eliphelet—nine in all. 9All these were the sons of David, besides his sons by his concubines. And Tamar was their sister.

The Kings of Judah

10Solomon's son was Rehoboam,
Abijah his son,
Asa his son,
Jehoshaphat his son,
11Jehoram[d] his son,
Ahaziah his son,
Joash his son,
12Amaziah his son,
Azariah his son,
Jotham his son,
13Ahaz his son,
Hezekiah his son,
Manasseh his son,
14Amon his son,
Josiah his son.

15The sons of Josiah:
Johanan the firstborn,
Jehoiakim the second son,
Zedekiah the third,
Shallum the fourth.

16The successors of Jehoiakim:
Jehoiachin[e] his son,
and Zedekiah.

The Royal Line After the Exile

17The descendants of Jehoiachin the captive:
Shealtiel his son, 18Malkiram, Pedaiah, Shenazzar, Jekamiah, Hoshama and Nedabiah.

19The sons of Pedaiah:
Zerubbabel and Shimei.

The sons of Zerubbabel:
Meshullam and Hananiah.
Shelomith was their sister.

20There were also five others:
Hashubah, Ohel, Berekiah, Hasadiah and Jushab-Hesed.

21The descendants of Hananiah:
Pelatiah and Jeshaiah, and the sons of Rephaiah, of Arnan, of Obadiah and of Shecaniah.

22The descendants of Shecaniah:
Shemaiah and his sons:
Hattush, Igal, Bariah, Neariah and Shaphat—six in all.

23The sons of Neariah:
Elioenai, Hizkiah and Azrikam—three in all.

24The sons of Elioenai:
Hodaviah, Eliashib, Pelaiah, Akkub, Johanan, Delaiah and Anani—seven in all.

Other Clans of Judah

4 The descendants of Judah:
Perez, Hezron, Carmi, Hur and Shobal.

2Reaiah son of Shobal was the father of Jahath, and Jahath the father of Ahumai and Lahad. These were the clans of the Zorathites.

3These were the sons[f] of Etam:
Jezreel, Ishma and Idbash. Their sister was named Hazzelelponi. 4Penuel was the father of Gedor, and Ezer the father of Hushah.

These were the descendants of Hur, the firstborn of Ephrathah and father[g] of Bethlehem.

5Ashhur the father of Tekoa had two wives, Helah and Naarah.

6Naarah bore him Ahuzzam, Hepher, Temeni and Haahashtari. These were the descendants of Naarah.

7The sons of Helah:
Zereth, Zohar, Ethnan, 8and Koz, who was the father of Anub and Hazzobebah and of the clans of Aharhel son of Harum.

9Jabez was more honorable than his brothers. His mother had named him

[a]5 Hebrew *Shimea,* a variant of *Shammua* [b]5 One Hebrew manuscript and Vulgate (see also Septuagint and 2 Samuel 11:3); most Hebrew manuscripts *Bathshua* [c]6 Two Hebrew manuscripts (see also 2 Samuel 5:15 and 1 Chron. 14:5); most Hebrew manuscripts *Elishama* [d]11 Hebrew *Joram,* a variant of *Jehoram* [e]16 Hebrew *Jeconiah,* a variant of *Jehoiachin;* also in verse 17 [f]3 Some Septuagint manuscripts (see also Vulgate); Hebrew *father* [g]4 *Father* may mean *civic leader* or *military leader;* also in verses 12, 14, 17, 18 and possibly elsewhere.

Jabez,[a] saying, "I gave birth to him in pain."
10 Jabez cried out to the God of Israel, "Oh,
that you would bless me and enlarge my
territory! Let your hand be with me, and keep
me from harm so that I will be free from
pain." And God granted his request.

11 Kelub, Shuhah's brother, was the father of Mehir, who was the father of
Eshton. 12 Eshton was the father of
Beth Rapha, Paseah and Tehinnah
the father of Ir Nahash.[b] These were
the men of Recah.

13 The sons of Kenaz:
Othniel and Seraiah.
The sons of Othniel:
Hathath and Meonothai.[c] 14 Meonothai was the father of Ophrah.
Seraiah was the father of Joab,
the father of Ge Harashim.[d] It was
called this because its people were
craftsmen.

15 The sons of Caleb son of Jephunneh:
Iru, Elah and Naam.
The son of Elah:
Kenaz.

16 The sons of Jehallelel:
Ziph, Ziphah, Tiria and Asarel.

17 The sons of Ezrah:
Jether, Mered, Epher and Jalon.
One of Mered's wives gave birth to
Miriam, Shammai and Ishbah the fa-
ther of Eshtemoa. 18 (His Judean wife
gave birth to Jered the father of Ge-
dor, Heber the father of Soco, and
Jekuthiel the father of Zanoah.)
These were the children of Phar-
aoh's daughter Bithiah, whom
Mered had married.

19 The sons of Hodiah's wife, the sister of
Naham:
the father of Keilah the Garmite, and
Eshtemoa the Maacathite.

20 The sons of Shimon:
Amnon, Rinnah, Ben-Hanan and Ti-
lon.
The descendants of Ishi:
Zoheth and Ben-Zoheth.

21 The sons of Shelah son of Judah:
Er the father of Lecah, Laadah the
father of Mareshah and the clans of
the linen workers at Beth Ashbea,
22 Jokim, the men of Cozeba, and
Joash and Saraph, who ruled in
Moab and Jashubi Lehem. (These
records are from ancient times.)
23 They were the potters who lived at
Netaim and Gederah; they stayed
there and worked for the king.

Simeon

24 The descendants of Simeon:
Nemuel, Jamin, Jarib, Zerah and
Shaul;
25 Shallum was Shaul's son, Mibsam
his son and Mishma his son.
26 The descendants of Mishma:
Hammuel his son, Zaccur his son
and Shimei his son.

27 Shimei had sixteen sons and six daughters, but his brothers did not have many children; so their entire clan did not become as
numerous as the people of Judah. 28 They
lived in Beersheba, Moladah, Hazar Shual,
29 Bilhah, Ezem, Tolad, 30 Bethuel, Hormah,
Ziklag, 31 Beth Marcaboth, Hazar Susim,
Beth Biri and Shaaraim. These were their
towns until the reign of David. 32 Their surrounding villages were Etam, Ain, Rimmon,
Token and Ashan—five towns— 33 and all
the villages around these towns as far as
Baalath.[e] These were their settlements. And
they kept a genealogical record.

34 Meshobab, Jamlech, Joshah son of
Amaziah, 35 Joel, Jehu son of Joshibiah,
the son of Seraiah, the son of Asiel,
36 also Elioenai, Jaakobah, Jeshohaiah,
Asaiah, Adiel, Jesimiel, Benaiah, 37 and
Ziza son of Shiphi, the son of Allon, the
son of Jedaiah, the son of Shimri, the
son of Shemaiah.

38 The men listed above by name were
leaders of their clans. Their families increased greatly, 39 and they went to the outskirts of Gedor to the east of the valley in
search of pasture for their flocks. 40 They
found rich, good pasture, and the land was
spacious, peaceful and quiet. Some Hamites
had lived there formerly.

41 The men whose names were listed came
in the days of Hezekiah king of Judah. They
attacked the Hamites in their dwellings and
also the Meunites who were there and completely destroyed[f] them, as is evident to this
day. Then they settled in their place, be-

[a]9 *Jabez* sounds like the Hebrew for *pain.* [b]12 Or *of the city of Nahash* [c]13 Some Septuagint manuscripts and Vulgate; Hebrew does not have *and Meonothai.* [d]14 *Ge Harashim* means *valley of craftsmen.* [e]33 Some Septuagint manuscripts (see also Joshua 19:8); Hebrew *Baal* [f]41 The Hebrew term refers to the irrevocable giving over of things or persons to the LORD, often by totally destroying them.

cause there was pasture for their flocks.
42And five hundred of these Simeonites, led
by Pelatiah, Neariah, Rephaiah and Uzziel,
the sons of Ishi, invaded the hill country of
Seir. 43They killed the remaining Amalekites
who had escaped, and they have lived there
to this day.

Reuben

5 The sons of Reuben the firstborn of Israel (he was the firstborn, but when he
defiled his father's marriage bed, his rights
as firstborn were given to the sons of Joseph
son of Israel; so he could not be listed in the
genealogical record in accordance with his
birthright, 2and though Judah was the
strongest of his brothers and a ruler came
from him, the rights of the firstborn belonged
to Joseph)— 3the sons of Reuben the firstborn of Israel:

Hanoch, Pallu, Hezron and Carmi.

4The descendants of Joel:

Shemaiah his son, Gog his son,
Shimei his son, 5Micah his son,
Reaiah his son, Baal his son,
6and Beerah his son, whom Tiglath-
Pileser[a] king of Assyria took into exile. Beerah was a leader of the Reubenites.

7Their relatives by clans, listed according to their genealogical records:

Jeiel the chief, Zechariah, 8and Bela
son of Azaz, the son of Shema, the
son of Joel. They settled in the area
from Aroer to Nebo and Baal Meon.
9To the east they occupied the land
up to the edge of the desert that extends to the Euphrates River, because their livestock had increased
in Gilead.

10During Saul's reign they waged
war against the Hagrites, who were
defeated at their hands; they occupied
the dwellings of the Hagrites
throughout the entire region east of
Gilead.

Gad

11The Gadites lived next to them in Bashan, as far as Salecah:

12Joel was the chief, Shapham the
second, then Janai and Shaphat, in
Bashan.

13Their relatives, by families, were:

Michael, Meshullam, Sheba, Jorai,
Jacan, Zia and Eber—seven in all.

14These were the sons of Abihail son
of Huri, the son of Jaroah, the son of
Gilead, the son of Michael, the son of
Jeshishai, the son of Jahdo, the son
of Buz.

15Ahi son of Abdiel, the son of Guni,
was head of their family.

16The Gadites lived in Gilead, in Bashan
and its outlying villages, and on all
the pasturelands of Sharon as far as
they extended.

17All these were entered in the genealogical records during the reigns of Jotham king
of Judah and Jeroboam king of Israel.

18The Reubenites, the Gadites and the
half-tribe of Manasseh had 44,760 men
ready for military service—able-bodied men
who could handle shield and sword, who
could use a bow, and who were trained for
battle. 19They waged war against the Hagrites, Jetur, Naphish and Nodab. 20They
were helped in fighting them, and God handed the Hagrites and all their allies over to
them, because they cried out to him during
the battle. He answered their prayers, because they trusted in him. 21They seized the
livestock of the Hagrites—fifty thousand
camels, two hundred fifty thousand sheep
and two thousand donkeys. They also took
one hundred thousand people captive, 22and
many others fell slain, because the battle
was God's. And they occupied the land until
the exile.

The Half-Tribe of Manasseh

23The people of the half-tribe of Manasseh
were numerous; they settled in the land from
Bashan to Baal Hermon, that is, to Senir
(Mount Hermon).

24These were the heads of their families:
Epher, Ishi, Eliel, Azriel, Jeremiah, Hodaviah
and Jahdiel. They were brave warriors, famous men, and heads of their families. 25But
they were unfaithful to the God of their fathers and prostituted themselves to the gods
of the peoples of the land, whom God had
destroyed before them. 26So the God of Israel stirred up the spirit of Pul king of Assyria
(that is, Tiglath-Pileser king of Assyria), who
took the Reubenites, the Gadites and the
half-tribe of Manasseh into exile. He took
them to Halah, Habor, Hara and the river of
Gozan, where they are to this day.

[a]6 Hebrew *Tilgath-Pilneser,* a variant of *Tiglath-Pileser;* also in verse 26

Levi

6 The sons of Levi:
Gershon, Kohath and Merari.
2The sons of Kohath:
Amram, Izhar, Hebron and Uzziel.
3The children of Amram:
Aaron, Moses and Miriam.
The sons of Aaron:
Nadab, Abihu, Eleazar and Ithamar.
4Eleazar was the father of Phinehas,
Phinehas the father of Abishua,
5Abishua the father of Bukki,
Bukki the father of Uzzi,
6Uzzi the father of Zerahiah,
Zerahiah the father of Meraioth,
7Meraioth the father of Amariah,
Amariah the father of Ahitub,
8Ahitub the father of Zadok,
Zadok the father of Ahimaaz,
9Ahimaaz the father of Azariah,
Azariah the father of Johanan,
10Johanan the father of Azariah (it was
he who served as priest in the temple Solomon built in Jerusalem),
11Azariah the father of Amariah,
Amariah the father of Ahitub,
12Ahitub the father of Zadok,
Zadok the father of Shallum,
13Shallum the father of Hilkiah,
Hilkiah the father of Azariah,
14Azariah the father of Seraiah,
and Seraiah the father of Jehozadak.
15Jehozadak was deported when the
LORD sent Judah and Jerusalem into
exile by the hand of Nebuchadnezzar.
16The sons of Levi:
Gershon,[a] Kohath and Merari.
17These are the names of the sons of
Gershon:
Libni and Shimei.
18The sons of Kohath:
Amram, Izhar, Hebron and Uzziel.
19The sons of Merari:
Mahli and Mushi.
These are the clans of the Levites listed
according to their fathers:
20Of Gershon:
Libni his son, Jehath his son,
Zimmah his son, 21Joah his son,
Iddo his son, Zerah his son
and Jeatherai his son.
22The descendants of Kohath:
Amminadab his son, Korah his son,
Assir his son, 23Elkanah his son,
Ebiasaph his son, Assir his son,
24Tahath his son, Uriel his son,
Uzziah his son and Shaul his son.
25The descendants of Elkanah:
Amasai, Ahimoth,
26Elkanah his son,[b] Zophai his son,
Nahath his son, 27Eliab his son,
Jeroham his son, Elkanah his son
and Samuel his son.[c]
28The sons of Samuel:
Joel[d] the firstborn
and Abijah the second son.
29The descendants of Merari:
Mahli, Libni his son,
Shimei his son, Uzzah his son,
30Shimea his son, Haggiah his son
and Asaiah his son.

The Temple Musicians

31These are the men David put in charge of
the music in the house of the LORD after the
ark came to rest there. 32They ministered
with music before the tabernacle, the Tent of
Meeting, until Solomon built the temple of
the LORD in Jerusalem. They performed their
duties according to the regulations laid down
for them.
33Here are the men who served, together
with their sons:
From the Kohathites:
Heman, the musician,
the son of Joel, the son of Samuel,
34the son of Elkanah, the son of Jeroham,
the son of Eliel, the son of Toah,
35the son of Zuph, the son of Elkanah,
the son of Mahath, the son of
Amasai,
36the son of Elkanah, the son of Joel,
the son of Azariah, the son of Zephaniah,
37the son of Tahath, the son of Assir,
the son of Ebiasaph, the son of
Korah,
38the son of Izhar, the son of Kohath,
the son of Levi, the son of Israel;

[a]*16* Hebrew *Gershom,* a variant of *Gershon;* also in verses 17, 20, 43, 62 and 71 [b]*26* Some Hebrew manuscripts, Septuagint and Syriac; most Hebrew manuscripts *Ahimoth 26and Elkanah. The sons of Elkanah:* [c]*27* Some Septuagint manuscripts (see also 1 Samuel 1:19,20 and 1 Chron. 6:33,34); Hebrew does not have *and Samuel his son.* [d]*28* Some Septuagint manuscripts and Syriac (see also 1 Samuel 8:2 and 1 Chron. 6:33); Hebrew does not have *Joel.*

[39]and Heman's associate Asaph, who served at his right hand:
Asaph son of Berekiah, the son of Shimea,
[40]the son of Michael, the son of Baaseiah,[a]
the son of Malkijah, [41]the son of Ethni,
the son of Zerah, the son of Adaiah,
[42]the son of Ethan, the son of Zimmah,
the son of Shimei, [43]the son of Jahath,
the son of Gershon, the son of Levi;
[44]and from their associates, the Merarites, at his left hand:
Ethan son of Kishi, the son of Abdi,
the son of Malluch, [45]the son of Hashabiah,
the son of Amaziah, the son of Hilkiah,
[46]the son of Amzi, the son of Bani,
the son of Shemer, [47]the son of Mahli,
the son of Mushi, the son of Merari,
the son of Levi.

[48]Their fellow Levites were assigned to all
the other duties of the tabernacle, the house
of God. [49]But Aaron and his descendants
were the ones who presented offerings on
the altar of burnt offering and on the altar of
incense in connection with all that was done
in the Most Holy Place, making atonement
for Israel, in accordance with all that Moses
the servant of God had commanded.

[50]These were the descendants of Aaron:
Eleazar his son, Phinehas his son,
Abishua his son, [51]Bukki his son,
Uzzi his son, Zerahiah his son,
[52]Meraioth his son, Amariah his son,
Ahitub his son, [53]Zadok his son
and Ahimaaz his son.

[54]These were the locations of their settlements allotted as their territory (they were assigned to the descendants of Aaron who were from the Kohathite clan, because the first lot was for them):

[55]They were given Hebron in Judah
with its surrounding pasturelands. [56]But
the fields and villages around the city
were given to Caleb son of Jephunneh.
[57]So the descendants of Aaron were
given Hebron (a city of refuge), and Libnah,[b] Jattir, Eshtemoa, [58]Hilen, Debir,
[59]Ashan, Juttah[c] and Beth Shemesh,
together with their pasturelands. [60]And
from the tribe of Benjamin they were
given Gibeon,[d] Geba, Alemeth and
Anathoth, together with their pasturelands.

These towns, which were distributed among the Kohathite clans, were thirteen in all.

[61]The rest of Kohath's descendants were allotted ten towns from the clans of half the tribe of Manasseh.

[62]The descendants of Gershon, clan by clan, were allotted thirteen towns from the tribes of Issachar, Asher and Naphtali, and from the part of the tribe of Manasseh that is in Bashan.

[63]The descendants of Merari, clan by clan, were allotted twelve towns from the tribes of Reuben, Gad and Zebulun.

[64]So the Israelites gave the Levites these
towns and their pasturelands. [65]From the
tribes of Judah, Simeon and Benjamin they
allotted the previously named towns.

[66]Some of the Kohathite clans were given as their territory towns from the tribe of Ephraim.

[67]In the hill country of Ephraim they
were given Shechem (a city of refuge),
and Gezer,[e] [68]Jokmeam, Beth Horon,
[69]Aijalon and Gath Rimmon, together
with their pasturelands.
[70]And from half the tribe of Manasseh
the Israelites gave Aner and Bileam, together with their pasturelands, to the rest of the Kohathite clans.

[71]The Gershonites received the following:
From the clan of the half-tribe of Manasseh
they received Golan in Bashan and also Ashtaroth, together with their pasturelands;
[72]from the tribe of Issachar
they received Kedesh, Daberath,
[73]Ramoth and Anem, together with
their pasturelands;
[74]from the tribe of Asher
they received Mashal, Abdon,

[a]40 Most Hebrew manuscripts; some Hebrew manuscripts, one Septuagint manuscript and Syriac *Maaseiah*
[b]57 See Joshua 21:13; Hebrew *given the cities of refuge: Hebron, Libnah.*
[c]59 Syriac (see also Septuagint and Joshua 21:16); Hebrew does not have *Juttah.*
[d]60 See Joshua 21:17; Hebrew does not have *Gibeon.*
[e]67 See Joshua 21:21; Hebrew *given the cities of refuge: Shechem, Gezer.*

[75]Hukok and Rehob, together with their pasturelands;
[76]and from the tribe of Naphtali
they received Kedesh in Galilee, Hammon and Kiriathaim, together with their pasturelands.

[77]The Merarites (the rest of the Levites) received the following:
From the tribe of Zebulun
they received Jokneam, Kartah,[a] Rimmono and Tabor, together with their pasturelands;
[78]from the tribe of Reuben across the Jordan east of Jericho
they received Bezer in the desert,
Jahzah, [79]Kedemoth and Mephaath,
together with their pasturelands;
[80]and from the tribe of Gad
they received Ramoth in Gilead,
Mahanaim, [81]Heshbon and Jazer,
together with their pasturelands.

Issachar

7 The sons of Issachar:
Tola, Puah, Jashub and Shimron—four in all.
[2]The sons of Tola:
Uzzi, Rephaiah, Jeriel, Jahmai, Ibsam and Samuel—heads of their families. During the reign of David, the descendants of Tola listed as fighting men in their genealogy numbered 22,600.
[3]The son of Uzzi:
Izrahiah.
The sons of Izrahiah:
Michael, Obadiah, Joel and Isshiah.
All five of them were chiefs. [4]According to their family genealogy, they had 36,000 men ready for battle, for they had many wives and children.
[5]The relatives who were fighting men belonging to all the clans of Issachar, as listed in their genealogy, were 87,000 in all.

Benjamin

[6]Three sons of Benjamin:
Bela, Beker and Jediael.
[7]The sons of Bela:
Ezbon, Uzzi, Uzziel, Jerimoth and Iri, heads of families—five in all. Their genealogical record listed 22,034 fighting men.
[8]The sons of Beker:
Zemirah, Joash, Eliezer, Elioenai, Omri, Jeremoth, Abijah, Anathoth and Alemeth. All these were the
sons of Beker. [9]Their genealogical
record listed the heads of families and 20,200 fighting men.
[10]The son of Jediael:
Bilhan.
The sons of Bilhan:
Jeush, Benjamin, Ehud, Kenaanah, Zethan, Tarshish and Ahishahar.
[11]All these sons of Jediael were heads of families. There were 17,200 fighting men ready to go out to war.
[12]The Shuppites and Huppites were the descendants of Ir, and the Hushites the descendants of Aher.

Naphtali

[13]The sons of Naphtali:
Jahziel, Guni, Jezer and Shillem[b]—the descendants of Bilhah.

Manasseh

[14]The descendants of Manasseh:
Asriel was his descendant through his Aramean concubine. She gave birth to Makir the father of Gilead.
[15]Makir took a wife from among the Huppites and Shuppites. His sister's name was Maacah.
Another descendant was named Zelophehad, who had only daughters.
[16]Makir's wife Maacah gave birth to a son and named him Peresh. His brother was named Sheresh, and his sons were Ulam and Rakem.
[17]The son of Ulam:
Bedan.
These were the sons of Gilead son of
Makir, the son of Manasseh. [18]His
sister Hammoleketh gave birth to Ishhod, Abiezer and Mahlah.
[19]The sons of Shemida were:
Ahian, Shechem, Likhi and Aniam.

Ephraim

[20]The descendants of Ephraim:
Shuthelah, Bered his son,
Tahath his son, Eleadah his son,
Tahath his son, [21]Zabad his son
and Shuthelah his son.

[a]77 See Septuagint and Joshua 21:34; Hebrew does not have *Jokneam, Kartah.* [b]13 Some Hebrew and Septuagint manuscripts (see also Gen. 46:24 and Num. 26:49); most Hebrew manuscripts *Shallum*

Ezer and Elead were killed by the
native-born men of Gath, when they
went down to seize their livestock.
22Their father Ephraim mourned for
them many days, and his relatives
came to comfort him. 23Then he lay
with his wife again, and she became
pregnant and gave birth to a son. He
named him Beriah,[a] because there
had been misfortune in his family. 24His
daughter was Sheerah, who built
Lower and Upper Beth Horon as well
as Uzzen Sheerah.

25Rephah was his son, Resheph his
son,[b]
Telah his son, Tahan his son,
26Ladan his son, Ammihud his son,
Elishama his son, 27Nun his son
and Joshua his son.

28Their lands and settlements included
Bethel and its surrounding villages, Naaran
to the east, Gezer and its villages to the west,
and Shechem and its villages all the way to
Ayyah and its villages. 29Along the borders of
Manasseh were Beth Shan, Taanach,
Megiddo and Dor, together with their vil-
lages. The descendants of Joseph son of
Israel lived in these towns.

Asher

30The sons of Asher:
Imnah, Ishvah, Ishvi and Beriah.
Their sister was Serah.
31The sons of Beriah:
Heber and Malkiel, who was the father of Birzaith.
32Heber was the father of Japhlet, Shomer and Hotham and of their sister
Shua.
33The sons of Japhlet:
Pasach, Bimhal and Ashvath.
These were Japhlet's sons.
34The sons of Shomer:
Ahi, Rohgah,[c] Hubbah and Aram.
35The sons of his brother Helem:
Zophah, Imna, Shelesh and Amal.
36The sons of Zophah:
Suah, Harnepher, Shual, Beri, Im-
rah, 37Bezer, Hod, Shamma, Shil-
shah, Ithran[d] and Beera.
38The sons of Jether:
Jephunneh, Pispah and Ara.
39The sons of Ulla:
Arah, Hanniel and Rizia.

40All these were descendants of Asher—
heads of families, choice men, brave warriors and outstanding leaders. The number of
men ready for battle, as listed in their genealogy, was 26,000.

The Genealogy of Saul the Benjamite

8 Benjamin was the father of Bela his firstborn,
Ashbel the second son, Aharah the
third,
2Nohah the fourth and Rapha the fifth.
3The sons of Bela were:
Addar, Gera, Abihud,[e] 4Abishua,
Naaman, Ahoah, 5Gera, Shephu-
phan and Huram.
6These were the descendants of Ehud,
who were heads of families of those
living in Geba and were deported to
Manahath:
7Naaman, Ahijah, and Gera, who deported them and who was the father
of Uzza and Ahihud.
8Sons were born to Shaharaim in Moab
after he had divorced his wives Hushim and Baara. 9By his wife Hodesh
he had Jobab, Zibia, Mesha, Malcam, 10Jeuz, Sakia and Mirmah.
These were his sons, heads of families. 11By Hushim he had Abitub and
Elpaal.
12The sons of Elpaal:
Eber, Misham, Shemed (who built
Ono and Lod with its surrounding villages), 13and Beriah and Shema,
who were heads of families of those
living in Aijalon and who drove out
the inhabitants of Gath.
14Ahio, Shashak, Jeremoth, 15Zebadiah,
Arad, Eder, 16Michael, Ishpah and
Joha were the sons of Beriah.
17Zebadiah, Meshullam, Hizki, Heber,
18Ishmerai, Izliah and Jobab were
the sons of Elpaal.
19Jakim, Zicri, Zabdi, 20Elienai, Zillethai,
Eliel, 21Adaiah, Beraiah and Shim-
rath were the sons of Shimei.
22Ishpan, Eber, Eliel, 23Abdon, Zicri, Hanan, 24Hananiah, Elam, Anthothijah,
25Iphdeiah and Penuel were the
sons of Shashak.
26Shamsherai, Shehariah, Athaliah,
27Jaareshiah, Elijah and Zicri were
the sons of Jeroham.

[a]23 *Beriah* sounds like the Hebrew for *misfortune.* [b]25 Some Septuagint manuscripts; Hebrew does not have *his son.* [c]34 Or *of his brother Shomer: Rohgah* [d]37 Possibly a variant of *Jether* [e]3 Or *Gera the father of Ehud*

[28]All these were heads of families, chiefs as listed in their genealogy, and they lived in Jerusalem.

[29]Jeiel[a] the father[b] of Gibeon lived in Gibeon.
His wife's name was Maacah, [30]and
his firstborn son was Abdon, followed by Zur, Kish, Baal, Ner,[c]
Nadab, [31]Gedor, Ahio, Zeker [32]and
Mikloth, who was the father of Shimeah. They too lived near their relatives in Jerusalem.

[33]Ner was the father of Kish, Kish the father of Saul, and Saul the father of Jonathan, Malki-Shua, Abinadab and Esh-Baal.[d]

[34]The son of Jonathan:
Merib-Baal,[e] who was the father of Micah.

[35]The sons of Micah:
Pithon, Melech, Tarea and Ahaz.
[36]Ahaz was the father of Jehoaddah, Jehoaddah was the father of Alemeth, Azmaveth and Zimri, and
Zimri was the father of Moza. [37]Moza
was the father of Binea; Raphah was his son, Eleasah his son and Azel his son.

[38]Azel had six sons, and these were their names:
Azrikam, Bokeru, Ishmael, Sheariah, Obadiah and Hanan. All these were the sons of Azel.

[39]The sons of his brother Eshek:
Ulam his firstborn, Jeush the second
son and Eliphelet the third. [40]The
sons of Ulam were brave warriors who could handle the bow. They had many sons and grandsons—150 in all.

All these were the descendants of Benjamin.

9 All Israel was listed in the genealogies recorded in the book of the kings of Israel.

The People in Jerusalem

The people of Judah were taken captive to Babylon because of their unfaithfulness.
[2]Now the first to resettle on their own property in their own towns were some Israelites, priests, Levites and temple servants.
[3]Those from Judah, from Benjamin, and from Ephraim and Manasseh who lived in Jerusalem were:

[4]Uthai son of Ammihud, the son of Omri, the son of Imri, the son of Bani, a descendant of Perez son of Judah.

[5]Of the Shilonites:
Asaiah the firstborn and his sons.

[6]Of the Zerahites:
Jeuel.
The people from Judah numbered 690.

[7]Of the Benjamites:
Sallu son of Meshullam, the son of Hodaviah, the son of Hassenuah;
[8]Ibneiah son of Jeroham; Elah son of Uzzi, the son of Micri; and Meshullam son of Shephatiah, the son of Reuel, the son of Ibnijah.
[9]The people from Benjamin, as listed in their genealogy, numbered 956. All these men were heads of their families.

[10]Of the priests:
Jedaiah; Jehoiarib; Jakin;
[11]Azariah son of Hilkiah, the son of Meshullam, the son of Zadok, the son of Meraioth, the son of Ahitub, the official in charge of the house of God;
[12]Adaiah son of Jeroham, the son of Pashhur, the son of Malkijah; and Maasai son of Adiel, the son of Jahzerah, the son of Meshullam, the son of Meshillemith, the son of Immer.
[13]The priests, who were heads of families, numbered 1,760. They were able men, responsible for ministering in the house of God.

[14]Of the Levites:
Shemaiah son of Hasshub, the son of Azrikam, the son of Hashabiah, a
Merarite; [15]Bakbakkar, Heresh, Galal and Mattaniah son of Mica, the
son of Zicri, the son of Asaph; [16]Obadiah son of Shemaiah, the son of Galal, the son of Jeduthun; and Berekiah son of Asa, the son of Elkanah, who lived in the villages of the Netophathites.

[17]The gatekeepers:
Shallum, Akkub, Talmon, Ahiman and their brothers, Shallum their
chief [18]being stationed at the King's Gate on the east, up to the present

[a]29 Some Septuagint manuscripts (see also 1 Chron. 9:35); Hebrew does not have *Jeiel.* [b]29 *Father* may mean *civic leader* or *military leader.* [c]30 Some Septuagint manuscripts (see also 1 Chron. 9:36); Hebrew does not have *Ner.* [d]33 Also known as *Ish-Bosheth* [e]34 Also known as *Mephibosheth*

time. These were the gatekeepers
belonging to the camp of the Levites.
19Shallum son of Kore, the son of
Ebiasaph, the son of Korah, and his
fellow gatekeepers from his family
(the Korahites) were responsible for
guarding the thresholds of the Tent[a]
just as their fathers had been responsible for guarding the entrance
to the dwelling of the LORD. 20In earlier times Phinehas son of Eleazar
was in charge of the gatekeepers,
and the LORD was with him. 21Zecha-
riah son of Meshelemiah was the
gatekeeper at the entrance to the
Tent of Meeting.
22Altogether, those chosen to be gatekeepers at the thresholds numbered 212.
They were registered by genealogy in their
villages. The gatekeepers had been assigned to their positions of trust by David and
Samuel the seer. 23They and their descendants were in charge of guarding the gates of
the house of the LORD—the house called the
Tent. 24The gatekeepers were on the four
sides: east, west, north and south. 25Their
brothers in their villages had to come from
time to time and share their duties for seven-
day periods. 26But the four principal gatekeepers, who were Levites, were entrusted
with the responsibility for the rooms and treasuries in the house of God. 27They would
spend the night stationed around the house
of God, because they had to guard it; and
they had charge of the key for opening it
each morning.
28Some of them were in charge of the articles used in the temple service; they counted
them when they were brought in and when
they were taken out. 29Others were assigned
to take care of the furnishings and all the
other articles of the sanctuary, as well as the
flour and wine, and the oil, incense and
spices. 30But some of the priests took care of
mixing the spices. 31A Levite named Mattithiah, the firstborn son of Shallum the Korahite, was entrusted with the responsibility for
baking the offering bread. 32Some of their
Kohathite brothers were in charge of preparing for every Sabbath the bread set out on
the table.
33Those who were musicians, heads of Levite families, stayed in the rooms of the temple and were exempt from other duties because they were responsible for the work
day and night.
34All these were heads of Levite families,
chiefs as listed in their genealogy, and they
lived in Jerusalem.

The Genealogy of Saul

35Jeiel the father[b] of Gibeon lived in
Gibeon.
His wife's name was Maacah, 36and
his firstborn son was Abdon, followed by Zur, Kish, Baal, Ner,
Nadab, 37Gedor, Ahio, Zechariah
and Mikloth. 38Mikloth was the father
of Shimeam. They too lived near
their relatives in Jerusalem.
39Ner was the father of Kish, Kish the
father of Saul, and Saul the father of
Jonathan, Malki-Shua, Abinadab
and Esh-Baal.[c]
40The son of Jonathan:
Merib-Baal,[d] who was the father of
Micah.
41The sons of Micah:
Pithon, Melech, Tahrea and Ahaz.[e]
42Ahaz was the father of Jadah,
Jadah[f] was the father of Alemeth,
Azmaveth and Zimri, and Zimri was
the father of Moza. 43Moza was the
father of Binea; Rephaiah was his
son, Eleasah his son and Azel his
son.
44Azel had six sons, and these were their
names:
Azrikam, Bokeru, Ishmael, Sheariah, Obadiah and Hanan. These
were the sons of Azel.

Saul Takes His Life

10 Now the Philistines fought against Israel; the Israelites fled before them,
and many fell slain on Mount Gilboa. 2The
Philistines pressed hard after Saul and his
sons, and they killed his sons Jonathan,
Abinadab and Malki-Shua. 3The fighting
grew fierce around Saul, and when the archers overtook him, they wounded him.
4Saul said to his armor-bearer, "Draw your
sword and run me through, or these uncircumcised fellows will come and abuse me."
But his armor-bearer was terrified and
would not do it; so Saul took his own sword

[a]*19* That is, the temple; also in verses 21 and 23 [b]*35* *Father* may mean *civic leader* or *military leader.* [c]*39* Also known as *Ish-Bosheth* [d]*40* Also known as *Mephibosheth* [e]*41* Vulgate and Syriac (see also Septuagint and 1 Chron. 8:35); Hebrew does not have *and Ahaz.* [f]*42* Some Hebrew manuscripts and Septuagint (see also 1 Chron. 8:36); most Hebrew manuscripts *Jarah, Jarah*

and fell on it. 5When the armor-bearer saw
that Saul was dead, he too fell on his sword
and died. 6So Saul and his three sons died,
and all his house died together.
7When all the Israelites in the valley saw
that the army had fled and that Saul and his
sons had died, they abandoned their towns
and fled. And the Philistines came and occupied them.
8The next day, when the Philistines came
to strip the dead, they found Saul and his
sons fallen on Mount Gilboa. 9They stripped
him and took his head and his armor, and
sent messengers throughout the land of the
Philistines to proclaim the news among their
idols and their people. 10They put his armor
in the temple of their gods and hung up his
head in the temple of Dagon.
11When all the inhabitants of Jabesh Gilead heard of everything the Philistines had
done to Saul, 12all their valiant men went and
took the bodies of Saul and his sons and
brought them to Jabesh. Then they buried
their bones under the great tree in Jabesh,
and they fasted seven days.
13Saul died because he was unfaithful to
the LORD; he did not keep the word of the
LORD and even consulted a medium for guidance, 14and did not inquire of the LORD. So
the LORD put him to death and turned the
kingdom over to David son of Jesse.

David Becomes King Over Israel

11 All Israel came together to David at
Hebron and said, "We are your own
flesh and blood. 2In the past, even while Saul
was king, you were the one who led Israel on
their military campaigns. And the LORD your
God said to you, 'You will shepherd my
people Israel, and you will become their
ruler.' "
3When all the elders of Israel had come to
King David at Hebron, he made a compact
with them at Hebron before the LORD, and
they anointed David king over Israel, as the
LORD had promised through Samuel.

David Conquers Jerusalem

4David and all the Israelites marched to
Jerusalem (that is, Jebus). The Jebusites
who lived there 5said to David, "You will not
get in here." Nevertheless, David captured
the fortress of Zion, the City of David.
6David had said, "Whoever leads the attack on the Jebusites will become command-
er-in-chief." Joab son of Zeruiah went up
first, and so he received the command.
7David then took up residence in the fortress, and so it was called the City of David.
8He built up the city around it, from the supporting terraces[a] to the surrounding wall,
while Joab restored the rest of the city. 9And
David became more and more powerful, because the LORD Almighty was with him.

David's Mighty Men

10These were the chiefs of David's mighty
men—they, together with all Israel, gave his
kingship strong support to extend it over the
whole land, as the LORD had promised—
11this is the list of David's mighty men:
Jashobeam,[b] a Hacmonite, was chief of
the officers[c]; he raised his spear against
three hundred men, whom he killed in one
encounter.
12Next to him was Eleazar son of Dodai the
Ahohite, one of the three mighty men. 13He
was with David at Pas Dammim when the
Philistines gathered there for battle. At a
place where there was a field full of barley,
the troops fled from the Philistines. 14But
they took their stand in the middle of the field.
They defended it and struck the Philistines
down, and the LORD brought about a great
victory.
15Three of the thirty chiefs came down to
David to the rock at the cave of Adullam,
while a band of Philistines was encamped in
the Valley of Rephaim. 16At that time David
was in the stronghold, and the Philistine garrison was at Bethlehem. 17David longed for
water and said, "Oh, that someone would
get me a drink of water from the well near the
gate of Bethlehem!" 18So the Three broke
through the Philistine lines, drew water from
the well near the gate of Bethlehem and carried it back to David. But he refused to drink
it; instead, he poured it out before the LORD.
19"God forbid that I should do this!" he said.
"Should I drink the blood of these men who
went at the risk of their lives?" Because they
risked their lives to bring it back, David would
not drink it.
Such were the exploits of the three mighty
men.
20Abishai the brother of Joab was chief of
the Three. He raised his spear against three
hundred men, whom he killed, and so he

[a]8 Or *the Millo* [b]11 Possibly a variant of *Jashob-Baal* (see also 2 Samuel 23:8) [c]11 Or *Thirty;* some Septuagint manuscripts *Three*

became as famous as the Three. 21He was
doubly honored above the Three and
became their commander, even though he
was not included among them.
22Benaiah son of Jehoiada was a valiant
fighter from Kabzeel, who performed great
exploits. He struck down two of Moab's best
men. He also went down into a pit on a
snowy day and killed a lion. 23And he struck
down an Egyptian who was seven and a half
feet[a] tall. Although the Egyptian had a spear
like a weaver's rod in his hand, Benaiah went
against him with a club. He snatched the
spear from the Egyptian's hand and killed
him with his own spear. 24Such were the
exploits of Benaiah son of Jehoiada; he too
was as famous as the three mighty men.
25He was held in greater honor than any of
the Thirty, but he was not included among
the Three. And David put him in charge of his
bodyguard.

26The mighty men were:
Asahel the brother of Joab,
Elhanan son of Dodo from Bethlehem,
27Shammoth the Harorite,
Helez the Pelonite,
28Ira son of Ikkesh from Tekoa,
Abiezer from Anathoth,
29Sibbecai the Hushathite,
Ilai the Ahohite,
30Maharai the Netophathite,
Heled son of Baanah the Netophathite,
31Ithai son of Ribai from Gibeah in Benjamin,
Benaiah the Pirathonite,
32Hurai from the ravines of Gaash,
Abiel the Arbathite,
33Azmaveth the Baharumite,
Eliahba the Shaalbonite,
34the sons of Hashem the Gizonite,
Jonathan son of Shagee the Hararite,
35Ahiam son of Sacar the Hararite,
Eliphal son of Ur,
36Hepher the Mekerathite,
Ahijah the Pelonite,
37Hezro the Carmelite,
Naarai son of Ezbai,
38Joel the brother of Nathan,
Mibhar son of Hagri,
39Zelek the Ammonite,
Naharai the Berothite, the armor-bearer of Joab son of Zeruiah,
40Ira the Ithrite,
Gareb the Ithrite,
41Uriah the Hittite,
Zabad son of Ahlai,
42Adina son of Shiza the Reubenite, who was chief of the Reubenites, and the thirty with him,
43Hanan son of Maacah,
Joshaphat the Mithnite,
44Uzzia the Ashterathite,
Shama and Jeiel the sons of Hotham the Aroerite,
45Jediael son of Shimri,
his brother Joha the Tizite,
46Eliel the Mahavite,
Jeribai and Joshaviah the sons of Elnaam,
Ithmah the Moabite,
47Eliel, Obed and Jaasiel the Mezobaite.

Warriors Join David

12 These were the men who came to
David at Ziklag, while he was banished from the presence of Saul son of Kish
(they were among the warriors who helped
him in battle; 2they were armed with bows
and were able to shoot arrows or to sling
stones right-handed or left-handed; they
were kinsmen of Saul from the tribe of Benjamin):

3Ahiezer their chief and Joash the sons
of Shemaah the Gibeathite; Jeziel and
Pelet the sons of Azmaveth; Beracah,
Jehu the Anathothite, 4and Ishmaiah the
Gibeonite, a mighty man among the
Thirty, who was a leader of the Thirty;
Jeremiah, Jahaziel, Johanan, Jozabad
the Gederathite, 5Eluzai, Jerimoth, Bealiah, Shemariah and Shephatiah the Haruphite; 6Elkanah, Isshiah, Azarel, Joezer and Jashobeam the Korahites; 7and
Joelah and Zebadiah the sons of Jeroham from Gedor.

8Some Gadites defected to David at his
stronghold in the desert. They were brave
warriors, ready for battle and able to handle
the shield and spear. Their faces were the
faces of lions, and they were as swift as
gazelles in the mountains.
9Ezer was the chief,
Obadiah the second in command, Eliab the third,

[a]23 Hebrew *five cubits* (about 2.3 meters)

10 Mishmannah the fourth, Jeremiah the
fifth,
11 Attai the sixth, Eliel the seventh,
12 Johanan the eighth, Elzabad the ninth,
13 Jeremiah the tenth and Macbannai the
eleventh.

14 These Gadites were army commanders;
the least was a match for a hundred, and the
greatest for a thousand. 15 It was they who
crossed the Jordan in the first month when it
was overflowing all its banks, and they put to
flight everyone living in the valleys, to the
east and to the west.

16 Other Benjamites and some men from
Judah also came to David in his stronghold.
17 David went out to meet them and said to
them, "If you have come to me in peace, to
help me, I am ready to have you unite with
me. But if you have come to betray me to my
enemies when my hands are free from violence, may the God of our fathers see it and
judge you."

18 Then the Spirit came upon Amasai, chief
of the Thirty, and he said:

"We are yours, O David!
We are with you, O son of Jesse!
Success, success to you,
and success to those who help you,
for your God will help you."

So David received them and made them
leaders of his raiding bands.

19 Some of the men of Manasseh defected
to David when he went with the Philistines to
fight against Saul. (He and his men did not
help the Philistines because, after consulta-
tion, their rulers sent him away. They said, "It
will cost us our heads if he deserts to his
master Saul.") 20 When David went to Ziklag,
these were the men of Manasseh who defected to him: Adnah, Jozabad, Jediael, Michael, Jozabad, Elihu and Zillethai, leaders
of units of a thousand in Manasseh. 21 They
helped David against raiding bands, for all of
them were brave warriors, and they were
commanders in his army. 22 Day after day
men came to help David, until he had a great
army, like the army of God.[a]

Others Join David at Hebron

23 These are the numbers of the men
armed for battle who came to David at Hebron to turn Saul's kingdom over to him, as
the LORD had said:

24 men of Judah, carrying shield and
spear—6,800 armed for battle;
25 men of Simeon, warriors ready for battle—7,100;
26 men of Levi—4,600, 27 including Jehoiada, leader of the family of Aaron,
with 3,700 men, 28 and Zadok, a
brave young warrior, with 22 officers
from his family;
29 men of Benjamin, Saul's kinsmen—
3,000, most of whom had remained
loyal to Saul's house until then;
30 men of Ephraim, brave warriors, famous in their own clans—20,800;
31 men of half the tribe of Manasseh, designated by name to come and make
David king—18,000;
32 men of Issachar, who understood the
times and knew what Israel should
do—200 chiefs, with all their relatives under their command;
33 men of Zebulun, experienced soldiers
prepared for battle with every type of
weapon, to help David with undivided loyalty—50,000;
34 men of Naphtali—1,000 officers, together with 37,000 men carrying
shields and spears;
35 men of Dan, ready for battle—28,600;
36 men of Asher, experienced soldiers
prepared for battle—40,000;
37 and from east of the Jordan, men of
Reuben, Gad and the half-tribe of
Manasseh, armed with every type of
weapon—120,000.

38 All these were fighting men who volunteered to serve in the ranks. They came to
Hebron fully determined to make David king
over all Israel. All the rest of the Israelites
were also of one mind to make David king.
39 The men spent three days there with David, eating and drinking, for their families had
supplied provisions for them. 40 Also, their
neighbors from as far away as Issachar,
Zebulun and Naphtali came bringing food on
donkeys, camels, mules and oxen. There
were plentiful supplies of flour, fig cakes, raisin cakes, wine, oil, cattle and sheep, for
there was joy in Israel.

Bringing Back the Ark

13 David conferred with each of his officers, the commanders of thousands
and commanders of hundreds. 2 He then said

[a] 22 Or *a great and mighty army*

to the whole assembly of Israel, "If it seems good to you and if it is the will of the LORD our God, let us send word far and wide to the rest of our brothers throughout the territories of Israel, and also to the priests and Levites who are with them in their towns and pasturelands, to come and join us. 3Let us bring the ark of our God back to us, for we did not inquire of[a] it[b] during the reign of Saul." 4The whole assembly agreed to do this, because it seemed right to all the people.

5So David assembled all the Israelites, from the Shihor River in Egypt to Lebo[c] Hamath, to bring the ark of God from Kiriath Jearim. 6David and all the Israelites with him went to Baalah of Judah (Kiriath Jearim) to bring up from there the ark of God the LORD, who is enthroned between the cherubim—the ark that is called by the Name.

7They moved the ark of God from Abinadab's house on a new cart, with Uzzah and Ahio guiding it. 8David and all the Israelites were celebrating with all their might before God, with songs and with harps, lyres, tambourines, cymbals and trumpets.

9When they came to the threshing floor of Kidon, Uzzah reached out his hand to steady the ark, because the oxen stumbled. 10The LORD's anger burned against Uzzah, and he struck him down because he had put his hand on the ark. So he died there before God.

11Then David was angry because the LORD's wrath had broken out against Uzzah, and to this day that place is called Perez Uzzah.[d]

12David was afraid of God that day and asked, "How can I ever bring the ark of God to me?" 13He did not take the ark to be with him in the City of David. Instead, he took it aside to the house of Obed-Edom the Gittite. 14The ark of God remained with the family of Obed-Edom in his house for three months, and the LORD blessed his household and everything he had.

David's House and Family

14 Now Hiram king of Tyre sent messengers to David, along with cedar logs, stonemasons and carpenters to build a palace for him. 2And David knew that the LORD had established him as king over Israel and that his kingdom had been highly exalted for the sake of his people Israel.

3In Jerusalem David took more wives and became the father of more sons and daughters. 4These are the names of the children born to him there: Shammua, Shobab, Nathan, Solomon, 5Ibhar, Elishua, Elpelet, 6Nogah, Nepheg, Japhia, 7Elishama, Beeliada[e] and Eliphelet.

David Defeats the Philistines

8When the Philistines heard that David had been anointed king over all Israel, they went up in full force to search for him, but David heard about it and went out to meet them. 9Now the Philistines had come and raided the Valley of Rephaim; 10so David inquired of God: "Shall I go and attack the Philistines? Will you hand them over to me?"

The LORD answered him, "Go, I will hand them over to you."

11So David and his men went up to Baal Perazim, and there he defeated them. He said, "As waters break out, God has broken out against my enemies by my hand." So that place was called Baal Perazim.[f] 12The Philistines had abandoned their gods there, and David gave orders to burn them in the fire.

13Once more the Philistines raided the valley; 14so David inquired of God again, and God answered him, "Do not go straight up, but circle around them and attack them in front of the balsam trees. 15As soon as you hear the sound of marching in the tops of the balsam trees, move out to battle, because that will mean God has gone out in front of you to strike the Philistine army." 16So David did as God commanded him, and they struck down the Philistine army, all the way from Gibeon to Gezer.

17So David's fame spread throughout every land, and the LORD made all the nations fear him.

The Ark Brought to Jerusalem

15 After David had constructed buildings for himself in the City of David, he prepared a place for the ark of God and pitched a tent for it. 2Then David said, "No one but the Levites may carry the ark of God, because the LORD chose them to carry the ark of the LORD and to minister before him forever."

3David assembled all Israel in Jerusalem to bring up the ark of the LORD to the place he

[a]3 Or *we neglected* [b]3 Or *him* [c]5 Or *to the entrance to* [d]11 *Perez Uzzah* means *outbreak against Uzzah.* [e]7 A variant of *Eliada* [f]11 *Baal Perazim* means *the lord who breaks out.*

had prepared for it. [4]He called together the descendants of Aaron and the Levites:

[5]From the descendants of Kohath,
Uriel the leader and 120 relatives;
[6]from the descendants of Merari,
Asaiah the leader and 220 relatives;
[7]from the descendants of Gershon,[a]
Joel the leader and 130 relatives;
[8]from the descendants of Elizaphan,
Shemaiah the leader and 200 relatives;
[9]from the descendants of Hebron,
Eliel the leader and 80 relatives;
[10]from the descendants of Uzziel,
Amminadab the leader and 112 relatives.

[11]Then David summoned Zadok and Abiathar the priests, and Uriel, Asaiah, Joel, Shemaiah, Eliel and Amminadab the Levites. [12]He said to them, "You are the heads of the Levitical families; you and your fellow Levites are to consecrate yourselves and bring up the ark of the LORD, the God of Israel, to the place I have prepared for it. [13]It was because you, the Levites, did not bring it up the first time that the LORD our God broke out in anger against us. We did not inquire of him about how to do it in the prescribed way." [14]So the priests and Levites consecrated themselves in order to bring up the ark of the LORD, the God of Israel. [15]And the Levites carried the ark of God with the poles on their shoulders, as Moses had commanded in accordance with the word of the LORD.

[16]David told the leaders of the Levites to appoint their brothers as singers to sing joyful songs, accompanied by musical instruments: lyres, harps and cymbals.

[17]So the Levites appointed Heman son of Joel; from his brothers, Asaph son of Berekiah; and from their brothers the Merarites, Ethan son of Kushaiah; [18]and with them their brothers next in rank: Zechariah,[b] Jaaziel, Shemiramoth, Jehiel, Unni, Eliab, Benaiah, Maaseiah, Mattithiah, Eliphelehu, Mikneiah, Obed-Edom and Jeiel,[c] the gatekeepers.

[19]The musicians Heman, Asaph and Ethan were to sound the bronze cymbals; [20]Zechariah, Aziel, Shemiramoth, Jehiel, Unni, Eliab, Maaseiah and Benaiah were to play the lyres according to *alamoth,*[d] [21]and Mattithiah, Eliphelehu, Mikneiah, Obed-Edom, Jeiel and Azaziah were to play the harps, directing according to *sheminith.*[d] [22]Kenaniah the head Levite was in charge of the singing; that was his responsibility because he was skillful at it.

[23]Berekiah and Elkanah were to be doorkeepers for the ark. [24]Shebaniah, Joshaphat, Nethanel, Amasai, Zechariah, Benaiah and Eliezer the priests were to blow trumpets before the ark of God. Obed-Edom and Jehiah were also to be doorkeepers for the ark.

[25]So David and the elders of Israel and the commanders of units of a thousand went to bring up the ark of the covenant of the LORD from the house of Obed-Edom, with rejoicing. [26]Because God had helped the Levites who were carrying the ark of the covenant of the LORD, seven bulls and seven rams were sacrificed. [27]Now David was clothed in a robe of fine linen, as were all the Levites who were carrying the ark, and as were the singers, and Kenaniah, who was in charge of the singing of the choirs. David also wore a linen ephod. [28]So all Israel brought up the ark of the covenant of the LORD with shouts, with the sounding of rams' horns and trumpets, and of cymbals, and the playing of lyres and harps.

[29]As the ark of the covenant of the LORD was entering the City of David, Michal daughter of Saul watched from a window. And when she saw King David dancing and celebrating, she despised him in her heart.

16 They brought the ark of God and set it inside the tent that David had pitched for it, and they presented burnt offerings and fellowship offerings[e] before God. [2]After David had finished sacrificing the burnt offerings and fellowship offerings, he blessed the people in the name of the LORD. [3]Then he gave a loaf of bread, a cake of dates and a cake of raisins to each Israelite man and woman.

[4]He appointed some of the Levites to minister before the ark of the LORD, to make petition, to give thanks, and to praise the LORD, the God of Israel: [5]Asaph was the chief, Zechariah second, then Jeiel, Shemiramoth, Jehiel, Mattithiah, Eliab, Benaiah, Obed-Edom and Jeiel. They were to play the lyres and harps, Asaph was to sound the cymbals, [6]and Benaiah and Jahaziel the priests were to blow the trumpets regularly before the ark of the covenant of God.

[a]*7* Hebrew *Gershom,* a variant of *Gershon* [b]*18* Three Hebrew manuscripts and most Septuagint manuscripts (see also verse 20 and 1 Chron. 16:5); most Hebrew manuscripts *Zechariah son and* or *Zechariah, Ben and* [c]*18* Hebrew; Septuagint (see also verse 21) *Jeiel and Azaziah* [d]*20,21* Probably a musical term
[e]*1* Traditionally *peace offerings;* also in verse 2

David's Psalm of Thanks

7That day David first committed to Asaph and his associates this psalm of thanks to the LORD:

8Give thanks to the LORD, call on his name;
 make known among the nations what
 he has done.
9Sing to him, sing praise to him;
 tell of all his wonderful acts.
10Glory in his holy name;
 let the hearts of those who seek the
 LORD rejoice.
11Look to the LORD and his strength;
 seek his face always.
12Remember the wonders he has done,
 his miracles, and the judgments he
 pronounced,
13O descendants of Israel his servant,
 O sons of Jacob, his chosen ones.

14He is the LORD our God;
 his judgments are in all the earth.
15He remembers[a] his covenant forever,
 the word he commanded, for a
 thousand generations,
16the covenant he made with Abraham,
 the oath he swore to Isaac.
17He confirmed it to Jacob as a decree,
 to Israel as an everlasting covenant:
18"To you I will give the land of Canaan
 as the portion you will inherit."

19When they were but few in number,
 few indeed, and strangers in it,
20they[b] wandered from nation to nation,
 from one kingdom to another.
21He allowed no man to oppress them;
 for their sake he rebuked kings:
22"Do not touch my anointed ones;
 do my prophets no harm."
23Sing to the LORD, all the earth;
 proclaim his salvation day after day.
24Declare his glory among the nations,
 his marvelous deeds among all
 peoples.
25For great is the LORD and most worthy of
 praise;
 he is to be feared above all gods.
26For all the gods of the nations are idols,
 but the LORD made the heavens.
27Splendor and majesty are before him;
 strength and joy in his dwelling place.
28Ascribe to the LORD, O families of nations,
 ascribe to the LORD glory and strength,
29 ascribe to the LORD the glory due his
 name.
Bring an offering and come before him;
 worship the LORD in the splendor of his[c]
 holiness.
30Tremble before him, all the earth!
 The world is firmly established; it
 cannot be moved.
31Let the heavens rejoice, let the earth be
 glad;
 let them say among the nations, "The
 LORD reigns!"
32Let the sea resound, and all that is in it;
 let the fields be jubilant, and everything
 in them!
33Then the trees of the forest will sing,
 they will sing for joy before the LORD,
 for he comes to judge the earth.

34Give thanks to the LORD, for he is good;
 his love endures forever.
35Cry out, "Save us, O God our Savior;
 gather us and deliver us from the
 nations,
that we may give thanks to your holy
 name,
 that we may glory in your praise."
36Praise be to the LORD, the God of Israel,
 from everlasting to everlasting.

Then all the people said "Amen" and "Praise the LORD."

37David left Asaph and his associates before the ark of the covenant of the LORD to
minister there regularly, according to each
day's requirements. 38He also left Obed-
Edom and his sixty-eight associates to minister with them. Obed-Edom son of Jeduthun, and also Hosah, were gatekeepers.
39David left Zadok the priest and his fellow
priests before the tabernacle of the LORD at
the high place in Gibeon 40to present burnt
offerings to the LORD on the altar of burnt
offering regularly, morning and evening, in
accordance with everything written in the
Law of the LORD, which he had given Israel.
41With them were Heman and Jeduthun and
the rest of those chosen and designated by
name to give thanks to the LORD, "for his love
endures forever." 42Heman and Jeduthun
were responsible for the sounding of the
trumpets and cymbals and for the playing of

[a] *15* Some Septuagint manuscripts (see also Psalm 105:8); Hebrew *Remember* [b] *18-20* One Hebrew manuscript, Septuagint and Vulgate (see also Psalm 105:12); most Hebrew manuscripts *inherit, / [19]though you are but few in number, / few indeed, and strangers in it." / [20]They* [c] *29* Or *LORD with the splendor of*

the other instruments for sacred song. The
sons of Jeduthun were stationed at the gate.
43Then all the people left, each for his own
home, and David returned home to bless his
family.

God's Promise to David

17 After David was settled in his palace,
he said to Nathan the prophet, "Here
I am, living in a palace of cedar, while the ark
of the covenant of the LORD is under a tent."
2Nathan replied to David, "Whatever you
have in mind, do it, for God is with you."
3That night the word of God came to Nathan, saying:

4"Go and tell my servant David, 'This
is what the LORD says: You are not the
one to build me a house to dwell in. 5I
have not dwelt in a house from the day I
brought Israel up out of Egypt to this
day. I have moved from one tent site to
another, from one dwelling place to another. 6Wherever I have moved with all
the Israelites, did I ever say to any of
their leaders[a] whom I commanded to
shepherd my people, "Why have you
not built me a house of cedar?" '
7"Now then, tell my servant David,
'This is what the LORD Almighty says: I
took you from the pasture and from following the flock, to be ruler over my
people Israel. 8I have been with you
wherever you have gone, and I have cut
off all your enemies from before you.
Now I will make your name like the
names of the greatest men of the earth.
9And I will provide a place for my people
Israel and will plant them so that they
can have a home of their own and no
longer be disturbed. Wicked people will
not oppress them anymore, as they did
at the beginning 10and have done ever
since the time I appointed leaders over
my people Israel. I will also subdue all
your enemies.
" 'I declare to you that the LORD will
build a house for you: 11When your days
are over and you go to be with your
fathers, I will raise up your offspring to
succeed you, one of your own sons, and
I will establish his kingdom. 12He is the
one who will build a house for me, and I
will establish his throne forever. 13I will
be his father, and he will be my son. I will
never take my love away from him, as I
took it away from your predecessor. 14I
will set him over my house and my kingdom forever; his throne will be established forever.' "

15Nathan reported to David all the words of
this entire revelation.

David's Prayer

16Then King David went in and sat before
the LORD, and he said:

"Who am I, O LORD God, and what is
my family, that you have brought me this
far? 17And as if this were not enough in
your sight, O God, you have spoken
about the future of the house of your
servant. You have looked on me as
though I were the most exalted of men,
O LORD God.
18"What more can David say to you
for honoring your servant? For you
know your servant, 19O LORD. For the
sake of your servant and according to
your will, you have done this great thing
and made known all these great promises.
20"There is no one like you, O LORD,
and there is no God but you, as we have
heard with our own ears. 21And who is
like your people Israel—the one nation
on earth whose God went out to redeem
a people for himself, and to make a
name for yourself, and to perform great
and awesome wonders by driving out
nations from before your people, whom
you redeemed from Egypt? 22You made
your people Israel your very own forever, and you, O LORD, have become
their God.
23"And now, LORD, let the promise you
have made concerning your servant
and his house be established forever.
Do as you promised, 24so that it will be
established and that your name will be
great forever. Then men will say, 'The
LORD Almighty, the God over Israel, is
Israel's God!' And the house of your servant David will be established before
you.
25"You, my God, have revealed to
your servant that you will build a house
for him. So your servant has found courage to pray to you. 26O LORD, you are
God! You have promised these good
things to your servant. 27Now you have

[a]6 Traditionally *judges*; also in verse 10

been pleased to bless the house of your
servant, that it may continue forever in
your sight; for you, O LORD, have
blessed it, and it will be blessed forever."

David's Victories

18 In the course of time, David defeated
the Philistines and subdued them,
and he took Gath and its surrounding villages from the control of the Philistines.
2David also defeated the Moabites, and
they became subject to him and brought tribute.
3Moreover, David fought Hadadezer king
of Zobah, as far as Hamath, when he went to
establish his control along the Euphrates
River. 4David captured a thousand of his
chariots, seven thousand charioteers and
twenty thousand foot soldiers. He hamstrung
all but a hundred of the chariot horses.
5When the Arameans of Damascus came
to help Hadadezer king of Zobah, David
struck down twenty-two thousand of them.
6He put garrisons in the Aramean kingdom of
Damascus, and the Arameans became subject to him and brought tribute. The LORD
gave David victory everywhere he went.
7David took the gold shields carried by the
officers of Hadadezer and brought them to
Jerusalem. 8From Tebah[a] and Cun, towns
that belonged to Hadadezer, David took a
great quantity of bronze, which Solomon
used to make the bronze Sea, the pillars and
various bronze articles.
9When Tou king of Hamath heard that David had defeated the entire army of Hadadezer king of Zobah, 10he sent his son Hadoram to King David to greet him and congratulate him on his victory in battle over
Hadadezer, who had been at war with Tou.
Hadoram brought all kinds of articles of gold
and silver and bronze.
11King David dedicated these articles to
the LORD, as he had done with the silver and
gold he had taken from all these nations:
Edom and Moab, the Ammonites and the
Philistines, and Amalek.
12Abishai son of Zeruiah struck down eighteen thousand Edomites in the Valley of Salt.
13He put garrisons in Edom, and all the
Edomites became subject to David. The
LORD gave David victory everywhere he
went.

David's Officials

14David reigned over all Israel, doing what
was just and right for all his people. 15Joab
son of Zeruiah was over the army; Jehosha
phat son of Ahilud was recorder; 16Zadok
son of Ahitub and Ahimelech[b] son of Abiathar were priests; Shavsha was secretary;
17Benaiah son of Jehoiada was over the
Kerethites and Pelethites; and David's sons
were chief officials at the king's side.

The Battle Against the Ammonites

19 In the course of time, Nahash king of
the Ammonites died, and his son
succeeded him as king. 2David thought, "I
will show kindness to Hanun son of Nahash,
because his father showed kindness to me."
So David sent a delegation to express his
sympathy to Hanun concerning his father.
When David's men came to Hanun in the
land of the Ammonites to express sympathy
to him, 3the Ammonite nobles said to Hanun,
"Do you think David is honoring your father
by sending men to you to express sympathy? Haven't his men come to you to explore
and spy out the country and overthrow it?"
4So Hanun seized David's men, shaved
them, cut off their garments in the middle at
the buttocks, and sent them away.
5When someone came and told David
about the men, he sent messengers to meet
them, for they were greatly humiliated. The
king said, "Stay at Jericho till your beards
have grown, and then come back."
6When the Ammonites realized that they
had become a stench in David's nostrils,
Hanun and the Ammonites sent a thousand
talents[c] of silver to hire chariots and charioteers from Aram Naharaim,[d] Aram Maacah
and Zobah. 7They hired thirty-two thousand
chariots and charioteers, as well as the king
of Maacah with his troops, who came and
camped near Medeba, while the Ammonites
were mustered from their towns and moved
out for battle.
8On hearing this, David sent Joab out with
the entire army of fighting men. 9The Ammonites came out and drew up in battle formation at the entrance to their city, while the
kings who had come were by themselves in
the open country.
10Joab saw that there were battle lines in
front of him and behind him; so he selected

[a]8 Hebrew *Tibhath*, a variant of *Tebah* [b]16 Some Hebrew manuscripts, Vulgate and Syriac (see also 2 Samuel 8:17); most Hebrew manuscripts *Abimelech* [c]6 That is, about 37 tons (about 34 metric tons) [d]6 That is, Northwest Mesopotamia

some of the best troops in Israel and deployed them against the Arameans. 11He put the rest of the men under the command of Abishai his brother, and they were deployed against the Ammonites. 12Joab said, "If the Arameans are too strong for me, then you are to rescue me; but if the Ammonites are too strong for you, then I will rescue you. 13Be strong and let us fight bravely for our people and the cities of our God. The LORD will do what is good in his sight."

14Then Joab and the troops with him advanced to fight the Arameans, and they fled before him. 15When the Ammonites saw that the Arameans were fleeing, they too fled before his brother Abishai and went inside the city. So Joab went back to Jerusalem.

16After the Arameans saw that they had been routed by Israel, they sent messengers and had Arameans brought from beyond the River,[a] with Shophach the commander of Hadadezer's army leading them.

17When David was told of this, he gathered all Israel and crossed the Jordan; he advanced against them and formed his battle lines opposite them. David formed his lines to meet the Arameans in battle, and they fought against him. 18But they fled before Israel, and David killed seven thousand of their charioteers and forty thousand of their foot soldiers. He also killed Shophach the commander of their army.

19When the vassals of Hadadezer saw that they had been defeated by Israel, they made peace with David and became subject to him.

So the Arameans were not willing to help the Ammonites anymore.

The Capture of Rabbah

20 In the spring, at the time when kings go off to war, Joab led out the armed forces. He laid waste the land of the Ammonites and went to Rabbah and besieged it, but David remained in Jerusalem. Joab attacked Rabbah and left it in ruins. 2David took the crown from the head of their king[b]—its weight was found to be a talent[c] of gold, and it was set with precious stones—and it was placed on David's head. He took a great quantity of plunder from the city 3and brought out the people who were there, consigning them to labor with saws and with iron picks and axes. David did this to all the Ammonite towns. Then David and his entire army returned to Jerusalem.

War With the Philistines

4In the course of time, war broke out with the Philistines, at Gezer. At that time Sibbecai the Hushathite killed Sippai, one of the descendants of the Rephaites, and the Philistines were subjugated.

5In another battle with the Philistines, Elhanan son of Jair killed Lahmi the brother of Goliath the Gittite, who had a spear with a shaft like a weaver's rod.

6In still another battle, which took place at Gath, there was a huge man with six fingers on each hand and six toes on each foot—twenty-four in all. He also was descended from Rapha. 7When he taunted Israel, Jonathan son of Shimea, David's brother, killed him.

8These were descendants of Rapha in Gath, and they fell at the hands of David and his men.

David Numbers the Fighting Men

21 Satan rose up against Israel and incited David to take a census of Israel. 2So David said to Joab and the commanders of the troops, "Go and count the Israelites from Beersheba to Dan. Then report back to me so that I may know how many there are."

3But Joab replied, "May the LORD multiply his troops a hundred times over. My lord the king, are they not all my lord's subjects? Why does my lord want to do this? Why should he bring guilt on Israel?"

4The king's word, however, overruled Joab; so Joab left and went throughout Israel and then came back to Jerusalem. 5Joab reported the number of the fighting men to David: In all Israel there were one million one hundred thousand men who could handle a sword, including four hundred and seventy thousand in Judah.

6But Joab did not include Levi and Benjamin in the numbering, because the king's command was repulsive to him. 7This command was also evil in the sight of God; so he punished Israel.

8Then David said to God, "I have sinned greatly by doing this. Now, I beg you, take away the guilt of your servant. I have done a very foolish thing."

9The LORD said to Gad, David's seer, 10"Go

[a]*16* That is, the Euphrates [b]*2* Or *of Milcom,* that is, Molech [c]*2* That is, about 75 pounds (about 34 kilograms)

and tell David, 'This is what the LORD says: I am giving you three options. Choose one of them for me to carry out against you.' "

11 So Gad went to David and said to him, "This is what the LORD says: 'Take your choice: 12 three years of famine, three months of being swept away[a] before your enemies, with their swords overtaking you, or three days of the sword of the LORD—days of plague in the land, with the angel of the LORD ravaging every part of Israel.' Now then, decide how I should answer the one who sent me."

13 David said to God, "I am in deep distress. Let me fall into the hands of the LORD, for his mercy is very great; but do not let me fall into the hands of men."

14 So the LORD sent a plague on Israel, and seventy thousand men of Israel fell dead. 15 And God sent an angel to destroy Jerusalem. But as the angel was doing so, the LORD saw it and was grieved because of the calamity and said to the angel who was destroying the people, "Enough! Withdraw your hand." The angel of the LORD was then standing at the threshing floor of Araunah[b] the Jebusite.

16 David looked up and saw the angel of the LORD standing between heaven and earth, with a drawn sword in his hand extended over Jerusalem. Then David and the elders, clothed in sackcloth, fell facedown.

17 David said to God, "Was it not I who ordered the fighting men to be counted? I am the one who has sinned and done wrong. These are but sheep. What have they done? O LORD my God, let your hand fall upon me and my family, but do not let this plague remain on your people."

18 Then the angel of the LORD ordered Gad to tell David to go up and build an altar to the LORD on the threshing floor of Araunah the Jebusite. 19 So David went up in obedience to the word that Gad had spoken in the name of the LORD.

20 While Araunah was threshing wheat, he turned and saw the angel; his four sons who were with him hid themselves. 21 Then David approached, and when Araunah looked and saw him, he left the threshing floor and bowed down before David with his face to the ground.

22 David said to him, "Let me have the site of your threshing floor so I can build an altar to the LORD, that the plague on the people may be stopped. Sell it to me at the full price."

23 Araunah said to David, "Take it! Let my lord the king do whatever pleases him. Look, I will give the oxen for the burnt offerings, the threshing sledges for the wood, and the wheat for the grain offering. I will give all this."

24 But King David replied to Araunah, "No, I insist on paying the full price. I will not take for the LORD what is yours, or sacrifice a burnt offering that costs me nothing."

25 So David paid Araunah six hundred shekels[c] of gold for the site. 26 David built an altar to the LORD there and sacrificed burnt offerings and fellowship offerings.[d] He called on the LORD, and the LORD answered him with fire from heaven on the altar of burnt offering.

27 Then the LORD spoke to the angel, and he put his sword back into its sheath. 28 At that time, when David saw that the LORD had answered him on the threshing floor of Araunah the Jebusite, he offered sacrifices there. 29 The tabernacle of the LORD, which Moses had made in the desert, and the altar of burnt offering were at that time on the high place at Gibeon. 30 But David could not go before it to inquire of God, because he was afraid of the sword of the angel of the LORD.

22 Then David said, "The house of the LORD God is to be here, and also the altar of burnt offering for Israel."

Preparations for the Temple

2 So David gave orders to assemble the aliens living in Israel, and from among them he appointed stonecutters to prepare dressed stone for building the house of God. 3 He provided a large amount of iron to make nails for the doors of the gateways and for the fittings, and more bronze than could be weighed. 4 He also provided more cedar logs than could be counted, for the Sidonians and Tyrians had brought large numbers of them to David.

5 David said, "My son Solomon is young and inexperienced, and the house to be built for the LORD should be of great magnificence and fame and splendor in the sight of all the nations. Therefore I will make preparations for it." So David made extensive preparations before his death.

[a] 12 Hebrew; Septuagint and Vulgate (see also 2 Samuel 24:13) *of fleeing* [b] 15 Hebrew *Ornan*, a variant of *Araunah*; also in verses 18-28 [c] 25 That is, about 15 pounds (about 7 kilograms) [d] 26 Traditionally *peace offerings*

6Then he called for his son Solomon and
charged him to build a house for the LORD,
the God of Israel. 7David said to Solomon:
"My son, I had it in my heart to build a house
for the Name of the LORD my God. 8But this
word of the LORD came to me: 'You have
shed much blood and have fought many
wars. You are not to build a house for my
Name, because you have shed much blood
on the earth in my sight. 9But you will have a
son who will be a man of peace and rest, and
I will give him rest from all his enemies on
every side. His name will be Solomon,[a] and I
will grant Israel peace and quiet during his
reign. 10He is the one who will build a house
for my Name. He will be my son, and I will be
his father. And I will establish the throne of
his kingdom over Israel forever.'

11"Now, my son, the LORD be with you, and
may you have success and build the house
of the LORD your God, as he said you would.
12May the LORD give you discretion and
understanding when he puts you in command over Israel, so that you may keep the
law of the LORD your God. 13Then you will
have success if you are careful to observe
the decrees and laws that the LORD gave
Moses for Israel. Be strong and courageous.
Do not be afraid or discouraged.

14"I have taken great pains to provide for
the temple of the LORD a hundred thousand
talents[b] of gold, a million talents[c] of silver,
quantities of bronze and iron too great to be
weighed, and wood and stone. And you may
add to them. 15You have many workmen:
stonecutters, masons and carpenters, as
well as men skilled in every kind of work 16in
gold and silver, bronze and iron—craftsmen
beyond number. Now begin the work, and
the LORD be with you."

17Then David ordered all the leaders of
Israel to help his son Solomon. 18He said to
them, "Is not the LORD your God with you?
And has he not granted you rest on every
side? For he has handed the inhabitants of
the land over to me, and the land is subject to
the LORD and to his people. 19Now devote
your heart and soul to seeking the LORD your
God. Begin to build the sanctuary of the LORD
God, so that you may bring the ark of the
covenant of the LORD and the sacred articles
belonging to God into the temple that will be
built for the Name of the LORD."

The Levites

23 When David was old and full of
years, he made his son Solomon
king over Israel.

2He also gathered together all the leaders
of Israel, as well as the priests and Levites.
3The Levites thirty years old or more were
counted, and the total number of men was
thirty-eight thousand. 4David said, "Of these,
twenty-four thousand are to supervise the
work of the temple of the LORD and six thousand are to be officials and judges. 5Four
thousand are to be gatekeepers and four
thousand are to praise the LORD with the
musical instruments I have provided for that
purpose."

6David divided the Levites into groups corresponding to the sons of Levi: Gershon,
Kohath and Merari.

Gershonites

7Belonging to the Gershonites:
Ladan and Shimei.
8The sons of Ladan:
Jehiel the first, Zetham and Joel—
three in all.
9The sons of Shimei:
Shelomoth, Haziel and Haran—
three in all.
These were the heads of the families
of Ladan.
10And the sons of Shimei:
Jahath, Ziza,[d] Jeush and Beriah.
These were the sons of Shimei—
four in all.
11Jahath was the first and Ziza the
second, but Jeush and Beriah did
not have many sons; so they were
counted as one family with one as-
signment.

Kohathites

12The sons of Kohath:
Amram, Izhar, Hebron and Uzziel—
four in all.
13The sons of Amram:
Aaron and Moses.
Aaron was set apart, he and his descendants forever, to consecrate the
most holy things, to offer sacrifices
before the LORD, to minister before
him and to pronounce blessings in

[a]9 *Solomon* sounds like and may be derived from the Hebrew for *peace.* [b]14 That is, about 3,750 tons (about 3,450 metric tons) [c]14 That is, about 37,500 tons (about 34,500 metric tons) [d]10 One Hebrew manuscript, Septuagint and Vulgate (see also verse 11); most Hebrew manuscripts *Zina*

his name forever. 14The sons of
Moses the man of God were counted
as part of the tribe of Levi.
15The sons of Moses:
Gershom and Eliezer.
16The descendants of Gershom:
Shubael was the first.
17The descendants of Eliezer:
Rehabiah was the first.
Eliezer had no other sons, but the
sons of Rehabiah were very numerous.
18The sons of Izhar:
Shelomith was the first.
19The sons of Hebron:
Jeriah the first, Amariah the second,
Jahaziel the third and Jekameam the
fourth.
20The sons of Uzziel:
Micah the first and Isshiah the second.

Merarites

21The sons of Merari:
Mahli and Mushi.
The sons of Mahli:
Eleazar and Kish.
22Eleazar died without having sons: he
had only daughters. Their cousins,
the sons of Kish, married them.
23The sons of Mushi:
Mahli, Eder and Jerimoth—three in
all.

24These were the descendants of Levi by
their families—the heads of families as they
were registered under their names and
counted individually, that is, the workers
twenty years old or more who served in the
temple of the LORD. 25For David had said,
"Since the LORD, the God of Israel, has
granted rest to his people and has come to
dwell in Jerusalem forever, 26the Levites no
longer need to carry the tabernacle or any of
the articles used in its service." 27According
to the last instructions of David, the Levites
were counted from those twenty years old or
more.

28The duty of the Levites was to help
Aaron's descendants in the service of the
temple of the LORD: to be in charge of the
courtyards, the side rooms, the purification
of all sacred things and the performance of
other duties at the house of God. 29They
were in charge of the bread set out on the
table, the flour for the grain offerings, the
unleavened wafers, the baking and the mixing, and all measurements of quantity and
size. 30They were also to stand every morning to thank and praise the LORD. They were
to do the same in the evening 31and whenever burnt offerings were presented to the
LORD on Sabbaths and at New Moon festivals
and at appointed feasts. They were to serve
before the LORD regularly in the proper number and in the way prescribed for them.

32And so the Levites carried out their responsibilities for the Tent of Meeting, for the
Holy Place and, under their brothers the descendants of Aaron, for the service of the
temple of the LORD.

The Divisions of Priests

24 These were the divisions of the sons
of Aaron:

The sons of Aaron were Nadab, Abihu,
Eleazar and Ithamar. 2But Nadab and Abihu
died before their father did, and they had no
sons; so Eleazar and Ithamar served as the
priests. 3With the help of Zadok a descendant of Eleazar and Ahimelech a descendant
of Ithamar, David separated them into divisions for their appointed order of ministering.
4A larger number of leaders were found
among Eleazar's descendants than among
Ithamar's, and they were divided accordingly: sixteen heads of families from Eleazar's descendants and eight heads of families from Ithamar's descendants. 5They divided them impartially by drawing lots, for
there were officials of the sanctuary and officials of God among the descendants of both
Eleazar and Ithamar.

6The scribe Shemaiah son of Nethanel, a
Levite, recorded their names in the presence
of the king and of the officials: Zadok the
priest, Ahimelech son of Abiathar and the
heads of families of the priests and of the
Levites—one family being taken from Eleazar and then one from Ithamar.

7The first lot fell to Jehoiarib,
the second to Jedaiah,
8the third to Harim,
the fourth to Seorim,
9the fifth to Malkijah,
the sixth to Mijamin,
10the seventh to Hakkoz,
the eighth to Abijah,
11the ninth to Jeshua,
the tenth to Shecaniah,
12the eleventh to Eliashib,
the twelfth to Jakim,

13the thirteenth to Huppah,
the fourteenth to Jeshebeab,
14the fifteenth to Bilgah,
the sixteenth to Immer,
15the seventeenth to Hezir,
the eighteenth to Happizzez,
16the nineteenth to Pethahiah,
the twentieth to Jehezkel,
17the twenty-first to Jakin,
the twenty-second to Gamul,
18the twenty-third to Delaiah
and the twenty-fourth to Maaziah.

19This was their appointed order of ministering when they entered the temple of the LORD, according to the regulations prescribed for them by their forefather Aaron, as the LORD, the God of Israel, had commanded him.

The Rest of the Levites

20As for the rest of the descendants of Levi:
from the sons of Amram: Shubael;
from the sons of Shubael: Jehdeiah.
21As for Rehabiah, from his sons:
Isshiah was the first.
22From the Izharites: Shelomoth;
from the sons of Shelomoth: Jahath.
23The sons of Hebron: Jeriah the first,[a]
Amariah the second, Jahaziel the
third and Jekameam the fourth.
24The son of Uzziel: Micah;
from the sons of Micah: Shamir.
25The brother of Micah: Isshiah;
from the sons of Isshiah: Zechariah.
26The sons of Merari: Mahli and Mushi.
The son of Jaaziah: Beno.
27The sons of Merari:
from Jaaziah: Beno, Shoham, Zaccur and Ibri.
28From Mahli: Eleazar, who had no sons.
29From Kish: the son of Kish:
Jerahmeel.
30And the sons of Mushi: Mahli, Eder and
Jerimoth.

These were the Levites, according to their
families. 31They also cast lots, just as their brothers the descendants of Aaron did, in the presence of King David and of Zadok, Ahimelech, and the heads of families of the priests and of the Levites. The families of the oldest brother were treated the same as those of the youngest.

The Singers

25 David, together with the commanders of the army, set apart some of the sons of Asaph, Heman and Jeduthun for the ministry of prophesying, accompanied by harps, lyres and cymbals. Here is the list of the men who performed this service:

2From the sons of Asaph:
Zaccur, Joseph, Nethaniah and Asarelah. The sons of Asaph were under the supervision of Asaph, who prophesied under the king's supervision.
3As for Jeduthun, from his sons:
Gedaliah, Zeri, Jeshaiah, Shimei,[b] Hashabiah and Mattithiah, six in all, under the supervision of their father Jeduthun, who prophesied, using the harp in thanking and praising the LORD.
4As for Heman, from his sons:
Bukkiah, Mattaniah, Uzziel, Shubael and Jerimoth; Hananiah, Hanani, Eliathah, Giddalti and Romamti-Ezer; Joshbekashah, Mallothi, Hothir and Mahazioth.
5All these were sons of Heman the king's seer. They were given him through the promises of God to exalt him.[c] God gave Heman fourteen sons and three daughters.

6All these men were under the supervision of their fathers for the music of the temple of the LORD, with cymbals, lyres and harps, for the ministry at the house of God. Asaph, Jeduthun and Heman were under the supervision of the king.
7Along with their relatives—all of them trained and skilled in music for the LORD—they numbered 288.
8Young and old alike, teacher as well as student, cast lots for their duties.

9The first lot, which was for Asaph, fell to Joseph,
his sons and relatives,[d] 12[e]
the second to Gedaliah,
he and his relatives and sons, 12
10the third to Zaccur,
his sons and relatives, 12
11the fourth to Izri,[f]
his sons and relatives, 12

[a]23 Two Hebrew manuscripts and some Septuagint manuscripts (see also 1 Chron. 23:19); most Hebrew manuscripts *The sons of Jeriah:* [b]3 One Hebrew manuscript and some Septuagint manuscripts (see also verse 17); most Hebrew manuscripts do not have *Shimei.* [c]5 Hebrew *exalt the horn* [d]9 See Septuagint; Hebrew does not have *his sons and relatives.* [e]9 See the total in verse 7; Hebrew does not have *twelve.*
[f]11 A variant of *Zeri*

12the fifth to Nethaniah,
his sons and relatives, 12
13the sixth to Bukkiah,
his sons and relatives, 12
14the seventh to Jesarelah,[a]
his sons and relatives, 12
15the eighth to Jeshaiah,
his sons and relatives, 12
16the ninth to Mattaniah,
his sons and relatives, 12
17the tenth to Shimei,
his sons and relatives, 12
18the eleventh to Azarel,[b]
his sons and relatives, 12
19the twelfth to Hashabiah,
his sons and relatives, 12
20the thirteenth to Shubael,
his sons and relatives, 12
21the fourteenth to Mattithiah,
his sons and relatives, 12
22the fifteenth to Jerimoth,
his sons and relatives, 12
23the sixteenth to Hananiah,
his sons and relatives, 12
24the seventeenth to Joshbekashah,
his sons and relatives, 12
25the eighteenth to Hanani,
his sons and relatives, 12
26the nineteenth to Mallothi,
his sons and relatives, 12
27the twentieth to Eliathah,
his sons and relatives, 12
28the twenty-first to Hothir,
his sons and relatives, 12
29the twenty-second to Giddalti,
his sons and relatives, 12
30the twenty-third to Mahazioth,
his sons and relatives, 12
31the twenty-fourth to Romamti-Ezer,
his sons and relatives, 12

The Gatekeepers

26 The divisions of the gatekeepers:
From the Korahites: Meshelemiah son of Kore, one of the sons of Asaph.
2Meshelemiah had sons:
Zechariah the firstborn,
Jediael the second,
Zebadiah the third,
Jathniel the fourth,
3Elam the fifth,
Jehohanan the sixth
and Eliehoenai the seventh.
4Obed-Edom also had sons:
Shemaiah the firstborn,
Jehozabad the second,
Joah the third,
Sacar the fourth,
Nethanel the fifth,
5Ammiel the sixth,
Issachar the seventh
and Peullethai the eighth.
(For God had blessed Obed-Edom.)

6His son Shemaiah also had sons, who
were leaders in their father's family
because they were very capable
men. 7The sons of Shemaiah: Othni,
Rephael, Obed and Elzabad; his
relatives Elihu and Semakiah were
also able men. 8All these were descendants of Obed-Edom; they and
their sons and their relatives were
capable men with the strength to do
the work—descendants of Obed-
Edom, 62 in all.
9Meshelemiah had sons and relatives,
who were able men—18 in all.

10Hosah the Merarite had sons: Shimri
the first (although he was not the
firstborn, his father had appointed
him the first), 11Hilkiah the second,
Tabaliah the third and Zechariah the
fourth. The sons and relatives of
Hosah were 13 in all.
12These divisions of the gatekeepers,
through their chief men, had duties for ministering in the temple of the LORD, just as their
relatives had. 13Lots were cast for each gate,
according to their families, young and old
alike.
14The lot for the East Gate fell to Shelemiah.[c] Then lots were cast for his son Zechariah, a wise counselor, and the lot for the
North Gate fell to him. 15The lot for the South
Gate fell to Obed-Edom, and the lot for the
storehouse fell to his sons. 16The lots for the
West Gate and the Shalleketh Gate on the
upper road fell to Shuppim and Hosah.
Guard was alongside of guard: 17There
were six Levites a day on the east, four a day
on the north, four a day on the south and two
at a time at the storehouse. 18As for the court
to the west, there were four at the road and
two at the court itself.
19These were the divisions of the gatekeepers who were descendants of Korah
and Merari.

[a] 14 A variant of *Asarelah* [b] 18 A variant of *Uzziel* [c] 14 A variant of *Meshelemiah*

The Treasurers and Other Officials

20Their fellow Levites were[a] in charge of
the treasuries of the house of God and the
treasuries for the dedicated things.
21The descendants of Ladan, who were
Gershonites through Ladan and who were
heads of families belonging to Ladan the
Gershonite, were Jehieli, 22the sons of
Jehieli, Zetham and his brother Joel. They
were in charge of the treasuries of the temple
of the LORD.
23From the Amramites, the Izharites, the
Hebronites and the Uzzielites:

24Shubael, a descendant of Gershom
son of Moses, was the officer in
charge of the treasuries. 25His relatives through Eliezer: Rehabiah his
son, Jeshaiah his son, Joram his
son, Zicri his son and Shelomith his
son. 26Shelomith and his relatives
were in charge of all the treasuries
for the things dedicated by King David, by the heads of families who
were the commanders of thousands
and commanders of hundreds, and
by the other army commanders.
27Some of the plunder taken in battle
they dedicated for the repair of the
temple of the LORD. 28And everything
dedicated by Samuel the seer and
by Saul son of Kish, Abner son of
Ner and Joab son of Zeruiah, and all
the other dedicated things were in
the care of Shelomith and his relatives.
29From the Izharites: Kenaniah and his
sons were assigned duties away
from the temple, as officials and
judges over Israel.
30From the Hebronites: Hashabiah and
his relatives—seventeen hundred
able men—were responsible in Israel west of the Jordan for all the
work of the LORD and for the king's
service. 31As for the Hebronites, Jeriah was their chief according to the
genealogical records of their families. In the fortieth year of David's
reign a search was made in the
records, and capable men among
the Hebronites were found at Jazer
in Gilead. 32Jeriah had twenty-seven
hundred relatives, who were able
men and heads of families, and King
David put them in charge of the Reubenites, the Gadites and the half-
tribe of Manasseh for every matter
pertaining to God and for the affairs
of the king.

Army Divisions

27 This is the list of the Israelites—
heads of families, commanders of
thousands and commanders of hundreds,
and their officers, who served the king in all
that concerned the army divisions that were
on duty month by month throughout the year.
Each division consisted of 24,000 men.

2In charge of the first division, for the first
month, was Jashobeam son of
Zabdiel. There were 24,000 men in his
division. 3He was a descendant of
Perez and chief of all the army officers
for the first month.
4In charge of the division for the second
month was Dodai the Ahohite; Mikloth
was the leader of his division. There
were 24,000 men in his division.
5The third army commander, for the third
month, was Benaiah son of Jehoiada
the priest. He was chief and there were
24,000 men in his division. 6This was
the Benaiah who was a mighty man
among the Thirty and was over the
Thirty. His son Ammizabad was in
charge of his division.
7The fourth, for the fourth month, was
Asahel the brother of Joab; his son
Zebadiah was his successor. There
were 24,000 men in his division.
8The fifth, for the fifth month, was the
commander Shamhuth the Izrahite.
There were 24,000 men in his division.
9The sixth, for the sixth month, was Ira the
son of Ikkesh the Tekoite. There were
24,000 men in his division.
10The seventh, for the seventh month, was
Helez the Pelonite, an Ephraimite.
There were 24,000 men in his division.
11The eighth, for the eighth month, was
Sibbecai the Hushathite, a Zerahite.
There were 24,000 men in his division.
12The ninth, for the ninth month, was Abiezer
the Anathothite, a Benjamite. There
were 24,000 men in his division.
13The tenth, for the tenth month, was
Maharai the Netophathite, a Zerahite.
There were 24,000 men in his division.

[a]20 Septuagint; Hebrew *As for the Levites, Ahijah was*

14The eleventh, for the eleventh month, was Benaiah the Pirathonite, an Ephraimite. There were 24,000 men in his division.
15The twelfth, for the twelfth month, was Heldai the Netophathite, from the family of Othniel. There were 24,000 men in his division.

Officers of the Tribes

16The officers over the tribes of Israel:

over the Reubenites: Eliezer son of Zicri;
over the Simeonites: Shephatiah son of Maacah;
17over Levi: Hashabiah son of Kemuel;
over Aaron: Zadok;
18over Judah: Elihu, a brother of David;
over Issachar: Omri son of Michael;
19over Zebulun: Ishmaiah son of Obadiah;
over Naphtali: Jerimoth son of Azriel;
20over the Ephraimites: Hoshea son of Azaziah;
over half the tribe of Manasseh: Joel son of Pedaiah;
21over the half-tribe of Manasseh in Gilead: Iddo son of Zechariah;
over Benjamin: Jaasiel son of Abner;
22over Dan: Azarel son of Jeroham.

These were the officers over the tribes of Israel.

23David did not take the number of the men
twenty years old or less, because the LORD
had promised to make Israel as numerous
as the stars in the sky. 24Joab son of Zeruiah
began to count the men but did not finish.
Wrath came on Israel on account of this
numbering, and the number was not entered
in the book[a] of the annals of King David.

The King's Overseers

25Azmaveth son of Adiel was in charge of
the royal storehouses.

Jonathan son of Uzziah was in charge of
the storehouses in the outlying districts, in
the towns, the villages and the watchtowers.
26Ezri son of Kelub was in charge of the
field workers who farmed the land.
27Shimei the Ramathite was in charge of
the vineyards.

Zabdi the Shiphmite was in charge of the
produce of the vineyards for the wine vats.
28Baal-Hanan the Gederite was in charge
of the olive and sycamore-fig trees in the
western foothills.

Joash was in charge of the supplies of
olive oil.
29Shitrai the Sharonite was in charge of the
herds grazing in Sharon.

Shaphat son of Adlai was in charge of the
herds in the valleys.
30Obil the Ishmaelite was in charge of the
camels.

Jehdeiah the Meronothite was in charge of
the donkeys.
31Jaziz the Hagrite was in charge of the
flocks.

All these were the officials in charge of
King David's property.

32Jonathan, David's uncle, was a counsel-
or, a man of insight and a scribe. Jehiel son
of Hacmoni took care of the king's sons.
33Ahithophel was the king's counselor.

Hushai the Arkite was the king's friend.
34Ahithophel was succeeded by Jehoiada
son of Benaiah and by Abiathar.

Joab was the commander of the royal
army.

David's Plans for the Temple

28 David summoned all the officials of
Israel to assemble at Jerusalem: the
officers over the tribes, the commanders of
the divisions in the service of the king, the
commanders of thousands and commanders of hundreds, and the officials in charge of
all the property and livestock belonging to
the king and his sons, together with the palace officials, the mighty men and all the
brave warriors.

2King David rose to his feet and said: "Listen to me, my brothers and my people. I had
it in my heart to build a house as a place of
rest for the ark of the covenant of the LORD,
for the footstool of our God, and I made plans
to build it. 3But God said to me, 'You are not
to build a house for my Name, because you
are a warrior and have shed blood.'

4"Yet the LORD, the God of Israel, chose me
from my whole family to be king over Israel
forever. He chose Judah as leader, and from
the house of Judah he chose my family, and
from my father's sons he was pleased to
make me king over all Israel. 5Of all my
sons—and the LORD has given me many—he
has chosen my son Solomon to sit on the
throne of the kingdom of the LORD over Israel.

[a]24 Septuagint; Hebrew *number*

6He said to me: 'Solomon your son is the one
who will build my house and my courts, for I
have chosen him to be my son, and I will be
his father. 7I will establish his kingdom forever if he is unswerving in carrying out my
commands and laws, as is being done at this
time.'

8"So now I charge you in the sight of all
Israel and of the assembly of the LORD, and in
the hearing of our God: Be careful to follow
all the commands of the LORD your God, that
you may possess this good land and pass it
on as an inheritance to your descendants
forever.

9"And you, my son Solomon, acknowledge the God of your father, and serve him
with wholehearted devotion and with a willing mind, for the LORD searches every heart
and understands every motive behind the
thoughts. If you seek him, he will be found by
you; but if you forsake him, he will reject you
forever. 10Consider now, for the LORD has
chosen you to build a temple as a sanctuary.
Be strong and do the work."

11Then David gave his son Solomon the
plans for the portico of the temple, its buildings, its storerooms, its upper parts, its inner
rooms and the place of atonement. 12He
gave him the plans of all that the Spirit had
put in his mind for the courts of the temple of
the LORD and all the surrounding rooms, for
the treasuries of the temple of God and for
the treasuries for the dedicated things. 13He
gave him instructions for the divisions of the
priests and Levites, and for all the work of
serving in the temple of the LORD, as well as
for all the articles to be used in its service.
14He designated the weight of gold for all the
gold articles to be used in various kinds of
service, and the weight of silver for all the
silver articles to be used in various kinds of
service: 15the weight of gold for the gold
lampstands and their lamps, with the weight
for each lampstand and its lamps; and the
weight of silver for each silver lampstand and
its lamps, according to the use of each lampstand; 16the weight of gold for each table for
consecrated bread; the weight of silver for
the silver tables; 17the weight of pure gold for
the forks, sprinkling bowls and pitchers; the
weight of gold for each gold dish; the weight
of silver for each silver dish; 18and the weight
of the refined gold for the altar of incense. He
also gave him the plan for the chariot, that is,
the cherubim of gold that spread their wings
and shelter the ark of the covenant of the
LORD.

19"All this," David said, "I have in writing
from the hand of the LORD upon me, and he
gave me understanding in all the details of
the plan."

20David also said to Solomon his son, "Be
strong and courageous, and do the work. Do
not be afraid or discouraged, for the LORD
God, my God, is with you. He will not fail you
or forsake you until all the work for the service of the temple of the LORD is finished.
21The divisions of the priests and Levites are
ready for all the work on the temple of God,
and every willing man skilled in any craft will
help you in all the work. The officials and
all the people will obey your every command."

Gifts for Building the Temple

29 Then King David said to the whole
assembly: "My son Solomon, the
one whom God has chosen, is young and
inexperienced. The task is great, because
this palatial structure is not for man but for
the LORD God. 2With all my resources I have
provided for the temple of my God—gold for
the gold work, silver for the silver, bronze for
the bronze, iron for the iron and wood for the
wood, as well as onyx for the settings, turquoise,[a] stones of various colors, and all
kinds of fine stone and marble—all of these
in large quantities. 3Besides, in my devotion
to the temple of my God I now give my personal treasures of gold and silver for the
temple of my God, over and above everything I have provided for this holy temple:
4three thousand talents[b] of gold (gold of
Ophir) and seven thousand talents[c] of refined silver, for the overlaying of the walls of
the buildings, 5for the gold work and the silver work, and for all the work to be done by
the craftsmen. Now, who is willing to consecrate himself today to the LORD?"

6Then the leaders of families, the officers
of the tribes of Israel, the commanders of
thousands and commanders of hundreds,
and the officials in charge of the king's work
gave willingly. 7They gave toward the work
on the temple of God five thousand talents[d]
and ten thousand darics[e] of gold, ten thousand talents[f] of silver, eighteen thousand

[a]2 The meaning of the Hebrew for this word is uncertain. [b]4 That is, about 110 tons (about 100 metric tons)
[c]4 That is, about 260 tons (about 240 metric tons) [d]7 That is, about 190 tons (about 170 metric tons)
[e]7 That is, about 185 pounds (about 84 kilograms) [f]7 That is, about 375 tons (about 345 metric tons)

talents[a] of bronze and a hundred thousand
talents[b] of iron. 8Any who had precious
stones gave them to the treasury of the temple of the LORD in the custody of Jehiel the
Gershonite. 9The people rejoiced at the willing response of their leaders, for they had
given freely and wholeheartedly to the LORD.
David the king also rejoiced greatly.

David's Prayer

10David praised the LORD in the presence
of the whole assembly, saying,

"Praise be to you, O LORD,
  God of our father Israel,
  from everlasting to everlasting.
11Yours, O LORD, is the greatness and the power
  and the glory and the majesty and the splendor,
  for everything in heaven and earth is yours.
Yours, O LORD, is the kingdom;
  you are exalted as head over all.
12Wealth and honor come from you;
  you are the ruler of all things.
In your hands are strength and power
  to exalt and give strength to all.
13Now, our God, we give you thanks,
  and praise your glorious name.

14"But who am I, and who are my people,
that we should be able to give as generously
as this? Everything comes from you, and we
have given you only what comes from your
hand. 15We are aliens and strangers in your
sight, as were all our forefathers. Our days
on earth are like a shadow, without hope. 16O
LORD our God, as for all this abundance that
we have provided for building you a temple
for your Holy Name, it comes from your
hand, and all of it belongs to you. 17I know,
my God, that you test the heart and are
pleased with integrity. All these things have I
given willingly and with honest intent. And
now I have seen with joy how willingly your
people who are here have given to you. 18O
LORD, God of our fathers Abraham, Isaac and
Israel, keep this desire in the hearts of your
people forever, and keep their hearts loyal to
you. 19And give my son Solomon the wholehearted devotion to keep your commands,
requirements and decrees and to do everything to build the palatial structure for which I
have provided."

20Then David said to the whole assembly,
"Praise the LORD your God." So they all
praised the LORD, the God of their fathers;
they bowed low and fell prostrate before the
LORD and the king.

Solomon Acknowledged as King

21The next day they made sacrifices to the
LORD and presented burnt offerings to him: a
thousand bulls, a thousand rams and a thousand male lambs, together with their drink
offerings, and other sacrifices in abundance
for all Israel. 22They ate and drank with great
joy in the presence of the LORD that day.

Then they acknowledged Solomon son of
David as king a second time, anointing him
before the LORD to be ruler and Zadok to be
priest. 23So Solomon sat on the throne of the
LORD as king in place of his father David. He
prospered and all Israel obeyed him. 24All the
officers and mighty men, as well as all of
King David's sons, pledged their submission
to King Solomon.

25The LORD highly exalted Solomon in the
sight of all Israel and bestowed on him royal
splendor such as no king over Israel ever
had before.

The Death of David

26David son of Jesse was king over all
Israel. 27He ruled over Israel forty years—
seven in Hebron and thirty-three in Jerusalem. 28He died at a good old age, having
enjoyed long life, wealth and honor. His son
Solomon succeeded him as king.

29As for the events of King David's reign,
from beginning to end, they are written in the
records of Samuel the seer, the records of
Nathan the prophet and the records of Gad
the seer, 30together with the details of his
reign and power, and the circumstances that
surrounded him and Israel and the kingdoms
of all the other lands.

[a]7 That is, about 675 tons (about 610 metric tons)
[b]7 That is, about 3,750 tons (about 3,450 metric tons)

2 Chronicles

Introduction:

Second Chronicles continues the history of David's royal line. Chapters 1–9 describe the building of the temple during Solomon's reign. Chapters 10–36 follow the history of the southern kingdom of Judah to the final destruction of Jerusalem and the people being taken captives to Babylon.

This book, like 1 Chronicles, shows that the people's relationship to God was most important. When the author wrote about the kings he measured them on the basis of their faithfulness to God. The reigns of evil kings are reported by the author quickly, while the reigns of good kings are described in more detail.

Outline of contents:

The reign of Solomon (1:1–9:31)
The kings of Judah (10:1–36:14)
The destruction of Jerusalem (36:15–23)

Solomon Asks for Wisdom

1 Solomon son of David established himself firmly over his kingdom, for the LORD
his God was with him and made him exceedingly great.
2Then Solomon spoke to all Israel—to the
commanders of thousands and commanders of hundreds, to the judges and to all the
leaders in Israel, the heads of families—
3and Solomon and the whole assembly went
to the high place at Gibeon, for God's Tent of
Meeting was there, which Moses the LORD's
servant had made in the desert. 4Now David
had brought up the ark of God from Kiriath
Jearim to the place he had prepared for it,
because he had pitched a tent for it in
Jerusalem. 5But the bronze altar that Bezalel
son of Uri, the son of Hur, had made was in
Gibeon in front of the tabernacle of the LORD;
so Solomon and the assembly inquired of
him there. 6Solomon went up to the bronze
altar before the LORD in the Tent of Meeting
and offered a thousand burnt offerings on it.
7That night God appeared to Solomon and
said to him, "Ask for whatever you want me
to give you."
8Solomon answered God, "You have
shown great kindness to David my father
and have made me king in his place. 9Now,
LORD God, let your promise to my father David be confirmed, for you have made me king
over a people who are as numerous as the
dust of the earth. 10Give me wisdom and
knowledge, that I may lead this people, for
who is able to govern this great people of
yours?"
11God said to Solomon, "Since this is your
heart's desire and you have not asked for
wealth, riches or honor, nor for the death of
your enemies, and since you have not asked
for a long life but for wisdom and knowledge
to govern my people over whom I have made
you king, 12therefore wisdom and knowledge
will be given you. And I will also give you
wealth, riches and honor, such as no king
who was before you ever had and none after
you will have."
13Then Solomon went to Jerusalem from
the high place at Gibeon, from before the
Tent of Meeting. And he reigned over Israel.
14Solomon accumulated chariots and
horses; he had fourteen hundred chariots
and twelve thousand horses,[a] which he kept
in the chariot cities and also with him in
Jerusalem. 15The king made silver and gold
as common in Jerusalem as stones, and cedar as plentiful as sycamore-fig trees in the
foothills. 16Solomon's horses were imported
from Egypt[b] and from Kue[c]—the royal merchants purchased them from Kue. 17They
imported a chariot from Egypt for six hun-

[a]14 Or *charioteers* [b]16 Or possibly *Muzur,* a region in Cilicia; also in verse 17 [c]16 Probably Cilicia

dred shekels[a] of silver, and a horse for a hundred and fifty.[b] They also exported them to all the kings of the Hittites and of the Arameans.

Preparations for Building the Temple

2 Solomon gave orders to build a temple for the Name of the LORD and a royal palace for himself. 2He conscripted seventy thousand men as carriers and eighty thousand as stonecutters in the hills and thirty-six hundred as foremen over them.

3Solomon sent this message to Hiram[c] king of Tyre:

"Send me cedar logs as you did for my father David when you sent him cedar to build a palace to live in. 4Now I am about to build a temple for the Name of the LORD my God and to dedicate it to him for burning fragrant incense before him, for setting out the consecrated bread regularly, and for making burnt offerings every morning and evening and on Sabbaths and New Moons and at the appointed feasts of the LORD our God. This is a lasting ordinance for Israel.

5"The temple I am going to build will be great, because our God is greater than all other gods. 6But who is able to build a temple for him, since the heavens, even the highest heavens, cannot contain him? Who then am I to build a temple for him, except as a place to burn sacrifices before him?

7"Send me, therefore, a man skilled to work in gold and silver, bronze and iron, and in purple, crimson and blue yarn, and experienced in the art of engraving, to work in Judah and Jerusalem with my skilled craftsmen, whom my father David provided.

8"Send me also cedar, pine and algum[d] logs from Lebanon, for I know that your men are skilled in cutting timber there. My men will work with yours 9to provide me with plenty of lumber, because the temple I build must be large and magnificent. 10I will give your servants, the woodsmen who cut the timber, twenty thousand cors[e] of ground wheat, twenty thousand cors of barley, twenty thousand baths[f] of wine and twenty thousand baths of olive oil."

11Hiram king of Tyre replied by letter to Solomon:

"Because the LORD loves his people, he has made you their king."

12And Hiram added:

"Praise be to the LORD, the God of Israel, who made heaven and earth! He has given King David a wise son, endowed with intelligence and discernment, who will build a temple for the LORD and a palace for himself.

13"I am sending you Huram-Abi, a man of great skill, 14whose mother was from Dan and whose father was from Tyre. He is trained to work in gold and silver, bronze and iron, stone and wood, and with purple and blue and crimson yarn and fine linen. He is experienced in all kinds of engraving and can execute any design given to him. He will work with your craftsmen and with those of my lord, David your father.

15"Now let my lord send his servants the wheat and barley and the olive oil and wine he promised, 16and we will cut all the logs from Lebanon that you need and will float them in rafts by sea down to Joppa. You can then take them up to Jerusalem."

17Solomon took a census of all the aliens who were in Israel, after the census his father David had taken; and they were found to be 153,600. 18He assigned 70,000 of them to be carriers and 80,000 to be stonecutters in the hills, with 3,600 foremen over them to keep the people working.

Solomon Builds the Temple

3 Then Solomon began to build the temple of the LORD in Jerusalem on Mount Moriah, where the LORD had appeared to his father David. It was on the threshing floor of Araunah[g] the Jebusite, the place provided by David. 2He began building on the second day of the second month in the fourth year of his reign.

3The foundation Solomon laid for building the temple of God was sixty cubits long and

[a] *17* That is, about 15 pounds (about 7 kilograms) [b] *17* That is, about 3 3/4 pounds (about 1.7 kilograms) [c] *3* Hebrew *Huram,* a variant of *Hiram;* also in verses 11 and 12 [d] *8* Probably a variant of *almug;* possibly juniper [e] *10* That is, probably about 125,000 bushels (about 4,400 kiloliters) [f] *10* That is, probably about 115,000 gallons (about 440 kiloliters) [g] *1* Hebrew *Ornan,* a variant of *Araunah*

twenty cubits wide[a] (using the cubit of the old
standard). 4The portico at the front of the
temple was twenty cubits[b] long across the
width of the building and twenty cubits[c] high.

He overlaid the inside with pure gold. 5He
paneled the main hall with pine and covered
it with fine gold and decorated it with palm
tree and chain designs. 6He adorned the
temple with precious stones. And the gold he
used was gold of Parvaim. 7He overlaid the
ceiling beams, doorframes, walls and doors
of the temple with gold, and he carved cherubim on the walls.

8He built the Most Holy Place, its length
corresponding to the width of the temple—
twenty cubits long and twenty cubits wide.
He overlaid the inside with six hundred talents[d] of fine gold. 9The gold nails weighed
fifty shekels.[e] He also overlaid the upper
parts with gold.

10In the Most Holy Place he made a pair of
sculptured cherubim and overlaid them with
gold. 11The total wingspan of the cherubim
was twenty cubits. One wing of the first cherub was five cubits[f] long and touched the
temple wall, while its other wing, also five
cubits long, touched the wing of the other
cherub. 12Similarly one wing of the second
cherub was five cubits long and touched the
other temple wall, and its other wing, also
five cubits long, touched the wing of the first
cherub. 13The wings of these cherubim extended twenty cubits. They stood on their
feet, facing the main hall.[g]

14He made the curtain of blue, purple and
crimson yarn and fine linen, with cherubim
worked into it.

15In the front of the temple he made two
pillars, which ⌊together⌋ were thirty-five cubits[h] long, each with a capital on top measuring five cubits. 16He made interwoven
chains[i] and put them on top of the pillars. He
also made a hundred pomegranates and attached them to the chains. 17He erected the
pillars in the front of the temple, one to the
south and one to the north. The one to the
south he named Jakin[j] and the one to the
north Boaz.[k]

The Temple's Furnishings

4 He made a bronze altar twenty cubits
long, twenty cubits wide and ten cubits
high.[l] 2He made the Sea of cast metal, circular in shape, measuring ten cubits from rim to
rim and five cubits[m] high. It took a line of thirty
cubits[n] to measure around it. 3Below the rim,
figures of bulls encircled it—ten to a cubit.[o]
The bulls were cast in two rows in one piece
with the Sea.

4The Sea stood on twelve bulls, three facing north, three facing west, three facing
south and three facing east. The Sea rested
on top of them, and their hindquarters were
toward the center. 5It was a handbreadth[p] in
thickness, and its rim was like the rim of a
cup, like a lily blossom. It held three thousand baths.[q]

6He then made ten basins for washing and
placed five on the south side and five on the
north. In them the things to be used for the
burnt offerings were rinsed, but the Sea was
to be used by the priests for washing.

7He made ten gold lampstands according
to the specifications for them and placed
them in the temple, five on the south side and
five on the north.

8He made ten tables and placed them in
the temple, five on the south side and five on
the north. He also made a hundred gold
sprinkling bowls.

9He made the courtyard of the priests, and
the large court and the doors for the court,
and overlaid the doors with bronze. 10He
placed the Sea on the south side, at the
southeast corner.

11He also made the pots and shovels and
sprinkling bowls.

So Huram finished the work he had undertaken for King Solomon in the temple of God:

12the two pillars;
the two bowl-shaped capitals on top of
the pillars;
the two sets of network decorating the
two bowl-shaped capitals on top of
the pillars;
13the four hundred pomegranates for the

a3 That is, about 90 feet (about 27 meters) long and 30 feet (about 9 meters) wide b4 That is, about 30 feet (about 9 meters); also in verses 8, 11 and 13 c4 Some Septuagint and Syriac manuscripts; Hebrew *and a hundred and twenty* d8 That is, about 23 tons (about 21 metric tons) e9 That is, about 1 1/4 pounds (about 0.6 kilogram) f11 That is, about 7 1/2 feet (about 2.3 meters); also in verse 15 g13 Or *facing inward* h15 That is, about 52 feet (about 16 meters) i16 Or possibly *made chains in the inner sanctuary*; the meaning of the Hebrew for this phrase is uncertain. j17 *Jakin* probably means *he establishes.* k17 *Boaz* probably means *in him is strength.* l1 That is, about 30 feet (about 9 meters) long and wide, and about 15 feet (about 4.5 meters) high m2 That is, about 7 1/2 feet (about 2.3 meters) n2 That is, about 45 feet (about 13.5 meters) o3 That is, about 1 1/2 feet (about 0.5 meter) p5 That is, about 3 inches (about 8 centimeters) q5 That is, about 17,500 gallons (about 66 kiloliters)

two sets of network (two rows of
pomegranates for each network,
decorating the bowl-shaped capitals
on top of the pillars);
14 the stands with their basins;
15 the Sea and the twelve bulls under it;
16 the pots, shovels, meat forks and all
related articles.

All the objects that Huram-Abi made for
King Solomon for the temple of the LORD
were of polished bronze. 17 The king had
them cast in clay molds in the plain of the
Jordan between Succoth and Zarethan.[a]
18 All these things that Solomon made
amounted to so much that the weight of the
bronze was not determined.
19 Solomon also made all the furnishings
that were in God's temple:

the golden altar;
the tables on which was the bread of
the Presence;
20 the lampstands of pure gold with their
lamps, to burn in front of the inner
sanctuary as prescribed;
21 the gold floral work and lamps and
tongs (they were solid gold);
22 the pure gold wick trimmers, sprinkling
bowls, dishes and censers; and the
gold doors of the temple: the inner
doors to the Most Holy Place and the
doors of the main hall.

5 When all the work Solomon had done for
the temple of the LORD was finished, he
brought in the things his father David had
dedicated—the silver and gold and all the
furnishings—and he placed them in the treasuries of God's temple.

The Ark Brought to the Temple

2 Then Solomon summoned to Jerusalem
the elders of Israel, all the heads of the tribes
and the chiefs of the Israelite families, to
bring up the ark of the LORD's covenant from
Zion, the City of David. 3 And all the men of
Israel came together to the king at the time of
the festival in the seventh month.
4 When all the elders of Israel had arrived,
the Levites took up the ark, 5 and they
brought up the ark and the Tent of Meeting
and all the sacred furnishings in it. The
priests, who were Levites, carried them up;
6 and King Solomon and the entire assembly
of Israel that had gathered about him were
before the ark, sacrificing so many sheep
and cattle that they could not be recorded or
counted.
7 The priests then brought the ark of the
LORD's covenant to its place in the inner
sanctuary of the temple, the Most Holy
Place, and put it beneath the wings of the
cherubim. 8 The cherubim spread their wings
over the place of the ark and covered the ark
and its carrying poles. 9 These poles were so
long that their ends, extending from the ark,
could be seen from in front of the inner sanctuary, but not from outside the Holy Place;
and they are still there today. 10 There was
nothing in the ark except the two tablets that
Moses had placed in it at Horeb, where the
LORD made a covenant with the Israelites after they came out of Egypt.
11 The priests then withdrew from the Holy
Place. All the priests who were there had
consecrated themselves, regardless of their
divisions. 12 All the Levites who were musicians—Asaph, Heman, Jeduthun and their
sons and relatives—stood on the east side of
the altar, dressed in fine linen and playing
cymbals, harps and lyres. They were accompanied by 120 priests sounding trumpets.
13 The trumpeters and singers joined in unison, as with one voice, to give praise and
thanks to the LORD. Accompanied by trumpets, cymbals and other instruments, they
raised their voices in praise to the LORD and
sang:

"He is good;
his love endures forever."

Then the temple of the LORD was filled with
a cloud, 14 and the priests could not perform
their service because of the cloud, for the
glory of the LORD filled the temple of God.
6 Then Solomon said, "The LORD has said
that he would dwell in a dark cloud; 2 I
have built a magnificent temple for you, a
place for you to dwell forever."
3 While the whole assembly of Israel was
standing there, the king turned around and
blessed them. 4 Then he said:

"Praise be to the LORD, the God of
Israel, who with his hands has fulfilled
what he promised with his mouth to my
father David. For he said, 5 'Since the
day I brought my people out of Egypt, I
have not chosen a city in any tribe of
Israel to have a temple built for my
Name to be there, nor have I chosen
anyone to be the leader over my people

[a] 17 Hebrew *Zeredatha,* a variant of *Zarethan*

Israel. 6But now I have chosen Jerusalem for my Name to be there, and I have chosen David to rule my people Israel.'

7"My father David had it in his heart to build a temple for the Name of the LORD, the God of Israel. 8But the LORD said to my father David, 'Because it was in your heart to build a temple for my Name, you did well to have this in your heart. 9Nevertheless, you are not the one to build the temple, but your son, who is your own flesh and blood—he is the one who will build the temple for my Name.'

10"The LORD has kept the promise he made. I have succeeded David my father and now I sit on the throne of Israel, just as the LORD promised, and I have built the temple for the Name of the LORD, the God of Israel. 11There I have placed the ark, in which is the covenant of the LORD that he made with the people of Israel."

Solomon's Prayer of Dedication

12Then Solomon stood before the altar of the LORD in front of the whole assembly of Israel and spread out his hands. 13Now he had made a bronze platform, five cubits[a] long, five cubits wide and three cubits[b] high, and had placed it in the center of the outer court. He stood on the platform and then knelt down before the whole assembly of Israel and spread out his hands toward heaven. 14He said:

"O LORD, God of Israel, there is no God like you in heaven or on earth—you who keep your covenant of love with your servants who continue wholeheartedly in your way. 15You have kept your promise to your servant David my father; with your mouth you have promised and with your hand you have fulfilled it—as it is today.

16"Now LORD, God of Israel, keep for your servant David my father the promises you made to him when you said, 'You shall never fail to have a man to sit before me on the throne of Israel, if only your sons are careful in all they do to walk before me according to my law, as you have done.' 17And now, O LORD, God of Israel, let your word that you promised your servant David come true.

18"But will God really dwell on earth with men? The heavens, even the highest heavens, cannot contain you. How much less this temple I have built! 19Yet give attention to your servant's prayer and his plea for mercy, O LORD my God. Hear the cry and the prayer that your servant is praying in your presence. 20May your eyes be open toward this temple day and night, this place of which you said you would put your Name there. May you hear the prayer your servant prays toward this place. 21Hear the supplications of your servant and of your people Israel when they pray toward this place. Hear from heaven, your dwelling place; and when you hear, forgive.

22"When a man wrongs his neighbor and is required to take an oath and he comes and swears the oath before your altar in this temple, 23then hear from heaven and act. Judge between your servants, repaying the guilty by bringing down on his own head what he has done. Declare the innocent not guilty and so establish his innocence.

24"When your people Israel have been defeated by an enemy because they have sinned against you and when they turn back and confess your name, praying and making supplication before you in this temple, 25then hear from heaven and forgive the sin of your people Israel and bring them back to the land you gave to them and their fathers.

26"When the heavens are shut up and there is no rain because your people have sinned against you, and when they pray toward this place and confess your name and turn from their sin because you have afflicted them, 27then hear from heaven and forgive the sin of your servants, your people Israel. Teach them the right way to live, and send rain on the land you gave your people for an inheritance.

28"When famine or plague comes to the land, or blight or mildew, locusts or grasshoppers, or when enemies besiege them in any of their cities, whatever disaster or disease may come, 29and when a prayer or plea is made by any of your people Israel—each one aware of his afflictions and pains, and spreading out his hands toward this temple— 30then hear from heaven, your

[a] 13 That is, about 7 1/2 feet (about 2.3 meters) [b] 13 That is, about 4 1/2 feet (about 1.3 meters)

dwelling place. Forgive, and deal with each man according to all he does, since you know his heart (for you alone know the hearts of men), [31]so that they will fear you and walk in your ways all the time they live in the land you gave our fathers.

[32]"As for the foreigner who does not belong to your people Israel but has come from a distant land because of your great name and your mighty hand and your outstretched arm—when he comes and prays toward this temple, [33]then hear from heaven, your dwelling place, and do whatever the foreigner asks of you, so that all the peoples of the earth may know your name and fear you, as do your own people Israel, and may know that this house I have built bears your Name.

[34]"When your people go to war against their enemies, wherever you send them, and when they pray to you toward this city you have chosen and the temple I have built for your Name, [35]then hear from heaven their prayer and their plea, and uphold their cause.

[36]"When they sin against you—for there is no one who does not sin—and you become angry with them and give them over to the enemy, who takes them captive to a land far away or near; [37]and if they have a change of heart in the land where they are held captive, and repent and plead with you in the land of their captivity and say, 'We have sinned, we have done wrong and acted wickedly'; [38]and if they turn back to you with all their heart and soul in the land of their captivity where they were taken, and pray toward the land you gave their fathers, toward the city you have chosen and toward the temple I have built for your Name; [39]then from heaven, your dwelling place, hear their prayer and their pleas, and uphold their cause. And forgive your people, who have sinned against you.

[40]"Now, my God, may your eyes be open and your ears attentive to the prayers offered in this place.

[41]"Now arise, O LORD God, and come
to your resting place,
you and the ark of your might.
May your priests, O LORD God, be
clothed with salvation,
may your saints rejoice in your
goodness.
[42]O LORD God, do not reject your
anointed one.
Remember the great love
promised to David your
servant."

The Dedication of the Temple

7 When Solomon finished praying, fire came down from heaven and consumed the burnt offering and the sacrifices, and the glory of the LORD filled the temple. [2]The priests could not enter the temple of the LORD because the glory of the LORD filled it. [3]When all the Israelites saw the fire coming down and the glory of the LORD above the temple, they knelt on the pavement with their faces to the ground, and they worshiped and gave thanks to the LORD, saying,

"He is good;
his love endures forever."

[4]Then the king and all the people offered sacrifices before the LORD. [5]And King Solomon offered a sacrifice of twenty-two thousand head of cattle and a hundred and twenty thousand sheep and goats. So the king and all the people dedicated the temple of God. [6]The priests took their positions, as did the Levites with the LORD's musical instruments, which King David had made for praising the LORD and which were used when he gave thanks, saying, "His love endures forever." Opposite the Levites, the priests blew their trumpets, and all the Israelites were standing.

[7]Solomon consecrated the middle part of the courtyard in front of the temple of the LORD, and there he offered burnt offerings and the fat of the fellowship offerings,[a] because the bronze altar he had made could not hold the burnt offerings, the grain offerings and the fat portions.

[8]So Solomon observed the festival at that time for seven days, and all Israel with him—a vast assembly, people from Lebo[b] Hamath to the Wadi of Egypt. [9]On the eighth day they held an assembly, for they had celebrated the dedication of the altar for seven days and the festival for seven days more. [10]On the twenty-third day of the seventh month he

[a]7 Traditionally *peace offerings* [b]8 Or *from the entrance to*

sent the people to their homes, joyful and
glad in heart for the good things the LORD had
done for David and Solomon and for his
people Israel.

The LORD Appears to Solomon

11When Solomon had finished the temple
of the LORD and the royal palace, and had
succeeded in carrying out all he had in mind
to do in the temple of the LORD and in his own
palace, 12the LORD appeared to him at night
and said:

"I have heard your prayer and have
chosen this place for myself as a temple
for sacrifices.

13"When I shut up the heavens so that
there is no rain, or command locusts to
devour the land or send a plague among
my people, 14if my people, who are
called by my name, will humble themselves and pray and seek my face and
turn from their wicked ways, then will I
hear from heaven and will forgive their
sin and will heal their land. 15Now my
eyes will be open and my ears attentive
to the prayers offered in this place. 16I
have chosen and consecrated this temple so that my Name may be there forever. My eyes and my heart will always
be there.

17"As for you, if you walk before me as
David your father did, and do all I command, and observe my decrees and
laws, 18I will establish your royal throne,
as I covenanted with David your father
when I said, 'You shall never fail to have
a man to rule over Israel.'

19"But if you[a] turn away and forsake
the decrees and commands I have giv-
en you[a] and go off to serve other gods
and worship them, 20then I will uproot
Israel from my land, which I have given
them, and will reject this temple I have
consecrated for my Name. I will make it
a byword and an object of ridicule
among all peoples. 21And though this
temple is now so imposing, all who pass
by will be appalled and say, 'Why has
the LORD done such a thing to this land
and to this temple?' 22People will answer, 'Because they have forsaken the
LORD, the God of their fathers, who
brought them out of Egypt, and have
embraced other gods, worshiping and
serving them—that is why he brought all
this disaster on them.' "

Solomon's Other Activities

8 At the end of twenty years, during which
Solomon built the temple of the LORD and
his own palace, 2Solomon rebuilt the villages
that Hiram[b] had given him, and settled Israelites in them. 3Solomon then went to
Hamath Zobah and captured it. 4He also built
up Tadmor in the desert and all the store
cities he had built in Hamath. 5He rebuilt Upper Beth Horon and Lower Beth Horon as
fortified cities, with walls and with gates and
bars, 6as well as Baalath and all his store
cities, and all the cities for his chariots and for
his horses[c]—whatever he desired to build in
Jerusalem, in Lebanon and throughout all
the territory he ruled.

7All the people left from the Hittites, Amorites, Perizzites, Hivites and Jebusites
(these peoples were not Israelites), 8that is,
their descendants remaining in the land,
whom the Israelites had not destroyed—
these Solomon conscripted for his slave labor force, as it is to this day. 9But Solomon
did not make slaves of the Israelites for his
work; they were his fighting men, commanders of his captains, and commanders of his
chariots and charioteers. 10They were also
King Solomon's chief officials—two hundred
and fifty officials supervising the men.

11Solomon brought Pharaoh's daughter up
from the City of David to the palace he had
built for her, for he said, "My wife must not
live in the palace of David king of Israel,
because the places the ark of the LORD has
entered are holy."

12On the altar of the LORD that he had built
in front of the portico, Solomon sacrificed
burnt offerings to the LORD, 13according to the
daily requirement for offerings commanded
by Moses for Sabbaths, New Moons and the
three annual feasts—the Feast of Unleavened Bread, the Feast of Weeks and the
Feast of Tabernacles. 14In keeping with the
ordinance of his father David, he appointed
the divisions of the priests for their duties,
and the Levites to lead the praise and to
assist the priests according to each day's
requirement. He also appointed the gatekeepers by divisions for the various gates,
because this was what David the man of God
had ordered. 15They did not deviate from the

[a]19 The Hebrew is plural. [b]2 Hebrew *Huram,* a variant of *Hiram;* also in verse 18 [c]6 Or *charioteers*

king's commands to the priests or to the Levites in any matter, including that of the treasuries.
16All Solomon's work was carried out, from
the day the foundation of the temple of the
LORD was laid until its completion. So the
temple of the LORD was finished.
17Then Solomon went to Ezion Geber and
Elath on the coast of Edom. 18And Hiram
sent him ships commanded by his own officers, men who knew the sea. These, with
Solomon's men, sailed to Ophir and brought
back four hundred and fifty talents[a] of gold,
which they delivered to King Solomon.

The Queen of Sheba Visits Solomon

9 When the queen of Sheba heard of Solomon's fame, she came to Jerusalem to
test him with hard questions. Arriving with a
very great caravan—with camels carrying
spices, large quantities of gold, and precious
stones—she came to Solomon and talked
with him about all she had on her mind.
2Solomon answered all her questions; nothing was too hard for him to explain to her.
3When the queen of Sheba saw the wisdom
of Solomon, as well as the palace he had
built, 4the food on his table, the seating of his
officials, the attending servants in their
robes, the cupbearers in their robes and the
burnt offerings he made at[b] the temple of the
LORD, she was overwhelmed.
5She said to the king, "The report I heard in
my own country about your achievements
and your wisdom is true. 6But I did not believe what they said until I came and saw with
my own eyes. Indeed, not even half the
greatness of your wisdom was told me; you
have far exceeded the report I heard. 7How
happy your men must be! How happy your
officials, who continually stand before you
and hear your wisdom! 8Praise be to the LORD
your God, who has delighted in you and
placed you on his throne as king to rule for
the LORD your God. Because of the love of
your God for Israel and his desire to uphold
them forever, he has made you king over
them, to maintain justice and righteousness."
9Then she gave the king 120 talents[c] of
gold, large quantities of spices, and precious
stones. There had never been such spices
as those the queen of Sheba gave to King
Solomon.
10(The men of Hiram and the men of Solomon brought gold from Ophir; they also
brought algumwood[d] and precious stones.
11The king used the algumwood to make
steps for the temple of the LORD and for the
royal palace, and to make harps and lyres for
the musicians. Nothing like them had ever
been seen in Judah.)
12King Solomon gave the queen of Sheba
all she desired and asked for; he gave her
more than she had brought to him. Then she
left and returned with her retinue to her own
country.

Solomon's Splendor

13The weight of the gold that Solomon received yearly was 666 talents,[e] 14not including the revenues brought in by merchants
and traders. Also all the kings of Arabia and
the governors of the land brought gold and
silver to Solomon.
15King Solomon made two hundred large
shields of hammered gold; six hundred
bekas[f] of hammered gold went into each
shield. 16He also made three hundred small
shields of hammered gold, with three hundred bekas[g] of gold in each shield. The king
put them in the Palace of the Forest of Lebanon.
17Then the king made a great throne inlaid
with ivory and overlaid with pure gold. 18The
throne had six steps, and a footstool of gold
was attached to it. On both sides of the seat
were armrests, with a lion standing beside
each of them. 19Twelve lions stood on the six
steps, one at either end of each step. Nothing like it had ever been made for any other
kingdom. 20All King Solomon's goblets were
gold, and all the household articles in the
Palace of the Forest of Lebanon were pure
gold. Nothing was made of silver, because
silver was considered of little value in Solomon's day. 21The king had a fleet of trading
ships[h] manned by Hiram's[i] men. Once
every three years it returned, carrying gold,
silver and ivory, and apes and baboons.
22King Solomon was greater in riches and
wisdom than all the other kings of the earth.
23All the kings of the earth sought audience
with Solomon to hear the wisdom God had

[a] 18 That is, about 17 tons (about 16 metric tons) [b] 4 Or *the ascent by which he went up to* [c] 9 That is, about 4 1/2 tons (about 4 metric tons) [d] 10 Probably a variant of *almugwood* [e] 13 That is, about 25 tons (about 23 metric tons) [f] 15 That is, about 7 1/2 pounds (about 3.5 kilograms) [g] 16 That is, about 3 3/4 pounds (about 1.7 kilograms) [h] 21 Hebrew *of ships that could go to Tarshish* [i] 21 Hebrew *Huram*, a variant of *Hiram*

put in his heart. [24]Year after year, everyone who came brought a gift—articles of silver and gold, and robes, weapons and spices, and horses and mules.

[25]Solomon had four thousand stalls for horses and chariots, and twelve thousand horses,[a] which he kept in the chariot cities and also with him in Jerusalem. [26]He ruled over all the kings from the River[b] to the land of the Philistines, as far as the border of Egypt. [27]The king made silver as common in Jerusalem as stones, and cedar as plentiful as sycamore-fig trees in the foothills. [28]Solomon's horses were imported from Egypt[c] and from all other countries.

Solomon's Death

[29]As for the other events of Solomon's reign, from beginning to end, are they not written in the records of Nathan the prophet, in the prophecy of Ahijah the Shilonite and in the visions of Iddo the seer concerning Jeroboam son of Nebat? [30]Solomon reigned in Jerusalem over all Israel forty years. [31]Then he rested with his fathers and was buried in the city of David his father. And Rehoboam his son succeeded him as king.

Israel Rebels Against Rehoboam

10 Rehoboam went to Shechem, for all the Israelites had gone there to make him king. [2]When Jeroboam son of Nebat heard this (he was in Egypt, where he had fled from King Solomon), he returned from Egypt. [3]So they sent for Jeroboam, and he and all Israel went to Rehoboam and said to him: [4]"Your father put a heavy yoke on us, but now lighten the harsh labor and the heavy yoke he put on us, and we will serve you."

[5]Rehoboam answered, "Come back to me in three days." So the people went away.

[6]Then King Rehoboam consulted the elders who had served his father Solomon during his lifetime. "How would you advise me to answer these people?" he asked.

[7]They replied, "If you will be kind to these people and please them and give them a favorable answer, they will always be your servants."

[8]But Rehoboam rejected the advice the elders gave him and consulted the young men who had grown up with him and were serving him. [9]He asked them, "What is your advice? How should we answer these people who say to me, 'Lighten the yoke your father put on us'?"

[10]The young men who had grown up with him replied, "Tell the people who have said to you, 'Your father put a heavy yoke on us, but make our yoke lighter'—tell them, 'My little finger is thicker than my father's waist. [11]My father laid on you a heavy yoke; I will make it even heavier. My father scourged you with whips; I will scourge you with scorpions.'"

[12]Three days later Jeroboam and all the people returned to Rehoboam, as the king had said, "Come back to me in three days." [13]The king answered them harshly. Rejecting the advice of the elders, [14]he followed the advice of the young men and said, "My father made your yoke heavy; I will make it even heavier. My father scourged you with whips; I will scourge you with scorpions." [15]So the king did not listen to the people, for this turn of events was from God, to fulfill the word the LORD had spoken to Jeroboam son of Nebat through Ahijah the Shilonite.

[16]When all Israel saw that the king refused to listen to them, they answered the king:

"What share do we have in David,
  what part in Jesse's son?
To your tents, O Israel!
  Look after your own house, O David!"

So all the Israelites went home. [17]But as for the Israelites who were living in the towns of Judah, Rehoboam still ruled over them.

[18]King Rehoboam sent out Adoniram,[d] who was in charge of forced labor, but the Israelites stoned him to death. King Rehoboam, however, managed to get into his chariot and escape to Jerusalem. [19]So Israel has been in rebellion against the house of David to this day.

11 When Rehoboam arrived in Jerusalem, he mustered the house of Judah and Benjamin—a hundred and eighty thousand fighting men—to make war against Israel and to regain the kingdom for Rehoboam.

[2]But this word of the LORD came to Shemaiah the man of God: [3]"Say to Rehoboam son of Solomon king of Judah and to all the Israelites in Judah and Benjamin, [4]'This is what the LORD says: Do not go up to fight against your brothers. Go home, every one of you,

[a]25 Or *charioteers* [b]26 That is, the Euphrates [c]28 Or possibly *Muzur,* a region in Cilicia
[d]18 Hebrew *Hadoram,* a variant of *Adoniram*

for this is my doing.' " So they obeyed the
words of the LORD and turned back from
marching against Jeroboam.

Rehoboam Fortifies Judah

5Rehoboam lived in Jerusalem and built
up towns for defense in Judah: 6Bethlehem,
Etam, Tekoa, 7Beth Zur, Soco, Adullam,
8Gath, Mareshah, Ziph, 9Adoraim, Lachish,
Azekah, 10Zorah, Aijalon and Hebron. These
were fortified cities in Judah and Benjamin.
11He strengthened their defenses and put
commanders in them, with supplies of food,
olive oil and wine. 12He put shields and
spears in all the cities, and made them
very strong. So Judah and Benjamin were
his.

13The priests and Levites from all their districts throughout Israel sided with him. 14The
Levites even abandoned their pasturelands
and property, and came to Judah and
Jerusalem because Jeroboam and his sons
had rejected them as priests of the LORD.
15And he appointed his own priests for the
high places and for the goat and calf idols he
had made. 16Those from every tribe of Israel
who set their hearts on seeking the LORD, the
God of Israel, followed the Levites to Jerusalem to offer sacrifices to the LORD, the God of
their fathers. 17They strengthened the kingdom of Judah and supported Rehoboam son
of Solomon three years, walking in the ways
of David and Solomon during this time.

Rehoboam's Family

18Rehoboam married Mahalath, who was
the daughter of David's son Jerimoth and of
Abihail, the daughter of Jesse's son Eliab.
19She bore him sons: Jeush, Shemariah and
Zaham. 20Then he married Maacah daughter
of Absalom, who bore him Abijah, Attai, Ziza
and Shelomith. 21Rehoboam loved Maacah
daughter of Absalom more than any of his
other wives and concubines. In all, he had
eighteen wives and sixty concubines,
twenty-eight sons and sixty daughters.

22Rehoboam appointed Abijah son of
Maacah to be the chief prince among his
brothers, in order to make him king. 23He
acted wisely, dispersing some of his sons
throughout the districts of Judah and Benjamin, and to all the fortified cities. He gave
them abundant provisions and took many
wives for them.

Shishak Attacks Jerusalem

12 After Rehoboam's position as king
was established and he had become
strong, he and all Israel[a] with him abandoned the law of the LORD. 2Because they
had been unfaithful to the LORD, Shishak king
of Egypt attacked Jerusalem in the fifth year
of King Rehoboam. 3With twelve hundred
chariots and sixty thousand horsemen and
the innumerable troops of Libyans, Sukkites
and Cushites[b] that came with him from
Egypt, 4he captured the fortified cities of
Judah and came as far as Jerusalem.

5Then the prophet Shemaiah came to
Rehoboam and to the leaders of Judah who
had assembled in Jerusalem for fear of Shishak, and he said to them, "This is what the
LORD says, 'You have abandoned me; therefore, I now abandon you to Shishak.' "

6The leaders of Israel and the king humbled themselves and said, "The LORD is
just."

7When the LORD saw that they humbled
themselves, this word of the LORD came to
Shemaiah: "Since they have humbled themselves, I will not destroy them but will soon
give them deliverance. My wrath will not be
poured out on Jerusalem through Shishak.
8They will, however, become subject to him,
so that they may learn the difference between serving me and serving the kings of
other lands."

9When Shishak king of Egypt attacked
Jerusalem, he carried off the treasures of the
temple of the LORD and the treasures of the
royal palace. He took everything, including
the gold shields Solomon had made. 10So
King Rehoboam made bronze shields to replace them and assigned these to the commanders of the guard on duty at the entrance
to the royal palace. 11Whenever the king
went to the LORD's temple, the guards went
with him, bearing the shields, and afterward
they returned them to the guardroom.

12Because Rehoboam humbled himself,
the LORD's anger turned from him, and he
was not totally destroyed. Indeed, there was
some good in Judah.

13King Rehoboam established himself
firmly in Jerusalem and continued as king.
He was forty-one years old when he became
king, and he reigned seventeen years in
Jerusalem, the city the LORD had chosen out
of all the tribes of Israel in which to put his

[a] *1* That is, Judah, as frequently in 2 Chronicles [b] *3* That is, people from the upper Nile region

Name. His mother's name was Naamah; she was an Ammonite. 14He did evil because he had not set his heart on seeking the LORD.

15As for the events of Rehoboam's reign, from beginning to end, are they not written in the records of Shemaiah the prophet and of Iddo the seer that deal with genealogies? There was continual warfare between Rehoboam and Jeroboam. 16Rehoboam rested with his fathers and was buried in the City of David. And Abijah his son succeeded him as king.

Abijah King of Judah

13 In the eighteenth year of the reign of Jeroboam, Abijah became king of Judah, 2and he reigned in Jerusalem three years. His mother's name was Maacah,[a] a daughter[b] of Uriel of Gibeah.

There was war between Abijah and Jeroboam. 3Abijah went into battle with a force of four hundred thousand able fighting men, and Jeroboam drew up a battle line against him with eight hundred thousand able troops.

4Abijah stood on Mount Zemaraim, in the hill country of Ephraim, and said, "Jeroboam and all Israel, listen to me! 5Don't you know that the LORD, the God of Israel, has given the kingship of Israel to David and his descendants forever by a covenant of salt? 6Yet Jeroboam son of Nebat, an official of Solomon son of David, rebelled against his master. 7Some worthless scoundrels gathered around him and opposed Rehoboam son of Solomon when he was young and indecisive and not strong enough to resist them.

8"And now you plan to resist the kingdom of the LORD, which is in the hands of David's descendants. You are indeed a vast army and have with you the golden calves that Jeroboam made to be your gods. 9But didn't you drive out the priests of the LORD, the sons of Aaron, and the Levites, and make priests of your own as the peoples of other lands do? Whoever comes to consecrate himself with a young bull and seven rams may become a priest of what are not gods.

10"As for us, the LORD is our God, and we have not forsaken him. The priests who serve the LORD are sons of Aaron, and the Levites assist them. 11Every morning and evening they present burnt offerings and fragrant incense to the LORD. They set out the bread on the ceremonially clean table and light the lamps on the gold lampstand every evening. We are observing the requirements of the LORD our God. But you have forsaken him. 12God is with us; he is our leader. His priests with their trumpets will sound the battle cry against you. Men of Israel, do not fight against the LORD, the God of your fathers, for you will not succeed."

13Now Jeroboam had sent troops around to the rear, so that while he was in front of Judah the ambush was behind them. 14Judah turned and saw that they were being attacked at both front and rear. Then they cried out to the LORD. The priests blew their trumpets 15and the men of Judah raised the battle cry. At the sound of their battle cry, God routed Jeroboam and all Israel before Abijah and Judah. 16The Israelites fled before Judah, and God delivered them into their hands. 17Abijah and his men inflicted heavy losses on them, so that there were five hundred thousand casualties among Israel's able men. 18The men of Israel were subdued on that occasion, and the men of Judah were victorious because they relied on the LORD, the God of their fathers.

19Abijah pursued Jeroboam and took from him the towns of Bethel, Jeshanah and Ephron, with their surrounding villages. 20Jeroboam did not regain power during the time of Abijah. And the LORD struck him down and he died.

21But Abijah grew in strength. He married fourteen wives and had twenty-two sons and sixteen daughters.

22The other events of Abijah's reign, what he did and what he said, are written in the annotations of the prophet Iddo.

14 And Abijah rested with his fathers and was buried in the City of David. Asa his son succeeded him as king, and in his days the country was at peace for ten years.

Asa King of Judah

2Asa did what was good and right in the eyes of the LORD his God. 3He removed the foreign altars and the high places, smashed the sacred stones and cut down the Asherah poles.[c] 4He commanded Judah to seek the LORD, the God of their fathers, and to obey his laws and commands. 5He removed the high

[a]2 Most Septuagint manuscripts and Syriac (see also 2 Chron. 11:20 and 1 Kings 15:2); Hebrew *Micaiah*
[b]2 Or *granddaughter* [c]3 That is, symbols of the goddess Asherah; here and elsewhere in 2 Chronicles

places and incense altars in every town in
Judah, and the kingdom was at peace under
him. 6He built up the fortified cities of Judah,
since the land was at peace. No one was at
war with him during those years, for the LORD
gave him rest.

7"Let us build up these towns," he said to
Judah, "and put walls around them, with towers, gates and bars. The land is still ours,
because we have sought the LORD our God;
we sought him and he has given us rest on
every side." So they built and prospered.

8Asa had an army of three hundred thousand men from Judah, equipped with large
shields and with spears, and two hundred
and eighty thousand from Benjamin, armed
with small shields and with bows. All these
were brave fighting men.

9Zerah the Cushite marched out against
them with a vast army[a] and three hundred
chariots, and came as far as Mareshah.
10Asa went out to meet him, and they took up
battle positions in the Valley of Zephathah
near Mareshah.

11Then Asa called to the LORD his God and
said, "LORD, there is no one like you to help
the powerless against the mighty. Help us, O
LORD our God, for we rely on you, and in your
name we have come against this vast army.
O LORD, you are our God; do not let man
prevail against you."

12The LORD struck down the Cushites before Asa and Judah. The Cushites fled, 13and
Asa and his army pursued them as far as
Gerar. Such a great number of Cushites fell
that they could not recover; they were
crushed before the LORD and his forces. The
men of Judah carried off a large amount of
plunder. 14They destroyed all the villages
around Gerar, for the terror of the LORD had
fallen upon them. They plundered all these
villages, since there was much booty there.
15They also attacked the camps of the herdsmen and carried off droves of sheep and
goats and camels. Then they returned to
Jerusalem.

Asa's Reform

15 The Spirit of God came upon Azariah
son of Oded. 2He went out to meet
Asa and said to him, "Listen to me, Asa and
all Judah and Benjamin. The LORD is with you
when you are with him. If you seek him, he
will be found by you, but if you forsake him,
he will forsake you. 3For a long time Israel
was without the true God, without a priest to
teach and without the law. 4But in their distress they turned to the LORD, the God of
Israel, and sought him, and he was found by
them. 5In those days it was not safe to travel
about, for all the inhabitants of the lands
were in great turmoil. 6One nation was being
crushed by another and one city by another,
because God was troubling them with every
kind of distress. 7But as for you, be strong
and do not give up, for your work will be
rewarded."

8When Asa heard these words and the
prophecy of Azariah son of[b] Oded the
prophet, he took courage. He removed the
detestable idols from the whole land of
Judah and Benjamin and from the towns he
had captured in the hills of Ephraim. He repaired the altar of the LORD that was in front of
the portico of the LORD's temple.

9Then he assembled all Judah and Benjamin and the people from Ephraim, Manasseh and Simeon who had settled among
them, for large numbers had come over to
him from Israel when they saw that the LORD
his God was with him.

10They assembled at Jerusalem in the
third month of the fifteenth year of Asa's
reign. 11At that time they sacrificed to the
LORD seven hundred head of cattle and
seven thousand sheep and goats from the
plunder they had brought back. 12They entered into a covenant to seek the LORD, the
God of their fathers, with all their heart and
soul. 13All who would not seek the LORD, the
God of Israel, were to be put to death,
whether small or great, man or woman.
14They took an oath to the LORD with loud
acclamation, with shouting and with trumpets and horns. 15All Judah rejoiced about
the oath because they had sworn it wholeheartedly. They sought God eagerly, and he
was found by them. So the LORD gave them
rest on every side.

16King Asa also deposed his grandmother
Maacah from her position as queen mother,
because she had made a repulsive Asherah
pole. Asa cut the pole down, broke it up and
burned it in the Kidron Valley. 17Although he
did not remove the high places from Israel,
Asa's heart was fully committed ⌞to the LORD⌟
all his life. 18He brought into the temple of

[a]9 Hebrew *with an army of a thousand thousands* or *with an army of thousands upon thousands* [b]8 Vulgate and Syriac (see also Septuagint and verse 1); Hebrew does not have *Azariah son of.*

God the silver and gold and the articles that he and his father had dedicated.

19There was no more war until the thirty-fifth year of Asa's reign.

Asa's Last Years

16 In the thirty-sixth year of Asa's reign Baasha king of Israel went up against Judah and fortified Ramah to prevent anyone from leaving or entering the territory of Asa king of Judah.

2Asa then took the silver and gold out of the treasuries of the LORD's temple and of his own palace and sent it to Ben-Hadad king of Aram, who was ruling in Damascus. 3"Let there be a treaty between me and you," he said, "as there was between my father and your father. See, I am sending you silver and gold. Now break your treaty with Baasha king of Israel so he will withdraw from me."

4Ben-Hadad agreed with King Asa and sent the commanders of his forces against the towns of Israel. They conquered Ijon, Dan, Abel Maim[a] and all the store cities of Naphtali. 5When Baasha heard this, he stopped building Ramah and abandoned his work. 6Then King Asa brought all the men of Judah, and they carried away from Ramah the stones and timber Baasha had been using. With them he built up Geba and Mizpah.

7At that time Hanani the seer came to Asa king of Judah and said to him: "Because you relied on the king of Aram and not on the LORD your God, the army of the king of Aram has escaped from your hand. 8Were not the Cushites[b] and Libyans a mighty army with great numbers of chariots and horsemen[c]? Yet when you relied on the LORD, he delivered them into your hand. 9For the eyes of the LORD range throughout the earth to strengthen those whose hearts are fully committed to him. You have done a foolish thing, and from now on you will be at war."

10Asa was angry with the seer because of this; he was so enraged that he put him in prison. At the same time Asa brutally oppressed some of the people.

11The events of Asa's reign, from beginning to end, are written in the book of the kings of Judah and Israel. 12In the thirty-ninth year of his reign Asa was afflicted with a disease in his feet. Though his disease was severe, even in his illness he did not seek help from the LORD, but only from the physicians. 13Then in the forty-first year of his reign Asa died and rested with his fathers. 14They buried him in the tomb that he had cut out for himself in the City of David. They laid him on a bier covered with spices and various blended perfumes, and they made a huge fire in his honor.

Jehoshaphat King of Judah

17 Jehoshaphat his son succeeded him as king and strengthened himself against Israel. 2He stationed troops in all the fortified cities of Judah and put garrisons in Judah and in the towns of Ephraim that his father Asa had captured.

3The LORD was with Jehoshaphat because in his early years he walked in the ways his father David had followed. He did not consult the Baals 4but sought the God of his father and followed his commands rather than the practices of Israel. 5The LORD established the kingdom under his control; and all Judah brought gifts to Jehoshaphat, so that he had great wealth and honor. 6His heart was devoted to the ways of the LORD; furthermore, he removed the high places and the Asherah poles from Judah.

7In the third year of his reign he sent his officials Ben-Hail, Obadiah, Zechariah, Nethanel and Micaiah to teach in the towns of Judah. 8With them were certain Levites—Shemaiah, Nethaniah, Zebadiah, Asahel, Shemiramoth, Jehonathan, Adonijah, Tobijah and Tob-Adonijah—and the priests Elishama and Jehoram. 9They taught throughout Judah, taking with them the Book of the Law of the LORD; they went around to all the towns of Judah and taught the people.

10The fear of the LORD fell on all the kingdoms of the lands surrounding Judah, so that they did not make war with Jehoshaphat. 11Some Philistines brought Jehoshaphat gifts and silver as tribute, and the Arabs brought him flocks: seven thousand seven hundred rams and seven thousand seven hundred goats.

12Jehoshaphat became more and more powerful; he built forts and store cities in Judah 13and had large supplies in the towns of Judah. He also kept experienced fighting men in Jerusalem. 14Their enrollment by families was as follows:

From Judah, commanders of units of 1,000:

[a]4 Also known as *Abel Beth Maacah* [b]8 That is, people from the upper Nile region [c]8 Or *charioteers*

Adnah the commander, with 300,000
fighting men;
15next, Jehohanan the commander,
with 280,000;
16next, Amasiah son of Zicri, who volunteered himself for the service of the
LORD, with 200,000.
17From Benjamin:
Eliada, a valiant soldier, with 200,000
men armed with bows and shields;
18next, Jehozabad, with 180,000 men
armed for battle.

19These were the men who served the king, besides those he stationed in the fortified cities throughout Judah.

Micaiah Prophesies Against Ahab

18 Now Jehoshaphat had great wealth and honor, and he allied himself with Ahab by marriage.
2Some years later he went down to visit Ahab in Samaria. Ahab slaughtered many sheep and cattle for him and the people with him and urged him to attack Ramoth Gilead.
3Ahab king of Israel asked Jehoshaphat king of Judah, "Will you go with me against Ramoth Gilead?"

Jehoshaphat replied, "I am as you are, and my people as your people; we will join you in the war."
4But Jehoshaphat also said to the king of Israel, "First seek the counsel of the LORD."

5So the king of Israel brought together the prophets—four hundred men—and asked them, "Shall we go to war against Ramoth Gilead, or shall I refrain?"

"Go," they answered, "for God will give it into the king's hand."

6But Jehoshaphat asked, "Is there not a prophet of the LORD here whom we can inquire of?"

7The king of Israel answered Jehoshaphat, "There is still one man through whom we can inquire of the LORD, but I hate him because he never prophesies anything good about me, but always bad. He is Micaiah son of Imlah."

"The king should not say that," Jehoshaphat replied.

8So the king of Israel called one of his officials and said, "Bring Micaiah son of Imlah at once."

9Dressed in their royal robes, the king of Israel and Jehoshaphat king of Judah were sitting on their thrones at the threshing floor by the entrance to the gate of Samaria, with all the prophets prophesying before them.
10Now Zedekiah son of Kenaanah had made iron horns, and he declared, "This is what the LORD says: 'With these you will gore the Arameans until they are destroyed.' "

11All the other prophets were prophesying the same thing. "Attack Ramoth Gilead and be victorious," they said, "for the LORD will give it into the king's hand."

12The messenger who had gone to summon Micaiah said to him, "Look, as one man the other prophets are predicting success for the king. Let your word agree with theirs, and speak favorably."

13But Micaiah said, "As surely as the LORD lives, I can tell him only what my God says."

14When he arrived, the king asked him, "Micaiah, shall we go to war against Ramoth Gilead, or shall I refrain?"

"Attack and be victorious," he answered, "for they will be given into your hand."

15The king said to him, "How many times must I make you swear to tell me nothing but the truth in the name of the LORD?"

16Then Micaiah answered, "I saw all Israel scattered on the hills like sheep without a shepherd, and the LORD said, 'These people have no master. Let each one go home in peace.' "

17The king of Israel said to Jehoshaphat, "Didn't I tell you that he never prophesies anything good about me, but only bad?"

18Micaiah continued, "Therefore hear the word of the LORD: I saw the LORD sitting on his throne with all the host of heaven standing on his right and on his left.
19And the LORD said, 'Who will entice Ahab king of Israel into attacking Ramoth Gilead and going to his death there?'

"One suggested this, and another that.
20Finally, a spirit came foreward, stood before the LORD and said, 'I will entice him.'

" 'By what means?' the LORD asked.

21" 'I will go and be a lying spirit in the mouths of all his prophets,' he said.

" 'You will succeed in enticing him,' said the LORD. 'Go and do it.'

22"So now the LORD has put a lying spirit in the mouths of these prophets of yours. The LORD has decreed disaster for you."

23Then Zedekiah son of Kenaanah went up and slapped Micaiah in the face. "Which way did the spirit from[a] the LORD go when he went from me to speak to you?" he asked.

[a]23 Or *Spirit of*

24Micaiah replied, "You will find out on the day you go to hide in an inner room."

25The king of Israel then ordered, "Take Micaiah and send him back to Amon the ruler of the city and to Joash the king's son, 26and say, 'This is what the king says: Put this fellow in prison and give him nothing but bread and water until I return safely.'"

27Micaiah declared, "If you ever return safely, the LORD has not spoken through me." Then he added, "Mark my words, all you people!"

Ahab Killed at Ramoth Gilead

28So the king of Israel and Jehoshaphat king of Judah went up to Ramoth Gilead. 29The king of Israel said to Jehoshaphat, "I will enter the battle in disguise, but you wear your royal robes." So the king of Israel disguised himself and went into battle.

30Now the king of Aram had ordered his chariot commanders, "Do not fight with anyone, small or great, except the king of Israel." 31When the chariot commanders saw Jehoshaphat, they thought, "This is the king of Israel." So they turned to attack him, but Jehoshaphat cried out, and the LORD helped him. God drew them away from him, 32for when the chariot commanders saw that he was not the king of Israel, they stopped pursuing him.

33But someone drew his bow at random and hit the king of Israel between the sections of his armor. The king told the chariot driver, "Wheel around and get me out of the fighting. I've been wounded." 34All day long the battle raged, and the king of Israel propped himself up in his chariot facing the Arameans until evening. Then at sunset he died.

19 When Jehoshaphat king of Judah returned safely to his palace in Jerusalem, 2Jehu the seer, the son of Hanani, went out to meet him and said to the king, "Should you help the wicked and love[a] those who hate the LORD? Because of this, the wrath of the LORD is upon you. 3There is, however, some good in you, for you have rid the land of the Asherah poles and have set your heart on seeking God."

Jehoshaphat Appoints Judges

4Jehoshaphat lived in Jerusalem, and he went out again among the people from Beersheba to the hill country of Ephraim and turned them back to the LORD, the God of their fathers. 5He appointed judges in the land, in each of the fortified cities of Judah. 6He told them, "Consider carefully what you do, because you are not judging for man but for the LORD, who is with you whenever you give a verdict. 7Now let the fear of the LORD be upon you. Judge carefully, for with the LORD our God there is no injustice or partiality or bribery."

8In Jerusalem also, Jehoshaphat appointed some of the Levites, priests and heads of Israelite families to administer the law of the LORD and to settle disputes. And they lived in Jerusalem. 9He gave them these orders: "You must serve faithfully and wholeheartedly in the fear of the LORD. 10In every case that comes before you from your fellow countrymen who live in the cities—whether bloodshed or other concerns of the law, commands, decrees or ordinances—you are to warn them not to sin against the LORD; otherwise his wrath will come on you and your brothers. Do this, and you will not sin.

11"Amariah the chief priest will be over you in any matter concerning the LORD, and Zebadiah son of Ishmael, the leader of the tribe of Judah, will be over you in any matter concerning the king, and the Levites will serve as officials before you. Act with courage, and may the LORD be with those who do well."

Jehoshaphat Defeats Moab and Ammon

20 After this, the Moabites and Ammonites with some of the Meunites[b] came to make war on Jehoshaphat.

2Some men came and told Jehoshaphat, "A vast army is coming against you from Edom,[c] from the other side of the Sea.[d] It is already in Hazazon Tamar" (that is, En Gedi). 3Alarmed, Jehoshaphat resolved to inquire of the LORD, and he proclaimed a fast for all Judah. 4The people of Judah came together to seek help from the LORD; indeed, they came from every town in Judah to seek him.

5Then Jehoshaphat stood up in the assembly of Judah and Jerusalem at the tem-

[a]2 Or *and make alliances with* [b]1 Some Septuagint manuscripts; Hebrew *Ammonites* [c]2 One Hebrew manuscript; most Hebrew manuscripts, Septuagint and Vulgate *Aram* [d]2 That is, the Dead Sea

ple of the LORD in the front of the new courtyard 6and said:

"O LORD, God of our fathers, are you not the God who is in heaven? You rule over all the kingdoms of the nations. Power and might are in your hand, and no one can withstand you. 7O our God, did you not drive out the inhabitants of this land before your people Israel and give it forever to the descendants of Abraham your friend? 8They have lived in it and have built in it a sanctuary for your Name, saying, 9'If calamity comes upon us, whether the sword of judgment, or plague or famine, we will stand in your presence before this temple that bears your Name and will cry out to you in our distress, and you will hear us and save us.'

10"But now here are men from Ammon, Moab and Mount Seir, whose territory you would not allow Israel to invade when they came from Egypt; so they turned away from them and did not destroy them. 11See how they are repaying us by coming to drive us out of the possession you gave us as an inheritance. 12O our God, will you not judge them? For we have no power to face this vast army that is attacking us. We do not know what to do, but our eyes are upon you."

13All the men of Judah, with their wives and children and little ones, stood there before the LORD.

14Then the Spirit of the LORD came upon Jahaziel son of Zechariah, the son of Benaiah, the son of Jeiel, the son of Mattaniah, a Levite and descendant of Asaph, as he stood in the assembly.

15He said: "Listen, King Jehoshaphat and all who live in Judah and Jerusalem! This is what the LORD says to you: 'Do not be afraid or discouraged because of this vast army. For the battle is not yours, but God's. 16Tomorrow march down against them. They will be climbing up by the Pass of Ziz, and you will find them at the end of the gorge in the Desert of Jeruel. 17You will not have to fight this battle. Take up your positions; stand firm and see the deliverance the LORD will give you, O Judah and Jerusalem. Do not be afraid; do not be discouraged. Go out to face them tomorrow, and the LORD will be with you.' "

18Jehoshaphat bowed with his face to the ground, and all the people of Judah and Jerusalem fell down in worship before the LORD. 19Then some Levites from the Kohathites and Korahites stood up and praised the LORD, the God of Israel, with very loud voice.

20Early in the morning they left for the Desert of Tekoa. As they set out, Jehoshaphat stood and said, "Listen to me, Judah and people of Jerusalem! Have faith in the LORD your God and you will be upheld; have faith in his prophets and you will be successful." 21After consulting the people, Jehoshaphat appointed men to sing to the LORD and to praise him for the splendor of his[a] holiness as they went out at the head of the army, saying:

"Give thanks to the LORD,
for his love endures forever."

22As they began to sing and praise, the LORD set ambushes against the men of Ammon and Moab and Mount Seir who were invading Judah, and they were defeated. 23The men of Ammon and Moab rose up against the men from Mount Seir to destroy and annihilate them. After they finished slaughtering the men from Seir, they helped to destroy one another.

24When the men of Judah came to the place that overlooks the desert and looked toward the vast army, they saw only dead bodies lying on the ground; no one had escaped. 25So Jehoshaphat and his men went to carry off their plunder, and they found among them a great amount of equipment and clothing[b] and also articles of value—more than they could take away. There was so much plunder that it took three days to collect it. 26On the fourth day they assembled in the Valley of Beracah, where they praised the LORD. This is why it is called the Valley of Beracah[c] to this day.

27Then, led by Jehoshaphat, all the men of Judah and Jerusalem returned joyfully to Jerusalem, for the LORD had given them cause to rejoice over their enemies. 28They entered Jerusalem and went to the temple of the LORD with harps and lutes and trumpets.

29The fear of God came upon all the kingdoms of the countries when they heard how the LORD had fought against the enemies of

[a]21 Or *him with the splendor of* [b]25 Some Hebrew manuscripts and Vulgate; most Hebrew manuscripts *corpses* [c]26 *Beracah* means *praise.*

Israel. 30And the kingdom of Jehoshaphat was at peace, for his God had given him rest on every side.

The End of Jehoshaphat's Reign

31So Jehoshaphat reigned over Judah. He was thirty-five years old when he became king of Judah, and he reigned in Jerusalem twenty-five years. His mother's name was Azubah daughter of Shilhi. 32He walked in the ways of his father Asa and did not stray from them; he did what was right in the eyes of the LORD. 33The high places, however, were not removed, and the people still had not set their hearts on the God of their fathers.

34The other events of Jehoshaphat's reign, from beginning to end, are written in the annals of Jehu son of Hanani, which are recorded in the book of the kings of Israel.

35Later, Jehoshaphat king of Judah made an alliance with Ahaziah king of Israel, who was guilty of wickedness. 36He agreed with him to construct a fleet of trading ships.[a] After these were built at Ezion Geber, 37Eliezer son of Dodavahu of Mareshah prophesied against Jehoshaphat, saying, "Because you have made an alliance with Ahaziah, the LORD will destroy what you have made." The ships were wrecked and were not able to set sail to trade.[b]

21 Then Jehoshaphat rested with his fathers and was buried with them in the City of David. And Jehoram his son succeeded him as king. 2Jehoram's brothers, the sons of Jehoshaphat, were Azariah, Jehiel, Zechariah, Azariahu, Michael and Shephatiah. All these were sons of Jehoshaphat king of Israel.[c] 3Their father had given them many gifts of silver and gold and articles of value, as well as fortified cities in Judah, but he had given the kingdom to Jehoram because he was his firstborn son.

Jehoram King of Judah

4When Jehoram established himself firmly over his father's kingdom, he put all his brothers to the sword along with some of the princes of Israel. 5Jehoram was thirty-two years old when he became king, and he reigned in Jerusalem eight years. 6He walked in the ways of the kings of Israel, as the house of Ahab had done, for he married a daughter of Ahab. He did evil in the eyes of the LORD. 7Nevertheless, because of the covenant the LORD had made with David, the LORD was not willing to destroy the house of David. He had promised to maintain a lamp for him and his descendants forever.

8In the time of Jehoram, Edom rebelled against Judah and set up its own king. 9So Jehoram went there with his officers and all his chariots. The Edomites surrounded him and his chariot commanders, but he rose up and broke through by night. 10To this day Edom has been in rebellion against Judah.

Libnah revolted at the same time, because Jehoram had forsaken the LORD, the God of his fathers. 11He had also built high places on the hills of Judah and had caused the people of Jerusalem to prostitute themselves and had led Judah astray.

12Jehoram received a letter from Elijah the prophet, which said:

> "This is what the LORD, the God of your father David, says: 'You have not walked in the ways of your father Jehoshaphat or of Asa king of Judah. 13But you have walked in the ways of the kings of Israel, and you have led Judah and the people of Jerusalem to prostitute themselves, just as the house of Ahab did. You have also murdered your own brothers, members of your father's house, men who were better than you. 14So now the LORD is about to strike your people, your sons, your wives and everything that is yours, with a heavy blow. 15You yourself will be very ill with a lingering disease of the bowels, until the disease causes your bowels to come out.' "

16The LORD aroused against Jehoram the hostility of the Philistines and of the Arabs who lived near the Cushites. 17They attacked Judah, invaded it and carried off all the goods found in the king's palace, together with his sons and wives. Not a son was left to him except Ahaziah,[d] the youngest.

18After all this, the LORD afflicted Jehoram with an incurable disease of the bowels. 19In the course of time, at the end of the second year, his bowels came out because of the disease, and he died in great pain. His people made no fire in his honor, as they had for his fathers.

20Jehoram was thirty-two years old when

[a]36 Hebrew *of ships that could go to Tarshish* [b]37 Hebrew *sail for Tarshish* [c]2 That is, Judah, as frequently in 2 Chronicles [d]17 Hebrew *Jehoahaz,* a variant of *Ahaziah*

he became king, and he reigned in Jerusalem eight years. He passed away, to no one's regret, and was buried in the City of David, but not in the tombs of the kings.

Ahaziah King of Judah

22 The people of Jerusalem made Ahaziah, Jehoram's youngest son, king in his place, since the raiders, who came with the Arabs into the camp, had killed all the older sons. So Ahaziah son of Jehoram king of Judah began to reign.

2Ahaziah was twenty-two[a] years old when he became king, and he reigned in Jerusalem one year. His mother's name was Athaliah, a granddaughter of Omri.

3He too walked in the ways of the house of Ahab, for his mother encouraged him in doing wrong. 4He did evil in the eyes of the LORD, as the house of Ahab had done, for after his father's death they became his advisers, to his undoing. 5He also followed their counsel when he went with Joram[b] son of Ahab king of Israel to war against Hazael king of Aram at Ramoth Gilead. The Arameans wounded Joram; 6so he returned to Jezreel to recover from the wounds they had inflicted on him at Ramoth[c] in his battle with Hazael king of Aram.

Then Ahaziah[d] son of Jehoram king of Judah went down to Jezreel to see Joram son of Ahab because he had been wounded.

7Through Ahaziah's visit to Joram, God brought about Ahaziah's downfall. When Ahaziah arrived, he went out with Joram to meet Jehu son of Nimshi, whom the LORD had anointed to destroy the house of Ahab. 8While Jehu was executing judgment on the house of Ahab, he found the princes of Judah and the sons of Ahaziah's relatives, who had been attending Ahaziah, and he killed them. 9He then went in search of Ahaziah, and his men captured him while he was hiding in Samaria. He was brought to Jehu and put to death. They buried him, for they said, "He was a son of Jehoshaphat, who sought the LORD with all his heart." So there was no one in the house of Ahaziah powerful enough to retain the kingdom.

Athaliah and Joash

10When Athaliah the mother of Ahaziah saw that her son was dead, she proceeded to destroy the whole royal family of the house of Judah. 11But Jehosheba,[e] the daughter of King Jehoram, took Joash son of Ahaziah and stole him away from among the royal princes who were about to be murdered and put him and his nurse in a bedroom. Because Jehosheba,[e] the daughter of King Jehoram and wife of the priest Jehoiada, was Ahaziah's sister, she hid the child from Athaliah so she could not kill him. 12He remained hidden with them at the temple of God for six years while Athaliah ruled the land.

23 In the seventh year Jehoiada showed his strength. He made a covenant with the commanders of units of a hundred: Azariah son of Jeroham, Ishmael son of Jehohanan, Azariah son of Obed, Maaseiah son of Adaiah, and Elishaphat son of Zicri. 2They went throughout Judah and gathered the Levites and the heads of Israelite families from all the towns. When they came to Jerusalem, 3the whole assembly made a covenant with the king at the temple of God.

Jehoiada said to them, "The king's son shall reign, as the LORD promised concerning the descendants of David. 4Now this is what you are to do: A third of you priests and Levites who are going on duty on the Sabbath are to keep watch at the doors, 5a third of you at the royal palace and a third at the Foundation Gate, and all the other men are to be in the courtyards of the temple of the LORD. 6No one is to enter the temple of the LORD except the priests and Levites on duty; they may enter because they are consecrated, but all the other men are to guard what the LORD has assigned to them.[f] 7The Levites are to station themselves around the king, each man with his weapons in his hand. Anyone who enters the temple must be put to death. Stay close to the king wherever he goes."

8The Levites and all the men of Judah did just as Jehoiada the priest ordered. Each one took his men—those who were going on duty on the Sabbath and those who were going off duty—for Jehoiada the priest had not released any of the divisions. 9Then he gave the commanders of units of a hundred the spears and the large and small shields that had belonged to King David and that

[a]2 Some Septuagint manuscripts and Syriac (see also 2 Kings 8:26); Hebrew *forty-two* [b]5 Hebrew *Jehoram,* a variant of *Joram;* also in verses 6 and 7 [c]6 Hebrew *Ramah,* a variant of *Ramoth* [d]6 Some Hebrew manuscripts, Septuagint, Vulgate and Syriac (see also 2 Kings 8:29); most Hebrew manuscripts *Azariah*
[e]11 Hebrew *Jehoshabeath,* a variant of *Jehosheba* [f]6 Or *to observe the LORD's command* ⌞*not to enter*⌟

were in the temple of God. 10He stationed all
the men, each with his weapon in his hand,
around the king—near the altar and the temple, from the south side to the north side of
the temple.
11Jehoiada and his sons brought out the
king's son and put the crown on him; they
presented him with a copy of the covenant
and proclaimed him king. They anointed him
and shouted, "Long live the king!"
12When Athaliah heard the noise of the
people running and cheering the king, she
went to them at the temple of the LORD. 13She
looked, and there was the king, standing by
his pillar at the entrance. The officers and the
trumpeters were beside the king, and all the
people of the land were rejoicing and blowing trumpets, and singers with musical instruments were leading the praises. Then
Athaliah tore her robes and shouted, "Treason! Treason!"
14Jehoiada the priest sent out the commanders of units of a hundred, who were in
charge of the troops, and said to them:
"Bring her out between the ranks[a] and put to
the sword anyone who follows her." For the
priest had said, "Do not put her to death at
the temple of the LORD." 15So they seized her
as she reached the entrance of the Horse
Gate on the palace grounds, and there they
put her to death.
16Jehoiada then made a covenant that he
and the people and the king[b] would be the
LORD's people. 17All the people went to the
temple of Baal and tore it down. They
smashed the altars and idols and killed Mattan the priest of Baal in front of the altars.
18Then Jehoiada placed the oversight of
the temple of the LORD in the hands of the
priests, who were Levites, to whom David
had made assignments in the temple, to
present the burnt offerings of the LORD as
written in the Law of Moses, with rejoicing
and singing, as David had ordered. 19He also
stationed doorkeepers at the gates of the
LORD's temple so that no one who was in any
way unclean might enter.
20He took with him the commanders of
hundreds, the nobles, the rulers of the
people and all the people of the land and
brought the king down from the temple of the
LORD. They went into the palace through the
Upper Gate and seated the king on the royal
throne, 21and all the people of the land rejoiced. And the city was quiet, because
Athaliah had been slain with the sword.

Joash Repairs the Temple

24 Joash was seven years old when he
became king, and he reigned in
Jerusalem forty years. His mother's name
was Zibiah; she was from Beersheba.
2Joash did what was right in the eyes of the
LORD all the years of Jehoiada the priest.
3Jehoiada chose two wives for him, and he
had sons and daughters.
4Some time later Joash decided to restore
the temple of the LORD. 5He called together
the priests and Levites and said to them, "Go
to the towns of Judah and collect the money
due annually from all Israel, to repair the
temple of your God. Do it now." But the Levites did not act at once.
6Therefore the king summoned Jehoiada
the chief priest and said to him, "Why haven't
you required the Levites to bring in from
Judah and Jerusalem the tax imposed by
Moses the servant of the LORD and by the
assembly of Israel for the Tent of the Testimony?"
7Now the sons of that wicked woman
Athaliah had broken into the temple of God
and had used even its sacred objects for the
Baals.
8At the king's command, a chest was
made and placed outside, at the gate of the
temple of the LORD. 9A proclamation was then
issued in Judah and Jerusalem that they
should bring to the LORD the tax that Moses
the servant of God had required of Israel in
the desert. 10All the officials and all the
people brought their contributions gladly,
dropping them into the chest until it was full.
11Whenever the chest was brought in by the
Levites to the king's officials and they saw
that there was a large amount of money, the
royal secretary and the officer of the chief
priest would come and empty the chest and
carry it back to its place. They did this regularly and collected a great amount of money.
12The king and Jehoiada gave it to the men
who carried out the work required for the
temple of the LORD. They hired masons and
carpenters to restore the LORD's temple, and
also workers in iron and bronze to repair the
temple.
13The men in charge of the work were diligent, and the repairs progressed under

[a] 14 Or *out from the precincts* [b] 16 Or *covenant between* ⌞*the* LORD⌟ *and the people and the king that they* (see 2 Kings 11:17)

them. They rebuilt the temple of God according to its original design and reinforced it.
14When they had finished, they brought the
rest of the money to the king and Jehoiada,
and with it were made articles for the LORD's
temple: articles for the service and for the
burnt offerings, and also dishes and other
objects of gold and silver. As long as Jehoiada lived, burnt offerings were presented
continually in the temple of the LORD.
15Now Jehoiada was old and full of years,
and he died at the age of a hundred and
thirty. 16He was buried with the kings in the
City of David, because of the good he had
done in Israel for God and his temple.

The Wickedness of Joash

17After the death of Jehoiada, the officials
of Judah came and paid homage to the king,
and he listened to them. 18They abandoned
the temple of the LORD, the God of their fathers, and worshiped Asherah poles and
idols. Because of their guilt, God's anger
came upon Judah and Jerusalem. 19Al-
though the LORD sent prophets to the people
to bring them back to him, and though they
testified against them, they would not listen.
20Then the Spirit of God came upon Zechariah son of Jehoiada the priest. He stood
before the people and said, "This is what
God says: 'Why do you disobey the LORD's
commands? You will not prosper. Because
you have forsaken the LORD, he has forsaken
you.' "
21But they plotted against him, and by order of the king they stoned him to death in
the courtyard of the LORD's temple. 22King
Joash did not remember the kindness Zechariah's father Jehoiada had shown him but
killed his son, who said as he lay dying, "May
the LORD see this and call you to account."
23At the turn of the year,[a] the army of Aram
marched against Joash; it invaded Judah
and Jerusalem and killed all the leaders of
the people. They sent all the plunder to their
king in Damascus. 24Although the Aramean
army had come with only a few men, the
LORD delivered into their hands a much larger
army. Because Judah had forsaken the
LORD, the God of their fathers, judgment was
executed on Joash. 25When the Arameans
withdrew, they left Joash severely wounded.
His officials conspired against him for murdering the son of Jehoiada the priest, and
they killed him in his bed. So he died and was
buried in the City of David, but not in the
tombs of the kings.
26Those who conspired against him were
Zabad,[b] son of Shimeath an Ammonite
woman, and Jehozabad, son of Shimrith[c] a
Moabite woman. 27The account of his sons,
the many prophecies about him, and the
record of the restoration of the temple of God
are written in the annotations on the book of
the kings. And Amaziah his son succeeded
him as king.

Amaziah King of Judah

25 Amaziah was twenty-five years old
when he became king, and he
reigned in Jerusalem twenty-nine years. His
mother's name was Jehoaddin[d]; she was
from Jerusalem. 2He did what was right in
the eyes of the LORD, but not wholeheartedly.
3After the kingdom was firmly in his control,
he executed the officials who had murdered
his father the king. 4Yet he did not put their
sons to death, but acted in accordance with
what is written in the Law, in the Book of
Moses, where the LORD commanded: "Fathers shall not be put to death for their children, nor children put to death for their fathers; each is to die for his own sins."[e]
5Amaziah called the people of Judah together and assigned them according to their
families to commanders of thousands and
commanders of hundreds for all Judah and
Benjamin. He then mustered those twenty
years old or more and found that there were
three hundred thousand men ready for military service, able to handle the spear and
shield. 6He also hired a hundred thousand
fighting men from Israel for a hundred talents[f] of silver.
7But a man of God came to him and said,
"O king, these troops from Israel must not
march with you, for the LORD is not with Israel—not with any of the people of Ephraim.
8Even if you go and fight courageously in
battle, God will overthrow you before the
enemy, for God has the power to help or to
overthrow."
9Amaziah asked the man of God, "But
what about the hundred talents I paid for
these Israelite troops?"
The man of God replied, "The LORD can
give you much more than that."
10So Amaziah dismissed the troops who

[a]23 Probably in the spring [b]26 A variant of *Jozabad* [c]26 A variant of *Shomer* [d]1 Hebrew *Jehoaddan,* a variant of *Jehoaddin* [e]4 Deut. 24:16 [f]6 That is, about 3 3/4 tons (about 3.4 metric tons); also in verse 9

had come to him from Ephraim and sent
them home. They were furious with Judah
and left for home in a great rage.
11 Amaziah then marshaled his strength
and led his army to the Valley of Salt, where
he killed ten thousand men of Seir. 12 The
army of Judah also captured ten thousand
men alive, took them to the top of a cliff and
threw them down so that all were dashed to
pieces.
13 Meanwhile the troops that Amaziah had
sent back and had not allowed to take part in
the war raided Judean towns from Samaria
to Beth Horon. They killed three thousand
people and carried off great quantities of
plunder.
14 When Amaziah returned from slaughtering the Edomites, he brought back the gods
of the people of Seir. He set them up as his
own gods, bowed down to them and burned
sacrifices to them. 15 The anger of the LORD
burned against Amaziah, and he sent a
prophet to him, who said, "Why do you consult this people's gods, which could not save
their own people from your hand?"
16 While he was still speaking, the king said
to him, "Have we appointed you an adviser
to the king? Stop! Why be struck down?"
So the prophet stopped but said, "I know
that God has determined to destroy you, because you have done this and have not listened to my counsel."
17 After Amaziah king of Judah consulted
his advisers, he sent this challenge to Jehoash[a] son of Jehoahaz, the son of Jehu,
king of Israel: "Come, meet me face to face."
18 But Jehoash king of Israel replied to
Amaziah king of Judah: "A thistle in Lebanon
sent a message to a cedar in Lebanon, 'Give
your daughter to my son in marriage.' Then a
wild beast in Lebanon came along and trampled the thistle underfoot. 19 You say to yourself that you have defeated Edom, and now
you are arrogant and proud. But stay at
home! Why ask for trouble and cause your
own downfall and that of Judah also?"
20 Amaziah, however, would not listen, for
God so worked that he might hand them over
to ⌞Jehoash⌟, because they sought the gods
of Edom. 21 So Jehoash king of Israel attacked. He and Amaziah king of Judah faced
each other at Beth Shemesh in Judah.
22 Judah was routed by Israel, and every man
fled to his home. 23 Jehoash king of Israel
captured Amaziah king of Judah, the son of
Joash, the son of Ahaziah,[b] at Beth Shemesh. Then Jehoash brought him to Jerusalem and broke down the wall of Jerusalem
from the Ephraim Gate to the Corner Gate—
a section about six hundred feet[c] long. 24 He
took all the gold and silver and all the articles
found in the temple of God that had been in
the care of Obed-Edom, together with the
palace treasures and the hostages, and returned to Samaria.
25 Amaziah son of Joash king of Judah
lived for fifteen years after the death of Jehoash son of Jehoahaz king of Israel. 26 As
for the other events of Amaziah's reign, from
beginning to end, are they not written in the
book of the kings of Judah and Israel?
27 From the time that Amaziah turned away
from following the LORD, they conspired
against him in Jerusalem and he fled to Lachish, but they sent men after him to Lachish
and killed him there. 28 He was brought back
by horse and was buried with his fathers in
the City of Judah.

Uzziah King of Judah

26 Then all the people of Judah took
Uzziah,[d] who was sixteen years old,
and made him king in place of his father
Amaziah. 2 He was the one who rebuilt Elath
and restored it to Judah after Amaziah rested with his fathers.
3 Uzziah was sixteen years old when he
became king, and he reigned in Jerusalem
fifty-two years. His mother's name was Jecoliah; she was from Jerusalem. 4 He did what
was right in the eyes of the LORD, just as his
father Amaziah had done. 5 He sought God
during the days of Zechariah, who instructed
him in the fear[e] of God. As long as he sought
the LORD, God gave him success.
6 He went to war against the Philistines and
broke down the walls of Gath, Jabneh and
Ashdod. He then rebuilt towns near Ashdod
and elsewhere among the Philistines. 7 God
helped him against the Philistines and
against the Arabs who lived in Gur Baal and
against the Meunites. 8 The Ammonites
brought tribute to Uzziah, and his fame
spread as far as the border of Egypt, because he had become very powerful.
9 Uzziah built towers in Jerusalem at the
Corner Gate, at the Valley Gate and at the
angle of the wall, and he fortified them. 10 He

[a] *17* Hebrew *Joash,* a variant of *Jehoash*; also in verses 18, 21, 23 and 25 [b] *23* Hebrew *Jehoahaz,* a variant of *Ahaziah* [c] *23* Hebrew *four hundred cubits* (about 180 meters) [d] *1* Also called *Azariah* [e] *5* Many Hebrew manuscripts, Septuagint and Syriac; other Hebrew manuscripts *vision*

also built towers in the desert and dug many
cisterns, because he had much livestock in
the foothills and in the plain. He had people
working his fields and vineyards in the hills
and in the fertile lands, for he loved the soil.
11Uzziah had a well-trained army, ready to
go out by divisions according to their numbers as mustered by Jeiel the secretary and
Maaseiah the officer under the direction of
Hananiah, one of the royal officials. 12The
total number of family leaders over the fighting men was 2,600. 13Under their command
was an army of 307,500 men trained for war,
a powerful force to support the king against
his enemies. 14Uzziah provided shields,
spears, helmets, coats of armor, bows and
slingstones for the entire army. 15In Jerusalem he made machines designed by skillful
men for use on the towers and on the corner
defenses to shoot arrows and hurl large
stones. His fame spread far and wide, for he
was greatly helped until he became powerful.
16But after Uzziah became powerful, his
pride led to his downfall. He was unfaithful to
the LORD his God, and entered the temple of
the LORD to burn incense on the altar of incense. 17Azariah the priest with eighty other
courageous priests of the LORD followed him
in. 18They confronted him and said, "It is not
right for you, Uzziah, to burn incense to the
LORD. That is for the priests, the descendants
of Aaron, who have been consecrated to
burn incense. Leave the sanctuary, for you
have been unfaithful; and you will not be
honored by the LORD God."
19Uzziah, who had a censer in his hand
ready to burn incense, became angry. While
he was raging at the priests in their presence
before the incense altar in the LORD's temple,
leprosy[a] broke out on his forehead. 20When
Azariah the chief priest and all the other
priests looked at him, they saw that he had
leprosy on his forehead, so they hurried him
out. Indeed, he himself was eager to leave,
because the LORD had afflicted him.
21King Uzziah had leprosy until the day he
died. He lived in a separate house[b] —
leprous, and excluded from the temple of the
LORD. Jotham his son had charge of the palace and governed the people of the land.
22The other events of Uzziah's reign, from
beginning to end, are recorded by the
prophet Isaiah son of Amoz. 23Uzziah rested
with his fathers and was buried near them in
a field for burial that belonged to the kings,
for people said, "He had leprosy." And Jotham his son succeeded him as king.

Jotham King of Judah

27 Jotham was twenty-five years old
when he became king, and he
reigned in Jerusalem sixteen years. His
mother's name was Jerusha daughter of
Zadok. 2He did what was right in the eyes of
the LORD, just as his father Uzziah had done,
but unlike him he did not enter the temple of
the LORD. The people, however, continued
their corrupt practices. 3Jotham rebuilt the
Upper Gate of the temple of the LORD and did
extensive work on the wall at the hill of Ophel. 4He built towns in the Judean hills and
forts and towers in the wooded areas.
5Jotham made war on the king of the Ammonites and conquered them. That year the
Ammonites paid him a hundred talents[c] of
silver, ten thousand cors[d] of wheat and ten
thousand cors of barley. The Ammonites
brought him the same amount also in the
second and third years.
6Jotham grew powerful because he
walked steadfastly before the LORD his God.
7The other events in Jotham's reign, including all his wars and the other things he
did, are written in the book of the kings of
Israel and Judah. 8He was twenty-five years
old when he became king, and he reigned in
Jerusalem sixteen years. 9Jotham rested
with his fathers and was buried in the City of
David. And Ahaz his son succeeded him as
king.

Ahaz King of Judah

28 Ahaz was twenty years old when he
became king, and he reigned in
Jerusalem sixteen years. Unlike David his
father, he did not do what was right in the
eyes of the LORD. 2He walked in the ways of
the kings of Israel and also made cast idols
for worshiping the Baals. 3He burned sacrifices in the Valley of Ben Hinnom and sacrificed his sons in the fire, following the detestable ways of the nations the LORD had driven
out before the Israelites. 4He offered sacrifices and burned incense at the high places,
on the hilltops and under every spreading
tree.
5Therefore the LORD his God handed him

[a]*19* The Hebrew word was used for various diseases affecting the skin—not necessarily leprosy; also in verses 20, 21 and 23. [b]*21* Or *in a house where he was relieved of responsibilities* [c]*5* That is, about 3 3/4 tons (about 3.4 metric tons) [d]*5* That is, probably about 62,000 bushels (about 2,200 kiloliters)

over to the king of Aram. The Arameans defeated him and took many of his people as
prisoners and brought them to Damascus.
He was also given into the hands of the
king of Israel, who inflicted heavy casualties
on him. 6In one day Pekah son of Remaliah
killed a hundred and twenty thousand soldiers in Judah—because Judah had forsak-
en the LORD, the God of their fathers. 7Zicri,
an Ephraimite warrior, killed Maaseiah the
king's son, Azrikam the officer in charge of
the palace, and Elkanah, second to the king.
8The Israelites took captive from their kinsmen two hundred thousand wives, sons and
daughters. They also took a great deal of
plunder, which they carried back to Samaria.
9But a prophet of the LORD named Oded
was there, and he went out to meet the army
when it returned to Samaria. He said to
them, "Because the LORD, the God of your
fathers, was angry with Judah, he gave them
into your hand. But you have slaughtered
them in a rage that reaches to heaven. 10And
now you intend to make the men and women
of Judah and Jerusalem your slaves. But
aren't you also guilty of sins against the LORD
your God? 11Now listen to me! Send back
your fellow countrymen you have taken as
prisoners, for the LORD's fierce anger rests on
you."
12Then some of the leaders in Ephraim—
Azariah son of Jehohanan, Berekiah son of
Meshillemoth, Jehizkiah son of Shallum, and
Amasa son of Hadlai—confronted those who
were arriving from the war. 13"You must not
bring those prisoners here," they said, "or
we will be guilty before the LORD. Do you
intend to add to our sin and guilt? For our
guilt is already great, and his fierce anger
rests on Israel."
14So the soldiers gave up the prisoners
and plunder in the presence of the officials
and all the assembly. 15The men designated
by name took the prisoners, and from the
plunder they clothed all who were naked.
They provided them with clothes and sandals, food and drink, and healing balm. All
those who were weak they put on donkeys.
So they took them back to their fellow countrymen at Jericho, the City of Palms, and
returned to Samaria.
16At that time King Ahaz sent to the king[a]
of Assyria for help. 17The Edomites had
again come and attacked Judah and carried
away prisoners, 18while the Philistines had
raided towns in the foothills and in the Negev
of Judah. They captured and occupied Beth
Shemesh, Aijalon and Gederoth, as well as
Soco, Timnah and Gimzo, with their surrounding villages. 19The LORD had humbled
Judah because of Ahaz king of Israel,[b] for he
had promoted wickedness in Judah and had
been most unfaithful to the LORD. 20Tiglath-
Pileser[c] king of Assyria came to him, but he
gave him trouble instead of help. 21Ahaz took
some of the things from the temple of the
LORD and from the royal palace and from the
princes and presented them to the king of
Assyria, but that did not help him.
22In his time of trouble King Ahaz became
even more unfaithful to the LORD. 23He offered sacrifices to the gods of Damascus,
who had defeated him; for he thought,
"Since the gods of the kings of Aram have
helped them, I will sacrifice to them so they
will help me." But they were his downfall and
the downfall of all Israel.
24Ahaz gathered together the furnishings
from the temple of God and took them
away.[d] He shut the doors of the LORD's temple and set up altars at every street corner in
Jerusalem. 25In every town in Judah he built
high places to burn sacrifices to other gods
and provoked the LORD, the God of his fathers, to anger.
26The other events of his reign and all his
ways, from beginning to end, are written in
the book of the kings of Judah and Israel.
27Ahaz rested with his fathers and was buried in the city of Jerusalem, but he was not
placed in the tombs of the kings of Israel.
And Hezekiah his son succeeded him as
king.

Hezekiah Purifies the Temple

29 Hezekiah was twenty-five years old
when he became king, and he
reigned in Jerusalem twenty-nine years. His
mother's name was Abijah daughter of Zechariah. 2He did what was right in the eyes of
the LORD, just as his father David had done.
3In the first month of the first year of his
reign, he opened the doors of the temple of
the LORD and repaired them. 4He brought in
the priests and the Levites, assembled them
in the square on the east side 5and said:
"Listen to me, Levites! Consecrate yourselves now and consecrate the temple of the

[a]16 One Hebrew manuscript, Septuagint and Vulgate (see also 2 Kings 16:7); most Hebrew manuscripts *kings*
[b]19 That is, Judah, as frequently in 2 Chronicles [c]20 Hebrew *Tilgath-Pilneser*, a variant of *Tiglath-Pileser*
[d]24 Or *and cut them up*

LORD, the God of your fathers. Remove all
defilement from the sanctuary. 6Our fathers
were unfaithful; they did evil in the eyes of
the LORD our God and forsook him. They
turned their faces away from the LORD's
dwelling place and turned their backs on
him. 7They also shut the doors of the portico
and put out the lamps. They did not burn
incense or present any burnt offerings at the
sanctuary to the God of Israel. 8Therefore,
the anger of the LORD has fallen on Judah
and Jerusalem; he has made them an object
of dread and horror and scorn, as you can
see with your own eyes. 9This is why our
fathers have fallen by the sword and why our
sons and daughters and our wives are in
captivity. 10Now I intend to make a covenant
with the LORD, the God of Israel, so that his
fierce anger will turn away from us. 11My
sons, do not be negligent now, for the LORD
has chosen you to stand before him and
serve him, to minister before him and to burn
incense."

12Then these Levites set to work:
from the Kohathites,
Mahath son of Amasai and Joel son of Azariah;
from the Merarites,
Kish son of Abdi and Azariah son of Jehallelel;
from the Gershonites,
Joah son of Zimmah and Eden son of Joah;
13from the descendants of Elizaphan,
Shimri and Jeiel;
from the descendants of Asaph,
Zechariah and Mattaniah;
14from the descendants of Heman,
Jehiel and Shimei;
from the descendants of Jeduthun,
Shemaiah and Uzziel.

15When they had assembled their brothers
and consecrated themselves, they went in to
purify the temple of the LORD, as the king had
ordered, following the word of the LORD.
16The priests went into the sanctuary of the
LORD to purify it. They brought out to the
courtyard of the LORD's temple everything unclean that they found in the temple of the
LORD. The Levites took it and carried it out to
the Kidron Valley. 17They began the consecration on the first day of the first month, and
by the eighth day of the month they reached
the portico of the LORD. For eight more days
they consecrated the temple of the LORD itself, finishing on the sixteenth day of the first
month.

18Then they went in to King Hezekiah and
reported: "We have purified the entire temple of the LORD, the altar of burnt offering with
all its utensils, and the table for setting out
the consecrated bread, with all its articles.
19We have prepared and consecrated all the
articles that King Ahaz removed in his unfaithfulness while he was king. They are now
in front of the LORD's altar."

20Early the next morning King Hezekiah
gathered the city officials together and went
up to the temple of the LORD. 21They brought
seven bulls, seven rams, seven male lambs
and seven male goats as a sin offering for
the kingdom, for the sanctuary and for
Judah. The king commanded the priests, the
descendants of Aaron, to offer these on the
altar of the LORD. 22So they slaughtered the
bulls, and the priests took the blood and
sprinkled it on the altar; next they slaughtered the rams and sprinkled their blood on
the altar; then they slaughtered the lambs
and sprinkled their blood on the altar. 23The
goats for the sin offering were brought before
the king and the assembly, and they laid their
hands on them. 24The priests then slaughtered the goats and presented their blood on
the altar for a sin offering to atone for all
Israel, because the king had ordered the
burnt offering and the sin offering for all Israel.

25He stationed the Levites in the temple of
the LORD with cymbals, harps and lyres in the
way prescribed by David and Gad the king's
seer and Nathan the prophet; this was commanded by the LORD through his prophets.
26So the Levites stood ready with David's
instruments, and the priests with their trumpets.

27Hezekiah gave the order to sacrifice the
burnt offering on the altar. As the offering
began, singing to the LORD began also, accompanied by trumpets and the instruments
of David king of Israel. 28The whole assembly bowed in worship, while the singers sang
and the trumpeters played. All this continued
until the sacrifice of the burnt offering was
completed.

29When the offerings were finished, the
king and everyone present with him knelt
down and worshiped. 30King Hezekiah and
his officials ordered the Levites to praise the
LORD with the words of David and of Asaph
the seer. So they sang praises with gladness
and bowed their heads and worshiped.

31Then Hezekiah said, "You have now
dedicated yourselves to the LORD. Come and

bring sacrifices and thank offerings to the
temple of the LORD." So the assembly
brought sacrifices and thank offerings, and
all whose hearts were willing brought burnt
offerings.
32The number of burnt offerings the assembly brought was seventy bulls, a hundred rams and two hundred male lambs—all
of them for burnt offerings to the LORD. 33The
animals consecrated as sacrifices amounted
to six hundred bulls and three thousand
sheep and goats. 34The priests, however,
were too few to skin all the burnt offerings; so
their kinsmen the Levites helped them until
the task was finished and until other priests
had been consecrated, for the Levites had
been more conscientious in consecrating
themselves than the priests had been.
35There were burnt offerings in abundance,
together with the fat of the fellowship offerings[a] and the drink offerings that accompanied the burnt offerings.
So the service of the temple of the LORD
was reestablished. 36Hezekiah and all the
people rejoiced at what God had brought
about for his people, because it was done so
quickly.

Hezekiah Celebrates the Passover

30 Hezekiah sent word to all Israel and
Judah and also wrote letters to
Ephraim and Manasseh, inviting them to
come to the temple of the LORD in Jerusalem
and celebrate the Passover to the LORD, the
God of Israel. 2The king and his officials and
the whole assembly in Jerusalem decided to
celebrate the Passover in the second month.
3They had not been able to celebrate it at the
regular time because not enough priests had
consecrated themselves and the people had
not assembled in Jerusalem. 4The plan
seemed right both to the king and to the
whole assembly. 5They decided to send a
proclamation throughout Israel, from Beersheba to Dan, calling the people to come to
Jerusalem and celebrate the Passover to the
LORD, the God of Israel. It had not been celebrated in large numbers according to what
was written.
6At the king's command, couriers went
throughout Israel and Judah with letters from
the king and from his officials, which read:

"People of Israel, return to the LORD,
the God of Abraham, Isaac and Israel,
that he may return to you who are left,
who have escaped from the hand of the
kings of Assyria. 7Do not be like your
fathers and brothers, who were unfaithful to the LORD, the God of their fathers,
so that he made them an object of horror, as you see. 8Do not be stiff-necked,
as your fathers were; submit to the LORD.
Come to the sanctuary, which he has
consecrated forever. Serve the LORD
your God, so that his fierce anger will
turn away from you. 9If you return to the
LORD, then your brothers and your children will be shown compassion by their
captors and will come back to this land,
for the LORD your God is gracious and
compassionate. He will not turn his face
from you if you return to him."

10The couriers went from town to town in
Ephraim and Manasseh, as far as Zebulun,
but the people scorned and ridiculed them.
11Nevertheless, some men of Asher, Manasseh and Zebulun humbled themselves
and went to Jerusalem. 12Also in Judah the
hand of God was on the people to give them
unity of mind to carry out what the king and
his officials had ordered, following the word
of the LORD.
13A very large crowd of people assembled
in Jerusalem to celebrate the Feast of Unleavened Bread in the second month. 14They
removed the altars in Jerusalem and cleared
away the incense altars and threw them into
the Kidron Valley.
15They slaughtered the Passover lamb on
the fourteenth day of the second month. The
priests and the Levites were ashamed and
consecrated themselves and brought burnt
offerings to the temple of the LORD. 16Then
they took up their regular positions as prescribed in the Law of Moses the man of God.
The priests sprinkled the blood handed to
them by the Levites. 17Since many in the
crowd had not consecrated themselves, the
Levites had to kill the Passover lambs for all
those who were not ceremonially clean and
could not consecrate ⌞their lambs⌟ to the
LORD. 18Although most of the many people
who came from Ephraim, Manasseh, Issachar and Zebulun had not purified themselves, yet they ate the Passover, contrary to
what was written. But Hezekiah prayed for
them, saying, "May the LORD, who is good,
pardon everyone 19who sets his heart on
seeking God—the LORD, the God of his fathers—even if he is not clean according to

[a]35 Traditionally *peace offerings*

the rules of the sanctuary." 20And the LORD heard Hezekiah and healed the people.

21The Israelites who were present in Jerusalem celebrated the Feast of Unleavened Bread for seven days with great rejoicing, while the Levites and priests sang to the LORD every day, accompanied by the LORD's instruments of praise.[a]

22Hezekiah spoke encouragingly to all the Levites, who showed good understanding of the service of the LORD. For the seven days they ate their assigned portion and offered fellowship offerings[b] and praised the LORD, the God of their fathers.

23The whole assembly then agreed to celebrate the festival seven more days; so for another seven days they celebrated joyfully. 24Hezekiah king of Judah provided a thousand bulls and seven thousand sheep and goats for the assembly, and the officials provided them with a thousand bulls and ten thousand sheep and goats. A great number of priests consecrated themselves. 25The entire assembly of Judah rejoiced, along with the priests and Levites and all who had assembled from Israel, including the aliens who had come from Israel and those who lived in Judah. 26There was great joy in Jerusalem, for since the days of Solomon son of David king of Israel there had been nothing like this in Jerusalem. 27The priests and the Levites stood to bless the people, and God heard them, for their prayer reached heaven, his holy dwelling place.

31 When all this had ended, the Israelites who were there went out to the towns of Judah, smashed the sacred stones and cut down the Asherah poles. They destroyed the high places and the altars throughout Judah and Benjamin and in Ephraim and Manasseh. After they had destroyed all of them, the Israelites returned to their own towns and to their own property.

Contributions for Worship

2Hezekiah assigned the priests and Levites to divisions—each of them according to their duties as priests or Levites—to offer burnt offerings and fellowship offerings,[b] to minister, to give thanks and to sing praises at the gates of the LORD's dwelling. 3The king contributed from his own possessions for the morning and evening burnt offerings and for the burnt offerings on the Sabbaths, New Moons and appointed feasts as written in the Law of the LORD. 4He ordered the people living in Jerusalem to give the portion due the priests and Levites so they could devote themselves to the Law of the LORD. 5As soon as the order went out, the Israelites generously gave the firstfruits of their grain, new wine, oil and honey and all that the fields produced. They brought a great amount, a tithe of everything. 6The men of Israel and Judah who lived in the towns of Judah also brought a tithe of their herds and flocks and a tithe of the holy things dedicated to the LORD their God, and they piled them in heaps. 7They began doing this in the third month and finished in the seventh month. 8When Hezekiah and his officials came and saw the heaps, they praised the LORD and blessed his people Israel.

9Hezekiah asked the priests and Levites about the heaps; 10and Azariah the chief priest, from the family of Zadok, answered, "Since the people began to bring their contributions to the temple of the LORD, we have had enough to eat and plenty to spare, because the LORD has blessed his people, and this great amount is left over."

11Hezekiah gave orders to prepare storerooms in the temple of the LORD, and this was done. 12Then they faithfully brought in the contributions, tithes and dedicated gifts. Conaniah, a Levite, was in charge of these things, and his brother Shimei was next in rank. 13Jehiel, Azaziah, Nahath, Asahel, Jerimoth, Jozabad, Eliel, Ismakiah, Mahath and Benaiah were supervisors under Conaniah and Shimei his brother, by appointment of King Hezekiah and Azariah the official in charge of the temple of God.

14Kore son of Imnah the Levite, keeper of the East Gate, was in charge of the freewill offerings given to God, distributing the contributions made to the LORD and also the consecrated gifts. 15Eden, Miniamin, Jeshua, Shemaiah, Amariah and Shecaniah assisted him faithfully in the towns of the priests, distributing to their fellow priests according to their divisions, old and young alike.

16In addition, they distributed to the males three years old or more whose names were in the genealogical records—all who would enter the temple of the LORD to perform the daily duties of their various tasks, according to their responsibilities and their divisions.

[a]21 Or *priests praised the LORD every day with resounding instruments belonging to the LORD*
[b]22,2 Traditionally *peace offerings*

17And they distributed to the priests enrolled
by their families in the genealogical records
and likewise to the Levites twenty years old
or more, according to their responsibilities
and their divisions. 18They included all the
little ones, the wives, and the sons and
daughters of the whole community listed in
these genealogical records. For they were
faithful in consecrating themselves.

19As for the priests, the descendants of
Aaron, who lived on the farm lands around
their towns or in any other towns, men were
designated by name to distribute portions to
every male among them and to all who were
recorded in the genealogies of the Levites.

20This is what Hezekiah did throughout
Judah, doing what was good and right and
faithful before the LORD his God. 21In everything that he undertook in the service of
God's temple and in obedience to the law
and the commands, he sought his God and
worked wholeheartedly. And so he prospered.

Sennacherib Threatens Jerusalem

32 After all that Hezekiah had so faithfully done, Sennacherib king of Assyria came and invaded Judah. He laid siege
to the fortified cities, thinking to conquer
them for himself. 2When Hezekiah saw that
Sennacherib had come and that he intended
to make war on Jerusalem, 3he consulted
with his officials and military staff about
blocking off the water from the springs outside the city, and they helped him. 4A large
force of men assembled, and they blocked
all the springs and the stream that flowed
through the land. "Why should the kings[a] of
Assyria come and find plenty of water?" they
said. 5Then he worked hard repairing all the
broken sections of the wall and building towers on it. He built another wall outside that
one and reinforced the supporting terraces[b]
of the City of David. He also made large
numbers of weapons and shields.

6He appointed military officers over the
people and assembled them before him in
the square at the city gate and encouraged
them with these words: 7"Be strong and
courageous. Do not be afraid or discouraged
because of the king of Assyria and the vast
army with him, for there is a greater power
with us than with him. 8With him is only the
arm of flesh, but with us is the LORD our God
to help us and to fight our battles." And the
people gained confidence from what Hezekiah the king of Judah said.

9Later, when Sennacherib king of Assyria
and all his forces were laying siege to Lachish, he sent his officers to Jerusalem with
this message for Hezekiah king of Judah and
for all the people of Judah who were there:

> 10"This is what Sennacherib king of
> Assyria says: On what are you basing
> your confidence, that you remain in
> Jerusalem under siege? 11When Heze-
> kiah says, 'The LORD our God will save
> us from the hand of the king of Assyria,'
> he is misleading you, to let you die of
> hunger and thirst. 12Did not Hezekiah
> himself remove this god's high places
> and altars, saying to Judah and Jerusa-
> lem, 'You must worship before one altar
> and burn sacrifices on it'?
>
> 13"Do you not know what I and my
> fathers have done to all the peoples of
> the other lands? Were the gods of those
> nations ever able to deliver their land
> from my hand? 14Who of all the gods of
> these nations that my fathers destroyed
> has been able to save his people from
> me? How then can your god deliver you
> from my hand? 15Now do not let Heze-
> kiah deceive you and mislead you like
> this. Do not believe him, for no god of
> any nation or kingdom has been able to
> deliver his people from my hand or the
> hand of my fathers. How much less will
> your god deliver you from my hand!"

16Sennacherib's officers spoke further
against the LORD God and against his servant
Hezekiah. 17The king also wrote letters insulting the LORD, the God of Israel, and saying this against him: "Just as the gods of the
peoples of the other lands did not rescue
their people from my hand, so the god of
Hezekiah will not rescue his people from my
hand." 18Then they called out in Hebrew to
the people of Jerusalem who were on the
wall, to terrify them and make them afraid in
order to capture the city. 19They spoke about
the God of Jerusalem as they did about the
gods of the other peoples of the world—the
work of men's hands.

20King Hezekiah and the prophet Isaiah
son of Amoz cried out in prayer to heaven
about this. 21And the LORD sent an angel, who
annihilated all the fighting men and the leaders and officers in the camp of the Assyrian

[a]4 Hebrew; Septuagint and Syriac *king* [b]5 Or *the Millo*

king. So he withdrew to his own land in disgrace. And when he went into the temple of
his god, some of his sons cut him down with
the sword.
22So the LORD saved Hezekiah and the
people of Jerusalem from the hand of Sennacherib king of Assyria and from the hand
of all others. He took care of them[a] on every
side. 23Many brought offerings to Jerusalem
for the LORD and valuable gifts for Hezekiah
king of Judah. From then on he was highly
regarded by all the nations.

Hezekiah's Pride, Success and Death

24In those days Hezekiah became ill and
was at the point of death. He prayed to the
LORD, who answered him and gave him a
miraculous sign. 25But Hezekiah's heart was
proud and he did not respond to the kindness
shown him; therefore the LORD's wrath was
on him and on Judah and Jerusalem. 26Then
Hezekiah repented of the pride of his heart,
as did the people of Jerusalem; therefore the
LORD's wrath did not come upon them during
the days of Hezekiah.
27Hezekiah had very great riches and hon-
or, and he made treasuries for his silver and
gold and for his precious stones, spices,
shields and all kinds of valuables. 28He also
made buildings to store the harvest of grain,
new wine and oil; and he made stalls for
various kinds of cattle, and pens for the
flocks. 29He built villages and acquired great
numbers of flocks and herds, for God had
given him very great riches.
30It was Hezekiah who blocked the upper
outlet of the Gihon spring and channeled the
water down to the west side of the City of
David. He succeeded in everything he undertook. 31But when envoys were sent by the
rulers of Babylon to ask him about the miraculous sign that had occurred in the land, God
left him to test him and to know everything
that was in his heart.
32The other events of Hezekiah's reign
and his acts of devotion are written in the
vision of the prophet Isaiah son of Amoz in
the book of the kings of Judah and Israel.
33Hezekiah rested with his fathers and was
buried on the hill where the tombs of David's
descendants are. All Judah and the people
of Jerusalem honored him when he died.
And Manasseh his son succeeded him as
king.

Manasseh King of Judah

33 Manasseh was twelve years old
when he became king, and he
reigned in Jerusalem fifty-five years. 2He did
evil in the eyes of the LORD, following the
detestable practices of the nations the LORD
had driven out before the Israelites. 3He rebuilt the high places his father Hezekiah had
demolished; he also erected altars to the
Baals and made Asherah poles. He bowed
down to all the starry hosts and worshiped
them. 4He built altars in the temple of the
LORD, of which the LORD had said, "My Name
will remain in Jerusalem forever." 5In both
courts of the temple of the LORD, he built
altars to all the starry hosts. 6He sacrificed
his sons in[b] the fire in the Valley of Ben
Hinnom, practiced sorcery, divination and
witchcraft, and consulted mediums and spiritists. He did much evil in the eyes of the
LORD, provoking him to anger.
7He took the carved image he had made
and put it in God's temple, of which God had
said to David and to his son Solomon, "In this
temple and in Jerusalem, which I have chosen out of all the tribes of Israel, I will put my
Name forever. 8I will not again make the feet
of the Israelites leave the land I assigned to
your forefathers, if only they will be careful to
do everything I commanded them concerning all the laws, decrees and ordinances giv-
en through Moses." 9But Manasseh led
Judah and the people of Jerusalem astray,
so that they did more evil than the nations the
LORD had destroyed before the Israelites.
10The LORD spoke to Manasseh and his
people, but they paid no attention. 11So the
LORD brought against them the army commanders of the king of Assyria, who took
Manasseh prisoner, put a hook in his nose,
bound him with bronze shackles and took
him to Babylon. 12In his distress he sought
the favor of the LORD his God and humbled
himself greatly before the God of his fathers.
13And when he prayed to him, the LORD was
moved by his entreaty and listened to his
plea; so he brought him back to Jerusalem
and to his kingdom. Then Manasseh knew
that the LORD is God.
14Afterward he rebuilt the outer wall of the
City of David, west of the Gihon spring in the
valley, as far as the entrance of the Fish Gate
and encircling the hill of Ophel; he also made
it much higher. He stationed military com-

[a]22 Hebrew; Septuagint and Vulgate *He gave them rest*

[b]6 Or *He made his sons pass through*

manders in all the fortified cities in Judah.

15He got rid of the foreign gods and removed the image from the temple of the LORD, as well as all the altars he had built on the temple hill and in Jerusalem; and he threw them out of the city. 16Then he restored the altar of the LORD and sacrificed fellowship offerings[a] and thank offerings on it, and told Judah to serve the LORD, the God of Israel. 17The people, however, continued to sacrifice at the high places, but only to the LORD their God.

18The other events of Manasseh's reign, including his prayer to his God and the words the seers spoke to him in the name of the LORD, the God of Israel, are written in the annals of the kings of Israel.[b] 19His prayer and how God was moved by his entreaty, as well as all his sins and unfaithfulness, and the sites where he built high places and set up Asherah poles and idols before he humbled himself—all are written in the records of the seers.[c] 20Manasseh rested with his fathers and was buried in his palace. And Amon his son succeeded him as king.

Amon King of Judah

21Amon was twenty-two years old when he became king, and he reigned in Jerusalem two years. 22He did evil in the eyes of the LORD, as his father Manasseh had done. Amon worshiped and offered sacrifices to all the idols Manasseh had made. 23But unlike his father Manasseh, he did not humble himself before the LORD; Amon increased his guilt.

24Amon's officials conspired against him and assassinated him in his palace. 25Then the people of the land killed all who had plotted against King Amon, and they made Josiah his son king in his place.

Josiah's Reforms

34 Josiah was eight years old when he became king, and he reigned in Jerusalem thirty-one years. 2He did what was right in the eyes of the LORD and walked in the ways of his father David, not turning aside to the right or to the left.

3In the eighth year of his reign, while he was still young, he began to seek the God of his father David. In his twelfth year he began to purge Judah and Jerusalem of high places, Asherah poles, carved idols and cast images. 4Under his direction the altars of the Baals were torn down; he cut to pieces the incense altars that were above them, and smashed the Asherah poles, the idols and the images. These he broke to pieces and scattered over the graves of those who had sacrificed to them. 5He burned the bones of the priests on their altars, and so he purged Judah and Jerusalem. 6In the towns of Manasseh, Ephraim and Simeon, as far as Naphtali, and in the ruins around them, 7he tore down the altars and the Asherah poles and crushed the idols to powder and cut to pieces all the incense altars throughout Israel. Then he went back to Jerusalem.

8In the eighteenth year of Josiah's reign, to purify the land and the temple, he sent Shaphan son of Azaliah and Maaseiah the ruler of the city, with Joah son of Joahaz, the recorder, to repair the temple of the LORD his God.

9They went to Hilkiah the high priest and gave him the money that had been brought into the temple of God, which the Levites who were the doorkeepers had collected from the people of Manasseh, Ephraim and the entire remnant of Israel and from all the people of Judah and Benjamin and the inhabitants of Jerusalem. 10Then they entrusted it to the men appointed to supervise the work on the LORD's temple. These men paid the workers who repaired and restored the temple. 11They also gave money to the carpenters and builders to purchase dressed stone, and timber for joists and beams for the buildings that the kings of Judah had allowed to fall into ruin.

12The men did the work faithfully. Over them to direct them were Jahath and Obadiah, Levites descended from Merari, and Zechariah and Meshullam, descended from Kohath. The Levites—all who were skilled in playing musical instruments— 13had charge of the laborers and supervised all the workers from job to job. Some of the Levites were secretaries, scribes and doorkeepers.

The Book of the Law Found

14While they were bringing out the money that had been taken into the temple of the LORD, Hilkiah the priest found the Book of the Law of the LORD that had been given through Moses. 15Hilkiah said to Shaphan the secre-

[a] *16* Traditionally *peace offerings* [b] *18* That is, Judah, as frequently in 2 Chron. [c] *19* One Hebrew manuscript and Septuagint; most Hebrew manuscripts *of Hozai*

tary, "I have found the Book of the Law in the temple of the LORD." He gave it to Shaphan.

[16]Then Shaphan took the book to the king and reported to him: "Your officials are doing everything that has been committed to them. [17]They have paid out the money that was in the temple of the LORD and have entrusted it to the supervisors and workers." [18]Then Shaphan the secretary informed the king, "Hilkiah the priest has given me a book." And Shaphan read from it in the presence of the king.

[19]When the king heard the words of the Law, he tore his robes. [20]He gave these orders to Hilkiah, Ahikam son of Shaphan, Abdon son of Micah,[a] Shaphan the secretary and Asaiah the king's attendant: [21]"Go and inquire of the LORD for me and for the remnant in Israel and Judah about what is written in this book that has been found. Great is the LORD's anger that is poured out on us because our fathers have not kept the word of the LORD; they have not acted in accordance with all that is written in this book."

[22]Hilkiah and those the king had sent with him[b] went to speak to the prophetess Huldah, who was the wife of Shallum son of Tokhath,[c] the son of Hasrah,[d] keeper of the wardrobe. She lived in Jerusalem, in the Second District.

[23]She said to them, "This is what the LORD, the God of Israel, says: Tell the man who sent you to me, [24]'This is what the LORD says: I am going to bring disaster on this place and its people—all the curses written in the book that has been read in the presence of the king of Judah. [25]Because they have forsaken me and burned incense to other gods and provoked me to anger by all that their hands have made,[e] my anger will be poured out on this place and will not be quenched.' [26]Tell the king of Judah, who sent you to inquire of the LORD, 'This is what the LORD, the God of Israel, says concerning the words you heard: [27]Because your heart was responsive and you humbled yourself before God when you heard what he spoke against this place and its people, and because you humbled yourself before me and tore your robes and wept in my presence, I have heard you, declares the LORD. [28]Now I will gather you to your fathers, and you will be buried in peace. Your eyes will not see all the disaster I am going to bring on this place and on those who live here.' "

So they took her answer back to the king.

[29]Then the king called together all the elders of Judah and Jerusalem. [30]He went up to the temple of the LORD with the men of Judah, the people of Jerusalem, the priests and the Levites—all the people from the least to the greatest. He read in their hearing all the words of the Book of the Covenant, which had been found in the temple of the LORD. [31]The king stood by his pillar and renewed the covenant in the presence of the LORD—to follow the LORD and keep his commands, regulations and decrees with all his heart and all his soul, and to obey the words of the covenant written in this book.

[32]Then he had everyone in Jerusalem and Benjamin pledge themselves to it; the people of Jerusalem did this in accordance with the covenant of God, the God of their fathers.

[33]Josiah removed all the detestable idols from all the territory belonging to the Israelites, and he had all who were present in Israel serve the LORD their God. As long as he lived, they did not fail to follow the LORD, the God of their fathers.

Josiah Celebrates the Passover

35 Josiah celebrated the Passover to the LORD in Jerusalem, and the Passover lamb was slaughtered on the fourteenth day of the first month. [2]He appointed the priests to their duties and encouraged them in the service of the LORD's temple. [3]He said to the Levites, who instructed all Israel and who had been consecrated to the LORD: "Put the sacred ark in the temple that Solomon son of David king of Israel built. It is not to be carried about on your shoulders. Now serve the LORD your God and his people Israel. [4]Prepare yourselves by families in your divisions, according to the directions written by David king of Israel and by his son Solomon.

[5]"Stand in the holy place with a group of Levites for each subdivision of the families of your fellow countrymen, the lay people. [6]Slaughter the Passover lambs, consecrate yourselves and prepare ⌞the lambs⌟ for your fellow countrymen, doing what the LORD commanded through Moses."

[7]Josiah provided for all the lay people who were there a total of thirty thousand sheep

[a]20 Also called *Acbor son of Micaiah* [b]22 One Hebrew manuscript, Vulgate and Syriac; most Hebrew manuscripts do not have *had sent with him.* [c]22 Also called *Tikvah* [d]22 Also called *Harhas* [e]25 Or *by everything they have done*

and goats for the Passover offerings, and
also three thousand cattle—all from the
king's own possessions.
8His officials also contributed voluntarily to
the people and the priests and Levites. Hilkiah, Zechariah and Jehiel, the administrators of God's temple, gave the priests
twenty-six hundred Passover offerings and
three hundred cattle. 9Also Conaniah along
with Shemaiah and Nethanel, his brothers,
and Hashabiah, Jeiel and Jozabad, the leaders of the Levites, provided five thousand
Passover offerings and five hundred head of
cattle for the Levites.
10The service was arranged and the
priests stood in their places with the Levites
in their divisions as the king had ordered.
11The Passover lambs were slaughtered,
and the priests sprinkled the blood handed to
them, while the Levites skinned the animals.
12They set aside the burnt offerings to give
them to the subdivisions of the families of the
people to offer to the LORD, as is written in the
Book of Moses. They did the same with the
cattle. 13They roasted the Passover animals
over the fire as prescribed, and boiled the
holy offerings in pots, caldrons and pans and
served them quickly to all the people. 14After
this, they made preparations for themselves
and for the priests, because the priests, the
descendants of Aaron, were sacrificing the
burnt offerings and the fat portions until
nightfall. So the Levites made preparations
for themselves and for the Aaronic priests.
15The musicians, the descendants of
Asaph, were in the places prescribed by David, Asaph, Heman and Jeduthun the king's
seer. The gatekeepers at each gate did not
need to leave their posts, because their fellow Levites made the preparations for them.
16So at that time the entire service of the
LORD was carried out for the celebration of
the Passover and the offering of burnt offerings on the altar of the LORD, as King Josiah
had ordered. 17The Israelites who were
present celebrated the Passover at that time
and observed the Feast of Unleavened
Bread for seven days. 18The Passover had
not been observed like this in Israel since the
days of the prophet Samuel; and none of the
kings of Israel had ever celebrated such a
Passover as did Josiah, with the priests, the
Levites and all Judah and Israel who were
there with the people of Jerusalem. 19This
Passover was celebrated in the eighteenth
year of Josiah's reign.

The Death of Josiah

20After all this, when Josiah had set the
temple in order, Neco king of Egypt went up
to fight at Carchemish on the Euphrates, and
Josiah marched out to meet him in battle.
21But Neco sent messengers to him, saying,
"What quarrel is there between you and me,
O king of Judah? It is not you I am attacking
at this time, but the house with which I am at
war. God has told me to hurry; so stop opposing God, who is with me, or he will destroy you."
22Josiah, however, would not turn away
from him, but disguised himself to engage
him in battle. He would not listen to what
Neco had said at God's command but went
to fight him on the plain of Megiddo.
23Archers shot King Josiah, and he told his
officers, "Take me away; I am badly wounded." 24So they took him out of his chariot, put
him in the other chariot he had and brought
him to Jerusalem, where he died. He was
buried in the tombs of his fathers, and all
Judah and Jerusalem mourned for him.
25Jeremiah composed laments for Josiah,
and to this day all the men and women singers commemorate Josiah in the laments.
These became a tradition in Israel and are
written in the Laments.
26The other events of Josiah's reign and
his acts of devotion, according to what is
written in the Law of the LORD— 27all the
events, from beginning to end, are written in
the book of the kings of Israel and Judah.

36 1And the people of the land took
Jehoahaz son of Josiah and made
him king in Jerusalem in place of his father.

Jehoahaz King of Judah

2Jehoahaz[a] was twenty-three years old
when he became king, and he reigned in
Jerusalem three months. 3The king of Egypt
dethroned him in Jerusalem and imposed on
Judah a levy of a hundred talents[b] of silver
and a talent[c] of gold. 4The king of Egypt
made Eliakim, a brother of Jehoahaz, king
over Judah and Jerusalem and changed
Eliakim's name to Jehoiakim. But Neco took
Eliakim's brother Jehoahaz and carried him
off to Egypt.

[a]2 Hebrew *Joahaz*, a variant of *Jehoahaz*; also in verse 4
[b]3 That is, about 3 3/4 tons (about 3.4 metric tons)
[c]3 That is, about 75 pounds (about 34 kilograms)

Jehoiakim King of Judah

5 Jehoiakim was twenty-five years old
when he became king, and he reigned in
Jerusalem eleven years. He did evil in the
eyes of the LORD his God. 6 Nebuchadnezzar
king of Babylon attacked him and bound him
with bronze shackles to take him to Babylon.
7 Nebuchadnezzar also took to Babylon articles from the temple of the LORD and put
them in his temple[a] there.
8 The other events of Jehoiakim's reign, the
detestable things he did and all that was
found against him, are written in the book of
the kings of Israel and Judah. And Jehoiachin his son succeeded him as king.

Jehoiachin King of Judah

9 Jehoiachin was eighteen[b] years old when
he became king, and he reigned in Jerusalem three months and ten days. He did evil in
the eyes of the LORD. 10 In the spring, King
Nebuchadnezzar sent for him and brought
him to Babylon, together with articles of
value from the temple of the LORD, and he
made Jehoiachin's uncle,[c] Zedekiah, king
over Judah and Jerusalem.

Zedekiah King of Judah

11 Zedekiah was twenty-one years old
when he became king, and he reigned in
Jerusalem eleven years. 12 He did evil in the
eyes of the LORD his God and did not humble
himself before Jeremiah the prophet, who
spoke the word of the LORD. 13 He also rebelled against King Nebuchadnezzar, who
had made him take an oath in God's name.
He became stiff-necked and hardened his
heart and would not turn to the LORD, the God
of Israel. 14 Furthermore, all the leaders of the
priests and the people became more and
more unfaithful, following all the detestable
practices of the nations and defiling the temple of the LORD, which he had consecrated in
Jerusalem.

The Fall of Jerusalem

15 The LORD, the God of their fathers, sent
word to them through his messengers again
and again, because he had pity on his
people and on his dwelling place. 16 But they
mocked God's messengers, despised his
words and scoffed at his prophets until the
wrath of the LORD was aroused against his
people and there was no remedy. 17 He
brought up against them the king of the Babylonians,[d] who killed their young men with
the sword in the sanctuary, and spared
neither young man nor young woman, old
man or aged. God handed all of them over to
Nebuchadnezzar. 18 He carried to Babylon all
the articles from the temple of God, both
large and small, and the treasures of the
LORD's temple and the treasures of the king
and his officials. 19 They set fire to God's temple and broke down the wall of Jerusalem;
they burned all the palaces and destroyed
everything of value there.
20 He carried into exile to Babylon the remnant, who escaped from the sword, and they
became servants to him and his sons until
the kingdom of Persia came to power. 21 The
land enjoyed its sabbath rests; all the time of
its desolation it rested, until the seventy
years were completed in fulfillment of the
word of the LORD spoken by Jeremiah.
22 In the first year of Cyrus king of Persia, in
order to fulfill the word of the LORD spoken by
Jeremiah, the LORD moved the heart of Cyrus
king of Persia to make a proclamation
throughout his realm and to put it in writing:

23 "This is what Cyrus king of Persia says:
" 'The LORD, the God of heaven, has
given me all the kingdoms of the earth
and he has appointed me to build a temple for him at Jerusalem in Judah. Anyone of his people among you—may the
LORD his God be with him, and let him go
up.' "

[a] *7* Or *palace* [b] *9* One Hebrew manuscript, some Septuagint manuscripts and Syriac (see also 2 Kings 24:8); most Hebrew manuscripts *eight* [c] *10* Hebrew *brother,* that is, relative (see 2 Kings 24:17) [d] *17* Or *Chaldeans*

Ezra

Introduction:

The book of Ezra tells about the return of the Jews from exile in Babylon. It begins in 539 B.C. with the decree of Cyrus, king of Persia, which allowed the people to go back to Jerusalem under the leadership of Zerubbabel. The people enthusiastically began rebuilding the temple and resumed sacrifices. But for eighteen years they were delayed by their enemies from the north. Finally, in 521 B.C. a decree from Darius, king of Persia, let them finish. The people completed and dedicated the temple in 515 B.C.

In 458 B.C. Ezra, the priest, returned to Jerusalem with another group of Babylonian exiles. He taught the people the law and reformed their religious life so the other nations around them could see they were God's chosen nation.

Ezra is the author of the books of Ezra and Nehemiah.

Outline of contents:

The first exiles return to the land of Judah (1:1–2:70)
The temple is rebuilt (3:1–6:22)
Ezra's return and ministry (7:1–10:44)

Cyrus Helps the Exiles to Return

1 In the first year of Cyrus king of Persia, in
order to fulfill the word of the LORD
spoken by Jeremiah, the LORD moved the
heart of Cyrus king of Persia to make a proclamation throughout his realm and to put it in
writing:

2"This is what Cyrus king of Persia says:
" 'The LORD, the God of heaven, has
given me all the kingdoms of the earth
and he has appointed me to build a temple for him at Jerusalem in Judah. 3Any-
one of his people among you—may his
God be with him, and let him go up to
Jerusalem in Judah and build the temple of the LORD, the God of Israel, the
God who is in Jerusalem. 4And the
people of any place where survivors
may now be living are to provide him
with silver and gold, with goods and livestock, and with freewill offerings for the
temple of God in Jerusalem.' "

5Then the family heads of Judah and Benjamin, and the priests and Levites—everyone whose heart God had moved—prepared
to go up and build the house of the LORD in
Jerusalem. 6All their neighbors assisted
them with articles of silver and gold, with
goods and livestock, and with valuable gifts,
in addition to all the freewill offerings. 7More-
over, King Cyrus brought out the articles belonging to the temple of the LORD, which
Nebuchadnezzar had carried away from
Jerusalem and had placed in the temple of
his god.[a] 8Cyrus king of Persia had them
brought by Mithredath the treasurer, who
counted them out to Sheshbazzar the prince
of Judah.

9This was the inventory:

gold dishes	30
silver dishes	1,000
silver pans[b]	29
10gold bowls	30
matching silver bowls	410
other articles	1,000

11In all, there were 5,400 articles of gold
and of silver. Sheshbazzar brought all these
along when the exiles came up from Babylon
to Jerusalem.

The List of the Exiles Who Returned

2 Now these are the people of the province who came up from the captivity of
the exiles, whom Nebuchadnezzar king of

[a]7 Or *gods* [b]9 The meaning of the Hebrew for this word is uncertain.

Babylon had taken captive to Babylon (they
returned to Jerusalem and Judah, each to
his own town, [2]in company with Zerubbabel,
Jeshua, Nehemiah, Seraiah, Reelaiah, Mordecai, Bilshan, Mispar, Bigvai, Rehum and Baanah):

The list of the men of the people of Israel:

[3]the descendants of Parosh 2,172
[4]of Shephatiah 372
[5]of Arah 775
[6]of Pahath-Moab (through the line of Jeshua and Joab) 2,812
[7]of Elam 1,254
[8]of Zattu 945
[9]of Zaccai 760
[10]of Bani 642
[11]of Bebai 623
[12]of Azgad 1,222
[13]of Adonikam 666
[14]of Bigvai 2,056
[15]of Adin 454
[16]of Ater (through Hezekiah) 98
[17]of Bezai 323
[18]of Jorah 112
[19]of Hashum 223
[20]of Gibbar 95

[21]the men of Bethlehem 123
[22]of Netophah 56
[23]of Anathoth 128
[24]of Azmaveth 42
[25]of Kiriath Jearim,[a] Kephirah and Beeroth 743
[26]of Ramah and Geba 621
[27]of Micmash 122
[28]of Bethel and Ai 223
[29]of Nebo 52
[30]of Magbish 156
[31]of the other Elam 1,254
[32]of Harim 320
[33]of Lod, Hadid and Ono 725
[34]of Jericho 345
[35]of Senaah 3,630

[36]The priests:

the descendants of Jedaiah (through the family of Jeshua) 973
[37]of Immer 1,052
[38]of Pashhur 1,247
[39]of Harim 1,017

[40]The Levites:

the descendants of Jeshua and Kadmiel (through the line of Hodaviah) 74

[41]The singers:

the descendants of Asaph 128

[42]The gatekeepers of the temple:

the descendants of Shallum, Ater, Talmon, Akkub, Hatita and Shobai 139

[43]The temple servants:

the descendants of
Ziha, Hasupha, Tabbaoth,
[44]Keros, Siaha, Padon,
[45]Lebanah, Hagabah, Akkub,
[46]Hagab, Shalmai, Hanan,
[47]Giddel, Gahar, Reaiah,
[48]Rezin, Nekoda, Gazzam,
[49]Uzza, Paseah, Besai,
[50]Asnah, Meunim, Nephussim,
[51]Bakbuk, Hakupha, Harhur,
[52]Bazluth, Mehida, Harsha,
[53]Barkos, Sisera, Temah,
[54]Neziah and Hatipha

[55]The descendants of the servants of Solomon:

the descendants of
Sotai, Hassophereth, Peruda,
[56]Jaala, Darkon, Giddel,
[57]Shephatiah, Hattil,
Pokereth-Hazzebaim and Ami

[58]The temple servants and the descendants of the servants of Solomon 392

[59]The following came up from the
towns of Tel Melah, Tel Harsha, Kerub,
Addon and Immer, but they could not
show that their families were descended
from Israel:

[60]The descendants of
Delaiah, Tobiah and Nekoda 652

[61]And from among the priests:

The descendants of
Hobaiah, Hakkoz and Barzillai (a man who had married a daughter of Barzillai the Gileadite and was called by that name).

[62]These searched for their family
records, but they could not find them
and so were excluded from the priesthood as unclean. [63]The governor ordered them not to eat any of the most

[a]25 See Septuagint (see also Neh. 7:29); Hebrew *Kiriath Arim.*

sacred food until there was a priest ministering with the Urim and Thummim.

64 The whole company numbered 42,360, 65 besides their 7,337 menservants and maidservants; and they also had 200 men and women singers. 66 They had 736 horses, 245 mules, 67 435 camels and 6,720 donkeys.

68 When they arrived at the house of the LORD in Jerusalem, some of the heads of the families gave freewill offerings toward the rebuilding of the house of God on its site. 69 According to their ability they gave to the treasury for this work 61,000 drachmas[a] of gold, 5,000 minas[b] of silver and 100 priestly garments.

70 The priests, the Levites, the singers, the gatekeepers and the temple servants settled in their own towns, along with some of the other people, and the rest of the Israelites settled in their towns.

Rebuilding the Altar

3 When the seventh month came and the Israelites had settled in their towns, the people assembled as one man in Jerusalem. 2 Then Jeshua son of Jozadak and his fellow priests and Zerubbabel son of Shealtiel and his associates began to build the altar of the God of Israel to sacrifice burnt offerings on it, in accordance with what is written in the Law of Moses the man of God. 3 Despite their fear of the peoples around them, they built the altar on its foundation and sacrificed burnt offerings on it to the LORD, both the morning and evening sacrifices. 4 Then in accordance with what is written, they celebrated the Feast of Tabernacles with the required number of burnt offerings prescribed for each day. 5 After that, they presented the regular burnt offerings, the New Moon sacrifices and the sacrifices for all the appointed sacred feasts of the LORD, as well as those brought as freewill offerings to the LORD. 6 On the first day of the seventh month they began to offer burnt offerings to the LORD, though the foundation of the LORD's temple had not yet been laid.

Rebuilding the Temple

7 Then they gave money to the masons and carpenters, and gave food and drink and oil to the people of Sidon and Tyre, so that they would bring cedar logs by sea from Lebanon to Joppa, as authorized by Cyrus king of Persia.

8 In the second month of the second year after their arrival at the house of God in Jerusalem, Zerubbabel son of Shealtiel, Jeshua son of Jozadak and the rest of their brothers (the priests and the Levites and all who had returned from the captivity to Jerusalem) began the work, appointing Levites twenty years of age and older to supervise the building of the house of the LORD. 9 Jeshua and his sons and brothers and Kadmiel and his sons (descendants of Hodaviah[c]) and the sons of Henadad and their sons and brothers—all Levites—joined together in supervising those working on the house of God.

10 When the builders laid the foundation of the temple of the LORD, the priests in their vestments and with trumpets, and the Levites (the sons of Asaph) with cymbals, took their places to praise the LORD, as prescribed by David king of Israel. 11 With praise and thanksgiving they sang to the LORD:

"He is good;
  his love to Israel endures forever."

And all the people gave a great shout of praise to the LORD, because the foundation of the house of the LORD was laid. 12 But many of the older priests and Levites and family heads, who had seen the former temple, wept aloud when they saw the foundation of this temple being laid, while many others shouted for joy. 13 No one could distinguish the sound of the shouts of joy from the sound of weeping, because the people made so much noise. And the sound was heard far away.

Opposition to the Rebuilding

4 When the enemies of Judah and Benjamin heard that the exiles were building a temple for the LORD, the God of Israel, 2 they came to Zerubbabel and to the heads of the families and said, "Let us help you build because, like you, we seek your God and have been sacrificing to him since the time of Esarhaddon king of Assyria, who brought us here."

3 But Zerubbabel, Jeshua and the rest of the heads of the families of Israel answered, "You have no part with us in building a tem-

[a] *69* That is, about 1,100 pounds (about 500 kilograms)
[b] *69* That is, about 3 tons (about 2.9 metric tons)
[c] *9* Hebrew *Yehudah,* probably a variant of *Hodaviah*

ple to our God. We alone will build it for the
LORD, the God of Israel, as King Cyrus, the
king of Persia, commanded us."
4Then the peoples around them set out to
discourage the people of Judah and make
them afraid to go on building.[a] 5They hired
counselors to work against them and frustrate their plans during the entire reign of
Cyrus king of Persia and down to the reign of
Darius king of Persia.

Later Opposition Under Xerxes and Artaxerxes

6At the beginning of the reign of Xerxes,[b]
they lodged an accusation against the
people of Judah and Jerusalem.
7And in the days of Artaxerxes king of
Persia, Bishlam, Mithredath, Tabeel and the
rest of his associates wrote a letter to Artaxerxes. The letter was written in Aramaic
script and in the Aramaic language.[c,d]
8Rehum the commanding officer and
Shimshai the secretary wrote a letter against
Jerusalem to Artaxerxes the king as follows:

9Rehum the commanding officer and
Shimshai the secretary, together with
the rest of their associates—the judges
and officials over the men from Tripolis,
Persia,[e] Erech and Babylon, the Elamites of Susa,
10and the other people
whom the great and honorable Ashurbanipal[f] deported and settled in the city
of Samaria and elsewhere in Trans-Euphrates.

11(This is a copy of the letter they sent
him.)

To King Artaxerxes,

From your servants, the men of Trans-Euphrates:

12The king should know that the Jews
who came up to us from you have gone
to Jerusalem and are rebuilding that rebellious and wicked city. They are restoring the walls and repairing the foundations.
13Furthermore, the king should know
that if this city is built and its walls are
restored, no more taxes, tribute or duty
will be paid, and the royal revenues will
suffer. 14Now since we are under obligation to the palace and it is not proper for
us to see the king dishonored, we are
sending this message to inform the king,
15so that a search may be made in the
archives of your predecessors. In these
records you will find that this city is a
rebellious city, troublesome to kings and
provinces, a place of rebellion from ancient times. That is why this city was
destroyed. 16We inform the king that if
this city is built and its walls are restored, you will be left with nothing in
Trans-Euphrates.

17The king sent this reply:

To Rehum the commanding officer,
Shimshai the secretary and the rest of
their associates living in Samaria and
elsewhere in Trans-Euphrates:

Greetings.

18The letter you sent us has been read
and translated in my presence. 19I issued an order and a search was made,
and it was found that this city has a long
history of revolt against kings and has
been a place of rebellion and sedition.
20Jerusalem has had powerful kings ruling over the whole of Trans-Euphrates,
and taxes, tribute and duty were paid to
them. 21Now issue an order to these
men to stop work, so that this city will not
be rebuilt until I so order. 22Be careful
not to neglect this matter. Why let this
threat grow, to the detriment of the royal
interests?

23As soon as the copy of the letter of King
Artaxerxes was read to Rehum and Shimshai the secretary and their associates, they
went immediately to the Jews in Jerusalem
and compelled them by force to stop.

24Thus the work on the house of God in
Jerusalem came to a standstill until the second year of the reign of Darius king of Persia.

Tattenai's Letter to Darius

5 Now Haggai the prophet and Zechariah
the prophet, a descendant of Iddo,
prophesied to the Jews in Judah and Jerusalem in the name of the God of Israel, who
was over them. 2Then Zerubbabel son of
Shealtiel and Jeshua son of Jozadak set to

[a]4 Or *and troubled them as they built* [b]6 Hebrew *Ahasuerus,* a variant of Xerxes' Persian name [c]7 Or *written in Aramaic and translated* [d]7 The text of Ezra 4:8—6:18 is in Aramaic. [e]9 Or *officials, magistrates and governors over the men from* [f]10 Aramaic *Osnappar, a variant of Ashurbanipal*

work to rebuild the house of God in Jerusalem. And the prophets of God were with them, helping them.

3At that time Tattenai, governor of Trans-Euphrates, and Shethar-Bozenai and their associates went to them and asked, "Who authorized you to rebuild this temple and restore this structure?" 4They also asked, "What are the names of the men constructing this building?"[a] 5But the eye of their God was watching over the elders of the Jews, and they were not stopped until a report could go to Darius and his written reply be received.

6This is a copy of the letter that Tattenai, governor of Trans-Euphrates, and Shethar-Bozenai and their associates, the officials of Trans-Euphrates, sent to King Darius. 7The report they sent him read as follows:

To King Darius:

Cordial greetings.

8The king should know that we went to the district of Judah, to the temple of the great God. The people are building it with large stones and placing the timbers in the walls. The work is being carried on with diligence and is making rapid progress under their direction.

9We questioned the elders and asked them, "Who authorized you to rebuild this temple and restore this structure?" 10We also asked them their names, so that we could write down the names of their leaders for your information.

11This is the answer they gave us:

"We are the servants of the God of heaven and earth, and we are rebuilding the temple that was built many years ago, one that a great king of Israel built and finished. 12But because our fathers angered the God of heaven, he handed them over to Nebuchadnezzar the Chaldean, king of Babylon, who destroyed this temple and deported the people to Babylon.

13"However, in the first year of Cyrus king of Babylon, King Cyrus issued a decree to rebuild this house of God. 14He even removed from the temple[b] of Babylon the gold and silver articles of the house of God, which Nebuchadnezzar had taken from the temple in Jerusalem and brought to the temple[b] in Babylon.

"Then King Cyrus gave them to a man named Sheshbazzar, whom he had appointed governor, 15and he told him, 'Take these articles and go and deposit them in the temple in Jerusalem. And rebuild the house of God on its site.' 16So this Sheshbazzar came and laid the foundations of the house of God in Jerusalem. From that day to the present it has been under construction but is not yet finished."

17Now if it pleases the king, let a search be made in the royal archives of Babylon to see if King Cyrus did in fact issue a decree to rebuild this house of God in Jerusalem. Then let the king send us his decision in this matter.

The Decree of Darius

6 King Darius then issued an order, and they searched in the archives stored in the treasury at Babylon. 2A scroll was found in the citadel of Ecbatana in the province of Media, and this was written on it:

Memorandum:

3In the first year of King Cyrus, the king issued a decree concerning the temple of God in Jerusalem:

Let the temple be rebuilt as a place to present sacrifices, and let its foundations be laid. It is to be ninety feet[c] high and ninety feet wide, 4with three courses of large stones and one of timbers. The costs are to be paid by the royal treasury. 5Also, the gold and silver articles of the house of God, which Nebuchadnezzar took from the temple in Jerusalem and brought to Babylon, are to be returned to their places in the temple in Jerusalem; they are to be deposited in the house of God.

6Now then, Tattenai, governor of Trans-Euphrates, and Shethar-Bozenai and you, their fellow officials of that province, stay away from there. 7Do not interfere with the work on this temple of God. Let the governor of the Jews and the Jewish elders rebuild this house of God on its site.

a4 See Septuagint; Aramaic *4We told them the names of the men constructing this building.* b14 Or *palace*
c3 Aramaic *sixty cubits* (about 27 meters)

8Moreover, I hereby decree what you
are to do for these elders of the Jews
in the construction of this house of
God:

The expenses of these men are to be
fully paid out of the royal treasury, from
the revenues of Trans-Euphrates, so
that the work will not stop. 9Whatever is
needed—young bulls, rams, male
lambs for burnt offerings to the God of
heaven, and wheat, salt, wine and oil,
as requested by the priests in Jerusalem—must be given them daily without
fail, 10so that they may offer sacrifices
pleasing to the God of heaven and pray
for the well-being of the king and his
sons.

11Furthermore, I decree that if anyone
changes this edict, a beam is to be
pulled from his house and he is to be
lifted up and impaled on it. And for this
crime his house is to be made a pile of
rubble. 12May God, who has caused his
Name to dwell there, overthrow any king
or people who lifts a hand to change this
decree or to destroy this temple in
Jerusalem.

I Darius have decreed it. Let it be carried out with diligence.

Completion and Dedication of the Temple

13Then, because of the decree King Darius
had sent, Tattenai, governor of Trans-Euphrates, and Shethear-Bozenai and their
associates carried it out with diligence. 14So
the elders of the Jews continued to build and
prosper under the preaching of Haggai the
prophet and Zechariah, a descendant of
Iddo. They finished building the temple according to the command of the God of Israel
and the decrees of Cyrus, Darius and Artaxerxes, kings of Persia. 15The temple was
completed on the third day of the month
Adar, in the sixth year of the reign of King
Darius.

16Then the people of Israel—the priests,
the Levites and the rest of the exiles—celebrated the dedication of the house of God
with joy. 17For the dedication of this house of
God they offered a hundred bulls, two hundred rams, four hundred male lambs and, as
a sin offering for all Israel, twelve male goats,
one for each of the tribes of Israel. 18And they
installed the priests in their divisions and the
Levites in their groups for the service of God
at Jerusalem, according to what is written in
the Book of Moses.

The Passover

19On the fourteenth day of the first month,
the exiles celebrated the Passover. 20The
priests and Levites had purified themselves
and were all ceremonially clean. The Levites
slaughtered the Passover lamb for all the
exiles, for their brothers the priests and for
themselves. 21So the Israelites who had returned from the exile ate it, together with all
who had separated themselves from the unclean practices of their Gentile neighbors in
order to seek the LORD, the God of Israel.
22For seven days they celebrated with joy the
Feast of Unleavened Bread, because the
LORD had filled them with joy by changing the
attitude of the king of Assyria, so that he
assisted them in the work on the house of
God, the God of Israel.

Ezra Comes to Jerusalem

7 After these things, during the reign of
Artaxerxes king of Persia, Ezra son of
Seraiah, the son of Azariah, the son of Hilkiah, 2the son of Shallum, the son of Zadok,
the son of Ahitub, 3the son of Amariah, the
son of Azariah, the son of Meraioth, 4the son
of Zerahiah, the son of Uzzi, the son of Bukki,
5the son of Abishua, the son of Phinehas, the
son of Eleazar, the son of Aaron the chief
priest— 6this Ezra came up from Babylon.
He was a teacher well versed in the Law of
Moses, which the LORD, the God of Israel,
had given. The king had granted him everything he asked, for the hand of the LORD his
God was on him. 7Some of the Israelites,
including priests, Levites, singers, gatekeepers and temple servants, also came up
to Jerusalem in the seventh year of King
Artaxerxes.

8Ezra arrived in Jerusalem in the fifth
month of the seventh year of the king. 9He
had begun his journey from Babylon on the
first day of the first month, and he arrived in
Jerusalem on the first day of the fifth month,
for the gracious hand of his God was on him.
10For Ezra had devoted himself to the study
and observance of the Law of the LORD, and
to teaching its decrees and laws in Israel.

King Artaxerxes' Letter to Ezra

11This is a copy of the letter King Artaxerxes had given to Ezra the priest and teacher, a

man learned in matters concerning the commands and decrees of the LORD for Israel:

12[a] Artaxerxes, king of kings,

To Ezra the priest, a teacher of the Law
of the God of heaven:

Greetings.

13 Now I decree that any of the Israelites in my kingdom, including priests
and Levites, who wish to go to Jerusalem with you, may go. 14 You are sent by
the king and his seven advisers to inquire about Judah and Jerusalem with
regard to the Law of your God, which is
in your hand. 15 Moreover, you are to
take with you the silver and gold that the
king and his advisers have freely given
to the God of Israel, whose dwelling is in
Jerusalem, 16 together with all the silver
and gold you may obtain from the province of Babylon, as well as the freewill
offerings of the people and priests for
the temple of their God in Jerusalem.
17 With this money be sure to buy bulls,
rams and male lambs, together with
their grain offerings and drink offerings,
and sacrifice them on the altar of the
temple of your God in Jerusalem.

18 You and your brother Jews may
then do whatever seems best with the
rest of the silver and gold, in accordance
with the will of your God. 19 Deliver to the
God of Jerusalem all the articles entrusted to you for worship in the temple
of your God. 20 And anything else
needed for the temple of your God that
you may have occasion to supply, you
may provide from the royal treasury.

21 Now I, King Artaxerxes, order all the
treasurers of Trans-Euphrates to provide with diligence whatever Ezra the
priest, a teacher of the Law of the God of
heaven, may ask of you— 22 up to a hundred talents[b] of silver, a hundred cors[c]
of wheat, a hundred baths[d] of wine, a
hundred baths[d] of olive oil, and salt
without limit. 23 Whatever the God of
heaven has prescribed, let it be done
with diligence for the temple of the God
of heaven. Why should there be wrath
against the realm of the king and of his
sons? 24 You are also to know that you
have no authority to impose taxes, tribute or duty on any of the priests, Levites,
singers, gatekeepers, temple servants
or other workers at this house of God.

25 And you, Ezra, in accordance with
the wisdom of your God, which you possess, appoint magistrates and judges to
administer justice to all the people of
Trans-Euphrates—all who know the
laws of your God. And you are to teach
any who do not know them. 26 Whoever
does not obey the law of your God and
the law of the king must surely be punished by death, banishment, confiscation of property, or imprisonment.

27 Praise be to the LORD, the God of our
fathers, who has put it into the king's heart to
bring honor to the house of the LORD in
Jerusalem in this way 28 and who has extended his good favor to me before the king
and his advisers and all the king's powerful
officials. Because the hand of the LORD my
God was on me, I took courage and gathered
leading men from Israel to go up with me.

List of the Family Heads Returning With Ezra

8 These are the family heads and those
registered with them who came up with
me from Babylon during the reign of King
Artaxerxes:

2 of the descendants of Phinehas, Gershom;
of the descendants of Ithamar, Daniel;
of the descendants of David, Hattush
3 of the descendants of Shecaniah;
of the descendants of Parosh, Zechariah, and with him were registered
150 men;
4 of the descendants of Pahath-Moab,
Eliehoenai son of Zerahiah, and with
him 200 men;
5 of the descendants of Zattu,[e] Shecaniah son of Jahaziel, and with him
300 men;
6 of the descendants of Adin, Ebed son
of Jonathan, and with him 50 men;
7 of the descendants of Elam, Jeshaiah
son of Athaliah, and with him 70
men;
8 of the descendants of Shephatiah,
Zebadiah son of Michael, and with
him 80 men;

[a] *12* The text of Ezra 7:12-26 is in Aramaic. [b] *22* That is, about 3 3/4 tons (about 3.4 metric tons) [c] *22* That is, probably about 600 bushels (about 22 kiloliters) [d] *22* That is, probably about 600 gallons (about 2.2 kiloliters) [e] *5* Some Septuagint manuscripts (also 1 Esdras 8:32); Hebrew does not have *Zattu.*

9of the descendants of Joab, Obadiah
son of Jehiel, and with him 218 men;
10of the descendants of Bani,[a] Shelomith
son of Josiphiah, and with him 160
men;
11of the descendants of Bebai, Zechariah
son of Bebai, and with him 28 men;
12of the descendants of Azgad, Johanan
son of Hakkatan, and with him 110
men;
13of the descendants of Adonikam, the
last ones, whose names were
Eliphelet, Jeuel and Shemaiah, and
with them 60 men;
14of the descendants of Bigvai, Uthai and
Zaccur, and with them 70 men.

The Return to Jerusalem

15I assembled them at the canal that flows
toward Ahava, and we camped there three
days. When I checked among the people
and the priests, I found no Levites there. 16So
I summoned Eliezer, Ariel, Shemaiah, Elnathan, Jarib, Elnathan, Nathan, Zechariah
and Meshullam, who were leaders, and Joiarib and Elnathan, who were men of learning,
17and I sent them to Iddo, the leader in Casiphia. I told them what to say to Iddo and his
kinsmen, the temple servants in Casiphia, so
that they might bring attendants to us for the
house of our God. 18Because the gracious
hand of our God was on us, they brought us
Sherebiah, a capable man, from the descendants of Mahli son of Levi, the son of
Israel, and Sherebiah's sons and brothers,
18 men; 19and Hashabiah, together with Jeshaiah from the descendants of Merari, and
his brothers and nephews, 20 men. 20They
also brought 220 of the temple servants—a
body that David and the officials had established to assist the Levites. All were registered by name.

21There, by the Ahava Canal, I proclaimed
a fast, so that we might humble ourselves
before our God and ask him for a safe journey for us and our children, with all our
possessions. 22I was ashamed to ask the
king for soldiers and horsemen to protect us
from enemies on the road, because we had
told the king, "The gracious hand of our God
is on everyone who looks to him, but his
great anger is against all who forsake him."
23So we fasted and petitioned our God about
this, and he answered our prayer.

24Then I set apart twelve of the leading
priests, together with Sherebiah, Hashabiah
and ten of their brothers, 25and I weighed out
to them the offering of silver and gold and the
articles that the king, his advisers, his officials and all Israel present there had donated
for the house of our God. 26I weighed out to
them 650 talents[b] of silver, silver articles
weighing 100 talents,[c] 100 talents[c] of gold,
2720 bowls of gold valued at 1,000 darics,[d]
and two fine articles of polished bronze, as
precious as gold.

28I said to them, "You as well as these
articles are consecrated to the LORD. The silver and gold are a freewill offering to the
LORD, the God of your fathers. 29Guard them
carefully until you weigh them out in the
chambers of the house of the LORD in Jerusalem before the leading priests and the Levites and the family heads of Israel." 30Then
the priests and Levites received the silver
and gold and sacred articles that had been
weighed out to be taken to the house of our
God in Jerusalem.

31On the twelfth day of the first month we
set out from the Ahava Canal to go to Jerusalem. The hand of our God was on us, and he
protected us from enemies and bandits
along the way. 32So we arrived in Jerusalem,
where we rested three days.

33On the fourth day, in the house of our
God, we weighed out the silver and gold and
the sacred articles into the hands of Meremoth son of Uriah, the priest. Eleazar son of
Phinehas was with him, and so were the
Levites Jozabad son of Jeshua and Noadiah
son of Binnui. 34Everything was accounted
for by number and weight, and the entire
weight was recorded at that time.

35Then the exiles who had returned from
captivity sacrificed burnt offerings to the God
of Israel: twelve bulls for all Israel, ninety-six
rams, seventy-seven male lambs and, as a
sin offering, twelve male goats. All this was a
burnt offering to the LORD. 36They also delivered the king's orders to the royal satraps
and to the governors of Trans-Euphrates,
who then gave assistance to the people and
to the house of God.

Ezra's Prayer About Intermarriage

9 After these things had been done, the
leaders came to me and said, "The
people of Israel, including the priests and the

[a]*10* Some Septuagint manuscripts (also 1 Esdras 8:36); Hebrew does not have *Bani.* [b]*26* That is, about 25 tons (about 22 metric tons) [c]*26* That is, about 3 3/4 tons (about 3.4 metric tons) [d]*27* That is, about 19 pounds (about 8.5 kilograms)

Levites, have not kept themselves separate
from the neighboring peoples with their detestable practices, like those of the Canaanites, Hittites, Perizzites, Jebusites, Ammonites, Moabites, Egyptians and Amorites.
2They have taken some of their daughters as
wives for themselves and their sons, and
have mingled the holy race with the peoples
around them. And the leaders and officials
have led the way in this unfaithfulness."

3When I heard this, I tore my tunic and
cloak, pulled hair from my head and beard
and sat down appalled. 4Then everyone who
trembled at the words of the God of Israel
gathered around me because of this unfaithfulness of the exiles. And I sat there appalled
until the evening sacrifice.

5Then, at the evening sacrifice, I rose from
my self-abasement, with my tunic and cloak
torn, and fell on my knees with my hands
spread out to the LORD my God 6and prayed:

"O my God, I am too ashamed and
disgraced to lift up my face to you, my
God, because our sins are higher than
our heads and our guilt has reached to
the heavens. 7From the days of our forefathers until now, our guilt has been
great. Because of our sins, we and our
kings and our priests have been subjected to the sword and captivity, to pillage and humiliation at the hand of foreign kings, as it is today.

8"But now, for a brief moment, the
LORD our God has been gracious in leaving us a remnant and giving us a firm
place in his sanctuary, and so our God
gives light to our eyes and a little relief in
our bondage. 9Though we are slaves,
our God has not deserted us in our
bondage. He has shown us kindness in
the sight of the kings of Persia: He has
granted us new life to rebuild the house
of our God and repair its ruins, and he
has given us a wall of protection in
Judah and Jerusalem.

10"But now, O our God, what can we
say after this? For we have disregarded
the commands 11you gave through your
servants the prophets when you said:
'The land you are entering to possess is
a land polluted by the corruption of its
peoples. By their detestable practices
they have filled it with their impurity from
one end to the other. 12Therefore, do not
give your daughters in marriage to their
sons or take their daughters for your
sons. Do not seek a treaty of friendship
with them at any time, that you may be
strong and eat the good things of the
land and leave it to your children as an
everlasting inheritance.'

13"What has happened to us is a result of our evil deeds and our great guilt,
and yet, our God, you have punished us
less than our sins have deserved and
have given us a remnant like this.
14Shall we again break your commands
and intermarry with the peoples who
commit such detestable practices?
Would you not be angry enough with us
to destroy us, leaving us no remnant or
survivor? 15O LORD, God of Israel, you
are righteous! We are left this day as a
remnant. Here we are before you in our
guilt, though because of it not one of us
can stand in your presence."

The People's Confession of Sin

10 While Ezra was praying and confessing, weeping and throwing himself
down before the house of God, a large crowd
of Israelites—men, women and children—
gathered around him. They too wept bitterly.
2Then Shecaniah son of Jehiel, one of the
descendants of Elam, said to Ezra, "We
have been unfaithful to our God by marrying
foreign women from the peoples around us.
But in spite of this, there is still hope for
Israel. 3Now let us make a covenant before
our God to send away all these women and
their children, in accordance with the counsel of my lord and of those who fear the
commands of our God. Let it be done according to the Law. 4Rise up; this matter is in
your hands. We will support you, so take
courage and do it."

5So Ezra rose up and put the leading
priests and Levites and all Israel under oath
to do what had been suggested. And they
took the oath. 6Then Ezra withdrew from before the house of God and went to the room
of Jehohanan son of Eliashib. While he was
there, he ate no food and drank no water,
because he continued to mourn over the unfaithfulness of the exiles.

7A proclamation was then issued throughout Judah and Jerusalem for all the exiles to
assemble in Jerusalem. 8Anyone who failed
to appear within three days would forfeit all
his property, in accordance with the decision
of the officials and elders, and would himself
be expelled from the assembly of the exiles.

[9]Within the three days, all the men of
Judah and Benjamin had gathered in
Jerusalem. And on the twentieth day of the
ninth month, all the people were sitting in the
square before the house of God, greatly distressed by the occasion and because of the
rain. [10]Then Ezra the priest stood up and
said to them, "You have been unfaithful; you
have married foreign women, adding to Israel's guilt. [11]Now make confession to the
LORD, the God of your fathers, and do his will.
Separate yourselves from the peoples
around you and from your foreign wives."

[12]The whole assembly responded with a
loud voice: "You are right! We must do as
you say. [13]But there are many people here
and it is the rainy season; so we cannot
stand outside. Besides, this matter cannot
be taken care of in a day or two, because we
have sinned greatly in this thing. [14]Let our
officials act for the whole assembly. Then let
everyone in our towns who has married a
foreign woman come at a set time, along with
the elders and judges of each town, until the
fierce anger of our God in this matter is
turned away from us." [15]Only Jonathan son
of Asahel and Jahzeiah son of Tikvah, supported by Meshullam and Shabbethai the
Levite, opposed this.

[16]So the exiles did as was proposed. Ezra
the priest selected men who were family
heads, one from each family division, and all
of them designated by name. On the first day
of the tenth month they sat down to investigate the cases, [17]and by the first day of the
first month they finished dealing with all the
men who had married foreign women.

Those Guilty of Intermarriage

[18]Among the descendants of the priests, the following had married foreign women:

From the descendants of Jeshua son of Jozadak, and his brothers: Maaseiah, Eliezer, Jarib and Gedaliah.
[19](They all gave their hands in pledge to put away their wives, and for their guilt they each presented a ram from the flock as a guilt offering.)

[20]From the descendants of Immer:
Hanani and Zebadiah.

[21]From the descendants of Harim:
Maaseiah, Elijah, Shemaiah, Jehiel and Uzziah.

[22]From the descendants of Pashhur:
Elioenai, Maaseiah, Ishmael, Nethanel, Jozabad and Elasah.

[23]Among the Levites:

Jozabad, Shimei, Kelaiah (that is Kelita), Pethahiah, Judah and Eliezer.

[24]From the singers:
Eliashib.

From the gatekeepers:
Shallum, Telem and Uri.

[25]And among the other Israelites:

From the descendants of Parosh:
Ramiah, Izziah, Malkijah, Mijamin, Eleazar, Malkijah and Benaiah.

[26]From the descendants of Elam:
Mattaniah, Zechariah, Jehiel, Abdi, Jeremoth and Elijah.

[27]From the descendants of Zattu:
Elioenai, Eliashib, Mattaniah, Jeremoth, Zabad and Aziza.

[28]From the descendants of Bebai:
Jehohanan, Hananiah, Zabbai and Athlai.

[29]From the descendants of Bani:
Meshullam, Malluch, Adaiah, Jashub, Sheal and Jeremoth.

[30]From the descendants of Pahath-Moab:
Adna, Kelal, Benaiah, Maaseiah, Mattaniah, Bezalel, Binnui and Manasseh.

[31]From the descendants of Harim:
Eliezer, Ishijah, Malkijah, Shemaiah,
Shimeon, [32]Benjamin, Malluch and
Shemariah.

[33]From the descendants of Hashum:
Mattenai, Mattattah, Zabad, Eliphelet, Jeremai, Manasseh and Shimei.

[34]From the descendants of Bani:
Maadai, Amram, Uel, [35]Benaiah, Be-
deiah, Keluhi, [36]Vaniah, Meremoth,
Eliashib, [37]Mattaniah, Mattenai and
Jaasu.

[38]From the descendants of Binnui:[a]
Shimei, [39]Shelemiah, Nathan,
Adaiah, [40]Macnadebai, Shashai,
Sharai, [41]Azarel, Shelemiah,
Shemariah, [42]Shallum, Amariah and
Joseph.

[a]*37,38* See Septuagint (also 1 Esdras 9:34); Hebrew *Jaasu* [38]*and Bani and Binnui,*

43From the descendants of Nebo:
Jeiel, Mattithiah, Zabad, Zebina,
Jaddai, Joel and Benaiah.

44All these had married foreign women,
and some of them had children by these
wives.[a]

[a]44 Or *and they sent them away with their children*

Nehemiah

Introduction:

Nehemiah continues the history of the Jews who returned from exile in Babylon. Nehemiah gave up his job as cupbearer to Artaxerxes, the Persian king, to become governor of Jerusalem. Nehemiah went to Jerusalem in 444 B.C., almost 100 years after the return of the first exiles. Nehemiah led the people in repairing the walls of Jerusalem and with Ezra provided leadership for the people. An important part of this book is the description of the importance of prayer to Nehemiah.

Outline of contents:

Nehemiah rebuilds the walls (1:1–7:3)
Change under Ezra (7:4–10:39)
Nehemiah's plans (11:1–13:31)

Nehemiah's Prayer

1 The words of Nehemiah son of Hacaliah:

In the month of Kislev in the twentieth
year, while I was in the citadel of Susa,
2Hanani, one of my brothers, came from
Judah with some other men, and I questioned them about the Jewish remnant that
survived the exile, and also about Jerusalem.
3They said to me, "Those who survived the
exile and are back in the province are in
great trouble and disgrace. The wall of
Jerusalem is broken down, and its gates
have been burned with fire."
4When I heard these things, I sat down and
wept. For some days I mourned and fasted
and prayed before the God of heaven. 5Then
I said:

"O LORD, God of heaven, the great
and awesome God, who keeps his covenant of love with those who love him
and obey his commands, 6let your ear
be attentive and your eyes open to hear
the prayer your servant is praying before you day and night for your servants,
the people of Israel. I confess the sins
we Israelites, including myself and my
father's house, have committed against
you. 7We have acted very wickedly
toward you. We have not obeyed the
commands, decrees and laws you gave
your servant Moses.

8"Remember the instruction you gave
your servant Moses, saying, 'If you are
unfaithful, I will scatter you among the
nations, 9but if you return to me and
obey my commands, then even if your
exiled people are at the farthest horizon,
I will gather them from there and bring
them to the place I have chosen as a
dwelling for my Name.'
10"They are your servants and your
people, whom you redeemed by your
great strength and your mighty hand.
11O Lord, let your ear be attentive to the
prayer of this your servant and to the
prayer of your servants who delight in
revering your name. Give your servant
success today by granting him favor in
the presence of this man."

I was cupbearer to the king.

Artaxerxes Sends Nehemiah to Jerusalem

2 In the month of Nisan in the twentieth
year of King Artaxerxes, when wine was
brought for him, I took the wine and gave it to
the king. I had not been sad in his presence
before; 2so the king asked me, "Why does
your face look so sad when you are not ill?
This can be nothing but sadness of heart."
I was very much afraid, 3but I said to the
king, "May the king live forever! Why should
my face not look sad when the city where my

fathers are buried lies in ruins, and its gates have been destroyed by fire?"

4The king said to me, "What is it you want?"

Then I prayed to the God of heaven, 5and I answered the king, "If it pleases the king and if your servant has found favor in his sight, let him send me to the city in Judah where my fathers are buried so that I can rebuild it."

6Then the king, with the queen sitting beside him, asked me, "How long will your journey take, and when will you get back?" It pleased the king to send me; so I set a time.

7I also said to him, "If it pleases the king, may I have letters to the governors of Trans-Euphrates, so that they will provide me safe-conduct until I arrive in Judah? 8And may I have a letter to Asaph, keeper of the king's forest, so he will give me timber to make beams for the gates of the citadel by the temple and for the city wall and for the residence I will occupy?" And because the gracious hand of my God was upon me, the king granted my requests. 9So I went to the governors of Trans-Euphrates and gave them the king's letters. The king had also sent army officers and cavalry with me.

10When Sanballat the Horonite and Tobiah the Ammonite official heard about this, they were very much disturbed that someone had come to promote the welfare of the Israelites.

Nehemiah Inspects Jerusalem's Walls

11I went to Jerusalem, and after staying there three days 12I set out during the night with a few men. I had not told anyone what my God had put in my heart to do for Jerusalem. There were no mounts with me except the one I was riding on.

13By night I went out through the Valley Gate toward the Jackal[a] Well and the Dung Gate, examining the walls of Jerusalem, which had been broken down, and its gates, which had been destroyed by fire. 14Then I moved on toward the Fountain Gate and the King's Pool, but there was not enough room for my mount to get through; 15so I went up the valley by night, examining the wall. Finally, I turned back and reentered through the Valley Gate. 16The officials did not know where I had gone or what I was doing, because as yet I had said nothing to the Jews or the priests or nobles or officials or any others who would be doing the work.

17Then I said to them, "You see the trouble we are in: Jerusalem lies in ruins, and its gates have been burned with fire. Come, let us rebuild the wall of Jerusalem, and we will no longer be in disgrace." 18I also told them about the gracious hand of my God upon me and what the king had said to me.

They replied, "Let us start rebuilding." So they began this good work.

19But when Sanballat the Horonite, Tobiah the Ammonite official and Geshem the Arab heard about it, they mocked and ridiculed us. "What is this you are doing?" they asked. "Are you rebelling against the king?"

20I answered them by saying, "The God of heaven will give us success. We his servants will start rebuilding, but as for you, you have no share in Jerusalem or any claim or historic right to it."

Builders of the Wall

3 Eliashib the high priest and his fellow priests went to work and rebuilt the Sheep Gate. They dedicated it and set its doors in place, building as far as the Tower of the Hundred, which they dedicated, and as far as the Tower of Hananel. 2The men of Jericho built the adjoining section, and Zaccur son of Imri built next to them.

3The Fish Gate was rebuilt by the sons of Hassenaah. They laid its beams and put its doors and bolts and bars in place. 4Meremoth son of Uriah, the son of Hakkoz, repaired the next section. Next to him Meshullam son of Berekiah, the son of Meshezabel, made repairs, and next to him Zadok son of Baana also made repairs. 5The next section was repaired by the men of Tekoa, but their nobles would not put their shoulders to the work under their supervisors.[b]

6The Jeshanah[c] Gate was repaired by Joiada son of Paseah and Meshullam son of Besodeiah. They laid its beams and put its doors and bolts and bars in place. 7Next to them, repairs were made by men from Gibeon and Mizpah—Melatiah of Gibeon and Jadon of Meronoth—places under the authority of the governor of Trans-Euphrates. 8Uzziel son of Harhaiah, one of the goldsmiths, repaired the next section; and Hananiah, one of the perfume-makers, made repairs next to

[a]13 Or *Serpent* or *Fig* [b]5 Or *their Lord* or *the governor* [c]6 Or *Old*

that. They restored[a] Jerusalem as far as the
Broad Wall. [9]Rephaiah son of Hur, ruler of a
half-district of Jerusalem, repaired the next
section. [10]Adjoining this, Jedaiah son of
Harumaph made repairs opposite his house,
and Hattush son of Hashabneiah made repairs next to him. [11]Malkijah son of Harim
and Hasshub son of Pahath-Moab repaired
another section and the Tower of the Ovens.
[12]Shallum son of Hallohesh, ruler of a half-
district of Jerusalem, repaired the next section with the help of his daughters.

[13]The Valley Gate was repaired by Hanun
and the residents of Zanoah. They rebuilt it
and put its doors and bolts and bars in place.
They also repaired five hundred yards[b] of
the wall as far as the Dung Gate.

[14]The Dung Gate was repaired by Malkijah
son of Recab, ruler of the district of Beth
Hakkerem. He rebuilt it and put its doors and
bolts and bars in place.

[15]The Fountain Gate was repaired by
Shallun son of Col-Hozeh, ruler of the district
of Mizpah. He rebuilt it, roofing it over and
putting its doors and bolts and bars in place.
He also repaired the wall of the Pool of Siloam,[c] by the King's Garden, as far as the
steps going down from the City of David.
[16]Beyond him, Nehemiah son of Azbuk, ruler
of a half-district of Beth Zur, made repairs up
to a point opposite the tombs[d] of David, as
far as the artificial pool and the House of the
Heroes.
[17]Next to him, the repairs were made by
the Levites under Rehum son of Bani. Beside him, Hashabiah, ruler of half the district
of Keilah, carried out repairs for his district.
[18]Next to him, the repairs were made by their
countrymen under Binnui[e] son of Henadad,
ruler of the other half-district of Keilah. [19]Next
to him, Ezer son of Jeshua, ruler of Mizpah,
repaired another section, from a point facing
the ascent to the armory as far as the angle.
[20]Next to him, Baruch son of Zabbai zealous-
ly repaired another section, from the angle to
the entrance of the house of Eliashib the high
priest. [21]Next to him, Meremoth son of Uriah,
the son of Hakkoz, repaired another section,
from the entrance of Eliashib's house to the
end of it.
[22]The repairs next to him were made by
the priests from the surrounding region.
[23]Beyond them, Benjamin and Hasshub
made repairs in front of their house; and next
to them, Azariah son of Maaseiah, the son of
Ananiah, made repairs beside his house.
[24]Next to him, Binnui son of Henadad repaired another section, from Azariah's
house to the angle and the corner, [25]and
Palal son of Uzai worked opposite the angle
and the tower projecting from the upper palace near the court of the guard. Next to him,
Pedaiah son of Parosh [26]and the temple servants living on the hill of Ophel made repairs
up to a point opposite the Water Gate toward
the east and the projecting tower. [27]Next to
them, the men of Tekoa repaired another
section, from the great projecting tower to
the wall of Ophel.

[28]Above the Horse Gate, the priests made
repairs, each in front of his own house.
[29]Next to them, Zadok son of Immer made
repairs opposite his house. Next to him,
Shemaiah son of Shecaniah, the guard at
the East Gate, made repairs. [30]Next to him,
Hananiah son of Shelemiah, and Hanun, the
sixth son of Zalaph, repaired another section. Next to them, Meshullam son of Berekiah made repairs opposite his living quarters. [31]Next to him, Malkijah, one of the goldsmiths, made repairs as far as the house of
the temple servants and the merchants, opposite the Inspection Gate, and as far as the
room above the corner; [32]and between the
room above the corner and the Sheep Gate
the goldsmiths and merchants made repairs.

Opposition to the Rebuilding

4 When Sanballat heard that we were rebuilding the wall, he became angry and
was greatly incensed. He ridiculed the Jews,
[2]and in the presence of his associates and
the army of Samaria, he said, "What are
those feeble Jews doing? Will they restore
their wall? Will they offer sacrifices? Will they
finish in a day? Can they bring the stones
back to life from those heaps of rubble—
burned as they are?"

[3]Tobiah the Ammonite, who was at his
side, said, "What they are building—if even a
fox climbed up on it, he would break down
their wall of stones!"

[4]Hear us, O our God, for we are despised.
Turn their insults back on their own heads.

[a]8 Or *They left out part of* [b]13 Hebrew *a thousand cubits* (about 450 meters) [c]15 Hebrew *Shelah,* a variant of *Shiloah,* that is, Siloam [d]16 Hebrew; Septuagint, some Vulgate manuscripts and Syriac *tomb*
[e]18 Two Hebrew manuscripts and Syriac (see also Septuagint and verse 24); most Hebrew manuscripts *Bavvai*

Give them over as plunder in a land of captivity. 5Do not cover up their guilt or blot out
their sins from your sight, for they have
thrown insults in the face of[a] the builders.

6So we rebuilt the wall till all of it reached
half its height, for the people worked with all
their heart.
7But when Sanballat, Tobiah, the Arabs,
the Ammonites and the men of Ashdod
heard that the repairs to Jerusalem's walls
had gone ahead and that the gaps were being closed, they were very angry. 8They all
plotted together to come and fight against
Jerusalem and stir up trouble against it. 9But
we prayed to our God and posted a guard
day and night to meet this threat.
10Meanwhile, the people in Judah said,
"The strength of the laborers is giving out,
and there is so much rubble that we cannot
rebuild the wall."
11Also our enemies said, "Before they
know it or see us, we will be right there
among them and will kill them and put an end
to the work."
12Then the Jews who lived near them
came and told us ten times over, "Wherever
you turn, they will attack us."
13Therefore I stationed some of the people
behind the lowest points of the wall at the
exposed places, posting them by families,
with their swords, spears and bows. 14After I
looked things over, I stood up and said to the
nobles, the officials and the rest of the
people, "Don't be afraid of them. Remember
the Lord, who is great and awesome, and
fight for your brothers, your sons and your
daughters, your wives and your homes."
15When our enemies heard that we were
aware of their plot and that God had frustrated it, we all returned to the wall, each to
his own work.
16From that day on, half of my men did the
work, while the other half were equipped with
spears, shields, bows and armor. The officers posted themselves behind all the
people of Judah 17who were building the
wall. Those who carried materials did their
work with one hand and held a weapon in the
other, 18and each of the builders wore his
sword at his side as he worked. But the man
who sounded the trumpet stayed with me.
19Then I said to the nobles, the officials
and the rest of the people, "The work is extensive and spread out, and we are widely
separated from each other along the wall.
20Wherever you hear the sound of the trumpet, join us there. Our God will fight for us!"
21So we continued the work with half the
men holding spears, from the first light of
dawn till the stars came out. 22At that time I
also said to the people, "Have every man
and his helper stay inside Jerusalem at
night, so they can serve us as guards by
night and workmen by day." 23Neither I nor
my brothers nor my men nor the guards with
me took off our clothes; each had his weapon, even when he went for water.[b]

Nehemiah Helps the Poor

5 Now the men and their wives raised a
great outcry against their Jewish brothers. 2Some were saying, "We and our sons
and daughters are numerous; in order for us
to eat and stay alive, we must get grain."
3Others were saying, "We are mortgaging
our fields, our vineyards and our homes to
get grain during the famine."
4Still others were saying, "We have had to
borrow money to pay the king's tax on our
fields and vineyards. 5Although we are of the
same flesh and blood as our countrymen
and though our sons are as good as theirs,
yet we have to subject our sons and daughters to slavery. Some of our daughters have
already been enslaved, but we are powerless, because our fields and our vineyards
belong to others."
6When I heard their outcry and these
charges, I was very angry. 7I pondered them
in my mind and then accused the nobles and
officials. I told them, "You are exacting usury
from your own countrymen!" So I called together a large meeting to deal with them
8and said: "As far as possible, we have
bought back our Jewish brothers who were
sold to the Gentiles. Now you are selling your
brothers, only for them to be sold back to us!"
They kept quiet, because they could find
nothing to say.
9So I continued, "What you are doing is not
right. Shouldn't you walk in the fear of our
God to avoid the reproach of our Gentile
enemies? 10I and my brothers and my men
are also lending the people money and
grain. But let the exacting of usury stop!
11Give back to them immediately their fields,
vineyards, olive groves and houses, and
also the usury you are charging them—the
hundredth part of the money, grain, new
wine and oil."

[a]5 Or *have provoked you to anger before*
[b]23 The meaning of the Hebrew for this clause is uncertain.

12"We will give it back," they said. "And we
will not demand anything more from them.
We will do as you say."

Then I summoned the priests and made
the nobles and officials take an oath to do
what they had promised. 13I also shook out
the folds of my robe and said, "In this way
may God shake out of his house and possessions every man who does not keep this
promise. So may such a man be shaken out
and emptied!"

At this the whole assembly said, "Amen,"
and praised the LORD. And the people did as
they had promised.

14Moreover, from the twentieth year of
King Artaxerxes, when I was appointed to be
their governor in the land of Judah, until his
thirty-second year—twelve years—neither I
nor my brothers ate the food allotted to the
governor. 15But the earlier governors—those
preceding me—placed a heavy burden on
the people and took forty shekels[a] of silver
from them in addition to food and wine. Their
assistants also lorded it over the people. But
out of reverence for God I did not act like
that. 16Instead, I devoted myself to the work
on this wall. All my men were assembled
there for the work; we[b] did not acquire any
land.

17Furthermore, a hundred and fifty Jews
and officials ate at my table, as well as those
who came to us from the surrounding nations. 18Each day one ox, six choice sheep
and some poultry were prepared for me, and
every ten days an abundant supply of wine of
all kinds. In spite of all this, I never demanded the food allotted to the governor, because
the demands were heavy on these people.

19Remember me with favor, O my God, for
all I have done for these people.

Further Opposition to the Rebuilding

6 When word came to Sanballat, Tobiah,
Geshem the Arab and the rest of our
enemies that I had rebuilt the wall and not a
gap was left in it—though up to that time I
had not set the doors in the gates— 2Sanbal-
lat and Geshem sent me this message:
"Come, let us meet together in one of the
villages[c] on the plain of Ono."

But they were scheming to harm me; 3so I
sent messengers to them with this reply: "I
am carrying on a great project and cannot go
down. Why should the work stop while I
leave it and go down to you?" 4Four times
they sent me the same message, and each
time I gave them the same answer.

5Then, the fifth time, Sanballat sent his
aide to me with the same message, and in
his hand was an unsealed letter 6in which
was written:

> "It is reported among the nations—
> and Geshem[d] says it is true—that you
> and the Jews are plotting to revolt, and
> therefore you are building the wall.
> Moreover, according to these reports
> you are about to become their king 7and
> have even appointed prophets to make
> this proclamation about you in Jerusa-
> lem: 'There is a king in Judah!' Now this
> report will get back to the king; so come,
> let us confer together."

8I sent him this reply: "Nothing like what
you are saying is happening; you are just
making it up out of your head."

9They were all trying to frighten us, thinking, "Their hands will get too weak for the
work, and it will not be completed."

⌞But I prayed,⌟ "Now strengthen my
hands."

10One day I went to the house of Shemaiah
son of Delaiah, the son of Mehetabel, who
was shut in at his home. He said, "Let us
meet in the house of God, inside the temple,
and let us close the temple doors, because
men are coming to kill you—by night they are
coming to kill you."

11But I said, "Should a man like me run
away? Or should one like me go into the
temple to save his life? I will not go!" 12I
realized that God had not sent him, but that
he had prophesied against me because Tobiah and Sanballat had hired him. 13He had
been hired to intimidate me so that I would
commit a sin by doing this, and then they
would give me a bad name to discredit me.

14Remember Tobiah and Sanballat, O my
God, because of what they have done;
remember also the prophetess Noadiah and
the rest of the prophets who have been trying
to intimidate me.

The Completion of the Wall

15So the wall was completed on the
twenty-fifth of Elul, in fifty-two days. 16When
all our enemies heard about this, all the sur-

[a]15 That is, about 1 pound (about 0.5 kilogram) [b]16 Most Hebrew manuscripts; some Hebrew manuscripts, Septuagint, Vulgate and Syriac *I* [c]2 Or *in Kephirim* [d]6 Hebrew *Gashmu,* a variant of *Geshem*

rounding nations were afraid and lost their
self-confidence, because they realized that
this work had been done with the help of our
God.
17Also, in those days the nobles of Judah
were sending many letters to Tobiah, and
replies from Tobiah kept coming to them.
18For many in Judah were under oath to him,
since he was son-in-law to Shecaniah son of
Arah, and his son Jehohanan had married
the daughter of Meshullam son of Berekiah.
19Moreover, they kept reporting to me his
good deeds and then telling him what I said.
And Tobiah sent letters to intimidate me.

7 After the wall had been rebuilt and I had
set the doors in place, the gatekeepers
and the singers and the Levites were appointed. 2I put in charge of Jerusalem my
brother Hanani, along with[a] Hananiah the
commander of the citadel, because he was a
man of integrity and feared God more than
most men do. 3I said to them, "The gates of
Jerusalem are not to be opened until the sun
is hot. While the gatekeepers are still on
duty, have them shut the doors and bar
them. Also appoint residents of Jerusalem
as guards, some at their posts and some
near their own houses."

The List of the Exiles Who Returned

4Now the city was large and spacious, but
there were few people in it, and the houses
had not yet been rebuilt. 5So my God put it
into my heart to assemble the nobles, the
officials and the common people for registra-
tion by families. I found the genealogical
record of those who had been the first to
return. This is what I found written there:

6These are the people of the province
who came up from the captivity of the
exiles whom Nebuchadnezzar king of
Babylon had taken captive (they returned to Jerusalem and Judah, each to
his own town, 7in company with Zerubbabel, Jeshua, Nehemiah, Azariah,
Raamiah, Nahamani, Mordecai, Bilshan, Mispereth, Bigvai, Nehum and
Baanah):

The list of the men of Israel:

8the descendants of Parosh 2,172
9of Shephatiah 372
10of Arah 652
11of Pahath-Moab (through the
line of Jeshua and Joab) 2,818
12of Elam 1,254
13of Zattu 845
14of Zaccai 760
15of Binnui 648
16of Bebai 628
17of Azgad 2,322
18of Adonikam 667
19of Bigvai 2,067
20of Adin 655
21of Ater (through Hezekiah) 98
22of Hashum 328
23of Bezai 324
24of Hariph 112
25of Gibeon 95

26the men of Bethlehem and
Netophah 188
27of Anathoth 128
28of Beth Azmaveth 42
29of Kiriath Jearim, Kephirah and
Beeroth 743
30of Ramah and Geba 621
31of Micmash 122
32of Bethel and Ai 123
33of the other Nebo 52
34of the other Elam 1,254
35of Harim 320
36of Jericho 345
37of Lod, Hadid and Ono 721
38of Senaah 3,930

39The priests:

the descendants of Jedaiah (through
the family of Jeshua) 973
40of Immer 1,052
41of Pashhur 1,247
42of Harim 1,017

43The Levites:

the descendants of Jeshua (through
Kadmiel through the line of
Hodaviah) 74

44The singers:

the descendants of Asaph 148

45The gatekeepers:

the descendants of
Shallum, Ater, Talmon, Akkub,
Hatita and Shobai 138

46The temple servants:

the descendants of
Ziha, Hasupha, Tabbaoth,
47Keros, Sia, Padon,
48Lebana, Hagaba, Shalmai,

[a]2 Or *Hanani, that is,*

49Hanan, Giddel, Gahar,
50Reaiah, Rezin, Nekoda,
51Gazzam, Uzza, Paseah,
52Besai, Meunim, Nephussim,
53Bakbuk, Hakupha, Harhur,
54Bazluth, Mehida, Harsha,
55Barkos, Sisera, Temah,
56Neziah and Hatipha

57The descendants of the servants of Solomon:

the descendants of
Sotai, Sophereth, Perida,
58Jaala, Darkon, Giddel,
59Shephatiah, Hattil,
Pokereth-Hazzebaim and Amon

60The temple servants and the descendants of the servants of Solomon 392

61The following came up from the
towns of Tel Melah, Tel Harsha, Kerub,
Addon and Immer, but they could not show that their families were descended from Israel:

62the descendants of
Delaiah, Tobiah and Nekoda 642

63And from among the priests:

the descendants of
Hobaiah, Hakkoz and Barzillai (a man who had married a daughter of Barzillai the Gileadite and was called by that name).

64These searched for their family
records, but they could not find them and so were excluded from the priesthood as unclean.
65The governor, therefore, ordered them not to eat any of the most sacred food until there should be a priest ministering with the Urim and Thummim.

66The whole company numbered 42,-
360, 67besides their 7,337 menservants and maidservants; and they also had 245 men and women singers.
68There
were 736 horses, 245 mules,[a]
69435
camels and 6,720 donkeys.

70Some of the heads of the families contributed to the work. The governor gave to the treasury 1,000 drachmas[b] of gold, 50 bowls and 530 garments for priests.
71Some of the heads of the families gave to the treasury for the work 20,000 drachmas[c] of gold and 2,200 minas[d] of silver.
72The total given by the rest of the people was 20,000 drachmas of gold, 2,000 minas[e] of silver and 67 garments for priests.

73The priests, the Levites, the gatekeepers, the singers and the temple servants, along with certain of the people and the rest of the Israelites, settled in their own towns.

Ezra Reads the Law

8 When the seventh month came and the Israelites had settled in their towns,
1all
the people assembled as one man in the square before the Water Gate. They told Ezra the scribe to bring out the Book of the Law of Moses, which the LORD had commanded for Israel.

2So on the first day of the seventh month Ezra the priest brought the Law before the assembly, which was made up of men and women and all who were able to understand.
3He read it aloud from daybreak till noon as he faced the square before the Water Gate in the presence of the men, women and others who could understand. And all the people listened attentively to the Book of the Law.

4Ezra the scribe stood on a high wooden platform built for the occasion. Beside him on his right stood Mattithiah, Shema, Anaiah, Uriah, Hilkiah and Maaseiah; and on his left were Pedaiah, Mishael, Malkijah, Hashum, Hashbaddanah, Zechariah and Meshullam.

5Ezra opened the book. All the people could see him because he was standing above them; and as he opened it, the people all stood up.
6Ezra praised the LORD, the great God; and all the people lifted their hands and responded, "Amen! Amen!" Then they bowed down and worshiped the LORD with their faces to the ground.

7The Levites—Jeshua, Bani, Sherebiah, Jamin, Akkub, Shabbethai, Hodiah, Maaseiah, Kelita, Azariah, Jozabad, Hanan and Pelaiah—instructed the people in the Law while the people were standing there.
8They
read from the Book of the Law of God, making it clear[f] and giving the meaning so that

[a] 68 Some Hebrew manuscripts (see also Ezra 2:66); most Hebrew manuscripts do not have this verse.
[b] 70 That is, about 19 pounds (about 8.5 kilograms)
[c] 71 That is, about 375 pounds (about 170 kilograms); also in verse 72
[d] 71 That is, about 1 1/3 tons (about 1.2 metric tons)
[e] 72 That is, about 1 1/4 tons (about 1.1 metric tons)
[f] 8 Or *God, translating it*

the people could understand what was being read.

9Then Nehemiah the governor, Ezra the priest and scribe, and the Levites who were instructing the people said to them all, "This day is sacred to the LORD your God. Do not mourn or weep." For all the people had been weeping as they listened to the words of the Law.

10Nehemiah said, "Go and enjoy choice food and sweet drinks, and send some to those who have nothing prepared. This day is sacred to our Lord. Do not grieve, for the joy of the LORD is your strength."

11The Levites calmed all the people, saying, "Be still, for this is a sacred day. Do not grieve."

12Then all the people went away to eat and drink, to send portions of food and to celebrate with great joy, because they now understood the words that had been made known to them.

13On the second day of the month, the heads of all the families, along with the priests and the Levites, gathered around Ezra the scribe to give attention to the words of the Law. 14They found written in the Law, which the LORD had commanded through Moses, that the Israelites were to live in booths during the feast of the seventh month 15and that they should proclaim this word and spread it throughout their towns and in Jerusalem: "Go out into the hill country and bring back branches from olive and wild olive trees, and from myrtles, palms and shade trees, to make booths"—as it is written.[a]

16So the people went out and brought back branches and built themselves booths on their own roofs, in their courtyards, in the courts of the house of God and in the square by the Water Gate and the one by the Gate of Ephraim. 17The whole company that had returned from exile built booths and lived in them. From the days of Joshua son of Nun until that day, the Israelites had not celebrated it like this. And their joy was very great.

18Day after day, from the first day to the last, Ezra read from the Book of the Law of God. They celebrated the feast for seven days, and on the eighth day, in accordance with the regulation, there was an assembly.

The Israelites Confess Their Sins

9 On the twenty-fourth day of the same month, the Israelites gathered together, fasting and wearing sackcloth and having dust on their heads. 2Those of Israelite descent had separated themselves from all foreigners. They stood in their places and confessed their sins and the wickedness of their fathers. 3They stood where they were and read from the Book of the Law of the LORD their God for a quarter of the day, and spent another quarter in confession and in worshiping the LORD their God. 4Standing on the stairs were the Levites—Jeshua, Bani, Kadmiel, Shebaniah, Bunni, Sherebiah, Bani and Kenani—who called with loud voices to the LORD their God. 5And the Levites—Jeshua, Kadmiel, Bani, Hashabneiah, Sherebiah, Hodiah, Shebaniah and Pethahiah—said: "Stand up and praise the LORD your God, who is from everlasting to everlasting.[b]"

"Blessed be your glorious name, and may it be exalted above all blessing and praise. 6You alone are the LORD. You made the heavens, even the highest heavens, and all their starry host, the earth and all that is on it, the seas and all that is in them. You give life to everything, and the multitudes of heaven worship you.

7"You are the LORD God, who chose Abram and brought him out of Ur of the Chaldeans and named him Abraham. 8You found his heart faithful to you, and you made a covenant with him to give to his descendants the land of the Canaanites, Hittites, Amorites, Perizzites, Jebusites and Girgashites. You have kept your promise because you are righteous.

9"You saw the suffering of our forefathers in Egypt; you heard their cry at the Red Sea.[c] 10You sent miraculous signs and wonders against Pharaoh, against all his officials and all the people of his land, for you knew how arrogantly the Egyptians treated them. You made a name for yourself, which remains to this day. 11You divided the sea before them, so that they passed through it on dry ground, but you hurled their pursuers into the depths, like a stone into mighty

[a] *15* See Lev. 23:37-40.
[b] *5* Or *God for ever and ever*
[c] *9* Hebrew *Yam Suph;* that is, Sea of Reeds

waters. [12]By day you led them with a
pillar of cloud, and by night with a pillar
of fire to give them light on the way they
were to take.

[13]"You came down on Mount Sinai;
you spoke to them from heaven. You
gave them regulations and laws that are
just and right, and decrees and commands that are good. [14]You made
known to them your holy Sabbath and
gave them commands, decrees and
laws through your servant Moses. [15]In
their hunger you gave them bread from
heaven and in their thirst you brought
them water from the rock; you told them
to go in and take possession of the land
you had sworn with uplifted hand to give
them.

[16]"But they, our forefathers, became
arrogant and stiff-necked, and did not
obey your commands. [17]They refused to
listen and failed to remember the miracles you performed among them. They
became stiff-necked and in their rebellion appointed a leader in order to return
to their slavery. But you are a forgiving
God, gracious and compassionate,
slow to anger and abounding in love.
Therefore you did not desert them,
[18]even when they cast for themselves
an image of a calf and said, 'This is your
god, who brought you up out of Egypt,'
or when they committed awful blasphemies.

[19]"Because of your great compassion
you did not abandon them in the desert.
By day the pillar of cloud did not cease
to guide them on their path, nor the pillar
of fire by night to shine on the way they
were to take. [20]You gave your good
Spirit to instruct them. You did not withhold your manna from their mouths, and
you gave them water for their thirst.
[21]For forty years you sustained them in
the desert; they lacked nothing, their
clothes did not wear out nor did their feet
become swollen.

[22]"You gave them kingdoms and nations, allotting to them even the remotest frontiers. They took over the country
of Sihon[a] king of Heshbon and the
country of Og king of Bashan. [23]You
made their sons as numerous as the
stars in the sky, and you brought them
into the land that you told their fathers to
enter and possess. [24]Their sons went in
and took possession of the land. You
subdued before them the Canaanites,
who lived in the land; you handed the
Canaanites over to them, along with
their kings and the peoples of the land,
to deal with them as they pleased.
[25]They captured fortified cities and fertile land; they took possession of
houses filled with all kinds of good
things, wells already dug, vineyards,
olive groves and fruit trees in abundance. They ate to the full and were
well-nourished; they reveled in your
great goodness.

[26]"But they were disobedient and rebelled against you; they put your law
behind their backs. They killed your
prophets, who had admonished them in
order to turn them back to you; they
committed awful blasphemies. [27]So you
handed them over to their enemies, who
oppressed them. But when they were
oppressed they cried out to you. From
heaven you heard them, and in your
great compassion you gave them deliverers, who rescued them from the hand
of their enemies.

[28]"But as soon as they were at rest,
they again did what was evil in your
sight. Then you abandoned them to the
hand of their enemies so that they ruled
over them. And when they cried out to
you again, you heard from heaven, and
in your compassion you delivered them
time after time.

[29]"You warned them to return to your
law, but they became arrogant and disobeyed your commands. They sinned
against your ordinances, by which a
man will live if he obeys them. Stubbornly they turned their backs on you,
became stiff-necked and refused to listen. [30]For many years you were patient
with them. By your Spirit you admonished them through your prophets. Yet
they paid no attention, so you handed
them over to the neighboring peoples.
[31]But in your great mercy you did not put
an end to them or abandon them, for
you are a gracious and merciful God.

[32]"Now therefore, O our God, the
great, mighty and awesome God, who

[a]*22* One Hebrew manuscript and Septuagint; most Hebrew manuscripts *Sihon, that is, the country of the*

keeps his covenant of love, do not let all
this hardship seem trifling in your
eyes—the hardship that has come upon
us, upon our kings and leaders, upon
our priests and prophets, upon our fathers and all your people, from the days
of the kings of Assyria until today. 33In all
that has happened to us, you have been
just; you have acted faithfully, while we
did wrong. 34Our kings, our leaders, our
priests and our fathers did not follow
your law; they did not pay attention to
your commands or the warnings you
gave them. 35Even while they were in
their kingdom, enjoying your great
goodness to them in the spacious and
fertile land you gave them, they did not
serve you or turn from their evil ways.
36"But see, we are slaves today,
slaves in the land you gave our forefathers so they could eat its fruit and the
other good things it produces. 37Be-
cause of our sins, its abundant harvest
goes to the kings you have placed over
us. They rule over our bodies and our
cattle as they please. We are in great
distress.

The Agreement of the People

38"In view of all this, we are making a binding agreement, putting it in writing, and our leaders, our Levites and our priests are affixing their seals to it."

10 Those who sealed it were:

Nehemiah the governor, the son of Hacaliah.

Zedekiah, 2Seraiah, Azariah, Jeremiah,
3Pashhur, Amariah, Malkijah,
4Hattush, Shebaniah, Malluch,
5Harim, Meremoth, Obadiah,
6Daniel, Ginnethon, Baruch,
7Meshullam, Abijah, Mijamin,
8Maaziah, Bilgai and Shemaiah.
These were the priests.

9The Levites:

Jeshua son of Azaniah, Binnui of the sons of Henadad, Kadmiel,
10and their associates: Shebaniah,
Hodiah, Kelita, Pelaiah, Hanan,
11Mica, Rehob, Hashabiah,
12Zaccur, Sherebiah, Shebaniah,
13Hodiah, Bani and Beninu.

14The leaders of the people:

Parosh, Pahath-Moab, Elam, Zattu, Bani,
15Bunni, Azgad, Bebai,
16Adonijah, Bigvai, Adin,
17Ater, Hezekiah, Azzur,
18Hodiah, Hashum, Bezai,
19Hariph, Anathoth, Nebai,
20Magpiash, Meshullam, Hezir,
21Meshezabel, Zadok, Jaddua,
22Pelatiah, Hanan, Anaiah,
23Hoshea, Hananiah, Hasshub,
24Hallohesh, Pilha, Shobek,
25Rehum, Hashabnah, Maaseiah,
26Ahiah, Hanan, Anan,
27Malluch, Harim and Baanah.

28"The rest of the people—priests, Levites, gatekeepers, singers, temple servants and all who separated themselves
from the neighboring peoples for the
sake of the Law of God, together with
their wives and all their sons and daughters who are able to understand— 29all
these now join their brothers the nobles,
and bind themselves with a curse and
an oath to follow the Law of God given
through Moses the servant of God and
to obey carefully all the commands,
regulations and decrees of the LORD our
Lord.
30"We promise not to give our daughters in marriage to the peoples around
us or take their daughters for our sons.
31"When the neighboring peoples
bring merchandise or grain to sell on the
Sabbath, we will not buy from them on
the Sabbath or on any holy day. Every
seventh year we will forgo working the
land and will cancel all debts.
32"We assume the responsibility for
carrying out the commands to give a
third of a shekel[a] each year for the service of the house of our God: 33for the
bread set out on the table; for the regular grain offerings and burnt offerings;
for the offerings on the Sabbaths, New
Moon festivals and appointed feasts; for
the holy offerings; for sin offerings to
make atonement for Israel; and for all
the duties of the house of our God.
34"We—the priests, the Levites and
the people—have cast lots to determine
when each of our families is to bring to

a32 That is, about 1/8 ounce (about 4 grams)

the house of our God at set times each
year a contribution of wood to burn on
the altar of the LORD our God, as it is
written in the Law.
35“We also assume responsibility for
bringing to the house of the LORD each
year the firstfruits of our crops and of
every fruit tree.
36“As it is also written in the Law, we
will bring the firstborn of our sons and of
our cattle, of our herds and of our flocks
to the house of our God, to the priests
ministering there.
37“Moreover, we will bring to the
storerooms of the house of our God, to
the priests, the first of our ground meal,
of our ⌊grain⌋ offerings, of the fruit of all
our trees and of our new wine and oil.
And we will bring a tithe of our crops to
the Levites, for it is the Levites who collect the tithes in all the towns where we
work. 38A priest descended from Aaron
is to accompany the Levites when they
receive the tithes, and the Levites are to
bring a tenth of the tithes up to the house
of our God, to the storerooms of the
treasury. 39The people of Israel, including the Levites, are to bring their contributions of grain, new wine and oil to the
storerooms where the articles for the
sanctuary are kept and where the ministering priests, the gatekeepers and the
singers stay.
“We will not neglect the house of our
God.”

The New Residents of Jerusalem

11 Now the leaders of the people settled
in Jerusalem, and the rest of the
people cast lots to bring one out of every ten
to live in Jerusalem, the holy city, while the
remaining nine were to stay in their own
towns. 2The people commended all the men
who volunteered to live in Jerusalem.
3These are the provincial leaders who settled in Jerusalem (now some Israelites,
priests, Levites, temple servants and descendants of Solomon’s servants lived in the
towns of Judah, each on his own property in
the various towns, 4while other people from
both Judah and Benjamin lived in Jerusalem):

From the descendants of Judah:

Athaiah son of Uzziah, the son of Zechariah, the son of Amariah, the son of
Shephatiah, the son of Mahalalel, a descendant of Perez; 5and Maaseiah son
of Baruch, the son of Col-Hozeh, the
son of Hazaiah, the son of Adaiah, the
son of Joiarib, the son of Zechariah, a
descendant of Shelah. 6The descendants of Perez who lived in Jerusalem
totaled 468 able men.

7From the descendants of Benjamin:

Sallu son of Meshullam, the son of
Joed, the son of Pedaiah, the son of
Kolaiah, the son of Maaseiah, the son of
Ithiel, the son of Jeshaiah, 8and his followers, Gabbai and Sallai—928 men.
9Joel son of Zicri was their chief officer,
and Judah son of Hassenuah was over
the Second District of the city.

10From the priests:

Jedaiah; the son of Joiarib; Jakin; 11Se-
raiah son of Hilkiah, the son of Meshullam, the son of Zadok, the son of
Meraioth, the son of Ahitub, supervisor
in the house of God, 12and their associates, who carried on work for the temple—822 men; Adaiah son of Jeroham,
the son of Pelaliah, the son of Amzi, the
son of Zechariah, the son of Pashhur,
the son of Malkijah, 13and his associates, who were heads of families—
242 men; Amashsai son of Azarel, the
son of Ahzai, the son of Meshillemoth,
the son of Immer, 14and his[a] associates,
who were able men—128. Their chief
officer was Zabdiel son of Haggedolim.

15From the Levites:

Shemaiah son of Hasshub, the son of
Azrikam, the son of Hashabiah, the son
of Bunni; 16Shabbethai and Jozabad,
two of the heads of the Levites, who had
charge of the outside work of the house
of God; 17Mattaniah son of Mica, the son
of Zabdi, the son of Asaph, the director
who led in thanksgiving and prayer;
Bakbukiah, second among his associates; and Abda son of Shammua, the
son of Galal, the son of Jeduthun. 18The
Levites in the holy city totaled 284.

19The gatekeepers:

Akkub, Talmon and their associates,
who kept watch at the gates—172 men.

[a] 14 Most Septuagint manuscripts; Hebrew *their*

20 The rest of the Israelites, with the priests
and Levites, were in all the towns of Judah,
each on his ancestral property.
21 The temple servants lived on the hill of
Ophel, and Ziha and Gishpa were in charge
of them.
22 The chief officer of the Levites in Jerusalem was Uzzi son of Bani, the son of Hashabiah, the son of Mattaniah, the son of Mica.
Uzzi was one of Asaph's descendants, who
were the singers responsible for the service
of the house of God. 23 The singers were under the king's orders, which regulated their
daily activity.
24 Pethahiah son of Meshezabel, one of the
descendants of Zerah son of Judah, was the
king's agent in all affairs relating to the
people.
25 As for the villages with their fields, some
of the people of Judah lived in Kiriath Arba
and its surrounding settlements, in Dibon
and its settlements, in Jekabzeel and its villages, 26 in Jeshua, in Moladah, in Beth Pelet,
27 in Hazar Shual, in Beersheba and its settlements, 28 in Ziklag, in Meconah and its settlements, 29 in En Rimmon, in Zorah, in Jarmuth, 30 Zanoah, Adullam and their villages,
in Lachish and its fields, and in Azekah and
its settlements. So they were living all the
way from Beersheba to the Valley of Hinnom.
31 The descendants of the Benjamites from
Geba lived in Micmash, Aija, Bethel and its
settlements, 32 in Anathoth, Nob and Ananiah, 33 in Hazor, Ramah and Gittaim, 34 in
Hadid, Zeboim and Neballat, 35 in Lod and
Ono, and in the Valley of the Craftsmen.
36 Some of the divisions of the Levites of
Judah settled in Benjamin.

Priests and Levites

12 These were the priests and Levites
who returned with Zerubbabel son of
Shealtiel and with Jeshua:

Seraiah, Jeremiah, Ezra,
2 Amariah, Malluch, Hattush,
3 Shecaniah, Rehum, Meremoth,
4 Iddo, Ginnethon,[a] Abijah,
5 Mijamin,[b] Moadiah, Bilgah,
6 Shemaiah, Joiarib, Jedaiah,
7 Sallu, Amok, Hilkiah and Jedaiah.

These were the leaders of the priests and
their associates in the days of Jeshua.

8 The Levites were Jeshua, Binnui, Kadmiel, Sherebiah, Judah, and also Mattaniah,
who, together with his associates, was in
charge of the songs of thanksgiving. 9 Bakbukiah and Unni, their associates, stood opposite them in the services.
10 Jeshua was the father of Joiakim,
Joiakim the father of Eliashib, Eliashib
the father of Joiada, 11 Joiada the father of
Jonathan, and Jonathan the father of Jaddua.
12 In the days of Joiakim, these were the
heads of the priestly families:

of Seraiah's family, Meraiah;
of Jeremiah's, Hananiah;
13 of Ezra's, Meshullam;
of Amariah's, Jehohanan;
14 of Malluch's, Jonathan;
of Shecaniah's,[c] Joseph;
15 of Harim's, Adna;
of Meremoth's,[d] Helkai;
16 of Iddo's, Zechariah;
of Ginnethon's, Meshullam;
17 of Abijah's, Zicri;
of Miniamin's and of Moadiah's, Piltai;
18 of Bilgah's, Shammua;
of Shemaiah's, Jehonathan;
19 of Joiarib's, Mattenai;
of Jedaiah's, Uzzi;
20 of Sallu's, Kallai;
of Amok's, Eber;
21 of Hilkiah's, Hashabiah;
of Jedaiah's, Nethanel.

22 The family heads of the Levites in the
days of Eliashib, Joiada, Johanan and Jaddua, as well as those of the priests, were
recorded in the reign of Darius the Persian.
23 The family heads among the descendants
of Levi up to the time of Johanan son of
Eliashib were recorded in the book of the
annals. 24 And the leaders of the Levites were
Hashabiah, Sherebiah, Jeshua son of Kadmiel, and their associates, who stood opposite them to give praise and thanksgiving,
one section responding to the other, as prescribed by David the man of God.
25 Mattaniah, Bakbukiah, Obadiah, Meshullam, Talmon and Akkub were gatekeepers who guarded the storerooms at the
gates. 26 They served in the days of Joiakim
son of Jeshua, the son of Jozadak, and in the
days of Nehemiah the governor and of Ezra
the priest and scribe.

[a] *4* Many Hebrew manuscripts and Vulgate (see also Neh. 12:16); most Hebrew manuscripts *Ginnethoi* [b] *5* A variant of *Miniamin* [c] *14* Very many Hebrew manuscripts, some Septuagint manuscripts and Syriac (see also Neh. 12:3); most Hebrew manuscripts *Shebaniah's* [d] *15* Some Septuagint manuscripts (see also Neh. 12:3); Hebrew *Meraioth's*

Dedication of the Wall of Jerusalem

27At the dedication of the wall of Jerusalem, the Levites were sought out from where they lived and were brought to Jerusalem to celebrate joyfully the dedication with songs of thanksgiving and with the music of cymbals, harps and lyres. 28The singers also were brought together from the region around Jerusalem—from the villages of the Netophathites, 29from Beth Gilgal, and from the area of Geba and Azmaveth, for the singers had built villages for themselves around Jerusalem. 30When the priests and Levites had purified themselves ceremonially, they purified the people, the gates and the wall.

31I had the leaders of Judah go up on top[a] of the wall. I also assigned two large choirs to give thanks. One was to proceed on top[b] of the wall to the right, toward the Dung Gate. 32Hoshaiah and half the leaders of Judah followed them, 33along with Azariah, Ezra, Meshullam, 34Judah, Benjamin, Shemaiah, Jeremiah, 35as well as some priests with trumpets, and also Zechariah son of Jonathan, the son of Shemaiah, the son of Mattaniah, the son of Micaiah, the son of Zaccur, the son of Asaph, 36and his associates—Shemaiah, Azarel, Milalai, Gilalai, Maai, Nethanel, Judah and Hanani—with musical instruments ⌊prescribed by⌋ David the man of God. Ezra the scribe led the procession. 37At the Fountain Gate they continued directly up the steps of the City of David on the ascent to the wall and passed above the house of David to the Water Gate on the east.

38The second choir proceeded in the opposite direction. I followed them on top[c] of the wall, together with half the people—past the Tower of the Ovens to the Broad Wall, 39over the Gate of Ephraim, the Jeshanah[d] Gate, the Fish Gate, the Tower of Hananel and the Tower of the Hundred, as far as the Sheep Gate. At the Gate of the Guard they stopped.

40The two choirs that gave thanks then took their places in the house of God; so did I, together with half the officials, 41as well as the priests—Eliakim, Maaseiah, Miniamin, Micaiah, Elioenai, Zechariah and Hananiah with their trumpets— 42and also Maaseiah, Shemaiah, Eleazar, Uzzi, Jehohanan, Malkijah, Elam and Ezer. The choirs sang under the direction of Jezrahiah. 43And on that day they offered great sacrifices, rejoicing because God had given them great joy. The women and children also rejoiced. The sound of rejoicing in Jerusalem could be heard far away.

44At that time men were appointed to be in charge of the storerooms for the contributions, firstfruits and tithes. From the fields around the towns they were to bring into the storerooms the portions required by the Law for the priests and the Levites, for Judah was pleased with the ministering priests and Levites. 45They performed the service of their God and the service of purification, as did also the singers and gatekeepers, according to the commands of David and his son Solomon. 46For long ago, in the days of David and Asaph, there had been directors for the singers and for the songs of praise and thanksgiving to God. 47So in the days of Zerubbabel and of Nehemiah, all Israel contributed the daily portions for the singers and gatekeepers. They also set aside the portion for the other Levites, and the Levites set aside the portion for the descendants of Aaron.

Nehemiah's Final Reforms

13 On that day the Book of Moses was read aloud in the hearing of the people and there it was found written that no Ammonite or Moabite should ever be admitted into the assembly of God, 2because they had not met the Israelites with food and water but had hired Balaam to call a curse down on them. (Our God, however, turned the curse into a blessing.) 3When the people heard this law, they excluded from Israel all who were of foreign descent.

4Before this, Eliashib the priest had been put in charge of the storerooms of the house of our God. He was closely associated with Tobiah, 5and he had provided him with a large room formerly used to store the grain offerings and incense and temple articles, and also the tithes of grain, new wine and oil prescribed for the Levites, singers and gatekeepers, as well as the contributions for the priests.

6But while all this was going on, I was not in Jerusalem, for in the thirty-second year of Artaxerxes king of Babylon I had returned to the king. Some time later I asked his permission 7and came back to Jerusalem. Here I learned about the evil thing Eliashib had done in providing Tobiah a room in the courts of the house of God. 8I was greatly displeased and threw all Tobiah's household

[a]31 Or *go alongside* [b]31 Or *proceed alongside* [c]38 Or *them alongside* [d]39 Or *Old*

goods out of the room. 9I gave orders to purify the rooms, and then I put back into them the equipment of the house of God, with the grain offerings and the incense.

10I also learned that the portions assigned to the Levites had not been given to them, and that all the Levites and singers responsible for the service had gone back to their own fields. 11So I rebuked the officials and asked them, "Why is the house of God neglected?" Then I called them together and stationed them at their posts.

12All Judah brought the tithes of grain, new wine and oil into the storerooms. 13I put Shelemiah the priest, Zadok the scribe, and a Levite named Pedaiah in charge of the storerooms and made Hanan son of Zaccur, the son of Mattaniah, their assistant, because these men were considered trustworthy. They were made responsible for distributing the supplies to their brothers.

14Remember me for this, O my God, and do not blot out what I have so faithfully done for the house of my God and its services.

15In those days I saw men in Judah treading winepresses on the Sabbath and bringing in grain and loading it on donkeys, together with wine, grapes, figs and all other kinds of loads. And they were bringing all this into Jerusalem on the Sabbath. Therefore I warned them against selling food on that day. 16Men from Tyre who lived in Jerusalem were bringing in fish and all kinds of merchandise and selling them in Jerusalem on the Sabbath to the people of Judah. 17I rebuked the nobles of Judah and said to them, "What is this wicked thing you are doing—desecrating the Sabbath day? 18Didn't your forefathers do the same things, so that our God brought all this calamity upon us and upon this city? Now you are stirring up more wrath against Israel by desecrating the Sabbath."

19When evening shadows fell on the gates of Jerusalem before the Sabbath, I ordered the doors to be shut and not opened until the Sabbath was over. I stationed some of my own men at the gates so that no load could be brought in on the Sabbath day. 20Once or twice the merchants and sellers of all kinds of goods spent the night outside Jerusalem. 21But I warned them and said, "Why do you spend the night by the wall? If you do this again, I will lay hands on you." From that time on they no longer came on the Sabbath. 22Then I commanded the Levites to purify themselves and go and guard the gates in order to keep the Sabbath day holy.

Remember me for this also, O my God, and show mercy to me according to your great love.

23Moreover, in those days I saw men of Judah who had married women from Ashdod, Ammon and Moab. 24Half of their children spoke the language of Ashdod or the language of one of the other peoples, and did not know how to speak the language of Judah. 25I rebuked them and called curses down on them. I beat some of the men and pulled out their hair. I made them take an oath in God's name and said: "You are not to give your daughters in marriage to their sons, nor are you to take their daughters in marriage for your sons or for yourselves. 26Was it not because of marriages like these that Solomon king of Israel sinned? Among the many nations there was no king like him. He was loved by his God, and God made him king over all Israel, but even he was led into sin by foreign women. 27Must we hear now that you too are doing all this terrible wickedness and are being unfaithful to our God by marrying foreign women?"

28One of the sons of Joiada son of Eliashib the high priest was son-in-law to Sanballat the Horonite. And I drove him away from me.

29Remember them, O my God, because they defiled the priestly office and the covenant of the priesthood and of the Levites.

30So I purified the priests and the Levites of everything foreign, and assigned them duties, each to his own task. 31I also made provision for contributions of wood at designated times, and for the firstfruits.

Remember me with favor, O my God.

Esther

Introduction:

The setting for the book of Esther is Susa, the Persian capital, during the time of Xerxes, who ruled Persia from 486–465 B.C. The book tells the story of a beautiful Jewish girl whom King Xerxes chose to be his queen. When Haman plotted to murder all the Jews, Queen Esther's cousin Mordecai persuaded Esther to try to save her people. Risking her own life, she appealed to the king and rescued the Jews.

Although the name of God does not appear in this book, his care for his chosen people is clearly shown. This exciting story of the rescue of the Jews is celebrated annually during the Feast of Purim, at which time the book of Esther is read out loud.

Outline of contents:

Queen Vashti Deposed

1 This is what happened during the time of
Xerxes,[a] the Xerxes who ruled over 127
provinces stretching from India to Cush[b]: 2At
that time King Xerxes reigned from his royal
throne in the citadel of Susa, 3and in the third
year of his reign he gave a banquet for all his
nobles and officials. The military leaders of
Persia and Media, the princes, and the nobles of the provinces were present.
4For a full 180 days he displayed the vast
wealth of his kingdom and the splendor and
glory of his majesty. 5When these days were
over, the king gave a banquet, lasting seven
days, in the enclosed garden of the king's
palace, for all the people from the least to the
greatest, who were in the citadel of Susa.
6The garden had hangings of white and blue
linen, fastened with cords of white linen and
purple material to silver rings on marble pillars. There were couches of gold and silver
on a mosaic pavement of porphyry, marble,
mother-of-pearl and other costly stones.
7Wine was served in goblets of gold, each
one different from the other, and the royal
wine was abundant, in keeping with the
king's liberality. 8By the king's command
each guest was allowed to drink in his own
way, for the king instructed all the wine stew-
ards to serve each man what he wished.
9Queen Vashti also gave a banquet for
the women in the royal palace of King
Xerxes.
10On the seventh day, when King Xerxes
was in high spirits from wine, he commanded
the seven eunuchs who served him—Mehu-
man, Biztha, Harbona, Bigtha, Abagtha, Ze-
thar and Carcas— 11to bring before him
Queen Vashti, wearing her royal crown, in
order to display her beauty to the people and
nobles, for she was lovely to look at. 12But
when the attendants delivered the king's
command, Queen Vashti refused to come.
Then the king became furious and burned
with anger.
13Since it was customary for the king to
consult experts in matters of law and justice,
he spoke with the wise men who understood
the times 14and were closest to the king—
Carshena, Shethar, Admatha, Tarshish,
Meres, Marsena and Memucan, the seven
nobles of Persia and Media who had special
access to the king and were highest in the
kingdom.
15"According to law, what must be done to
Queen Vashti?" he asked. "She has not

[a] 1 Hebrew *Ahasuerus,* a variant of Xerxes' name; here and throughout Esther [b] 1 That is, the upper Nile region

obeyed the command of King Xerxes that
the eunuchs have taken to her."
16Then Memucan replied in the presence
of the king and the nobles, "Queen Vashti
has done wrong, not only against the king
but also against all the nobles and the peoples of all the provinces of King Xerxes. 17For
the queen's conduct will become known to
all the women, and so they will despise their
husbands and say, 'King Xerxes commanded Queen Vashti to be brought before
him, but she would not come.' 18This very
day the Persian and Median women of the
nobility who have heard about the queen's
conduct will respond to all the king's nobles
in the same way. There will be no end of
disrespect and discord.
19"Therefore, if it pleases the king, let him
issue a royal decree and let it be written in
the laws of Persia and Media, which cannot
be repealed, that Vashti is never again to
enter the presence of King Xerxes. Also let
the king give her royal position to someone
else who is better than she. 20Then when the
king's edict is proclaimed throughout all his
vast realm, all the women will respect their
husbands, from the least to the greatest."
21The king and his nobles were pleased
with this advice, so the king did as Memucan
proposed. 22He sent dispatches to all parts of
the kingdom, to each province in its own
script and to each people in its own language, proclaiming in each people's tongue
that every man should be ruler over his own
household.

Esther Made Queen

2 Later when the anger of King Xerxes had
subsided, he remembered Vashti and
what she had done and what he had decreed
about her. 2Then the king's personal attendants proposed, "Let a search be made for
beautiful young virgins for the king. 3Let the
king appoint commissioners in every province of his realm to bring all these beautiful
girls into the harem at the citadel of Susa. Let
them be placed under the care of Hegai, the
king's eunuch, who is in charge of the
women; and let beauty treatments be given
to them. 4Then let the girl who pleases the
king be queen instead of Vashti." This advice appealed to the king, and he followed it.
5Now there was in the citadel of Susa a
Jew of the tribe of Benjamin, named Mordecai son of Jair, the son of Shimei, the son
of Kish, 6who had been carried into exile
from Jerusalem by Nebuchadnezzar king of
Babylon, among those taken captive with
Jehoiachin[a] king of Judah. 7Mordecai had a
cousin named Hadassah, whom he had
brought up because she had neither father
nor mother. This girl, who was also known as
Esther, was lovely in form and features, and
Mordecai had taken her as his own daughter
when her father and mother died.
8When the king's order and edict had been
proclaimed, many girls were brought to the
citadel of Susa and put under the care of
Hegai. Esther also was taken to the king's
palace and entrusted to Hegai, who had
charge of the harem. 9The girl pleased him
and won his favor. Immediately he provided
her with her beauty treatments and special
food. He assigned to her seven maids selected from the king's palace and moved her
and her maids into the best place in the
harem.
10Esther had not revealed her nationality
and family background, because Mordecai
had forbidden her to do so. 11Every day he
walked back and forth near the courtyard of
the harem to find out how Esther was and
what was happening to her.
12Before a girl's turn came to go in to King
Xerxes, she had to complete twelve months
of beauty treatments prescribed for the
women, six months with oil of myrrh and six
with perfumes and cosmetics. 13And this is
how she would go to the king: Anything she
wanted was given her to take with her from
the harem to the king's palace. 14In the evening she would go there and in the morning
return to another part of the harem to the
care of Shaashgaz, the king's eunuch who
was in charge of the concubines. She would
not return to the king unless he was pleased
with her and summoned her by name.
15When the turn came for Esther (the girl
Mordecai had adopted, the daughter of his
uncle Abihail) to go to the king, she asked for
nothing other than what Hegai, the king's
eunuch who was in charge of the harem,
suggested. And Esther won the favor of
everyone who saw her. 16She was taken to
King Xerxes in the royal residence in the
tenth month, the month of Tebeth, in the
seventh year of his reign.
17Now the king was attracted to Esther
more than to any of the other women, and
she won his favor and approval more than

[a]6 Hebrew *Jeconiah,* a variant of *Jehoiachin*

any of the other virgins. So he set a royal crown on her head and made her queen instead of Vashti. 18And the king gave a great banquet, Esther's banquet, for all his nobles and officials. He proclaimed a holiday throughout the provinces and distributed gifts with royal liberality.

Mordecai Uncovers a Conspiracy

19When the virgins were assembled a second time, Mordecai was sitting at the king's gate. 20But Esther had kept secret her family background and nationality just as Mordecai had told her to do, for she continued to follow Mordecai's instructions as she had done when he was bringing her up.

21During the time Mordecai was sitting at the king's gate, Bigthana[a] and Teresh, two of the king's officers who guarded the doorway, became angry and conspired to assassinate King Xerxes. 22But Mordecai found out about the plot and told Queen Esther, who in turn reported it to the king, giving credit to Mordecai. 23And when the report was investigated and found to be true, the two officials were hanged on a gallows.[b] All this was recorded in the book of the annals in the presence of the king.

Haman's Plot to Destroy the Jews

3 After these events, King Xerxes honored Haman son of Hammedatha, the Agagite, elevating him and giving him a seat of honor higher than that of all the other nobles. 2All the royal officials at the king's gate knelt down and paid honor to Haman, for the king had commanded this concerning him. But Mordecai would not kneel down or pay him honor.

3Then the royal officials at the king's gate asked Mordecai, "Why do you disobey the king's command?" 4Day after day they spoke to him but he refused to comply. Therefore they told Haman about it to see whether Mordecai's behavior would be tolerated, for he had told them he was a Jew.

5When Haman saw that Mordecai would not kneel down or pay him honor, he was enraged. 6Yet having learned who Mordecai's people were, he scorned the idea of killing only Mordecai. Instead Haman looked for a way to destroy all Mordecai's people, the Jews, throughout the whole kingdom of Xerxes.

7In the twelfth year of King Xerxes, in the first month, the month of Nisan, they cast the *pur* (that is, the lot) in the presence of Haman to select a day and month. And the lot fell on[c] the twelfth month, the month of Adar.

8Then Haman said to King Xerxes, "There is a certain people dispersed and scattered among the peoples in all the provinces of your kingdom whose customs are different from those of all other people and who do not obey the king's laws; it is not in the king's best interest to tolerate them. 9If it pleases the king, let a decree be issued to destroy them, and I will put ten thousand talents[d] of silver into the royal treasury for the men who carry out this business."

10So the king took his signet ring from his finger and gave it to Haman son of Hammedatha, the Agagite, the enemy of the Jews. 11"Keep the money," the king said to Haman, "and do with the people as you please."

12Then on the thirteenth day of the first month the royal secretaries were summoned. They wrote out in the script of each province and in the language of each people all Haman's orders to the king's satraps, the governors of the various provinces and the nobles of the various peoples. These were written in the name of King Xerxes himself and sealed with his own ring. 13Dispatches were sent by couriers to all the king's provinces with the order to destroy, kill and annihilate all the Jews—young and old, women and little children—on a single day, the thirteenth day of the twelfth month, the month of Adar, and to plunder their goods. 14A copy of the text of the edict was to be issued as law in every province and made known to the people of every nationality so they would be ready for that day.

15Spurred on by the king's command, the couriers went out, and the edict was issued in the citadel of Susa. The king and Haman sat down to drink, but the city of Susa was bewildered.

Mordecai Persuades Esther to Help

4 When Mordecai learned of all that had been done, he tore his clothes, put on sackcloth and ashes, and went out into the city, wailing loudly and bitterly. 2But he went only as far as the king's gate, because no one clothed in sackcloth was allowed to en-

[a]21 Hebrew *Bigthan,* a variant of *Bigthana* [b]23 Or *were hung* (or *impaled*) *on poles;* similarly elsewhere in Esther [c]7 Septuagint; Hebrew does not have *And the lot fell on.* [d]9 That is, about 375 tons (about 345 metric tons)

ter it. 3In every province to which the edict
and order of the king came, there was great
mourning among the Jews, with fasting,
weeping and wailing. Many lay in sackcloth
and ashes.

4When Esther's maids and eunuchs came
and told her about Mordecai, she was in
great distress. She sent clothes for him to put
on instead of his sackcloth, but he would not
accept them. 5Then Esther summoned Hathach, one of the king's eunuchs assigned to
attend her, and ordered him to find out what
was troubling Mordecai and why.

6So Hathach went out to Mordecai in the
open square of the city in front of the king's
gate. 7Mordecai told him everything that had
happened to him, including the exact amount
of money Haman had promised to pay into
the royal treasury for the destruction of the
Jews. 8He also gave him a copy of the text of
the edict for their annihilation, which had
been published in Susa, to show to Esther
and explain it to her, and he told him to urge
her to go into the king's presence to beg for
mercy and plead with him for her people.

9Hathach went back and reported to Esther what Mordecai had said. 10Then she
instructed him to say to Mordecai, 11"All the
king's officials and the people of the royal
provinces know that for any man or woman
who approaches the king in the inner court
without being summoned the king has but
one law: that he be put to death. The only
exception to this is for the king to extend the
gold scepter to him and spare his life. But
thirty days have passed since I was called to
go to the king."

12When Esther's words were reported to
Mordecai, 13he sent back this answer: "Do
not think that because you are in the king's
house you alone of all the Jews will escape.
14For if you remain silent at this time, relief
and deliverance for the Jews will arise from
another place, but you and your father's
family will perish. And who knows but that
you have come to royal position for such a
time as this?"

15Then Esther sent this reply to Mordecai:
16"Go, gather together all the Jews who are
in Susa, and fast for me. Do not eat or drink
for three days, night or day. I and my maids
will fast as you do. When this is done, I will go
to the king, even though it is against the law.
And if I perish, I perish."

17So Mordecai went away and carried out
all of Esther's instructions.

Esther's Request to the King

5 On the third day Esther put on her royal
robes and stood in the inner court of the
palace, in front of the king's hall. The king
was sitting on his royal throne in the hall,
facing the entrance. 2When he saw Queen
Esther standing in the court, he was pleased
with her and held out to her the gold scepter
that was in his hand. So Esther approached
and touched the tip of the scepter.

3Then the king asked, "What is it, Queen
Esther? What is your request? Even up to
half the kingdom, it will be given you."

4"If it pleases the king," replied Esther,
"let the king, together with Haman, come
today to a banquet I have prepared for
him."

5"Bring Haman at once," the king said, "so
that we may do what Esther asks."

So the king and Haman went to the banquet Esther had prepared. 6As they were
drinking wine, the king again asked Esther,
"Now what is your petition? It will be given
you. And what is your request? Even up to
half the kingdom, it will be granted."

7Esther replied, "My petition and my request is this: 8If the king regards me with
favor and if it pleases the king to grant my
petition and fulfill my request, let the king and
Haman come tomorrow to the banquet I will
prepare for them. Then I will answer the
king's question."

Haman's Rage Against Mordecai

9Haman went out that day happy and in
high spirits. But when he saw Mordecai at
the king's gate and observed that he neither
rose nor showed fear in his presence, he
was filled with rage against Mordecai.
10Nevertheless, Haman restrained himself
and went home.

Calling together his friends and Zeresh,
his wife, 11Haman boasted to them about his
vast wealth, his many sons, and all the ways
the king had honored him and how he had
elevated him above the other nobles and
officials. 12"And that's not all," Haman
added. "I'm the only person Queen Esther
invited to accompany the king to the banquet
she gave. And she has invited me along with
the king tomorrow. 13But all this gives me no
satisfaction as long as I see that Jew Mordecai sitting at the king's gate."

14His wife Zeresh and all his friends said to

him, "Have a gallows built, seventy-five feet[a]
high, and ask the king in the morning to have
Mordecai hanged on it. Then go with the king
to the dinner and be happy." This suggestion
delighted Haman, and he had the gallows
built.

Mordecai Honored

6 That night the king could not sleep; so he
ordered the book of the chronicles, the
record of his reign, to be brought in and read
to him. 2It was found recorded there that
Mordecai had exposed Bigthana and Teresh, two of the king's officers who guarded
the doorway, who had conspired to assassinate King Xerxes.
3"What honor and recognition has Mordecai received for this?" the king asked.
"Nothing has been done for him," his attendants answered.
4The king said, "Who is in the court?" Now
Haman had just entered the outer court of
the palace to speak to the king about hanging Mordecai on the gallows he had erected
for him.
5His attendants answered, "Haman is
standing in the court."
"Bring him in," the king ordered.
6When Haman entered, the king asked
him, "What should be done for the man the
king delights to honor?"
Now Haman thought to himself, "Who is
there that the king would rather honor than
me?" 7So he answered the king, "For the
man the king delights to honor, 8have them
bring a royal robe the king has worn and a
horse the king has ridden, one with a royal
crest placed on its head. 9Then let the robe
and horse be entrusted to one of the king's
most noble princes. Let them robe the man
the king delights to honor, and lead him on
the horse through the city streets, proclaiming before him, 'This is what is done for the
man the king delights to honor!' "
10"Go at once," the king commanded Haman. "Get the robe and the horse and do just
as you have suggested for Mordecai the
Jew, who sits at the king's gate. Do not neglect anything you have recommended."
11So Haman got the robe and the horse.
He robed Mordecai, and led him on
horseback through the city streets, proclaiming before him, "This is what is done for the
man the king delights to honor!"
12Afterward Mordecai returned to the
king's gate. But Haman rushed home, with
his head covered in grief, 13and told Zeresh
his wife and all his friends everything that
had happened to him.
His advisers and his wife Zeresh said to
him, "Since Mordecai, before whom your
downfall has started, is of Jewish origin, you
cannot stand against him—you will surely
come to ruin!" 14While they were still talking
with him, the king's eunuchs arrived and hurried Haman away to the banquet Esther had
prepared.

Haman Hanged

7 So the king and Haman went to dine with
Queen Esther, 2and as they were drinking wine on that second day, the king again
asked, "Queen Esther, what is your petition?
It will be given you. What is your request?
Even up to half the kingdom, it will be
granted."
3Then Queen Esther answered, "If I have
found favor with you, O king, and if it pleases
your majesty, grant me my life—this is my
petition. And spare my people—this is my
request. 4For I and my people have been
sold for destruction and slaughter and annihilation. If we had merely been sold as
male and female slaves, I would have kept
quiet, because no such distress would justify
disturbing the king.[b]"
5King Xerxes asked Queen Esther, "Who
is he? Where is the man who has dared to do
such a thing?"
6Esther said, "The adversary and enemy
is this vile Haman."
Then Haman was terrified before the king
and queen. 7The king got up in a rage, left his
wine and went out into the palace garden.
But Haman, realizing that the king had already decided his fate, stayed behind to beg
Queen Esther for his life.
8Just as the king returned from the palace
garden to the banquet hall, Haman was falling on the couch where Esther was reclining.
The king exclaimed, "Will he even molest
the queen while she is with me in the
house?"
As soon as the word left the king's mouth,
they covered Haman's face. 9Then Harbona,
one of the eunuchs attending the king, said,
"A gallows seventy-five feet[a] high stands by

[a] 14,9 Hebrew *fifty cubits* (about 23 meters) [b] 4 Or *quiet, but the compensation our adversary offers cannot be compared with the loss the king would suffer*

Haman's house. He had it made for Mordecai, who spoke up to help the king."
The king said, "Hang him on it!" 10So they
hanged Haman on the gallows he had prepared for Mordecai. Then the king's fury subsided.

The King's Edict in Behalf of the Jews

8 That same day King Xerxes gave Queen
Esther the estate of Haman, the enemy
of the Jews. And Mordecai came into the
presence of the king, for Esther had told how
he was related to her. 2The king took off his
signet ring, which he had reclaimed from Haman, and presented it to Mordecai. And Esther appointed him over Haman's estate.
3Esther again pleaded with the king, falling
at his feet and weeping. She begged him to
put an end to the evil plan of Haman the
Agagite, which he had devised against the
Jews. 4Then the king extended the gold
scepter to Esther and she arose and stood
before him.
5"If it pleases the king," she said, "and if he
regards me with favor and thinks it the right
thing to do, and if he is pleased with me, let
an order be written overruling the dispatches
that Haman son of Hammedatha, the Agagite, devised and wrote to destroy the Jews in
all the king's provinces. 6For how can I bear
to see disaster fall on my people? How can I
bear to see the destruction of my family?"
7King Xerxes replied to Queen Esther and
to Mordecai the Jew, "Because Haman attacked the Jews, I have given his estate to
Esther, and they have hanged him on the
gallows. 8Now write another decree in the
king's name in behalf of the Jews as seems
best to you, and seal it with the king's signet
ring—for no document written in the king's
name and sealed with his ring can be
revoked."
9At once the royal secretaries were summoned—on the twenty-third day of the third
month, the month of Sivan. They wrote out
all Mordecai's orders to the Jews, and to the
satraps, governors and nobles of the 127
provinces stretching from India to Cush.[a]
These orders were written in the script of
each province and the language of each
people and also to the Jews in their own
script and language. 10Mordecai wrote in the
name of King Xerxes, sealed the dispatches
with the king's signet ring, and sent them by
mounted couriers, who rode fast horses
especially bred for the king.
11The king's edict granted the Jews in
every city the right to assemble and protect
themselves; to destroy, kill and annihilate
any armed force of any nationality or province that might attack them and their women
and children; and to plunder the property of
their enemies. 12The day appointed for the
Jews to do this in all the provinces of King
Xerxes was the thirteenth day of the twelfth
month, the month of Adar. 13A copy of the
text of the edict was to be issued as law in
every province and made known to the
people of every nationality so that the Jews
would be ready on that day to avenge themselves on their enemies.
14The couriers, riding the royal horses,
raced out, spurred on by the king's command. And the edict was also issued in the
citadel of Susa.
15Mordecai left the king's presence wearing royal garments of blue and white, a large
crown of gold and a purple robe of fine linen.
And the city of Susa held a joyous celebration. 16For the Jews it was a time of happiness and joy, gladness and honor. 17In every
province and in every city, wherever the
edict of the king went, there was joy and
gladness among the Jews, with feasting and
celebrating. And many people of other nationalities became Jews because fear of the
Jews had seized them.

Triumph of the Jews

9 On the thirteenth day of the twelfth
month, the month of Adar, the edict commanded by the king was to be carried out. On
this day the enemies of the Jews had hoped
to overpower them, but now the tables were
turned and the Jews got the upper hand over
those who hated them. 2The Jews assembled in their cities in all the provinces of King
Xerxes to attack those seeking their destruction. No one could stand against them, because the people of all the other nationalities
were afraid of them. 3And all the nobles of
the provinces, the satraps, the governors
and the king's administrators helped the
Jews, because fear of Mordecai had seized
them. 4Mordecai was prominent in the palace; his reputation spread throughout the
provinces, and he became more and more
powerful.

[a]9 That is, the upper Nile region

5The Jews struck down all their enemies
with the sword, killing and destroying them,
and they did what they pleased to those who
hated them. 6In the citadel of Susa, the Jews
killed and destroyed five hundred men.
7They also killed Parshandatha, Dalphon,
Aspatha, 8Poratha, Adalia, Aridatha, 9Par-
mashta, Arisai, Aridai and Vaizatha, 10the
ten sons of Haman son of Hammedatha, the
enemy of the Jews. But they did not lay their
hands on the plunder.

11The number of those slain in the citadel
of Susa was reported to the king that same
day. 12The king said to Queen Esther, "The
Jews have killed and destroyed five hundred
men and the ten sons of Haman in the citadel
of Susa. What have they done in the rest of
the king's provinces? Now what is your petition? It will be given you. What is your request? It will also be granted."

13"If it pleases the king," Esther answered,
"give the Jews in Susa permission to carry
out this day's edict tomorrow also, and let
Haman's ten sons be hanged on gallows."

14So the king commanded that this be
done. An edict was issued in Susa, and they
hanged the ten sons of Haman. 15The Jews
in Susa came together on the fourteenth day
of the month of Adar, and they put to death in
Susa three hundred men, but they did not lay
their hands on the plunder.

16Meanwhile, the remainder of the Jews
who were in the king's provinces also assembled to protect themselves and get relief
from their enemies. They killed seventy-five
thousand of them but did not lay their hands
on the plunder. 17This happened on the thirteenth day of the month of Adar, and on the
fourteenth they rested and made it a day of
feasting and joy.

Purim Celebrated

18The Jews in Susa, however, had assembled on the thirteenth and fourteenth, and
then on the fifteenth they rested and made it
a day of feasting and joy.

19That is why rural Jews—those living in
villages—observe the fourteenth of the
month of Adar as a day of joy and feasting, a
day for giving presents to each other.

20Mordecai recorded these events, and he
sent letters to all the Jews throughout the
provinces of King Xerxes, near and far, 21to
have them celebrate annually the fourteenth
and fifteenth days of the month of Adar 22as
the time when the Jews got relief from their
enemies, and as the month when their sorrow was turned into joy and their mourning
into a day of celebration. He wrote them to
observe the days as days of feasting and joy
and giving presents of food to one another
and gifts to the poor.

23So the Jews agreed to continue the celebration they had begun, doing what Mordecai had written to them. 24For Haman son
of Hammedatha, the Agagite, the enemy of
all the Jews, had plotted against the Jews to
destroy them and had cast the *pur* (that is,
the lot) for their ruin and destruction. 25But
when the plot came to the king's attention,[a]
he issued written orders that the evil scheme
Haman had devised against the Jews should
come back onto his own head, and that he
and his sons should be hanged on the gallows. 26(Therefore these days were called
Purim, from the word *pur*.) Because of everything written in this letter and because of
what they had seen and what had happened
to them, 27the Jews took it upon themselves
to establish the custom that they and their
descendants and all who join them should
without fail observe these two days every
year, in the way prescribed and at the time
appointed. 28These days should be remembered and observed in every generation by
every family, and in every province and in
every city. And these days of Purim should
never cease to be celebrated by the Jews,
nor should the memory of them die out
among their descendants.

29So Queen Esther, daughter of Abihail,
along with Mordecai the Jew, wrote with full
authority to confirm this second letter concerning Purim. 30And Mordecai sent letters
to all the Jews in the 127 provinces of the
kingdom of Xerxes—words of goodwill and
assurance— 31to establish these days of
Purim at their designated times, as Mordecai
the Jew and Queen Esther had decreed for
them, and as they had established for themselves and their descendants in regard to
their times of fasting and lamentation. 32Es-
ther's decree confirmed these regulations
about Purim, and it was written down in the
records.

The Greatness of Mordecai

10 King Xerxes imposed tribute
throughout the empire, to its distant
shores. 2And all his acts of power and might,

[a]25 *Or when Esther came before the king*

together with a full account of the greatness of Mordecai to which the king had raised him, are they not written in the book of the annals of the kings of Media and Persia? 3Mordecai the Jew was second in rank to King Xerxes, preeminent among the Jews, and held in high esteem by his many fellow Jews, because he worked for the good of his people and spoke up for the welfare of all the Jews.

Job

Introduction:

The book of Job is named for its main character, a righteous man who was very rich. Even after losing everything he owned and suffering from a terrible sickness, Job still confessed his love for God.

The book questions the reasons for suffering, especially the suffering of people who love God and are good. Job's friends insisted he was suffering as punishment for his sin. Job defended himself by insisting that he had done nothing seriously wrong and then expressed his trust in God.

Then God spoke and showed his mighty power. Job finally admitted that God is too great and wonderful for us to understand.

Outline of contents:

Prologue

1 In the land of Uz there lived a man
whose name was Job. This man was
blameless and upright; he feared God and
shunned evil. 2He had seven sons and three
daughters, 3and he owned seven thousand
sheep, three thousand camels, five hundred
yoke of oxen and five hundred donkeys, and
had a large number of servants. He was the
greatest man among all the people of the
East.
4His sons used to take turns holding feasts
in their homes, and they would invite their
three sisters to eat and drink with them.
5When a period of feasting had run its
course, Job would send and have them purified. Early in the morning he would sacrifice
a burnt offering for each of them, thinking,
"Perhaps my children have sinned and
cursed God in their hearts." This was Job's
regular custom.

Job's First Test

6One day the angels[a] came to present
themselves before the LORD, and Satan[b] also
came with them. 7The LORD said to Satan,
"Where have you come from?"
Satan answered the LORD, "From roaming
through the earth and going back and forth in
it."
8Then the LORD said to Satan, "Have you
considered my servant Job? There is no one
on earth like him; he is blameless and upright, a man who fears God and shuns evil."
9"Does Job fear God for nothing?" Satan
replied. 10"Have you not put a hedge around
him and his household and everything he
has? You have blessed the work of his
hands, so that his flocks and herds are
spread throughout the land. 11But stretch out
your hand and strike everything he has, and
he will surely curse you to your face."
12The LORD said to Satan, "Very well, then,
everything he has is in your hands, but on the
man himself do not lay a finger."
Then Satan went out from the presence of
the LORD.
13One day when Job's sons and daughters
were feasting and drinking wine at the oldest
brother's house, 14a messenger came to Job

[a]6 Hebrew *the sons of God* [b]6 *Satan* means *accuser.*

and said, "The oxen were plowing and the
donkeys were grazing nearby, 15and the Sabeans attacked and carried them off. They
put the servants to the sword, and I am the
only one who has escaped to tell you!"
16While he was still speaking, another
messenger came and said, "The fire of God
fell from the sky and burned up the sheep
and the servants, and I am the only one who
has escaped to tell you!"
17While he was still speaking, another
messenger came and said, "The Chaldeans
formed three raiding parties and swept down
on your camels and carried them off. They
put the servants to the sword, and I am the
only one who has escaped to tell you!"
18While he was still speaking, yet another
messenger came and said, "Your sons and
daughters were feasting and drinking wine at
the oldest brother's house, 19when suddenly
a mighty wind swept in from the desert and
struck the four corners of the house. It collapsed on them and they are dead, and I am
the only one who has escaped to tell you!"
20At this, Job got up and tore his robe and
shaved his head. Then he fell to the ground
in worship 21and said:

"Naked I came from my mother's womb,
and naked I will depart.[a]
The LORD gave and the LORD has taken
away;
may the name of the LORD be praised."

22In all this, Job did not sin by charging
God with wrongdoing.

Job's Second Test

2 On another day the angels[b] came to
present themselves before the LORD, and
Satan also came with them to present himself before him. 2And the LORD said to Satan,
"Where have you come from?"
Satan answered the LORD, "From roaming
through the earth and going back and forth in
it."
3Then the LORD said to Satan, "Have you
considered my servant Job? There is no one
on earth like him; he is blameless and upright, a man who fears God and shuns evil.
And he still maintains his integrity, though
you incited me against him to ruin him without any reason."
4"Skin for skin!" Satan replied. "A man will
give all he has for his own life. 5But stretch
out your hand and strike his flesh and bones,
and he will surely curse you to your face."
6The LORD said to Satan, "Very well, then,
he is in your hands; but you must spare his
life."
7So Satan went out from the presence of
the LORD and afflicted Job with painful sores
from the soles of his feet to the top of his
head. 8Then Job took a piece of broken pottery and scraped himself with it as he sat
among the ashes.
9His wife said to him, "Are you still holding
on to your integrity? Curse God and die!"
10He replied, "You are talking like a foolish[c] woman. Shall we accept good from
God, and not trouble?"
In all this, Job did not sin in what he said.

Job's Three Friends

11When Job's three friends, Eliphaz the
Temanite, Bildad the Shuhite and Zophar the
Naamathite, heard about all the troubles that
had come upon him, they set out from their
homes and met together by agreement to go
and sympathize with him and comfort him.
12When they saw him from a distance, they
could hardly recognize him; they began to
weep aloud, and they tore their robes and
sprinkled dust on their heads. 13Then they
sat on the ground with him for seven days
and seven nights. No one said a word to him,
because they saw how great his suffering
was.

Job Speaks

3 After this, Job opened his mouth and
cursed the day of his birth. 2He said:

3"May the day of my birth perish,
and the night it was said, 'A boy is
born!'
4That day—may it turn to darkness;
may God above not care about it;
may no light shine upon it.
5May darkness and deep shadow[d] claim it
once more;
may a cloud settle over it;
may blackness overwhelm its light.
6That night—may thick darkness seize it;
may it not be included among the days
of the year
nor be entered in any of the months.
7May that night be barren;
may no shout of joy be heard in it.

[a]21 Or *will return there* [b]1 Hebrew *the sons of God* [c]10 The Hebrew word rendered *foolish* denotes
moral deficiency. [d]5 Or *and the shadow of death*

8May those who curse days[a] curse that day,
those who are ready to rouse Leviathan.
9May its morning stars become dark;
may it wait for daylight in vain
and not see the first rays of dawn,
10for it did not shut the doors of the womb on me
to hide trouble from my eyes.

11"Why did I not perish at birth,
and die as I came from the womb?
12Why were there knees to receive me
and breasts that I might be nursed?
13For now I would be lying down in peace;
I would be asleep and at rest
14with kings and counselors of the earth,
who built for themselves places now lying in ruins,
15with rulers who had gold,
who filled their houses with silver.
16Or why was I not hidden in the ground like a stillborn child,
like an infant who never saw the light of day?
17There the wicked cease from turmoil,
and there the weary are at rest.
18Captives also enjoy their ease;
they no longer hear the slave driver's shout.
19The small and the great are there,
and the slave is freed from his master.

20"Why is light given to those in misery,
and life to the bitter of soul,
21to those who long for death that does not come,
who search for it more than for hidden treasure,
22who are filled with gladness
and rejoice when they reach the grave?
23Why is life given to a man
whose way is hidden,
whom God has hedged in?
24For sighing comes to me instead of food;
my groans pour out like water.
25What I feared has come upon me;
what I dreaded has happened to me.
26I have no peace, no quietness;
I have no rest, but only turmoil."

Eliphaz

4 Then Eliphaz the Temanite replied:

2"If someone ventures a word with you,
will you be impatient?
But who can keep from speaking?
3Think how you have instructed many,
how you have strengthened feeble hands.
4Your words have supported those who stumbled;
you have strengthened faltering knees.
5But now trouble comes to you, and you are discouraged;
it strikes you, and you are dismayed.
6Should not your piety be your confidence
and your blameless ways your hope?

7"Consider now: Who, being innocent, has ever perished?
Where were the upright ever destroyed?
8As I have observed, those who plow evil
and those who sow trouble reap it.
9At the breath of God they are destroyed;
at the blast of his anger they perish.
10The lions may roar and growl,
yet the teeth of the great lions are broken.
11The lion perishes for lack of prey,
and the cubs of the lioness are scattered.

12"A word was secretly brought to me,
my ears caught a whisper of it.
13Amid disquieting dreams in the night,
when deep sleep falls on men,
14fear and trembling seized me
and made all my bones shake.
15A spirit glided past my face,
and the hair on my body stood on end.
16It stopped,
but I could not tell what it was.
A form stood before my eyes,
and I heard a hushed voice:
17'Can a mortal be more righteous than God?
Can a man be more pure than his Maker?
18If God places no trust in his servants,
if he charges his angels with error,
19how much more those who live in houses of clay,
whose foundations are in the dust,
who are crushed more readily than a moth!
20Between dawn and dusk they are broken to pieces;
unnoticed, they perish forever.
21Are not the cords of their tent pulled up,
so that they die without wisdom?'[b]

[a]8 Or *the sea* [b]21 Some interpreters end the quotation after verse 17.

5 "Call if you will, but who will answer
you?
To which of the holy ones will you turn?
2Resentment kills a fool,
and envy slays the simple.
3I myself have seen a fool taking root,
but suddenly his house was cursed.
4His children are far from safety,
crushed in court without a defender.
5The hungry consume his harvest,
taking it even from among thorns,
and the thirsty pant after his wealth.
6For hardship does not spring from the
soil,
nor does trouble sprout from the
ground.
7Yet man is born to trouble
as surely as sparks fly upward.

8"But if it were I, I would appeal to God;
I would lay my cause before him.
9He performs wonders that cannot be
fathomed,
miracles that cannot be counted.
10He bestows rain on the earth;
he sends water upon the countryside.
11The lowly he sets on high,
and those who mourn are lifted to
safety.
12He thwarts the plans of the crafty,
so that their hands achieve no success.
13He catches the wise in their craftiness,
and the schemes of the wily are swept
away.
14Darkness comes upon them in the
daytime;
at noon they grope as in the night.
15He saves the needy from the sword in
their mouth;
he saves them from the clutches of the
powerful.
16So the poor have hope,
and injustice shuts its mouth.

17"Blessed is the man whom God corrects;
so do not despise the discipline of the
Almighty.[a]
18For he wounds, but he also binds up;
he injures, but his hands also heal.
19From six calamities he will rescue you;
in seven no harm will befall you.
20In famine he will ransom you from death,
and in battle from the stroke of the
sword.
21You will be protected from the lash of the
tongue,
and need not fear when destruction
comes.
22You will laugh at destruction and famine,
and need not fear the beasts of the
earth.
23For you will have a covenant with the
stones of the field,
and the wild animals will be at peace
with you.
24You will know that your tent is secure;
you will take stock of your property and
find nothing missing.
25You will know that your children will be
many,
and your descendants like the grass of
the earth.
26You will come to the grave in full vigor,
like sheaves gathered in season.

27"We have examined this, and it is true.
So hear it and apply it to yourself."

Job

6 Then Job replied:

2"If only my anguish could be weighed
and all my misery be placed on the
scales!
3It would surely outweigh the sand of the
seas—
no wonder my words have been
impetuous.
4The arrows of the Almighty are in me,
my spirit drinks in their poison;
God's terrors are marshaled against
me.
5Does a wild donkey bray when it has
grass,
or an ox bellow when it has fodder?
6Is tasteless food eaten without salt,
or is there flavor in the white of an
egg[b]?
7I refuse to touch it;
such food makes me ill.

8"Oh, that I might have my request,
that God would grant what I hope for,
9that God would be willing to crush me,
to let loose his hand and cut me off!
10Then I would still have this consolation—
my joy in unrelenting pain—
that I had not denied the words of the
Holy One.

11"What strength do I have, that I should
still hope?

[a]17 Hebrew *Shaddai;* here and throughout Job

[b]6 The meaning of the Hebrew for this phrase is uncertain.

What prospects, that I should be patient?
12Do I have the strength of stone?
Is my flesh bronze?
13Do I have any power to help myself,
now that success has been driven from me?

14"A despairing man should have the devotion of his friends,
even though he forsakes the fear of the Almighty.
15But my brothers are as undependable as intermittent streams,
as the streams that overflow
16when darkened by thawing ice
and swollen with melting snow,
17but that cease to flow in the dry season,
and in the heat vanish from their channels.
18Caravans turn aside from their routes;
they go up into the wasteland and perish.
19The caravans of Tema look for water,
the traveling merchants of Sheba look in hope.
20They are distressed, because they had been confident;
they arrive there, only to be disappointed.
21Now you too have proved to be of no help;
you see something dreadful and are afraid.
22Have I ever said, 'Give something on my behalf,
pay a ransom for me from your wealth,
23deliver me from the hand of the enemy,
ransom me from the clutches of the ruthless'?

24"Teach me, and I will be quiet;
show me where I have been wrong.
25How painful are honest words!
But what do your arguments prove?
26Do you mean to correct what I say,
and treat the words of a despairing man as wind?
27You would even cast lots for the fatherless
and barter away your friend.

28"But now be so kind as to look at me.
Would I lie to your face?
29Relent, do not be unjust;
reconsider, for my integrity is at stake.[a]
30Is there any wickedness on my lips?
Can my mouth not discern malice?

7 "Does not man have hard service on earth?
Are not his days like those of a hired man?
2Like a slave longing for the evening shadows,
or a hired man waiting eagerly for his wages,
3so I have been allotted months of futility,
and nights of misery have been assigned to me.
4When I lie down I think, 'How long before I get up?'
The night drags on, and I toss till dawn.
5My body is clothed with worms and scabs,
my skin is broken and festering.

6"My days are swifter than a weaver's shuttle,
and they come to an end without hope.
7Remember, O God, that my life is but a breath;
my eyes will never see happiness again.
8The eye that now sees me will see me no longer;
you will look for me, but I will be no more.
9As a cloud vanishes and is gone,
so he who goes down to the grave[b]
does not return.
10He will never come to his house again;
his place will know him no more.

11"Therefore I will not keep silent;
I will speak out in the anguish of my spirit,
I will complain in the bitterness of my soul.
12Am I the sea, or the monster of the deep,
that you put me under guard?
13When I think my bed will comfort me
and my couch will ease my complaint,
14even then you frighten me with dreams
and terrify me with visions,
15so that I prefer strangling and death,
rather than this body of mine.
16I despise my life; I would not live forever.
Let me alone; my days have no meaning.

17"What is man that you make so much of him,
that you give him so much attention,

[a]29 Or *my righteousness still stands* [b]9 Hebrew *Sheol*

[18]that you examine him every morning
and test him every moment?
[19]Will you never look away from me,
or let me alone even for an instant?
[20]If I have sinned, what have I done to you,
O watcher of men?
Why have you made me your target?
Have I become a burden to you?[a]
[21]Why do you not pardon my offenses
and forgive my sins?
For I will soon lie down in the dust;
you will search for me, but I will be no
more."

Bildad

8 Then Bildad the Shuhite replied:

[2]"How long will you say such things?
Your words are a blustering wind.
[3]Does God pervert justice?
Does the Almighty pervert what is
right?
[4]When your children sinned against him,
he gave them over to the penalty of
their sin.
[5]But if you will look to God
and plead with the Almighty,
[6]if you are pure and upright,
even now he will rouse himself on your
behalf
and restore you to your rightful place.
[7]Your beginnings will seem humble,
so prosperous will your future be.

[8]"Ask the former generations
and find out what their fathers learned,
[9]for we were born only yesterday and
know nothing,
and our days on earth are but a
shadow.
[10]Will they not instruct you and tell you?
Will they not bring forth words from
their understanding?
[11]Can papyrus grow tall where there is no
marsh?
Can reeds thrive without water?
[12]While still growing and uncut,
they wither more quickly than grass.
[13]Such is the destiny of all who forget God;
so perishes the hope of the godless.
[14]What he trusts in is fragile[b];
what he relies on is a spider's web.
[15]He leans on his web, but it gives way;
he clings to it, but it does not hold.
[16]He is like a well-watered plant in the
sunshine,
spreading its shoots over the garden;
[17]it entwines its roots around a pile of rocks
and looks for a place among the
stones.
[18]But when it is torn from its spot,
that place disowns it and says, 'I never
saw you.'
[19]Surely its life withers away,
and[c] from the soil other plants grow.

[20]"Surely God does not reject a blameless
man
or strengthen the hands of evildoers.
[21]He will yet fill your mouth with laughter
and your lips with shouts of joy.
[22]Your enemies will be clothed in shame,
and the tents of the wicked will be no
more."

Job

9 Then Job replied:

[2]"Indeed, I know that this is true.
But how can a mortal be righteous
before God?
[3]Though one wished to dispute with him,
he could not answer him one time out
of a thousand.
[4]His wisdom is profound, his power is
vast.
Who has resisted him and come out
unscathed?
[5]He moves mountains without their
knowing it
and overturns them in his anger.
[6]He shakes the earth from its place
and makes its pillars tremble.
[7]He speaks to the sun and it does not
shine;
he seals off the light of the stars.
[8]He alone stretches out the heavens
and treads on the waves of the sea.
[9]He is the Maker of the Bear and Orion,
the Pleiades and the constellations of
the south.
[10]He performs wonders that cannot be
fathomed,
miracles that cannot be counted.
[11]When he passes me, I cannot see him;
when he goes by, I cannot perceive
him.
[12]If he snatches away, who can stop him?

[a]20 A few manuscripts of the Masoretic Text, an ancient Hebrew scribal tradition and Septuagint; most manuscripts of the Masoretic Text *I have become a burden to myself.* [b]14 The meaning of the Hebrew for this word is uncertain. [c]19 Or *Surely all the joy it has / is that*

Who can say to him, 'What are you
doing?'
13God does not restrain his anger;
even the cohorts of Rahab cowered at
his feet.

14"How then can I dispute with him?
How can I find words to argue with
him?
15Though I were innocent, I could not
answer him;
I could only plead with my Judge for
mercy.
16Even if I summoned him and he
responded,
I do not believe he would give me a
hearing.
17He would crush me with a storm
and multiply my wounds for no reason.
18He would not let me regain my breath
but would overwhelm me with misery.
19If it is a matter of strength, he is mighty!
And if it is a matter of justice, who will
summon him[a]?
20Even if I were innocent, my mouth would
condemn me;
if I were blameless, it would pronounce
me guilty.

21"Although I am blameless,
I have no concern for myself;
I despise my own life.
22It is all the same; that is why I say,
'He destroys both the blameless and
the wicked.'
23When a scourge brings sudden death,
he mocks the despair of the innocent.
24When a land falls into the hands of the
wicked,
he blindfolds its judges.
If it is not he, then who is it?

25"My days are swifter than a runner;
they fly away without a glimpse of joy.
26They skim past like boats of papyrus,
like eagles swooping down on their
prey.
27If I say, 'I will forget my complaint,
I will change my expression, and smile,'
28I still dread all my sufferings,
for I know you will not hold me
innocent.
29Since I am already found guilty,
why should I struggle in vain?
30Even if I washed myself with soap[b]
and my hands with washing soda,
31you would plunge me into a slime pit
so that even my clothes would detest
me.

32"He is not a man like me that I might
answer him,
that we might confront each other in
court.
33If only there were someone to arbitrate
between us,
to lay his hand upon us both,
34someone to remove God's rod from me,
so that his terror would frighten me no
more.
35Then I would speak up without fear of
him,
but as it now stands with me, I cannot.

10 "I loathe my very life;
therefore I will give free rein to my
complaint
and speak out in the bitterness of my
soul.
2I will say to God: Do not condemn me,
but tell me what charges you have
against me.
3Does it please you to oppress me,
to spurn the work of your hands,
while you smile on the schemes of the
wicked?
4Do you have eyes of flesh?
Do you see as a mortal sees?
5Are your days like those of a mortal
or your years like those of a man,
6that you must search out my faults
and probe after my sin—
7though you know that I am not guilty
and that no one can rescue me from
your hand?

8"Your hands shaped me and made me.
Will you now turn and destroy me?
9Remember that you molded me like clay.
Will you now turn me to dust again?
10Did you not pour me out like milk
and curdle me like cheese,
11clothe me with skin and flesh
and knit me together with bones and
sinews?
12You gave me life and showed me
kindness,
and in your providence watched over
my spirit.

13"But this is what you concealed in your
heart,
and I know that this was in your mind:
14If I sinned, you would be watching me

[a]19 See Septuagint; Hebrew *me.* [b]30 Or *snow*

and would not let my offense go
unpunished.
15If I am guilty—woe to me!
Even if I am innocent, I cannot lift my
head,
for I am full of shame
and drowned in[a] my affliction.
16If I hold my head high, you stalk me like a
lion
and again display your awesome power
against me.
17You bring new witnesses against me
and increase your anger toward me;
your forces come against me wave
upon wave.

18"Why then did you bring me out of the
womb?
I wish I had died before any eye saw
me.
19If only I had never come into being,
or had been carried straight from the
womb to the grave!
20Are not my few days almost over?
Turn away from me so I can have a
moment's joy
21before I go to the place of no return,
to the land of gloom and deep
shadow,[b]
22to the land of deepest night,
of deep shadow and disorder,
where even the light is like darkness."

Zophar

11 Then Zophar the Naamathite replied:
2"Are all these words to go
unanswered?
Is this talker to be vindicated?
3Will your idle talk reduce men to silence?
Will no one rebuke you when you
mock?
4You say to God, 'My beliefs are flawless
and I am pure in your sight.'
5Oh, how I wish that God would speak,
that he would open his lips against you
6and disclose to you the secrets of
wisdom,
for true wisdom has two sides.
Know this: God has even forgotten
some of your sin.

7"Can you fathom the mysteries of God?
Can you probe the limits of the
Almighty?
8They are higher than the heavens—what
can you do?
They are deeper than the depths of the
grave[c]—what can you know?
9Their measure is longer than the earth
and wider than the sea.

10"If he comes along and confines you in
prison
and convenes a court, who can oppose
him?
11Surely he recognizes deceitful men;
and when he sees evil, does he not
take note?
12But a witless man can no more become
wise
than a wild donkey's colt can be born a
man.[d]

13"Yet if you devote your heart to him
and stretch out your hands to him,
14if you put away the sin that is in your
hand
and allow no evil to dwell in your tent,
15then you will lift up your face without
shame;
you will stand firm and without fear.
16You will surely forget your trouble,
recalling it only as waters gone by.
17Life will be brighter than noonday,
and darkness will become like morning.
18You will be secure, because there is
hope;
you will look about you and take your
rest in safety.
19You will lie down, with no one to make
you afraid,
and many will court your favor.
20But the eyes of the wicked will fail,
and escape will elude them;
their hope will become a dying gasp."

Job

12 Then Job replied:
2"Doubtless you are the people,
and wisdom will die with you!
3But I have a mind as well as you;
I am not inferior to you.
Who does not know all these things?

4"I have become a laughingstock to my
friends,
though I called upon God and he
answered—

[a]15 *Or and aware of* [b]21 *Or and the shadow of death*; also in verse 22 [c]8 Hebrew *than Sheol*
[d]12 *Or wild donkey can be born tame*

a mere laughingstock, though righteous
and blameless!
5Men at ease have contempt for
misfortune
as the fate of those whose feet are
slipping.
6The tents of marauders are undisturbed,
and those who provoke God are
secure—
those who carry their god in their
hands.[a]

7"But ask the animals, and they will teach
you,
or the birds of the air, and they will tell
you;
8or speak to the earth, and it will teach
you,
or let the fish of the sea inform you.
9Which of all these does not know
that the hand of the LORD has done
this?
10In his hand is the life of every creature
and the breath of all mankind.
11Does not the ear test words
as the tongue tastes food?
12Is not wisdom found among the aged?
Does not long life bring understanding?

13"To God belong wisdom and power;
counsel and understanding are his.
14What he tears down cannot be rebuilt;
the man he imprisons cannot be
released.
15If he holds back the waters, there is
drought;
if he lets them loose, they devastate
the land.
16To him belong strength and victory;
both deceived and deceiver are his.
17He leads counselors away stripped
and makes fools of judges.
18He takes off the shackles put on by kings
and ties a loincloth[b] around their waist.
19He leads priests away stripped
and overthrows men long established.
20He silences the lips of trusted advisers
and takes away the discernment of
elders.
21He pours contempt on nobles
and disarms the mighty.
22He reveals the deep things of darkness
and brings deep shadows into the light.
23He makes nations great, and destroys
them;
he enlarges nations, and disperses
them.
24He deprives the leaders of the earth of
their reason;
he sends them wandering through a
trackless waste.
25They grope in darkness with no light;
he makes them stagger like drunkards.

13 "My eyes have seen all this,
my ears have heard and
understood it.
2What you know, I also know;
I am not inferior to you.
3But I desire to speak to the Almighty
and to argue my case with God.
4You, however, smear me with lies;
you are worthless physicians, all of
you!
5If only you would be altogether silent!
For you, that would be wisdom.
6Hear now my argument;
listen to the plea of my lips.
7Will you speak wickedly on God's behalf?
Will you speak deceitfully for him?
8Will you show him partiality?
Will you argue the case for God?
9Would it turn out well if he examined
you?
Could you deceive him as you might
deceive men?
10He would surely rebuke you
if you secretly showed partiality.
11Would not his splendor terrify you?
Would not the dread of him fall on you?
12Your maxims are proverbs of ashes;
your defenses are defenses of clay.

13"Keep silent and let me speak;
then let come to me what may.
14Why do I put myself in jeopardy
and take my life in my hands?
15Though he slay me, yet will I hope in him;
I will surely[c] defend my ways to his
face.
16Indeed, this will turn out for my
deliverance,
for no godless man would dare come
before him!
17Listen carefully to my words;
let your ears take in what I say.
18Now that I have prepared my case,
I know I will be vindicated.
19Can anyone bring charges against me?
If so, I will be silent and die.

[a]6 Or *secure / in what God's hand brings them*
[b]18 Or *shackles of kings / and ties a belt*
[c]15 Or *He will surely slay me; I have no hope — / yet I will*

20 "Only grant me these two things, O God,
and then I will not hide from you:
21 Withdraw your hand far from me,
and stop frightening me with your terrors.
22 Then summon me and I will answer,
or let me speak, and you reply.
23 How many wrongs and sins have I committed?
Show me my offense and my sin.
24 Why do you hide your face
and consider me your enemy?
25 Will you torment a windblown leaf?
Will you chase after dry chaff?
26 For you write down bitter things against me
and make me inherit the sins of my youth.
27 You fasten my feet in shackles;
you keep close watch on all my paths
by putting marks on the soles of my feet.

28 "So man wastes away like something rotten,
like a garment eaten by moths.

14 "Man born of woman
is of few days and full of trouble.
2 He springs up like a flower and withers away;
like a fleeting shadow, he does not endure.
3 Do you fix your eye on such a one?
Will you bring him[a] before you for judgment?
4 Who can bring what is pure from the impure?
No one!
5 Man's days are determined;
you have decreed the number of his months
and have set limits he cannot exceed.
6 So look away from him and let him alone,
till he has put in his time like a hired man.

7 "At least there is hope for a tree:
If it is cut down, it will sprout again,
and its new shoots will not fail.
8 Its roots may grow old in the ground
and its stump die in the soil,
9 yet at the scent of water it will bud
and put forth shoots like a plant.
10 But man dies and is laid low;
he breathes his last and is no more.
11 As water disappears from the sea
or a riverbed becomes parched and dry,
12 so man lies down and does not rise;
till the heavens are no more, men will not awake
or be roused from their sleep.

13 "If only you would hide me in the grave[b]
and conceal me till your anger has passed!
If only you would set me a time
and then remember me!
14 If a man dies, will he live again?
All the days of my hard service
I will wait for my renewal[c] to come.
15 You will call and I will answer you;
you will long for the creature your hands have made.
16 Surely then you will count my steps
but not keep track of my sin.
17 My offenses will be sealed up in a bag;
you will cover over my sin.

18 "But as a mountain erodes and crumbles
and as a rock is moved from its place,
19 as water wears away stones
and torrents wash away the soil,
so you destroy man's hope.
20 You overpower him once for all, and he is gone;
you change his countenance and send him away.
21 If his sons are honored, he does not know it;
if they are brought low, he does not see it.
22 He feels but the pain of his own body
and mourns only for himself."

Eliphaz

15 Then Eliphaz the Temanite replied:
2 "Would a wise man answer with empty notions
or fill his belly with the hot east wind?
3 Would he argue with useless words,
with speeches that have no value?
4 But you even undermine piety
and hinder devotion to God.
5 Your sin prompts your mouth;
you adopt the tongue of the crafty.
6 Your own mouth condemns you, not mine;
your own lips testify against you.

7 "Are you the first man ever born?
Were you brought forth before the hills?

[a] 3 Septuagint, Vulgate and Syriac; Hebrew *me* [b] 13 Hebrew *Sheol* [c] 14 Or *release*

8Do you listen in on God's council?
Do you limit wisdom to yourself?
9What do you know that we do not know?
What insights do you have that we do not have?
10The gray-haired and the aged are on our side,
men even older than your father.
11Are God's consolations not enough for you,
words spoken gently to you?
12Why has your heart carried you away,
and why do your eyes flash,
13so that you vent your rage against God
and pour out such words from your mouth?

14"What is man, that he could be pure,
or one born of woman, that he could be righteous?
15If God places no trust in his holy ones,
if even the heavens are not pure in his eyes,
16how much less man, who is vile and corrupt,
who drinks up evil like water!

17"Listen to me and I will explain to you;
let me tell you what I have seen,
18what wise men have declared,
hiding nothing received from their fathers
19(to whom alone the land was given
when no alien passed among them):
20All his days the wicked man suffers torment,
the ruthless through all the years stored up for him.
21Terrifying sounds fill his ears;
when all seems well, marauders attack him.
22He despairs of escaping the darkness;
he is marked for the sword.
23He wanders about—food for vultures[a];
he knows the day of darkness is at hand.
24Distress and anguish fill him with terror;
they overwhelm him, like a king poised to attack,
25because he shakes his fist at God
and vaunts himself against the Almighty,
26defiantly charging against him
with a thick, strong shield.

27"Though his face is covered with fat
and his waist bulges with flesh,
28he will inhabit ruined towns
and houses where no one lives,
houses crumbling to rubble.
29He will no longer be rich and his wealth will not endure,
nor will his possessions spread over the land.
30He will not escape the darkness;
a flame will wither his shoots,
and the breath of God's mouth will carry him away.
31Let him not deceive himself by trusting what is worthless,
for he will get nothing in return.
32Before his time he will be paid in full,
and his branches will not flourish.
33He will be like a vine stripped of its unripe grapes,
like an olive tree shedding its blossoms.
34For the company of the godless will be barren,
and fire will consume the tents of those who love bribes.
35They conceive trouble and give birth to evil;
their womb fashions deceit."

Job

16 Then Job replied:
2"I have heard many things like these;
miserable comforters are you all!
3Will your long-winded speeches never end?
What ails you that you keep on arguing?
4I also could speak like you,
if you were in my place;
I could make fine speeches against you
and shake my head at you.
5But my mouth would encourage you;
comfort from my lips would bring you relief.

6"Yet if I speak, my pain is not relieved;
and if I refrain, it does not go away.
7Surely, O God, you have worn me out;
you have devastated my entire household.
8You have bound me—and it has become a witness;
my gauntness rises up and testifies against me.
9God assails me and tears me in his anger

[a]23 Or *about, looking for food*

and gnashes his teeth at me;
my opponent fastens on me his piercing eyes.
10 Men open their mouths to jeer at me;
they strike my cheek in scorn
and unite together against me.
11 God has turned me over to evil men
and thrown me into the clutches of the wicked.
12 All was well with me, but he shattered me;
he seized me by the neck and crushed me.
He has made me his target;
13 his archers surround me.
Without pity, he pierces my kidneys
and spills my gall on the ground.
14 Again and again he bursts upon me;
he rushes at me like a warrior.

15 "I have sewed sackcloth over my skin
and buried my brow in the dust.
16 My face is red with weeping,
deep shadows ring my eyes;
17 yet my hands have been free of violence
and my prayer is pure.

18 "O earth, do not cover my blood;
may my cry never be laid to rest!
19 Even now my witness is in heaven;
my advocate is on high.
20 My intercessor is my friend[a]
as my eyes pour out tears to God;
21 on behalf of a man he pleads with God
as a man pleads for his friend.

22 "Only a few years will pass
before I go on the journey of no return.

17 1 My spirit is broken,
my days are cut short,
the grave awaits me.
2 Surely mockers surround me;
my eyes must dwell on their hostility.

3 "Give me, O God, the pledge you demand.
Who else will put up security for me?
4 You have closed their minds to understanding;
therefore you will not let them triumph.
5 If a man denounces his friends for reward,
the eyes of his children will fail.

6 "God has made me a byword to everyone,
a man in whose face people spit.
7 My eyes have grown dim with grief;
my whole frame is but a shadow.
8 Upright men are appalled at this;
the innocent are aroused against the ungodly.
9 Nevertheless, the righteous will hold to their ways,
and those with clean hands will grow stronger.

10 "But come on, all of you, try again!
I will not find a wise man among you.
11 My days have passed, my plans are shattered,
and so are the desires of my heart.
12 These men turn night into day;
in the face of darkness they say, 'Light is near.'
13 If the only home I hope for is the grave,[b]
if I spread out my bed in darkness,
14 if I say to corruption, 'You are my father,'
and to the worm, 'My mother' or 'My sister,'
15 where then is my hope?
Who can see any hope for me?
16 Will it go down to the gates of death[b]?
Will we descend together into the dust?"

Bildad

18 Then Bildad the Shuhite replied:
2 "When will you end these speeches?
Be sensible, and then we can talk.
3 Why are we regarded as cattle
and considered stupid in your sight?
4 You who tear yourself to pieces in your anger,
is the earth to be abandoned for your sake?
Or must the rocks be moved from their place?

5 "The lamp of the wicked is snuffed out;
the flame of his fire stops burning.
6 The light in his tent becomes dark;
the lamp beside him goes out.
7 The vigor of his step is weakened;
his own schemes throw him down.
8 His feet thrust him into a net
and he wanders into its mesh.
9 A trap seizes him by the heel;
a snare holds him fast.
10 A noose is hidden for him on the ground;
a trap lies in his path.
11 Terrors startle him on every side
and dog his every step.

[a] *20* Or *My friends treat me with scorn* [b] *13,16* Hebrew *Sheol*

12Calamity is hungry for him;
disaster is ready for him when he falls.
13It eats away parts of his skin;
death's firstborn devours his limbs.
14He is torn from the security of his tent
and marched off to the king of terrors.
15Fire resides[a] in his tent;
burning sulfur is scattered over his dwelling.
16His roots dry up below
and his branches wither above.
17The memory of him perishes from the earth;
he has no name in the land.
18He is driven from light into darkness
and is banished from the world.
19He has no offspring or descendants among his people,
no survivor where once he lived.
20Men of the west are appalled at his fate;
men of the east are seized with horror.
21Surely such is the dwelling of an evil man;
such is the place of one who knows not God."

Job

19 Then Job replied:

2"How long will you torment me
and crush me with words?
3Ten times now you have reproached me;
shamelessly you attack me.
4If it is true that I have gone astray,
my error remains my concern alone.
5If indeed you would exalt yourselves above me
and use my humiliation against me,
6then know that God has wronged me
and drawn his net around me.

7"Though I cry, 'I've been wronged!' I get no response;
though I call for help, there is no justice.
8He has blocked my way so I cannot pass;
he has shrouded my paths in darkness.
9He has stripped me of my honor
and removed the crown from my head.
10He tears me down on every side till I am gone;
he uproots my hope like a tree.
11His anger burns against me;
he counts me among his enemies.
12His troops advance in force;
they build a siege ramp against me
and encamp around my tent.

13"He has alienated my brothers from me;
my acquaintances are completely estranged from me.
14My kinsmen have gone away;
my friends have forgotten me.
15My guests and my maidservants count me a stranger;
they look upon me as an alien.
16I summon my servant, but he does not answer,
though I beg him with my own mouth.
17My breath is offensive to my wife;
I am loathsome to my own brothers.
18Even the little boys scorn me;
when I appear, they ridicule me.
19All my intimate friends detest me;
those I love have turned against me.
20I am nothing but skin and bones;
I have escaped with only the skin of my teeth.[b]

21"Have pity on me, my friends, have pity,
for the hand of God has struck me.
22Why do you pursue me as God does?
Will you never get enough of my flesh?

23"Oh, that my words were recorded,
that they were written on a scroll,
24that they were inscribed with an iron tool on[c] lead,
or engraved in rock forever!
25I know that my Redeemer[d] lives,
and that in the end he will stand upon the earth.[e]
26And after my skin has been destroyed,
yet[f] in[g] my flesh I will see God;
27I myself will see him
with my own eyes—I, and not another.
How my heart yearns within me!

28"If you say, 'How we will hound him,
since the root of the trouble lies in him,[h]'
29you should fear the sword yourselves;
for wrath will bring punishment by the sword,
and then you will know that there is judgment.[i]"

[a]15 Or *Nothing he had remains* [b]20 Or *only my gums* [c]24 Or *and* [d]25 Or *defender* [e]25 Or *upon my grave* [f]26 Or *And after I awake, / though this* ⌊*body*⌋ *has been destroyed, / then* [g]26 Or */ apart from* [h]28 Many Hebrew manuscripts, Septuagint and Vulgate; most Hebrew manuscripts *me* [i]29 Or */ that you may come to know the Almighty*

Zophar

20 Then Zophar the Naamathite replied:
2"My troubled thoughts prompt me to answer
because I am greatly disturbed.
3I hear a rebuke that dishonors me,
and my understanding inspires me to reply.

4"Surely you know how it has been from of old,
ever since man[a] was placed on the earth,
5that the mirth of the wicked is brief,
the joy of the godless lasts but a moment.
6Though his pride reaches to the heavens
and his head touches the clouds,
7he will perish forever, like his own dung;
those who have seen him will say, 'Where is he?'
8Like a dream he flies away, no more to be found,
banished like a vision of the night.
9The eye that saw him will not see him again;
his place will look on him no more.
10His children must make amends to the poor;
his own hands must give back his wealth.
11The youthful vigor that fills his bones
will lie with him in the dust.

12"Though evil is sweet in his mouth
and he hides it under his tongue,
13though he cannot bear to let it go
and keeps it in his mouth,
14yet his food will turn sour in his stomach;
it will become the venom of serpents within him.
15He will spit out the riches he swallowed;
God will make his stomach vomit them up.
16He will suck the poison of serpents;
the fangs of an adder will kill him.
17He will not enjoy the streams,
the rivers flowing with honey and cream.
18What he toiled for he must give back uneaten;
he will not enjoy the profit from his trading.
19For he has oppressed the poor and left them destitute;
he has seized houses he did not build.

20"Surely he will have no respite from his craving;
he cannot save himself by his treasure.
21Nothing is left for him to devour;
his prosperity will not endure.
22In the midst of his plenty, distress will overtake him;
the full force of misery will come upon him.
23When he has filled his belly,
God will vent his burning anger against him
and rain down his blows upon him.
24Though he flees from an iron weapon,
a bronze-tipped arrow pierces him.
25He pulls it out of his back,
the gleaming point out of his liver.
Terrors will come over him;
26 total darkness lies in wait for his treasures.
A fire unfanned will consume him
and devour what is left in his tent.
27The heavens will expose his guilt;
the earth will rise up against him.
28A flood will carry off his house,
rushing waters[b] on the day of God's wrath.
29Such is the fate God allots the wicked,
the heritage appointed for them by God."

Job

21 Then Job replied:
2"Listen carefully to my words;
let this be the consolation you give me.
3Bear with me while I speak,
and after I have spoken, mock on.

4"Is my complaint directed to man?
Why should I not be impatient?
5Look at me and be astonished;
clap your hand over your mouth.
6When I think about this, I am terrified;
trembling seizes my body.
7Why do the wicked live on,
growing old and increasing in power?
8They see their children established around them,
their offspring before their eyes.
9Their homes are safe and free from fear;
the rod of God is not upon them.
10Their bulls never fail to breed;
their cows calve and do not miscarry.

[a]4 Or *Adam* [b]28 Or *The possessions in his house will be carried off, / washed away*

11They send forth their children as a flock;
their little ones dance about.
12They sing to the music of tambourine and harp;
they make merry to the sound of the flute.
13They spend their years in prosperity
and go down to the grave[a] in peace.[b]
14Yet they say to God, 'Leave us alone!
We have no desire to know your ways.
15Who is the Almighty, that we should serve him?
What would we gain by praying to him?'
16But their prosperity is not in their own hands,
so I stand aloof from the counsel of the wicked.

17"Yet how often is the lamp of the wicked snuffed out?
How often does calamity come upon them,
the fate God allots in his anger?
18How often are they like straw before the wind,
like chaff swept away by a gale?
19It is said, 'God stores up a man's punishment for his sons.'
Let him repay the man himself, so that he will know it!
20Let his own eyes see his destruction;
let him drink of the wrath of the Almighty.[c]
21For what does he care about the family he leaves behind
when his allotted months come to an end?

22"Can anyone teach knowledge to God,
since he judges even the highest?
23One man dies in full vigor,
completely secure and at ease,
24his body[d] well nourished,
his bones rich with marrow.
25Another man dies in bitterness of soul,
never having enjoyed anything good.
26Side by side they lie in the dust,
and worms cover them both.

27"I know full well what you are thinking,
the schemes by which you would wrong me.
28You say, 'Where now is the great man's house,
the tents where wicked men lived?'
29Have you never questioned those who travel?
Have you paid no regard to their accounts—
30that the evil man is spared from the day of calamity,
that he is delivered from[e] the day of wrath?
31Who denounces his conduct to his face?
Who repays him for what he has done?
32He is carried to the grave,
and watch is kept over his tomb.
33The soil in the valley is sweet to him;
all men follow after him,
and a countless throng goes[f] before him.

34"So how can you console me with your nonsense?
Nothing is left of your answers but falsehood!"

Eliphaz

22 Then Eliphaz the Temanite replied:
2"Can a man be of benefit to God?
Can even a wise man benefit him?
3What pleasure would it give the Almighty if you were righteous?
What would he gain if your ways were blameless?

4"Is it for your piety that he rebukes you
and brings charges against you?
5Is not your wickedness great?
Are not your sins endless?
6You demanded security from your brothers for no reason;
you stripped men of their clothing, leaving them naked.
7You gave no water to the weary
and you withheld food from the hungry,
8though you were a powerful man, owning land—
an honored man, living on it.
9And you sent widows away empty-handed
and broke the strength of the fatherless.
10That is why snares are all around you,
why sudden peril terrifies you,
11why it is so dark you cannot see,
and why a flood of water covers you.

[a]13 Hebrew *Sheol* [b]13 Or *in an instant* [c]17-20 Verses 17 and 18 may be taken as exclamations and 19 and 20 as declarations. [d]24 The meaning of the Hebrew for this word is uncertain. [e]30 Or *man is reserved for the day of calamity, / that he is brought forth to* [f]33 Or / *as a countless throng went*

12"Is not God in the heights of heaven?
And see how lofty are the highest stars!
13Yet you say, 'What does God know?
Does he judge through such darkness?
14Thick clouds veil him, so he does not see us
as he goes about in the vaulted heavens.'
15Will you keep to the old path
that evil men have trod?
16They were carried off before their time,
their foundations washed away by a flood.
17They said to God, 'Leave us alone!
What can the Almighty do to us?'
18Yet it was he who filled their houses with good things,
so I stand aloof from the counsel of the wicked.

19"The righteous see their ruin and rejoice;
the innocent mock them, saying,
20'Surely our foes are destroyed,
and fire devours their wealth.'

21"Submit to God and be at peace with him;
in this way prosperity will come to you.
22Accept instruction from his mouth
and lay up his words in your heart.
23If you return to the Almighty, you will be restored:
If you remove wickedness far from your tent
24and assign your nuggets to the dust,
your gold of Ophir to the rocks in the ravines,
25then the Almighty will be your gold,
the choicest silver for you.
26Surely then you will find delight in the Almighty
and will lift up your face to God.
27You will pray to him, and he will hear you,
and you will fulfill your vows.
28What you decide on will be done,
and light will shine on your ways.
29When men are brought low and you say,
'Lift them up!'
then he will save the downcast.
30He will deliver even one who is not innocent,
who will be delivered through the cleanness of your hands."

Job

23 Then Job replied:

2"Even today my complaint is bitter;
his hand[a] is heavy in spite of[b] my groaning.
3If only I knew where to find him;
if only I could go to his dwelling!
4I would state my case before him
and fill my mouth with arguments.
5I would find out what he would answer me,
and consider what he would say.
6Would he oppose me with great power?
No, he would not press charges against me.
7There an upright man could present his case before him,
and I would be delivered forever from my judge.

8"But if I go to the east, he is not there;
if I go to the west, I do not find him.
9When he is at work in the north, I do not see him;
when he turns to the south, I catch no glimpse of him.
10But he knows the way that I take;
when he has tested me, I will come forth as gold.
11My feet have closely followed his steps;
I have kept to his way without turning aside.
12I have not departed from the commands of his lips;
I have treasured the words of his mouth more than my daily bread.

13"But he stands alone, and who can oppose him?
He does whatever he pleases.
14He carries out his decree against me,
and many such plans he still has in store.
15That is why I am terrified before him;
when I think of all this, I fear him.
16God has made my heart faint;
the Almighty has terrified me.
17Yet I am not silenced by the darkness,
by the thick darkness that covers my face.

[a]2 Septuagint and Syriac; Hebrew / *the hand on me* [b]2 Or *heavy on me in*

24 "Why does the Almighty not set
times for judgment?
Why must those who know him look in
vain for such days?
2 Men move boundary stones;
they pasture flocks they have stolen.
3 They drive away the orphan's donkey
and take the widow's ox in pledge.
4 They thrust the needy from the path
and force all the poor of the land into
hiding.
5 Like wild donkeys in the desert,
the poor go about their labor of foraging
food;
the wasteland provides food for their
children.
6 They gather fodder in the fields
and glean in the vineyards of the
wicked.
7 Lacking clothes, they spend the night
naked;
they have nothing to cover themselves
in the cold.
8 They are drenched by mountain rains
and hug the rocks for lack of shelter.
9 The fatherless child is snatched from the
breast;
the infant of the poor is seized for a
debt.
10 Lacking clothes, they go about naked;
they carry the sheaves, but still go
hungry.
11 They crush olives among the terraces[a];
they tread the winepresses, yet suffer
thirst.
12 The groans of the dying rise from the city,
and the souls of the wounded cry out
for help.
But God charges no one with
wrongdoing.

13 "There are those who rebel against the
light,
who do not know its ways
or stay in its paths.
14 When daylight is gone, the murderer
rises up
and kills the poor and needy;
in the night he steals forth like a thief.
15 The eye of the adulterer watches for
dusk;
he thinks, 'No eye will see me,'
and he keeps his face concealed.
16 In the dark, men break into houses,
but by day they shut themselves in;
they want nothing to do with the light.
17 For all of them, deep darkness is their
morning[b];
they make friends with the terrors of
darkness.[c]

18 "Yet they are foam on the surface of the
water;
their portion of the land is cursed,
so that no one goes to the vineyards.
19 As heat and drought snatch away the
melted snow,
so the grave[d] snatches away those
who have sinned.
20 The womb forgets them,
the worm feasts on them;
evil men are no longer remembered
but are broken like a tree.
21 They prey on the barren and childless
woman,
and to the widow show no kindness.
22 But God drags away the mighty by his
power;
though they become established, they
have no assurance of life.
23 He may let them rest in a feeling of
security,
but his eyes are on their ways.
24 For a little while they are exalted, and
then they are gone;
they are brought low and gathered up
like all others;
they are cut off like heads of grain.

25 "If this is not so, who can prove me false
and reduce my words to nothing?"

Bildad

25 Then Bildad the Shuhite replied:

2 "Dominion and awe belong to God;
he establishes order in the heights of
heaven.
3 Can his forces be numbered?
Upon whom does his light not rise?
4 How then can a man be righteous before
God?
How can one born of woman be pure?
5 If even the moon is not bright
and the stars are not pure in his eyes,
6 how much less man, who is but a
maggot—
a son of man, who is only a worm!"

[a] *11* Or *olives between the millstones;* the meaning of the Hebrew for this word is uncertain. [b] *17* Or *them, their morning is like the shadow of death* [c] *17* Or *of the shadow of death* [d] *19* Hebrew *Sheol*

Job

26 Then Job replied:
2"How you have helped the powerless!
How you have saved the arm that is feeble!
3What advice you have offered to one without wisdom!
And what great insight you have displayed!
4Who has helped you utter these words?
And whose spirit spoke from your mouth?

5"The dead are in deep anguish,
those beneath the waters and all that live in them.
6Death[a] is naked before God;
Destruction[b] lies uncovered.
7He spreads out the northern ⌞skies⌟ over empty space;
he suspends the earth over nothing.
8He wraps up the waters in his clouds,
yet the clouds do not burst under their weight.
9He covers the face of the full moon,
spreading his clouds over it.
10He marks out the horizon on the face of the waters
for a boundary between light and darkness.
11The pillars of the heavens quake,
aghast at his rebuke.
12By his power he churned up the sea;
by his wisdom he cut Rahab to pieces.
13By his breath the skies became fair;
his hand pierced the gliding serpent.
14And these are but the outer fringe of his works;
how faint the whisper we hear of him!
Who then can understand the thunder of his power?"

27 And Job continued his discourse:
2"As surely as God lives, who has denied me justice,
the Almighty, who has made me taste bitterness of soul,
3as long as I have life within me,
the breath of God in my nostrils,
4my lips will not speak wickedness,
and my tongue will utter no deceit.
5I will never admit you are in the right;
till I die, I will not deny my integrity.
6I will maintain my righteousness and never let go of it;
my conscience will not reproach me as long as I live.

7"May my enemies be like the wicked,
my adversaries like the unjust!
8For what hope has the godless when he is cut off,
when God takes away his life?
9Does God listen to his cry
when distress comes upon him?
10Will he find delight in the Almighty?
Will he call upon God at all times?

11"I will teach you about the power of God;
the ways of the Almighty I will not conceal.
12You have all seen this yourselves.
Why then this meaningless talk?

13"Here is the fate God allots to the wicked,
the heritage a ruthless man receives from the Almighty:
14However many his children, their fate is the sword;
his offspring will never have enough to eat.
15The plague will bury those who survive him,
and their widows will not weep for them.
16Though he heaps up silver like dust
and clothes like piles of clay,
17what he lays up the righteous will wear,
and the innocent will divide his silver.
18The house he builds is like a moth's cocoon,
like a hut made by a watchman.
19He lies down wealthy, but will do so no more;
when he opens his eyes, all is gone.
20Terrors overtake him like a flood;
a tempest snatches him away in the night.
21The east wind carries him off, and he is gone;
it sweeps him out of his place.
22It hurls itself against him without mercy
as he flees headlong from its power.
23It claps its hands in derision
and hisses him out of his place.

28 "There is a mine for silver
and a place where gold is refined.
2Iron is taken from the earth,

[a]6 Hebrew *Sheol* [b]6 Hebrew *Abaddon*

and copper is smelted from ore.
3Man puts an end to the darkness;
he searches the farthest recesses
for ore in the blackest darkness.
4Far from where people dwell he cuts a shaft,
in places forgotten by the foot of man;
far from men he dangles and sways.
5The earth, from which food comes,
is transformed below as by fire;
6sapphires[a] come from its rocks,
and its dust contains nuggets of gold.
7No bird of prey knows that hidden path,
no falcon's eye has seen it.
8Proud beasts do not set foot on it,
and no lion prowls there.
9Man's hand assaults the flinty rock
and lays bare the roots of the mountains.
10He tunnels through the rock;
his eyes see all its treasures.
11He searches[b] the sources of the rivers
and brings hidden things to light.

12"But where can wisdom be found?
Where does understanding dwell?
13Man does not comprehend its worth;
it cannot be found in the land of the living.
14The deep says, 'It is not in me';
the sea says, 'It is not with me.'
15It cannot be bought with the finest gold,
nor can its price be weighed in silver.
16It cannot be bought with the gold of Ophir,
with precious onyx or sapphires.
17Neither gold nor crystal can compare with it,
nor can it be had for jewels of gold.
18Coral and jasper are not worthy of mention;
the price of wisdom is beyond rubies.
19The topaz of Cush cannot compare with it;
it cannot be bought with pure gold.

20"Where then does wisdom come from?
Where does understanding dwell?
21It is hidden from the eyes of every living thing,
concealed even from the birds of the air.
22Destruction[c] and Death say,
'Only a rumor of it has reached our ears.'
23God understands the way to it
and he alone knows where it dwells,
24for he views the ends of the earth
and sees everything under the heavens.
25When he established the force of the wind
and measured out the waters,
26when he made a decree for the rain
and a path for the thunderstorm,
27then he looked at wisdom and appraised it;
he confirmed it and tested it.
28And he said to man,
'The fear of the Lord—that is wisdom,
and to shun evil is understanding.' "

29 Job continued his discourse:

2"How I long for the months gone by,
for the days when God watched over me,
3when his lamp shone upon my head
and by his light I walked through darkness!
4Oh, for the days when I was in my prime,
when God's intimate friendship blessed my house,
5when the Almighty was still with me
and my children were around me,
6when my path was drenched with cream
and the rock poured out for me streams of olive oil.

7"When I went to the gate of the city
and took my seat in the public square,
8the young men saw me and stepped aside
and the old men rose to their feet;
9the chief men refrained from speaking
and covered their mouths with their hands;
10the voices of the nobles were hushed,
and their tongues stuck to the roof of their mouths.
11Whoever heard me spoke well of me,
and those who saw me commended me,
12because I rescued the poor who cried for help,
and the fatherless who had none to assist him.
13The man who was dying blessed me;
I made the widow's heart sing.

[a]6 Or *lapis lazuli*; also in verse 16 [b]11 Septuagint, Aquila and Vulgate; Hebrew *He dams up* [c]22 Hebrew *Abaddon*

14I put on righteousness as my clothing;
justice was my robe and my turban.
15I was eyes to the blind
and feet to the lame.
16I was a father to the needy;
I took up the case of the stranger.
17I broke the fangs of the wicked
and snatched the victims from their teeth.

18"I thought, 'I will die in my own house,
my days as numerous as the grains of sand.
19My roots will reach to the water,
and the dew will lie all night on my branches.
20My glory will remain fresh in me,
the bow ever new in my hand.'

21"Men listened to me expectantly,
waiting in silence for my counsel.
22After I had spoken, they spoke no more;
my words fell gently on their ears.
23They waited for me as for showers
and drank in my words as the spring rain.
24When I smiled at them, they scarcely believed it;
the light of my face was precious to them.[a]
25I chose the way for them and sat as their chief;
I dwelt as a king among his troops;
I was like one who comforts mourners.

30 "But now they mock me,
men younger than I,
whose fathers I would have disdained
to put with my sheep dogs.
2Of what use was the strength of their hands to me,
since their vigor had gone from them?
3Haggard from want and hunger,
they roamed[b] the parched land
in desolate wastelands at night.
4In the brush they gathered salt herbs,
and their food[c] was the root of the broom tree.
5They were banished from their fellow men,
shouted at as if they were thieves.
6They were forced to live in the dry stream beds,
among the rocks and in holes in the ground.
7They brayed among the bushes
and huddled in the undergrowth.
8A base and nameless brood,
they were driven out of the land.

9"And now their sons mock me in song;
I have become a byword among them.
10They detest me and keep their distance;
they do not hesitate to spit in my face.
11Now that God has unstrung my bow and afflicted me,
they throw off restraint in my presence.
12On my right the tribe[d] attacks;
they lay snares for my feet,
they build their siege ramps against me.
13They break up my road;
they succeed in destroying me—
without anyone's helping them.[e]
14They advance as through a gaping breach;
amid the ruins they come rolling in.
15Terrors overwhelm me;
my dignity is driven away as by the wind,
my safety vanishes like a cloud.

16"And now my life ebbs away;
days of suffering grip me.
17Night pierces my bones;
my gnawing pains never rest.
18In his great power ⌞God⌟ becomes like clothing to me[f];
he binds me like the neck of my garment.
19He throws me into the mud,
and I am reduced to dust and ashes.

20"I cry out to you, O God, but you do not answer;
I stand up, but you merely look at me.
21You turn on me ruthlessly;
with the might of your hand you attack me.
22You snatch me up and drive me before the wind;
you toss me about in the storm.
23I know you will bring me down to death,
to the place appointed for all the living.

24"Surely no one lays a hand on a broken man
when he cries for help in his distress.
25Have I not wept for those in trouble?
Has not my soul grieved for the poor?

[a]*24* The meaning of the Hebrew for this clause is uncertain. [b]*3* Or *gnawed* [c]*4* Or *fuel* [d]*12* The meaning of the Hebrew for this word is uncertain. [e]*13* Or *me. / 'No one can help him,' ⌞they say⌟.*
[f]*18* Hebrew; Septuagint *⌞God⌟ grasps my clothing*

[26]Yet when I hoped for good, evil came;
when I looked for light, then came darkness.
[27]The churning inside me never stops;
days of suffering confront me.
[28]I go about blackened, but not by the sun;
I stand up in the assembly and cry for help.
[29]I have become a brother of jackals,
a companion of owls.
[30]My skin grows black and peels;
my body burns with fever.
[31]My harp is tuned to mourning,
and my flute to the sound of wailing.

31 "I made a covenant with my eyes
not to look lustfully at a girl.
[2]For what is man's lot from God above,
his heritage from the Almighty on high?
[3]Is it not ruin for the wicked,
disaster for those who do wrong?
[4]Does he not see my ways
and count my every step?

[5]"If I have walked in falsehood
or my foot has hurried after deceit—
[6]let God weigh me in honest scales
and he will know that I am blameless—
[7]if my steps have turned from the path,
if my heart has been led by my eyes,
or if my hands have been defiled,
[8]then may others eat what I have sown,
and may my crops be uprooted.

[9]"If my heart has been enticed by a woman,
or if I have lurked at my neighbor's door,
[10]then may my wife grind another man's grain,
and may other men sleep with her.
[11]For that would have been shameful,
a sin to be judged.
[12]It is a fire that burns to Destruction[a];
it would have uprooted my harvest.

[13]"If I have denied justice to my menservants and maidservants
when they had a grievance against me,
[14]what will I do when God confronts me?
What will I answer when called to account?
[15]Did not he who made me in the womb make them?
Did not the same one form us both within our mothers?

[16]"If I have denied the desires of the poor
or let the eyes of the widow grow weary,
[17]if I have kept my bread to myself,
not sharing it with the fatherless—
[18]but from my youth I reared him as would a father,
and from my birth I guided the widow—
[19]if I have seen anyone perishing for lack of clothing,
or a needy man without a garment,
[20]and his heart did not bless me
for warming him with the fleece from my sheep,
[21]if I have raised my hand against the fatherless,
knowing that I had influence in court,
[22]then let my arm fall from the shoulder,
let it be broken off at the joint.
[23]For I dreaded destruction from God,
and for fear of his splendor I could not do such things.

[24]"If I have put my trust in gold
or said to pure gold, 'You are my security,'
[25]if I have rejoiced over my great wealth,
the fortune my hands had gained,
[26]if I have regarded the sun in its radiance
or the moon moving in splendor,
[27]so that my heart was secretly enticed
and my hand offered them a kiss of homage,
[28]then these also would be sins to be judged,
for I would have been unfaithful to God on high.

[29]"If I have rejoiced at my enemy's misfortune
or gloated over the trouble that came to him—
[30]I have not allowed my mouth to sin
by invoking a curse against his life—
[31]if the men of my household have never said,
'Who has not had his fill of Job's meat?'—
[32]but no stranger had to spend the night in the street,
for my door was always open to the traveler—
[33]if I have concealed my sin as men do,[b]
by hiding my guilt in my heart
[34]because I so feared the crowd
and so dreaded the contempt of the clans

[a]12 Hebrew *Abaddon* [b]33 Or *as Adam did*

that I kept silent and would not go
outside

[35]("Oh, that I had someone to hear me!
I sign now my defense—let the
Almighty answer me;
let my accuser put his indictment in
writing.
[36]Surely I would wear it on my shoulder,
I would put it on like a crown.
[37]I would give him an account of my every
step;
like a prince I would approach him.)—

[38]"if my land cries out against me
and all its furrows are wet with tears,
[39]if I have devoured its yield without
payment
or broken the spirit of its tenants,
[40]then let briers come up instead of wheat
and weeds instead of barley."

The words of Job are ended.

Elihu

32 So these three men stopped answering Job, because he was righteous in
his own eyes. [2]But Elihu son of Barakel the
Buzite, of the family of Ram, became very
angry with Job for justifying himself rather
than God. [3]He was also angry with the three
friends, because they had found no way to
refute Job, and yet had condemned him.[a]
[4]Now Elihu had waited before speaking to
Job because they were older than he. [5]But
when he saw that the three men had nothing
more to say, his anger was aroused.
[6]So Elihu son of Barakel the Buzite said:

"I am young in years,
and you are old;
that is why I was fearful,
not daring to tell you what I know.
[7]I thought, 'Age should speak;
advanced years should teach wisdom.'
[8]But it is the spirit[b] in a man,
the breath of the Almighty, that gives
him understanding.
[9]It is not only the old[c] who are wise,
not only the aged who understand what
is right.

[10]"Therefore I say: Listen to me;
I too will tell you what I know.
[11]I waited while you spoke,
I listened to your reasoning;
while you were searching for words,
[12] I gave you my full attention.
But not one of you has proved Job wrong;
none of you has answered his
arguments.
[13]Do not say, 'We have found wisdom;
let God refute him, not man.'
[14]But Job has not marshaled his words
against me,
and I will not answer him with your
arguments.

[15]"They are dismayed and have no more to
say;
words have failed them.
[16]Must I wait, now that they are silent,
now that they stand there with no
reply?
[17]I too will have my say;
I too will tell what I know.
[18]For I am full of words,
and the spirit within me compels me;
[19]inside I am like bottled-up wine,
like new wineskins ready to burst.
[20]I must speak and find relief;
I must open my lips and reply.
[21]I will show partiality to no one,
nor will I flatter any man;
[22]for if I were skilled in flattery,
my Maker would soon take me away.

33 "But now, Job, listen to my words;
pay attention to everything I say.
[2]I am about to open my mouth;
my words are on the tip of my tongue.
[3]My words come from an upright heart;
my lips sincerely speak what I know.
[4]The Spirit of God has made me;
the breath of the Almighty gives me life.
[5]Answer me then, if you can;
prepare yourself and confront me.
[6]I am just like you before God;
I too have been taken from clay.
[7]No fear of me should alarm you,
nor should my hand be heavy upon
you.

[8]"But you have said in my hearing—
I heard the very words—
[9]'I am pure and without sin;
I am clean and free from guilt.
[10]Yet God has found fault with me;
he considers me his enemy.
[11]He fastens my feet in shackles;
he keeps close watch on all my paths.'

[12]"But I tell you, in this you are not right,

[a]3 Masoretic Text; an ancient Hebrew scribal tradition *Job, and so had condemned God* [b]8 Or *Spirit*; also in verse 18 [c]9 Or *many*; or *great*

for God is greater than man.
13Why do you complain to him
that he answers none of man's
words[a]?
14For God does speak—now one way, now
another—
though man may not perceive it.
15In a dream, in a vision of the night,
when deep sleep falls on men
as they slumber in their beds,
16he may speak in their ears
and terrify them with warnings,
17to turn man from wrongdoing
and keep him from pride,
18to preserve his soul from the pit,[b]
his life from perishing by the sword.[c]
19Or a man may be chastened on a bed of
pain
with constant distress in his bones,
20so that his very being finds food repulsive
and his soul loathes the choicest meal.
21His flesh wastes away to nothing,
and his bones, once hidden, now stick
out.
22His soul draws near to the pit,[d]
and his life to the messengers of
death.[e]

23"Yet if there is an angel on his side
as a mediator, one out of a thousand,
to tell a man what is right for him,
24to be gracious to him and say,
'Spare him from going down to the pit[f];
I have found a ransom for him'—
25then his flesh is renewed like a child's;
it is restored as in the days of his youth.
26He prays to God and finds favor with him,
he sees God's face and shouts for joy;
he is restored by God to his righteous
state.
27Then he comes to men and says,
'I sinned, and perverted what was right,
but I did not get what I deserved.
28He redeemed my soul from going down
to the pit,[g]
and I will live to enjoy the light.'

29"God does all these things to a man—
twice, even three times—
30to turn back his soul from the pit,[h]
that the light of life may shine on him.

31"Pay attention, Job, and listen to me;
be silent, and I will speak.
32If you have anything to say, answer me;
speak up, for I want you to be cleared.
33But if not, then listen to me;
be silent, and I will teach you wisdom."

34 Then Elihu said:
2"Hear my words, you wise men;
listen to me, you men of learning.
3For the ear tests words
as the tongue tastes food.
4Let us discern for ourselves what is right;
let us learn together what is good.

5"Job says, 'I am innocent,
but God denies me justice.
6Although I am right,
I am considered a liar;
although I am guiltless,
his arrow inflicts an incurable wound.'
7What man is like Job,
who drinks scorn like water?
8He keeps company with evildoers;
he associates with wicked men.
9For he says, 'It profits a man nothing
when he tries to please God.'

10"So listen to me, you men of
understanding.
Far be it from God to do evil,
from the Almighty to do wrong.
11He repays a man for what he has done;
he brings upon him what his conduct
deserves.
12It is unthinkable that God would do
wrong,
that the Almighty would pervert justice.
13Who appointed him over the earth?
Who put him in charge of the whole
world?
14If it were his intention
and he withdrew his spirit[i] and breath,
15all mankind would perish together
and man would return to the dust.

16"If you have understanding, hear this;
listen to what I say.
17Can he who hates justice govern?
Will you condemn the just and mighty
One?
18Is he not the One who says to kings, 'You
are worthless,'
and to nobles, 'You are wicked,'
19who shows no partiality to princes
and does not favor the rich over the
poor,

[a]13 *Or that he does not answer for any of his actions* [b]18 *Or preserve him from the grave* [c]18 *Or from crossing the River* [d]22 *Or He draws near to the grave* [e]22 *Or to the dead* [f]24 *Or grave* [g]28 *Or redeemed me from going down to the grave* [h]30 *Or turn him back from the grave* [i]14 *Or Spirit*

for they are all the work of his hands?
20They die in an instant, in the middle of the night;
the people are shaken and they pass away;
the mighty are removed without human hand.
21"His eyes are on the ways of men;
he sees their every step.
22There is no dark place, no deep shadow,
where evildoers can hide.
23God has no need to examine men further,
that they should come before him for judgment.
24Without inquiry he shatters the mighty
and sets up others in their place.
25Because he takes note of their deeds,
he overthrows them in the night and they are crushed.
26He punishes them for their wickedness
where everyone can see them,
27because they turned from following him
and had no regard for any of his ways.
28They caused the cry of the poor to come before him,
so that he heard the cry of the needy.
29But if he remains silent, who can condemn him?
If he hides his face, who can see him?
Yet he is over man and nation alike,
30 to keep a godless man from ruling,
from laying snares for the people.

31"Suppose a man says to God,
'I am guilty but will offend no more.
32Teach me what I cannot see;
if I have done wrong, I will not do so again.'
33Should God then reward you on your terms,
when you refuse to repent?
You must decide, not I;
so tell me what you know.

34"Men of understanding declare,
wise men who hear me say to me,
35'Job speaks without knowledge;
his words lack insight.'
36Oh, that Job might be tested to the utmost
for answering like a wicked man!
37To his sin he adds rebellion;
scornfully he claps his hands among us
and multiplies his words against God."

35 Then Elihu said:

2"Do you think this is just?
You say, 'I will be cleared by God.[a]'
3Yet you ask him, 'What profit is it to me,[b]
and what do I gain by not sinning?'

4"I would like to reply to you
and to your friends with you.
5Look up at the heavens and see;
gaze at the clouds so high above you.
6If you sin, how does that affect him?
If your sins are many, what does that do to him?
7If you are righteous, what do you give to him,
or what does he receive from your hand?
8Your wickedness affects only a man like yourself,
and your righteousness only the sons of men.

9"Men cry out under a load of oppression;
they plead for relief from the arm of the powerful.
10But no one says, 'Where is God my Maker,
who gives songs in the night,
11who teaches more to us than to[c] the beasts of the earth
and makes us wiser than[d] the birds of the air?'
12He does not answer when men cry out
because of the arrogance of the wicked.
13Indeed, God does not listen to their empty plea;
the Almighty pays no attention to it.
14How much less, then, will he listen
when you say that you do not see him,
that your case is before him
and you must wait for him,
15and further, that his anger never punishes
and he does not take the least notice of wickedness.[e]
16So Job opens his mouth with empty talk;
without knowledge he multiplies words."

36 Elihu continued:

2"Bear with me a little longer and I will show you

[a]2 Or *My righteousness is more than God's* [b]3 Or *you* [c]11 Or *teaches us by* [d]11 Or *us wise by*
[e]15 Symmachus, Theodotion and Vulgate; the meaning of the Hebrew for this word is uncertain.

that there is more to be said in God's
behalf.
3I get my knowledge from afar;
I will ascribe justice to my Maker.
4Be assured that my words are not false;
one perfect in knowledge is with you.

5"God is mighty, but does not despise
men;
he is mighty, and firm in his purpose.
6He does not keep the wicked alive
but gives the afflicted their rights.
7He does not take his eyes off the
righteous;
he enthrones them with kings
and exalts them forever.
8But if men are bound in chains,
held fast by cords of affliction,
9he tells them what they have done—
that they have sinned arrogantly.
10He makes them listen to correction
and commands them to repent of their
evil.
11If they obey and serve him,
they will spend the rest of their days in
prosperity
and their years in contentment.
12But if they do not listen,
they will perish by the sword[a]
and die without knowledge.

13"The godless in heart harbor resentment;
even when he fetters them, they do not
cry for help.
14They die in their youth,
among male prostitutes of the shrines.
15But those who suffer he delivers in their
suffering;
he speaks to them in their affliction.

16"He is wooing you from the jaws of
distress
to a spacious place free from
restriction,
to the comfort of your table laden with
choice food.
17But now you are laden with the judgment
due the wicked;
judgment and justice have taken hold
of you.
18Be careful that no one entices you by
riches;
do not let a large bribe turn you aside.
19Would your wealth
or even all your mighty efforts
sustain you so you would not be in
distress?
20Do not long for the night,
to drag people away from their homes.[b]
21Beware of turning to evil,
which you seem to prefer to affliction.

22"God is exalted in his power.
Who is a teacher like him?
23Who has prescribed his ways for him,
or said to him, 'You have done wrong'?
24Remember to extol his work,
which men have praised in song.
25All mankind has seen it;
men gaze on it from afar.
26How great is God—beyond our
understanding!
The number of his years is past finding
out.

27"He draws up the drops of water,
which distill as rain to the streams[c];
28the clouds pour down their moisture
and abundant showers fall on mankind.
29Who can understand how he spreads out
the clouds,
how he thunders from his pavilion?
30See how he scatters his lightning about
him,
bathing the depths of the sea.
31This is the way he governs[d] the nations
and provides food in abundance.
32He fills his hands with lightning
and commands it to strike its mark.
33His thunder announces the coming
storm;
even the cattle make known its
approach.[e]

37 "At this my heart pounds
and leaps from its place.
2Listen! Listen to the roar of his voice,
to the rumbling that comes from his
mouth.
3He unleashes his lightning beneath the
whole heaven
and sends it to the ends of the earth.
4After that comes the sound of his roar;
he thunders with his majestic voice.
When his voice resounds,
he holds nothing back.
5God's voice thunders in marvelous ways;
he does great things beyond our
understanding.
6He says to the snow, 'Fall on the earth,'

[a] 12 Or *will cross the River* [b] 20 The meaning of the Hebrew for verses 18-20 is uncertain. [c] 27 Or *distill from the mist as rain* [d] 31 Or *nourishes* [e] 33 Or *announces his coming— / the One zealous against evil*

and to the rain shower, 'Be a mighty
downpour.'
7So that all men he has made may know
his work,
he stops every man from his labor.[a]
8The animals take cover;
they remain in their dens.
9The tempest comes out from its chamber,
the cold from the driving winds.
10The breath of God produces ice,
and the broad waters become frozen.
11He loads the clouds with moisture;
he scatters his lightning through them.
12At his direction they swirl around
over the face of the whole earth
to do whatever he commands them.
13He brings the clouds to punish men,
or to water his earth[b] and show his
love.

14"Listen to this, Job;
stop and consider God's wonders.
15Do you know how God controls the
clouds
and makes his lightning flash?
16Do you know how the clouds hang
poised,
those wonders of him who is perfect in
knowledge?
17You who swelter in your clothes
when the land lies hushed under the
south wind,
18can you join him in spreading out the
skies,
hard as a mirror of cast bronze?

19"Tell us what we should say to him;
we cannot draw up our case because
of our darkness.
20Should he be told that I want to speak?
Would any man ask to be swallowed
up?
21Now no one can look at the sun,
bright as it is in the skies
after the wind has swept them clean.
22Out of the north he comes in golden
splendor;
God comes in awesome majesty.
23The Almighty is beyond our reach and
exalted in power;
in his justice and great righteousness,
he does not oppress.
24Therefore, men revere him,
for does he not have regard for all the
wise in heart?[c]"

The Lord Speaks

38 Then the Lord answered Job out of
the storm. He said:

2"Who is this that darkens my counsel
with words without knowledge?
3Brace yourself like a man;
I will question you,
and you shall answer me.

4"Where were you when I laid the earth's
foundation?
Tell me, if you understand.
5Who marked off its dimensions? Surely
you know!
Who stretched a measuring line
across it?
6On what were its footings set,
or who laid its cornerstone—
7while the morning stars sang together
and all the angels[d] shouted for joy?

8"Who shut up the sea behind doors
when it burst forth from the womb,
9when I made the clouds its garment
and wrapped it in thick darkness,
10when I fixed limits for it
and set its doors and bars in place,
11when I said, 'This far you may come and
no farther;
here is where your proud waves halt'?

12"Have you ever given orders to the
morning,
or shown the dawn its place,
13that it might take the earth by the edges
and shake the wicked out of it?
14The earth takes shape like clay under a
seal;
its features stand out like those of a
garment.
15The wicked are denied their light,
and their upraised arm is broken.

16"Have you journeyed to the springs of the
sea
or walked in the recesses of the deep?
17Have the gates of death been shown to
you?
Have you seen the gates of the shadow
of death[e]?
18Have you comprehended the vast
expanses of the earth?
Tell me, if you know all this.

[a]7 Or / *he fills all men with fear by his power* [b]13 Or *to favor them* [c]24 Or *for he does not have regard for any who think they are wise.* [d]7 Hebrew *the sons of God* [e]17 Or *gates of deep shadows*

19"What is the way to the abode of light?
And where does darkness reside?
20Can you take them to their places?
Do you know the paths to their dwellings?
21Surely you know, for you were already born!
You have lived so many years!

22"Have you entered the storehouses of the snow
or seen the storehouses of the hail,
23which I reserve for times of trouble,
for days of war and battle?
24What is the way to the place where the lightning is dispersed,
or the place where the east winds are scattered over the earth?
25Who cuts a channel for the torrents of rain,
and a path for the thunderstorm,
26to water a land where no man lives,
a desert with no one in it,
27to satisfy a desolate wasteland
and make it sprout with grass?
28Does the rain have a father?
Who fathers the drops of dew?
29From whose womb comes the ice?
Who gives birth to the frost from the heavens
30when the waters become hard as stone,
when the surface of the deep is frozen?

31"Can you bind the beautiful[a] Pleiades?
Can you loose the cords of Orion?
32Can you bring forth the constellations in their seasons[b]
or lead out the Bear[c] with its cubs?
33Do you know the laws of the heavens?
Can you set up ⌞God's[d]⌟ dominion over the earth?

34"Can you raise your voice to the clouds
and cover yourself with a flood of water?
35Do you send the lightning bolts on their way?
Do they report to you, 'Here we are'?
36Who endowed the heart[e] with wisdom
or gave understanding to the mind[e]?
37Who has the wisdom to count the clouds?
Who can tip over the water jars of the heavens
38when the dust becomes hard
and the clods of earth stick together?

39"Do you hunt the prey for the lioness
and satisfy the hunger of the lions
40when they crouch in their dens
or lie in wait in a thicket?
41Who provides food for the raven
when its young cry out to God
and wander about for lack of food?

39

"Do you know when the mountain goats give birth?
Do you watch when the doe bears her fawn?
2Do you count the months till they bear?
Do you know the time they give birth?
3They crouch down and bring forth their young;
their labor pains are ended.
4Their young thrive and grow strong in the wilds;
they leave and do not return.

5"Who let the wild donkey go free?
Who untied his ropes?
6I gave him the wasteland as his home,
the salt flats as his habitat.
7He laughs at the commotion in the town;
he does not hear a driver's shout.
8He ranges the hills for his pasture
and searches for any green thing.

9"Will the wild ox consent to serve you?
Will he stay by your manger at night?
10Can you hold him to the furrow with a harness?
Will he till the valleys behind you?
11Will you rely on him for his great strength?
Will you leave your heavy work to him?
12Can you trust him to bring in your grain
and gather it to your threshing floor?

13"The wings of the ostrich flap joyfully,
but they cannot compare with the pinions and feathers of the stork.
14She lays her eggs on the ground
and lets them warm in the sand,
15unmindful that a foot may crush them,
that some wild animal may trample them.
16She treats her young harshly, as if they were not hers;
she cares not that her labor was in vain,
17for God did not endow her with wisdom
or give her a share of good sense.

[a]31 Or *the twinkling;* or *the chains of the* [b]32 Or *the morning star in its season* [c]32 Or *out Leo*
[d]33 Or *his;* or *their* [e]36 The meaning of the Hebrew for this word is uncertain.

[18]Yet when she spreads her feathers to run,
she laughs at horse and rider.

[19]"Do you give the horse his strength
or clothe his neck with a flowing mane?
[20]Do you make him leap like a locust,
striking terror with his proud snorting?
[21]He paws fiercely, rejoicing in his strength,
and charges into the fray.
[22]He laughs at fear, afraid of nothing;
he does not shy away from the sword.
[23]The quiver rattles against his side,
along with the flashing spear and lance.
[24]In frenzied excitement he eats up the ground;
he cannot stand still when the trumpet sounds.
[25]At the blast of the trumpet he snorts, 'Aha!'
He catches the scent of battle from afar,
the shout of commanders and the battle cry.

[26]"Does the hawk take flight by your wisdom
and spread his wings toward the south?
[27]Does the eagle soar at your command
and build his nest on high?
[28]He dwells on a cliff and stays there at night;
a rocky crag is his stronghold.
[29]From there he seeks out his food;
his eyes detect it from afar.
[30]His young ones feast on blood,
and where the slain are, there is he."

40 The LORD said to Job:

[2]"Will the one who contends with the Almighty correct him?
Let him who accuses God answer him!"

[3]Then Job answered the LORD:

[4]"I am unworthy—how can I reply to you?
I put my hand over my mouth.
[5]I spoke once, but I have no answer—
twice, but I will say no more."

[6]Then the LORD spoke to Job out of the storm:

[7]"Brace yourself like a man;
I will question you,
and you shall answer me.

[8]"Would you discredit my justice?
Would you condemn me to justify yourself?
[9]Do you have an arm like God's,
and can your voice thunder like his?
[10]Then adorn yourself with glory and splendor,
and clothe yourself in honor and majesty.
[11]Unleash the fury of your wrath,
look at every proud man and bring him low,
[12]look at every proud man and humble him,
crush the wicked where they stand.
[13]Bury them all in the dust together;
shroud their faces in the grave.
[14]Then I myself will admit to you
that your own right hand can save you.

[15]"Look at the behemoth,[a]
which I made along with you
and which feeds on grass like an ox.
[16]What strength he has in his loins,
what power in the muscles of his belly!
[17]His tail[b] sways like a cedar;
the sinews of his thighs are close-knit.
[18]His bones are tubes of bronze,
his limbs like rods of iron.
[19]He ranks first among the works of God,
yet his Maker can approach him with his sword.
[20]The hills bring him their produce,
and all the wild animals play nearby.
[21]Under the lotus plants he lies,
hidden among the reeds in the marsh.
[22]The lotuses conceal him in their shadow;
the poplars by the stream surround him.
[23]When the river rages, he is not alarmed;
he is secure, though the Jordan should surge against his mouth.
[24]Can anyone capture him by the eyes,[c]
or trap him and pierce his nose?

41 "Can you pull in the leviathan[d] with a fishhook
or tie down his tongue with a rope?
[2]Can you put a cord through his nose
or pierce his jaw with a hook?
[3]Will he keep begging you for mercy?
Will he speak to you with gentle words?
[4]Will he make an agreement with you
for you to take him as your slave for life?

[a] 15 Possibly the hippopotamus or the elephant [b] 17 Possibly trunk [c] 24 Or *by a water hole*
[d] 1 Possibly the crocodile

5Can you make a pet of him like a bird
or put him on a leash for your girls?
6Will traders barter for him?
Will they divide him up among the
merchants?
7Can you fill his hide with harpoons
or his head with fishing spears?
8If you lay a hand on him,
you will remember the struggle and
never do it again!
9Any hope of subduing him is false;
the mere sight of him is overpowering.
10No one is fierce enough to rouse him.
Who then is able to stand against me?
11Who has a claim against me that I must
pay?
Everything under heaven belongs
to me.

12"I will not fail to speak of his limbs,
his strength and his graceful form.
13Who can strip off his outer coat?
Who would approach him with a bridle?
14Who dares open the doors of his mouth,
ringed about with his fearsome teeth?
15His back has[a] rows of shields
tightly sealed together;
16each is so close to the next
that no air can pass between.
17They are joined fast to one another;
they cling together and cannot be
parted.
18His snorting throws out flashes of light;
his eyes are like the rays of dawn.
19Firebrands stream from his mouth;
sparks of fire shoot out.
20Smoke pours from his nostrils
as from a boiling pot over a fire of
reeds.
21His breath sets coals ablaze,
and flames dart from his mouth.
22Strength resides in his neck;
dismay goes before him.
23The folds of his flesh are tightly joined;
they are firm and immovable.
24His chest is hard as rock,
hard as a lower millstone.
25When he rises up, the mighty are
terrified;
they retreat before his thrashing.
26The sword that reaches him has no
effect,
nor does the spear or the dart or the
javelin.
27Iron he treats like straw
and bronze like rotten wood.
28Arrows do not make him flee;
slingstones are like chaff to him.
29A club seems to him but a piece of straw;
he laughs at the rattling of the lance.
30His undersides are jagged potsherds,
leaving a trail in the mud like a
threshing sledge.
31He makes the depths churn like a boiling
caldron
and stirs up the sea like a pot of
ointment.
32Behind him he leaves a glistening wake;
one would think the deep had white
hair.
33Nothing on earth is his equal—
a creature without fear.
34He looks down on all that are haughty;
he is king over all that are proud."

Job

42 Then Job replied to the LORD:

2"I know that you can do all things;
no plan of yours can be thwarted.
3⌞You asked,⌟ 'Who is this that obscures
my counsel without knowledge?'
Surely I spoke of things I did not
understand,
things too wonderful for me to know.

4⌞"You said,⌟ 'Listen now, and I will speak;
I will question you,
and you shall answer me.'
5My ears had heard of you
but now my eyes have seen you.
6Therefore I despise myself
and repent in dust and ashes."

Epilogue

7After the LORD had said these things to
Job, he said to Eliphaz the Temanite, "I am
angry with you and your two friends, because you have not spoken of me what is
right, as my servant Job has. 8So now take
seven bulls and seven rams and go to my
servant Job and sacrifice a burnt offering for
yourselves. My servant Job will pray for you,
and I will accept his prayer and not deal with
you according to your folly. You have not
spoken of me what is right, as my servant
Job has." 9So Eliphaz the Temanite, Bildad
the Shuhite and Zophar the Naamathite did
what the LORD told them; and the LORD accepted Job's prayer.
10After Job had prayed for his friends, the

[a] *15* Or *His pride is his*

LORD made him prosperous again and gave
him twice as much as he had before. 11All his
brothers and sisters and everyone who had
known him before came and ate with him in
his house. They comforted and consoled him
over all the trouble the LORD had brought
upon him, and each one gave him a piece of
silver[a] and a gold ring.

12The LORD blessed the latter part of Job's
life more than the first. He had fourteen thousand sheep, six thousand camels, a thousand yoke of oxen and a thousand donkeys.
13And he also had seven sons and three
daughters. 14The first daughter he named
Jemimah, the second Keziah and the third
Keren-Happuch. 15Nowhere in all the land
were there found women as beautiful as
Job's daughters, and their father granted
them an inheritance along with their brothers.

16After this, Job lived a hundred and forty
years; he saw his children and their children
to the fourth generation. 17And so he died,
old and full of years.

[a] 11 Hebrew *him a kesitah;* a kesitah was a unit of money of unknown weight and value.

Psalms

Introduction:

The Psalms are poems or songs of praise, worship, thankfulness, and repentance, and each one of them is complete by itself. They also show a variety of feelings, emotions, attitudes and interests.

Of the 150 Psalms, one hundred of them are thought to be written by the following authors: David—73; Asaph—12; Sons of Korah—10; Moses—1; Heman the Ezrahite—1; Ethan the Ezrahite—1; and one or two by Solomon. The rest of the Psalms have no recorded author.

Because the Psalms are written by so many people, from different time periods, and they show such a variety of emotions they have had a world-wide appeal and are familiar and loved by many people.

Hebrew poetry often uses pairs of lines. The second line either repeats the thought of the first or gives an opposite. Look for these pairs of lines as you read the Psalms.

Outline of contents:

Book I: Psalms 1–41
Book II: Psalms 42–72
Book III: Psalms 73–89
Book IV: Psalms 90–106
Book V: Psalms 107–150

BOOK I

Psalms 1-41

Psalm 1

1Blessed is the man
who does not walk in the counsel of the wicked
or stand in the way of sinners
or sit in the seat of mockers.
2But his delight is in the law of the LORD,
and on his law he meditates day and night.
3He is like a tree planted by streams of water,
which yields its fruit in season
and whose leaf does not wither.
Whatever he does prospers.

4Not so the wicked!
They are like chaff
that the wind blows away.
5Therefore the wicked will not stand in the judgment,
nor sinners in the assembly of the righteous.
6For the LORD watches over the way of the righteous,
but the way of the wicked will perish.

Psalm 2

1Why do the nations conspire[a]
and the peoples plot in vain?
2The kings of the earth take their stand
and the rulers gather together
against the LORD
and against his Anointed One.[b]
3"Let us break their chains," they say,
"and throw off their fetters."

4The One enthroned in heaven laughs;
the Lord scoffs at them.
5Then he rebukes them in his anger
and terrifies them in his wrath, saying,
6"I have installed my King[c]
on Zion, my holy hill."

7I will proclaim the decree of the LORD:

[a]1 Hebrew; Septuagint *rage* [b]2 Or *anointed one* [c]6 Or *king*

He said to me, "You are my Son[a];
today I have become your Father.[b]
8Ask of me,
and I will make the nations your inheritance,
the ends of the earth your possession.
9You will rule them with an iron scepter[c];
you will dash them to pieces like pottery."

10Therefore, you kings, be wise;
be warned, you rulers of the earth.
11Serve the LORD with fear
and rejoice with trembling.
12Kiss the Son, lest he be angry
and you be destroyed in your way,
for his wrath can flare up in a moment.
Blessed are all who take refuge in him.

Psalm 3

A psalm of David. When he fled from his son Absalom.

1O LORD, how many are my foes!
How many rise up against me!
2Many are saying of me,
"God will not deliver him." *Selah*[d]

3But you are a shield around me, O LORD;
you bestow glory on me and lift[e] up my head.
4To the LORD I cry aloud,
and he answers me from his holy hill. *Selah*

5I lie down and sleep;
I wake again, because the LORD sustains me.
6I will not fear the tens of thousands
drawn up against me on every side.

7Arise, O LORD!
Deliver me, O my God!
Strike all my enemies on the jaw;
break the teeth of the wicked.

8From the LORD comes deliverance.
May your blessing be on your people. *Selah*

Psalm 4

For the director of music. With stringed instruments. A psalm of David.

1Answer me when I call to you,
O my righteous God.
Give me relief from my distress;
be merciful to me and hear my prayer.

2How long, O men, will you turn my glory into shame[f]?
How long will you love delusions and seek false gods[g]? *Selah*
3Know that the LORD has set apart the godly for himself;
the LORD will hear when I call to him.

4In your anger do not sin;
when you are on your beds,
search your hearts and be silent. *Selah*
5Offer right sacrifices
and trust in the LORD.

6Many are asking, "Who can show us any good?"
Let the light of your face shine upon us, O LORD.
7You have filled my heart with greater joy
than when their grain and new wine abound.
8I will lie down and sleep in peace,
for you alone, O LORD,
make me dwell in safety.

Psalm 5

For the director of music. For flutes. A psalm of David.

1Give ear to my words, O LORD,
consider my sighing.
2Listen to my cry for help,
my King and my God,
for to you I pray.
3In the morning, O LORD, you hear my voice;
in the morning I lay my requests before you
and wait in expectation.

[a]7 Or *son*; also in verse 12 [b]7 Or *have begotten you* [c]9 Or *will break them with a rod of iron* [d]2 A word of uncertain meaning, occurring frequently in the Psalms; possibly a musical term [e]3 Or *LORD, / my Glorious One, who lifts* [f]2 Or *you dishonor my Glorious One* [g]2 Or *seek lies*

[4]You are not a God who takes pleasure in evil;
with you the wicked cannot dwell.
[5]The arrogant cannot stand in your presence;
you hate all who do wrong.
[6]You destroy those who tell lies;
bloodthirsty and deceitful men
the LORD abhors.

[7]But I, by your great mercy,
will come into your house;
in reverence will I bow down
toward your holy temple.
[8]Lead me, O LORD, in your righteousness
because of my enemies—
make straight your way before me.

[9]Not a word from their mouth can be trusted;
their heart is filled with destruction.
Their throat is an open grave;
with their tongue they speak deceit.
[10]Declare them guilty, O God!
Let their intrigues be their downfall.
Banish them for their many sins,
for they have rebelled against you.

[11]But let all who take refuge in you be glad;
let them ever sing for joy.
Spread your protection over them,
that those who love your name may rejoice in you.
[12]For surely, O LORD, you bless the righteous;
you surround them with your favor as with a shield.

Psalm 6

For the director of music. With stringed instruments. According to *sheminith*.[a] A psalm of David.

[1]O LORD, do not rebuke me in your anger
or discipline me in your wrath.
[2]Be merciful to me, LORD, for I am faint;
O LORD, heal me, for my bones are in agony.
[3]My soul is in anguish.
How long, O LORD, how long?

[4]Turn, O LORD, and deliver me;
save me because of your unfailing love.
[5]No one remembers you when he is dead.
Who praises you from the grave[b]?
[6]I am worn out from groaning;
all night long I flood my bed with weeping
and drench my couch with tears.
[7]My eyes grow weak with sorrow;
they fail because of all my foes.

[8]Away from me, all you who do evil,
for the LORD has heard my weeping.
[9]The LORD has heard my cry for mercy;
the LORD accepts my prayer.
[10]All my enemies will be ashamed and dismayed;
they will turn back in sudden disgrace.

Psalm 7

A *shiggaion*[c] of David, which he sang to the LORD concerning Cush, a Benjamite.

[1]O LORD my God, I take refuge in you;
save and deliver me from all who pursue me,
[2]or they will tear me like a lion
and rip me to pieces with no one to rescue me.

[3]O LORD my God, if I have done this
and there is guilt on my hands—
[4]if I have done evil to him who is at peace with me
or without cause have robbed my foe—
[5]then let my enemy pursue and overtake me;
let him trample my life to the ground
and make me sleep in the dust. *Selah*

[6]Arise, O LORD, in your anger;
rise up against the rage of my enemies.
Awake, my God; decree justice.
[7]Let the assembled peoples gather around you.
Rule over them from on high;
[8] let the LORD judge the peoples.
Judge me, O LORD, according to my righteousness,
according to my integrity, O Most High.
[9]O righteous God,
who searches minds and hearts,
bring to an end the violence of the wicked
and make the righteous secure.

[10]My shield[d] is God Most High,
who saves the upright in heart.

[a]Title: Probably a musical term [b]5 Hebrew *Sheol* [c]Title: Probably a literary or musical term [d]10 Or *sovereign*

11God is a righteous judge,
a God who expresses his wrath every day.
12If he does not relent,
he[a] will sharpen his sword;
he will bend and string his bow.
13He has prepared his deadly weapons;
he makes ready his flaming arrows.

14He who is pregnant with evil
and conceives trouble gives birth to disillusionment.
15He who digs a hole and scoops it out
falls into the pit he has made.
16The trouble he causes recoils on himself;
his violence comes down on his own head.

17I will give thanks to the LORD because of his righteousness
and will sing praise to the name of the LORD Most High.

Psalm 8

For the director of music. According to *gittith*.[b] A psalm of David.

1O LORD, our Lord,
how majestic is your name in all the earth!

You have set your glory
above the heavens.
2From the lips of children and infants
you have ordained praise[c]
because of your enemies,
to silence the foe and the avenger.

3When I consider your heavens,
the work of your fingers,
the moon and the stars,
which you have set in place,
4what is man that you are mindful of him,
the son of man that you care for him?
5You made him a little lower than the heavenly beings[d]
and crowned him with glory and honor.

6You made him ruler over the works of your hands;
you put everything under his feet:
7all flocks and herds,
and the beasts of the field,
8the birds of the air,
and the fish of the sea,
all that swim the paths of the seas.

9O LORD, our Lord,
how majestic is your name in all the earth!

Psalm 9[e]

For the director of music. To ⌞the tune of⌟ "The Death of the Son." A psalm of David.

1I will praise you, O LORD, with all my heart;
I will tell of all your wonders.
2I will be glad and rejoice in you;
I will sing praise to your name, O Most High.

3My enemies turn back;
they stumble and perish before you.
4For you have upheld my right and my cause;
you have sat on your throne, judging righteously.
5You have rebuked the nations and destroyed the wicked;
you have blotted out their name for ever and ever.
6Endless ruin has overtaken the enemy,
you have uprooted their cities;
even the memory of them has perished.

7The LORD reigns forever;
he has established his throne for judgment.
8He will judge the world in righteousness;
he will govern the peoples with justice.
9The LORD is a refuge for the oppressed,
a stronghold in times of trouble.
10Those who know your name will trust in you,
for you, LORD, have never forsaken those who seek you.

11Sing praises to the LORD, enthroned in Zion;
proclaim among the nations what he has done.
12For he who avenges blood remembers;
he does not ignore the cry of the afflicted.

13O LORD, see how my enemies persecute me!

[a]12 Or *If a man does not repent, / God* [b]Title: Probably a musical term [c]2 Or *strength* [d]5 Or *than God* [e]Psalms 9 and 10 may have been originally a single acrostic poem, the stanzas of which begin with the successive letters of the Hebrew alphabet. In the Septuagint they constitute one psalm.

Have mercy and lift me up from the gates of death,
[14]that I may declare your praises
in the gates of the Daughter of Zion
and there rejoice in your salvation.
[15]The nations have fallen into the pit they have dug;
their feet are caught in the net they have hidden.
[16]The LORD is known by his justice;
the wicked are ensnared by the work of their hands. *Higgaion.*[a] *Selah*
[17]The wicked return to the grave,[b]
all the nations that forget God.
[18]But the needy will not always be forgotten,
nor the hope of the afflicted ever perish.

[19]Arise, O LORD, let not man triumph;
let the nations be judged in your presence.
[20]Strike them with terror, O LORD;
let the nations know they are but men. *Selah*

Psalm 10[c]

[1]Why, O LORD, do you stand far off?
Why do you hide yourself in times of trouble?

[2]In his arrogance the wicked man hunts down the weak,
who are caught in the schemes he devises.
[3]He boasts of the cravings of his heart;
he blesses the greedy and reviles the LORD.
[4]In his pride the wicked does not seek him;
in all his thoughts there is no room for God.
[5]His ways are always prosperous;
he is haughty and your laws are far from him;
he sneers at all his enemies.
[6]He says to himself, "Nothing will shake me;
I'll always be happy and never have trouble."
[7]His mouth is full of curses and lies and threats;
trouble and evil are under his tongue.
[8]He lies in wait near the villages;
from ambush he murders the innocent,
watching in secret for his victims.
[9]He lies in wait like a lion in cover;
he lies in wait to catch the helpless;
he catches the helpless and drags them off in his net.
[10]His victims are crushed, they collapse;
they fall under his strength.
[11]He says to himself, "God has forgotten;
he covers his face and never sees."

[12]Arise, LORD! Lift up your hand, O God.
Do not forget the helpless.
[13]Why does the wicked man revile God?
Why does he say to himself,
"He won't call me to account"?
[14]But you, O God, do see trouble and grief;
you consider it to take it in hand.
The victim commits himself to you;
you are the helper of the fatherless.
[15]Break the arm of the wicked and evil man;
call him to account for his wickedness
that would not be found out.

[16]The LORD is King for ever and ever;
the nations will perish from his land.
[17]You hear, O LORD, the desire of the afflicted;
you encourage them, and you listen to their cry,
[18]defending the fatherless and the oppressed,
in order that man, who is of the earth,
may terrify no more.

Psalm 11

For the director of music. Of David.

[1]In the LORD I take refuge.
How then can you say to me:
"Flee like a bird to your mountain.
[2]For look, the wicked bend their bows;
they set their arrows against the strings
to shoot from the shadows
at the upright in heart.
[3]When the foundations are being destroyed,
what can the righteous do[d]?"

[4]The LORD is in his holy temple;
the LORD is on his heavenly throne.

[a]*16* Or *Meditation;* possibly a musical notation [b]*17* Hebrew *Sheol* [c]Psalms 9 and 10 may have been originally a single acrostic poem, the stanzas of which begin with the successive letters of the Hebrew alphabet. In the Septuagint they constitute one psalm. [d]*3* Or *what is the Righteous One doing*

He observes the sons of men;
his eyes examine them.
5The LORD examines the righteous,
but the wicked[a] and those who love violence
his soul hates.
6On the wicked he will rain
fiery coals and burning sulfur;
a scorching wind will be their lot.

7For the LORD is righteous,
he loves justice;
upright men will see his face.

Psalm 12

For the director of music. According to *sheminith.*[b] A psalm of David.

1Help, LORD, for the godly are no more;
the faithful have vanished from among men.
2Everyone lies to his neighbor;
their flattering lips speak with deception.
3May the LORD cut off all flattering lips
and every boastful tongue
4that says, "We will triumph with our tongues;
we own our lips[c]—who is our master?"

5"Because of the oppression of the weak
and the groaning of the needy,
I will now arise," says the LORD.
"I will protect them from those who malign them."
6And the words of the LORD are flawless,
like silver refined in a furnace of clay,
purified seven times.

7O LORD, you will keep us safe
and protect us from such people forever.
8The wicked freely strut about
when what is vile is honored among men.

Psalm 13

For the director of music. A psalm of David.

1How long, O LORD? Will you forget me forever?
How long will you hide your face from me?
2How long must I wrestle with my thoughts
and every day have sorrow in my heart?
How long will my enemy triumph over me?

3Look on me and answer, O LORD my God.
Give light to my eyes, or I will sleep in death;
4my enemy will say, "I have overcome him,"
and my foes will rejoice when I fall.

5But I trust in your unfailing love;
my heart rejoices in your salvation.
6I will sing to the LORD,
for he has been good to me.

Psalm 14

For the director of music. Of David.

1The fool[d] says in his heart,
"There is no God."
They are corrupt, their deeds are vile;
there is no one who does good.

2The LORD looks down from heaven
on the sons of men
to see if there are any who understand,
any who seek God.
3All have turned aside,
they have together become corrupt;
there is no one who does good,
not even one.

4Will evildoers never learn—
those who devour my people as men eat bread
and who do not call on the LORD?
5There they are, overwhelmed with dread,
for God is present in the company of the righteous.
6You evildoers frustrate the plans of the poor,
but the LORD is their refuge.

7Oh, that salvation for Israel would come out of Zion!
When the LORD restores the fortunes of his people,
let Jacob rejoice and Israel be glad!

[a]5 Or *The LORD, the Righteous One, examines the wicked, /* [b]Title: Probably a musical term [c]4 Or */ our lips are our plowshares* [d]1 The Hebrew words rendered *fool* in Psalms denote one who is morally deficient.

Psalm 15

A psalm of David.

[1]LORD, who may dwell in your sanctuary?
Who may live on your holy hill?

[2]He whose walk is blameless
and who does what is righteous,
who speaks the truth from his heart
[3] and has no slander on his tongue,
who does his neighbor no wrong
and casts no slur on his fellowman,
[4]who despises a vile man
but honors those who fear the LORD,
who keeps his oath
even when it hurts,
[5]who lends his money without usury
and does not accept a bribe against the innocent.

He who does these things
will never be shaken.

Psalm 16

A *miktam*[a] of David.

[1]Keep me safe, O God,
for in you I take refuge.

[2]I said to the LORD, "You are my Lord;
apart from you I have no good thing."
[3]As for the saints who are in the land,
they are the glorious ones in whom is all my delight.[b]
[4]The sorrows of those will increase
who run after other gods.
I will not pour out their libations of blood
or take up their names on my lips.

[5]LORD, you have assigned me my portion and my cup;
you have made my lot secure.
[6]The boundary lines have fallen for me in pleasant places;
surely I have a delightful inheritance.

[7]I will praise the LORD, who counsels me;
even at night my heart instructs me.
[8]I have set the LORD always before me.
Because he is at my right hand,
I will not be shaken.

[9]Therefore my heart is glad and my tongue rejoices;
my body also will rest secure,
[10]because you will not abandon me to the grave,[c]
nor will you let your Holy One[d] see decay.
[11]You have made[e] known to me the path of life;
you will fill me with joy in your presence,
with eternal pleasures at your right hand.

Psalm 17

A prayer of David.

[1]Hear, O LORD, my righteous plea;
listen to my cry.
Give ear to my prayer—
it does not rise from deceitful lips.
[2]May my vindication come from you;
may your eyes see what is right.

[3]Though you probe my heart and examine me at night,
though you test me, you will find nothing;
I have resolved that my mouth will not sin.
[4]As for the deeds of men—
by the word of your lips
I have kept myself
from the ways of the violent.
[5]My steps have held to your paths;
my feet have not slipped.

[6]I call on you, O God, for you will answer me;
give ear to me and hear my prayer.
[7]Show the wonder of your great love,
you who save by your right hand
those who take refuge in you from their foes.
[8]Keep me as the apple of your eye;
hide me in the shadow of your wings
[9]from the wicked who assail me,
from my mortal enemies who surround me.

[10]They close up their callous hearts,
and their mouths speak with arrogance.
[11]They have tracked me down, they now surround me,
with eyes alert, to throw me to the ground.
[12]They are like a lion hungry for prey,

[a]Title: Probably a literary or musical term [b]3 Or *As for the pagan priests who are in the land / and the nobles in whom all delight, I said:* [c]10 Hebrew *Sheol* [d]10 Or *your faithful one* [e]11 Or *You will make*

like a great lion crouching in cover.

13Rise up, O LORD, confront them, bring them down;
rescue me from the wicked by your sword.
14O LORD, by your hand save me from such men,
from men of this world whose reward is in this life.

You still the hunger of those you cherish;
their sons have plenty,
and they store up wealth for their children.
15And I—in righteousness I will see your face;
when I awake, I will be satisfied with seeing your likeness.

Psalm 18

For the director of music. Of David the servant of the LORD. He sang to the LORD the words of this song when the LORD delivered him from the hand of all his enemies and from the hand of Saul. He said:

1I love you, O LORD, my strength.

2The LORD is my rock, my fortress and my deliverer;
my God is my rock, in whom I take refuge.
He is my shield and the horn[a] of my salvation, my stronghold.
3I call to the LORD, who is worthy of praise,
and I am saved from my enemies.

4The cords of death entangled me;
the torrents of destruction overwhelmed me.
5The cords of the grave[b] coiled around me;
the snares of death confronted me.
6In my distress I called to the LORD;
I cried to my God for help.
From his temple he heard my voice;
my cry came before him, into his ears.

7The earth trembled and quaked,
and the foundations of the mountains shook;
they trembled because he was angry.
8Smoke rose from his nostrils;
consuming fire came from his mouth,
burning coals blazed out of it.
9He parted the heavens and came down;
dark clouds were under his feet.
10He mounted the cherubim and flew;
he soared on the wings of the wind.
11He made darkness his covering, his canopy around him—
the dark rain clouds of the sky.
12Out of the brightness of his presence clouds advanced,
with hailstones and bolts of lightning.
13The LORD thundered from heaven;
the voice of the Most High resounded.[c]
14He shot his arrows and scattered ⌞the enemies⌟,
great bolts of lightning and routed them.
15The valleys of the sea were exposed
and the foundations of the earth laid bare
at your rebuke, O LORD,
at the blast of breath from your nostrils.

16He reached down from on high and took hold of me;
he drew me out of deep waters.
17He rescued me from my powerful enemy,
from my foes, who were too strong for me.
18They confronted me in the day of my disaster,
but the LORD was my support.
19He brought me out into a spacious place;
he rescued me because he delighted in me.

20The LORD has dealt with me according to my righteousness;
according to the cleanness of my hands he has rewarded me.
21For I have kept the ways of the LORD;
I have not done evil by turning from my God.
22All his laws are before me;
I have not turned away from his decrees.
23I have been blameless before him
and have kept myself from sin.
24The LORD has rewarded me according to my righteousness,
according to the cleanness of my hands in his sight.

25To the faithful you show yourself faithful,
to the blameless you show yourself blameless,

[a]2 *Horn* here symbolizes strength. [b]5 Hebrew *Sheol* [c]13 Some Hebrew manuscripts and Septuagint (see also 2 Samuel 22:14); most Hebrew manuscripts *resounded, / amid hailstones and bolts of lightning*

26to the pure you show yourself pure,
but to the crooked you show yourself shrewd.
27You save the humble
but bring low those whose eyes are haughty.
28You, O LORD, keep my lamp burning;
my God turns my darkness into light.
29With your help I can advance against a troop[a];
with my God I can scale a wall.

30As for God, his way is perfect;
the word of the LORD is flawless.
He is a shield
for all who take refuge in him.
31For who is God besides the LORD?
And who is the Rock except our God?
32It is God who arms me with strength
and makes my way perfect.
33He makes my feet like the feet of a deer;
he enables me to stand on the heights.
34He trains my hands for battle;
my arms can bend a bow of bronze.
35You give me your shield of victory,
and your right hand sustains me;
you stoop down to make me great.
36You broaden the path beneath me,
so that my ankles do not turn.

37I pursued my enemies and overtook them;
I did not turn back till they were destroyed.
38I crushed them so that they could not rise;
they fell beneath my feet.
39You armed me with strength for battle;
you made my adversaries bow at my feet.
40You made my enemies turn their backs in flight,
and I destroyed my foes.
41They cried for help, but there was no one to save them—
to the LORD, but he did not answer.
42I beat them as fine as dust borne on the wind;
I poured them out like mud in the streets.
43You have delivered me from the attacks of the people;
you have made me the head of nations;
people I did not know are subject to me.
44As soon as they hear me, they obey me;
foreigners cringe before me.
45They all lose heart;
they come trembling from their strongholds.

46The LORD lives! Praise be to my Rock!
Exalted be God my Savior!
47He is the God who avenges me,
who subdues nations under me,
48 who saves me from my enemies.
You exalted me above my foes;
from violent men you rescued me.
49Therefore I will praise you among the nations, O LORD;
I will sing praises to your name.
50He gives his king great victories;
he shows unfailing kindness to his anointed,
to David and his descendants forever.

Psalm 19

For the director of music. A psalm of David.

1The heavens declare the glory of God;
the skies proclaim the work of his hands.
2Day after day they pour forth speech;
night after night they display knowledge.
3There is no speech or language
where their voice is not heard.[b]
4Their voice[c] goes out into all the earth,
their words to the ends of the world.

In the heavens he has pitched a tent for the sun,
5 which is like a bridegroom coming forth from his pavilion,
like a champion rejoicing to run his course.
6It rises at one end of the heavens
and makes its circuit to the other;
nothing is hidden from its heat.

7The law of the LORD is perfect,
reviving the soul.
The statutes of the LORD are trustworthy,
making wise the simple.
8The precepts of the LORD are right,
giving joy to the heart.
The commands of the LORD are radiant,
giving light to the eyes.

[a]29 Or *can run through a barricade* [b]3 Or *They have no speech, there are no words; / no sound is heard from them* [c]4 Septuagint, Jerome and Syriac; Hebrew *line*

9The fear of the LORD is pure,
enduring forever.
The ordinances of the LORD are sure
and altogether righteous.
10They are more precious than gold,
than much pure gold;
they are sweeter than honey,
than honey from the comb.
11By them is your servant warned;
in keeping them there is great reward.

12Who can discern his errors?
Forgive my hidden faults.
13Keep your servant also from willful sins;
may they not rule over me.
Then will I be blameless,
innocent of great transgression.

14May the words of my mouth and the meditation of my heart
be pleasing in your sight,
O LORD, my Rock and my Redeemer.

Psalm 20

For the director of music. A psalm of David.

1May the LORD answer you when you are in distress;
may the name of the God of Jacob protect you.
2May he send you help from the sanctuary
and grant you support from Zion.
3May he remember all your sacrifices
and accept your burnt offerings. *Selah*
4May he give you the desire of your heart
and make all your plans succeed.
5We will shout for joy when you are victorious
and will lift up our banners in the name of our God.
May the LORD grant all your requests.

6Now I know that the LORD saves his anointed;
he answers him from his holy heaven
with the saving power of his right hand.
7Some trust in chariots and some in horses,
but we trust in the name of the LORD our God.
8They are brought to their knees and fall,
but we rise up and stand firm.

9O LORD, save the king!
Answer[a] us when we call!

Psalm 21

For the director of music. A psalm of David.

1O LORD, the king rejoices in your strength.
How great is his joy in the victories you give!
2You have granted him the desire of his heart
and have not withheld the request of his lips. *Selah*
3You welcomed him with rich blessings
and placed a crown of pure gold on his head.
4He asked you for life, and you gave it to him—
length of days, for ever and ever.
5Through the victories you gave, his glory is great;
you have bestowed on him splendor and majesty.
6Surely you have granted him eternal blessings
and made him glad with the joy of your presence.
7For the king trusts in the LORD;
through the unfailing love of the Most High
he will not be shaken.

8Your hand will lay hold on all your enemies;
your right hand will seize your foes.
9At the time of your appearing
you will make them like a fiery furnace.
In his wrath the LORD will swallow them up,
and his fire will consume them.
10You will destroy their descendants from the earth,
their posterity from mankind.
11Though they plot evil against you
and devise wicked schemes, they cannot succeed;
12for you will make them turn their backs
when you aim at them with drawn bow.

13Be exalted, O LORD, in your strength;
we will sing and praise your might.

[a]9 Or *save! / O King, answer*

Psalm 22

For the director of music. To ⌊the tune of⌋ "The Doe of the Morning." A psalm of David.

1My God, my God, why have you forsaken
me?
Why are you so far from saving me,
so far from the words of my groaning?
2O my God, I cry out by day, but you do
not answer,
by night, and am not silent.

3Yet you are enthroned as the Holy One;
you are the praise of Israel.[a]
4In you our fathers put their trust;
they trusted and you delivered them.
5They cried to you and were saved;
in you they trusted and were not
disappointed.

6But I am a worm and not a man,
scorned by men and despised by the
people.
7All who see me mock me;
they hurl insults, shaking their heads:
8"He trusts in the LORD;
let the LORD rescue him.
Let him deliver him,
since he delights in him."
9Yet you brought me out of the womb;
you made me trust in you
even at my mother's breast.
10From birth I was cast upon you;
from my mother's womb you have been
my God.
11Do not be far from me,
for trouble is near
and there is no one to help.

12Many bulls surround me;
strong bulls of Bashan encircle me.
13Roaring lions tearing their prey
open their mouths wide against me.
14I am poured out like water,
and all my bones are out of joint.
My heart has turned to wax;
it has melted away within me.
15My strength is dried up like a potsherd,
and my tongue sticks to the roof of my
mouth;
you lay me[b] in the dust of death.
16Dogs have surrounded me;
a band of evil men has encircled me,
they have pierced[c] my hands and my
feet.
17I can count all my bones;
people stare and gloat over me.
18They divide my garments among them
and cast lots for my clothing.

19But you, O LORD, be not far off;
O my Strength, come quickly to help
me.
20Deliver my life from the sword,
my precious life from the power of the
dogs.
21Rescue me from the mouth of the lions;
save[d] me from the horns of the wild
oxen.

22I will declare your name to my brothers;
in the congregation I will praise you.
23You who fear the LORD, praise him!
All you descendants of Jacob, honor
him!
Revere him, all you descendants of
Israel!
24For he has not despised or disdained
the suffering of the afflicted one;
he has not hidden his face from him
but has listened to his cry for help.

25From you comes the theme of my praise
in the great assembly;
before those who fear you[e] will I fulfill
my vows.
26The poor will eat and be satisfied;
they who seek the LORD will praise
him—
may your hearts live forever!
27All the ends of the earth
will remember and turn to the LORD,
and all the families of the nations
will bow down before him,
28for dominion belongs to the LORD
and he rules over the nations.

29All the rich of the earth will feast and
worship;
all who go down to the dust will kneel
before him—
those who cannot keep themselves
alive.
30Posterity will serve him;
future generations will be told about the
Lord.
31They will proclaim his righteousness
to a people yet unborn—
for he has done it.

[a]3 Or *Yet you are holy, / enthroned on the praises of Israel* [b]15 Or */ I am laid* [c]16 Some Hebrew manuscripts, Septuagint and Syriac; most Hebrew manuscripts */ like the lion,* [d]21 Or */ you have heard* [e]25 Hebrew *him*

Psalm 23

A psalm of David.

1The LORD is my shepherd, I shall not be in want.
2 He makes me lie down in green pastures,
he leads me beside quiet waters,
3 he restores my soul.
He guides me in paths of righteousness
for his name's sake.
4Even though I walk
through the valley of the shadow of death,[a]
I will fear no evil,
for you are with me;
your rod and your staff,
they comfort me.

5You prepare a table before me
in the presence of my enemies.
You anoint my head with oil;
my cup overflows.
6Surely goodness and love will follow me
all the days of my life,
and I will dwell in the house of the LORD
forever.

Psalm 24

Of David. A psalm.

1The earth is the LORD's, and everything in it,
the world, and all who live in it;
2for he founded it upon the seas
and established it upon the waters.

3Who may ascend the hill of the LORD?
Who may stand in his holy place?
4He who has clean hands and a pure heart,
who does not lift up his soul to an idol
or swear by what is false.[b]
5He will receive blessing from the LORD
and vindication from God his Savior.
6Such is the generation of those who seek him,
who seek your face, O God of Jacob.[c] *Selah*

7Lift up your heads, O you gates;
be lifted up, you ancient doors,
that the King of glory may come in.
8Who is this King of glory?
The LORD strong and mighty,
the LORD mighty in battle.
9Lift up your heads, O you gates;
lift them up, you ancient doors,
that the King of glory may come in.
10Who is he, this King of glory?
The LORD Almighty—
he is the King of glory. *Selah*

Psalm 25[d]

Of David.

1To you, O LORD, I lift up my soul;
2 in you I trust, O my God.
Do not let me be put to shame,
nor let my enemies triumph over me.
3No one whose hope is in you
will ever be put to shame,
but they will be put to shame
who are treacherous without excuse.

4Show me your ways, O LORD,
teach me your paths;
5guide me in your truth and teach me,
for you are God my Savior,
and my hope is in you all day long.
6Remember, O LORD, your great mercy and love,
for they are from of old.
7Remember not the sins of my youth
and my rebellious ways;
according to your love remember me,
for you are good, O LORD.

8Good and upright is the LORD;
therefore he instructs sinners in his ways.
9He guides the humble in what is right
and teaches them his way.
10All the ways of the LORD are loving and faithful
for those who keep the demands of his covenant.
11For the sake of your name, O LORD,
forgive my iniquity, though it is great.
12Who, then, is the man that fears the LORD?
He will instruct him in the way chosen for him.
13He will spend his days in prosperity,

[a]4 Or *through the darkest valley* [b]4 Or *swear falsely* [c]6 Two Hebrew manuscripts and Syriac (see also Septuagint); most Hebrew manuscripts *face, Jacob* [d]This psalm is an acrostic poem, the verses of which begin with the successive letters of the Hebrew alphabet.

and his descendants will inherit the
land.
14The LORD confides in those who fear him;
he makes his covenant known to them.
15My eyes are ever on the LORD,
for only he will release my feet from the
snare.

16Turn to me and be gracious to me,
for I am lonely and afflicted.
17The troubles of my heart have multiplied;
free me from my anguish.
18Look upon my affliction and my distress
and take away all my sins.
19See how my enemies have increased
and how fiercely they hate me!
20Guard my life and rescue me;
let me not be put to shame,
for I take refuge in you.
21May integrity and uprightness protect me,
because my hope is in you.

22Redeem Israel, O God,
from all their troubles!

Psalm 26

Of David.

1Vindicate me, O LORD,
for I have led a blameless life;
I have trusted in the LORD
without wavering.
2Test me, O LORD, and try me,
examine my heart and my mind;
3for your love is ever before me,
and I walk continually in your truth.
4I do not sit with deceitful men,
nor do I consort with hypocrites;
5I abhor the assembly of evildoers
and refuse to sit with the wicked.
6I wash my hands in innocence,
and go about your altar, O LORD,
7proclaiming aloud your praise
and telling of all your wonderful deeds.
8I love the house where you live, O LORD,
the place where your glory dwells.

9Do not take away my soul along with
sinners,
my life with bloodthirsty men,
10in whose hands are wicked schemes,
whose right hands are full of bribes.
11But I lead a blameless life;
redeem me and be merciful to me.

12My feet stand on level ground;
in the great assembly I will praise the
LORD.

Psalm 27

Of David.

1The LORD is my light and my salvation—
whom shall I fear?
The LORD is the stronghold of my life—
of whom shall I be afraid?
2When evil men advance against me
to devour my flesh,[a]
when my enemies and my foes attack
me,
they will stumble and fall.
3Though an army besiege me,
my heart will not fear;
though war break out against me,
even then will I be confident.

4One thing I ask of the LORD,
this is what I seek:
that I may dwell in the house of the LORD
all the days of my life,
to gaze upon the beauty of the LORD
and to seek him in his temple.
5For in the day of trouble
he will keep me safe in his dwelling;
he will hide me in the shelter of his
tabernacle
and set me high upon a rock.
6Then my head will be exalted
above the enemies who surround me;
at his tabernacle will I sacrifice with
shouts of joy;
I will sing and make music to the LORD.

7Hear my voice when I call, O LORD;
be merciful to me and answer me.
8My heart says of you, "Seek his[b] face!"
Your face, LORD, I will seek.
9Do not hide your face from me,
do not turn your servant away in anger;
you have been my helper.
Do not reject me or forsake me,
O God my Savior.
10Though my father and mother forsake
me,
the LORD will receive me.
11Teach me your way, O LORD;
lead me in a straight path
because of my oppressors.
12Do not turn me over to the desire of my
foes,

[a]2 Or *to slander me* [b]8 Or *To you, O my heart, he has said, "Seek my*

for false witnesses rise up against me,
breathing out violence.

13 I am still confident of this:
I will see the goodness of the LORD
in the land of the living.
14 Wait for the LORD;
be strong and take heart
and wait for the LORD.

Psalm 28

Of David.

1 To you I call, O LORD my Rock;
do not turn a deaf ear to me.
For if you remain silent,
I will be like those who have gone down to the pit.
2 Hear my cry for mercy
as I call to you for help,
as I lift up my hands
toward your Most Holy Place.

3 Do not drag me away with the wicked,
with those who do evil,
who speak cordially with their neighbors
but harbor malice in their hearts.
4 Repay them for their deeds
and for their evil work;
repay them for what their hands have done
and bring back upon them what they deserve.
5 Since they show no regard for the works of the LORD
and what his hands have done,
he will tear them down
and never build them up again.

6 Praise be to the LORD,
for he has heard my cry for mercy.
7 The LORD is my strength and my shield;
my heart trusts in him, and I am helped.
My heart leaps for joy
and I will give thanks to him in song.

8 The LORD is the strength of his people,
a fortress of salvation for his anointed one.
9 Save your people and bless your inheritance;
be their shepherd and carry them forever.

Psalm 29

A psalm of David.

1 Ascribe to the LORD, O mighty ones,
ascribe to the LORD glory and strength.
2 Ascribe to the LORD the glory due his name;
worship the LORD in the splendor of his[a] holiness.

3 The voice of the LORD is over the waters;
the God of glory thunders,
the LORD thunders over the mighty waters.
4 The voice of the LORD is powerful;
the voice of the LORD is majestic.
5 The voice of the LORD breaks the cedars;
the LORD breaks in pieces the cedars of Lebanon.
6 He makes Lebanon skip like a calf,
Sirion[b] like a young wild ox.
7 The voice of the LORD strikes
with flashes of lightning.
8 The voice of the LORD shakes the desert;
the LORD shakes the Desert of Kadesh.
9 The voice of the LORD twists the oaks[c]
and strips the forests bare.
And in his temple all cry, "Glory!"

10 The LORD sits[d] enthroned over the flood;
the LORD is enthroned as King forever.
11 The LORD gives strength to his people;
the LORD blesses his people with peace.

Psalm 30

A psalm. A song. For the dedication of the temple.[e] Of David.

1 I will exalt you, O LORD,
for you lifted me out of the depths
and did not let my enemies gloat over me.
2 O LORD my God, I called to you for help
and you healed me.
3 O LORD, you brought me up from the grave[f];
you spared me from going down into the pit.

4 Sing to the LORD, you saints of his;

[a] 2 Or *LORD with the splendor of* [b] 6 That is, Mount Hermon [c] 9 Or *LORD makes the deer give birth*
[d] 10 Or *sat* [e] Title: Or *palace* [f] 3 Hebrew *Sheol*

praise his holy name.
5For his anger lasts only a moment,
but his favor lasts a lifetime;
weeping may remain for a night,
but rejoicing comes in the morning.

6When I felt secure, I said,
"I will never be shaken."
7O LORD, when you favored me,
you made my mountain[a] stand firm;
but when you hid your face,
I was dismayed.

8To you, O LORD, I called;
to the Lord I cried for mercy:
9"What gain is there in my destruction,[b]
in my going down into the pit?
Will the dust praise you?
Will it proclaim your faithfulness?
10Hear, O LORD, and be merciful to me;
O LORD, be my help."
11You turned my wailing into dancing;
you removed my sackcloth and clothed me with joy,
12that my heart may sing to you and not be silent.
O LORD my God, I will give you thanks forever.

Psalm 31

For the director of music. A psalm of David.

1In you, O LORD, I have taken refuge;
let me never be put to shame;
deliver me in your righteousness.
2Turn your ear to me,
come quickly to my rescue;
be my rock of refuge,
a strong fortress to save me.
3Since you are my rock and my fortress,
for the sake of your name lead and guide me.
4Free me from the trap that is set for me,
for you are my refuge.
5Into your hands I commit my spirit;
redeem me, O LORD, the God of truth.

6I hate those who cling to worthless idols;
I trust in the LORD.
7I will be glad and rejoice in your love,
for you saw my affliction
and knew the anguish of my soul.
8You have not handed me over to the enemy
but have set my feet in a spacious place.

9Be merciful to me, O LORD, for I am in distress;
my eyes grow weak with sorrow,
my soul and my body with grief.
10My life is consumed by anguish
and my years by groaning;
my strength fails because of my affliction,[c]
and my bones grow weak.
11Because of all my enemies,
I am the utter contempt of my neighbors;
I am a dread to my friends—
those who see me on the street flee from me.
12I am forgotten by them as though I were dead;
I have become like broken pottery.
13For I hear the slander of many;
there is terror on every side;
they conspire against me
and plot to take my life.
14But I trust in you, O LORD;
I say, "You are my God."
15My times are in your hands;
deliver me from my enemies
and from those who pursue me.
16Let your face shine on your servant;
save me in your unfailing love.
17Let me not be put to shame, O LORD,
for I have cried out to you;
but let the wicked be put to shame
and lie silent in the grave.[d]
18Let their lying lips be silenced,
for with pride and contempt
they speak arrogantly against the righteous.

19How great is your goodness,
which you have stored up for those who fear you,
which you bestow in the sight of men
on those who take refuge in you.
20In the shelter of your presence you hide them
from the intrigues of men;
in your dwelling you keep them safe
from accusing tongues.

21Praise be to the LORD,
for he showed his wonderful love to me
when I was in a besieged city.

[a]7 Or *hill country* [b]9 Or *there if I am silenced* [c]10 Or *guilt* [d]17 Hebrew *Sheol*

22In my alarm I said,
"I am cut off from your sight!"
Yet you heard my cry for mercy
when I called to you for help.

23Love the LORD, all his saints!
The LORD preserves the faithful,
but the proud he pays back in full.
24Be strong and take heart,
all you who hope in the LORD.

Psalm 32

Of David. A *maskil.*[a]

1Blessed is he
whose transgressions are forgiven,
whose sins are covered.
2Blessed is the man
whose sin the LORD does not count against him
and in whose spirit is no deceit.

3When I kept silent,
my bones wasted away
through my groaning all day long.
4For day and night
your hand was heavy upon me;
my strength was sapped
as in the heat of summer. *Selah*
5Then I acknowledged my sin to you
and did not cover up my iniquity.
I said, "I will confess
my transgressions to the LORD"—
and you forgave
the guilt of my sin. *Selah*

6Therefore let everyone who is godly pray to you
while you may be found;
surely when the mighty waters rise,
they will not reach him.
7You are my hiding place;
you will protect me from trouble
and surround me with songs of deliverance. *Selah*

8I will instruct you and teach you in the way you should go;
I will counsel you and watch over you.
9Do not be like the horse or the mule,
which have no understanding
but must be controlled by bit and bridle
or they will not come to you.
10Many are the woes of the wicked,
but the LORD's unfailing love
surrounds the man who trusts in him.

11Rejoice in the LORD and be glad, you righteous;
sing, all you who are upright in heart!

Psalm 33

1Sing joyfully to the LORD, you righteous;
it is fitting for the upright to praise him.
2Praise the LORD with the harp;
make music to him on the ten-stringed lyre.
3Sing to him a new song;
play skillfully, and shout for joy.

4For the word of the LORD is right and true;
he is faithful in all he does.
5The LORD loves righteousness and justice;
the earth is full of his unfailing love.

6By the word of the LORD were the heavens made,
their starry host by the breath of his mouth.
7He gathers the waters of the sea into jars[b];
he puts the deep into storehouses.
8Let all the earth fear the LORD;
let all the people of the world revere him.
9For he spoke, and it came to be;
he commanded, and it stood firm.
10The LORD foils the plans of the nations;
he thwarts the purposes of the peoples.
11But the plans of the LORD stand firm forever,
the purposes of his heart through all generations.

12Blessed is the nation whose God is the LORD,
the people he chose for his inheritance.
13From heaven the LORD looks down
and sees all mankind;
14from his dwelling place he watches
all who live on earth—
15he who forms the hearts of all,
who considers everything they do.
16No king is saved by the size of his army;
no warrior escapes by his great strength.
17A horse is a vain hope for deliverance;
despite all its great strength it cannot save.
18But the eyes of the LORD are on those who fear him,

[a]Title: Probably a literary or musical term [b]7 Or *sea as into a heap*

on those whose hope is in his unfailing
love,
19to deliver them from death
and keep them alive in famine.

20We wait in hope for the LORD;
he is our help and our shield.
21In him our hearts rejoice,
for we trust in his holy name.
22May your unfailing love rest upon us,
O LORD,
even as we put our hope in you.

Psalm 34[a]

Of David. When he pretended to be insane before Abimelech, who drove him away, and he left.

1I will extol the LORD at all times;
his praise will always be on my lips.
2My soul will boast in the LORD;
let the afflicted hear and rejoice.
3Glorify the LORD with me;
let us exalt his name together.

4I sought the LORD, and he answered me;
he delivered me from all my fears.
5Those who look to him are radiant;
their faces are never covered with
shame.
6This poor man called, and the LORD heard
him;
he saved him out of all his troubles.
7The angel of the LORD encamps around
those who fear him,
and he delivers them.

8Taste and see that the LORD is good;
blessed is the man who takes refuge in
him.
9Fear the LORD, you his saints,
for those who fear him lack nothing.
10The lions may grow weak and hungry,
but those who seek the LORD lack no
good thing.

11Come, my children, listen to me;
I will teach you the fear of the LORD.
12Whoever of you loves life
and desires to see many good days,
13keep your tongue from evil
and your lips from speaking lies.
14Turn from evil and do good;
seek peace and pursue it.

15The eyes of the LORD are on the righteous
and his ears are attentive to their cry;
16the face of the LORD is against those who
do evil,
to cut off the memory of them from the
earth.

17The righteous cry out, and the LORD hears
them;
he delivers them from all their troubles.
18The LORD is close to the brokenhearted
and saves those who are crushed in
spirit.

19A righteous man may have many
troubles,
but the LORD delivers him from them all;
20he protects all his bones,
not one of them will be broken.

21Evil will slay the wicked;
the foes of the righteous will be
condemned.
22The LORD redeems his servants;
no one will be condemned who takes
refuge in him.

Psalm 35

Of David.

1Contend, O LORD, with those who contend
with me;
fight against those who fight against
me.
2Take up shield and buckler;
arise and come to my aid.
3Brandish spear and javelin[b]
against those who pursue me.
Say to my soul,
"I am your salvation."

4May those who seek my life
be disgraced and put to shame;
may those who plot my ruin
be turned back in dismay.
5May they be like chaff before the wind,
with the angel of the LORD driving them
away;
6may their path be dark and slippery,
with the angel of the LORD pursuing
them.
7Since they hid their net for me without
cause
and without cause dug a pit for me,
8may ruin overtake them by surprise—
may the net they hid entangle them,

[a]This psalm is an acrostic poem, the verses of which begin with the successive letters of the Hebrew alphabet.
[b]3 Or *and block the way*

may they fall into the pit, to their ruin.
9Then my soul will rejoice in the LORD
and delight in his salvation.
10My whole being will exclaim,
"Who is like you, O LORD?
You rescue the poor from those too strong for them,
the poor and needy from those who rob them."

11Ruthless witnesses come forward;
they question me on things I know nothing about.
12They repay me evil for good
and leave my soul forlorn.
13Yet when they were ill, I put on sackcloth
and humbled myself with fasting.
When my prayers returned to me unanswered,
14 I went about mourning
as though for my friend or brother.
I bowed my head in grief
as though weeping for my mother.
15But when I stumbled, they gathered in glee;
attackers gathered against me when I was unaware.
They slandered me without ceasing.
16Like the ungodly they maliciously mocked[a];
they gnashed their teeth at me.
17O Lord, how long will you look on?
Rescue my life from their ravages,
my precious life from these lions.
18I will give you thanks in the great assembly;
among throngs of people I will praise you.

19Let not those gloat over me
who are my enemies without cause;
let not those who hate me without reason
maliciously wink the eye.
20They do not speak peaceably,
but devise false accusations
against those who live quietly in the land.
21They gape at me and say, "Aha! Aha!
With our own eyes we have seen it."

22O LORD, you have seen this; be not silent.
Do not be far from me, O Lord.
23Awake, and rise to my defense!
Contend for me, my God and Lord.
24Vindicate me in your righteousness,
O LORD my God;
do not let them gloat over me.
25Do not let them think, "Aha, just what we wanted!"
or say, "We have swallowed him up."

26May all who gloat over my distress
be put to shame and confusion;
may all who exalt themselves over me
be clothed with shame and disgrace.
27May those who delight in my vindication
shout for joy and gladness;
may they always say, "The LORD be exalted,
who delights in the well-being of his servant."
28My tongue will speak of your righteousness
and of your praises all day long.

Psalm 36

For the director of music. Of David the servant of the LORD.

1An oracle is within my heart
concerning the sinfulness of the wicked:[b]
There is no fear of God
before his eyes.
2For in his own eyes he flatters himself
too much to detect or hate his sin.
3The words of his mouth are wicked and deceitful;
he has ceased to be wise and to do good.
4Even on his bed he plots evil;
he commits himself to a sinful course
and does not reject what is wrong.

5Your love, O LORD, reaches to the heavens,
your faithfulness to the skies.
6Your righteousness is like the mighty mountains,
your justice like the great deep.
O LORD, you preserve both man and beast.
7 How priceless is your unfailing love!
Both high and low among men
find[c] refuge in the shadow of your wings.
8They feast on the abundance of your house;
you give them drink from your river of delights.

[a]16 Septuagint; Hebrew may mean *ungodly circle of mockers.* [b]1 Or *heart: / Sin proceeds from the wicked.*
[c]7 Or *love, O God! / Men find;* or *love! / Both heavenly beings and men / find*

9For with you is the fountain of life;
in your light we see light.

10Continue your love to those who know you,
your righteousness to the upright in heart.
11May the foot of the proud not come against me,
nor the hand of the wicked drive me away.
12See how the evildoers lie fallen—
thrown down, not able to rise!

Psalm 37[a]

Of David.

1Do not fret because of evil men
or be envious of those who do wrong;
2for like the grass they will soon wither,
like green plants they will soon die away.
3Trust in the LORD and do good;
dwell in the land and enjoy safe pasture.
4Delight yourself in the LORD
and he will give you the desires of your heart.
5Commit your way to the LORD;
trust in him and he will do this:
6He will make your righteousness shine like the dawn,
the justice of your cause like the noonday sun.
7Be still before the LORD and wait patiently for him;
do not fret when men succeed in their ways,
when they carry out their wicked schemes.
8Refrain from anger and turn from wrath;
do not fret—it leads only to evil.
9For evil men will be cut off,
but those who hope in the LORD will inherit the land.

10A little while, and the wicked will be no more;
though you look for them, they will not be found.
11But the meek will inherit the land
and enjoy great peace.

12The wicked plot against the righteous
and gnash their teeth at them;
13but the Lord laughs at the wicked,
for he knows their day is coming.

14The wicked draw the sword
and bend the bow
to bring down the poor and needy,
to slay those whose ways are upright.
15But their swords will pierce their own hearts,
and their bows will be broken.

16Better the little that the righteous have
than the wealth of many wicked;
17for the power of the wicked will be broken,
but the LORD upholds the righteous.

18The days of the blameless are known to the LORD,
and their inheritance will endure forever.
19In times of disaster they will not wither;
in days of famine they will enjoy plenty.

20But the wicked will perish:
The LORD's enemies will be like the beauty of the fields,
they will vanish—vanish like smoke.

21The wicked borrow and do not repay,
but the righteous give generously;
22those the LORD blesses will inherit the land,
but those he curses will be cut off.

23If the LORD delights in a man's way,
he makes his steps firm;
24though he stumble, he will not fall,
for the LORD upholds him with his hand.

25I was young and now I am old,
yet I have never seen the righteous forsaken
or their children begging bread.
26They are always generous and lend freely;
their children will be blessed.

27Turn from evil and do good;
then you will dwell in the land forever.
28For the LORD loves the just
and will not forsake his faithful ones.

They will be protected forever,
but the offspring of the wicked will be cut off;

[a]This psalm is an acrostic poem, the stanzas of which begin with the successive letters of the Hebrew alphabet.

[29]the righteous will inherit the land
and dwell in it forever.

[30]The mouth of the righteous man utters
wisdom,
and his tongue speaks what is just.
[31]The law of his God is in his heart;
his feet do not slip.

[32]The wicked lie in wait for the righteous,
seeking their very lives;
[33]but the LORD will not leave them in their
power
or let them be condemned when
brought to trial.

[34]Wait for the LORD
and keep his way.
He will exalt you to inherit the land;
when the wicked are cut off, you will
see it.

[35]I have seen a wicked and ruthless man
flourishing like a green tree in its native
soil,
[36]but he soon passed away and was no
more;
though I looked for him, he could not be
found.

[37]Consider the blameless, observe the
upright;
there is a future[a] for the man of peace.
[38]But all sinners will be destroyed;
the future[b] of the wicked will be cut off.

[39]The salvation of the righteous comes
from the LORD;
he is their stronghold in time of trouble.
[40]The LORD helps them and delivers them;
he delivers them from the wicked and
saves them,
because they take refuge in him.

Psalm 38

A psalm of David. A petition.

[1]O LORD, do not rebuke me in your anger
or discipline me in your wrath.
[2]For your arrows have pierced me,
and your hand has come down upon
me.
[3]Because of your wrath there is no health
in my body;
my bones have no soundness because
of my sin.
[4]My guilt has overwhelmed me
like a burden too heavy to bear.

[5]My wounds fester and are loathsome
because of my sinful folly.
[6]I am bowed down and brought very low;
all day long I go about mourning.
[7]My back is filled with searing pain;
there is no health in my body.
[8]I am feeble and utterly crushed;
I groan in anguish of heart.

[9]All my longings lie open before you,
O Lord;
my sighing is not hidden from you.
[10]My heart pounds, my strength fails me;
even the light has gone from my eyes.
[11]My friends and companions avoid me
because of my wounds;
my neighbors stay far away.
[12]Those who seek my life set their traps,
those who would harm me talk of my
ruin;
all day long they plot deception.

[13]I am like a deaf man, who cannot hear,
like a mute, who cannot open his
mouth;
[14]I have become like a man who does not
hear,
whose mouth can offer no reply.
[15]I wait for you, O LORD;
you will answer, O Lord my God.
[16]For I said, "Do not let them gloat
or exalt themselves over me when my
foot slips."

[17]For I am about to fall,
and my pain is ever with me.
[18]I confess my iniquity;
I am troubled by my sin.
[19]Many are those who are my vigorous
enemies;
those who hate me without reason are
numerous.
[20]Those who repay my good with evil
slander me when I pursue what is
good.

[21]O LORD, do not forsake me;
be not far from me, O my God.
[22]Come quickly to help me,
O Lord my Savior.

[a]*37 Or there will be posterity* [b]*38 Or posterity*

Psalm 39

For the director of music. For Jeduthun.
A psalm of David.

[1]I said, "I will watch my ways
and keep my tongue from sin;
I will put a muzzle on my mouth
as long as the wicked are in my
presence."
[2]But when I was silent and still,
not even saying anything good,
my anguish increased.
[3]My heart grew hot within me,
and as I meditated, the fire burned;
then I spoke with my tongue:

[4]"Show me, O LORD, my life's end
and the number of my days;
let me know how fleeting is my life.
[5]You have made my days a mere
handbreadth;
the span of my years is as nothing
before you.
Each man's life is but a breath. *Selah*
[6]Man is a mere phantom as he goes to
and fro:
He bustles about, but only in vain;
he heaps up wealth, not knowing who
will get it.

[7]"But now, Lord, what do I look for?
My hope is in you.
[8]Save me from all my transgressions;
do not make me the scorn of fools.
[9]I was silent; I would not open my mouth,
for you are the one who has done this.
[10]Remove your scourge from me;
I am overcome by the blow of your
hand.
[11]You rebuke and discipline men for their
sin;
you consume their wealth like a moth—
each man is but a breath.
Selah

[12]"Hear my prayer, O LORD,
listen to my cry for help;
be not deaf to my weeping.
For I dwell with you as an alien,
a stranger, as all my fathers were.
[13]Look away from me, that I may rejoice
again
before I depart and am no more."

Psalm 40

For the director of music. Of David. A psalm.

[1]I waited patiently for the LORD;
he turned to me and heard my cry.
[2]He lifted me out of the slimy pit,
out of the mud and mire;
he set my feet on a rock
and gave me a firm place to stand.
[3]He put a new song in my mouth,
a hymn of praise to our God.
Many will see and fear
and put their trust in the LORD.

[4]Blessed is the man
who makes the LORD his trust,
who does not look to the proud,
to those who turn aside to false
gods.[a]
[5]Many, O LORD my God,
are the wonders you have done.
The things you planned for us
no one can recount to you;
were I to speak and tell of them,
they would be too many to declare.

[6]Sacrifice and offering you did not
desire,
but my ears you have pierced[b,c];
burnt offerings and sin offerings
you did not require.
[7]Then I said, "Here I am, I have come—
it is written about me in the scroll.[d]
[8]I desire to do your will, O my God;
your law is within my heart."

[9]I proclaim righteousness in the great
assembly;
I do not seal my lips,
as you know, O LORD.
[10]I do not hide your righteousness in my
heart;
I speak of your faithfulness and
salvation.
I do not conceal your love and your truth
from the great assembly.

[11]Do not withhold your mercy from me,
O LORD;
may your love and your truth always
protect me.
[12]For troubles without number surround
me;

[a]4 Or *to falsehood* [b]6 Hebrew; Septuagint *but a body you have prepared for me* (see also Symmachus and Theodotion) [c]6 Or *opened* [d]7 Or *come / with the scroll written for me*

my sins have overtaken me, and I
cannot see.
They are more than the hairs of my head,
and my heart fails within me.

13Be pleased, O LORD, to save me;
O LORD, come quickly to help me.
14May all who seek to take my life
be put to shame and confusion;
may all who desire my ruin
be turned back in disgrace.
15May those who say to me, "Aha! Aha!"
be appalled at their own shame.
16But may all who seek you
rejoice and be glad in you;
may those who love your salvation
always say,
"The LORD be exalted!"

17Yet I am poor and needy;
may the Lord think of me.
You are my help and my deliverer;
O my God, do not delay.

Psalm 41

For the director of music. A psalm of David.

1Blessed is he who has regard for the
weak;
the LORD delivers him in times of
trouble.
2The LORD will protect him and preserve
his life;
he will bless him in the land
and not surrender him to the desire of
his foes.
3The LORD will sustain him on his sickbed
and restore him from his bed of illness.

4I said, "O LORD, have mercy on me;
heal me, for I have sinned against
you."
5My enemies say of me in malice,
"When will he die and his name
perish?"
6Whenever one comes to see me,
he speaks falsely, while his heart
gathers slander;
then he goes out and spreads it
abroad.

7All my enemies whisper together against
me;
they imagine the worst for me, saying,
8"A vile disease has beset him;
he will never get up from the place
where he lies."
9Even my close friend, whom I trusted,
he who shared my bread,
has lifted up his heel against me.

10But you, O LORD, have mercy on me;
raise me up, that I may repay them.
11I know that you are pleased with me,
for my enemy does not triumph over
me.
12In my integrity you uphold me
and set me in your presence forever.

13Praise be to the LORD, the God of Israel,
from everlasting to everlasting.
Amen and Amen.

BOOK II

Psalms 42-72

Psalm 42[a]

For the director of music. A *maskil*[b] of the Sons of Korah.

1As the deer pants for streams of water,
so my soul pants for you, O God.
2My soul thirsts for God, for the living God.
When can I go and meet with God?
3My tears have been my food
day and night,
while men say to me all day long,
"Where is your God?"
4These things I remember
as I pour out my soul:
how I used to go with the multitude,
leading the procession to the house of
God,
with shouts of joy and thanksgiving
among the festive throng.

5Why are you downcast, O my soul?
Why so disturbed within me?
Put your hope in God,
for I will yet praise him,
my Savior and 6my God.

My[c] soul is downcast within me;
therefore I will remember you
from the land of the Jordan,

[a]In many Hebrew manuscripts Psalms 42 and 43 constitute one psalm. [b]Title: Probably a literary or musical term [c]5,6 A few Hebrew manuscripts, Septuagint and Syriac; most Hebrew manuscripts *praise him for his saving help.* / 6O *my God, my*

the heights of Hermon—from Mount Mizar.
7Deep calls to deep
in the roar of your waterfalls;
all your waves and breakers
have swept over me.

8By day the LORD directs his love,
at night his song is with me—
a prayer to the God of my life.

9I say to God my Rock,
"Why have you forgotten me?
Why must I go about mourning,
oppressed by the enemy?"
10My bones suffer mortal agony
as my foes taunt me,
saying to me all day long,
"Where is your God?"

11Why are you downcast, O my soul?
Why so disturbed within me?
Put your hope in God,
for I will yet praise him,
my Savior and my God.

Psalm 43[a]

1Vindicate me, O God,
and plead my cause against an ungodly nation;
rescue me from deceitful and wicked men.
2You are God my stronghold.
Why have you rejected me?
Why must I go about mourning,
oppressed by the enemy?
3Send forth your light and your truth,
let them guide me;
let them bring me to your holy mountain,
to the place where you dwell.
4Then will I go to the altar of God,
to God, my joy and my delight.
I will praise you with the harp,
O God, my God.

5Why are you downcast, O my soul?
Why so disturbed within me?
Put your hope in God,
for I will yet praise him,
my Savior and my God.

Psalm 44

For the director of music. Of the Sons of Korah. A *maskil.*[b]

1We have heard with our ears, O God;
our fathers have told us
what you did in their days,
in days long ago.
2With your hand you drove out the nations
and planted our fathers;
you crushed the peoples
and made our fathers flourish.
3It was not by their sword that they won the land,
nor did their arm bring them victory;
it was your right hand, your arm,
and the light of your face, for you loved them.

4You are my King and my God,
who decrees[c] victories for Jacob.
5Through you we push back our enemies;
through your name we trample our foes.
6I do not trust in my bow,
my sword does not bring me victory;
7but you give us victory over our enemies,
you put our adversaries to shame.
8In God we make our boast all day long,
and we will praise your name forever.
Selah

9But now you have rejected and humbled us;
you no longer go out with our armies.
10You made us retreat before the enemy,
and our adversaries have plundered us.
11You gave us up to be devoured like sheep
and have scattered us among the nations.
12You sold your people for a pittance,
gaining nothing from their sale.

13You have made us a reproach to our neighbors,
the scorn and derision of those around us.

[a]In many Hebrew manuscripts Psalms 42 and 43 constitute one psalm. [b]Title: Probably a literary or musical term [c]4 Septuagint, Aquila and Syriac; Hebrew *King, O God; / command*

14You have made us a byword among the nations;
the peoples shake their heads at us.
15My disgrace is before me all day long,
and my face is covered with shame
16at the taunts of those who reproach and revile me,
because of the enemy, who is bent on revenge.

17All this happened to us,
though we had not forgotten you
or been false to your covenant.
18Our hearts had not turned back;
our feet had not strayed from your path.
19But you crushed us and made us a haunt for jackals
and covered us over with deep darkness.

20If we had forgotten the name of our God
or spread out our hands to a foreign god,
21would not God have discovered it,
since he knows the secrets of the heart?
22Yet for your sake we face death all day long;
we are considered as sheep to be slaughtered.

23Awake, O Lord! Why do you sleep?
Rouse yourself! Do not reject us forever.
24Why do you hide your face
and forget our misery and oppression?

25We are brought down to the dust;
our bodies cling to the ground.
26Rise up and help us;
redeem us because of your unfailing love.

Psalm 45

For the director of music. To ⌞the tune of⌟ "Lilies." Of the Sons of Korah. A *maskil.*[a] A wedding song.

1My heart is stirred by a noble theme
as I recite my verses for the king;
my tongue is the pen of a skillful writer.

2You are the most excellent of men
and your lips have been anointed with grace,
since God has blessed you forever.
3Gird your sword upon your side, O mighty one;
clothe yourself with splendor and majesty.
4In your majesty ride forth victoriously
in behalf of truth, humility and righteousness;
let your right hand display awesome deeds.
5Let your sharp arrows pierce the hearts of the king's enemies;
let the nations fall beneath your feet.
6Your throne, O God, will last for ever and ever;
a scepter of justice will be the scepter of your kingdom.
7You love righteousness and hate wickedness;
therefore God, your God, has set you above your companions
by anointing you with the oil of joy.
8All your robes are fragrant with myrrh and aloes and cassia;
from palaces adorned with ivory
the music of the strings makes you glad.
9Daughters of kings are among your honored women;
at your right hand is the royal bride in gold of Ophir.

10Listen, O daughter, consider and give ear:
Forget your people and your father's house.
11The king is enthralled by your beauty;
honor him, for he is your lord.
12The Daughter of Tyre will come with a gift,[b]
men of wealth will seek your favor.

13All glorious is the princess within ⌞her chamber⌟;
her gown is interwoven with gold.
14In embroidered garments she is led to the king;
her virgin companions follow her
and are brought to you.
15They are led in with joy and gladness;
they enter the palace of the king.

16Your sons will take the place of your fathers;
you will make them princes throughout the land.

[a]Title: Probably a literary or musical term
[b]12 Or *A Tyrian robe is among the gifts*

17 I will perpetuate your memory through all generations;
therefore the nations will praise you for ever and ever.

Psalm 46

For the director of music. Of the Sons of Korah. According to *alamoth*.[a] A song.

1 God is our refuge and strength,
an ever-present help in trouble.
2 Therefore we will not fear, though the earth give way
and the mountains fall into the heart of the sea,
3 though its waters roar and foam
and the mountains quake with their surging. *Selah*

4 There is a river whose streams make glad the city of God,
the holy place where the Most High dwells.
5 God is within her, she will not fall;
God will help her at break of day.
6 Nations are in uproar, kingdoms fall;
he lifts his voice, the earth melts.

7 The LORD Almighty is with us;
the God of Jacob is our fortress. *Selah*

8 Come and see the works of the LORD,
the desolations he has brought on the earth.
9 He makes wars cease to the ends of the earth;
he breaks the bow and shatters the spear,
he burns the shields[b] with fire.
10 "Be still, and know that I am God;
I will be exalted among the nations,
I will be exalted in the earth."

11 The LORD Almighty is with us;
the God of Jacob is our fortress. *Selah*

Psalm 47

For the director of music. Of the Sons of Korah. A psalm.

1 Clap your hands, all you nations;
shout to God with cries of joy.
2 How awesome is the LORD Most High,
the great King over all the earth!
3 He subdued nations under us,
peoples under our feet.
4 He chose our inheritance for us,
the pride of Jacob, whom he loved. *Selah*

5 God has ascended amid shouts of joy,
the LORD amid the sounding of trumpets.
6 Sing praises to God, sing praises;
sing praises to our King, sing praises.

7 For God is the King of all the earth;
sing to him a psalm[c] of praise.
8 God reigns over the nations;
God is seated on his holy throne.
9 The nobles of the nations assemble
as the people of the God of Abraham,
for the kings[d] of the earth belong to God;
he is greatly exalted.

Psalm 48

A song. A psalm of the Sons of Korah.

1 Great is the LORD, and most worthy of praise,
in the city of our God, his holy mountain.
2 It is beautiful in its loftiness,
the joy of the whole earth.
Like the utmost heights of Zaphon[e] is Mount Zion,
the[f] city of the Great King.
3 God is in her citadels;
he has shown himself to be her fortress.

4 When the kings joined forces,
when they advanced together,
5 they saw ⌞her⌟ and were astounded;
they fled in terror.
6 Trembling seized them there,
pain like that of a woman in labor.
7 You destroyed them like ships of Tarshish
shattered by an east wind.

8 As we have heard,
so have we seen
in the city of the LORD Almighty,
in the city of our God:
God makes her secure forever. *Selah*

[a] Title: Probably a musical term [b] 9 Or *chariots* [c] 7 Or *a maskil* (probably a literary or musical term) [d] 9 Or *shields* [e] 2 *Zaphon* can refer to a sacred mountain or the direction north. [f] 2 Or *earth, / Mount Zion, on the northern side / of the*

9Within your temple, O God,
we meditate on your unfailing love.
10Like your name, O God,
your praise reaches to the ends of the earth;
your right hand is filled with righteousness.
11Mount Zion rejoices,
the villages of Judah are glad
because of your judgments.

12Walk about Zion, go around her,
count her towers,
13consider well her ramparts,
view her citadels,
that you may tell of them to the next generation.
14For this God is our God for ever and ever;
he will be our guide even to the end.

Psalm 49

For the director of music. Of the Sons of Korah. A psalm.

1Hear this, all you peoples;
listen, all who live in this world,
2both low and high,
rich and poor alike:
3My mouth will speak words of wisdom;
the utterance from my heart will give understanding.
4I will turn my ear to a proverb;
with the harp I will expound my riddle:

5Why should I fear when evil days come,
when wicked deceivers surround me—
6those who trust in their wealth
and boast of their great riches?
7No man can redeem the life of another
or give to God a ransom for him—
8the ransom for a life is costly,
no payment is ever enough—
9that he should live on forever
and not see decay.

10For all can see that wise men die;
the foolish and the senseless alike perish
and leave their wealth to others.
11Their tombs will remain their houses[a] forever,
their dwellings for endless generations,
though they had[b] named lands after themselves.

12But man, despite his riches, does not endure;
he is[c] like the beasts that perish.

13This is the fate of those who trust in themselves,
and of their followers, who approve their sayings. *Selah*
14Like sheep they are destined for the grave,[d]
and death will feed on them.
The upright will rule over them in the morning;
their forms will decay in the grave,[d]
far from their princely mansions.
15But God will redeem my life[e] from the grave;
he will surely take me to himself. *Selah*
16Do not be overawed when a man grows rich,
when the splendor of his house increases;
17for he will take nothing with him when he dies,
his splendor will not descend with him.
18Though while he lived he counted himself blessed—
and men praise you when you prosper—
19he will join the generation of his fathers,
who will never see the light ⌞of life⌟.

20A man who has riches without understanding
is like the beasts that perish.

Psalm 50

A psalm of Asaph.

1The Mighty One, God, the LORD,
speaks and summons the earth
from the rising of the sun to the place where it sets.
2From Zion, perfect in beauty,
God shines forth.
3Our God comes and will not be silent;
a fire devours before him,
and around him a tempest rages.
4He summons the heavens above,

[a] 11 Septuagint and Syriac; Hebrew *In their thoughts their houses will remain* [b] 11 Or / *for they have*
[c] 12 Hebrew; Septuagint and Syriac read verse 12 the same as verse 20. [d] 14 Hebrew *Sheol;* also in verse 15
[e] 15 Or *soul*

and the earth, that he may judge his
people:
5"Gather to me my consecrated ones,
who made a covenant with me by
sacrifice."
6And the heavens proclaim his
righteousness,
for God himself is judge. *Selah*

7"Hear, O my people, and I will speak,
O Israel, and I will testify against you:
I am God, your God.
8I do not rebuke you for your sacrifices
or your burnt offerings, which are ever
before me.
9I have no need of a bull from your stall
or of goats from your pens,
10for every animal of the forest is mine,
and the cattle on a thousand hills.
11I know every bird in the mountains,
and the creatures of the field are mine.
12If I were hungry I would not tell you,
for the world is mine, and all that is in it.
13Do I eat the flesh of bulls
or drink the blood of goats?
14Sacrifice thank offerings to God,
fulfill your vows to the Most High,
15and call upon me in the day of trouble;
I will deliver you, and you will honor
me."

16But to the wicked, God says:

"What right have you to recite my laws
or take my covenant on your lips?
17You hate my instruction
and cast my words behind you.
18When you see a thief, you join with him;
you throw in your lot with adulterers.
19You use your mouth for evil
and harness your tongue to deceit.
20You speak continually against your
brother
and slander your own mother's son.
21These things you have done and I kept
silent;
you thought I was altogether[a] like you.
But I will rebuke you
and accuse you to your face.

22"Consider this, you who forget God,
or I will tear you to pieces, with none to
rescue:
23He who sacrifices thank offerings honors
me,
and he prepares the way
so that I may show him[b] the salvation
of God."

Psalm 51

For the director of music. A psalm of David. When the prophet Nathan came to him after David had committed adultery with Bathsheba.

1Have mercy on me, O God,
according to your unfailing love;
according to your great compassion
blot out my transgressions.
2Wash away all my iniquity
and cleanse me from my sin.
3For I know my transgressions,
and my sin is always before me.
4Against you, you only, have I sinned
and done what is evil in your sight,
so that you are proved right when you
speak
and justified when you judge.
5Surely I was sinful at birth,
sinful from the time my mother
conceived me.
6Surely you desire truth in the inner
parts[c];
you teach[d] me wisdom in the inmost
place.

7Cleanse me with hyssop, and I will be
clean;
wash me, and I will be whiter than
snow.
8Let me hear joy and gladness;
let the bones you have crushed rejoice.
9Hide your face from my sins
and blot out all my iniquity.

10Create in me a pure heart, O God,
and renew a steadfast spirit within me.
11Do not cast me from your presence
or take your Holy Spirit from me.
12Restore to me the joy of your salvation
and grant me a willing spirit, to sustain
me.

13Then I will teach transgressors your
ways,
and sinners will turn back to you.
14Save me from bloodguilt, O God,
the God who saves me,
and my tongue will sing of your
righteousness.

[a]21 Or *thought the 'I AM' was* [b]23 Or *and to him who considers his way / I will show* [c]6 The meaning of the Hebrew for this phrase is uncertain. [d]6 Or *you desired . . . ; / you taught*

15O Lord, open my lips,
and my mouth will declare your praise.
16You do not delight in sacrifice, or I would bring it;
you do not take pleasure in burnt offerings.
17The sacrifices of God are[a] a broken spirit;
a broken and contrite heart,
O God, you will not despise.

18In your good pleasure make Zion prosper;
build up the walls of Jerusalem.
19Then there will be righteous sacrifices,
whole burnt offerings to delight you;
then bulls will be offered on your altar.

Psalm 52

For the director of music. A *maskil*[b] of David. When Doeg the Edomite had gone to Saul and told him: "David has gone to the house of Ahimelech."

1Why do you boast of evil, you mighty man?
Why do you boast all day long,
you who are a disgrace in the eyes of God?
2Your tongue plots destruction;
it is like a sharpened razor,
you who practice deceit.
3You love evil rather than good,
falsehood rather than speaking the truth. *Selah*
4You love every harmful word,
O you deceitful tongue!
5Surely God will bring you down to everlasting ruin:
He will snatch you up and tear you from your tent;
he will uproot you from the land of the living. *Selah*
6The righteous will see and fear;
they will laugh at him, saying,
7"Here now is the man
who did not make God his stronghold
but trusted in his great wealth
and grew strong by destroying others!"

8But I am like an olive tree
flourishing in the house of God;
I trust in God's unfailing love
for ever and ever.
9I will praise you forever for what you have done;
in your name I will hope, for your name is good.
I will praise you in the presence of your saints.

Psalm 53

For the director of music. According to *mahalath*.[c] A *maskil*[b] of David.

1The fool says in his heart,
"There is no God."
They are corrupt, and their ways are vile;
there is no one who does good.

2God looks down from heaven
on the sons of men
to see if there are any who understand,
any who seek God.
3Everyone has turned away,
they have together become corrupt;
there is no one who does good,
not even one.

4Will the evildoers never learn—
those who devour my people as men eat bread
and who do not call on God?
5There they were, overwhelmed with dread,
where there was nothing to dread.
God scattered the bones of those who attacked you;
you put them to shame, for God despised them.

6Oh, that salvation for Israel would come out of Zion!
When God restores the fortunes of his people,
let Jacob rejoice and Israel be glad!

Psalm 54

For the director of music. With stringed instruments. A *maskil*[b] of David. When the Ziphites had gone to Saul and said, "Is not David hiding among us?"

1Save me, O God, by your name;
vindicate me by your might.
2Hear my prayer, O God;
listen to the words of my mouth.

[a]17 Or *My sacrifice, O God, is* [b]Title: Probably a literary or musical term [c]Title: Probably a musical term

3Strangers are attacking me;
ruthless men seek my life—
men without regard for God. *Selah*
4Surely God is my help;
the Lord is the one who sustains me.

5Let evil recoil on those who slander me;
in your faithfulness destroy them.

6I will sacrifice a freewill offering to you;
I will praise your name, O LORD,
for it is good.
7For he has delivered me from all my troubles,
and my eyes have looked in triumph on my foes.

Psalm 55

For the director of music. With stringed instruments. A *maskil*[a] of David.

1Listen to my prayer, O God,
do not ignore my plea;
2 hear me and answer me.
My thoughts trouble me and I am distraught
3 at the voice of the enemy,
at the stares of the wicked;
for they bring down suffering upon me
and revile me in their anger.

4My heart is in anguish within me;
the terrors of death assail me.
5Fear and trembling have beset me;
horror has overwhelmed me.
6I said, "Oh, that I had the wings of a dove!
I would fly away and be at rest—
7I would flee far away
and stay in the desert; *Selah*
8I would hurry to my place of shelter,
far from the tempest and storm."

9Confuse the wicked, O Lord, confound their speech,
for I see violence and strife in the city.
10Day and night they prowl about on its walls;
malice and abuse are within it.
11Destructive forces are at work in the city;
threats and lies never leave its streets.

12If an enemy were insulting me,
I could endure it;
if a foe were raising himself against me,
I could hide from him.
13But it is you, a man like myself,
my companion, my close friend,
14with whom I once enjoyed sweet fellowship
as we walked with the throng at the house of God.

15Let death take my enemies by surprise;
let them go down alive to the grave,[b]
for evil finds lodging among them.
16But I call to God,
and the LORD saves me.
17Evening, morning and noon
I cry out in distress,
and he hears my voice.
18He ransoms me unharmed
from the battle waged against me,
even though many oppose me.
19God, who is enthroned forever,
will hear them and afflict them— *Selah*
men who never change their ways
and have no fear of God.

20My companion attacks his friends;
he violates his covenant.
21His speech is smooth as butter,
yet war is in his heart;
his words are more soothing than oil,
yet they are drawn swords.

22Cast your cares on the LORD
and he will sustain you;
he will never let the righteous fall.
23But you, O God, will bring down the wicked
into the pit of corruption;
bloodthirsty and deceitful men
will not live out half their days.

But as for me, I trust in you.

Psalm 56

For the director of music. To ⌞the tune of⌟ "A Dove on Distant Oaks." Of David. A *miktam*.[a] When the Philistines had seized him in Gath.

1Be merciful to me, O God, for men hotly pursue me;
all day long they press their attack.
2My slanderers pursue me all day long;
many are attacking me in their pride.
3When I am afraid,
I will trust in you.
4In God, whose word I praise,

[a]Title: Probably a literary or musical term [b]15 Hebrew *Sheol*

in God I trust; I will not be afraid.
What can mortal man do to me?

5All day long they twist my words;
they are always plotting to harm me.
6They conspire, they lurk,
they watch my steps,
eager to take my life.
7On no account let them escape;
in your anger, O God, bring down the nations.
8Record my lament;
list my tears on your scroll[a]—
are they not in your record?

9Then my enemies will turn back
when I call for help.
By this I will know that God is for me.
10In God, whose word I praise,
in the LORD, whose word I praise—
11in God I trust; I will not be afraid.
What can man do to me?

12I am under vows to you, O God;
I will present my thank offerings to you.
13For you have delivered me[b] from death
and my feet from stumbling,
that I may walk before God
in the light of life.[c]

Psalm 57

For the director of music. ⌞To the tune of⌟ "Do Not Destroy." Of David. A *miktam.*[d] When he had fled from Saul into the cave.

1Have mercy on me, O God, have mercy on me,
for in you my soul takes refuge.
I will take refuge in the shadow of your wings
until the disaster has passed.

2I cry out to God Most High,
to God, who fulfills ⌞his purpose⌟ for me.
3He sends from heaven and saves me,
rebuking those who hotly pursue me;
Selah
God sends his love and his faithfulness.

4I am in the midst of lions;
I lie among ravenous beasts—
men whose teeth are spears and arrows,
whose tongues are sharp swords.

5Be exalted, O God, above the heavens;
let your glory be over all the earth.

6They spread a net for my feet—
I was bowed down in distress.
They dug a pit in my path—
but they have fallen into it themselves.
Selah

7My heart is steadfast, O God,
my heart is steadfast;
I will sing and make music.
8Awake, my soul!
Awake, harp and lyre!
I will awaken the dawn.

9I will praise you, O Lord, among the nations;
I will sing of you among the peoples.
10For great is your love, reaching to the heavens;
your faithfulness reaches to the skies.

11Be exalted, O God, above the heavens;
let your glory be over all the earth.

Psalm 58

For the director of music. ⌞To the tune of⌟ "Do Not Destroy." Of David. A *miktam.*[d]

1Do you rulers indeed speak justly?
Do you judge uprightly among men?
2No, in your heart you devise injustice,
and your hands mete out violence on the earth.
3Even from birth the wicked go astray;
from the womb they are wayward and speak lies.
4Their venom is like the venom of a snake,
like that of a cobra that has stopped its ears,
5that will not heed the tune of the charmer,
however skillful the enchanter may be.

6Break the teeth in their mouths, O God;
tear out, O LORD, the fangs of the lions!
7Let them vanish like water that flows away;
when they draw the bow, let their arrows be blunted.
8Like a slug melting away as it moves along,
like a stillborn child, may they not see the sun.

9Before your pots can feel ⌞the heat of⌟ the thorns—

[a]8 Or *I put my tears in your wineskin* [b]13 Or *my soul* [c]13 Or *the land of the living* [d]Title: Probably a literary or musical term

whether they be green or dry—the
wicked will be swept away.[a]
10The righteous will be glad when they are
avenged,
when they bathe their feet in the blood
of the wicked.
11Then men will say,
"Surely the righteous still are rewarded;
surely there is a God who judges the
earth."

Psalm 59

For the director of music. To the tune of "Do Not Destroy." Of David. A *miktam*.[b] When Saul had sent men to watch David's house in order to kill him.

1Deliver me from my enemies, O God;
protect me from those who rise up
against me.
2Deliver me from evildoers
and save me from bloodthirsty men.

3See how they lie in wait for me!
Fierce men conspire against me
for no offense or sin of mine, O LORD.
4I have done no wrong, yet they are ready
to attack me.
Arise to help me; look on my plight!
5O LORD God Almighty, the God of Israel,
rouse yourself to punish all the nations;
show no mercy to wicked traitors.
Selah

6They return at evening,
snarling like dogs,
and prowl about the city.
7See what they spew from their mouths—
they spew out swords from their lips,
and they say, "Who can hear us?"
8But you, O LORD, laugh at them;
you scoff at all those nations.

9O my Strength, I watch for you;
you, O God, are my fortress, 10my
loving God.

God will go before me
and will let me gloat over those who
slander me.
11But do not kill them, O Lord our shield,[c]
or my people will forget.
In your might make them wander about,
and bring them down.
12For the sins of their mouths,
for the words of their lips,
let them be caught in their pride.
For the curses and lies they utter,
13 consume them in wrath,
consume them till they are no more.
Then it will be known to the ends of the
earth
that God rules over Jacob. *Selah*

14They return at evening,
snarling like dogs,
and prowl about the city.
15They wander about for food
and howl if not satisfied.
16But I will sing of your strength,
in the morning I will sing of your love;
for you are my fortress,
my refuge in times of trouble.

17O my Strength, I sing praise to you;
you, O God, are my fortress, my loving
God.

Psalm 60

For the director of music. To the tune of "The Lily of the Covenant." A *miktam*[b] of David. For teaching. When he fought Aram Naharaim[d] and Aram Zobah,[e] and when Joab returned and struck down twelve thousand Edomites in the Valley of Salt.

1You have rejected us, O God, and burst
forth upon us;
you have been angry—now restore us!
2You have shaken the land and torn it
open;
mend its fractures, for it is quaking.
3You have shown your people desperate
times;
you have given us wine that makes us
stagger.

4But for those who fear you, you have
raised a banner
to be unfurled against the bow. *Selah*

5Save us and help us with your right hand,
that those you love may be delivered.
6God has spoken from his sanctuary:
"In triumph I will parcel out Shechem
and measure off the Valley of Succoth.
7Gilead is mine, and Manasseh is mine;
Ephraim is my helmet,
Judah my scepter.
8Moab is my washbasin,

[a]9 The meaning of the Hebrew for this verse is uncertain. [b]Title: Probably a literary or musical term
[c]11 Or *sovereign* [d]Title: That is, Arameans of Northwest Mesopotamia [e]Title: That is, Arameans of central Syria

upon Edom I toss my sandal;
over Philistia I shout in triumph."

9Who will bring me to the fortified city?
Who will lead me to Edom?
10Is it not you, O God, you who have rejected us
and no longer go out with our armies?
11Give us aid against the enemy,
for the help of man is worthless.
12With God we will gain the victory,
and he will trample down our enemies.

Psalm 61

For the director of music. With stringed instruments. Of David.

1Hear my cry, O God;
listen to my prayer.

2From the ends of the earth I call to you,
I call as my heart grows faint;
lead me to the rock that is higher than I.
3For you have been my refuge,
a strong tower against the foe.

4I long to dwell in your tent forever
and take refuge in the shelter of your wings. *Selah*
5For you have heard my vows, O God;
you have given me the heritage of those who fear your name.

6Increase the days of the king's life,
his years for many generations.
7May he be enthroned in God's presence forever;
appoint your love and faithfulness to protect him.

8Then will I ever sing praise to your name
and fulfill my vows day after day.

Psalm 62

For the director of music. For Jeduthun. A psalm of David.

1My soul finds rest in God alone;
my salvation comes from him.
2He alone is my rock and my salvation;
he is my fortress, I will never be shaken.

3How long will you assault a man?
Would all of you throw him down—
this leaning wall, this tottering fence?
4They fully intend to topple him
from his lofty place;
they take delight in lies.
With their mouths they bless,
but in their hearts they curse. *Selah*

5Find rest, O my soul, in God alone;
my hope comes from him.
6He alone is my rock and my salvation;
he is my fortress, I will not be shaken.
7My salvation and my honor depend on God[a];
he is my mighty rock, my refuge.
8Trust in him at all times, O people;
pour out your hearts to him,
for God is our refuge. *Selah*

9Lowborn men are but a breath,
the highborn are but a lie;
if weighed on a balance, they are nothing;
together they are only a breath.
10Do not trust in extortion
or take pride in stolen goods;
though your riches increase,
do not set your heart on them.

11One thing God has spoken,
two things have I heard:
that you, O God, are strong,
12 and that you, O Lord, are loving.
Surely you will reward each person
according to what he has done.

Psalm 63

A psalm of David. When he was in the Desert of Judah.

1O God, you are my God,
earnestly I seek you;
my soul thirsts for you,
my body longs for you,
in a dry and weary land
where there is no water.

2I have seen you in the sanctuary
and beheld your power and your glory.
3Because your love is better than life,
my lips will glorify you.
4I will praise you as long as I live,
and in your name I will lift up my hands.
5My soul will be satisfied as with the richest of foods;
with singing lips my mouth will praise you.

6On my bed I remember you;

[a]7 Or / *God Most High is my salvation and my honor*

I think of you through the watches of
the night.
7 Because you are my help,
I sing in the shadow of your wings.
8 My soul clings to you;
your right hand upholds me.

9 They who seek my life will be destroyed;
they will go down to the depths of the
earth.
10 They will be given over to the sword
and become food for jackals.
11 But the king will rejoice in God;
all who swear by God's name will
praise him,
while the mouths of liars will be
silenced.

Psalm 64

For the director of music. A psalm of David.

1 Hear me, O God, as I voice my
complaint;
protect my life from the threat of the
enemy.
2 Hide me from the conspiracy of the
wicked,
from that noisy crowd of evildoers.

3 They sharpen their tongues like swords
and aim their words like deadly arrows.
4 They shoot from ambush at the innocent
man;
they shoot at him suddenly, without
fear.

5 They encourage each other in evil plans,
they talk about hiding their snares;
they say, "Who will see them[a]?"
6 They plot injustice and say,
"We have devised a perfect plan!"
Surely the mind and heart of man are
cunning.

7 But God will shoot them with arrows;
suddenly they will be struck down.
8 He will turn their own tongues against
them
and bring them to ruin;
all who see them will shake their heads
in scorn.

9 All mankind will fear;
they will proclaim the works of God
and ponder what he has done.

10 Let the righteous rejoice in the LORD
and take refuge in him;
let all the upright in heart praise him!

Psalm 65

For the director of music. A psalm of David.
A song.

1 Praise awaits[b] you, O God, in Zion;
to you our vows will be fulfilled.
2 O you who hear prayer,
to you all men will come.
3 When we were overwhelmed by sins,
you forgave[c] our transgressions.
4 Blessed are those you choose
and bring near to live in your courts!
We are filled with the good things of your
house,
of your holy temple.

5 You answer us with awesome deeds of
righteousness,
O God our Savior,
the hope of all the ends of the earth
and of the farthest seas,
6 who formed the mountains by your
power,
having armed yourself with strength,
7 who stilled the roaring of the seas,
the roaring of their waves,
and the turmoil of the nations.
8 Those living far away fear your wonders;
where morning dawns and evening
fades
you call forth songs of joy.

9 You care for the land and water it;
you enrich it abundantly.
The streams of God are filled with water
to provide the people with grain,
for so you have ordained it.[d]
10 You drench its furrows
and level its ridges;
you soften it with showers
and bless its crops.
11 You crown the year with your bounty,
and your carts overflow with
abundance.
12 The grasslands of the desert overflow;
the hills are clothed with gladness.
13 The meadows are covered with flocks
and the valleys are mantled with grain;
they shout for joy and sing.

[a]5 Or *us* [b]1 Or *befits;* the meaning of the Hebrew for this word is uncertain. [c]3 Or *made atonement for*
[d]9 Or *for that is how you prepare the land*

Psalm 66

For the director of music. A song. A psalm.

1Shout with joy to God, all the earth!
2 Sing the glory of his name;
make his praise glorious!
3Say to God, "How awesome are your deeds!
So great is your power
that your enemies cringe before you.
4All the earth bows down to you;
they sing praise to you,
they sing praise to your name." *Selah*

5Come and see what God has done,
how awesome his works in man's behalf!
6He turned the sea into dry land,
they passed through the waters on foot—
come, let us rejoice in him.
7He rules forever by his power,
his eyes watch the nations—
let not the rebellious rise up against him. *Selah*

8Praise our God, O peoples,
let the sound of his praise be heard;
9he has preserved our lives
and kept our feet from slipping.
10For you, O God, tested us;
you refined us like silver.
11You brought us into prison
and laid burdens on our backs.
12You let men ride over our heads;
we went through fire and water,
but you brought us to a place of abundance.

13I will come to your temple with burnt offerings
and fulfill my vows to you—
14vows my lips promised and my mouth spoke
when I was in trouble.
15I will sacrifice fat animals to you
and an offering of rams;
I will offer bulls and goats. *Selah*

16Come and listen, all you who fear God;
let me tell you what he has done for me.
17I cried out to him with my mouth;
his praise was on my tongue.
18If I had cherished sin in my heart,
the Lord would not have listened;
19but God has surely listened
and heard my voice in prayer.
20Praise be to God,
who has not rejected my prayer
or withheld his love from me!

Psalm 67

For the director of music. With stringed instruments. A psalm. A song.

1May God be gracious to us and bless us
and make his face shine upon us, *Selah*
2that your ways may be known on earth,
your salvation among all nations.

3May the peoples praise you, O God;
may all the peoples praise you.
4May the nations be glad and sing for joy,
for you rule the peoples justly
and guide the nations of the earth. *Selah*
5May the peoples praise you, O God;
may all the peoples praise you.

6Then the land will yield its harvest,
and God, our God, will bless us.
7God will bless us,
and all the ends of the earth will fear him.

Psalm 68

For the director of music. Of David. A psalm. A song.

1May God arise, may his enemies be scattered;
may his foes flee before him.
2As smoke is blown away by the wind,
may you blow them away;
as wax melts before the fire,
may the wicked perish before God.
3But may the righteous be glad
and rejoice before God;
may they be happy and joyful.

4Sing to God, sing praise to his name,
extol him who rides on the clouds[a]—
his name is the LORD—
and rejoice before him.
5A father to the fatherless, a defender of widows,
is God in his holy dwelling.
6God sets the lonely in families,[b]

[a]4 Or / *prepare the way for him who rides through the deserts*
[b]6 Or *the desolate in a homeland*

he leads forth the prisoners with
singing;
but the rebellious live in a sun-scorched
land.

7When you went out before your people,
O God,
when you marched through the
wasteland, *Selah*
8the earth shook,
the heavens poured down rain,
before God, the One of Sinai,
before God, the God of Israel.
9You gave abundant showers, O God;
you refreshed your weary inheritance.
10Your people settled in it,
and from your bounty, O God, you
provided for the poor.

11The Lord announced the word,
and great was the company of those
who proclaimed it:
12"Kings and armies flee in haste;
in the camps men divide the plunder.
13Even while you sleep among the
campfires,[a]
the wings of ⌊my⌋ dove are sheathed
with silver,
its feathers with shining gold."
14When the Almighty[b] scattered the kings
in the land,
it was like snow fallen on Zalmon.

15The mountains of Bashan are majestic
mountains;
rugged are the mountains of Bashan.
16Why gaze in envy, O rugged mountains,
at the mountain where God chooses to
reign,
where the LORD himself will dwell
forever?
17The chariots of God are tens of
thousands
and thousands of thousands;
the Lord ⌊has come⌋ from Sinai into his
sanctuary.
18When you ascended on high,
you led captives in your train;
you received gifts from men,
even from[c] the rebellious—
that you,[d] O LORD God, might dwell
there.

19Praise be to the Lord, to God our Savior,
who daily bears our burdens. *Selah*
20Our God is a God who saves;
from the Sovereign LORD comes escape
from death.

21Surely God will crush the heads of his
enemies,
the hairy crowns of those who go on in
their sins.
22The Lord says, "I will bring them from
Bashan;
I will bring them from the depths of the
sea,
23that you may plunge your feet in the
blood of your foes,
while the tongues of your dogs have
their share."

24Your procession has come into view,
O God,
the procession of my God and King into
the sanctuary.
25In front are the singers, after them the
musicians;
with them are the maidens playing
tambourines.
26Praise God in the great congregation;
praise the LORD in the assembly of
Israel.
27There is the little tribe of Benjamin,
leading them,
there the great throng of Judah's
princes,
and there the princes of Zebulun and of
Naphtali.

28Summon your power, O God[e];
show us your strength, O God, as you
have done before.
29Because of your temple at Jerusalem
kings will bring you gifts.
30Rebuke the beast among the reeds,
the herd of bulls among the calves of
the nations.
Humbled, may it bring bars of silver.
Scatter the nations who delight in war.
31Envoys will come from Egypt;
Cush[f] will submit herself to God.

32Sing to God, O kingdoms of the earth,
sing praise to the Lord, *Selah*
33to him who rides the ancient skies above,
who thunders with mighty voice.
34Proclaim the power of God,
whose majesty is over Israel,
whose power is in the skies.
35You are awesome, O God, in your
sanctuary;

[a]13 Or *saddlebags* [b]14 Hebrew *Shaddai* [c]18 Or *gifts for men, / even* [d]18 Or *they* [e]28 Many Hebrew manuscripts, Septuagint and Syriac; most Hebrew manuscripts *Your God has summoned power for you*
[f]31 That is, the upper Nile region

the God of Israel gives power and
strength to his people.

Praise be to God!

Psalm 69

For the director of music. To ⌞the tune of⌟ "Lilies." Of David.

1 Save me, O God,
for the waters have come up to my neck.
2 I sink in the miry depths,
where there is no foothold.
I have come into the deep waters;
the floods engulf me.
3 I am worn out calling for help;
my throat is parched.
My eyes fail,
looking for my God.
4 Those who hate me without reason
outnumber the hairs of my head;
many are my enemies without cause,
those who seek to destroy me.
I am forced to restore
what I did not steal.

5 You know my folly, O God;
my guilt is not hidden from you.

6 May those who hope in you
not be disgraced because of me,
O Lord, the LORD Almighty;
may those who seek you
not be put to shame because of me,
O God of Israel.
7 For I endure scorn for your sake,
and shame covers my face.
8 I am a stranger to my brothers,
an alien to my own mother's sons;
9 for zeal for your house consumes me,
and the insults of those who insult you fall on me.
10 When I weep and fast,
I must endure scorn;
11 when I put on sackcloth,
people make sport of me.
12 Those who sit at the gate mock me,
and I am the song of the drunkards.

13 But I pray to you, O LORD,
in the time of your favor;
in your great love, O God,
answer me with your sure salvation.
14 Rescue me from the mire,
do not let me sink;
deliver me from those who hate me,
from the deep waters.
15 Do not let the floodwaters engulf me
or the depths swallow me up
or the pit close its mouth over me.
16 Answer me, O LORD, out of the goodness of your love;
in your great mercy turn to me.
17 Do not hide your face from your servant;
answer me quickly, for I am in trouble.
18 Come near and rescue me;
redeem me because of my foes.

19 You know how I am scorned, disgraced and shamed;
all my enemies are before you.
20 Scorn has broken my heart
and has left me helpless;
I looked for sympathy, but there was none,
for comforters, but I found none.
21 They put gall in my food
and gave me vinegar for my thirst.

22 May the table set before them become a snare;
may it become retribution and[a] a trap.
23 May their eyes be darkened so they cannot see,
and their backs be bent forever.
24 Pour out your wrath on them;
let your fierce anger overtake them.
25 May their place be deserted;
let there be no one to dwell in their tents.
26 For they persecute those you wound
and talk about the pain of those you hurt.
27 Charge them with crime upon crime;
do not let them share in your salvation.
28 May they be blotted out of the book of life
and not be listed with the righteous.

29 I am in pain and distress;
may your salvation, O God, protect me.

30 I will praise God's name in song
and glorify him with thanksgiving.
31 This will please the LORD more than an ox,
more than a bull with its horns and hoofs.
32 The poor will see and be glad—
you who seek God, may your hearts live!
33 The LORD hears the needy

[a]22 Or *snare / and their fellowship become*

and does not despise his captive
people.
34Let heaven and earth praise him,
the seas and all that move in them,
35for God will save Zion
and rebuild the cities of Judah.
Then people will settle there and
possess it;
36 the children of his servants will
inherit it,
and those who love his name will
dwell there.

Psalm 70

For the director of music. Of David.
A petition.

1Hasten, O God, to save me;
O LORD, come quickly to help me.
2May those who seek my life
be put to shame and confusion;
may all who desire my ruin
be turned back in disgrace.
3May those who say to me, "Aha! Aha!"
turn back because of their shame.
4But may all who seek you
rejoice and be glad in you;
may those who love your salvation
always say,
"Let God be exalted!"

5Yet I am poor and needy;
come quickly to me, O God.
You are my help and my deliverer;
O LORD, do not delay.

Psalm 71

1In you, O LORD, I have taken refuge;
let me never be put to shame.
2Rescue me and deliver me in your
righteousness;
turn your ear to me and save me.
3Be my rock of refuge,
to which I can always go;
give the command to save me,
for you are my rock and my fortress.
4Deliver me, O my God, from the hand of
the wicked,
from the grasp of evil and cruel men.

5For you have been my hope,
O Sovereign LORD,
my confidence since my youth.
6From birth I have relied on you;
you brought me forth from my mother's
womb.
I will ever praise you.
7I have become like a portent to many,
but you are my strong refuge.
8My mouth is filled with your praise,
declaring your splendor all day long.

9Do not cast me away when I am old;
do not forsake me when my strength is
gone.
10For my enemies speak against me;
those who wait to kill me conspire
together.
11They say, "God has forsaken him;
pursue him and seize him,
for no one will rescue him."
12Be not far from me, O God;
come quickly, O my God, to help me.
13May my accusers perish in shame;
may those who want to harm me
be covered with scorn and disgrace.

14But as for me, I will always have hope;
I will praise you more and more.
15My mouth will tell of your righteousness,
of your salvation all day long,
though I know not its measure.
16I will come and proclaim your mighty
acts, O Sovereign LORD;
I will proclaim your righteousness,
yours alone.
17Since my youth, O God, you have taught
me,
and to this day I declare your
marvelous deeds.
18Even when I am old and gray,
do not forsake me, O God,
till I declare your power to the next
generation,
your might to all who are to come.

19Your righteousness reaches to the skies,
O God,
you who have done great things.
Who, O God, is like you?
20Though you have made me see troubles,
many and bitter,
you will restore my life again;
from the depths of the earth
you will again bring me up.
21You will increase my honor
and comfort me once again.

22I will praise you with the harp
for your faithfulness, O my God;
I will sing praise to you with the lyre,

O Holy One of Israel.
[23]My lips will shout for joy
when I sing praise to you—
I, whom you have redeemed.
[24]My tongue will tell of your righteous acts
all day long,
for those who wanted to harm me
have been put to shame and confusion.

Psalm 72

Of Solomon.

[1]Endow the king with your justice, O God,
the royal son with your righteousness.
[2]He will[a] judge your people in
righteousness,
your afflicted ones with justice.
[3]The mountains will bring prosperity to the
people,
the hills the fruit of righteousness.
[4]He will defend the afflicted among the
people
and save the children of the needy;
he will crush the oppressor.

[5]He will endure[b] as long as the sun,
as long as the moon, through all
generations.
[6]He will be like rain falling on a mown
field,
like showers watering the earth.
[7]In his days the righteous will flourish;
prosperity will abound till the moon is
no more.

[8]He will rule from sea to sea
and from the River[c] to the ends of the
earth.[d]
[9]The desert tribes will bow before him
and his enemies will lick the dust.
[10]The kings of Tarshish and of distant
shores
will bring tribute to him;
the kings of Sheba and Seba
will present him gifts.
[11]All kings will bow down to him
and all nations will serve him.

[12]For he will deliver the needy who cry out,
the afflicted who have no one to help.
[13]He will take pity on the weak and the
needy
and save the needy from death.
[14]He will rescue them from oppression and
violence,
for precious is their blood in his sight.

[15]Long may he live!
May gold from Sheba be given him.
May people ever pray for him
and bless him all day long.
[16]Let grain abound throughout the land;
on the tops of the hills may it sway.
Let its fruit flourish like Lebanon;
let it thrive like the grass of the field.
[17]May his name endure forever;
may it continue as long as the sun.

All nations will be blessed through him,
and they will call him blessed.

[18]Praise be to the LORD God, the God of
Israel,
who alone does marvelous deeds.
[19]Praise be to his glorious name forever;
may the whole earth be filled with his
glory.
Amen and Amen.

[20]This concludes the prayers of David son
of Jesse.

BOOK III

Psalms 73-89

Psalm 73

A psalm of Asaph.

[1]Surely God is good to Israel,
to those who are pure in heart.

[2]But as for me, my feet had almost
slipped;
I had nearly lost my foothold.
[3]For I envied the arrogant
when I saw the prosperity of the
wicked.

[4]They have no struggles;
their bodies are healthy and strong.[e]
[5]They are free from the burdens common
to man;
they are not plagued by human ills.
[6]Therefore pride is their necklace;

[a]2 Or *May he*; similarly in verses 3-11 and 17 [b]5 Septuagint; Hebrew *You will be feared* [c]8 That is, the Euphrates [d]8 Or *the end of the land* [e]4 With a different word division of the Hebrew; Masoretic Text *struggles at their death; / their bodies are healthy*

they clothe themselves with violence.
7From their callous hearts comes iniquity[a];
the evil conceits of their minds know no limits.
8They scoff, and speak with malice;
in their arrogance they threaten oppression.
9Their mouths lay claim to heaven,
and their tongues take possession of the earth.
10Therefore their people turn to them
and drink up waters in abundance.[b]
11They say, "How can God know?
Does the Most High have knowledge?"

12This is what the wicked are like—
always carefree, they increase in wealth.
13Surely in vain have I kept my heart pure;
in vain have I washed my hands in innocence.
14All day long I have been plagued;
I have been punished every morning.

15If I had said, "I will speak thus,"
I would have betrayed your children.
16When I tried to understand all this,
it was oppressive to me
17till I entered the sanctuary of God;
then I understood their final destiny.

18Surely you place them on slippery ground;
you cast them down to ruin.
19How suddenly are they destroyed,
completely swept away by terrors!
20As a dream when one awakes,
so when you arise, O Lord,
you will despise them as fantasies.

21When my heart was grieved
and my spirit embittered,
22I was senseless and ignorant;
I was a brute beast before you.

23Yet I am always with you;
you hold me by my right hand.
24You guide me with your counsel,
and afterward you will take me into glory.
25Whom have I in heaven but you?
And earth has nothing I desire besides you.
26My flesh and my heart may fail,
but God is the strength of my heart
and my portion forever.

27Those who are far from you will perish;
you destroy all who are unfaithful to you.
28But as for me, it is good to be near God.
I have made the Sovereign LORD my refuge;
I will tell of all your deeds.

Psalm 74

A *maskil*[c] of Asaph.

1Why have you rejected us forever, O God?
Why does your anger smolder against the sheep of your pasture?
2Remember the people you purchased of old,
the tribe of your inheritance, whom you redeemed—
Mount Zion, where you dwelt.
3Turn your steps toward these everlasting ruins,
all this destruction the enemy has brought on the sanctuary.

4Your foes roared in the place where you met with us;
they set up their standards as signs.
5They behaved like men wielding axes
to cut through a thicket of trees.
6They smashed all the carved paneling
with their axes and hatchets.
7They burned your sanctuary to the ground;
they defiled the dwelling place of your Name.
8They said in their hearts, "We will crush them completely!"
They burned every place where God was worshiped in the land.
9We are given no miraculous signs;
no prophets are left,
and none of us knows how long this will be.

10How long will the enemy mock you, O God?
Will the foe revile your name forever?
11Why do you hold back your hand, your right hand?
Take it from the folds of your garment and destroy them!

12But you, O God, are my king from of old;

[a]7 Syriac (see also Septuagint); Hebrew *Their eyes bulge with fat* [b]*10* The meaning of the Hebrew for this verse is uncertain. [c]Title: Probably a literary or musical term

you bring salvation upon the earth.
13It was you who split open the sea by your power;
you broke the heads of the monster in the waters.
14It was you who crushed the heads of Leviathan
and gave him as food to the creatures of the desert.
15It was you who opened up springs and streams;
you dried up the ever flowing rivers.
16The day is yours, and yours also the night;
you established the sun and moon.
17It was you who set all the boundaries of the earth;
you made both summer and winter.

18Remember how the enemy has mocked you, O LORD,
how foolish people have reviled your name.
19Do not hand over the life of your dove to wild beasts;
do not forget the lives of your afflicted people forever.
20Have regard for your covenant,
because haunts of violence fill the dark places of the land.
21Do not let the oppressed retreat in disgrace;
may the poor and needy praise your name.
22Rise up, O God, and defend your cause;
remember how fools mock you all day long.
23Do not ignore the clamor of your adversaries,
the uproar of your enemies, which rises continually.

Psalm 75

For the director of music. ⌞To the tune of⌟ "Do Not Destroy." A psalm of Asaph. A song.

1We give thanks to you, O God,
we give thanks, for your Name is near;
men tell of your wonderful deeds.
2You say, "I choose the appointed time;
it is I who judge uprightly.
3When the earth and all its people quake,
it is I who hold its pillars firm. *Selah*
4To the arrogant I say, 'Boast no more,'
and to the wicked, 'Do not lift up your horns.
5Do not lift your horns against heaven;
do not speak with outstretched neck.' "

6No one from the east or the west
or from the desert can exalt a man.
7But it is God who judges:
He brings one down, he exalts another.
8In the hand of the LORD is a cup
full of foaming wine mixed with spices;
he pours it out, and all the wicked of the earth
drink it down to its very dregs.

9As for me, I will declare this forever;
I will sing praise to the God of Jacob.
10I will cut off the horns of all the wicked,
but the horns of the righteous will be lifted up.

Psalm 76

For the director of music. With stringed instruments. A psalm of Asaph. A song.

1In Judah God is known;
his name is great in Israel.
2His tent is in Salem,
his dwelling place in Zion.
3There he broke the flashing arrows,
the shields and the swords, the weapons of war. *Selah*

4You are resplendent with light,
more majestic than mountains rich with game.
5Valiant men lie plundered,
they sleep their last sleep;
not one of the warriors
can lift his hands.
6At your rebuke, O God of Jacob,
both horse and chariot lie still.
7You alone are to be feared.
Who can stand before you when you are angry?
8From heaven you pronounced judgment,
and the land feared and was quiet—
9when you, O God, rose up to judge,
to save all the afflicted of the land. *Selah*
10Surely your wrath against men brings you praise,
and the survivors of your wrath are restrained.[a]

[a] 10 Or *Surely the wrath of men brings you praise, / and with the remainder of wrath you arm yourself*

11Make vows to the LORD your God and
fulfill them;
let all the neighboring lands
bring gifts to the One to be feared.
12He breaks the spirit of rulers;
he is feared by the kings of the earth.

Psalm 77

For the director of music. For Jeduthun.
Of Asaph. A psalm.

1I cried out to God for help;
I cried out to God to hear me.
2When I was in distress, I sought the Lord;
at night I stretched out untiring hands
and my soul refused to be comforted.

3I remembered you, O God, and I
groaned;
I mused, and my spirit grew faint. *Selah*
4You kept my eyes from closing;
I was too troubled to speak.
5I thought about the former days,
the years of long ago;
6I remembered my songs in the night.
My heart mused and my spirit inquired:

7"Will the Lord reject forever?
Will he never show his favor again?
8Has his unfailing love vanished forever?
Has his promise failed for all time?
9Has God forgotten to be merciful?
Has he in anger withheld his
compassion?" *Selah*

10Then I thought, "To this I will appeal:
the years of the right hand of the Most
High."
11I will remember the deeds of the LORD;
yes, I will remember your miracles of
long ago.
12I will meditate on all your works
and consider all your mighty deeds.

13Your ways, O God, are holy.
What god is so great as our God?
14You are the God who performs miracles;
you display your power among the
peoples.
15With your mighty arm you redeemed your
people,
the descendants of Jacob and Joseph.
Selah

16The waters saw you, O God,
the waters saw you and writhed;
the very depths were convulsed.
17The clouds poured down water,
the skies resounded with thunder;
your arrows flashed back and forth.
18Your thunder was heard in the whirlwind,
your lightning lit up the world;
the earth trembled and quaked.
19Your path led through the sea,
your way through the mighty waters,
though your footprints were not seen.

20You led your people like a flock
by the hand of Moses and Aaron.

Psalm 78

A *maskil*[a] of Asaph.

1O my people, hear my teaching;
listen to the words of my mouth.
2I will open my mouth in parables,
I will utter hidden things, things from of
old—
3what we have heard and known,
what our fathers have told us.
4We will not hide them from their children;
we will tell the next generation
the praiseworthy deeds of the LORD,
his power, and the wonders he has
done.
5He decreed statutes for Jacob
and established the law in Israel,
which he commanded our forefathers
to teach their children,
6so the next generation would know them,
even the children yet to be born,
and they in turn would tell their
children.
7Then they would put their trust in God
and would not forget his deeds
but would keep his commands.
8They would not be like their forefathers—
a stubborn and rebellious generation,
whose hearts were not loyal to God,
whose spirits were not faithful to him.

9The men of Ephraim, though armed with
bows,
turned back on the day of battle;
10they did not keep God's covenant
and refused to live by his law.
11They forgot what he had done,
the wonders he had shown them.
12He did miracles in the sight of their
fathers
in the land of Egypt, in the region of
Zoan.

[a]Title: Probably a literary or musical term

13He divided the sea and led them through;
he made the water stand firm like a wall.
14He guided them with the cloud by day
and with light from the fire all night.
15He split the rocks in the desert
and gave them water as abundant as the seas;
16he brought streams out of a rocky crag
and made water flow down like rivers.

17But they continued to sin against him,
rebelling in the desert against the Most High.
18They willfully put God to the test
by demanding the food they craved.
19They spoke against God, saying,
"Can God spread a table in the desert?
20When he struck the rock, water gushed out,
and streams flowed abundantly.
But can he also give us food?
Can he supply meat for his people?"
21When the LORD heard them, he was very angry;
his fire broke out against Jacob,
and his wrath rose against Israel,
22for they did not believe in God
or trust in his deliverance.
23Yet he gave a command to the skies above
and opened the doors of the heavens;
24he rained down manna for the people to eat,
he gave them the grain of heaven.
25Men ate the bread of angels;
he sent them all the food they could eat.
26He let loose the east wind from the heavens
and led forth the south wind by his power.
27He rained meat down on them like dust,
flying birds like sand on the seashore.
28He made them come down inside their camp,
all around their tents.
29They ate till they had more than enough,
for he had given them what they craved.
30But before they turned from the food they craved,
even while it was still in their mouths,
31God's anger rose against them;
he put to death the sturdiest among them,
cutting down the young men of Israel.

32In spite of all this, they kept on sinning;
in spite of his wonders, they did not believe.
33So he ended their days in futility
and their years in terror.
34Whenever God slew them, they would seek him;
they eagerly turned to him again.
35They remembered that God was their Rock,
that God Most High was their Redeemer.
36But then they would flatter him with their mouths,
lying to him with their tongues;
37their hearts were not loyal to him,
they were not faithful to his covenant.
38Yet he was merciful;
he forgave their iniquities
and did not destroy them.
Time after time he restrained his anger
and did not stir up his full wrath.
39He remembered that they were but flesh,
a passing breeze that does not return.

40How often they rebelled against him in the desert
and grieved him in the wasteland!
41Again and again they put God to the test;
they vexed the Holy One of Israel.
42They did not remember his power—
the day he redeemed them from the oppressor,
43the day he displayed his miraculous signs in Egypt,
his wonders in the region of Zoan.
44He turned their rivers to blood;
they could not drink from their streams.
45He sent swarms of flies that devoured them,
and frogs that devastated them.
46He gave their crops to the grasshopper,
their produce to the locust.
47He destroyed their vines with hail
and their sycamore-figs with sleet.
48He gave over their cattle to the hail,
their livestock to bolts of lightning.
49He unleashed against them his hot anger,
his wrath, indignation and hostility—
a band of destroying angels.
50He prepared a path for his anger;
he did not spare them from death
but gave them over to the plague.
51He struck down all the firstborn of Egypt,
the firstfruits of manhood in the tents of Ham.

[52]But he brought his people out like a flock;
he led them like sheep through the desert.
[53]He guided them safely, so they were unafraid;
but the sea engulfed their enemies.
[54]Thus he brought them to the border of his holy land,
to the hill country his right hand had taken.
[55]He drove out nations before them
and allotted their lands to them as an inheritance;
he settled the tribes of Israel in their homes.

[56]But they put God to the test
and rebelled against the Most High;
they did not keep his statutes.
[57]Like their fathers they were disloyal and faithless,
as unreliable as a faulty bow.
[58]They angered him with their high places;
they aroused his jealousy with their idols.
[59]When God heard them, he was very angry;
he rejected Israel completely.
[60]He abandoned the tabernacle of Shiloh,
the tent he had set up among men.
[61]He sent ⌊the ark of⌋ his might into captivity,
his splendor into the hands of the enemy.
[62]He gave his people over to the sword;
he was very angry with his inheritance.
[63]Fire consumed their young men,
and their maidens had no wedding songs;
[64]their priests were put to the sword,
and their widows could not weep.

[65]Then the Lord awoke as from sleep,
as a man wakes from the stupor of wine.
[66]He beat back his enemies;
he put them to everlasting shame.
[67]Then he rejected the tents of Joseph,
he did not choose the tribe of Ephraim;
[68]but he chose the tribe of Judah,
Mount Zion, which he loved.
[69]He built his sanctuary like the heights,
like the earth that he established forever.
[70]He chose David his servant
and took him from the sheep pens;
[71]from tending the sheep he brought him
to be the shepherd of his people Jacob,
of Israel his inheritance.
[72]And David shepherded them with integrity of heart;
with skillful hands he led them.

Psalm 79

A psalm of Asaph.

[1]O God, the nations have invaded your inheritance;
they have defiled your holy temple,
they have reduced Jerusalem to rubble.
[2]They have given the dead bodies of your servants
as food to the birds of the air,
the flesh of your saints to the beasts of the earth.
[3]They have poured out blood like water
all around Jerusalem,
and there is no one to bury the dead.
[4]We are objects of reproach to our neighbors,
of scorn and derision to those around us.

[5]How long, O LORD? Will you be angry forever?
How long will your jealousy burn like fire?
[6]Pour out your wrath on the nations
that do not acknowledge you,
on the kingdoms
that do not call on your name;
[7]for they have devoured Jacob
and destroyed his homeland.
[8]Do not hold against us the sins of the fathers;
may your mercy come quickly to meet us,
for we are in desperate need.
[9]Help us, O God our Savior,
for the glory of your name;
deliver us and forgive our sins
for your name's sake.
[10]Why should the nations say,
"Where is their God?"
Before our eyes, make known among the nations
that you avenge the outpoured blood of your servants.
[11]May the groans of the prisoners come before you;
by the strength of your arm
preserve those condemned to die.

[12]Pay back into the laps of our neighbors
seven times
the reproach they have hurled at you,
O Lord.
[13]Then we your people, the sheep of your
pasture,
will praise you forever;
from generation to generation
we will recount your praise.

Psalm 80

For the director of music. To ⌞the tune of⌟ "The Lilies of the Covenant." Of Asaph. A psalm.

[1]Hear us, O Shepherd of Israel,
you who lead Joseph like a flock;
you who sit enthroned between the
cherubim, shine forth
[2] before Ephraim, Benjamin and
Manasseh.
Awaken your might;
come and save us.

[3]Restore us, O God;
make your face shine upon us,
that we may be saved.

[4]O LORD God Almighty,
how long will your anger smolder
against the prayers of your people?
[5]You have fed them with the bread of
tears;
you have made them drink tears by the
bowlful.
[6]You have made us a source of contention
to our neighbors,
and our enemies mock us.

[7]Restore us, O God Almighty;
make your face shine upon us,
that we may be saved.

[8]You brought a vine out of Egypt;
you drove out the nations and planted
it.
[9]You cleared the ground for it,
and it took root and filled the land.
[10]The mountains were covered with its
shade,
the mighty cedars with its branches.
[11]It sent out its boughs to the Sea,[a]
its shoots as far as the River.[b]

[12]Why have you broken down its walls
so that all who pass by pick its grapes?
[13]Boars from the forest ravage it
and the creatures of the field feed on it.
[14]Return to us, O God Almighty!
Look down from heaven and see!
Watch over this vine,
[15] the root your right hand has planted,
the son[c] you have raised up for
yourself.

[16]Your vine is cut down, it is burned with
fire;
at your rebuke your people perish.
[17]Let your hand rest on the man at your
right hand,
the son of man you have raised up for
yourself.
[18]Then we will not turn away from you;
revive us, and we will call on your
name.

[19]Restore us, O LORD God Almighty;
make your face shine upon us,
that we may be saved.

Psalm 81

For the director of music. According to *gittith.*[d] Of Asaph.

[1]Sing for joy to God our strength;
shout aloud to the God of Jacob!
[2]Begin the music, strike the tambourine,
play the melodious harp and lyre.

[3]Sound the ram's horn at the New Moon,
and when the moon is full, on the day
of our Feast;
[4]this is a decree for Israel,
an ordinance of the God of Jacob.
[5]He established it as a statute for Joseph
when he went out against Egypt,
where we heard a language we did not
understand.[e]

[6]He says, "I removed the burden from
their shoulders;
their hands were set free from the
basket.
[7]In your distress you called and I rescued
you,
I answered you out of a thundercloud;
I tested you at the waters of Meribah.
Selah
[8]"Hear, O my people, and I will warn
you—

[a]11 Probably the Mediterranean [b]11 That is, the Euphrates [c]15 Or *branch* [d]Title: Probably a musical term [e]5 Or / *and we heard a voice we had not known*

if you would but listen to me, O Israel!
[9]You shall have no foreign god among you;
you shall not bow down to an alien god.
[10]I am the LORD your God,
who brought you up out of Egypt.
Open wide your mouth and I will fill it.

[11]"But my people would not listen to me;
Israel would not submit to me.
[12]So I gave them over to their stubborn hearts
to follow their own devices.

[13]"If my people would but listen to me,
if Israel would follow my ways,
[14]how quickly would I subdue their enemies
and turn my hand against their foes!
[15]Those who hate the LORD would cringe before him,
and their punishment would last forever.
[16]But you would be fed with the finest of wheat;
with honey from the rock I would satisfy you."

Psalm 82

A psalm of Asaph.

[1]God presides in the great assembly;
he gives judgment among the "gods":

[2]"How long will you[a] defend the unjust
and show partiality to the wicked? *Selah*
[3]Defend the cause of the weak and fatherless;
maintain the rights of the poor and oppressed.
[4]Rescue the weak and needy;
deliver them from the hand of the wicked.

[5]"They know nothing, they understand nothing.
They walk about in darkness;
all the foundations of the earth are shaken.

[6]"I said, 'You are "gods";
you are all sons of the Most High.'
[7]But you will die like mere men;
you will fall like every other ruler."

[8]Rise up, O God, judge the earth,
for all the nations are your inheritance.

Psalm 83

A song. A psalm of Asaph.

[1]O God, do not keep silent;
be not quiet, O God, be not still.
[2]See how your enemies are astir,
how your foes rear their heads.
[3]With cunning they conspire against your people;
they plot against those you cherish.
[4]"Come," they say, "let us destroy them as a nation,
that the name of Israel be remembered no more."

[5]With one mind they plot together;
they form an alliance against you—
[6]the tents of Edom and the Ishmaelites,
of Moab and the Hagrites,
[7]Gebal,[b] Ammon and Amalek,
Philistia, with the people of Tyre.
[8]Even Assyria has joined them
to lend strength to the descendants of Lot. *Selah*

[9]Do to them as you did to Midian,
as you did to Sisera and Jabin at the river Kishon,
[10]who perished at Endor
and became like refuse on the ground.
[11]Make their nobles like Oreb and Zeeb,
all their princes like Zebah and Zalmunna,
[12]who said, "Let us take possession
of the pasturelands of God."

[13]Make them like tumbleweed, O my God,
like chaff before the wind.
[14]As fire consumes the forest
or a flame sets the mountains ablaze,
[15]so pursue them with your tempest
and terrify them with your storm.
[16]Cover their faces with shame
so that men will seek your name, O LORD.

[17]May they ever be ashamed and dismayed;
may they perish in disgrace.
[18]Let them know that you, whose name is the LORD—
that you alone are the Most High over all the earth.

[a]2 The Hebrew is plural. [b]7 That is, Byblos

Psalm 84

For the director of music. According to *gittith*.[a] Of the Sons of Korah. A psalm.

[1]How lovely is your dwelling place,
O LORD Almighty!
[2]My soul yearns, even faints,
for the courts of the LORD;
my heart and my flesh cry out
for the living God.

[3]Even the sparrow has found a home,
and the swallow a nest for herself,
where she may have her young—
a place near your altar,
O LORD Almighty, my King and my God.
[4]Blessed are those who dwell in your house;
they are ever praising you. *Selah*

[5]Blessed are those whose strength is in you,
who have set their hearts on pilgrimage.
[6]As they pass through the Valley of Baca,
they make it a place of springs;
the autumn rains also cover it with pools.[b]
[7]They go from strength to strength,
till each appears before God in Zion.

[8]Hear my prayer, O LORD God Almighty;
listen to me, O God of Jacob. *Selah*
[9]Look upon our shield,[c] O God;
look with favor on your anointed one.

[10]Better is one day in your courts
than a thousand elsewhere;
I would rather be a doorkeeper in the house of my God
than dwell in the tents of the wicked.
[11]For the LORD God is a sun and shield;
the LORD bestows favor and honor;
no good thing does he withhold
from those whose walk is blameless.

[12]O LORD Almighty,
blessed is the man who trusts in you.

Psalm 85

For the director of music. Of the Sons of Korah. A psalm.

[1]You showed favor to your land, O LORD;
you restored the fortunes of Jacob.
[2]You forgave the iniquity of your people
and covered all their sins. *Selah*
[3]You set aside all your wrath
and turned from your fierce anger.

[4]Restore us again, O God our Savior,
and put away your displeasure toward us.
[5]Will you be angry with us forever?
Will you prolong your anger through all generations?
[6]Will you not revive us again,
that your people may rejoice in you?
[7]Show us your unfailing love, O LORD,
and grant us your salvation.

[8]I will listen to what God the LORD will say;
he promises peace to his people, his saints—
but let them not return to folly.
[9]Surely his salvation is near those who fear him,
that his glory may dwell in our land.

[10]Love and faithfulness meet together;
righteousness and peace kiss each other.
[11]Faithfulness springs forth from the earth,
and righteousness looks down from heaven.
[12]The LORD will indeed give what is good,
and our land will yield its harvest.
[13]Righteousness goes before him
and prepares the way for his steps.

Psalm 86

A prayer of David.

[1]Hear, O LORD, and answer me,
for I am poor and needy.
[2]Guard my life, for I am devoted to you.
You are my God; save your servant
who trusts in you.
[3]Have mercy on me, O Lord,
for I call to you all day long.
[4]Bring joy to your servant,
for to you, O Lord,
I lift up my soul.

[5]You are forgiving and good, O Lord,
abounding in love to all who call to you.
[6]Hear my prayer, O LORD;
listen to my cry for mercy.
[7]In the day of my trouble I will call to you,
for you will answer me.

[a]Title: Probably a musical term [b]6 Or *blessings* [c]9 Or *sovereign*

8Among the gods there is none like you,
O Lord;
no deeds can compare with yours.
9All the nations you have made
will come and worship before you,
O Lord;
they will bring glory to your name.
10For you are great and do marvelous
deeds;
you alone are God.

11Teach me your way, O LORD,
and I will walk in your truth;
give me an undivided heart,
that I may fear your name.
12I will praise you, O Lord my God, with all
my heart;
I will glorify your name forever.
13For great is your love toward me;
you have delivered me from the depths
of the grave.[a]

14The arrogant are attacking me, O God;
a band of ruthless men seeks my life—
men without regard for you.
15But you, O Lord, are a compassionate
and gracious God,
slow to anger, abounding in love and
faithfulness.
16Turn to me and have mercy on me;
grant your strength to your servant
and save the son of your maidservant.[b]
17Give me a sign of your goodness,
that my enemies may see it and be put
to shame,
for you, O LORD, have helped me and
comforted me.

Psalm 87

Of the Sons of Korah. A psalm. A song.

1He has set his foundation on the holy
mountain;
2 the LORD loves the gates of Zion
more than all the dwellings of Jacob.
3Glorious things are said of you,
O city of God: *Selah*
4"I will record Rahab[c] and Babylon
among those who acknowledge me—
Philistia too, and Tyre, along with
Cush[d]—
and will say, 'This[e] one was born in
Zion.' "
5Indeed, of Zion it will be said,
"This one and that one were born in
her,
and the Most High himself will establish
her."
6The LORD will write in the register of the
peoples:
"This one was born in Zion." *Selah*
7As they make music they will sing,
"All my fountains are in you."

Psalm 88

A song. A psalm of the Sons of Korah. For the director of music. According to *mahalath leannoth*.[f] A *maskil*[g] of Heman the Ezrahite.

1O LORD, the God who saves me,
day and night I cry out before you.
2May my prayer come before you;
turn your ear to my cry.

3For my soul is full of trouble
and my life draws near the grave.[a]
4I am counted among those who go down
to the pit;
I am like a man without strength.
5I am set apart with the dead,
like the slain who lie in the grave,
whom you remember no more,
who are cut off from your care.

6You have put me in the lowest pit,
in the darkest depths.
7Your wrath lies heavily upon me;
you have overwhelmed me with all your
waves. *Selah*
8You have taken from me my closest
friends
and have made me repulsive to them.
I am confined and cannot escape;
9 my eyes are dim with grief.

I call to you, O LORD, every day;
I spread out my hands to you.
10Do you show your wonders to the dead?
Do those who are dead rise up and
praise you? *Selah*
11Is your love declared in the grave,
your faithfulness in Destruction[h]?
12Are your wonders known in the place of
darkness,

[a]*13,3* Hebrew *Sheol* [b]*16* Or *save your faithful son* [c]*4* A poetic name for Egypt [d]*4* That is, the upper Nile region [e]*4* Or *"O Rahab and Babylon, / Philistia, Tyre and Cush, / I will record concerning those who acknowledge me: / 'This* [f]Title: Possibly a tune, "The Suffering of Affliction" [g]Title: Probably a literary or musical term [h]*11* Hebrew *Abaddon*

or your righteous deeds in the land of oblivion?

13But I cry to you for help, O LORD;
in the morning my prayer comes before you.
14Why, O LORD, do you reject me
and hide your face from me?
15From my youth I have been afflicted and close to death;
I have suffered your terrors and am in despair.
16Your wrath has swept over me;
your terrors have destroyed me.
17All day long they surround me like a flood;
they have completely engulfed me.
18You have taken my companions and loved ones from me;
the darkness is my closest friend.

Psalm 89

A *maskil*[a] of Ethan the Ezrahite.

1I will sing of the LORD's great love forever;
with my mouth I will make your faithfulness known through all generations.
2I will declare that your love stands firm forever,
that you established your faithfulness in heaven itself.
3You said, "I have made a covenant with my chosen one,
I have sworn to David my servant,
4'I will establish your line forever
and make your throne firm through all generations.'" *Selah*

5The heavens praise your wonders, O LORD,
your faithfulness too, in the assembly of the holy ones.
6For who in the skies above can compare with the LORD?
Who is like the LORD among the heavenly beings?
7In the council of the holy ones God is greatly feared;
he is more awesome than all who surround him.
8O LORD God Almighty, who is like you?
You are mighty, O LORD, and your faithfulness surrounds you.

9You rule over the surging sea;
when its waves mount up, you still them.
10You crushed Rahab like one of the slain;
with your strong arm you scattered your enemies.
11The heavens are yours, and yours also the earth;
you founded the world and all that is in it.
12You created the north and the south;
Tabor and Hermon sing for joy at your name.
13Your arm is endued with power;
your hand is strong, your right hand exalted.

14Righteousness and justice are the foundation of your throne;
love and faithfulness go before you.
15Blessed are those who have learned to acclaim you,
who walk in the light of your presence, O LORD.
16They rejoice in your name all day long;
they exult in your righteousness.
17For you are their glory and strength,
and by your favor you exalt our horn.[b]
18Indeed, our shield[c] belongs to the LORD,
our king to the Holy One of Israel.

19Once you spoke in a vision,
to your faithful people you said:
"I have bestowed strength on a warrior;
I have exalted a young man from among the people.
20I have found David my servant;
with my sacred oil I have anointed him.
21My hand will sustain him;
surely my arm will strengthen him.
22No enemy will subject him to tribute;
no wicked man will oppress him.
23I will crush his foes before him
and strike down his adversaries.
24My faithful love will be with him,
and through my name his horn[d] will be exalted.
25I will set his hand over the sea,
his right hand over the rivers.
26He will call out to me, 'You are my Father,

[a]Title: Probably a literary or musical term [b]17 *Horn* here symbolizes strong one. [c]18 Or *sovereign*
[d]24 *Horn* here symbolizes strength.

my God, the Rock my Savior.'
27I will also appoint him my firstborn,
the most exalted of the kings of the earth.
28I will maintain my love to him forever,
and my covenant with him will never fail.
29I will establish his line forever,
his throne as long as the heavens endure.

30"If his sons forsake my law
and do not follow my statutes,
31if they violate my decrees
and fail to keep my commands,
32I will punish their sin with the rod,
their iniquity with flogging;
33but I will not take my love from him,
nor will I ever betray my faithfulness.
34I will not violate my covenant
or alter what my lips have uttered.
35Once for all, I have sworn by my holiness—
and I will not lie to David—
36that his line will continue forever
and his throne endure before me like the sun;
37it will be established forever like the moon,
the faithful witness in the sky." *Selah*

38But you have rejected, you have spurned,
you have been very angry with your anointed one.
39You have renounced the covenant with your servant
and have defiled his crown in the dust.
40You have broken through all his walls
and reduced his strongholds to ruins.
41All who pass by have plundered him;
he has become the scorn of his neighbors.
42You have exalted the right hand of his foes;
you have made all his enemies rejoice.
43You have turned back the edge of his sword
and have not supported him in battle.
44You have put an end to his splendor
and cast his throne to the ground.
45You have cut short the days of his youth;
you have covered him with a mantle of shame. *Selah*

46How long, O LORD? Will you hide yourself forever?
How long will your wrath burn like fire?
47Remember how fleeting is my life.
For what futility you have created all men!
48What man can live and not see death,
or save himself from the power of the grave[a]? *Selah*
49O Lord, where is your former great love,
which in your faithfulness you swore to David?
50Remember, Lord, how your servant has[b] been mocked,
how I bear in my heart the taunts of all the nations,
51the taunts with which your enemies have mocked, O LORD,
with which they have mocked every step of your anointed one.

52Praise be to the LORD forever!
Amen and Amen.

BOOK IV

Psalms 90-106

Psalm 90

A prayer of Moses the man of God.

1Lord, you have been our dwelling place
throughout all generations.
2Before the mountains were born
or you brought forth the earth and the world,
from everlasting to everlasting you are God.

3You turn men back to dust,
saying, "Return to dust, O sons of men."
4For a thousand years in your sight
are like a day that has just gone by,
or like a watch in the night.
5You sweep men away in the sleep of death;
they are like the new grass of the morning—
6though in the morning it springs up new,
by evening it is dry and withered.

7We are consumed by your anger
and terrified by your indignation.
8You have set our iniquities before you,
our secret sins in the light of your presence.

[a]48 Hebrew *Sheol* [b]50 Or *your servants have*

[9]All our days pass away under your wrath;
we finish our years with a moan.
[10]The length of our days is seventy years—
or eighty, if we have the strength;
yet their span[a] is but trouble and sorrow,
for they quickly pass, and we fly away.

[11]Who knows the power of your anger?
For your wrath is as great as the fear
that is due you.
[12]Teach us to number our days aright,
that we may gain a heart of wisdom.

[13]Relent, O LORD! How long will it be?
Have compassion on your servants.
[14]Satisfy us in the morning with your
unfailing love,
that we may sing for joy and be glad all
our days.
[15]Make us glad for as many days as you
have afflicted us,
for as many years as we have seen
trouble.
[16]May your deeds be shown to your
servants,
your splendor to their children.

[17]May the favor[b] of the Lord our God rest
upon us;
establish the work of our hands for
us—
yes, establish the work of our hands.

Psalm 91

[1]He who dwells in the shelter of the Most
High
will rest in the shadow of the Almighty.[c]
[2]I will say[d] of the LORD, "He is my refuge
and my fortress,
my God, in whom I trust."

[3]Surely he will save you from the fowler's
snare
and from the deadly pestilence.
[4]He will cover you with his feathers,
and under his wings you will find
refuge;
his faithfulness will be your shield and
rampart.
[5]You will not fear the terror of night,
nor the arrow that flies by day,
[6]nor the pestilence that stalks in the
darkness,
nor the plague that destroys at midday.
[7]A thousand may fall at your side,
ten thousand at your right hand,
but it will not come near you.
[8]You will only observe with your eyes
and see the punishment of the wicked.

[9]If you make the Most High your
dwelling—
even the LORD, who is my refuge—
[10]then no harm will befall you,
no disaster will come near your tent.
[11]For he will command his angels
concerning you
to guard you in all your ways;
[12]they will lift you up in their hands,
so that you will not strike your foot
against a stone.
[13]You will tread upon the lion and the
cobra;
you will trample the great lion and the
serpent.

[14]"Because he loves me," says the LORD, "I
will rescue him;
I will protect him, for he acknowledges
my name.
[15]He will call upon me, and I will answer
him;
I will be with him in trouble,
I will deliver him and honor him.
[16]With long life will I satisfy him
and show him my salvation."

Psalm 92

A psalm. A song. For the Sabbath day.

[1]It is good to praise the LORD
and make music to your name, O Most
High,
[2]to proclaim your love in the morning
and your faithfulness at night,
[3]to the music of the ten-stringed lyre
and the melody of the harp.
[4]For you make me glad by your deeds,
O LORD;
I sing for joy at the works of your
hands.
[5]How great are your works, O LORD,
how profound your thoughts!
[6]The senseless man does not know,
fools do not understand,
[7]that though the wicked spring up like
grass
and all evildoers flourish,
they will be forever destroyed.

[8]But you, O LORD, are exalted forever.

[a]10 Or *yet the best of them* [b]17 Or *beauty* [c]1 Hebrew *Shaddai* [d]2 Or *He says*

9For surely your enemies, O LORD,
surely your enemies will perish;
all evildoers will be scattered.
10You have exalted my horn[a] like that of a wild ox;
fine oils have been poured upon me.
11My eyes have seen the defeat of my adversaries;
my ears have heard the rout of my wicked foes.

12The righteous will flourish like a palm tree,
they will grow like a cedar of Lebanon;
13planted in the house of the LORD,
they will flourish in the courts of our God.
14They will still bear fruit in old age,
they will stay fresh and green,
15proclaiming, "The LORD is upright;
he is my Rock, and there is no wickedness in him."

Psalm 93

1The LORD reigns, he is robed in majesty;
the LORD is robed in majesty
and is armed with strength.
The world is firmly established;
it cannot be moved.
2Your throne was established long ago;
you are from all eternity.

3The seas have lifted up, O LORD,
the seas have lifted up their voice;
the seas have lifted up their pounding waves.
4Mightier than the thunder of the great waters,
mightier than the breakers of the sea—
the LORD on high is mighty.

5Your statutes stand firm;
holiness adorns your house
for endless days, O LORD.

Psalm 94

1O LORD, the God who avenges,
O God who avenges, shine forth.
2Rise up, O Judge of the earth;
pay back to the proud what they deserve.
3How long will the wicked, O LORD,
how long will the wicked be jubilant?
4They pour out arrogant words;
all the evildoers are full of boasting.
5They crush your people, O LORD;
they oppress your inheritance.
6They slay the widow and the alien;
they murder the fatherless.
7They say, "The LORD does not see;
the God of Jacob pays no heed."

8Take heed, you senseless ones among the people;
you fools, when will you become wise?
9Does he who implanted the ear not hear?
Does he who formed the eye not see?
10Does he who disciplines nations not punish?
Does he who teaches man lack knowledge?
11The LORD knows the thoughts of man;
he knows that they are futile.

12Blessed is the man you discipline, O LORD,
the man you teach from your law;
13you grant him relief from days of trouble,
till a pit is dug for the wicked.
14For the LORD will not reject his people;
he will never forsake his inheritance.
15Judgment will again be founded on righteousness,
and all the upright in heart will follow it.

16Who will rise up for me against the wicked?
Who will take a stand for me against evildoers?
17Unless the LORD had given me help,
I would soon have dwelt in the silence of death.
18When I said, "My foot is slipping,"
your love, O LORD, supported me.
19When anxiety was great within me,
your consolation brought joy to my soul.

20Can a corrupt throne be allied with you—
one that brings on misery by its decrees?
21They band together against the righteous
and condemn the innocent to death.
22But the LORD has become my fortress,
and my God the rock in whom I take refuge.
23He will repay them for their sins
and destroy them for their wickedness;
the LORD our God will destroy them.

[a]10 *Horn* here symbolizes strength.

Psalm 95

1Come, let us sing for joy to the LORD;
let us shout aloud to the Rock of our salvation.
2Let us come before him with thanksgiving
and extol him with music and song.

3For the LORD is the great God,
the great King above all gods.
4In his hand are the depths of the earth,
and the mountain peaks belong to him.
5The sea is his, for he made it,
and his hands formed the dry land.

6Come, let us bow down in worship,
let us kneel before the LORD our Maker;
7for he is our God
and we are the people of his pasture,
the flock under his care.

Today, if you hear his voice,
8 do not harden your hearts as you did at Meribah,[a]
as you did that day at Massah[b] in the desert,
9where your fathers tested and tried me,
though they had seen what I did.
10For forty years I was angry with that generation;
I said, "They are a people whose hearts go astray,
and they have not known my ways."
11So I declared on oath in my anger,
"They shall never enter my rest."

Psalm 96

1Sing to the LORD a new song;
sing to the LORD, all the earth.
2Sing to the LORD, praise his name;
proclaim his salvation day after day.
3Declare his glory among the nations,
his marvelous deeds among all peoples.

4For great is the LORD and most worthy of praise;
he is to be feared above all gods.
5For all the gods of the nations are idols,
but the LORD made the heavens.
6Splendor and majesty are before him;
strength and glory are in his sanctuary.

7Ascribe to the LORD, O families of nations,
ascribe to the LORD glory and strength.
8Ascribe to the LORD the glory due his name;
bring an offering and come into his courts.
9Worship the LORD in the splendor of his[c] holiness;
tremble before him, all the earth.

10Say among the nations, "The LORD reigns."
The world is firmly established, it cannot be moved;
he will judge the peoples with equity.
11Let the heavens rejoice, let the earth be glad;
let the sea resound, and all that is in it;
12 let the fields be jubilant, and everything in them.
Then all the trees of the forest will sing for joy;
13 they will sing before the LORD, for he comes,
he comes to judge the earth.
He will judge the world in righteousness
and the peoples in his truth.

Psalm 97

1The LORD reigns, let the earth be glad;
let the distant shores rejoice.
2Clouds and thick darkness surround him;
righteousness and justice are the foundation of his throne.
3Fire goes before him
and consumes his foes on every side.
4His lightning lights up the world;
the earth sees and trembles.
5The mountains melt like wax before the LORD,
before the Lord of all the earth.
6The heavens proclaim his righteousness,
and all the peoples see his glory.

7All who worship images are put to shame,
those who boast in idols—
worship him, all you gods!

8Zion hears and rejoices
and the villages of Judah are glad
because of your judgments, O LORD.
9For you, O LORD, are the Most High over all the earth;
you are exalted far above all gods.

[a]8 *Meribah* means *quarreling.* [b]8 *Massah* means *testing.* [c]9 Or LORD *with the splendor of*

10Let those who love the LORD hate evil,
for he guards the lives of his faithful ones
and delivers them from the hand of the wicked.
11Light is shed upon the righteous
and joy on the upright in heart.
12Rejoice in the LORD, you who are righteous,
and praise his holy name.

Psalm 98

A psalm.

1Sing to the LORD a new song,
for he has done marvelous things;
his right hand and his holy arm
have worked salvation for him.
2The LORD has made his salvation known
and revealed his righteousness to the nations.
3He has remembered his love
and his faithfulness to the house of Israel;
all the ends of the earth have seen
the salvation of our God.

4Shout for joy to the LORD, all the earth,
burst into jubilant song with music;
5make music to the LORD with the harp,
with the harp and the sound of singing,
6with trumpets and the blast of the ram's horn—
shout for joy before the LORD, the King.

7Let the sea resound, and everything in it,
the world, and all who live in it.
8Let the rivers clap their hands,
let the mountains sing together for joy;
9let them sing before the LORD,
for he comes to judge the earth.
He will judge the world in righteousness
and the peoples with equity.

Psalm 99

1The LORD reigns,
let the nations tremble;
he sits enthroned between the cherubim,
let the earth shake.
2Great is the LORD in Zion;
he is exalted over all the nations.
3Let them praise your great and awesome name—
he is holy.

4The King is mighty, he loves justice—
you have established equity;
in Jacob you have done
what is just and right.
5Exalt the LORD our God
and worship at his footstool;
he is holy.

6Moses and Aaron were among his priests,
Samuel was among those who called on his name;
they called on the LORD
and he answered them.
7He spoke to them from the pillar of cloud;
they kept his statutes and the decrees he gave them.

8O LORD our God,
you answered them;
you were to Israel[a] a forgiving God,
though you punished their misdeeds.[b]
9Exalt the LORD our God
and worship at his holy mountain,
for the LORD our God is holy.

Psalm 100

A psalm. For giving thanks.

1Shout for joy to the LORD, all the earth.
2 Worship the LORD with gladness;
come before him with joyful songs.
3Know that the LORD is God.
It is he who made us, and we are his[c];
we are his people, the sheep of his pasture.

4Enter his gates with thanksgiving
and his courts with praise;
give thanks to him and praise his name.
5For the LORD is good and his love endures forever;
his faithfulness continues through all generations.

Psalm 101

Of David. A psalm.

1I will sing of your love and justice;
to you, O LORD, I will sing praise.
2I will be careful to lead a blameless life—
when will you come to me?

I will walk in my house

[a]8 Hebrew *them* [b]8 Or / *an avenger of the wrongs done to them* [c]3 Or *and not we ourselves*

with blameless heart.
[3]I will set before my eyes
no vile thing.

The deeds of faithless men I hate;
they will not cling to me.
[4]Men of perverse heart shall be far from me;
I will have nothing to do with evil.

[5]Whoever slanders his neighbor in secret,
him will I put to silence;
whoever has haughty eyes and a proud heart,
him will I not endure.

[6]My eyes will be on the faithful in the land,
that they may dwell with me;
he whose walk is blameless
will minister to me.

[7]No one who practices deceit
will dwell in my house;
no one who speaks falsely
will stand in my presence.

[8]Every morning I will put to silence
all the wicked in the land;
I will cut off every evildoer
from the city of the LORD.

Psalm 102

A prayer of an afflicted man. When he is faint and pours out his lament before the LORD.

[1]Hear my prayer, O LORD;
let my cry for help come to you.
[2]Do not hide your face from me
when I am in distress.
Turn your ear to me;
when I call, answer me quickly.

[3]For my days vanish like smoke;
my bones burn like glowing embers.
[4]My heart is blighted and withered like grass;
I forget to eat my food.
[5]Because of my loud groaning
I am reduced to skin and bones.
[6]I am like a desert owl,
like an owl among the ruins.
[7]I lie awake; I have become
like a bird alone on a roof.
[8]All day long my enemies taunt me;
those who rail against me use my name as a curse.
[9]For I eat ashes as my food
and mingle my drink with tears
[10]because of your great wrath,
for you have taken me up and thrown me aside.
[11]My days are like the evening shadow;
I wither away like grass.

[12]But you, O LORD, sit enthroned forever;
your renown endures through all generations.
[13]You will arise and have compassion on Zion,
for it is time to show favor to her;
the appointed time has come.
[14]For her stones are dear to your servants;
her very dust moves them to pity.
[15]The nations will fear the name of the LORD,
all the kings of the earth will revere your glory.
[16]For the LORD will rebuild Zion
and appear in his glory.
[17]He will respond to the prayer of the destitute;
he will not despise their plea.

[18]Let this be written for a future generation,
that a people not yet created may praise the LORD:
[19]"The LORD looked down from his sanctuary on high,
from heaven he viewed the earth,
[20]to hear the groans of the prisoners
and release those condemned to death."
[21]So the name of the LORD will be declared in Zion
and his praise in Jerusalem
[22]when the peoples and the kingdoms
assemble to worship the LORD.

[23]In the course of my life[a] he broke my strength;
he cut short my days.
[24]So I said:
"Do not take me away, O my God, in the midst of my days;
your years go on through all generations.
[25]In the beginning you laid the foundations of the earth,
and the heavens are the work of your hands.
[26]They will perish, but you remain;
they will all wear out like a garment.

[a]23 Or *By his power*

Like clothing you will change them
and they will be discarded.
27But you remain the same,
and your years will never end.
28The children of your servants will live in
your presence;
their descendants will be established
before you."

Psalm 103

Of David.

1Praise the LORD, O my soul;
all my inmost being, praise his holy
name.
2Praise the LORD, O my soul,
and forget not all his benefits—
3who forgives all your sins
and heals all your diseases,
4who redeems your life from the pit
and crowns you with love and
compassion,
5who satisfies your desires with good
things
so that your youth is renewed like the
eagle's.

6The LORD works righteousness
and justice for all the oppressed.

7He made known his ways to Moses,
his deeds to the people of Israel:
8The LORD is compassionate and gracious,
slow to anger, abounding in love.
9He will not always accuse,
nor will he harbor his anger forever;
10he does not treat us as our sins deserve
or repay us according to our iniquities.
11For as high as the heavens are above the
earth,
so great is his love for those who fear
him;
12as far as the east is from the west,
so far has he removed our
transgressions from us.
13As a father has compassion on his
children,
so the LORD has compassion on those
who fear him;
14for he knows how we are formed,
he remembers that we are dust.
15As for man, his days are like grass,
he flourishes like a flower of the field;
16the wind blows over it and it is gone,
and its place remembers it no more.
17But from everlasting to everlasting
the LORD's love is with those who fear
him,
and his righteousness with their
children's children—
18with those who keep his covenant
and remember to obey his precepts.

19The LORD has established his throne in
heaven,
and his kingdom rules over all.

20Praise the LORD, you his angels,
you mighty ones who do his bidding,
who obey his word.
21Praise the LORD, all his heavenly hosts,
you his servants who do his will.
22Praise the LORD, all his works
everywhere in his dominion.

Praise the LORD, O my soul.

Psalm 104

1Praise the LORD, O my soul.

O LORD my God, you are very great;
you are clothed with splendor and
majesty.
2He wraps himself in light as with a
garment;
he stretches out the heavens like a tent
3 and lays the beams of his upper
chambers on their waters.
He makes the clouds his chariot
and rides on the wings of the wind.
4He makes winds his messengers,[a]
flames of fire his servants.

5He set the earth on its foundations;
it can never be moved.
6You covered it with the deep as with a
garment;
the waters stood above the mountains.
7But at your rebuke the waters fled,
at the sound of your thunder they took
to flight;
8they flowed over the mountains,
they went down into the valleys,
to the place you assigned for them.
9You set a boundary they cannot cross;
never again will they cover the earth.

10He makes springs pour water into the
ravines;
it flows between the mountains.

[a]4 Or *angels*

11 They give water to all the beasts of the field;
the wild donkeys quench their thirst.
12 The birds of the air nest by the waters;
they sing among the branches.
13 He waters the mountains from his upper chambers;
the earth is satisfied by the fruit of his work.
14 He makes grass grow for the cattle,
and plants for man to cultivate—
bringing forth food from the earth:
15 wine that gladdens the heart of man,
oil to make his face shine,
and bread that sustains his heart.
16 The trees of the LORD are well watered,
the cedars of Lebanon that he planted.
17 There the birds make their nests;
the stork has its home in the pine trees.
18 The high mountains belong to the wild goats;
the crags are a refuge for the coneys.[a]

19 The moon marks off the seasons,
and the sun knows when to go down.
20 You bring darkness, it becomes night,
and all the beasts of the forest prowl.
21 The lions roar for their prey
and seek their food from God.
22 The sun rises, and they steal away;
they return and lie down in their dens.
23 Then man goes out to his work,
to his labor until evening.

24 How many are your works, O LORD!
In wisdom you made them all;
the earth is full of your creatures.
25 There is the sea, vast and spacious,
teeming with creatures beyond number—
living things both large and small.
26 There the ships go to and fro,
and the leviathan, which you formed to frolic there.

27 These all look to you
to give them their food at the proper time.
28 When you give it to them,
they gather it up;
when you open your hand,
they are satisfied with good things.
29 When you hide your face,
they are terrified;
when you take away their breath,
they die and return to the dust.
30 When you send your Spirit,
they are created,
and you renew the face of the earth.

31 May the glory of the LORD endure forever;
may the LORD rejoice in his works—
32 he who looks at the earth, and it trembles,
who touches the mountains, and they smoke.

33 I will sing to the LORD all my life;
I will sing praise to my God as long as I live.
34 May my meditation be pleasing to him,
as I rejoice in the LORD.
35 But may sinners vanish from the earth
and the wicked be no more.

Praise the LORD, O my soul.

Praise the LORD.[b]

Psalm 105

1 Give thanks to the LORD, call on his name;
make known among the nations what he has done.
2 Sing to him, sing praise to him;
tell of all his wonderful acts.
3 Glory in his holy name;
let the hearts of those who seek the LORD rejoice.
4 Look to the LORD and his strength;
seek his face always.

5 Remember the wonders he has done,
his miracles, and the judgments he pronounced,
6 O descendants of Abraham his servant,
O sons of Jacob, his chosen ones.
7 He is the LORD our God;
his judgments are in all the earth.

8 He remembers his covenant forever,
the word he commanded, for a thousand generations,
9 the covenant he made with Abraham,
the oath he swore to Isaac.
10 He confirmed it to Jacob as a decree,
to Israel as an everlasting covenant:
11 "To you I will give the land of Canaan
as the portion you will inherit."

12 When they were but few in number,
few indeed, and strangers in it,
13 they wandered from nation to nation,

[a] *18* That is, the hyrax or rock badger
[b] *35* Hebrew *Hallelu Yah*; in the Septuagint this line stands at the beginning of Psalm 105.

from one kingdom to another.
14He allowed no one to oppress them;
for their sake he rebuked kings:
15"Do not touch my anointed ones;
do my prophets no harm."

16He called down famine on the land
and destroyed all their supplies of food;
17and he sent a man before them—
Joseph, sold as a slave.
18They bruised his feet with shackles,
his neck was put in irons,
19till what he foretold came to pass,
till the word of the LORD proved him true.
20The king sent and released him,
the ruler of peoples set him free.
21He made him master of his household,
ruler over all he possessed,
22to instruct his princes as he pleased
and teach his elders wisdom.

23Then Israel entered Egypt;
Jacob lived as an alien in the land of Ham.
24The LORD made his people very fruitful;
he made them too numerous for their foes,
25whose hearts he turned to hate his people,
to conspire against his servants.
26He sent Moses his servant,
and Aaron, whom he had chosen.
27They performed his miraculous signs among them,
his wonders in the land of Ham.
28He sent darkness and made the land dark—
for had they not rebelled against his words?
29He turned their waters into blood,
causing their fish to die.
30Their land teemed with frogs,
which went up into the bedrooms of their rulers.
31He spoke, and there came swarms of flies,
and gnats throughout their country.
32He turned their rain into hail,
with lightning throughout their land;
33he struck down their vines and fig trees
and shattered the trees of their country.
34He spoke, and the locusts came,
grasshoppers without number;
35they ate up every green thing in their land,
ate up the produce of their soil.
36Then he struck down all the firstborn in their land,
the firstfruits of all their manhood.

37He brought out Israel, laden with silver and gold,
and from among their tribes no one faltered.
38Egypt was glad when they left,
because dread of Israel had fallen on them.
39He spread out a cloud as a covering,
and a fire to give light at night.
40They asked, and he brought them quail
and satisfied them with the bread of heaven.
41He opened the rock, and water gushed out;
like a river it flowed in the desert.

42For he remembered his holy promise
given to his servant Abraham.
43He brought out his people with rejoicing,
his chosen ones with shouts of joy;
44he gave them the lands of the nations,
and they fell heir to what others had toiled for—
45that they might keep his precepts
and observe his laws.

Praise the LORD.[a]

Psalm 106

1Praise the LORD.[b]

Give thanks to the LORD, for he is good;
his love endures forever.
2Who can proclaim the mighty acts of the LORD
or fully declare his praise?
3Blessed are they who maintain justice,
who constantly do what is right.
4Remember me, O LORD, when you show favor to your people,
come to my aid when you save them,
5that I may enjoy the prosperity of your chosen ones,
that I may share in the joy of your nation
and join your inheritance in giving praise.

6We have sinned, even as our fathers did;
we have done wrong and acted wickedly.

[a] 45 Hebrew *Hallelu Yah* [b] 1 Hebrew *Hallelu Yah*; also in verse 48

7When our fathers were in Egypt,
they gave no thought to your miracles;
they did not remember your many kindnesses,
and they rebelled by the sea, the Red Sea.[a]
8Yet he saved them for his name's sake,
to make his mighty power known.
9He rebuked the Red Sea, and it dried up;
he led them through the depths as through a desert.
10He saved them from the hand of the foe;
from the hand of the enemy he redeemed them.
11The waters covered their adversaries;
not one of them survived.
12Then they believed his promises
and sang his praise.

13But they soon forgot what he had done
and did not wait for his counsel.
14In the desert they gave in to their craving;
in the wasteland they put God to the test.
15So he gave them what they asked for,
but sent a wasting disease upon them.

16In the camp they grew envious of Moses
and of Aaron, who was consecrated to the LORD.
17The earth opened up and swallowed Dathan;
it buried the company of Abiram.
18Fire blazed among their followers;
a flame consumed the wicked.

19At Horeb they made a calf
and worshiped an idol cast from metal.
20They exchanged their Glory
for an image of a bull, which eats grass.
21They forgot the God who saved them,
who had done great things in Egypt,
22miracles in the land of Ham
and awesome deeds by the Red Sea.
23So he said he would destroy them—
had not Moses, his chosen one,
stood in the breach before him
to keep his wrath from destroying them.

24Then they despised the pleasant land;
they did not believe his promise.
25They grumbled in their tents
and did not obey the LORD.
26So he swore to them with uplifted hand
that he would make them fall in the desert,
27make their descendants fall among the nations
and scatter them throughout the lands.

28They yoked themselves to the Baal of Peor
and ate sacrifices offered to lifeless gods;
29they provoked the LORD to anger by their wicked deeds,
and a plague broke out among them.
30But Phinehas stood up and intervened,
and the plague was checked.
31This was credited to him as righteousness
for endless generations to come.

32By the waters of Meribah they angered the LORD,
and trouble came to Moses because of them;
33for they rebelled against the Spirit of God,
and rash words came from Moses' lips.[b]

34They did not destroy the peoples
as the LORD had commanded them,
35but they mingled with the nations
and adopted their customs.
36They worshiped their idols,
which became a snare to them.
37They sacrificed their sons
and their daughters to demons.
38They shed innocent blood,
the blood of their sons and daughters,
whom they sacrificed to the idols of Canaan,
and the land was desecrated by their blood.
39They defiled themselves by what they did;
by their deeds they prostituted themselves.

40Therefore the LORD was angry with his people
and abhorred his inheritance.
41He handed them over to the nations,
and their foes ruled over them.
42Their enemies oppressed them
and subjected them to their power.
43Many times he delivered them,
but they were bent on rebellion
and they wasted away in their sin.

[a]7 Hebrew *Yam Suph;* that is, Sea of Reeds; also in verses 9 and 22 [b]33 Or *against his spirit, / and rash words came from his lips*

44But he took note of their distress
when he heard their cry;
45for their sake he remembered his covenant
and out of his great love he relented.
46He caused them to be pitied
by all who held them captive.

47Save us, O LORD our God,
and gather us from the nations,
that we may give thanks to your holy name
and glory in your praise.

48Praise be to the LORD, the God of Israel,
from everlasting to everlasting.
Let all the people say, "Amen!"

Praise the LORD.

BOOK V

Psalms 107-150

Psalm 107

1Give thanks to the LORD, for he is good;
his love endures forever.
2Let the redeemed of the LORD say this—
those he redeemed from the hand of the foe,
3those he gathered from the lands,
from east and west, from north and south.[a]
4Some wandered in desert wastelands,
finding no way to a city where they could settle.
5They were hungry and thirsty,
and their lives ebbed away.
6Then they cried out to the LORD in their trouble,
and he delivered them from their distress.
7He led them by a straight way
to a city where they could settle.
8Let them give thanks to the LORD for his unfailing love
and his wonderful deeds for men,
9for he satisfies the thirsty
and fills the hungry with good things.

10Some sat in darkness and the deepest gloom,
prisoners suffering in iron chains,
11for they had rebelled against the words of God
and despised the counsel of the Most High.
12So he subjected them to bitter labor;
they stumbled, and there was no one to help.
13Then they cried to the LORD in their trouble,
and he saved them from their distress.
14He brought them out of darkness and the deepest gloom
and broke away their chains.
15Let them give thanks to the LORD for his unfailing love
and his wonderful deeds for men,
16for he breaks down gates of bronze
and cuts through bars of iron.

17Some became fools through their rebellious ways
and suffered affliction because of their iniquities.
18They loathed all food
and drew near the gates of death.
19Then they cried to the LORD in their trouble,
and he saved them from their distress.
20He sent forth his word and healed them;
he rescued them from the grave.
21Let them give thanks to the LORD for his unfailing love
and his wonderful deeds for men.
22Let them sacrifice thank offerings
and tell of his works with songs of joy.

23Others went out on the sea in ships;
they were merchants on the mighty waters.
24They saw the works of the LORD,
his wonderful deeds in the deep.
25For he spoke and stirred up a tempest
that lifted high the waves.
26They mounted up to the heavens and went down to the depths;
in their peril their courage melted away.
27They reeled and staggered like drunken men;
they were at their wits' end.
28Then they cried out to the LORD in their trouble,
and he brought them out of their distress.
29He stilled the storm to a whisper;
the waves of the sea were hushed.

[a]3 Hebrew *north and the sea*

30They were glad when it grew calm,
and he guided them to their desired haven.
31Let them give thanks to the LORD for his unfailing love
and his wonderful deeds for men.
32Let them exalt him in the assembly of the people
and praise him in the council of the elders.

33He turned rivers into a desert,
flowing springs into thirsty ground,
34and fruitful land into a salt waste,
because of the wickedness of those who lived there.
35He turned the desert into pools of water
and the parched ground into flowing springs;
36there he brought the hungry to live,
and they founded a city where they could settle.
37They sowed fields and planted vineyards
that yielded a fruitful harvest;
38he blessed them, and their numbers greatly increased,
and he did not let their herds diminish.

39Then their numbers decreased, and they were humbled
by oppression, calamity and sorrow;
40he who pours contempt on nobles
made them wander in a trackless waste.
41But he lifted the needy out of their affliction
and increased their families like flocks.
42The upright see and rejoice,
but all the wicked shut their mouths.

43Whoever is wise, let him heed these things
and consider the great love of the LORD.

Psalm 108

A song. A psalm of David.

1My heart is steadfast, O God;
I will sing and make music with all my soul.
2Awake, harp and lyre!
I will awaken the dawn.
3I will praise you, O LORD, among the nations;
I will sing of you among the peoples.
4For great is your love, higher than the heavens;
your faithfulness reaches to the skies.
5Be exalted, O God, above the heavens,
and let your glory be over all the earth.

6Save us and help us with your right hand,
that those you love may be delivered.
7God has spoken from his sanctuary:
"In triumph I will parcel out Shechem
and measure off the Valley of Succoth.
8Gilead is mine, Manasseh is mine;
Ephraim is my helmet,
Judah my scepter.
9Moab is my washbasin,
upon Edom I toss my sandal;
over Philistia I shout in triumph."

10Who will bring me to the fortified city?
Who will lead me to Edom?
11Is it not you, O God, you who have rejected us
and no longer go out with our armies?
12Give us aid against the enemy,
for the help of man is worthless.
13With God we will gain the victory,
and he will trample down our enemies.

Psalm 109

For the director of music. Of David. A psalm.

1O God, whom I praise,
do not remain silent,
2for wicked and deceitful men
have opened their mouths against me;
they have spoken against me with lying tongues.
3With words of hatred they surround me;
they attack me without cause.
4In return for my friendship they accuse me,
but I am a man of prayer.
5They repay me evil for good,
and hatred for my friendship.

6Appoint[a] an evil man[b] to oppose him;
let an accuser[c] stand at his right hand.
7When he is tried, let him be found guilty,
and may his prayers condemn him.
8May his days be few;
may another take his place of leadership.
9May his children be fatherless
and his wife a widow.
10May his children be wandering beggars;

[a]6 Or ⌊They say:⌋ "Appoint (with quotation marks at the end of verse 19) [b]6 Or *the Evil One* [c]6 Or *let Satan*

may they be driven[a] from their ruined
homes.
11May a creditor seize all he has;
may strangers plunder the fruits of his
labor.
12May no one extend kindness to him
or take pity on his fatherless children.
13May his descendants be cut off,
their names blotted out from the next
generation.
14May the iniquity of his fathers be
remembered before the LORD;
may the sin of his mother never be
blotted out.
15May their sins always remain before the
LORD,
that he may cut off the memory of them
from the earth.

16For he never thought of doing a kindness,
but hounded to death the poor
and the needy and the brokenhearted.
17He loved to pronounce a curse—
may it[b] come on him;
he found no pleasure in blessing—
may it be[c] far from him.
18He wore cursing as his garment;
it entered into his body like water,
into his bones like oil.
19May it be like a cloak wrapped about him,
like a belt tied forever around him.
20May this be the LORD's payment to my
accusers,
to those who speak evil of me.

21But you, O Sovereign LORD,
deal well with me for your name's sake;
out of the goodness of your love,
deliver me.
22For I am poor and needy,
and my heart is wounded within me.
23I fade away like an evening shadow;
I am shaken off like a locust.
24My knees give way from fasting;
my body is thin and gaunt.
25I am an object of scorn to my accusers;
when they see me, they shake their
heads.

26Help me, O LORD my God;
save me in accordance with your love.
27Let them know that it is your hand,
that you, O LORD, have done it.
28They may curse, but you will bless;
when they attack they will be put to
shame,
but your servant will rejoice.
29My accusers will be clothed with disgrace
and wrapped in shame as in a cloak.

30With my mouth I will greatly extol the
LORD;
in the great throng I will praise him.
31For he stands at the right hand of the
needy one,
to save his life from those who
condemn him.

Psalm 110

Of David. A psalm.

1The LORD says to my Lord:
"Sit at my right hand
until I make your enemies
a footstool for your feet."
2The LORD will extend your mighty scepter
from Zion;
you will rule in the midst of your
enemies.
3Your troops will be willing
on your day of battle.
Arrayed in holy majesty,
from the womb of the dawn
you will receive the dew of your youth.[d]

4The LORD has sworn
and will not change his mind:
"You are a priest forever,
in the order of Melchizedek."

5The Lord is at your right hand;
he will crush kings on the day of his
wrath.
6He will judge the nations, heaping up the
dead
and crushing the rulers of the whole
earth.
7He will drink from a brook beside the
way[e];
therefore he will lift up his head.

Psalm 111[f]

1Praise the LORD.[g]

I will extol the LORD with all my heart

[a] *10* Septuagint; Hebrew *sought* [b] *17* Or *curse, / and it has* [c] *17* Or *blessing, / and it is* [d] *3* Or / *your young men will come to you like the dew* [e] *7* Or / *The One who grants succession will set him in authority*
[f] This psalm is an acrostic poem, the lines of which begin with the successive letters of the Hebrew alphabet.
[g] *1* Hebrew *Hallelu Yah*

in the council of the upright and in the assembly.

2Great are the works of the LORD;
they are pondered by all who delight in them.
3Glorious and majestic are his deeds,
and his righteousness endures forever.
4He has caused his wonders to be remembered;
the LORD is gracious and compassionate.
5He provides food for those who fear him;
he remembers his covenant forever.
6He has shown his people the power of his works,
giving them the lands of other nations.
7The works of his hands are faithful and just;
all his precepts are trustworthy.
8They are steadfast for ever and ever,
done in faithfulness and uprightness.
9He provided redemption for his people;
he ordained his covenant forever—
holy and awesome is his name.

10The fear of the LORD is the beginning of wisdom;
all who follow his precepts have good understanding.
To him belongs eternal praise.

Psalm 112[a]

1Praise the LORD.[b]

Blessed is the man who fears the LORD,
who finds great delight in his commands.

2His children will be mighty in the land;
the generation of the upright will be blessed.
3Wealth and riches are in his house,
and his righteousness endures forever.
4Even in darkness light dawns for the upright,
for the gracious and compassionate and righteous man.[c]
5Good will come to him who is generous and lends freely,
who conducts his affairs with justice.
6Surely he will never be shaken;
a righteous man will be remembered forever.
7He will have no fear of bad news;
his heart is steadfast, trusting in the LORD.
8His heart is secure, he will have no fear;
in the end he will look in triumph on his foes.
9He has scattered abroad his gifts to the poor,
his righteousness endures forever;
his horn[d] will be lifted high in honor.

10The wicked man will see and be vexed,
he will gnash his teeth and waste away;
the longings of the wicked will come to nothing.

Psalm 113

1Praise the LORD.[e]

Praise, O servants of the LORD,
praise the name of the LORD.
2Let the name of the LORD be praised,
both now and forevermore.
3From the rising of the sun to the place where it sets,
the name of the LORD is to be praised.

4The LORD is exalted over all the nations,
his glory above the heavens.
5Who is like the LORD our God,
the One who sits enthroned on high,
6who stoops down to look
on the heavens and the earth?

7He raises the poor from the dust
and lifts the needy from the ash heap;
8he seats them with princes,
with the princes of their people.
9He settles the barren woman in her home
as a happy mother of children.

Praise the LORD.

Psalm 114

1When Israel came out of Egypt,
the house of Jacob from a people of foreign tongue,
2Judah became God's sanctuary,
Israel his dominion.

3The sea looked and fled,
the Jordan turned back;
4the mountains skipped like rams,
the hills like lambs.

[a]This psalm is an acrostic poem, the lines of which begin with the successive letters of the Hebrew alphabet.
[b]1 Hebrew *Hallelu Yah* [c]4 Or *1 for ⌊the LORD⌋ is gracious and compassionate and righteous* [d]9 *Horn* here symbolizes dignity. [e]1 Hebrew *Hallelu Yah*; also in verse 9

5Why was it, O sea, that you fled,
O Jordan, that you turned back,
6you mountains, that you skipped like rams,
you hills, like lambs?

7Tremble, O earth, at the presence of the Lord,
at the presence of the God of Jacob,
8who turned the rock into a pool,
the hard rock into springs of water.

Psalm 115

1Not to us, O LORD, not to us
but to your name be the glory,
because of your love and faithfulness.

2Why do the nations say,
"Where is their God?"
3Our God is in heaven;
he does whatever pleases him.
4But their idols are silver and gold,
made by the hands of men.
5They have mouths, but cannot speak,
eyes, but they cannot see;
6they have ears, but cannot hear,
noses, but they cannot smell;
7they have hands, but cannot feel,
feet, but they cannot walk;
nor can they utter a sound with their throats.
8Those who make them will be like them,
and so will all who trust in them.

9O house of Israel, trust in the LORD—
he is their help and shield.
10O house of Aaron, trust in the LORD—
he is their help and shield.
11You who fear him, trust in the LORD—
he is their help and shield.

12The LORD remembers us and will bless us:
He will bless the house of Israel,
he will bless the house of Aaron,
13he will bless those who fear the LORD—
small and great alike.

14May the LORD make you increase,
both you and your children.
15May you be blessed by the LORD,
the Maker of heaven and earth.

16The highest heavens belong to the LORD,
but the earth he has given to man.
17It is not the dead who praise the LORD,
those who go down to silence;
18it is we who extol the LORD,
both now and forevermore.

Praise the LORD.[a]

Psalm 116

1I love the LORD, for he heard my voice;
he heard my cry for mercy.
2Because he turned his ear to me,
I will call on him as long as I live.

3The cords of death entangled me,
the anguish of the grave[b] came upon me;
I was overcome by trouble and sorrow.
4Then I called on the name of the LORD:
"O LORD, save me!"

5The LORD is gracious and righteous;
our God is full of compassion.
6The LORD protects the simplehearted;
when I was in great need, he saved me.

7Be at rest once more, O my soul,
for the LORD has been good to you.

8For you, O LORD, have delivered my soul from death,
my eyes from tears,
my feet from stumbling,
9that I may walk before the LORD
in the land of the living.
10I believed; therefore[c] I said,
"I am greatly afflicted."
11And in my dismay I said,
"All men are liars."

12How can I repay the LORD
for all his goodness to me?
13I will lift up the cup of salvation
and call on the name of the LORD.
14I will fulfill my vows to the LORD
in the presence of all his people.

15Precious in the sight of the LORD
is the death of his saints.
16O LORD, truly I am your servant;
I am your servant, the son of your maidservant[d];
you have freed me from my chains.

17I will sacrifice a thank offering to you
and call on the name of the LORD.
18I will fulfill my vows to the LORD

[a]18 Hebrew *Hallelu Yah* [b]3 Hebrew *Sheol* [c]10 Or *believed even when* [d]16 Or *servant, your faithful son*

in the presence of all his people,
[19]in the courts of the house of the LORD—
in your midst, O Jerusalem.

Praise the LORD.[a]

Psalm 117

[1]Praise the LORD, all you nations;
extol him, all you peoples.
[2]For great is his love toward us,
and the faithfulness of the LORD
endures forever.

Praise the LORD.[a]

Psalm 118

[1]Give thanks to the LORD, for he is good;
his love endures forever.

[2]Let Israel say:
"His love endures forever."
[3]Let the house of Aaron say:
"His love endures forever."
[4]Let those who fear the LORD say:
"His love endures forever."

[5]In my anguish I cried to the LORD,
and he answered by setting me free.
[6]The LORD is with me; I will not be afraid.
What can man do to me?
[7]The LORD is with me; he is my helper.
I will look in triumph on my enemies.

[8]It is better to take refuge in the LORD
than to trust in man.
[9]It is better to take refuge in the LORD
than to trust in princes.

[10]All the nations surrounded me,
but in the name of the LORD I cut them
off.
[11]They surrounded me on every side,
but in the name of the LORD I cut them
off.
[12]They swarmed around me like bees,
but they died out as quickly as burning
thorns;
in the name of the LORD I cut them off.

[13]I was pushed back and about to fall,
but the LORD helped me.
[14]The LORD is my strength and my song;
he has become my salvation.

[15]Shouts of joy and victory
resound in the tents of the righteous:
"The LORD's right hand has done mighty
things!
[16] The LORD's right hand is lifted high;
the LORD's right hand has done mighty
things!"

[17]I will not die but live,
and will proclaim what the LORD has
done.
[18]The LORD has chastened me severely,
but he has not given me over to death.

[19]Open for me the gates of righteousness;
I will enter and give thanks to the LORD.
[20]This is the gate of the LORD
through which the righteous may enter.
[21]I will give you thanks, for you answered
me;
you have become my salvation.

[22]The stone the builders rejected
has become the capstone;
[23]the LORD has done this,
and it is marvelous in our eyes.
[24]This is the day the LORD has made;
let us rejoice and be glad in it.

[25]O LORD, save us;
O LORD, grant us success.
[26]Blessed is he who comes in the name of
the LORD.
From the house of the LORD we bless
you.[b]
[27]The LORD is God,
and he has made his light shine upon
us.
With boughs in hand, join in the festal
procession
up[c] to the horns of the altar.

[28]You are my God, and I will give you
thanks;
you are my God, and I will exalt you.

[29]Give thanks to the LORD, for he is good;
his love endures forever.

Psalm 119[d]

א Aleph

[1]Blessed are they whose ways are
blameless,
who walk according to the law of the
LORD.

[a]19,2 Hebrew *Hallelu Yah* [b]26 The Hebrew is plural. [c]27 Or *Bind the festal sacrifice with ropes / and take it* [d]This psalm is an acrostic poem; the verses of each stanza begin with the same letter of the Hebrew alphabet.

2Blessed are they who keep his statutes
and seek him with all their heart.
3They do nothing wrong;
they walk in his ways.
4You have laid down precepts
that are to be fully obeyed.
5Oh, that my ways were steadfast
in obeying your decrees!
6Then I would not be put to shame
when I consider all your commands.
7I will praise you with an upright heart
as I learn your righteous laws.
8I will obey your decrees;
do not utterly forsake me.

ב Beth

9How can a young man keep his way
pure?
By living according to your word.
10I seek you with all my heart;
do not let me stray from your
commands.
11I have hidden your word in my heart
that I might not sin against you.
12Praise be to you, O LORD;
teach me your decrees.
13With my lips I recount
all the laws that come from your
mouth.
14I rejoice in following your statutes
as one rejoices in great riches.
15I meditate on your precepts
and consider your ways.
16I delight in your decrees;
I will not neglect your word.

ג Gimel

17Do good to your servant, and I will live;
I will obey your word.
18Open my eyes that I may see
wonderful things in your law.
19I am a stranger on earth;
do not hide your commands from me.
20My soul is consumed with longing
for your laws at all times.
21You rebuke the arrogant, who are cursed
and who stray from your commands.
22Remove from me scorn and contempt,
for I keep your statutes.
23Though rulers sit together and slander
me,
your servant will meditate on your
decrees.
24Your statutes are my delight;
they are my counselors.

ד Daleth

25I am laid low in the dust;
preserve my life according to your
word.
26I recounted my ways and you answered
me;
teach me your decrees.
27Let me understand the teaching of your
precepts;
then I will meditate on your wonders.
28My soul is weary with sorrow;
strengthen me according to your word.
29Keep me from deceitful ways;
be gracious to me through your law.
30I have chosen the way of truth;
I have set my heart on your laws.
31I hold fast to your statutes, O LORD;
do not let me be put to shame.
32I run in the path of your commands,
for you have set my heart free.

ה He

33Teach me, O LORD, to follow your
decrees;
then I will keep them to the end.
34Give me understanding, and I will keep
your law
and obey it with all my heart.
35Direct me in the path of your commands,
for there I find delight.
36Turn my heart toward your statutes
and not toward selfish gain.
37Turn my eyes away from worthless
things;
preserve my life according to your
word.[a]
38Fulfill your promise to your servant,
so that you may be feared.
39Take away the disgrace I dread,
for your laws are good.
40How I long for your precepts!
Preserve my life in your righteousness.

ו Waw

41May your unfailing love come to me,
O LORD,
your salvation according to your
promise;
42then I will answer the one who taunts me,
for I trust in your word.

[a]37 Two manuscripts of the Masoretic Text and Dead Sea Scrolls; most manuscripts of the Masoretic Text *life in your way*

43Do not snatch the word of truth from my
mouth,
for I have put my hope in your laws.
44I will always obey your law,
for ever and ever.
45I will walk about in freedom,
for I have sought out your precepts.
46I will speak of your statutes before kings
and will not be put to shame,
47for I delight in your commands
because I love them.
48I lift up my hands to[a] your commands,
which I love,
and I meditate on your decrees.

ז Zayin

49Remember your word to your servant,
for you have given me hope.
50My comfort in my suffering is this:
Your promise preserves my life.
51The arrogant mock me without restraint,
but I do not turn from your law.
52I remember your ancient laws, O LORD,
and I find comfort in them.
53Indignation grips me because of the
wicked,
who have forsaken your law.
54Your decrees are the theme of my song
wherever I lodge.
55In the night I remember your name,
O LORD,
and I will keep your law.
56This has been my practice:
I obey your precepts.

ח Heth

57You are my portion, O LORD;
I have promised to obey your words.
58I have sought your face with all my heart;
be gracious to me according to your
promise.
59I have considered my ways
and have turned my steps to your
statutes.
60I will hasten and not delay
to obey your commands.
61Though the wicked bind me with ropes,
I will not forget your law.
62At midnight I rise to give you thanks
for your righteous laws.
63I am a friend to all who fear you,
to all who follow your precepts.
64The earth is filled with your love, O LORD;
teach me your decrees.

ט Teth

65Do good to your servant
according to your word, O LORD.
66Teach me knowledge and good
judgment,
for I believe in your commands.
67Before I was afflicted I went astray,
but now I obey your word.
68You are good, and what you do is good;
teach me your decrees.
69Though the arrogant have smeared me
with lies,
I keep your precepts with all my heart.
70Their hearts are callous and unfeeling,
but I delight in your law.
71It was good for me to be afflicted
so that I might learn your decrees.
72The law from your mouth is more
precious to me
than thousands of pieces of silver and
gold.

י Yodh

73Your hands made me and formed me;
give me understanding to learn your
commands.
74May those who fear you rejoice when
they see me,
for I have put my hope in your word.
75I know, O LORD, that your laws are
righteous,
and in faithfulness you have afflicted
me.
76May your unfailing love be my comfort,
according to your promise to your
servant.
77Let your compassion come to me that I
may live,
for your law is my delight.
78May the arrogant be put to shame for
wronging me without cause;
but I will meditate on your precepts.
79May those who fear you turn to me,
those who understand your statutes.
80May my heart be blameless toward your
decrees,
that I may not be put to shame.

כ Kaph

81My soul faints with longing for your
salvation,
but I have put my hope in your word.
82My eyes fail, looking for your promise;

[a]48 Or *for*

I say, "When will you comfort me?"
83Though I am like a wineskin in the smoke,
I do not forget your decrees.
84How long must your servant wait?
When will you punish my persecutors?
85The arrogant dig pitfalls for me,
contrary to your law.
86All your commands are trustworthy;
help me, for men persecute me without cause.
87They almost wiped me from the earth,
but I have not forsaken your precepts.
88Preserve my life according to your love,
and I will obey the statutes of your mouth.

ל Lamedh

89Your word, O LORD, is eternal;
it stands firm in the heavens.
90Your faithfulness continues through all generations;
you established the earth, and it endures.
91Your laws endure to this day,
for all things serve you.
92If your law had not been my delight,
I would have perished in my affliction.
93I will never forget your precepts,
for by them you have preserved my life.
94Save me, for I am yours;
I have sought out your precepts.
95The wicked are waiting to destroy me,
but I will ponder your statutes.
96To all perfection I see a limit;
but your commands are boundless.

מ Mem

97Oh, how I love your law!
I meditate on it all day long.
98Your commands make me wiser than my enemies,
for they are ever with me.
99I have more insight than all my teachers,
for I meditate on your statutes.
100I have more understanding than the elders,
for I obey your precepts.
101I have kept my feet from every evil path
so that I might obey your word.
102I have not departed from your laws,
for you yourself have taught me.
103How sweet are your words to my taste,
sweeter than honey to my mouth!
104I gain understanding from your precepts;
therefore I hate every wrong path.

נ Nun

105Your word is a lamp to my feet
and a light for my path.
106I have taken an oath and confirmed it,
that I will follow your righteous laws.
107I have suffered much;
preserve my life, O LORD, according to your word.
108Accept, O LORD, the willing praise of my mouth,
and teach me your laws.
109Though I constantly take my life in my hands,
I will not forget your law.
110The wicked have set a snare for me,
but I have not strayed from your precepts.
111Your statutes are my heritage forever;
they are the joy of my heart.
112My heart is set on keeping your decrees
to the very end.

ס Samekh

113I hate double-minded men,
but I love your law.
114You are my refuge and my shield;
I have put my hope in your word.
115Away from me, you evildoers,
that I may keep the commands of my God!
116Sustain me according to your promise, and I will live;
do not let my hopes be dashed.
117Uphold me, and I will be delivered;
I will always have regard for your decrees.
118You reject all who stray from your decrees,
for their deceitfulness is in vain.
119All the wicked of the earth you discard like dross;
therefore I love your statutes.
120My flesh trembles in fear of you;
I stand in awe of your laws.

ע Ayin

121I have done what is righteous and just;
do not leave me to my oppressors.
122Ensure your servant's well-being;
let not the arrogant oppress me.
123My eyes fail, looking for your salvation,
looking for your righteous promise.
124Deal with your servant according to your love
and teach me your decrees.

125I am your servant; give me discernment
that I may understand your statutes.
126It is time for you to act, O LORD;
your law is being broken.
127Because I love your commands
more than gold, more than pure gold,
128and because I consider all your precepts
right,
I hate every wrong path.

פ Pe

129Your statutes are wonderful;
therefore I obey them.
130The unfolding of your words gives light;
it gives understanding to the simple.
131I open my mouth and pant,
longing for your commands.
132Turn to me and have mercy on me,
as you always do to those who love
your name.
133Direct my footsteps according to your
word;
let no sin rule over me.
134Redeem me from the oppression of men,
that I may obey your precepts.
135Make your face shine upon your servant
and teach me your decrees.
136Streams of tears flow from my eyes,
for your law is not obeyed.

צ Tsadhe

137Righteous are you, O LORD,
and your laws are right.
138The statutes you have laid down are
righteous;
they are fully trustworthy.
139My zeal wears me out,
for my enemies ignore your words.
140Your promises have been thoroughly
tested,
and your servant loves them.
141Though I am lowly and despised,
I do not forget your precepts.
142Your righteousness is everlasting
and your law is true.
143Trouble and distress have come upon
me,
but your commands are my delight.
144Your statutes are forever right;
give me understanding that I may live.

ק Qoph

145I call with all my heart; answer me,
O LORD,
and I will obey your decrees.
146I call out to you; save me
and I will keep your statutes.
147I rise before dawn and cry for help;
I have put my hope in your word.
148My eyes stay open through the watches
of the night,
that I may meditate on your promises.
149Hear my voice in accordance with your
love;
preserve my life, O LORD, according to
your laws.
150Those who devise wicked schemes are
near,
but they are far from your law.
151Yet you are near, O LORD,
and all your commands are true.
152Long ago I learned from your statutes
that you established them to last
forever.

ר Resh

153Look upon my suffering and deliver me,
for I have not forgotten your law.
154Defend my cause and redeem me;
preserve my life according to your
promise.
155Salvation is far from the wicked,
for they do not seek out your decrees.
156Your compassion is great, O LORD;
preserve my life according to your laws.
157Many are the foes who persecute me,
but I have not turned from your
statutes.
158I look on the faithless with loathing,
for they do not obey your word.
159See how I love your precepts;
preserve my life, O LORD, according to
your love.
160All your words are true;
all your righteous laws are eternal.

ש Sin and Shin

161Rulers persecute me without cause,
but my heart trembles at your word.
162I rejoice in your promise
like one who finds great spoil.
163I hate and abhor falsehood
but I love your law.
164Seven times a day I praise you
for your righteous laws.
165Great peace have they who love your
law,
and nothing can make them stumble.
166I wait for your salvation, O LORD,
and I follow your commands.

167 I obey your statutes,
for I love them greatly.
168 I obey your precepts and your statutes,
for all my ways are known to you.

ת Taw

169 May my cry come before you, O LORD;
give me understanding according to your word.
170 May my supplication come before you;
deliver me according to your promise.
171 May my lips overflow with praise,
for you teach me your decrees.
172 May my tongue sing of your word,
for all your commands are righteous.
173 May your hand be ready to help me,
for I have chosen your precepts.
174 I long for your salvation, O LORD,
and your law is my delight.
175 Let me live that I may praise you,
and may your laws sustain me.
176 I have strayed like a lost sheep.
Seek your servant,
for I have not forgotten your commands.

Psalm 120

A song of ascents.

1 I call on the LORD in my distress,
and he answers me.
2 Save me, O LORD, from lying lips
and from deceitful tongues.

3 What will he do to you,
and what more besides, O deceitful tongue?
4 He will punish you with a warrior's sharp arrows,
with burning coals of the broom tree.

5 Woe to me that I dwell in Meshech,
that I live among the tents of Kedar!
6 Too long have I lived
among those who hate peace.
7 I am a man of peace;
but when I speak, they are for war.

Psalm 121

A song of ascents.

1 I lift up my eyes to the hills—
where does my help come from?
2 My help comes from the LORD,
the Maker of heaven and earth.

3 He will not let your foot slip—
he who watches over you will not slumber;
4 indeed, he who watches over Israel
will neither slumber nor sleep.

5 The LORD watches over you—
the LORD is your shade at your right hand;
6 the sun will not harm you by day,
nor the moon by night.

7 The LORD will keep you from all harm—
he will watch over your life;
8 the LORD will watch over your coming and going
both now and forevermore.

Psalm 122

A song of ascents. Of David.

1 I rejoiced with those who said to me,
"Let us go to the house of the LORD."
2 Our feet are standing
in your gates, O Jerusalem.

3 Jerusalem is built like a city
that is closely compacted together.
4 That is where the tribes go up,
the tribes of the LORD,
to praise the name of the LORD
according to the statute given to Israel.
5 There the thrones for judgment stand,
the thrones of the house of David.

6 Pray for the peace of Jerusalem:
"May those who love you be secure.
7 May there be peace within your walls
and security within your citadels."
8 For the sake of my brothers and friends,
I will say, "Peace be within you."
9 For the sake of the house of the LORD our God,
I will seek your prosperity.

Psalm 123

A song of ascents.

1 I lift up my eyes to you,
to you whose throne is in heaven.
2 As the eyes of slaves look to the hand of their master,
as the eyes of a maid look to the hand of her mistress,
so our eyes look to the LORD our God,
till he shows us his mercy.

3Have mercy on us, O LORD, have mercy
on us,
for we have endured much contempt.
4We have endured much ridicule from the
proud,
much contempt from the arrogant.

Psalm 124

A song of ascents. Of David.

1If the LORD had not been on our side—
let Israel say—
2if the LORD had not been on our side
when men attacked us,
3when their anger flared against us,
they would have swallowed us alive;
4the flood would have engulfed us,
the torrent would have swept over us,
5the raging waters
would have swept us away.

6Praise be to the LORD,
who has not let us be torn by their
teeth.
7We have escaped like a bird
out of the fowler's snare;
the snare has been broken,
and we have escaped.
8Our help is in the name of the LORD,
the Maker of heaven and earth.

Psalm 125

A song of ascents.

1Those who trust in the LORD are like
Mount Zion,
which cannot be shaken but endures
forever.
2As the mountains surround Jerusalem,
so the LORD surrounds his people
both now and forevermore.

3The scepter of the wicked will not remain
over the land allotted to the righteous,
for then the righteous might use
their hands to do evil.

4Do good, O LORD, to those who are good,
to those who are upright in heart.
5But those who turn to crooked ways
the LORD will banish with the evildoers.

Peace be upon Israel.

Psalm 126

A song of ascents.

1When the LORD brought back the captives
to[a] Zion,
we were like men who dreamed.[b]
2Our mouths were filled with laughter,
our tongues with songs of joy.
Then it was said among the nations,
"The LORD has done great things for
them."
3The LORD has done great things for us,
and we are filled with joy.

4Restore our fortunes,[c] O LORD,
like streams in the Negev.
5Those who sow in tears
will reap with songs of joy.
6He who goes out weeping,
carrying seed to sow,
will return with songs of joy,
carrying sheaves with him.

Psalm 127

A song of ascents. Of Solomon.

1Unless the LORD builds the house,
its builders labor in vain.
Unless the LORD watches over the city,
the watchmen stand guard in vain.
2In vain you rise early
and stay up late,
toiling for food to eat—
for he grants sleep to[d] those he loves.

3Sons are a heritage from the LORD,
children a reward from him.
4Like arrows in the hands of a warrior
are sons born in one's youth.
5Blessed is the man
whose quiver is full of them.
They will not be put to shame
when they contend with their enemies
in the gate.

Psalm 128

A song of ascents.

1Blessed are all who fear the LORD,
who walk in his ways.
2You will eat the fruit of your labor;

[a] 1 Or *LORD restored the fortunes of* [b] 1 Or *men restored to health* [c] 4 Or *Bring back our captives*
[d] 2 Or *eat— / for while they sleep he provides for*

blessings and prosperity will be yours.
3Your wife will be like a fruitful vine
within your house;
your sons will be like olive shoots
around your table.
4Thus is the man blessed
who fears the LORD.

5May the LORD bless you from Zion
all the days of your life;
may you see the prosperity of Jerusalem,
6 and may you live to see your children's children.

Peace be upon Israel.

Psalm 129

A song of ascents.

1They have greatly oppressed me from my youth—
let Israel say—
2they have greatly oppressed me from my youth,
but they have not gained the victory over me.
3Plowmen have plowed my back
and made their furrows long.
4But the LORD is righteous;
he has cut me free from the cords of the wicked.

5May all who hate Zion
be turned back in shame.
6May they be like grass on the roof,
which withers before it can grow;
7with it the reaper cannot fill his hands,
nor the one who gathers fill his arms.
8May those who pass by not say,
"The blessing of the LORD be upon you;
we bless you in the name of the LORD."

Psalm 130

A song of ascents.

1Out of the depths I cry to you, O LORD;
2 O Lord, hear my voice.
Let your ears be attentive
to my cry for mercy.

3If you, O LORD, kept a record of sins,
O Lord, who could stand?
4But with you there is forgiveness;
therefore you are feared.

5I wait for the LORD, my soul waits,
and in his word I put my hope.
6My soul waits for the Lord
more than watchmen wait for the morning,
more than watchmen wait for the morning.

7O Israel, put your hope in the LORD,
for with the LORD is unfailing love
and with him is full redemption.
8He himself will redeem Israel
from all their sins.

Psalm 131

A song of ascents. Of David.

1My heart is not proud, O LORD,
my eyes are not haughty;
I do not concern myself with great matters
or things too wonderful for me.
2But I have stilled and quieted my soul;
like a weaned child with its mother,
like a weaned child is my soul within me.

3O Israel, put your hope in the LORD
both now and forevermore.

Psalm 132

A song of ascents.

1O LORD, remember David
and all the hardships he endured.

2He swore an oath to the LORD
and made a vow to the Mighty One of Jacob:
3"I will not enter my house
or go to my bed—
4I will allow no sleep to my eyes,
no slumber to my eyelids,
5till I find a place for the LORD,
a dwelling for the Mighty One of Jacob."

6We heard it in Ephrathah,
we came upon it in the fields of Jaar[a]:[b]
7"Let us go to his dwelling place;
let us worship at his footstool—
8arise, O LORD, and come to your resting place,
you and the ark of your might.

[a]6 That is, Kiriath Jearim [b]6 Or *heard of it in Ephrathah, / we found it in the fields of Jaar.* (And no quotes around verses 7-9)

9May your priests be clothed with
righteousness;
may your saints sing for joy."

10For the sake of David your servant,
do not reject your anointed one.

11The LORD swore an oath to David,
a sure oath that he will not revoke:
"One of your own descendants
I will place on your throne—
12if your sons keep my covenant
and the statutes I teach them,
then their sons will sit
on your throne for ever and ever."

13For the LORD has chosen Zion,
he has desired it for his dwelling:
14"This is my resting place for ever and
ever;
here I will sit enthroned, for I have
desired it—
15I will bless her with abundant provisions;
her poor will I satisfy with food.
16I will clothe her priests with salvation,
and her saints will ever sing for joy.

17"Here I will make a horn[a] grow for David
and set up a lamp for my anointed one.
18I will clothe his enemies with shame,
but the crown on his head will be
resplendent."

Psalm 133

A song of ascents. Of David.

1How good and pleasant it is
when brothers live together in unity!
2It is like precious oil poured on the head,
running down on the beard,
running down on Aaron's beard,
down upon the collar of his robes.
3It is as if the dew of Hermon
were falling on Mount Zion.
For there the LORD bestows his blessing,
even life forevermore.

Psalm 134

A song of ascents.

1Praise the LORD, all you servants of the
LORD
who minister by night in the house of
the LORD.
2Lift up your hands in the sanctuary
and praise the LORD.

3May the LORD, the Maker of heaven and
earth,
bless you from Zion.

Psalm 135

1Praise the LORD.[b]

Praise the name of the LORD;
praise him, you servants of the LORD,
2you who minister in the house of the
LORD,
in the courts of the house of our God.

3Praise the LORD, for the LORD is good;
sing praise to his name, for that is
pleasant.
4For the LORD has chosen Jacob to be his
own,
Israel to be his treasured possession.

5I know that the LORD is great,
that our Lord is greater than all gods.
6The LORD does whatever pleases him,
in the heavens and on the earth,
in the seas and all their depths.
7He makes clouds rise from the ends of
the earth;
he sends lightning with the rain
and brings out the wind from his
storehouses.

8He struck down the firstborn of Egypt,
the firstborn of men and animals.
9He sent his signs and wonders into your
midst, O Egypt,
against Pharaoh and all his servants.
10He struck down many nations
and killed mighty kings—
11Sihon king of the Amorites,
Og king of Bashan
and all the kings of Canaan—
12and he gave their land as an inheritance,
an inheritance to his people Israel.

13Your name, O LORD, endures forever,
your renown, O LORD, through all
generations.
14For the LORD will vindicate his people
and have compassion on his servants.

15The idols of the nations are silver and
gold,
made by the hands of men.
16They have mouths, but cannot speak,
eyes, but they cannot see;

[a] 17 *Horn* here symbolizes strong one, that is, king.

[b] 1 Hebrew *Hallelu Yah*; also in verses 3 and 21

17they have ears, but cannot hear,
nor is there breath in their mouths.
18Those who make them will be like them,
and so will all who trust in them.

19O house of Israel, praise the LORD;
O house of Aaron, praise the LORD;
20O house of Levi, praise the LORD;
you who fear him, praise the LORD.
21Praise be to the LORD from Zion,
to him who dwells in Jerusalem.

Praise the LORD.

Psalm 136

1Give thanks to the LORD, for he is good.
His love endures forever.
2Give thanks to the God of gods.
His love endures forever.
3Give thanks to the Lord of lords:
His love endures forever.

4to him who alone does great wonders,
His love endures forever.
5who by his understanding made the heavens,
His love endures forever.
6who spread out the earth upon the waters,
His love endures forever.
7who made the great lights—
His love endures forever.
8the sun to govern the day,
His love endures forever.
9the moon and stars to govern the night;
His love endures forever.

10to him who struck down the firstborn of Egypt
His love endures forever.
11and brought Israel out from among them
His love endures forever.
12with a mighty hand and outstretched arm;
His love endures forever.

13to him who divided the Red Sea[a] asunder
His love endures forever.
14and brought Israel through the midst of it,
His love endures forever.
15but swept Pharaoh and his army into the Red Sea;
His love endures forever.

16to him who led his people through the desert,
His love endures forever.
17who struck down great kings,
His love endures forever.
18and killed mighty kings—
His love endures forever.
19Sihon king of the Amorites
His love endures forever.
20and Og king of Bashan—
His love endures forever.
21and gave their land as an inheritance,
His love endures forever.
22an inheritance to his servant Israel;
His love endures forever.

23to the One who remembered us in our low estate
His love endures forever.
24and freed us from our enemies,
His love endures forever.
25and who gives food to every creature.
His love endures forever.

26Give thanks to the God of heaven.
His love endures forever.

Psalm 137

1By the rivers of Babylon we sat and wept
when we remembered Zion.
2There on the poplars
we hung our harps,
3for there our captors asked us for songs,
our tormentors demanded songs of joy;
they said, "Sing us one of the songs of Zion!"

4How can we sing the songs of the LORD
while in a foreign land?
5If I forget you, O Jerusalem,
may my right hand forget ⌞its skill⌟.
6May my tongue cling to the roof of my mouth
if I do not remember you,
if I do not consider Jerusalem
my highest joy.

7Remember, O LORD, what the Edomites did
on the day Jerusalem fell.
"Tear it down," they cried,
"tear it down to its foundations!"

8O Daughter of Babylon, doomed to destruction,
happy is he who repays you
for what you have done to us—
9he who seizes your infants
and dashes them against the rocks.

[a]*13* Hebrew *Yam Suph;* that is, Sea of Reeds; also in verse 15

Psalm 138

Of David.

1I will praise you, O LORD, with all my
heart;
before the "gods" I will sing your
praise.
2I will bow down toward your holy temple
and will praise your name
for your love and your faithfulness,
for you have exalted above all things
your name and your word.
3When I called, you answered me;
you made me bold and stouthearted.

4May all the kings of the earth praise you,
O LORD,
when they hear the words of your
mouth.
5May they sing of the ways of the LORD,
for the glory of the LORD is great.

6Though the LORD is on high, he looks
upon the lowly,
but the proud he knows from afar.
7Though I walk in the midst of trouble,
you preserve my life;
you stretch out your hand against the
anger of my foes,
with your right hand you save me.
8The LORD will fulfill ⌞his purpose⌟ for me;
your love, O LORD, endures forever—
do not abandon the works of your
hands.

Psalm 139

For the director of music. Of David. A psalm.

1O LORD, you have searched me
and you know me.
2You know when I sit and when I rise;
you perceive my thoughts from afar.
3You discern my going out and my lying
down;
you are familiar with all my ways.
4Before a word is on my tongue
you know it completely, O LORD.

5You hem me in—behind and before;
you have laid your hand upon me.
6Such knowledge is too wonderful for me,
too lofty for me to attain.

7Where can I go from your Spirit?
Where can I flee from your presence?
8If I go up to the heavens, you are there;
if I make my bed in the depths,[a] you
are there.
9If I rise on the wings of the dawn,
if I settle on the far side of the sea,
10even there your hand will guide me,
your right hand will hold me fast.

11If I say, "Surely the darkness will hide me
and the light become night around me,"
12even the darkness will not be dark to you;
the night will shine like the day,
for darkness is as light to you.

13For you created my inmost being;
you knit me together in my mother's
womb.
14I praise you because I am fearfully and
wonderfully made;
your works are wonderful,
I know that full well.
15My frame was not hidden from you
when I was made in the secret place.
When I was woven together in the depths
of the earth,
16 your eyes saw my unformed body.
All the days ordained for me
were written in your book
before one of them came to be.

17How precious to[b] me are your thoughts,
O God!
How vast is the sum of them!
18Were I to count them,
they would outnumber the grains of
sand.
When I awake,
I am still with you.

19If only you would slay the wicked, O God!
Away from me, you bloodthirsty men!
20They speak of you with evil intent;
your adversaries misuse your name.
21Do I not hate those who hate you,
O LORD,
and abhor those who rise up against
you?
22I have nothing but hatred for them;
I count them my enemies.

23Search me, O God, and know my heart;
test me and know my anxious thoughts.
24See if there is any offensive way in me,
and lead me in the way everlasting.

[a]8 Hebrew *Sheol* [b]17 Or *concerning*

Psalm 140

For the director of music. A psalm of David.

1Rescue me, O LORD, from evil men;
protect me from men of violence,
2who devise evil plans in their hearts
and stir up war every day.
3They make their tongues as sharp as a serpent's;
the poison of vipers is on their lips. *Selah*

4Keep me, O LORD, from the hands of the wicked;
protect me from men of violence
who plan to trip my feet.
5Proud men have hidden a snare for me;
they have spread out the cords of their net
and have set traps for me along my path. *Selah*

6O LORD, I say to you, "You are my God."
Hear, O LORD, my cry for mercy.
7O Sovereign LORD, my strong deliverer,
who shields my head in the day of battle—
8do not grant the wicked their desires, O LORD;
do not let their plans succeed,
or they will become proud. *Selah*

9Let the heads of those who surround me
be covered with the trouble their lips have caused.
10Let burning coals fall upon them;
may they be thrown into the fire,
into miry pits, never to rise.
11Let slanderers not be established in the land;
may disaster hunt down men of violence.

12I know that the LORD secures justice for the poor
and upholds the cause of the needy.
13Surely the righteous will praise your name
and the upright will live before you.

Psalm 141

A psalm of David.

1O LORD, I call to you; come quickly to me.
Hear my voice when I call to you.
2May my prayer be set before you like incense;
may the lifting up of my hands be like the evening sacrifice.

3Set a guard over my mouth, O LORD;
keep watch over the door of my lips.
4Let not my heart be drawn to what is evil,
to take part in wicked deeds
with men who are evildoers;
let me not eat of their delicacies.

5Let a righteous man[a] strike me—it is a kindness;
let him rebuke me—it is oil on my head.
My head will not refuse it.

Yet my prayer is ever against the deeds of evildoers;
6 their rulers will be thrown down from the cliffs,
and the wicked will learn that my words were well spoken.
7⌞They will say,⌟ "As one plows and breaks up the earth,
so our bones have been scattered at the mouth of the grave.[b]"

8But my eyes are fixed on you, O Sovereign LORD;
in you I take refuge—do not give me over to death.
9Keep me from the snares they have laid for me,
from the traps set by evildoers.
10Let the wicked fall into their own nets,
while I pass by in safety.

Psalm 142

A *maskil*[c] of David. When he was in the cave. A prayer.

1I cry aloud to the LORD;
I lift up my voice to the LORD for mercy.
2I pour out my complaint before him;
before him I tell my trouble.

3When my spirit grows faint within me,
it is you who know my way.
In the path where I walk
men have hidden a snare for me.
4Look to my right and see;
no one is concerned for me.
I have no refuge;
no one cares for my life.

[a]5 Or *Let the Righteous One* [b]7 Hebrew *Sheol* [c]Title: Probably a literary or musical term

[5]I cry to you, O LORD;
I say, "You are my refuge,
my portion in the land of the living."
[6]Listen to my cry,
for I am in desperate need;
rescue me from those who pursue me,
for they are too strong for me.
[7]Set me free from my prison,
that I may praise your name.

Then the righteous will gather about me
because of your goodness to me.

Psalm 143

A psalm of David.

[1]O LORD, hear my prayer,
listen to my cry for mercy;
in your faithfulness and righteousness
come to my relief.
[2]Do not bring your servant into judgment,
for no one living is righteous before you.
[3]The enemy pursues me,
he crushes me to the ground;
he makes me dwell in darkness
like those long dead.
[4]So my spirit grows faint within me;
my heart within me is dismayed.
[5]I remember the days of long ago;
I meditate on all your works
and consider what your hands have done.
[6]I spread out my hands to you;
my soul thirsts for you like a parched land. *Selah*

[7]Answer me quickly, O LORD;
my spirit fails.
Do not hide your face from me
or I will be like those who go down to the pit.
[8]Let the morning bring me word of your unfailing love,
for I have put my trust in you.
Show me the way I should go,
for to you I lift up my soul.
[9]Rescue me from my enemies, O LORD,
for I hide myself in you.
[10]Teach me to do your will,
for you are my God;
may your good Spirit
lead me on level ground.

[11]For your name's sake, O LORD, preserve my life;
in your righteousness, bring me out of trouble.
[12]In your unfailing love, silence my enemies;
destroy all my foes,
for I am your servant.

Psalm 144

Of David.

[1]Praise be to the LORD my Rock,
who trains my hands for war,
my fingers for battle.
[2]He is my loving God and my fortress,
my stronghold and my deliverer,
my shield, in whom I take refuge,
who subdues peoples[a] under me.

[3]O LORD, what is man that you care for him,
the son of man that you think of him?
[4]Man is like a breath;
his days are like a fleeting shadow.

[5]Part your heavens, O LORD, and come down;
touch the mountains, so that they smoke.
[6]Send forth lightning and scatter ⌞the enemies⌟;
shoot your arrows and rout them.
[7]Reach down your hand from on high;
deliver me and rescue me
from the mighty waters,
from the hands of foreigners
[8]whose mouths are full of lies,
whose right hands are deceitful.

[9]I will sing a new song to you, O God;
on the ten-stringed lyre I will make music to you,
[10]to the One who gives victory to kings,
who delivers his servant David from the deadly sword.

[11]Deliver me and rescue me
from the hands of foreigners
whose mouths are full of lies,
whose right hands are deceitful.

[12]Then our sons in their youth
will be like well-nurtured plants,
and our daughters will be like pillars

[a]2 Many manuscripts of the Masoretic Text, Dead Sea Scrolls, Aquila, Jerome and Syriac; most manuscripts of the Masoretic Text *subdues my people*

carved to adorn a palace.
13Our barns will be filled
with every kind of provision.
Our sheep will increase by thousands,
by tens of thousands in our fields;
14 our oxen will draw heavy loads.[a]
There will be no breaching of walls,
no going into captivity,
no cry of distress in our streets.

15Blessed are the people of whom this is true;
blessed are the people whose God is the LORD.

Psalm 145[b]

A psalm of praise. Of David.

1I will exalt you, my God the King;
I will praise your name for ever and ever.
2Every day I will praise you
and extol your name for ever and ever.

3Great is the LORD and most worthy of praise;
his greatness no one can fathom.
4One generation will commend your works to another;
they will tell of your mighty acts.
5They will speak of the glorious splendor of your majesty,
and I will meditate on your wonderful works.[c]
6They will tell of the power of your awesome works,
and I will proclaim your great deeds.
7They will celebrate your abundant goodness
and joyfully sing of your righteousness.

8The LORD is gracious and compassionate,
slow to anger and rich in love.
9The LORD is good to all;
he has compassion on all he has made.
10All you have made will praise you, O LORD;
your saints will extol you.
11They will tell of the glory of your kingdom
and speak of your might,
12so that all men may know of your mighty acts
and the glorious splendor of your kingdom.
13Your kingdom is an everlasting kingdom,
and your dominion endures through all generations.

The LORD is faithful to all his promises
and loving toward all he has made.[d]
14The LORD upholds all those who fall
and lifts up all who are bowed down.
15The eyes of all look to you,
and you give them their food at the proper time.
16You open your hand
and satisfy the desires of every living thing.

17The LORD is righteous in all his ways
and loving toward all he has made.
18The LORD is near to all who call on him,
to all who call on him in truth.
19He fulfills the desires of those who fear him;
he hears their cry and saves them.
20The LORD watches over all who love him,
but all the wicked he will destroy.

21My mouth will speak in praise of the LORD.
Let every creature praise his holy name
for ever and ever.

Psalm 146

1Praise the LORD.[e]

Praise the LORD, O my soul.
2 I will praise the LORD all my life;
I will sing praise to my God as long as I live.

3Do not put your trust in princes,
in mortal men, who cannot save.
4When their spirit departs, they return to the ground;
on that very day their plans come to nothing.

5Blessed is he whose help is the God of Jacob,
whose hope is in the LORD his God,
6the Maker of heaven and earth,

[a] 14 Or *our chieftains will be firmly established* [b] This psalm is an acrostic poem, the verses of which (including verse 13b) begin with the successive letters of the Hebrew alphabet. [c] 5 Dead Sea Scrolls and Syriac (see also Septuagint); Masoretic Text *On the glorious splendor of your majesty / and on your wonderful works I will meditate* [d] 13 One manuscript of the Masoretic Text, Dead Sea Scrolls and Syriac (see also Septuagint); most manuscripts of the Masoretic Text do not have the last two lines of verse 13. [e] 1 Hebrew *Hallelu Yah*; also in verse 10

the sea, and everything in them—
the LORD, who remains faithful forever.
7He upholds the cause of the oppressed
and gives food to the hungry.
The LORD sets prisoners free,
8 the LORD gives sight to the blind,
the LORD lifts up those who are bowed
down,
the LORD loves the righteous.
9The LORD watches over the alien
and sustains the fatherless and the
widow,
but he frustrates the ways of the
wicked.

10The LORD reigns forever,
your God, O Zion, for all generations.

Praise the LORD.

Psalm 147

1Praise the LORD.[a]

How good it is to sing praises to our God,
how pleasant and fitting to praise him!

2The LORD builds up Jerusalem;
he gathers the exiles of Israel.
3He heals the brokenhearted
and binds up their wounds.

4He determines the number of the stars
and calls them each by name.
5Great is our Lord and mighty in power;
his understanding has no limit.
6The LORD sustains the humble
but casts the wicked to the ground.

7Sing to the LORD with thanksgiving;
make music to our God on the harp.
8He covers the sky with clouds;
he supplies the earth with rain
and makes grass grow on the hills.
9He provides food for the cattle
and for the young ravens when they
call.

10His pleasure is not in the strength of the
horse,
nor his delight in the legs of a man;
11the LORD delights in those who fear him,
who put their hope in his unfailing love.

12Extol the LORD, O Jerusalem;
praise your God, O Zion,
13for he strengthens the bars of your gates
and blesses your people within you.
14He grants peace to your borders
and satisfies you with the finest of
wheat.

15He sends his command to the earth;
his word runs swiftly.
16He spreads the snow like wool
and scatters the frost like ashes.
17He hurls down his hail like pebbles.
Who can withstand his icy blast?
18He sends his word and melts them;
he stirs up his breezes, and the waters
flow.

19He has revealed his word to Jacob,
his laws and decrees to Israel.
20He has done this for no other nation;
they do not know his laws.

Praise the LORD.

Psalm 148

1Praise the LORD.[b]

Praise the LORD from the heavens,
praise him in the heights above.
2Praise him, all his angels,
praise him, all his heavenly hosts.
3Praise him, sun and moon,
praise him, all you shining stars.
4Praise him, you highest heavens
and you waters above the skies.
5Let them praise the name of the LORD,
for he commanded and they were
created.
6He set them in place for ever and ever;
he gave a decree that will never pass
away.

7Praise the LORD from the earth,
you great sea creatures and all ocean
depths,
8lightning and hail, snow and clouds,
stormy winds that do his bidding,
9you mountains and all hills,
fruit trees and all cedars,
10wild animals and all cattle,
small creatures and flying birds,
11kings of the earth and all nations,
you princes and all rulers on earth,
12young men and maidens,
old men and children.

13Let them praise the name of the LORD,
for his name alone is exalted;
his splendor is above the earth and the
heavens.

[a] 1 Hebrew *Hallelu Yah*; also in verse 20

[b] 1 Hebrew *Hallelu Yah*; also in verse 14

14He has raised up for his people a horn,[a]
the praise of all his saints,
of Israel, the people close to his heart.

Praise the LORD.

Psalm 149

1Praise the LORD.[b]

Sing to the LORD a new song,
his praise in the assembly of the saints.

2Let Israel rejoice in their Maker;
let the people of Zion be glad in their King.
3Let them praise his name with dancing
and make music to him with tambourine and harp.
4For the LORD takes delight in his people;
he crowns the humble with salvation.
5Let the saints rejoice in this honor
and sing for joy on their beds.

6May the praise of God be in their mouths
and a double-edged sword in their hands,
7to inflict vengeance on the nations
and punishment on the peoples,
8to bind their kings with fetters,
their nobles with shackles of iron,
9to carry out the sentence written against them.
This is the glory of all his saints.

Praise the LORD.

Psalm 150

1Praise the LORD.[c]

Praise God in his sanctuary;
praise him in his mighty heavens.
2Praise him for his acts of power;
praise him for his surpassing greatness.
3Praise him with the sounding of the trumpet,
praise him with the harp and lyre,
4praise him with tambourine and dancing,
praise him with the strings and flute,
5praise him with the clash of cymbals,
praise him with resounding cymbals.

6Let everything that has breath praise the LORD.

Praise the LORD.

[a] 14 *Horn* here symbolizes strong one, that is, king. [b] 1 Hebrew *Hallelu Yah*; also in verse 9 [c] 1 Hebrew *Hallelu Yah*; also in verse 6

Proverbs

Introduction:

Proverbs is a collection of wise sayings and good advice for daily living. The book begins by reminding us that "The fear of the LORD is the beginning of knowledge" (1:7). The first four chapters go on to discuss the importance of wisdom.

Following this, the author includes a collection of short and powerful two-line sayings that cover many different subjects including: marriage, social behavior, friendship, justice, folly, poverty, wealth, family, love, laziness, and warnings against drinking and adultery.

Many of these proverbs came from King Solomon. Others were copied by the men of Hezekiah. Agur and Lemuel wrote the last two chapters.

Outline of contents:

Instructions on wisdom and foolishness (1:1–9:18)
The proverbs of Solomon (10:1–22:16)
Sayings of the wise (22:17–24:34)
More proverbs of Solomon (25:1–29:27)
Sayings of Agur and Lemuel (30:1–31:31)

Prologue: Purpose and Theme

1 The proverbs of Solomon son of David,
king of Israel:

2for attaining wisdom and discipline;
for understanding words of insight;
3for acquiring a disciplined and prudent life,
doing what is right and just and fair;
4for giving prudence to the simple,
knowledge and discretion to the young—
5let the wise listen and add to their learning,
and let the discerning get guidance—
6for understanding proverbs and parables,
the sayings and riddles of the wise.

7The fear of the LORD is the beginning of knowledge,
but fools[a] despise wisdom and discipline.

Exhortations to Embrace Wisdom

Warning Against Enticement

8Listen, my son, to your father's instruction
and do not forsake your mother's teaching.
9They will be a garland to grace your head
and a chain to adorn your neck.

10My son, if sinners entice you,
do not give in to them.
11If they say, "Come along with us;
let's lie in wait for someone's blood,
let's waylay some harmless soul;
12let's swallow them alive, like the grave,[b]
and whole, like those who go down to the pit;
13we will get all sorts of valuable things
and fill our houses with plunder;
14throw in your lot with us,
and we will share a common purse"—

[a]7 The Hebrew words rendered *fool* in Proverbs, and often elsewhere in the Old Testament, denote one who is morally deficient. [b]12 Hebrew *Sheol*

15my son, do not go along with them,
do not set foot on their paths;
16for their feet rush into sin,
they are swift to shed blood.
17How useless to spread a net
in full view of all the birds!
18These men lie in wait for their own blood;
they waylay only themselves!
19Such is the end of all who go after
ill-gotten gain;
it takes away the lives of those who
get it.

Warning Against Rejecting Wisdom

20Wisdom calls aloud in the street,
she raises her voice in the public
squares;
21at the head of the noisy streets[a] she cries
out,
in the gateways of the city she makes
her speech:

22"How long will you simple ones[b] love
your simple ways?
How long will mockers delight in
mockery
and fools hate knowledge?
23If you had responded to my rebuke,
I would have poured out my heart to
you
and made my thoughts known to you.
24But since you rejected me when I called
and no one gave heed when I stretched
out my hand,
25since you ignored all my advice
and would not accept my rebuke,
26I in turn will laugh at your disaster;
I will mock when calamity overtakes
you—
27when calamity overtakes you like a
storm,
when disaster sweeps over you like a
whirlwind,
when distress and trouble overwhelm
you.

28"Then they will call to me but I will not
answer;
they will look for me but will not find
me.
29Since they hated knowledge
and did not choose to fear the LORD,
30since they would not accept my advice
and spurned my rebuke,
31they will eat the fruit of their ways
and be filled with the fruit of their
schemes.
32For the waywardness of the simple will
kill them,
and the complacency of fools will
destroy them;
33but whoever listens to me will live in
safety
and be at ease, without fear of harm."

Moral Benefits of Wisdom

2 My son, if you accept my words
and store up my commands within you,
2turning your ear to wisdom
and applying your heart to
understanding,
3and if you call out for insight
and cry aloud for understanding,
4and if you look for it as for silver
and search for it as for hidden treasure,
5then you will understand the fear of the
LORD
and find the knowledge of God.
6For the LORD gives wisdom,
and from his mouth come knowledge
and understanding.
7He holds victory in store for the upright,
he is a shield to those whose walk is
blameless,
8for he guards the course of the just
and protects the way of his faithful
ones.

9Then you will understand what is right
and just
and fair—every good path.
10For wisdom will enter your heart,
and knowledge will be pleasant to your
soul.
11Discretion will protect you,
and understanding will guard you.

12Wisdom will save you from the ways of
wicked men,
from men whose words are perverse,
13who leave the straight paths
to walk in dark ways,
14who delight in doing wrong
and rejoice in the perverseness of evil,
15whose paths are crooked
and who are devious in their ways.

16It will save you also from the adulteress,
from the wayward wife with her
seductive words,

[a]21 Hebrew; Septuagint / *on the tops of the walls* [b]22 The Hebrew word rendered *simple* in Proverbs generally denotes one without moral direction and inclined to evil.

17who has left the partner of her youth
and ignored the covenant she made
before God.[a]
18For her house leads down to death
and her paths to the spirits of the dead.
19None who go to her return
or attain the paths of life.

20Thus you will walk in the ways of good
men
and keep to the paths of the righteous.
21For the upright will live in the land,
and the blameless will remain in it;
22but the wicked will be cut off from the
land,
and the unfaithful will be torn from it.

Further Benefits of Wisdom

3 My son, do not forget my teaching,
but keep my commands in your heart,
2for they will prolong your life many years
and bring you prosperity.

3Let love and faithfulness never leave you;
bind them around your neck,
write them on the tablet of your heart.
4Then you will win favor and a good name
in the sight of God and man.

5Trust in the LORD with all your heart
and lean not on your own
understanding;
6in all your ways acknowledge him,
and he will make your paths straight.[b]

7Do not be wise in your own eyes;
fear the LORD and shun evil.
8This will bring health to your body
and nourishment to your bones.

9Honor the LORD with your wealth,
with the firstfruits of all your crops;
10then your barns will be filled to
overflowing,
and your vats will brim over with new
wine.

11My son, do not despise the LORD's
discipline
and do not resent his rebuke,
12because the LORD disciplines those he
loves,
as a father[c] the son he delights in.

13Blessed is the man who finds wisdom,
the man who gains understanding,
14for she is more profitable than silver
and yields better returns than gold.
15She is more precious than rubies;
nothing you desire can compare with
her.
16Long life is in her right hand;
in her left hand are riches and honor.
17Her ways are pleasant ways,
and all her paths are peace.
18She is a tree of life to those who embrace
her;
those who lay hold of her will be
blessed.

19By wisdom the LORD laid the earth's
foundations,
by understanding he set the heavens in
place;
20by his knowledge the deeps were
divided,
and the clouds let drop the dew.

21My son, preserve sound judgment and
discernment,
do not let them out of your sight;
22they will be life for you,
an ornament to grace your neck.
23Then you will go on your way in safety,
and your foot will not stumble;
24when you lie down, you will not be afraid;
when you lie down, your sleep will be
sweet.
25Have no fear of sudden disaster
or of the ruin that overtakes the wicked,
26for the LORD will be your confidence
and will keep your foot from being
snared.

27Do not withhold good from those who
deserve it,
when it is in your power to act.
28Do not say to your neighbor,
"Come back later; I'll give it
tomorrow"—
when you now have it with you.
29Do not plot harm against your neighbor,
who lives trustfully near you.
30Do not accuse a man for no reason—
when he has done you no harm.

31Do not envy a violent man
or choose any of his ways,
32for the LORD detests a perverse man
but takes the upright into his
confidence.

33The LORD's curse is on the house of the
wicked,

[a]17 Or *covenant of her God* [b]6 Or *will direct your paths* [c]12 Hebrew; Septuagint / *and he punishes*

but he blesses the home of the
righteous.
34He mocks proud mockers
but gives grace to the humble.
35The wise inherit honor,
but fools he holds up to shame.

Wisdom Is Supreme

4 Listen, my sons, to a father's
instruction;
pay attention and gain understanding.
2I give you sound learning,
so do not forsake my teaching.
3When I was a boy in my father's house,
still tender, and an only child of my
mother,
4he taught me and said,
"Lay hold of my words with all your
heart;
keep my commands and you will live.
5Get wisdom, get understanding;
do not forget my words or swerve from
them.
6Do not forsake wisdom, and she will
protect you;
love her, and she will watch over you.
7Wisdom is supreme; therefore get
wisdom.
Though it cost all you have,[a] get
understanding.
8Esteem her, and she will exalt you;
embrace her, and she will honor you.
9She will set a garland of grace on your
head
and present you with a crown of
splendor."
10Listen, my son, accept what I say,
and the years of your life will be many.
11I guide you in the way of wisdom
and lead you along straight paths.
12When you walk, your steps will not be
hampered;
when you run, you will not stumble.
13Hold on to instruction, do not let it go;
guard it well, for it is your life.
14Do not set foot on the path of the wicked
or walk in the way of evil men.
15Avoid it, do not travel on it;
turn from it and go on your way.
16For they cannot sleep till they do evil;
they are robbed of slumber till they
make someone fall.
17They eat the bread of wickedness
and drink the wine of violence.
18The path of the righteous is like the first
gleam of dawn,
shining ever brighter till the full light of
day.
19But the way of the wicked is like deep
darkness;
they do not know what makes them
stumble.
20My son, pay attention to what I say;
listen closely to my words.
21Do not let them out of your sight,
keep them within your heart;
22for they are life to those who find them
and health to a man's whole body.
23Above all else, guard your heart,
for it is the wellspring of life.
24Put away perversity from your mouth;
keep corrupt talk far from your lips.
25Let your eyes look straight ahead,
fix your gaze directly before you.
26Make level[b] paths for your feet
and take only ways that are firm.
27Do not swerve to the right or the left;
keep your foot from evil.

Warning Against Adultery

5 My son, pay attention to my wisdom,
listen well to my words of insight,
2that you may maintain discretion
and your lips may preserve knowledge.
3For the lips of an adulteress drip honey,
and her speech is smoother than oil;
4but in the end she is bitter as gall,
sharp as a double-edged sword.
5Her feet go down to death;
her steps lead straight to the grave.[c]
6She gives no thought to the way of life;
her paths are crooked, but she knows it
not.
7Now then, my sons, listen to me;
do not turn aside from what I say.
8Keep to a path far from her,
do not go near the door of her house,
9lest you give your best strength to others
and your years to one who is cruel,
10lest strangers feast on your wealth
and your toil enrich another man's
house.
11At the end of your life you will groan,
when your flesh and body are spent.
12You will say, "How I hated discipline!
How my heart spurned correction!
13I would not obey my teachers

[a]7 Or *Whatever else you get* [b]26 Or *Consider the* [c]5 Hebrew *Sheol*

or listen to my instructors.
14I have come to the brink of utter ruin
in the midst of the whole assembly."

15Drink water from your own cistern,
running water from your own well.
16Should your springs overflow in the streets,
your streams of water in the public squares?
17Let them be yours alone,
never to be shared with strangers.
18May your fountain be blessed,
and may you rejoice in the wife of your youth.
19A loving doe, a graceful deer—
may her breasts satisfy you always,
may you ever be captivated by her love.
20Why be captivated, my son, by an adulteress?
Why embrace the bosom of another man's wife?

21For a man's ways are in full view of the LORD,
and he examines all his paths.
22The evil deeds of a wicked man ensnare him;
the cords of his sin hold him fast.
23He will die for lack of discipline,
led astray by his own great folly.

Warnings Against Folly

6 My son, if you have put up security for your neighbor,
if you have struck hands in pledge for another,
2if you have been trapped by what you said,
ensnared by the words of your mouth,
3then do this, my son, to free yourself,
since you have fallen into your neighbor's hands:
Go and humble yourself;
press your plea with your neighbor!
4Allow no sleep to your eyes,
no slumber to your eyelids.
5Free yourself, like a gazelle from the hand of the hunter,
like a bird from the snare of the fowler.

6Go to the ant, you sluggard;
consider its ways and be wise!
7It has no commander,
no overseer or ruler,
8yet it stores its provisions in summer
and gathers its food at harvest.

9How long will you lie there, you sluggard?
When will you get up from your sleep?
10A little sleep, a little slumber,
a little folding of the hands to rest—
11and poverty will come on you like a bandit
and scarcity like an armed man.[a]

12A scoundrel and villain,
who goes about with a corrupt mouth,
13 who winks with his eye,
signals with his feet
and motions with his fingers,
14 who plots evil with deceit in his heart—
he always stirs up dissension.
15Therefore disaster will overtake him in an instant;
he will suddenly be destroyed—without remedy.

16There are six things the LORD hates,
seven that are detestable to him:
17 haughty eyes,
a lying tongue,
hands that shed innocent blood,
18 a heart that devises wicked schemes,
feet that are quick to rush into evil,
19 a false witness who pours out lies
and a man who stirs up dissension among brothers.

Warning Against Adultery

20My son, keep your father's commands
and do not forsake your mother's teaching.
21Bind them upon your heart forever;
fasten them around your neck.
22When you walk, they will guide you;
when you sleep, they will watch over you;
when you awake, they will speak to you.
23For these commands are a lamp,
this teaching is a light,
and the corrections of discipline
are the way to life,
24keeping you from the immoral woman,
from the smooth tongue of the wayward wife.
25Do not lust in your heart after her beauty
or let her captivate you with her eyes,

[a] 11 Or *like a vagrant / and scarcity like a beggar*

[26]for the prostitute reduces you to a loaf of bread,
and the adulteress preys upon your very life.
[27]Can a man scoop fire into his lap
without his clothes being burned?
[28]Can a man walk on hot coals
without his feet being scorched?
[29]So is he who sleeps with another man's wife;
no one who touches her will go unpunished.

[30]Men do not despise a thief if he steals
to satisfy his hunger when he is starving.
[31]Yet if he is caught, he must pay sevenfold,
though it costs him all the wealth of his house.
[32]But a man who commits adultery lacks judgment;
whoever does so destroys himself.
[33]Blows and disgrace are his lot,
and his shame will never be wiped away;
[34]for jealousy arouses a husband's fury,
and he will show no mercy when he takes revenge.
[35]He will not accept any compensation;
he will refuse the bribe, however great it is.

Warning Against the Adulteress

7 My son, keep my words
and store up my commands within you.
[2]Keep my commands and you will live;
guard my teachings as the apple of your eye.
[3]Bind them on your fingers;
write them on the tablet of your heart.
[4]Say to wisdom, "You are my sister,"
and call understanding your kinsman;
[5]they will keep you from the adulteress,
from the wayward wife with her seductive words.

[6]At the window of my house
I looked out through the lattice.
[7]I saw among the simple,
I noticed among the young men,
a youth who lacked judgment.
[8]He was going down the street near her corner,
walking along in the direction of her house
[9]at twilight, as the day was fading,
as the dark of night set in.

[10]Then out came a woman to meet him,
dressed like a prostitute and with crafty intent.
[11](She is loud and defiant,
her feet never stay at home;
[12]now in the street, now in the squares,
at every corner she lurks.)
[13]She took hold of him and kissed him
and with a brazen face she said:

[14]"I have fellowship offerings[a] at home;
today I fulfilled my vows.
[15]So I came out to meet you;
I looked for you and have found you!
[16]I have covered my bed
with colored linens from Egypt.
[17]I have perfumed my bed
with myrrh, aloes and cinnamon.
[18]Come, let's drink deep of love till morning;
let's enjoy ourselves with love!
[19]My husband is not at home;
he has gone on a long journey.
[20]He took his purse filled with money
and will not be home till full moon."

[21]With persuasive words she led him astray;
she seduced him with her smooth talk.
[22]All at once he followed her
like an ox going to the slaughter,
like a deer[b] stepping into a noose[c]
[23] till an arrow pierces his liver,
like a bird darting into a snare,
little knowing it will cost him his life.

[24]Now then, my sons, listen to me;
pay attention to what I say.
[25]Do not let your heart turn to her ways
or stray into her paths.
[26]Many are the victims she has brought down;
her slain are a mighty throng.
[27]Her house is a highway to the grave,[d]
leading down to the chambers of death.

Wisdom's Call

8 Does not wisdom call out?
Does not understanding raise her voice?

[a]*14* Traditionally *peace offerings* [b]*22* Syriac (see also Septuagint); Hebrew *fool* [c]*22* The meaning of the Hebrew for this line is uncertain. [d]*27* Hebrew *Sheol*

2On the heights along the way,
where the paths meet, she takes her stand;
3beside the gates leading into the city,
at the entrances, she cries aloud:
4"To you, O men, I call out;
I raise my voice to all mankind.
5You who are simple, gain prudence;
you who are foolish, gain understanding.
6Listen, for I have worthy things to say;
I open my lips to speak what is right.
7My mouth speaks what is true,
for my lips detest wickedness.
8All the words of my mouth are just;
none of them is crooked or perverse.
9To the discerning all of them are right;
they are faultless to those who have knowledge.
10Choose my instruction instead of silver,
knowledge rather than choice gold,
11for wisdom is more precious than rubies,
and nothing you desire can compare with her.

12"I, wisdom, dwell together with prudence;
I possess knowledge and discretion.
13To fear the LORD is to hate evil;
I hate pride and arrogance,
evil behavior and perverse speech.
14Counsel and sound judgment are mine;
I have understanding and power.
15By me kings reign
and rulers make laws that are just;
16by me princes govern,
and all nobles who rule on earth.[a]
17I love those who love me,
and those who seek me find me.
18With me are riches and honor,
enduring wealth and prosperity.
19My fruit is better than fine gold;
what I yield surpasses choice silver.
20I walk in the way of righteousness,
along the paths of justice,
21bestowing wealth on those who love me
and making their treasuries full.

22"The LORD brought me forth[b] as the first of his works,[c]
before his deeds of old;
23I was appointed[d] from eternity,
from the beginning, before the world began.
24When there were no oceans, I was given birth,
when there were no springs abounding with water;
25before the mountains were settled in place,
before the hills, I was given birth,
26before he made the earth or its fields
or any of the dust of the world.
27I was there when he set the heavens in place,
when he marked out the horizon on the face of the deep,
28when he established the clouds above
and fixed securely the fountains of the deep,
29when he gave the sea its boundary
so the waters would not overstep his command,
and when he marked out the foundations of the earth.
30 Then I was the craftsman at his side.
I was filled with delight day after day,
rejoicing always in his presence,
31rejoicing in his whole world
and delighting in mankind.

32"Now then, my sons, listen to me;
blessed are those who keep my ways.
33Listen to my instruction and be wise;
do not ignore it.
34Blessed is the man who listens to me,
watching daily at my doors,
waiting at my doorway.
35For whoever finds me finds life
and receives favor from the LORD.
36But whoever fails to find me harms himself;
all who hate me love death."

Invitations of Wisdom and of Folly

9 Wisdom has built her house;
she has hewn out its seven pillars.
2She has prepared her meat and mixed her wine;
she has also set her table.
3She has sent out her maids, and she calls
from the highest point of the city.
4"Let all who are simple come in here!"
she says to those who lack judgment.
5"Come, eat my food
and drink the wine I have mixed.
6Leave your simple ways and you will live;
walk in the way of understanding.

[a]16 Many Hebrew manuscripts and Septuagint; most Hebrew manuscripts *and nobles—all righteous rulers*
[b]22 Or *The LORD brought me forth* [c]22 Or *way;* or *dominion* [d]23 Or *fashioned*

7"Whoever corrects a mocker invites insult;
whoever rebukes a wicked man incurs abuse.
8Do not rebuke a mocker or he will hate you;
rebuke a wise man and he will love you.
9Instruct a wise man and he will be wiser still;
teach a righteous man and he will add to his learning.

10"The fear of the LORD is the beginning of wisdom,
and knowledge of the Holy One is understanding.
11For through me your days will be many,
and years will be added to your life.
12If you are wise, your wisdom will reward you;
if you are a mocker, you alone will suffer."

13The woman Folly is loud;
she is undisciplined and without knowledge.
14She sits at the door of her house,
on a seat at the highest point of the city,
15calling out to those who pass by,
who go straight on their way.
16"Let all who are simple come in here!"
she says to those who lack judgment.
17"Stolen water is sweet;
food eaten in secret is delicious!"
18But little do they know that the dead are there,
that her guests are in the depths of the grave.[a]

Proverbs of Solomon

10 The proverbs of Solomon:

A wise son brings joy to his father,
but a foolish son grief to his mother.

2Ill-gotten treasures are of no value,
but righteousness delivers from death.

3The LORD does not let the righteous go hungry
but he thwarts the craving of the wicked.

4Lazy hands make a man poor,
but diligent hands bring wealth.

5He who gathers crops in summer is a wise son,
but he who sleeps during harvest is a disgraceful son.

6Blessings crown the head of the righteous,
but violence overwhelms the mouth of the wicked.[b]

7The memory of the righteous will be a blessing,
but the name of the wicked will rot.

8The wise in heart accept commands,
but a chattering fool comes to ruin.

9The man of integrity walks securely,
but he who takes crooked paths will be found out.

10He who winks maliciously causes grief,
and a chattering fool comes to ruin.

11The mouth of the righteous is a fountain of life,
but violence overwhelms the mouth of the wicked.

12Hatred stirs up dissension,
but love covers over all wrongs.

13Wisdom is found on the lips of the discerning,
but a rod is for the back of him who lacks judgment.

14Wise men store up knowledge,
but the mouth of a fool invites ruin.

15The wealth of the rich is their fortified city,
but poverty is the ruin of the poor.

16The wages of the righteous bring them life,
but the income of the wicked brings them punishment.

17He who heeds discipline shows the way to life,
but whoever ignores correction leads others astray.

18He who conceals his hatred has lying lips,
and whoever spreads slander is a fool.

19When words are many, sin is not absent,
but he who holds his tongue is wise.

20The tongue of the righteous is choice silver,

[a] 18 Hebrew *Sheol* [b] 6 Or *but the mouth of the wicked conceals violence*; also in verse 11

but the heart of the wicked is of little value.

21The lips of the righteous nourish many,
but fools die for lack of judgment.

22The blessing of the LORD brings wealth,
and he adds no trouble to it.

23A fool finds pleasure in evil conduct,
but a man of understanding delights in wisdom.

24What the wicked dreads will overtake him;
what the righteous desire will be granted.

25When the storm has swept by, the wicked are gone,
but the righteous stand firm forever.

26As vinegar to the teeth and smoke to the eyes,
so is a sluggard to those who send him.

27The fear of the LORD adds length to life,
but the years of the wicked are cut short.

28The prospect of the righteous is joy,
but the hopes of the wicked come to nothing.

29The way of the LORD is a refuge for the righteous,
but it is the ruin of those who do evil.

30The righteous will never be uprooted,
but the wicked will not remain in the land.

31The mouth of the righteous brings forth wisdom,
but a perverse tongue will be cut out.

32The lips of the righteous know what is fitting,
but the mouth of the wicked only what is perverse.

11 The LORD abhors dishonest scales,
but accurate weights are his delight.

2When pride comes, then comes disgrace,
but with humility comes wisdom.

3The integrity of the upright guides them,
but the unfaithful are destroyed by their duplicity.

4Wealth is worthless in the day of wrath,
but righteousness delivers from death.

5The righteousness of the blameless makes a straight way for them,
but the wicked are brought down by their own wickedness.

6The righteousness of the upright delivers them,
but the unfaithful are trapped by evil desires.

7When a wicked man dies, his hope perishes;
all he expected from his power comes to nothing.

8The righteous man is rescued from trouble,
and it comes on the wicked instead.

9With his mouth the godless destroys his neighbor,
but through knowledge the righteous escape.

10When the righteous prosper, the city rejoices;
when the wicked perish, there are shouts of joy.

11Through the blessing of the upright a city is exalted,
but by the mouth of the wicked it is destroyed.

12A man who lacks judgment derides his neighbor,
but a man of understanding holds his tongue.

13A gossip betrays a confidence,
but a trustworthy man keeps a secret.

14For lack of guidance a nation falls,
but many advisers make victory sure.

15He who puts up security for another will surely suffer,
but whoever refuses to strike hands in pledge is safe.

16A kindhearted woman gains respect,
but ruthless men gain only wealth.

17A kind man benefits himself,
but a cruel man brings trouble on himself.

18The wicked man earns deceptive wages,
but he who sows righteousness reaps a sure reward.

19The truly righteous man attains life,

but he who pursues evil goes to his
death.

20The LORD detests men of perverse heart
but he delights in those whose ways
are blameless.

21Be sure of this: The wicked will not go
unpunished,
but those who are righteous will go
free.

22Like a gold ring in a pig's snout
is a beautiful woman who shows no
discretion.

23The desire of the righteous ends only in
good,
but the hope of the wicked only in
wrath.

24One man gives freely, yet gains even
more;
another withholds unduly, but comes to
poverty.

25A generous man will prosper;
he who refreshes others will himself be
refreshed.

26People curse the man who hoards grain,
but blessing crowns him who is willing
to sell.

27He who seeks good finds good will,
but evil comes to him who searches
for it.

28Whoever trusts in his riches will fall,
but the righteous will thrive like a green
leaf.

29He who brings trouble on his family will
inherit only wind,
and the fool will be servant to the wise.

30The fruit of the righteous is a tree of life,
and he who wins souls is wise.

31If the righteous receive their due on
earth,
how much more the ungodly and the
sinner!

12 Whoever loves discipline loves
knowledge,
but he who hates correction is stupid.

2A good man obtains favor from the LORD,
but the LORD condemns a crafty man.

3A man cannot be established through
wickedness,
but the righteous cannot be uprooted.

4A wife of noble character is her
husband's crown,
but a disgraceful wife is like decay in
his bones.

5The plans of the righteous are just,
but the advice of the wicked is
deceitful.

6The words of the wicked lie in wait for
blood,
but the speech of the upright rescues
them.

7Wicked men are overthrown and are no
more,
but the house of the righteous stands
firm.

8A man is praised according to his
wisdom,
but men with warped minds are
despised.

9Better to be a nobody and yet have a
servant
than pretend to be somebody and have
no food.

10A righteous man cares for the needs of
his animal,
but the kindest acts of the wicked are
cruel.

11He who works his land will have
abundant food,
but he who chases fantasies lacks
judgment.

12The wicked desire the plunder of evil
men,
but the root of the righteous flourishes.

13An evil man is trapped by his sinful talk,
but a righteous man escapes trouble.

14From the fruit of his lips a man is filled
with good things
as surely as the work of his hands
rewards him.

15The way of a fool seems right to him,
but a wise man listens to advice.

16A fool shows his annoyance at once,
but a prudent man overlooks an insult.

17A truthful witness gives honest testimony,
but a false witness tells lies.

18Reckless words pierce like a sword,
but the tongue of the wise brings
healing.

19Truthful lips endure forever,
but a lying tongue lasts only a moment.

20There is deceit in the hearts of those who plot evil,
but joy for those who promote peace.

21No harm befalls the righteous,
but the wicked have their fill of trouble.

22The LORD detests lying lips,
but he delights in men who are truthful.

23A prudent man keeps his knowledge to himself,
but the heart of fools blurts out folly.

24Diligent hands will rule,
but laziness ends in slave labor.

25An anxious heart weighs a man down,
but a kind word cheers him up.

26A righteous man is cautious in friendship,[a]
but the way of the wicked leads them astray.

27The lazy man does not roast[b] his game,
but the diligent man prizes his possessions.

28In the way of righteousness there is life;
along that path is immortality.

13 A wise son heeds his father's instruction,
but a mocker does not listen to rebuke.

2From the fruit of his lips a man enjoys good things,
but the unfaithful have a craving for violence.

3He who guards his lips guards his life,
but he who speaks rashly will come to ruin.

4The sluggard craves and gets nothing,
but the desires of the diligent are fully satisfied.

5The righteous hate what is false,
but the wicked bring shame and disgrace.

6Righteousness guards the man of integrity,
but wickedness overthrows the sinner.

7One man pretends to be rich, yet has nothing;
another pretends to be poor, yet has great wealth.

8A man's riches may ransom his life,
but a poor man hears no threat.

9The light of the righteous shines brightly,
but the lamp of the wicked is snuffed out.

10Pride only breeds quarrels,
but wisdom is found in those who take advice.

11Dishonest money dwindles away,
but he who gathers money little by little makes it grow.

12Hope deferred makes the heart sick,
but a longing fulfilled is a tree of life.

13He who scorns instruction will pay for it,
but he who respects a command is rewarded.

14The teaching of the wise is a fountain of life,
turning a man from the snares of death.

15Good understanding wins favor,
but the way of the unfaithful is hard.[c]

16Every prudent man acts out of knowledge,
but a fool exposes his folly.

17A wicked messenger falls into trouble,
but a trustworthy envoy brings healing.

18He who ignores discipline comes to poverty and shame,
but whoever heeds correction is honored.

19A longing fulfilled is sweet to the soul,
but fools detest turning from evil.

20He who walks with the wise grows wise,
but a companion of fools suffers harm.

21Misfortune pursues the sinner,
but prosperity is the reward of the righteous.

22A good man leaves an inheritance for his children's children,
but a sinner's wealth is stored up for the righteous.

23A poor man's field may produce abundant food,
but injustice sweeps it away.

[a]26 Or *man is a guide to his neighbor* [b]27 The meaning of the Hebrew for this word is uncertain. [c]15 Or *unfaithful does not endure*

24He who spares the rod hates his son,
but he who loves him is careful to
discipline him.

25The righteous eat to their hearts' content,
but the stomach of the wicked goes
hungry.

14 The wise woman builds her house,
but with her own hands the foolish
one tears hers down.

2He whose walk is upright fears the LORD,
but he whose ways are devious
despises him.

3A fool's talk brings a rod to his back,
but the lips of the wise protect them.

4Where there are no oxen, the manger is
empty,
but from the strength of an ox comes
an abundant harvest.

5A truthful witness does not deceive,
but a false witness pours out lies.

6The mocker seeks wisdom and finds
none,
but knowledge comes easily to the
discerning.

7Stay away from a foolish man,
for you will not find knowledge on his
lips.

8The wisdom of the prudent is to give
thought to their ways,
but the folly of fools is deception.

9Fools mock at making amends for sin,
but goodwill is found among the
upright.

10Each heart knows its own bitterness,
and no one else can share its joy.

11The house of the wicked will be
destroyed,
but the tent of the upright will flourish.

12There is a way that seems right to a man,
but in the end it leads to death.

13Even in laughter the heart may ache,
and joy may end in grief.

14The faithless will be fully repaid for their
ways,
and the good man rewarded for his.

15A simple man believes anything,
but a prudent man gives thought to his
steps.

16A wise man fears the LORD and shuns
evil,
but a fool is hotheaded and reckless.

17A quick-tempered man does foolish
things,
and a crafty man is hated.

18The simple inherit folly,
but the prudent are crowned with
knowledge.

19Evil men will bow down in the presence
of the good,
and the wicked at the gates of the
righteous.

20The poor are shunned even by their
neighbors,
but the rich have many friends.

21He who despises his neighbor sins,
but blessed is he who is kind to the
needy.

22Do not those who plot evil go astray?
But those who plan what is good find[a]
love and faithfulness.

23All hard work brings a profit,
but mere talk leads only to poverty.

24The wealth of the wise is their crown,
but the folly of fools yields folly.

25A truthful witness saves lives,
but a false witness is deceitful.

26He who fears the LORD has a secure
fortress,
and for his children it will be a refuge.

27The fear of the LORD is a fountain of life,
turning a man from the snares of death.

28A large population is a king's glory,
but without subjects a prince is ruined.

29A patient man has great understanding,
but a quick-tempered man displays
folly.

30A heart at peace gives life to the body,
but envy rots the bones.

31He who oppresses the poor shows
contempt for their Maker,
but whoever is kind to the needy
honors God.

[a]22 Or *show*

32When calamity comes, the wicked are brought down,
but even in death the righteous have a refuge.

33Wisdom reposes in the heart of the discerning
and even among fools she lets herself be known.[a]

34Righteousness exalts a nation,
but sin is a disgrace to any people.

35A king delights in a wise servant,
but a shameful servant incurs his wrath.

15 A gentle answer turns away wrath,
but a harsh word stirs up anger.

2The tongue of the wise commends knowledge,
but the mouth of the fool gushes folly.

3The eyes of the LORD are everywhere,
keeping watch on the wicked and the good.

4The tongue that brings healing is a tree of life,
but a deceitful tongue crushes the spirit.

5A fool spurns his father's discipline,
but whoever heeds correction shows prudence.

6The house of the righteous contains great treasure,
but the income of the wicked brings them trouble.

7The lips of the wise spread knowledge;
not so the hearts of fools.

8The LORD detests the sacrifice of the wicked,
but the prayer of the upright pleases him.

9The LORD detests the way of the wicked
but he loves those who pursue righteousness.

10Stern discipline awaits him who leaves the path;
he who hates correction will die.

11Death and Destruction[b] lie open before the LORD—
how much more the hearts of men!

12A mocker resents correction;
he will not consult the wise.

13A happy heart makes the face cheerful,
but heartache crushes the spirit.

14The discerning heart seeks knowledge,
but the mouth of a fool feeds on folly.

15All the days of the oppressed are wretched,
but the cheerful heart has a continual feast.

16Better a little with the fear of the LORD
than great wealth with turmoil.

17Better a meal of vegetables where there is love
than a fattened calf with hatred.

18A hot-tempered man stirs up dissension,
but a patient man calms a quarrel.

19The way of the sluggard is blocked with thorns,
but the path of the upright is a highway.

20A wise son brings joy to his father,
but a foolish man despises his mother.

21Folly delights a man who lacks judgment,
but a man of understanding keeps a straight course.

22Plans fail for lack of counsel,
but with many advisers they succeed.

23A man finds joy in giving an apt reply—
and how good is a timely word!

24The path of life leads upward for the wise
to keep him from going down to the grave.[c]

25The LORD tears down the proud man's house
but he keeps the widow's boundaries intact.

26The LORD detests the thoughts of the wicked,
but those of the pure are pleasing to him.

27A greedy man brings trouble to his family,
but he who hates bribes will live.

28The heart of the righteous weighs its answers,
but the mouth of the wicked gushes evil.

[a]33 Hebrew; Septuagint and Syriac / *but in the heart of fools she is not known* [b]11 Hebrew *Sheol and Abaddon* [c]24 Hebrew *Sheol*

[29]The LORD is far from the wicked
but he hears the prayer of the
righteous.

[30]A cheerful look brings joy to the heart,
and good news gives health to the
bones.

[31]He who listens to a life-giving rebuke
will be at home among the wise.

[32]He who ignores discipline despises
himself,
but whoever heeds correction gains
understanding.

[33]The fear of the LORD teaches a man
wisdom,[a]
and humility comes before honor.

16 To man belong the plans of the
heart,
but from the LORD comes the reply of
the tongue.

[2]All a man's ways seem innocent to him,
but motives are weighed by the LORD.

[3]Commit to the LORD whatever you do,
and your plans will succeed.

[4]The LORD works out everything for his
own ends—
even the wicked for a day of disaster.

[5]The LORD detests all the proud of heart.
Be sure of this: They will not go
unpunished.

[6]Through love and faithfulness sin is
atoned for;
through the fear of the LORD a man
avoids evil.

[7]When a man's ways are pleasing to the
LORD,
he makes even his enemies live at
peace with him.

[8]Better a little with righteousness
than much gain with injustice.

[9]In his heart a man plans his course,
but the LORD determines his steps.

[10]The lips of a king speak as an oracle,
and his mouth should not betray
justice.

[11]Honest scales and balances are from the
LORD;
all the weights in the bag are of his
making.

[12]Kings detest wrongdoing,
for a throne is established through
righteousness.

[13]Kings take pleasure in honest lips;
they value a man who speaks the truth.

[14]A king's wrath is a messenger of death,
but a wise man will appease it.

[15]When a king's face brightens, it means
life;
his favor is like a rain cloud in spring.

[16]How much better to get wisdom than
gold,
to choose understanding rather than
silver!

[17]The highway of the upright avoids evil;
he who guards his way guards his life.

[18]Pride goes before destruction,
a haughty spirit before a fall.

[19]Better to be lowly in spirit and among the
oppressed
than to share plunder with the proud.

[20]Whoever gives heed to instruction
prospers,
and blessed is he who trusts in the
LORD.

[21]The wise in heart are called discerning,
and pleasant words promote
instruction.[b]

[22]Understanding is a fountain of life to
those who have it,
but folly brings punishment to fools.

[23]A wise man's heart guides his mouth,
and his lips promote instruction.[c]

[24]Pleasant words are a honeycomb,
sweet to the soul and healing to the
bones.

[25]There is a way that seems right to a man,
but in the end it leads to death.

[26]The laborer's appetite works for him;
his hunger drives him on.

[27]A scoundrel plots evil,
and his speech is like a scorching fire.

[28]A perverse man stirs up dissension,

[a]33 Or *Wisdom teaches the fear of the LORD*
[b]21 Or *words make a man persuasive*
[c]23 Or *mouth / and makes his lips persuasive*

and a gossip separates close friends.

29A violent man entices his neighbor
and leads him down a path that is not good.

30He who winks with his eye is plotting perversity;
he who purses his lips is bent on evil.

31Gray hair is a crown of splendor;
it is attained by a righteous life.

32Better a patient man than a warrior,
a man who controls his temper than one who takes a city.

33The lot is cast into the lap,
but its every decision is from the LORD.

17

Better a dry crust with peace and quiet
than a house full of feasting,[a] with strife.

2A wise servant will rule over a disgraceful son,
and will share the inheritance as one of the brothers.

3The crucible for silver and the furnace for gold,
but the LORD tests the heart.

4A wicked man listens to evil lips;
a liar pays attention to a malicious tongue.

5He who mocks the poor shows contempt for their Maker;
whoever gloats over disaster will not go unpunished.

6Children's children are a crown to the aged,
and parents are the pride of their children.

7Arrogant[b] lips are unsuited to a fool—
how much worse lying lips to a ruler!

8A bribe is a charm to the one who gives it;
wherever he turns, he succeeds.

9He who covers over an offense promotes love,
but whoever repeats the matter separates close friends.

10A rebuke impresses a man of discernment
more than a hundred lashes a fool.

11An evil man is bent only on rebellion;
a merciless official will be sent against him.

12Better to meet a bear robbed of her cubs
than a fool in his folly.

13If a man pays back evil for good,
evil will never leave his house.

14Starting a quarrel is like breaching a dam;
so drop the matter before a dispute breaks out.

15Acquitting the guilty and condemning the innocent—
the LORD detests them both.

16Of what use is money in the hand of a fool,
since he has no desire to get wisdom?

17A friend loves at all times,
and a brother is born for adversity.

18A man lacking in judgment strikes hands in pledge
and puts up security for his neighbor.

19He who loves a quarrel loves sin;
he who builds a high gate invites destruction.

20A man of perverse heart does not prosper;
he whose tongue is deceitful falls into trouble.

21To have a fool for a son brings grief;
there is no joy for the father of a fool.

22A cheerful heart is good medicine,
but a crushed spirit dries up the bones.

23A wicked man accepts a bribe in secret
to pervert the course of justice.

24A discerning man keeps wisdom in view,
but a fool's eyes wander to the ends of the earth.

25A foolish son brings grief to his father
and bitterness to the one who bore him.

26It is not good to punish an innocent man,
or to flog officials for their integrity.

27A man of knowledge uses words with restraint,
and a man of understanding is even-tempered.

28Even a fool is thought wise if he keeps silent,

[a] 1 Hebrew *sacrifices* [b] 7 Or *Eloquent*

and discerning if he holds his tongue.

18 An unfriendly man pursues selfish
ends;
he defies all sound judgment.

2A fool finds no pleasure in understanding
but delights in airing his own opinions.

3When wickedness comes, so does
contempt,
and with shame comes disgrace.

4The words of a man's mouth are deep
waters,
but the fountain of wisdom is a bubbling
brook.

5It is not good to be partial to the wicked
or to deprive the innocent of justice.

6A fool's lips bring him strife,
and his mouth invites a beating.

7A fool's mouth is his undoing,
and his lips are a snare to his soul.

8The words of a gossip are like choice
morsels;
they go down to a man's inmost parts.

9One who is slack in his work
is brother to one who destroys.

10The name of the LORD is a strong tower;
the righteous run to it and are safe.

11The wealth of the rich is their fortified city;
they imagine it an unscalable wall.

12Before his downfall a man's heart is
proud,
but humility comes before honor.

13He who answers before listening—
that is his folly and his shame.

14A man's spirit sustains him in sickness,
but a crushed spirit who can bear?

15The heart of the discerning acquires
knowledge;
the ears of the wise seek it out.

16A gift opens the way for the giver
and ushers him into the presence of the
great.

17The first to present his case seems right,
till another comes forward and
questions him.

18Casting the lot settles disputes
and keeps strong opponents apart.

19An offended brother is more unyielding
than a fortified city,
and disputes are like the barred gates
of a citadel.

20From the fruit of his mouth a man's
stomach is filled;
with the harvest from his lips he is
satisfied.

21The tongue has the power of life and
death,
and those who love it will eat its fruit.

22He who finds a wife finds what is good
and receives favor from the LORD.

23A poor man pleads for mercy,
but a rich man answers harshly.

24A man of many companions may come to
ruin,
but there is a friend who sticks closer
than a brother.

19 Better a poor man whose walk is
blameless
than a fool whose lips are perverse.

2It is not good to have zeal without
knowledge,
nor to be hasty and miss the way.

3A man's own folly ruins his life,
yet his heart rages against the LORD.

4Wealth brings many friends,
but a poor man's friend deserts him.

5A false witness will not go unpunished,
and he who pours out lies will not go
free.

6Many curry favor with a ruler,
and everyone is the friend of a man
who gives gifts.

7A poor man is shunned by all his
relatives—
how much more do his friends avoid
him!
Though he pursues them with pleading,
they are nowhere to be found.[a]

8He who gets wisdom loves his own soul;
he who cherishes understanding
prospers.

9A false witness will not go unpunished,
and he who pours out lies will perish.

10It is not fitting for a fool to live in luxury—

[a]7 The meaning of the Hebrew for this sentence is uncertain.

how much worse for a slave to rule
over princes!

11 A man's wisdom gives him patience;
it is to his glory to overlook an offense.

12 A king's rage is like the roar of a lion,
but his favor is like dew on the grass.

13 A foolish son is his father's ruin,
and a quarrelsome wife is like a
constant dripping.

14 Houses and wealth are inherited from
parents,
but a prudent wife is from the LORD.

15 Laziness brings on deep sleep,
and the shiftless man goes hungry.

16 He who obeys instructions guards his life,
but he who is contemptuous of his
ways will die.

17 He who is kind to the poor lends to the
LORD,
and he will reward him for what he has
done.

18 Discipline your son, for in that there is
hope;
do not be a willing party to his death.

19 A hot-tempered man must pay the
penalty;
if you rescue him, you will have to do it
again.

20 Listen to advice and accept instruction,
and in the end you will be wise.

21 Many are the plans in a man's heart,
but it is the LORD's purpose that
prevails.

22 What a man desires is unfailing love[a];
better to be poor than a liar.

23 The fear of the LORD leads to life:
Then one rests content, untouched by
trouble.

24 The sluggard buries his hand in the dish;
he will not even bring it back to his
mouth!

25 Flog a mocker, and the simple will learn
prudence;
rebuke a discerning man, and he will
gain knowledge.

26 He who robs his father and drives out his
mother
is a son who brings shame and
disgrace.

27 Stop listening to instruction, my son,
and you will stray from the words of
knowledge.

28 A corrupt witness mocks at justice,
and the mouth of the wicked gulps
down evil.

29 Penalties are prepared for mockers,
and beatings for the backs of fools.

20 Wine is a mocker and beer a
brawler;
whoever is led astray by them is not
wise.

2 A king's wrath is like the roar of a lion;
he who angers him forfeits his life.

3 It is to a man's honor to avoid strife,
but every fool is quick to quarrel.

4 A sluggard does not plow in season;
so at harvest time he looks but finds
nothing.

5 The purposes of a man's heart are deep
waters,
but a man of understanding draws
them out.

6 Many a man claims to have unfailing
love,
but a faithful man who can find?

7 The righteous man leads a blameless life;
blessed are his children after him.

8 When a king sits on his throne to judge,
he winnows out all evil with his eyes.

9 Who can say, "I have kept my heart pure;
I am clean and without sin"?

10 Differing weights and differing
measures—
the LORD detests them both.

11 Even a child is known by his actions,
by whether his conduct is pure and
right.

12 Ears that hear and eyes that see—
the LORD has made them both.

13 Do not love sleep or you will grow poor;
stay awake and you will have food to
spare.

[a]22 Or *A man's greed is his shame*

14"It's no good, it's no good!" says the buyer;
then off he goes and boasts about his purchase.

15Gold there is, and rubies in abundance,
but lips that speak knowledge are a rare jewel.

16Take the garment of one who puts up security for a stranger;
hold it in pledge if he does it for a wayward woman.

17Food gained by fraud tastes sweet to a man,
but he ends up with a mouth full of gravel.

18Make plans by seeking advice;
if you wage war, obtain guidance.

19A gossip betrays a confidence;
so avoid a man who talks too much.

20If a man curses his father or mother,
his lamp will be snuffed out in pitch darkness.

21An inheritance quickly gained at the beginning
will not be blessed at the end.

22Do not say, "I'll pay you back for this wrong!"
Wait for the LORD, and he will deliver you.

23The LORD detests differing weights,
and dishonest scales do not please him.

24A man's steps are directed by the LORD.
How then can anyone understand his own way?

25It is a trap for a man to dedicate something rashly
and only later to consider his vows.

26A wise king winnows out the wicked;
he drives the threshing wheel over them.

27The lamp of the LORD searches the spirit of a man[a];
it searches out his inmost being.

28Love and faithfulness keep a king safe;
through love his throne is made secure.

29The glory of young men is their strength,
gray hair the splendor of the old.

30Blows and wounds cleanse away evil,
and beatings purge the inmost being.

21 The king's heart is in the hand of the LORD;
he directs it like a watercourse wherever he pleases.

2All a man's ways seem right to him,
but the LORD weighs the heart.

3To do what is right and just
is more acceptable to the LORD than sacrifice.

4Haughty eyes and a proud heart,
the lamp of the wicked, are sin!

5The plans of the diligent lead to profit
as surely as haste leads to poverty.

6A fortune made by a lying tongue
is a fleeting vapor and a deadly snare.[b]

7The violence of the wicked will drag them away,
for they refuse to do what is right.

8The way of the guilty is devious,
but the conduct of the innocent is upright.

9Better to live on a corner of the roof
than share a house with a quarrelsome wife.

10The wicked man craves evil;
his neighbor gets no mercy from him.

11When a mocker is punished, the simple gain wisdom;
when a wise man is instructed, he gets knowledge.

12The Righteous One[c] takes note of the house of the wicked
and brings the wicked to ruin.

13If a man shuts his ears to the cry of the poor,
he too will cry out and not be answered.

14A gift given in secret soothes anger,
and a bribe concealed in the cloak pacifies great wrath.

15When justice is done, it brings joy to the righteous
but terror to evildoers.

[a]27 Or *The spirit of man is the LORD's lamp* [b]6 Some Hebrew manuscripts, Septuagint and Vulgate; most Hebrew manuscripts *vapor for those who seek death* [c]12 Or *The righteous man*

16A man who strays from the path of
understanding
comes to rest in the company of the
dead.

17He who loves pleasure will become poor;
whoever loves wine and oil will never
be rich.

18The wicked become a ransom for the
righteous,
and the unfaithful for the upright.

19Better to live in a desert
than with a quarrelsome and
ill-tempered wife.

20In the house of the wise are stores of
choice food and oil,
but a foolish man devours all he has.

21He who pursues righteousness and love
finds life, prosperity[a] and honor.

22A wise man attacks the city of the mighty
and pulls down the stronghold in which
they trust.

23He who guards his mouth and his tongue
keeps himself from calamity.

24The proud and arrogant man—"Mocker"
is his name;
he behaves with overweening pride.

25The sluggard's craving will be the death
of him,
because his hands refuse to work.
26All day long he craves for more,
but the righteous give without sparing.
27The sacrifice of the wicked is
detestable—
how much more so when brought with
evil intent!

28A false witness will perish,
and whoever listens to him will be
destroyed forever.[b]

29A wicked man puts up a bold front,
but an upright man gives thought to his
ways.

30There is no wisdom, no insight, no plan
that can succeed against the LORD.

31The horse is made ready for the day of
battle,
but victory rests with the LORD.

22 A good name is more desirable
than great riches;
to be esteemed is better than silver or
gold.

2Rich and poor have this in common:
The LORD is the Maker of them all.

3A prudent man sees danger and takes
refuge,
but the simple keep going and suffer
for it.

4Humility and the fear of the LORD
bring wealth and honor and life.

5In the paths of the wicked lie thorns and
snares,
but he who guards his soul stays far
from them.

6Train[c] a child in the way he should go,
and when he is old he will not turn
from it.

7The rich rule over the poor,
and the borrower is servant to the
lender.

8He who sows wickedness reaps trouble,
and the rod of his fury will be
destroyed.

9A generous man will himself be blessed,
for he shares his food with the poor.

10Drive out the mocker, and out goes strife;
quarrels and insults are ended.

11He who loves a pure heart and whose
speech is gracious
will have the king for his friend.

12The eyes of the LORD keep watch over
knowledge,
but he frustrates the words of the
unfaithful.

13The sluggard says, "There is a lion
outside!"
or, "I will be murdered in the streets!"

14The mouth of an adulteress is a deep
pit;
he who is under the LORD's wrath will
fall into it.

15Folly is bound up in the heart of a child,
but the rod of discipline will drive it far
from him.

16He who oppresses the poor to increase
his wealth
and he who gives gifts to the rich—both
come to poverty.

[a]21 Or *righteousness* [b]28 Or / *but the words of an obedient man will live on* [c]6 Or *Start*

Sayings of the Wise

17Pay attention and listen to the sayings of the wise;
apply your heart to what I teach,
18for it is pleasing when you keep them in your heart
and have all of them ready on your lips.
19So that your trust may be in the LORD,
I teach you today, even you.
20Have I not written thirty[a] sayings for you,
sayings of counsel and knowledge,
21teaching you true and reliable words,
so that you can give sound answers
to him who sent you?

22Do not exploit the poor because they are poor
and do not crush the needy in court,
23for the LORD will take up their case
and will plunder those who plunder them.

24Do not make friends with a hot-tempered man,
do not associate with one easily angered,
25or you may learn his ways
and get yourself ensnared.

26Do not be a man who strikes hands in pledge
or puts up security for debts;
27if you lack the means to pay,
your very bed will be snatched from under you.

28Do not move an ancient boundary stone
set up by your forefathers.

29Do you see a man skilled in his work?
He will serve before kings;
he will not serve before obscure men.

23 When you sit to dine with a ruler,
note well what[b] is before you,
2and put a knife to your throat
if you are given to gluttony.
3Do not crave his delicacies,
for that food is deceptive.

4Do not wear yourself out to get rich;
have the wisdom to show restraint.
5Cast but a glance at riches, and they are gone,
for they will surely sprout wings
and fly off to the sky like an eagle.

6Do not eat the food of a stingy man,
do not crave his delicacies;
7for he is the kind of man
who is always thinking about the cost.[c]
"Eat and drink," he says to you,
but his heart is not with you.
8You will vomit up the little you have eaten
and will have wasted your compliments.

9Do not speak to a fool,
for he will scorn the wisdom of your words.

10Do not move an ancient boundary stone
or encroach on the fields of the fatherless,
11for their Defender is strong;
he will take up their case against you.

12Apply your heart to instruction
and your ears to words of knowledge.

13Do not withhold discipline from a child;
if you punish him with the rod, he will not die.
14Punish him with the rod
and save his soul from death.[d]

15My son, if your heart is wise,
then my heart will be glad;
16my inmost being will rejoice
when your lips speak what is right.

17Do not let your heart envy sinners,
but always be zealous for the fear of the LORD.
18There is surely a future hope for you,
and your hope will not be cut off.

19Listen, my son, and be wise,
and keep your heart on the right path.
20Do not join those who drink too much wine
or gorge themselves on meat,
21for drunkards and gluttons become poor,
and drowsiness clothes them in rags.

22Listen to your father, who gave you life,
and do not despise your mother when she is old.
23Buy the truth and do not sell it;
get wisdom, discipline and understanding.
24The father of a righteous man has great joy;
he who has a wise son delights in him.
25May your father and mother be glad;
may she who gave you birth rejoice!

[a]20 Or *not formerly written;* or *not written excellent* [b]1 Or *who* [c]7 Or *for as he thinks within himself, / so he is;* or *for as he puts on a feast, / so he is* [d]14 Hebrew *Sheol*

26My son, give me your heart
and let your eyes keep to my ways,
27for a prostitute is a deep pit
and a wayward wife is a narrow well.
28Like a bandit she lies in wait,
and multiplies the unfaithful among men.

29Who has woe? Who has sorrow?
Who has strife? Who has complaints?
Who has needless bruises? Who has bloodshot eyes?
30Those who linger over wine,
who go to sample bowls of mixed wine.
31Do not gaze at wine when it is red,
when it sparkles in the cup,
when it goes down smoothly!
32In the end it bites like a snake
and poisons like a viper.
33Your eyes will see strange sights
and your mind imagine confusing things.
34You will be like one sleeping on the high seas,
lying on top of the rigging.
35"They hit me," you will say, "but I'm not hurt!
They beat me, but I don't feel it!
When will I wake up
so I can find another drink?"

24 Do not envy wicked men,
do not desire their company;
2for their hearts plot violence,
and their lips talk about making trouble.

3By wisdom a house is built,
and through understanding it is established;
4through knowledge its rooms are filled
with rare and beautiful treasures.

5A wise man has great power,
and a man of knowledge increases strength;
6for waging war you need guidance,
and for victory many advisers.

7Wisdom is too high for a fool;
in the assembly at the gate he has nothing to say.

8He who plots evil
will be known as a schemer.
9The schemes of folly are sin,
and men detest a mocker.

10If you falter in times of trouble,
how small is your strength!
11Rescue those being led away to death;
hold back those staggering toward slaughter.
12If you say, "But we knew nothing about this,"
does not he who weighs the heart perceive it?
Does not he who guards your life know it?
Will he not repay each person
according to what he has done?

13Eat honey, my son, for it is good;
honey from the comb is sweet to your taste.
14Know also that wisdom is sweet to your soul;
if you find it, there is a future hope for you,
and your hope will not be cut off.

15Do not lie in wait like an outlaw against a righteous man's house,
do not raid his dwelling place;
16for though a righteous man falls seven times, he rises again,
but the wicked are brought down by calamity.

17Do not gloat when your enemy falls;
when he stumbles, do not let your heart rejoice,
18or the LORD will see and disapprove
and turn his wrath away from him.

19Do not fret because of evil men
or be envious of the wicked,
20for the evil man has no future hope,
and the lamp of the wicked will be snuffed out.

21Fear the LORD and the king, my son,
and do not join with the rebellious,
22for those two will send sudden destruction upon them,
and who knows what calamities they can bring?

Further Sayings of the Wise

23These also are sayings of the wise:

To show partiality in judging is not good:
24Whoever says to the guilty, "You are innocent"—
peoples will curse him and nations denounce him.
25But it will go well with those who convict the guilty,
and rich blessing will come upon them.

26An honest answer
is like a kiss on the lips.

[27]Finish your outdoor work
and get your fields ready;
after that, build your house.

[28]Do not testify against your neighbor
without cause,
or use your lips to deceive.
[29]Do not say, "I'll do to him as he has done
to me;
I'll pay that man back for what he did."

[30]I went past the field of the sluggard,
past the vineyard of the man who lacks
judgment;
[31]thorns had come up everywhere,
the ground was covered with weeds,
and the stone wall was in ruins.
[32]I applied my heart to what I observed
and learned a lesson from what
I saw:
[33]A little sleep, a little slumber,
a little folding of the hands to rest—
[34]and poverty will come on you like a
bandit
and scarcity like an armed man.[a]

More Proverbs of Solomon

25 These are more proverbs of Solomon, copied by the men of Hezekiah king of Judah:

[2]It is the glory of God to conceal a matter;
to search out a matter is the glory of
kings.
[3]As the heavens are high and the earth is
deep,
so the hearts of kings are
unsearchable.

[4]Remove the dross from the silver,
and out comes material for[b] the
silversmith;
[5]remove the wicked from the king's
presence,
and his throne will be established
through righteousness.

[6]Do not exalt yourself in the king's
presence,
and do not claim a place among great
men;
[7]it is better for him to say to you, "Come
up here,"
than for him to humiliate you before a
nobleman.

What you have seen with your eyes
[8] do not bring[c] hastily to court,
for what will you do in the end
if your neighbor puts you to shame?
[9]If you argue your case with a neighbor,
do not betray another man's
confidence,
[10]or he who hears it may shame you
and you will never lose your bad
reputation.

[11]A word aptly spoken
is like apples of gold in settings of
silver.

[12]Like an earring of gold or an ornament of
fine gold
is a wise man's rebuke to a listening
ear.

[13]Like the coolness of snow at harvest time
is a trustworthy messenger to those
who send him;
he refreshes the spirit of his masters.

[14]Like clouds and wind without rain
is a man who boasts of gifts he does
not give.

[15]Through patience a ruler can be
persuaded,
and a gentle tongue can break a bone.

[16]If you find honey, eat just enough—
too much of it, and you will vomit.
[17]Seldom set foot in your neighbor's
house—
too much of you, and he will hate you.

[18]Like a club or a sword or a sharp arrow
is the man who gives false testimony
against his neighbor.

[19]Like a bad tooth or a lame foot
is reliance on the unfaithful in times of
trouble.

[20]Like one who takes away a garment on a
cold day,
or like vinegar poured on soda,
is one who sings songs to a heavy
heart.

[21]If your enemy is hungry, give him food to
eat;
if he is thirsty, give him water to drink.
[22]In doing this, you will heap burning coals
on his head,
and the LORD will reward you.

[a]*34 Or like a vagrant / and scarcity like a beggar* [b]*4 Or comes a vessel from* [c]*7,8 Or nobleman / on whom you had set your eyes. / 8Do not go*

23As a north wind brings rain,
so a sly tongue brings angry looks.

24Better to live on a corner of the roof
than share a house with a quarrelsome wife.

25Like cold water to a weary soul
is good news from a distant land.

26Like a muddied spring or a polluted well
is a righteous man who gives way to the wicked.

27It is not good to eat too much honey,
nor is it honorable to seek one's own honor.

28Like a city whose walls are broken down
is a man who lacks self-control.

26 Like snow in summer or rain in harvest,
honor is not fitting for a fool.

2Like a fluttering sparrow or a darting swallow,
an undeserved curse does not come to rest.

3A whip for the horse, a halter for the donkey,
and a rod for the backs of fools!

4Do not answer a fool according to his folly,
or you will be like him yourself.

5Answer a fool according to his folly,
or he will be wise in his own eyes.

6Like cutting off one's feet or drinking violence
is the sending of a message by the hand of a fool.

7Like a lame man's legs that hang limp
is a proverb in the mouth of a fool.

8Like tying a stone in a sling
is the giving of honor to a fool.

9Like a thornbush in a drunkard's hand
is a proverb in the mouth of a fool.

10Like an archer who wounds at random
is he who hires a fool or any passer-by.

11As a dog returns to its vomit,
so a fool repeats his folly.

12Do you see a man wise in his own eyes?
There is more hope for a fool than for him.

13The sluggard says, "There is a lion in the road,
a fierce lion roaming the streets!"

14As a door turns on its hinges,
so a sluggard turns on his bed.

15The sluggard buries his hand in the dish;
he is too lazy to bring it back to his mouth.

16The sluggard is wiser in his own eyes
than seven men who answer discreetly.

17Like one who seizes a dog by the ears
is a passer-by who meddles in a quarrel not his own.

18Like a madman shooting
firebrands or deadly arrows
19is a man who deceives his neighbor
and says, "I was only joking!"

20Without wood a fire goes out;
without gossip a quarrel dies down.

21As charcoal to embers and as wood to fire,
so is a quarrelsome man for kindling strife.

22The words of a gossip are like choice morsels;
they go down to a man's inmost parts.

23Like a coating of glaze[a] over earthenware
are fervent lips with an evil heart.

24A malicious man disguises himself with his lips,
but in his heart he harbors deceit.
25Though his speech is charming, do not believe him,
for seven abominations fill his heart.
26His malice may be concealed by deception,
but his wickedness will be exposed in the assembly.

27If a man digs a pit, he will fall into it;
if a man rolls a stone, it will roll back on him.

28A lying tongue hates those it hurts,
and a flattering mouth works ruin.

27 Do not boast about tomorrow,
for you do not know what a day may bring forth.

[a]23 With a different word division of the Hebrew; Masoretic Text *of silver dross*

[2]Let another praise you, and not your own mouth;
someone else, and not your own lips.

[3]Stone is heavy and sand a burden,
but provocation by a fool is heavier than both.

[4]Anger is cruel and fury overwhelming,
but who can stand before jealousy?

[5]Better is open rebuke
than hidden love.

[6]Wounds from a friend can be trusted,
but an enemy multiplies kisses.

[7]He who is full loathes honey,
but to the hungry even what is bitter tastes sweet.

[8]Like a bird that strays from its nest
is a man who strays from his home.

[9]Perfume and incense bring joy to the heart,
and the pleasantness of one's friend springs from his earnest counsel.

[10]Do not forsake your friend and the friend of your father,
and do not go to your brother's house when disaster strikes you—
better a neighbor nearby than a brother far away.

[11]Be wise, my son, and bring joy to my heart;
then I can answer anyone who treats me with contempt.

[12]The prudent see danger and take refuge,
but the simple keep going and suffer for it.

[13]Take the garment of one who puts up security for a stranger;
hold it in pledge if he does it for a wayward woman.

[14]If a man loudly blesses his neighbor early in the morning,
it will be taken as a curse.

[15]A quarrelsome wife is like
a constant dripping on a rainy day;
[16]restraining her is like restraining the wind
or grasping oil with the hand.

[17]As iron sharpens iron,
so one man sharpens another.

[18]He who tends a fig tree will eat its fruit,
and he who looks after his master will be honored.

[19]As water reflects a face,
so a man's heart reflects the man.

[20]Death and Destruction[a] are never satisfied,
and neither are the eyes of man.

[21]The crucible for silver and the furnace for gold,
but man is tested by the praise he receives.

[22]Though you grind a fool in a mortar,
grinding him like grain with a pestle,
you will not remove his folly from him.

[23]Be sure you know the condition of your flocks,
give careful attention to your herds;
[24]for riches do not endure forever,
and a crown is not secure for all generations.
[25]When the hay is removed and new growth appears
and the grass from the hills is gathered in,
[26]the lambs will provide you with clothing,
and the goats with the price of a field.
[27]You will have plenty of goats' milk
to feed you and your family
and to nourish your servant girls.

28

The wicked man flees though no one pursues,
but the righteous are as bold as a lion.

[2]When a country is rebellious, it has many rulers,
but a man of understanding and knowledge maintains order.

[3]A ruler[b] who oppresses the poor
is like a driving rain that leaves no crops.

[4]Those who forsake the law praise the wicked,
but those who keep the law resist them.

[5]Evil men do not understand justice,
but those who seek the LORD understand it fully.

[6]Better a poor man whose walk is blameless
than a rich man whose ways are perverse.

[a]*20* Hebrew *Sheol and Abaddon* [b]*3* Or *A poor man*

7He who keeps the law is a discerning
son,
but a companion of gluttons disgraces
his father.

8He who increases his wealth by
exorbitant interest
amasses it for another, who will be kind
to the poor.

9If anyone turns a deaf ear to the law,
even his prayers are detestable.

10He who leads the upright along an evil
path
will fall into his own trap,
but the blameless will receive a good
inheritance.

11A rich man may be wise in his own eyes,
but a poor man who has discernment
sees through him.

12When the righteous triumph, there is
great elation;
but when the wicked rise to power, men
go into hiding.

13He who conceals his sins does not
prosper,
but whoever confesses and renounces
them finds mercy.

14Blessed is the man who always fears the
LORD,
but he who hardens his heart falls into
trouble.

15Like a roaring lion or a charging bear
is a wicked man ruling over a helpless
people.

16A tyrannical ruler lacks judgment,
but he who hates ill-gotten gain will
enjoy a long life.

17A man tormented by the guilt of murder
will be a fugitive till death;
let no one support him.

18He whose walk is blameless is kept safe,
but he whose ways are perverse will
suddenly fall.

19He who works his land will have
abundant food,
but the one who chases fantasies will
have his fill of poverty.

20A faithful man will be richly blessed,
but one eager to get rich will not go
unpunished.

21To show partiality is not good—
yet a man will do wrong for a piece of
bread.

22A stingy man is eager to get rich
and is unaware that poverty awaits him.

23He who rebukes a man will in the end
gain more favor
than he who has a flattering tongue.

24He who robs his father or mother
and says, "It's not wrong"—
he is partner to him who destroys.

25A greedy man stirs up dissension,
but he who trusts in the LORD will
prosper.

26He who trusts in himself is a fool,
but he who walks in wisdom is kept
safe.

27He who gives to the poor will lack
nothing,
but he who closes his eyes to them
receives many curses.

28When the wicked rise to power, people
go into hiding;
but when the wicked perish, the
righteous thrive.

29 A man who remains stiff-necked
after many rebukes
will suddenly be destroyed—without
remedy.

2When the righteous thrive, the people
rejoice;
when the wicked rule, the people
groan.

3A man who loves wisdom brings joy to
his father,
but a companion of prostitutes
squanders his wealth.

4By justice a king gives a country stability,
but one who is greedy for bribes tears it
down.

5Whoever flatters his neighbor
is spreading a net for his feet.

6An evil man is snared by his own sin,
but a righteous one can sing and be
glad.

7The righteous care about justice for the
poor,
but the wicked have no such concern.

8Mockers stir up a city,
but wise men turn away anger.

9If a wise man goes to court with a fool,
the fool rages and scoffs, and there is no peace.

10Bloodthirsty men hate a man of integrity
and seek to kill the upright.

11A fool gives full vent to his anger,
but a wise man keeps himself under control.

12If a ruler listens to lies,
all his officials become wicked.

13The poor man and the oppressor have this in common:
The LORD gives sight to the eyes of both.

14If a king judges the poor with fairness,
his throne will always be secure.

15The rod of correction imparts wisdom,
but a child left to himself disgraces his mother.

16When the wicked thrive, so does sin,
but the righteous will see their downfall.

17Discipline your son, and he will give you peace;
he will bring delight to your soul.

18Where there is no revelation, the people cast off restraint;
but blessed is he who keeps the law.

19A servant cannot be corrected by mere words;
though he understands, he will not respond.

20Do you see a man who speaks in haste?
There is more hope for a fool than for him.

21If a man pampers his servant from youth,
he will bring grief[a] in the end.

22An angry man stirs up dissension,
and a hot-tempered one commits many sins.

23A man's pride brings him low,
but a man of lowly spirit gains honor.

24The accomplice of a thief is his own enemy;
he is put under oath and dare not testify.

25Fear of man will prove to be a snare,
but whoever trusts in the LORD is kept safe.

26Many seek an audience with a ruler,
but it is from the LORD that man gets justice.

27The righteous detest the dishonest;
the wicked detest the upright.

Sayings of Agur

30 The sayings of Agur son of Jakeh—an oracle[b]:

This man declared to Ithiel,
to Ithiel and to Ucal:[c]

2"I am the most ignorant of men;
I do not have a man's understanding.
3I have not learned wisdom,
nor have I knowledge of the Holy One.
4Who has gone up to heaven and come down?
Who has gathered up the wind in the hollow of his hands?
Who has wrapped up the waters in his cloak?
Who has established all the ends of the earth?
What is his name, and the name of his son?
Tell me if you know!

5"Every word of God is flawless;
he is a shield to those who take refuge in him.
6Do not add to his words,
or he will rebuke you and prove you a liar.

7"Two things I ask of you, O LORD;
do not refuse me before I die:
8Keep falsehood and lies far from me;
give me neither poverty nor riches,
but give me only my daily bread.
9Otherwise, I may have too much and disown you
and say, 'Who is the LORD?'
Or I may become poor and steal,
and so dishonor the name of my God.

10"Do not slander a servant to his master,
or he will curse you, and you will pay for it.

11"There are those who curse their fathers

[a]21 The meaning of the Hebrew for this word is uncertain. [b]1 Or *Jakeh of Massa* [c]1 Masoretic Text; with a different word division of the Hebrew *declared, "I am weary, O God; / I am weary, O God, and faint.*

and do not bless their mothers;
12those who are pure in their own eyes
and yet are not cleansed of their filth;
13those whose eyes are ever so haughty,
whose glances are so disdainful;
14those whose teeth are swords
and whose jaws are set with knives
to devour the poor from the earth,
the needy from among mankind.

15"The leech has two daughters.
'Give! Give!' they cry.

"There are three things that are never satisfied,
four that never say, 'Enough!':
16the grave,[a] the barren womb,
land, which is never satisfied with water,
and fire, which never says, 'Enough!'

17"The eye that mocks a father,
that scorns obedience to a mother,
will be pecked out by the ravens of the valley,
will be eaten by the vultures.

18"There are three things that are too amazing for me,
four that I do not understand:
19the way of an eagle in the sky,
the way of a snake on a rock,
the way of a ship on the high seas,
and the way of a man with a maiden.

20"This is the way of an adulteress:
She eats and wipes her mouth
and says, 'I've done nothing wrong.'

21"Under three things the earth trembles,
under four it cannot bear up:
22a servant who becomes king,
a fool who is full of food,
23an unloved woman who is married,
and a maidservant who displaces her mistress.

24"Four things on earth are small,
yet they are extremely wise:
25Ants are creatures of little strength,
yet they store up their food in the summer;
26coneys[b] are creatures of little power,
yet they make their home in the crags;
27locusts have no king,
yet they advance together in ranks;
28a lizard can be caught with the hand,
yet it is found in kings' palaces.

29"There are three things that are stately in their stride,
four that move with stately bearing:
30a lion, mighty among beasts,
who retreats before nothing;
31a strutting rooster, a he-goat,
and a king with his army around him.[c]

32"If you have played the fool and exalted yourself,
or if you have planned evil,
clap your hand over your mouth!
33For as churning the milk produces butter,
and as twisting the nose produces blood,
so stirring up anger produces strife."

Sayings of King Lemuel

31 The sayings of King Lemuel—an oracle[d] his mother taught him:

2"O my son, O son of my womb,
O son of my vows,[e]
3do not spend your strength on women,
your vigor on those who ruin kings.

4"It is not for kings, O Lemuel—
not for kings to drink wine,
not for rulers to crave beer,
5lest they drink and forget what the law decrees,
and deprive all the oppressed of their rights.
6Give beer to those who are perishing,
wine to those who are in anguish;
7let them drink and forget their poverty
and remember their misery no more.

8"Speak up for those who cannot speak for themselves,
for the rights of all who are destitute.
9Speak up and judge fairly;
defend the rights of the poor and needy."

Epilogue: The Wife of Noble Character

10[f]A wife of noble character who can find?
She is worth far more than rubies.
11Her husband has full confidence in her
and lacks nothing of value.

[a] 16 Hebrew *Sheol* [b] 26 That is, the hyrax or rock badger [c] 31 Or *king secure against revolt* [d] 1 Or *of Lemuel king of Massa, which* [e] 2 Or */ the answer to my prayers* [f] 10 Verses 10-31 are an acrostic, each verse beginning with a successive letter of the Hebrew alphabet.

12She brings him good, not harm,
all the days of her life.
13She selects wool and flax
and works with eager hands.
14She is like the merchant ships,
bringing her food from afar.
15She gets up while it is still dark;
she provides food for her family
and portions for her servant girls.
16She considers a field and buys it;
out of her earnings she plants a vineyard.
17She sets about her work vigorously;
her arms are strong for her tasks.
18She sees that her trading is profitable,
and her lamp does not go out at night.
19In her hand she holds the distaff
and grasps the spindle with her fingers.
20She opens her arms to the poor
and extends her hands to the needy.
21When it snows, she has no fear for her household;
for all of them are clothed in scarlet.
22She makes coverings for her bed;
she is clothed in fine linen and purple.
23Her husband is respected at the city gate,
where he takes his seat among the elders of the land.
24She makes linen garments and sells them,
and supplies the merchants with sashes.
25She is clothed with strength and dignity;
she can laugh at the days to come.
26She speaks with wisdom,
and faithful instruction is on her tongue.
27She watches over the affairs of her household
and does not eat the bread of idleness.
28Her children arise and call her blessed;
her husband also, and he praises her:
29"Many women do noble things,
but you surpass them all."
30Charm is deceptive, and beauty is fleeting;
but a woman who fears the LORD is to be praised.
31Give her the reward she has earned,
and let her works bring her praise at the city gate.

Ecclesiastes

Introduction:

Ecclesiastes studies the meaning of life. The "Teacher" looks at wisdom, pleasure, work, power, riches, religion, and other things. All of these have some value and are useful in the proper time and place, but they have lasting value only if God is at the center of man's life. Reverence and respect for God and a real devotion in serving God are the most important in making life have meaning. Without God, the "Teacher" says, "everything is meaningless."

Outline of contents:

Everything Is Meaningless

1 The words of the Teacher,[a] son of David, king in Jerusalem:

2"Meaningless! Meaningless!"
says the Teacher.
"Utterly meaningless!
Everything is meaningless."

3What does man gain from all his labor
at which he toils under the sun?
4Generations come and generations go,
but the earth remains forever.
5The sun rises and the sun sets,
and hurries back to where it rises.
6The wind blows to the south
and turns to the north;
round and round it goes,
ever returning on its course.
7All streams flow into the sea,
yet the sea is never full.
To the place the streams come from,
there they return again.
8All things are wearisome,
more than one can say.
The eye never has enough of seeing,
nor the ear its fill of hearing.
9What has been will be again,
what has been done will be done again;
there is nothing new under the sun.
10Is there anything of which one can say,
"Look! This is something new"?
It was here already, long ago;
it was here before our time.
11There is no remembrance of men of old,
and even those who are yet to come
will not be remembered
by those who follow.

Wisdom Is Meaningless

12I, the Teacher, was king over Israel in
Jerusalem. 13I devoted myself to study and
to explore by wisdom all that is done under
heaven. What a heavy burden God has laid
on men! 14I have seen all the things that are
done under the sun; all of them are meaningless, a chasing after the wind.

15What is twisted cannot be straightened;
what is lacking cannot be counted.

16I thought to myself, "Look, I have grown
and increased in wisdom more than anyone
who has ruled over Jerusalem before me; I
have experienced much of wisdom and
knowledge." 17Then I applied myself to the
understanding of wisdom, and also of madness and folly, but I learned that this, too, is a
chasing after the wind.

[a] 1 Or *leader of the assembly;* also in verses 2 and 12

18 For with much wisdom comes much
sorrow;
the more knowledge, the more grief.

Pleasures Are Meaningless

2 I thought in my heart, "Come now, I will
test you with pleasure to find out what is
good." But that also proved to be meaningless. 2 "Laughter," I said, "is foolish. And
what does pleasure accomplish?" 3 I tried
cheering myself with wine, and embracing
folly—my mind still guiding me with wisdom.
I wanted to see what was worthwhile for men
to do under heaven during the few days of
their lives.

4 I undertook great projects: I built houses
for myself and planted vineyards. 5 I made
gardens and parks and planted all kinds of
fruit trees in them. 6 I made reservoirs to
water groves of flourishing trees. 7 I bought
male and female slaves and had other
slaves who were born in my house. I also
owned more herds and flocks than anyone in
Jerusalem before me. 8 I amassed silver and
gold for myself, and the treasure of kings and
provinces. I acquired men and women singers, and a harem[a] as well—the delights of
the heart of man. 9 I became greater by far
than anyone in Jerusalem before me. In all
this my wisdom stayed with me.

10 I denied myself nothing my eyes desired;
I refused my heart no pleasure.
My heart took delight in all my work,
and this was the reward for all my
labor.
11 Yet when I surveyed all that my hands
had done
and what I had toiled to achieve,
everything was meaningless, a chasing
after the wind;
nothing was gained under the sun.

Wisdom and Folly Are Meaningless

12 Then I turned my thoughts to consider
wisdom,
and also madness and folly.
What more can the king's successor do
than what has already been done?
13 I saw that wisdom is better than folly,
just as light is better than darkness.
14 The wise man has eyes in his head,
while the fool walks in the darkness;
but I came to realize
that the same fate overtakes them
both.

15 Then I thought in my heart,
"The fate of the fool will overtake me
also.
What then do I gain by being wise?"
I said in my heart,
"This too is meaningless."
16 For the wise man, like the fool, will not be
long remembered;
in days to come both will be forgotten.
Like the fool, the wise man too must die!

Toil Is Meaningless

17 So I hated life, because the work that is
done under the sun was grievous to me. All
of it is meaningless, a chasing after the wind.
18 I hated all the things I had toiled for under
the sun, because I must leave them to the
one who comes after me. 19 And who knows
whether he will be a wise man or a fool? Yet
he will have control over all the work into
which I have poured my effort and skill under
the sun. This too is meaningless. 20 So my
heart began to despair over all my toilsome
labor under the sun. 21 For a man may do his
work with wisdom, knowledge and skill, and
then he must leave all he owns to someone
who has not worked for it. This too is meaningless and a great misfortune. 22 What does
a man get for all the toil and anxious striving
with which he labors under the sun? 23 All his
days his work is pain and grief; even at night
his mind does not rest. This too is meaningless.

24 A man can do nothing better than to eat
and drink and find satisfaction in his work.
This too, I see, is from the hand of God, 25 for
without him, who can eat or find enjoyment?
26 To the man who pleases him, God gives
wisdom, knowledge and happiness, but to
the sinner he gives the task of gathering and
storing up wealth to hand it over to the one
who pleases God. This too is meaningless, a
chasing after the wind.

A Time for Everything

3 There is a time for everything,
and a season for every activity under
heaven:
2 a time to be born and a time to die,
a time to plant and a time to uproot,

[a] 8 The meaning of the Hebrew for this phrase is uncertain.

3 a time to kill and a time to heal,
a time to tear down and a time to build,
4 a time to weep and a time to laugh,
a time to mourn and a time to dance,
5 a time to scatter stones and a time to
gather them,
a time to embrace and a time to refrain,
6 a time to search and a time to give up,
a time to keep and a time to throw
away,
7 a time to tear and a time to mend,
a time to be silent and a time to speak,
8 a time to love and a time to hate,
a time for war and a time for peace.

9What does the worker gain from his toil?
10I have seen the burden God has laid on
men. 11He has made everything beautiful in
its time. He has also set eternity in the hearts
of men; yet they cannot fathom what God
has done from beginning to end. 12I know
that there is nothing better for men than to be
happy and do good while they live. 13That
everyone may eat and drink, and find satisfaction in all his toil—this is the gift of God. 14I
know that everything God does will endure
forever; nothing can be added to it and nothing taken from it. God does it so that men will
revere him.

15Whatever is has already been,
and what will be has been before;
and God will call the past to account.[a]

16And I saw something else under the sun:

In the place of judgment—wickedness
was there,
in the place of justice—wickedness was
there.

17I thought in my heart,

"God will bring to judgment
both the righteous and the wicked,
for there will be a time for every activity,
a time for every deed."

18I also thought, "As for men, God tests
them so that they may see that they are like
the animals. 19Man's fate is like that of the
animals; the same fate awaits them both: As
one dies, so dies the other. All have the
same breath[b]; man has no advantage over
the animal. Everything is meaningless. 20All
go to the same place; all come from dust,
and to dust all return. 21Who knows if the
spirit of man rises upward and if the spirit of
the animal[c] goes down into the earth?"

22So I saw that there is nothing better for a
man than to enjoy his work, because that is
his lot. For who can bring him to see what will
happen after him?

Oppression, Toil, Friendlessness

4 Again I looked and saw all the oppression that was taking place under the sun:

I saw the tears of the oppressed—
and they have no comforter;
power was on the side of their
oppressors—
and they have no comforter.
2And I declared that the dead,
who had already died,
are happier than the living,
who are still alive.
3But better than both
is he who has not yet been,
who has not seen the evil
that is done under the sun.

4And I saw that all labor and all achieve-
ment spring from man's envy of his neighbor.
This too is meaningless, a chasing after the
wind.

5The fool folds his hands
and ruins himself.
6Better one handful with tranquillity
than two handfuls with toil
and chasing after the wind.

7Again I saw something meaningless under the sun:

8There was a man all alone;
he had neither son nor brother.
There was no end to his toil,
yet his eyes were not content with his
wealth.
"For whom am I toiling," he asked,
"and why am I depriving myself of
enjoyment?"
This too is meaningless—
a miserable business!

9Two are better than one,
because they have a good return for
their work:
10If one falls down,
his friend can help him up.
But pity the man who falls

[a] 15 Or *God calls back the past* [b] 19 Or *spirit* [c] 21 Or *Who knows the spirit of man, which rises upward, or the spirit of the animal, which*

and has no one to help him up!
11Also, if two lie down together, they will
keep warm.
But how can one keep warm alone?
12Though one may be overpowered,
two can defend themselves.
A cord of three strands is not quickly
broken.

Advancement Is Meaningless

13Better a poor but wise youth than an old
but foolish king who no longer knows how to
take warning. 14The youth may have come
from prison to the kingship, or he may have
been born in poverty within his kingdom. 15I
saw that all who lived and walked under the
sun followed the youth, the king's successor.
16There was no end to all the people who
were before them. But those who came later
were not pleased with the successor. This
too is meaningless, a chasing after the wind.

Stand in Awe of God

5 Guard your steps when you go to the house of God. Go near to listen rather than to offer the sacrifice of fools, who do not know that they do wrong.

2Do not be quick with your mouth,
do not be hasty in your heart
to utter anything before God.
God is in heaven
and you are on earth,
so let your words be few.
3As a dream comes when there are many
cares,
so the speech of a fool when there are
many words.

4When you make a vow to God, do not
delay in fulfilling it. He has no pleasure in
fools; fulfill your vow. 5It is better not to vow
than to make a vow and not fulfill it. 6Do not
let your mouth lead you into sin. And do not
protest to the ⌊temple⌋ messenger, "My vow
was a mistake." Why should God be angry at
what you say and destroy the work of your
hands? 7Much dreaming and many words
are meaningless. Therefore stand in awe of
God.

Riches Are Meaningless

8If you see the poor oppressed in a district,
and justice and rights denied, do not be surprised at such things; for one official is eyed
by a higher one, and over them both are
others higher still. 9The increase from the
land is taken by all; the king himself profits
from the fields.

10Whoever loves money never has money
enough;
whoever loves wealth is never satisfied
with his income.
This too is meaningless.
11As goods increase,
so do those who consume them.
And what benefit are they to the owner
except to feast his eyes on them?

12The sleep of a laborer is sweet,
whether he eats little or much,
but the abundance of a rich man
permits him no sleep.

13I have seen a grievous evil under the
sun:

wealth hoarded to the harm of its owner,
14 or wealth lost through some misfortune,
so that when he has a son
there is nothing left for him.
15Naked a man comes from his mother's
womb,
and as he comes, so he departs.
He takes nothing from his labor
that he can carry in his hand.

16This too is a grievous evil:

As a man comes, so he departs,
and what does he gain,
since he toils for the wind?
17All his days he eats in darkness,
with great frustration, affliction and
anger.

18Then I realized that it is good and proper
for a man to eat and drink, and to find satisfaction in his toilsome labor under the sun
during the few days of life God has given
him—for this is his lot. 19Moreover, when
God gives any man wealth and possessions,
and enables him to enjoy them, to accept his
lot and be happy in his work—this is a gift of
God. 20He seldom reflects on the days of his
life, because God keeps him occupied with
gladness of heart.

6 I have seen another evil under the sun, and it weighs heavily on men: 2God
gives a man wealth, possessions and honor,
so that he lacks nothing his heart desires, but
God does not enable him to enjoy them, and
a stranger enjoys them instead. This is
meaningless, a grievous evil.
3A man may have a hundred children and

live many years; yet no matter how long he
lives, if he cannot enjoy his prosperity and
does not receive proper burial, I say that a
stillborn child is better off than he. [4]It comes
without meaning, it departs in darkness, and
in darkness its name is shrouded. [5]Though it
never saw the sun or knew anything, it has
more rest than does that man— [6]even if he
lives a thousand years twice over but fails to
enjoy his prosperity. Do not all go to the
same place?

[7]All man's efforts are for his mouth,
yet his appetite is never satisfied.
[8]What advantage has a wise man
over a fool?
What does a poor man gain
by knowing how to conduct himself
before others?
[9]Better what the eye sees
than the roving of the appetite.
This too is meaningless,
a chasing after the wind.

[10]Whatever exists has already been
named,
and what man is has been known;
no man can contend
with one who is stronger than he.
[11]The more the words,
the less the meaning,
and how does that profit anyone?

[12]For who knows what is good for a man in
life, during the few and meaningless days he
passes through like a shadow? Who can tell
him what will happen under the sun after he
is gone?

Wisdom

7 A good name is better than fine
perfume,
and the day of death better than the
day of birth.
[2]It is better to go to a house of mourning
than to go to a house of feasting,
for death is the destiny of every man;
the living should take this to heart.
[3]Sorrow is better than laughter,
because a sad face is good for the
heart.
[4]The heart of the wise is in the house of
mourning,
but the heart of fools is in the house of
pleasure.
[5]It is better to heed a wise man's rebuke
than to listen to the song of fools.
[6]Like the crackling of thorns under the pot,
so is the laughter of fools.
This too is meaningless.

[7]Extortion turns a wise man into a fool,
and a bribe corrupts the heart.

[8]The end of a matter is better than its
beginning,
and patience is better than pride.
[9]Do not be quickly provoked in your spirit,
for anger resides in the lap of fools.

[10]Do not say, "Why were the old days
better than these?"
For it is not wise to ask such questions.

[11]Wisdom, like an inheritance, is a good
thing
and benefits those who see the sun.
[12]Wisdom is a shelter
as money is a shelter,
but the advantage of knowledge is this:
that wisdom preserves the life of its
possessor.

[13]Consider what God has done:

Who can straighten
what he has made crooked?
[14]When times are good, be happy;
but when times are bad, consider:
God has made the one
as well as the other.
Therefore, a man cannot discover
anything about his future.

[15]In this meaningless life of mine I have
seen both of these:

a righteous man perishing in his
righteousness,
and a wicked man living long in his
wickedness.
[16]Do not be overrighteous,
neither be overwise—
why destroy yourself?
[17]Do not be overwicked,
and do not be a fool—
why die before your time?
[18]It is good to grasp the one
and not let go of the other.
The man who fears God will avoid all
⌊extremes⌋.[a]
[19]Wisdom makes one wise man more
powerful
than ten rulers in a city.

[a]*18 Or will follow them both*

20 There is not a righteous man on earth
who does what is right and never sins.

21 Do not pay attention to every word
people say,
or you may hear your servant cursing
you—
22 for you know in your heart
that many times you yourself have
cursed others.

23 All this I tested by wisdom and I said,

"I am determined to be wise"—
but this was beyond me.
24 Whatever wisdom may be,
it is far off and most profound—
who can discover it?
25 So I turned my mind to understand,
to investigate and to search out wisdom
and the scheme of things
and to understand the stupidity of
wickedness
and the madness of folly.

26 I find more bitter than death
the woman who is a snare,
whose heart is a trap
and whose hands are chains.
The man who pleases God will escape
her,
but the sinner she will ensnare.

27 "Look," says the Teacher,[a] "this is what
I have discovered:

"Adding one thing to another to discover
the scheme of things—
28 while I was still searching
but not finding—
I found one ⌊upright⌋ man among a
thousand,
but not one ⌊upright⌋ woman among
them all.
29 This only have I found:
God made mankind upright,
but men have gone in search of many
schemes."

8

Who is like the wise man?
Who knows the explanation of things?
Wisdom brightens a man's face
and changes its hard appearance.

Obey the King

2 Obey the king's command, I say, because
you took an oath before God. 3 Do not be in a
hurry to leave the king's presence. Do not
stand up for a bad cause, for he will do whatever he pleases. 4 Since a king's word is supreme, who can say to him, "What are you
doing?"

5 Whoever obeys his command will come
to no harm,
and the wise heart will know the proper
time and procedure.
6 For there is a proper time and procedure
for every matter,
though a man's misery weighs heavily
upon him.
7 Since no man knows the future,
who can tell him what is to come?
8 No man has power over the wind to
contain it[b];
so no one has power over the day of
his death.
As no one is discharged in time of war,
so wickedness will not release those
who practice it.

9 All this I saw, as I applied my mind to
everything done under the sun. There is a
time when a man lords it over others to his
own[c] hurt. 10 Then too, I saw the wicked buried—those who used to come and go from
the holy place and receive praise[d] in the city
where they did this. This too is meaningless.
11 When the sentence for a crime is not
quickly carried out, the hearts of the people
are filled with schemes to do wrong. 12 Although a wicked man commits a hundred
crimes and still lives a long time, I know that
it will go better with God-fearing men, who
are reverent before God. 13 Yet because the
wicked do not fear God, it will not go well with
them, and their days will not lengthen like a
shadow.

14 There is something else meaningless
that occurs on earth: righteous men who get
what the wicked deserve, and wicked men
who get what the righteous deserve. This
too, I say, is meaningless. 15 So I commend
the enjoyment of life, because nothing is better for a man under the sun than to eat and
drink and be glad. Then joy will accompany
him in his work all the days of the life God has
given him under the sun.

16 When I applied my mind to know wisdom
and to observe man's labor on earth—his
eyes not seeing sleep day or night— 17 then I
saw all that God has done. No one can comprehend what goes on under the sun. De-

[a] 27 Or *leader of the assembly* [b] 8 Or *over his spirit to retain it* [c] 9 Or *to their* [d] 10 Some Hebrew manuscripts and Septuagint (Aquila); most Hebrew manuscripts *and are forgotten*

spite all his efforts to search it out, man cannot discover its meaning. Even if a wise man claims he knows, he cannot really comprehend it.

A Common Destiny for All

9 So I reflected on all this and concluded
that the righteous and the wise and what
they do are in God's hands, but no man
knows whether love or hate awaits him. 2All
share a common destiny—the righteous and
the wicked, the good and the bad,[a] the clean
and the unclean, those who offer sacrifices
and those who do not.

As it is with the good man,
so with the sinner;
as it is with those who take oaths,
so with those who are afraid to take
them.

3This is the evil in everything that happens
under the sun: The same destiny overtakes
all. The hearts of men, moreover, are full of
evil and there is madness in their hearts
while they live, and afterward they join the
dead. 4Anyone who is among the living has
hope[b]—even a live dog is better off than a
dead lion!

5For the living know that they will die,
but the dead know nothing;
they have no further reward,
and even the memory of them is
forgotten.
6Their love, their hate
and their jealousy have long since
vanished;
never again will they have a part
in anything that happens under the sun.

7Go, eat your food with gladness, and
drink your wine with a joyful heart, for it is
now that God favors what you do. 8Always
be clothed in white, and always anoint your
head with oil. 9Enjoy life with your wife,
whom you love, all the days of this meaningless life that God has given you under the
sun— all your meaningless days. For this is
your lot in life and in your toilsome labor
under the sun. 10Whatever your hand finds to
do, do it with all your might, for in the grave,[c]
where you are going, there is neither working
nor planning nor knowledge nor wisdom.

11I have seen something else under the
sun:

The race is not to the swift
or the battle to the strong,
nor does food come to the wise
or wealth to the brilliant
or favor to the learned;
but time and chance happen to them all.

12Moreover, no man knows when his hour
will come:

As fish are caught in a cruel net,
or birds are taken in a snare,
so men are trapped by evil times
that fall unexpectedly upon them.

Wisdom Better Than Folly

13I also saw under the sun this example of
wisdom that greatly impressed me: 14There
was once a small city with only a few people
in it. And a powerful king came against it,
surrounded it and built huge siegeworks
against it. 15Now there lived in that city a man
poor but wise, and he saved the city by his
wisdom. But nobody remembered that poor
man. 16So I said, "Wisdom is better than
strength." But the poor man's wisdom is despised, and his words are no longer heeded.

17The quiet words of the wise are more to
be heeded
than the shouts of a ruler of fools.
18Wisdom is better than weapons of war,
but one sinner destroys much good.

10 As dead flies give perfume a bad
smell,
so a little folly outweighs wisdom and
honor.
2The heart of the wise inclines to the right,
but the heart of the fool to the left.
3Even as he walks along the road,
the fool lacks sense
and shows everyone how stupid he is.
4If a ruler's anger rises against you,
do not leave your post;
calmness can lay great errors to rest.

5There is an evil I have seen under the
sun,
the sort of error that arises from a ruler:
6Fools are put in many high positions,
while the rich occupy the low ones.
7I have seen slaves on horseback,
while princes go on foot like slaves.
8Whoever digs a pit may fall into it;

[a]2 Septuagint (Aquila), Vulgate and Syriac; Hebrew does not have *and the bad.* [b]4 Or *What then is to be chosen? With all who live, there is hope* [c]10 Hebrew *Sheol*

whoever breaks through a wall may be
bitten by a snake.
9Whoever quarries stones may be injured
by them;
whoever splits logs may be
endangered by them.

10If the ax is dull
and its edge unsharpened,
more strength is needed
but skill will bring success.
11If a snake bites before it is charmed,
there is no profit for the charmer.

12Words from a wise man's mouth are
gracious,
but a fool is consumed by his own lips.
13At the beginning his words are folly;
at the end they are wicked madness—
14 and the fool multiplies words.

No one knows what is coming—
who can tell him what will happen after
him?

15A fool's work wearies him;
he does not know the way to town.

16Woe to you, O land whose king was a
servant[a]
and whose princes feast in the
morning.
17Blessed are you, O land whose king is of
noble birth
and whose princes eat at a proper
time—
for strength and not for drunkenness.

18If a man is lazy, the rafters sag;
if his hands are idle, the house leaks.

19A feast is made for laughter,
and wine makes life merry,
but money is the answer for everything.

20Do not revile the king even in your
thoughts,
or curse the rich in your bedroom,
because a bird of the air may carry your
words,
and a bird on the wing may report what
you say.

Bread Upon the Waters

11 Cast your bread upon the waters,
for after many days you will find it
again.
2Give portions to seven, yes to eight,
for you do not know what disaster may
come upon the land.

3If clouds are full of water,
they pour rain upon the earth.
Whether a tree falls to the south or to the
north,
in the place where it falls, there will it
lie.
4Whoever watches the wind will not plant;
whoever looks at the clouds will not
reap.

5As you do not know the path of the wind,
or how the body is formed[b] in a
mother's womb,
so you cannot understand the work of
God,
the Maker of all things.

6Sow your seed in the morning,
and at evening let not your hands be
idle,
for you do not know which will succeed,
whether this or that,
or whether both will do equally well.

Remember Your Creator While Young

7Light is sweet,
and it pleases the eyes to see the sun.
8However many years a man may live,
let him enjoy them all.
But let him remember the days of
darkness,
for they will be many.
Everything to come is meaningless.

9Be happy, young man, while you are
young,
and let your heart give you joy in the
days of your youth.
Follow the ways of your heart
and whatever your eyes see,
but know that for all these things
God will bring you to judgment.
10So then, banish anxiety from your heart
and cast off the troubles of your body,
for youth and vigor are meaningless.

12 Remember your Creator
in the days of your youth,
before the days of trouble come
and the years approach when you will
say,
"I find no pleasure in them"—

[a]16 Or *king is a child* [b]5 Or *know how life* (or *the spirit*) / *enters the body being formed*

2before the sun and the light
and the moon and the stars grow dark,
and the clouds return after the rain;
3when the keepers of the house tremble,
and the strong men stoop,
when the grinders cease because they
are few,
and those looking through the windows
grow dim;
4when the doors to the street are closed
and the sound of grinding fades;
when men rise up at the sound of birds,
but all their songs grow faint;
5when men are afraid of heights
and of dangers in the streets;
when the almond tree blossoms
and the grasshopper drags himself
along
and desire no longer is stirred.
Then man goes to his eternal home
and mourners go about the streets.

6Remember him—before the silver cord is
severed,
or the golden bowl is broken;
before the pitcher is shattered at the
spring,
or the wheel broken at the well,
7and the dust returns to the ground it
came from,
and the spirit returns to God who
gave it.

8"Meaningless! Meaningless!" says the
Teacher.[a]
"Everything is meaningless!"

The Conclusion of the Matter

9Not only was the Teacher wise, but also
he imparted knowledge to the people. He
pondered and searched out and set in order
many proverbs. 10The Teacher searched to
find just the right words, and what he wrote
was upright and true.
11The words of the wise are like goads,
their collected sayings like firmly embedded
nails—given by one Shepherd. 12Be warned,
my son, of anything in addition to them.
Of making many books there is no end,
and much study wearies the body.

13Now all has been heard;
here is the conclusion of the matter:
Fear God and keep his commandments,
for this is the whole ⌊duty⌋ of man.
14For God will bring every deed into
judgment,
including every hidden thing,
whether it is good or evil.

[a]8 Or *the leader of the assembly*; also in verses 9 and 10

Song of Songs

Introduction:

Although some scholars view Song of Songs as being a picture of Christ's love for his people, the more accepted view of Song of Songs is that it is a collection of love poems between a lover and his beloved. It is a beautiful picture of ideal human love and marriage.

Outline of contents:

---

1 Solomon's Song of Songs.

Beloved[a]

2Let him kiss me with the kisses of his mouth—
for your love is more delightful than wine.
3Pleasing is the fragrance of your perfumes;
your name is like perfume poured out.
No wonder the maidens love you!
4Take me away with you—let us hurry!
Let the king bring me into his chambers.

Friends

We rejoice and delight in you[b];
we will praise your love more than wine.

Beloved

How right they are to adore you!

5Dark am I, yet lovely,
O daughters of Jerusalem,
dark like the tents of Kedar,
like the tent curtains of Solomon.[c]
6Do not stare at me because I am dark,
because I am darkened by the sun.
My mother's sons were angry with me
and made me take care of the vineyards;
my own vineyard I have neglected.
7Tell me, you whom I love, where you graze your flock
and where you rest your sheep at midday.
Why should I be like a veiled woman
beside the flocks of your friends?

Friends

8If you do not know, most beautiful of women,
follow the tracks of the sheep
and graze your young goats
by the tents of the shepherds.

Lover

9I liken you, my darling, to a mare
harnessed to one of the chariots of Pharaoh.
10Your cheeks are beautiful with earrings,
your neck with strings of jewels.
11We will make you earrings of gold,
studded with silver.

Beloved

12While the king was at his table,
my perfume spread its fragrance.

---

[a]Primarily on the basis of the gender of the Hebrew pronouns used, male and female speakers are indicated in the margins by the captions *Lover* and *Beloved* respectively. The words of others are marked *Friends.* In some instances the divisions and their captions are debatable. [b]*4* The Hebrew is masculine singular. [c]*5* Or *Salma*

13My lover is to me a sachet of myrrh
resting between my breasts.
14My lover is to me a cluster of henna blossoms
from the vineyards of En Gedi.

Lover

15How beautiful you are, my darling!
Oh, how beautiful!
Your eyes are doves.

Beloved

16How handsome you are, my lover!
Oh, how charming!
And our bed is verdant.

Lover

17The beams of our house are cedars;
our rafters are firs.

Beloved[a]

2 I am a rose[b] of Sharon,
a lily of the valleys.

Lover

2Like a lily among thorns
is my darling among the maidens.

Beloved

3Like an apple tree among the trees of the forest
is my lover among the young men.
I delight to sit in his shade,
and his fruit is sweet to my taste.
4He has taken me to the banquet hall,
and his banner over me is love.
5Strengthen me with raisins,
refresh me with apples,
for I am faint with love.
6His left arm is under my head,
and his right arm embraces me.
7Daughters of Jerusalem, I charge you
by the gazelles and by the does of the field:
Do not arouse or awaken love
until it so desires.

8Listen! My lover!
Look! Here he comes,
leaping across the mountains,
bounding over the hills.
9My lover is like a gazelle or a young stag.
Look! There he stands behind our wall,
gazing through the windows,
peering through the lattice.
10My lover spoke and said to me,
"Arise, my darling,
my beautiful one, and come with me.
11See! The winter is past;
the rains are over and gone.
12Flowers appear on the earth;
the season of singing has come,
the cooing of doves
is heard in our land.
13The fig tree forms its early fruit;
the blossoming vines spread their fragrance.
Arise, come, my darling;
my beautiful one, come with me."

Lover

14My dove in the clefts of the rock,
in the hiding places on the mountainside,
show me your face,
let me hear your voice;
for your voice is sweet,
and your face is lovely.
15Catch for us the foxes,
the little foxes
that ruin the vineyards,
our vineyards that are in bloom.

Beloved

16My lover is mine and I am his;
he browses among the lilies.
17Until the day breaks
and the shadows flee,
turn, my lover,
and be like a gazelle
or like a young stag
on the rugged hills.[c]

3 All night long on my bed
I looked for the one my heart loves;
I looked for him but did not find him.
2I will get up now and go about the city,
through its streets and squares;
I will search for the one my heart loves.
So I looked for him but did not find him.
3The watchmen found me
as they made their rounds in the city.
"Have you seen the one my heart loves?"
4Scarcely had I passed them
when I found the one my heart loves.
I held him and would not let him go
till I had brought him to my mother's house,

[a] 1 Or *Lover* [b] 1 Possibly a member of the crocus family [c] 17 Or *the hills of Bether*

to the room of the one who conceived
me.
5Daughters of Jerusalem, I charge you
by the gazelles and by the does of the
field:
Do not arouse or awaken love
until it so desires.

6Who is this coming up from the desert
like a column of smoke,
perfumed with myrrh and incense
made from all the spices of the
merchant?
7Look! It is Solomon's carriage,
escorted by sixty warriors,
the noblest of Israel,
8all of them wearing the sword,
all experienced in battle,
each with his sword at his side,
prepared for the terrors of the night.
9King Solomon made for himself the
carriage;
he made it of wood from Lebanon.
10Its posts he made of silver,
its base of gold.
Its seat was upholstered with purple,
its interior lovingly inlaid
by[a] the daughters of Jerusalem.
11Come out, you daughters of Zion,
and look at King Solomon wearing the
crown,
the crown with which his mother
crowned him
on the day of his wedding,
the day his heart rejoiced.

Lover

4 How beautiful you are, my darling!
Oh, how beautiful!
Your eyes behind your veil are doves.
Your hair is like a flock of goats
descending from Mount Gilead.
2Your teeth are like a flock of sheep just
shorn,
coming up from the washing.
Each has its twin;
not one of them is alone.
3Your lips are like a scarlet ribbon;
your mouth is lovely.
Your temples behind your veil
are like the halves of a pomegranate.
4Your neck is like the tower of David,
built with elegance[b];
on it hang a thousand shields,
all of them shields of warriors.
5Your two breasts are like two fawns,
like twin fawns of a gazelle
that browse among the lilies.
6Until the day breaks
and the shadows flee,
I will go to the mountain of myrrh
and to the hill of incense.
7All beautiful you are, my darling;
there is no flaw in you.

8Come with me from Lebanon, my bride,
come with me from Lebanon.
Descend from the crest of Amana,
from the top of Senir, the summit of
Hermon,
from the lions' dens
and the mountain haunts of the
leopards.
9You have stolen my heart, my sister, my
bride;
you have stolen my heart
with one glance of your eyes,
with one jewel of your necklace.
10How delightful is your love, my sister, my
bride!
How much more pleasing is your love
than wine,
and the fragrance of your perfume than
any spice!
11Your lips drop sweetness as the
honeycomb, my bride;
milk and honey are under your tongue.
The fragrance of your garments is like
that of Lebanon.
12You are a garden locked up, my sister,
my bride;
you are a spring enclosed, a sealed
fountain.
13Your plants are an orchard of
pomegranates
with choice fruits,
with henna and nard,
14 nard and saffron,
calamus and cinnamon,
with every kind of incense tree,
with myrrh and aloes
and all the finest spices.
15You are[c] a garden fountain,
a well of flowing water
streaming down from Lebanon.

Beloved

16Awake, north wind,
and come, south wind!
Blow on my garden,

[a] 10 Or *its inlaid interior a gift of love / from*
[b] 4 The meaning of the Hebrew for this word is uncertain.
[c] 15 Or *I am* (spoken by the *Beloved*)

that its fragrance may spread abroad.
Let my lover come into his garden
and taste its choice fruits.

Lover

5 I have come into my garden, my sister,
my bride;
I have gathered my myrrh with my
spice.
I have eaten my honeycomb and my
honey;
I have drunk my wine and my milk.

Friends

Eat, O friends, and drink;
drink your fill, O lovers.

Beloved

2I slept but my heart was awake.
Listen! My lover is knocking:
"Open to me, my sister, my darling,
my dove, my flawless one.
My head is drenched with dew,
my hair with the dampness of the
night."
3I have taken off my robe—
must I put it on again?
I have washed my feet—
must I soil them again?
4My lover thrust his hand through the
latch-opening;
my heart began to pound for him.
5I arose to open for my lover,
and my hands dripped with myrrh,
my fingers with flowing myrrh,
on the handles of the lock.
6I opened for my lover,
but my lover had left; he was gone.
My heart sank at his departure.[a]
I looked for him but did not find him.
I called him but he did not answer.
7The watchmen found me
as they made their rounds in the city.
They beat me, they bruised me;
they took away my cloak,
those watchmen of the walls!
8O daughters of Jerusalem, I charge
you—
if you find my lover,
what will you tell him?
Tell him I am faint with love.

Friends

9How is your beloved better than others,
most beautiful of women?
How is your beloved better than others,
that you charge us so?

Beloved

10My lover is radiant and ruddy,
outstanding among ten thousand.
11His head is purest gold;
his hair is wavy
and black as a raven.
12His eyes are like doves
by the water streams,
washed in milk,
mounted like jewels.
13His cheeks are like beds of spice
yielding perfume.
His lips are like lilies
dripping with myrrh.
14His arms are rods of gold
set with chrysolite.
His body is like polished ivory
decorated with sapphires.[b]
15His legs are pillars of marble
set on bases of pure gold.
His appearance is like Lebanon,
choice as its cedars.
16His mouth is sweetness itself;
he is altogether lovely.
This is my lover, this my friend,
O daughters of Jerusalem.

Friends

6 Where has your lover gone,
most beautiful of women?
Which way did your lover turn,
that we may look for him with you?

Beloved

2My lover has gone down to his garden,
to the beds of spices,
to browse in the gardens
and to gather lilies.
3I am my lover's and my lover is mine;
he browses among the lilies.

Lover

4You are beautiful, my darling, as Tirzah,
lovely as Jerusalem,
majestic as troops with banners.
5Turn your eyes from me;
they overwhelm me.
Your hair is like a flock of goats
descending from Gilead.
6Your teeth are like a flock of sheep
coming up from the washing.
Each has its twin,

[a]6 Or *heart had gone out to him when he spoke*
[b]14 Or *lapis lazuli*

not one of them is alone.
7Your temples behind your veil
are like the halves of a pomegranate.
8Sixty queens there may be,
and eighty concubines,
and virgins beyond number;
9but my dove, my perfect one, is unique,
the only daughter of her mother,
the favorite of the one who bore her.
The maidens saw her and called her
blessed;
the queens and concubines praised
her.

Friends

10Who is this that appears like the dawn,
fair as the moon, bright as the sun,
majestic as the stars in procession?

Lover

11I went down to the grove of nut trees
to look at the new growth in the valley,
to see if the vines had budded
or the pomegranates were in bloom.
12Before I realized it,
my desire set me among the royal
chariots of my people.[a]

Friends

13Come back, come back, O Shulammite;
come back, come back, that we may
gaze on you!

Lover

Why would you gaze on the Shulammite
as on the dance of Mahanaim?

7 How beautiful your sandaled feet,
O prince's daughter!
Your graceful legs are like jewels,
the work of a craftsman's hands.
2Your navel is a rounded goblet
that never lacks blended wine.
Your waist is a mound of wheat
encircled by lilies.
3Your breasts are like two fawns,
twins of a gazelle.
4Your neck is like an ivory tower.
Your eyes are the pools of Heshbon
by the gate of Bath Rabbim.
Your nose is like the tower of Lebanon
looking toward Damascus.
5Your head crowns you like Mount
Carmel.
Your hair is like royal tapestry;
the king is held captive by its tresses.
6How beautiful you are and how pleasing,
O love, with your delights!
7Your stature is like that of the palm,
and your breasts like clusters of fruit.
8I said, "I will climb the palm tree;
I will take hold of its fruit."
May your breasts be like the clusters of
the vine,
the fragrance of your breath like
apples,
9 and your mouth like the best wine.

Beloved

May the wine go straight to my lover,
flowing gently over lips and teeth.[b]
10I belong to my lover,
and his desire is for me.
11Come, my lover, let us go to the
countryside,
let us spend the night in the
villages.[c]
12Let us go early to the vineyards
to see if the vines have budded,
if their blossoms have opened,
and if the pomegranates are in bloom—
there I will give you my love.
13The mandrakes send out their fragrance,
and at our door is every delicacy,
both new and old,
that I have stored up for you, my lover.

8 If only you were to me like a brother,
who was nursed at my mother's
breasts!
Then, if I found you outside,
I would kiss you,
and no one would despise me.
2I would lead you
and bring you to my mother's house—
she who has taught me.
I would give you spiced wine to drink,
the nectar of my pomegranates.
3His left arm is under my head
and his right arm embraces me.
4Daughters of Jerusalem, I charge you:
Do not arouse or awaken love
until it so desires.

Friends

5Who is this coming up from the desert
leaning on her lover?

[a]12 Or *among the chariots of Amminadab;* or *among the chariots of the people of the prince* [b]9 Septuagint, Aquila, Vulgate and Syriac; Hebrew *lips of sleepers* [c]11 Or *henna bushes*

Beloved

Under the apple tree I roused you;
there your mother conceived you,
there she who was in labor gave you birth.
6 Place me like a seal over your heart,
like a seal on your arm;
for love is as strong as death,
its jealousy[a] unyielding as the grave.[b]
It burns like blazing fire,
like a mighty flame.[c]
7 Many waters cannot quench love;
rivers cannot wash it away.
If one were to give
all the wealth of his house for love,
it[d] would be utterly scorned.

Friends

8 We have a young sister,
and her breasts are not yet grown.
What shall we do for our sister
for the day she is spoken for?
9 If she is a wall,
we will build towers of silver on her.
If she is a door,
we will enclose her with panels of cedar.

Beloved

10 I am a wall,
and my breasts are like towers.
Thus I have become in his eyes
like one bringing contentment.
11 Solomon had a vineyard in Baal Hamon;
he let out his vineyard to tenants.
Each was to bring for its fruit
a thousand shekels[e] of silver.
12 But my own vineyard is mine to give;
the thousand shekels are for you, O Solomon,
and two hundred[f] are for those who tend its fruit.

Lover

13 You who dwell in the gardens
with friends in attendance,
let me hear your voice!

Beloved

14 Come away, my lover,
and be like a gazelle
or like a young stag
on the spice-laden mountains.

[a]6 Or *ardor* [b]6 Hebrew *Sheol* [c]6 Or / *like the very flame of the* LORD [d]7 Or *he* [e]11 That is, about 25 pounds (about 11.5 kilograms); also in verse 12 [f]12 That is, about 5 pounds (about 2.3 kilograms)

Isaiah

Introduction:

Isaiah prophesied in Judah during the reigns of Kings Uzziah, Jotham, Ahaz, and Hezekiah. According to tradition Isaiah was martyred under Manasseh, the wicked son of Hezekiah, about 680 B.C.

Isaiah repeatedly warned the people that Jerusalem and Judah would be judged because of their wickedness. In chapter 39 he predicted the Babylonian exile. But he also held to the hope that the kingdom would be restored again.

Beginning in chapter 40 Isaiah offered comfort with these promises from God: 1) the Babylonian exiles would be allowed to return to Jerusalem; 2) a righteous, suffering servant would bring salvation; 3) God would set up a new, righteous kingdom.

Outline of contents:

Judgment and hope of restoration (1:1–6:13)
Hopes in Assyria or God (7:1–12:6)
Prophecies about nations (13:1–23:18)
Israel's judgment and deliverance (24:1–27:13)
Warnings and Zion restored (28:1–35:10)
King Hezekiah withstands Assyria (36:1–39:8)
Promises of divine deliverance (40:1–56:8)
The final kingdom established (56:9–66:24)

---

1 The vision concerning Judah and
Jerusalem that Isaiah son of Amoz saw
during the reigns of Uzziah, Jotham, Ahaz
and Hezekiah, kings of Judah.

A Rebellious Nation

2Hear, O heavens! Listen, O earth!
For the LORD has spoken:
"I reared children and brought them up,
but they have rebelled against me.
3The ox knows his master,
the donkey his owner's manger,
but Israel does not know,
my people do not understand."

4Ah, sinful nation,
a people loaded with guilt,
a brood of evildoers,
children given to corruption!
They have forsaken the LORD;
they have spurned the Holy One of Israel
and turned their backs on him.

5Why should you be beaten anymore?
Why do you persist in rebellion?
Your whole head is injured,
your whole heart afflicted.
6From the sole of your foot to the top of your head
there is no soundness—
only wounds and welts
and open sores,
not cleansed or bandaged
or soothed with oil.

7Your country is desolate,
your cities burned with fire;
your fields are being stripped by foreigners
right before you,
laid waste as when overthrown by strangers.
8The Daughter of Zion is left
like a shelter in a vineyard,
like a hut in a field of melons,
like a city under siege.
9Unless the LORD Almighty
had left us some survivors,
we would have become like Sodom,
we would have been like Gomorrah.

10Hear the word of the LORD,
you rulers of Sodom;

listen to the law of our God,
you people of Gomorrah!
11"The multitude of your sacrifices—
what are they to me?" says the LORD.
"I have more than enough of burnt offerings,
of rams and the fat of fattened animals;
I have no pleasure
in the blood of bulls and lambs and goats.
12When you come to appear before me,
who has asked this of you,
this trampling of my courts?
13Stop bringing meaningless offerings!
Your incense is detestable to me.
New Moons, Sabbaths and convocations—
I cannot bear your evil assemblies.
14Your New Moon festivals and your appointed feasts
my soul hates.
They have become a burden to me;
I am weary of bearing them.
15When you spread out your hands in prayer,
I will hide my eyes from you;
even if you offer many prayers,
I will not listen.
Your hands are full of blood;
16 wash and make yourselves clean.
Take your evil deeds
out of my sight!
Stop doing wrong,
17 learn to do right!
Seek justice,
encourage the oppressed.[a]
Defend the cause of the fatherless,
plead the case of the widow.

18"Come now, let us reason together,"
says the LORD.
"Though your sins are like scarlet,
they shall be as white as snow;
though they are red as crimson,
they shall be like wool.
19If you are willing and obedient,
you will eat the best from the land;
20but if you resist and rebel,
you will be devoured by the sword."
For the mouth of the LORD has spoken.

21See how the faithful city
has become a harlot!
She once was full of justice;
righteousness used to dwell in her—
but now murderers!
22Your silver has become dross,
your choice wine is diluted with water.
23Your rulers are rebels,
companions of thieves;
they all love bribes
and chase after gifts.
They do not defend the cause of the fatherless;
the widow's case does not come before them.
24Therefore the Lord, the LORD Almighty,
the Mighty One of Israel, declares:
"Ah, I will get relief from my foes
and avenge myself on my enemies.
25I will turn my hand against you;
I will thoroughly purge away your dross
and remove all your impurities.
26I will restore your judges as in days of old,
your counselors as at the beginning.
Afterward you will be called
the City of Righteousness,
the Faithful City."

27Zion will be redeemed with justice,
her penitent ones with righteousness.
28But rebels and sinners will both be broken,
and those who forsake the LORD will perish.
29"You will be ashamed because of the sacred oaks
in which you have delighted;
you will be disgraced because of the gardens
that you have chosen.
30You will be like an oak with fading leaves,
like a garden without water.
31The mighty man will become tinder
and his work a spark;
both will burn together,
with no one to quench the fire."

The Mountain of the LORD

2 This is what Isaiah son of Amoz saw concerning Judah and Jerusalem:

2In the last days

the mountain of the LORD's temple will be established
as chief among the mountains;
it will be raised above the hills,
and all nations will stream to it.

[a]17 Or / *rebuke the oppressor*

3Many peoples will come and say,
"Come, let us go up to the mountain of the LORD,
to the house of the God of Jacob.
He will teach us his ways,
so that we may walk in his paths."
The law will go out from Zion,
the word of the LORD from Jerusalem.
4He will judge between the nations
and will settle disputes for many peoples.
They will beat their swords into plowshares
and their spears into pruning hooks.
Nation will not take up sword against nation,
nor will they train for war anymore.

5Come, O house of Jacob,
let us walk in the light of the LORD.

The Day of the LORD

6You have abandoned your people,
the house of Jacob.
They are full of superstitions from the East;
they practice divination like the Philistines
and clasp hands with pagans.
7Their land is full of silver and gold;
there is no end to their treasures.
Their land is full of horses;
there is no end to their chariots.
8Their land is full of idols;
they bow down to the work of their hands,
to what their fingers have made.
9So man will be brought low
and mankind humbled—
do not forgive them.[a]

10Go into the rocks,
hide in the ground
from dread of the LORD
and the splendor of his majesty!
11The eyes of the arrogant man will be humbled
and the pride of men brought low;
the LORD alone will be exalted in that day.

12The LORD Almighty has a day in store
for all the proud and lofty,
for all that is exalted
(and they will be humbled),
13for all the cedars of Lebanon, tall and lofty,
and all the oaks of Bashan,
14for all the towering mountains
and all the high hills,
15for every lofty tower
and every fortified wall,
16for every trading ship[b]
and every stately vessel.
17The arrogance of man will be brought low
and the pride of men humbled;
the LORD alone will be exalted in that day,
18 and the idols will totally disappear.

19Men will flee to caves in the rocks
and to holes in the ground
from dread of the LORD
and the splendor of his majesty,
when he rises to shake the earth.
20In that day men will throw away
to the rodents and bats
their idols of silver and idols of gold,
which they made to worship.
21They will flee to caverns in the rocks
and to the overhanging crags
from dread of the LORD
and the splendor of his majesty,
when he rises to shake the earth.

22Stop trusting in man,
who has but a breath in his nostrils.
Of what account is he?

Judgment on Jerusalem and Judah

3 See now, the Lord,
the LORD Almighty,
is about to take from Jerusalem and Judah
both supply and support:
all supplies of food and all supplies of water,
2 the hero and warrior,
the judge and prophet,
the soothsayer and elder,
3the captain of fifty and man of rank,
the counselor, skilled craftsman and clever enchanter.

4I will make boys their officials;
mere children will govern them.
5People will oppress each other—
man against man, neighbor against neighbor.
The young will rise up against the old,
the base against the honorable.

6A man will seize one of his brothers
at his father's home, and say,
"You have a cloak, you be our leader;

[a]9 Or *not raise them up* [b]16 Hebrew *every ship of Tarshish*

take charge of this heap of ruins!"
7But in that day he will cry out,
"I have no remedy.
I have no food or clothing in my house;
do not make me the leader of the people."

8Jerusalem staggers,
Judah is falling;
their words and deeds are against the LORD,
defying his glorious presence.
9The look on their faces testifies against them;
they parade their sin like Sodom;
they do not hide it.
Woe to them!
They have brought disaster upon themselves.

10Tell the righteous it will be well with them,
for they will enjoy the fruit of their deeds.
11Woe to the wicked! Disaster is upon them!
They will be paid back for what their hands have done.

12Youths oppress my people,
women rule over them.
O my people, your guides lead you astray;
they turn you from the path.

13The LORD takes his place in court;
he rises to judge the people.
14The LORD enters into judgment
against the elders and leaders of his people:
"It is you who have ruined my vineyard;
the plunder from the poor is in your houses.
15What do you mean by crushing my people
and grinding the faces of the poor?"
declares the Lord, the LORD Almighty.

16The LORD says,
"The women of Zion are haughty,
walking along with outstretched necks,
flirting with their eyes,
tripping along with mincing steps,
with ornaments jingling on their ankles.
17Therefore the Lord will bring sores on the heads of the women of Zion;
the LORD will make their scalps bald."

18In that day the Lord will snatch away their
finery: the bangles and headbands and cres-
cent necklaces, 19the earrings and bracelets
and veils, 20the headdresses and ankle
chains and sashes, the perfume bottles and
charms, 21the signet rings and nose rings,
22the fine robes and the capes and cloaks,
the purses 23and mirrors, and the linen garments and tiaras and shawls.

24Instead of fragrance there will be a stench;
instead of a sash, a rope;
instead of well-dressed hair, baldness;
instead of fine clothing, sackcloth;
instead of beauty, branding.
25Your men will fall by the sword,
your warriors in battle.
26The gates of Zion will lament and mourn;
destitute, she will sit on the ground.

4 In that day seven women
will take hold of one man
and say, "We will eat our own food
and provide our own clothes;
only let us be called by your name.
Take away our disgrace!"

The Branch of the LORD

2In that day the Branch of the LORD will be
beautiful and glorious, and the fruit of the
land will be the pride and glory of the survivors in Israel. 3Those who are left in Zion,
who remain in Jerusalem, will be called holy,
all who are recorded among the living in
Jerusalem. 4The Lord will wash away the filth
of the women of Zion; he will cleanse the
bloodstains from Jerusalem by a spirit[a] of
judgment and a spirit[a] of fire. 5Then the LORD
will create over all of Mount Zion and over
those who assemble there a cloud of smoke
by day and a glow of flaming fire by night;
over all the glory will be a canopy. 6It will be a
shelter and shade from the heat of the day,
and a refuge and hiding place from the storm
and rain.

The Song of the Vineyard

5 I will sing for the one I love
a song about his vineyard:
My loved one had a vineyard
on a fertile hillside.
2He dug it up and cleared it of stones
and planted it with the choicest vines.
He built a watchtower in it

[a]4 Or *the Spirit*

and cut out a winepress as well.
Then he looked for a crop of good grapes,
but it yielded only bad fruit.

3"Now you dwellers in Jerusalem and men of Judah,
judge between me and my vineyard.
4What more could have been done for my vineyard
than I have done for it?
When I looked for good grapes,
why did it yield only bad?
5Now I will tell you
what I am going to do to my vineyard:
I will take away its hedge,
and it will be destroyed;
I will break down its wall,
and it will be trampled.
6I will make it a wasteland,
neither pruned nor cultivated,
and briers and thorns will grow there.
I will command the clouds
not to rain on it."

7The vineyard of the LORD Almighty
is the house of Israel,
and the men of Judah
are the garden of his delight.
And he looked for justice, but saw bloodshed;
for righteousness, but heard cries of distress.

Woes and Judgments

8Woe to you who add house to house
and join field to field
till no space is left
and you live alone in the land.

9The LORD Almighty has declared in my hearing:

"Surely the great houses will become desolate,
the fine mansions left without occupants.
10A ten-acre[a] vineyard will produce only a bath[b] of wine,
a homer[c] of seed only an ephah[d] of grain."

11Woe to those who rise early in the morning
to run after their drinks,
who stay up late at night
till they are inflamed with wine.
12They have harps and lyres at their banquets,
tambourines and flutes and wine,
but they have no regard for the deeds of the LORD,
no respect for the work of his hands.
13Therefore my people will go into exile
for lack of understanding;
their men of rank will die of hunger
and their masses will be parched with thirst.
14Therefore the grave[e] enlarges its appetite
and opens its mouth without limit;
into it will descend their nobles and masses
with all their brawlers and revelers.
15So man will be brought low
and mankind humbled,
the eyes of the arrogant humbled.
16But the LORD Almighty will be exalted by his justice,
and the holy God will show himself holy by his righteousness.
17Then sheep will graze as in their own pasture;
lambs will feed[f] among the ruins of the rich.

18Woe to those who draw sin along with cords of deceit,
and wickedness as with cart ropes,
19to those who say, "Let God hurry,
let him hasten his work
so we may see it.
Let it approach,
let the plan of the Holy One of Israel come,
so we may know it."

20Woe to those who call evil good
and good evil,
who put darkness for light
and light for darkness,
who put bitter for sweet
and sweet for bitter.

21Woe to those who are wise in their own eyes
and clever in their own sight.

22Woe to those who are heroes at drinking wine
and champions at mixing drinks,

[a] 10 Hebrew *ten-yoke,* that is, the land plowed by 10 yoke of oxen in one day [b] 10 That is, probably about 6 gallons (about 22 liters) [c] 10 That is, probably about 6 bushels (about 220 liters) [d] 10 That is, probably about 3/5 bushel (about 22 liters) [e] 14 Hebrew *Sheol* [f] 17 Septuagint; Hebrew / *strangers will eat*

23who acquit the guilty for a bribe,
but deny justice to the innocent.
24Therefore, as tongues of fire lick up straw
and as dry grass sinks down in the flames,
so their roots will decay
and their flowers blow away like dust;
for they have rejected the law of the LORD Almighty
and spurned the word of the Holy One of Israel.
25Therefore the LORD's anger burns against his people;
his hand is raised and he strikes them down.
The mountains shake,
and the dead bodies are like refuse in the streets.

Yet for all this, his anger is not turned away,
his hand is still upraised.

26He lifts up a banner for the distant nations,
he whistles for those at the ends of the earth.
Here they come,
swiftly and speedily!
27Not one of them grows tired or stumbles,
not one slumbers or sleeps;
not a belt is loosened at the waist,
not a sandal thong is broken.
28Their arrows are sharp,
all their bows are strung;
their horses' hoofs seem like flint,
their chariot wheels like a whirlwind.
29Their roar is like that of the lion,
they roar like young lions;
they growl as they seize their prey
and carry it off with no one to rescue.
30In that day they will roar over it
like the roaring of the sea.
And if one looks at the land,
he will see darkness and distress;
even the light will be darkened by the clouds.

Isaiah's Commission

6 In the year that King Uzziah died, I saw
the Lord seated on a throne, high and
exalted, and the train of his robe filled the
temple. 2Above him were seraphs, each with
six wings: With two wings they covered their
faces, with two they covered their feet, and
with two they were flying. 3And they were
calling to one another:

"Holy, holy, holy is the LORD Almighty;
the whole earth is full of his glory."

4At the sound of their voices the doorposts
and thresholds shook and the temple was
filled with smoke.
5"Woe to me!" I cried. "I am ruined! For I
am a man of unclean lips, and I live among a
people of unclean lips, and my eyes have
seen the King, the LORD Almighty."
6Then one of the seraphs flew to me with a
live coal in his hand, which he had taken with
tongs from the altar. 7With it he touched my
mouth and said, "See, this has touched your
lips; your guilt is taken away and your sin
atoned for."
8Then I heard the voice of the Lord saying,
"Whom shall I send? And who will go for
us?"
And I said, "Here am I. Send me!"
9He said, "Go and tell this people:

" 'Be ever hearing, but never understanding;
be ever seeing, but never perceiving.'
10Make the heart of this people calloused;
make their ears dull
and close their eyes.[a]
Otherwise they might see with their eyes,
hear with their ears,
understand with their hearts,
and turn and be healed."

11Then I said, "For how long, O Lord?"
And he answered:

"Until the cities lie ruined
and without inhabitant,
until the houses are left deserted
and the fields ruined and ravaged,
12until the LORD has sent everyone far away
and the land is utterly forsaken.
13And though a tenth remains in the land,
it will again be laid waste.
But as the terebinth and oak
leave stumps when they are cut down,
so the holy seed will be the stump in the land."

The Sign of Immanuel

7 When Ahaz son of Jotham, the son of
Uzziah, was king of Judah, King Rezin of
Aram and Pekah son of Remaliah king of

[a]9,10 Hebrew; Septuagint *'You will be ever hearing, but never understanding; / you will be ever seeing, but never perceiving.' / 10This people's heart has become calloused; / they hardly hear with their ears, / and they have closed their eyes*

Israel marched up to fight against Jerusalem, but they could not overpower it.
2Now the house of David was told, "Aram
has allied itself with[a] Ephraim"; so the hearts
of Ahaz and his people were shaken, as the
trees of the forest are shaken by the wind.
3Then the LORD said to Isaiah, "Go out, you
and your son Shear-Jashub,[b] to meet Ahaz
at the end of the aqueduct of the Upper Pool,
on the road to the Washerman's Field. 4Say
to him, 'Be careful, keep calm and don't be
afraid. Do not lose heart because of these
two smoldering stubs of firewood—because
of the fierce anger of Rezin and Aram and of
the son of Remaliah. 5Aram, Ephraim and
Remaliah's son have plotted your ruin, saying, 6"Let us invade Judah; let us tear it apart
and divide it among ourselves, and make the
son of Tabeel king over it." 7Yet this is what
the Sovereign LORD says:

" 'It will not take place,
it will not happen,
8for the head of Aram is Damascus,
and the head of Damascus is only
Rezin.
Within sixty-five years
Ephraim will be too shattered to be a
people.
9The head of Ephraim is Samaria,
and the head of Samaria is only
Remaliah's son.
If you do not stand firm in your faith,
you will not stand at all.' "

10Again the LORD spoke to Ahaz, 11"Ask the
LORD your God for a sign, whether in the
deepest depths or in the highest heights."
12But Ahaz said, "I will not ask; I will not put
the LORD to the test."
13Then Isaiah said, "Hear now, you house
of David! Is it not enough to try the patience
of men? Will you try the patience of my God
also? 14Therefore the Lord himself will give
you[c] a sign: The virgin will be with child and
will give birth to a son, and[d] will call him
Immanuel.[e] 15He will eat curds and honey
when he knows enough to reject the wrong
and choose the right. 16But before the boy
knows enough to reject the wrong and
choose the right, the land of the two kings
you dread will be laid waste. 17The LORD will
bring on you and on your people and on the
house of your father a time unlike any since
Ephraim broke away from Judah—he will
bring the king of Assyria."
18In that day the LORD will whistle for flies
from the distant streams of Egypt and for
bees from the land of Assyria. 19They will all
come and settle in the steep ravines and in
the crevices in the rocks, on all the thornbushes and at all the water holes. 20In that
day the Lord will use a razor hired from
beyond the River[f]—the king of Assyria—to
shave your head and the hair of your legs,
and to take off your beards also. 21In that
day, a man will keep alive a young cow and
two goats. 22And because of the abundance
of the milk they give, he will have curds to
eat. All who remain in the land will eat curds
and honey. 23In that day, in every place
where there were a thousand vines worth a
thousand silver shekels,[g] there will be only
briers and thorns. 24Men will go there with
bow and arrow, for the land will be covered
with briers and thorns. 25As for all the hills
once cultivated by the hoe, you will no longer
go there for fear of the briers and thorns; they
will become places where cattle are turned
loose and where sheep run.

Assyria, the LORD's Instrument

8 The LORD said to me, "Take a large scroll
and write on it with an ordinary pen:
Maher-Shalal-Hash-Baz.[h] 2And I will call in
Uriah the priest and Zechariah son of
Jeberekiah as reliable witnesses for me."
3Then I went to the prophetess, and she
conceived and gave birth to a son. And the
LORD said to me, "Name him Maher-Shalal-
Hash-Baz. 4Before the boy knows how to say
'My father' or 'My mother,' the wealth of
Damascus and the plunder of Samaria will
be carried off by the king of Assyria."
5The LORD spoke to me again:

6"Because this people has rejected
the gently flowing waters of Shiloah
and rejoices over Rezin
and the son of Remaliah,
7therefore the Lord is about to bring
against them
the mighty floodwaters of the River[f]—
the king of Assyria with all his pomp.
It will overflow all its channels,
run over all its banks
8and sweep on into Judah, swirling over it,

[a]2 Or *has set up camp in* [b]3 *Shear-Jashub* means *a remnant will return.* [c]14 The Hebrew is plural. [d]14 Masoretic Text; Dead Sea Scrolls *and he* or *and they* [e]14 *Immanuel* means *God with us.* [f]20,7 That is, the Euphrates [g]23 That is, about 25 pounds (about 11.5 kilograms) [h]1 *Maher-Shalal-Hash-Baz* means *quick to the plunder, swift to the spoil*; also in verse 3.

passing through it and reaching up to
the neck.
Its outspread wings will cover the breadth
of your land,
O Immanuel[a]!"

9Raise the war cry,[b] you nations, and be
shattered!
Listen, all you distant lands.
Prepare for battle, and be shattered!
Prepare for battle, and be shattered!
10Devise your strategy, but it will be
thwarted;
propose your plan, but it will not stand,
for God is with us.[c]

Fear God

11The LORD spoke to me with his strong
hand upon me, warning me not to follow the
way of this people. He said:

12"Do not call conspiracy
everything that these people call
conspiracy[d];
do not fear what they fear,
and do not dread it.
13The LORD Almighty is the one you are to
regard as holy,
he is the one you are to fear,
he is the one you are to dread,
14and he will be a sanctuary;
but for both houses of Israel he will be
a stone that causes men to stumble
and a rock that makes them fall.
And for the people of Jerusalem he will
be
a trap and a snare.
15Many of them will stumble;
they will fall and be broken,
they will be snared and captured."

16Bind up the testimony
and seal up the law among my
disciples.
17I will wait for the LORD,
who is hiding his face from the house of
Jacob.
I will put my trust in him.

18Here am I, and the children the LORD has
given me. We are signs and symbols in Israel from the LORD Almighty, who dwells on
Mount Zion.
19When men tell you to consult mediums
and spiritists, who whisper and mutter,
should not a people inquire of their God?
Why consult the dead on behalf of the living?
20To the law and to the testimony! If they do
not speak according to this word, they have
no light of dawn. 21Distressed and hungry,
they will roam through the land; when they
are famished, they will become enraged and,
looking upward, will curse their king and their
God. 22Then they will look toward the earth
and see only distress and darkness and fearful gloom, and they will be thrust into utter
darkness.

To Us a Child Is Born

9 Nevertheless, there will be no more
gloom for those who were in distress. In
the past he humbled the land of Zebulun and
the land of Naphtali, but in the future he will
honor Galilee of the Gentiles, by the way of
the sea, along the Jordan—

2The people walking in darkness
have seen a great light;
on those living in the land of the shadow
of death[e]
a light has dawned.
3You have enlarged the nation
and increased their joy;
they rejoice before you
as people rejoice at the harvest,
as men rejoice
when dividing the plunder.
4For as in the day of Midian's defeat,
you have shattered
the yoke that burdens them,
the bar across their shoulders,
the rod of their oppressor.
5Every warrior's boot used in battle
and every garment rolled in blood
will be destined for burning,
will be fuel for the fire.
6For to us a child is born,
to us a son is given,
and the government will be on his
shoulders.
And he will be called
Wonderful Counselor,[f] Mighty God,
Everlasting Father, Prince of Peace.
7Of the increase of his government and
peace
there will be no end.
He will reign on David's throne
and over his kingdom,
establishing and upholding it
with justice and righteousness

[a]8 *Immanuel* means *God with us.* [b]9 Or *Do your worst* [c]10 Hebrew *Immanuel* [d]12 Or *Do not call for a treaty / every time these people call for a treaty* [e]2 Or *land of darkness* [f]6 Or *Wonderful, Counselor*

from that time on and forever.
The zeal of the LORD Almighty
will accomplish this.

The LORD's Anger Against Israel

8The Lord has sent a message against Jacob;
it will fall on Israel.
9All the people will know it—
Ephraim and the inhabitants of Samaria—
who say with pride
and arrogance of heart,
10"The bricks have fallen down,
but we will rebuild with dressed stone;
the fig trees have been felled,
but we will replace them with cedars."
11But the LORD has strengthened Rezin's foes against them
and has spurred their enemies on.
12Arameans from the east and Philistines from the west
have devoured Israel with open mouth.

Yet for all this, his anger is not turned away,
his hand is still upraised.

13But the people have not returned to him who struck them,
nor have they sought the LORD Almighty.
14So the LORD will cut off from Israel both head and tail,
both palm branch and reed in a single day;
15the elders and prominent men are the head,
the prophets who teach lies are the tail.
16Those who guide this people mislead them,
and those who are guided are led astray.
17Therefore the Lord will take no pleasure in the young men,
nor will he pity the fatherless and widows,
for everyone is ungodly and wicked,
every mouth speaks vileness.

Yet for all this, his anger is not turned away,
his hand is still upraised.

18Surely wickedness burns like a fire;
it consumes briers and thorns,
it sets the forest thickets ablaze,
so that it rolls upward in a column of smoke.
19By the wrath of the LORD Almighty
the land will be scorched
and the people will be fuel for the fire;
no one will spare his brother.
20On the right they will devour,
but still be hungry;
on the left they will eat,
but not be satisfied.
Each will feed on the flesh of his own offspring[a]:
21 Manasseh will feed on Ephraim, and Ephraim on Manasseh;
together they will turn against Judah.

Yet for all this, his anger is not turned away,
his hand is still upraised.

10 Woe to those who make unjust laws,
to those who issue oppressive decrees,
2to deprive the poor of their rights
and withhold justice from the oppressed of my people,
making widows their prey
and robbing the fatherless.
3What will you do on the day of reckoning,
when disaster comes from afar?
To whom will you run for help?
Where will you leave your riches?
4Nothing will remain but to cringe among the captives
or fall among the slain.

Yet for all this, his anger is not turned away,
his hand is still upraised.

God's Judgment on Assyria

5"Woe to the Assyrian, the rod of my anger,
in whose hand is the club of my wrath!
6I send him against a godless nation,
I dispatch him against a people who anger me,
to seize loot and snatch plunder,
and to trample them down like mud in the streets.
7But this is not what he intends,
this is not what he has in mind;
his purpose is to destroy,
to put an end to many nations.
8'Are not my commanders all kings?' he says.

[a]20 Or *arm*

9 'Has not Calno fared like Carchemish?
Is not Hamath like Arpad,
and Samaria like Damascus?
10 As my hand seized the kingdoms of the idols,
kingdoms whose images excelled those of Jerusalem and Samaria—
11 shall I not deal with Jerusalem and her images
as I dealt with Samaria and her idols?' "

12 When the Lord has finished all his work
against Mount Zion and Jerusalem, he will
say, "I will punish the king of Assyria for the
willful pride of his heart and the haughty look
in his eyes. 13 For he says:

" 'By the strength of my hand I have done this,
and by my wisdom, because I have understanding.
I removed the boundaries of nations,
I plundered their treasures;
like a mighty one I subdued[a] their kings.
14 As one reaches into a nest,
so my hand reached for the wealth of the nations;
as men gather abandoned eggs,
so I gathered all the countries;
not one flapped a wing,
or opened its mouth to chirp.' "

15 Does the ax raise itself above him who swings it,
or the saw boast against him who uses it?
As if a rod were to wield him who lifts it up,
or a club brandish him who is not wood!
16 Therefore, the Lord, the LORD Almighty,
will send a wasting disease upon his sturdy warriors;
under his pomp a fire will be kindled
like a blazing flame.
17 The Light of Israel will become a fire,
their Holy One a flame;
in a single day it will burn and consume
his thorns and his briers.
18 The splendor of his forests and fertile fields
it will completely destroy,
as when a sick man wastes away.
19 And the remaining trees of his forests will be so few
that a child could write them down.

The Remnant of Israel

20 In that day the remnant of Israel,
the survivors of the house of Jacob,
will no longer rely on him
who struck them down
but will truly rely on the LORD,
the Holy One of Israel.
21 A remnant will return,[b] a remnant of Jacob
will return to the Mighty God.
22 Though your people, O Israel, be like the sand by the sea,
only a remnant will return.
Destruction has been decreed,
overwhelming and righteous.
23 The Lord, the LORD Almighty, will carry out
the destruction decreed upon the whole land.

24 Therefore, this is what the Lord, the LORD
Almighty, says:

"O my people who live in Zion,
do not be afraid of the Assyrians,
who beat you with a rod
and lift up a club against you, as Egypt did.
25 Very soon my anger against you will end
and my wrath will be directed to their destruction."

26 The LORD Almighty will lash them with a whip,
as when he struck down Midian at the rock of Oreb;
and he will raise his staff over the waters,
as he did in Egypt.
27 In that day their burden will be lifted from your shoulders,
their yoke from your neck;
the yoke will be broken
because you have grown so fat.[c]

28 They enter Aiath;
they pass through Migron;
they store supplies at Micmash.
29 They go over the pass, and say,
"We will camp overnight at Geba."
Ramah trembles;
Gibeah of Saul flees.

[a] *13* Or / *I subdued the mighty,*
[b] *21* Hebrew *shear-jashub*; also in verse 22
[c] *27* Hebrew; Septuagint *broken / from your shoulders*

[30]Cry out, O Daughter of Gallim!
Listen, O Laishah!
Poor Anathoth!
[31]Madmenah is in flight;
the people of Gebim take cover.
[32]This day they will halt at Nob;
they will shake their fist
at the mount of the Daughter of Zion,
at the hill of Jerusalem.

[33]See, the Lord, the LORD Almighty,
will lop off the boughs with great power.
The lofty trees will be felled,
the tall ones will be brought low.
[34]He will cut down the forest thickets with an ax;
Lebanon will fall before the Mighty One.

The Branch From Jesse

11 A shoot will come up from the stump of Jesse;
from his roots a Branch will bear fruit.
[2]The Spirit of the LORD will rest on him—
the Spirit of wisdom and of understanding,
the Spirit of counsel and of power,
the Spirit of knowledge and of the fear of the LORD—
[3]and he will delight in the fear of the LORD.
He will not judge by what he sees with his eyes,
or decide by what he hears with his ears;
[4]but with righteousness he will judge the needy,
with justice he will give decisions for the poor of the earth.
He will strike the earth with the rod of his mouth;
with the breath of his lips he will slay the wicked.
[5]Righteousness will be his belt
and faithfulness the sash around his waist.
[6]The wolf will live with the lamb,
the leopard will lie down with the goat,
the calf and the lion and the yearling[a] together;
and a little child will lead them.
[7]The cow will feed with the bear,
their young will lie down together,
and the lion will eat straw like the ox.
[8]The infant will play near the hole of the cobra,
and the young child put his hand into the viper's nest.
[9]They will neither harm nor destroy
on all my holy mountain,
for the earth will be full of the knowledge of the LORD
as the waters cover the sea.

[10]In that day the Root of Jesse will stand as
a banner for the peoples; the nations will rally
to him, and his place of rest will be glorious.
[11]In that day the Lord will reach out his hand
a second time to reclaim the remnant that is
left of his people from Assyria, from Lower
Egypt, from Upper Egypt,[b] from Cush,[c] from
Elam, from Babylonia,[d] from Hamath and
from the islands of the sea.

[12]He will raise a banner for the nations
and gather the exiles of Israel;
he will assemble the scattered people of Judah
from the four quarters of the earth.
[13]Ephraim's jealousy will vanish,
and Judah's enemies[e] will be cut off;
Ephraim will not be jealous of Judah,
nor Judah hostile toward Ephraim.
[14]They will swoop down on the slopes of Philistia to the west;
together they will plunder the people to the east.
They will lay hands on Edom and Moab,
and the Ammonites will be subject to them.
[15]The LORD will dry up
the gulf of the Egyptian sea;
with a scorching wind he will sweep his hand
over the Euphrates River.[f]
He will break it up into seven streams
so that men can cross over in sandals.
[16]There will be a highway for the remnant of his people
that is left from Assyria,
as there was for Israel
when they came up from Egypt.

Songs of Praise

12 In that day you will say:
"I will praise you, O LORD.
Although you were angry with me,
your anger has turned away
and you have comforted me.
[2]Surely God is my salvation;
I will trust and not be afraid.

[a]6 Hebrew; Septuagint *lion will feed* [b]11 Hebrew *from Pathros* [c]11 That is, the upper Nile region
[d]11 Hebrew *Shinar* [e]13 Or *hostility* [f]15 Hebrew *the River*

The LORD, the LORD, is my strength and
my song;
he has become my salvation."
3 With joy you will draw water
from the wells of salvation.

4 In that day you will say:

"Give thanks to the LORD, call on his
name;
make known among the nations what
he has done,
and proclaim that his name is exalted.
5 Sing to the LORD, for he has done glorious
things;
let this be known to all the world.
6 Shout aloud and sing for joy, people of
Zion,
for great is the Holy One of Israel
among you."

A Prophecy Against Babylon

13 An oracle concerning Babylon that Isaiah son of Amoz saw:

2 Raise a banner on a bare hilltop,
shout to them;
beckon to them
to enter the gates of the nobles.
3 I have commanded my holy ones;
I have summoned my warriors to carry
out my wrath—
those who rejoice in my triumph.

4 Listen, a noise on the mountains,
like that of a great multitude!
Listen, an uproar among the kingdoms,
like nations massing together!
The LORD Almighty is mustering
an army for war.
5 They come from faraway lands,
from the ends of the heavens—
the LORD and the weapons of his wrath—
to destroy the whole country.

6 Wail, for the day of the LORD is near;
it will come like destruction from the
Almighty.[a]
7 Because of this, all hands will go limp,
every man's heart will melt.
8 Terror will seize them,
pain and anguish will grip them;
they will writhe like a woman in labor.
They will look aghast at each other,
their faces aflame.

9 See, the day of the LORD is coming
—a cruel day, with wrath and fierce
anger—
to make the land desolate
and destroy the sinners within it.
10 The stars of heaven and their
constellations
will not show their light.
The rising sun will be darkened
and the moon will not give its light.
11 I will punish the world for its evil,
the wicked for their sins.
I will put an end to the arrogance of the
haughty
and will humble the pride of the
ruthless.
12 I will make man scarcer than pure gold,
more rare than the gold of Ophir.
13 Therefore I will make the heavens
tremble;
and the earth will shake from its place
at the wrath of the LORD Almighty,
in the day of his burning anger.

14 Like a hunted gazelle,
like sheep without a shepherd,
each will return to his own people,
each will flee to his native land.
15 Whoever is captured will be thrust
through;
all who are caught will fall by the sword.
16 Their infants will be dashed to pieces
before their eyes;
their houses will be looted and their
wives ravished.

17 See, I will stir up against them the
Medes,
who do not care for silver
and have no delight in gold.
18 Their bows will strike down the young
men;
they will have no mercy on infants
nor will they look with compassion on
children.
19 Babylon, the jewel of kingdoms,
the glory of the Babylonians'[b] pride,
will be overthrown by God
like Sodom and Gomorrah.
20 She will never be inhabited
or lived in through all generations;
no Arab will pitch his tent there,
no shepherd will rest his flocks there.
21 But desert creatures will lie there,
jackals will fill her houses;
there the owls will dwell,

[a] 6 Hebrew *Shaddai* [b] 19 Or *Chaldeans'*

and there the wild goats will leap about.
22Hyenas will howl in her strongholds,
jackals in her luxurious palaces.
Her time is at hand,
and her days will not be prolonged.

14 The LORD will have compassion on Jacob;
once again he will choose Israel
and will settle them in their own land.
Aliens will join them
and unite with the house of Jacob.
2Nations will take them
and bring them to their own place.
And the house of Israel will possess the nations
as menservants and maidservants in the LORD's land.
They will make captives of their captors
and rule over their oppressors.

3On the day the LORD gives you relief from
suffering and turmoil and cruel bondage,
4you will take up this taunt against the king of
Babylon:

How the oppressor has come to an end!
How his fury[a] has ended!
5The LORD has broken the rod of the wicked,
the scepter of the rulers,
6which in anger struck down peoples
with unceasing blows,
and in fury subdued nations
with relentless aggression.
7All the lands are at rest and at peace;
they break into singing.
8Even the pine trees and the cedars of Lebanon
exult over you and say,
"Now that you have been laid low,
no woodsman comes to cut us down."
9The grave[b] below is all astir
to meet you at your coming;
it rouses the spirits of the departed to greet you—
all those who were leaders in the world;
it makes them rise from their thrones—
all those who were kings over the nations.
10They will all respond,
they will say to you,
"You also have become weak, as we are;
you have become like us."
11All your pomp has been brought down to the grave,
along with the noise of your harps;
maggots are spread out beneath you
and worms cover you.

12How you have fallen from heaven,
O morning star, son of the dawn!
You have been cast down to the earth,
you who once laid low the nations!
13You said in your heart,
"I will ascend to heaven;
I will raise my throne
above the stars of God;
I will sit enthroned on the mount of assembly,
on the utmost heights of the sacred mountain.[c]
14I will ascend above the tops of the clouds;
I will make myself like the Most High."
15But you are brought down to the grave,
to the depths of the pit.

16Those who see you stare at you,
they ponder your fate:
"Is this the man who shook the earth
and made kingdoms tremble,
17the man who made the world a desert,
who overthrew its cities
and would not let his captives go home?"

18All the kings of the nations lie in state,
each in his own tomb.
19But you are cast out of your tomb
like a rejected branch;
you are covered with the slain,
with those pierced by the sword,
those who descend to the stones of the pit.
Like a corpse trampled underfoot,
20 you will not join them in burial,
for you have destroyed your land
and killed your people.

The offspring of the wicked
will never be mentioned again.
21Prepare a place to slaughter his sons
for the sins of their forefathers;
they are not to rise to inherit the land
and cover the earth with their cities.

22"I will rise up against them,"
declares the LORD Almighty.

[a]4 Dead Sea Scrolls, Septuagint and Syriac; the meaning of the word in the Masoretic Text is uncertain.
[b]9 Hebrew *Sheol*; also in verses 11 and 15 [c]13 Or *the north;* Hebrew *Zaphon*

"I will cut off from Babylon her name and survivors,
her offspring and descendants,"
declares the LORD.
23"I will turn her into a place for owls
and into swampland;
I will sweep her with the broom of destruction,"
declares the LORD Almighty.

A Prophecy Against Assyria

24The LORD Almighty has sworn,

"Surely, as I have planned, so it will be,
and as I have purposed, so it will stand.
25I will crush the Assyrian in my land;
on my mountains I will trample him down.
His yoke will be taken from my people,
and his burden removed from their shoulders."
26This is the plan determined for the whole world;
this is the hand stretched out over all nations.
27For the LORD Almighty has purposed, and who can thwart him?
His hand is stretched out, and who can turn it back?

A Prophecy Against the Philistines

28This oracle came in the year King Ahaz died:

29Do not rejoice, all you Philistines,
that the rod that struck you is broken;
from the root of that snake will spring up a viper,
its fruit will be a darting, venomous serpent.
30The poorest of the poor will find pasture,
and the needy will lie down in safety.
But your root I will destroy by famine;
it will slay your survivors.

31Wail, O gate! Howl, O city!
Melt away, all you Philistines!
A cloud of smoke comes from the north,
and there is not a straggler in its ranks.
32What answer shall be given
to the envoys of that nation?
"The LORD has established Zion,
and in her his afflicted people will find refuge."

A Prophecy Against Moab

15 An oracle concerning Moab:

Ar in Moab is ruined,
destroyed in a night!
Kir in Moab is ruined,
destroyed in a night!
2Dibon goes up to its temple,
to its high places to weep;
Moab wails over Nebo and Medeba.
Every head is shaved
and every beard cut off.
3In the streets they wear sackcloth;
on the roofs and in the public squares
they all wail,
prostrate with weeping.
4Heshbon and Elealeh cry out,
their voices are heard all the way to Jahaz.
Therefore the armed men of Moab cry out,
and their hearts are faint.

5My heart cries out over Moab;
her fugitives flee as far as Zoar,
as far as Eglath Shelishiyah.
They go up the way to Luhith,
weeping as they go;
on the road to Horonaim
they lament their destruction.
6The waters of Nimrim are dried up
and the grass is withered;
the vegetation is gone
and nothing green is left.
7So the wealth they have acquired and stored up
they carry away over the Ravine of the Poplars.
8Their outcry echoes along the border of Moab;
their wailing reaches as far as Eglaim,
their lamentation as far as Beer Elim.
9Dimon's[a] waters are full of blood,
but I will bring still more upon Dimon[a]—
a lion upon the fugitives of Moab
and upon those who remain in the land.

16 Send lambs as tribute
to the ruler of the land,
from Sela, across the desert,
to the mount of the Daughter of Zion.
2Like fluttering birds
pushed from the nest,

[a]9 Masoretic Text; Dead Sea Scrolls, some Septuagint manuscripts and Vulgate *Dibon*

so are the women of Moab
at the fords of the Arnon.

3"Give us counsel,
render a decision.
Make your shadow like night—
at high noon.
Hide the fugitives,
do not betray the refugees.
4Let the Moabite fugitives stay with you;
be their shelter from the destroyer."

The oppressor will come to an end,
and destruction will cease;
the aggressor will vanish from the land.
5In love a throne will be established;
in faithfulness a man will sit on it—
one from the house[a] of David—
one who in judging seeks justice
and speeds the cause of
righteousness.

6We have heard of Moab's pride—
her overweening pride and conceit,
her pride and her insolence—
but her boasts are empty.
7Therefore the Moabites wail,
they wail together for Moab.
Lament and grieve
for the men[b] of Kir Hareseth.
8The fields of Heshbon wither,
the vines of Sibmah also.
The rulers of the nations
have trampled down the choicest vines,
which once reached Jazer
and spread toward the desert.
Their shoots spread out
and went as far as the sea.
9So I weep, as Jazer weeps,
for the vines of Sibmah.
O Heshbon, O Elealeh,
I drench you with tears!
The shouts of joy over your ripened fruit
and over your harvests have been
stilled.
10Joy and gladness are taken away from
the orchards;
no one sings or shouts in the
vineyards;
no one treads out wine at the presses,
for I have put an end to the shouting.
11My heart laments for Moab like a harp,
my inmost being for Kir Hareseth.
12When Moab appears at her high place,
she only wears herself out;
when she goes to her shrine to pray,
it is to no avail.

13This is the word the LORD has already
spoken concerning Moab. 14But now the
LORD says: "Within three years, as a servant
bound by contract would count them, Moab's
splendor and all her many people will be
despised, and her survivors will be very few
and feeble."

An Oracle Against Damascus

17 An oracle concerning Damascus:
"See, Damascus will no longer be a
city
but will become a heap of ruins.
2The cities of Aroer will be deserted
and left to flocks, which will lie down,
with no one to make them afraid.
3The fortified city will disappear from
Ephraim,
and royal power from Damascus;
the remnant of Aram will be
like the glory of the Israelites,"
declares the LORD Almighty.

4"In that day the glory of Jacob will fade;
the fat of his body will waste away.
5It will be as when a reaper gathers the
standing grain
and harvests the grain with his arm—
as when a man gleans heads of grain
in the Valley of Rephaim.
6Yet some gleanings will remain,
as when an olive tree is beaten,
leaving two or three olives on the topmost
branches,
four or five on the fruitful boughs,"
declares the LORD,
the God of Israel.

7In that day men will look to their Maker
and turn their eyes to the Holy One of
Israel.
8They will not look to the altars,
the work of their hands,
and they will have no regard for the
Asherah poles[c]
and the incense altars their fingers
have made.

9In that day their strong cities, which they
left because of the Israelites, will be like
places abandoned to thickets and undergrowth. And all will be desolation.

10You have forgotten God your Savior;
you have not remembered the Rock,
your fortress.

[a]5 Hebrew *tent* [b]7 Or "*raisin cakes*," a wordplay [c]8 That is, symbols of the goddess Asherah

Therefore, though you set out the finest plants
and plant imported vines,
11 though on the day you set them out, you make them grow,
and on the morning when you plant them, you bring them to bud,
yet the harvest will be as nothing
in the day of disease and incurable pain.

12 Oh, the raging of many nations—
they rage like the raging sea!
Oh, the uproar of the peoples—
they roar like the roaring of great waters!
13 Although the peoples roar like the roar of surging waters,
when he rebukes them they flee far away,
driven before the wind like chaff on the hills,
like tumbleweed before a gale.
14 In the evening, sudden terror!
Before the morning, they are gone!
This is the portion of those who loot us,
the lot of those who plunder us.

A Prophecy Against Cush

18 Woe to the land of whirring wings[a]
along the rivers of Cush,[b]
2 which sends envoys by sea
in papyrus boats over the water.

Go, swift messengers,
to a people tall and smooth-skinned,
to a people feared far and wide,
an aggressive nation of strange speech,
whose land is divided by rivers.

3 All you people of the world,
you who live on the earth,
when a banner is raised on the mountains,
you will see it,
and when a trumpet sounds,
you will hear it.
4 This is what the LORD says to me:
"I will remain quiet and will look on from my dwelling place,
like shimmering heat in the sunshine,
like a cloud of dew in the heat of harvest."
5 For, before the harvest, when the blossom is gone
and the flower becomes a ripening grape,
he will cut off the shoots with pruning knives,
and cut down and take away the spreading branches.
6 They will all be left to the mountain birds of prey
and to the wild animals;
the birds will feed on them all summer,
the wild animals all winter.

7 At that time gifts will be brought to the
LORD Almighty

from a people tall and smooth-skinned,
from a people feared far and wide,
an aggressive nation of strange speech,
whose land is divided by rivers—

the gifts will be brought to Mount Zion, the
place of the Name of the LORD Almighty.

A Prophecy About Egypt

19 An oracle concerning Egypt:

See, the LORD rides on a swift cloud
and is coming to Egypt.
The idols of Egypt tremble before him,
and the hearts of the Egyptians melt within them.

2 "I will stir up Egyptian against Egyptian—
brother will fight against brother,
neighbor against neighbor,
city against city,
kingdom against kingdom.
3 The Egyptians will lose heart,
and I will bring their plans to nothing;
they will consult the idols and the spirits of the dead,
the mediums and the spiritists.
4 I will hand the Egyptians over
to the power of a cruel master,
and a fierce king will rule over them,"
declares the Lord, the LORD Almighty.

5 The waters of the river will dry up,
and the riverbed will be parched and dry.
6 The canals will stink;
the streams of Egypt will dwindle and dry up.
The reeds and rushes will wither,
7 also the plants along the Nile,
at the mouth of the river.

[a] *1* Or *of locusts* [b] *1* That is, the upper Nile region

Every sown field along the Nile
will become parched, will blow away
and be no more.
8The fishermen will groan and lament,
all who cast hooks into the Nile;
those who throw nets on the water
will pine away.
9Those who work with combed flax will
despair,
the weavers of fine linen will lose hope.
10The workers in cloth will be dejected,
and all the wage earners will be sick at
heart.

11The officials of Zoan are nothing but
fools;
the wise counselors of Pharaoh give
senseless advice.
How can you say to Pharaoh,
"I am one of the wise men,
a disciple of the ancient kings"?
12Where are your wise men now?
Let them show you and make known
what the LORD Almighty
has planned against Egypt.
13The officials of Zoan have become fools,
the leaders of Memphis[a] are deceived;
the cornerstones of her peoples
have led Egypt astray.
14The LORD has poured into them
a spirit of dizziness;
they make Egypt stagger in all that she
does,
as a drunkard staggers around in his
vomit.
15There is nothing Egypt can do—
head or tail, palm branch or reed.

16In that day the Egyptians will be like
women. They will shudder with fear at the
uplifted hand that the LORD Almighty raises
against them. 17And the land of Judah will
bring terror to the Egyptians; everyone to
whom Judah is mentioned will be terrified,
because of what the LORD Almighty is planning against them.
18In that day five cities in Egypt will speak
the language of Canaan and swear allegiance to the LORD Almighty. One of them will
be called the City of Destruction.[b]
19In that day there will be an altar to the
LORD in the heart of Egypt, and a monument
to the LORD at its border. 20It will be a sign and
witness to the LORD Almighty in the land of
Egypt. When they cry out to the LORD because of their oppressors, he will send them
a savior and defender, and he will rescue
them. 21So the LORD will make himself known
to the Egyptians, and in that day they will
acknowledge the LORD. They will worship
with sacrifices and grain offerings; they will
make vows to the LORD and keep them. 22The
LORD will strike Egypt with a plague; he will
strike them and heal them. They will turn to
the LORD, and he will respond to their pleas
and heal them.
23In that day there will be a highway from
Egypt to Assyria. The Assyrians will go to
Egypt and the Egyptians to Assyria. The
Egyptians and Assyrians will worship together. 24In that day Israel will be the third,
along with Egypt and Assyria, a blessing on
the earth. 25The LORD Almighty will bless
them, saying, "Blessed be Egypt my people,
Assyria my handiwork, and Israel my inheritance."

A Prophecy Against Egypt and Cush

20 In the year that the supreme commander, sent by Sargon king of Assyria, came to Ashdod and attacked and
captured it— 2at that time the LORD spoke
through Isaiah son of Amoz. He said to him,
"Take off the sackcloth from your body and
the sandals from your feet." And he did so,
going around stripped and barefoot.
3Then the LORD said, "Just as my servant
Isaiah has gone stripped and barefoot for
three years, as a sign and portent against
Egypt and Cush,[c] 4so the king of Assyria will
lead away stripped and barefoot the Egyptian captives and Cushite exiles, young and
old, with buttocks bared—to Egypt's shame.
5Those who trusted in Cush and boasted in
Egypt will be afraid and put to shame. 6In that
day the people who live on this coast will say,
'See what has happened to those we relied
on, those we fled to for help and deliverance
from the king of Assyria! How then can we
escape?' "

A Prophecy Against Babylon

21 An oracle concerning the Desert by
the Sea:

Like whirlwinds sweeping through the
southland,

[a] *13* Hebrew *Noph* [b] *18* Most manuscripts of the Masoretic Text; some manuscripts of the Masoretic Text, Dead Sea Scrolls and Vulgate *City of the Sun* (that is, Heliopolis) [c] *3* That is, the upper Nile region; also in verse 5

an invader comes from the desert,
from a land of terror.

2A dire vision has been shown to me:
The traitor betrays, the looter takes loot.
Elam, attack! Media, lay siege!
I will bring to an end all the groaning she caused.

3At this my body is racked with pain,
pangs seize me, like those of a woman in labor;
I am staggered by what I hear,
I am bewildered by what I see.
4My heart falters,
fear makes me tremble;
the twilight I longed for
has become a horror to me.

5They set the tables,
they spread the rugs,
they eat, they drink!
Get up, you officers,
oil the shields!

6This is what the Lord says to me:

"Go, post a lookout
and have him report what he sees.
7When he sees chariots
with teams of horses,
riders on donkeys
or riders on camels,
let him be alert,
fully alert."

8And the lookout[a] shouted,

"Day after day, my lord, I stand on the watchtower;
every night I stay at my post.
9Look, here comes a man in a chariot
with a team of horses.
And he gives back the answer:
'Babylon has fallen, has fallen!
All the images of its gods
lie shattered on the ground!' "

10O my people, crushed on the threshing floor,
I tell you what I have heard
from the LORD Almighty,
from the God of Israel.

A Prophecy Against Edom

11An oracle concerning Dumah[b]:

Someone calls to me from Seir,
"Watchman, what is left of the night?
Watchman, what is left of the night?"
12The watchman replies,
"Morning is coming, but also the night.
If you would ask, then ask;
and come back yet again."

A Prophecy Against Arabia

13An oracle concerning Arabia:

You caravans of Dedanites,
who camp in the thickets of Arabia,
14 bring water for the thirsty;
you who live in Tema,
bring food for the fugitives.
15They flee from the sword,
from the drawn sword,
from the bent bow
and from the heat of battle.

16This is what the Lord says to me: "Within
one year, as a servant bound by contract
would count it, all the pomp of Kedar will
come to an end. 17The survivors of the bow-
men, the warriors of Kedar, will be few." The
LORD, the God of Israel, has spoken.

A Prophecy About Jerusalem

22 An oracle concerning the Valley of Vision:

What troubles you now,
that you have all gone up on the roofs,
2O town full of commotion,
O city of tumult and revelry?
Your slain were not killed by the sword,
nor did they die in battle.
3All your leaders have fled together;
they have been captured without using the bow.
All you who were caught were taken prisoner together,
having fled while the enemy was still far away.
4Therefore I said, "Turn away from me;
let me weep bitterly.
Do not try to console me
over the destruction of my people."

5The Lord, the LORD Almighty, has a day
of tumult and trampling and terror
in the Valley of Vision,
a day of battering down walls
and of crying out to the mountains.
6Elam takes up the quiver,
with her charioteers and horses;

[a]8 Dead Sea Scrolls and Syriac; Masoretic Text *A lion*

[b]11 *Dumah* means *silence* or *stillness*, a wordplay on *Edom*.

Kir uncovers the shield.
7Your choicest valleys are full of chariots,
and horsemen are posted at the city gates;
8 the defenses of Judah are stripped away.

And you looked in that day
to the weapons in the Palace of the Forest;
9you saw that the City of David
had many breaches in its defenses;
you stored up water
in the Lower Pool.
10You counted the buildings in Jerusalem
and tore down houses to strengthen the wall.
11You built a reservoir between the two walls
for the water of the Old Pool,
but you did not look to the One who made it,
or have regard for the One who planned it long ago.

12The Lord, the LORD Almighty,
called you on that day
to weep and to wail,
to tear out your hair and put on sackcloth.
13But see, there is joy and revelry,
slaughtering of cattle and killing of sheep,
eating of meat and drinking of wine!
"Let us eat and drink," you say,
"for tomorrow we die!"

14The LORD Almighty has revealed this in
my hearing: "Till your dying day this sin will
not be atoned for," says the Lord, the LORD
Almighty.

15This is what the Lord, the LORD Almighty,
says:

"Go, say to this steward,
to Shebna, who is in charge of the palace:
16What are you doing here and who gave you permission
to cut out a grave for yourself here,
hewing your grave on the height
and chiseling your resting place in the rock?
17"Beware, the LORD is about to take firm hold of you
and hurl you away, O you mighty man.
18He will roll you up tightly like a ball
and throw you into a large country.
There you will die
and there your splendid chariots will remain—
you disgrace to your master's house!
19I will depose you from your office,
and you will be ousted from your position.

20"In that day I will summon my servant,
Eliakim son of Hilkiah. 21I will clothe him with
your robe and fasten your sash around him
and hand your authority over to him. He will
be a father to those who live in Jerusalem
and to the house of Judah. 22I will place on
his shoulder the key to the house of David;
what he opens no one can shut, and what he
shuts no one can open. 23I will drive him like
a peg into a firm place; he will be a seat[a] of
honor for the house of his father. 24All the
glory of his family will hang on him: its offspring and offshoots—all its lesser vessels,
from the bowls to all the jars.

25"In that day," declares the LORD Almighty, "the peg driven into the firm place
will give way; it will be sheared off and will
fall, and the load hanging on it will be cut
down." The LORD has spoken.

A Prophecy About Tyre

23 An oracle concerning Tyre:

Wail, O ships of Tarshish!
For Tyre is destroyed
and left without house or harbor.
From the land of Cyprus[b]
word has come to them.

2Be silent, you people of the island
and you merchants of Sidon,
whom the seafarers have enriched.
3On the great waters
came the grain of the Shihor;
the harvest of the Nile[c] was the revenue of Tyre,
and she became the marketplace of the nations.

4Be ashamed, O Sidon, and you, O fortress of the sea,
for the sea has spoken:
"I have neither been in labor nor given birth;

[a]23 Or *throne* [b]1,12 Hebrew *Kittim* [c]2,3 Masoretic Text; one Dead Sea Scroll *Sidon, / who cross over the sea; / your envoys* [3]*are on the great waters. / The grain of the Shihor, / the harvest of the Nile,*

I have neither reared sons nor brought
up daughters."
5When word comes to Egypt,
they will be in anguish at the report
from Tyre.

6Cross over to Tarshish;
wail, you people of the island.
7Is this your city of revelry,
the old, old city,
whose feet have taken her
to settle in far-off lands?
8Who planned this against Tyre,
the bestower of crowns,
whose merchants are princes,
whose traders are renowned in the
earth?
9The LORD Almighty planned it,
to bring low the pride of all glory
and to humble all who are renowned on
the earth.

10Till[a] your land as along the Nile,
O Daughter of Tarshish,
for you no longer have a harbor.
11The LORD has stretched out his hand over
the sea
and made its kingdoms tremble.
He has given an order concerning
Phoenicia[b]
that her fortresses be destroyed.
12He said, "No more of your reveling,
O Virgin Daughter of Sidon, now
crushed!

"Up, cross over to Cyprus[c];
even there you will find no rest."
13Look at the land of the Babylonians,[d]
this people that is now of no account!
The Assyrians have made it
a place for desert creatures;
they raised up their siege towers,
they stripped its fortresses bare
and turned it into a ruin.

14Wail, you ships of Tarshish;
your fortress is destroyed!

15At that time Tyre will be forgotten for seventy years, the span of a king's life. But at the
end of these seventy years, it will happen to
Tyre as in the song of the prostitute:

16"Take up a harp, walk through the city,
O prostitute forgotten;
play the harp well, sing many a song,
so that you will be remembered."

17At the end of seventy years, the LORD will
deal with Tyre. She will return to her hire as a
prostitute and will ply her trade with all the
kingdoms on the face of the earth. 18Yet her
profit and her earnings will be set apart for
the LORD; they will not be stored up or hoarded. Her profits will go to those who live before
the LORD, for abundant food and fine clothes.

The LORD's Devastation of the Earth

24 See, the LORD is going to lay waste
the earth
and devastate it;
he will ruin its face
and scatter its inhabitants—
2it will be the same
for priest as for people,
for master as for servant,
for mistress as for maid,
for seller as for buyer,
for borrower as for lender,
for debtor as for creditor.
3The earth will be completely laid waste
and totally plundered.
The LORD has spoken this word.

4The earth dries up and withers,
the world languishes and withers,
the exalted of the earth languish.
5The earth is defiled by its people;
they have disobeyed the laws,
violated the statutes
and broken the everlasting covenant.
6Therefore a curse consumes the earth;
its people must bear their guilt.
Therefore earth's inhabitants are burned
up,
and very few are left.
7The new wine dries up and the vine
withers;
all the merrymakers groan.
8The gaiety of the tambourines is stilled,
the noise of the revelers has stopped,
the joyful harp is silent.
9No longer do they drink wine with a song;
the beer is bitter to its drinkers.
10The ruined city lies desolate;
the entrance to every house is barred.
11In the streets they cry out for wine;
all joy turns to gloom,
all gaiety is banished from the earth.
12The city is left in ruins,
its gate is battered to pieces.
13So will it be on the earth

[a]*10* Dead Sea Scrolls and some Septuagint manuscripts; Masoretic Text *Go through* [b]*11* Hebrew *Canaan*
[c]*12* Hebrew *Kittim* [d]*13* Or *Chaldeans*

and among the nations,
as when an olive tree is beaten,
or as when gleanings are left after the grape harvest.
14They raise their voices, they shout for joy;
from the west they acclaim the LORD's majesty.
15Therefore in the east give glory to the LORD;
exalt the name of the LORD, the God of Israel,
in the islands of the sea.
16From the ends of the earth we hear singing:
"Glory to the Righteous One."

But I said, "I waste away, I waste away!
Woe to me!
The treacherous betray!
With treachery the treacherous betray!"
17Terror and pit and snare await you,
O people of the earth.
18Whoever flees at the sound of terror
will fall into a pit;
whoever climbs out of the pit
will be caught in a snare.

The floodgates of the heavens are opened,
the foundations of the earth shake.
19The earth is broken up,
the earth is split asunder,
the earth is thoroughly shaken.
20The earth reels like a drunkard,
it sways like a hut in the wind;
so heavy upon it is the guilt of its rebellion
that it falls—never to rise again.

21In that day the LORD will punish
the powers in the heavens above
and the kings on the earth below.
22They will be herded together
like prisoners bound in a dungeon;
they will be shut up in prison
and be punished[a] after many days.
23The moon will be abashed, the sun ashamed;
for the LORD Almighty will reign
on Mount Zion and in Jerusalem,
and before its elders, gloriously.

Praise to the LORD

25 O LORD, you are my God;
I will exalt you and praise your name,
for in perfect faithfulness
you have done marvelous things,
things planned long ago.
2You have made the city a heap of rubble,
the fortified town a ruin,
the foreigners' stronghold a city no more;
it will never be rebuilt.
3Therefore strong peoples will honor you;
cities of ruthless nations will revere you.
4You have been a refuge for the poor,
a refuge for the needy in his distress,
a shelter from the storm
and a shade from the heat.
For the breath of the ruthless
is like a storm driving against a wall
5 and like the heat of the desert.
You silence the uproar of foreigners;
as heat is reduced by the shadow of a cloud,
so the song of the ruthless is stilled.

6On this mountain the LORD Almighty will prepare
a feast of rich food for all peoples,
a banquet of aged wine—
the best of meats and the finest of wines.
7On this mountain he will destroy
the shroud that enfolds all peoples,
the sheet that covers all nations;
8 he will swallow up death forever.
The Sovereign LORD will wipe away the tears
from all faces;
he will remove the disgrace of his people
from all the earth.
The LORD has spoken.

9In that day they will say,

"Surely this is our God;
we trusted in him, and he saved us.
This is the LORD, we trusted in him;
let us rejoice and be glad in his salvation."

10The hand of the LORD will rest on this mountain;
but Moab will be trampled under him
as straw is trampled down in the manure.
11They will spread out their hands in it,
as a swimmer spreads out his hands to swim.
God will bring down their pride
despite the cleverness[b] of their hands.

[a]22 Or *released* [b]11 The meaning of the Hebrew for this word is uncertain.

12He will bring down your high fortified
walls
and lay them low;
he will bring them down to the ground,
to the very dust.

A Song of Praise

26 In that day this song will be sung in the land of Judah:

We have a strong city;
God makes salvation
its walls and ramparts.
2Open the gates
that the righteous nation may enter,
the nation that keeps faith.
3You will keep in perfect peace
him whose mind is steadfast,
because he trusts in you.
4Trust in the LORD forever,
for the LORD, the LORD, is the Rock
eternal.
5He humbles those who dwell on high,
he lays the lofty city low;
he levels it to the ground
and casts it down to the dust.
6Feet trample it down—
the feet of the oppressed,
the footsteps of the poor.

7The path of the righteous is level;
O upright One, you make the way of
the righteous smooth.
8Yes, LORD, walking in the way of your
laws,[a]
we wait for you;
your name and renown
are the desire of our hearts.
9My soul yearns for you in the night;
in the morning my spirit longs for you.
When your judgments come upon the
earth,
the people of the world learn
righteousness.
10Though grace is shown to the wicked,
they do not learn righteousness;
even in a land of uprightness they go on
doing evil
and regard not the majesty of the LORD.
11O LORD, your hand is lifted high,
but they do not see it.
Let them see your zeal for your people
and be put to shame;
let the fire reserved for your enemies
consume them.

12LORD, you establish peace for us;
all that we have accomplished you
have done for us.
13O LORD, our God, other lords besides you
have ruled over us,
but your name alone do we honor.
14They are now dead, they live no more;
those departed spirits do not rise.
You punished them and brought them to
ruin;
you wiped out all memory of them.
15You have enlarged the nation, O LORD;
you have enlarged the nation.
You have gained glory for yourself;
you have extended all the borders of
the land.

16LORD, they came to you in their distress;
when you disciplined them,
they could barely whisper a prayer.[b]
17As a woman with child and about to give
birth
writhes and cries out in her pain,
so were we in your presence, O LORD.
18We were with child, we writhed in pain,
but we gave birth to wind.
We have not brought salvation to the
earth;
we have not given birth to people of the
world.

19But your dead will live;
their bodies will rise.
You who dwell in the dust,
wake up and shout for joy.
Your dew is like the dew of the morning;
the earth will give birth to her dead.

20Go, my people, enter your rooms
and shut the doors behind you;
hide yourselves for a little while
until his wrath has passed by.
21See, the LORD is coming out of his
dwelling
to punish the people of the earth for
their sins.
The earth will disclose the blood shed
upon her;
she will conceal her slain no longer.

Deliverance of Israel

27 In that day,
the LORD will punish with his sword,
his fierce, great and powerful sword,
Leviathan the gliding serpent,
Leviathan the coiling serpent;
he will slay the monster of the sea.

[a]8 Or *judgments* [b]16 The meaning of the Hebrew for this clause is uncertain.

[2]In that day—

"Sing about a fruitful vineyard:
3 I, the LORD, watch over it;
I water it continually.
I guard it day and night
so that no one may harm it.
4 I am not angry.
If only there were briers and thorns
confronting me!
I would march against them in battle;
I would set them all on fire.
[5]Or else let them come to me for refuge;
let them make peace with me,
yes, let them make peace with me."

[6]In days to come Jacob will take root,
Israel will bud and blossom
and fill all the world with fruit.

[7]Has ⌞the LORD⌟ struck her
as he struck down those who struck
her?
Has she been killed
as those were killed who killed her?
[8]By warfare[a] and exile you contend with
her—
with his fierce blast he drives her out,
as on a day the east wind blows.
[9]By this, then, will Jacob's guilt be atoned
for,
and this will be the full fruitage of the
removal of his sin:
When he makes all the altar stones
to be like chalk stones crushed to
pieces,
no Asherah poles[b] or incense altars
will be left standing.
[10]The fortified city stands desolate,
an abandoned settlement, forsaken like
the desert;
there the calves graze,
there they lie down;
they strip its branches bare.
[11]When its twigs are dry, they are broken
off
and women come and make fires with
them.
For this is a people without
understanding;
so their Maker has no compassion on
them,
and their Creator shows them no favor.

[12]In that day the LORD will thresh from the
flowing Euphrates[c] to the Wadi of Egypt, and
you, O Israelites, will be gathered up one by
one. [13]And in that day a great trumpet will
sound. Those who were perishing in Assyria
and those who were exiled in Egypt will
come and worship the LORD on the holy
mountain in Jerusalem.

Woe to Ephraim

28 Woe to that wreath, the pride of
Ephraim's drunkards,
to the fading flower, his glorious
beauty,
set on the head of a fertile valley—
to that city, the pride of those laid low
by wine!
[2]See, the Lord has one who is powerful
and strong.
Like a hailstorm and a destructive wind,
like a driving rain and a flooding
downpour,
he will throw it forcefully to the ground.
[3]That wreath, the pride of Ephraim's
drunkards,
will be trampled underfoot.
[4]That fading flower, his glorious beauty,
set on the head of a fertile valley,
will be like a fig ripe before harvest—
as soon as someone sees it and takes
it in his hand,
he swallows it.

[5]In that day the LORD Almighty
will be a glorious crown,
a beautiful wreath
for the remnant of his people.
[6]He will be a spirit of justice
to him who sits in judgment,
a source of strength
to those who turn back the battle at the
gate.

[7]And these also stagger from wine
and reel from beer:
Priests and prophets stagger from beer
and are befuddled with wine;
they reel from beer,
they stagger when seeing visions,
they stumble when rendering decisions.
[8]All the tables are covered with vomit
and there is not a spot without filth.

[9]"Who is it he is trying to teach?
To whom is he explaining his
message?
To children weaned from their milk,

[a]*8* See Septuagint; the meaning of the Hebrew for this word is uncertain. [b]*9* That is, symbols of the goddess Asherah [c]*12* Hebrew *River*

to those just taken from the breast?
10For it is:
Do and do, do and do,
rule on rule, rule on rule[a];
a little here, a little there."

11Very well then, with foreign lips and strange tongues
God will speak to this people,
12to whom he said,
"This is the resting place, let the weary rest";
and, "This is the place of repose"—
but they would not listen.
13So then, the word of the LORD to them will become:
Do and do, do and do,
rule on rule, rule on rule;
a little here, a little there—
so that they will go and fall backward,
be injured and snared and captured.

14Therefore hear the word of the LORD, you scoffers
who rule this people in Jerusalem.
15You boast, "We have entered into a covenant with death,
with the grave[b] we have made an agreement.
When an overwhelming scourge sweeps by,
it cannot touch us,
for we have made a lie our refuge
and falsehood[c] our hiding place."

16So this is what the Sovereign LORD says:

"See, I lay a stone in Zion,
a tested stone,
a precious cornerstone for a sure foundation;
the one who trusts will never be dismayed.
17I will make justice the measuring line
and righteousness the plumb line;
hail will sweep away your refuge, the lie,
and water will overflow your hiding place.
18Your covenant with death will be annulled;
your agreement with the grave will not stand.
When the overwhelming scourge sweeps by,
you will be beaten down by it.
19As often as it comes it will carry you away;
morning after morning, by day and by night,
it will sweep through."

The understanding of this message
will bring sheer terror.
20The bed is too short to stretch out on,
the blanket too narrow to wrap around you.
21The LORD will rise up as he did at Mount Perazim,
he will rouse himself as in the Valley of Gibeon—
to do his work, his strange work,
and perform his task, his alien task.
22Now stop your mocking,
or your chains will become heavier;
the Lord, the LORD Almighty, has told me
of the destruction decreed against the whole land.

23Listen and hear my voice;
pay attention and hear what I say.
24When a farmer plows for planting, does he plow continually?
Does he keep on breaking up and harrowing the soil?
25When he has leveled the surface,
does he not sow caraway and scatter cummin?
Does he not plant wheat in its place,[d]
barley in its plot,[d]
and spelt in its field?
26His God instructs him
and teaches him the right way.

27Caraway is not threshed with a sledge,
nor is a cartwheel rolled over cummin;
caraway is beaten out with a rod,
and cummin with a stick.
28Grain must be ground to make bread;
so one does not go on threshing it forever.
Though he drives the wheels of his threshing cart over it,
his horses do not grind it.
29All this also comes from the LORD Almighty,
wonderful in counsel and magnificent in wisdom.

[a]10 Hebrew / *sav lasav sav lasav / kav lakav kav lakav* (possibly meaningless sounds; perhaps a mimicking of the prophet's words); also in verse 13 [b]15 Hebrew *Sheol*; also in verse 18 [c]15 Or *false gods* [d]25 The meaning of the Hebrew for this word is uncertain.

Woe to David's City

29 Woe to you, Ariel, Ariel,
the city where David settled!
Add year to year
and let your cycle of festivals go on.
2Yet I will besiege Ariel;
she will mourn and lament,
she will be to me like an altar hearth.[a]
3I will encamp against you all around;
I will encircle you with towers
and set up my siege works against you.
4Brought low, you will speak from the ground;
your speech will mumble out of the dust.
Your voice will come ghostlike from the earth;
out of the dust your speech will whisper.

5But your many enemies will become like fine dust,
the ruthless hordes like blown chaff.
Suddenly, in an instant,
6 the LORD Almighty will come
with thunder and earthquake and great noise,
with windstorm and tempest and flames of a devouring fire.
7Then the hordes of all the nations that fight against Ariel,
that attack her and her fortress and besiege her,
will be as it is with a dream,
with a vision in the night—
8as when a hungry man dreams that he is eating,
but he awakens, and his hunger remains;
as when a thirsty man dreams that he is drinking,
but he awakens faint, with his thirst unquenched.
So will it be with the hordes of all the nations
that fight against Mount Zion.

9Be stunned and amazed,
blind yourselves and be sightless;
be drunk, but not from wine,
stagger, but not from beer.
10The LORD has brought over you a deep sleep:
He has sealed your eyes (the prophets);
he has covered your heads (the seers).

11For you this whole vision is nothing but
words sealed in a scroll. And if you give the
scroll to someone who can read, and say to
him, "Read this, please," he will answer, "I
can't; it is sealed." 12Or if you give the scroll
to someone who cannot read, and say,
"Read this, please," he will answer, "I don't
know how to read."

13The Lord says:

"These people come near to me with their mouth
and honor me with their lips,
but their hearts are far from me.
Their worship of me
is made up only of rules taught by men.[b]
14Therefore once more I will astound these people
with wonder upon wonder;
the wisdom of the wise will perish,
the intelligence of the intelligent will vanish."
15Woe to those who go to great depths
to hide their plans from the LORD,
who do their work in darkness and think,
"Who sees us? Who will know?"
16You turn things upside down,
as if the potter were thought to be like the clay!
Shall what is formed say to him who formed it,
"He did not make me"?
Can the pot say of the potter,
"He knows nothing"?

17In a very short time, will not Lebanon be turned into a fertile field
and the fertile field seem like a forest?
18In that day the deaf will hear the words of the scroll,
and out of gloom and darkness
the eyes of the blind will see.
19Once more the humble will rejoice in the LORD;
the needy will rejoice in the Holy One of Israel.
20The ruthless will vanish,
the mockers will disappear,
and all who have an eye for evil will be cut down—
21those who with a word make a man out to be guilty,

[a]2 The Hebrew for *altar hearth* sounds like the Hebrew for *Ariel.* [b]13 Hebrew; Septuagint *They worship me in vain; / their teachings are but rules taught by men*

who ensnare the defender in court
and with false testimony deprive the
innocent of justice.

22Therefore this is what the LORD, who redeemed Abraham, says to the house of
Jacob:

"No longer will Jacob be ashamed;
no longer will their faces grow pale.
23When they see among them their
children,
the work of my hands,
they will keep my name holy;
they will acknowledge the holiness of
the Holy One of Jacob,
and will stand in awe of the God of
Israel.
24Those who are wayward in spirit will gain
understanding;
those who complain will accept
instruction."

Woe to the Obstinate Nation

30 "Woe to the obstinate children,"
declares the LORD,
"to those who carry out plans that are not
mine,
forming an alliance, but not by my
Spirit,
heaping sin upon sin;
2who go down to Egypt
without consulting me;
who look for help to Pharaoh's protection,
to Egypt's shade for refuge.
3But Pharaoh's protection will be to your
shame,
Egypt's shade will bring you disgrace.
4Though they have officials in Zoan
and their envoys have arrived in
Hanes,
5everyone will be put to shame
because of a people useless to them,
who bring neither help nor advantage,
but only shame and disgrace."

6An oracle concerning the animals of the
Negev:

Through a land of hardship and distress,
of lions and lionesses,
of adders and darting snakes,
the envoys carry their riches on donkeys'
backs,
their treasures on the humps of camels,
to that unprofitable nation,
7 to Egypt, whose help is utterly useless.
Therefore I call her
Rahab the Do-Nothing.

8Go now, write it on a tablet for them,
inscribe it on a scroll,
that for the days to come
it may be an everlasting witness.
9These are rebellious people, deceitful
children,
children unwilling to listen to the LORD's
instruction.
10They say to the seers,
"See no more visions!"
and to the prophets,
"Give us no more visions of what is
right!
Tell us pleasant things,
prophesy illusions.
11Leave this way,
get off this path,
and stop confronting us
with the Holy One of Israel!"

12Therefore, this is what the Holy One of
Israel says:

"Because you have rejected this
message,
relied on oppression
and depended on deceit,
13this sin will become for you
like a high wall, cracked and bulging,
that collapses suddenly, in an instant.
14It will break in pieces like pottery,
shattered so mercilessly
that among its pieces not a fragment will
be found
for taking coals from a hearth
or scooping water out of a cistern."

15This is what the Sovereign LORD, the Holy
One of Israel, says:

"In repentance and rest is your salvation,
in quietness and trust is your strength,
but you would have none of it.
16You said, 'No, we will flee on horses.'
Therefore you will flee!
You said, 'We will ride off on swift
horses.'
Therefore your pursuers will be swift!
17A thousand will flee
at the threat of one;
at the threat of five
you will all flee away,
till you are left
like a flagstaff on a mountaintop,
like a banner on a hill."
18Yet the LORD longs to be gracious to you;

he rises to show you compassion.
For the LORD is a God of justice.
Blessed are all who wait for him!

19O people of Zion, who live in Jerusalem,
you will weep no more. How gracious he will
be when you cry for help! As soon as he
hears, he will answer you. 20Although the
Lord gives you the bread of adversity and the
water of affliction, your teachers will be hidden no more; with your own eyes you will see
them. 21Whether you turn to the right or to the
left, your ears will hear a voice behind you,
saying, "This is the way; walk in it." 22Then
you will defile your idols overlaid with silver
and your images covered with gold; you will
throw them away like a menstrual cloth and
say to them, "Away with you!"

23He will also send you rain for the seed
you sow in the ground, and the food that
comes from the land will be rich and plentiful.
In that day your cattle will graze in broad
meadows. 24The oxen and donkeys that
work the soil will eat fodder and mash,
spread out with fork and shovel. 25In the day
of great slaughter, when the towers fall,
streams of water will flow on every high
mountain and every lofty hill. 26The moon will
shine like the sun, and the sunlight will be
seven times brighter, like the light of seven
full days, when the LORD binds up the bruises
of his people and heals the wounds he inflicted.

27See, the Name of the LORD comes from afar,
with burning anger and dense clouds of smoke;
his lips are full of wrath,
and his tongue is a consuming fire.
28His breath is like a rushing torrent,
rising up to the neck.
He shakes the nations in the sieve of destruction;
he places in the jaws of the peoples
a bit that leads them astray.
29And you will sing
as on the night you celebrate a holy festival;
your hearts will rejoice
as when people go up with flutes
to the mountain of the LORD,
to the Rock of Israel.
30The LORD will cause men to hear his majestic voice
and will make them see his arm coming down
with raging anger and consuming fire,
with cloudburst, thunderstorm and hail.
31The voice of the LORD will shatter Assyria;
with his scepter he will strike them down.
32Every stroke the LORD lays on them
with his punishing rod
will be to the music of tambourines and harps,
as he fights them in battle with the blows of his arm.
33Topheth has long been prepared;
it has been made ready for the king.
Its fire pit has been made deep and wide,
with an abundance of fire and wood;
the breath of the LORD,
like a stream of burning sulfur,
sets it ablaze.

Woe to Those Who Rely on Egypt

31 Woe to those who go down to Egypt for help,
who rely on horses,
who trust in the multitude of their chariots
and in the great strength of their horsemen,
but do not look to the Holy One of Israel,
or seek help from the LORD.
2Yet he too is wise and can bring disaster;
he does not take back his words.
He will rise up against the house of the wicked,
against those who help evildoers.
3But the Egyptians are men and not God;
their horses are flesh and not spirit.
When the LORD stretches out his hand,
he who helps will stumble,
he who is helped will fall;
both will perish together.

4This is what the LORD says to me:

"As a lion growls,
a great lion over his prey—
and though a whole band of shepherds
is called together against him,
he is not frightened by their shouts
or disturbed by their clamor—
so the LORD Almighty will come down
to do battle on Mount Zion and on its heights.
5Like birds hovering overhead,
the LORD Almighty will shield Jerusalem;
he will shield it and deliver it,
he will 'pass over' it and will rescue it."

6Return to him you have so greatly revolt-

ed against, O Israelites. [7]For in that day
every one of you will reject the idols of silver
and gold your sinful hands have made.

[8]"Assyria will fall by a sword that is not of man;
a sword, not of mortals, will devour them.
They will flee before the sword
and their young men will be put to forced labor.
[9]Their stronghold will fall because of terror;
at sight of the battle standard their commanders will panic,"
declares the LORD,
whose fire is in Zion,
whose furnace is in Jerusalem.

The Kingdom of Righteousness

32 See, a king will reign in righteousness
and rulers will rule with justice.
[2]Each man will be like a shelter from the wind
and a refuge from the storm,
like streams of water in the desert
and the shadow of a great rock in a thirsty land.

[3]Then the eyes of those who see will no longer be closed,
and the ears of those who hear will listen.
[4]The mind of the rash will know and understand,
and the stammering tongue will be fluent and clear.
[5]No longer will the fool be called noble
nor the scoundrel be highly respected.
[6]For the fool speaks folly,
his mind is busy with evil:
He practices ungodliness
and spreads error concerning the LORD;
the hungry he leaves empty
and from the thirsty he withholds water.
[7]The scoundrel's methods are wicked,
he makes up evil schemes
to destroy the poor with lies,
even when the plea of the needy is just.
[8]But the noble man makes noble plans,
and by noble deeds he stands.

The Women of Jerusalem

[9]You women who are so complacent,
rise up and listen to me;
you daughters who feel secure,
hear what I have to say!
[10]In little more than a year
you who feel secure will tremble;
the grape harvest will fail,
and the harvest of fruit will not come.
[11]Tremble, you complacent women;
shudder, you daughters who feel secure!
Strip off your clothes,
put sackcloth around your waists.
[12]Beat your breasts for the pleasant fields,
for the fruitful vines
[13]and for the land of my people,
a land overgrown with thorns and briers—
yes, mourn for all houses of merriment
and for this city of revelry.
[14]The fortress will be abandoned,
the noisy city deserted;
citadel and watchtower will become a wasteland forever,
the delight of donkeys, a pasture for flocks,
[15]till the Spirit is poured upon us from on high,
and the desert becomes a fertile field,
and the fertile field seems like a forest.
[16]Justice will dwell in the desert
and righteousness live in the fertile field.
[17]The fruit of righteousness will be peace;
the effect of righteousness will be quietness and confidence forever.
[18]My people will live in peaceful dwelling places,
in secure homes,
in undisturbed places of rest.
[19]Though hail flattens the forest
and the city is leveled completely,
[20]how blessed you will be,
sowing your seed by every stream,
and letting your cattle and donkeys range free.

Distress and Help

33 Woe to you, O destroyer,
you who have not been destroyed!
Woe to you, O traitor,
you who have not been betrayed!
When you stop destroying,
you will be destroyed;
when you stop betraying,
you will be betrayed.

[2]O LORD, be gracious to us;
we long for you.

Be our strength every morning,
our salvation in time of distress.
3At the thunder of your voice, the peoples flee;
when you rise up, the nations scatter.
4Your plunder, O nations, is harvested as by young locusts;
like a swarm of locusts men pounce on it.

5The LORD is exalted, for he dwells on high;
he will fill Zion with justice and righteousness.
6He will be the sure foundation for your times,
a rich store of salvation and wisdom and knowledge;
the fear of the LORD is the key to this treasure.[a]

7Look, their brave men cry aloud in the streets;
the envoys of peace weep bitterly.
8The highways are deserted,
no travelers are on the roads.
The treaty is broken,
its witnesses[b] are despised,
no one is respected.
9The land mourns[c] and wastes away,
Lebanon is ashamed and withers;
Sharon is like the Arabah,
and Bashan and Carmel drop their leaves.

10"Now will I arise," says the LORD.
"Now will I be exalted;
now will I be lifted up.
11You conceive chaff,
you give birth to straw;
your breath is a fire that consumes you.
12The peoples will be burned as if to lime;
like cut thornbushes they will be set ablaze."

13You who are far away, hear what I have done;
you who are near, acknowledge my power!
14The sinners in Zion are terrified;
trembling grips the godless:
"Who of us can dwell with the consuming fire?
Who of us can dwell with everlasting burning?"
15He who walks righteously
and speaks what is right,
who rejects gain from extortion
and keeps his hand from accepting bribes,
who stops his ears against plots of murder
and shuts his eyes against contemplating evil—
16this is the man who will dwell on the heights,
whose refuge will be the mountain fortress.
His bread will be supplied,
and water will not fail him.

17Your eyes will see the king in his beauty
and view a land that stretches afar.
18In your thoughts you will ponder the former terror:
"Where is that chief officer?
Where is the one who took the revenue?
Where is the officer in charge of the towers?"
19You will see those arrogant people no more,
those people of an obscure speech,
with their strange, incomprehensible tongue.

20Look upon Zion, the city of our festivals;
your eyes will see Jerusalem,
a peaceful abode, a tent that will not be moved;
its stakes will never be pulled up,
nor any of its ropes broken.
21There the LORD will be our Mighty One.
It will be like a place of broad rivers and streams.
No galley with oars will ride them,
no mighty ship will sail them.
22For the LORD is our judge,
the LORD is our lawgiver,
the LORD is our king;
it is he who will save us.

23Your rigging hangs loose:
The mast is not held secure,
the sail is not spread.
Then an abundance of spoils will be divided
and even the lame will carry off plunder.
24No one living in Zion will say, "I am ill";
and the sins of those who dwell there will be forgiven.

[a]6 Or *is a treasure from him* [b]8 Dead Sea Scrolls; Masoretic Text / *the cities* [c]9 Or *dries up*

Judgment Against the Nations

34 Come near, you nations, and listen;
pay attention, you peoples!
Let the earth hear, and all that is in it,
the world, and all that comes out of it!
2The LORD is angry with all nations;
his wrath is upon all their armies.
He will totally destroy[a] them,
he will give them over to slaughter.
3Their slain will be thrown out,
their dead bodies will send up a stench;
the mountains will be soaked with their blood.
4All the stars of the heavens will be dissolved
and the sky rolled up like a scroll;
all the starry host will fall
like withered leaves from the vine,
like shriveled figs from the fig tree.

5My sword has drunk its fill in the heavens;
see, it descends in judgment on Edom,
the people I have totally destroyed.
6The sword of the LORD is bathed in blood,
it is covered with fat—
the blood of lambs and goats,
fat from the kidneys of rams.
For the LORD has a sacrifice in Bozrah
and a great slaughter in Edom.
7And the wild oxen will fall with them,
the bull calves and the great bulls.
Their land will be drenched with blood,
and the dust will be soaked with fat.

8For the LORD has a day of vengeance,
a year of retribution, to uphold Zion's cause.
9Edom's streams will be turned into pitch,
her dust into burning sulfur;
her land will become blazing pitch!
10It will not be quenched night and day;
its smoke will rise forever.
From generation to generation it will lie desolate;
no one will ever pass through it again.
11The desert owl[b] and screech owl[b] will possess it;
the great owl[b] and the raven will nest there.
God will stretch out over Edom
the measuring line of chaos
and the plumb line of desolation.
12Her nobles will have nothing there to be called a kingdom,
all her princes will vanish away.
13Thorns will overrun her citadels,
nettles and brambles her strongholds.
She will become a haunt for jackals,
a home for owls.
14Desert creatures will meet with hyenas,
and wild goats will bleat to each other;
there the night creatures will also repose
and find for themselves places of rest.
15The owl will nest there and lay eggs,
she will hatch them, and care for her young under the shadow of her wings;
there also the falcons will gather,
each with its mate.

16Look in the scroll of the LORD and read:

None of these will be missing,
not one will lack her mate.
For it is his mouth that has given the order,
and his Spirit will gather them together.
17He allots their portions;
his hand distributes them by measure.
They will possess it forever
and dwell there from generation to generation.

Joy of the Redeemed

35 The desert and the parched land will be glad;
the wilderness will rejoice and blossom.
Like the crocus, 2it will burst into bloom;
it will rejoice greatly and shout for joy.
The glory of Lebanon will be given to it,
the splendor of Carmel and Sharon;
they will see the glory of the LORD,
the splendor of our God.

3Strengthen the feeble hands,
steady the knees that give way;
4say to those with fearful hearts,
"Be strong, do not fear;
your God will come,
he will come with vengeance;
with divine retribution
he will come to save you."

5Then will the eyes of the blind be opened
and the ears of the deaf unstopped.
6Then will the lame leap like a deer,
and the mute tongue shout for joy.
Water will gush forth in the wilderness
and streams in the desert.
7The burning sand will become a pool,

[a]2 The Hebrew term refers to the irrevocable giving over of things or persons to the LORD, often by totally destroying them; also in verse 5. [b]11 The precise identification of these birds is uncertain.

the thirsty ground bubbling springs.
In the haunts where jackals once lay,
grass and reeds and papyrus will grow.

8And a highway will be there;
it will be called the Way of Holiness.
The unclean will not journey on it;
it will be for those who walk in that
Way;
wicked fools will not go about on it.[a]
9No lion will be there,
nor will any ferocious beast get up on it;
they will not be found there.
But only the redeemed will walk there,
10 and the ransomed of the LORD will
return.
They will enter Zion with singing;
everlasting joy will crown their heads.
Gladness and joy will overtake them,
and sorrow and sighing will flee away.

Sennacherib Threatens Jerusalem

36 In the fourteenth year of King Hezekiah's reign, Sennacherib king of Assyria attacked all the fortified cities of Judah
and captured them. 2Then the king of Assyria
sent his field commander with a large army
from Lachish to King Hezekiah at Jerusalem.
When the commander stopped at the aqueduct of the Upper Pool, on the road to the
Washerman's Field, 3Eliakim son of Hilkiah
the palace administrator, Shebna the secretary, and Joah son of Asaph the recorder
went out to him.

4The field commander said to them, "Tell
Hezekiah,

" 'This is what the great king, the king
of Assyria, says: On what are you basing this confidence of yours? 5You say
you have strategy and military
strength—but you speak only empty
words. On whom are you depending,
that you rebel against me? 6Look now,
you are depending on Egypt, that splintered reed of a staff, which pierces a
man's hand and wounds him if he leans
on it! Such is Pharaoh king of Egypt to
all who depend on him. 7And if you say
to me, "We are depending on the LORD
our God"—isn't he the one whose high
places and altars Hezekiah removed,
saying to Judah and Jerusalem, "You
must worship before this altar"?

8" 'Come now, make a bargain with
my master, the king of Assyria: I will give
you two thousand horses—if you can
put riders on them! 9How then can you
repulse one officer of the least of my
master's officials, even though you are
depending on Egypt for chariots and
horsemen? 10Furthermore, have I come
to attack and destroy this land without
the LORD? The LORD himself told me to
march against this country and destroy
it.' "

11Then Eliakim, Shebna and Joah said to
the field commander, "Please speak to your
servants in Aramaic, since we understand it.
Don't speak to us in Hebrew in the hearing of
the people on the wall."

12But the commander replied, "Was it only
to your master and you that my master sent
me to say these things, and not to the men
sitting on the wall—who, like you, will have
to eat their own filth and drink their own
urine?"

13Then the commander stood and called
out in Hebrew, "Hear the words of the great
king, the king of Assyria! 14This is what the
king says: Do not let Hezekiah deceive you.
He cannot deliver you! 15Do not let Hezekiah
persuade you to trust in the LORD when he
says, 'The LORD will surely deliver us; this city
will not be given into the hand of the king of
Assyria.'

16"Do not listen to Hezekiah. This is what
the king of Assyria says: Make peace with
me and come out to me. Then every one of
you will eat from his own vine and fig tree and
drink water from his own cistern, 17until I
come and take you to a land like your own—
a land of grain and new wine, a land of bread
and vineyards.

18"Do not let Hezekiah mislead you when
he says, 'The LORD will deliver us.' Has the
god of any nation ever delivered his land
from the hand of the king of Assyria?
19Where are the gods of Hamath and Arpad?
Where are the gods of Sepharvaim? Have
they rescued Samaria from my hand? 20Who
of all the gods of these countries has been
able to save his land from me? How then can
the LORD deliver Jerusalem from my hand?"

21But the people remained silent and said
nothing in reply, because the king had commanded, "Do not answer him."

22Then Eliakim son of Hilkiah the palace
administrator, Shebna the secretary, and

[a]8 Or / *the simple will not stray from it*

Joah son of Asaph the recorder went to
Hezekiah, with their clothes torn, and told
him what the field commander had said.

Jerusalem's Deliverance Foretold

37 When King Hezekiah heard this, he
tore his clothes and put on sackcloth
and went into the temple of the LORD. 2He
sent Eliakim the palace administrator, Shebna the secretary, and the leading priests, all
wearing sackcloth, to the prophet Isaiah son
of Amoz. 3They told him, "This is what Hezekiah says: This day is a day of distress and
rebuke and disgrace, as when children come
to the point of birth and there is no strength to
deliver them. 4It may be that the LORD your
God will hear the words of the field commander, whom his master, the king of Assyria, has sent to ridicule the living God, and
that he will rebuke him for the words the LORD
your God has heard. Therefore pray for the
remnant that still survives."

5When King Hezekiah's officials came to
Isaiah, 6Isaiah said to them, "Tell your master, 'This is what the LORD says: Do not be
afraid of what you have heard—those words
with which the underlings of the king of Assyria have blasphemed me. 7Listen! I am
going to put a spirit in him so that when he
hears a certain report, he will return to his
own country, and there I will have him cut
down with the sword.' "

8When the field commander heard that the
king of Assyria had left Lachish, he withdrew
and found the king fighting against Libnah.

9Now Sennacherib received a report that
Tirhakah, the Cushite[a] king ⌞of Egypt⌟, was
marching out to fight against him. When he
heard it, he sent messengers to Hezekiah
with this word: 10"Say to Hezekiah king of
Judah: Do not let the god you depend on
deceive you when he says, 'Jerusalem will
not be handed over to the king of Assyria.'
11Surely you have heard what the kings of
Assyria have done to all the countries, destroying them completely. And will you be
delivered? 12Did the gods of the nations that
were destroyed by my forefathers deliver
them—the gods of Gozan, Haran, Rezeph
and the people of Eden who were in Tel
Assar? 13Where is the king of Hamath, the
king of Arpad, the king of the city of Sepharvaim, or of Hena or Ivvah?"

Hezekiah's Prayer

14Hezekiah received the letter from the
messengers and read it. Then he went up to
the temple of the LORD and spread it out before the LORD. 15And Hezekiah prayed to the
LORD: 16"O LORD Almighty, God of Israel, enthroned between the cherubim, you alone
are God over all the kingdoms of the earth.
You have made heaven and earth. 17Give
ear, O LORD, and hear; open your eyes, O
LORD, and see; listen to all the words Sennacherib has sent to insult the living God.

18"It is true, O LORD, that the Assyrian kings
have laid waste all these peoples and their
lands. 19They have thrown their gods into the
fire and destroyed them, for they were not
gods but only wood and stone, fashioned by
human hands. 20Now, O LORD our God, deliver us from his hand, so that all kingdoms
on earth may know that you alone, O LORD,
are God.[b]"

Sennacherib's Fall

21Then Isaiah son of Amoz sent a message to Hezekiah: "This is what the LORD, the
God of Israel, says: Because you have
prayed to me concerning Sennacherib king
of Assyria, 22this is the word the LORD has
spoken against him:

"The Virgin Daughter of Zion
    despises and mocks you.
The Daughter of Jerusalem
    tosses her head as you flee.
23Who is it you have insulted and
        blasphemed?
    Against whom have you raised your
        voice
and lifted your eyes in pride?
    Against the Holy One of Israel!
24By your messengers
    you have heaped insults on the Lord.
And you have said,
    'With my many chariots
I have ascended the heights of the
        mountains,
    the utmost heights of Lebanon.
I have cut down its tallest cedars,
    the choicest of its pines.
I have reached its remotest heights,
    the finest of its forests.
25I have dug wells in foreign lands[c]
    and drunk the water there.

[a]9 That is, from the upper Nile region [b]20 Dead Sea Scrolls (see also 2 Kings 19:19); Masoretic Text *alone are the LORD* [c]25 Dead Sea Scrolls (see also 2 Kings 19:24); Masoretic Text does not have *in foreign lands.*

With the soles of my feet
  I have dried up all the streams of
    Egypt.'
[26]"Have you not heard?
  Long ago I ordained it.
In days of old I planned it;
  now I have brought it to pass,
that you have turned fortified cities
  into piles of stone.
[27]Their people, drained of power,
  are dismayed and put to shame.
They are like plants in the field,
  like tender green shoots,
like grass sprouting on the roof,
  scorched[a] before it grows up.

[28]"But I know where you stay
  and when you come and go
  and how you rage against me.
[29]Because you rage against me
  and because your insolence has
    reached my ears,
I will put my hook in your nose
  and my bit in your mouth,
and I will make you return
  by the way you came.

[30]"This will be the sign for you, O Hezekiah:

"This year you will eat what grows by
    itself,
  and the second year what springs from
    that.
But in the third year sow and reap,
  plant vineyards and eat their fruit.
[31]Once more a remnant of the house of
    Judah
  will take root below and bear fruit
    above.
[32]For out of Jerusalem will come a
    remnant,
  and out of Mount Zion a band of
    survivors.
The zeal of the LORD Almighty
  will accomplish this.

[33]"Therefore this is what the LORD says
concerning the king of Assyria:

"He will not enter this city
  or shoot an arrow here.
He will not come before it with shield
  or build a siege ramp against it.
[34]By the way that he came he will return;
  he will not enter this city,"
    declares the LORD.
[35]"I will defend this city and save it,
  for my sake and for the sake of David
    my servant!"

[36]Then the angel of the LORD went out and
put to death a hundred and eighty-five thousand men in the Assyrian camp. When the
people got up the next morning—there were
all the dead bodies! [37]So Sennacherib king
of Assyria broke camp and withdrew. He returned to Nineveh and stayed there.
[38]One day, while he was worshiping in the
temple of his god Nisroch, his sons Adrammelech and Sharezer cut him down with the
sword, and they escaped to the land of Ararat. And Esarhaddon his son succeeded him
as king.

Hezekiah's Illness

38 In those days Hezekiah became ill
and was at the point of death. The
prophet Isaiah son of Amoz went to him and
said, "This is what the LORD says: Put your
house in order, because you are going to die;
you will not recover."
[2]Hezekiah turned his face to the wall and
prayed to the LORD, [3]"Remember, O LORD,
how I have walked before you faithfully and
with wholehearted devotion and have done
what is good in your eyes." And Hezekiah
wept bitterly.
[4]Then the word of the LORD came to Isaiah:
[5]"Go and tell Hezekiah, 'This is what the
LORD, the God of your father David, says: I
have heard your prayer and seen your tears;
I will add fifteen years to your life. [6]And I will
deliver you and this city from the hand of the
king of Assyria. I will defend this city.
[7]" 'This is the LORD's sign to you that the
LORD will do what he has promised: [8]I will
make the shadow cast by the sun go back
the ten steps it has gone down on the stairway of Ahaz.' " So the sunlight went back the
ten steps it had gone down.

[9]A writing of Hezekiah king of Judah after
his illness and recovery:

[10]I said, "In the prime of my life
  must I go through the gates of death[b]
  and be robbed of the rest of my
    years?"
[11]I said, "I will not again see the LORD,

[a]*27* Some manuscripts of the Masoretic Text, Dead Sea Scrolls and some Septuagint manuscripts (see also 2 Kings 19:26); most manuscripts of the Masoretic Text *roof / and terraced fields* [b]*10* Hebrew *Sheol*

the LORD, in the land of the living;
no longer will I look on mankind,
or be with those who now dwell in this world.[a]
12Like a shepherd's tent my house
has been pulled down and taken from me.
Like a weaver I have rolled up my life,
and he has cut me off from the loom;
day and night you made an end of me.
13I waited patiently till dawn,
but like a lion he broke all my bones;
day and night you made an end of me.
14I cried like a swift or thrush,
I moaned like a mourning dove.
My eyes grew weak as I looked to the heavens.
I am troubled; O Lord, come to my aid!"

15But what can I say?
He has spoken to me, and he himself has done this.
I will walk humbly all my years
because of this anguish of my soul.
16Lord, by such things men live;
and my spirit finds life in them too.
You restored me to health
and let me live.
17Surely it was for my benefit
that I suffered such anguish.
In your love you kept me
from the pit of destruction;
you have put all my sins
behind your back.
18For the grave[b] cannot praise you,
death cannot sing your praise;
those who go down to the pit
cannot hope for your faithfulness.
19The living, the living—they praise you,
as I am doing today;
fathers tell their children
about your faithfulness.

20The LORD will save me,
and we will sing with stringed instruments
all the days of our lives
in the temple of the LORD.

21Isaiah had said, "Prepare a poultice of
figs and apply it to the boil, and he will recover."
22Hezekiah had asked, "What will be the
sign that I will go up to the temple of the
LORD?"

Envoys From Babylon

39 At that time Merodach-Baladan son
of Baladan king of Babylon sent
Hezekiah letters and a gift, because he had
heard of his illness and recovery. 2Hezekiah
received the envoys gladly and showed
them what was in his storehouses—the silver, the gold, the spices, the fine oil, his entire armory and everything found among his
treasures. There was nothing in his palace or
in all his kingdom that Hezekiah did not show
them.
3Then Isaiah the prophet went to King
Hezekiah and asked, "What did those men
say, and where did they come from?"
"From a distant land," Hezekiah replied.
"They came to me from Babylon."
4The prophet asked, "What did they see in
your palace?"
"They saw everything in my palace,"
Hezekiah said. "There is nothing among my
treasures that I did not show them."
5Then Isaiah said to Hezekiah, "Hear the
word of the LORD Almighty: 6The time will
surely come when everything in your palace,
and all that your fathers have stored up until
this day, will be carried off to Babylon. Nothing will be left, says the LORD. 7And some of
your descendants, your own flesh and blood
who will be born to you, will be taken away,
and they will become eunuchs in the palace
of the king of Babylon."
8"The word of the LORD you have spoken is
good," Hezekiah replied. For he thought,
"There will be peace and security in my lifetime."

Comfort for God's People

40 Comfort, comfort my people,
says your God.
2Speak tenderly to Jerusalem,
and proclaim to her
that her hard service has been completed,
that her sin has been paid for,
that she has received from the LORD's hand
double for all her sins.

3A voice of one calling:
"In the desert prepare
the way for the LORD[c];
make straight in the wilderness

[a] 11 A few Hebrew manuscripts; most Hebrew manuscripts *in the place of cessation* [b] 18 Hebrew *Sheol*
[c] 3 Or *A voice of one calling in the desert: / "Prepare the way for the LORD*

a highway for our God.[a]
[4]Every valley shall be raised up,
every mountain and hill made low;
the rough ground shall become level,
the rugged places a plain.
[5]And the glory of the LORD will be revealed,
and all mankind together will see it.
For the mouth of the LORD has
spoken."

[6]A voice says, "Cry out."
And I said, "What shall I cry?"

"All men are like grass,
and all their glory is like the flowers of
the field.
[7]The grass withers and the flowers fall,
because the breath of the LORD blows
on them.
Surely the people are grass.
[8]The grass withers and the flowers fall,
but the word of our God stands
forever."
[9]You who bring good tidings to Zion,
go up on a high mountain.
You who bring good tidings to
Jerusalem,[b]
lift up your voice with a shout,
lift it up, do not be afraid;
say to the towns of Judah,
"Here is your God!"
[10]See, the Sovereign LORD comes with
power,
and his arm rules for him.
See, his reward is with him,
and his recompense accompanies him.
[11]He tends his flock like a shepherd:
He gathers the lambs in his arms
and carries them close to his heart;
he gently leads those that have young.

[12]Who has measured the waters in the
hollow of his hand,
or with the breadth of his hand marked
off the heavens?
Who has held the dust of the earth in a
basket,
or weighed the mountains on the
scales
and the hills in a balance?
[13]Who has understood the mind[c] of the
LORD,
or instructed him as his counselor?
[14]Whom did the LORD consult to enlighten
him,
and who taught him the right way?
Who was it that taught him knowledge
or showed him the path of
understanding?

[15]Surely the nations are like a drop in a
bucket;
they are regarded as dust on the
scales;
he weighs the islands as though they
were fine dust.
[16]Lebanon is not sufficient for altar fires,
nor its animals enough for burnt
offerings.
[17]Before him all the nations are as nothing;
they are regarded by him as worthless
and less than nothing.

[18]To whom, then, will you compare God?
What image will you compare him to?
[19]As for an idol, a craftsman casts it,
and a goldsmith overlays it with gold
and fashions silver chains for it.
[20]A man too poor to present such an
offering
selects wood that will not rot.
He looks for a skilled craftsman
to set up an idol that will not topple.

[21]Do you not know?
Have you not heard?
Has it not been told you from the
beginning?
Have you not understood since the
earth was founded?
[22]He sits enthroned above the circle of the
earth,
and its people are like grasshoppers.
He stretches out the heavens like a
canopy,
and spreads them out like a tent to
live in.
[23]He brings princes to naught
and reduces the rulers of this world to
nothing.
[24]No sooner are they planted,
no sooner are they sown,
no sooner do they take root in the
ground,
than he blows on them and they wither,
and a whirlwind sweeps them away like
chaff.

[25]"To whom will you compare me?
Or who is my equal?" says the Holy
One.

[a]3 Hebrew; Septuagint *make straight the paths of our God*
high mountain. / O Jerusalem, bringer of good tidings
[b]9 Or *O Zion, bringer of good tidings, / go up on a*
[c]13 Or *Spirit*; or *spirit*

26 Lift your eyes and look to the heavens:
Who created all these?
He who brings out the starry host one by one,
and calls them each by name.
Because of his great power and mighty strength,
not one of them is missing.

27 Why do you say, O Jacob,
and complain, O Israel,
"My way is hidden from the LORD;
my cause is disregarded by my God"?
28 Do you not know?
Have you not heard?
The LORD is the everlasting God,
the Creator of the ends of the earth.
He will not grow tired or weary,
and his understanding no one can fathom.
29 He gives strength to the weary
and increases the power of the weak.
30 Even youths grow tired and weary,
and young men stumble and fall;
31 but those who hope in the LORD
will renew their strength.
They will soar on wings like eagles;
they will run and not grow weary,
they will walk and not be faint.

The Helper of Israel

41 "Be silent before me, you islands!
Let the nations renew their strength!
Let them come forward and speak;
let us meet together at the place of judgment.

2 "Who has stirred up one from the east,
calling him in righteousness to his service[a]?
He hands nations over to him
and subdues kings before him.
He turns them to dust with his sword,
to windblown chaff with his bow.
3 He pursues them and moves on unscathed,
by a path his feet have not traveled before.
4 Who has done this and carried it through,
calling forth the generations from the beginning?
I, the LORD—with the first of them
and with the last—I am he."

5 The islands have seen it and fear;
the ends of the earth tremble.
They approach and come forward;
6 each helps the other
and says to his brother, "Be strong!"
7 The craftsman encourages the goldsmith,
and he who smooths with the hammer
spurs on him who strikes the anvil.
He says of the welding, "It is good."
He nails down the idol so it will not topple.

8 "But you, O Israel, my servant,
Jacob, whom I have chosen,
you descendants of Abraham my friend,
9 I took you from the ends of the earth,
from its farthest corners I called you.
I said, 'You are my servant';
I have chosen you and have not rejected you.
10 So do not fear, for I am with you;
do not be dismayed, for I am your God.
I will strengthen you and help you;
I will uphold you with my righteous right hand.

11 "All who rage against you
will surely be ashamed and disgraced;
those who oppose you
will be as nothing and perish.
12 Though you search for your enemies,
you will not find them.
Those who wage war against you
will be as nothing at all.
13 For I am the LORD, your God,
who takes hold of your right hand
and says to you, Do not fear;
I will help you.
14 Do not be afraid, O worm Jacob,
O little Israel,
for I myself will help you," declares the LORD,
your Redeemer, the Holy One of Israel.
15 "See, I will make you into a threshing sledge,
new and sharp, with many teeth.
You will thresh the mountains and crush them,
and reduce the hills to chaff.
16 You will winnow them, the wind will pick them up,
and a gale will blow them away.
But you will rejoice in the LORD
and glory in the Holy One of Israel.

17 "The poor and needy search for water,
but there is none;

[a]2 Or / *whom victory meets at every step*

their tongues are parched with thirst.
But I the LORD will answer them;
I, the God of Israel, will not forsake them.
18I will make rivers flow on barren heights,
and springs within the valleys.
I will turn the desert into pools of water,
and the parched ground into springs.
19I will put in the desert
the cedar and the acacia, the myrtle and the olive.
I will set pines in the wasteland,
the fir and the cypress together,
20so that people may see and know,
may consider and understand,
that the hand of the LORD has done this,
that the Holy One of Israel has created it.

21"Present your case," says the LORD.
"Set forth your arguments," says Jacob's King.
22"Bring in ⌊your idols⌋ to tell us
what is going to happen.
Tell us what the former things were,
so that we may consider them
and know their final outcome.
Or declare to us the things to come,
23 tell us what the future holds,
so we may know that you are gods.
Do something, whether good or bad,
so that we will be dismayed and filled with fear.
24But you are less than nothing
and your works are utterly worthless;
he who chooses you is detestable.

25"I have stirred up one from the north, and he comes—
one from the rising sun who calls on my name.
He treads on rulers as if they were mortar,
as if he were a potter treading the clay.
26Who told of this from the beginning, so we could know,
or beforehand, so we could say, 'He was right'?
No one told of this,
no one foretold it,
no one heard any words from you.
27I was the first to tell Zion, 'Look, here they are!'
I gave to Jerusalem a messenger of good tidings.
28I look but there is no one—
no one among them to give counsel,
no one to give answer when I ask them.
29See, they are all false!
Their deeds amount to nothing;
their images are but wind and confusion.

The Servant of the LORD

42 "Here is my servant, whom I uphold,
my chosen one in whom I delight;
I will put my Spirit on him
and he will bring justice to the nations.
2He will not shout or cry out,
or raise his voice in the streets.
3A bruised reed he will not break,
and a smoldering wick he will not snuff out.
In faithfulness he will bring forth justice;
4 he will not falter or be discouraged
till he establishes justice on earth.
In his law the islands will put their hope."

5This is what God the LORD says—
he who created the heavens and stretched them out,
who spread out the earth and all that comes out of it,
who gives breath to its people,
and life to those who walk on it:
6"I, the LORD, have called you in righteousness;
I will take hold of your hand.
I will keep you and will make you
to be a covenant for the people
and a light for the Gentiles,
7to open eyes that are blind,
to free captives from prison
and to release from the dungeon those who sit in darkness.

8"I am the LORD; that is my name!
I will not give my glory to another
or my praise to idols.
9See, the former things have taken place,
and new things I declare;
before they spring into being
I announce them to you."

Song of Praise to the LORD

10Sing to the LORD a new song,
his praise from the ends of the earth,
you who go down to the sea, and all that is in it,
you islands, and all who live in them.

11Let the desert and its towns raise their voices;
let the settlements where Kedar lives rejoice.
Let the people of Sela sing for joy;
let them shout from the mountaintops.
12Let them give glory to the LORD
and proclaim his praise in the islands.
13The LORD will march out like a mighty man,
like a warrior he will stir up his zeal;
with a shout he will raise the battle cry
and will triumph over his enemies.

14"For a long time I have kept silent,
I have been quiet and held myself back.
But now, like a woman in childbirth,
I cry out, I gasp and pant.
15I will lay waste the mountains and hills
and dry up all their vegetation;
I will turn rivers into islands
and dry up the pools.
16I will lead the blind by ways they have not known,
along unfamiliar paths I will guide them;
I will turn the darkness into light before them
and make the rough places smooth.
These are the things I will do;
I will not forsake them.
17But those who trust in idols,
who say to images, 'You are our gods,'
will be turned back in utter shame.

Israel Blind and Deaf

18"Hear, you deaf;
look, you blind, and see!
19Who is blind but my servant,
and deaf like the messenger I send?
Who is blind like the one committed to me,
blind like the servant of the LORD?
20You have seen many things, but have paid no attention;
your ears are open, but you hear nothing."
21It pleased the LORD
for the sake of his righteousness
to make his law great and glorious.
22But this is a people plundered and looted,
all of them trapped in pits
or hidden away in prisons.
They have become plunder,
with no one to rescue them;
they have been made loot,
with no one to say, "Send them back."
23Which of you will listen to this
or pay close attention in time to come?
24Who handed Jacob over to become loot,
and Israel to the plunderers?
Was it not the LORD,
against whom we have sinned?
For they would not follow his ways;
they did not obey his law.
25So he poured out on them his burning anger,
the violence of war.
It enveloped them in flames, yet they did not understand;
it consumed them, but they did not take it to heart.

Israel's Only Savior

43 But now, this is what the LORD says—
he who created you, O Jacob,
he who formed you, O Israel:
"Fear not, for I have redeemed you;
I have summoned you by name; you are mine.
2When you pass through the waters,
I will be with you;
and when you pass through the rivers,
they will not sweep over you.
When you walk through the fire,
you will not be burned;
the flames will not set you ablaze.
3For I am the LORD, your God,
the Holy One of Israel, your Savior;
I give Egypt for your ransom,
Cush[a] and Seba in your stead.
4Since you are precious and honored in my sight,
and because I love you,
I will give men in exchange for you,
and people in exchange for your life.
5Do not be afraid, for I am with you;
I will bring your children from the east
and gather you from the west.
6I will say to the north, 'Give them up!'
and to the south, 'Do not hold them back.'
Bring my sons from afar
and my daughters from the ends of the earth—
7everyone who is called by my name,
whom I created for my glory,
whom I formed and made."

[a]3 That is, the upper Nile region

8 Lead out those who have eyes but are blind,
who have ears but are deaf.
9 All the nations gather together
and the peoples assemble.
Which of them foretold this
and proclaimed to us the former things?
Let them bring in their witnesses to prove they were right,
so that others may hear and say, "It is true."
10 "You are my witnesses," declares the LORD,
"and my servant whom I have chosen,
so that you may know and believe me
and understand that I am he.
Before me no god was formed,
nor will there be one after me.
11 I, even I, am the LORD,
and apart from me there is no savior.
12 I have revealed and saved and proclaimed—
I, and not some foreign god among you.
You are my witnesses," declares the LORD, "that I am God.
13 Yes, and from ancient days I am he.
No one can deliver out of my hand.
When I act, who can reverse it?"

God's Mercy and Israel's Unfaithfulness

14 This is what the LORD says—
your Redeemer, the Holy One of Israel:
"For your sake I will send to Babylon
and bring down as fugitives all the Babylonians,[a]
in the ships in which they took pride.
15 I am the LORD, your Holy One,
Israel's Creator, your King."

16 This is what the LORD says—
he who made a way through the sea,
a path through the mighty waters,
17 who drew out the chariots and horses,
the army and reinforcements together,
and they lay there, never to rise again,
extinguished, snuffed out like a wick:
18 "Forget the former things;
do not dwell on the past.
19 See, I am doing a new thing!
Now it springs up; do you not perceive it?
I am making a way in the desert
and streams in the wasteland.
20 The wild animals honor me,
the jackals and the owls,
because I provide water in the desert
and streams in the wasteland,
to give drink to my people, my chosen,
21 the people I formed for myself
that they may proclaim my praise.

22 "Yet you have not called upon me, O Jacob,
you have not wearied yourselves for me, O Israel.
23 You have not brought me sheep for burnt offerings,
nor honored me with your sacrifices.
I have not burdened you with grain offerings
nor wearied you with demands for incense.
24 You have not bought any fragrant calamus for me,
or lavished on me the fat of your sacrifices.
But you have burdened me with your sins
and wearied me with your offenses.

25 "I, even I, am he who blots out
your transgressions, for my own sake,
and remembers your sins no more.
26 Review the past for me,
let us argue the matter together;
state the case for your innocence.
27 Your first father sinned;
your spokesmen rebelled against me.
28 So I will disgrace the dignitaries of your temple,
and I will consign Jacob to destruction[b]
and Israel to scorn.

Israel the Chosen

44 "But now listen, O Jacob, my servant,
Israel, whom I have chosen.
2 This is what the LORD says—
he who made you, who formed you in the womb,
and who will help you:
Do not be afraid, O Jacob, my servant,
Jeshurun, whom I have chosen.
3 For I will pour water on the thirsty land,
and streams on the dry ground;
I will pour out my Spirit on your offspring,
and my blessing on your descendants.

[a] 14 Or *Chaldeans* [b] 28 The Hebrew term refers to the irrevocable giving over of things or persons to the LORD, often by totally destroying them.

4They will spring up like grass in a
meadow,
like poplar trees by flowing streams.
5One will say, 'I belong to the LORD';
another will call himself by the name of
Jacob;
still another will write on his hand, 'The
LORD's,'
and will take the name Israel.

The LORD, Not Idols

6"This is what the LORD says—
Israel's King and Redeemer, the LORD
Almighty:
I am the first and I am the last;
apart from me there is no God.
7Who then is like me? Let him proclaim it.
Let him declare and lay out before me
what has happened since I established
my ancient people,
and what is yet to come—
yes, let him foretell what will come.
8Do not tremble, do not be afraid.
Did I not proclaim this and foretell it
long ago?
You are my witnesses. Is there any God
besides me?
No, there is no other Rock; I know not
one."

9All who make idols are nothing,
and the things they treasure are
worthless.
Those who would speak up for them are
blind;
they are ignorant, to their own shame.
10Who shapes a god and casts an idol,
which can profit him nothing?
11He and his kind will be put to shame;
craftsmen are nothing but men.
Let them all come together and take their
stand;
they will be brought down to terror and
infamy.

12The blacksmith takes a tool
and works with it in the coals;
he shapes an idol with hammers,
he forges it with the might of his arm.
He gets hungry and loses his strength;
he drinks no water and grows faint.
13The carpenter measures with a line
and makes an outline with a marker;
he roughs it out with chisels
and marks it with compasses.
He shapes it in the form of man,
of man in all his glory,
that it may dwell in a shrine.
14He cut down cedars,
or perhaps took a cypress or oak.
He let it grow among the trees of the
forest,
or planted a pine, and the rain made it
grow.
15It is man's fuel for burning;
some of it he takes and warms himself,
he kindles a fire and bakes bread.
But he also fashions a god and worships
it;
he makes an idol and bows down to it.
16Half of the wood he burns in the fire;
over it he prepares his meal,
he roasts his meat and eats his fill.
He also warms himself and says,
"Ah! I am warm; I see the fire."
17From the rest he makes a god, his idol;
he bows down to it and worships.
He prays to it and says,
"Save me; you are my god."
18They know nothing, they understand
nothing;
their eyes are plastered over so they
cannot see,
and their minds closed so they cannot
understand.
19No one stops to think,
no one has the knowledge or
understanding to say,
"Half of it I used for fuel;
I even baked bread over its coals,
I roasted meat and I ate.
Shall I make a detestable thing from what
is left?
Shall I bow down to a block of wood?"
20He feeds on ashes, a deluded heart
misleads him;
he cannot save himself, or say,
"Is not this thing in my right hand a
lie?"

21"Remember these things, O Jacob,
for you are my servant, O Israel.
I have made you, you are my servant;
O Israel, I will not forget you.
22I have swept away your offenses like a
cloud,
your sins like the morning mist.
Return to me,
for I have redeemed you."

23Sing for joy, O heavens, for the LORD has
done this;
shout aloud, O earth beneath.
Burst into song, you mountains,

you forests and all your trees,
for the LORD has redeemed Jacob,
he displays his glory in Israel.

Jerusalem to Be Inhabited

24"This is what the LORD says—
your Redeemer, who formed you in the womb:

I am the LORD,
who has made all things,
who alone stretched out the heavens,
who spread out the earth by myself,

25who foils the signs of false prophets
and makes fools of diviners,
who overthrows the learning of the wise
and turns it into nonsense,
26who carries out the words of his servants
and fulfills the predictions of his messengers,

who says of Jerusalem, 'It shall be inhabited,'
of the towns of Judah, 'They shall be built,'
and of their ruins, 'I will restore them,'
27who says to the watery deep, 'Be dry,
and I will dry up your streams,'
28who says of Cyrus, 'He is my shepherd
and will accomplish all that I please;
he will say of Jerusalem, "Let it be rebuilt,"
and of the temple, "Let its foundations be laid." '

45 "This is what the LORD says to his anointed,
to Cyrus, whose right hand I take hold of
to subdue nations before him
and to strip kings of their armor,
to open doors before him
so that gates will not be shut:
2I will go before you
and will level the mountains[a];
I will break down gates of bronze
and cut through bars of iron.
3I will give you the treasures of darkness,
riches stored in secret places,
so that you may know that I am the LORD,
the God of Israel, who summons you by name.
4For the sake of Jacob my servant,
of Israel my chosen,
I summon you by name
and bestow on you a title of honor,
though you do not acknowledge me.
5I am the LORD, and there is no other;
apart from me there is no God.
I will strengthen you,
though you have not acknowledged me,
6so that from the rising of the sun
to the place of its setting
men may know there is none besides me.
I am the LORD, and there is no other.
7I form the light and create darkness,
I bring prosperity and create disaster;
I, the LORD, do all these things.

8"You heavens above, rain down righteousness;
let the clouds shower it down.
Let the earth open wide,
let salvation spring up,
let righteousness grow with it;
I, the LORD, have created it.

9"Woe to him who quarrels with his Maker,
to him who is but a potsherd among the potsherds on the ground.
Does the clay say to the potter,
'What are you making?'
Does your work say,
'He has no hands'?
10Woe to him who says to his father,
'What have you begotten?'
or to his mother,
'What have you brought to birth?'

11"This is what the LORD says—
the Holy One of Israel, and its Maker:
Concerning things to come,
do you question me about my children,
or give me orders about the work of my hands?
12It is I who made the earth
and created mankind upon it.
My own hands stretched out the heavens;
I marshaled their starry hosts.
13I will raise up Cyrus[b] in my righteousness:
I will make all his ways straight.
He will rebuild my city
and set my exiles free,
but not for a price or reward,
says the LORD Almighty."

14This is what the LORD says:

"The products of Egypt and the merchandise of Cush,[c]

[a]2 Dead Sea Scrolls and Septuagint; the meaning of the word in the Masoretic Text is uncertain. [b]13 Hebrew *him* [c]14 That is, the upper Nile region

and those tall Sabeans—
they will come over to you
and will be yours;
they will trudge behind you,
coming over to you in chains.
They will bow down before you
and plead with you, saying,
'Surely God is with you, and there is no other;
there is no other god.' "

15 Truly you are a God who hides himself,
O God and Savior of Israel.
16 All the makers of idols will be put to shame and disgraced;
they will go off into disgrace together.
17 But Israel will be saved by the LORD
with an everlasting salvation;
you will never be put to shame or disgraced,
to ages everlasting.

18 For this is what the LORD says—
he who created the heavens,
he is God;
he who fashioned and made the earth,
he founded it;
he did not create it to be empty,
but formed it to be inhabited—
he says:
"I am the LORD,
and there is no other.
19 I have not spoken in secret,
from somewhere in a land of darkness;
I have not said to Jacob's descendants,
'Seek me in vain.'
I, the LORD, speak the truth;
I declare what is right.

20 "Gather together and come;
assemble, you fugitives from the nations.
Ignorant are those who carry about idols of wood,
who pray to gods that cannot save.
21 Declare what is to be, present it—
let them take counsel together.
Who foretold this long ago,
who declared it from the distant past?
Was it not I, the LORD?
And there is no God apart from me,
a righteous God and a Savior;
there is none but me.

22 "Turn to me and be saved,
all you ends of the earth;
for I am God, and there is no other.
23 By myself I have sworn,
my mouth has uttered in all integrity
a word that will not be revoked:
Before me every knee will bow;
by me every tongue will swear.
24 They will say of me, 'In the LORD alone
are righteousness and strength.' "
All who have raged against him
will come to him and be put to shame.
25 But in the LORD all the descendants of Israel
will be found righteous and will exult.

Gods of Babylon

46 Bel bows down, Nebo stoops low;
their idols are borne by beasts of burden.[a]
The images that are carried about are burdensome,
a burden for the weary.
2 They stoop and bow down together;
unable to rescue the burden,
they themselves go off into captivity.

3 "Listen to me, O house of Jacob,
all you who remain of the house of Israel,
you whom I have upheld since you were conceived,
and have carried since your birth.
4 Even to your old age and gray hairs
I am he, I am he who will sustain you.
I have made you and I will carry you;
I will sustain you and I will rescue you.

5 "To whom will you compare me or count me equal?
To whom will you liken me that we may be compared?
6 Some pour out gold from their bags
and weigh out silver on the scales;
they hire a goldsmith to make it into a god,
and they bow down and worship it.
7 They lift it to their shoulders and carry it;
they set it up in its place, and there it stands.
From that spot it cannot move.
Though one cries out to it, it does not answer;
it cannot save him from his troubles.

8 "Remember this, fix it in mind,
take it to heart, you rebels.
9 Remember the former things, those of long ago;

[a] 1 Or *are but beasts and cattle*

I am God, and there is no other;
I am God, and there is none like me.
10I make known the end from the beginning,
from ancient times, what is still to come.
I say: My purpose will stand,
and I will do all that I please.
11From the east I summon a bird of prey;
from a far-off land, a man to fulfill my purpose.
What I have said, that will I bring about;
what I have planned, that will I do.
12Listen to me, you stubborn-hearted,
you who are far from righteousness.
13I am bringing my righteousness near,
it is not far away;
and my salvation will not be delayed.
I will grant salvation to Zion,
my splendor to Israel.

The Fall of Babylon

47 "Go down, sit in the dust,
Virgin Daughter of Babylon;
sit on the ground without a throne,
Daughter of the Babylonians.[a]
No more will you be called
tender or delicate.
2Take millstones and grind flour;
take off your veil.
Lift up your skirts, bare your legs,
and wade through the streams.
3Your nakedness will be exposed
and your shame uncovered.
I will take vengeance;
I will spare no one."

4Our Redeemer—the LORD Almighty is his name—
is the Holy One of Israel.

5"Sit in silence, go into darkness,
Daughter of the Babylonians;
no more will you be called
queen of kingdoms.
6I was angry with my people
and desecrated my inheritance;
I gave them into your hand,
and you showed them no mercy.
Even on the aged
you laid a very heavy yoke.
7You said, 'I will continue forever—
the eternal queen!'
But you did not consider these things
or reflect on what might happen.

8"Now then, listen, you wanton creature,
lounging in your security
and saying to yourself,
'I am, and there is none besides me.
I will never be a widow
or suffer the loss of children.'
9Both of these will overtake you
in a moment, on a single day:
loss of children and widowhood.
They will come upon you in full measure,
in spite of your many sorceries
and all your potent spells.
10You have trusted in your wickedness
and have said, 'No one sees me.'
Your wisdom and knowledge mislead you
when you say to yourself,
'I am, and there is none besides me.'
11Disaster will come upon you,
and you will not know how to conjure it away.
A calamity will fall upon you
that you cannot ward off with a ransom;
a catastrophe you cannot foresee
will suddenly come upon you.

12"Keep on, then, with your magic spells
and with your many sorceries,
which you have labored at since childhood.
Perhaps you will succeed,
perhaps you will cause terror.
13All the counsel you have received has only worn you out!
Let your astrologers come forward,
those stargazers who make predictions month by month,
let them save you from what is coming upon you.
14Surely they are like stubble;
the fire will burn them up.
They cannot even save themselves
from the power of the flame.
Here are no coals to warm anyone;
here is no fire to sit by.
15That is all they can do for you—
these you have labored with
and trafficked with since childhood.
Each of them goes on in his error;
there is not one that can save you.

Stubborn Israel

48 "Listen to this, O house of Jacob,
you who are called by the name of Israel

[a] 1 Or *Chaldeans;* also in verse 5

and come from the line of Judah,
you who take oaths in the name of the LORD
and invoke the God of Israel—
but not in truth or righteousness—
2you who call yourselves citizens of the holy city
and rely on the God of Israel—
the LORD Almighty is his name:
3I foretold the former things long ago,
my mouth announced them and I made them known;
then suddenly I acted, and they came to pass.
4For I knew how stubborn you were;
the sinews of your neck were iron,
your forehead was bronze.
5Therefore I told you these things long ago;
before they happened I announced them to you
so that you could not say,
'My idols did them;
my wooden image and metal god ordained them.'
6You have heard these things; look at them all.
Will you not admit them?

"From now on I will tell you of new things,
of hidden things unknown to you.
7They are created now, and not long ago;
you have not heard of them before today.
So you cannot say,
'Yes, I knew of them.'
8You have neither heard nor understood;
from of old your ear has not been open.
Well do I know how treacherous you are;
you were called a rebel from birth.
9For my own name's sake I delay my wrath;
for the sake of my praise I hold it back from you,
so as not to cut you off.
10See, I have refined you, though not as silver;
I have tested you in the furnace of affliction.
11For my own sake, for my own sake, I do this.
How can I let myself be defamed?
I will not yield my glory to another.

Israel Freed

12"Listen to me, O Jacob,
Israel, whom I have called:
I am he;
I am the first and I am the last.
13My own hand laid the foundations of the earth,
and my right hand spread out the heavens;
when I summon them,
they all stand up together.

14"Come together, all of you, and listen:
Which of ⌞the idols⌟ has foretold these things?
The LORD's chosen ally
will carry out his purpose against Babylon;
his arm will be against the Babylonians.[a]
15I, even I, have spoken;
yes, I have called him.
I will bring him,
and he will succeed in his mission.

16"Come near me and listen to this:

"From the first announcement I have not spoken in secret;
at the time it happens, I am there."

And now the Sovereign LORD has sent me,
with his Spirit.

17This is what the LORD says—
your Redeemer, the Holy One of Israel:
"I am the LORD your God,
who teaches you what is best for you,
who directs you in the way you should go.
18If only you had paid attention to my commands,
your peace would have been like a river,
your righteousness like the waves of the sea.
19Your descendants would have been like the sand,
your children like its numberless grains;
their name would never be cut off
nor destroyed from before me."

20Leave Babylon,
flee from the Babylonians!

[a]14 Or *Chaldeans;* also in verse 20

Announce this with shouts of joy
and proclaim it.
Send it out to the ends of the earth;
say, "The LORD has redeemed his servant Jacob."
21 They did not thirst when he led them through the deserts;
he made water flow for them from the rock;
he split the rock
and water gushed out.

22 "There is no peace," says the LORD, "for the wicked."

The Servant of the LORD

49 Listen to me, you islands;
hear this, you distant nations:
Before I was born the LORD called me;
from my birth he has made mention of my name.
2 He made my mouth like a sharpened sword,
in the shadow of his hand he hid me;
he made me into a polished arrow
and concealed me in his quiver.
3 He said to me, "You are my servant,
Israel, in whom I will display my splendor."
4 But I said, "I have labored to no purpose;
I have spent my strength in vain and for nothing.
Yet what is due me is in the LORD's hand,
and my reward is with my God."

5 And now the LORD says—
he who formed me in the womb to be his servant
to bring Jacob back to him
and gather Israel to himself,
for I am honored in the eyes of the LORD
and my God has been my strength—
6 he says:
"It is too small a thing for you to be my servant
to restore the tribes of Jacob
and bring back those of Israel I have kept.
I will also make you a light for the Gentiles,
that you may bring my salvation to the ends of the earth."

7 This is what the LORD says—
the Redeemer and Holy One of Israel—
to him who was despised and abhorred by the nation,
to the servant of rulers:
"Kings will see you and rise up,
princes will see and bow down,
because of the LORD, who is faithful,
the Holy One of Israel, who has chosen you."

Restoration of Israel

8 This is what the LORD says:

"In the time of my favor I will answer you,
and in the day of salvation I will help you;
I will keep you and will make you
to be a covenant for the people,
to restore the land
and to reassign its desolate inheritances,
9 to say to the captives, 'Come out,'
and to those in darkness, 'Be free!'

"They will feed beside the roads
and find pasture on every barren hill.
10 They will neither hunger nor thirst,
nor will the desert heat or the sun beat upon them.
He who has compassion on them will guide them
and lead them beside springs of water.
11 I will turn all my mountains into roads,
and my highways will be raised up.
12 See, they will come from afar—
some from the north, some from the west,
some from the region of Aswan.[a]"

13 Shout for joy, O heavens;
rejoice, O earth;
burst into song, O mountains!
For the LORD comforts his people
and will have compassion on his afflicted ones.

14 But Zion said, "The LORD has forsaken me,
the Lord has forgotten me."

15 "Can a mother forget the baby at her breast
and have no compassion on the child she has borne?
Though she may forget,
I will not forget you!

[a] 12 Dead Sea Scrolls; Masoretic Text *Sinim*

[16]See, I have engraved you on the palms
of my hands;
your walls are ever before me.
[17]Your sons hasten back,
and those who laid you waste depart
from you.
[18]Lift up your eyes and look around;
all your sons gather and come to you.
As surely as I live," declares the LORD,
"you will wear them all as ornaments;
you will put them on, like a bride.

[19]"Though you were ruined and made
desolate
and your land laid waste,
now you will be too small for your people,
and those who devoured you will be far
away.
[20]The children born during your
bereavement
will yet say in your hearing,
'This place is too small for us;
give us more space to live in.'
[21]Then you will say in your heart,
'Who bore me these?
I was bereaved and barren;
I was exiled and rejected.
Who brought these up?
I was left all alone,
but these—where have they come
from?' "

[22]This is what the Sovereign LORD says:

"See, I will beckon to the Gentiles,
I will lift up my banner to the peoples;
they will bring your sons in their arms
and carry your daughters on their
shoulders.
[23]Kings will be your foster fathers,
and their queens your nursing mothers.
They will bow down before you with their
faces to the ground;
they will lick the dust at your feet.
Then you will know that I am the LORD;
those who hope in me will not be
disappointed."

[24]Can plunder be taken from warriors,
or captives rescued from the fierce[a]?

[25]But this is what the LORD says:

"Yes, captives will be taken from warriors,
and plunder retrieved from the fierce;
I will contend with those who contend with
you,
and your children I will save.
[26]I will make your oppressors eat their own
flesh;
they will be drunk on their own blood,
as with wine.
Then all mankind will know
that I, the LORD, am your Savior,
your Redeemer, the Mighty One of
Jacob."

Israel's Sin and the Servant's Obedience

50 This is what the LORD says:

"Where is your mother's certificate
of divorce
with which I sent her away?
Or to which of my creditors
did I sell you?
Because of your sins you were sold;
because of your transgressions your
mother was sent away.
[2]When I came, why was there no one?
When I called, why was there no one to
answer?
Was my arm too short to ransom you?
Do I lack the strength to rescue you?
By a mere rebuke I dry up the sea,
I turn rivers into a desert;
their fish rot for lack of water
and die of thirst.
[3]I clothe the sky with darkness
and make sackcloth its covering."

[4]The Sovereign LORD has given me an
instructed tongue,
to know the word that sustains the
weary.
He wakens me morning by morning,
wakens my ear to listen like one being
taught.
[5]The Sovereign LORD has opened my ears,
and I have not been rebellious;
I have not drawn back.
[6]I offered my back to those who beat me,
my cheeks to those who pulled out my
beard;
I did not hide my face
from mocking and spitting.
[7]Because the Sovereign LORD helps me,
I will not be disgraced.
Therefore have I set my face like flint,
and I know I will not be put to shame.
[8]He who vindicates me is near.
Who then will bring charges against
me?
Let us face each other!

[a]24 Dead Sea Scrolls, Vulgate and Syriac (see also Septuagint and verse 25); Masoretic Text *righteous*

Who is my accuser?
Let him confront me!
9It is the Sovereign LORD who helps me.
Who is he that will condemn me?
They will all wear out like a garment;
the moths will eat them up.

10Who among you fears the LORD
and obeys the word of his servant?
Let him who walks in the dark,
who has no light,
trust in the name of the LORD
and rely on his God.
11But now, all you who light fires
and provide yourselves with flaming torches,
go, walk in the light of your fires
and of the torches you have set ablaze.
This is what you shall receive from my hand:
You will lie down in torment.

Everlasting Salvation for Zion

51 "Listen to me, you who pursue righteousness
and who seek the LORD:
Look to the rock from which you were cut
and to the quarry from which you were hewn;
2look to Abraham, your father,
and to Sarah, who gave you birth.
When I called him he was but one,
and I blessed him and made him many.
3The LORD will surely comfort Zion
and will look with compassion on all her ruins;
he will make her deserts like Eden,
her wastelands like the garden of the LORD.
Joy and gladness will be found in her,
thanksgiving and the sound of singing.

4"Listen to me, my people;
hear me, my nation:
The law will go out from me;
my justice will become a light to the nations.
5My righteousness draws near speedily,
my salvation is on the way,
and my arm will bring justice to the nations.
The islands will look to me
and wait in hope for my arm.
6Lift up your eyes to the heavens,
look at the earth beneath;
the heavens will vanish like smoke,
the earth will wear out like a garment
and its inhabitants die like flies.
But my salvation will last forever,
my righteousness will never fail.

7"Hear me, you who know what is right,
you people who have my law in your hearts:
Do not fear the reproach of men
or be terrified by their insults.
8For the moth will eat them up like a garment;
the worm will devour them like wool.
But my righteousness will last forever,
my salvation through all generations."

9Awake, awake! Clothe yourself with strength,
O arm of the LORD;
awake, as in days gone by,
as in generations of old.
Was it not you who cut Rahab to pieces,
who pierced that monster through?
10Was it not you who dried up the sea,
the waters of the great deep,
who made a road in the depths of the sea
so that the redeemed might cross over?
11The ransomed of the LORD will return.
They will enter Zion with singing;
everlasting joy will crown their heads.
Gladness and joy will overtake them,
and sorrow and sighing will flee away.

12"I, even I, am he who comforts you.
Who are you that you fear mortal men,
the sons of men, who are but grass,
13that you forget the LORD your Maker,
who stretched out the heavens
and laid the foundations of the earth,
that you live in constant terror every day
because of the wrath of the oppressor,
who is bent on destruction?
For where is the wrath of the oppressor?
14 The cowering prisoners will soon be set free;
they will not die in their dungeon,
nor will they lack bread.
15For I am the LORD your God,
who churns up the sea so that its waves roar—
the LORD Almighty is his name.
16I have put my words in your mouth
and covered you with the shadow of my hand—
I who set the heavens in place,
who laid the foundations of the earth,

and who say to Zion, 'You are my
people.'"

The Cup of the LORD's Wrath

17 Awake, awake!
Rise up, O Jerusalem,
you who have drunk from the hand of the
LORD
the cup of his wrath,
you who have drained to its dregs
the goblet that makes men stagger.
18 Of all the sons she bore
there was none to guide her;
of all the sons she reared
there was none to take her by the
hand.
19 These double calamities have come upon
you—
who can comfort you?—
ruin and destruction, famine and sword—
who can[a] console you?
20 Your sons have fainted;
they lie at the head of every street,
like antelope caught in a net.
They are filled with the wrath of the LORD
and the rebuke of your God.

21 Therefore hear this, you afflicted one,
made drunk, but not with wine.
22 This is what your Sovereign LORD says,
your God, who defends his people:
"See, I have taken out of your hand
the cup that made you stagger;
from that cup, the goblet of my wrath,
you will never drink again.
23 I will put it into the hands of your
tormentors,
who said to you,
'Fall prostrate that we may walk over
you.'
And you made your back like the ground,
like a street to be walked over."

52 Awake, awake, O Zion,
clothe yourself with strength.
Put on your garments of splendor,
O Jerusalem, the holy city.
The uncircumcised and defiled
will not enter you again.
2 Shake off your dust;
rise up, sit enthroned, O Jerusalem.
Free yourself from the chains on your
neck,
O captive Daughter of Zion.

3 For this is what the LORD says:

"You were sold for nothing,
and without money you will be
redeemed."

4 For this is what the Sovereign LORD says:

"At first my people went down to Egypt to
live;
lately, Assyria has oppressed them.

5 "And now what do I have here?" declares
the LORD.

"For my people have been taken away for
nothing,
and those who rule them mock,[b]"
declares the LORD.
"And all day long
my name is constantly blasphemed.
6 Therefore my people will know my name;
therefore in that day they will know
that it is I who foretold it.
Yes, it is I."

7 How beautiful on the mountains
are the feet of those who bring good
news,
who proclaim peace,
who bring good tidings,
who proclaim salvation,
who say to Zion,
"Your God reigns!"
8 Listen! Your watchmen lift up their voices;
together they shout for joy.
When the LORD returns to Zion,
they will see it with their own eyes.
9 Burst into songs of joy together,
you ruins of Jerusalem,
for the LORD has comforted his people,
he has redeemed Jerusalem.
10 The LORD will lay bare his holy arm
in the sight of all the nations,
and all the ends of the earth will see
the salvation of our God.

11 Depart, depart, go out from there!
Touch no unclean thing!
Come out from it and be pure,
you who carry the vessels of the LORD.
12 But you will not leave in haste
or go in flight;
for the LORD will go before you,
the God of Israel will be your rear
guard.

[a] *19* Dead Sea Scrolls, Septuagint, Vulgate and Syriac; Masoretic Text / *how can I* [b] *5* Dead Sea Scrolls and Vulgate; Masoretic Text *wail*

The Suffering and Glory of the Servant

13See, my servant will act wisely[a];
he will be raised and lifted up and highly exalted.
14Just as there were many who were appalled at him[b]—
his appearance was so disfigured beyond that of any man
and his form marred beyond human likeness—
15so will he sprinkle many nations,[c]
and kings will shut their mouths because of him.
For what they were not told, they will see,
and what they have not heard, they will understand.

53 Who has believed our message
and to whom has the arm of the LORD been revealed?
2He grew up before him like a tender shoot,
and like a root out of dry ground.
He had no beauty or majesty to attract us to him,
nothing in his appearance that we should desire him.
3He was despised and rejected by men,
a man of sorrows, and familiar with suffering.
Like one from whom men hide their faces
he was despised, and we esteemed him not.

4Surely he took up our infirmities
and carried our sorrows,
yet we considered him stricken by God,
smitten by him, and afflicted.
5But he was pierced for our transgressions,
he was crushed for our iniquities;
the punishment that brought us peace was upon him,
and by his wounds we are healed.
6We all, like sheep, have gone astray,
each of us has turned to his own way;
and the LORD has laid on him
the iniquity of us all.

7He was oppressed and afflicted,
yet he did not open his mouth;
he was led like a lamb to the slaughter,
and as a sheep before her shearers is silent,
so he did not open his mouth.
8By oppression[d] and judgment he was taken away.
And who can speak of his descendants?
For he was cut off from the land of the living;
for the transgression of my people he was stricken.[e]
9He was assigned a grave with the wicked,
and with the rich in his death,
though he had done no violence,
nor was any deceit in his mouth.

10Yet it was the LORD's will to crush him and cause him to suffer,
and though the LORD makes[f] his life a guilt offering,
he will see his offspring and prolong his days,
and the will of the LORD will prosper in his hand.
11After the suffering of his soul,
he will see the light ⌞of life⌟[g] and be satisfied[h];
by his knowledge[i] my righteous servant will justify many,
and he will bear their iniquities.
12Therefore I will give him a portion among the great,[j]
and he will divide the spoils with the strong,[k]
because he poured out his life unto death,
and was numbered with the transgressors.
For he bore the sin of many,
and made intercession for the transgressors.

The Future Glory of Zion

54 "Sing, O barren woman,
you who never bore a child;
burst into song, shout for joy,
you who were never in labor;
because more are the children of the desolate woman

[a]13 Or *will prosper* [b]14 Hebrew *you* [c]15 Hebrew; Septuagint *so will many nations marvel at him* [d]8 Or *From arrest* [e]8 Or *away. / Yet who of his generation considered / that he was cut off from the land of the living / for the transgression of my people, / to whom the blow was due?* [f]10 Hebrew *though you make* [g]11 Dead Sea Scrolls (see also Septuagint); Masoretic Text does not have *the light ⌞of life⌟.* [h]11 Or (with Masoretic Text) *11He will see the result of the suffering of his soul / and be satisfied* [i]11 Or *by knowledge of him* [j]12 Or *many* [k]12 Or *numerous*

than of her who has a husband,"
says the LORD.
2"Enlarge the place of your tent,
stretch your tent curtains wide,
do not hold back;
lengthen your cords,
strengthen your stakes.
3For you will spread out to the right and to the left;
your descendants will dispossess nations
and settle in their desolate cities.

4"Do not be afraid; you will not suffer shame.
Do not fear disgrace; you will not be humiliated.
You will forget the shame of your youth
and remember no more the reproach of your widowhood.
5For your Maker is your husband—
the LORD Almighty is his name—
the Holy One of Israel is your Redeemer;
he is called the God of all the earth.
6The LORD will call you back
as if you were a wife deserted and distressed in spirit—
a wife who married young,
only to be rejected," says your God.
7"For a brief moment I abandoned you,
but with deep compassion I will bring you back.
8In a surge of anger
I hid my face from you for a moment,
but with everlasting kindness
I will have compassion on you,"
says the LORD your Redeemer.

9"To me this is like the days of Noah,
when I swore that the waters of Noah would never again cover the earth.
So now I have sworn not to be angry with you,
never to rebuke you again.
10Though the mountains be shaken
and the hills be removed,
yet my unfailing love for you will not be shaken
nor my covenant of peace be removed,"
says the LORD, who has compassion on you.

11"O afflicted city, lashed by storms and not comforted,
I will build you with stones of turquoise,[a]
your foundations with sapphires.[b]
12I will make your battlements of rubies,
your gates of sparkling jewels,
and all your walls of precious stones.
13All your sons will be taught by the LORD,
and great will be your children's peace.
14In righteousness you will be established:
Tyranny will be far from you;
you will have nothing to fear.
Terror will be far removed;
it will not come near you.
15If anyone does attack you, it will not be my doing;
whoever attacks you will surrender to you.

16"See, it is I who created the blacksmith
who fans the coals into flame
and forges a weapon fit for its work.
And it is I who have created the destroyer to work havoc;
17 no weapon forged against you will prevail,
and you will refute every tongue that accuses you.
This is the heritage of the servants of the LORD,
and this is their vindication from me,"
declares the LORD.

Invitation to the Thirsty

55 "Come, all you who are thirsty,
come to the waters;
and you who have no money,
come, buy and eat!
Come, buy wine and milk
without money and without cost.
2Why spend money on what is not bread,
and your labor on what does not satisfy?
Listen, listen to me, and eat what is good,
and your soul will delight in the richest of fare.
3Give ear and come to me;
hear me, that your soul may live.
I will make an everlasting covenant with you,
my faithful love promised to David.
4See, I have made him a witness to the peoples,
a leader and commander of the peoples.

[a] 11 The meaning of the Hebrew for this word is uncertain. [b] 11 Or *lapis lazuli*

5Surely you will summon nations you know not,
and nations that do not know you will hasten to you,
because of the LORD your God,
the Holy One of Israel,
for he has endowed you with splendor."

6Seek the LORD while he may be found;
call on him while he is near.
7Let the wicked forsake his way
and the evil man his thoughts.
Let him turn to the LORD, and he will have mercy on him,
and to our God, for he will freely pardon.

8"For my thoughts are not your thoughts,
neither are your ways my ways,"
declares the LORD.
9"As the heavens are higher than the earth,
so are my ways higher than your ways
and my thoughts than your thoughts.
10As the rain and the snow
come down from heaven,
and do not return to it
without watering the earth
and making it bud and flourish,
so that it yields seed for the sower and bread for the eater,
11so is my word that goes out from my mouth:
It will not return to me empty,
but will accomplish what I desire
and achieve the purpose for which I sent it.
12You will go out in joy
and be led forth in peace;
the mountains and hills
will burst into song before you,
and all the trees of the field
will clap their hands.
13Instead of the thornbush will grow the pine tree,
and instead of briers the myrtle will grow.
This will be for the LORD's renown,
for an everlasting sign,
which will not be destroyed."

Salvation for Others

56 This is what the LORD says:
"Maintain justice
and do what is right,
for my salvation is close at hand
and my righteousness will soon be revealed.
2Blessed is the man who does this,
the man who holds it fast,
who keeps the Sabbath without desecrating it,
and keeps his hand from doing any evil."
3Let no foreigner who has bound himself to the LORD say,
"The LORD will surely exclude me from his people."
And let not any eunuch complain,
"I am only a dry tree."

4For this is what the LORD says:

"To the eunuchs who keep my Sabbaths,
who choose what pleases me
and hold fast to my covenant—
5to them I will give within my temple and its walls
a memorial and a name
better than sons and daughters;
I will give them an everlasting name
that will not be cut off.
6And foreigners who bind themselves to the LORD
to serve him,
to love the name of the LORD,
and to worship him,
all who keep the Sabbath without desecrating it
and who hold fast to my covenant—
7these I will bring to my holy mountain
and give them joy in my house of prayer.
Their burnt offerings and sacrifices
will be accepted on my altar;
for my house will be called
a house of prayer for all nations."
8The Sovereign LORD declares—
he who gathers the exiles of Israel:
"I will gather still others to them
besides those already gathered."

God's Accusation Against the Wicked

9Come, all you beasts of the field,
come and devour, all you beasts of the forest!
10Israel's watchmen are blind,
they all lack knowledge;
they are all mute dogs,
they cannot bark;
they lie around and dream,
they love to sleep.

11They are dogs with mighty appetites;
they never have enough.
They are shepherds who lack understanding;
they all turn to their own way,
each seeks his own gain.
12"Come," each one cries, "let me get wine!
Let us drink our fill of beer!
And tomorrow will be like today,
or even far better."

57 The righteous perish,
and no one ponders it in his heart;
devout men are taken away,
and no one understands
that the righteous are taken away
to be spared from evil.
2Those who walk uprightly
enter into peace;
they find rest as they lie in death.

3"But you—come here, you sons of a sorceress,
you offspring of adulterers and prostitutes!
4Whom are you mocking?
At whom do you sneer
and stick out your tongue?
Are you not a brood of rebels,
the offspring of liars?
5You burn with lust among the oaks
and under every spreading tree;
you sacrifice your children in the ravines
and under the overhanging crags.
6⌊The idols⌋ among the smooth stones of the ravines are your portion;
they, they are your lot.
Yes, to them you have poured out drink offerings
and offered grain offerings.
In the light of these things, should I relent?
7You have made your bed on a high and lofty hill;
there you went up to offer your sacrifices.
8Behind your doors and your doorposts
you have put your pagan symbols.
Forsaking me, you uncovered your bed,
you climbed into it and opened it wide;
you made a pact with those whose beds you love,
and you looked on their nakedness.
9You went to Molech[a] with olive oil
and increased your perfumes.
You sent your ambassadors[b] far away;
you descended to the grave[c] itself!
10You were wearied by all your ways,
but you would not say, 'It is hopeless.'
You found renewal of your strength,
and so you did not faint.

11"Whom have you so dreaded and feared
that you have been false to me,
and have neither remembered me
nor pondered this in your hearts?
Is it not because I have long been silent
that you do not fear me?
12I will expose your righteousness and your works,
and they will not benefit you.
13When you cry out for help,
let your collection ⌊of idols⌋ save you!
The wind will carry all of them off,
a mere breath will blow them away.
But the man who makes me his refuge
will inherit the land
and possess my holy mountain."

Comfort for the Contrite

14And it will be said:

"Build up, build up, prepare the road!
Remove the obstacles out of the way of my people."
15For this is what the high and lofty One says—
he who lives forever, whose name is holy:
"I live in a high and holy place,
but also with him who is contrite and lowly in spirit,
to revive the spirit of the lowly
and to revive the heart of the contrite.
16I will not accuse forever,
nor will I always be angry,
for then the spirit of man would grow faint before me—
the breath of man that I have created.
17I was enraged by his sinful greed;
I punished him, and hid my face in anger,
yet he kept on in his willful ways.
18I have seen his ways, but I will heal him;
I will guide him and restore comfort to him,
19 creating praise on the lips of the mourners in Israel.
Peace, peace, to those far and near,"
says the LORD. "And I will heal them."

a9 Or *to the king* b9 Or *idols* c9 Hebrew *Sheol*

20But the wicked are like the tossing sea,
which cannot rest,
whose waves cast up mire and mud.
21"There is no peace," says my God, "for
the wicked."

True Fasting

58 "Shout it aloud, do not hold back.
Raise your voice like a trumpet.
Declare to my people their rebellion
and to the house of Jacob their sins.
2For day after day they seek me out;
they seem eager to know my ways,
as if they were a nation that does what is
right
and has not forsaken the commands of
its God.
They ask me for just decisions
and seem eager for God to come near
them.
3'Why have we fasted,' they say,
'and you have not seen it?
Why have we humbled ourselves,
and you have not noticed?'

"Yet on the day of your fasting, you do as
you please
and exploit all your workers.
4Your fasting ends in quarreling and strife,
and in striking each other with wicked
fists.
You cannot fast as you do today
and expect your voice to be heard on
high.
5Is this the kind of fast I have chosen,
only a day for a man to humble
himself?
Is it only for bowing one's head like a
reed
and for lying on sackcloth and ashes?
Is that what you call a fast,
a day acceptable to the LORD?

6"Is not this the kind of fasting I have
chosen:
to loose the chains of injustice
and untie the cords of the yoke,
to set the oppressed free
and break every yoke?
7Is it not to share your food with the
hungry
and to provide the poor wanderer with
shelter—
when you see the naked, to clothe him,
and not to turn away from your own
flesh and blood?
8Then your light will break forth like the
dawn,
and your healing will quickly appear;
then your righteousness[a] will go before
you,
and the glory of the LORD will be your
rear guard.
9Then you will call, and the LORD will
answer;
you will cry for help, and he will say:
Here am I.

"If you do away with the yoke of
oppression,
with the pointing finger and malicious
talk,
10and if you spend yourselves in behalf of
the hungry
and satisfy the needs of the oppressed,
then your light will rise in the darkness,
and your night will become like the
noonday.
11The LORD will guide you always;
he will satisfy your needs in a
sun-scorched land
and will strengthen your frame.
You will be like a well-watered garden,
like a spring whose waters never fail.
12Your people will rebuild the ancient ruins
and will raise up the age-old
foundations;
you will be called Repairer of Broken
Walls,
Restorer of Streets with Dwellings.

13"If you keep your feet from breaking the
Sabbath
and from doing as you please on my
holy day,
if you call the Sabbath a delight
and the LORD's holy day honorable,
and if you honor it by not going your own
way
and not doing as you please or
speaking idle words,
14then you will find your joy in the LORD,
and I will cause you to ride on the
heights of the land
and to feast on the inheritance of your
father Jacob."
The mouth of the LORD has
spoken.

Sin, Confession and Redemption

59 Surely the arm of the LORD is not too
short to save,

[a]8 *Or your righteous One*

nor his ear too dull to hear.
2But your iniquities have separated
you from your God;
your sins have hidden his face from you,
so that he will not hear.
3For your hands are stained with blood,
your fingers with guilt.
Your lips have spoken lies,
and your tongue mutters wicked things.
4No one calls for justice;
no one pleads his case with integrity.
They rely on empty arguments and speak
lies;
they conceive trouble and give birth to
evil.
5They hatch the eggs of vipers
and spin a spider's web.
Whoever eats their eggs will die,
and when one is broken, an adder is
hatched.
6Their cobwebs are useless for clothing;
they cannot cover themselves with
what they make.
Their deeds are evil deeds,
and acts of violence are in their hands.
7Their feet rush into sin;
they are swift to shed innocent blood.
Their thoughts are evil thoughts;
ruin and destruction mark their ways.
8The way of peace they do not know;
there is no justice in their paths.
They have turned them into crooked
roads;
no one who walks in them will know
peace.

9So justice is far from us,
and righteousness does not reach us.
We look for light, but all is darkness;
for brightness, but we walk in deep
shadows.
10Like the blind we grope along the wall,
feeling our way like men without eyes.
At midday we stumble as if it were
twilight;
among the strong, we are like the dead.
11We all growl like bears;
we moan mournfully like doves.
We look for justice, but find none;
for deliverance, but it is far away.

12For our offenses are many in your sight,
and our sins testify against us.
Our offenses are ever with us,
and we acknowledge our iniquities:
13rebellion and treachery against the LORD,
turning our backs on our God,
fomenting oppression and revolt,
uttering lies our hearts have conceived.
14So justice is driven back,
and righteousness stands at a
distance;
truth has stumbled in the streets,
honesty cannot enter.
15Truth is nowhere to be found,
and whoever shuns evil becomes a
prey.

The LORD looked and was displeased
that there was no justice.
16He saw that there was no one,
he was appalled that there was no one
to intervene;
so his own arm worked salvation for him,
and his own righteousness sustained
him.
17He put on righteousness as his
breastplate,
and the helmet of salvation on his
head;
he put on the garments of vengeance
and wrapped himself in zeal as in a
cloak.
18According to what they have done,
so will he repay
wrath to his enemies
and retribution to his foes;
he will repay the islands their due.
19From the west, men will fear the name of
the LORD,
and from the rising of the sun, they will
revere his glory.
For he will come like a pent-up flood
that the breath of the LORD drives
along.[a]

20"The Redeemer will come to Zion,
to those in Jacob who repent of their
sins,"
declares the LORD.

21"As for me, this is my covenant with
them," says the LORD. "My Spirit, who is on
you, and my words that I have put in your
mouth will not depart from your mouth, or
from the mouths of your children, or from the
mouths of their descendants from this time
on and forever," says the LORD.

The Glory of Zion

60 "Arise, shine, for your light has
come,

[a]19 Or *When the enemy comes in like a flood, / the Spirit of the LORD will put him to flight*

and the glory of the LORD rises upon
you.
[2]See, darkness covers the earth
and thick darkness is over the peoples,
but the LORD rises upon you
and his glory appears over you.
[3]Nations will come to your light,
and kings to the brightness of your
dawn.

[4]"Lift up your eyes and look about you:
All assemble and come to you;
your sons come from afar,
and your daughters are carried on the
arm.
[5]Then you will look and be radiant,
your heart will throb and swell with joy;
the wealth on the seas will be brought to
you,
to you the riches of the nations will
come.
[6]Herds of camels will cover your land,
young camels of Midian and Ephah.
And all from Sheba will come,
bearing gold and incense
and proclaiming the praise of the LORD.
[7]All Kedar's flocks will be gathered to you,
the rams of Nebaioth will serve you;
they will be accepted as offerings on my
altar,
and I will adorn my glorious temple.

[8]"Who are these that fly along like clouds,
like doves to their nests?
[9]Surely the islands look to me;
in the lead are the ships of Tarshish,[a]
bringing your sons from afar,
with their silver and gold,
to the honor of the LORD your God,
the Holy One of Israel,
for he has endowed you with
splendor.

[10]"Foreigners will rebuild your walls,
and their kings will serve you.
Though in anger I struck you,
in favor I will show you compassion.
[11]Your gates will always stand open,
they will never be shut, day or night,
so that men may bring you the wealth of
the nations—
their kings led in triumphal procession.
[12]For the nation or kingdom that will not
serve you will perish;
it will be utterly ruined.

[13]"The glory of Lebanon will come to you,
the pine, the fir and the cypress
together,
to adorn the place of my sanctuary;
and I will glorify the place of my feet.
[14]The sons of your oppressors will come
bowing before you;
all who despise you will bow down at
your feet
and will call you the City of the LORD,
Zion of the Holy One of Israel.

[15]"Although you have been forsaken and
hated,
with no one traveling through,
I will make you the everlasting pride
and the joy of all generations.
[16]You will drink the milk of nations
and be nursed at royal breasts.
Then you will know that I, the LORD, am
your Savior,
your Redeemer, the Mighty One of
Jacob.
[17]Instead of bronze I will bring you gold,
and silver in place of iron.
Instead of wood I will bring you bronze,
and iron in place of stones.
I will make peace your governor
and righteousness your ruler.
[18]No longer will violence be heard in your
land,
nor ruin or destruction within your
borders,
but you will call your walls Salvation
and your gates Praise.
[19]The sun will no more be your light by
day,
nor will the brightness of the moon
shine on you,
for the LORD will be your everlasting light,
and your God will be your glory.
[20]Your sun will never set again,
and your moon will wane no more;
the LORD will be your everlasting light,
and your days of sorrow will end.
[21]Then will all your people be righteous
and they will possess the land
forever.
They are the shoot I have planted,
the work of my hands,
for the display of my splendor.
[22]The least of you will become a thousand,
the smallest a mighty nation.
I am the LORD;
in its time I will do this swiftly."

[a]9 *Or the trading ships*

The Year of the LORD's Favor

61 The Spirit of the Sovereign LORD is
on me,
because the LORD has anointed me
to preach good news to the poor.
He has sent me to bind up the
brokenhearted,
to proclaim freedom for the captives
and release from darkness for the
prisoners,[a]
2to proclaim the year of the LORD's favor
and the day of vengeance of our God,
to comfort all who mourn,
3 and provide for those who grieve in
Zion—
to bestow on them a crown of beauty
instead of ashes,
the oil of gladness
instead of mourning,
and a garment of praise
instead of a spirit of despair.
They will be called oaks of righteousness,
a planting of the LORD
for the display of his splendor.

4They will rebuild the ancient ruins
and restore the places long devastated;
they will renew the ruined cities
that have been devastated for
generations.
5Aliens will shepherd your flocks;
foreigners will work your fields and
vineyards.
6And you will be called priests of the LORD,
you will be named ministers of our God.
You will feed on the wealth of nations,
and in their riches you will boast.

7Instead of their shame
my people will receive a double portion,
and instead of disgrace
they will rejoice in their inheritance;
and so they will inherit a double portion in
their land,
and everlasting joy will be theirs.

8"For I, the LORD, love justice;
I hate robbery and iniquity.
In my faithfulness I will reward them
and make an everlasting covenant with
them.
9Their descendants will be known among
the nations
and their offspring among the peoples.
All who see them will acknowledge
that they are a people the LORD has
blessed."
10I delight greatly in the LORD;
my soul rejoices in my God.
For he has clothed me with garments of
salvation
and arrayed me in a robe of
righteousness,
as a bridegroom adorns his head like a
priest,
and as a bride adorns herself with her
jewels.
11For as the soil makes the sprout come up
and a garden causes seeds to grow,
so the Sovereign LORD will make
righteousness and praise
spring up before all nations.

Zion's New Name

62 For Zion's sake I will not keep
silent,
for Jerusalem's sake I will not remain
quiet,
till her righteousness shines out like the
dawn,
her salvation like a blazing torch.
2The nations will see your righteousness,
and all kings your glory;
you will be called by a new name
that the mouth of the LORD will bestow.
3You will be a crown of splendor in the
LORD's hand,
a royal diadem in the hand of your God.
4No longer will they call you Deserted,
or name your land Desolate.
But you will be called Hephzibah,[b]
and your land Beulah[c];
for the LORD will take delight in you,
and your land will be married.
5As a young man marries a maiden,
so will your sons[d] marry you;
as a bridegroom rejoices over his bride,
so will your God rejoice over you.

6I have posted watchmen on your walls,
O Jerusalem;
they will never be silent day or night.
You who call on the LORD,
give yourselves no rest,
7and give him no rest till he establishes
Jerusalem
and makes her the praise of the earth.

8The LORD has sworn by his right hand

[a] 1 Hebrew; Septuagint *the blind* [b] 4 *Hephzibah* means *my delight is in her.* [c] 4 *Beulah* means *married.*
[d] 5 Or *Builder*

and by his mighty arm:
"Never again will I give your grain
as food for your enemies,
and never again will foreigners drink the
new wine
for which you have toiled;
9but those who harvest it will eat it
and praise the LORD,
and those who gather the grapes will
drink it
in the courts of my sanctuary."

10Pass through, pass through the gates!
Prepare the way for the people.
Build up, build up the highway!
Remove the stones.
Raise a banner for the nations.

11The LORD has made proclamation
to the ends of the earth:
"Say to the Daughter of Zion,
'See, your Savior comes!
See, his reward is with him,
and his recompense accompanies
him.' "
12They will be called the Holy People,
the Redeemed of the LORD;
and you will be called Sought After,
the City No Longer Deserted.

God's Day of Vengeance and Redemption

63 Who is this coming from Edom,
from Bozrah, with his garments
stained crimson?
Who is this, robed in splendor,
striding forward in the greatness of his
strength?

"It is I, speaking in righteousness,
mighty to save."

2Why are your garments red,
like those of one treading the
winepress?

3"I have trodden the winepress alone;
from the nations no one was with me.
I trampled them in my anger
and trod them down in my wrath;
their blood spattered my garments,
and I stained all my clothing.
4For the day of vengeance was in my
heart,
and the year of my redemption has
come.
5I looked, but there was no one to help,
I was appalled that no one gave
support;
so my own arm worked salvation for me,
and my own wrath sustained me.
6I trampled the nations in my anger;
in my wrath I made them drunk
and poured their blood on the ground."

Praise and Prayer

7I will tell of the kindnesses of the LORD,
the deeds for which he is to be praised,
according to all the LORD has done for
us—
yes, the many good things he has done
for the house of Israel,
according to his compassion and many
kindnesses.
8He said, "Surely they are my people,
sons who will not be false to me";
and so he became their Savior.
9In all their distress he too was distressed,
and the angel of his presence saved
them.
In his love and mercy he redeemed them;
he lifted them up and carried them
all the days of old.
10Yet they rebelled
and grieved his Holy Spirit.
So he turned and became their enemy
and he himself fought against them.

11Then his people recalled[a] the days of old,
the days of Moses and his people—
where is he who brought them through
the sea,
with the shepherd of his flock?
Where is he who set
his Holy Spirit among them,
12who sent his glorious arm of power
to be at Moses' right hand,
who divided the waters before them,
to gain for himself everlasting renown,
13who led them through the depths?
Like a horse in open country,
they did not stumble;
14like cattle that go down to the plain,
they were given rest by the Spirit of the
LORD.
This is how you guided your people
to make for yourself a glorious name.

15Look down from heaven and see
from your lofty throne, holy and
glorious.
Where are your zeal and your might?

[a]11 Or *But may he recall*

Your tenderness and compassion are
withheld from us.
16But you are our Father,
though Abraham does not know us
or Israel acknowledge us;
you, O LORD, are our Father,
our Redeemer from of old is your
name.
17Why, O LORD, do you make us wander
from your ways
and harden our hearts so we do not
revere you?
Return for the sake of your servants,
the tribes that are your inheritance.
18For a little while your people possessed
your holy place,
but now our enemies have trampled
down your sanctuary.
19We are yours from of old;
but you have not ruled over them,
they have not been called by your
name.[a]

64 Oh, that you would rend the
heavens and come down,
that the mountains would tremble
before you!
2As when fire sets twigs ablaze
and causes water to boil,
come down to make your name known to
your enemies
and cause the nations to quake before
you!
3For when you did awesome things that
we did not expect,
you came down, and the mountains
trembled before you.
4Since ancient times no one has heard,
no ear has perceived,
no eye has seen any God besides you,
who acts on behalf of those who wait
for him.
5You come to the help of those who gladly
do right,
who remember your ways.
But when we continued to sin against
them,
you were angry.
How then can we be saved?
6All of us have become like one who is
unclean,
and all our righteous acts are like filthy
rags;
we all shrivel up like a leaf,
and like the wind our sins sweep us
away.
7No one calls on your name
or strives to lay hold of you;
for you have hidden your face from us
and made us waste away because of
our sins.
8Yet, O LORD, you are our Father.
We are the clay, you are the potter;
we are all the work of your hand.
9Do not be angry beyond measure,
O LORD;
do not remember our sins forever.
Oh, look upon us, we pray,
for we are all your people.
10Your sacred cities have become a desert;
even Zion is a desert, Jerusalem a
desolation.
11Our holy and glorious temple, where our
fathers praised you,
has been burned with fire,
and all that we treasured lies in ruins.
12After all this, O LORD, will you hold
yourself back?
Will you keep silent and punish us
beyond measure?

Judgment and Salvation

65 "I revealed myself to those who did
not ask for me;
I was found by those who did not seek
me.
To a nation that did not call on my name,
I said, 'Here am I, here am I.'
2All day long I have held out my hands
to an obstinate people,
who walk in ways not good,
pursuing their own imaginations—
3a people who continually provoke me
to my very face,
offering sacrifices in gardens
and burning incense on altars of brick;
4who sit among the graves
and spend their nights keeping secret
vigil;
who eat the flesh of pigs,
and whose pots hold broth of unclean
meat;
5who say, 'Keep away; don't come near
me,
for I am too sacred for you!'
Such people are smoke in my nostrils,
a fire that keeps burning all day.

[a] 19 Or *We are like those you have never ruled, / like those never called by your name*

6"See, it stands written before me:
I will not keep silent but will pay back in full;
I will pay it back into their laps—
7both your sins and the sins of your fathers,"
says the LORD.
"Because they burned sacrifices on the mountains
and defied me on the hills,
I will measure into their laps
the full payment for their former deeds."

8This is what the LORD says:

"As when juice is still found in a cluster of grapes
and men say, 'Don't destroy it,
there is yet some good in it,'
so will I do in behalf of my servants;
I will not destroy them all.
9I will bring forth descendants from Jacob,
and from Judah those who will possess my mountains;
my chosen people will inherit them,
and there will my servants live.
10Sharon will become a pasture for flocks,
and the Valley of Achor a resting place for herds,
for my people who seek me.

11"But as for you who forsake the LORD
and forget my holy mountain,
who spread a table for Fortune
and fill bowls of mixed wine for Destiny,
12I will destine you for the sword,
and you will all bend down for the slaughter;
for I called but you did not answer,
I spoke but you did not listen.
You did evil in my sight
and chose what displeases me."

13Therefore this is what the Sovereign LORD says:

"My servants will eat,
but you will go hungry;
my servants will drink,
but you will go thirsty;
my servants will rejoice,
but you will be put to shame.
14My servants will sing
out of the joy of their hearts,
but you will cry out
from anguish of heart
and wail in brokenness of spirit.
15You will leave your name
to my chosen ones as a curse;
the Sovereign LORD will put you to death,
but to his servants he will give another name.
16Whoever invokes a blessing in the land
will do so by the God of truth;
he who takes an oath in the land
will swear by the God of truth.
For the past troubles will be forgotten
and hidden from my eyes.

New Heavens and a New Earth

17"Behold, I will create
new heavens and a new earth.
The former things will not be remembered,
nor will they come to mind.
18But be glad and rejoice forever
in what I will create,
for I will create Jerusalem to be a delight
and its people a joy.
19I will rejoice over Jerusalem
and take delight in my people;
the sound of weeping and of crying
will be heard in it no more.

20"Never again will there be in it
an infant who lives but a few days,
or an old man who does not live out his years;
he who dies at a hundred
will be thought a mere youth;
he who fails to reach[a] a hundred
will be considered accursed.
21They will build houses and dwell in them;
they will plant vineyards and eat their fruit.
22No longer will they build houses and others live in them,
or plant and others eat.
For as the days of a tree,
so will be the days of my people;
my chosen ones will long enjoy
the works of their hands.
23They will not toil in vain
or bear children doomed to misfortune;
for they will be a people blessed by the LORD,
they and their descendants with them.
24Before they call I will answer;
while they are still speaking I will hear.
25The wolf and the lamb will feed together,
and the lion will eat straw like the ox,
but dust will be the serpent's food.

[a]20 Or / *the sinner who reaches*

They will neither harm nor destroy
on all my holy mountain,"
says the LORD.

Judgment and Hope

66 This is what the LORD says:
"Heaven is my throne,
and the earth is my footstool.
Where is the house you will build for me?
Where will my resting place be?
2Has not my hand made all these things,
and so they came into being?"
declares the LORD.

"This is the one I esteem:
he who is humble and contrite in spirit,
and trembles at my word.
3But whoever sacrifices a bull
is like one who kills a man,
and whoever offers a lamb,
like one who breaks a dog's neck;
whoever makes a grain offering
is like one who presents pig's blood,
and whoever burns memorial incense,
like one who worships an idol.
They have chosen their own ways,
and their souls delight in their
abominations;
4so I also will choose harsh treatment for
them
and will bring upon them what they
dread.
For when I called, no one answered,
when I spoke, no one listened.
They did evil in my sight
and chose what displeases me."
5Hear the word of the LORD,
you who tremble at his word:
"Your brothers who hate you,
and exclude you because of my name,
have said,
'Let the LORD be glorified,
that we may see your joy!'
Yet they will be put to shame.
6Hear that uproar from the city,
hear that noise from the temple!
It is the sound of the LORD
repaying his enemies all they deserve.

7"Before she goes into labor,
she gives birth;
before the pains come upon her,
she delivers a son.
8Who has ever heard of such a thing?
Who has ever seen such things?
Can a country be born in a day
or a nation be brought forth in a
moment?
Yet no sooner is Zion in labor
than she gives birth to her children.
9Do I bring to the moment of birth
and not give delivery?" says the LORD.
"Do I close up the womb
when I bring to delivery?" says your
God.
10"Rejoice with Jerusalem and be glad for
her,
all you who love her;
rejoice greatly with her,
all you who mourn over her.
11For you will nurse and be satisfied
at her comforting breasts;
you will drink deeply
and delight in her overflowing
abundance."

12For this is what the LORD says:
"I will extend peace to her like a river,
and the wealth of nations like a flooding
stream;
you will nurse and be carried on her arm
and dandled on her knees.
13As a mother comforts her child,
so will I comfort you;
and you will be comforted over
Jerusalem."

14When you see this, your heart will rejoice
and you will flourish like grass;
the hand of the LORD will be made known
to his servants,
but his fury will be shown to his foes.
15See, the LORD is coming with fire,
and his chariots are like a whirlwind;
he will bring down his anger with fury,
and his rebuke with flames of fire.
16For with fire and with his sword
the LORD will execute judgment upon all
men,
and many will be those slain by the
LORD.

17"Those who consecrate and purify themselves to go into the gardens, following the
one in the midst of[a] those who eat the flesh
of pigs and rats and other abominable
things—they will meet their end together,"
declares the LORD.
18"And I, because of their actions and their

[a]17 *Or gardens behind one of your temples, and*

imaginations, am about to come[b] and gather
all nations and tongues, and they will come
and see my glory.
19"I will set a sign among them, and I will
send some of those who survive to the nations—to Tarshish, to the Libyans[b] and Lydi-
ans (famous as archers), to Tubal and
Greece, and to the distant islands that have
not heard of my fame or seen my glory. They
will proclaim my glory among the nations.
20And they will bring all your brothers, from
all the nations, to my holy mountain in
Jerusalem as an offering to the LORD—on
horses, in chariots and wagons, and on
mules and camels," says the LORD. "They will
bring them, as the Israelites bring their grain
offerings, to the temple of the LORD in ceremonially clean vessels. 21And I will select
some of them also to be priests and Levites,"
says the LORD.

22"As the new heavens and the new earth
that I make will endure before me," declares
the LORD, "so will your name and descendants endure. 23From one New Moon to another and from one Sabbath to another, all
mankind will come and bow down before
me," says the LORD. 24"And they will go out
and look upon the dead bodies of those who
rebelled against me; their worm will not die,
nor will their fire be quenched, and they will
be loathsome to all mankind."

[a]18 The meaning of the Hebrew for this clause is uncertain. [b]19 Some Septuagint manuscripts *Put* (Libyans); Hebrew *Pul*

Jeremiah

Introduction:

Jeremiah, like Isaiah, was a young man called by God to warn Judah about its wickedness. He spent the first twenty years of his ministry under Josiah, a good king who tried to bring the people of Judah back to God. After this Jeremiah was often in danger from political and religious leaders who were angry because of his messages. Through all this God protected Jeremiah so he could continue to warn the wicked and comfort those who trusted in God.

After Jerusalem was destroyed in 586 B.C., Jeremiah chose to remain with the people, and eventually went with them to Egypt.

Since the messages of Jeremiah are not arranged in chronological order, it is helpful to read the history of Judah as found in Kings and Chronicles to better understand Jeremiah's messages.

Outline of contents:

The call of Jeremiah (1:1–19)
The sinful condition of Judah (2:1–6:30)
The temple, the law and the covenant (7:1–12:17)
The certainty of captivity (13:1–18:23)
Jeremiah confronts the leaders (19:1–29:32)
The promise of restoration (30:1–33:26)
The kingdom falls apart (34:1–39:18)
The trip to Egypt (40:1–45:5)
Messages concerning foreign nations (46:1–51:64)
The fall of Jerusalem (52:1–34)

---

1 The words of Jeremiah son of Hilkiah,
one of the priests at Anathoth in the territory of Benjamin. 2The word of the LORD
came to him in the thirteenth year of the reign
of Josiah son of Amon king of Judah, 3and
through the reign of Jehoiakim son of Josiah
king of Judah, down to the fifth month of the
eleventh year of Zedekiah son of Josiah king
of Judah, when the people of Jerusalem
went into exile.

The Call of Jeremiah

4The word of the LORD came to me, saying,

5"Before I formed you in the womb I
knew[a] you,
before you were born I set you apart;
I appointed you as a prophet to the
nations."

6"Ah, Sovereign LORD," I said, "I do not
know how to speak; I am only a child."
7But the LORD said to me, "Do not say, 'I am
only a child.' You must go to everyone I send
you to and say whatever I command you.
8Do not be afraid of them, for I am with you
and will rescue you," declares the LORD.
9Then the LORD reached out his hand and
touched my mouth and said to me, "Now, I
have put my words in your mouth. 10See,
today I appoint you over nations and kingdoms to uproot and tear down, to destroy
and overthrow, to build and to plant."
11The word of the LORD came to me: "What
do you see, Jeremiah?"

"I see the branch of an almond tree," I
replied.

12The LORD said to me, "You have seen
correctly, for I am watching[b] to see that my
word is fulfilled."
13The word of the LORD came to me again:
"What do you see?"

"I see a boiling pot, tilting away from the
north," I answered.

14The LORD said to me, "From the north

[a]5 Or *chose* [b]12 The Hebrew for *watching* sounds like the Hebrew for *almond tree.*

disaster will be poured out on all who live in
the land. [15]I am about to summon all the
peoples of the northern kingdoms," declares
the LORD.

"Their kings will come and set up their thrones
in the entrance of the gates of Jerusalem;
they will come against all her surrounding walls
and against all the towns of Judah.
[16]I will pronounce my judgments on my people
because of their wickedness in forsaking me,
in burning incense to other gods
and in worshiping what their hands have made.

[17]"Get yourself ready! Stand up and say to
them whatever I command you. Do not be
terrified by them, or I will terrify you before
them. [18]Today I have made you a fortified
city, an iron pillar and a bronze wall to stand
against the whole land—against the kings of
Judah, its officials, its priests and the people
of the land. [19]They will fight against you but
will not overcome you, for I am with you and
will rescue you," declares the LORD.

Israel Forsakes God

2 The word of the LORD came to me: [2]"Go
and proclaim in the hearing of Jerusalem:

" 'I remember the devotion of your youth,
how as a bride you loved me
and followed me through the desert,
through a land not sown.
[3]Israel was holy to the LORD,
the firstfruits of his harvest;
all who devoured her were held guilty,
and disaster overtook them,' "
declares the LORD.

[4]Hear the word of the LORD, O house of Jacob,
all you clans of the house of Israel.

[5]This is what the LORD says:

"What fault did your fathers find in me,
that they strayed so far from me?
They followed worthless idols
and became worthless themselves.
[6]They did not ask, 'Where is the LORD,
who brought us up out of Egypt
and led us through the barren wilderness,
through a land of deserts and rifts,
a land of drought and darkness,[a]
a land where no one travels and no one lives?'
[7]I brought you into a fertile land
to eat its fruit and rich produce.
But you came and defiled my land
and made my inheritance detestable.
[8]The priests did not ask,
'Where is the LORD?'
Those who deal with the law did not know me;
the leaders rebelled against me.
The prophets prophesied by Baal,
following worthless idols.

[9]"Therefore I bring charges against you again,"
declares the LORD.
"And I will bring charges against your children's children.
[10]Cross over to the coasts of Kittim[b] and look,
send to Kedar[c] and observe closely;
see if there has ever been anything like this:
[11]Has a nation ever changed its gods?
(Yet they are not gods at all.)
But my people have exchanged their[d] Glory
for worthless idols.
[12]Be appalled at this, O heavens,
and shudder with great horror,"
declares the LORD.
[13]"My people have committed two sins:
They have forsaken me,
the spring of living water,
and have dug their own cisterns,
broken cisterns that cannot hold water.
[14]Is Israel a servant, a slave by birth?
Why then has he become plunder?
[15]Lions have roared;
they have growled at him.
They have laid waste his land;
his towns are burned and deserted.
[16]Also, the men of Memphis[e] and Tahpanhes
have shaved the crown of your head.[f]
[17]Have you not brought this on yourselves
by forsaking the LORD your God
when he led you in the way?
[18]Now why go to Egypt

[a]6 Or *and the shadow of death* [b]10 That is, Cyprus and western coastlands [c]10 The home of Bedouin tribes in the Syro-Arabian desert [d]11 Masoretic Text; an ancient Hebrew scribal tradition *my* [e]16 Hebrew *Noph* [f]16 Or *have cracked your skull*

to drink water from the Shihor[a]?
And why go to Assyria
to drink water from the River[b]?
19Your wickedness will punish you;
your backsliding will rebuke you.
Consider then and realize
how evil and bitter it is for you
when you forsake the LORD your God
and have no awe of me,"
declares the Lord,
the LORD Almighty.

20"Long ago you broke off your yoke
and tore off your bonds;
you said, 'I will not serve you!'
Indeed, on every high hill
and under every spreading tree
you lay down as a prostitute.
21I had planted you like a choice vine
of sound and reliable stock.
How then did you turn against me
into a corrupt, wild vine?
22Although you wash yourself with soda
and use an abundance of soap,
the stain of your guilt is still before me,"
declares the Sovereign LORD.
23"How can you say, 'I am not defiled;
I have not run after the Baals'?
See how you behaved in the valley;
consider what you have done.
You are a swift she-camel
running here and there,
24a wild donkey accustomed to the desert,
sniffing the wind in her craving—
in her heat who can restrain her?
Any males that pursue her need not tire
themselves;
at mating time they will find her.
25Do not run until your feet are bare
and your throat is dry.
But you said, 'It's no use!
I love foreign gods,
and I must go after them.'

26"As a thief is disgraced when he is
caught,
so the house of Israel is disgraced—
they, their kings and their officials,
their priests and their prophets.
27They say to wood, 'You are my father,'
and to stone, 'You gave me birth.'
They have turned their backs to me
and not their faces;
yet when they are in trouble, they say,
'Come and save us!'
28Where then are the gods you made for
yourselves?
Let them come if they can save you
when you are in trouble!
For you have as many gods
as you have towns, O Judah.

29"Why do you bring charges against me?
You have all rebelled against me,"
declares the LORD.
30"In vain I punished your people;
they did not respond to correction.
Your sword has devoured your prophets
like a ravening lion.

31"You of this generation, consider the
word of the LORD:

"Have I been a desert to Israel
or a land of great darkness?
Why do my people say, 'We are free to
roam;
we will come to you no more'?
32Does a maiden forget her jewelry,
a bride her wedding ornaments?
Yet my people have forgotten me,
days without number.
33How skilled you are at pursuing love!
Even the worst of women can learn
from your ways.
34On your clothes men find
the lifeblood of the innocent poor,
though you did not catch them
breaking in.
Yet in spite of all this
35 you say, 'I am innocent;
he is not angry with me.'
But I will pass judgment on you
because you say, 'I have not sinned.'
36Why do you go about so much,
changing your ways?
You will be disappointed by Egypt
as you were by Assyria.
37You will also leave that place
with your hands on your head,
for the LORD has rejected those you trust;
you will not be helped by them.

3 "If a man divorces his wife
and she leaves him and marries
another man,
should he return to her again?
Would not the land be completely
defiled?

[a] 18 That is, a branch of the Nile [b] 18 That is, the Euphrates

But you have lived as a prostitute with
many lovers—
would you now return to me?"
declares the LORD.
[2]"Look up to the barren heights and see.
Is there any place where you have not
been ravished?
By the roadside you sat waiting for lovers,
sat like a nomad[a] in the desert.
You have defiled the land
with your prostitution and wickedness.
[3]Therefore the showers have been
withheld,
and no spring rains have fallen.
Yet you have the brazen look of a
prostitute;
you refuse to blush with shame.
[4]Have you not just called to me:
'My Father, my friend from my youth,
[5]will you always be angry?
Will your wrath continue forever?'
This is how you talk,
but you do all the evil you can."

Unfaithful Israel

[6]During the reign of King Josiah, the LORD
said to me, "Have you seen what faithless
Israel has done? She has gone up on every
high hill and under every spreading tree and
has committed adultery there. [7]I thought that
after she had done all this she would return
to me but she did not, and her unfaithful
sister Judah saw it. [8]I gave faithless Israel
her certificate of divorce and sent her away
because of all her adulteries. Yet I saw that
her unfaithful sister Judah had no fear; she
also went out and committed adultery. [9]Be-
cause Israel's immorality mattered so little to
her, she defiled the land and committed
adultery with stone and wood. [10]In spite of all
this, her unfaithful sister Judah did not return
to me with all her heart, but only in pretense,"
declares the LORD.

[11]The LORD said to me, "Faithless Israel is
more righteous than unfaithful Judah. [12]Go,
proclaim this message toward the north:

" 'Return, faithless Israel,' declares the
LORD,
'I will frown on you no longer,
for I am merciful,' declares the LORD,
'I will not be angry forever.
[13]Only acknowledge your guilt—
you have rebelled against the LORD
your God,
you have scattered your favors to foreign
gods
under every spreading tree,
and have not obeyed me,' "
declares the LORD.

[14]"Return, faithless people," declares the
LORD, "for I am your husband. I will choose
you—one from a town and two from a clan—
and bring you to Zion. [15]Then I will give you
shepherds after my own heart, who will lead
you with knowledge and understanding. [16]In
those days, when your numbers have increased greatly in the land," declares the
LORD, "men will no longer say, 'The ark of the
covenant of the LORD.' It will never enter their
minds or be remembered; it will not be
missed, nor will another one be made. [17]At
that time they will call Jerusalem The Throne
of the LORD, and all nations will gather in
Jerusalem to honor the name of the LORD. No
longer will they follow the stubbornness of
their evil hearts. [18]In those days the house of
Judah will join the house of Israel, and together they will come from a northern land to
the land I gave your forefathers as an inheritance.

[19]"I myself said,

" 'How gladly would I treat you like sons
and give you a desirable land,
the most beautiful inheritance of any
nation.'
I thought you would call me 'Father'
and not turn away from following me.
[20]But like a woman unfaithful to her
husband,
so you have been unfaithful to me,
O house of Israel,"
declares the LORD.

[21]A cry is heard on the barren heights,
the weeping and pleading of the people
of Israel,
because they have perverted their ways
and have forgotten the LORD their God.

[22]"Return, faithless people;
I will cure you of backsliding."

"Yes, we will come to you,
for you are the LORD our God.
[23]Surely the ⌞idolatrous⌟ commotion on the
hills
and mountains is a deception;
surely in the LORD our God
is the salvation of Israel.

[a]2 Or *an Arab*

[24]From our youth shameful gods have consumed
the fruits of our fathers' labor—
their flocks and herds,
their sons and daughters.
[25]Let us lie down in our shame,
and let our disgrace cover us.
We have sinned against the LORD our God,
both we and our fathers;
from our youth till this day
we have not obeyed the LORD our God."

4 "If you will return, O Israel,
return to me,"
declares the LORD.
"If you put your detestable idols out of my sight
and no longer go astray,
[2]and if in a truthful, just and righteous way
you swear, 'As surely as the LORD lives,'
then the nations will be blessed by him
and in him they will glory."

[3]This is what the LORD says to the men of
Judah and to Jerusalem:

"Break up your unplowed ground
and do not sow among thorns.
[4]Circumcise yourselves to the LORD,
circumcise your hearts,
you men of Judah and people of Jerusalem,
or my wrath will break out and burn like fire
because of the evil you have done—
burn with no one to quench it.

Disaster From the North

[5]"Announce in Judah and proclaim in Jerusalem and say:
'Sound the trumpet throughout the land!'
Cry aloud and say:
'Gather together!
Let us flee to the fortified cities!'
[6]Raise the signal to go to Zion!
Flee for safety without delay!
For I am bringing disaster from the north,
even terrible destruction."

[7]A lion has come out of his lair;
a destroyer of nations has set out.
He has left his place
to lay waste your land.
Your towns will lie in ruins
without inhabitant.
[8]So put on sackcloth,
lament and wail,
for the fierce anger of the LORD
has not turned away from us.

[9]"In that day," declares the LORD,
"the king and the officials will lose heart,
the priests will be horrified,
and the prophets will be appalled."

[10]Then I said, "Ah, Sovereign LORD, how
completely you have deceived this people
and Jerusalem by saying, 'You will have
peace,' when the sword is at our throats."
[11]At that time this people and Jerusalem
will be told, "A scorching wind from the barren heights in the desert blows toward my
people, but not to winnow or cleanse; [12]a
wind too strong for that comes from me.[a]
Now I pronounce my judgments against
them."

[13]Look! He advances like the clouds,
his chariots come like a whirlwind,
his horses are swifter than eagles.
Woe to us! We are ruined!
[14]O Jerusalem, wash the evil from your heart and be saved.
How long will you harbor wicked thoughts?
[15]A voice is announcing from Dan,
proclaiming disaster from the hills of Ephraim.
[16]"Tell this to the nations,
proclaim it to Jerusalem:
'A besieging army is coming from a distant land,
raising a war cry against the cities of Judah.
[17]They surround her like men guarding a field,
because she has rebelled against me,' "
declares the LORD.
[18]"Your own conduct and actions
have brought this upon you.
This is your punishment.
How bitter it is!
How it pierces to the heart!"

[19]Oh, my anguish, my anguish!
I writhe in pain.
Oh, the agony of my heart!
My heart pounds within me,

[a]12 Or *comes at my command*

I cannot keep silent.
For I have heard the sound of the trumpet;
I have heard the battle cry.
20Disaster follows disaster;
the whole land lies in ruins.
In an instant my tents are destroyed,
my shelter in a moment.
21How long must I see the battle standard
and hear the sound of the trumpet?

22"My people are fools;
they do not know me.
They are senseless children;
they have no understanding.
They are skilled in doing evil;
they know not how to do good."

23I looked at the earth,
and it was formless and empty;
and at the heavens,
and their light was gone.
24I looked at the mountains,
and they were quaking;
all the hills were swaying.
25I looked, and there were no people;
every bird in the sky had flown away.
26I looked, and the fruitful land was a desert;
all its towns lay in ruins
before the LORD, before his fierce anger.

27This is what the LORD says:

"The whole land will be ruined,
though I will not destroy it completely.
28Therefore the earth will mourn
and the heavens above grow dark,
because I have spoken and will not relent,
I have decided and will not turn back."

29At the sound of horsemen and archers
every town takes to flight.
Some go into the thickets;
some climb up among the rocks.
All the towns are deserted;
no one lives in them.

30What are you doing, O devastated one?
Why dress yourself in scarlet
and put on jewels of gold?
Why shade your eyes with paint?
You adorn yourself in vain.
Your lovers despise you;
they seek your life.

31I hear a cry as of a woman in labor,
a groan as of one bearing her first child—
the cry of the Daughter of Zion gasping for breath,
stretching out her hands and saying,
"Alas! I am fainting;
my life is given over to murderers."

Not One Is Upright

5 "Go up and down the streets of Jerusalem,
look around and consider,
search through her squares.
If you can find but one person
who deals honestly and seeks the truth,
I will forgive this city.
2Although they say, 'As surely as the LORD lives,'
still they are swearing falsely."

3O LORD, do not your eyes look for truth?
You struck them, but they felt no pain;
you crushed them, but they refused correction.
They made their faces harder than stone
and refused to repent.
4I thought, "These are only the poor;
they are foolish,
for they do not know the way of the LORD,
the requirements of their God.
5So I will go to the leaders
and speak to them;
surely they know the way of the LORD,
the requirements of their God."
But with one accord they too had broken off the yoke
and torn off the bonds.
6Therefore a lion from the forest will attack them,
a wolf from the desert will ravage them,
a leopard will lie in wait near their towns
to tear to pieces any who venture out,
for their rebellion is great
and their backslidings many.

7"Why should I forgive you?
Your children have forsaken me
and sworn by gods that are not gods.
I supplied all their needs,
yet they committed adultery
and thronged to the houses of prostitutes.
8They are well-fed, lusty stallions,
each neighing for another man's wife.
9Should I not punish them for this?"
declares the LORD.

"Should I not avenge myself
on such a nation as this?

10"Go through her vineyards and ravage them,
but do not destroy them completely.
Strip off her branches,
for these people do not belong to the LORD.
11The house of Israel and the house of Judah
have been utterly unfaithful to me,"
declares the LORD.

12They have lied about the LORD;
they said, "He will do nothing!
No harm will come to us;
we will never see sword or famine.
13The prophets are but wind
and the word is not in them;
so let what they say be done to them."

14Therefore this is what the LORD God Almighty says:

"Because the people have spoken these words,
I will make my words in your mouth a fire
and these people the wood it consumes.
15O house of Israel," declares the LORD,
"I am bringing a distant nation against you—
an ancient and enduring nation,
a people whose language you do not know,
whose speech you do not understand.
16Their quivers are like an open grave;
all of them are mighty warriors.
17They will devour your harvests and food,
devour your sons and daughters;
they will devour your flocks and herds,
devour your vines and fig trees.
With the sword they will destroy
the fortified cities in which you trust.

18"Yet even in those days," declares the
LORD, "I will not destroy you completely.
19And when the people ask, 'Why has the
LORD our God done all this to us?' you will tell
them, 'As you have forsaken me and served
foreign gods in your own land, so now you
will serve foreigners in a land not your own.'

20"Announce this to the house of Jacob
and proclaim it in Judah:
21Hear this, you foolish and senseless people,
who have eyes but do not see,
who have ears but do not hear:
22Should you not fear me?" declares the LORD.
"Should you not tremble in my presence?
I made the sand a boundary for the sea,
an everlasting barrier it cannot cross.
The waves may roll, but they cannot prevail;
they may roar, but they cannot cross it.
23But these people have stubborn and rebellious hearts;
they have turned aside and gone away.
24They do not say to themselves,
'Let us fear the LORD our God,
who gives autumn and spring rains in season,
who assures us of the regular weeks of harvest.'
25Your wrongdoings have kept these away;
your sins have deprived you of good.

26"Among my people are wicked men
who lie in wait like men who snare birds
and like those who set traps to catch men.
27Like cages full of birds,
their houses are full of deceit;
they have become rich and powerful
28 and have grown fat and sleek.
Their evil deeds have no limit;
they do not plead the case of the fatherless to win it,
they do not defend the rights of the poor.
29Should I not punish them for this?"
declares the LORD.
"Should I not avenge myself
on such a nation as this?

30"A horrible and shocking thing
has happened in the land:
31The prophets prophesy lies,
the priests rule by their own authority,
and my people love it this way.
But what will you do in the end?

Jerusalem Under Siege

6 "Flee for safety, people of Benjamin!
Flee from Jerusalem!
Sound the trumpet in Tekoa!
Raise the signal over Beth Hakkerem!
For disaster looms out of the north,
even terrible destruction.
2I will destroy the Daughter of Zion,
so beautiful and delicate.

3Shepherds with their flocks will come
against her;
they will pitch their tents around her,
each tending his own portion."

4"Prepare for battle against her!
Arise, let us attack at noon!
But, alas, the daylight is fading,
and the shadows of evening grow long.
5So arise, let us attack at night
and destroy her fortresses!"

6This is what the LORD Almighty says:

"Cut down the trees
and build siege ramps against
Jerusalem.
This city must be punished;
it is filled with oppression.
7As a well pours out its water,
so she pours out her wickedness.
Violence and destruction resound in her;
her sickness and wounds are ever
before me.
8Take warning, O Jerusalem,
or I will turn away from you
and make your land desolate
so no one can live in it."

9This is what the LORD Almighty says:

"Let them glean the remnant of Israel
as thoroughly as a vine;
pass your hand over the branches again,
like one gathering grapes."

10To whom can I speak and give warning?
Who will listen to me?
Their ears are closed[a]
so they cannot hear.
The word of the LORD is offensive to them;
they find no pleasure in it.
11But I am full of the wrath of the LORD,
and I cannot hold it in.

"Pour it out on the children in the street
and on the young men gathered
together;
both husband and wife will be caught in it,
and the old, those weighed down with
years.
12Their houses will be turned over to
others,
together with their fields and their
wives,
when I stretch out my hand
against those who live in the land,"
declares the LORD.
13"From the least to the greatest,
all are greedy for gain;
prophets and priests alike,
all practice deceit.
14They dress the wound of my people
as though it were not serious.
'Peace, peace,' they say,
when there is no peace.
15Are they ashamed of their loathsome
conduct?
No, they have no shame at all;
they do not even know how to blush.
So they will fall among the fallen;
they will be brought down when I
punish them,"
says the LORD.

16This is what the LORD says:

"Stand at the crossroads and look;
ask for the ancient paths,
ask where the good way is, and walk in it,
and you will find rest for your souls.
But you said, 'We will not walk in it.'
17I appointed watchmen over you and said,
'Listen to the sound of the trumpet!'
But you said, 'We will not listen.'
18Therefore hear, O nations;
observe, O witnesses,
what will happen to them.
19Hear, O earth:
I am bringing disaster on this people,
the fruit of their schemes,
because they have not listened to my
words
and have rejected my law.
20What do I care about incense from Sheba
or sweet calamus from a distant land?
Your burnt offerings are not acceptable;
your sacrifices do not please me."

21Therefore this is what the LORD says:

"I will put obstacles before this people.
Fathers and sons alike will stumble
over them;
neighbors and friends will perish."

22This is what the LORD says:

"Look, an army is coming
from the land of the north;
a great nation is being stirred up
from the ends of the earth.
23They are armed with bow and spear;
they are cruel and show no mercy.
They sound like the roaring sea
as they ride on their horses;
they come like men in battle formation

[a]10 Hebrew *uncircumcised*

to attack you, O Daughter of Zion."

24We have heard reports about them,
and our hands hang limp.
Anguish has gripped us,
pain like that of a woman in labor.
25Do not go out to the fields
or walk on the roads,
for the enemy has a sword,
and there is terror on every side.
26O my people, put on sackcloth
and roll in ashes;
mourn with bitter wailing
as for an only son,
for suddenly the destroyer
will come upon us.

27"I have made you a tester of metals
and my people the ore,
that you may observe
and test their ways.
28They are all hardened rebels,
going about to slander.
They are bronze and iron;
they all act corruptly.
29The bellows blow fiercely
to burn away the lead with fire,
but the refining goes on in vain;
the wicked are not purged out.
30They are called rejected silver,
because the LORD has rejected them."

False Religion Worthless

7 This is the word that came to Jeremiah
from the LORD: 2"Stand at the gate of the
LORD's house and there proclaim this message:

" 'Hear the word of the LORD, all you people
of Judah who come through these gates to
worship the LORD. 3This is what the LORD Almighty, the God of Israel, says: Reform your
ways and your actions, and I will let you live
in this place. 4Do not trust in deceptive words
and say, "This is the temple of the LORD, the
temple of the LORD, the temple of the LORD!"
5If you really change your ways and your
actions and deal with each other justly, 6if
you do not oppress the alien, the fatherless
or the widow and do not shed innocent blood
in this place, and if you do not follow other
gods to your own harm, 7then I will let you live
in this place, in the land I gave your forefathers for ever and ever. 8But look, you are
trusting in deceptive words that are worthless.

9" 'Will you steal and murder, commit adultery and perjury,[a] burn incense to Baal and
follow other gods you have not known, 10and
then come and stand before me in this
house, which bears my Name, and say, "We
are safe"—safe to do all these detestable
things? 11Has this house, which bears my
Name, become a den of robbers to you? But
I have been watching! declares the LORD.

12" 'Go now to the place in Shiloh where I
first made a dwelling for my Name, and see
what I did to it because of the wickedness of
my people Israel. 13While you were doing all
these things, declares the LORD, I spoke to
you again and again, but you did not listen; I
called you, but you did not answer. 14There-
fore, what I did to Shiloh I will now do to the
house that bears my Name, the temple you
trust in, the place I gave to you and your
fathers. 15I will thrust you from my presence,
just as I did all your brothers, the people of
Ephraim.'

16"So do not pray for this people nor offer
any plea or petition for them; do not plead
with me, for I will not listen to you. 17Do you
not see what they are doing in the towns of
Judah and in the streets of Jerusalem? 18The
children gather wood, the fathers light the
fire, and the women knead the dough and
make cakes of bread for the Queen of
Heaven. They pour out drink offerings to
other gods to provoke me to anger. 19But am
I the one they are provoking? declares the
LORD. Are they not rather harming themselves, to their own shame?

20" 'Therefore this is what the Sovereign
LORD says: My anger and my wrath will be
poured out on this place, on man and beast,
on the trees of the field and on the fruit of the
ground, and it will burn and not be quenched.

21" 'This is what the LORD Almighty, the
God of Israel, says: Go ahead, add your
burnt offerings to your other sacrifices and
eat the meat yourselves! 22For when I
brought your forefathers out of Egypt and
spoke to them, I did not just give them commands about burnt offerings and sacrifices,
23but I gave them this command: Obey me,
and I will be your God and you will be my
people. Walk in all the ways I command you,
that it may go well with you. 24But they did not
listen or pay attention; instead, they followed
the stubborn inclinations of their evil hearts.
They went backward and not forward.
25From the time your forefathers left Egypt
until now, day after day, again and again I

a9 Or *and swear by false gods*

sent you my servants the prophets. 26But
they did not listen to me or pay attention.
They were stiff-necked and did more evil
than their forefathers.'

27"When you tell them all this, they will not
listen to you; when you call to them, they will
not answer. 28Therefore say to them, 'This is
the nation that has not obeyed the LORD its
God or responded to correction. Truth has
perished; it has vanished from their lips.
29Cut off your hair and throw it away; take up
a lament on the barren heights, for the LORD
has rejected and abandoned this generation
that is under his wrath.

The Valley of Slaughter

30" 'The people of Judah have done evil in
my eyes, declares the LORD. They have set
up their detestable idols in the house that
bears my Name and have defiled it. 31They
have built the high places of Topheth in the
Valley of Ben Hinnom to burn their sons and
daughters in the fire—something I did not
command, nor did it enter my mind. 32So
beware, the days are coming, declares the
LORD, when people will no longer call it
Topheth or the Valley of Ben Hinnom, but the
Valley of Slaughter, for they will bury the
dead in Topheth until there is no more room.
33Then the carcasses of this people will
become food for the birds of the air and the
beasts of the earth, and there will be no one
to frighten them away. 34I will bring an end to
the sounds of joy and gladness and to the
voices of bride and bridegroom in the towns
of Judah and the streets of Jerusalem, for
the land will become desolate.

8 " 'At that time, declares the LORD, the
bones of the kings and officials of Judah,
the bones of the priests and prophets, and
the bones of the people of Jerusalem will be
removed from their graves. 2They will be exposed to the sun and the moon and all the
stars of the heavens, which they have loved
and served and which they have followed
and consulted and worshiped. They will not
be gathered up or buried, but will be like
refuse lying on the ground. 3Wherever I banish them, all the survivors of this evil nation
will prefer death to life, declares the LORD
Almighty.'

Sin and Punishment

4"Say to them, 'This is what the LORD says:

" 'When men fall down, do they not get up?
When a man turns away, does he not return?
5Why then have these people turned away?
Why does Jerusalem always turn away?
They cling to deceit;
they refuse to return.
6I have listened attentively,
but they do not say what is right.
No one repents of his wickedness,
saying, "What have I done?"
Each pursues his own course
like a horse charging into battle.
7Even the stork in the sky
knows her appointed seasons,
and the dove, the swift and the thrush
observe the time of their migration.
But my people do not know
the requirements of the LORD.

8" 'How can you say, "We are wise,
for we have the law of the LORD,"
when actually the lying pen of the scribes
has handled it falsely?
9The wise will be put to shame;
they will be dismayed and trapped.
Since they have rejected the word of the LORD,
what kind of wisdom do they have?
10Therefore I will give their wives to other men
and their fields to new owners.
From the least to the greatest,
all are greedy for gain;
prophets and priests alike,
all practice deceit.
11They dress the wound of my people
as though it were not serious.
"Peace, peace," they say,
when there is no peace.
12Are they ashamed of their loathsome conduct?
No, they have no shame at all;
they do not even know how to blush.
So they will fall among the fallen;
they will be brought down when they are punished,
says the LORD.

13" 'I will take away their harvest,
declares the LORD.
There will be no grapes on the vine.
There will be no figs on the tree,
and their leaves will wither.
What I have given them

will be taken from them.[a]' "

[14]"Why are we sitting here?
Gather together!
Let us flee to the fortified cities
and perish there!
For the LORD our God has doomed us to perish
and given us poisoned water to drink,
because we have sinned against him.
[15]We hoped for peace
but no good has come,
for a time of healing
but there was only terror.
[16]The snorting of the enemy's horses
is heard from Dan;
at the neighing of their stallions
the whole land trembles.
They have come to devour
the land and everything in it,
the city and all who live there."

[17]"See, I will send venomous snakes among you,
vipers that cannot be charmed,
and they will bite you,"
declares the LORD.

[18]O my Comforter[b] in sorrow,
my heart is faint within me.
[19]Listen to the cry of my people
from a land far away:
"Is the LORD not in Zion?
Is her King no longer there?"

"Why have they provoked me to anger with their images,
with their worthless foreign idols?"

[20]"The harvest is past,
the summer has ended,
and we are not saved."

[21]Since my people are crushed, I am crushed;
I mourn, and horror grips me.
[22]Is there no balm in Gilead?
Is there no physician there?
Why then is there no healing
for the wound of my people?

9 [1]Oh, that my head were a spring of water
and my eyes a fountain of tears!
I would weep day and night
for the slain of my people.
[2]Oh, that I had in the desert
a lodging place for travelers,
so that I might leave my people
and go away from them;
for they are all adulterers,
a crowd of unfaithful people.

[3]"They make ready their tongue
like a bow, to shoot lies;
it is not by truth
that they triumph[c] in the land.
They go from one sin to another;
they do not acknowledge me,"
declares the LORD.
[4]"Beware of your friends;
do not trust your brothers.
For every brother is a deceiver,[d]
and every friend a slanderer.
[5]Friend deceives friend,
and no one speaks the truth.
They have taught their tongues to lie;
they weary themselves with sinning.
[6]You[e] live in the midst of deception;
in their deceit they refuse to acknowledge me,"
declares the LORD.

[7]Therefore this is what the LORD Almighty
says:

"See, I will refine and test them,
for what else can I do
because of the sin of my people?
[8]Their tongue is a deadly arrow;
it speaks with deceit.
With his mouth each speaks cordially to his neighbor,
but in his heart he sets a trap for him.
[9]Should I not punish them for this?"
declares the LORD.
"Should I not avenge myself
on such a nation as this?"

[10]I will weep and wail for the mountains
and take up a lament concerning the desert pastures.
They are desolate and untraveled,
and the lowing of cattle is not heard.
The birds of the air have fled
and the animals are gone.

[11]"I will make Jerusalem a heap of ruins,
a haunt of jackals;
and I will lay waste the towns of Judah
so no one can live there."

[12]What man is wise enough to understand
this? Who has been instructed by the LORD
and can explain it? Why has the land been

[a] *13* The meaning of the Hebrew for this sentence is uncertain. [b] *18* The meaning of the Hebrew for this word is uncertain. [c] *3* Or *lies; / they are not valiant for truth* [d] *4* Or *a deceiving Jacob* [e] *6* That is, Jeremiah (the Hebrew is singular)

ruined and laid waste like a desert that no
one can cross?
13The LORD said, "It is because they have
forsaken my law, which I set before them;
they have not obeyed me or followed my law.
14Instead, they have followed the stubbornness of their hearts; they have followed the
Baals, as their fathers taught them."
15Therefore, this is what the LORD Almighty,
the God of Israel, says: "See, I will make this
people eat bitter food and drink poisoned
water. 16I will scatter them among nations
that neither they nor their fathers have
known, and I will pursue them with the sword
until I have destroyed them."

17This is what the LORD Almighty says:

"Consider now! Call for the wailing
women to come;
send for the most skillful of them.
18Let them come quickly
and wail over us
till our eyes overflow with tears
and water streams from our eyelids.
19The sound of wailing is heard from Zion:
'How ruined we are!
How great is our shame!
We must leave our land
because our houses are in ruins.' "

20Now, O women, hear the word of the
LORD;
open your ears to the words of his
mouth.
Teach your daughters how to wail;
teach one another a lament.
21Death has climbed in through our
windows
and has entered our fortresses;
it has cut off the children from the streets
and the young men from the public
squares.

22Say, "This is what the LORD declares:

" 'The dead bodies of men will lie
like refuse on the open field,
like cut grain behind the reaper,
with no one to gather them.' "

23This is what the LORD says:

"Let not the wise man boast of his
wisdom
or the strong man boast of his strength
or the rich man boast of his riches,
24but let him who boasts boast about this:
that he understands and knows me,
that I am the LORD, who exercises
kindness,
justice and righteousness on earth,
for in these I delight,"
declares the LORD.

25"The days are coming," declares the
LORD, "when I will punish all who are circumcised only in the flesh— 26Egypt, Judah,
Edom, Ammon, Moab and all who live in the
desert in distant places.[a] For all these nations are really uncircumcised, and even the
whole house of Israel is uncircumcised in
heart."

God and Idols

10 Hear what the LORD says to you, O
house of Israel. 2This is what the
LORD says:

"Do not learn the ways of the nations
or be terrified by signs in the sky,
though the nations are terrified by
them.
3For the customs of the peoples are
worthless;
they cut a tree out of the forest,
and a craftsman shapes it with his
chisel.
4They adorn it with silver and gold;
they fasten it with hammer and nails
so it will not totter.
5Like a scarecrow in a melon patch,
their idols cannot speak;
they must be carried
because they cannot walk.
Do not fear them;
they can do no harm
nor can they do any good."

6No one is like you, O LORD;
you are great,
and your name is mighty in power.
7Who should not revere you,
O King of the nations?
This is your due.
Among all the wise men of the nations
and in all their kingdoms,
there is no one like you.
8They are all senseless and foolish;
they are taught by worthless wooden
idols.
9Hammered silver is brought from
Tarshish
and gold from Uphaz.
What the craftsman and goldsmith have
made

[a]26 Or *desert and who clip the hair by their foreheads*

is then dressed in blue and purple—
all made by skilled workers.
10But the LORD is the true God;
he is the living God, the eternal King.
When he is angry, the earth trembles;
the nations cannot endure his wrath.

11"Tell them this: 'These gods, who did not
make the heavens and the earth, will perish
from the earth and from under the heavens.' "[a]

12But God made the earth by his power;
he founded the world by his wisdom
and stretched out the heavens by his understanding.
13When he thunders, the waters in the heavens roar;
he makes clouds rise from the ends of the earth.
He sends lightning with the rain
and brings out the wind from his storehouses.

14Everyone is senseless and without knowledge;
every goldsmith is shamed by his idols.
His images are a fraud;
they have no breath in them.
15They are worthless, the objects of mockery;
when their judgment comes, they will perish.
16He who is the Portion of Jacob is not like these,
for he is the Maker of all things,
including Israel, the tribe of his inheritance—
the LORD Almighty is his name.

Coming Destruction

17Gather up your belongings to leave the land,
you who live under siege.
18For this is what the LORD says:
"At this time I will hurl out
those who live in this land;
I will bring distress on them
so that they may be captured."

19Woe to me because of my injury!
My wound is incurable!
Yet I said to myself,
"This is my sickness, and I must endure it."
20My tent is destroyed;
all its ropes are snapped.
My sons are gone from me and are no more;
no one is left now to pitch my tent
or to set up my shelter.
21The shepherds are senseless
and do not inquire of the LORD;
so they do not prosper
and all their flock is scattered.
22Listen! The report is coming—
a great commotion from the land of the north!
It will make the towns of Judah desolate,
a haunt of jackals.

Jeremiah's Prayer

23I know, O LORD, that a man's life is not his own;
it is not for man to direct his steps.
24Correct me, LORD, but only with justice—
not in your anger,
lest you reduce me to nothing.
25Pour out your wrath on the nations
that do not acknowledge you,
on the peoples who do not call on your name.
For they have devoured Jacob;
they have devoured him completely
and destroyed his homeland.

The Covenant Is Broken

11 This is the word that came to Jeremiah from the LORD: 2"Listen to the
terms of this covenant and tell them to the
people of Judah and to those who live in
Jerusalem. 3Tell them that this is what the
LORD, the God of Israel, says: 'Cursed is the
man who does not obey the terms of this
covenant— 4the terms I commanded your
forefathers when I brought them out of
Egypt, out of the iron-smelting furnace.' I
said, 'Obey me and do everything I command you, and you will be my people, and I
will be your God. 5Then I will fulfill the oath I
swore to your forefathers, to give them a land
flowing with milk and honey'—the land you
possess today."

I answered, "Amen, LORD."

6The LORD said to me, "Proclaim all these
words in the towns of Judah and in the
streets of Jerusalem: 'Listen to the terms of
this covenant and follow them. 7From the
time I brought your forefathers up from Egypt
until today, I warned them again and again,
saying, "Obey me." 8But they did not listen or
pay attention; instead, they followed the

[a]11 The text of this verse is in Aramaic.

stubbornness of their evil hearts. So I
brought on them all the curses of the covenant I had commanded them to follow but
that they did not keep.' "
[9]Then the LORD said to me, "There is a
conspiracy among the people of Judah and
those who live in Jerusalem. [10]They have
returned to the sins of their forefathers, who
refused to listen to my words. They have
followed other gods to serve them. Both the
house of Israel and the house of Judah have
broken the covenant I made with their forefathers. [11]Therefore this is what the LORD
says: 'I will bring on them a disaster they
cannot escape. Although they cry out to me,
I will not listen to them. [12]The towns of Judah
and the people of Jerusalem will go and cry
out to the gods to whom they burn incense,
but they will not help them at all when disaster strikes. [13]You have as many gods as you
have towns, O Judah; and the altars you
have set up to burn incense to that shameful
god Baal are as many as the streets of
Jerusalem.'

[14]"Do not pray for this people nor offer any
plea or petition for them, because I will not
listen when they call to me in the time of their
distress.

[15]"What is my beloved doing in my temple
as she works out her evil schemes with many?
Can consecrated meat avert ⌞your punishment⌟?
When you engage in your wickedness,
then you rejoice.[a]"

[16]The LORD called you a thriving olive tree
with fruit beautiful in form.
But with the roar of a mighty storm
he will set it on fire,
and its branches will be broken.

[17]The LORD Almighty, who planted you, has
decreed disaster for you, because the house
of Israel and the house of Judah have done
evil and provoked me to anger by burning
incense to Baal.

Plot Against Jeremiah

[18]Because the LORD revealed their plot to
me, I knew it, for at that time he showed me
what they were doing. [19]I had been like a
gentle lamb led to the slaughter; I did not
realize that they had plotted against me, saying,

"Let us destroy the tree and its fruit;
let us cut him off from the land of the living,
that his name be remembered no more."
[20]But, O LORD Almighty, you who judge righteously
and test the heart and mind,
let me see your vengeance upon them,
for to you I have committed my cause.

[21]"Therefore this is what the LORD says
about the men of Anathoth who are seeking
your life and saying, 'Do not prophesy in the
name of the LORD or you will die by our
hands'— [22]therefore this is what the LORD
Almighty says: 'I will punish them. Their
young men will die by the sword, their sons
and daughters by famine. [23]Not even a remnant will be left to them, because I will bring
disaster on the men of Anathoth in the year
of their punishment.' "

Jeremiah's Complaint

12 You are always righteous, O LORD,
when I bring a case before you.
Yet I would speak with you about your justice:
Why does the way of the wicked prosper?
Why do all the faithless live at ease?
[2]You have planted them, and they have taken root;
they grow and bear fruit.
You are always on their lips
but far from their hearts.
[3]Yet you know me, O LORD;
you see me and test my thoughts about you.
Drag them off like sheep to be butchered!
Set them apart for the day of slaughter!
[4]How long will the land lie parched[b]
and the grass in every field be withered?
Because those who live in it are wicked,
the animals and birds have perished.
Moreover, the people are saying,
"He will not see what happens to us."

God's Answer

[5]"If you have raced with men on foot
and they have worn you out,
how can you compete with horses?
If you stump in safe country,[c]

[a]15 Or *Could consecrated meat avert your punishment? / Then you would rejoice* [b]4 Or *land mourn*
[c]5 Or *If you put your trust in a land of safety*

how will you manage in the thickets by[a]
the Jordan?
6Your brothers, your own family—
even they have betrayed you;
they have raised a loud cry against
you.
Do not trust them,
though they speak well of you.

7"I will forsake my house,
abandon my inheritance;
I will give the one I love
into the hands of her enemies.
8My inheritance has become to me
like a lion in the forest.
She roars at me;
therefore I hate her.
9Has not my inheritance become to me
like a speckled bird of prey
that other birds of prey surround and
attack?
Go and gather all the wild beasts;
bring them to devour.
10Many shepherds will ruin my vineyard
and trample down my field;
they will turn my pleasant field
into a desolate wasteland.
11It will be made a wasteland,
parched and desolate before me;
the whole land will be laid waste
because there is no one who cares.
12Over all the barren heights in the desert
destroyers will swarm,
for the sword of the LORD will devour
from one end of the land to the other;
no one will be safe.
13They will sow wheat but reap thorns;
they will wear themselves out but gain
nothing.
So bear the shame of your harvest
because of the LORD's fierce anger."

14This is what the LORD says: "As for all my
wicked neighbors who seize the inheritance I
gave my people Israel, I will uproot them
from their lands and I will uproot the house of
Judah from among them. 15But after I uproot
them, I will again have compassion and will
bring each of them back to his own inheritance and his own country. 16And if they
learn well the ways of my people and swear
by my name, saying, 'As surely as the LORD
lives'—even as they once taught my people
to swear by Baal—then they will be established among my people. 17But if any nation
does not listen, I will completely uproot and
destroy it," declares the LORD.

A Linen Belt

13 This is what the LORD said to me: "Go
and buy a linen belt and put it around
your waist, but do not let it touch water." 2So
I bought a belt, as the LORD directed, and put
it around my waist.
3Then the word of the LORD came to me a
second time: 4"Take the belt you bought and
are wearing around your waist, and go now
to Perath[b] and hide it there in a crevice in the
rocks." 5So I went and hid it at Perath, as the
LORD told me.
6Many days later the LORD said to me, "Go
now to Perath and get the belt I told you to
hide there." 7So I went to Perath and dug up
the belt and took it from the place where I
had hidden it, but now it was ruined and
completely useless.
8Then the word of the LORD came to me:
9"This is what the LORD says: 'In the same
way I will ruin the pride of Judah and the
great pride of Jerusalem. 10These wicked
people, who refuse to listen to my words,
who follow the stubbornness of their hearts
and go after other gods to serve and worship
them, will be like this belt—completely useless! 11For as a belt is bound around a man's
waist, so I bound the whole house of Israel
and the whole house of Judah to me,' declares the LORD, 'to be my people for my
renown and praise and honor. But they have
not listened.'

Wineskins

12"Say to them: 'This is what the LORD, the
God of Israel, says: Every wineskin should
be filled with wine.' And if they say to you,
'Don't we know that every wineskin should
be filled with wine?' 13then tell them, 'This is
what the LORD says: I am going to fill with
drunkenness all who live in this land, including the kings who sit on David's throne, the
priests, the prophets and all those living in
Jerusalem. 14I will smash them one against
the other, fathers and sons alike, declares
the LORD. I will allow no pity or mercy or compassion to keep me from destroying them.'"

Threat of Captivity

15Hear and pay attention,

[a]5 Or *the flooding of* [b]4 Or possibly *the Euphrates*; also in verses 5-7

do not be arrogant,
for the LORD has spoken.
16Give glory to the LORD your God
before he brings the darkness,
before your feet stumble
on the darkening hills.
You hope for light,
but he will turn it to thick darkness
and change it to deep gloom.
17But if you do not listen,
I will weep in secret
because of your pride;
my eyes will weep bitterly,
overflowing with tears,
because the LORD's flock will be taken captive.

18Say to the king and to the queen mother,
"Come down from your thrones,
for your glorious crowns
will fall from your heads."
19The cities in the Negev will be shut up,
and there will be no one to open them.
All Judah will be carried into exile,
carried completely away.

20Lift up your eyes and see
those who are coming from the north.
Where is the flock that was entrusted to you,
the sheep of which you boasted?
21What will you say when ⌊the LORD⌋ sets over you
those you cultivated as your special allies?
Will not pain grip you
like that of a woman in labor?
22And if you ask yourself,
"Why has this happened to me?"—
it is because of your many sins
that your skirts have been torn off
and your body mistreated.
23Can the Ethiopian[a] change his skin
or the leopard its spots?
Neither can you do good
who are accustomed to doing evil.

24"I will scatter you like chaff
driven by the desert wind.
25This is your lot,
the portion I have decreed for you,"
declares the LORD,
"because you have forgotten me
and trusted in false gods.
26I will pull up your skirts over your face
that your shame may be seen—
27your adulteries and lustful neighings,
your shameless prostitution!
I have seen your detestable acts
on the hills and in the fields.
Woe to you, O Jerusalem!
How long will you be unclean?"

Drought, Famine, Sword

14 This is the word of the LORD to Jeremiah concerning the drought:

2"Judah mourns,
her cities languish;
they wail for the land,
and a cry goes up from Jerusalem.
3The nobles send their servants for water;
they go to the cisterns
but find no water.
They return with their jars unfilled;
dismayed and despairing,
they cover their heads.
4The ground is cracked
because there is no rain in the land;
the farmers are dismayed
and cover their heads.
5Even the doe in the field
deserts her newborn fawn
because there is no grass.
6Wild donkeys stand on the barren heights
and pant like jackals;
their eyesight fails
for lack of pasture."

7Although our sins testify against us,
O LORD, do something for the sake of your name.
For our backsliding is great;
we have sinned against you.
8O Hope of Israel,
its Savior in times of distress,
why are you like a stranger in the land,
like a traveler who stays only a night?
9Why are you like a man taken by surprise,
like a warrior powerless to save?
You are among us, O LORD,
and we bear your name;
do not forsake us!

10This is what the LORD says about this
people:

"They greatly love to wander;
they do not restrain their feet.
So the LORD does not accept them;
he will now remember their wickedness
and punish them for their sins."

11Then the LORD said to me, "Do not pray

[a]23 Hebrew *Cushite* (probably a person from the upper Nile region)

for the well-being of this people. 12Although
they fast, I will not listen to their cry; though
they offer burnt offerings and grain offerings,
I will not accept them. Instead, I will destroy
them with the sword, famine and plague."
13But I said, "Ah, Sovereign LORD, the
prophets keep telling them, 'You will not see
the sword or suffer famine. Indeed, I will give
you lasting peace in this place.' "
14Then the LORD said to me, "The prophets
are prophesying lies in my name. I have not
sent them or appointed them or spoken to
them. They are prophesying to you false visions, divinations, idolatries[a] and the delusions of their own minds. 15Therefore, this is
what the LORD says about the prophets who
are prophesying in my name: I did not send
them, yet they are saying, 'No sword or famine will touch this land.' Those same prophets will perish by sword and famine. 16And
the people they are prophesying to will be
thrown out into the streets of Jerusalem because of the famine and sword. There will be
no one to bury them or their wives, their sons
or their daughters. I will pour out on them the
calamity they deserve.

17"Speak this word to them:

" 'Let my eyes overflow with tears
night and day without ceasing;
for my virgin daughter—my people—
has suffered a grievous wound,
a crushing blow.
18If I go into the country,
I see those slain by the sword;
if I go into the city,
I see the ravages of famine.
Both prophet and priest
have gone to a land they know not.' "
19Have you rejected Judah completely?
Do you despise Zion?
Why have you afflicted us
so that we cannot be healed?
We hoped for peace
but no good has come,
for a time of healing
but there is only terror.
20O LORD, we acknowledge our wickedness
and the guilt of our fathers;
we have indeed sinned against you.
21For the sake of your name do not despise
us;
do not dishonor your glorious throne.
Remember your covenant with us
and do not break it.
22Do any of the worthless idols of the
nations bring rain?
Do the skies themselves send down
showers?
No, it is you, O LORD our God.
Therefore our hope is in you,
for you are the one who does all this.

15 Then the LORD said to me: "Even if
Moses and Samuel were to stand before me, my heart would not go out to this
people. Send them away from my presence!
Let them go! 2And if they ask you, 'Where
shall we go?' tell them, 'This is what the LORD
says:

" 'Those destined for death, to death;
those for the sword, to the sword;
those for starvation, to starvation;
those for captivity, to captivity.'

3"I will send four kinds of destroyers
against them," declares the LORD, "the sword
to kill and the dogs to drag away and the
birds of the air and the beasts of the earth to
devour and destroy. 4I will make them abhorrent to all the kingdoms of the earth because
of what Manasseh son of Hezekiah king of
Judah did in Jerusalem.

5"Who will have pity on you,
O Jerusalem?
Who will mourn for you?
Who will stop to ask how you are?
6You have rejected me," declares the
LORD.
"You keep on backsliding.
So I will lay hands on you and destroy
you;
I can no longer show compassion.
7I will winnow them with a winnowing fork
at the city gates of the land.
I will bring bereavement and destruction
on my people,
for they have not changed their ways.
8I will make their widows more numerous
than the sand of the sea.
At midday I will bring a destroyer
against the mothers of their young
men;
suddenly I will bring down on them
anguish and terror.
9The mother of seven will grow faint
and breathe her last.
Her sun will set while it is still day;
she will be disgraced and humiliated.
I will put the survivors to the sword

a14 Or *visions, worthless divinations*

before their enemies,"
declares the LORD.

10Alas, my mother, that you gave me birth,
a man with whom the whole land
strives and contends!
I have neither lent nor borrowed,
yet everyone curses me.

11The LORD said,

"Surely I will deliver you for a good
purpose;
surely I will make your enemies plead
with you
in times of disaster and times of
distress.
12"Can a man break iron—
iron from the north—or bronze?
13Your wealth and your treasures
I will give as plunder, without charge,
because of all your sins
throughout your country.
14I will enslave you to your enemies
in[a] a land you do not know,
for my anger will kindle a fire
that will burn against you."
15You understand, O LORD;
remember me and care for me.
Avenge me on my persecutors.
You are long-suffering—do not take me
away;
think of how I suffer reproach for your
sake.
16When your words came, I ate them;
they were my joy and my heart's
delight,
for I bear your name,
O LORD God Almighty.
17I never sat in the company of revelers,
never made merry with them;
I sat alone because your hand was on me
and you had filled me with indignation.
18Why is my pain unending
and my wound grievous and incurable?
Will you be to me like a deceptive brook,
like a spring that fails?

19Therefore this is what the LORD says:

"If you repent, I will restore you
that you may serve me;
if you utter worthy, not worthless, words,
you will be my spokesman.
Let this people turn to you,
but you must not turn to them.
20I will make you a wall to this people,
a fortified wall of bronze;
they will fight against you
but will not overcome you,
for I am with you
to rescue and save you,"
declares the LORD.
21"I will save you from the hands of the
wicked
and redeem you from the grasp of the
cruel."

Day of Disaster

16 Then the word of the LORD came to
me: 2"You must not marry and have
sons or daughters in this place." 3For this is
what the LORD says about the sons and
daughters born in this land and about the
women who are their mothers and the men
who are their fathers: 4"They will die of deadly diseases. They will not be mourned or
buried but will be like refuse lying on the
ground. They will perish by sword and famine, and their dead bodies will become food
for the birds of the air and the beasts of the
earth."
5For this is what the LORD says: "Do not
enter a house where there is a funeral meal;
do not go to mourn or show sympathy, because I have withdrawn my blessing, my
love and my pity from this people," declares
the LORD. 6"Both high and low will die in this
land. They will not be buried or mourned, and
no one will cut himself or shave his head for
them. 7No one will offer food to comfort those
who mourn for the dead—not even for a father or a mother—nor will anyone give them
a drink to console them.
8"And do not enter a house where there is
feasting and sit down to eat and drink. 9For
this is what the LORD Almighty, the God of
Israel, says: Before your eyes and in your
days I will bring an end to the sounds of joy
and gladness and to the voices of bride and
bridegroom in this place.
10"When you tell these people all this and
they ask you, 'Why has the LORD decreed
such a great disaster against us? What
wrong have we done? What sin have we
committed against the LORD our God?' 11then
say to them, 'It is because your fathers forsook me,' declares the LORD, 'and followed
other gods and served and worshiped them.
They forsook me and did not keep my law.

[a]14 Some Hebrew manuscripts, Septuagint and Syriac (see also Jer. 17:4); most Hebrew manuscripts *I will cause your enemies to bring you / into*

12But you have behaved more wickedly than
your fathers. See how each of you is following the stubbornness of his evil heart instead
of obeying me. 13So I will throw you out of this
land into a land neither you nor your fathers
have known, and there you will serve other
gods day and night, for I will show you no
favor.'

14"However, the days are coming," declares the LORD, "when men will no longer
say, 'As surely as the LORD lives, who
brought the Israelites up out of Egypt,' 15but
they will say, 'As surely as the LORD lives,
who brought the Israelites up out of the land
of the north and out of all the countries where
he had banished them.' For I will restore
them to the land I gave their forefathers.

16"But now I will send for many fishermen,"
declares the LORD, "and they will catch them.
After that I will send for many hunters, and
they will hunt them down on every mountain
and hill and from the crevices of the rocks.
17My eyes are on all their ways; they are not
hidden from me, nor is their sin concealed
from my eyes. 18I will repay them double for
their wickedness and their sin, because they
have defiled my land with the lifeless forms
of their vile images and have filled my inheritance with their detestable idols."

19O LORD, my strength and my fortress,
 my refuge in time of distress,
to you the nations will come
 from the ends of the earth and say,
"Our fathers possessed nothing but false gods,
 worthless idols that did them no good.
20Do men make their own gods?
 Yes, but they are not gods!"

21"Therefore I will teach them—
 this time I will teach them
 my power and might.
Then they will know
 that my name is the LORD.

17 "Judah's sin is engraved with an iron tool,
 inscribed with a flint point,
on the tablets of their hearts
 and on the horns of their altars.
2Even their children remember
 their altars and Asherah poles[a]
beside the spreading trees
 and on the high hills.
3My mountain in the land
 and your[b] wealth and all your treasures
I will give away as plunder,
 together with your high places,
 because of sin throughout your country.
4Through your own fault you will lose
 the inheritance I gave you.
I will enslave you to your enemies
 in a land you do not know,
for you have kindled my anger,
 and it will burn forever."

5This is what the LORD says:

"Cursed is the one who trusts in man,
 who depends on flesh for his strength
 and whose heart turns away from the LORD.
6He will be like a bush in the wastelands;
 he will not see prosperity when it comes.
He will dwell in the parched places of the desert,
 in a salt land where no one lives.

7"But blessed is the man who trusts in the LORD,
 whose confidence is in him.
8He will be like a tree planted by the water
 that sends out its roots by the stream.
It does not fear when heat comes;
 its leaves are always green.
It has no worries in a year of drought
 and never fails to bear fruit."

9The heart is deceitful above all things
 and beyond cure.
 Who can understand it?

10"I the LORD search the heart
 and examine the mind,
to reward a man according to his conduct,
 according to what his deeds deserve."

11Like a partridge that hatches eggs it did not lay
 is the man who gains riches by unjust means.
When his life is half gone, they will desert him,
 and in the end he will prove to be a fool.

12A glorious throne, exalted from the beginning,
 is the place of our sanctuary.
13O LORD, the hope of Israel,
 all who forsake you will be put to shame.
Those who turn away from you will be written in the dust

[a]2 That is, symbols of the goddess Asherah

[b]2,3 Or *hills* / [3]*and the mountains of the land. / Your*

because they have forsaken the LORD,
the spring of living water.

14Heal me, O LORD, and I will be healed;
save me and I will be saved,
for you are the one I praise.
15They keep saying to me,
"Where is the word of the LORD?
Let it now be fulfilled!"
16I have not run away from being your
shepherd;
you know I have not desired the day of
despair.
What passes my lips is open before
you.
17Do not be a terror to me;
you are my refuge in the day of
disaster.
18Let my persecutors be put to shame,
but keep me from shame;
let them be terrified,
but keep me from terror.
Bring on them the day of disaster;
destroy them with double destruction.

Keeping the Sabbath Holy

19This is what the LORD said to me: "Go and
stand at the gate of the people, through
which the kings of Judah go in and out; stand
also at all the other gates of Jerusalem.
20Say to them, 'Hear the word of the LORD, O
kings of Judah and all people of Judah and
everyone living in Jerusalem who come
through these gates. 21This is what the LORD
says: Be careful not to carry a load on the
Sabbath day or bring it through the gates of
Jerusalem. 22Do not bring a load out of your
houses or do any work on the Sabbath, but
keep the Sabbath day holy, as I commanded
your forefathers. 23Yet they did not listen or
pay attention; they were stiff-necked and
would not listen or respond to discipline.
24But if you are careful to obey me, declares
the LORD, and bring no load through the gates
of this city on the Sabbath, but keep the
Sabbath day holy by not doing any work on it,
25then kings who sit on David's throne will
come through the gates of this city with their
officials. They and their officials will come
riding in chariots and on horses, accompanied by the men of Judah and those living
in Jerusalem, and this city will be inhabited
forever. 26People will come from the towns of
Judah and the villages around Jerusalem,
from the territory of Benjamin and the western foothills, from the hill country and the
Negev, bringing burnt offerings and sacrifices, grain offerings, incense and thank offerings to the house of the LORD. 27But if you
do not obey me to keep the Sabbath day holy
by not carrying any load as you come
through the gates of Jerusalem on the Sabbath day, then I will kindle an unquenchable
fire in the gates of Jerusalem that will consume her fortresses.' "

At the Potter's House

18 This is the word that came to Jeremiah from the LORD: 2"Go down to the
potter's house, and there I will give you my
message." 3So I went down to the potter's
house, and I saw him working at the wheel.
4But the pot he was shaping from the clay
was marred in his hands; so the potter
formed it into another pot, shaping it as
seemed best to him.

5Then the word of the LORD came to me:
6"O house of Israel, can I not do with you as
this potter does?" declares the LORD. "Like
clay in the hand of the potter, so are you in
my hand, O house of Israel. 7If at any time I
announce that a nation or kingdom is to be
uprooted, torn down and destroyed, 8and if
that nation I warned repents of its evil, then I
will relent and not inflict on it the disaster I
had planned. 9And if at another time I announce that a nation or kingdom is to be built
up and planted, 10and if it does evil in my
sight and does not obey me, then I will reconsider the good I had intended to do for it.

11"Now therefore say to the people of
Judah and those living in Jerusalem, 'This is
what the LORD says: Look! I am preparing a
disaster for you and devising a plan against
you. So turn from your evil ways, each one of
you, and reform your ways and your actions.'
12But they will reply, 'It's no use. We will
continue with our own plans; each of us will
follow the stubbornness of his evil heart.' "

13Therefore this is what the LORD says:

"Inquire among the nations:
Who has ever heard anything like this?
A most horrible thing has been done
by Virgin Israel.
14Does the snow of Lebanon
ever vanish from its rocky slopes?
Do its cool waters from distant sources
ever cease to flow?[a]
15Yet my people have forgotten me;
they burn incense to worthless idols,

[a]14 The meaning of the Hebrew for this sentence is uncertain.

which made them stumble in their ways
and in the ancient paths.
They made them walk in bypaths
and on roads not built up.
16Their land will be laid waste,
an object of lasting scorn;
all who pass by will be appalled
and will shake their heads.
17Like a wind from the east,
I will scatter them before their enemies;
I will show them my back and not my face
in the day of their disaster."

18They said, "Come, let's make plans
against Jeremiah; for the teaching of the law
by the priest will not be lost, nor will counsel
from the wise, nor the word from the prophets. So come, let's attack him with our
tongues and pay no attention to anything he
says."

19Listen to me, O LORD;
hear what my accusers are saying!
20Should good be repaid with evil?
Yet they have dug a pit for me.
Remember that I stood before you
and spoke in their behalf
to turn your wrath away from them.
21So give their children over to famine;
hand them over to the power of the
sword.
Let their wives be made childless and
widows;
let their men be put to death,
their young men slain by the sword in
battle.
22Let a cry be heard from their houses
when you suddenly bring invaders
against them,
for they have dug a pit to capture me
and have hidden snares for my feet.
23But you know, O LORD,
all their plots to kill me.
Do not forgive their crimes
or blot out their sins from your sight.
Let them be overthrown before you;
deal with them in the time of your
anger.

19 This is what the LORD says: "Go and
buy a clay jar from a potter. Take
along some of the elders of the people and of
the priests 2and go out to the Valley of Ben
Hinnom, near the entrance of the Potsherd
Gate. There proclaim the words I tell you,
3and say, 'Hear the word of the LORD, O kings
of Judah and people of Jerusalem. This is
what the LORD Almighty, the God of Israel,
says: Listen! I am going to bring a disaster on
this place that will make the ears of everyone
who hears of it tingle. 4For they have forsak-
en me and made this a place of foreign gods;
they have burned sacrifices in it to gods that
neither they nor their fathers nor the kings of
Judah ever knew, and they have filled this
place with the blood of the innocent. 5They
have built the high places of Baal to burn
their sons in the fire as offerings to Baal—
something I did not command or mention,
nor did it enter my mind. 6So beware, the
days are coming, declares the LORD, when
people will no longer call this place Topheth
or the Valley of Ben Hinnom, but the Valley of
Slaughter.

7" 'In this place I will ruin[a] the plans of
Judah and Jerusalem. I will make them fall
by the sword before their enemies, at the
hands of those who seek their lives, and I will
give their carcasses as food to the birds of
the air and the beasts of the earth. 8I will
devastate this city and make it an object of
scorn; all who pass by will be appalled and
will scoff because of all its wounds. 9I will
make them eat the flesh of their sons and
daughters, and they will eat one another's
flesh during the stress of the siege imposed
on them by the enemies who seek their
lives.'

10"Then break the jar while those who go
with you are watching, 11and say to them,
'This is what the LORD Almighty says: I will
smash this nation and this city just as this
potter's jar is smashed and cannot be repaired. They will bury the dead in Topheth
until there is no more room. 12This is what I
will do to this place and to those who live
here, declares the LORD. I will make this city
like Topheth. 13The houses in Jerusalem and
those of the kings of Judah will be defiled like
this place, Topheth—all the houses where
they burned incense on the roofs to all the
starry hosts and poured out drink offerings to
other gods.' "

14Jeremiah then returned from Topheth,
where the LORD had sent him to prophesy,
and stood in the court of the LORD's temple
and said to all the people, 15"This is what the
LORD Almighty, the God of Israel, says: 'Listen! I am going to bring on this city and the
villages around it every disaster I pronounced against them, because they were

[a]7 The Hebrew for *ruin* sounds like the Hebrew for *jar* (see verses 1 and 10).

stiff-necked and would not listen to my
words.' "

Jeremiah and Pashhur

20 When the priest Pashhur son of Immer, the chief officer in the temple of
the LORD, heard Jeremiah prophesying these
things, 2he had Jeremiah the prophet beaten
and put in the stocks at the Upper Gate of
Benjamin at the LORD's temple. 3The next
day, when Pashhur released him from the
stocks, Jeremiah said to him, "The LORD's
name for you is not Pashhur, but Magor-Missabib.[a] 4For this is what the LORD says: 'I will
make you a terror to yourself and to all your
friends; with your own eyes you will see them
fall by the sword of their enemies. I will hand
all Judah over to the king of Babylon, who will
carry them away to Babylon or put them to
the sword. 5I will hand over to their enemies
all the wealth of this city—all its products, all
its valuables and all the treasures of the
kings of Judah. They will take it away as
plunder and carry it off to Babylon. 6And you,
Pashhur, and all who live in your house will
go into exile to Babylon. There you will die
and be buried, you and all your friends to
whom you have prophesied lies.' "

Jeremiah's Complaint

7O LORD, you deceived[b] me, and I was
deceived[b];
you overpowered me and prevailed.
I am ridiculed all day long;
everyone mocks me.
8Whenever I speak, I cry out
proclaiming violence and destruction.
So the word of the LORD has brought me
insult and reproach all day long.
9But if I say, "I will not mention him
or speak any more in his name,"
his word is in my heart like a fire,
a fire shut up in my bones.
I am weary of holding it in;
indeed, I cannot.
10I hear many whispering,
"Terror on every side!
Report him! Let's report him!"
All my friends
are waiting for me to slip, saying,
"Perhaps he will be deceived;
then we will prevail over him
and take our revenge on him."
11But the LORD is with me like a mighty
warrior;
so my persecutors will stumble and not
prevail.
They will fail and be thoroughly
disgraced;
their dishonor will never be forgotten.
12O LORD Almighty, you who examine the
righteous
and probe the heart and mind,
let me see your vengeance upon them,
for to you I have committed my cause.

13Sing to the LORD!
Give praise to the LORD!
He rescues the life of the needy
from the hands of the wicked.

14Cursed be the day I was born!
May the day my mother bore me not be
blessed!
15Cursed be the man who brought my
father the news,
who made him very glad, saying,
"A child is born to you—a son!"
16May that man be like the towns
the LORD overthrew without pity.
May he hear wailing in the morning,
a battle cry at noon.
17For he did not kill me in the womb,
with my mother as my grave,
her womb enlarged forever.
18Why did I ever come out of the womb
to see trouble and sorrow
and to end my days in shame?

God Rejects Zedekiah's Request

21 The word came to Jeremiah from the
LORD when King Zedekiah sent to him
Pashhur son of Malkijah and the priest Zephaniah son of Maaseiah. They said: 2"Inquire
now of the LORD for us because Nebuchadnezzar[c] king of Babylon is attacking us.
Perhaps the LORD will perform wonders for us
as in times past so that he will withdraw from
us."
3But Jeremiah answered them, "Tell
Zedekiah, 4'This is what the LORD, the God of
Israel, says: I am about to turn against you
the weapons of war that are in your hands,
which you are using to fight the king of Babylon and the Babylonians[d] who are outside
the wall besieging you. And I will gather them
inside this city. 5I myself will fight against you

[a]3 *Magor-Missabib* means *terror on every side.* [b]7 Or *persuaded* [c]2 Hebrew *Nebuchadrezzar,* of which *Nebuchadnezzar* is a variant; here and often in Jeremiah and Ezekiel [d]4 Or *Chaldeans*; also in verse 9

with an outstretched hand and a mighty arm
in anger and fury and great wrath. 6I will
strike down those who live in this city—both
men and animals—and they will die of a terrible plague. 7After that, declares the LORD, I
will hand over Zedekiah king of Judah, his
officials and the people in this city who survive the plague, sword and famine, to Nebuchadnezzar king of Babylon and to their enemies who seek their lives. He will put them to
the sword; he will show them no mercy or pity
or compassion.'

8"Furthermore, tell the people, 'This is
what the LORD says: See, I am setting before
you the way of life and the way of death.
9Whoever stays in this city will die by the
sword, famine or plague. But whoever goes
out and surrenders to the Babylonians who
are besieging you will live; he will escape
with his life. 10I have determined to do this
city harm and not good, declares the LORD. It
will be given into the hands of the king of
Babylon, and he will destroy it with fire.'

11"Moreover, say to the royal house of
Judah, 'Hear the word of the LORD; 12O house
of David, this is what the LORD says:

" 'Administer justice every morning;
 rescue from the hand of his oppressor
 the one who has been robbed,
or my wrath will break out and burn like
  fire
 because of the evil you have done—
 burn with no one to quench it.
13I am against you, ⌊Jerusalem,⌋
 you who live above this valley
 on the rocky plateau,
   declares the LORD—
you who say, "Who can come against
  us?
 Who can enter our refuge?"
14I will punish you as your deeds deserve,
   declares the LORD.
I will kindle a fire in your forests
 that will consume everything around
  you.' "

Judgment Against Evil Kings

22 This is what the LORD says: "Go down
to the palace of the king of Judah and
proclaim this message there: 2'Hear the
word of the LORD, O king of Judah, you who
sit on David's throne—you, your officials and
your people who come through these gates.
3This is what the LORD says: Do what is just
and right. Rescue from the hand of his oppressor the one who has been robbed. Do no
wrong or violence to the alien, the fatherless
or the widow, and do not shed innocent
blood in this place. 4For if you are careful to
carry out these commands, then kings who
sit on David's throne will come through the
gates of this palace, riding in chariots and on
horses, accompanied by their officials and
their people. 5But if you do not obey these
commands, declares the LORD, I swear by
myself that this palace will become a ruin.' "

6For this is what the LORD says about the
palace of the king of Judah:

"Though you are like Gilead to me,
 like the summit of Lebanon,
I will surely make you like a desert,
 like towns not inhabited.
7I will send destroyers against you,
 each man with his weapons,
and they will cut up your fine cedar
  beams
 and throw them into the fire.

8"People from many nations will pass by
this city and will ask one another, 'Why has
the LORD done such a thing to this great city?'
9And the answer will be: 'Because they have
forsaken the covenant of the LORD their God
and have worshiped and served other
gods.' "

10Do not weep for the dead ⌊king⌋ or mourn
  his loss;
 rather, weep bitterly for him who is
  exiled,
because he will never return
 nor see his native land again.

11For this is what the LORD says about Shallum[a] son of Josiah, who succeeded his father as king of Judah but has gone from this
place: "He will never return. 12He will die in
the place where they have led him captive;
he will not see this land again."

13"Woe to him who builds his palace by
  unrighteousness,
 his upper rooms by injustice,
making his countrymen work for nothing,
 not paying them for their labor.
14He says, 'I will build myself a great
  palace
 with spacious upper rooms.'
So he makes large windows in it,
 panels it with cedar
 and decorates it in red.

[a]11 Also called *Jehoahaz*

[15]"Does it make you a king
to have more and more cedar?
Did not your father have food and drink?
He did what was right and just,
so all went well with him.
[16]He defended the cause of the poor and needy,
and so all went well.
Is that not what it means to know me?"
declares the LORD.
[17]"But your eyes and your heart
are set only on dishonest gain,
on shedding innocent blood
and on oppression and extortion."

[18]Therefore this is what the LORD says about
Jehoiakim son of Josiah king of Judah:

"They will not mourn for him:
'Alas, my brother! Alas, my sister!'
They will not mourn for him:
'Alas, my master! Alas, his splendor!'
[19]He will have the burial of a donkey—
dragged away and thrown
outside the gates of Jerusalem."

[20]"Go up to Lebanon and cry out,
let your voice be heard in Bashan,
cry out from Abarim,
for all your allies are crushed.
[21]I warned you when you felt secure,
but you said, 'I will not listen!'
This has been your way from your youth;
you have not obeyed me.
[22]The wind will drive all your shepherds away,
and your allies will go into exile.
Then you will be ashamed and disgraced
because of all your wickedness.
[23]You who live in 'Lebanon,[a]'
who are nestled in cedar buildings,
how you will groan when pangs come upon you,
pain like that of a woman in labor!

[24]"As surely as I live," declares the LORD,
"even if you, Jehoiachin[b] son of Jehoiakim
king of Judah, were a signet ring on my right
hand, I would still pull you off. [25]I will hand
you over to those who seek your life, those
you fear—to Nebuchadnezzar king of Babylon and to the Babylonians.[c] [26]I will hurl you
and the mother who gave you birth into another country, where neither of you was
born, and there you both will die. [27]You will
never come back to the land you long to
return to."

[28]Is this man Jehoiachin a despised, broken pot,
an object no one wants?
Why will he and his children be hurled out,
cast into a land they do not know?
[29]O land, land, land,
hear the word of the LORD!
[30]This is what the LORD says:
"Record this man as if childless,
a man who will not prosper in his lifetime,
for none of his offspring will prosper,
none will sit on the throne of David
or rule anymore in Judah."

The Righteous Branch

23 "Woe to the shepherds who are destroying and scattering the sheep of
my pasture!" declares the LORD. [2]Therefore
this is what the LORD, the God of Israel, says
to the shepherds who tend my people: "Because you have scattered my flock and
driven them away and have not bestowed
care on them, I will bestow punishment on
you for the evil you have done," declares the
LORD. [3]"I myself will gather the remnant of my
flock out of all the countries where I have
driven them and will bring them back to their
pasture, where they will be fruitful and increase in number. [4]I will place shepherds
over them who will tend them, and they will
no longer be afraid or terrified, nor will any be
missing," declares the LORD.

[5]"The days are coming," declares the LORD,
"when I will raise up to David[d] a righteous Branch,
a King who will reign wisely
and do what is just and right in the land.
[6]In his days Judah will be saved
and Israel will live in safety.
This is the name by which he will be called:
The LORD Our Righteousness.

[7]"So then, the days are coming," declares
the LORD, "when people will no longer say,
'As surely as the LORD lives, who brought the

[a]23 That is, the palace in Jerusalem (see 1 Kings 7:2) [b]24 Hebrew *Coniah,* a variant of *Jehoiachin;* also in verse 28 [c]25 Or *Chaldeans* [d]5 Or *up from David's line*

Israelites up out of Egypt,' [8]but they will say,
'As surely as the LORD lives, who brought the
descendants of Israel up out of the land of
the north and out of all the countries where
he had banished them.' Then they will live in
their own land."

Lying Prophets

[9]Concerning the prophets:

My heart is broken within me;
all my bones tremble.
I am like a drunken man,
like a man overcome by wine,
because of the LORD
and his holy words.
[10]The land is full of adulterers;
because of the curse[a] the land lies parched[b]
and the pastures in the desert are withered.
The ⌊prophets⌋ follow an evil course
and use their power unjustly.

[11]"Both prophet and priest are godless;
even in my temple I find their wickedness,"
declares the LORD.
[12]"Therefore their path will become slippery;
they will be banished to darkness
and there they will fall.
I will bring disaster on them
in the year they are punished,"
declares the LORD.
[13]"Among the prophets of Samaria
I saw this repulsive thing:
They prophesied by Baal
and led my people Israel astray.
[14]And among the prophets of Jerusalem
I have seen something horrible:
They commit adultery and live a lie.
They strengthen the hands of evildoers,
so that no one turns from his wickedness.
They are all like Sodom to me;
the people of Jerusalem are like Gomorrah."

[15]Therefore, this is what the LORD Almighty
says concerning the prophets:

"I will make them eat bitter food
and drink poisoned water,
because from the prophets of Jerusalem
ungodliness has spread throughout the land."

[16]This is what the LORD Almighty says:

"Do not listen to what the prophets are prophesying to you;
they fill you with false hopes.
They speak visions from their own minds,
not from the mouth of the LORD.
[17]They keep saying to those who despise me,
'The LORD says: You will have peace.'
And to all who follow the stubbornness of their hearts
they say, 'No harm will come to you.'
[18]But which of them has stood in the council of the LORD
to see or to hear his word?
Who has listened and heard his word?
[19]See, the storm of the LORD
will burst out in wrath,
a whirlwind swirling down
on the heads of the wicked.
[20]The anger of the LORD will not turn back
until he fully accomplishes
the purposes of his heart.
In days to come
you will understand it clearly.
[21]I did not send these prophets,
yet they have run with their message;
I did not speak to them,
yet they have prophesied.
[22]But if they had stood in my council,
they would have proclaimed my words to my people
and would have turned them from their evil ways
and from their evil deeds.

[23]"Am I only a God nearby,"
declares the LORD,
"and not a God far away?
[24]Can anyone hide in secret places
so that I cannot see him?"
declares the LORD.
"Do not I fill heaven and earth?"
declares the LORD.

[25]"I have heard what the prophets say who
prophesy lies in my name. They say, 'I had a
dream! I had a dream!' [26]How long will this
continue in the hearts of these lying prophets, who prophesy the delusions of their own
minds? [27]They think the dreams they tell one
another will make my people forget my
name, just as their fathers forgot my name
through Baal worship. [28]Let the prophet who
has a dream tell his dream, but let the one
who has my word speak it faithfully. For what

[a] 10 Or *because of these things* [b] 10 Or *land mourns*

has straw to do with grain?" declares the
LORD. 29"Is not my word like fire," declares
the LORD, "and like a hammer that breaks a
rock in pieces?
30"Therefore," declares the LORD, "I am
against the prophets who steal from one another words supposedly from me. 31Yes,"
declares the LORD, "I am against the prophets who wag their own tongues and yet declare, 'The LORD declares.' 32Indeed, I am
against those who prophesy false dreams,"
declares the LORD. "They tell them and lead
my people astray with their reckless lies, yet
I did not send or appoint them. They do not
benefit these people in the least," declares
the LORD.

False Oracles and False Prophets

33"When these people, or a prophet or a
priest, ask you, 'What is the oracle[a] of the
LORD?' say to them, 'What oracle?[b] I will forsake you, declares the LORD.' 34If a prophet or
a priest or anyone else claims, 'This is the
oracle of the LORD,' I will punish that man and
his household. 35This is what each of you
keeps on saying to his friend or relative:
'What is the LORD's answer?' or 'What has
the LORD spoken?' 36But you must not mention 'the oracle of the LORD' again, because
every man's own word becomes his oracle
and so you distort the words of the living
God, the LORD Almighty, our God. 37This is
what you keep saying to a prophet: 'What is
the LORD's answer to you?' or 'What has the
LORD spoken?' 38Although you claim, 'This is
the oracle of the LORD,' this is what the LORD
says: You used the words, 'This is the oracle
of the LORD,' even though I told you that you
must not claim, 'This is the oracle of the
LORD.' 39Therefore, I will surely forget you
and cast you out of my presence along with
the city I gave to you and your fathers. 40I will
bring upon you everlasting disgrace—everlasting shame that will not be forgotten."

Two Baskets of Figs

24 After Jehoiachin[c] son of Jehoiakim
king of Judah and the officials, the
craftsmen and the artisans of Judah were
carried into exile from Jerusalem to Babylon
by Nebuchadnezzar king of Babylon, the
LORD showed me two baskets of figs placed
in front of the temple of the LORD. 2One basket had very good figs, like those that ripen
early; the other basket had very poor figs, so
bad they could not be eaten.
3Then the LORD asked me, "What do you
see, Jeremiah?"
"Figs," I answered. "The good ones are
very good, but the poor ones are so bad they
cannot be eaten."
4Then the word of the LORD came to me:
5"This is what the LORD, the God of Israel,
says: 'Like these good figs, I regard as good
the exiles from Judah, whom I sent away
from this place to the land of the Babylonians.[d] 6My eyes will watch over them for
their good, and I will bring them back to this
land. I will build them up and not tear them
down; I will plant them and not uproot them.
7I will give them a heart to know me, that I am
the LORD. They will be my people, and I will be
their God, for they will return to me with all
their heart.
8" 'But like the poor figs, which are so bad
they cannot be eaten,' says the LORD, 'so will
I deal with Zedekiah king of Judah, his officials and the survivors from Jerusalem,
whether they remain in this land or live in
Egypt. 9I will make them abhorrent and an
offense to all the kingdoms of the earth, a
reproach and a byword, an object of ridicule
and cursing, wherever I banish them. 10I will
send the sword, famine and plague against
them until they are destroyed from the land I
gave to them and their fathers.' "

Seventy Years of Captivity

25 The word came to Jeremiah concerning all the people of Judah in the
fourth year of Jehoiakim son of Josiah king of
Judah, which was the first year of Nebuchadnezzar king of Babylon. 2So Jeremiah
the prophet said to all the people of Judah
and to all those living in Jerusalem: 3For
twenty-three years—from the thirteenth year
of Josiah son of Amon king of Judah until this
very day—the word of the LORD has come to
me and I have spoken to you again and
again, but you have not listened.
4And though the LORD has sent all his servants the prophets to you again and again,
you have not listened or paid any attention.
5They said, "Turn now, each of you, from
your evil ways and your evil practices, and
you can stay in the land the LORD gave to you
and your fathers for ever and ever. 6Do not
follow other gods to serve and worship them;

[a]33 Or *burden* (see Septuagint and Vulgate) [b]33 Hebrew; Septuagint and Vulgate *'You are the burden.* (The Hebrew for *oracle* and *burden* is the same.) [c]1 Hebrew *Jeconiah,* a variant of *Jehoiachin* [d]5 Or *Chaldeans*

do not provoke me to anger with what your hands have made. Then I will not harm you."

7"But you did not listen to me," declares the LORD, "and you have provoked me with what your hands have made, and you have brought harm to yourselves."

8Therefore the LORD Almighty says this: "Because you have not listened to my words, 9I will summon all the peoples of the north and my servant Nebuchadnezzar king of Babylon," declares the LORD, "and I will bring them against this land and its inhabitants and against all the surrounding nations. I will completely destroy[a] them and make them an object of horror and scorn, and an everlasting ruin. 10I will banish from them the sounds of joy and gladness, the voices of bride and bridegroom, the sound of millstones and the light of the lamp. 11This whole country will become a desolate wasteland, and these nations will serve the king of Babylon seventy years.

12"But when the seventy years are fulfilled, I will punish the king of Babylon and his nation, the land of the Babylonians,[b] for their guilt," declares the LORD, "and will make it desolate forever. 13I will bring upon that land all the things I have spoken against it, all that are written in this book and prophesied by Jeremiah against all the nations. 14They themselves will be enslaved by many nations and great kings; I will repay them according to their deeds and the work of their hands."

The Cup of God's Wrath

15This is what the LORD, the God of Israel, said to me: "Take from my hand this cup filled with the wine of my wrath and make all the nations to whom I send you drink it. 16When they drink it, they will stagger and go mad because of the sword I will send among them."

17So I took the cup from the LORD's hand and made all the nations to whom he sent me drink it: 18Jerusalem and the towns of Judah, its kings and officials, to make them a ruin and an object of horror and scorn and cursing, as they are today; 19Pharaoh king of Egypt, his attendants, his officials and all his people, 20and all the foreign people there; all the kings of Uz; all the kings of the Philistines (those of Ashkelon, Gaza, Ekron, and the people left at Ashdod); 21Edom, Moab and Ammon; 22all the kings of Tyre and Sidon; the kings of the coastlands across the sea; 23Dedan, Tema, Buz and all who are in distant places[c]; 24all the kings of Arabia and all the kings of the foreign people who live in the desert; 25all the kings of Zimri, Elam and Media; 26and all the kings of the north, near and far, one after the other—all the kingdoms on the face of the earth. And after all of them, the king of Sheshach[d] will drink it too.

27"Then tell them, 'This is what the LORD Almighty, the God of Israel, says: Drink, get drunk and vomit, and fall to rise no more because of the sword I will send among you.' 28But if they refuse to take the cup from your hand and drink, tell them, 'This is what the LORD Almighty says: You must drink it! 29See, I am beginning to bring disaster on the city that bears my Name, and will you indeed go unpunished? You will not go unpunished, for I am calling down a sword upon all who live on the earth, declares the LORD Almighty.'

30"Now prophesy all these words against them and say to them:

" 'The LORD will roar from on high;
he will thunder from his holy dwelling
and roar mightily against his land.
He will shout like those who tread the grapes,
shout against all who live on the earth.
31The tumult will resound to the ends of the earth,
for the LORD will bring charges against the nations;
he will bring judgment on all mankind
and put the wicked to the sword,' "
declares the LORD.

32This is what the LORD Almighty says:

"Look! Disaster is spreading
from nation to nation;
a mighty storm is rising
from the ends of the earth."

33At that time those slain by the LORD will be everywhere—from one end of the earth to the other. They will not be mourned or gathered up or buried, but will be like refuse lying on the ground.

34Weep and wail, you shepherds;
roll in the dust, you leaders of the flock.
For your time to be slaughtered has come;

[a]9 The Hebrew term refers to the irrevocable giving over of things or persons to the LORD, often by totally destroying them. [b]12 Or *Chaldeans* [c]23 Or *who clip the hair by their foreheads* [d]26 *Sheshach* is a cryptogram for Babylon.

you will fall and be shattered like fine
pottery.
35The shepherds will have nowhere to flee,
the leaders of the flock no place to
escape.
36Hear the cry of the shepherds,
the wailing of the leaders of the flock,
for the LORD is destroying their pasture.
37The peaceful meadows will be laid waste
because of the fierce anger of the LORD.
38Like a lion he will leave his lair,
and their land will become desolate
because of the sword[a] of the oppressor
and because of the LORD's fierce anger.

Jeremiah Threatened With Death

26 Early in the reign of Jehoiakim son of
Josiah king of Judah, this word came
from the LORD: 2"This is what the LORD says:
Stand in the courtyard of the LORD's house
and speak to all the people of the towns of
Judah who come to worship in the house of
the LORD. Tell them everything I command
you; do not omit a word. 3Perhaps they will
listen and each will turn from his evil way.
Then I will relent and not bring on them the
disaster I was planning because of the evil
they have done. 4Say to them, 'This is what
the LORD says: If you do not listen to me and
follow my law, which I have set before you,
5and if you do not listen to the words of my
servants the prophets, whom I have sent to
you again and again (though you have not
listened), 6then I will make this house like
Shiloh and this city an object of cursing
among all the nations of the earth.' "
7The priests, the prophets and all the
people heard Jeremiah speak these words in
the house of the LORD. 8But as soon as Jeremiah finished telling all the people everything
the LORD had commanded him to say, the
priests, the prophets and all the people
seized him and said, "You must die! 9Why do
you prophesy in the LORD's name that this
house will be like Shiloh and this city will be
desolate and deserted?" And all the people
crowded around Jeremiah in the house of
the LORD.
10When the officials of Judah heard about
these things, they went up from the royal
palace to the house of the LORD and took their
places at the entrance of the New Gate of the
LORD's house. 11Then the priests and the
prophets said to the officials and all the
people, "This man should be sentenced to
death because he has prophesied against
this city. You have heard it with your own
ears!"
12Then Jeremiah said to all the officials
and all the people: "The LORD sent me to
prophesy against this house and this city all
the things you have heard. 13Now reform
your ways and your actions and obey the
LORD your God. Then the LORD will relent and
not bring the disaster he has pronounced
against you. 14As for me, I am in your hands;
do with me whatever you think is good and
right. 15Be assured, however, that if you put
me to death, you will bring the guilt of innocent blood on yourselves and on this city and
on those who live in it, for in truth the LORD
has sent me to you to speak all these words
in your hearing."
16Then the officials and all the people said
to the priests and the prophets, "This man
should not be sentenced to death! He has
spoken to us in the name of the LORD our
God."
17Some of the elders of the land stepped
forward and said to the entire assembly of
people, 18"Micah of Moresheth prophesied in
the days of Hezekiah king of Judah. He told
all the people of Judah, 'This is what the LORD
Almighty says:

" 'Zion will be plowed like a field,
Jerusalem will become a heap of
rubble,
the temple hill a mound overgrown with
thickets.'[b]

19"Did Hezekiah king of Judah or anyone
else in Judah put him to death? Did not
Hezekiah fear the LORD and seek his favor?
And did not the LORD relent, so that he did not
bring the disaster he pronounced against
them? We are about to bring a terrible disaster on ourselves!"
20(Now Uriah son of Shemaiah from Kiriath
Jearim was another man who prophesied in
the name of the LORD; he prophesied the
same things against this city and this land as
Jeremiah did. 21When King Jehoiakim and
all his officers and officials heard his words,
the king sought to put him to death. But Uriah
heard of it and fled in fear to Egypt. 22King
Jehoiakim, however, sent Elnathan son of
Acbor to Egypt, along with some other men.
23They brought Uriah out of Egypt and took

[a]*38* Some Hebrew manuscripts and Septuagint (see also Jer. 46:16 and 50:16); most Hebrew manuscripts *anger*
[b]*18* Micah 3:12

him to King Jehoiakim, who had him struck
down with a sword and his body thrown into
the burial place of the common people.)
24Furthermore, Ahikam son of Shaphan
supported Jeremiah, and so he was not
handed over to the people to be put to death.

Judah to Serve Nebuchadnezzar

27 Early in the reign of Zedekiah[a] son of
Josiah king of Judah, this word came
to Jeremiah from the LORD: 2This is what the
LORD said to me: "Make a yoke out of straps
and crossbars and put it on your neck. 3Then
send word to the kings of Edom, Moab, Ammon, Tyre and Sidon through the envoys
who have come to Jerusalem to Zedekiah
king of Judah. 4Give them a message for
their masters and say, 'This is what the LORD
Almighty, the God of Israel, says: "Tell this to
your masters: 5With my great power and outstretched arm I made the earth and its
people and the animals that are on it, and I
give it to anyone I please. 6Now I will hand all
your countries over to my servant Nebuchadnezzar king of Babylon; I will make even
the wild animals subject to him. 7All nations
will serve him and his son and his grandson
until the time for his land comes; then many
nations and great kings will subjugate him.
8" ' "If, however, any nation or kingdom will
not serve Nebuchadnezzar king of Babylon
or bow its neck under his yoke, I will punish
that nation with the sword, famine and
plague, declares the LORD, until I destroy it by
his hand. 9So do not listen to your prophets,
your diviners, your interpreters of dreams,
your mediums or your sorcerers who tell you,
'You will not serve the king of Babylon.'
10They prophesy lies to you that will only
serve to remove you far from your lands; I will
banish you and you will perish. 11But if any
nation will bow its neck under the yoke of the
king of Babylon and serve him, I will let that
nation remain in its own land to till it and to
live there, declares the LORD." ' "
12I gave the same message to Zedekiah
king of Judah. I said, "Bow your neck under
the yoke of the king of Babylon; serve him
and his people, and you will live. 13Why will
you and your people die by the sword, famine and plague with which the LORD has
threatened any nation that will not serve the
king of Babylon? 14Do not listen to the words
of the prophets who say to you, 'You will not
serve the king of Babylon,' for they are
prophesying lies to you. 15'I have not sent
them,' declares the LORD. 'They are prophesying lies in my name. Therefore, I will banish you and you will perish, both you and the
prophets who prophesy to you.' "
16Then I said to the priests and all these
people, "This is what the LORD says: Do not
listen to the prophets who say, 'Very soon
now the articles from the LORD's house will be
brought back from Babylon.' They are
prophesying lies to you. 17Do not listen to
them. Serve the king of Babylon, and you will
live. Why should this city become a ruin? 18If
they are prophets and have the word of the
LORD, let them plead with the LORD Almighty
that the furnishings remaining in the house of
the LORD and in the palace of the king of
Judah and in Jerusalem not be taken to Babylon. 19For this is what the LORD Almighty
says about the pillars, the Sea, the movable
stands and the other furnishings that are left
in this city, 20which Nebuchadnezzar king of
Babylon did not take away when he carried
Jehoiachin[b] son of Jehoiakim king of Judah
into exile from Jerusalem to Babylon, along
with all the nobles of Judah and Jerusalem—
21yes, this is what the LORD Almighty, the God
of Israel, says about the things that are left in
the house of the LORD and in the palace of the
king of Judah and in Jerusalem: 22'They will
be taken to Babylon and there they will remain until the day I come for them,' declares
the LORD. 'Then I will bring them back and
restore them to this place.' "

The False Prophet Hananiah

28 In the fifth month of that same year,
the fourth year, early in the reign of
Zedekiah king of Judah, the prophet Hananiah son of Azzur, who was from Gibeon,
said to me in the house of the LORD in the
presence of the priests and all the people:
2"This is what the LORD Almighty, the God of
Israel, says: 'I will break the yoke of the king
of Babylon. 3Within two years I will bring
back to this place all the articles of the LORD's
house that Nebuchadnezzar king of Babylon
removed from here and took to Babylon. 4I
will also bring back to this place Jehoiachin[b]
son of Jehoiakim king of Judah and all the
other exiles from Judah who went to Babylon,' declares the LORD, 'for I will break the
yoke of the king of Babylon.' "

[a] *1* A few Hebrew manuscripts and Syriac (see also Jer. 27:3, 12 and 28:1); most Hebrew manuscripts *Jehoiakim* (Most Septuagint manuscripts do not have this verse.)
[b] *20,4* Hebrew *Jeconiah,* a variant of *Jehoiachin*

5Then the prophet Jeremiah replied to the
prophet Hananiah before the priests and all
the people who were standing in the house
of the LORD. 6He said, "Amen! May the LORD
do so! May the LORD fulfill the words you have
prophesied by bringing the articles of the
LORD's house and all the exiles back to this
place from Babylon. 7Nevertheless, listen to
what I have to say in your hearing and in the
hearing of all the people: 8From early times
the prophets who preceded you and me
have prophesied war, disaster and plague
against many countries and great kingdoms.
9But the prophet who prophesies peace will
be recognized as one truly sent by the LORD
only if his prediction comes true."
10Then the prophet Hananiah took the
yoke off the neck of the prophet Jeremiah
and broke it, 11and he said before all the
people, "This is what the LORD says: 'In the
same way will I break the yoke of Nebuchadnezzar king of Babylon off the neck of
all the nations within two years.' " At this, the
prophet Jeremiah went on his way.
12Shortly after the prophet Hananiah had
broken the yoke off the neck of the prophet
Jeremiah, the word of the LORD came to Jeremiah: 13"Go and tell Hananiah, 'This is what
the LORD says: You have broken a wooden
yoke, but in its place you will get a yoke of
iron. 14This is what the LORD Almighty, the
God of Israel, says: I will put an iron yoke on
the necks of all these nations to make them
serve Nebuchadnezzar king of Babylon, and
they will serve him. I will even give him control over the wild animals.' "
15Then the prophet Jeremiah said to
Hananiah the prophet, "Listen, Hananiah!
The LORD has not sent you, yet you have
persuaded this nation to trust in lies. 16There-
fore, this is what the LORD says: 'I am about to
remove you from the face of the earth. This
very year you are going to die, because you
have preached rebellion against the LORD.' "
17In the seventh month of that same year,
Hananiah the prophet died.

A Letter to the Exiles

29 This is the text of the letter that the
prophet Jeremiah sent from Jerusa-
lem to the surviving elders among the exiles
and to the priests, the prophets and all the
other people Nebuchadnezzar had carried
into exile from Jerusalem to Babylon. 2(This
was after King Jehoiachin[a] and the queen
mother, the court officials and the leaders of
Judah and Jerusalem, the craftsmen and the
artisans had gone into exile from Jerusalem.) 3He entrusted the letter to Elasah son
of Shaphan and to Gemariah son of Hilkiah,
whom Zedekiah king of Judah sent to King
Nebuchadnezzar in Babylon. It said:

4This is what the LORD Almighty, the
God of Israel, says to all those I carried
into exile from Jerusalem to Babylon:
5"Build houses and settle down; plant
gardens and eat what they produce.
6Marry and have sons and daughters;
find wives for your sons and give your
daughters in marriage, so that they too
may have sons and daughters. Increase
in number there; do not decrease. 7Also,
seek the peace and prosperity of the city
to which I have carried you into exile.
Pray to the LORD for it, because if it prospers, you too will prosper." 8Yes, this is
what the LORD Almighty, the God of Israel, says: "Do not let the prophets and
diviners among you deceive you. Do not
listen to the dreams you encourage
them to have. 9They are prophesying
lies to you in my name. I have not sent
them," declares the LORD.
10This is what the LORD says: "When
seventy years are completed for Babylon, I will come to you and fulfill my
gracious promise to bring you back to
this place. 11For I know the plans I have
for you," declares the LORD, "plans to
prosper you and not to harm you, plans
to give you hope and a future. 12Then
you will call upon me and come and pray
to me, and I will listen to you. 13You will
seek me and find me when you seek me
with all your heart. 14I will be found by
you," declares the LORD, "and will bring
you back from captivity.[b] I will gather
you from all the nations and places
where I have banished you," declares
the LORD, "and will bring you back to the
place from which I carried you into exile."
15You may say, "The LORD has raised
up prophets for us in Babylon," 16but this
is what the LORD says about the king
who sits on David's throne and all the
people who remain in this city, your
countrymen who did not go with you into
exile— 17yes, this is what the LORD Al-

[a]2 Hebrew *Jeconiah,* a variant of *Jehoiachin* [b]14 Or *will restore your fortunes*

mighty says: "I will send the sword, famine and plague against them and I will
make them like poor figs that are so bad
they cannot be eaten. 18I will pursue
them with the sword, famine and plague
and will make them abhorrent to all the
kingdoms of the earth and an object of
cursing and horror, of scorn and reproach, among all the nations where I
drive them. 19For they have not listened
to my words," declares the LORD, "words
that I sent to them again and again by
my servants the prophets. And you exiles have not listened either," declares
the LORD.

20Therefore, hear the word of the
LORD, all you exiles whom I have sent
away from Jerusalem to Babylon. 21This
is what the LORD Almighty, the God of
Israel, says about Ahab son of Kolaiah
and Zedekiah son of Maaseiah, who are
prophesying lies to you in my name: "I
will hand them over to Nebuchadnezzar
king of Babylon, and he will put them to
death before your very eyes. 22Because
of them, all the exiles from Judah who
are in Babylon will use this curse: 'The
LORD treat you like Zedekiah and Ahab,
whom the king of Babylon burned in the
fire.' 23For they have done outrageous
things in Israel; they have committed
adultery with their neighbors' wives and
in my name have spoken lies, which I
did not tell them to do. I know it and am
a witness to it," declares the LORD.

Message to Shemaiah

24Tell Shemaiah the Nehelamite, 25"This is
what the LORD Almighty, the God of Israel,
says: You sent letters in your own name to all
the people in Jerusalem, to Zephaniah son
of Maaseiah the priest, and to all the other
priests. You said to Zephaniah, 26'The LORD
has appointed you priest in place of Jehoiada to be in charge of the house of the LORD;
you should put any madman who acts like a
prophet into the stocks and neck-irons. 27So
why have you not reprimanded Jeremiah
from Anathoth, who poses as a prophet
among you? 28He has sent this message to
us in Babylon: It will be a long time. Therefore build houses and settle down; plant gardens and eat what they produce.' "

29Zephaniah the priest, however, read the
letter to Jeremiah the prophet. 30Then the
word of the LORD came to Jeremiah: 31"Send
this message to all the exiles: 'This is what
the LORD says about Shemaiah the Nehelamite: Because Shemaiah has prophesied to
you, even though I did not send him, and has
led you to believe a lie, 32this is what the LORD
says: I will surely punish Shemaiah the
Nehelamite and his descendants. He will
have no one left among this people, nor will
he see the good things I will do for my
people, declares the LORD, because he has
preached rebellion against me.' "

Restoration of Israel

30 This is the word that came to Jeremiah from the LORD: 2"This is what
the LORD, the God of Israel, says: 'Write in a
book all the words I have spoken to you.
3The days are coming,' declares the LORD,
'when I will bring my people Israel and Judah
back from captivity[a] and restore them to the
land I gave their forefathers to possess,'
says the LORD."

4These are the words the LORD spoke concerning Israel and Judah: 5"This is what the
LORD says:

" 'Cries of fear are heard—
terror, not peace.
6Ask and see:
Can a man bear children?
Then why do I see every strong man
with his hands on his stomach like a
woman in labor,
every face turned deathly pale?
7How awful that day will be!
None will be like it.
It will be a time of trouble for Jacob,
but he will be saved out of it.

8" 'In that day,' declares the LORD
Almighty,
'I will break the yoke off their necks
and will tear off their bonds;
no longer will foreigners enslave them.
9Instead, they will serve the LORD their
God
and David their king,
whom I will raise up for them.

10" 'So do not fear, O Jacob my servant;
do not be dismayed, O Israel,'
declares the LORD.
'I will surely save you out of a distant
place,

[a]3 *Or will restore the fortunes of my people Israel and Judah*

your descendants from the land of their
exile.
Jacob will again have peace and security,
and no one will make him afraid.
11I am with you and will save you,'
declares the LORD.
'Though I completely destroy all the
nations
among which I scatter you,
I will not completely destroy you.
I will discipline you but only with justice;
I will not let you go entirely
unpunished.'

12"This is what the LORD says:

" 'Your wound is incurable,
your injury beyond healing.
13There is no one to plead your cause,
no remedy for your sore,
no healing for you.
14All your allies have forgotten you;
they care nothing for you.
I have struck you as an enemy would
and punished you as would the cruel,
because your guilt is so great
and your sins so many.
15Why do you cry out over your wound,
your pain that has no cure?
Because of your great guilt and many
sins
I have done these things to you.

16" 'But all who devour you will be
devoured;
all your enemies will go into exile.
Those who plunder you will be plundered;
all who make spoil of you I will despoil.
17But I will restore you to health
and heal your wounds,'
declares the LORD,
'because you are called an outcast,
Zion for whom no one cares.'

18"This is what the LORD says:

" 'I will restore the fortunes of Jacob's
tents
and have compassion on his dwellings;
the city will be rebuilt on her ruins,
and the palace will stand in its proper
place.
19From them will come songs of
thanksgiving
and the sound of rejoicing.
I will add to their numbers,
and they will not be decreased;
I will bring them honor,
and they will not be disdained.
20Their children will be as in days of old,
and their community will be established
before me;
I will punish all who oppress them.
21Their leader will be one of their own;
their ruler will arise from among them.
I will bring him near and he will come
close to me,
for who is he who will devote himself
to be close to me?'
declares the LORD.
22" 'So you will be my people,
and I will be your God.' "

23See, the storm of the LORD
will burst out in wrath,
a driving wind swirling down
on the heads of the wicked.
24The fierce anger of the LORD will not turn
back
until he fully accomplishes
the purposes of his heart.
In days to come
you will understand this.

31 "At that time," declares the LORD, "I
will be the God of all the clans of
Israel, and they will be my people."

2This is what the LORD says:

"The people who survive the sword
will find favor in the desert;
I will come to give rest to Israel."

3The LORD appeared to us in the past,[a]
saying:

"I have loved you with an everlasting
love;
I have drawn you with loving-kindness.
4I will build you up again
and you will be rebuilt, O Virgin Israel.
Again you will take up your tambourines
and go out to dance with the joyful.
5Again you will plant vineyards
on the hills of Samaria;
the farmers will plant them
and enjoy their fruit.
6There will be a day when watchmen cry
out
on the hills of Ephraim,
'Come, let us go up to Zion,
to the LORD our God.' "

7This is what the LORD says:

"Sing with joy for Jacob;

[a]3 Or *LORD has appeared to us from afar*

shout for the foremost of the nations.
Make your praises heard, and say,
'O LORD, save your people,
the remnant of Israel.'
8See, I will bring them from the land of the north
and gather them from the ends of the earth.
Among them will be the blind and the lame,
expectant mothers and women in labor;
a great throng will return.
9They will come with weeping;
they will pray as I bring them back.
I will lead them beside streams of water
on a level path where they will not stumble,
because I am Israel's father,
and Ephraim is my firstborn son.

10"Hear the word of the LORD, O nations;
proclaim it in distant coastlands:
'He who scattered Israel will gather them
and will watch over his flock like a shepherd.'
11For the LORD will ransom Jacob
and redeem them from the hand of those stronger than they.
12They will come and shout for joy on the heights of Zion;
they will rejoice in the bounty of the LORD—
the grain, the new wine and the oil,
the young of the flocks and herds.
They will be like a well-watered garden,
and they will sorrow no more.
13Then maidens will dance and be glad,
young men and old as well.
I will turn their mourning into gladness;
I will give them comfort and joy instead of sorrow.
14I will satisfy the priests with abundance,
and my people will be filled with my bounty,"
declares the LORD.

15This is what the LORD says:

"A voice is heard in Ramah,
mourning and great weeping,
Rachel weeping for her children
and refusing to be comforted,
because her children are no more."

16This is what the LORD says:

"Restrain your voice from weeping
and your eyes from tears,
for your work will be rewarded,"
declares the LORD.
"They will return from the land of the enemy.
17So there is hope for your future,"
declares the LORD.
"Your children will return to their own land.

18"I have surely heard Ephraim's moaning:
'You disciplined me like an unruly calf,
and I have been disciplined.
Restore me, and I will return,
because you are the LORD my God.
19After I strayed,
I repented;
after I came to understand,
I beat my breast.
I was ashamed and humiliated
because I bore the disgrace of my youth.'
20Is not Ephraim my dear son,
the child in whom I delight?
Though I often speak against him,
I still remember him.
Therefore my heart yearns for him;
I have great compassion for him,"
declares the LORD.

21"Set up road signs;
put up guideposts.
Take note of the highway,
the road that you take.
Return, O Virgin Israel,
return to your towns.
22How long will you wander,
O unfaithful daughter?
The LORD will create a new thing on earth—
a woman will surround[a] a man."

23This is what the LORD Almighty, the God
of Israel, says: "When I bring them back from
captivity,[b] the people in the land of Judah
and in its towns will once again use these
words: 'The LORD bless you, O righteous
dwelling, O sacred mountain.' 24People will
live together in Judah and all its towns—
farmers and those who move about with their
flocks. 25I will refresh the weary and satisfy
the faint."

26At this I awoke and looked around. My
sleep had been pleasant to me.

27"The days are coming," declares the
LORD, "when I will plant the house of Israel
and the house of Judah with the offspring of
men and of animals. 28Just as I watched over

[a]22 Or *will go about* ⌊*seeking*⌋; or *will protect*
[b]23 Or *I restore their fortunes*

them to uproot and tear down, and to overthrow, destroy and bring disaster, so I will
watch over them to build and to plant," declares the LORD. 29"In those days people will
no longer say,

'The fathers have eaten sour grapes,
and the children's teeth are set on
edge.'

30Instead, everyone will die for his own sin;
whoever eats sour grapes—his own teeth
will be set on edge.

31"The time is coming," declares the LORD,
"when I will make a new covenant
with the house of Israel
and with the house of Judah.
32It will not be like the covenant
I made with their forefathers
when I took them by the hand
to lead them out of Egypt,
because they broke my covenant,
though I was a husband to[a] them,[b]"
declares the LORD.
33"This is the covenant I will make with the
house of Israel
after that time," declares the LORD.
"I will put my law in their minds
and write it on their hearts.
I will be their God,
and they will be my people.
34No longer will a man teach his neighbor,
or a man his brother, saying, 'Know the
LORD,'
because they will all know me,
from the least of them to the greatest,"
declares the LORD.
"For I will forgive their wickedness
and will remember their sins no more."

35This is what the LORD says,

he who appoints the sun
to shine by day,
who decrees the moon and stars
to shine by night,
who stirs up the sea
so that its waves roar—
the LORD Almighty is his name:
36"Only if these decrees vanish from my
sight,"
declares the LORD,
"will the descendants of Israel ever cease
to be a nation before me."

37This is what the LORD says:

"Only if the heavens above can be
measured
and the foundations of the earth below
be searched out
will I reject all the descendants of Israel
because of all they have done,"
declares the LORD.

38"The days are coming," declares the
LORD, "when this city will be rebuilt for me
from the Tower of Hananel to the Corner
Gate. 39The measuring line will stretch from
there straight to the hill of Gareb and then
turn to Goah. 40The whole valley where dead
bodies and ashes are thrown, and all the
terraces out to the Kidron Valley on the east
as far as the corner of the Horse Gate, will be
holy to the LORD. The city will never again be
uprooted or demolished."

Jeremiah Buys a Field

32 This is the word that came to Jeremiah from the LORD in the tenth year
of Zedekiah king of Judah, which was the
eighteenth year of Nebuchadnezzar. 2The
army of the king of Babylon was then besieging Jerusalem, and Jeremiah the prophet
was confined in the courtyard of the guard in
the royal palace of Judah.

3Now Zedekiah king of Judah had imprisoned him there, saying, "Why do you
prophesy as you do? You say, 'This is what
the LORD says: I am about to hand this city
over to the king of Babylon, and he will capture it. 4Zedekiah king of Judah will not escape out of the hands of the Babylonians[c]
but will certainly be handed over to the king
of Babylon, and will speak with him face to
face and see him with his own eyes. 5He will
take Zedekiah to Babylon, where he will remain until I deal with him, declares the LORD.
If you fight against the Babylonians, you will
not succeed.' "

6Jeremiah said, "The word of the LORD
came to me: 7Hanamel son of Shallum your
uncle is going to come to you and say, 'Buy
my field at Anathoth, because as nearest
relative it is your right and duty to buy it.'

8"Then, just as the LORD had said, my
cousin Hanamel came to me in the courtyard
of the guard and said, 'Buy my field at Anathoth in the territory of Benjamin. Since it is
your right to redeem it and possess it, buy it
for yourself.'

[a]32 Hebrew; Septuagint and Syriac / *and I turned away from* [b]32 Or *was their master* [c]4 Or *Chaldeans;* also in verses 5, 24, 25, 28, 29 and 43

"I knew that this was the word of the LORD;
9so I bought the field at Anathoth from my
cousin Hanamel and weighed out for him
seventeen shekels[a] of silver. 10I signed and
sealed the deed, had it witnessed, and
weighed out the silver on the scales. 11I took
the deed of purchase—the sealed copy containing the terms and conditions, as well as
the unsealed copy— 12and I gave this deed
to Baruch son of Neriah, the son of Mahseiah, in the presence of my cousin Hanamel
and of the witnesses who had signed the
deed and of all the Jews sitting in the courtyard of the guard.

13"In their presence I gave Baruch these
instructions: 14'This is what the LORD Almighty, the God of Israel, says: Take these
documents, both the sealed and unsealed
copies of the deed of purchase, and put them
in a clay jar so they will last a long time. 15For
this is what the LORD Almighty, the God of
Israel, says: Houses, fields and vineyards
will again be bought in this land.'

16"After I had given the deed of purchase
to Baruch son of Neriah, I prayed to the LORD:

17"Ah, Sovereign LORD, you have made
the heavens and the earth by your great
power and outstretched arm. Nothing is
too hard for you. 18You show love to
thousands but bring the punishment for
the fathers' sins into the laps of their
children after them. O great and powerful God, whose name is the LORD Almighty, 19great are your purposes and
mighty are your deeds. Your eyes are
open to all the ways of men; you reward
everyone according to his conduct and
as his deeds deserve. 20You performed
miraculous signs and wonders in Egypt
and have continued them to this day,
both in Israel and among all mankind,
and have gained the renown that is still
yours. 21You brought your people Israel
out of Egypt with signs and wonders, by
a mighty hand and an outstretched arm
and with great terror. 22You gave them
this land you had sworn to give their
forefathers, a land flowing with milk and
honey. 23They came in and took
possession of it, but they did not obey
you or follow your law; they did not do
what you commanded them to do. So
you brought all this disaster upon them.

24"See how the siege ramps are built
up to take the city. Because of the
sword, famine and plague, the city will
be handed over to the Babylonians who
are attacking it. What you said has happened, as you now see. 25And though
the city will be handed over to the Babylonians, you, O Sovereign LORD, say to
me, 'Buy the field with silver and have
the transaction witnessed.' "

26Then the word of the LORD came to Jeremiah: 27"I am the LORD, the God of all mankind. Is anything too hard for me? 28There-
fore, this is what the LORD says: I am about to
hand this city over to the Babylonians and to
Nebuchadnezzar king of Babylon, who will
capture it. 29The Babylonians who are attacking this city will come in and set it on fire;
they will burn it down, along with the houses
where the people provoked me to anger by
burning incense on the roofs to Baal and by
pouring out drink offerings to other gods.

30"The people of Israel and Judah have
done nothing but evil in my sight from their
youth; indeed, the people of Israel have
done nothing but provoke me with what their
hands have made, declares the LORD. 31From
the day it was built until now, this city has so
aroused my anger and wrath that I must remove it from my sight. 32The people of Israel
and Judah have provoked me by all the evil
they have done—they, their kings and officials, their priests and prophets, the men of
Judah and the people of Jerusalem. 33They
turned their backs to me and not their faces;
though I taught them again and again, they
would not listen or respond to discipline.
34They set up their abominable idols in the
house that bears my Name and defiled it.
35They built high places for Baal in the Valley
of Ben Hinnom to sacrifice their sons and
daughters[b] to Molech, though I never commanded, nor did it enter my mind, that they
should do such a detestable thing and so
make Judah sin.

36"You are saying about this city, 'By the
sword, famine and plague it will be handed
over to the king of Babylon'; but this is what
the LORD, the God of Israel, says: 37I will surely gather them from all the lands where I
banish them in my furious anger and great
wrath; I will bring them back to this place and
let them live in safety. 38They will be my
people, and I will be their God. 39I will give
them singleness of heart and action, so that
they will always fear me for their own good
and the good of their children after them. 40I

[a]9 That is, about 7 ounces (about 200 grams)

[b]35 Or *to make their sons and daughters pass through* ⌞*the fire*⌟

will make an everlasting covenant with them:
I will never stop doing good to them, and I will
inspire them to fear me, so that they will
never turn away from me. [41]I will rejoice in
doing them good and will assuredly plant
them in this land with all my heart and soul.
[42]"This is what the LORD says: As I have
brought all this great calamity on this people,
so I will give them all the prosperity I have
promised them. [43]Once more fields will be
bought in this land of which you say, 'It is a
desolate waste, without men or animals, for
it has been handed over to the Babylonians.'
[44]Fields will be bought for silver, and deeds
will be signed, sealed and witnessed in the
territory of Benjamin, in the villages around
Jerusalem, in the towns of Judah and in the
towns of the hill country, of the western foothills and of the Negev, because I will restore
their fortunes,[a] declares the LORD."

Promise of Restoration

33 While Jeremiah was still confined in
the courtyard of the guard, the word
of the LORD came to him a second time:
[2]"This is what the LORD says, he who made
the earth, the LORD who formed it and established it—the LORD is his name: [3]'Call to me
and I will answer you and tell you great and
unsearchable things you do not know.' [4]For
this is what the LORD, the God of Israel, says
about the houses in this city and the royal
palaces of Judah that have been torn down
to be used against the siege ramps and the
sword [5]in the fight with the Babylonians[b]:
'They will be filled with the dead bodies of the
men I will slay in my anger and wrath. I will
hide my face from this city because of all its
wickedness.
[6]" 'Nevertheless, I will bring health and
healing to it; I will heal my people and will let
them enjoy abundant peace and security. [7]I
will bring Judah and Israel back from captivity[c] and will rebuild them as they were before.
[8]I will cleanse them from all the sin they have
committed against me and will forgive all
their sins of rebellion against me. [9]Then this
city will bring me renown, joy, praise and
honor before all nations on earth that hear of
all the good things I do for it; and they will be
in awe and will tremble at the abundant prosperity and peace I provide for it.'
[10]"This is what the LORD says: 'You say
about this place, "It is a desolate waste, without men or animals." Yet in the towns of
Judah and the streets of Jerusalem that are
deserted, inhabited by neither men nor animals, there will be heard once more [11]the
sounds of joy and gladness, the voices of
bride and bridegroom, and the voices of
those who bring thank offerings to the house
of the LORD, saying,

"Give thanks to the LORD Almighty,
  for the LORD is good;
  his love endures forever."

For I will restore the fortunes of the land as
they were before,' says the LORD.
[12]"This is what the LORD Almighty says: 'In
this place, desolate and without men or animals—in all its towns there will again be pastures for shepherds to rest their flocks. [13]In
the towns of the hill country, of the western
foothills and of the Negev, in the territory of
Benjamin, in the villages around Jerusalem
and in the towns of Judah, flocks will again
pass under the hand of the one who counts
them,' says the LORD.
[14]" 'The days are coming,' declares the
LORD, 'when I will fulfill the gracious promise I
made to the house of Israel and to the house
of Judah.

[15]" 'In those days and at that time
  I will make a righteous Branch sprout
    from David's line;
  he will do what is just and right in the
    land.
[16]In those days Judah will be saved
  and Jerusalem will live in safety.
This is the name by which it[d] will be
    called:
  The LORD Our Righteousness.'

[17]For this is what the LORD says: 'David will
never fail to have a man to sit on the throne of
the house of Israel, [18]nor will the priests, who
are Levites, ever fail to have a man to stand
before me continually to offer burnt offerings,
to burn grain offerings and to present sacrifices.' "
[19]The word of the LORD came to Jeremiah:
[20]"This is what the LORD says: 'If you can
break my covenant with the day and my covenant with the night, so that day and night no
longer come at their appointed time, [21]then
my covenant with David my servant—and
my covenant with the Levites who are priests

[a]44 *Or will bring them back from captivity* [b]5 *Or Chaldeans* [c]7 *Or will restore the fortunes of Judah and Israel* [d]16 *Or he*

ministering before me—can be broken and David will no longer have a descendant to reign on his throne. [22]I will make the descendants of David my servant and the Levites who minister before me as countless as the stars of the sky and as measureless as the sand on the seashore.' "

[23]The word of the LORD came to Jeremiah: [24]"Have you not noticed that these people are saying, 'The LORD has rejected the two kingdoms[a] he chose'? So they despise my people and no longer regard them as a nation. [25]This is what the LORD says: 'If I have not established my covenant with day and night and the fixed laws of heaven and earth, [26]then I will reject the descendants of Jacob and David my servant and will not choose one of his sons to rule over the descendants of Abraham, Isaac and Jacob. For I will restore their fortunes[b] and have compassion on them.' "

Warning to Zedekiah

34 While Nebuchadnezzar king of Babylon and all his army and all the kingdoms and peoples in the empire he ruled were fighting against Jerusalem and all its surrounding towns, this word came to Jeremiah from the LORD: [2]"This is what the LORD, the God of Israel, says: Go to Zedekiah king of Judah and tell him, 'This is what the LORD says: I am about to hand this city over to the king of Babylon, and he will burn it down. [3]You will not escape from his grasp but will surely be captured and handed over to him. You will see the king of Babylon with your own eyes, and he will speak with you face to face. And you will go to Babylon.

[4]" 'Yet hear the promise of the LORD, O Zedekiah king of Judah. This is what the LORD says concerning you: You will not die by the sword; [5]you will die peacefully. As people made a funeral fire in honor of your fathers, the former kings who preceded you, so they will make a fire in your honor and lament, "Alas, O master!" I myself make this promise, declares the LORD.' "

[6]Then Jeremiah the prophet told all this to Zedekiah king of Judah, in Jerusalem, [7]while the army of the king of Babylon was fighting against Jerusalem and the other cities of Judah that were still holding out—Lachish and Azekah. These were the only fortified cities left in Judah.

Freedom for Slaves

[8]The word came to Jeremiah from the LORD after King Zedekiah had made a covenant with all the people in Jerusalem to proclaim freedom for the slaves. [9]Everyone was to free his Hebrew slaves, both male and female; no one was to hold a fellow Jew in bondage. [10]So all the officials and people who entered into this covenant agreed that they would free their male and female slaves and no longer hold them in bondage. They agreed, and set them free. [11]But afterward they changed their minds and took back the slaves they had freed and enslaved them again.

[12]Then the word of the LORD came to Jeremiah: [13]"This is what the LORD, the God of Israel, says: I made a covenant with your forefathers when I brought them out of Egypt, out of the land of slavery. I said, [14]'Every seventh year each of you must free any fellow Hebrew who has sold himself to you. After he has served you six years, you must let him go free.'[c] Your fathers, however, did not listen to me or pay attention to me. [15]Recently you repented and did what is right in my sight: Each of you proclaimed freedom to his countrymen. You even made a covenant before me in the house that bears my Name. [16]But now you have turned around and profaned my name; each of you has taken back the male and female slaves you had set free to go where they wished. You have forced them to become your slaves again.

[17]"Therefore, this is what the LORD says: You have not obeyed me; you have not proclaimed freedom for your fellow countrymen. So I now proclaim 'freedom' for you, declares the LORD—'freedom' to fall by the sword, plague and famine. I will make you abhorrent to all the kingdoms of the earth. [18]The men who have violated my covenant and have not fulfilled the terms of the covenant they made before me, I will treat like the calf they cut in two and then walked between its pieces. [19]The leaders of Judah and Jerusalem, the court officials, the priests and all the people of the land who walked between the pieces of the calf, [20]I will hand over to their enemies who seek their lives. Their dead bodies will become food for the birds of the air and the beasts of the earth.

[21]"I will hand Zedekiah king of Judah and

[a]24 *Or families* [b]26 *Or will bring them back from captivity* [c]14 Deut. 15:12

his officials over to their enemies who seek
their lives, to the army of the king of Babylon,
which has withdrawn from you. 22I am going
to give the order, declares the LORD, and I will
bring them back to this city. They will fight
against it, take it and burn it down. And I will
lay waste the towns of Judah so no one can
live there."

The Recabites

35 This is the word that came to Jeremiah from the LORD during the reign
of Jehoiakim son of Josiah king of Judah:
2"Go to the Recabite family and invite them
to come to one of the side rooms of the
house of the LORD and give them wine to
drink."

3So I went to get Jaazaniah son of Jeremiah, the son of Habazziniah, and his brothers and all his sons—the whole family of the
Recabites. 4I brought them into the house of
the LORD, into the room of the sons of Hanan
son of Igdaliah the man of God. It was next to
the room of the officials, which was over that
of Maaseiah son of Shallum the doorkeeper.
5Then I set bowls full of wine and some cups
before the men of the Recabite family and
said to them, "Drink some wine."

6But they replied, "We do not drink wine,
because our forefather Jonadab son of
Recab gave us this command: 'Neither you
nor your descendants must ever drink wine.
7Also you must never build houses, sow
seed or plant vineyards; you must never
have any of these things, but must always
live in tents. Then you will live a long time in
the land where you are nomads.' 8We have
obeyed everything our forefather Jonadab
son of Recab commanded us. Neither we
nor our wives nor our sons and daughters
have ever drunk wine 9or built houses to live
in or had vineyards, fields or crops. 10We
have lived in tents and have fully obeyed
everything our forefather Jonadab commanded us. 11But when Nebuchadnezzar
king of Babylon invaded this land, we said,
'Come, we must go to Jerusalem to escape
the Babylonian[a] and Aramean armies.' So
we have remained in Jerusalem."

12Then the word of the LORD came to Jeremiah, saying: 13"This is what the LORD Almighty, the God of Israel, says: Go and tell
the men of Judah and the people of Jerusalem, 'Will you not learn a lesson and obey my
words?' declares the LORD. 14'Jonadab son of
Recab ordered his sons not to drink wine and
this command has been kept. To this day
they do not drink wine, because they obey
their forefather's command. But I have
spoken to you again and again, yet you have
not obeyed me. 15Again and again I sent all
my servants the prophets to you. They said,
"Each of you must turn from your wicked
ways and reform your actions; do not follow
other gods to serve them. Then you will live
in the land I have given to you and your
fathers." But you have not paid attention or
listened to me. 16The descendants of Jonadab son of Recab have carried out the command their forefather gave them, but these
people have not obeyed me.'

17"Therefore, this is what the LORD God
Almighty, the God of Israel, says: 'Listen! I
am going to bring on Judah and on everyone
living in Jerusalem every disaster I pronounced against them. I spoke to them, but
they did not listen; I called to them, but they
did not answer.' "

18Then Jeremiah said to the family of the
Recabites, "This is what the LORD Almighty,
the God of Israel, says: 'You have obeyed
the command of your forefather Jonadab
and have followed all his instructions and
have done everything he ordered.' 19There-
fore, this is what the LORD Almighty, the God
of Israel, says: 'Jonadab son of Recab will
never fail to have a man to serve me.' "

Jehoiakim Burns Jeremiah's Scroll

36 In the fourth year of Jehoiakim son of
Josiah king of Judah, this word came
to Jeremiah from the LORD: 2"Take a scroll
and write on it all the words I have spoken to
you concerning Israel, Judah and all the
other nations from the time I began speaking
to you in the reign of Josiah till now. 3Per-
haps when the people of Judah hear about
every disaster I plan to inflict on them, each
of them will turn from his wicked way; then I
will forgive their wickedness and their sin."

4So Jeremiah called Baruch son of Neriah,
and while Jeremiah dictated all the words the
LORD had spoken to him, Baruch wrote them
on the scroll. 5Then Jeremiah told Baruch, "I
am restricted; I cannot go to the LORD's temple. 6So you go to the house of the LORD on a
day of fasting and read to the people from the

[a] 11 Or *Chaldean*

scroll the words of the LORD that you wrote as I dictated. Read them to all the people of Judah who come in from their towns. 7Perhaps they will bring their petition before the LORD, and each will turn from his wicked ways, for the anger and wrath pronounced against this people by the LORD are great."

8Baruch son of Neriah did everything Jeremiah the prophet told him to do; at the LORD's temple he read the words of the LORD from the scroll. 9In the ninth month of the fifth year of Jehoiakim son of Josiah king of Judah, a time of fasting before the LORD was proclaimed for all the people in Jerusalem and those who had come from the towns of Judah. 10From the room of Gemariah son of Shaphan the secretary, which was in the upper courtyard at the entrance of the New Gate of the temple, Baruch read to all the people at the LORD's temple the words of Jeremiah from the scroll.

11When Micaiah son of Gemariah, the son of Shaphan, heard all the words of the LORD from the scroll, 12he went down to the secretary's room in the royal palace, where all the officials were sitting: Elishama the secretary, Delaiah son of Shemaiah, Elnathan son of Acbor, Gemariah son of Shaphan, Zedekiah son of Hananiah, and all the other officials. 13After Micaiah told them everything he had heard Baruch read to the people from the scroll, 14all the officials sent Jehudi son of Nethaniah, the son of Shelemiah, the son of Cushi, to say to Baruch, "Bring the scroll from which you have read to the people and come." So Baruch son of Neriah went to them with the scroll in his hand. 15They said to him, "Sit down, please, and read it to us."

So Baruch read it to them. 16When they heard all these words, they looked at each other in fear and said to Baruch, "We must report all these words to the king." 17Then they asked Baruch, "Tell us, how did you come to write all this? Did Jeremiah dictate it?"

18"Yes," Baruch replied, "he dictated all these words to me, and I wrote them in ink on the scroll."

19Then the officials said to Baruch, "You and Jeremiah, go and hide. Don't let anyone know where you are."

20After they put the scroll in the room of Elishama the secretary, they went to the king in the courtyard and reported everything to him. 21The king sent Jehudi to get the scroll, and Jehudi brought it from the room of Elishama the secretary and read it to the king and all the officials standing beside him. 22It was the ninth month and the king was sitting in the winter apartment, with a fire burning in the firepot in front of him. 23Whenever Jehudi had read three or four columns of the scroll, the king cut them off with a scribe's knife and threw them into the firepot, until the entire scroll was burned in the fire. 24The king and all his attendants who heard all these words showed no fear, nor did they tear their clothes. 25Even though Elnathan, Delaiah and Gemariah urged the king not to burn the scroll, he would not listen to them. 26Instead, the king commanded Jerahmeel, a son of the king, Seraiah son of Azriel and Shelemiah son of Abdeel to arrest Baruch the scribe and Jeremiah the prophet. But the LORD had hidden them.

27After the king burned the scroll containing the words that Baruch had written at Jeremiah's dictation, the word of the LORD came to Jeremiah: 28"Take another scroll and write on it all the words that were on the first scroll, which Jehoiakim king of Judah burned up. 29Also tell Jehoiakim king of Judah, 'This is what the LORD says: You burned that scroll and said, "Why did you write on it that the king of Babylon would certainly come and destroy this land and cut off both men and animals from it?" 30Therefore, this is what the LORD says about Jehoiakim king of Judah: He will have no one to sit on the throne of David; his body will be thrown out and exposed to the heat by day and the frost by night. 31I will punish him and his children and his attendants for their wickedness; I will bring on them and those living in Jerusalem and the people of Judah every disaster I pronounced against them, because they have not listened.' "

32So Jeremiah took another scroll and gave it to the scribe Baruch son of Neriah, and as Jeremiah dictated, Baruch wrote on it all the words of the scroll that Jehoiakim king of Judah had burned in the fire. And many similar words were added to them.

Jeremiah in Prison

37 Zedekiah son of Josiah was made king of Judah by Nebuchadnezzar king of Babylon; he reigned in place of Jehoiachin[a] son of Jehoiakim. 2Neither he nor his attendants nor the people of the land

[a] 1 Hebrew *Coniah,* a variant of *Jehoiachin*

paid any attention to the words the LORD had
spoken through Jeremiah the prophet.
3King Zedekiah, however, sent Jehucal
son of Shelemiah with the priest Zephaniah
son of Maaseiah to Jeremiah the prophet
with this message: "Please pray to the LORD
our God for us."
4Now Jeremiah was free to come and go
among the people, for he had not yet been
put in prison. 5Pharaoh's army had marched
out of Egypt, and when the Babylonians[a]
who were besieging Jerusalem heard the
report about them, they withdrew from
Jerusalem.
6Then the word of the LORD came to Jeremiah the prophet: 7"This is what the LORD, the
God of Israel, says: Tell the king of Judah,
who sent you to inquire of me, 'Pharaoh's
army, which has marched out to support you,
will go back to its own land, to Egypt. 8Then
the Babylonians will return and attack this
city; they will capture it and burn it down.'
9"This is what the LORD says: Do not deceive yourselves, thinking, 'The Babylonians
will surely leave us.' They will not! 10Even if
you were to defeat the entire Babylonian[b]
army that is attacking you and only wounded
men were left in their tents, they would come
out and burn this city down."
11After the Babylonian army had withdrawn from Jerusalem because of Pharaoh's army, 12Jeremiah started to leave the
city to go to the territory of Benjamin to get
his share of the property among the people
there. 13But when he reached the Benjamin
Gate, the captain of the guard, whose name
was Irijah son of Shelemiah, the son of
Hananiah, arrested him and said, "You are
deserting to the Babylonians!"
14"That's not true!" Jeremiah said. "I am
not deserting to the Babylonians." But Irijah
would not listen to him; instead, he arrested
Jeremiah and brought him to the officials.
15They were angry with Jeremiah and had
him beaten and imprisoned in the house of
Jonathan the secretary, which they had
made into a prison.
16Jeremiah was put into a vaulted cell in a
dungeon, where he remained a long time.
17Then King Zedekiah sent for him and had
him brought to the palace, where he asked
him privately, "Is there any word from the
LORD?"
"Yes," Jeremiah replied, "you will be
handed over to the king of Babylon."
18Then Jeremiah said to King Zedekiah,
"What crime have I committed against you or
your officials or this people, that you have put
me in prison? 19Where are your prophets
who prophesied to you, 'The king of Babylon
will not attack you or this land'? 20But now,
my lord the king, please listen. Let me bring
my petition before you: Do not send me back
to the house of Jonathan the secretary, or I
will die there."
21King Zedekiah then gave orders for Jeremiah to be placed in the courtyard of the
guard and given bread from the street of the
bakers each day until all the bread in the city
was gone. So Jeremiah remained in the
courtyard of the guard.

Jeremiah Thrown Into a Cistern

38 Shephatiah son of Mattan, Gedaliah
son of Pashhur, Jehucal[c] son of
Shelemiah, and Pashhur son of Malkijah
heard what Jeremiah was telling all the
people when he said, 2"This is what the LORD
says: 'Whoever stays in this city will die by
the sword, famine or plague, but whoever
goes over to the Babylonians[d] will live. He
will escape with his life; he will live.' 3And this
is what the LORD says: 'This city will certainly
be handed over to the army of the king of
Babylon, who will capture it.' "
4Then the officials said to the king, "This
man should be put to death. He is discourag-
ing the soldiers who are left in this city, as
well as all the people, by the things he is
saying to them. This man is not seeking the
good of these people but their ruin."
5"He is in your hands," King Zedekiah answered. "The king can do nothing to oppose
you."
6So they took Jeremiah and put him into
the cistern of Malkijah, the king's son, which
was in the courtyard of the guard. They lowered Jeremiah by ropes into the cistern; it
had no water in it, only mud, and Jeremiah
sank down into the mud.
7But Ebed-Melech, a Cushite,[e] an official[f]
in the royal palace, heard that they had put
Jeremiah into the cistern. While the king was
sitting in the Benjamin Gate, 8Ebed-Melech
went out of the palace and said to him, 9"My
lord the king, these men have acted wickedly

[a] 5 Or *Chaldeans;* also in verses 8, 9, 13 and 14 [b] 10 Or *Chaldean;* also in verse 11 [c] 1 Hebrew *Jucal,* a variant of *Jehucal* [d] 2 Or *Chaldeans*; also in verses 18, 19 and 23 [e] 7 Probably from the upper Nile region [f] 7 Or *a eunuch*

in all they have done to Jeremiah the
prophet. They have thrown him into a cistern, where he will starve to death when
there is no longer any bread in the city."
10Then the king commanded Ebed-Melech
the Cushite, "Take thirty men from here with
you and lift Jeremiah the prophet out of the
cistern before he dies."
11So Ebed-Melech took the men with him
and went to a room under the treasury in the
palace. He took some old rags and worn-out
clothes from there and let them down with
ropes to Jeremiah in the cistern. 12Ebed-
Melech the Cushite said to Jeremiah, "Put
these old rags and worn-out clothes under
your arms to pad the ropes." Jeremiah did
so, 13and they pulled him up with the ropes
and lifted him out of the cistern. And Jeremiah remained in the courtyard of the guard.

Zedekiah Questions Jeremiah Again

14Then King Zedekiah sent for Jeremiah
the prophet and had him brought to the third
entrance to the temple of the LORD. "I am
going to ask you something," the king said to
Jeremiah. "Do not hide anything from me."
15Jeremiah said to Zedekiah, "If I give you
an answer, will you not kill me? Even if I did
give you counsel, you would not listen to
me."
16But King Zedekiah swore this oath secretly to Jeremiah: "As surely as the LORD
lives, who has given us breath, I will neither
kill you nor hand you over to those who are
seeking your life."
17Then Jeremiah said to Zedekiah, "This is
what the LORD God Almighty, the God of Israel, says: 'If you surrender to the officers of
the king of Babylon, your life will be spared
and this city will not be burned down; you and
your family will live. 18But if you will not surrender to the officers of the king of Babylon,
this city will be handed over to the Babylonians and they will burn it down; you yourself
will not escape from their hands.' "
19King Zedekiah said to Jeremiah, "I am
afraid of the Jews who have gone over to the
Babylonians, for the Babylonians may hand
me over to them and they will mistreat me."
20"They will not hand you over," Jeremiah
replied. "Obey the LORD by doing what I tell
you. Then it will go well with you, and your life
will be spared. 21But if you refuse to surrender, this is what the LORD has revealed to me:
22All the women left in the palace of the king
of Judah will be brought out to the officials of
the king of Babylon. Those women will say to
you:

" 'They misled you and overcame you—
those trusted friends of yours.
Your feet are sunk in the mud;
your friends have deserted you.'

23"All your wives and children will be
brought out to the Babylonians. You yourself
will not escape from their hands but will be
captured by the king of Babylon; and this city
will[a] be burned down."
24Then Zedekiah said to Jeremiah, "Do
not let anyone know about this conversation,
or you may die. 25If the officials hear that I
talked with you, and they come to you and
say, 'Tell us what you said to the king and
what the king said to you; do not hide it from
us or we will kill you,' 26then tell them, 'I was
pleading with the king not to send me back to
Jonathan's house to die there.' "
27All the officials did come to Jeremiah and
question him, and he told them everything
the king had ordered him to say. So they said
no more to him, for no one had heard his
conversation with the king.
28And Jeremiah remained in the courtyard
of the guard until the day Jerusalem was
captured.

The Fall of Jerusalem

39 This is how Jerusalem was taken: 1In
the ninth year of Zedekiah king of
Judah, in the tenth month, Nebuchadnezzar
king of Babylon marched against Jerusalem
with his whole army and laid siege to it. 2And
on the ninth day of the fourth month of Zedekiah's eleventh year, the city wall was broken
through. 3Then all the officials of the king of
Babylon came and took seats in the Middle
Gate: Nergal-Sharezer of Samgar, Nebo-
Sarsekim[b] a chief officer, Nergal-Sharezer a
high official and all the other officials of the
king of Babylon. 4When Zedekiah king of
Judah and all the soldiers saw them, they
fled; they left the city at night by way of the
king's garden, through the gate between the
two walls, and headed toward the Arabah.[c]
5But the Babylonian[d] army pursued them
and overtook Zedekiah in the plains of Jericho. They captured him and took him to
Nebuchadnezzar king of Babylon at Riblah

[a]23 Or *and you will cause this city to* [b]3 Or *Nergal-Sharezer, Samgar-Nebo, Sarsekim* [c]4 Or *the Jordan Valley* [d]5 Or *Chaldean*

in the land of Hamath, where he pronounced sentence on him. 6There at Riblah the king of Babylon slaughtered the sons of Zedekiah before his eyes and also killed all the nobles of Judah. 7Then he put out Zedekiah's eyes and bound him with bronze shackles to take him to Babylon.

8The Babylonians[a] set fire to the royal palace and the houses of the people and broke down the walls of Jerusalem. 9Nebuzaradan commander of the imperial guard carried into exile to Babylon the people who remained in the city, along with those who had gone over to him, and the rest of the people. 10But Nebuzaradan the commander of the guard left behind in the land of Judah some of the poor people, who owned nothing; and at that time he gave them vineyards and fields.

11Now Nebuchadnezzar king of Babylon had given these orders about Jeremiah through Nebuzaradan commander of the imperial guard: 12"Take him and look after him; don't harm him but do for him whatever he asks." 13So Nebuzaradan the commander of the guard, Nebushazban a chief officer, Nergal-Sharezer a high official and all the other officers of the king of Babylon 14sent and had Jeremiah taken out of the courtyard of the guard. They turned him over to Gedaliah son of Ahikam, the son of Shaphan, to take him back to his home. So he remained among his own people.

15While Jeremiah had been confined in the courtyard of the guard, the word of the LORD came to him: 16"Go and tell Ebed-Melech the Cushite, 'This is what the LORD Almighty, the God of Israel, says: I am about to fulfill my words against this city through disaster, not prosperity. At that time they will be fulfilled before your eyes. 17But I will rescue you on that day, declares the LORD; you will not be handed over to those you fear. 18I will save you; you will not fall by the sword but will escape with your life, because you trust in me, declares the LORD.' "

Jeremiah Freed

40 The word came to Jeremiah from the LORD after Nebuzaradan commander of the imperial guard had released him at Ramah. He had found Jeremiah bound in chains among all the captives from Jerusalem and Judah who were being carried into exile to Babylon. 2When the commander of the guard found Jeremiah, he said to him, "The LORD your God decreed this disaster for this place. 3And now the LORD has brought it about; he has done just as he said he would. All this happened because you people sinned against the LORD and did not obey him. 4But today I am freeing you from the chains on your wrists. Come with me to Babylon, if you like, and I will look after you; but if you do not want to, then don't come. Look, the whole country lies before you; go wherever you please." 5However, before Jeremiah turned to go,[b] Nebuzaradan added, "Go back to Gedaliah son of Ahikam, the son of Shaphan, whom the king of Babylon has appointed over the towns of Judah, and live with him among the people, or go anywhere else you please."

Then the commander gave him provisions and a present and let him go. 6So Jeremiah went to Gedaliah son of Ahikam at Mizpah and stayed with him among the people who were left behind in the land.

Gedaliah Assassinated

7When all the army officers and their men who were still in the open country heard that the king of Babylon had appointed Gedaliah son of Ahikam as governor over the land and had put him in charge of the men, women and children who were the poorest in the land and who had not been carried into exile to Babylon, 8they came to Gedaliah at Mizpah—Ishmael son of Nethaniah, Johanan and Jonathan the sons of Kareah, Seraiah son of Tanhumeth, the sons of Ephai the Netophathite, and Jaazaniah[c] the son of the Maacathite, and their men. 9Gedaliah son of Ahikam, the son of Shaphan, took an oath to reassure them and their men. "Do not be afraid to serve the Babylonians,[d]" he said. "Settle down in the land and serve the king of Babylon, and it will go well with you. 10I myself will stay at Mizpah to represent you before the Babylonians who come to us, but you are to harvest the wine, summer fruit and oil, and put them in your storage jars, and live in the towns you have taken over."

11When all the Jews in Moab, Ammon, Edom and all the other countries heard that the king of Babylon had left a remnant in Judah and had appointed Gedaliah son of Ahikam, the son of Shaphan, as governor over them, 12they all came back to the land of

[a]8 Or *Chaldeans* [b]5 Or *Jeremiah answered* [c]8 Hebrew *Jezaniah,* a variant of *Jaazaniah* [d]9 Or *Chaldeans;* also in verse 10

Judah, to Gedaliah at Mizpah, from all the countries where they had been scattered. And they harvested an abundance of wine and summer fruit.

13Johanan son of Kareah and all the army officers still in the open country came to Gedaliah at Mizpah 14and said to him, "Don't you know that Baalis king of the Ammonites has sent Ishmael son of Nethaniah to take your life?" But Gedaliah son of Ahikam did not believe them.

15Then Johanan son of Kareah said privately to Gedaliah in Mizpah, "Let me go and kill Ishmael son of Nethaniah, and no one will know it. Why should he take your life and cause all the Jews who are gathered around you to be scattered and the remnant of Judah to perish?"

16But Gedaliah son of Ahikam said to Johanan son of Kareah, "Don't do such a thing! What you are saying about Ishmael is not true."

41 In the seventh month Ishmael son of Nethaniah, the son of Elishama, who was of royal blood and had been one of the king's officers, came with ten men to Gedaliah son of Ahikam at Mizpah. While they were eating together there, 2Ishmael son of Nethaniah and the ten men who were with him got up and struck down Gedaliah son of Ahikam, the son of Shaphan, with the sword, killing the one whom the king of Babylon had appointed as governor over the land. 3Ishmael also killed all the Jews who were with Gedaliah at Mizpah, as well as the Babylonian[a] soldiers who were there.

4The day after Gedaliah's assassination, before anyone knew about it, 5eighty men who had shaved off their beards, torn their clothes and cut themselves came from Shechem, Shiloh and Samaria, bringing grain offerings and incense with them to the house of the LORD. 6Ishmael son of Nethaniah went out from Mizpah to meet them, weeping as he went. When he met them, he said, "Come to Gedaliah son of Ahikam." 7When they went into the city, Ishmael son of Nethaniah and the men who were with him slaughtered them and threw them into a cistern. 8But ten of them said to Ishmael, "Don't kill us! We have wheat and barley, oil and honey, hidden in a field." So he let them alone and did not kill them with the others. 9Now the cistern where he threw all the bodies of the men he had killed along with Gedaliah was the one King Asa had made as part of his defense against Baasha king of Israel. Ishmael son of Nethaniah filled it with the dead.

10Ishmael made captives of all the rest of the people who were in Mizpah—the king's daughters along with all the others who were left there, over whom Nebuzaradan commander of the imperial guard had appointed Gedaliah son of Ahikam. Ishmael son of Nethaniah took them captive and set out to cross over to the Ammonites.

11When Johanan son of Kareah and all the army officers who were with him heard about all the crimes Ishmael son of Nethaniah had committed, 12they took all their men and went to fight Ishmael son of Nethaniah. They caught up with him near the great pool in Gibeon. 13When all the people Ishmael had with him saw Johanan son of Kareah and the army officers who were with him, they were glad. 14All the people Ishmael had taken captive at Mizpah turned and went over to Johanan son of Kareah. 15But Ishmael son of Nethaniah and eight of his men escaped from Johanan and fled to the Ammonites.

Flight to Egypt

16Then Johanan son of Kareah and all the army officers who were with him led away all the survivors from Mizpah whom he had recovered from Ishmael son of Nethaniah after he had assassinated Gedaliah son of Ahikam: the soldiers, women, children and court officials he had brought from Gibeon. 17And they went on, stopping at Geruth Kimham near Bethlehem on their way to Egypt 18to escape the Babylonians.[b] They were afraid of them because Ishmael son of Nethaniah had killed Gedaliah son of Ahikam, whom the king of Babylon had appointed as governor over the land.

42 Then all the army officers, including Johanan son of Kareah and Jezaniah[c] son of Hoshaiah, and all the people from the least to the greatest approached 2Jeremiah the prophet and said to him, "Please hear our petition and pray to the LORD your God for this entire remnant. For as you now see, though we were once many, now only a few are left. 3Pray that the LORD your God will tell us where we should go and what we should do."

4"I have heard you," replied Jeremiah the prophet. "I will certainly pray to the LORD your God as you have requested; I will tell you

[a]3 Or *Chaldean* [b]18 Or *Chaldeans* [c]1 Hebrew; Septuagint (see also 43:2) *Azariah*

everything the LORD says and will keep nothing back from you."
5Then they said to Jeremiah, "May the
LORD be a true and faithful witness against us
if we do not act in accordance with everything the LORD your God sends you to tell us.
6Whether it is favorable or unfavorable, we
will obey the LORD our God, to whom we are
sending you, so that it will go well with us, for
we will obey the LORD our God."
7Ten days later the word of the LORD came
to Jeremiah. 8So he called together Johanan
son of Kareah and all the army officers who
were with him and all the people from the
least to the greatest. 9He said to them, "This
is what the LORD, the God of Israel, to whom
you sent me to present your petition, says:
10'If you stay in this land, I will build you up
and not tear you down; I will plant you and
not uproot you, for I am grieved over the
disaster I have inflicted on you. 11Do not be
afraid of the king of Babylon, whom you now
fear. Do not be afraid of him, declares the
LORD, for I am with you and will save you and
deliver you from his hands. 12I will show you
compassion so that he will have compassion
on you and restore you to your land.'
13"However, if you say, 'We will not stay in
this land,' and so disobey the LORD your God,
14and if you say, 'No, we will go and live in
Egypt, where we will not see war or hear the
trumpet or be hungry for bread,' 15then hear
the word of the LORD, O remnant of Judah.
This is what the LORD Almighty, the God of
Israel, says: 'If you are determined to go to
Egypt and you do go to settle there, 16then
the sword you fear will overtake you there,
and the famine you dread will follow you into
Egypt, and there you will die. 17Indeed, all
who are determined to go to Egypt to settle
there will die by the sword, famine and
plague; not one of them will survive or escape the disaster I will bring on them.' 18This
is what the LORD Almighty, the God of Israel,
says: 'As my anger and wrath have been
poured out on those who lived in Jerusalem,
so will my wrath be poured out on you when
you go to Egypt. You will be an object of
cursing and horror, of condemnation and reproach; you will never see this place again.'
19"O remnant of Judah, the LORD has told
you, 'Do not go to Egypt.' Be sure of this: I
warn you today 20that you made a fatal mistake[a] when you sent me to the LORD your
God and said, 'Pray to the LORD our God for
us; tell us everything he says and we will do
it.' 21I have told you today, but you still have
not obeyed the LORD your God in all he sent
me to tell you. 22So now, be sure of this: You
will die by the sword, famine and plague in
the place where you want to go to settle."

43 When Jeremiah finished telling the
people all the words of the LORD their
God—everything the LORD had sent him to
tell them— 2Azariah son of Hoshaiah and
Johanan son of Kareah and all the arrogant
men said to Jeremiah, "You are lying! The
LORD our God has not sent you to say, 'You
must not go to Egypt to settle there.' 3But
Baruch son of Neriah is inciting you against
us to hand us over to the Babylonians,[b] so
they may kill us or carry us into exile to Babylon."
4So Johanan son of Kareah and all the
army officers and all the people disobeyed
the LORD's command to stay in the land of
Judah. 5Instead, Johanan son of Kareah and
all the army officers led away all the remnant
of Judah who had come back to live in the
land of Judah from all the nations where they
had been scattered. 6They also led away all
the men, women and children and the king's
daughters whom Nebuzaradan commander
of the imperial guard had left with Gedaliah
son of Ahikam, the son of Shaphan, and
Jeremiah the prophet and Baruch son of Neriah. 7So they entered Egypt in disobedience
to the LORD and went as far as Tahpanhes.
8In Tahpanhes the word of the LORD came
to Jeremiah: 9"While the Jews are watching,
take some large stones with you and bury
them in clay in the brick pavement at the
entrance to Pharaoh's palace in Tahpanhes.
10Then say to them, 'This is what the LORD
Almighty, the God of Israel, says: I will send
for my servant Nebuchadnezzar king of Babylon, and I will set his throne over these
stones I have buried here; he will spread his
royal canopy above them. 11He will come
and attack Egypt, bringing death to those
destined for death, captivity to those destined for captivity, and the sword to those
destined for the sword. 12He[c] will set fire to
the temples of the gods of Egypt; he will burn
their temples and take their gods captive. As
a shepherd wraps his garment around him,
so will he wrap Egypt around himself and
depart from there unscathed. 13There in the
temple of the sun[d] in Egypt he will demolish

[a]20 Or *you erred in your hearts* [b]3 Or *Chaldeans* [c]12 Or *I* [d]13 Or *in Heliopolis*

the sacred pillars and will burn down the
temples of the gods of Egypt.' "

Disaster Because of Idolatry

44 This word came to Jeremiah concerning all the Jews living in Lower
Egypt—in Migdol, Tahpanhes and Memphis[a]—and in Upper Egypt[b]: 2"This is what
the LORD Almighty, the God of Israel, says:
You saw the great disaster I brought on
Jerusalem and on all the towns of Judah.
Today they lie deserted and in ruins 3be-
cause of the evil they have done. They provoked me to anger by burning incense and
by worshiping other gods that neither they
nor you nor your fathers ever knew. 4Again
and again I sent my servants the prophets,
who said, 'Do not do this detestable thing
that I hate!' 5But they did not listen or pay
attention; they did not turn from their wickedness or stop burning incense to other gods.
6Therefore, my fierce anger was poured out;
it raged against the towns of Judah and the
streets of Jerusalem and made them the
desolate ruins they are today.

7"Now this is what the LORD God Almighty,
the God of Israel, says: Why bring such great
disaster on yourselves by cutting off from
Judah the men and women, the children and
infants, and so leave yourselves without a
remnant? 8Why provoke me to anger with
what your hands have made, burning incense to other gods in Egypt, where you
have come to live? You will destroy yourselves and make yourselves an object of
cursing and reproach among all the nations
on earth. 9Have you forgotten the wickedness committed by your fathers and by the
kings and queens of Judah and the wickedness committed by you and your wives in the
land of Judah and the streets of Jerusalem?
10To this day they have not humbled themselves or shown reverence, nor have they
followed my law and the decrees I set before
you and your fathers.

11"Therefore, this is what the LORD Almighty, the God of Israel, says: I am determined to bring disaster on you and to destroy
all Judah. 12I will take away the remnant of
Judah who were determined to go to Egypt
to settle there. They will all perish in Egypt;
they will fall by the sword or die from famine.
From the least to the greatest, they will die by
sword or famine. They will become an object
of cursing and horror, of condemnation and
reproach. 13I will punish those who live in
Egypt with the sword, famine and plague, as
I punished Jerusalem. 14None of the remnant of Judah who have gone to live in Egypt
will escape or survive to return to the land of
Judah, to which they long to return and live;
none will return except a few fugitives."

15Then all the men who knew that their
wives were burning incense to other gods,
along with all the women who were present—a large assembly—and all the people
living in Lower and Upper Egypt,[c] said to
Jeremiah, 16"We will not listen to the message you have spoken to us in the name of
the LORD! 17We will certainly do everything
we said we would: We will burn incense to
the Queen of Heaven and will pour out drink
offerings to her just as we and our fathers,
our kings and our officials did in the towns of
Judah and in the streets of Jerusalem. At
that time we had plenty of food and were well
off and suffered no harm. 18But ever since we
stopped burning incense to the Queen of
Heaven and pouring out drink offerings to
her, we have had nothing and have been
perishing by sword and famine."

19The women added, "When we burned
incense to the Queen of Heaven and poured
out drink offerings to her, did not our husbands know that we were making cakes like
her image and pouring out drink offerings to
her?"

20Then Jeremiah said to all the people,
both men and women, who were answering
him, 21"Did not the LORD remember and think
about the incense burned in the towns of
Judah and the streets of Jerusalem by you
and your fathers, your kings and your officials and the people of the land? 22When the
LORD could no longer endure your wicked
actions and the detestable things you did,
your land became an object of cursing and a
desolate waste without inhabitants, as it is
today. 23Because you have burned incense
and have sinned against the LORD and have
not obeyed him or followed his law or his
decrees or his stipulations, this disaster has
come upon you, as you now see."

24Then Jeremiah said to all the people,
including the women, "Hear the word of the
LORD, all you people of Judah in Egypt. 25This
is what the LORD Almighty, the God of Israel,
says: You and your wives have shown by
your actions what you promised when you
said, 'We will certainly carry out the vows we

[a] *1* Hebrew *Noph* [b] *1* Hebrew *in Pathros* [c] *15* Hebrew *in Egypt and Pathros*

made to burn incense and pour out drink
offerings to the Queen of Heaven.'
"Go ahead then, do what you promised!
Keep your vows! 26But hear the word of the
LORD, all Jews living in Egypt: 'I swear by my
great name,' says the LORD, 'that no one from
Judah living anywhere in Egypt will ever
again invoke my name or swear, "As surely
as the Sovereign LORD lives." 27For I am
watching over them for harm, not for good;
the Jews in Egypt will perish by sword and
famine until they are all destroyed. 28Those
who escape the sword and return to the land
of Judah from Egypt will be very few. Then
the whole remnant of Judah who came to live
in Egypt will know whose word will stand—
mine or theirs.
29" 'This will be the sign to you that I will
punish you in this place,' declares the LORD,
'so that you will know that my threats of harm
against you will surely stand.' 30This is what
the LORD says: 'I am going to hand Pharaoh
Hophra king of Egypt over to his enemies
who seek his life, just as I handed Zedekiah
king of Judah over to Nebuchadnezzar king
of Babylon, the enemy who was seeking his
life.' "

A Message to Baruch

45 This is what Jeremiah the prophet
told Baruch son of Neriah in the
fourth year of Jehoiakim son of Josiah king of
Judah, after Baruch had written on a scroll
the words Jeremiah was then dictating:
2"This is what the LORD, the God of Israel,
says to you, Baruch: 3You said, 'Woe to me!
The LORD has added sorrow to my pain; I am
worn out with groaning and find no rest.' "
4⌊The LORD said,⌋ "Say this to him: 'This is
what the LORD says: I will overthrow what I
have built and uproot what I have planted,
throughout the land. 5Should you then seek
great things for yourself? Seek them not. For
I will bring disaster on all people, declares
the LORD, but wherever you go I will let you
escape with your life.' "

A Message About Egypt

46 This is the word of the LORD that came
to Jeremiah the prophet concerning
the nations:

2Concerning Egypt:

This is the message against the army of
Pharaoh Neco king of Egypt, which was defeated at Carchemish on the Euphrates River by Nebuchadnezzar king of Babylon in the
fourth year of Jehoiakim son of Josiah king of
Judah:

3"Prepare your shields, both large and
small,
and march out for battle!
4Harness the horses,
mount the steeds!
Take your positions
with helmets on!
Polish your spears,
put on your armor!
5What do I see?
They are terrified,
they are retreating,
their warriors are defeated.
They flee in haste
without looking back,
and there is terror on every side,"
declares the LORD.
6"The swift cannot flee
nor the strong escape.
In the north by the River Euphrates
they stumble and fall.

7"Who is this that rises like the Nile,
like rivers of surging waters?
8Egypt rises like the Nile,
like rivers of surging waters.
She says, 'I will rise and cover the earth;
I will destroy cities and their people.'
9Charge, O horses!
Drive furiously, O charioteers!
March on, O warriors—
men of Cush[a] and Put who carry
shields,
men of Lydia who draw the bow.
10But that day belongs to the Lord, the LORD
Almighty—
a day of vengeance, for vengeance on
his foes.
The sword will devour till it is satisfied,
till it has quenched its thirst with blood.
For the Lord, the LORD Almighty, will offer
sacrifice
in the land of the north by the River
Euphrates.

11"Go up to Gilead and get balm,
O Virgin Daughter of Egypt.
But you multiply remedies in vain;
there is no healing for you.
12The nations will hear of your shame;
your cries will fill the earth.

[a]9 That is, the upper Nile region

One warrior will stumble over another;
both will fall down together."

[13]This is the message the LORD spoke to
Jeremiah the prophet about the coming of
Nebuchadnezzar king of Babylon to attack
Egypt:

[14]"Announce this in Egypt, and proclaim it
in Migdol;
proclaim it also in Memphis[a] and
Tahpanhes:
'Take your positions and get ready,
for the sword devours those around
you.'
[15]Why will your warriors be laid low?
They cannot stand, for the LORD will
push them down.
[16]They will stumble repeatedly;
they will fall over each other.
They will say, 'Get up, let us go back
to our own people and our native lands,
away from the sword of the oppressor.'
[17]There they will exclaim,
'Pharaoh king of Egypt is only a loud
noise;
he has missed his opportunity.'

[18]"As surely as I live," declares the King,
whose name is the LORD Almighty,
"one will come who is like Tabor among
the mountains,
like Carmel by the sea.
[19]Pack your belongings for exile,
you who live in Egypt,
for Memphis will be laid waste
and lie in ruins without inhabitant.

[20]"Egypt is a beautiful heifer,
but a gadfly is coming
against her from the north.
[21]The mercenaries in her ranks
are like fattened calves.
They too will turn and flee together,
they will not stand their ground,
for the day of disaster is coming upon
them,
the time for them to be punished.
[22]Egypt will hiss like a fleeing serpent
as the enemy advances in force;
they will come against her with axes,
like men who cut down trees.
[23]They will chop down her forest,"
declares the LORD,
"dense though it be.
They are more numerous than locusts,
they cannot be counted.
[24]The Daughter of Egypt will be put to
shame,
handed over to the people of the
north."

[25]The LORD Almighty, the God of Israel,
says: "I am about to bring punishment on
Amon god of Thebes,[b] on Pharaoh, on
Egypt and her gods and her kings, and on
those who rely on Pharaoh. [26]I will hand
them over to those who seek their lives, to
Nebuchadnezzar king of Babylon and his officers. Later, however, Egypt will be inhabited as in times past," declares the LORD.

[27]"Do not fear, O Jacob my servant;
do not be dismayed, O Israel.
I will surely save you out of a distant
place,
your descendants from the land of their
exile.
Jacob will again have peace and security,
and no one will make him afraid.
[28]Do not fear, O Jacob my servant,
for I am with you," declares the LORD.
"Though I completely destroy all the
nations
among which I scatter you,
I will not completely destroy you.
I will discipline you but only with justice;
I will not let you go entirely
unpunished."

A Message About the Philistines

47 This is the word of the LORD that came
to Jeremiah the prophet concerning
the Philistines before Pharaoh attacked
Gaza:

[2]This is what the LORD says:

"See how the waters are rising in the
north;
they will become an overflowing torrent.
They will overflow the land and everything
in it,
the towns and those who live in them.
The people will cry out;
all who dwell in the land will wail
[3]at the sound of the hoofs of galloping
steeds,
at the noise of enemy chariots
and the rumble of their wheels.
Fathers will not turn to help their children;
their hands will hang limp.
[4]For the day has come

[a]14 Hebrew *Noph*; also in verse 19 [b]25 Hebrew *No*

to destroy all the Philistines
and to cut off all survivors
who could help Tyre and Sidon.
The LORD is about to destroy the Philistines,
the remnant from the coasts of Caphtor.[a]
5Gaza will shave her head in mourning;
Ashkelon will be silenced.
O remnant on the plain,
how long will you cut yourselves?

6" 'Ah, sword of the LORD,' you cry,
'how long till you rest?
Return to your scabbard;
cease and be still.'
7But how can it rest
when the LORD has commanded it,
when he has ordered it
to attack Ashkelon and the coast?"

A Message About Moab

48 Concerning Moab:

This is what the LORD Almighty, the God of Israel, says:

"Woe to Nebo, for it will be ruined.
Kiriathaim will be disgraced and captured;
the stronghold[b] will be disgraced and shattered.
2Moab will be praised no more;
in Heshbon[c] men will plot her downfall:
'Come, let us put an end to that nation.'
You too, O Madmen,[d] will be silenced;
the sword will pursue you.
3Listen to the cries from Horonaim,
cries of great havoc and destruction.
4Moab will be broken;
her little ones will cry out.[e]
5They go up the way to Luhith,
weeping bitterly as they go;
on the road down to Horonaim
anguished cries over the destruction are heard.
6Flee! Run for your lives;
become like a bush[f] in the desert.
7Since you trust in your deeds and riches,
you too will be taken captive,
and Chemosh will go into exile,
together with his priests and officials.
8The destroyer will come against every town,
and not a town will escape.
The valley will be ruined
and the plateau destroyed,
because the LORD has spoken.
9Put salt on Moab,
for she will be laid waste[g];
her towns will become desolate,
with no one to live in them.

10"A curse on him who is lax in doing the LORD's work!
A curse on him who keeps his sword from bloodshed!

11"Moab has been at rest from youth,
like wine left on its dregs,
not poured from one jar to another—
she has not gone into exile.
So she tastes as she did,
and her aroma is unchanged.
12But days are coming,"
declares the LORD,
"when I will send men who pour from jars,
and they will pour her out;
they will empty her jars
and smash her jugs.
13Then Moab will be ashamed of Chemosh,
as the house of Israel was ashamed
when they trusted in Bethel.

14"How can you say, 'We are warriors,
men valiant in battle'?
15Moab will be destroyed and her towns invaded;
her finest young men will go down in the slaughter,"
declares the King, whose name is the LORD Almighty.
16"The fall of Moab is at hand;
her calamity will come quickly.
17Mourn for her, all who live around her,
all who know her fame;
say, 'How broken is the mighty scepter,
how broken the glorious staff!'

18"Come down from your glory
and sit on the parched ground,
O inhabitants of the Daughter of Dibon,
for he who destroys Moab
will come up against you
and ruin your fortified cities.
19Stand by the road and watch,
you who live in Aroer.
Ask the man fleeing and the woman escaping,
ask them, 'What has happened?'

[a]4 That is, Crete [b]1 Or / *Misgab* [c]2 The Hebrew for *Heshbon* sounds like the Hebrew for *plot.*
[d]2 The name of the Moabite town Madmen sounds like the Hebrew for *be silenced.* [e]4 Hebrew; Septuagint / *proclaim it to Zoar* [f]6 Or *like Aroer* [g]9 Or *Give wings to Moab, / for she will fly away*

20Moab is disgraced, for she is shattered.
Wail and cry out!
Announce by the Arnon
that Moab is destroyed.
21Judgment has come to the plateau—
to Holon, Jahzah and Mephaath,
22 to Dibon, Nebo and Beth Diblathaim,
23 to Kiriathaim, Beth Gamul and Beth Meon,
24 to Kerioth and Bozrah—
to all the towns of Moab, far and near.
25Moab's horn[a] is cut off;
her arm is broken,"
declares the LORD.

26"Make her drunk,
for she has defied the LORD.
Let Moab wallow in her vomit;
let her be an object of ridicule.
27Was not Israel the object of your ridicule?
Was she caught among thieves,
that you shake your head in scorn
whenever you speak of her?
28Abandon your towns and dwell among the rocks,
you who live in Moab.
Be like a dove that makes its nest
at the mouth of a cave.

29"We have heard of Moab's pride—
her overweening pride and conceit,
her pride and arrogance
and the haughtiness of her heart.
30I know her insolence but it is futile,"
declares the LORD,
"and her boasts accomplish nothing.
31Therefore I wail over Moab,
for all Moab I cry out,
I moan for the men of Kir Hareseth.
32I weep for you, as Jazer weeps,
O vines of Sibmah.
Your branches spread as far as the sea;
they reached as far as the sea of Jazer.
The destroyer has fallen
on your ripened fruit and grapes.
33Joy and gladness are gone
from the orchards and fields of Moab.
I have stopped the flow of wine from the presses;
no one treads them with shouts of joy.
Although there are shouts,
they are not shouts of joy.

34"The sound of their cry rises
from Heshbon to Elealeh and Jahaz,
from Zoar as far as Horonaim and Eglath Shelishiyah,
for even the waters of Nimrim are dried up.
35In Moab I will put an end
to those who make offerings on the high places
and burn incense to their gods,"
declares the LORD.
36"So my heart laments for Moab like a flute;
it laments like a flute for the men of Kir Hareseth.
The wealth they acquired is gone.
37Every head is shaved
and every beard cut off;
every hand is slashed
and every waist is covered with sackcloth.
38On all the roofs in Moab
and in the public squares
there is nothing but mourning,
for I have broken Moab
like a jar that no one wants,"
declares the LORD.
39"How shattered she is! How they wail!
How Moab turns her back in shame!
Moab has become an object of ridicule,
an object of horror to all those around her."

40This is what the LORD says:

"Look! An eagle is swooping down,
spreading its wings over Moab.
41Kerioth[b] will be captured
and the strongholds taken.
In that day the hearts of Moab's warriors
will be like the heart of a woman in labor.
42Moab will be destroyed as a nation
because she defied the LORD.
43Terror and pit and snare await you,
O people of Moab,"
declares the LORD.
44"Whoever flees from the terror
will fall into a pit,
whoever climbs out of the pit
will be caught in a snare;
for I will bring upon Moab
the year of her punishment,"
declares the LORD.

45"In the shadow of Heshbon
the fugitives stand helpless,
for a fire has gone out from Heshbon,
a blaze from the midst of Sihon;
it burns the foreheads of Moab,
the skulls of the noisy boasters.

[a]25 *Horn* here symbolizes strength. [b]41 Or *The cities*

[46]Woe to you, O Moab!
The people of Chemosh are destroyed;
your sons are taken into exile
and your daughters into captivity.

[47]"Yet I will restore the fortunes of Moab
in days to come,"
declares the LORD.

Here ends the judgment on Moab.

A Message About Ammon

49 Concerning the Ammonites:

This is what the LORD says:

"Has Israel no sons?
Has she no heirs?
Why then has Molech[a] taken possession
of Gad?
Why do his people live in its towns?
[2]But the days are coming,"
declares the LORD,
"when I will sound the battle cry
against Rabbah of the Ammonites;
it will become a mound of ruins,
and its surrounding villages will be set
on fire.
Then Israel will drive out
those who drove her out,"
says the LORD.
[3]"Wail, O Heshbon, for Ai is destroyed!
Cry out, O inhabitants of Rabbah!
Put on sackcloth and mourn;
rush here and there inside the walls,
for Molech will go into exile,
together with his priests and officials.
[4]Why do you boast of your valleys,
boast of your valleys so fruitful?
O unfaithful daughter,
you trust in your riches and say,
'Who will attack me?'
[5]I will bring terror on you
from all those around you,"
declares the Lord,
the LORD Almighty.
"Every one of you will be driven away,
and no one will gather the fugitives.

[6]"Yet afterward, I will restore the fortunes
of the Ammonites,"
declares the LORD.

A Message About Edom

[7]Concerning Edom:

This is what the LORD Almighty says:

"Is there no longer wisdom in Teman?
Has counsel perished from the
prudent?
Has their wisdom decayed?
[8]Turn and flee, hide in deep caves,
you who live in Dedan,
for I will bring disaster on Esau
at the time I punish him.
[9]If grape pickers came to you,
would they not leave a few grapes?
If thieves came during the night,
would they not steal only as much as
they wanted?
[10]But I will strip Esau bare;
I will uncover his hiding places,
so that he cannot conceal himself.
His children, relatives and neighbors will
perish,
and he will be no more.
[11]Leave your orphans; I will protect their
lives.
Your widows too can trust in me."

[12]This is what the LORD says: "If those who
do not deserve to drink the cup must drink it,
why should you go unpunished? You will not
go unpunished, but must drink it. [13]I swear by
myself," declares the LORD, "that Bozrah will
become a ruin and an object of horror, of
reproach and of cursing; and all its towns will
be in ruins forever."

[14]I have heard a message from the LORD:
An envoy was sent to the nations to
say,
"Assemble yourselves to attack it!
Rise up for battle!"

[15]"Now I will make you small among the
nations,
despised among men.
[16]The terror you inspire
and the pride of your heart have
deceived you,
you who live in the clefts of the rocks,
who occupy the heights of the hill.
Though you build your nest as high as the
eagle's,
from there I will bring you down,"
declares the LORD.
[17]"Edom will become an object of horror;
all who pass by will be appalled and will
scoff
because of all its wounds.
[18]As Sodom and Gomorrah were
overthrown,
along with their neighboring towns,"
says the LORD,

[a] *1* Or *their king;* Hebrew *malcam;* also in verse 3

"so no one will live there;
no man will dwell in it.

19"Like a lion coming up from Jordan's thickets
to a rich pastureland,
I will chase Edom from its land in an instant.
Who is the chosen one I will appoint for this?
Who is like me and who can challenge me?
And what shepherd can stand against me?"
20Therefore, hear what the LORD has planned against Edom,
what he has purposed against those who live in Teman:
The young of the flock will be dragged away;
he will completely destroy their pasture because of them.
21At the sound of their fall the earth will tremble;
their cry will resound to the Red Sea.[a]
22Look! An eagle will soar and swoop down,
spreading its wings over Bozrah.
In that day the hearts of Edom's warriors
will be like the heart of a woman in labor.

A Message About Damascus

23Concerning Damascus:

"Hamath and Arpad are dismayed,
for they have heard bad news.
They are disheartened,
troubled like[b] the restless sea.
24Damascus has become feeble,
she has turned to flee
and panic has gripped her;
anguish and pain have seized her,
pain like that of a woman in labor.
25Why has the city of renown not been abandoned,
the town in which I delight?
26Surely, her young men will fall in the streets;
all her soldiers will be silenced in that day,"
declares the LORD Almighty.
27"I will set fire to the walls of Damascus;
it will consume the fortresses of Ben-Hadad."

A Message About Kedar and Hazor

28Concerning Kedar and the kingdoms of Hazor, which Nebuchadnezzar king of Babylon attacked:

This is what the LORD says:

"Arise, and attack Kedar
and destroy the people of the East.
29Their tents and their flocks will be taken;
their shelters will be carried off
with all their goods and camels.
Men will shout to them,
'Terror on every side!'

30"Flee quickly away!
Stay in deep caves, you who live in Hazor,"
declares the LORD.
"Nebuchadnezzar king of Babylon has plotted against you;
he has devised a plan against you.

31"Arise and attack a nation at ease,
which lives in confidence,"
declares the LORD,
"a nation that has neither gates nor bars;
its people live alone.
32Their camels will become plunder,
and their large herds will be booty.
I will scatter to the winds those who are in distant places[c]
and will bring disaster on them from every side,"
declares the LORD.
33"Hazor will become a haunt of jackals,
a desolate place forever.
No one will live there;
no man will dwell in it."

A Message About Elam

34This is the word of the LORD that came to Jeremiah the prophet concerning Elam, early in the reign of Zedekiah king of Judah:

35This is what the LORD Almighty says:

"See, I will break the bow of Elam,
the mainstay of their might.
36I will bring against Elam the four winds
from the four quarters of the heavens;
I will scatter them to the four winds,
and there will not be a nation
where Elam's exiles do not go.
37I will shatter Elam before their foes,
before those who seek their lives;

[a]21 Hebrew *Yam Suph;* that is, Sea of Reeds [b]23 Hebrew *on* or *by* [c]32 Or *who clip the hair by their foreheads*

I will bring disaster upon them,
even my fierce anger,"
declares the LORD.
"I will pursue them with the sword
until I have made an end of them.
38 I will set my throne in Elam
and destroy her king and officials,"
declares the LORD.

39 "Yet I will restore the fortunes of Elam
in days to come,"
declares the LORD.

A Message About Babylon

50 This is the word the LORD spoke
through Jeremiah the prophet concerning Babylon and the land of the Babylonians[a]:

2 "Announce and proclaim among the
nations,
lift up a banner and proclaim it;
keep nothing back, but say,
'Babylon will be captured;
Bel will be put to shame,
Marduk filled with terror.
Her images will be put to shame
and her idols filled with terror.'
3 A nation from the north will attack her
and lay waste her land.
No one will live in it;
both men and animals will flee away.

4 "In those days, at that time,"
declares the LORD,
"the people of Israel and the people of
Judah together
will go in tears to seek the LORD their
God.
5 They will ask the way to Zion
and turn their faces toward it.
They will come and bind themselves to
the LORD
in an everlasting covenant
that will not be forgotten.

6 "My people have been lost sheep;
their shepherds have led them astray
and caused them to roam on the
mountains.
They wandered over mountain and hill
and forgot their own resting place.
7 Whoever found them devoured them;
their enemies said, 'We are not guilty,
for they sinned against the LORD, their true
pasture,
the LORD, the hope of their fathers.'

8 "Flee out of Babylon;
leave the land of the Babylonians,
and be like the goats that lead the
flock.
9 For I will stir up and bring against
Babylon
an alliance of great nations from the
land of the north.
They will take up their positions against
her,
and from the north she will be captured.
Their arrows will be like skilled warriors
who do not return empty-handed.
10 So Babylonia[b] will be plundered;
all who plunder her will have their fill,"
declares the LORD.

11 "Because you rejoice and are glad,
you who pillage my inheritance,
because you frolic like a heifer threshing
grain
and neigh like stallions,
12 your mother will be greatly ashamed;
she who gave you birth will be
disgraced.
She will be the least of the nations—
a wilderness, a dry land, a desert.
13 Because of the LORD's anger she will not
be inhabited
but will be completely desolate.
All who pass Babylon will be horrified and
scoff
because of all her wounds.

14 "Take up your positions around Babylon,
all you who draw the bow.
Shoot at her! Spare no arrows,
for she has sinned against the LORD.
15 Shout against her on every side!
She surrenders, her towers fall,
her walls are torn down.
Since this is the vengeance of the LORD,
take vengeance on her;
do to her as she has done to others.
16 Cut off from Babylon the sower,
and the reaper with his sickle at
harvest.
Because of the sword of the oppressor
let everyone return to his own people,
let everyone flee to his own land.

17 "Israel is a scattered flock
that lions have chased away.
The first to devour him
was the king of Assyria;
the last to crush his bones

[a] *1* Or *Chaldeans*; also in verses 8, 25, 35 and 45 [b] *10* Or *Chaldea*

was Nebuchadnezzar king of Babylon."

18Therefore this is what the LORD Almighty,
the God of Israel, says:

"I will punish the king of Babylon and his land
as I punished the king of Assyria.
19But I will bring Israel back to his own pasture
and he will graze on Carmel and Bashan;
his appetite will be satisfied
on the hills of Ephraim and Gilead.
20In those days, at that time,"
declares the LORD,
"search will be made for Israel's guilt,
but there will be none,
and for the sins of Judah,
but none will be found,
for I will forgive the remnant I spare.

21"Attack the land of Merathaim
and those who live in Pekod.
Pursue, kill and completely destroy[a] them,"
declares the LORD.
"Do everything I have commanded you.
22The noise of battle is in the land,
the noise of great destruction!
23How broken and shattered
is the hammer of the whole earth!
How desolate is Babylon
among the nations!
24I set a trap for you, O Babylon,
and you were caught before you knew it;
you were found and captured
because you opposed the LORD.
25The LORD has opened his arsenal
and brought out the weapons of his wrath,
for the Sovereign LORD Almighty has work to do
in the land of the Babylonians.
26Come against her from afar.
Break open her granaries;
pile her up like heaps of grain.
Completely destroy her
and leave her no remnant.
27Kill all her young bulls;
let them go down to the slaughter!
Woe to them! For their day has come,
the time for them to be punished.
28Listen to the fugitives and refugees from Babylon
declaring in Zion
how the LORD our God has taken vengeance,
vengeance for his temple.

29"Summon archers against Babylon,
all those who draw the bow.
Encamp all around her;
let no one escape.
Repay her for her deeds;
do to her as she has done.
For she has defied the LORD,
the Holy One of Israel.
30Therefore, her young men will fall in the streets;
all her soldiers will be silenced in that day,"
declares the LORD.
31"See, I am against you, O arrogant one,"
declares the Lord, the LORD Almighty,
"for your day has come,
the time for you to be punished.
32The arrogant one will stumble and fall
and no one will help her up;
I will kindle a fire in her towns
that will consume all who are around her."

33This is what the LORD Almighty says:

"The people of Israel are oppressed,
and the people of Judah as well.
All their captors hold them fast,
refusing to let them go.
34Yet their Redeemer is strong;
the LORD Almighty is his name.
He will vigorously defend their cause
so that he may bring rest to their land,
but unrest to those who live in Babylon.

35"A sword against the Babylonians!"
declares the LORD—
"against those who live in Babylon
and against her officials and wise men!
36A sword against her false prophets!
They will become fools.
A sword against her warriors!
They will be filled with terror.
37A sword against her horses and chariots
and all the foreigners in her ranks!
They will become women.
A sword against her treasures!
They will be plundered.
38A drought on[b] her waters!
They will dry up.

[a]21 The Hebrew term refers to the irrevocable giving over of things or persons to the LORD, often by totally destroying them; also in verse 26. [b]38 Or *A sword against*

For it is a land of idols,
idols that will go mad with terror.

39 "So desert creatures and hyenas will live there,
and there the owl will dwell.
It will never again be inhabited
or lived in from generation to generation.
40 As God overthrew Sodom and Gomorrah
along with their neighboring towns,"
declares the LORD,
"so no one will live there;
no man will dwell in it.

41 "Look! An army is coming from the north;
a great nation and many kings
are being stirred up from the ends of the earth.
42 They are armed with bows and spears;
they are cruel and without mercy.
They sound like the roaring sea
as they ride on their horses;
they come like men in battle formation
to attack you, O Daughter of Babylon.
43 The king of Babylon has heard reports about them,
and his hands hang limp.
Anguish has gripped him,
pain like that of a woman in labor.
44 Like a lion coming up from Jordan's thickets
to a rich pastureland,
I will chase Babylon from its land in an instant.
Who is the chosen one I will appoint for this?
Who is like me and who can challenge me?
And what shepherd can stand against me?"
45 Therefore, hear what the LORD has planned against Babylon,
what he has purposed against the land of the Babylonians:
The young of the flock will be dragged away;
he will completely destroy their pasture because of them.
46 At the sound of Babylon's capture the earth will tremble;
its cry will resound among the nations.

51

This is what the LORD says:
"See, I will stir up the spirit of a destroyer
against Babylon and the people of Leb Kamai.[a]
2 I will send foreigners to Babylon
to winnow her and to devastate her land;
they will oppose her on every side
in the day of her disaster.
3 Let not the archer string his bow,
nor let him put on his armor.
Do not spare her young men;
completely destroy[b] her army.
4 They will fall down slain in Babylon,[c]
fatally wounded in her streets.
5 For Israel and Judah have not been forsaken
by their God, the LORD Almighty,
though their land[d] is full of guilt
before the Holy One of Israel.

6 "Flee from Babylon!
Run for your lives!
Do not be destroyed because of her sins.
It is time for the LORD's vengeance;
he will pay her what she deserves.
7 Babylon was a gold cup in the LORD's hand;
she made the whole earth drunk.
The nations drank her wine;
therefore they have now gone mad.
8 Babylon will suddenly fall and be broken.
Wail over her!
Get balm for her pain;
perhaps she can be healed.

9 " 'We would have healed Babylon,
but she cannot be healed;
let us leave her and each go to his own land,
for her judgment reaches to the skies,
it rises as high as the clouds.'

10 " 'The LORD has vindicated us;
come, let us tell in Zion
what the LORD our God has done.'

11 "Sharpen the arrows,
take up the shields!
The LORD has stirred up the kings of the Medes,

[a] *1 Leb Kamai* is a cryptogram for Chaldea, that is, Babylonia. [b] *3* The Hebrew term refers to the irrevocable giving over of things or persons to the LORD, often by totally destroying them. [c] *4* Or *Chaldea* [d] *5* Or / *and the land ⌊of the Babylonians⌋*

because his purpose is to destroy Babylon.
The LORD will take vengeance,
vengeance for his temple.
12Lift up a banner against the walls of Babylon!
Reinforce the guard,
station the watchmen,
prepare an ambush!
The LORD will carry out his purpose,
his decree against the people of Babylon.
13You who live by many waters
and are rich in treasures,
your end has come,
the time for you to be cut off.
14The LORD Almighty has sworn by himself:
I will surely fill you with men, as with a swarm of locusts,
and they will shout in triumph over you.

15"He made the earth by his power;
he founded the world by his wisdom
and stretched out the heavens by his understanding.
16When he thunders, the waters in the heavens roar;
he makes clouds rise from the ends of the earth.
He sends lightning with the rain
and brings out the wind from his storehouses.

17"Every man is senseless and without knowledge;
every goldsmith is shamed by his idols.
His images are a fraud;
they have no breath in them.
18They are worthless, the objects of mockery;
when their judgment comes, they will perish.
19He who is the Portion of Jacob is not like these,
for he is the Maker of all things,
including the tribe of his inheritance—
the LORD Almighty is his name.

20"You are my war club,
my weapon for battle—
with you I shatter nations,
with you I destroy kingdoms,
21with you I shatter horse and rider,
with you I shatter chariot and driver,
22with you I shatter man and woman,
with you I shatter old man and youth,
with you I shatter young man and maiden,
23with you I shatter shepherd and flock,
with you I shatter farmer and oxen,
with you I shatter governors and officials.

24"Before your eyes I will repay Babylon
and all who live in Babylonia[a] for all the
wrong they have done in Zion," declares the
LORD.

25"I am against you, O destroying mountain,
you who destroy the whole earth,"
declares the LORD.
"I will stretch out my hand against you,
roll you off the cliffs,
and make you a burned-out mountain.
26No rock will be taken from you for a cornerstone,
nor any stone for a foundation,
for you will be desolate forever,"
declares the LORD.

27"Lift up a banner in the land!
Blow the trumpet among the nations!
Prepare the nations for battle against her;
summon against her these kingdoms:
Ararat, Minni and Ashkenaz.
Appoint a commander against her;
send up horses like a swarm of locusts.
28Prepare the nations for battle against her—
the kings of the Medes,
their governors and all their officials,
and all the countries they rule.
29The land trembles and writhes,
for the LORD's purposes against Babylon stand—
to lay waste the land of Babylon
so that no one will live there.
30Babylon's warriors have stopped fighting;
they remain in their strongholds.
Their strength is exhausted;
they have become like women.
Her dwellings are set on fire;
the bars of her gates are broken.
31One courier follows another
and messenger follows messenger
to announce to the king of Babylon
that his entire city is captured,
32the river crossings seized,
the marshes set on fire,
and the soldiers terrified."

[a]24 Or *Chaldea;* also in verse 35

[33]This is what the LORD Almighty, the God of Israel, says:

"The Daughter of Babylon is like a
threshing floor
at the time it is trampled;
the time to harvest her will soon come."

[34]"Nebuchadnezzar king of Babylon has
devoured us,
he has thrown us into confusion,
he has made us an empty jar.
Like a serpent he has swallowed us
and filled his stomach with our
delicacies,
and then has spewed us out.
[35]May the violence done to our flesh[a] be
upon Babylon,"
say the inhabitants of Zion.
"May our blood be on those who live in
Babylonia,"
says Jerusalem.

[36]Therefore, this is what the LORD says:

"See, I will defend your cause
and avenge you;
I will dry up her sea
and make her springs dry.
[37]Babylon will be a heap of ruins,
a haunt of jackals,
an object of horror and scorn,
a place where no one lives.
[38]Her people all roar like young lions,
they growl like lion cubs.
[39]But while they are aroused,
I will set out a feast for them
and make them drunk,
so that they shout with laughter—
then sleep forever and not awake,"
declares the LORD.
[40]"I will bring them down
like lambs to the slaughter,
like rams and goats.

[41]"How Sheshach[b] will be captured,
the boast of the whole earth seized!
What a horror Babylon will be
among the nations!
[42]The sea will rise over Babylon;
its roaring waves will cover her.
[43]Her towns will be desolate,
a dry and desert land,
a land where no one lives,
through which no man travels.
[44]I will punish Bel in Babylon
and make him spew out what he has
swallowed.
The nations will no longer stream to him.
And the wall of Babylon will fall.

[45]"Come out of her, my people!
Run for your lives!
Run from the fierce anger of the LORD.
[46]Do not lose heart or be afraid
when rumors are heard in the land;
one rumor comes this year, another the
next,
rumors of violence in the land
and of ruler against ruler.
[47]For the time will surely come
when I will punish the idols of Babylon;
her whole land will be disgraced
and her slain will all lie fallen within her.
[48]Then heaven and earth and all that is in
them
will shout for joy over Babylon,
for out of the north
destroyers will attack her,"
declares the LORD.

[49]"Babylon must fall because of Israel's
slain,
just as the slain in all the earth
have fallen because of Babylon.
[50]You who have escaped the sword,
leave and do not linger!
Remember the LORD in a distant land,
and think on Jerusalem."

[51]"We are disgraced,
for we have been insulted
and shame covers our faces,
because foreigners have entered
the holy places of the LORD's house."

[52]"But days are coming," declares the
LORD,
"when I will punish her idols,
and throughout her land
the wounded will groan.
[53]Even if Babylon reaches the sky
and fortifies her lofty stronghold,
I will send destroyers against her,"
declares the LORD.

[54]"The sound of a cry comes from Babylon,
the sound of great destruction
from the land of the Babylonians.[c]
[55]The LORD will destroy Babylon;
he will silence her noisy din.
Waves ⌊of enemies⌋ will rage like great
waters;
the roar of their voices will resound.
[56]A destroyer will come against Babylon;
her warriors will be captured,

[a]35 Or *done to us and to our children* [b]41 *Sheshach* is a cryptogram for Babylon. [c]54 Or *Chaldeans*

and their bows will be broken.
For the LORD is a God of retribution;
he will repay in full.
57I will make her officials and wise men
drunk,
her governors, officers and warriors as
well;
they will sleep forever and not awake,"
declares the King, whose name is the
LORD Almighty.

58This is what the LORD Almighty says:

"Babylon's thick wall will be leveled
and her high gates set on fire;
the peoples exhaust themselves for
nothing,
the nations' labor is only fuel for the
flames."

59This is the message Jeremiah gave to
the staff officer Seraiah son of Neriah, the
son of Mahseiah, when he went to Babylon
with Zedekiah king of Judah in the fourth
year of his reign. 60Jeremiah had written on a
scroll about all the disasters that would come
upon Babylon—all that had been recorded
concerning Babylon. 61He said to Seraiah,
"When you get to Babylon, see that you read
all these words aloud. 62Then say, 'O LORD,
you have said you will destroy this place, so
that neither man nor animal will live in it; it will
be desolate forever.' 63When you finish reading this scroll, tie a stone to it and throw it into
the Euphrates. 64Then say, 'So will Babylon
sink to rise no more because of the disaster I
will bring upon her. And her people will fall.' "

The words of Jeremiah end here.

The Fall of Jerusalem

52 Zedekiah was twenty-one years old
when he became king, and he
reigned in Jerusalem eleven years. His
mother's name was Hamutal daughter of
Jeremiah; she was from Libnah. 2He did evil
in the eyes of the LORD, just as Jehoiakim had
done. 3It was because of the LORD's anger
that all this happened to Jerusalem and
Judah, and in the end he thrust them from his
presence.
Now Zedekiah rebelled against the king of
Babylon.
4So in the ninth year of Zedekiah's reign,
on the tenth day of the tenth month, Nebuchadnezzar king of Babylon marched
against Jerusalem with his whole army. They
camped outside the city and built siege
works all around it. 5The city was kept under
siege until the eleventh year of King Zedekiah.
6By the ninth day of the fourth month the
famine in the city had become so severe that
there was no food for the people to eat.
7Then the city wall was broken through, and
the whole army fled. They left the city at night
through the gate between the two walls near
the king's garden, though the Babylonians[a]
were surrounding the city. They fled toward
the Arabah,[b] 8but the Babylonian[c] army pursued King Zedekiah and overtook him in the
plains of Jericho. All his soldiers were separated from him and scattered, 9and he was
captured.
He was taken to the king of Babylon at
Riblah in the land of Hamath, where he pronounced sentence on him. 10There at Riblah
the king of Babylon slaughtered the sons of
Zedekiah before his eyes; he also killed all
the officials of Judah. 11Then he put out
Zedekiah's eyes, bound him with bronze
shackles and took him to Babylon, where
he put him in prison till the day of his
death.
12On the tenth day of the fifth month, in the
nineteenth year of Nebuchadnezzar king of
Babylon, Nebuzaradan commander of the
imperial guard, who served the king of Babylon, came to Jerusalem. 13He set fire to the
temple of the LORD, the royal palace and all
the houses of Jerusalem. Every important
building he burned down. 14The whole Babylonian army under the commander of the
imperial guard broke down all the walls
around Jerusalem. 15Nebuzaradan the commander of the guard carried into exile some
of the poorest people and those who remained in the city, along with the rest of the
craftsmen[d] and those who had gone over to
the king of Babylon. 16But Nebuzaradan left
behind the rest of the poorest people of the
land to work the vineyards and fields.
17The Babylonians broke up the bronze
pillars, the movable stands and the bronze
Sea that were at the temple of the LORD and
they carried all the bronze to Babylon.
18They also took away the pots, shovels,
wick trimmers, sprinkling bowls, dishes and

[a] 7 Or *Chaldeans;* also in verse 17 [b] 7 Or *the Jordan Valley* [c] 8 Or *Chaldean;* also in verse 14
[d] 15 Or *populace*

all the bronze articles used in the temple
service. 19The commander of the imperial
guard took away the basins, censers, sprinkling bowls, pots, lampstands, dishes and
bowls used for drink offerings—all that were
made of pure gold or silver.

20The bronze from the two pillars, the Sea
and the twelve bronze bulls under it, and the
movable stands, which King Solomon had
made for the temple of the LORD, was more
than could be weighed. 21Each of the pillars
was eighteen cubits high and twelve cubits in
circumference[a]; each was four fingers thick,
and hollow. 22The bronze capital on top of
the one pillar was five cubits[b] high and was
decorated with a network and pomegranates
of bronze all around. The other pillar, with its
pomegranates, was similar. 23There were
ninety-six pomegranates on the sides; the
total number of pomegranates above the
surrounding network was a hundred.

24The commander of the guard took as
prisoners Seraiah the chief priest, Zephaniah the priest next in rank and the three
doorkeepers. 25Of those still in the city, he
took the officer in charge of the fighting men,
and seven royal advisers. He also took the
secretary who was chief officer in charge of
conscripting the people of the land and sixty
of his men who were found in the city. 26Neb-
uzaradan the commander took them all and
brought them to the king of Babylon at Riblah. 27There at Riblah, in the land of Hamath,
the king had them executed.

So Judah went into captivity, away from
her land. 28This is the number of the people
Nebuchadnezzar carried into exile:

in the seventh year, 3,023 Jews;
29in Nebuchadnezzar's eighteenth year,
832 people from Jerusalem;
30in his twenty-third year,
745 Jews taken into exile by Nebuzaradan
the commander of the imperial guard.
There were 4,600 people in all.

Jehoiachin Released

31In the thirty-seventh year of the exile of
Jehoiachin king of Judah, in the year Evil-
Merodach[c] became king of Babylon, he
released Jehoiachin king of Judah and freed
him from prison on the twenty-fifth day of the
twelfth month. 32He spoke kindly to him and
gave him a seat of honor higher than those of
the other kings who were with him in Babylon. 33So Jehoiachin put aside his prison
clothes and for the rest of his life ate regularly
at the king's table. 34Day by day the king of
Babylon gave Jehoiachin a regular allowance as long as he lived, till the day of his
death.

[a]21 That is, about 27 feet (about 8.1 meters) high and 18 feet (about 5.4 meters) in circumference [b]22 That is, about 7 1/2 feet (about 2.3 meters) [c]31 Also called *Amel-Marduk*

Lamentations

Introduction:

The title of this book means "funeral songs." The author was probably Jeremiah, and he was grieving about the destruction of Jerusalem.

In the original language, Hebrew, the twenty-two verses in each of chapters 1, 2, and 4 use the twenty-two letters of the Hebrew alphabet to start the verse. The third chapter has sixty-six verses and every third verse starts a new letter of the Hebrew alphabet. This is called an acrostic.

Jeremiah reflects here on the total destruction that has happened to Jerusalem and the temple. But he recognizes that all of this is the judgment of a righteous God. Knowing that God is merciful he appeals for mercy in prayer to God.

Outline of contents:

Jerusalem's total destruction (1:1–22)
God's anger—search for comfort (2:1–22)
Thoughts on suffering—hope in God (3:1–66)
The old glory of Jerusalem—present misery (4:1–22)
A prayer for God's mercy (5:1–22)

1[a] How deserted lies the city,
once so full of people!
How like a widow is she,
who once was great among the nations!
She who was queen among the provinces
has now become a slave.

2Bitterly she weeps at night,
tears are upon her cheeks.
Among all her lovers
there is none to comfort her.
All her friends have betrayed her;
they have become her enemies.

3After affliction and harsh labor,
Judah has gone into exile.
She dwells among the nations;
she finds no resting place.
All who pursue her have overtaken her
in the midst of her distress.

4The roads to Zion mourn,
for no one comes to her appointed feasts.
All her gateways are desolate,
her priests groan,
her maidens grieve,
and she is in bitter anguish.

5Her foes have become her masters;
her enemies are at ease.
The LORD has brought her grief
because of her many sins.
Her children have gone into exile,
captive before the foe.

6All the splendor has departed
from the Daughter of Zion.
Her princes are like deer
that find no pasture;
in weakness they have fled
before the pursuer.

7In the days of her affliction and wandering
Jerusalem remembers all the treasures
that were hers in days of old.
When her people fell into enemy hands,
there was no one to help her.
Her enemies looked at her
and laughed at her destruction.

8Jerusalem has sinned greatly
and so has become unclean.
All who honored her despise her,
for they have seen her nakedness;
she herself groans
and turns away.

[a]This chapter is an acrostic poem, the verses of which begin with the successive letters of the Hebrew alphabet.

[9]Her filthiness clung to her skirts;
she did not consider her future.
Her fall was astounding;
there was none to comfort her.
"Look, O LORD, on my affliction,
for the enemy has triumphed."

[10]The enemy laid hands
on all her treasures;
she saw pagan nations
enter her sanctuary—
those you had forbidden
to enter your assembly.

[11]All her people groan
as they search for bread;
they barter their treasures for food
to keep themselves alive.
"Look, O LORD, and consider,
for I am despised."

[12]"Is it nothing to you, all you who pass by?
Look around and see.
Is any suffering like my suffering
that was inflicted on me,
that the LORD brought on me
in the day of his fierce anger?

[13]"From on high he sent fire,
sent it down into my bones.
He spread a net for my feet
and turned me back.
He made me desolate,
faint all the day long.

[14]"My sins have been bound into a yoke[a];
by his hands they were woven
together.
They have come upon my neck
and the Lord has sapped my strength.
He has handed me over
to those I cannot withstand.

[15]"The Lord has rejected
all the warriors in my midst;
he has summoned an army against me
to[b] crush my young men.
In his winepress the Lord has trampled
the Virgin Daughter of Judah.

[16]"This is why I weep
and my eyes overflow with tears.
No one is near to comfort me,
no one to restore my spirit.
My children are destitute
because the enemy has prevailed."

[17]Zion stretches out her hands,
but there is no one to comfort her.
The LORD has decreed for Jacob
that his neighbors become his foes;
Jerusalem has become
an unclean thing among them.

[18]"The LORD is righteous,
yet I rebelled against his command.
Listen, all you peoples;
look upon my suffering.
My young men and maidens
have gone into exile.

[19]"I called to my allies
but they betrayed me.
My priests and my elders
perished in the city
while they searched for food
to keep themselves alive.

[20]"See, O LORD, how distressed I am!
I am in torment within,
and in my heart I am disturbed,
for I have been most rebellious.
Outside, the sword bereaves;
inside, there is only death.

[21]"People have heard my groaning,
but there is no one to comfort me.
All my enemies have heard of my
distress;
they rejoice at what you have done.
May you bring the day you have
announced
so they may become like me.

[22]"Let all their wickedness come before
you;
deal with them
as you have dealt with me
because of all my sins.
My groans are many
and my heart is faint."

2

[c]How the Lord has covered the
Daughter of Zion
with the cloud of his anger[d]!
He has hurled down the splendor of Israel
from heaven to earth;
he has not remembered his footstool
in the day of his anger.

[2]Without pity the Lord has swallowed up
all the dwellings of Jacob;
in his wrath he has torn down
the strongholds of the Daughter of
Judah.

[a]14 Most Hebrew manuscripts; Septuagint *He kept watch over my sins* [b]15 Or *has set a time for me / when he will* [c]This chapter is an acrostic poem, the verses of which begin with the successive letters of the Hebrew alphabet. [d]1 Or *How the Lord in his anger / has treated the Daughter of Zion with contempt*

He has brought her kingdom and its princes
down to the ground in dishonor.

3In fierce anger he has cut off
every horn[a] of Israel.
He has withdrawn his right hand
at the approach of the enemy.
He has burned in Jacob like a flaming fire
that consumes everything around it.

4Like an enemy he has strung his bow;
his right hand is ready.
Like a foe he has slain
all who were pleasing to the eye;
he has poured out his wrath like fire
on the tent of the Daughter of Zion.

5The Lord is like an enemy;
he has swallowed up Israel.
He has swallowed up all her palaces
and destroyed her strongholds.
He has multiplied mourning and lamentation
for the Daughter of Judah.

6He has laid waste his dwelling like a garden;
he has destroyed his place of meeting.
The LORD has made Zion forget
her appointed feasts and her Sabbaths;
in his fierce anger he has spurned
both king and priest.

7The Lord has rejected his altar
and abandoned his sanctuary.
He has handed over to the enemy
the walls of her palaces;
they have raised a shout in the house of the LORD
as on the day of an appointed feast.

8The LORD determined to tear down
the wall around the Daughter of Zion.
He stretched out a measuring line
and did not withhold his hand from destroying.
He made ramparts and walls lament;
together they wasted away.

9Her gates have sunk into the ground;
their bars he has broken and destroyed.
Her king and her princes are exiled among the nations,
the law is no more,
and her prophets no longer find
visions from the LORD.

10The elders of the Daughter of Zion
sit on the ground in silence;
they have sprinkled dust on their heads
and put on sackcloth.
The young women of Jerusalem
have bowed their heads to the ground.

11My eyes fail from weeping,
I am in torment within,
my heart is poured out on the ground
because my people are destroyed,
because children and infants faint
in the streets of the city.

12They say to their mothers,
"Where is bread and wine?"
as they faint like wounded men
in the streets of the city,
as their lives ebb away
in their mothers' arms.

13What can I say for you?
With what can I compare you,
O Daughter of Jerusalem?
To what can I liken you,
that I may comfort you,
O Virgin Daughter of Zion?
Your wound is as deep as the sea.
Who can heal you?

14The visions of your prophets
were false and worthless;
they did not expose your sin
to ward off your captivity.
The oracles they gave you
were false and misleading.

15All who pass your way
clap their hands at you;
they scoff and shake their heads
at the Daughter of Jerusalem:
"Is this the city that was called
the perfection of beauty,
the joy of the whole earth?"

16All your enemies open their mouths
wide against you;
they scoff and gnash their teeth
and say, "We have swallowed her up.
This is the day we have waited for;
we have lived to see it."

17The LORD has done what he planned;
he has fulfilled his word,
which he decreed long ago.
He has overthrown you without pity,
he has let the enemy gloat over you,
he has exalted the horn[b] of your foes.

[a]3 Or *all the strength;* or *every king; horn* here symbolizes strength. [b]17 *Horn* here symbolizes strength.

18The hearts of the people
cry out to the Lord.
O wall of the Daughter of Zion,
let your tears flow like a river
day and night;
give yourself no relief,
your eyes no rest.

19Arise, cry out in the night,
as the watches of the night begin;
pour out your heart like water
in the presence of the Lord.
Lift up your hands to him
for the lives of your children,
who faint from hunger
at the head of every street.

20"Look, O LORD, and consider:
Whom have you ever treated like this?
Should women eat their offspring,
the children they have cared for?
Should priest and prophet be killed
in the sanctuary of the Lord?

21"Young and old lie together
in the dust of the streets;
my young men and maidens
have fallen by the sword.
You have slain them in the day of your
anger;
you have slaughtered them without
pity.

22"As you summon to a feast day,
so you summoned against me terrors
on every side.
In the day of the LORD's anger
no one escaped or survived;
those I cared for and reared,
my enemy has destroyed."

3

I[a] am the man who has seen affliction
by the rod of his wrath.
2He has driven me away and made me
walk
in darkness rather than light;
3indeed, he has turned his hand against
me
again and again, all day long.

4He has made my skin and my flesh grow
old
and has broken my bones.
5He has besieged me and surrounded me
with bitterness and hardship.
6He has made me dwell in darkness
like those long dead.

7He has walled me in so I cannot escape;
he has weighed me down with chains.
8Even when I call out or cry for help,
he shuts out my prayer.
9He has barred my way with blocks of
stone;
he has made my paths crooked.

10Like a bear lying in wait,
like a lion in hiding,
11he dragged me from the path and
mangled me
and left me without help.
12He drew his bow
and made me the target for his arrows.

13He pierced my heart
with arrows from his quiver.
14I became the laughingstock of all my
people;
they mock me in song all day long.
15He has filled me with bitter herbs
and sated me with gall.

16He has broken my teeth with gravel;
he has trampled me in the dust.
17I have been deprived of peace;
I have forgotten what prosperity is.
18So I say, "My splendor is gone
and all that I had hoped from the LORD."

19I remember my affliction and my
wandering,
the bitterness and the gall.
20I well remember them,
and my soul is downcast within me.
21Yet this I call to mind
and therefore I have hope:

22Because of the LORD's great love we are
not consumed,
for his compassions never fail.
23They are new every morning;
great is your faithfulness.
24I say to myself, "The LORD is my portion;
therefore I will wait for him."

25The LORD is good to those whose hope is
in him,
to the one who seeks him;
26it is good to wait quietly
for the salvation of the LORD.
27It is good for a man to bear the yoke
while he is young.

28Let him sit alone in silence,
for the LORD has laid it on him.
29Let him bury his face in the dust—

[a]This chapter is an acrostic poem; the verses of each stanza begin with the successive letters of the Hebrew alphabet, and the verses within each stanza begin with the same letter.

there may yet be hope.
30Let him offer his cheek to one who would strike him,
and let him be filled with disgrace.

31For men are not cast off
by the Lord forever.
32Though he brings grief, he will show compassion,
so great is his unfailing love.
33For he does not willingly bring affliction
or grief to the children of men.

34To crush underfoot
all prisoners in the land,
35to deny a man his rights
before the Most High,
36to deprive a man of justice—
would not the Lord see such things?

37Who can speak and have it happen
if the Lord has not decreed it?
38Is it not from the mouth of the Most High
that both calamities and good things come?
39Why should any living man complain
when punished for his sins?

40Let us examine our ways and test them,
and let us return to the LORD.
41Let us lift up our hearts and our hands
to God in heaven, and say:
42"We have sinned and rebelled
and you have not forgiven.

43"You have covered yourself with anger
and pursued us;
you have slain without pity.
44You have covered yourself with a cloud
so that no prayer can get through.
45You have made us scum and refuse
among the nations.

46"All our enemies have opened their mouths
wide against us.
47We have suffered terror and pitfalls,
ruin and destruction."
48Streams of tears flow from my eyes
because my people are destroyed.

49My eyes will flow unceasingly,
without relief,
50until the LORD looks down
from heaven and sees.
51What I see brings grief to my soul
because of all the women of my city.

52Those who were my enemies without cause
hunted me like a bird.
53They tried to end my life in a pit
and threw stones at me;
54the waters closed over my head,
and I thought I was about to be cut off.

55I called on your name, O LORD,
from the depths of the pit.
56You heard my plea: "Do not close your ears
to my cry for relief."
57You came near when I called you,
and you said, "Do not fear."

58O Lord, you took up my case;
you redeemed my life.
59You have seen, O LORD, the wrong done to me.
Uphold my cause!
60You have seen the depth of their vengeance,
all their plots against me.

61O LORD, you have heard their insults,
all their plots against me—
62what my enemies whisper and mutter
against me all day long.
63Look at them! Sitting or standing,
they mock me in their songs.

64Pay them back what they deserve, O LORD,
for what their hands have done.
65Put a veil over their hearts,
and may your curse be on them!
66Pursue them in anger and destroy them
from under the heavens of the LORD.

4 [a] How the gold has lost its luster,
the fine gold become dull!
The sacred gems are scattered
at the head of every street.

2How the precious sons of Zion,
once worth their weight in gold,
are now considered as pots of clay,
the work of a potter's hands!

3Even jackals offer their breasts
to nurse their young,
but my people have become heartless
like ostriches in the desert.

4Because of thirst the infant's tongue
sticks to the roof of its mouth;

[a]This chapter is an acrostic poem, the verses of which begin with the successive letters of the Hebrew alphabet.

the children beg for bread,
but no one gives it to them.

5 Those who once ate delicacies
are destitute in the streets.
Those nurtured in purple
now lie on ash heaps.

6 The punishment of my people
is greater than that of Sodom,
which was overthrown in a moment
without a hand turned to help her.

7 Their princes were brighter than snow
and whiter than milk,
their bodies more ruddy than rubies,
their appearance like sapphires.[a]

8 But now they are blacker than soot;
they are not recognized in the streets.
Their skin has shriveled on their bones;
it has become as dry as a stick.

9 Those killed by the sword are better off
than those who die of famine;
racked with hunger, they waste away
for lack of food from the field.

10 With their own hands compassionate
women
have cooked their own children,
who became their food
when my people were destroyed.

11 The LORD has given full vent to his wrath;
he has poured out his fierce anger.
He kindled a fire in Zion
that consumed her foundations.

12 The kings of the earth did not believe,
nor did any of the world's people,
that enemies and foes could enter
the gates of Jerusalem.

13 But it happened because of the sins of
her prophets
and the iniquities of her priests,
who shed within her
the blood of the righteous.

14 Now they grope through the streets
like men who are blind.
They are so defiled with blood
that no one dares to touch their
garments.

15 "Go away! You are unclean!" men cry to
them.
"Away! Away! Don't touch us!"
When they flee and wander about,
people among the nations say,
"They can stay here no longer."

16 The LORD himself has scattered them;
he no longer watches over them.
The priests are shown no honor,
the elders no favor.

17 Moreover, our eyes failed,
looking in vain for help;
from our towers we watched
for a nation that could not save us.

18 Men stalked us at every step,
so we could not walk in our streets.
Our end was near, our days were
numbered,
for our end had come.

19 Our pursuers were swifter
than eagles in the sky;
they chased us over the mountains
and lay in wait for us in the desert.

20 The LORD's anointed, our very life breath,
was caught in their traps.
We thought that under his shadow
we would live among the nations.

21 Rejoice and be glad, O Daughter of
Edom,
you who live in the land of Uz.
But to you also the cup will be passed;
you will be drunk and stripped naked.

22 O Daughter of Zion, your punishment will
end;
he will not prolong your exile.
But, O Daughter of Edom, he will punish
your sin
and expose your wickedness.

5 Remember, O LORD, what has
happened to us;
look, and see our disgrace.
2 Our inheritance has been turned over to
aliens,
our homes to foreigners.
3 We have become orphans and
fatherless,
our mothers like widows.
4 We must buy the water we drink;
our wood can be had only at a price.
5 Those who pursue us are at our heels;
we are weary and find no rest.
6 We submitted to Egypt and Assyria
to get enough bread.
7 Our fathers sinned and are no more,
and we bear their punishment.
8 Slaves rule over us,

[a]7 Or *lapis lazuli*

and there is none to free us from their
hands.
9We get our bread at the risk of our lives
because of the sword in the desert.
10Our skin is hot as an oven,
feverish from hunger.
11Women have been ravished in Zion,
and virgins in the towns of Judah.
12Princes have been hung up by their
hands;
elders are shown no respect.
13Young men toil at the millstones;
boys stagger under loads of wood.
14The elders are gone from the city gate;
the young men have stopped their
music.
15Joy is gone from our hearts;
our dancing has turned to mourning.
16The crown has fallen from our head.
Woe to us, for we have sinned!
17Because of this our hearts are faint,
because of these things our eyes grow
dim
18for Mount Zion, which lies desolate,
with jackals prowling over it.

19You, O LORD, reign forever;
your throne endures from generation to
generation.
20Why do you always forget us?
Why do you forsake us so long?
21Restore us to yourself, O LORD, that we
may return;
renew our days as of old
22unless you have utterly rejected us
and are angry with us beyond measure.

Ezekiel

Introduction:

This book is named after the prophet Ezekiel, which means "God is strong." His messages are dated between the years 593–571 B.C. and were given to his fellow exiles in Babylonian captivity.

Born in 623 B.C. to a priestly family, Ezekiel grew up in the surroundings of the temple in Jerusalem. In 597 B.C. he was included in the exile to Babylon. It was in 593 B.C. that he was called by God in a divine revelation to be a prophet.

During the first part of his ministry Ezekiel proclaimed basically the same message given by Jeremiah—Jerusalem and the temple were doomed to destruction because of the sinfulness and idolatry of the people.

After the news reached Babylon that Jerusalem actually had been destroyed in 586 B.C. Ezekiel proclaimed a new message of hope and restoration—God would regather the Israelites from the ends of the earth and re-establish them in their own land. The nations who challenged Israel's return would be defeated and judged.

Outline of contents:

Ezekiel's call (1:1–3:27)
Jerusalem's sinful condition and doom (4:1–24:27)
Foreign nations in prophecy (25:1–32:32)
Hopes for restoration (33:1–39:29)
Israel restored to Palestine (40:1–48:35)

The Living Creatures and the Glory of the LORD

1 In the[a] thirtieth year, in the fourth month
on the fifth day, while I was among the
exiles by the Kebar River, the heavens were
opened and I saw visions of God.
2 On the fifth of the month—it was the fifth
year of the exile of King Jehoiachin— 3 the
word of the LORD came to Ezekiel the priest,
the son of Buzi,[b] by the Kebar River in the
land of the Babylonians.[c] There the hand of
the LORD was upon him.
4 I looked, and I saw a windstorm coming
out of the north—an immense cloud with
flashing lightning and surrounded by brilliant
light. The center of the fire looked like glowing metal, 5 and in the fire was what looked
like four living creatures. In appearance their
form was that of a man, 6 but each of them
had four faces and four wings. 7 Their legs
were straight; their feet were like those of a
calf and gleamed like burnished bronze.
8 Under their wings on their four sides they
had the hands of a man. All four of them had
faces and wings, 9 and their wings touched
one another. Each one went straight ahead;
they did not turn as they moved.
10 Their faces looked like this: Each of the
four had the face of a man, and on the right
side each had the face of a lion, and on the
left the face of an ox; each also had the face
of an eagle. 11 Such were their faces. Their
wings were spread out upward; each had
two wings, one touching the wing of another
creature on either side, and two wings covering its body. 12 Each one went straight ahead.
Wherever the spirit would go, they would go,
without turning as they went. 13 The appearance of the living creatures was like burning
coals of fire or like torches. Fire moved back
and forth among the creatures; it was bright,
and lightning flashed out of it. 14 The creatures sped back and forth like flashes of lightning.
15 As I looked at the living creatures, I saw a
wheel on the ground beside each creature

---

[a] 1 Or ⌊my⌋ [b] 3 Or *Ezekiel son of Buzi the priest* [c] 3 Or *Chaldeans*

with its four faces. [16]This was the appearance and structure of the wheels: They sparkled like chrysolite, and all four looked alike. Each appeared to be made like a wheel intersecting a wheel. [17]As they moved, they would go in any one of the four directions the creatures faced; the wheels did not turn about[a] as the creatures went. [18]Their rims were high and awesome, and all four rims were full of eyes all around.

[19]When the living creatures moved, the wheels beside them moved; and when the living creatures rose from the ground, the wheels also rose. [20]Wherever the spirit would go, they would go, and the wheels would rise along with them, because the spirit of the living creatures was in the wheels. [21]When the creatures moved, they also moved; when the creatures stood still, they also stood still; and when the creatures rose from the ground, the wheels rose along with them, because the spirit of the living creatures was in the wheels.

[22]Spread out above the heads of the living creatures was what looked like an expanse, sparkling like ice, and awesome. [23]Under the expanse their wings were stretched out one toward the other, and each had two wings covering its body. [24]When the creatures moved, I heard the sound of their wings, like the roar of rushing waters, like the voice of the Almighty,[b] like the tumult of an army. When they stood still, they lowered their wings.

[25]Then there came a voice from above the expanse over their heads as they stood with lowered wings. [26]Above the expanse over their heads was what looked like a throne of sapphire,[c] and high above on the throne was a figure like that of a man. [27]I saw that from what appeared to be his waist up he looked like glowing metal, as if full of fire, and that from there down he looked like fire; and brilliant light surrounded him. [28]Like the appearance of a rainbow in the clouds on a rainy day, so was the radiance around him.

This was the appearance of the likeness of the glory of the LORD. When I saw it, I fell facedown, and I heard the voice of one speaking.

Ezekiel's Call

2 He said to me, "Son of man, stand up on your feet and I will speak to you." [2]As he spoke, the Spirit came into me and raised me to my feet, and I heard him speaking to me.

[3]He said: "Son of man, I am sending you to the Israelites, to a rebellious nation that has rebelled against me; they and their fathers have been in revolt against me to this very day. [4]The people to whom I am sending you are obstinate and stubborn. Say to them, 'This is what the Sovereign LORD says.' [5]And whether they listen or fail to listen—for they are a rebellious house—they will know that a prophet has been among them. [6]And you, son of man, do not be afraid of them or their words. Do not be afraid, though briers and thorns are all around you and you live among scorpions. Do not be afraid of what they say or terrified by them, though they are a rebellious house. [7]You must speak my words to them, whether they listen or fail to listen, for they are rebellious. [8]But you, son of man, listen to what I say to you. Do not rebel like that rebellious house; open your mouth and eat what I give you."

[9]Then I looked, and I saw a hand stretched out to me. In it was a scroll, [10]which he unrolled before me. On both sides of it were written words of lament and mourning and woe.

3 And he said to me, "Son of man, eat what is before you, eat this scroll; then go and speak to the house of Israel." [2]So I opened my mouth, and he gave me the scroll to eat.

[3]Then he said to me, "Son of man, eat this scroll I am giving you and fill your stomach with it." So I ate it, and it tasted as sweet as honey in my mouth.

[4]He then said to me: "Son of man, go now to the house of Israel and speak my words to them. [5]You are not being sent to a people of obscure speech and difficult language, but to the house of Israel— [6]not to many peoples of obscure speech and difficult language, whose words you cannot understand. Surely if I had sent you to them, they would have listened to you. [7]But the house of Israel is not willing to listen to you because they are not willing to listen to me, for the whole house of Israel is hardened and obstinate. [8]But I will make you as unyielding and hardened as they are. [9]I will make your forehead like the hardest stone, harder than flint. Do not be afraid of them or terrified by them, though they are a rebellious house."

[10]And he said to me, "Son of man, listen carefully and take to heart all the words I

[a]17 Or *aside* [b]24 Hebrew *Shaddai* [c]26 Or *lapis lazuli*

speak to you. 11Go now to your countrymen in exile and speak to them. Say to them, 'This is what the Sovereign LORD says,' whether they listen or fail to listen."

12Then the Spirit lifted me up, and I heard behind me a loud rumbling sound—May the glory of the LORD be praised in his dwelling place!— 13the sound of the wings of the living creatures brushing against each other and the sound of the wheels beside them, a loud rumbling sound. 14The Spirit then lifted me up and took me away, and I went in bitterness and in the anger of my spirit, with the strong hand of the LORD upon me. 15I came to the exiles who lived at Tel Abib near the Kebar River. And there, where they were living, I sat among them for seven days—overwhelmed.

Warning to Israel

16At the end of seven days the word of the LORD came to me: 17"Son of man, I have made you a watchman for the house of Israel; so hear the word I speak and give them warning from me. 18When I say to a wicked man, 'You will surely die,' and you do not warn him or speak out to dissuade him from his evil ways in order to save his life, that wicked man will die for[a] his sin, and I will hold you accountable for his blood. 19But if you do warn the wicked man and he does not turn from his wickedness or from his evil ways, he will die for his sin; but you will have saved yourself.

20"Again, when a righteous man turns from his righteousness and does evil, and I put a stumbling block before him, he will die. Since you did not warn him, he will die for his sin. The righteous things he did will not be remembered, and I will hold you accountable for his blood. 21But if you do warn the righteous man not to sin and he does not sin, he will surely live because he took warning, and you will have saved yourself."

22The hand of the LORD was upon me there, and he said to me, "Get up and go out to the plain, and there I will speak to you." 23So I got up and went out to the plain. And the glory of the LORD was standing there, like the glory I had seen by the Kebar River, and I fell facedown.

24Then the Spirit came into me and raised me to my feet. He spoke to me and said: "Go, shut yourself inside your house. 25And you, son of man, they will tie with ropes; you will be bound so that you cannot go out among the people. 26I will make your tongue stick to the roof of your mouth so that you will be silent and unable to rebuke them, though they are a rebellious house. 27But when I speak to you, I will open your mouth and you shall say to them, 'This is what the Sovereign LORD says.' Whoever will listen let him listen, and whoever will refuse let him refuse; for they are a rebellious house.

Siege of Jerusalem Symbolized

4 "Now, son of man, take a clay tablet, put it in front of you and draw the city of Jerusalem on it. 2Then lay siege to it: Erect siege works against it, build a ramp up to it, set up camps against it and put battering rams around it. 3Then take an iron pan, place it as an iron wall between you and the city and turn your face toward it. It will be under siege, and you shall besiege it. This will be a sign to the house of Israel.

4"Then lie on your left side and put the sin of the house of Israel upon yourself.[b] You are to bear their sin for the number of days you lie on your side. 5I have assigned you the same number of days as the years of their sin. So for 390 days you will bear the sin of the house of Israel.

6"After you have finished this, lie down again, this time on your right side, and bear the sin of the house of Judah. I have assigned you 40 days, a day for each year. 7Turn your face toward the siege of Jerusalem and with bared arm prophesy against her. 8I will tie you up with ropes so that you cannot turn from one side to the other until you have finished the days of your siege.

9"Take wheat and barley, beans and lentils, millet and spelt; put them in a storage jar and use them to make bread for yourself. You are to eat it during the 390 days you lie on your side. 10Weigh out twenty shekels[c] of food to eat each day and eat it at set times. 11Also measure out a sixth of a hin[d] of water and drink it at set times. 12Eat the food as you would a barley cake; bake it in the sight of the people, using human excrement for fuel." 13The LORD said, "In this way the people of Israel will eat defiled food among the nations where I will drive them."

14Then I said, "Not so, Sovereign LORD! I have never defiled myself. From my youth

[a] *18* Or *in;* also in verses 19 and 20 [b] *4* Or *your side* [c] *10* That is, about 8 ounces (about 0.2 kilogram)
[d] *11* That is, about 2/3 quart (about 0.6 liter)

until now I have never eaten anything found
dead or torn by wild animals. No unclean
meat has ever entered my mouth."
15"Very well," he said, "I will let you bake
your bread over cow manure instead of human excrement."
16He then said to me: "Son of man, I will
cut off the supply of food in Jerusalem. The
people will eat rationed food in anxiety and
drink rationed water in despair, 17for food
and water will be scarce. They will be appalled at the sight of each other and will
waste away because of[a] their sin.
5 "Now, son of man, take a sharp sword
and use it as a barber's razor to shave
your head and your beard. Then take a set of
scales and divide up the hair. 2When the
days of your siege come to an end, burn a
third of the hair with fire inside the city. Take
a third and strike it with the sword all around
the city. And scatter a third to the wind. For I
will pursue them with drawn sword. 3But take
a few strands of hair and tuck them away in
the folds of your garment. 4Again, take a few
of these and throw them into the fire and burn
them up. A fire will spread from there to the
whole house of Israel.
5"This is what the Sovereign LORD says:
This is Jerusalem, which I have set in the
center of the nations, with countries all
around her. 6Yet in her wickedness she has
rebelled against my laws and decrees more
than the nations and countries around her.
She has rejected my laws and has not followed my decrees.
7"Therefore this is what the Sovereign
LORD says: You have been more unruly than
the nations around you and have not followed my decrees or kept my laws. You have
not even[b] conformed to the standards of the
nations around you.
8"Therefore this is what the Sovereign
LORD says: I myself am against you, Jerusalem, and I will inflict punishment on you in the
sight of the nations. 9Because of all your
detestable idols, I will do to you what I have
never done before and will never do again.
10Therefore in your midst fathers will eat their
children, and children will eat their fathers. I
will inflict punishment on you and will scatter
all your survivors to the winds. 11Therefore
as surely as I live, declares the Sovereign
LORD, because you have defiled my sanctuary with all your vile images and detestable
practices, I myself will withdraw my favor; I
will not look on you with pity or spare you. 12A
third of your people will die of the plague or
perish by famine inside you; a third will fall by
the sword outside your walls; and a third I will
scatter to the winds and pursue with drawn
sword.
13"Then my anger will cease and my wrath
against them will subside, and I will be
avenged. And when I have spent my wrath
upon them, they will know that I the LORD
have spoken in my zeal.
14"I will make you a ruin and a reproach
among the nations around you, in the sight of
all who pass by. 15You will be a reproach and
a taunt, a warning and an object of horror to
the nations around you when I inflict punishment on you in anger and in wrath and with
stinging rebuke. I the LORD have spoken.
16When I shoot at you with my deadly and
destructive arrows of famine, I will shoot to
destroy you. I will bring more and more famine upon you and cut off your supply of food.
17I will send famine and wild beasts against
you, and they will leave you childless.
Plague and bloodshed will sweep through
you, and I will bring the sword against you. I
the LORD have spoken."

A Prophecy Against the Mountains of Israel

6 The word of the LORD came to me: 2"Son
of man, set your face against the mountains of Israel; prophesy against them 3and
say: 'O mountains of Israel, hear the word of
the Sovereign LORD. This is what the Sovereign LORD says to the mountains and hills, to
the ravines and valleys: I am about to bring a
sword against you, and I will destroy your
high places. 4Your altars will be demolished
and your incense altars will be smashed; and
I will slay your people in front of your idols. 5I
will lay the dead bodies of the Israelites in
front of their idols, and I will scatter your
bones around your altars. 6Wherever you
live, the towns will be laid waste and the high
places demolished, so that your altars will be
laid waste and devastated, your idols
smashed and ruined, your incense altars
broken down, and what you have made
wiped out. 7Your people will fall slain among
you, and you will know that I am the LORD.
8" 'But I will spare some, for some of you
will escape the sword when you are scattered among the lands and nations. 9Then in

[a]17 Or *away in* [b]7 Most Hebrew manuscripts; some Hebrew manuscripts and Syriac *You have*

the nations where they have been carried captive, those who escape will remember me—how I have been grieved by their adulterous hearts, which have turned away from me, and by their eyes, which have lusted after their idols. They will loathe themselves for the evil they have done and for all their detestable practices. 10And they will know that I am the LORD; I did not threaten in vain to bring this calamity on them.

11" 'This is what the Sovereign LORD says: Strike your hands together and stamp your feet and cry out "Alas!" because of all the wicked and detestable practices of the house of Israel, for they will fall by the sword, famine and plague. 12He that is far away will die of the plague, and he that is near will fall by the sword, and he that survives and is spared will die of famine. So will I spend my wrath upon them. 13And they will know that I am the LORD, when their people lie slain among their idols around their altars, on every high hill and on all the mountaintops, under every spreading tree and every leafy oak—places where they offered fragrant incense to all their idols. 14And I will stretch out my hand against them and make the land a desolate waste from the desert to Diblah[a]—wherever they live. Then they will know that I am the LORD.' "

The End Has Come

7 The word of the LORD came to me: 2"Son of man, this is what the Sovereign LORD says to the land of Israel: The end! The end has come upon the four corners of the land. 3The end is now upon you and I will unleash my anger against you. I will judge you according to your conduct and repay you for all your detestable practices. 4I will not look on you with pity or spare you; I will surely repay you for your conduct and the detestable practices among you. Then you will know that I am the LORD.

5"This is what the Sovereign LORD says: Disaster! An unheard-of[b] disaster is coming. 6The end has come! The end has come! It has roused itself against you. It has come! 7Doom has come upon you—you who dwell in the land. The time has come, the day is near; there is panic, not joy, upon the mountains. 8I am about to pour out my wrath on you and spend my anger against you; I will judge you according to your conduct and repay you for all your detestable practices. 9I will not look on you with pity or spare you; I will repay you in accordance with your conduct and the detestable practices among you. Then you will know that it is I the LORD who strikes the blow.

10"The day is here! It has come! Doom has burst forth, the rod has budded, arrogance has blossomed! 11Violence has grown into[c] a rod to punish wickedness; none of the people will be left, none of that crowd—no wealth, nothing of value. 12The time has come, the day has arrived. Let not the buyer rejoice nor the seller grieve, for wrath is upon the whole crowd. 13The seller will not recover the land he has sold as long as both of them live, for the vision concerning the whole crowd will not be reversed. Because of their sins, not one of them will preserve his life. 14Though they blow the trumpet and get everything ready, no one will go into battle, for my wrath is upon the whole crowd.

15"Outside is the sword, inside are plague and famine; those in the country will die by the sword, and those in the city will be devoured by famine and plague. 16All who survive and escape will be in the mountains, moaning like doves of the valleys, each because of his sins. 17Every hand will go limp, and every knee will become as weak as water. 18They will put on sackcloth and be clothed with terror. Their faces will be covered with shame and their heads will be shaved. 19They will throw their silver into the streets, and their gold will be an unclean thing. Their silver and gold will not be able to save them in the day of the LORD's wrath. They will not satisfy their hunger or fill their stomachs with it, for it has made them stumble into sin. 20They were proud of their beautiful jewelry and used it to make their detestable idols and vile images. Therefore I will turn these into an unclean thing for them. 21I will hand it all over as plunder to foreigners and as loot to the wicked of the earth, and they will defile it. 22I will turn my face away from them, and they will desecrate my treasured place; robbers will enter it and desecrate it.

23"Prepare chains, because the land is full of bloodshed and the city is full of violence. 24I will bring the most wicked of the nations to take possession of their houses; I will put an end to the pride of the mighty, and their sanc-

[a] 14 Most Hebrew manuscripts; a few Hebrew manuscripts *Riblah* [b] 5 Most Hebrew manuscripts; some Hebrew manuscripts and Syriac *Disaster after* [c] 11 Or *The violent one has become*

tuaries will be desecrated. 25When terror comes, they will seek peace, but there will be none. 26Calamity upon calamity will come, and rumor upon rumor. They will try to get a vision from the prophet; the teaching of the law by the priest will be lost, as will the counsel of the elders. 27The king will mourn, the prince will be clothed with despair, and the hands of the people of the land will tremble. I will deal with them according to their conduct, and by their own standards I will judge them. Then they will know that I am the LORD."

Idolatry in the Temple

8 In the sixth year, in the sixth month on the fifth day, while I was sitting in my house and the elders of Judah were sitting before me, the hand of the Sovereign LORD came upon me there. 2I looked, and I saw a figure like that of a man.[a] From what appeared to be his waist down he was like fire, and from there up his appearance was as bright as glowing metal. 3He stretched out what looked like a hand and took me by the hair of my head. The Spirit lifted me up between earth and heaven and in visions of God he took me to Jerusalem, to the entrance to the north gate of the inner court, where the idol that provokes to jealousy stood. 4And there before me was the glory of the God of Israel, as in the vision I had seen in the plain.

5Then he said to me, "Son of man, look toward the north." So I looked, and in the entrance north of the gate of the altar I saw this idol of jealousy.

6And he said to me, "Son of man, do you see what they are doing—the utterly detestable things the house of Israel is doing here, things that will drive me far from my sanctuary? But you will see things that are even more detestable."

7Then he brought me to the entrance to the court. I looked, and I saw a hole in the wall. 8He said to me, "Son of man, now dig into the wall." So I dug into the wall and saw a doorway there.

9And he said to me, "Go in and see the wicked and detestable things they are doing here." 10So I went in and looked, and I saw portrayed all over the walls all kinds of crawling things and detestable animals and all the idols of the house of Israel. 11In front of them stood seventy elders of the house of Israel, and Jaazaniah son of Shaphan was standing among them. Each had a censer in his hand, and a fragrant cloud of incense was rising.

12He said to me, "Son of man, have you seen what the elders of the house of Israel are doing in the darkness, each at the shrine of his own idol? They say, 'The LORD does not see us; the LORD has forsaken the land.'" 13Again, he said, "You will see them doing things that are even more detestable."

14Then he brought me to the entrance to the north gate of the house of the LORD, and I saw women sitting there, mourning for Tammuz. 15He said to me, "Do you see this, son of man? You will see things that are even more detestable than this."

16He then brought me into the inner court of the house of the LORD, and there at the entrance to the temple, between the portico and the altar, were about twenty-five men. With their backs toward the temple of the LORD and their faces toward the east, they were bowing down to the sun in the east.

17He said to me, "Have you seen this, son of man? Is it a trivial matter for the house of Judah to do the detestable things they are doing here? Must they also fill the land with violence and continually provoke me to anger? Look at them putting the branch to their nose! 18Therefore I will deal with them in anger; I will not look on them with pity or spare them. Although they shout in my ears, I will not listen to them."

Idolaters Killed

9 Then I heard him call out in a loud voice, "Bring the guards of the city here, each with a weapon in his hand." 2And I saw six men coming from the direction of the upper gate, which faces north, each with a deadly weapon in his hand. With them was a man clothed in linen who had a writing kit at his side. They came in and stood beside the bronze altar.

3Now the glory of the God of Israel went up from above the cherubim, where it had been, and moved to the threshold of the temple. Then the LORD called to the man clothed in linen who had the writing kit at his side 4and said to him, "Go throughout the city of Jerusalem and put a mark on the foreheads of those who grieve and lament over all the detestable things that are done in it."

5As I listened, he said to the others, "Follow him through the city and kill, without

[a]2 Or *saw a fiery figure*

showing pity or compassion. 6Slaughter old
men, young men and maidens, women and
children, but do not touch anyone who has
the mark. Begin at my sanctuary." So they
began with the elders who were in front of the
temple.

7Then he said to them, "Defile the temple
and fill the courts with the slain. Go!" So they
went out and began killing throughout the
city. 8While they were killing and I was left
alone, I fell facedown, crying out, "Ah, Sovereign LORD! Are you going to destroy the
entire remnant of Israel in this outpouring of
your wrath on Jerusalem?"

9He answered me, "The sin of the house of
Israel and Judah is exceedingly great; the
land is full of bloodshed and the city is full of
injustice. They say, 'The LORD has forsaken
the land; the LORD does not see.' 10So I will
not look on them with pity or spare them, but
I will bring down on their own heads what
they have done."

11Then the man in linen with the writing kit
at his side brought back word, saying, "I
have done as you commanded."

The Glory Departs From the Temple

10 I looked, and I saw the likeness of a
throne of sapphire[a] above the expanse that was over the heads of the cherubim. 2The LORD said to the man clothed in
linen, "Go in among the wheels beneath the
cherubim. Fill your hands with burning coals
from among the cherubim and scatter them
over the city." And as I watched, he went in.

3Now the cherubim were standing on the
south side of the temple when the man went
in, and a cloud filled the inner court. 4Then
the glory of the LORD rose from above the
cherubim and moved to the threshold of the
temple. The cloud filled the temple, and the
court was full of the radiance of the glory of
the LORD. 5The sound of the wings of the
cherubim could be heard as far away as the
outer court, like the voice of God Almighty[b]
when he speaks.

6When the LORD commanded the man in
linen, "Take fire from among the wheels,
from among the cherubim," the man went in
and stood beside a wheel. 7Then one of the
cherubim reached out his hand to the fire
that was among them. He took up some of it
and put it into the hands of the man in linen,
who took it and went out. 8(Under the wings
of the cherubim could be seen what looked
like the hands of a man.)

9I looked, and I saw beside the cherubim
four wheels, one beside each of the cherubim; the wheels sparkled like chrysolite.
10As for their appearance, the four of them
looked alike; each was like a wheel intersecting a wheel. 11As they moved, they would go
in any one of the four directions the cherubim
faced; the wheels did not turn about[c] as the
cherubim went. The cherubim went in whatever direction the head faced, without turning as they went. 12Their entire bodies, including their backs, their hands and their
wings, were completely full of eyes, as were
their four wheels. 13I heard the wheels being
called "the whirling wheels." 14Each of the
cherubim had four faces: One face was that
of a cherub, the second the face of a man,
the third the face of a lion, and the fourth the
face of an eagle.

15Then the cherubim rose upward. These
were the living creatures I had seen by the
Kebar River. 16When the cherubim moved,
the wheels beside them moved; and when
the cherubim spread their wings to rise from
the ground, the wheels did not leave their
side. 17When the cherubim stood still, they
also stood still; and when the cherubim rose,
they rose with them, because the spirit of the
living creatures was in them.

18Then the glory of the LORD departed from
over the threshold of the temple and stopped
above the cherubim. 19While I watched, the
cherubim spread their wings and rose from
the ground, and as they went, the wheels
went with them. They stopped at the entrance to the east gate of the LORD's house,
and the glory of the God of Israel was above
them.

20These were the living creatures I had
seen beneath the God of Israel by the Kebar
River, and I realized that they were cherubim. 21Each had four faces and four wings,
and under their wings was what looked like
the hands of a man. 22Their faces had the
same appearance as those I had seen by the
Kebar River. Each one went straight ahead.

Judgment on Israel's Leaders

11 Then the Spirit lifted me up and
brought me to the gate of the house
of the LORD that faces east. There at the entrance to the gate were twenty-five men, and

[a] 1 Or *lapis lazuli* [b] 5 Hebrew *El-Shaddai* [c] 11 Or *aside*

I saw among them Jaazaniah son of Azzur and Pelatiah son of Benaiah, leaders of the people. 2The LORD said to me, "Son of man, these are the men who are plotting evil and giving wicked advice in this city. 3They say, 'Will it not soon be time to build houses?[a] This city is a cooking pot, and we are the meat.' 4Therefore prophesy against them; prophesy, son of man."

5Then the Spirit of the LORD came upon me, and he told me to say: "This is what the LORD says: That is what you are saying, O house of Israel, but I know what is going through your mind. 6You have killed many people in this city and filled its streets with the dead.

7"Therefore this is what the Sovereign LORD says: The bodies you have thrown there are the meat and this city is the pot, but I will drive you out of it. 8You fear the sword, and the sword is what I will bring against you, declares the Sovereign LORD. 9I will drive you out of the city and hand you over to foreigners and inflict punishment on you. 10You will fall by the sword, and I will execute judgment on you at the borders of Israel. Then you will know that I am the LORD. 11This city will not be a pot for you, nor will you be the meat in it; I will execute judgment on you at the borders of Israel. 12And you will know that I am the LORD, for you have not followed my decrees or kept my laws but have conformed to the standards of the nations around you."

13Now as I was prophesying, Pelatiah son of Benaiah died. Then I fell facedown and cried out in a loud voice, "Ah, Sovereign LORD! Will you completely destroy the remnant of Israel?"

14The word of the LORD came to me: 15"Son of man, your brothers—your brothers who are your blood relatives[b] and the whole house of Israel—are those of whom the people of Jerusalem have said, 'They are[c] far away from the LORD; this land was given to us as our possession.'

Promised Return of Israel

16"Therefore say: 'This is what the Sovereign LORD says: Although I sent them far away among the nations and scattered them among the countries, yet for a little while I have been a sanctuary for them in the countries where they have gone.'

17"Therefore say: 'This is what the Sovereign LORD says: I will gather you from the nations and bring you back from the countries where you have been scattered, and I will give you back the land of Israel again.'

18"They will return to it and remove all its vile images and detestable idols. 19I will give them an undivided heart and put a new spirit in them; I will remove from them their heart of stone and give them a heart of flesh. 20Then they will follow my decrees and be careful to keep my laws. They will be my people, and I will be their God. 21But as for those whose hearts are devoted to their vile images and detestable idols, I will bring down on their own heads what they have done, declares the Sovereign LORD."

22Then the cherubim, with the wheels beside them, spread their wings, and the glory of the God of Israel was above them. 23The glory of the LORD went up from within the city and stopped above the mountain east of it. 24The Spirit lifted me up and brought me to the exiles in Babylonia[d] in the vision given by the Spirit of God.

Then the vision I had seen went up from me, 25and I told the exiles everything the LORD had shown me.

The Exile Symbolized

12 The word of the LORD came to me: 2"Son of man, you are living among a rebellious people. They have eyes to see but do not see and ears to hear but do not hear, for they are a rebellious people.

3"Therefore, son of man, pack your belongings for exile and in the daytime, as they watch, set out and go from where you are to another place. Perhaps they will understand, though they are a rebellious house. 4During the daytime, while they watch, bring out your belongings packed for exile. Then in the evening, while they are watching, go out like those who go into exile. 5While they watch, dig through the wall and take your belongings out through it. 6Put them on your shoulder as they are watching and carry them out at dusk. Cover your face so that you cannot see the land, for I have made you a sign to the house of Israel."

7So I did as I was commanded. During the day I brought out my things packed for exile. Then in the evening I dug through the wall with my hands. I took my belongings out at dusk, carrying them on my shoulders while they watched.

[a] 3 Or *This is not the time to build houses.* [b] 15 Or *are in exile with you* (see Septuagint and Syriac) [c] 15 Or *those to whom the people of Jerusalem have said, 'Stay* [d] 24 Or *Chaldea*

8In the morning the word of the LORD came
to me: 9"Son of man, did not that rebellious
house of Israel ask you, 'What are you doing?'
10"Say to them, 'This is what the Sovereign
LORD says: This oracle concerns the prince in
Jerusalem and the whole house of Israel
who are there.' 11Say to them, 'I am a sign to
you.'
"As I have done, so it will be done to them.
They will go into exile as captives.
12"The prince among them will put his
things on his shoulder at dusk and leave, and
a hole will be dug in the wall for him to go
through. He will cover his face so that he
cannot see the land. 13I will spread my net for
him, and he will be caught in my snare; I will
bring him to Babylonia, the land of the Chaldeans, but he will not see it, and there he will
die. 14I will scatter to the winds all those
around him—his staff and all his troops—
and I will pursue them with drawn sword.
15"They will know that I am the LORD, when
I disperse them among the nations and scatter them through the countries. 16But I will
spare a few of them from the sword, famine
and plague, so that in the nations where they
go they may acknowledge all their detestable practices. Then they will know that I am
the LORD."
17The word of the LORD came to me: 18"Son
of man, tremble as you eat your food, and
shudder in fear as you drink your water.
19Say to the people of the land: 'This is what
the Sovereign LORD says about those living in
Jerusalem and in the land of Israel: They will
eat their food in anxiety and drink their water
in despair, for their land will be stripped of
everything in it because of the violence of all
who live there. 20The inhabited towns will be
laid waste and the land will be desolate.
Then you will know that I am the LORD.' "
21The word of the LORD came to me: 22"Son
of man, what is this proverb you have in the
land of Israel: 'The days go by and every
vision comes to nothing'? 23Say to them,
'This is what the Sovereign LORD says: I am
going to put an end to this proverb, and they
will no longer quote it in Israel.' Say to them,
'The days are near when every vision will be
fulfilled. 24For there will be no more false
visions or flattering divinations among the
people of Israel. 25But I the LORD will speak
what I will, and it shall be fulfilled without
delay. For in your days, you rebellious
house, I will fulfill whatever I say, declares
the Sovereign LORD.' "
26The word of the LORD came to me: 27"Son
of man, the house of Israel is saying, 'The
vision he sees is for many years from now,
and he prophesies about the distant future.'
28"Therefore say to them, 'This is what the
Sovereign LORD says: None of my words will
be delayed any longer; whatever I say will be
fulfilled, declares the Sovereign LORD.' "

False Prophets Condemned

13 The word of the LORD came to me:
2"Son of man, prophesy against the
prophets of Israel who are now prophesying.
Say to those who prophesy out of their own
imagination: 'Hear the word of the LORD!
3This is what the Sovereign LORD says: Woe
to the foolish[a] prophets who follow their own
spirit and have seen nothing! 4Your prophets, O Israel, are like jackals among ruins.
5You have not gone up to the breaks in the
wall to repair it for the house of Israel so that
it will stand firm in the battle on the day of the
LORD. 6Their visions are false and their divinations a lie. They say, "The LORD declares,"
when the LORD has not sent them; yet they
expect their words to be fulfilled. 7Have you
not seen false visions and uttered lying divinations when you say, "The LORD declares,"
though I have not spoken?
8" 'Therefore this is what the Sovereign
LORD says: Because of your false words and
lying visions, I am against you, declares the
Sovereign LORD. 9My hand will be against the
prophets who see false visions and utter lying divinations. They will not belong to the
council of my people or be listed in the
records of the house of Israel, nor will they
enter the land of Israel. Then you will know
that I am the Sovereign LORD.
10" 'Because they lead my people astray,
saying, "Peace," when there is no peace,
and because, when a flimsy wall is built, they
cover it with whitewash, 11therefore tell those
who cover it with whitewash that it is going to
fall. Rain will come in torrents, and I will send
hailstones hurtling down, and violent winds
will burst forth. 12When the wall collapses,
will people not ask you, "Where is the whitewash you covered it with?"
13" 'Therefore this is what the Sovereign
LORD says: In my wrath I will unleash a violent
wind, and in my anger hailstones and torrents of rain will fall with destructive fury. 14I

[a]3 Or *wicked*

will tear down the wall you have covered with
whitewash and will level it to the ground so
that its foundation will be laid bare. When it[a]
falls, you will be destroyed in it; and you will
know that I am the LORD. 15So I will spend my
wrath against the wall and against those who
covered it with whitewash. I will say to you,
"The wall is gone and so are those who
whitewashed it, 16those prophets of Israel
who prophesied to Jerusalem and saw visions of peace for her when there was no
peace, declares the Sovereign LORD." '

17"Now, son of man, set your face against
the daughters of your people who prophesy
out of their own imagination. Prophesy
against them 18and say, 'This is what the
Sovereign LORD says: Woe to the women
who sew magic charms on all their wrists and
make veils of various lengths for their heads
in order to ensnare people. Will you ensnare
the lives of my people but preserve your
own? 19You have profaned me among my
people for a few handfuls of barley and
scraps of bread. By lying to my people, who
listen to lies, you have killed those who
should not have died and have spared those
who should not live.

20" 'Therefore this is what the Sovereign
LORD says: I am against your magic charms
with which you ensnare people like birds and
I will tear them from your arms; I will set free
the people that you ensnare like birds. 21I will
tear off your veils and save my people from
your hands, and they will no longer fall prey
to your power. Then you will know that I am
the LORD. 22Because you disheartened the
righteous with your lies, when I had brought
them no grief, and because you encouraged
the wicked not to turn from their evil ways
and so save their lives, 23therefore you will
no longer see false visions or practice divination. I will save my people from your hands.
And then you will know that I am the
LORD.' "

Idolaters Condemned

14 Some of the elders of Israel came to
me and sat down in front of me.
2Then the word of the LORD came to me:
3"Son of man, these men have set up idols in
their hearts and put wicked stumbling blocks
before their faces. Should I let them inquire
of me at all? 4Therefore speak to them and
tell them, 'This is what the Sovereign LORD
says: When any Israelite sets up idols in his
heart and puts a wicked stumbling block before his face and then goes to a prophet, I the
LORD will answer him myself in keeping with
his great idolatry. 5I will do this to recapture
the hearts of the people of Israel, who have
all deserted me for their idols.'

6"Therefore say to the house of Israel,
'This is what the Sovereign LORD says: Repent! Turn from your idols and renounce all
your detestable practices!

7" 'When any Israelite or any alien living in
Israel separates himself from me and sets up
idols in his heart and puts a wicked stumbling
block before his face and then goes to a
prophet to inquire of me, I the LORD will answer him myself. 8I will set my face against
that man and make him an example and a
byword. I will cut him off from my people.
Then you will know that I am the LORD.

9" 'And if the prophet is enticed to utter a
prophecy, I the LORD have enticed that
prophet, and I will stretch out my hand
against him and destroy him from among my
people Israel. 10They will bear their guilt—
the prophet will be as guilty as the one who
consults him. 11Then the people of Israel will
no longer stray from me, nor will they defile
themselves anymore with all their sins. They
will be my people, and I will be their God,
declares the Sovereign LORD.' "

Judgment Inescapable

12The word of the LORD came to me: 13"Son
of man, if a country sins against me by being
unfaithful and I stretch out my hand against it
to cut off its food supply and send famine
upon it and kill its men and their animals,
14even if these three men—Noah, Daniel[b]
and Job—were in it, they could save only
themselves by their righteousness, declares
the Sovereign LORD.

15"Or if I send wild beasts through that
country and they leave it childless and it
becomes desolate so that no one can pass
through it because of the beasts, 16as surely
as I live, declares the Sovereign LORD, even if
these three men were in it, they could not
save their own sons or daughters. They
alone would be saved, but the land would be
desolate.

17"Or if I bring a sword against that country
and say, 'Let the sword pass throughout the
land,' and I kill its men and their animals, 18as

[a] 14 Or *the city* [b] 14 Or *Danel;* the Hebrew spelling may suggest a person other than the prophet Daniel; also in verse 20.

surely as I live, declares the Sovereign LORD,
even if these three men were in it, they could
not save their own sons or daughters. They
alone would be saved.
19"Or if I send a plague into that land and
pour out my wrath upon it through bloodshed, killing its men and their animals, 20as
surely as I live, declares the Sovereign LORD,
even if Noah, Daniel and Job were in it, they
could save neither son nor daughter. They
would save only themselves by their righteousness.
21"For this is what the Sovereign LORD
says: How much worse will it be when I send
against Jerusalem my four dreadful judgments—sword and famine and wild beasts
and plague—to kill its men and their animals!
22Yet there will be some survivors—sons
and daughters who will be brought out of it.
They will come to you, and when you see
their conduct and their actions, you will be
consoled regarding the disaster I have
brought upon Jerusalem—every disaster I
have brought upon it. 23You will be consoled
when you see their conduct and their actions, for you will know that I have done nothing in it without cause, declares the Sovereign LORD."

Jerusalem, A Useless Vine

15 The word of the LORD came to me:
2"Son of man, how is the wood of a
vine better than that of a branch on any of the
trees in the forest? 3Is wood ever taken from
it to make anything useful? Do they make
pegs from it to hang things on? 4And after it is
thrown on the fire as fuel and the fire burns
both ends and chars the middle, is it then
useful for anything? 5If it was not useful for
anything when it was whole, how much less
can it be made into something useful when
the fire has burned it and it is charred?
6"Therefore this is what the Sovereign
LORD says: As I have given the wood of the
vine among the trees of the forest as fuel for
the fire, so will I treat the people living in
Jerusalem. 7I will set my face against them.
Although they have come out of the fire, the
fire will yet consume them. And when I set
my face against them, you will know that I am
the LORD. 8I will make the land desolate because they have been unfaithful, declares
the Sovereign LORD."

An Allegory of Unfaithful Jerusalem

16 The word of the LORD came to me:
2"Son of man, confront Jerusalem
with her detestable practices 3and say, 'This
is what the Sovereign LORD says to Jerusalem: Your ancestry and birth were in the land
of the Canaanites; your father was an Amorite and your mother a Hittite. 4On the day
you were born your cord was not cut, nor
were you washed with water to make you
clean, nor were you rubbed with salt or
wrapped in cloths. 5No one looked on you
with pity or had compassion enough to do
any of these things for you. Rather, you were
thrown out into the open field, for on the day
you were born you were despised.
6" 'Then I passed by and saw you kicking
about in your blood, and as you lay there in
your blood I said to you, "Live!"[a] 7I made you
grow like a plant of the field. You grew up and
developed and became the most beautiful
of jewels.[b] Your breasts were formed and
your hair grew, you who were naked and
bare.
8" 'Later I passed by, and when I looked at
you and saw that you were old enough for
love, I spread the corner of my garment over
you and covered your nakedness. I gave you
my solemn oath and entered into a covenant
with you, declares the Sovereign LORD, and
you became mine.
9" 'I bathed[c] you with water and washed
the blood from you and put ointments on you.
10I clothed you with an embroidered dress
and put leather sandals on you. I dressed
you in fine linen and covered you with costly
garments. 11I adorned you with jewelry: I put
bracelets on your arms and a necklace
around your neck, 12and I put a ring on your
nose, earrings on your ears and a beautiful
crown on your head. 13So you were adorned
with gold and silver; your clothes were of fine
linen and costly fabric and embroidered
cloth. Your food was fine flour, honey and
olive oil. You became very beautiful and rose
to be a queen. 14And your fame spread
among the nations on account of your beauty, because the splendor I had given you
made your beauty perfect, declares the Sovereign LORD.
15" 'But you trusted in your beauty and
used your fame to become a prostitute. You
lavished your favors on anyone who passed

[a]6 A few Hebrew manuscripts, Septuagint and Syriac; most Hebrew manuscripts *"Live!" And as you lay there in your blood I said to you, "Live!"* [b]7 *Or became mature* [c]9 *Or I had bathed*

by and your beauty became his.[a] 16You took some of your garments to make gaudy high places, where you carried on your prostitution. Such things should not happen, nor should they ever occur. 17You also took the fine jewelry I gave you, the jewelry made of my gold and silver, and you made for yourself male idols and engaged in prostitution with them. 18And you took your embroidered clothes to put on them, and you offered my oil and incense before them. 19Also the food I provided for you—the fine flour, olive oil and honey I gave you to eat—you offered as fragrant incense before them. That is what happened, declares the Sovereign LORD.

20" 'And you took your sons and daughters whom you bore to me and sacrificed them as food to the idols. Was your prostitution not enough? 21You slaughtered my children and sacrificed them[b] to the idols. 22In all your detestable practices and your prostitution you did not remember the days of your youth, when you were naked and bare, kicking about in your blood.

23" 'Woe! Woe to you, declares the Sovereign LORD. In addition to all your other wickedness, 24you built a mound for yourself and made a lofty shrine in every public square. 25At the head of every street you built your lofty shrines and degraded your beauty, offering your body with increasing promiscuity to anyone who passed by. 26You engaged in prostitution with the Egyptians, your lustful neighbors, and provoked me to anger with your increasing promiscuity. 27So I stretched out my hand against you and reduced your territory; I gave you over to the greed of your enemies, the daughters of the Philistines, who were shocked by your lewd conduct. 28You engaged in prostitution with the Assyrians too, because you were insatiable; and even after that, you still were not satisfied. 29Then you increased your promiscuity to include Babylonia,[c] a land of merchants, but even with this you were not satisfied.

30" 'How weak-willed you are, declares the Sovereign LORD, when you do all these things, acting like a brazen prostitute! 31When you built your mounds at the head of every street and made your lofty shrines in every public square, you were unlike a prostitute, because you scorned payment.

32" 'You adulterous wife! You prefer strangers to your own husband! 33Every prostitute receives a fee, but you give gifts to all your lovers, bribing them to come to you from everywhere for your illicit favors. 34So in your prostitution you are the opposite of others; no one runs after you for your favors. You are the very opposite, for you give payment and none is given to you.

35" 'Therefore, you prostitute, hear the word of the LORD! 36This is what the Sovereign LORD says: Because you poured out your wealth[d] and exposed your nakedness in your promiscuity with your lovers, and because of all your detestable idols, and because you gave them your children's blood, 37therefore I am going to gather all your lovers, with whom you found pleasure, those you loved as well as those you hated. I will gather them against you from all around and will strip you in front of them, and they will see all your nakedness. 38I will sentence you to the punishment of women who commit adultery and who shed blood; I will bring upon you the blood vengeance of my wrath and jealous anger. 39Then I will hand you over to your lovers, and they will tear down your mounds and destroy your lofty shrines. They will strip you of your clothes and take your fine jewelry and leave you naked and bare. 40They will bring a mob against you, who will stone you and hack you to pieces with their swords. 41They will burn down your houses and inflict punishment on you in the sight of many women. I will put a stop to your prostitution, and you will no longer pay your lovers. 42Then my wrath against you will subside and my jealous anger will turn away from you; I will be calm and no longer angry.

43" 'Because you did not remember the days of your youth but enraged me with all these things, I will surely bring down on your head what you have done, declares the Sovereign LORD. Did you not add lewdness to all your other detestable practices?

44" 'Everyone who quotes proverbs will quote this proverb about you: "Like mother, like daughter." 45You are a true daughter of your mother, who despised her husband and her children; and you are a true sister of your sisters, who despised their husbands and their children. Your mother was a Hittite and your father an Amorite. 46Your older sister was Samaria, who lived to the north of you with her daughters; and your younger sister,

[a]*15* Most Hebrew manuscripts; one Hebrew manuscript (see some Septuagint manuscripts) *by. Such a thing should not happen* [b]*21* Or *and made them pass through* ⌞*the fire*⌟ [c]*29* Or *Chaldea* [d]*36* Or *lust*

who lived to the south of you with her daughters, was Sodom. 47You not only walked in
their ways and copied their detestable practices, but in all your ways you soon became
more depraved than they. 48As surely as I
live, declares the Sovereign LORD, your sister
Sodom and her daughters never did what
you and your daughters have done.

49" 'Now this was the sin of your sister
Sodom: She and her daughters were arrogant, overfed and unconcerned; they did not
help the poor and needy. 50They were
haughty and did detestable things before
me. Therefore I did away with them as you
have seen. 51Samaria did not commit half the
sins you did. You have done more detestable things than they, and have made your
sisters seem righteous by all these things
you have done. 52Bear your disgrace, for you
have furnished some justification for your
sisters. Because your sins were more vile
than theirs, they appear more righteous than
you. So then, be ashamed and bear your
disgrace, for you have made your sisters
appear righteous.

53" 'However, I will restore the fortunes of
Sodom and her daughters and of Samaria
and her daughters, and your fortunes along
with them, 54so that you may bear your disgrace and be ashamed of all you have done
in giving them comfort. 55And your sisters,
Sodom with her daughters and Samaria with
her daughters, will return to what they were
before; and you and your daughters will return to what you were before. 56You would
not even mention your sister Sodom in the
day of your pride, 57before your wickedness
was uncovered. Even so, you are now
scorned by the daughters of Edom[a] and all
her neighbors and the daughters of the Philistines—all those around you who despise
you. 58You will bear the consequences of
your lewdness and your detestable practices, declares the LORD.

59" 'This is what the Sovereign LORD says: I
will deal with you as you deserve, because
you have despised my oath by breaking the
covenant. 60Yet I will remember the covenant I made with you in the days of your
youth, and I will establish an everlasting covenant with you. 61Then you will remember
your ways and be ashamed when you receive your sisters, both those who are older
than you and those who are younger. I will
give them to you as daughters, but not on the
basis of my covenant with you. 62So I will
establish my covenant with you, and you will
know that I am the LORD. 63Then, when I
make atonement for you for all you have
done, you will remember and be ashamed
and never again open your mouth because
of your humiliation, declares the Sovereign
LORD.' "

Two Eagles and a Vine

17 The word of the LORD came to me:
2"Son of man, set forth an allegory
and tell the house of Israel a parable. 3Say to
them, 'This is what the Sovereign LORD says:
A great eagle with powerful wings, long
feathers and full plumage of varied colors
came to Lebanon. Taking hold of the top of a
cedar, 4he broke off its topmost shoot and
carried it away to a land of merchants, where
he planted it in a city of traders.

5" 'He took some of the seed of your land
and put it in fertile soil. He planted it like a
willow by abundant water, 6and it sprouted
and became a low, spreading vine. Its
branches turned toward him, but its roots
remained under it. So it became a vine and
produced branches and put out leafy
boughs.

7" 'But there was another great eagle with
powerful wings and full plumage. The vine
now sent out its roots toward him from the
plot where it was planted and stretched out
its branches to him for water. 8It had been
planted in good soil by abundant water so
that it would produce branches, bear fruit
and become a splendid vine.'

9"Say to them, 'This is what the Sovereign
LORD says: Will it thrive? Will it not be uprooted and stripped of its fruit so that it withers?
All its new growth will wither. It will not take a
strong arm or many people to pull it up by the
roots. 10Even if it is transplanted, will it
thrive? Will it not wither completely when the
east wind strikes it—wither away in the plot
where it grew?' "

11Then the word of the LORD came to me:
12"Say to this rebellious house, 'Do you not
know what these things mean?' Say to them:
'The king of Babylon went to Jerusalem and
carried off her king and her nobles, bringing
them back with him to Babylon. 13Then he
took a member of the royal family and made
a treaty with him, putting him under oath. He
also carried away the leading men of the
land, 14so that the kingdom would be brought

[a]57 Many Hebrew manuscripts and Syriac; most Hebrew manuscripts, Septuagint and Vulgate *Aram*

low, unable to rise again, surviving only by
keeping his treaty. 15But the king rebelled
against him by sending his envoys to Egypt
to get horses and a large army. Will he succeed? Will he who does such things escape?
Will he break the treaty and yet escape?
16" 'As surely as I live, declares the Sovereign LORD, he shall die in Babylon, in the land
of the king who put him on the throne, whose
oath he despised and whose treaty he broke.
17Pharaoh with his mighty army and great
horde will be of no help to him in war, when
ramps are built and siege works erected to
destroy many lives. 18He despised the oath
by breaking the covenant. Because he had
given his hand in pledge and yet did all these
things, he shall not escape.
19" 'Therefore this is what the Sovereign
LORD says: As surely as I live, I will bring
down on his head my oath that he despised
and my covenant that he broke. 20I will
spread my net for him, and he will be caught
in my snare. I will bring him to Babylon and
execute judgment upon him there because
he was unfaithful to me. 21All his fleeing
troops will fall by the sword, and the survivors will be scattered to the winds. Then you
will know that I the LORD have spoken.
22" 'This is what the Sovereign LORD says: I
myself will take a shoot from the very top of a
cedar and plant it; I will break off a tender
sprig from its topmost shoots and plant it on a
high and lofty mountain. 23On the mountain
heights of Israel I will plant it; it will produce
branches and bear fruit and become a splendid cedar. Birds of every kind will nest in it;
they will find shelter in the shade of its
branches. 24All the trees of the field will know
that I the LORD bring down the tall tree and
make the low tree grow tall. I dry up the
green tree and make the dry tree flourish.
" 'I the LORD have spoken, and I will do it.' "

The Soul Who Sins Will Die

18 The word of the LORD came to me:
2"What do you people mean by quot-
ing this proverb about the land of Israel:

" 'The fathers eat sour grapes,
and the children's teeth are set on
edge'?

3"As surely as I live, declares the Sovereign LORD, you will no longer quote this proverb in Israel. 4For every living soul belongs to
me, the father as well as the son—both alike
belong to me. The soul who sins is the one
who will die.

5"Suppose there is a righteous man
who does what is just and right.
6He does not eat at the mountain shrines
or look to the idols of the house of
Israel.
He does not defile his neighbor's wife
or lie with a woman during her period.
7He does not oppress anyone,
but returns what he took in pledge for a
loan.
He does not commit robbery
but gives his food to the hungry
and provides clothing for the naked.
8He does not lend at usury
or take excessive interest.[a]
He withholds his hand from doing wrong
and judges fairly between man and
man.
9He follows my decrees
and faithfully keeps my laws.
That man is righteous;
he will surely live,
declares the Sovereign LORD.

10"Suppose he has a violent son, who
sheds blood or does any of these other
things[b] 11(though the father has done none
of them):

"He eats at the mountain shrines.
He defiles his neighbor's wife.
12He oppresses the poor and needy.
He commits robbery.
He does not return what he took in
pledge.
He looks to the idols.
He does detestable things.
13He lends at usury and takes excessive
interest.

Will such a man live? He will not! Because he
has done all these detestable things, he will
surely be put to death and his blood will be
on his own head.
14"But suppose this son has a son who
sees all the sins his father commits, and
though he sees them, he does not do such
things:

15"He does not eat at the mountain shrines
or look to the idols of the house of
Israel.
He does not defile his neighbor's wife.
16He does not oppress anyone

[a]8 Or *take interest;* similarly in verses 13 and 17 [b]10 Or *things to a brother*

or require a pledge for a loan.
He does not commit robbery
but gives his food to the hungry
and provides clothing for the naked.
17He withholds his hand from sin[a]
and takes no usury or excessive
interest.
He keeps my laws and follows my
decrees.

He will not die for his father's sin; he will
surely live. 18But his father will die for his own
sin, because he practiced extortion, robbed
his brother and did what was wrong among
his people.
19"Yet you ask, 'Why does the son not
share the guilt of his father?' Since the son
has done what is just and right and has been
careful to keep all my decrees, he will surely
live. 20The soul who sins is the one who will
die. The son will not share the guilt of the
father, nor will the father share the guilt of the
son. The righteousness of the righteous man
will be credited to him, and the wickedness of
the wicked will be charged against him.
21"But if a wicked man turns away from all
the sins he has committed and keeps all my
decrees and does what is just and right, he
will surely live; he will not die. 22None of the
offenses he has committed will be remembered against him. Because of the righteous
things he has done, he will live. 23Do I take
any pleasure in the death of the wicked?
declares the Sovereign Lord. Rather, am I
not pleased when they turn from their ways
and live?
24"But if a righteous man turns from his
righteousness and commits sin and does the
same detestable things the wicked man
does, will he live? None of the righteous
things he has done will be remembered. Because of the unfaithfulness he is guilty of and
because of the sins he has committed, he
will die.
25"Yet you say, 'The way of the Lord is not
just.' Hear, O house of Israel: Is my way
unjust? Is it not your ways that are unjust?
26If a righteous man turns from his righteousness and commits sin, he will die for it; because of the sin he has committed he will die.
27But if a wicked man turns away from the
wickedness he has committed and does
what is just and right, he will save his life.
28Because he considers all the offenses he
has committed and turns away from them,
he will surely live; he will not die. 29Yet the
house of Israel says, 'The way of the Lord is
not just.' Are my ways unjust, O house of
Israel? Is it not your ways that are unjust?
30"Therefore, O house of Israel, I will judge
you, each one according to his ways, declares the Sovereign Lord. Repent! Turn
away from all your offenses; then sin will not
be your downfall. 31Rid yourselves of all the
offenses you have committed, and get a new
heart and a new spirit. Why will you die, O
house of Israel? 32For I take no pleasure in
the death of anyone, declares the Sovereign
Lord. Repent and live!

A Lament for Israel's Princes

19 "Take up a lament concerning the
princes of Israel 2and say:

" 'What a lioness was your mother
among the lions!
She lay down among the young lions
and reared her cubs.
3She brought up one of her cubs,
and he became a strong lion.
He learned to tear the prey
and he devoured men.
4The nations heard about him,
and he was trapped in their pit.
They led him with hooks
to the land of Egypt.

5" 'When she saw her hope unfulfilled,
her expectation gone,
she took another of her cubs
and made him a strong lion.
6He prowled among the lions,
for he was now a strong lion.
He learned to tear the prey
and he devoured men.
7He broke down[b] their strongholds
and devastated their towns.
The land and all who were in it
were terrified by his roaring.
8Then the nations came against him,
those from regions round about.
They spread their net for him,
and he was trapped in their pit.
9With hooks they pulled him into a cage
and brought him to the king of Babylon.
They put him in prison,
so his roar was heard no longer
on the mountains of Israel.

10" 'Your mother was like a vine in your
vineyard[c]

[a] 17 Septuagint (see also verse 8); Hebrew *from the poor* [b] 7 Targum (see Septuagint); Hebrew *He knew*
[c] 10 Two Hebrew manuscripts; most Hebrew manuscripts *your blood*

planted by the water;
it was fruitful and full of branches
because of abundant water.
11Its branches were strong,
fit for a ruler's scepter.
It towered high
above the thick foliage,
conspicuous for its height
and for its many branches.
12But it was uprooted in fury
and thrown to the ground.
The east wind made it shrivel,
it was stripped of its fruit;
its strong branches withered
and fire consumed them.
13Now it is planted in the desert,
in a dry and thirsty land.
14Fire spread from one of its main[a]
branches
and consumed its fruit.
No strong branch is left on it
fit for a ruler's scepter.'

This is a lament and is to be used as a lament."

Rebellious Israel

20 In the seventh year, in the fifth month
on the tenth day, some of the elders
of Israel came to inquire of the LORD, and they
sat down in front of me.

2Then the word of the LORD came to me:
3"Son of man, speak to the elders of Israel
and say to them, 'This is what the Sovereign
LORD says: Have you come to inquire of me?
As surely as I live, I will not let you inquire of
me, declares the Sovereign LORD.'

4"Will you judge them? Will you judge
them, son of man? Then confront them with
the detestable practices of their fathers 5and
say to them: 'This is what the Sovereign LORD
says: On the day I chose Israel, I swore with
uplifted hand to the descendants of the
house of Jacob and revealed myself to them
in Egypt. With uplifted hand I said to them, "I
am the LORD your God." 6On that day I swore
to them that I would bring them out of Egypt
into a land I had searched out for them, a
land flowing with milk and honey, the most
beautiful of all lands. 7And I said to them,
"Each of you, get rid of the vile images you
have set your eyes on, and do not defile
yourselves with the idols of Egypt. I am the
LORD your God."

8" 'But they rebelled against me and would
not listen to me; they did not get rid of the vile
images they had set their eyes on, nor did
they forsake the idols of Egypt. So I said I
would pour out my wrath on them and spend
my anger against them in Egypt. 9But for the
sake of my name I did what would keep it
from being profaned in the eyes of the nations they lived among and in whose sight I
had revealed myself to the Israelites by
bringing them out of Egypt. 10Therefore I led
them out of Egypt and brought them into the
desert. 11I gave them my decrees and made
known to them my laws, for the man who
obeys them will live by them. 12Also I gave
them my Sabbaths as a sign between us, so
they would know that I the LORD made them
holy.

13" 'Yet the people of Israel rebelled
against me in the desert. They did not follow
my decrees but rejected my laws—although
the man who obeys them will live by them—
and they utterly desecrated my Sabbaths.
So I said I would pour out my wrath on them
and destroy them in the desert. 14But for the
sake of my name I did what would keep it
from being profaned in the eyes of the nations in whose sight I had brought them out.
15Also with uplifted hand I swore to them in
the desert that I would not bring them into the
land I had given them—a land flowing with
milk and honey, most beautiful of all lands—
16because they rejected my laws and did not
follow my decrees and desecrated my Sabbaths. For their hearts were devoted to their
idols. 17Yet I looked on them with pity and did
not destroy them or put an end to them in the
desert. 18I said to their children in the desert,
"Do not follow the statutes of your fathers or
keep their laws or defile yourselves with their
idols. 19I am the LORD your God; follow my
decrees and be careful to keep my laws.
20Keep my Sabbaths holy, that they may be a
sign between us. Then you will know that I
am the LORD your God."

21" 'But the children rebelled against me:
They did not follow my decrees, they were
not careful to keep my laws—although the
man who obeys them will live by them—and
they desecrated my Sabbaths. So I said I
would pour out my wrath on them and spend
my anger against them in the desert. 22But I
withheld my hand, and for the sake of my
name I did what would keep it from being
profaned in the eyes of the nations in whose
sight I had brought them out. 23Also with
uplifted hand I swore to them in the desert

[a]14 Or *from under its*

that I would disperse them among the nations and scatter them through the countries, 24because they had not obeyed my laws but had rejected my decrees and desecrated my Sabbaths, and their eyes ⌞lusted⌟ after their fathers' idols. 25I also gave them over to statutes that were not good and laws they could not live by; 26I let them become defiled through their gifts—the sacrifice of every firstborn[a]—that I might fill them with horror so they would know that I am the LORD.'

27"Therefore, son of man, speak to the people of Israel and say to them, 'This is what the Sovereign LORD says: In this also your fathers blasphemed me by forsaking me: 28When I brought them into the land I had sworn to give them and they saw any high hill or any leafy tree, there they offered their sacrifices, made offerings that provoked me to anger, presented their fragrant incense and poured out their drink offerings. 29Then I said to them: What is this high place you go to?' " (It is called Bamah[b] to this day.)

Judgment and Restoration

30"Therefore say to the house of Israel: 'This is what the Sovereign LORD says: Will you defile yourselves the way your fathers did and lust after their vile images? 31When you offer your gifts—the sacrifice of your sons in[c] the fire—you continue to defile yourselves with all your idols to this day. Am I to let you inquire of me, O house of Israel? As surely as I live, declares the Sovereign LORD, I will not let you inquire of me.

32" 'You say, "We want to be like the nations, like the peoples of the world, who serve wood and stone." But what you have in mind will never happen. 33As surely as I live, declares the Sovereign LORD, I will rule over you with a mighty hand and an outstretched arm and with outpoured wrath. 34I will bring you from the nations and gather you from the countries where you have been scattered—with a mighty hand and an outstretched arm and with outpoured wrath. 35I will bring you into the desert of the nations and there, face to face, I will execute judgment upon you. 36As I judged your fathers in the desert of the land of Egypt, so I will judge you, declares the Sovereign LORD. 37I will take note of you as you pass under my rod, and I will bring you into the bond of the covenant. 38I will purge you of those who revolt and rebel against me. Although I will bring them out of the land where they are living, yet they will not enter the land of Israel. Then you will know that I am the LORD.

39" 'As for you, O house of Israel, this is what the Sovereign LORD says: Go and serve your idols, every one of you! But afterward you will surely listen to me and no longer profane my holy name with your gifts and idols. 40For on my holy mountain, the high mountain of Israel, declares the Sovereign LORD, there in the land the entire house of Israel will serve me, and there I will accept them. There I will require your offerings and your choice gifts,[d] along with all your holy sacrifices. 41I will accept you as fragrant incense when I bring you out from the nations and gather you from the countries where you have been scattered, and I will show myself holy among you in the sight of the nations. 42Then you will know that I am the LORD, when I bring you into the land of Israel, the land I had sworn with uplifted hand to give to your fathers. 43There you will remember your conduct and all the actions by which you have defiled yourselves, and you will loathe yourselves for all the evil you have done. 44You will know that I am the LORD, when I deal with you for my name's sake and not according to your evil ways and your corrupt practices, O house of Israel, declares the Sovereign LORD.' "

Prophecy Against the South

45The word of the LORD came to me: 46"Son of man, set your face toward the south; preach against the south and prophesy against the forest of the southland. 47Say to the southern forest: 'Hear the word of the LORD. This is what the Sovereign LORD says: I am about to set fire to you, and it will consume all your trees, both green and dry. The blazing flame will not be quenched, and every face from south to north will be scorched by it. 48Everyone will see that I the LORD have kindled it; it will not be quenched.' "

49Then I said, "Ah, Sovereign LORD! They are saying of me, 'Isn't he just telling parables?' "

Babylon, God's Sword of Judgment

21 The word of the LORD came to me: 2"Son of man, set your face against

[a]26 Or *—making every firstborn pass through ⌞the fire⌟* [b]29 *Bamah* means *high place.* [c]31 Or *—making your sons pass through* [d]40 Or *and the gifts of your firstfruits*

Jerusalem and preach against the sanctuary. Prophesy against the land of Israel 3and
say to her: 'This is what the LORD says: I am
against you. I will draw my sword from its
scabbard and cut off from you both the righteous and the wicked. 4Because I am going to
cut off the righteous and the wicked, my
sword will be unsheathed against everyone
from south to north. 5Then all people will
know that I the LORD have drawn my sword
from its scabbard; it will not return again.'
6"Therefore groan, son of man! Groan before them with broken heart and bitter grief.
7And when they ask you, 'Why are you
groaning?' you shall say, 'Because of the
news that is coming. Every heart will melt
and every hand go limp; every spirit will
become faint and every knee become as
weak as water.' It is coming! It will surely take
place, declares the Sovereign LORD."
8The word of the LORD came to me: 9"Son
of man, prophesy and say, 'This is what the
Lord says:

" 'A sword, a sword,
sharpened and polished—
10sharpened for the slaughter,
polished to flash like lightning!

" 'Shall we rejoice in the scepter of my son
⌊Judah⌋? The sword despises every such
stick.

11" 'The sword is appointed to be polished,
to be grasped with the hand;
it is sharpened and polished,
made ready for the hand of the slayer.
12Cry out and wail, son of man,
for it is against my people;
it is against all the princes of Israel.
They are thrown to the sword
along with my people.
Therefore beat your breast.

13" 'Testing will surely come. And what if
the scepter ⌊of Judah⌋, which the sword despises, does not continue? declares the Sovereign LORD.'

14"So then, son of man, prophesy
and strike your hands together.
Let the sword strike twice,
even three times.
It is a sword for slaughter—
a sword for great slaughter,
closing in on them from every side.
15So that hearts may melt
and the fallen be many,
I have stationed the sword for slaughter[a]
at all their gates.
Oh! It is made to flash like lightning,
it is grasped for slaughter.
16O sword, slash to the right,
then to the left,
wherever your blade is turned.
17I too will strike my hands together,
and my wrath will subside.
I the LORD have spoken."

18The word of the LORD came to me: 19"Son
of man, mark out two roads for the sword of
the king of Babylon to take, both starting
from the same country. Make a signpost
where the road branches off to the city.
20Mark out one road for the sword to come
against Rabbah of the Ammonites and another against Judah and fortified Jerusalem.
21For the king of Babylon will stop at the fork
in the road, at the junction of the two roads,
to seek an omen: He will cast lots with arrows, he will consult his idols, he will examine the liver. 22Into his right hand will come
the lot for Jerusalem, where he is to set up
battering rams, to give the command to
slaughter, to sound the battle cry, to set battering rams against the gates, to build a ramp
and to erect siege works. 23It will seem like a
false omen to those who have sworn allegiance to him, but he will remind them of their
guilt and take them captive.
24"Therefore this is what the Sovereign
LORD says: 'Because you people have
brought to mind your guilt by your open rebellion, revealing your sins in all that you
do—because you have done this, you will be
taken captive.
25" 'O profane and wicked prince of Israel,
whose day has come, whose time of punishment has reached its climax, 26this is what
the Sovereign LORD says: Take off the turban, remove the crown. It will not be as it
was: The lowly will be exalted and the exalted will be brought low. 27A ruin! A ruin! I will
make it a ruin! It will not be restored until he
comes to whom it rightfully belongs; to him I
will give it.'
28"And you, son of man, prophesy and
say, 'This is what the Sovereign LORD says
about the Ammonites and their insults:

" 'A sword, a sword,
drawn for the slaughter,
polished to consume
and to flash like lightning!

[a]15 Septuagint; the meaning of the Hebrew for this word is uncertain.

29Despite false visions concerning you
and lying divinations about you,
it will be laid on the necks
of the wicked who are to be slain,
whose day has come,
whose time of punishment has reached
its climax.
30Return the sword to its scabbard.
In the place where you were created,
in the land of your ancestry,
I will judge you.
31I will pour out my wrath upon you
and breathe out my fiery anger against
you;
I will hand you over to brutal men,
men skilled in destruction.
32You will be fuel for the fire,
your blood will be shed in your land,
you will be remembered no more;
for I the LORD have spoken.' "

Jerusalem's Sins

22 The word of the LORD came to me:
2"Son of man, will you judge her? Will
you judge this city of bloodshed? Then confront her with all her detestable practices
3and say: 'This is what the Sovereign LORD
says: O city that brings on herself doom by
shedding blood in her midst and defiles herself by making idols, 4you have become
guilty because of the blood you have shed
and have become defiled by the idols you
have made. You have brought your days to a
close, and the end of your years has come.
Therefore I will make you an object of scorn
to the nations and a laughingstock to all the
countries. 5Those who are near and those
who are far away will mock you, O infamous
city, full of turmoil.
6" 'See how each of the princes of Israel
who are in you uses his power to shed blood.
7In you they have treated father and mother
with contempt; in you they have oppressed
the alien and mistreated the fatherless and
the widow. 8You have despised my holy
things and desecrated my Sabbaths. 9In you
are slanderous men bent on shedding blood;
in you are those who eat at the mountain
shrines and commit lewd acts. 10In you are
those who dishonor their fathers' bed; in you
are those who violate women during their
period, when they are ceremonially unclean.
11In you one man commits a detestable offense with his neighbor's wife, another
shamefully defiles his daughter-in-law, and
another violates his sister, his own father's
daughter. 12In you men accept bribes to shed
blood; you take usury and excessive interest[a] and make unjust gain from your neighbors by extortion. And you have forgotten
me, declares the Sovereign LORD.
13" 'I will surely strike my hands together at
the unjust gain you have made and at the
blood you have shed in your midst. 14Will
your courage endure or your hands be
strong in the day I deal with you? I the LORD
have spoken, and I will do it. 15I will disperse
you among the nations and scatter you
through the countries; and I will put an end to
your uncleanness. 16When you have been
defiled[b] in the eyes of the nations, you will
know that I am the LORD.' "
17Then the word of the LORD came to me:
18"Son of man, the house of Israel has
become dross to me; all of them are the
copper, tin, iron and lead left inside a furnace. They are but the dross of silver.
19Therefore this is what the Sovereign LORD
says: 'Because you have all become dross, I
will gather you into Jerusalem. 20As men
gather silver, copper, iron, lead and tin into a
furnace to melt it with a fiery blast, so will I
gather you in my anger and my wrath and put
you inside the city and melt you. 21I will gather you and I will blow on you with my fiery
wrath, and you will be melted inside her. 22As
silver is melted in a furnace, so you will be
melted inside her, and you will know that I the
LORD have poured out my wrath upon you.' "
23Again the word of the LORD came to me:
24"Son of man, say to the land, 'You are a
land that has had no rain or showers[c] in the
day of wrath.' 25There is a conspiracy of her
princes[d] within her like a roaring lion tearing
its prey; they devour people, take treasures
and precious things and make many widows
within her. 26Her priests do violence to my
law and profane my holy things; they do not
distinguish between the holy and the common; they teach that there is no difference
between the unclean and the clean; and they
shut their eyes to the keeping of my Sabbaths, so that I am profaned among them.
27Her officials within her are like wolves tearing their prey; they shed blood and kill people
to make unjust gain. 28Her prophets whitewash these deeds for them by false visions
and lying divinations. They say, 'This is what

[a]12 Or *usury and interest* [b]16 Or *When I have allotted you your inheritance* [c]24 Septuagint; Hebrew *has not been cleansed or rained on* [d]25 Septuagint; Hebrew *prophets*

the Sovereign LORD says'—when the LORD has not spoken. [29]The people of the land practice extortion and commit robbery; they oppress the poor and needy and mistreat the alien, denying them justice.

[30]"I looked for a man among them who would build up the wall and stand before me in the gap on behalf of the land so I would not have to destroy it, but I found none. [31]So I will pour out my wrath on them and consume them with my fiery anger, bringing down on their own heads all they have done, declares the Sovereign LORD."

Two Adulterous Sisters

23 The word of the LORD came to me: [2]"Son of man, there were two women, daughters of the same mother. [3]They became prostitutes in Egypt, engaging in prostitution from their youth. In that land their breasts were fondled and their virgin bosoms caressed. [4]The older was named Oholah, and her sister was Oholibah. They were mine and gave birth to sons and daughters. Oholah is Samaria, and Oholibah is Jerusalem.

[5]"Oholah engaged in prostitution while she was still mine; and she lusted after her lovers, the Assyrians—warriors [6]clothed in blue, governors and commanders, all of them handsome young men, and mounted horsemen. [7]She gave herself as a prostitute to all the elite of the Assyrians and defiled herself with all the idols of everyone she lusted after. [8]She did not give up the prostitution she began in Egypt, when during her youth men slept with her, caressed her virgin bosom and poured out their lust upon her.

[9]"Therefore I handed her over to her lovers, the Assyrians, for whom she lusted. [10]They stripped her naked, took away her sons and daughters and killed her with the sword. She became a byword among women, and punishment was inflicted on her.

[11]"Her sister Oholibah saw this, yet in her lust and prostitution she was more depraved than her sister. [12]She too lusted after the Assyrians—governors and commanders, warriors in full dress, mounted horsemen, all handsome young men. [13]I saw that she too defiled herself; both of them went the same way.

[14]"But she carried her prostitution still further. She saw men portrayed on a wall, figures of Chaldeans[a] portrayed in red, [15]with belts around their waists and flowing turbans on their heads; all of them looked like Babylonian chariot officers, natives of Chaldea.[b] [16]As soon as she saw them, she lusted after them and sent messengers to them in Chaldea. [17]Then the Babylonians came to her, to the bed of love, and in their lust they defiled her. After she had been defiled by them, she turned away from them in disgust. [18]When she carried on her prostitution openly and exposed her nakedness, I turned away from her in disgust, just as I had turned away from her sister. [19]Yet she became more and more promiscuous as she recalled the days of her youth, when she was a prostitute in Egypt. [20]There she lusted after her lovers, whose genitals were like those of donkeys and whose emission was like that of horses. [21]So you longed for the lewdness of your youth, when in Egypt your bosom was caressed and your young breasts fondled.[c]

[22]"Therefore, Oholibah, this is what the Sovereign LORD says: I will stir up your lovers against you, those you turned away from in disgust, and I will bring them against you from every side— [23]the Babylonians and all the Chaldeans, the men of Pekod and Shoa and Koa, and all the Assyrians with them, handsome young men, all of them governors and commanders, chariot officers and men of high rank, all mounted on horses. [24]They will come against you with weapons,[d] chariots and wagons and with a throng of people; they will take up positions against you on every side with large and small shields and with helmets. I will turn you over to them for punishment, and they will punish you according to their standards. [25]I will direct my jealous anger against you, and they will deal with you in fury. They will cut off your noses and your ears, and those of you who are left will fall by the sword. They will take away your sons and daughters, and those of you who are left will be consumed by fire. [26]They will also strip you of your clothes and take your fine jewelry. [27]So I will put a stop to the lewdness and prostitution you began in Egypt. You will not look on these things with longing or remember Egypt anymore.

[28]"For this is what the Sovereign LORD says: I am about to hand you over to those you hate, to those you turned away from in

[a]*14* Or *Babylonians* [b]*15* Or *Babylonia;* also in verse 16 [c]*21* Syriac (see also verse 3); Hebrew *caressed because of your young breasts* [d]*24* The meaning of the Hebrew for this word is uncertain.

disgust. 29They will deal with you in hatred
and take away everything you have worked
for. They will leave you naked and bare, and
the shame of your prostitution will be exposed. Your lewdness and promiscuity
30have brought this upon you, because you
lusted after the nations and defiled yourself
with their idols. 31You have gone the way of
your sister; so I will put her cup into your
hand.
32"This is what the Sovereign LORD says:

"You will drink your sister's cup,
a cup large and deep;
it will bring scorn and derision,
for it holds so much.
33You will be filled with drunkenness and
sorrow,
the cup of ruin and desolation,
the cup of your sister Samaria.
34You will drink it and drain it dry;
you will dash it to pieces
and tear your breasts.

I have spoken, declares the Sovereign LORD.

35"Therefore this is what the Sovereign
LORD says: Since you have forgotten me and
thrust me behind your back, you must bear
the consequences of your lewdness and
prostitution."
36The LORD said to me: "Son of man, will
you judge Oholah and Oholibah? Then confront them with their detestable practices,
37for they have committed adultery and
blood is on their hands. They committed
adultery with their idols; they even sacrificed
their children, whom they bore to me,[a] as
food for them. 38They have also done this to
me: At that same time they defiled my sanctuary and desecrated my Sabbaths. 39On the
very day they sacrificed their children to their
idols, they entered my sanctuary and desecrated it. That is what they did in my house.
40"They even sent messengers for men
who came from far away, and when they
arrived you bathed yourself for them, painted
your eyes and put on your jewelry. 41You sat
on an elegant couch, with a table spread
before it on which you had placed the incense and oil that belonged to me.
42"The noise of a carefree crowd was
around her; Sabeans[b] were brought from the
desert along with men from the rabble, and
they put bracelets on the arms of the woman
and her sister and beautiful crowns on their
heads. 43Then I said about the one worn out
by adultery, 'Now let them use her as a prostitute, for that is all she is.' 44And they slept
with her. As men sleep with a prostitute, so
they slept with those lewd women, Oholah
and Oholibah. 45But righteous men will sentence them to the punishment of women who
commit adultery and shed blood, because
they are adulterous and blood is on their
hands.
46"This is what the Sovereign LORD says:
Bring a mob against them and give them
over to terror and plunder. 47The mob will
stone them and cut them down with their
swords; they will kill their sons and daughters and burn down their houses.
48"So I will put an end to lewdness in the
land, that all women may take warning and
not imitate you. 49You will suffer the penalty
for your lewdness and bear the consequences of your sins of idolatry. Then you
will know that I am the Sovereign LORD."

The Cooking Pot

24 In the ninth year, in the tenth month
on the tenth day, the word of the LORD
came to me: 2"Son of man, record this date,
this very date, because the king of Babylon
has laid siege to Jerusalem this very day.
3Tell this rebellious house a parable and say
to them: 'This is what the Sovereign LORD
says:

" 'Put on the cooking pot; put it on
and pour water into it.
4Put into it the pieces of meat,
all the choice pieces—the leg and the
shoulder.
Fill it with the best of these bones;
5 take the pick of the flock.
Pile wood beneath it for the bones;
bring it to a boil
and cook the bones in it.

6" 'For this is what the Sovereign LORD says:

" 'Woe to the city of bloodshed,
to the pot now encrusted,
whose deposit will not go away!
Empty it piece by piece
without casting lots for them.

7" 'For the blood she shed is in her midst:
She poured it on the bare rock;
she did not pour it on the ground,
where the dust would cover it.
8To stir up wrath and take revenge
I put her blood on the bare rock,

[a]37 Or *even made the children they bore to me pass through* ⌊*the fire*⌋ [b]42 Or *drunkards*

so that it would not be covered.
9" 'Therefore this is what the Sovereign LORD
says:

" 'Woe to the city of bloodshed!
I, too, will pile the wood high.
10So heap on the wood
and kindle the fire.
Cook the meat well,
mixing in the spices;
and let the bones be charred.
11Then set the empty pot on the coals
till it becomes hot and its copper glows
so its impurities may be melted
and its deposit burned away.
12It has frustrated all efforts;
its heavy deposit has not been
removed,
not even by fire.

13" 'Now your impurity is lewdness. Because I tried to cleanse you but you would
not be cleansed from your impurity, you will
not be clean again until my wrath against you
has subsided.

14" 'I the LORD have spoken. The time has
come for me to act. I will not hold back; I will
not have pity, nor will I relent. You will be
judged according to your conduct and your
actions, declares the Sovereign LORD.' "

Ezekiel's Wife Dies

15The word of the LORD came to me: 16"Son
of man, with one blow I am about to take
away from you the delight of your eyes. Yet
do not lament or weep or shed any tears.
17Groan quietly; do not mourn for the dead.
Keep your turban fastened and your sandals
on your feet; do not cover the lower part of
your face or eat the customary food ⌊of
mourners⌋."

18So I spoke to the people in the morning,
and in the evening my wife died. The next
morning I did as I had been commanded.

19Then the people asked me, "Won't you
tell us what these things have to do with us?"

20So I said to them, "The word of the LORD
came to me: 21Say to the house of Israel,
'This is what the Sovereign LORD says: I am
about to desecrate my sanctuary—the
stronghold in which you take pride, the delight of your eyes, the object of your affection. The sons and daughters you left behind
will fall by the sword. 22And you will do as I
have done. You will not cover the lower part
of your face or eat the customary food ⌊of
mourners⌋. 23You will keep your turbans on
your heads and your sandals on your feet.
You will not mourn or weep but will waste
away because of[a] your sins and groan
among yourselves. 24Ezekiel will be a sign to
you; you will do just as he has done. When
this happens, you will know that I am the
Sovereign LORD.'

25"And you, son of man, on the day I take
away their stronghold, their joy and glory, the
delight of their eyes, their heart's desire, and
their sons and daughters as well— 26on that
day a fugitive will come to tell you the news.
27At that time your mouth will be opened; you
will speak with him and will no longer be
silent. So you will be a sign to them, and they
will know that I am the LORD."

A Prophecy Against Ammon

25 The word of the LORD came to me:
2"Son of man, set your face against
the Ammonites and prophesy against them.
3Say to them, 'Hear the word of the Sovereign LORD. This is what the Sovereign LORD
says: Because you said "Aha!" over my
sanctuary when it was desecrated and over
the land of Israel when it was laid waste and
over the people of Judah when they went
into exile, 4therefore I am going to give you to
the people of the East as a possession. They
will set up their camps and pitch their tents
among you; they will eat your fruit and drink
your milk. 5I will turn Rabbah into a pasture
for camels and Ammon into a resting place
for sheep. Then you will know that I am the
LORD. 6For this is what the Sovereign LORD
says: Because you have clapped your hands
and stamped your feet, rejoicing with all the
malice of your heart against the land of Israel, 7therefore I will stretch out my hand
against you and give you as plunder to the
nations. I will cut you off from the nations and
exterminate you from the countries. I will destroy you, and you will know that I am the
LORD.' "

A Prophecy Against Moab

8"This is what the Sovereign LORD says:
'Because Moab and Seir said, "Look, the
house of Judah has become like all the other
nations," 9therefore I will expose the flank of
Moab, beginning at its frontier towns—Beth
Jeshimoth, Baal Meon and Kiriathaim—the
glory of that land. 10I will give Moab along

[a]23 Or *away in*

with the Ammonites to the people of the East
as a possession, so that the Ammonites will
not be remembered among the nations;
11and I will inflict punishment on Moab. Then
they will know that I am the LORD.' "

A Prophecy Against Edom

12"This is what the Sovereign LORD says:
'Because Edom took revenge on the house
of Judah and became very guilty by doing so,
13therefore this is what the Sovereign LORD
says: I will stretch out my hand against Edom
and kill its men and their animals. I will lay it
waste, and from Teman to Dedan they will
fall by the sword. 14I will take vengeance on
Edom by the hand of my people Israel, and
they will deal with Edom in accordance with
my anger and my wrath; they will know my
vengeance, declares the Sovereign LORD.' "

A Prophecy Against Philistia

15"This is what the Sovereign LORD says:
'Because the Philistines acted in vengeance
and took revenge with malice in their hearts,
and with ancient hostility sought to destroy
Judah, 16therefore this is what the Sovereign
LORD says: I am about to stretch out my hand
against the Philistines, and I will cut off the
Kerethites and destroy those remaining
along the coast. 17I will carry out great vengeance on them and punish them in my
wrath. Then they will know that I am the LORD,
when I take vengeance on them.' "

A Prophecy Against Tyre

26 In the eleventh year, on the first day
of the month, the word of the LORD
came to me: 2"Son of man, because Tyre
has said of Jerusalem, 'Aha! The gate to the
nations is broken, and its doors have swung
open to me; now that she lies in ruins I will
prosper,' 3therefore this is what the Sovereign LORD says: I am against you, O Tyre,
and I will bring many nations against you, like
the sea casting up its waves. 4They will destroy the walls of Tyre and pull down her
towers; I will scrape away her rubble and
make her a bare rock. 5Out in the sea she will
become a place to spread fishnets, for I have
spoken, declares the Sovereign LORD. She
will become plunder for the nations, 6and her
settlements on the mainland will be ravaged
by the sword. Then they will know that I am
the LORD.
7"For this is what the Sovereign LORD says:
From the north I am going to bring against
Tyre Nebuchadnezzar[a] king of Babylon,
king of kings, with horses and chariots, with
horsemen and a great army. 8He will ravage
your settlements on the mainland with the
sword; he will set up siege works against
you, build a ramp up to your walls and raise
his shields against you. 9He will direct the
blows of his battering rams against your
walls and demolish your towers with his
weapons. 10His horses will be so many that
they will cover you with dust. Your walls will
tremble at the noise of the war horses, wagons and chariots when he enters your gates
as men enter a city whose walls have been
broken through. 11The hoofs of his horses
will trample all your streets; he will kill your
people with the sword, and your strong pillars will fall to the ground. 12They will plunder
your wealth and loot your merchandise; they
will break down your walls and demolish
your fine houses and throw your stones, timber and rubble into the sea. 13I will put an end
to your noisy songs, and the music of your
harps will be heard no more. 14I will make
you a bare rock, and you will become a place
to spread fishnets. You will never be rebuilt,
for I the LORD have spoken, declares the Sovereign LORD.
15"This is what the Sovereign LORD says to
Tyre: Will not the coastlands tremble at the
sound of your fall, when the wounded groan
and the slaughter takes place in you? 16Then
all the princes of the coast will step down
from their thrones and lay aside their robes
and take off their embroidered garments.
Clothed with terror, they will sit on the
ground, trembling every moment, appalled
at you. 17Then they will take up a lament
concerning you and say to you:

" 'How you are destroyed, O city of
renown,
peopled by men of the sea!
You were a power on the seas,
you and your citizens;
you put your terror
on all who lived there.
18Now the coastlands tremble
on the day of your fall;
the islands in the sea
are terrified at your collapse.'

19"This is what the Sovereign LORD says:
When I make you a desolate city, like cities
no longer inhabited, and when I bring the

a7 Hebrew *Nebuchadrezzar,* of which *Nebuchadnezzar* is a variant; here and often in Ezekiel and Jeremiah

ocean depths over you and its vast waters
cover you, 20 then I will bring you down with
those who go down to the pit, to the people of
long ago. I will make you dwell in the earth
below, as in ancient ruins, with those who go
down to the pit, and you will not return or take
your place[a] in the land of the living. 21 I will
bring you to a horrible end and you will be no
more. You will be sought, but you will never
again be found, declares the Sovereign
LORD."

A Lament for Tyre

27 The word of the LORD came to me:
2 "Son of man, take up a lament concerning Tyre. 3 Say to Tyre, situated at the
gateway to the sea, merchant of peoples on
many coasts, 'This is what the Sovereign
LORD says:

" 'You say, O Tyre,
  "I am perfect in beauty."
4 Your domain was on the high seas;
  your builders brought your beauty to
    perfection.
5 They made all your timbers
  of pine trees from Senir[b];
they took a cedar from Lebanon
  to make a mast for you.
6 Of oaks from Bashan
  they made your oars;
of cypress wood[c] from the coasts of
    Cyprus[d]
  they made your deck, inlaid with ivory.
7 Fine embroidered linen from Egypt was
    your sail
  and served as your banner;
your awnings were of blue and purple
  from the coasts of Elishah.
8 Men of Sidon and Arvad were your
    oarsmen;
  your skilled men, O Tyre, were aboard
    as your seamen.
9 Veteran craftsmen of Gebal[e] were on
    board
  as shipwrights to caulk your seams.
All the ships of the sea and their sailors
  came alongside to trade for your wares.

10 " 'Men of Persia, Lydia and Put
  served as soldiers in your army.
They hung their shields and helmets on
    your walls,
  bringing you splendor.
11 Men of Arvad and Helech
  manned your walls on every side;
men of Gammad
  were in your towers.
They hung their shields around your
    walls;
  they brought your beauty to perfection.

12 " 'Tarshish did business with you because of your great wealth of goods; they
exchanged silver, iron, tin and lead for your
merchandise.
13 " 'Greece, Tubal and Meshech traded
with you; they exchanged slaves and articles
of bronze for your wares.
14 " 'Men of Beth Togarmah exchanged
work horses, war horses and mules for your
merchandise.
15 " 'The men of Rhodes[f] traded with you,
and many coastlands were your customers;
they paid you with ivory tusks and ebony.
16 " 'Aram[g] did business with you because
of your many products; they exchanged turquoise, purple fabric, embroidered work, fine
linen, coral and rubies for your merchandise.
17 " 'Judah and Israel traded with you; they
exchanged wheat from Minnith and confec-
tions,[h] honey, oil and balm for your wares.
18 " 'Damascus, because of your many
products and great wealth of goods, did
business with you in wine from Helbon and
wool from Zahar.
19 " 'Danites and Greeks from Uzal bought
your merchandise; they exchanged wrought
iron, cassia and calamus for your wares.
20 " 'Dedan traded in saddle blankets with
you.
21 " 'Arabia and all the princes of Kedar
were your customers; they did business with
you in lambs, rams and goats.
22 " 'The merchants of Sheba and Raamah
traded with you; for your merchandise they
exchanged the finest of all kinds of spices
and precious stones, and gold.
23 " 'Haran, Canneh and Eden and merchants of Sheba, Asshur and Kilmad traded
with you. 24 In your marketplace they traded
with you beautiful garments, blue fabric, embroidered work and multicolored rugs with
cords twisted and tightly knotted.

25 " 'The ships of Tarshish serve
  as carriers for your wares.
You are filled with heavy cargo

[a]20 Septuagint; Hebrew *return, and I will give glory* [b]5 That is, Hermon [c]6 Targum; the Masoretic Text has a different division of the consonants. [d]6 Hebrew *Kittim* [e]9 That is, Byblos [f]15 Septuagint; Hebrew *Dedan* [g]16 Most Hebrew manuscripts; some Hebrew manuscripts and Syriac *Edom* [h]17 The meaning of the Hebrew for this word is uncertain.

in the heart of the sea.
26Your oarsmen take you
out to the high seas.
But the east wind will break you to pieces
in the heart of the sea.
27Your wealth, merchandise and wares,
your mariners, seamen and
shipwrights,
your merchants and all your soldiers,
and everyone else on board
will sink into the heart of the sea
on the day of your shipwreck.
28The shorelands will quake
when your seamen cry out.
29All who handle the oars
will abandon their ships;
the mariners and all the seamen
will stand on the shore.
30They will raise their voice
and cry bitterly over you;
they will sprinkle dust on their heads
and roll in ashes.
31They will shave their heads because of
you
and will put on sackcloth.
They will weep over you with anguish of
soul
and with bitter mourning.
32As they wail and mourn over you,
they will take up a lament concerning
you:
"Who was ever silenced like Tyre,
surrounded by the sea?"
33When your merchandise went out on the
seas,
you satisfied many nations;
with your great wealth and your wares
you enriched the kings of the earth.
34Now you are shattered by the sea
in the depths of the waters;
your wares and all your company
have gone down with you.
35All who live in the coastlands
are appalled at you;
their kings shudder with horror
and their faces are distorted with fear.
36The merchants among the nations hiss at
you;
you have come to a horrible end
and will be no more.' "

A Prophecy Against the King of Tyre

28 The word of the LORD came to me:
2"Son of man, say to the ruler of Tyre,
'This is what the Sovereign LORD says:

" 'In the pride of your heart
you say, "I am a god;
I sit on the throne of a god
in the heart of the seas."
But you are a man and not a god,
though you think you are as wise as a
god.
3Are you wiser than Daniel[a]?
Is no secret hidden from you?
4By your wisdom and understanding
you have gained wealth for yourself
and amassed gold and silver
in your treasuries.
5By your great skill in trading
you have increased your wealth,
and because of your wealth
your heart has grown proud.

6" 'Therefore this is what the Sovereign
LORD says:

" 'Because you think you are wise,
as wise as a god,
7I am going to bring foreigners against
you,
the most ruthless of nations;
they will draw their swords against your
beauty and wisdom
and pierce your shining splendor.
8They will bring you down to the pit,
and you will die a violent death
in the heart of the seas.
9Will you then say, "I am a god,"
in the presence of those who kill you?
You will be but a man, not a god,
in the hands of those who slay you.
10You will die the death of the
uncircumcised
at the hands of foreigners.

I have spoken, declares the Sovereign
LORD.' "

11The word of the LORD came to me: 12"Son
of man, take up a lament concerning the king
of Tyre and say to him: 'This is what the
Sovereign LORD says:

" 'You were the model of perfection,
full of wisdom and perfect in beauty.
13You were in Eden,
the garden of God;
every precious stone adorned you:
ruby, topaz and emerald,
chrysolite, onyx and jasper,

[a]3 Or *Danel;* the Hebrew spelling may suggest a person other than the prophet Daniel.

sapphire,[a] turquoise and beryl.[b]
Your settings and mountings[c] were made of gold;
on the day you were created they were prepared.
14 You were anointed as a guardian cherub,
for so I ordained you.
You were on the holy mount of God;
you walked among the fiery stones.
15 You were blameless in your ways
from the day you were created
till wickedness was found in you.
16 Through your widespread trade
you were filled with violence,
and you sinned.
So I drove you in disgrace from the mount of God,
and I expelled you, O guardian cherub,
from among the fiery stones.
17 Your heart became proud
on account of your beauty,
and you corrupted your wisdom
because of your splendor.
So I threw you to the earth;
I made a spectacle of you before kings.
18 By your many sins and dishonest trade
you have desecrated your sanctuaries.
So I made a fire come out from you,
and it consumed you,
and I reduced you to ashes on the ground
in the sight of all who were watching.
19 All the nations who knew you
are appalled at you;
you have come to a horrible end
and will be no more.' "

A Prophecy Against Sidon

20 The word of the LORD came to me: 21 "Son
of man, set your face against Sidon; prophesy against her 22 and say: 'This is what the
Sovereign LORD says:

" 'I am against you, O Sidon,
and I will gain glory within you.
They will know that I am the LORD,
when I inflict punishment on her
and show myself holy within her.
23 I will send a plague upon her
and make blood flow in her streets.
The slain will fall within her,
with the sword against her on every side.
Then they will know that I am the LORD.

24 " 'No longer will the people of Israel have
malicious neighbors who are painful briers
and sharp thorns. Then they will know that I
am the Sovereign LORD.

25 " 'This is what the Sovereign LORD says:
When I gather the people of Israel from the
nations where they have been scattered, I
will show myself holy among them in the
sight of the nations. Then they will live in their
own land, which I gave to my servant Jacob.
26 They will live there in safety and will build
houses and plant vineyards; they will live in
safety when I inflict punishment on all their
neighbors who maligned them. Then they
will know that I am the LORD their God.' "

A Prophecy Against Egypt

29 In the tenth year, in the tenth month
on the twelfth day, the word of the
LORD came to me: 2 "Son of man, set your
face against Pharaoh king of Egypt and
prophesy against him and against all Egypt.
3 Speak to him and say: 'This is what the
Sovereign LORD says:

" 'I am against you, Pharaoh king of Egypt,
you great monster lying among your streams.
You say, "The Nile is mine;
I made it for myself."
4 But I will put hooks in your jaws
and make the fish of your streams stick to your scales.
I will pull you out from among your streams,
with all the fish sticking to your scales.
5 I will leave you in the desert,
you and all the fish of your streams.
You will fall on the open field
and not be gathered or picked up.
I will give you as food
to the beasts of the earth and the birds of the air.

6 Then all who live in Egypt will know that I am
the LORD.

" 'You have been a staff of reed for the
house of Israel. 7 When they grasped you
with their hands, you splintered and you tore
open their shoulders; when they leaned on
you, you broke and their backs were
wrenched.[d]

[a] 13 Or *lapis lazuli* [b] 13 The precise identification of some of these precious stones is uncertain. [c] 13 The meaning of the Hebrew for this phrase is uncertain. [d] 7 Syriac (see also Septuagint and Vulgate); Hebrew *and you caused their backs to stand*

8" 'Therefore this is what the Sovereign
LORD says: I will bring a sword against you
and kill your men and their animals. 9Egypt
will become a desolate wasteland. Then they
will know that I am the LORD.

" 'Because you said, "The Nile is mine; I
made it," 10therefore I am against you and
against your streams, and I will make the
land of Egypt a ruin and a desolate waste
from Migdol to Aswan, as far as the border of
Cush.[a] 11No foot of man or animal will pass
through it; no one will live there for forty
years. 12I will make the land of Egypt desolate among devastated lands, and her cities
will lie desolate forty years among ruined
cities. And I will disperse the Egyptians
among the nations and scatter them through
the countries.

13" 'Yet this is what the Sovereign LORD
says: At the end of forty years I will gather the
Egyptians from the nations where they were
scattered. 14I will bring them back from captivity and return them to Upper Egypt,[b] the
land of their ancestry. There they will be a
lowly kingdom. 15It will be the lowliest of kingdoms and will never again exalt itself above
the other nations. I will make it so weak that it
will never again rule over the nations.
16Egypt will no longer be a source of confidence for the people of Israel but will be a
reminder of their sin in turning to her for help.
Then they will know that I am the Sovereign
LORD.' "

17In the twenty-seventh year, in the first
month on the first day, the word of the LORD
came to me: 18"Son of man, Nebuchadnezzar king of Babylon drove his army in a hard
campaign against Tyre; every head was
rubbed bare and every shoulder made raw.
Yet he and his army got no reward from the
campaign he led against Tyre. 19Therefore
this is what the Sovereign LORD says: I am
going to give Egypt to Nebuchadnezzar king
of Babylon, and he will carry off its wealth. He
will loot and plunder the land as pay for his
army. 20I have given him Egypt as a reward
for his efforts because he and his army did it
for me, declares the Sovereign LORD.

21"On that day I will make a horn[c] grow for
the house of Israel, and I will open your
mouth among them. Then they will know that
I am the LORD."

A Lament for Egypt

30 The word of the LORD came to me:
2"Son of man, prophesy and say:
'This is what the Sovereign LORD says:

" 'Wail and say,
  "Alas for that day!"
3For the day is near,
  the day of the LORD is near—
a day of clouds,
  a time of doom for the nations.
4A sword will come against Egypt,
  and anguish will come upon Cush.[d]
When the slain fall in Egypt,
  her wealth will be carried away
  and her foundations torn down.

5Cush and Put, Lydia and all Arabia, Libya[e]
and the people of the covenant land will fall
by the sword along with Egypt.

6" 'This is what the LORD says:

" 'The allies of Egypt will fall
  and her proud strength will fail.
From Migdol to Aswan
  they will fall by the sword within her,
    declares the Sovereign LORD.
7" 'They will be desolate
  among desolate lands,
and their cities will lie
  among ruined cities.
8Then they will know that I am the LORD,
  when I set fire to Egypt
  and all her helpers are crushed.

9" 'On that day messengers will go out
from me in ships to frighten Cush out of her
complacency. Anguish will take hold of them
on the day of Egypt's doom, for it is sure to
come.

10" 'This is what the Sovereign LORD says:

" 'I will put an end to the hordes of Egypt
  by the hand of Nebuchadnezzar king of
    Babylon.
11He and his army—the most ruthless of
    nations—
  will be brought in to destroy the land.
They will draw their swords against
    Egypt
  and fill the land with the slain.
12I will dry up the streams of the Nile
  and sell the land to evil men;
by the hand of foreigners

[a] 10 That is, the upper Nile region
[b] 14 Hebrew *to Pathros*
[c] 21 *Horn* here symbolizes strength.
[d] 4 That is, the upper Nile region; also in verses 5 and 9
[e] 5 Hebrew *Cub*

I will lay waste the land and everything
in it.

I the LORD have spoken.

13" 'This is what the Sovereign LORD says:

" 'I will destroy the idols
and put an end to the images in
Memphis.[a]
No longer will there be a prince in Egypt,
and I will spread fear throughout the
land.
14I will lay waste Upper Egypt,[b]
set fire to Zoan
and inflict punishment on Thebes.[c]
15I will pour out my wrath on Pelusium,[d]
the stronghold of Egypt,
and cut off the hordes of Thebes.
16I will set fire to Egypt;
Pelusium will writhe in agony.
Thebes will be taken by storm;
Memphis will be in constant distress.
17The young men of Heliopolis[e] and
Bubastis[f]
will fall by the sword,
and the cities themselves will go into
captivity.
18Dark will be the day at Tahpanhes
when I break the yoke of Egypt;
there her proud strength will come to
an end.
She will be covered with clouds,
and her villages will go into captivity.
19So I will inflict punishment on Egypt,
and they will know that I am the LORD.' "

20In the eleventh year, in the first month on
the seventh day, the word of the LORD came
to me: 21"Son of man, I have broken the arm
of Pharaoh king of Egypt. It has not been
bound up for healing or put in a splint so as to
become strong enough to hold a sword.
22Therefore this is what the Sovereign LORD
says: I am against Pharaoh king of Egypt. I
will break both his arms, the good arm as
well as the broken one, and make the sword
fall from his hand. 23I will disperse the Egyptians among the nations and scatter them
through the countries. 24I will strengthen the
arms of the king of Babylon and put my
sword in his hand, but I will break the arms of
Pharaoh, and he will groan before him like a
mortally wounded man. 25I will strengthen
the arms of the king of Babylon, but the arms
of Pharaoh will fall limp. Then they will know
that I am the LORD, when I put my sword into
the hand of the king of Babylon and he bran-
dishes it against Egypt. 26I will disperse the
Egyptians among the nations and scatter
them through the countries. Then they will
know that I am the LORD."

A Cedar in Lebanon

31 In the eleventh year, in the third
month on the first day, the word of the
LORD came to me: 2"Son of man, say to Pharaoh king of Egypt and to his hordes:

" 'Who can be compared with you in
majesty?
3Consider Assyria, once a cedar in
Lebanon,
with beautiful branches overshadowing
the forest;
it towered on high,
its top above the thick foliage.
4The waters nourished it,
deep springs made it grow tall;
their streams flowed
all around its base
and sent their channels
to all the trees of the field.
5So it towered higher
than all the trees of the field;
its boughs increased
and its branches grew long,
spreading because of abundant
waters.
6All the birds of the air
nested in its boughs,
all the beasts of the field
gave birth under its branches;
all the great nations
lived in its shade.
7It was majestic in beauty,
with its spreading boughs,
for its roots went down
to abundant waters.
8The cedars in the garden of God
could not rival it,
nor could the pine trees
equal its boughs,
nor could the plane trees
compare with its branches—
no tree in the garden of God
could match its beauty.
9I made it beautiful
with abundant branches,

[a]*13* Hebrew *Noph;* also in verse 16 [b]*14* Hebrew *waste Pathros* [c]*14* Hebrew *No;* also in verses 15 and 16 [d]*15* Hebrew *Sin;* also in verse 16 [e]*17* Hebrew *Awen* (or *On*) [f]*17* Hebrew *Pi Beseth*

the envy of all the trees of Eden
in the garden of God.

10“ 'Therefore this is what the Sovereign
LORD says: Because it towered on high, lifting
its top above the thick foliage, and because it
was proud of its height, 11I handed it over to
the ruler of the nations, for him to deal with
according to its wickedness. I cast it aside,
12and the most ruthless of foreign nations cut
it down and left it. Its boughs fell on the
mountains and in all the valleys; its branches
lay broken in all the ravines of the land. All
the nations of the earth came out from under
its shade and left it. 13All the birds of the air
settled on the fallen tree, and all the beasts of
the field were among its branches. 14There-
fore no other trees by the waters are ever to
tower proudly on high, lifting their tops above
the thick foliage. No other trees so well-
watered are ever to reach such a height; they
are all destined for death, for the earth
below, among mortal men, with those who
go down to the pit.

15“ 'This is what the Sovereign LORD says:
On the day it was brought down to the grave[a]
I covered the deep springs with mourning for
it; I held back its streams, and its abundant
waters were restrained. Because of it I
clothed Lebanon with gloom, and all the
trees of the field withered away. 16I made the
nations tremble at the sound of its fall when I
brought it down to the grave with those who
go down to the pit. Then all the trees of Eden,
the choicest and best of Lebanon, all the
trees that were well-watered, were consoled
in the earth below. 17Those who lived in its
shade, its allies among the nations, had also
gone down to the grave with it, joining those
killed by the sword.

18“ 'Which of the trees of Eden can be
compared with you in splendor and majesty?
Yet you, too, will be brought down with the
trees of Eden to the earth below; you will lie
among the uncircumcised, with those killed
by the sword.

“ 'This is Pharaoh and all his hordes, declares the Sovereign LORD.' ”

A Lament for Pharaoh

32 In the twelfth year, in the twelfth
month on the first day, the word of the
LORD came to me: 2“Son of man, take up a
lament concerning Pharaoh king of Egypt
and say to him:

“ 'You are like a lion among the nations;
you are like a monster in the seas
thrashing about in your streams,
churning the water with your feet
and muddying the streams.

3“ 'This is what the Sovereign LORD says:

“ 'With a great throng of people
I will cast my net over you,
and they will haul you up in my net.
4I will throw you on the land
and hurl you on the open field.
I will let all the birds of the air settle on
you
and all the beasts of the earth gorge
themselves on you.
5I will spread your flesh on the mountains
and fill the valleys with your remains.
6I will drench the land with your flowing
blood
all the way to the mountains,
and the ravines will be filled with your
flesh.
7When I snuff you out, I will cover the
heavens
and darken their stars;
I will cover the sun with a cloud,
and the moon will not give its light.
8All the shining lights in the heavens
I will darken over you;
I will bring darkness over your land,
declares the Sovereign LORD.
9I will trouble the hearts of many peoples
when I bring about your destruction
among the nations,
among[b] lands you have not known.
10I will cause many peoples to be appalled
at you,
and their kings will shudder with horror
because of you
when I brandish my sword before them.
On the day of your downfall
each of them will tremble
every moment for his life.

11“ 'For this is what the Sovereign LORD
says:

“ 'The sword of the king of Babylon
will come against you.
12I will cause your hordes to fall
by the swords of mighty men—
the most ruthless of all nations.
They will shatter the pride of Egypt,

[a]15 Hebrew *Sheol*; also in verses 16 and 17
[b]9 Hebrew; Septuagint *bring you into captivity among the nations, / to*

and all her hordes will be overthrown.
13I will destroy all her cattle
from beside abundant waters
no longer to be stirred by the foot of man
or muddied by the hoofs of cattle.
14Then I will let her waters settle
and make her streams flow like oil,
declares the Sovereign LORD.
15When I make Egypt desolate
and strip the land of everything in it,
when I strike down all who live there,
then they will know that I am the LORD.'

16"This is the lament they will chant for her.
The daughters of the nations will chant it; for
Egypt and all her hordes they will chant it,
declares the Sovereign LORD."

17In the twelfth year, on the fifteenth day of
the month, the word of the LORD came to me:
18"Son of man, wail for the hordes of Egypt
and consign to the earth below both her and
the daughters of mighty nations, with those
who go down to the pit. 19Say to them, 'Are
you more favored than others? Go down and
be laid among the uncircumcised.' 20They
will fall among those killed by the sword. The
sword is drawn; let her be dragged off with all
her hordes. 21From within the grave[a] the
mighty leaders will say of Egypt and her allies, 'They have come down and they lie with
the uncircumcised, with those killed by the
sword.'

22"Assyria is there with her whole army;
she is surrounded by the graves of all her
slain, all who have fallen by the sword.
23Their graves are in the depths of the pit and
her army lies around her grave. All who had
spread terror in the land of the living are
slain, fallen by the sword.

24"Elam is there, with all her hordes
around her grave. All of them are slain, fallen
by the sword. All who had spread terror in the
land of the living went down uncircumcised
to the earth below. They bear their shame
with those who go down to the pit. 25A bed is
made for her among the slain, with all her
hordes around her grave. All of them are
uncircumcised, killed by the sword. Because
their terror had spread in the land of the
living, they bear their shame with those who
go down to the pit; they are laid among the
slain.

26"Meshech and Tubal are there, with all
their hordes around their graves. All of them
are uncircumcised, killed by the sword because they spread their terror in the land of
the living. 27Do they not lie with the other
uncircumcised warriors who have fallen,
who went down to the grave with their weapons of war, whose swords were placed under their heads? The punishment for their
sins rested on their bones, though the terror
of these warriors had stalked through the
land of the living.

28"You too, O Pharaoh, will be broken and
will lie among the uncircumcised, with those
killed by the sword.

29"Edom is there, her kings and all her
princes; despite their power, they are laid
with those killed by the sword. They lie with
the uncircumcised, with those who go down
to the pit.

30"All the princes of the north and all the
Sidonians are there; they went down with the
slain in disgrace despite the terror caused by
their power. They lie uncircumcised with
those killed by the sword and bear their
shame with those who go down to the pit.

31"Pharaoh—he and all his army—will see
them and he will be consoled for all his
hordes that were killed by the sword, declares the Sovereign LORD. 32Although I had
him spread terror in the land of the living,
Pharaoh and all his hordes will be laid
among the uncircumcised, with those killed
by the sword, declares the Sovereign LORD."

Ezekiel a Watchman

33 The word of the LORD came to me:
2"Son of man, speak to your countrymen and say to them: 'When I bring the
sword against a land, and the people of the
land choose one of their men and make him
their watchman, 3and he sees the sword
coming against the land and blows the trumpet to warn the people, 4then if anyone hears
the trumpet but does not take warning and
the sword comes and takes his life, his blood
will be on his own head. 5Since he heard the
sound of the trumpet but did not take warning, his blood will be on his own head. If he
had taken warning, he would have saved
himself. 6But if the watchman sees the sword
coming and does not blow the trumpet to
warn the people and the sword comes and
takes the life of one of them, that man will be
taken away because of his sin, but I will hold
the watchman accountable for his blood.'

7"Son of man, I have made you a watchman for the house of Israel; so hear the word

[a]21 Hebrew *Sheol*; also in verse 27

I speak and give them warning from me.
8When I say to the wicked, 'O wicked man,
you will surely die,' and you do not speak out
to dissuade him from his ways, that wicked
man will die for[a] his sin, and I will hold you
accountable for his blood. 9But if you do warn
the wicked man to turn from his ways and he
does not do so, he will die for his sin, but you
will have saved yourself.
10"Son of man, say to the house of Israel,
'This is what you are saying: "Our offenses
and sins weigh us down, and we are wasting
away because of[b] them. How then can we
live?"' 11Say to them, 'As surely as I live,
declares the Sovereign LORD, I take no pleasure in the death of the wicked, but rather
that they turn from their ways and live. Turn!
Turn from your evil ways! Why will you die, O
house of Israel?'
12"Therefore, son of man, say to your
countrymen, 'The righteousness of the righteous man will not save him when he disobeys, and the wickedness of the wicked
man will not cause him to fall when he turns
from it. The righteous man, if he sins, will not
be allowed to live because of his former
righteousness.' 13If I tell the righteous man
that he will surely live, but then he trusts in
his righteousness and does evil, none of the
righteous things he has done will be remembered; he will die for the evil he has done.
14And if I say to the wicked man, 'You will
surely die,' but he then turns away from his
sin and does what is just and right— 15if he
gives back what he took in pledge for a loan,
returns what he has stolen, follows the decrees that give life, and does no evil, he will
surely live; he will not die. 16None of the sins
he has committed will be remembered
against him. He has done what is just and
right; he will surely live.
17"Yet your countrymen say, 'The way of
the Lord is not just.' But it is their way that is
not just. 18If a righteous man turns from his
righteousness and does evil, he will die for it.
19And if a wicked man turns away from his
wickedness and does what is just and right,
he will live by doing so. 20Yet, O house of
Israel, you say, 'The way of the Lord is not
just.' But I will judge each of you according to
his own ways."

Jerusalem's Fall Explained

21In the twelfth year of our exile, in the
tenth month on the fifth day, a man who had
escaped from Jerusalem came to me and
said, "The city has fallen!" 22Now the evening before the man arrived, the hand of the
LORD was upon me, and he opened my
mouth before the man came to me in the
morning. So my mouth was opened and I
was no longer silent.
23Then the word of the LORD came to me:
24"Son of man, the people living in those
ruins in the land of Israel are saying, 'Abraham was only one man, yet he possessed
the land. But we are many; surely the land
has been given to us as our possession.'
25Therefore say to them, 'This is what the
Sovereign LORD says: Since you eat meat
with the blood still in it and look to your idols
and shed blood, should you then possess
the land? 26You rely on your sword, you do
detestable things, and each of you defiles his
neighbor's wife. Should you then possess
the land?'
27"Say this to them: 'This is what the Sovereign LORD says: As surely as I live, those
who are left in the ruins will fall by the sword,
those out in the country I will give to the wild
animals to be devoured, and those in strongholds and caves will die of a plague. 28I will
make the land a desolate waste, and her
proud strength will come to an end, and the
mountains of Israel will become desolate so
that no one will cross them. 29Then they will
know that I am the LORD, when I have made
the land a desolate waste because of all the
detestable things they have done.'
30"As for you, son of man, your countrymen are talking together about you by the
walls and at the doors of the houses, saying
to each other, 'Come and hear the message
that has come from the LORD.' 31My people
come to you, as they usually do, and sit before you to listen to your words, but they do
not put them into practice. With their mouths
they express devotion, but their hearts are
greedy for unjust gain. 32Indeed, to them you
are nothing more than one who sings love
songs with a beautiful voice and plays an
instrument well, for they hear your words but
do not put them into practice.
33"When all this comes true—and it surely
will—then they will know that a prophet has
been among them."

Shepherds and Sheep

34 The word of the LORD came to me:
2"Son of man, prophesy against the

[a]8 Or *in*; also in verse 9 [b]10 Or *away in*

shepherds of Israel; prophesy and say to them: 'This is what the Sovereign LORD says: Woe to the shepherds of Israel who only take care of themselves! Should not shepherds take care of the flock? 3You eat the curds, clothe yourselves with the wool and slaughter the choice animals, but you do not take care of the flock. 4You have not strengthened the weak or healed the sick or bound up the injured. You have not brought back the strays or searched for the lost. You have ruled them harshly and brutally. 5So they were scattered because there was no shepherd, and when they were scattered they became food for all the wild animals. 6My sheep wandered over all the mountains and on every high hill. They were scattered over the whole earth, and no one searched or looked for them.

7" 'Therefore, you shepherds, hear the word of the LORD: 8As surely as I live, declares the Sovereign LORD, because my flock lacks a shepherd and so has been plundered and has become food for all the wild animals, and because my shepherds did not search for my flock but cared for themselves rather than for my flock, 9therefore, O shepherds, hear the word of the LORD: 10This is what the Sovereign LORD says: I am against the shepherds and will hold them accountable for my flock. I will remove them from tending the flock so that the shepherds can no longer feed themselves. I will rescue my flock from their mouths, and it will no longer be food for them.

11" 'For this is what the Sovereign LORD says: I myself will search for my sheep and look after them. 12As a shepherd looks after his scattered flock when he is with them, so will I look after my sheep. I will rescue them from all the places where they were scattered on a day of clouds and darkness. 13I will bring them out from the nations and gather them from the countries, and I will bring them into their own land. I will pasture them on the mountains of Israel, in the ravines and in all the settlements in the land. 14I will tend them in a good pasture, and the mountain heights of Israel will be their grazing land. There they will lie down in good grazing land, and there they will feed in a rich pasture on the mountains of Israel. 15I myself will tend my sheep and have them lie down, declares the Sovereign LORD. 16I will search for the lost and bring back the strays. I will bind up the injured and strengthen the weak, but the sleek and the strong I will destroy. I will shepherd the flock with justice.

17" 'As for you, my flock, this is what the Sovereign LORD says: I will judge between one sheep and another, and between rams and goats. 18Is it not enough for you to feed on the good pasture? Must you also trample the rest of your pasture with your feet? Is it not enough for you to drink clear water? Must you also muddy the rest with your feet? 19Must my flock feed on what you have trampled and drink what you have muddied with your feet?

20" 'Therefore this is what the Sovereign LORD says to them: See, I myself will judge between the fat sheep and the lean sheep. 21Because you shove with flank and shoulder, butting all the weak sheep with your horns until you have driven them away, 22I will save my flock, and they will no longer be plundered. I will judge between one sheep and another. 23I will place over them one shepherd, my servant David, and he will tend them; he will tend them and be their shepherd. 24I the LORD will be their God, and my servant David will be prince among them. I the LORD have spoken.

25" 'I will make a covenant of peace with them and rid the land of wild beasts so that they may live in the desert and sleep in the forests in safety. 26I will bless them and the places surrounding my hill.[a] I will send down showers in season; there will be showers of blessing. 27The trees of the field will yield their fruit and the ground will yield its crops; the people will be secure in their land. They will know that I am the LORD, when I break the bars of their yoke and rescue them from the hands of those who enslaved them. 28They will no longer be plundered by the nations, nor will wild animals devour them. They will live in safety, and no one will make them afraid. 29I will provide for them a land renowned for its crops, and they will no longer be victims of famine in the land or bear the scorn of the nations. 30Then they will know that I, the LORD their God, am with them and that they, the house of Israel, are my people, declares the Sovereign LORD. 31You my sheep, the sheep of my pasture, are people, and I am your God, declares the Sovereign LORD.' "

a26 Or *I will make them and the places surrounding my hill a blessing*

A Prophecy Against Edom

35 The word of the LORD came to me: 2"Son of man, set your face against Mount Seir; prophesy against it 3and say: 'This is what the Sovereign LORD says: I am against you, Mount Seir, and I will stretch out my hand against you and make you a desolate waste. 4I will turn your towns into ruins and you will be desolate. Then you will know that I am the LORD.

5" 'Because you harbored an ancient hostility and delivered the Israelites over to the sword at the time of their calamity, the time their punishment reached its climax, 6therefore as surely as I live, declares the Sovereign LORD, I will give you over to bloodshed and it will pursue you. Since you did not hate bloodshed, bloodshed will pursue you. 7I will make Mount Seir a desolate waste and cut off from it all who come and go. 8I will fill your mountains with the slain; those killed by the sword will fall on your hills and in your valleys and in all your ravines. 9I will make you desolate forever; your towns will not be inhabited. Then you will know that I am the LORD.

10" 'Because you have said, "These two nations and countries will be ours and we will take possession of them," even though I the LORD was there, 11therefore as surely as I live, declares the Sovereign LORD, I will treat you in accordance with the anger and jealousy you showed in your hatred of them and I will make myself known among them when I judge you. 12Then you will know that I the LORD have heard all the contemptible things you have said against the mountains of Israel. You said, "They have been laid waste and have been given over to us to devour." 13You boasted against me and spoke against me without restraint, and I heard it. 14This is what the Sovereign LORD says: While the whole earth rejoices, I will make you desolate. 15Because you rejoiced when the inheritance of the house of Israel became desolate, that is how I will treat you. You will be desolate, O Mount Seir, you and all of Edom. Then they will know that I am the LORD.' "

A Prophecy to the Mountains of Israel

36 "Son of man, prophesy to the mountains of Israel and say, 'O mountains of Israel, hear the word of the LORD. 2This is what the Sovereign LORD says: The enemy said of you, "Aha! The ancient heights have become our possession." ' 3Therefore prophesy and say, 'This is what the Sovereign LORD says: Because they ravaged and hounded you from every side so that you became the possession of the rest of the nations and the object of people's malicious talk and slander, 4therefore, O mountains of Israel, hear the word of the Sovereign LORD: This is what the Sovereign LORD says to the mountains and hills, to the ravines and valleys, to the desolate ruins and the deserted towns that have been plundered and ridiculed by the rest of the nations around you— 5this is what the Sovereign LORD says: In my burning zeal I have spoken against the rest of the nations, and against all Edom, for with glee and with malice in their hearts they made my land their own possession so that they might plunder its pastureland.' 6Therefore prophesy concerning the land of Israel and say to the mountains and hills, to the ravines and valleys: 'This is what the Sovereign LORD says: I speak in my jealous wrath because you have suffered the scorn of the nations. 7Therefore this is what the Sovereign LORD says: I swear with uplifted hand that the nations around you will also suffer scorn.

8" 'But you, O mountains of Israel, will produce branches and fruit for my people Israel, for they will soon come home. 9I am concerned for you and will look on you with favor; you will be plowed and sown, 10and I will multiply the number of people upon you, even the whole house of Israel. The towns will be inhabited and the ruins rebuilt. 11I will increase the number of men and animals upon you, and they will be fruitful and become numerous. I will settle people on you as in the past and will make you prosper more than before. Then you will know that I am the LORD. 12I will cause people, my people Israel, to walk upon you. They will possess you, and you will be their inheritance; you will never again deprive them of their children.

13" 'This is what the Sovereign LORD says: Because people say to you, "You devour men and deprive your nation of its children," 14therefore you will no longer devour men or make your nation childless, declares the Sovereign LORD. 15No longer will I make you hear the taunts of the nations, and no longer will you suffer the scorn of the peoples or cause your nation to fall, declares the Sovereign LORD.' "

16Again the word of the LORD came to me: 17"Son of man, when the people of Israel were living in their own land, they defiled it by their conduct and their actions. Their conduct was like a woman's monthly uncleanness in my sight. 18So I poured out my wrath on them because they had shed blood in the land and because they had defiled it with their idols. 19I dispersed them among the nations, and they were scattered through the countries; I judged them according to their conduct and their actions. 20And wherever they went among the nations they profaned my holy name, for it was said of them, 'These are the LORD's people, and yet they had to leave his land.' 21I had concern for my holy name, which the house of Israel profaned among the nations where they had gone.

22"Therefore say to the house of Israel, 'This is what the Sovereign LORD says: It is not for your sake, O house of Israel, that I am going to do these things, but for the sake of my holy name, which you have profaned among the nations where you have gone. 23I will show the holiness of my great name, which has been profaned among the nations, the name you have profaned among them. Then the nations will know that I am the LORD, declares the Sovereign LORD, when I show myself holy through you before their eyes.

24" 'For I will take you out of the nations; I will gather you from all the countries and bring you back into your own land. 25I will sprinkle clean water on you, and you will be clean; I will cleanse you from all your impurities and from all your idols. 26I will give you a new heart and put a new spirit in you; I will remove from you your heart of stone and give you a heart of flesh. 27And I will put my Spirit in you and move you to follow my decrees and be careful to keep my laws. 28You will live in the land I gave your forefathers; you will be my people, and I will be your God. 29I will save you from all your uncleanness. I will call for the grain and make it plentiful and will not bring famine upon you. 30I will increase the fruit of the trees and the crops of the field, so that you will no longer suffer disgrace among the nations because of famine. 31Then you will remember your evil ways and wicked deeds, and you will loathe yourselves for your sins and detestable practices. 32I want you to know that I am not doing this for your sake, declares the Sovereign LORD. Be ashamed and disgraced for your conduct, O house of Israel!

33" 'This is what the Sovereign LORD says: On the day I cleanse you from all your sins, I will resettle your towns, and the ruins will be rebuilt. 34The desolate land will be cultivated instead of lying desolate in the sight of all who pass through it. 35They will say, "This land that was laid waste has become like the garden of Eden; the cities that were lying in ruins, desolate and destroyed, are now fortified and inhabited." 36Then the nations around you that remain will know that I the LORD have rebuilt what was destroyed and have replanted what was desolate. I the LORD have spoken, and I will do it.'

37"This is what the Sovereign LORD says: Once again I will yield to the plea of the house of Israel and do this for them: I will make their people as numerous as sheep, 38as numerous as the flocks for offerings at Jerusalem during her appointed feasts. So will the ruined cities be filled with flocks of people. Then they will know that I am the LORD."

The Valley of Dry Bones

37 The hand of the LORD was upon me, and he brought me out by the Spirit of the LORD and set me in the middle of a valley; it was full of bones. 2He led me back and forth among them, and I saw a great many bones on the floor of the valley, bones that were very dry. 3He asked me, "Son of man, can these bones live?"

I said, "O Sovereign LORD, you alone know."

4Then he said to me, "Prophesy to these bones and say to them, 'Dry bones, hear the word of the LORD! 5This is what the Sovereign LORD says to these bones: I will make breath[a] enter you, and you will come to life. 6I will attach tendons to you and make flesh come upon you and cover you with skin; I will put breath in you, and you will come to life. Then you will know that I am the LORD.' "

7So I prophesied as I was commanded. And as I was prophesying, there was a noise, a rattling sound, and the bones came together, bone to bone. 8I looked, and tendons and flesh appeared on them and skin covered them, but there was no breath in them.

9Then he said to me, "Prophesy to the breath; prophesy, son of man, and say to it, 'This is what the Sovereign LORD says: Come from the four winds, O breath, and breathe

[a]5 The Hebrew for this word can also mean *wind* or *spirit* (see verses 6-14).

into these slain, that they may live.' " 10So I prophesied as he commanded me, and breath entered them; they came to life and stood up on their feet—a vast army.

11Then he said to me: "Son of man, these bones are the whole house of Israel. They say, 'Our bones are dried up and our hope is gone; we are cut off.' 12Therefore prophesy and say to them: 'This is what the Sovereign LORD says: O my people, I am going to open your graves and bring you up from them; I will bring you back to the land of Israel. 13Then you, my people, will know that I am the LORD, when I open your graves and bring you up from them. 14I will put my Spirit in you and you will live, and I will settle you in your own land. Then you will know that I the LORD have spoken, and I have done it, declares the LORD.' "

One Nation Under One King

15The word of the LORD came to me: 16"Son of man, take a stick of wood and write on it, 'Belonging to Judah and the Israelites associated with him.' Then take another stick of wood, and write on it, 'Ephraim's stick, belonging to Joseph and all the house of Israel associated with him.' 17Join them together into one stick so that they will become one in your hand.

18"When your countrymen ask you, 'Won't you tell us what you mean by this?' 19say to them, 'This is what the Sovereign LORD says: I am going to take the stick of Joseph—which is in Ephraim's hand—and of the Israelite tribes associated with him, and join it to Judah's stick, making them a single stick of wood, and they will become one in my hand.' 20Hold before their eyes the sticks you have written on 21and say to them, 'This is what the Sovereign LORD says: I will take the Israelites out of the nations where they have gone. I will gather them from all around and bring them back into their own land. 22I will make them one nation in the land, on the mountains of Israel. There will be one king over all of them and they will never again be two nations or be divided into two kingdoms. 23They will no longer defile themselves with their idols and vile images or with any of their offenses, for I will save them from all their sinful backsliding,[a] and I will cleanse them. They will be my people, and I will be their God.

24" 'My servant David will be king over them, and they will all have one shepherd. They will follow my laws and be careful to keep my decrees. 25They will live in the land I gave to my servant Jacob, the land where your fathers lived. They and their children and their children's children will live there forever, and David my servant will be their prince forever. 26I will make a covenant of peace with them; it will be an everlasting covenant. I will establish them and increase their numbers, and I will put my sanctuary among them forever. 27My dwelling place will be with them; I will be their God, and they will be my people. 28Then the nations will know that I the LORD make Israel holy, when my sanctuary is among them forever.' "

A Prophecy Against Gog

38 The word of the LORD came to me: 2"Son of man, set your face against Gog, of the land of Magog, the chief prince of[b] Meshech and Tubal; prophesy against him 3and say: 'This is what the Sovereign LORD says: I am against you, O Gog, chief prince of[c] Meshech and Tubal. 4I will turn you around, put hooks in your jaws and bring you out with your whole army—your horses, your horsemen fully armed, and a great horde with large and small shields, all of them brandishing their swords. 5Persia, Cush[d] and Put will be with them, all with shields and helmets, 6also Gomer with all its troops, and Beth Togarmah from the far north with all its troops—the many nations with you.

7" 'Get ready; be prepared, you and all the hordes gathered about you, and take command of them. 8After many days you will be called to arms. In future years you will invade a land that has recovered from war, whose people were gathered from many nations to the mountains of Israel, which had long been desolate. They had been brought out from the nations, and now all of them live in safety. 9You and all your troops and the many nations with you will go up, advancing like a storm; you will be like a cloud covering the land.

10" 'This is what the Sovereign LORD says: On that day thoughts will come into your mind and you will devise an evil scheme. 11You will say, "I will invade a land of unwalled villages; I will attack a peaceful and

[a]23 Many Hebrew manuscripts (see also Septuagint); most Hebrew manuscripts *all their dwelling places where they sinned* [b]2 Or *the prince of Rosh,* [c]3 Or *Gog, prince of Rosh,* [d]5 That is, the upper Nile region

unsuspecting people—all of them living without walls and without gates and bars. 12I will plunder and loot and turn my hand against the resettled ruins and the people gathered from the nations, rich in livestock and goods, living at the center of the land." 13Sheba and Dedan and the merchants of Tarshish and all her villages[a] will say to you, "Have you come to plunder? Have you gathered your hordes to loot, to carry off silver and gold, to take away livestock and goods and to seize much plunder?" '

14"Therefore, son of man, prophesy and say to Gog: 'This is what the Sovereign LORD says: In that day, when my people Israel are living in safety, will you not take notice of it? 15You will come from your place in the far north, you and many nations with you, all of them riding on horses, a great horde, a mighty army. 16You will advance against my people Israel like a cloud that covers the land. In days to come, O Gog, I will bring you against my land, so that the nations may know me when I show myself holy through you before their eyes.

17" 'This is what the Sovereign LORD says: Are you not the one I spoke of in former days by my servants the prophets of Israel? At that time they prophesied for years that I would bring you against them. 18This is what will happen in that day: When Gog attacks the land of Israel, my hot anger will be aroused, declares the Sovereign LORD. 19In my zeal and fiery wrath I declare that at that time there shall be a great earthquake in the land of Israel. 20The fish of the sea, the birds of the air, the beasts of the field, every creature that moves along the ground, and all the people on the face of the earth will tremble at my presence. The mountains will be overturned, the cliffs will crumble and every wall will fall to the ground. 21I will summon a sword against Gog on all my mountains, declares the Sovereign LORD. Every man's sword will be against his brother. 22I will execute judgment upon him with plague and bloodshed; I will pour down torrents of rain, hailstones and burning sulfur on him and on his troops and on the many nations with him. 23And so I will show my greatness and my holiness, and I will make myself known in the sight of many nations. Then they will know that I am the LORD.'

39 "Son of man, prophesy against Gog and say: 'This is what the Sovereign LORD says: I am against you, O Gog, chief prince of[b] Meshech and Tubal. 2I will turn you around and drag you along. I will bring you from the far north and send you against the mountains of Israel. 3Then I will strike your bow from your left hand and make your arrows drop from your right hand. 4On the mountains of Israel you will fall, you and all your troops and the nations with you. I will give you as food to all kinds of carrion birds and to the wild animals. 5You will fall in the open field, for I have spoken, declares the Sovereign LORD. 6I will send fire on Magog and on those who live in safety in the coastlands, and they will know that I am the LORD.

7" 'I will make known my holy name among my people Israel. I will no longer let my holy name be profaned, and the nations will know that I the LORD am the Holy One in Israel. 8It is coming! It will surely take place, declares the Sovereign LORD. This is the day I have spoken of.

9" 'Then those who live in the towns of Israel will go out and use the weapons for fuel and burn them up—the small and large shields, the bows and arrows, the war clubs and spears. For seven years they will use them for fuel. 10They will not need to gather wood from the fields or cut it from the forests, because they will use the weapons for fuel. And they will plunder those who plundered them and loot those who looted them, declares the Sovereign LORD.

11" 'On that day I will give Gog a burial place in Israel, in the valley of those who travel east toward[c] the Sea.[d] It will block the way of travelers, because Gog and all his hordes will be buried there. So it will be called the Valley of Hamon Gog.[e]

12" 'For seven months the house of Israel will be burying them in order to cleanse the land. 13All the people of the land will bury them, and the day I am glorified will be a memorable day for them, declares the Sovereign LORD.

14" 'Men will be regularly employed to cleanse the land. Some will go throughout the land and, in addition to them, others will bury those that remain on the ground. At the end of the seven months they will begin their search. 15As they go through the land and

[a] 13 Or *her strong lions* [b] 1 Or *Gog, prince of Rosh,* [c] 11 Or *of* [d] 11 That is, the Dead Sea [e] 11 *Hamon Gog* means *hordes of Gog.*

one of them sees a human bone, he will set
up a marker beside it until the gravediggers
have buried it in the Valley of Hamon Gog.
16(Also a town called Hamonah[a] will be
there.) And so they will cleanse the land.'
17"Son of man, this is what the Sovereign
LORD says: Call out to every kind of bird and
all the wild animals: 'Assemble and come
together from all around to the sacrifice I am
preparing for you, the great sacrifice on the
mountains of Israel. There you will eat flesh
and drink blood. 18You will eat the flesh of
mighty men and drink the blood of the
princes of the earth as if they were rams and
lambs, goats and bulls—all of them fattened
animals from Bashan. 19At the sacrifice I am
preparing for you, you will eat fat till you are
glutted and drink blood till you are drunk. 20At
my table you will eat your fill of horses and
riders, mighty men and soldiers of every
kind,' declares the Sovereign LORD.
21"I will display my glory among the nations, and all the nations will see the punishment I inflict and the hand I lay upon them.
22From that day forward the house of Israel
will know that I am the LORD their God. 23And
the nations will know that the people of Israel
went into exile for their sin, because they
were unfaithful to me. So I hid my face from
them and handed them over to their enemies, and they all fell by the sword. 24I dealt
with them according to their uncleanness
and their offenses, and I hid my face from
them.
25"Therefore this is what the Sovereign
LORD says: I will now bring Jacob back from
captivity[b] and will have compassion on all
the people of Israel, and I will be zealous for
my holy name. 26They will forget their shame
and all the unfaithfulness they showed
toward me when they lived in safety in their
land with no one to make them afraid.
27When I have brought them back from the
nations and have gathered them from the
countries of their enemies, I will show myself
holy through them in the sight of many nations. 28Then they will know that I am the
LORD their God, for though I sent them into
exile among the nations, I will gather them to
their own land, not leaving any behind. 29I will
no longer hide my face from them, for I will
pour out my Spirit on the house of Israel,
declares the Sovereign LORD."

The New Temple Area

40 In the twenty-fifth year of our exile, at
the beginning of the year, on the
tenth of the month, in the fourteenth year
after the fall of the city—on that very day the
hand of the LORD was upon me and he took
me there. 2In visions of God he took me to
the land of Israel and set me on a very high
mountain, on whose south side were some
buildings that looked like a city. 3He took me
there, and I saw a man whose appearance
was like bronze; he was standing in the gateway with a linen cord and a measuring rod in
his hand. 4The man said to me, "Son of man,
look with your eyes and hear with your ears
and pay attention to everything I am going to
show you, for that is why you have been
brought here. Tell the house of Israel everything you see."

The East Gate to the Outer Court

5I saw a wall completely surrounding the
temple area. The length of the measuring
rod in the man's hand was six long cubits,
each of which was a cubit[c] and a handbreadth.[d] He measured the wall; it was one
measuring rod thick and one rod high.
6Then he went to the gate facing east. He
climbed its steps and measured the threshold of the gate; it was one rod deep.[e] 7The
alcoves for the guards were one rod long and
one rod wide, and the projecting walls between the alcoves were five cubits thick. And
the threshold of the gate next to the portico
facing the temple was one rod deep.
8Then he measured the portico of the gateway; 9it[f] was eight cubits deep and its jambs
were two cubits thick. The portico of the
gateway faced the temple.
10Inside the east gate were three alcoves
on each side; the three had the same measurements, and the faces of the projecting
walls on each side had the same measurements. 11Then he measured the width of
the entrance to the gateway; it was ten cubits
and its length was thirteen cubits. 12In front of
each alcove was a wall one cubit high, and
the alcoves were six cubits square. 13Then

[a]16 *Hamonah* means *horde.* [b]25 Or *now restore the fortunes of Jacob* [c]5 The common cubit was about 1 1/2 feet (about 0.5 meter). [d]5 That is, about 3 inches (about 8 centimeters) [e]6 Septuagint; Hebrew *deep, the first threshold, one rod deep* [f]8,9 Many Hebrew manuscripts, Septuagint, Vulgate and Syriac; most Hebrew manuscripts *gateway facing the temple; it was one rod deep. 9Then he measured the portico of the gateway; it*

he measured the gateway from the top of the rear wall of one alcove to the top of the opposite one; the distance was twenty-five cubits from one parapet opening to the opposite one. 14He measured along the faces of the projecting walls all around the inside of the gateway—sixty cubits. The measurement was up to the portico[a] facing the courtyard.[b] 15The distance from the entrance of the gateway to the far end of its portico was fifty cubits. 16The alcoves and the projecting walls inside the gateway were surmounted by narrow parapet openings all around, as was the portico; the openings all around faced inward. The faces of the projecting walls were decorated with palm trees.

The Outer Court

17Then he brought me into the outer court. There I saw some rooms and a pavement that had been constructed all around the court; there were thirty rooms along the pavement. 18It abutted the sides of the gateways and was as wide as they were long; this was the lower pavement. 19Then he measured the distance from the inside of the lower gateway to the outside of the inner court; it was a hundred cubits on the east side as well as on the north.

The North Gate

20Then he measured the length and width of the gate facing north, leading into the outer court. 21Its alcoves—three on each side—its projecting walls and its portico had the same measurements as those of the first gateway. It was fifty cubits long and twenty-five cubits wide. 22Its openings, its portico and its palm tree decorations had the same measurements as those of the gate facing east. Seven steps led up to it, with its portico opposite them. 23There was a gate to the inner court facing the north gate, just as there was on the east. He measured from one gate to the opposite one; it was a hundred cubits.

The South Gate

24Then he led me to the south side and I saw a gate facing south. He measured its jambs and its portico, and they had the same measurements as the others. 25The gateway and its portico had narrow openings all around, like the openings of the others. It was fifty cubits long and twenty-five cubits wide. 26Seven steps led up to it, with its portico opposite them; it had palm tree decorations on the faces of the projecting walls on each side. 27The inner court also had a gate facing south, and he measured from this gate to the outer gate on the south side; it was a hundred cubits.

Gates to the Inner Court

28Then he brought me into the inner court through the south gate, and he measured the south gate; it had the same measurements as the others. 29Its alcoves, its projecting walls and its portico had the same measurements as the others. The gateway and its portico had openings all around. It was fifty cubits long and twenty-five cubits wide. 30(The porticoes of the gateways around the inner court were twenty-five cubits wide and five cubits deep.) 31Its portico faced the outer court; palm trees decorated its jambs, and eight steps led up to it.

32Then he brought me to the inner court on the east side, and he measured the gateway; it had the same measurements as the others. 33Its alcoves, its projecting walls and its portico had the same measurements as the others. The gateway and its portico had openings all around. It was fifty cubits long and twenty-five cubits wide. 34Its portico faced the outer court; palm trees decorated the jambs on either side, and eight steps led up to it.

35Then he brought me to the north gate and measured it. It had the same measurements as the others, 36as did its alcoves, its projecting walls and its portico, and it had openings all around. It was fifty cubits long and twenty-five cubits wide. 37Its portico[c] faced the outer court; palm trees decorated the jambs on either side, and eight steps led up to it.

The Rooms for Preparing Sacrifices

38A room with a doorway was by the portico in each of the inner gateways, where the burnt offerings were washed. 39In the portico of the gateway were two tables on each side, on which the burnt offerings, sin offerings and guilt offerings were slaughtered. 40By the outside wall of the portico of the gateway, near the steps at the entrance to the north gateway were two tables, and on the other

[a]14 Septuagint; Hebrew *projecting wall* [b]14 The meaning of the Hebrew for this verse is uncertain.
[c]37 Septuagint (see also verses 31 and 34); Hebrew *jambs*

side of the steps were two tables. 41So there
were four tables on one side of the gateway
and four on the other—eight tables in all—on
which the sacrifices were slaughtered.
42There were also four tables of dressed
stone for the burnt offerings, each a cubit
and a half long, a cubit and a half wide and a
cubit high. On them were placed the utensils
for slaughtering the burnt offerings and the
other sacrifices. 43And double-pronged
hooks, each a handbreadth long, were attached to the wall all around. The tables
were for the flesh of the offerings.

Rooms for the Priests

44Outside the inner gate, within the inner
court, were two rooms, one[a] at the side of
the north gate and facing south, and another
at the side of the south[b] gate and facing
north. 45He said to me, "The room facing
south is for the priests who have charge of
the temple, 46and the room facing north is for
the priests who have charge of the altar.
These are the sons of Zadok, who are the
only Levites who may draw near to the LORD
to minister before him."

47Then he measured the court: It was
square—a hundred cubits long and a hundred cubits wide. And the altar was in front of
the temple.

The Temple

48He brought me to the portico of the temple and measured the jambs of the portico;
they were five cubits wide on either side. The
width of the entrance was fourteen cubits
and its projecting walls were[c] three cubits
wide on either side. 49The portico was twenty
cubits wide, and twelve[d] cubits from front to
back. It was reached by a flight of stairs,[e]
and there were pillars on each side of the
jambs.

41 Then the man brought me to the outer sanctuary and measured the
jambs; the width of the jambs was six cubits[f]
on each side.[g] 2The entrance was ten cubits
wide, and the projecting walls on each side
of it were five cubits wide. He also measured
the outer sanctuary; it was forty cubits long
and twenty cubits wide.

3Then he went into the inner sanctuary and
measured the jambs of the entrance; each
was two cubits wide. The entrance was six
cubits wide, and the projecting walls on each
side of it were seven cubits wide. 4And he
measured the length of the inner sanctuary;
it was twenty cubits, and its width was twenty
cubits across the end of the outer sanctuary.
He said to me, "This is the Most Holy Place."

5Then he measured the wall of the temple;
it was six cubits thick, and each side room
around the temple was four cubits wide. 6The
side rooms were on three levels, one above
another, thirty on each level. There were
ledges all around the wall of the temple to
serve as supports for the side rooms, so that
the supports were not inserted into the wall
of the temple. 7The side rooms all around the
temple were wider at each successive level.
The structure surrounding the temple was
built in ascending stages, so that the rooms
widened as one went upward. A stairway
went up from the lowest floor to the top floor
through the middle floor.

8I saw that the temple had a raised base all
around it, forming the foundation of the side
rooms. It was the length of the rod, six long
cubits. 9The outer wall of the side rooms was
five cubits thick. The open area between the
side rooms of the temple 10and the ⌊priests'⌋
rooms was twenty cubits wide all around the
temple. 11There were entrances to the side
rooms from the open area, one on the north
and another on the south; and the base adjoining the open area was five cubits wide all
around.

12The building facing the temple courtyard
on the west side was seventy cubits wide.
The wall of the building was five cubits thick
all around, and its length was ninety cubits.

13Then he measured the temple; it was a
hundred cubits long, and the temple courtyard and the building with its walls were also
a hundred cubits long. 14The width of the
temple courtyard on the east, including the
front of the temple, was a hundred cubits.

15Then he measured the length of the
building facing the courtyard at the rear of
the temple, including its galleries on each
side; it was a hundred cubits.

The outer sanctuary, the inner sanctuary
and the portico facing the court, 16as well as
the thresholds and the narrow windows and
galleries around the three of them—everything beyond and including the threshold
was covered with wood. The floor, the wall

[a]44 Septuagint; Hebrew *were rooms for singers, which were* [b]44 Septuagint; Hebrew *east*
[c]48 Septuagint; Hebrew *entrance was* [d]49 Septuagint; Hebrew *eleven* [e]49 Hebrew; Septuagint *Ten steps led up to it* [f]1 The common cubit was about 1 1/2 feet (about 0.5 meter). [g]1 One Hebrew manuscript and Septuagint; most Hebrew manuscripts *side, the width of the tent*

up to the windows, and the windows were
covered. 17In the space above the outside of
the entrance to the inner sanctuary and on
the walls at regular intervals all around the
inner and outer sanctuary 18were carved
cherubim and palm trees. Palm trees alternated with cherubim. Each cherub had two
faces: 19the face of a man toward the palm
tree on one side and the face of a lion toward
the palm tree on the other. They were carved
all around the whole temple. 20From the floor
to the area above the entrance, cherubim
and palm trees were carved on the wall of the
outer sanctuary.

21The outer sanctuary had a rectangular
doorframe, and the one at the front of the
Most Holy Place was similar. 22There was a
wooden altar three cubits high and two cubits square[a]; its corners, its base[b] and its
sides were of wood. The man said to me,
"This is the table that is before the LORD."
23Both the outer sanctuary and the Most Holy
Place had double doors. 24Each door had
two leaves—two hinged leaves for each
door. 25And on the doors of the outer sanctuary were carved cherubim and palm trees
like those carved on the walls, and there was
a wooden overhang on the front of the portico. 26On the sidewalls of the portico were
narrow windows with palm trees carved on
each side. The side rooms of the temple also
had overhangs.

Rooms for the Priests

42 Then the man led me northward into
the outer court and brought me to the
rooms opposite the temple courtyard and opposite the outer wall on the north side. 2The
building whose door faced north was a hundred cubits[c] long and fifty cubits wide. 3Both
in the section twenty cubits from the inner
court and in the section opposite the pavement of the outer court, gallery faced gallery
at the three levels. 4In front of the rooms was
an inner passageway ten cubits wide and a
hundred cubits[d] long. Their doors were on
the north. 5Now the upper rooms were nar-
rower, for the galleries took more space from
them than from the rooms on the lower and
middle floors of the building. 6The rooms on
the third floor had no pillars, as the courts
had; so they were smaller in floor space than
those on the lower and middle floors. 7There
was an outer wall parallel to the rooms and
the outer court; it extended in front of the
rooms for fifty cubits. 8While the row of
rooms on the side next to the outer court was
fifty cubits long, the row on the side nearest
the sanctuary was a hundred cubits long.
9The lower rooms had an entrance on the
east side as one enters them from the outer
court.

10On the south side[e] along the length of
the wall of the outer court, adjoining the temple courtyard and opposite the outer wall,
were rooms 11with a passageway in front of
them. These were like the rooms on the
north; they had the same length and width,
with similar exits and dimensions. Similar to
the doorways on the north 12were the doorways of the rooms on the south. There was a
doorway at the beginning of the passageway
that was parallel to the corresponding wall
extending eastward, by which one enters the
rooms.

13Then he said to me, "The north and
south rooms facing the temple courtyard are
the priests' rooms, where the priests who
approach the LORD will eat the most holy offerings. There they will put the most holy
offerings—the grain offerings, the sin offerings and the guilt offerings—for the place is
holy. 14Once the priests enter the holy precincts, they are not to go into the outer court
until they leave behind the garments in which
they minister, for these are holy. They are to
put on other clothes before they go near the
places that are for the people."

15When he had finished measuring what
was inside the temple area, he led me out by
the east gate and measured the area all
around: 16He measured the east side with
the measuring rod; it was five hundred cubits.[f] 17He measured the north side; it was
five hundred cubits[g] by the measuring rod.
18He measured the south side; it was five
hundred cubits by the measuring rod. 19Then
he turned to the west side and measured; it
was five hundred cubits by the measuring
rod. 20So he measured the area on all four
sides. It had a wall around it, five hundred
cubits long and five hundred cubits wide, to
separate the holy from the common.

The Glory Returns to the Temple

43 Then the man brought me to the gate
facing east, 2and I saw the glory of
the God of Israel coming from the east. His

[a]22 Septuagint; Hebrew *long* [b]22 Septuagint; Hebrew *length* [c]2 The common cubit was about 1 1/2 feet (about 0.5 meter). [d]4 Septuagint and Syriac; Hebrew *and one cubit* [e]10 Septuagint; Hebrew *Eastward* [f]16 See Septuagint of verse 17; Hebrew *rods;* also in verses 18 and 19. [g]17 Septuagint; Hebrew *rods*

voice was like the roar of rushing waters, and
the land was radiant with his glory. 3The vision I saw was like the vision I had seen
when he[a] came to destroy the city and like
the visions I had seen by the Kebar River,
and I fell facedown. 4The glory of the LORD
entered the temple through the gate facing
east. 5Then the Spirit lifted me up and
brought me into the inner court, and the glory
of the LORD filled the temple.

6While the man was standing beside me, I
heard someone speaking to me from inside
the temple. 7He said: "Son of man, this is the
place of my throne and the place for the
soles of my feet. This is where I will live
among the Israelites forever. The house of
Israel will never again defile my holy name—
neither they nor their kings—by their prostitution[b] and the lifeless idols[c] of their kings at
their high places. 8When they placed their
threshold next to my threshold and their
doorposts beside my doorposts, with only a
wall between me and them, they defiled my
holy name by their detestable practices. So I
destroyed them in my anger. 9Now let them
put away from me their prostitution and the
lifeless idols of their kings, and I will live
among them forever.

10"Son of man, describe the temple to the
people of Israel, that they may be ashamed
of their sins. Let them consider the plan,
11and if they are ashamed of all they have
done, make known to them the design of the
temple—its arrangement, its exits and entrances—its whole design and all its regulations[d] and laws. Write these down before
them so that they may be faithful to its design
and follow all its regulations.

12"This is the law of the temple: All the
surrounding area on top of the mountain will
be most holy. Such is the law of the temple.

The Altar

13"These are the measurements of the altar in long cubits, that cubit being a cubit[e]
and a handbreadth[f]: Its gutter is a cubit deep
and a cubit wide, with a rim of one span[g]
around the edge. And this is the height of the
altar: 14From the gutter on the ground up to
the lower ledge it is two cubits high and a
cubit wide, and from the smaller ledge up to
the larger ledge it is four cubits high and a
cubit wide. 15The altar hearth is four cubits
high, and four horns project upward from the
hearth. 16The altar hearth is square, twelve
cubits long and twelve cubits wide. 17The
upper ledge also is square, fourteen cubits
long and fourteen cubits wide, with a rim of
half a cubit and a gutter of a cubit all around.
The steps of the altar face east."

18Then he said to me, "Son of man, this is
what the Sovereign LORD says: These will be
the regulations for sacrificing burnt offerings
and sprinkling blood upon the altar when it is
built: 19You are to give a young bull as a sin
offering to the priests, who are Levites, of the
family of Zadok, who come near to minister
before me, declares the Sovereign LORD.
20You are to take some of its blood and put it
on the four horns of the altar and on the four
corners of the upper ledge and all around the
rim, and so purify the altar and make atonement for it. 21You are to take the bull for the
sin offering and burn it in the designated part
of the temple area outside the sanctuary.

22"On the second day you are to offer a
male goat without defect for a sin offering,
and the altar is to be purified as it was purified with the bull. 23When you have finished
purifying it, you are to offer a young bull and
a ram from the flock, both without defect.
24You are to offer them before the LORD, and
the priests are to sprinkle salt on them and
sacrifice them as a burnt offering to the LORD.

25"For seven days you are to provide a
male goat daily for a sin offering; you are also
to provide a young bull and a ram from the
flock, both without defect. 26For seven days
they are to make atonement for the altar and
cleanse it; thus they will dedicate it. 27At the
end of these days, from the eighth day on,
the priests are to present your burnt offerings
and fellowship offerings[h] on the altar. Then I
will accept you, declares the Sovereign
LORD."

The Prince, the Levites, the Priests

44 Then the man brought me back to the
outer gate of the sanctuary, the one
facing east, and it was shut. 2The LORD said
to me, "This gate is to remain shut. It must
not be opened; no one may enter through it.
It is to remain shut because the LORD, the
God of Israel, has entered through it. 3The

[a]3 Some Hebrew manuscripts and Vulgate; most Hebrew manuscripts *I* [b]7 Or *their spiritual adultery;* also in verse 9 [c]7 Or *the corpses;* also in verse 9 [d]11 Some Hebrew manuscripts and Septuagint; most Hebrew manuscripts *regulations and its whole design* [e]13 The common cubit was about 1 1/2 feet (about 0.5 meter). [f]13 That is, about 3 inches (about 8 centimeters) [g]13 That is, about 9 inches (about 22 centimeters) [h]27 Traditionally *peace offerings*

prince himself is the only one who may sit
inside the gateway to eat in the presence of
the LORD. He is to enter by way of the portico
of the gateway and go out the same way."
4Then the man brought me by way of the
north gate to the front of the temple. I looked
and saw the glory of the LORD filling the temple of the LORD, and I fell facedown.
5The LORD said to me, "Son of man, look
carefully, listen closely and give attention to
everything I tell you concerning all the regulations regarding the temple of the LORD.
Give attention to the entrance of the temple
and all the exits of the sanctuary. 6Say to the
rebellious house of Israel, 'This is what the
Sovereign LORD says: Enough of your detestable practices, O house of Israel! 7In addition
to all your other detestable practices, you
brought foreigners uncircumcised in heart
and flesh into my sanctuary, desecrating my
temple while you offered me food, fat and
blood, and you broke my covenant. 8Instead
of carrying out your duty in regard to my holy
things, you put others in charge of my sanctuary. 9This is what the Sovereign LORD says:
No foreigner uncircumcised in heart and
flesh is to enter my sanctuary, not even the
foreigners who live among the Israelites.
10" 'The Levites who went far from me
when Israel went astray and who wandered
from me after their idols must bear the
consequences of their sin. 11They may serve
in my sanctuary, having charge of the gates
of the temple and serving in it; they may
slaughter the burnt offerings and sacrifices
for the people and stand before the people
and serve them. 12But because they served
them in the presence of their idols and made
the house of Israel fall into sin, therefore I
have sworn with uplifted hand that they must
bear the consequences of their sin, declares
the Sovereign LORD. 13They are not to come
near to serve me as priests or come near any
of my holy things or my most holy offerings;
they must bear the shame of their detestable
practices. 14Yet I will put them in charge of
the duties of the temple and all the work that
is to be done in it.
15" 'But the priests, who are Levites and
descendants of Zadok and who faithfully carried out the duties of my sanctuary when the
Israelites went astray from me, are to come
near to minister before me; they are to stand
before me to offer sacrifices of fat and blood,
declares the Sovereign LORD. 16They alone
are to enter my sanctuary; they alone are to
come near my table to minister before me
and perform my service.
17" 'When they enter the gates of the inner
court, they are to wear linen clothes; they
must not wear any woolen garment while
ministering at the gates of the inner court or
inside the temple. 18They are to wear linen
turbans on their heads and linen undergarments around their waists. They must not
wear anything that makes them perspire.
19When they go out into the outer court
where the people are, they are to take off the
clothes they have been ministering in and
are to leave them in the sacred rooms, and
put on other clothes, so that they do not
consecrate the people by means of their garments.
20" 'They must not shave their heads or let
their hair grow long, but they are to keep the
hair of their heads trimmed. 21No priest is to
drink wine when he enters the inner court.
22They must not marry widows or divorced
women; they may marry only virgins of Israelite descent or widows of priests. 23They are
to teach my people the difference between
the holy and the common and show them
how to distinguish between the unclean and
the clean.
24" 'In any dispute, the priests are to serve
as judges and decide it according to my ordinances. They are to keep my laws and my
decrees for all my appointed feasts, and they
are to keep my Sabbaths holy.
25" 'A priest must not defile himself by going near a dead person; however, if the dead
person was his father or mother, son or
daughter, brother or unmarried sister, then
he may defile himself. 26After he is cleansed,
he must wait seven days. 27On the day he
goes into the inner court of the sanctuary to
minister in the sanctuary, he is to offer a sin
offering for himself, declares the Sovereign
LORD.
28" 'I am to be the only inheritance the
priests have. You are to give them no
possession in Israel; I will be their possession. 29They will eat the grain offerings, the
sin offerings and the guilt offerings; and
everything in Israel devoted[a] to the LORD will
belong to them. 30The best of all the firstfruits
and of all your special gifts will belong to the
priests. You are to give them the first portion
of your ground meal so that a blessing may
rest on your household. 31The priests must

[a]29 The Hebrew term refers to the irrevocable giving over of things or persons to the LORD.

not eat anything, bird or animal, found dead or torn by wild animals.

Division of the Land

45 " 'When you allot the land as an inheritance, you are to present to the LORD a portion of the land as a sacred district, 25,000 cubits long and 20,000[a] cubits wide; the entire area will be holy. 2 Of this, a section 500 cubits square is to be for the sanctuary, with 50 cubits around it for open land. 3 In the sacred district, measure off a section 25,000 cubits[b] long and 10,000 cubits[c] wide. In it will be the sanctuary, the Most Holy Place. 4 It will be the sacred portion of the land for the priests, who minister in the sanctuary and who draw near to minister before the LORD. It will be a place for their houses as well as a holy place for the sanctuary. 5 An area 25,000 cubits long and 10,000 cubits wide will belong to the Levites, who serve in the temple, as their possession for towns to live in.[d]

6 " 'You are to give the city as its property an area 5,000 cubits wide and 25,000 cubits long, adjoining the sacred portion; it will belong to the whole house of Israel.

7 " 'The prince will have the land bordering each side of the area formed by the sacred district and the property of the city. It will extend westward from the west side and eastward from the east side, running lengthwise from the western to the eastern border parallel to one of the tribal portions. 8 This land will be his possession in Israel. And my princes will no longer oppress my people but will allow the house of Israel to possess the land according to their tribes.

9 " 'This is what the Sovereign LORD says: You have gone far enough, O princes of Israel! Give up your violence and oppression and do what is just and right. Stop dispossessing my people, declares the Sovereign LORD. 10 You are to use accurate scales, an accurate ephah[e] and an accurate bath.[f] 11 The ephah and the bath are to be the same size, the bath containing a tenth of a homer[g] and the ephah a tenth of a homer; the homer is to be the standard measure for both. 12 The shekel[h] is to consist of twenty gerahs. Twenty shekels plus twenty-five shekels plus fifteen shekels equal one mina.[i]

Offerings and Holy Days

13 " 'This is the special gift you are to offer: a sixth of an ephah from each homer of wheat and a sixth of an ephah from each homer of barley. 14 The prescribed portion of oil, measured by the bath, is a tenth of a bath from each cor (which consists of ten baths or one homer, for ten baths are equivalent to a homer). 15 Also one sheep is to be taken from every flock of two hundred from the well-watered pastures of Israel. These will be used for the grain offerings, burnt offerings and fellowship offerings[j] to make atonement for the people, declares the Sovereign LORD. 16 All the people of the land will participate in this special gift for the use of the prince in Israel. 17 It will be the duty of the prince to provide the burnt offerings, grain offerings and drink offerings at the festivals, the New Moons and the Sabbaths—at all the appointed feasts of the house of Israel. He will provide the sin offerings, grain offerings, burnt offerings and fellowship offerings to make atonement for the house of Israel.

18 " 'This is what the Sovereign LORD says: In the first month on the first day you are to take a young bull without defect and purify the sanctuary. 19 The priest is to take some of the blood of the sin offering and put it on the doorposts of the temple, on the four corners of the upper ledge of the altar and on the gateposts of the inner court. 20 You are to do the same on the seventh day of the month for anyone who sins unintentionally or through ignorance; so you are to make atonement for the temple.

21 " 'In the first month on the fourteenth day you are to observe the Passover, a feast lasting seven days, during which you shall eat bread made without yeast. 22 On that day the prince is to provide a bull as a sin offering for himself and for all the people of the land. 23 Every day during the seven days of the Feast he is to provide seven bulls and seven rams without defect as a burnt offering to the LORD, and a male goat for a sin offering. 24 He is to provide as a grain offering an ephah for each bull and an ephah for each ram, along with a hin[k] of oil for each ephah.

25 " 'During the seven days of the Feast,

---

[a] 1 Septuagint (see also verses 3 and 5 and 48:9); Hebrew *10,000*
[b] 3 That is, about 7 miles (about 12 kilometers)
[c] 3 That is, about 3 miles (about 5 kilometers)
[d] 5 Septuagint; Hebrew *temple; they will have as their possession 20 rooms*
[e] 10 An ephah was a dry measure.
[f] 10 A bath was a liquid measure.
[g] 11 A homer was a dry measure.
[h] 12 A shekel weighed about 2/5 ounce (about 11.5 grams).
[i] 12 That is, 60 shekels; the common mina was 50 shekels.
[j] 15 Traditionally *peace offerings*; also in verse 17
[k] 24 That is, probably about 4 quarts (about 4 liters)

which begins in the seventh month on the
fifteenth day, he is to make the same provision for sin offerings, burnt offerings, grain
offerings and oil.

46 " 'This is what the Sovereign LORD
says: The gate of the inner court facing east is to be shut on the six working days,
but on the Sabbath day and on the day of the
New Moon it is to be opened. 2The prince is
to enter from the outside through the portico
of the gateway and stand by the gatepost.
The priests are to sacrifice his burnt offering
and his fellowship offerings.[a] He is to worship at the threshold of the gateway and then
go out, but the gate will not be shut until
evening. 3On the Sabbaths and New Moons
the people of the land are to worship in the
presence of the LORD at the entrance to that
gateway. 4The burnt offering the prince
brings to the LORD on the Sabbath day is to be
six male lambs and a ram, all without defect.
5The grain offering given with the ram is to be
an ephah,[b] and the grain offering with the
lambs is to be as much as he pleases, along
with a hin[c] of oil for each ephah. 6On the day
of the New Moon he is to offer a young bull,
six lambs and a ram, all without defect. 7He is
to provide as a grain offering one ephah with
the bull, one ephah with the ram, and with the
lambs as much as he wants to give, along
with a hin of oil with each ephah. 8When the
prince enters, he is to go in through the portico of the gateway, and he is to come out the
same way.

9" 'When the people of the land come before the LORD at the appointed feasts, whoever enters by the north gate to worship is to
go out the south gate; and whoever enters by
the south gate is to go out the north gate. No
one is to return through the gate by which he
entered, but each is to go out the opposite
gate. 10The prince is to be among them, going in when they go in and going out when
they go out.

11" 'At the festivals and the appointed
feasts, the grain offering is to be an ephah
with a bull, an ephah with a ram, and with the
lambs as much as one pleases, along with a
hin of oil for each ephah. 12When the prince
provides a freewill offering to the LORD—
whether a burnt offering or fellowship offerings—the gate facing east is to be opened
for him. He shall offer his burnt offering or his
fellowship offerings as he does on the Sabbath day. Then he shall go out, and after he
has gone out, the gate will be shut.

13" 'Every day you are to provide a year-
old lamb without defect for a burnt offering to
the LORD; morning by morning you shall provide it. 14You are also to provide with it morning by morning a grain offering, consisting of
a sixth of an ephah with a third of a hin of oil
to moisten the flour. The presenting of this
grain offering to the LORD is a lasting ordinance. 15So the lamb and the grain offering
and the oil shall be provided morning by
morning for a regular burnt offering.

16" 'This is what the Sovereign LORD says:
If the prince makes a gift from his inheritance
to one of his sons, it will also belong to his
descendants; it is to be their property by inheritance. 17If, however, he makes a gift from
his inheritance to one of his servants, the
servant may keep it until the year of freedom;
then it will revert to the prince. His inheritance belongs to his sons only; it is theirs.
18The prince must not take any of the inheritance of the people, driving them off their
property. He is to give his sons their inheritance out of his own property, so that none of
my people will be separated from his property.' "

19Then the man brought me through the
entrance at the side of the gate to the sacred
rooms facing north, which belonged to the
priests, and showed me a place at the western end. 20He said to me, "This is the place
where the priests will cook the guilt offering
and the sin offering and bake the grain offering, to avoid bringing them into the outer
court and consecrating the people."

21He then brought me to the outer court
and led me around to its four corners, and I
saw in each corner another court. 22In the
four corners of the outer court were enclosed[d] courts, forty cubits long and thirty
cubits wide; each of the courts in the four
corners was the same size. 23Around the
inside of each of the four courts was a ledge
of stone, with places for fire built all around
under the ledge. 24He said to me, "These are
the kitchens where those who minister at the
temple will cook the sacrifices of the people."

The River From the Temple

47 The man brought me back to the entrance of the temple, and I saw water
coming out from under the threshold of the

[a]2 Traditionally *peace offerings*; also in verse 12
[b]5 That is, probably about 3/5 bushel (about 22 liters)
[c]5 That is, probably about 4 quarts (about 4 liters)
[d]22 The meaning of the Hebrew for this word is uncertain.

temple toward the east (for the temple faced
east). The water was coming down from under the south side of the temple, south of the
altar. 2He then brought me out through the
north gate and led me around the outside to
the outer gate facing east, and the water was
flowing from the south side.

3As the man went eastward with a measuring line in his hand, he measured off a thousand cubits[a] and then led me through water
that was ankle-deep. 4He measured off another thousand cubits and led me through
water that was knee-deep. He measured off
another thousand and led me through water
that was up to the waist. 5He measured off
another thousand, but now it was a river that
I could not cross, because the water had
risen and was deep enough to swim in—a
river that no one could cross. 6He asked me,
"Son of man, do you see this?"

Then he led me back to the bank of the
river. 7When I arrived there, I saw a great
number of trees on each side of the river. 8He
said to me, "This water flows toward the
eastern region and goes down into the Arabah,[b] where it enters the Sea.[c] When it emp-
ties into the Sea,[c] the water there becomes
fresh. 9Swarms of living creatures will live
wherever the river flows. There will be large
numbers of fish, because this water flows
there and makes the salt water fresh; so
where the river flows everything will live.
10Fishermen will stand along the shore; from
En Gedi to En Eglaim there will be places for
spreading nets. The fish will be of many
kinds—like the fish of the Great Sea.[d] 11But
the swamps and marshes will not become
fresh; they will be left for salt. 12Fruit trees of
all kinds will grow on both banks of the river.
Their leaves will not wither, nor will their fruit
fail. Every month they will bear, because the
water from the sanctuary flows to them.
Their fruit will serve for food and their leaves
for healing."

The Boundaries of the Land

13This is what the Sovereign LORD says:
"These are the boundaries by which you are
to divide the land for an inheritance among
the twelve tribes of Israel, with two portions
for Joseph. 14You are to divide it equally
among them. Because I swore with uplifted
hand to give it to your forefathers, this land
will become your inheritance.

15"This is to be the boundary of the land:

"On the north side it will run from the Great
Sea by the Hethlon road past Lebo[e]
Hamath to Zedad, 16Berothah[f] and
Sibraim (which lies on the border
between Damascus and Hamath), as
far as Hazer Hatticon, which is on the
border of Hauran. 17The boundary will
extend from the sea to Hazar Enan,[g]
along the northern border of Damascus, with the border of Hamath
to the north. This will be the north
boundary.

18"On the east side the boundary will run
between Hauran and Damascus,
along the northern border of Damascus, with the border of Hamath
and as far as Tamar.[h] This will be the
east boundary.

19"On the south side it will run from Tamar as
far as the waters of Meribah Kadesh,
then along the Wadi ⌊of Egypt⌋ to the
Great Sea. This will be the south
boundary.

20"On the west side, the Great Sea will be the
boundary to a point opposite Lebo[i]
Hamath. This will be the west
boundary.

21"You are to distribute this land among
yourselves according to the tribes of Israel.
22You are to allot it as an inheritance for
yourselves and for the aliens who have settled among you and who have children. You
are to consider them as native-born Israelites; along with you they are to be allotted an
inheritance among the tribes of Israel. 23In
whatever tribe the alien settles, there you are
to give him his inheritance," declares the
Sovereign LORD.

The Division of the Land

48 "These are the tribes, listed by
name: At the northern frontier, Dan
will have one portion; it will follow the Hethlon
road to Lebo[j] Hamath; Hazar Enan and the
northern border of Damascus next to
Hamath will be part of its border from the
east side to the west side.

[a]3 That is, about 1,500 feet (about 450 meters) [b]8 Or *the Jordan Valley* [c]8 That is, the Dead Sea
[d]10 That is, the Mediterranean; also in verses 15, 19 and 20 [e]15 Or *past the entrance to* [f]15,16 See
Septuagint and Ezekiel 48:1; Hebrew *road to go into Zedad,* [16]*Hamath, Berothah* [g]17 Hebrew *Enon,* a variant
of *Enan* [h]18 Septuagint and Syriac; Hebrew *Israel. You will measure to the eastern sea* [i]20 Or *opposite
the entrance to* [j]1 Or *to the entrance to*

2"Asher will have one portion; it will border the territory of Dan from east to west.

3"Naphtali will have one portion; it will border the territory of Asher from east to west.

4"Manasseh will have one portion; it will border the territory of Naphtali from east to west.

5"Ephraim will have one portion; it will border the territory of Manasseh from east to west.

6"Reuben will have one portion; it will border the territory of Ephraim from east to west.

7"Judah will have one portion; it will border the territory of Reuben from east to west.

8"Bordering the territory of Judah from east to west will be the portion you are to present as a special gift. It will be 25,000 cubits[a] wide, and its length from east to west will equal one of the tribal portions; the sanctuary will be in the center of it.

9"The special portion you are to offer to the LORD will be 25,000 cubits long and 10,000 cubits[b] wide. 10This will be the sacred portion for the priests. It will be 25,000 cubits long on the north side, 10,000 cubits wide on the west side, 10,000 cubits wide on the east side and 25,000 cubits long on the south side. In the center of it will be the sanctuary of the LORD. 11This will be for the consecrated priests, the Zadokites, who were faithful in serving me and did not go astray as the Levites did when the Israelites went astray. 12It will be a special gift to them from the sacred portion of the land, a most holy portion, bordering the territory of the Levites.

13"Alongside the territory of the priests, the Levites will have an allotment 25,000 cubits long and 10,000 cubits wide. Its total length will be 25,000 cubits and its width 10,000 cubits. 14They must not sell or exchange any of it. This is the best of the land and must not pass into other hands, because it is holy to the LORD.

15"The remaining area, 5,000 cubits wide and 25,000 cubits long, will be for the common use of the city, for houses and for pastureland. The city will be in the center of it 16and will have these measurements: the north side 4,500 cubits, the south side 4,500 cubits, the east side 4,500 cubits, and the west side 4,500 cubits. 17The pastureland for the city will be 250 cubits on the north, 250 cubits on the south, 250 cubits on the east, and 250 cubits on the west. 18What remains of the area, bordering on the sacred portion and running the length of it, will be 10,000 cubits on the east side and 10,000 cubits on the west side. Its produce will supply food for the workers of the city. 19The workers from the city who farm it will come from all the tribes of Israel. 20The entire portion will be a square, 25,000 cubits on each side. As a special gift you will set aside the sacred portion, along with the property of the city.

21"What remains on both sides of the area formed by the sacred portion and the city property will belong to the prince. It will extend eastward from the 25,000 cubits of the sacred portion to the eastern border, and westward from the 25,000 cubits to the western border. Both these areas running the length of the tribal portions will belong to the prince, and the sacred portion with the temple sanctuary will be in the center of them. 22So the property of the Levites and the property of the city will lie in the center of the area that belongs to the prince. The area belonging to the prince will lie between the border of Judah and the border of Benjamin.

23"As for the rest of the tribes: Benjamin will have one portion; it will extend from the east side to the west side.

24"Simeon will have one portion; it will border the territory of Benjamin from east to west.

25"Issachar will have one portion; it will border the territory of Simeon from east to west.

26"Zebulun will have one portion; it will border the territory of Issachar from east to west.

27"Gad will have one portion; it will border the territory of Zebulun from east to west.

28"The southern boundary of Gad will run south from Tamar to the waters of Meribah Kadesh, then along the Wadi ⌞of Egypt⌟ to the Great Sea.[c]

29"This is the land you are to allot as an inheritance to the tribes of Israel, and these will be their portions," declares the Sovereign LORD.

The Gates of the City

30"These will be the exits of the city: Beginning on the north side, which is 4,500 cubits long, 31the gates of the city will be named after the tribes of Israel. The three gates on

[a] *8* That is, about 7 miles (about 12 kilometers) [b] *9* That is, about 3 miles (about 5 kilometers) [c] *28* That is, the Mediterranean

the north side will be the gate of Reuben, the
gate of Judah and the gate of Levi.
32"On the east side, which is 4,500 cubits
long, will be three gates: the gate of Joseph,
the gate of Benjamin and the gate of Dan.
33"On the south side, which measures
4,500 cubits, will be three gates: the gate
of Simeon, the gate of Issachar and the gate
of Zebulun.
34"On the west side, which is 4,500 cubits
long, will be three gates: the gate of Gad, the
gate of Asher and the gate of Naphtali.
35"The distance all around will be 18,000
cubits.

"And the name of the city from that time on
will be:

THE LORD IS THERE."

Daniel

Introduction:

Daniel has traditionally been named the author of this book. The entire book tells of the experiences of Daniel and his friends and the divine revelation that came to Daniel in dreams and visions during his lifetime (about 605–530 B.C.).

Daniel was taken hostage from Jerusalem in 605 B.C. to the Babylonian court. After telling and interpreting Nebuchadnezzar's dream he was given a position of power. He wrote this book during Israel's captivity to encourage the people to trust in God who controls all of history.

In the last six chapters of this book, Daniel describes his visions of the rise and fall of earthly kingdoms and finally the rise of an everlasting kingdom.

Outline of contents:

Daniel's Training in Babylon

1 In the third year of the reign of Jehoiakim
king of Judah, Nebuchadnezzar king of
Babylon came to Jerusalem and besieged it.
2 And the Lord delivered Jehoiakim king of
Judah into his hand, along with some of the
articles from the temple of God. These he
carried off to the temple of his god in Babylonia[a] and put in the treasure house of his god.
3 Then the king ordered Ashpenaz, chief of
his court officials, to bring in some of the
Israelites from the royal family and the nobility— 4 young men without any physical defect,
handsome, showing aptitude for every kind
of learning, well informed, quick to understand, and qualified to serve in the king's
palace. He was to teach them the language
and literature of the Babylonians.[b] 5 The king
assigned them a daily amount of food and
wine from the king's table. They were to be
trained for three years, and after that they
were to enter the king's service.
6 Among these were some from Judah:
Daniel, Hananiah, Mishael and Azariah.
7 The chief official gave them new names: to
Daniel, the name Belteshazzar; to Hananiah, Shadrach; to Mishael, Meshach; and to
Azariah, Abednego.
8 But Daniel resolved not to defile himself
with the royal food and wine, and he asked
the chief official for permission not to defile
himself this way. 9 Now God had caused the
official to show favor and sympathy to Daniel, 10 but the official told Daniel, "I am afraid
of my lord the king, who has assigned your[c]
food and drink. Why should he see you looking worse than the other young men your
age? The king would then have my head
because of you."
11 Daniel then said to the guard whom the
chief official had appointed over Daniel,
Hananiah, Mishael and Azariah, 12 "Please
test your servants for ten days: Give us nothing but vegetables to eat and water to drink.
13 Then compare our appearance with that of
the young men who eat the royal food, and
treat your servants in accordance with what
you see." 14 So he agreed to this and tested
them for ten days.
15 At the end of the ten days they looked
healthier and better nourished than any of
the young men who ate the royal food. 16 So

[a]2 Hebrew *Shinar* [b]4 Or *Chaldeans* [c]10 The Hebrew for *your* and *you* in this verse is plural.

the guard took away their choice food and
the wine they were to drink and gave them
vegetables instead.
17To these four young men God gave
knowledge and understanding of all kinds of
literature and learning. And Daniel could understand visions and dreams of all kinds.
18At the end of the time set by the king to
bring them in, the chief official presented
them to Nebuchadnezzar. 19The king talked
with them, and he found none equal to Daniel, Hananiah, Mishael and Azariah; so they
entered the king's service. 20In every matter
of wisdom and understanding about which
the king questioned them, he found them ten
times better than all the magicians and enchanters in his whole kingdom.
21And Daniel remained there until the first
year of King Cyrus.

Nebuchadnezzar's Dream

2 In the second year of his reign, Nebuchadnezzar had dreams; his mind was
troubled and he could not sleep. 2So the king
summoned the magicians, enchanters, sorcerers and astrologers[a] to tell him what he
had dreamed. When they came in and stood
before the king, 3he said to them, "I have had
a dream that troubles me and I want to know
what it means.[b]"
4Then the astrologers answered the king
in Aramaic,[c] "O king, live forever! Tell your
servants the dream, and we will interpret it."
5The king replied to the astrologers, "This
is what I have firmly decided: If you do not tell
me what my dream was and interpret it, I will
have you cut into pieces and your houses
turned into piles of rubble. 6But if you tell me
the dream and explain it, you will receive
from me gifts and rewards and great honor.
So tell me the dream and interpret it for me."
7Once more they replied, "Let the king tell
his servants the dream, and we will interpret
it."
8Then the king answered, "I am certain
that you are trying to gain time, because you
realize that this is what I have firmly decided:
9If you do not tell me the dream, there is just
one penalty for you. You have conspired to
tell me misleading and wicked things, hoping
the situation will change. So then, tell me the
dream, and I will know that you can interpret
it for me."
10The astrologers answered the king,
"There is not a man on earth who can do
what the king asks! No king, however great
and mighty, has ever asked such a thing of
any magician or enchanter or astrologer.
11What the king asks is too difficult. No one
can reveal it to the king except the gods, and
they do not live among men."
12This made the king so angry and furious
that he ordered the execution of all the wise
men of Babylon. 13So the decree was issued
to put the wise men to death, and men were
sent to look for Daniel and his friends to put
them to death.
14When Arioch, the commander of the
king's guard, had gone out to put to death the
wise men of Babylon, Daniel spoke to him
with wisdom and tact. 15He asked the king's
officer, "Why did the king issue such a harsh
decree?" Arioch then explained the matter to
Daniel. 16At this, Daniel went in to the king
and asked for time, so that he might interpret
the dream for him.
17Then Daniel returned to his house and
explained the matter to his friends Hananiah,
Mishael and Azariah. 18He urged them to
plead for mercy from the God of heaven concerning this mystery, so that he and his
friends might not be executed with the rest of
the wise men of Babylon. 19During the night
the mystery was revealed to Daniel in a vision. Then Daniel praised the God of heaven
20and said:

"Praise be to the name of God for ever
and ever;
wisdom and power are his.
21He changes times and seasons;
he sets up kings and deposes them.
He gives wisdom to the wise
and knowledge to the discerning.
22He reveals deep and hidden things;
he knows what lies in darkness,
and light dwells with him.
23I thank and praise you, O God of my
fathers:
You have given me wisdom and power,
you have made known to me what we
asked of you,
you have made known to us the dream
of the king."

Daniel Interprets the Dream

24Then Daniel went to Arioch, whom the
king had appointed to execute the wise men

[a]2 Or *Chaldeans*; also in verses 4, 5 and 10
[b]3 Or *was*
[c]4 The text from here through chapter 7 is in Aramaic.

of Babylon, and said to him, "Do not execute
the wise men of Babylon. Take me to the
king, and I will interpret his dream for him."
25Arioch took Daniel to the king at once
and said, "I have found a man among the
exiles from Judah who can tell the king what
his dream means."
26The king asked Daniel (also called Belteshazzar), "Are you able to tell me what I saw
in my dream and interpret it?"
27Daniel replied, "No wise man, enchanter, magician or diviner can explain to the king
the mystery he has asked about, 28but there
is a God in heaven who reveals mysteries.
He has shown King Nebuchadnezzar what
will happen in days to come. Your dream and
the visions that passed through your mind as
you lay on your bed are these:
29"As you were lying there, O king, your
mind turned to things to come, and the revealer of mysteries showed you what is going to happen. 30As for me, this mystery has
been revealed to me, not because I have
greater wisdom than other living men, but so
that you, O king, may know the interpretation
and that you may understand what went
through your mind.
31"You looked, O king, and there before
you stood a large statue—an enormous,
dazzling statue, awesome in appearance.
32The head of the statue was made of pure
gold, its chest and arms of silver, its belly and
thighs of bronze, 33its legs of iron, its feet
partly of iron and partly of baked clay.
34While you were watching, a rock was cut
out, but not by human hands. It struck the
statue on its feet of iron and clay and
smashed them. 35Then the iron, the clay, the
bronze, the silver and the gold were broken
to pieces at the same time and became like
chaff on a threshing floor in the summer. The
wind swept them away without leaving a
trace. But the rock that struck the statue
became a huge mountain and filled the
whole earth.
36"This was the dream, and now we will
interpret it to the king. 37You, O king, are the
king of kings. The God of heaven has given
you dominion and power and might and
glory; 38in your hands he has placed mankind and the beasts of the field and the birds
of the air. Wherever they live, he has made
you ruler over them all. You are that head of
gold.
39"After you, another kingdom will rise, inferior to yours. Next, a third kingdom, one of
bronze, will rule over the whole earth. 40Fi-
nally, there will be a fourth kingdom, strong
as iron—for iron breaks and smashes everything—and as iron breaks things to pieces,
so it will crush and break all the others. 41Just
as you saw that the feet and toes were partly
of baked clay and partly of iron, so this will be
a divided kingdom; yet it will have some of
the strength of iron in it, even as you saw iron
mixed with clay. 42As the toes were partly
iron and partly clay, so this kingdom will be
partly strong and partly brittle. 43And just as
you saw the iron mixed with baked clay, so
the people will be a mixture and will not remain united, any more than iron mixes with
clay.
44"In the time of those kings, the God of
heaven will set up a kingdom that will never
be destroyed, nor will it be left to another
people. It will crush all those kingdoms and
bring them to an end, but it will itself endure
forever. 45This is the meaning of the vision of
the rock cut out of a mountain, but not by
human hands—a rock that broke the iron,
the bronze, the clay, the silver and the gold to
pieces.
"The great God has shown the king what
will take place in the future. The dream is true
and the interpretation is trustworthy."
46Then King Nebuchadnezzar fell prostrate before Daniel and paid him honor and
ordered that an offering and incense be
presented to him. 47The king said to Daniel,
"Surely your God is the God of gods and the
Lord of kings and a revealer of mysteries, for
you were able to reveal this mystery."
48Then the king placed Daniel in a high
position and lavished many gifts on him. He
made him ruler over the entire province of
Babylon and placed him in charge of all its
wise men. 49Moreover, at Daniel's request
the king appointed Shadrach, Meshach and
Abednego administrators over the province
of Babylon, while Daniel himself remained at
the royal court.

The Image of Gold and the Fiery Furnace

3 King Nebuchadnezzar made an image
of gold, ninety feet high and nine feet[a]
wide, and set it up on the plain of Dura in the
province of Babylon. 2He then summoned
the satraps, prefects, governors, advisers,

[a] 1 Aramaic *sixty cubits high and six cubits wide* (about 27 meters high and 2.7 meters wide)

treasurers, judges, magistrates and all the
other provincial officials to come to the dedication of the image he had set up. 3So the
satraps, prefects, governors, advisers, treasurers, judges, magistrates and all the other
provincial officials assembled for the dedication of the image that King Nebuchadnezzar
had set up, and they stood before it.

4Then the herald loudly proclaimed, "This
is what you are commanded to do, O peoples, nations and men of every language:
5As soon as you hear the sound of the horn,
flute, zither, lyre, harp, pipes and all kinds of
music, you must fall down and worship the
image of gold that King Nebuchadnezzar
has set up. 6Whoever does not fall down and
worship will immediately be thrown into a
blazing furnace."

7Therefore, as soon as they heard the
sound of the horn, flute, zither, lyre, harp and
all kinds of music, all the peoples, nations
and men of every language fell down and
worshiped the image of gold that King Nebuchadnezzar had set up.

8At this time some astrologers[a] came forward and denounced the Jews. 9They said to
King Nebuchadnezzar, "O king, live forever!
10You have issued a decree, O king, that
everyone who hears the sound of the horn,
flute, zither, lyre, harp, pipes and all kinds of
music must fall down and worship the image
of gold, 11and that whoever does not fall
down and worship will be thrown into a blazing furnace. 12But there are some Jews
whom you have set over the affairs of the
province of Babylon—Shadrach, Meshach
and Abednego—who pay no attention to
you, O king. They neither serve your gods
nor worship the image of gold you have set
up."

13Furious with rage, Nebuchadnezzar
summoned Shadrach, Meshach and Abednego. So these men were brought before the
king, 14and Nebuchadnezzar said to them,
"Is it true, Shadrach, Meshach and Abednego, that you do not serve my gods or worship the image of gold I have set up? 15Now
when you hear the sound of the horn, flute,
zither, lyre, harp, pipes and all kinds of music, if you are ready to fall down and worship
the image I made, very good. But if you do
not worship it, you will be thrown immediately into a blazing furnace. Then what god
will be able to rescue you from my hand?"

16Shadrach, Meshach and Abednego replied to the king, "O Nebuchadnezzar, we do
not need to defend ourselves before you in
this matter. 17If we are thrown into the blazing
furnace, the God we serve is able to save us
from it, and he will rescue us from your hand,
O king. 18But even if he does not, we want
you to know, O king, that we will not serve
your gods or worship the image of gold you
have set up."

19Then Nebuchadnezzar was furious with
Shadrach, Meshach and Abednego, and his
attitude toward them changed. He ordered
the furnace heated seven times hotter than
usual 20and commanded some of the strongest soldiers in his army to tie up Shadrach,
Meshach and Abednego and throw them into
the blazing furnace. 21So these men, wearing their robes, trousers, turbans and other
clothes, were bound and thrown into the
blazing furnace. 22The king's command was
so urgent and the furnace so hot that the
flames of the fire killed the soldiers who took
up Shadrach, Meshach and Abednego,
23and these three men, firmly tied, fell into
the blazing furnace.

24Then King Nebuchadnezzar leaped to
his feet in amazement and asked his advisers, "Weren't there three men that we tied up
and threw into the fire?"

They replied, "Certainly, O king."

25He said, "Look! I see four men walking
around in the fire, unbound and unharmed,
and the fourth looks like a son of the gods."

26Nebuchadnezzar then approached the
opening of the blazing furnace and shouted,
"Shadrach, Meshach and Abednego, servants of the Most High God, come out! Come
here!"

So Shadrach, Meshach and Abednego
came out of the fire, 27and the satraps, prefects, governors and royal advisers crowded
around them. They saw that the fire had not
harmed their bodies, nor was a hair of their
heads singed; their robes were not
scorched, and there was no smell of fire on
them.

28Then Nebuchadnezzar said, "Praise be
to the God of Shadrach, Meshach and Abednego, who has sent his angel and rescued
his servants! They trusted in him and defied
the king's command and were willing to give
up their lives rather than serve or worship
any god except their own God. 29Therefore I
decree that the people of any nation or language who say anything against the God of

[a]8 Or *Chaldeans*

Shadrach, Meshach and Abednego be cut
into pieces and their houses be turned into
piles of rubble, for no other god can save in
this way."
30Then the king promoted Shadrach, Meshach and Abednego in the province of Babylon.

Nebuchadnezzar's Dream of a Tree

4 King Nebuchadnezzar,

To the peoples, nations and men of
every language, who live in all the world:

May you prosper greatly!

2It is my pleasure to tell you about the
miraculous signs and wonders that the
Most High God has performed for me.

3How great are his signs,
how mighty his wonders!
His kingdom is an eternal kingdom;
his dominion endures from generation
to generation.

4I, Nebuchadnezzar, was at home in
my palace, contented and prosperous.
5I had a dream that made me afraid. As
I was lying in my bed, the images and
visions that passed through my mind
terrified me. 6So I commanded that all
the wise men of Babylon be brought before me to interpret the dream for me.
7When the magicians, enchanters, astrologers[a] and diviners came, I told
them the dream, but they could not interpret it for me. 8Finally, Daniel came
into my presence and I told him the
dream. (He is called Belteshazzar, after
the name of my god, and the spirit of the
holy gods is in him.)
9I said, "Belteshazzar, chief of the
magicians, I know that the spirit of the
holy gods is in you, and no mystery is
too difficult for you. Here is my dream;
interpret it for me. 10These are the visions I saw while lying in my bed: I
looked, and there before me stood a
tree in the middle of the land. Its height
was enormous. 11The tree grew large
and strong and its top touched the sky; it
was visible to the ends of the earth. 12Its
leaves were beautiful, its fruit abundant,
and on it was food for all. Under it the
beasts of the field found shelter, and the
birds of the air lived in its branches; from
it every creature was fed.
13"In the visions I saw while lying in
my bed, I looked, and there before me
was a messenger,[b] a holy one, coming
down from heaven. 14He called in a loud
voice: 'Cut down the tree and trim off its
branches; strip off its leaves and scatter
its fruit. Let the animals flee from under it
and the birds from its branches. 15But let
the stump and its roots, bound with iron
and bronze, remain in the ground, in the
grass of the field.
" 'Let him be drenched with the dew of
heaven, and let him live with the animals
among the plants of the earth. 16Let his
mind be changed from that of a man and
let him be given the mind of an animal,
till seven times[c] pass by for him.
17" 'The decision is announced by
messengers, the holy ones declare the
verdict, so that the living may know that
the Most High is sovereign over the
kingdoms of men and gives them to
anyone he wishes and sets over them
the lowliest of men.'
18"This is the dream that I, King Nebuchadnezzar, had. Now, Belteshazzar,
tell me what it means, for none of the
wise men in my kingdom can interpret it
for me. But you can, because the spirit
of the holy gods is in you."

Daniel Interprets the Dream

19Then Daniel (also called Beltesha z-
zar) was greatly perplexed for a time,
and his thoughts terrified him. So the
king said, "Belteshazzar, do not let the
dream or its meaning alarm you."
Belteshazzar answered, "My lord, if
only the dream applied to your enemies
and its meaning to your adversaries!
20The tree you saw, which grew large
and strong, with its top touching the sky,
visible to the whole earth, 21with beautiful leaves and abundant fruit, providing
food for all, giving shelter to the beasts
of the field, and having nesting places in
its branches for the birds of the air—
22you, O king, are that tree! You have
become great and strong; your greatness has grown until it reaches the sky,
and your dominion extends to distant
parts of the earth.
23"You, O king, saw a messenger, a
holy one, coming down from heaven
and saying, 'Cut down the tree and de-

[a]7 Or *Chaldeans* [b]13 Or *watchman*; also in verses 17 and 23 [c]16 Or *years*; also in verses 23, 25 and 32

stroy it, but leave the stump, bound with
iron and bronze, in the grass of the field,
while its roots remain in the ground. Let
him be drenched with the dew of
heaven; let him live like the wild animals, until seven times pass by for him.'
24 "This is the interpretation, O king,
and this is the decree the Most High has
issued against my lord the king: 25 You
will be driven away from people and will
live with the wild animals; you will eat
grass like cattle and be drenched with
the dew of heaven. Seven times will
pass by for you until you acknowledge
that the Most High is sovereign over the
kingdoms of men and gives them to
anyone he wishes. 26 The command to
leave the stump of the tree with its roots
means that your kingdom will be restored to you when you acknowledge
that Heaven rules. 27 Therefore, O king,
be pleased to accept my advice: Renounce your sins by doing what is right,
and your wickedness by being kind to
the oppressed. It may be that then your
prosperity will continue."

The Dream Is Fulfilled

28 All this happened to King Nebuchadnezzar. 29 Twelve months later, as
the king was walking on the roof of the
royal palace of Babylon, 30 he said, "Is
not this the great Babylon I have built as
the royal residence, by my mighty power
and for the glory of my majesty?"
31 The words were still on his lips when
a voice came from heaven, "This is
what is decreed for you, King Nebuchadnezzar: Your royal authority has
been taken from you. 32 You will be
driven away from people and will live
with the wild animals; you will eat grass
like cattle. Seven times will pass by for
you until you acknowledge that the Most
High is sovereign over the kingdoms of
men and gives them to anyone he
wishes."
33 Immediately what had been said
about Nebuchadnezzar was fulfilled. He
was driven away from people and ate
grass like cattle. His body was drenched
with the dew of heaven until his hair
grew like the feathers of an eagle and
his nails like the claws of a bird.
34 At the end of that time, I, Nebuchadnezzar, raised my eyes toward
heaven, and my sanity was restored.
Then I praised the Most High; I honored
and glorified him who lives forever.

His dominion is an eternal dominion;
his kingdom endures from generation
to generation.
35 All the peoples of the earth
are regarded as nothing.
He does as he pleases
with the powers of heaven
and the peoples of the earth.
No one can hold back his hand
or say to him: "What have you done?"

36 At the same time that my sanity was
restored, my honor and splendor were
returned to me for the glory of my kingdom. My advisers and nobles sought
me out, and I was restored to my throne
and became even greater than before.
37 Now I, Nebuchadnezzar, praise and
exalt and glorify the King of heaven, because everything he does is right and all
his ways are just. And those who walk in
pride he is able to humble.

The Writing on the Wall

5 King Belshazzar gave a great banquet
for a thousand of his nobles and drank
wine with them. 2 While Belshazzar was
drinking his wine, he gave orders to bring in
the gold and silver goblets that Nebuchadnezzar his father[a] had taken from the
temple in Jerusalem, so that the king and his
nobles, his wives and his concubines might
drink from them. 3 So they brought in the gold
goblets that had been taken from the temple
of God in Jerusalem, and the king and his
nobles, his wives and his concubines drank
from them. 4 As they drank the wine, they
praised the gods of gold and silver, of
bronze, iron, wood and stone.
5 Suddenly the fingers of a human hand
appeared and wrote on the plaster of the
wall, near the lampstand in the royal palace.
The king watched the hand as it wrote. 6 His
face turned pale and he was so frightened
that his knees knocked together and his legs
gave way.
7 The king called out for the enchanters,
astrologers[b] and diviners to be brought and
said to these wise men of Babylon, "Whoever reads this writing and tells me what it
means will be clothed in purple and have a

[a]2 Or *ancestor;* or *predecessor,* also in verses 11, 13 and 18 [b]7 Or *Chaldeans*; also in verse 11

gold chain placed around his neck, and he will be made the third highest ruler in the kingdom."

8Then all the king's wise men came in, but they could not read the writing or tell the king what it meant. 9So King Belshazzar became even more terrified and his face grew more pale. His nobles were baffled.

10The queen,[a] hearing the voices of the king and his nobles, came into the banquet hall. "O king, live forever!" she said. "Don't be alarmed! Don't look so pale! 11There is a man in your kingdom who has the spirit of the holy gods in him. In the time of your father he was found to have insight and intelligence and wisdom like that of the gods. King Nebuchadnezzar your father—your father the king, I say—appointed him chief of the magicians, enchanters, astrologers and diviners. 12This man Daniel, whom the king called Belteshazzar, was found to have a keen mind and knowledge and understanding, and also the ability to interpret dreams, explain riddles and solve difficult problems. Call for Daniel, and he will tell you what the writing means."

13So Daniel was brought before the king, and the king said to him, "Are you Daniel, one of the exiles my father the king brought from Judah? 14I have heard that the spirit of the gods is in you and that you have insight, intelligence and outstanding wisdom. 15The wise men and enchanters were brought before me to read this writing and tell me what it means, but they could not explain it. 16Now I have heard that you are able to give interpretations and to solve difficult problems. If you can read this writing and tell me what it means, you will be clothed in purple and have a gold chain placed around your neck, and you will be made the third highest ruler in the kingdom."

17Then Daniel answered the king, "You may keep your gifts for yourself and give your rewards to someone else. Nevertheless, I will read the writing for the king and tell him what it means.

18"O king, the Most High God gave your father Nebuchadnezzar sovereignty and greatness and glory and splendor. 19Because of the high position he gave him, all the peoples and nations and men of every language dreaded and feared him. Those the king wanted to put to death, he put to death; those he wanted to spare, he spared; those he wanted to promote, he promoted; and those he wanted to humble, he humbled. 20But when his heart became arrogant and hardened with pride, he was deposed from his royal throne and stripped of his glory. 21He was driven away from people and given the mind of an animal; he lived with the wild donkeys and ate grass like cattle; and his body was drenched with the dew of heaven, until he acknowledged that the Most High God is sovereign over the kingdoms of men and sets over them anyone he wishes.

22"But you his son,[b] O Belshazzar, have not humbled yourself, though you knew all this. 23Instead, you have set yourself up against the Lord of heaven. You had the goblets from his temple brought to you, and you and your nobles, your wives and your concubines drank wine from them. You praised the gods of silver and gold, of bronze, iron, wood and stone, which cannot see or hear or understand. But you did not honor the God who holds in his hand your life and all your ways. 24Therefore he sent the hand that wrote the inscription.

25"This is the inscription that was written:

MENE, MENE, TEKEL, PARSIN[c]

26"This is what these words mean:

Mene[d]: God has numbered the days of your reign and brought it to an end.

27*Tekel*[e]: You have been weighed on the scales and found wanting.

28*Peres*[f]: Your kingdom is divided and given to the Medes and Persians."

29Then at Belshazzar's command, Daniel was clothed in purple, a gold chain was placed around his neck, and he was proclaimed the third highest ruler in the kingdom.

30That very night Belshazzar, king of the Babylonians,[g] was slain, 31and Darius the Mede took over the kingdom, at the age of sixty-two.

Daniel in the Den of Lions

6 It pleased Darius to appoint 120 satraps to rule throughout the kingdom, 2with three administrators over them, one of whom

[a]10 Or *queen mother* [b]22 Or *descendant;* or *successor* [c]25 Aramaic *UPARSIN* (that is, *AND PARSIN*) [d]26 *Mene* can mean *numbered* or *mina* (a unit of money). [e]27 *Tekel* can mean *weighed* or *shekel.* [f]28 *Peres* (the singular of *Parsin*) can mean *divided* or *Persia* or *a half mina* or *a half shekel.* [g]30 Or *Chaldeans*

was Daniel. The satraps were made accountable to them so that the king might not
suffer loss. 3Now Daniel so distinguished
himself among the administrators and the
satraps by his exceptional qualities that the
king planned to set him over the whole kingdom. 4At this, the administrators and the satraps tried to find grounds for charges
against Daniel in his conduct of government
affairs, but they were unable to do so. They
could find no corruption in him, because he
was trustworthy and neither corrupt nor negligent. 5Finally these men said, "We will never find any basis for charges against this
man Daniel unless it has something to do
with the law of his God."

6So the administrators and the satraps
went as a group to the king and said: "O King
Darius, live forever! 7The royal administrators, prefects, satraps, advisers and governors have all agreed that the king should
issue an edict and enforce the decree that
anyone who prays to any god or man during
the next thirty days, except to you, O king,
shall be thrown into the lions' den. 8Now, O
king, issue the decree and put it in writing so
that it cannot be altered—in accordance with
the laws of the Medes and Persians, which
cannot be repealed." 9So King Darius put the
decree in writing.

10Now when Daniel learned that the decree had been published, he went home to
his upstairs room where the windows
opened toward Jerusalem. Three times a
day he got down on his knees and prayed,
giving thanks to his God, just as he had done
before. 11Then these men went as a group
and found Daniel praying and asking God for
help. 12So they went to the king and spoke to
him about his royal decree: "Did you not
publish a decree that during the next thirty
days anyone who prays to any god or man
except to you, O king, would be thrown into
the lions' den?"

The king answered, "The decree stands
—in accordance with the laws of the Medes
and Persians, which cannot be repealed."

13Then they said to the king, "Daniel, who
is one of the exiles from Judah, pays no
attention to you, O king, or to the decree you
put in writing. He still prays three times a
day." 14When the king heard this, he was
greatly distressed; he was determined to
rescue Daniel and made every effort until
sundown to save him.

15Then the men went as a group to the king
and said to him, "Remember, O king, that
according to the law of the Medes and Persians no decree or edict that the king issues
can be changed."

16So the king gave the order, and they
brought Daniel and threw him into the lions'
den. The king said to Daniel, "May your God,
whom you serve continually, rescue you!"

17A stone was brought and placed over the
mouth of the den, and the king sealed it with
his own signet ring and with the rings of his
nobles, so that Daniel's situation might not
be changed. 18Then the king returned to his
palace and spent the night without eating
and without any entertainment being brought
to him. And he could not sleep.

19At the first light of dawn, the king got up
and hurried to the lions' den. 20When he
came near the den, he called to Daniel in an
anguished voice, "Daniel, servant of the living God, has your God, whom you serve
continually, been able to rescue you from the
lions?"

21Daniel answered, "O king, live forever!
22My God sent his angel, and he shut the
mouths of the lions. They have not hurt me,
because I was found innocent in his sight.
Nor have I ever done any wrong before you,
O king."

23The king was overjoyed and gave orders
to lift Daniel out of the den. And when Daniel
was lifted from the den, no wound was found
on him, because he had trusted in his God.

24At the king's command, the men who
had falsely accused Daniel were brought in
and thrown into the lions' den, along with
their wives and children. And before they
reached the floor of the den, the lions overpowered them and crushed all their bones.

25Then King Darius wrote to all the peoples, nations and men of every language
throughout the land:

"May you prosper greatly!

26"I issue a decree that in every part of
my kingdom people must fear and reverence the God of Daniel.

"For he is the living God
and he endures forever;
his kingdom will not be destroyed,
his dominion will never end.
27He rescues and he saves;
he performs signs and wonders
in the heavens and on the earth.
He has rescued Daniel
from the power of the lions."

28So Daniel prospered during the reign of

Darius and the reign of Cyrus[a] the Persian.

Daniel's Dream of Four Beasts

7 In the first year of Belshazzar king of
Babylon, Daniel had a dream, and visions passed through his mind as he was
lying on his bed. He wrote down the sub-
stance of his dream.
2Daniel said: "In my vision at night I
looked, and there before me were the four
winds of heaven churning up the great sea.
3Four great beasts, each different from the
others, came up out of the sea.
4"The first was like a lion, and it had the
wings of an eagle. I watched until its wings
were torn off and it was lifted from the ground
so that it stood on two feet like a man, and
the heart of a man was given to it.
5"And there before me was a second
beast, which looked like a bear. It was raised
up on one of its sides, and it had three ribs in
its mouth between its teeth. It was told, 'Get
up and eat your fill of flesh!'
6"After that, I looked, and there before me
was another beast, one that looked like a
leopard. And on its back it had four wings like
those of a bird. This beast had four heads,
and it was given authority to rule.
7"After that, in my vision at night I looked,
and there before me was a fourth beast—terrifying and frightening and very powerful. It
had large iron teeth; it crushed and devoured
its victims and trampled underfoot whatever
was left. It was different from all the former
beasts, and it had ten horns.
8"While I was thinking about the horns,
there before me was another horn, a little
one, which came up among them; and three
of the first horns were uprooted before it.
This horn had eyes like the eyes of a man
and a mouth that spoke boastfully.
9"As I looked,

"thrones were set in place,
  and the Ancient of Days took his seat.
His clothing was as white as snow;
  the hair of his head was white like wool.
His throne was flaming with fire,
  and its wheels were all ablaze.
10A river of fire was flowing,
  coming out from before him.
Thousands upon thousands attended him;
  ten thousand times ten thousand stood
    before him.
The court was seated,
  and the books were opened.

11"Then I continued to watch because of
the boastful words the horn was speaking. I
kept looking until the beast was slain and its
body destroyed and thrown into the blazing
fire. 12(The other beasts had been stripped of
their authority, but were allowed to live for a
period of time.)
13"In my vision at night I looked, and there
before me was one like a son of man, coming
with the clouds of heaven. He approached
the Ancient of Days and was led into his
presence. 14He was given authority, glory
and sovereign power; all peoples, nations
and men of every language worshiped him.
His dominion is an everlasting dominion that
will not pass away, and his kingdom is one
that will never be destroyed.

The Interpretation of the Dream

15"I, Daniel, was troubled in spirit, and the
visions that passed through my mind disturbed me. 16I approached one of those
standing there and asked him the true meaning of all this.
"So he told me and gave me the interpretation of these things: 17'The four great
beasts are four kingdoms that will rise from
the earth. 18But the saints of the Most High
will receive the kingdom and will possess it
forever—yes, for ever and ever.'
19"Then I wanted to know the true meaning
of the fourth beast, which was different from
all the others and most terrifying, with its iron
teeth and bronze claws—the beast that
crushed and devoured its victims and trampled underfoot whatever was left. 20I also
wanted to know about the ten horns on its
head and about the other horn that came up,
before which three of them fell—the horn
that looked more imposing than the others
and that had eyes and a mouth that spoke
boastfully. 21As I watched, this horn was
waging war against the saints and defeating
them, 22until the Ancient of Days came and
pronounced judgment in favor of the saints
of the Most High, and the time came when
they possessed the kingdom.
23"He gave me this explanation: 'The
fourth beast is a fourth kingdom that will appear on earth. It will be different from all the
other kingdoms and will devour the whole
earth, trampling it down and crushing it.
24The ten horns are ten kings who will come
from this kingdom. After them another king
will arise, different from the earlier ones; he

[a]28 Or *Darius, that is, the reign of Cyrus*

will subdue three kings. 25He will speak against the Most High and oppress his saints and try to change the set times and the laws. The saints will be handed over to him for a time, times and half a time.[a]

26" 'But the court will sit, and his power will be taken away and completely destroyed forever. 27Then the sovereignty, power and greatness of the kingdoms under the whole heaven will be handed over to the saints, the people of the Most High. His kingdom will be an everlasting kingdom, and all rulers will worship and obey him.'

28"This is the end of the matter. I, Daniel, was deeply troubled by my thoughts, and my face turned pale, but I kept the matter to myself."

Daniel's Vision of a Ram and a Goat

8 In the third year of King Belshazzar's reign, I, Daniel, had a vision, after the one that had already appeared to me. 2In my vision I saw myself in the citadel of Susa in the province of Elam; in the vision I was beside the Ulai Canal. 3I looked up, and there before me was a ram with two horns, standing beside the canal, and the horns were long. One of the horns was longer than the other but grew up later. 4I watched the ram as he charged toward the west and the north and the south. No animal could stand against him, and none could rescue from his power. He did as he pleased and became great.

5As I was thinking about this, suddenly a goat with a prominent horn between his eyes came from the west, crossing the whole earth without touching the ground. 6He came toward the two-horned ram I had seen standing beside the canal and charged at him in great rage. 7I saw him attack the ram furiously, striking the ram and shattering his two horns. The ram was powerless to stand against him; the goat knocked him to the ground and trampled on him, and none could rescue the ram from his power. 8The goat became very great, but at the height of his power his large horn was broken off, and in its place four prominent horns grew up toward the four winds of heaven.

9Out of one of them came another horn, which started small but grew in power to the south and to the east and toward the Beautiful Land. 10It grew until it reached the host of the heavens, and it threw some of the starry host down to the earth and trampled on them. 11It set itself up to be as great as the Prince of the host; it took away the daily sacrifice from him, and the place of his sanctuary was brought low. 12Because of rebellion, the host ⌞of the saints⌟[b] and the daily sacrifice were given over to it. It prospered in everything it did, and truth was thrown to the ground.

13Then I heard a holy one speaking, and another holy one said to him, "How long will it take for the vision to be fulfilled—the vision concerning the daily sacrifice, the rebellion that causes desolation, and the surrender of the sanctuary and of the host that will be trampled underfoot?"

14He said to me, "It will take 2,300 evenings and mornings; then the sanctuary will be reconsecrated."

The Interpretation of the Vision

15While I, Daniel, was watching the vision and trying to understand it, there before me stood one who looked like a man. 16And I heard a man's voice from the Ulai calling, "Gabriel, tell this man the meaning of the vision."

17As he came near the place where I was standing, I was terrified and fell prostrate. "Son of man," he said to me, "understand that the vision concerns the time of the end."

18While he was speaking to me, I was in a deep sleep, with my face to the ground. Then he touched me and raised me to my feet.

19He said: "I am going to tell you what will happen later in the time of wrath, because the vision concerns the appointed time of the end.[c] 20The two-horned ram that you saw represents the kings of Media and Persia. 21The shaggy goat is the king of Greece, and the large horn between his eyes is the first king. 22The four horns that replaced the one that was broken off represent four kingdoms that will emerge from his nation but will not have the same power.

23"In the latter part of their reign, when rebels have become completely wicked, a stern-faced king, a master of intrigue, will arise. 24He will become very strong, but not by his own power. He will cause astounding devastation and will succeed in whatever he does. He will destroy the mighty men and the

[a]25 Or *for a year, two years and half a year at the appointed time*
[b]12 Or *rebellion, the armies*
[c]19 Or *because the end will be*

holy people. 25 He will cause deceit to prosper, and he will consider himself superior. When they feel secure, he will destroy many and take his stand against the Prince of princes. Yet he will be destroyed, but not by human power.

26 "The vision of the evenings and mornings that has been given you is true, but seal up the vision, for it concerns the distant future."

27 I, Daniel, was exhausted and lay ill for several days. Then I got up and went about the king's business. I was appalled by the vision; it was beyond understanding.

Daniel's Prayer

9 In the first year of Darius son of Xerxes[a] (a Mede by descent), who was made ruler over the Babylonian[b] kingdom— 2 in the first year of his reign, I, Daniel, understood from the Scriptures, according to the word of the LORD given to Jeremiah the prophet, that the desolation of Jerusalem would last seventy years. 3 So I turned to the Lord God and pleaded with him in prayer and petition, in fasting, and in sackcloth and ashes.

4 I prayed to the LORD my God and confessed:

> "O Lord, the great and awesome God, who keeps his covenant of love with all who love him and obey his commands, 5 we have sinned and done wrong. We have been wicked and have rebelled; we have turned away from your commands and laws. 6 We have not listened to your servants the prophets, who spoke in your name to our kings, our princes and our fathers, and to all the people of the land.
>
> 7 "Lord, you are righteous, but this day we are covered with shame—the men of Judah and people of Jerusalem and all Israel, both near and far, in all the countries where you have scattered us because of our unfaithfulness to you. 8 O LORD, we and our kings, our princes and our fathers are covered with shame because we have sinned against you. 9 The Lord our God is merciful and forgiving, even though we have rebelled against him; 10 we have not obeyed the LORD our God or kept the laws he gave us through his servants the prophets. 11 All Israel has transgressed your law and turned away, refusing to obey you.
>
> "Therefore the curses and sworn judgments written in the Law of Moses, the servant of God, have been poured out on us, because we have sinned against you. 12 You have fulfilled the words spoken against us and against our rulers by bringing upon us great disaster. Under the whole heaven nothing has ever been done like what has been done to Jerusalem. 13 Just as it is written in the Law of Moses, all this disaster has come upon us, yet we have not sought the favor of the LORD our God by turning from our sins and giving attention to your truth. 14 The LORD did not hesitate to bring the disaster upon us, for the LORD our God is righteous in everything he does; yet we have not obeyed him.
>
> 15 "Now, O Lord our God, who brought your people out of Egypt with a mighty hand and who made for yourself a name that endures to this day, we have sinned, we have done wrong. 16 O Lord, in keeping with all your righteous acts, turn away your anger and your wrath from Jerusalem, your city, your holy hill. Our sins and the iniquities of our fathers have made Jerusalem and your people an object of scorn to all those around us.
>
> 17 "Now, our God, hear the prayers and petitions of your servant. For your sake, O Lord, look with favor on your desolate sanctuary. 18 Give ear, O God, and hear; open your eyes and see the desolation of the city that bears your Name. We do not make requests of you because we are righteous, but because of your great mercy. 19 O Lord, listen! O Lord, forgive! O Lord, hear and act! For your sake, O my God, do not delay, because your city and your people bear your Name."

The Seventy "Sevens"

20 While I was speaking and praying, confessing my sin and the sin of my people Israel and making my request to the LORD my God for his holy hill— 21 while I was still in prayer, Gabriel, the man I had seen in the earlier vision, came to me in swift flight about the time of the evening sacrifice. 22 He instructed me and said to me, "Daniel, I have now come to give you insight and understanding. 23 As soon as you began to pray, an

[a] 1 Hebrew *Ahasuerus* [b] 1 Or *Chaldean*

answer was given, which I have come to tell
you, for you are highly esteemed. Therefore,
consider the message and understand the
vision:
24“Seventy ‘sevens’[a] are decreed for your
people and your holy city to finish[b] transgression, to put an end to sin, to atone for
wickedness, to bring in everlasting righteousness, to seal up vision and prophecy
and to anoint the most holy.[c]
25“Know and understand this: From the
issuing of the decree[d] to restore and rebuild
Jerusalem until the Anointed One,[e] the ruler,
comes, there will be seven ‘sevens,’ and sixty-two ‘sevens.’ It will be rebuilt with streets
and a trench, but in times of trouble. 26After
the sixty-two ‘sevens,’ the Anointed One will
be cut off and will have nothing.[f] The people
of the ruler who will come will destroy the city
and the sanctuary. The end will come like a
flood: War will continue until the end, and
desolations have been decreed. 27He will
confirm a covenant with many for one
‘seven.’[g] In the middle of the ‘seven’[g] he will
put an end to sacrifice and offering. And on a
wing ⌞of the temple⌟ he will set up an abomination that causes desolation, until the end
that is decreed is poured out on him.[h]”[i]

Daniel’s Vision of a Man

10 In the third year of Cyrus king of
Persia, a revelation was given to
Daniel (who was called Belteshazzar). Its
message was true and it concerned a great
war.[j] The understanding of the message
came to him in a vision.
2At that time I, Daniel, mourned for three
weeks. 3I ate no choice food; no meat or wine
touched my lips; and I used no lotions at all
until the three weeks were over.
4On the twenty-fourth day of the first
month, as I was standing on the bank of the
great river, the Tigris, 5I looked up and there
before me was a man dressed in linen, with a
belt of the finest gold around his waist. 6His
body was like chrysolite, his face like lightning, his eyes like flaming torches, his arms
and legs like the gleam of burnished bronze,
and his voice like the sound of a multitude.
7I, Daniel, was the only one who saw the
vision; the men with me did not see it, but
such terror overwhelmed them that they fled
and hid themselves. 8So I was left alone,
gazing at this great vision; I had no strength
left, my face turned deathly pale and I was
helpless. 9Then I heard him speaking, and as
I listened to him, I fell into a deep sleep, my
face to the ground.
10A hand touched me and set me trembling
on my hands and knees. 11He said, “Daniel,
you who are highly esteemed, consider carefully the words I am about to speak to you,
and stand up, for I have now been sent to
you.” And when he said this to me, I stood up
trembling.
12Then he continued, “Do not be afraid,
Daniel. Since the first day that you set your
mind to gain understanding and to humble
yourself before your God, your words were
heard, and I have come in response to them.
13But the prince of the Persian kingdom resisted me twenty-one days. Then Michael,
one of the chief princes, came to help me,
because I was detained there with the king of
Persia. 14Now I have come to explain to you
what will happen to your people in the future,
for the vision concerns a time yet to come.”
15While he was saying this to me, I bowed
with my face toward the ground and was
speechless. 16Then one who looked like a
man[k] touched my lips, and I opened my
mouth and began to speak. I said to the one
standing before me, “I am overcome with
anguish because of the vision, my lord, and I
am helpless. 17How can I, your servant, talk
with you, my lord? My strength is gone and I
can hardly breathe.”
18Again the one who looked like a man
touched me and gave me strength. 19“Do not
be afraid, O man highly esteemed,” he said.
“Peace! Be strong now; be strong.”
When he spoke to me, I was strengthened
and said, “Speak, my lord, since you have
given me strength.”
20So he said, “Do you know why I have
come to you? Soon I will return to fight
against the prince of Persia, and when I go,
the prince of Greece will come; 21but first I
will tell you what is written in the Book of
Truth. (No one supports me against them
11 except Michael, your prince. 1And in
the first year of Darius the Mede, I

[a]24 Or *‘weeks’*; also in verses 25 and 26 [b]24 Or *restrain* [c]24 Or *Most Holy Place;* or *most holy One* [d]25 Or *word* [e]25 Or *an anointed one*; also in verse 26 [f]26 Or *off and will have no one;* or *off, but not for himself* [g]27 Or *‘week’* [h]27 Or *it* [i]27 Or *And one who causes desolation will come upon the pinnacle of the abominable ⌞temple⌟, until the end that is decreed is poured out on the desolated ⌞city⌟* [j]1 Or *true and burdensome* [k]16 Most manuscripts of the Masoretic Text; one manuscript of the Masoretic Text, Dead Sea Scrolls and Septuagint *Then something that looked like a man’s hand*

took my stand to support and protect him.)

The Kings of the South and the North

2"Now then, I tell you the truth: Three more
kings will appear in Persia, and then a fourth,
who will be far richer than all the others.
When he has gained power by his wealth, he
will stir up everyone against the kingdom of
Greece. 3Then a mighty king will appear,
who will rule with great power and do as he
pleases. 4After he has appeared, his empire
will be broken up and parceled out toward
the four winds of heaven. It will not go to his
descendants, nor will it have the power he
exercised, because his empire will be
uprooted and given to others.
5"The king of the South will become
strong, but one of his commanders will
become even stronger than he and will rule
his own kingdom with great power. 6After
some years, they will become allies. The
daughter of the king of the South will go to
the king of the North to make an alliance, but
she will not retain her power, and he and his
power[a] will not last. In those days she will be
handed over, together with her royal escort
and her father[b] and the one who supported
her.
7"One from her family line will arise to take
her place. He will attack the forces of the king
of the North and enter his fortress; he will
fight against them and be victorious. 8He will
also seize their gods, their metal images and
their valuable articles of silver and gold and
carry them off to Egypt. For some years he
will leave the king of the North alone. 9Then
the king of the North will invade the realm of
the king of the South but will retreat to his
own country. 10His sons will prepare for war
and assemble a great army, which will
sweep on like an irresistible flood and carry
the battle as far as his fortress.
11"Then the king of the South will march
out in a rage and fight against the king of the
North, who will raise a large army, but it will
be defeated. 12When the army is carried off,
the king of the South will be filled with pride
and will slaughter many thousands, yet he
will not remain triumphant. 13For the king of
the North will muster another army, larger
than the first; and after several years, he will
advance with a huge army fully equipped.
14"In those times many will rise against the
king of the South. The violent men among
your own people will rebel in fulfillment of the
vision, but without success. 15Then the king
of the North will come and build up siege
ramps and will capture a fortified city. The
forces of the South will be powerless to resist; even their best troops will not have the
strength to stand. 16The invader will do as he
pleases; no one will be able to stand against
him. He will establish himself in the Beautiful
Land and will have the power to destroy it.
17He will determine to come with the might of
his entire kingdom and will make an alliance
with the king of the South. And he will give
him a daughter in marriage in order to overthrow the kingdom, but his plans[c] will not
succeed or help him. 18Then he will turn his
attention to the coastlands and will take
many of them, but a commander will put an
end to his insolence and will turn his insolence back upon him. 19After this, he will turn
back toward the fortresses of his own country but will stumble and fall, to be seen no
more.
20"His successor will send out a tax collector to maintain the royal splendor. In a few
years, however, he will be destroyed, yet not
in anger or in battle.
21"He will be succeeded by a contemptible
person who has not been given the honor of
royalty. He will invade the kingdom when its
people feel secure, and he will seize it
through intrigue. 22Then an overwhelming
army will be swept away before him; both it
and a prince of the covenant will be destroyed. 23After coming to an agreement with
him, he will act deceitfully, and with only a
few people he will rise to power. 24When the
richest provinces feel secure, he will invade
them and will achieve what neither his fathers nor his forefathers did. He will distribute plunder, loot and wealth among his followers. He will plot the overthrow of fortresses—but only for a time.
25"With a large army he will stir up his
strength and courage against the king of the
South. The king of the South will wage war
with a large and very powerful army, but he
will not be able to stand because of the plots
devised against him. 26Those who eat from
the king's provisions will try to destroy him;
his army will be swept away, and many will
fall in battle. 27The two kings, with their
hearts bent on evil, will sit at the same table
and lie to each other, but to no avail, because
an end will still come at the appointed time.
28The king of the North will return to his own

[a]6 Or *offspring* [b]6 Or *child* (see Vulgate and Syriac) [c]17 Or *but she*

country with great wealth, but his heart will
be set against the holy covenant. He will take
action against it and then return to his own
country.
29"At the appointed time he will invade the
South again, but this time the outcome will
be different from what it was before. 30Ships
of the western coastlands[a] will oppose him,
and he will lose heart. Then he will turn back
and vent his fury against the holy covenant.
He will return and show favor to those who
forsake the holy covenant.
31"His armed forces will rise up to desecrate the temple fortress and will abolish the
daily sacrifice. Then they will set up the
abomination that causes desolation. 32With
flattery he will corrupt those who have violated the covenant, but the people who know
their God will firmly resist him.
33"Those who are wise will instruct many,
though for a time they will fall by the sword or
be burned or captured or plundered. 34When
they fall, they will receive a little help, and
many who are not sincere will join them.
35Some of the wise will stumble, so that they
may be refined, purified and made spotless
until the time of the end, for it will still come at
the appointed time.

The King Who Exalts Himself

36"The king will do as he pleases. He will
exalt and magnify himself above every god
and will say unheard-of things against the
God of gods. He will be successful until the
time of wrath is completed, for what has
been determined must take place. 37He will
show no regard for the gods of his fathers or
for the one desired by women, nor will he
regard any god, but will exalt himself above
them all. 38Instead of them, he will honor a
god of fortresses; a god unknown to his fathers he will honor with gold and silver, with
precious stones and costly gifts. 39He will
attack the mightiest fortresses with the help
of a foreign god and will greatly honor those
who acknowledge him. He will make them
rulers over many people and will distribute
the land at a price.[b]
40"At the time of the end the king of the
South will engage him in battle, and the king
of the North will storm out against him with
chariots and cavalry and a great fleet of
ships. He will invade many countries and
sweep through them like a flood. 41He will
also invade the Beautiful Land. Many countries will fall, but Edom, Moab and the leaders of Ammon will be delivered from his
hand. 42He will extend his power over many
countries; Egypt will not escape. 43He will
gain control of the treasures of gold and silver and all the riches of Egypt, with the Libyans and Nubians in submission. 44But reports from the east and the north will alarm
him, and he will set out in a great rage to
destroy and annihilate many. 45He will pitch
his royal tents between the seas at[c] the
beautiful holy mountain. Yet he will come to
his end, and no one will help him.

The End Times

12 "At that time Michael, the great
prince who protects your people, will
arise. There will be a time of distress such as
has not happened from the beginning of nations until then. But at that time your people—everyone whose name is found written
in the book—will be delivered. 2Multitudes
who sleep in the dust of the earth will awake:
some to everlasting life, others to shame and
everlasting contempt. 3Those who are wise[d]
will shine like the brightness of the heavens,
and those who lead many to righteousness,
like the stars for ever and ever. 4But you,
Daniel, close up and seal the words of the
scroll until the time of the end. Many will go
here and there to increase knowledge."

5Then I, Daniel, looked, and there before
me stood two others, one on this bank of the
river and one on the opposite bank. 6One of
them said to the man clothed in linen, who
was above the waters of the river, "How long
will it be before these astonishing things are
fulfilled?"
7The man clothed in linen, who was above
the waters of the river, lifted his right hand
and his left hand toward heaven, and I heard
him swear by him who lives forever, saying,
"It will be for a time, times and half a time.[e]
When the power of the holy people has been
finally broken, all these things will be completed."
8I heard, but I did not understand. So I
asked, "My lord, what will the outcome of all
this be?"
9He replied, "Go your way, Daniel, because the words are closed up and sealed
until the time of the end. 10Many will be puri-

[a]30 Hebrew *of Kittim* [b]39 Or *land for a reward* [c]45 Or *the sea and* [d]3 Or *who impart wisdom*
[e]7 Or *a year, two years and half a year*

fied, made spotless and refined, but the
wicked will continue to be wicked. None of
the wicked will understand, but those who
are wise will understand.
[11]"From the time that the daily sacrifice is
abolished and the abomination that causes
desolation is set up, there will be 1,290 days.
[12]Blessed is the one who waits for and
reaches the end of the 1,335 days.
[13]"As for you, go your way till the end. You
will rest, and then at the end of the days you
will rise to receive your allotted inheritance."

Hosea

Introduction:

The prophet Hosea was a citizen of the northern kingdom, which he commonly called Ephraim. He probably began his ministry before King Jeroboam II died in 753 B.C. and may have given his messages shortly before the fall of Samaria in 722 B.C.

Chapters 1–3 tell about Hosea's love for his unfaithful wife, Gomer. Her unfaithfulness is a picture of Israel's unfaithfulness in her covenant relationship with God. Instead of responding in thankfulness and love to God for all their blessings, the Israelites used their crops as offerings to idols. The injustice and mistreatment of others reflected their lack of love for God as well as for their fellow citizens.

Outline of contents:

Hosea's experience in family life (1:1–3:5)
Israel's sin (4:1–6:3)
Punishment for Israel (6:4–10:15)
God's judgment and mercy (11:1–14:9)

---

1 The word of the LORD that came to Hosea
son of Beeri during the reigns of Uzziah,
Jotham, Ahaz and Hezekiah, kings of Judah,
and during the reign of Jeroboam son of Jehoash[a] king of Israel:

Hosea's Wife and Children

2When the LORD began to speak through
Hosea, the LORD said to him, "Go, take to
yourself an adulterous wife and children of
unfaithfulness, because the land is guilty of
the vilest adultery in departing from the
LORD." 3So he married Gomer daughter of
Diblaim, and she conceived and bore him a
son.
4Then the LORD said to Hosea, "Call him
Jezreel, because I will soon punish the
house of Jehu for the massacre at Jezreel,
and I will put an end to the kingdom of Israel.
5In that day I will break Israel's bow in the
Valley of Jezreel."
6Gomer conceived again and gave birth to
a daughter. Then the LORD said to Hosea,
"Call her Lo-Ruhamah,[b] for I will no longer
show love to the house of Israel, that I should
at all forgive them. 7Yet I will show love to the
house of Judah; and I will save them—not by
bow, sword or battle, or by horses and horsemen, but by the LORD their God."
8After she had weaned Lo-Ruhamah, Gomer had another son. 9Then the LORD said,
"Call him Lo-Ammi,[c] for you are not my
people, and I am not your God.
10"Yet the Israelites will be like the sand on
the seashore, which cannot be measured or
counted. In the place where it was said to
them, 'You are not my people,' they will be
called 'sons of the living God.' 11The people
of Judah and the people of Israel will be
reunited, and they will appoint one leader
and will come up out of the land, for great will
be the day of Jezreel.

2 "Say of your brothers, 'My people,' and
of your sisters, 'My loved one.'

Israel Punished and Restored

2"Rebuke your mother, rebuke her,
for she is not my wife,
and I am not her husband.
Let her remove the adulterous look from her face
and the unfaithfulness from between her breasts.
3Otherwise I will strip her naked
and make her as bare as on the day she was born;
I will make her like a desert,

a1 Hebrew *Joash,* a variant of *Jehoash* *b6 Lo-Ruhamah* means *not loved.* *c9 Lo-Ammi* means *not my people.*

turn her into a parched land,
and slay her with thirst.
4I will not show my love to her children,
because they are the children of adultery.
5Their mother has been unfaithful
and has conceived them in disgrace.
She said, 'I will go after my lovers,
who give me my food and my water,
my wool and my linen, my oil and my drink.'
6Therefore I will block her path with thornbushes;
I will wall her in so that she cannot find her way.
7She will chase after her lovers but not catch them;
she will look for them but not find them.
Then she will say,
'I will go back to my husband as at first,
for then I was better off than now.'
8She has not acknowledged that I was the one
who gave her the grain, the new wine and oil,
who lavished on her the silver and gold—
which they used for Baal.

9"Therefore I will take away my grain when it ripens,
and my new wine when it is ready.
I will take back my wool and my linen,
intended to cover her nakedness.
10So now I will expose her lewdness
before the eyes of her lovers;
no one will take her out of my hands.
11I will stop all her celebrations:
her yearly festivals, her New Moons,
her Sabbath days—all her appointed feasts.
12I will ruin her vines and her fig trees,
which she said were her pay from her lovers;
I will make them a thicket,
and wild animals will devour them.
13I will punish her for the days
she burned incense to the Baals;
she decked herself with rings and jewelry,
and went after her lovers,
but me she forgot,"
declares the LORD.

14"Therefore I am now going to allure her;
I will lead her into the desert
and speak tenderly to her.
15There I will give her back her vineyards,
and will make the Valley of Achor[a] a door of hope.
There she will sing[b] as in the days of her youth,
as in the day she came up out of Egypt.

16"In that day," declares the LORD,
"you will call me 'my husband';
you will no longer call me 'my master.[c]'
17I will remove the names of the Baals from her lips;
no longer will their names be invoked.
18In that day I will make a covenant for them
with the beasts of the field and the birds of the air
and the creatures that move along the ground.
Bow and sword and battle
I will abolish from the land,
so that all may lie down in safety.
19I will betroth you to me forever;
I will betroth you in[d] righteousness and justice,
in[e] love and compassion.
20I will betroth you in faithfulness,
and you will acknowledge the LORD.

21"In that day I will respond,"
declares the LORD—
"I will respond to the skies,
and they will respond to the earth;
22and the earth will respond to the grain,
the new wine and oil,
and they will respond to Jezreel.[f]
23I will plant her for myself in the land;
I will show my love to the one I called 'Not my loved one.[g]'
I will say to those called 'Not my people,[h]'
'You are my people';
and they will say, 'You are my God.' "

Hosea's Reconciliation With His Wife

3 The LORD said to me, "Go, show your
love to your wife again, though she is
loved by another and is an adulteress. Love
her as the LORD loves the Israelites, though
they turn to other gods and love the sacred
raisin cakes."
2So I bought her for fifteen shekels[i] of
silver and about a homer and a lethek[j] of
barley. 3Then I told her, "You are to live with[k]

[a] 15 *Achor* means *trouble.* [b] 15 Or *respond* [c] 16 Hebrew *baal* [d] 19 Or *with*; also in verse 20
[e] 19 Or *with* [f] 22 *Jezreel* means *God plants.* [g] 23 Hebrew *Lo-Ruhamah* [h] 23 Hebrew *Lo-Ammi*
[i] 2 That is, about 6 ounces (about 170 grams) [j] 2 That is, probably about 10 bushels (about 330 liters)
[k] 3 Or *wait for*

me many days; you must not be a prostitute
or be intimate with any man, and I will live
with[a] you."
4For the Israelites will live many days without king or prince, without sacrifice or sacred
stones, without ephod or idol. 5Afterward the
Israelites will return and seek the LORD their
God and David their king. They will come
trembling to the LORD and to his blessings in
the last days.

The Charge Against Israel

4 Hear the word of the LORD, you
Israelites,
because the LORD has a charge to bring
against you who live in the land:
"There is no faithfulness, no love,
no acknowledgment of God in the land.
2There is only cursing,[b] lying and murder,
stealing and adultery;
they break all bounds,
and bloodshed follows bloodshed.
3Because of this the land mourns,[c]
and all who live in it waste away;
the beasts of the field and the birds of the
air
and the fish of the sea are dying.

4"But let no man bring a charge,
let no man accuse another,
for your people are like those
who bring charges against a priest.
5You stumble day and night,
and the prophets stumble with you.
So I will destroy your mother—
6 my people are destroyed from lack of
knowledge.

"Because you have rejected knowledge,
I also reject you as my priests;
because you have ignored the law of your
God,
I also will ignore your children.
7The more the priests increased,
the more they sinned against me;
they exchanged[d] their[e] Glory for
something disgraceful.
8They feed on the sins of my people
and relish their wickedness.
9And it will be: Like people, like priests.
I will punish both of them for their ways
and repay them for their deeds.

10"They will eat but not have enough;
they will engage in prostitution but not
increase,
because they have deserted the LORD
to give themselves 11to prostitution,
to old wine and new,
which take away the understanding 12of
my people.
They consult a wooden idol
and are answered by a stick of wood.
A spirit of prostitution leads them astray;
they are unfaithful to their God.
13They sacrifice on the mountaintops
and burn offerings on the hills,
under oak, poplar and terebinth,
where the shade is pleasant.
Therefore your daughters turn to
prostitution
and your daughters-in-law to adultery.

14"I will not punish your daughters
when they turn to prostitution,
nor your daughters-in-law
when they commit adultery,
because the men themselves consort
with harlots
and sacrifice with shrine prostitutes—
a people without understanding will
come to ruin!

15"Though you commit adultery, O Israel,
let not Judah become guilty.

"Do not go to Gilgal;
do not go up to Beth Aven.[f]
And do not swear, 'As surely as the
LORD lives!'
16The Israelites are stubborn,
like a stubborn heifer.
How then can the LORD pasture them
like lambs in a meadow?
17Ephraim is joined to idols;
leave him alone!
18Even when their drinks are gone,
they continue their prostitution;
their rulers dearly love shameful ways.
19A whirlwind will sweep them away,
and their sacrifices will bring them
shame.

Judgment Against Israel

5 "Hear this, you priests!
Pay attention, you Israelites!
Listen, O royal house!
This judgment is against you:

[a]3 Or *wait for* [b]2 That is, to pronounce a curse upon [c]3 Or *dries up* [d]7 Syriac and an ancient Hebrew scribal tradition; Masoretic Text *I will exchange* [e]7 Masoretic Text; an ancient Hebrew scribal tradition *my* [f]15 *Beth Aven* means *house of wickedness* (a name for Bethel, which means *house of God*).

You have been a snare at Mizpah,
a net spread out on Tabor.
2The rebels are deep in slaughter.
I will discipline all of them.
3I know all about Ephraim;
Israel is not hidden from me.
Ephraim, you have now turned to
prostitution;
Israel is corrupt.

4"Their deeds do not permit them
to return to their God.
A spirit of prostitution is in their heart;
they do not acknowledge the LORD.
5Israel's arrogance testifies against them;
the Israelites, even Ephraim, stumble in
their sin;
Judah also stumbles with them.
6When they go with their flocks and herds
to seek the LORD,
they will not find him;
he has withdrawn himself from them.
7They are unfaithful to the LORD;
they give birth to illegitimate children.
Now their New Moon festivals
will devour them and their fields.

8"Sound the trumpet in Gibeah,
the horn in Ramah.
Raise the battle cry in Beth Aven[a];
lead on, O Benjamin.
9Ephraim will be laid waste
on the day of reckoning.
Among the tribes of Israel
I proclaim what is certain.
10Judah's leaders are like those
who move boundary stones.
I will pour out my wrath on them
like a flood of water.
11Ephraim is oppressed,
trampled in judgment,
intent on pursuing idols.[b]
12I am like a moth to Ephraim,
like rot to the people of Judah.

13"When Ephraim saw his sickness,
and Judah his sores,
then Ephraim turned to Assyria,
and sent to the great king for help.
But he is not able to cure you,
not able to heal your sores.
14For I will be like a lion to Ephraim,
like a great lion to Judah.
I will tear them to pieces and go away;
I will carry them off, with no one to
rescue them.
15Then I will go back to my place
until they admit their guilt.
And they will seek my face;
in their misery they will earnestly seek
me."

Israel Unrepentant

6 "Come, let us return to the LORD.
He has torn us to pieces
but he will heal us;
he has injured us
but he will bind up our wounds.
2After two days he will revive us;
on the third day he will restore us,
that we may live in his presence.
3Let us acknowledge the LORD;
let us press on to acknowledge him.
As surely as the sun rises,
he will appear;
he will come to us like the winter rains,
like the spring rains that water the
earth."

4"What can I do with you, Ephraim?
What can I do with you, Judah?
Your love is like the morning mist,
like the early dew that disappears.
5Therefore I cut you in pieces with my
prophets,
I killed you with the words of my mouth;
my judgments flashed like lightning
upon you.
6For I desire mercy, not sacrifice,
and acknowledgment of God rather
than burnt offerings.
7Like Adam,[c] they have broken the
covenant—
they were unfaithful to me there.
8Gilead is a city of wicked men,
stained with footprints of blood.
9As marauders lie in ambush for a man,
so do bands of priests;
they murder on the road to Shechem,
committing shameful crimes.
10I have seen a horrible thing
in the house of Israel.
There Ephraim is given to prostitution
and Israel is defiled.

11"Also for you, Judah,
a harvest is appointed.

"Whenever I would restore the fortunes
of my people,
7 1whenever I would heal Israel,
the sins of Ephraim are exposed

[a]8 *Beth Aven* means *house of wickedness* (a name for Bethel, which means *house of God*). [b]11 The meaning of the Hebrew for this word is uncertain. [c]7 Or *As at Adam;* or *Like men*

and the crimes of Samaria revealed.
They practice deceit,
thieves break into houses,
bandits rob in the streets;
2but they do not realize
that I remember all their evil deeds.
Their sins engulf them;
they are always before me.

3"They delight the king with their wickedness,
the princes with their lies.
4They are all adulterers,
burning like an oven
whose fire the baker need not stir
from the kneading of the dough till it rises.
5On the day of the festival of our king
the princes become inflamed with wine,
and he joins hands with the mockers.
6Their hearts are like an oven;
they approach him with intrigue.
Their passion smolders all night;
in the morning it blazes like a flaming fire.
7All of them are hot as an oven;
they devour their rulers.
All their kings fall,
and none of them calls on me.

8"Ephraim mixes with the nations;
Ephraim is a flat cake not turned over.
9Foreigners sap his strength,
but he does not realize it.
His hair is sprinkled with gray,
but he does not notice.
10Israel's arrogance testifies against him,
but despite all this
he does not return to the LORD his God
or search for him.

11"Ephraim is like a dove,
easily deceived and senseless—
now calling to Egypt,
now turning to Assyria.
12When they go, I will throw my net over them;
I will pull them down like birds of the air.
When I hear them flocking together,
I will catch them.
13Woe to them,
because they have strayed from me!
Destruction to them,
because they have rebelled against me!
I long to redeem them
but they speak lies against me.
14They do not cry out to me from their hearts
but wail upon their beds.
They gather together[a] for grain and new wine
but turn away from me.
15I trained them and strengthened them,
but they plot evil against me.
16They do not turn to the Most High;
they are like a faulty bow.
Their leaders will fall by the sword
because of their insolent words.
For this they will be ridiculed
in the land of Egypt.

Israel to Reap the Whirlwind

8 "Put the trumpet to your lips!
An eagle is over the house of the LORD
because the people have broken my covenant
and rebelled against my law.
2Israel cries out to me,
'O our God, we acknowledge you!'
3But Israel has rejected what is good;
an enemy will pursue him.
4They set up kings without my consent;
they choose princes without my approval.
With their silver and gold
they make idols for themselves
to their own destruction.
5Throw out your calf-idol, O Samaria!
My anger burns against them.
How long will they be incapable of purity?
6 They are from Israel!
This calf—a craftsman has made it;
it is not God.
It will be broken in pieces,
that calf of Samaria.

7"They sow the wind
and reap the whirlwind.
The stalk has no head;
it will produce no flour.
Were it to yield grain,
foreigners would swallow it up.
8Israel is swallowed up;
now she is among the nations
like a worthless thing.
9For they have gone up to Assyria
like a wild donkey wandering alone.
Ephraim has sold herself to lovers.

[a]14 Most Hebrew manuscripts; some Hebrew manuscripts and Septuagint *They slash themselves*

[10]Although they have sold themselves
among the nations,
I will now gather them together.
They will begin to waste away
under the oppression of the mighty
king.

[11]"Though Ephraim built many altars for sin
offerings,
these have become altars for sinning.
[12]I wrote for them the many things of my
law,
but they regarded them as something
alien.
[13]They offer sacrifices given to me
and they eat the meat,
but the LORD is not pleased with them.
Now he will remember their wickedness
and punish their sins:
They will return to Egypt.
[14]Israel has forgotten his Maker
and built palaces;
Judah has fortified many towns.
But I will send fire upon their cities
that will consume their fortresses."

Punishment for Israel

9 Do not rejoice, O Israel;
do not be jubilant like the other nations.
For you have been unfaithful to your God;
you love the wages of a prostitute
at every threshing floor.
[2]Threshing floors and winepresses will not
feed the people;
the new wine will fail them.
[3]They will not remain in the LORD's land;
Ephraim will return to Egypt
and eat unclean[a] food in Assyria.
[4]They will not pour out wine offerings to
the LORD,
nor will their sacrifices please him.
Such sacrifices will be to them like the
bread of mourners;
all who eat them will be unclean.
This food will be for themselves;
it will not come into the temple of the
LORD.

[5]What will you do on the day of your
appointed feasts,
on the festival days of the LORD?
[6]Even if they escape from destruction,
Egypt will gather them,
and Memphis will bury them.
Their treasures of silver will be taken over
by briers,
and thorns will overrun their tents.
[7]The days of punishment are coming,
the days of reckoning are at hand.
Let Israel know this.
Because your sins are so many
and your hostility so great,
the prophet is considered a fool,
the inspired man a maniac.
[8]The prophet, along with my God,
is the watchman over Ephraim,[b]
yet snares await him on all his paths,
and hostility in the house of his God.
[9]They have sunk deep into corruption,
as in the days of Gibeah.
God will remember their wickedness
and punish them for their sins.

[10]"When I found Israel,
it was like finding grapes in the desert;
when I saw your fathers,
it was like seeing the early fruit on the
fig tree.
But when they came to Baal Peor,
they consecrated themselves to that
shameful idol
and became as vile as the thing they
loved.
[11]Ephraim's glory will fly away like a bird—
no birth, no pregnancy, no conception.
[12]Even if they rear children,
I will bereave them of every one.
Woe to them
when I turn away from them!
[13]I have seen Ephraim, like Tyre,
planted in a pleasant place.
But Ephraim will bring out
their children to the slayer."

[14]Give them, O LORD—
what will you give them?
Give them wombs that miscarry
and breasts that are dry.

[15]"Because of all their wickedness in
Gilgal,
I hated them there.
Because of their sinful deeds,
I will drive them out of my house.
I will no longer love them;
all their leaders are rebellious.
[16]Ephraim is blighted,
their root is withered,
they yield no fruit.
Even if they bear children,
I will slay their cherished offspring."

[17]My God will reject them

[a]3 That is, ceremonially unclean [b]8 Or *The prophet is the watchman over Ephraim, / the people of my God*

because they have not obeyed him;
they will be wanderers among the nations.

10 Israel was a spreading vine;
he brought forth fruit for himself.
As his fruit increased,
he built more altars;
as his land prospered,
he adorned his sacred stones.
2Their heart is deceitful,
and now they must bear their guilt.
The LORD will demolish their altars
and destroy their sacred stones.

3Then they will say, "We have no king
because we did not revere the LORD.
But even if we had a king,
what could he do for us?"
4They make many promises,
take false oaths
and make agreements;
therefore lawsuits spring up
like poisonous weeds in a plowed field.
5The people who live in Samaria fear
for the calf-idol of Beth Aven.[a]
Its people will mourn over it,
and so will its idolatrous priests,
those who had rejoiced over its splendor,
because it is taken from them into exile.
6It will be carried to Assyria
as tribute for the great king.
Ephraim will be disgraced;
Israel will be ashamed of its wooden idols.[b]
7Samaria and its king will float away
like a twig on the surface of the waters.
8The high places of wickedness[c] will be destroyed—
it is the sin of Israel.
Thorns and thistles will grow up
and cover their altars.
Then they will say to the mountains,
"Cover us!"
and to the hills, "Fall on us!"

9"Since the days of Gibeah, you have sinned, O Israel,
and there you have remained.[d]
Did not war overtake
the evildoers in Gibeah?
10When I please, I will punish them;
nations will be gathered against them
to put them in bonds for their double sin.
11Ephraim is a trained heifer
that loves to thresh;
so I will put a yoke
on her fair neck.
I will drive Ephraim,
Judah must plow,
and Jacob must break up the ground.
12Sow for yourselves righteousness,
reap the fruit of unfailing love,
and break up your unplowed ground;
for it is time to seek the LORD,
until he comes
and showers righteousness on you.
13But you have planted wickedness,
you have reaped evil,
you have eaten the fruit of deception.
Because you have depended on your own strength
and on your many warriors,
14the roar of battle will rise against your people,
so that all your fortresses will be devastated—
as Shalman devastated Beth Arbel on the day of battle,
when mothers were dashed to the ground with their children.
15Thus will it happen to you, O Bethel,
because your wickedness is great.
When that day dawns,
the king of Israel will be completely destroyed.

God's Love for Israel

11 "When Israel was a child, I loved him,
and out of Egypt I called my son.
2But the more I[e] called Israel,
the further they went from me.[f]
They sacrificed to the Baals
and they burned incense to images.
3It was I who taught Ephraim to walk,
taking them by the arms;
but they did not realize
it was I who healed them.
4I led them with cords of human kindness,
with ties of love;
I lifted the yoke from their neck
and bent down to feed them.

5"Will they not return to Egypt
and will not Assyria rule over them
because they refuse to repent?

[a]5 *Beth Aven* means *house of wickedness* (a name for Bethel, which means *house of God*). [b]6 Or *its counsel*
[c]8 Hebrew *aven*, a reference to Beth Aven (a derogatory name for Bethel) [d]9 Or *there a stand was taken*
[e]2 Some Septuagint manuscripts; Hebrew *they* [f]2 Septuagint; Hebrew *them*

6Swords will flash in their cities,
will destroy the bars of their gates
and put an end to their plans.
7My people are determined to turn from me.
Even if they call to the Most High,
he will by no means exalt them.

8"How can I give you up, Ephraim?
How can I hand you over, Israel?
How can I treat you like Admah?
How can I make you like Zeboiim?
My heart is changed within me;
all my compassion is aroused.
9I will not carry out my fierce anger,
nor will I turn and devastate Ephraim.
For I am God, and not man—
the Holy One among you.
I will not come in wrath.[a]
10They will follow the LORD;
he will roar like a lion.
When he roars,
his children will come trembling from the west.
11They will come trembling
like birds from Egypt,
like doves from Assyria.
I will settle them in their homes,"
declares the LORD.

Israel's Sin

12Ephraim has surrounded me with lies,
the house of Israel with deceit.
And Judah is unruly against God,
even against the faithful Holy One.

12 1Ephraim feeds on the wind;
he pursues the east wind all day
and multiplies lies and violence.
He makes a treaty with Assyria
and sends olive oil to Egypt.
2The LORD has a charge to bring against Judah;
he will punish Jacob[b] according to his ways
and repay him according to his deeds.
3In the womb he grasped his brother's heel;
as a man he struggled with God.
4He struggled with the angel and overcame him;
he wept and begged for his favor.
He found him at Bethel
and talked with him there—
5the LORD God Almighty,
the LORD is his name of renown!
6But you must return to your God;
maintain love and justice,
and wait for your God always.

7The merchant uses dishonest scales;
he loves to defraud.
8Ephraim boasts,
"I am very rich; I have become wealthy.
With all my wealth they will not find in me
any iniquity or sin."

9"I am the LORD your God,
⌞who brought you⌟ out of[c] Egypt;
I will make you live in tents again,
as in the days of your appointed feasts.
10I spoke to the prophets,
gave them many visions
and told parables through them."

11Is Gilead wicked?
Its people are worthless!
Do they sacrifice bulls in Gilgal?
Their altars will be like piles of stones
on a plowed field.
12Jacob fled to the country of Aram[d];
Israel served to get a wife,
and to pay for her he tended sheep.
13The LORD used a prophet to bring Israel up from Egypt,
by a prophet he cared for him.
14But Ephraim has bitterly provoked him to anger;
his Lord will leave upon him the guilt of his bloodshed
and will repay him for his contempt.

The LORD's Anger Against Israel

13 When Ephraim spoke, men trembled;
he was exalted in Israel.
But he became guilty of Baal worship and died.
2Now they sin more and more;
they make idols for themselves from their silver,
cleverly fashioned images,
all of them the work of craftsmen.
It is said of these people,
"They offer human sacrifice
and kiss[e] the calf-idols."
3Therefore they will be like the morning mist,
like the early dew that disappears,
like chaff swirling from a threshing floor,
like smoke escaping through a window.

[a]9 Or *come against any city* [b]2 *Jacob* means *he grasps the heel* (figuratively, *he deceives*). [c]9 Or *God / ever since you were in* [d]12 That is, Northwest Mesopotamia [e]2 Or *"Men who sacrifice / kiss*

4 "But I am the LORD your God,
  ⌊who brought you⌋ out of[a] Egypt.
You shall acknowledge no God but me,
  no Savior except me.
5 I cared for you in the desert,
  in the land of burning heat.
6 When I fed them, they were satisfied;
  when they were satisfied, they became proud;
  then they forgot me.
7 So I will come upon them like a lion,
  like a leopard I will lurk by the path.
8 Like a bear robbed of her cubs,
  I will attack them and rip them open.
Like a lion I will devour them;
  a wild animal will tear them apart.

9 "You are destroyed, O Israel,
  because you are against me, against your helper.
10 Where is your king, that he may save you?
  Where are your rulers in all your towns,
of whom you said,
  'Give me a king and princes'?
11 So in my anger I gave you a king,
  and in my wrath I took him away.
12 The guilt of Ephraim is stored up,
  his sins are kept on record.
13 Pains as of a woman in childbirth come to him,
  but he is a child without wisdom;
when the time arrives,
  he does not come to the opening of the womb.

14 "I will ransom them from the power of the grave[b];
  I will redeem them from death.
Where, O death, are your plagues?
  Where, O grave,[b] is your destruction?

"I will have no compassion,
15   even though he thrives among his brothers.
An east wind from the LORD will come,
  blowing in from the desert;
his spring will fail
  and his well dry up.
His storehouse will be plundered
  of all its treasures.
16 The people of Samaria must bear their guilt,
  because they have rebelled against their God.
They will fall by the sword;
  their little ones will be dashed to the ground,
  their pregnant women ripped open."

Repentance to Bring Blessing

14 Return, O Israel, to the LORD your God.
  Your sins have been your downfall!
2 Take words with you
  and return to the LORD.
Say to him:
  "Forgive all our sins
and receive us graciously,
  that we may offer the fruit of our lips.[c]
3 Assyria cannot save us;
  we will not mount war-horses.
We will never again say 'Our gods'
  to what our own hands have made,
  for in you the fatherless find compassion."

4 "I will heal their waywardness
  and love them freely,
  for my anger has turned away from them.
5 I will be like the dew to Israel;
  he will blossom like a lily.
Like a cedar of Lebanon
  he will send down his roots;
6   his young shoots will grow.
His splendor will be like an olive tree,
  his fragrance like a cedar of Lebanon.
7 Men will dwell again in his shade.
  He will flourish like the grain.
He will blossom like a vine,
  and his fame will be like the wine from Lebanon.
8 O Ephraim, what more have I[d] to do with idols?
  I will answer him and care for him.
I am like a green pine tree;
  your fruitfulness comes from me."
9 Who is wise? He will realize these things.
  Who is discerning? He will understand them.
The ways of the LORD are right;
  the righteous walk in them,
  but the rebellious stumble in them.

[a] 4 Or *God / ever since you were in* [b] 14 Hebrew *Sheol* [c] 2 Or *offer our lips as sacrifices of bulls*
[d] 8 Or *What more has Ephraim*

Joel

Introduction:

Although the name Joel was common in the Old Testament, nothing is known about this prophet beyond what the book says—he was the son of Pethuel.

In this book Joel gives a detailed description of a severe locust plague that hit Palestine. In this event he saw a sign for the final judgment and warned the people to turn to God in repentance. Joel announced that the "day of the LORD" was coming and would bring even greater judgment.

Outline of contents:

An invasion of locusts (1:1–12)
A call to repentance (1:13–20)
Warnings and God's promise (2:1–32)
God's final judgment and rule (3:1–21)

---

1 The word of the LORD that came to Joel son of Pethuel.

An Invasion of Locusts

2Hear this, you elders;
listen, all who live in the land.
Has anything like this ever happened in your days
or in the days of your forefathers?
3Tell it to your children,
and let your children tell it to their children,
and their children to the next generation.
4What the locust swarm has left
the great locusts have eaten;
what the great locusts have left
the young locusts have eaten;
what the young locusts have left
other locusts[a] have eaten.

5Wake up, you drunkards, and weep!
Wail, all you drinkers of wine;
wail because of the new wine,
for it has been snatched from your lips.
6A nation has invaded my land,
powerful and without number;
it has the teeth of a lion,
the fangs of a lioness.
7It has laid waste my vines
and ruined my fig trees.
It has stripped off their bark
and thrown it away,
leaving their branches white.

8Mourn like a virgin[b] in sackcloth
grieving for the husband[c] of her youth.
9Grain offerings and drink offerings
are cut off from the house of the LORD.
The priests are in mourning,
those who minister before the LORD.
10The fields are ruined,
the ground is dried up[d];
the grain is destroyed,
the new wine is dried up,
the oil fails.
11Despair, you farmers,
wail, you vine growers;
grieve for the wheat and the barley,
because the harvest of the field is destroyed.
12The vine is dried up
and the fig tree is withered;
the pomegranate, the palm and the apple tree—
all the trees of the field—are dried up.
Surely the joy of mankind
is withered away.

A Call to Repentance

13Put on sackcloth, O priests, and mourn;
wail, you who minister before the altar.

[a]4 The precise meaning of the four Hebrew words used here for locusts is uncertain. [b]8 Or *young woman* [c]8 Or *betrothed* [d]10 Or *ground mourns*

Come, spend the night in sackcloth,
you who minister before my God;
for the grain offerings and drink offerings
are withheld from the house of your God.
14Declare a holy fast;
call a sacred assembly.
Summon the elders
and all who live in the land
to the house of the LORD your God,
and cry out to the LORD.

15Alas for that day!
For the day of the LORD is near;
it will come like destruction from the Almighty.[a]

16Has not the food been cut off
before our very eyes—
joy and gladness
from the house of our God?
17The seeds are shriveled
beneath the clods.[b]
The storehouses are in ruins,
the granaries have been broken down,
for the grain has dried up.
18How the cattle moan!
The herds mill about
because they have no pasture;
even the flocks of sheep are suffering.

19To you, O LORD, I call,
for fire has devoured the open pastures
and flames have burned up all the trees of the field.
20Even the wild animals pant for you;
the streams of water have dried up
and fire has devoured the open pastures.

An Army of Locusts

2 Blow the trumpet in Zion;
sound the alarm on my holy hill.
Let all who live in the land tremble,
for the day of the LORD is coming.
It is close at hand—
2 a day of darkness and gloom,
a day of clouds and blackness.
Like dawn spreading across the mountains
a large and mighty army comes,
such as never was of old
nor ever will be in ages to come.

3Before them fire devours,
behind them a flame blazes.
Before them the land is like the garden of Eden,
behind them, a desert waste—
nothing escapes them.
4They have the appearance of horses;
they gallop along like cavalry.
5With a noise like that of chariots
they leap over the mountaintops,
like a crackling fire consuming stubble,
like a mighty army drawn up for battle.

6At the sight of them, nations are in anguish;
every face turns pale.
7They charge like warriors;
they scale walls like soldiers.
They all march in line,
not swerving from their course.
8They do not jostle each other;
each marches straight ahead.
They plunge through defenses
without breaking ranks.
9They rush upon the city;
they run along the wall.
They climb into the houses;
like thieves they enter through the windows.

10Before them the earth shakes,
the sky trembles,
the sun and moon are darkened,
and the stars no longer shine.
11The LORD thunders
at the head of his army;
his forces are beyond number,
and mighty are those who obey his command.
The day of the LORD is great;
it is dreadful.
Who can endure it?

Rend Your Heart

12"Even now," declares the LORD,
"return to me with all your heart,
with fasting and weeping and mourning."

13Rend your heart
and not your garments.
Return to the LORD your God,
for he is gracious and compassionate,
slow to anger and abounding in love,
and he relents from sending calamity.
14Who knows? He may turn and have pity
and leave behind a blessing—

[a] 15 Hebrew *Shaddai* [b] 17 The meaning of the Hebrew for this word is uncertain.

grain offerings and drink offerings
for the LORD your God.

15Blow the trumpet in Zion,
declare a holy fast,
call a sacred assembly.
16Gather the people,
consecrate the assembly;
bring together the elders,
gather the children,
those nursing at the breast.
Let the bridegroom leave his room
and the bride her chamber.
17Let the priests, who minister before the LORD,
weep between the temple porch and the altar.
Let them say, "Spare your people, O LORD.
Do not make your inheritance an object of scorn,
a byword among the nations.
Why should they say among the peoples,
'Where is their God?' "

The LORD's Answer

18Then the LORD will be jealous for his land
and take pity on his people.

19The LORD will reply[a] to them:

"I am sending you grain, new wine and oil,
enough to satisfy you fully;
never again will I make you
an object of scorn to the nations.

20"I will drive the northern army far from you,
pushing it into a parched and barren land,
with its front columns going into the eastern sea[b]
and those in the rear into the western sea.[c]
And its stench will go up;
its smell will rise."

Surely he has done great things.[d]
21 Be not afraid, O land;
be glad and rejoice.
Surely the LORD has done great things.
22 Be not afraid, O wild animals,
for the open pastures are becoming green.
The trees are bearing their fruit;
the fig tree and the vine yield their riches.
23Be glad, O people of Zion,
rejoice in the LORD your God,
for he has given you
the autumn rains in righteousness.[e]
He sends you abundant showers,
both autumn and spring rains, as before.
24The threshing floors will be filled with grain;
the vats will overflow with new wine and oil.

25"I will repay you for the years the locusts have eaten—
the great locust and the young locust,
the other locusts and the locust swarm[f]—
my great army that I sent among you.
26You will have plenty to eat, until you are full,
and you will praise the name of the LORD your God,
who has worked wonders for you;
never again will my people be shamed.
27Then you will know that I am in Israel,
that I am the LORD your God,
and that there is no other;
never again will my people be shamed.

The Day of the LORD

28"And afterward,
I will pour out my Spirit on all people.
Your sons and daughters will prophesy,
your old men will dream dreams,
your young men will see visions.
29Even on my servants, both men and women,
I will pour out my Spirit in those days.
30I will show wonders in the heavens
and on the earth,
blood and fire and billows of smoke.
31The sun will be turned to darkness
and the moon to blood
before the coming of the great and dreadful day of the LORD.
32And everyone who calls
on the name of the LORD will be saved;
for on Mount Zion and in Jerusalem
there will be deliverance,
as the LORD has said,
among the survivors
whom the LORD calls.

[a]*18,19* Or *LORD was jealous . . . / and took pity . . . / [19]The LORD replied* [b]*20* That is, the Dead Sea [c]*20* That is, the Mediterranean [d]*20* Or *rise. / Surely it has done great things."* [e]*23* Or / *the teacher for righteousness:* [f]*25* The precise meaning of the four Hebrew words used here for locusts is uncertain.

The Nations Judged

3 "In those days and at that time,
when I restore the fortunes of Judah
and Jerusalem,
2I will gather all nations
and bring them down to the Valley of
Jehoshaphat.[a]
There I will enter into judgment against
them
concerning my inheritance, my people
Israel,
for they scattered my people among the
nations
and divided up my land.
3They cast lots for my people
and traded boys for prostitutes;
they sold girls for wine
that they might drink.

4"Now what have you against me, O Tyre
and Sidon and all you regions of Philistia?
Are you repaying me for something I have
done? If you are paying me back, I will swiftly
and speedily return on your own heads what
you have done. 5For you took my silver and
my gold and carried off my finest treasures to
your temples. 6You sold the people of Judah
and Jerusalem to the Greeks, that you might
send them far from their homeland.
7"See, I am going to rouse them out of the
places to which you sold them, and I will
return on your own heads what you have
done. 8I will sell your sons and daughters to
the people of Judah, and they will sell them
to the Sabeans, a nation far away." The LORD
has spoken.

9Proclaim this among the nations:
Prepare for war!
Rouse the warriors!
Let all the fighting men draw near and
attack.
10Beat your plowshares into swords
and your pruning hooks into spears.
Let the weakling say,
"I am strong!"
11Come quickly, all you nations from every
side,
and assemble there.

Bring down your warriors, O LORD!
12"Let the nations be roused;
let them advance into the Valley of
Jehoshaphat,
for there I will sit
to judge all the nations on every side.
13Swing the sickle,
for the harvest is ripe.
Come, trample the grapes,
for the winepress is full
and the vats overflow—
so great is their wickedness!"
14Multitudes, multitudes
in the valley of decision!
For the day of the LORD is near
in the valley of decision.
15The sun and moon will be darkened,
and the stars no longer shine.
16The LORD will roar from Zion
and thunder from Jerusalem;
the earth and the sky will tremble.
But the LORD will be a refuge for his
people,
a stronghold for the people of Israel.

Blessings for God's People

17"Then you will know that I, the LORD your
God,
dwell in Zion, my holy hill.
Jerusalem will be holy;
never again will foreigners invade her.

18"In that day the mountains will drip new
wine,
and the hills will flow with milk;
all the ravines of Judah will run with
water.
A fountain will flow out of the LORD's
house
and will water the valley of acacias.[b]
19But Egypt will be desolate,
Edom a desert waste,
because of violence done to the people of
Judah,
in whose land they shed innocent
blood.
20Judah will be inhabited forever
and Jerusalem through all generations.
21Their bloodguilt, which I have not
pardoned,
I will pardon."
The LORD dwells in Zion!

[a]2 *Jehoshaphat* means *the LORD judges;* also in verse 12.
[b]18 Or *Valley of Shittim*

Amos

Introduction:

The author's name, Amos, means "burden" or "burdenbearer." Amos was a shepherd called by God to be a prophet in the northern cities of Israel, during a time of riches and wealth for the northern kingdom.

He announced God's judgment on the people for turning away from God, for being cruel to the poor, and for living selfishly.

In a series of five visions, Amos saw the day of doom as being close. He warned the people that they were to prepare to meet God. For those who loved God, however, Amos had a word of hope. The day was coming when the kingdom of David would be re-established and God's people would dwell in safety.

Outline of contents:

Judgment on Israel's neighbors (1:1–2:5)
Judgment on Israel (2:6–16)
Israel's guilt (3:1–6:14)
The five visions (7:1–9:10)
Israel's restoration (9:11–15)

---

1 The words of Amos, one of the shepherds of Tekoa—what he saw concerning Israel two years before the earthquake, when Uzziah was king of Judah and Jeroboam son of Jehoash[a] was king of Israel.
2 He said:

"The LORD roars from Zion
and thunders from Jerusalem;
the pastures of the shepherds dry up,[b]
and the top of Carmel withers."

Judgment on Israel's Neighbors

3 This is what the LORD says:

"For three sins of Damascus,
even for four, I will not turn back ⌞my wrath⌟.
Because she threshed Gilead
with sledges having iron teeth,
4 I will send fire upon the house of Hazael
that will consume the fortresses of Ben-Hadad.
5 I will break down the gate of Damascus;
I will destroy the king who is in[c] the Valley of Aven[d]
and the one who holds the scepter in Beth Eden.
The people of Aram will go into exile to Kir,"
says the LORD.

6 This is what the LORD says:

"For three sins of Gaza,
even for four, I will not turn back ⌞my wrath⌟.
Because she took captive whole communities
and sold them to Edom,
7 I will send fire upon the walls of Gaza
that will consume her fortresses.
8 I will destroy the king[e] of Ashdod
and the one who holds the scepter in Ashkelon.
I will turn my hand against Ekron,
till the last of the Philistines is dead,"
says the Sovereign LORD.

9 This is what the LORD says:

"For three sins of Tyre,
even for four, I will not turn back ⌞my wrath⌟.
Because she sold whole communities of captives to Edom,
disregarding a treaty of brotherhood,

[a] 1 Hebrew *Joash,* a variant of *Jehoash* [b] 2 Or *shepherds mourn* [c] 5 Or *the inhabitants of* [d] 5 *Aven* means *wickedness.* [e] 8 Or *inhabitants*

10I will send fire upon the walls of Tyre
that will consume her fortresses."

11This is what the LORD says:

"For three sins of Edom,
even for four, I will not turn back ⌞my
wrath⌟.
Because he pursued his brother with a
sword,
stifling all compassion,[a]
because his anger raged continually
and his fury flamed unchecked,
12I will send fire upon Teman
that will consume the fortresses of
Bozrah."

13This is what the LORD says:

"For three sins of Ammon,
even for four, I will not turn back ⌞my
wrath⌟.
Because he ripped open the pregnant
women of Gilead
in order to extend his borders,
14I will set fire to the walls of Rabbah
that will consume her fortresses
amid war cries on the day of battle,
amid violent winds on a stormy day.
15Her king[b] will go into exile,
he and his officials together,"
says the LORD.

2 This is what the LORD says:

"For three sins of Moab,
even for four, I will not turn back ⌞my
wrath⌟.
Because he burned, as if to lime,
the bones of Edom's king,
2I will send fire upon Moab
that will consume the fortresses of
Kerioth.[c]
Moab will go down in great tumult
amid war cries and the blast of the
trumpet.
3I will destroy her ruler
and kill all her officials with him,"
says the LORD.

4This is what the LORD says:

"For three sins of Judah,
even for four, I will not turn back ⌞my
wrath⌟.
Because they have rejected the law of the
LORD
and have not kept his decrees,
because they have been led astray by
false gods,[d]
the gods[e] their ancestors followed,
5I will send fire upon Judah
that will consume the fortresses of
Jerusalem."

Judgment on Israel

6This is what the LORD says:

"For three sins of Israel,
even for four, I will not turn back ⌞my
wrath⌟.
They sell the righteous for silver,
and the needy for a pair of sandals.
7They trample on the heads of the poor
as upon the dust of the ground
and deny justice to the oppressed.
Father and son use the same girl
and so profane my holy name.
8They lie down beside every altar
on garments taken in pledge.
In the house of their god
they drink wine taken as fines.

9"I destroyed the Amorite before them,
though he was tall as the cedars
and strong as the oaks.
I destroyed his fruit above
and his roots below.

10"I brought you up out of Egypt,
and I led you forty years in the desert
to give you the land of the Amorites.
11I also raised up prophets from among
your sons
and Nazirites from among your young
men.
Is this not true, people of Israel?"
declares the LORD.
12"But you made the Nazirites drink wine
and commanded the prophets not to
prophesy.

13"Now then, I will crush you
as a cart crushes when loaded with
grain.
14The swift will not escape,
the strong will not muster their strength,
and the warrior will not save his life.
15The archer will not stand his ground,
the fleet-footed soldier will not get
away,
and the horseman will not save his life.
16Even the bravest warriors

[a] 11 Or *sword / and destroyed his allies* [b] 15 Or / *Molech;* Hebrew *malcam* [c] 2 Or *of her cities* [d] 4 Or *by lies* [e] 4 Or *lies*

will flee naked on that day,"
declares the LORD.

Witnesses Summoned Against Israel

3 Hear this word the LORD has spoken against you, O people of Israel—against the whole family I brought up out of Egypt:

2"You only have I chosen
of all the families of the earth;
therefore I will punish you
for all your sins."

3Do two walk together
unless they have agreed to do so?
4Does a lion roar in the thicket
when he has no prey?
Does he growl in his den
when he has caught nothing?
5Does a bird fall into a trap on the ground
where no snare has been set?
Does a trap spring up from the earth
when there is nothing to catch?
6When a trumpet sounds in a city,
do not the people tremble?
When disaster comes to a city,
has not the LORD caused it?

7Surely the Sovereign LORD does nothing
without revealing his plan
to his servants the prophets.

8The lion has roared—
who will not fear?
The Sovereign LORD has spoken—
who can but prophesy?

9Proclaim to the fortresses of Ashdod
and to the fortresses of Egypt:
"Assemble yourselves on the mountains
of Samaria;
see the great unrest within her
and the oppression among her people."

10"They do not know how to do right,"
declares the LORD,
"who hoard plunder and loot in their
fortresses."

11Therefore this is what the Sovereign
LORD says:

"An enemy will overrun the land;
he will pull down your strongholds
and plunder your fortresses."

12This is what the LORD says:

"As a shepherd saves from the lion's
mouth
only two leg bones or a piece of an ear,
so will the Israelites be saved,
those who sit in Samaria
on the edge of their beds
and in Damascus on their couches.[a]"

13"Hear this and testify against the house
of Jacob," declares the Lord, the LORD God
Almighty.

14"On the day I punish Israel for her sins,
I will destroy the altars of Bethel;
the horns of the altar will be cut off
and fall to the ground.
15I will tear down the winter house
along with the summer house;
the houses adorned with ivory will be
destroyed
and the mansions will be demolished,"
declares the LORD.

Israel Has Not Returned to God

4 Hear this word, you cows of Bashan on
Mount Samaria,
you women who oppress the poor and
crush the needy
and say to your husbands, "Bring us
some drinks!"
2The Sovereign LORD has sworn by his
holiness:
"The time will surely come
when you will be taken away with hooks,
the last of you with fishhooks.
3You will each go straight out
through breaks in the wall,
and you will be cast out toward
Harmon,[b]"
declares the LORD.

4"Go to Bethel and sin;
go to Gilgal and sin yet more.
Bring your sacrifices every morning,
your tithes every three years.[c]
5Burn leavened bread as a thank offering
and brag about your freewill offerings—
boast about them, you Israelites,
for this is what you love to do,"
declares the Sovereign LORD.

6"I gave you empty stomachs[d] in every
city
and lack of bread in every town,

[a]12 The meaning of the Hebrew for this line is uncertain.
[b]3 Masoretic Text; with a different word division of the Hebrew (see Septuagint) *out, O mountain of oppression*
[c]4 Or *tithes on the third day*
[d]6 Hebrew *you cleanness of teeth*

yet you have not returned to me,"
declares the LORD.

7"I also withheld rain from you
when the harvest was still three months away.
I sent rain on one town,
but withheld it from another.
One field had rain;
another had none and dried up.
8People staggered from town to town for water
but did not get enough to drink,
yet you have not returned to me,"
declares the LORD.

9"Many times I struck your gardens and vineyards,
I struck them with blight and mildew.
Locusts devoured your fig and olive trees,
yet you have not returned to me,"
declares the LORD.

10"I sent plagues among you
as I did to Egypt.
I killed your young men with the sword,
along with your captured horses.
I filled your nostrils with the stench of your camps,
yet you have not returned to me,"
declares the LORD.

11"I overthrew some of you
as I[a] overthrew Sodom and Gomorrah.
You were like a burning stick snatched from the fire,
yet you have not returned to me,"
declares the LORD.

12"Therefore this is what I will do to you, Israel,
and because I will do this to you,
prepare to meet your God, O Israel."

13He who forms the mountains,
creates the wind,
and reveals his thoughts to man,
he who turns dawn to darkness,
and treads the high places of the earth—
the LORD God Almighty is his name.

A Lament and Call to Repentance

5 Hear this word, O house of Israel, this lament I take up concerning you:

2"Fallen is Virgin Israel,
never to rise again,
deserted in her own land,
with no one to lift her up."

3This is what the Sovereign LORD says:

"The city that marches out a thousand strong for Israel
will have only a hundred left;
the town that marches out a hundred strong
will have only ten left."

4This is what the LORD says to the house of Israel:

"Seek me and live;
5 do not seek Bethel,
do not go to Gilgal,
do not journey to Beersheba.
For Gilgal will surely go into exile,
and Bethel will be reduced to nothing.[b]"
6Seek the LORD and live,
or he will sweep through the house of Joseph like a fire;
it will devour,
and Bethel will have no one to quench it.

7You who turn justice into bitterness
and cast righteousness to the ground
8(he who made the Pleiades and Orion,
who turns blackness into dawn
and darkens day into night,
who calls for the waters of the sea
and pours them out over the face of the land—
the LORD is his name—
9he flashes destruction on the stronghold
and brings the fortified city to ruin),
10you hate the one who reproves in court
and despise him who tells the truth.

11You trample on the poor
and force him to give you grain.
Therefore, though you have built stone mansions,
you will not live in them;
though you have planted lush vineyards,
you will not drink their wine.
12For I know how many are your offenses
and how great your sins.

You oppress the righteous and take bribes
and you deprive the poor of justice in the courts.

[a]11 Hebrew *God* [b]5 Or *grief;* or *wickedness*; Hebrew *aven,* a reference to Beth Aven (a derogatory name for Bethel)

13Therefore the prudent man keeps quiet in such times,
for the times are evil.

14Seek good, not evil,
that you may live.
Then the LORD God Almighty will be with you,
just as you say he is.
15Hate evil, love good;
maintain justice in the courts.
Perhaps the LORD God Almighty will have mercy
on the remnant of Joseph.

16Therefore this is what the Lord, the LORD
God Almighty, says:

"There will be wailing in all the streets
and cries of anguish in every public square.
The farmers will be summoned to weep
and the mourners to wail.
17There will be wailing in all the vineyards,
for I will pass through your midst,"
says the LORD.

The Day of the LORD

18Woe to you who long
for the day of the LORD!
Why do you long for the day of the LORD?
That day will be darkness, not light.
19It will be as though a man fled from a lion
only to meet a bear,
as though he entered his house
and rested his hand on the wall
only to have a snake bite him.
20Will not the day of the LORD be darkness, not light—
pitch-dark, without a ray of brightness?

21"I hate, I despise your religious feasts;
I cannot stand your assemblies.
22Even though you bring me burnt offerings
and grain offerings,
I will not accept them.
Though you bring choice fellowship offerings,[a]
I will have no regard for them.
23Away with the noise of your songs!
I will not listen to the music of your harps.
24But let justice roll on like a river,
righteousness like a never-failing stream!

25"Did you bring me sacrifices and offerings
forty years in the desert, O house of Israel?
26You have lifted up the shrine of your king,
the pedestal of your idols,
the star of your god[b]—
which you made for yourselves.
27Therefore I will send you into exile
beyond Damascus,"
says the LORD, whose name is God Almighty.

Woe to the Complacent

6 Woe to you who are complacent in Zion,
and to you who feel secure on Mount Samaria,
you notable men of the foremost nation,
to whom the people of Israel come!
2Go to Calneh and look at it;
go from there to great Hamath,
and then go down to Gath in Philistia.
Are they better off than your two kingdoms?
Is their land larger than yours?
3You put off the evil day
and bring near a reign of terror.
4You lie on beds inlaid with ivory
and lounge on your couches.
You dine on choice lambs
and fattened calves.
5You strum away on your harps like David
and improvise on musical instruments.
6You drink wine by the bowlful
and use the finest lotions,
but you do not grieve over the ruin of Joseph.
7Therefore you will be among the first to go into exile;
your feasting and lounging will end.

The LORD Abhors the Pride of Israel

8The Sovereign LORD has sworn by himself—the LORD God Almighty declares:

"I abhor the pride of Jacob
and detest his fortresses;
I will deliver up the city
and everything in it."

9If ten men are left in one house, they too
will die. 10And if a relative who is to burn the
bodies comes to carry them out of the house

[a]22 Traditionally *peace offerings* [b]26 Or *lifted up Sakkuth your king / and Kaiwan your idols, / your star-gods*; Septuagint *lifted up the shrine of Molech / and the star of your god Rephan, / their idols*

and asks anyone still hiding there, "Is anyone with you?" and he says, "No," then he will say, "Hush! We must not mention the name of the LORD."

[11]For the LORD has given the command,
and he will smash the great house into pieces
and the small house into bits.

[12]Do horses run on the rocky crags?
Does one plow there with oxen?
But you have turned justice into poison
and the fruit of righteousness into bitterness—
[13]you who rejoice in the conquest of Lo Debar[a]
and say, "Did we not take Karnaim[b] by our own strength?"

[14]For the LORD God Almighty declares,
"I will stir up a nation against you,
O house of Israel,
that will oppress you all the way
from Lebo[c] Hamath to the valley of the Arabah."

Locusts, Fire and a Plumb Line

7 This is what the Sovereign LORD showed
me: He was preparing swarms of locusts
after the king's share had been harvested
and just as the second crop was coming up.
[2]When they had stripped the land clean, I
cried out, "Sovereign LORD, forgive! How can
Jacob survive? He is so small!"
[3]So the LORD relented.
"This will not happen," the LORD said.
[4]This is what the Sovereign LORD showed
me: The Sovereign LORD was calling for judgment by fire; it dried up the great deep and
devoured the land. [5]Then I cried out, "Sovereign LORD, I beg you, stop! How can Jacob
survive? He is so small!"
[6]So the LORD relented.
"This will not happen either," the Sovereign LORD said.

[7]This is what he showed me: The Lord was
standing by a wall that had been built true to
plumb, with a plumb line in his hand. [8]And
the LORD asked me, "What do you see,
Amos?"
"A plumb line," I replied.
Then the Lord said, "Look, I am setting a
plumb line among my people Israel; I will
spare them no longer.

[9]"The high places of Isaac will be destroyed
and the sanctuaries of Israel will be ruined;
with my sword I will rise against the house of Jeroboam."

Amos and Amaziah

[10]Then Amaziah the priest of Bethel sent a
message to Jeroboam king of Israel: "Amos
is raising a conspiracy against you in the
very heart of Israel. The land cannot bear all
his words. [11]For this is what Amos is saying:

" 'Jeroboam will die by the sword,
and Israel will surely go into exile,
away from their native land.' "

[12]Then Amaziah said to Amos, "Get out,
you seer! Go back to the land of Judah. Earn
your bread there and do your prophesying
there. [13]Don't prophesy anymore at Bethel,
because this is the king's sanctuary and the
temple of the kingdom."
[14]Amos answered Amaziah, "I was neither
a prophet nor a prophet's son, but I was a
shepherd, and I also took care of sycamore-fig trees. [15]But the LORD took me from tending
the flock and said to me, 'Go, prophesy to my
people Israel.' [16]Now then, hear the word of
the LORD. You say,

" 'Do not prophesy against Israel,
and stop preaching against the house of Isaac.'

[17]"Therefore this is what the LORD says:

" 'Your wife will become a prostitute in the city,
and your sons and daughters will fall by the sword.
Your land will be measured and divided up,
and you yourself will die in a pagan[d] country.
And Israel will certainly go into exile,
away from their native land.' "

A Basket of Ripe Fruit

8 This is what the Sovereign LORD showed
me: a basket of ripe fruit. [2]"What do you
see, Amos?" he asked.
"A basket of ripe fruit," I answered.
Then the LORD said to me, "The time is ripe

[a] 13 *Lo Debar* means *nothing.* [b] 13 *Karnaim* means *horns; horn* here symbolizes strength. [c] 14 Or *from the entrance to* [d] 17 Hebrew *an unclean*

for my people Israel; I will spare them no
longer.
3"In that day," declares the Sovereign
LORD, "the songs in the temple will turn to
wailing.[a] Many, many bodies—flung everywhere! Silence!"

4Hear this, you who trample the needy
and do away with the poor of the land,

5saying,

"When will the New Moon be over
that we may sell grain,
and the Sabbath be ended
that we may market wheat?"—
skimping the measure,
boosting the price
and cheating with dishonest scales,
6buying the poor with silver
and the needy for a pair of sandals,
selling even the sweepings with the
wheat.

7The LORD has sworn by the Pride of
Jacob: "I will never forget anything they have
done.

8"Will not the land tremble for this,
and all who live in it mourn?
The whole land will rise like the Nile;
it will be stirred up and then sink
like the river of Egypt.

9"In that day," declares the Sovereign
LORD,

"I will make the sun go down at noon
and darken the earth in broad daylight.
10I will turn your religious feasts into
mourning
and all your singing into weeping.
I will make all of you wear sackcloth
and shave your heads.
I will make that time like mourning for an
only son
and the end of it like a bitter day.

11"The days are coming," declares the
Sovereign LORD,
"when I will send a famine through the
land—
not a famine of food or a thirst for water,
but a famine of hearing the words of
the LORD.
12Men will stagger from sea to sea
and wander from north to east,
searching for the word of the LORD,
but they will not find it.

13"In that day

"the lovely young women and strong
young men
will faint because of thirst.
14They who swear by the shame[b] of
Samaria,
or say, 'As surely as your god lives,
O Dan,'
or, 'As surely as the god[c] of Beersheba
lives'—
they will fall,
never to rise again."

Israel to Be Destroyed

9 I saw the Lord standing by the altar, and
he said:

"Strike the tops of the pillars
so that the thresholds shake.
Bring them down on the heads of all the
people;
those who are left I will kill with the
sword.
Not one will get away,
none will escape.
2Though they dig down to the depths of
the grave,[d]
from there my hand will take them.
Though they climb up to the heavens,
from there I will bring them down.
3Though they hide themselves on the top
of Carmel,
there I will hunt them down and seize
them.
Though they hide from me at the bottom
of the sea,
there I will command the serpent to bite
them.
4Though they are driven into exile by their
enemies,
there I will command the sword to slay
them.
I will fix my eyes upon them
for evil and not for good."

5The Lord, the LORD Almighty,
he who touches the earth and it melts,
and all who live in it mourn—
the whole land rises like the Nile,
then sinks like the river of Egypt—
6he who builds his lofty palace[e] in the
heavens
and sets its foundation[f] on the earth,

[a]3 Or *"the temple singers will wail* [b]14 Or *by Ashima;* or *by the idol* [c]14 Or *power* [d]2 Hebrew *to Sheol* [e]6 The meaning of the Hebrew for this phrase is uncertain. [f]6 The meaning of the Hebrew for this word is uncertain.

who calls for the waters of the sea
and pours them out over the face of the land—
the LORD is his name.

7"Are not you Israelites
the same to me as the Cushites[a]?"
declares the LORD.
"Did I not bring Israel up from Egypt,
the Philistines from Caphtor[b]
and the Arameans from Kir?

8"Surely the eyes of the Sovereign LORD
are on the sinful kingdom.
I will destroy it
from the face of the earth—
yet I will not totally destroy
the house of Jacob,"
declares the LORD.
9"For I will give the command,
and I will shake the house of Israel
among all the nations
as grain is shaken in a sieve,
and not a pebble will reach the ground.
10All the sinners among my people
will die by the sword,
all those who say,
'Disaster will not overtake or meet us.'

Israel's Restoration

11"In that day I will restore
David's fallen tent.
I will repair its broken places,
restore its ruins,
and build it as it used to be,
12so that they may possess the remnant of Edom
and all the nations that bear my name,[c]"
declares the LORD,
who will do these things.

13"The days are coming," declares the LORD,

"when the reaper will be overtaken by the plowman
and the planter by the one treading grapes.
New wine will drip from the mountains
and flow from all the hills.
14I will bring back my exiled[d] people Israel;
they will rebuild the ruined cities and live in them.
They will plant vineyards and drink their wine;
they will make gardens and eat their fruit.
15I will plant Israel in their own land,
never again to be uprooted
from the land I have given them,"

says the LORD your God.

[a] 7 That is, people from the upper Nile region [b] 7 That is, Crete [c] 12 Hebrew; Septuagint *so that the remnant of men / and all the nations that bear my name may seek ⌞the Lord⌟* [d] 14 Or *will restore the fortunes of my*

Obadiah

Introduction:

The name Obadiah means "servant of Jehovah." Nothing more is known about this prophet than this short book containing his prophecy.

Obadiah is a book of prophecy against the nation of Edom. This country had invaded and plundered Jerusalem at least four times, so Obadiah announced God's judgment against them and prophesied that their kingdom would be destroyed.

The Edomites are heard of no more after the destruction of Jerusalem in A.D. 70.

Outline of contents:

The doom of Edom (1–14)
Edom in the day of the Lord (15–21)

1The vision of Obadiah.

This is what the Sovereign LORD says about Edom—

We have heard a message from the LORD:
An envoy was sent to the nations to say,
"Rise, and let us go against her for battle"—

2"See, I will make you small among the nations;
you will be utterly despised.
3The pride of your heart has deceived you,
you who live in the clefts of the rocks[a]
and make your home on the heights,
you who say to yourself,
'Who can bring me down to the ground?'
4Though you soar like the eagle
and make your nest among the stars,
from there I will bring you down,"
declares the LORD.
5"If thieves came to you,
if robbers in the night—
Oh, what a disaster awaits you—
would they not steal only as much as they wanted?
If grape pickers came to you,
would they not leave a few grapes?
6But how Esau will be ransacked,
his hidden treasures pillaged!
7All your allies will force you to the border;
your friends will deceive and overpower you;
those who eat your bread will set a trap for you,[b]
but you will not detect it.

8"In that day," declares the LORD,
"will I not destroy the wise men of Edom,
men of understanding in the mountains of Esau?
9Your warriors, O Teman, will be terrified,
and everyone in Esau's mountains
will be cut down in the slaughter.
10Because of the violence against your brother Jacob,
you will be covered with shame;
you will be destroyed forever.
11On the day you stood aloof
while strangers carried off his wealth
and foreigners entered his gates
and cast lots for Jerusalem,
you were like one of them.
12You should not look down on your brother
in the day of his misfortune,
nor rejoice over the people of Judah
in the day of their destruction,
nor boast so much
in the day of their trouble.

[a]3 Or *of Sela* [b]7 The meaning of the Hebrew for this clause is uncertain.

13You should not march through the gates
of my people
in the day of their disaster,
nor look down on them in their calamity
in the day of their disaster,
nor seize their wealth
in the day of their disaster.
14You should not wait at the crossroads
to cut down their fugitives,
nor hand over their survivors
in the day of their trouble.
15"The day of the LORD is near
for all nations.
As you have done, it will be done to you;
your deeds will return upon your own
head.
16Just as you drank on my holy hill,
so all the nations will drink
continually;
they will drink and drink
and be as if they had never been.
17But on Mount Zion will be deliverance;
it will be holy,
and the house of Jacob
will possess its inheritance.
18The house of Jacob will be a fire
and the house of Joseph a flame;
the house of Esau will be stubble,
and they will set it on fire and
consume it.
There will be no survivors
from the house of Esau."
The LORD has spoken.

19People from the Negev will occupy
the mountains of Esau,
and people from the foothills will possess
the land of the Philistines.
They will occupy the fields of Ephraim
and Samaria,
and Benjamin will possess Gilead.
20This company of Israelite exiles who are
in Canaan
will possess ⌊the land⌋ as far as
Zarephath;
the exiles from Jerusalem who are in
Sepharad
will possess the towns of the Negev.
21Deliverers will go up on[a] Mount Zion
to govern the mountains of Esau.
And the kingdom will be the LORD's.

[a]21 *Or from*

Jonah

Introduction:
Jonah was a prophet whom God called to preach in the foreign city of Nineveh. Jonah tried to run away from God and was swallowed by a great fish.
When the fish returned him to land, Jonah went to Nineveh and warned the people about God's judgment. Jonah learned, to his dismay, that God would forgive even a heathen city if the people were sorry for their sins.

Outline of contents:
Jonah flees from the Lord (1:1–17)
Jonah's prayer and deliverance (2:1–10)
Jonah goes to Nineveh (3:1–10)
Jonah's anger at the Lord's mercy (4:1–11)

Jonah Flees From the Lord

1 The word of the LORD came to Jonah son
of Amittai: 2"Go to the great city of Nineveh and preach against it, because its
wickedness has come up before me."
3But Jonah ran away from the LORD and
headed for Tarshish. He went down to Joppa, where he found a ship bound for that
port. After paying the fare, he went aboard
and sailed for Tarshish to flee from the
LORD.
4Then the LORD sent a great wind on the
sea, and such a violent storm arose that the
ship threatened to break up. 5All the sailors
were afraid and each cried out to his own
god. And they threw the cargo into the sea to
lighten the ship.
But Jonah had gone below deck, where he
lay down and fell into a deep sleep. 6The
captain went to him and said, "How can you
sleep? Get up and call on your god! Maybe
he will take notice of us, and we will not
perish."
7Then the sailors said to each other,
"Come, let us cast lots to find out who is
responsible for this calamity." They cast lots
and the lot fell on Jonah.
8So they asked him, "Tell us, who is responsible for making all this trouble for us?
What do you do? Where do you come from?
What is your country? From what people are
you?"
9He answered, "I am a Hebrew and I worship the LORD, the God of heaven, who made
the sea and the land."
10This terrified them and they asked,
"What have you done?" (They knew he was
running away from the LORD, because he had
already told them so.)
11The sea was getting rougher and rougher. So they asked him, "What should we do
to you to make the sea calm down for
us?"
12"Pick me up and throw me into the sea,"
he replied, "and it will become calm. I know
that it is my fault that this great storm has
come upon you."
13Instead, the men did their best to row
back to land. But they could not, for the sea
grew even wilder than before. 14Then they
cried to the LORD, "O LORD, please do not let
us die for taking this man's life. Do not hold
us accountable for killing an innocent man,
for you, O LORD, have done as you pleased."
15Then they took Jonah and threw him overboard, and the raging sea grew calm. 16At
this the men greatly feared the LORD, and
they offered a sacrifice to the LORD and made
vows to him.
17But the LORD provided a great fish to
swallow Jonah, and Jonah was inside the
fish three days and three nights.

Jonah's Prayer

2 From inside the fish Jonah prayed to the
LORD his God. 2He said:

"In my distress I called to the LORD,
and he answered me.

From the depths of the grave[a] I called for
help,
and you listened to my cry.
3You hurled me into the deep,
into the very heart of the seas,
and the currents swirled about me;
all your waves and breakers
swept over me.
4I said, 'I have been banished
from your sight;
yet I will look again
toward your holy temple.'
5The engulfing waters threatened me,[b]
the deep surrounded me;
seaweed was wrapped around my
head.
6To the roots of the mountains I sank
down;
the earth beneath barred me in
forever.
But you brought my life up from the pit,
O LORD my God.

7"When my life was ebbing away,
I remembered you, LORD,
and my prayer rose to you,
to your holy temple.

8"Those who cling to worthless idols
forfeit the grace that could be theirs.
9But I, with a song of thanksgiving,
will sacrifice to you.
What I have vowed I will make good.
Salvation comes from the LORD."

10And the LORD commanded the fish, and it
vomited Jonah onto dry land.

Jonah Goes to Nineveh

3 Then the word of the LORD came to
Jonah a second time: 2"Go to the great
city of Nineveh and proclaim to it the message I give you."
3Jonah obeyed the word of the LORD and
went to Nineveh. Now Nineveh was a very
important city—a visit required three days.
4On the first day, Jonah started into the city.
He proclaimed: "Forty more days and Nineveh will be overturned." 5The Ninevites believed God. They declared a fast, and all of
them, from the greatest to the least, put on
sackcloth.
6When the news reached the king of Nineveh, he rose from his throne, took off his
royal robes, covered himself with sackcloth
and sat down in the dust. 7Then he issued a
proclamation in Nineveh:

"By the decree of the king and his nobles:

Do not let any man or beast, herd or
flock, taste anything; do not let them eat
or drink. 8But let man and beast be
covered with sackcloth. Let everyone
call urgently on God. Let them give up
their evil ways and their violence. 9Who
knows? God may yet relent and with
compassion turn from his fierce anger
so that we will not perish."

10When God saw what they did and how
they turned from their evil ways, he had compassion and did not bring upon them the
destruction he had threatened.

Jonah's Anger at the LORD's Compassion

4 But Jonah was greatly displeased and
became angry. 2He prayed to the LORD,
"O LORD, is this not what I said when I was
still at home? That is why I was so quick to
flee to Tarshish. I knew that you are a gracious and compassionate God, slow to anger and abounding in love, a God who relents from sending calamity. 3Now, O LORD,
take away my life, for it is better for me to die
than to live."
4But the LORD replied, "Have you any right
to be angry?"
5Jonah went out and sat down at a place
east of the city. There he made himself a
shelter, sat in its shade and waited to see
what would happen to the city. 6Then the
LORD God provided a vine and made it grow
up over Jonah to give shade for his head to
ease his discomfort, and Jonah was very
happy about the vine. 7But at dawn the next
day God provided a worm, which chewed the
vine so that it withered. 8When the sun rose,
God provided a scorching east wind, and the
sun blazed on Jonah's head so that he grew
faint. He wanted to die, and said, "It would be
better for me to die than to live."
9But God said to Jonah, "Do you have a
right to be angry about the vine?"
"I do," he said. "I am angry enough to
die."

[a]2 Hebrew *Sheol* [b]5 Or *waters were at my throat*

[10]But the LORD said, "You have been concerned about this vine, though you did not
tend it or make it grow. It sprang up overnight
and died overnight. [11]But Nineveh has more
than a hundred and twenty thousand people
who cannot tell their right hand from their left,
and many cattle as well. Should I not be
concerned about that great city?"

Micah

Introduction:

This book contains the writings of the prophet Micah who lived in the countryside of Judah during the reigns of Jotham, Ahaz and Hezekiah. Micah warned about God's judgment against the capital cities of both kingdoms, Jerusalem and Samaria, because of the sinfulness of their rulers, prophets and priests. The poor were oppressed and people's lives did not show that they belonged to a holy God.

But Micah promised the restoration of Zion and a kingdom of peace for those who trusted in God. He prophesied that a ruler born in Bethlehem would set up a kingdom that would last forever.

Outline of contents:

---

1 The word of the LORD that came to Micah of Moresheth during the reigns of Jotham, Ahaz and Hezekiah, kings of Judah—the vision he saw concerning Samaria and Jerusalem.

2Hear, O peoples, all of you,
listen, O earth and all who are in it,
that the Sovereign LORD may witness against you,
the Lord from his holy temple.

Judgment Against Samaria and Jerusalem

3Look! The LORD is coming from his dwelling place;
he comes down and treads the high places of the earth.
4The mountains melt beneath him
and the valleys split apart,
like wax before the fire,
like water rushing down a slope.
5All this is because of Jacob's transgression,
because of the sins of the house of Israel.
What is Jacob's transgression?
Is it not Samaria?
What is Judah's high place?
Is it not Jerusalem?

6"Therefore I will make Samaria a heap of rubble,
a place for planting vineyards.
I will pour her stones into the valley
and lay bare her foundations.
7All her idols will be broken to pieces;
all her temple gifts will be burned with fire;
I will destroy all her images.
Since she gathered her gifts from the wages of prostitutes,
as the wages of prostitutes they will again be used."

Weeping and Mourning

8Because of this I will weep and wail;
I will go about barefoot and naked.
I will howl like a jackal
and moan like an owl.
9For her wound is incurable;
it has come to Judah.
It[a] has reached the very gate of my people,
even to Jerusalem itself.
10Tell it not in Gath[b];
weep not at all.[c]
In Beth Ophrah[d]

[a]9 Or *He* [b]10 *Gath* sounds like the Hebrew for *tell.* [c]10 Hebrew; Septuagint may suggest *not in Acco.* The Hebrew for *in Acco* sounds like the Hebrew for *weep.* [d]10 *Beth Ophrah* means *house of dust.*

roll in the dust.
[11]Pass on in nakedness and shame,
you who live in Shaphir.[a]
Those who live in Zaanan[b]
will not come out.
Beth Ezel is in mourning;
its protection is taken from you.
[12]Those who live in Maroth[c] writhe in pain,
waiting for relief,
because disaster has come from the LORD,
even to the gate of Jerusalem.
[13]You who live in Lachish,[d]
harness the team to the chariot.
You were the beginning of sin
to the Daughter of Zion,
for the transgressions of Israel
were found in you.
[14]Therefore you will give parting gifts
to Moresheth Gath.
The town of Aczib[e] will prove deceptive
to the kings of Israel.
[15]I will bring a conqueror against you
who live in Mareshah.[f]
He who is the glory of Israel
will come to Adullam.
[16]Shave your heads in mourning
for the children in whom you delight;
make yourselves as bald as the vulture,
for they will go from you into exile.

Man's Plans and God's

2 Woe to those who plan iniquity,
to those who plot evil on their beds!
At morning's light they carry it out
because it is in their power to do it.
[2]They covet fields and seize them,
and houses, and take them.
They defraud a man of his home,
a fellowman of his inheritance.

[3]Therefore, the LORD says:

"I am planning disaster against this people,
from which you cannot save yourselves.
You will no longer walk proudly,
for it will be a time of calamity.
[4]In that day men will ridicule you;
they will taunt you with this mournful song:
'We are utterly ruined;
my people's possession is divided up.
He takes it from me!
He assigns our fields to traitors.' "
[5]Therefore you will have no one in the assembly of the LORD
to divide the land by lot.

False Prophets

[6]"Do not prophesy," their prophets say.
"Do not prophesy about these things;
disgrace will not overtake us."
[7]Should it be said, O house of Jacob:
"Is the Spirit of the LORD angry?
Does he do such things?"
"Do not my words do good
to him whose ways are upright?
[8]Lately my people have risen up
like an enemy.
You strip off the rich robe
from those who pass by without a care,
like men returning from battle.
[9]You drive the women of my people
from their pleasant homes.
You take away my blessing
from their children forever.
[10]Get up, go away!
For this is not your resting place,
because it is defiled,
it is ruined, beyond all remedy.
[11]If a liar and deceiver comes and says,
'I will prophesy for you plenty of wine and beer,'
he would be just the prophet for this people!

Deliverance Promised

[12]"I will surely gather all of you, O Jacob;
I will surely bring together the remnant of Israel.
I will bring them together like sheep in a pen,
like a flock in its pasture;
the place will throng with people.
[13]One who breaks open the way will go up before them;
they will break through the gate and go out.
Their king will pass through before them,
the LORD at their head."

[a]11 *Shaphir* means *pleasant.* [b]11 *Zaanan* sounds like the Hebrew for *come out.* [c]12 *Maroth* sounds like the Hebrew for *bitter.* [d]13 *Lachish* sounds like the Hebrew for *team.* [e]14 *Aczib* means *deception.* [f]15 *Mareshah* sounds like the Hebrew for *conqueror.*

Leaders and Prophets Rebuked

3 Then I said,
"Listen, you leaders of Jacob,
you rulers of the house of Israel.
Should you not know justice,
2 you who hate good and love evil;
who tear the skin from my people
and the flesh from their bones;
3 who eat my people's flesh,
strip off their skin
and break their bones in pieces;
who chop them up like meat for the pan,
like flesh for the pot?"

4 Then they will cry out to the LORD,
but he will not answer them.
At that time he will hide his face from them
because of the evil they have done.

5 This is what the LORD says:

"As for the prophets
who lead my people astray,
if one feeds them,
they proclaim 'peace';
if he does not,
they prepare to wage war against him.
6 Therefore night will come over you,
without visions,
and darkness, without divination.
The sun will set for the prophets,
and the day will go dark for them.
7 The seers will be ashamed
and the diviners disgraced.
They will all cover their faces
because there is no answer from God."

8 But as for me, I am filled with power,
with the Spirit of the LORD,
and with justice and might,
to declare to Jacob his transgression,
to Israel his sin.
9 Hear this, you leaders of the house of Jacob,
you rulers of the house of Israel,
who despise justice
and distort all that is right;
10 who build Zion with bloodshed,
and Jerusalem with wickedness.
11 Her leaders judge for a bribe,
her priests teach for a price,
and her prophets tell fortunes for money.
Yet they lean upon the LORD and say,
"Is not the LORD among us?
No disaster will come upon us."
12 Therefore because of you,
Zion will be plowed like a field,
Jerusalem will become a heap of rubble,
the temple hill a mound overgrown with thickets.

The Mountain of the LORD

4 In the last days
the mountain of the LORD's temple will be established
as chief among the mountains;
it will be raised above the hills,
and peoples will stream to it.

2 Many nations will come and say,

"Come, let us go up to the mountain of the LORD,
to the house of the God of Jacob.
He will teach us his ways,
so that we may walk in his paths."
The law will go out from Zion,
the word of the LORD from Jerusalem.
3 He will judge between many peoples
and will settle disputes for strong nations far and wide.
They will beat their swords into plowshares
and their spears into pruning hooks.
Nation will not take up sword against nation,
nor will they train for war anymore.
4 Every man will sit under his own vine
and under his own fig tree,
and no one will make them afraid,
for the LORD Almighty has spoken.
5 All the nations may walk
in the name of their gods;
we will walk in the name of the LORD
our God for ever and ever.

The LORD's Plan

6 "In that day," declares the LORD,

"I will gather the lame;
I will assemble the exiles
and those I have brought to grief.
7 I will make the lame a remnant,
those driven away a strong nation.
The LORD will rule over them in Mount Zion
from that day and forever.
8 As for you, O watchtower of the flock,
O stronghold[a] of the Daughter of Zion,

[a]8 Or *hill*

the former dominion will be restored to you;
kingship will come to the Daughter of Jerusalem."

9Why do you now cry aloud—
have you no king?
Has your counselor perished,
that pain seizes you like that of a woman in labor?
10Writhe in agony, O Daughter of Zion,
like a woman in labor,
for now you must leave the city
to camp in the open field.
You will go to Babylon;
there you will be rescued.
There the LORD will redeem you
out of the hand of your enemies.

11But now many nations
are gathered against you.
They say, "Let her be defiled,
let our eyes gloat over Zion!"
12But they do not know
the thoughts of the LORD;
they do not understand his plan,
he who gathers them like sheaves to the threshing floor.

13"Rise and thresh, O Daughter of Zion,
for I will give you horns of iron;
I will give you hoofs of bronze
and you will break to pieces many nations."
You will devote their ill-gotten gains to the LORD,
their wealth to the Lord of all the earth.

A Promised Ruler From Bethlehem

5 Marshal your troops, O city of troops,[a]
for a siege is laid against us.
They will strike Israel's ruler
on the cheek with a rod.

2"But you, Bethlehem Ephrathah,
though you are small among the clans[b] of Judah,
out of you will come for me
one who will be ruler over Israel,
whose origins[c] are from of old,
from ancient times.[d]"

3Therefore Israel will be abandoned
until the time when she who is in labor gives birth
and the rest of his brothers return
to join the Israelites.

4He will stand and shepherd his flock
in the strength of the LORD,
in the majesty of the name of the LORD his God.
And they will live securely, for then his greatness
will reach to the ends of the earth.
5 And he will be their peace.

Deliverance and Destruction

When the Assyrian invades our land
and marches through our fortresses,
we will raise against him seven shepherds,
even eight leaders of men.
6They will rule[e] the land of Assyria with the sword,
the land of Nimrod with drawn sword.[f]
He will deliver us from the Assyrian
when he invades our land
and marches into our borders.

7The remnant of Jacob will be
in the midst of many peoples
like dew from the LORD,
like showers on the grass,
which do not wait for man
or linger for mankind.
8The remnant of Jacob will be among the nations,
in the midst of many peoples,
like a lion among the beasts of the forest,
like a young lion among flocks of sheep,
which mauls and mangles as it goes,
and no one can rescue.
9Your hand will be lifted up in triumph over your enemies,
and all your foes will be destroyed.

10"In that day," declares the LORD,

"I will destroy your horses from among you
and demolish your chariots.
11I will destroy the cities of your land
and tear down all your strongholds.
12I will destroy your witchcraft
and you will no longer cast spells.
13I will destroy your carved images
and your sacred stones from among you;
you will no longer bow down

[a]1 Or *Strengthen your walls, O walled city* [b]2 Or *rulers* [c]2 Hebrew *goings out* [d]2 Or *from days of eternity* [e]6 Or *crush* [f]6 Or *Nimrod in its gates*

to the work of your hands.
[14]I will uproot from among you your
Asherah poles[a]
and demolish your cities.
[15]I will take vengeance in anger and wrath
upon the nations that have not obeyed
me."

The LORD's Case Against Israel

6 Listen to what the LORD says:
"Stand up, plead your case before the
mountains;
let the hills hear what you have to say.
[2]Hear, O mountains, the LORD's
accusation;
listen, you everlasting foundations of
the earth.
For the LORD has a case against his
people;
he is lodging a charge against Israel.

[3]"My people, what have I done to you?
How have I burdened you? Answer me.
[4]I brought you up out of Egypt
and redeemed you from the land of
slavery.
I sent Moses to lead you,
also Aaron and Miriam.
[5]My people, remember
what Balak king of Moab counseled
and what Balaam son of Beor
answered.
Remember ⌊your journey⌋ from Shittim to
Gilgal,
that you may know the righteous acts
of the LORD."

[6]With what shall I come before the LORD
and bow down before the exalted God?
Shall I come before him with burnt
offerings,
with calves a year old?
[7]Will the LORD be pleased with thousands
of rams,
with ten thousand rivers of oil?
Shall I offer my firstborn for my
transgression,
the fruit of my body for the sin of my
soul?
[8]He has showed you, O man, what is
good.
And what does the LORD require of you?
To act justly and to love mercy
and to walk humbly with your God.

Israel's Guilt and Punishment

[9]Listen! The LORD is calling to the city—
and to fear your name is wisdom—
"Heed the rod and the One who
appointed it.[b]
[10]Am I still to forget, O wicked house,
your ill-gotten treasures
and the short ephah,[c] which is
accursed?
[11]Shall I acquit a man with dishonest
scales,
with a bag of false weights?
[12]Her rich men are violent;
her people are liars
and their tongues speak deceitfully.
[13]Therefore, I have begun to destroy you,
to ruin you because of your sins.
[14]You will eat but not be satisfied;
your stomach will still be empty.[d]
You will store up but save nothing,
because what you save I will give to the
sword.
[15]You will plant but not harvest;
you will press olives but not use the oil
on yourselves,
you will crush grapes but not drink the
wine.
[16]You have observed the statutes of Omri
and all the practices of Ahab's house,
and you have followed their traditions.
Therefore I will give you over to ruin
and your people to derision;
you will bear the scorn of the nations.[e]"

Israel's Misery

7 What misery is mine!
I am like one who gathers summer
fruit
at the gleaning of the vineyard;
there is no cluster of grapes to eat,
none of the early figs that I crave.
[2]The godly have been swept from the
land;
not one upright man remains.
All men lie in wait to shed blood;
each hunts his brother with a net.
[3]Both hands are skilled in doing evil;
the ruler demands gifts,
the judge accepts bribes,
the powerful dictate what they desire—
they all conspire together.
[4]The best of them is like a brier,

[a]14 That is, symbols of the goddess Asherah [b]9 The meaning of the Hebrew for this line is uncertain.
[c]10 An ephah was a dry measure. [d]14 The meaning of the Hebrew for this word is uncertain.
[e]16 Septuagint; Hebrew *scorn due my people*

the most upright worse than a thorn
hedge.
The day of your watchmen has come,
the day God visits you.
Now is the time of their confusion.
5Do not trust a neighbor;
put no confidence in a friend.
Even with her who lies in your embrace
be careful of your words.
6For a son dishonors his father,
a daughter rises up against her mother,
a daughter-in-law against her
mother-in-law—
a man's enemies are the members of
his own household.

7But as for me, I watch in hope for the
LORD,
I wait for God my Savior;
my God will hear me.

Israel Will Rise

8Do not gloat over me, my enemy!
Though I have fallen, I will rise.
Though I sit in darkness,
the LORD will be my light.
9Because I have sinned against him,
I will bear the LORD's wrath,
until he pleads my case
and establishes my right.
He will bring me out into the light;
I will see his righteousness.
10Then my enemy will see it
and will be covered with shame,
she who said to me,
"Where is the LORD your God?"
My eyes will see her downfall;
even now she will be trampled
underfoot
like mire in the streets.

11The day for building your walls will come,
the day for extending your boundaries.
12In that day people will come to you
from Assyria and the cities of Egypt,
even from Egypt to the Euphrates
and from sea to sea
and from mountain to mountain.
13The earth will become desolate because
of its inhabitants,
as the result of their deeds.

Prayer and Praise

14Shepherd your people with your staff,
the flock of your inheritance,
which lives by itself in a forest,
in fertile pasturelands.[a]
Let them feed in Bashan and Gilead
as in days long ago.

15"As in the days when you came out of
Egypt,
I will show them my wonders."

16Nations will see and be ashamed,
deprived of all their power.
They will lay their hands on their mouths
and their ears will become deaf.
17They will lick dust like a snake,
like creatures that crawl on the ground.
They will come trembling out of their
dens;
they will turn in fear to the LORD our
God
and will be afraid of you.
18Who is a God like you,
who pardons sin and forgives the
transgression
of the remnant of his inheritance?
You do not stay angry forever
but delight to show mercy.
19You will again have compassion on us;
you will tread our sins underfoot
and hurl all our iniquities into the
depths of the sea.
20You will be true to Jacob,
and show mercy to Abraham,
as you pledged on oath to our fathers
in days long ago.

[a]14 *Or in the middle of Carmel*

Nahum

Introduction:
Nahum was a prophet in the last half of the seventh century B.C. He prophesied at the same time as Zephaniah, Jeremiah, and Habakkuk.
Nahum is a book of prophecy against Nineveh, the capital of Assyria. The prophet describes the cruelty of the Assyrians as they conquered nation after nation. He predicts the seige and destruction of Nineveh and the end of the kingdom of Assyria.
Nahum's only advice to Judah was that they observe their religious feasts, since the Assyrians would never again threaten Jerusalem.

Outline of contents:

---

1 An oracle concerning Nineveh. The book of the vision of Nahum the Elkoshite.

The LORD's Anger Against Nineveh

2 The LORD is a jealous and avenging God;
the LORD takes vengeance and is filled with wrath.
The LORD takes vengeance on his foes
and maintains his wrath against his enemies.
3 The LORD is slow to anger and great in power;
the LORD will not leave the guilty unpunished.
His way is in the whirlwind and the storm,
and clouds are the dust of his feet.
4 He rebukes the sea and dries it up;
he makes all the rivers run dry.
Bashan and Carmel wither
and the blossoms of Lebanon fade.
5 The mountains quake before him
and the hills melt away.
The earth trembles at his presence,
the world and all who live in it.
6 Who can withstand his indignation?
Who can endure his fierce anger?
His wrath is poured out like fire;
the rocks are shattered before him.

7 The LORD is good,
a refuge in times of trouble.
He cares for those who trust in him,
8 but with an overwhelming flood
he will make an end of ⌞Nineveh⌟;
he will pursue his foes into darkness.

9 Whatever they plot against the LORD
he[a] will bring to an end;
trouble will not come a second time.
10 They will be entangled among thorns
and drunk from their wine;
they will be consumed like dry stubble.[b]
11 From you, ⌞O Nineveh,⌟ has one come forth
who plots evil against the LORD
and counsels wickedness.

12 This is what the LORD says:

"Although they have allies and are numerous,
they will be cut off and pass away.
Although I have afflicted you, ⌞O Judah,⌟
I will afflict you no more.
13 Now I will break their yoke from your neck
and tear your shackles away."

14 The LORD has given a command concerning you, ⌞Nineveh⌟:
"You will have no descendants to bear your name.

[a] 9 Or *What do you foes plot against the LORD? / He*
[b] 10 The meaning of the Hebrew for this verse is uncertain.

I will destroy the carved images and cast idols
that are in the temple of your gods.
I will prepare your grave,
for you are vile."

15 Look, there on the mountains,
the feet of one who brings good news,
who proclaims peace!
Celebrate your festivals, O Judah,
and fulfill your vows.
No more will the wicked invade you;
they will be completely destroyed.

Nineveh to Fall

2 An attacker advances against you, ⌊Nineveh⌋.
Guard the fortress,
watch the road,
brace yourselves,
marshal all your strength!

2 The LORD will restore the splendor of Jacob
like the splendor of Israel,
though destroyers have laid them waste
and have ruined their vines.

3 The shields of his soldiers are red;
the warriors are clad in scarlet.
The metal on the chariots flashes
on the day they are made ready;
the spears of pine are brandished.[a]
4 The chariots storm through the streets,
rushing back and forth through the squares.
They look like flaming torches;
they dart about like lightning.

5 He summons his picked troops,
yet they stumble on their way.
They dash to the city wall;
the protective shield is put in place.
6 The river gates are thrown open
and the palace collapses.
7 It is decreed[b] that ⌊the city⌋
be exiled and carried away.
Its slave girls moan like doves
and beat upon their breasts.
8 Nineveh is like a pool,
and its water is draining away.
"Stop! Stop!" they cry,
but no one turns back.
9 Plunder the silver!
Plunder the gold!
The supply is endless,
the wealth from all its treasures!
10 She is pillaged, plundered, stripped!
Hearts melt, knees give way,
bodies tremble, every face grows pale.

11 Where now is the lions' den,
the place where they fed their young,
where the lion and lioness went,
and the cubs, with nothing to fear?
12 The lion killed enough for his cubs
and strangled the prey for his mate,
filling his lairs with the kill
and his dens with the prey.

13 "I am against you,"
declares the LORD Almighty.
"I will burn up your chariots in smoke,
and the sword will devour your young lions.
I will leave you no prey on the earth.
The voices of your messengers
will no longer be heard."

Woe to Nineveh

3 Woe to the city of blood,
full of lies,
full of plunder,
never without victims!
2 The crack of whips,
the clatter of wheels,
galloping horses
and jolting chariots!
3 Charging cavalry,
flashing swords
and glittering spears!
Many casualties,
piles of dead,
bodies without number,
people stumbling over the corpses—
4 all because of the wanton lust of a harlot,
alluring, the mistress of sorceries,
who enslaved nations by her prostitution
and peoples by her witchcraft.

5 "I am against you," declares the LORD Almighty.
"I will lift your skirts over your face.
I will show the nations your nakedness
and the kingdoms your shame.
6 I will pelt you with filth,
I will treat you with contempt
and make you a spectacle.
7 All who see you will flee from you and say,

[a] 3 Hebrew; Septuagint and Syriac / *the horsemen rush to and fro* [b] 7 The meaning of the Hebrew for this word is uncertain.

'Nineveh is in ruins—who will mourn for her?'
Where can I find anyone to comfort you?"

8Are you better than Thebes,[a]
situated on the Nile,
with water around her?
The river was her defense,
the waters her wall.
9Cush[b] and Egypt were her boundless strength;
Put and Libya were among her allies.
10Yet she was taken captive
and went into exile.
Her infants were dashed to pieces
at the head of every street.
Lots were cast for her nobles,
and all her great men were put in chains.
11You too will become drunk;
you will go into hiding
and seek refuge from the enemy.

12All your fortresses are like fig trees
with their first ripe fruit;
when they are shaken,
the figs fall into the mouth of the eater.
13Look at your troops—
they are all women!
The gates of your land
are wide open to your enemies;
fire has consumed their bars.

14Draw water for the siege,
strengthen your defenses!
Work the clay,
tread the mortar,
repair the brickwork!
15There the fire will devour you;
the sword will cut you down
and, like grasshoppers, consume you.
Multiply like grasshoppers,
multiply like locusts!
16You have increased the number of your merchants
till they are more than the stars of the sky,
but like locusts they strip the land
and then fly away.
17Your guards are like locusts,
your officials like swarms of locusts
that settle in the walls on a cold day—
but when the sun appears they fly away,
and no one knows where.

18O king of Assyria, your shepherds[c] slumber;
your nobles lie down to rest.
Your people are scattered on the mountains
with no one to gather them.
19Nothing can heal your wound;
your injury is fatal.
Everyone who hears the news about you
claps his hands at your fall,
for who has not felt
your endless cruelty?

[a]8 Hebrew *No Amon* [b]9 That is, the upper Nile region [c]18 Or *rulers*

Habakkuk

Introduction:

Habakkuk was written as a dialogue or conversation between God and the prophet. Habakkuk saw that the leaders in Judah were oppressing the poor, so he asked the question as to why God allowed those wicked people to prosper. When God told him that the Babylonians would come to punish Judah, Habakkuk became more concerned. He did not understand how God could use the Babylonians, who were actually more wicked than the wicked Jews, to bring judgment on God's chosen people. God's answer was that the just would live by faith in God and that they had the assurance that God was doing what was right. God told Habakkuk that in due time the Babylonians too would be judged and that justice would come about for the people of God. Habakkuk ends his book with a prayer of praise.

Outline of contents:

---

1 The oracle that Habakkuk the prophet received.

Habakkuk's Complaint

2How long, O LORD, must I call for help,
but you do not listen?
Or cry out to you, "Violence!"
but you do not save?
3Why do you make me look at injustice?
Why do you tolerate wrong?
Destruction and violence are before me;
there is strife, and conflict abounds.
4Therefore the law is paralyzed,
and justice never prevails.
The wicked hem in the righteous,
so that justice is perverted.

The LORD's Answer

5"Look at the nations and watch—
and be utterly amazed.
For I am going to do something in your days
that you would not believe,
even if you were told.
6I am raising up the Babylonians,[a]
that ruthless and impetuous people,
who sweep across the whole earth
to seize dwelling places not their own.
7They are a feared and dreaded people;
they are a law to themselves
and promote their own honor.
8Their horses are swifter than leopards,
fiercer than wolves at dusk.
Their cavalry gallops headlong;
their horsemen come from afar.
They fly like a vulture swooping to devour;
9 they all come bent on violence.
Their hordes[b] advance like a desert wind
and gather prisoners like sand.
10They deride kings
and scoff at rulers.
They laugh at all fortified cities;
they build earthen ramps and capture them.
11Then they sweep past like the wind and go on—
guilty men, whose own strength is their god."

Habakkuk's Second Complaint

12O LORD, are you not from everlasting?
My God, my Holy One, we will not die.
O LORD, you have appointed them to execute judgment;

[a]6 Or *Chaldeans* [b]9 The meaning of the Hebrew for this word is uncertain.

O Rock, you have ordained them to
punish.
13Your eyes are too pure to look on evil;
you cannot tolerate wrong.
Why then do you tolerate the
treacherous?
Why are you silent while the wicked
swallow up those more righteous than
themselves?
14You have made men like fish in the sea,
like sea creatures that have no ruler.
15The wicked foe pulls all of them up with
hooks,
he catches them in his net,
he gathers them up in his dragnet;
and so he rejoices and is glad.
16Therefore he sacrifices to his net
and burns incense to his dragnet,
for by his net he lives in luxury
and enjoys the choicest food.
17Is he to keep on emptying his net,
destroying nations without mercy?

2 I will stand at my watch
and station myself on the ramparts;
I will look to see what he will say to me,
and what answer I am to give to this
complaint.[a]

The Lord's Answer

2Then the Lord replied:

"Write down the revelation
and make it plain on tablets
so that a herald[b] may run with it.
3For the revelation awaits an appointed
time;
it speaks of the end
and will not prove false.
Though it linger, wait for it;
it[c] will certainly come and will not
delay.

4"See, he is puffed up;
his desires are not upright—
but the righteous will live by his faith[d]—
5indeed, wine betrays him;
he is arrogant and never at rest.
Because he is as greedy as the grave[e]
and like death is never satisfied,
he gathers to himself all the nations
and takes captive all the peoples.

6"Will not all of them taunt him with ridicule
and scorn, saying,

" 'Woe to him who piles up stolen goods
and makes himself wealthy by
extortion!
How long must this go on?'
7Will not your debtors[f] suddenly arise?
Will they not wake up and make you
tremble?
Then you will become their victim.
8Because you have plundered many
nations,
the peoples who are left will plunder
you.
For you have shed man's blood;
you have destroyed lands and cities
and everyone in them.

9"Woe to him who builds his realm by
unjust gain
to set his nest on high,
to escape the clutches of ruin!
10You have plotted the ruin of many
peoples,
shaming your own house and forfeiting
your life.
11The stones of the wall will cry out,
and the beams of the woodwork will
echo it.

12"Woe to him who builds a city with
bloodshed
and establishes a town by crime!
13Has not the Lord Almighty determined
that the people's labor is only fuel for
the fire,
that the nations exhaust themselves for
nothing?
14For the earth will be filled with the
knowledge of the glory of the
Lord,
as the waters cover the sea.

15"Woe to him who gives drink to his
neighbors,
pouring it from the wineskin till they are
drunk,
so that he can gaze on their naked
bodies.
16You will be filled with shame instead of
glory.
Now it is your turn! Drink and be
exposed[g]!
The cup from the Lord's right hand is
coming around to you,
and disgrace will cover your glory.

[a]*1* Or *and what to answer when I am rebuked* [b]*2* Or *so that whoever reads it* [c]*3* Or *Though he linger, wait for him; / he* [d]*4* Or *faithfulness* [e]*5* Hebrew *Sheol* [f]*7* Or *creditors* [g]*16* Masoretic Text; Dead Sea Scrolls, Aquila, Vulgate and Syriac (see also Septuagint) *and stagger*

17The violence you have done to Lebanon
will overwhelm you,
and your destruction of animals will
terrify you.
For you have shed man's blood;
you have destroyed lands and cities
and everyone in them.

18"Of what value is an idol, since a man
has carved it?
Or an image that teaches lies?
For he who makes it trusts in his own
creation;
he makes idols that cannot speak.
19Woe to him who says to wood, 'Come to
life!'
Or to lifeless stone, 'Wake up!'
Can it give guidance?
It is covered with gold and silver;
there is no breath in it.
20But the LORD is in his holy temple;
let all the earth be silent before him."

Habakkuk's Prayer

3 A prayer of Habakkuk the prophet. On *shigionoth.*[a]

2LORD, I have heard of your fame;
I stand in awe of your deeds, O LORD.
Renew them in our day,
in our time make them known;
in wrath remember mercy.

3God came from Teman,
the Holy One from Mount Paran.
Selah[b]
His glory covered the heavens
and his praise filled the earth.
4His splendor was like the sunrise;
rays flashed from his hand,
where his power was hidden.
5Plague went before him;
pestilence followed his steps.
6He stood, and shook the earth;
he looked, and made the nations
tremble.
The ancient mountains crumbled
and the age-old hills collapsed.
His ways are eternal.
7I saw the tents of Cushan in distress,
the dwellings of Midian in anguish.

8Were you angry with the rivers, O LORD?
Was your wrath against the streams?
Did you rage against the sea
when you rode with your horses
and your victorious chariots?
9You uncovered your bow,
you called for many arrows. *Selah*
You split the earth with rivers;
10 the mountains saw you and writhed.
Torrents of water swept by;
the deep roared
and lifted its waves on high.

11Sun and moon stood still in the heavens
at the glint of your flying arrows,
at the lightning of your flashing spear.
12In wrath you strode through the earth
and in anger you threshed the nations.
13You came out to deliver your people,
to save your anointed one.
You crushed the leader of the land of
wickedness,
you stripped him from head to foot.
Selah
14With his own spear you pierced his head
when his warriors stormed out to
scatter us,
gloating as though about to devour
the wretched who were in hiding.
15You trampled the sea with your horses,
churning the great waters.

16I heard and my heart pounded,
my lips quivered at the sound;
decay crept into my bones,
and my legs trembled.
Yet I will wait patiently for the day of
calamity
to come on the nation invading us.
17Though the fig tree does not bud
and there are no grapes on the vines,
though the olive crop fails
and the fields produce no food,
though there are no sheep in the pen
and no cattle in the stalls,
18yet I will rejoice in the LORD,
I will be joyful in God my Savior.

19The Sovereign LORD is my strength;
he makes my feet like the feet of a
deer,
he enables me to go on the heights.

For the director of music. On my stringed
instruments.

[a]1 Probably a literary or musical term [b]3 A word of uncertain meaning; possibly a musical term; also in verses 9 and 13

Zephaniah

Introduction:

Zephaniah's ministry is dated in the reign of Josiah (640–609 B.C.). He warned that the day of the Lord would bring judgment on Judah and Jerusalem and he called the Jews to return to God.

Zephaniah then predicted that Judah's neighboring nations would be destroyed as well. With a note of hope, he promised that God would bring his people home.

Outline of contents:

God's judgment announced (1:1–2:3)
Judgment against the nations (2:4–15)
The future of Jerusalem (3:1–20)

---

1 The word of the LORD that came to Zephaniah son of Cushi, the son of Gedaliah,
the son of Amariah, the son of Hezekiah,
during the reign of Josiah son of Amon king
of Judah:

Warning of Coming Destruction

2"I will sweep away everything
from the face of the earth,"
declares the LORD.
3"I will sweep away both men and animals;
I will sweep away the birds of the air
and the fish of the sea.
The wicked will have only heaps of rubble[a]
when I cut off man from the face of the earth,"
declares the LORD.

Against Judah

4"I will stretch out my hand against Judah
and against all who live in Jerusalem.
I will cut off from this place every remnant of Baal,
the names of the pagan and the idolatrous priests—
5those who bow down on the roofs
to worship the starry host,
those who bow down and swear by the LORD
and who also swear by Molech,[b]
6those who turn back from following the LORD
and neither seek the LORD nor inquire of him.
7Be silent before the Sovereign LORD,
for the day of the LORD is near.
The LORD has prepared a sacrifice;
he has consecrated those he has invited.
8On the day of the LORD's sacrifice
I will punish the princes
and the king's sons
and all those clad
in foreign clothes.
9On that day I will punish
all who avoid stepping on the threshold,[c]
who fill the temple of their gods
with violence and deceit.

10"On that day," declares the LORD,
"a cry will go up from the Fish Gate,
wailing from the New Quarter,
and a loud crash from the hills.
11Wail, you who live in the market district[d];
all your merchants will be wiped out,
all who trade with[e] silver will be ruined.
12At that time I will search Jerusalem with lamps
and punish those who are complacent,
who are like wine left on its dregs,
who think, 'The LORD will do nothing,
either good or bad.'

[a]3 The meaning of the Hebrew for this line is uncertain. [b]5 Hebrew *Malcam,* that is, Milcom [c]9 See 1 Samuel 5:5. [d]11 Or *the Mortar* [e]11 Or *in*

13 Their wealth will be plundered,
their houses demolished.
They will build houses
but not live in them;
they will plant vineyards
but not drink the wine.

The Great Day of the Lord

14 "The great day of the Lord is near—
near and coming quickly.
Listen! The cry on the day of the Lord will be bitter,
the shouting of the warrior there.
15 That day will be a day of wrath,
a day of distress and anguish,
a day of trouble and ruin,
a day of darkness and gloom,
a day of clouds and blackness,
16 a day of trumpet and battle cry
against the fortified cities
and against the corner towers.
17 I will bring distress on the people
and they will walk like blind men,
because they have sinned against the Lord.
Their blood will be poured out like dust
and their entrails like filth.
18 Neither their silver nor their gold
will be able to save them
on the day of the Lord's wrath.
In the fire of his jealousy
the whole world will be consumed,
for he will make a sudden end
of all who live in the earth."

2 Gather together, gather together,
O shameful nation,
2 before the appointed time arrives
and that day sweeps on like chaff,
before the fierce anger of the Lord comes upon you,
before the day of the Lord's wrath comes upon you.
3 Seek the Lord, all you humble of the land,
you who do what he commands.
Seek righteousness, seek humility;
perhaps you will be sheltered
on the day of the Lord's anger.

Against Philistia

4 Gaza will be abandoned
and Ashkelon left in ruins.
At midday Ashdod will be emptied
and Ekron uprooted.
5 Woe to you who live by the sea,
O Kerethite people;
the word of the Lord is against you,
O Canaan, land of the Philistines.

"I will destroy you,
and none will be left."

6 The land by the sea, where the Kerethites[a] dwell,
will be a place for shepherds and sheep pens.
7 It will belong to the remnant of the house of Judah;
there they will find pasture.
In the evening they will lie down
in the houses of Ashkelon.
The Lord their God will care for them;
he will restore their fortunes.[b]

Against Moab and Ammon

8 "I have heard the insults of Moab
and the taunts of the Ammonites,
who insulted my people
and made threats against their land.
9 Therefore, as surely as I live,"
declares the Lord Almighty, the God of Israel,
"surely Moab will become like Sodom,
the Ammonites like Gomorrah—
a place of weeds and salt pits,
a wasteland forever.
The remnant of my people will plunder them;
the survivors of my nation will inherit their land."
10 This is what they will get in return for their pride,
for insulting and mocking the people of the Lord Almighty.
11 The Lord will be awesome to them
when he destroys all the gods of the land.
The nations on every shore will worship him,
every one in its own land.

Against Cush

12 "You too, O Cushites,[c]
will be slain by my sword."

[a]6 The meaning of the Hebrew for this word is uncertain. [b]7 Or *will bring back their captives* [c]12 That is, people from the upper Nile region

Against Assyria

13He will stretch out his hand against the north
and destroy Assyria,
leaving Nineveh utterly desolate
and dry as the desert.
14Flocks and herds will lie down there,
creatures of every kind.
The desert owl and the screech owl
will roost on her columns.
Their calls will echo through the windows,
rubble will be in the doorways,
the beams of cedar will be exposed.
15This is the carefree city
that lived in safety.
She said to herself,
"I am, and there is none besides me."
What a ruin she has become,
a lair for wild beasts!
All who pass by her scoff
and shake their fists.

The Future of Jerusalem

3 Woe to the city of oppressors,
rebellious and defiled!
2She obeys no one,
she accepts no correction.
She does not trust in the LORD,
she does not draw near to her God.
3Her officials are roaring lions,
her rulers are evening wolves,
who leave nothing for the morning.
4Her prophets are arrogant;
they are treacherous men.
Her priests profane the sanctuary
and do violence to the law.
5The LORD within her is righteous;
he does no wrong.
Morning by morning he dispenses his justice,
and every new day he does not fail,
yet the unrighteous know no shame.

6"I have cut off nations;
their strongholds are demolished.
I have left their streets deserted,
with no one passing through.
Their cities are destroyed;
no one will be left—no one at all.
7I said to the city,
'Surely you will fear me
and accept correction!'
Then her dwelling would not be cut off,
nor all my punishments come upon her.
But they were still eager
to act corruptly in all they did.
8Therefore wait for me," declares the LORD,
"for the day I will stand up to testify.[a]
I have decided to assemble the nations,
to gather the kingdoms
and to pour out my wrath on them—
all my fierce anger.
The whole world will be consumed
by the fire of my jealous anger.

9"Then will I purify the lips of the peoples,
that all of them may call on the name of the LORD
and serve him shoulder to shoulder.
10From beyond the rivers of Cush[b]
my worshipers, my scattered people,
will bring me offerings.
11On that day you will not be put to shame
for all the wrongs you have done to me,
because I will remove from this city
those who rejoice in their pride.
Never again will you be haughty
on my holy hill.
12But I will leave within you
the meek and humble,
who trust in the name of the LORD.
13The remnant of Israel will do no wrong;
they will speak no lies,
nor will deceit be found in their mouths.
They will eat and lie down
and no one will make them afraid."

14Sing, O Daughter of Zion;
shout aloud, O Israel!
Be glad and rejoice with all your heart,
O Daughter of Jerusalem!
15The LORD has taken away your punishment,
he has turned back your enemy.
The LORD, the King of Israel, is with you;
never again will you fear any harm.
16On that day they will say to Jerusalem,
"Do not fear, O Zion;
do not let your hands hang limp.
17The LORD your God is with you,
he is mighty to save.
He will take great delight in you,
he will quiet you with his love,
he will rejoice over you with singing."

18"The sorrows for the appointed feasts

[a] *8* Septuagint and Syriac; Hebrew *will rise up to plunder*
[b] *10* That is, the upper Nile region

I will remove from you;
they are a burden and a reproach to
you.[a]
19At that time I will deal
with all who oppressed you;
I will rescue the lame
and gather those who have been
scattered.
I will give them praise and honor
in every land where they were put to
shame.
20At that time I will gather you;
at that time I will bring you home.
I will give you honor and praise
among all the peoples of the earth
when I restore your fortunes[b]
before your very eyes,"
says the LORD.

[a]18 Or *"I will gather you who mourn for the appointed feasts; / your reproach is a burden to you* [b]20 Or *I bring back your captives*

Haggai

Introduction:

Eighteen years had passed since Cyrus's decree in 538 B.C. had allowed the Jews to return from exile to Jerusalem. Because they were busy building their own homes, the people still had not finished building God's temple.

Haggai's message was that the time had come to build the house of the Lord. Under the leadership of Zerubbabel and Joshua and with Haggai's prodding the temple was rebuilt during the years 520–515 B.C.

Haggai told the people that the glory of the temple they were building would be greater than that of the former temple, even though the building itself would be less to look at. This temple would be greater because God would fill this house with his glory.

Outline of contents:

The call to rebuild the temple (1:1–15)
Hopes for the new temple (2:1–9)
Promised blessings (2:10–19)
God's final triumph (2:20–23)

A Call to Build the House of the LORD

1 In the second year of King Darius, on the
first day of the sixth month, the word of
the LORD came through the prophet Haggai to
Zerubbabel son of Shealtiel, governor of
Judah, and to Joshua[a] son of Jehozadak,
the high priest:
2This is what the LORD Almighty says:
"These people say, 'The time has not yet
come for the LORD's house to be built.' "
3Then the word of the LORD came through
the prophet Haggai: 4"Is it a time for you
yourselves to be living in your paneled
houses, while this house remains a ruin?"
5Now this is what the LORD Almighty says:
"Give careful thought to your ways. 6You
have planted much, but have harvested little.
You eat, but never have enough. You drink,
but never have your fill. You put on
clothes, but are not warm. You earn wages,
only to put them in a purse with holes
in it."
7This is what the LORD Almighty says:
"Give careful thought to your ways. 8Go up
into the mountains and bring down timber
and build the house, so that I may take pleasure in it and be honored," says the LORD.
9"You expected much, but see, it turned out
to be little. What you brought home, I blew
away. Why?" declares the LORD Almighty.
"Because of my house, which remains a
ruin, while each of you is busy with his own
house. 10Therefore, because of you the
heavens have withheld their dew and the
earth its crops. 11I called for a drought on the
fields and the mountains, on the grain, the
new wine, the oil and whatever the ground
produces, on men and cattle, and on the
labor of your hands."

12Then Zerubbabel son of Shealtiel,
Joshua son of Jehozadak, the high priest,
and the whole remnant of the people obeyed
the voice of the LORD their God and the message of the prophet Haggai, because the
LORD their God had sent him. And the people
feared the LORD.
13Then Haggai, the LORD's messenger,
gave this message of the LORD to the people:
"I am with you," declares the LORD. 14So the
LORD stirred up the spirit of Zerubbabel son of
Shealtiel, governor of Judah, and the spirit of
Joshua son of Jehozadak, the high priest,
and the spirit of the whole remnant of the
people. They came and began to work on the
house of the LORD Almighty, their God, 15on

[a] 1 A variant of *Jeshua;* here and elsewhere in Haggai

the twenty-fourth day of the sixth month in the second year of King Darius.

The Promised Glory of the New House

2 On the twenty-first day of the seventh month, the word of the LORD came through the prophet Haggai: 2"Speak to Zerubbabel son of Shealtiel, governor of Judah, to Joshua son of Jehozadak, the high priest, and to the remnant of the people. Ask them, 3'Who of you is left who saw this house in its former glory? How does it look to you now? Does it not seem to you like nothing? 4But now be strong, O Zerubbabel,' declares the LORD. 'Be strong, O Joshua son of Jehozadak, the high priest. Be strong, all you people of the land,' declares the LORD, 'and work. For I am with you,' declares the LORD Almighty. 5'This is what I covenanted with you when you came out of Egypt. And my Spirit remains among you. Do not fear.'

6"This is what the LORD Almighty says: 'In a little while I will once more shake the heavens and the earth, the sea and the dry land. 7I will shake all nations, and the desired of all nations will come, and I will fill this house with glory,' says the LORD Almighty. 8'The silver is mine and the gold is mine,' declares the LORD Almighty. 9'The glory of this present house will be greater than the glory of the former house,' says the LORD Almighty. 'And in this place I will grant peace,' declares the LORD Almighty."

Blessings for a Defiled People

10On the twenty-fourth day of the ninth month, in the second year of Darius, the word of the LORD came to the prophet Haggai: 11"This is what the LORD Almighty says: 'Ask the priests what the law says: 12If a person carries consecrated meat in the fold of his garment, and that fold touches some bread or stew, some wine, oil or other food, does it become consecrated?' "

The priests answered, "No."

13Then Haggai said, "If a person defiled by contact with a dead body touches one of these things, does it become defiled?"

"Yes," the priests replied, "it becomes defiled."

14Then Haggai said, " 'So it is with this people and this nation in my sight,' declares the LORD. 'Whatever they do and whatever they offer there is defiled.

15" 'Now give careful thought to this from this day on[a]—consider how things were before one stone was laid on another in the LORD's temple. 16When anyone came to a heap of twenty measures, there were only ten. When anyone went to a wine vat to draw fifty measures, there were only twenty. 17I struck all the work of your hands with blight, mildew and hail, yet you did not turn to me,' declares the LORD. 18'From this day on, from this twenty-fourth day of the ninth month, give careful thought to the day when the foundation of the LORD's temple was laid. Give careful thought: 19Is there yet any seed left in the barn? Until now, the vine and the fig tree, the pomegranate and the olive tree have not borne fruit.

" 'From this day on I will bless you.' "

Zerubbabel the LORD's Signet Ring

20The word of the LORD came to Haggai a second time on the twenty-fourth day of the month: 21"Tell Zerubbabel governor of Judah that I will shake the heavens and the earth. 22I will overturn royal thrones and shatter the power of the foreign kingdoms. I will overthrow chariots and their drivers; horses and their riders will fall, each by the sword of his brother.

23" 'On that day,' declares the LORD Almighty, 'I will take you, my servant Zerubbabel son of Shealtiel,' declares the LORD, 'and I will make you like my signet ring, for I have chosen you,' declares the LORD Almighty."

[a]15 *Or to the days past*

Zechariah

Introduction:
Zechariah's prophecies began two months after Haggai's first message (520 B.C.).

In his opening message Zechariah warned the people who had just begun rebuilding the temple that they were to listen to God's message through the prophets. They were also to keep a close relationship with God so that there would be no further judgment.

This opening message is followed by visions that offered encouragement to the builders at a time when they were ready to give up. Zechariah comforted them by telling them God had a long-range plan for Israel.

In chapters 7 and 8 Zechariah called the people to obey God by acting fairly and mercifully to one another. God wanted obedience in his relationship with them.

Chapters 9 through 14 tell of the coming Messiah, the last judgment and the long-range growth of the final kingdom.

Outline of contents:

A Call to Return to the LORD

1 In the eighth month of the second year of
Darius, the word of the LORD came to the
prophet Zechariah son of Berekiah, the son
of Iddo:
2"The LORD was very angry with your forefathers. 3Therefore tell the people: This is
what the LORD Almighty says: 'Return to me,'
declares the LORD Almighty, 'and I will return
to you,' says the LORD Almighty. 4Do not be
like your forefathers, to whom the earlier
prophets proclaimed: This is what the LORD
Almighty says: 'Turn from your evil ways and
your evil practices.' But they would not listen
or pay attention to me, declares the LORD.
5Where are your forefathers now? And the
prophets, do they live forever? 6But did not
my words and my decrees, which I commanded my servants the prophets, overtake
your forefathers?
"Then they repented and said, 'The LORD
Almighty has done to us what our ways and
practices deserve, just as he determined to
do.' "

The Man Among the Myrtle Trees

7On the twenty-fourth day of the eleventh
month, the month of Shebat, in the second
year of Darius, the word of the LORD came to
the prophet Zechariah son of Berekiah, the
son of Iddo.
8During the night I had a vision—and there
before me was a man riding a red horse! He
was standing among the myrtle trees in a
ravine. Behind him were red, brown and
white horses.
9I asked, "What are these, my lord?"
The angel who was talking with me answered, "I will show you what they are."
10Then the man standing among the myrtle trees explained, "They are the ones the
LORD has sent to go throughout the earth."
11And they reported to the angel of the
LORD, who was standing among the myrtle
trees, "We have gone throughout the earth
and found the whole world at rest and in
peace."
12Then the angel of the LORD said, "LORD
Almighty, how long will you withhold mercy

from Jerusalem and from the towns of
Judah, which you have been angry with
these seventy years?" 13So the LORD spoke
kind and comforting words to the angel who
talked with me.
14Then the angel who was speaking to me
said, "Proclaim this word: This is what the
LORD Almighty says: 'I am very jealous for
Jerusalem and Zion, 15but I am very angry
with the nations that feel secure. I was only a
little angry, but they added to the calamity.'
16"Therefore, this is what the LORD says: 'I
will return to Jerusalem with mercy, and
there my house will be rebuilt. And the measuring line will be stretched out over Jerusalem,' declares the LORD Almighty.
17"Proclaim further: This is what the LORD
Almighty says: 'My towns will again overflow
with prosperity, and the LORD will again comfort Zion and choose Jerusalem.' "

Four Horns and Four Craftsmen

18Then I looked up—and there before me
were four horns! 19I asked the angel who was
speaking to me, "What are these?"
He answered me, "These are the horns
that scattered Judah, Israel and Jerusalem."
20Then the LORD showed me four craftsmen. 21I asked, "What are these coming to
do?"
He answered, "These are the horns that
scattered Judah so that no one could raise
his head, but the craftsmen have come to
terrify them and throw down these horns of
the nations who lifted up their horns against
the land of Judah to scatter its people."

A Man With a Measuring Line

2 Then I looked up—and there before me
was a man with a measuring line in his
hand! 2I asked, "Where are you going?"
He answered me, "To measure Jerusalem, to find out how wide and how long it is."
3Then the angel who was speaking to me
left, and another angel came to meet him
4and said to him: "Run, tell that young man,
'Jerusalem will be a city without walls because of the great number of men and livestock in it. 5And I myself will be a wall of fire
around it,' declares the LORD, 'and I will be its
glory within.'
6"Come! Come! Flee from the land of the
north," declares the LORD, "for I have scattered you to the four winds of heaven," declares the LORD.
7"Come, O Zion! Escape, you who live in
the Daughter of Babylon!" 8For this is what
the LORD Almighty says: "After he has honored me and has sent me against the nations
that have plundered you—for whoever
touches you touches the apple of his eye— 9I
will surely raise my hand against them so
that their slaves will plunder them.[a] Then
you will know that the LORD Almighty has sent
me.
10"Shout and be glad, O Daughter of Zion.
For I am coming, and I will live among you,"
declares the LORD. 11"Many nations will be
joined with the LORD in that day and will
become my people. I will live among you and
you will know that the LORD Almighty has sent
me to you. 12The LORD will inherit Judah as
his portion in the holy land and will again
choose Jerusalem. 13Be still before the LORD,
all mankind, because he has roused himself
from his holy dwelling."

Clean Garments for the High Priest

3 Then he showed me Joshua[b] the high
priest standing before the angel of the
LORD, and Satan[c] standing at his right side to
accuse him. 2The LORD said to Satan, "The
LORD rebuke you, Satan! The LORD, who has
chosen Jerusalem, rebuke you! Is not this
man a burning stick snatched from the fire?"
3Now Joshua was dressed in filthy clothes
as he stood before the angel. 4The angel
said to those who were standing before him,
"Take off his filthy clothes."
Then he said to Joshua, "See, I have tak-
en away your sin, and I will put rich garments
on you."
5Then I said, "Put a clean turban on his
head." So they put a clean turban on his
head and clothed him, while the angel of the
LORD stood by.
6The angel of the LORD gave this charge to
Joshua: 7"This is what the LORD Almighty
says: 'If you will walk in my ways and keep
my requirements, then you will govern my
house and have charge of my courts, and I
will give you a place among these standing
here.
8" 'Listen, O high priest Joshua and your
associates seated before you, who are men
symbolic of things to come: I am going to

[a]8,9 Or *says after . . . eye:* 9"*I . . . plunder them."*
[b]1 A variant of *Jeshua;* here and elsewhere in Zechariah
[c]1 *Satan* means *accuser.*

bring my servant, the Branch. 9See, the stone I have set in front of Joshua! There are seven eyes[a] on that one stone, and I will engrave an inscription on it,' says the LORD Almighty, 'and I will remove the sin of this land in a single day.

10" 'In that day each of you will invite his neighbor to sit under his vine and fig tree,' declares the LORD Almighty."

The Gold Lampstand and the Two Olive Trees

4 Then the angel who talked with me returned and wakened me, as a man is wakened from his sleep. 2He asked me, "What do you see?"

I answered, "I see a solid gold lampstand with a bowl at the top and seven lights on it, with seven channels to the lights. 3Also there are two olive trees by it, one on the right of the bowl and the other on its left."

4I asked the angel who talked with me, "What are these, my lord?"

5He answered, "Do you not know what these are?"

"No, my lord," I replied.

6So he said to me, "This is the word of the LORD to Zerubbabel: 'Not by might nor by power, but by my Spirit,' says the LORD Almighty.

7"What[b] are you, O mighty mountain? Before Zerubbabel you will become level ground. Then he will bring out the capstone to shouts of 'God bless it! God bless it!' "

8Then the word of the LORD came to me: 9"The hands of Zerubbabel have laid the foundation of this temple; his hands will also complete it. Then you will know that the LORD Almighty has sent me to you.

10"Who despises the day of small things? Men will rejoice when they see the plumb line in the hand of Zerubbabel.

"(These seven are the eyes of the LORD, which range throughout the earth.)"

11Then I asked the angel, "What are these two olive trees on the right and the left of the lampstand?"

12Again I asked him, "What are these two olive branches beside the two gold pipes that pour out golden oil?"

13He replied, "Do you not know what these are?"

"No, my lord," I said.

14So he said, "These are the two who are anointed to[c] serve the Lord of all the earth."

The Flying Scroll

5 I looked again—and there before me was a flying scroll!

2He asked me, "What do you see?"

I answered, "I see a flying scroll, thirty feet long and fifteen feet wide.[d]"

3And he said to me, "This is the curse that is going out over the whole land; for according to what it says on one side, every thief will be banished, and according to what it says on the other, everyone who swears falsely will be banished. 4The LORD Almighty declares, 'I will send it out, and it will enter the house of the thief and the house of him who swears falsely by my name. It will remain in his house and destroy it, both its timbers and its stones.' "

The Woman in a Basket

5Then the angel who was speaking to me came forward and said to me, "Look up and see what this is that is appearing."

6I asked, "What is it?"

He replied, "It is a measuring basket.[e]" And he added, "This is the iniquity[f] of the people throughout the land."

7Then the cover of lead was raised, and there in the basket sat a woman! 8He said, "This is wickedness," and he pushed her back into the basket and pushed the lead cover down over its mouth.

9Then I looked up—and there before me were two women, with the wind in their wings! They had wings like those of a stork, and they lifted up the basket between heaven and earth.

10"Where are they taking the basket?" I asked the angel who was speaking to me.

11He replied, "To the country of Babylonia[g] to build a house for it. When it is ready, the basket will be set there in its place."

Four Chariots

6 I looked up again—and there before me were four chariots coming out from between two mountains—mountains of bronze! 2The first chariot had red horses, the second black, 3the third white, and the fourth dappled—all of them powerful. 4I asked the

[a] 9 Or *facets* [b] 7 Or *Who* [c] 14 Or *two who bring oil and* [d] 2 Hebrew *twenty cubits long and ten cubits wide* (about 9 meters long and 4.5 meters wide) [e] 6 Hebrew *an ephah*; also in verses 7-11 [f] 6 Or *appearance* [g] 11 Hebrew *Shinar*

angel who was speaking to me, "What are these, my lord?"

5 The angel answered me, "These are the four spirits[a] of heaven, going out from standing in the presence of the Lord of the whole world. 6 The one with the black horses is going toward the north country, the one with the white horses toward the west,[b] and the one with the dappled horses toward the south."

7 When the powerful horses went out, they were straining to go throughout the earth. And he said, "Go throughout the earth!" So they went throughout the earth.

8 Then he called to me, "Look, those going toward the north country have given my Spirit[c] rest in the land of the north."

A Crown for Joshua

9 The word of the LORD came to me: 10 "Take ⌊silver and gold⌋ from the exiles Heldai, Tobijah and Jedaiah, who have arrived from Babylon. Go the same day to the house of Josiah son of Zephaniah. 11 Take the silver and gold and make a crown, and set it on the head of the high priest, Joshua son of Jehozadak. 12 Tell him this is what the LORD Almighty says: 'Here is the man whose name is the Branch, and he will branch out from his place and build the temple of the LORD. 13 It is he who will build the temple of the LORD, and he will be clothed with majesty and will sit and rule on his throne. And he will be a priest on his throne. And there will be harmony between the two.' 14 The crown will be given to Heldai,[d] Tobijah, Jedaiah and Hen[e] son of Zephaniah as a memorial in the temple of the LORD. 15 Those who are far away will come and help to build the temple of the LORD, and you will know that the LORD Almighty has sent me to you. This will happen if you diligently obey the LORD your God."

Justice and Mercy, Not Fasting

7 In the fourth year of King Darius, the word of the LORD came to Zechariah on the fourth day of the ninth month, the month of Kislev. 2 The people of Bethel had sent Sharezer and Regem-Melech, together with their men, to entreat the LORD 3 by asking the priests of the house of the LORD Almighty and the prophets, "Should I mourn and fast in the fifth month, as I have done for so many years?"

4 Then the word of the LORD Almighty came to me: 5 "Ask all the people of the land and the priests, 'When you fasted and mourned in the fifth and seventh months for the past seventy years, was it really for me that you fasted? 6 And when you were eating and drinking, were you not just feasting for yourselves? 7 Are these not the words the LORD proclaimed through the earlier prophets when Jerusalem and its surrounding towns were at rest and prosperous, and the Negev and the western foothills were settled?' "

8 And the word of the LORD came again to Zechariah: 9 "This is what the LORD Almighty says: 'Administer true justice; show mercy and compassion to one another. 10 Do not oppress the widow or the fatherless, the alien or the poor. In your hearts do not think evil of each other.'

11 "But they refused to pay attention; stubbornly they turned their backs and stopped up their ears. 12 They made their hearts as hard as flint and would not listen to the law or to the words that the LORD Almighty had sent by his Spirit through the earlier prophets. So the LORD Almighty was very angry.

13 " 'When I called, they did not listen; so when they called, I would not listen,' says the LORD Almighty. 14 'I scattered them with a whirlwind among all the nations, where they were strangers. The land was left so desolate behind them that no one could come or go. This is how they made the pleasant land desolate.' "

The LORD Promises to Bless Jerusalem

8 Again the word of the LORD Almighty came to me. 2 This is what the LORD Almighty says: "I am very jealous for Zion; I am burning with jealousy for her."

3 This is what the LORD says: "I will return to Zion and dwell in Jerusalem. Then Jerusalem will be called the City of Truth, and the mountain of the LORD Almighty will be called the Holy Mountain."

4 This is what the LORD Almighty says: "Once again men and women of ripe old age will sit in the streets of Jerusalem, each with cane in hand because of his age. 5 The city streets will be filled with boys and girls playing there."

6 This is what the LORD Almighty says: "It may seem marvelous to the remnant of this people at that time, but will it seem marvelous to me?" declares the LORD Almighty.

[a]5 Or *winds* [b]6 Or *horses after them* [c]8 Or *spirit* [d]14 Syriac; Hebrew *Helem* [e]14 Or *and the gracious one, the*

7This is what the LORD Almighty says: "I will
save my people from the countries of the
east and the west. 8I will bring them back to
live in Jerusalem; they will be my people, and
I will be faithful and righteous to them as their
God."
9This is what the LORD Almighty says: "You
who now hear these words spoken by the
prophets who were there when the foundation was laid for the house of the LORD Almighty, let your hands be strong so that the
temple may be built. 10Before that time there
were no wages for man or beast. No one
could go about his business safely because
of his enemy, for I had turned every man
against his neighbor. 11But now I will not deal
with the remnant of this people as I did in the
past," declares the LORD Almighty.
12"The seed will grow well, the vine will
yield its fruit, the ground will produce its
crops, and the heavens will drop their dew. I
will give all these things as an inheritance to
the remnant of this people. 13As you have
been an object of cursing among the nations,
O Judah and Israel, so will I save you, and
you will be a blessing. Do not be afraid, but
let your hands be strong."
14This is what the LORD Almighty says:
"Just as I had determined to bring disaster
upon you and showed no pity when your
fathers angered me," says the LORD Almighty, 15"so now I have determined to do
good again to Jerusalem and Judah. Do not
be afraid. 16These are the things you are to
do: Speak the truth to each other, and render
true and sound judgment in your courts; 17do
not plot evil against your neighbor, and do
not love to swear falsely. I hate all this,"
declares the LORD.
18Again the word of the LORD Almighty
came to me. 19This is what the LORD Almighty
says: "The fasts of the fourth, fifth, seventh
and tenth months will become joyful and glad
occasions and happy festivals for Judah.
Therefore love truth and peace."
20This is what the LORD Almighty says:
"Many peoples and the inhabitants of many
cities will yet come, 21and the inhabitants of
one city will go to another and say, 'Let us go
at once to entreat the LORD and seek the LORD
Almighty. I myself am going.' 22And many
peoples and powerful nations will come to
Jerusalem to seek the LORD Almighty and to
entreat him."
23This is what the LORD Almighty says: "In
those days ten men from all languages and
nations will take firm hold of one Jew by the
hem of his robe and say, 'Let us go with you,
because we have heard that God is with
you.' "

Judgment on Israel's Enemies

An Oracle

9 The word of the LORD is against the
land of Hadrach
and will rest upon Damascus—
for the eyes of men and all the tribes of
Israel
are on the LORD—[a]
2and upon Hamath too, which borders
on it,
and upon Tyre and Sidon, though they
are very skillful.
3Tyre has built herself a stronghold;
she has heaped up silver like dust,
and gold like the dirt of the streets.
4But the Lord will take away her
possessions
and destroy her power on the sea,
and she will be consumed by fire.
5Ashkelon will see it and fear;
Gaza will writhe in agony,
and Ekron too, for her hope will wither.
Gaza will lose her king
and Ashkelon will be deserted.
6Foreigners will occupy Ashdod,
and I will cut off the pride of the
Philistines.
7I will take the blood from their mouths,
the forbidden food from between their
teeth.
Those who are left will belong to our God
and become leaders in Judah,
and Ekron will be like the Jebusites.
8But I will defend my house
against marauding forces.
Never again will an oppressor overrun my
people,
for now I am keeping watch.

The Coming of Zion's King

9Rejoice greatly, O Daughter of Zion!
Shout, Daughter of Jerusalem!
See, your king[b] comes to you,
righteous and having salvation,
gentle and riding on a donkey,
on a colt, the foal of a donkey.
10I will take away the chariots from Ephraim
and the war-horses from Jerusalem,

[a] 1 Or *Damascus. / For the eye of the LORD is on all mankind, / as well as on the tribes of Israel,*   [b] 9 Or *King*

and the battle bow will be broken.
He will proclaim peace to the nations.
His rule will extend from sea to sea
and from the River[a] to the ends of the
earth.[b]
11 As for you, because of the blood of my
covenant with you,
I will free your prisoners from the
waterless pit.
12 Return to your fortress, O prisoners of
hope;
even now I announce that I will restore
twice as much to you.
13 I will bend Judah as I bend my bow
and fill it with Ephraim.
I will rouse your sons, O Zion,
against your sons, O Greece,
and make you like a warrior's sword.

The LORD Will Appear

14 Then the LORD will appear over them;
his arrow will flash like lightning.
The Sovereign LORD will sound the
trumpet;
he will march in the storms of the
south,
15 and the LORD Almighty will shield them.
They will destroy
and overcome with slingstones.
They will drink and roar as with wine;
they will be full like a bowl
used for sprinkling[c] the corners of the
altar.
16 The LORD their God will save them on that
day
as the flock of his people.
They will sparkle in his land
like jewels in a crown.
17 How attractive and beautiful they will be!
Grain will make the young men thrive,
and new wine the young women.

The LORD Will Care for Judah

10 Ask the LORD for rain in the
springtime;
it is the LORD who makes the storm
clouds.
He gives showers of rain to men,
and plants of the field to everyone.
2 The idols speak deceit,
diviners see visions that lie;
they tell dreams that are false,
they give comfort in vain.
Therefore the people wander like sheep
oppressed for lack of a shepherd.

3 "My anger burns against the shepherds,
and I will punish the leaders;
for the LORD Almighty will care
for his flock, the house of Judah,
and make them like a proud horse in
battle.
4 From Judah will come the cornerstone,
from him the tent peg,
from him the battle bow,
from him every ruler.
5 Together they[d] will be like mighty men
trampling the muddy streets in battle.
Because the LORD is with them,
they will fight and overthrow the
horsemen.

6 "I will strengthen the house of Judah
and save the house of Joseph.
I will restore them
because I have compassion on them.
They will be as though
I had not rejected them,
for I am the LORD their God
and I will answer them.
7 The Ephraimites will become like mighty
men,
and their hearts will be glad as with
wine.
Their children will see it and be joyful;
their hearts will rejoice in the LORD.
8 I will signal for them
and gather them in.
Surely I will redeem them;
they will be as numerous as before.
9 Though I scatter them among the
peoples,
yet in distant lands they will remember
me.
They and their children will survive,
and they will return.
10 I will bring them back from Egypt
and gather them from Assyria.
I will bring them to Gilead and Lebanon,
and there will not be room enough for
them.
11 They will pass through the sea of trouble;
the surging sea will be subdued
and all the depths of the Nile will
dry up.
Assyria's pride will be brought down
and Egypt's scepter will pass away.
12 I will strengthen them in the LORD

[a] 10 That is, the Euphrates [b] 10 *Or the end of the land* [c] 15 *Or bowl, / like* [d] 4,5 *Or ruler, all of them together. / 5 They*

and in his name they will walk,"
declares the LORD.

11 Open your doors, O Lebanon,
so that fire may devour your cedars!
2Wail, O pine tree, for the cedar has fallen;
the stately trees are ruined!
Wail, oaks of Bashan;
the dense forest has been cut down!
3Listen to the wail of the shepherds;
their rich pastures are destroyed!
Listen to the roar of the lions;
the lush thicket of the Jordan is ruined!

Two Shepherds

4This is what the LORD my God says: "Pasture the flock marked for slaughter. 5Their
buyers slaughter them and go unpunished.
Those who sell them say, 'Praise the LORD, I
am rich!' Their own shepherds do not spare
them. 6For I will no longer have pity on the
people of the land," declares the LORD. "I will
hand everyone over to his neighbor and his
king. They will oppress the land, and I will not
rescue them from their hands."

7So I pastured the flock marked for slaughter, particularly the oppressed of the flock.
Then I took two staffs and called one Favor
and the other Union, and I pastured the flock.
8In one month I got rid of the three shepherds.

The flock detested me, and I grew weary
of them 9and said, "I will not be your shepherd. Let the dying die, and the perishing
perish. Let those who are left eat one another's flesh."

10Then I took my staff called Favor and
broke it, revoking the covenant I had made
with all the nations. 11It was revoked on that
day, and so the afflicted of the flock who
were watching me knew it was the word of
the LORD.

12I told them, "If you think it best, give me
my pay; but if not, keep it." So they paid me
thirty pieces of silver.

13And the LORD said to me, "Throw it to the
potter"—the handsome price at which they
priced me! So I took the thirty pieces of silver
and threw them into the house of the LORD to
the potter.

14Then I broke my second staff called
Union, breaking the brotherhood between
Judah and Israel.

15Then the LORD said to me, "Take again
the equipment of a foolish shepherd. 16For I
am going to raise up a shepherd over the
land who will not care for the lost, or seek the
young, or heal the injured, or feed the
healthy, but will eat the meat of the choice
sheep, tearing off their hoofs.

17"Woe to the worthless shepherd,
who deserts the flock!
May the sword strike his arm and his right
eye!
May his arm be completely withered,
his right eye totally blinded!"

Jerusalem's Enemies to Be Destroyed

An Oracle

12 This is the word of the LORD concerning Israel. The LORD, who stretches
out the heavens, who lays the foundation of
the earth, and who forms the spirit of man
within him, declares: 2"I am going to make
Jerusalem a cup that sends all the surrounding peoples reeling. Judah will be besieged
as well as Jerusalem. 3On that day, when all
the nations of the earth are gathered against
her, I will make Jerusalem an immovable
rock for all the nations. All who try to move it
will injure themselves. 4On that day I will
strike every horse with panic and its rider
with madness," declares the LORD. "I will
keep a watchful eye over the house of
Judah, but I will blind all the horses of the
nations. 5Then the leaders of Judah will say
in their hearts, 'The people of Jerusalem are
strong, because the LORD Almighty is their
God.'

6"On that day I will make the leaders of
Judah like a firepot in a woodpile, like a flaming torch among sheaves. They will consume right and left all the surrounding peoples, but Jerusalem will remain intact in her
place.

7"The LORD will save the dwellings of
Judah first, so that the honor of the house of
David and of Jerusalem's inhabitants may
not be greater than that of Judah. 8On that
day the LORD will shield those who live in
Jerusalem, so that the feeblest among them
will be like David, and the house of David will
be like God, like the Angel of the LORD going
before them. 9On that day I will set out to
destroy all the nations that attack Jerusalem.

Mourning for the One They Pierced

10"And I will pour out on the house of David
and the inhabitants of Jerusalem a spirit[a] of
grace and supplication. They will look on[b]

[a] 10 Or *the Spirit* [b] 10 Or *to*

me, the one they have pierced, and they will
mourn for him as one mourns for an only
child, and grieve bitterly for him as one
grieves for a firstborn son. 11On that day the
weeping in Jerusalem will be great, like the
weeping of Hadad Rimmon in the plain of
Megiddo. 12The land will mourn, each clan by
itself, with their wives by themselves: the
clan of the house of David and their wives,
the clan of the house of Nathan and their
wives, 13the clan of the house of Levi and
their wives, the clan of Shimei and their
wives, 14and all the rest of the clans and their
wives.

Cleansing From Sin

13 "On that day a fountain will be
opened to the house of David and the
inhabitants of Jerusalem, to cleanse them
from sin and impurity.

2"On that day, I will banish the names of
the idols from the land, and they will be
remembered no more," declares the LORD
Almighty. "I will remove both the prophets
and the spirit of impurity from the land. 3And
if anyone still prophesies, his father and
mother, to whom he was born, will say to
him, 'You must die, because you have told
lies in the LORD's name.' When he prophesies, his own parents will stab him.

4"On that day every prophet will be
ashamed of his prophetic vision. He will not
put on a prophet's garment of hair in order to
deceive. 5He will say, 'I am not a prophet. I
am a farmer; the land has been my livelihood
since my youth.[a] 6If someone asks him,
'What are these wounds on your body[b]?' he
will answer, 'The wounds I was given at the
house of my friends.'

The Shepherd Struck, the Sheep Scattered

7"Awake, O sword, against my shepherd,
against the man who is close to me!"
declares the LORD Almighty.
"Strike the shepherd,
and the sheep will be scattered,
and I will turn my hand against the little
ones.
8In the whole land," declares the LORD,
"two-thirds will be struck down and
perish;
yet one-third will be left in it.
9This third I will bring into the fire;
I will refine them like silver
and test them like gold.
They will call on my name
and I will answer them;
I will say, 'They are my people,'
and they will say, 'The LORD is our
God.' "

The LORD Comes and Reigns

14 A day of the LORD is coming when
your plunder will be divided among
you.

2I will gather all the nations to Jerusalem to
fight against it; the city will be captured, the
houses ransacked, and the women raped.
Half of the city will go into exile, but the rest of
the people will not be taken from the city.
3Then the LORD will go out and fight against
those nations, as he fights in the day of battle. 4On that day his feet will stand on the
Mount of Olives, east of Jerusalem, and the
Mount of Olives will be split in two from east
to west, forming a great valley, with half of
the mountain moving north and half moving
south. 5You will flee by my mountain valley,
for it will extend to Azel. You will flee as you
fled from the earthquake[c] in the days of
Uzziah king of Judah. Then the LORD my
God will come, and all the holy ones with
him.

6On that day there will be no light, no cold
or frost. 7It will be a unique day, without daytime or nighttime—a day known to the LORD.
When evening comes, there will be light.

8On that day living water will flow out from
Jerusalem, half to the eastern sea[d] and half
to the western sea,[e] in summer and in winter.

9The LORD will be king over the whole
earth. On that day there will be one LORD, and
his name the only name.

10The whole land, from Geba to Rimmon,
south of Jerusalem, will become like the Arabah. But Jerusalem will be raised up and
remain in its place, from the Benjamin Gate
to the site of the First Gate, to the Corner
Gate, and from the Tower of Hananel to the
royal winepresses. 11It will be inhabited; never again will it be destroyed. Jerusalem will
be secure.

12This is the plague with which the LORD will
strike all the nations that fought against

[a]5 Or *farmer; a man sold me in my youth* [b]6 Or *wounds between your hands* [c]5 Or [5]*My mountain valley will be blocked and will extend to Azel. It will be blocked as it was blocked because of the earthquake* [d]8 That is, the Dead Sea [e]8 That is, the Mediterranean

Jerusalem: Their flesh will rot while they are still standing on their feet, their eyes will rot in their sockets, and their tongues will rot in their mouths. 13On that day men will be stricken by the LORD with great panic. Each man will seize the hand of another, and they will attack each other. 14Judah too will fight at Jerusalem. The wealth of all the surrounding nations will be collected—great quantities of gold and silver and clothing. 15A similar plague will strike the horses and mules, the camels and donkeys, and all the animals in those camps.

16Then the survivors from all the nations that have attacked Jerusalem will go up year after year to worship the King, the LORD Almighty, and to celebrate the Feast of Tabernacles. 17If any of the peoples of the earth do not go up to Jerusalem to worship the King, the LORD Almighty, they will have no rain. 18If the Egyptian people do not go up and take part, they will have no rain. The LORD[a] will bring on them the plague he inflicts on the nations that do not go up to celebrate the Feast of Tabernacles. 19This will be the punishment of Egypt and the punishment of all the nations that do not go up to celebrate the Feast of Tabernacles.

20On that day HOLY TO THE LORD will be inscribed on the bells of the horses, and the cooking pots in the LORD's house will be like the sacred bowls in front of the altar. 21Every pot in Jerusalem and Judah will be holy to the LORD Almighty, and all who come to sacrifice will take some of the pots and cook in them. And on that day there will no longer be a Canaanite[b] in the house of the LORD Almighty.

[a]18 *Or part, then the LORD* [b]21 *Or merchant*

Malachi

Introduction:

This book records the messages of the prophet, Malachi, who lived during the second half of the fifth century B.C., after the temple had been rebuilt. The Jews' religious life was not in good condition—they had married foreign women, failed to give God what they should have, and even left God.

Malachi's chief concern was that the Israelites' relationship to God was not as it should be. They had forgotten God and treated him with dishonor. They failed to do what God required of them. Because of this, there would be judgment, but the God-fearing people did not need to worry because they were in God's book and would enjoy God's salvation forever.

Outline of contents:

God's love for Israel (1:1–5)
Israel insults God (1:6–2:16)
God's judgment and promise (2:17–4:6)

---

1 An oracle: The word of the LORD to Israel through Malachi.[a]

Jacob Loved, Esau Hated

2"I have loved you," says the LORD.

"But you ask, 'How have you loved us?'

"Was not Esau Jacob's brother?" the LORD says. "Yet I have loved Jacob, 3but Esau I have hated, and I have turned his mountains into a wasteland and left his inheritance to the desert jackals."

4Edom may say, "Though we have been crushed, we will rebuild the ruins."

But this is what the LORD Almighty says: "They may build, but I will demolish. They will be called the Wicked Land, a people always under the wrath of the LORD. 5You will see it with your own eyes and say, 'Great is the LORD—even beyond the borders of Israel!'

Blemished Sacrifices

6"A son honors his father, and a servant his master. If I am a father, where is the honor due me? If I am a master, where is the respect due me?" says the LORD Almighty. "It is you, O priests, who show contempt for my name.

"But you ask, 'How have we shown contempt for your name?'

7"You place defiled food on my altar.

"But you ask, 'How have we defiled you?'

"By saying that the LORD's table is contemptible. 8When you bring blind animals for sacrifice, is that not wrong? When you sacrifice crippled or diseased animals, is that not wrong? Try offering them to your governor! Would he be pleased with you? Would he accept you?" says the LORD Almighty.

9"Now implore God to be gracious to us. With such offerings from your hands, will he accept you?"—says the LORD Almighty.

10"Oh, that one of you would shut the temple doors, so that you would not light useless fires on my altar! I am not pleased with you," says the LORD Almighty, "and I will accept no offering from your hands. 11My name will be great among the nations, from the rising to the setting of the sun. In every place incense and pure offerings will be brought to my name, because my name will be great among the nations," says the LORD Almighty.

12"But you profane it by saying of the Lord's table, 'It is defiled,' and of its food, 'It is contemptible.' 13And you say, 'What a burden!' and you sniff at it contemptuously," says the LORD Almighty.

"When you bring injured, crippled or diseased animals and offer them as sacrifices, should I accept them from your

[a]1 *Malachi* means *my messenger.*

hands?" says the LORD. 14"Cursed is the
cheat who has an acceptable male in his
flock and vows to give it, but then sacrifices a
blemished animal to the Lord. For I am a
great king," says the LORD Almighty, "and my
name is to be feared among the nations.

Admonition for the Priests

2 "And now this admonition is for you, O
priests. 2If you do not listen, and if you do
not set your heart to honor my name," says
the LORD Almighty, "I will send a curse upon
you, and I will curse your blessings. Yes, I
have already cursed them, because you
have not set your heart to honor me.
3"Because of you I will rebuke[a] your descendants[b]; I will spread on your faces the
offal from your festival sacrifices, and you
will be carried off with it. 4And you will know
that I have sent you this admonition so that
my covenant with Levi may continue," says
the LORD Almighty. 5"My covenant was with
him, a covenant of life and peace, and I gave
them to him; this called for reverence and he
revered me and stood in awe of my name.
6True instruction was in his mouth and nothing false was found on his lips. He walked
with me in peace and uprightness, and
turned many from sin.
7"For the lips of a priest ought to preserve
knowledge, and from his mouth men should
seek instruction—because he is the messenger of the LORD Almighty. 8But you have
turned from the way and by your teaching
have caused many to stumble; you have violated the covenant with Levi," says the LORD
Almighty. 9"So I have caused you to be despised and humiliated before all the people,
because you have not followed my ways but
have shown partiality in matters of the law."

Judah Unfaithful

10Have we not all one Father[c]? Did not one
God create us? Why do we profane the covenant of our fathers by breaking faith with
one another?
11Judah has broken faith. A detestable
thing has been committed in Israel and in
Jerusalem: Judah has desecrated the sanctuary the LORD loves, by marrying the daughter of a foreign god. 12As for the man who
does this, whoever he may be, may the LORD
cut him off from the tents of Jacob[d]—even
though he brings offerings to the LORD Almighty.
13Another thing you do: You flood the
LORD's altar with tears. You weep and wail
because he no longer pays attention to your
offerings or accepts them with pleasure from
your hands. 14You ask, "Why?" It is because
the LORD is acting as the witness between
you and the wife of your youth, because you
have broken faith with her, though she is
your partner, the wife of your marriage covenant.
15Has not ⌊the LORD⌋ made them one? In
flesh and spirit they are his. And why one?
Because he was seeking godly offspring.[e]
So guard yourself in your spirit, and do not
break faith with the wife of your youth.
16"I hate divorce," says the LORD God of
Israel, "and I hate a man's covering himself[f]
with violence as well as with his garment,"
says the LORD Almighty.
So guard yourself in your spirit, and do not
break faith.

The Day of Judgment

17You have wearied the LORD with your
words.
"How have we wearied him?" you ask.
By saying, "All who do evil are good in the
eyes of the LORD, and he is pleased with
them" or "Where is the God of justice?"
3 "See, I will send my messenger, who will
prepare the way before me. Then suddenly the Lord you are seeking will come to
his temple; the messenger of the covenant,
whom you desire, will come," says the LORD
Almighty.
2But who can endure the day of his coming? Who can stand when he appears? For
he will be like a refiner's fire or a launderer's
soap. 3He will sit as a refiner and purifier of
silver; he will purify the Levites and refine
them like gold and silver. Then the LORD will
have men who will bring offerings in righteousness, 4and the offerings of Judah and
Jerusalem will be acceptable to the LORD, as
in days gone by, as in former years.
5"So I will come near to you for judgment. I
will be quick to testify against sorcerers,
adulterers and perjurers, against those who
defraud laborers of their wages, who oppress the widows and the fatherless, and

[a]3 Or *cut off* (see Septuagint) [b]3 Or *will blight your grain* [c]10 Or *father* [d]12 Or *12May the LORD cut off from the tents of Jacob anyone who gives testimony in behalf of the man who does this* [e]15 Or *15But the one ⌊who is our father⌋ did not do this, not as long as life remained in him. And what was he seeking? An offspring from God* [f]16 Or *his wife*

deprive aliens of justice, but do not fear me,"
says the LORD Almighty.

Robbing God

6"I the LORD do not change. So you, O
descendants of Jacob, are not destroyed.
7Ever since the time of your forefathers you
have turned away from my decrees and
have not kept them. Return to me, and I will
return to you," says the LORD Almighty.

"But you ask, 'How are we to return?'

8"Will a man rob God? Yet you rob me.

"But you ask, 'How do we rob you?'

"In tithes and offerings. 9You are under a
curse—the whole nation of you—because
you are robbing me. 10Bring the whole tithe
into the storehouse, that there may be food
in my house. Test me in this," says the LORD
Almighty, "and see if I will not throw open the
floodgates of heaven and pour out so much
blessing that you will not have room enough
for it. 11I will prevent pests from devouring
your crops, and the vines in your fields will
not cast their fruit," says the LORD Almighty.
12"Then all the nations will call you blessed,
for yours will be a delightful land," says the
LORD Almighty.

13"You have said harsh things against
me," says the LORD.

"Yet you ask, 'What have we said against
you?'

14"You have said, 'It is futile to serve God.
What did we gain by carrying out his requirements and going about like mourners
before the LORD Almighty? 15But now we call
the arrogant blessed. Certainly the evildoers
prosper, and even those who challenge God
escape.' "

16Then those who feared the LORD talked
with each other, and the LORD listened and
heard. A scroll of remembrance was written
in his presence concerning those who feared
the LORD and honored his name.

17"They will be mine," says the LORD Almighty, "in the day when I make up my treasured possession.[a] I will spare them, just as
in compassion a man spares his son who
serves him. 18And you will again see the distinction between the righteous and the
wicked, between those who serve God and
those who do not.

The Day of the LORD

4 "Surely the day is coming; it will burn like
a furnace. All the arrogant and every
evildoer will be stubble, and that day that is
coming will set them on fire," says the LORD
Almighty. "Not a root or a branch will be left
to them. 2But for you who revere my name,
the sun of righteousness will rise with healing in its wings. And you will go out and leap
like calves released from the stall. 3Then you
will trample down the wicked; they will be
ashes under the soles of your feet on the day
when I do these things," says the LORD Almighty.

4"Remember the law of my servant
Moses, the decrees and laws I gave him at
Horeb for all Israel.

5"See, I will send you the prophet Elijah
before that great and dreadful day of the
LORD comes. 6He will turn the hearts of the
fathers to their children, and the hearts of the
children to their fathers; or else I will come
and strike the land with a curse."

[a]17 Or *Almighty, "my treasured possession, in the day when I act*

The New Testament

Matthew

Introduction:

The book of Matthew tells of the good news that the long-awaited Messiah had come to save people—both Jews and Gentiles. Matthew, one of the twelve disciples, is believed to be the author of this book. It was probably written sometime before the Romans destroyed the temple in Jerusalem in A.D. 70.

Although Mark and Luke also wrote about Jesus' life, Matthew's Gospel had some special things that are different from the others. Matthew uses much of the Gospel to show that Jesus is the promised Messiah of the Old Testament. Matthew quotes the Old Testament often and uses the phrase "kingdom of heaven" from the Old Testament frequently. Because of this many people think he was writing his Gospel to Jewish people.

Matthew also presents Christ as the great teacher who helps us understand God's law and tells the people about the kingdom of God and what it is. Most of Christ's teachings are found in the following five places:

1. The Sermon on the Mount (5:1–7:27)
2. Instruction to the disciples (10:5–42)
3. Teaching through parables (13:3–52)
4. The meaning of discipleship (18:1–35)
5. Teachings about the end of time and the coming of the kingdom of heaven (24:4–25:46)

Outline of contents:

- Background and preparation (1:1–4:25)
- The Galilean ministry (5:1–18:35)
  - The Sermon on the Mount (5:1–7:29)
  - The ministry through miracles (8:1–10:42)
  - Teaching through parables (11:1–13:52)
  - Opposition and withdrawal (13:53–16:12)
  - Jesus as the son of God (16:13–18:35)
- The final period (19:1–28:20)
  - Toward Jerusalem (19:1–20:34)
  - The triumphal entry (21:1–17)
  - Christ as teacher (21:18–25:46)
  - Trial, death and burial (26:1–27:66)
  - Resurrection and ascension (28:1–20)

The Genealogy of Jesus

1 A record of the genealogy of Jesus Christ the son of David, the son of Abraham:

2Abraham was the father of Isaac,
Isaac the father of Jacob,
Jacob the father of Judah and his brothers,
3Judah the father of Perez and Zerah, whose mother was Tamar,
Perez the father of Hezron,
Hezron the father of Ram,
4Ram the father of Amminadab,
Amminadab the father of Nahshon,
Nahshon the father of Salmon,
5Salmon the father of Boaz, whose mother was Rahab,
Boaz the father of Obed, whose mother was Ruth,
Obed the father of Jesse,
6and Jesse the father of King David.

David was the father of Solomon, whose
mother had been Uriah's wife,
7 Solomon the father of Rehoboam,
Rehoboam the father of Abijah,
Abijah the father of Asa,
8 Asa the father of Jehoshaphat,
Jehoshaphat the father of Jehoram,
Jehoram the father of Uzziah,
9 Uzziah the father of Jotham,
Jotham the father of Ahaz,
Ahaz the father of Hezekiah,
10 Hezekiah the father of Manasseh,
Manasseh the father of Amon,
Amon the father of Josiah,
11 and Josiah the father of Jeconiah[a]
and his brothers at the time of the
exile to Babylon.

12 After the exile to Babylon:
Jeconiah was the father of Shealtiel,
Shealtiel the father of Zerubbabel,
13 Zerubbabel the father of Abiud,
Abiud the father of Eliakim,
Eliakim the father of Azor,
14 Azor the father of Zadok,
Zadok the father of Akim,
Akim the father of Eliud,
15 Eliud the father of Eleazar,
Eleazar the father of Matthan,
Matthan the father of Jacob,
16 and Jacob the father of Joseph, the
husband of Mary, of whom was born
Jesus, who is called Christ.

17 Thus there were fourteen generations in
all from Abraham to David, fourteen from
David to the exile to Babylon, and fourteen
from the exile to the Christ.[b]

The Birth of Jesus Christ

18 This is how the birth of Jesus Christ
came about: His mother Mary was pledged
to be married to Joseph, but before they
came together, she was found to be with
child through the Holy Spirit. 19 Because Joseph her husband was a righteous man and
did not want to expose her to public disgrace,
he had in mind to divorce her quietly.

20 But after he had considered this, an angel of the Lord appeared to him in a dream
and said, "Joseph son of David, do not be
afraid to take Mary home as your wife, because what is conceived in her is from the
Holy Spirit. 21 She will give birth to a son, and
you are to give him the name Jesus,[c] because he will save his people from their
sins."

22 All this took place to fulfill what the Lord
had said through the prophet: 23 "The virgin
will be with child and will give birth to a son,
and they will call him Immanuel"[d]—which
means, "God with us."

24 When Joseph woke up, he did what the
angel of the Lord had commanded him and
took Mary home as his wife. 25 But he had no
union with her until she gave birth to a son.
And he gave him the name Jesus.

The Visit of the Magi

2 After Jesus was born in Bethlehem in
Judea, during the time of King Herod,
Magi[e] from the east came to Jerusalem 2 and
asked, "Where is the one who has been born
king of the Jews? We saw his star in the
east[f] and have come to worship him."

3 When King Herod heard this he was disturbed, and all Jerusalem with him. 4 When
he had called together all the people's chief
priests and teachers of the law, he asked
them where the Christ[g] was to be born. 5 "In
Bethlehem in Judea," they replied, "for this
is what the prophet has written:

6 " 'But you, Bethlehem, in the land of
Judah,
are by no means least among the
rulers of Judah;
for out of you will come a ruler
who will be the shepherd of my people
Israel.'[h]"

7 Then Herod called the Magi secretly and
found out from them the exact time the star
had appeared. 8 He sent them to Bethlehem
and said, "Go and make a careful search for
the child. As soon as you find him, report to
me, so that I too may go and worship him."

9 After they had heard the king, they went
on their way, and the star they had seen in
the east[i] went ahead of them until it stopped
over the place where the child was. 10 When
they saw the star, they were overjoyed. 11 On
coming to the house, they saw the child with
his mother Mary, and they bowed down and
worshiped him. Then they opened their treasures and presented him with gifts of gold
and of incense and of myrrh. 12 And having
been warned in a dream not to go back to

[a] *11* That is, Jehoiachin; also in verse 12 [b] *17* Or *Messiah.* "The Christ" (Greek) and "the Messiah" (Hebrew) both mean "the Anointed One." [c] *21* *Jesus* is the Greek form of *Joshua,* which means *the Lord saves.* [d] *23* Isaiah 7:14 [e] *1* Traditionally *Wise Men* [f] *2* Or *star when it rose* [g] *4* Or *Messiah* [h] *6* Micah 5:2 [i] *9* Or *seen when it rose*

Herod, they returned to their country by another route.

The Escape to Egypt

13When they had gone, an angel of the
Lord appeared to Joseph in a dream. "Get
up," he said, "take the child and his mother
and escape to Egypt. Stay there until I tell
you, for Herod is going to search for the child
to kill him."

14So he got up, took the child and his
mother during the night and left for Egypt,
15where he stayed until the death of Herod.
And so was fulfilled what the Lord had said
through the prophet: "Out of Egypt I called
my son."[a]

16When Herod realized that he had been
outwitted by the Magi, he was furious, and he
gave orders to kill all the boys in Bethlehem
and its vicinity who were two years old and
under, in accordance with the time he had
learned from the Magi. 17Then what was said
through the prophet Jeremiah was fulfilled:

18"A voice is heard in Ramah,
weeping and great mourning,
Rachel weeping for her children
and refusing to be comforted,
because they are no more."[b]

The Return to Nazareth

19After Herod died, an angel of the Lord
appeared in a dream to Joseph in Egypt
20and said, "Get up, take the child and his
mother and go to the land of Israel, for those
who were trying to take the child's life are
dead."

21So he got up, took the child and his
mother and went to the land of Israel. 22But
when he heard that Archelaus was reigning
in Judea in place of his father Herod, he was
afraid to go there. Having been warned in a
dream, he withdrew to the district of Galilee,
23and he went and lived in a town called
Nazareth. So was fulfilled what was said
through the prophets: "He will be called a
Nazarene."

John the Baptist Prepares the Way

3 In those days John the Baptist came,
preaching in the Desert of Judea 2and
saying, "Repent, for the kingdom of heaven
is near." 3This is he who was spoken of
through the prophet Isaiah:

"A voice of one calling in the desert,
'Prepare the way for the Lord,
make straight paths for him.' "[c]

4John's clothes were made of camel's hair,
and he had a leather belt around his waist.
His food was locusts and wild honey.
5People went out to him from Jerusalem and
all Judea and the whole region of the Jordan.
6Confessing their sins, they were baptized
by him in the Jordan River.

7But when he saw many of the Pharisees
and Sadducees coming to where he was
baptizing, he said to them: "You brood of
vipers! Who warned you to flee from the
coming wrath? 8Produce fruit in keeping with
repentance. 9And do not think you can say to
yourselves, 'We have Abraham as our father.' I tell you that out of these stones God
can raise up children for Abraham. 10The ax
is already at the root of the trees, and every
tree that does not produce good fruit will be
cut down and thrown into the fire.

11"I baptize you with[d] water for repentance. But after me will come one who is
more powerful than I, whose sandals I am
not fit to carry. He will baptize you with the
Holy Spirit and with fire. 12His winnowing fork
is in his hand, and he will clear his threshing
floor, gathering his wheat into the barn and
burning up the chaff with unquenchable fire."

The Baptism of Jesus

13Then Jesus came from Galilee to the
Jordan to be baptized by John. 14But John
tried to deter him, saying, "I need to be baptized by you, and do you come to me?"

15Jesus replied, "Let it be so now; it is
proper for us to do this to fulfill all righteousness." Then John consented.

16As soon as Jesus was baptized, he went
up out of the water. At that moment heaven
was opened, and he saw the Spirit of God
descending like a dove and lighting on him.
17And a voice from heaven said, "This is my
Son, whom I love; with him I am well
pleased."

The Temptation of Jesus

4 Then Jesus was led by the Spirit into the
desert to be tempted by the devil. 2After
fasting forty days and forty nights, he was
hungry. 3The tempter came to him and said,
"If you are the Son of God, tell these stones
to become bread."

4Jesus answered, "It is written: 'Man does

[a] *15* Hosea 11:1 [b] *18* Jer. 31:15 [c] *3* Isaiah 40:3 [d] *11* Or *in*

not live on bread alone, but on every word
that comes from the mouth of God.'[a]"
5Then the devil took him to the holy city
and had him stand on the highest point of the
temple. 6"If you are the Son of God," he said,
"throw yourself down. For it is written:

" 'He will command his angels concerning
you,
and they will lift you up in their hands,
so that you will not strike your foot against
a stone.'[b]"

7Jesus answered him, "It is also written:
'Do not put the Lord your God to the test.'[c]"
8Again, the devil took him to a very high
mountain and showed him all the kingdoms
of the world and their splendor. 9"All this I will
give you," he said, "if you will bow down and
worship me."
10Jesus said to him, "Away from me, Satan! For it is written: 'Worship the Lord your
God, and serve him only.'[d]"
11Then the devil left him, and angels came
and attended him.

Jesus Begins to Preach

12When Jesus heard that John had been
put in prison, he returned to Galilee. 13Leav-
ing Nazareth, he went and lived in Capernaum, which was by the lake in the area of
Zebulun and Naphtali— 14to fulfill what was
said through the prophet Isaiah:

15"Land of Zebulun and land of Naphtali,
the way to the sea, along the Jordan,
Galilee of the Gentiles—
16the people living in darkness
have seen a great light;
on those living in the land of the shadow
of death
a light has dawned."[e]

17From that time on Jesus began to
preach, "Repent, for the kingdom of heaven
is near."

The Calling of the First Disciples

18As Jesus was walking beside the Sea of
Galilee, he saw two brothers, Simon called
Peter and his brother Andrew. They were
casting a net into the lake, for they were
fishermen. 19"Come, follow me," Jesus said,
"and I will make you fishers of men." 20At
once they left their nets and followed him.
21Going on from there, he saw two other
brothers, James son of Zebedee and his
brother John. They were in a boat with their
father Zebedee, preparing their nets. Jesus
called them, 22and immediately they left the
boat and their father and followed him.

Jesus Heals the Sick

23Jesus went throughout Galilee, teaching
in their synagogues, preaching the good
news of the kingdom, and healing every disease and sickness among the people.
24News about him spread all over Syria, and
people brought to him all who were ill with
various diseases, those suffering severe
pain, the demon-possessed, those having
seizures, and the paralyzed, and he healed
them. 25Large crowds from Galilee, the
Decapolis,[f] Jerusalem, Judea and the region across the Jordan followed him.

The Beatitudes

5 Now when he saw the crowds, he went
up on a mountainside and sat down. His
disciples came to him, 2and he began to
teach them, saying:

3"Blessed are the poor in spirit,
for theirs is the kingdom of heaven.
4Blessed are those who mourn,
for they will be comforted.
5Blessed are the meek,
for they will inherit the earth.
6Blessed are those who hunger and thirst
for righteousness,
for they will be filled.
7Blessed are the merciful,
for they will be shown mercy.
8Blessed are the pure in heart,
for they will see God.
9Blessed are the peacemakers,
for they will be called sons of God.
10Blessed are those who are persecuted
because of righteousness,
for theirs is the kingdom of heaven.

11"Blessed are you when people insult
you, persecute you and falsely say all kinds
of evil against you because of me. 12Rejoice
and be glad, because great is your reward in
heaven, for in the same way they persecuted
the prophets who were before you.

Salt and Light

13"You are the salt of the earth. But if the
salt loses its saltiness, how can it be made

[a] *4* Deut. 8:3 [b] *6* Psalm 91:11,12 [c] *7* Deut. 6:16 [d] *10* Deut. 6:13 [e] *16* Isaiah 9:1,2 [f] *25* That is, the Ten Cities

salty again? It is no longer good for anything, except to be thrown out and trampled by men.

14"You are the light of the world. A city on a hill cannot be hidden. 15Neither do people light a lamp and put it under a bowl. Instead they put it on its stand, and it gives light to everyone in the house. 16In the same way, let your light shine before men, that they may see your good deeds and praise your Father in heaven.

The Fulfillment of the Law

17"Do not think that I have come to abolish the Law or the Prophets; I have not come to abolish them but to fulfill them. 18I tell you the truth, until heaven and earth disappear, not the smallest letter, not the least stroke of a pen, will by any means disappear from the Law until everything is accomplished. 19Anyone who breaks one of the least of these commandments and teaches others to do the same will be called least in the kingdom of heaven, but whoever practices and teaches these commands will be called great in the kingdom of heaven. 20For I tell you that unless your righteousness surpasses that of the Pharisees and the teachers of the law, you will certainly not enter the kingdom of heaven.

Murder

21"You have heard that it was said to the people long ago, 'Do not murder,[a] and anyone who murders will be subject to judgment.' 22But I tell you that anyone who is angry with his brother[b] will be subject to judgment. Again, anyone who says to his brother, 'Raca,[c]' is answerable to the Sanhedrin. But anyone who says, 'You fool!' will be in danger of the fire of hell.

23"Therefore, if you are offering your gift at the altar and there remember that your brother has something against you, 24leave your gift there in front of the altar. First go and be reconciled to your brother; then come and offer your gift.

25"Settle matters quickly with your adversary who is taking you to court. Do it while you are still with him on the way, or he may hand you over to the judge, and the judge may hand you over to the officer, and you may be thrown into prison. 26I tell you the truth, you will not get out until you have paid the last penny.[d]

Adultery

27"You have heard that it was said, 'Do not commit adultery.'[e] 28But I tell you that anyone who looks at a woman lustfully has already committed adultery with her in his heart. 29If your right eye causes you to sin, gouge it out and throw it away. It is better for you to lose one part of your body than for your whole body to be thrown into hell. 30And if your right hand causes you to sin, cut it off and throw it away. It is better for you to lose one part of your body than for your whole body to go into hell.

Divorce

31"It has been said, 'Anyone who divorces his wife must give her a certificate of divorce.'[f] 32But I tell you that anyone who divorces his wife, except for marital unfaithfulness, causes her to become an adulteress, and anyone who marries the divorced woman commits adultery.

Oaths

33"Again, you have heard that it was said to the people long ago, 'Do not break your oath, but keep the oaths you have made to the Lord.' 34But I tell you, Do not swear at all: either by heaven, for it is God's throne; 35or by the earth, for it is his footstool; or by Jerusalem, for it is the city of the Great King. 36And do not swear by your head, for you cannot make even one hair white or black. 37Simply let your 'Yes' be 'Yes,' and your 'No,' 'No'; anything beyond this comes from the evil one.

An Eye for an Eye

38"You have heard that it was said, 'Eye for eye, and tooth for tooth.'[g] 39But I tell you, Do not resist an evil person. If someone strikes you on the right cheek, turn to him the other also. 40And if someone wants to sue you and take your tunic, let him have your cloak as well. 41If someone forces you to go one mile, go with him two miles. 42Give to the one who asks you, and do not turn away from the one who wants to borrow from you.

[a] *21* Exodus 20:13 [b] *22* Some manuscripts *brother without cause* [c] *22* An Aramaic term of contempt
[d] *26* Greek *kodrantes* [e] *27* Exodus 20:14 [f] *31* Deut. 24:1 [g] *38* Exodus 21:24; Lev. 24:20; Deut. 19:21

Love for Enemies

43"You have heard that it was said, 'Love your neighbor[a] and hate your enemy.' 44But I tell you: Love your enemies[b] and pray for those who persecute you, 45that you may be sons of your Father in heaven. He causes his sun to rise on the evil and the good, and sends rain on the righteous and the unrighteous. 46If you love those who love you, what reward will you get? Are not even the tax collectors doing that? 47And if you greet only your brothers, what are you doing more than others? Do not even pagans do that? 48Be perfect, therefore, as your heavenly Father is perfect.

Giving to the Needy

6 "Be careful not to do your 'acts of righteousness' before men, to be seen by them. If you do, you will have no reward from your Father in heaven.

2"So when you give to the needy, do not announce it with trumpets, as the hypocrites do in the synagogues and on the streets, to be honored by men. I tell you the truth, they have received their reward in full. 3But when you give to the needy, do not let your left hand know what your right hand is doing, 4so that your giving may be in secret. Then your Father, who sees what is done in secret, will reward you.

Prayer

5"And when you pray, do not be like the hypocrites, for they love to pray standing in the synagogues and on the street corners to be seen by men. I tell you the truth, they have received their reward in full. 6But when you pray, go into your room, close the door and pray to your Father, who is unseen. Then your Father, who sees what is done in secret, will reward you. 7And when you pray, do not keep on babbling like pagans, for they think they will be heard because of their many words. 8Do not be like them, for your Father knows what you need before you ask him.

9"This, then, is how you should pray:

" 'Our Father in heaven,
hallowed be your name,
10your kingdom come,
your will be done
on earth as it is in heaven.
11Give us today our daily bread.
12Forgive us our debts,
as we also have forgiven our debtors.
13And lead us not into temptation,
but deliver us from the evil one.[c]'

14For if you forgive men when they sin against you, your heavenly Father will also forgive you. 15But if you do not forgive men their sins, your Father will not forgive your sins.

Fasting

16"When you fast, do not look somber as the hypocrites do, for they disfigure their faces to show men they are fasting. I tell you the truth, they have received their reward in full. 17But when you fast, put oil on your head and wash your face, 18so that it will not be obvious to men that you are fasting, but only to your Father, who is unseen; and your Father, who sees what is done in secret, will reward you.

Treasures in Heaven

19"Do not store up for yourselves treasures on earth, where moth and rust destroy, and where thieves break in and steal. 20But store up for yourselves treasures in heaven, where moth and rust do not destroy, and where thieves do not break in and steal. 21For where your treasure is, there your heart will be also.

22"The eye is the lamp of the body. If your eyes are good, your whole body will be full of light. 23But if your eyes are bad, your whole body will be full of darkness. If then the light within you is darkness, how great is that darkness!

24"No one can serve two masters. Either he will hate the one and love the other, or he will be devoted to the one and despise the other. You cannot serve both God and Money.

Do Not Worry

25"Therefore I tell you, do not worry about your life, what you will eat or drink; or about your body, what you will wear. Is not life more important than food, and the body more important than clothes? 26Look at the birds of the air; they do not sow or reap or store away in barns, and yet your heavenly Father feeds them. Are you not much more valuable than

[a]43 Lev. 19:18 [b]44 Some late manuscripts *enemies, bless those who curse you, do good to those who hate you* [c]13 Or *from evil;* some late manuscripts *one, / for yours is the kingdom and the power and the glory forever. Amen.*

they? 27Who of you by worrying can add a
single hour to his life[a]?
28"And why do you worry about clothes?
See how the lilies of the field grow. They do
not labor or spin. 29Yet I tell you that not even
Solomon in all his splendor was dressed like
one of these. 30If that is how God clothes the
grass of the field, which is here today and
tomorrow is thrown into the fire, will he not
much more clothe you, O you of little faith?
31So do not worry, saying, 'What shall we
eat?' or 'What shall we drink?' or 'What shall
we wear?' 32For the pagans run after all
these things, and your heavenly Father
knows that you need them. 33But seek first
his kingdom and his righteousness, and all
these things will be given to you as well.
34Therefore do not worry about tomorrow, for
tomorrow will worry about itself. Each day
has enough trouble of its own.

Judging Others

7 "Do not judge, or you too will be judged.
2For in the same way you judge others,
you will be judged, and with the measure you
use, it will be measured to you.
3"Why do you look at the speck of sawdust
in your brother's eye and pay no attention to
the plank in your own eye? 4How can you say
to your brother, 'Let me take the speck out of
your eye,' when all the time there is a plank in
your own eye? 5You hypocrite, first take the
plank out of your own eye, and then you will
see clearly to remove the speck from your
brother's eye.
6"Do not give dogs what is sacred; do not
throw your pearls to pigs. If you do, they may
trample them under their feet, and then turn
and tear you to pieces.

Ask, Seek, Knock

7"Ask and it will be given to you; seek and
you will find; knock and the door will be
opened to you. 8For everyone who asks receives; he who seeks finds; and to him who
knocks, the door will be opened.
9"Which of you, if his son asks for bread,
will give him a stone? 10Or if he asks for a
fish, will give him a snake? 11If you, then,
though you are evil, know how to give good
gifts to your children, how much more will
your Father in heaven give good gifts to
those who ask him! 12So in everything, do to
others what you would have them do to you,
for this sums up the Law and the Prophets.

The Narrow and Wide Gates

13"Enter through the narrow gate. For wide
is the gate and broad is the road that leads to
destruction, and many enter through it. 14But
small is the gate and narrow the road that
leads to life, and only a few find it.

A Tree and Its Fruit

15"Watch out for false prophets. They
come to you in sheep's clothing, but inwardly
they are ferocious wolves. 16By their fruit you
will recognize them. Do people pick grapes
from thornbushes, or figs from thistles?
17Likewise every good tree bears good fruit,
but a bad tree bears bad fruit. 18A good tree
cannot bear bad fruit, and a bad tree cannot
bear good fruit. 19Every tree that does not
bear good fruit is cut down and thrown into
the fire. 20Thus, by their fruit you will recognize them.
21"Not everyone who says to me, 'Lord,
Lord,' will enter the kingdom of heaven, but
only he who does the will of my Father who is
in heaven. 22Many will say to me on that day,
'Lord, Lord, did we not prophesy in your
name, and in your name drive out demons
and perform many miracles?' 23Then I will tell
them plainly, 'I never knew you. Away from
me, you evildoers!'

The Wise and Foolish Builders

24"Therefore everyone who hears these
words of mine and puts them into practice is
like a wise man who built his house on the
rock. 25The rain came down, the streams
rose, and the winds blew and beat against
that house; yet it did not fall, because it had
its foundation on the rock. 26But everyone
who hears these words of mine and does not
put them into practice is like a foolish man
who built his house on sand. 27The rain came
down, the streams rose, and the winds blew
and beat against that house, and it fell with a
great crash."

28When Jesus had finished saying these
things, the crowds were amazed at his
teaching, 29because he taught as one who
had authority, and not as their teachers of
the law.

The Man With Leprosy

8 When he came down from the mountainside, large crowds followed him. 2A man

[a]27 Or *single cubit to his height*

with leprosy[a] came and knelt before him and
said, "Lord, if you are willing, you can make
me clean."
3Jesus reached out his hand and touched
the man. "I am willing," he said. "Be clean!"
Immediately he was cured[b] of his leprosy.
4Then Jesus said to him, "See that you don't
tell anyone. But go, show yourself to the
priest and offer the gift Moses commanded,
as a testimony to them."

The Faith of the Centurion

5When Jesus had entered Capernaum, a
centurion came to him, asking for help.
6"Lord," he said, "my servant lies at home
paralyzed and in terrible suffering."
7Jesus said to him, "I will go and heal him."
8The centurion replied, "Lord, I do not deserve to have you come under my roof. But
just say the word, and my servant will be
healed. 9For I myself am a man under authority, with soldiers under me. I tell this one,
'Go,' and he goes; and that one, 'Come,' and
he comes. I say to my servant, 'Do this,' and
he does it."
10When Jesus heard this, he was astonished and said to those following him, "I tell
you the truth, I have not found anyone in
Israel with such great faith. 11I say to you that
many will come from the east and the west,
and will take their places at the feast with
Abraham, Isaac and Jacob in the kingdom of
heaven. 12But the subjects of the kingdom
will be thrown outside, into the darkness,
where there will be weeping and gnashing of
teeth."
13Then Jesus said to the centurion, "Go! It
will be done just as you believed it would."
And his servant was healed at that very hour.

Jesus Heals Many

14When Jesus came into Peter's house, he
saw Peter's mother-in-law lying in bed with a
fever. 15He touched her hand and the fever
left her, and she got up and began to wait on
him.
16When evening came, many who were
demon-possessed were brought to him, and
he drove out the spirits with a word and
healed all the sick. 17This was to fulfill what
was spoken through the prophet Isaiah:

"He took up our infirmities
and carried our diseases."[c]

The Cost of Following Jesus

18When Jesus saw the crowd around him,
he gave orders to cross to the other side of
the lake. 19Then a teacher of the law came to
him and said, "Teacher, I will follow you
wherever you go."
20Jesus replied, "Foxes have holes and
birds of the air have nests, but the Son of
Man has no place to lay his head."
21Another disciple said to him, "Lord, first
let me go and bury my father."
22But Jesus told him, "Follow me, and let
the dead bury their own dead."

Jesus Calms the Storm

23Then he got into the boat and his disciples followed him. 24Without warning, a furious storm came up on the lake, so that the
waves swept over the boat. But Jesus was
sleeping. 25The disciples went and woke
him, saying, "Lord, save us! We're going to
drown!"
26He replied, "You of little faith, why are
you so afraid?" Then he got up and rebuked
the winds and the waves, and it was completely calm.
27The men were amazed and asked,
"What kind of man is this? Even the winds
and the waves obey him!"

The Healing of Two Demon-possessed Men

28When he arrived at the other side in the
region of the Gadarenes,[d] two demon-possessed men coming from the tombs met him.
They were so violent that no one could pass
that way. 29"What do you want with us, Son
of God?" they shouted. "Have you come
here to torture us before the appointed
time?"
30Some distance from them a large herd of
pigs was feeding. 31The demons begged
Jesus, "If you drive us out, send us into the
herd of pigs."
32He said to them, "Go!" So they came out
and went into the pigs, and the whole herd
rushed down the steep bank into the lake
and died in the water. 33Those tending the
pigs ran off, went into the town and reported
all this, including what had happened to the
demon-possessed men. 34Then the whole
town went out to meet Jesus. And when they

[a]2 The Greek word was used for various diseases affecting the skin—not necessarily leprosy. [b]3 Greek *made clean* [c]17 Isaiah 53:4 [d]28 Some manuscripts *Gergesenes;* others *Gerasenes*

saw him, they pleaded with him to leave their
region.

Jesus Heals a Paralytic

9 Jesus stepped into a boat, crossed over
and came to his own town. 2Some men
brought to him a paralytic, lying on a mat.
When Jesus saw their faith, he said to the
paralytic, "Take heart, son; your sins are forgiven."
3At this, some of the teachers of the law
said to themselves, "This fellow is blaspheming!"
4Knowing their thoughts, Jesus said, "Why
do you entertain evil thoughts in your hearts?
5Which is easier: to say, 'Your sins are forgiven,' or to say, 'Get up and walk'? 6But so
that you may know that the Son of Man has
authority on earth to forgive sins. . . ." Then
he said to the paralytic, "Get up, take your
mat and go home." 7And the man got up and
went home. 8When the crowd saw this, they
were filled with awe; and they praised God,
who had given such authority to men.

The Calling of Matthew

9As Jesus went on from there, he saw a
man named Matthew sitting at the tax collector's booth. "Follow me," he told him, and
Matthew got up and followed him.
10While Jesus was having dinner at Matthew's house, many tax collectors and "sinners" came and ate with him and his disciples. 11When the Pharisees saw this, they
asked his disciples, "Why does your teacher
eat with tax collectors and 'sinners'?"
12On hearing this, Jesus said, "It is not the
healthy who need a doctor, but the sick.
13But go and learn what this means: 'I desire
mercy, not sacrifice.'[a] For I have not come to
call the righteous, but sinners."

Jesus Questioned About Fasting

14Then John's disciples came and asked
him, "How is it that we and the Pharisees
fast, but your disciples do not fast?"
15Jesus answered, "How can the guests of
the bridegroom mourn while he is with them?
The time will come when the bridegroom will
be taken from them; then they will fast.
16"No one sews a patch of unshrunk cloth
on an old garment, for the patch will pull
away from the garment, making the tear
worse. 17Neither do men pour new wine into
old wineskins. If they do, the skins will burst,
the wine will run out and the wineskins will be
ruined. No, they pour new wine into new
wineskins, and both are preserved."

A Dead Girl and a Sick Woman

18While he was saying this, a ruler came
and knelt before him and said, "My daughter
has just died. But come and put your hand on
her, and she will live." 19Jesus got up and
went with him, and so did his disciples.
20Just then a woman who had been subject to bleeding for twelve years came up
behind him and touched the edge of his
cloak. 21She said to herself, "If I only touch
his cloak, I will be healed."
22Jesus turned and saw her. "Take heart,
daughter," he said, "your faith has healed
you." And the woman was healed from that
moment.
23When Jesus entered the ruler's house
and saw the flute players and the noisy
crowd, 24he said, "Go away. The girl is not
dead but asleep." But they laughed at him.
25After the crowd had been put outside, he
went in and took the girl by the hand, and she
got up. 26News of this spread through all that
region.

Jesus Heals the Blind and Mute

27As Jesus went on from there, two blind
men followed him, calling out, "Have mercy
on us, Son of David!"
28When he had gone indoors, the blind
men came to him, and he asked them, "Do
you believe that I am able to do this?"
"Yes, Lord," they replied.
29Then he touched their eyes and said,
"According to your faith will it be done to
you"; 30and their sight was restored. Jesus
warned them sternly, "See that no one
knows about this." 31But they went out and
spread the news about him all over that region.
32While they were going out, a man who
was demon-possessed and could not talk
was brought to Jesus. 33And when the demon was driven out, the man who had been
mute spoke. The crowd was amazed and
said, "Nothing like this has ever been seen in
Israel."
34But the Pharisees said, "It is by the
prince of demons that he drives out demons."

[a] *13* Hosea 6:6

The Workers Are Few

35Jesus went through all the towns and villages, teaching in their synagogues, preaching the good news of the kingdom and healing every disease and sickness. 36When he saw the crowds, he had compassion on them, because they were harassed and helpless, like sheep without a shepherd. 37Then he said to his disciples, "The harvest is plentiful but the workers are few. 38Ask the Lord of the harvest, therefore, to send out workers into his harvest field."

Jesus Sends Out the Twelve

10 He called his twelve disciples to him and gave them authority to drive out evil[a] spirits and to heal every disease and sickness.

2These are the names of the twelve apostles: first, Simon (who is called Peter) and his brother Andrew; James son of Zebedee, and his brother John; 3Philip and Bartholomew; Thomas and Matthew the tax collector; James son of Alphaeus, and Thaddaeus; 4Simon the Zealot and Judas Iscariot, who betrayed him.

5These twelve Jesus sent out with the following instructions: "Do not go among the Gentiles or enter any town of the Samaritans. 6Go rather to the lost sheep of Israel. 7As you go, preach this message: 'The kingdom of heaven is near.' 8Heal the sick, raise the dead, cleanse those who have leprosy,[b] drive out demons. Freely you have received, freely give. 9Do not take along any gold or silver or copper in your belts; 10take no bag for the journey, or extra tunic, or sandals or a staff; for the worker is worth his keep.

11"Whatever town or village you enter, search for some worthy person there and stay at his house until you leave. 12As you enter the home, give it your greeting. 13If the home is deserving, let your peace rest on it; if it is not, let your peace return to you. 14If anyone will not welcome you or listen to your words, shake the dust off your feet when you leave that home or town. 15I tell you the truth, it will be more bearable for Sodom and Gomorrah on the day of judgment than for that town. 16I am sending you out like sheep among wolves. Therefore be as shrewd as snakes and as innocent as doves.

17"Be on your guard against men; they will hand you over to the local councils and flog you in their synagogues. 18On my account you will be brought before governors and kings as witnesses to them and to the Gentiles. 19But when they arrest you, do not worry about what to say or how to say it. At that time you will be given what to say, 20for it will not be you speaking, but the Spirit of your Father speaking through you.

21"Brother will betray brother to death, and a father his child; children will rebel against their parents and have them put to death. 22All men will hate you because of me, but he who stands firm to the end will be saved. 23When you are persecuted in one place, flee to another. I tell you the truth, you will not finish going through the cities of Israel before the Son of Man comes.

24"A student is not above his teacher, nor a servant above his master. 25It is enough for the student to be like his teacher, and the servant like his master. If the head of the house has been called Beelzebub,[c] how much more the members of his household!

26"So do not be afraid of them. There is nothing concealed that will not be disclosed, or hidden that will not be made known. 27What I tell you in the dark, speak in the daylight; what is whispered in your ear, proclaim from the roofs. 28Do not be afraid of those who kill the body but cannot kill the soul. Rather, be afraid of the One who can destroy both soul and body in hell. 29Are not two sparrows sold for a penny[d]? Yet not one of them will fall to the ground apart from the will of your Father. 30And even the very hairs of your head are all numbered. 31So don't be afraid; you are worth more than many sparrows.

32"Whoever acknowledges me before men, I will also acknowledge him before my Father in heaven. 33But whoever disowns me before men, I will disown him before my Father in heaven.

34"Do not suppose that I have come to bring peace to the earth. I did not come to bring peace, but a sword. 35For I have come to turn

" 'a man against his father,
a daughter against her mother,
a daughter-in-law against her
mother-in-law—
36 a man's enemies will be the members
of his own household.'[e]

[a] 1 Greek *unclean* [b] 8 The Greek word was used for various diseases affecting the skin—not necessarily leprosy. [c] 25 Greek *Beezeboul* or *Beelzeboul* [d] 29 Greek *an assarion* [e] 36 Micah 7:6

37"Anyone who loves his father or mother
more than me is not worthy of me; anyone
who loves his son or daughter more than me
is not worthy of me; 38and anyone who does
not take his cross and follow me is not worthy
of me. 39Whoever finds his life will lose it, and
whoever loses his life for my sake will find it.
40"He who receives you receives me, and
he who receives me receives the one who
sent me. 41Anyone who receives a prophet
because he is a prophet will receive a
prophet's reward, and anyone who receives
a righteous man because he is a righteous
man will receive a righteous man's reward.
42And if anyone gives even a cup of cold
water to one of these little ones because he
is my disciple, I tell you the truth, he will
certainly not lose his reward."

Jesus and John the Baptist

11 After Jesus had finished instructing
his twelve disciples, he went on from
there to teach and preach in the towns of
Galilee.[a]
2When John heard in prison what Christ
was doing, he sent his disciples 3to ask him,
"Are you the one who was to come, or should
we expect someone else?"
4Jesus replied, "Go back and report to
John what you hear and see: 5The blind receive sight, the lame walk, those who have
leprosy[b] are cured, the deaf hear, the dead
are raised, and the good news is preached to
the poor. 6Blessed is the man who does not
fall away on account of me."
7As John's disciples were leaving, Jesus
began to speak to the crowd about John:
"What did you go out into the desert to see?
A reed swayed by the wind? 8If not, what did
you go out to see? A man dressed in fine
clothes? No, those who wear fine clothes are
in kings' palaces. 9Then what did you go out
to see? A prophet? Yes, I tell you, and more
than a prophet. 10This is the one about whom
it is written:

" 'I will send my messenger ahead of you,
who will prepare your way before you.'[c]

11I tell you the truth: Among those born of
women there has not risen anyone greater
than John the Baptist; yet he who is least in
the kingdom of heaven is greater than he.
12From the days of John the Baptist until
now, the kingdom of heaven has been forcefully advancing, and forceful men lay hold of
it. 13For all the Prophets and the Law prophesied until John. 14And if you are willing to
accept it, he is the Elijah who was to come.
15He who has ears, let him hear.
16"To what can I compare this generation?
They are like children sitting in the marketplaces and calling out to others:

17" 'We played the flute for you,
and you did not dance;
we sang a dirge,
and you did not mourn.'

18For John came neither eating nor drinking,
and they say, 'He has a demon.' 19The Son
of Man came eating and drinking, and they
say, 'Here is a glutton and a drunkard, a
friend of tax collectors and "sinners." ' But
wisdom is proved right by her actions."

Woe on Unrepentant Cities

20Then Jesus began to denounce the cities in which most of his miracles had been
performed, because they did not repent.
21"Woe to you, Korazin! Woe to you, Bethsaida! If the miracles that were performed in
you had been performed in Tyre and Sidon,
they would have repented long ago in sackcloth and ashes. 22But I tell you, it will be
more bearable for Tyre and Sidon on the day
of judgment than for you. 23And you, Capernaum, will you be lifted up to the skies? No,
you will go down to the depths.[d] If the miracles that were performed in you had been
performed in Sodom, it would have remained
to this day. 24But I tell you that it will be more
bearable for Sodom on the day of judgment
than for you."

Rest for the Weary

25At that time Jesus said, "I praise you,
Father, Lord of heaven and earth, because
you have hidden these things from the wise
and learned, and revealed them to little children. 26Yes, Father, for this was your good
pleasure.
27"All things have been committed to me
by my Father. No one knows the Son except
the Father, and no one knows the Father
except the Son and those to whom the Son
chooses to reveal him.
28"Come to me, all you who are weary and
burdened, and I will give you rest. 29Take my
yoke upon you and learn from me, for I am

[a] *1* Greek *in their towns* [b] *5* The Greek word was used for various diseases affecting the skin—not necessarily leprosy. [c] *10* Mal. 3:1 [d] *23* Greek *Hades*

gentle and humble in heart, and you will find
rest for your souls. 30For my yoke is easy and
my burden is light."

Lord of the Sabbath

12 At that time Jesus went through the
grainfields on the Sabbath. His disciples were hungry and began to pick some
heads of grain and eat them. 2When the
Pharisees saw this, they said to him, "Look!
Your disciples are doing what is unlawful on
the Sabbath."

3He answered, "Haven't you read what
David did when he and his companions were
hungry? 4He entered the house of God, and
he and his companions ate the consecrated
bread—which was not lawful for them to do,
but only for the priests. 5Or haven't you read
in the Law that on the Sabbath the priests in
the temple desecrate the day and yet are
innocent? 6I tell you that one[a] greater than
the temple is here. 7If you had known what
these words mean, 'I desire mercy, not sacrifice,'[b] you would not have condemned the
innocent. 8For the Son of Man is Lord of the
Sabbath."

9Going on from that place, he went into
their synagogue, 10and a man with a shriveled hand was there. Looking for a reason to
accuse Jesus, they asked him, "Is it lawful to
heal on the Sabbath?"

11He said to them, "If any of you has a
sheep and it falls into a pit on the Sabbath,
will you not take hold of it and lift it out?
12How much more valuable is a man than a
sheep! Therefore it is lawful to do good on
the Sabbath."

13Then he said to the man, "Stretch out
your hand." So he stretched it out and it was
completely restored, just as sound as the
other. 14But the Pharisees went out and plotted how they might kill Jesus.

God's Chosen Servant

15Aware of this, Jesus withdrew from that
place. Many followed him, and he healed all
their sick, 16warning them not to tell who he
was. 17This was to fulfill what was spoken
through the prophet Isaiah:

18"Here is my servant whom I have
chosen,
the one I love, in whom I delight;
I will put my Spirit on him,
and he will proclaim justice to the
nations.
19He will not quarrel or cry out;
no one will hear his voice in the streets.
20A bruised reed he will not break,
and a smoldering wick he will not snuff
out,
till he leads justice to victory.
21 In his name the nations will put their
hope."[c]

Jesus and Beelzebub

22Then they brought him a demon-possessed man who was blind and mute, and
Jesus healed him, so that he could both talk
and see. 23All the people were astonished
and said, "Could this be the Son of David?"

24But when the Pharisees heard this, they
said, "It is only by Beelzebub,[d] the prince of
demons, that this fellow drives out demons."

25Jesus knew their thoughts and said to
them, "Every kingdom divided against itself
will be ruined, and every city or household
divided against itself will not stand. 26If Satan
drives out Satan, he is divided against himself. How then can his kingdom stand? 27And
if I drive out demons by Beelzebub, by whom
do your people drive them out? So then, they
will be your judges. 28But if I drive out demons by the Spirit of God, then the kingdom
of God has come upon you.

29"Or again, how can anyone enter a
strong man's house and carry off his possessions unless he first ties up the strong man?
Then he can rob his house.

30"He who is not with me is against me,
and he who does not gather with me scatters. 31And so I tell you, every sin and blasphemy will be forgiven men, but the blasphemy against the Spirit will not be forgiven.
32Anyone who speaks a word against the
Son of Man will be forgiven, but anyone who
speaks against the Holy Spirit will not be
forgiven, either in this age or in the age to
come.

33"Make a tree good and its fruit will be
good, or make a tree bad and its fruit will be
bad, for a tree is recognized by its fruit. 34You
brood of vipers, how can you who are evil
say anything good? For out of the overflow of
the heart the mouth speaks. 35The good man
brings good things out of the good stored up

[a] 6 Or *something;* also in verses 41 and 42 [b] 7 Hosea 6:6 [c] 21 Isaiah 42:1-4 [d] 24 Greek *Beezeboul*
or *Beelzeboul*; also in verse 27

in him, and the evil man brings evil things out
of the evil stored up in him. 36But I tell you
that men will have to give account on the day
of judgment for every careless word they
have spoken. 37For by your words you will be
acquitted, and by your words you will be condemned."

The Sign of Jonah

38Then some of the Pharisees and teachers of the law said to him, "Teacher, we want
to see a miraculous sign from you."

39He answered, "A wicked and adulterous
generation asks for a miraculous sign! But
none will be given it except the sign of the
prophet Jonah. 40For as Jonah was three
days and three nights in the belly of a huge
fish, so the Son of Man will be three days and
three nights in the heart of the earth. 41The
men of Nineveh will stand up at the judgment
with this generation and condemn it; for they
repented at the preaching of Jonah, and now
one[a] greater than Jonah is here. 42The
Queen of the South will rise at the judgment
with this generation and condemn it; for she
came from the ends of the earth to listen to
Solomon's wisdom, and now one greater
than Solomon is here.

43"When an evil[b] spirit comes out of a
man, it goes through arid places seeking rest
and does not find it. 44Then it says, 'I will
return to the house I left.' When it arrives, it
finds the house unoccupied, swept clean
and put in order. 45Then it goes and takes
with it seven other spirits more wicked than
itself, and they go in and live there. And the
final condition of that man is worse than the
first. That is how it will be with this wicked
generation."

Jesus' Mother and Brothers

46While Jesus was still talking to the
crowd, his mother and brothers stood outside, wanting to speak to him. 47Someone
told him, "Your mother and brothers are
standing outside, wanting to speak to you."[c]

48He replied to him, "Who is my mother,
and who are my brothers?" 49Pointing to his
disciples, he said, "Here are my mother and
my brothers. 50For whoever does the will of
my Father in heaven is my brother and sister
and mother."

The Parable of the Sower

13 That same day Jesus went out of the
house and sat by the lake. 2Such
large crowds gathered around him that he
got into a boat and sat in it, while all the
people stood on the shore. 3Then he told
them many things in parables, saying: "A
farmer went out to sow his seed. 4As he was
scattering the seed, some fell along the path,
and the birds came and ate it up. 5Some fell
on rocky places, where it did not have much
soil. It sprang up quickly, because the soil
was shallow. 6But when the sun came up,
the plants were scorched, and they withered
because they had no root. 7Other seed fell
among thorns, which grew up and choked
the plants. 8Still other seed fell on good soil,
where it produced a crop—a hundred, sixty
or thirty times what was sown. 9He who has
ears, let him hear."

10The disciples came to him and asked,
"Why do you speak to the people in parables?"

11He replied, "The knowledge of the secrets of the kingdom of heaven has been
given to you, but not to them. 12Whoever has
will be given more, and he will have an abundance. Whoever does not have, even what
he has will be taken from him. 13This is why I
speak to them in parables:

"Though seeing, they do not see;
  though hearing, they do not hear or
    understand.

14In them is fulfilled the prophecy of Isaiah:

" 'You will be ever hearing but never
    understanding;
  you will be ever seeing but never
    perceiving.
15For this people's heart has become
    calloused;
  they hardly hear with their ears,
  and they have closed their eyes.
Otherwise they might see with their eyes,
  hear with their ears,
  understand with their hearts
and turn, and I would heal them.'[d]

16But blessed are your eyes because they
see, and your ears because they hear. 17For
I tell you the truth, many prophets and right-

[a] 41 Or *something*; also in verse 42 [b] 43 Greek *unclean* [c] 47 Some manuscripts do not have verse 47.
[d] 15 Isaiah 6:9,10

eous men longed to see what you see but did
not see it, and to hear what you hear but did
not hear it.

18“Listen then to what the parable of the
sower means: 19When anyone hears the
message about the kingdom and does not
understand it, the evil one comes and
snatches away what was sown in his heart.
This is the seed sown along the path. 20The
one who received the seed that fell on rocky
places is the man who hears the word and at
once receives it with joy. 21But since he has
no root, he lasts only a short time. When
trouble or persecution comes because of the
word, he quickly falls away. 22The one who
received the seed that fell among the thorns
is the man who hears the word, but the worries of this life and the deceitfulness of
wealth choke it, making it unfruitful. 23But the
one who received the seed that fell on good
soil is the man who hears the word and understands it. He produces a crop, yielding a
hundred, sixty or thirty times what was
sown.”

The Parable of the Weeds

24Jesus told them another parable: “The
kingdom of heaven is like a man who sowed
good seed in his field. 25But while everyone
was sleeping, his enemy came and sowed
weeds among the wheat, and went away.
26When the wheat sprouted and formed
heads, then the weeds also appeared.

27“The owner’s servants came to him and
said, ‘Sir, didn’t you sow good seed in your
field? Where then did the weeds come
from?’

28“ ‘An enemy did this,’ he replied.

“The servants asked him, ‘Do you want us
to go and pull them up?’

29“ ‘No,’ he answered, ‘because while you
are pulling the weeds, you may root up the
wheat with them. 30Let both grow together
until the harvest. At that time I will tell the
harvesters: First collect the weeds and tie
them in bundles to be burned; then gather
the wheat and bring it into my barn.’ ”

The Parables of the Mustard Seed and the Yeast

31He told them another parable: “The kingdom of heaven is like a mustard seed, which
a man took and planted in his field. 32Though
it is the smallest of all your seeds, yet when it
grows, it is the largest of garden plants and
becomes a tree, so that the birds of the air
come and perch in its branches.”

33He told them still another parable: “The
kingdom of heaven is like yeast that a
woman took and mixed into a large amount[a]
of flour until it worked all through the dough.”

34Jesus spoke all these things to the crowd
in parables; he did not say anything to them
without using a parable. 35So was fulfilled
what was spoken through the prophet:

“I will open my mouth in parables,
I will utter things hidden since the
creation of the world.”[b]

The Parable of the Weeds Explained

36Then he left the crowd and went into the
house. His disciples came to him and said,
“Explain to us the parable of the weeds in the
field.”

37He answered, “The one who sowed the
good seed is the Son of Man. 38The field is
the world, and the good seed stands for the
sons of the kingdom. The weeds are the
sons of the evil one, 39and the enemy who
sows them is the devil. The harvest is the
end of the age, and the harvesters are angels.

40“As the weeds are pulled up and burned
in the fire, so it will be at the end of the age.
41The Son of Man will send out his angels,
and they will weed out of his kingdom everything that causes sin and all who do evil.
42They will throw them into the fiery furnace,
where there will be weeping and gnashing of
teeth. 43Then the righteous will shine like the
sun in the kingdom of their Father. He who
has ears, let him hear.

The Parables of the Hidden Treasure and the Pearl

44“The kingdom of heaven is like treasure
hidden in a field. When a man found it, he hid
it again, and then in his joy went and sold all
he had and bought that field.

45“Again, the kingdom of heaven is like a
merchant looking for fine pearls. 46When he
found one of great value, he went away and
sold everything he had and bought it.

The Parable of the Net

47“Once again, the kingdom of heaven is
like a net that was let down into the lake and
caught all kinds of fish. 48When it was full, the

[a]33 Greek *three satas* (probably about 1/2 bushel or 22 liters) [b]35 Psalm 78:2

fishermen pulled it up on the shore. Then they sat down and collected the good fish in baskets, but threw the bad away. 49This is how it will be at the end of the age. The angels will come and separate the wicked from the righteous 50and throw them into the fiery furnace, where there will be weeping and gnashing of teeth.

51"Have you understood all these things?" Jesus asked.

"Yes," they replied.

52He said to them, "Therefore every teacher of the law who has been instructed about the kingdom of heaven is like the owner of a house who brings out of his storeroom new treasures as well as old."

A Prophet Without Honor

53When Jesus had finished these parables, he moved on from there. 54Coming to his hometown, he began teaching the people in their synagogue, and they were amazed. "Where did this man get this wisdom and these miraculous powers?" they asked. 55"Isn't this the carpenter's son? Isn't his mother's name Mary, and aren't his brothers James, Joseph, Simon and Judas? 56Aren't all his sisters with us? Where then did this man get all these things?" 57And they took offense at him.

But Jesus said to them, "Only in his hometown and in his own house is a prophet without honor."

58And he did not do many miracles there because of their lack of faith.

John the Baptist Beheaded

14 At that time Herod the tetrarch heard the reports about Jesus, 2and he said to his attendants, "This is John the Baptist; he has risen from the dead! That is why miraculous powers are at work in him."

3Now Herod had arrested John and bound him and put him in prison because of Herodias, his brother Philip's wife, 4for John had been saying to him: "It is not lawful for you to have her." 5Herod wanted to kill John, but he was afraid of the people, because they considered him a prophet.

6On Herod's birthday the daughter of Herodias danced for them and pleased Herod so much 7that he promised with an oath to give her whatever she asked. 8Prompted by her mother, she said, "Give me here on a platter the head of John the Baptist." 9The king was distressed, but because of his oaths and his dinner guests, he ordered that her request be granted 10and had John beheaded in the prison. 11His head was brought in on a platter and given to the girl, who carried it to her mother. 12John's disciples came and took his body and buried it. Then they went and told Jesus.

Jesus Feeds the Five Thousand

13When Jesus heard what had happened, he withdrew by boat privately to a solitary place. Hearing of this, the crowds followed him on foot from the towns. 14When Jesus landed and saw a large crowd, he had compassion on them and healed their sick.

15As evening approached, the disciples came to him and said, "This is a remote place, and it's already getting late. Send the crowds away, so they can go to the villages and buy themselves some food."

16Jesus replied, "They do not need to go away. You give them something to eat."

17"We have here only five loaves of bread and two fish," they answered.

18"Bring them here to me," he said. 19And he directed the people to sit down on the grass. Taking the five loaves and the two fish and looking up to heaven, he gave thanks and broke the loaves.Then he gave them to the disciples, and the disciples gave them to the people. 20They all ate and were satisfied, and the disciples picked up twelve basketfuls of broken pieces that were left over. 21The number of those who ate was about five thousand men, besides women and children.

Jesus Walks on the Water

22Immediately Jesus made the disciples get into the boat and go on ahead of him to the other side, while he dismissed the crowd. 23After he had dismissed them, he went up on a mountainside by himself to pray. When evening came, he was there alone, 24but the boat was already a considerable distance[a] from land, buffeted by the waves because the wind was against it.

25During the fourth watch of the night Jesus went out to them, walking on the lake. 26When the disciples saw him walking on the lake, they were terrified. "It's a ghost," they said, and cried out in fear.

27But Jesus immediately said to them: "Take courage! It is I. Don't be afraid."

[a]24 Greek *many stadia*

28“Lord, if it's you,” Peter replied, “tell me
to come to you on the water.”
29“Come,” he said.
Then Peter got down out of the boat,
walked on the water and came toward
Jesus. 30But when he saw the wind, he was
afraid and, beginning to sink, cried out,
“Lord, save me!”
31Immediately Jesus reached out his hand
and caught him. “You of little faith,” he said,
“why did you doubt?”
32And when they climbed into the boat, the
wind died down. 33Then those who were in
the boat worshiped him, saying, “Truly you
are the Son of God.”
34When they had crossed over, they landed at Gennesaret. 35And when the men of
that place recognized Jesus, they sent word
to all the surrounding country. People
brought all their sick to him 36and begged him
to let the sick just touch the edge of his cloak,
and all who touched him were healed.

Clean and Unclean

15 Then some Pharisees and teachers
of the law came to Jesus from
Jerusalem and asked, 2“Why do your disciples break the tradition of the elders? They
don't wash their hands before they eat!”
3Jesus replied, “And why do you break the
command of God for the sake of your tradition? 4For God said, ‘Honor your father and
mother’[a] and ‘Anyone who curses his father
or mother must be put to death.’[b] 5But you
say that if a man says to his father or mother,
‘Whatever help you might otherwise have
received from me is a gift devoted to God,’
6he is not to ‘honor his father[c]’ with it. Thus
you nullify the word of God for the sake of
your tradition. 7You hypocrites! Isaiah was
right when he prophesied about you:

8“ ‘These people honor me with their lips,
but their hearts are far from me.
9They worship me in vain;
their teachings are but rules taught by
men.’[d]”

10Jesus called the crowd to him and said,
“Listen and understand. 11What goes into a
man's mouth does not make him ‘unclean,’
but what comes out of his mouth, that is what
makes him ‘unclean.’ ”
12Then the disciples came to him and
asked, “Do you know that the Pharisees
were offended when they heard this?”
13He replied, “Every plant that my heavenly Father has not planted will be pulled up by
the roots. 14Leave them; they are blind
guides.[e] If a blind man leads a blind man,
both will fall into a pit.”
15Peter said, “Explain the parable to us.”
16“Are you still so dull?” Jesus asked
them. 17“Don't you see that whatever enters
the mouth goes into the stomach and then
out of the body? 18But the things that come
out of the mouth come from the heart, and
these make a man ‘unclean.’ 19For out of the
heart come evil thoughts, murder, adultery,
sexual immorality, theft, false testimony,
slander. 20These are what make a man ‘unclean’; but eating with unwashed hands does
not make him ‘unclean.’ ”

The Faith of the Canaanite Woman

21Leaving that place, Jesus withdrew to
the region of Tyre and Sidon. 22A Canaanite
woman from that vicinity came to him, crying
out, “Lord, Son of David, have mercy on me!
My daughter is suffering terribly from demon-
possession.”
23Jesus did not answer a word. So his disciples came to him and urged him, “Send her
away, for she keeps crying out after us.”
24He answered, “I was sent only to the lost
sheep of Israel.”
25The woman came and knelt before him.
“Lord, help me!” she said.
26He replied, “It is not right to take the
children's bread and toss it to their dogs.”
27“Yes, Lord,” she said, “but even the
dogs eat the crumbs that fall from their masters' table.”
28Then Jesus answered, “Woman, you
have great faith! Your request is granted.”
And her daughter was healed from that very
hour.

Jesus Feeds the Four Thousand

29Jesus left there and went along the Sea
of Galilee. Then he went up on a mountainside and sat down. 30Great crowds came to
him, bringing the lame, the blind, the crippled, the mute and many others, and laid
them at his feet; and he healed them. 31The
people were amazed when they saw the
mute speaking, the crippled made well, the

[a] 4 Exodus 20:12; Deut. 5:16 [b] 4 Exodus 21:17; Lev. 20:9 [c] 6 Some manuscripts *father or his mother*
[d] 9 Isaiah 29:13 [e] 14 Some manuscripts *guides of the blind*

lame walking and the blind seeing. And they
praised the God of Israel.
32Jesus called his disciples to him and
said, "I have compassion for these people;
they have already been with me three days
and have nothing to eat. I do not want to
send them away hungry, or they may collapse on the way."
33His disciples answered, "Where could
we get enough bread in this remote place to
feed such a crowd?"
34"How many loaves do you have?" Jesus
asked.
"Seven," they replied, "and a few small
fish."
35He told the crowd to sit down on the
ground. 36Then he took the seven loaves and
the fish, and when he had given thanks, he
broke them and gave them to the disciples,
and they in turn to the people. 37They all ate
and were satisfied. Afterward the disciples
picked up seven basketfuls of broken pieces
that were left over. 38The number of those
who ate was four thousand, besides women
and children. 39After Jesus had sent the
crowd away, he got into the boat and went to
the vicinity of Magadan.

The Demand for a Sign

16 The Pharisees and Sadducees came
to Jesus and tested him by asking
him to show them a sign from heaven.
2He replied,[a] "When evening comes, you
say, 'It will be fair weather, for the sky is red,'
3and in the morning, 'Today it will be stormy,
for the sky is red and overcast.' You know
how to interpret the appearance of the sky,
but you cannot interpret the signs of the
times. 4A wicked and adulterous generation
looks for a miraculous sign, but none will be
given it except the sign of Jonah." Jesus
then left them and went away.

The Yeast of the Pharisees and Sadducees

5When they went across the lake, the disciples forgot to take bread. 6"Be careful,"
Jesus said to them. "Be on your guard
against the yeast of the Pharisees and Sadducees."
7They discussed this among themselves
and said, "It is because we didn't bring any
bread."
8Aware of their discussion, Jesus asked,
"You of little faith, why are you talking among
yourselves about having no bread? 9Do you
still not understand? Don't you remember
the five loaves for the five thousand, and how
many basketfuls you gathered? 10Or the
seven loaves for the four thousand, and how
many basketfuls you gathered? 11How is it
you don't understand that I was not talking to
you about bread? But be on your guard
against the yeast of the Pharisees and Sadducees." 12Then they understood that he
was not telling them to guard against the
yeast used in bread, but against the teaching
of the Pharisees and Sadducees.

Peter's Confession of Christ

13When Jesus came to the region of Caesarea Philippi, he asked his disciples, "Who
do people say the Son of Man is?"
14They replied, "Some say John the Baptist; others say Elijah; and still others, Jeremiah or one of the prophets."
15"But what about you?" he asked. "Who
do you say I am?"
16Simon Peter answered, "You are the
Christ,[b] the Son of the living God."
17Jesus replied, "Blessed are you, Simon
son of Jonah, for this was not revealed to you
by man, but by my Father in heaven. 18And I
tell you that you are Peter,[c] and on this rock
I will build my church, and the gates of
Hades[d] will not overcome it.[e] 19I will give you
the keys of the kingdom of heaven; whatever
you bind on earth will be[f] bound in heaven,
and whatever you loose on earth will be[f]
loosed in heaven." 20Then he warned his
disciples not to tell anyone that he was the
Christ.

Jesus Predicts His Death

21From that time on Jesus began to explain to his disciples that he must go to
Jerusalem and suffer many things at the
hands of the elders, chief priests and teachers of the law, and that he must be killed and
on the third day be raised to life.
22Peter took him aside and began to
rebuke him. "Never, Lord!" he said. "This
shall never happen to you!"
23Jesus turned and said to Peter, "Get behind me, Satan! You are a stumbling block to
me; you do not have in mind the things of
God, but the things of men."
24Then Jesus said to his disciples, "If any-

[a]2 Some early manuscripts do not have the rest of verse 2 and all of verse 3. [b]16 Or *Messiah; also in* verse 20 [c]18 *Peter* means *rock.* [d]18 Or *hell* [e]18 Or *not prove stronger than it* [f]19 Or *have been*

one would come after me, he must deny
himself and take up his cross and follow me.
25For whoever wants to save his life[a] will lose
it, but whoever loses his life for me will find it.
26What good will it be for a man if he gains
the whole world, yet forfeits his soul? Or
what can a man give in exchange for his
soul? 27For the Son of Man is going to come
in his Father's glory with his angels, and then
he will reward each person according to
what he has done. 28I tell you the truth, some
who are standing here will not taste death
before they see the Son of Man coming in his
kingdom."

The Transfiguration

17 After six days Jesus took with him
Peter, James and John the brother of
James, and led them up a high mountain by
themselves. 2There he was transfigured before them. His face shone like the sun, and
his clothes became as white as the light.
3Just then there appeared before them
Moses and Elijah, talking with Jesus.

4Peter said to Jesus, "Lord, it is good for us
to be here. If you wish, I will put up three
shelters—one for you, one for Moses and
one for Elijah."

5While he was still speaking, a bright cloud
enveloped them, and a voice from the cloud
said, "This is my Son, whom I love; with him
I am well pleased. Listen to him!"

6When the disciples heard this, they fell
facedown to the ground, terrified. 7But Jesus
came and touched them. "Get up," he said.
"Don't be afraid." 8When they looked up,
they saw no one except Jesus.

9As they were coming down the mountain,
Jesus instructed them, "Don't tell anyone
what you have seen, until the Son of Man
has been raised from the dead."

10The disciples asked him, "Why then do
the teachers of the law say that Elijah must
come first?"

11Jesus replied, "To be sure, Elijah comes
and will restore all things. 12But I tell you,
Elijah has already come, and they did not
recognize him, but have done to him everything they wished. In the same way the Son
of Man is going to suffer at their hands."
13Then the disciples understood that he
was talking to them about John the Baptist.

The Healing of a Boy With a Demon

14When they came to the crowd, a man
approached Jesus and knelt before him.
15"Lord, have mercy on my son," he said.
"He has seizures and is suffering greatly. He
often falls into the fire or into the water. 16I
brought him to your disciples, but they could
not heal him."

17"O unbelieving and perverse generation," Jesus replied, "how long shall I stay
with you? How long shall I put up with you?
Bring the boy here to me." 18Jesus rebuked
the demon, and it came out of the boy, and
he was healed from that moment.

19Then the disciples came to Jesus in private and asked, "Why couldn't we drive it
out?"

20He replied, "Because you have so little
faith. I tell you the truth, if you have faith as
small as a mustard seed, you can say to this
mountain, 'Move from here to there' and it
will move. Nothing will be impossible for
you.[b]"

22When they came together in Galilee, he
said to them, "The Son of Man is going to be
betrayed into the hands of men. 23They will
kill him, and on the third day he will be raised
to life." And the disciples were filled with
grief.

The Temple Tax

24After Jesus and his disciples arrived in
Capernaum, the collectors of the two-drachma tax came to Peter and asked, "Doesn't
your teacher pay the temple tax[c]?"

25"Yes, he does," he replied.

When Peter came into the house, Jesus
was the first to speak. "What do you think,
Simon?" he asked. "From whom do the
kings of the earth collect duty and taxes—
from their own sons or from others?"

26"From others," Peter answered.

"Then the sons are exempt," Jesus said to
him. 27"But so that we may not offend them,
go to the lake and throw out your line. Take
the first fish you catch; open its mouth and
you will find a four-drachma coin. Take it and
give it to them for my tax and yours."

[a]25 The Greek word means either *life* or *soul;* also in verse 26. [b]20 Some manuscripts *you.* [21]*But this kind does not go out except by prayer and fasting.* [c]24 Greek *the two drachmas*

The Greatest in the Kingdom of Heaven

18 At that time the disciples came to
Jesus and asked, "Who is the greatest in the kingdom of heaven?"
2He called a little child and had him stand
among them. 3And he said: "I tell you the
truth, unless you change and become like
little children, you will never enter the kingdom of heaven. 4Therefore, whoever humbles himself like this child is the greatest in
the kingdom of heaven.
5"And whoever welcomes a little child like
this in my name welcomes me. 6But if anyone causes one of these little ones who believe in me to sin, it would be better for him to
have a large millstone hung around his neck
and to be drowned in the depths of the sea.
7"Woe to the world because of the things
that cause people to sin! Such things must
come, but woe to the man through whom
they come! 8If your hand or your foot causes
you to sin, cut it off and throw it away. It is
better for you to enter life maimed or crippled
than to have two hands or two feet and be
thrown into eternal fire. 9And if your eye
causes you to sin, gouge it out and throw it
away. It is better for you to enter life with one
eye than to have two eyes and be thrown into
the fire of hell.

The Parable of the Lost Sheep

10"See that you do not look down on one of
these little ones. For I tell you that their angels in heaven always see the face of my
Father in heaven.[a]
12"What do you think? If a man owns a
hundred sheep, and one of them wanders
away, will he not leave the ninety-nine on the
hills and go to look for the one that wandered
off? 13And if he finds it, I tell you the truth, he
is happier about that one sheep than about
the ninety-nine that did not wander off. 14In
the same way your Father in heaven is not
willing that any of these little ones should be
lost.

A Brother Who Sins Against You

15"If your brother sins against you,[b] go and
show him his fault, just between the two of
you. If he listens to you, you have won your
brother over. 16But if he will not listen, take
one or two others along, so that 'every matter
may be established by the testimony of two
or three witnesses.'[c] 17If he refuses to listen
to them, tell it to the church; and if he refuses
to listen even to the church, treat him as you
would a pagan or a tax collector.
18"I tell you the truth, whatever you bind on
earth will be[d] bound in heaven, and whatever you loose on earth will be[d] loosed in
heaven.
19"Again, I tell you that if two of you on
earth agree about anything you ask for, it will
be done for you by my Father in heaven.
20For where two or three come together in
my name, there am I with them."

The Parable of the Unmerciful Servant

21Then Peter came to Jesus and asked,
"Lord, how many times shall I forgive my
brother when he sins against me? Up to
seven times?"
22Jesus answered, "I tell you, not seven
times, but seventy-seven times.[e]
23"Therefore, the kingdom of heaven is
like a king who wanted to settle accounts
with his servants. 24As he began the settlement, a man who owed him ten thousand
talents[f] was brought to him. 25Since he was
not able to pay, the master ordered that he
and his wife and his children and all that he
had be sold to repay the debt.
26"The servant fell on his knees before
him. 'Be patient with me,' he begged, 'and I
will pay back everything.' 27The servant's
master took pity on him, canceled the debt
and let him go.
28"But when that servant went out, he
found one of his fellow servants who owed
him a hundred denarii.[g] He grabbed him and
began to choke him. 'Pay back what you owe
me!' he demanded.
29"His fellow servant fell to his knees and
begged him, 'Be patient with me, and I will
pay you back.'
30"But he refused. Instead, he went off and
had the man thrown into prison until he could
pay the debt. 31When the other servants saw
what had happened, they were greatly distressed and went and told their master
everything that had happened.
32"Then the master called the servant in.
'You wicked servant,' he said, 'I canceled all
that debt of yours because you begged me
to. 33Shouldn't you have had mercy on your

[a] *10* Some manuscripts *heaven.* *11The Son of Man came to save what was lost.* [b] *15* Some manuscripts do not have *against you.* [c] *16* Deut. 19:15 [d] *18* Or *have been* [e] *22* Or *seventy times seven* [f] *24* That is, millions of dollars [g] *28* That is, a few dollars

fellow servant just as I had on you?' 34In anger his master turned him over to the jailers to be tortured, until he should pay back all he owed.

35"This is how my heavenly Father will treat each of you unless you forgive your brother from your heart."

Divorce

19 When Jesus had finished saying these things, he left Galilee and went into the region of Judea to the other side of the Jordan. 2Large crowds followed him, and he healed them there.

3Some Pharisees came to him to test him. They asked, "Is it lawful for a man to divorce his wife for any and every reason?"

4"Haven't you read," he replied, "that at the beginning the Creator 'made them male and female,'[a] 5and said, 'For this reason a man will leave his father and mother and be united to his wife, and the two will become one flesh'[b]? 6So they are no longer two, but one. Therefore what God has joined together, let man not separate."

7"Why then," they asked, "did Moses command that a man give his wife a certificate of divorce and send her away?"

8Jesus replied, "Moses permitted you to divorce your wives because your hearts were hard. But it was not this way from the beginning. 9I tell you that anyone who divorces his wife, except for marital unfaithfulness, and marries another woman commits adultery."

10The disciples said to him, "If this is the situation between a husband and wife, it is better not to marry."

11Jesus replied, "Not everyone can accept this word, but only those to whom it has been given. 12For some are eunuchs because they were born that way; others were made that way by men; and others have renounced marriage[c] because of the kingdom of heaven. The one who can accept this should accept it."

The Little Children and Jesus

13Then little children were brought to Jesus for him to place his hands on them and pray for them. But the disciples rebuked those who brought them.

14Jesus said, "Let the little children come to me, and do not hinder them, for the kingdom of heaven belongs to such as these." 15When he had placed his hands on them, he went on from there.

The Rich Young Man

16Now a man came up to Jesus and asked, "Teacher, what good thing must I do to get eternal life?"

17"Why do you ask me about what is good?" Jesus replied. "There is only One who is good. If you want to enter life, obey the commandments."

18"Which ones?" the man inquired.

Jesus replied, " 'Do not murder, do not commit adultery, do not steal, do not give false testimony, 19honor your father and mother,'[d] and 'love your neighbor as yourself.'[e]"

20"All these I have kept," the young man said. "What do I still lack?"

21Jesus answered, "If you want to be perfect, go, sell your possessions and give to the poor, and you will have treasure in heaven. Then come, follow me."

22When the young man heard this, he went away sad, because he had great wealth.

23Then Jesus said to his disciples, "I tell you the truth, it is hard for a rich man to enter the kingdom of heaven. 24Again I tell you, it is easier for a camel to go through the eye of a needle than for a rich man to enter the kingdom of God."

25When the disciples heard this, they were greatly astonished and asked, "Who then can be saved?"

26Jesus looked at them and said, "With man this is impossible, but with God all things are possible."

27Peter answered him, "We have left everything to follow you! What then will there be for us?"

28Jesus said to them, "I tell you the truth, at the renewal of all things, when the Son of Man sits on his glorious throne, you who have followed me will also sit on twelve thrones, judging the twelve tribes of Israel. 29And everyone who has left houses or brothers or sisters or father or mother[f] or children or fields for my sake will receive a hundred times as much and will inherit eternal life. 30But many who are first will be last, and many who are last will be first.

[a] *4* Gen. 1:27 [b] *5* Gen. 2:24 [c] *12* Or *have made themselves eunuchs* [d] *19* Exodus 20:12-16; Deut. 5:16-20 [e] *19* Lev. 19:18 [f] *29* Some manuscripts *mother or wife*

The Parable of the Workers in the Vineyard

20 "For the kingdom of heaven is like a landowner who went out early in the morning to hire men to work in his vineyard. 2He agreed to pay them a denarius for the day and sent them into his vineyard.

3"About the third hour he went out and saw others standing in the marketplace doing nothing. 4He told them, 'You also go and work in my vineyard, and I will pay you whatever is right.' 5So they went.

"He went out again about the sixth hour and the ninth hour and did the same thing. 6About the eleventh hour he went out and found still others standing around. He asked them, 'Why have you been standing here all day long doing nothing?'

7" 'Because no one has hired us,' they answered.

"He said to them, 'You also go and work in my vineyard.'

8"When evening came, the owner of the vineyard said to his foreman, 'Call the workers and pay them their wages, beginning with the last ones hired and going on to the first.'

9"The workers who were hired about the eleventh hour came and each received a denarius. 10So when those came who were hired first, they expected to receive more. But each one of them also received a denarius. 11When they received it, they began to grumble against the landowner. 12'These men who were hired last worked only one hour,' they said, 'and you have made them equal to us who have borne the burden of the work and the heat of the day.'

13"But he answered one of them, 'Friend, I am not being unfair to you. Didn't you agree to work for a denarius? 14Take your pay and go. I want to give the man who was hired last the same as I gave you. 15Don't I have the right to do what I want with my own money? Or are you envious because I am generous?'

16"So the last will be first, and the first will be last."

Jesus Again Predicts His Death

17Now as Jesus was going up to Jerusalem, he took the twelve disciples aside and said to them, 18"We are going up to Jerusalem, and the Son of Man will be betrayed to the chief priests and the teachers of the law. They will condemn him to death 19and will turn him over to the Gentiles to be mocked and flogged and crucified. On the third day he will be raised to life!"

A Mother's Request

20Then the mother of Zebedee's sons came to Jesus with her sons and, kneeling down, asked a favor of him.

21"What is it you want?" he asked.

She said, "Grant that one of these two sons of mine may sit at your right and the other at your left in your kingdom."

22"You don't know what you are asking," Jesus said to them. "Can you drink the cup I am going to drink?"

"We can," they answered.

23Jesus said to them, "You will indeed drink from my cup, but to sit at my right or left is not for me to grant. These places belong to those for whom they have been prepared by my Father."

24When the ten heard about this, they were indignant with the two brothers. 25Jesus called them together and said, "You know that the rulers of the Gentiles lord it over them, and their high officials exercise authority over them. 26Not so with you. Instead, whoever wants to become great among you must be your servant, 27and whoever wants to be first must be your slave— 28just as the Son of Man did not come to be served, but to serve, and to give his life as a ransom for many."

Two Blind Men Receive Sight

29As Jesus and his disciples were leaving Jericho, a large crowd followed him. 30Two blind men were sitting by the roadside, and when they heard that Jesus was going by, they shouted, "Lord, Son of David, have mercy on us!"

31The crowd rebuked them and told them to be quiet, but they shouted all the louder, "Lord, Son of David, have mercy on us!"

32Jesus stopped and called them. "What do you want me to do for you?" he asked.

33"Lord," they answered, "we want our sight."

34Jesus had compassion on them and touched their eyes. Immediately they received their sight and followed him.

The Triumphal Entry

21 As they approached Jerusalem and came to Bethphage on the Mount of Olives, Jesus sent two disciples, 2saying to them, "Go to the village ahead of you, and at

once you will find a donkey tied there, with
her colt by her. Untie them and bring them to
me. 3If anyone says anything to you, tell him
that the Lord needs them, and he will send
them right away."
4This took place to fulfill what was spoken
through the prophet:

5"Say to the Daughter of Zion,
'See, your king comes to you,
gentle and riding on a donkey,
on a colt, the foal of a donkey.' "[a]

6The disciples went and did as Jesus had
instructed them. 7They brought the donkey
and the colt, placed their cloaks on them,
and Jesus sat on them. 8A very large crowd
spread their cloaks on the road, while others
cut branches from the trees and spread them
on the road. 9The crowds that went ahead of
him and those that followed shouted,

"Hosanna[b] to the Son of David!"

"Blessed is he who comes in the name of
the Lord!"[c]

"Hosanna[b] in the highest!"

10When Jesus entered Jerusalem, the
whole city was stirred and asked, "Who is
this?"
11The crowds answered, "This is Jesus,
the prophet from Nazareth in Galilee."

Jesus at the Temple

12Jesus entered the temple area and
drove out all who were buying and selling
there. He overturned the tables of the money
changers and the benches of those selling
doves. 13"It is written," he said to them, " 'My
house will be called a house of prayer,'[d] but
you are making it a 'den of robbers.'[e]"
14The blind and the lame came to him at
the temple, and he healed them. 15But when
the chief priests and the teachers of the law
saw the wonderful things he did and the children shouting in the temple area, "Hosanna
to the Son of David," they were indignant.
16"Do you hear what these children are
saying?" they asked him.
"Yes," replied Jesus, "have you never
read,

" 'From the lips of children and infants
you have ordained praise'[f]?"

17And he left them and went out of the city
to Bethany, where he spent the night.

The Fig Tree Withers

18Early in the morning, as he was on his
way back to the city, he was hungry. 19See-
ing a fig tree by the road, he went up to it but
found nothing on it except leaves. Then he
said to it, "May you never bear fruit again!"
Immediately the tree withered.
20When the disciples saw this, they were
amazed. "How did the fig tree wither so
quickly?" they asked.
21Jesus replied, "I tell you the truth, if you
have faith and do not doubt, not only can you
do what was done to the fig tree, but also you
can say to this mountain, 'Go, throw yourself
into the sea,' and it will be done. 22If you
believe, you will receive whatever you ask
for in prayer."

The Authority of Jesus Questioned

23Jesus entered the temple courts, and,
while he was teaching, the chief priests and
the elders of the people came to him. "By
what authority are you doing these things?"
they asked. "And who gave you this authority?"
24Jesus replied, "I will also ask you one
question. If you answer me, I will tell you by
what authority I am doing these things.
25John's baptism—where did it come from?
Was it from heaven, or from men?"
They discussed it among themselves and
said, "If we say, 'From heaven,' he will ask,
'Then why didn't you believe him?' 26But if we
say, 'From men'—we are afraid of the
people, for they all hold that John was a
prophet."
27So they answered Jesus, "We don't
know."
Then he said, "Neither will I tell you by
what authority I am doing these things.

The Parable of the Two Sons

28"What do you think? There was a man
who had two sons. He went to the first and
said, 'Son, go and work today in the vineyard.'
29" 'I will not,' he answered, but later he
changed his mind and went.
30"Then the father went to the other son

[a] *5* Zech. 9:9 [b] *9* A Hebrew expression meaning "Save!" which became an exclamation of praise; also in verse 15 [c] *9* Psalm 118:26 [d] *13* Isaiah 56:7 [e] *13* Jer. 7:11 [f] *16* Psalm 8:2

and said the same thing. He answered, 'I will,
sir,' but he did not go.
31"Which of the two did what his father
wanted?"
"The first," they answered.
Jesus said to them, "I tell you the truth, the
tax collectors and the prostitutes are entering the kingdom of God ahead of you. 32For
John came to you to show you the way of
righteousness, and you did not believe him,
but the tax collectors and the prostitutes did.
And even after you saw this, you did not
repent and believe him.

The Parable of the Tenants

33"Listen to another parable: There was a
landowner who planted a vineyard. He put a
wall around it, dug a winepress in it and built
a watchtower. Then he rented the vineyard
to some farmers and went away on a journey. 34When the harvest time approached,
he sent his servants to the tenants to collect
his fruit.
35"The tenants seized his servants; they
beat one, killed another, and stoned a third.
36Then he sent other servants to them, more
than the first time, and the tenants treated
them the same way. 37Last of all, he sent his
son to them. 'They will respect my son,' he
said.
38"But when the tenants saw the son, they
said to each other, 'This is the heir. Come,
let's kill him and take his inheritance.' 39So
they took him and threw him out of the vineyard and killed him.
40"Therefore, when the owner of the vineyard comes, what will he do to those tenants?"
41"He will bring those wretches to a
wretched end," they replied, "and he will rent
the vineyard to other tenants, who will give
him his share of the crop at harvest time."
42Jesus said to them, "Have you never
read in the Scriptures:

" 'The stone the builders rejected
has become the capstone[a];
the Lord has done this,
and it is marvelous in our eyes'[b]?

43"Therefore I tell you that the kingdom of
God will be taken away from you and given to
a people who will produce its fruit. 44He who
falls on this stone will be broken to pieces,
but he on whom it falls will be crushed."[c]
45When the chief priests and the Pharisees heard Jesus' parables, they knew he
was talking about them. 46They looked for a
way to arrest him, but they were afraid of the
crowd because the people held that he was a
prophet.

The Parable of the Wedding Banquet

22 Jesus spoke to them again in parables, saying: 2"The kingdom of
heaven is like a king who prepared a wedding banquet for his son. 3He sent his servants to those who had been invited to the
banquet to tell them to come, but they
refused to come.
4"Then he sent some more servants and
said, 'Tell those who have been invited that I
have prepared my dinner: My oxen and fattened cattle have been butchered, and
everything is ready. Come to the wedding
banquet.'
5"But they paid no attention and went off—
one to his field, another to his business. 6The
rest seized his servants, mistreated them
and killed them. 7The king was enraged. He
sent his army and destroyed those murderers and burned their city.
8"Then he said to his servants, 'The wedding banquet is ready, but those I invited did
not deserve to come. 9Go to the street corners and invite to the banquet anyone you
find.' 10So the servants went out into the
streets and gathered all the people they
could find, both good and bad, and the wedding hall was filled with guests.
11"But when the king came in to see the
guests, he noticed a man there who was not
wearing wedding clothes. 12'Friend,' he
asked, 'how did you get in here without wedding clothes?' The man was speechless.
13"Then the king told the attendants, 'Tie
him hand and foot, and throw him outside,
into the darkness, where there will be weeping and gnashing of teeth.'
14"For many are invited, but few are chosen."

Paying Taxes to Caesar

15Then the Pharisees went out and laid
plans to trap him in his words. 16They sent
their disciples to him along with the Herodians. "Teacher," they said, "we know you are
a man of integrity and that you teach the way
of God in accordance with the truth. You
aren't swayed by men, because you pay no
attention to who they are. 17Tell us then, what

[a]42 Or *cornerstone* [b]42 Psalm 118:22,23 [c]44 Some manuscripts do not have verse 44.

is your opinion? Is it right to pay taxes to
Caesar or not?"
18But Jesus, knowing their evil intent, said,
"You hypocrites, why are you trying to trap
me? 19Show me the coin used for paying the
tax." They brought him a denarius, 20and he
asked them, "Whose portrait is this? And
whose inscription?"
21"Caesar's," they replied.
Then he said to them, "Give to Caesar
what is Caesar's, and to God what is God's."
22When they heard this, they were
amazed. So they left him and went away.

Marriage at the Resurrection

23That same day the Sadducees, who say
there is no resurrection, came to him with a
question. 24"Teacher," they said, "Moses
told us that if a man dies without having children, his brother must marry the widow and
have children for him. 25Now there were
seven brothers among us. The first one married and died, and since he had no children,
he left his wife to his brother. 26The same
thing happened to the second and third
brother, right on down to the seventh. 27Fi-
nally, the woman died. 28Now then, at the
resurrection, whose wife will she be of the
seven, since all of them were married to
her?"
29Jesus replied, "You are in error because
you do not know the Scriptures or the power
of God. 30At the resurrection people will
neither marry nor be given in marriage; they
will be like the angels in heaven. 31But about
the resurrection of the dead—have you not
read what God said to you, 32'I am the God of
Abraham, the God of Isaac, and the God of
Jacob'[a]? He is not the God of the dead but
of the living."
33When the crowds heard this, they were
astonished at his teaching.

The Greatest Commandment

34Hearing that Jesus had silenced the
Sadducees, the Pharisees got together.
35One of them, an expert in the law, tested
him with this question: 36"Teacher, which is
the greatest commandment in the Law?"
37Jesus replied: " 'Love the Lord your God
with all your heart and with all your soul and
with all your mind.'[b] 38This is the first and
greatest commandment. 39And the second is
like it: 'Love your neighbor as yourself.'[c] 40All
the Law and the Prophets hang on these two
commandments."

Whose Son Is the Christ?

41While the Pharisees were gathered together, Jesus asked them, 42"What do you
think about the Christ[d]? Whose son is he?"
"The son of David," they replied.
43He said to them, "How is it then that
David, speaking by the Spirit, calls him
'Lord'? For he says,

44" 'The Lord said to my Lord:
"Sit at my right hand
until I put your enemies
under your feet." '[e]

45If then David calls him 'Lord,' how can he
be his son?" 46No one could say a word in
reply, and from that day on no one dared to
ask him any more questions.

Seven Woes

23 Then Jesus said to the crowds and to
his disciples: 2"The teachers of the
law and the Pharisees sit in Moses' seat. 3So
you must obey them and do everything they
tell you. But do not do what they do, for they
do not practice what they preach. 4They tie
up heavy loads and put them on men's
shoulders, but they themselves are not willing to lift a finger to move them.
5"Everything they do is done for men to
see: They make their phylacteries[f] wide and
the tassels on their garments long; 6they love
the place of honor at banquets and the most
important seats in the synagogues; 7they
love to be greeted in the marketplaces and to
have men call them 'Rabbi.'
8"But you are not to be called 'Rabbi,' for
you have only one Master and you are all
brothers. 9And do not call anyone on earth
'father,' for you have one Father, and he is in
heaven. 10Nor are you to be called 'teacher,'
for you have one Teacher, the Christ.[d] 11The
greatest among you will be your servant.
12For whoever exalts himself will be humbled, and whoever humbles himself will be
exalted.
13"Woe to you, teachers of the law and
Pharisees, you hypocrites! You shut the
kingdom of heaven in men's faces. You

[a] *32* Exodus 3:6 [b] *37* Deut. 6:5 [c] *39* Lev. 19:18 [d] *42,10* Or *Messiah* [e] *44* Psalm 110:1
[f] *5* That is, boxes containing Scripture verses, worn on forehead and arm

yourselves do not enter, nor will you let those
enter who are trying to.[a]

15"Woe to you, teachers of the law and
Pharisees, you hypocrites! You travel over
land and sea to win a single convert, and
when he becomes one, you make him twice
as much a son of hell as you are.

16"Woe to you, blind guides! You say, 'If
anyone swears by the temple, it means nothing; but if anyone swears by the gold of the
temple, he is bound by his oath.' 17You blind
fools! Which is greater: the gold, or the temple that makes the gold sacred? 18You also
say, 'If anyone swears by the altar, it means
nothing; but if anyone swears by the gift on it,
he is bound by his oath.' 19You blind men!
Which is greater: the gift, or the altar that
makes the gift sacred? 20Therefore, he who
swears by the altar swears by it and by
everything on it. 21And he who swears by the
temple swears by it and by the one who
dwells in it. 22And he who swears by heaven
swears by God's throne and by the one who
sits on it.

23"Woe to you, teachers of the law and
Pharisees, you hypocrites! You give a tenth
of your spices—mint, dill and cummin. But
you have neglected the more important matters of the law—justice, mercy and faithfulness. You should have practiced the latter,
without neglecting the former. 24You blind
guides! You strain out a gnat but swallow a
camel.

25"Woe to you, teachers of the law and
Pharisees, you hypocrites! You clean the
outside of the cup and dish, but inside they
are full of greed and self-indulgence. 26Blind
Pharisee! First clean the inside of the cup
and dish, and then the outside also will be
clean.

27"Woe to you, teachers of the law and
Pharisees, you hypocrites! You are like
whitewashed tombs, which look beautiful on
the outside but on the inside are full of dead
men's bones and everything unclean. 28In
the same way, on the outside you appear to
people as righteous but on the inside you are
full of hypocrisy and wickedness.

29"Woe to you, teachers of the law and
Pharisees, you hypocrites! You build tombs
for the prophets and decorate the graves of
the righteous. 30And you say, 'If we had lived
in the days of our forefathers, we would not
have taken part with them in shedding the
blood of the prophets.' 31So you testify
against yourselves that you are the descendants of those who murdered the prophets.
32Fill up, then, the measure of the sin of your
forefathers!

33"You snakes! You brood of vipers! How
will you escape being condemned to hell?
34Therefore I am sending you prophets and
wise men and teachers. Some of them you
will kill and crucify; others you will flog in your
synagogues and pursue from town to town.
35And so upon you will come all the righteous
blood that has been shed on earth, from the
blood of righteous Abel to the blood of Zechariah son of Berekiah, whom you murdered
between the temple and the altar. 36I tell you
the truth, all this will come upon this generation.

37"O Jerusalem, Jerusalem, you who kill
the prophets and stone those sent to you,
how often I have longed to gather your children together, as a hen gathers her chicks
under her wings, but you were not willing.
38Look, your house is left to you desolate.
39For I tell you, you will not see me again until
you say, 'Blessed is he who comes in the
name of the Lord.'[b]"

Signs of the End of the Age

24 Jesus left the temple and was walking away when his disciples came up
to him to call his attention to its buildings.
2"Do you see all these things?" he asked. "I
tell you the truth, not one stone here will be
left on another; every one will be thrown
down."

3As Jesus was sitting on the Mount of Olives, the disciples came to him privately.
"Tell us," they said, "when will this happen,
and what will be the sign of your coming and
of the end of the age?"

4Jesus answered: "Watch out that no one
deceives you. 5For many will come in my
name, claiming, 'I am the Christ,[c]' and will
deceive many. 6You will hear of wars and
rumors of wars, but see to it that you are not
alarmed. Such things must happen, but the
end is still to come. 7Nation will rise against
nation, and kingdom against kingdom. There
will be famines and earthquakes in various
places. 8All these are the beginning of birth
pains.

9"Then you will be handed over to be persecuted and put to death, and you will be

[a]13 Some manuscripts *to.* [14]*Woe to you, teachers of the law and Pharisees, you hypocrites! You devour widows' houses and for a show make lengthy prayers. Therefore you will be punished more severely.*
[b]39 Psalm 118:26 [c]5 Or *Messiah;* also in verse 23

hated by all nations because of me. 10At that
time many will turn away from the faith and
will betray and hate each other, 11and many
false prophets will appear and deceive many
people. 12Because of the increase of wickedness, the love of most will grow cold, 13but he
who stands firm to the end will be saved.
14And this gospel of the kingdom will be
preached in the whole world as a testimony
to all nations, and then the end will come.

15"So when you see standing in the holy
place 'the abomination that causes desolation,'[a] spoken of through the prophet Daniel—let the reader understand— 16then let
those who are in Judea flee to the mountains. 17Let no one on the roof of his house go
down to take anything out of the house. 18Let
no one in the field go back to get his cloak.
19How dreadful it will be in those days for
pregnant women and nursing mothers!
20Pray that your flight will not take place in
winter or on the Sabbath. 21For then there
will be great distress, unequaled from the
beginning of the world until now—and never
to be equaled again. 22If those days had not
been cut short, no one would survive, but for
the sake of the elect those days will be shortened. 23At that time if anyone says to you,
'Look, here is the Christ!' or, 'There he is!' do
not believe it. 24For false Christs and false
prophets will appear and perform great signs
and miracles to deceive even the elect—if
that were possible. 25See, I have told you
ahead of time.

26"So if anyone tells you, 'There he is, out
in the desert,' do not go out; or, 'Here he is, in
the inner rooms,' do not believe it. 27For as
lightning that comes from the east is visible
even in the west, so will be the coming of the
Son of Man. 28Wherever there is a carcass,
there the vultures will gather.

29"Immediately after the distress of those
days

" 'the sun will be darkened,
and the moon will not give its light;
the stars will fall from the sky,
and the heavenly bodies will be
shaken.'[b]

30"At that time the sign of the Son of Man
will appear in the sky, and all the nations of
the earth will mourn. They will see the Son of
Man coming on the clouds of the sky, with
power and great glory. 31And he will send his
angels with a loud trumpet call, and they will
gather his elect from the four winds, from one
end of the heavens to the other.

32"Now learn this lesson from the fig tree:
As soon as its twigs get tender and its leaves
come out, you know that summer is near.
33Even so, when you see all these things,
you know that it[c] is near, right at the door. 34I
tell you the truth, this generation[d] will certainly not pass away until all these things
have happened. 35Heaven and earth will
pass away, but my words will never pass
away.

The Day and Hour Unknown

36"No one knows about that day or hour,
not even the angels in heaven, nor the Son,[e]
but only the Father. 37As it was in the days of
Noah, so it will be at the coming of the Son of
Man. 38For in the days before the flood,
people were eating and drinking, marrying
and giving in marriage, up to the day Noah
entered the ark; 39and they knew nothing
about what would happen until the flood
came and took them all away. That is how it
will be at the coming of the Son of Man.
40Two men will be in the field; one will be
taken and the other left. 41Two women will be
grinding with a hand mill; one will be taken
and the other left.

42"Therefore keep watch, because you do
not know on what day your Lord will come.
43But understand this: If the owner of the
house had known at what time of night the
thief was coming, he would have kept watch
and would not have let his house be broken
into. 44So you also must be ready, because
the Son of Man will come at an hour when
you do not expect him.

45"Who then is the faithful and wise servant, whom the master has put in charge of
the servants in his household to give them
their food at the proper time? 46It will be good
for that servant whose master finds him doing so when he returns. 47I tell you the truth,
he will put him in charge of all his possessions. 48But suppose that servant is wicked
and says to himself, 'My master is staying
away a long time,' 49and he then begins to
beat his fellow servants and to eat and drink
with drunkards. 50The master of that servant
will come on a day when he does not expect
him and at an hour he is not aware of. 51He
will cut him to pieces and assign him a place

[a] *15* Daniel 9:27; 11:31; 12:11 [b] *29* Isaiah 13:10; 34:4 [c] *33* Or *he* [d] *34* Or *race* [e] *36* Some manuscripts do not have *nor the Son.*

with the hypocrites, where there will be
weeping and gnashing of teeth.

The Parable of the Ten Virgins

25 "At that time the kingdom of heaven
will be like ten virgins who took their
lamps and went out to meet the bridegroom.
2Five of them were foolish and five were
wise. 3The foolish ones took their lamps but
did not take any oil with them. 4The wise,
however, took oil in jars along with their
lamps. 5The bridegroom was a long time in
coming, and they all became drowsy and fell
asleep.
6"At midnight the cry rang out: 'Here's the
bridegroom! Come out to meet him!'
7"Then all the virgins woke up and trimmed
their lamps. 8The foolish ones said to the
wise, 'Give us some of your oil; our lamps are
going out.'
9" 'No,' they replied, 'there may not be
enough for both us and you. Instead, go to
those who sell oil and buy some for yourselves.'
10"But while they were on their way to buy
the oil, the bridegroom arrived. The virgins
who were ready went in with him to the wedding banquet. And the door was shut.
11"Later the others also came. 'Sir! Sir!'
they said. 'Open the door for us!'
12"But he replied, 'I tell you the truth, I don't
know you.'
13"Therefore keep watch, because you do
not know the day or the hour.

The Parable of the Talents

14"Again, it will be like a man going on a
journey, who called his servants and entrusted his property to them. 15To one he
gave five talents[a] of money, to another two
talents, and to another one talent, each according to his ability. Then he went on his
journey. 16The man who had received the
five talents went at once and put his money
to work and gained five more. 17So also, the
one with the two talents gained two more.
18But the man who had received the one
talent went off, dug a hole in the ground and
hid his master's money.
19"After a long time the master of those
servants returned and settled accounts with
them. 20The man who had received the five
talents brought the other five. 'Master,' he
said, 'you entrusted me with five talents.
See, I have gained five more.'
21"His master replied, 'Well done, good
and faithful servant! You have been faithful
with a few things; I will put you in charge of
many things. Come and share your master's
happiness!'
22"The man with the two talents also came.
'Master,' he said, 'you entrusted me with two
talents; see, I have gained two more.'
23"His master replied, 'Well done, good
and faithful servant! You have been faithful
with a few things; I will put you in charge of
many things. Come and share your master's
happiness!'
24"Then the man who had received the
one talent came. 'Master,' he said, 'I knew
that you are a hard man, harvesting where
you have not sown and gathering where you
have not scattered seed. 25So I was afraid
and went out and hid your talent in the
ground. See, here is what belongs to you.'
26"His master replied, 'You wicked, lazy
servant! So you knew that I harvest where I
have not sown and gather where I have not
scattered seed? 27Well then, you should
have put my money on deposit with the
bankers, so that when I returned I would
have received it back with interest.
28" 'Take the talent from him and give it to
the one who has the ten talents. 29For everyone who has will be given more, and he will
have an abundance. Whoever does not
have, even what he has will be taken from
him. 30And throw that worthless servant outside, into the darkness, where there will be
weeping and gnashing of teeth.'

The Sheep and the Goats

31"When the Son of Man comes in his
glory, and all the angels with him, he will sit
on his throne in heavenly glory. 32All the nations will be gathered before him, and he will
separate the people one from another as a
shepherd separates the sheep from the
goats. 33He will put the sheep on his right and
the goats on his left.
34"Then the King will say to those on his
right, 'Come, you who are blessed by my
Father; take your inheritance, the kingdom
prepared for you since the creation of the
world. 35For I was hungry and you gave me
something to eat, I was thirsty and you gave
me something to drink, I was a stranger and
you invited me in, 36I needed clothes and you
clothed me, I was sick and you looked after
me, I was in prison and you came to visit me.'

[a] *15* A talent was worth more than a thousand dollars.

37"Then the righteous will answer him,
'Lord, when did we see you hungry and feed
you, or thirsty and give you something to
drink? 38When did we see you a stranger and
invite you in, or needing clothes and clothe
you? 39When did we see you sick or in prison
and go to visit you?'

40"The King will reply, 'I tell you the truth,
whatever you did for one of the least of these
brothers of mine, you did for me.'

41"Then he will say to those on his left,
'Depart from me, you who are cursed, into
the eternal fire prepared for the devil and his
angels. 42For I was hungry and you gave me
nothing to eat, I was thirsty and you gave me
nothing to drink, 43I was a stranger and you
did not invite me in, I needed clothes and you
did not clothe me, I was sick and in prison
and you did not look after me.'

44"They also will answer, 'Lord, when did
we see you hungry or thirsty or a stranger or
needing clothes or sick or in prison, and did
not help you?'

45"He will reply, 'I tell you the truth, whatever you did not do for one of the least of
these, you did not do for me.'

46"Then they will go away to eternal punishment, but the righteous to eternal life."

The Plot Against Jesus

26 When Jesus had finished saying all
these things, he said to his disciples,
2"As you know, the Passover is two days
away—and the Son of Man will be handed
over to be crucified."

3Then the chief priests and the elders of
the people assembled in the palace of the
high priest, whose name was Caiaphas,
4and they plotted to arrest Jesus in some sly
way and kill him. 5"But not during the Feast,"
they said, "or there may be a riot among the
people."

Jesus Anointed at Bethany

6While Jesus was in Bethany in the home
of a man known as Simon the Leper, 7a
woman came to him with an alabaster jar of
very expensive perfume, which she poured
on his head as he was reclining at the table.

8When the disciples saw this, they were
indignant. "Why this waste?" they asked.
9"This perfume could have been sold at a
high price and the money given to the poor."

10Aware of this, Jesus said to them, "Why
are you bothering this woman? She has
done a beautiful thing to me. 11The poor you
will always have with you, but you will not
always have me. 12When she poured this
perfume on my body, she did it to prepare me
for burial. 13I tell you the truth, wherever this
gospel is preached throughout the world,
what she has done will also be told, in memory of her."

Judas Agrees to Betray Jesus

14Then one of the Twelve—the one called
Judas Iscariot—went to the chief priests
15and asked, "What are you willing to give
me if I hand him over to you?" So they counted out for him thirty silver coins. 16From then
on Judas watched for an opportunity to hand
him over.

The Lord's Supper

17On the first day of the Feast of Unleavened Bread, the disciples came to Jesus and
asked, "Where do you want us to make
preparations for you to eat the Passover?"

18He replied, "Go into the city to a certain
man and tell him, 'The Teacher says: My
appointed time is near. I am going to celebrate the Passover with my disciples at your
house.' " 19So the disciples did as Jesus had
directed them and prepared the Passover.

20When evening came, Jesus was reclining at the table with the Twelve. 21And while
they were eating, he said, "I tell you the truth,
one of you will betray me."

22They were very sad and began to say to
him one after the other, "Surely not I, Lord?"

23Jesus replied, "The one who has dipped
his hand into the bowl with me will betray me.
24The Son of Man will go just as it is written
about him. But woe to that man who betrays
the Son of Man! It would be better for him if
he had not been born."

25Then Judas, the one who would betray
him, said, "Surely not I, Rabbi?"

Jesus answered, "Yes, it is you."[a]

26While they were eating, Jesus took
bread, gave thanks and broke it, and gave it
to his disciples, saying, "Take and eat; this is
my body."

27Then he took the cup, gave thanks and
offered it to them, saying, "Drink from it, all of
you. 28This is my blood of the[b] covenant,
which is poured out for many for the forgiveness of sins. 29I tell you, I will not drink of this
fruit of the vine from now on until that day

[a]25 Or *"You yourself have said it"* [b]28 Some manuscripts *the new*

when I drink it anew with you in my Father's
kingdom."
30When they had sung a hymn, they went
out to the Mount of Olives.

Jesus Predicts Peter's Denial

31Then Jesus told them, "This very night
you will all fall away on account of me, for it is
written:

" 'I will strike the shepherd,
and the sheep of the flock will be
scattered.'[a]

32But after I have risen, I will go ahead of you
into Galilee."
33Peter replied, "Even if all fall away on
account of you, I never will."
34"I tell you the truth," Jesus answered,
"this very night, before the rooster crows,
you will disown me three times."
35But Peter declared, "Even if I have to die
with you, I will never disown you." And all the
other disciples said the same.

Gethsemane

36Then Jesus went with his disciples to a
place called Gethsemane, and he said to
them, "Sit here while I go over there and
pray." 37He took Peter and the two sons of
Zebedee along with him, and he began to be
sorrowful and troubled. 38Then he said to
them, "My soul is overwhelmed with sorrow
to the point of death. Stay here and keep
watch with me."
39Going a little farther, he fell with his face
to the ground and prayed, "My Father, if it is
possible, may this cup be taken from me. Yet
not as I will, but as you will."
40Then he returned to his disciples and
found them sleeping. "Could you men not
keep watch with me for one hour?" he asked
Peter. 41"Watch and pray so that you will not
fall into temptation. The spirit is willing, but
the body is weak."
42He went away a second time and
prayed, "My Father, if it is not possible for
this cup to be taken away unless I drink it,
may your will be done."
43When he came back, he again found
them sleeping, because their eyes were
heavy. 44So he left them and went away once
more and prayed the third time, saying the
same thing.
45Then he returned to the disciples and
said to them, "Are you still sleeping and resting? Look, the hour is near, and the Son of
Man is betrayed into the hands of sinners.
46Rise, let us go! Here comes my betrayer!"

Jesus Arrested

47While he was still speaking, Judas, one
of the Twelve, arrived. With him was a large
crowd armed with swords and clubs, sent
from the chief priests and the elders of the
people. 48Now the betrayer had arranged a
signal with them: "The one I kiss is the man;
arrest him." 49Going at once to Jesus, Judas
said, "Greetings, Rabbi!" and kissed him.
50Jesus replied, "Friend, do what you
came for."[b]
Then the men stepped forward, seized
Jesus and arrested him. 51With that, one of
Jesus' companions reached for his sword,
drew it out and struck the servant of the high
priest, cutting off his ear.
52"Put your sword back in its place," Jesus
said to him, "for all who draw the sword will
die by the sword. 53Do you think I cannot call
on my Father, and he will at once put at my
disposal more than twelve legions of angels?
54But how then would the Scriptures be fulfilled that say it must happen in this way?"
55At that time Jesus said to the crowd,
"Am I leading a rebellion, that you have
come out with swords and clubs to capture
me? Every day I sat in the temple courts
teaching, and you did not arrest me. 56But
this has all taken place that the writings of the
prophets might be fulfilled." Then all the disciples deserted him and fled.

Before the Sanhedrin

57Those who had arrested Jesus took him
to Caiaphas, the high priest, where the
teachers of the law and the elders had assembled. 58But Peter followed him at a distance, right up to the courtyard of the high
priest. He entered and sat down with the
guards to see the outcome.
59The chief priests and the whole Sanhedrin were looking for false evidence against
Jesus so that they could put him to death.
60But they did not find any, though many
false witnesses came forward.
Finally two came forward 61and declared,
"This fellow said, 'I am able to destroy the
temple of God and rebuild it in three days.' "
62Then the high priest stood up and said to
Jesus, "Are you not going to answer? What
is this testimony that these men are bringing

[a] *31* Zech. 13:7 [b] *50* Or *"Friend, why have you come?"*

against you?" 63But Jesus remained silent.
The high priest said to him, "I charge you
under oath by the living God: Tell us if you
are the Christ,[a] the Son of God."
64"Yes, it is as you say," Jesus replied.
"But I say to all of you: In the future you will
see the Son of Man sitting at the right hand of
the Mighty One and coming on the clouds of
heaven."
65Then the high priest tore his clothes and
said, "He has spoken blasphemy! Why do
we need any more witnesses? Look, now
you have heard the blasphemy. 66What do
you think?"
"He is worthy of death," they answered.
67Then they spit in his face and struck him
with their fists. Others slapped him 68and
said, "Prophesy to us, Christ. Who hit you?"

Peter Disowns Jesus

69Now Peter was sitting out in the courtyard, and a servant girl came to him. "You
also were with Jesus of Galilee," she said.
70But he denied it before them all. "I don't
know what you're talking about," he said.
71Then he went out to the gateway, where
another girl saw him and said to the people
there, "This fellow was with Jesus of Nazareth."
72He denied it again, with an oath: "I don't
know the man!"
73After a little while, those standing there
went up to Peter and said, "Surely you are
one of them, for your accent gives you
away."
74Then he began to call down curses on
himself and he swore to them, "I don't know
the man!"
Immediately a rooster crowed. 75Then Peter remembered the word Jesus had spoken:
"Before the rooster crows, you will disown
me three times." And he went outside and
wept bitterly.

Judas Hangs Himself

27 Early in the morning, all the chief
priests and the elders of the people
came to the decision to put Jesus to death.
2They bound him, led him away and handed
him over to Pilate, the governor.
3When Judas, who had betrayed him, saw
that Jesus was condemned, he was seized
with remorse and returned the thirty silver
coins to the chief priests and the elders. 4"I
have sinned," he said, "for I have betrayed
innocent blood."
"What is that to us?" they replied. "That's
your responsibility."
5So Judas threw the money into the temple
and left. Then he went away and hanged
himself.
6The chief priests picked up the coins and
said, "It is against the law to put this into the
treasury, since it is blood money." 7So they
decided to use the money to buy the potter's
field as a burial place for foreigners. 8That is
why it has been called the Field of Blood to
this day. 9Then what was spoken by Jeremiah the prophet was fulfilled: "They took
the thirty silver coins, the price set on him by
the people of Israel, 10and they used them to
buy the potter's field, as the Lord commanded me."[b]

Jesus Before Pilate

11Meanwhile Jesus stood before the governor, and the governor asked him, "Are you
the king of the Jews?"
"Yes, it is as you say," Jesus replied.
12When he was accused by the chief
priests and the elders, he gave no answer.
13Then Pilate asked him, "Don't you hear the
testimony they are bringing against you?"
14But Jesus made no reply, not even to a
single charge—to the great amazement of
the governor.
15Now it was the governor's custom at the
Feast to release a prisoner chosen by the
crowd. 16At that time they had a notorious
prisoner, called Barabbas. 17So when the
crowd had gathered, Pilate asked them,
"Which one do you want me to release to
you: Barabbas, or Jesus who is called
Christ?" 18For he knew it was out of envy that
they had handed Jesus over to him.
19While Pilate was sitting on the judge's
seat, his wife sent him this message: "Don't
have anything to do with that innocent man,
for I have suffered a great deal today in a
dream because of him."
20But the chief priests and the elders persuaded the crowd to ask for Barabbas and to
have Jesus executed.
21"Which of the two do you want me to
release to you?" asked the governor.
"Barabbas," they answered.
22"What shall I do, then, with Jesus who is
called Christ?" Pilate asked.

[a]63 Or *Messiah*; also in verse 68 [b]10 See Zech. 11:12,13; Jer. 19:1-13; 32:6-9.

They all answered, "Crucify him!"

23"Why? What crime has he committed?" asked Pilate.

But they shouted all the louder, "Crucify him!"

24When Pilate saw that he was getting nowhere, but that instead an uproar was starting, he took water and washed his hands in front of the crowd. "I am innocent of this man's blood," he said. "It is your responsibility!"

25All the people answered, "Let his blood be on us and on our children!"

26Then he released Barabbas to them. But he had Jesus flogged, and handed him over to be crucified.

The Soldiers Mock Jesus

27Then the governor's soldiers took Jesus into the Praetorium and gathered the whole company of soldiers around him. 28They stripped him and put a scarlet robe on him, 29and then twisted together a crown of thorns and set it on his head. They put a staff in his right hand and knelt in front of him and mocked him. "Hail, king of the Jews!" they said. 30They spit on him, and took the staff and struck him on the head again and again. 31After they had mocked him, they took off the robe and put his own clothes on him. Then they led him away to crucify him.

The Crucifixion

32As they were going out, they met a man from Cyrene, named Simon, and they forced him to carry the cross. 33They came to a place called Golgotha (which means The Place of the Skull). 34There they offered Jesus wine to drink, mixed with gall; but after tasting it, he refused to drink it. 35When they had crucified him, they divided up his clothes by casting lots.[a] 36And sitting down, they kept watch over him there. 37Above his head they placed the written charge against him: THIS IS JESUS, THE KING OF THE JEWS. 38Two robbers were crucified with him, one on his right and one on his left. 39Those who passed by hurled insults at him, shaking their heads 40and saying, "You who are going to destroy the temple and build it in three days, save yourself! Come down from the cross, if you are the Son of God!"

41In the same way the chief priests, the teachers of the law and the elders mocked him. 42"He saved others," they said, "but he can't save himself! He's the King of Israel! Let him come down now from the cross, and we will believe in him. 43He trusts in God. Let God rescue him now if he wants him, for he said, 'I am the Son of God.' " 44In the same way the robbers who were crucified with him also heaped insults on him.

The Death of Jesus

45From the sixth hour until the ninth hour darkness came over all the land. 46About the ninth hour Jesus cried out in a loud voice, *"Eloi, Eloi,[b] lama sabachthani?"*—which means, "My God, my God, why have you forsaken me?"[c]

47When some of those standing there heard this, they said, "He's calling Elijah."

48Immediately one of them ran and got a sponge. He filled it with wine vinegar, put it on a stick, and offered it to Jesus to drink. 49The rest said, "Now leave him alone. Let's see if Elijah comes to save him."

50And when Jesus had cried out again in a loud voice, he gave up his spirit.

51At that moment the curtain of the temple was torn in two from top to bottom. The earth shook and the rocks split. 52The tombs broke open and the bodies of many holy people who had died were raised to life. 53They came out of the tombs, and after Jesus' resurrection they went into the holy city and appeared to many people.

54When the centurion and those with him who were guarding Jesus saw the earthquake and all that had happened, they were terrified, and exclaimed, "Surely he was the Son[d] of God!"

55Many women were there, watching from a distance. They had followed Jesus from Galilee to care for his needs. 56Among them were Mary Magdalene, Mary the mother of James and Joses, and the mother of Zebedee's sons.

The Burial of Jesus

57As evening approached, there came a rich man from Arimathea, named Joseph, who had himself become a disciple of Jesus. 58Going to Pilate, he asked for Jesus' body, and Pilate ordered that it be given to him. 59Joseph took the body, wrapped it in a clean linen cloth, 60and placed it in his own new tomb that he had cut out of the rock. He

[a]35 A few late manuscripts *lots that the word spoken by the prophet might be fulfilled: "They divided my garments among themselves and cast lots for my clothing"* (Psalm 22:18) [b]46 Some manuscripts *Eli, Eli* [c]46 Psalm 22:1 [d]54 Or *a son*

rolled a big stone in front of the entrance to
the tomb and went away. [61]Mary Magdalene
and the other Mary were sitting there opposite the tomb.

The Guard at the Tomb

[62]The next day, the one after Preparation
Day, the chief priests and the Pharisees
went to Pilate. [63]"Sir," they said, "we remember that while he was still alive that deceiver
said, 'After three days I will rise again.' [64]So
give the order for the tomb to be made secure until the third day. Otherwise, his disciples may come and steal the body and tell
the people that he has been raised from the
dead. This last deception will be worse than
the first."

[65]"Take a guard," Pilate answered. "Go,
make the tomb as secure as you know how."
[66]So they went and made the tomb secure by
putting a seal on the stone and posting the
guard.

The Resurrection

28 After the Sabbath, at dawn on the
first day of the week, Mary Magdalene and the other Mary went to look at the
tomb.

[2]There was a violent earthquake, for an
angel of the Lord came down from heaven
and, going to the tomb, rolled back the stone
and sat on it. [3]His appearance was like lightning, and his clothes were white as snow.
[4]The guards were so afraid of him that they
shook and became like dead men.

[5]The angel said to the women, "Do not be
afraid, for I know that you are looking for
Jesus, who was crucified. [6]He is not here; he
has risen, just as he said. Come and see the
place where he lay. [7]Then go quickly and tell
his disciples: 'He has risen from the dead
and is going ahead of you into Galilee. There
you will see him.' Now I have told you."

[8]So the women hurried away from the
tomb, afraid yet filled with joy, and ran to tell
his disciples. [9]Suddenly Jesus met them.
"Greetings," he said. They came to him,
clasped his feet and worshiped him. [10]Then
Jesus said to them, "Do not be afraid. Go
and tell my brothers to go to Galilee; there
they will see me."

The Guards' Report

[11]While the women were on their way,
some of the guards went into the city and
reported to the chief priests everything that
had happened. [12]When the chief priests had
met with the elders and devised a plan, they
gave the soldiers a large sum of money,
[13]telling them, "You are to say, 'His disciples
came during the night and stole him away
while we were asleep.' [14]If this report gets to
the governor, we will satisfy him and keep
you out of trouble." [15]So the soldiers took the
money and did as they were instructed. And
this story has been widely circulated among
the Jews to this very day.

The Great Commission

[16]Then the eleven disciples went to Galilee, to the mountain where Jesus had told
them to go. [17]When they saw him, they worshiped him; but some doubted. [18]Then Jesus
came to them and said, "All authority in
heaven and on earth has been given to me.
[19]Therefore go and make disciples of all nations, baptizing them in[a] the name of the
Father and of the Son and of the Holy Spirit,
[20]and teaching them to obey everything I
have commanded you. And surely I am with
you always, to the very end of the age."

[a]19 Or *into;* see Acts 8:16; 19:5; Romans 6:3; 1 Cor. 1:13; 10:2 and Gal. 3:27.

Mark

Introduction:

Mark, the author of this Gospel, probably was the first to write down the events of Jesus' life. It is believed that he is the same person who worked for many years as a missionary with Paul and Barnabas.

The book of Mark, which stresses facts and actions rather than themes or topics, is the most exciting account of the life of Christ among the Gospels. Although it is the shortest of the four Gospels, it is often the most detailed. From the beginning Mark tells the stories of Christ's ministry, especially his miracles.

Mark shows Jesus as a man of action and authority. He spends one third of the book telling the events of Christ's last week on earth, ending with the Savior's death and resurrection.

Outline of contents:

Background and preparation (1:1–13)
Ministry of healing and teaching (1:14–8:26)
Jesus and his disciples (8:27–10:45)
Jericho and Jerusalem (10:46–13:37)
Passion and death of Christ (14:1–15:47)
The resurrected Christ and his followers (16:1–20)

John the Baptist Prepares the Way

1 The beginning of the gospel about Jesus Christ, the Son of God.[a]

2It is written in Isaiah the prophet:

"I will send my messenger ahead of you,
who will prepare your way"[b]—
3"a voice of one calling in the desert,
'Prepare the way for the Lord,
make straight paths for him.' "[c]

4And so John came, baptizing in the desert region and preaching a baptism of repentance for the forgiveness of sins. 5The whole Judean countryside and all the people of Jerusalem went out to him. Confessing their sins, they were baptized by him in the Jordan River. 6John wore clothing made of camel's hair, with a leather belt around his waist, and he ate locusts and wild honey. 7And this was his message: "After me will come one more powerful than I, the thongs of whose sandals I am not worthy to stoop down and untie. 8I baptize you with[d] water, but he will baptize you with the Holy Spirit."

The Baptism and Temptation of Jesus

9At that time Jesus came from Nazareth in Galilee and was baptized by John in the Jordan. 10As Jesus was coming up out of the water, he saw heaven being torn open and the Spirit descending on him like a dove. 11And a voice came from heaven: "You are my Son, whom I love; with you I am well pleased."

12At once the Spirit sent him out into the desert, 13and he was in the desert forty days, being tempted by Satan. He was with the wild animals, and angels attended him.

The Calling of the First Disciples

14After John was put in prison, Jesus went into Galilee, proclaiming the good news of God. 15"The time has come," he said. "The kingdom of God is near. Repent and believe the good news!"

16As Jesus walked beside the Sea of Galilee, he saw Simon and his brother Andrew casting a net into the lake, for they were fishermen. 17"Come, follow me," Jesus said, "and I will make you fishers of men." 18At

[a] 1 Some manuscripts do not have *the Son of God.* [b] 2 Mal. 3:1 [c] 3 Isaiah 40:3 [d] 8 Or *in*

once they left their nets and followed him.

19When he had gone a little farther, he saw James son of Zebedee and his brother John in a boat, preparing their nets. 20Without delay he called them, and they left their father Zebedee in the boat with the hired men and followed him.

Jesus Drives Out an Evil Spirit

21They went to Capernaum, and when the Sabbath came, Jesus went into the synagogue and began to teach. 22The people were amazed at his teaching, because he taught them as one who had authority, not as the teachers of the law. 23Just then a man in their synagogue who was possessed by an evil[a] spirit cried out, 24"What do you want with us, Jesus of Nazareth? Have you come to destroy us? I know who you are—the Holy One of God!"

25"Be quiet!" said Jesus sternly. "Come out of him!" 26The evil spirit shook the man violently and came out of him with a shriek.

27The people were all so amazed that they asked each other, "What is this? A new teaching—and with authority! He even gives orders to evil spirits and they obey him." 28News about him spread quickly over the whole region of Galilee.

Jesus Heals Many

29As soon as they left the synagogue, they went with James and John to the home of Simon and Andrew. 30Simon's mother-in-law was in bed with a fever, and they told Jesus about her. 31So he went to her, took her hand and helped her up. The fever left her and she began to wait on them.

32That evening after sunset the people brought to Jesus all the sick and demon-possessed. 33The whole town gathered at the door, 34and Jesus healed many who had various diseases. He also drove out many demons, but he would not let the demons speak because they knew who he was.

Jesus Prays in a Solitary Place

35Very early in the morning, while it was still dark, Jesus got up, left the house and went off to a solitary place, where he prayed. 36Simon and his companions went to look for him, 37and when they found him, they exclaimed: "Everyone is looking for you!"

38Jesus replied, "Let us go somewhere else—to the nearby villages—so I can preach there also. That is why I have come." 39So he traveled throughout Galilee, preaching in their synagogues and driving out demons.

A Man With Leprosy

40A man with leprosy[b] came to him and begged him on his knees, "If you are willing, you can make me clean."

41Filled with compassion, Jesus reached out his hand and touched the man. "I am willing," he said. "Be clean!" 42Immediately the leprosy left him and he was cured.

43Jesus sent him away at once with a strong warning: 44"See that you don't tell this to anyone. But go, show yourself to the priest and offer the sacrifices that Moses commanded for your cleansing, as a testimony to them." 45Instead he went out and began to talk freely, spreading the news. As a result, Jesus could no longer enter a town openly but stayed outside in lonely places. Yet the people still came to him from everywhere.

Jesus Heals a Paralytic

2 A few days later, when Jesus again entered Capernaum, the people heard that he had come home. 2So many gathered that there was no room left, not even outside the door, and he preached the word to them. 3Some men came, bringing to him a paralytic, carried by four of them. 4Since they could not get him to Jesus because of the crowd, they made an opening in the roof above Jesus and, after digging through it, lowered the mat the paralyzed man was lying on. 5When Jesus saw their faith, he said to the paralytic, "Son, your sins are forgiven."

6Now some teachers of the law were sitting there, thinking to themselves, 7"Why does this fellow talk like that? He's blaspheming! Who can forgive sins but God alone?"

8Immediately Jesus knew in his spirit that this was what they were thinking in their hearts, and he said to them, "Why are you thinking these things? 9Which is easier: to say to the paralytic, 'Your sins are forgiven,' or to say, 'Get up, take your mat and walk'? 10But that you may know that the Son of Man has authority on earth to forgive sins . . . ." He said to the paralytic, 11"I tell you, get up, take your mat and go home." 12He got up,

[a]23 Greek *unclean*; also in verses 26 and 27

[b]40 The Greek word was used for various diseases affecting the skin—not necessarily leprosy.

took his mat and walked out in full view of
them all. This amazed everyone and they
praised God, saying, "We have never seen
anything like this!"

The Calling of Levi

13Once again Jesus went out beside the
lake. A large crowd came to him, and he
began to teach them. 14As he walked along,
he saw Levi son of Alphaeus sitting at the tax
collector's booth. "Follow me," Jesus told
him, and Levi got up and followed him.

15While Jesus was having dinner at Levi's
house, many tax collectors and "sinners"
were eating with him and his disciples, for
there were many who followed him. 16When
the teachers of the law who were Pharisees
saw him eating with the "sinners" and tax
collectors, they asked his disciples: "Why
does he eat with tax collectors and 'sinners'?"

17On hearing this, Jesus said to them, "It is
not the healthy who need a doctor, but the
sick. I have not come to call the righteous,
but sinners."

Jesus Questioned About Fasting

18Now John's disciples and the Pharisees
were fasting. Some people came and asked
Jesus, "How is it that John's disciples and
the disciples of the Pharisees are fasting, but
yours are not?"

19Jesus answered, "How can the guests of
the bridegroom fast while he is with them?
They cannot, so long as they have him with
them. 20But the time will come when the
bridegroom will be taken from them, and on
that day they will fast.

21"No one sews a patch of unshrunk cloth
on an old garment. If he does, the new piece
will pull away from the old, making the tear
worse. 22And no one pours new wine into old
wineskins. If he does, the wine will burst the
skins, and both the wine and the wineskins
will be ruined. No, he pours new wine into
new wineskins."

Lord of the Sabbath

23One Sabbath Jesus was going through
the grainfields, and as his disciples walked
along, they began to pick some heads of
grain. 24The Pharisees said to him, "Look,
why are they doing what is unlawful on the
Sabbath?"

25He answered, "Have you never read
what David did when he and his companions
were hungry and in need? 26In the days of
Abiathar the high priest, he entered the
house of God and ate the consecrated
bread, which is lawful only for priests to eat.
And he also gave some to his companions."

27Then he said to them, "The Sabbath was
made for man, not man for the Sabbath. 28So
the Son of Man is Lord even of the Sabbath."

3 Another time he went into the synagogue, and a man with a shriveled hand
was there. 2Some of them were looking for a
reason to accuse Jesus, so they watched
him closely to see if he would heal him on the
Sabbath. 3Jesus said to the man with the
shriveled hand, "Stand up in front of everyone."

4Then Jesus asked them, "Which is lawful
on the Sabbath: to do good or to do evil, to
save life or to kill?" But they remained silent.

5He looked around at them in anger and,
deeply distressed at their stubborn hearts,
said to the man, "Stretch out your hand." He
stretched it out, and his hand was completely
restored. 6Then the Pharisees went out and
began to plot with the Herodians how they
might kill Jesus.

Crowds Follow Jesus

7Jesus withdrew with his disciples to the
lake, and a large crowd from Galilee followed. 8When they heard all he was doing,
many people came to him from Judea,
Jerusalem, Idumea, and the regions across
the Jordan and around Tyre and Sidon. 9Be-
cause of the crowd he told his disciples to
have a small boat ready for him, to keep the
people from crowding him. 10For he had
healed many, so that those with diseases
were pushing forward to touch him. 11When-
ever the evil[a] spirits saw him, they fell down
before him and cried out, "You are the Son of
God." 12But he gave them strict orders not to
tell who he was.

The Appointing of the Twelve Apostles

13Jesus went up on a mountainside and
called to him those he wanted, and they
came to him. 14He appointed twelve—designating them apostles[b]—that they might be
with him and that he might send them out to
preach 15and to have authority to drive out
demons. 16These are the twelve he appointed: Simon (to whom he gave the name
Peter); 17James son of Zebedee and his

[a] *11* Greek *unclean*; also in verse 30 [b] *14* Some manuscripts do not have *designating them apostles*.

brother John (to them he gave the name
Boanerges, which means Sons of Thunder);
18Andrew, Philip, Bartholomew, Matthew,
Thomas, James son of Alphaeus, Thaddaeus, Simon the Zealot 19and Judas Iscariot, who betrayed him.

Jesus and Beelzebub

20Then Jesus entered a house, and again
a crowd gathered, so that he and his disciples were not even able to eat. 21When his
family heard about this, they went to take
charge of him, for they said, "He is out of his
mind."

22And the teachers of the law who came
down from Jerusalem said, "He is possessed by Beelzebub[a]! By the prince of demons he is driving out demons."

23So Jesus called them and spoke to them
in parables: "How can Satan drive out Satan? 24If a kingdom is divided against itself,
that kingdom cannot stand. 25If a house is
divided against itself, that house cannot
stand. 26And if Satan opposes himself and is
divided, he cannot stand; his end has come.
27In fact, no one can enter a strong man's
house and carry off his possessions unless
he first ties up the strong man. Then he can
rob his house. 28I tell you the truth, all the sins
and blasphemies of men will be forgiven
them. 29But whoever blasphemes against
the Holy Spirit will never be forgiven; he is
guilty of an eternal sin."

30He said this because they were saying,
"He has an evil spirit."

Jesus' Mother and Brothers

31Then Jesus' mother and brothers arrived. Standing outside, they sent someone
in to call him. 32A crowd was sitting around
him, and they told him, "Your mother and
brothers are outside looking for you."

33"Who are my mother and my brothers?"
he asked.

34Then he looked at those seated in a circle around him and said, "Here are my
mother and my brothers! 35Whoever does
God's will is my brother and sister and
mother."

The Parable of the Sower

4 Again Jesus began to teach by the lake.
The crowd that gathered around him
was so large that he got into a boat and sat in
it out on the lake, while all the people were
along the shore at the water's edge. 2He
taught them many things by parables, and in
his teaching said: 3"Listen! A farmer went out
to sow his seed. 4As he was scattering the
seed, some fell along the path, and the birds
came and ate it up. 5Some fell on rocky
places, where it did not have much soil. It
sprang up quickly, because the soil was
shallow. 6But when the sun came up, the
plants were scorched, and they withered because they had no root. 7Other seed fell
among thorns, which grew up and choked
the plants, so that they did not bear grain.
8Still other seed fell on good soil. It came up,
grew and produced a crop, multiplying thirty,
sixty, or even a hundred times."

9Then Jesus said, "He who has ears to
hear, let him hear."

10When he was alone, the Twelve and the
others around him asked him about the parables. 11He told them, "The secret of the kingdom of God has been given to you. But to
those on the outside everything is said in
parables 12so that,

" 'they may be ever seeing but never
perceiving,
and ever hearing but never
understanding;
otherwise they might turn and be
forgiven!'[b]"

13Then Jesus said to them, "Don't you understand this parable? How then will you understand any parable? 14The farmer sows
the word. 15Some people are like seed along
the path, where the word is sown. As soon as
they hear it, Satan comes and takes away
the word that was sown in them. 16Others,
like seed sown on rocky places, hear the
word and at once receive it with joy. 17But
since they have no root, they last only a short
time. When trouble or persecution comes
because of the word, they quickly fall away.
18Still others, like seed sown among thorns,
hear the word; 19but the worries of this life,
the deceitfulness of wealth and the desires
for other things come in and choke the word,
making it unfruitful. 20Others, like seed sown
on good soil, hear the word, accept it, and
produce a crop—thirty, sixty or even a hundred times what was sown."

A Lamp on a Stand

21He said to them, "Do you bring in a lamp
to put it under a bowl or a bed? Instead, don't

[a] *22* Greek *Beezeboul* or *Beelzeboul*   [b] *12* Isaiah 6:9,10

you put it on its stand? 22For whatever is
hidden is meant to be disclosed, and whatever is concealed is meant to be brought out
into the open. 23If anyone has ears to hear,
let him hear."
24"Consider carefully what you hear," he
continued. "With the measure you use, it will
be measured to you—and even more.
25Whoever has will be given more; whoever
does not have, even what he has will be
taken from him."

The Parable of the Growing Seed

26He also said, "This is what the kingdom
of God is like. A man scatters seed on the
ground. 27Night and day, whether he sleeps
or gets up, the seed sprouts and grows,
though he does not know how. 28All by itself
the soil produces grain—first the stalk, then
the head, then the full kernel in the head.
29As soon as the grain is ripe, he puts the
sickle to it, because the harvest has come."

The Parable of the Mustard Seed

30Again he said, "What shall we say the
kingdom of God is like, or what parable shall
we use to describe it? 31It is like a mustard
seed, which is the smallest seed you plant in
the ground. 32Yet when planted, it grows and
becomes the largest of all garden plants,
with such big branches that the birds of the
air can perch in its shade."
33With many similar parables Jesus spoke
the word to them, as much as they could
understand. 34He did not say anything to
them without using a parable. But when he
was alone with his own disciples, he explained everything.

Jesus Calms the Storm

35That day when evening came, he said to
his disciples, "Let us go over to the other
side." 36Leaving the crowd behind, they took
him along, just as he was, in the boat. There
were also other boats with him. 37A furious
squall came up, and the waves broke over
the boat, so that it was nearly swamped.
38Jesus was in the stern, sleeping on a cush-
ion. The disciples woke him and said to him,
"Teacher, don't you care if we drown?"
39He got up, rebuked the wind and said to
the waves, "Quiet! Be still!" Then the wind
died down and it was completely calm.
40He said to his disciples, "Why are you so
afraid? Do you still have no faith?"
41They were terrified and asked each
other, "Who is this? Even the wind and the
waves obey him!"

The Healing of a Demon-possessed Man

5 They went across the lake to the region
of the Gerasenes.[a] 2When Jesus got out
of the boat, a man with an evil[b] spirit came
from the tombs to meet him. 3This man lived
in the tombs, and no one could bind him any
more, not even with a chain. 4For he had
often been chained hand and foot, but he
tore the chains apart and broke the irons on
his feet. No one was strong enough to subdue him. 5Night and day among the tombs
and in the hills he would cry out and cut
himself with stones.
6When he saw Jesus from a distance, he
ran and fell on his knees in front of him. 7He
shouted at the top of his voice, "What do you
want with me, Jesus, Son of the Most High
God? Swear to God that you won't torture
me!" 8For Jesus had said to him, "Come out
of this man, you evil spirit!"
9Then Jesus asked him, "What is your
name?"
"My name is Legion," he replied, "for we
are many." 10And he begged Jesus again
and again not to send them out of the area.
11A large herd of pigs was feeding on the
nearby hillside. 12The demons begged
Jesus, "Send us among the pigs; allow us to
go into them." 13He gave them permission,
and the evil spirits came out and went into
the pigs. The herd, about two thousand in
number, rushed down the steep bank into
the lake and were drowned.
14Those tending the pigs ran off and reported this in the town and countryside, and
the people went out to see what had happened. 15When they came to Jesus, they
saw the man who had been possessed by
the legion of demons, sitting there, dressed
and in his right mind; and they were afraid.
16Those who had seen it told the people what
had happened to the demon-possessed
man—and told about the pigs as well. 17Then
the people began to plead with Jesus to
leave their region.
18As Jesus was getting into the boat, the
man who had been demon-possessed
begged to go with him. 19Jesus did not let
him, but said, "Go home to your family and

[a] *1* Some manuscripts *Gadarenes;* other manuscripts *Gergesenes*
[b] *2* Greek *unclean*; also in verses 8 and 13

tell them how much the Lord has done for
you, and how he has had mercy on you."
20So the man went away and began to tell in
the Decapolis[a] how much Jesus had done
for him. And all the people were amazed.

A Dead Girl and a Sick Woman

21When Jesus had again crossed over by
boat to the other side of the lake, a large
crowd gathered around him while he was by
the lake. 22Then one of the synagogue rulers, named Jairus, came there. Seeing
Jesus, he fell at his feet 23and pleaded earnestly with him, "My little daughter is dying.
Please come and put your hands on her so
that she will be healed and live." 24So Jesus
went with him.

A large crowd followed and pressed
around him. 25And a woman was there who
had been subject to bleeding for twelve
years. 26She had suffered a great deal under
the care of many doctors and had spent all
she had, yet instead of getting better she
grew worse. 27When she heard about Jesus,
she came up behind him in the crowd and
touched his cloak, 28because she thought, "If
I just touch his clothes, I will be healed."
29Immediately her bleeding stopped and she
felt in her body that she was freed from her
suffering.

30At once Jesus realized that power had
gone out from him. He turned around in the
crowd and asked, "Who touched my
clothes?"

31"You see the people crowding against
you," his disciples answered, "and yet you
can ask, 'Who touched me?' "

32But Jesus kept looking around to see
who had done it. 33Then the woman, knowing what had happened to her, came and fell
at his feet and, trembling with fear, told him
the whole truth. 34He said to her, "Daughter,
your faith has healed you. Go in peace and
be freed from your suffering."

35While Jesus was still speaking, some
men came from the house of Jairus, the
synagogue ruler. "Your daughter is dead,"
they said. "Why bother the teacher any
more?"

36Ignoring what they said, Jesus told the
synagogue ruler, "Don't be afraid; just believe."

37He did not let anyone follow him except
Peter, James and John the brother of
James. 38When they came to the home of the
synagogue ruler, Jesus saw a commotion,
with people crying and wailing loudly. 39He
went in and said to them, "Why all this commotion and wailing? The child is not dead but
asleep." 40But they laughed at him.

After he put them all out, he took the child's
father and mother and the disciples who
were with him, and went in where the child
was. 41He took her by the hand and said to
her, *"Talitha koum!"* (which means, "Little
girl, I say to you, get up!"). 42Immediately the
girl stood up and walked around (she was
twelve years old). At this they were completely astonished. 43He gave strict orders
not to let anyone know about this, and told
them to give her something to eat.

A Prophet Without Honor

6 Jesus left there and went to his hometown, accompanied by his disciples.
2When the Sabbath came, he began to teach
in the synagogue, and many who heard him
were amazed.

"Where did this man get these things?"
they asked. "What's this wisdom that has
been given him, that he even does miracles!
3Isn't this the carpenter? Isn't this Mary's son
and the brother of James, Joseph,[b] Judas
and Simon? Aren't his sisters here with us?"
And they took offense at him.

4Jesus said to them, "Only in his hometown, among his relatives and in his own
house is a prophet without honor." 5He could
not do any miracles there, except lay his
hands on a few sick people and heal them.
6And he was amazed at their lack of faith.

Jesus Sends Out the Twelve

Then Jesus went around teaching from
village to village. 7Calling the Twelve to him,
he sent them out two by two and gave them
authority over evil[c] spirits.

8These were his instructions: "Take nothing for the journey except a staff—no bread,
no bag, no money in your belts. 9Wear sandals but not an extra tunic. 10Whenever you
enter a house, stay there until you leave that
town. 11And if any place will not welcome you
or listen to you, shake the dust off your feet
when you leave, as a testimony against
them."

12They went out and preached that people
should repent. 13They drove out many demons and anointed many sick people with oil
and healed them.

[a]20 That is, the Ten Cities [b]3 Greek *Joses*, a variant of *Joseph* [c]7 Greek *unclean*

John the Baptist Beheaded

14King Herod heard about this, for Jesus'
name had become well known. Some were
saying,[a] "John the Baptist has been raised
from the dead, and that is why miraculous
powers are at work in him."

15Others said, "He is Elijah."

And still others claimed, "He is a prophet,
like one of the prophets of long ago."

16But when Herod heard this, he said,
"John, the man I beheaded, has been raised
from the dead!"

17For Herod himself had given orders to
have John arrested, and he had him bound
and put in prison. He did this because of
Herodias, his brother Philip's wife, whom he
had married. 18For John had been saying to
Herod, "It is not lawful for you to have your
brother's wife." 19So Herodias nursed a
grudge against John and wanted to kill him.
But she was not able to, 20because Herod
feared John and protected him, knowing him
to be a righteous and holy man. When Herod
heard John, he was greatly puzzled[b]; yet he
liked to listen to him.

21Finally the opportune time came. On his
birthday Herod gave a banquet for his high
officials and military commanders and the
leading men of Galilee. 22When the daughter
of Herodias came in and danced, she
pleased Herod and his dinner guests.

The king said to the girl, "Ask me for anything you want, and I'll give it to you." 23And
he promised her with an oath, "Whatever
you ask I will give you, up to half my kingdom."

24She went out and said to her mother,
"What shall I ask for?"

"The head of John the Baptist," she answered.

25At once the girl hurried in to the king with
the request: "I want you to give me right now
the head of John the Baptist on a platter."

26The king was greatly distressed, but because of his oaths and his dinner guests, he
did not want to refuse her. 27So he immediately sent an executioner with orders to bring
John's head. The man went, beheaded John
in the prison, 28and brought back his head on
a platter. He presented it to the girl, and she
gave it to her mother. 29On hearing of this,
John's disciples came and took his body and
laid it in a tomb.

Jesus Feeds the Five Thousand

30The apostles gathered around Jesus
and reported to him all they had done and
taught. 31Then, because so many people
were coming and going that they did not
even have a chance to eat, he said to them,
"Come with me by yourselves to a quiet
place and get some rest."

32So they went away by themselves in a
boat to a solitary place. 33But many who saw
them leaving recognized them and ran on
foot from all the towns and got there ahead of
them. 34When Jesus landed and saw a large
crowd, he had compassion on them, because they were like sheep without a shepherd. So he began teaching them many
things.

35By this time it was late in the day, so his
disciples came to him. "This is a remote
place," they said, "and it's already very late.
36Send the people away so they can go to
the surrounding countryside and villages
and buy themselves something to eat."

37But he answered, "You give them something to eat."

They said to him, "That would take eight
months of a man's wages[c]! Are we to go and
spend that much on bread and give it to them
to eat?"

38"How many loaves do you have?" he
asked. "Go and see."

When they found out, they said, "Five—
and two fish."

39Then Jesus directed them to have all the
people sit down in groups on the green
grass. 40So they sat down in groups of hundreds and fifties. 41Taking the five loaves and
the two fish and looking up to heaven, he
gave thanks and broke the loaves. Then he
gave them to his disciples to set before the
people. He also divided the two fish among
them all. 42They all ate and were satisfied,
43and the disciples picked up twelve basketfuls of broken pieces of bread and fish. 44The
number of the men who had eaten was five
thousand.

Jesus Walks on the Water

45Immediately Jesus made his disciples
get into the boat and go on ahead of him to
Bethsaida, while he dismissed the crowd.
46After leaving them, he went up on a mountainside to pray.

[a]14 Some early manuscripts *He was saying* [b]20 Some early manuscripts *he did many things* [c]37 Greek *take two hundred denarii*

47When evening came, the boat was in the middle of the lake, and he was alone on land. 48He saw the disciples straining at the oars, because the wind was against them. About the fourth watch of the night he went out to them, walking on the lake. He was about to pass by them, 49but when they saw him walking on the lake, they thought he was a ghost. They cried out, 50because they all saw him and were terrified.

Immediately he spoke to them and said, "Take courage! It is I. Don't be afraid." 51Then he climbed into the boat with them, and the wind died down. They were completely amazed, 52for they had not understood about the loaves; their hearts were hardened.

53When they had crossed over, they landed at Gennesaret and anchored there. 54As soon as they got out of the boat, people recognized Jesus. 55They ran throughout that whole region and carried the sick on mats to wherever they heard he was. 56And wherever he went—into villages, towns or countryside—they placed the sick in the marketplaces. They begged him to let them touch even the edge of his cloak, and all who touched him were healed.

Clean and Unclean

7 The Pharisees and some of the teachers of the law who had come from Jerusalem gathered around Jesus and 2saw some of his disciples eating food with hands that were "unclean," that is, unwashed. 3(The Pharisees and all the Jews do not eat unless they give their hands a ceremonial washing, holding to the tradition of the elders. 4When they come from the marketplace they do not eat unless they wash. And they observe many other traditions, such as the washing of cups, pitchers and kettles.[a])

5So the Pharisees and teachers of the law asked Jesus, "Why don't your disciples live according to the tradition of the elders instead of eating their food with 'unclean' hands?"

6He replied, "Isaiah was right when he prophesied about you hypocrites; as it is written:

" 'These people honor me with their lips,
but their hearts are far from me.
7They worship me in vain;
their teachings are but rules taught by men.'[b]

8You have let go of the commands of God and are holding on to the traditions of men."

9And he said to them: "You have a fine way of setting aside the commands of God in order to observe[c] your own traditions! 10For Moses said, 'Honor your father and your mother,'[d] and, 'Anyone who curses his father or mother must be put to death.'[e] 11But you say that if a man says to his father or mother: 'Whatever help you might otherwise have received from me is Corban' (that is, a gift devoted to God), 12then you no longer let him do anything for his father or mother. 13Thus you nullify the word of God by your tradition that you have handed down. And you do many things like that."

14Again Jesus called the crowd to him and said, "Listen to me, everyone, and understand this. 15Nothing outside a man can make him 'unclean' by going into him. Rather, it is what comes out of a man that makes him 'unclean.'[f]"

17After he had left the crowd and entered the house, his disciples asked him about this parable. 18"Are you so dull?" he asked. "Don't you see that nothing that enters a man from the outside can make him 'unclean'? 19For it doesn't go into his heart but into his stomach, and then out of his body." (In saying this, Jesus declared all foods "clean.")

20He went on: "What comes out of a man is what makes him 'unclean.' 21For from within, out of men's hearts, come evil thoughts, sexual immorality, theft, murder, adultery, 22greed, malice, deceit, lewdness, envy, slander, arrogance and folly. 23All these evils come from inside and make a man 'unclean.' "

The Faith of a Syrophoenician Woman

24Jesus left that place and went to the vicinity of Tyre.[g] He entered a house and did not want anyone to know it; yet he could not keep his presence secret. 25In fact, as soon as she heard about him, a woman whose little daughter was possessed by an evil[h] spirit came and fell at his feet. 26The woman was a Greek, born in Syrian Phoenicia. She

[a]4 Some early manuscripts *pitchers, kettles and dining couches* [b]6,7 Isaiah 29:13 [c]9 Some manuscripts *set up* [d]10 Exodus 20:12; Deut. 5:16 [e]10 Exodus 21:17; Lev. 20:9 [f]15 Some early manuscripts *'unclean.' [16]If anyone has ears to hear, let him hear.* [g]24 Many early manuscripts *Tyre and Sidon* [h]25 Greek *unclean*

begged Jesus to drive the demon out of her
daughter.
27“First let the children eat all they want,”
he told her, “for it is not right to take the
children's bread and toss it to their dogs.”
28“Yes, Lord,” she replied, “but even the
dogs under the table eat the children's
crumbs.”
29Then he told her, “For such a reply, you
may go; the demon has left your daughter.”
30She went home and found her child lying
on the bed, and the demon gone.

The Healing of a Deaf and Mute Man

31Then Jesus left the vicinity of Tyre and
went through Sidon, down to the Sea of Galilee and into the region of the Decapolis.[a]
32There some people brought to him a man
who was deaf and could hardly talk, and they
begged him to place his hand on the man.
33After he took him aside, away from the
crowd, Jesus put his fingers into the man's
ears. Then he spit and touched the man's
tongue. 34He looked up to heaven and with a
deep sigh said to him, *“Ephphatha!”* (which
means, “Be opened!”). 35At this, the man's
ears were opened, his tongue was loosened
and he began to speak plainly.
36Jesus commanded them not to tell anyone. But the more he did so, the more they
kept talking about it. 37People were overwhelmed with amazement. “He has done
everything well,” they said. “He even makes
the deaf hear and the mute speak.”

Jesus Feeds the Four Thousand

8 During those days another large crowd
gathered. Since they had nothing to eat,
Jesus called his disciples to him and said, 2“I
have compassion for these people; they
have already been with me three days and
have nothing to eat. 3If I send them home
hungry, they will collapse on the way, because some of them have come a long distance.”
4His disciples answered, “But where in this
remote place can anyone get enough bread
to feed them?”
5“How many loaves do you have?” Jesus
asked.
“Seven,” they replied.
6He told the crowd to sit down on the
ground. When he had taken the seven
loaves and given thanks, he broke them and
gave them to his disciples to set before the
people, and they did so. 7They had a few
small fish as well; he gave thanks for them
also and told the disciples to distribute them.
8The people ate and were satisfied. Afterward the disciples picked up seven basketfuls of broken pieces that were left over.
9About four thousand men were present.
And having sent them away, 10he got into the
boat with his disciples and went to the region
of Dalmanutha.
11The Pharisees came and began to question Jesus. To test him, they asked him for a
sign from heaven. 12He sighed deeply and
said, “Why does this generation ask for a
miraculous sign? I tell you the truth, no sign
will be given to it.” 13Then he left them, got
back into the boat and crossed to the other
side.

The Yeast of the Pharisees and Herod

14The disciples had forgotten to bring
bread, except for one loaf they had with them
in the boat. 15“Be careful,” Jesus warned
them. “Watch out for the yeast of the Pharisees and that of Herod.”
16They discussed this with one another
and said, “It is because we have no bread.”
17Aware of their discussion, Jesus asked
them: “Why are you talking about having no
bread? Do you still not see or understand?
Are your hearts hardened? 18Do you have
eyes but fail to see, and ears but fail to hear?
And don't you remember? 19When I broke
the five loaves for the five thousand, how
many basketfuls of pieces did you pick up?”
“Twelve,” they replied.
20“And when I broke the seven loaves for
the four thousand, how many basketfuls of
pieces did you pick up?”
They answered, “Seven.”
21He said to them, “Do you still not understand?”

The Healing of a Blind Man at Bethsaida

22They came to Bethsaida, and some
people brought a blind man and begged
Jesus to touch him. 23He took the blind man
by the hand and led him outside the village.
When he had spit on the man's eyes and put
his hands on him, Jesus asked, “Do you see
anything?”
24He looked up and said, “I see people;
they look like trees walking around.”

[a]31 That is, the Ten Cities

25Once more Jesus put his hands on the
man's eyes. Then his eyes were opened, his
sight was restored, and he saw everything
clearly. 26Jesus sent him home, saying,
"Don't go into the village.[a]"

Peter's Confession of Christ

27Jesus and his disciples went on to the
villages around Caesarea Philippi. On the
way he asked them, "Who do people say I
am?"
28They replied, "Some say John the Baptist; others say Elijah; and still others, one of
the prophets."
29"But what about you?" he asked. "Who
do you say I am?"
Peter answered, "You are the Christ.[b]"
30Jesus warned them not to tell anyone
about him.

Jesus Predicts His Death

31He then began to teach them that the
Son of Man must suffer many things and be
rejected by the elders, chief priests and
teachers of the law, and that he must be
killed and after three days rise again. 32He
spoke plainly about this, and Peter took him
aside and began to rebuke him.
33But when Jesus turned and looked at his
disciples, he rebuked Peter. "Get behind me,
Satan!" he said. "You do not have in mind
the things of God, but the things of men."
34Then he called the crowd to him along
with his disciples and said: "If anyone would
come after me, he must deny himself and
take up his cross and follow me. 35For whoever wants to save his life[c] will lose it, but
whoever loses his life for me and for the
gospel will save it. 36What good is it for a man
to gain the whole world, yet forfeit his soul?
37Or what can a man give in exchange for his
soul? 38If anyone is ashamed of me and my
words in this adulterous and sinful generation, the Son of Man will be ashamed of him
when he comes in his Father's glory with the
holy angels."

9 And he said to them, "I tell you the truth,
some who are standing here will not
taste death before they see the kingdom of
God come with power."

The Transfiguration

2After six days Jesus took Peter, James
and John with him and led them up a high
mountain, where they were all alone. There
he was transfigured before them. 3His
clothes became dazzling white, whiter than
anyone in the world could bleach them. 4And
there appeared before them Elijah and
Moses, who were talking with Jesus.
5Peter said to Jesus, "Rabbi, it is good for
us to be here. Let us put up three shelters—
one for you, one for Moses and one for Elijah." 6(He did not know what to say, they
were so frightened.)
7Then a cloud appeared and enveloped
them, and a voice came from the cloud:
"This is my Son, whom I love. Listen to him!"
8Suddenly, when they looked around, they
no longer saw anyone with them except
Jesus.
9As they were coming down the mountain,
Jesus gave them orders not to tell anyone
what they had seen until the Son of Man had
risen from the dead. 10They kept the matter
to themselves, discussing what "rising from
the dead" meant.
11And they asked him, "Why do the teachers of the law say that Elijah must come
first?"
12Jesus replied, "To be sure, Elijah does
come first, and restores all things. Why then
is it written that the Son of Man must suffer
much and be rejected? 13But I tell you, Elijah
has come, and they have done to him everything they wished, just as it is written about
him."

The Healing of a Boy With an Evil Spirit

14When they came to the other disciples,
they saw a large crowd around them and the
teachers of the law arguing with them. 15As
soon as all the people saw Jesus, they were
overwhelmed with wonder and ran to greet
him.
16"What are you arguing with them
about?" he asked.
17A man in the crowd answered, "Teacher,
I brought you my son, who is possessed by a
spirit that has robbed him of speech.
18Whenever it seizes him, it throws him to the
ground. He foams at the mouth, gnashes his
teeth and becomes rigid. I asked your disciples to drive out the spirit, but they could
not."
19"O unbelieving generation," Jesus re-

[a]*26* Some manuscripts *Don't go and tell anyone in the village* [b]*29* Or *Messiah*. "The Christ" (Greek) and "the Messiah" (Hebrew) both mean "the Anointed One." [c]*35* The Greek word means either *life* or *soul*; also in verse 36.

plied, "how long shall I stay with you? How
long shall I put up with you? Bring the boy to
me."
20So they brought him. When the spirit saw
Jesus, it immediately threw the boy into a
convulsion. He fell to the ground and rolled
around, foaming at the mouth.
21Jesus asked the boy's father, "How long
has he been like this?"
"From childhood," he answered. 22"It has
often thrown him into fire or water to kill him.
But if you can do anything, take pity on us
and help us."
23" 'If you can'?" said Jesus. "Everything is
possible for him who believes."
24Immediately the boy's father exclaimed,
"I do believe; help me overcome my unbelief!"
25When Jesus saw that a crowd was running to the scene, he rebuked the evil[a] spirit.
"You deaf and mute spirit," he said, "I command you, come out of him and never enter
him again."
26The spirit shrieked, convulsed him violently and came out. The boy looked so
much like a corpse that many said, "He's
dead." 27But Jesus took him by the hand and
lifted him to his feet, and he stood up.
28After Jesus had gone indoors, his disciples asked him privately, "Why couldn't we
drive it out?"
29He replied, "This kind can come out only
by prayer.[b]"
30They left that place and passed through
Galilee. Jesus did not want anyone to know
where they were, 31because he was teaching his disciples. He said to them, "The Son
of Man is going to be betrayed into the hands
of men. They will kill him, and after three
days he will rise." 32But they did not understand what he meant and were afraid to ask
him about it.

Who Is the Greatest?

33They came to Capernaum. When he was
in the house, he asked them, "What were
you arguing about on the road?" 34But they
kept quiet because on the way they had argued about who was the greatest.
35Sitting down, Jesus called the Twelve
and said, "If anyone wants to be first, he
must be the very last, and the servant of all."
36He took a little child and had him stand
among them. Taking him in his arms, he said
to them, 37"Whoever welcomes one of these
little children in my name welcomes me; and
whoever welcomes me does not welcome
me but the one who sent me."

Whoever Is Not Against Us Is for Us

38"Teacher," said John, "we saw a man
driving out demons in your name and we told
him to stop, because he was not one of us."
39"Do not stop him," Jesus said. "No one
who does a miracle in my name can in the
next moment say anything bad about me,
40for whoever is not against us is for us. 41I
tell you the truth, anyone who gives you a
cup of water in my name because you belong to Christ will certainly not lose his reward.

Causing to Sin

42"And if anyone causes one of these little
ones who believe in me to sin, it would be
better for him to be thrown into the sea with a
large millstone tied around his neck. 43If your
hand causes you to sin, cut it off. It is better
for you to enter life maimed than with two
hands to go into hell, where the fire never
goes out.[c] 45And if your foot causes you to
sin, cut it off. It is better for you to enter life
crippled than to have two feet and be thrown
into hell.[d] 47And if your eye causes you to
sin, pluck it out. It is better for you to enter the
kingdom of God with one eye than to have
two eyes and be thrown into hell, 48where

" 'their worm does not die,
and the fire is not quenched.'[e]

49Everyone will be salted with fire.
50"Salt is good, but if it loses its saltiness,
how can you make it salty again? Have salt
in yourselves, and be at peace with each
other."

Divorce

10 Jesus then left that place and went
into the region of Judea and across
the Jordan. Again crowds of people came to
him, and as was his custom, he taught them.
2Some Pharisees came and tested him by
asking, "Is it lawful for a man to divorce his
wife?"
3"What did Moses command you?" he replied.
4They said, "Moses permitted a man to

[a]25 Greek *unclean* [b]29 Some manuscripts *prayer and fasting* [c]43 Some manuscripts *out,* [44]*where / " 'their worm does not die, / and the fire is not quenched.'* [d]45 Some manuscripts *hell,* [46]*where / " 'their worm does not die, / and the fire is not quenched.'* [e]48 Isaiah 66:24

write a certificate of divorce and send her
away."
5"It was because your hearts were hard
that Moses wrote you this law," Jesus replied. 6"But at the beginning of creation God
'made them male and female.'[a] 7'For this
reason a man will leave his father and
mother and be united to his wife,[b] 8and the
two will become one flesh.'[c] So they are no
longer two, but one. 9Therefore what God
has joined together, let man not separate."
10When they were in the house again, the
disciples asked Jesus about this. 11He answered, "Anyone who divorces his wife and
marries another woman commits adultery
against her. 12And if she divorces her husband and marries another man, she commits
adultery."

The Little Children and Jesus

13People were bringing little children to
Jesus to have him touch them, but the disciples rebuked them. 14When Jesus saw this,
he was indignant. He said to them, "Let the
little children come to me, and do not hinder
them, for the kingdom of God belongs to
such as these. 15I tell you the truth, anyone
who will not receive the kingdom of God like
a little child will never enter it." 16And he took
the children in his arms, put his hands on
them and blessed them.

The Rich Young Man

17As Jesus started on his way, a man ran
up to him and fell on his knees before him.
"Good teacher," he asked, "what must I do
to inherit eternal life?"
18"Why do you call me good?" Jesus answered. "No one is good—except God
alone. 19You know the commandments: 'Do
not murder, do not commit adultery, do not
steal, do not give false testimony, do not
defraud, honor your father and mother.'[d]"
20"Teacher," he declared, "all these I have
kept since I was a boy."
21Jesus looked at him and loved him. "One
thing you lack," he said. "Go, sell everything
you have and give to the poor, and you will
have treasure in heaven. Then come, follow
me."
22At this the man's face fell. He went away
sad, because he had great wealth.
23Jesus looked around and said to his disciples, "How hard it is for the rich to enter the
kingdom of God!"
24The disciples were amazed at his words.
But Jesus said again, "Children, how hard it
is[e] to enter the kingdom of God! 25It is easier
for a camel to go through the eye of a needle
than for a rich man to enter the kingdom of
God."
26The disciples were even more amazed,
and said to each other, "Who then can be
saved?"
27Jesus looked at them and said, "With
man this is impossible, but not with God; all
things are possible with God."
28Peter said to him, "We have left everything to follow you!"
29"I tell you the truth," Jesus replied, "no
one who has left home or brothers or sisters
or mother or father or children or fields for me
and the gospel 30will fail to receive a hundred
times as much in this present age (homes,
brothers, sisters, mothers, children and
fields—and with them, persecutions) and in
the age to come, eternal life. 31But many who
are first will be last, and the last first."

Jesus Again Predicts His Death

32They were on their way up to Jerusalem,
with Jesus leading the way, and the disciples
were astonished, while those who followed
were afraid. Again he took the Twelve aside
and told them what was going to happen to
him. 33"We are going up to Jerusalem," he
said, "and the Son of Man will be betrayed to
the chief priests and teachers of the law.
They will condemn him to death and will
hand him over to the Gentiles, 34who will
mock him and spit on him, flog him and kill
him. Three days later he will rise."

The Request of James and John

35Then James and John, the sons of Zebedee, came to him. "Teacher," they said, "we
want you to do for us whatever we ask."
36"What do you want me to do for you?" he
asked.
37They replied, "Let one of us sit at your
right and the other at your left in your glory."
38"You don't know what you are asking,"
Jesus said. "Can you drink the cup I drink or
be baptized with the baptism I am baptized
with?"
39"We can," they answered.

[a]*6* Gen. 1:27 [b]*7* Some early manuscripts do not have *and be united to his wife.* [c]*8* Gen. 2:24
[d]*19* Exodus 20:12-16; Deut. 5:16-20 [e]*24* Some manuscripts *is for those who trust in riches*

Jesus said to them, "You will drink the cup
I drink and be baptized with the baptism I am
baptized with, 40but to sit at my right or left is
not for me to grant. These places belong to
those for whom they have been prepared."
41When the ten heard about this, they
became indignant with James and John.
42Jesus called them together and said, "You
know that those who are regarded as rulers
of the Gentiles lord it over them, and their
high officials exercise authority over them.
43Not so with you. Instead, whoever wants to
become great among you must be your servant, 44and whoever wants to be first must be
slave of all. 45For even the Son of Man did
not come to be served, but to serve, and to
give his life as a ransom for many."

Blind Bartimaeus Receives His Sight

46Then they came to Jericho. As Jesus
and his disciples, together with a large
crowd, were leaving the city, a blind man,
Bartimaeus (that is, the Son of Timaeus),
was sitting by the roadside begging. 47When
he heard that it was Jesus of Nazareth, he
began to shout, "Jesus, Son of David, have
mercy on me!"
48Many rebuked him and told him to be
quiet, but he shouted all the more, "Son of
David, have mercy on me!"
49Jesus stopped and said, "Call him."
So they called to the blind man, "Cheer up!
On your feet! He's calling you." 50Throwing
his cloak aside, he jumped to his feet and
came to Jesus.
51"What do you want me to do for you?"
Jesus asked him.
The blind man said, "Rabbi, I want to see."
52"Go," said Jesus, "your faith has healed
you." Immediately he received his sight and
followed Jesus along the road.

The Triumphal Entry

11 As they approached Jerusalem and
came to Bethphage and Bethany at
the Mount of Olives, Jesus sent two of his
disciples, 2saying to them, "Go to the village
ahead of you, and just as you enter it, you will
find a colt tied there, which no one has ever
ridden. Untie it and bring it here. 3If anyone
asks you, 'Why are you doing this?' tell him,
'The Lord needs it and will send it back here
shortly.' "
4They went and found a colt outside in the
street, tied at a doorway. As they untied it,
5some people standing there asked, "What
are you doing, untying that colt?" 6They answered as Jesus had told them to, and the
people let them go. 7When they brought the
colt to Jesus and threw their cloaks over it,
he sat on it. 8Many people spread their
cloaks on the road, while others spread
branches they had cut in the fields. 9Those
who went ahead and those who followed
shouted,

"Hosanna![a]"

"Blessed is he who comes in the name of
the Lord!"[b]

10"Blessed is the coming kingdom of our
father David!"

"Hosanna in the highest!"

11Jesus entered Jerusalem and went to
the temple. He looked around at everything,
but since it was already late, he went out to
Bethany with the Twelve.

Jesus Clears the Temple

12The next day as they were leaving Bethany, Jesus was hungry. 13Seeing in the distance a fig tree in leaf, he went to find out if it
had any fruit. When he reached it, he found
nothing but leaves, because it was not the
season for figs. 14Then he said to the tree,
"May no one ever eat fruit from you again."
And his disciples heard him say it.
15On reaching Jerusalem, Jesus entered
the temple area and began driving out those
who were buying and selling there. He overturned the tables of the money changers and
the benches of those selling doves, 16and
would not allow anyone to carry merchandise through the temple courts. 17And as he
taught them, he said, "Is it not written:

" 'My house will be called
a house of prayer for all nations'[c]?

But you have made it 'a den of robbers.'[d]"
18The chief priests and the teachers of the
law heard this and began looking for a way to
kill him, for they feared him, because the
whole crowd was amazed at his teaching.
19When evening came, they[e] went out of
the city.

[a]9 A Hebrew expression meaning "Save!" which became an exclamation of praise; also in verse 10
[b]9 Psalm 118:25,26 [c]17 Isaiah 56:7 [d]17 Jer. 7:11 [e]19 Some early manuscripts *he*

The Withered Fig Tree

20In the morning, as they went along, they
saw the fig tree withered from the roots.
21Peter remembered and said to Jesus,
"Rabbi, look! The fig tree you cursed has
withered!"

22"Have[a] faith in God," Jesus answered.
23"I tell you the truth, if anyone says to this
mountain, 'Go, throw yourself into the sea,'
and does not doubt in his heart but believes
that what he says will happen, it will be done
for him. 24Therefore I tell you, whatever you
ask for in prayer, believe that you have received it, and it will be yours. 25And when you
stand praying, if you hold anything against
anyone, forgive him, so that your Father in
heaven may forgive you your sins.[b]"

The Authority of Jesus Questioned

27They arrived again in Jerusalem, and
while Jesus was walking in the temple
courts, the chief priests, the teachers of the
law and the elders came to him. 28"By what
authority are you doing these things?" they
asked. "And who gave you authority to do
this?"

29Jesus replied, "I will ask you one question. Answer me, and I will tell you by what
authority I am doing these things. 30John's
baptism—was it from heaven, or from men?
Tell me!"

31They discussed it among themselves
and said, "If we say, 'From heaven,' he will
ask, 'Then why didn't you believe him?' 32But
if we say, 'From men'. . . ." (They feared the
people, for everyone held that John really
was a prophet.)

33So they answered Jesus, "We don't
know."

Jesus said, "Neither will I tell you by what
authority I am doing these things."

The Parable of the Tenants

12 He then began to speak to them in
parables: "A man planted a vineyard.
He put a wall around it, dug a pit for the
winepress and built a watchtower. Then he
rented the vineyard to some farmers and
went away on a journey. 2At harvest time he
sent a servant to the tenants to collect from
them some of the fruit of the vineyard. 3But
they seized him, beat him and sent him away
empty-handed. 4Then he sent another servant to them; they struck this man on the
head and treated him shamefully. 5He sent
still another, and that one they killed. He sent
many others; some of them they beat, others
they killed.

6"He had one left to send, a son, whom he
loved. He sent him last of all, saying, 'They
will respect my son.'

7"But the tenants said to one another, 'This
is the heir. Come, let's kill him, and the inheritance will be ours.' 8So they took him and
killed him, and threw him out of the vineyard.

9"What then will the owner of the vineyard
do? He will come and kill those tenants and
give the vineyard to others. 10Haven't you
read this scripture:

" 'The stone the builders rejected
  has become the capstone[c];
11the Lord has done this,
  and it is marvelous in our eyes'[d]?"

12Then they looked for a way to arrest him
because they knew he had spoken the parable against them. But they were afraid of the
crowd; so they left him and went away.

Paying Taxes to Caesar

13Later they sent some of the Pharisees
and Herodians to Jesus to catch him in his
words. 14They came to him and said,
"Teacher, we know you are a man of integrity. You aren't swayed by men, because you
pay no attention to who they are; but you
teach the way of God in accordance with the
truth. Is it right to pay taxes to Caesar or not?
15Should we pay or shouldn't we?"

But Jesus knew their hypocrisy. "Why are
you trying to trap me?" he asked. "Bring me
a denarius and let me look at it." 16They
brought the coin, and he asked them,
"Whose portrait is this? And whose inscription?"

"Caesar's," they replied.

17Then Jesus said to them, "Give to Caesar what is Caesar's and to God what is
God's."

And they were amazed at him.

Marriage at the Resurrection

18Then the Sadducees, who say there is
no resurrection, came to him with a question.
19"Teacher," they said, "Moses wrote for us
that if a man's brother dies and leaves a wife
but no children, the man must marry the
widow and have children for his brother.

[a]22 Some early manuscripts *If you have* [b]25 Some manuscripts *sins.* *26But if you do not forgive, neither will your Father who is in heaven forgive your sins.* [c]10 Or *cornerstone* [d]11 Psalm 118:22,23

20Now there were seven brothers. The first one married and died without leaving any children. 21The second one married the widow, but he also died, leaving no child. It was the same with the third. 22In fact, none of the seven left any children. Last of all, the woman died too. 23At the resurrection[a] whose wife will she be, since the seven were married to her?"

24Jesus replied, "Are you not in error because you do not know the Scriptures or the power of God? 25When the dead rise, they will neither marry nor be given in marriage; they will be like the angels in heaven. 26Now about the dead rising—have you not read in the book of Moses, in the account of the bush, how God said to him, 'I am the God of Abraham, the God of Isaac, and the God of Jacob'[b]? 27He is not the God of the dead, but of the living. You are badly mistaken!"

The Greatest Commandment

28One of the teachers of the law came and heard them debating. Noticing that Jesus had given them a good answer, he asked him, "Of all the commandments, which is the most important?"

29"The most important one," answered Jesus, "is this: 'Hear, O Israel, the Lord our God, the Lord is one.[c] 30Love the Lord your God with all your heart and with all your soul and with all your mind and with all your strength.'[d] 31The second is this: 'Love your neighbor as yourself.'[e] There is no commandment greater than these."

32"Well said, teacher," the man replied. "You are right in saying that God is one and there is no other but him. 33To love him with all your heart, with all your understanding and with all your strength, and to love your neighbor as yourself is more important than all burnt offerings and sacrifices."

34When Jesus saw that he had answered wisely, he said to him, "You are not far from the kingdom of God." And from then on no one dared ask him any more questions.

Whose Son Is the Christ?

35While Jesus was teaching in the temple courts, he asked, "How is it that the teachers of the law say that the Christ[f] is the son of David? 36David himself, speaking by the Holy Spirit, declared:

"'The Lord said to my Lord:
"Sit at my right hand
until I put your enemies
under your feet."'[g]

37David himself calls him 'Lord.' How then can he be his son?"

The large crowd listened to him with delight.

38As he taught, Jesus said, "Watch out for the teachers of the law. They like to walk around in flowing robes and be greeted in the marketplaces, 39and have the most important seats in the synagogues and the places of honor at banquets. 40They devour widows' houses and for a show make lengthy prayers. Such men will be punished most severely."

The Widow's Offering

41Jesus sat down opposite the place where the offerings were put and watched the crowd putting their money into the temple treasury. Many rich people threw in large amounts. 42But a poor widow came and put in two very small copper coins,[h] worth only a fraction of a penny.[i]

43Calling his disciples to him, Jesus said, "I tell you the truth, this poor widow has put more into the treasury than all the others. 44They all gave out of their wealth; but she, out of her poverty, put in everything—all she had to live on."

Signs of the End of the Age

13 As he was leaving the temple, one of his disciples said to him, "Look, Teacher! What massive stones! What magnificent buildings!"

2"Do you see all these great buildings?" replied Jesus. "Not one stone here will be left on another; every one will be thrown down."

3As Jesus was sitting on the Mount of Olives opposite the temple, Peter, James, John and Andrew asked him privately, 4"Tell us, when will these things happen? And what will be the sign that they are all about to be fulfilled?"

5Jesus said to them: "Watch out that no one deceives you. 6Many will come in my name, claiming, 'I am he,' and will deceive many. 7When you hear of wars and rumors of wars, do not be alarmed. Such things must

[a]23 Some manuscripts *resurrection, when men rise from the dead,* [b]26 Exodus 3:6 [c]29 Or *the Lord our God is one Lord* [d]30 Deut. 6:4,5 [e]31 Lev. 19:18 [f]35 Or *Messiah* [g]36 Psalm 110:1 [h]42 Greek *two lepta* [i]42 Greek *kodrantes*

happen, but the end is still to come. 8Nation
will rise against nation, and kingdom against
kingdom. There will be earthquakes in various places, and famines. These are the beginning of birth pains.
9"You must be on your guard. You will be
handed over to the local councils and
flogged in the synagogues. On account of
me you will stand before governors and
kings as witnesses to them. 10And the gospel
must first be preached to all nations.
11Whenever you are arrested and brought to
trial, do not worry beforehand about what to
say. Just say whatever is given you at the
time, for it is not you speaking, but the Holy
Spirit.
12"Brother will betray brother to death, and
a father his child. Children will rebel against
their parents and have them put to death.
13All men will hate you because of me, but he
who stands firm to the end will be saved.
14"When you see 'the abomination that
causes desolation'[a] standing where it[b] does
not belong—let the reader understand—
then let those who are in Judea flee to the
mountains. 15Let no one on the roof of his
house go down or enter the house to take
anything out. 16Let no one in the field go back
to get his cloak. 17How dreadful it will be in
those days for pregnant women and nursing
mothers! 18Pray that this will not take place in
winter, 19because those will be days of distress unequaled from the beginning, when
God created the world, until now—and never
to be equaled again. 20If the Lord had not cut
short those days, no one would survive. But
for the sake of the elect, whom he has chosen, he has shortened them. 21At that time if
anyone says to you, 'Look, here is the
Christ[c]!' or, 'Look, there he is!' do not believe
it. 22For false Christs and false prophets will
appear and perform signs and miracles to
deceive the elect—if that were possible. 23So
be on your guard; I have told you everything
ahead of time.
24"But in those days, following that distress,

" 'the sun will be darkened,
 and the moon will not give its light;
25the stars will fall from the sky,
 and the heavenly bodies will be
  shaken.'[d]

26"At that time men will see the Son of Man
coming in clouds with great power and glory.
27And he will send his angels and gather his
elect from the four winds, from the ends of
the earth to the ends of the heavens.
28"Now learn this lesson from the fig tree:
As soon as its twigs get tender and its leaves
come out, you know that summer is near.
29Even so, when you see these things happening, you know that it is near, right at the
door. 30I tell you the truth, this generation[e]
will certainly not pass away until all these
things have happened. 31Heaven and earth
will pass away, but my words will never pass
away.

The Day and Hour Unknown

32"No one knows about that day or hour,
not even the angels in heaven, nor the Son,
but only the Father. 33Be on guard! Be alert[f]!
You do not know when that time will come.
34It's like a man going away: He leaves his
house and puts his servants in charge, each
with his assigned task, and tells the one at
the door to keep watch.
35"Therefore keep watch because you do
not know when the owner of the house will
come back—whether in the evening, or at
midnight, or when the rooster crows, or at
dawn. 36If he comes suddenly, do not let him
find you sleeping. 37What I say to you, I say
to everyone: 'Watch!' "

Jesus Anointed at Bethany

14 Now the Passover and the Feast of
Unleavened Bread were only two
days away, and the chief priests and the
teachers of the law were looking for some sly
way to arrest Jesus and kill him. 2"But not
during the Feast," they said, "or the people
may riot."
3While he was in Bethany, reclining at the
table in the home of a man known as Simon
the Leper, a woman came with an alabaster
jar of very expensive perfume, made of pure
nard. She broke the jar and poured the perfume on his head.
4Some of those present were saying indig-
nantly to one another, "Why this waste of
perfume? 5It could have been sold for more
than a year's wages[g] and the money given to
the poor." And they rebuked her harshly.
6"Leave her alone," said Jesus. "Why are
you bothering her? She has done a beautiful
thing to me. 7The poor you will always have

[a]14 Daniel 9:27; 11:31; 12:11 [b]14 Or *he*; also in verse 29 [c]21 Or *Messiah* [d]25 Isaiah 13:10; 34:4
[e]30 Or *race* [f]33 Some manuscripts *alert and pray* [g]5 Greek *than three hundred denarii*

with you, and you can help them any time
you want. But you will not always have me.
8She did what she could. She poured perfume on my body beforehand to prepare for
my burial. 9I tell you the truth, wherever the
gospel is preached throughout the world,
what she has done will also be told, in memory of her."
10Then Judas Iscariot, one of the Twelve,
went to the chief priests to betray Jesus to
them. 11They were delighted to hear this and
promised to give him money. So he watched
for an opportunity to hand him over.

The Lord's Supper

12On the first day of the Feast of Unleavened Bread, when it was customary to sacrifice the Passover lamb, Jesus' disciples
asked him, "Where do you want us to go and
make preparations for you to eat the Passover?"
13So he sent two of his disciples, telling
them, "Go into the city, and a man carrying a
jar of water will meet you. Follow him. 14Say
to the owner of the house he enters, 'The
Teacher asks: Where is my guest room,
where I may eat the Passover with my disciples?' 15He will show you a large upper room,
furnished and ready. Make preparations for
us there."
16The disciples left, went into the city and
found things just as Jesus had told them. So
they prepared the Passover.
17When evening came, Jesus arrived with
the Twelve. 18While they were reclining at
the table eating, he said, "I tell you the truth,
one of you will betray me—one who is eating
with me."
19They were saddened, and one by one
they said to him, "Surely not I?"
20"It is one of the Twelve," he replied, "one
who dips bread into the bowl with me. 21The
Son of Man will go just as it is written about
him. But woe to that man who betrays the
Son of Man! It would be better for him if he
had not been born."
22While they were eating, Jesus took
bread, gave thanks and broke it, and gave it
to his disciples, saying, "Take it; this is my
body."
23Then he took the cup, gave thanks and
offered it to them, and they all drank from it.
24"This is my blood of the[a] covenant,
which is poured out for many," he said to
them. 25"I tell you the truth, I will not drink
again of the fruit of the vine until that day
when I drink it anew in the kingdom of God."
26When they had sung a hymn, they went
out to the Mount of Olives.

Jesus Predicts Peter's Denial

27"You will all fall away," Jesus told them,
"for it is written:

" 'I will strike the shepherd,
and the sheep will be scattered.'[b]

28But after I have risen, I will go ahead of you
into Galilee."
29Peter declared, "Even if all fall away, I
will not."
30"I tell you the truth," Jesus answered,
"today—yes, tonight—before the rooster
crows twice[c] you yourself will disown me
three times."
31But Peter insisted emphatically, "Even if
I have to die with you, I will never disown
you." And all the others said the same.

Gethsemane

32They went to a place called Gethsemane, and Jesus said to his disciples, "Sit here
while I pray." 33He took Peter, James and
John along with him, and he began to be
deeply distressed and troubled. 34"My soul is
overwhelmed with sorrow to the point of
death," he said to them. "Stay here and keep
watch."
35Going a little farther, he fell to the ground
and prayed that if possible the hour might
pass from him. 36"*Abba*,[d] Father," he said,
"everything is possible for you. Take this cup
from me. Yet not what I will, but what you
will."
37Then he returned to his disciples and
found them sleeping. "Simon," he said to
Peter, "are you asleep? Could you not keep
watch for one hour? 38Watch and pray so
that you will not fall into temptation. The spirit
is willing, but the body is weak."
39Once more he went away and prayed the
same thing. 40When he came back, he again
found them sleeping, because their eyes
were heavy. They did not know what to say
to him.
41Returning the third time, he said to them,
"Are you still sleeping and resting? Enough!
The hour has come. Look, the Son of Man is

[a]*24* Some manuscripts *the new* [b]*27* Zech. 13:7 [c]*30* Some early manuscripts do not have *twice.*
[d]*36* Aramaic for *Father*

betrayed into the hands of sinners. 42Rise!
Let us go! Here comes my betrayer!"

Jesus Arrested

43Just as he was speaking, Judas, one of
the Twelve, appeared. With him was a crowd
armed with swords and clubs, sent from the
chief priests, the teachers of the law, and the
elders.
44Now the betrayer had arranged a signal
with them: "The one I kiss is the man; arrest
him and lead him away under guard." 45Go-
ing at once to Jesus, Judas said, "Rabbi!"
and kissed him. 46The men seized Jesus and
arrested him. 47Then one of those standing
near drew his sword and struck the servant
of the high priest, cutting off his ear.
48"Am I leading a rebellion," said Jesus,
"that you have come out with swords and
clubs to capture me? 49Every day I was with
you, teaching in the temple courts, and you
did not arrest me. But the Scriptures must be
fulfilled." 50Then everyone deserted him and
fled.
51A young man, wearing nothing but a
linen garment, was following Jesus. When
they seized him, 52he fled naked, leaving his
garment behind.

Before the Sanhedrin

53They took Jesus to the high priest, and
all the chief priests, elders and teachers of
the law came together. 54Peter followed him
at a distance, right into the courtyard of the
high priest. There he sat with the guards and
warmed himself at the fire.
55The chief priests and the whole Sanhedrin were looking for evidence against Jesus
so that they could put him to death, but they
did not find any. 56Many testified falsely
against him, but their statements did not
agree.
57Then some stood up and gave this false
testimony against him: 58"We heard him say,
'I will destroy this man-made temple and in
three days will build another, not made by
man.'" 59Yet even then their testimony did
not agree.
60Then the high priest stood up before
them and asked Jesus, "Are you not going to
answer? What is this testimony that these
men are bringing against you?" 61But Jesus
remained silent and gave no answer.
Again the high priest asked him, "Are you
the Christ,[a] the Son of the Blessed One?"
62"I am," said Jesus. "And you will see the
Son of Man sitting at the right hand of the
Mighty One and coming on the clouds of
heaven."
63The high priest tore his clothes. "Why do
we need any more witnesses?" he asked.
64"You have heard the blasphemy. What do
you think?"
They all condemned him as worthy of
death. 65Then some began to spit at him;
they blindfolded him, struck him with their
fists, and said, "Prophesy!" And the guards
took him and beat him.

Peter Disowns Jesus

66While Peter was below in the courtyard,
one of the servant girls of the high priest
came by. 67When she saw Peter warming
himself, she looked closely at him.
"You also were with that Nazarene,
Jesus," she said.
68But he denied it. "I don't know or understand what you're talking about," he said,
and went out into the entryway.[b]
69When the servant girl saw him there, she
said again to those standing around, "This
fellow is one of them." 70Again he denied it.
After a little while, those standing near
said to Peter, "Surely you are one of them,
for you are a Galilean."
71He began to call down curses on himself,
and he swore to them, "I don't know this man
you're talking about."
72Immediately the rooster crowed the second time.[c] Then Peter remembered the word
Jesus had spoken to him: "Before the rooster crows twice[d] you will disown me three
times." And he broke down and wept.

Jesus Before Pilate

15 Very early in the morning, the chief
priests, with the elders, the teachers
of the law and the whole Sanhedrin, reached
a decision. They bound Jesus, led him away
and handed him over to Pilate.
2"Are you the king of the Jews?" asked
Pilate.
"Yes, it is as you say," Jesus replied.
3The chief priests accused him of many
things. 4So again Pilate asked him, "Aren't
you going to answer? See how many things
they are accusing you of."

[a]*61* Or *Messiah* [b]*68* Some early manuscripts *entryway and the rooster crowed* [c]*72* Some early manuscripts do not have *the second time.* [d]*72* Some early manuscripts do not have *twice.*

5But Jesus still made no reply, and Pilate was amazed.

6Now it was the custom at the Feast to release a prisoner whom the people requested. 7A man called Barabbas was in prison with the insurrectionists who had committed murder in the uprising. 8The crowd came up and asked Pilate to do for them what he usually did.

9"Do you want me to release to you the king of the Jews?" asked Pilate, 10knowing it was out of envy that the chief priests had handed Jesus over to him. 11But the chief priests stirred up the crowd to have Pilate release Barabbas instead.

12"What shall I do, then, with the one you call the king of the Jews?" Pilate asked them.

13"Crucify him!" they shouted.

14"Why? What crime has he committed?" asked Pilate.

But they shouted all the louder, "Crucify him!"

15Wanting to satisfy the crowd, Pilate released Barabbas to them. He had Jesus flogged, and handed him over to be crucified.

The Soldiers Mock Jesus

16The soldiers led Jesus away into the palace (that is, the Praetorium) and called together the whole company of soldiers. 17They put a purple robe on him, then twisted together a crown of thorns and set it on him. 18And they began to call out to him, "Hail, king of the Jews!" 19Again and again they struck him on the head with a staff and spit on him. Falling on their knees, they paid homage to him. 20And when they had mocked him, they took off the purple robe and put his own clothes on him. Then they led him out to crucify him.

The Crucifixion

21A certain man from Cyrene, Simon, the father of Alexander and Rufus, was passing by on his way in from the country, and they forced him to carry the cross. 22They brought Jesus to the place called Golgotha (which means The Place of the Skull). 23Then they offered him wine mixed with myrrh, but he did not take it. 24And they crucified him. Dividing up his clothes, they cast lots to see what each would get.

25It was the third hour when they crucified him. 26The written notice of the charge against him read: THE KING OF THE JEWS. 27They crucified two robbers with him, one on his right and one on his left.[a] 29Those who passed by hurled insults at him, shaking their heads and saying, "So! You who are going to destroy the temple and build it in three days, 30come down from the cross and save yourself!"

31In the same way the chief priests and the teachers of the law mocked him among themselves. "He saved others," they said, "but he can't save himself! 32Let this Christ,[b] this King of Israel, come down now from the cross, that we may see and believe." Those crucified with him also heaped insults on him.

The Death of Jesus

33At the sixth hour darkness came over the whole land until the ninth hour. 34And at the ninth hour Jesus cried out in a loud voice, *"Eloi, Eloi, lama sabachthani?"*—which means, "My God, my God, why have you forsaken me?"[c]

35When some of those standing near heard this, they said, "Listen, he's calling Elijah."

36One man ran, filled a sponge with wine vinegar, put it on a stick, and offered it to Jesus to drink. "Now leave him alone. Let's see if Elijah comes to take him down," he said.

37With a loud cry, Jesus breathed his last.

38The curtain of the temple was torn in two from top to bottom. 39And when the centurion, who stood there in front of Jesus, heard his cry and[d] saw how he died, he said, "Surely this man was the Son[e] of God!"

40Some women were watching from a distance. Among them were Mary Magdalene, Mary the mother of James the younger and of Joses, and Salome. 41In Galilee these women had followed him and cared for his needs. Many other women who had come up with him to Jerusalem were also there.

The Burial of Jesus

42It was Preparation Day (that is, the day before the Sabbath). So as evening approached, 43Joseph of Arimathea, a prominent member of the Council, who was himself waiting for the kingdom of God, went

[a]27 Some manuscripts *left,* [28]*and the scripture was fulfilled which says, "He was counted with the lawless ones"* (Isaiah 53:12) [b]32 Or *Messiah* [c]34 Psalm 22:1 [d]39 Some manuscripts do not have *heard his cry and.* [e]39 Or *a son*

boldly to Pilate and asked for Jesus' body.
44Pilate was surprised to hear that he was
already dead. Summoning the centurion, he
asked him if Jesus had already died. 45When
he learned from the centurion that it was so,
he gave the body to Joseph. 46So Joseph
bought some linen cloth, took down the
body, wrapped it in the linen, and placed it in
a tomb cut out of rock. Then he rolled a stone
against the entrance of the tomb. 47Mary
Magdalene and Mary the mother of Joses
saw where he was laid.

The Resurrection

16 When the Sabbath was over, Mary
Magdalene, Mary the mother of
James, and Salome bought spices so that
they might go to anoint Jesus' body. 2Very
early on the first day of the week, just after
sunrise, they were on their way to the tomb
3and they asked each other, "Who will roll
the stone away from the entrance of the
tomb?"

4But when they looked up, they saw that
the stone, which was very large, had been
rolled away. 5As they entered the tomb, they
saw a young man dressed in a white robe
sitting on the right side, and they were
alarmed.

6"Don't be alarmed," he said. "You are
looking for Jesus the Nazarene, who was
crucified. He has risen! He is not here. See
the place where they laid him. 7But go, tell his
disciples and Peter, 'He is going ahead of
you into Galilee. There you will see him, just
as he told you.' "

8Trembling and bewildered, the women
went out and fled from the tomb. They said
nothing to anyone, because they were
afraid.

[The most reliable early manuscripts and other ancient witnesses do not have Mark 16:9-20.]

9When Jesus rose early on the first day of
the week, he appeared first to Mary Magdalene, out of whom he had driven seven demons. 10She went and told those who had
been with him and who were mourning and
weeping. 11When they heard that Jesus was
alive and that she had seen him, they did not
believe it.

12Afterward Jesus appeared in a different
form to two of them while they were walking
in the country. 13These returned and reported it to the rest; but they did not believe
them either.

14Later Jesus appeared to the Eleven as
they were eating; he rebuked them for their
lack of faith and their stubborn refusal to
believe those who had seen him after he had
risen.

15He said to them, "Go into all the world
and preach the good news to all creation.
16Whoever believes and is baptized will be
saved, but whoever does not believe will be
condemned. 17And these signs will accompany those who believe: In my name they will
drive out demons; they will speak in new
tongues; 18they will pick up snakes with their
hands; and when they drink deadly poison, it
will not hurt them at all; they will place their
hands on sick people, and they will get well."

19After the Lord Jesus had spoken to them,
he was taken up into heaven and he sat at
the right hand of God. 20Then the disciples
went out and preached everywhere, and the
Lord worked with them and confirmed his
word by the signs that accompanied it.

Luke

Introduction:

Luke, the longest of the Gospels, was written by the same author as the book of Acts. Luke's writing shows him to be a highly educated man, who wrote from a Greek background and viewpoint.

Luke tells us in the first four verses of his book that he wrote this Gospel so we would have the true and complete story of Jesus' life. He wrote the fullest, most orderly story of his life.

One of Luke's interests in writing this book was to show that Jesus loved all kinds of people. He often wrote about and identified by name the women Christ met and spoke to. He also gave more attention to children than any other gospel writer. In the parables especially, he wrote about the poor and oppressed. Jesus is shown by Luke as an actual person in history who "came to seek and to save what was lost" (19:10).

The theme of joy is felt throughout this book—from the song of Mary and later the angels at Jesus' birth to the disciples who "returned to Jerusalem with great joy" after Christ's ascension. It is obvious that Luke wanted to tell the good news of Christ and show that his coming brought joy as well as hope and salvation to a sinful world.

Outline of contents:

Introduction

1 Many have undertaken to draw up an
account of the things that have been fulfilled[a] among us, 2just as they were handed
down to us by those who from the first were
eyewitnesses and servants of the word.
3Therefore, since I myself have carefully investigated everything from the beginning, it
seemed good also to me to write an orderly
account for you, most excellent Theophilus,
4so that you may know the certainty of the
things you have been taught.

The Birth of John the Baptist Foretold

5In the time of Herod king of Judea there
was a priest named Zechariah, who belonged to the priestly division of Abijah; his
wife Elizabeth was also a descendant of
Aaron. 6Both of them were upright in the
sight of God, observing all the Lord's commandments and regulations blamelessly.
7But they had no children, because Elizabeth
was barren; and they were both well along in
years.

8Once when Zechariah's division was on
duty and he was serving as priest before
God, 9he was chosen by lot, according to the
custom of the priesthood, to go into the temple of the Lord and burn incense. 10And when
the time for the burning of incense came, all
the assembled worshipers were praying outside.

11Then an angel of the Lord appeared to
him, standing at the right side of the altar of
incense. 12When Zechariah saw him, he was
startled and was gripped with fear. 13But the

[a] 1 Or *been surely believed*

angel said to him: "Do not be afraid, Zechariah; your prayer has been heard. Your wife
Elizabeth will bear you a son, and you are to
give him the name John. 14He will be a joy
and delight to you, and many will rejoice because of his birth, 15for he will be great in the
sight of the Lord. He is never to take wine or
other fermented drink, and he will be filled
with the Holy Spirit even from birth.[a] 16Many
of the people of Israel will he bring back to
the Lord their God. 17And he will go on before
the Lord, in the spirit and power of Elijah, to
turn the hearts of the fathers to their children
and the disobedient to the wisdom of the
righteous—to make ready a people prepared for the Lord."

18Zechariah asked the angel, "How can I
be sure of this? I am an old man and my wife
is well along in years."

19The angel answered, "I am Gabriel. I
stand in the presence of God, and I have
been sent to speak to you and to tell you this
good news. 20And now you will be silent and
not able to speak until the day this happens,
because you did not believe my words,
which will come true at their proper time."

21Meanwhile, the people were waiting for
Zechariah and wondering why he stayed so
long in the temple. 22When he came out, he
could not speak to them. They realized he
had seen a vision in the temple, for he kept
making signs to them but remained unable to
speak.

23When his time of service was completed,
he returned home. 24After this his wife Elizabeth became pregnant and for five months
remained in seclusion. 25"The Lord has done
this for me," she said. "In these days he has
shown his favor and taken away my disgrace
among the people."

The Birth of Jesus Foretold

26In the sixth month, God sent the angel
Gabriel to Nazareth, a town in Galilee, 27to a
virgin pledged to be married to a man named
Joseph, a descendant of David. The virgin's
name was Mary. 28The angel went to her and
said, "Greetings, you who are highly favored! The Lord is with you."

29Mary was greatly troubled at his words
and wondered what kind of greeting this
might be. 30But the angel said to her, "Do not
be afraid, Mary, you have found favor with
God. 31You will be with child and give birth to
a son, and you are to give him the name
Jesus. 32He will be great and will be called
the Son of the Most High. The Lord God will
give him the throne of his father David, 33and
he will reign over the house of Jacob forever;
his kingdom will never end."

34"How will this be," Mary asked the angel,
"since I am a virgin?"

35The angel answered, "The Holy Spirit
will come upon you, and the power of the
Most High will overshadow you. So the holy
one to be born will be called[b] the Son of God.
36Even Elizabeth your relative is going to
have a child in her old age, and she who was
said to be barren is in her sixth month. 37For
nothing is impossible with God."

38"I am the Lord's servant," Mary answered. "May it be to me as you have said."
Then the angel left her.

Mary Visits Elizabeth

39At that time Mary got ready and hurried
to a town in the hill country of Judea, 40where
she entered Zechariah's home and greeted
Elizabeth. 41When Elizabeth heard Mary's
greeting, the baby leaped in her womb, and
Elizabeth was filled with the Holy Spirit. 42In a
loud voice she exclaimed: "Blessed are you
among women, and blessed is the child you
will bear! 43But why am I so favored, that the
mother of my Lord should come to me? 44As
soon as the sound of your greeting reached
my ears, the baby in my womb leaped for joy.
45Blessed is she who has believed that what
the Lord has said to her will be accomplished!"

Mary's Song

46And Mary said:

"My soul glorifies the Lord
47 and my spirit rejoices in God my
Savior,
48for he has been mindful
of the humble state of his servant.
From now on all generations will call me
blessed,
49 for the Mighty One has done great
things for me—
holy is his name.
50His mercy extends to those who fear him,
from generation to generation.
51He has performed mighty deeds with his
arm;
he has scattered those who are proud
in their inmost thoughts.

[a]15 *Or from his mother's womb* [b]35 *Or So the child to be born will be called holy,*

52 He has brought down rulers from their
thrones
but has lifted up the humble.
53 He has filled the hungry with good things
but has sent the rich away empty.
54 He has helped his servant Israel,
remembering to be merciful
55 to Abraham and his descendants forever,
even as he said to our fathers."

56 Mary stayed with Elizabeth for about
three months and then returned home.

The Birth of John the Baptist

57 When it was time for Elizabeth to have
her baby, she gave birth to a son. 58 Her
neighbors and relatives heard that the Lord
had shown her great mercy, and they shared
her joy.
59 On the eighth day they came to circumcise the child, and they were going to name
him after his father Zechariah, 60 but his
mother spoke up and said, "No! He is to be
called John."
61 They said to her, "There is no one
among your relatives who has that name."
62 Then they made signs to his father, to
find out what he would like to name the child.
63 He asked for a writing tablet, and to everyone's astonishment he wrote, "His name is
John." 64 Immediately his mouth was opened
and his tongue was loosed, and he began to
speak, praising God. 65 The neighbors were
all filled with awe, and throughout the hill
country of Judea people were talking about
all these things. 66 Everyone who heard this
wondered about it, asking, "What then is this
child going to be?" For the Lord's hand was
with him.

Zechariah's Song

67 His father Zechariah was filled with the
Holy Spirit and prophesied:

68 "Praise be to the Lord, the God of Israel,
because he has come and has
redeemed his people.
69 He has raised up a horn[a] of salvation
for us
in the house of his servant David
70 (as he said through his holy prophets of
long ago),
71 salvation from our enemies
and from the hand of all who hate us—
72 to show mercy to our fathers
and to remember his holy covenant,
73 the oath he swore to our father
Abraham:
74 to rescue us from the hand of our
enemies,
and to enable us to serve him without
fear
75 in holiness and righteousness before
him all our days.

76 And you, my child, will be called a
prophet of the Most High;
for you will go on before the Lord to
prepare the way for him,
77 to give his people the knowledge of
salvation
through the forgiveness of their sins,
78 because of the tender mercy of our God,
by which the rising sun will come to us
from heaven
79 to shine on those living in darkness
and in the shadow of death,
to guide our feet into the path of peace."

80 And the child grew and became strong in
spirit; and he lived in the desert until he appeared publicly to Israel.

The Birth of Jesus

2 In those days Caesar Augustus issued a
decree that a census should be taken of
the entire Roman world. 2 (This was the first
census that took place while Quirinius was
governor of Syria.) 3 And everyone went to
his own town to register.
4 So Joseph also went up from the town of
Nazareth in Galilee to Judea, to Bethlehem
the town of David, because he belonged to
the house and line of David. 5 He went there
to register with Mary, who was pledged to be
married to him and was expecting a child.
6 While they were there, the time came for the
baby to be born, 7 and she gave birth to her
firstborn, a son. She wrapped him in cloths
and placed him in a manger, because there
was no room for them in the inn.

The Shepherds and the Angels

8 And there were shepherds living out in the
fields nearby, keeping watch over their flocks
at night. 9 An angel of the Lord appeared to
them, and the glory of the Lord shone around
them, and they were terrified. 10 But the angel
said to them, "Do not be afraid. I bring you
good news of great joy that will be for all the
people. 11 Today in the town of David a Savior

[a] 69 *Horn* here symbolizes strength.

has been born to you; he is Christ[a] the Lord.
12This will be a sign to you: You will find a
baby wrapped in cloths and lying in a manger."
13Suddenly a great company of the heavenly host appeared with the angel, praising
God and saying,

14"Glory to God in the highest,
and on earth peace to men on whom
his favor rests."

15When the angels had left them and gone
into heaven, the shepherds said to one another, "Let's go to Bethlehem and see this
thing that has happened, which the Lord has
told us about."
16So they hurried off and found Mary and
Joseph, and the baby, who was lying in the
manger. 17When they had seen him, they
spread the word concerning what had been
told them about this child, 18and all who
heard it were amazed at what the shepherds
said to them. 19But Mary treasured up all
these things and pondered them in her heart.
20The shepherds returned, glorifying and
praising God for all the things they had heard
and seen, which were just as they had been
told.

Jesus Presented in the Temple

21On the eighth day, when it was time to
circumcise him, he was named Jesus, the
name the angel had given him before he had
been conceived.
22When the time of their purification according to the Law of Moses had been completed, Joseph and Mary took him to Jerusalem to present him to the Lord 23(as it is
written in the Law of the Lord, "Every firstborn male is to be consecrated to the
Lord"[b]), 24and to offer a sacrifice in keeping
with what is said in the Law of the Lord: "a
pair of doves or two young pigeons."[c]
25Now there was a man in Jerusalem
called Simeon, who was righteous and devout. He was waiting for the consolation of
Israel, and the Holy Spirit was upon him. 26It
had been revealed to him by the Holy Spirit
that he would not die before he had seen the
Lord's Christ. 27Moved by the Spirit, he went
into the temple courts. When the parents
brought in the child Jesus to do for him what
the custom of the Law required, 28Simeon
took him in his arms and praised God, saying:

29"Sovereign Lord, as you have promised,
you now dismiss[d] your servant in
peace.
30For my eyes have seen your salvation,
31 which you have prepared in the sight of
all people,
32a light for revelation to the Gentiles
and for glory to your people Israel."

33The child's father and mother marveled
at what was said about him. 34Then Simeon
blessed them and said to Mary, his mother:
"This child is destined to cause the falling
and rising of many in Israel, and to be a sign
that will be spoken against, 35so that the
thoughts of many hearts will be revealed.
And a sword will pierce your own soul too."
36There was also a prophetess, Anna, the
daughter of Phanuel, of the tribe of Asher.
She was very old; she had lived with her
husband seven years after her marriage,
37and then was a widow until she was eighty-
four.[e] She never left the temple but worshiped night and day, fasting and praying.
38Coming up to them at that very moment,
she gave thanks to God and spoke about the
child to all who were looking forward to the
redemption of Jerusalem.
39When Joseph and Mary had done everything required by the Law of the Lord, they
returned to Galilee to their own town of Nazareth. 40And the child grew and became
strong; he was filled with wisdom, and the
grace of God was upon him.

The Boy Jesus at the Temple

41Every year his parents went to Jerusalem for the Feast of the Passover. 42When he
was twelve years old, they went up to the
Feast, according to the custom. 43After the
Feast was over, while his parents were returning home, the boy Jesus stayed behind
in Jerusalem, but they were unaware of it.
44Thinking he was in their company, they
traveled on for a day. Then they began looking for him among their relatives and friends.
45When they did not find him, they went back
to Jerusalem to look for him. 46After three
days they found him in the temple courts,
sitting among the teachers, listening to them
and asking them questions. 47Everyone who

[a]*11* Or *Messiah.* "The Christ" (Greek) and "the Messiah" (Hebrew) both mean "the Anointed One"; also in verse 26. [b]*23* Exodus 13:2,12 [c]*24* Lev. 12:8 [d]*29* Or *promised, / now dismiss* [e]*37* Or *widow for eighty-four years*

heard him was amazed at his understanding
and his answers. 48When his parents saw
him, they were astonished. His mother said
to him, "Son, why have you treated us like
this? Your father and I have been anxiously
searching for you."
49"Why were you searching for me?" he
asked. "Didn't you know I had to be in my
Father's house?" 50But they did not understand what he was saying to them.
51Then he went down to Nazareth with
them and was obedient to them. But his
mother treasured all these things in her
heart. 52And Jesus grew in wisdom and stature, and in favor with God and men.

John the Baptist Prepares the Way

3 In the fifteenth year of the reign of Tiberi-
us Caesar—when Pontius Pilate was
governor of Judea, Herod tetrarch of Galilee,
his brother Philip tetrarch of Iturea and
Traconitis, and Lysanias tetrarch of Abilene— 2during the high priesthood of Annas
and Caiaphas, the word of God came to
John son of Zechariah in the desert. 3He
went into all the country around the Jordan,
preaching a baptism of repentance for the
forgiveness of sins. 4As is written in the book
of the words of Isaiah the prophet:

"A voice of one calling in the desert,
'Prepare the way for the Lord,
make straight paths for him.
5Every valley shall be filled in,
every mountain and hill made low.
The crooked roads shall become straight,
the rough ways smooth.
6And all mankind will see God's
salvation.' "[a]

7John said to the crowds coming out to be
baptized by him, "You brood of vipers! Who
warned you to flee from the coming wrath?
8Produce fruit in keeping with repentance.
And do not begin to say to yourselves, 'We
have Abraham as our father.' For I tell you
that out of these stones God can raise up
children for Abraham. 9The ax is already at
the root of the trees, and every tree that does
not produce good fruit will be cut down and
thrown into the fire."
10"What should we do then?" the crowd
asked.
11John answered, "The man with two tunics should share with him who has none,
and the one who has food should do the
same."
12Tax collectors also came to be baptized.
"Teacher," they asked, "what should we
do?"
13"Don't collect any more than you are required to," he told them.
14Then some soldiers asked him, "And
what should we do?"
He replied, "Don't extort money and don't
accuse people falsely—be content with your
pay."
15The people were waiting expectantly and
were all wondering in their hearts if John
might possibly be the Christ.[b] 16John answered them all, "I baptize you with[c] water.
But one more powerful than I will come, the
thongs of whose sandals I am not worthy to
untie. He will baptize you with the Holy Spirit
and with fire. 17His winnowing fork is in his
hand to clear his threshing floor and to gather the wheat into his barn, but he will burn up
the chaff with unquenchable fire." 18And with
many other words John exhorted the people
and preached the good news to them.
19But when John rebuked Herod the tetrarch because of Herodias, his brother's
wife, and all the other evil things he had
done, 20Herod added this to them all: He
locked John up in prison.

The Baptism and Genealogy of Jesus

21When all the people were being baptized, Jesus was baptized too. And as he
was praying, heaven was opened 22and the
Holy Spirit descended on him in bodily form
like a dove. And a voice came from heaven:
"You are my Son, whom I love; with you I am
well pleased."
23Now Jesus himself was about thirty
years old when he began his ministry. He
was the son, so it was thought, of Joseph,

the son of Heli, 24the son of Matthat,
the son of Levi, the son of Melki,
the son of Jannai, the son of Joseph,
25the son of Mattathias, the son of Amos,
the son of Nahum, the son of Esli,
the son of Naggai, 26the son of Maath,
the son of Mattathias, the son of
Semein,
the son of Josech, the son of Joda,
27the son of Joanan, the son of Rhesa,

[a]6 Isaiah 40:3-5 [b]15 Or *Messiah* [c]16 Or *in*

the son of Zerubbabel, the son of
Shealtiel,
the son of Neri, [28]the son of Melki,
the son of Addi, the son of Cosam,
the son of Elmadam, the son of Er,
[29]the son of Joshua, the son of Eliezer,
the son of Jorim, the son of Matthat,
the son of Levi, [30]the son of Simeon,
the son of Judah, the son of Joseph,
the son of Jonam, the son of Eliakim,
[31]the son of Melea, the son of Menna,
the son of Mattatha, the son of Nathan,
the son of David, [32]the son of Jesse,
the son of Obed, the son of Boaz,
the son of Salmon,[a] the son of
Nahshon,
[33]the son of Amminadab, the son of
Ram,[b]
the son of Hezron, the son of Perez,
the son of Judah, [34]the son of Jacob,
the son of Isaac, the son of Abraham,
the son of Terah, the son of Nahor,
[35]the son of Serug, the son of Reu,
the son of Peleg, the son of Eber,
the son of Shelah, [36]the son of Cainan,
the son of Arphaxad, the son of Shem,
the son of Noah, the son of Lamech,
[37]the son of Methuselah, the son of
Enoch,
the son of Jared, the son of Mahalalel,
the son of Kenan, [38]the son of Enosh,
the son of Seth, the son of Adam,
the son of God.

The Temptation of Jesus

4 Jesus, full of the Holy Spirit, returned
from the Jordan and was led by the Spirit
in the desert, [2]where for forty days he was
tempted by the devil. He ate nothing during
those days, and at the end of them he was
hungry.
[3]The devil said to him, "If you are the Son
of God, tell this stone to become bread."
[4]Jesus answered, "It is written: 'Man does
not live on bread alone.'[c]"
[5]The devil led him up to a high place and
showed him in an instant all the kingdoms of
the world. [6]And he said to him, "I will give you
all their authority and splendor, for it has
been given to me, and I can give it to anyone
I want to. [7]So if you worship me, it will all be
yours."
[8]Jesus answered, "It is written: 'Worship
the Lord your God and serve him only.'[d]"
[9]The devil led him to Jerusalem and had
him stand on the highest point of the temple.
"If you are the Son of God," he said, "throw
yourself down from here. [10]For it is written:

" 'He will command his angels concerning
you
to guard you carefully;
[11]they will lift you up in their hands,
so that you will not strike your foot
against a stone.'[e]"

[12]Jesus answered, "It says: 'Do not put the
Lord your God to the test.'[f]"
[13]When the devil had finished all this
tempting, he left him until an opportune time.

Jesus Rejected at Nazareth

[14]Jesus returned to Galilee in the power of
the Spirit, and news about him spread
through the whole countryside. [15]He taught
in their synagogues, and everyone praised
him.
[16]He went to Nazareth, where he had been
brought up, and on the Sabbath day he went
into the synagogue, as was his custom. And
he stood up to read. [17]The scroll of the
prophet Isaiah was handed to him. Unrolling
it, he found the place where it is written:

[18]"The Spirit of the Lord is on me,
because he has anointed me
to preach good news to the poor.
He has sent me to proclaim freedom for
the prisoners
and recovery of sight for the blind,
to release the oppressed,
[19] to proclaim the year of the Lord's
favor."[g]

[20]Then he rolled up the scroll, gave it back
to the attendant and sat down. The eyes of
everyone in the synagogue were fastened
on him, [21]and he began by saying to them,
"Today this scripture is fulfilled in your hearing."
[22]All spoke well of him and were amazed at
the gracious words that came from his lips.
"Isn't this Joseph's son?" they asked.
[23]Jesus said to them, "Surely you will
quote this proverb to me: 'Physician, heal
yourself! Do here in your hometown what we
have heard that you did in Capernaum.' "
[24]"I tell you the truth," he continued, "no
prophet is accepted in his hometown. [25]I assure you that there were many widows in

[a]*32* Some early manuscripts *Sala* [b]*33* Some manuscripts *Amminadab, the son of Admin, the son of Arni;* other manuscripts vary widely. [c]*4* Deut. 8:3 [d]*8* Deut. 6:13 [e]*11* Psalm 91:11,12 [f]*12* Deut. 6:16 [g]*19* Isaiah 61:1,2

Israel in Elijah's time, when the sky was shut
for three and a half years and there was a
severe famine throughout the land. 26Yet Elijah was not sent to any of them, but to a
widow in Zarephath in the region of Sidon.
27And there were many in Israel with leprosy[a] in the time of Elisha the prophet, yet
not one of them was cleansed—only Naaman the Syrian."

28All the people in the synagogue were
furious when they heard this. 29They got up,
drove him out of the town, and took him to
the brow of the hill on which the town was
built, in order to throw him down the cliff.
30But he walked right through the crowd and
went on his way.

Jesus Drives Out an Evil Spirit

31Then he went down to Capernaum, a
town in Galilee, and on the Sabbath began to
teach the people. 32They were amazed at his
teaching, because his message had authority.

33In the synagogue there was a man possessed by a demon, an evil[b] spirit. He cried
out at the top of his voice, 34"Ha! What do
you want with us, Jesus of Nazareth? Have
you come to destroy us? I know who you
are—the Holy One of God!"

35"Be quiet!" Jesus said sternly. "Come
out of him!" Then the demon threw the man
down before them all and came out without
injuring him.

36All the people were amazed and said to
each other, "What is this teaching? With authority and power he gives orders to evil
spirits and they come out!" 37And the news
about him spread throughout the surrounding area.

Jesus Heals Many

38Jesus left the synagogue and went to the
home of Simon. Now Simon's mother-in-law
was suffering from a high fever, and they
asked Jesus to help her. 39So he bent over
her and rebuked the fever, and it left her. She
got up at once and began to wait on them.

40When the sun was setting, the people
brought to Jesus all who had various kinds of
sickness, and laying his hands on each one,
he healed them. 41Moreover, demons came
out of many people, shouting, "You are the
Son of God!" But he rebuked them and
would not allow them to speak, because they
knew he was the Christ.[c]

42At daybreak Jesus went out to a solitary
place. The people were looking for him and
when they came to where he was, they tried
to keep him from leaving them. 43But he said,
"I must preach the good news of the kingdom of God to the other towns also, because
that is why I was sent." 44And he kept on
preaching in the synagogues of Judea.[d]

The Calling of the First Disciples

5 One day as Jesus was standing by the
Lake of Gennesaret,[e] with the people
crowding around him and listening to the
word of God, 2he saw at the water's edge two
boats, left there by the fishermen, who were
washing their nets. 3He got into one of the
boats, the one belonging to Simon, and
asked him to put out a little from shore. Then
he sat down and taught the people from the
boat.

4When he had finished speaking, he said
to Simon, "Put out into deep water, and let
down[f] the nets for a catch."

5Simon answered, "Master, we've worked
hard all night and haven't caught anything.
But because you say so, I will let down the
nets."

6When they had done so, they caught such
a large number of fish that their nets began to
break. 7So they signaled their partners in the
other boat to come and help them, and they
came and filled both boats so full that they
began to sink.

8When Simon Peter saw this, he fell at
Jesus' knees and said, "Go away from me,
Lord; I am a sinful man!" 9For he and all his
companions were astonished at the catch of
fish they had taken, 10and so were James
and John, the sons of Zebedee, Simon's
partners.

Then Jesus said to Simon, "Don't be
afraid; from now on you will catch men." 11So
they pulled their boats up on shore, left
everything and followed him.

The Man With Leprosy

12While Jesus was in one of the towns, a
man came along who was covered with leprosy.[a] When he saw Jesus, he fell with his
face to the ground and begged him, "Lord, if
you are willing, you can make me clean."

[a] 27,12 The Greek word was used for various diseases affecting the skin—not necessarily leprosy. [b] 33 Greek *unclean*; also in verse 36 [c] 41 Or *Messiah* [d] 44 Or *the land of the Jews;* some manuscripts *Galilee* [e] 1 That is, Sea of Galilee [f] 4 The Greek verb is plural.

13 Jesus reached out his hand and touched
the man. "I am willing," he said. "Be clean!"
And immediately the leprosy left him.
14 Then Jesus ordered him, "Don't tell anyone, but go, show yourself to the priest and
offer the sacrifices that Moses commanded
for your cleansing, as a testimony to them."
15 Yet the news about him spread all the
more, so that crowds of people came to hear
him and to be healed of their sicknesses.
16 But Jesus often withdrew to lonely places
and prayed.

Jesus Heals a Paralytic

17 One day as he was teaching, Pharisees
and teachers of the law, who had come from
every village of Galilee and from Judea and
Jerusalem, were sitting there. And the power
of the Lord was present for him to heal the
sick. 18 Some men came carrying a paralytic
on a mat and tried to take him into the house
to lay him before Jesus. 19 When they could
not find a way to do this because of the
crowd, they went up on the roof and lowered
him on his mat through the tiles into the middle of the crowd, right in front of Jesus.
20 When Jesus saw their faith, he said,
"Friend, your sins are forgiven."
21 The Pharisees and the teachers of the
law began thinking to themselves, "Who is
this fellow who speaks blasphemy? Who can
forgive sins but God alone?"
22 Jesus knew what they were thinking and
asked, "Why are you thinking these things in
your hearts? 23 Which is easier: to say, 'Your
sins are forgiven,' or to say, 'Get up and
walk'? 24 But that you may know that the Son
of Man has authority on earth to forgive
sins. . . ." He said to the paralyzed man, "I
tell you, get up, take your mat and go home."
25 Immediately he stood up in front of them,
took what he had been lying on and went
home praising God. 26 Everyone was
amazed and gave praise to God. They were
filled with awe and said, "We have seen
remarkable things today."

The Calling of Levi

27 After this, Jesus went out and saw a tax
collector by the name of Levi sitting at his tax
booth. "Follow me," Jesus said to him, 28 and
Levi got up, left everything and followed him.
29 Then Levi held a great banquet for Jesus
at his house, and a large crowd of tax collectors and others were eating with them. 30 But
the Pharisees and the teachers of the law
who belonged to their sect complained to his
disciples, "Why do you eat and drink with tax
collectors and 'sinners'?"
31 Jesus answered them, "It is not the
healthy who need a doctor, but the sick. 32 I
have not come to call the righteous, but sinners to repentance."

Jesus Questioned About Fasting

33 They said to him, "John's disciples often
fast and pray, and so do the disciples of the
Pharisees, but yours go on eating and drinking."
34 Jesus answered, "Can you make the
guests of the bridegroom fast while he is with
them? 35 But the time will come when the
bridegroom will be taken from them; in those
days they will fast."
36 He told them this parable: "No one tears
a patch from a new garment and sews it on
an old one. If he does, he will have torn the
new garment, and the patch from the new
will not match the old. 37 And no one pours
new wine into old wineskins. If he does, the
new wine will burst the skins, the wine will
run out and the wineskins will be ruined.
38 No, new wine must be poured into new
wineskins. 39 And no one after drinking old
wine wants the new, for he says, 'The old is
better.' "

Lord of the Sabbath

6 One Sabbath Jesus was going through
the grainfields, and his disciples began
to pick some heads of grain, rub them in their
hands and eat the kernels. 2 Some of the
Pharisees asked, "Why are you doing what
is unlawful on the Sabbath?"
3 Jesus answered them, "Have you never
read what David did when he and his companions were hungry? 4 He entered the
house of God, and taking the consecrated
bread, he ate what is lawful only for priests to
eat. And he also gave some to his companions." 5 Then Jesus said to them, "The Son of
Man is Lord of the Sabbath."
6 On another Sabbath he went into the
synagogue and was teaching, and a man
was there whose right hand was shriveled.
7 The Pharisees and the teachers of the law
were looking for a reason to accuse Jesus,
so they watched him closely to see if he
would heal on the Sabbath. 8 But Jesus knew
what they were thinking and said to the man
with the shriveled hand, "Get up and stand in
front of everyone." So he got up and stood
there.
9 Then Jesus said to them, "I ask you,

which is lawful on the Sabbath: to do good or
to do evil, to save life or to destroy it?"
10He looked around at them all, and then
said to the man, "Stretch out your hand." He
did so, and his hand was completely restored. 11But they were furious and began to
discuss with one another what they might do
to Jesus.

The Twelve Apostles

12One of those days Jesus went out to a
mountainside to pray, and spent the night
praying to God. 13When morning came, he
called his disciples to him and chose twelve
of them, whom he also designated apostles:
14Simon (whom he named Peter), his brother
Andrew, James, John, Philip, Bartholomew,
15Matthew, Thomas, James son of Alphaeus, Simon who was called the Zealot,
16Judas son of James, and Judas Iscariot,
who became a traitor.

Blessings and Woes

17He went down with them and stood on a
level place. A large crowd of his disciples
was there and a great number of people from
all over Judea, from Jerusalem, and from the
coast of Tyre and Sidon, 18who had come to
hear him and to be healed of their diseases.
Those troubled by evil[a] spirits were cured,
19and the people all tried to touch him, because power was coming from him and healing them all.
20Looking at his disciples, he said:

"Blessed are you who are poor,
for yours is the kingdom of God.
21Blessed are you who hunger now,
for you will be satisfied.
Blessed are you who weep now,
for you will laugh.
22Blessed are you when men hate you,
when they exclude you and insult you
and reject your name as evil,
because of the Son of Man.

23"Rejoice in that day and leap for joy, because great is your reward in heaven. For
that is how their fathers treated the prophets.

24"But woe to you who are rich,
for you have already received your
comfort.
25Woe to you who are well fed now,
for you will go hungry.
Woe to you who laugh now,
for you will mourn and weep.
26Woe to you when all men speak well of
you,
for that is how their fathers treated the
false prophets.

Love for Enemies

27"But I tell you who hear me: Love your
enemies, do good to those who hate you,
28bless those who curse you, pray for those
who mistreat you. 29If someone strikes you
on one cheek, turn to him the other also. If
someone takes your cloak, do not stop him
from taking your tunic. 30Give to everyone
who asks you, and if anyone takes what belongs to you, do not demand it back. 31Do to
others as you would have them do to you.
32"If you love those who love you, what
credit is that to you? Even 'sinners' love
those who love them. 33And if you do good to
those who are good to you, what credit is that
to you? Even 'sinners' do that. 34And if you
lend to those from whom you expect repay-
ment, what credit is that to you? Even 'sinners' lend to 'sinners,' expecting to be repaid
in full. 35But love your enemies, do good to
them, and lend to them without expecting to
get anything back. Then your reward will be
great, and you will be sons of the Most High,
because he is kind to the ungrateful and
wicked. 36Be merciful, just as your Father is
merciful.

Judging Others

37"Do not judge, and you will not be
judged. Do not condemn, and you will not be
condemned. Forgive, and you will be forgiven. 38Give, and it will be given to you. A
good measure, pressed down, shaken together and running over, will be poured into
your lap. For with the measure you use, it will
be measured to you."
39He also told them this parable: "Can a
blind man lead a blind man? Will they not
both fall into a pit? 40A student is not above
his teacher, but everyone who is fully trained
will be like his teacher.
41"Why do you look at the speck of sawdust in your brother's eye and pay no attention to the plank in your own eye? 42How can
you say to your brother, 'Brother, let me take
the speck out of your eye,' when you yourself
fail to see the plank in your own eye? You
hypocrite, first take the plank out of your eye,
and then you will see clearly to remove the
speck from your brother's eye.

[a] 18 Greek *unclean*

A Tree and Its Fruit

43“No good tree bears bad fruit, nor does a
bad tree bear good fruit. 44Each tree is recognized by its own fruit. People do not pick figs
from thornbushes, or grapes from briers.
45The good man brings good things out of the
good stored up in his heart, and the evil man
brings evil things out of the evil stored up in
his heart. For out of the overflow of his heart
his mouth speaks.

The Wise and Foolish Builders

46“Why do you call me, ‘Lord, Lord,’ and do
not do what I say? 47I will show you what he
is like who comes to me and hears my words
and puts them into practice. 48He is like a
man building a house, who dug down deep
and laid the foundation on rock. When a
flood came, the torrent struck that house but
could not shake it, because it was well built.
49But the one who hears my words and does
not put them into practice is like a man who
built a house on the ground without a foundation. The moment the torrent struck that
house, it collapsed and its destruction was
complete.”

The Faith of the Centurion

7 When Jesus had finished saying all this
in the hearing of the people, he entered
Capernaum. 2There a centurion's servant,
whom his master valued highly, was sick and
about to die. 3The centurion heard of Jesus
and sent some elders of the Jews to him,
asking him to come and heal his servant.
4When they came to Jesus, they pleaded
earnestly with him, “This man deserves to
have you do this, 5because he loves our nation and has built our synagogue.” 6So Jesus
went with them.

He was not far from the house when the
centurion sent friends to say to him: “Lord,
don't trouble yourself, for I do not deserve to
have you come under my roof. 7That is why I
did not even consider myself worthy to come
to you. But say the word, and my servant will
be healed. 8For I myself am a man under
authority, with soldiers under me. I tell this
one, ‘Go,’ and he goes; and that one,
‘Come,’ and he comes. I say to my servant,
‘Do this,’ and he does it.”

9When Jesus heard this, he was amazed
at him, and turning to the crowd following
him, he said, “I tell you, I have not found such
great faith even in Israel.” 10Then the men
who had been sent returned to the house
and found the servant well.

Jesus Raises a Widow's Son

11Soon afterward, Jesus went to a town
called Nain, and his disciples and a large
crowd went along with him. 12As he approached the town gate, a dead person was
being carried out—the only son of his
mother, and she was a widow. And a large
crowd from the town was with her. 13When
the Lord saw her, his heart went out to her
and he said, “Don't cry.”

14Then he went up and touched the coffin,
and those carrying it stood still. He said,
“Young man, I say to you, get up!” 15The
dead man sat up and began to talk, and
Jesus gave him back to his mother.

16They were all filled with awe and praised
God. “A great prophet has appeared among
us,” they said. “God has come to help his
people.” 17This news about Jesus spread
throughout Judea[a] and the surrounding
country.

Jesus and John the Baptist

18John's disciples told him about all these
things. Calling two of them, 19he sent them to
the Lord to ask, “Are you the one who was to
come, or should we expect someone else?”

20When the men came to Jesus, they said,
“John the Baptist sent us to you to ask, ‘Are
you the one who was to come, or should we
expect someone else?’ ”

21At that very time Jesus cured many who
had diseases, sicknesses and evil spirits,
and gave sight to many who were blind. 22So
he replied to the messengers, “Go back and
report to John what you have seen and
heard: The blind receive sight, the lame
walk, those who have leprosy[b] are cured,
the deaf hear, the dead are raised, and the
good news is preached to the poor.
23Blessed is the man who does not fall away
on account of me.”

24After John's messengers left, Jesus began to speak to the crowd about John: “What
did you go out into the desert to see? A reed
swayed by the wind? 25If not, what did you go
out to see? A man dressed in fine clothes?
No, those who wear expensive clothes and
indulge in luxury are in palaces. 26But what
did you go out to see? A prophet? Yes, I tell

[a] 17 Or *the land of the Jews* [b] 22 The Greek word was used for various diseases affecting the skin—not necessarily leprosy.

you, and more than a prophet. 27This is the one about whom it is written:

" 'I will send my messenger ahead of you,
who will prepare your way before you.'[a]

28I tell you, among those born of women there is no one greater than John; yet the one who is least in the kingdom of God is greater than he."

29(All the people, even the tax collectors, when they heard Jesus' words, acknowledged that God's way was right, because they had been baptized by John. 30But the Pharisees and experts in the law rejected God's purpose for themselves, because they had not been baptized by John.)

31"To what, then, can I compare the people of this generation? What are they like? 32They are like children sitting in the marketplace and calling out to each other:

" 'We played the flute for you,
and you did not dance;
we sang a dirge,
and you did not cry.'

33For John the Baptist came neither eating bread nor drinking wine, and you say, 'He has a demon.' 34The Son of Man came eating and drinking, and you say, 'Here is a glutton and a drunkard, a friend of tax collectors and "sinners." ' 35But wisdom is proved right by all her children."

Jesus Anointed by a Sinful Woman

36Now one of the Pharisees invited Jesus to have dinner with him, so he went to the Pharisee's house and reclined at the table. 37When a woman who had lived a sinful life in that town learned that Jesus was eating at the Pharisee's house, she brought an alabaster jar of perfume, 38and as she stood behind him at his feet weeping, she began to wet his feet with her tears. Then she wiped them with her hair, kissed them and poured perfume on them.

39When the Pharisee who had invited him saw this, he said to himself, "If this man were a prophet, he would know who is touching him and what kind of woman she is—that she is a sinner."

40Jesus answered him, "Simon, I have something to tell you."

"Tell me, teacher," he said.

41"Two men owed money to a certain moneylender. One owed him five hundred denarii,[b] and the other fifty. 42Neither of them had the money to pay him back, so he canceled the debts of both. Now which of them will love him more?"

43Simon replied, "I suppose the one who had the bigger debt canceled."

"You have judged correctly," Jesus said.

44Then he turned toward the woman and said to Simon, "Do you see this woman? I came into your house. You did not give me any water for my feet, but she wet my feet with her tears and wiped them with her hair. 45You did not give me a kiss, but this woman, from the time I entered, has not stopped kissing my feet. 46You did not put oil on my head, but she has poured perfume on my feet. 47Therefore, I tell you, her many sins have been forgiven—for she loved much. But he who has been forgiven little loves little."

48Then Jesus said to her, "Your sins are forgiven."

49The other guests began to say among themselves, "Who is this who even forgives sins?"

50Jesus said to the woman, "Your faith has saved you; go in peace."

The Parable of the Sower

8 After this, Jesus traveled about from one town and village to another, proclaiming the good news of the kingdom of God. The Twelve were with him, 2and also some women who had been cured of evil spirits and diseases: Mary (called Magdalene) from whom seven demons had come out; 3Joanna the wife of Cuza, the manager of Herod's household; Susanna; and many others. These women were helping to support them out of their own means.

4While a large crowd was gathering and people were coming to Jesus from town after town, he told this parable: 5"A farmer went out to sow his seed. As he was scattering the seed, some fell along the path; it was trampled on, and the birds of the air ate it up. 6Some fell on rock, and when it came up, the plants withered because they had no moisture. 7Other seed fell among thorns, which grew up with it and choked the plants. 8Still other seed fell on good soil. It came up and yielded a crop, a hundred times more than was sown."

When he said this, he called out, "He who has ears to hear, let him hear."

9His disciples asked him what this parable

[a]27 Mal. 3:1 [b]41 A denarius was a coin worth about a day's wages.

meant. 10He said, "The knowledge of the
secrets of the kingdom of God has been giv-
en to you, but to others I speak in parables,
so that,

> " 'though seeing, they may not see;
> though hearing, they may not
> understand.'[a]

11"This is the meaning of the parable: The
seed is the word of God. 12Those along the
path are the ones who hear, and then the
devil comes and takes away the word from
their hearts, so that they may not believe and
be saved. 13Those on the rock are the ones
who receive the word with joy when they
hear it, but they have no root. They believe
for a while, but in the time of testing they fall
away. 14The seed that fell among thorns
stands for those who hear, but as they go on
their way they are choked by life's worries,
riches and pleasures, and they do not mature. 15But the seed on good soil stands for
those with a noble and good heart, who hear
the word, retain it, and by persevering produce a crop.

A Lamp on a Stand

16"No one lights a lamp and hides it in a jar
or puts it under a bed. Instead, he puts it on a
stand, so that those who come in can see the
light. 17For there is nothing hidden that will
not be disclosed, and nothing concealed that
will not be known or brought out into the
open. 18Therefore consider carefully how
you listen. Whoever has will be given more;
whoever does not have, even what he thinks
he has will be taken from him."

Jesus' Mother and Brothers

19Now Jesus' mother and brothers came
to see him, but they were not able to get near
him because of the crowd. 20Someone told
him, "Your mother and brothers are standing
outside, wanting to see you."

21He replied, "My mother and brothers are
those who hear God's word and put it into
practice."

Jesus Calms the Storm

22One day Jesus said to his disciples,
"Let's go over to the other side of the lake."
So they got into a boat and set out. 23As they
sailed, he fell asleep. A squall came down on
the lake, so that the boat was being
swamped, and they were in great danger.

24The disciples went and woke him, saying, "Master, Master, we're going to drown!"

He got up and rebuked the wind and the
raging waters; the storm subsided, and all
was calm. 25"Where is your faith?" he asked
his disciples.

In fear and amazement they asked one
another, "Who is this? He commands even
the winds and the water, and they obey him."

The Healing of a Demon-possessed Man

26They sailed to the region of the Gerasenes,[b] which is across the lake from Galilee. 27When Jesus stepped ashore, he was
met by a demon-possessed man from the
town. For a long time this man had not worn
clothes or lived in a house, but had lived in
the tombs. 28When he saw Jesus, he cried
out and fell at his feet, shouting at the top of
his voice, "What do you want with me, Jesus,
Son of the Most High God? I beg you, don't
torture me!" 29For Jesus had commanded
the evil[c] spirit to come out of the man. Many
times it had seized him, and though he was
chained hand and foot and kept under guard,
he had broken his chains and had been
driven by the demon into solitary places.

30Jesus asked him, "What is your name?"

"Legion," he replied, because many demons had gone into him. 31And they begged
him repeatedly not to order them to go into
the Abyss.

32A large herd of pigs was feeding there on
the hillside. The demons begged Jesus to let
them go into them, and he gave them permission. 33When the demons came out of the
man, they went into the pigs, and the herd
rushed down the steep bank into the lake
and was drowned.

34When those tending the pigs saw what
had happened, they ran off and reported this
in the town and countryside, 35and the
people went out to see what had happened.
When they came to Jesus, they found the
man from whom the demons had gone out,
sitting at Jesus' feet, dressed and in his right
mind; and they were afraid. 36Those who had
seen it told the people how the demon-possessed man had been cured. 37Then all the
people of the region of the Gerasenes asked
Jesus to leave them, because they were

[a] *10* Isaiah 6:9 [b] *26* Some manuscripts *Gadarenes*; other manuscripts *Gergesenes;* also in verse 37
[c] *29* Greek *unclean*

overcome with fear. So he got into the boat
and left.
38The man from whom the demons had
gone out begged to go with him, but Jesus
sent him away, saying, 39"Return home and
tell how much God has done for you." So the
man went away and told all over town how
much Jesus had done for him.

A Dead Girl and a Sick Woman

40Now when Jesus returned, a crowd welcomed him, for they were all expecting him.
41Then a man named Jairus, a ruler of the
synagogue, came and fell at Jesus' feet,
pleading with him to come to his house 42be-
cause his only daughter, a girl of about
twelve, was dying.
As Jesus was on his way, the crowds almost crushed him. 43And a woman was there
who had been subject to bleeding for twelve
years,[a] but no one could heal her. 44She
came up behind him and touched the edge of
his cloak, and immediately her bleeding
stopped.
45"Who touched me?" Jesus asked.
When they all denied it, Peter said, "Master, the people are crowding and pressing
against you."
46But Jesus said, "Someone touched me; I
know that power has gone out from me."
47Then the woman, seeing that she could
not go unnoticed, came trembling and fell at
his feet. In the presence of all the people, she
told why she had touched him and how she
had been instantly healed. 48Then he said to
her, "Daughter, your faith has healed you.
Go in peace."
49While Jesus was still speaking, someone
came from the house of Jairus, the synagogue ruler. "Your daughter is dead," he
said. "Don't bother the teacher any more."
50Hearing this, Jesus said to Jairus, "Don't
be afraid; just believe, and she will be
healed."
51When he arrived at the house of Jairus,
he did not let anyone go in with him except
Peter, John and James, and the child's father and mother. 52Meanwhile, all the people
were wailing and mourning for her. "Stop
wailing," Jesus said. "She is not dead but
asleep."
53They laughed at him, knowing that she
was dead. 54But he took her by the hand and
said, "My child, get up!" 55Her spirit returned,
and at once she stood up. Then Jesus told
them to give her something to eat. 56Her parents were astonished, but he ordered them
not to tell anyone what had happened.

Jesus Sends Out the Twelve

9 When Jesus had called the Twelve together, he gave them power and authority to drive out all demons and to cure diseases, 2and he sent them out to preach the
kingdom of God and to heal the sick. 3He told
them: "Take nothing for the journey—no
staff, no bag, no bread, no money, no extra
tunic. 4Whatever house you enter, stay there
until you leave that town. 5If people do not
welcome you, shake the dust off your feet
when you leave their town, as a testimony
against them." 6So they set out and went
from village to village, preaching the gospel
and healing people everywhere.
7Now Herod the tetrarch heard about all
that was going on. And he was perplexed,
because some were saying that John had
been raised from the dead, 8others that Elijah had appeared, and still others that one of
the prophets of long ago had come back to
life. 9But Herod said, "I beheaded John.
Who, then, is this I hear such things about?"
And he tried to see him.

Jesus Feeds the Five Thousand

10When the apostles returned, they reported to Jesus what they had done. Then he
took them with him and they withdrew by
themselves to a town called Bethsaida, 11but
the crowds learned about it and followed
him. He welcomed them and spoke to them
about the kingdom of God, and healed those
who needed healing.
12Late in the afternoon the Twelve came to
him and said, "Send the crowd away so they
can go to the surrounding villages and countryside and find food and lodging, because
we are in a remote place here."
13He replied, "You give them something to
eat."
They answered, "We have only five loaves
of bread and two fish—unless we go and buy
food for all this crowd." 14(About five thousand men were there.)
But he said to his disciples, "Have them sit
down in groups of about fifty each." 15The
disciples did so, and everybody sat down.
16Taking the five loaves and the two fish and
looking up to heaven, he gave thanks and
broke them. Then he gave them to the disci-

[a]43 Many manuscripts *years, and she had spent all she had on doctors*

ples to set before the people. 17They all ate
and were satisfied, and the disciples picked
up twelve basketfuls of broken pieces that
were left over.

Peter's Confession of Christ

18Once when Jesus was praying in private
and his disciples were with him, he asked
them, "Who do the crowds say I am?"

19They replied, "Some say John the Baptist; others say Elijah; and still others, that
one of the prophets of long ago has come
back to life."

20"But what about you?" he asked. "Who
do you say I am?"

Peter answered, "The Christ[a] of God."

21Jesus strictly warned them not to tell this
to anyone. 22And he said, "The Son of Man
must suffer many things and be rejected by
the elders, chief priests and teachers of the
law, and he must be killed and on the third
day be raised to life."

23Then he said to them all: "If anyone
would come after me, he must deny himself
and take up his cross daily and follow me.
24For whoever wants to save his life will lose
it, but whoever loses his life for me will save
it. 25What good is it for a man to gain the
whole world, and yet lose or forfeit his very
self? 26If anyone is ashamed of me and my
words, the Son of Man will be ashamed of
him when he comes in his glory and in the
glory of the Father and of the holy angels. 27I
tell you the truth, some who are standing
here will not taste death before they see the
kingdom of God."

The Transfiguration

28About eight days after Jesus said this, he
took Peter, John and James with him and
went up onto a mountain to pray. 29As he
was praying, the appearance of his face
changed, and his clothes became as bright
as a flash of lightning. 30Two men, Moses
and Elijah, 31appeared in glorious splendor,
talking with Jesus. They spoke about his departure, which he was about to bring to fulfillment at Jerusalem. 32Peter and his companions were very sleepy, but when they
became fully awake, they saw his glory and
the two men standing with him. 33As the men
were leaving Jesus, Peter said to him, "Master, it is good for us to be here. Let us put up
three shelters—one for you, one for Moses
and one for Elijah." (He did not know what he
was saying.)

34While he was speaking, a cloud appeared and enveloped them, and they were
afraid as they entered the cloud. 35A voice
came from the cloud, saying, "This is my
Son, whom I have chosen; listen to him."
36When the voice had spoken, they found
that Jesus was alone. The disciples kept this
to themselves, and told no one at that time
what they had seen.

The Healing of a Boy With an Evil Spirit

37The next day, when they came down
from the mountain, a large crowd met him.
38A man in the crowd called out, "Teacher, I
beg you to look at my son, for he is my only
child. 39A spirit seizes him and he suddenly
screams; it throws him into convulsions so
that he foams at the mouth. It scarcely ever
leaves him and is destroying him. 40I begged
your disciples to drive it out, but they could
not."

41"O unbelieving and perverse generation," Jesus replied, "how long shall I stay
with you and put up with you? Bring your son
here."

42Even while the boy was coming, the demon threw him to the ground in a convulsion.
But Jesus rebuked the evil[b] spirit, healed the
boy and gave him back to his father. 43And
they were all amazed at the greatness of
God.

While everyone was marveling at all that
Jesus did, he said to his disciples, 44"Listen
carefully to what I am about to tell you: The
Son of Man is going to be betrayed into the
hands of men." 45But they did not understand what this meant. It was hidden from
them, so that they did not grasp it, and they
were afraid to ask him about it.

Who Will Be the Greatest?

46An argument started among the disciples as to which of them would be the greatest. 47Jesus, knowing their thoughts, took a
little child and had him stand beside him.
48Then he said to them, "Whoever welcomes
this little child in my name welcomes me; and
whoever welcomes me welcomes the one
who sent me. For he who is least among you
all—he is the greatest."

[a]20 Or *Messiah* [b]42 Greek *unclean*

49"Master," said John, "we saw a man
driving out demons in your name and we
tried to stop him, because he is not one of
us."

50"Do not stop him," Jesus said, "for whoever is not against you is for you."

Samaritan Opposition

51As the time approached for him to be
taken up to heaven, Jesus resolutely set out
for Jerusalem. 52And he sent messengers on
ahead, who went into a Samaritan village to
get things ready for him; 53but the people
there did not welcome him, because he was
heading for Jerusalem. 54When the disciples
James and John saw this, they asked, "Lord,
do you want us to call fire down from heaven
to destroy them[a]?" 55But Jesus turned and
rebuked them, 56and[b] they went to another
village.

The Cost of Following Jesus

57As they were walking along the road, a
man said to him, "I will follow you wherever
you go."

58Jesus replied, "Foxes have holes and
birds of the air have nests, but the Son of
Man has no place to lay his head."

59He said to another man, "Follow me."

But the man replied, "Lord, first let me go
and bury my father."

60Jesus said to him, "Let the dead bury
their own dead, but you go and proclaim the
kingdom of God."

61Still another said, "I will follow you, Lord;
but first let me go back and say good-by to
my family."

62Jesus replied, "No one who puts his
hand to the plow and looks back is fit for
service in the kingdom of God."

Jesus Sends Out the Seventy-two

10 After this the Lord appointed seventy-two[c] others and sent them two by
two ahead of him to every town and place
where he was about to go. 2He told them,
"The harvest is plentiful, but the workers are
few. Ask the Lord of the harvest, therefore, to
send out workers into his harvest field. 3Go! I
am sending you out like lambs among
wolves. 4Do not take a purse or bag or sandals; and do not greet anyone on the road.

5"When you enter a house, first say,
'Peace to this house.' 6If a man of peace is
there, your peace will rest on him; if not, it will
return to you. 7Stay in that house, eating and
drinking whatever they give you, for the
worker deserves his wages. Do not move
around from house to house.

8"When you enter a town and are welcomed, eat what is set before you. 9Heal the
sick who are there and tell them, 'The kingdom of God is near you.' 10But when you
enter a town and are not welcomed, go into
its streets and say, 11'Even the dust of your
town that sticks to our feet we wipe off
against you. Yet be sure of this: The kingdom
of God is near.' 12I tell you, it will be more
bearable on that day for Sodom than for that
town.

13"Woe to you, Korazin! Woe to you, Bethsaida! For if the miracles that were performed in you had been performed in Tyre
and Sidon, they would have repented long
ago, sitting in sackcloth and ashes. 14But it
will be more bearable for Tyre and Sidon at
the judgment than for you. 15And you, Capernaum, will you be lifted up to the skies? No,
you will go down to the depths.[d]

16"He who listens to you listens to me; he
who rejects you rejects me; but he who rejects me rejects him who sent me."

17The seventy-two returned with joy and
said, "Lord, even the demons submit to us in
your name."

18He replied, "I saw Satan fall like lightning
from heaven. 19I have given you authority to
trample on snakes and scorpions and to
overcome all the power of the enemy; nothing will harm you. 20However, do not rejoice
that the spirits submit to you, but rejoice that
your names are written in heaven."

21At that time Jesus, full of joy through the
Holy Spirit, said, "I praise you, Father, Lord
of heaven and earth, because you have hidden these things from the wise and learned,
and revealed them to little children. Yes, Father, for this was your good pleasure.

22"All things have been committed to me
by my Father. No one knows who the Son is
except the Father, and no one knows who
the Father is except the Son and those to
whom the Son chooses to reveal him."

23Then he turned to his disciples and said
privately, "Blessed are the eyes that see
what you see. 24For I tell you that many
prophets and kings wanted to see what you

[a]54 Some manuscripts *them, even as Elijah did* [b]55,56 Some manuscripts *them. And he said, "You do not know what kind of spirit you are of, for the Son of Man did not come to destroy men's lives, but to save them." 56And*
[c]1 Some manuscripts *seventy*; also in verse 17 [d]15 Greek *Hades*

see but did not see it, and to hear what you
hear but did not hear it."

The Parable of the Good Samaritan

25 On one occasion an expert in the law
stood up to test Jesus. "Teacher," he asked,
"what must I do to inherit eternal life?"
26 "What is written in the Law?" he replied.
"How do you read it?"
27 He answered: " 'Love the Lord your God
with all your heart and with all your soul and
with all your strength and with all your
mind'[a]; and, 'Love your neighbor as yourself.'[b]"
28 "You have answered correctly," Jesus
replied. "Do this and you will live."
29 But he wanted to justify himself, so he
asked Jesus, "And who is my neighbor?"
30 In reply Jesus said: "A man was going
down from Jerusalem to Jericho, when he
fell into the hands of robbers. They stripped
him of his clothes, beat him and went away,
leaving him half dead. 31 A priest happened to
be going down the same road, and when he
saw the man, he passed by on the other side.
32 So too, a Levite, when he came to the
place and saw him, passed by on the other
side. 33 But a Samaritan, as he traveled,
came where the man was; and when he saw
him, he took pity on him. 34 He went to him
and bandaged his wounds, pouring on oil
and wine. Then he put the man on his own
donkey, took him to an inn and took care of
him. 35 The next day he took out two silver
coins[c] and gave them to the innkeeper.
'Look after him,' he said, 'and when I return,
I will reimburse you for any extra expense
you may have.'
36 "Which of these three do you think was a
neighbor to the man who fell into the hands
of robbers?"
37 The expert in the law replied, "The one
who had mercy on him."
Jesus told him, "Go and do likewise."

At the Home of Martha and Mary

38 As Jesus and his disciples were on their
way, he came to a village where a woman
named Martha opened her home to him.
39 She had a sister called Mary, who sat at the
Lord's feet listening to what he said. 40 But
Martha was distracted by all the preparations
that had to be made. She came to him and
asked, "Lord, don't you care that my sister
has left me to do the work by myself? Tell her
to help me!"
41 "Martha, Martha," the Lord answered,
"you are worried and upset about many
things, 42 but only one thing is needed.[d] Mary
has chosen what is better, and it will not be
taken away from her."

Jesus' Teaching on Prayer

11 One day Jesus was praying in a certain place. When he finished, one of
his disciples said to him, "Lord, teach us to
pray, just as John taught his disciples."
2 He said to them, "When you pray, say:

" 'Father,[e]
hallowed be your name,
your kingdom come.[f]
3 Give us each day our daily bread.
4 Forgive us our sins,
for we also forgive everyone who sins
against us.[g]
And lead us not into temptation.[h]' "

5 Then he said to them, "Suppose one of
you has a friend, and he goes to him at midnight and says, 'Friend, lend me three loaves
of bread, 6 because a friend of mine on a
journey has come to me, and I have nothing
to set before him.'
7 "Then the one inside answers, 'Don't
bother me. The door is already locked, and
my children are with me in bed. I can't get up
and give you anything.' 8 I tell you, though he
will not get up and give him the bread because he is his friend, yet because of the
man's boldness[i] he will get up and give him
as much as he needs.
9 "So I say to you: Ask and it will be given to
you; seek and you will find; knock and the
door will be opened to you. 10 For everyone
who asks receives; he who seeks finds; and
to him who knocks, the door will be opened.
11 "Which of you fathers, if your son asks
for[j] a fish, will give him a snake instead?
12 Or if he asks for an egg, will give him a
scorpion? 13 If you then, though you are evil,
know how to give good gifts to your children,
how much more will your Father in heaven
give the Holy Spirit to those who ask him!"

[a]27 Deut. 6:5 [b]27 Lev. 19:18 [c]35 Greek *two denarii* [d]42 Some manuscripts *but few things are needed—or only one* [e]2 Some manuscripts *Our Father in heaven* [f]2 Some manuscripts *come. May your will be done on earth as it is in heaven.* [g]4 Greek *everyone who is indebted to us* [h]4 Some manuscripts *temptation but deliver us from the evil one* [i]8 Or *persistence* [j]11 Some manuscripts *for bread, will give him a stone; or if he asks for*

Jesus and Beelzebub

14Jesus was driving out a demon that was mute. When the demon left, the man who had been mute spoke, and the crowd was amazed. 15But some of them said, "By Beelzebub,[a] the prince of demons, he is driving out demons." 16Others tested him by asking for a sign from heaven.

17Jesus knew their thoughts and said to them: "Any kingdom divided against itself will be ruined, and a house divided against itself will fall. 18If Satan is divided against himself, how can his kingdom stand? I say this because you claim that I drive out demons by Beelzebub. 19Now if I drive out demons by Beelzebub, by whom do your followers drive them out? So then, they will be your judges. 20But if I drive out demons by the finger of God, then the kingdom of God has come to you.

21"When a strong man, fully armed, guards his own house, his possessions are safe. 22But when someone stronger attacks and overpowers him, he takes away the armor in which the man trusted and divides up the spoils.

23"He who is not with me is against me, and he who does not gather with me, scatters.

24"When an evil[b] spirit comes out of a man, it goes through arid places seeking rest and does not find it. Then it says, 'I will return to the house I left.' 25When it arrives, it finds the house swept clean and put in order. 26Then it goes and takes seven other spirits more wicked than itself, and they go in and live there. And the final condition of that man is worse than the first."

27As Jesus was saying these things, a woman in the crowd called out, "Blessed is the mother who gave you birth and nursed you."

28He replied, "Blessed rather are those who hear the word of God and obey it."

The Sign of Jonah

29As the crowds increased, Jesus said, "This is a wicked generation. It asks for a miraculous sign, but none will be given it except the sign of Jonah. 30For as Jonah was a sign to the Ninevites, so also will the Son of Man be to this generation. 31The Queen of the South will rise at the judgment with the men of this generation and condemn them; for she came from the ends of the earth to listen to Solomon's wisdom, and now one[c] greater than Solomon is here. 32The men of Nineveh will stand up at the judgment with this generation and condemn it; for they repented at the preaching of Jonah, and now one greater than Jonah is here.

The Lamp of the Body

33"No one lights a lamp and puts it in a place where it will be hidden, or under a bowl. Instead he puts it on its stand, so that those who come in may see the light. 34Your eye is the lamp of your body. When your eyes are good, your whole body also is full of light. But when they are bad, your body also is full of darkness. 35See to it, then, that the light within you is not darkness. 36Therefore, if your whole body is full of light, and no part of it dark, it will be completely lighted, as when the light of a lamp shines on you."

Six Woes

37When Jesus had finished speaking, a Pharisee invited him to eat with him; so he went in and reclined at the table. 38But the Pharisee, noticing that Jesus did not first wash before the meal, was surprised.

39Then the Lord said to him, "Now then, you Pharisees clean the outside of the cup and dish, but inside you are full of greed and wickedness. 40You foolish people! Did not the one who made the outside make the inside also? 41But give what is inside ⌞the dish⌟[d] to the poor, and everything will be clean for you.

42"Woe to you Pharisees, because you give God a tenth of your mint, rue and all other kinds of garden herbs, but you neglect justice and the love of God. You should have practiced the latter without leaving the former undone.

43"Woe to you Pharisees, because you love the most important seats in the synagogues and greetings in the marketplaces.

44"Woe to you, because you are like unmarked graves, which men walk over without knowing it."

45One of the experts in the law answered him, "Teacher, when you say these things, you insult us also."

46Jesus replied, "And you experts in the law, woe to you, because you load people down with burdens they can hardly carry,

[a] 15 Greek *Beezeboul* or *Beelzeboul*; also in verses 18 and 19 [b] 24 Greek *unclean* [c] 31 Or *something*; also in verse 32 [d] 41 Or *what you have*

and you yourselves will not lift one finger to
help them.
47“Woe to you, because you build tombs
for the prophets, and it was your forefathers
who killed them. 48So you testify that you
approve of what your forefathers did; they
killed the prophets, and you build their
tombs. 49Because of this, God in his wisdom
said, ‘I will send them prophets and apostles,
some of whom they will kill and others they
will persecute.’ 50Therefore this generation
will be held responsible for the blood of all
the prophets that has been shed since the
beginning of the world, 51from the blood of
Abel to the blood of Zechariah, who was
killed between the altar and the sanctuary.
Yes, I tell you, this generation will be held
responsible for it all.
52“Woe to you experts in the law, because
you have taken away the key to knowledge.
You yourselves have not entered, and you
have hindered those who were entering.”
53When Jesus left there, the Pharisees
and the teachers of the law began to oppose
him fiercely and to besiege him with questions, 54waiting to catch him in something he
might say.

Warnings and Encouragements

12 Meanwhile, when a crowd of many
thousands had gathered, so that they
were trampling on one another, Jesus began
to speak first to his disciples, saying: “Be on
your guard against the yeast of the Pharisees, which is hypocrisy. 2There is nothing
concealed that will not be disclosed, or hidden that will not be made known. 3What you
have said in the dark will be heard in the
daylight, and what you have whispered in the
ear in the inner rooms will be proclaimed
from the roofs.
4“I tell you, my friends, do not be afraid of
those who kill the body and after that can do
no more. 5But I will show you whom you
should fear: Fear him who, after the killing of
the body, has power to throw you into hell.
Yes, I tell you, fear him. 6Are not five sparrows sold for two pennies[a]? Yet not one of
them is forgotten by God. 7Indeed, the very
hairs of your head are all numbered. Don’t be
afraid; you are worth more than many sparrows.
8“I tell you, whoever acknowledges me before men, the Son of Man will also acknowledge him before the angels of God. 9But he
who disowns me before men will be disowned before the angels of God. 10And
everyone who speaks a word against the
Son of Man will be forgiven, but anyone who
blasphemes against the Holy Spirit will not
be forgiven.
11“When you are brought before synagogues, rulers and authorities, do not worry
about how you will defend yourselves or
what you will say, 12for the Holy Spirit will
teach you at that time what you should say.”

The Parable of the Rich Fool

13Someone in the crowd said to him,
“Teacher, tell my brother to divide the inheritance with me.”
14Jesus replied, “Man, who appointed me
a judge or an arbiter between you?” 15Then
he said to them, “Watch out! Be on your
guard against all kinds of greed; a man’s life
does not consist in the abundance of his
possessions.”
16And he told them this parable: “The
ground of a certain rich man produced a
good crop. 17He thought to himself, ‘What
shall I do? I have no place to store my crops.’
18“Then he said, ‘This is what I’ll do. I will
tear down my barns and build bigger ones,
and there I will store all my grain and my
goods. 19And I’ll say to myself, “You have
plenty of good things laid up for many years.
Take life easy; eat, drink and be merry.” ’
20“But God said to him, ‘You fool! This very
night your life will be demanded from you.
Then who will get what you have prepared
for yourself?’
21“This is how it will be with anyone who
stores up things for himself but is not rich
toward God.”

Do Not Worry

22Then Jesus said to his disciples: “Therefore I tell you, do not worry about your life,
what you will eat; or about your body, what
you will wear. 23Life is more than food, and
the body more than clothes. 24Consider the
ravens: They do not sow or reap, they have
no storeroom or barn; yet God feeds them.
And how much more valuable you are than
birds! 25Who of you by worrying can add a
single hour to his life[b]? 26Since you cannot
do this very little thing, why do you worry
about the rest?
27“Consider how the lilies grow. They do
not labor or spin. Yet I tell you, not even

[a]6 Greek *two assaria* [b]25 Or *single cubit to his height*

Solomon in all his splendor was dressed like one of these. 28If that is how God clothes the grass of the field, which is here today, and tomorrow is thrown into the fire, how much more will he clothe you, O you of little faith! 29And do not set your heart on what you will eat or drink; do not worry about it. 30For the pagan world runs after all such things, and your Father knows that you need them. 31But seek his kingdom, and these things will be given to you as well.

32"Do not be afraid, little flock, for your Father has been pleased to give you the kingdom. 33Sell your possessions and give to the poor. Provide purses for yourselves that will not wear out, a treasure in heaven that will not be exhausted, where no thief comes near and no moth destroys. 34For where your treasure is, there your heart will be also.

Watchfulness

35"Be dressed ready for service and keep your lamps burning, 36like men waiting for their master to return from a wedding banquet, so that when he comes and knocks they can immediately open the door for him. 37It will be good for those servants whose master finds them watching when he comes. I tell you the truth, he will dress himself to serve, will have them recline at the table and will come and wait on them. 38It will be good for those servants whose master finds them ready, even if he comes in the second or third watch of the night. 39But understand this: If the owner of the house had known at what hour the thief was coming, he would not have let his house be broken into. 40You also must be ready, because the Son of Man will come at an hour when you do not expect him."

41Peter asked, "Lord, are you telling this parable to us, or to everyone?"

42The Lord answered, "Who then is the faithful and wise manager, whom the master puts in charge of his servants to give them their food allowance at the proper time? 43It will be good for that servant whom the master finds doing so when he returns. 44I tell you the truth, he will put him in charge of all his possessions. 45But suppose the servant says to himself, 'My master is taking a long time in coming,' and he then begins to beat the menservants and maidservants and to eat and drink and get drunk. 46The master of that servant will come on a day when he does not expect him and at an hour he is not aware of. He will cut him to pieces and assign him a place with the unbelievers.

47"That servant who knows his master's will and does not get ready or does not do what his master wants will be beaten with many blows. 48But the one who does not know and does things deserving punishment will be beaten with few blows. From everyone who has been given much, much will be demanded; and from the one who has been entrusted with much, much more will be asked.

Not Peace but Division

49"I have come to bring fire on the earth, and how I wish it were already kindled! 50But I have a baptism to undergo, and how distressed I am until it is completed! 51Do you think I came to bring peace on earth? No, I tell you, but division. 52From now on there will be five in one family divided against each other, three against two and two against three. 53They will be divided, father against son and son against father, mother against daughter and daughter against mother, mother-in-law against daughter-in-law and daughter-in-law against mother-in-law."

Interpreting the Times

54He said to the crowd: "When you see a cloud rising in the west, immediately you say, 'It's going to rain,' and it does. 55And when the south wind blows, you say, 'It's going to be hot,' and it is. 56Hypocrites! You know how to interpret the appearance of the earth and the sky. How is it that you don't know how to interpret this present time?

57"Why don't you judge for yourselves what is right? 58As you are going with your adversary to the magistrate, try hard to be reconciled to him on the way, or he may drag you off to the judge, and the judge turn you over to the officer, and the officer throw you into prison. 59I tell you, you will not get out until you have paid the last penny.[a]"

Repent or Perish

13 Now there were some present at that time who told Jesus about the Galileans whose blood Pilate had mixed with their sacrifices. 2Jesus answered, "Do you think that these Galileans were worse sinners than all the other Galileans because

[a]59 Greek *lepton*

they suffered this way? [3]I tell you, no! But
unless you repent, you too will all perish. [4]Or
those eighteen who died when the tower in
Siloam fell on them—do you think they were
more guilty than all the others living in
Jerusalem? [5]I tell you, no! But unless you
repent, you too will all perish."
[6]Then he told this parable: "A man had a
fig tree, planted in his vineyard, and he went
to look for fruit on it, but did not find any. [7]So
he said to the man who took care of the
vineyard, 'For three years now I've been
coming to look for fruit on this fig tree and
haven't found any. Cut it down! Why should it
use up the soil?'
[8]" 'Sir,' the man replied, 'leave it alone for
one more year, and I'll dig around it and
fertilize it. [9]If it bears fruit next year, fine! If
not, then cut it down.' "

A Crippled Woman Healed on the Sabbath

[10]On a Sabbath Jesus was teaching in one
of the synagogues, [11]and a woman was
there who had been crippled by a spirit for
eighteen years. She was bent over and
could not straighten up at all. [12]When Jesus
saw her, he called her forward and said to
her, "Woman, you are set free from your
infirmity." [13]Then he put his hands on her,
and immediately she straightened up and
praised God.
[14]Indignant because Jesus had healed on
the Sabbath, the synagogue ruler said to the
people, "There are six days for work. So
come and be healed on those days, not on
the Sabbath."
[15]The Lord answered him, "You hypocrites! Doesn't each of you on the Sabbath
untie his ox or donkey from the stall and lead
it out to give it water? [16]Then should not this
woman, a daughter of Abraham, whom Satan has kept bound for eighteen long years,
be set free on the Sabbath day from what
bound her?"
[17]When he said this, all his opponents
were humiliated, but the people were delighted with all the wonderful things he was doing.

The Parables of the Mustard Seed and the Yeast

[18]Then Jesus asked, "What is the kingdom
of God like? What shall I compare it to? [19]It is
like a mustard seed, which a man took and
planted in his garden. It grew and became a
tree, and the birds of the air perched in its
branches."
[20]Again he asked, "What shall I compare
the kingdom of God to? [21]It is like yeast that
a woman took and mixed into a large
amount[a] of flour until it worked all through
the dough."

The Narrow Door

[22]Then Jesus went through the towns and
villages, teaching as he made his way to
Jerusalem. [23]Someone asked him, "Lord,
are only a few people going to be saved?"
He said to them, [24]"Make every effort to
enter through the narrow door, because
many, I tell you, will try to enter and will not
be able to. [25]Once the owner of the house
gets up and closes the door, you will stand
outside knocking and pleading, 'Sir, open the
door for us.'
"But he will answer, 'I don't know you or
where you come from.'
[26]"Then you will say, 'We ate and drank
with you, and you taught in our streets.'
[27]"But he will reply, 'I don't know you or
where you come from. Away from me, all you
evildoers!'
[28]"There will be weeping there, and
gnashing of teeth, when you see Abraham,
Isaac and Jacob and all the prophets in the
kingdom of God, but you yourselves thrown
out. [29]People will come from east and west
and north and south, and will take their
places at the feast in the kingdom of God.
[30]Indeed there are those who are last who
will be first, and first who will be last."

Jesus' Sorrow for Jerusalem

[31]At that time some Pharisees came to
Jesus and said to him, "Leave this place and
go somewhere else. Herod wants to kill
you."
[32]He replied, "Go tell that fox, 'I will drive
out demons and heal people today and tomorrow, and on the third day I will reach my
goal.' [33]In any case, I must keep going today
and tomorrow and the next day—for surely
no prophet can die outside Jerusalem!
[34]"O Jerusalem, Jerusalem, you who kill
the prophets and stone those sent to you,
how often I have longed to gather your children together, as a hen gathers her chicks
under her wings, but you were not willing!
[35]Look, your house is left to you desolate. I

[a]21 Greek *three satas* (probably about 1/2 bushel or 22 liters)

tell you, you will not see me again until you
say, 'Blessed is he who comes in the name
of the Lord.'[a]"

Jesus at a Pharisee's House

14 One Sabbath, when Jesus went to
eat in the house of a prominent
Pharisee, he was being carefully watched.
2There in front of him was a man suffering
from dropsy. 3Jesus asked the Pharisees
and experts in the law, "Is it lawful to heal on
the Sabbath or not?" 4But they remained silent. So taking hold of the man, he healed
him and sent him away.
5Then he asked them, "If one of you has a
son[b] or an ox that falls into a well on the
Sabbath day, will you not immediately pull
him out?" 6And they had nothing to say.
7When he noticed how the guests picked
the places of honor at the table, he told them
this parable: 8"When someone invites you to
a wedding feast, do not take the place of
honor, for a person more distinguished than
you may have been invited. 9If so, the host
who invited both of you will come and say to
you, 'Give this man your seat.' Then, humiliated, you will have to take the least important
place. 10But when you are invited, take the
lowest place, so that when your host comes,
he will say to you, 'Friend, move up to a
better place.' Then you will be honored in the
presence of all your fellow guests. 11For
everyone who exalts himself will be humbled, and he who humbles himself will be
exalted."
12Then Jesus said to his host, "When you
give a luncheon or dinner, do not invite your
friends, your brothers or relatives, or your
rich neighbors; if you do, they may invite you
back and so you will be repaid. 13But when
you give a banquet, invite the poor, the crippled, the lame, the blind, 14and you will be
blessed. Although they cannot repay you,
you will be repaid at the resurrection of the
righteous."

The Parable of the Great Banquet

15When one of those at the table with him
heard this, he said to Jesus, "Blessed is the
man who will eat at the feast in the kingdom
of God."
16Jesus replied: "A certain man was preparing a great banquet and invited many
guests. 17At the time of the banquet he sent
his servant to tell those who had been invited, 'Come, for everything is now ready.'
18"But they all alike began to make excuses. The first said, 'I have just bought a
field, and I must go and see it. Please excuse
me.'
19"Another said, 'I have just bought five
yoke of oxen, and I'm on my way to try them
out. Please excuse me.'
20"Still another said, 'I just got married, so
I can't come.'
21"The servant came back and reported
this to his master. Then the owner of the
house became angry and ordered his servant, 'Go out quickly into the streets and
alleys of the town and bring in the poor, the
crippled, the blind and the lame.'
22" 'Sir,' the servant said, 'what you ordered has been done, but there is still room.'
23"Then the master told his servant, 'Go
out to the roads and country lanes and make
them come in, so that my house will be full.
24I tell you, not one of those men who were
invited will get a taste of my banquet.' "

The Cost of Being a Disciple

25Large crowds were traveling with Jesus,
and turning to them he said: 26"If anyone
comes to me and does not hate his father
and mother, his wife and children, his brothers and sisters—yes, even his own life—he
cannot be my disciple. 27And anyone who
does not carry his cross and follow me cannot be my disciple.
28"Suppose one of you wants to build a
tower. Will he not first sit down and estimate
the cost to see if he has enough money to
complete it? 29For if he lays the foundation
and is not able to finish it, everyone who sees
it will ridicule him, 30saying, 'This fellow began to build and was not able to finish.'
31"Or suppose a king is about to go to war
against another king. Will he not first sit down
and consider whether he is able with ten
thousand men to oppose the one coming
against him with twenty thousand? 32If he is
not able, he will send a delegation while the
other is still a long way off and will ask for
terms of peace. 33In the same way, any of
you who does not give up everything he has
cannot be my disciple.
34"Salt is good, but if it loses its saltiness,
how can it be made salty again? 35It is fit
neither for the soil nor for the manure pile; it
is thrown out.

"He who has ears to hear, let him hear."

[a] *35* Psalm 118:26 [b] *5* Some manuscripts *donkey*

The Parable of the Lost Sheep

15 Now the tax collectors and "sinners"
were all gathering around to hear
him. 2But the Pharisees and the teachers of
the law muttered, "This man welcomes sinners and eats with them."
3Then Jesus told them this parable: 4"Suppose one of you has a hundred sheep and
loses one of them. Does he not leave the
ninety-nine in the open country and go after
the lost sheep until he finds it? 5And when he
finds it, he joyfully puts it on his shoulders
6and goes home. Then he calls his friends
and neighbors together and says, 'Rejoice
with me; I have found my lost sheep.' 7I tell
you that in the same way there will be more
rejoicing in heaven over one sinner who repents than over ninety-nine righteous persons who do not need to repent.

The Parable of the Lost Coin

8"Or suppose a woman has ten silver
coins[a] and loses one. Does she not light a
lamp, sweep the house and search carefully
until she finds it? 9And when she finds it, she
calls her friends and neighbors together and
says, 'Rejoice with me; I have found my lost
coin.' 10In the same way, I tell you, there is
rejoicing in the presence of the angels of
God over one sinner who repents."

The Parable of the Lost Son

11Jesus continued: "There was a man who
had two sons. 12The younger one said to his
father, 'Father, give me my share of the estate.' So he divided his property between
them.
13"Not long after that, the younger son got
together all he had, set off for a distant country and there squandered his wealth in wild
living. 14After he had spent everything, there
was a severe famine in that whole country,
and he began to be in need. 15So he went
and hired himself out to a citizen of that country, who sent him to his fields to feed pigs.
16He longed to fill his stomach with the pods
that the pigs were eating, but no one gave
him anything.
17"When he came to his senses, he said,
'How many of my father's hired men have
food to spare, and here I am starving to
death! 18I will set out and go back to my
father and say to him: Father, I have sinned
against heaven and against you. 19I am no
longer worthy to be called your son; make
me like one of your hired men.' 20So he got
up and went to his father.
"But while he was still a long way off, his
father saw him and was filled with compassion for him; he ran to his son, threw his arms
around him and kissed him.
21"The son said to him, 'Father, I have
sinned against heaven and against you. I am
no longer worthy to be called your son.[b]'
22"But the father said to his servants,
'Quick! Bring the best robe and put it on him.
Put a ring on his finger and sandals on his
feet. 23Bring the fattened calf and kill it. Let's
have a feast and celebrate. 24For this son of
mine was dead and is alive again; he was
lost and is found.' So they began to celebrate.
25"Meanwhile, the older son was in the
field. When he came near the house, he
heard music and dancing. 26So he called one
of the servants and asked him what was
going on. 27'Your brother has come,' he replied, 'and your father has killed the fattened
calf because he has him back safe and
sound.'
28"The older brother became angry and
refused to go in. So his father went out and
pleaded with him. 29But he answered his father, 'Look! All these years I've been slaving
for you and never disobeyed your orders.
Yet you never gave me even a young goat so
I could celebrate with my friends. 30But when
this son of yours who has squandered your
property with prostitutes comes home, you
kill the fattened calf for him!'
31" 'My son,' the father said, 'you are always with me, and everything I have is
yours. 32But we had to celebrate and be glad,
because this brother of yours was dead and
is alive again; he was lost and is found.' "

The Parable of the Shrewd Manager

16 Jesus told his disciples: "There was
a rich man whose manager was
accused of wasting his possessions. 2So he
called him in and asked him, 'What is this I
hear about you? Give an account of your
management, because you cannot be manager any longer.'
3"The manager said to himself, 'What shall
I do now? My master is taking away my job.
I'm not strong enough to dig, and I'm
ashamed to beg— 4I know what I'll do so

[a]8 Greek *ten drachmas*, each worth about a day's wages

[b]21 Some early manuscripts *son. Make me like one of your hired men.*

that, when I lose my job here, people will
welcome me into their houses.'
5"So he called in each one of his master's
debtors. He asked the first, 'How much do
you owe my master?'
6" 'Eight hundred gallons[a] of olive oil,' he
replied.
"The manager told him, 'Take your bill, sit
down quickly, and make it four hundred.'
7"Then he asked the second, 'And how
much do you owe?'
" 'A thousand bushels[b] of wheat,' he replied.
"He told him, 'Take your bill and make it
eight hundred.'
8"The master commended the dishonest
manager because he had acted shrewdly.
For the people of this world are more shrewd
in dealing with their own kind than are the
people of the light. 9I tell you, use worldly
wealth to gain friends for yourselves, so that
when it is gone, you will be welcomed into
eternal dwellings.
10"Whoever can be trusted with very little
can also be trusted with much, and whoever
is dishonest with very little will also be dishonest with much. 11So if you have not been
trustworthy in handling worldly wealth, who
will trust you with true riches? 12And if you
have not been trustworthy with someone
else's property, who will give you property of
your own?
13"No servant can serve two masters.
Either he will hate the one and love the other,
or he will be devoted to the one and despise
the other. You cannot serve both God and
Money."
14The Pharisees, who loved money, heard
all this and were sneering at Jesus. 15He said
to them, "You are the ones who justify yourselves in the eyes of men, but God knows
your hearts. What is highly valued among
men is detestable in God's sight.

Additional Teachings

16"The Law and the Prophets were proclaimed until John. Since that time, the good
news of the kingdom of God is being
preached, and everyone is forcing his way
into it. 17It is easier for heaven and earth to
disappear than for the least stroke of a pen to
drop out of the Law.
18"Anyone who divorces his wife and marries another woman commits adultery, and
the man who marries a divorced woman
commits adultery.

The Rich Man and Lazarus

19"There was a rich man who was dressed
in purple and fine linen and lived in luxury
every day. 20At his gate was laid a beggar
named Lazarus, covered with sores 21and
longing to eat what fell from the rich man's
table. Even the dogs came and licked his
sores.
22"The time came when the beggar died
and the angels carried him to Abraham's
side. The rich man also died and was buried.
23In hell,[c] where he was in torment, he
looked up and saw Abraham far away, with
Lazarus by his side. 24So he called to him,
'Father Abraham, have pity on me and send
Lazarus to dip the tip of his finger in water
and cool my tongue, because I am in agony
in this fire.'
25"But Abraham replied, 'Son, remember
that in your lifetime you received your good
things, while Lazarus received bad things,
but now he is comforted here and you are in
agony. 26And besides all this, between us
and you a great chasm has been fixed, so
that those who want to go from here to you
cannot, nor can anyone cross over from
there to us.'
27"He answered, 'Then I beg you, father,
send Lazarus to my father's house, 28for I
have five brothers. Let him warn them, so
that they will not also come to this place of
torment.'
29"Abraham replied, 'They have Moses
and the Prophets; let them listen to them.'
30" 'No, father Abraham,' he said, 'but if
someone from the dead goes to them, they
will repent.'
31"He said to him, 'If they do not listen to
Moses and the Prophets, they will not be
convinced even if someone rises from the
dead.' "

Sin, Faith, Duty

17 Jesus said to his disciples: "Things
that cause people to sin are bound to
come, but woe to that person through whom
they come. 2It would be better for him to be
thrown into the sea with a millstone tied
around his neck than for him to cause one of
these little ones to sin. 3So watch yourselves.
"If your brother sins, rebuke him, and if he

[a]6 Greek *one hundred batous* (probably about 3 kiloliters) [b]7 Greek *one hundred korous* (probably about 35 kiloliters) [c]23 Greek *Hades*

repents, forgive him. 4If he sins against you seven times in a day, and seven times comes back to you and says, 'I repent,' forgive him."

5The apostles said to the Lord, "Increase our faith!"

6He replied, "If you have faith as small as a mustard seed, you can say to this mulberry tree, 'Be uprooted and planted in the sea,' and it will obey you.

7"Suppose one of you had a servant plowing or looking after the sheep. Would he say to the servant when he comes in from the field, 'Come along now and sit down to eat'? 8Would he not rather say, 'Prepare my supper, get yourself ready and wait on me while I eat and drink; after that you may eat and drink'? 9Would he thank the servant because he did what he was told to do? 10So you also, when you have done everything you were told to do, should say, 'We are unworthy servants; we have only done our duty.' "

Ten Healed of Leprosy

11Now on his way to Jerusalem, Jesus traveled along the border between Samaria and Galilee. 12As he was going into a village, ten men who had leprosy[a] met him. They stood at a distance 13and called out in a loud voice, "Jesus, Master, have pity on us!"

14When he saw them, he said, "Go, show yourselves to the priests." And as they went, they were cleansed.

15One of them, when he saw he was healed, came back, praising God in a loud voice. 16He threw himself at Jesus' feet and thanked him—and he was a Samaritan.

17Jesus asked, "Were not all ten cleansed? Where are the other nine? 18Was no one found to return and give praise to God except this foreigner?" 19Then he said to him, "Rise and go; your faith has made you well."

The Coming of the Kingdom of God

20Once, having been asked by the Pharisees when the kingdom of God would come, Jesus replied, "The kingdom of God does not come with your careful observation, 21nor will people say, 'Here it is,' or 'There it is,' because the kingdom of God is within[b] you."

22Then he said to his disciples, "The time is coming when you will long to see one of the days of the Son of Man, but you will not see it. 23Men will tell you, 'There he is!' or 'Here he is!' Do not go running off after them. 24For the Son of Man in his day[c] will be like the lightning, which flashes and lights up the sky from one end to the other. 25But first he must suffer many things and be rejected by this generation.

26"Just as it was in the days of Noah, so also will it be in the days of the Son of Man. 27People were eating, drinking, marrying and being given in marriage up to the day Noah entered the ark. Then the flood came and destroyed them all.

28"It was the same in the days of Lot. People were eating and drinking, buying and selling, planting and building. 29But the day Lot left Sodom, fire and sulfur rained down from heaven and destroyed them all.

30"It will be just like this on the day the Son of Man is revealed. 31On that day no one who is on the roof of his house, with his goods inside, should go down to get them. Likewise, no one in the field should go back for anything. 32Remember Lot's wife! 33Whoever tries to keep his life will lose it, and whoever loses his life will preserve it. 34I tell you, on that night two people will be in one bed; one will be taken and the other left. 35Two women will be grinding grain together; one will be taken and the other left.[d]"

37"Where, Lord?" they asked.

He replied, "Where there is a dead body, there the vultures will gather."

The Parable of the Persistent Widow

18 Then Jesus told his disciples a parable to show them that they should always pray and not give up. 2He said: "In a certain town there was a judge who neither feared God nor cared about men. 3And there was a widow in that town who kept coming to him with the plea, 'Grant me justice against my adversary.'

4"For some time he refused. But finally he said to himself, 'Even though I don't fear God or care about men, 5yet because this widow keeps bothering me, I will see that she gets justice, so that she won't eventually wear me out with her coming!' "

6And the Lord said, "Listen to what the unjust judge says. 7And will not God bring about justice for his chosen ones, who cry out to him day and night? Will he keep putting them off? 8I tell you, he will see that they

[a]*12* The Greek word was used for various diseases affecting the skin—not necessarily leprosy. [b]*21* Or *among*
[c]*24* Some manuscripts do not have *in his day.* [d]*35* Some manuscripts *left.* [36]*Two men will be in the field; one will be taken and the other left.*

get justice, and quickly. However, when the
Son of Man comes, will he find faith on the
earth?"

The Parable of the Pharisee and the Tax Collector

9To some who were confident of their own
righteousness and looked down on everybody else, Jesus told this parable: 10"Two
men went up to the temple to pray, one a
Pharisee and the other a tax collector. 11The
Pharisee stood up and prayed about[a] himself: 'God, I thank you that I am not like other
men—robbers, evildoers, adulterers—or
even like this tax collector. 12I fast twice a
week and give a tenth of all I get.'
13"But the tax collector stood at a distance.
He would not even look up to heaven, but
beat his breast and said, 'God, have mercy
on me, a sinner.'
14"I tell you that this man, rather than the
other, went home justified before God. For
everyone who exalts himself will be humbled, and he who humbles himself will be
exalted."

The Little Children and Jesus

15People were also bringing babies to
Jesus to have him touch them. When the
disciples saw this, they rebuked them. 16But
Jesus called the children to him and said,
"Let the little children come to me, and do not
hinder them, for the kingdom of God belongs
to such as these. 17I tell you the truth, anyone
who will not receive the kingdom of God like
a little child will never enter it."

The Rich Ruler

18A certain ruler asked him, "Good
teacher, what must I do to inherit eternal
life?"
19"Why do you call me good?" Jesus answered. "No one is good—except God
alone. 20You know the commandments: 'Do
not commit adultery, do not murder, do not
steal, do not give false testimony, honor your
father and mother.'[b]"
21"All these I have kept since I was a boy,"
he said.
22When Jesus heard this, he said to him,
"You still lack one thing. Sell everything you
have and give to the poor, and you will have
treasure in heaven. Then come, follow me."
23When he heard this, he became very
sad, because he was a man of great wealth.
24Jesus looked at him and said, "How hard it
is for the rich to enter the kingdom of God!
25Indeed, it is easier for a camel to go
through the eye of a needle than for a rich
man to enter the kingdom of God."
26Those who heard this asked, "Who then
can be saved?"
27Jesus replied, "What is impossible with
men is possible with God."
28Peter said to him, "We have left all we
had to follow you!"
29"I tell you the truth," Jesus said to them,
"no one who has left home or wife or brothers or parents or children for the sake of the
kingdom of God 30will fail to receive many
times as much in this age and, in the age to
come, eternal life."

Jesus Again Predicts His Death

31Jesus took the Twelve aside and told
them, "We are going up to Jerusalem, and
everything that is written by the prophets
about the Son of Man will be fulfilled. 32He
will be handed over to the Gentiles. They will
mock him, insult him, spit on him, flog him
and kill him. 33On the third day he will rise
again."
34The disciples did not understand any of
this. Its meaning was hidden from them, and
they did not know what he was talking about.

A Blind Beggar Receives His Sight

35As Jesus approached Jericho, a blind
man was sitting by the roadside begging.
36When he heard the crowd going by, he
asked what was happening. 37They told him,
"Jesus of Nazareth is passing by."
38He called out, "Jesus, Son of David,
have mercy on me!"
39Those who led the way rebuked him and
told him to be quiet, but he shouted all the
more, "Son of David, have mercy on me!"
40Jesus stopped and ordered the man to
be brought to him. When he came near,
Jesus asked him, 41"What do you want me to
do for you?"
"Lord, I want to see," he replied.
42Jesus said to him, "Receive your sight;
your faith has healed you." 43Immediately he
received his sight and followed Jesus, praising God. When all the people saw it, they
also praised God.

[a] *11* Or *to* [b] *20* Exodus 20:12-16; Deut. 5:16-20

Zacchaeus the Tax Collector

19 Jesus entered Jericho and was passing through. 2A man was there by the
name of Zacchaeus; he was a chief tax collector and was wealthy. 3He wanted to see
who Jesus was, but being a short man he
could not, because of the crowd. 4So he ran
ahead and climbed a sycamore-fig tree to
see him, since Jesus was coming that way.
5When Jesus reached the spot, he looked
up and said to him, "Zacchaeus, come down
immediately. I must stay at your house today." 6So he came down at once and welcomed him gladly.
7All the people saw this and began to mutter, "He has gone to be the guest of a 'sinner.' "
8But Zacchaeus stood up and said to the
Lord, "Look, Lord! Here and now I give half of
my possessions to the poor, and if I have
cheated anybody out of anything, I will pay
back four times the amount."
9Jesus said to him, "Today salvation has
come to this house, because this man, too, is
a son of Abraham. 10For the Son of Man
came to seek and to save what was lost."

The Parable of the Ten Minas

11While they were listening to this, he went
on to tell them a parable, because he was
near Jerusalem and the people thought that
the kingdom of God was going to appear at
once. 12He said: "A man of noble birth went
to a distant country to have himself appointed king and then to return. 13So he
called ten of his servants and gave them ten
minas.[a] 'Put this money to work,' he said,
'until I come back.'
14"But his subjects hated him and sent a
delegation after him to say, 'We don't want
this man to be our king.'
15"He was made king, however, and returned home. Then he sent for the servants
to whom he had given the money, in order to
find out what they had gained with it.
16"The first one came and said, 'Sir, your
mina has earned ten more.'
17" 'Well done, my good servant!' his master replied. 'Because you have been trustworthy in a very small matter, take charge of
ten cities.'
18"The second came and said, 'Sir, your
mina has earned five more.'
19"His master answered, 'You take charge
of five cities.'
20"Then another servant came and said,
'Sir, here is your mina; I have kept it laid
away in a piece of cloth. 21I was afraid of you,
because you are a hard man. You take out
what you did not put in and reap what you did
not sow.'
22"His master replied, 'I will judge you by
your own words, you wicked servant! You
knew, did you, that I am a hard man, taking
out what I did not put in, and reaping what I
did not sow? 23Why then didn't you put my
money on deposit, so that when I came back,
I could have collected it with interest?'
24"Then he said to those standing by,
'Take his mina away from him and give it to
the one who has ten minas.'
25" 'Sir,' they said, 'he already has ten!'
26"He replied, 'I tell you that to everyone
who has, more will be given, but as for the
one who has nothing, even what he has will
be taken away. 27But those enemies of mine
who did not want me to be king over them—
bring them here and kill them in front of
me.' "

The Triumphal Entry

28After Jesus had said this, he went on
ahead, going up to Jerusalem. 29As he approached Bethphage and Bethany at the hill
called the Mount of Olives, he sent two of his
disciples, saying to them, 30"Go to the village
ahead of you, and as you enter it, you will
find a colt tied there, which no one has ever
ridden. Untie it and bring it here. 31If anyone
asks you, 'Why are you untying it?' tell him,
'The Lord needs it.' "
32Those who were sent ahead went and
found it just as he had told them. 33As they
were untying the colt, its owners asked them,
"Why are you untying the colt?"
34They replied, "The Lord needs it."
35They brought it to Jesus, threw their
cloaks on the colt and put Jesus on it. 36As he
went along, people spread their cloaks on
the road.
37When he came near the place where the
road goes down the Mount of Olives, the
whole crowd of disciples began joyfully to
praise God in loud voices for all the miracles
they had seen:

38"Blessed is the king who comes in the
name of the Lord!"[b]

"Peace in heaven and glory in the
highest!"

[a] 13 A mina was about three months' wages. [b] 38 Psalm 118:26

39Some of the Pharisees in the crowd said
to Jesus, "Teacher, rebuke your disciples!"
40"I tell you," he replied, "if they keep quiet,
the stones will cry out."
41As he approached Jerusalem and saw
the city, he wept over it 42and said, "If you,
even you, had only known on this day what
would bring you peace—but now it is hidden
from your eyes. 43The days will come upon
you when your enemies will build an em-
bankment against you and encircle you and
hem you in on every side. 44They will dash
you to the ground, you and the children within your walls. They will not leave one stone
on another, because you did not recognize
the time of God's coming to you."

Jesus at the Temple

45Then he entered the temple area and
began driving out those who were selling.
46"It is written," he said to them, " 'My house
will be a house of prayer'[a]; but you have
made it 'a den of robbers.'[b]"
47Every day he was teaching at the temple.
But the chief priests, the teachers of the law
and the leaders among the people were trying to kill him. 48Yet they could not find any
way to do it, because all the people hung on
his words.

The Authority of Jesus Questioned

20 One day as he was teaching the
people in the temple courts and
preaching the gospel, the chief priests and
the teachers of the law, together with the
elders, came up to him. 2"Tell us by what
authority you are doing these things," they
said. "Who gave you this authority?"
3He replied, "I will also ask you a question.
Tell me, 4John's baptism—was it from
heaven, or from men?"
5They discussed it among themselves and
said, "If we say, 'From heaven,' he will ask,
'Why didn't you believe him?' 6But if we say,
'From men,' all the people will stone us, because they are persuaded that John was a
prophet."
7So they answered, "We don't know where
it was from."
8Jesus said, "Neither will I tell you by what
authority I am doing these things."

The Parable of the Tenants

9He went on to tell the people this parable:
"A man planted a vineyard, rented it to some
farmers and went away for a long time. 10At
harvest time he sent a servant to the tenants
so they would give him some of the fruit of
the vineyard. But the tenants beat him and
sent him away empty-handed. 11He sent another servant, but that one also they beat
and treated shamefully and sent away empty-handed. 12He sent still a third, and they
wounded him and threw him out.
13"Then the owner of the vineyard said,
'What shall I do? I will send my son, whom I
love; perhaps they will respect him.'
14"But when the tenants saw him, they
talked the matter over. 'This is the heir,' they
said. 'Let's kill him, and the inheritance will
be ours.' 15So they threw him out of the vineyard and killed him.
"What then will the owner of the vineyard
do to them? 16He will come and kill those
tenants and give the vineyard to others."
When the people heard this, they said,
"May this never be!"
17Jesus looked directly at them and asked,
"Then what is the meaning of that which is
written:

" 'The stone the builders rejected
has become the capstone'[c,d]?

18Everyone who falls on that stone will be
broken to pieces, but he on whom it falls will
be crushed."
19The teachers of the law and the chief
priests looked for a way to arrest him
immediately, because they knew he had
spoken this parable against them. But they
were afraid of the people.

Paying Taxes to Caesar

20Keeping a close watch on him, they sent
spies, who pretended to be honest. They
hoped to catch Jesus in something he said
so that they might hand him over to the
power and authority of the governor. 21So the
spies questioned him: "Teacher, we know
that you speak and teach what is right, and
that you do not show partiality but teach the
way of God in accordance with the truth. 22Is
it right for us to pay taxes to Caesar or not?"
23He saw through their duplicity and said to
them, 24"Show me a denarius. Whose portrait and inscription are on it?"
25"Caesar's," they replied.
He said to them, "Then give to Caesar
what is Caesar's, and to God what is God's."
26They were unable to trap him in what he

[a] 46 Isaiah 56:7 [b] 46 Jer. 7:11 [c] 17 Or *cornerstone* [d] 17 Psalm 118:22

had said there in public. And astonished by his answer, they became silent.

The Resurrection and Marriage

27Some of the Sadducees, who say there is no resurrection, came to Jesus with a question. 28"Teacher," they said, "Moses wrote for us that if a man's brother dies and leaves a wife but no children, the man must marry the widow and have children for his brother. 29Now there were seven brothers. The first one married a woman and died childless. 30The second 31and then the third married her, and in the same way the seven died, leaving no children. 32Finally, the woman died too. 33Now then, at the resurrection whose wife will she be, since the seven were married to her?"

34Jesus replied, "The people of this age marry and are given in marriage. 35But those who are considered worthy of taking part in that age and in the resurrection from the dead will neither marry nor be given in marriage, 36and they can no longer die; for they are like the angels. They are God's children, since they are children of the resurrection. 37But in the account of the bush, even Moses showed that the dead rise, for he calls the Lord 'the God of Abraham, and the God of Isaac, and the God of Jacob.'[a] 38He is not the God of the dead, but of the living, for to him all are alive."

39Some of the teachers of the law responded, "Well said, teacher!" 40And no one dared to ask him any more questions.

Whose Son Is the Christ?

41Then Jesus said to them, "How is it that they say the Christ[b] is the Son of David? 42David himself declares in the Book of Psalms:

" 'The Lord said to my Lord:
 "Sit at my right hand
43until I make your enemies
 a footstool for your feet." '[c]

44David calls him 'Lord.' How then can he be his son?"

45While all the people were listening, Jesus said to his disciples, 46"Beware of the teachers of the law. They like to walk around in flowing robes and love to be greeted in the marketplaces and have the most important seats in the synagogues and the places of honor at banquets. 47They devour widows' houses and for a show make lengthy prayers. Such men will be punished most severely."

The Widow's Offering

21 As he looked up, Jesus saw the rich putting their gifts into the temple treasury. 2He also saw a poor widow put in two very small copper coins.[d] 3"I tell you the truth," he said, "this poor widow has put in more than all the others. 4All these people gave their gifts out of their wealth; but she out of her poverty put in all she had to live on."

Signs of the End of the Age

5Some of his disciples were remarking about how the temple was adorned with beautiful stones and with gifts dedicated to God. But Jesus said, 6"As for what you see here, the time will come when not one stone will be left on another; every one of them will be thrown down."

7"Teacher," they asked, "when will these things happen? And what will be the sign that they are about to take place?"

8He replied: "Watch out that you are not deceived. For many will come in my name, claiming, 'I am he,' and, 'The time is near.' Do not follow them. 9When you hear of wars and revolutions, do not be frightened. These things must happen first, but the end will not come right away."

10Then he said to them: "Nation will rise against nation, and kingdom against kingdom. 11There will be great earthquakes, famines and pestilences in various places, and fearful events and great signs from heaven.

12"But before all this, they will lay hands on you and persecute you. They will deliver you to synagogues and prisons, and you will be brought before kings and governors, and all on account of my name. 13This will result in your being witnesses to them. 14But make up your mind not to worry beforehand how you will defend yourselves. 15For I will give you words and wisdom that none of your adversaries will be able to resist or contradict. 16You will be betrayed even by parents, brothers, relatives and friends, and they will put some of you to death. 17All men will hate you because of me. 18But not a hair of your head will perish. 19By standing firm you will gain life.

20"When you see Jerusalem being surrounded by armies, you will know that its

[a]37 Exodus 3:6 [b]41 Or *Messiah* [c]43 Psalm 110:1 [d]2 Greek *two lepta*

desolation is near. 21Then let those who are
in Judea flee to the mountains, let those in
the city get out, and let those in the country
not enter the city. 22For this is the time of
punishment in fulfillment of all that has been
written. 23How dreadful it will be in those
days for pregnant women and nursing
mothers! There will be great distress in the
land and wrath against this people. 24They
will fall by the sword and will be taken as
prisoners to all the nations. Jerusalem will be
trampled on by the Gentiles until the times of
the Gentiles are fulfilled.

25"There will be signs in the sun, moon and
stars. On the earth, nations will be in anguish
and perplexity at the roaring and tossing of
the sea. 26Men will faint from terror, apprehensive of what is coming on the world, for
the heavenly bodies will be shaken. 27At that
time they will see the Son of Man coming in a
cloud with power and great glory. 28When
these things begin to take place, stand up
and lift up your heads, because your redemption is drawing near."

29He told them this parable: "Look at the fig
tree and all the trees. 30When they sprout
leaves, you can see for yourselves and know
that summer is near. 31Even so, when you
see these things happening, you know that
the kingdom of God is near.

32"I tell you the truth, this generation[a] will
certainly not pass away until all these things
have happened. 33Heaven and earth will
pass away, but my words will never pass
away.

34"Be careful, or your hearts will be
weighed down with dissipation, drunkenness and the anxieties of life, and that day
will close on you unexpectedly like a trap.
35For it will come upon all those who live on
the face of the whole earth. 36Be always on
the watch, and pray that you may be able to
escape all that is about to happen, and that
you may be able to stand before the Son of
Man."

37Each day Jesus was teaching at the temple, and each evening he went out to spend
the night on the hill called the Mount of Olives, 38and all the people came early in the
morning to hear him at the temple.

Judas Agrees to Betray Jesus

22 Now the Feast of Unleavened Bread,
called the Passover, was approach-
ing, 2and the chief priests and the teachers of
the law were looking for some way to get rid
of Jesus, for they were afraid of the people.
3Then Satan entered Judas, called Iscariot,
one of the Twelve. 4And Judas went to the
chief priests and the officers of the temple
guard and discussed with them how he
might betray Jesus. 5They were delighted
and agreed to give him money. 6He consented, and watched for an opportunity to hand
Jesus over to them when no crowd was
present.

The Last Supper

7Then came the day of Unleavened Bread
on which the Passover lamb had to be sacrificed. 8Jesus sent Peter and John, saying,
"Go and make preparations for us to eat the
Passover."

9"Where do you want us to prepare for it?"
they asked.

10He replied, "As you enter the city, a man
carrying a jar of water will meet you. Follow
him to the house that he enters, 11and say to
the owner of the house, 'The Teacher asks:
Where is the guest room, where I may eat
the Passover with my disciples?' 12He will
show you a large upper room, all furnished.
Make preparations there."

13They left and found things just as Jesus
had told them. So they prepared the Passover.

14When the hour came, Jesus and his
apostles reclined at the table. 15And he said
to them, "I have eagerly desired to eat this
Passover with you before I suffer. 16For I tell
you, I will not eat it again until it finds fulfillment in the kingdom of God."

17After taking the cup, he gave thanks and
said, "Take this and divide it among you.
18For I tell you I will not drink again of the fruit
of the vine until the kingdom of God comes."

19And he took bread, gave thanks and
broke it, and gave it to them, saying, "This is
my body given for you; do this in remembrance of me."

20In the same way, after the supper he took
the cup, saying, "This cup is the new covenant in my blood, which is poured out for
you. 21But the hand of him who is going to
betray me is with mine on the table. 22The
Son of Man will go as it has been decreed,
but woe to that man who betrays him."
23They began to question among themselves which of them it might be who would
do this.

[a]32 Or *race*

24Also a dispute arose among them as to
which of them was considered to be greatest. 25Jesus said to them, "The kings of the
Gentiles lord it over them; and those who
exercise authority over them call themselves
Benefactors. 26But you are not to be like that.
Instead, the greatest among you should be
like the youngest, and the one who rules like
the one who serves. 27For who is greater, the
one who is at the table or the one who
serves? Is it not the one who is at the table?
But I am among you as one who serves.
28You are those who have stood by me in my
trials. 29And I confer on you a kingdom, just
as my Father conferred one on me, 30so that
you may eat and drink at my table in my
kingdom and sit on thrones, judging the
twelve tribes of Israel.

31"Simon, Simon, Satan has asked to sift
you[a] as wheat. 32But I have prayed for you,
Simon, that your faith may not fail. And when
you have turned back, strengthen your
brothers."

33But he replied, "Lord, I am ready to go
with you to prison and to death."

34Jesus answered, "I tell you, Peter, before the rooster crows today, you will deny
three times that you know me."

35Then Jesus asked them, "When I sent
you without purse, bag or sandals, did you
lack anything?"

"Nothing," they answered.

36He said to them, "But now if you have a
purse, take it, and also a bag; and if you don't
have a sword, sell your cloak and buy one.
37It is written: 'And he was numbered with the
transgressors'[b]; and I tell you that this must
be fulfilled in me. Yes, what is written about
me is reaching its fulfillment."

38The disciples said, "See, Lord, here are
two swords."

"That is enough," he replied.

Jesus Prays on the Mount of Olives

39Jesus went out as usual to the Mount of
Olives, and his disciples followed him. 40On
reaching the place, he said to them, "Pray
that you will not fall into temptation." 41He
withdrew about a stone's throw beyond
them, knelt down and prayed, 42"Father, if
you are willing, take this cup from me; yet not
my will, but yours be done." 43An angel from
heaven appeared to him and strengthened
him. 44And being in anguish, he prayed more
earnestly, and his sweat was like drops of
blood falling to the ground.[c]

45When he rose from prayer and went
back to the disciples, he found them asleep,
exhausted from sorrow. 46"Why are you
sleeping?" he asked them. "Get up and pray
so that you will not fall into temptation."

Jesus Arrested

47While he was still speaking a crowd
came up, and the man who was called
Judas, one of the Twelve, was leading them.
He approached Jesus to kiss him, 48but
Jesus asked him, "Judas, are you betraying
the Son of Man with a kiss?"

49When Jesus' followers saw what was going to happen, they said, "Lord, should we
strike with our swords?" 50And one of them
struck the servant of the high priest, cutting
off his right ear.

51But Jesus answered, "No more of this!"
And he touched the man's ear and healed
him.

52Then Jesus said to the chief priests, the
officers of the temple guard, and the elders,
who had come for him, "Am I leading a rebellion, that you have come with swords and
clubs? 53Every day I was with you in the
temple courts, and you did not lay a hand on
me. But this is your hour—when darkness
reigns."

Peter Disowns Jesus

54Then seizing him, they led him away and
took him into the house of the high priest.
Peter followed at a distance. 55But when they
had kindled a fire in the middle of the courtyard and had sat down together, Peter sat
down with them. 56A servant girl saw him
seated there in the firelight. She looked
closely at him and said, "This man was with
him."

57But he denied it. "Woman, I don't know
him," he said.

58A little later someone else saw him and
said, "You also are one of them."

"Man, I am not!" Peter replied.

59About an hour later another asserted,
"Certainly this fellow was with him, for he is a
Galilean."

60Peter replied, "Man, I don't know what
you're talking about!" Just as he was speaking, the rooster crowed. 61The Lord turned
and looked straight at Peter. Then Peter
remembered the word the Lord had spoken

[a] *31* The Greek is plural. [b] *37* Isaiah 53:12 [c] *44* Some early manuscripts do not have verses 43 and 44.

to him: "Before the rooster crows today, you
will disown me three times." 62And he went
outside and wept bitterly.

The Guards Mock Jesus

63The men who were guarding Jesus began mocking and beating him. 64They blindfolded him and demanded, "Prophesy! Who
hit you?" 65And they said many other insulting things to him.

Jesus Before Pilate and Herod

66At daybreak the council of the elders of
the people, both the chief priests and teachers of the law, met together, and Jesus was
led before them. 67"If you are the Christ,[a]"
they said, "tell us."

Jesus answered, "If I tell you, you will not
believe me, 68and if I asked you, you would
not answer. 69But from now on, the Son of
Man will be seated at the right hand of the
mighty God."

70They all asked, "Are you then the Son of
God?"

He replied, "You are right in saying I am."

71Then they said, "Why do we need any
more testimony? We have heard it from his
own lips."

23 Then the whole assembly rose and
led him off to Pilate. 2And they began
to accuse him, saying, "We have found this
man subverting our nation. He opposes payment of taxes to Caesar and claims to be
Christ,[b] a king."

3So Pilate asked Jesus, "Are you the king
of the Jews?"

"Yes, it is as you say," Jesus replied.

4Then Pilate announced to the chief
priests and the crowd, "I find no basis for a
charge against this man."

5But they insisted, "He stirs up the people
all over Judea[c] by his teaching. He started in
Galilee and has come all the way here."

6On hearing this, Pilate asked if the man
was a Galilean. 7When he learned that Jesus
was under Herod's jurisdiction, he sent him
to Herod, who was also in Jerusalem at that
time.

8When Herod saw Jesus, he was greatly
pleased, because for a long time he had
been wanting to see him. From what he had
heard about him, he hoped to see him perform some miracle. 9He plied him with many
questions, but Jesus gave him no answer.
10The chief priests and the teachers of the
law were standing there, vehemently accusing him. 11Then Herod and his soldiers ridiculed and mocked him. Dressing him in an
elegant robe, they sent him back to Pilate.
12That day Herod and Pilate became
friends—before this they had been enemies.

13Pilate called together the chief priests,
the rulers and the people, 14and said to them,
"You brought me this man as one who was
inciting the people to rebellion. I have examined him in your presence and have found no
basis for your charges against him. 15Neither
has Herod, for he sent him back to us; as you
can see, he has done nothing to deserve
death. 16Therefore, I will punish him and then
release him.[d]"

18With one voice they cried out, "Away
with this man! Release Barabbas to us!"
19(Barabbas had been thrown into prison for
an insurrection in the city, and for murder.)

20Wanting to release Jesus, Pilate appealed to them again. 21But they kept shouting, "Crucify him! Crucify him!"

22For the third time he spoke to them:
"Why? What crime has this man committed?
I have found in him no grounds for the death
penalty. Therefore I will have him punished
and then release him."

23But with loud shouts they insistently demanded that he be crucified, and their
shouts prevailed. 24So Pilate decided to
grant their demand. 25He released the man
who had been thrown into prison for insurrection and murder, the one they asked for,
and surrendered Jesus to their will.

The Crucifixion

26As they led him away, they seized Simon
from Cyrene, who was on his way in from the
country, and put the cross on him and made
him carry it behind Jesus. 27A large number
of people followed him, including women
who mourned and wailed for him. 28Jesus
turned and said to them, "Daughters of
Jerusalem, do not weep for me; weep for
yourselves and for your children. 29For the
time will come when you will say, 'Blessed
are the barren women, the wombs that never
bore and the breasts that never nursed!'
30Then

" 'they will say to the mountains, "Fall on
us!"
and to the hills, "Cover us!" '[e]

[a]67 Or *Messiah* [b]2 Or *Messiah;* also in verses 35 and 39 [c]5 Or *over the land of the Jews* [d]16 Some manuscripts *him."* [17] *Now he was obliged to release one man to them at the Feast.* [e]30 Hosea 10:8

31For if men do these things when the tree is
green, what will happen when it is dry?"
32Two other men, both criminals, were
also led out with him to be executed. 33When
they came to the place called the Skull, there
they crucified him, along with the criminals—
one on his right, the other on his left. 34Jesus
said, "Father, forgive them, for they do not
know what they are doing."[a] And they divided up his clothes by casting lots.
35The people stood watching, and the rulers even sneered at him. They said, "He
saved others; let him save himself if he is the
Christ of God, the Chosen One."
36The soldiers also came up and mocked
him. They offered him wine vinegar 37and
said, "If you are the king of the Jews, save
yourself."
38There was a written notice above him,
which read: THIS IS THE KING OF THE JEWS.
39One of the criminals who hung there
hurled insults at him: "Aren't you the Christ?
Save yourself and us!"
40But the other criminal rebuked him.
"Don't you fear God," he said, "since you are
under the same sentence? 41We are punished justly, for we are getting what our
deeds deserve. But this man has done nothing wrong."
42Then he said, "Jesus, remember me
when you come into your kingdom.[b]"
43Jesus answered him, "I tell you the truth,
today you will be with me in paradise."

Jesus' Death

44It was now about the sixth hour, and
darkness came over the whole land until the
ninth hour, 45for the sun stopped shining.
And the curtain of the temple was torn in two.
46Jesus called out with a loud voice, "Father,
into your hands I commit my spirit." When he
had said this, he breathed his last.
47The centurion, seeing what had happened, praised God and said, "Surely this
was a righteous man." 48When all the people
who had gathered to witness this sight saw
what took place, they beat their breasts and
went away. 49But all those who knew him,
including the women who had followed him
from Galilee, stood at a distance, watching
these things.

Jesus' Burial

50Now there was a man named Joseph, a
member of the Council, a good and upright
man, 51who had not consented to their decision and action. He came from the Judean
town of Arimathea and he was waiting for the
kingdom of God. 52Going to Pilate, he asked
for Jesus' body. 53Then he took it down,
wrapped it in linen cloth and placed it in a
tomb cut in the rock, one in which no one had
yet been laid. 54It was Preparation Day, and
the Sabbath was about to begin.
55The women who had come with Jesus
from Galilee followed Joseph and saw the
tomb and how his body was laid in it. 56Then
they went home and prepared spices and
perfumes. But they rested on the Sabbath in
obedience to the commandment.

The Resurrection

24 On the first day of the week, very
early in the morning, the women took
the spices they had prepared and went to the
tomb. 2They found the stone rolled away
from the tomb, 3but when they entered, they
did not find the body of the Lord Jesus.
4While they were wondering about this, suddenly two men in clothes that gleamed like
lightning stood beside them. 5In their fright
the women bowed down with their faces to
the ground, but the men said to them, "Why
do you look for the living among the dead?
6He is not here; he has risen! Remember
how he told you, while he was still with you in
Galilee: 7'The Son of Man must be delivered
into the hands of sinful men, be crucified and
on the third day be raised again.' " 8Then
they remembered his words.
9When they came back from the tomb,
they told all these things to the Eleven and to
all the others. 10It was Mary Magdalene,
Joanna, Mary the mother of James, and the
others with them who told this to the apostles. 11But they did not believe the women,
because their words seemed to them like
nonsense. 12Peter, however, got up and ran
to the tomb. Bending over, he saw the strips
of linen lying by themselves, and he went
away, wondering to himself what had happened.

On the Road to Emmaus

13Now that same day two of them were
going to a village called Emmaus, about

[a]34 Some early manuscripts do not have this sentence. [b]42 Some manuscripts *come with your kingly power*

seven miles[a] from Jerusalem. 14They were talking with each other about everything that had happened. 15As they talked and discussed these things with each other, Jesus himself came up and walked along with them; 16but they were kept from recognizing him.

17He asked them, "What are you discussing together as you walk along?"

They stood still, their faces downcast. 18One of them, named Cleopas, asked him, "Are you only a visitor to Jerusalem and do not know the things that have happened there in these days?"

19"What things?" he asked.

"About Jesus of Nazareth," they replied. "He was a prophet, powerful in word and deed before God and all the people. 20The chief priests and our rulers handed him over to be sentenced to death, and they crucified him; 21but we had hoped that he was the one who was going to redeem Israel. And what is more, it is the third day since all this took place. 22In addition, some of our women amazed us. They went to the tomb early this morning 23but didn't find his body. They came and told us that they had seen a vision of angels, who said he was alive. 24Then some of our companions went to the tomb and found it just as the women had said, but him they did not see."

25He said to them, "How foolish you are, and how slow of heart to believe all that the prophets have spoken! 26Did not the Christ[b] have to suffer these things and then enter his glory?" 27And beginning with Moses and all the Prophets, he explained to them what was said in all the Scriptures concerning himself.

28As they approached the village to which they were going, Jesus acted as if he were going farther. 29But they urged him strongly, "Stay with us, for it is nearly evening; the day is almost over." So he went in to stay with them.

30When he was at the table with them, he took bread, gave thanks, broke it and began to give it to them. 31Then their eyes were opened and they recognized him, and he disappeared from their sight. 32They asked each other, "Were not our hearts burning within us while he talked with us on the road and opened the Scriptures to us?"

33They got up and returned at once to Jerusalem. There they found the Eleven and those with them, assembled together 34and saying, "It is true! The Lord has risen and has appeared to Simon." 35Then the two told what had happened on the way, and how Jesus was recognized by them when he broke the bread.

Jesus Appears to the Disciples

36While they were still talking about this, Jesus himself stood among them and said to them, "Peace be with you."

37They were startled and frightened, thinking they saw a ghost. 38He said to them, "Why are you troubled, and why do doubts rise in your minds? 39Look at my hands and my feet. It is I myself! Touch me and see; a ghost does not have flesh and bones, as you see I have."

40When he had said this, he showed them his hands and feet. 41And while they still did not believe it because of joy and amazement, he asked them, "Do you have anything here to eat?" 42They gave him a piece of broiled fish, 43and he took it and ate it in their presence.

44He said to them, "This is what I told you while I was still with you: Everything must be fulfilled that is written about me in the Law of Moses, the Prophets and the Psalms."

45Then he opened their minds so they could understand the Scriptures. 46He told them, "This is what is written: The Christ will suffer and rise from the dead on the third day, 47and repentance and forgiveness of sins will be preached in his name to all nations, beginning at Jerusalem. 48You are witnesses of these things. 49I am going to send you what my Father has promised; but stay in the city until you have been clothed with power from on high."

The Ascension

50When he had led them out to the vicinity of Bethany, he lifted up his hands and blessed them. 51While he was blessing them, he left them and was taken up into heaven. 52Then they worshiped him and returned to Jerusalem with great joy. 53And they stayed continually at the temple, praising God.

[a] *13* Greek *sixty stadia* (about 11 kilometers)

[b] *26* Or *Messiah*; also in verse 46

John

Introduction:

The fourth Gospel was also written by one of Jesus' twelve disciples—John, "The disciple whom Jesus loved." John wrote this Gospel sometime between A.D. 90–100 so that "you may believe that Jesus is the Christ, the Son of God, and that by believing you may have life in his name" (John 20:31).

Although the book of John gives a general outline of the life and work of Jesus Christ, it is very different from the other three Gospels. John reports five miracles that are not reported by the other Gospels. Only two of the miracles reported in the other Gospels are reported in John. This book contains no parables and seems to stress Jesus' relationships with individuals.

The purpose of this Gospel is to report the signs, usually called miracles in other Gospels. The signs that John reports give proof that Christ is God and has supernatural powers. Although John gives much attention to proving that Jesus is the Son of God he also shows often that Jesus was very much a human by showing that he was tired, sad, hungry and loving.

Outline of contents:

The Word Became Flesh

1 In the beginning was the Word, and the
Word was with God, and the Word was
God. 2He was with God in the beginning.
3Through him all things were made; without him nothing was made that has been
made. 4In him was life, and that life was
the light of men. 5The light shines in the
darkness, but the darkness has not understood[a] it.
6There came a man who was sent from
God; his name was John. 7He came as a
witness to testify concerning that light, so
that through him all men might believe. 8He
himself was not the light; he came only as a
witness to the light. 9The true light that gives
light to every man was coming into the
world.[b]
10He was in the world, and though the
world was made through him, the world did
not recognize him. 11He came to that which
was his own, but his own did not receive him.
12Yet to all who received him, to those who
believed in his name, he gave the right to
become children of God— 13children born
not of natural descent,[c] nor of human decision or a husband's will, but born of God.
14The Word became flesh and made his
dwelling among us. We have seen his glory,
the glory of the One and Only,[d] who came
from the Father, full of grace and truth.
15John testifies concerning him. He cries
out, saying, "This was he of whom I said, 'He
who comes after me has surpassed me because he was before me.' " 16From the fullness of his grace we have all received one
blessing after another. 17For the law was giv-
en through Moses; grace and truth came
through Jesus Christ. 18No one has ever
seen God, but God the One and Only,[d,e]

[a]5 Or *darkness, and the darkness has not overcome* [b]9 Or *This was the true light that gives light to every man who comes into the world* [c]*13* Greek *of bloods* [d]*14,18* Or *the Only Begotten* [e]*18* Some manuscripts *but the only* (or *only begotten*) *Son*

who is at the Father's side, has made him
known.

John the Baptist Denies Being the Christ

19Now this was John's testimony when the
Jews of Jerusalem sent priests and Levites
to ask him who he was. 20He did not fail to
confess, but confessed freely, "I am not the
Christ.[a]"

21They asked him, "Then who are you?
Are you Elijah?"

He said, "I am not."

"Are you the Prophet?"

He answered, "No."

22Finally they said, "Who are you? Give us
an answer to take back to those who sent us.
What do you say about yourself?"

23John replied in the words of Isaiah the
prophet, "I am the voice of one calling in the
desert, 'Make straight the way for the
Lord.' "[b]

24Now some Pharisees who had been sent
25questioned him, "Why then do you baptize
if you are not the Christ, nor Elijah, nor the
Prophet?"

26"I baptize with[c] water," John replied,
"but among you stands one you do not know.
27He is the one who comes after me, the
thongs of whose sandals I am not worthy to
untie."

28This all happened at Bethany on the
other side of the Jordan, where John was
baptizing.

Jesus the Lamb of God

29The next day John saw Jesus coming
toward him and said, "Look, the Lamb of
God, who takes away the sin of the world!
30This is the one I meant when I said, 'A man
who comes after me has surpassed me because he was before me.' 31I myself did not
know him, but the reason I came baptizing
with water was that he might be revealed to
Israel."

32Then John gave this testimony: "I saw
the Spirit come down from heaven as a dove
and remain on him. 33I would not have known
him, except that the one who sent me to
baptize with water told me, 'The man on
whom you see the Spirit come down and
remain is he who will baptize with the Holy
Spirit.' 34I have seen and I testify that this is
the Son of God."

Jesus' First Disciples

35The next day John was there again with
two of his disciples. 36When he saw Jesus
passing by, he said, "Look, the Lamb of
God!"

37When the two disciples heard him say
this, they followed Jesus. 38Turning around,
Jesus saw them following and asked, "What
do you want?"

They said, "Rabbi" (which means
Teacher), "where are you staying?"

39"Come," he replied, "and you will see."

So they went and saw where he was staying, and spent that day with him. It was about
the tenth hour.

40Andrew, Simon Peter's brother, was one
of the two who heard what John had said and
who had followed Jesus. 41The first thing Andrew did was to find his brother Simon and
tell him, "We have found the Messiah" (that
is, the Christ). 42And he brought him to
Jesus.

Jesus looked at him and said, "You are
Simon son of John. You will be called
Cephas" (which, when translated, is Pe-
ter[d]).

Jesus Calls Philip and Nathanael

43The next day Jesus decided to leave for
Galilee. Finding Philip, he said to him, "Follow me."

44Philip, like Andrew and Peter, was from
the town of Bethsaida. 45Philip found Nathanael and told him, "We have found the
one Moses wrote about in the Law, and
about whom the prophets also wrote—Jesus
of Nazareth, the son of Joseph."

46"Nazareth! Can anything good come
from there?" Nathanael asked.

"Come and see," said Philip.

47When Jesus saw Nathanael approach-
ing, he said of him, "Here is a true Israelite, in
whom there is nothing false."

48"How do you know me?" Nathanael
asked.

Jesus answered, "I saw you while you
were still under the fig tree before Philip
called you."

49Then Nathanael declared, "Rabbi, you
are the Son of God; you are the King of
Israel."

50Jesus said, "You believe[e] because I told
you I saw you under the fig tree. You shall

[a]20 Or *Messiah.* "The Christ" (Greek) and "the Messiah" (Hebrew) both mean "the Anointed One"; also in verse 25. [b]23 Isaiah 40:3 [c]26 Or *in;* also in verses 31 and 33 [d]42 Both *Cephas* (Aramaic) and *Peter* (Greek) mean *rock.* [e]50 Or *Do you believe . . .?*

see greater things than that." 51He then added, "I tell you[a] the truth, you[a] shall see heaven open, and the angels of God ascending and descending on the Son of Man."

Jesus Changes Water to Wine

2 On the third day a wedding took place at Cana in Galilee. Jesus' mother was there, 2and Jesus and his disciples had also been invited to the wedding. 3When the wine was gone, Jesus' mother said to him, "They have no more wine."

4"Dear woman, why do you involve me?" Jesus replied. "My time has not yet come."

5His mother said to the servants, "Do whatever he tells you."

6Nearby stood six stone water jars, the kind used by the Jews for ceremonial washing, each holding from twenty to thirty gallons.[b]

7Jesus said to the servants, "Fill the jars with water"; so they filled them to the brim.

8Then he told them, "Now draw some out and take it to the master of the banquet."

They did so, 9and the master of the banquet tasted the water that had been turned into wine. He did not realize where it had come from, though the servants who had drawn the water knew. Then he called the bridegroom aside 10and said, "Everyone brings out the choice wine first and then the cheaper wine after the guests have had too much to drink; but you have saved the best till now."

11This, the first of the miraculous signs, Jesus performed at Cana in Galilee. He thus revealed his glory, and his disciples put their faith in him.

Jesus Clears the Temple

12After this he went down to Capernaum with his mother and brothers and his disciples. There they stayed for a few days.

13When it was almost time for the Jewish Passover, Jesus went up to Jerusalem. 14In the temple courts he found men selling cattle, sheep and doves, and others sitting at tables exchanging money. 15So he made a whip out of cords, and drove all from the temple area, both sheep and cattle; he scattered the coins of the money changers and overturned their tables. 16To those who sold doves he said, "Get these out of here! How dare you turn my Father's house into a market!"

17His disciples remembered that it is written: "Zeal for your house will consume me."[c]

18Then the Jews demanded of him, "What miraculous sign can you show us to prove your authority to do all this?"

19Jesus answered them, "Destroy this temple, and I will raise it again in three days."

20The Jews replied, "It has taken forty-six years to build this temple, and you are going to raise it in three days?" 21But the temple he had spoken of was his body. 22After he was raised from the dead, his disciples recalled what he had said. Then they believed the Scripture and the words that Jesus had spoken.

23Now while he was in Jerusalem at the Passover Feast, many people saw the miraculous signs he was doing and believed in his name.[d] 24But Jesus would not entrust himself to them, for he knew all men. 25He did not need man's testimony about man, for he knew what was in a man.

Jesus Teaches Nicodemus

3 Now there was a man of the Pharisees named Nicodemus, a member of the Jewish ruling council. 2He came to Jesus at night and said, "Rabbi, we know you are a teacher who has come from God. For no one could perform the miraculous signs you are doing if God were not with him."

3In reply Jesus declared, "I tell you the truth, no one can see the kingdom of God unless he is born again.[e]"

4"How can a man be born when he is old?" Nicodemus asked. "Surely he cannot enter a second time into his mother's womb to be born!"

5Jesus answered, "I tell you the truth, no one can enter the kingdom of God unless he is born of water and the Spirit. 6Flesh gives birth to flesh, but the Spirit[f] gives birth to spirit. 7You should not be surprised at my saying, 'You[a] must be born again.' 8The wind blows wherever it pleases. You hear its sound, but you cannot tell where it comes from or where it is going. So it is with everyone born of the Spirit."

9"How can this be?" Nicodemus asked.

10"You are Israel's teacher," said Jesus, "and do you not understand these things? 11I tell you the truth, we speak of what we know,

[a]51,7 The Greek is plural. [b]6 Greek *two or three metretes* (probably about 75 to 115 liters)
[c]17 Psalm 69:9 [d]23 Or *and believed in him* [e]3 Or *born from above;* also in verse 7 [f]6 Or *but spirit*

and we testify to what we have seen, but still you people do not accept our testimony. 12I have spoken to you of earthly things and you do not believe; how then will you believe if I speak of heavenly things? 13No one has ever gone into heaven except the one who came from heaven—the Son of Man.[a] 14Just as Moses lifted up the snake in the desert, so the Son of Man must be lifted up, 15that everyone who believes in him may have eternal life.[b]

16"For God so loved the world that he gave his one and only Son,[c] that whoever believes in him shall not perish but have eternal life. 17For God did not send his Son into the world to condemn the world, but to save the world through him. 18Whoever believes in him is not condemned, but whoever does not believe stands condemned already because he has not believed in the name of God's one and only Son.[d] 19This is the verdict: Light has come into the world, but men loved darkness instead of light because their deeds were evil. 20Everyone who does evil hates the light, and will not come into the light for fear that his deeds will be exposed. 21But whoever lives by the truth comes into the light, so that it may be seen plainly that what he has done has been done through God."[e]

John the Baptist's Testimony About Jesus

22After this, Jesus and his disciples went out into the Judean countryside, where he spent some time with them, and baptized. 23Now John also was baptizing at Aenon near Salim, because there was plenty of water, and people were constantly coming to be baptized. 24(This was before John was put in prison.) 25An argument developed between some of John's disciples and a certain Jew[f] over the matter of ceremonial washing. 26They came to John and said to him, "Rabbi, that man who was with you on the other side of the Jordan—the one you testified about—well, he is baptizing, and everyone is going to him."

27To this John replied, "A man can receive only what is given him from heaven. 28You yourselves can testify that I said, 'I am not the Christ[g] but am sent ahead of him.' 29The bride belongs to the bridegroom. The friend who attends the bridegroom waits and listens for him, and is full of joy when he hears the bridegroom's voice. That joy is mine, and it is now complete. 30He must become greater; I must become less.

31"The one who comes from above is above all; the one who is from the earth belongs to the earth, and speaks as one from the earth. The one who comes from heaven is above all. 32He testifies to what he has seen and heard, but no one accepts his testimony. 33The man who has accepted it has certified that God is truthful. 34For the one whom God has sent speaks the words of God, for God[h] gives the Spirit without limit. 35The Father loves the Son and has placed everything in his hands. 36Whoever believes in the Son has eternal life, but whoever rejects the Son will not see life, for God's wrath remains on him."[i]

Jesus Talks With a Samaritan Woman

4 The Pharisees heard that Jesus was gaining and baptizing more disciples than John, 2although in fact it was not Jesus who baptized, but his disciples. 3When the Lord learned of this, he left Judea and went back once more to Galilee.

4Now he had to go through Samaria. 5So he came to a town in Samaria called Sychar, near the plot of ground Jacob had given to his son Joseph. 6Jacob's well was there, and Jesus, tired as he was from the journey, sat down by the well. It was about the sixth hour.

7When a Samaritan woman came to draw water, Jesus said to her, "Will you give me a drink?" 8(His disciples had gone into the town to buy food.)

9The Samaritan woman said to him, "You are a Jew and I am a Samaritan woman. How can you ask me for a drink?" (For Jews do not associate with Samaritans.[j])

10Jesus answered her, "If you knew the gift of God and who it is that asks you for a drink, you would have asked him and he would have given you living water."

11"Sir," the woman said, "you have nothing to draw with and the well is deep. Where can you get this living water? 12Are you greater than our father Jacob, who gave us the well and drank from it himself, as did also his sons and his flocks and herds?"

13Jesus answered, "Everyone who drinks this water will be thirsty again, 14but whoever

[a]13 Some manuscripts *Man, who is in heaven* [b]15 Or *believes may have eternal life in him* [c]16 Or *his only begotten Son:* [d]18 Or *God's only begotten Son* [e]21 Some interpreters end the quotation after verse 15. [f]25 Some manuscripts *and certain Jews* [g]28 Or *Messiah* [h]34 Greek *he* [i]36 Some interpreters end the quotation after verse 30. [j]9 Or *do not use dishes Samaritans have used*

drinks the water I give him will never thirst. Indeed, the water I give him will become in him a spring of water welling up to eternal life."

15 The woman said to him, "Sir, give me this water so that I won't get thirsty and have to keep coming here to draw water."

16 He told her, "Go, call your husband and come back."

17 "I have no husband," she replied.

Jesus said to her, "You are right when you say you have no husband. 18 The fact is, you have had five husbands, and the man you now have is not your husband. What you have just said is quite true."

19 "Sir," the woman said, "I can see that you are a prophet. 20 Our fathers worshiped on this mountain, but you Jews claim that the place where we must worship is in Jerusalem."

21 Jesus declared, "Believe me, woman, a time is coming when you will worship the Father neither on this mountain nor in Jerusalem. 22 You Samaritans worship what you do not know; we worship what we do know, for salvation is from the Jews. 23 Yet a time is coming and has now come when the true worshipers will worship the Father in spirit and truth, for they are the kind of worshipers the Father seeks. 24 God is spirit, and his worshipers must worship in spirit and in truth."

25 The woman said, "I know that Messiah" (called Christ) "is coming. When he comes, he will explain everything to us."

26 Then Jesus declared, "I who speak to you am he."

The Disciples Rejoin Jesus

27 Just then his disciples returned and were surprised to find him talking with a woman. But no one asked, "What do you want?" or "Why are you talking with her?"

28 Then, leaving her water jar, the woman went back to the town and said to the people, 29 "Come, see a man who told me everything I ever did. Could this be the Christ[a]?" 30 They came out of the town and made their way toward him.

31 Meanwhile his disciples urged him, "Rabbi, eat something."

32 But he said to them, "I have food to eat that you know nothing about."

33 Then his disciples said to each other, "Could someone have brought him food?"

34 "My food," said Jesus, "is to do the will of him who sent me and to finish his work. 35 Do you not say, 'Four months more and then the harvest'? I tell you, open your eyes and look at the fields! They are ripe for harvest. 36 Even now the reaper draws his wages, even now he harvests the crop for eternal life, so that the sower and the reaper may be glad together. 37 Thus the saying 'One sows and another reaps' is true. 38 I sent you to reap what you have not worked for. Others have done the hard work, and you have reaped the benefits of their labor."

Many Samaritans Believe

39 Many of the Samaritans from that town believed in him because of the woman's testimony, "He told me everything I ever did." 40 So when the Samaritans came to him, they urged him to stay with them, and he stayed two days. 41 And because of his words many more became believers.

42 They said to the woman, "We no longer believe just because of what you said; now we have heard for ourselves, and we know that this man really is the Savior of the world."

Jesus Heals the Official's Son

43 After the two days he left for Galilee. 44 (Now Jesus himself had pointed out that a prophet has no honor in his own country.) 45 When he arrived in Galilee, the Galileans welcomed him. They had seen all that he had done in Jerusalem at the Passover Feast, for they also had been there.

46 Once more he visited Cana in Galilee, where he had turned the water into wine. And there was a certain royal official whose son lay sick at Capernaum. 47 When this man heard that Jesus had arrived in Galilee from Judea, he went to him and begged him to come and heal his son, who was close to death.

48 "Unless you people see miraculous signs and wonders," Jesus told him, "you will never believe."

49 The royal official said, "Sir, come down before my child dies."

50 Jesus replied, "You may go. Your son will live."

The man took Jesus at his word and departed. 51 While he was still on the way, his servants met him with the news that his boy was living. 52 When he inquired as to the time

[a]29 Or *Messiah*

when his son got better, they said to him,
"The fever left him yesterday at the seventh
hour."
[53]Then the father realized that this was the
exact time at which Jesus had said to him,
"Your son will live." So he and all his household believed.
[54]This was the second miraculous sign
that Jesus performed, having come from
Judea to Galilee.

The Healing at the Pool

5 Some time later, Jesus went up to
Jerusalem for a feast of the Jews. [2]Now
there is in Jerusalem near the Sheep Gate a
pool, which in Aramaic is called Bethesda[a]
and which is surrounded by five covered
colonnades. [3]Here a great number of disabled people used to lie—the blind, the
lame, the paralyzed.[b] [5]One who was there
had been an invalid for thirty-eight years.
[6]When Jesus saw him lying there and
learned that he had been in this condition for
a long time, he asked him, "Do you want to
get well?"
[7]"Sir," the invalid replied, "I have no one to
help me into the pool when the water is
stirred. While I am trying to get in, someone
else goes down ahead of me."
[8]Then Jesus said to him, "Get up! Pick up
your mat and walk." [9]At once the man was
cured; he picked up his mat and walked.
The day on which this took place was a
Sabbath, [10]and so the Jews said to the man
who had been healed, "It is the Sabbath; the
law forbids you to carry your mat."
[11]But he replied, "The man who made me
well said to me, 'Pick up your mat and
walk.'"
[12]So they asked him, "Who is this fellow
who told you to pick it up and walk?"
[13]The man who was healed had no idea
who it was, for Jesus had slipped away into
the crowd that was there.
[14]Later Jesus found him at the temple and
said to him, "See, you are well again. Stop
sinning or something worse may happen to
you." [15]The man went away and told the
Jews that it was Jesus who had made him
well.

Life Through the Son

[16]So, because Jesus was doing these
things on the Sabbath, the Jews persecuted
him. [17]Jesus said to them, "My Father is always at his work to this very day, and I, too,
am working." [18]For this reason the Jews tried
all the harder to kill him; not only was he
breaking the Sabbath, but he was even calling God his own Father, making himself
equal with God.
[19]Jesus gave them this answer: "I tell you
the truth, the Son can do nothing by himself;
he can do only what he sees his Father doing, because whatever the Father does the
Son also does. [20]For the Father loves the
Son and shows him all he does. Yes, to your
amazement he will show him even greater
things than these. [21]For just as the Father
raises the dead and gives them life, even so
the Son gives life to whom he is pleased to
give it. [22]Moreover, the Father judges no
one, but has entrusted all judgment to the
Son, [23]that all may honor the Son just as they
honor the Father. He who does not honor the
Son does not honor the Father, who sent
him.
[24]"I tell you the truth, whoever hears my
word and believes him who sent me has
eternal life and will not be condemned; he
has crossed over from death to life. [25]I tell
you the truth, a time is coming and has now
come when the dead will hear the voice of
the Son of God and those who hear will live.
[26]For as the Father has life in himself, so he
has granted the Son to have life in himself.
[27]And he has given him authority to judge
because he is the Son of Man.
[28]"Do not be amazed at this, for a time is
coming when all who are in their graves will
hear his voice [29]and come out—those who
have done good will rise to live, and those
who have done evil will rise to be condemned. [30]By myself I can do nothing; I
judge only as I hear, and my judgment is just,
for I seek not to please myself but him who
sent me.

Testimonies About Jesus

[31]"If I testify about myself, my testimony is
not valid. [32]There is another who testifies in
my favor, and I know that his testimony about
me is valid.
[33]"You have sent to John and he has testified to the truth. [34]Not that I accept human
testimony; but I mention it that you may be

[a]2 Some manuscripts *Bethzatha;* other manuscripts *Bethsaida* [b]3 Some less important manuscripts *paralyzed—and they waited for the moving of the waters.* [4]*From time to time an angel of the Lord would come down and stir up the waters. The first one into the pool after each such disturbance would be cured of whatever disease he had.*

saved. 35John was a lamp that burned and
gave light, and you chose for a time to enjoy
his light.
36"I have testimony weightier than that of
John. For the very work that the Father has
given me to finish, and which I am doing,
testifies that the Father has sent me. 37And
the Father who sent me has himself testified
concerning me. You have never heard his
voice nor seen his form, 38nor does his word
dwell in you, for you do not believe the one
he sent. 39You diligently study[a] the Scriptures because you think that by them you
possess eternal life. These are the Scriptures that testify about me, 40yet you refuse
to come to me to have life.
41"I do not accept praise from men, 42but I
know you. I know that you do not have the
love of God in your hearts. 43I have come in
my Father's name, and you do not accept
me; but if someone else comes in his own
name, you will accept him. 44How can you
believe if you accept praise from one another, yet make no effort to obtain the praise
that comes from the only God[b]?
45"But do not think I will accuse you before
the Father. Your accuser is Moses, on whom
your hopes are set. 46If you believed Moses,
you would believe me, for he wrote about
me. 47But since you do not believe what he
wrote, how are you going to believe what I
say?"

Jesus Feeds the Five Thousand

6 Some time after this, Jesus crossed to
the far shore of the Sea of Galilee (that
is, the Sea of Tiberias), 2and a great crowd of
people followed him because they saw the
miraculous signs he had performed on the
sick. 3Then Jesus went up on a mountainside and sat down with his disciples. 4The
Jewish Passover Feast was near.
5When Jesus looked up and saw a great
crowd coming toward him, he said to Philip,
"Where shall we buy bread for these people
to eat?" 6He asked this only to test him, for
he already had in mind what he was going to
do.
7Philip answered him, "Eight months'
wages[c] would not buy enough bread for
each one to have a bite!"
8Another of his disciples, Andrew, Simon
Peter's brother, spoke up, 9"Here is a boy
with five small barley loaves and two small
fish, but how far will they go among so
many?"
10Jesus said, "Have the people sit down."
There was plenty of grass in that place, and
the men sat down, about five thousand of
them. 11Jesus then took the loaves, gave
thanks, and distributed to those who were
seated as much as they wanted. He did the
same with the fish.
12When they had all had enough to eat, he
said to his disciples, "Gather the pieces that
are left over. Let nothing be wasted." 13So
they gathered them and filled twelve baskets
with the pieces of the five barley loaves left
over by those who had eaten.
14After the people saw the miraculous sign
that Jesus did, they began to say, "Surely
this is the Prophet who is to come into the
world." 15Jesus, knowing that they intended
to come and make him king by force, withdrew again to a mountain by himself.

Jesus Walks on the Water

16When evening came, his disciples went
down to the lake, 17where they got into a boat
and set off across the lake for Capernaum.
By now it was dark, and Jesus had not yet
joined them. 18A strong wind was blowing
and the waters grew rough. 19When they had
rowed three or three and a half miles,[d] they
saw Jesus approaching the boat, walking on
the water; and they were terrified. 20But he
said to them, "It is I; don't be afraid." 21Then
they were willing to take him into the boat,
and immediately the boat reached the shore
where they were heading.
22The next day the crowd that had stayed
on the opposite shore of the lake realized
that only one boat had been there, and that
Jesus had not entered it with his disciples,
but that they had gone away alone. 23Then
some boats from Tiberias landed near the
place where the people had eaten the bread
after the Lord had given thanks. 24Once the
crowd realized that neither Jesus nor his disciples were there, they got into the boats and
went to Capernaum in search of Jesus.

Jesus the Bread of Life

25When they found him on the other side of
the lake, they asked him, "Rabbi, when did
you get here?"
26Jesus answered, "I tell you the truth, you
are looking for me, not because you saw

[a]39 Or *Study diligently* (the imperative) [b]44 Some early manuscripts *the Only One* [c]7 Greek *two hundred denarii* [d]19 Greek *rowed twenty-five or thirty stadia* (about 5 or 6 kilometers)

miraculous signs but because you ate the loaves and had your fill. 27Do not work for food that spoils, but for food that endures to eternal life, which the Son of Man will give you. On him God the Father has placed his seal of approval."

28Then they asked him, "What must we do to do the works God requires?"

29Jesus answered, "The work of God is this: to believe in the one he has sent."

30So they asked him, "What miraculous sign then will you give that we may see it and believe you? What will you do? 31Our forefathers ate the manna in the desert; as it is written: 'He gave them bread from heaven to eat.'[a]"

32Jesus said to them, "I tell you the truth, it is not Moses who has given you the bread from heaven, but it is my Father who gives you the true bread from heaven. 33For the bread of God is he who comes down from heaven and gives life to the world."

34"Sir," they said, "from now on give us this bread."

35Then Jesus declared, "I am the bread of life. He who comes to me will never go hungry, and he who believes in me will never be thirsty. 36But as I told you, you have seen me and still you do not believe. 37All that the Father gives me will come to me, and whoever comes to me I will never drive away. 38For I have come down from heaven not to do my will but to do the will of him who sent me. 39And this is the will of him who sent me, that I shall lose none of all that he has given me, but raise them up at the last day. 40For my Father's will is that everyone who looks to the Son and believes in him shall have eternal life, and I will raise him up at the last day."

41At this the Jews began to grumble about him because he said, "I am the bread that came down from heaven." 42They said, "Is this not Jesus, the son of Joseph, whose father and mother we know? How can he now say, 'I came down from heaven'?"

43"Stop grumbling among yourselves," Jesus answered. 44"No one can come to me unless the Father who sent me draws him, and I will raise him up at the last day. 45It is written in the Prophets: 'They will all be taught by God.'[b] Everyone who listens to the Father and learns from him comes to me. 46No one has seen the Father except the one who is from God; only he has seen the Father. 47I tell you the truth, he who believes has everlasting life. 48I am the bread of life. 49Your forefathers ate the manna in the desert, yet they died. 50But here is the bread that comes down from heaven, which a man may eat and not die. 51I am the living bread that came down from heaven. If anyone eats of this bread, he will live forever. This bread is my flesh, which I will give for the life of the world."

52Then the Jews began to argue sharply among themselves, "How can this man give us his flesh to eat?"

53Jesus said to them, "I tell you the truth, unless you eat the flesh of the Son of Man and drink his blood, you have no life in you. 54Whoever eats my flesh and drinks my blood has eternal life, and I will raise him up at the last day. 55For my flesh is real food and my blood is real drink. 56Whoever eats my flesh and drinks my blood remains in me, and I in him. 57Just as the living Father sent me and I live because of the Father, so the one who feeds on me will live because of me. 58This is the bread that came down from heaven. Your forefathers ate manna and died, but he who feeds on this bread will live forever." 59He said this while teaching in the synagogue in Capernaum.

Many Disciples Desert Jesus

60On hearing it, many of his disciples said, "This is a hard teaching. Who can accept it?"

61Aware that his disciples were grumbling about this, Jesus said to them, "Does this offend you? 62What if you see the Son of Man ascend to where he was before! 63The Spirit gives life; the flesh counts for nothing. The words I have spoken to you are spirit[c] and they are life. 64Yet there are some of you who do not believe." For Jesus had known from the beginning which of them did not believe and who would betray him. 65He went on to say, "This is why I told you that no one can come to me unless the Father has enabled him."

66From this time many of his disciples turned back and no longer followed him.

67"You do not want to leave too, do you?" Jesus asked the Twelve.

68Simon Peter answered him, "Lord, to whom shall we go? You have the words of eternal life. 69We believe and know that you are the Holy One of God."

70Then Jesus replied, "Have I not chosen you, the Twelve? Yet one of you is a devil!"

[a]*31* Exodus 16:4; Neh. 9:15; Psalm 78:24,25 [b]*45* Isaiah 54:13 [c]*63* Or *Spirit*

71(He meant Judas, the son of Simon Iscariot, who, though one of the Twelve, was later
to betray him.)

Jesus goes to the Feast of Tabernacles

7 After this, Jesus went around in Galilee,
purposely staying away from Judea because the Jews there were waiting to take
his life. 2But when the Jewish Feast of Tabernacles was near, 3Jesus' brothers said to
him, "You ought to leave here and go to
Judea, so that your disciples may see the
miracles you do. 4No one who wants to
become a public figure acts in secret. Since
you are doing these things, show yourself to
the world." 5For even his own brothers did
not believe in him.

6Therefore Jesus told them, "The right
time for me has not yet come; for you any
time is right. 7The world cannot hate you, but
it hates me because I testify that what it does
is evil. 8You go to the Feast. I am not yet[a]
going up to this Feast, because for me the
right time has not yet come." 9Having said
this, he stayed in Galilee.

10However, after his brothers had left for
the Feast, he went also, not publicly, but in
secret. 11Now at the Feast the Jews were
watching for him and asking, "Where is that
man?"

12Among the crowds there was widespread whispering about him. Some said,
"He is a good man."

Others replied, "No, he deceives the
people." 13But no one would say anything
publicly about him for fear of the Jews.

Jesus Teaches at the Feast

14Not until halfway through the Feast did
Jesus go up to the temple courts and begin
to teach. 15The Jews were amazed and
asked, "How did this man get such learning
without having studied?"

16Jesus answered, "My teaching is not my
own. It comes from him who sent me. 17If
anyone chooses to do God's will, he will find
out whether my teaching comes from God or
whether I speak on my own. 18He who
speaks on his own does so to gain honor for
himself, but he who works for the honor of
the one who sent him is a man of truth; there
is nothing false about him. 19Has not Moses
given you the law? Yet not one of you keeps
the law. Why are you trying to kill me?"

20"You are demon-possessed," the crowd
answered. "Who is trying to kill you?"

21Jesus said to them, "I did one miracle,
and you are all astonished. 22Yet, because
Moses gave you circumcision (though actually it did not come from Moses, but from the
patriarchs), you circumcise a child on the
Sabbath. 23Now if a child can be circumcised
on the Sabbath so that the law of Moses may
not be broken, why are you angry with me for
healing the whole man on the Sabbath?
24Stop judging by mere appearances, and
make a right judgment."

Is Jesus the Christ?

25At that point some of the people of
Jerusalem began to ask, "Isn't this the man
they are trying to kill? 26Here he is, speaking
publicly, and they are not saying a word to
him. Have the authorities really concluded
that he is the Christ[b]? 27But we know where
this man is from; when the Christ comes, no
one will know where he is from."

28Then Jesus, still teaching in the temple
courts, cried out, "Yes, you know me, and
you know where I am from. I am not here on
my own, but he who sent me is true. You do
not know him, 29but I know him because I am
from him and he sent me."

30At this they tried to seize him, but no one
laid a hand on him, because his time had not
yet come. 31Still, many in the crowd put their
faith in him. They said, "When the Christ
comes, will he do more miraculous signs
than this man?"

32The Pharisees heard the crowd whispering such things about him. Then the chief
priests and the Pharisees sent temple
guards to arrest him.

33Jesus said, "I am with you for only a
short time, and then I go to the one who sent
me. 34You will look for me, but you will
not find me; and where I am, you cannot
come."

35The Jews said to one another, "Where
does this man intend to go that we cannot
find him? Will he go where our people live
scattered among the Greeks, and teach the
Greeks? 36What did he mean when he said,
'You will look for me, but you will not find me,'
and 'Where I am, you cannot come'?"

37On the last and greatest day of the Feast,
Jesus stood and said in a loud voice, "If
anyone is thirsty, let him come to me and

[a]8 Some early manuscripts do not have *yet.*
[b]26 Or *Messiah*; also in verses 27, 31, 41 and 42

drink. 38Whoever believes in me, as[a] the Scripture has said, streams of living water will flow from within him." 39By this he meant the Spirit, whom those who believed in him were later to receive. Up to that time the Spirit had not been given, since Jesus had not yet been glorified.

40On hearing his words, some of the people said, "Surely this man is the Prophet."

41Others said, "He is the Christ."

Still others asked, "How can the Christ come from Galilee? 42Does not the Scripture say that the Christ will come from David's family[b] and from Bethlehem, the town where David lived?" 43Thus the people were divided because of Jesus. 44Some wanted to seize him, but no one laid a hand on him.

Unbelief of the Jewish Leaders

45Finally the temple guards went back to the chief priests and Pharisees, who asked them, "Why didn't you bring him in?"

46"No one ever spoke the way this man does," the guards declared.

47"You mean he has deceived you also?" the Pharisees retorted. 48"Has any of the rulers or of the Pharisees believed in him? 49No! But this mob that knows nothing of the law—there is a curse on them."

50Nicodemus, who had gone to Jesus earlier and who was one of their own number, asked, 51"Does our law condemn anyone without first hearing him to find out what he is doing?"

52They replied, "Are you from Galilee, too? Look into it, and you will find that a prophet[c] does not come out of Galilee."

[The earliest and most reliable manuscripts and other ancient witnesses do not have John 7:53-8:11.]

53Then each went to his own home.

8 But Jesus went to the Mount of Olives. 2At dawn he appeared again in the temple courts, where all the people gathered around him, and he sat down to teach them. 3The teachers of the law and the Pharisees brought in a woman caught in adultery. They made her stand before the group 4and said to Jesus, "Teacher, this woman was caught in the act of adultery. 5In the Law Moses commanded us to stone such women. Now what do you say?" 6They were using this question as a trap, in order to have a basis for accusing him.

But Jesus bent down and started to write on the ground with his finger. 7When they kept on questioning him, he straightened up and said to them, "If any one of you is without sin, let him be the first to throw a stone at her." 8Again he stooped down and wrote on the ground.

9At this, those who heard began to go away one at a time, the older ones first, until only Jesus was left, with the woman still standing there. 10Jesus straightened up and asked her, "Woman, where are they? Has no one condemned you?"

11"No one, sir," she said.

"Then neither do I condemn you," Jesus declared. "Go now and leave your life of sin."

The Validity of Jesus' Testimony

12When Jesus spoke again to the people, he said, "I am the light of the world. Whoever follows me will never walk in darkness, but will have the light of life."

13The Pharisees challenged him, "Here you are, appearing as your own witness; your testimony is not valid."

14Jesus answered, "Even if I testify on my own behalf, my testimony is valid, for I know where I came from and where I am going. But you have no idea where I come from or where I am going. 15You judge by human standards; I pass judgment on no one. 16But if I do judge, my decisions are right, because I am not alone. I stand with the Father, who sent me. 17In your own Law it is written that the testimony of two men is valid. 18I am one who testifies for myself; my other witness is the Father, who sent me."

19Then they asked him, "Where is your father?"

"You do not know me or my Father," Jesus replied. "If you knew me, you would know my Father also." 20He spoke these words while teaching in the temple area near the place where the offerings were put. Yet no one seized him, because his time had not yet come.

21Once more Jesus said to them, "I am

[a]37,38 Or / *If anyone is thirsty, let him come to me. / And let him drink,* 38*who believes in me. / As* [b]42 Greek *seed* [c]52 Two early manuscripts *the Prophet*

going away, and you will look for me, and you will die in your sin. Where I go, you cannot come."

22This made the Jews ask, "Will he kill himself? Is that why he says, 'Where I go, you cannot come'?"

23But he continued, "You are from below; I am from above. You are of this world; I am not of this world. 24I told you that you would die in your sins; if you do not believe that I am ⌊the one I claim to be⌋,[a] you will indeed die in your sins."

25"Who are you?" they asked.

"Just what I have been claiming all along," Jesus replied. 26"I have much to say in judgment of you. But he who sent me is reliable, and what I have heard from him I tell the world."

27They did not understand that he was telling them about his Father. 28So Jesus said, "When you have lifted up the Son of Man, then you will know that I am ⌊the one I claim to be⌋ and that I do nothing on my own but speak just what the Father has taught me. 29The one who sent me is with me; he has not left me alone, for I always do what pleases him." 30Even as he spoke, many put their faith in him.

The Children of Abraham

31To the Jews who had believed him, Jesus said, "If you hold to my teaching, you are really my disciples. 32Then you will know the truth, and the truth will set you free."

33They answered him, "We are Abraham's descendants[b] and have never been slaves of anyone. How can you say that we shall be set free?"

34Jesus replied, "I tell you the truth, everyone who sins is a slave to sin. 35Now a slave has no permanent place in the family, but a son belongs to it forever. 36So if the Son sets you free, you will be free indeed. 37I know you are Abraham's descendants. Yet you are ready to kill me, because you have no room for my word. 38I am telling you what I have seen in the Father's presence, and you do what you have heard from your father.[c]"

39"Abraham is our father," they answered.

"If you were Abraham's children," said Jesus, "then you would[d] do the things Abraham did. 40As it is, you are determined to kill me, a man who has told you the truth that I heard from God. Abraham did not do such things. 41You are doing the things your own father does."

"We are not illegitimate children," they protested. "The only Father we have is God himself."

The Children of the Devil

42Jesus said to them, "If God were your Father, you would love me, for I came from God and now am here. I have not come on my own; but he sent me. 43Why is my language not clear to you? Because you are unable to hear what I say. 44You belong to your father, the devil, and you want to carry out your father's desire. He was a murderer from the beginning, not holding to the truth, for there is no truth in him. When he lies, he speaks his native language, for he is a liar and the father of lies. 45Yet because I tell the truth, you do not believe me! 46Can any of you prove me guilty of sin? If I am telling the truth, why don't you believe me? 47He who belongs to God hears what God says. The reason you do not hear is that you do not belong to God."

The Claims of Jesus About Himself

48The Jews answered him, "Aren't we right in saying that you are a Samaritan and demon-possessed?"

49"I am not possessed by a demon," said Jesus, "but I honor my Father and you dishonor me. 50I am not seeking glory for myself; but there is one who seeks it, and he is the judge. 51I tell you the truth, if anyone keeps my word, he will never see death."

52At this the Jews exclaimed, "Now we know that you are demon-possessed! Abraham died and so did the prophets, yet you say that if anyone keeps your word, he will never taste death. 53Are you greater than our father Abraham? He died, and so did the prophets. Who do you think you are?"

54Jesus replied, "If I glorify myself, my glory means nothing. My Father, whom you claim as your God, is the one who glorifies me. 55Though you do not know him, I know him. If I said I did not, I would be a liar like you, but I do know him and keep his word. 56Your father Abraham rejoiced at the thought of seeing my day; he saw it and was glad."

57"You are not yet fifty years old," the Jews said to him, "and you have seen Abraham!"

[a]*24* Or *I am he*; also in verse 28 [b]*33* Greek *seed;* also in verse 37 [c]*38* Or *presence. Therefore do what you have heard from the Father.* [d]*39* Some early manuscripts *"If you are Abraham's children," said Jesus, "then*

58"I tell you the truth," Jesus answered,
"before Abraham was born, I am!" 59At this,
they picked up stones to stone him, but
Jesus hid himself, slipping away from the
temple grounds.

Jesus Heals a Man Born Blind

9 As he went along, he saw a man blind
from birth. 2His disciples asked him,
"Rabbi, who sinned, this man or his parents,
that he was born blind?"
3"Neither this man nor his parents sinned,"
said Jesus, "but this happened so that the
work of God might be displayed in his life.
4As long as it is day, we must do the work of
him who sent me. Night is coming, when no
one can work. 5While I am in the world, I am
the light of the world."
6Having said this, he spit on the ground,
made some mud with the saliva, and put it on
the man's eyes. 7"Go," he told him, "wash in
the Pool of Siloam" (this word means Sent).
So the man went and washed, and came
home seeing.
8His neighbors and those who had formerly seen him begging asked, "Isn't this the
same man who used to sit and beg?" 9Some
claimed that he was.
Others said, "No, he only looks like him."
But he himself insisted, "I am the man."
10"How then were your eyes opened?"
they demanded.
11He replied, "The man they call Jesus
made some mud and put it on my eyes. He
told me to go to Siloam and wash. So I went
and washed, and then I could see."
12"Where is this man?" they asked him.
"I don't know," he said.

The Pharisees Investigate the Healing

13They brought to the Pharisees the man
who had been blind. 14Now the day on which
Jesus had made the mud and opened the
man's eyes was a Sabbath. 15Therefore the
Pharisees also asked him how he had received his sight. "He put mud on my eyes,"
the man replied, "and I washed, and now I
see."
16Some of the Pharisees said, "This man
is not from God, for he does not keep the
Sabbath."
But others asked, "How can a sinner do
such miraculous signs?" So they were divided.
17Finally they turned again to the blind
man, "What have you to say about him? It
was your eyes he opened."
The man replied, "He is a prophet."
18The Jews still did not believe that he had
been blind and had received his sight until
they sent for the man's parents. 19"Is this
your son?" they asked. "Is this the one you
say was born blind? How is it that now he can
see?"
20"We know he is our son," the parents
answered, "and we know he was born blind.
21But how he can see now, or who opened
his eyes, we don't know. Ask him. He is of
age; he will speak for himself." 22His parents
said this because they were afraid of the
Jews, for already the Jews had decided that
anyone who acknowledged that Jesus was
the Christ[a] would be put out of the synagogue. 23That was why his parents said, "He
is of age; ask him."
24A second time they summoned the man
who had been blind. "Give glory to God,[b]"
they said. "We know this man is a sinner."
25He replied, "Whether he is a sinner or
not, I don't know. One thing I do know. I was
blind but now I see!"
26Then they asked him, "What did he do to
you? How did he open your eyes?"
27He answered, "I have told you already
and you did not listen. Why do you want to
hear it again? Do you want to become his
disciples, too?"
28Then they hurled insults at him and said,
"You are this fellow's disciple! We are disciples of Moses! 29We know that God spoke to
Moses, but as for this fellow, we don't even
know where he comes from."
30The man answered, "Now that is
remarkable! You don't know where he
comes from, yet he opened my eyes. 31We
know that God does not listen to sinners. He
listens to the godly man who does his will.
32Nobody has ever heard of opening the
eyes of a man born blind. 33If this man were
not from God, he could do nothing."
34To this they replied, "You were steeped
in sin at birth; how dare you lecture us!" And
they threw him out.

Spiritual Blindness

35Jesus heard that they had thrown him
out, and when he found him, he said, "Do
you believe in the Son of Man?"
36"Who is he, sir?" the man asked. "Tell
me so that I may believe in him."

[a]22 Or *Messiah* [b]24 A solemn charge to tell the truth (see Joshua 7:19)

37Jesus said, "You have now seen him; in fact, he is the one speaking with you."

38Then the man said, "Lord, I believe," and he worshiped him.

39Jesus said, "For judgment I have come into this world, so that the blind will see and those who see will become blind."

40Some Pharisees who were with him heard him say this and asked, "What? Are we blind too?"

41Jesus said, "If you were blind, you would not be guilty of sin; but now that you claim you can see, your guilt remains.

The Shepherd and His Flock

10 "I tell you the truth, the man who does not enter the sheep pen by the gate, but climbs in by some other way, is a thief and a robber. 2The man who enters by the gate is the shepherd of his sheep. 3The watchman opens the gate for him, and the sheep listen to his voice. He calls his own sheep by name and leads them out. 4When he has brought out all his own, he goes on ahead of them, and his sheep follow him because they know his voice. 5But they will never follow a stranger; in fact, they will run away from him because they do not recognize a stranger's voice." 6Jesus used this figure of speech, but they did not understand what he was telling them.

7Therefore Jesus said again, "I tell you the truth, I am the gate for the sheep. 8All who ever came before me were thieves and robbers, but the sheep did not listen to them. 9I am the gate; whoever enters through me will be saved.[a] He will come in and go out, and find pasture. 10The thief comes only to steal and kill and destroy; I have come that they may have life, and have it to the full.

11"I am the good shepherd. The good shepherd lays down his life for the sheep. 12The hired hand is not the shepherd who owns the sheep. So when he sees the wolf coming, he abandons the sheep and runs away. Then the wolf attacks the flock and scatters it. 13The man runs away because he is a hired hand and cares nothing for the sheep.

14"I am the good shepherd; I know my sheep and my sheep know me— 15just as the Father knows me and I know the Father—and I lay down my life for the sheep. 16I have other sheep that are not of this sheep pen. I must bring them also. They too will listen to my voice, and there shall be one flock and one shepherd. 17The reason my Father loves me is that I lay down my life—only to take it up again. 18No one takes it from me, but I lay it down of my own accord. I have authority to lay it down and authority to take it up again. This command I received from my Father."

19At these words the Jews were again divided. 20Many of them said, "He is demon-possessed and raving mad. Why listen to him?"

21But others said, "These are not the sayings of a man possessed by a demon. Can a demon open the eyes of the blind?"

The Unbelief of the Jews

22Then came the Feast of Dedication[b] at Jerusalem. It was winter, 23and Jesus was in the temple area walking in Solomon's Colonnade. 24The Jews gathered around him, saying, "How long will you keep us in suspense? If you are the Christ,[c] tell us plainly."

25Jesus answered, "I did tell you, but you do not believe. The miracles I do in my Father's name speak for me, 26but you do not believe because you are not my sheep. 27My sheep listen to my voice; I know them, and they follow me. 28I give them eternal life, and they shall never perish; no one can snatch them out of my hand. 29My Father, who has given them to me, is greater than all[d]; no one can snatch them out of my Father's hand. 30I and the Father are one."

31Again the Jews picked up stones to stone him, 32but Jesus said to them, "I have shown you many great miracles from the Father. For which of these do you stone me?"

33"We are not stoning you for any of these," replied the Jews, "but for blasphemy, because you, a mere man, claim to be God."

34Jesus answered them, "Is it not written in your Law, 'I have said you are gods'[e]? 35If he called them 'gods,' to whom the word of God came—and the Scripture cannot be broken— 36what about the one whom the Father set apart as his very own and sent into the world? Why then do you accuse me of blasphemy because I said, 'I am God's Son'? 37Do not believe me unless I do what my Father does. 38But if I do it, even though you do not believe me, believe the miracles, that

[a]9 Or *kept safe* [b]22 That is, Hanukkah [c]24 Or *Messiah* [d]29 Many early manuscripts *What my Father has given me is greater than all* [e]34 Psalm 82:6

you may know and understand that the Father is in me, and I in the Father." 39Again
they tried to seize him, but he escaped their
grasp.
40Then Jesus went back across the Jordan
to the place where John had been baptizing
in the early days. Here he stayed 41and many
people came to him. They said, "Though
John never performed a miraculous sign, all
that John said about this man was true."
42And in that place many believed in Jesus.

The Death of Lazarus

11 Now a man named Lazarus was sick.
He was from Bethany, the village of
Mary and her sister Martha. 2This Mary,
whose brother Lazarus now lay sick, was the
same one who poured perfume on the Lord
and wiped his feet with her hair. 3So the
sisters sent word to Jesus, "Lord, the one
you love is sick."
4When he heard this, Jesus said, "This
sickness will not end in death. No, it is for
God's glory so that God's Son may be glorified through it." 5Jesus loved Martha and her
sister and Lazarus. 6Yet when he heard that
Lazarus was sick, he stayed where he was
two more days.
7Then he said to his disciples, "Let us go
back to Judea."
8"But Rabbi," they said, "a short while ago
the Jews tried to stone you, and yet you are
going back there?"
9Jesus answered, "Are there not twelve
hours of daylight? A man who walks by day
will not stumble, for he sees by this world's
light. 10It is when he walks by night that he
stumbles, for he has no light."
11After he had said this, he went on to tell
them, "Our friend Lazarus has fallen asleep;
but I am going there to wake him up."
12His disciples replied, "Lord, if he sleeps,
he will get better." 13Jesus had been speaking of his death, but his disciples thought he
meant natural sleep.
14So then he told them plainly, "Lazarus is
dead, 15and for your sake I am glad I was not
there, so that you may believe. But let us go
to him."
16Then Thomas (called Didymus) said to
the rest of the disciples, "Let us also go, that
we may die with him."

Jesus Comforts the Sisters

17On his arrival, Jesus found that Lazarus
had already been in the tomb for four days.
18Bethany was less than two miles[a] from
Jerusalem, 19and many Jews had come to
Martha and Mary to comfort them in the loss
of their brother. 20When Martha heard that
Jesus was coming, she went out to meet
him, but Mary stayed at home.
21"Lord," Martha said to Jesus, "if you had
been here, my brother would not have died.
22But I know that even now God will give you
whatever you ask."
23Jesus said to her, "Your brother will rise
again."
24Martha answered, "I know he will rise
again in the resurrection at the last day."
25Jesus said to her, "I am the resurrection
and the life. He who believes in me will live,
even though he dies; 26and whoever lives
and believes in me will never die. Do you
believe this?"
27"Yes, Lord," she told him, "I believe that
you are the Christ,[b] the Son of God, who was
to come into the world."
28And after she had said this, she went
back and called her sister Mary aside. "The
Teacher is here," she said, "and is asking for
you." 29When Mary heard this, she got up
quickly and went to him. 30Now Jesus had
not yet entered the village, but was still at the
place where Martha had met him. 31When
the Jews who had been with Mary in the
house, comforting her, noticed how quickly
she got up and went out, they followed her,
supposing she was going to the tomb to
mourn there.
32When Mary reached the place where
Jesus was and saw him, she fell at his feet
and said, "Lord, if you had been here, my
brother would not have died."
33When Jesus saw her weeping, and the
Jews who had come along with her also
weeping, he was deeply moved in spirit and
troubled. 34"Where have you laid him?" he
asked.
"Come and see, Lord," they replied.
35Jesus wept.
36Then the Jews said, "See how he loved
him!"
37But some of them said, "Could not he
who opened the eyes of the blind man have
kept this man from dying?"

Jesus Raises Lazarus From the Dead

38Jesus, once more deeply moved, came
to the tomb. It was a cave with a stone laid

[a]18 Greek *fifteen stadia* (about 3 kilometers) [b]27 Or *Messiah*

across the entrance. 39“Take away the stone,” he said.

“But, Lord,” said Martha, the sister of the dead man, “by this time there is a bad odor, for he has been there four days.”

40Then Jesus said, “Did I not tell you that if you believed, you would see the glory of God?”

41So they took away the stone. Then Jesus looked up and said, “Father, I thank you that you have heard me. 42I knew that you always hear me, but I said this for the benefit of the people standing here, that they may believe that you sent me.”

43When he had said this, Jesus called in a loud voice, “Lazarus, come out!” 44The dead man came out, his hands and feet wrapped with strips of linen, and a cloth around his face.

Jesus said to them, “Take off the grave clothes and let him go.”

The Plot to Kill Jesus

45Therefore many of the Jews who had come to visit Mary, and had seen what Jesus did, put their faith in him. 46But some of them went to the Pharisees and told them what Jesus had done. 47Then the chief priests and the Pharisees called a meeting of the Sanhedrin.

“What are we accomplishing?” they asked. “Here is this man performing many miraculous signs. 48If we let him go on like this, everyone will believe in him, and then the Romans will come and take away both our place[a] and our nation.”

49Then one of them, named Caiaphas, who was high priest that year, spoke up, “You know nothing at all! 50You do not realize that it is better for you that one man die for the people than that the whole nation perish.”

51He did not say this on his own, but as high priest that year he prophesied that Jesus would die for the Jewish nation, 52and not only for that nation but also for the scattered children of God, to bring them together and make them one. 53So from that day on they plotted to take his life.

54Therefore Jesus no longer moved about publicly among the Jews. Instead he withdrew to a region near the desert, to a village called Ephraim, where he stayed with his disciples.

55When it was almost time for the Jewish Passover, many went up from the country to Jerusalem for their ceremonial cleansing before the Passover. 56They kept looking for Jesus, and as they stood in the temple area they asked one another, “What do you think? Isn’t he coming to the Feast at all?” 57But the chief priests and Pharisees had given orders that if anyone found out where Jesus was, he should report it so that they might arrest him.

Jesus Anointed at Bethany

12 Six days before the Passover, Jesus arrived at Bethany, where Lazarus lived, whom Jesus had raised from the dead. 2Here a dinner was given in Jesus’ honor. Martha served, while Lazarus was among those reclining at the table with him. 3Then Mary took about a pint[b] of pure nard, an expensive perfume; she poured it on Jesus’ feet and wiped his feet with her hair. And the house was filled with the fragrance of the perfume.

4But one of his disciples, Judas Iscariot, who was later to betray him, objected, 5“Why wasn’t this perfume sold and the money given to the poor? It was worth a year’s wages.[c]” 6He did not say this because he cared about the poor but because he was a thief; as keeper of the money bag, he used to help himself to what was put into it.

7“Leave her alone,” Jesus replied. “⌊It was intended⌋ that she should save this perfume for the day of my burial. 8You will always have the poor among you, but you will not always have me.”

9Meanwhile a large crowd of Jews found out that Jesus was there and came, not only because of him but also to see Lazarus, whom he had raised from the dead. 10So the chief priests made plans to kill Lazarus as well, 11for on account of him many of the Jews were going over to Jesus and putting their faith in him.

The Triumphal Entry

12The next day the great crowd that had come for the Feast heard that Jesus was on his way to Jerusalem. 13They took palm branches and went out to meet him, shouting,

“Hosanna![d]”

[a]48 Or *temple* [b]3 Greek *a litra* (probably about 0.5 liter) [c]5 Greek *three hundred denarii* [d]13 A Hebrew expression meaning “Save!” which became an exclamation of praise

"Blessed is he who comes in the name of
the Lord!"[a]

"Blessed is the King of Israel!"

14 Jesus found a young donkey and sat upon
it, as it is written,

15 "Do not be afraid, O Daughter of Zion;
see, your king is coming,
seated on a donkey's colt."[b]

16 At first his disciples did not understand
all this. Only after Jesus was glorified did
they realize that these things had been written about him and that they had done these
things to him.

17 Now the crowd that was with him when
he called Lazarus from the tomb and raised
him from the dead continued to spread the
word. 18 Many people, because they had
heard that he had given this miraculous sign,
went out to meet him. 19 So the Pharisees
said to one another, "See, this is getting us
nowhere. Look how the whole world has
gone after him!"

Jesus Predicts His Death

20 Now there were some Greeks among
those who went up to worship at the Feast.
21 They came to Philip, who was from Bethsaida in Galilee, with a request. "Sir," they
said, "we would like to see Jesus." 22 Philip
went to tell Andrew; Andrew and Philip in
turn told Jesus.

23 Jesus replied, "The hour has come for
the Son of Man to be glorified. 24 I tell you the
truth, unless a kernel of wheat falls to the
ground and dies, it remains only a single
seed. But if it dies, it produces many seeds.
25 The man who loves his life will lose it, while
the man who hates his life in this world will
keep it for eternal life. 26 Whoever serves me
must follow me; and where I am, my servant
also will be. My Father will honor the one who
serves me.

27 "Now my heart is troubled, and what
shall I say? 'Father, save me from this hour'?
No, it was for this very reason I came to this
hour. 28 Father, glorify your name!"

Then a voice came from heaven, "I have
glorified it, and will glorify it again." 29 The
crowd that was there and heard it said it had
thundered; others said an angel had spoken
to him.

30 Jesus said, "This voice was for your benefit, not mine. 31 Now is the time for judgment
on this world; now the prince of this world will
be driven out. 32 But I, when I am lifted up
from the earth, will draw all men to myself."
33 He said this to show the kind of death he
was going to die.

34 The crowd spoke up, "We have heard
from the Law that the Christ[c] will remain
forever, so how can you say, 'The Son of
Man must be lifted up'? Who is this 'Son of
Man'?"

35 Then Jesus told them, "You are going to
have the light just a little while longer. Walk
while you have the light, before darkness
overtakes you. The man who walks in the
dark does not know where he is going. 36 Put
your trust in the light while you have it, so that
you may become sons of light." When he
had finished speaking, Jesus left and hid
himself from them.

The Jews Continue in Their Unbelief

37 Even after Jesus had done all these miraculous signs in their presence, they still
would not believe in him. 38 This was to fulfill
the word of Isaiah the prophet:

"Lord, who has believed our message
and to whom has the arm of the Lord
been revealed?"[d]

39 For this reason they could not believe,
because, as Isaiah says elsewhere:

40 "He has blinded their eyes
and deadened their hearts,
so they can neither see with their eyes,
nor understand with their hearts,
nor turn—and I would heal them."[e]

41 Isaiah said this because he saw Jesus'
glory and spoke about him.

42 Yet at the same time many even among
the leaders believed in him. But because of
the Pharisees they would not confess their
faith for fear they would be put out of the
synagogue; 43 for they loved praise from men
more than praise from God.

44 Then Jesus cried out, "When a man believes in me, he does not believe in me only,
but in the one who sent me. 45 When he looks
at me, he sees the one who sent me. 46 I have
come into the world as a light, so that no one
who believes in me should stay in darkness.

47 "As for the person who hears my words
but does not keep them, I do not judge him.
For I did not come to judge the world, but to
save it. 48 There is a judge for the one who

[a] *13* Psalm 118:25, 26 [b] *15* Zech. 9:9 [c] *34* Or *Messiah* [d] *38* Isaiah 53:1 [e] *40* Isaiah 6:10

rejects me and does not accept my words; that very word which I spoke will condemn him at the last day. [49]For I did not speak of my own accord, but the Father who sent me commanded me what to say and how to say it. [50]I know that his command leads to eternal life. So whatever I say is just what the Father has told me to say."

Jesus Washes His Disciples' Feet

13 It was just before the Passover Feast. Jesus knew that the time had come for him to leave this world and go to the Father. Having loved his own who were in the world, he now showed them the full extent of his love.[a]

[2]The evening meal was being served, and the devil had already prompted Judas Iscariot, son of Simon, to betray Jesus. [3]Jesus knew that the Father had put all things under his power, and that he had come from God and was returning to God; [4]so he got up from the meal, took off his outer clothing, and wrapped a towel around his waist. [5]After that, he poured water into a basin and began to wash his disciples' feet, drying them with the towel that was wrapped around him.

[6]He came to Simon Peter, who said to him, "Lord, are you going to wash my feet?"

[7]Jesus replied, "You do not realize now what I am doing, but later you will understand."

[8]"No," said Peter, "you shall never wash my feet."

Jesus answered, "Unless I wash you, you have no part with me."

[9]"Then, Lord," Simon Peter replied, "not just my feet but my hands and my head as well!"

[10]Jesus answered, "A person who has had a bath needs only to wash his feet; his whole body is clean. And you are clean, though not every one of you." [11]For he knew who was going to betray him, and that was why he said not every one was clean.

[12]When he had finished washing their feet, he put on his clothes and returned to his place. "Do you understand what I have done for you?" he asked them. [13]"You call me 'Teacher' and 'Lord,' and rightly so, for that is what I am. [14]Now that I, your Lord and Teacher, have washed your feet, you also should wash one another's feet. [15]I have set you an example that you should do as I have done for you. [16]I tell you the truth, no servant is greater than his master, nor is a messenger greater than the one who sent him. [17]Now that you know these things, you will be blessed if you do them.

Jesus Predicts His Betrayal

[18]"I am not referring to all of you; I know those I have chosen. But this is to fulfill the scripture: 'He who shares my bread has lifted up his heel against me.'[b]

[19]"I am telling you now before it happens, so that when it does happen you will believe that I am He. [20]I tell you the truth, whoever accepts anyone I send accepts me; and whoever accepts me accepts the one who sent me."

[21]After he had said this, Jesus was troubled in spirit and testified, "I tell you the truth, one of you is going to betray me."

[22]His disciples stared at one another, at a loss to know which of them he meant. [23]One of them, the disciple whom Jesus loved, was reclining next to him. [24]Simon Peter motioned to this disciple and said, "Ask him which one he means."

[25]Leaning back against Jesus, he asked him, "Lord, who is it?"

[26]Jesus answered, "It is the one to whom I will give this piece of bread when I have dipped it in the dish." Then, dipping the piece of bread, he gave it to Judas Iscariot, son of Simon. [27]As soon as Judas took the bread, Satan entered into him.

"What you are about to do, do quickly," Jesus told him, [28]but no one at the meal understood why Jesus said this to him. [29]Since Judas had charge of the money, some thought Jesus was telling him to buy what was needed for the Feast, or to give something to the poor. [30]As soon as Judas had taken the bread, he went out. And it was night.

Jesus Predicts Peter's Denial

[31]When he was gone, Jesus said, "Now is the Son of Man glorified and God is glorified in him. [32]If God is glorified in him,[c] God will glorify the Son in himself, and will glorify him at once.

[33]"My children, I will be with you only a little longer. You will look for me, and just as I told the Jews, so I tell you now: Where I am going, you cannot come.

[a] *1* Or *he loved them to the last* [b] *18* Psalm 41:9 [c] *32* Many early manuscripts do not have *If God is glorified in him.*

34"A new command I give you: Love one another. As I have loved you, so you must love one another. 35By this all men will know that you are my disciples, if you love one another."

36Simon Peter asked him, "Lord, where are you going?"

Jesus replied, "Where I am going, you cannot follow now, but you will follow later."

37Peter asked, "Lord, why can't I follow you now? I will lay down my life for you."

38Then Jesus answered, "Will you really lay down your life for me? I tell you the truth, before the rooster crows, you will disown me three times!

Jesus Comforts His Disciples

14 "Do not let your hearts be troubled. Trust in God[a]; trust also in me. 2In my Father's house are many rooms; if it were not so, I would have told you. I am going there to prepare a place for you. 3And if I go and prepare a place for you, I will come back and take you to be with me that you also may be where I am. 4You know the way to the place where I am going."

Jesus the Way to the Father

5Thomas said to him, "Lord, we don't know where you are going, so how can we know the way?"

6Jesus answered, "I am the way and the truth and the life. No one comes to the Father except through me. 7If you really knew me, you would know[b] my Father as well. From now on, you do know him and have seen him."

8Philip said, "Lord, show us the Father and that will be enough for us."

9Jesus answered: "Don't you know me, Philip, even after I have been among you such a long time? Anyone who has seen me has seen the Father. How can you say, 'Show us the Father'? 10Don't you believe that I am in the Father, and that the Father is in me? The words I say to you are not just my own. Rather, it is the Father, living in me, who is doing his work. 11Believe me when I say that I am in the Father and the Father is in me; or at least believe on the evidence of the miracles themselves. 12I tell you the truth, anyone who has faith in me will do what I have been doing. He will do even greater things than these, because I am going to the Father. 13And I will do whatever you ask in my name, so that the Son may bring glory to the Father. 14You may ask me for anything in my name, and I will do it.

Jesus Promises the Holy Spirit

15"If you love me, you will obey what I command. 16And I will ask the Father, and he will give you another Counselor to be with you forever— 17the Spirit of truth. The world cannot accept him, because it neither sees him nor knows him. But you know him, for he lives with you and will be[c] in you. 18I will not leave you as orphans; I will come to you. 19Before long, the world will not see me anymore, but you will see me. Because I live, you also will live. 20On that day you will realize that I am in my Father, and you are in me, and I am in you. 21Whoever has my commands and obeys them, he is the one who loves me. He who loves me will be loved by my Father, and I too will love him and show myself to him."

22Then Judas (not Judas Iscariot) said, "But, Lord, why do you intend to show yourself to us and not to the world?"

23Jesus replied, "If anyone loves me, he will obey my teaching. My Father will love him, and we will come to him and make our home with him. 24He who does not love me will not obey my teaching. These words you hear are not my own; they belong to the Father who sent me.

25"All this I have spoken while still with you. 26But the Counselor, the Holy Spirit, whom the Father will send in my name, will teach you all things and will remind you of everything I have said to you. 27Peace I leave with you; my peace I give you. I do not give to you as the world gives. Do not let your hearts be troubled and do not be afraid.

28"You heard me say, 'I am going away and I am coming back to you.' If you loved me, you would be glad that I am going to the Father, for the Father is greater than I. 29I have told you now before it happens, so that when it does happen you will believe. 30I will not speak with you much longer, for the prince of this world is coming. He has no hold on me, 31but the world must learn that I love the Father and that I do exactly what my Father has commanded me.

"Come now; let us leave.

[a] *1* Or *You trust in God* [b] *7* Some early manuscripts *If you really have known me, you will know* [c] *17* Some early manuscripts *and is*

The Vine and the Branches

15 "I am the true vine, and my Father is the gardener. 2He cuts off every branch in me that bears no fruit, while every branch that does bear fruit he prunes[a] so that it will be even more fruitful. 3You are already clean because of the word I have spoken to you. 4Remain in me, and I will remain in you. No branch can bear fruit by itself; it must remain in the vine. Neither can you bear fruit unless you remain in me.

5"I am the vine; you are the branches. If a man remains in me and I in him, he will bear much fruit; apart from me you can do nothing. 6If anyone does not remain in me, he is like a branch that is thrown away and withers; such branches are picked up, thrown into the fire and burned. 7If you remain in me and my words remain in you, ask whatever you wish, and it will be given you. 8This is to my Father's glory, that you bear much fruit, showing yourselves to be my disciples.

9"As the Father has loved me, so have I loved you. Now remain in my love. 10If you obey my commands, you will remain in my love, just as I have obeyed my Father's commands and remain in his love. 11I have told you this so that my joy may be in you and that your joy may be complete. 12My command is this: Love each other as I have loved you. 13Greater love has no one than this, that he lay down his life for his friends. 14You are my friends if you do what I command. 15I no longer call you servants, because a servant does not know his master's business. Instead, I have called you friends, for everything that I learned from my Father I have made known to you. 16You did not choose me, but I chose you and appointed you to go and bear fruit—fruit that will last. Then the Father will give you whatever you ask in my name. 17This is my command: Love each other.

The World Hates the Disciples

18"If the world hates you, keep in mind that it hated me first. 19If you belonged to the world, it would love you as its own. As it is, you do not belong to the world, but I have chosen you out of the world. That is why the world hates you. 20Remember the words I spoke to you: 'No servant is greater than his master.'[b] If they persecuted me, they will persecute you also. If they obeyed my teaching, they will obey yours also. 21They will treat you this way because of my name, for they do not know the One who sent me. 22If I had not come and spoken to them, they would not be guilty of sin. Now, however, they have no excuse for their sin. 23He who hates me hates my Father as well. 24If I had not done among them what no one else did, they would not be guilty of sin. But now they have seen these miracles, and yet they have hated both me and my Father. 25But this is to fulfill what is written in their Law: 'They hated me without reason.'[c]

26"When the Counselor comes, whom I will send to you from the Father, the Spirit of truth who goes out from the Father, he will testify about me. 27And you also must testify, for you have been with me from the beginning.

16 "All this I have told you so that you will not go astray. 2They will put you out of the synagogue; in fact, a time is coming when anyone who kills you will think he is offering a service to God. 3They will do such things because they have not known the Father or me. 4I have told you this, so that when the time comes you will remember that I warned you. I did not tell you this at first because I was with you.

The Work of the Holy Spirit

5"Now I am going to him who sent me, yet none of you asks me, 'Where are you going?' 6Because I have said these things, you are filled with grief. 7But I tell you the truth: It is for your good that I am going away. Unless I go away, the Counselor will not come to you; but if I go, I will send him to you. 8When he comes, he will convict the world of guilt[d] in regard to sin and righteousness and judgment: 9in regard to sin, because men do not believe in me; 10in regard to righteousness, because I am going to the Father, where you can see me no longer; 11and in regard to judgment, because the prince of this world now stands condemned.

12"I have much more to say to you, more than you can now bear. 13But when he, the Spirit of truth, comes, he will guide you into all truth. He will not speak on his own; he will speak only what he hears, and he will tell you what is yet to come. 14He will bring glory to me by taking from what is mine and making it known to you. 15All that belongs to the Father

a2 The Greek for *prunes* also means *cleans.* b20 John 13:16 c25 Psalms 35:19; 69:4 d8 Or *will expose the guilt of the world*

is mine. That is why I said the Spirit will take
from what is mine and make it known to you.
16"In a little while you will see me no more,
and then after a little while you will see me."

The Disciples' Grief Will Turn to Joy

17Some of his disciples said to one another, "What does he mean by saying, 'In a
little while you will see me no more, and then
after a little while you will see me,' and 'Because I am going to the Father'?" 18They
kept asking, "What does he mean by 'a little
while'? We don't understand what he is saying."
19Jesus saw that they wanted to ask him
about this, so he said to them, "Are you asking one another what I meant when I said, 'In
a little while you will see me no more, and
then after a little while you will see me'? 20I
tell you the truth, you will weep and mourn
while the world rejoices. You will grieve, but
your grief will turn to joy. 21A woman giving
birth to a child has pain because her time has
come; but when her baby is born she forgets
the anguish because of her joy that a child is
born into the world. 22So with you: Now is
your time of grief, but I will see you again and
you will rejoice, and no one will take away
your joy. 23In that day you will no longer ask
me anything. I tell you the truth, my Father
will give you whatever you ask in my name.
24Until now you have not asked for anything
in my name. Ask and you will receive, and
your joy will be complete.
25"Though I have been speaking figuratively, a time is coming when I will no longer
use this kind of language but will tell you
plainly about my Father. 26In that day you will
ask in my name. I am not saying that I will ask
the Father on your behalf. 27No, the Father
himself loves you because you have loved
me and have believed that I came from God.
28I came from the Father and entered the
world; now I am leaving the world and going
back to the Father."
29Then Jesus' disciples said, "Now you
are speaking clearly and without figures of
speech. 30Now we can see that you know all
things and that you do not even need to have
anyone ask you questions. This makes us
believe that you came from God."
31"You believe at last!"[a] Jesus answered.
32"But a time is coming, and has come, when
you will be scattered, each to his own home.
You will leave me all alone. Yet I am not
alone, for my Father is with me.
33"I have told you these things, so that in
me you may have peace. In this world you
will have trouble. But take heart! I have overcome the world."

Jesus Prays for Himself

17 After Jesus said this, he looked
toward heaven and prayed:
"Father, the time has come. Glorify
your Son, that your Son may glorify you.
2For you granted him authority over all
people that he might give eternal life to
all those you have given him. 3Now this
is eternal life: that they may know you,
the only true God, and Jesus Christ,
whom you have sent. 4I have brought
you glory on earth by completing the
work you gave me to do. 5And now, Father, glorify me in your presence with
the glory I had with you before the world
began.

Jesus Prays for His Disciples

6"I have revealed you[b] to those whom
you gave me out of the world. They were
yours; you gave them to me and they
have obeyed your word. 7Now they
know that everything you have given me
comes from you. 8For I gave them the
words you gave me and they accepted
them. They knew with certainty that I
came from you, and they believed that
you sent me. 9I pray for them. I am not
praying for the world, but for those you
have given me, for they are yours. 10All I
have is yours, and all you have is mine.
And glory has come to me through
them. 11I will remain in the world no
longer, but they are still in the world, and
I am coming to you. Holy Father, protect
them by the power of your name—the
name you gave me—so that they may
be one as we are one. 12While I was with
them, I protected them and kept them
safe by that name you gave me. None
has been lost except the one doomed to
destruction so that Scripture would be
fulfilled.
13"I am coming to you now, but I say
these things while I am still in the world,
so that they may have the full measure

[a]31 Or *"Do you now believe?"* [b]6 Greek *your name;* also in verse 26

of my joy within them. 14I have given
them your word and the world has hated
them, for they are not of the world any
more than I am of the world. 15My prayer
is not that you take them out of the world
but that you protect them from the evil
one. 16They are not of the world, even as
I am not of it. 17Sanctify[a] them by the
truth; your word is truth. 18As you sent
me into the world, I have sent them into
the world. 19For them I sanctify myself,
that they too may be truly sanctified.

Jesus Prays for All Believers

20"My prayer is not for them alone. I
pray also for those who will believe in
me through their message, 21that all of
them may be one, Father, just as you
are in me and I am in you. May they also
be in us so that the world may believe
that you have sent me. 22I have given
them the glory that you gave me, that
they may be one as we are one: 23I in
them and you in me. May they be
brought to complete unity to let the
world know that you sent me and have
loved them even as you have loved me.

24"Father, I want those you have giv-
en me to be with me where I am, and to
see my glory, the glory you have given
me because you loved me before the
creation of the world.

25"Righteous Father, though the
world does not know you, I know you,
and they know that you have sent me.
26I have made you known to them, and
will continue to make you known in order that the love you have for me may be
in them and that I myself may be in
them."

Jesus Arrested

18 When he had finished praying, Jesus
left with his disciples and crossed the
Kidron Valley. On the other side there was
an olive grove, and he and his disciples went
into it.

2Now Judas, who betrayed him, knew the
place, because Jesus had often met there
with his disciples. 3So Judas came to the
grove, guiding a detachment of soldiers and
some officials from the chief priests and
Pharisees. They were carrying torches, lan-
terns and weapons.

4Jesus, knowing all that was going to happen to him, went out and asked them, "Who
is it you want?"

5"Jesus of Nazareth," they replied.

"I am he," Jesus said. (And Judas the
traitor was standing there with them.) 6When
Jesus said, "I am he," they drew back and
fell to the ground.

7Again he asked them, "Who is it you
want?"

And they said, "Jesus of Nazareth."

8"I told you that I am he," Jesus answered.
"If you are looking for me, then let these men
go." 9This happened so that the words he
had spoken would be fulfilled: "I have not lost
one of those you gave me."[b]

10Then Simon Peter, who had a sword,
drew it and struck the high priest's servant,
cutting off his right ear. (The servant's name
was Malchus.)

11Jesus commanded Peter, "Put your
sword away! Shall I not drink the cup the
Father has given me?"

Jesus Taken to Annas

12Then the detachment of soldiers with its
commander and the Jewish officials arrested
Jesus. They bound him 13and brought him
first to Annas, who was the father-in-law of
Caiaphas, the high priest that year. 14Caia-
phas was the one who had advised the Jews
that it would be good if one man died for the
people.

Peter's First Denial

15Simon Peter and another disciple were
following Jesus. Because this disciple was
known to the high priest, he went with Jesus
into the high priest's courtyard, 16but Peter
had to wait outside at the door. The other
disciple, who was known to the high priest,
came back, spoke to the girl on duty there
and brought Peter in.

17"You are not one of his disciples, are
you?" the girl at the door asked Peter.

He replied, "I am not."

18It was cold, and the servants and officials
stood around a fire they had made to keep
warm. Peter also was standing with them,
warming himself.

The High Priest Questions Jesus

19Meanwhile, the high priest questioned
Jesus about his disciples and his teaching.

20"I have spoken openly to the world,"
Jesus replied. "I always taught in syna-

[a]17 Greek *hagiazo (set apart for sacred use* or *make holy)*; also in verse 19 [b]9 John 6:39

gogues or at the temple, where all the Jews
come together. I said nothing in secret.
[21]Why question me? Ask those who heard
me. Surely they know what I said."
[22]When Jesus said this, one of the officials
nearby struck him in the face. "Is this the way
you answer the high priest?" he demanded.
[23]"If I said something wrong," Jesus replied, "testify as to what is wrong. But if I
spoke the truth, why did you strike me?"
[24]Then Annas sent him, still bound, to Caiaphas the high priest.[a]

Peter's Second and Third Denials

[25]As Simon Peter stood warming himself,
he was asked, "You are not one of his disciples, are you?"
He denied it, saying, "I am not."
[26]One of the high priest's servants, a relative of the man whose ear Peter had cut off,
challenged him, "Didn't I see you with him in
the olive grove?" [27]Again Peter denied it,
and at that moment a rooster began to crow.

Jesus Before Pilate

[28]Then the Jews led Jesus from Caiaphas
to the palace of the Roman governor. By now
it was early morning, and to avoid ceremonial uncleanness the Jews did not enter the
palace; they wanted to be able to eat the
Passover. [29]So Pilate came out to them and
asked, "What charges are you bringing
against this man?"
[30]"If he were not a criminal," they replied,
"we would not have handed him over to
you."
[31]Pilate said, "Take him yourselves and
judge him by your own law."
"But we have no right to execute anyone,"
the Jews objected. [32]This happened so that
the words Jesus had spoken indicating the
kind of death he was going to die would be
fulfilled.
[33]Pilate then went back inside the palace,
summoned Jesus and asked him, "Are you
the king of the Jews?"
[34]"Is that your own idea," Jesus asked, "or
did others talk to you about me?"
[35]"Am I a Jew?" Pilate replied. "It was your
people and your chief priests who handed
you over to me. What is it you have done?"
[36]Jesus said, "My kingdom is not of this
world. If it were, my servants would fight to
prevent my arrest by the Jews. But now my
kingdom is from another place."
[37]"You are a king, then!" said Pilate.
Jesus answered, "You are right in saying I
am a king. In fact, for this reason I was born,
and for this I came into the world, to testify to
the truth. Everyone on the side of truth listens to me."
[38]"What is truth?" Pilate asked. With this
he went out again to the Jews and said, "I
find no basis for a charge against him. [39]But
it is your custom for me to release to you one
prisoner at the time of the Passover. Do you
want me to release 'the king of the Jews'?"
[40]They shouted back, "No, not him! Give
us Barabbas!" Now Barabbas had taken part
in a rebellion.

Jesus Sentenced to be Crucified

19 Then Pilate took Jesus and had him
flogged. [2]The soldiers twisted together a crown of thorns and put it on his
head. They clothed him in a purple robe [3]and
went up to him again and again, saying,
"Hail, king of the Jews!" And they struck him
in the face.
[4]Once more Pilate came out and said to
the Jews, "Look, I am bringing him out to you
to let you know that I find no basis for a
charge against him." [5]When Jesus came out
wearing the crown of thorns and the purple
robe, Pilate said to them, "Here is the man!"
[6]As soon as the chief priests and their officials saw him, they shouted, "Crucify! Crucify!"
But Pilate answered, "You take him and
crucify him. As for me, I find no basis for a
charge against him."
[7]The Jews insisted, "We have a law, and
according to that law he must die, because
he claimed to be the Son of God."
[8]When Pilate heard this, he was even
more afraid, [9]and he went back inside the
palace. "Where do you come from?" he
asked Jesus, but Jesus gave him no answer.
[10]"Do you refuse to speak to me?" Pilate
said. "Don't you realize I have power either
to free you or to crucify you?"
[11]Jesus answered, "You would have no
power over me if it were not given to you from
above. Therefore the one who handed me
over to you is guilty of a greater sin."
[12]From then on, Pilate tried to set Jesus
free, but the Jews kept shouting, "If you let
this man go, you are no friend of Caesar.
Anyone who claims to be a king opposes
Caesar."

[a]24 Or *(Now Annas had sent him, still bound, to Caiaphas the high priest.)*

13When Pilate heard this, he brought
Jesus out and sat down on the judge's seat
at a place known as the Stone Pavement
(which in Aramaic is Gabbatha). 14It was the
day of Preparation of Passover Week, about
the sixth hour.

"Here is your king," Pilate said to the
Jews.

15But they shouted, "Take him away! Take
him away! Crucify him!"

"Shall I crucify your king?" Pilate asked.

"We have no king but Caesar," the chief
priests answered.

16Finally Pilate handed him over to them to
be crucified.

The Crucifixion

So the soldiers took charge of Jesus.
17Carrying his own cross, he went out to the
place of the Skull (which in Aramaic is called
Golgotha). 18Here they crucified him, and
with him two others—one on each side and
Jesus in the middle.

19Pilate had a notice prepared and fastened to the cross. It read: JESUS OF NAZARETH,
THE KING OF THE JEWS. 20Many of the Jews read
this sign, for the place where Jesus was
crucified was near the city, and the sign was
written in Aramaic, Latin and Greek. 21The
chief priests of the Jews protested to Pilate,
"Do not write 'The King of the Jews,' but that
this man claimed to be king of the Jews."

22Pilate answered, "What I have written, I
have written."

23When the soldiers crucified Jesus, they
took his clothes, dividing them into four
shares, one for each of them, with the under-
garment remaining. This garment was
seamless, woven in one piece from top to
bottom.

24"Let's not tear it," they said to one another. "Let's decide by lot who will get it."

This happened that the scripture might be
fulfilled which said,

"They divided my garments among them
and cast lots for my clothing."[a]

So this is what the soldiers did.

25Near the cross of Jesus stood his
mother, his mother's sister, Mary the wife of
Clopas, and Mary Magdalene. 26When
Jesus saw his mother there, and the disciple
whom he loved standing nearby, he said to
his mother, "Dear woman, here is your son,"
27and to the disciple, "Here is your mother."
From that time on, this disciple took her into
his home.

The Death of Jesus

28Later, knowing that all was now completed, and so that the Scripture would be
fulfilled, Jesus said, "I am thirsty." 29A jar of
wine vinegar was there, so they soaked a
sponge in it, put the sponge on a stalk of the
hyssop plant, and lifted it to Jesus' lips.
30When he had received the drink, Jesus
said, "It is finished." With that, he bowed his
head and gave up his spirit.

31Now it was the day of Preparation, and
the next day was to be a special Sabbath.
Because the Jews did not want the bodies
left on the crosses during the Sabbath, they
asked Pilate to have the legs broken and the
bodies taken down. 32The soldiers therefore
came and broke the legs of the first man who
had been crucified with Jesus, and then
those of the other. 33But when they came to
Jesus and found that he was already dead,
they did not break his legs. 34Instead, one of
the soldiers pierced Jesus' side with a spear,
bringing a sudden flow of blood and water.
35The man who saw it has given testimony,
and his testimony is true. He knows that he
tells the truth, and he testifies so that you
also may believe. 36These things happened
so that the scripture would be fulfilled: "Not
one of his bones will be broken,"[b] 37and, as
another scripture says, "They will look on the
one they have pierced."[c]

The Burial of Jesus

38Later, Joseph of Arimathea asked Pilate
for the body of Jesus. Now Joseph was a
disciple of Jesus, but secretly because he
feared the Jews. With Pilate's permission, he
came and took the body away. 39He was
accompanied by Nicodemus, the man who
earlier had visited Jesus at night. Nicodemus
brought a mixture of myrrh and aloes, about
seventy-five pounds.[d] 40Taking Jesus' body,
the two of them wrapped it, with the spices, in
strips of linen. This was in accordance with
Jewish burial customs. 41At the place where
Jesus was crucified, there was a garden,
and in the garden a new tomb, in which no
one had ever been laid. 42Because it was the
Jewish day of Preparation and since the
tomb was nearby, they laid Jesus there.

[a]*24* Psalm 22:18 [b]*36* Exodus 12:46; Num. 9:12; Psalm 34:20 [c]*37* Zech. 12:10 [d]*39* Greek *a hundred litrai* (about 34 kilograms)

The Empty Tomb

20 Early on the first day of the week, while it was still dark, Mary Magdalene went to the tomb and saw that the stone had been removed from the entrance. 2So she came running to Simon Peter and the other disciple, the one Jesus loved, and said, "They have taken the Lord out of the tomb, and we don't know where they have put him!"

3So Peter and the other disciple started for the tomb. 4Both were running, but the other disciple outran Peter and reached the tomb first. 5He bent over and looked in at the strips of linen lying there but did not go in. 6Then Simon Peter, who was behind him, arrived and went into the tomb. He saw the strips of linen lying there, 7as well as the burial cloth that had been around Jesus' head. The cloth was folded up by itself, separate from the linen. 8Finally the other disciple, who had reached the tomb first, also went inside. He saw and believed. 9(They still did not understand from Scripture that Jesus had to rise from the dead.)

Jesus Appears to Mary Magdalene

10Then the disciples went back to their homes, 11but Mary stood outside the tomb crying. As she wept, she bent over to look into the tomb 12and saw two angels in white, seated where Jesus' body had been, one at the head and the other at the foot.

13They asked her, "Woman, why are you crying?"

"They have taken my Lord away," she said, "and I don't know where they have put him." 14At this, she turned around and saw Jesus standing there, but she did not realize that it was Jesus.

15"Woman," he said, "why are you crying? Who is it you are looking for?"

Thinking he was the gardener, she said, "Sir, if you have carried him away, tell me where you have put him, and I will get him."

16Jesus said to her, "Mary."

She turned toward him and cried out in Aramaic, "Rabboni!" (which means Teacher).

17Jesus said, "Do not hold on to me, for I have not yet returned to the Father. Go instead to my brothers and tell them, 'I am returning to my Father and your Father, to my God and your God.' "

18Mary Magdalene went to the disciples with the news: "I have seen the Lord!" And she told them that he had said these things to her.

Jesus Appears to His Disciples

19On the evening of that first day of the week, when the disciples were together, with the doors locked for fear of the Jews, Jesus came and stood among them and said, "Peace be with you!" 20After he said this, he showed them his hands and side. The disciples were overjoyed when they saw the Lord.

21Again Jesus said, "Peace be with you! As the Father has sent me, I am sending you." 22And with that he breathed on them and said, "Receive the Holy Spirit. 23If you forgive anyone his sins, they are forgiven; if you do not forgive them, they are not forgiven."

Jesus Appears to Thomas

24Now Thomas (called Didymus), one of the Twelve, was not with the disciples when Jesus came. 25So the other disciples told him, "We have seen the Lord!"

But he said to them, "Unless I see the nail marks in his hands and put my finger where the nails were, and put my hand into his side, I will not believe it."

26A week later his disciples were in the house again, and Thomas was with them. Though the doors were locked, Jesus came and stood among them and said, "Peace be with you!" 27Then he said to Thomas, "Put your finger here; see my hands. Reach out your hand and put it into my side. Stop doubting and believe."

28Thomas said to him, "My Lord and my God!"

29Then Jesus told him, "Because you have seen me, you have believed; blessed are those who have not seen and yet have believed."

30Jesus did many other miraculous signs in the presence of his disciples, which are not recorded in this book. 31But these are written that you may[a] believe that Jesus is the Christ, the Son of God, and that by believing you may have life in his name.

Jesus and the Miraculous Catch of Fish

21 Afterward Jesus appeared again to his disciples, by the Sea of Tiberias.[b]

[a] *31* Some manuscripts *may continue to* [b] *1* That is, Sea of Galilee

It happened this way: 2Simon Peter, Thomas (called Didymus), Nathanael from Cana in Galilee, the sons of Zebedee, and two other disciples were together. 3"I'm going out to fish," Simon Peter told them, and they said, "We'll go with you." So they went out and got into the boat, but that night they caught nothing.

4Early in the morning, Jesus stood on the shore, but the disciples did not realize that it was Jesus.

5He called out to them, "Friends, haven't you any fish?"

"No," they answered.

6He said, "Throw your net on the right side of the boat and you will find some." When they did, they were unable to haul the net in because of the large number of fish.

7Then the disciple whom Jesus loved said to Peter, "It is the Lord!" As soon as Simon Peter heard him say, "It is the Lord," he wrapped his outer garment around him (for he had taken it off) and jumped into the water. 8The other disciples followed in the boat, towing the net full of fish, for they were not far from shore, about a hundred yards.[a] 9When they landed, they saw a fire of burning coals there with fish on it, and some bread.

10Jesus said to them, "Bring some of the fish you have just caught."

11Simon Peter climbed aboard and dragged the net ashore. It was full of large fish, 153, but even with so many the net was not torn. 12Jesus said to them, "Come and have breakfast." None of the disciples dared ask him, "Who are you?" They knew it was the Lord. 13Jesus came, took the bread and gave it to them, and did the same with the fish. 14This was now the third time Jesus appeared to his disciples after he was raised from the dead.

Jesus Reinstates Peter

15When they had finished eating, Jesus said to Simon Peter, "Simon son of John, do you truly love me more than these?"

"Yes, Lord," he said, "you know that I love you."

Jesus said, "Feed my lambs."

16Again Jesus said, "Simon son of John, do you truly love me?"

He answered, "Yes, Lord, you know that I love you."

Jesus said, "Take care of my sheep."

17The third time he said to him, "Simon son of John, do you love me?"

Peter was hurt because Jesus asked him the third time, "Do you love me?" He said, "Lord, you know all things; you know that I love you."

Jesus said, "Feed my sheep. 18I tell you the truth, when you were younger you dressed yourself and went where you wanted; but when you are old you will stretch out your hands, and someone else will dress you and lead you where you do not want to go." 19Jesus said this to indicate the kind of death by which Peter would glorify God. Then he said to him, "Follow me!"

20Peter turned and saw that the disciple whom Jesus loved was following them. (This was the one who had leaned back against Jesus at the supper and had said, "Lord, who is going to betray you?") 21When Peter saw him, he asked, "Lord, what about him?"

22Jesus answered, "If I want him to remain alive until I return, what is that to you? You must follow me." 23Because of this, the rumor spread among the brothers that this disciple would not die. But Jesus did not say that he would not die; he only said, "If I want him to remain alive until I return, what is that to you?"

24This is the disciple who testifies to these things and who wrote them down. We know that his testimony is true.

25Jesus did many other things as well. If every one of them were written down, I suppose that even the whole world would not have room for the books that would be written.

[a]8 Greek *about two hundred cubits* (about 90 meters)

Acts

Introduction:

The Acts of the Apostles is the second part of Luke's history. It was written so we would have the true story of how the Christian church began and grew.

This book especially tells about the work of two of the apostles—Peter and Paul. Peter is the central person involved in beginning the church in Jerusalem and Paul is the important missionary who went out to nearby countries to tell others about Christ. Acts can also be called "The Acts of the Holy Spirit" because it teaches about the coming and work of the Spirit.

The book of Acts teaches three things about the early church: 1) what the message of the early church was; 2) how the Jews rejected this message and how God sent the apostles to the Gentiles, who accepted the Gospel; and 3) how the early church was treated by the local and Roman governments.

Outline of contents:

Jesus Taken Up Into Heaven

1 In my former book, Theophilus, I wrote
about all that Jesus began to do and to
teach 2until the day he was taken up to
heaven, after giving instructions through the
Holy Spirit to the apostles he had chosen.
3After his suffering, he showed himself to
these men and gave many convincing proofs
that he was alive. He appeared to them over
a period of forty days and spoke about the
kingdom of God. 4On one occasion, while he
was eating with them, he gave them this
command: "Do not leave Jerusalem, but wait
for the gift my Father promised, which you
have heard me speak about. 5For John baptized with[a] water, but in a few days you will
be baptized with the Holy Spirit."
6So when they met together, they asked
him, "Lord, are you at this time going to restore the kingdom to Israel?"
7He said to them: "It is not for you to know
the times or dates the Father has set by his
own authority. 8But you will receive power
when the Holy Spirit comes on you; and you
will be my witnesses in Jerusalem, and in all
Judea and Samaria, and to the ends of the
earth."
9After he said this, he was taken up before
their very eyes, and a cloud hid him from
their sight.
10They were looking intently up into the sky
as he was going, when suddenly two men
dressed in white stood beside them. 11"Men
of Galilee," they said, "why do you stand
here looking into the sky? This same Jesus,
who has been taken from you into heaven,
will come back in the same way you have
seen him go into heaven."

Matthias Chosen to Replace Judas

12Then they returned to Jerusalem from
the hill called the Mount of Olives, a Sabbath
day's walk[b] from the city. 13When they arrived, they went upstairs to the room where

[a]5 Or *in*   [b]12 That is, about 3/4 mile (about 1,100 meters)

they were staying. Those present were Peter, John, James and Andrew; Philip and
Thomas, Bartholomew and Matthew; James
son of Alphaeus and Simon the Zealot, and
Judas son of James. 14They all joined together constantly in prayer, along with the
women and Mary the mother of Jesus, and
with his brothers.

15In those days Peter stood up among the
believers[a] (a group numbering about a hundred and twenty) 16and said, "Brothers, the
Scripture had to be fulfilled which the Holy
Spirit spoke long ago through the mouth of
David concerning Judas, who served as
guide for those who arrested Jesus— 17he
was one of our number and shared in this
ministry."

18(With the reward he got for his wickedness, Judas bought a field; there he fell
headlong, his body burst open and all his
intestines spilled out. 19Everyone in Jerusalem heard about this, so they called that field
in their language Akeldama, that is, Field of
Blood.)

20"For," said Peter, "it is written in the book
of Psalms,

" 'May his place be deserted;
let there be no one to dwell in it,'[b]

and,

" 'May another take his place of
leadership.'[c]

21Therefore it is necessary to choose one of
the men who have been with us the whole
time the Lord Jesus went in and out among
us, 22beginning from John's baptism to the
time when Jesus was taken up from us. For
one of these must become a witness with us
of his resurrection."

23So they proposed two men: Joseph
called Barsabbas (also known as Justus)
and Matthias. 24Then they prayed, "Lord,
you know everyone's heart. Show us which
of these two you have chosen 25to take over
this apostolic ministry, which Judas left to go
where he belongs." 26Then they cast lots,
and the lot fell to Matthias; so he was added
to the eleven apostles.

The Holy Spirit Comes at Pentecost

2 When the day of Pentecost came, they
were all together in one place. 2Sudden-
ly a sound like the blowing of a violent wind
came from heaven and filled the whole
house where they were sitting. 3They saw
what seemed to be tongues of fire that separated and came to rest on each of them. 4All
of them were filled with the Holy Spirit and
began to speak in other tongues[d] as the
Spirit enabled them.

5Now there were staying in Jerusalem
God-fearing Jews from every nation under
heaven. 6When they heard this sound, a
crowd came together in bewilderment, because each one heard them speaking in his
own language. 7Utterly amazed, they asked:
"Are not all these men who are speaking
Galileans? 8Then how is it that each of us
hears them in his own native language?
9Parthians, Medes and Elamites; residents
of Mesopotamia, Judea and Cappadocia,
Pontus and Asia, 10Phrygia and Pamphylia,
Egypt and the parts of Libya near Cyrene;
visitors from Rome 11(both Jews and converts to Judaism); Cretans and Arabs—we
hear them declaring the wonders of God in
our own tongues!" 12Amazed and perplexed,
they asked one another, "What does this
mean?"

13Some, however, made fun of them and
said, "They have had too much wine.[e]"

Peter Addresses the Crowd

14Then Peter stood up with the Eleven,
raised his voice and addressed the crowd:
"Fellow Jews and all of you who live in
Jerusalem, let me explain this to you; listen
carefully to what I say. 15These men are not
drunk, as you suppose. It's only nine in the
morning! 16No, this is what was spoken by
the prophet Joel:

17" 'In the last days, God says,
I will pour out my Spirit on all people.
Your sons and daughters will prophesy,
your young men will see visions,
your old men will dream dreams.
18Even on my servants, both men and
women,
I will pour out my Spirit in those days,
and they will prophesy.
19I will show wonders in the heaven above
and signs on the earth below,
blood and fire and billows of smoke.
20The sun will be turned to darkness
and the moon to blood

[a]*15* Greek *brothers* [b]*20* Psalm 69:25 [c]*20* Psalm 109:8 [d]*4* Or *languages*; also in verse 11
[e]*13* Or *sweet wine*

before the coming of the great and
glorious day of the Lord.
21 And everyone who calls
on the name of the Lord will be saved.'[a]

22"Men of Israel, listen to this: Jesus of
Nazareth was a man accredited by God to
you by miracles, wonders and signs, which
God did among you through him, as you
yourselves know. 23This man was handed
over to you by God's set purpose and foreknowledge; and you, with the help of wicked
men,[b] put him to death by nailing him to the
cross. 24But God raised him from the dead,
freeing him from the agony of death, because it was impossible for death to keep its
hold on him. 25David said about him:

" 'I saw the Lord always before me.
Because he is at my right hand,
I will not be shaken.
26Therefore my heart is glad and my
tongue rejoices;
my body also will live in hope,
27because you will not abandon me to the
grave,
nor will you let your Holy One see
decay.
28You have made known to me the paths of
life;
you will fill me with joy in your
presence.'[c]

29"Brothers, I can tell you confidently that
the patriarch David died and was buried, and
his tomb is here to this day. 30But he was a
prophet and knew that God had promised
him on oath that he would place one of his
descendants on his throne. 31Seeing what
was ahead, he spoke of the resurrection of
the Christ,[d] that he was not abandoned to
the grave, nor did his body see decay. 32God
has raised this Jesus to life, and we are all
witnesses of the fact. 33Exalted to the right
hand of God, he has received from the Father the promised Holy Spirit and has poured
out what you now see and hear. 34For David
did not ascend to heaven, and yet he said,

" 'The Lord said to my Lord:
"Sit at my right hand
35until I make your enemies
a footstool for your feet." '[e]

36"Therefore let all Israel be assured of
this: God has made this Jesus, whom you
crucified, both Lord and Christ."

37When the people heard this, they were
cut to the heart and said to Peter and the
other apostles, "Brothers, what shall we
do?"

38Peter replied, "Repent and be baptized,
every one of you, in the name of Jesus Christ
for the forgiveness of your sins. And you will
receive the gift of the Holy Spirit. 39The promise is for you and your children and for all
who are far off—for all whom the Lord our
God will call."

40With many other words he warned them;
and he pleaded with them, "Save yourselves
from this corrupt generation." 41Those who
accepted his message were baptized, and
about three thousand were added to their
number that day.

The Fellowship of the Believers

42They devoted themselves to the apostles' teaching and to the fellowship, to the
breaking of bread and to prayer. 43Everyone
was filled with awe, and many wonders and
miraculous signs were done by the apostles.
44All the believers were together and had
everything in common. 45Selling their
possessions and goods, they gave to anyone as he had need. 46Every day they continued to meet together in the temple courts.
They broke bread in their homes and ate
together with glad and sincere hearts,
47praising God and enjoying the favor of all
the people. And the Lord added to their number daily those who were being saved.

Peter Heals the Crippled Beggar

3 One day Peter and John were going up
to the temple at the time of prayer—at
three in the afternoon. 2Now a man crippled
from birth was being carried to the temple
gate called Beautiful, where he was put
every day to beg from those going into the
temple courts. 3When he saw Peter and
John about to enter, he asked them for
money. 4Peter looked straight at him, as did
John. Then Peter said, "Look at us!" 5So the
man gave them his attention, expecting to
get something from them.

6Then Peter said, "Silver or gold I do not
have, but what I have I give you. In the name

[a]21 Joel 2:28-32 [b]23 Or *of those not having the law* (that is, Gentiles) [c]28 Psalm 16:8-11 [d]31 Or *Messiah.* "The Christ" (Greek) and "the Messiah" (Hebrew) both mean "the Anointed One"; also in verse 36. [e]35 Psalm 110:1

of Jesus Christ of Nazareth, walk." 7Taking him by the right hand, he helped him up, and instantly the man's feet and ankles became strong. 8He jumped to his feet and began to walk. Then he went with them into the temple courts, walking and jumping, and praising God. 9When all the people saw him walking and praising God, 10they recognized him as the same man who used to sit begging at the temple gate called Beautiful, and they were filled with wonder and amazement at what had happened to him.

Peter Speaks to the Onlookers

11While the beggar held on to Peter and John, all the people were astonished and came running to them in the place called Solomon's Colonnade. 12When Peter saw this, he said to them: "Men of Israel, why does this surprise you? Why do you stare at us as if by our own power or godliness we had made this man walk? 13The God of Abraham, Isaac and Jacob, the God of our fathers, has glorified his servant Jesus. You handed him over to be killed, and you disowned him before Pilate, though he had decided to let him go. 14You disowned the Holy and Righteous One and asked that a murderer be released to you. 15You killed the author of life, but God raised him from the dead. We are witnesses of this. 16By faith in the name of Jesus, this man whom you see and know was made strong. It is Jesus' name and the faith that comes through him that has given this complete healing to him, as you can all see.

17"Now, brothers, I know that you acted in ignorance, as did your leaders. 18But this is how God fulfilled what he had foretold through all the prophets, saying that his Christ[a] would suffer. 19Repent, then, and turn to God, so that your sins may be wiped out, that times of refreshing may come from the Lord, 20and that he may send the Christ, who has been appointed for you—even Jesus. 21He must remain in heaven until the time comes for God to restore everything, as he promised long ago through his holy prophets. 22For Moses said, 'The Lord your God will raise up for you a prophet like me from among your own people; you must listen to everything he tells you. 23Anyone who does not listen to him will be completely cut off from among his people.'[b]

24"Indeed, all the prophets from Samuel on, as many as have spoken, have foretold these days. 25And you are heirs of the prophets and of the covenant God made with your fathers. He said to Abraham, 'Through your offspring all peoples on earth will be blessed.'[c] 26When God raised up his servant, he sent him first to you to bless you by turning each of you from your wicked ways."

Peter and John Before the Sanhedrin

4 The priests and the captain of the temple guard and the Sadducees came up to Peter and John while they were speaking to the people. 2They were greatly disturbed because the apostles were teaching the people and proclaiming in Jesus the resurrection of the dead. 3They seized Peter and John, and because it was evening, they put them in jail until the next day. 4But many who heard the message believed, and the number of men grew to about five thousand.

5The next day the rulers, elders and teachers of the law met in Jerusalem. 6Annas the high priest was there, and so were Caiaphas, John, Alexander and the other men of the high priest's family. 7They had Peter and John brought before them and began to question them: "By what power or what name did you do this?"

8Then Peter, filled with the Holy Spirit, said to them: "Rulers and elders of the people! 9If we are being called to account today for an act of kindness shown to a cripple and are asked how he was healed, 10then know this, you and all the people of Israel: It is by the name of Jesus Christ of Nazareth, whom you crucified but whom God raised from the dead, that this man stands before you healed. 11He is

" 'the stone you builders rejected,
which has become the capstone.[d][e]

12Salvation is found in no one else, for there is no other name under heaven given to men by which we must be saved."

13When they saw the courage of Peter and John and realized that they were unschooled, ordinary men, they were astonished and they took note that these men had been with Jesus. 14But since they could see the man who had been healed standing there with them, there was nothing they could say. 15So they ordered them to with-

[a]*18* Or *Messiah*; also in verse 20 [b]*23* Deut. 18:15,18,19 [c]*25* Gen. 22:18; 26:4 [d]*11* Or *cornerstone*
[e]*11* Psalm 118:22

draw from the Sanhedrin and then conferred
together. 16“What are we going to do with
these men?” they asked. “Everybody living
in Jerusalem knows they have done an outstanding miracle, and we cannot deny it.
17But to stop this thing from spreading any
further among the people, we must warn
these men to speak no longer to anyone in
this name.”
18Then they called them in again and commanded them not to speak or teach at all in
the name of Jesus. 19But Peter and John
replied, “Judge for yourselves whether it is
right in God’s sight to obey you rather than
God. 20For we cannot help speaking about
what we have seen and heard.”
21After further threats they let them go.
They could not decide how to punish them,
because all the people were praising God for
what had happened. 22For the man who was
miraculously healed was over forty years
old.

The Believers’ Prayer

23On their release, Peter and John went
back to their own people and reported all that
the chief priests and elders had said to them.
24When they heard this, they raised their
voices together in prayer to God. “Sovereign
Lord,” they said, “you made the heaven and
the earth and the sea, and everything in
them. 25You spoke by the Holy Spirit through
the mouth of your servant, our father David:

“ ‘Why do the nations rage
and the peoples plot in vain?
26The kings of the earth take their stand
and the rulers gather together
against the Lord
and against his Anointed One.[a][b]

27Indeed Herod and Pontius Pilate met together with the Gentiles and the people[c] of
Israel in this city to conspire against your
holy servant Jesus, whom you anointed.
28They did what your power and will had decided beforehand should happen. 29Now,
Lord, consider their threats and enable your
servants to speak your word with great boldness. 30Stretch out your hand to heal and
perform miraculous signs and wonders
through the name of your holy servant
Jesus.”
31After they prayed, the place where they
were meeting was shaken. And they were all
filled with the Holy Spirit and spoke the word
of God boldly.

The Believers Share Their Possessions

32All the believers were one in heart and
mind. No one claimed that any of his possessions was his own, but they shared everything they had. 33With great power the apostles continued to testify to the resurrection of
the Lord Jesus, and much grace was upon
them all. 34There were no needy persons
among them. For from time to time those
who owned lands or houses sold them,
brought the money from the sales 35and put it
at the apostles’ feet, and it was distributed to
anyone as he had need.
36Joseph, a Levite from Cyprus, whom the
apostles called Barnabas (which means Son
of Encouragement), 37sold a field he owned
and brought the money and put it at the
apostles’ feet.

Ananias and Sapphira

5 Now a man named Ananias, together
with his wife Sapphira, also sold a piece
of property. 2With his wife’s full knowledge
he kept back part of the money for himself,
but brought the rest and put it at the apostles’
feet.
3Then Peter said, “Ananias, how is it that
Satan has so filled your heart that you have
lied to the Holy Spirit and have kept for yourself some of the money you received for the
land? 4Didn’t it belong to you before it was
sold? And after it was sold, wasn’t the money
at your disposal? What made you think of
doing such a thing? You have not lied to men
but to God.”
5When Ananias heard this, he fell down
and died. And great fear seized all who
heard what had happened. 6Then the young
men came forward, wrapped up his body,
and carried him out and buried him.
7About three hours later his wife came in,
not knowing what had happened. 8Peter
asked her, “Tell me, is this the price you and
Ananias got for the land?”
“Yes,” she said, “that is the price.”
9Peter said to her, “How could you agree
to test the Spirit of the Lord? Look! The feet
of the men who buried your husband are

[a]26 That is, Christ or Messiah [b]26 Psalm 2:1,2 [c]27 The Greek is plural.

at the door, and they will carry you out also."
10 At that moment she fell down at his feet
and died. Then the young men came in and,
finding her dead, carried her out and buried
her beside her husband. 11 Great fear seized
the whole church and all who heard about
these events.

The Apostles Heal Many

12 The apostles performed many miraculous signs and wonders among the people.
And all the believers used to meet together in
Solomon's Colonnade. 13 No one else dared
join them, even though they were highly regarded by the people. 14 Nevertheless, more
and more men and women believed in the
Lord and were added to their number. 15 As a
result, people brought the sick into the
streets and laid them on beds and mats so
that at least Peter's shadow might fall on
some of them as he passed by. 16 Crowds
gathered also from the towns around Jerusalem, bringing their sick and those tormented
by evil[a] spirits, and all of them were healed.

The Apostles Persecuted

17 Then the high priest and all his associates, who were members of the party of the
Sadducees, were filled with jealousy. 18 They
arrested the apostles and put them in the
public jail. 19 But during the night an angel of
the Lord opened the doors of the jail and
brought them out. 20 "Go, stand in the temple
courts," he said, "and tell the people the full
message of this new life."
21 At daybreak they entered the temple
courts, as they had been told, and began to
teach the people.

When the high priest and his associates
arrived, they called together the Sanhedrin—the full assembly of the elders of Israel—and sent to the jail for the apostles. 22 But
on arriving at the jail, the officers did not find
them there. So they went back and reported,
23 "We found the jail securely locked, with the
guards standing at the doors; but when we
opened them, we found no one inside." 24 On
hearing this report, the captain of the temple
guard and the chief priests were puzzled,
wondering what would come of this.
25 Then someone came and said, "Look!
The men you put in jail are standing in the
temple courts teaching the people." 26 At
that, the captain went with his officers and
brought the apostles. They did not use force,
because they feared that the people would
stone them.
27 Having brought the apostles, they made
them appear before the Sanhedrin to be
questioned by the high priest. 28 "We gave
you strict orders not to teach in this name,"
he said. "Yet you have filled Jerusalem with
your teaching and are determined to make
us guilty of this man's blood."
29 Peter and the other apostles replied:
"We must obey God rather than men! 30 The
God of our fathers raised Jesus from the
dead—whom you had killed by hanging him
on a tree. 31 God exalted him to his own right
hand as Prince and Savior that he might give
repentance and forgiveness of sins to Israel.
32 We are witnesses of these things, and so is
the Holy Spirit, whom God has given to those
who obey him."
33 When they heard this, they were furious
and wanted to put them to death. 34 But a
Pharisee named Gamaliel, a teacher of the
law, who was honored by all the people,
stood up in the Sanhedrin and ordered that
the men be put outside for a little while.
35 Then he addressed them: "Men of Israel,
consider carefully what you intend to do to
these men. 36 Some time ago Theudas appeared, claiming to be somebody, and about
four hundred men rallied to him. He was
killed, all his followers were dispersed, and it
all came to nothing. 37 After him, Judas the
Galilean appeared in the days of the census
and led a band of people in revolt. He too
was killed, and all his followers were scattered. 38 Therefore, in the present case I advise you: Leave these men alone! Let them
go! For if their purpose or activity is of human
origin, it will fail. 39 But if it is from God, you will
not be able to stop these men; you will only
find yourselves fighting against God."
40 His speech persuaded them. They called
the apostles in and had them flogged. Then
they ordered them not to speak in the name
of Jesus, and let them go.
41 The apostles left the Sanhedrin, rejoicing
because they had been counted worthy of
suffering disgrace for the Name. 42 Day after
day, in the temple courts and from house to
house, they never stopped teaching and proclaiming the good news that Jesus is the
Christ.[b]

[a] 16 Greek *unclean* [b] 42 Or *Messiah*

The Choosing of the Seven

6 In those days when the number of disciples was increasing, the Grecian Jews
among them complained against the Hebra-
ic Jews because their widows were being
overlooked in the daily distribution of food.
2So the Twelve gathered all the disciples together and said, "It would not be right for us
to neglect the ministry of the word of God in
order to wait on tables. 3Brothers, choose
seven men from among you who are known
to be full of the Spirit and wisdom. We will
turn this responsibility over to them 4and will
give our attention to prayer and the ministry
of the word."
5This proposal pleased the whole group.
They chose Stephen, a man full of faith and
of the Holy Spirit; also Philip, Procorus, Nica-
nor, Timon, Parmenas, and Nicolas from Antioch, a convert to Judaism. 6They presented
these men to the apostles, who prayed and
laid their hands on them.
7So the word of God spread. The number
of disciples in Jerusalem increased rapidly,
and a large number of priests became obedient to the faith.

Stephen Seized

8Now Stephen, a man full of God's grace
and power, did great wonders and miraculous signs among the people. 9Opposition
arose, however, from members of the Synagogue of the Freedmen (as it was
called)—Jews of Cyrene and Alexandria as
well as the provinces of Cilicia and Asia.
These men began to argue with Stephen,
10but they could not stand up against his
wisdom or the Spirit by whom he spoke.
11Then they secretly persuaded some men
to say, "We have heard Stephen speak
words of blasphemy against Moses and
against God."
12So they stirred up the people and the
elders and the teachers of the law. They
seized Stephen and brought him before the
Sanhedrin. 13They produced false witnesses, who testified, "This fellow never
stops speaking against this holy place and
against the law. 14For we have heard him say
that this Jesus of Nazareth will destroy this
place and change the customs Moses handed down to us."
15All who were sitting in the Sanhedrin
looked intently at Stephen, and they saw that
his face was like the face of an angel.

Stephen's Speech to the Sanhedrin

7 Then the high priest asked him, "Are
these charges true?"
2To this he replied: "Brothers and fathers,
listen to me! The God of glory appeared to
our father Abraham while he was still in
Mesopotamia, before he lived in Haran.
3'Leave your country and your people,' God
said, 'and go to the land I will show you.'[a]
4"So he left the land of the Chaldeans and
settled in Haran. After the death of his father,
God sent him to this land where you are now
living. 5He gave him no inheritance here, not
even a foot of ground. But God promised him
that he and his descendants after him would
possess the land, even though at that time
Abraham had no child. 6God spoke to him in
this way: 'Your descendants will be
strangers in a country not their own, and they
will be enslaved and mistreated four hundred
years. 7But I will punish the nation they serve
as slaves,' God said, 'and afterward they will
come out of that country and worship me in
this place.'[b] 8Then he gave Abraham the
covenant of circumcision. And Abraham
became the father of Isaac and circumcised
him eight days after his birth. Later Isaac
became the father of Jacob, and Jacob
became the father of the twelve patriarchs.
9"Because the patriarchs were jealous of
Joseph, they sold him as a slave into Egypt.
But God was with him 10and rescued him
from all his troubles. He gave Joseph wisdom and enabled him to gain the goodwill of
Pharaoh king of Egypt; so he made him ruler
over Egypt and all his palace.
11"Then a famine struck all Egypt and Canaan, bringing great suffering, and our fathers could not find food. 12When Jacob
heard that there was grain in Egypt, he sent
our fathers on their first visit. 13On their second visit, Joseph told his brothers who he
was, and Pharaoh learned about Joseph's
family. 14After this, Joseph sent for his father
Jacob and his whole family, seventy-five in
all. 15Then Jacob went down to Egypt, where
he and our fathers died. 16Their bodies were
brought back to Shechem and placed in the
tomb that Abraham had bought from the
sons of Hamor at Shechem for a certain sum
of money.
17"As the time drew near for God to fulfill
his promise to Abraham, the number of our
people in Egypt greatly increased. 18Then
another king, who knew nothing about Jo-

[a]3 Gen. 12:1 [b]7 Gen. 15:13,14

seph, became ruler of Egypt. 19He dealt treacherously with our people and oppressed our forefathers by forcing them to throw out their newborn babies so that they would die.

20"At that time Moses was born, and he was no ordinary child.[a] For three months he was cared for in his father's house. 21When he was placed outside, Pharaoh's daughter took him and brought him up as her own son. 22Moses was educated in all the wisdom of the Egyptians and was powerful in speech and action.

23"When Moses was forty years old, he decided to visit his fellow Israelites. 24He saw one of them being mistreated by an Egyptian, so he went to his defense and avenged him by killing the Egyptian. 25Moses thought that his own people would realize that God was using him to rescue them, but they did not. 26The next day Moses came upon two Israelites who were fighting. He tried to reconcile them by saying, 'Men, you are brothers; why do you want to hurt each other?'

27"But the man who was mistreating the other pushed Moses aside and said, 'Who made you ruler and judge over us? 28Do you want to kill me as you killed the Egyptian yesterday?'[b] 29When Moses heard this, he fled to Midian, where he settled as a foreigner and had two sons.

30"After forty years had passed, an angel appeared to Moses in the flames of a burning bush in the desert near Mount Sinai. 31When he saw this, he was amazed at the sight. As he went over to look more closely, he heard the Lord's voice: 32'I am the God of your fathers, the God of Abraham, Isaac and Jacob.'[c] Moses trembled with fear and did not dare to look.

33"Then the Lord said to him, 'Take off your sandals; the place where you are standing is holy ground. 34I have indeed seen the oppression of my people in Egypt. I have heard their groaning and have come down to set them free. Now come, I will send you back to Egypt.'[d]

35"This is the same Moses whom they had rejected with the words, 'Who made you ruler and judge?' He was sent to be their ruler and deliverer by God himself, through the angel who appeared to him in the bush. 36He led them out of Egypt and did wonders and miraculous signs in Egypt, at the Red Sea[e] and for forty years in the desert.

37"This is that Moses who told the Israelites, 'God will send you a prophet like me from your own people.'[f] 38He was in the assembly in the desert, with the angel who spoke to him on Mount Sinai, and with our fathers; and he received living words to pass on to us.

39"But our fathers refused to obey him. Instead, they rejected him and in their hearts turned back to Egypt. 40They told Aaron, 'Make us gods who will go before us. As for this fellow Moses who led us out of Egypt—we don't know what has happened to him!'[g] 41That was the time they made an idol in the form of a calf. They brought sacrifices to it and held a celebration in honor of what their hands had made. 42But God turned away and gave them over to the worship of the heavenly bodies. This agrees with what is written in the book of the prophets:

" 'Did you bring me sacrifices and
    offerings
  forty years in the desert, O house of
    Israel?
43You have lifted up the shrine of Molech
  and the star of your god Rephan,
  the idols you made to worship.
Therefore I will send you into exile'[h]
    beyond Babylon.

44"Our forefathers had the tabernacle of the Testimony with them in the desert. It had been made as God directed Moses, according to the pattern he had seen. 45Having received the tabernacle, our fathers under Joshua brought it with them when they took the land from the nations God drove out before them. It remained in the land until the time of David, 46who enjoyed God's favor and asked that he might provide a dwelling place for the God of Jacob.[i] 47But it was Solomon who built the house for him.

48"However, the Most High does not live in houses made by men. As the prophet says:

49" 'Heaven is my throne,
  and the earth is my footstool.
What kind of house will you build for me?
    says the Lord.
  Or where will my resting place be?

[a]20 Or *was fair in the sight of God* [b]28 Exodus 2:14 [c]32 Exodus 3:6 [d]34 Exodus 3:5,7,8,10 [e]36 That is, Sea of Reeds [f]37 Deut. 18:15 [g]40 Exodus 32:1 [h]43 Amos 5:25-27 [i]46 Some early manuscripts *the house of Jacob*

50 Has not my hand made all these
things?'[a]

51 "You stiff-necked people, with uncircumcised hearts and ears! You are just like your
fathers: You always resist the Holy Spirit!
52 Was there ever a prophet your fathers did
not persecute? They even killed those who
predicted the coming of the Righteous One.
And now you have betrayed and murdered
him— 53 you who have received the law that
was put into effect through angels but have
not obeyed it."

The Stoning of Stephen

54 When they heard this, they were furious
and gnashed their teeth at him. 55 But Stephen, full of the Holy Spirit, looked up to
heaven and saw the glory of God, and Jesus
standing at the right hand of God. 56 "Look,"
he said, "I see heaven open and the Son of
Man standing at the right hand of God."
57 At this they covered their ears and, yell-
ing at the top of their voices, they all rushed
at him, 58 dragged him out of the city and
began to stone him. Meanwhile, the witnesses laid their clothes at the feet of a
young man named Saul.
59 While they were stoning him, Stephen
prayed, "Lord Jesus, receive my spirit."
60 Then he fell on his knees and cried out,
"Lord, do not hold this sin against them."
When he had said this, he fell asleep.

8 And Saul was there, giving approval to
his death.

The Church Persecuted and Scattered

On that day a great persecution broke out
against the church at Jerusalem, and all except the apostles were scattered throughout
Judea and Samaria. 2 Godly men buried Stephen and mourned deeply for him. 3 But Saul
began to destroy the church. Going from
house to house, he dragged off men and
women and put them in prison.

Philip in Samaria

4 Those who had been scattered preached
the word wherever they went. 5 Philip went
down to a city in Samaria and proclaimed the
Christ[b] there. 6 When the crowds heard Philip
and saw the miraculous signs he did, they all
paid close attention to what he said. 7 With
shrieks, evil[c] spirits came out of many, and
many paralytics and cripples were healed.
8 So there was great joy in that city.

Simon the Sorcerer

9 Now for some time a man named Simon
had practiced sorcery in the city and amazed
all the people of Samaria. He boasted that he
was someone great, 10 and all the people,
both high and low, gave him their attention
and exclaimed, "This man is the divine
power known as the Great Power." 11 They
followed him because he had amazed them
for a long time with his magic. 12 But when
they believed Philip as he preached the good
news of the kingdom of God and the name of
Jesus Christ, they were baptized, both men
and women. 13 Simon himself believed and
was baptized. And he followed Philip everywhere, astonished by the great signs and
miracles he saw.
14 When the apostles in Jerusalem heard
that Samaria had accepted the word of God,
they sent Peter and John to them. 15 When
they arrived, they prayed for them that they
might receive the Holy Spirit, 16 because the
Holy Spirit had not yet come upon any of
them; they had simply been baptized into[d]
the name of the Lord Jesus. 17 Then Peter
and John placed their hands on them, and
they received the Holy Spirit.
18 When Simon saw that the Spirit was giv-
en at the laying on of the apostles' hands, he
offered them money 19 and said, "Give me
also this ability so that everyone on whom I
lay my hands may receive the Holy Spirit."
20 Peter answered: "May your money perish with you, because you thought you could
buy the gift of God with money! 21 You have
no part or share in this ministry, because
your heart is not right before God. 22 Repent
of this wickedness and pray to the Lord. Perhaps he will forgive you for having such a
thought in your heart. 23 For I see that you are
full of bitterness and captive to sin."
24 Then Simon answered, "Pray to the Lord
for me so that nothing you have said may
happen to me."
25 When they had testified and proclaimed
the word of the Lord, Peter and John returned to Jerusalem, preaching the gospel in
many Samaritan villages.

Philip and the Ethiopian

26 Now an angel of the Lord said to Philip,
"Go south to the road—the desert road—
that goes down from Jerusalem to Gaza."
27 So he started out, and on his way he met

[a] *50* Isaiah 66:1,2 [b] *5* Or *Messiah* [c] *7* Greek *unclean* [d] *16* Or *in*

an Ethiopian[a] eunuch, an important official in charge of all the treasury of Candace, queen of the Ethiopians. This man had gone to Jerusalem to worship, 28and on his way home was sitting in his chariot reading the book of Isaiah the prophet. 29The Spirit told Philip, "Go to that chariot and stay near it."

30Then Philip ran up to the chariot and heard the man reading Isaiah the prophet. "Do you understand what you are reading?" Philip asked.

31"How can I," he said, "unless someone explains it to me?" So he invited Philip to come up and sit with him.

32The eunuch was reading this passage of Scripture:

"He was led like a sheep to the slaughter,
 and as a lamb before the shearer is
  silent,
 so he did not open his mouth.
33In his humiliation he was deprived of
  justice.
 Who can speak of his descendants?
 For his life was taken from the earth."[b]

34The eunuch asked Philip, "Tell me, please, who is the prophet talking about, himself or someone else?" 35Then Philip began with that very passage of Scripture and told him the good news about Jesus.

36As they traveled along the road, they came to some water and the eunuch said, "Look, here is water. Why shouldn't I be baptized?"[c] 38And he gave orders to stop the chariot. Then both Philip and the eunuch went down into the water and Philip baptized him. 39When they came up out of the water, the Spirit of the Lord suddenly took Philip away, and the eunuch did not see him again, but went on his way rejoicing. 40Philip, however, appeared at Azotus and traveled about, preaching the gospel in all the towns until he reached Caesarea.

Saul's Conversion

9 Meanwhile, Saul was still breathing out murderous threats against the Lord's disciples. He went to the high priest 2and asked him for letters to the synagogues in Damascus, so that if he found any there who belonged to the Way, whether men or women, he might take them as prisoners to Jerusalem. 3As he neared Damascus on his journey, suddenly a light from heaven flashed around him. 4He fell to the ground and heard a voice say to him, "Saul, Saul, why do you persecute me?"

5"Who are you, Lord?" Saul asked.

"I am Jesus, whom you are persecuting," he replied. 6"Now get up and go into the city, and you will be told what you must do."

7The men traveling with Saul stood there speechless; they heard the sound but did not see anyone. 8Saul got up from the ground, but when he opened his eyes he could see nothing. So they led him by the hand into Damascus. 9For three days he was blind, and did not eat or drink anything.

10In Damascus there was a disciple named Ananias. The Lord called to him in a vision, "Ananias!"

"Yes, Lord," he answered.

11The Lord told him, "Go to the house of Judas on Straight Street and ask for a man from Tarsus named Saul, for he is praying. 12In a vision he has seen a man named Ananias come and place his hands on him to restore his sight."

13"Lord," Ananias answered, "I have heard many reports about this man and all the harm he has done to your saints in Jerusalem. 14And he has come here with authority from the chief priests to arrest all who call on your name."

15But the Lord said to Ananias, "Go! This man is my chosen instrument to carry my name before the Gentiles and their kings and before the people of Israel. 16I will show him how much he must suffer for my name."

17Then Ananias went to the house and entered it. Placing his hands on Saul, he said, "Brother Saul, the Lord—Jesus, who appeared to you on the road as you were coming here—has sent me so that you may see again and be filled with the Holy Spirit." 18Immediately, something like scales fell from Saul's eyes, and he could see again. He got up and was baptized, 19and after taking some food, he regained his strength.

Saul in Damascus and Jerusalem

Saul spent several days with the disciples in Damascus. 20At once he began to preach in the synagogues that Jesus is the Son of God. 21All those who heard him were astonished and asked, "Isn't he the man who raised havoc in Jerusalem among those who call on this name? And hasn't he come here

[a] *27* That is, from the upper Nile region [b] *33* Isaiah 53:7,8 [c] *36* Some late manuscripts *baptized?" 37Philip said, "If you believe with all your heart, you may." The eunuch answered, "I believe that Jesus Christ is the Son of God."*

to take them as prisoners to the chief priests?" 22Yet Saul grew more and more powerful and baffled the Jews living in Damascus by proving that Jesus is the Christ.[a]

23After many days had gone by, the Jews conspired to kill him, 24but Saul learned of their plan. Day and night they kept close watch on the city gates in order to kill him. 25But his followers took him by night and lowered him in a basket through an opening in the wall.

26When he came to Jerusalem, he tried to join the disciples, but they were all afraid of him, not believing that he really was a disciple. 27But Barnabas took him and brought him to the apostles. He told them how Saul on his journey had seen the Lord and that the Lord had spoken to him, and how in Damascus he had preached fearlessly in the name of Jesus. 28So Saul stayed with them and moved about freely in Jerusalem, speaking boldly in the name of the Lord. 29He talked and debated with the Grecian Jews, but they tried to kill him. 30When the brothers learned of this, they took him down to Caesarea and sent him off to Tarsus.

31Then the church throughout Judea, Galilee and Samaria enjoyed a time of peace. It was strengthened; and encouraged by the Holy Spirit, it grew in numbers, living in the fear of the Lord.

Aeneas and Dorcas

32As Peter traveled about the country, he went to visit the saints in Lydda. 33There he found a man named Aeneas, a paralytic who had been bedridden for eight years. 34"Aeneas," Peter said to him, "Jesus Christ heals you. Get up and take care of your mat." Immediately Aeneas got up. 35All those who lived in Lydda and Sharon saw him and turned to the Lord.

36In Joppa there was a disciple named Tabitha (which, when translated, is Dorcas[b]), who was always doing good and helping the poor. 37About that time she became sick and died, and her body was washed and placed in an upstairs room. 38Lydda was near Joppa; so when the disciples heard that Peter was in Lydda, they sent two men to him and urged him, "Please come at once!"

39Peter went with them, and when he arrived he was taken upstairs to the room. All the widows stood around him, crying and showing him the robes and other clothing that Dorcas had made while she was still with them.

40Peter sent them all out of the room; then he got down on his knees and prayed. Turning toward the dead woman, he said, "Tabitha, get up." She opened her eyes, and seeing Peter she sat up. 41He took her by the hand and helped her to her feet. Then he called the believers and the widows and presented her to them alive. 42This became known all over Joppa, and many people believed in the Lord. 43Peter stayed in Joppa for some time with a tanner named Simon.

Cornelius Calls for Peter

10 At Caesarea there was a man named Cornelius, a centurion in what was known as the Italian Regiment. 2He and all his family were devout and God-fearing; he gave generously to those in need and prayed to God regularly. 3One day at about three in the afternoon he had a vision. He distinctly saw an angel of God, who came to him and said, "Cornelius!"

4Cornelius stared at him in fear. "What is it, Lord?" he asked.

The angel answered, "Your prayers and gifts to the poor have come up as a memorial offering before God. 5Now send men to Joppa to bring back a man named Simon who is called Peter. 6He is staying with Simon the tanner, whose house is by the sea."

7When the angel who spoke to him had gone, Cornelius called two of his servants and a devout soldier who was one of his attendants. 8He told them everything that had happened and sent them to Joppa.

Peter's Vision

9About noon the following day as they were on their journey and approaching the city, Peter went up on the roof to pray. 10He became hungry and wanted something to eat, and while the meal was being prepared, he fell into a trance. 11He saw heaven opened and something like a large sheet being let down to earth by its four corners. 12It contained all kinds of four-footed animals, as well as reptiles of the earth and birds of the air. 13Then a voice told him, "Get up, Peter. Kill and eat."

14"Surely not, Lord!" Peter replied. "I have never eaten anything impure or unclean."

15The voice spoke to him a second time,

[a]22 Or *Messiah* [b]36 Both *Tabitha* (Aramaic) and *Dorcas* (Greek) mean *gazelle*.

"Do not call anything impure that God has
made clean."
16This happened three times, and immediately the sheet was taken back to heaven.
17While Peter was wondering about the
meaning of the vision, the men sent by Cornelius found out where Simon's house was
and stopped at the gate. 18They called out,
asking if Simon who was known as Peter
was staying there.
19While Peter was still thinking about the
vision, the Spirit said to him, "Simon, three[a]
men are looking for you. 20So get up and go
downstairs. Do not hesitate to go with them,
for I have sent them."
21Peter went down and said to the men,
"I'm the one you're looking for. Why have
you come?"
22The men replied, "We have come from
Cornelius the centurion. He is a righteous
and God-fearing man, who is respected by
all the Jewish people. A holy angel told him
to have you come to his house so that he
could hear what you have to say." 23Then
Peter invited the men into the house to be his
guests.

Peter at Cornelius' House

The next day Peter started out with them,
and some of the brothers from Joppa went
along. 24The following day he arrived in
Caesarea. Cornelius was expecting them
and had called together his relatives and
close friends. 25As Peter entered the house,
Cornelius met him and fell at his feet in reverence. 26But Peter made him get up. "Stand
up," he said, "I am only a man myself."
27Talking with him, Peter went inside and
found a large gathering of people. 28He said
to them: "You are well aware that it is against
our law for a Jew to associate with a Gentile
or visit him. But God has shown me that I
should not call any man impure or unclean.
29So when I was sent for, I came without
raising any objection. May I ask why you sent
for me?"
30Cornelius answered: "Four days ago I
was in my house praying at this hour, at three
in the afternoon. Suddenly a man in shining
clothes stood before me 31and said, 'Cornelius, God has heard your prayer and remembered your gifts to the poor. 32Send to Joppa
for Simon who is called Peter. He is a guest
in the home of Simon the tanner, who lives
by the sea.' 33So I sent for you immediately,
and it was good of you to come. Now we are
all here in the presence of God to listen to
everything the Lord has commanded you to
tell us."
34Then Peter began to speak: "I now realize how true it is that God does not show
favoritism 35but accepts men from every nation who fear him and do what is right. 36You
know the message God sent to the people of
Israel, telling the good news of peace
through Jesus Christ, who is Lord of all.
37You know what has happened throughout
Judea, beginning in Galilee after the baptism
that John preached— 38how God anointed
Jesus of Nazareth with the Holy Spirit and
power, and how he went around doing good
and healing all who were under the power of
the devil, because God was with him.
39"We are witnesses of everything he did
in the country of the Jews and in Jerusalem.
They killed him by hanging him on a tree,
40but God raised him from the dead on the
third day and caused him to be seen. 41He
was not seen by all the people, but by witnesses whom God had already chosen—by
us who ate and drank with him after he rose
from the dead. 42He commanded us to
preach to the people and to testify that he is
the one whom God appointed as judge of the
living and the dead. 43All the prophets testify
about him that everyone who believes in him
receives forgiveness of sins through his
name."
44While Peter was still speaking these
words, the Holy Spirit came on all who heard
the message. 45The circumcised believers
who had come with Peter were astonished
that the gift of the Holy Spirit had been
poured out even on the Gentiles. 46For they
heard them speaking in tongues[b] and praising God.
Then Peter said, 47"Can anyone keep
these people from being baptized with
water? They have received the Holy Spirit
just as we have." 48So he ordered that they
be baptized in the name of Jesus Christ.
Then they asked Peter to stay with them for a
few days.

Peter Explains His Actions

11 The apostles and the brothers
throughout Judea heard that the
Gentiles also had received the word of God.
2So when Peter went up to Jerusalem, the
circumcised believers criticized him 3and

[a] *19* One early manuscript *two;* other manuscripts do not have the number. [b] *46* Or *other languages*

said, "You went into the house of uncircumcised men and ate with them."
4Peter began and explained everything to
them precisely as it had happened: 5"I was in
the city of Joppa praying, and in a trance I
saw a vision. I saw something like a large
sheet being let down from heaven by its four
corners, and it came down to where I was. 6I
looked into it and saw four-footed animals of
the earth, wild beasts, reptiles, and birds of
the air. 7Then I heard a voice telling me, 'Get
up, Peter. Kill and eat.'
8"I replied, 'Surely not, Lord! Nothing impure or unclean has ever entered my mouth.'
9"The voice spoke from heaven a second
time, 'Do not call anything impure that God
has made clean.' 10This happened three
times, and then it was all pulled up to heaven
again.
11"Right then three men who had been
sent to me from Caesarea stopped at the
house where I was staying. 12The Spirit told
me to have no hesitation about going with
them. These six brothers also went with me,
and we entered the man's house. 13He told
us how he had seen an angel appear in his
house and say, 'Send to Joppa for Simon
who is called Peter. 14He will bring you a
message through which you and all your
household will be saved.'
15"As I began to speak, the Holy Spirit
came on them as he had come on us at the
beginning. 16Then I remembered what the
Lord had said: 'John baptized with[a] water,
but you will be baptized with the Holy Spirit.'
17So if God gave them the same gift as he
gave us, who believed in the Lord Jesus
Christ, who was I to think that I could oppose
God?"
18When they heard this, they had no further objections and praised God, saying, "So
then, God has granted even the Gentiles
repentance unto life."

The Church in Antioch

19Now those who had been scattered by
the persecution in connection with Stephen
traveled as far as Phoenicia, Cyprus and
Antioch, telling the message only to Jews.
20Some of them, however, men from Cyprus
and Cyrene, went to Antioch and began to
speak to Greeks also, telling them the good
news about the Lord Jesus. 21The Lord's
hand was with them, and a great number of
people believed and turned to the Lord.
22News of this reached the ears of the
church at Jerusalem, and they sent Barnabas to Antioch. 23When he arrived and
saw the evidence of the grace of God, he
was glad and encouraged them all to remain
true to the Lord with all their hearts. 24He was
a good man, full of the Holy Spirit and faith,
and a great number of people were brought
to the Lord.
25Then Barnabas went to Tarsus to look
for Saul, 26and when he found him, he
brought him to Antioch. So for a whole year
Barnabas and Saul met with the church and
taught great numbers of people. The disciples were called Christians first at Antioch.
27During this time some prophets came
down from Jerusalem to Antioch. 28One of
them, named Agabus, stood up and through
the Spirit predicted that a severe famine
would spread over the entire Roman world.
(This happened during the reign of Claudius.) 29The disciples, each according to his
ability, decided to provide help for the brothers living in Judea. 30This they did, sending
their gift to the elders by Barnabas and Saul.

Peter's Miraculous Escape From Prison

12 It was about this time that King Herod
arrested some who belonged to the
church, intending to persecute them. 2He
had James, the brother of John, put to death
with the sword. 3When he saw that this
pleased the Jews, he proceeded to seize
Peter also. This happened during the Feast
of Unleavened Bread. 4After arresting him,
he put him in prison, handing him over to be
guarded by four squads of four soldiers
each. Herod intended to bring him out for
public trial after the Passover.
5So Peter was kept in prison, but the
church was earnestly praying to God for him.
6The night before Herod was to bring him
to trial, Peter was sleeping between two soldiers, bound with two chains, and sentries
stood guard at the entrance. 7Suddenly an
angel of the Lord appeared and a light shone
in the cell. He struck Peter on the side and
woke him up. "Quick, get up!" he said, and
the chains fell off Peter's wrists.
8Then the angel said to him, "Put on your
clothes and sandals." And Peter did so.
"Wrap your cloak around you and follow
me," the angel told him. 9Peter followed him

[a]16 Or *in*

out of the prison, but he had no idea that
what the angel was doing was really happening; he thought he was seeing a vision.
10They passed the first and second guards
and came to the iron gate leading to the city.
It opened for them by itself, and they went
through it. When they had walked the length
of one street, suddenly the angel left him.
11Then Peter came to himself and said,
"Now I know without a doubt that the Lord
sent his angel and rescued me from Herod's
clutches and from everything the Jewish
people were anticipating."
12When this had dawned on him, he went
to the house of Mary the mother of John, also
called Mark, where many people had gathered and were praying. 13Peter knocked at
the outer entrance, and a servant girl named
Rhoda came to answer the door. 14When
she recognized Peter's voice, she was so
overjoyed she ran back without opening it
and exclaimed, "Peter is at the door!"
15"You're out of your mind," they told her.
When she kept insisting that it was so, they
said, "It must be his angel."
16But Peter kept on knocking, and when
they opened the door and saw him, they
were astonished. 17Peter motioned with his
hand for them to be quiet and described how
the Lord had brought him out of prison. "Tell
James and the brothers about this," he said,
and then he left for another place.
18In the morning, there was no small commotion among the soldiers as to what had
become of Peter. 19After Herod had a
thorough search made for him and did not
find him, he cross-examined the guards and
ordered that they be executed.

Herod's Death

Then Herod went from Judea to Caesarea
and stayed there a while. 20He had been
quarreling with the people of Tyre and Sidon;
they now joined together and sought an
audience with him. Having secured the support of Blastus, a trusted personal servant of
the king, they asked for peace, because they
depended on the king's country for their food
supply.
21On the appointed day Herod, wearing his
royal robes, sat on his throne and delivered a
public address to the people. 22They shouted, "This is the voice of a god, not of a man."
23Immediately, because Herod did not give
praise to God, an angel of the Lord struck
him down, and he was eaten by worms and
died.
24But the word of God continued to increase and spread.
25When Barnabas and Saul had finished
their mission, they returned from[a] Jerusalem, taking with them John, also called Mark.

Barnabas and Saul Sent Off

13 In the church at Antioch there were
prophets and teachers: Barnabas,
Simeon called Niger, Lucius of Cyrene,
Manaen (who had been brought up with Herod the tetrarch) and Saul. 2While they were
worshiping the Lord and fasting, the Holy
Spirit said, "Set apart for me Barnabas and
Saul for the work to which I have called
them." 3So after they had fasted and prayed,
they placed their hands on them and sent
them off.

On Cyprus

4The two of them, sent on their way by the
Holy Spirit, went down to Seleucia and sailed
from there to Cyprus. 5When they arrived at
Salamis, they proclaimed the word of God in
the Jewish synagogues. John was with them
as their helper.
6They traveled through the whole island
until they came to Paphos. There they met a
Jewish sorcerer and false prophet named
Bar-Jesus, 7who was an attendant of the proconsul, Sergius Paulus. The proconsul, an
intelligent man, sent for Barnabas and Saul
because he wanted to hear the word of God.
8But Elymas the sorcerer (for that is what his
name means) opposed them and tried to
turn the proconsul from the faith. 9Then Saul,
who was also called Paul, filled with the Holy
Spirit, looked straight at Elymas and said,
10"You are a child of the devil and an enemy
of everything that is right! You are full of all
kinds of deceit and trickery. Will you never
stop perverting the right ways of the Lord?
11Now the hand of the Lord is against you.
You are going to be blind, and for a time you
will be unable to see the light of the sun."
Immediately mist and darkness came over
him, and he groped about, seeking someone
to lead him by the hand. 12When the proconsul saw what had happened, he believed, for
he was amazed at the teaching about the
Lord.

[a]25 Some manuscripts *to*

In Pisidian Antioch

13From Paphos, Paul and his companions
sailed to Perga in Pamphylia, where John
left them to return to Jerusalem. 14From Perga they went on to Pisidian Antioch. On the
Sabbath they entered the synagogue and
sat down. 15After the reading from the Law
and the Prophets, the synagogue rulers sent
word to them, saying, "Brothers, if you have
a message of encouragement for the people,
please speak."
16Standing up, Paul motioned with his
hand and said: "Men of Israel and you Gentiles who worship God, listen to me! 17The
God of the people of Israel chose our fathers;
he made the people prosper during their stay
in Egypt, with mighty power he led them out
of that country, 18he endured their conduct[a]
for about forty years in the desert, 19he overthrew seven nations in Canaan and gave
their land to his people as their inheritance.
20All this took about 450 years.
"After this, God gave them judges until the
time of Samuel the prophet. 21Then the
people asked for a king, and he gave them
Saul son of Kish, of the tribe of Benjamin,
who ruled forty years. 22After removing Saul,
he made David their king. He testified concerning him: 'I have found David son of
Jesse a man after my own heart; he will do
everything I want him to do.'
23"From this man's descendants God has
brought to Israel the Savior Jesus, as he
promised. 24Before the coming of Jesus,
John preached repentance and baptism to
all the people of Israel. 25As John was completing his work, he said: 'Who do you think I
am? I am not that one. No, but he is coming
after me, whose sandals I am not worthy to
untie.'
26"Brothers, children of Abraham, and you
God-fearing Gentiles, it is to us that this message of salvation has been sent. 27The
people of Jerusalem and their rulers did not
recognize Jesus, yet in condemning him
they fulfilled the words of the prophets that
are read every Sabbath. 28Though they
found no proper ground for a death sentence, they asked Pilate to have him executed. 29When they had carried out all that was
written about him, they took him down from
the tree and laid him in a tomb. 30But God
raised him from the dead, 31and for many
days he was seen by those who had traveled
with him from Galilee to Jerusalem. They are
now his witnesses to our people.
32"We tell you the good news: What God
promised our fathers 33he has fulfilled for us,
their children, by raising up Jesus. As it is
written in the second Psalm:

" 'You are my Son;
today I have become your Father.'[b,c]

34The fact that God raised him from the dead,
never to decay, is stated in these words:

" 'I will give you the holy and sure
blessings promised to David.'[d]

35So it is stated elsewhere:

" 'You will not let your Holy One see
decay.'[e]

36"For when David had served God's purpose in his own generation, he fell asleep; he
was buried with his fathers and his body
decayed. 37But the one whom God raised
from the dead did not see decay.
38"Therefore, my brothers, I want you to
know that through Jesus the forgiveness of
sins is proclaimed to you. 39Through him
everyone who believes is justified from
everything you could not be justified from by
the law of Moses. 40Take care that what the
prophets have said does not happen to you:

41" 'Look, you scoffers,
wonder and perish,
for I am going to do something in your
days
that you would never believe,
even if someone told you.'[f]"

42As Paul and Barnabas were leaving the
synagogue, the people invited them to speak
further about these things on the next Sabbath. 43When the congregation was dismissed, many of the Jews and devout converts to Judaism followed Paul and Barnabas, who talked with them and urged them
to continue in the grace of God.
44On the next Sabbath almost the whole
city gathered to hear the word of the Lord.
45When the Jews saw the crowds, they were
filled with jealousy and talked abusively
against what Paul was saying.
46Then Paul and Barnabas answered
them boldly: "We had to speak the word of
God to you first. Since you reject it and do not
consider yourselves worthy of eternal life, we

[a]*18* Some manuscripts *and cared for them* 33 Or *have begotten you* [c]*33* Psalm 2:7
[d]*34* Isaiah 55:3 [e]*35* Psalm 16:10 [f]*41* Hab. 1:5

now turn to the Gentiles. 47For this is what the Lord has commanded us:

> " 'I have made you[a] a light for the
> Gentiles,
> that you[a] may bring salvation to the
> ends of the earth.'[b]"

48When the Gentiles heard this, they were glad and honored the word of the Lord; and all who were appointed for eternal life believed.

49The word of the Lord spread through the whole region. 50But the Jews incited the God-fearing women of high standing and the leading men of the city. They stirred up persecution against Paul and Barnabas, and expelled them from their region. 51So they shook the dust from their feet in protest against them and went to Iconium. 52And the disciples were filled with joy and with the Holy Spirit.

In Iconium

14 At Iconium Paul and Barnabas went as usual into the Jewish synagogue. There they spoke so effectively that a great number of Jews and Gentiles believed. 2But the Jews who refused to believe stirred up the Gentiles and poisoned their minds against the brothers. 3So Paul and Barnabas spent considerable time there, speaking boldly for the Lord, who confirmed the message of his grace by enabling them to do miraculous signs and wonders. 4The people of the city were divided; some sided with the Jews, others with the apostles. 5There was a plot afoot among the Gentiles and Jews, together with their leaders, to mistreat them and stone them. 6But they found out about it and fled to the Lycaonian cities of Lystra and Derbe and to the surrounding country, 7where they continued to preach the good news.

In Lystra and Derbe

8In Lystra there sat a man crippled in his feet, who was lame from birth and had never walked. 9He listened to Paul as he was speaking. Paul looked directly at him, saw that he had faith to be healed 10and called out, "Stand up on your feet!" At that, the man jumped up and began to walk.

11When the crowd saw what Paul had done, they shouted in the Lycaonian language, "The gods have come down to us in human form!" 12Barnabas they called Zeus, and Paul they called Hermes because he was the chief speaker. 13The priest of Zeus, whose temple was just outside the city, brought bulls and wreaths to the city gates because he and the crowd wanted to offer sacrifices to them.

14But when the apostles Barnabas and Paul heard of this, they tore their clothes and rushed out into the crowd, shouting: 15"Men, why are you doing this? We too are only men, human like you. We are bringing you good news, telling you to turn from these worthless things to the living God, who made heaven and earth and sea and everything in them. 16In the past, he let all nations go their own way. 17Yet he has not left himself without testimony: He has shown kindness by giving you rain from heaven and crops in their seasons; he provides you with plenty of food and fills your hearts with joy." 18Even with these words, they had difficulty keeping the crowd from sacrificing to them.

19Then some Jews came from Antioch and Iconium and won the crowd over. They stoned Paul and dragged him outside the city, thinking he was dead. 20But after the disciples had gathered around him, he got up and went back into the city. The next day he and Barnabas left for Derbe.

The Return to Antioch in Syria

21They preached the good news in that city and won a large number of disciples. Then they returned to Lystra, Iconium and Antioch, 22strengthening the disciples and encouraging them to remain true to the faith. "We must go through many hardships to enter the kingdom of God," they said. 23Paul and Barnabas appointed elders[c] for them in each church and, with prayer and fasting, committed them to the Lord, in whom they had put their trust. 24After going through Pisidia, they came into Pamphylia, 25and when they had preached the word in Perga, they went down to Attalia.

26From Attalia they sailed back to Antioch, where they had been committed to the grace of God for the work they had now completed. 27On arriving there, they gathered the church together and reported all that God had done through them and how he had opened the

[a] *47* The Greek is singular. [b] *47* Isaiah 49:6 [c] *23* Or *Barnabas ordained elders*; or *Barnabas had elders elected*

door of faith to the Gentiles. 28And they stayed there a long time with the disciples.

The Council at Jerusalem

15 Some men came down from Judea to Antioch and were teaching the brothers: "Unless you are circumcised, according to the custom taught by Moses, you cannot be saved." 2This brought Paul and Barnabas into sharp dispute and debate with them. So Paul and Barnabas were appointed, along with some other believers, to go up to Jerusalem to see the apostles and elders about this question. 3The church sent them on their way, and as they traveled through Phoenicia and Samaria, they told how the Gentiles had been converted. This news made all the brothers very glad. 4When they came to Jerusalem, they were welcomed by the church and the apostles and elders, to whom they reported everything God had done through them.

5Then some of the believers who belonged to the party of the Pharisees stood up and said, "The Gentiles must be circumcised and required to obey the law of Moses."

6The apostles and elders met to consider this question. 7After much discussion, Peter got up and addressed them: "Brothers, you know that some time ago God made a choice among you that the Gentiles might hear from my lips the message of the gospel and believe. 8God, who knows the heart, showed that he accepted them by giving the Holy Spirit to them, just as he did to us. 9He made no distinction between us and them, for he purified their hearts by faith. 10Now then, why do you try to test God by putting on the necks of the disciples a yoke that neither we nor our fathers have been able to bear? 11No! We believe it is through the grace of our Lord Jesus that we are saved, just as they are."

12The whole assembly became silent as they listened to Barnabas and Paul telling about the miraculous signs and wonders God had done among the Gentiles through them. 13When they finished, James spoke up: "Brothers, listen to me. 14Simon[a] has described to us how God at first showed his concern by taking from the Gentiles a people for himself. 15The words of the prophets are in agreement with this, as it is written:

16" 'After this I will return
and rebuild David's fallen tent.
Its ruins I will rebuild,
and I will restore it,
17that the remnant of men may seek the Lord,
and all the Gentiles who bear my name,
says the Lord, who does these things'[b]
18 that have been known for ages.[c]

19"It is my judgment, therefore, that we should not make it difficult for the Gentiles who are turning to God. 20Instead we should write to them, telling them to abstain from food polluted by idols, from sexual immorality, from the meat of strangled animals and from blood. 21For Moses has been preached in every city from the earliest times and is read in the synagogues on every Sabbath."

The Council's Letter to Gentile Believers

22Then the apostles and elders, with the whole church, decided to choose some of their own men and send them to Antioch with Paul and Barnabas. They chose Judas (called Barsabbas) and Silas, two men who were leaders among the brothers. 23With them they sent the following letter:

The apostles and elders, your brothers,

To the Gentile believers in Antioch, Syria and Cilicia:

Greetings.

24We have heard that some went out from us without our authorization and disturbed you, troubling your minds by what they said. 25So we all agreed to choose some men and send them to you with our dear friends Barnabas and Paul— 26men who have risked their lives for the name of our Lord Jesus Christ. 27Therefore we are sending Judas and Silas to confirm by word of mouth what we are writing. 28It seemed good to the Holy Spirit and to us not to burden you with anything beyond the following requirements: 29You are to abstain from food sacrificed to idols, from blood, from the meat of strangled animals and from sexual immorality. You will do well to avoid these things.

Farewell.

[a] *14* Greek *Simeon,* a variant of *Simon;* that is, Peter [b] *17* Amos 9:11,12 [c] *17,18* Some manuscripts *things'— / 18known to the Lord for ages is his work*

30The men were sent off and went down to Antioch, where they gathered the church together and delivered the letter. 31The people read it and were glad for its encouraging message. 32Judas and Silas, who themselves were prophets, said much to encourage and strengthen the brothers. 33After spending some time there, they were sent off by the brothers with the blessing of peace to return to those who had sent them.[a] 35But Paul and Barnabas remained in Antioch, where they and many others taught and preached the word of the Lord.

Disagreement Between Paul and Barnabas

36Some time later Paul said to Barnabas, "Let us go back and visit the brothers in all the towns where we preached the word of the Lord and see how they are doing." 37Barnabas wanted to take John, also called Mark, with them, 38but Paul did not think it wise to take him, because he had deserted them in Pamphylia and had not continued with them in the work. 39They had such a sharp disagreement that they parted company. Barnabas took Mark and sailed for Cyprus, 40but Paul chose Silas and left, commended by the brothers to the grace of the Lord. 41He went through Syria and Cilicia, strengthening the churches.

Timothy Joins Paul and Silas

16 He came to Derbe and then to Lystra, where a disciple named Timothy lived, whose mother was a Jewess and a believer, but whose father was a Greek. 2The brothers at Lystra and Iconium spoke well of him. 3Paul wanted to take him along on the journey, so he circumcised him because of the Jews who lived in that area, for they all knew that his father was a Greek. 4As they traveled from town to town, they delivered the decisions reached by the apostles and elders in Jerusalem for the people to obey. 5So the churches were strengthened in the faith and grew daily in numbers.

Paul's Vision of the Man of Macedonia

6Paul and his companions traveled throughout the region of Phrygia and Galatia, having been kept by the Holy Spirit from preaching the word in the province of Asia. 7When they came to the border of Mysia, they tried to enter Bithynia, but the Spirit of Jesus would not allow them to. 8So they passed by Mysia and went down to Troas. 9During the night Paul had a vision of a man of Macedonia standing and begging him, "Come over to Macedonia and help us." 10After Paul had seen the vision, we got ready at once to leave for Macedonia, concluding that God had called us to preach the gospel to them.

Lydia's Conversion in Philippi

11From Troas we put out to sea and sailed straight for Samothrace, and the next day on to Neapolis. 12From there we traveled to Philippi, a Roman colony and the leading city of that district of Macedonia. And we stayed there several days.

13On the Sabbath we went outside the city gate to the river, where we expected to find a place of prayer. We sat down and began to speak to the women who had gathered there. 14One of those listening was a woman named Lydia, a dealer in purple cloth from the city of Thyatira, who was a worshiper of God. The Lord opened her heart to respond to Paul's message. 15When she and the members of her household were baptized, she invited us to her home. "If you consider me a believer in the Lord," she said, "come and stay at my house." And she persuaded us.

Paul and Silas in Prison

16Once when we were going to the place of prayer, we were met by a slave girl who had a spirit by which she predicted the future. She earned a great deal of money for her owners by fortune-telling. 17This girl followed Paul and the rest of us, shouting, "These men are servants of the Most High God, who are telling you the way to be saved." 18She kept this up for many days. Finally Paul became so troubled that he turned around and said to the spirit, "In the name of Jesus Christ I command you to come out of her!" At that moment the spirit left her.

19When the owners of the slave girl realized that their hope of making money was gone, they seized Paul and Silas and dragged them into the marketplace to face the authorities. 20They brought them before the magistrates and said, "These men are Jews, and are throwing our city into an uproar 21by advocating customs unlawful for us Romans to accept or practice."

[a]33 Some manuscripts *them,* 34*but Silas decided to remain there*

22The crowd joined in the attack against Paul and Silas, and the magistrates ordered them to be stripped and beaten. 23After they had been severely flogged, they were thrown into prison, and the jailer was commanded to guard them carefully. 24Upon receiving such orders, he put them in the inner cell and fastened their feet in the stocks.

25About midnight Paul and Silas were praying and singing hymns to God, and the other prisoners were listening to them. 26Suddenly there was such a violent earthquake that the foundations of the prison were shaken. At once all the prison doors flew open, and everybody's chains came loose. 27The jailer woke up, and when he saw the prison doors open, he drew his sword and was about to kill himself because he thought the prisoners had escaped. 28But Paul shouted, "Don't harm yourself! We are all here!"

29The jailer called for lights, rushed in and fell trembling before Paul and Silas. 30He then brought them out and asked, "Sirs, what must I do to be saved?"

31They replied, "Believe in the Lord Jesus, and you will be saved—you and your household." 32Then they spoke the word of the Lord to him and to all the others in his house. 33At that hour of the night the jailer took them and washed their wounds; then immediately he and all his family were baptized. 34The jailer brought them into his house and set a meal before them; he was filled with joy because he had come to believe in God—he and his whole family.

35When it was daylight, the magistrates sent their officers to the jailer with the order: "Release those men." 36The jailer told Paul, "The magistrates have ordered that you and Silas be released. Now you can leave. Go in peace."

37But Paul said to the officers: "They beat us publicly without a trial, even though we are Roman citizens, and threw us into prison. And now do they want to get rid of us quietly? No! Let them come themselves and escort us out."

38The officers reported this to the magistrates, and when they heard that Paul and Silas were Roman citizens, they were alarmed. 39They came to appease them and escorted them from the prison, requesting them to leave the city. 40After Paul and Silas came out of the prison, they went to Lydia's house, where they met with the brothers and encouraged them. Then they left.

In Thessalonica

17 When they had passed through Amphipolis and Apollonia, they came to Thessalonica, where there was a Jewish synagogue. 2As his custom was, Paul went into the synagogue, and on three Sabbath days he reasoned with them from the Scriptures, 3explaining and proving that the Christ[a] had to suffer and rise from the dead. "This Jesus I am proclaiming to you is the Christ,[a]" he said. 4Some of the Jews were persuaded and joined Paul and Silas, as did a large number of God-fearing Greeks and not a few prominent women.

5But the Jews were jealous; so they rounded up some bad characters from the marketplace, formed a mob and started a riot in the city. They rushed to Jason's house in search of Paul and Silas in order to bring them out to the crowd.[b] 6But when they did not find them, they dragged Jason and some other brothers before the city officials, shouting: "These men who have caused trouble all over the world have now come here, 7and Jason has welcomed them into his house. They are all defying Caesar's decrees, saying that there is another king, one called Jesus." 8When they heard this, the crowd and the city officials were thrown into turmoil. 9Then they made Jason and the others post bond and let them go.

In Berea

10As soon as it was night, the brothers sent Paul and Silas away to Berea. On arriving there, they went to the Jewish synagogue. 11Now the Bereans were of more noble character than the Thessalonians, for they received the message with great eagerness and examined the Scriptures every day to see if what Paul said was true. 12Many of the Jews believed, as did also a number of prominent Greek women and many Greek men.

13When the Jews in Thessalonica learned that Paul was preaching the word of God at Berea, they went there too, agitating the crowds and stirring them up. 14The brothers immediately sent Paul to the coast, but Silas and Timothy stayed at Berea. 15The men who escorted Paul brought him to Athens

[a]3 Or *Messiah* [b]5 Or *the assembly of the people*

and then left with instructions for Silas and
Timothy to join him as soon as possible.

In Athens

[16]While Paul was waiting for them in
Athens, he was greatly distressed to see that
the city was full of idols. [17]So he reasoned in
the synagogue with the Jews and the God-
fearing Greeks, as well as in the marketplace
day by day with those who happened to be
there. [18]A group of Epicurean and Stoic
philosophers began to dispute with him.
Some of them asked, "What is this babbler
trying to say?" Others remarked, "He seems
to be advocating foreign gods." They said
this because Paul was preaching the good
news about Jesus and the resurrection.
[19]Then they took him and brought him to a
meeting of the Areopagus, where they said
to him, "May we know what this new teaching is that you are presenting? [20]You are
bringing some strange ideas to our ears, and
we want to know what they mean." [21](All the
Athenians and the foreigners who lived there
spent their time doing nothing but talking
about and listening to the latest ideas.)

[22]Paul then stood up in the meeting of the
Areopagus and said: "Men of Athens! I see
that in every way you are very religious. [23]For
as I walked around and looked carefully at
your objects of worship, I even found an altar
with this inscription: TO AN UNKNOWN GOD. Now
what you worship as something unknown I
am going to proclaim to you.

[24]"The God who made the world and
everything in it is the Lord of heaven and
earth and does not live in temples built by
hands. [25]And he is not served by human
hands, as if he needed anything, because he
himself gives all men life and breath and
everything else. [26]From one man he made
every nation of men, that they should inhabit
the whole earth; and he determined the
times set for them and the exact places
where they should live. [27]God did this so that
men would seek him and perhaps reach out
for him and find him, though he is not far from
each one of us. [28]'For in him we live and
move and have our being.' As some of your
own poets have said, 'We are his offspring.'

[29]"Therefore since we are God's offspring,
we should not think that the divine being is
like gold or silver or stone—an image made
by man's design and skill. [30]In the past God
overlooked such ignorance, but now he commands all people everywhere to repent.
[31]For he has set a day when he will judge the
world with justice by the man he has appointed. He has given proof of this to all men
by raising him from the dead."

[32]When they heard about the resurrection
of the dead, some of them sneered, but others said, "We want to hear you again on this
subject." [33]At that, Paul left the Council. [34]A
few men became followers of Paul and believed. Among them was Dionysius, a member of the Areopagus, also a woman named
Damaris, and a number of others.

In Corinth

18 After this, Paul left Athens and went
to Corinth. [2]There he met a Jew
named Aquila, a native of Pontus, who had
recently come from Italy with his wife Priscilla, because Claudius had ordered all the
Jews to leave Rome. Paul went to see them,
[3]and because he was a tentmaker as they
were, he stayed and worked with them.
[4]Every Sabbath he reasoned in the synagogue, trying to persuade Jews and Greeks.

[5]When Silas and Timothy came from
Macedonia, Paul devoted himself exclusively to preaching, testifying to the Jews that
Jesus was the Christ.[a] [6]But when the Jews
opposed Paul and became abusive, he
shook out his clothes in protest and said to
them, "Your blood be on your own heads! I
am clear of my responsibility. From now on I
will go to the Gentiles."

[7]Then Paul left the synagogue and went
next door to the house of Titius Justus, a
worshiper of God. [8]Crispus, the synagogue
ruler, and his entire household believed in
the Lord; and many of the Corinthians who
heard him believed and were baptized.

[9]One night the Lord spoke to Paul in a
vision: "Do not be afraid; keep on speaking,
do not be silent. [10]For I am with you, and no
one is going to attack and harm you, because I have many people in this city." [11]So
Paul stayed for a year and a half, teaching
them the word of God.

[12]While Gallio was proconsul of Achaia,
the Jews made a united attack on Paul and
brought him into court. [13]"This man," they
charged, "is persuading the people to worship God in ways contrary to the law."

[14]Just as Paul was about to speak, Gallio
said to the Jews, "If you Jews were making a
complaint about some misdemeanor or seri-

[a]5 Or *Messiah;* also in verse 28

ous crime, it would be reasonable for me to listen to you. 15But since it involves questions about words and names and your own law—settle the matter yourselves. I will not be a judge of such things." 16So he had them ejected from the court. 17Then they all turned on Sosthenes the synagogue ruler and beat him in front of the court. But Gallio showed no concern whatever.

Priscilla, Aquila and Apollos

18Paul stayed on in Corinth for some time. Then he left the brothers and sailed for Syria, accompanied by Priscilla and Aquila. Before he sailed, he had his hair cut off at Cenchrea because of a vow he had taken. 19They arrived at Ephesus, where Paul left Priscilla and Aquila. He himself went into the synagogue and reasoned with the Jews. 20When they asked him to spend more time with them, he declined. 21But as he left, he promised, "I will come back if it is God's will." Then he set sail from Ephesus. 22When he landed at Caesarea, he went up and greeted the church and then went down to Antioch.

23After spending some time in Antioch, Paul set out from there and traveled from place to place throughout the region of Galatia and Phrygia, strengthening all the disciples.

24Meanwhile a Jew named Apollos, a native of Alexandria, came to Ephesus. He was a learned man, with a thorough knowledge of the Scriptures. 25He had been instructed in the way of the Lord, and he spoke with great fervor[a] and taught about Jesus accurately, though he knew only the baptism of John. 26He began to speak boldly in the synagogue. When Priscilla and Aquila heard him, they invited him to their home and explained to him the way of God more adequately.

27When Apollos wanted to go to Achaia, the brothers encouraged him and wrote to the disciples there to welcome him. On arriving, he was a great help to those who by grace had believed. 28For he vigorously refuted the Jews in public debate, proving from the Scriptures that Jesus was the Christ.

Paul in Ephesus

19 While Apollos was at Corinth, Paul took the road through the interior and arrived at Ephesus. There he found some disciples 2and asked them, "Did you receive the Holy Spirit when[b] you believed?"

They answered, "No, we have not even heard that there is a Holy Spirit."

3So Paul asked, "Then what baptism did you receive?"

"John's baptism," they replied.

4Paul said, "John's baptism was a baptism of repentance. He told the people to believe in the one coming after him, that is, in Jesus." 5On hearing this, they were baptized into[c] the name of the Lord Jesus. 6When Paul placed his hands on them, the Holy Spirit came on them, and they spoke in tongues[d] and prophesied. 7There were about twelve men in all.

8Paul entered the synagogue and spoke boldly there for three months, arguing persuasively about the kingdom of God. 9But some of them became obstinate; they refused to believe and publicly maligned the Way. So Paul left them. He took the disciples with him and had discussions daily in the lecture hall of Tyrannus. 10This went on for two years, so that all the Jews and Greeks who lived in the province of Asia heard the word of the Lord.

11God did extraordinary miracles through Paul, 12so that even handkerchiefs and aprons that had touched him were taken to the sick, and their illnesses were cured and the evil spirits left them.

13Some Jews who went around driving out evil spirits tried to invoke the name of the Lord Jesus over those who were demon-possessed. They would say, "In the name of Jesus, whom Paul preaches, I command you to come out." 14Seven sons of Sceva, a Jewish chief priest, were doing this. 15⌞One day⌟ the evil spirit answered them, "Jesus I know, and I know about Paul, but who are you?" 16Then the man who had the evil spirit jumped on them and overpowered them all. He gave them such a beating that they ran out of the house naked and bleeding.

17When this became known to the Jews and Greeks living in Ephesus, they were all seized with fear, and the name of the Lord Jesus was held in high honor. 18Many of those who believed now came and openly confessed their evil deeds. 19A number who had practiced sorcery brought their scrolls together and burned them publicly. When they calculated the value of the scrolls, the

[a]25 Or *with fervor in the Spirit* [b]2 Or *after* [c]5 Or *in* [d]6 Or *other languages*

total came to fifty thousand drachmas.[a] 20In this way the word of the Lord spread widely and grew in power.

21After all this had happened, Paul decided to go to Jerusalem, passing through Macedonia and Achaia. "After I have been there," he said, "I must visit Rome also." 22He sent two of his helpers, Timothy and Erastus, to Macedonia, while he stayed in the province of Asia a little longer.

The Riot in Ephesus

23About that time there arose a great disturbance about the Way. 24A silversmith named Demetrius, who made silver shrines of Artemis, brought in no little business for the craftsmen. 25He called them together, along with the workmen in related trades, and said: "Men, you know we receive a good income from this business. 26And you see and hear how this fellow Paul has convinced and led astray large numbers of people here in Ephesus and in practically the whole province of Asia. He says that man-made gods are no gods at all. 27There is danger not only that our trade will lose its good name, but also that the temple of the great goddess Artemis will be discredited, and the goddess herself, who is worshiped throughout the province of Asia and the world, will be robbed of her divine majesty."

28When they heard this, they were furious and began shouting: "Great is Artemis of the Ephesians!" 29Soon the whole city was in an uproar. The people seized Gaius Aristarchus, Paul's traveling companions from Macedonia, and rushed as one man into the theater. 30Paul wanted to appear before the crowd, but the disciples would not let him. 31Even some of the officials of the province, friends of Paul, sent him a message begging him not to venture into the theater.

32The assembly was in confusion: Some were shouting one thing, some another. Most of the people did not even know why they were there. 33The Jews pushed Alexander to the front, and some of the crowd shouted instructions to him. He motioned for silence in order to make a defense before the people. 34But when they realized he was a Jew, they all shouted in unison for about two hours: "Great is Artemis of the Ephesians!"

35The city clerk quieted the crowd and said: "Men of Ephesus, doesn't all the world know that the city of Ephesus is the guardian of the temple of the great Artemis and of her image, which fell from heaven? 36Therefore, since these facts are undeniable, you ought to be quiet and not do anything rash. 37You have brought these men here, though they have neither robbed temples nor blasphemed our goddess. 38If, then, Demetrius and his fellow craftsmen have a grievance against anybody, the courts are open and there are proconsuls. They can press charges. 39If there is anything further you want to bring up, it must be settled in a legal assembly. 40As it is, we are in danger of being charged with rioting because of today's events. In that case we would not be able to account for this commotion, since there is no reason for it." 41After he had said this, he dismissed the assembly.

Through Macedonia and Greece

20 When the uproar had ended, Paul sent for the disciples and, after encouraging them, said good-by and set out for Macedonia. 2He traveled through that area, speaking many words of encouragement to the people, and finally arrived in Greece, 3where he stayed three months. Because the Jews made a plot against him just as he was about to sail for Syria, he decided to go back through Macedonia. 4He was accompanied by Sopater son of Pyrrhus from Berea, Aristarchus and Secundus from Thessalonica, Gaius from Derbe, Timothy also, and Tychicus and Trophimus from the province of Asia. 5These men went on ahead and waited for us at Troas. 6But we sailed from Philippi after the Feast of Unleavened Bread, and five days later joined the others at Troas, where we stayed seven days.

Eutychus Raised From the Dead at Troas

7On the first day of the week we came together to break bread. Paul spoke to the people and, because he intended to leave the next day, kept on talking until midnight. 8There were many lamps in the upstairs room where we were meeting. 9Seated in a window was a young man named Eutychus, who was sinking into a deep sleep as Paul talked on and on. When he was sound asleep, he fell to the ground from the third story and was picked up dead. 10Paul went down, threw himself on the young man and

[a] *19* A drachma was a silver coin worth about a day's wages.

put his arms around him. "Don't be
alarmed," he said. "He's alive!" 11Then he
went upstairs again and broke bread and
ate. After talking until daylight, he left. 12The
people took the young man home alive and
were greatly comforted.

Paul's Farewell to the Ephesian Elders

13We went on ahead to the ship and sailed
for Assos, where we were going to take Paul
aboard. He had made this arrangement because he was going there on foot. 14When he
met us at Assos, we took him aboard and
went on to Mitylene. 15The next day we set
sail from there and arrived off Kios. The day
after that we crossed over to Samos, and on
the following day arrived at Miletus. 16Paul
had decided to sail past Ephesus to avoid
spending time in the province of Asia, for he
was in a hurry to reach Jerusalem, if possible, by the day of Pentecost.

17From Miletus, Paul sent to Ephesus for
the elders of the church. 18When they arrived, he said to them: "You know how I lived
the whole time I was with you, from the first
day I came into the province of Asia. 19I
served the Lord with great humility and with
tears, although I was severely tested by the
plots of the Jews. 20You know that I have not
hesitated to preach anything that would be
helpful to you but have taught you publicly
and from house to house. 21I have declared
to both Jews and Greeks that they must turn
to God in repentance and have faith in our
Lord Jesus.

22"And now, compelled by the Spirit, I am
going to Jerusalem, not knowing what will
happen to me there. 23I only know that in
every city the Holy Spirit warns me that prison and hardships are facing me. 24However,
I consider my life worth nothing to me, if only
I may finish the race and complete the task
the Lord Jesus has given me—the task of
testifying to the gospel of God's grace.

25"Now I know that none of you among
whom I have gone about preaching the kingdom will ever see me again. 26Therefore, I
declare to you today that I am innocent of the
blood of all men. 27For I have not hesitated to
proclaim to you the whole will of God. 28Keep
watch over yourselves and all the flock of
which the Holy Spirit has made you overseers.[a] Be shepherds of the church of God,[b]
which he bought with his own blood. 29I know
that after I leave, savage wolves will come in
among you and will not spare the flock.
30Even from your own number men will arise
and distort the truth in order to draw away
disciples after them. 31So be on your guard!
Remember that for three years I never
stopped warning each of you night and day
with tears.

32"Now I commit you to God and to the
word of his grace, which can build you up
and give you an inheritance among all those
who are sanctified. 33I have not coveted anyone's silver or gold or clothing. 34You yourselves know that these hands of mine have
supplied my own needs and the needs of my
companions. 35In everything I did, I showed
you that by this kind of hard work we must
help the weak, remembering the words the
Lord Jesus himself said: 'It is more blessed
to give than to receive.' "

36When he had said this, he knelt down
with all of them and prayed. 37They all wept
as they embraced him and kissed him.
38What grieved them most was his statement
that they would never see his face again.
Then they accompanied him to the ship.

On to Jerusalem

21 After we had torn ourselves away
from them, we put out to sea and
sailed straight to Cos. The next day we went
to Rhodes and from there to Patara. 2We
found a ship crossing over to Phoenicia,
went on board and set sail. 3After sighting
Cyprus and passing to the south of it, we
sailed on to Syria. We landed at Tyre, where
our ship was to unload its cargo. 4Finding the
disciples there, we stayed with them seven
days. Through the Spirit they urged Paul not
to go on to Jerusalem. 5But when our time
was up, we left and continued on our way. All
the disciples and their wives and children
accompanied us out of the city, and there on
the beach we knelt to pray. 6After saying
good-by to each other, we went aboard the
ship, and they returned home.

7We continued our voyage from Tyre and
landed at Ptolemais, where we greeted the
brothers and stayed with them for a day.
8Leaving the next day, we reached Caesarea and stayed at the house of Philip the
evangelist, one of the Seven. 9He had four
unmarried daughters who prophesied.

10After we had been there a number of
days, a prophet named Agabus came down
from Judea. 11Coming over to us, he took

[a]28 Traditionally *bishops* [b]28 Many manuscripts *of the Lord*

Paul's belt, tied his own hands and feet with
it and said, "The Holy Spirit says, 'In this way
the Jews of Jerusalem will bind the owner of
this belt and will hand him over to the Gentiles.' "

12When we heard this, we and the people
there pleaded with Paul not to go up to
Jerusalem. 13Then Paul answered, "Why are
you weeping and breaking my heart? I am
ready not only to be bound, but also to die in
Jerusalem for the name of the Lord Jesus."
14When he would not be dissuaded, we gave
up and said, "The Lord's will be done."

15After this, we got ready and went up to
Jerusalem. 16Some of the disciples from
Caesarea accompanied us and brought us
to the home of Mnason, where we were to
stay. He was a man from Cyprus and one of
the early disciples.

Paul's Arrival at Jerusalem

17When we arrived at Jerusalem, the
brothers received us warmly. 18The next day
Paul and the rest of us went to see James,
and all the elders were present. 19Paul greeted them and reported in detail what God had
done among the Gentiles through his ministry.

20When they heard this, they praised God.
Then they said to Paul: "You see, brother,
how many thousands of Jews have believed,
and all of them are zealous for the law.
21They have been informed that you teach all
the Jews who live among the Gentiles to turn
away from Moses, telling them not to circumcise their children or live according to our
customs. 22What shall we do? They will certainly hear that you have come, 23so do what
we tell you. There are four men with us who
have made a vow. 24Take these men, join in
their purification rites and pay their expenses, so that they can have their heads
shaved. Then everybody will know there is
no truth in these reports about you, but that
you yourself are living in obedience to the
law. 25As for the Gentile believers, we have
written to them our decision that they should
abstain from food sacrificed to idols, from
blood, from the meat of strangled animals
and from sexual immorality."

26The next day Paul took the men and purified himself along with them. Then he went to
the temple to give notice of the date when the
days of purification would end and the offering would be made for each of them.

Paul Arrested

27When the seven days were nearly over,
some Jews from the province of Asia saw
Paul at the temple. They stirred up the whole
crowd and seized him, 28shouting, "Men of
Israel, help us! This is the man who teaches
all men everywhere against our people and
our law and this place. And besides, he has
brought Greeks into the temple area and
defiled this holy place." 29(They had previously seen Trophimus the Ephesian in the
city with Paul and assumed that Paul had
brought him into the temple area.)

30The whole city was aroused, and the
people came running from all directions.
Seizing Paul, they dragged him from the
temple, and immediately the gates were
shut. 31While they were trying to kill him,
news reached the commander of the Roman
troops that the whole city of Jerusalem was
in an uproar. 32He at once took some officers
and soldiers and ran down to the crowd.
When the rioters saw the commander and
his soldiers, they stopped beating Paul.

33The commander came up and arrested
him and ordered him to be bound with two
chains. Then he asked who he was and what
he had done. 34Some in the crowd shouted
one thing and some another, and since the
commander could not get at the truth because of the uproar, he ordered that Paul be
taken into the barracks. 35When Paul
reached the steps, the violence of the mob
was so great he had to be carried by the
soldiers. 36The crowd that followed kept
shouting, "Away with him!"

Paul Speaks to the Crowd

37As the soldiers were about to take Paul
into the barracks, he asked the commander,
"May I say something to you?"

"Do you speak Greek?" he replied.
38"Aren't you the Egyptian who started a revolt and led four thousand terrorists out into
the desert some time ago?"

39Paul answered, "I am a Jew, from Tarsus in Cilicia, a citizen of no ordinary city.
Please let me speak to the people."

40Having received the commander's permission, Paul stood on the steps and motioned to the crowd. When they were all si-
22 lent, he said to them in Aramaic[a]:
1"Brothers and fathers, listen now to
my defense."

[a]*40* Or possibly *Hebrew;* also in 22:2

2When they heard him speak to them in
Aramaic, they became very quiet.
Then Paul said: 3"I am a Jew, born in Tarsus of Cilicia, but brought up in this city.
Under Gamaliel I was thoroughly trained in
the law of our fathers and was just as zealous for God as any of you are today. 4I persecuted the followers of this Way to their death,
arresting both men and women and throwing
them into prison, 5as also the high priest and
all the Council can testify. I even obtained
letters from them to their brothers in Damascus, and went there to bring these people as
prisoners to Jerusalem to be punished.
6"About noon as I came near Damascus,
suddenly a bright light from heaven flashed
around me. 7I fell to the ground and heard a
voice say to me, 'Saul! Saul! Why do you
persecute me?'
8" 'Who are you, Lord?' I asked.
" 'I am Jesus of Nazareth, whom you are
persecuting,' he replied. 9My companions
saw the light, but they did not understand the
voice of him who was speaking to me.
10" 'What shall I do, Lord?' I asked.
" 'Get up,' the Lord said, 'and go into
Damascus. There you will be told all that you
have been assigned to do.' 11My companions led me by the hand into Damascus,
because the brilliance of the light had blinded me.
12"A man named Ananias came to see me.
He was a devout observer of the law and
highly respected by all the Jews living there.
13He stood beside me and said, 'Brother
Saul, receive your sight!' And at that very
moment I was able to see him.
14"Then he said: 'The God of our fathers
has chosen you to know his will and to see
the Righteous One and to hear words from
his mouth. 15You will be his witness to all
men of what you have seen and heard. 16And
now what are you waiting for? Get up, be
baptized and wash your sins away, calling
on his name.'
17"When I returned to Jerusalem and was
praying at the temple, I fell into a trance
18and saw the Lord speaking. 'Quick!' he
said to me. 'Leave Jerusalem immediately,
because they will not accept your testimony
about me.'
19" 'Lord,' I replied, 'these men know that I
went from one synagogue to another to im-
prison and beat those who believe in you.
20And when the blood of your martyr[a] Stephen was shed, I stood there giving my approval and guarding the clothes of those who
were killing him.'
21"Then the Lord said to me, 'Go; I will
send you far away to the Gentiles.' "

Paul the Roman Citizen

22The crowd listened to Paul until he said
this. Then they raised their voices and shouted, "Rid the earth of him! He's not fit to live!"
23As they were shouting and throwing off
their cloaks and flinging dust into the air,
24the commander ordered Paul to be taken
into the barracks. He directed that he be
flogged and questioned in order to find out
why the people were shouting at him like
this. 25As they stretched him out to flog him,
Paul said to the centurion standing there, "Is
it legal for you to flog a Roman citizen who
hasn't even been found guilty?"
26When the centurion heard this, he went
to the commander and reported it. "What are
you going to do?" he asked. "This man is a
Roman citizen."
27The commander went to Paul and
asked, "Tell me, are you a Roman citizen?"
"Yes, I am," he answered.
28Then the commander said, "I had to pay
a big price for my citizenship."
"But I was born a citizen," Paul replied.
29Those who were about to question him
withdrew immediately. The commander himself was alarmed when he realized that he
had put Paul, a Roman citizen, in chains.

Before the Sanhedrin

30The next day, since the commander
wanted to find out exactly why Paul was being accused by the Jews, he released him
and ordered the chief priests and all the Sanhedrin to assemble. Then he brought Paul
and had him stand before them.

23 Paul looked straight at the Sanhedrin
and said, "My brothers, I have fulfilled my duty to God in all good conscience
to this day." 2At this the high priest Ananias
ordered those standing near Paul to strike
him on the mouth. 3Then Paul said to him,
"God will strike you, you whitewashed wall!
You sit there to judge me according to the
law, yet you yourself violate the law by commanding that I be struck!"
4Those who were standing near Paul said,
"You dare to insult God's high priest?"
5Paul replied, "Brothers, I did not realize

[a]20 Or *witness*

that he was the high priest; for it is written: 'Do not speak evil about the ruler of your people.'[a]"

6Then Paul, knowing that some of them were Sadducees and the others Pharisees, called out in the Sanhedrin, "My brothers, I am a Pharisee, the son of a Pharisee. I stand on trial because of my hope in the resurrection of the dead." 7When he said this, a dispute broke out between the Pharisees and the Sadducees, and the assembly was divided. 8(The Sadducees say that there is no resurrection, and that there are neither angels nor spirits, but the Pharisees acknowledge them all.)

9There was a great uproar, and some of the teachers of the law who were Pharisees stood up and argued vigorously. "We find nothing wrong with this man," they said. "What if a spirit or an angel has spoken to him?" 10The dispute became so violent that the commander was afraid Paul would be torn to pieces by them. He ordered the troops to go down and take him away from them by force and bring him into the barracks.

11The following night the Lord stood near Paul and said, "Take courage! As you have testified about me in Jerusalem, so you must also testify in Rome."

The Plot to Kill Paul

12The next morning the Jews formed a conspiracy and bound themselves with an oath not to eat or drink until they had killed Paul. 13More than forty men were involved in this plot. 14They went to the chief priests and elders and said, "We have taken a solemn oath not to eat anything until we have killed Paul. 15Now then, you and the Sanhedrin petition the commander to bring him before you on the pretext of wanting more accurate information about his case. We are ready to kill him before he gets here."

16But when the son of Paul's sister heard of this plot, he went into the barracks and told Paul.

17Then Paul called one of the centurions and said, "Take this young man to the commander; he has something to tell him." 18So he took him to the commander.

The centurion said, "Paul, the prisoner, sent for me and asked me to bring this young man to you because he has something to tell you."

19The commander took the young man by the hand, drew him aside and asked, "What is it you want to tell me?"

20He said: "The Jews have agreed to ask you to bring Paul before the Sanhedrin tomorrow on the pretext of wanting more accurate information about him. 21Don't give in to them, because more than forty of them are waiting in ambush for him. They have taken an oath not to eat or drink until they have killed him. They are ready now, waiting for your consent to their request."

22The commander dismissed the young man and cautioned him, "Don't tell anyone that you have reported this to me."

Paul Transferred to Caesarea

23Then he called two of his centurions and ordered them, "Get ready a detachment of two hundred soldiers, seventy horsemen and two hundred spearmen[b] to go to Caesarea at nine tonight. 24Provide mounts for Paul so that he may be taken safely to Governor Felix."

25He wrote a letter as follows:

> 26Claudius Lysias,
>
> To His Excellency, Governor Felix:
>
> Greetings.
>
> 27This man was seized by the Jews and they were about to kill him, but I came with my troops and rescued him, for I had learned that he is a Roman citizen. 28I wanted to know why they were accusing him, so I brought him to their Sanhedrin. 29I found that the accusation had to do with questions about their law, but there was no charge against him that deserved death or imprisonment. 30When I was informed of a plot to be carried out against the man, I sent him to you at once. I also ordered his accusers to present to you their case against him.

31So the soldiers, carrying out their orders, took Paul with them during the night and brought him as far as Antipatris. 32The next day they let the cavalry go on with him, while they returned to the barracks. 33When the cavalry arrived in Caesarea, they delivered the letter to the governor and handed Paul over to him. 34The governor read the letter

[a]*5* Exodus 22:28 [b]*23* The meaning of the Greek for this word is uncertain.

and asked what province he was from.
Learning that he was from Cilicia, 35he said,
"I will hear your case when your accusers
get here." Then he ordered that Paul be kept
under guard in Herod's palace.

The Trial Before Felix

24 Five days later the high priest
Ananias went down to Caesarea with
some of the elders and a lawyer named Tertullus, and they brought their charges
against Paul before the governor. 2When
Paul was called in, Tertullus presented his
case before Felix: "We have enjoyed a long
period of peace under you, and your fore-
sight has brought about reforms in this nation. 3Everywhere and in every way, most
excellent Felix, we acknowledge this with
profound gratitude. 4But in order not to weary
you further, I would request that you be kind
enough to hear us briefly.

5"We have found this man to be a troublemaker, stirring up riots among the Jews
all over the world. He is a ringleader of the
Nazarene sect 6and even tried to desecrate
the temple; so we seized him. 8By[a] examining him yourself you will be able to learn the
truth about all these charges we are bringing
against him."

9The Jews joined in the accusation, as-
serting that these things were true.

10When the governor motioned for him to
speak, Paul replied: "I know that for a number of years you have been a judge over this
nation; so I gladly make my defense. 11You
can easily verify that no more than twelve
days ago I went up to Jerusalem to worship.
12My accusers did not find me arguing with
anyone at the temple, or stirring up a crowd
in the synagogues or anywhere else in the
city. 13And they cannot prove to you the
charges they are now making against me.
14However, I admit that I worship the God of
our fathers as a follower of the Way, which
they call a sect. I believe everything that
agrees with the Law and that is written in the
Prophets, 15and I have the same hope in God
as these men, that there will be a resurrection of both the righteous and the wicked.
16So I strive always to keep my conscience
clear before God and man.

17"After an absence of several years, I
came to Jerusalem to bring my people gifts
for the poor and to present offerings. 18I was
ceremonially clean when they found me in
the temple courts doing this. There was no
crowd with me, nor was I involved in any
disturbance. 19But there are some Jews from
the province of Asia, who ought to be here
before you and bring charges if they have
anything against me. 20Or these who are
here should state what crime they found in
me when I stood before the Sanhedrin—
21unless it was this one thing I shouted as I
stood in their presence: 'It is concerning the
resurrection of the dead that I am on trial
before you today.' "

22Then Felix, who was well acquainted
with the Way, adjourned the proceedings.
"When Lysias the commander comes," he
said, "I will decide your case." 23He ordered
the centurion to keep Paul under guard but to
give him some freedom and permit his
friends to take care of his needs.

24Several days later Felix came with his
wife Drusilla, who was a Jewess. He sent for
Paul and listened to him as he spoke about
faith in Christ Jesus. 25As Paul discoursed on
righteousness, self-control and the judgment
to come, Felix was afraid and said, "That's
enough for now! You may leave. When I find
it convenient, I will send for you." 26At the
same time he was hoping that Paul would
offer him a bribe, so he sent for him frequently and talked with him.

27When two years had passed, Felix was
succeeded by Porcius Festus, but because
Felix wanted to grant a favor to the Jews, he
left Paul in prison.

The Trial Before Festus

25 Three days after arriving in the province, Festus went up from Caesarea
to Jerusalem, 2where the chief priests and
Jewish leaders appeared before him and
presented the charges against Paul. 3They
urgently requested Festus, as a favor to
them, to have Paul transferred to Jerusalem,
for they were preparing an ambush to kill him
along the way. 4Festus answered, "Paul is
being held at Caesarea, and I myself am
going there soon. 5Let some of your leaders
come with me and press charges against the
man there, if he has done anything wrong."

6After spending eight or ten days with
them, he went down to Caesarea, and the
next day he convened the court and ordered
that Paul be brought before him. 7When Paul

[a]6-8 Some manuscripts *him and wanted to judge him according to our law. 7But the commander, Lysias, came and with the use of much force snatched him from our hands 8and ordered his accusers to come before you. By*

appeared, the Jews who had come down from Jerusalem stood around him, bringing many serious charges against him, which they could not prove.

8Then Paul made his defense: "I have done nothing wrong against the law of the Jews or against the temple or against Caesar."

9Festus, wishing to do the Jews a favor, said to Paul, "Are you willing to go up to Jerusalem and stand trial before me there on these charges?"

10Paul answered: "I am now standing before Caesar's court, where I ought to be tried. I have not done any wrong to the Jews, as you yourself know very well. 11If, however, I am guilty of doing anything deserving death, I do not refuse to die. But if the charges brought against me by these Jews are not true, no one has the right to hand me over to them. I appeal to Caesar!"

12After Festus had conferred with his council, he declared: "You have appealed to Caesar. To Caesar you will go!"

Festus Consults King Agrippa

13A few days later King Agrippa and Bernice arrived at Caesarea to pay their respects to Festus. 14Since they were spending many days there, Festus discussed Paul's case with the king. He said: "There is a man here whom Felix left as a prisoner. 15When I went to Jerusalem, the chief priests and elders of the Jews brought charges against him and asked that he be condemned.

16"I told them that it is not the Roman custom to hand over any man before he has faced his accusers and has had an opportunity to defend himself against their charges. 17When they came here with me, I did not delay the case, but convened the court the next day and ordered the man to be brought in. 18When his accusers got up to speak, they did not charge him with any of the crimes I had expected. 19Instead, they had some points of dispute with him about their own religion and about a dead man named Jesus who Paul claimed was alive. 20I was at a loss how to investigate such matters; so I asked if he would be willing to go to Jerusalem and stand trial there on these charges. 21When Paul made his appeal to be held over for the Emperor's decision, I ordered him held until I could send him to Caesar."

22Then Agrippa said to Festus, "I would like to hear this man myself."

He replied, "Tomorrow you will hear him."

Paul Before Agrippa

23The next day Agrippa and Bernice came with great pomp and entered the audience room with the high ranking officers and the leading men of the city. At the command of Festus, Paul was brought in. 24Festus said: "King Agrippa, and all who are present with us, you see this man! The whole Jewish community has petitioned me about him in Jerusalem and here in Caesarea, shouting that he ought not to live any longer. 25I found he had done nothing deserving of death, but because he made his appeal to the Emperor I decided to send him to Rome. 26But I have nothing definite to write to His Majesty about him. Therefore I have brought him before all of you, and especially before you, King Agrippa, so that as a result of this investigation I may have something to write. 27For I think it is unreasonable to send on a prisoner without specifying the charges against him."

26 Then Agrippa said to Paul, "You have permission to speak for yourself."

So Paul motioned with his hand and began his defense: 2"King Agrippa, I consider myself fortunate to stand before you today as I make my defense against all the accusations of the Jews, 3and especially so because you are well acquainted with all the Jewish customs and controversies. Therefore, I beg you to listen to me patiently.

4"The Jews all know the way I have lived ever since I was a child, from the beginning of my life in my own country, and also in Jerusalem. 5They have known me for a long time and can testify, if they are willing, that according to the strictest sect of our religion, I lived as a Pharisee. 6And now it is because of my hope in what God has promised our fathers that I am on trial today. 7This is the promise our twelve tribes are hoping to see fulfilled as they earnestly serve God day and night. O king, it is because of this hope that the Jews are accusing me. 8Why should any of you consider it incredible that God raises the dead?

9"I too was convinced that I ought to do all that was possible to oppose the name of Jesus of Nazareth. 10And that is just what I did in Jerusalem. On the authority of the chief priests I put many of the saints in prison, and when they were put to death, I cast my vote against them. 11Many a time I went from one synagogue to another to have them

punished, and I tried to force them to blaspheme. In my obsession against them, I
even went to foreign cities to persecute
them.
12"On one of these journeys I was going to
Damascus with the authority and commission of the chief priests. 13About noon, O
king, as I was on the road, I saw a light from
heaven, brighter than the sun, blazing
around me and my companions. 14We all fell
to the ground, and I heard a voice saying to
me in Aramaic,[a] 'Saul, Saul, why do you
persecute me? It is hard for you to kick
against the goads.'
15"Then I asked, 'Who are you, Lord?'
" 'I am Jesus, whom you are persecuting,'
the Lord replied. 16'Now get up and stand on
your feet. I have appeared to you to appoint
you as a servant and as a witness of what
you have seen of me and what I will show
you. 17I will rescue you from your own people
and from the Gentiles. I am sending you to
them 18to open their eyes and turn them from
darkness to light, and from the power of Satan to God, so that they may receive forgiveness of sins and a place among those who
are sanctified by faith in me.'
19"So then, King Agrippa, I was not
disobedient to the vision from heaven. 20First
to those in Damascus, then to those in
Jerusalem and in all Judea, and to the Gentiles also, I preached that they should repent
and turn to God and prove their repentance
by their deeds. 21That is why the Jews seized
me in the temple courts and tried to kill me.
22But I have had God's help to this very day,
and so I stand here and testify to small and
great alike. I am saying nothing beyond what
the prophets and Moses said would happen— 23that the Christ[b] would suffer and, as
the first to rise from the dead, would proclaim
light to his own people and to the Gentiles."
24At this point Festus interrupted Paul's
defense. "You are out of your mind, Paul!"
he shouted. "Your great learning is driving
you insane."
25"I am not insane, most excellent Festus," Paul replied. "What I am saying is true
and reasonable. 26The king is familiar with
these things, and I can speak freely to him. I
am convinced that none of this has escaped
his notice, because it was not done in a corner. 27King Agrippa, do you believe the
prophets? I know you do."
28Then Agrippa said to Paul, "Do you think
that in such a short time you can persuade
me to be a Christian?"
29Paul replied, "Short time or long—I pray
God that not only you but all who are listening to me today may become what I am,
except for these chains."
30The king rose, and with him the governor
and Bernice and those sitting with them.
31They left the room, and while talking with
one another, they said, "This man is not doing anything that deserves death or imprisonment."
32Agrippa said to Festus, "This man could
have been set free if he had not appealed to
Caesar."

Paul Sails for Rome

27 When it was decided that we would
sail for Italy, Paul and some other
prisoners were handed over to a centurion
named Julius, who belonged to the Imperial
Regiment. 2We boarded a ship from
Adramyttium about to sail for ports along the
coast of the province of Asia, and we put out
to sea. Aristarchus, a Macedonian from
Thessalonica, was with us.
3The next day we landed at Sidon; and
Julius, in kindness to Paul, allowed him to go
to his friends so they might provide for his
needs. 4From there we put out to sea again
and passed to the lee of Cyprus because the
winds were against us. 5When we had sailed
across the open sea off the coast of Cilicia
and Pamphylia, we landed at Myra in Lycia.
6There the centurion found an Alexandrian
ship sailing for Italy and put us on board. 7We
made slow headway for many days and had
difficulty arriving off Cnidus. When the wind
did not allow us to hold our course, we sailed
to the lee of Crete, opposite Salmone. 8We
moved along the coast with difficulty and
came to a place called Fair Havens, near the
town of Lasea.
9Much time had been lost, and sailing had
already become dangerous because by now
it was after the Fast.[c] So Paul warned them,
10"Men, I can see that our voyage is going to
be disastrous and bring great loss to ship
and cargo, and to our own lives also." 11But
the centurion, instead of listening to what
Paul said, followed the advice of the pilot and
of the owner of the ship. 12Since the harbor
was unsuitable to winter in, the majority decided that we should sail on, hoping to reach
Phoenix and winter there. This was a harbor

[a] *14* Or *Hebrew* [b] *23* Or *Messiah* [c] *9* That is, the Day of Atonement (Yom Kippur)

in Crete, facing both southwest and northwest.

The Storm

13When a gentle south wind began to blow,
they thought they had obtained what they
wanted; so they weighed anchor and sailed
along the shore of Crete. 14Before very long,
a wind of hurricane force, called the
"northeaster," swept down from the island.
15The ship was caught by the storm and
could not head into the wind; so we gave way
to it and were driven along. 16As we passed
to the lee of a small island called Cauda, we
were hardly able to make the lifeboat secure.
17When the men had hoisted it aboard, they
passed ropes under the ship itself to hold it
together. Fearing that they would run
aground on the sandbars of Syrtis, they lowered the sea anchor and let the ship be
driven along. 18We took such a violent battering from the storm that the next day they
began to throw the cargo overboard. 19On
the third day, they threw the ship's tackle
overboard with their own hands. 20When
neither sun nor stars appeared for many
days and the storm continued raging, we
finally gave up all hope of being saved.

21After the men had gone a long time without food, Paul stood up before them and
said: "Men, you should have taken my advice not to sail from Crete; then you would
have spared yourselves this damage and
loss. 22But now I urge you to keep up your
courage, because not one of you will be lost;
only the ship will be destroyed. 23Last night
an angel of the God whose I am and whom I
serve stood beside me 24and said, 'Do not be
afraid, Paul. You must stand trial before
Caesar; and God has graciously given you
the lives of all who sail with you.' 25So keep
up your courage, men, for I have faith in God
that it will happen just as he told me. 26Never-
theless, we must run aground on some island."

The Shipwreck

27On the fourteenth night we were still being driven across the Adriatic[a] Sea, when
about midnight the sailors sensed they were
approaching land. 28They took soundings
and found that the water was a hundred and
twenty feet[b] deep. A short time later they
took soundings again and found it was ninety
feet[c] deep. 29Fearing that we would be
dashed against the rocks, they dropped four
anchors from the stern and prayed for daylight. 30In an attempt to escape from the ship,
the sailors let the lifeboat down into the sea,
pretending they were going to lower some
anchors from the bow. 31Then Paul said to
the centurion and the soldiers, "Unless these
men stay with the ship, you cannot be
saved." 32So the soldiers cut the ropes that
held the lifeboat and let it fall away.

33Just before dawn Paul urged them all to
eat. "For the last fourteen days," he said,
"you have been in constant suspense and
have gone without food—you haven't eaten
anything. 34Now I urge you to take some
food. You need it to survive. Not one of you
will lose a single hair from his head." 35After
he said this, he took some bread and gave
thanks to God in front of them all. Then he
broke it and began to eat. 36They were all
encouraged and ate some food themselves.
37Altogether there were 276 of us on board.
38When they had eaten as much as they
wanted, they lightened the ship by throwing
the grain into the sea.

39When daylight came, they did not recognize the land, but they saw a bay with a
sandy beach, where they decided to run the
ship aground if they could. 40Cutting loose
the anchors, they left them in the sea and at
the same time untied the ropes that held the
rudders. Then they hoisted the foresail to the
wind and made for the beach. 41But the ship
struck a sandbar and ran aground. The bow
stuck fast and would not move, and the stern
was broken to pieces by the pounding of the
surf.

42The soldiers planned to kill the prisoners
to prevent any of them from swimming away
and escaping. 43But the centurion wanted to
spare Paul's life and kept them from carrying
out their plan. He ordered those who could
swim to jump overboard first and get to land.
44The rest were to get there on planks or on
pieces of the ship. In this way everyone
reached land in safety.

Ashore on Malta

28 Once safely on shore, we found out
that the island was called Malta. 2The
islanders showed us unusual kindness.
They built a fire and welcomed us all because it was raining and cold. 3Paul gathered

[a]27 In ancient times the name referred to an area extending well south of Italy. [b]28 Greek *twenty orguias* (about 37 meters) [c]28 Greek *fifteen orguias* (about 27 meters)

a pile of brushwood and, as he put it on the
fire, a viper, driven out by the heat, fastened
itself on his hand. 4When the islanders saw
the snake hanging from his hand, they said
to each other, "This man must be a murderer; for though he escaped from the sea,
Justice has not allowed him to live." 5But
Paul shook the snake off into the fire and
suffered no ill effects. 6The people expected
him to swell up or suddenly fall dead, but
after waiting a long time and seeing nothing
unusual happen to him, they changed their
minds and said he was a god.

7There was an estate nearby that belonged to Publius, the chief official of the
island. He welcomed us to his home and for
three days entertained us hospitably. 8His
father was sick in bed, suffering from fever
and dysentery. Paul went in to see him and,
after prayer, placed his hands on him and
healed him. 9When this had happened, the
rest of the sick on the island came and were
cured. 10They honored us in many ways and
when we were ready to sail, they furnished
us with the supplies we needed.

Arrival at Rome

11After three months we put out to sea in a
ship that had wintered in the island. It was an
Alexandrian ship with the figurehead of the
twin gods Castor and Pollux. 12We put in at
Syracuse and stayed there three days.
13From there we set sail and arrived at
Rhegium. The next day the south wind came
up, and on the following day we reached
Puteoli. 14There we found some brothers
who invited us to spend a week with them.
And so we came to Rome. 15The brothers
there had heard that we were coming, and
they traveled as far as the Forum of Appius
and the Three Taverns to meet us. At the
sight of these men Paul thanked God and
was encouraged. 16When we got to Rome,
Paul was allowed to live by himself, with a
soldier to guard him.

Paul Preaches at Rome Under Guard

17Three days later he called together the
leaders of the Jews. When they had assembled, Paul said to them: "My brothers, although I have done nothing against our
people or against the customs of our ancestors, I was arrested in Jerusalem and handed over to the Romans. 18They examined me
and wanted to release me, because I was
not guilty of any crime deserving death. 19But
when the Jews objected, I was compelled to
appeal to Caesar—not that I had any charge
to bring against my own people. 20For this
reason I have asked to see you and talk with
you. It is because of the hope of Israel that I
am bound with this chain."

21They replied, "We have not received any
letters from Judea concerning you, and none
of the brothers who have come from there
has reported or said anything bad about you.
22But we want to hear what your views are,
for we know that people everywhere are talking against this sect."

23They arranged to meet Paul on a certain
day, and came in even larger numbers to the
place where he was staying. From morning
till evening he explained and declared to
them the kingdom of God and tried to convince them about Jesus from the Law of
Moses and from the Prophets. 24Some were
convinced by what he said, but others would
not believe. 25They disagreed among themselves and began to leave after Paul had
made this final statement: "The Holy Spirit
spoke the truth to your forefathers when he
said through Isaiah the prophet:

26" 'Go to this people and say,
"You will be ever hearing but never
understanding;
you will be ever seeing but never
perceiving."
27For this people's heart has become
calloused;
they hardly hear with their ears,
and they have closed their eyes.
Otherwise they might see with their eyes,
hear with their ears,
understand with their hearts
and turn, and I would heal them.'[a]

28"Therefore I want you to know that God's
salvation has been sent to the Gentiles, and
they will listen!"[b]

30For two whole years Paul stayed there in
his own rented house and welcomed all who
came to see him. 31Boldly and without hindrance he preached the kingdom of God and
taught about the Lord Jesus Christ.

[a]27 Isaiah 6:9,10 [b]28 Some manuscripts *listen!" 29After he said this, the Jews left, arguing vigorously among themselves.*

Romans

Introduction:

This letter was written by Paul to the church in Rome in A.D. 56 or 57 as he was finishing his third missionary journey. Paul had hoped to first go to Jerusalem and then on to Rome and Spain. He probably wrote this letter in preparation for his visit.

The theme of this letter is righteousness. Paul teaches in this letter that: 1) no human being is righteous; 2) Jesus Christ is perfectly righteous; 3) if we have faith in Jesus, we are freed from the power of sin, given a new life, and returned to a right relationship with God; 4) we should live Christian lives that are "holy and pleasing to God."

Outline of contents:

Introduction (1:1–17)
No one is righteous (1:18–3:20)
Righteousness through faith (3:21–8:39)
Israel in God's plan (9:1–11:36)
Christian living and relationships (12:1–15:13)
Conclusion and greetings (15:14–16:27)

---

1 Paul, a servant of Christ Jesus, called to
be an apostle and set apart for the gospel of God— 2the gospel he promised
beforehand through his prophets in the Holy
Scriptures 3regarding his Son, who as to his
human nature was a descendant of David,
4and who through the Spirit[a] of holiness was
declared with power to be the Son of God[b]
by his resurrection from the dead: Jesus
Christ our Lord. 5Through him and for his
name's sake, we received grace and apostleship to call people from among all the
Gentiles to the obedience that comes from
faith. 6And you also are among those who
are called to belong to Jesus Christ.

7To all in Rome who are loved by God and
called to be saints:

Grace and peace to you from God our
Father and from the Lord Jesus Christ.

Paul's Longing to Visit Rome

8First, I thank my God through Jesus
Christ for all of you, because your faith is
being reported all over the world. 9God,
whom I serve with my whole heart in preaching the gospel of his Son, is my witness how
constantly I remember you 10in my prayers at
all times; and I pray that now at last by God's
will the way may be opened for me to come
to you.

11I long to see you so that I may impart to
you some spiritual gift to make you strong—
12that is, that you and I may be mutually
encouraged by each other's faith. 13I do not
want you to be unaware, brothers, that I
planned many times to come to you (but
have been prevented from doing so until
now) in order that I might have a harvest
among you, just as I have had among the
other Gentiles.

14I am obligated both to Greeks and non-
Greeks, both to the wise and the foolish.
15That is why I am so eager to preach the
gospel also to you who are at Rome.

16I am not ashamed of the gospel, because it is the power of God for the salvation
of everyone who believes: first for the Jew,
then for the Gentile. 17For in the gospel a
righteousness from God is revealed, a righteousness that is by faith from first to last,[c]
just as it is written: "The righteous will live by
faith."[d]

[a]4 Or *who as to his spirit* [b]4 Or *was appointed to be the Son of God with power* [c]17 Or *is from faith to faith* [d]17 Hab. 2:4

God's Wrath Against Mankind

[18]The wrath of God is being revealed from heaven against all the godlessness and wickedness of men who suppress the truth by their wickedness, [19]since what may be known about God is plain to them, because God has made it plain to them. [20]For since the creation of the world God's invisible qualities—his eternal power and divine nature—have been clearly seen, being understood from what has been made, so that men are without excuse.

[21]For although they knew God, they neither glorified him as God nor gave thanks to him, but their thinking became futile and their foolish hearts were darkened. [22]Although they claimed to be wise, they became fools [23]and exchanged the glory of the immortal God for images made to look like mortal man and birds and animals and reptiles.

[24]Therefore God gave them over in the sinful desires of their hearts to sexual impurity for the degrading of their bodies with one another. [25]They exchanged the truth of God for a lie, and worshiped and served created things rather than the Creator—who is forever praised. Amen.

[26]Because of this, God gave them over to shameful lusts. Even their women exchanged natural relations for unnatural ones. [27]In the same way the men also abandoned natural relations with women and were inflamed with lust for one another. Men committed indecent acts with other men, and received in themselves the due penalty for their perversion.

[28]Furthermore, since they did not think it worthwhile to retain the knowledge of God, he gave them over to a depraved mind, to do what ought not to be done. [29]They have become filled with every kind of wickedness, evil, greed and depravity. They are full of envy, murder, strife, deceit and malice. They are gossips, [30]slanderers, God-haters, insolent, arrogant and boastful; they invent ways of doing evil; they disobey their parents; [31]they are senseless, faithless, heartless, ruthless. [32]Although they know God's righteous decree that those who do such things deserve death, they not only continue to do these very things but also approve of those who practice them.

God's Righteous Judgment

2 You, therefore, have no excuse, you who pass judgment on someone else, for at whatever point you judge the other, you are condemning yourself, because you who pass judgment do the same things. [2]Now we know that God's judgment against those who do such things is based on truth. [3]So when you, a mere man, pass judgment on them and yet do the same things, do you think you will escape God's judgment? [4]Or do you show contempt for the riches of his kindness, tolerance and patience, not realizing that God's kindness leads you toward repentance?

[5]But because of your stubbornness and your unrepentant heart, you are storing up wrath against yourself for the day of God's wrath, when his righteous judgment will be revealed. [6]God "will give to each person according to what he has done."[a] [7]To those who by persistence in doing good seek glory, honor and immortality, he will give eternal life. [8]But for those who are self-seeking and who reject the truth and follow evil, there will be wrath and anger. [9]There will be trouble and distress for every human being who does evil: first for the Jew, then for the Gentile; [10]but glory, honor and peace for everyone who does good: first for the Jew, then for the Gentile. [11]For God does not show favoritism.

[12]All who sin apart from the law will also perish apart from the law, and all who sin under the law will be judged by the law. [13]For it is not those who hear the law who are righteous in God's sight, but it is those who obey the law who will be declared righteous. [14](Indeed, when Gentiles, who do not have the law, do by nature things required by the law, they are a law for themselves, even though they do not have the law, [15]since they show that the requirements of the law are written on their hearts, their consciences also bearing witness, and their thoughts now accusing, now even defending them.) [16]This will take place on the day when God will judge men's secrets through Jesus Christ, as my gospel declares.

The Jews and the Law

[17]Now you, if you call yourself a Jew; if you rely on the law and brag about your relation-

[a]6 Psalm 62:12; Prov. 24:12

ship to God; 18if you know his will and approve of what is superior because you are
instructed by the law; 19if you are convinced
that you are a guide for the blind, a light for
those who are in the dark, 20an instructor of
the foolish, a teacher of infants, because you
have in the law the embodiment of knowledge and truth— 21you, then, who teach others, do you not teach yourself? You who
preach against stealing, do you steal? 22You
who say that people should not commit adultery, do you commit adultery? You who abhor idols, do you rob temples? 23You who
brag about the law, do you dishonor God by
breaking the law? 24As it is written: "God's
name is blasphemed among the Gentiles because of you."[a]

25Circumcision has value if you observe
the law, but if you break the law, you have
become as though you had not been circumcised. 26If those who are not circumcised
keep the law's requirements, will they not be
regarded as though they were circumcised?
27The one who is not circumcised physically
and yet obeys the law will condemn you who,
even though you have the[b] written code and
circumcision, are a lawbreaker.

28A man is not a Jew if he is only one
outwardly, nor is circumcision merely outward and physical. 29No, a man is a Jew if he
is one inwardly; and circumcision is circumcision of the heart, by the Spirit, not by the
written code. Such a man's praise is not from
men, but from God.

God's Faithfulness

3 What advantage, then, is there in being
a Jew, or what value is there in circumcision? 2Much in every way! First of all, they
have been entrusted with the very words of
God.

3What if some did not have faith? Will their
lack of faith nullify God's faithfulness? 4Not at
all! Let God be true, and every man a liar. As
it is written:

"So that you may be proved right when
you speak
and prevail when you judge."[c]

5But if our unrighteousness brings out
God's righteousness more clearly, what
[illegible]hall we say? That God is unjust in bringing
[illegible]wrath on us? (I am using a human argu-
[illegible] 6Certainly not! If that were so, how
could God judge the world? 7Someone might
argue, "If my falsehood enhances God's
truthfulness and so increases his glory, why
am I still condemned as a sinner?" 8Why not
say—as we are being slanderously reported
as saying and as some claim that we
say—"Let us do evil that good may result"?
Their condemnation is deserved.

No One Is Righteous

9What shall we conclude then? Are we any
better[d]? Not at all! We have already made
the charge that Jews and Gentiles alike are
all under sin. 10As it is written:

"There is no one righteous, not even one;
11 there is no one who understands,
no one who seeks God.
12All have turned away,
they have together become worthless;
there is no one who does good,
not even one."[e]
13"Their throats are open graves;
their tongues practice deceit."[f]
"The poison of vipers is on their lips."[g]
14 "Their mouths are full of cursing and
bitterness."[h]
15"Their feet are swift to shed blood;
16 ruin and misery mark their ways,
17and the way of peace they do not
know."[i]
18 "There is no fear of God before their
eyes."[j]

19Now we know that whatever the law
says, it says to those who are under the law,
so that every mouth may be silenced and the
whole world held accountable to God.
20Therefore no one will be declared righteous in his sight by observing the law; rather,
through the law we become conscious of sin.

Righteousness Through Faith

21But now a righteousness from God,
apart from law, has been made known, to
which the Law and the Prophets testify.
22This righteousness from God comes
through faith in Jesus Christ to all who believe. There is no difference, 23for all have
sinned and fall short of the glory of God,
24and are justified freely by his grace through
the redemption that came by Christ Jesus.
25God presented him as a sacrifice of atonement,[k] through faith in his blood. He did this
to demonstrate his justice, because in his

[illegible]2:5; Ezek. 36:22 [b]27 Or *who, by means of a* [c]4 Psalm 51:4 [d]9 Or *worse*
[illegible]4:1-3; 53:1-3; Eccles. 7:20 [f]13 Psalm 5:9 [g]13 Psalm 140:3 [h]14 Psalm 10:7
[illegible] [j]18 Psalm 36:1 [k]25 Or *as the one who would turn aside his wrath, taking away sin*

forbearance he had left the sins committed beforehand unpunished— [26]he did it to demonstrate his justice at the present time, so as to be just and the one who justifies those who have faith in Jesus.

[27]Where, then, is boasting? It is excluded. On what principle? On that of observing the law? No, but on that of faith. [28]For we maintain that a man is justified by faith apart from observing the law. [29]Is God the God of Jews only? Is he not the God of Gentiles too? Yes, of Gentiles too, [30]since there is only one God, who will justify the circumcised by faith and the uncircumcised through that same faith. [31]Do we, then, nullify the law by this faith? Not at all! Rather, we uphold the law.

Abraham Justified by Faith

4 What then shall we say that Abraham, our forefather, discovered in this matter? [2]If, in fact, Abraham was justified by works, he had something to boast about—but not before God. [3]What does the Scripture say? "Abraham believed God, and it was credited to him as righteousness."[a]

[4]Now when a man works, his wages are not credited to him as a gift, but as an obligation. [5]However, to the man who does not work but trusts God who justifies the wicked, his faith is credited as righteousness. [6]David says the same thing when he speaks of the blessedness of the man to whom God credits righteousness apart from works:

[7]"Blessed are they
whose transgressions are forgiven,
whose sins are covered.
[8]Blessed is the man
whose sin the Lord will never count
against him."[b]

[9]Is this blessedness only for the circumcised, or also for the uncircumcised? We have been saying that Abraham's faith was credited to him as righteousness. [10]Under what circumstances was it credited? Was it after he was circumcised, or before? It was not after, but before! [11]And he received the sign of circumcision, a seal of the righteousness that he had by faith while he was still uncircumcised. So then, he is the father of all who believe but have not been circumcised, in order that righteousness might be credited to them. [12]And he is also the father of the circumcised who not only are circumcised but who also walk in the footsteps of the faith that our father Abraham had before he was circumcised.

[13]It was not through law that Abraham and his offspring received the promise that he would be heir of the world, but through the righteousness that comes by faith. [14]For if those who live by law are heirs, faith has no value and the promise is worthless, [15]because law brings wrath. And where there is no law there is no transgression.

[16]Therefore, the promise comes by faith, so that it may be by grace and may be guaranteed to all Abraham's offspring—not only to those who are of the law but also to those who are of the faith of Abraham. He is the father of us all. [17]As it is written: "I have made you a father of many nations."[c] He is our father in the sight of God, in whom he believed—the God who gives life to the dead and calls things that are not as though they were.

[18]Against all hope, Abraham in hope believed and so became the father of many nations, just as it had been said to him, "So shall your offspring be."[d] [19]Without weakening in his faith, he faced the fact that his body was as good as dead—since he was about a hundred years old—and that Sarah's womb was also dead. [20]Yet he did not waver through unbelief regarding the promise of God, but was strengthened in his faith and gave glory to God, [21]being fully persuaded that God had power to do what he had promised. [22]This is why "it was credited to him as righteousness." [23]The words "it was credited to him" were written not for him alone, [24]but also for us, to whom God will credit righteousness—for us who believe in him who raised Jesus our Lord from the dead. [25]He was delivered over to death for our sins and was raised to life for our justification.

Peace and Joy

5 Therefore, since we have been justified through faith, we[e] have peace with God through our Lord Jesus Christ, [2]through whom we have gained access by faith into this grace in which we now stand. And we[e] rejoice in the hope of the glory of God. [3]Not only so, but we[e] also rejoice in our sufferings, because we know that suffering produces perseverance; [4]perseverance, character; and character, hope. [5]And hope does not disappoint us, because God has poured

[a] *3* Gen. 15:6; also in verse 22 [b] *8* Psalm 32:1,2 [c] *17* Gen. 17:5 [d] *18* Gen. 15:5 [e] *1,2,3* Or *let us*

out his love into our hearts by the Holy Spirit,
whom he has given us.
6You see, at just the right time, when we
were still powerless, Christ died for the
ungodly. 7Very rarely will anyone die for a
righteous man, though for a good man
someone might possibly dare to die. 8But
God demonstrates his own love for us in this:
While we were still sinners, Christ died for
us.
9Since we have now been justified by his
blood, how much more shall we be saved
from God's wrath through him! 10For if, when
we were God's enemies, we were reconciled
to him through the death of his Son, how
much more, having been reconciled, shall
we be saved through his life! 11Not only is
this so, but we also rejoice in God through
our Lord Jesus Christ, through whom we
have now received reconciliation.

Death Through Adam, Life Through Christ

12Therefore, just as sin entered the world
through one man, and death through sin,
and in this way death came to all men, because all sinned— 13for before the law was
given, sin was in the world. But sin is not
taken into account when there is no law.
14Nevertheless, death reigned from the time
of Adam to the time of Moses, even over
those who did not sin by breaking a command, as did Adam, who was a pattern of the
one to come.
15But the gift is not like the trespass. For if
the many died by the trespass of the one
man, how much more did God's grace and
the gift that came by the grace of the one
man, Jesus Christ, overflow to the many!
16Again, the gift of God is not like the result of
the one man's sin: The judgment followed
one sin and brought condemnation, but the
gift followed many trespasses and brought
justification. 17For if, by the trespass of the
one man, death reigned through that one
man, how much more will those who receive
God's abundant provision of grace and of the
gift of righteousness reign in life through the
one man, Jesus Christ.
18Consequently, just as the result of one
trespass was condemnation for all men, so
also the result of one act of righteousness
was justification that brings life for all men.
19For just as through the disobedience of the
one man the many were made sinners, so
also through the obedience of the one man
the many will be made righteous.
20The law was added so that the trespass
might increase. But where sin increased,
grace increased all the more, 21so that, just
as sin reigned in death, so also grace might
reign through righteousness to bring eternal
life through Jesus Christ our Lord.

Dead to Sin, Alive in Christ

6 What shall we say, then? Shall we go on
sinning so that grace may increase? 2By
no means! We died to sin; how can we live in
it any longer? 3Or don't you know that all of
us who were baptized into Christ Jesus were
baptized into his death? 4We were therefore
buried with him through baptism into death in
order that, just as Christ was raised from the
dead through the glory of the Father, we too
may live a new life.
5If we have been united with him like this in
his death, we will certainly also be united
with him in his resurrection. 6For we know
that our old self was crucified with him so that
the body of sin might be done away with,[a]
that we should no longer be slaves to sin—
7because anyone who has died has been
freed from sin.
8Now if we died with Christ, we believe that
we will also live with him. 9For we know that
since Christ was raised from the dead, he
cannot die again; death no longer has mastery over him. 10The death he died, he died to
sin once for all; but the life he lives, he lives to
God.
11In the same way, count yourselves dead
to sin but alive to God in Christ Jesus.
12Therefore do not let sin reign in your mortal
body so that you obey its evil desires. 13Do
not offer the parts of your body to sin, as
instruments of wickedness, but rather offer
yourselves to God, as those who have been
brought from death to life; and offer the parts
of your body to him as instruments of righteousness. 14For sin shall not be your master,
because you are not under law, but under
grace.

Slaves to Righteousness

15What then? Shall we sin because we are
not under law but under grace? By no
means! 16Don't you know that when you offer
yourselves to someone to obey him as
slaves, you are slaves to the one whom you
obey—whether you are slaves to sin, which

[a]6 Or *be rendered powerless*

leads to death, or to obedience, which leads
to righteousness? 17But thanks be to God
that, though you used to be slaves to sin, you
wholeheartedly obeyed the form of teaching
to which you were entrusted. 18You have
been set free from sin and have become
slaves to righteousness.

19I put this in human terms because you
are weak in your natural selves. Just as you
used to offer the parts of your body in slavery
to impurity and to ever-increasing wickedness, so now offer them in slavery to righteousness leading to holiness. 20When you
were slaves to sin, you were free from the
control of righteousness. 21What benefit did
you reap at that time from the things you are
now ashamed of? Those things result in
death! 22But now that you have been set free
from sin and have become slaves to God,
the benefit you reap leads to holiness, and
the result is eternal life. 23For the wages of
sin is death, but the gift of God is eternal life
in[a] Christ Jesus our Lord.

An Illustration From Marriage

7 Do you not know, brothers—for I am
speaking to men who know the law—
that the law has authority over a man only as
long as he lives? 2For example, by law a
married woman is bound to her husband as
long as he is alive, but if her husband dies,
she is released from the law of marriage. 3So
then, if she marries another man while her
husband is still alive, she is called an adulteress. But if her husband dies, she is released
from that law and is not an adulteress, even
though she marries another man.

4So, my brothers, you also died to the law
through the body of Christ, that you might
belong to another, to him who was raised
from the dead, in order that we might bear
fruit to God. 5For when we were controlled by
the sinful nature,[b] the sinful passions
aroused by the law were at work in our bodies, so that we bore fruit for death. 6But now,
by dying to what once bound us, we have
been released from the law so that we serve
in the new way of the Spirit, and not in the old
way of the written code.

Struggling With Sin

7What shall we say, then? Is the law sin?
Certainly not! Indeed I would not have known
what sin was except through the law. For I
would not have known what coveting really
was if the law had not said, "Do not covet."[c]
8But sin, seizing the opportunity afforded by
the commandment, produced in me every
kind of covetous desire. For apart from law,
sin is dead. 9Once I was alive apart from law;
but when the commandment came, sin
sprang to life and I died. 10I found that the
very commandment that was intended to
bring life actually brought death. 11For sin,
seizing the opportunity afforded by the commandment, deceived me, and through the
commandment put me to death. 12So then,
the law is holy, and the commandment is
holy, righteous and good.

13Did that which is good, then, become
death to me? By no means! But in order that
sin might be recognized as sin, it produced
death in me through what was good, so that
through the commandment sin might
become utterly sinful.

14We know that the law is spiritual; but I am
unspiritual, sold as a slave to sin. 15I do not
understand what I do. For what I want to do I
do not do, but what I hate I do. 16And if I do
what I do not want to do, I agree that the law
is good. 17As it is, it is no longer I myself who
do it, but it is sin living in me. 18I know that
nothing good lives in me, that is, in my sinful
nature.[d] For I have the desire to do what is
good, but I cannot carry it out. 19For what I do
is not the good I want to do; no, the evil I do
not want to do—this I keep on doing. 20Now if
I do what I do not want to do, it is no longer I
who do it, but it is sin living in me that does it.

21So I find this law at work: When I want to
do good, evil is right there with me. 22For in
my inner being I delight in God's law; 23but I
see another law at work in the members of
my body, waging war against the law of my
mind and making me a prisoner of the law of
sin at work within my members. 24What a
wretched man I am! Who will rescue me from
this body of death? 25Thanks be to God—
through Jesus Christ our Lord!

So then, I myself in my mind am a slave to
God's law, but in the sinful nature a slave to
the law of sin.

Life Through the Spirit

8 Therefore, there is now no condemnation for those who are in Christ Jesus,[e]
2because through Christ Jesus the law of the
Spirit of life set me free from the law of sin

[a]*23* Or *through* [b]*5* Or *the flesh;* also in verse 25 [c]*7* Exodus 20:17; Deut. 5:21 [d]*18* Or *my flesh*
[e]*1* Some later manuscripts *Jesus, who do not live according to the sinful nature but according to the Spirit,*

and death. 3For what the law was powerless
to do in that it was weakened by the sinful
nature,[a] God did by sending his own Son in
the likeness of sinful man to be a sin offering.[b] And so he condemned sin in sinful
man,[c] 4in order that the righteous requirements of the law might be fully met in
us, who do not live according to the sinful
nature but according to the Spirit.

5Those who live according to the sinful nature have their minds set on what that nature
desires; but those who live in accordance
with the Spirit have their minds set on what
the Spirit desires. 6The mind of sinful man[d] is
death, but the mind controlled by the Spirit is
life and peace; 7the sinful mind[e] is hostile to
God. It does not submit to God's law, nor can
it do so. 8Those controlled by the sinful nature cannot please God.

9You, however, are controlled not by the
sinful nature but by the Spirit, if the Spirit of
God lives in you. And if anyone does not
have the Spirit of Christ, he does not belong
to Christ. 10But if Christ is in you, your body is
dead because of sin, yet your spirit is alive
because of righteousness. 11And if the Spirit
of him who raised Jesus from the dead is
living in you, he who raised Christ from the
dead will also give life to your mortal bodies
through his Spirit, who lives in you.

12Therefore, brothers, we have an obligation—but it is not to the sinful nature, to live
according to it. 13For if you live according to
the sinful nature, you will die; but if by the
Spirit you put to death the misdeeds of the
body, you will live, 14because those who are
led by the Spirit of God are sons of God.
15For you did not receive a spirit that makes
you a slave again to fear, but you received
the Spirit of sonship.[f] And by him we cry,
"*Abba*,[g] Father." 16The Spirit himself testifies with our spirit that we are God's children.
17Now if we are children, then we are heirs—
heirs of God and co-heirs with Christ, if indeed we share in his sufferings in order that
we may also share in his glory.

Future Glory

18I consider that our present sufferings are
not worth comparing with the glory that will
be revealed in us. 19The creation waits in
eager expectation for the sons of God to be
revealed. 20For the creation was subjected to
frustration, not by its own choice, but by the
will of the one who subjected it, in hope
21that[h] the creation itself will be liberated
from its bondage to decay and brought into
the glorious freedom of the children of God.

22We know that the whole creation has
been groaning as in the pains of childbirth
right up to the present time. 23Not only so, but
we ourselves, who have the firstfruits of the
Spirit, groan inwardly as we wait eagerly for
our adoption as sons, the redemption of our
bodies. 24For in this hope we were saved.
But hope that is seen is no hope at all. Who
hopes for what he already has? 25But if we
hope for what we do not yet have, we wait for
it patiently.

26In the same way, the Spirit helps us in
our weakness. We do not know what we
ought to pray for, but the Spirit himself intercedes for us with groans that words cannot
express. 27And he who searches our hearts
knows the mind of the Spirit, because the
Spirit intercedes for the saints in accordance
with God's will.

More Than Conquerors

28And we know that in all things God works
for the good of those who love him,[i] who[j]
have been called according to his purpose.
29For those God foreknew he also predestined to be conformed to the likeness of his
Son, that he might be the firstborn among
many brothers. 30And those he predestined,
he also called; those he called, he also justified; those he justified, he also glorified.

31What, then, shall we say in response to
this? If God is for us, who can be against us?
32He who did not spare his own Son, but
gave him up for us all—how will he not also,
along with him, graciously give us all things?
33Who will bring any charge against those
whom God has chosen? It is God who justifies. 34Who is he that condemns? Christ
Jesus, who died—more than that, who was
raised to life—is at the right hand of God and
is also interceding for us. 35Who shall separate us from the love of Christ? Shall trouble
or hardship or persecution or famine or
nakedness or danger or sword? 36As it is
written:

[a]3 Or *the flesh;* also in verses 4, 5, 8, 9, 12 and 13 [b]3 Or *man, for sin* [c]3 Or *in the flesh* [d]6 Or *mind set on the flesh* [e]7 Or *the mind set on the flesh* [f]15 Or *adoption* [g]15 Aramaic for *Father*
[h]20,21 Or *subjected it in hope.* [21]*For* [i]28 Some manuscripts *And we know that all things work together for good to those who love God* [j]28 Or *works together with those who love him to bring about what is good—with those who*

"For your sake we face death all day
long;
we are considered as sheep to be
slaughtered."[a]

37No, in all these things we are more than
conquerors through him who loved us. 38For
I am convinced that neither death nor life,
neither angels nor demons,[b] neither the
present nor the future, nor any powers,
39neither height nor depth, nor anything else
in all creation, will be able to separate us
from the love of God that is in Christ Jesus
our Lord.

God's Sovereign Choice

9 I speak the truth in Christ—I am not lying, my conscience confirms it in the
Holy Spirit— 2I have great sorrow and unceasing anguish in my heart. 3For I could
wish that I myself were cursed and cut off
from Christ for the sake of my brothers, those
of my own race, 4the people of Israel. Theirs
is the adoption as sons; theirs the divine
glory, the covenants, the receiving of the
law, the temple worship and the promises.
5Theirs are the patriarchs, and from them is
traced the human ancestry of Christ, who is
God over all, forever praised![c] Amen.

6It is not as though God's word had failed.
For not all who are descended from Israel
are Israel. 7Nor because they are his descendants are they all Abraham's children.
On the contrary, "It is through Isaac that your
offspring will be reckoned."[d] 8In other words,
it is not the natural children who are God's
children, but it is the children of the promise
who are regarded as Abraham's offspring.
9For this was how the promise was stated:
"At the appointed time I will return, and Sarah will have a son."[e]

10Not only that, but Rebekah's children
had one and the same father, our father
Isaac. 11Yet, before the twins were born or
had done anything good or bad—in order
that God's purpose in election might stand:
12not by works but by him who calls—she
was told, "The older will serve the younger."[f] 13Just as it is written: "Jacob I loved,
but Esau I hated."[g]

14What then shall we say? Is God unjust?
Not at all! 15For he says to Moses,

"I will have mercy on whom I have mercy,
and I will have compassion on whom I
have compassion."[h]

16It does not, therefore, depend on man's
desire or effort, but on God's mercy. 17For
the Scripture says to Pharaoh: "I raised you
up for this very purpose, that I might display
my power in you and that my name might be
proclaimed in all the earth."[i] 18Therefore
God has mercy on whom he wants to have
mercy, and he hardens whom he wants to
harden.

19One of you will say to me: "Then why
does God still blame us? For who resists his
will?" 20But who are you, O man, to talk back
to God? "Shall what is formed say to him
who formed it, 'Why did you make me like
this?' "[j] 21Does not the potter have the right
to make out of the same lump of clay some
pottery for noble purposes and some for
common use?

22What if God, choosing to show his wrath
and make his power known, bore with great
patience the objects of his wrath—prepared
for destruction? 23What if he did this to make
the riches of his glory known to the objects of
his mercy, whom he prepared in advance for
glory— 24even us, whom he also called, not
only from the Jews but also from the Gentiles? 25As he says in Hosea:

"I will call them 'my people' who are not
my people;
and I will call her 'my loved one' who is
not my loved one,"[k]

26and,

"It will happen that in the very place
where it was said to them,
'You are not my people,'
they will be called 'sons of the living
God.' "[l]

27Isaiah cries out concerning Israel:

"Though the number of the Israelites be
like the sand by the sea,
only the remnant will be saved.
28For the Lord will carry out
his sentence on earth with speed and
finality."[m]

29It is just as Isaiah said previously:

"Unless the Lord Almighty
had left us descendants,

[a]*36* Psalm 44:22 [b]*38* Or *nor heavenly rulers* [c]*5* Or *Christ, who is over all. God be forever praised!* Or *Christ. God who is over all be forever praised!* [d]*7* Gen. 21:12 [e]*9* Gen. 18:10,14 [f]*12* Gen. 25:23 [g]*13* Mal. 1:2,3 [h]*15* Exodus 33:19 [i]*17* Exodus 9:16 [j]*20* Isaiah 29:16; 45:9 [k]*25* Hosea 2:23 [l]*26* Hosea 1:10 [m]*28* Isaiah 10:22,23

we would have become like Sodom,
we would have been like Gomorrah."[a]

Israel's Unbelief

30What then shall we say? That the Gentiles, who did not pursue righteousness,
have obtained it, a righteousness that is by
faith; 31but Israel, who pursued a law of righteousness, has not attained it. 32Why not?
Because they pursued it not by faith but as if
it were by works. They stumbled over the
"stumbling stone." 33As it is written:

"See, I lay in Zion a stone that causes
men to stumble
and a rock that makes them fall,
and the one who trusts in him will never
be put to shame."[b]

10 Brothers, my heart's desire and
prayer to God for the Israelites is that
they may be saved. 2For I can testify about
them that they are zealous for God, but their
zeal is not based on knowledge. 3Since they
did not know the righteousness that comes
from God and sought to establish their own,
they did not submit to God's righteousness.
4Christ is the end of the law so that there may
be righteousness for everyone who believes.
5Moses describes in this way the righteousness that is by the law: "The man who
does these things will live by them."[c] 6But
the righteousness that is by faith says: "Do
not say in your heart, 'Who will ascend into
heaven?'[d] " (that is, to bring Christ down)
7"or 'Who will descend into the deep?'[e]"
(that is, to bring Christ up from the dead).
8But what does it say? "The word is near
you; it is in your mouth and in your heart,"[f]
that is, the word of faith we are proclaiming:
9That if you confess with your mouth, "Jesus
is Lord," and believe in your heart that God
raised him from the dead, you will be saved.
10For it is with your heart that you believe and
are justified, and it is with your mouth that
you confess and are saved. 11As the Scripture says, "Anyone who trusts in him will
never be put to shame."[g] 12For there is no
difference between Jew and Gentile—the
same Lord is Lord of all and richly blesses all
who call on him, 13for, "Everyone who calls
on the name of the Lord will be saved."[h]
14How, then, can they call on the one they
have not believed in? And how can they believe in the one of whom they have not
heard? And how can they hear without
someone preaching to them? 15And how can
they preach unless they are sent? As it is
written, "How beautiful are the feet of those
who bring good news!"[i]
16But not all the Israelites accepted the
good news. For Isaiah says, "Lord, who has
believed our message?"[j] 17Consequently,
faith comes from hearing the message, and
the message is heard through the word of
Christ. 18But I ask: Did they not hear? Of
course they did:

"Their voice has gone out into all the
earth,
their words to the ends of the world."[k]

19Again I ask: Did Israel not understand?
First, Moses says,

"I will make you envious by those who
are not a nation;
I will make you angry by a nation that
has no understanding."[l]

20And Isaiah boldly says,

"I was found by those who did not seek
me;
I revealed myself to those who did not
ask for me."[m]

21But concerning Israel he says,

"All day long I have held out my hands
to a disobedient and obstinate
people."[n]

The Remnant of Israel

11 I ask then: Did God reject his people?
By no means! I am an Israelite myself, a descendant of Abraham, from the
tribe of Benjamin. 2God did not reject his
people, whom he foreknew. Don't you know
what the Scripture says in the passage about
Elijah—how he appealed to God against Israel: 3"Lord, they have killed your prophets
and torn down your altars; I am the only one
left, and they are trying to kill me"[o]? 4And
what was God's answer to him? "I have reserved for myself seven thousand who have
not bowed the knee to Baal."[p] 5So too, at the
present time there is a remnant chosen by
grace. 6And if by grace, then it is no longer by

a29 Isaiah 1:9 b33 Isaiah 8:14; 28:16 c5 Lev. 18:5 d6 Deut. 30:12 e7 Deut. 30:13
f8 Deut. 30:14 g11 Isaiah 28:16 h13 Joel 2:32 i15 Isaiah 52:7 j16 Isaiah 53:1
k18 Psalm 19:4 l19 Deut. 32:21 m20 Isaiah 65:1 n21 Isaiah 65:2 o3 1 Kings 19:10,14
p4 1 Kings 19:18

works; if it were, grace would no longer be
grace.[a]
7What then? What Israel sought so earnestly it did not obtain, but the elect did. The
others were hardened, 8as it is written:

"God gave them a spirit of stupor,
eyes so that they could not see
and ears so that they could not hear,
to this very day."[b]

9And David says:

"May their table become a snare and a
trap,
a stumbling block and a retribution for
them.
10May their eyes be darkened so they
cannot see,
and their backs be bent forever."[c]

Ingrafted Branches

11Again I ask: Did they stumble so as to fall
beyond recovery? Not at all! Rather, because of their transgression, salvation has
come to the Gentiles to make Israel envious.
12But if their transgression means riches for
the world, and their loss means riches for the
Gentiles, how much greater riches will their
fullness bring!
13I am talking to you Gentiles. Inasmuch as
I am the apostle to the Gentiles, I make much
of my ministry 14in the hope that I may somehow arouse my own people to envy and save
some of them. 15For if their rejection is the
reconciliation of the world, what will their acceptance be but life from the dead? 16If the
part of the dough offered as firstfruits is holy,
then the whole batch is holy; if the root is
holy, so are the branches.
17If some of the branches have been broken off, and you, though a wild olive shoot,
have been grafted in among the others and
now share in the nourishing sap from the
olive root, 18do not boast over those
branches. If you do, consider this: You do not
support the root, but the root supports you.
19You will say then, "Branches were broken
off so that I could be grafted in." 20Granted.
But they were broken off because of unbelief, and you stand by faith. Do not be
arrogant, but be afraid. 21For if God did not
spare the natural branches, he will not spare
you either.
22Consider therefore the kindness and
sternness of God: sternness to those who
fell, but kindness to you, provided that you
continue in his kindness. Otherwise, you
also will be cut off. 23And if they do not persist
in unbelief, they will be grafted in, for God is
able to graft them in again. 24After all, if you
were cut out of an olive tree that is wild by
nature, and contrary to nature were grafted
into a cultivated olive tree, how much more
readily will these, the natural branches, be
grafted into their own olive tree!

All Israel Will Be Saved

25I do not want you to be ignorant of this
mystery, brothers, so that you may not be
conceited: Israel has experienced a hardening in part until the full number of the Gentiles
has come in. 26And so all Israel will be saved,
as it is written:

"The deliverer will come from Zion;
he will turn godlessness away from
Jacob.
27And this is[d] my covenant with them
when I take away their sins."[e]

28As far as the gospel is concerned, they
are enemies on your account; but as far as
election is concerned, they are loved on account of the patriarchs, 29for God's gifts and
his call are irrevocable. 30Just as you who
were at one time disobedient to God have
now received mercy as a result of their disobedience, 31so they too have now become
disobedient in order that they too may now[f]
receive mercy as a result of God's mercy to
you. 32For God has bound all men over to
disobedience so that he may have mercy on
them all.

Doxology

33Oh, the depth of the riches of the wisdom
and[g] knowledge of God!
How unsearchable his judgments,
and his paths beyond tracing out!
34"Who has known the mind of the Lord?
Or who has been his counselor?"[h]
35"Who has ever given to God,
that God should repay him?"[i]
36For from him and through him and to him
are all things.
To him be the glory forever! Amen.

[a]*6* Some manuscripts *by grace. But if by works, then it is no longer grace; if it were, work would no longer be work.*
[b]*8* Deut. 29:4; Isaiah 29:10
[c]*10* Psalm 69:22,23
[d]*27* Or *will be*
[e]*27* Isaiah 59:20,21; 27:9; Jer. 31:33,34
[f]*31* Some manuscripts do not have *now.*
[g]*33* Or *riches and the wisdom and the*
[h]*34* Isaiah 40:13
[i]*35* Job 41:11

Living Sacrifices

12 Therefore, I urge you, brothers, in view of God's mercy, to offer your bodies as living sacrifices, holy and pleasing to God—this is your spiritual[a] act of worship. 2Do not conform any longer to the pattern of this world, but be transformed by the renewing of your mind. Then you will be able to test and approve what God's will is—his good, pleasing and perfect will.

3For by the grace given me I say to every one of you: Do not think of yourself more highly than you ought, but rather think of yourself with sober judgment, in accordance with the measure of faith God has given you. 4Just as each of us has one body with many members, and these members do not all have the same function, 5so in Christ we who are many form one body, and each member belongs to all the others. 6We have different gifts, according to the grace given us. If a man's gift is prophesying, let him use it in proportion to his[b] faith. 7If it is serving, let him serve; if it is teaching, let him teach; 8if it is encouraging, let him encourage; if it is contributing to the needs of others, let him give generously; if it is leadership, let him govern diligently; if it is showing mercy, let him do it cheerfully.

Love

9Love must be sincere. Hate what is evil; cling to what is good. 10Be devoted to one another in brotherly love. Honor one another above yourselves. 11Never be lacking in zeal, but keep your spiritual fervor, serving the Lord. 12Be joyful in hope, patient in affliction, faithful in prayer. 13Share with God's people who are in need. Practice hospitality.

14Bless those who persecute you; bless and do not curse. 15Rejoice with those who rejoice; mourn with those who mourn. 16Live in harmony with one another. Do not be proud, but be willing to associate with people of low position.[c] Do not be conceited.

17Do not repay anyone evil for evil. Be careful to do what is right in the eyes of everybody. 18If it is possible, as far as it depends on you, live at peace with everyone. 19Do not take revenge, my friends, but leave room for God's wrath, for it is written: "It is mine to avenge; I will repay,"[d] says the Lord. 20On the contrary:

"If your enemy is hungry, feed him;
if he is thirsty, give him something to drink.
In doing this, you will heap burning coals on his head."[e]

21Do not be overcome by evil, but overcome evil with good.

Submission to the Authorities

13 Everyone must submit himself to the governing authorities, for there is no authority except that which God has established. The authorities that exist have been established by God. 2Consequently, he who rebels against the authority is rebelling against what God has instituted, and those who do so will bring judgment on themselves. 3For rulers hold no terror for those who do right, but for those who do wrong. Do you want to be free from fear of the one in authority? Then do what is right and he will commend you. 4For he is God's servant to do you good. But if you do wrong, be afraid, for he does not bear the sword for nothing. He is God's servant, an agent of wrath to bring punishment on the wrongdoer. 5Therefore, it is necessary to submit to the authorities, not only because of possible punishment but also because of conscience.

6This is also why you pay taxes, for the authorities are God's servants, who give their full time to governing. 7Give everyone what you owe him: If you owe taxes, pay taxes; if revenue, then revenue; if respect, then respect; if honor, then honor.

Love, for the Day Is Near

8Let no debt remain outstanding, except the continuing debt to love one another, for he who loves his fellowman has fulfilled the law. 9The commandments, "Do not commit adultery," "Do not murder," "Do not steal," "Do not covet,"[f] and whatever other commandment there may be, are summed up in this one rule: "Love your neighbor as yourself."[g] 10Love does no harm to its neighbor. Therefore love is the fulfillment of the law.

11And do this, understanding the present time. The hour has come for you to wake up from your slumber, because our salvation is nearer now than when we first believed. 12The night is nearly over; the day is almost

[a] *1* Or *reasonable* [b] *6* Or *in agreement with the* [c] *16* Or *willing to do menial work* [d] *19* Deut. 32:35
[e] *20* Prov. 25:21,22 [f] *9* Exodus 20:13-15,17; Deut. 5:17-19,21 [g] *9* Lev. 19:18

here. So let us put aside the deeds of darkness and put on the armor of light. [13]Let us behave decently, as in the daytime, not in orgies and drunkenness, not in sexual immorality and debauchery, not in dissension and jealousy. [14]Rather, clothe yourselves with the Lord Jesus Christ, and do not think about how to gratify the desires of the sinful nature.[a]

The Weak and the Strong

14 Accept him whose faith is weak, without passing judgment on disputable matters. [2]One man's faith allows him to eat everything, but another man, whose faith is weak, eats only vegetables. [3]The man who eats everything must not look down on him who does not, and the man who does not eat everything must not condemn the man who does, for God has accepted him. [4]Who are you to judge someone else's servant? To his own master he stands or falls. And he will stand, for the Lord is able to make him stand.

[5]One man considers one day more sacred than another; another man considers every day alike. Each one should be fully convinced in his own mind. [6]He who regards one day as special, does so to the Lord. He who eats meat, eats to the Lord, for he gives thanks to God; and he who abstains, does so to the Lord and gives thanks to God. [7]For none of us lives to himself alone and none of us dies to himself alone. [8]If we live, we live to the Lord; and if we die, we die to the Lord. So, whether we live or die, we belong to the Lord.

[9]For this very reason, Christ died and returned to life so that he might be the Lord of both the dead and the living. [10]You, then, why do you judge your brother? Or why do you look down on your brother? For we will all stand before God's judgment seat. [11]It is written:

" 'As surely as I live,' says the Lord,
'every knee will bow before me;
every tongue will confess to God.' "[b]

[12]So then, each of us will give an account of himself to God.

[13]Therefore let us stop passing judgment on one another. Instead, make up your mind not to put any stumbling block or obstacle in your brother's way. [14]As one who is in the Lord Jesus, I am fully convinced that no food[c] is unclean in itself. But if anyone regards something as unclean, then for him it is unclean. [15]If your brother is distressed because of what you eat, you are no longer acting in love. Do not by your eating destroy your brother for whom Christ died. [16]Do not allow what you consider good to be spoken of as evil. [17]For the kingdom of God is not a matter of eating and drinking, but of righteousness, peace and joy in the Holy Spirit, [18]because anyone who serves Christ in this way is pleasing to God and approved by men.

[19]Let us therefore make every effort to do what leads to peace and to mutual edification. [20]Do not destroy the work of God for the sake of food. All food is clean, but it is wrong for a man to eat anything that causes someone else to stumble. [21]It is better not to eat meat or drink wine or to do anything else that will cause your brother to fall.

[22]So whatever you believe about these things keep between yourself and God. Blessed is the man who does not condemn himself by what he approves. [23]But the man who has doubts is condemned if he eats, because his eating is not from faith; and everything that does not come from faith is sin.

15 We who are strong ought to bear with the failings of the weak and not to please ourselves. [2]Each of us should please his neighbor for his good, to build him up. [3]For even Christ did not please himself but, as it is written: "The insults of those who insult you have fallen on me."[d] [4]For everything that was written in the past was written to teach us, so that through endurance and the encouragement of the Scriptures we might have hope.

[5]May the God who gives endurance and encouragement give you a spirit of unity among yourselves as you follow Christ Jesus, [6]so that with one heart and mouth you may glorify the God and Father of our Lord Jesus Christ.

[7]Accept one another, then, just as Christ accepted you, in order to bring praise to God. [8]For I tell you that Christ has become a servant of the Jews[e] on behalf of God's truth, to confirm the promises made to the patriarchs [9]so that the Gentiles may glorify God for his mercy, as it is written:

[a]14 Or *the flesh* [b]11 Isaiah 45:23 [c]14 Or *that nothing* [d]3 Psalm 69:9 [e]8 Greek *circumcision*

"Therefore I will praise you among the
Gentiles;
I will sing hymns to your name."[a]

10Again, it says,

"Rejoice, O Gentiles, with his people."[b]

11And again,

"Praise the Lord, all you Gentiles,
and sing praises to him, all you
peoples."[c]

12And again, Isaiah says,

"The Root of Jesse will spring up,
one who will arise to rule over the
nations;
the Gentiles will hope in him."[d]

13May the God of hope fill you with all joy
and peace as you trust in him, so that you
may overflow with hope by the power of the
Holy Spirit.

Paul the Minister to the Gentiles

14I myself am convinced, my brothers, that
you yourselves are full of goodness, complete in knowledge and competent to instruct
one another. 15I have written you quite boldly
on some points, as if to remind you of them
again, because of the grace God gave me
16to be a minister of Christ Jesus to the Gentiles with the priestly duty of proclaiming the
gospel of God, so that the Gentiles might
become an offering acceptable to God,
sanctified by the Holy Spirit.

17Therefore I glory in Christ Jesus in my
service to God. 18I will not venture to speak of
anything except what Christ has accomplished through me in leading the Gentiles to
obey God by what I have said and done—
19by the power of signs and miracles,
through the power of the Spirit. So from
Jerusalem all the way around to Illyricum, I
have fully proclaimed the gospel of Christ.
20It has always been my ambition to preach
the gospel where Christ was not known, so
that I would not be building on someone
else's foundation. 21Rather, as it is written:

"Those who were not told about him will
see,
and those who have not heard will
understand."[e]

22This is why I have often been hindered
from coming to you.

Paul's Plan to Visit Rome

23But now that there is no more place for
me to work in these regions, and since I have
been longing for many years to see you, 24I
plan to do so when I go to Spain. I hope to
visit you while passing through and to have
you assist me on my journey there, after I
have enjoyed your company for a while.
25Now, however, I am on my way to Jerusalem in the service of the saints there. 26For
Macedonia and Achaia were pleased to
make a contribution for the poor among the
saints in Jerusalem. 27They were pleased to
do it, and indeed they owe it to them. For if
the Gentiles have shared in the Jews' spiritual blessings, they owe it to the Jews to
share with them their material blessings.
28So after I have completed this task and
have made sure that they have received this
fruit, I will go to Spain and visit you on the
way. 29I know that when I come to you, I will
come in the full measure of the blessing of
Christ.

30I urge you, brothers, by our Lord Jesus
Christ and by the love of the Spirit, to join me
in my struggle by praying to God for me.
31Pray that I may be rescued from the unbelievers in Judea and that my service in
Jerusalem may be acceptable to the saints
there, 32so that by God's will I may come to
you with joy and together with you be refreshed. 33The God of peace be with you all.
Amen.

Personal Greetings

16 I commend to you our sister Phoebe,
a servant[f] of the church in Cenchrea. 2I ask you to receive her in the Lord in
a way worthy of the saints and to give her
any help she may need from you, for she has
been a great help to many people, including
me.

3Greet Priscilla[g] and Aquila, my fellow
workers in Christ Jesus. 4They risked
their lives for me. Not only I but all the
churches of the Gentiles are grateful to
them.
5Greet also the church that meets at their
house.

[a] 9 2 Samuel 22:50; Psalm 18:49 [b] 10 Deut. 32:43 [c] 11 Psalm 117:1 [d] 12 Isaiah 11:10
[e] 21 Isaiah 52:15 [f] 1 Or *deaconess* [g] 3 Greek *Prisca*, a variant of *Priscilla*

Greet my dear friend Epenetus, who was the first convert to Christ in the province of Asia.
[6]Greet Mary, who worked very hard for you.
[7]Greet Andronicus and Junias, my relatives who have been in prison with me. They are outstanding among the apostles, and they were in Christ before I was.
[8]Greet Ampliatus, whom I love in the Lord.
[9]Greet Urbanus, our fellow worker in Christ, and my dear friend Stachys.
[10]Greet Apelles, tested and approved in Christ.
Greet those who belong to the household of Aristobulus.
[11]Greet Herodion, my relative.
Greet those in the household of Narcissus who are in the Lord.
[12]Greet Tryphena and Tryphosa, those women who work hard in the Lord.
Greet my dear friend Persis, another woman who has worked very hard in the Lord.
[13]Greet Rufus, chosen in the Lord, and his mother, who has been a mother to me, too.
[14]Greet Asyncritus, Phlegon, Hermes, Patrobas, Hermas and the brothers with them.
[15]Greet Philologus, Julia, Nereus and his sister, and Olympas and all the saints with them.
[16]Greet one another with a holy kiss.
All the churches of Christ send greetings.

[17]I urge you, brothers, to watch out for
those who cause divisions and put obstacles
in your way that are contrary to the teaching
you have learned. Keep away from them.
[18]For such people are not serving our Lord
Christ, but their own appetites. By smooth
talk and flattery they deceive the minds of
naive people. [19]Everyone has heard about
your obedience, so I am full of joy over you;
but I want you to be wise about what is good,
and innocent about what is evil.

[20]The God of peace will soon crush Satan
under your feet.

The grace of our Lord Jesus be with you.

[21]Timothy, my fellow worker, sends his
greetings to you, as do Lucius, Jason and
Sosipater, my relatives.

[22]I, Tertius, who wrote down this letter,
greet you in the Lord.

[23]Gaius, whose hospitality I and the whole
church here enjoy, sends you his greetings.

Erastus, who is the city's director of public
works, and our brother Quartus send you
their greetings.[a]

[25]Now to him who is able to establish you
by my gospel and the proclamation of Jesus
Christ, according to the revelation of the
mystery hidden for long ages past, [26]but now
revealed and made known through the prophetic writings by the command of the eternal God, so that all nations might believe and
obey him— [27]to the only wise God be glory
forever through Jesus Christ! Amen.

[a]23 Some manuscripts *their greetings.* [24]*May the grace of our Lord Jesus Christ be with all of you. Amen.*

I Corinthians

Introduction:

This letter was written by Paul to the church in Corinth, probably in the winter of A.D. 55. It was while he was in Ephesus that he sent this letter in response to a letter from the Corinthian church.

Located on the Mediterranean, the city of Corinth was a wealthy trading center. It was also a wicked city and was known for that throughout the Roman world. Because the church in Corinth was new it was hard for the Christians there not to act like their neighbors, so the church had some problems.

The Christians in Corinth were not getting along with one another—they were taking sides. Some of them were living very sinful lives. Paul wrote this letter to scold them and teach them how Christians should act. He tried to teach practical lessons about the Christian life so that people in Corinth would know right from wrong.

Outline of contents:

Greetings and thanksgiving (1:1–9)
Divisions in the church (1:10–4:21)
Sexual immorality and lawsuits (5:1–6:20)
Marriage (7:1–40)
Christian rights and responsibility (8:1–11:1)
Christians in public worship (11:2–34)
Place and importance of spiritual gifts (12:1–14:40)
The resurrection of Christ and believers (15:1–58)
Conclusion (16:1–24)

---

1 Paul, called to be an apostle of Christ
Jesus by the will of God, and our brother
Sosthenes,

2To the church of God in Corinth, to those
sanctified in Christ Jesus and called to be
holy, together with all those everywhere who
call on the name of our Lord Jesus Christ—
their Lord and ours:

3Grace and peace to you from God our
Father and the Lord Jesus Christ.

Thanksgiving

4I always thank God for you because of his
grace given you in Christ Jesus. 5For in him
you have been enriched in every way—in all
your speaking and in all your knowledge—
6because our testimony about Christ was
confirmed in you. 7Therefore you do not lack
any spiritual gift as you eagerly wait for our
Lord Jesus Christ to be revealed. 8He will
keep you strong to the end, so that you will
be blameless on the day of our Lord Jesus
Christ. 9God, who has called you into fellowship with his Son Jesus Christ our Lord, is
faithful.

Divisions in the Church

10I appeal to you, brothers, in the name of
our Lord Jesus Christ, that all of you agree
with one another so that there may be no
divisions among you and that you may be
perfectly united in mind and thought. 11My
brothers, some from Chloe's household
have informed me that there are quarrels
among you. 12What I mean is this: One of
you says, "I follow Paul"; another, "I follow
Apollos"; another, "I follow Cephas[a]"; still
another, "I follow Christ."

13Is Christ divided? Was Paul crucified for
you? Were you baptized into[b] the name of
Paul? 14I am thankful that I did not baptize
any of you except Crispus and Gaius, 15so no
one can say that you were baptized into my

[a] *12* That is, Peter [b] *13* Or *in*; also in verse 15

name. 16(Yes, I also baptized the household
of Stephanas; beyond that, I don't remember
if I baptized anyone else.) 17For Christ did not
send me to baptize, but to preach the gospel—not with words of human wisdom, lest
the cross of Christ be emptied of its power.

Christ the Wisdom and Power of God

18For the message of the cross is foolishness to those who are perishing, but to us
who are being saved it is the power of God.
19For it is written:

"I will destroy the wisdom of the wise;
the intelligence of the intelligent I will
frustrate."[a]

20Where is the wise man? Where is the
scholar? Where is the philosopher of this
age? Has not God made foolish the wisdom
of the world? 21For since in the wisdom of
God the world through its wisdom did not
know him, God was pleased through the
foolishness of what was preached to save
those who believe. 22Jews demand miraculous signs and Greeks look for wisdom, 23but
we preach Christ crucified: a stumbling block
to Jews and foolishness to Gentiles, 24but to
those whom God has called, both Jews and
Greeks, Christ the power of God and the
wisdom of God. 25For the foolishness of God
is wiser than man's wisdom, and the weakness of God is stronger than man's strength.
26Brothers, think of what you were when
you were called. Not many of you were wise
by human standards; not many were influential; not many were of noble birth. 27But God
chose the foolish things of the world to
shame the wise; God chose the weak things
of the world to shame the strong. 28He chose
the lowly things of this world and the despised things—and the things that are not—
to nullify the things that are, 29so that no one
may boast before him. 30It is because of him
that you are in Christ Jesus, who has
become for us wisdom from God—that is,
our righteousness, holiness and redemption.
31Therefore, as it is written: "Let him who
boasts boast in the Lord."[b]

2 When I came to you, brothers, I did not
come with eloquence or superior wisdom as I proclaimed to you the testimony
about God.[c] 2For I resolved to know nothing
while I was with you except Jesus Christ and
him crucified. 3I came to you in weakness
and fear, and with much trembling. 4My message and my preaching were not with wise
and persuasive words, but with a demonstration of the Spirit's power, 5so that your faith
might not rest on men's wisdom, but on
God's power.

Wisdom From the Spirit

6We do, however, speak a message of
wisdom among the mature, but not the wisdom of this age or of the rulers of this age,
who are coming to nothing. 7No, we speak of
God's secret wisdom, a wisdom that has
been hidden and that God destined for our
glory before time began. 8None of the rulers
of this age understood it, for if they had, they
would not have crucified the Lord of glory.
9However, as it is written:

"No eye has seen,
no ear has heard,
no mind has conceived
what God has prepared for those who
love him"[d]—

10but God has revealed it to us by his Spirit.
The Spirit searches all things, even the
deep things of God. 11For who among men
knows the thoughts of a man except the
man's spirit within him? In the same way no
one knows the thoughts of God except the
Spirit of God. 12We have not received the
spirit of the world but the Spirit who is from
God, that we may understand what God has
freely given us. 13This is what we speak, not
in words taught us by human wisdom but in
words taught by the Spirit, expressing spiritual truths in spiritual words.[e] 14The man
without the Spirit does not accept the things
that come from the Spirit of God, for they are
foolishness to him, and he cannot understand them, because they are spiritually discerned. 15The spiritual man makes judgments about all things, but he himself is not
subject to any man's judgment:

16"For who has known the mind of the Lord
that he may instruct him?"[f]

But we have the mind of Christ.

On Divisions in the Church

3 Brothers, I could not address you as
spiritual but as worldly—mere infants in

[a] 19 Isaiah 29:14 [b] 31 Jer. 9:24 [c] 1 Some manuscripts *as I proclaimed to you God's mystery*
[d] 9 Isaiah 64:4 [e] 13 Or *Spirit, interpreting spiritual truths to spiritual men* [f] 16 Isaiah 40:13

Christ. [2]I gave you milk, not solid food, for
you were not yet ready for it. Indeed, you are
still not ready. [3]You are still worldly. For
since there is jealousy and quarreling among
you, are you not worldly? Are you not acting
like mere men? [4]For when one says, "I follow
Paul," and another, "I follow Apollos," are
you not mere men?

[5]What, after all, is Apollos? And what is
Paul? Only servants, through whom you
came to believe—as the Lord has assigned
to each his task. [6]I planted the seed, Apollos
watered it, but God made it grow. [7]So neither
he who plants nor he who waters is anything,
but only God, who makes things grow. [8]The
man who plants and the man who waters
have one purpose, and each will be rewarded according to his own labor. [9]For we
are God's fellow workers; you are God's
field, God's building.

[10]By the grace God has given me, I laid a
foundation as an expert builder, and someone else is building on it. But each one
should be careful how he builds. [11]For no
one can lay any foundation other than the
one already laid, which is Jesus Christ. [12]If
any man builds on this foundation using
gold, silver, costly stones, wood, hay or
straw, [13]his work will be shown for what it is,
because the Day will bring it to light. It will be
revealed with fire, and the fire will test the
quality of each man's work. [14]If what he has
built survives, he will receive his reward. [15]If
it is burned up, he will suffer loss; he himself
will be saved, but only as one escaping
through the flames.

[16]Don't you know that you yourselves are
God's temple and that God's Spirit lives in
you? [17]If anyone destroys God's temple,
God will destroy him; for God's temple is
sacred, and you are that temple.

[18]Do not deceive yourselves. If any one of
you thinks he is wise by the standards of this
age, he should become a "fool" so that he
may become wise. [19]For the wisdom of this
world is foolishness in God's sight. As it is
written: "He catches the wise in their craftiness"[a]; [20]and again, "The Lord knows that
the thoughts of the wise are futile."[b] [21]So
then, no more boasting about men! All things
are yours, [22]whether Paul or Apollos or Cephas[c] or the world or life or death or the
present or the future—all are yours, [23]and
you are of Christ, and Christ is of God.

Apostles of Christ

4 So then, men ought to regard us as servants of Christ and as those entrusted
with the secret things of God. [2]Now it is required that those who have been given a
trust must prove faithful. [3]I care very little if I
am judged by you or by any human court;
indeed, I do not even judge myself. [4]My conscience is clear, but that does not make me
innocent. It is the Lord who judges me.
[5]Therefore judge nothing before the appointed time; wait till the Lord comes. He will
bring to light what is hidden in darkness and
will expose the motives of men's hearts. At
that time each will receive his praise from
God.

[6]Now, brothers, I have applied these
things to myself and Apollos for your benefit,
so that you may learn from us the meaning of
the saying, "Do not go beyond what is written." Then you will not take pride in one man
over against another. [7]For who makes you
different from anyone else? What do you
have that you did not receive? And if you did
receive it, why do you boast as though you
did not?

[8]Already you have all you want! Already
you have become rich! You have become
kings—and that without us! How I wish that
you really had become kings so that we
might be kings with you! [9]For it seems to me
that God has put us apostles on display at
the end of the procession, like men condemned to die in the arena. We have been
made a spectacle to the whole universe, to
angels as well as to men. [10]We are fools for
Christ, but you are so wise in Christ! We are
weak, but you are strong! You are honored,
we are dishonored! [11]To this very hour we go
hungry and thirsty, we are in rags, we are
brutally treated, we are homeless. [12]We
work hard with our own hands. When we are
cursed, we bless; when we are persecuted,
we endure it; [13]when we are slandered, we
answer kindly. Up to this moment we have
become the scum of the earth, the refuse of
the world.

[14]I am not writing this to shame you, but to
warn you, as my dear children. [15]Even
though you have ten thousand guardians in
Christ, you do not have many fathers, for in
Christ Jesus I became your father through
the gospel. [16]Therefore I urge you to imitate

[a]*19* Job 5:13 [b]*20* Psalm 94:11 [c]*22* That is, Peter

me. 17For this reason I am sending to you
Timothy, my son whom I love, who is faithful
in the Lord. He will remind you of my way of
life in Christ Jesus, which agrees with what I
teach everywhere in every church.
18Some of you have become arrogant, as if
I were not coming to you. 19But I will come to
you very soon, if the Lord is willing, and then
I will find out not only how these arrogant
people are talking, but what power they
have. 20For the kingdom of God is not a matter of talk but of power. 21What do you prefer? Shall I come to you with a whip, or in love
and with a gentle spirit?

Expel the Immoral Brother!

5 It is actually reported that there is sexual
immorality among you, and of a kind that
does not occur even among pagans: A man
has his father's wife. 2And you are proud!
Shouldn't you rather have been filled with
grief and have put out of your fellowship the
man who did this? 3Even though I am not
physically present, I am with you in spirit.
And I have already passed judgment on the
one who did this, just as if I were present.
4When you are assembled in the name of our
Lord Jesus and I am with you in spirit, and
the power of our Lord Jesus is present,
5hand this man over to Satan, so that the
sinful nature[a] may be destroyed and his
spirit saved on the day of the Lord.
6Your boasting is not good. Don't you
know that a little yeast works through the
whole batch of dough? 7Get rid of the old
yeast that you may be a new batch without
yeast—as you really are. For Christ, our
Passover lamb, has been sacrificed. 8There-
fore let us keep the Festival, not with the old
yeast, the yeast of malice and wickedness,
but with bread without yeast, the bread of
sincerity and truth.
9I have written you in my letter not to associate with sexually immoral people— 10not at
all meaning the people of this world who are
immoral, or the greedy and swindlers, or
idolaters. In that case you would have to
leave this world. 11But now I am writing you
that you must not associate with anyone who
calls himself a brother but is sexually immoral or greedy, an idolater or a slanderer, a
drunkard or a swindler. With such a man do
not even eat.
12What business is it of mine to judge
those outside the church? Are you not to
judge those inside? 13God will judge those
outside. "Expel the wicked man from among
you."[b]

Lawsuits Among Believers

6 If any of you has a dispute with another,
dare he take it before the ungodly for
judgment instead of before the saints? 2Do
you not know that the saints will judge the
world? And if you are to judge the world, are
you not competent to judge trivial cases?
3Do you not know that we will judge angels?
How much more the things of this life!
4Therefore, if you have disputes about such
matters, appoint as judges even men of little
account in the church![c] 5I say this to shame
you. Is it possible that there is nobody among
you wise enough to judge a dispute between
believers? 6But instead, one brother goes to
law against another—and this in front of unbelievers!
7The very fact that you have lawsuits
among you means you have been completely defeated already. Why not rather be
wronged? Why not rather be cheated? 8In-
stead, you yourselves cheat and do wrong,
and you do this to your brothers.
9Do you not know that the wicked will not
inherit the kingdom of God? Do not be deceived: Neither the sexually immoral nor
idolaters nor adulterers nor male prostitutes
nor homosexual offenders 10nor thieves nor
the greedy nor drunkards nor slanderers nor
swindlers will inherit the kingdom of God.
11And that is what some of you were. But you
were washed, you were sanctified, you were
justified in the name of the Lord Jesus Christ
and by the Spirit of our God.

Sexual Immorality

12"Everything is permissible for me"—but
not everything is beneficial. "Everything is
permissible for me"—but I will not be mastered by anything. 13"Food for the stomach
and the stomach for food"—but God will destroy them both. The body is not meant for
sexual immorality, but for the Lord, and the
Lord for the body. 14By his power God raised
the Lord from the dead, and he will raise us
also. 15Do you not know that your bodies are

[a]*5* Or *that his body*; or *that the flesh* [b]*13* Deut. 17:7; 19:19; 21:21; 22:21,24; 24:7 [c]*4* Or *matters, do you appoint as judges men of little account in the church?*

members of Christ himself? Shall I then take
the members of Christ and unite them with a
prostitute? Never! 16Do you not know that he
who unites himself with a prostitute is one
with her in body? For it is said, "The two will
become one flesh."[a] 17But he who unites
himself with the Lord is one with him in spirit.

18Flee from sexual immorality. All other
sins a man commits are outside his body, but
he who sins sexually sins against his own
body. 19Do you not know that your body is a
temple of the Holy Spirit, who is in you, whom
you have received from God? You are not
your own; 20you were bought at a price.
Therefore honor God with your body.

Marriage

7 Now for the matters you wrote about: It is
good for a man not to marry.[b] 2But since
there is so much immorality, each man
should have his own wife, and each woman
her own husband. 3The husband should fulfill his marital duty to his wife, and likewise
the wife to her husband. 4The wife's body
does not belong to her alone but also to her
husband. In the same way, the husband's
body does not belong to him alone but also to
his wife. 5Do not deprive each other except
by mutual consent and for a time, so that you
may devote yourselves to prayer. Then
come together again so that Satan will not
tempt you because of your lack of self-control. 6I say this as a concession, not as a
command. 7I wish that all men were as I am.
But each man has his own gift from God; one
has this gift, another has that.

8Now to the unmarried and the widows I
say: It is good for them to stay unmarried, as
I am. 9But if they cannot control themselves,
they should marry, for it is better to marry
than to burn with passion.

10To the married I give this command (not
I, but the Lord): A wife must not separate
from her husband. 11But if she does, she
must remain unmarried or else be reconciled
to her husband. And a husband must not
divorce his wife.

12To the rest I say this (I, not the Lord): If
any brother has a wife who is not a believer
and she is willing to live with him, he must not
divorce her. 13And if a woman has a husband
who is not a believer and he is willing to live
with her, she must not divorce him. 14For the
unbelieving husband has been sanctified
through his wife, and the unbelieving wife
has been sanctified through her believing
husband. Otherwise your children would be
unclean, but as it is, they are holy.

15But if the unbeliever leaves, let him do
so. A believing man or woman is not bound in
such circumstances; God has called us to
live in peace. 16How do you know, wife,
whether you will save your husband? Or,
how do you know, husband, whether you will
save your wife?

17Nevertheless, each one should retain
the place in life that the Lord assigned to him
and to which God has called him. This is the
rule I lay down in all the churches. 18Was a
man already circumcised when he was
called? He should not become uncircumcised. Was a man uncircumcised when he
was called? He should not be circumcised.
19Circumcision is nothing and uncircumcision is nothing. Keeping God's commands is
what counts. 20Each one should remain in
the situation which he was in when God
called him. 21Were you a slave when you
were called? Don't let it trouble you—
although if you can gain your freedom, do so.
22For he who was a slave when he was
called by the Lord is the Lord's freedman;
similarly, he who was a free man when he
was called is Christ's slave. 23You were
bought at a price; do not become slaves of
men. 24Brothers, each man, as responsible
to God, should remain in the situation God
called him to.

25Now about virgins: I have no command
from the Lord, but I give a judgment as one
who by the Lord's mercy is trustworthy. 26Be-
cause of the present crisis, I think that it is
good for you to remain as you are. 27Are you
married? Do not seek a divorce. Are you
unmarried? Do not look for a wife. 28But if
you do marry, you have not sinned; and if a
virgin marries, she has not sinned. But those
who marry will face many troubles in this life,
and I want to spare you this.

29What I mean, brothers, is that the time is
short. From now on those who have wives
should live as if they had none; 30those who
mourn, as if they did not; those who are happy, as if they were not; those who buy something, as if it were not theirs to keep; 31those
who use the things of the world, as if not
engrossed in them. For this world in its
present form is passing away.

32I would like you to be free from concern.

[a] *16* Gen. 2:24 [b] *1* Or "*It is good for a man not to have sexual relations with a woman.*"

An unmarried man is concerned about the
Lord's affairs—how he can please the Lord.
33But a married man is concerned about the
affairs of this world—how he can please his
wife— 34and his interests are divided. An
unmarried woman or virgin is concerned
about the Lord's affairs: Her aim is to be
devoted to the Lord in both body and spirit.
But a married woman is concerned about the
affairs of this world—how she can please her
husband. 35I am saying this for your own
good, not to restrict you, but that you may live
in a right way in undivided devotion to the
Lord.

36If anyone thinks he is acting improperly
toward the virgin he is engaged to, and if she
is getting along in years and he feels he
ought to marry, he should do as he wants. He
is not sinning. They should get married. 37But
the man who has settled the matter in his
own mind, who is under no compulsion but
has control over his own will, and who has
made up his mind not to marry the virgin—
this man also does the right thing. 38So then,
he who marries the virgin does right, but he
who does not marry her does even better.[a]

39A woman is bound to her husband as
long as he lives. But if her husband dies, she
is free to marry anyone she wishes, but he
must belong to the Lord. 40In my judgment,
she is happier if she stays as she is—and I
think that I too have the Spirit of God.

Food Sacrificed to Idols

8 Now about food sacrificed to idols: We
know that we all possess knowledge.[b]
Knowledge puffs up, but love builds up. 2The
man who thinks he knows something does
not yet know as he ought to know. 3But the
man who loves God is known by God.

4So then, about eating food sacrificed to
idols: We know that an idol is nothing at all in
the world and that there is no God but one.
5For even if there are so-called gods,
whether in heaven or on earth (as indeed
there are many "gods" and many "lords"),
6yet for us there is but one God, the Father,
from whom all things came and for whom we
live; and there is but one Lord, Jesus Christ,
through whom all things came and through
whom we live.

7But not everyone knows this. Some
people are still so accustomed to idols that
when they eat such food they think of it as
having been sacrificed to an idol, and since
their conscience is weak, it is defiled. 8But
food does not bring us near to God; we are
no worse if we do not eat, and no better if
we do.

9Be careful, however, that the exercise of
your freedom does not become a stumbling
block to the weak. 10For if anyone with a
weak conscience sees you who have this
knowledge eating in an idol's temple, won't
he be emboldened to eat what has been
sacrificed to idols? 11So this weak brother,
for whom Christ died, is destroyed by your
knowledge. 12When you sin against your
brothers in this way and wound their weak
conscience, you sin against Christ. 13There-
fore, if what I eat causes my brother to fall
into sin, I will never eat meat again, so that I
will not cause him to fall.

The Rights of an Apostle

9 Am I not free? Am I not an apostle? Have
I not seen Jesus our Lord? Are you not
the result of my work in the Lord? 2Even
though I may not be an apostle to others,
surely I am to you! For you are the seal of my
apostleship in the Lord.

3This is my defense to those who sit in
judgment on me. 4Don't we have the right to
food and drink? 5Don't we have the right to
take a believing wife along with us, as do the
other apostles and the Lord's brothers and
Cephas[c]? 6Or is it only I and Barnabas who
must work for a living?

7Who serves as a soldier at his own expense? Who plants a vineyard and does not
eat of its grapes? Who tends a flock and
does not drink of the milk? 8Do I say this
merely from a human point of view? Doesn't
the Law say the same thing? 9For it is written
in the Law of Moses: "Do not muzzle an ox
while it is treading out the grain."[d] Is it about
oxen that God is concerned? 10Surely he
says this for us, doesn't he? Yes, this was
written for us, because when the plowman
plows and the thresher threshes, they ought
to do so in the hope of sharing in the harvest.
11If we have sown spiritual seed among you,

[a]36-38 Or *36If anyone thinks he is not treating his daughter properly, and if she is getting along in years, and he feels she ought to marry, he should do as he wants. He is not sinning. He should let her get married. 37But the man who has settled the matter in his own mind, who is under no compulsion but has control over his own will, and who has made up his mind to keep the virgin unmarried—this man also does the right thing. 38So then, he who gives his virgin in marriage does right, but he who does not give her in marriage does even better.* [b]1 Or *"We all possess knowledge," as you say* [c]5 That is, Peter [d]9 Deut. 25:4

is it too much if we reap a material harvest from you? [12]If others have this right of support from you, shouldn't we have it all the more?

But we did not use this right. On the contrary, we put up with anything rather than hinder the gospel of Christ. [13]Don't you know that those who work in the temple get their food from the temple, and those who serve at the altar share in what is offered on the altar? [14]In the same way, the Lord has commanded that those who preach the gospel should receive their living from the gospel.

[15]But I have not used any of these rights. And I am not writing this in the hope that you will do such things for me. I would rather die than have anyone deprive me of this boast. [16]Yet when I preach the gospel, I cannot boast, for I am compelled to preach. Woe to me if I do not preach the gospel! [17]If I preach voluntarily, I have a reward; if not voluntarily, I am simply discharging the trust committed to me. [18]What then is my reward? Just this: that in preaching the gospel I may offer it free of charge, and so not make use of my rights in preaching it.

[19]Though I am free and belong to no man, I make myself a slave to everyone, to win as many as possible. [20]To the Jews I became like a Jew, to win the Jews. To those under the law I became like one under the law (though I myself am not under the law), so as to win those under the law. [21]To those not having the law I became like one not having the law (though I am not free from God's law but am under Christ's law), so as to win those not having the law. [22]To the weak I became weak, to win the weak. I have become all things to all men so that by all possible means I might save some. [23]I do all this for the sake of the gospel, that I may share in its blessings.

[24]Do you not know that in a race all the runners run, but only one gets the prize? Run in such a way as to get the prize. [25]Everyone who competes in the games goes into strict training. They do it to get a crown that will not last; but we do it to get a crown that will last forever. [26]Therefore I do not run like a man running aimlessly; I do not fight like a man beating the air. [27]No, I beat my body and make it my slave so that after I have preached to others, I myself will not be disqualified for the prize.

Warnings From Israel's History

10 For I do not want you to be ignorant of the fact, brothers, that our forefathers were all under the cloud and that they all passed through the sea. [2]They were all baptized into Moses in the cloud and in the sea. [3]They all ate the same spiritual food [4]and drank the same spiritual drink; for they drank from the spiritual rock that accompanied them, and that rock was Christ. [5]Nevertheless, God was not pleased with most of them; their bodies were scattered over the desert.

[6]Now these things occurred as examples[a] to keep us from setting our hearts on evil things as they did. [7]Do not be idolaters, as some of them were; as it is written: "The people sat down to eat and drink and got up to indulge in pagan revelry."[b] [8]We should not commit sexual immorality, as some of them did—and in one day twenty-three thousand of them died. [9]We should not test the Lord, as some of them did—and were killed by snakes. [10]And do not grumble, as some of them did—and were killed by the destroying angel.

[11]These things happened to them as examples and were written down as warnings for us, on whom the fulfillment of the ages has come. [12]So, if you think you are standing firm, be careful that you don't fall! [13]No temptation has seized you except what is common to man. And God is faithful; he will not let you be tempted beyond what you can bear. But when you are tempted, he will also provide a way out so that you can stand up under it.

Idol Feasts and the Lord's Supper

[14]Therefore, my dear friends, flee from idolatry. [15]I speak to sensible people; judge for yourselves what I say. [16]Is not the cup of thanksgiving for which we give thanks a participation in the blood of Christ? And is not the bread that we break a participation in the body of Christ? [17]Because there is one loaf, we, who are many, are one body, for we all partake of the one loaf.

[18]Consider the people of Israel: Do not those who eat the sacrifices participate in the altar? [19]Do I mean then that a sacrifice offered to an idol is anything, or that an idol is anything? [20]No, but the sacrifices of pagans

[a]6 Or *types*; also in verse 11 [b]7 Exodus 32:6

are offered to demons, not to God, and I do
not want you to be participants with demons.
21You cannot drink the cup of the Lord and
the cup of demons too; you cannot have a
part in both the Lord's table and the table of
demons. 22Are we trying to arouse the Lord's
jealousy? Are we stronger than he?

The Believer's Freedom

23"Everything is permissible"—but not
everything is beneficial. "Everything is permissible"—but
not everything is constructive.
24Nobody should seek his own good,
but the good of others.

25Eat anything sold in the meat market
without raising questions of conscience,
26for, "The earth is the Lord's, and everything
in it."[a]

27If some unbeliever invites you to a meal
and you want to go, eat whatever is put before
you without raising questions of conscience.
28But if anyone says to you, "This
has been offered in sacrifice," then do not
eat it, both for the sake of the man who told
you and for conscience' sake[b]— 29the other
man's conscience, I mean, not yours. For
why should my freedom be judged by another's
conscience? 30If I take part in the
meal with thankfulness, why am I denounced
because of something I thank God for?

31So whether you eat or drink or whatever
you do, do it all for the glory of God. 32Do not
cause anyone to stumble, whether Jews,
Greeks or the church of God— 33even as I try
to please everybody in every way. For I am
not seeking my own good but the good of
11 many, so that they may be saved.
1Follow my example, as I follow the
example of Christ.

Propriety in Worship

2I praise you for remembering me in everything
and for holding to the teachings,[c] just
as I passed them on to you.

3Now I want you to realize that the head of
every man is Christ, and the head of the
woman is man, and the head of Christ is
God. 4Every man who prays or prophesies
with his head covered dishonors his head.
5And every woman who prays or prophesies
with her head uncovered dishonors her
head—it is just as though her head were
shaved. 6If a woman does not cover her
head, she should have her hair cut off; and if
it is a disgrace for a woman to have her hair
cut or shaved off, she should cover her head.
7A man ought not to cover his head,[d] since
he is the image and glory of God; but the
woman is the glory of man. 8For man did not
come from woman, but woman from man;
9neither was man created for woman, but
woman for man. 10For this reason, and because
of the angels, the woman ought to
have a sign of authority on her head.

11In the Lord, however, woman is not independent
of man, nor is man independent of
woman. 12For as woman came from man, so
also man is born of woman. But everything
comes from God. 13Judge for yourselves: Is
it proper for a woman to pray to God with her
head uncovered? 14Does not the very nature
of things teach you that if a man has long
hair, it is a disgrace to him, 15but that if a
woman has long hair, it is her glory? For long
hair is given to her as a covering. 16If anyone
wants to be contentious about this, we have
no other practice—nor do the churches of
God.

The Lord's Supper

17In the following directives I have no
praise for you, for your meetings do more
harm than good. 18In the first place, I hear
that when you come together as a church,
there are divisions among you, and to some
extent I believe it. 19No doubt there have to
be differences among you to show which of
you have God's approval. 20When you come
together, it is not the Lord's Supper you eat,
21for as you eat, each of you goes ahead
without waiting for anybody else. One remains
hungry, another gets drunk. 22Don't
you have homes to eat and drink in? Or do
you despise the church of God and humiliate
those who have nothing? What shall I say to
you? Shall I praise you for this? Certainly
not!

23For I received from the Lord what I also
passed on to you: The Lord Jesus, on the
night he was betrayed, took bread, 24and
when he had given thanks, he broke it and
said, "This is my body, which is for you; do
this in remembrance of me." 25In the same

[a]26 Psalm 24:1 [b]28 Some manuscripts *conscience' sake, for "the earth is the Lord's and everything in it"*
[c]2 Or *traditions* [d]4-7 Or *4Every man who prays or prophesies with long hair dishonors his head. 5And every woman who prays or prophesies with no covering ⌞of hair⌟ on her head dishonors her head—she is just like one of the "shorn women." 6If a woman has no covering, let her be for now with short hair, but since it is a disgrace for a woman to have her hair shorn or shaved, she should grow it again. 7A man ought not to have long hair*

way, after supper he took the cup, saying, "This cup is the new covenant in my blood; do this, whenever you drink it, in remembrance of me." 26For whenever you eat this bread and drink this cup, you proclaim the Lord's death until he comes.

27Therefore, whoever eats the bread or drinks the cup of the Lord in an unworthy manner will be guilty of sinning against the body and blood of the Lord. 28A man ought to examine himself before he eats of the bread and drinks of the cup. 29For anyone who eats and drinks without recognizing the body of the Lord eats and drinks judgment on himself. 30That is why many among you are weak and sick, and a number of you have fallen asleep. 31But if we judged ourselves, we would not come under judgment. 32When we are judged by the Lord, we are being disciplined so that we will not be condemned with the world.

33So then, my brothers, when you come together to eat, wait for each other. 34If anyone is hungry, he should eat at home, so that when you meet together it may not result in judgment.

And when I come I will give further directions.

Spiritual Gifts

12 Now about spiritual gifts, brothers, I do not want you to be ignorant. 2You know that when you were pagans, somehow or other you were influenced and led astray to mute idols. 3Therefore I tell you that no one who is speaking by the Spirit of God says, "Jesus be cursed," and no one can say, "Jesus is Lord," except by the Holy Spirit.

4There are different kinds of gifts, but the same Spirit. 5There are different kinds of service, but the same Lord. 6There are different kinds of working, but the same God works all of them in all men.

7Now to each one the manifestation of the Spirit is given for the common good. 8To one there is given through the Spirit the message of wisdom, to another the message of knowledge by means of the same Spirit, 9to another faith by the same Spirit, to another gifts of healing by that one Spirit, 10to another miraculous powers, to another prophecy, to another distinguishing between spirits, to another speaking in different kinds of tongues,[a] and to still another the interpretation of tongues.[a] 11All these are the work of one and the same Spirit, and he gives them to each one, just as he determines.

One Body, Many Parts

12The body is a unit, though it is made up of many parts; and though all its parts are many, they form one body. So it is with Christ. 13For we were all baptized by[b] one Spirit into one body—whether Jews or Greeks, slave or free—and we were all given the one Spirit to drink.

14Now the body is not made up of one part but of many. 15If the foot should say, "Because I am not a hand, I do not belong to the body," it would not for that reason cease to be part of the body. 16And if the ear should say, "Because I am not an eye, I do not belong to the body," it would not for that reason cease to be part of the body. 17If the whole body were an eye, where would the sense of hearing be? If the whole body were an ear, where would the sense of smell be? 18But in fact God has arranged the parts in the body, every one of them, just as he wanted them to be. 19If they were all one part, where would the body be? 20As it is, there are many parts, but one body.

21The eye cannot say to the hand, "I don't need you!" And the head cannot say to the feet, "I don't need you!" 22On the contrary, those parts of the body that seem to be weaker are indispensable, 23and the parts that we think are less honorable we treat with special honor. And the parts that are unpresentable are treated with special modesty, 24while our presentable parts need no special treatment. But God has combined the members of the body and has given greater honor to the parts that lacked it, 25so that there should be no division in the body, but that its parts should have equal concern for each other. 26If one part suffers, every part suffers with it; if one part is honored, every part rejoices with it.

27Now you are the body of Christ, and each one of you is a part of it. 28And in the church God has appointed first of all apostles, second prophets, third teachers, then workers of miracles, also those having gifts of healing, those able to help others, those with gifts of administration, and those speaking in different kinds of tongues. 29Are all apostles? Are all prophets? Are all teachers? Do all work miracles? 30Do all have gifts of healing? Do

[a] *10* Or *languages*; also in verse 28 [b] *13* Or *with*; or *in*

all speak in tongues[a]? Do all interpret? 31 But eagerly desire[b] the greater gifts.

Love

And now I will show you the most excellent way.

13 If I speak in the tongues[c] of men and of angels, but have not love, I am only a resounding gong or a clanging cymbal. 2 If I have the gift of prophecy and can fathom all mysteries and all knowledge, and if I have a faith that can move mountains, but have not love, I am nothing. 3 If I give all I possess to the poor and surrender my body to the flames,[d] but have not love, I gain nothing.

4 Love is patient, love is kind. It does not envy, it does not boast, it is not proud. 5 It is not rude, it is not self-seeking, it is not easily angered, it keeps no record of wrongs. 6 Love does not delight in evil but rejoices with the truth. 7 It always protects, always trusts, always hopes, always perseveres.

8 Love never fails. But where there are prophecies, they will cease; where there are tongues, they will be stilled; where there is knowledge, it will pass away. 9 For we know in part and we prophesy in part, 10 but when perfection comes, the imperfect disappears. 11 When I was a child, I talked like a child, I thought like a child, I reasoned like a child. When I became a man, I put childish ways behind me. 12 Now we see but a poor reflection as in a mirror; then we shall see face to face. Now I know in part; then I shall know fully, even as I am fully known.

13 And now these three remain: faith, hope and love. But the greatest of these is love.

Gifts of Prophecy and Tongues

14 Follow the way of love and eagerly desire spiritual gifts, especially the gift of prophecy. 2 For anyone who speaks in a tongue[e] does not speak to men but to God. Indeed, no one understands him; he utters mysteries with his spirit.[f] 3 But everyone who prophesies speaks to men for their strengthening, encouragement and comfort. 4 He who speaks in a tongue edifies himself, but he who prophesies edifies the church. 5 I would like every one of you to speak in tongues,[g] but I would rather have you prophesy. He who prophesies is greater than one who speaks in tongues,[g] unless he interprets, so that the church may be edified.

6 Now, brothers, if I come to you and speak in tongues, what good will I be to you, unless I bring you some revelation or knowledge or prophecy or word of instruction? 7 Even in the case of lifeless things that make sounds, such as the flute or harp, how will anyone know what tune is being played unless there is a distinction in the notes? 8 Again, if the trumpet does not sound a clear call, who will get ready for battle? 9 So it is with you. Unless you speak intelligible words with your tongue, how will anyone know what you are saying? You will just be speaking into the air. 10 Undoubtedly there are all sorts of languages in the world, yet none of them is without meaning. 11 If then I do not grasp the meaning of what someone is saying, I am a foreigner to the speaker, and he is a foreigner to me. 12 So it is with you. Since you are eager to have spiritual gifts, try to excel in gifts that build up the church.

13 For this reason anyone who speaks in a tongue should pray that he may interpret what he says. 14 For if I pray in a tongue, my spirit prays, but my mind is unfruitful. 15 So what shall I do? I will pray with my spirit, but I will also pray with my mind; I will sing with my spirit, but I will also sing with my mind. 16 If you are praising God with your spirit, how can one who finds himself among those who do not understand[h] say "Amen" to your thanksgiving, since he does not know what you are saying? 17 You may be giving thanks well enough, but the other man is not edified.

18 I thank God that I speak in tongues more than all of you. 19 But in the church I would rather speak five intelligible words to instruct others than ten thousand words in a tongue.

20 Brothers, stop thinking like children. In regard to evil be infants, but in your thinking be adults. 21 In the Law it is written:

"Through men of strange tongues
  and through the lips of foreigners
I will speak to this people,
  but even then they will not listen to
    me,"[i]

says the Lord.

22 Tongues, then, are a sign, not for believers but for unbelievers; prophecy, how-

[a]30 Or *other languages* [b]31 Or *But you are eagerly desiring* [c]1 Or *languages* [d]3 Some early manuscripts *body that I may boast* [e]2 Or *another language;* also in verses 4, 13, 14, 19, 26 and 27 [f]2 Or *by the Spirit* [g]5 Or *other languages;* also in verses 6, 18, 22, 23 and 39 [h]16 Or *among the inquirers* [i]21 Isaiah 28:11,12

ever, is for believers, not for unbelievers.
23So if the whole church comes together and
everyone speaks in tongues, and some who
do not understand[a] or some unbelievers
come in, will they not say that you are out of
your mind? 24But if an unbeliever or someone who does not understand[b] comes in
while everybody is prophesying, he will be
convinced by all that he is a sinner and will
be judged by all, 25and the secrets of his
heart will be laid bare. So he will fall down
and worship God, exclaiming, "God is really
among you!"

Orderly Worship

26What then shall we say, brothers? When
you come together, everyone has a hymn, or
a word of instruction, a revelation, a tongue
or an interpretation. All of these must be
done for the strengthening of the church. 27If
anyone speaks in a tongue, two—or at the
most three—should speak, one at a time,
and someone must interpret. 28If there is no
interpreter, the speaker should keep quiet in
the church and speak to himself and God.
29Two or three prophets should speak, and
the others should weigh carefully what is
said. 30And if a revelation comes to someone
who is sitting down, the first speaker should
stop. 31For you can all prophesy in turn so
that everyone may be instructed and encouraged. 32The spirits of prophets are subject to
the control of prophets. 33For God is not a
God of disorder but of peace.

As in all the congregations of the saints,
34women should remain silent in the
churches. They are not allowed to speak, but
must be in submission, as the Law says. 35If
they want to inquire about something, they
should ask their own husbands at home; for
it is disgraceful for a woman to speak in the
church.

36Did the word of God originate with you?
Or are you the only people it has reached?
37If anybody thinks he is a prophet or spiritually gifted, let him acknowledge that what I
am writing to you is the Lord's command. 38If
he ignores this, he himself will be ignored.[c]
39Therefore, my brothers, be eager to
prophesy, and do not forbid speaking in
tongues. 40But everything should be done in
a fitting and orderly way.

The Resurrection of Christ

15 Now, brothers, I want to remind you
of the gospel I preached to you,
which you received and on which you have
taken your stand. 2By this gospel you are
saved, if you hold firmly to the word I
preached to you. Otherwise, you have believed in vain.

3For what I received I passed on to you as
of first importance[d]: that Christ died for our
sins according to the Scriptures, 4that he was
buried, that he was raised on the third day
according to the Scriptures, 5and that he appeared to Peter,[e] and then to the Twelve.
6After that, he appeared to more than five
hundred of the brothers at the same time,
most of whom are still living, though some
have fallen asleep. 7Then he appeared to
James, then to all the apostles, 8and last of
all he appeared to me also, as to one abnor-
mally born.

9For I am the least of the apostles and do
not even deserve to be called an apostle,
because I persecuted the church of God.
10But by the grace of God I am what I am, and
his grace to me was not without effect. No, I
worked harder than all of them—yet not I, but
the grace of God that was with me.
11Whether, then, it was I or they, this is
what we preach, and this is what you believed.

The Resurrection of the Dead

12But if it is preached that Christ has been
raised from the dead, how can some of you
say that there is no resurrection of the dead?
13If there is no resurrection of the dead, then
not even Christ has been raised. 14And if
Christ has not been raised, our preaching is
useless and so is your faith. 15More than that,
we are then found to be false witnesses
about God, for we have testified about God
that he raised Christ from the dead. But he
did not raise him if in fact the dead are not
raised. 16For if the dead are not raised, then
Christ has not been raised either. 17And if
Christ has not been raised, your faith is futile;
you are still in your sins. 18Then those also
who have fallen asleep in Christ are lost. 19If
only for this life we have hope in Christ, we
are to be pitied more than all men.

20But Christ has indeed been raised from

[a]23 Or *some inquirers* [b]24 Or *or some inquirer* [c]38 Some manuscripts *If he is ignorant of this, let him be ignorant* [d]3 Or *you at the first* [e]5 Greek *Cephas*

the dead, the firstfruits of those who have
fallen asleep. 21For since death came
through a man, the resurrection of the dead
comes also through a man. 22For as in Adam
all die, so in Christ all will be made alive.
23But each in his own turn: Christ, the firstfruits; then, when he comes, those who belong to him. 24Then the end will come, when
he hands over the kingdom to God the Father after he has destroyed all dominion, authority and power. 25For he must reign until
he has put all his enemies under his feet.
26The last enemy to be destroyed is death.
27For he "has put everything under his
feet."[a] Now when it says that "everything"
has been put under him, it is clear that this
does not include God himself, who put
everything under Christ. 28When he has
done this, then the Son himself will be made
subject to him who put everything under him,
so that God may be all in all.

29Now if there is no resurrection, what will
those do who are baptized for the dead? If
the dead are not raised at all, why are people
baptized for them? 30And as for us, why do
we endanger ourselves every hour? 31I die
every day—I mean that, brothers—just as
surely as I glory over you in Christ Jesus our
Lord. 32If I fought wild beasts in Ephesus for
merely human reasons, what have I gained?
If the dead are not raised,

"Let us eat and drink,
for tomorrow we die."[b]

33Do not be misled: "Bad company corrupts
good character." 34Come back to your
senses as you ought, and stop sinning; for
there are some who are ignorant of God—I
say this to your shame.

The Resurrection Body

35But someone may ask, "How are the
dead raised? With what kind of body will they
come?" 36How foolish! What you sow does
not come to life unless it dies. 37When you
sow, you do not plant the body that will be,
but just a seed, perhaps of wheat or of something else. 38But God gives it a body as he
has determined, and to each kind of seed he
gives its own body. 39All flesh is not the
same: Men have one kind of flesh, animals
have another, birds another and fish another. 40There are also heavenly bodies and
there are earthly bodies; but the splendor of
the heavenly bodies is one kind, and the
splendor of the earthly bodies is another.
41The sun has one kind of splendor, the
moon another and the stars another; and
star differs from star in splendor.

42So will it be with the resurrection of the
dead. The body that is sown is perishable, it
is raised imperishable; 43it is sown in dishon-
or, it is raised in glory; it is sown in weakness,
it is raised in power; 44it is sown a natural
body, it is raised a spiritual body.

If there is a natural body, there is also a
spiritual body. 45So it is written: "The first
man Adam became a living being"[c]; the last
Adam, a life-giving spirit. 46The spiritual did
not come first, but the natural, and after that
the spiritual. 47The first man was of the dust
of the earth, the second man from heaven.
48As was the earthly man, so are those who
are of the earth; and as is the man from
heaven, so also are those who are of
heaven. 49And just as we have borne the
likeness of the earthly man, so shall we[d]
bear the likeness of the man from heaven.

50I declare to you, brothers, that flesh and
blood cannot inherit the kingdom of God, nor
does the perishable inherit the imperishable.
51Listen, I tell you a mystery: We will not all
sleep, but we will all be changed— 52in a
flash, in the twinkling of an eye, at the last
trumpet. For the trumpet will sound, the dead
will be raised imperishable, and we will be
changed. 53For the perishable must clothe
itself with the imperishable, and the mortal
with immortality. 54When the perishable has
been clothed with the imperishable, and the
mortal with immortality, then the saying that
is written will come true: "Death has been
swallowed up in victory."[e]

55"Where, O death, is your victory?
Where, O death, is your sting?"[f]

56The sting of death is sin, and the power of
sin is the law. 57But thanks be to God! He
gives us the victory through our Lord Jesus
Christ.

58Therefore, my dear brothers, stand firm.
Let nothing move you. Always give yourselves fully to the work of the Lord, because
you know that your labor in the Lord is not in
vain.

[a] *27* Psalm 8:6 [b] *32* Isaiah 22:13 [c] *45* Gen. 2:7 [d] *49* Some early manuscripts *so let us*
[e] *54* Isaiah 25:8 [f] *55* Hosea 13:14

The Collection for God's People

16 Now about the collection for God's
people: Do what I told the Galatian
churches to do. 2On the first day of every
week, each one of you should set aside a
sum of money in keeping with his income,
saving it up, so that when I come no collec-
tions will have to be made. 3Then, when I
arrive, I will give letters of introduction to the
men you approve and send them with your
gift to Jerusalem. 4If it seems advisable for
me to go also, they will accompany me.

Personal Requests

5After I go through Macedonia, I will come
to you—for I will be going through Macedonia. 6Perhaps I will stay with you awhile, or
even spend the winter, so that you can help
me on my journey, wherever I go. 7I do not
want to see you now and make only a passing visit; I hope to spend some time with you,
if the Lord permits. 8But I will stay on at Ephesus until Pentecost, 9because a great door
for effective work has opened to me, and
there are many who oppose me.

10If Timothy comes, see to it that he has
nothing to fear while he is with you, for he is
carrying on the work of the Lord, just as I am.
11No one, then, should refuse to accept him.
Send him on his way in peace so that he may
return to me. I am expecting him along with
the brothers.

12Now about our brother Apollos: I strongly
urged him to go to you with the brothers. He
was quite unwilling to go now, but he will go
when he has the opportunity.

13Be on your guard; stand firm in the faith;
be men of courage; be strong. 14Do everything in love.

15You know that the household of Stephanas were the first converts in Achaia, and
they have devoted themselves to the service
of the saints. I urge you, brothers, 16to submit
to such as these and to everyone who joins
in the work, and labors at it. 17I was glad
when Stephanas, Fortunatus and Achaicus
arrived, because they have supplied what
was lacking from you. 18For they refreshed
my spirit and yours also. Such men deserve
recognition.

Final Greetings

19The churches in the province of Asia
send you greetings. Aquila and Priscilla[a]
greet you warmly in the Lord, and so does
the church that meets at their house. 20All the
brothers here send you greetings. Greet one
another with a holy kiss.

21I, Paul, write this greeting in my own
hand.

22If anyone does not love the Lord—a
curse be on him. Come, O Lord[b]!

23The grace of the Lord Jesus be with you.

24My love to all of you in Christ Jesus.
Amen.[c]

[a]19 Greek *Prisca*, a variant of *Priscilla* [b]22 In Aramaic the expression *Come, O Lord* is *Marana tha.*
[c]24 Some manuscripts do not have *Amen.*

2 Corinthians

Introduction:

The letter known as 2 Corinthians seems to have been written a few months after the first letter. The divisions and problems that were present in 1 Corinthians were still in the church at Corinth. Paul himself may have made a quick trip to Corinth, but left rather quickly because some of the members in the church there refused to change or believe that Paul was an apostle of God.

After returning to Macedonia, Paul felt much better when Titus brought him the good news that the people in the Corinthian church had seen their problems and sins and were willing to change. It was at this time that Paul wrote his second letter to the Corinthians.

The first part of this letter tells how happy and thankful Paul was when he heard that the Corinthians were sorry for the way they had acted and were now trying to live the way God wanted them to.

In the second part of the letter, Paul defends himself against the people who were angry with him and who were saying untrue things about him.

Outline of contents:

Introduction (1:1–11)
Paul as God's messenger (1:12–7:16)
Generosity in giving (8:1–9:15)
Paul as an apostle (10:1–13:10)
Conclusion (13:11–14)

---

1 Paul, an apostle of Christ Jesus by the
will of God, and Timothy our brother,

To the church of God in Corinth, together
with all the saints throughout Achaia:

[2]Grace and peace to you from God our
Father and the Lord Jesus Christ.

The God of All Comfort

[3]Praise be to the God and Father of our
Lord Jesus Christ, the Father of compassion
and the God of all comfort, [4]who comforts us
in all our troubles, so that we can comfort
those in any trouble with the comfort we ourselves have received from God. [5]For just as
the sufferings of Christ flow over into our
lives, so also through Christ our comfort
overflows. [6]If we are distressed, it is for your
comfort and salvation; if we are comforted, it
is for your comfort, which produces in you
patient endurance of the same sufferings we
suffer. [7]And our hope for you is firm, because
we know that just as you share in our sufferings, so also you share in our comfort.

[8]We do not want you to be uninformed,
brothers, about the hardships we suffered in
the province of Asia. We were under great
pressure, far beyond our ability to endure, so
that we despaired even of life. [9]Indeed, in our
hearts we felt the sentence of death. But this
happened that we might not rely on ourselves but on God, who raises the dead.
[10]He has delivered us from such a deadly
peril, and he will deliver us. On him we have
set our hope that he will continue to deliver
us, [11]as you help us by your prayers. Then
many will give thanks on our[a] behalf for the
gracious favor granted us in answer to the
prayers of many.

Paul's Change of Plans

[12]Now this is our boast: Our conscience
testifies that we have conducted ourselves in
the world, and especially in our relations with
you, in the holiness and sincerity that are
from God. We have done so not according to
worldly wisdom but according to God's
grace. [13]For we do not write you anything

[a]11 Many manuscripts *your*

you cannot read or understand. And I hope that, [14]as you have understood us in part, you will come to understand fully that you can boast of us just as we will boast of you in the day of the Lord Jesus.

[15]Because I was confident of this, I planned to visit you first so that you might benefit twice. [16]I planned to visit you on my way to Macedonia and to come back to you from Macedonia, and then to have you send me on my way to Judea. [17]When I planned this, did I do it lightly? Or do I make my plans in a worldly manner so that in the same breath I say, "Yes, yes" and "No, no"?

[18]But as surely as God is faithful, our message to you is not "Yes" and "No." [19]For the Son of God, Jesus Christ, who was preached among you by me and Silas[a] and Timothy, was not "Yes" and "No," but in him it has always been "Yes." [20]For no matter how many promises God has made, they are "Yes" in Christ. And so through him the "Amen" is spoken by us to the glory of God. [21]Now it is God who makes both us and you stand firm in Christ. He anointed us, [22]set his seal of ownership on us, and put his Spirit in our hearts as a deposit, guaranteeing what is to come.

[23]I call God as my witness that it was in order to spare you that I did not return to Corinth. [24]Not that we lord it over your faith, but we work with you for your joy, because it

2 is by faith you stand firm. [1]So I made up my mind that I would not make another painful visit to you. [2]For if I grieve you, who is left to make me glad but you whom I have grieved? [3]I wrote as I did so that when I came I should not be distressed by those who ought to make me rejoice. I had confidence in all of you, that you would all share my joy. [4]For I wrote you out of great distress and anguish of heart and with many tears, not to grieve you but to let you know the depth of my love for you.

Forgiveness for the Sinner

[5]If anyone has caused grief, he has not so much grieved me as he has grieved all of you, to some extent—not to put it too severely. [6]The punishment inflicted on him by the majority is sufficient for him. [7]Now instead, you ought to forgive and comfort him, so that he will not be overwhelmed by excessive sorrow. [8]I urge you, therefore, to reaffirm your love for him. [9]The reason I wrote you was to see if you would stand the test and be obedient in everything. [10]If you forgive anyone, I also forgive him. And what I have forgiven—if there was anything to forgive—I have forgiven in the sight of Christ for your sake, [11]in order that Satan might not outwit us. For we are not unaware of his schemes.

Ministers of the New Covenant

[12]Now when I went to Troas to preach the gospel of Christ and found that the Lord had opened a door for me, [13]I still had no peace of mind, because I did not find my brother Titus there. So I said good-by to them and went on to Macedonia.

[14]But thanks be to God, who always leads us in triumphal procession in Christ and through us spreads everywhere the fragrance of the knowledge of him. [15]For we are to God the aroma of Christ among those who are being saved and those who are perishing. [16]To the one we are the smell of death; to the other, the fragrance of life. And who is equal to such a task? [17]Unlike so many, we do not peddle the word of God for profit. On the contrary, in Christ we speak before God with sincerity, like men sent from God.

3 Are we beginning to commend ourselves again? Or do we need, like some people, letters of recommendation to you or from you? [2]You yourselves are our letter, written on our hearts, known and read by everybody. [3]You show that you are a letter from Christ, the result of our ministry, written not with ink but with the Spirit of the living God, not on tablets of stone but on tablets of human hearts.

[4]Such confidence as this is ours through Christ before God. [5]Not that we are competent in ourselves to claim anything for ourselves, but our competence comes from God. [6]He has made us competent as ministers of a new covenant—not of the letter but of the Spirit; for the letter kills, but the Spirit gives life.

The Glory of the New Covenant

[7]Now if the ministry that brought death, which was engraved in letters on stone, came with glory, so that the Israelites could not look steadily at the face of Moses because of its glory, fading though it was, [8]will not the ministry of the Spirit be even more glorious? [9]If the ministry that condemns men

[a]19 Greek *Silvanus*, a variant of *Silas*

is glorious, how much more glorious is the
ministry that brings righteousness! 10For
what was glorious has no glory now in comparison with the surpassing glory. 11And if
what was fading away came with glory, how
much greater is the glory of that which lasts!
12Therefore, since we have such a hope,
we are very bold. 13We are not like Moses,
who would put a veil over his face to keep the
Israelites from gazing at it while the radiance
was fading away. 14But their minds were
made dull, for to this day the same veil remains when the old covenant is read. It has
not been removed, because only in Christ is
it taken away. 15Even to this day when
Moses is read, a veil covers their hearts.
16But whenever anyone turns to the Lord, the
veil is taken away. 17Now the Lord is the
Spirit, and where the Spirit of the Lord is,
there is freedom. 18And we, who with unveiled faces all reflect[a] the Lord's glory, are
being transformed into his likeness with
ever-increasing glory, which comes from
the Lord, who is the Spirit.

Treasures in Jars of Clay

4 Therefore, since through God's mercy
we have this ministry, we do not lose
heart. 2Rather, we have renounced secret
and shameful ways; we do not use deception, nor do we distort the word of God. On
the contrary, by setting forth the truth plainly
we commend ourselves to every man's conscience in the sight of God. 3And even if our
gospel is veiled, it is veiled to those who are
perishing. 4The god of this age has blinded
the minds of unbelievers, so that they cannot
see the light of the gospel of the glory of
Christ, who is the image of God. 5For we do
not preach ourselves, but Jesus Christ as
Lord, and ourselves as your servants for
Jesus' sake. 6For God, who said, "Let light
shine out of darkness,"[b] made his light shine
in our hearts to give us the light of the knowledge of the glory of God in the face of Christ.
7But we have this treasure in jars of clay to
show that this all-surpassing power is from
God and not from us. 8We are hard pressed
on every side, but not crushed; perplexed,
but not in despair; 9persecuted, but not abandoned; struck down, but not destroyed. 10We
always carry around in our body the death of
Jesus, so that the life of Jesus may also be
revealed in our body. 11For we who are alive
are always being given over to death for
Jesus' sake, so that his life may be revealed
in our mortal body. 12So then, death is at
work in us, but life is at work in you.
13It is written: "I believed; therefore I have
spoken."[c] With that same spirit of faith we
also believe and therefore speak, 14because
we know that the one who raised the Lord
Jesus from the dead will also raise us with
Jesus and present us with you in his presence. 15All this is for your benefit, so that the
grace that is reaching more and more people
may cause thanksgiving to overflow to the
glory of God.
16Therefore we do not lose heart. Though
outwardly we are wasting away, yet inwardly
we are being renewed day by day. 17For our
light and momentary troubles are achieving
for us an eternal glory that far outweighs
them all. 18So we fix our eyes not on what is
seen, but on what is unseen. For what is
seen is temporary, but what is unseen is
eternal.

Our Heavenly Dwelling

5 Now we know that if the earthly tent we
live in is destroyed, we have a building
from God, an eternal house in heaven, not
built by human hands. 2Meanwhile we groan,
longing to be clothed with our heavenly
dwelling, 3because when we are clothed, we
will not be found naked. 4For while we are in
this tent, we groan and are burdened, because we do not wish to be unclothed but to
be clothed with our heavenly dwelling, so
that what is mortal may be swallowed up by
life. 5Now it is God who has made us for this
very purpose and has given us the Spirit as a
deposit, guaranteeing what is to come.
6Therefore we are always confident and
know that as long as we are at home in the
body we are away from the Lord. 7We live by
faith, not by sight. 8We are confident, I say,
and would prefer to be away from the body
and at home with the Lord. 9So we make it
our goal to please him, whether we are at
home in the body or away from it. 10For we
must all appear before the judgment seat of
Christ, that each one may receive what is
due him for the things done while in the body,
whether good or bad.

The Ministry of Reconciliation

11Since, then, we know what it is to fear the
Lord, we try to persuade men. What we are is
plain to God, and I hope it is also plain to your

[a] 18 Or *contemplate* [b] 6 Gen. 1:3 [c] 13 Psalm 116:10

conscience. 12We are not trying to commend
ourselves to you again, but are giving you an
opportunity to take pride in us, so that you
can answer those who take pride in what is
seen rather than in what is in the heart. 13If
we are out of our mind, it is for the sake of
God; if we are in our right mind, it is for you.
14For Christ's love compels us, because we
are convinced that one died for all, and
therefore all died. 15And he died for all, that
those who live should no longer live for themselves but for him who died for them and was
raised again.

16So from now on we regard no one from a
worldly point of view. Though we once regarded Christ in this way, we do so no
longer. 17Therefore, if anyone is in Christ, he
is a new creation; the old has gone, the new
has come! 18All this is from God, who reconciled us to himself through Christ and gave
us the ministry of reconciliation: 19that God
was reconciling the world to himself in Christ,
not counting men's sins against them. And
he has committed to us the message of
reconciliation. 20We are therefore Christ's
ambassadors, as though God were making
his appeal through us. We implore you on
Christ's behalf: Be reconciled to God. 21God
made him who had no sin to be sin[a] for us, so
that in him we might become the righteousness of God.

6 As God's fellow workers we urge you not
to receive God's grace in vain. 2For he
says,

> "In the time of my favor I heard you,
> and in the day of salvation I helped
> you."[b]

I tell you, now is the time of God's favor, now
is the day of salvation.

Paul's Hardships

3We put no stumbling block in anyone's
path, so that our ministry will not be discredited. 4Rather, as servants of God we commend ourselves in every way: in great endurance; in troubles, hardships and distresses;
5in beatings, imprisonments and riots; in
hard work, sleepless nights and hunger; 6in
purity, understanding, patience and kindness; in the Holy Spirit and in sincere love;
7in truthful speech and in the power of God;
with weapons of righteousness in the right
hand and in the left; 8through glory and dishonor, bad report and good report; genuine,
yet regarded as impostors; 9known, yet regarded as unknown; dying, and yet we live
on; beaten, and yet not killed; 10sorrowful,
yet always rejoicing; poor, yet making many
rich; having nothing, and yet possessing
everything.

11We have spoken freely to you, Corinthians, and opened wide our hearts to you.
12We are not withholding our affection from
you, but you are withholding yours from us.
13As a fair exchange—I speak as to my children—open wide your hearts also.

Do Not Be Yoked With Unbelievers

14Do not be yoked together with unbelievers. For what do righteousness and wickedness have in common? Or what fellowship
can light have with darkness? 15What harmony is there between Christ and Belial[c]?
What does a believer have in common with
an unbeliever? 16What agreement is there
between the temple of God and idols? For
we are the temple of the living God. As God
has said: "I will live with them and walk
among them, and I will be their God, and they
will be my people."[d]

> 17"Therefore come out from them
> and be separate,
> says the Lord.
> Touch no unclean thing,
> and I will receive you."[e]
> 18"I will be a Father to you,
> and you will be my sons and daughters,
> says the Lord Almighty."[f]

7 Since we have these promises, dear
friends, let us purify ourselves from
everything that contaminates body and
spirit, perfecting holiness out of reverence
for God.

Paul's Joy

2Make room for us in your hearts. We have
wronged no one, we have corrupted no one,
we have exploited no one. 3I do not say this
to condemn you; I have said before that you
have such a place in our hearts that we
would live or die with you. 4I have great confidence in you; I take great pride in you. I am
greatly encouraged; in all our troubles my joy
knows no bounds.

5For when we came into Macedonia, this
body of ours had no rest, but we were

[a] *21* Or *be a sin offering* [b] *2* Isaiah 49:8 [c] *15* Greek *Beliar,* a variant of *Belial* [d] *16* Lev. 26:12; Jer. 32:38; Ezek. 37:27 [e] *17* Isaiah 52:11; Ezek. 20:34,41 [f] *18* 2 Samuel 7:14; 7:8

harassed at every turn—conflicts on the outside, fears within. 6But God, who comforts
the downcast, comforted us by the coming of
Titus, 7and not only by his coming but also by
the comfort you had given him. He told us
about your longing for me, your deep sorrow,
your ardent concern for me, so that my joy
was greater than ever.

8Even if I caused you sorrow by my letter, I
do not regret it. Though I did regret it—I see
that my letter hurt you, but only for a little
while— 9yet now I am happy, not because
you were made sorry, but because your sorrow led you to repentance. For you became
sorrowful as God intended and so were not
harmed in any way by us. 10Godly sorrow
brings repentance that leads to salvation and
leaves no regret, but worldly sorrow brings
death. 11See what this godly sorrow has produced in you: what earnestness, what eagerness to clear yourselves, what indignation,
what alarm, what longing, what concern,
what readiness to see justice done. At every
point you have proved yourselves to be innocent in this matter. 12So even though I wrote
to you, it was not on account of the one who
did the wrong or of the injured party, but
rather that before God you could see for
yourselves how devoted to us you are. 13By
all this we are encouraged.

In addition to our own encouragement, we
were especially delighted to see how happy
Titus was, because his spirit has been refreshed by all of you. 14I had boasted to him
about you, and you have not embarrassed
me. But just as everything we said to you
was true, so our boasting about you to Titus
has proved to be true as well. 15And his affection for you is all the greater when he
remembers that you were all obedient, receiving him with fear and trembling. 16I am
glad I can have complete confidence in you.

Generosity Encouraged

8 And now, brothers, we want you to know
about the grace that God has given the
Macedonian churches. 2Out of the most
severe trial, their overflowing joy and their
extreme poverty welled up in rich generosity.
3For I testify that they gave as much as they
were able, and even beyond their ability. Entirely on their own, 4they urgently pleaded
with us for the privilege of sharing in this
service to the saints. 5And they did not do as
we expected, but they gave themselves first
to the Lord and then to us in keeping with
God's will. 6So we urged Titus, since he had
earlier made a beginning, to bring also to
completion this act of grace on your part.
7But just as you excel in everything—in faith,
in speech, in knowledge, in complete earnestness and in your love for us[a]—see that
you also excel in this grace of giving.

8I am not commanding you, but I want to
test the sincerity of your love by comparing it
with the earnestness of others. 9For you
know the grace of our Lord Jesus Christ, that
though he was rich, yet for your sakes he
became poor, so that you through his poverty might become rich.

10And here is my advice about what is best
for you in this matter: Last year you were the
first not only to give but also to have the
desire to do so. 11Now finish the work, so that
your eager willingness to do it may be
matched by your completion of it, according
to your means. 12For if the willingness is
there, the gift is acceptable according to
what one has, not according to what he does
not have.

13Our desire is not that others might be
relieved while you are hard pressed, but that
there might be equality. 14At the present time
your plenty will supply what they need, so
that in turn their plenty will supply what you
need. Then there will be equality, 15as it is
written: "He who gathered much did not
have too much, and he who gathered little
did not have too little."[b]

Titus Sent to Corinth

16I thank God, who put into the heart of
Titus the same concern I have for you. 17For
Titus not only welcomed our appeal, but he is
coming to you with much enthusiasm and on
his own initiative. 18And we are sending
along with him the brother who is praised by
all the churches for his service to the gospel.
19What is more, he was chosen by the
churches to accompany us as we carry the
offering, which we administer in order to hon-
or the Lord himself and to show our eagerness to help. 20We want to avoid any criticism of the way we administer this liberal gift.
21For we are taking pains to do what is right,
not only in the eyes of the Lord but also in the
eyes of men.

22In addition, we are sending with them our
brother who has often proved to us in many
ways that he is zealous, and now even more

[a]7 Some manuscripts *in our love for you* [b]15 Exodus 16:18

so because of his great confidence in you.
23As for Titus, he is my partner and fellow
worker among you; as for our brothers, they
are representatives of the churches and an
honor to Christ. 24Therefore show these men
the proof of your love and the reason for our
pride in you, so that the churches can see it.

9 There is no need for me to write to you
about this service to the saints. 2For I
know your eagerness to help, and I have
been boasting about it to the Macedonians,
telling them that since last year you in Achaia
were ready to give; and your enthusiasm has
stirred most of them to action. 3But I am
sending the brothers in order that our boasting about you in this matter should not prove
hollow, but that you may be ready, as I said
you would be. 4For if any Macedonians come
with me and find you unprepared, we—not to
say anything about you—would be ashamed
of having been so confident. 5So I thought it
necessary to urge the brothers to visit you in
advance and finish the arrangements for the
generous gift you had promised. Then it will
be ready as a generous gift, not as one
grudgingly given.

Sowing Generously

6Remember this: Whoever sows sparingly
will also reap sparingly, and whoever sows
generously will also reap generously. 7Each
man should give what he has decided in his
heart to give, not reluctantly or under compulsion, for God loves a cheerful giver. 8And
God is able to make all grace abound to you,
so that in all things at all times, having all that
you need, you will abound in every good
work. 9As it is written:

> "He has scattered abroad his gifts to the poor;
> his righteousness endures forever."[a]

10Now he who supplies seed to the sower
and bread for food will also supply and increase your store of seed and will enlarge
the harvest of your righteousness. 11You will
be made rich in every way so that you can be
generous on every occasion, and through us
your generosity will result in thanksgiving to
God.

12This service that you perform is not only
supplying the needs of God's people but is
also overflowing in many expressions of
thanks to God. 13Because of the service by
which you have proved yourselves, men will
praise God for the obedience that accompanies your confession of the gospel of Christ,
and for your generosity in sharing with them
and with everyone else. 14And in their
prayers for you their hearts will go out to you,
because of the surpassing grace God has
given you. 15Thanks be to God for his indescribable gift!

Paul's Defense of His Ministry

10 By the meekness and gentleness of
Christ, I appeal to you—I, Paul, who
am "timid" when face to face with you, but
"bold" when away! 2I beg you that when I
come I may not have to be as bold as I
expect to be toward some people who think
that we live by the standards of this world.
3For though we live in the world, we do not
wage war as the world does. 4The weapons
we fight with are not the weapons of the
world. On the contrary, they have divine
power to demolish strongholds. 5We demolish arguments and every pretension that
sets itself up against the knowledge of God,
and we take captive every thought to make it
obedient to Christ. 6And we will be ready to
punish every act of disobedience, once your
obedience is complete.

7You are looking only on the surface of
things.[b] If anyone is confident that he belongs to Christ, he should consider again
that we belong to Christ just as much as he.
8For even if I boast somewhat freely about
the authority the Lord gave us for building
you up rather than pulling you down, I will not
be ashamed of it. 9I do not want to seem to
be trying to frighten you with my letters. 10For
some say, "His letters are weighty and forceful, but in person he is unimpressive and his
speaking amounts to nothing." 11Such
people should realize that what we are in our
letters when we are absent, we will be in our
actions when we are present.

12We do not dare to classify or compare
ourselves with some who commend themselves. When they measure themselves by
themselves and compare themselves with
themselves, they are not wise. 13We, however, will not boast beyond proper limits, but
will confine our boasting to the field God has
assigned to us, a field that reaches even to
you. 14We are not going too far in our boasting, as would be the case if we had not come
to you, for we did get as far as you with the
gospel of Christ. 15Neither do we go beyond

[a]9 Psalm 112:9 [b]7 Or *Look at the obvious facts*

our limits by boasting of work done by others.[a] Our hope is that, as your faith continues to grow, our area of activity among you
will greatly expand, 16so that we can preach
the gospel in the regions beyond you. For we
do not want to boast about work already
done in another man's territory. 17But, "Let
him who boasts boast in the Lord."[b] 18For it
is not the one who commends himself who is
approved, but the one whom the Lord commends.

Paul and the False Apostles

11 I hope you will put up with a little of
my foolishness; but you are already
doing that. 2I am jealous for you with a godly
jealousy. I promised you to one husband, to
Christ, so that I might present you as a pure
virgin to him. 3But I am afraid that just as Eve
was deceived by the serpent's cunning, your
minds may somehow be led astray from your
sincere and pure devotion to Christ. 4For if
someone comes to you and preaches a
Jesus other than the Jesus we preached, or
if you receive a different spirit from the one
you received, or a different gospel from the
one you accepted, you put up with it easily
enough. 5But I do not think I am in the least
inferior to those "super-apostles." 6I may not
be a trained speaker, but I do have knowledge. We have made this perfectly clear to
you in every way.

7Was it a sin for me to lower myself in order
to elevate you by preaching the gospel of
God to you free of charge? 8I robbed other
churches by receiving support from them so
as to serve you. 9And when I was with you
and needed something, I was not a burden to
anyone, for the brothers who came from
Macedonia supplied what I needed. I have
kept myself from being a burden to you in
any way, and will continue to do so. 10As
surely as the truth of Christ is in me, nobody
in the regions of Achaia will stop this boasting of mine. 11Why? Because I do not love
you? God knows I do! 12And I will keep on
doing what I am doing in order to cut the
ground from under those who want an opportunity to be considered equal with us in
the things they boast about.

13For such men are false apostles, deceitful workmen, masquerading as apostles of
Christ. 14And no wonder, for Satan himself
masquerades as an angel of light. 15It is not
surprising, then, if his servants masquerade
as servants of righteousness. Their end will
be what their actions deserve.

Paul Boasts About His Sufferings

16I repeat: Let no one take me for a fool.
But if you do, then receive me just as you
would a fool, so that I may do a little boasting.
17In this self-confident boasting I am not talking as the Lord would, but as a fool. 18Since
many are boasting in the way the world does,
I too will boast. 19You gladly put up with fools
since you are so wise! 20In fact, you even put
up with anyone who enslaves you or exploits
you or takes advantage of you or pushes
himself forward or slaps you in the face. 21To
my shame I admit that we were too weak for
that!

What anyone else dares to boast about—I
am speaking as a fool—I also dare to boast
about. 22Are they Hebrews? So am I. Are
they Israelites? So am I. Are they Abraham's
descendants? So am I. 23Are they servants
of Christ? (I am out of my mind to talk like
this.) I am more. I have worked much harder,
been in prison more frequently, been flogged
more severely, and been exposed to death
again and again. 24Five times I received from
the Jews the forty lashes minus one. 25Three
times I was beaten with rods, once I was
stoned, three times I was shipwrecked, I
spent a night and a day in the open sea, 26I
have been constantly on the move. I have
been in danger from rivers, in danger from
bandits, in danger from my own countrymen,
in danger from Gentiles; in danger in the city,
in danger in the country, in danger at sea;
and in danger from false brothers. 27I have
labored and toiled and have often gone without sleep; I have known hunger and thirst
and have often gone without food; I have
been cold and naked. 28Besides everything
else, I face daily the pressure of my concern
for all the churches. 29Who is weak, and I do
not feel weak? Who is led into sin, and I do
not inwardly burn?

30If I must boast, I will boast of the things
that show my weakness. 31The God and Father of the Lord Jesus, who is to be praised
forever, knows that I am not lying. 32In
Damascus the governor under King Aretas
had the city of the Damascenes guarded in

[a] *13-15* Or *13We, however, will not boast about things that cannot be measured, but we will boast according to the standard of measurement that the God of measure has assigned us—a measurement that relates even to you. 14 . . . . 15Neither do we boast about things that cannot be measured in regard to the work done by others.*
[b] *17* Jer. 9:24

order to arrest me. [33]But I was lowered in a basket from a window in the wall and slipped through his hands.

Paul's Vision and His Thorn

12 I must go on boasting. Although there is nothing to be gained, I will go on to visions and revelations from the Lord. [2]I know a man in Christ who fourteen years ago was caught up to the third heaven. Whether it was in the body or out of the body I do not know—God knows. [3]And I know that this man—whether in the body or apart from the body I do not know, but God knows— [4]was caught up to paradise. He heard inexpressible things, things that man is not permitted to tell. [5]I will boast about a man like that, but I will not boast about myself, except about my weaknesses. [6]Even if I should choose to boast, I would not be a fool, because I would be speaking the truth. But I refrain, so no one will think more of me than is warranted by what I do or say.

[7]To keep me from becoming conceited because of these surpassingly great revelations, there was given me a thorn in my flesh, a messenger of Satan, to torment me. [8]Three times I pleaded with the Lord to take it away from me. [9]But he said to me, "My grace is sufficient for you, for my power is made perfect in weakness." Therefore I will boast all the more gladly about my weaknesses, so that Christ's power may rest on me. [10]That is why, for Christ's sake, I delight in weaknesses, in insults, in hardships, in persecutions, in difficulties. For when I am weak, then I am strong.

Paul's Concern for the Corinthians

[11]I have made a fool of myself, but you drove me to it. I ought to have been commended by you, for I am not in the least inferior to the "super-apostles," even though I am nothing. [12]The things that mark an apostle—signs, wonders and miracles—were done among you with great perseverance. [13]How were you inferior to the other churches, except that I was never a burden to you? Forgive me this wrong!

[14]Now I am ready to visit you for the third time, and I will not be a burden to you, because what I want is not your possessions but you. After all, children should not have to save up for their parents, but parents for their children. [15]So I will very gladly spend for you everything I have and expend myself as well. If I love you more, will you love me less? [16]Be that as it may, I have not been a burden to you. Yet, crafty fellow that I am, I caught you by trickery! [17]Did I exploit you through any of the men I sent you? [18]I urged Titus to go to you and I sent our brother with him. Titus did not exploit you, did he? Did we not act in the same spirit and follow the same course?

[19]Have you been thinking all along that we have been defending ourselves to you? We have been speaking in the sight of God as those in Christ; and everything we do, dear friends, is for your strengthening. [20]For I am afraid that when I come I may not find you as I want you to be, and you may not find me as you want me to be. I fear that there may be quarreling, jealousy, outbursts of anger, factions, slander, gossip, arrogance and disorder. [21]I am afraid that when I come again my God will humble me before you, and I will be grieved over many who have sinned earlier and have not repented of the impurity, sexual sin and debauchery in which they have indulged.

Final Warnings

13 This will be my third visit to you. "Every matter must be established by the testimony of two or three witnesses."[a] [2]I already gave you a warning when I was with you the second time. I now repeat it while absent: On my return I will not spare those who sinned earlier or any of the others, [3]since you are demanding proof that Christ is speaking through me. He is not weak in dealing with you, but is powerful among you. [4]For to be sure, he was crucified in weakness, yet he lives by God's power. Likewise, we are weak in him, yet by God's power we will live with him to serve you.

[5]Examine yourselves to see whether you are in the faith; test yourselves. Do you not realize that Christ Jesus is in you—unless, of course, you fail the test? [6]And I trust that you will discover that we have not failed the test. [7]Now we pray to God that you will not do anything wrong. Not that people will see that we have stood the test but that you will do what is right even though we may seem to have failed. [8]For we cannot do anything against the truth, but only for the truth. [9]We are glad whenever we are weak but you are strong; and our prayer is for your perfection.

[a] 1 Deut. 19:15

[10]This is why I write these things when I am absent, that when I come I may not have to be harsh in my use of authority—the authority the Lord gave me for building you up, not for tearing you down.

Final Greetings

[11]Finally, brothers, good-by. Aim for perfection, listen to my appeal, be of one mind, live in peace. And the God of love and peace will be with you.

[12]Greet one another with a holy kiss. [13]All
the saints send their greetings.

[14]May the grace of the Lord Jesus Christ, and the love of God, and the fellowship of the Holy Spirit be with you all.

Galatians

Introduction:

Paul wrote this letter to the Christian churches in the Roman province of Galatia. These churches were being confused by false teachers called Judaizers, who were teaching the gentile Christians that they were not really saved unless they obeyed all the Jewish laws—such as circumcision, eating special foods, and celebrating Jewish feast days. This group also said that Paul did not have God's authority and, therefore, was not to be listened to.

Paul begins the letter by telling the Galatians what gospel it is that he preaches and that his authority is from God. We cannot be saved from our sins by obeying the law; we are saved only by believing in Jesus Christ, Paul adds. Christians are free to live by the law of love, not the law of Moses. Faith, says Paul, must be shown in love and believers must live by the Spirit.

Outline of contents:

---

1 Paul, an apostle—sent not from men nor
by man, but by Jesus Christ and God the
Father, who raised him from the dead— 2and
all the brothers with me,

To the churches in Galatia:

3Grace and peace to you from God our
Father and the Lord Jesus Christ, 4who gave
himself for our sins to rescue us from the
present evil age, according to the will of our
God and Father, 5to whom be glory for ever
and ever. Amen.

No Other Gospel

6I am astonished that you are so quickly
deserting the one who called you by the
grace of Christ and are turning to a different
gospel— 7which is really no gospel at all.
Evidently some people are throwing you into
confusion and are trying to pervert the gospel of Christ. 8But even if we or an angel from
heaven should preach a gospel other than
the one we preached to you, let him be eternally condemned! 9As we have already said,
so now I say again: If anybody is preaching
to you a gospel other than what you accepted, let him be eternally condemned!

10Am I now trying to win the approval of
men, or of God? Or am I trying to please
men? If I were still trying to please men, I
would not be a servant of Christ.

Paul Called by God

11I want you to know, brothers, that the
gospel I preached is not something that man
made up. 12I did not receive it from any man,
nor was I taught it; rather, I received it by
revelation from Jesus Christ.

13For you have heard of my previous way
of life in Judaism, how intensely I persecuted
the church of God and tried to destroy it. 14I
was advancing in Judaism beyond many
Jews of my own age and was extremely
zealous for the traditions of my fathers. 15But
when God, who set me apart from birth[a] and
called me by his grace, was pleased 16to
reveal his Son in me so that I might preach
him among the Gentiles, I did not consult any
man, 17nor did I go up to Jerusalem to see
those who were apostles before I was, but I
went immediately into Arabia and later returned to Damascus.

18Then after three years, I went up to
Jerusalem to get acquainted with Peter[b] and

[a]15 Or *from my mother's womb* [b]18 Greek *Cephas*

stayed with him fifteen days. 19I saw none of
the other apostles—only James, the Lord's
brother. 20I assure you before God that what
I am writing you is no lie. 21Later I went to
Syria and Cilicia. 22I was personally unknown to the churches of Judea that are in
Christ. 23They only heard the report: "The
man who formerly persecuted us is now
preaching the faith he once tried to destroy."
24And they praised God because of me.

Paul Accepted by the Apostles

2 Fourteen years later I went up again to
Jerusalem, this time with Barnabas. I
took Titus along also. 2I went in response to a
revelation and set before them the gospel
that I preach among the Gentiles. But I did
this privately to those who seemed to be
leaders, for fear that I was running or had run
my race in vain. 3Yet not even Titus, who was
with me, was compelled to be circumcised,
even though he was a Greek. 4⌊This matter
arose⌋ because some false brothers had infiltrated our ranks to spy on the freedom we
have in Christ Jesus and to make us slaves.
5We did not give in to them for a moment, so
that the truth of the gospel might remain with
you.

6As for those who seemed to be important—whatever they were makes no difference to me; God does not judge by external
appearance—those men added nothing to
my message. 7On the contrary, they saw that
I had been entrusted with the task of preaching the gospel to the Gentiles,[a] just as Peter
had been to the Jews.[b] 8For God, who was at
work in the ministry of Peter as an apostle to
the Jews, was also at work in my ministry as
an apostle to the Gentiles. 9James, Peter[c]
and John, those reputed to be pillars, gave
me and Barnabas the right hand of fellowship when they recognized the grace given
to me. They agreed that we should go to the
Gentiles, and they to the Jews. 10All they
asked was that we should continue to
remember the poor, the very thing I was eager to do.

Paul Opposes Peter

11When Peter came to Antioch, I opposed
him to his face, because he was clearly in the
wrong. 12Before certain men came from
James, he used to eat with the Gentiles. But
when they arrived, he began to draw back
and separate himself from the Gentiles because he was afraid of those who belonged
to the circumcision group. 13The other Jews
joined him in his hypocrisy, so that by their
hypocrisy even Barnabas was led astray.

14When I saw that they were not acting in
line with the truth of the gospel, I said to
Peter in front of them all, "You are a Jew, yet
you live like a Gentile and not like a Jew.
How is it, then, that you force Gentiles to
follow Jewish customs?

15"We who are Jews by birth and not 'Gentile sinners' 16know that a man is not justified
by observing the law, but by faith in Jesus
Christ. So we, too, have put our faith in Christ
Jesus that we may be justified by faith in
Christ and not by observing the law, because
by observing the law no one will be justified.

17"If, while we seek to be justified in Christ,
it becomes evident that we ourselves are
sinners, does that mean that Christ promotes sin? Absolutely not! 18If I rebuild what
I destroyed, I prove that I am a lawbreaker.
19For through the law I died to the law so that
I might live for God. 20I have been crucified
with Christ and I no longer live, but Christ
lives in me. The life I live in the body, I live by
faith in the Son of God, who loved me and
gave himself for me. 21I do not set aside the
grace of God, for if righteousness could be
gained through the law, Christ died for nothing!"[d]

Faith or Observance of the Law

3 You foolish Galatians! Who has bewitched you? Before your very eyes
Jesus Christ was clearly portrayed as crucified. 2I would like to learn just one thing from
you: Did you receive the Spirit by observing
the law, or by believing what you heard? 3Are
you so foolish? After beginning with the
Spirit, are you now trying to attain your goal
by human effort? 4Have you suffered so
much for nothing—if it really was for nothing? 5Does God give you his Spirit and work
miracles among you because you observe
the law, or because you believe what you
heard?

6Consider Abraham: "He believed God,
and it was credited to him as righteousness."[e] 7Understand, then, that those who
believe are children of Abraham. 8The Scripture foresaw that God would justify the Gentiles by faith, and announced the gospel in

[a]7 Greek *uncircumcised* [b]7 Greek *circumcised;* also in verses 8 and 9 [c]9 Greek *Cephas;* also in verses 11 and 14 [d]21 Some interpreters end the quotation after verse 14. [e]6 Gen. 15:6

advance to Abraham: "All nations will be
blessed through you."[a] 9So those who have
faith are blessed along with Abraham, the
man of faith.

10All who rely on observing the law are
under a curse, for it is written: "Cursed is
everyone who does not continue to do everything written in the Book of the Law."[b]
11Clearly no one is justified before God by
the law, because, "The righteous will live by
faith."[c] 12The law is not based on faith; on
the contrary, "The man who does these
things will live by them."[d] 13Christ redeemed
us from the curse of the law by becoming a
curse for us, for it is written: "Cursed is
everyone who is hung on a tree."[e] 14He redeemed us in order that the blessing given to
Abraham might come to the Gentiles through
Christ Jesus, so that by faith we might receive the promise of the Spirit.

The Law and the Promise

15Brothers, let me take an example from
everyday life. Just as no one can set aside or
add to a human covenant that has been duly
established, so it is in this case. 16The promises were spoken to Abraham and to his
seed. The Scripture does not say "and to
seeds," meaning many people, but "and to
your seed,"[f] meaning one person, who is
Christ. 17What I mean is this: The law, introduced 430 years later, does not set aside the
covenant previously established by God and
thus do away with the promise. 18For if the
inheritance depends on the law, then it no
longer depends on a promise; but God in his
grace gave it to Abraham through a promise.

19What, then, was the purpose of the law?
It was added because of transgressions until
the Seed to whom the promise referred had
come. The law was put into effect through
angels by a mediator. 20A mediator, however, does not represent just one party; but
God is one.

21Is the law, therefore, opposed to the
promises of God? Absolutely not! For if a law
had been given that could impart life, then
righteousness would certainly have come by
the law. 22But the Scripture declares that the
whole world is a prisoner of sin, so that what
was promised, being given through faith in
Jesus Christ, might be given to those who
believe.

23Before this faith came, we were held
prisoners by the law, locked up until faith
should be revealed. 24So the law was put in
charge to lead us to Christ[g] that we might be
justified by faith. 25Now that faith has come,
we are no longer under the supervision of the
law.

Sons of God

26You are all sons of God through faith in
Christ Jesus, 27for all of you who were baptized into Christ have clothed yourselves
with Christ. 28There is neither Jew nor Greek,
slave nor free, male nor female, for you are
all one in Christ Jesus. 29If you belong to
Christ, then you are Abraham's seed, and
heirs according to the promise.

4 What I am saying is that as long as the
heir is a child, he is no different from a
slave, although he owns the whole estate.
2He is subject to guardians and trustees until
the time set by his father. 3So also, when we
were children, we were in slavery under the
basic principles of the world. 4But when the
time had fully come, God sent his Son, born
of a woman, born under law, 5to redeem
those under law, that we might receive the
full rights of sons. 6Because you are sons,
God sent the Spirit of his Son into our hearts,
the Spirit who calls out, "*Abba*,[h] Father." 7So
you are no longer a slave, but a son; and
since you are a son, God has made you also
an heir.

Paul's Concern for the Galatians

8Formerly, when you did not know God,
you were slaves to those who by nature are
not gods. 9But now that you know God—or
rather are known by God—how is it that you
are turning back to those weak and miserable principles? Do you wish to be enslaved
by them all over again? 10You are observing
special days and months and seasons and
years! 11I fear for you, that somehow I have
wasted my efforts on you.

12I plead with you, brothers, become like
me, for I became like you. You have done me
no wrong. 13As you know, it was because of
an illness that I first preached the gospel to
you. 14Even though my illness was a trial to
you, you did not treat me with contempt or
scorn. Instead, you welcomed me as if I were
an angel of God, as if I were Christ Jesus
himself. 15What has happened to all your
joy? I can testify that, if you could have done

[a] *8* Gen. 12:3; 18:18; 22:18 [b] *10* Deut. 27:26 [c] *11* Hab. 2:4 [d] *12* Lev. 18:5 [e] *13* Deut. 21:23
[f] *16* Gen. 12:7; 13:15; 24:7 [g] *24* Or *charge until Christ came* [h] *6* Aramaic for *Father*

so, you would have torn out your eyes and given them to me. [16]Have I now become your enemy by telling you the truth?

[17]Those people are zealous to win you over, but for no good. What they want is to alienate you ⌊from us⌋, so that you may be zealous for them. [18]It is fine to be zealous, provided the purpose is good, and to be so always and not just when I am with you. [19]My dear children, for whom I am again in the pains of childbirth until Christ is formed in you, [20]how I wish I could be with you now and change my tone, because I am perplexed about you!

Hagar and Sarah

[21]Tell me, you who want to be under the law, are you not aware of what the law says? [22]For it is written that Abraham had two sons, one by the slave woman and the other by the free woman. [23]His son by the slave woman was born in the ordinary way; but his son by the free woman was born as the result of a promise.

[24]These things may be taken figuratively, for the women represent two covenants. One covenant is from Mount Sinai and bears children who are to be slaves: This is Hagar. [25]Now Hagar stands for Mount Sinai in Arabia and corresponds to the present city of Jerusalem, because she is in slavery with her children. [26]But the Jerusalem that is above is free, and she is our mother. [27]For it is written:

"Be glad, O barren woman,
  who bears no children;
break forth and cry aloud,
  you who have no labor pains;
because more are the children of the
    desolate woman
  than of her who has a husband."[a]

[28]Now you, brothers, like Isaac, are children of promise. [29]At that time the son born in the ordinary way persecuted the son born by the power of the Spirit. It is the same now. [30]But what does the Scripture say? "Get rid of the slave woman and her son, for the slave woman's son will never share in the inheritance with the free woman's son."[b] [31]Therefore, brothers, we are not children of the slave woman, but of the free woman.

Freedom in Christ

5 It is for freedom that Christ has set us free. Stand firm, then, and do not let yourselves be burdened again by a yoke of slavery.

[2]Mark my words! I, Paul, tell you that if you let yourselves be circumcised, Christ will be of no value to you at all. [3]Again I declare to every man who lets himself be circumcised that he is obligated to obey the whole law. [4]You who are trying to be justified by law have been alienated from Christ; you have fallen away from grace. [5]But by faith we eagerly await through the Spirit the righteousness for which we hope. [6]For in Christ Jesus neither circumcision nor uncircumcision has any value. The only thing that counts is faith expressing itself through love.

[7]You were running a good race. Who cut in on you and kept you from obeying the truth? [8]That kind of persuasion does not come from the one who calls you. [9]"A little yeast works through the whole batch of dough." [10]I am confident in the Lord that you will take no other view. The one who is throwing you into confusion will pay the penalty, whoever he may be. [11]Brothers, if I am still preaching circumcision, why am I still being persecuted? In that case the offense of the cross has been abolished. [12]As for those agitators, I wish they would go the whole way and emasculate themselves!

[13]You, my brothers, were called to be free. But do not use your freedom to indulge the sinful nature[c]; rather, serve one another in love. [14]The entire law is summed up in a single command: "Love your neighbor as yourself."[d] [15]If you keep on biting and devouring each other, watch out or you will be destroyed by each other.

Life by the Spirit

[16]So I say, live by the Spirit, and you will not gratify the desires of the sinful nature. [17]For the sinful nature desires what is contrary to the Spirit, and the Spirit what is contrary to the sinful nature. They are in conflict with each other, so that you do not do what you want. [18]But if you are led by the Spirit, you are not under law.

[19]The acts of the sinful nature are obvious: sexual immorality, impurity and debauchery; [20]idolatry and witchcraft; hatred, discord,

[a]*27* Isaiah 54:1 [b]*30* Gen. 21:10 [c]*13* Or *the flesh;* also in verses 16, 17, 19 and 24 [d]*14* Lev. 19:18

jealousy, fits of rage, selfish ambition, dissensions, factions 21and envy; drunkenness,
orgies, and the like. I warn you, as I did
before, that those who live like this will not
inherit the kingdom of God.
22But the fruit of the Spirit is love, joy,
peace, patience, kindness, goodness, faithfulness, 23gentleness and self-control.
Against such things there is no law. 24Those
who belong to Christ Jesus have crucified
the sinful nature with its passions and desires. 25Since we live by the Spirit, let us
keep in step with the Spirit. 26Let us not
become conceited, provoking and envying
each other.

Doing Good to All

6 Brothers, if someone is caught in a sin,
you who are spiritual should restore him
gently. But watch yourself, or you also may
be tempted. 2Carry each other's burdens,
and in this way you will fulfill the law of Christ.
3If anyone thinks he is something when he is
nothing, he deceives himself. 4Each one
should test his own actions. Then he can
take pride in himself, without comparing himself to somebody else, 5for each one should
carry his own load.
6Anyone who receives instruction in the
word must share all good things with his instructor.
7Do not be deceived: God cannot be
mocked. A man reaps what he sows. 8The
one who sows to please his sinful nature,
from that nature[a] will reap destruction; the
one who sows to please the Spirit, from the
Spirit will reap eternal life. 9Let us not
become weary in doing good, for at the
proper time we will reap a harvest if we do
not give up. 10Therefore, as we have opportunity, let us do good to all people, especially
to those who belong to the family of believers.

Not Circumcision but a New Creation

11See what large letters I use as I write to
you with my own hand!
12Those who want to make a good impres-
sion outwardly are trying to compel you to be
circumcised. The only reason they do this is
to avoid being persecuted for the cross of
Christ. 13Not even those who are circumcised obey the law, yet they want you to be
circumcised that they may boast about your
flesh. 14May I never boast except in the cross
of our Lord Jesus Christ, through which[b] the
world has been crucified to me, and I to the
world. 15Neither circumcision nor uncircumcision means anything; what counts is a new
creation. 16Peace and mercy to all who follow
this rule, even to the Israel of God.
17Finally, let no one cause me trouble, for I
bear on my body the marks of Jesus.
18The grace of our Lord Jesus Christ be
with your spirit, brothers. Amen.

[a]8 Or *his flesh, from the flesh* [b]14 Or *whom*

Ephesians

Introduction:

This letter was written by Paul during his two-year imprisonment in Rome (about A.D. 60). This letter probably was sent not just to the church at Ephesus but to all the Christian churches near Ephesus. Ephesus was a large, important city at that time, so it was a natural center for the Christian churches.

One of Paul's themes in Ephesians is that of unity and God's purpose "to bring all things in heaven and on earth together under one head, even Christ." Because of this unity, Paul wrote, all Christians are one family in Jesus, and they should act with love toward each other. He gives believers instructions on how to "live a life of love" by addressing the husband-wife, parent-children, and slave-master relationships.

In this letter Paul also writes about the church—not a church building in a certain place but the church that is made up of all Christians who have ever lived. We call this "the church universal." He compares Christ's relationship to the church to the body, a building, and a wife.

Outline of contents:

Greetings (1:1,2)
Christ and the church (1:3–3:21)
Conduct of the believer (4:1–6:9)
The Christian's warfare (6:10–20)
Conclusion (6:21–24)

---

1 Paul, an apostle of Christ Jesus by the will of God,

To the saints in Ephesus,[a] the faithful[b] in Christ Jesus:

2Grace and peace to you from God our Father and the Lord Jesus Christ.

Spiritual Blessings in Christ

3Praise be to the God and Father of our Lord Jesus Christ, who has blessed us in the heavenly realms with every spiritual blessing
in Christ. 4For he chose us in him before the creation of the world to be holy and blameless in his sight. In love
5he[c] predestined us to be adopted as his sons through Jesus Christ, in accordance with his pleasure and will—
6to the praise of his glorious grace, which he has freely given us in the One he
loves. 7In him we have redemption through his blood, the forgiveness of sins, in accordance with the riches of God's grace
8that he lavished on us with all wisdom and understanding.
9And he[d] made known to us the mystery of his will according to his good pleasure, which he purposed in Christ,
10to be put into effect when the times will have reached their fulfillment—to bring all things in heaven and on earth together under one head, even Christ.

11In him we were also chosen,[e] having been predestined according to the plan of him who works out everything in conformity with the purpose of his will,
12in order that we, who were the first to hope in Christ, might be for the praise of his glory.
13And you also were included in Christ when you heard the word of truth, the gospel of your salvation. Having believed, you were marked in him with a seal, the promised Holy Spirit,
14who is a deposit guaranteeing our inheritance until the redemption of those who are God's possession—to the praise of his glory.

Thanksgiving and Prayer

15For this reason, ever since I heard about

[a] 1 Some early manuscripts do not have *in Ephesus.* [b] 1 Or *believers who are* [c] 4,5 Or *sight in love.* [5]*He* [d] 8,9 Or *us. With all wisdom and understanding,* [9]*he* [e] 11 Or *were made heirs*

your faith in the Lord Jesus and your love for all the saints, [16]I have not stopped giving thanks for you, remembering you in my prayers. [17]I keep asking that the God of our Lord Jesus Christ, the glorious Father, may give you the Spirit[a] of wisdom and revelation, so that you may know him better. [18]I pray also that the eyes of your heart may be enlightened in order that you may know the hope to which he has called you, the riches of his glorious inheritance in the saints, [19]and his incomparably great power for us who believe. That power is like the working of his mighty strength, [20]which he exerted in Christ when he raised him from the dead and seated him at his right hand in the heavenly realms, [21]far above all rule and authority, power and dominion, and every title that can be given, not only in the present age but also in the one to come. [22]And God placed all things under his feet and appointed him to be head over everything for the church, [23]which is his body, the fullness of him who fills everything in every way.

Made Alive in Christ

2 As for you, you were dead in your transgressions and sins, [2]in which you used to live when you followed the ways of this world and of the ruler of the kingdom of the air, the spirit who is now at work in those who are disobedient. [3]All of us also lived among them at one time, gratifying the cravings of our sinful nature[b] and following its desires and thoughts. Like the rest, we were by nature objects of wrath. [4]But because of his great love for us, God, who is rich in mercy, [5]made us alive with Christ even when we were dead in transgressions—it is by grace you have been saved. [6]And God raised us up with Christ and seated us with him in the heavenly realms in Christ Jesus, [7]in order that in the coming ages he might show the incomparable riches of his grace, expressed in his kindness to us in Christ Jesus. [8]For it is by grace you have been saved, through faith—and this not from yourselves, it is the gift of God— [9]not by works, so that no one can boast. [10]For we are God's workmanship, created in Christ Jesus to do good works, which God prepared in advance for us to do.

One in Christ

[11]Therefore, remember that formerly you who are Gentiles by birth and called "uncircumcised" by those who call themselves "the circumcision" (that done in the body by the hands of men)— [12]remember that at that time you were separate from Christ, excluded from citizenship in Israel and foreigners to the covenants of the promise, without hope and without God in the world. [13]But now in Christ Jesus you who once were far away have been brought near through the blood of Christ.

[14]For he himself is our peace, who has made the two one and has destroyed the barrier, the dividing wall of hostility, [15]by abolishing in his flesh the law with its commandments and regulations. His purpose was to create in himself one new man out of the two, thus making peace, [16]and in this one body to reconcile both of them to God through the cross, by which he put to death their hostility. [17]He came and preached peace to you who were far away and peace to those who were near. [18]For through him we both have access to the Father by one Spirit.

[19]Consequently, you are no longer foreigners and aliens, but fellow citizens with God's people and members of God's household, [20]built on the foundation of the apostles and prophets, with Christ Jesus himself as the chief cornerstone. [21]In him the whole building is joined together and rises to become a holy temple in the Lord. [22]And in him you too are being built together to become a dwelling in which God lives by his Spirit.

Paul the Preacher to the Gentiles

3 For this reason I, Paul, the prisoner of Christ Jesus for the sake of you Gentiles—

[2]Surely you have heard about the administration of God's grace that was given to me for you, [3]that is, the mystery made known to me by revelation, as I have already written briefly. [4]In reading this, then, you will be able to understand my insight into the mystery of Christ, [5]which was not made known to men in other generations as it has now been revealed by the Spirit to God's holy apostles and prophets. [6]This mystery is that through the gospel the Gentiles are heirs together with Israel, members together of one body, and sharers together in the promise in Christ Jesus.

[7]I became a servant of this gospel by the

[a]17 Or *a spirit* [b]3 Or *our flesh*

gift of God's grace given me through the working of his power. 8Although I am less than the least of all God's people, this grace was given me: to preach to the Gentiles the unsearchable riches of Christ, 9and to make plain to everyone the administration of this mystery, which for ages past was kept hidden in God, who created all things. 10His intent was that now, through the church, the manifold wisdom of God should be made known to the rulers and authorities in the heavenly realms, 11according to his eternal purpose which he accomplished in Christ Jesus our Lord. 12In him and through faith in him we may approach God with freedom and confidence. 13I ask you, therefore, not to be discouraged because of my sufferings for you, which are your glory.

A Prayer for the Ephesians

14For this reason I kneel before the Father, 15from whom his whole family[a] in heaven and on earth derives its name. 16I pray that out of his glorious riches he may strengthen you with power through his Spirit in your inner being, 17so that Christ may dwell in your hearts through faith. And I pray that you, being rooted and established in love, 18may have power, together with all the saints, to grasp how wide and long and high and deep is the love of Christ, 19and to know this love that surpasses knowledge—that you may be filled to the measure of all the fullness of God.

20Now to him who is able to do immeasurably more than all we ask or imagine, according to his power that is at work within us, 21to him be glory in the church and in Christ Jesus throughout all generations, for ever and ever! Amen.

Unity in the Body of Christ

4 As a prisoner for the Lord, then, I urge you to live a life worthy of the calling you have received. 2Be completely humble and gentle; be patient, bearing with one another in love. 3Make every effort to keep the unity of the Spirit through the bond of peace. 4There is one body and one Spirit— just as you were called to one hope when you were called— 5one Lord, one faith, one baptism; 6one God and Father of all, who is over all and through all and in all.

7But to each one of us grace has been given as Christ apportioned it. 8This is why it[b] says:

"When he ascended on high,
he led captives in his train
and gave gifts to men."[c]

9(What does "he ascended" mean except that he also descended to the lower, earthly regions[d]? 10He who descended is the very one who ascended higher than all the heavens, in order to fill the whole universe.) 11It was he who gave some to be apostles, some to be prophets, some to be evangelists, and some to be pastors and teachers, 12to prepare God's people for works of service, so that the body of Christ may be built up 13until we all reach unity in the faith and in the knowledge of the Son of God and become mature, attaining to the whole measure of the fullness of Christ.

14Then we will no longer be infants, tossed back and forth by the waves, and blown here and there by every wind of teaching and by the cunning and craftiness of men in their deceitful scheming. 15Instead, speaking the truth in love, we will in all things grow up into him who is the Head, that is, Christ. 16From him the whole body, joined and held together by every supporting ligament, grows and builds itself up in love, as each part does its work.

Living as Children of Light

17So I tell you this, and insist on it in the Lord, that you must no longer live as the Gentiles do, in the futility of their thinking. 18They are darkened in their understanding and separated from the life of God because of the ignorance that is in them due to the hardening of their hearts. 19Having lost all sensitivity, they have given themselves over to sensuality so as to indulge in every kind of impurity, with a continual lust for more.

20You, however, did not come to know Christ that way. 21Surely you heard of him and were taught in him in accordance with the truth that is in Jesus. 22You were taught, with regard to your former way of life, to put off your old self, which is being corrupted by its deceitful desires; 23to be made new in the attitude of your minds; 24and to put on the new self, created to be like God in true righteousness and holiness.

25Therefore each of you must put off false-

[a]15 Or *whom all fatherhood* [b]8 Or *God* [c]8 Psalm 68:18 [d]9 Or *the depths of the earth*

hood and speak truthfully to his neighbor, for we are all members of one body. 26"In your anger do not sin"[a]: Do not let the sun go down while you are still angry, 27and do not give the devil a foothold. 28He who has been stealing must steal no longer, but must work, doing something useful with his own hands, that he may have something to share with those in need.

29Do not let any unwholesome talk come out of your mouths, but only what is helpful for building others up according to their needs, that it may benefit those who listen. 30And do not grieve the Holy Spirit of God, with whom you were sealed for the day of redemption. 31Get rid of all bitterness, rage and anger, brawling and slander, along with every form of malice. 32Be kind and compassionate to one another, forgiving each other, just as in Christ God forgave you.

5 Be imitators of God, therefore, as dearly loved children 2and live a life of love, just as Christ loved us and gave himself up for us as a fragrant offering and sacrifice to God.

3But among you there must not be even a hint of sexual immorality, or of any kind of impurity, or of greed, because these are improper for God's holy people. 4Nor should there be obscenity, foolish talk or coarse joking, which are out of place, but rather thanksgiving. 5For of this you can be sure: No immoral, impure or greedy person—such a man is an idolater—has any inheritance in the kingdom of Christ and of God.[b] 6Let no one deceive you with empty words, for because of such things God's wrath comes on those who are disobedient. 7Therefore do not be partners with them.

8For you were once darkness, but now you are light in the Lord. Live as children of light 9(for the fruit of the light consists in all goodness, righteousness and truth) 10and find out what pleases the Lord. 11Have nothing to do with the fruitless deeds of darkness, but rather expose them. 12For it is shameful even to mention what the disobedient do in secret. 13But everything exposed by the light becomes visible, 14for it is light that makes everything visible. This is why it is said:

"Wake up, O sleeper,
  rise from the dead,
and Christ will shine on you."

15Be very careful, then, how you live—not as unwise but as wise, 16making the most of every opportunity, because the days are evil. 17Therefore do not be foolish, but understand what the Lord's will is. 18Do not get drunk on wine, which leads to debauchery. Instead, be filled with the Spirit. 19Speak to one another with psalms, hymns and spiritual songs. Sing and make music in your heart to the Lord, 20always giving thanks to God the Father for everything, in the name of our Lord Jesus Christ.

21Submit to one another out of reverence for Christ.

Wives and Husbands

22Wives, submit to your husbands as to the Lord. 23For the husband is the head of the wife as Christ is the head of the church, his body, of which he is the Savior. 24Now as the church submits to Christ, so also wives should submit to their husbands in everything.

25Husbands, love your wives, just as Christ loved the church and gave himself up for her 26to make her holy, cleansing[c] her by the washing with water through the word, 27and to present her to himself as a radiant church, without stain or wrinkle or any other blemish, but holy and blameless. 28In this same way, husbands ought to love their wives as their own bodies. He who loves his wife loves himself. 29After all, no one ever hated his own body, but he feeds and cares for it, just as Christ does the church— 30for we are members of his body. 31"For this reason a man will leave his father and mother and be united to his wife, and the two will become one flesh."[d] 32This is a profound mystery—but I am talking about Christ and the church. 33However, each one of you also must love his wife as he loves himself, and the wife must respect her husband.

Children and Parents

6 Children, obey your parents in the Lord, for this is right. 2"Honor your father and mother"—which is the first commandment with a promise— 3"that it may go well with you and that you may enjoy long life on the earth."[e]

4Fathers, do not exasperate your children; instead, bring them up in the training and instruction of the Lord.

[a] 26 Psalm 4:4 [b] 5 Or *kingdom of the Christ and God* [c] 26 Or *having cleansed* [d] 31 Gen. 2:24
[e] 3 Deut. 5:16

Slaves and Masters

5Slaves, obey your earthly masters with
respect and fear, and with sincerity of heart,
just as you would obey Christ. 6Obey them
not only to win their favor when their eye is
on you, but like slaves of Christ, doing the will
of God from your heart. 7Serve wholeheartedly, as if you were serving the Lord, not
men, 8because you know that the Lord will
reward everyone for whatever good he does,
whether he is slave or free.

9And masters, treat your slaves in the
same way. Do not threaten them, since you
know that he who is both their Master and
yours is in heaven, and there is no favoritism
with him.

The Armor of God

10Finally, be strong in the Lord and in his
mighty power. 11Put on the full armor of God
so that you can take your stand against the
devil's schemes. 12For our struggle is not
against flesh and blood, but against the rulers, against the authorities, against the powers of this dark world and against the spiritual
forces of evil in the heavenly realms.
13Therefore put on the full armor of God, so
that when the day of evil comes, you may be
able to stand your ground, and after you
have done everything, to stand. 14Stand firm
then, with the belt of truth buckled around
your waist, with the breastplate of righteousness in place, 15and with your feet fitted with
the readiness that comes from the gospel of
peace. 16In addition to all this, take up the
shield of faith, with which you can extinguish
all the flaming arrows of the evil one. 17Take
the helmet of salvation and the sword of the
Spirit, which is the word of God. 18And pray in
the Spirit on all occasions with all kinds of
prayers and requests. With this in mind, be
alert and always keep on praying for all the
saints.

19Pray also for me, that whenever I open
my mouth, words may be given me so that I
will fearlessly make known the mystery of
the gospel, 20for which I am an ambassador
in chains. Pray that I may declare it fearlessly, as I should.

Final Greetings

21Tychicus, the dear brother and faithful
servant in the Lord, will tell you everything,
so that you also may know how I am and
what I am doing. 22I am sending him to you
for this very purpose, that you may know how
we are, and that he may encourage you.

23Peace to the brothers, and love with faith
from God the Father and the Lord Jesus
Christ. 24Grace to all who love our Lord
Jesus Christ with an undying love.

Philippians

Introduction:

Philippians, as well as Colossians, Philemon, and Ephesians, was written by Paul while he was in prison in Rome about A.D. 60. The Philippians had sent Epaphroditus to Paul with a gift. While Epaphroditus was in Rome, he became sick, and the Philippian Christians were worried about him. After he was better, Paul sent him back to Philippi with this letter.

Paul's strong feelings of love for the Philippians is felt throughout this letter and this is the most personal of Paul's letters written to a church. Paul tells of his thankfulness for the love and helpfulness of the Philippians.

Even though Paul was writing from prison this letter is full of joy. The words "joy" or "rejoice" are used fourteen times. Paul here gives his own testimony to the meaning of his present life when he writes "For to me, to live is Christ and to die is gain" (1:21).

As in his other letters Paul gives words of encouragement and instructions for living in harmony with others and in obedience to God.

Outline of contents:

- Introduction (1:1–11)
- Paul's circumstances and concern (1:12–30)
- Imitating Christ's humility (2:1–18)
- Paul's messengers (2:19–30)
- Warnings and advice (3:1–4:20)
- Conclusion (4:21–23)

---

1 Paul and Timothy, servants of Christ
Jesus,

To all the saints in Christ Jesus at Philippi,
together with the overseers[a] and deacons:

2Grace and peace to you from God our
Father and the Lord Jesus Christ.

Thanksgiving and Prayer

3I thank my God every time I remember
you. 4In all my prayers for all of you, I always
pray with joy 5because of your partnership in
the gospel from the first day until now, 6being
confident of this, that he who began a good
work in you will carry it on to completion until
the day of Christ Jesus.

7It is right for me to feel this way about all of
you, since I have you in my heart; for whether
I am in chains or defending and confirming
the gospel, all of you share in God's grace
with me. 8God can testify how I long for all of
you with the affection of Christ Jesus.

9And this is my prayer: that your love may
abound more and more in knowledge and
depth of insight, 10so that you may be able to
discern what is best and may be pure and
blameless until the day of Christ, 11filled with
the fruit of righteousness that comes through
Jesus Christ—to the glory and praise of God.

Paul's Chains Advance the Gospel

12Now I want you to know, brothers, that
what has happened to me has really served
to advance the gospel. 13As a result, it has
become clear throughout the whole palace
guard[b] and to everyone else that I am in
chains for Christ. 14Because of my chains,
most of the brothers in the Lord have been
encouraged to speak the word of God more
courageously and fearlessly.

15It is true that some preach Christ out of
envy and rivalry, but others out of goodwill.
16The latter do so in love, knowing that I am
put here for the defense of the gospel. 17The
former preach Christ out of selfish ambition,
not sincerely, supposing that they can stir up

[a] 1 Traditionally *bishops* [b] 13 Or *whole palace*

trouble for me while I am in chains.[a] 18But
what does it matter? The important thing is
that in every way, whether from false motives or true, Christ is preached. And because of this I rejoice.

Yes, and I will continue to rejoice, 19for I
know that through your prayers and the help
given by the Spirit of Jesus Christ, what has
happened to me will turn out for my deliverance.[b] 20I eagerly expect and hope that I will
in no way be ashamed, but will have sufficient courage so that now as always Christ
will be exalted in my body, whether by life or
by death. 21For to me, to live is Christ and to
die is gain. 22If I am to go on living in the
body, this will mean fruitful labor for me. Yet
what shall I choose? I do not know! 23I am
torn between the two: I desire to depart and
be with Christ, which is better by far; 24but it is
more necessary for you that I remain in the
body. 25Convinced of this, I know that I will
remain, and I will continue with all of you for
your progress and joy in the faith, 26so that
through my being with you again your joy in
Christ Jesus will overflow on account of
me.

27Whatever happens, conduct yourselves
in a manner worthy of the gospel of Christ.
Then, whether I come and see you or only
hear about you in my absence, I will know
that you stand firm in one spirit, contending
as one man for the faith of the gospel 28with-
out being frightened in any way by those who
oppose you. This is a sign to them that they
will be destroyed, but that you will be
saved—and that by God. 29For it has been
granted to you on behalf of Christ not only to
believe on him, but also to suffer for him,
30since you are going through the same
struggle you saw I had, and now hear that I
still have.

Imitating Christ's Humility

2 If you have any encouragement from being united with Christ, if any comfort from
his love, if any fellowship with the Spirit, if
any tenderness and compassion, 2then
make my joy complete by being like-minded,
having the same love, being one in spirit and
purpose. 3Do nothing out of selfish ambition
or vain conceit, but in humility consider others better than yourselves. 4Each of you
should look not only to your own interests,
but also to the interests of others.

5Your attitude should be the same as that
of Christ Jesus:

6Who, being in very nature[c] God,
did not consider equality with God
something to be grasped,
7but made himself nothing,
taking the very nature[d] of a servant,
being made in human likeness.
8And being found in appearance as a
man,
he humbled himself
and became obedient to death—
even death on a cross!
9Therefore God exalted him to the highest
place
and gave him the name that is above
every name,
10that at the name of Jesus every knee
should bow,
in heaven and on earth and under the
earth,
11and every tongue confess that Jesus
Christ is Lord,
to the glory of God the Father.

Shining as Stars

12Therefore, my dear friends, as you have
always obeyed—not only in my presence,
but now much more in my absence—continue to work out your salvation with fear and
trembling, 13for it is God who works in you to
will and to act according to his good purpose.

14Do everything without complaining or arguing, 15so that you may become blameless
and pure, children of God without fault in a
crooked and depraved generation, in which
you shine like stars in the universe 16as you
hold out[e] the word of life—in order that I may
boast on the day of Christ that I did not run or
labor for nothing. 17But even if I am being
poured out like a drink offering on the sacrifice and service coming from your faith, I am
glad and rejoice with all of you. 18So you too
should be glad and rejoice with me.

Timothy and Epaphroditus

19I hope in the Lord Jesus to send Timothy
to you soon, that I also may be cheered when
I receive news about you. 20I have no one
else like him, who takes a genuine interest in
your welfare. 21For everyone looks out for his
own interests, not those of Jesus Christ.

[a] *16,17* Some late manuscripts have verses 16 and 17 in reverse order. [b] *19* Or *salvation* [c] *6* Or *in the form of* [d] *7* Or *the form* [e] *16* Or *hold on to*

22But you know that Timothy has proved himself, because as a son with his father he has served with me in the work of the gospel. 23I hope, therefore, to send him as soon as I see how things go with me. 24And I am confident in the Lord that I myself will come soon.

25But I think it is necessary to send back to you Epaphroditus, my brother, fellow worker and fellow soldier, who is also your messenger, whom you sent to take care of my needs. 26For he longs for all of you and is distressed because you heard he was ill. 27Indeed he was ill, and almost died. But God had mercy on him, and not on him only but also on me, to spare me sorrow upon sorrow. 28Therefore I am all the more eager to send him, so that when you see him again you may be glad and I may have less anxiety. 29Welcome him in the Lord with great joy, and honor men like him, 30because he almost died for the work of Christ, risking his life to make up for the help you could not give me.

No Confidence in the Flesh

3 Finally, my brothers, rejoice in the Lord! It is no trouble for me to write the same things to you again, and it is a safeguard for you.

2Watch out for those dogs, those men who do evil, those mutilators of the flesh. 3For it is we who are the circumcision, we who worship by the Spirit of God, who glory in Christ Jesus, and who put no confidence in the flesh— 4though I myself have reasons for such confidence.

If anyone else thinks he has reasons to put confidence in the flesh, I have more: 5circumcised on the eighth day, of the people of Israel, of the tribe of Benjamin, a Hebrew of Hebrews; in regard to the law, a Pharisee; 6as for zeal, persecuting the church; as for legalistic righteousness, faultless.

7But whatever was to my profit I now consider loss for the sake of Christ. 8What is more, I consider everything a loss compared to the surpassing greatness of knowing Christ Jesus my Lord, for whose sake I have lost all things. I consider them rubbish, that I may gain Christ 9and be found in him, not having a righteousness of my own that comes from the law, but that which is through faith in Christ—the righteousness that comes from God and is by faith. 10I want to know Christ and the power of his resurrection and the fellowship of sharing in his sufferings, becoming like him in his death, 11and so, somehow, to attain to the resurrection from the dead.

Pressing on Toward the Goal

12Not that I have already obtained all this, or have already been made perfect, but I press on to take hold of that for which Christ Jesus took hold of me. 13Brothers, I do not consider myself yet to have taken hold of it. But one thing I do: Forgetting what is behind and straining toward what is ahead, 14I press on toward the goal to win the prize for which God has called me heavenward in Christ Jesus.

15All of us who are mature should take such a view of things. And if on some point you think differently, that too God will make clear to you. 16Only let us live up to what we have already attained.

17Join with others in following my example, brothers, and take note of those who live according to the pattern we gave you. 18For, as I have often told you before and now say again even with tears, many live as enemies of the cross of Christ. 19Their destiny is destruction, their god is their stomach, and their glory is in their shame. Their mind is on earthly things. 20But our citizenship is in heaven. And we eagerly await a Savior from there, the Lord Jesus Christ, 21who, by the power that enables him to bring everything under his control, will transform our lowly bodies so that they will be like his glorious body.

4 Therefore, my brothers, you whom I love and long for, my joy and crown, that is how you should stand firm in the Lord, dear friends!

Exhortations

2I plead with Euodia and I plead with Syntyche to agree with each other in the Lord. 3Yes, and I ask you, loyal yokefellow,[a] help these women who have contended at my side in the cause of the gospel, along with Clement and the rest of my fellow workers, whose names are in the book of life.

4Rejoice in the Lord always. I will say it again: Rejoice! 5Let your gentleness be evident to all. The Lord is near. 6Do not be anxious about anything, but in everything, by prayer and petition, with thanksgiving, present your requests to God. 7And the

[a]3 Or *loyal Syzygus*

peace of God, which transcends all understanding, will guard your hearts and your
minds in Christ Jesus.
[8]Finally, brothers, whatever is true, whatever is noble, whatever is right, whatever is
pure, whatever is lovely, whatever is admirable—if anything is excellent or praiseworthy—think about such things. [9]Whatever
you have learned or received or heard from
me, or seen in me—put it into practice. And
the God of peace will be with you.

Thanks for Their Gifts

[10]I rejoice greatly in the Lord that at last
you have renewed your concern for me. Indeed, you have been concerned, but you
had no opportunity to show it. [11]I am not
saying this because I am in need, for I have
learned to be content whatever the circumstances. [12]I know what it is to be in need, and
I know what it is to have plenty. I have
learned the secret of being content in any
and every situation, whether well fed or hungry, whether living in plenty or in want. [13]I can
do everything through him who gives me
strength.
[14]Yet it was good of you to share in my
troubles. [15]Moreover, as you Philippians
know, in the early days of your acquaintance
with the gospel, when I set out from Macedonia, not one church shared with me in the
matter of giving and receiving, except you
only; [16]for even when I was in Thessalonica,
you sent me aid again and again when I was
in need. [17]Not that I am looking for a gift, but
I am looking for what may be credited to your
account. [18]I have received full payment and
even more; I am amply supplied, now that I
have received from Epaphroditus the gifts
you sent. They are a fragrant offering, an
acceptable sacrifice, pleasing to God. [19]And
my God will meet all your needs according to
his glorious riches in Christ Jesus.
[20]To our God and Father be glory for ever
and ever. Amen.

Final Greetings

[21]Greet all the saints in Christ Jesus. The
brothers who are with me send greetings.
[22]All the saints send you greetings, especially those who belong to Caesar's household.
[23]The grace of the Lord Jesus Christ be
with your spirit. Amen.[a]

[a]*23* Some manuscripts do not have *Amen*.

Colossians

Introduction:

Colossians is the third letter written from prison in Rome (about A.D. 60). Epaphras had come to Rome and told Paul that there were false teachers in Colosse who were telling the people that the Christian faith was incomplete. They were teaching the Colossians to worship angels and to follow special rules and ceremonies.

Paul wrote to the Colossians to oppose these false teachers. He reminded them that Jesus is supreme over everything, that his death is all we need to save us from our sins, and that through him we are free from man-made rules.

Outline of contents:

---

1 Paul, an apostle of Christ Jesus by the
will of God, and Timothy our brother,

2To the holy and faithful[a] brothers in Christ
at Colosse:

Grace and peace to you from God our
Father.[b]

Thanksgiving and Prayer

3We always thank God, the Father of our
Lord Jesus Christ, when we pray for you,
4because we have heard of your faith in
Christ Jesus and of the love you have for all
the saints— 5the faith and love that spring
from the hope that is stored up for you in
heaven and that you have already heard
about in the word of truth, the gospel 6that
has come to you. All over the world this gospel is bearing fruit and growing, just as it has
been doing among you since the day you
heard it and understood God's grace in all its
truth. 7You learned it from Epaphras, our
dear fellow servant, who is a faithful minister
of Christ on our[c] behalf, 8and who also told
us of your love in the Spirit.

9For this reason, since the day we heard
about you, we have not stopped praying for
you and asking God to fill you with the knowledge of his will through all spiritual wisdom
and understanding. 10And we pray this in
order that you may live a life worthy of the
Lord and may please him in every way: bearing fruit in every good work, growing in the
knowledge of God, 11being strengthened
with all power according to his glorious might
so that you may have great endurance and
patience, and joyfully 12giving thanks to the
Father, who has qualified you[d] to share in
the inheritance of the saints in the kingdom
of light. 13For he has rescued us from the
dominion of darkness and brought us into
the kingdom of the Son he loves, 14in whom
we have redemption,[e] the forgiveness of
sins.

The Supremacy of Christ

15He is the image of the invisible God, the
firstborn over all creation. 16For by him all
things were created: things in heaven and on
earth, visible and invisible, whether thrones
or powers or rulers or authorities; all things
were created by him and for him. 17He is
before all things, and in him all things hold
together. 18And he is the head of the body,
the church; he is the beginning and the firstborn from among the dead, so that in everything he might have the supremacy. 19For
God was pleased to have all his fullness

[a]2 Or *believing* [b]2 Some manuscripts *Father and the Lord Jesus Christ* [c]7 Some manuscripts *your*
[d]12 Some manuscripts *us* [e]14 A few late manuscripts *redemption through his blood*

dwell in him, 20and through him to reconcile
to himself all things, whether things on earth
or things in heaven, by making peace
through his blood, shed on the cross.

21Once you were alienated from God and
were enemies in your minds because of[a]
your evil behavior. 22But now he has reconciled you by Christ's physical body through
death to present you holy in his sight, without
blemish and free from accusation— 23if you
continue in your faith, established and firm,
not moved from the hope held out in the
gospel. This is the gospel that you heard and
that has been proclaimed to every creature
under heaven, and of which I, Paul, have
become a servant.

Paul's Labor for the Church

24Now I rejoice in what was suffered for
you, and I fill up in my flesh what is still
lacking in regard to Christ's afflictions, for the
sake of his body, which is the church. 25I
have become its servant by the commission
God gave me to present to you the word of
God in its fullness— 26the mystery that has
been kept hidden for ages and generations,
but is now disclosed to the saints. 27To them
God has chosen to make known among the
Gentiles the glorious riches of this mystery,
which is Christ in you, the hope of glory.
28We proclaim him, admonishing and
teaching everyone with all wisdom, so that
we may present everyone perfect in Christ.
29To this end I labor, struggling with all his
energy, which so powerfully works in me.

2 I want you to know how much I am struggling for you and for those at Laodicea,
and for all who have not met me personally.
2My purpose is that they may be encouraged
in heart and united in love, so that they may
have the full riches of complete understanding, in order that they may know the mystery
of God, namely, Christ, 3in whom are hidden
all the treasures of wisdom and knowledge.
4I tell you this so that no one may deceive
you by fine-sounding arguments. 5For
though I am absent from you in body, I am
present with you in spirit and delight to see
how orderly you are and how firm your faith
in Christ is.

Freedom From Human Regulations Through Life With Christ

6So then, just as you received Christ Jesus
as Lord, continue to live in him, 7rooted and
built up in him, strengthened in the faith as
you were taught, and overflowing with thankfulness.

8See to it that no one takes you captive
through hollow and deceptive philosophy,
which depends on human tradition and the
basic principles of this world rather than on
Christ.

9For in Christ all the fullness of the Deity
lives in bodily form, 10and you have been
given fullness in Christ, who is the head over
every power and authority. 11In him you were
also circumcised, in the putting off of the
sinful nature,[b] not with a circumcision done
by the hands of men but with the circumcision done by Christ, 12having been buried
with him in baptism and raised with him
through your faith in the power of God, who
raised him from the dead.

13When you were dead in your sins and in
the uncircumcision of your sinful nature,[c]
God made you[d] alive with Christ. He forgave
us all our sins, 14having canceled the written
code, with its regulations, that was against
us and that stood opposed to us; he took it
away, nailing it to the cross. 15And having
disarmed the powers and authorities, he
made a public spectacle of them, triumphing
over them by the cross.[e]

16Therefore do not let anyone judge you by
what you eat or drink, or with regard to a
religious festival, a New Moon celebration or
a Sabbath day. 17These are a shadow of the
things that were to come; the reality, however, is found in Christ. 18Do not let anyone
who delights in false humility and the worship of angels disqualify you for the prize.
Such a person goes into great detail about
what he has seen, and his unspiritual mind
puffs him up with idle notions. 19He has lost
connection with the Head, from whom the
whole body, supported and held together by
its ligaments and sinews, grows as God
causes it to grow.

20Since you died with Christ to the basic
principles of this world, why, as though you
still belonged to it, do you submit to its rules:
21"Do not handle! Do not taste! Do not
touch!"? 22These are all destined to perish
with use, because they are based on human
commands and teachings. 23Such regulations indeed have an appearance of wisdom,
with their self-imposed worship, their false

[a]21 Or *minds, as shown by* [b]11 Or *the flesh* [c]13 Or *your flesh* [d]13 Some manuscripts *us*
[e]15 Or *them in him*

humility and their harsh treatment of the body, but they lack any value in restraining sensual indulgence.

Rules for Holy Living

3 Since, then, you have been raised with Christ, set your hearts on things above, where Christ is seated at the right hand of God. 2Set your minds on things above, not on earthly things. 3For you died, and your life is now hidden with Christ in God. 4When Christ, who is your[a] life, appears, then you also will appear with him in glory.

5Put to death, therefore, whatever belongs to your earthly nature: sexual immorality, impurity, lust, evil desires and greed, which is idolatry. 6Because of these, the wrath of God is coming.[b] 7You used to walk in these ways, in the life you once lived. 8But now you must rid yourselves of all such things as these: anger, rage, malice, slander, and filthy language from your lips. 9Do not lie to each other, since you have taken off your old self with its practices 10and have put on the new self, which is being renewed in knowledge in the image of its Creator. 11Here there is no Greek or Jew, circumcised or uncircumcised, barbarian, Scythian, slave or free, but Christ is all, and is in all.

12Therefore, as God's chosen people, holy and dearly loved, clothe yourselves with compassion, kindness, humility, gentleness and patience. 13Bear with each other and forgive whatever grievances you may have against one another. Forgive as the Lord forgave you. 14And over all these virtues put on love, which binds them all together in perfect unity.

15Let the peace of Christ rule in your hearts, since as members of one body you were called to peace. And be thankful. 16Let the word of Christ dwell in you richly as you teach and admonish one another with all wisdom, and as you sing psalms, hymns and spiritual songs with gratitude in your hearts to God. 17And whatever you do, whether in word or deed, do it all in the name of the Lord Jesus, giving thanks to God the Father through him.

Rules for Christian Households

18Wives, submit to your husbands, as is fitting in the Lord.

19Husbands, love your wives and do not be harsh with them.

20Children, obey your parents in everything, for this pleases the Lord.

21Fathers, do not embitter your children, or they will become discouraged.

22Slaves, obey your earthly masters in everything; and do it, not only when their eye is on you and to win their favor, but with sincerity of heart and reverence for the Lord. 23Whatever you do, work at it with all your heart, as working for the Lord, not for men, 24since you know that you will receive an inheritance from the Lord as a reward. It is the Lord Christ you are serving. 25Anyone who does wrong will be repaid for his wrong, and there is no favoritism.

4 Masters, provide your slaves with what is right and fair, because you know that you also have a Master in heaven.

Further Instructions

2Devote yourselves to prayer, being watchful and thankful. 3And pray for us, too, that God may open a door for our message, so that we may proclaim the mystery of Christ, for which I am in chains. 4Pray that I may proclaim it clearly, as I should. 5Be wise in the way you act toward outsiders; make the most of every opportunity. 6Let your conversation be always full of grace, seasoned with salt, so that you may know how to answer everyone.

Final Greetings

7Tychicus will tell you all the news about me. He is a dear brother, a faithful minister and fellow servant in the Lord. 8I am sending him to you for the express purpose that you may know about our[c] circumstances and that he may encourage your hearts. 9He is coming with Onesimus, our faithful and dear brother, who is one of you. They will tell you everything that is happening here.

10My fellow prisoner Aristarchus sends you his greetings, as does Mark, the cousin of Barnabas. (You have received instructions about him; if he comes to you, welcome him.) 11Jesus, who is called Justus, also sends greetings. These are the only Jews among my fellow workers for the kingdom of God, and they have proved a comfort to me. 12Epaphras, who is one of you and a servant

[a]4 Some manuscripts *our* [b]6 Some early manuscripts *coming on those who are disobedient* [c]8 Some manuscripts *that he may know about your*

of Christ Jesus, sends greetings. He is always wrestling in prayer for you, that you
may stand firm in all the will of God, mature
and fully assured. 13I vouch for him that he is
working hard for you and for those at Laodicea and Hierapolis. 14Our dear friend Luke,
the doctor, and Demas send greetings.
15Give my greetings to the brothers at Laodicea, and to Nympha and the church in her
house.

16After this letter has been read to you, see
that it is also read in the church of the Laodi-
ceans and that you in turn read the letter
from Laodicea.

17Tell Archippus: "See to it that you complete the work you have received in the
Lord."

18I, Paul, write this greeting in my own
hand. Remember my chains. Grace be with
you.

I Thessalonians

Introduction:

Paul started the church at Thessalonica on his second missionary journey. He taught there for about three weeks, but then had to leave because the Jews were opposing him so strongly. On hearing from Timothy about the conditions in Thessalonica, Paul wrote this letter from Corinth to encourage the Thessalonians and to teach them more about Christianity (A.D. 51).

Paul begins by praising the Thessalonians for being brave and not giving up their faith "in spite of severe suffering." He instructs them "how to live in order to please God." And he teaches them about Jesus' second coming. He explains that the time of Jesus' coming is secret, so they should keep working hard until he comes.

Outline of contents:

Introduction and thanksgiving (1:1–10)
Paul's ministry in the church (2:1–3:13)
Instructions on the Lord's coming (4:1–5:11)
Conclusion (5:12–28)

---

1 Paul, Silas[a] and Timothy,

To the church of the Thessalonians in
God the Father and the Lord Jesus Christ:

Grace and peace to you.[b]

Thanksgiving for the Thessalonians' Faith

2We always thank God for all of you, men-
tioning you in our prayers. 3We continually
remember before our God and Father your
work produced by faith, your labor prompted
by love, and your endurance inspired by
hope in our Lord Jesus Christ.
4For we know, brothers loved by God, that
he has chosen you, 5because our gospel
came to you not simply with words, but also
with power, with the Holy Spirit and with
deep conviction. You know how we lived
among you for your sake. 6You became
imitators of us and of the Lord; in spite of
severe suffering, you welcomed the message with the joy given by the Holy Spirit.
7And so you became a model to all the believers in Macedonia and Achaia. 8The
Lord's message rang out from you not only in
Macedonia and Achaia—your faith in God
has become known everywhere. Therefore
we do not need to say anything about it, 9for
they themselves report what kind of recep-
tion you gave us. They tell how you turned to
God from idols to serve the living and true
God, 10and to wait for his Son from heaven,
whom he raised from the dead—Jesus, who
rescues us from the coming wrath.

Paul's Ministry in Thessalonica

2 You know, brothers, that our visit to you
was not a failure. 2We had previously
suffered and been insulted in Philippi, as you
know, but with the help of our God we dared
to tell you his gospel in spite of strong opposition. 3For the appeal we make does not
spring from error or impure motives, nor are
we trying to trick you. 4On the contrary, we
speak as men approved by God to be entrusted with the gospel. We are not trying to
please men but God, who tests our hearts.
5You know we never used flattery, nor did we
put on a mask to cover up greed—God is our
witness. 6We were not looking for praise
from men, not from you or anyone else.
As apostles of Christ we could have been
a burden to you, 7but we were gentle among
you, like a mother caring for her little children. 8We loved you so much that we were

[a] *1* Greek *Silvanus,* a variant of *Silas*
[b] *1* Some early manuscripts *you from God our Father and the Lord Jesus Christ*

delighted to share with you not only the gospel of God but our lives as well, because you
had become so dear to us. 9Surely you
remember, brothers, our toil and hardship;
we worked night and day in order not to be a
burden to anyone while we preached the
gospel of God to you.

10You are witnesses, and so is God, of how
holy, righteous and blameless we were
among you who believed. 11For you know
that we dealt with each of you as a father
deals with his own children, 12encouraging,
comforting and urging you to live lives worthy
of God, who calls you into his kingdom and
glory.

13And we also thank God continually because, when you received the word of God,
which you heard from us, you accepted it not
as the word of men, but as it actually is, the
word of God, which is at work in you who
believe. 14For you, brothers, became imitators of God's churches in Judea, which are in
Christ Jesus: You suffered from your own
countrymen the same things those churches
suffered from the Jews, 15who killed the Lord
Jesus and the prophets and also drove us
out. They displease God and are hostile to all
men 16in their effort to keep us from speaking
to the Gentiles so that they may be saved. In
this way they always heap up their sins to the
limit. The wrath of God has come upon them
at last.[a]

Paul's Longing to See the Thessalonians

17But, brothers, when we were torn away
from you for a short time (in person, not in
thought), out of our intense longing we made
every effort to see you. 18For we wanted to
come to you—certainly I, Paul, did, again
and again—but Satan stopped us. 19For
what is our hope, our joy, or the crown in
which we will glory in the presence of our
Lord Jesus when he comes? Is it not you?
20Indeed, you are our glory and joy.

3 So when we could stand it no longer, we
thought it best to be left by ourselves in
Athens. 2We sent Timothy, who is our brother and God's fellow worker[b] in spreading the
gospel of Christ, to strengthen and encourage you in your faith, 3so that no one would
be unsettled by these trials. You know quite
well that we were destined for them. 4In fact,
when we were with you, we kept telling you
that we would be persecuted. And it turned
out that way, as you well know. 5For this
reason, when I could stand it no longer, I sent
to find out about your faith. I was afraid that in
some way the tempter might have tempted
you and our efforts might have been useless.

Timothy's Encouraging Report

6But Timothy has just now come to us from
you and has brought good news about your
faith and love. He has told us that you always
have pleasant memories of us and that you
long to see us, just as we also long to see
you. 7Therefore, brothers, in all our distress
and persecution we were encouraged about
you because of your faith. 8For now we really
live, since you are standing firm in the Lord.
9How can we thank God enough for you in
return for all the joy we have in the presence
of our God because of you? 10Night and day
we pray most earnestly that we may see you
again and supply what is lacking in your faith.

11Now may our God and Father himself
and our Lord Jesus clear the way for us to
come to you. 12May the Lord make your love
increase and overflow for each other and for
everyone else, just as ours does for you.
13May he strengthen your hearts so that you
will be blameless and holy in the presence of
our God and Father when our Lord Jesus
comes with all his holy ones.

Living to Please God

4 Finally, brothers, we instructed you how
to live in order to please God, as in fact
you are living. Now we ask you and urge you
in the Lord Jesus to do this more and more.
2For you know what instructions we gave you
by the authority of the Lord Jesus.

3It is God's will that you should be sanctified: that you should avoid sexual immorality;
4that each of you should learn to control his
own body[c] in a way that is holy and honorable, 5not in passionate lust like the heathen,
who do not know God; 6and that in this matter no one should wrong his brother or take
advantage of him. The Lord will punish men
for all such sins, as we have already told you
and warned you. 7For God did not call us to
be impure, but to live a holy life. 8Therefore,
he who rejects this instruction does not reject
man but God, who gives you his Holy Spirit.

9Now about brotherly love we do not need
to write to you, for you yourselves have been

[a] 16 Or *them fully* [b] 2 Some manuscripts *brother and fellow worker;* other manuscripts *brother and God's servant* [c] 4 Or *learn to live with his own wife;* or *learn to acquire a wife*

taught by God to love each other. 10And in
fact, you do love all the brothers throughout
Macedonia. Yet we urge you, brothers, to do
so more and more.
11Make it your ambition to lead a quiet life,
to mind your own business and to work with
your hands, just as we told you, 12so that
your daily life may win the respect of outsiders and so that you will not be dependent on
anybody.

The Coming of the Lord

13Brothers, we do not want you to be ignorant about those who fall asleep, or to grieve
like the rest of men, who have no hope. 14We
believe that Jesus died and rose again and
so we believe that God will bring with Jesus
those who have fallen asleep in him. 15Ac-
cording to the Lord's own word, we tell you
that we who are still alive, who are left till the
coming of the Lord, will certainly not precede
those who have fallen asleep. 16For the Lord
himself will come down from heaven, with a
loud command, with the voice of the archangel and with the trumpet call of God, and
the dead in Christ will rise first. 17After that,
we who are still alive and are left will be
caught up together with them in the clouds to
meet the Lord in the air. And so we will be
with the Lord forever. 18Therefore encourage
each other with these words.

5 Now, brothers, about times and dates
we do not need to write to you, 2for you
know very well that the day of the Lord will
come like a thief in the night. 3While people
are saying, "Peace and safety," destruction
will come on them suddenly, as labor pains
on a pregnant woman, and they will not escape.
4But you, brothers, are not in darkness so
that this day should surprise you like a thief.
5You are all sons of the light and sons of the
day. We do not belong to the night or to the
darkness. 6So then, let us not be like others,
who are asleep, but let us be alert and self-
controlled. 7For those who sleep, sleep at
night, and those who get drunk, get drunk at
night. 8But since we belong to the day, let us
be self-controlled, putting on faith and love
as a breastplate, and the hope of salvation
as a helmet. 9For God did not appoint us to
suffer wrath but to receive salvation through
our Lord Jesus Christ. 10He died for us so
that, whether we are awake or asleep, we
may live together with him. 11Therefore encourage one another and build each other
up, just as in fact you are doing.

Final Instructions

12Now we ask you, brothers, to respect
those who work hard among you, who are
over you in the Lord and who admonish you.
13Hold them in the highest regard in love
because of their work. Live in peace with
each other. 14And we urge you, brothers,
warn those who are idle, encourage the timid, help the weak, be patient with everyone.
15Make sure that nobody pays back wrong
for wrong, but always try to be kind to each
other and to everyone else.
16Be joyful always; 17pray continually;
18give thanks in all circumstances, for this is
God's will for you in Christ Jesus.
19Do not put out the Spirit's fire; 20do not
treat prophecies with contempt. 21Test
everything. Hold on to the good. 22Avoid
every kind of evil.
23May God himself, the God of peace,
sanctify you through and through. May your
whole spirit, soul and body be kept blameless at the coming of our Lord Jesus Christ.
24The one who calls you is faithful and he will
do it.

25Brothers, pray for us. 26Greet all the
brothers with a holy kiss. 27I charge you before the Lord to have this letter read to all the
brothers.
28The grace of our Lord Jesus Christ be
with you.

2 Thessalonians

Introduction:

Second Thessalonians was sent from Corinth a few months after the first letter. Some people had misunderstood Paul and were sure Jesus was coming very soon. In fact, they had stopped working and were just waiting for Jesus.

Paul writes the Thessalonians again and describes to them what Jesus' second coming will be like. He also reminds them to keep working hard until Jesus comes and to use their time wisely.

Outline of contents:

Paul's personal concern (1:1–12)
Conditions for the Lord's coming (2:1–17)
Strong advice and a blessing (3:1–18)

---

1 Paul, Silas[a] and Timothy,
To the church of the Thessalonians in
God our Father and the Lord Jesus Christ:
2Grace and peace to you from God the
Father and the Lord Jesus Christ.

Thanksgiving and Prayer

3We ought always to thank God for you,
brothers, and rightly so, because your faith is
growing more and more, and the love every
one of you has for each other is increasing.
4Therefore, among God's churches we
boast about your perseverance and faith in
all the persecutions and trials you are enduring.
5All this is evidence that God's judgment is
right, and as a result you will be counted
worthy of the kingdom of God, for which you
are suffering. 6God is just: He will pay back
trouble to those who trouble you 7and give
relief to you who are troubled, and to us as
well. This will happen when the Lord Jesus is
revealed from heaven in blazing fire with his
powerful angels. 8He will punish those who
do not know God and do not obey the gospel
of our Lord Jesus. 9They will be punished
with everlasting destruction and shut out
from the presence of the Lord and from the
majesty of his power 10on the day he comes
to be glorified in his holy people and to be
marveled at among all those who have believed. This includes you, because you believed our testimony to you.
11With this in mind, we constantly pray for
you, that our God may count you worthy of
his calling, and that by his power he may
fulfill every good purpose of yours and every
act prompted by your faith. 12We pray this so
that the name of our Lord Jesus may be
glorified in you, and you in him, according to
the grace of our God and the Lord Jesus
Christ.[b]

The Man of Lawlessness

2 Concerning the coming of our Lord
Jesus Christ and our being gathered to
him, we ask you, brothers, 2not to become
easily unsettled or alarmed by some prophecy, report or letter supposed to have come
from us, saying that the day of the Lord has
already come. 3Don't let anyone deceive you
in any way, for ⌊that day will not come⌋ until
the rebellion occurs and the man of lawlessness[c] is revealed, the man doomed to destruction. 4He will oppose and will exalt himself over everything that is called God or is
worshiped, so that he sets himself up in
God's temple, proclaiming himself to be
God.
5Don't you remember that when I was with
you I used to tell you these things? 6And now
you know what is holding him back, so that
he may be revealed at the proper time. 7For

[a] 1 Greek *Silvanus*, a variant of *Silas* [b] 12 Or *God and Lord, Jesus Christ* [c] 3 Some manuscripts *sin*

the secret power of lawlessness is already at work; but the one who now holds it back will continue to do so till he is taken out of the way. 8And then the lawless one will be revealed, whom the Lord Jesus will overthrow with the breath of his mouth and destroy by the splendor of his coming. 9The coming of the lawless one will be in accordance with the work of Satan displayed in all kinds of counterfeit miracles, signs and wonders, 10and in every sort of evil that deceives those who are perishing. They perish because they refused to love the truth and so be saved. 11For this reason God sends them a powerful delusion so that they will believe the lie 12and so that all will be condemned who have not believed the truth but have delighted in wickedness.

Stand Firm

13But we ought always to thank God for you, brothers loved by the Lord, because from the beginning God chose you[a] to be saved through the sanctifying work of the Spirit and through belief in the truth. 14He called you to this through our gospel, that you might share in the glory of our Lord Jesus Christ. 15So then, brothers, stand firm and hold to the teachings[b] we passed on to you, whether by word of mouth or by letter.

16May our Lord Jesus Christ himself and God our Father, who loved us and by his grace gave us eternal encouragement and good hope, 17encourage your hearts and strengthen you in every good deed and word.

Request for Prayer

3 Finally, brothers, pray for us that the message of the Lord may spread rapidly and be honored, just as it was with you. 2And pray that we may be delivered from wicked and evil men, for not everyone has faith. 3But the Lord is faithful, and he will strengthen and protect you from the evil one. 4We have confidence in the Lord that you are doing and will continue to do the things we command. 5May the Lord direct your hearts into God's love and Christ's perseverance.

Warning Against Idleness

6In the name of the Lord Jesus Christ, we command you, brothers, to keep away from every brother who is idle and does not live according to the teaching[c] you received from us. 7For you yourselves know how you ought to follow our example. We were not idle when we were with you, 8nor did we eat anyone's food without paying for it. On the contrary, we worked night and day, laboring and toiling so that we would not be a burden to any of you. 9We did this, not because we do not have the right to such help, but in order to make ourselves a model for you to follow. 10For even when we were with you, we gave you this rule: "If a man will not work, he shall not eat."

11We hear that some among you are idle. They are not busy; they are busybodies. 12Such people we command and urge in the Lord Jesus Christ to settle down and earn the bread they eat. 13And as for you, brothers, never tire of doing what is right.

14If anyone does not obey our instruction in this letter, take special note of him. Do not associate with him, in order that he may feel ashamed. 15Yet do not regard him as an enemy, but warn him as a brother.

Final Greetings

16Now may the Lord of peace himself give you peace at all times and in every way. The Lord be with all of you.

17I, Paul, write this greeting in my own hand, which is the distinguishing mark in all my letters. This is how I write.

18The grace of our Lord Jesus Christ be with you all.

[a]13 Some manuscripts *because God chose you as his firstfruits* [b]15 Or *traditions* [c]6 Or *tradition*

I Timothy

Introduction:

First and Second Timothy and Titus are commonly called the pastoral letters and were written by Paul. They are called pastoral letters because they deal with the qualifications and duties of pastors.

Timothy was born at Lystra and had a Greek father and a Jewish mother (who taught him the Scriptures from childhood). He went with Paul on his second missionary journey and from then on helped Paul in his work. At the time Paul wrote this letter, Timothy was working as the teacher and leader of the church at Ephesus.

Timothy was quite young to have the important job of leading a church, so Paul wrote this very personal letter to him. In this letter Paul gives him help and advice for his work. He warns him of false teachers and their teachings that are opposite God's commands. Because of Paul's deep care for Timothy he offers him advice on how to be a "man of God."

Outline of contents:

Introduction (1:1–17)
Instructions for the church (1:18–3:16)
Personal instructions for Timothy (4:1–6:21)

---

1 Paul, an apostle of Christ Jesus by the
command of God our Savior and of
Christ Jesus our hope,

2To Timothy my true son in the faith:

Grace, mercy and peace from God the Father and Christ Jesus our Lord.

Warning Against False Teachers of the Law

3As I urged you when I went into Macedonia, stay there in Ephesus so that you may
command certain men not to teach false
doctrines any longer 4nor to devote themselves to myths and endless genealogies.
These promote controversies rather than
God's work—which is by faith. 5The goal of
this command is love, which comes from a
pure heart and a good conscience and a
sincere faith. 6Some have wandered away
from these and turned to meaningless talk.
7They want to be teachers of the law, but
they do not know what they are talking about
or what they so confidently affirm.

8We know that the law is good if one uses
it properly. 9We also know that law[a] is made
not for the righteous but for lawbreakers and
rebels, the ungodly and sinful, the unholy
and irreligious; for those who kill their fathers
or mothers, for murderers, 10for adulterers
and perverts, for slave traders and liars and
perjurers—and for whatever else is contrary
to the sound doctrine 11that conforms to the
glorious gospel of the blessed God, which he
entrusted to me.

The Lord's Grace to Paul

12I thank Christ Jesus our Lord, who has
given me strength, that he considered me
faithful, appointing me to his service. 13Even
though I was once a blasphemer and a persecutor and a violent man, I was shown
mercy because I acted in ignorance and unbelief. 14The grace of our Lord was poured
out on me abundantly, along with the faith
and love that are in Christ Jesus.

15Here is a trustworthy saying that deserves full acceptance: Christ Jesus came
into the world to save sinners—of whom I am
the worst. 16But for that very reason I was
shown mercy so that in me, the worst of
sinners, Christ Jesus might display his unlimited patience as an example for those
who would believe on him and receive eter-

[a]9 *Or that the law*

nal life. 17Now to the King eternal, immortal, invisible, the only God, be honor and glory for ever and ever. Amen.

18Timothy, my son, I give you this instruction in keeping with the prophecies once made about you, so that by following them you may fight the good fight, 19holding on to faith and a good conscience. Some have rejected these and so have shipwrecked their faith. 20Among them are Hymenaeus and Alexander, whom I have handed over to Satan to be taught not to blaspheme.

Instructions on Worship

2 I urge, then, first of all, that requests, prayers, intercession and thanksgiving be made for everyone— 2for kings and all those in authority, that we may live peaceful and quiet lives in all godliness and holiness. 3This is good, and pleases God our Savior, 4who wants all men to be saved and to come to a knowledge of the truth. 5For there is one God and one mediator between God and men, the man Christ Jesus, 6who gave himself as a ransom for all men—the testimony given in its proper time. 7And for this purpose I was appointed a herald and an apostle—I am telling the truth, I am not lying—and a teacher of the true faith to the Gentiles.

8I want men everywhere to lift up holy hands in prayer, without anger or disputing.

9I also want women to dress modestly, with decency and propriety, not with braided hair or gold or pearls or expensive clothes, 10but with good deeds, appropriate for women who profess to worship God.

11A woman should learn in quietness and full submission. 12I do not permit a woman to teach or to have authority over a man; she must be silent. 13For Adam was formed first, then Eve. 14And Adam was not the one deceived; it was the woman who was deceived and became a sinner. 15But women[a] will be saved[b] through childbearing—if they continue in faith, love and holiness with propriety.

Overseers and Deacons

3 Here is a trustworthy saying: If anyone sets his heart on being an overseer,[c] he desires a noble task. 2Now the overseer must be above reproach, the husband of but one wife, temperate, self-controlled, respectable, hospitable, able to teach, 3not given to drunkenness, not violent but gentle, not quarrelsome, not a lover of money. 4He must manage his own family well and see that his children obey him with proper respect. 5(If anyone does not know how to manage his own family, how can he take care of God's church?) 6He must not be a recent convert, or he may become conceited and fall under the same judgment as the devil. 7He must also have a good reputation with outsiders, so that he will not fall into disgrace and into the devil's trap.

8Deacons, likewise, are to be men worthy of respect, sincere, not indulging in much wine, and not pursuing dishonest gain. 9They must keep hold of the deep truths of the faith with a clear conscience. 10They must first be tested; and then if there is nothing against them, let them serve as deacons.

11In the same way, their wives[d] are to be women worthy of respect, not malicious talkers but temperate and trustworthy in everything.

12A deacon must be the husband of but one wife and must manage his children and his household well. 13Those who have served well gain an excellent standing and great assurance in their faith in Christ Jesus.

14Although I hope to come to you soon, I am writing you these instructions so that, 15if I am delayed, you will know how people ought to conduct themselves in God's household, which is the church of the living God, the pillar and foundation of the truth. 16Beyond all question, the mystery of godliness is great:

He[e] appeared in a body,[f]
  was vindicated by the Spirit,
was seen by angels,
  was preached among the nations,
was believed on in the world,
  was taken up in glory.

Instructions to Timothy

4 The Spirit clearly says that in later times some will abandon the faith and follow deceiving spirits and things taught by demons. 2Such teachings come through hypocritical liars, whose consciences have been seared as with a hot iron. 3They forbid people to marry and order them to abstain from certain foods, which God created to be received with thanksgiving by those who be-

[a] 15 Greek *she* [b] 15 Or *restored* [c] 1 Traditionally *bishop;* also in verse 2 [d] 11 Or *way, deaconesses*
[e] 16 Some manuscripts *God* [f] 16 Or *in the flesh*

lieve and who know the truth. 4For everything
God created is good, and nothing is to be
rejected if it is received with thanksgiving,
5because it is consecrated by the word of
God and prayer.

6If you point these things out to the brothers, you will be a good minister of Christ
Jesus, brought up in the truths of the faith
and of the good teaching that you have followed. 7Have nothing to do with godless
myths and old wives' tales; rather, train yourself to be godly. 8For physical training is of
some value, but godliness has value for all
things, holding promise for both the present
life and the life to come.

9This is a trustworthy saying that deserves
full acceptance 10(and for this we labor and
strive), that we have put our hope in the living
God, who is the Savior of all men, and especially of those who believe.

11Command and teach these things.
12Don't let anyone look down on you because you are young, but set an example for
the believers in speech, in life, in love, in faith
and in purity. 13Until I come, devote yourself
to the public reading of Scripture, to preaching and to teaching. 14Do not neglect your
gift, which was given you through a prophetic
message when the body of elders laid their
hands on you.

15Be diligent in these matters; give yourself wholly to them, so that everyone may
see your progress. 16Watch your life and
doctrine closely. Persevere in them, because if you do, you will save both yourself
and your hearers.

Advice About Widows, Elders and Slaves

5 Do not rebuke an older man harshly, but
exhort him as if he were your father.
Treat younger men as brothers, 2older
women as mothers, and younger women as
sisters, with absolute purity.

3Give proper recognition to those widows
who are really in need. 4But if a widow has
children or grandchildren, these should learn
first of all to put their religion into practice by
caring for their own family and so repaying
their parents and grandparents, for this is
pleasing to God. 5The widow who is really in
need and left all alone puts her hope in God
and continues night and day to pray and to
ask God for help. 6But the widow who lives
for pleasure is dead even while she lives.
7Give the people these instructions, too, so
that no one may be open to blame. 8If anyone does not provide for his relatives, and
especially for his immediate family, he has
denied the faith and is worse than an unbeliever.

9No widow may be put on the list of widows
unless she is over sixty, has been faithful to
her husband,[a] 10and is well known for her
good deeds, such as bringing up children,
showing hospitality, washing the feet of the
saints, helping those in trouble and devoting
herself to all kinds of good deeds.

11As for younger widows, do not put them
on such a list. For when their sensual desires
overcome their dedication to Christ, they
want to marry. 12Thus they bring judgment
on themselves, because they have broken
their first pledge. 13Besides, they get into the
habit of being idle and going about from
house to house. And not only do they
become idlers, but also gossips and busybodies, saying things they ought not to. 14So
I counsel younger widows to marry, to have
children, to manage their homes and to give
the enemy no opportunity for slander.
15Some have in fact already turned away to
follow Satan.

16If any woman who is a believer has widows in her family, she should help them and
not let the church be burdened with them, so
that the church can help those widows who
are really in need.

17The elders who direct the affairs of the
church well are worthy of double honor,
especially those whose work is preaching
and teaching. 18For the Scripture says, "Do
not muzzle the ox while it is treading out the
grain,"[b] and "The worker deserves his
wages."[c] 19Do not entertain an accusation
against an elder unless it is brought by two or
three witnesses. 20Those who sin are to be
rebuked publicly, so that the others may take
warning.

21I charge you, in the sight of God and
Christ Jesus and the elect angels, to keep
these instructions without partiality, and to
do nothing out of favoritism.

22Do not be hasty in the laying on of hands,
and do not share in the sins of others. Keep
yourself pure.

23Stop drinking only water, and use a little
wine because of your stomach and your frequent illnesses.

24The sins of some men are obvious,

[a]9 Or *has had but one husband* [b]18 Deut. 25:4 [c]18 Luke 10:7

reaching the place of judgment ahead of them; the sins of others trail behind them. 25In the same way, good deeds are obvious, and even those that are not cannot be hidden.

6 All who are under the yoke of slavery should consider their masters worthy of full respect, so that God's name and our teaching may not be slandered. 2Those who have believing masters are not to show less respect for them because they are brothers. Instead, they are to serve them even better, because those who benefit from their service are believers, and dear to them. These are the things you are to teach and urge on them.

Love of Money

3If anyone teaches false doctrines and does not agree to the sound instruction of our Lord Jesus Christ and to godly teaching, 4he is conceited and understands nothing. He has an unhealthy interest in controversies and quarrels about words that result in envy, strife, malicious talk, evil suspicions 5and constant friction between men of corrupt mind, who have been robbed of the truth and who think that godliness is a means to financial gain.

6But godliness with contentment is great gain. 7For we brought nothing into the world, and we can take nothing out of it. 8But if we have food and clothing, we will be content with that. 9People who want to get rich fall into temptation and a trap and into many foolish and harmful desires that plunge men into ruin and destruction. 10For the love of money is a root of all kinds of evil. Some people, eager for money, have wandered from the faith and pierced themselves with many griefs.

Paul's Charge to Timothy

11But you, man of God, flee from all this, and pursue righteousness, godliness, faith, love, endurance and gentleness. 12Fight the good fight of the faith. Take hold of the eternal life to which you were called when you made your good confession in the presence of many witnesses. 13In the sight of God, who gives life to everything, and of Christ Jesus, who while testifying before Pontius Pilate made the good confession, I charge you 14to keep this command without spot or blame until the appearing of our Lord Jesus Christ, 15which God will bring about in his own time—God, the blessed and only Ruler, the King of kings and Lord of lords, 16who alone is immortal and who lives in unapproachable light, whom no one has seen or can see. To him be honor and might forever. Amen.

17Command those who are rich in this present world not to be arrogant nor to put their hope in wealth, which is so uncertain, but to put their hope in God, who richly provides us with everything for our enjoyment. 18Command them to do good, to be rich in good deeds, and to be generous and willing to share. 19In this way they will lay up treasure for themselves as a firm foundation for the coming age, so that they may take hold of the life that is truly life.

20Timothy, guard what has been entrusted to your care. Turn away from godless chatter and the opposing ideas of what is falsely called knowledge, 21which some have professed and in so doing have wandered from the faith.

Grace be with you.

2 Timothy

Introduction:

It seems probable that Paul was arrested again sometime after writing I Timothy and Titus, and that he wrote this second letter to Timothy from Rome where he was being held a prisoner.

In this letter Paul seems to know that there is little chance of his getting out of prison and that he will soon die. It is for these reasons that he writes to Timothy.

Paul wants not only to see Timothy again but also to encourage Timothy because he would have to continue Paul's missionary work after his death.

Paul gives Timothy more instructions on how to lead a church and warns him to stay away from false teachers. He urges Timothy to be faithful to true Christian teachings.

Outline of contents:

Greeting (1:1,2)
Encouragement to be faithful (1:3–2:13)
The false and the true way (2:14–3:9)
Paul's charge to Timothy (3:10–4:8)
Conclusion (4:9–22)

---

1 Paul, an apostle of Christ Jesus by the
will of God, according to the promise of
life that is in Christ Jesus,

2To Timothy, my dear son:

Grace, mercy and peace from God the
Father and Christ Jesus our Lord.

Encouragement to Be Faithful

3I thank God, whom I serve, as my forefathers did, with a clear conscience, as night
and day I constantly remember you in my
prayers. 4Recalling your tears, I long to see
you, so that I may be filled with joy. 5I have
been reminded of your sincere faith, which
first lived in your grandmother Lois and in
your mother Eunice and, I am persuaded,
now lives in you also. 6For this reason I
remind you to fan into flame the gift of God,
which is in you through the laying on of my
hands. 7For God did not give us a spirit of
timidity, but a spirit of power, of love and of
self-discipline.

8So do not be ashamed to testify about our
Lord, or ashamed of me his prisoner. But join
with me in suffering for the gospel, by the
power of God, 9who has saved us and called
us to a holy life—not because of anything we
have done but because of his own purpose
and grace. This grace was given us in Christ
Jesus before the beginning of time, 10but it
has now been revealed through the appearing of our Savior, Christ Jesus, who has destroyed death and has brought life and immortality to light through the gospel. 11And of
this gospel I was appointed a herald and an
apostle and a teacher. 12That is why I am
suffering as I am. Yet I am not ashamed,
because I know whom I have believed, and
am convinced that he is able to guard what I
have entrusted to him for that day.

13What you heard from me, keep as the
pattern of sound teaching, with faith and love
in Christ Jesus. 14Guard the good deposit
that was entrusted to you—guard it with the
help of the Holy Spirit who lives in us.

15You know that everyone in the province
of Asia has deserted me, including Phygelus
and Hermogenes.

16May the Lord show mercy to the household of Onesiphorus, because he often refreshed me and was not ashamed of my
chains. 17On the contrary, when he was in
Rome, he searched hard for me until he
found me. 18May the Lord grant that he will
find mercy from the Lord on that day! You

know very well in how many ways he helped me in Ephesus.

2 You then, my son, be strong in the grace that is in Christ Jesus. 2And the things you have heard me say in the presence of many witnesses entrust to reliable men who will also be qualified to teach others. 3Endure hardship with us like a good soldier of Christ Jesus. 4No one serving as a soldier gets involved in civilian affairs—he wants to please his commanding officer. 5Similarly, if anyone competes as an athlete, he does not receive the victor's crown unless he competes according to the rules. 6The hardworking farmer should be the first to receive a share of the crops. 7Reflect on what I am saying, for the Lord will give you insight into all this.

8Remember Jesus Christ, raised from the dead, descended from David. This is my gospel, 9for which I am suffering even to the point of being chained like a criminal. But God's word is not chained. 10Therefore I endure everything for the sake of the elect, that they too may obtain the salvation that is in Christ Jesus, with eternal glory.

11Here is a trustworthy saying:

If we died with him,
  we will also live with him;
12if we endure,
  we will also reign with him.
If we disown him,
  he will also disown us;
13if we are faithless,
  he will remain faithful,
  for he cannot disown himself.

A Workman Approved by God

14Keep reminding them of these things. Warn them before God against quarreling about words; it is of no value, and only ruins those who listen. 15Do your best to present yourself to God as one approved, a workman who does not need to be ashamed and who correctly handles the word of truth. 16Avoid godless chatter, because those who indulge in it will become more and more ungodly. 17Their teaching will spread like gangrene. Among them are Hymenaeus and Philetus, 18who have wandered away from the truth. They say that the resurrection has already taken place, and they destroy the faith of some. 19Nevertheless, God's solid foundation stands firm, sealed with this inscription: "The Lord knows those who are his,"[a] and, "Everyone who confesses the name of the Lord must turn away from wickedness."

20In a large house there are articles not only of gold and silver, but also of wood and clay; some are for noble purposes and some for ignoble. 21If a man cleanses himself from the latter, he will be an instrument for noble purposes, made holy, useful to the Master and prepared to do any good work.

22Flee the evil desires of youth, and pursue righteousness, faith, love and peace, along with those who call on the Lord out of a pure heart. 23Don't have anything to do with foolish and stupid arguments, because you know they produce quarrels. 24And the Lord's servant must not quarrel; instead, he must be kind to everyone, able to teach, not resentful. 25Those who oppose him he must gently instruct, in the hope that God will grant them repentance leading them to a knowledge of the truth, 26and that they will come to their senses and escape from the trap of the devil, who has taken them captive to do his will.

Godlessness in the Last Days

3 But mark this: There will be terrible times in the last days. 2People will be lovers of themselves, lovers of money, boastful, proud, abusive, disobedient to their parents, ungrateful, unholy, 3without love, unforgiving, slanderous, without self-control, brutal, not lovers of the good, 4treacherous, rash, conceited, lovers of pleasure rather than lovers of God— 5having a form of godliness but denying its power. Have nothing to do with them.

6They are the kind who worm their way into homes and gain control over weak-willed women, who are loaded down with sins and are swayed by all kinds of evil desires, 7always learning but never able to acknowledge the truth. 8Just as Jannes and Jambres opposed Moses, so also these men oppose the truth—men of depraved minds, who, as far as the faith is concerned, are rejected. 9But they will not get very far because, as in the case of those men, their folly will be clear to everyone.

Paul's Charge to Timothy

10You, however, know all about my teaching, my way of life, my purpose, faith, patience, love, endurance, 11persecutions, sufferings—what kinds of things happened to

[a]19 Num. 16:5 (see Septuagint)

me in Antioch, Iconium and Lystra, the persecutions I endured. Yet the Lord rescued
me from all of them. 12In fact, everyone who
wants to live a godly life in Christ Jesus will
be persecuted, 13while evil men and impostors will go from bad to worse, deceiving and
being deceived. 14But as for you, continue in
what you have learned and have become
convinced of, because you know those from
whom you learned it, 15and how from infancy
you have known the holy Scriptures, which
are able to make you wise for salvation
through faith in Christ Jesus. 16All Scripture
is God-breathed and is useful for teaching,
rebuking, correcting and training in righteousness, 17so that the man of God may be
thoroughly equipped for every good work.
4 In the presence of God and of Christ
Jesus, who will judge the living and the
dead, and in view of his appearing and his
kingdom, I give you this charge: 2Preach the
Word; be prepared in season and out of season; correct, rebuke and encourage—with
great patience and careful instruction. 3For
the time will come when men will not put up
with sound doctrine. Instead, to suit their
own desires, they will gather around them a
great number of teachers to say what their
itching ears want to hear. 4They will turn their
ears away from the truth and turn aside to
myths. 5But you, keep your head in all situations, endure hardship, do the work of an
evangelist, discharge all the duties of your
ministry.
6For I am already being poured out like a
drink offering, and the time has come for my
departure. 7I have fought the good fight, I
have finished the race, I have kept the faith.
8Now there is in store for me the crown of
righteousness, which the Lord, the righteous
Judge, will award to me on that day—and not
only to me, but also to all who have longed
for his appearing.

Personal Remarks

9Do your best to come to me quickly, 10for
Demas, because he loved this world, has
deserted me and has gone to Thessalonica.
Crescens has gone to Galatia, and Titus to
Dalmatia. 11Only Luke is with me. Get Mark
and bring him with you, because he is helpful
to me in my ministry. 12I sent Tychicus to
Ephesus. 13When you come, bring the cloak
that I left with Carpus at Troas, and my
scrolls, especially the parchments.
14Alexander the metalworker did me a
great deal of harm. The Lord will repay him
for what he has done. 15You too should be on
your guard against him, because he strongly
opposed our message.
16At my first defense, no one came to my
support, but everyone deserted me. May it
not be held against them. 17But the Lord
stood at my side and gave me strength, so
that through me the message might be fully
proclaimed and all the Gentiles might hear it.
And I was delivered from the lion's mouth.
18The Lord will rescue me from every evil
attack and will bring me safely to his heavenly kingdom. To him be glory for ever and
ever. Amen.

Final Greetings

19Greet Priscilla[a] and Aquila and the
household of Onesiphorus. 20Erastus stayed
in Corinth, and I left Trophimus sick in Miletus. 21Do your best to get here before winter.
Eubulus greets you, and so do Pudens,
Linus, Claudia and all the brothers.
22The Lord be with your spirit. Grace be
with you.

[a]19 Greek *Prisca,* a variant of *Priscilla*

Titus

Introduction:

Titus was another friend and helper of Paul's. He had traveled with Paul on some of his missionary journeys, and was working as the leader of the church on Crete. This letter is similar to the two letters to Timothy.

The church in Crete seems to have been an unorganized church and made up of people who needed much instruction in being Christians. Paul tells Titus and the church how God's people should behave. He tells Titus to teach the people the truth of God and instructs him in how to be a good leader of the church.

Outline of contents:

---

1 Paul, a servant of God and an apostle of
Jesus Christ for the faith of God's elect
and the knowledge of the truth that leads to
godliness— 2a faith and knowledge resting
on the hope of eternal life, which God, who
does not lie, promised before the beginning
of time, 3and at his appointed season he
brought his word to light through the preaching entrusted to me by the command of God
our Savior,

4To Titus, my true son in our common faith:

Grace and peace from God the Father and
Christ Jesus our Savior.

Titus' Task on Crete

5The reason I left you in Crete was that you
might straighten out what was left unfinished
and appoint[a] elders in every town, as I directed you. 6An elder must be blameless, the
husband of but one wife, a man whose children believe and are not open to the charge
of being wild and disobedient. 7Since an
overseer[b] is entrusted with God's work, he
must be blameless—not overbearing, not
quick-tempered, not given to drunkenness,
not violent, not pursuing dishonest gain.
8Rather he must be hospitable, one who
loves what is good, who is self-controlled,
upright, holy and disciplined. 9He must hold
firmly to the trustworthy message as it has
been taught, so that he can encourage others by sound doctrine and refute those who
oppose it.

10For there are many rebellious people,
mere talkers and deceivers, especially those
of the circumcision group. 11They must be
silenced, because they are ruining whole
households by teaching things they ought
not to teach—and that for the sake of dishonest gain. 12Even one of their own prophets
has said, "Cretans are always liars, evil
brutes, lazy gluttons." 13This testimony is
true. Therefore, rebuke them sharply, so that
they will be sound in the faith 14and will pay
no attention to Jewish myths or to the commands of those who reject the truth. 15To the
pure, all things are pure, but to those who are
corrupted and do not believe, nothing is
pure. In fact, both their minds and consciences are corrupted. 16They claim to
know God, but by their actions they deny
him. They are detestable, disobedient and
unfit for doing anything good.

What Must Be Taught to Various Groups

2 You must teach what is in accord with
sound doctrine. 2Teach the older men to

[a]5 Or *ordain* [b]7 Traditionally *bishop*

be temperate, worthy of respect, self-controlled, and sound in faith, in love and in endurance.

3 Likewise, teach the older women to be reverent in the way they live, not to be slanderers or addicted to much wine, but to teach what is good. 4 Then they can train the younger women to love their husbands and children, 5 to be self-controlled and pure, to be busy at home, to be kind, and to be subject to their husbands, so that no one will malign the word of God.

6 Similarly, encourage the young men to be self-controlled. 7 In everything set them an example by doing what is good. In your teaching show integrity, seriousness 8 and soundness of speech that cannot be condemned, so that those who oppose you may be ashamed because they have nothing bad to say about us.

9 Teach slaves to be subject to their masters in everything, to try to please them, not to talk back to them, 10 and not to steal from them, but to show that they can be fully trusted, so that in every way they will make the teaching about God our Savior attractive.

11 For the grace of God that brings salvation has appeared to all men. 12 It teaches us to say "No" to ungodliness and worldly passions, and to live self-controlled, upright and godly lives in this present age, 13 while we wait for the blessed hope—the glorious appearing of our great God and Savior, Jesus Christ, 14 who gave himself for us to redeem us from all wickedness and to purify for himself a people that are his very own, eager to do what is good.

15 These, then, are the things you should teach. Encourage and rebuke with all authority. Do not let anyone despise you.

Doing What Is Good

3 Remind the people to be subject to rulers and authorities, to be obedient, to be ready to do whatever is good, 2 to slander no one, to be peaceable and considerate, and to show true humility toward all men.

3 At one time we too were foolish, disobedient, deceived and enslaved by all kinds of passions and pleasures. We lived in malice and envy, being hated and hating one another. 4 But when the kindness and love of God our Savior appeared, 5 he saved us, not because of righteous things we had done, but because of his mercy. He saved us through the washing of rebirth and renewal by the Holy Spirit, 6 whom he poured out on us generously through Jesus Christ our Savior, 7 so that, having been justified by his grace, we might become heirs having the hope of eternal life. 8 This is a trustworthy saying. And I want you to stress these things, so that those who have trusted in God may be careful to devote themselves to doing what is good. These things are excellent and profitable for everyone.

9 But avoid foolish controversies and genealogies and arguments and quarrels about the law, because these are unprofitable and useless. 10 Warn a divisive person once, and then warn him a second time. After that, have nothing to do with him. 11 You may be sure that such a man is warped and sinful; he is self-condemned.

Final Remarks

12 As soon as I send Artemas or Tychicus to you, do your best to come to me at Nicopolis, because I have decided to winter there. 13 Do everything you can to help Zenas the lawyer and Apollos on their way and see that they have everything they need. 14 Our people must learn to devote themselves to doing what is good, in order that they may provide for daily necessities and not live unproductive lives.

15 Everyone with me sends you greetings. Greet those who love us in the faith.

Grace be with you all.

Philemon

Introduction:

Philemon was a leader of the church at Colosse and a friend of Paul's. Philemon's slave, Onesimus, had stolen money from him and had run away to Rome. While he was there he met Paul and became a Christian.

Paul sends Onesimus back to Philemon with this letter. He begs Philemon to forgive Onesimus and to treat him as a brother in Christ instead of a runaway slave.

This short letter, along with Ephesians, Colossians, and Philippians are often called the prison letters because they were written while Paul was in prison in Rome for the first time (about A.D. 59–61).

Outline of contents:

Greetings (1–3)
Paul's concern and love (4–7)
Paul's plea for Onesimus (8–22)
Farewell (23–25)

1Paul, a prisoner of Christ Jesus, and Timothy our brother,

To Philemon our dear friend and fellow
worker, 2to Apphia our sister, to Archippus
our fellow soldier and to the church that
meets in your home:

3Grace to you and peace from God our
Father and the Lord Jesus Christ.

Thanksgiving and Prayer

4I always thank my God as I remember you
in my prayers, 5because I hear about your
faith in the Lord Jesus and your love for all
the saints. 6I pray that you may be active in
sharing your faith, so that you will have a full
understanding of every good thing we have
in Christ. 7Your love has given me great joy
and encouragement, because you, brother,
have refreshed the hearts of the saints.

Paul's Plea for Onesimus

8Therefore, although in Christ I could be
bold and order you to do what you ought to
do, 9yet I appeal to you on the basis of love.
I then, as Paul—an old man and now also a
prisoner of Christ Jesus— 10I appeal to you
for my son Onesimus,[a] who became my son
while I was in chains. 11Formerly he was
useless to you, but now he has become useful both to you and to me.

12I am sending him—who is my very
heart—back to you. 13I would have liked to
keep him with me so that he could take your
place in helping me while I am in chains for
the gospel. 14But I did not want to do anything without your consent, so that any favor
you do will be spontaneous and not forced.
15Perhaps the reason he was separated
from you for a little while was that you might
have him back for good— 16no longer as a
slave, but better than a slave, as a dear
brother. He is very dear to me but even dearer to you, both as a man and as a brother in
the Lord.

17So if you consider me a partner, welcome him as you would welcome me. 18If he
has done you any wrong or owes you anything, charge it to me. 19I, Paul, am writing
this with my own hand. I will pay it back—not
to mention that you owe me your very self. 20I
do wish, brother, that I may have some benefit from you in the Lord; refresh my heart in
Christ. 21Confident of your obedience, I write
to you, knowing that you will do even more
than I ask.

[a] 10 *Onesimus* means *useful.*

22And one thing more: Prepare a guest
room for me, because I hope to be restored
to you in answer to your prayers.

23Epaphras, my fellow prisoner in Christ
Jesus, sends you greetings. 24And so do
Mark, Aristarchus, Demas and Luke, my fel-
low workers.

25The grace of the Lord Jesus Christ be
with your spirit.

Hebrews

Introduction:

Although the author of Hebrews is unknown, this book was probably written in the late A.D. 60's. During this time persecution was a real problem for the church in Rome. This letter was most likely written to the Jewish Christians in either Palestine or Rome who were ready to give up their faith and return to the Jewish faith because of persecution.

The book of Hebrews was written to teach these Jewish Christians that the Christian faith is better in every way than the Jewish faith. Christ is from God and is better than the angels, Moses and Joshua, any priest, and he is the only complete sacrifice. The author shows how Jesus completed the Jewish faith by making the final sacrifice for sin. After his death, none of the Old Testament sacrifices were needed. Chapter 11—the famous chapter on men and women of faith in Old Testament times—must have given these persecuted Christians great hope and helped them to have faith and trust in God.

Outline of contents:

Christ—God's complete revelation (1:1–3)
Christ—superior to the angels (1:4–2:18)
Christ—superior to Moses and Joshua (3:1–4:13)
Christ—the superior intercessor or priest (4:14–7:28)
Christ's superior covenant and sacrifice (8:1–10:18)
The practical appeal (10:19–12:29)
Concluding advice (13:1–25)

The Son Superior to Angels

1 In the past God spoke to our forefathers
through the prophets at many times and
in various ways, 2but in these last days he
has spoken to us by his Son, whom he appointed heir of all things, and through whom
he made the universe. 3The Son is the radiance of God's glory and the exact representation of his being, sustaining all things by his
powerful word. After he had provided purification for sins, he sat down at the right hand
of the Majesty in heaven. 4So he became as
much superior to the angels as the name he
has inherited is superior to theirs.
5For to which of the angels did God ever
say,

"You are my Son;
today I have become your Father[a]"[b]?

Or again,

"I will be his Father,
and he will be my Son"[c]?

6And again, when God brings his firstborn
into the world, he says,

"Let all God's angels worship him."[d]

7In speaking of the angels he says,

"He makes his angels winds,
his servants flames of fire."[e]

8But about the Son he says,

"Your throne, O God, will last for ever and
ever,
and righteousness will be the scepter of
your kingdom.
9You have loved righteousness and hated
wickedness;
therefore God, your God, has set you
above your companions
by anointing you with the oil of joy."[f]

10He also says,

"In the beginning, O Lord, you laid the
foundations of the earth,

[a]5 Or *have begotten you* [b]5 Psalm 2:7 [c]5 2 Samuel 7:14; 1 Chron. 17:13 [d]6 Deut. 32:43 (see Dead Sea Scrolls and Septuagint) [e]7 Psalm 104:4 [f]9 Psalm 45:6,7

and the heavens are the work of your
hands.
11They will perish, but you remain;
they will all wear out like a garment.
12You will roll them up like a robe;
like a garment they will be changed.
But you remain the same,
and your years will never end."[a]

13To which of the angels did God ever say,

"Sit at my right hand
until I make your enemies
a footstool for your feet"[b]?

14Are not all angels ministering spirits sent to
serve those who will inherit salvation?

Warning to Pay Attention

2 We must pay more careful attention,
therefore, to what we have heard, so that
we do not drift away. 2For if the message
spoken by angels was binding, and every
violation and disobedience received its just
punishment, 3how shall we escape if we ignore such a great salvation? This salvation,
which was first announced by the Lord, was
confirmed to us by those who heard him.
4God also testified to it by signs, wonders
and various miracles, and gifts of the Holy
Spirit distributed according to his will.

Jesus Made Like His Brothers

5It is not to angels that he has subjected
the world to come, about which we are
speaking. 6But there is a place where someone has testified:

"What is man that you are mindful of him,
the son of man that you care for him?
7You made him a little[c] lower than the
angels;
you crowned him with glory and honor
8 and put everything under his feet."[d]

In putting everything under him, God left
nothing that is not subject to him. Yet at
present we do not see everything subject to
him. 9But we see Jesus, who was made a
little lower than the angels, now crowned
with glory and honor because he suffered
death, so that by the grace of God he might
taste death for everyone.

10In bringing many sons to glory, it was
fitting that God, for whom and through whom
everything exists, should make the author of
their salvation perfect through suffering.
11Both the one who makes men holy and
those who are made holy are of the same
family. So Jesus is not ashamed to call them
brothers. 12He says,

"I will declare your name to my brothers;
in the presence of the congregation I
will sing your praises."[e]

13And again,

"I will put my trust in him."[f]

And again he says,

"Here am I, and the children God has
given me."[g]

14Since the children have flesh and blood,
he too shared in their humanity so that by his
death he might destroy him who holds the
power of death—that is, the devil— 15and
free those who all their lives were held in
slavery by their fear of death. 16For surely it is
not angels he helps, but Abraham's descendants. 17For this reason he had to be
made like his brothers in every way, in order
that he might become a merciful and faithful
high priest in service to God, and that he
might make atonement for[h] the sins of the
people. 18Because he himself suffered when
he was tempted, he is able to help those who
are being tempted.

Jesus Greater Than Moses

3 Therefore, holy brothers, who share in
the heavenly calling, fix your thoughts on
Jesus, the apostle and high priest whom we
confess. 2He was faithful to the one who appointed him, just as Moses was faithful in all
God's house. 3Jesus has been found worthy
of greater honor than Moses, just as the
builder of a house has greater honor than the
house itself. 4For every house is built by
someone, but God is the builder of everything. 5Moses was faithful as a servant in all
God's house, testifying to what would be
said in the future. 6But Christ is faithful as a
son over God's house. And we are his
house, if we hold on to our courage and the
hope of which we boast.

Warning Against Unbelief

7So, as the Holy Spirit says:

"Today, if you hear his voice,

[a]*12* Psalm 102:25-27 [b]*13* Psalm 110:1 [c]*7* Or *him for a little while;* also in verse 9 [d]*8* Psalm 8:4-6
[e]*12* Psalm 22:22 [f]*13* Isaiah 8:17 [g]*13* Isaiah 8:18 [h]*17* Or *and that he might turn aside God's wrath, taking away*

8 do not harden your hearts
as you did in the rebellion,
during the time of testing in the desert,
9where your fathers tested and tried me
and for forty years saw what I did.
10That is why I was angry with that
generation,
and I said, 'Their hearts are always
going astray,
and they have not known my ways.'
11So I declared on oath in my anger,
'They shall never enter my rest.' "[a]

12See to it, brothers, that none of you has a
sinful, unbelieving heart that turns away from
the living God. 13But encourage one another
daily, as long as it is called Today, so that
none of you may be hardened by sin's deceitfulness. 14We have come to share in
Christ if we hold firmly till the end the confidence we had at first. 15As has just been
said:

"Today, if you hear his voice,
do not harden your hearts
as you did in the rebellion."[b]

16Who were they who heard and rebelled?
Were they not all those Moses led out of
Egypt? 17And with whom was he angry for
forty years? Was it not with those who
sinned, whose bodies fell in the desert?
18And to whom did God swear that they
would never enter his rest if not to those who
disobeyed[c]? 19So we see that they were not
able to enter, because of their unbelief.

A Sabbath-Rest for the People of God

4 Therefore, since the promise of entering
his rest still stands, let us be careful that
none of you be found to have fallen short of
it. 2For we also have had the gospel
preached to us, just as they did; but the message they heard was of no value to them,
because those who heard did not combine it
with faith.[d] 3Now we who have believed enter that rest, just as God has said,

"So I declared on oath in my anger,
'They shall never enter my rest.' "[e]

And yet his work has been finished since the
creation of the world. 4For somewhere he
has spoken about the seventh day in these
words: "And on the seventh day God rested
from all his work."[f] 5And again in the passage above he says, "They shall never enter
my rest."

6It still remains that some will enter that
rest, and those who formerly had the gospel
preached to them did not go in, because of
their disobedience. 7Therefore God again
set a certain day, calling it Today, when a
long time later he spoke through David, as
was said before:

"Today, if you hear his voice,
do not harden your hearts."[b]

8For if Joshua had given them rest, God
would not have spoken later about another
day. 9There remains, then, a Sabbath-rest
for the people of God; 10for anyone who enters God's rest also rests from his own work,
just as God did from his. 11Let us, therefore,
make every effort to enter that rest, so that
no one will fall by following their example of
disobedience.

12For the word of God is living and active.
Sharper than any double-edged sword, it
penetrates even to dividing soul and spirit,
joints and marrow; it judges the thoughts and
attitudes of the heart. 13Nothing in all creation is hidden from God's sight Everything is
uncovered and laid bare before the eyes of
him to whom we must give account.

Jesus the Great High Priest

14Therefore, since we have a great high
priest who has gone through the heavens,[g]
Jesus the Son of God, let us hold firmly to the
faith we profess. 15For we do not have a high
priest who is unable to sympathize with our
weaknesses, but we have one who has been
tempted in every way, just as we are—yet
was without sin. 16Let us then approach the
throne of grace with confidence, so that we
may receive mercy and find grace to help us
in our time of need.

5 Every high priest is selected from among
men and is appointed to represent them
in matters related to God, to offer gifts and
sacrifices for sins. 2He is able to deal gently
with those who are ignorant and are going
astray, since he himself is subject to weakness. 3This is why he has to offer sacrifices
for his own sins, as well as for the sins of the
people.

4No one takes this honor upon himself; he
must be called by God, just as Aaron was.

[a] *11* Psalm 95:7-11 [b] *15,7* Psalm 95:7,8 [c] *18* Or *disbelieved* [d] *2* Many manuscripts *because they did not share in the faith of those who obeyed* [e] *3* Psalm 95:11; also in verse 5 [f] *4* Gen. 2:2 [g] *14* Or *gone into heaven*

5So Christ also did not take upon himself the glory of becoming a high priest. But God said to him,

"You are my Son;
today I have become your Father.[a]"[b]

6And he says in another place,

"You are a priest forever,
in the order of Melchizedek."[c]

7During the days of Jesus' life on earth, he offered up prayers and petitions with loud cries and tears to the one who could save him from death, and he was heard because of his reverent submission. 8Although he was a son, he learned obedience from what he suffered 9and, once made perfect, he became the source of eternal salvation for all who obey him 10and was designated by God to be high priest in the order of Melchizedek.

Warning Against Falling Away

11We have much to say about this, but it is hard to explain because you are slow to learn. 12In fact, though by this time you ought to be teachers, you need someone to teach you the elementary truths of God's word all over again. You need milk, not solid food! 13Anyone who lives on milk, being still an infant, is not acquainted with the teaching about righteousness. 14But solid food is for the mature, who by constant use have trained themselves to distinguish good from evil.

6 Therefore let us leave the elementary teachings about Christ and go on to maturity, not laying again the foundation of repentance from acts that lead to death,[d] and of faith in God, 2instruction about baptisms, the laying on of hands, the resurrection of the dead, and eternal judgment. 3And God permitting, we will do so.

4It is impossible for those who have once been enlightened, who have tasted the heavenly gift, who have shared in the Holy Spirit, 5who have tasted the goodness of the word of God and the powers of the coming age, 6if they fall away, to be brought back to repentance, because[e] to their loss they are crucifying the Son of God all over again and subjecting him to public disgrace.

7Land that drinks in the rain often falling on it and that produces a crop useful to those for whom it is farmed receives the blessing of God. 8But land that produces thorns and thistles is worthless and is in danger of being cursed. In the end it will be burned.

9Even though we speak like this, dear friends, we are confident of better things in your case—things that accompany salvation. 10God is not unjust; he will not forget your work and the love you have shown him as you have helped his people and continue to help them. 11We want each of you to show this same diligence to the very end, in order to make your hope sure. 12We do not want you to become lazy, but to imitate those who through faith and patience inherit what has been promised.

The Certainty of God's Promise

13When God made his promise to Abraham, since there was no one greater for him to swear by, he swore by himself, 14saying, "I will surely bless you and give you many descendants."[f] 15And so after waiting patiently, Abraham received what was promised.

16Men swear by someone greater than themselves, and the oath confirms what is said and puts an end to all argument. 17Because God wanted to make the unchanging nature of his purpose very clear to the heirs of what was promised, he confirmed it with an oath. 18God did this so that, by two unchangeable things in which it is impossible for God to lie, we who have fled to take hold of the hope offered to us may be greatly encouraged. 19We have this hope as an anchor for the soul, firm and secure. It enters the inner sanctuary behind the curtain, 20where Jesus, who went before us, has entered on our behalf. He has become a high priest forever, in the order of Melchizedek.

Melchizedek the Priest

7 This Melchizedek was king of Salem and priest of God Most High. He met Abraham returning from the defeat of the kings and blessed him, 2and Abraham gave him a tenth of everything. First, his name means "king of righteousness"; then also, "king of Salem" means "king of peace." 3Without father or mother, without genealogy, without beginning of days or end of life, like the Son of God he remains a priest forever.

4Just think how great he was: Even the patriarch Abraham gave him a tenth of the plunder! 5Now the law requires the descend-

[a]5 Or *have begotten you* [b]5 Psalm 2:7 [c]6 Psalm 110:4 [d]1 Or *from useless rituals* [e]6 Or *repentance while* [f]14 Gen. 22:17

ants of Levi who become priests to collect a
tenth from the people—that is, their brothers—even though their brothers are descended from Abraham. 6This man, however, did not trace his descent from Levi, yet
he collected a tenth from Abraham and
blessed him who had the promises. 7And
without doubt the lesser person is blessed by
the greater. 8In the one case, the tenth is
collected by men who die; but in the other
case, by him who is declared to be living.
9One might even say that Levi, who collects
the tenth, paid the tenth through Abraham,
10because when Melchizedek met Abraham,
Levi was still in the body of his ancestor.

Jesus Like Melchizedek

11If perfection could have been attained
through the Levitical priesthood (for on the
basis of it the law was given to the people),
why was there still need for another priest to
come—one in the order of Melchizedek, not
in the order of Aaron? 12For when there is a
change of the priesthood, there must also be
a change of the law. 13He of whom these
things are said belonged to a different tribe,
and no one from that tribe has ever served at
the altar. 14For it is clear that our Lord descended from Judah, and in regard to that
tribe Moses said nothing about priests.
15And what we have said is even more clear
if another priest like Melchizedek appears,
16one who has become a priest not on the
basis of a regulation as to his ancestry but on
the basis of the power of an indestructible
life. 17For it is declared:

"You are a priest forever,
  in the order of Melchizedek."[a]

18The former regulation is set aside because it was weak and useless 19(for the law
made nothing perfect), and a better hope is
introduced, by which we draw near to God.
20And it was not without an oath! Others
became priests without any oath, 21but he
became a priest with an oath when God said
to him:

"The Lord has sworn
  and will not change his mind:
'You are a priest forever.' "[a]

22Because of this oath, Jesus has become
the guarantee of a better covenant.
23Now there have been many of those
priests, since death prevented them from
continuing in office; 24but because Jesus
lives forever, he has a permanent priesthood. 25Therefore he is able to save completely[b] those who come to God through
him, because he always lives to intercede for
them.

26Such a high priest meets our need—one
who is holy, blameless, pure, set apart from
sinners, exalted above the heavens. 27Unlike
the other high priests, he does not need to
offer sacrifices day after day, first for his own
sins, and then for the sins of the people. He
sacrificed for their sins once for all when he
offered himself. 28For the law appoints as
high priests men who are weak; but the oath,
which came after the law, appointed the Son,
who has been made perfect forever.

The High Priest of a New Covenant

8 The point of what we are saying is this:
We do have such a high priest, who sat
down at the right hand of the throne of the
Majesty in heaven, 2and who serves in the
sanctuary, the true tabernacle set up by the
Lord, not by man.

3Every high priest is appointed to offer
both gifts and sacrifices, and so it was
necessary for this one also to have something to offer. 4If he were on earth, he would
not be a priest, for there are already men
who offer the gifts prescribed by the law.
5They serve at a sanctuary that is a copy and
shadow of what is in heaven. This is why
Moses was warned when he was about to
build the tabernacle: "See to it that you make
everything according to the pattern shown
you on the mountain."[c] 6But the ministry
Jesus has received is as superior to theirs as
the covenant of which he is mediator is superior to the old one, and it is founded on better
promises.

7For if there had been nothing wrong with
that first covenant, no place would have
been sought for another. 8But God found
fault with the people and said[d]:

"The time is coming, declares the Lord,
  when I will make a new covenant
with the house of Israel
  and with the house of Judah.
9It will not be like the covenant
  I made with their forefathers
when I took them by the hand

[a]*17,21* Psalm 110:4 [b]*25* Or *forever* [c]*5* Exodus 25:40 [d]*8* Some manuscripts may be translated *fault and said to the people.*

to lead them out of Egypt,
because they did not remain faithful to my covenant,
and I turned away from them,
declares the Lord.
[10]This is the covenant I will make with the house of Israel
after that time, declares the Lord.
I will put my laws in their minds
and write them on their hearts.
I will be their God,
and they will be my people.
[11]No longer will a man teach his neighbor,
or a man his brother, saying, 'Know the Lord,'
because they will all know me,
from the least of them to the greatest.
[12]For I will forgive their wickedness
and will remember their sins no more."[a]

[13]By calling this covenant "new," he has
made the first one obsolete; and what is obsolete and aging will soon disappear.

Worship in the Earthly Tabernacle

9 Now the first covenant had regulations
for worship and also an earthly sanctuary. [2]A tabernacle was set up. In its first room
were the lampstand, the table and the consecrated bread; this was called the Holy
Place. [3]Behind the second curtain was a
room called the Most Holy Place, [4]which had
the golden altar of incense and the gold-cov-
ered ark of the covenant. This ark contained
the gold jar of manna, Aaron's staff that had
budded, and the stone tablets of the covenant. [5]Above the ark were the cherubim of
the Glory, overshadowing the atonement
cover.[b] But we cannot discuss these things
in detail now.

[6]When everything had been arranged like
this, the priests entered regularly into the
outer room to carry on their ministry. [7]But
only the high priest entered the inner room,
and that only once a year, and never without
blood, which he offered for himself and for
the sins the people had committed in ignorance. [8]The Holy Spirit was showing by this
that the way into the Most Holy Place had not
yet been disclosed as long as the first tabernacle was still standing. [9]This is an illustra-
tion for the present time, indicating that the
gifts and sacrifices being offered were not
able to clear the conscience of the worshiper. [10]They are only a matter of food and drink
and various ceremonial washings—external
regulations applying until the time of the new
order.

The Blood of Christ

[11]When Christ came as high priest of the
good things that are already here,[c] he went
through the greater and more perfect tabernacle that is not man-made, that is to say, not
a part of this creation. [12]He did not enter by
means of the blood of goats and calves; but
he entered the Most Holy Place once for all
by his own blood, having obtained eternal
redemption. [13]The blood of goats and bulls
and the ashes of a heifer sprinkled on those
who are ceremonially unclean sanctify them
so that they are outwardly clean. [14]How
much more, then, will the blood of Christ,
who through the eternal Spirit offered himself
unblemished to God, cleanse our consciences from acts that lead to death,[d] so
that we may serve the living God!

[15]For this reason Christ is the mediator of a
new covenant, that those who are called
may receive the promised eternal inheritance—now that he has died as a ransom to
set them free from the sins committed under
the first covenant.

[16]In the case of a will,[e] it is necessary to
prove the death of the one who made it,
[17]because a will is in force only when somebody has died; it never takes effect while the
one who made it is living. [18]This is why even
the first covenant was not put into effect without blood. [19]When Moses had proclaimed
every commandment of the law to all the
people, he took the blood of calves, together
with water, scarlet wool and branches of hyssop, and sprinkled the scroll and all the
people. [20]He said, "This is the blood of the
covenant, which God has commanded you
to keep."[f] [21]In the same way, he sprinkled
with the blood both the tabernacle and
everything used in its ceremonies. [22]In fact,
the law requires that nearly everything be
cleansed with blood, and without the shedding of blood there is no forgiveness.

[23]It was necessary, then, for the copies of
the heavenly things to be purified with these
sacrifices, but the heavenly things themselves with better sacrifices than these.
[24]For Christ did not enter a man-made sanctuary that was only a copy of the true one; he

[a] *12* Jer. 31:31-34 [b] *5* Traditionally *the mercy seat* [c] *11* Some early manuscripts *are to come* [d] *14* Or *from useless rituals* [e] *16* Same Greek word as *covenant*; also in verse 17 [f] *20* Exodus 24:8

entered heaven itself, now to appear for us in
God's presence. 25Nor did he enter heaven
to offer himself again and again, the way the
high priest enters the Most Holy Place every
year with blood that is not his own. 26Then
Christ would have had to suffer many times
since the creation of the world. But now he
has appeared once for all at the end of the
ages to do away with sin by the sacrifice of
himself. 27Just as man is destined to die
once, and after that to face judgment, 28so
Christ was sacrificed once to take away the
sins of many people; and he will appear a
second time, not to bear sin, but to bring
salvation to those who are waiting for him.

Christ's Sacrifice Once for All

10 The law is only a shadow of the good
things that are coming—not the realities themselves. For this reason it can never,
by the same sacrifices repeated endlessly
year after year, make perfect those who
draw near to worship. 2If it could, would they
not have stopped being offered? For the
worshipers would have been cleansed once
for all, and would no longer have felt guilty for
their sins. 3But those sacrifices are an annual
reminder of sins, 4because it is impossible
for the blood of bulls and goats to take away
sins.

5Therefore, when Christ came into the
world, he said:

"Sacrifice and offering you did not desire,
but a body you prepared for me;
6with burnt offerings and sin offerings
you were not pleased.
7Then I said, 'Here I am—it is written
about me in the scroll—
I have come to do your will, O God.' "[a]

8First he said, "Sacrifices and offerings,
burnt offerings and sin offerings you did not
desire, nor were you pleased with them" (although the law required them to be made).
9Then he said, "Here I am, I have come to do
your will." He sets aside the first to establish
the second. 10And by that will, we have been
made holy through the sacrifice of the body
of Jesus Christ once for all.

11Day after day every priest stands and
performs his religious duties; again and
again he offers the same sacrifices, which
can never take away sins. 12But when this
priest had offered for all time one sacrifice for
sins, he sat down at the right hand of God.
13Since that time he waits for his enemies to
be made his footstool, 14because by one
sacrifice he has made perfect forever those
who are being made holy.

15The Holy Spirit also testifies to us about
this. First he says:

16"This is the covenant I will make with
them
after that time, says the Lord.
I will put my laws in their hearts,
and I will write them on their minds."[b]

17Then he adds:

"Their sins and lawless acts
I will remember no more."[c]

18And where these have been forgiven, there
is no longer any sacrifice for sin.

A Call to Persevere

19Therefore, brothers, since we have confidence to enter the Most Holy Place by the
blood of Jesus, 20by a new and living way
opened for us through the curtain, that is, his
body, 21and since we have a great priest over
the house of God, 22let us draw near to God
with a sincere heart in full assurance of faith,
having our hearts sprinkled to cleanse us
from a guilty conscience and having our bodies washed with pure water. 23Let us hold
unswervingly to the hope we profess, for he
who promised is faithful. 24And let us consider how we may spur one another on
toward love and good deeds. 25Let us not
give up meeting together, as some are in the
habit of doing, but let us encourage one
another—and all the more as you see the
Day approaching.

26If we deliberately keep on sinning after
we have received the knowledge of the truth,
no sacrifice for sins is left, 27but only a fearful
expectation of judgment and of raging fire
that will consume the enemies of God.
28Anyone who rejected the law of Moses
died without mercy on the testimony of two or
three witnesses. 29How much more severely
do you think a man deserves to be punished
who has trampled the Son of God under foot,
who has treated as an unholy thing the blood
of the covenant that sanctified him, and who
has insulted the Spirit of grace? 30For we
know him who said, "It is mine to avenge; I
will repay,"[d] and again, "The Lord will judge

[a] *7* Psalm 40:6-8 (see Septuagint) [b] *16* Jer. 31:33 [c] *17* Jer. 31:34 [d] *30* Deut. 32:35

his people."[a] 31It is a dreadful thing to fall into the hands of the living God.

32Remember those earlier days after you had received the light, when you stood your ground in a great contest in the face of suffering. 33Sometimes you were publicly exposed to insult and persecution; at other times you stood side by side with those who were so treated. 34You sympathized with those in prison and joyfully accepted the confiscation of your property, because you knew that you yourselves had better and lasting possessions.

35So do not throw away your confidence; it will be richly rewarded. 36You need to persevere so that when you have done the will of God, you will receive what he has promised. 37For in just a very little while,

"He who is coming will come and will not
delay.
38 But my righteous one[b] will live by faith.
And if he shrinks back,
I will not be pleased with him."[c]

39But we are not of those who shrink back and are destroyed, but of those who believe and are saved.

By Faith

11 Now faith is being sure of what we hope for and certain of what we do not see. 2This is what the ancients were commended for.

3By faith we understand that the universe was formed at God's command, so that what is seen was not made out of what was visible.

4By faith Abel offered God a better sacrifice than Cain did. By faith he was commended as a righteous man, when God spoke well of his offerings. And by faith he still speaks, even though he is dead.

5By faith Enoch was taken from this life, so that he did not experience death; he could not be found, because God had taken him away. For before he was taken, he was commended as one who pleased God. 6And without faith it is impossible to please God, because anyone who comes to him must believe that he exists and that he rewards those who earnestly seek him.

7By faith Noah, when warned about things not yet seen, in holy fear built an ark to save his family. By his faith he condemned the world and became heir of the righteousness that comes by faith.

8By faith Abraham, when called to go to a place he would later receive as his inheritance, obeyed and went, even though he did not know where he was going. 9By faith he made his home in the promised land like a stranger in a foreign country; he lived in tents, as did Isaac and Jacob, who were heirs with him of the same promise. 10For he was looking forward to the city with foundations, whose architect and builder is God.

11By faith Abraham, even though he was past age—and Sarah herself was barren—was enabled to become a father because he[d] considered him faithful who had made the promise. 12And so from this one man, and he as good as dead, came descendants as numerous as the stars in the sky and as countless as the sand on the seashore.

13All these people were still living by faith when they died. They did not receive the things promised; they only saw them and welcomed them from a distance. And they admitted that they were aliens and strangers on earth. 14People who say such things show that they are looking for a country of their own. 15If they had been thinking of the country they had left, they would have had opportunity to return. 16Instead, they were longing for a better country—a heavenly one. Therefore God is not ashamed to be called their God, for he has prepared a city for them.

17By faith Abraham, when God tested him, offered Isaac as a sacrifice. He who had received the promises was about to sacrifice his one and only son, 18even though God had said to him, "It is through Isaac that your offspring[e] will be reckoned."[f] 19Abraham reasoned that God could raise the dead, and figuratively speaking, he did receive Isaac back from death.

20By faith Isaac blessed Jacob and Esau in regard to their future.

21By faith Jacob, when he was dying, blessed each of Joseph's sons, and worshiped as he leaned on the top of his staff.

22By faith Joseph, when his end was near, spoke about the exodus of the Israelites from Egypt and gave instructions about his bones.

23By faith Moses' parents hid him for three months after he was born, because they saw

[a] *30* Deut. 32:36; Psalm 135:14 [b] *38* One early manuscript *But the righteous* [c] *38* Hab. 2:3,4 [d] *11* Or *By faith even Sarah, who was past age, was enabled to bear children because she* [e] *18* Greek *seed* [f] *18* Gen. 21:12

he was no ordinary child, and they were not afraid of the king's edict.

24By faith Moses, when he had grown up, refused to be known as the son of Pharaoh's daughter. 25He chose to be mistreated along with the people of God rather than to enjoy the pleasures of sin for a short time. 26He regarded disgrace for the sake of Christ as of greater value than the treasures of Egypt, because he was looking ahead to his reward. 27By faith he left Egypt, not fearing the king's anger; he persevered because he saw him who is invisible. 28By faith he kept the Passover and the sprinkling of blood, so that the destroyer of the firstborn would not touch the firstborn of Israel.

29By faith the people passed through the Red Sea[a] as on dry land; but when the Egyptians tried to do so, they were drowned.

30By faith the walls of Jericho fell, after the people had marched around them for seven days.

31By faith the prostitute Rahab, because she welcomed the spies, was not killed with those who were disobedient.[b]

32And what more shall I say? I do not have time to tell about Gideon, Barak, Samson, Jephthah, David, Samuel and the prophets, 33who through faith conquered kingdoms, administered justice, and gained what was promised; who shut the mouths of lions, 34quenched the fury of the flames, and escaped the edge of the sword; whose weakness was turned to strength; and who became powerful in battle and routed foreign armies. 35Women received back their dead, raised to life again. Others were tortured and refused to be released, so that they might gain a better resurrection. 36Some faced jeers and flogging, while still others were chained and put in prison. 37They were stoned[c]; they were sawed in two; they were put to death by the sword. They went about in sheepskins and goatskins, destitute, persecuted and mistreated— 38the world was not worthy of them. They wandered in deserts and mountains, and in caves and holes in the ground.

39These were all commended for their faith, yet none of them received what had been promised. 40God had planned something better for us so that only together with us would they be made perfect.

God Disciplines His Sons

12 Therefore, since we are surrounded by such a great cloud of witnesses, let us throw off everything that hinders and the sin that so easily entangles, and let us run with perseverance the race marked out for us. 2Let us fix our eyes on Jesus, the author and perfecter of our faith, who for the joy set before him endured the cross, scorning its shame, and sat down at the right hand of the throne of God. 3Consider him who endured such opposition from sinful men, so that you will not grow weary and lose heart.

4In your struggle against sin, you have not yet resisted to the point of shedding your blood. 5And you have forgotten that word of encouragement that addresses you as sons:

"My son, do not make light of the Lord's
discipline,
and do not lose heart when he rebukes
you,
6because the Lord disciplines those he
loves,
and he punishes everyone he accepts
as a son."[d]

7Endure hardship as discipline; God is treating you as sons. For what son is not disciplined by his father? 8If you are not disciplined (and everyone undergoes discipline), then you are illegitimate children and not true sons. 9Moreover, we have all had human fathers who disciplined us and we respected them for it. How much more should we submit to the Father of our spirits and live! 10Our fathers disciplined us for a little while as they thought best; but God disciplines us for our good, that we may share in his holiness. 11No discipline seems pleasant at the time, but painful. Later on, however, it produces a harvest of righteousness and peace for those who have been trained by it.

12Therefore, strengthen your feeble arms and weak knees. 13"Make level paths for your feet,"[e] so that the lame may not be disabled, but rather healed.

Warning Against Refusing God

14Make every effort to live in peace with all

[a]*29* That is, Sea of Reeds [b]*31* Or *unbelieving* [c]*37* Some early manuscripts *stoned; they were put to the test;* [d]*6* Prov. 3:11,12 [e]*13* Prov. 4:26

men and to be holy; without holiness no one will see the Lord. 15See to it that no one misses the grace of God and that no bitter root grows up to cause trouble and defile many. 16See that no one is sexually immoral, or is godless like Esau, who for a single meal sold his inheritance rights as the oldest son. 17Afterward, as you know, when he wanted to inherit this blessing, he was rejected. He could bring about no change of mind, though he sought the blessing with tears.

18You have not come to a mountain that can be touched and that is burning with fire; to darkness, gloom and storm; 19to a trumpet blast or to such a voice speaking words that those who heard it begged that no further word be spoken to them, 20because they could not bear what was commanded: "If even an animal touches the mountain, it must be stoned."[a] 21The sight was so terrifying that Moses said, "I am trembling with fear."[b]

22But you have come to Mount Zion, to the heavenly Jerusalem, the city of the living God. You have come to thousands upon thousands of angels in joyful assembly, 23to the church of the firstborn, whose names are written in heaven. You have come to God, the judge of all men, to the spirits of righteous men made perfect, 24to Jesus the mediator of a new covenant, and to the sprinkled blood that speaks a better word than the blood of Abel.

25See to it that you do not refuse him who speaks. If they did not escape when they refused him who warned them on earth, how much less will we, if we turn away from him who warns us from heaven? 26At that time his voice shook the earth, but now he has promised, "Once more I will shake not only the earth but also the heavens."[c] 27The words "once more" indicate the removing of what can be shaken—that is, created things—so that what cannot be shaken may remain.

28Therefore, since we are receiving a kingdom that cannot be shaken, let us be thankful, and so worship God acceptably with reverence and awe, 29for our "God is a consuming fire."[d]

Concluding Exhortations

13 Keep on loving each other as brothers. 2Do not forget to entertain strangers, for by so doing some people have entertained angels without knowing it. 3Remember those in prison as if you were their fellow prisoners, and those who are mistreated as if you yourselves were suffering.

4Marriage should be honored by all, and the marriage bed kept pure, for God will judge the adulterer and all the sexually immoral. 5Keep your lives free from the love of money and be content with what you have, because God has said,

> "Never will I leave you;
> never will I forsake you."[e]

6So we say with confidence,

> "The Lord is my helper; I will not be
> afraid.
> What can man do to me?"[f]

7Remember your leaders, who spoke the word of God to you. Consider the outcome of their way of life and imitate their faith. 8Jesus Christ is the same yesterday and today and forever.

9Do not be carried away by all kinds of strange teachings. It is good for our hearts to be strengthened by grace, not by ceremonial foods, which are of no value to those who eat them. 10We have an altar from which those who minister at the tabernacle have no right to eat.

11The high priest carries the blood of animals into the Most Holy Place as a sin offering, but the bodies are burned outside the camp. 12And so Jesus also suffered outside the city gate to make the people holy through his own blood. 13Let us, then, go to him outside the camp, bearing the disgrace he bore. 14For here we do not have an enduring city, but we are looking for the city that is to come.

15Through Jesus, therefore, let us continually offer to God a sacrifice of praise—the fruit of lips that confess his name. 16And do not forget to do good and to share with others, for with such sacrifices God is pleased.

17Obey your leaders and submit to their authority. They keep watch over you as men who must give an account. Obey them so that their work will be a joy, not a burden, for that would be of no advantage to you.

18Pray for us. We are sure that we have a clear conscience and desire to live honor-

a20 Exodus 19:12,13 *b21* Deut. 9:19 *c26* Haggai 2:6 *d29* Deut. 4:24 *e5* Deut. 31:6
f6 Psalm 118:6,7

ably in every way. [19]I particularly urge you to
pray so that I may be restored to you soon.
[20]May the God of peace, who through the
blood of the eternal covenant brought back
from the dead our Lord Jesus, that great
Shepherd of the sheep, [21]equip you with
everything good for doing his will, and may
he work in us what is pleasing to him,
through Jesus Christ, to whom be glory for
ever and ever. Amen.

[22]Brothers, I urge you to bear with my word
of exhortation, for I have written you only a
short letter.
[23]I want you to know that our brother Timothy has been released. If he arrives soon, I
will come with him to see you.
[24]Greet all your leaders and all God's
people. Those from Italy send you their
greetings.
[25]Grace be with you all.

James

Introduction:

The book of James may be the earliest of the New Testament letters, written about A.D. 48. This letter written by the brother of Jesus and one of the leaders of the church in Jerusalem, was addressed to Christians everywhere. The seven books of the New Testament from James through Jude are called the general letters because they are addressed to Christians in general and not to a special church.

James wrote this letter to teach Christians the practice of Christianity. He insists that if we have real faith, we will show it by acting like Christians. He gives practical advice on things like anger and quarreling, showing favoritism, controlling the tongue, boasting, patience and prayer.

Outline of contents:

---

1 James, a servant of God and of the Lord
Jesus Christ,

To the twelve tribes scattered among the
nations:

Greetings.

Trials and Temptations

[2]Consider it pure joy, my brothers, whenever you face trials of many kinds, [3]because
you know that the testing of your faith develops perseverance. [4]Perseverance must finish its work so that you may be mature and
complete, not lacking anything. [5]If any of you
lacks wisdom, he should ask God, who gives
generously to all without finding fault, and it
will be given to him. [6]But when he asks, he
must believe and not doubt, because he who
doubts is like a wave of the sea, blown and
tossed by the wind. [7]That man should not
think he will receive anything from the Lord;
[8]he is a double-minded man, unstable in all
he does.

[9]The brother in humble circumstances
ought to take pride in his high position. [10]But
the one who is rich should take pride in his
low position, because he will pass away like
a wild flower. [11]For the sun rises with scorching heat and withers the plant; its blossom
falls and its beauty is destroyed. In the same
way, the rich man will fade away even while
he goes about his business.

[12]Blessed is the man who perseveres under trial, because when he has stood the
test, he will receive the crown of life that God
has promised to those who love him.

[13]When tempted, no one should say, "God
is tempting me." For God cannot be tempted
by evil, nor does he tempt anyone; [14]but
each one is tempted when, by his own evil
desire, he is dragged away and enticed.
[15]Then, after desire has conceived, it gives
birth to sin; and sin, when it is full-grown,
gives birth to death.

[16]Don't be deceived, my dear brothers.
[17]Every good and perfect gift is from above,
coming down from the Father of the heavenly lights, who does not change like shifting
shadows. [18]He chose to give us birth through
the word of truth, that we might be a kind of
firstfruits of all he created.

Listening and Doing

[19]My dear brothers, take note of this:
Everyone should be quick to listen, slow to
speak and slow to become angry, [20]for
man's anger does not bring about the righteous life that God desires. [21]Therefore, get
rid of all moral filth and the evil that is so

prevalent and humbly accept the word
planted in you, which can save you.
22Do not merely listen to the word, and so
deceive yourselves. Do what it says. 23Any-
one who listens to the word but does not do
what it says is like a man who looks at his
face in a mirror 24and, after looking at himself, goes away and immediately forgets
what he looks like. 25But the man who looks
intently into the perfect law that gives freedom, and continues to do this, not forgetting
what he has heard, but doing it—he will be
blessed in what he does.
26If anyone considers himself religious and
yet does not keep a tight rein on his tongue,
he deceives himself and his religion is worthless. 27Religion that God our Father accepts
as pure and faultless is this: to look after
orphans and widows in their distress and to
keep oneself from being polluted by the
world.

Favoritism Forbidden

2 My brothers, as believers in our glorious
Lord Jesus Christ, don't show favoritism.
2Suppose a man comes into your meeting
wearing a gold ring and fine clothes, and a
poor man in shabby clothes also comes in.
3If you show special attention to the man
wearing fine clothes and say, "Here's a good
seat for you," but say to the poor man, "You
stand there" or "Sit on the floor by my feet,"
4have you not discriminated among yourselves and become judges with evil
thoughts?
5Listen, my dear brothers: Has not God
chosen those who are poor in the eyes of the
world to be rich in faith and to inherit the
kingdom he promised those who love him?
6But you have insulted the poor. Is it not the
rich who are exploiting you? Are they not the
ones who are dragging you into court? 7Are
they not the ones who are slandering the
noble name of him to whom you belong?
8If you really keep the royal law found in
Scripture, "Love your neighbor as yourself,"[a] you are doing right. 9But if you show
favoritism, you sin and are convicted by the
law as lawbreakers. 10For whoever keeps
the whole law and yet stumbles at just one
point is guilty of breaking all of it. 11For he
who said, "Do not commit adultery,"[b] also
said, "Do not murder."[c] If you do not commit
adultery but do commit murder, you have
become a lawbreaker.
12Speak and act as those who are going to
be judged by the law that gives freedom,
13because judgment without mercy will be
shown to anyone who has not been merciful.
Mercy triumphs over judgment!

Faith and Deeds

14What good is it, my brothers, if a man
claims to have faith but has no deeds? Can
such faith save him? 15Suppose a brother or
sister is without clothes and daily food. 16If
one of you says to him, "Go, I wish you well;
keep warm and well fed," but does nothing
about his physical needs, what good is it?
17In the same way, faith by itself, if it is not
accompanied by action, is dead.
18But someone will say, "You have faith; I
have deeds."
Show me your faith without deeds, and I
will show you my faith by what I do. 19You
believe that there is one God. Good! Even
the demons believe that—and shudder.
20You foolish man, do you want evidence
that faith without deeds is useless[d]? 21Was
not our ancestor Abraham considered righteous for what he did when he offered his son
Isaac on the altar? 22You see that his faith
and his actions were working together, and
his faith was made complete by what he did.
23And the scripture was fulfilled that says,
"Abraham believed God, and it was credited
to him as righteousness,"[e] and he was
called God's friend. 24You see that a person
is justified by what he does and not by faith
alone.
25In the same way, was not even Rahab
the prostitute considered righteous for what
she did when she gave lodging to the spies
and sent them off in a different direction?
26As the body without the spirit is dead, so
faith without deeds is dead.

Taming the Tongue

3 Not many of you should presume to be
teachers, my brothers, because you
know that we who teach will be judged more
strictly. 2We all stumble in many ways. If anyone is never at fault in what he says, he is a
perfect man, able to keep his whole body in
check.
3When we put bits into the mouths of

[a]*8* Lev. 19:18 [b]*11* Exodus 20:14; Deut. 5:18 [c]*11* Exodus 20:13; Deut. 5:17 [d]*20* Some early manuscripts *dead* [e]*23* Gen. 15:6

horses to make them obey us, we can turn
the whole animal. 4Or take ships as an example. Although they are so large and are
driven by strong winds, they are steered by a
very small rudder wherever the pilot wants to
go. 5Likewise the tongue is a small part of the
body, but it makes great boasts. Consider
what a great forest is set on fire by a small
spark. 6The tongue also is a fire, a world of
evil among the parts of the body. It corrupts
the whole person, sets the whole course of
his life on fire, and is itself set on fire by hell.
7All kinds of animals, birds, reptiles and
creatures of the sea are being tamed and
have been tamed by man, 8but no man can
tame the tongue. It is a restless evil, full of
deadly poison.
9With the tongue we praise our Lord and
Father, and with it we curse men, who have
been made in God's likeness. 10Out of the
same mouth come praise and cursing. My
brothers, this should not be. 11Can both fresh
water and salt[a] water flow from the same
spring? 12My brothers, can a fig tree bear
olives, or a grapevine bear figs? Neither can
a salt spring produce fresh water.

Two Kinds of Wisdom

13Who is wise and understanding among
you? Let him show it by his good life, by
deeds done in the humility that comes from
wisdom. 14But if you harbor bitter envy and
selfish ambition in your hearts, do not boast
about it or deny the truth. 15Such "wisdom"
does not come down from heaven but is
earthly, unspiritual, of the devil. 16For where
you have envy and selfish ambition, there
you find disorder and every evil practice.
17But the wisdom that comes from heaven
is first of all pure; then peace-loving, considerate, submissive, full of mercy and good
fruit, impartial and sincere. 18Peacemakers
who sow in peace raise a harvest of righteousness.

Submit Yourselves to God

4 What causes fights and quarrels among
you? Don't they come from your desires
that battle within you? 2You want something
but don't get it. You kill and covet, but you
cannot have what you want. You quarrel and
fight. You do not have, because you do not
ask God. 3When you ask, you do not receive,
because you ask with wrong motives, that
you may spend what you get on your pleasures.
4You adulterous people, don't you know
that friendship with the world is hatred
toward God? Anyone who chooses to be a
friend of the world becomes an enemy of
God. 5Or do you think Scripture says without
reason that the spirit he caused to live in us
envies intensely?[b] 6But he gives us more
grace. That is why Scripture says:

"God opposes the proud
  but gives grace to the humble."[c]

7Submit yourselves, then, to God. Resist
the devil, and he will flee from you. 8Come
near to God and he will come near to you.
Wash your hands, you sinners, and purify
your hearts, you double-minded. 9Grieve,
mourn and wail. Change your laughter to
mourning and your joy to gloom. 10Humble
yourselves before the Lord, and he will lift
you up.
11Brothers, do not slander one another.
Anyone who speaks against his brother or
judges him speaks against the law and
judges it. When you judge the law, you are
not keeping it, but sitting in judgment on it.
12There is only one Lawgiver and Judge, the
one who is able to save and destroy. But
you—who are you to judge your neighbor?

Boasting About Tomorrow

13Now listen, you who say, "Today or tomorrow we will go to this or that city, spend a
year there, carry on business and make
money." 14Why, you do not even know what
will happen tomorrow. What is your life? You
are a mist that appears for a little while and
then vanishes. 15Instead, you ought to say,
"If it is the Lord's will, we will live and do this
or that." 16As it is, you boast and brag. All
such boasting is evil. 17Anyone, then, who
knows the good he ought to do and doesn't
do it, sins.

Warning to Rich Oppressors

5 Now listen, you rich people, weep and
wail because of the misery that is coming upon you. 2Your wealth has rotted, and
moths have eaten your clothes. 3Your gold
and silver are corroded. Their corrosion will
testify against you and eat your flesh like fire.
You have hoarded wealth in the last days.
4Look! The wages you failed to pay the work-

[a] 11 Greek *bitter* (see also verse 14) [b] 5 Or *that God jealously longs for the spirit that he made to live in us;* or *that the Spirit he caused to live in us longs jealously* [c] 6 Prov. 3:34

men who mowed your fields are crying out
against you. The cries of the harvesters have
reached the ears of the Lord Almighty. 5You
have lived on earth in luxury and self-indulgence. You have fattened yourselves in the
day of slaughter.[a] 6You have condemned
and murdered innocent men, who were not
opposing you.

Patience in Suffering

7Be patient, then, brothers, until the Lord's
coming. See how the farmer waits for the
land to yield its valuable crop and how patient he is for the autumn and spring rains.
8You too, be patient and stand firm, because
the Lord's coming is near. 9Don't grumble
against each other, brothers, or you will be
judged. The Judge is standing at the door!
10Brothers, as an example of patience in
the face of suffering, take the prophets who
spoke in the name of the Lord. 11As you
know, we consider blessed those who have
persevered. You have heard of Job's perseverance and have seen what the Lord finally
brought about. The Lord is full of compassion and mercy.
12Above all, my brothers, do not swear—
not by heaven or by earth or by anything
else. Let your "Yes" be yes, and your "No,"
no, or you will be condemned.

The Prayer of Faith

13Is any one of you in trouble? He should
pray. Is anyone happy? Let him sing songs
of praise. 14Is any one of you sick? He should
call the elders of the church to pray over him
and anoint him with oil in the name of the
Lord. 15And the prayer offered in faith will
make the sick person well; the Lord will raise
him up. If he has sinned, he will be forgiven.
16Therefore confess your sins to each other
and pray for each other so that you may be
healed. The prayer of a righteous man is
powerful and effective.
17Elijah was a man just like us. He prayed
earnestly that it would not rain, and it did not
rain on the land for three and a half years.
18Again he prayed, and the heavens gave
rain, and the earth produced its crops.
19My brothers, if one of you should wander
from the truth and someone should bring him
back, 20remember this: Whoever turns a sinner from the error of his way will save him
from death and cover over a multitude of
sins.

[a]5 Or *yourselves as in a day of feasting*

I Peter

Introduction:
First Peter was written by Peter, one of Jesus' twelve disciples, to the Christians who lived in the northern part of Asia Minor. These Christians were being persecuted for their faith, so Peter wrote to encourage them.

He urges them to remember how much Jesus suffered for them and to follow his example by trusting God to care for them. Because God chose them to be his people and because Jesus suffered and died for them, Peter tells these Christians they should live holy lives. He goes on to tell them how they can live as Christians in this sinful world and have hope for the future.

Outline of contents:

Greetings (1:1,2)
Praise to God for salvation (1:3–12)
Holy living (1:13–2:12)
Conduct of the believer (2:13–4:11)
Ministry through suffering (4:12–5:11)
Conclusion (5:12–14)

---

1 Peter, an apostle of Jesus Christ,
To God's elect, strangers in the world,
scattered throughout Pontus, Galatia, Cappadocia, Asia and Bithynia, 2who have been
chosen according to the foreknowledge of
God the Father, through the sanctifying work
of the Spirit, for obedience to Jesus Christ
and sprinkling by his blood:

Grace and peace be yours in abundance.

Praise to God for a Living Hope

3Praise be to the God and Father of our
Lord Jesus Christ! In his great mercy he has
given us new birth into a living hope through
the resurrection of Jesus Christ from the
dead, 4and into an inheritance that can never
perish, spoil or fade—kept in heaven for you,
5who through faith are shielded by God's
power until the coming of the salvation that is
ready to be revealed in the last time. 6In this
you greatly rejoice, though now for a little
while you may have had to suffer grief in all
kinds of trials. 7These have come so that
your faith—of greater worth than gold, which
perishes even though refined by fire—may
be proved genuine and may result in praise,
glory and honor when Jesus Christ is revealed. 8Though you have not seen him, you
love him; and even though you do not see
him now, you believe in him and are filled
with an inexpressible and glorious joy, 9for
you are receiving the goal of your faith, the
salvation of your souls.

10Concerning this salvation, the prophets,
who spoke of the grace that was to come to
you, searched intently and with the greatest
care, 11trying to find out the time and circumstances to which the Spirit of Christ in them
was pointing when he predicted the sufferings of Christ and the glories that would follow. 12It was revealed to them that they were
not serving themselves but you, when they
spoke of the things that have now been told
you by those who have preached the gospel
to you by the Holy Spirit sent from heaven.
Even angels long to look into these things.

Be Holy

13Therefore, prepare your minds for action; be self-controlled; set your hope fully on
the grace to be given you when Jesus Christ
is revealed. 14As obedient children, do not
conform to the evil desires you had when you
lived in ignorance. 15But just as he who
called you is holy, so be holy in all you do;

16for it is written: "Be holy, because I am
holy."[a]
17Since you call on a Father who judges
each man's work impartially, live your lives
as strangers here in reverent fear. 18For you
know that it was not with perishable things
such as silver or gold that you were redeemed from the empty way of life handed
down to you from your forefathers, 19but with
the precious blood of Christ, a lamb without
blemish or defect. 20He was chosen before
the creation of the world, but was revealed in
these last times for your sake. 21Through him
you believe in God, who raised him from the
dead and glorified him, and so your faith and
hope are in God.
22Now that you have purified yourselves
by obeying the truth so that you have sincere
love for your brothers, love one another
deeply, from the heart.[b] 23For you have been
born again, not of perishable seed, but of
imperishable, through the living and enduring word of God. 24For,

"All men are like grass,
and all their glory is like the flowers of
the field;
the grass withers and the flowers fall,
25 but the word of the Lord stands
forever."[c]

And this is the word that was preached to
you.

2 Therefore, rid yourselves of all malice
and all deceit, hypocrisy, envy, and slander of every kind. 2Like newborn babies,
crave pure spiritual milk, so that by it you
may grow up in your salvation, 3now that you
have tasted that the Lord is good.

The Living Stone and a Chosen People

4As you come to him, the living Stone—
rejected by men but chosen by God and precious to him— 5you also, like living stones,
are being built into a spiritual house to be a
holy priesthood, offering spiritual sacrifices
acceptable to God through Jesus Christ.
6For in Scripture it says:

"See, I lay a stone in Zion,
a chosen and precious cornerstone,
and the one who trusts in him
will never be put to shame."[d]

7Now to you who believe, this stone is precious. But to those who do not believe,

"The stone the builders rejected
has become the capstone.[e]"[f]

8and,

"A stone that causes men to stumble
and a rock that makes them fall."[g]

They stumble because they disobey the
message—which is also what they were
destined for.
9But you are a chosen people, a royal
priesthood, a holy nation, a people belonging
to God, that you may declare the praises of
him who called you out of darkness into his
wonderful light. 10Once you were not a
people, but now you are the people of God;
once you had not received mercy, but now
you have received mercy.
11Dear friends, I urge you, as aliens and
strangers in the world, to abstain from sinful
desires, which war against your soul. 12Live
such good lives among the pagans that,
though they accuse you of doing wrong, they
may see your good deeds and glorify God on
the day he visits us.

Submission to Rulers and Masters

13Submit yourselves for the Lord's sake
to every authority instituted among men:
whether to the king, as the supreme authority, 14or to governors, who are sent by him to
punish those who do wrong and to commend
those who do right. 15For it is God's will that
by doing good you should silence the ignorant talk of foolish men. 16Live as free men,
but do not use your freedom as a cover-up
for evil; live as servants of God. 17Show
proper respect to everyone: Love the brotherhood of believers, fear God, honor the
king.
18Slaves, submit yourselves to your masters with all respect, not only to those who
are good and considerate, but also to those
who are harsh. 19For it is commendable if a
man bears up under the pain of unjust suffering because he is conscious of God. 20But
how is it to your credit if you receive a beating
for doing wrong and endure it? But if you
suffer for doing good and you endure it, this
is commendable before God. 21To this you
were called, because Christ suffered for you,
leaving you an example, that you should follow in his steps.

[a]*16* Lev. 11:44,45; 19:2; 20:7 [b]*22* Some early manuscripts *from a pure heart* [c]*25* Isaiah 40:6-8
[d]*6* Isaiah 28:16 [e]*7* Or *cornerstone* [f]*7* Psalm 118:22 [g]*8* Isaiah 8:14

22"He committed no sin,
and no deceit was found in his
mouth."[a]
23When they hurled their insults at him, he
did not retaliate; when he suffered, he made
no threats. Instead, he entrusted himself to
him who judges justly. 24He himself bore our
sins in his body on the tree, so that we might
die to sins and live for righteousness; by his
wounds you have been healed. 25For you
were like sheep going astray, but now you
have returned to the Shepherd and Overseer
of your souls.

Wives and Husbands

3 Wives, in the same way be submissive
to your husbands so that, if any of them
do not believe the word, they may be won
over without words by the behavior of their
wives, 2when they see the purity and reverence of your lives. 3Your beauty should not
come from outward adornment, such as
braided hair and the wearing of gold jewelry
and fine clothes. 4Instead, it should be that of
your inner self, the unfading beauty of a gentle and quiet spirit, which is of great worth in
God's sight. 5For this is the way the holy
women of the past who put their hope in God
used to make themselves beautiful. They
were submissive to their own husbands, 6like
Sarah, who obeyed Abraham and called him
her master. You are her daughters if you do
what is right and do not give way to fear.
7Husbands, in the same way be considerate as you live with your wives, and treat
them with respect as the weaker partner and
as heirs with you of the gracious gift of life, so
that nothing will hinder your prayers.

Suffering for Doing Good

8Finally, all of you, live in harmony with one
another; be sympathetic, love as brothers,
be compassionate and humble. 9Do not
repay evil with evil or insult with insult, but
with blessing, because to this you were
called so that you may inherit a blessing.
10For,

"Whoever would love life
and see good days
must keep his tongue from evil
and his lips from deceitful speech.
11He must turn from evil and do good;
he must seek peace and pursue it.
12For the eyes of the Lord are on the
righteous
and his ears are attentive to their
prayer,
but the face of the Lord is against those
who do evil."[b]

13Who is going to harm you if you are eager to do good? 14But even if you should
suffer for what is right, you are blessed. "Do
not fear what they fear[c]; do not be frightened."[d] 15But in your hearts set apart Christ
as Lord. Always be prepared to give an answer to everyone who asks you to give the
reason for the hope that you have. But do
this with gentleness and respect, 16keeping a
clear conscience, so that those who speak
maliciously against your good behavior in
Christ may be ashamed of their slander. 17It
is better, if it is God's will, to suffer for doing
good than for doing evil. 18For Christ died for
sins once for all, the righteous for the unrighteous, to bring you to God. He was put to
death in the body but made alive by the
Spirit, 19through whom[e] also he went and
preached to the spirits in prison 20who disobeyed long ago when God waited patiently
in the days of Noah while the ark was being
built. In it only a few people, eight in all, were
saved through water, 21and this water symbolizes baptism that now saves you also—
not the removal of dirt from the body but the
pledge[f] of a good conscience toward God. It
saves you by the resurrection of Jesus
Christ, 22who has gone into heaven and is at
God's right hand—with angels, authorities
and powers in submission to him.

Living for God

4 Therefore, since Christ suffered in his
body, arm yourselves also with the same
attitude, because he who has suffered in his
body is done with sin. 2As a result, he does
not live the rest of his earthly life for evil
human desires, but rather for the will of God.
3For you have spent enough time in the past
doing what pagans choose to do—living in
debauchery, lust, drunkenness, orgies, carousing and detestable idolatry. 4They think
it strange that you do not plunge with them
into the same flood of dissipation, and they
heap abuse on you. 5But they will have to
give account to him who is ready to judge the

[a] 22 Isaiah 53:9 [b] 12 Psalm 34:12-16 [c] 14 Or *not fear their threats* [d] 14 Isaiah 8:12 [e] 18,19 Or *alive in the spirit, 19through which* [f] 21 Or *response*

living and the dead. 6For this is the reason the gospel was preached even to those who are now dead, so that they might be judged according to men in regard to the body, but live according to God in regard to the spirit.

7The end of all things is near. Therefore be clear minded and self-controlled so that you can pray. 8Above all, love each other deeply, because love covers over a multitude of sins. 9Offer hospitality to one another without grumbling. 10Each one should use whatever gift he has received to serve others, faithfully administering God's grace in its various forms. 11If anyone speaks, he should do it as one speaking the very words of God. If anyone serves, he should do it with the strength God provides, so that in all things God may be praised through Jesus Christ. To him be the glory and the power for ever and ever. Amen.

Suffering for Being a Christian

12Dear friends, do not be surprised at the painful trial you are suffering, as though something strange were happening to you. 13But rejoice that you participate in the sufferings of Christ, so that you may be overjoyed when his glory is revealed. 14If you are insulted because of the name of Christ, you are blessed, for the Spirit of glory and of God rests on you. 15If you suffer, it should not be as a murderer or thief or any other kind of criminal, or even as a meddler. 16However, if you suffer as a Christian, do not be ashamed, but praise God that you bear that name. 17For it is time for judgment to begin with the family of God; and if it begins with us, what will the outcome be for those who do not obey the gospel of God? 18And,

> "If it is hard for the righteous to be saved,
> what will become of the ungodly and
> the sinner?"[a]

19So then, those who suffer according to God's will should commit themselves to their faithful Creator and continue to do good.

To Elders and Young Men

5 To the elders among you, I appeal as a fellow elder, a witness of Christ's sufferings and one who also will share in the glory to be revealed: 2Be shepherds of God's flock that is under your care, serving as overseers—not because you must, but because you are willing, as God wants you to be; not greedy for money, but eager to serve; 3not lording it over those entrusted to you, but being examples to the flock. 4And when the Chief Shepherd appears, you will receive the crown of glory that will never fade away.

5Young men, in the same way be submissive to those who are older. All of you, clothe yourselves with humility toward one another, because,

> "God opposes the proud
> but gives grace to the humble."[b]

6Humble yourselves, therefore, under God's mighty hand, that he may lift you up in due time. 7Cast all your anxiety on him because he cares for you.

8Be self-controlled and alert. Your enemy the devil prowls around like a roaring lion looking for someone to devour. 9Resist him, standing firm in the faith, because you know that your brothers throughout the world are undergoing the same kind of sufferings.

10And the God of all grace, who called you to his eternal glory in Christ, after you have suffered a little while, will himself restore you and make you strong, firm and steadfast. 11To him be the power for ever and ever. Amen.

Final Greetings

12With the help of Silas,[c] whom I regard as a faithful brother, I have written to you briefly, encouraging you and testifying that this is the true grace of God. Stand fast in it.

13She who is in Babylon, chosen together with you, sends you her greetings, and so does my son Mark. 14Greet one another with a kiss of love.

Peace to all of you who are in Christ.

[a] *18* Prov. 11:31 [b] *5* Prov. 3:34 [c] *12* Greek *Silvanus,* a variant of *Silas*

2 Peter

Introduction:

Second Peter was written about A.D. 66 to the same group of Christians as Peter's first letter. These Christians were now not in danger of persecution but were in danger of being confused by false teachers.

Peter reminds the Christians that the best way to resist false teachers is to grow in the knowledge and practice of the Christian faith. He warns them that God would destroy the false teachers. Because Jesus will certainly keep his promise to come again, Peter reminds these Christians to live "holy and godly lives."

Outline of contents:

---

1 Simon Peter, a servant and apostle of
Jesus Christ,

To those who through the righteousness
of our God and Savior Jesus Christ have
received a faith as precious as ours:

2Grace and peace be yours in abundance
through the knowledge of God and of Jesus
our Lord.

Making One's Calling and Election Sure

3His divine power has given us everything
we need for life and godliness through our
knowledge of him who called us by his own
glory and goodness. 4Through these he has
given us his very great and precious promises, so that through them you may participate in the divine nature and escape the
corruption in the world caused by evil desires.

5For this very reason, make every effort to
add to your faith goodness; and to goodness, knowledge; 6and to knowledge, self-
control; and to self-control, perseverance;
and to perseverance, godliness; 7and to godliness, brotherly kindness; and to brotherly
kindness, love. 8For if you possess these
qualities in increasing measure, they will
keep you from being ineffective and unproductive in your knowledge of our Lord Jesus
Christ. 9But if anyone does not have them,
he is nearsighted and blind, and has forgotten that he has been cleansed from his past
sins.

10Therefore, my brothers, be all the more
eager to make your calling and election sure.
For if you do these things, you will never fall,
11and you will receive a rich welcome into the
eternal kingdom of our Lord and Savior
Jesus Christ.

Prophecy of Scripture

12So I will always remind you of these
things, even though you know them and are
firmly established in the truth you now have.
13I think it is right to refresh your memory as
long as I live in the tent of this body, 14be-
cause I know that I will soon put it aside, as
our Lord Jesus Christ has made clear to me.
15And I will make every effort to see that after
my departure you will always be able to
remember these things.

16We did not follow cleverly invented stories when we told you about the power and
coming of our Lord Jesus Christ, but we were
eyewitnesses of his majesty. 17For he received honor and glory from God the Father
when the voice came to him from the Majestic Glory, saying, "This is my Son, whom I

love; with him I am well pleased."[a] 18We ourselves heard this voice that came from heaven when we were with him on the sacred mountain.

19And we have the word of the prophets made more certain, and you will do well to pay attention to it, as to a light shining in a dark place, until the day dawns and the morning star rises in your hearts. 20Above all, you must understand that no prophecy of Scripture came about by the prophet's own interpretation. 21For prophecy never had its origin in the will of man, but men spoke from God as they were carried along by the Holy Spirit.

False Teachers and Their Destruction

2 But there were also false prophets among the people, just as there will be false teachers among you. They will secretly introduce destructive heresies, even denying the sovereign Lord who bought them—bringing swift destruction on themselves. 2Many will follow their shameful ways and will bring the way of truth into disrepute. 3In their greed these teachers will exploit you with stories they have made up. Their condemnation has long been hanging over them, and their destruction has not been sleeping.

4For if God did not spare angels when they sinned, but sent them to hell,[b] putting them into gloomy dungeons[c] to be held for judgment; 5if he did not spare the ancient world when he brought the flood on its ungodly people, but protected Noah, a preacher of righteousness, and seven others; 6if he condemned the cities of Sodom and Gomorrah by burning them to ashes, and made them an example of what is going to happen to the ungodly; 7and if he rescued Lot, a righteous man, who was distressed by the filthy lives of lawless men 8(for that righteous man, living among them day after day, was tormented in his righteous soul by the lawless deeds he saw and heard)— 9if this is so, then the Lord knows how to rescue godly men from trials and to hold the unrighteous for the day of judgment, while continuing their punishment.[d] 10This is especially true of those who follow the corrupt desire of the sinful nature[e] and despise authority.

Bold and arrogant, these men are not afraid to slander celestial beings; 11yet even angels, although they are stronger and more powerful, do not bring slanderous accusations against such beings in the presence of the Lord. 12But these men blaspheme in matters they do not understand. They are like brute beasts, creatures of instinct, born only to be caught and destroyed, and like beasts they too will perish.

13They will be paid back with harm for the harm they have done. Their idea of pleasure is to carouse in broad daylight. They are blots and blemishes, reveling in their pleasures while they feast with you.[f] 14With eyes full of adultery, they never stop sinning; they seduce the unstable; they are experts in greed—an accursed brood! 15They have left the straight way and wandered off to follow the way of Balaam son of Beor, who loved the wages of wickedness. 16But he was rebuked for his wrongdoing by a donkey—a beast without speech—who spoke with a man's voice and restrained the prophet's madness.

17These men are springs without water and mists driven by a storm. Blackest darkness is reserved for them. 18For they mouth empty, boastful words and, by appealing to the lustful desires of sinful human nature, they entice people who are just escaping from those who live in error. 19They promise them freedom, while they themselves are slaves of depravity—for a man is a slave to whatever has mastered him. 20If they have escaped the corruption of the world by knowing our Lord and Savior Jesus Christ and are again entangled in it and overcome, they are worse off at the end than they were at the beginning. 21It would have been better for them not to have known the way of righteousness, than to have known it and then to turn their backs on the sacred command that was passed on to them. 22Of them the proverbs are true: "A dog returns to its vomit,"[g] and, "A sow that is washed goes back to her wallowing in the mud."

The Day of the Lord

3 Dear friends, this is now my second letter to you. I have written both of them as reminders to stimulate you to wholesome thinking. 2I want you to recall the words spoken in the past by the holy prophets and the command given by our Lord and Savior through your apostles.

[a] 17 Matt. 17:5; Mark 9:7; Luke 9:35 [b] 4 Greek *Tartarus* [c] 4 Some manuscripts *into chains of darkness* [d] 9 Or *unrighteous for punishment until the day of judgment* [e] 10 Or *the flesh* [f] 13 Some manuscripts *in their love feasts* [g] 22 Prov. 26:11

3First of all, you must understand that in
the last days scoffers will come, scoffing and
following their own evil desires. 4They will
say, "Where is this 'coming' he promised?
Ever since our fathers died, everything goes
on as it has since the beginning of creation."
5But they deliberately forget that long ago by
God's word the heavens existed and the
earth was formed out of water and by water.
6By these waters also the world of that time
was deluged and destroyed. 7By the same
word the present heavens and earth are reserved for fire, being kept for the day of judgment and destruction of ungodly men.

8But do not forget this one thing, dear
friends: With the Lord a day is like a thousand years, and a thousand years are like a
day. 9The Lord is not slow in keeping his
promise, as some understand slowness. He
is patient with you, not wanting anyone to
perish, but everyone to come to repentance.

10But the day of the Lord will come like a
thief. The heavens will disappear with a roar;
the elements will be destroyed by fire, and
the earth and everything in it will be laid
bare.[a]

11Since everything will be destroyed in this
way, what kind of people ought you to be?
You ought to live holy and godly lives 12as
you look forward to the day of God and
speed its coming.[b] That day will bring about
the destruction of the heavens by fire, and
the elements will melt in the heat. 13But in
keeping with his promise we are looking forward to a new heaven and a new earth, the
home of righteousness.

14So then, dear friends, since you are looking forward to this, make every effort to be
found spotless, blameless and at peace with
him. 15Bear in mind that our Lord's patience
means salvation, just as our dear brother
Paul also wrote you with the wisdom that
God gave him. 16He writes the same way in
all his letters, speaking in them of these matters. His letters contain some things that are
hard to understand, which ignorant and unstable people distort, as they do the other
Scriptures, to their own destruction.

17Therefore, dear friends, since you already know this, be on your guard so that
you may not be carried away by the error of
lawless men and fall from your secure position. 18But grow in the grace and knowledge
of our Lord and Savior Jesus Christ. To him
be glory both now and forever! Amen.

[a] 10 Some manuscripts *be burned up*   [b] 12 Or *as you wait eagerly for the day of God to come*

I John

Introduction:

First, Second and Third John were written by John, the beloved disciple, who also wrote the fourth Gospel. All four books may have been written about the same time, probably about A.D. 90.

The first letter of John was written to warn Christians about dangerous false teachers who were trying to mislead them. These teachers were teaching that the man Jesus was not the Christ, the Son of God. They said that God did not become a man. John tells the Christians he is writing because it is very important to know and believe that Jesus Christ is both God and man.

John also encourages these Christians to keep their faith in Christ strong and to continue loving one another. He says Christians can know they are God's children if they love one another and if they obey God's commands.

Outline of contents:

Introduction (1:1–4)
Walking in the light (1:5–2:29)
Love must fill our life (3:1–4:21)
Faith and freedom from doubts (5:1–12)
Conclusion (5:13–21)

The Word of Life

1 That which was from the beginning, which we have heard, which we have seen with our eyes, which we have looked at and our hands have touched—this we proclaim concerning the Word of life. [2]The life appeared; we have seen it and testify to it, and we proclaim to you the eternal life, which was with the Father and has appeared to us. [3]We proclaim to you what we have seen and heard, so that you also may have fellowship with us. And our fellowship is with the Father and with his Son, Jesus Christ. [4]We write this to make our[a] joy complete.

Walking in the Light

[5]This is the message we have heard from him and declare to you: God is light; in him there is no darkness at all. [6]If we claim to have fellowship with him yet walk in the darkness, we lie and do not live by the truth. [7]But if we walk in the light, as he is in the light, we have fellowship with one another, and the blood of Jesus, his Son, purifies us from all[b] sin.

[8]If we claim to be without sin, we deceive ourselves and the truth is not in us. [9]If we confess our sins, he is faithful and just and will forgive us our sins and purify us from all unrighteousness. [10]If we claim we have not sinned, we make him out to be a liar and his word has no place in our lives.

2 My dear children, I write this to you so that you will not sin. But if anybody does sin, we have one who speaks to the Father in our defense—Jesus Christ, the Righteous One. [2]He is the atoning sacrifice for our sins, and not only for ours but also for[c] the sins of the whole world.

[3]We know that we have come to know him if we obey his commands. [4]The man who says, "I know him," but does not do what he commands is a liar, and the truth is not in him. [5]But if anyone obeys his word, God's love[d] is truly made complete in him. This is how we know we are in him: [6]Whoever claims to live in him must walk as Jesus did.

[7]Dear friends, I am not writing you a new command but an old one, which you have had since the beginning. This old command

[a]4 Some manuscripts *your* [b]7 Or *every* [c]2 Or *He is the one who turns aside God's wrath, taking away our sins, and not only ours but also* [d]5 Or *word, love for God*

is the message you have heard. 8Yet I am writing you a new command; its truth is seen in him and you, because the darkness is passing and the true light is already shining.

9Anyone who claims to be in the light but hates his brother is still in the darkness. 10Whoever loves his brother lives in the light, and there is nothing in him[a] to make him stumble. 11But whoever hates his brother is in the darkness and walks around in the darkness; he does not know where he is going, because the darkness has blinded him.

12I write to you, dear children,
  because your sins have been forgiven
    on account of his name.
13I write to you, fathers,
  because you have known him who is
    from the beginning.
I write to you, young men,
  because you have overcome the evil
    one.
I write to you, dear children,
  because you have known the Father.
14I write to you, fathers,
  because you have known him who is
    from the beginning.
I write to you, young men,
  because you are strong,
  and the word of God lives in you,
  and you have overcome the evil one.

Do Not Love the World

15Do not love the world or anything in the world. If anyone loves the world, the love of the Father is not in him. 16For everything in the world—the cravings of sinful man, the lust of his eyes and the boasting of what he has and does—comes not from the Father but from the world. 17The world and its desires pass away, but the man who does the will of God lives forever.

Warning Against Antichrists

18Dear children, this is the last hour; and as you have heard that the antichrist is coming, even now many antichrists have come. This is how we know it is the last hour. 19They went out from us, but they did not really belong to us. For if they had belonged to us, they would have remained with us; but their going showed that none of them belonged to us.

20But you have an anointing from the Holy One, and all of you know the truth.[b] 21I do not write to you because you do not know the truth, but because you do know it and because no lie comes from the truth. 22Who is the liar? It is the man who denies that Jesus is the Christ. Such a man is the antichrist—he denies the Father and the Son. 23No one who denies the Son has the Father; whoever acknowledges the Son has the Father also.

24See that what you have heard from the beginning remains in you. If it does, you also will remain in the Son and in the Father. 25And this is what he promised us—even eternal life.

26I am writing these things to you about those who are trying to lead you astray. 27As for you, the anointing you received from him remains in you, and you do not need anyone to teach you. But as his anointing teaches you about all things and as that anointing is real, not counterfeit—just as it has taught you, remain in him.

Children of God

28And now, dear children, continue in him, so that when he appears we may be confident and unashamed before him at his coming.

29If you know that he is righteous, you know that everyone who does what is right has been born of him.

3 How great is the love the Father has lavished on us, that we should be called children of God! And that is what we are! The reason the world does not know us is that it did not know him. 2Dear friends, now we are children of God, and what we will be has not yet been made known. But we know that when he appears,[c] we shall be like him, for we shall see him as he is. 3Everyone who has this hope in him purifies himself, just as he is pure.

4Everyone who sins breaks the law; in fact, sin is lawlessness. 5But you know that he appeared so that he might take away our sins. And in him is no sin. 6No one who lives in him keeps on sinning. No one who continues to sin has either seen him or known him.

7Dear children, do not let anyone lead you astray. He who does what is right is righteous, just as he is righteous. 8He who does what is sinful is of the devil, because the devil has been sinning from the beginning. The reason the Son of God appeared was to destroy the devil's work. 9No one who is born of God will continue to sin, because God's seed

[a] *10* Or *it* [b] *20* Some manuscripts *and you know all things* [c] *2* Or *when it is made known*

remains in him; he cannot go on sinning,
because he has been born of God. 10This is
how we know who the children of God are
and who the children of the devil are: Anyone
who does not do what is right is not a child of
God; nor is anyone who does not love his
brother.

Love One Another

11This is the message you heard from the
beginning: We should love one another.
12Do not be like Cain, who belonged to the
evil one and murdered his brother. And why
did he murder him? Because his own actions
were evil and his brother's were righteous.
13Do not be surprised, my brothers, if the
world hates you. 14We know that we have
passed from death to life, because we love
our brothers. Anyone who does not love remains in death. 15Anyone who hates his
brother is a murderer, and you know that no
murderer has eternal life in him.

16This is how we know what love is: Jesus
Christ laid down his life for us. And we ought
to lay down our lives for our brothers. 17If
anyone has material possessions and sees
his brother in need but has no pity on him,
how can the love of God be in him? 18Dear
children, let us not love with words or tongue
but with actions and in truth. 19This then is
how we know that we belong to the truth, and
how we set our hearts at rest in his presence
20whenever our hearts condemn us. For God
is greater than our hearts, and he knows
everything.

21Dear friends, if our hearts do not condemn us, we have confidence before God
22and receive from him anything we ask, because we obey his commands and do what
pleases him. 23And this is his command: to
believe in the name of his Son, Jesus Christ,
and to love one another as he commanded
us. 24Those who obey his commands live in
him, and he in them. And this is how we know
that he lives in us: We know it by the Spirit he
gave us.

Test the Spirits

4 Dear friends, do not believe every spirit,
but test the spirits to see whether they
are from God, because many false prophets
have gone out into the world. 2This is how
you can recognize the Spirit of God: Every
spirit that acknowledges that Jesus Christ
has come in the flesh is from God, 3but every
spirit that does not acknowledge Jesus is not
from God. This is the spirit of the antichrist,
which you have heard is coming and even
now is already in the world.

4You, dear children, are from God and
have overcome them, because the one who
is in you is greater than the one who is in the
world. 5They are from the world and therefore speak from the viewpoint of the world,
and the world listens to them. 6We are from
God, and whoever knows God listens to us;
but whoever is not from God does not listen
to us. This is how we recognize the Spirit[a] of
truth and the spirit of falsehood.

God's Love and Ours

7Dear friends, let us love one another, for
love comes from God. Everyone who loves
has been born of God and knows God.
8Whoever does not love does not know God,
because God is love. 9This is how God
showed his love among us: He sent his one
and only Son[b] into the world that we might
live through him. 10This is love: not that we
loved God, but that he loved us and sent his
Son as an atoning sacrifice for[c] our sins.
11Dear friends, since God so loved us, we
also ought to love one another. 12No one has
ever seen God; but if we love one another,
God lives in us and his love is made complete in us.

13We know that we live in him and he in us,
because he has given us of his Spirit. 14And
we have seen and testify that the Father has
sent his Son to be the Savior of the world. 15If
anyone acknowledges that Jesus is the Son
of God, God lives in him and he in God.
16And so we know and rely on the love God
has for us.

God is love. Whoever lives in love lives in
God, and God in him. 17In this way, love is
made complete among us so that we will
have confidence on the day of judgment,
because in this world we are like him.
18There is no fear in love. But perfect love
drives out fear, because fear has to do with
punishment. The one who fears is not made
perfect in love.

19We love because he first loved us. 20If
anyone says, "I love God," yet hates his
brother, he is a liar. For anyone who does not
love his brother, whom he has seen, cannot
love God, whom he has not seen. 21And he

[a]6 Or *spirit* [b]9 Or *his only begotten Son* [c]10 Or *as the one who would turn aside his wrath, taking away*

has given us this command: Whoever loves God must also love his brother.

Faith in the Son of God

5 Everyone who believes that Jesus is the Christ is born of God, and everyone who loves the father loves his child as well. 2This is how we know that we love the children of God: by loving God and carrying out his commands. 3This is love for God: to obey his commands. And his commands are not burdensome, 4for everyone born of God overcomes the world. This is the victory that has overcome the world, even our faith. 5Who is it that overcomes the world? Only he who believes that Jesus is the Son of God.

6This is the one who came by water and blood—Jesus Christ. He did not come by water only, but by water and blood. And it is the Spirit who testifies, because the Spirit is the truth. 7For there are three that testify: 8the[a] Spirit, the water and the blood; and the three are in agreement. 9We accept man's testimony, but God's testimony is greater because it is the testimony of God, which he has given about his Son. 10Anyone who believes in the Son of God has this testimony in his heart. Anyone who does not believe God has made him out to be a liar, because he has not believed the testimony God has given about his Son. 11And this is the testimony: God has given us eternal life, and this life is in his Son. 12He who has the Son has life; he who does not have the Son of God does not have life.

Concluding Remarks

13I write these things to you who believe in the name of the Son of God so that you may know that you have eternal life. 14This is the confidence we have in approaching God: that if we ask anything according to his will, he hears us. 15And if we know that he hears us—whatever we ask—we know that we have what we asked of him.

16If anyone sees his brother commit a sin that does not lead to death, he should pray and God will give him life. I refer to those whose sin does not lead to death. There is a sin that leads to death. I am not saying that he should pray about that. 17All wrongdoing is sin, and there is sin that does not lead to death.

18We know that anyone born of God does not continue to sin; the one who was born of God keeps him safe, and the evil one cannot harm him. 19We know that we are children of God, and that the whole world is under the control of the evil one. 20We know also that the Son of God has come and has given us understanding, so that we may know him who is true. And we are in him who is true—even in his Son Jesus Christ. He is the true God and eternal life.

21Dear children, keep yourselves from idols.

[a]7,8 Late manuscripts of the Vulgate *testify in heaven: the Father, the Word and the Holy Spirit, and these three are one. 8And there are three that testify on earth: the* (not found in any Greek manuscript before the sixteenth century)

2 John

Introduction:

John wrote this letter to "the chosen lady and her children." He might have meant either a Christian woman and her family or a church and its members.

In this letter John writes how important it is for Christians to love one another. He says that to love means to obey God's commandments, and God's commandments tell us to live lives of love.

John again emphasizes the importance of the doctrine that Jesus is God's Son and both man and God. Christians should separate themselves from those who teach that Jesus is not God's Son.

Outline of contents:

Greeting (1–3)
Advice and warning (4–11)
Conclusion (12,13)

1The elder,

To the chosen lady and her children,
whom I love in the truth—and not I only, but
also all who know the truth— 2because of the
truth, which lives in us and will be with us
forever:

3Grace, mercy and peace from God the
Father and from Jesus Christ, the Father's
Son, will be with us in truth and love.

4It has given me great joy to find some of
your children walking in the truth, just as the
Father commanded us. 5And now, dear lady,
I am not writing you a new command but one
we have had from the beginning. I ask that
we love one another. 6And this is love: that
we walk in obedience to his commands. As
you have heard from the beginning, his command is that you walk in love.

7Many deceivers, who do not acknowledge Jesus Christ as coming in the flesh,
have gone out into the world. Any such person is the deceiver and the antichrist. 8Watch
out that you do not lose what you have
worked for, but that you may be rewarded
fully. 9Anyone who runs ahead and does not
continue in the teaching of Christ does not
have God; whoever continues in the teaching has both the Father and the Son. 10If
anyone comes to you and does not bring this
teaching, do not take him into your house or
welcome him. 11Anyone who welcomes him
shares in his wicked work.

12I have much to write to you, but I do not
want to use paper and ink. Instead, I hope to
visit you and talk with you face to face, so
that our joy may be complete.

13The children of your chosen sister send
their greetings.

3 John

Introduction:
Third John was written to Gaius, a friend of John's and a leader in the church. There was a man named Diotrephes in Gaius' church who was refusing to welcome God's messengers. John writes this letter to praise and thank Gaius for his help and to scold Diotrephes for not cooperating. John promises to come to this church soon to deal with this matter himself.

Outline of contents:

Greeting (1–4)
Encouragement for Gaius (5–8)
A scolding for Diotrephes (9,10)
Praise for Demetrius (11,12)
Conclusion (13–15)

1The elder,

To my dear friend Gaius, whom I love in
the truth.

2Dear friend, I pray that you may enjoy
good health and that all may go well with you,
even as your soul is getting along well. 3It
gave me great joy to have some brothers
come and tell about your faithfulness to the
truth and how you continue to walk in the
truth. 4I have no greater joy than to hear that
my children are walking in the truth.
5Dear friend, you are faithful in what you
are doing for the brothers, even though they
are strangers to you. 6They have told the
church about your love. You will do well to
send them on their way in a manner worthy
of God. 7It was for the sake of the Name that
they went out, receiving no help from the
pagans. 8We ought therefore to show hospitality to such men so that we may work together for the truth.
9I wrote to the church, but Diotrephes, who
loves to be first, will have nothing to do with
us. 10So if I come, I will call attention to what
he is doing, gossiping maliciously about us.
Not satisfied with that, he refuses to welcome the brothers. He also stops those who
want to do so and puts them out of the
church.
11Dear friend, do not imitate what is evil but
what is good. Anyone who does what is good
is from God. Anyone who does what is evil
has not seen God. 12Demetrius is well
spoken of by everyone—and even by the
truth itself. We also speak well of him, and
you know that our testimony is true.
13I have much to write you, but I do not
want to do so with pen and ink. 14I hope
to see you soon, and we will talk face to
face.

Peace to you. The friends here send their
greetings. Greet the friends there by name.

Jude

Introduction:

Jude, like James, was a brother of Jesus. He wrote to warn Christians about the same false teachers Peter wrote about in his second letter. These false teachers were not only teaching that Jesus was not the Son of God; they were also leading the people to live sinful lives. Jude warns that God will punish and destroy these false teachers just as he had punished sinners in the Old Testament.

Outline of contents:

Introduction (1,2)
Warnings against false teachers (3–16)
Warning and conclusion (17–25)

1Jude, a servant of Jesus Christ and a brother of James,

To those who have been called, who are loved by God the Father and kept by[a] Jesus Christ:

2Mercy, peace and love be yours in abundance.

The Sin and Doom of Godless Men

3Dear friends, although I was very eager to write to you about the salvation we share, I felt I had to write and urge you to contend for the faith that was once for all entrusted to the saints. 4For certain men whose condemnation was written about[b] long ago have secretly slipped in among you. They are godless men, who change the grace of our God into a license for immorality and deny Jesus Christ our only Sovereign and Lord.

5Though you already know all this, I want to remind you that the Lord[c] delivered his people out of Egypt, but later destroyed those who did not believe. 6And the angels who did not keep their positions of authority but abandoned their own home—these he has kept in darkness, bound with everlasting chains for judgment on the great Day. 7In a similar way, Sodom and Gomorrah and the surrounding towns gave themselves up to sexual immorality and perversion. They serve as an example of those who suffer the punishment of eternal fire.

8In the very same way, these dreamers pollute their own bodies, reject authority and slander celestial beings. 9But even the archangel Michael, when he was disputing with the devil about the body of Moses, did not dare to bring a slanderous accusation against him, but said, "The Lord rebuke you!" 10Yet these men speak abusively against whatever they do not understand; and what things they do understand by instinct, like unreasoning animals—these are the very things that destroy them.

11Woe to them! They have taken the way of Cain; they have rushed for profit into Balaam's error; they have been destroyed in Korah's rebellion.

12These men are blemishes at your love feasts, eating with you without the slightest qualm—shepherds who feed only themselves. They are clouds without rain, blown along by the wind; autumn trees, without fruit and uprooted—twice dead. 13They are wild waves of the sea, foaming up their shame; wandering stars, for whom blackest darkness has been reserved forever.

14Enoch, the seventh from Adam, prophesied about these men: "See, the Lord is coming with thousands upon thousands of his holy ones 15to judge everyone, and to convict all the ungodly of all the ungodly acts they have done in the ungodly way, and of all the harsh words ungodly sinners have spoken against him." 16These men are grumblers

[a]1 Or *for;* or *in* [b]4 Or *men who were marked out for condemnation* [c]5 Some early manuscripts *Jesus*

and faultfinders; they follow their own evil desires; they boast about themselves and flatter others for their own advantage.

A Call to Persevere

[17]But, dear friends, remember what the apostles of our Lord Jesus Christ foretold. [18]They said to you, "In the last times there will be scoffers who will follow their own ungodly desires." [19]These are the men who divide you, who follow mere natural instincts and do not have the Spirit.

[20]But you, dear friends, build yourselves up in your most holy faith and pray in the Holy Spirit. [21]Keep yourselves in God's love as you wait for the mercy of our Lord Jesus Christ to bring you to eternal life.

[22]Be merciful to those who doubt; [23]snatch others from the fire and save them; to others show mercy, mixed with fear—hating even the clothing stained by corrupted flesh.

Doxology

[24]To him who is able to keep you from falling and to present you before his glorious presence without fault and with great joy— [25]to the only God our Savior be glory, majesty, power and authority, through Jesus Christ our Lord, before all ages, now and forevermore! Amen.

Revelation

Introduction:
The book of Revelation was written by the apostle John during his exile on the island of Patmos. John's purpose in writing this book was to give hope and encouragement to those Christians who were suffering severe persecution for their faith in Jesus Christ. These Christians needed to know that God controls whatever happens here on earth.

Through the imagery and symbols, even though they are sometimes difficult to understand, one thing is made clear, Jesus Christ is the Lord and ruler over everyone and everything—even powerful human governments. He is clearly in control and will someday judge and punish what is evil, even Satan. He will also establish an everlasting kingdom with a new heaven and a new earth.

Outline of contents:

Christ reveals himself to John (1:1–20)
Letters to the seven churches (2:1–3:22)
The heavenly throne (4:1–5:14)
The seven seals (6:1–8:5)
The seven trumpets (8:6–11:19)
The seven figures (12:1–14:20)
The bowls of wrath (15:1–16:21)
Babylon judged (17:1–19:10)
Beast and false prophet judged (19:11–21)
Satan judged (20:1–3)
Thousand-year reign (20:4–6)
Rebellion and final judgment (20:7–15)
New heaven, new earth, new Jerusalem (21:1–22:5)
Conclusion (22:6–21)

Prologue

1 The revelation of Jesus Christ, which
God gave him to show his servants what
must soon take place. He made it known by
sending his angel to his servant John, [2]who
testifies to everything he saw—that is, the
word of God and the testimony of Jesus
Christ. [3]Blessed is the one who reads the
words of this prophecy, and blessed are
those who hear it and take to heart what is
written in it, because the time is near.

Greetings and Doxology

[4]John,

To the seven churches in the province of Asia:

Grace and peace to you from him who is,
and who was, and who is to come, and from
the seven spirits[a] before his throne, [5]and
from Jesus Christ, who is the faithful witness,
the firstborn from the dead, and the ruler of
the kings of the earth.

To him who loves us and has freed us from
our sins by his blood, [6]and has made us to be
a kingdom and priests to serve his God and
Father—to him be glory and power for ever
and ever! Amen.

[7]Look, he is coming with the clouds,
and every eye will see him,
even those who pierced him;
and all the peoples of the earth will
mourn because of him.
So shall it be! Amen.

[8]"I am the Alpha and the Omega," says

[a]4 Or *the sevenfold Spirit*

the Lord God, "who is, and who was, and
who is to come, the Almighty."

One Like a Son of Man

9I, John, your brother and companion in
the suffering and kingdom and patient endurance that are ours in Jesus, was on the island of Patmos because of the word of God
and the testimony of Jesus. 10On the Lord's
Day I was in the Spirit, and I heard behind me
a loud voice like a trumpet, 11which said:
"Write on a scroll what you see and send it to
the seven churches: to Ephesus, Smyrna,
Pergamum, Thyatira, Sardis, Philadelphia
and Laodicea."

12I turned around to see the voice that was
speaking to me. And when I turned I saw
seven golden lampstands, 13and among the
lampstands was someone "like a son of
man,"[a] dressed in a robe reaching down to
his feet and with a golden sash around his
chest. 14His head and hair were white like
wool, as white as snow, and his eyes were
like blazing fire. 15His feet were like bronze
glowing in a furnace, and his voice was like
the sound of rushing waters. 16In his right
hand he held seven stars, and out of his
mouth came a sharp double-edged sword.
His face was like the sun shining in all its
brilliance.

17When I saw him, I fell at his feet as
though dead. Then he placed his right hand
on me and said: "Do not be afraid. I am the
First and the Last. 18I am the Living One; I
was dead, and behold I am alive for ever and
ever! And I hold the keys of death and
Hades.

19"Write, therefore, what you have seen,
what is now and what will take place later.
20The mystery of the seven stars that you
saw in my right hand and of the seven golden
lampstands is this: The seven stars are the
angels[b] of the seven churches, and the
seven lampstands are the seven churches.

To the Church in Ephesus

2 "To the angel[c] of the church in Ephesus
write:

These are the words of him who holds
the seven stars in his right hand and
walks among the seven golden lampstands: 2I know your deeds, your hard
work and your perseverance. I know
that you cannot tolerate wicked men,
that you have tested those who claim to
be apostles but are not, and have found
them false. 3You have persevered and
have endured hardships for my name,
and have not grown weary.

4Yet I hold this against you: You have
forsaken your first love. 5Remember the
height from which you have fallen! Repent and do the things you did at first. If
you do not repent, I will come to you and
remove your lampstand from its place.
6But you have this in your favor: You
hate the practices of the Nicolaitans,
which I also hate.

7He who has an ear, let him hear what
the Spirit says to the churches. To him
who overcomes, I will give the right to
eat from the tree of life, which is in the
paradise of God.

To the Church in Smyrna

8"To the angel of the church in Smyrna write:

These are the words of him who is the
First and the Last, who died and came to
life again. 9I know your afflictions and
your poverty—yet you are rich! I know
the slander of those who say they are
Jews and are not, but are a synagogue
of Satan. 10Do not be afraid of what you
are about to suffer. I tell you, the devil
will put some of you in prison to test you,
and you will suffer persecution for ten
days. Be faithful, even to the point of
death, and I will give you the crown of
life.

11He who has an ear, let him hear
what the Spirit says to the churches. He
who overcomes will not be hurt at all by
the second death.

To the Church in Pergamum

12"To the angel of the church in Pergamum
write:

These are the words of him who has
the sharp, double-edged sword. 13I
know where you live—where Satan has
his throne. Yet you remain true to my
name. You did not renounce your faith
in me, even in the days of Antipas, my
faithful witness, who was put to death in
your city—where Satan lives.

14Nevertheless, I have a few things
against you: You have people there who
hold to the teaching of Balaam, who
taught Balak to entice the Israelites to

[a] *13* Daniel 7:13 [b] *20* Or *messengers* [c] *1* Or *messenger;* also in verses 8, 12 and 18

sin by eating food sacrificed to idols and
by committing sexual immorality. 15Like-
wise you also have those who hold to
the teaching of the Nicolaitans. 16Re-
pent therefore! Otherwise, I will soon
come to you and will fight against them
with the sword of my mouth.

17He who has an ear, let him hear
what the Spirit says to the churches. To
him who overcomes, I will give some of
the hidden manna. I will also give him a
white stone with a new name written on
it, known only to him who receives it.

To the Church in Thyatira

18"To the angel of the church in Thyatira
write:

These are the words of the Son of
God, whose eyes are like blazing fire
and whose feet are like burnished
bronze. 19I know your deeds, your love
and faith, your service and perseverance, and that you are now doing more
than you did at first.

20Nevertheless, I have this against
you: You tolerate that woman Jezebel,
who calls herself a prophetess. By her
teaching she misleads my servants into
sexual immorality and the eating of food
sacrificed to idols. 21I have given her
time to repent of her immorality, but she
is unwilling. 22So I will cast her on a bed
of suffering, and I will make those who
commit adultery with her suffer intensely, unless they repent of her ways. 23I will
strike her children dead. Then all the
churches will know that I am he who
searches hearts and minds, and I will
repay each of you according to your
deeds. 24Now I say to the rest of you in
Thyatira, to you who do not hold to her
teaching and have not learned Satan's
so-called deep secrets (I will not impose
any other burden on you): 25Only hold
on to what you have until I come.

26To him who overcomes and does
my will to the end, I will give authority
over the nations—

27'He will rule them with an iron
scepter;
he will dash them to pieces like
pottery'[a]—

just as I have received authority from my
Father. 28I will also give him the morning
star. 29He who has an ear, let him hear
what the Spirit says to the churches.

To the Church in Sardis

3 "To the angel[b] of the church in Sardis
write:

These are the words of him who holds
the seven spirits[c] of God and the seven
stars. I know your deeds; you have a
reputation of being alive, but you are
dead. 2Wake up! Strengthen what remains and is about to die, for I have not
found your deeds complete in the sight
of my God. 3Remember, therefore, what
you have received and heard; obey it,
and repent. But if you do not wake up, I
will come like a thief, and you will not
know at what time I will come to you.

4Yet you have a few people in Sardis
who have not soiled their clothes. They
will walk with me, dressed in white, for
they are worthy. 5He who overcomes
will, like them, be dressed in white. I will
never blot out his name from the book of
life, but will acknowledge his name before my Father and his angels. 6He who
has an ear, let him hear what the Spirit
says to the churches.

To the Church in Philadelphia

7"To the angel of the church in Philadelphia
write:

These are the words of him who is
holy and true, who holds the key of David. What he opens no one can shut,
and what he shuts no one can open. 8I
know your deeds. See, I have placed
before you an open door that no one can
shut. I know that you have little strength,
yet you have kept my word and have not
denied my name. 9I will make those who
are of the synagogue of Satan, who
claim to be Jews though they are not,
but are liars—I will make them come
and fall down at your feet and acknowledge that I have loved you. 10Since you
have kept my command to endure patiently, I will also keep you from the hour
of trial that is going to come upon the
whole world to test those who live on the
earth.

11I am coming soon. Hold on to what
you have, so that no one will take your
crown. 12Him who overcomes I will

[a]27 Psalm 2:9 [b]1 Or *messenger;* also in verses 7 and 14 [c]1 Or *the sevenfold Spirit*

make a pillar in the temple of my God. Never again will he leave it. I will write on him the name of my God and the name of the city of my God, the new Jerusalem, which is coming down out of heaven from my God; and I will also write on him my new name. 13He who has an ear, let him hear what the Spirit says to the churches.

To the Church in Laodicea

14"To the angel of the church in Laodicea write:

These are the words of the Amen, the faithful and true witness, the ruler of God's creation. 15I know your deeds, that you are neither cold nor hot. I wish you were either one or the other! 16So, because you are lukewarm—neither hot nor cold—I am about to spit you out of my mouth. 17You say, 'I am rich; I have acquired wealth and do not need a thing.' But you do not realize that you are wretched, pitiful, poor, blind and naked. 18I counsel you to buy from me gold refined in the fire, so you can become rich; and white clothes to wear, so you can cover your shameful nakedness; and salve to put on your eyes, so you can see.

19Those whom I love I rebuke and discipline. So be earnest, and repent. 20Here I am! I stand at the door and knock. If anyone hears my voice and opens the door, I will come in and eat with him, and he with me.

21To him who overcomes, I will give the right to sit with me on my throne, just as I overcame and sat down with my Father on his throne. 22He who has an ear, let him hear what the Spirit says to the churches."

The Throne in Heaven

4 After this I looked, and there before me was a door standing open in heaven. And the voice I had first heard speaking to me like a trumpet said, "Come up here, and I will show you what must take place after this." 2At once I was in the Spirit, and there before me was a throne in heaven with someone sitting on it. 3And the one who sat there had the appearance of jasper and carnelian. A rainbow, resembling an emerald, encircled the throne. 4Surrounding the throne were twenty-four other thrones, and seated on them were twenty-four elders. They were dressed in white and had crowns of gold on their heads. 5From the throne came flashes of lightning, rumblings and peals of thunder. Before the throne, seven lamps were blazing. These are the seven spirits[a] of God. 6Also before the throne there was what looked like a sea of glass, clear as crystal.

In the center, around the throne, were four living creatures, and they were covered with eyes, in front and in back. 7The first living creature was like a lion, the second was like an ox, the third had a face like a man, the fourth was like a flying eagle. 8Each of the four living creatures had six wings and was covered with eyes all around, even under his wings. Day and night they never stop saying:

"Holy, holy, holy
is the Lord God Almighty,
who was, and is, and is to come."

9Whenever the living creatures give glory, honor and thanks to him who sits on the throne and who lives for ever and ever, 10the twenty-four elders fall down before him who sits on the throne, and worship him who lives for ever and ever. They lay their crowns before the throne and say:

11"You are worthy, our Lord and God,
to receive glory and honor and power,
for you created all things,
and by your will they were created
and have their being."

The Scroll and the Lamb

5 Then I saw in the right hand of him who sat on the throne a scroll with writing on both sides and sealed with seven seals. 2And I saw a mighty angel proclaiming in a loud voice, "Who is worthy to break the seals and open the scroll?" 3But no one in heaven or on earth or under the earth could open the scroll or even look inside it. 4I wept and wept because no one was found who was worthy to open the scroll or look inside. 5Then one of the elders said to me, "Do not weep! See, the Lion of the tribe of Judah, the Root of David, has triumphed. He is able to open the scroll and its seven seals."

6Then I saw a Lamb, looking as if it had been slain, standing in the center of the throne, encircled by the four living creatures

a5 Or *the sevenfold Spirit*

and the elders. He had seven horns and
seven eyes, which are the seven spirits[a] of
God sent out into all the earth. 7He came and
took the scroll from the right hand of him who
sat on the throne. 8And when he had taken it,
the four living creatures and the twenty-four
elders fell down before the Lamb. Each one
had a harp and they were holding golden
bowls full of incense, which are the prayers
of the saints. 9And they sang a new song:

"You are worthy to take the scroll
and to open its seals,
because you were slain,
and with your blood you purchased
men for God
from every tribe and language and
people and nation.
10You have made them to be a kingdom
and priests to serve our God,
and they will reign on the earth."

11Then I looked and heard the voice of
many angels, numbering thousands upon
thousands, and ten thousand times ten thousand. They encircled the throne and the living creatures and the elders. 12In a loud
voice they sang:

"Worthy is the Lamb, who was slain,
to receive power and wealth and wisdom
and strength
and honor and glory and praise!"

13Then I heard every creature in heaven
and on earth and under the earth and on the
sea, and all that is in them, singing:

"To him who sits on the throne and to the
Lamb
be praise and honor and glory and power,
for ever and ever!"

14The four living creatures said, "Amen," and
the elders fell down and worshiped.

The Seals

6 I watched as the Lamb opened the first
of the seven seals. Then I heard one of
the four living creatures say in a voice like
thunder, "Come!" 2I looked, and there before
me was a white horse! Its rider held a bow,
and he was given a crown, and he rode out
as a conqueror bent on conquest.

3When the Lamb opened the second seal,
I heard the second living creature say,
"Come!" 4Then another horse came out, a
fiery red one. Its rider was given power to
take peace from the earth and to make men
slay each other. To him was given a large
sword.

5When the Lamb opened the third seal, I
heard the third living creature say, "Come!" I
looked, and there before me was a black
horse! Its rider was holding a pair of scales in
his hand. 6Then I heard what sounded like a
voice among the four living creatures, saying, "A quart[b] of wheat for a day's wages,[c]
and three quarts of barley for a day's
wages,[c] and do not damage the oil and the
wine!"

7When the Lamb opened the fourth seal, I
heard the voice of the fourth living creature
say, "Come!" 8I looked, and there before me
was a pale horse! Its rider was named Death,
and Hades was following close behind him.
They were given power over a fourth of the
earth to kill by sword, famine and plague,
and by the wild beasts of the earth.

9When he opened the fifth seal, I saw under the altar the souls of those who had been
slain because of the word of God and the
testimony they had maintained. 10They
called out in a loud voice, "How long, Sovereign Lord, holy and true, until you judge the
inhabitants of the earth and avenge our
blood?" 11Then each of them was given a
white robe, and they were told to wait a little
longer, until the number of their fellow servants and brothers who were to be killed as
they had been was completed.

12I watched as he opened the sixth seal.
There was a great earthquake. The sun
turned black like sackcloth made of goat
hair, the whole moon turned blood red, 13and
the stars in the sky fell to earth, as late figs
drop from a fig tree when shaken by a strong
wind. 14The sky receded like a scroll, rolling
up, and every mountain and island was removed from its place.

15Then the kings of the earth, the princes,
the generals, the rich, the mighty, and every
slave and every free man hid in caves and
among the rocks of the mountains. 16They
called to the mountains and the rocks, "Fall
on us and hide us from the face of him who
sits on the throne and from the wrath of the
Lamb! 17For the great day of their wrath has
come, and who can stand?"

144,000 Sealed

7 After this I saw four angels standing at
the four corners of the earth, holding

[a]6 Or *the sevenfold Spirit* [b]6 Greek *a choinix* (probably about a liter) [c]6 Greek *a denarius*

back the four winds of the earth to prevent
any wind from blowing on the land or on the
sea or on any tree. 2Then I saw another angel coming up from the east, having the seal
of the living God. He called out in a loud
voice to the four angels who had been given
power to harm the land and the sea: 3"Do not
harm the land or the sea or the trees until we
put a seal on the foreheads of the servants of
our God." 4Then I heard the number of those
who were sealed: 144,000 from all the tribes
of Israel.

5From the tribe of Judah 12,000 were
sealed,
from the tribe of Reuben 12,000,
from the tribe of Gad 12,000,
6from the tribe of Asher 12,000,
from the tribe of Naphtali 12,000,
from the tribe of Manasseh 12,000,
7from the tribe of Simeon 12,000,
from the tribe of Levi 12,000,
from the tribe of Issachar 12,000,
8from the tribe of Zebulun 12,000,
from the tribe of Joseph 12,000,
from the tribe of Benjamin 12,000.

The Great Multitude in White Robes

9After this I looked and there before me
was a great multitude that no one could
count, from every nation, tribe, people and
language, standing before the throne and in
front of the Lamb. They were wearing white
robes and were holding palm branches in
their hands. 10And they cried out in a loud
voice:

"Salvation belongs to our God,
who sits on the throne,
and to the Lamb."

11All the angels were standing around the
throne and around the elders and the four
living creatures. They fell down on their
faces before the throne and worshiped God,
12saying:

"Amen!
Praise and glory
and wisdom and thanks and honor
and power and strength
be to our God for ever and ever.
Amen!"

13Then one of the elders asked me,
"These in white robes—who are they, and
where did they come from?"
14I answered, "Sir, you know."
And he said, "These are they who have
come out of the great tribulation; they have
washed their robes and made them white in
the blood of the Lamb. 15Therefore,

"they are before the throne of God
and serve him day and night in his
temple;
and he who sits on the throne will spread
his tent over them.
16Never again will they hunger;
never again will they thirst.
The sun will not beat upon them,
nor any scorching heat.
17For the Lamb at the center of the throne
will be their shepherd;
he will lead them to springs of living
water.
And God will wipe away every tear from
their eyes."

The Seventh Seal and the Golden Censer

8 When he opened the seventh seal, there
was silence in heaven for about half an
hour.
2And I saw the seven angels who stand
before God, and to them were given seven
trumpets.
3Another angel, who had a golden censer,
came and stood at the altar. He was given
much incense to offer, with the prayers of all
the saints, on the golden altar before the
throne. 4The smoke of the incense, together
with the prayers of the saints, went up before
God from the angel's hand. 5Then the angel
took the censer, filled it with fire from the
altar, and hurled it on the earth; and there
came peals of thunder, rumblings, flashes of
lightning and an earthquake.

The Trumpets

6Then the seven angels who had the
seven trumpets prepared to sound them.
7The first angel sounded his trumpet, and
there came hail and fire mixed with blood,
and it was hurled down upon the earth. A
third of the earth was burned up, a third of the
trees were burned up, and all the green
grass was burned up.
8The second angel sounded his trumpet,
and something like a huge mountain, all
ablaze, was thrown into the sea. A third of
the sea turned into blood, 9a third of the living
creatures in the sea died, and a third of the
ships were destroyed.
10The third angel sounded his trumpet,

and a great star, blazing like a torch, fell from
the sky on a third of the rivers and on the
springs of water— 11the name of the star is
Wormwood.[a] A third of the waters turned
bitter, and many people died from the waters
that had become bitter.
12The fourth angel sounded his trumpet,
and a third of the sun was struck, a third of
the moon, and a third of the stars, so that a
third of them turned dark. A third of the day
was without light, and also a third of the
night.
13As I watched, I heard an eagle that was
flying in midair call out in a loud voice: "Woe!
Woe! Woe to the inhabitants of the earth,
because of the trumpet blasts about to be
sounded by the other three angels!"
9 The fifth angel sounded his trumpet, and
I saw a star that had fallen from the sky
to the earth. The star was given the key to
the shaft of the Abyss. 2When he opened the
Abyss, smoke rose from it like the smoke
from a gigantic furnace. The sun and sky
were darkened by the smoke from the
Abyss. 3And out of the smoke locusts came
down upon the earth and were given power
like that of scorpions of the earth. 4They were
told not to harm the grass of the earth or any
plant or tree, but only those people who did
not have the seal of God on their foreheads.
5They were not given power to kill them, but
only to torture them for five months. And the
agony they suffered was like that of the sting
of a scorpion when it strikes a man. 6During
those days men will seek death, but will not
find it; they will long to die, but death will
elude them.
7The locusts looked like horses prepared
for battle. On their heads they wore something like crowns of gold, and their faces
resembled human faces. 8Their hair was like
women's hair, and their teeth were like lions'
teeth. 9They had breastplates like breastplates of iron, and the sound of their wings
was like the thundering of many horses and
chariots rushing into battle. 10They had tails
and stings like scorpions, and in their tails
they had power to torment people for five
months. 11They had as king over them the
angel of the Abyss, whose name in Hebrew
is Abaddon, and in Greek, Apollyon.[b]
12The first woe is past; two other woes are
yet to come.
13The sixth angel sounded his trumpet,
and I heard a voice coming from the horns[c]
of the golden altar that is before God. 14It
said to the sixth angel who had the trumpet,
"Release the four angels who are bound at
the great river Euphrates." 15And the four
angels who had been kept ready for this very
hour and day and month and year were
released to kill a third of mankind. 16The
number of the mounted troops was two hundred million. I heard their number.
17The horses and riders I saw in my vision
looked like this: Their breastplates were fiery
red, dark blue, and yellow as sulfur. The
heads of the horses resembled the heads of
lions, and out of their mouths came fire,
smoke and sulfur. 18A third of mankind was
killed by the three plagues of fire, smoke and
sulfur that came out of their mouths. 19The
power of the horses was in their mouths and
in their tails; for their tails were like snakes,
having heads with which they inflict injury.
20The rest of mankind that were not killed
by these plagues still did not repent of the
work of their hands; they did not stop worshiping demons, and idols of gold, silver,
bronze, stone and wood—idols that cannot
see or hear or walk. 21Nor did they repent of
their murders, their magic arts, their sexual
immorality or their thefts.

The Angel and the Little Scroll

10 Then I saw another mighty angel
coming down from heaven. He was
robed in a cloud, with a rainbow above his
head; his face was like the sun, and his legs
were like fiery pillars. 2He was holding a little
scroll, which lay open in his hand. He planted
his right foot on the sea and his left foot on
the land, 3and he gave a loud shout like the
roar of a lion. When he shouted, the voices of
the seven thunders spoke. 4And when the
seven thunders spoke, I was about to write;
but I heard a voice from heaven say, "Seal
up what the seven thunders have said and
do not write it down."
5Then the angel I had seen standing on the
sea and on the land raised his right hand to
heaven. 6And he swore by him who lives for
ever and ever, who created the heavens and
all that is in them, the earth and all that is in it,
and the sea and all that is in it, and said,
"There will be no more delay! 7But in the
days when the seventh angel is about to
sound his trumpet, the mystery of God will be
accomplished, just as he announced to his
servants the prophets."

[a]*11* That is, Bitterness [b]*11* *Abaddon* and *Apollyon* mean *Destroyer.* [c]*13* That is, projections

8Then the voice that I had heard from
heaven spoke to me once more: "Go, take
the scroll that lies open in the hand of the
angel who is standing on the sea and on the
land."
9So I went to the angel and asked him to
give me the little scroll. He said to me, "Take
it and eat it. It will turn your stomach sour, but
in your mouth it will be as sweet as honey."
10I took the little scroll from the angel's hand
and ate it. It tasted as sweet as honey in my
mouth, but when I had eaten it, my stomach
turned sour. 11Then I was told, "You must
prophesy again about many peoples, nations, languages and kings."

The Two Witnesses

11 I was given a reed like a measuring
rod and was told, "Go and measure
the temple of God and the altar, and count
the worshipers there. 2But exclude the outer
court; do not measure it, because it has been
given to the Gentiles. They will trample on
the holy city for 42 months. 3And I will give
power to my two witnesses, and they will
prophesy for 1,260 days, clothed in sackcloth." 4These are the two olive trees and the
two lampstands that stand before the Lord of
the earth. 5If anyone tries to harm them, fire
comes from their mouths and devours their
enemies. This is how anyone who wants to
harm them must die. 6These men have
power to shut up the sky so that it will not rain
during the time they are prophesying; and
they have power to turn the waters into blood
and to strike the earth with every kind of
plague as often as they want.
7Now when they have finished their testimony, the beast that comes up from the
Abyss will attack them, and overpower and
kill them. 8Their bodies will lie in the street of
the great city, which is figuratively called
Sodom and Egypt, where also their Lord was
crucified. 9For three and a half days men
from every people, tribe, language and nation will gaze on their bodies and refuse them
burial. 10The inhabitants of the earth will
gloat over them and will celebrate by sending each other gifts, because these two
prophets had tormented those who live on
the earth.
11But after the three and a half days a
breath of life from God entered them, and
they stood on their feet, and terror struck
those who saw them. 12Then they heard a
loud voice from heaven saying to them,
"Come up here." And they went up to
heaven in a cloud, while their enemies
looked on.
13At that very hour there was a severe
earthquake and a tenth of the city collapsed.
Seven thousand people were killed in the
earthquake, and the survivors were terrified
and gave glory to the God of heaven.
14The second woe has passed; the third
woe is coming soon.

The Seventh Trumpet

15The seventh angel sounded his trumpet,
and there were loud voices in heaven, which
said:

"The kingdom of the world has become
the kingdom of our Lord and of
his Christ,
and he will reign for ever and ever."

16And the twenty-four elders, who were seated on their thrones before God, fell on their
faces and worshiped God, 17saying:

"We give thanks to you, Lord God
Almighty,
the One who is and who was,
because you have taken your great
power
and have begun to reign.
18The nations were angry;
and your wrath has come.
The time has come for judging the dead,
and for rewarding your servants the
prophets
and your saints and those who reverence
your name,
both small and great—
and for destroying those who destroy the
earth."

19Then God's temple in heaven was
opened, and within his temple was seen the
ark of his covenant. And there came flashes
of lightning, rumblings, peals of thunder, an
earthquake and a great hailstorm.

The Woman and the Dragon

12 A great and wondrous sign appeared
in heaven: a woman clothed with the
sun, with the moon under her feet and a
crown of twelve stars on her head. 2She was
pregnant and cried out in pain as she was
about to give birth. 3Then another sign appeared in heaven: an enormous red dragon
with seven heads and ten horns and seven
crowns on his heads. 4His tail swept a third of
the stars out of the sky and flung them to the
earth. The dragon stood in front of the

woman who was about to give birth, so that
he might devour her child the moment it was
born. 5She gave birth to a son, a male child,
who will rule all the nations with an iron scepter. And her child was snatched up to God
and to his throne. 6The woman fled into the
desert to a place prepared for her by God,
where she might be taken care of for 1,260
days.

7And there was war in heaven. Michael
and his angels fought against the dragon,
and the dragon and his angels fought back.
8But he was not strong enough, and they lost
their place in heaven. 9The great dragon was
hurled down—that ancient serpent called the
devil, or Satan, who leads the whole world
astray. He was hurled to the earth, and his
angels with him.

10Then I heard a loud voice in heaven say:

"Now have come the salvation and the
power and the kingdom of our
God,
and the authority of his Christ.
For the accuser of our brothers,
who accuses them before our God day
and night,
has been hurled down.
11They overcame him
by the blood of the Lamb
and by the word of their testimony;
they did not love their lives so much
as to shrink from death.
12Therefore rejoice, you heavens
and you who dwell in them!
But woe to the earth and the sea,
because the devil has gone down to
you!
He is filled with fury,
because he knows that his time is
short."

13When the dragon saw that he had been
hurled to the earth, he pursued the woman
who had given birth to the male child. 14The
woman was given the two wings of a great
eagle, so that she might fly to the place prepared for her in the desert, where she would
be taken care of for a time, times and half a
time, out of the serpent's reach. 15Then from
his mouth the serpent spewed water like a
river, to overtake the woman and sweep her
away with the torrent. 16But the earth helped
the woman by opening its mouth and swal-
lowing the river that the dragon had spewed
out of his mouth. 17Then the dragon was
enraged at the woman and went off to make
war against the rest of her offspring—those
who obey God's commandments and hold to
13 the testimony of Jesus. 1And the
dragon[a] stood on the shore of the
sea.

The Beast out of the Sea

And I saw a beast coming out of the sea.
He had ten horns and seven heads, with ten
crowns on his horns, and on each head a
blasphemous name. 2The beast I saw
resembled a leopard, but had feet like those
of a bear and a mouth like that of a lion. The
dragon gave the beast his power and his
throne and great authority. 3One of the
heads of the beast seemed to have had a
fatal wound, but the fatal wound had been
healed. The whole world was astonished
and followed the beast. 4Men worshiped the
dragon because he had given authority to
the beast, and they also worshiped the beast
and asked, "Who is like the beast? Who can
make war against him?"

5The beast was given a mouth to utter
proud words and blasphemies and to exercise his authority for forty-two months. 6He
opened his mouth to blaspheme God, and to
slander his name and his dwelling place and
those who live in heaven. 7He was given
power to make war against the saints and to
conquer them. And he was given authority
over every tribe, people, language and nation. 8All inhabitants of the earth will worship
the beast—all whose names have not been
written in the book of life belonging to the
Lamb that was slain from the creation of the
world.[b]

9He who has an ear, let him hear.

10If anyone is to go into captivity,
into captivity he will go.
If anyone is to be killed[c] with the sword,
with the sword he will be killed.

This calls for patient endurance and faithfulness on the part of the saints.

The Beast out of the Earth

11Then I saw another beast, coming out of
the earth. He had two horns like a lamb, but
he spoke like a dragon. 12He exercised all
the authority of the first beast on his behalf,
and made the earth and its inhabitants wor-

[a] *1* Some late manuscripts *And I* [b] *8* Or *written from the creation of the world in the book of life belonging to the Lamb that was slain* [c] *10* Some manuscripts *anyone kills*

ship the first beast, whose fatal wound had
been healed. 13And he performed great and
miraculous signs, even causing fire to come
down from heaven to earth in full view of
men. 14Because of the signs he was given
power to do on behalf of the first beast, he
deceived the inhabitants of the earth. He ordered them to set up an image in honor of the
beast who was wounded by the sword and
yet lived. 15He was given power to give
breath to the image of the first beast, so that
it could speak and cause all who refused to
worship the image to be killed. 16He also
forced everyone, small and great, rich and
poor, free and slave, to receive a mark on his
right hand or on his forehead, 17so that no
one could buy or sell unless he had the mark,
which is the name of the beast or the number
of his name.

18This calls for wisdom. If anyone has insight, let him calculate the number of the
beast, for it is man's number. His number is
666.

The Lamb and the 144,000

14 Then I looked, and there before me
was the Lamb, standing on Mount
Zion, and with him 144,000 who had his
name and his Father's name written on their
foreheads. 2And I heard a sound from
heaven like the roar of rushing waters and
like a loud peal of thunder. The sound I heard
was like that of harpists playing their harps.
3And they sang a new song before the throne
and before the four living creatures and the
elders. No one could learn the song except
the 144,000 who had been redeemed from
the earth. 4These are those who did not
defile themselves with women, for they kept
themselves pure. They follow the Lamb
wherever he goes. They were purchased
from among men and offered as firstfruits to
God and the Lamb. 5No lie was found in their
mouths; they are blameless.

The Three Angels

6Then I saw another angel flying in midair,
and he had the eternal gospel to proclaim to
those who live on the earth—to every nation,
tribe, language and people. 7He said in a
loud voice, "Fear God and give him glory,
because the hour of his judgment has come.
Worship him who made the heavens, the
earth, the sea and the springs of water."

8A second angel followed and said,
"Fallen! Fallen is Babylon the Great, which
made all the nations drink the maddening
wine of her adulteries."

9A third angel followed them and said in a
loud voice: "If anyone worships the beast
and his image and receives his mark on the
forehead or on the hand, 10he, too, will drink
of the wine of God's fury, which has been
poured full strength into the cup of his wrath.
He will be tormented with burning sulfur in
the presence of the holy angels and of the
Lamb. 11And the smoke of their torment rises
for ever and ever. There is no rest day or
night for those who worship the beast and his
image, or for anyone who receives the mark
of his name." 12This calls for patient endurance on the part of the saints who obey
God's commandments and remain faithful to
Jesus.

13Then I heard a voice from heaven say,
"Write: Blessed are the dead who die in the
Lord from now on."

"Yes," says the Spirit, "they will rest from
their labor, for their deeds will follow them."

The Harvest of the Earth

14I looked, and there before me was a
white cloud, and seated on the cloud was
one "like a son of man"[a] with a crown of gold
on his head and a sharp sickle in his hand.
15Then another angel came out of the temple
and called in a loud voice to him who was
sitting on the cloud, "Take your sickle and
reap, because the time to reap has come, for
the harvest of the earth is ripe." 16So he who
was seated on the cloud swung his sickle
over the earth, and the earth was harvested.

17Another angel came out of the temple in
heaven, and he too had a sharp sickle. 18Still
another angel, who had charge of the fire,
came from the altar and called in a loud voice
to him who had the sharp sickle, "Take your
sharp sickle and gather the clusters of
grapes from the earth's vine, because its
grapes are ripe." 19The angel swung his sickle on the earth, gathered its grapes and
threw them into the great winepress of God's
wrath. 20They were trampled in the winepress outside the city, and blood flowed out
of the press, rising as high as the horses'
bridles for a distance of 1,600 stadia.[b]

Seven Angels With Seven Plagues

15 I saw in heaven another great and
marvelous sign: seven angels with

[a] 14 Daniel 7:13 [b] 20 That is, about 180 miles (about 300 kilometers)

the seven last plagues—last, because with
them God's wrath is completed. 2And I saw
what looked like a sea of glass mixed with
fire and, standing beside the sea, those who
had been victorious over the beast and his
image and over the number of his name.
They held harps given them by God 3and
sang the song of Moses the servant of God
and the song of the Lamb:

"Great and marvelous are your deeds,
  Lord God Almighty.
Just and true are your ways,
  King of the ages.
4Who will not fear you, O Lord,
  and bring glory to your name?
For you alone are holy.
All nations will come
  and worship before you,
for your righteous acts have been
    revealed."

5After this I looked and in heaven the temple, that is, the tabernacle of the Testimony,
was opened. 6Out of the temple came the
seven angels with the seven plagues. They
were dressed in clean, shining linen and
wore golden sashes around their chests.
7Then one of the four living creatures gave to
the seven angels seven golden bowls filled
with the wrath of God, who lives for ever and
ever. 8And the temple was filled with smoke
from the glory of God and from his power,
and no one could enter the temple until the
seven plagues of the seven angels were
completed.

The Seven Bowls of God's Wrath

16 Then I heard a loud voice from the
temple saying to the seven angels,
"Go, pour out the seven bowls of God's
wrath on the earth."

2The first angel went and poured out his
bowl on the land, and ugly and painful sores
broke out on the people who had the mark of
the beast and worshiped his image.

3The second angel poured out his bowl on
the sea, and it turned into blood like that of a
dead man, and every living thing in the sea
died.

4The third angel poured out his bowl on the
rivers and springs of water, and they became
blood. 5Then I heard the angel in charge of
the waters say:

"You are just in these judgments,
  you who are and who were, the Holy
    One,
  because you have so judged;
6for they have shed the blood of your
    saints and prophets,
  and you have given them blood to drink
    as they deserve."

7And I heard the altar respond:

"Yes, Lord God Almighty,
  true and just are your judgments."

8The fourth angel poured out his bowl on
the sun, and the sun was given power to
scorch people with fire. 9They were seared
by the intense heat and they cursed the
name of God, who had control over these
plagues, but they refused to repent and glorify him.

10The fifth angel poured out his bowl on the
throne of the beast, and his kingdom was
plunged into darkness. Men gnawed their
tongues in agony 11and cursed the God of
heaven because of their pains and their
sores, but they refused to repent of what they
had done.

12The sixth angel poured out his bowl on
the great river Euphrates, and its water was
dried up to prepare the way for the kings from
the East. 13Then I saw three evil[a] spirits that
looked like frogs; they came out of the mouth
of the dragon, out of the mouth of the beast
and out of the mouth of the false prophet.
14They are spirits of demons performing miraculous signs, and they go out to the kings
of the whole world, to gather them for the
battle on the great day of God Almighty.

15"Behold, I come like a thief! Blessed is he
who stays awake and keeps his clothes with
him, so that he may not go naked and be
shamefully exposed."

16Then they gathered the kings together to
the place that in Hebrew is called Armageddon.

17The seventh angel poured out his bowl
into the air, and out of the temple came a
loud voice from the throne, saying, "It is
done!" 18Then there came flashes of lightning, rumblings, peals of thunder and a
severe earthquake. No earthquake like it has
ever occurred since man has been on earth,
so tremendous was the quake. 19The great
city split into three parts, and the cities of the
nations collapsed. God remembered Babylon the Great and gave her the cup filled

[a]13 Greek *unclean*

with the wine of the fury of his wrath. 20Every
island fled away and the mountains could not
be found. 21From the sky huge hailstones of
about a hundred pounds each fell upon men.
And they cursed God on account of the
plague of hail, because the plague was so
terrible.

The Woman on the Beast

17 One of the seven angels who had the
seven bowls came and said to me,
"Come, I will show you the punishment of the
great prostitute, who sits on many waters.
2With her the kings of the earth committed
adultery and the inhabitants of the earth
were intoxicated with the wine of her adulteries."

3Then the angel carried me away in the
Spirit into a desert. There I saw a woman
sitting on a scarlet beast that was covered
with blasphemous names and had seven
heads and ten horns. 4The woman was
dressed in purple and scarlet, and was glittering with gold, precious stones and pearls.
She held a golden cup in her hand, filled with
abominable things and the filth of her adulteries. 5This title was written on her forehead:

MYSTERY
BABYLON THE GREAT
THE MOTHER OF PROSTITUTES
AND OF THE ABOMINATIONS OF THE EARTH.

6I saw that the woman was drunk with the
blood of the saints, the blood of those who
bore testimony to Jesus.

When I saw her, I was greatly astonished.
7Then the angel said to me: "Why are you
astonished? I will explain to you the mystery
of the woman and of the beast she rides,
which has the seven heads and ten horns.
8The beast, which you saw, once was, now is
not, and will come up out of the Abyss and go
to his destruction. The inhabitants of the
earth whose names have not been written in
the book of life from the creation of the world
will be astonished when they see the beast,
because he once was, now is not, and yet
will come.

9"This calls for a mind with wisdom. The
seven heads are seven hills on which the
woman sits. 10They are also seven kings.
Five have fallen, one is, the other has not yet
come; but when he does come, he must remain for a little while. 11The beast who once
was, and now is not, is an eighth king. He
belongs to the seven and is going to his
destruction.

12"The ten horns you saw are ten kings
who have not yet received a kingdom, but
who for one hour will receive authority as
kings along with the beast. 13They have one
purpose and will give their power and authority to the beast. 14They will make war against
the Lamb, but the Lamb will overcome them
because he is Lord of lords and King of
kings—and with him will be his called, chosen and faithful followers."

15Then the angel said to me, "The waters
you saw, where the prostitute sits, are peoples, multitudes, nations and languages.
16The beast and the ten horns you saw will
hate the prostitute. They will bring her to ruin
and leave her naked; they will eat her flesh
and burn her with fire. 17For God has put it
into their hearts to accomplish his purpose
by agreeing to give the beast their power to
rule, until God's words are fulfilled. 18The
woman you saw is the great city that rules
over the kings of the earth."

The Fall of Babylon

18 After this I saw another angel coming
down from heaven. He had great authority, and the earth was illuminated by his
splendor. 2With a mighty voice he shouted:

"Fallen! Fallen is Babylon the Great!
She has become a home for demons
and a haunt for every evil[a] spirit,
a haunt for every unclean and
detestable bird.
3For all the nations have drunk
the maddening wine of her adulteries.
The kings of the earth committed adultery
with her,
and the merchants of the earth grew
rich from her excessive luxuries."

4Then I heard another voice from heaven
say:

"Come out of her, my people,
so that you will not share in her sins,
so that you will not receive any of her
plagues;
5for her sins are piled up to heaven,
and God has remembered her crimes.
6Give back to her as she has given;
pay her back double for what she has
done.

[a]2 Greek *unclean*

Mix her a double portion from her own
cup.
7Give her as much torture and grief
as the glory and luxury she gave
herself.
In her heart she boasts,
'I sit as queen; I am not a widow,
and I will never mourn.'
8Therefore in one day her plagues will
overtake her:
death, mourning and famine.
She will be consumed by fire,
for mighty is the Lord God who judges
her.

9"When the kings of the earth who committed adultery with her and shared her luxury
see the smoke of her burning, they will weep
and mourn over her. 10Terrified at her torment, they will stand far off and cry:

" 'Woe! Woe, O great city,
O Babylon, city of power!
In one hour your doom has come!'

11"The merchants of the earth will weep
and mourn over her because no one buys
their cargoes any more— 12cargoes of gold,
silver, precious stones and pearls; fine linen,
purple, silk and scarlet cloth; every sort of
citron wood, and articles of every kind made
of ivory, costly wood, bronze, iron and marble; 13cargoes of cinnamon and spice, of incense, myrrh and frankincense, of wine and
olive oil, of fine flour and wheat; cattle and
sheep; horses and carriages; and bodies
and souls of men.
14"They will say, 'The fruit you longed for is
gone from you. All your riches and splendor
have vanished, never to be recovered.'
15The merchants who sold these things and
gained their wealth from her will stand far off,
terrified at her torment. They will weep and
mourn 16and cry out:

" 'Woe! Woe, O great city,
dressed in fine linen, purple and
scarlet,
and glittering with gold, precious stones
and pearls!
17In one hour such great wealth has been
brought to ruin!'

"Every sea captain, and all who travel by
ship, the sailors, and all who earn their living
from the sea, will stand far off. 18When they
see the smoke of her burning, they will exclaim, 'Was there ever a city like this great
city?' 19They will throw dust on their heads,
and with weeping and mourning cry out:

" 'Woe! Woe, O great city,
where all who had ships on the sea
became rich through her wealth!
In one hour she has been brought to ruin!
20Rejoice over her, O heaven!
Rejoice, saints and apostles and
prophets!
God has judged her for the way she
treated you.' "

21Then a mighty angel picked up a boulder
the size of a large millstone and threw it into
the sea, and said:

"With such violence
the great city of Babylon will be thrown
down,
never to be found again.
22The music of harpists and musicians,
flute players and trumpeters,
will never be heard in you again.
No workman of any trade
will ever be found in you again.
The sound of a millstone
will never be heard in you again.
23The light of a lamp
will never shine in you again.
The voice of bridegroom and bride
will never be heard in you again.
Your merchants were the world's great
men.
By your magic spell all the nations were
led astray.
24In her was found the blood of prophets
and of the saints,
and of all who have been killed on the
earth."

Hallelujah!

19 After this I heard what sounded like
the roar of a great multitude in
heaven shouting:

"Hallelujah!
Salvation and glory and power belong to
our God,
2 for true and just are his judgments.
He has condemned the great prostitute
who corrupted the earth by her
adulteries.
He has avenged on her the blood of his
servants."

3And again they shouted:

"Hallelujah!
The smoke from her goes up for ever and
ever."

4The twenty-four elders and the four living
creatures fell down and worshiped God, who
was seated on the throne. And they cried:

"Amen, Hallelujah!"

5Then a voice came from the throne, saying:

"Praise our God,
all you his servants,
you who fear him,
both small and great!"

6Then I heard what sounded like a great
multitude, like the roar of rushing waters and
like loud peals of thunder, shouting:

"Hallelujah!
For our Lord God Almighty reigns.
7Let us rejoice and be glad
and give him glory!
For the wedding of the Lamb has come,
and his bride has made herself ready.
8Fine linen, bright and clean,
was given her to wear."
(Fine linen stands for the righteous acts of
the saints.)

9Then the angel said to me, "Write:
'Blessed are those who are invited to the
wedding supper of the Lamb!'" And he
added, "These are the true words of God."
10At this I fell at his feet to worship him. But
he said to me, "Do not do it! I am a fellow
servant with you and with your brothers who
hold to the testimony of Jesus. Worship God!
For the testimony of Jesus is the spirit of
prophecy."

The Rider on the White Horse

11I saw heaven standing open and there
before me was a white horse, whose rider is
called Faithful and True. With justice he
judges and makes war. 12His eyes are like
blazing fire, and on his head are many
crowns. He has a name written on him that
no one knows but he himself. 13He is dressed
in a robe dipped in blood, and his name is the
Word of God. 14The armies of heaven were
following him, riding on white horses and
dressed in fine linen, white and clean. 15Out
of his mouth comes a sharp sword with
which to strike down the nations. "He will rule
them with an iron scepter."[a] He treads the
winepress of the fury of the wrath of God
Almighty. 16On his robe and on his thigh he
has this name written:

KING OF KINGS AND LORD OF LORDS.

17And I saw an angel standing in the sun,
who cried in a loud voice to all the birds flying
in midair, "Come, gather together for the
great supper of God, 18so that you may eat
the flesh of kings, generals, and mighty men,
of horses and their riders, and the flesh of all
people, free and slave, small and great."
19Then I saw the beast and the kings of the
earth and their armies gathered together to
make war against the rider on the horse and
his army. 20But the beast was captured, and
with him the false prophet who had performed the miraculous signs on his behalf.
With these signs he had deluded those who
had received the mark of the beast and worshiped his image. The two of them were
thrown alive into the fiery lake of burning
sulfur. 21The rest of them were killed with the
sword that came out of the mouth of the rider
on the horse, and all the birds gorged themselves on their flesh.

The Thousand Years

20 And I saw an angel coming down out
of heaven, having the key to the
Abyss and holding in his hand a great chain.
2He seized the dragon, that ancient serpent,
who is the devil, or Satan, and bound him for
a thousand years. 3He threw him into the
Abyss, and locked and sealed it over him, to
keep him from deceiving the nations anymore until the thousand years were ended.
After that, he must be set free for a short
time.
4I saw thrones on which were seated those
who had been given authority to judge. And I
saw the souls of those who had been beheaded because of their testimony for Jesus
and because of the word of God. They had
not worshiped the beast or his image and
had not received his mark on their foreheads
or their hands. They came to life and reigned
with Christ a thousand years. 5(The rest of
the dead did not come to life until the thousand years were ended.) This is the first
resurrection. 6Blessed and holy are those
who have part in the first resurrection. The
second death has no power over them, but

[a] 15 Psalm 2:9

they will be priests of God and of Christ and
will reign with him for a thousand years.

Satan's Doom

7When the thousand years are over, Satan
will be released from his prison 8and will go
out to deceive the nations in the four corners
of the earth—Gog and Magog—to gather
them for battle. In number they are like the
sand on the seashore. 9They marched
across the breadth of the earth and surrounded the camp of God's people, the city
he loves. But fire came down from heaven
and devoured them. 10And the devil, who
deceived them, was thrown into the lake of
burning sulfur, where the beast and the false
prophet had been thrown. They will be tormented day and night for ever and ever.

The Dead Are Judged

11Then I saw a great white throne and him
who was seated on it. Earth and sky fled from
his presence, and there was no place for
them. 12And I saw the dead, great and small,
standing before the throne, and books were
opened. Another book was opened, which is
the book of life. The dead were judged according to what they had done as recorded in
the books. 13The sea gave up the dead that
were in it, and death and Hades gave up the
dead that were in them, and each person
was judged according to what he had done.
14Then death and Hades were thrown into
the lake of fire. The lake of fire is the second
death. 15If anyone's name was not found
written in the book of life, he was thrown into
the lake of fire.

The New Jerusalem

21 Then I saw a new heaven and a new
earth, for the first heaven and the first
earth had passed away, and there was no
longer any sea. 2I saw the Holy City, the new
Jerusalem, coming down out of heaven from
God, prepared as a bride beautifully dressed
for her husband. 3And I heard a loud voice
from the throne saying, "Now the dwelling of
God is with men, and he will live with them.
They will be his people, and God himself will
be with them and be their God. 4He will wipe
every tear from their eyes. There will be no
more death or mourning or crying or pain, for
the old order of things has passed away."
5He who was seated on the throne said, "I
am making everything new!" Then he said,
"Write this down, for these words are trustworthy and true."
6He said to me: "It is done. I am the Alpha
and the Omega, the Beginning and the End.
To him who is thirsty I will give to drink without cost from the spring of the water of life.
7He who overcomes will inherit all this, and I
will be his God and he will be my son. 8But
the cowardly, the unbelieving, the vile, the
murderers, the sexually immoral, those who
practice magic arts, the idolaters and all liars—their place will be in the fiery lake of
burning sulfur. This is the second death."
9One of the seven angels who had the
seven bowls full of the seven last plagues
came and said to me, "Come, I will show you
the bride, the wife of the Lamb." 10And he
carried me away in the Spirit to a mountain
great and high, and showed me the Holy
City, Jerusalem, coming down out of heaven
from God. 11It shone with the glory of God,
and its brilliance was like that of a very precious jewel, like a jasper, clear as crystal. 12It
had a great, high wall with twelve gates, and
with twelve angels at the gates. On the gates
were written the names of the twelve tribes of
Israel. 13There were three gates on the east,
three on the north, three on the south and
three on the west. 14The wall of the city had
twelve foundations, and on them were the
names of the twelve apostles of the Lamb.
15The angel who talked with me had a
measuring rod of gold to measure the city, its
gates and its walls. 16The city was laid out
like a square, as long as it was wide. He
measured the city with the rod and found it to
be 12,000 stadia[a] in length, and as wide and
high as it is long. 17He measured its wall and
it was 144 cubits[b] thick,[c] by man's measurement, which the angel was using. 18The
wall was made of jasper, and the city of pure
gold, as pure as glass. 19The foundations of
the city walls were decorated with every kind
of precious stone. The first foundation was
jasper, the second sapphire, the third chal-
cedony, the fourth emerald, 20the fifth sard-
onyx, the sixth carnelian, the seventh
chrysolite, the eighth beryl, the ninth topaz,
the tenth chrysoprase, the eleventh jacinth,
and the twelfth amethyst.[d] 21The twelve
gates were twelve pearls, each gate made of
a single pearl. The great street of the city was
of pure gold, like transparent glass.

[a] *16* That is, about 1,400 miles (about 2,200 kilometers) [b] *17* That is, about 200 feet (about 65 meters)
[c] *17* Or *high* [d] *20* The precise identification of some of these precious stones is uncertain.

22I did not see a temple in the city, because the Lord God Almighty and the Lamb are its temple. 23The city does not need the sun or the moon to shine on it, for the glory of God gives it light, and the Lamb is its lamp. 24The nations will walk by its light, and the kings of the earth will bring their splendor into it. 25On no day will its gates ever be shut, for there will be no night there. 26The glory and honor of the nations will be brought into it. 27Nothing impure will ever enter it, nor will anyone who does what is shameful or deceitful, but only those whose names are written in the Lamb's book of life.

The River of Life

22 Then the angel showed me the river of the water of life, as clear as crystal, flowing from the throne of God and of the Lamb 2down the middle of the great street of the city. On each side of the river stood the tree of life, bearing twelve crops of fruit, yielding its fruit every month. And the leaves of the tree are for the healing of the nations. 3No longer will there be any curse. The throne of God and of the Lamb will be in the city, and his servants will serve him. 4They will see his face, and his name will be on their foreheads. 5There will be no more night. They will not need the light of a lamp or the light of the sun, for the Lord God will give them light. And they will reign for ever and ever.

6The angel said to me, "These words are trustworthy and true. The Lord, the God of the spirits of the prophets, sent his angel to show his servants the things that must soon take place."

Jesus Is Coming

7"Behold, I am coming soon! Blessed is he who keeps the words of the prophecy in this book."

8I, John, am the one who heard and saw these things. And when I had heard and seen them, I fell down to worship at the feet of the angel who had been showing them to me. 9But he said to me, "Do not do it! I am a fellow servant with you and with your brothers the prophets and of all who keep the words of this book. Worship God!"

10Then he told me, "Do not seal up the words of the prophecy of this book, because the time is near. 11Let him who does wrong continue to do wrong; let him who is vile continue to be vile; let him who does right continue to do right; and let him who is holy continue to be holy."

12"Behold, I am coming soon! My reward is with me, and I will give to everyone according to what he has done. 13I am the Alpha and the Omega, the First and the Last, the Beginning and the End.

14"Blessed are those who wash their robes, that they may have the right to the tree of life and may go through the gates into the city. 15Outside are the dogs, those who practice magic arts, the sexually immoral, the murderers, the idolaters and everyone who loves and practices falsehood.

16"I, Jesus, have sent my angel to give you[a] this testimony for the churches. I am the Root and the Offspring of David, and the bright Morning Star."

17The Spirit and the bride say, "Come!" And let him who hears say, "Come!" Whoever is thirsty, let him come; and whoever wishes, let him take the free gift of the water of life.

18I warn everyone who hears the words of the prophecy of this book: If anyone adds anything to them, God will add to him the plagues described in this book. 19And if anyone takes words away from this book of prophecy, God will take away from him his share in the tree of life and in the holy city, which are described in this book.

20He who testifies to these things says, "Yes, I am coming soon."

Amen. Come, Lord Jesus.

21The grace of the Lord Jesus be with God's people. Amen.

[a]*16* The Greek is plural.

Table of Weights and Measures

BIBLICAL UNIT		AMERICAN EQUIVALENT	METRIC EQUIVALENT
WEIGHTS			
talent	*(60 minas)*	75 pounds	34 kilograms
mina	*(50 shekels)*	1 1/4 pounds	0.6 kilogram
shekel	*(2 bekas)*	2/5 ounce	11.5 grams
pim	*(2/3 shekel)*	1/3 ounce	7.6 grams
beka	*(10 gerahs)*	1/5 ounce	6 grams
gerah		1/50 ounce	0.6 gram
LENGTH			
cubit		18 inches	0.5 meter
span		9 inches	23 centimeters
handbreadth		3 inches	8 centimeters
CAPACITY			
Dry Measure			
cor [homer]	*(10 ephahs)*	6 bushels	220 liters
lethek	*(5 ephahs)*	3 bushels	110 liters
ephah	*(10 omers)*	1/2 bushel	22 liters
seah	*(1/3 ephah)*	7 quarts	7.3 liters
omer	*(1/10 ephah)*	2 quarts	2 liters
cab	*(1/18 ephah)*	1 quart	1 liter
Liquid Measure			
bath	*(1 ephah)*	6 gallons	22 liters
hin	*(1/6 bath)*	4 quarts	4 liters
log	*(1/72 bath)*	1/3 quart	0.3 liter

The figures of the table are calculated on the basis of a shekel equaling 11.5 grams, a cubit equaling 18 inches and an ephah equaling 22 liters. The quart referred to is either a dry quart (slightly larger than a liter) or a liquid quart (slightly smaller than a liter), whichever is applicable. The ton referred to in the footnotes is the American ton of 2,000 pounds.

This table is based upon the best available information, but it is not intended to be mathematically precise; like the measurement equivalents in the footnotes, it merely gives approximate amounts and distances. Weights and measures differed somewhat at various times and places in the ancient world. There is uncertainty particularly about the ephah and the bath; further discoveries may give more light on these units of capacity.

Concordance

The NIV Mini-Concordance

Grand Rapids, Michigan

Introduction

The NIV Concordance, created by Edward W. Goodrick and John R. Kohlenberger III, has been developed specifically for use with the New International Version. Like all concordances, it is a special index which contains an alphabetical listing of words used in the Bible text. By looking up key words, readers can find verses and passages for which they remember a word or two but not their location.

This concordance contains 5,000 word entries, with some 35,000 Scripture references. Each word entry is followed by the Scripture references in which that particular word is found, as well as by a brief excerpt from the surrounding context. The first letter of the entry word is italicized to conserve space and to allow for a longer context excerpt. Variant spellings due to number and tense and compound forms follow the entry in parentheses, and direct the reader to check other forms of that word in locating a passage.

This concordance contains a number of "block entries," which highlight some of the key events and characteristics in the lives of certain Bible figures. The descriptive phrases replace the brief context surrounding each occurrence of the name. In those instances where more than one Bible character has the same name, that name is placed under one block entry, and each person is given a number (1), (2), etc. Insignificant names are not included.

Word or block entries marked with an asterisk (*) list every verse in the Bible in which the word appears.

This concordance is a valuable tool for Bible study. While one of its key purposes is to help the reader find forgotten references to verses, it can also be used to do word studies and to locate and trace biblical themes. Be sure to use this concordance as more than just a verse finder. Whenever you look up a verse, aim to discover the intended meaning of the verse in context. Give special attention to the flow of thought from the beginning of the passage to the end.

ABBREVIATIONS FOR THE BOOKS OF THE BIBLE

Genesis	Ge	Nahum	Na
Exodus	Ex	Habbakuk	Hab
Leviticus	Lev	Zephaniah	Zep
Numbers	Nu	Haggai	Hag
Deuteronomy	Dt	Zechariah	Zec
Joshua	Jos	Malachi	Mal
Judges	Jdg	Matthew	Mt
Ruth	Ru	Mark	Mk
I Samuel	I Sa	Luke	Lk
2 Samuel	2Sa	John	Jn
I Kings	I Ki	Acts	Ac
2 Kings	2Ki	Romans	Ro
I Chronicles	I Ch	I Corinthians	I Co
2 Chronicles	2Ch	2 Corinthians	2Co
Ezra	Ezr	Galatians	Gal
Nehemiah	Ne	Ephesians	Eph
Esther	Est	Philippians	Php
Job	Job	Colossians	Col
Psalms	Ps	I Thessalonians	I Th
Proverbs	Pr	2 Thessalonians	2Th
Ecclesiastes	Ecc	I Timothy	I Ti
Song of Songs	SS	2 Timothy	2Ti
Isaiah	Isa	Titus	Tit
Jeremiah	Jer	Philemon	Phm
Lamentations	La	Hebrews	Heb
Ezekiel	Eze	James	Jas
Daniel	Da	I Peter	I Pe
Hosea	Hos	2 Peter	2Pe
Joel	Joel	I John	I Jn
Amos	Am	2 John	2Jn
Obadiah	Ob	3 John	3Jn
Jonah	Jnh	Jude	Jude
Micah	Mic	Revelation	Rev

AARON

Genealogy of (Ex 6:16-20; Jos 21:4, 10; 1Ch 6:3-15).

Priesthood of (Ex 28:1; Nu 17; Heb 5:1-4; 7), garments (Ex 28; 39), consecration (Ex 29), ordination (Lev 8).

Spokesman for Moses (Ex 4:14-16, 27-31; 7:1-2). Supported Moses' hands in battle (Ex 17:8-13). Built golden calf (Ex 32; Dt 9:20). Talked against Moses (Nu 12). Priesthood opposed (Nu 16); staff budded (Nu 17). Forbidden to enter land (Nu 20:1-12). Death (Nu 20:22-29; 33:38-39).

ABADDON*

Rev 9:11 whose name in Hebrew is *A*,

ABANDON (ABANDONED)

Dt 4:31 he will not *a* or destroy you
1Ki 6:13 and will not *a* my people Israel."
Ne 9:19 compassion you did not *a* them
9:31 an end to them or *a* them,
Ps 16:10 you will not *a* me to the grave,
Ac 2:27 you will not *a* me to the grave,
1Ti 4:1 in later times some will *a* the faith

ABANDONED (ABANDON)

Ge 24:27 who has not *a* his kindness
2Co 4:9 persecuted, but not *a*; struck down,

ABBA*

Mk 14:36 "*A*, Father," he said, "everything is
Ro 8:15 And by him we cry, "*A*, Father."
Gal 4:6 the Spirit who calls out, "*A*, Father

ABEDNEGO

Deported to Babylon with Daniel (Da 1:1-6). Name changed from Azariah (Da 1:7). Refused defilement by food (Da 1:8-20). Refused idol worship (Da 3:1-12); saved from furnace (Da 3:13-30).

ABEL

Second son of Adam (Ge 4:2). Offered proper sacrifice (Ge 4:4; Heb 11:4). Murdered by Cain (Ge 4:8; Mt 23:35; Lk 11:51; 1Jn 3:12).

ABHOR (ABHORS)

Lev 26:30 of your idols, and I will *a* you.
Dt 7:26 Utterly *a* and detest it,
Ps 26:5 I *a* the assembly of evildoers
119:163 I hate and *a* falsehood
139:21 and *a* those who rise up against you
Am 6:8 "I *a* the pride of Jacob
Ro 2:22 You who *a* idols, do you rob

ABHORS (ABHOR)

Pr 11:1 The LORD *a* dishonest scales,

ABIATHAR

High priest in days of Saul and David (1Sa 22; 2Sa 15; 1Ki 1-2; Mk 2:26). Escaped Saul's slaughter of priests (1Sa 22:18-23). Supported David in Absalom's revolt (2Sa 15:24-29). Supported Adonijah (1Ki 1:7-42); deposed by Solomon (1Ki 2:22-35; cf. 1Sa 2:31-35).

ABIDE see REMAIN

ABIGAIL

1. Sister of David (1Ch 2:16-17).

2. Wife of Nabal (1Sa 25:30); pled for his life with David (1Sa 25:14-35). Became David's wife after Nabal's death (1Sa 25:36-42); bore him Kileab (2Sa 3:3) also known as Daniel (1Ch 3:1).

ABIHU

Son of Aaron (Ex 6:23; 24:1, 9); killed for offering unauthorized fire (Lev 10; Nu 3:2-4; 1Ch 24:1-2).

ABIJAH

1. Second son of Samuel (1Ch 6:28); a corrupt judge (1Sa 8:1-5).

2. An Aaronic priest (1Ch 24:10; Lk 1:5).

3. Son of Jeroboam I of Israel; died as prophesied by Ahijah (1Ki 14:1-18).

4. Son of Rehoboam; king of Judah who fought Jeroboam I attempting to reunite the kingdom (1Ki 14:31-15:8; 2Ch 12:16-14:1; Mt 1:7).

ABILITY (ABLE)

Ex 35:34 tribe of Dan, the *a* to teach others.
Dt 8:18 for it is he who gives you the *a*
Ezr 2:69 According to their *a* they gave
Mt 25:15 one talent, each according to his *a*.
Ac 11:29 disciples, each according to his *a*,
2Co 1:8 far beyond our *a* to endure,
8:3 were able, and even beyond their *a*.

ABIMELECH

1. King of Gerar who took Abraham's wife Sarah, believing her to be his sister (Ge 20). Later made a covenant with Abraham (Ge 21:22-33).

2. King of Gerar who took Isaac's wife Rebekah, believing her to be his sister (Ge 26:1-11). Later made a covenant with Isaac (Ge 26:12-31).

3. Son of Gideon (Jdg 8:31). Attempted to make himself king (Jdg 9).

ABISHAG*

Shunammite virgin; attendant of David in his old age (1Ki 1:1-15; 2:17-22).

ABISHAI

Son of Zeruiah, David's sister (1Sa 26:6; 1Ch 2:16). One of David's chief warriors (1Ch 11:15-21): against Edom (1Ch 18:12-13), Ammon (2Sa 10), Absalom (2Sa 18), Sheba (2Sa 20). Wanted to kill Saul (1Sa 26), killed Abner (2Sa 2:18-27; 3:22-39), wanted to kill Shimei (2Sa 16:5-13; 19:16-23).

ABLE (ABILITY ENABLE ENABLED ENABLES ENABLING)

Nu 14:16 'The LORD was not *a*
1Ch 29:14 that we should be *a* to give
2Ch 2:6 who is *a* to build a temple for him,
Eze 7:19 and gold will not be *a* to save them
Da 3:17 the God we serve is *a* to save us
4:37 walk in pride he is *a* to humble.
Mt 9:28 "Do you believe that I am *a*
Lk 13:24 will try to enter and will not be *a* to
14:30 to build and was not *a* to finish.'
21:15 none of your adversaries will be *a*
21:36 and that you may be *a* to stand
Ac 5:39 you will not be *a* to stop these men;
Ro 8:39 will be *a* to separate us
14:4 for the Lord is *a* to make him stand
16:25 to him who is *a* to establish you
2Co 9:8 God is *a* to make all grace abound
Eph 3:20 him who is *a* to do immeasurably
6:13 you may be *a* to stand your ground,
1Ti 3:2 respectable, hospitable, *a* to teach,
2Ti 1:12 and am convinced that he is *a*
2:24 kind to everyone, *a* to teach,
3:15 which are *a* to make you wise
Heb 2:18 he is *a* to help those who are being
7:25 he is *a* to save completely
Jas 3:2 *a* to keep his whole body in check.
Jude :24 To him who is *a* to keep you
Rev 5:5 He is *a* to open the scroll

ABNER

Cousin of Saul and commander of his army (1Sa 14:50; 17:55-57; 26). Made Ish-Bosheth king after Saul (2Sa 2:8-10), but later defected to David (2Sa 3:6-21). Killed Asahel (2Sa 2:18-32), for which he was killed by Joab and Abishai (2Sa 3:22-39).

ABOLISH (ABOLISHED ABOLISHING)

Hos 2:18 I will *a* from the land,
Mt 5:17 that I have come to *a* the Law

ABOLISHED (ABOLISH)

Gal 5:11 the offense of the cross has been *a*.

ABOLISHING* (ABOLISH)

Eph 2:15 by *a* in his flesh the law

ABOMINATION*

Da 11:31 set up the *a* that causes desolation.
12:11 *a* that causes desolation is set up,
Mt 24:15 the holy place 'the *a* that causes
Mk 13:14 you see 'the *a* that causes

ABOUND (ABOUNDING)

2Co 9:8 able to make all grace *a* to you,
9:8 you will *a* in every good work.
Php 1:9 that your love may *a* more

ABOUNDING (ABOUND)

Ex 34:6 slow to anger, *a* in love
Nu 14:18 *a* in love and forgiving sin
Ne 9:17 slow to anger and *a* in love.
Ps 86:5 *a* in love to all who call to you.
86:15 slow to anger, *a* in love
Ps 103:8 slow to anger, *a* in love.
Joel 2:13 slow to anger and *a* in love,
Jnh 4:2 slow to anger and *a* in love,

ABRAHAM

Abram, son of Terah (Ge 11:26-27), husband of Sarah (Ge 11:29).

Covenant relation with the LORD (Ge 12:1-3; 13:14-17; 15; 17; 22:15-18; Ex 2:24; Ne 9:8; Ps 105; Mic 7:20; Lk 1:68-75; Ro 4; Heb 6:13-15).

Called from Ur, via Haran, to Canaan (Ge 12:1; Ac 7:2-4; Heb 11:8-10). Moved to Egypt, nearly lost Sarah to Pharoah (Ge 12:10-20). Divided the land with Lot; settled in Hebron (Ge 13). Saved Lot from four kings (Ge 14:1-16); blessed by Melchizedek (Ge 14:17-20; Heb 7:1-20). Declared righteous by faith (Ge 15:6; Ro 4:3; Gal 3:6-9). Fathered Ishmael by Hagar (Ge 16).

Name changed from Abram (Ge 17:5; Ne 9:7). Circumcised (Ge 17; Ro 4:9-12). Entertained three visitors (Ge 18); promised a son by Sarah (Ge 18:9-15; 17:16). Questioned destruction of Sodom and Gomorrah (Ge 18:16-33). Moved to Gerar; nearly lost Sarah to Abimelech (Ge 20). Fathered Isaac by Sarah (Ge 21:1-7; Ac 7:8; Heb 11:11-12); sent away Hagar and Ishmael (Ge 21:8-21; Gal 4:22-30). Covenant with Abimelech (Ge 21:22-32). Tested by offering Isaac (Ge 22; Heb 11:17-19; Jas 2:21-24). Sarah died; bought field of Ephron for burial (Ge 23). Secured wife for Isaac (Ge 24). Fathered children by Keturah (Ge 25:1-6; 1Ch 1:32-33). Death (Ge 25:7-11).

Called servant of God (Ge 26:24), friend of God (2Ch 20:7; Isa 41:8; Jas 2:23), prophet (Ge 20:7), father of Israel (Ex 3:15; Isa 51:2; Mt 3:9; Jn 8:39-58).

ABRAM see ABRAHAM

ABSALOM

Son of David by Maacah (2Sa 3:3; 1Ch 3:2). Killed Amnon for rape of his sister Tamar; banished by David (2Sa 13). Returned to Jerusalem; received by David (2Sa 14). Rebelled against David; siezed kingdom (2Sa 15-17). Killed (2Sa 18).

ABSENT

Col 2:5 though I am *a* from you in body,

ABSOLUTE*

1Ti 5:2 women as sisters, with *a* purity.

ABSTAIN (ABSTAINS)

Ex 19:15 *A* from sexual relations."
Nu 6:3 he must *a* from wine and other
Ac 15:20 them to *a* from food polluted
1Pe 2:11 to *a* from sinful desires,

ABSTAINS* (ABSTAIN)

Ro 14:6 thanks to God; and he who *a*,

ABUNDANCE (ABUNDANT)

Ge 41:29 Seven years of great *a* are coming
Job 36:31 and provides food in *a*.
Ps 66:12 but you brought us to a place of *a*.
Ecc 5:12 but the *a* of a rich man
Isa 66:11 and delight in her overflowing *a*."
Jer 2:22 and use an *a* of soap,
Mt 13:12 given more, and he will have an *a*.
25:29 given more, and he will have an *a*.
Lk 12:15 consist in the *a* of his possessions."
1Pe 1:2 Grace and peace be yours in *a*.
2Pe 1:2 yours in *a* through the knowledge
Jude :2 peace and love be yours in *a*.

ABUNDANT (ABUNDANCE)

Dt 28:11 will grant you *a* prosperity—
32:2 like *a* rain on tender plants.
Job 36:28 and *a* showers fall on mankind.
Ps 68:9 You gave *a* showers, O God;
78:15 gave them water as *a* as the seas;
132:15 I will bless her with *a* provisions;
145:7 will celebrate your *a* goodness
Pr 12:11 works his land will have *a* food,
28:19 works his land will have *a* food,
Jer 33:9 and will tremble at the *a* prosperity
Ro 5:17 who receive God's *a* provision

ABUSIVE

2Ti 3:2 *a*, disobedient to their parents,

ABYSS*

Lk 8:31 not to order them to go into the *A*.

Rev 9: 1 the key to the shaft of the A.
9: 2 When he opened the A, smoke rose
9: 2 darkened by the smoke from the A.
9: 11 king over them the angel of the A,
11: 7 up from the A will attack them,
17: 8 and will come up out of the A
20: 1 having the key to the A
20: 3 He threw him into the A,

ACCEPT (ACCEPTABLE ACCEPTANCE ACCEPTED ACCEPTS)

Ex 23: 8 "Do not a a bribe,
Dt 16: 19 Do not a a bribe, for a bribe blinds
Job 42: 8 and I will a his prayer and not deal
Pr 10: 8 The wise in heart a commands,
19: 20 Listen to advice and a instruction,
Ro 15: 7 A one another, then, just
Jas 1: 21 humbly a the word planted in you,

ACCEPTABLE (ACCEPT)

Pr 21: 3 is more a to the LORD

ACCEPTANCE* (ACCEPT)

Ro 11: 15 what will their a be but life
1Ti 1: 15 saying that deserves full a:
4: 9 saying that deserves full a

ACCEPTED (ACCEPT)

Ge 4: 7 will you not be a? But if you do not
Job 42: 9 and the LORD a Job's prayer.
Lk 4: 24 "no prophet is a in his hometown.
Gal 1: 9 you a gospel other than what you a,

ACCEPTS (ACCEPT)

Ps 6: 9 the LORD a my prayer.
Jn 13: 20 whoever a anyone I send a me;
13: 20 whoever a me a the one who sent

ACCESS

Ro 5: 2 through whom we have gained a
Eph 2: 18 For through him we both have a

ACCOMPANIED (ACCOMPANY)

1Co 10: 4 from the spiritual rock that a them,
Jas 2: 17 if it is not a by action, is dead.

ACCOMPANIES (ACCOMPANY)

2Co 9: 13 obedience that a your confession

ACCOMPANY (ACCOMPANIED ACCOMPANIES)

Dt 28: 2 a you if you obey the LORD your
Mk 16: 17 these signs will a those who believe
Heb 6: 9 your case—things that a salvation.

ACCOMPLISH

Ecc 2: 2 And what does pleasure a?"
Isa 44: 28 and will a all that I please;
55: 11 but will a what I desire

ACCORD

Nu 24: 13 not do anything of my own a,
Jn 10: 18 but I lay it down of my own a.
12: 49 For I did not speak of my own a,

ACCOUNT (ACCOUNTABLE)

Ge 2: 4 This is the a of the heavens
5: 1 This is the written a of Adam's line
6: 9 This is the a of Noah.
10: 1 This is the a of Shem, Ham
11: 10 This is the a of Shem.
11: 27 This is the a of Terah.
25: 12 This is the a of Abraham's son
25: 19 This is the a of Abraham's son
36: 1 This is the a of Esau (that is, Edom
36: 9 This is the a of Esau the father
37: 2 This is the a of Jacob.
Mt 12: 36 to give a on the day of judgment
Lk 16: 2 Give an a of your management,
Ro 14: 12 each of us will give an a of himself
Heb 4: 13 of him to whom we must give a.

ACCOUNTABLE* (ACCOUNT)

Eze 3: 18 and I will hold you a for his blood.
3: 20 and I will hold you a for his blood.
33: 6 but I will hold the watchman a
33: 8 and I will hold you a for his blood.
34: 10 and will hold them a for my flock.
Da 6: 2 The satraps were made a to them
Jnh 1: 14 Do not hold us a for killing
Ro 3: 19 and the whole world held a to God.

ACCURATE

Dt 25: 15 You must have a and honest
Pr 11: 1 but a weights are his delight.

ACCURSED (CURSE)

2Pe 2: 14 experts in greed—an a brood!

ACCUSATION (ACCUSE)

1Ti 5: 19 Do not entertain an a

ACCUSATIONS (ACCUSE)

2Pe 2: 11 do not bring slanderous a

ACCUSE (ACCUSATION ACCUSATIONS ACCUSER ACCUSES ACCUSING)

Pr 3: 30 Do not a a man for no reason—
Lk 3: 14 and don't a people falsely—

ACCUSER (ACCUSE)

Jn 5: 45 Your a is Moses, on whom your
Rev 12: 10 For the a of our brothers,

ACCUSES (ACCUSE)

Job 40: 2 Let him who a God answer him!"
Rev 12: 10 who a them before our God day

ACCUSING (ACCUSE)

Ro 2: 15 and their thoughts now a,

ACHAN*

Sin at Jericho caused defeat at Ai; stoned (Jos 7; 22:20; 1Ch 2:7).

ACHE*

Pr 14: 13 Even in laughter the heart may a,

ACHIEVE

Isa 55: 11 a the purpose for which I sent it.

ACHISH

King of Gath before whom David feigned insanity (1Sa 21:10-15). Later "ally" of David (2Sa 27-29).

ACKNOWLEDGE (ACKNOWLEDGED ACKNOWLEDGES)

Pr 3: 6 in all your ways a him,
Jer 3: 13 Only a your guilt—
Hos 6: 3 let us press on to a him.
Mt 10: 32 a him before my Father in heaven.
Lk 12: 8 a him before the angels of God.
1Jn 4: 3 spirit that does not a Jesus is not

ACKNOWLEDGED (ACKNOWLEDGE)

Lk 7: 29 a that God's way was right,

ACKNOWLEDGES* (ACKNOWLEDGE)

Ps 91: 14 for he a my name.
Mt 10: 32 "Whoever a me before men,
Lk 12: 8 whoever a me before men,
1Jn 2: 23 whoever a the Son has the Father
4: 2 Every spirit that a that Jesus Christ
4: 15 If anyone a that Jesus is the Son

ACQUIRES (ACQUIRING)

Pr 18: 15 of the discerning a knowledge;

ACQUIRING* (ACQUIRES)

Pr 1: 3 for a a disciplined and prudent life,

ACQUIT (ACQUITTING)

Ex 23: 7 to death, for I will not a the guilty.

ACQUITTING* (ACQUIT)

Dt 25: 1 a the innocent and condemning
Pr 17: 15 A the guilty and condemning

ACT (ACTION ACTIONS ACTIVE ACTIVITY ACTS)

Ps 119: 126 It is time for you to a, O LORD;

ACTION (ACT)

2Co 9: 2 has stirred most of them to a.
Jas 2: 17 if it is not accompanied by a,
1Pe 1: 13 minds for a; be self-controlled;

ACTIONS (ACT)

Mt 11: 19 wisdom is proved right by her a."
Gal 6: 4 Each one should test his own a.
Tit 1: 16 but by their a they deny him.

ACTIVE* (ACT)

Phm : 6 I pray that you may be a
Heb 4: 12 For the word of God is living and a

ACTIVITY (ACT)

Ecc 3: 1 a season for every a under heaven:
3: 17 for there will be a time for every a,

ACTS (ACT)

1Ch 16: 9 tell of all his wonderful a.
Ps 71: 16 proclaim your mighty a,
71: 24 tell of your righteous a
105: 2 tell of all his wonderful a.
106: 2 Who can proclaim the mighty a
145: 4 they will tell of your mighty a.
145: 12 all men may know of your mighty a
150: 2 Praise him for his a of power;
Isa 64: 6 all our righteous a are like filthy
Mt 6: 1 not to do your 'a of righteousness'

ADAM

1. First man (Ge 1:26-2:25; Ro 5:14; 1Ti 2:13). Sin of (Ge 3; Hos 6:7; Ro 5:12-21). Children of (Ge 4:1-5:5). Death of (Ge 5:5; Ro 5:12-21; 1Co 15:22).
2. City (Jos 3:16).

ADD (ADDED)

Dt 4: 2 Do not a to what I command you
12: 32 do not a to it or take away from it.
Pr 1: 5 let the wise listen and a
9: 9 he will a to his learning.
30: 6 Do not a to his words,
Mt 6: 27 by worrying can a a single hour
Lk 12: 25 by worrying can a a single hour
Rev 22: 18 God will a to him the plagues

ADDED (ADD)

Ecc 3: 14 nothing can be a to it and nothing
Ac 2: 47 Lord a to their number daily those
Ro 5: 20 The law was a so that the trespass
Gal 3: 19 It was a because of transgressions

ADDICTED*

Tit 2: 3 to be slanderers or a to much wine,

ADMINISTRATION*

1Co 12: 28 with gifts of a, and those speaking
Eph 3: 2 Surely you have heard about the a
3: 9 to everyone the a of this mystery,

ADMIRABLE*

Php 4: 8 whatever is lovely, whatever is a—

ADMIT

Hos 5: 15 until they a their guilt.

ADMONISH* (ADMONISHING)

Col 3: 16 and a one another with all wisdom,
1Th 5: 12 you in the Lord and who a you.

ADMONISHING* (ADMONISH)

Col 1: 28 a and teaching everyone

ADONIJAH

1. Son of David by Haggith (2Sa 3:4; 1Ch 3:2). Attempted to be king after David; killed by Solomon's order (1Ki 1-2).
2. Levite; teacher of the Law (2Ch 17:8).

ADOPTED (ADOPTION)

Eph 1: 5 In love he predestined us to be a

ADOPTION* (ADOPTED)

Ro 8: 23 as we wait eagerly for our a as sons,
9: 4 Theirs is the a as sons; theirs

ADORE*

SS 1: 4 How right they are to a you!

ADORNMENT* (ADORNS)

1Pe 3: 3 should not come from outward a,

ADORNS* (ADORNMENT)

Ps 93: 5 holiness a your house
Isa 61: 10 as a bride a herself with her jewels.
61: 10 bridegroom a his head like a priest,

ADULTERER (ADULTERY)

Lev 20: 10 both the a and the adulteress must
Heb 13: 4 for God will judge the a

ADULTERERS (ADULTERY)

1Co 6: 9 idolaters nor a nor male prostitutes
1Ti 1: 10 for murderers, for a and perverts,

ADULTERESS (ADULTERY)

Hos 3: 1 she is loved by another and is an a.

ADULTERIES (ADULTERY)

Jer 3: 8 sent her away because of all her a.

ADULTEROUS (ADULTERY)

Mk 8:38 in this *a* and sinful generation,
Jas 4: 4 You *a* people, don't you know that

ADULTERY (ADULTERER ADULTERERS ADULTERESS ADULTERIES ADULTEROUS)

Ex 20:14 "You shall not commit *a*.
Dt 5:18 "You shall not commit *a*.
Mt 5:27 that it was said, 'Do not commit *a*.'
5:28 lustfully has already committed *a*
5:32 the divorced woman commits *a*.
15:19 murder, *a*, sexual immorality, theft
19: 9 marries another woman commits *a*
19:18 do not commit *a*, do not steal,
Mk 7:21 theft, murder, *a*, greed, malice,
10:11 marries another woman commits *a*
10:12 another man, she commits *a*."
10:19 do not commit *a*, do not steal,
Lk 16:18 a divorced woman commits *a*.
16:18 marries another woman commits *a*
18:20 'Do not commit *a*, do not murder,
Jn 8: 4 woman was caught in the act of *a*.
Rev 18: 3 of the earth committed *a* with her,

ADULTS*

1Co 14:20 but in your thinking be *a*.

ADVANCE (ADVANCED)

Ps 18:29 With your help I can *a*
Php 1:12 has really served to *a* the gospel.

ADVANCED (ADVANCE)

Job 32: 7 *a* years should teach wisdom.'

ADVANTAGE

Ex 22:22 "Do not take *a* of a widow
Dt 24:14 Do not take *a* of a hired man who is
Ro 3: 1 What *a*, then, is there
2Co 11:20 or exploits you or takes *a* of you
1Th 4: 6 should wrong his brother or take *a*

ADVERSITY*

Pr 17:17 and a brother is born for *a*.
Isa 30:20 the Lord gives you the bread of *a*

ADVICE (ADVISERS)

1Ki 12: 8 rejected the *a* the elders
12:14 he followed the *a* of the young men
2Ch 10: 8 rejected the *a* the elders
Pr 12: 5 but the *a* of the wicked is deceitful.
12:15 but a wise man listens to *a*.
19:20 Listen to *a* and accept instruction,
20:18 Make plans by seeking *a*;

ADVISERS (ADVICE)

Pr 11:14 but many *a* make victory sure.

ADVOCATE*

Job 16:19 my *a* is on high.

AFFLICTED (AFFLICTION)

Job 2: 7 and *a* Job with painful sores
36: 6 but gives the *a* their rights.
Ps 9:12 he does not ignore the cry of the *a*.
9:18 nor the hope of the *a* ever perish.
119: 67 Before I was *a* I went astray,
119: 71 It was good for me to be *a*
119: 75 and in faithfulness you have *a* me.
Isa 49:13 will have compassion on his *a* ones.
53: 4 smitten by him, and *a*.
53: 7 He was oppressed and *a*,
Na 1:12 Although I have *a* you, ⌊O Judah,⌋

AFFLICTION (AFFLICTED AFFLICTIONS)

Dt 16: 3 bread of *a*, because you left Egypt
Ps 107: 41 he lifted the needy out of their *a*
Isa 30:20 of adversity and the water of *a*,
48:10 in the furnace of *a*.
La 3:33 For he does not willingly bring *a*
Ro 12:12 patient in *a*, faithful in prayer.

AFFLICTIONS (AFFLICTION)

Col 1:24 lacking in regard to Christ's *a*,

AFRAID (FEAR)

Ge 3:10 and I was *a* because I was naked;
26:24 Do not be *a*, for I am with you;
Ex 2:14 Then Moses was *a* and thought,
3: 6 because he was *a* to look at God.
Dt 1:21 Do not be *a*; do not be discouraged
1:29 "Do not be terrified; do not be *a*
20: 1 do not be *a* of them,
20: 3 Do not be fainthearted or *a*;
2Ki 25:24 "Do not be *a* of the Babylonian
1Ch 13:12 David was *a* of God that day
Ps 27: 1 of whom shall I be *a*?
56: 3 When I am *a*, / I will trust in you.
56: 4 in God I trust; I will not be *a*.
Pr 3:24 lie down, you will not be *a*;
Isa 10:24 do not be *a* of the Assyrians,
12: 2 I will trust and not be *a*.
44: 8 Do not tremble, do not be *a*.
Jer 1: 8 Do not be *a* of them, for I am
Mt 8:26 You of little faith, why are you so *a*
10:28 be *a* of the One who can destroy
10:31 So don't be *a*; you are worth more
Mk 5:36 "Don't be *a*; just believe."
Lk 9:34 and they were *a* as they entered
Jn 14:27 hearts be troubled and do not be *a*.
Ac 27:24 beside me and said, 'Do not be *a*,
Ro 11:20 Do not be arrogant, but be *a*.
Heb 13: 6 Lord is my helper; I will not be *a*.

AGAG (AGAGITE)

King of Amalekites not killed by Saul (1Sa 15).

AGAGITE (AGAG)

Est 8: 3 to the evil plan of Haman the *A*,

AGED (AGES)

Job 12:12 Is not wisdom found among the *a*?
Pr 17: 6 children are a crown to the *a*,

AGES (AGED)

Ro 16:25 the mystery hidden for long *a* past,
Eph 2: 7 that in the coming *a* he might show
3: 9 which for *a* past was kept hidden
Col 1:26 that has been kept hidden for *a*
Rev 15: 3 King of the *a*.

AGONY

Lk 16:24 because I am in *a* in this fire.'
Rev 16:10 Men gnawed their tongues in *a*

AGREE (AGREEMENT AGREES)

Mt 18:19 on earth *a* about anything you ask
Ro 7:16 want to do, I *a* that the law is good.
Php 4: 2 with Syntyche to *a* with each other

AGREEMENT (AGREE)

2Co 6:16 What *a* is there between the temple

AGREES* (AGREE)

Ac 7:42 This *a* with what is written
24:14 I believe everything that *a*
1Co 4:17 which *a* with what I teach

AGRIPPA*

Descendant of Herod; king before whom Paul pled his case in Caesarea (Ac 25:13-26:32).

AHAB

1. Son of Omri; king of Israel (1Ki 16:28-22:40), husband of Jezebel (1Ki 16:31). Promoted Baal worship (1Ki 16:31-33); opposed by Elijah (1Ki 17:1; 18; 21), a prophet (1Ki 20:35-43), Micaiah (1Ki 22:1-28). Defeated Ben-Hadad (1Ki 20). Killed for failing to kill Ben-Hadad and for murder of Naboth (1Ki 20:35-21:40).

2. A false prophet (Jer 29:21-22).

AHAZ

1. Son of Jotham; king of Judah, (2Ki 16; 2Ch 28). Idolatry of (2Ki 16:3-4, 10-18; 2Ch 28:1-4, 22-25). Defeated by Aram and Israel (2Ki 16:5-6; 2Ch 28:5-15). Sought help from Assyria rather than the LORD (2Ki 16:7-9; 2Ch 28:16-21; Isa 7).

2. Benjamite, descendant of Saul (1Ch 8:35-36).

AHAZIAH

1. Son of Ahab; king of Israel (1Ki 22:51-2Ki 1:18; 2Ch 20:35-37). Made an unsuccessful alliance with Jehoshaphat of Judah (2Ch 20:35-37). Died for seeking Baal rather than the LORD (1Ki 1).

2. Son of Jehoram; king of Judah (2Ki 8:25-29; 9:14-29), also called Jehoahaz (2Ch 21:17-22:9; 25:23). Killed by Jehu while visiting Joram (2Ki 9:14-29; 2Ch 22:1-9).

AHIJAH

1Sa 14:18 Saul said to *A*, "Bring the ark
1Ki 14: 2 *A* the prophet is there—the one

AHIMELECH

1. Priest who helped David in his flight from Saul (1Sa 21-22).

2. One of David's warriors (1Sa 26:6).

AHITHOPHEL

One of David's counselors who sided with Absalom (2Sa 15:12, 31-37; 1Ch 27:33-34); committed suicide when his advice was ignored (2Sa 16:15-17:23).

AI

Jos 7: 4 they were routed by the men of *A*,
8:28 So Joshua burned *A* and made it

AID

Isa 38:14 troubled; O Lord, come to my *a*!"
Php 4:16 you sent me *a* again and again

AIM

1Co 7:34 Her *a* is to be devoted to the Lord
2Co 13:11 *A* for perfection, listen

AIR

Mt 8:20 and birds of the *a* have nests,
Lk 9:58 and birds of the *a* have nests,
1Co 9:26 not fight like a man beating the *a*.
14: 9 You will just be speaking into the *a*
Eph 2: 2 of the ruler of the kingdom of the *a*,
1Th 4:17 clouds to meet the Lord in the *a*.

ALABASTER*

Mt 26: 7 came to him with an *a* jar
Mk 14: 3 a woman came with an *a* jar
Lk 7:37 she brought an *a* jar of perfume,

ALARM (ALARMED)

2Co 7:11 indignation, what *a*, what longing,

ALARMED (ALARM)

Mk 13: 7 and rumors of wars, do not be *a*.
2Th 2: 2 not to become easily unsettled or *a*

ALERT*

Jos 8: 4 All of you be on the *a*.
Ps 17:11 with eyes *a*, to throw me
Isa 21: 7 let him be *a*, / fully *a*."
Mk 13:33 Be *a*! You do not know
Eph 6:18 be *a* and always keep on praying
1Th 5: 6 but let us be *a* and self-controlled.
1Pe 5: 8 Be self-controlled and *a*.

ALIEN (ALIENATED ALIENS)

Ex 22:21 "Do not mistreat an *a*
Lev 24:22 are to have the same law for the *a*
Ps 146: 9 The LORD watches over the *a*

ALIENATED (ALIEN)

Gal 5: 4 by law have been *a* from Christ;
Col 1:21 Once you were *a* from God

ALIENS (ALIEN)

Ex 23: 9 know how it feels to be *a*,
1Pe 2:11 as *a* and strangers in the world,

ALIVE (LIVE)

1Sa 2: 6 LORD brings death and makes *a*;
Lk 24:23 vision of angels, who said he was *a*.
Ac 1: 3 convincing proofs that he was *a*.
Ro 6:11 but *a* to God in Christ Jesus.
1Co 15:22 so in Christ all will be made *a*.
Eph 2: 5 made us *a* with Christ

ALMIGHTY (MIGHT)

Ge 17: 1 "I am God *A*; walk before me
Ex 6: 3 to Isaac and to Jacob as God *A*,
Ru 1:20 the *A* has made my life very bitter.
Job 11: 7 Can you probe the limits of the *A*?
33: 4 the breath of the *A* gives me life.
Ps 89: 8 O LORD God *A*, who is like you?
91: 1 will rest in the shadow of the *A*.
Isa 6: 3 "Holy, holy, holy is the LORD *A*;
45:13 says the LORD *A*."
47: 4 the LORD *A* is his name—
48: 2 the LORD *A* is his name:
51:15 the LORD *A* is his name.
54: 5 the LORD *A* is his name—
Am 5:14 the LORD God *A* will be with you,
5:15 the LORD God *A* will have mercy
Rev 4: 8 holy is the Lord God *A*, who was,
19: 6 For our Lord God *A* reigns.

ALMS see GIVING, (acts of) RIGHTEOUSNESS

ALPHA*

Rev 1: 8 "I am the *A* and the Omega,"
21: 6 I am the *A* and the Omega,

Rev 22:13 I am the *A* and the Omega,

ALTAR

Ge 8:20 Then Noah built an *a* to the LORD
12: 7 So he built an *a* there to the LORD
13:18 where he built an *a* to the LORD.
22: 9 Abraham built an *a* there
22: 9 his son Isaac and laid him on the *a*,
26:25 Isaac built an *a* there and called
35: 1 and build an *a* there to God,
Ex 17:15 Moses built an *a* and called it
27: 1 "Build an *a* of acacia wood,
30: 1 "Make an *a* of acacia wood
37:25 They made the *a* of incense out
Dt 27: 5 an *a* to the LORD your God, an *a*
Jos 8:30 on Mount Ebal an *a* to the LORD,
22:10 built an imposing *a* there
Jdg 6:24 So Gideon built an *a* to the LORD
21: 4 the next day the people built an *a*
1Sa 7:17 he built an *a* there to the LORD.
14:35 Then Saul built an *a* to the LORD;
2Sa 24:25 David built an *a* to the LORD
1Ki 12:33 sacrifices on the *a* he had built
13: 2 "O *a*, *a*! This is what the LORD
16:32 He set up an *a* for Baal
18:30 and he repaired the *a* of the LORD
2Ki 16:11 So Uriah the priest built an *a*
1Ch 21:26 David built an *a* to the LORD
2Ch 4: 1 made a bronze *a* twenty cubits
4:19 the golden *a*; the tables
15: 8 He repaired the *a* of the LORD
32:12 'You must worship before one *a*
33:16 he restored the *a* of the LORD
Ezr 3: 2 to build the *a* of the God of Israel
Isa 6: 6 taken with tongs from the *a*.
Eze 40:47 the *a* was in front of the temple.
Mt 5:23 if you are offering your gift at the *a*
Ac 17:23 found an *a* with this inscription:
Heb 13:10 We have an *a* from which those
Rev 6: 9 I saw under the *a* the souls

ALTER*

Ps 89:34 or *a* what my lips have uttered.

ALWAYS

Dt 15:11 There will *a* be poor people
Ps 16: 8 I have set the LORD *a* before me.
51: 3 and my sin is *a* before me.
Pr 23: 7 who is *a* thinking about the cost.
Mt 26:11 The poor you will *a* have with you,
28:20 And surely I am with you *a*,
Mk 14: 7 The poor you will *a* have with you,
Jn 12: 8 You will *a* have the poor
1Co 13: 7 *a* protects, *a* trusts, *a* hopes, *a*
Php 4: 4 Rejoice in the Lord *a*.
1Pe 3:15 *A* be prepared to give an answer

AMALEKITES

Ex 17: 8 *A* came and attacked the Israelites
1Sa 15: 2 'I will punish the *A*

AMASA

Nephew of David (1Ch 2:17). Commander of Absalom's forces (2Sa 17:24-27). Returned to David (2Sa 19:13). Killed by Joab (2Sa 20:4-13).

AMASSES*

Pr 28: 8 *a* it for another, who will be kind

AMAZED

Mt 7:28 the crowds were *a* at his teaching,
Mk 6: 6 And he was *a* at their lack of faith.
10:24 The disciples were *a* at his words.
Ac 2: 7 Utterly *a*, they asked: "Are not all
13:12 for he was *a* at the teaching about

AMAZIAH

1. Son of Joash; king of Judah (2Ki 14; 2Ch 25). Defeated Edom (2Ki 14:7; 2Ch 25:5-13); defeated by Israel for worshiping Edom's gods (2Ki 14:8-14; 2Ch 25:14-24).

2. Idolatrous priest who opposed Amos (Am 7:10-17).

AMBASSADOR* (AMBASSADORS)

Eph 6:20 for which I am an *a* in chains.

AMBASSADORS (AMBASSADOR)

2Co 5:20 We are therefore Christ's *a*,

AMBITION*

Ro 15:20 It has always been my *a*
Gal 5:20 fits of rage, selfish *a*, dissensions,
Php 1:17 preach Christ out of selfish *a*,
2: 3 Do nothing out of selfish *a*
1Th 4:11 Make it your *a* to lead a quiet life,
Jas 3:14 and selfish *a* in your hearts,
3:16 where you have envy and selfish *a*,

AMENDS

Pr 14: 9 Fools mock at making *a* for sin,

AMNON

Firstborn of David (2Sa 3:2; 1Ch 3:1). Killed by Absalom for raping his sister Tamar (2Sa 13).

AMON

1. Son of Manasseh; king of Judah (2Ki 21:18-26; 1Ch 3:14; 2Ch 33:21-25).

2. Ruler of Samaria under Ahab (1Ki 22:26; 2Ch 18:25).

AMOS

1. Prophet from Tekoa (Am 1:1; 7:10-17).

2. Ancestor of Jesus (Lk 3:25).

ANAK (ANAKITES)

Nu 13:28 even saw descendants of *A* there.

ANAKITES (ANAK)

Dt 1:28 We even saw the *A* there.' "
2:10 and numerous, and as tall as the *A*.
9: 2 "Who can stand up against the *A*?"

ANANIAS

1. Husband of Sapphira; died for lying to God (Ac 5:1-11).

2. Disciple who baptized Saul (Ac 9:10-19).

3. High priest at Paul's arrest (Ac 22:30-24:1).

ANCESTORS (ANCESTRY)

1Ki 19: 4 I am no better than my *a*."

ANCESTRY (ANCESTORS)

Ro 9: 5 from them is traced the human *a*

ANCHOR

Heb 6:19 We have this hope as an *a*

ANCIENT

Da 7: 9 and the *A* of Days took his seat.
7:13 He approached the *A* of Days
7:22 until the *A* of Days came

ANDREW*

Apostle; brother of Simon Peter (Mt 4:18; 10:2; Mk 1:16-18, 29; 3:18; 13:3; Lk 6:14; Jn 1:35-44; 6:8-9; 12:22; Ac 1:13).

ANGEL (ANGELS ARCHANGEL)

Ge 16: 7 The *a* of the LORD found Hagar
22:11 But the *a* of the LORD called out
Ex 23:20 I am sending an *a* ahead of you
Nu 22:23 When the donkey saw the *a*
Jdg 2: 1 The *a* of the LORD went up
6:22 Gideon realized that it was the *a*
13:15 Manoah said to the *a* of the LORD
2Sa 24:16 The *a* of the LORD was then
1Ki 19: 7 The *a* of the LORD came back
2Ki 19:35 That night the *a* of the LORD went
Ps 34: 7 The *a* of the LORD encamps
Hos 12: 4 He struggled with the *a*
Mt 2:13 an *a* of the Lord appeared
28: 2 for an *a* of the Lord came
Lk 1:26 God sent the *a* Gabriel
2: 9 An *a* of the Lord appeared to them,
22:43 An *a* from heaven appeared to him
Ac 6:15 his face was like the face of an *a*.
12: 7 Suddenly an *a* of the Lord
2Co 11:14 Satan himself masquerades as an *a*
Gal 1: 8 or an *a* from heaven should preach

ANGELS (ANGEL)

Ps 91:11 command his *a* concerning you
Mt 4: 6 command his *a* concerning you,
13:39 of the age, and the harvesters are *a*.
13:49 The *a* will come and separate
18:10 For I tell you that their *a*
25:41 prepared for the devil and his *a*.
Lk 4:10 command his *a* concerning you
20:36 for they are like the *a*.
1Co 6: 3 you not know that we will judge *a*?
13: 1 in the tongues of men and of *a*,
Col 2:18 and the worship of *a* disqualify you
Heb 1: 4 as much superior to the *a*
1: 6 "Let all God's *a* worship him."
1: 7 "He makes his *a* winds,
1:14 Are not all *a* ministering spirits
2: 7 made him a little lower than the *a*;
2: 9 was made a little lower than the *a*,
Heb 13: 2 some people have entertained *a*
1Pe 1:12 Even *a* long to look
2Pe 2: 4 For if God did not spare *a*
Jude : 6 *a* who did not keep their positions

ANGER (ANGERED ANGRY)

Ex 15: 7 You unleashed your burning *a*;
22:24 My *a* will be aroused, and I will kill
32:10 alone so that my *a* may burn
32:11 "why should your *a* burn
32:12 Turn from your fierce *a*; relent
32:19 his *a* burned and he threw
34: 6 slow to *a*, abounding in love
Lev 26:28 then in my *a* I will be hostile
Nu 14:18 slow to *a*, abounding in love
25:11 has turned my *a* away
32:10 LORD's *a* was aroused that day
32:13 The LORD's *a* burned
Dt 9:19 I feared the *a* and wrath
29:28 In furious *a* and in great wrath
Jdg 14:19 Burning with *a*, he went up
2Sa 12: 5 David burned with *a*
2Ki 22:13 Great is the LORD's *a* that burns
Ne 9:17 slow to *a* and abounding in love.
Ps 30: 5 For his *a* lasts only a moment,
78:38 Time after time he restrained his *a*
86:15 slow to *a*, abounding in love
90: 7 We are consumed by your *a*
103: 8 slow to *a*, abounding in love.
Pr 15: 1 but a harsh word stirs up *a*.
29:11 A fool gives full vent to his *a*,
30:33 so stirring up *a* produces strife."
Jnh 4: 2 slow to *a* and abounding in love,
Eph 4:26 "In your *a* do not sin": Do not let
Jas 1:20 for man's *a* does not bring about

ANGERED (ANGER)

Pr 22:24 do not associate with one easily *a*,
1Co 13: 5 it is not easily *a*, it keeps no record

ANGRY (ANGER)

Ps 2:12 Kiss the Son, lest he be *a*
95:10 For forty years I was *a*
Pr 29:22 An *a* man stirs up dissension,
Mt 5:22 But I tell you that anyone who is *a*
Jas 1:19 slow to speak and slow to become *a*

ANGUISH

Ps 118: 5 In my *a* I cried to the LORD,
Jer 4:19 Oh, my *a*, my *a*!
Zep 1:15 a day of distress and *a*,
Lk 21:25 nations will be in *a* and perplexity
22:44 in *a*, he prayed more earnestly,
Ro 9: 2 and unceasing *a* in my heart.

ANIMALS

Ge 1:24 wild *a*, each according to its kind."
7:16 The *a* going in were male
Dt 14: 4 These are the *a* you may eat: the ox
Job 12: 7 ask the *a*, and they will teach you,
Isa 43:20 The wild *a* honor me,

ANNOUNCE (ANNOUNCED)

Mt 6: 2 give to the needy, do not *a* it

ANNOUNCED (ANNOUNCE)

Isa 48: 5 before they happened I *a* them
Gal 3: 8 and *a* the gospel in advance

ANNOYANCE*

Pr 12:16 A fool shows his *a* at once,

ANNUAL*

Ex 30:10 This *a* atonement must be made
Jdg 21:19 there is the *a* festival of the LORD
1Sa 1:21 family to offer the *a* sacrifice
2:19 husband to offer the *a* sacrifice.
20: 6 an *a* sacrifice is being made there
2Ch 8:13 New Moons and the three *a* feasts
Heb 10: 3 those sacrifices are an *a* reminder

ANOINT (ANOINTED ANOINTING)

Ex 30:26 use it to *a* the Tent of Meeting,
30:30 "*A* Aaron and his sons
1Sa 9:16 *A* him leader over my people Israel
15: 1 to *a* you king over his people Israel;
2Ki 9: 3 what the LORD says: I *a* you king
Ps 23: 5 You *a* my head with oil;
Da 9:24 prophecy and to *a* the most holy.
Jas 5:14 and *a* him with oil in the name

ANOINTED (ANOINT)

1Ch 16:22 "Do not touch my *a* ones;
Ps 105:15 "Do not touch my *a* ones;
Isa 61: 1 because the LORD has *a* me

Da 9:26 the A One will be cut off
Lk 4:18 because he has a me
Ac 10:38 how God a Jesus of Nazareth

ANOINTING (ANOINT)
Lev 8:12 some of the a oil on Aaron's head
1Ch 29:22 a him before the LORD to be ruler
Ps 45:7 by a you with the oil of joy.
Heb 1:9 by a you with the oil of joy."
1Jn 2:20 you have an a from the Holy One,
2:27 about all things and as that a is real,

ANT* (ANTS)
Pr 6:6 Go to the a, you sluggard;

ANTICHRIST* (ANTICHRISTS)
1Jn 2:18 have heard that the a is coming,
2:22 a man is the a—he denies
4:3 of the a, which you have heard is
2Jn :7 person is the deceiver and the a.

ANTICHRISTS* (ANTICHRIST)
1Jn 2:18 even now many a have come.

ANTIOCH
Ac 11:26 were called Christians first at A.

ANTS* (ANT)
Pr 30:25 A are creatures of little strength,

ANXIETIES* (ANXIOUS)
Lk 21:34 drunkenness and the a of life,

ANXIETY (ANXIOUS)
1Pe 5:7 Cast all your a on him

ANXIOUS (ANXIETIES ANXIETY)
Pr 12:25 An a heart weighs a man down,
Php 4:6 Do not be a about anything,

APOLLOS*
Christian from Alexandria, learned in the Scriptures; instructed by Aquila and Priscilla (Ac 18:24-28). Ministered with Paul at Corinth (Ac 19:1; 1Co 1:12; 3; Tit 3:13).

APOLLYON*
Rev 9:11 is Abaddon, and in Greek, A.

APOSTLE (APOSTLES APOSTLES')
Ro 11:13 as I am the a to the Gentiles,
1Co 9:1 Am I not an a? Have I not seen
2Co 12:12 The things that mark an a—signs,
Gal 2:8 of Peter as an a to the Jews,
1Ti 2:7 was appointed a herald and an a—
2Ti 1:11 I was appointed a herald and an a
Heb 3:1 a and high priest whom we confess.

APOSTLES (APOSTLE)
See also Andrew, Bartholomew, James, John, Judas, Matthew, Matthias, Nathanael, Paul, Peter, Philip, Simon, Thaddaeus, Thomas.
Mk 3:14 twelve—designating them a—
Lk 11:49 'I will send them prophets and a,
Ac 1:26 so he was added to the eleven a.
2:43 signs were done by the a.
1Co 12:28 God has appointed first of all a,
15:9 For I am the least of the a
2Co 11:13 masquerading as a of Christ.
Eph 2:20 built on the foundation of the a
4:11 It was he who gave some to be a,
Rev 21:14 names of the twelve a of the Lamb.

APOSTLES' (APOSTLE)
Ac 5:2 the rest and put it at the a' feet.
8:18 at the laying on of the a' hands,

APPEAL
Ac 25:11 I a to Caesar!" After Festus had
Phm :9 yet I a to you on the basis of love.

APPEAR (APPEARANCE APPEARANCES APPEARED APPEARING APPEARS)
Ge 1:9 to one place, and let dry ground a."
Lev 16:2 I a in the cloud over the atonement
Mt 24:30 of the Son of Man will a in the sky,
Mk 13:22 false prophets will a and perform
Lk 19:11 of God was going to a at once.
2Co 5:10 we must all a before the judgment
Col 3:4 also will a with him in glory.
Heb 9:24 now to a for us in God's presence.
9:28 and he will a a second time,

APPEARANCE (APPEAR)
1Sa 16:7 Man looks at the outward a,
Isa 52:14 his a was so disfigured beyond that
53:2 in his a that we should desire him.
Gal 2:6 God does not judge by external a—

APPEARANCES* (APPEAR)
Jn 7:24 Stop judging by mere a,

APPEARED (APPEAR)
Nu 14:10 glory of the LORD a at the Tent
Mt 1:20 an angel of the Lord a to him
Lk 2:9 An angel of the Lord a to them,
1Co 15:5 and that he a to Peter,
Heb 9:26 now he has a once for all at the end

APPEARING (APPEAR)
1Ti 6:14 until the a of our Lord Jesus Christ,
2Ti 1:10 through the a of our Savior,
4:8 to all who have longed for his a.
Tit 2:13 the glorious a of our great God

APPEARS (APPEAR)
Mal 3:2 Who can stand when he a?
Col 3:4 When Christ, who is your life, a,
1Pe 5:4 And when the Chief Shepherd a,
1Jn 3:2 But we know that when he a,

APPETITE
Pr 16:26 The laborer's a works for him;
Ecc 6:7 yet his a is never satisfied.
Jer 50:19 his a will be satisfied

APPLES
Pr 25:11 is like a of gold in settings of silver.

APPLY (APPLYING)
Pr 22:17 a your heart to what I teach,
23:12 A your heart to instruction

APPLYING (APPLY)
Pr 2:2 and a your heart to understanding,

APPOINT (APPOINTED)
Ps 61:7 a your love and faithfulness
1Th 5:9 For God did not a us
Tit 1:5 and a elders in every town,

APPOINTED (APPOINT)
Dt 1:15 a them to have authority over you
Pr 8:23 I was a from eternity,
Da 11:27 an end will still come at the a time.
Hab 2:3 For the revelation awaits an a time;
Jn 15:16 Chose you and a you to go
Ro 9:9 "At the a time I will return,

APPROACH (APPROACHING)
Ex 24:2 but Moses alone is to a the LORD;
Eph 3:12 in him we may a God with freedom
Heb 4:16 Let us then a the throne of grace

APPROACHING (APPROACH)
Heb 10:25 all the more as you see the Day a.
1Jn 5:14 is the confidence we have in a God:

APPROPRIATE
1Ti 2:10 a for women who profess

APPROVAL (APPROVE)
Jdg 18:6 Your journey has the LORD's a."
Jn 6:27 the Father has placed his seal of a."
1Co 11:19 to show which of you have God's a
Gal 1:10 trying to win the a of men,

APPROVE (APPROVAL APPROVED APPROVES)
Ro 2:18 if you know his will and a
12:2 and a what God's will is—

APPROVED* (APPROVE)
Ro 14:18 pleasing to God and a by men.
16:10 Greet Apelles, tested and a
2Co 10:18 who commends himself who is a,
1Th 2:4 as men a by God to be entrusted
2Ti 2:15 to present yourself to God as one a,

APPROVES* (APPROVE)
Ro 14:22 not condemn himself by what he a.

APT*
Pr 15:23 A man finds joy in giving an a reply

AQUILA*
Husband of Priscilla; co-worker with Paul, instructor of Apollos (Ac 18; Ro 16:3; 1Co 16:19; 2Ti 4:19).

ARABIA
Gal 1:17 but I went immediately into A
4:25 Hagar stands for Mount Sinai in A

ARARAT
Ge 8:4 came to rest on the mountains of A.

ARAUNAH
2Sa 24:16 threshing floor of A the Jebusite.

ARBITER* (ARBITRATE)
Lk 12:14 who appointed me a judge or an a

ARBITRATE* (ARBITER)
Job 9:33 If only there were someone to a

ARCHANGEL* (ANGEL)
1Th 4:16 with the voice of the a
Jude :9 a Michael, when he was disputing

ARCHER
Pr 26:10 Like an a who wounds at random

ARCHIPPUS*
Col 4:17 Tell A: "See to it that you complete
Phm :2 to A our fellow soldier

ARCHITECT*
Heb 11:10 whose a and builder is God.

AREOPAGUS*
Ac 17:19 brought him to a meeting of the A,
17:22 up in the meeting of the A
17:34 of the A, also a woman named

ARGUE (ARGUMENT ARGUMENTS)
Job 13:3 and to a my case with God.
13:8 Will you a the case for God?
Pr 25:9 If you a your case with a neighbor,

ARGUMENT (ARGUE)
Heb 6:16 is said and puts an end to all a.

ARGUMENTS (ARGUE)
Isa 41:21 "Set forth your a," says Jacob's
Col 2:4 you by fine-sounding a.
2Ti 2:23 to do with foolish and stupid a,
Tit 3:9 and a and quarrels about the law,

ARK
Ge 6:14 So make yourself an a
Ex 25:21 and put in the a the Testimony,
Dt 10:5 put the tablets in the a I had made,
1Sa 4:11 The a of God was captured,
7:2 that the a remained at Kiriath
2Sa 6:17 They brought the a of the LORD
1Ki 8:9 There was nothing in the a
1Ch 13:9 out his hand to steady the a,
2Ch 35:3 "Put the sacred a in the temple that
Heb 9:4 This a contained the gold jar
11:7 in holy fear built an a
Rev 11:19 within his temple was seen the a

ARM (ARMY)
Nu 11:23 "Is the LORD's a too short?
Dt 4:34 hand and an outstretched a,
7:19 mighty hand and outstretched a,
Ps 44:3 it was your right hand, your a,
98:1 his right hand and his holy a
Jer 27:5 outstretched a I made the earth
1Pe 4:1 a yourselves also with the same

ARMAGEDDON*
Rev 16:16 that in Hebrew is called A.

ARMIES (ARMY)
1Sa 17:26 Philistine that he should defy the a
Rev 19:14 a of heaven were following him,

ARMOR (ARMY)
1Ki 20:11 on his a should not boast like one
Jer 46:4 put on your a!
Ro 13:12 deeds of darkness and put on the a
Eph 6:11 Put on the full a of God
6:13 Therefore put on the full a of God,

ARMS (ARMY)
Dt 33:27 underneath are the everlasting a.
Ps 18:32 It is God who a me with strength
Pr 31:17 her a are strong for her tasks.
31:20 She opens her a to the poor
Isa 40:11 He gathers the lambs in his a
Mk 10:16 And he took the children in his a,
Heb 12:12 strengthen your feeble a

ARMY (ARM ARMIES ARMOR ARMS)
Ps 33:16 No king is saved by the size of his *a*
Joel 2: 2 a large and mighty *a* comes,
2: 5 like a mighty *a* drawn up for battle.
2:11 thunders at the head of his *a;*
Rev 19:19 the rider on the horse and his *a.*

AROMA
Ge 8:21 The LORD smelled the pleasing *a*
Ex 29:18 a pleasing *a,* an offering made
Lev 3:16 made by fire, a pleasing *a.*
2Co 2:15 For we are to God the *a* of Christ

AROUSE (AROUSED)
Ro 11:14 I may somehow *a* my own people

AROUSED (AROUSE)
Ps 78:58 they *a* his jealousy with their idols.

ARRANGED
1Co 12:18 But in fact God has *a* the parts

ARRAYED*
Ps 110: 3 *A* in holy majesty,
Isa 61:10 and *a* me in a robe of righteousness

ARREST
Mt 10:19 But when they *a* you, do not worry

ARROGANCE (ARROGANT)
1Sa 2: 3 or let your mouth speak such *a,*
Pr 8:13 I hate pride and *a,*
Mk 7:22 lewdness, envy, slander, *a* and folly
2Co 12:20 slander, gossip, *a* and disorder.

ARROGANT (ARROGANCE)
Ps 5: 5 The *a* cannot stand
119: 78 May the *a* be put to shame
Pr 17: 7 *A* lips are unsuited to a fool—
21:24 *a* man—"Mocker" is his name;
Ro 1:30 God-haters, insolent, *a*
11:20 Do not be *a,* but be afraid.
1Ti 6:17 in this present world not to be *a*

ARROW (ARROWS)
Ps 91: 5 nor the *a* that flies by day,
Pr 25:18 Like a club or a sword or a sharp *a*

ARROWS (ARROW)
Ps 64: 3 and aim their words like deadly *a.*
64: 7 But God will shoot them with *a;*
127: 4 Like *a* in the hands of a warrior
Pr 26:18 firebrands or deadly *a*
Eph 6:16 you can extinguish all the flaming *a*

ARTAXERXES
King of Persia; allowed rebuilding of temple under Ezra (Ezr 4; 7), and of walls of Jerusalem under his cupbearer Nehemiah (Ne 2; 5:14; 13:6).

ARTEMIS
Ac 19:28 "Great is *A* of the Ephesians!"

ASA
King of Judah (1Ki 15:8-24; 1Ch 3:10; 2Ch 14-16). Godly reformer (2Ch 15); in later years defeated Israel with help of Aram, not the LORD (1Ki 15:16-22; 2Ch 16).

ASAHEL
1. Nephew of David, one of his warriors (2Sa 23:24; 1Ch 2:16; 11:26; 27:7). Killed by Abner (2Sa 2); avenged by Joab (2Sa 3:22-39).
2. Levite; teacher (2Ch 17:8).

ASAPH
1. Recorder to Hezekiah (2Ki 18:18, 37; Isa 36:3, 22).
2. Levitical musician (1Ch 6:39; 15:17-19; 16:4-7, 37). Sons of (1Ch 25; 2Ch 5:12; 20:14; 29:13; 35:15; Ezr 2:41; 3:10; Ne 7:44; 11:17; 12:27-47). Psalms of (2Ch 29:30; Ps 50; 73-83).

ASCEND* (ASCENDED ASCENDING)
Dt 30:12 "Who will *a* into heaven to get it
Ps 24: 3 Who may *a* the hill of the LORD?
Isa 14:13 "I will *a* to heaven;
14:14 I will *a* above the tops of the clouds
Jn 6:62 of Man *a* to where he was before!
Ac 2:34 For David did not *a* to heaven,
Ro 10: 6 'Who will *a* into heaven?' " (that is,

ASCENDED (ASCEND)
Ps 68:18 When you *a* on high,
Eph 4: 8 "When he *a* on high,

ASCENDING (ASCEND)
Ge 28:12 and the angels of God were *a*
Jn 1:51 and the angels of God *a*

ASCRIBE*
1Ch 16:28 *A* to the LORD, O families
16:28 *a* to the LORD glory and strength,
16:29 *a* to the LORD the glory due his
Job 36: 3 I will *a* justice to my Maker.
Ps 29: 1 *A* to the LORD, O mighty ones,
29: 1 *a* to the LORD glory and strength.
29: 2 *A* to the LORD the glory due his
96: 7 *A* to the LORD, O families
96: 7 *a* to the LORD glory and strength.
96: 8 *A* to the LORD the glory due his

ASHAMED (SHAME)
Mk 8:38 If anyone is *a* of me and my words
Lk 9:26 If anyone is *a* of me and my words,
Ro 1:16 I am not *a* of the gospel,
2Ti 1: 8 So do not be *a* to testify about our
2:15 who does not need to be *a*

ASHER
Son of Jacob by Zilpah (Ge 30:13; 35:26; 46:17; Ex 1:4; 1Ch 2:2). Tribe of blessed (Ge 49:20; Dt 33:24-25), numbered (Nu 1:40-41; 26:44-47), allotted land (Jos 10:24-31; Eze 48:2), failed to fully possess (Jdg 1:31-32), failed to support Deborah (Jdg 5:17), supported Gideon (Jdg 6:35; 7:23) and David (1Ch 12:36), 12,000 from (Rev 7:6).

ASHERAH (ASHERAHS)
Ex 34:13 and cut down their *A* poles.
1Ki 18:19 the four hundred prophets of *A,*

ASHERAHS* (ASHERAH)
Jdg 3: 7 and served the Baals and the *A.*

ASHES
Job 42: 6 and repent in dust and *a.*"
Mt 11:21 ago in sackcloth and *a.*

ASHTORETHS
Jdg 2:13 and served Baal and the *A.*
1Sa 7: 4 put away their Baals and *A,*

ASLEEP (SLEEP)
1Co 15:18 who have fallen *a* in Christ are lost.
1Th 4:13 be ignorant about those who fall *a,*

ASSEMBLY
Ps 1: 5 nor sinners in the *a* of the righteous
35:18 I will give you thanks in the great *a*
82: 1 God presides in the great *a;*
149: 1 his praise in the *a* of the saints.

ASSIGNED
1Ki 7:14 and did all the work *a* to him.
Mk 13:34 with his *a* task, and tells the one
1Co 3: 5 as the Lord has *a* to each his task.
7:17 place in life that the Lord *a* to him
2Co 10:13 to the field God has *a* to us,

ASSOCIATE
Pr 22:24 do not *a* with one easily angered,
Jn 4: 9 (For Jews do not *a* with Samaritans
Ac 10:28 law for a Jew to *a* with a Gentile
Ro 12:16 but be willing to *a* with people
1Co 5: 9 to *a* with sexually immoral people
5:11 am writing you that you must not *a*
2Th 3:14 Do not *a* with him,

ASSURANCE (ASSURED)
Heb 10:22 with a sincere heart in full *a* of faith

ASSURED (ASSURANCE)
Col 4:12 the will of God, mature and fully *a.*

ASTRAY
Ps 119: 67 Before I was afflicted I went *a,*
Pr 10:17 ignores correction leads others *a.*
20: 1 whoever is led *a* by them is not
Isa 53: 6 We all, like sheep, have gone *a,*
Jer 50: 6 their shepherds have led them *a*
Jn 16: 1 you so that you will not go *a.*
1Pe 2:25 For you were like sheep going *a,*
1Jn 3: 7 do not let anyone lead you *a.*

ASTROLOGERS
Isa 47:13 Let your *a* come forward,
Da 2: 2 *a* to tell him what he had dreamed.

ATE (EAT)
Ge 3: 6 wisdom, she took some and *a* it.
27:25 Jacob brought it to him and he *a;*
2Sa 9:11 Mephibosheth *a* at David's table
Ps 78:25 Men *a* the bread of angels;
Jer 15:16 When your words came, I *a* them;
Eze 3: 3 So I *a* it, and it tasted as sweet
Mt 14:20 They all *a* and were satisfied,
15:37 They all *a* and were satisfied.
Mk 6:42 They all *a* and were satisfied,
Lk 9:17 They all *a* and were satisfied,

ATHALIAH
Granddaughter of Omri; wife of Jehoram and mother of Ahaziah; encouraged their evil ways (2Ki 8:18, 27; 2Ch 22:2). At death of Ahaziah she made herself queen, killing all his sons but Joash (2Ki 11:1-3; 2Ch 22:10-12); killed six years later when Joash was revealed (2Ki 11:4-16; 2Ch 23:1-15).

ATHLETE*
2Ti 2: 5 if anyone competes as an *a,*

ATONE* (ATONEMENT)
Ex 30:15 to the LORD to *a* for your lives.
2Ch 29:24 for a sin offering to *a* for all Israel,
Da 9:24 an end to sin, to *a* for wickedness,

ATONED* (ATONEMENT)
Dt 21: 8 And the bloodshed will be *a* for.
1Sa 3:14 guilt of Eli's house will never be *a*
Pr 16: 6 faithfulness sin is *a* for;
Isa 6: 7 guilt is taken away and your sin *a*
22:14 your dying day this sin will not be *a*
27: 9 then, will Jacob's guilt be *a* for,

ATONEMENT (ATONE ATONED)
Ex 25:17 "Make an *a* cover of pure gold—
30:10 Once a year Aaron shall make *a*
Lev 17:11 it is the blood that makes *a*
23:27 this seventh month is the Day of *A.*
Nu 25:13 and made *a* for the Israelites."
Ro 3:25 presented him as a sacrifice of *a,*
Heb 2:17 that he might make *a* for the sins

ATTACK
Ps 109: 3 they *a* me without cause.

ATTAINED
Php 3:16 up to what we have already *a.*
Heb 7:11 If perfection could have been *a*

ATTENTION (ATTENTIVE)
Pr 4: 1 pay *a* and gain understanding.
4:20 My son, pay *a* to what I say;
5: 1 My son, pay *a* to my wisdom,
7:24 pay *a* to what I say.
22:17 Pay *a* and listen to the sayings
Ecc 7:21 Do not pay *a* to every word people
Isa 42:20 many things, but have paid no *a;*
Tit 1:14 and will pay no *a* to Jewish myths
Heb 2: 1 We must pay more careful *a,*

ATTENTIVE (ATTENTION)
Ne 1:11 let your ear be *a* to the prayer
1Pe 3:12 and his ears are *a* to their prayer,

ATTITUDE (ATTITUDES)
Eph 4:23 new in the *a* of your minds;
Php 2: 5 Your *a* should be the same
1Pe 4: 1 yourselves also with the same *a,*

ATTITUDES (ATTITUDE)
Heb 4:12 it judges the thoughts and *a*

ATTRACTIVE
Tit 2:10 teaching about God our Savior *a.*

AUDIENCE
Pr 29:26 Many seek an *a* with a ruler,

AUTHORITIES (AUTHORITY)
Ro 13: 1 *a* that exist have been established
13: 5 it is necessary to submit to the *a,*
13: 6 for the *a* are God's servants,
Eph 3:10 and *a* in the heavenly realms,
6:12 but against the rulers, against the *a,*
Col 1:16 thrones or powers or rulers or *a;*
2:15 having disarmed the powers and *a,*

Tit 3: 1 people to be subject to rulers and *a*,
1Pe 3:22 *a* and powers in submission to him.

AUTHORITY (AUTHORITIES)

Mt 7:29 because he taught as one who had *a*
9: 6 the Son of Man has *a* on earth
28:18 "All *a* in heaven and on earth has
Mk 1:22 he taught them as one who had *a*,
2:10 the Son of Man has *a* on earth
Lk 4:32 because his message had *a*.
5:24 the Son of Man has *a* on earth
Jn 10:18 *a* to lay it down and *a*
Ac 1: 7 the Father has set by his own *a*.
Ro 7: 1 that the law has *a* over a man only
13: 1 for there is no *a* except that which
13: 2 rebels against the *a* is rebelling
1Co 11:10 to have a sign of *a* on her head.
15:24 he has destroyed all dominion, *a*
1Ti 2: 2 for kings and all those in *a*,
2:12 to teach or to have *a* over a man;
Tit 2:15 Encourage and rebuke with all *a*.
Heb 13:17 your leaders and submit to their *a*.

AUTUMN*

Dt 11:14 both *a* and spring rains,
Ps 84: 6 the *a* rains also cover it with pools.
Jer 5:24 who gives *a* and spring rains
Joel 2:23 both *a* and spring rains, as before.
Jas 5: 7 and how patient he is for the *a*
Jude :12 blown along by the wind; *a* trees,

AVENGE (VENGEANCE)

Lev 26:25 sword upon you to *a* the breaking
Dt 32:35 It is mine to *a*; I will repay.
32:43 for he will *a* the blood
Ro 12:19 "It is mine to *a*; I will repay,"
Heb 10:30 "It is mine to *a*; I will repay,"
Rev 6:10 of the earth and *a* our blood?"

AVENGER (VENGEANCE)

Nu 35:27 the *a* of blood may kill the accused
Jos 20: 3 find protection from the *a* of blood.
Ps 8: 2 to silence the foe and the *a*.

AVENGES (VENGEANCE)

Ps 94: 1 O LORD, the God who *a*,

AVENGING (VENGEANCE)

1Sa 25:26 and from *a* yourself with your own
Na 1: 2 The LORD is a jealous and *a* God;

AVOID (AVOIDS)

Pr 4:15 *A* it, do not travel on it;
20: 3 It is to a man's honor to *a* strife,
20:19 so *a* a man who talks too much.
Ecc 7:18 who fears God will *a* all extremes.
1Th 4: 3 you should *a* sexual immorality;
5:22 *A* every kind of evil.
2Ti 2:16 *A* godless chatter, because those
Tit 3: 9 But *a* foolish controversies

AVOIDS* (AVOID)

Pr 16: 6 of the LORD a man *a* evil.
16:17 The highway of the upright *a* evil;

AWAITS (WAIT)

Pr 15:10 Stern discipline *a* him who leaves
28:22 and is unaware that poverty *a* him.

AWAKE (WAKE)

Ps 17:15 when I *a*, I will be satisfied
Pr 6:22 when you *a*, they will speak to you.

AWARD*

2Ti 4: 8 will *a* to me on that day—

AWARE

Ex 34:29 he was not *a* that his face was
Mt 24:50 and at an hour he is not *a* of.
Lk 12:46 and at an hour he is not *a* of.

AWE* (AWESOME OVERAWED)

1Sa 12:18 So all the people stood in *a*
1Ki 3:28 they held the king in *a*,
Job 25: 2 "Dominion and *a* belong to God;
Ps 119:120 I stand in *a* of your laws.
Ecc 5: 7 Therefore stand in *a* of God.
Isa 29:23 will stand in *a* of the God of Israel.
Jer 2:19 and have no *a* of me,"
33: 9 they will be in *a* and will tremble
Hab 3: 2 I stand in *a* of your deeds,
Mal 2: 5 and stood in *a* of my name.
Mt 9: 8 they were filled with *a*;
Lk 1:65 The neighbors were all filled with *a*
5:26 They were filled with *a* and said,
Lk 7:16 They were all filled with *a*
Ac 2:43 Everyone was filled with *a*,
Heb 12:28 acceptably with reverence and *a*,

AWESOME* (AWE)

Ge 28:17 and said, "How *a* is this place!
Ex 15:11 *a* in glory,
34:10 among will see how *a* is the work
Dt 4:34 or by great and *a* deeds,
7:21 is among you, is a great and *a* God.
10:17 the great God, mighty and *a*,
10:21 and *a* wonders you saw
28:58 revere this glorious and *a* name—
34:12 performed the *a* deeds that Moses
Jdg 13: 6 like an angel of God, very *a*.
2Sa 7:23 *a* wonders by driving out nations
1Ch 17:21 *a* wonders by driving out nations
Ne 1: 5 of heaven, the great and *a* God,
4:14 and *a*, and fight for your brothers,
9:32 the great, mighty and *a* God,
Job 10:16 again display your *a* power
37:22 God comes in *a* majesty.
Ps 45: 4 let your right hand display *a* deeds.
47: 2 How *a* is the LORD Most High,
65: 5 us with *a* deeds of righteousness,
66: 3 to God, "How *a* are your deeds!
66: 5 how *a* his works in man's behalf!
68:35 You are *a*, O God,
89: 7 he is more *a* than all who surround
99: 3 praise your great and *a* name—
106:22 and *a* deeds by the Red Sea.
111: 9 holy and *a* is his name.
145: 6 of the power of your *a* works,
Isa 64: 3 when you did *a* things that we did
Eze 1:18 Their rims were high and *a*,
1:22 expanse, sparkling like ice, and *a*.
Da 2:31 dazzling statue, *a* in appearance.
9: 4 "O Lord, the great and *a* God,
Zep 2:11 The LORD will be *a* to them

AX

Mt 3:10 The *a* is already at the root
Lk 3: 9 The *a* is already at the root

BAAL

Jdg 6:25 Tear down your father's altar to *B*
1Ki 16:32 *B* in the temple of *B* that he built
18:25 Elijah said to the prophets of *B*,
19:18 knees have not bowed down to *B*
2Ki 10:28 Jehu destroyed *B* worship in Israel.
Jer 19: 5 places of *B* to burn their sons
Ro 11: 4 have not bowed the knee to *B*."

BAASHA

King of Israel (1Ki 15:16-16:7; 2Ch 16:1-6).

BABBLER* (BABBLING)

Ac 17:18 "What is this *b* trying to say?"

BABBLING* (BABBLER)

Mt 6: 7 do not keep on *b* like pagans,

BABIES* (BABY)

Ge 25:22 The *b* jostled each other within her
Ex 2: 6 "This is one of the Hebrew *b*,"
Lk 18:15 also bringing *b* to Jesus
Ac 7:19 them to throw out their newborn *b*
1Pe 2: 2 Like newborn *b*, crave pure

BABY* (BABIES BABY'S)

Ex 2: 6 She opened it and saw the *b*.
2: 7 women to nurse the *b* for you?"
2: 9 So the woman took the *b*
2: 9 "Take this *b* and nurse him for me,
1Ki 3:17 I had a *b* while she was there
3:18 was born, this woman also had a *b*.
3:26 give her the living *b*! Don't kill him
3:27 Give the living *b* to the first woman
Isa 49:15 "Can a mother forget the *b*
Lk 1:41 the *b* leaped in her womb,
1:44 the *b* in my womb leaped for joy.
1:57 time for Elizabeth to have her *b*,
2: 6 the time came for the *b* to be born,
2:12 You will find a *b* wrapped in strips
2:16 the *b*, who was lying in the manger.
Jn 16:21 but when her *b* is born she forgets

BABY'S* (BABY)

Ex 2: 8 the girl went and got the *b* mother.

BABYLON

Ps 137: 1 By the rivers of *B* we sat and wept
Jer 29:10 seventy years are completed for *B*,
51:37 *B* will be a heap of ruins,
Rev 14: 8 "Fallen! Fallen is *B* the Great,
Rev 17: 5 MYSTERY *B* THE GREAT

BACKS

2Pe 2:21 and then to turn their *b*

BACKSLIDING* (BACKSLIDINGS)

Jer 2:19 your *b* will rebuke you.
3:22 I will cure you of *b*."
14: 7 For our *b* is great;
15: 6 "You keep on *b*.
Eze 37:23 them from all their sinful *b*,

BACKSLIDINGS* (BACKSLIDING)

Jer 5: 6 and their *b* many.

BALAAM

Prophet who attempted to curse Israel (Nu 22-24; Dt 23:4-5; 2Pe 2:15; Jude 11). Killed in Israel's vengeance on Midianites (Nu 31:8; Jos 13:22).

BALAK

Moabite king who hired Balaam to curse Israel (Nu 22-24; Jos 24:9).

BALDHEAD

2Ki 2:23 "Go on up, you *b*!" they said.

BALM

Jer 8:22 Is there no *b* in Gilead?

BANISH (BANISHED)

Jer 25:10 I will *b* from them the sounds of joy

BANISHED (BANISH)

Dt 30: 4 Even if you have been *b*

BANNER

Ex 17:15 and called it The LORD is my *B*.
SS 2: 4 and his *b* over me is love.
Isa 11:10 the Root of Jesse will stand as a *b*

BANQUET

SS 2: 4 He has taken me to the *b* hall,
Lk 14:13 when you give a *b*, invite the poor,

BAPTISM* (BAPTIZE)

Mt 21:25 John's *b*—where did it come from?
Mk 1: 4 and preaching a *b* of repentance
10:38 baptized with the *b* I am baptized
10:39 baptized with the *b* I am baptized
11:30 John's *b*—was it from heaven,
Lk 3: 3 preaching a *b* of repentance
12:50 But I have a *b* to undergo,
20: 4 John's *b*—was it from heaven,
Ac 1:22 beginning from John's *b*
10:37 after the *b* that John preached—
13:24 and *b* to all the people of Israel.
18:25 though he knew only the *b* of John.
19: 3 did you receive?" "John's *b*,"
19: 3 "Then what *b* did you receive?"
19: 4 "John's *b* was a *b* of repentance.
Ro 6: 4 with him through *b* into death
Eph 4: 5 one Lord, one faith, one *b*;
Col 2:12 having been buried with him in *b*
1Pe 3:21 this water symbolizes *b* that now

BAPTISMS* (BAPTIZE)

Heb 6: 2 instruction about *b*, the laying

BAPTIZE* (BAPTISM BAPTISMS BAPTIZED BAPTIZING)

Mt 3:11 He will *b* you with the Holy Spirit
3:11 "I *b* you with water for repentance.
Mk 1: 8 I *b* you with water, but he will
1: 8 he will *b* you with the Holy Spirit."
Lk 3:16 He will *b* you with the Holy Spirit
3:16 John answered them all, "I *b* you
Jn 1:25 "Why then do you *b*
1:26 nor the Prophet?" "I *b* with water,"
1:33 and remain is he who will *b*
1:33 me to *b* with water told me,
1Co 1:14 I am thankful that I did not *b* any
1:17 For Christ did not send me to *b*,

BAPTIZED* (BAPTIZE)

Mt 3: 6 they were *b* by him in the Jordan
3:13 to the Jordan to be *b* by John.
3:14 saying, "I need to be *b* by you,
3:16 as Jesus was *b*, he went up out
Mk 1: 5 they were *b* by him in the Jordan
1: 9 and was *b* by John in the Jordan.
10:38 or be *b* with the baptism I am
10:38 with the baptism I am *b* with?"
10:39 and be *b* with the baptism I am

Mk 10:39 with the baptism I am *b* with,
16:16 believes and is *b* will be saved,
Lk 3: 7 to the crowds coming out to be *b*
3:12 Tax collectors also came to be *b*.
3:21 were being *b*, Jesus was *b* too.
7:29 because they had been *b* by John.
7:30 they had not been *b* by John.)
Jn 3:22 spent some time with them, and *b*.
3:23 were constantly coming to be *b*.
4: 2 in fact it was not Jesus who *b*,
Ac 1: 5 For John *b* with water,
1: 5 but in a few days you will be *b*
2:38 Repent and be *b*, every one of you,
2:41 who accepted his message were *b*,
8:12 they were *b*, both men and women.
8:13 Simon himself believed and was *b*.
8:16 they had simply been *b*
8:36 Why shouldn't I be *b*?"
8:38 into the water and Philip *b* him.
9:18 was *b*, and after taking some food,
10:47 people from being *b* with water?
10:48 So he ordered that they be *b*
11:16 what the Lord had said, 'John *b*
11:16 you will be *b* with the Holy Spirit.'
16:15 members of her household were *b*,
16:33 he and all his family were *b*.
18: 8 heard him believed and were *b*.
19: 5 they were *b* into the name
22:16 be *b* and wash your sins away,
Ro 6: 3 *b* into Christ Jesus were *b*
1Co 1:13 Were you *b* into the name of Paul?
1:15 so no one can say that you were *b*
1:16 I also *b* the household of Stephanas
1:16 I don't remember if I *b* anyone else
10: 2 They were all *b* into Moses
12:13 For we were all *b* by one Spirit
15:29 what will those do who are *b*
15:29 why are people *b* for them?
Gal 3:27 all of you who were *b*

BAPTIZING* (BAPTIZE)

Mt 3: 7 coming to where he was *b*,
28:19 *b* them in the name of the Father
Mk 1: 4 *b* in the desert region
Jn 1:28 of the Jordan, where John was *b*.
1:31 but the reason I came *b*
3:23 also was *b* at Aenon near Salim,
3:26 he is *b*, and everyone is going
4: 1 and *b* more disciples than John,
10:40 to the place where John had been *b*

BAR-JESUS*

Ac 13: 6 and false prophet named *B*,

BARABBAS

Mt 27:26 Then he released *B* to them.

BARAK*

Judge who fought with Deborah against Canaanites (Jdg 4-5; 1Sa 12:11; Heb 11:32).

BARBARIAN*

Col 3:11 circumcised or uncircumcised, *b*,

BARBS*

Nu 33:55 allow to remain will become *b*

BARE

Hos 2: 3 as *b* as on the day she was born;
Heb 4:13 and laid *b* before the eyes of him

BARNABAS*

Disciple, originally Joseph (Ac 4:36), prophet (Ac 13:1), apostle (Ac 14:14). Brought Paul to apostles (Ac 9:27), Antioch (Ac 11:22-29; Gal 2:1-13), on the first missionary journey (Ac 13-14). Together at Jerusalem Council, they separated over John Mark (Ac 15). Later co-workers (1Co 9:6; Col 4:10).

BARREN

Ge 11:30 Sarai was *b*; she had no children.
29:31 her womb, but Rachel was *b*.
Ps 113: 9 He settles the *b* woman
Isa 54: 1 "Sing, O *b* woman,
Lk 1: 7 children, because Elizabeth was *b*;
Gal 4:27 "Be glad, O *b* woman,
Heb 11:11 and Sarah herself was *b*—

BARTHOLOMEW*

Apostle (Mt 10:3; Mk 3:18; Lk 6:14; Ac 1:13). Possibly also known as Nathanael (Jn 1:45-49; 21:2).

BARUCH

Jeremiah's secretary (Jer 32:12-16; 36; 43:1-6; 45:1-2).

BARZILLAI

1. Gileadite who aided David during Absalom's revolt (2Sa 17:27; 19:31-39).
2. Son-in-law of 1. (Ezr 2:61; Ne 7:63).

BASHAN

Jos 22: 7 Moses had given land in *B*,
Ps 22:12 strong bulls of *B* encircle me.

BASIN

Ex 30:18 "Make a bronze *b*,

BASKET

Ex 2: 3 she got a papyrus *b* for him
Ac 9:25 him in a *b* through an opening
2Co 11:33 I was lowered in a *b* from a window

BATCH*

Ro 11:16 then the whole *b* is holy;
1Co 5: 6 through the whole *b* of dough?
5: 7 old yeast that you may be a new *b*
Gal 5: 9 through the whole *b* of dough."

BATH (BATHING)

Jn 13:10 person who has had a *b* needs only

BATHING (BATH)

2Sa 11: 2 From the roof he saw a woman *b*.

BATHSHEBA*

Wife of Uriah who committed adultery with and became wife of David (2Sa 11), mother of Solomon (2Sa 12:24; 1Ki 1-2; 1Ch 3:5).

BATTLE (BATTLES)

1Sa 17:47 for the *b* is the LORD's,
2Ch 20:15 For the *b* is not yours, but God's.
Ps 24: 8 the LORD mighty in *b*.
Ecc 9:11 or the *b* to the strong,
Isa 31: 4 down to do *b* on Mount Zion
Eze 13: 5 in the *b* on the day of the LORD.
Rev 16:14 them for the *b* on the great day
20: 8 and Magog—to gather them for *b*.

BATTLES* (BATTLE)

1Sa 8:20 to go out before us and fight our *b*."
18:17 and fight the *b* of the LORD."
25:28 because he fights the LORD's *b*.
2Ch 32: 8 God to help us and to fight our *b*."

BEAR (BEARING BEARS BIRTH BIRTHRIGHT BORE BORN CHILDBEARING CHILDBIRTH FIRSTBORN NEWBORN REBIRTH)

Ge 4:13 punishment is more than I can *b*.
Ps 38: 4 like a burden too heavy to *b*.
Isa 11: 7 The cow will feed with the *b*,
53:11 and he will *b* their iniquities.
Da 7: 5 beast, which looked like a *b*.
Mt 7:18 A good tree cannot *b* bad fruit,
Jn 15: 2 branch that does *b* fruit he prunes
15: 8 glory, that you *b* much fruit,
15:16 appointed you to go and *b* fruit—
Ro 7: 4 in order that we might *b* fruit
15: 1 ought to *b* with the failings
1Co 10:13 tempted beyond what you can *b*.
Col 3:13 *B* with each other and forgive

BEARD

Lev 19:27 or clip off the edges of your *b*.
Isa 50: 6 to those who pulled out my *b*;

BEARING (BEAR)

Eph 4: 2 *b* with one another in love.
Col 1:10 *b* fruit in every good work,
Heb 13:13 outside the camp, *b* the disgrace he

BEARS (BEAR)

1Ki 8:43 house I have built *b* your Name.
Ps 68:19 who daily *b* our burdens.

BEAST (BEASTS)

Rev 13:18 him calculate the number of the *b*,
16: 2 people who had the mark of the *b*
19:20 who had received the mark of the *b*

BEASTS (BEAST)

Da 7: 3 Four great *b*, each different
1Co 15:32 If I fought wild *b* in Ephesus

BEAT (BEATEN BEATING BEATINGS)

Isa 2: 4 They will *b* their swords
Joel 3:10 *B* your plowshares into swords
Mic 4: 3 They will *b* their swords
1Co 9:27 I *b* my body and make it my slave

BEATEN (BEAT)

Lk 12:47 do what his master wants will be *b*
12:48 deserving punishment will be *b*
2Co 11:25 Three times I was *b* with rods,

BEATING (BEAT)

1Co 9:26 I do not fight like a man *b* the air.
1Pe 2:20 if you receive a *b* for doing wrong

BEATINGS (BEAT)

Pr 19:29 and *b* for the backs of fools.

BEAUTIFUL* (BEAUTY)

Ge 6: 2 that the daughters of men were *b*,
12:11 "I know what a *b* woman you are.
12:14 saw that she was a very *b* woman.
24:16 The girl was very *b*, a virgin;
26: 7 of Rebekah, because she is *b*."
29:17 Rachel was lovely in form, and *b*.
49:21 that bears *b* fawns.
Nu 24: 5 "How *b* are your tents, O Jacob,
Dt 21:11 among the captives a *b* woman
Jos 7:21 saw in the plunder a *b* robe
1Sa 25: 3 was an intelligent and *b* woman,
2Sa 11: 2 The woman was very *b*,
13: 1 the *b* sister of Absalom son
14:27 and she became a *b* woman.
1Ki 1: 3 throughout Israel for a *b* girl
1: 4 The girl was very *b*; she took care
Est 2: 2 for *b* young virgins for the king.
2: 3 realm to bring all these *b* girls
Job 38:31 "Can you bind the *b* Pleiades?
42:15 land were there found women as *b*
Ps 48: 2 It is *b* in its loftiness,
Pr 11:22 is a *b* woman who shows no
24: 4 filled with rare and *b* treasures.
Ecc 3:11 He has made everything *b*
SS 1: 8 *Lover* If you do not know, most *b*
1:10 Your cheeks are *b* with earrings,
1:15 Oh, how *b*!
1:15 *Lover* How *b* you are, my darling!
2:10 my *b* one, and come with me.
2:13 my *b* one, come with me."
4: 1 How *b* you are, my darling!
4: 1 Oh, how *b*!
4: 7 All *b* you are, my darling;
5: 9 most *b* of women?
6: 1 most *b* of women?
6: 4 *Lover* You are *b*, my darling,
7: 1 How *b* your sandaled feet,
7: 6 How *b* you are and how pleasing,
Isa 4: 2 of the LORD will be *b*
28: 5 a *b* wreath
52: 7 How *b* on the mountains
Jer 3:19 the most *b* inheritance
6: 2 so *b* and delicate.
11:16 with fruit *b* in form.
46:20 "Egypt is a *b* heifer,
Eze 7:20 They were proud of their *b* jewelry
16: 7 and became the most *b* of jewels.
16:12 and a *b* crown on your head.
16:13 You became very *b* and rose
20: 6 and honey, the most *b* of all lands.
20:15 and honey, most *b* of all lands—
23:42 and *b* crowns on their heads.
27:24 traded with you *b* garments,
31: 3 with *b* branches overshadowing
31: 9 I made it *b*
33:32 who sings love songs with a *b* voice
Da 4:12 Its leaves were *b*, its fruit abundant
4:21 with *b* leaves and abundant fruit,
8: 9 to the east and toward the *B* Land.
11:16 will establish himself in the *B* Land
11:41 He will also invade the *B* Land.
11:45 the seas at the *b* holy mountain.
Zec 9:17 How attractive and *b* they will be!
Mt 23:27 which look *b* on the outside
26:10 She has done a *b* thing to me.
Mk 14: 6 She has done a *b* thing to me.
Lk 21: 5 temple was adorned with *b* stones
Ac 3: 2 carried to the temple gate called *B*,
3:10 at the temple gate called *B*,
Ro 10:15 "How *b* are the feet
1Pe 3: 5 in God used to make themselves *b*.

BEAUTY* (BEAUTIFUL)

Est 1:11 order to display her *b* to the people
2: 3 let *b* treatments be given to them.

Est 2: 9 her with her *b* treatments
2: 12 months of *b* treatments prescribed
Ps 27: 4 to gaze upon the *b* of the LORD
37: 20 LORD's enemies will be like the *b*
45: 11 The king is enthralled by your *b;*
50: 2 From Zion, perfect in *b,*
Pr 6: 25 lust in your heart after her *b*
31: 30 is deceptive, and *b* is fleeting;
Isa 3: 24 instead of *b,* branding.
28: 1 to the fading flower, his glorious *b,*
28: 4 That fading flower, his glorious *b,*
33: 17 Your eyes will see the king in his *b*
53: 2 He had no *b* or majesty
61: 3 to bestow on them a crown of *b*
La 2: 15 the perfection of *b,*
Eze 16: 14 had given you made your *b* perfect,
16: 14 the nations on account of your *b,*
16: 15 passed by and your *b* became his.
16: 15 " 'But you trusted in your *b*
16: 25 lofty shrines and degraded your *b,*
27: 3 "I am perfect in *b."*
27: 4 your builders brought your *b*
27: 11 they brought your *b* to perfection.
28: 7 draw their swords against your *b*
28: 12 full of wisdom and perfect in *b.*
28: 17 proud on account of your *b,*
31: 7 It was majestic in *b,*
31: 8 could match its *b.*
Jas 1: 11 blossom falls and its *b* is destroyed.
1Pe 3: 3 Your *b* should not come
3: 4 the unfading *b* of a gentle

BED (SICKBED)

Isa 28: 20 The *b* is too short to stretch out on,
Lk 11: 7 and my children are with me in *b.*
17: 34 night two people will be in one *b;*
Heb 13: 4 and the marriage *b* kept pure,

BEELZEBUB*

Mt 10: 25 of the house has been called *B,*
12: 24 "It is only by *B,* the prince
12: 27 And if I drive out demons by *B,*
Mk 3: 22 possessed by *B!* By the prince
Lk 11: 15 "By *B,* the prince of demons,
11: 18 claim that I drive out demons by *B.*
11: 19 Now if I drive out demons by *B,*

BEER

Pr 20: 1 Wine is a mocker and *b* a brawler;

BEERSHEBA

Ge 21: 14 and wandered in the desert of *B.*
Jdg 20: 1 all the Israelites from Dan to *B*
1Sa 3: 20 to *B* recognized that Samuel was
2Sa 3: 10 and Judah from Dan to *B."*
17: 11 Let all Israel, from Dan to *B*—
24: 2 the tribes of Israel from Dan to *B*
24: 15 of the people from Dan to *B* died.
1Ki 4: 25 from Dan to *B,* lived in safety,
1Ch 21: 2 count the Israelites from *B* to Dan.
2Ch 30: 5 throughout Israel, from *B* to Dan,

BEFALLS*

Pr 12: 21 No harm *b* the righteous,

BEGGING

Ps 37: 25 or their children *b* bread.
Ac 16: 9 of Macedonia standing and *b* him,

BEGINNING

Ge 1: 1 In the *b* God created the heavens
Ps 102: 25 In the *b* you laid the foundations
111: 10 of the LORD is the *b* of wisdom;
Pr 1: 7 of the LORD is the *b* of knowledge
9: 10 of the LORD is the *b* of wisdom,
Ecc 3: 11 fathom what God has done from *b*
Isa 40: 21 Has it not been told you from the *b*
46: 10 I make known the end from the *b,*
Mt 24: 8 All these are the *b* of birth pains.
Lk 1: 3 investigated everything from the *b,*
Jn 1: 1 In the *b* was the Word,
1Jn 1: 1 That which was from the *b,*
Rev 21: 6 and the Omega, the *B* and the End.
22: 13 and the Last, the *B* and the End.

BEHAVE (BEHAVIOR)

Ro 13: 13 Let us *b* decently, as in the daytime

BEHAVIOR (BEHAVE)

1Pe 3: 1 without words by the *b* of their wives,
3: 16 maliciously against your good *b*

BEHEMOTH*

Job 40: 15 "Look at the *b,*

BELIEVE (BELIEVED BELIEVER BELIEVERS BELIEVES BELIEVING)

Ex 4: 1 "What if they do not *b* me
1Ki 10: 7 I did not *b* these things until I came
2Ch 9: 6 But I did not *b* what they said
Ps 78: 32 of his wonders, they did not *b.*
Hab 1: 5 that you would not *b,*
Mt 18: 6 one of these little ones who *b* in me
21: 22 If you *b,* you will receive whatever
27: 42 from the cross, and we will *b* in him
Mk 1: 15 Repent and *b* the good news!"
5: 36 ruler, "Don't be afraid; just *b."*
9: 24 "I do *b;* help me overcome my
9: 42 one of these little ones who *b* in me
11: 24 *b* that you have received it,
15: 32 the cross, that we may see and *b."*
16: 16 but whoever does not *b* will be
16: 17 signs will accompany those who *b:*
Lk 8: 12 so that they may not *b* and be saved.
8: 13 They *b* for a while, but in the time
8: 50 just *b,* and she will be healed."
22: 67 you will not *b* me,
24: 25 to *b* all that the prophets have
Jn 1: 7 that through him all men might *b.*
3: 18 does not *b* stands condemned
4: 42 "We no longer *b* just
5: 38 for you do not *b* the one he sent.
5: 46 believed Moses, you would *b* me,
6: 29 to *b* in the one he has sent."
6: 69 We *b* and know that you are
7: 5 his own brothers did not *b* in him.
8: 24 if you do not *b* that I am the one I
9: 35 "Do you *b* in the Son of Man?"
9: 36 "Tell me so that I may *b* in him."
9: 38 "Lord, I *b,"* and he worshiped him.
10: 26 you do not *b* because you are not
10: 37 Do not *b* me unless I do what my
10: 38 you do not *b* me, *b* the miracles,
11: 27 "I *b* that you are the Christ,
12: 37 they still would not *b* in him.
12: 39 For this reason they could not *b,*
12: 44 in me, he does not *b* in me only,
13: 19 does happen you will *b* that I am
14: 10 Don't you *b* that I am in the Father
14: 11 *B* me when I say that I am
14: 11 or at least *b* on the evidence
16: 30 This makes us *b* that you came
16: 31 "You *b* at last!" Jesus answered.
17: 21 that the world may *b* that you have
19: 35 he testifies so that you also may *b.*
20: 27 Stop doubting and *b."*
20: 31 written that you may *b* that Jesus is
Ac 16: 31 They replied, "*B* in the Lord Jesus,
19: 4 the people to *b* in the one coming
24: 14 I *b* everything that agrees
26: 27 Agrippa, do you *b* the prophets?
Ro 3: 22 faith in Jesus Christ to all who *b.*
4: 11 he is the father of all who *b*
10: 9 *b* in your heart that God raised him
10: 10 For it is with your heart that you *b*
10: 14 And how can they *b* in the one
16: 26 so that all nations might *b*
1Co 1: 21 preached to save those who *b.*
Gal 3: 22 might be given to those who *b.*
Php 1: 29 of Christ not only to *b* on him,
1Th 4: 14 We *b* that Jesus died and rose again
2Th 2: 11 delusion so that they will *b* the lie
1Ti 4: 10 and especially of those who *b.*
Tit 1: 6 a man whose children *b*
Heb 11: 6 comes to him must *b* that he exists
Jas 1: 6 But when he asks, he must *b*
2: 19 Even the demons *b* that—
2: 19 You *b* that there is one God.
1Pe 2: 7 to you who *b,* this stone is precious
1Jn 3: 23 to *b* in the name of his Son,
4: 1 Dear friends, do not *b* every spirit,
5: 13 things to you who *b* in the name

BELIEVED (BELIEVE)

Ge 15: 6 Abram *b* the LORD, and he
Ex 4: 31 signs before the people, and they *b.*
Isa 53: 1 Who has *b* our message
Jnh 3: 5 The Ninevites *b* God.
Lk 1: 45 is she who has *b* that what the Lord
Jn 1: 12 to those who *b* in his name,
2: 22 Then they *b* the Scripture
3: 18 because he has not *b* in the name
5: 46 If you *b* Moses, you would believe
7: 39 whom those who *b*
11: 40 "Did I not tell you that if you *b,*
12: 38 "Lord, who has *b* our message
20: 8 He saw and *b.*
20: 29 who have not seen and yet have *b."*
Ac 13: 48 were appointed for eternal life *b.*
Ac 19: 2 the Holy Spirit when you *b?"*
Ro 4: 3 Scripture say? "Abraham *b* God,
10: 14 call on the one they have not *b* in?
10: 16 "Lord, who has *b* our message?"
1Co 15: 2 Otherwise, you have *b* in vain.
Gal 3: 6 Consider Abraham: "He *b* God,
2Th 2: 12 who have not *b* the truth
1Ti 3: 16 was *b* on in the world,
2Ti 1: 12 because I know whom I have *b,*
Jas 2: 23 that says, "Abraham *b* God,

BELIEVER* (BELIEVE)

1Ki 18: 3 (Obadiah was a devout *b*
Ac 16: 1 whose mother was a Jewess and a *b*
16: 15 "If you consider me a *b* in the Lord
1Co 7: 12 brother has a wife who is not a *b*
7: 13 has a husband who is not a *b*
2Co 6: 15 What does a *b* have in common
1Ti 5: 16 any woman who is a *b* has widows

BELIEVERS* (BELIEVE)

Jn 4: 41 of his words many more became *b.*
Ac 1: 15 among the *b* (a group numbering
2: 44 All the *b* were together
4: 32 All the *b* were one in heart
5: 12 And all the *b* used to meet together
9: 41 he called the *b* and the widows
10: 45 The circumcised *b* who had come
11: 2 the circumcised *b* criticized him
15: 2 along with some other *b,*
15: 5 Then some of the *b* who belonged
15: 23 To the Gentile *b* in Antioch,
21: 25 for the Gentile *b,* we have written
1Co 6: 5 to judge a dispute between *b?*
14: 22 is for *b,* not for unbelievers.
14: 22 not for *b* but for unbelievers;
Gal 6: 10 who belong to the family of *b.*
1Th 1: 7 a model to all the *b* in Macedonia
1Ti 4: 12 set an example for the *b* in speech,
6: 2 benefit from their service are *b,*
Jas 2: 1 *b* in our glorious Lord Jesus Christ,
1Pe 2: 17 Love the brotherhood of *b,*

BELIEVES* (BELIEVE)

Pr 14: 15 A simple man *b* anything,
Mk 9: 23 is possible for him who *b."*
11: 23 *b* that what he says will happen,
16: 16 Whoever *b* and is baptized will be
Jn 3: 15 that everyone who *b*
3: 16 that whoever *b* in him shall not
3: 18 Whoever *b* in him is not
3: 36 Whoever *b* in the Son has eternal
5: 24 *b* him who sent me has eternal life
6: 35 and he who *b* in me will never be
6: 40 and *b* in him shall have eternal life,
6: 47 he who *b* has everlasting life.
7: 38 Whoever *b* in me, as the Scripture
11: 25 He who *b* in me will live, even
11: 26 and *b* in me will never die.
12: 44 Jesus cried out, "When a man *b*
12: 46 so that no one who *b*
Ac 10: 43 about him that everyone who *b*
13: 39 him everyone who *b* is justified
Ro 1: 16 for the salvation of everyone who *b*
10: 4 righteousness for everyone who *b.*
1Jn 5: 1 Everyone who *b* that Jesus is
5: 5 Only he who *b* that Jesus is the Son
5: 10 Anyone who *b* in the Son

BELIEVING* (BELIEVE)

Jn 20: 31 and that by *b* you may have life
Ac 9: 26 not *b* that he really was a disciple.
1Co 7: 14 sanctified through her *b* husband.
7: 15 A *b* man or woman is not bound
9: 5 right to take a *b* wife along with us,
Gal 3: 2 or by *b* what you heard? Are you
1Ti 6: 2 Those who have *b* masters are not

BELLY

Ge 3: 14 You will crawl on your *b*
Da 2: 32 its *b* and thighs of bronze,
Mt 12: 40 three nights in the *b* of a huge fish,

BELONG (BELONGING BELONGS)

Ge 40: 8 "Do not interpretations *b* to God?
Lev 25: 55 for the Israelites *b* to me
Dt 10: 14 LORD your God *b* the heavens,
29: 29 The secret things *b*
Job 12: 13 "To God *b* wisdom and power;
12: 16 To him *b* strength and victory;
25: 2 "Dominion and awe *b* to God;
Ps 47: 9 for the kings of the earth *b* to God;
95: 4 and the mountain peaks *b* to him.
115: 16 The highest heavens *b*
Jer 5: 10 for these people do not *b*

Jn 8:44 You *b* to your father, the devil,
15:19 As it is, you do not *b* to the world,
Ro 1:6 called to *b* to Jesus Christ.
7:4 that you might *b* to another,
8:9 of Christ, he does not *b* to Christ.
14:8 we live or die, we *b* to the Lord.
1Co 7:39 but he must *b* to the Lord.
15:23 when he comes, those who *b*
Gal 3:29 If you *b* to Christ, then you are
5:24 Those who *b* to Christ Jesus have
1Th 5:5 We do not *b* to the night
5:8 But since we *b* to the day, let us be
1Jn 3:19 then is how we know that we *b*

BELONGING (BELONG)

1Pe 2:9 a holy nation, a people *b* to God,

BELONGS (BELONG)

Lev 27:30 *b* to the LORD; it is holy
Dt 1:17 of any man, for judgment *b* to God.
Job 41:11 Everything under heaven *b* to me.
Ps 22:28 for dominion *b* to the LORD
89:18 Indeed, our shield *b* to the LORD,
111:10 To him *b* eternal praise.
Eze 18:4 For every living soul *b* to me,
Jn 8:47 He who *b* to God hears what God
Ro 12:5 each member *b* to all the others.
Rev 7:10 "Salvation *b* to our God,

BELOVED* (LOVE)

Dt 33:12 "Let the *b* of the LORD rest secure
SS 5:9 How is your *b* better than others,
5:9 *Friends* How is your *b* better
Jer 11:15 "What is my *b* doing in my temple

BELSHAZZAR

King of Babylon in days of Daniel (Da 5).

BELT

Ex 12:11 with your cloak tucked into your *b*,
1Ki 18:46 and, tucking his cloak into his *b*,
2Ki 4:29 "Tuck your cloak into your *b*,
9:1 "Tuck your cloak into your *b*,
Isa 11:5 Righteousness will be his *b*
Eph 6:14 with the *b* of truth buckled

BENEFICIAL* (BENEFIT)

1Co 6:12 for me"—but not everything is *b*.
10:23 but not everything is *b*.

BENEFIT (BENEFICIAL BENEFITS)

Job 22:2 "Can a man be of *b* to God?
Isa 38:17 Surely it was for my *b*
Ro 6:22 the *b* you reap leads to holiness,
2Co 4:15 All this is for your *b*,

BENEFITS (BENEFIT)

Ps 103:2 and forget not all his *b*.
Jn 4:38 you have reaped the *b* of their labor

BENJAMIN

Twelfth son of Jacob by Rachel (Ge 35:16-24; 46:19-21; 1Ch 2:2). Jacob refused to send him to Egypt, but relented (Ge 42-45). Tribe of blessed (Ge 49:27; Dt 33:12), numbered (Nu 1:37; 26:41), allotted land (Jos 18:11-28; Eze 48:23), failed to fully possess (Jdg 1:21), nearly obliterated (Jdg 20-21), sided with Ish-Bosheth (2Sa 2), but turned to David (1Ch 12:2, 29). 12,000 from (Rev 7:8).

BEREANS*

Ac 17:11 the *B* were of more noble character

BESTOWING* (BESTOWS)

Pr 8:21 *b* wealth on those who love me

BESTOWS (BESTOWING)

Ps 84:11 the LORD *b* favor and honor;

BETHANY

Mk 11:1 and *B* at the Mount of Olives,

BETHEL

Ge 28:19 He called that place *B*,

BETHLEHEM

Ru 1:19 went on until they came to *B*.
1Sa 16:1 I am sending you to Jesse of *B*.
2Sa 23:15 from the well near the gate of *B*!"
Mic 5:2 "But you, *B* Ephrathah,
Mt 2:1 After Jesus was born in *B* in Judea,
2:6 " 'But you, *B*, in the land of Judah,

BETHPHAGE

Mt 21:1 came to *B* on the Mount of Olives,

BETHSAIDA

Jn 12:21 who was from *B* in Galilee,

BETRAY (BETRAYED BETRAYS)

Ps 89:33 nor will I ever *b* my faithfulness.
Pr 25:9 do not *b* another man's confidence,
Mt 10:21 "Brother will *b* brother to death,
26:21 the truth, one of you will *b* me."

BETRAYED (BETRAY)

Mt 27:4 "for I have *b* innocent blood."

BETRAYS (BETRAY)

Pr 11:13 A gossip *b* a confidence,
20:19 A gossip *b* a confidence;

BEULAH*

Isa 62:4 and your land *B*;

BEWITCHED*

Gal 3:1 foolish Galatians! Who has *b* you?

BEZALEL

Judahite craftsman in charge of building the tabernacle (Ex 31:1-11; 35:30-39:31).

BIDDING*

Ps 103:20 you mighty ones who do his *b*,
148:8 stormy winds that do his *b*,

BILDAD

One of Job's friends (Job 8; 18; 25).

BILHAH

Servant of Rachel, mother of Jacob's sons Dan and Naphtali (Ge 30:1-7; 35:25; 46:23-25).

BIND (BINDS BOUND)

Dt 6:8 and *b* them on your foreheads.
Pr 3:3 *b* them around your neck,
6:21 *B* them upon your heart forever;
7:3 *B* them on your fingers;
Isa 61:1 me to *b* up the brokenhearted,
Mt 16:19 whatever you *b* on earth will be

BINDS (BIND)

Ps 147:3 and *b* up their wounds.
Isa 30:26 when the LORD *b* up the bruises

BIRD (BIRDS)

Pr 27:8 Like a *b* that strays from its nest
Ecc 10:20 a *b* of the air may carry your words,

BIRDS (BIRD)

Mt 8:20 and *b* of the air have nests,
Lk 9:58 and *b* of the air have nests,

BIRTH (BEAR)

Ps 51:5 Surely I was sinful at *b*,
58:3 Even from *b* the wicked go astray;
Isa 26:18 but we gave *b* to wind.
Mt 1:18 This is how the *b* of Jesus Christ
24:8 these are the beginning of *b* pains.
Jn 3:6 Flesh gives *b* to flesh, but the Spirit
1Pe 1:3 great mercy he has given us new *b*

BIRTHRIGHT (BEAR)

Ge 25:34 So Esau despised his *b*.

BISHOP see OVERSEER

BITTEN

Nu 21:8 anyone who is *b* can look at it

BITTER (BITTERNESS EMBITTER)

Ex 12:8 along with *b* herbs, and bread made
Pr 27:7 what is *b* tastes sweet.

BITTERNESS (BITTER)

Pr 14:10 Each heart knows its own *b*,
17:25 and *b* to the one who bore him.
Ro 3:14 full of cursing and *b*."
Eph 4:31 Get rid of all *b*, rage and anger,

BLACK

Zec 6:6 The one with the *b* horses is going
Rev 6:5 and there before me was a *b* horse!

BLAMELESS* (BLAMELESSLY)

Ge 6:9 *b* among the people of his time,
17:1 walk before me and be *b*.
Dt 18:13 You must be *b* before the LORD
2Sa 22:24 I have been *b* before him
22:26 to the *b* you show yourself *b*,
Job 1:1 This man was *b* and upright;
1:8 one on earth like him; he is *b*
2:3 one on earth like him; he is *b*
4:6 and your *b* ways your hope?
8:20 God does not reject a *b* man
9:20 if I were *b*, it would pronounce me
9:21 "Although I am *b*,
9:22 'He destroys both the *b*
12:4 though righteous and *b*!
22:3 gain if your ways were *b*?
31:6 and he will know that I am *b*—
Ps 15:2 He whose walk is *b*
18:23 I have been *b* before him
18:25 to the *b* you show yourself *b*,
19:13 Then will I be *b*,
26:1 for I have led a *b* life;
26:11 But I lead a *b* life;
37:18 The days of the *b* are known
37:37 Consider the *b*, observe the upright
84:11 from those whose walk is *b*.
101:2 I will be careful to lead a *b* life—
101:2 house with *b* heart.
101:6 he whose walk is *b*
119:1 Blessed are they whose ways are *b*,
119:80 May my heart be *b*
Pr 2:7 a shield to those whose walk is *b*,
2:21 and the *b* will remain in it;
11:5 of the *b* makes a straight way
11:20 in those whose ways are *b*.
19:1 Better a poor man whose walk is *b*
20:7 The righteous man leads a *b* life;
28:6 Better a poor man whose walk is *b*
28:10 *b* will receive a good inheritance.
28:18 He whose walk is *b* is kept safe,
Eze 28:15 You were *b* in your ways
1Co 1:8 so that you will be *b* on the day
Eph 1:4 world to be holy and *b* in his sight.
5:27 any other blemish, but holy and *b*.
Php 1:10 and *b* until the day of Christ,
2:15 so that you may become *b* and pure
1Th 2:10 and *b* we were among you who
3:13 hearts so that you will be *b*
5:23 and body be kept *b* at the coming
Tit 1:6 An elder must be *b*, the husband of
1:7 he must be *b*—not overbearing,
Heb 7:26 *b*, pure, set apart from sinners,
2Pe 3:14 effort to be found spotless, *b*
Rev 14:5 found in their mouths; they are *b*.

BLAMELESSLY* (BLAMELESS)

Lk 1:6 commandments and regulations *b*.

BLASPHEME* (BLASPHEMED BLASPHEMER BLASPHEMES BLASPHEMIES BLASPHEMING BLASPHEMOUS BLASPHEMY)

Ex 22:28 "Do not *b* God or curse the ruler
Ac 26:11 and I tried to force them to *b*.
1Ti 1:20 over to Satan to be taught not to *b*.
2Pe 2:12 these men *b* in matters they do not
Rev 13:6 He opened his mouth to *b* God,

BLASPHEMED* (BLASPHEME)

Lev 24:11 of the Israelite woman *b* the Name
2Ki 19:6 of the king of Assyria have *b* me.
19:22 Who is it you have insulted and *b*?
Isa 37:6 of the king of Assyria have *b* me.
37:23 Who is it you have insulted and *b*?
52:5 my name is constantly *b*.
Eze 20:27 your fathers *b* me by forsaking me:
Ac 19:37 robbed temples nor *b* our goddess.
Ro 2:24 name is *b* among the Gentiles

BLASPHEMER* (BLASPHEME)

Lev 24:14 "Take the *b* outside the camp.
24:23 they took the *b* outside the camp
1Ti 1:13 I was once a *b* and a persecutor

BLASPHEMES* (BLASPHEME)

Lev 24:16 anyone who *b* the name
24:16 native-born, when he *b* the Name,
Nu 15:30 native-born or alien, *b* the LORD,
Mk 3:29 whoever *b* against the Holy Spirit
Lk 12:10 but anyone who *b* against the Holy

BLASPHEMIES* (BLASPHEME)

Ne 9:18 or when they committed awful *b*.
9:26 to you; they committed awful *b*.
Mk 3:28 and *b* of men will be forgiven them.
Rev 13:5 and *b* and to exercise his authority

BLASPHEMING* (BLASPHEME)
Mt 9: 3 "This fellow is *b!*" Knowing their
Mk 2: 7 He's *b!* Who can forgive sins

BLASPHEMOUS* (BLASPHEME)
Rev 13: 1 and on each head a *b* name.
17: 3 that was covered with *b* names

BLASPHEMY* (BLASPHEME)
Mt 12:31 and *b* will be forgiven men,
12:31 the *b* against the Spirit will not be
26:65 Look, now you have heard the *b*.
26:65 "He has spoken *b!* Why do we
Mk 14:64 "You have heard the *b*.
Lk 5:21 "Who is this fellow who speaks *b?*
Jn 10:33 replied the Jews, "but for *b*,
10:36 Why then do you accuse me of *b*
Ac 6:11 words of *b* against Moses

BLAST*
Ex 15: 8 By the *b* of your nostrils
19:13 horn sounds a long *b* may they go
19:16 and a very loud trumpet *b*.
Nu 10: 5 When a trumpet *b* is sounded,
10: 6 At the sounding of a second *b*,
10: 6 The *b* will be the signal
10: 9 sound a *b* on the trumpets.
Jos 6: 5 you hear them sound a long *b*
6:16 the priests sounded the trumpet *b*,
2Sa 22:16 at the *b* of breath from his nostrils.
Job 4: 9 at the *b* of his anger they perish.
39:25 At the *b* of the trumpet he snorts,
Ps 18:15 the *b* of breath from your nostrils.
98: 6 and the *b* of the ram's horn—
147: 17 Who can withstand his icy *b?*
Isa 27: 8 with his fierce *b* he drives her out,
Eze 22:20 a furnace to melt it with a fiery *b*,
Am 2: 2 tumult amid war cries and the *b*
Heb 12:19 to a trumpet *b* or to such a voice

BLEATING*
1Sa 15:14 "What then is this *b* of sheep

BLEMISH (BLEMISHES)
Lev 22:21 be without defect or *b*
Eph 5:27 or wrinkle or any other *b*,
Col 1:22 without *b* and free from accusation
1Pe 1:19 a lamb without *b* or defect.

BLEMISHES* (BLEMISH)
2Pe 2:13 and *b*, reveling in their pleasures
Jude :12 These men are *b* at your love feasts

BLESS (BLESSED BLESSES BLESSING BLESSINGS)
Ge 12: 3 I will *b* those who *b* you,
32:26 not let you go unless you *b* me."
Dt 7:13 He will love you and *b* you
33:11 *B* all his skills, O LORD,
Ps 72:15 and *b* him all day long.
Ro 12:14 Bless those who persecute you; *b*

BLESSED (BLESS)
Ge 1:22 God *b* them and said, "Be fruitful
2: 3 And God *b* the seventh day
22:18 nations on earth will be *b*,
Nu 24: 9 "May those who bless you be *b*
1Ch 17:27 have *b* it, and it will be *b* forever."
Ps 1: 1 *B* is the man
2:12 *B* are all who take refuge in him.
32: 2 *B* is the man
33:12 *B* is the nation whose God is
40: 4 *B* is the man
41: 1 *B* is he who has regard for the weak
84: 5 *B* are those whose strength is
89:15 *B* are those who have learned
94:12 *B* is the man you discipline,
106: 3 *B* are they who maintain justice,
112: 1 *B* is the man who fears the LORD,
118: 26 *B* is he who comes in the name
119: 1 *B* are they whose ways are
119: 2 *B* are they who keep his statutes
127: 5 *B* is the man
Pr 3:13 *B* is the man who finds wisdom,
8:34 *B* is the man who listens to me,
28:20 A faithful man will be richly *b*,
29:18 but *b* is he who keeps the law.
31:28 Her children arise and call her *b*;
Isa 30:18 *B* are all who wait for him!
Mal 3:12 Then all the nations will call you *b*,
3:15 But now we call the arrogant *b*.
Mt 5: 3 saying: "*B* are the poor in spirit,
5: 4 *B* are those who mourn,
5: 5 *B* are the meek,
Mt 5: 6 *B* are those who hunger
5: 7 *B* are the merciful,
5: 8 *B* are the pure in heart,
5: 9 *B* are the peacemakers,
5:10 *B* are those who are persecuted
5:11 "*B* are you when people insult you,
Lk 1:48 on all generations will call me *b*,
Jn 12:13 "*B* is he who comes in the name
Ac 20:35 'It is more *b* to give than to receive
Tit 2:13 while we wait for the *b* hope—
Jas 1:12 *B* is the man who perseveres
Rev 1: 3 *B* is the one who reads the words
22: 7 *B* is he who keeps the words
22:14 "*B* are those who wash their robes,

BLESSES (BLESS)
Ps 29:11 the LORD *b* his people with peace.
Ro 10:12 and richly *b* all who call on him,

BLESSING (BLESS)
Ge 27: 4 so that I may give you my *b*
Dt 23: 5 turned the curse into a *b* for you,
33: 1 This is the *b* that Moses the man
Pr 10:22 The *b* of the LORD brings wealth,
Eze 34:26 there will be showers of *b*.

BLESSINGS (BLESS)
Dt 11:29 proclaim on Mount Gerizim the *b*,
Jos 8:34 all the words of the law—the *b*
Pr 10: 6 *B* crown the head of the righteous,
Ro 15:27 shared in the Jews' spiritual *b*,

BLIND (BLINDED)
Mt 15:14 a *b* man leads a *b* man, both will fall
23:16 "Woe to you, *b* guides! You say,
Mk 10:46 a *b* man, Bartimaeus (that is,
Lk 6:39 "Can a *b* man lead a *b* man?
Jn 9:25 I was *b* but now I see!"

BLINDED (BLIND)
Jn 12:40 elsewhere: "He has *b* their eyes
2Co 4: 4 The god of this age has *b* the minds

BLOOD (BLOODSHED BLOODTHIRSTY)
Ge 4:10 Your brother's *b* cries out to me
9: 6 "Whoever sheds the *b* of man,
Ex 12:13 and when I see the *b*, I will pass
24: 8 "This is the *b* of the covenant that
Lev 16:15 and take its *b* behind the curtain
17:11 For the life of a creature is in the *b*,
Dt 12:23 eat the *b*, because the *b* is the life,
Ps 72:14 for precious is their *b* in his sight.
Pr 6:17 hands that shed innocent *b*,
Isa 1:11 pleasure in the *b* of bulls and lambs
Mt 26:28 This is my *b* of the covenant,
27:24 "I am innocent of this man's *b*,"
Mk 14:24 "This is my *b* of the covenant,
Lk 22:44 drops of *b* falling to the ground.
Jn 6:53 of the Son of Man and drink his *b*,
Ac 15:20 of strangled animals and from *b*.
20:26 innocent of the *b* of all men.
Ro 3:25 of atonement, through faith in his *b*
5: 9 have now been justified by his *b*,
1Co 11:25 cup is the new covenant in my *b*;
Eph 1: 7 we have redemption through his *b*,
2:13 near through the *b* of Christ.
Col 1:20 by making peace through his *b*,
Heb 9: 7 once a year, and never without *b*,
9:12 once for all by his own *b*,
9:20 "This is the *b* of the covenant,
9:22 of *b* there is no forgiveness.
12:24 word than the *b* of Abel.
1Pe 1:19 but with the precious *b* of Christ,
1Jn 1: 7 and the *b* of Jesus, his Son,
Rev 1: 5 has freed us from our sins by his *b*,
5: 9 with your *b* you purchased men
7:14 white in the *b* of the Lamb.
12:11 him by the *b* of the Lamb
19:13 He is dressed in a robe dipped in *b*,

BLOODSHED (BLOOD)
Jer 48:10 on him who keeps his sword from *b*
Eze 35: 6 did not hate *b*, *b* will pursue you.
Hab 2:12 to him who builds a city with *b*

BLOODTHIRSTY* (BLOOD)
Ps 5: 6 *b* and deceitful men
26: 9 my life with *b* men,
55:23 *b* and deceitful men
59: 2 and save me from *b* men.
139: 19 Away from me, you *b* men!
Pr 29:10 *B* men hate a man of integrity

BLOSSOM
Isa 35: 1 the wilderness will rejoice and *b*.

BLOT (BLOTS)
Ex 32:32 then *b* me out of the book you have
Ps 51: 1 *b* out my transgressions.
Rev 3: 5 I will never *b* out his name

BLOTS (BLOT)
Isa 43:25 "I, even I, am he who *b* out

BLOWN
Eph 4:14 and *b* here and there by every wind
Jas 1: 6 doubts is like a wave of the sea, *b*
Jude :12 without rain, *b* along by the wind;

BLUSH
Jer 6:15 they do not even know how to *b*.

BOAST (BOASTS)
1Ki 20:11 armor should not *b* like one who
Ps 34: 2 My soul will *b* in the LORD;
44: 8 In God we make our *b* all day long,
Pr 27: 1 Do not *b* about tomorrow,
Jer 9:23 or the rich man *b* of his riches,
1Co 1:31 Let him who boasts *b* in the Lord."
2Co 10:17 Let him who boasts *b* in the Lord."
11:30 I do not inwardly burn? If I must *b*,
Gal 6:14 May I never *b* except in the cross
Eph 2: 9 not by works, so that no one can *b*.

BOASTS (BOAST)
Jer 9:24 but let him who *b* boast about this:

BOAZ
Wealthy Bethlehemite who showed favor to Ruth (Ru 2), married her (Ru 4). Ancestor of David (Ru 4:18-22; 1Ch 2:12-15), Jesus (Mt 1:5-16; Lk 3:23-32).

BODIES (BODY)
Isa 26:19 their *b* will rise.
Ro 12: 1 to offer your *b* as living sacrifices,
1Co 6:15 not know that your *b* are members
Eph 5:28 to love their wives as their own *b*.

BODILY (BODY)
Col 2: 9 of the Deity lives in *b* form,

BODY (BODIES BODILY EMBODIMENT)
Zec 13: 6 What are these wounds on your *b?*'
Mt 10:28 afraid of those who kill the *b*
26:26 saying, "Take and eat; this is my *b*
26:41 spirit is willing, but the *b* is weak."
Mk 14:22 saying, "Take it; this is my *b*."
Lk 22:19 saying, "This is my *b* given for you;
Jn 13:10 wash his feet; his whole *b* is clean.
Ro 6:13 Do not offer the parts of your *b*
12: 4 us has one *b* with many members,
1Co 6:19 not know that your *b* is a temple
6:20 Therefore honor God with your *b*.
11:24 "This is my *b*, which is for you;
12:12 The *b* is a unit, though it is made up
12:13 baptized by one Spirit into one *b*—
15:44 a natural *b*, it is raised a spiritual *b*.
Eph 1:23 which is his *b*, the fullness
4:25 for we are all members of one *b*.
5:30 for we are members of his *b*.
Php 1:20 Christ will be exalted in my *b*,
Col 1:24 sake of his *b*, which is the church.

BOLD (BOLDNESS)
Ps 138: 3 you made me *b* and stouthearted.
Pr 21:29 A wicked man puts up a *b* front,
28: 1 but the righteous are as *b* as a lion.

BOLDNESS* (BOLD)
Lk 11: 8 of the man's *b* he will get up
Ac 4:29 to speak your word with great *b*.

BONDAGE
Ezr 9: 9 God has not deserted us in our *b*.

BONES
Ge 2:23 "This is now bone of my *b*
Ps 22:14 and all my *b* are out of joint.
22:17 I can count all my *b*;
Eze 37: 1 middle of a valley; it was full of *b*.
Jn 19:36 "Not one of his *b* will be broken,"

BOOK (BOOKS)
Ex 32:33 against me I will blot out of my *b*.
Jos 1: 8 Do not let this *B* of the Law depart
2Ki 22: 8 "I have found the *B* of the Law
2Ch 34:15 "I have found the *B* of the Law
Ne 8: 8 They read from the *B* of the Law
Ps 69:28 May they be blotted out of the *b*

Da 12: 1 name is found written in the *b*—
Jn 20:30 which are not recorded in this *b.*
Php 4: 3 whose names are in the *b* of life.
Rev 3: 5 never blot out his name from the *b*
20:12 *b* was opened, which is the *b*
20:15 was not found written in the *b*
21:27 written in the Lamb's *b* of life.
22:18 him the plagues described in this *b.*

BOOKS* (BOOK)

Ecc 12:12 Of making many *b* there is no end,
Da 7:10 and the *b* were opened.
Jn 21:25 for the *b* that would be written.
Rev 20:12 the throne, and *b* were opened.
20:12 they had done as recorded in the *b.*

BORE (BEAR)

Isa 53:12 For he *b* the sin of many,
1Pe 2:24 He himself *b* our sins in his body

BORN (BEAR)

Ecc 3: 2 a time to be *b* and a time to die,
Isa 9: 6 For to us a child is *b,*
66: 8 Can a country be *b* in a day
Lk 2:11 of David a Savior has been *b* to you
Jn 3: 3 see the kingdom of God unless he is *b* again.
3: 4 How can a man be *b* when he is old
3: 5 unless he is *b* of water
3: 7 at my saying, 'You must be *b* again
3: 8 it is with everyone *b* of the Spirit."
1Pe 1:23 For you have been *b* again,
1Jn 3: 9 because he has been *b* of God.
4: 7 Everyone who loves has been *b*
5: 1 believes that Jesus is the Christ is *b*
5: 4 for everyone *b* of God overcomes
5:18 We know that anyone *b*

BORROWER

Pr 22: 7 and the *b* is servant to the lender.

BOTHER (BOTHERING)

Lk 11: 7 one inside answers, 'Don't *b* me.

BOTHERING (BOTHER)

Lk 18: 5 yet because this widow keeps *b* me,

BOUGHT (BUY)

Ac 20:28 which he *b* with his own blood.
1Co 6:20 You are not your own; you were *b*
7:23 You were *b* at a price; do not
2Pe 2: 1 the sovereign Lord who *b* them—

BOUND (BIND)

Is 56: 3 Let no foreigner who has *b* himself
Mt 16:19 bind on earth will be *b* in heaven,
18:18 bind on earth will be *b* in heaven,
Ro 7: 2 by law a married woman is *b*
1Co 7:39 A woman is *b* to her husband
Jude : 6 *b* with everlasting chains
Rev 20: 2 and *b* him for a thousand years.

BOUNDARY (BOUNDS)

Nu 34: 3 your southern *b* will start
Pr 23:10 Do not move an ancient *b* stone
Hos 5:10 who move *b* stones.

BOUNDS (BOUNDARY)

2Co 7: 4 all our troubles my joy knows no *b.*

BOUNTY*

Ge 49:26 than the *b* of the age-old hills.
Dt 28:12 heavens, the storehouse of his *b,*
1Ki 10:13 he had given her out of his royal *b.*
Ps 65:11 You crown the year with your *b,*
68:10 from your *b,* O God, you provided
Jer 31:12 rejoice in the *b* of the LORD—
31:14 my people will be filled with my *b*

BOW (BOWED BOWS)

Dt 5: 9 You shall not *b* down to them
1Ki 22:34 But someone drew his *b* at random
Ps 5: 7 in reverence will I *b* down
44: 6 I do not trust in my *b,*
95: 6 Come, let us *b* down in worship,
138: 2 I will *b* down toward your holy
Isa 44:19 Shall I *b* down to a block of wood?"
45:23 Before me every knee will *b;*
Ro 14:11 'every knee will *b* before me;
Php 2:10 name of Jesus every knee should *b,*

BOWED (BOW)

Ps 145:14 and lifts up all who are *b* down.
146: 8 the LORD lifts up those who are *b*

BOWS (BOW)

Isa 44:15 he makes an idol and *b* down to it.
44:17 he *b* down to it and worships.

BOY (BOY'S BOYS)

Ge 21:17 God heard the *b* crying,
22:12 not lay a hand on the *b*
Jdg 13: 5 *b* is to be a Nazirite,
1Sa 2:11 *b* ministered before the LORD.
3: 8 the LORD was calling the *b.*
Isa 7:16 before the *b* knows enough
Mt 17:18 demon, and it came out of the *b*
Lk 2:43 the *b* Jesus stayed behind

BOY'S (BOY)

1Ki 17:22 the *b* life returned to him
2Ki 4:34 the *b* body grew warm

BOYS (BOY)

Ge 25:24 twin *b* in her womb
Ex 1:18 they let the *b* live.

BRACE*

Job 38: 3 *B* yourself like a man;
40: 7 out of the storm: "*B* yourself like
Na 2: 1 *b* yourselves,

BRAG*

Am 4: 5 and *b* about your freewill offerings
Ro 2:17 *b* about your relationship to God;
2:23 temples? You who *b* about the law,
Jas 4:16 As it is, you boast and *b.*

BRAIDED

1Ti 2: 9 not with *b* hair or gold or pearls
1Pe 3: 3 as *b* hair and the wearing

BRANCH (BRANCHES)

Isa 4: 2 In that day the *B* of the LORD will
Jer 23: 5 up to David a righteous *B,*
33:15 I will make a righteous *B* sprout
Zec 3: 8 going to bring my servant, the *B.*
6:12 is the man whose name is the *B,*
Jn 15: 2 while every *b* that does bear fruit
15: 4 No *b* can bear fruit by itself;

BRANCHES (BRANCH)

Jn 15: 5 "I am the vine; you are the *b.*
Ro 11:21 if God did not spare the natural *b,*

BRAVE

2Sa 2: 7 Now then, be strong and *b,*
13:28 you this order? Be strong and *b.*"

BREACH (BREAK)

Ps 106:23 stood in the *b* before him

BREACHING (BREAK)

Pr 17:14 Starting a quarrel is like *b* a dam;

BREAD

Ex 12: 8 and *b* made without yeast.
23:15 the Feast of Unleavened *B;*
25:30 Put the *b* of the Presence
Dt 8: 3 that man does not live on *b* alone
Ps 78:25 Men ate the *b* of angels;
Pr 30: 8 but give me only my daily *b.*
Ecc 11: 1 Cast your *b* upon the waters,
Isa 55: 2 Why spend money on what is not *b*
Mt 4: 3 tell these stones to become *b.*"
4: 4 'Man does not live on *b* alone,
6:11 Give us today our daily *b.*
26:26 Jesus took *b,* gave thanks
Mk 14:22 Jesus took *b,* gave thanks
Lk 4: 3 tell this stone to become *b.*"
4: 4 'Man does not live on *b* alone.' "
9:13 "We have only five loaves of *b*
11: 3 Give us each day our daily *b.*
22:19 And he took *b,* gave thanks
Jn 6:33 For the *b* of God is he who comes
6:35 Jesus declared, "I am the *b* of life.
6:41 "I am the *b* that came
6:48 I am the *b* of life.
6:51 I am the living *b* that came
6:51 This *b* is my flesh, which I will give
21:13 took the *b* and gave it to them,
1Co 10:16 And is not the *b* that we break
11:23 took *b,* and when he had given
11:26 For whenever you eat this *b*

BREAK (BREACH BREACHING BREAKERS BREAKING BREAKS BROKE BROKEN BROKENNESS)

Nu 30: 2 he must not *b* his word
Jdg 2: 1 'I will never *b* my covenant
Pr 25:15 and a gentle tongue can *b* a bone.
Isa 42: 3 A bruised reed he will not *b,*
Mal 2:15 and do not *b* faith with the wife
Mt 12:20 A bruised reed he will not *b,*
Ac 20: 7 week we came together to *b* bread.
1Co 10:16 the bread that we *b* a participation
Rev 5: 2 "Who is worthy to *b* the seals

BREAKERS* (BREAK)

Ps 42: 7 all your waves and *b*
93: 4 mightier than the *b* of the sea—
Jnh 2: 3 all your waves and *b*

BREAKING (BREAK)

Jos 9:20 fall on us for *b* the oath we swore
Eze 16:59 oath by *b* the covenant.
17:18 the oath by *b* the covenant.
Ac 2:42 to the *b* of bread and to prayer.
Jas 2:10 at just one point is guilty of *b* all

BREAKS (BREAK)

Jer 23:29 "and like a hammer that *b* a rock
1Jn 3: 4 Everyone who sins *b* the law;

BREASTPIECE (BREASTPLATE)

Ex 28:15 Fashion a *b* for making decisions—

BREASTPLATE* (BREASTPIECE)

Isa 59:17 He put on righteousness as his *b,*
Eph 6:14 with the *b* of righteousness in place
1Th 5: 8 putting on faith and love as a *b,*

BREASTS

La 4: 3 Even jackals offer their *b*

BREATH (BREATHED GOD-BREATHED)

Ge 2: 7 into his nostrils the *b* of life,

BREATHED (BREATH)

Ge 2: 7 *b* into his nostrils the breath of life,
Mk 15:37 With a loud cry, Jesus *b* his last.
Jn 20:22 And with that he *b* on them

BREEDS*

Pr 13:10 Pride only *b* quarrels,

BRIBE

Ex 23: 8 "Do not accept a *b,*
Dt 16:19 for a *b* blinds the eyes of the wise
27:25 "Cursed is the man who accepts a *b*
Pr 6:35 will refuse the *b,* however great it

BRIDE

Isa 62: 5 as a bridegroom rejoices over his *b,*
Rev 19: 7 and his *b* has made herself ready.
21: 2 as a *b* beautifully dressed
21: 9 I will show you the *b,* the wife
22:17 The Spirit and the *b* say, "Come!"

BRIDEGROOM

Ps 19: 5 which is like a *b* coming forth
Mt 25: 1 and went out to meet the *b.*
25: 5 The *b* was a long time in coming,

BRIGHTENS* (BRIGHTNESS)

Pr 16:15 When a king's face *b,* it means life;
Ecc 8: 1 Wisdom *b* a man's face

BRIGHTER (BRIGHTNESS)

Pr 4:18 shining ever *b* till the full light

BRIGHTNESS* (BRIGHTENS BRIGHTER)

2Sa 22:13 Out of the *b* of his presence
23: 4 like the *b* after rain
Ps 18:12 of the *b* of his presence clouds
Isa 59: 9 for *b,* but we walk in deep shadows.
60: 3 and kings to the *b* of your dawn.
60:19 will the *b* of the moon shine on you
Da 12: 3 who are wise will shine like the *b*
Am 5:20 pitch-dark, without a ray of *b?*

BRILLIANCE* (BRILLIANT)

Ac 22:11 the *b* of the light had blinded me.
Rev 1:16 was like the sun shining in all its *b.*
21:11 its *b* was like that of a very precious

BRILLIANT* (BRILLIANCE)

Ecc 9:11 or wealth to the *b*
Eze 1: 4 and surrounded by *b* light.
1:27 and *b* light surrounded him.

BRINK*

Pr 5:14 I have come to the *b* of utter ruin

BRITTLE

Da 2:42 will be partly strong and partly *b*.

BROAD

Mt 7:13 and *b* is the road that leads

BROKE (BREAK)

Mt 26:26 took bread, gave thanks and *b* it,
Mk 14:22 took bread, gave thanks and *b* it,
Ac 2:46 They *b* bread in their homes
20:11 he went upstairs again and *b* bread
1Co 11:24 when he had given thanks, he *b* it

BROKEN (BREAK)

Ps 34:20 not one of them will be *b*.
51:17 The sacrifices of God are a *b* spirit;
Ecc 4:12 of three strands is not quickly *b*.
Lk 20:18 on that stone will be *b* to pieces,
Jn 7:23 the law of Moses may not be *b*,
10:35 and the Scripture cannot be *b*—
19:36 "Not one of his bones will be *b*,"
Ro 11:20 they were *b* off because of unbelief,

BROKENHEARTED* (HEART)

Ps 34:18 The LORD is close to the *b*
109:16 and the needy and the *b*.
147:3 He heals the *b*
Isa 61:1 He has sent me to bind up the *b*,

BROKENNESS* (BREAK)

Isa 65:14 and wail in *b* of spirit.

BRONZE

Ex 27:2 and overlay the altar with *b*.
30:18 "Make a *b* basin, with its *b* stand,
Nu 21:9 So Moses made a *b* snake
Da 2:32 and thighs of *b*, its legs of iron,
10:6 legs like the gleam of burnished *b*,
Rev 1:15 His feet were like *b* glowing
2:18 whose feet are like burnished *b*.

BROTHER (BROTHER'S BROTHERHOOD BROTHERLY BROTHERS)

Pr 17:17 and a *b* is born for adversity.
18:24 a friend who sticks closer than a *b*.
27:10 neighbor nearby than a *b* far away.
Mt 5:24 and be reconciled to your *b*;
18:15 "If your *b* sins against you,
Mk 3:35 Whoever does God's will is my *b*
Lk 17:3 "If your *b* sins, rebuke him,
Ro 14:15 not by your eating destroy your *b*
14:21 anything else that will cause your *b*
1Co 8:13 if what I eat causes my *b* to fall
2Th 3:6 away from every *b* who is idle
3:15 as an enemy, but warn him as a *b*.
Phm :16 but better than a slave, as a dear *b*.
Jas 2:15 Suppose a *b* or sister is
4:11 Anyone who speaks against his *b*
1Jn 2:9 hates his *b* is still in the darkness.
2:10 Whoever loves his *b* lives
2:11 But whoever hates his *b* is
3:10 is anyone who does not love his *b*.
3:15 who hates his *b* is a murderer,
3:17 material possessions and sees his *b*
4:20 For anyone who does not love his *b*
4:20 yet hates his *b*, he is a liar.
4:21 loves God must also love his *b*.
5:16 If anyone sees his *b* commit a sin

BROTHER'S (BROTHER)

Ge 4:9 "Am I my *b* keeper?" The LORD
Mt 7:5 remove the speck from your *b* eye.
Ro 14:13 or obstacle in your *b* way.

BROTHERHOOD (BROTHER)

1Pe 2:17 Love the *b* of believers, fear God,

BROTHERLY* (BROTHER)

Ro 12:10 devoted to one another in *b* love.
1Th 4:9 Now about *b* love we do not need
2Pe 1:7 and to godliness, *b* kindness;
1:7 kindness; and to *b* kindness,

BROTHERS (BROTHER)

Jos 1:14 You are to help your *b*
Ps 133:1 is when *b* live together in unity!
Pr 6:19 who stirs up dissension among *b*.
Mt 12:49 "Here are my mother and my *b*.
19:29 everyone who has left houses or *b*
25:40 one of the least of these *b* of mine,
Mk 3:33 "Who are my mother and my *b*?"
10:29 or *b* or sisters or mother or father
Lk 21:16 You will be betrayed even by parents, *b*,
22:32 turned back, strengthen your *b*."
Jn 7:5 his own *b* did not believe in him.
Ac 15:32 to encourage and strengthen the *b*.
Ro 9:3 off from Christ for the sake of my *b*
1Co 8:12 sin against your *b* in this way
2Co 11:26 and in danger from false *b*.
Gal 2:4 some false *b* had infiltrated our
1Th 4:10 you do love all the *b*
5:26 Greet all the *b* with a holy kiss.
1Ti 6:2 for them because they are *b*.
Heb 2:11 Jesus is not ashamed to call them *b*.
2:17 to be made like his *b* in every way,
13:1 Keep on loving each other as *b*.
1Pe 1:22 you have sincere love for your *b*,
3:8 be sympathetic, love as *b*,
1Jn 3:14 death to life, because we love our *b*.
3:16 to lay down our lives for our *b*.
3Jn :10 he refuses to welcome the *b*.
Rev 12:10 For the accuser of our *b*,

BROW

Ge 3:19 By the sweat of your *b*

BRUISED (BRUISES)

Isa 42:3 A *b* reed he will not break,
Mt 12:20 A *b* reed he will not break,

BRUISES (BRUISED)

Isa 30:26 when the LORD binds up the *b*

BRUTAL (BRUTE)

2Ti 3:3 slanderous, without self-control, *b*,

BRUTE* (BRUTAL)

Ps 73:22 I was a *b* beast before you.
2Pe 2:12 They are like *b* beasts, creatures

BUBBLING*

Pr 18:4 the fountain of wisdom is a *b* brook
Isa 35:7 the thirsty ground *b* springs.

BUCKET*

Isa 40:15 the nations are like a drop in a *b*;

BUCKLED* (BUCKLER)

Eph 6:14 belt of truth *b* around your waist,

BUCKLER* (BUCKLED)

Ps 35:2 Take up shield and *b*;

BUD (BUDDED)

Isa 27:6 Israel will *b* and blossom

BUDDED (BUD)

Heb 9:4 Aaron's staff that had *b*,

BUILD (BUILDER BUILDERS BUILDING BUILDS BUILT REBUILD REBUILT)

2Sa 7:5 Are you the one to *b* me a house
1Ki 6:1 he began to *b* the temple
Ecc 3:3 a time to tear down and a time to *b*,
Mt 16:18 and on this rock I will *b* my church,
Ac 20:32 which can *b* you up and give you
Ro 15:2 neighbor for his good, to *b* him up.
1Co 14:12 excel in gifts that *b* up the church.
1Th 5:11 one another and *b* each other up,
Jude :20 *b* yourselves up in your most holy

BUILDER* (BUILD)

1Co 3:10 I laid a foundation as an expert *b*,
Heb 3:3 the *b* of a house has greater honor
3:4 but God is the *b* of everything.
11:10 whose architect and *b* is God.

BUILDERS (BUILD)

Ps 118:22 The stone the *b* rejected
Mt 21:42 " 'The stone the *b* rejected
Mk 12:10 " 'The stone the *b* rejected
Lk 20:17 " 'The stone the *b* rejected
Ac 4:11 " 'the stone you *b* rejected,
1Pe 2:7 "The stone the *b* rejected

BUILDING (BUILD)

Ezr 3:8 to supervise the *b* of the house
Ne 4:17 of Judah who were *b* the wall.
Ro 15:20 so that I would not be *b*
1Co 3:9 you are God's field, God's *b*.
2Co 5:1 we have a *b* from God, an eternal
10:8 us for *b* you up rather
13:10 the Lord gave me for *b* you up,
Eph 2:21 him the whole *b* is joined together
4:29 helpful for *b* others up according

BUILDS (BUILD)

Ps 127:1 Unless the LORD *b* the house,
Pr 14:1 The wise woman *b* her house,
1Co 3:10 one should be careful how he *b*.
3:12 If any man *b* on this foundation
8:1 Knowledge puffs up, but love *b* up.
Eph 4:16 grows and *b* itself up in love,

BUILT (BUILD)

1Ki 6:14 So Solomon *b* the temple
Mt 7:24 is like a wise man who *b* his house
Lk 6:49 is like a man who *b* a house
Ac 17:24 does not live in temples *b* by hands.
1Co 3:14 If what he has *b* survives, he will
2Co 5:1 in heaven, not *b* by human hands.
Eph 2:20 *b* on the foundation of the apostles
4:12 the body of Christ may be *b* up
Col 2:7 live in him, rooted and *b* up in him,
1Pe 2:5 are being *b* into a spiritual house

BULL (BULLS)

Lev 4:3 bring to the LORD a young *b*

BULLS (BULL)

1Ki 7:25 The Sea stood on twelve *b*,
Heb 10:4 it is impossible for the blood of *b*

BURDEN (BURDENED BURDENS BURDENSOME)

Ps 38:4 like a *b* too heavy to bear.
Ecc 1:13 What a heavy *b* God has laid
Mt 11:30 my yoke is easy and my *b* is light."
Ac 15:28 to us not to *b* you with anything
2Co 11:9 from being a *b* to you in any way,
12:14 and I will not be a *b* to you,
1Th 2:9 day in order not to be a *b* to anyone
2Th 3:8 so that we would not be a *b* to any
Heb 13:17 not a *b*, for that would be

BURDENED* (BURDEN)

Isa 43:23 have not *b* you with grain offerings
43:24 But you have *b* me with your sins
Mic 6:3 How have I *b* you? Answer me.
Mt 11:28 all you who are weary and *b*,
2Co 5:4 are in this tent, we groan and are *b*,
Gal 5:1 do not let yourselves be *b* again
1Ti 5:16 not let the church be *b* with them,

BURDENS (BURDEN)

Ps 68:19 who daily bears our *b*.
Lk 11:46 down with *b* they can hardly carry,
Gal 6:2 Carry each other's *b*,

BURDENSOME (BURDEN)

1Jn 5:3 And his commands are not *b*,

BURIED (BURY)

Ru 1:17 die I will die, and there I will be *b*.
Ro 6:4 *b* with him through baptism
1Co 15:4 that he was *b*, that he was raised
Col 2:12 having been *b* with him in baptism

BURN (BURNING BURNT)

Dt 7:5 and *b* their idols in the fire.
Ps 79:5 long will your jealousy *b* like fire?
1Co 7:9 to marry than to *b* with passion.

BURNING (BURN)

Ex 27:20 so that the lamps may be kept *b*.
Lev 6:9 the fire must be kept *b* on the altar.
Ps 18:28 You, O LORD, keep my lamp *b*;
Pr 25:22 you will heap *b* coals on his head,
Ro 12:20 you will heap *b* coals on his head."
Rev 19:20 alive into the fiery lake of *b* sulfur.

BURNISHED*

1Ki 7:45 of the LORD were of *b* bronze.
Eze 1:7 and gleamed like *b* bronze.
Da 10:6 and legs like the gleam of *b* bronze,
Rev 2:18 and whose feet are like *b* bronze.

BURNT (BURN)

Ge 8:20 he sacrificed *b* offerings on it.
22:2 as a *b* offering on one
Ex 10:25 and *b* offerings to present
18:12 brought a *b* offering and other
40:6 Place the altar of *b* offering in front
Lev 1:3 " 'If the offering is a *b* offering
Jos 8:31 offered to the LORD *b* offerings
Jdg 6:26 offer the second bull as a *b* offering
13:16 But if you prepare a *b* offering,
1Ki 3:4 offered a thousand *b* offerings
9:25 year Solomon sacrificed *b* offerings
10:5 and the *b* offerings he made
Ezr 3:2 Israel to sacrifice *b* offerings on it,
Eze 43:18 for sacrificing *b* offerings

BURST

Ps 98: 4 b into jubilant song with music;
Isa 44: 23 B into song, you mountains,
49: 13 b into song, O mountains!
52: 9 B into songs of joy together,
54: 1 b into song, shout for joy,
55: 12 will b into song before you,

BURY (BURIED)

Mt 8: 22 and let the dead b their own dead."
Lk 9: 60 "Let the dead b their own dead,

BUSH

Ex 3: 2 the b was on fire it did not burn up.
Mk 12: 26 the account of the b, how God said
Lk 20: 37 But in the account of the b,
Ac 7: 35 who appeared to him in the b.

BUSINESS

Ecc 4: 8 a miserable b!
Da 8: 27 and went about the king's b.
1Co 5: 12 What b is it of mine to judge those
1Th 4: 11 to mind your own b and to work
Jas 1: 11 even while he goes about his b.

BUSY*

1Ki 18: 27 Perhaps he is deep in thought, or b,
20: 40 While your servant was b here
Isa 32: 6 his mind is b with evil:
Hag 1: 9 of you is b with his own house.
2Th 3: 11 They are not b; they are
Tit 2: 5 to be b at home, to be kind,

BUSYBODIES*

2Th 3: 11 They are not busy; they are b.
1Ti 5: 13 b, saying things they ought not to.

BUY (BOUGHT BUYS)

Pr 23: 23 B the truth and do not sell it;
Isa 55: 1 Come, b wine and milk
Rev 13: 17 so that no one could b or sell

BUYS (BUY)

Pr 31: 16 She considers a field and b it;

BYWORD (WORD)

1Ki 9: 7 Israel will then become a b
Ps 44: 14 You have made us a b
Joel 2: 17 a b among the nations.

CAESAR

Mt 22: 21 "Give to C what is Caesar's,

CAIN

Firstborn of Adam (Ge 4:1), murdered brother Abel (Ge 4:1-16; 1Jn 3:12).

CAKE

Hos 7: 8 Ephraim is a flat c not turned over.

CALEB

Judahite who spied out Canaan (Nu 13:6); allowed to enter land because of faith (Nu 13:30-14:38; Dt 1:36). Possessed Hebron (Jdg 14:6-15:19).

CALF

Ex 32: 4 into an idol cast in the shape of a c,
Pr 15: 17 than a fattened c with hatred.
Lk 15: 23 Bring the fattened c and kill it.
Ac 7: 41 made an idol in the form of a c.

CALL (CALLED CALLING CALLS)

1Ki 18: 24 I will c on the name of the LORD.
2Ki 5: 11 c on the name of the LORD his
1Ch 16: 8 to the LORD, c on his name;
Ps 105: 1 to the LORD, c on his name;
116: 13 and c on the name of the LORD.
116: 17 and c on the name of the LORD.
145: 18 near to all who c on him,
Pr 31: 28 children arise and c her blessed;
Isa 5: 20 Woe to those who c evil good
12: 4 to the LORD, c on his name;
55: 6 c on him while he is near.
65: 24 Before they c I will answer;
Jer 33: 3 'C to me and I will answer you
Zep 3: 9 that all of them may c on the name
Zec 13: 9 They will c on my name
Mt 9: 13 come to c the righteous,
Mk 2: 17 I have not come to c the righteous,
Lk 5: 32 I have not come to c the righteous,
Ac 2: 39 all whom the Lord our God will c."
9: 14 to arrest all who c on your name."
9: 21 among those who c on this name?
Ro 10: 12 and richly blesses all who c on him,
11: 29 gifts and his c are irrevocable.
1Co 1: 2 with all those everywhere who c
1Th 4: 7 For God did not c us to be impure,
2Ti 2: 22 along with those who c

CALLED (CALL)

Ge 2: 23 she shall be c 'woman,'
5: 2 he blessed them and c them "man
12: 8 and c on the name of the LORD.
21: 33 and there he c upon the name
26: 25 and c on the name of the LORD.
1Sa 3: 5 and said, "Here I am; you c me."
2Ch 7: 14 if my people, who are c
Ps 34: 6 This poor man c, and the LORD
116: 4 Then I c on the name of the LORD
Isa 56: 7 for my house will be c
La 3: 55 I c on your name, O LORD,
Hos 11: 1 and out of Egypt I c my son.
Mt 1: 16 was born Jesus, who is c Christ.
2: 15 "Out of Egypt I c my son."
21: 13 " 'My house will be c a house
Mk 11: 17 " 'My house will be c
Lk 1: 32 will be c the Son of the Most High.
1: 35 to be born will be c the Son of God.
Ro 1: 1 c to be an apostle and set apart
1: 6 among those who are c to belong
1: 7 loved by God and c to be saints:
8: 28 who have been c according
8: 30 And those he predestined, he also c
1Co 1: 1 c to be an apostle of Christ Jesus
1: 2 in Christ Jesus and c to be holy,
1: 24 but to those whom God has c,
1: 26 of what you were when you were c.
7: 15 God has c us to live in peace.
7: 17 and to which God has c him.
Gal 1: 6 deserting the one who c you
1: 15 from birth and c me by his grace,
5: 13 You, my brothers, were c to be free
Eph 1: 18 the hope to which he has c you,
4: 4 as you were c to one hope
Col 3: 15 of one body you were c to peace.
2Th 2: 14 He c you to this through our gospel
1Ti 6: 12 life to which you were c
2Ti 1: 9 who has saved us and c us
Heb 9: 15 that those who are c may receive
1Pe 1: 15 But just as he who c you is holy,
2: 9 of him who c you out of darkness
3: 9 to this you were c so that you may
5: 10 who c you to his eternal glory
2Pe 1: 3 of him who c us by his own glory
Jude : 1 To those who have been c,

CALLING (CALL)

Isa 40: 3 A voice of one c:
Mt 3: 3 "A voice of one c in the desert,
Mk 1: 3 "a voice of one c in the desert,
10: 49 Cheer up! On your feet! He's c you
Lk 3: 4 "A voice of one c in the desert,
Jn 1: 23 I am the voice of one c in the desert
Ac 22: 16 wash your sins away, c on his name
Eph 4: 1 worthy of the c you have received.
2Th 1: 11 may count you worthy of his c,
2Pe 1: 10 all the more eager to make your c

CALLOUS* (CALLOUSED)

Ps 17: 10 They close up their c hearts,
73: 7 From their c hearts comes iniquity;
119: 70 Their hearts are c and unfeeling,

CALLOUSED* (CALLOUS)

Isa 6: 10 Make the heart of this people c;
Mt 13: 15 this people's heart has become c;
Ac 28: 27 this people's heart has become c;

CALLS (CALL)

Ps 147: 4 and c them each by name.
Isa 40: 26 and c them each by name.
Joel 2: 32 And everyone who c
Mt 22: 43 speaking by the Spirit, c him 'Lord
Jn 10: 3 He c his own sheep by name
Ac 2: 21 And everyone who c
Ro 10: 13 "Everyone who c on the name
1Th 2: 12 who c you into his kingdom
5: 24 The one who c you is faithful

CALM (CALMS)

Ps 107: 30 They were glad when it grew c,
Isa 7: 4 keep c and don't be afraid.
Eze 16: 42 I will be c and no longer angry.

CALMS* (CALM)

Pr 15: 18 but a patient man c a quarrel.

CAMEL

Mt 19: 24 it is easier for a c to go
23: 24 strain out a gnat but swallow a c.
Mk 10: 25 It is easier for a c to go
Lk 18: 25 it is easier for a c to go

CAMP (ENCAMPS)

Heb 13: 13 outside the c, bearing the disgrace

CANAAN (CANAANITE CANAANITES)

Ge 10: 15 C was the father of Sidon his
Lev 14: 34 "When you enter the land of C,
25: 38 of Egypt to give you the land of C
Nu 13: 2 men to explore the land of C,
33: 51 'When you cross the Jordan into C,
Jdg 4: 2 a king of C, who reigned in Hazor.
1Ch 16: 18 "To you I will give the land of C
Ps 105: 11 "To you I will give the land of C
Ac 13: 19 he overthrew seven nations in C

CANAANITE (CANAAN)

Ge 10: 18 Later the C clans scattered
28: 1 "Do not marry a C woman.
Jos 5: 1 all the C kings along the seacoast
Jdg 1: 32 lived among the C inhabitants

CANAANITES (CANAAN)

Ex 33: 2 before you and drive out the C,

CANCEL (CANCELED)

Dt 15: 1 seven years you must c debts.

CANCELED (CANCEL)

Mt 18: 27 pity on him, c the debt
Lk 7: 42 so he c the debts of both.
Col 2: 14 having c the written code,

CANDLESTICKS see LAMPSTANDS

CANOPY*

2Sa 22: 12 He made darkness his c
2Ki 16: 18 away the Sabbath c that had been
Ps 18: 11 made darkness his covering, his c
Isa 4: 5 over all the glory will be a c.
40: 22 stretches out the heavens like a c,
Jer 43: 10 he will spread his royal c

CAPERNAUM

Mt 4: 13 Nazareth, he went and lived in C,
Jn 6: 59 teaching in the synagogue in C.

CAPITAL

Dt 21: 22 guilty of a c offense is put to death

CAPSTONE* (STONE)

Ps 118: 22 has become the c;
Zec 4: 7 he will bring out the c to shouts
Mt 21: 42 has become the c;
Mk 12: 10 has become the c;
Lk 20: 17 has become the c'?
Ac 4: 11 which has become the c.'
1Pe 2: 7 has become the c,"

CAPTIVATE* (CAPTIVE)

Pr 6: 25 or let her c you with her eyes,

CAPTIVATED* (CAPTIVE)

Pr 5: 19 may you ever be c by her love.
5: 20 Why be c, my son, by an adulteress

CAPTIVE (CAPTIVATE CAPTIVATED CAPTIVES CAPTIVITY CAPTURED)

Ac 8: 23 full of bitterness and c to sin."
2Co 10: 5 and we take c every thought
Col 2: 8 See to it that no one takes you c
2Ti 2: 26 who has taken them c to do his will.

CAPTIVES (CAPTIVE)

Ps 68: 18 you led c in your train;
Isa 61: 1 to proclaim freedom for the c
Eph 4: 8 he led c in his train

CAPTIVITY (CAPTIVE)

Dt 28: 41 because they will go into c.
2Ki 25: 21 So Judah went into c, away
Jer 30: 3 Israel and Judah back from c
52: 27 So Judah went into c, away
Eze 29: 14 I will bring them back from c

CAPTURED (CAPTIVE)

1Sa 4: 11 The ark of God was c,
2Sa 5: 7 David c the fortress of Zion,
2Ki 17: 6 the king of Assyria c Samaria

CARCASS
Jdg 14: 9 taken the honey from the lion's c.
Mt 24:28 there is a c, there the vultures

CARE (CAREFUL CARES CARING)
Ps 8: 4 the son of man that you c for him?
65: 9 You c for the land and water it;
144: 3 what is man that you c for him,
Pr 29: 7 The righteous c about justice
Mk 5:26 deal under the c of many doctors
Lk 10:34 him to an inn and took c of him.
18: 4 I don't fear God or c about men,
Jn 21:16 Jesus said, "Take c of my sheep."
1Ti 3: 5 how can he take c of God's church
6:20 what has been entrusted to your c.
Heb 2: 6 the son of man that you c for him?
1Pe 5: 2 of God's flock that is under your c,

CAREFUL* (CARE)
Ge 31:24 "Be c not to say anything to Jacob,
31:29 'Be c not to say anything to Jacob,
Ex 19:12 'Be c that you do not go up
23:13 "Be c to do everything I have said
34:12 Be c not to make a treaty
34:15 "Be c not to make a treaty
Lev 18: 4 and be c to follow my decrees.
25:18 " 'Follow my decrees and be c
26: 3 and are c to obey my commands,
Dt 2: 4 afraid of you, but be very c.
4: 9 before you today? Only be c,
4:23 Be c not to forget the covenant
5:32 So be c to do what the LORD your
6: 3 be c to obey so that it may go well
6:12 be c that you do not forget
6:25 And if we are c to obey all this law
7:12 attention to these laws and are c
8: 1 Be c to follow every command I am
8:11 Be c that you do not forget
11:16 Be c, or you will be enticed
12: 1 and laws you must be c to follow
12:13 Be c not to sacrifice your burnt
12:19 Be c not to neglect the Levites
12:28 Be c to obey all these regulations I
12:30 be c not to be ensnared
15: 5 are c to follow all these commands
15: 9 Be c not to harbor this wicked
17:10 Be c to do everything they direct
24: 8 cases of leprous diseases be very c
Jos 1: 7 Be c to obey all the law my servant
1: 8 so that you may be c
22: 5 But be very c to keep
23: 6 be c to obey all that is written
23:11 be very c to love the LORD your
1Ki 8:25 if only your sons are c in all they do
2Ki 10:31 Yet Jehu was not c to keep the law
17:37 You must always be c
21: 8 if only they will be c
1Ch 22:13 if you are c to observe the decrees
28: 8 Be c to follow all the commands
2Ch 6:16 if only your sons are c in all they do
33: 8 if only they will be c
Ezr 4:22 Be c not to neglect this matter.
Job 36:18 Be c that no one entices you
Ps 101: 2 I will be c to lead a blameless life—
Pr 13:24 he who loves him is c
27:23 give c attention to your herds;
Isa 7: 4 Be c, keep calm and don't be afraid.
Jer 17:21 Be c not to carry a load
17:24 But if you are c to obey me,
22: 4 For if you are c to carry out these
Eze 11:20 will follow my decrees and be c
18:19 has been c to keep all my decrees,
20:19 follow my decrees and be c
20:21 they were not c to keep my laws—
36:27 you to follow my decrees and be c
37:24 and be c to keep my decrees.
Mic 7: 5 be c of your words.
Hag 1: 5 "Give c thought to your ways.
1: 7 "Give c thought to your ways.
2:15 give c thought to this from this day
2:18 Give c thought: Is there yet any
2:18 give c thought to the day
Mt 2: 8 and make a c search for the child.
6: 1 "Be c not to do your 'acts
16: 6 "Be c," Jesus said to them.
Mk 8:15 "Be c," Jesus warned them.
Lk 21:34 Be c, or your hearts will be weighed
Ro 12:17 Be c to do what is right in the eyes
1Co 3:10 each one should be c how he builds
8: 9 Be c, however, that the exercise
10:12 standing firm, be c that you don't
Eph 5:15 Be very c, then, how you live—
2Ti 4: 2 great patience and c instruction.
Tit 3: 8 may be c to devote themselves
Heb 2: 1 We must pay more c attention,
4: 1 let us be c that none

CARELESS*
Mt 12:36 for every c word they have spoken.

CARES* (CARE)
Dt 11:12 It is a land the LORD your God c
Job 39:16 she c not that her labor was in vain,
Ps 55:22 Cast your c on the LORD
142: 4 no one c for my life.
Pr 12:10 A righteous man c for the needs
Ecc 5: 3 when there are many c,
Jer 12:11 because there is no one who c.
30:17 Zion for whom no one c.'
Na 1: 7 He c for those who trust in him,
Jn 10:13 and c nothing for the sheep.
Eph 5:29 but he feeds and c for it, just
1Pe 5: 7 on him because he c for you.

CARING* (CARE)
1Th 2: 7 like a mother c for her little
1Ti 5: 4 practice by c for their own family

CARNAL see SINFUL, UNSPIRITUAL, WORLDLY

CARPENTER (CARPENTER'S)
Mk 6: 3 does miracles! Isn't this the c?

CARPENTER'S* (CARPENTER)
Mt 13:55 "Isn't this the c son? Isn't his

CARRIED (CARRY)
Ex 19: 4 and how I c you on eagles' wings
Dt 1:31 how the LORD your God c you,
Isa 53: 4 and c our sorrows,
63: 9 he lifted them up and c them
Mt 8:17 and c our diseases."
Heb 13: 9 Do not be c away by all kinds
2Pe 1:21 as they were c along by the Holy
3:17 so that you may not be c away

CARRIES (CARRY)
Dt 32:11 and c them on its pinions.
Isa 40:11 and c them close to his heart;

CARRY (CARRIED CARRIES CARRYING)
Lev 16:22 goat will c on itself all their sins
26:15 and fail to c out all my commands
Isa 46: 4 I have made you and I will c you;
Lk 14:27 anyone who does not c his cross
Gal 6: 2 C each other's burdens,
6: 5 for each one should c his own load.

CARRYING (CARRY)
Jn 19:17 C his own cross, he went out
1Jn 5: 2 loving God and c out his

CARVED (CARVES)
Nu 33:52 Destroy all their c images
Mic 5:13 I will destroy your c images

CARVES* (CARVED)
Dt 27:15 "Cursed is the man who c an image

CASE
Pr 18:17 to present his c seems right,
22:23 for the LORD will take up their c
23:11 he will take up their c against you.

CAST (CASTING)
Ex 34:17 "Do not make c idols.
Lev 16: 8 He is to c lots for the two goats—
Ps 22:18 and c lots for my clothing.
55:22 C your cares on the LORD
Pr 16:33 The lot is c into the lap,
Ecc 11: 1 C your bread upon the waters,
Jn 19:24 and c lots for my clothing."
1Pe 5: 7 C all your anxiety on him

CASTING (CAST)
Pr 18:18 C the lot settles disputes
Mt 27:35 divided up his clothes by c lots.

CATCH (CATCHES CAUGHT)
Lk 5: 4 and let down the nets for a c."
5:10 from now on you will c men."

CATCHES (CATCH)
Job 5:13 He c the wise in their craftiness,
1Co 3:19 "He c the wise in their craftiness";

CATTLE
Ps 50:10 and the c on a thousand hills.

CAUGHT (CATCH)
Ge 22:13 there in a thicket he saw a ram c
2Co 12: 2 who fourteen years ago was c up
1Th 4:17 and are left will be c up together with them

CAUSE (CAUSES)
Pr 24:28 against your neighbor without c,
Ecc 8: 3 Do not stand up for a bad c,
Mt 18: 7 of the things that c people to sin!
Ro 14:21 else that will c your brother
1Co 10:32 Do not c anyone to stumble,

CAUSES (CAUSE)
Ps 7:16 The trouble he c recoils on himself,
Isa 8:14 a stone that c men to stumble
Mt 5:29 If your right eye c you to sin,
5:30 And if your right hand c you to sin,
18: 6 if anyone c one of these little ones
18: 8 or your foot c you to sin,
Ro 14:20 to eat anything that c someone else
1Co 8:13 if what I eat c my brother to fall
1Pe 2: 8 "A stone that c men to stumble

CAUTIOUS*
Pr 12:26 A righteous man is c in friendship,

CEASE
Ps 46: 9 He makes wars c to the ends

CELEBRATE*
Ex 10: 9 we are to c a festival to the LORD
12:14 generations to come you shall c it
12:17 C this day as a lasting ordinance
12:17 "C the Feast of Unleavened Bread,
12:47 community of Israel must c it.
12:48 to c the LORD's Passover must
23:14 are to c a festival to me.
23:15 "C the Feast of Unleavened Bread;
23:16 "C the Feast of Harvest
23:16 "C the Feast of Ingathering
34:18 "C the Feast of Unleavened Bread.
34:22 "C the Feast of Weeks
Lev 23:39 c the festival to the LORD
23:41 C this as a festival to the LORD
23:41 for the generations to come; c it
Nu 9: 2 "Have the Israelites c the Passover
9: 3 C it at the appointed time,
9: 4 told the Israelites to c the Passover,
9: 6 of them could not c the Passover
9:10 they may still c the LORD's
9:11 are to c it on the fourteenth day
9:12 When they c the Passover,
9:13 on a journey fails to c the Passover,
9:14 to c the LORD's Passover must do
29:12 C a festival to the LORD
Dt 16: 1 c the Passover of the LORD your
16:10 Then c the Feast of Weeks
16:13 C the Feast of Tabernacles
16:15 For seven days c the Feast
Jdg 16:23 to Dagon their god and to c,
2Sa 6:21 the LORD's people Israel—I will c
2Ki 23:21 "C the Passover to the LORD your
2Ch 30: 1 and c the Passover to the LORD,
30: 2 decided to c the Passover
30: 3 able to c it at the regular time
30: 5 and c the Passover to the LORD,
30:13 in Jerusalem to c the Feast
30:23 to c the festival seven more days;
Ne 8:12 of food and to c with great joy,
12:27 to c joyfully the dedication
Est 9:21 to have them c annually
Ps 145: 7 They will c your abundant
Isa 30:29 as on the night you c a holy festival
Na 1:15 C your festivals, O Judah,
Zec 14:16 and to c the Feast of Tabernacles.
14:18 up to c the Feast of Tabernacles.
14:19 up to c the Feast of Tabernacles.
Mt 26:18 I am going to c the Passover
Lk 15:23 Let's have a feast and c.
15:24 So they began to c.
15:29 goat so I could c with my friends.
15:32 But we had to c and be glad,
Rev 11:10 will c by sending each other gifts,

CELESTIAL*
2Pe 2:10 afraid to slander c beings;
Jude : 8 authority and slander c beings.

CENSER (CENSERS)
Lev 16:12 is to take a c full of burning coals
Rev 8: 3 Another angel, who had a golden c,

CENSERS (CENSER)

Nu 16: 6 Take *c* and tomorrow put fire

CENTURION

Mt 8: 5 had entered Capernaum, a *c* came
27:54 When the *c* and those
Mk 15:39 And when the *c*, who stood there
Lk 7: 3 The *c* heard of Jesus and sent some
23:47 The *c*, seeing what had happened,
Ac 10: 1 a *c* in what was known
27: 1 handed over to a *c* named Julius,

CEPHAS* (PETER)

Jn 1:42 You will be called *C*" (which,
1Co 1:12 another, "I follow *C*"; still another,
3:22 Paul or Apollos or *C* or the world
9: 5 and the Lord's brothers and *C*?

CEREMONIAL* (CEREMONY)

Lev 14: 2 at the time of his *c* cleansing,
15:13 off seven days for his *c* cleansing;
Mk 7: 3 they give their hands a *c* washing,
Jn 2: 6 used by the Jews for *c* washing,
3:25 Jew over the matter of *c* washing.
11:55 to Jerusalem for their *c* cleansing
18:28 to avoid *c* uncleanness the Jews did
Heb 9:10 drink and various *c* washings—
13: 9 not by *c* foods, which are

CEREMONIALLY* (CEREMONY)

Lev 4:12 outside the camp to a place *c* clean,
5: 2 touches anything *c* unclean—
6:11 the camp to a place that is *c* clean.
7:19 anyone *c* clean may eat it.
7:19 touches anything *c* unclean must
10:14 Eat them in a *c* clean place;
11: 4 not have a split hoof; it is *c* unclean
12: 2 birth to a son will be *c* unclean
12: 7 and then she will be *c* clean
13: 3 he shall pronounce him *c* unclean.
14: 8 with water; then he will be *c* clean.
15:28 and after that she will be *c* clean.
15:33 lies with a woman who is *c* unclean.
17:15 he will be *c* unclean till evening.
21: 1 must not make himself *c* unclean
22: 3 of your descendants is *c* unclean
27:11 he vowed is a *c* unclean animal—
Nu 5: 2 who is *c* unclean because of a dead
6: 7 must not make himself *c* unclean
8: 6 Israelites and make them *c* clean.
9: 6 they were *c* unclean on account
9:13 But if a man who is *c* clean
18:11 household who is *c* clean may eat
18:13 household who is *c* clean may eat
19: 7 but he will be *c* unclean till evening
19: 9 and put them in a *c* clean place
19:18 Then a man who is *c* clean is
Dt 12:15 Both the *c* unclean and the clean
12:22 Both the *c* unclean and the clean
14: 7 they are *c* unclean for you.
15:22 Both the *c* unclean and the clean
1Sa 20:26 to David to make him *c* unclean—
2Ch 13:11 the bread on the *c* clean table
30:17 for all those who were not *c* clean
Ezr 6:20 themselves and were all *c* clean.
Ne 12:30 Levites had purified themselves *c*,
Isa 66:20 of the LORD in *c* clean vessels.
Eze 22:10 period, when they are *c* unclean.
Ac 24:18 I was *c* clean when they found me
Heb 9:13 those who are *c* unclean sanctify

CEREMONY* (CEREMONIAL CEREMONIALLY)

Ge 50:11 Egyptians are holding a solemn *c*
Ex 12:25 as he promised, observe this *c*.
12:26 'What does this *c* mean to you?'
13: 5 are to observe this *c* in this month:

CERTAIN (CERTAINTY)

2Pe 1:19 word of the prophets made more *c*,

CERTAINTY* (CERTAIN)

Lk 1: 4 so that you may know the *c*
Jn 17: 8 They knew with *c* that I came

CERTIFICATE* (CERTIFIED)

Dt 24: 1 and he writes her a *c* of divorce,
24: 3 and writes her a *c* of divorce,
Isa 50: 1 "Where is your mother's *c*
Jer 3: 8 I gave faithless Israel her *c*
Mt 5:31 divorces his wife must give her a *c*
19: 7 that a man give his wife a *c*
Mk 10: 4 a man to write a *c* of divorce

CERTIFIED* (CERTIFICATE)

Jn 3:33 has accepted it has *c* that God is

CHAFF

Ps 1: 4 They are like *c*
35: 5 May they be like *c* before the wind,
Da 2:35 became like *c* on a threshing floor
Mt 3:12 up the *c* with unquenchable fire."

CHAINED (CHAINS)

2Ti 2: 9 But God's word is not *c*.

CHAINS (CHAINED)

Eph 6:20 for which I am an ambassador in *c*.
Col 4:18 Remember my *c*.
2Ti 1:16 and was not ashamed of my *c*.
Jude : 6 with everlasting *c* for judgment

CHAMPION

Ps 19: 5 like a *c* rejoicing to run his course.

CHANCE

Ecc 9:11 but time and *c* happen to them all.

CHANGE (CHANGED)

1Sa 15:29 of Israel does not lie or *c* his mind;
Ps 110: 4 and will not *c* his mind:
Jer 7: 5 If you really *c* your ways
Mal 3: 6 "I the LORD do not *c*.
Mt 18: 3 unless you *c* and become like little
Heb 7:21 and will not *c* his mind:
Jas 1:17 who does not *c* like shifting

CHANGED (CHANGE)

1Sa 10: 6 you will be *c* into a different person
Hos 11: 8 My heart is *c* within me;
1Co 15:51 but we will all be *c*— in a flash,

CHARACTER*

Ru 3:11 that you are a woman of noble *c*.
Pr 12: 4 of noble *c* is her husband's crown,
31:10 A wife of noble *c* who can find?
Ac 17:11 noble *c* than the Thessalonians,
Ro 5: 4 perseverance, *c*; and *c*, hope.
1Co 15:33 "Bad company corrupts good *c*."

CHARGE (CHARGES)

Job 34:13 him in *c* of the whole world?
Ro 8:33 Who will bring any *c*
1Co 9:18 the gospel I may offer it free of *c*,
2Co 11: 7 the gospel of God to you free of *c*?
2Ti 4: 1 I give you this *c*: Preach the Word;
Phm :18 or owes you anything, *c* it to me.

CHARGES (CHARGE)

Isa 50: 8 Who then will bring *c* against me?

CHARIOT (CHARIOTS)

2Ki 2:11 suddenly a *c* of fire and horses
Ps 104: 3 He makes the clouds his *c*
Ac 8:28 sitting in his *c* reading the book

CHARIOTS (CHARIOT)

2Ki 6:17 and *c* of fire all around Elisha.
Ps 20: 7 Some trust in *c* and some in horses,
68:17 The *c* of God are tens of thousands

CHARITY see LOVE

CHARM* (CHARMING)

Pr 17: 8 bribe is a *c* to the one who gives it;
31:30 *C* is deceptive, and beauty is

CHARMING* (CHARM)

Pr 26:25 his speech is *c*, do not believe
SS 1:16 Oh, how *c*!

CHASE (CHASES)

Lev 26: 8 Five of you will *c* a hundred,

CHASES* (CHASE)

Pr 12:11 he who *c* fantasies lacks judgment.
28:19 one who *c* fantasies will have his

CHASM*

Lk 16:26 and you a great *c* has been fixed,

CHATTER* (CHATTERING)

1Ti 6:20 Turn away from godless *c*
2Ti 2:16 Avoid godless *c*, because those

CHATTERING* (CHATTER)

Pr 10: 8 but a *c* fool comes to ruin.
10:10 and a *c* fool comes to ruin.

CHEAT* (CHEATED CHEATING CHEATS)

Mal 1:14 "Cursed is the *c* who has
1Co 6: 8 you yourselves *c* and do wrong,

CHEATED* (CHEAT)

Ge 31: 7 yet your father has *c* me
1Sa 12: 3 Whom have I *c*? Whom have I
12: 4 "You have not *c* or oppressed us,"
Lk 19: 8 if I have *c* anybody out of anything,
1Co 6: 7 Why not rather be *c*? Instead,

CHEATING* (CHEAT)

Am 8: 5 and *c* with dishonest scales,

CHEATS* (CHEAT)

Lev 6: 2 or if he *c* him, or if he finds lost

CHEEK (CHEEKS)

Mt 5:39 someone strikes you on the right *c*,
Lk 6:29 If someone strikes you on one *c*,

CHEEKS (CHEEK)

Isa 50: 6 my *c* to those who pulled out my

CHEERFUL* (CHEERS)

Pr 15:13 A happy heart makes the face *c*,
15:15 but the *c* heart has a continual feast
15:30 A *c* look brings joy to the heart,
17:22 A *c* heart is good medicine,
2Co 9: 7 for God loves a *c* giver.

CHEERS (CHEERFUL)

Pr 12:25 but a kind word *c* him up.

CHEMOSH

2Ki 23:13 for *C* the vile god of Moab,

CHERISH (CHERISHED CHERISHES)

Ps 17:14 You still the hunger of those you *c*;

CHERISHED (CHERISH)

Ps 66:18 If I had *c* sin in my heart,

CHERISHES* (CHERISH)

Pr 19: 8 he who *c* understanding prospers.

CHERUB (CHERUBIM)

Ex 25:19 Make one *c* on one end
Eze 28:14 You were anointed as a guardian *c*,

CHERUBIM (CHERUB)

Ge 3:24 side of the Garden of Eden *c*
1Sa 4: 4 who is enthroned between the *c*.
2Sa 6: 2 enthroned between the *c* that are
22:11 He mounted the *c* and flew;
1Ki 6:23 a pair of *c* of olive wood,
2Ki 19:15 of Israel, enthroned between the *c*,
1Ch 13: 6 who is enthroned between the *c*—
Ps 18:10 He mounted the *c* and flew;
80: 1 who sit enthroned between the *c*,
99: 1 he sits enthroned between the *c*,
Isa 37:16 of Israel, enthroned between the *c*,
Eze 10: 1 was over the heads of the *c*.

CHEST

Ex 25:10 "Have them make a *c*
2Ki 12: 9 Jehoiada the priest took a *c*
Da 2:32 its *c* and arms of silver, its belly
Rev 1:13 with a golden sash around his *c*.

CHEWS

Lev 11: 3 divided and that *c* the cud.

CHIEF

1Pe 5: 4 And when the *C* Shepherd appears,

CHILD (CHILDISH CHILDREN CHILDREN'S GRANDCHILDREN)

Pr 20:11 Even a *c* is known by his actions,
22: 6 Train a *c* in the way he should go,
22:15 Folly is bound up in the heart of a *c*
23:13 not withhold discipline from a *c*;
29:15 *c* left to himself disgraces his mother.
Isa 7:14 The virgin will be with *c*
9: 6 For to us a *c* is born,
11: 6 and a little *c* will lead them.
66:13 As a mother comforts her *c*,
Mt 1:23 "The virgin will be with *c*
18: 2 He called a little *c* and had him
Lk 1:42 and blessed is the *c* you will bear!
1:80 And the *c* grew and became strong
1Co 13:11 When I was a *c*, I talked like a *c*,
1Jn 5: 1 who loves the father loves his *c*

CHILDBEARING (BEAR)
Ge 3:16 greatly increase your pains in *c;*

CHILDBIRTH (BEAR)
Gal 4:19 the pains of *c* until Christ is formed

CHILDISH* (CHILD)
1Co 13:11 When I became a man, I put *c* ways

CHILDREN (CHILD)
Ex 20:5 punishing the *c* for the sin
Dt 4:9 Teach them to your *c*
6:7 Impress them on your *c.*
11:19 them to your *c,* talking about them
14:1 You are the *c* of the LORD your
24:16 nor *c* put to death for their fathers;
30:19 so that you and your *c* may live
32:46 so that you may command your *c*
Job 1:5 "Perhaps my *c* have sinned
Ps 8:2 From the lips of *c* and infants
78:5 forefathers to teach their *c,*
Pr 17:6 Children's *c* are a crown
20:7 blessed are his *c* after him.
31:28 Her *c* arise and call her blessed;
Joel 1:3 Tell it to your *c,*
Mal 4:6 the hearts of the fathers to their *c,*
Mt 7:11 how to give good gifts to your *c,*
11:25 and revealed them to little *c.*
18:3 you change and become like little *c*
19:14 "Let the little *c* come to me,
21:16 " 'From the lips of *c* and infants
Mk 9:37 one of these little *c* in my name
10:14 "Let the little *c* come to me,
10:16 And he took the *c* in his arms,
13:12 *C* will rebel against their parents
Lk 10:21 and revealed them to little *c.*
18:16 "Let the little *c* come to me,
Jn 1:12 the right to become *c* of God—
Ac 2:39 The promise is for you and your *c*
Ro 8:16 with our spirit that we are God's *c.*
1Co 14:20 Brothers, stop thinking like *c.*
2Co 12:14 parents, but parents for their *c.*
Eph 6:1 *C,* obey your parents in the Lord,
6:4 do not exasperate your *c;* instead,
Col 3:20 *C,* obey your parents in everything,
3:21 Fathers, do not embitter your *c,*
1Ti 3:4 and see that his *c* obey him
3:12 and must manage his *c* and his
5:10 bringing up *c,* showing hospitality,
Heb 2:13 and the *c* God has given me."
1Jn 3:1 that we should be called *c* of God!

CHILDREN'S (CHILD)
Isa 54:13 and great will be your *c* peace.

CHOKE
Mk 4:19 come in and *c* the word,

CHOOSE (CHOOSES CHOSE CHOSEN)
Dt 30:19 Now *c* life, so that you
Jos 24:15 then *c* for yourselves this day
Pr 8:10 *C* my instruction instead of silver,
16:16 to *c* understanding rather
Jn 15:16 You did not *c* me, but I chose you

CHOOSES (CHOOSE)
Mt 11:27 to whom the Son *c* to reveal him.
Lk 10:22 to whom the Son *c* to reveal him."
Jn 7:17 If anyone *c* to do God's will,

CHOSE (CHOOSE)
Ge 13:11 So Lot *c* for himself the whole plain
Ps 33:12 the people he *c* for his inheritance.
Jn 15:16 but I *c* you and appointed you to go
1Co 1:27 But God *c* the foolish things
Eph 1:4 he *c* us in him before the creation
2Th 2:13 from the beginning God *c* you

CHOSEN (CHOOSE)
Isa 41:8 Jacob, whom I have *c,*
Mt 22:14 For many are invited, but few are *c*
Lk 10:42 Mary has *c* what is better,
23:35 the Christ of God, the *C* One."
Jn 15:19 but I have *c* you out of the world.
1Pe 1:20 He was *c* before the creation
2:9 But you are a *c* people, a royal

CHRIST (CHRIST'S CHRISTIAN CHRISTIANS CHRISTS)
Mt 1:16 was born Jesus, who is called *C.*
16:16 Peter answered, "You are the *C,*
22:42 "What do you think about the *C?*
Mk 1:1 of the gospel about Jesus *C,*
8:29 Peter answered, "You are the *C.*"
14:61 "Are you the *C,* the Son
Lk 9:20 Peter answered, "The *C* of God."
Jn 1:41 found the Messiah" (that is, the *C).*
20:31 you may believe that Jesus is the *C,*
Ac 2:36 you crucified, both Lord and *C.*"
5:42 the good news that Jesus is the *C.*
9:22 by proving that Jesus is the *C.*
9:34 said to him, "Jesus *C* heals you.
17:3 proving that the *C* had to suffer
18:28 the Scriptures that Jesus was the *C.*
26:23 that the *C* would suffer and,
Ro 1:4 from the dead: Jesus *C* our Lord.
3:22 comes through faith in Jesus *C*
5:1 God through our Lord Jesus *C,*
5:6 we were still powerless, *C* died
5:8 While we were still sinners, *C* died
5:11 in God through our Lord Jesus *C,*
5:17 life through the one man, Jesus *C.*
6:4 as *C* was raised from the dead
6:9 that since *C* was raised
6:23 life in *C* Jesus our Lord.
7:4 to the law through the body of *C,*
8:1 for those who are in *C* Jesus,
8:9 Spirit of *C,* he does not belong to *C.*
8:17 heirs of God and co-heirs with *C,*
8:34 Who is he that condemns? *C* Jesus,
8:35 us from the love of *C?*
9:5 is traced the human ancestry of *C,*
10:4 *C* is the end of the law
12:5 so in *C* we who are many form one
13:14 yourselves with the Lord Jesus *C,*
14:9 *C* died and returned to life
15:3 For even *C* did not please himself
15:5 yourselves as you follow *C* Jesus,
15:7 then, just as *C* accepted you,
16:18 people are not serving our Lord *C,*
1Co 1:2 to those sanctified in *C* Jesus
1:7 for our Lord Jesus *C* to be revealed.
1:13 Is *C* divided? Was Paul crucified
1:17 For *C* did not send me to baptize,
1:23 but we preach *C* crucified:
1:30 of him that you are in *C* Jesus,
2:2 except Jesus *C* and him crucified.
3:11 one already laid, which is Jesus *C.*
5:7 For *C,* our Passover lamb,
6:15 bodies are members of *C* himself?
8:6 and there is but one Lord, Jesus *C,*
8:12 conscience, you sin against *C.*
10:4 them, and that rock was *C.*
11:1 as I follow the example of *C.*
11:3 the head of every man is *C,*
12:27 Now you are the body of *C,*
15:3 that *C* died for our sins according
15:14 And if *C* has not been raised,
15:22 so in *C* all will be made alive.
15:57 victory through our Lord Jesus *C.*
2Co 1:5 as the sufferings of *C* flow
2:14 us in triumphal procession in *C*
3:3 show that you are a letter from *C,*
3:14 because only in *C* is it taken away.
4:4 light of the gospel of the glory of *C,*
4:5 not preach ourselves, but Jesus *C*
4:6 of the glory of God in the face of *C.*
5:10 before the judgment seat of *C,*
5:17 Therefore, if anyone is in *C,*
6:15 What harmony is there between *C*
10:1 the meekness and gentleness of *C,*
11:2 you to one husband, to *C,*
Gal 1:7 are trying to pervert the gospel of *C*
2:4 on the freedom we have in *C* Jesus
2:16 but by faith in Jesus *C.*
2:17 does that mean that *C* promotes sin
2:20 I have been crucified with *C*
2:21 *C* died for nothing!" You foolish
3:13 *C* redeemed us from the curse
3:16 meaning one person, who is *C.*
3:26 of God through faith in *C* Jesus,
4:19 of childbirth until *C* is formed
5:1 for freedom that *C* has set us free.
5:4 by law have been alienated from *C;*
5:24 to *C* Jesus have crucified the sinful
6:14 in the cross of our Lord Jesus *C,*
Eph 1:3 with every spiritual blessing in *C.*
1:10 together under one head, even *C.*
1:20 which he exerted in *C*
2:5 made us alive with *C*
2:10 created in *C* Jesus
2:12 time you were separate from *C,*
2:20 with *C* Jesus himself as the chief
3:8 the unsearchable riches of *C,*
3:17 so that *C* may dwell in your hearts
4:7 has been given as *C* apportioned it.
4:13 measure of the fullness of *C.*
4:15 into him who is the Head, that is, *C*
4:32 just as in *C* God forgave you.
Eph 5:2 as *C* loved us and gave himself up
5:21 out of reverence for *C.*
5:23 as *C* is the head of the church,
5:25 just as *C* loved the church
Php 1:18 motives or true, *C* is preached.
1:21 to live is *C* and to die is gain.
1:23 I desire to depart and be with *C,*
1:27 worthy of the gospel of *C.*
1:29 on behalf of *C* not only to believe
2:5 be the same as that of *C* Jesus:
3:7 now consider loss for the sake of *C.*
3:10 I want to know *C* and the power
3:18 as enemies of the cross of *C.*
4:19 to his glorious riches in *C* Jesus.
Col 1:4 heard of your faith in *C* Jesus
1:27 which is *C* in you, the hope of glory
1:28 may present everyone perfect in *C.*
2:2 the mystery of God, namely, *C,*
2:6 as you received *C* Jesus as Lord,
2:9 For in *C* all the fullness
2:13 God made you alive with *C.*
2:17 the reality, however, is found in *C.*
3:1 then, you have been raised with *C,*
3:3 and your life is now hidden with *C*
3:15 Let the peace of *C* rule
1Th 5:9 through our Lord Jesus *C.*
2Th 2:1 the coming of our Lord Jesus *C*
2:14 in the glory of our Lord Jesus *C.*
1Ti 1:12 I thank *C* Jesus our Lord, who has
1:15 *C* Jesus came into the world
1:16 *C* Jesus might display his unlimited
2:5 the man *C* Jesus, who gave himself
2Ti 1:9 us in *C* Jesus before the beginning
1:10 appearing of our Savior, *C* Jesus,
2:1 in the grace that is in *C* Jesus.
2:3 us like a good soldier of *C* Jesus.
2:8 Remember Jesus *C,* raised
2:10 the salvation that is in *C* Jesus,
3:12 life in *C* Jesus will be persecuted,
3:15 salvation through faith in *C* Jesus.
4:1 presence of God and of *C* Jesus,
Tit 2:13 our great God and Savior, Jesus *C,*
Heb 3:6 But *C* is faithful as a son
3:14 to share in *C* if we hold firmly
5:5 So *C* also did not take
6:1 the elementary teachings about *C*
9:11 When *C* came as high priest
9:14 more, then, will the blood of *C,*
9:15 For this reason *C* is the mediator
9:24 For *C* did not enter a man-made
9:26 Then *C* would have had
9:28 so *C* was sacrificed once
10:10 of the body of Jesus *C* once for all.
13:8 Jesus *C* is the same yesterday
1Pe 1:2 for obedience to Jesus *C*
1:3 of Jesus *C* from the dead,
1:11 he predicted the sufferings of *C*
1:19 but with the precious blood of *C,*
2:21 because *C* suffered for you,
3:15 in your hearts set apart *C* as Lord.
3:18 For *C* died for sins once for all,
3:21 you by the resurrection of Jesus *C,*
4:13 participate in the sufferings of *C,*
4:14 insulted because of the name of *C,*
2Pe 1:1 and Savior Jesus *C* have received
1:16 and coming of our Lord Jesus *C,*
1Jn 2:1 Jesus *C,* the Righteous One.
2:22 man who denies that Jesus is the *C.*
3:16 Jesus *C* laid down his life for us.
3:23 in the name of his Son, Jesus *C,*
4:2 that Jesus *C* has come
5:1 believes that Jesus is the *C* is born
5:20 even in his Son Jesus *C.*
2Jn :9 teaching of *C* does not have God;
Jude :4 deny Jesus *C* our only Sovereign
Rev 1:1 The revelation of Jesus *C,*
1:5 from Jesus *C,* who is the faithful
11:15 kingdom of our Lord and of his *C,*
20:4 reigned with *C* a thousand years.
20:6 they will be priests of God and of *C*

CHRIST'S (CHRIST)
1Co 9:21 from God's law but am under *C* law
2Co 5:14 For *C* love compels us,
5:20 We are therefore *C* ambassadors,
12:9 so that *C* power may rest on me.
Col 1:22 by *C* physical body through death

CHRISTIAN* (CHRIST)
Ac 26:28 you can persuade me to be a *C?*"
1Pe 4:16 as a *C,* do not be ashamed,

CHRISTIANS* (CHRIST)
Ac 11:26 The disciples were called *C* first

CHRISTS* (CHRIST)
Mt 24:24 For false *C* and false prophets will
Mk 13:22 For false *C* and false prophets will

CHURCH
Mt 16:18 and on this rock I will build my *c,*
18:17 if he refuses to listen even to the *c,*
Ac 20:28 Be shepherds of the *c* of God,
1Co 5:12 of mine to judge those outside the *c*
14:4 but he who prophesies edifies the *c.*
14:12 to excel in gifts that build up the *c.*
14:26 done for the strengthening of the *c.*
15:9 because I persecuted the *c* of God.
Gal 1:13 how intensely I persecuted the *c*
Eph 5:23 as Christ is the head of the *c,*
Col 1:18 he is the head of the body, the *c;*
1:24 the sake of his body, which is the *c.*

CHURNING
Pr 30:33 For as *c* the milk produces butter,

CIRCLE
Isa 40:22 enthroned above the *c* of the earth,

CIRCUMCISE (CIRCUMCISED CIRCUMCISION)
Dt 10:16 *C* your hearts, therefore,

CIRCUMCISED (CIRCUMCISE)
Ge 17:10 Every male among you shall be *c.*
17:12 who is eight days old must be *c,*
Jos 5:3 and *c* the Israelites at Gibeath
Gal 5:2 that if you let yourselves be *c,*

CIRCUMCISION (CIRCUMCISE)
Ro 2:25 *C* has value if you observe the law,
2:29 and *c* is *c* of the heart, by the Spirit,
1Co 7:19 *C* is nothing and uncircumcision is

CIRCUMSTANCES
Php 4:11 to be content whatever the *c.*
1Th 5:18 continually; give thanks in all *c,*

CITIES (CITY)
Lk 19:17 small matter, take charge of ten *c.'*
19:19 'You take charge of five *c.'*

CITIZENS (CITIZENSHIP)
Eph 2:19 but fellow *c* with God's people

CITIZENSHIP* (CITIZENS)
Ac 22:28 "I had to pay a big price for my *c.*"
Eph 2:12 excluded from *c* in Israel
Php 3:20 But our *c* is in heaven.

CITY (CITIES)
Mt 5:14 A *c* on a hill cannot be hidden.
Ac 18:10 I have many people in this *c.*"
Heb 13:14 here we do not have an enduring *c,*
Rev 21:2 saw the Holy *C,* the new

CIVILIAN*
2Ti 2:4 a soldier gets involved in *c* affairs—

CLAIM (CLAIMS RECLAIM)
Pr 25:6 do not *c* a place among great men;
1Jn 1:6 If we *c* to have fellowship
1:8 If we *c* to be without sin, we
1:10 If we *c* we have not sinned,

CLAIMS (CLAIM)
Jas 2:14 if a man *c* to have faith
1Jn 2:6 Whoever *c* to live in him must walk
2:9 Anyone who *c* to be in the light

CLANGING*
1Co 13:1 a resounding gong or a *c* cymbal.

CLAP* (CLAPPED CLAPS)
Job 21:5 *c* your hand over your mouth.
Ps 47:1 *C* your hands, all you nations;
98:8 Let the rivers *c* their hands,
Pr 30:32 *c* your hand over your mouth!
Isa 55:12 will *c* their hands.
La 2:15 *c* their hands at you;

CLAPPED* (CLAP)
2Ki 11:12 and the people *c* their hands
Eze 25:6 Because you have *c* your hands

CLAPS* (CLAP)
Job 27:23 It *c* its hands in derision
34:37 scornfully he *c* his hands among us
Na 3:19 *c* his hands at your fall,

CLASSIFY*
2Co 10:12 dare to *c* or compare ourselves

CLAUDIUS
Ac 11:28 happened during the reign of *C.)*
18:2 because *C* had ordered all the Jews

CLAY
Isa 45:9 Does the *c* say to the potter,
64:8 We are the *c,* you are the potter;
Jer 18:6 "Like *c* in the hand of the potter,
La 4:2 are now considered as pots of *c,*
Da 2:33 partly of iron and partly of baked *c.*
Ro 9:21 of the same lump of *c* some pottery
2Co 4:7 we have this treasure in jars of *c*
2Ti 2:20 and *c;* some are for noble purposes

CLEAN (CLEANNESS CLEANSE CLEANSED CLEANSES CLEANSING)
Ge 7:2 seven of every kind of *c* animal,
Lev 4:12 the camp to a place ceremonially *c,*
16:30 you will be *c* from all your sins.
Ps 24:4 He who has *c* hands and a pure
51:7 with hyssop, and I will be *c;*
Pr 20:9 I am *c* and without sin"?
Eze 36:25 I will sprinkle *c* water on you,
Mt 8:2 are willing, you can make me *c.*"
12:44 the house unoccupied, swept *c*
23:25 You *c* the outside of the cup
Mk 7:19 Jesus declared all foods *"c.")*
Jn 13:10 to wash his feet; his whole body is *c*
15:3 are already *c* because of the word
Ac 10:15 impure that God has made *c.*"
Ro 14:20 All food is *c,* but it is wrong

CLEANNESS (CLEAN)
2Sa 22:25 according to my *c* in his sight.

CLEANSE (CLEAN)
Ps 51:2 and *c* me from my sin.
51:7 *C* me with hyssop, and I will be
Pr 20:30 Blows and wounds *c* away evil,
Heb 9:14 *c* our consciences from acts that
10:22 having our hearts sprinkled to *c* us

CLEANSED (CLEAN)
Heb 9:22 requires that nearly everything be *c*
2Pe 1:9 has forgotten that he has been *c*

CLEANSES* (CLEAN)
2Ti 2:21 If a man *c* himself from the latter,

CLEANSING (CLEAN)
Eph 5:26 *c* her by the washing with water

CLEFT*
Ex 33:22 I will put you in a *c* in the rock

CLEVER
Isa 5:21 and *c* in their own sight.

CLING
Ro 12:9 Hate what is evil; *c* to what is good.

CLINGS
Ps 63:8 My soul *c* to you;

CLOAK
Ex 12:11 with your *c* tucked into your belt,
2Ki 4:29 "Tuck your *c* into your belt,
9:1 "Tuck your *c* into your belt,
Mt 5:40 let him have your *c* as well.

CLOSE (CLOSER CLOSES)
2Ki 11:8 Stay *c* to the king wherever he goes
2Ch 23:7 Stay *c* to the king wherever he goes
Ps 34:18 LORD is *c* to the brokenhearted
148:14 of Israel, the people *c* to his heart.
Isa 40:11 and carries them *c* to his heart;
Jer 30:21 himself to be *c* to me?'

CLOSER (CLOSE)
Ex 3:5 "Do not come any *c,*" God said.
Pr 18:24 there is a friend who sticks *c*

CLOSES (CLOSE)
Pr 28:27 he who *c* his eyes to them receives

CLOTHE (CLOTHED CLOTHES CLOTHING)
Ps 45:3 *c* yourself with splendor
Isa 52:1 *c* yourself with strength.
Ro 13:14 *c* yourselves with the Lord Jesus
Col 3:12 *c* yourselves with compassion,
1Pe 5:5 *c* yourselves with humility

CLOTHED (CLOTHE)
Ps 30:11 removed my sackcloth and *c* me
104:1 you are *c* with splendor
Pr 31:22 she is *c* in fine linen and purple.
31:25 She is *c* with strength and dignity;
Isa 61:10 For he has *c* me with garments
Lk 24:49 until you have been *c* with power
Gal 3:27 into Christ have *c* yourselves

CLOTHES (CLOTHE)
Dt 8:4 Your *c* did not wear out
Mt 6:25 the body more important than *c?*
6:28 "And why do you worry about *c?*
27:35 they divided up his *c* by casting lots
Jn 11:44 Take off the grave *c* and let him go

CLOTHING (CLOTHE)
Dt 22:5 A woman must not wear men's *c,*
Job 29:14 I put on righteousness as my *c;*
Ps 22:18 and cast lots for my *c.*
Mt 7:15 They come to you in sheep's *c,*
1Ti 6:8 But if we have food and *c,*

CLOUD (CLOUDS)
Ex 13:21 them in a pillar of *c* to guide them
1Ki 18:44 *c* as small as a man's hand is rising
Pr 16:15 his favor is like a rain *c* in spring.
Isa 19:1 See, the LORD rides on a swift *c*
Lk 21:27 of Man coming in a *c* with power
Heb 12:1 by such a great *c* of witnesses,
Rev 14:14 seated on the *c* was one "like a son

CLOUDS (CLOUD)
Dt 33:26 and on the *c* in his majesty.
Ps 68:4 extol him who rides on the *c*—
104:3 He makes the *c* his chariot
Pr 25:14 Like *c* and wind without rain
Da 7:13 coming with the *c* of heaven.
Mt 24:30 of Man coming on the *c* of the sky,
26:64 and coming on the *c* of heaven."
Mk 13:26 coming in *c* with great power
1Th 4:17 with them in the *c* to meet the Lord
Rev 1:7 Look, he is coming with the *c,*

CLUB
Pr 25:18 Like a *c* or a sword or a sharp arrow

CO-HEIRS* (INHERIT)
Ro 8:17 heirs of God and *c* with Christ,

COALS
Pr 25:22 you will heap burning *c* on his head
Ro 12:20 you will heap burning *c* on his head

COARSE*
Eph 5:4 or *c* joking, which are out of place,

CODE*
Ro 2:27 even though you have the written *c*
2:29 by the Spirit, not by the written *c.*
7:6 not in the old way of the written *c.*
Col 2:14 having canceled the written *c,*

COINS
Mt 26:15 out for him thirty silver *c.*
Lk 15:8 suppose a woman has ten silver *c*

COLD
Pr 25:25 Like *c* water to a weary soul
Mt 10:42 if anyone gives even a cup of *c* water
24:12 the love of most will grow *c,*

COLLECTION
1Co 16:1 Now about the *c* for God's people:

COLT
Zec 9:9 on a *c,* the foal of a donkey.
Mt 21:5 on a *c,* the foal of a donkey.'"

COMB
Ps 19:10 than honey from the *c.*

COMFORT* (COMFORTED COMFORTER COMFORTERS COMFORTING COMFORTS)
Ge 5:29 "He will *c* us in the labor
37:35 and daughters came to *c* him,
Ru 2:13 "You have given me *c*
1Ch 7:22 and his relatives came to *c* him.
Job 2:11 sympathize with him and *c* him.
7:13 When I think my bed will *c* me
16:5 *c* from my lips would bring you
36:16 to the *c* of your table laden
Ps 23:4 rod and your staff, they *c* me.
71:21 and *c* me once again.

Ps 119: 50 My c in my suffering is this:
119: 52 and I find c in them.
119: 76 May your unfailing love be my c,
119: 82 I say, "When will you c me?"
Isa 40: 1 C, c my people,
51: 3 The LORD will surely c Zion
51: 19 who can c you?—
57: 18 I will guide him and restore c
61: 2 to c all who mourn,
66: 13 so will I c you;
Jer 16: 7 food to c those who mourn
31: 13 I will give them c and joy instead
La 1: 2 there is none to c her.
1: 9 there was none to c her.
1: 16 No one is near to c me,
1: 17 but there is no one to c her.
1: 21 but there is no one to c me.
2: 13 that I may c you,
Eze 16: 54 all you have done in giving them c.
Na 3: 7 Where can I find anyone to c you?"
Zec 1: 17 and the LORD will again c Zion
10: 2 they give c in vain.
Lk 6: 24 you have already received your c.
Jn 11: 19 and Mary to c them in the loss
1Co 14: 3 encouragement and c.
2Co 1: 3 of compassion and the God of all c,
1: 4 so that we can c those
1: 4 with the c we ourselves have
1: 5 through Christ our c overflows.
1: 6 if we are comforted, it is for your c,
1: 6 it is for your c and salvation;
1: 7 so also you share in our c.
2: 7 you ought to forgive and c him,
7: 7 also by the c you had given him.
Php 2: 1 if any c from his love,
Col 4: 11 and they have proved a c to me.

COMFORTED* (COMFORT)

Ge 24: 67 Isaac was c after his mother's death
37: 35 comfort him, but he refused to be c.
2Sa 12: 24 Then David c his wife Bathsheba,
Job 42: 11 They c and consoled him
Ps 77: 2 and my soul refused to be c.
86: 17 have helped me and c me.
Isa 12: 1 and you have c me.
52: 9 for the LORD has c his people,
54: 11 lashed by storms and not c,
66: 13 and you will be c over Jerusalem."
Jer 31: 15 and refusing to be c,
Mt 2: 18 and refusing to be c,
5: 4 for they will be c.
Lk 16: 25 but now he is c here and you are
Ac 20: 12 man home alive and were greatly c.
2Co 1: 6 if we are c, it is for your comfort,
7: 6 c us by the coming of Titus,

COMFORTER* (COMFORT)

Ecc 4: 1 and they have no c;
4: 1 and they have no c.
Jer 8: 18 O my C in sorrow,

COMFORTERS* (COMFORT)

Job 16: 2 miserable c are you all!
Ps 69: 20 for c, but I found none.

COMFORTING* (COMFORT)

Isa 66: 11 satisfied at her c breasts;
Zec 1: 13 c words to the angel who talked
Jn 11: 31 c her, noticed how quickly she got
1Th 2: 12 c and urging you to live lives

COMFORTS* (COMFORT)

Job 29: 25 I was like one who c mourners.
Isa 49: 13 For the LORD c his people
51: 12 "I, even I, am he who c you.
66: 13 As a mother c her child,
2Co 1: 4 who c us in all our troubles,
7: 6 But God, who c the downcast,

COMMAND (COMMANDED COMMANDING COMMANDENT COMMANDMENTS COMMANDS)

Ex 7: 2 You are to say everything I c you,
Nu 14: 41 are you disobeying the LORD's c?
24: 13 to go beyond the c of the LORD—
Dt 4: 2 Do not add to what I c you
8: 1 to follow every c I am giving you
12: 32 See that you do all I c you;
15: 11 I c you to be openhanded
30: 16 For I c you today to love
32: 46 so that you may c your children
Ps 91: 11 For he will c his angels concerning
Pr 13: 13 but he who respects a c is rewarded
Ecc 8: 2 Obey the king's c, I say,
Jer 1: 7 you to and say whatever I c you.
Jer 1: 17 and say to them whatever I c you.
7: 23 Walk in all the ways I c you,
11: 4 Obey me and do everything I c you
26: 2 Tell them everything I c you;
Joel 2: 11 mighty are those who obey his c.
Mt 4: 6 He will c his angels concerning you
15: 3 why do you break the c of God
Lk 4: 10 " 'He will c his angels concerning
Jn 14: 15 love me, you will obey what I c.
15: 12 My c is this: Love each other
15: 14 friends if you do what I c.
15: 17 This is my c: Love each other.
1Co 14: 37 writing to you is the Lord's c.
Gal 5: 14 law is summed up in a single c:
1Ti 1: 5 goal of this c is love, which comes
6: 14 to you keep this c without spot
6: 17 C those who are rich
Heb 11: 3 universe was formed at God's c,
2Pe 2: 21 on the sacred c that was passed
3: 2 and the c given by our Lord
1Jn 2: 7 I am not writing you a new c
3: 23 this is his c: to believe in the name
4: 21 And he has given us this c:
2Jn : 6 his c is that you walk in love.

COMMANDED (COMMAND)

Ge 2: 16 And the LORD God c the man,
7: 5 Noah did all that the LORD c him.
50: 12 Jacob's sons did as he had c them:
Ex 7: 6 did just as the LORD c them.
19: 7 all the words the LORD had c him
Dt 4: 5 laws as the LORD my God c me,
6: 24 The LORD c us to obey all these
Jos 1: 9 Have I not c you? Be strong
1: 16 Whatever you have c us we will do,
2Sa 5: 25 So David did as the LORD c him,
2Ki 17: 13 the entire Law that I c your fathers
21: 8 careful to do everything I c them
2Ch 33: 8 do everything I c them concerning
Ps 33: 9 he c, and it stood firm.
78: 5 which he c our forefathers
148: 5 for he c and they were created.
Mt 28: 20 to obey everything I have c you.
1Co 9: 14 Lord has c that those who preach
1Jn 3: 23 and to love one another as he c us.
2Jn : 4 in the truth, just as the Father c us.

COMMANDING (COMMAND)

2Ti 2: 4 he wants to please his c officer.

COMMANDMENT* (COMMAND)

Jos 22: 5 But be very careful to keep the c
Mt 22: 36 which is the greatest c in the Law?"
22: 38 This is the first and greatest c.
Mk 12: 31 There is no c greater than these."
Lk 23: 56 the Sabbath in obedience to the c.
Jn 13: 34 "A new c I give you: Love one
Ro 7: 8 the opportunity afforded by the c,
7: 9 when the c came, sin sprang to life
7: 10 that the very c that was intended
7: 11 and through the c put me to death.
7: 11 the opportunity afforded by the c,
7: 12 and the c is holy, righteous
7: 13 through the c sin might become
13: 9 and whatever other c there may be,
Eph 6: 2 which is the first c with a promise
Heb 9: 19 Moses had proclaimed every c

COMMANDMENTS* (COMMAND)

Ex 20: 6 who love me and keep my c.
34: 28 of the covenant—the Ten C.
Dt 4: 13 to you his covenant, the Ten C,
5: 10 who love me and keep my c.
5: 22 These are the c the LORD
6: 6 These c that I give you today are
9: 10 were all the c the LORD
10: 4 The Ten C he had proclaimed
Ecc 12: 13 Fear God and keep his c,
Mt 5: 19 one of the least of these c
19: 17 If you want to enter life, obey the c
22: 40 the Prophets hang on these two c."
Mk 10: 19 You know the c: 'Do not murder,
12: 28 "Of all the c, which is the most
Lk 1: 6 observing all the Lord's c
18: 20 You know the c: 'Do not commit
Ro 13: 9 The c, "Do not commit adultery,"
Eph 2: 15 in his flesh the law with its c
Rev 12: 17 those who obey God's c
14: 12 part of the saints who obey God's c

COMMANDS (COMMAND)

Ex 24: 12 and c I have written for their
25: 22 give you all my c for the Israelites.
34: 32 gave them all the c the LORD had
Lev 22: 31 "Keep my c and follow them.
Nu 15: 39 and so you will remember all the c
Dt 7: 9 those who love him and keep his c.
7: 11 Therefore, take care to follow the c
11: 1 decrees, his laws and his c always.
11: 27 the blessing if you obey the c
28: 1 carefully follow all his c I give you
30: 10 LORD your God and keep his c
Jos 22: 5 to walk in all his ways, to obey his c
1Ki 2: 3 and keep his decrees and c,
8: 58 in all his ways and to keep the c,
8: 61 to live by his decrees and obey his c
1Ch 28: 7 unswerving in carrying out my c
29: 19 devotion to keep your c,
2Ch 31: 21 in obedience to the law and the c,
Ne 1: 5 those who love him and obey his c,
Ps 78: 7 but would keep his c.
112: 1 who finds great delight in his c.
119: 10 do not let me stray from your c.
119: 32 I run in the path of your c,
119: 35 Direct me in the path of your c,
119: 47 for I delight in your c
119: 48 I lift up my hands to your c,
119: 73 me understanding to learn your c.
119: 86 All your c are trustworthy;
119: 96 but your c are boundless.
119: 98 Your c make me wiser
119: 115 that I may keep the c of my God!
119: 127 Because I love your c
119: 131 longing for your c.
119: 143 but your c are my delight.
119: 151 and all your c are true.
119: 172 for all your c are righteous.
119: 176 for I have not forgotten your c.
Pr 2: 1 and store up my c within you,
3: 1 but keep my c in your heart,
6: 23 For these c are a lamp,
10: 8 The wise in heart accept c,
Isa 48: 18 you had paid attention to my c,
Da 9: 4 all who love him and obey his c,
Mt 5: 19 teaches these c will be called great
Mk 7: 8 You have let go of the c of God
7: 9 way of setting aside the c of God
Jn 14: 21 Whoever has my c and obeys them,
15: 10 If you obey my c, you will remain
Ac 17: 30 but now he c all people everywhere
1Co 7: 19 Keeping God's c is what counts.
1Jn 2: 3 come to know him if we obey his c.
2: 4 but does not do what he c is a liar,
3: 22 we obey his c and do what pleases
3: 24 Those who obey his c live in him,
5: 2 loving God and carrying out his c.
5: 3 And his c are not burdensome,
5: 3 This is love for God: to obey his c.
2Jn : 6 that we walk in obedience to his c.

COMMEMORATE

Ex 12: 14 "This is a day you are to c;

COMMEND* (COMMENDABLE COMMENDED COMMENDS)

Ps 145: 4 One generation will c your works
Ecc 8: 15 So I c the enjoyment of life,
Ro 13: 3 do what is right and he will c you.
16: 1 I c to you our sister Phoebe,
2Co 3: 1 beginning to c ourselves again?
4: 2 the truth plainly we c ourselves
5: 12 trying to c ourselves to you again,
6: 4 as servants of God we c ourselves
10: 12 with some who c themselves.
1Pe 2: 14 and to c those who do right.

COMMENDABLE* (COMMEND)

1Pe 2: 19 For it is c if a man bears up
2: 20 you endure it, this is c before God.

COMMENDED* (COMMEND)

Ne 11: 2 The people c all the men who
Job 29: 11 and those who saw me c me,
Lk 16: 8 master c the dishonest manager
Ac 15: 40 c by the brothers to the grace
2Co 12: 11 I ought to have been c by you,
Heb 11: 2 This is what the ancients were c for
11: 4 By faith he was c as a righteous
11: 5 he was c as one who pleased God.
11: 39 These were all c for their faith,

COMMENDS* (COMMEND)

Pr 15: 2 of the wise c knowledge,
2Co 10: 18 but the one whom the Lord c.
10: 18 not the one who c himself who is

COMMIT (COMMITS COMMITTED)

Ex 20: 14 "You shall not c adultery.
Dt 5: 18 "You shall not c adultery.
1Sa 7: 3 and c yourselves to the LORD

Ps 31: 5 Into your hands I *c* my spirit;
37: 5 *C* your way to the LORD;
Pr 16: 3 *C* to the LORD whatever you do,
Mt 5:27 that it was said, 'Do not *c* adultery.'
5:32 causes her to *c* adultery,
19:18 do not *c* adultery, do not steal,
Mk 10:19 do not *c* adultery, do not steal,
Lk 18:20 'Do not *c* adultery, do not murder,
23:46 into your hands I *c* my spirit."
Ac 20:32 I *c* you to God and to the word
Ro 2:22 do you *c* adultery? You who abhor
2:22 that people should not *c* adultery,
13: 9 "Do not *c* adultery,"
1Co 10: 8 We should not *c* sexual immorality,
Jas 2:11 do not *c* adultery but do *c* murder,
1Pe 4:19 to God's will should *c* themselves
Rev 2:22 I will make those who *c* adultery

COMMITS (COMMIT)
Pr 6:32 man who *c* adultery lacks
29:22 a hot-tempered one *c* many sins.
Ecc 8:12 a wicked man *c* a hundred crimes
Eze 18:12 He *c* robbery.
18:14 who sees all the sins his father *c*,
18:24 from his righteousness and *c* sin
18:26 from his righteousness and *c* sin,
22:11 you one man *c* a detestable offense
Mt 5:32 the divorced woman *c* adultery.
19: 9 marries another woman *c* adultery
Mk 10:11 marries another woman *c* adultery
10:12 another man, she *c* adultery."
Lk 16:18 a divorced woman *c* adultery.
16:18 marries another woman *c* adultery,

COMMITTED (COMMIT)
Nu 5: 7 and must confess the sin he has *c*.
1Ki 8:61 But your hearts must be fully *c*
15:14 Asa's heart was fully *c*
2Ch 16: 9 those whose hearts are fully *c*
Mt 5:28 lustfully has already *c* adultery
11:27 "All things have been *c* to me
Lk 10:22 "All things have been *c* to me
Ac 14:23 *c* them to the Lord,
14:26 where they had been *c* to the grace
1Co 9:17 I am simply discharging the trust *c*
2Co 5:19 And he has *c* to us the message
1Pe 2:22 "He *c* no sin,
Rev 17: 2 the kings of the earth *c* adultery
18: 3 of the earth *c* adultery with her,
18: 9 kings of the earth who *c* adultery

COMMON
Ge 11: 1 had one language and a *c* speech.
Lev 10:10 between the holy and the *c*,
Pr 22: 2 Rich and poor have this in *c*:
29:13 the oppressor have this in *c*:
Ac 2:44 together and had everything in *c*.
1Co 10:13 has seized you except what is *c*
2Co 6:14 and wickedness have in *c*?

COMPANION (COMPANIONS)
Ps 55:13 my *c*, my close friend,
55:20 My *c* attacks his friends;
Pr 13:20 but a *c* of fools suffers harm.
28: 7 a *c* of gluttons disgraces his father.
29: 3 *c* of prostitutes squanders his
Rev 1: 9 your brother and *c* in the suffering

COMPANIONS (COMPANION)
Ps 45: 7 your God, has set you above your *c*
Pr 18:24 A man of many *c* may come to ruin
Heb 1: 9 your God, has set you above your *c*

COMPANY
Ps 14: 5 present in the *c* of the righteous.
Pr 21:16 comes to rest in the *c* of the dead.
24: 1 do not desire their *c*;
Jer 15:17 I never sat in the *c* of revelers,
1Co 15:33 "Bad *c* corrupts good character."

COMPARE* (COMPARED COMPARING COMPARISON)
Job 28:17 Neither gold nor crystal can *c*
28:19 The topaz of Cush cannot *c* with it;
39:13 but they cannot *c* with the pinions
Ps 86: 8 no deeds can *c* with yours.
89: 6 skies above can *c* with the LORD?
Pr 3:15 nothing you desire can *c* with her.
8:11 nothing you desire can *c* with her.
Isa 40:18 To whom, then, will you *c* God?
40:18 What image will you *c* him to?
40:25 "To whom will you *c* me?
46: 5 "To whom will you *c* me
La 2:13 With what can I *c* you,
Eze 31: 8 *c* with its branches—
Da 1:13 Then *c* our appearance with that
Mt 11:16 "To what can I *c* this generation?
Lk 7:31 I *c* the people of this generation?
13:18 What shall I *c* it to? It is like
13:20 What shall I *c* the kingdom of God
2Co 10:12 and *c* themselves with themselves,
10:12 or *c* ourselves with some who

COMPARED* (COMPARE)
Jdg 8: 2 What have I accomplished *c* to you
8: 3 What was I able to do *c* to you?"
Isa 46: 5 you liken me that we may be *c*?
Eze 31: 2 Who can be *c* with you in majesty?
31:18 the trees of Eden can be *c* with you
Php 3: 8 I consider everything a loss *c*

COMPARING* (COMPARE)
Ro 8:18 present sufferings are not worth *c*
2Co 8: 8 the sincerity of your love by *c* it
Gal 6: 4 without *c* himself to somebody else

COMPARISON* (COMPARE)
2Co 3:10 now in *c* with the surpassing glory.

COMPASSION* (COMPASSIONATE COMPASSIONS)
Ex 33:19 I will have *c* on whom I will have *c*.
Dt 13:17 he will show you mercy, have *c*
28:54 man among you will have no *c*
30: 3 restore your fortunes and have *c*
32:36 and have *c* on his servants
Jdg 2:18 for the LORD had *c* on them
1Ki 3:26 son was alive was filled with *c*
2Ki 13:23 and had *c* and showed concern
2Ch 30: 9 and your children will be shown *c*
Ne 9:19 of your great *c* you did not
9:27 and in your great *c* you gave them
9:28 in your *c* you delivered them time
Ps 51: 1 according to your great *c*
77: 9 Has he in anger withheld his *c*?"
90:13 Have *c* on your servants.
102:13 You will arise and have *c* on Zion,
103: 4 and crowns you with love and *c*.
103:13 As a father has *c* on his children,
103:13 so the LORD has *c*
116: 5 our God is full of *c*.
119:77 Let your *c* come to me that I may
119:156 Your *c* is great, O LORD;
135:14 and have *c* on his servants.
145: 9 he has *c* on all he has made.
Isa 13:18 will they look with *c* on children.
14: 1 The LORD will have *c* on Jacob;
27:11 so their Maker has no *c* on them,
30:18 he rises to show you *c*.
49:10 He who has *c* on them will guide
49:13 and will have *c* on his afflicted ones
49:15 and have no *c* on the child she has
51: 3 and will look with *c* on all her ruins
54: 7 with deep *c* I will bring you back.
54: 8 I will have *c* on you,"
54:10 says the LORD, who has *c* on you.
60:10 in favor I will show you *c*.
63: 7 to his *c* and many kindnesses.
63:15 and *c* are withheld from us.
Jer 12:15 I will again have *c* and will bring
13:14 *c* to keep me from destroying them
15: 6 I can no longer show *c*.
21: 7 show them no mercy or pity or *c*.'
30:18 and have *c* on his dwellings;
31:20 I have great *c* for him,"
33:26 restore their fortunes and have *c*
42:12 I will show you *c* so that he will
42:12 so that he will have *c* on you
La 3:32 he brings grief, he will show *c*,
Eze 9: 5 without showing pity or *c*.
16: 5 or had *c* enough to do any
39:25 and will have *c* on all the people
Hos 2:19 in love and *c*.
11: 8 all my *c* is aroused.
13:14 "I will have no *c*,
14: 3 for in you the fatherless find *c*."
Am 1:11 stifling all *c*,
Jnh 3: 9 with *c* turn from his fierce anger
3:10 he had *c* and did not bring
Mic 7:19 You will again have *c* on us;
Zec 7: 9 show mercy and *c* to one another.
10: 6 because I have *c* on them.
Mal 3:17 as in *c* a man spares his son who
Mt 9:36 When he saw the crowds, he had *c*
14:14 he had *c* on them and healed their
15:32 "I have *c* for these people;
20:34 Jesus had *c* on them and touched
Mk 1:41 with *c*, Jesus reached out his hand
6:34 and saw a large crowd, he had *c*
8: 2 "I have *c* for these people;
Lk 15:20 and was filled with *c* for him;
Ro 9:15 and I will have *c* on whom I have *c*
2Co 1: 3 the Father of *c* and the God
Php 2: 1 and *c*, then make my joy complete
Col 3:12 clothe yourselves with *c*, kindness,
Jas 5:11 The Lord is full of *c* and mercy.

COMPASSIONATE* (COMPASSION)
Ex 22:27 out to me, I will hear, for I am *c*.
34: 6 the LORD, the *c* and gracious God
2Ch 30: 9 LORD your God is gracious and *c*.
Ne 9:17 gracious and *c*, slow to anger
Ps 86:15 O Lord, are a *c* and gracious God,
103: 8 The LORD is *c* and gracious,
111: 4 the LORD is gracious and *c*.
112: 4 the gracious and *c* and righteous
145: 8 The LORD is gracious and *c*,
La 4:10 With their own hands *c* women
Joel 2:13 for he is gracious and *c*,
Jnh 4: 2 that you are a gracious and *c* God,
Eph 4:32 Be kind and *c* to one another,
1Pe 3: 8 love as brothers, be *c* and humble.

COMPASSIONS* (COMPASSION)
La 3:22 for his *c* never fail.

COMPELLED (COMPULSION)
Ac 20:22 "And now, *c* by the Spirit,
1Co 9:16 I cannot boast, for I am *c* to preach.

COMPELS (COMPULSION)
Job 32:18 and the spirit within me *c* me;
2Co 5:14 For Christ's love *c* us, because we

COMPETENCE* (COMPETENT)
2Co 3: 5 but our *c* comes from God.

COMPETENT* (COMPETENCE)
Ro 15:14 and *c* to instruct one another.
1Co 6: 2 are you not *c* to judge trivial cases?
2Co 3: 5 Not that we are *c* in ourselves to claim
3: 6 He has made us *c* as ministers

COMPETES*
1Co 9:25 Everyone who *c* in the games goes
2Ti 2: 5 Similarly, if anyone *c* as an athlete,
2: 5 unless he *c* according to the rules.

COMPLACENCY* (COMPLACENT)
Pr 1:32 and the *c* of fools will destroy them
Eze 30: 9 ships to frighten Cush out of her *c*.

COMPLACENT* (COMPLACENCY)
Isa 32: 9 You women who are so *c*,
32:11 Tremble, you *c* women;
Am 6: 1 Woe to you who are *c* in Zion,
Zep 1:12 and punish those who are *c*,

COMPLAINING*
Php 2:14 Do everything without *c* or arguing

COMPLETE
Dt 16:15 your hands, and your joy will be *c*.
Jn 3:29 That joy is mine, and it is now *c*.
15:11 and that your joy may be *c*.
16:24 will receive, and your joy will be *c*.
17:23 May they be brought to *c* unity
Ac 20:24 *c* the task the Lord Jesus has given
Php 2: 2 then make my joy *c*
Col 4:17 to it that you *c* the work you have
Jas 1: 4 so that you may be mature and *c*,
2:22 his faith was made *c* by what he did
1Jn 1: 4 We write this to make our joy *c*.
2: 5 God's love is truly made *c* in him.
4:12 and his love is made *c* in us.
4:17 love is made *c* among us
2Jn :12 to face, so that our joy may be *c*.

COMPLIMENTS*
Pr 23: 8 and will have wasted your *c*.

COMPREHEND* (COMPREHENDED)
Job 28:13 Man does not *c* its worth;
Ecc 8:17 No one can *c* what goes
8:17 he knows, he cannot really *c* it.

COMPREHENDED* (COMPREHEND)
Job 38:18 Have you *c* the vast expanses

COMPULSION (COMPELLED COMPELS)
2Co 9: 7 not reluctantly or under *c*,

CONCEAL (CONCEALED CONCEALS)
Ps 40:10 I do not *c* your love and your truth
Pr 25: 2 It is the glory of God to *c* a matter;

CONCEALED (CONCEAL)
Jer 16:17 nor is their sin *c* from my eyes.
Mt 10:26 There is nothing *c* that will not be
Mk 4:22 and whatever is *c* is meant
Lk 8:17 nothing *c* that will not be known
12: 2 There is nothing *c* that will not be

CONCEALS* (CONCEAL)
Pr 10:18 He who *c* his hatred has lying lips,
28:13 He who *c* his sins does not prosper,

CONCEIT* (CONCEITED CONCEITS)
Isa 16: 6 her overweening pride and *c*,
Jer 48:29 her overweening pride and *c*,
Php 2: 3 out of selfish ambition or vain *c*,

CONCEITED* (CONCEIT)
1Sa 17:28 I know how *c* you are and how
Ro 11:25 brothers, so that you may not be *c*:
12:16 Do not be *c*.
2Co 12: 7 To keep me from becoming *c*
Gal 5:26 Let us not become *c*, provoking
1Ti 3: 6 or he may become *c* and fall
6: 4 he is *c* and understands nothing.
2Ti 3: 4 of the good, treacherous, rash, *c*,

CONCEITS* (CONCEIT)
Ps 73: 7 evil *c* of their minds know no

CONCEIVED (CONCEIVES)
Ps 51: 5 from the time my mother *c* me.
Mt 1:20 what is *c* in her is from the Holy
1Co 2: 9 no mind has *c*
Jas 1:15 after desire has *c*, it gives birth

CONCEIVES* (CONCEIVED)
Ps 7:14 *c* trouble gives birth

CONCERN* (CONCERNED)
Ge 39: 6 he did not *c* himself with anything
39: 8 "my master does not *c* himself
1Sa 23:21 "The LORD bless you for your *c*
2Ki 13:23 and had compassion and showed *c*
Job 9:21 I have no *c* for myself;
19: 4 my error remains my *c* alone.
Ps 131: 1 I do not *c* myself with great matters
Pr 29: 7 but the wicked have no such *c*.
Eze 36:21 I had *c* for my holy name, which
Ac 15:14 God at first showed his *c* by taking
18:17 But Gallio showed no *c* whatever.
1Co 7:32 I would like you to be free from *c*.
12:25 that its parts should have equal *c*
2Co 7: 7 your deep sorrow, your ardent *c*
7:11 what alarm, what longing, what *c*,
8:16 of Titus the same *c* I have for you.
11:28 of my *c* for all the churches.
Php 4:10 at last you have renewed your *c*

CONCERNED (CONCERN)
Ex 2:25 Israelites and was *c* about them.
Ps 142: 4 no one is *c* for me.
Jnh 4:10 "You have been *c* about this vine,
4:11 Should I not be *c* about that great
1Co 7:32 An unmarried man is *c* about
9: 9 Is it about oxen that God is *c*?
Php 4:10 you have been *c*, but you had no

CONCESSION*
1Co 7: 6 I say this as a *c*, not as a command.

CONDEMN* (CONDEMNATION CONDEMNED CONDEMNING CONDEMNS)
Job 9:20 innocent, my mouth would *c* me;
10: 2 I will say to God: Do not *c* me,
34:17 Will you *c* the just and mighty One
34:29 if he remains silent, who can *c* him?
40: 8 Would you *c* me to justify yourself?
Ps 94:21 and *c* the innocent to death.
109: 7 and may his prayers *c* him.
109: 31 from those who *c* him.
Isa 50: 9 Who is he that will *c* me?
Mt 12:41 with this generation and *c* it;
12:42 with this generation and *c* it;
20:18 They will *c* him to death
Mk 10:33 They will *c* him to death
Lk 6:37 Do not *c*, and you will not be
11:31 men of this generation and *c* them;
11:32 with this generation and *c* it;
Jn 3:17 Son into the world to *c* the world,
7:51 "Does our law *c* anyone
8:11 "Then neither do I *c* you,"
12:48 very word which I spoke will *c* him
Ro 2:27 yet obeys the law will *c* you who,
14: 3 everything must not *c* the man who
Ro 14:22 is the man who does not *c* himself
2Co 7: 3 this to *c* you; I have said
1Jn 3:20 presence whenever our hearts *c* us.
3:21 if our hearts do not *c* us,

CONDEMNATION* (CONDEMN)
Jer 42:18 of *c* and reproach; you will never
44:12 and horror, of *c* and reproach.
Ro 3: 8 may result"? Their *c* is deserved.
5:16 followed one sin and brought *c*,
5:18 of one trespass was *c* for all men,
8: 1 there is now no *c* for those who are
2Pe 2: 3 Their *c* has long been hanging
Jude : 4 certain men whose *c* was written

CONDEMNED* (CONDEMN)
Dt 13:17 of those *c* things shall be found
Job 32: 3 to refute Job, and yet had *c* him.
Ps 34:21 the foes of the righteous will be *c*.
34:22 will be *c* who takes refuge in him.
37:33 let them be *c* when brought to trial.
79:11 preserve those *c* to die.
102: 20 and release those *c* to death."
Mt 12: 7 you would not have *c* the innocent.
12:37 and by your words you will be *c*."
23:33 How will you escape being *c* to hell
27: 3 betrayed him, saw that Jesus was *c*,
Mk 14:64 They all *c* him as worthy of death.
16:16 whoever does not believe will be *c*.
Lk 6:37 condemn, and you will not be *c*.
Jn 3:18 Whoever believes in him is not *c*,
3:18 does not believe stands *c* already
5:24 has eternal life and will not be *c*;
5:29 who have done evil will rise to be *c*.
8:10 Has no one *c* you?" "No one, sir,"
16:11 prince of this world now stands *c*.
Ac 25:15 against him and asked that he be *c*.
Ro 3: 7 why am I still *c* as a sinner?"
8: 3 And so he *c* sin in sinful man,
14:23 But the man who has doubts is *c*
1Co 4: 9 like men *c* to die in the arena.
11:32 disciplined so that we will not be *c*
Gal 1: 8 let him be eternally *c*! As we have
1: 9 let him be eternally *c*! Am I now
2Th 2:12 that all will be *c* who have not
Tit 2: 8 of speech that cannot be *c*,
Heb 11: 7 By his faith he *c* the world
Jas 5: 6 You have *c* and murdered innocent
5:12 and your "No," no, or you will be *c*
2Pe 2: 6 if he *c* the cities of Sodom
Rev 19: 2 He has *c* the great prostitute

CONDEMNING* (CONDEMN)
Dt 25: 1 the innocent and *c* the guilty.
1Ki 8:32 *c* the guilty and bringing
Pr 17:15 the guilty and *c* the innocent—
Ac 13:27 yet in *c* him they fulfilled the words
Ro 2: 1 judge the other, you are *c* yourself,

CONDEMNS* (CONDEMN)
Job 15: 6 Your own mouth *c* you, not mine;
Pr 12: 2 but the LORD *c* a crafty man.
Ro 8:34 Who is he that *c*? Christ Jesus,
2Co 3: 9 the ministry that *c* men is glorious,

CONDITION
Pr 27:23 Be sure you know the *c*

CONDUCT (CONDUCTED CONDUCTS)
Pr 10:23 A fool finds pleasure in evil *c*,
20:11 by whether his *c* is pure and right.
21: 8 but the *c* of the innocent is upright.
Ecc 6: 8 how to *c* himself before others?
Jer 4:18 "Your own *c* and actions
17:10 to reward a man according to his *c*,
Eze 7: 3 I will judge you according to your *c*
Php 1:27 *c* yourselves in a manner worthy
1Ti 3:15 to *c* themselves in God's household

CONDUCTED* (CONDUCT)
2Co 1:12 testifies that we have *c* ourselves

CONDUCTS* (CONDUCT)
Ps 112: 5 who *c* his affairs with justice.

CONFESS* (CONFESSED CONFESSES CONFESSING CONFESSION)
Lev 5: 5 he must *c* in what way he has
16:21 and *c* over it all the wickedness
26:40 " 'But if they will *c* their sins
Nu 5: 7 must *c* the sin he has committed.
1Ki 8:33 back to you and *c* your name,
8:35 toward this place and *c* your name
2Ch 6:24 they turn back and *c* your name,
6:26 toward this place and *c* your name
Ne 1: 6 I *c* the sins we Israelites, including
Ps 32: 5 I said, "I will *c*
38:18 I *c* my iniquity;
Jn 1:20 fail to *c*, but confessed freely,
12:42 they would not *c* their faith
Ro 10: 9 That if you *c* with your mouth,
10:10 it is with your mouth that you *c*
14:11 every tongue will *c* to God.' "
Php 2:11 every tongue *c* that Jesus Christ is
Heb 3: 1 and high priest whom we *c*.
13:15 the fruit of lips that *c* his name.
Jas 5:16 Therefore *c* your sins to each other
1Jn 1: 9 If we *c* our sins, he is faithful

CONFESSED* (CONFESS)
1Sa 7: 6 day they fasted and there they *c*,
Ne 9: 2 in their places and *c* their sins
Da 9: 4 to the LORD my God and *c*:
Jn 1:20 but *c* freely, "I am not the Christ."
Ac 19:18 and openly *c* their evil deeds.

CONFESSES* (CONFESS)
Pr 28:13 whoever *c* and renounces them
2Ti 2:19 and, "Everyone who *c* the name

CONFESSING* (CONFESS)
Ezr 10: 1 While Ezra was praying and *c*,
Da 9:20 *c* my sin and the sin
Mt 3: 6 *C* their sins, they were baptized
Mk 1: 5 *C* their sins, they were baptized

CONFESSION* (CONFESS)
Ezr 10:11 Now make *c* to the LORD,
Ne 9: 3 and spent another quarter in *c*
2Co 9:13 obedience that accompanies your *c*
1Ti 6:12 called when you made your good *c*
6:13 Pontius Pilate made the good *c*,

CONFIDENCE* (CONFIDENT)
Jdg 9:26 and its citizens put their *c* in him.
2Ki 18:19 On what are you basing this *c*
2Ch 32: 8 And the people gained *c*
32:10 On what are you basing your *c*,
Job 4: 6 Should not your piety be your *c*
Ps 71: 5 my *c* since my youth.
Pr 3:26 for the LORD will be your *c*
3:32 but takes the upright into his *c*.
11:13 A gossip betrays a *c*,
20:19 A gossip betrays a *c*;
25: 9 do not betray another man's *c*,
31:11 Her husband has full *c* in her
Isa 32:17 will be quietness and *c* forever.
36: 4 On what are you basing this *c*
Jer 17: 7 whose *c* is in him.
49:31 which lives in *c*,"
Eze 29:16 a source of *c* for the people of Israel
Mic 7: 5 put no *c* in a friend.
2Co 2: 3 I had *c* in all of you, that you would
3: 4 Such *c* as this is ours
7: 4 I have great *c* in you; I take great
7:16 I am glad I can have complete *c*
8:22 so because of his great *c* in you.
Eph 3:12 God with freedom and *c*.
Php 3: 3 and who put no *c* in the flesh—
3: 4 I myself have reasons for such *c*.
3: 4 reasons to put *c* in the flesh,
2Th 3: 4 We have *c* in the Lord that you are
Heb 3:14 till the end the *c* we had at first.
4:16 the throne of grace with *c*,
10:19 since we have *c* to enter the Most
10:35 So do not throw away your *c*;
13: 6 So we say with *c*,
1Jn 3:21 we have *c* before God and receive
4:17 us so that we will have *c* on the day
5:14 This is the *c* we have

CONFIDENT* (CONFIDENCE)
Job 6:20 because they had been *c*;
Ps 27: 3 even then will I be *c*.
27:13 I am still *c* of this:
Lk 18: 9 To some who were *c*
2Co 1:15 Because I was *c* of this, I planned
5: 6 Therefore we are always *c*
5: 8 We are *c*, I say, and would prefer
9: 4 ashamed of having been so *c*.
10: 7 If anyone is *c* that he belongs
Gal 5:10 I am *c* in the Lord that you will
Php 1: 6 day until now, being *c* of this,
2:24 I am *c* in the Lord that I myself will
Phm :21 *C* of your obedience, I write to you,
Heb 6: 9 we are *c* of better things
1Jn 2:28 that when he appears we may be *c*

CONFIDES*
Ps 25:14 The LORD *c* in those who fear him

CONFORM* (CONFORMED CONFORMITY CONFORMS)
Ro 12: 2 Do not c any longer to the pattern
1Pe 1: 14 do not c to the evil desires you had

CONFORMED* (CONFORM)
Eze 5: 7 c to the standards of the nations
11: 12 but have c to the standards
Ro 8: 29 predestined to be c to the likeness

CONFORMITY* (CONFORM)
Eph 1: 11 in c with the purpose of his will,

CONFORMS* (CONFORM)
1Ti 1: 11 to the sound doctrine that c

CONQUEROR* (CONQUERORS)
Mic 1: 15 I will bring a c against you
Rev 6: 2 he rode out as a c bent on conquest.

CONQUERORS (CONQUEROR)
Ro 8: 37 than c through him who loved us.

CONSCIENCE* (CONSCIENCE-STRICKEN CONSCIENCES CONSCIENTIOUS)
Ge 20: 5 I have done this with a clear c
20: 6 I know you did this with a clear c,
1Sa 25: 31 have on his c the staggering burden
Job 27: 6 my c will not reproach me as long
Ac 23: 1 to God in all good c to this day."
24: 16 to keep my c clear before God
Ro 9: 1 my c confirms it in the Holy Spirit
13: 5 punishment but also because of c.
1Co 4: 4 My c is clear, but that does not
8: 7 since their c is weak, it is defiled.
8: 10 with a weak c sees you who have
8: 12 in this way and wound their weak c
10: 25 without raising questions of c,
10: 27 you without raising questions of c.
10: 28 man who told you and for c' sake—
10: 29 freedom be judged by another's c?
10: 29 the other man's c, I mean,
2Co 1: 12 Our c testifies that we have
4: 2 to every man's c in the sight of God
5: 11 and I hope it is also plain to your c.
1Ti 1: 5 and a good c and a sincere faith.
1: 19 holding on to faith and a good c.
3: 9 truths of the faith with a clear c.
2Ti 1: 3 as my forefathers did, with a clear c
Heb 9: 9 able to clear the c of the worshiper.
10: 22 to cleanse us from a guilty c
13: 18 We are sure that we have a clear c
1Pe 3: 16 and respect, keeping a clear c,
3: 21 the pledge of a good c toward God.

CONSCIENCE-STRICKEN* (CONSCIENCE)
1Sa 24: 5 David was c for having cut
2Sa 24: 10 David was c after he had counted

CONSCIENCES* (CONSCIENCE)
Ro 2: 15 their c also bearing witness,
1Ti 4: 2 whose c have been seared
Tit 1: 15 their minds and c are corrupted.
Heb 9: 14 cleanse our c from acts that lead

CONSCIENTIOUS* (CONSCIENCE)
2Ch 29: 34 for the Levites had been more c

CONSCIOUS*
Ro 3: 20 through the law we become c of sin
1Pe 2: 19 of unjust suffering because he is c

CONSECRATE (CONSECRATED)
Ex 13: 2 "C to me every firstborn male.
40: 9 c it and all its furnishings,
Lev 20: 7 " 'C yourselves and be holy,
25: 10 C the fiftieth year and proclaim
1Ch 15: 12 fellow Levites are to c yourselves

CONSECRATED (CONSECRATE)
Ex 29: 43 and the place will be c by my glory.
Lev 8: 30 So he c Aaron and his garments
2Ch 7: 16 c this temple so that my Name may
Lk 2: 23 is to be c to the Lord"),
1Ti 4: 5 because it is c by the word of God

CONSENT
1Co 7: 5 except by mutual c and for a time,

CONSIDER (CONSIDERATE CONSIDERED CONSIDERS)
1Sa 12: 24 c what great things he has done
16: 7 "Do not c his appearance
2Ch 19: 6 "C carefully what you do,
Job 37: 14 stop and c God's wonders.
Ps 8: 3 When I c your heavens,
77: 12 and c all your mighty deeds.
107: 43 and c the great love of the LORD.
143: 5 and c what your hands have done.
Pr 6: 6 c its ways and be wise!
20: 25 and only later to c his vows.
Ecc 7: 13 C what God has done:
Lk 12: 24 C the ravens: They do not sow
12: 27 about the rest? "C how the lilies
Php 2: 3 but in humility c others better
3: 8 I c everything a loss compared
Heb 10: 24 And let us c how we may spur one
Jas 1: 2 C it pure joy, my brothers,

CONSIDERATE* (CONSIDER)
Tit 3: 2 to be peaceable and c,
Jas 3: 17 then peace-loving, c, submissive,
1Pe 2: 18 only to those who are good and c,
3: 7 in the same way be c as you live

CONSIDERED (CONSIDER)
Job 1: 8 "Have you c my servant Job?
2: 3 "Have you c my servant Job?
Ps 44: 22 we are c as sheep to be slaughtered.
Isa 53: 4 yet we c him stricken by God,
Ro 8: 36 we are c as sheep to be slaughtered

CONSIDERS (CONSIDER)
Pr 31: 16 She c a field and buys it;
Ro 14: 5 One man c one day more sacred
Jas 1: 26 If anyone c himself religious

CONSIST (CONSISTS)
Lk 12: 15 a man's life does not c

CONSISTS (CONSIST)
Eph 5: 9 fruit of the light c in all goodness,

CONSOLATION
Ps 94: 19 your c brought joy to my soul.

CONSPIRE
Ps 2: 1 Why do the nations c

CONSTANT
Dt 28: 66 You will live in c suspense,
Pr 19: 13 wife is like a c dripping.
27: 15 a c dripping on a rainy day;
Ac 27: 33 "you have been in c suspense
Heb 5: 14 by c use have trained themselves

CONSTRUCTIVE*
1Co 10: 23 but not everything is c.

CONSULT
Pr 15: 12 he will not c the wise.
Gal 1: 16 I did not c any man, nor did I go up

CONSUME (CONSUMES CONSUMING)
Jn 2: 17 "Zeal for your house will c me."

CONSUMES (CONSUME)
Ps 69: 9 for zeal for your house c me,

CONSUMING (CONSUME)
Dt 4: 24 For the LORD your God is a c fire,
Heb 12: 29 and awe, for our "God is a c fire."

CONTAIN* (CONTAINED CONTAINS)
1Ki 8: 27 the highest heaven, cannot c you.
2Ch 2: 6 the highest heavens, cannot c him?
6: 18 the highest heavens, cannot c you.
Ecc 8: 8 power over the wind to c it;
2Pe 3: 16 His letters c some things that are

CONTAINED (CONTAIN)
Heb 9: 4 This ark c the gold jar of manna,

CONTAINS (CONTAIN)
Pr 15: 6 of the righteous c great treasure,

CONTAMINATES*
2Co 7: 1 from everything that c body

CONTEMPT
Pr 14: 31 He who oppresses the poor shows c
17: 5 He who mocks the poor shows c
18: 3 When wickedness comes, so does c
Da 12: 2 others to shame and everlasting c.
Mal 1: 6 O priests, who show c for my name.
Ro 2: 4 Or do you show c for the riches
Gal 4: 14 you did not treat me with c
1Th 5: 20 do not treat prophecies with c.

CONTEND (CONTENDED CONTENDING CONTENTIOUS)
Ge 6: 3 "My Spirit will not c
Ps 35: 1 C, O LORD, with those who
Isa 49: 25 I will c with those who c with you,
Jude : 3 you to c for the faith that was once

CONTENDED (CONTEND)
Php 4: 3 help these women who have c

CONTENDING* (CONTEND)
Php 1: 27 c as one man for the faith

CONTENT* (CONTENTMENT)
Jos 7: 7 If only we had been c to stay
Pr 13: 25 The righteous eat to their hearts' c,
19: 23 one rests c, untouched by trouble.
Ecc 4: 8 yet his eyes were not c
Lk 3: 14 don't accuse people falsely—be c
Php 4: 11 to be c whatever the circumstances
4: 12 I have learned the secret of being c
1Ti 6: 8 and clothing, we will be c with that.
Heb 13: 5 and be c with what you have,

CONTENTIOUS* (CONTEND)
1Co 11: 16 If anyone wants to be c about this,

CONTENTMENT* (CONTENT)
Job 36: 11 and their years in c.
SS 8: 10 like one bringing c.
1Ti 6: 6 But godliness with c is great gain.

CONTEST*
Heb 10: 32 in a great c in the face of suffering.

CONTINUAL (CONTINUE)
Pr 15: 15 but the cheerful heart has a c feast.
Eph 4: 19 of impurity, with a c lust for more.

CONTINUE (CONTINUAL CONTINUES CONTINUING)
1Ki 8: 23 servants who c wholeheartedly
2Ch 6: 14 servants who c wholeheartedly
Ps 36: 10 C your love to those who know you
Ac 13: 43 urged them to c in the grace of God
Ro 11: 22 provided that you c in his kindness.
Gal 3: 10 Cursed is everyone who does not c
Php 2: 12 c to work out your salvation
Col 1: 23 if you c in your faith, established
2: 6 received Christ Jesus as Lord, c
1Ti 2: 15 if they c in faith, love and holiness
2Ti 3: 14 c in what you have learned
1Jn 2: 28 And now, dear children, c in him,
3: 9 born of God will c to sin,
5: 18 born of God does not c to sin;
2Jn : 9 and does not c in the teaching
Rev 22: 11 and let him who is holy c to be holy
22: 11 let him who does right c to do right;

CONTINUES (CONTINUE)
Ps 100: 5 c through all generations.
119: 90 Your faithfulness c
2Co 10: 15 Our hope is that, as your faith c
1Jn 3: 6 No one who c to sin has

CONTINUING (CONTINUE)
Ro 13: 8 the c debt to love one another,

CONTRIBUTION (CONTRIBUTIONS)
Ro 15: 26 pleased to make a c for the poor

CONTRIBUTIONS (CONTRIBUTION)
2Ch 24: 10 all the people brought their c gladly
31: 12 they faithfully brought in the c,

CONTRITE*
Ps 51: 17 a broken and c heart,
Isa 57: 15 also with him who is c and lowly
57: 15 and to revive the heart of the c.
66: 2 he who is humble and c in spirit,

CONTROL (CONTROLLED CONTROLS SELF-CONTROL SELF-CONTROLLED)
Pr 29: 11 a wise man keeps himself under c.
1Co 7: 9 But if they cannot c themselves,
7: 37 but has c over his own will,
1Th 4: 4 you should learn to c his own body

CONTROLLED (CONTROL)
Ps 32: 9 but must be c by bit and bridle
Ro 8: 6 but the mind c by the Spirit is life
8: 8 Those c by the sinful nature cannot

CONTROLS* (CONTROL)

Job 37: 15 you know how God *c* the clouds
Pr 16: 32 a man who *c* his temper

CONTROVERSIES*

Ac 26: 3 with all the Jewish customs and *c.*
1Ti 1: 4 These promote *c* rather
6: 4 He has an unhealthy interest in *c*
Tit 3: 9 But avoid foolish *c* and genealogies

CONVERSATION

Col 4: 6 Let your *c* be always full of grace,

CONVERT

1Ti 3: 6 He must not be a recent *c,*

CONVICT (CONVICTION)

Pr 24: 25 with those who *c* the guilty,
Jn 16: 8 he will *c* the world of guilt in regard
Jude : 15 and to *c* all the ungodly

CONVICTION* (CONVICT)

1Th 1: 5 the Holy Spirit and with deep *c.*

CONVINCE* (CONVINCED CONVINCING)

Ac 28: 23 and tried to *c* them about Jesus

CONVINCED* (CONVINCE)

Ge 45: 28 "I'm *c!* My son Joseph is still alive.
Lk 16: 31 will not be *c* even if someone rises
Ac 19: 26 and hear how this fellow Paul has *c*
26: 9 "I too was *c* that I ought
26: 26 I am *c* that none of this has escaped
28: 24 Some were *c* by what he said,
Ro 2: 19 if you are *c* that you are a guide
8: 38 For I am *c* that neither death
14: 5 Each one should be fully *c*
14: 14 I am fully *c* that no food is unclean
15: 14 I myself am *c,* my brothers,
1Co 14: 24 he will be *c* by all that he is a sinner
2Co 5: 14 we are *c* that one died for all,
Php 1: 25 *C* of this, I know that I will remain,
2Ti 1: 12 and am *c* that he is able
3: 14 have learned and have become *c*

CONVINCING* (CONVINCE)

Ac 1: 3 and gave many *c* proofs that he was

COOLNESS*

Pr 25: 13 Like the *c* of snow at harvest time

COPIES (COPY)

Heb 9: 23 for the *c* of the heavenly things

COPY (COPIES)

Dt 17: 18 for himself on a scroll a *c* of this law
Heb 8: 5 They serve at a sanctuary that is a *c*
9: 24 sanctuary that was only a *c*

CORBAN*

Mk 7: 11 received from me is *C'* (that is,

CORD (CORDS)

Jos 2: 18 you have tied this scarlet *c*
Ecc 4: 12 *c* of three strands is not quickly

CORDS (CORD)

Pr 5: 22 the *c* of his sin hold him fast.
Isa 54: 2 lengthen your *c,*
Hos 11: 4 them with *c* of human kindness,

CORINTH

Ac 18: 1 Paul left Athens and went to *C.*
1Co 1: 2 To the church of God in *C,*
2Co 1: 1 To the church of God in *C,*

CORNELIUS*

Roman to whom Peter preached; first Gentile Christian (Ac 10).

CORNER (CORNERS)

Ru 3: 9 "Spread the *c* of your garment
Pr 21: 9 Better to live on a *c* of the roof
25: 24 Better to live on a *c* of the roof
Ac 26: 26 because it was not done in a *c.*

CORNERS (CORNER)

Mt 6: 5 on the street *c* to be seen by men.
22: 9 Go to the street *c* and invite

CORNERSTONE* (STONE)

Job 38: 6 or who laid its *c*—
Isa 28: 16 a precious *c* for a sure foundation;
Jer 51: 26 rock will be taken from you for a *c,*
Zec 10: 4 From Judah will come the *c,*
Eph 2: 20 Christ Jesus himself as the chief *c.*
1Pe 2: 6 a chosen and precious *c,*

CORRECT* (CORRECTED CORRECTING CORRECTION CORRECTIONS CORRECTS)

Job 6: 26 Do you mean to *c* what I say,
40: 2 contends with the Almighty *c* him?
Jer 10: 24 *C* me, LORD, but only with justice
2Ti 4: 2 *c,* rebuke and encourage—

CORRECTED* (CORRECT)

Pr 29: 19 A servant cannot be *c*

CORRECTING* (CORRECT)

2Ti 3: 16 *c* and training in righteousness,

CORRECTION* (CORRECT)

Lev 26: 23 things you do not accept my *c*
Job 36: 10 He makes them listen to *c*
Pr 5: 12 How my heart spurned *c!*
10: 17 whoever ignores *c* leads others
12: 1 but he who hates *c* is stupid.
13: 18 but whoever heeds *c* is honored.
15: 5 whoever heeds *c* shows prudence.
15: 10 he who hates *c* will die.
15: 12 A mocker resents *c;*
15: 32 whoever heeds *c* gains
29: 15 The rod of *c* imparts wisdom,
Jer 2: 30 they did not respond to *c.*
5: 3 crushed them, but they refused *c.*
7: 28 LORD its God or responded to *c.*
Zep 3: 2 she accepts no *c.*
3: 7 you will fear me / and accept *c!'*

CORRECTIONS* (CORRECT)

Pr 6: 23 and the *c* of discipline

CORRECTS* (CORRECT)

Job 5: 17 "Blessed is the man whom God *c;*
Pr 9: 7 Whoever *c* a mocker invites insult;

CORRUPT (CORRUPTED CORRUPTION CORRUPTS)

Ge 6: 11 Now the earth was *c* in God's sight
Ps 14: 1 They are *c,* their deeds are vile;
14: 3 they have together become *c;*
Pr 4: 24 keep *c* talk far from your lips.
6: 12 who goes about with a *c* mouth,
19: 28 A *c* witness mocks at justice,

CORRUPTED (CORRUPT)

2Co 7: 2 wronged no one, we have *c* no one,
Tit 1: 15 but to those who are *c* and do not

CORRUPTION (CORRUPT)

2Pe 1: 4 escape the *c* in the world caused
2: 20 If they have escaped the *c*

CORRUPTS* (CORRUPT)

Ecc 7: 7 and a bribe *c* the heart.
1Co 15: 33 "Bad company *c* good character."
Jas 3: 6 It *c* the whole person, sets

COST (COSTS)

Nu 16: 38 sinned at the *c* of their lives.
Pr 4: 7 Though it *c* all you have, get
7: 23 little knowing it will *c* him his life.
Isa 55: 1 milk without money and without *c.*
Lk 14: 28 and estimate the *c* to see
Rev 21: 6 to drink without *c* from the spring

COSTS (COST)

Pr 6: 31 it *c* him all the wealth of his house.

COUNCIL

Ps 89: 7 In the *c* of the holy ones God is
107: 32 and praise him in the *c* of the elders

COUNSEL (COUNSELOR COUNSELS)

1Ki 22: 5 "First seek the *c* of the LORD."
2Ch 18: 4 "First seek the *c* of the LORD."
Job 38: 2 "Who is this that darkens my *c*
42: 3 'Who is this that obscures my *c*
Ps 1: 1 walk in the *c* of the wicked
73: 24 You guide me with your *c,*
107: 11 despised the *c* of the Most High.
Pr 8: 14 *C* and sound judgment are mine;
15: 22 Plans fail for lack of *c,*
27: 9 from his earnest *c.*
Isa 28: 29 wonderful in *c* and magnificent
1Ti 5: 14 So I *c* younger widows to marry,
Rev 3: 18 I *c* you to buy from me gold refined

COUNSELOR (COUNSEL)

Isa 9: 6 Wonderful *C,* Mighty God,
Jn 14: 16 he will give you another *C* to be
14: 26 But the *C,* the Holy Spirit,
15: 26 "When the *C* comes, whom I will
16: 7 the *C* will not come to you;
Ro 11: 34 Or who has been his *c?"*

COUNSELS (COUNSEL)

Ps 16: 7 I will praise the LORD, who *c* me;

COUNT (COUNTED COUNTING COUNTS)

Ps 22: 17 I can *c* all my bones;
Ro 4: 8 whose sin the Lord will never *c*
6: 11 *c* yourselves dead to sin
2Th 1: 11 that our God may *c* you worthy

COUNTED (COUNT)

Ac 5: 41 because they had been *c* worthy
2Th 1: 5 and as a result you will be *c* worthy

COUNTERFEIT*

2Th 2: 9 displayed in all kinds of *c* miracles,
1Jn 2: 27 not *c*—just as it has taught you,

COUNTING (COUNT)

2Co 5: 19 not *c* men's sins against them.

COUNTRY

Pr 28: 2 When a *c* is rebellious, it has many
29: 4 By justice a king gives a *c* stability,
Isa 66: 8 Can a *c* be born in a day
Lk 15: 13 off for a distant *c* and there
Jn 4: 44 prophet has no honor in his own *c.)*
2Co 11: 26 in danger in the *c,* in danger at sea;
Heb 11: 14 looking for a *c* of their own.

COUNTRYMEN

2Co 11: 26 danger from my own *c,* in danger

COUNTS (COUNT)

Jn 6: 63 The Spirit gives life; the flesh *c*
1Co 7: 19 God's commands is what *c.*
Gal 5: 6 only thing that *c* is faith expressing

COURAGE* (COURAGEOUS)

Jos 2: 11 everyone's *c* failed because of you,
5: 1 and they no longer had the *c*
2Sa 4: 1 he lost *c,* and all Israel became
7: 27 So your servant has found *c*
1Ch 17: 25 So your servant has found *c* to pray
2Ch 15: 8 son of Oded the prophet, he took *c.*
19: 11 Act with *c,* and may the LORD be
Ezr 7: 28 I took *c* and gathered leading men
10: 4 We will support you, so take *c*
Ps 107: 26 in their peril their *c* melted away.
Eze 22: 14 Will your *c* endure or your hands
Da 11: 25 and *c* against the king of the South.
Mt 14: 27 said to them: "Take *c!*
Mk 6: 50 spoke to them and said, "Take *c!*
Ac 4: 13 When they saw the *c* of Peter
23: 11 "Take *c!* As you have testified
27: 22 now I urge you to keep up your *c,*
27: 25 So keep up your *c,* men,
1Co 16: 13 stand firm in the faith; be men of *c;*
Php 1: 20 will have sufficient *c* so that now
Heb 3: 6 if we hold on to our *c* and the hope

COURAGEOUS* (COURAGE)

Dt 31: 6 Be strong and *c.*
31: 7 of all Israel, "Be strong and *c,*
31: 23 son of Nun: "Be strong and *c,*
Jos 1: 6 and *c,* because you will lead these
1: 7 Be strong and very *c.*
1: 9 commanded you? Be strong and *c.*
1: 18 Only be strong and *c!"*
10: 25 Be strong and *c.*
1Ch 22: 13 Be strong and *c.*
28: 20 "Be strong and *c,* and do the work.
2Ch 26: 17 priest with eighty other *c* priests
32: 7 with these words: "Be strong and *c.*

COURSE

Ps 19: 5 a champion rejoicing to run his *c.*
Pr 2: 8 for he guards the *c* of the just
15: 21 of understanding keeps a straight *c.*
16: 9 In his heart a man plans his *c,*
17: 23 to pervert the *c* of justice.
Jas 3: 6 sets the whole *c* of his life on fire,

COURT (COURTS)

Pr 22: 22 and do not crush the needy in *c,*
25: 8 do not bring hastily to *c,*
Mt 5: 25 adversary who is taking you to *c.*

1Co 4: 3 judged by you or by any human c;

COURTS (COURT)

Ps 84:10 Better is one day in your c
100: 4 and his c with praise;
Am 5:15 maintain justice in the c.
Zec 8:16 and sound judgment in your c;

COURTYARD

Ex 27: 9 "Make a c for the tabernacle.

COUSIN

Col 4:10 as does Mark, the c of Barnabas.

COVENANT (COVENANTS)

Ge 9: 9 "I now establish my c with you
17: 2 I will confirm my c between me
Ex 19: 5 if you obey me fully and keep my c,
24: 7 Then he took the Book of the C
Dt 4:13 declared to you his c, the Ten
29: 1 in addition to the c he had made
Jdg 2: 1 'I will never break my c with you,
1Sa 23:18 of them made a c before the LORD
1Ki 8:21 in which is the c of the LORD that
8:23 you who keep your c of love
2Ki 23: 2 the words of the Book of the C,
1Ch 16:15 He remembers his c forever,
2Ch 6:14 you who keep your c of love
34:30 the words of the Book of the C,
Ne 1: 5 who keeps his c of love
Job 31: 1 "I made a c with my eyes
Ps 105: 8 He remembers his c forever,
Pr 2:17 ignored the c she made before God
Isa 42: 6 you to be a c for the people
61: 8 make an everlasting c with them.
Jer 11: 2 "Listen to the terms of this c
31:31 "when I will make a new c
31:32 It will not be like the c
31:33 "This is the c I will make
Eze 37:26 I will make a c of peace with them;
Da 9:27 He will confirm a c with many
Hos 6: 7 Like Adam, they have broken the c
Mal 2:14 the wife of your marriage c.
3: 1 of the c, whom you desire,
Mt 26:28 blood of the c, which is poured out
Mk 14:24 "This is my blood of the c,
Lk 22:20 "This cup is the new c in my blood,
1Co 11:25 "This cup is the new c in my blood;
2Co 3: 6 as ministers of a new c—
Gal 4:24 One c is from Mount Sinai
Heb 8: 6 as the c of which he is mediator is
8: 8 when I will make a new c
9:15 Christ is the mediator of a new c,
12:24 to Jesus the mediator of a new c,

COVENANTS (COVENANT)

Ro 9: 4 theirs the divine glory, the c,
Gal 4:24 for the women represent two c.

COVER (COVER-UP COVERED COVERING COVERINGS COVERS)

Ex 25:17 "Make an atonement c of pure gold
25:21 Place the c on top of the ark
33:22 and c you with my hand
Lev 16: 2 in the cloud over the atonement c.
Ps 32: 5 and did not c up my iniquity.
91: 4 He will c you with his feathers,
Hos 10: 8 say to the mountains, "C us!"
Lk 23:30 and to the hills, "C us!"'
1Co 11: 6 If a woman does not c her head,
11: 6 shaved off, she should c her head.
11: 7 A man ought not to c his head,
Jas 5:20 and cover a multitude of sins.

COVER-UP* (COVER)

1Pe 2:16 but do not use your freedom as a c

COVERED (COVER)

Ps 32: 1 whose sins are c.
85: 2 and c all their sins.
Isa 6: 2 With two wings they c their faces,
51:16 c you with the shadow of my hand
Ro 4: 7 whose sins are c.
1Co 11: 4 with his head c dishonors his head.

COVERING (COVER)

1Co 11:15 For long hair is given to her as a c.

COVERINGS (COVER)

Ge 3: 7 and made c for themselves.
Pr 31:22 She makes c for her bed;

COVERS (COVER)

Pr 10:12 but love c over all wrongs.
17: 9 He who c over an offense promotes
2Co 3:15 Moses is read, a veil c their hearts.
1Pe 4: 8 love c over a multitude of sins.

COVET* (COVETED COVETING COVETOUS)

Ex 20:17 You shall not c your neighbor's
20:17 "You shall not c your neighbor's
34:24 and no one will c your land
Dt 5:21 "You shall not c your neighbor's
7:25 Do not c the silver and gold
Mic 2: 2 They c fields and seize them,
Ro 7: 7 if the law had not said, "Do not c."
13: 9 "Do not steal," "Do not c,"
Jas 4: 2 c, but you cannot have what you

COVETED* (COVET)

Jos 7:21 weighing fifty shekels, I c them
Ac 20:33 I have not c anyone's silver or gold

COVETING

Ro 7: 7 what c really was if the law

COVETOUS* (COVET)

Ro 7: 8 in me every kind of c desire.

COWARDLY*

Rev 21: 8 But the c, the unbelieving, the vile,

COWS

Ge 41: 2 of the river there came up seven c,
Ex 25: 5 skins dyed red and hides of sea c;
Nu 4: 6 are to cover this with hides of sea c,
1Sa 6: 7 Hitch the c to the cart,

CRAFTINESS* (CRAFTY)

Job 5:13 He catches the wise in their c,
1Co 3:19 "He catches the wise in their c";
Eph 4:14 and c of men in their deceitful

CRAFTSMAN

Pr 8:30 Then I was the c at his side.

CRAFTY* (CRAFTINESS)

Ge 3: 1 the serpent was more c than any
1Sa 23:22 They tell me he is very c.
Job 5:12 He thwarts the plans of the c,
15: 5 you adopt the tongue of the c.
Pr 7:10 like a prostitute and with c intent.
12: 2 but the LORD condemns a c man.
14:17 and a c man is hated.
2Co 12:16 c fellow that I am, I caught you

CRAVE* (CRAVED CRAVES CRAVING CRAVINGS)

Nu 11: 4 with them began to c other food,
Dt 12:20 you c meat and say, "I would like
Pr 23: 3 Do not c his delicacies,
23: 6 do not c his delicacies;
31: 4 not for rulers to c beer,
Mic 7: 1 none of the early figs that I c.
1Pe 2: 2 newborn babies, c pure spiritual

CRAVED* (CRAVE)

Nu 11:34 the people who had c other food.
Ps 78:18 by demanding the food they c.
78:29 for he had given them what they c.
78:30 turned from the food they c,

CRAVES* (CRAVE)

Pr 13: 4 The sluggard c and gets nothing,
21:10 The wicked man c evil;
21:26 All day long he c for more,

CRAVING* (CRAVE)

Job 20:20 he will have no respite from his c;
Ps 106:14 In the desert they gave in to their c;
Pr 10: 3 but he thwarts the c of the wicked.
13: 2 the unfaithful have a c for violence.
21:25 The sluggard's c will be the death
Jer 2:24 sniffing the wind in her c—

CRAVINGS* (CRAVE)

Ps 10: 3 He boasts of the c of his heart;
Eph 2: 3 gratifying the c of our sinful nature
1Jn 2:16 in the world—the c of sinful man,

CRAWL

Ge 3:14 You will c on your belly

CREATE* (CREATED CREATES CREATING CREATION CREATOR)

Ps 51:10 C in me a pure heart, O God,
Isa 4: 5 Then the LORD will c over all
45: 7 I bring prosperity and c disaster;
45: 7 I form the light and c darkness,
45:18 he did not c it to be empty,
65:17 "Behold, I will c new heavens
65:18 for I will c Jerusalem to be a delight
65:18 forever in what I will c,
Jer 31:22 The LORD will c a new thing
Mal 2:10 one Father? Did not one God c us?
Eph 2:15 His purpose was to c

CREATED* (CREATE)

Ge 1: 1 In the beginning God c the heavens
1:21 God c the great creatures of the sea
1:27 So God c man in his own image,
1:27 in the image of God he c him;
1:27 male and female he c them.
2: 4 and the earth when they were c.
5: 1 When God c man, he made him
5: 2 He c them male and female
5: 2 when they were c, he called them
6: 7 whom I have c, from the face
Dt 4:32 from the day God c man
Ps 89:12 You c the north and the south;
89:47 what futility you have c all men!
102:18 a people not yet c may praise
104:30 you send your Spirit, / they are c,
139:13 For you c my inmost being;
148: 5 for he commanded and they were c
Isa 40:26 Who c all these?
41:20 that the Holy One of Israel has c it.
42: 5 he who c the heavens and stretched
43: 1 he who c you, O Jacob,
43: 7 whom I c for my glory,
45: 8 I, the LORD, have c it.
45:12 and c mankind upon it.
45:18 he who c the heavens,
48: 7 They are c now, and not long ago;
54:16 And it is I who have c the destroyer
54:16 "See, it is I who c the blacksmith
57:16 the breath of man that I have c.
Eze 21:30 In the place where you were c,
28:13 the day you were c they were
28:15 ways from the day you were c
Mk 13:19 when God c the world, until now—
Ro 1:25 and served c things rather
1Co 11: 9 neither was man c for woman,
Eph 2:10 c in Christ Jesus to do good works,
3: 9 hidden in God, who c all things.
4:24 c to be like God in true
Col 1:16 For by him all things were c:
1:16 all things were c by him
1Ti 4: 3 which God c to be received
4: 4 For everything God c is good,
Heb 12:27 c things—so that what cannot be
Jas 1:18 a kind of firstfruits of all he c.
Rev 4:11 and by your will they were c
4:11 for you c all things,
10: 6 who c the heavens and all that is

CREATES* (CREATE)

Am 4:13 c the wind,

CREATING* (CREATE)

Ge 2: 3 the work of c that he had done.
Isa 57:19 c praise on the lips of the mourners

CREATION* (CREATE)

Hab 2:18 he who makes it trusts in his own c;
Mt 13:35 hidden since the c of the world."
25:34 for you since the c of the world.
Mk 10: 6 of c God 'made them male
16:15 and preach the good news to all c.
Jn 17:24 me before the c of the world.
Ro 1:20 For since the c of the world God's
8:19 The c waits in eager expectation
8:20 For the c was subjected
8:21 in hope that the c itself will be
8:22 that the whole c has been groaning
8:39 depth, nor anything else in all c,
2Co 5:17 he is a new c; the old has gone,
Gal 6:15 anything; what counts is a new c.
Eph 1: 4 us in him before the c of the world
Col 1:15 God, the firstborn over all c.
Heb 4: 3 finished since the c of the world.
4:13 Nothing in all c is hidden
9:11 that is to say, not a part of this c.
9:26 times since the c of the world.
1Pe 1:20 chosen before the c of the world,
2Pe 3: 4 as it has since the beginning of c."
Rev 3:14 true witness, the ruler of God's c.
13: 8 slain from the c of the world.
17: 8 life from the c of the world will be

CREATOR* (CREATE)

Ge 14:19 C of heaven and earth.
14:22 God Most High, C of heaven
Dt 32: 6 Is he not your Father, your C,

Ecc 12: 1 Remember your *C*
Isa 27: 11 and their *C* shows them no favor.
40: 28 the *C* of the ends of the earth.
43: 15 Israel's *C*, your King."
Mt 19: 4 the beginning the *C* 'made them
Ro 1: 25 created things rather than the *C*—
Col 3: 10 in knowledge in the image of its *C*.
1Pe 4: 19 themselves to their faithful *C*

CREATURE (CREATURES)

Lev 17: 11 For the life of a *c* is in the blood,
17: 14 the life of every *c* is its blood.
Ps 136: 25 and who gives food to every *c*.
Eze 1: 15 beside each *c* with its four faces.
Rev 4: 7 The first living *c* was like a lion,

CREATURES (CREATURE)

Ge 6: 19 bring into the ark two of all living *c*,
8: 21 again will I destroy all living *c*,
Ps 104: 24 the earth is full of your *c*.
Eze 1: 5 was what looked like four living *c*.

CREDIT (CREDITED CREDITOR CREDITS)

Lk 6: 33 what *c* is that to you? Even
Ro 4: 24 to whom God will *c* righteousness
1Pe 2: 20 it to your *c* if you receive a beating

CREDITED (CREDIT)

Ge 15: 6 and he *c* it to him as righteousness.
Ps 106: 31 This was *c* to him as righteousness
Eze 18: 20 of the righteous man will be *c*
Ro 4: 3 and it was *c* to him as righteousness
4: 4 his wages are not *c* to him as a gift,
4: 5 his faith is *c* as righteousness.
4: 9 saying that Abraham's faith was *c*
4: 23 The words "it was *c*
Gal 3: 6 and it was *c* to him as righteousness
Php 4: 17 for what may be *c* to your account.
Jas 2: 23 and it was *c* to him as righteousness

CREDITOR (CREDIT)

Dt 15: 2 Every *c* shall cancel the loan he has

CREDITS (CREDIT)

Ro 4: 6 whom God *c* righteousness apart

CRETANS (CRETE)

Tit 1: 12 "*C* are always liars, evil brutes,

CRETE (CRETANS)

Ac 27: 12 harbor in *C*, facing both southwest

CRIED (CRY)

Ex 2: 23 groaned in their slavery and *c* out,
14: 10 They were terrified and *c* out
Nu 20: 16 but when we *c* out to the LORD,
Jos 24: 7 But they *c* to the LORD for help,
Jdg 3: 9 But when they *c* out to the LORD,
3: 15 Again the Israelites *c* out
4: 3 they *c* to the LORD for help.
6: 6 the Israelites that they *c* out
10: 12 Maonites oppressed you and you *c*
1Sa 7: 9 He *c* out to the LORD
12: 8 they *c* to the LORD for help,
12: 10 They *c* out to the LORD and said,
Ps 18: 6 I *c* to my God for help.

CRIMINALS

Lk 23: 32 both *c*, were also led out with him

CRIMSON

Isa 1: 18 though they are red as *c*,
63: 1 with his garments stained *c*?

CRIPPLED

2Sa 9: 3 of Jonathan; he is *c* in both feet."
Mk 9: 45 better for you to enter life *c*

CRISIS*

1Co 7: 26 of the present *c*, I think that it is

CRITICISM*

2Co 8: 20 We want to avoid any *c*

CROOKED*

Dt 32: 5 but a warped and *c* generation.
2Sa 22: 27 to the *c* you show yourself shrewd.
Ps 18: 26 to the *c* you show yourself shrewd.
125: 5 But those who turn to *c* ways
Pr 2: 15 whose paths are *c*
5: 6 her paths are *c*, but she knows it
8: 8 none of them is *c* or perverse.
10: 9 he who takes *c* paths will be found
Ecc 7: 13 what he has made *c*?
Isa 59: 8 have turned them into *c* roads;
La 3: 9 he has made my paths *c*.
Lk 3: 5 The *c* roads shall become straight,
Php 2: 15 children of God without fault in a *c*

CROP (CROPS)

Mt 13: 8 where it produced a *c*—a hundred,
21: 41 share of the *c* at harvest time."

CROPS (CROP)

Pr 3: 9 with the firstfruits of all your *c*;
10: 5 He who gathers *c* in summer is
28: 3 like a driving rain that leaves no *c*.
2Ti 2: 6 the first to receive a share of the *c*.

CROSS (CROSSED CROSSING)

Dt 4: 21 swore that I would not *c* the Jordan
12: 10 But you will *c* the Jordan
Mt 10: 38 and anyone who does not take his *c*
16: 24 and take up his *c* and follow me.
Mk 8: 34 and take up his *c* and follow me.
Lk 9: 23 take up his *c* daily and follow me.
14: 27 anyone who does not carry his *c*
Jn 19: 17 Carrying his own *c*, he went out
Ac 2: 23 to death by nailing him to the *c*.
1Co 1: 17 lest the *c* of Christ be emptied
1: 18 the message of the *c* is foolishness
Gal 5: 11 offense of the *c* has been abolished.
6: 12 persecuted for the *c* of Christ.
6: 14 in the *c* of our Lord Jesus Christ,
Eph 2: 16 both of them to God through the *c*,
Php 2: 8 even death on a *c*!
3: 18 as enemies of the *c* of Christ.
Col 1: 20 through his blood, shed on the *c*.
2: 14 he took it away, nailing it to the *c*.
2: 15 triumphing over them by the *c*.
Heb 12: 2 set before him endured the *c*,

CROSSED (CROSS)

Jos 4: 7 When it *c* the Jordan, the waters
Jn 5: 24 he has *c* over from death to life.

CROSSING (CROSS)

Ge 48: 14 he was the younger, and *c* his arms,

CROSSROADS (ROAD)

Jer 6: 16 "Stand at the *c* and look;

CROUCHING

Ge 4: 7 sin is *c* at your door; it desires

CROWD (CROWDS)

Ex 23: 2 Do not follow the *c* in doing wrong.

CROWDS (CROWD)

Mt 9: 36 he saw the *c*, he had compassion

CROWED (CROWS)

Mt 26: 74 the man!" Immediately a rooster *c*.

CROWN (CROWNED CROWNS)

Pr 4: 9 present you with a *c* of splendor."
10: 6 Blessings *c* the head
12: 4 noble character is her husband's *c*,
16: 31 Gray hair is a *c* of splendor;
17: 6 Children's children are a *c*
Isa 35: 10 everlasting joy will *c* their heads.
51: 11 everlasting joy will *c* their heads.
61: 3 to bestow on them a *c* of beauty
62: 3 You will be a *c* of splendor
Eze 16: 12 and a beautiful *c* on your head.
Zec 9: 16 like jewels in a *c*.
Mt 27: 29 and then twisted together a *c* of thorns
Mk 15: 17 then twisted together a *c* of thorns
Jn 19: 2 The soldiers twisted together a *c*
19: 5 When Jesus came out wearing the *c*
1Co 9: 25 it to get a *c* that will last forever.
9: 25 it to get a *c* that will not last;
Php 4: 1 and long for, my joy and *c*,
1Th 2: 19 or the *c* in which we will glory
2Ti 2: 5 he does not receive the victor's *c*
4: 8 store for me the *c* of righteousness,
Jas 1: 12 he will receive the *c*
1Pe 5: 4 you will receive the *c*
Rev 2: 10 and I will give you the *c* of life.
3: 11 so that no one will take your *c*.
14: 14 a son of man" with a *c* of gold

CROWNED* (CROWN)

Ps 8: 5 and *c* him with glory and honor.
Pr 14: 18 the prudent are *c* with knowledge.
SS 3: 11 crown with which his mother *c* him
Heb 2: 7 you *c* him with glory and honor
2: 9 now *c* with glory and honor

CROWNS (CROWN)

Ps 103: 4 and *c* me with love and compassion
149: 4 he *c* the humble with salvation.
Pr 11: 26 blessing *c* him who is willing to sell.
Rev 4: 4 and had *c* of gold on their heads.
4: 10 They lay their *c* before the throne
12: 3 ten horns and seven *c* on his heads.
19: 12 and on his head are many *c*.

CROWS (CROWED)

Mt 26: 34 this very night, before the rooster *c*

CRUCIFIED* (CRUCIFY)

Mt 20: 19 to be mocked and flogged and *c*.
26: 2 of Man will be handed over to be *c*
27: 26 and handed him over to be *c*.
27: 35 When they had *c* him, they divided
27: 38 Two robbers were *c* with him,
27: 44 same way the robbers who were *c*
28: 5 looking for Jesus, who was *c*.
Mk 15: 15 and handed him over to be *c*.
15: 24 And they *c* him.
15: 25 the third hour when they *c* him.
15: 27 They *c* two robbers with him,
15: 32 Those *c* with him also heaped
16: 6 for Jesus the Nazarene, who was *c*.
Lk 23: 23 insistently demanded that he be *c*,
23: 33 *c* him, along with the criminals—
24: 7 be *c* and on the third day be raised
24: 20 sentenced to death, and they *c* him;
Jn 19: 16 him over to them to be *c*.
19: 18 Here they *c* him, and with him two
19: 20 for the place where Jesus was *c* was
19: 23 When the soldiers *c* Jesus,
19: 32 of the first man who had been *c*
19: 41 At the place where Jesus was *c*,
Ac 2: 36 whom you *c*, both Lord and Christ
4: 10 whom you *c* but whom God raised
Ro 6: 6 For we know that our old self was *c*
1Co 1: 13 Is Christ divided? Was Paul *c*
1: 23 but we preach Christ *c*: a stumbling
2: 2 except Jesus Christ and him *c*.
2: 8 they would not have *c* the Lord
2Co 13: 4 to be sure, he was *c* in weakness,
Gal 2: 20 I have been *c* with Christ
3: 1 Christ was clearly portrayed as *c*.
5: 24 Christ Jesus have *c* the sinful
6: 14 which the world has been *c*
Rev 11: 8 where also their Lord was *c*.

CRUCIFY* (CRUCIFIED CRUCIFYING)

Mt 23: 34 Some of them you will kill and *c*;
27: 22 They all answered, "*C* him!" "Why
27: 23 they shouted all the louder, "*C* him
27: 31 Then they led him away to *c* him.
Mk 15: 13 "*C* him!" they shouted.
15: 14 they shouted all the louder, "*C* him
15: 20 Then they led him out to *c* him.
Lk 23: 21 they kept shouting, "*C* him! *C* him
Jn 19: 6 they shouted, "*C*! *C*!"
19: 6 "You take him and *c* him.
19: 10 either to free you or to *c* you?"
19: 15 Crucify him!" "Shall I *c* your king
19: 15 away! Take him away! *C* him!"

CRUCIFYING* (CRUCIFY)

Heb 6: 6 to their loss they are *c* the Son

CRUSH (CRUSHED)

Ge 3: 15 he will *c* your head,
Isa 53: 10 it was the LORD's will to *c* him
Ro 16: 20 The God of peace will soon *c* Satan

CRUSHED (CRUSH)

Ps 34: 18 and saves those who are *c* in spirit.
Pr 17: 22 but a *c* spirit dries up the bones.
18: 14 but a *c* spirit who can bear?
Isa 53: 5 he was *c* for our iniquities;
2Co 4: 8 not *c*; perplexed, but not in despair;

CRY (CRIED)

Ex 2: 23 *c* for help because of their slavery
Ps 5: 2 Listen to my *c* for help,
34: 15 and his ears are attentive to their *c*;
40: 1 he turned to me and heard my *c*.
130: 1 Out of the depths I *c* to you,
Pr 21: 13 to the *c* of the poor,
La 2: 18 *c* out to the Lord.
Hab 2: 11 The stones of the wall will *c* out,
Lk 19: 40 keep quiet, the stones will *c* out."

CUNNING

2Co 11: 3 deceived by the serpent's *c*,
Eph 4: 14 and by the *c* and craftiness of men

CUP

Ps 23: 5 my *c* overflows.
Isa 51:22 from that *c*, the goblet of my wrath,
51:22 the *c* that made you stagger;
Mt 10:42 if anyone gives even a *c* of cold water
20:22 "Can you drink the *c* I am going
23:25 You clean the outside of the *c*
23:26 First clean the inside of the *c*
26:27 Then he took the *c*, gave thanks
26:39 may this *c* be taken from me.
26:42 possible for this *c* to be taken away
Mk 9:41 anyone who gives you a *c* of water
10:38 "Can you drink the *c* I drink
10:39 "You will drink the *c* I drink
14:23 Then he took the *c*, gave thanks
14:36 Take this *c* from me.
Lk 11:39 Pharisees clean the outside of the *c*
22:17 After taking the *c*, he gave thanks
22:20 after the supper he took the *c*,
22:20 "This *c* is the new covenant
22:42 if you are willing, take this *c*
Jn 18:11 I not drink the *c* the Father has
1Co 10:16 Is not the *c* of thanksgiving
10:21 the *c* of the Lord and the *c*
11:25 after supper he took the *c*, saying,
11:25 "This *c* is the new covenant

CUPBEARER

Ge 40: 1 the *c* and the baker of the king
Ne 1:11 I was *c* to the king.

CURE (CURED)

Jer 17: 9 and beyond *c*.
30:15 your pain that has no *c*?
Hos 5:13 But he is not able to *c* you,
Lk 9: 1 out all demons and to *c* diseases,

CURED (CURE)

Mt 11: 5 those who have leprosy are *c*,
Lk 6:18 troubled by evil spirits were *c*,

CURSE (ACCURSED CURSED CURSES CURSING)

Ge 4:11 Now you are under a *c*
8:21 "Never again will I *c* the ground
12: 3 and whoever curses you I will *c*;
Dt 11:26 before you today a blessing and a *c*
11:28 the *c* if you disobey the commands
21:23 hung on a tree is under God's *c*.
23: 5 turned the *c* into a blessing for you,
Job 1:11 he will surely *c* you to your face."
2: 5 he will surely *c* you to your face."
2: 9 *C* God and die!" He replied,
Ps 109: 28 They may *c*, but you will bless;
Pr 3:33 The LORD's *c* is on the house
24:24 peoples will *c* him and nations
Mal 2: 2 and I will *c* your blessings.
Lk 6:28 bless those who *c* you, pray
Ro 12:14 persecute you; bless and do not *c*.
Gal 3:10 on observing the law are under a *c*,
3:13 of the law by becoming a *c* for us,
Jas 3: 9 with it we *c* men, who have been
Rev 22: 3 No longer will there be any *c*.

CURSED (CURSE)

Ge 3:17 "*C* is the ground because of you;
Dt 27:15 "*C* is the man who carves an image
27:16 "*C* is the man who dishonors his
27:17 "*C* is the man who moves his
27:18 "*C* is the man who leads the blind
27:19 *C* is the man who withholds justice
27:20 "*C* is the man who sleeps
27:21 "*C* is the man who has sexual
27:22 "*C* is the man who sleeps
27:23 "*C* is the man who sleeps
27:24 "*C* is the man who kills his
27:25 "*C* is the man who accepts a bribe
27:26 "*C* is the man who does not uphold
Jer 17: 5 "*C* is the one who trusts in man,
Mal 1:14 "*C* is the cheat who has
Ro 9: 3 I could wish that I myself were *c*
1Co 4:12 When we are *c*, we bless;
12: 3 "Jesus be *c*," and no one can say,
Gal 3:10 "*C* is everyone who does not
3:13 *C* is everyone who is hung on a tree

CURSES (CURSE)

Ex 21:17 "Anyone who *c* his father
Lev 20: 9 " 'If anyone *c* his father or mother,
Nu 5:23 is to write these *c* on a scroll
Jos 8:34 the blessings and the *c*—just
Pr 20:20 If a man *c* his father or mother,
28:27 to them receives many *c*.
Mt 15: 4 and 'Anyone who *c* his father
Mk 7:10 and, 'Anyone who *c* his father

CURSING (CURSE)

Ps 109: 18 He wore *c* as his garment;
Ro 3:14 "Their mouths are full of *c*
Jas 3:10 the same mouth come praise and *c*.

CURTAIN

Ex 26:31 "Make a *c* of blue, purple
26:33 The *c* will separate the Holy Place
Mt 27:51 At that moment the *c*
Mk 15:38 The *c* of the temple was torn in two
Lk 23:45 the *c* of the temple was torn in two.
Heb 6:19 the inner sanctuary behind the *c*,
9: 3 Behind the second *c* was a room
10:20 opened for us through the *c*,

CUSTOM

Job 1: 5 This was Job's regular *c*.
Mk 10: 1 and as was his *c*, he taught them.
Lk 4:16 into the synagogue, as was his *c*.
Ac 17: 2 As his *c* was, Paul went

CUT

Lev 19:27 " 'Do not *c* the hair at the sides
21: 5 of their beards or *c* their bodies.
1Ki 3:25 "*C* the living child in two
Isa 51: 1 to the rock from which you were *c*
53: 8 For he was *c* off from the land
Da 2:45 of the rock *c* out of a mountain,
9:26 the Anointed One will be *c* off
Mt 3:10 not produce good fruit will be *c*
24:22 If those days had not been *c* short,
1Co 11: 6 for a woman to have her hair *c*

CYMBAL* (CYMBALS)

1Co 13: 1 a resounding gong or a clanging *c*.

CYMBALS (CYMBAL)

1Ch 15:16 instruments: lyres, harps and *c*.
2Ch 5:12 dressed in fine linen and playing *c*,
Ps 150: 5 praise him with resounding *c*.

CYRUS

Persian king who allowed exiles to return (2Ch 36:22-Ezr 1:8), to rebuild temple (Ezr 5:13-6:14), as appointed by the LORD (Isa 44:28-45:13).

DAGON

Jdg 16:23 offer a great sacrifice to *D* their god
1Sa 5: 2 Dagon's temple and set it beside *D*.

DAMASCUS

Ac 9: 3 As he neared *D* on his journey,

DAN

1. Son of Jacob by Bilhah (Ge 30:4-6; 35:25; 46:23). Tribe of blessed (Ge 49:16-17; Dt 33:22), numbered (Nu 1:39; 26:43), allotted land (Jos 19:40-48; Eze 48:1), failed to fully possess (Jdg 1:34-35), failed to support Deborah (Jdg 5:17), possessed Laish/Dan (Jdg 18).

2. Northernmost city in Israel (Ge 14:14; Jdg 18; 20:1).

DANCE (DANCED DANCING)

Ecc 3: 4 a time to mourn and a time to *d*,
Mt 11:17 and you did not *d*;

DANCED (DANCE)

2Sa 6:14 *d* before the LORD
Mk 6:22 of Herodias came in and *d*,

DANCING (DANCE)

Ps 30:11 You turned my wailing into *d*;
149: 3 Let them praise his name with *d*

DANGER

Pr 22: 3 A prudent man sees *d*
27:12 The prudent see *d* and take refuge,
Mt 5:22 will be in *d* of the fire of hell.
Ro 8:35 famine or nakedness or *d* or sword?
2Co 11:26 I have been in *d* from rivers,

DANIEL

1. Hebrew exile to Babylon, name changed to Belteshazzar (Da 1:6-7). Refused to eat unclean food (Da 1:8-21). Interpreted Nebuchadnezzar's dreams (Da 2; 4), writing on the wall (Da 5). Thrown into lion's den (Da 6). Visions of (Da 7-12).

2. Son of David (1Ch 3:1).

DARIUS

1. King of Persia (Ezr 4:5), allowed rebuilding of temple (Ezr 5-6).

2. Mede who conquered Babylon (Da 5:31).

DARK (DARKENED DARKENS DARKNESS)

Job 34:22 There is no *d* place, no deep
Ps 18: 9 *d* clouds were under his feet.
Pr 31:15 She gets up while it is still *d*;
SS 1: 6 Do not stare at me because I am *d*,
Jn 12:35 in the *d* does not know where he is
Ro 2:19 a light for those who are in the *d*,
2Pe 1:19 as to a light shining in a *d* place,

DARKENED (DARK)

Joel 2:10 the sun and moon are *d*,
Mt 24:29 " 'the sun will be *d*,
Ro 1:21 and their foolish hearts were *d*.
Eph 4:18 They are *d* in their understanding

DARKENS (DARK)

Job 38: 2 "Who is this that *d* my counsel

DARKNESS (DARK)

Ge 1: 2 *d* was over the surface of the deep,
1: 4 he separated the light from the *d*.
Ex 10:22 and total *d* covered all Egypt
20:21 approached the thick *d* where God
2Sa 22:29 the LORD turns my *d* into light.
Ps 18:28 my God turns my *d* into light.
91: 6 the pestilence that stalks in the *d*,
112: 4 Even in *d* light dawns
139: 12 even the *d* will not be dark to you;
Pr 4:19 the way of the wicked is like deep *d*
Isa 5:20 and light for *d*,
42:16 I will turn the *d* into light
45: 7 I form the light and create *d*,
58:10 then your light will rise in the *d*,
61: 1 and release from *d*,
Joel 2:31 The sun will be turned to *d*
Mt 4:16 the people living in *d*
6:23 how great is that *d*!"No one can
Lk 11:34 are bad, your body also is full of *d*.
23:44 and *d* came over the whole land
Jn 1: 5 The light shines in the *d*,
3:19 but men loved *d* instead of light
Ac 2:20 The sun will be turned to *d*
2Co 4: 6 who said, "Let light shine out of *d*
6:14 fellowship can light have with *d*?
Eph 5: 8 For you were once *d*, but now you
5:11 to do with the fruitless deeds of *d*,
1Pe 2: 9 out of *d* into his wonderful light.
2Pe 2:17 Blackest *d* is reserved for them.
1Jn 1: 5 in him there is no *d* at all.
2: 9 but hates his brother is still in the *d*.
Jude : 6 in *d*, bound with everlasting chains
:13 for whom blackest *d* has been

DASH

Ps 2: 9 you will *d* them to pieces like

DAUGHTER (DAUGHTERS)

Ex 1:10 she took him to Pharaoh's *d*
Jdg 11:48 to commemorate the *d* of Jephthah
Est 2: 7 Mordecai had taken her as his own *d*
Ps 9:14 praises in the gates of the *D* of Zion
137: 8 O *D* of Babylon, doomed
Isa 62:11 "Say to the *D* of Zion,
Zec 9: 9 Shout, *D* of Jerusalem!
Mk 5:34 "*D*, your faith has healed you.
7:29 the demon has left your *d*.

DAUGHTERS (DAUGHTER)

Ge 6: 2 the *d* of men were beautiful,
19:36 Lot's *d* became pregnant
Nu 36:10 Zelophehad's *d* did as the LORD
Joel 2:28 sons and *d* will prophesy,

DAVID

Son of Jesse (Ru 4:17-22; 1Ch 2:13-15), ancestor of Jesus (Mt 1:1-17; Lk 3:31). Wives and children (1Sa 18; 25:39-44; 2Sa 3:2-5; 5:13-16; 11:27; 1Ch 3:1-9).

Anointed king by Samuel (1Sa 16:1-13). Musician to Saul (1Sa 16:14-23; 18:10). Killed Goliath (1Sa 17). Relation with Jonathan (1Sa 18:1-4; 19-20; 23:16-18; 2Sa 1). Disfavor of Saul (1Sa 18:6-23:29). Spared Saul's life (1Sa 24; 26). Among Philistines (1Sa 21:10-14; 27-30). Lament for Saul and Jonathan (2Sa 1).

Anointed king of Judah (2Sa 2:1-11). Conflict with house of Saul (2Sa 2-4). Anointed king of Israel (2Sa 5:1-4; 1Ch 11:1-3). Conquered Jerusalem (2Sa 6; 1Ch 13; 15-16). The LORD promised eternal dynasty (2Sa 7; 1Ch 17; Ps 132). Showed kindness to Mephibosheth (2Sa 9). Adultery with Bathsheba, murder of Uriah (2Sa 11-12). Son Amnon raped daughter Tamar; killed by Absalom (2Sa 13). Absalom's revolt (2Sa 14-17); death (2Sa 18). Sheba's revolt (2Sa 20). Victories: Philistines (2Sa 5:17-25; 1Ch 14:8-17; 2Sa 21:15-22; 1Ch 20:4-8), Ammonites (2Sa 10; 1Ch 19), various (2Sa 8; 1Ch 18). Mighty men (2Sa 23:8-39; 1Ch 11-12). Punished for numbering army (2Sa 24; 1Ch 21). Appointed Solomon king (1Ki 1:28-2:9). Prepared for building of temple (1Ch 22-29). Last words (2Sa 23:1-7). Death (1Ki 2:10-12, 1Ch 29:28).

Psalmist (Mt 22:43-45), musician (Am 6:5), prophet (2Sa 23:2-7; Ac 1:16; 2:30).

Psalms of: 2 (Ac 4:25), 3-32, 34-41, 51-65, 68-70, 86, 95 (Heb 4:7), 101, 103, 108-110, 122, 124, 131, 133, 138-145.

DAWN (DAWNED DAWNS)

Ps 37: 6 your righteousness shine like the *d*,
Pr 4: 18 is like the first gleam of *d*,
Isa 14: 12 O morning star, son of the *d!*
Am 4: 13 he who turns *d* to darkness,
5: 8 who turns blackness into *d*

DAWNED (DAWN)

Isa 9: 2 a light has *d*.
Mt 4: 16 a light has *d*."

DAWNS* (DAWN)

Ps 65: 8 where morning *d* and evening
112: 4 in darkness light *d* for the upright,
Hos 10: 15 When that day *d*,
2Pe 1: 19 until the day *d* and the morning

DAY (DAYS)

Ge 1: 5 God called the light "*d*,"
1: 5 and there was morning—the first *d*
1: 8 there was morning—the second *d*.
1: 13 there was morning—the third *d*.
1: 19 there was morning—the fourth *d*.
1: 23 there was morning—the fifth *d*.
1: 31 there was morning—the sixth *d*.
2: 2 so on the seventh *d* he rested
8: 22 *d* and night
Ex 16: 30 the people rested on the seventh *d*.
20: 8 "Remember the Sabbath *d*
Lev 16: 30 on this *d* atonement will be made
23: 28 because it is the *D* of Atonement,
Nu 14: 14 before them in a pillar of cloud by *d*
Jos 1: 8 meditate on it *d* and night,
2Ki 7: 9 This is a *d* of good news
25: 30 *D* by *d* the king gave Jehoiachin
1Ch 16: 23 proclaim his salvation *d* after *d*.
Ne 8: 18 *D* after *d*, from the first *d*
Ps 84: 10 Better is one *d* in your courts
96: 2 proclaim his salvation *d* after *d*.
118: 24 This is the *d* the LORD has made;
Pr 27: 1 not know what a *d* may bring forth.
Isa 13: 9 a cruel *d*, with wrath and fierce
Jer 46: 10 But that *d* belongs to the Lord,
50: 31 "for your *d* has come,
Eze 30: 2 "Alas for that *d!*"
Joel 1: 15 "Alas for that *d!*
2: 31 and dreadful *d* of the LORD.
Am 3: 14 On the *d* I punish Israel for her sins
5: 20 Will not the *d* of the LORD be
Ob : 15 "The *d* of the LORD is near
Zep 1: 14 The great *d* of the LORD is near—
Zec 2: 11 joined with the LORD in that *d*
14: 1 A *d* of the LORD is coming
14: 7 It will be a unique *d*,
Mal 4: 5 dreadful *d* of the LORD comes.
Mt 24: 38 up to the *d* Noah entered the ark;
Lk 11: 3 Give us each *d* our daily bread.
17: 24 in his *d* will be like the lightning,
Ac 5: 42 *D* after *d*, in the temple courts
17: 11 examined the Scriptures every *d*
17: 17 as in the marketplace *d* by *d*
Ro 14: 5 man considers every *d* alike.
1Co 5: 5 his spirit saved on the *d* of the Lord
2Co 4: 16 we are being renewed *d* by *d*.
11: 25 I spent a night and a *d*
1Th 5: 2 for you know very well that the *d*
5: 4 so that this *d* should surprise you
2Th 2: 2 saying that the *d* of the Lord has
Heb 7: 27 need to offer sacrifices *d* after *d*,
2Pe 3: 8 With the Lord a *d* is like
3: 10 *d* of the Lord will come like a thief.
Rev 6: 17 For the great *d* of their wrath has
16: 14 on the great *d* of God Almighty.

DAYS (DAY)

Dt 17: 19 he is to read it all the *d* of his life
32: 7 Remember the *d* of old;
Ps 23: 6 all the *d* of my life,
34: 12 and desires to see many good *d*,
39: 5 have made my *d* a mere
90: 10 The length of our *d* is seventy years
90: 12 Teach us to number our *d* aright,
103: 15 As for man, his *d* are like grass,
128: 5 all the *d* of your life;
Pr 31: 12 all the *d* of her life.
Ecc 9: 9 all the *d* of this meaningless life
12: 1 Creator in the *d* of your youth,
Isa 38: 20 all the *d* of our lives
Da 7: 9 and the Ancient of *D* took his seat.
7: 13 He approached the Ancient of *D*
7: 22 until the Ancient of *D* came
Hos 3: 5 and to his blessings in the last *d*.
Joel 2: 29 I will pour out my Spirit in those *d*.
Mic 4: 1 In the last *d*
Lk 19: 43 The *d* will come upon you
Ac 2: 17 by the prophet Joel: " 'In the last *d*,
2Ti 3: 1 will be terrible times in the last *d*.
Heb 1: 2 in these last *d* he has spoken to us
2Pe 3: 3 that in the last *d* scoffers will come,

DAZZLING*

Da 2: 31 *d* statue, awesome in appearance.
Mk 9: 3 His clothes became *d* white,

DEACON* (DEACONS)

1Ti 3: 12 A *d* must be the husband of

DEACONS* (DEACON)

Php 1: 1 together with the overseers and *d*:
1Ti 3: 8 *D*, likewise, are to be men worthy
3: 10 against them, let them serve as *d*.

DEAD (DIE)

Lev 17: 15 who eats anything found *d*
Dt 18: 11 or spiritist or who consults the *d*.
Isa 8: 19 Why consult the *d* on behalf
Mt 8: 22 and let the *d* bury their own *d*."
28: 7 'He has risen from the *d*
Lk 15: 24 For this son of mine was *d*
24: 46 rise from the *d* on the third day,
Ro 6: 11 count yourselves *d* to sin
1Co 15: 29 do who are baptized for the *d?*
Eph 2: 1 you were *d* in your transgressions
1Th 4: 16 and the *d* in Christ will rise first.
Jas 2: 17 is not accompanied by action, is *d*.
2: 26 so faith without deeds is *d*.
Rev 14: 13 Blessed are the *d* who die
20: 12 And I saw the *d*, great and small,

DEADENED* (DIE)

Jn 12: 40 and *d* their hearts,

DEAR* (DEARER)

2Sa 1: 26 you were very *d* to me.
Ps 102: 14 For her stones are *d*
Jer 31: 20 Is not Ephraim my *d* son,
Jn 2: 4 "*D* woman, why do you involve me
19: 26 he said to his mother, "*D* woman,
Ac 15: 25 to you with our *d* friends Barnabas
Ro 16: 5 Greet my *d* friend Epenetus,
16: 9 in Christ, and my *d* friend Stachys.
16: 12 Greet my *d* friend Persis, another
1Co 4: 14 but to warn you, as my *d* children.
10: 14 my *d* friends, flee from idolatry.
15: 58 Therefore, my *d* brothers,
2Co 7: 1 we have these promises, *d* friends,
12: 19 and everything we do, *d* friends,
Gal 4: 19 My *d* children, for whom I am
Eph 6: 21 the *d* brother and faithful servant
Php 2: 12 my *d* friends, as you have always
4: 1 firm in the Lord, *d* friends!
Col 1: 7 Epaphras, our *d* fellow servant,
4: 7 He is a *d* brother, a faithful
4: 9 our faithful and *d* brother,
4: 14 Our *d* friend Luke, the doctor,
1Th 2: 8 because you had become so *d* to us.
1Ti 6: 2 their service are believers, and *d*
2Ti 1: 2 To Timothy, my *d* son: Grace,
Phm 1 To Philemon our *d* friend
: 16 He is very *d* to me but
: 16 better than a slave, as a *d* brother.
Heb 6: 9 we speak like this, *d* friends,
Jas 1: 16 Don't be deceived, my *d* brothers.
1: 19 My *d* brothers, take note of this:
2: 5 thoughts? Listen, my *d* brothers:
1Pe 2: 11 *D* friends, I urge you, as aliens
4: 12 *D* friends, do not be surprised
2Pe 3: 1 *D* friends, this is now my second
3: 8 not forget this one thing, *d* friends:
3: 14 *d* friends, since you are looking
3: 15 just as our *d* brother Paul
3: 17 *d* friends, since you already know
1Jn 2: 1 My *d* children, I write this to you
2: 7 *D* friends, I am not writing you
2: 12 I write to you, *d* children,
2: 13 I write to you, *d* children,
2: 18 *D* children, this is the last hour;
2: 28 *d* children, continue in him,
3: 2 *D* friends, now we are children
3: 7 *D* children, do not let anyone lead
3: 18 love of God be in him? *D* children,
3: 21 *D* friends, if our hearts do not
4: 1 *D* friends, do not believe every
4: 4 *d* children, are from God
4: 7 *D* friends, let us love one another,
4: 11 *D* friends, since God so loved us,
5: 21 *D* children, keep yourselves
2Jn : 5 *d* lady, I am not writing you a new
3Jn : 1 The elder, To my *d* friend Gaius,
: 2 *D* friend, I pray that you may enjoy
: 5 *D* friend, you are faithful
: 11 *D* friend, do not imitate what is evil
Jude : 3 *D* friends, although I was very
: 17 But, *d* friends, remember what
: 20 *d* friends, build yourselves up

DEARER* (DEAR)

Phm : 16 dear to me but even *d* to you,

DEATH (DIE)

Ex 21: 12 kills him shall surely be put to *d*.
Nu 35: 16 the murderer shall be put to *d*.
Dt 30: 19 set before you life and *d*,
Ru 1: 17 if anything but *d* separates you
2Ki 4: 40 O man of God, there is *d* in the pot
Job 26: 6 *D* is naked before God;
Ps 23: 4 the valley of the shadow of *d*,
44: 22 for your sake we face *d* all day long
89: 48 What man can live and not see *d*,
116: 15 is the *d* of his saints.
Pr 8: 36 all who hate me love *d*."
11: 19 he who pursues evil goes to his *d*.
14: 12 but in the end it leads to *d*.
15: 11 *D* and Destruction lie open
16: 25 but in the end it leads to *d*.
18: 21 tongue has the power of life and *d*,
19: 18 do not be a willing party to his *d*.
23: 14 and save his soul from *d*.
Ecc 7: 2 for *d* is the destiny of every man;
Isa 25: 8 he will swallow up *d* forever.
53: 12 he poured out his life unto *d*,
Eze 18: 23 pleasure in the *d* of the wicked?
18: 32 pleasure in the *d* of anyone,
33: 11 pleasure in the *d* of the wicked,
Hos 13: 14 Where, O *d*, are your plagues?
Jn 5: 24 he has crossed over from *d* to life.
Ro 4: 25 delivered over to *d* for our sins
5: 12 and in this way *d* came to all men,
5: 14 *d* reigned from the time of Adam
6: 3 Jesus were baptized into his *d?*
6: 23 For the wages of sin is *d*,
7: 24 me from this body of *d?*
8: 13 put to *d* the misdeeds of the body,
8: 36 your sake we face *d* all day long;
1Co 15: 21 For since *d* came through a man,
15: 26 The last enemy to be destroyed is *d*
15: 55 Where, O *d*, is your sting?"
2Ti 1: 10 who has destroyed *d* and has
Heb 2: 14 him who holds the power of *d*—
1Jn 5: 16 There is a sin that leads to *d*.
Rev 1: 18 And I hold the keys of *d* and Hades
2: 11 hurt at all by the second *d*.
20: 6 The second *d* has no power
20: 14 The lake of fire is the second *d*.
20: 14 Then *d* and Hades were thrown
21: 4 There will be no more *d*
21: 8 This is the second *d*."

DEBAUCHERY*

Ro 13: 13 not in sexual immorality and *d*,
2Co 12: 21 and *d* in which they have indulged.
Gal 5: 19 impurity and *d*; idolatry
Eph 5: 18 drunk on wine, which leads to *d*.
1Pe 4: 3 living in *d*, lust, drunkenness,

DEBORAH*

1. Prophetess who led Israel to victory over Canaanites (Jdg 4-5).
2. Rebekah's nurse (Ge 35:8).

DEBT* (DEBTOR DEBTORS DEBTS)

Dt 15: 3 must cancel any *d* your brother
24: 6 the upper one—as security for a *d*,

1Sa 22: 2 or in *d* or discontented gathered
Job 24: 9 of the poor is seized for a *d*.
Mt 18:25 that he had be sold to repay the *d*.
18:27 canceled the *d* and let him go.
18:30 into prison until he could pay the *d*.
18:32 'I canceled all that *d* of yours
Lk 7:43 who had the bigger *d* canceled."
Ro 13: 8 Let no *d* remain outstanding,
13: 8 continuing *d* to love one another,

DEBTOR* (DEBT)

Isa 24: 2 for *d* as for creditor.

DEBTORS* (DEBT)

Hab 2: 7 Will not your *d* suddenly arise?
Mt 6:12 as we also have forgiven our *d*.
Lk 16: 5 called in each one of his master's *d*.

DEBTS* (DEBT)

Dt 15: 1 seven years you must cancel *d*.
15: 2 time for canceling *d* has been
15: 9 the year for canceling *d*, is near,"
31:10 in the year for canceling *d*,
2Ki 4: 7 "Go, sell the oil and pay your *d*.
Ne 10:31 the land and will cancel all *d*.
Pr 22:26 or puts up security for *d*;
Mt 6:12 Forgive us our *d*,
Lk 7:42 so he canceled the *d* of both.

DECAY*

Ps 16:10 will you let your Holy One see *d*.
49: 9 and not see *d*.
49:14 their forms will *d* in the grave,
Pr 12: 4 a disgraceful wife is like *d*
Isa 5:24 so their roots will *d*
Hab 3:16 *d* crept into my bones,
Ac 2:27 will you let your Holy One see *d*.
2:31 to the grave, nor did his body see *d*.
13:34 never to *d*, is stated in these words:
13:35 will not let your Holy One see *d*.'
13:37 raised from the dead did not see *d*.
Ro 8:21 liberated from its bondage to *d*

DECEIT (DECEIVE)

Ps 5: 9 with their tongue they speak *d*.
Isa 53: 9 nor was any *d* in his mouth.
Da 8:25 He will cause *d* to prosper,
Zep 3:13 nor will *d* be found in their mouths.
Mk 7:22 greed, malice, *d*, lewdness, envy,
Ac 13:10 You are full of all kinds of *d*
Ro 1:29 murder, strife, *d* and malice.
3:13 their tongues practice *d*."
1Pe 2: 1 yourselves of all malice and all *d*,
2:22 and no *d* was found in his mouth."

DECEITFUL (DECEIVE)

Jer 17: 9 The heart is *d* above all things
Hos 10: 2 Their heart is *d*,
2Co 11:13 men are false apostles, *d* workmen,
Eph 4:14 of men in their *d* scheming.
4:22 is being corrupted by its *d* desires;
1Pe 3:10 and his lips from *d* speech.
Rev 21:27 who does what is shameful or *d*,

DECEITFULNESS* (DECEIVE)

Ps 119:118 for their *d* is in vain.
Mt 13:22 and the *d* of wealth choke it,
Mk 4:19 the *d* of wealth and the desires
Heb 3:13 of you may be hardened by sin's *d*.

DECEIVE (DECEIT DECEITFUL DECEITFULNESS DECEIVED DECEIVER DECEIVERS DECEIVES DECEIVING DECEPTION DECEPTIVE)

Lev 19:11 " 'Do not *d* one another.
Pr 14: 5 A truthful witness does not *d*,
24:28 or use your lips to *d*.
Jer 37: 9 Do not *d* yourselves, thinking,
Zec 13: 4 garment of hair in order to *d*.
Mt 24: 5 'I am the Christ,' and will *d* many.
24:11 will appear and *d* many people.
24:24 and miracles to *d* even the elect—
Mk 13: 6 'I am he,' and will *d* many.
13:22 and miracles to *d* the elect—
Ro 16:18 and flattery they *d* the minds
1Co 3:18 Do not *d* yourselves.
Eph 5: 6 Let no one *d* you with empty words
Col 2: 4 this so that no one may *d* you
2Th 2: 3 Don't let anyone *d* you in any way,
Jas 1:22 to the word, and so *d* yourselves.
1Jn 1: 8 we *d* ourselves and the truth is not
Rev 20: 8 and will go out to *d* the nations

DECEIVED (DECEIVE)

Ge 3:13 "The serpent *d* me, and I ate."
Lk 21: 8 "Watch out that you are not *d*.
1Co 6: 9 the kingdom of God? Do not be *d*:
2Co 11: 3 Eve was *d* by the serpent's cunning
Gal 6: 7 Do not be *d*: God cannot be
1Ti 2:14 And Adam was not the one *d*;
2Ti 3:13 to worse, deceiving and being *d*.
Tit 3: 3 *d* and enslaved by all kinds
Jas 1:16 Don't be *d*, my dear brothers.
Rev 13:14 he *d* the inhabitants of the earth.
20:10 And the devil, who *d* them,

DECEIVER (DECEIVE)

Mt 27:63 while he was still alive that *d* said,
2Jn : 7 Any such person is the *d*

DECEIVERS* (DECEIVE)

Ps 49: 5 when wicked *d* surround me—
Tit 1:10 and *d*, especially those
2Jn : 7 Many *d*, who do not acknowledge

DECEIVES (DECEIVE)

Pr 26:19 is a man who *d* his neighbor
Mt 24: 4 "Watch out that no one *d* you.
Mk 13: 5 "Watch out that no one *d* you.
Gal 6: 3 when he is nothing, he *d* himself.
2Th 2:10 sort of evil that *d* those who are
Jas 1:26 he *d* himself and his religion is

DECEIVING* (DECEIVE)

Lev 6: 2 by *d* his neighbor about something
1Ti 4: 1 follow *d* spirits and things taught
2Ti 3:13 go from bad to worse, *d*
Rev 20: 3 him from *d* the nations anymore

DECENCY* (DECENTLY)

1Ti 2: 9 women to dress modestly, with *d*

DECENTLY* (DECENCY)

Ro 13:13 Let us behave *d*, as in the daytime,

DECEPTION (DECEIVE)

Pr 14: 8 but the folly of fools is *d*.
26:26 His malice may be concealed by *d*,
Mt 27:64 This last *d* will be worse
2Co 4: 2 we do not use *d*, nor do we distort

DECEPTIVE (DECEIVE)

Pr 11:18 The wicked man earns *d* wages,
31:30 Charm is *d*, and beauty is fleeting;
Jer 7: 4 Do not trust in *d* words and say,
Col 2: 8 through hollow and *d* philosophy,

DECIDED (DECISION)

2Co 9: 7 man should give what he has *d*

DECISION (DECIDED)

Ex 28:29 heart on the breastpiece of *d*
Joel 3:14 multitudes in the valley of *d*!

DECLARE (DECLARED DECLARING)

1Ch 16:24 *D* his glory among the nations,
Ps 19: 1 The heavens *d* the glory of God;
96: 3 *D* his glory among the nations,
Isa 42: 9 and new things I *d*;

DECLARED (DECLARE)

Mk 7:19 Jesus *d* all foods "clean.")
Ro 2:13 the law who will be *d* righteous.
3:20 no one will be *d* righteous

DECLARING (DECLARE)

Ps 71: 8 *d* your splendor all day long.
Ac 2:11 we hear them *d* the wonders

DECREE (DECREED DECREES)

Ex 15:25 There the LORD made a *d*
1Ch 16:17 He confirmed it to Jacob as a *d*,
Ps 2: 7 I will proclaim the *d* of the LORD:
7: 6 Awake, my God; *d* justice.
81: 4 this is a *d* for Israel,
148: 6 he gave a *d* that will never pass
Da 4:24 and this is the *d* the Most High has
Lk 2: 1 Augustus issued a *d* that a census
Ro 1:32 know God's righteous *d* that those

DECREED (DECREE)

Ps 78: 5 He *d* statutes for Jacob
Jer 40: 2 LORD your God *d* this disaster
La 3:37 happen if the Lord has not *d* it?
Da 9:24 "Seventy 'sevens' are *d*
9:26 and desolations have been *d*.
Lk 22:22 Son of Man will go as it has been *d*,

DECREES (DECREE)

Ge 26: 5 my commands, my *d* and my laws
Ex 15:26 to his commands and keep all his *d*,
18:16 inform them of God's *d* and laws."
18:20 Teach them the *d* and laws,
Lev 10:11 Israelites all the *d* the LORD has
18: 4 and be careful to follow my *d*.
18: 5 Keep my *d* and laws,
18:26 you must keep my *d* and my laws.
Ps 119: 12 teach me your *d*.
119: 16 I delight in your *d*;
119: 48 and I meditate on your *d*.
119:112 My heart is set on keeping your *d*

DEDICATE (DEDICATED DEDICATION)

Nu 6:12 He must *d* himself to the LORD
Pr 20:25 for a man to *d* something rashly

DEDICATED (DEDICATE)

Lev 21:12 he has been *d* by the anointing oil
Nu 6: 9 thus defiling the hair he has *d*,
6:18 shave off the hair that he *d*.
18: 6 *d* to the LORD to do the work
1Ki 8:63 and all the Israelites *d* the temple
2Ch 29:31 "You have now *d* yourselves
Ne 3: 1 They *d* it and set its doors in place,

DEDICATION (DEDICATE)

Nu 6:19 shaved off the hair of his *d*,
Jn 10:22 came the Feast of *D* at Jerusalem.
1Ti 5:11 sensual desires overcome their *d*

DEED (DEEDS)

Jer 32:10 and sealed the *d*, had it witnessed,
32:16 After I had given the *d* of purchase
Col 3:17 you do, whether in word or *d*,
2Th 2:17 and strengthen you in every good *d*

DEEDS (DEED)

Dt 3:24 or on earth who can do the *d*
4:34 or by great and awesome *d*,
34:12 the awesome *d* that Moses
1Sa 2: 3 and by him *d* are weighed.
1Ch 16:24 his marvelous *d* among all peoples.
Job 34:25 Because he takes note of their *d*,
Ps 26: 7 and telling of all your wonderful *d*.
45: 4 right hand display awesome *d*.
65: 5 with awesome *d* of righteousness,
66: 3 "How awesome are your *d*!
71:17 day I declare your marvelous *d*.
72:18 who alone does marvelous *d*.
73:28 I will tell of all your *d*.
75: 1 men tell of your wonderful *d*.
77:11 I will remember the *d* of the LORD
77:12 and consider all your mighty *d*.
78: 4 the praiseworthy *d* of the LORD,
78: 7 and would not forget his *d*
86: 8 no *d* can compare with yours.
86:10 you are great and do marvelous *d*;
88:12 or your righteous *d* in the land
90:16 May your *d* be shown
92: 4 For you make me glad by your *d*,
96: 3 his marvelous *d* among all peoples.
107: 8 and his wonderful *d* for men,
107: 15 and his wonderful *d* for men,
107: 21 and his wonderful *d* for men.
107: 24 his wonderful *d* in the deep.
107: 31 and his wonderful *d* for men.
111: 3 Glorious and majestic are his *d*,
145: 6 and I will proclaim your great *d*.
Jer 32:19 purposes and mighty are your *d*.
Hab 3: 2 I stand in awe of your *d*, O LORD.
Mt 5:16 that they may see your good *d*
Lk 1:51 He has performed mighty *d*
23:41 we are getting what our *d* deserve.
Ac 26:20 prove their repentance by their *d*.
1Ti 6:18 rich in good *d*, and to be generous
Heb 10:24 on toward love and good *d*.
Jas 2:14 claims to have faith but has no *d*?
2:18 Show me your faith without *d*,
2:20 faith without *d* is useless?
2:26 so faith without *d* is dead.
1Pe 2:12 they may see your good *d*
Rev 2:19 I know your *d*, your love and faith,
2:23 each of you according to your *d*.
3: 1 I know your *d*; you have
3: 2 I have not found your *d* complete
3: 8 I know your *d*.
3:15 I know your *d*, that you are neither
14:13 for their *d* will follow them."
15: 3 "Great and marvelous are your *d*,

DEEP (DEPTH DEPTHS)

Ge 1: 2 was over the surface of the *d*,
8: 2 Now the springs of the *d*
Ps 42: 7 *D* calls to *d*
Lk 5: 4 to Simon, "Put out into *d* water,

1Co 2:10 all things, even the *d* things
1Ti 3:9 hold of the *d* truths of the faith

DEER

Ps 42:1 As the *d* pants for streams of water,

DEFAMED*

Isa 48:11 How can I let myself be *d*?

DEFEATED

1Co 6:7 have been completely *d* already.

DEFEND (DEFENDED DEFENDER DEFENDING DEFENDS DEFENSE)

Ps 72:4 He will *d* the afflicted
74:22 Rise up, O God, and *d* your cause;
82:2 "How long will you *d* the unjust
82:3 *D* the cause of the weak
119:154 *D* my cause and redeem me;
Pr 31:9 *d* the rights of the poor and needy
Isa 1:17 *D* the cause of the fatherless,
1:23 They do not *d* the cause
Jer 5:28 they do not *d* the rights of the poor.
50:34 He will vigorously *d* their cause

DEFENDED (DEFEND)

Jer 22:16 He *d* the cause of the poor

DEFENDER (DEFEND)

Ex 22:2 the *d* is not guilty of bloodshed;
Ps 68:5 to the fatherless, a *d* of widows,
Pr 23:11 for their *D* is strong;

DEFENDING (DEFEND)

Ps 10:18 *d* the fatherless and the oppressed,
Ro 2:15 now accusing, now even *d* them.)
Php 1:7 or *d* and confirming the gospel,

DEFENDS* (DEFEND)

Dt 10:18 He *d* the cause of the fatherless
33:7 With his own hands he *d* his cause.
Isa 51:22 your God, who *d* his people:

DEFENSE (DEFEND)

Ps 35:23 Awake, and rise to my *d*!
Php 1:16 here for the *d* of the gospel.
1Jn 2:1 speaks to the Father in our *d*—

DEFERRED*

Pr 13:12 Hope *d* makes the heart sick,

DEFIED

1Sa 17:45 armies of Israel, whom you have *d*.
1Ki 13:26 the man of God who *d* the word

DEFILE (DEFILED)

Da 1:8 Daniel resolved not to *d* himself
Rev 14:4 are those who did not *d* themselves

DEFILED (DEFILE)

Isa 24:5 The earth is *d* by its people;

DEFRAUD

Lev 19:13 Do not *d* your neighbor or rob him.
Mk 10:19 do not *d*, honor your father

DEITY*

Col 2:9 of the *D* lives in bodily form,

DELAY

Ecc 5:4 vow to God, do not *d* in fulfilling it.
Isa 48:9 my own name's sake I *d* my wrath;
Heb 10:37 is coming will come and will not *d*.
Rev 10:6 and said, "There will be no more *d*!

DELICACIES

Ps 141:4 let me not eat of their *d*.
Pr 23:3 Do not crave his *d*,
23:6 do not crave his *d*;

DELICIOUS*

Pr 9:17 food eaten in secret is *d*!"

DELIGHT* (DELIGHTED DELIGHTFUL DELIGHTING DELIGHTS)

Lev 26:31 and I will take no *d* in the pleasing
Dt 30:9 The LORD will again *d* in you
1Sa 2:1 for I *d* in your deliverance.
15:22 "Does the LORD *d*
Ne 1:11 the prayer of your servants who *d*
Job 22:26 Surely then you will find *d*
27:10 Will he find *d* in the Almighty?
Ps 1:2 But his *d* is in the law of the LORD
16:3 in whom is all my *d*.
35:9 and *d* in his salvation.
35:27 those who *d* in my vindication
37:4 *D* yourself in the LORD
43:4 to God, my joy and my *d*.
51:16 You do not *d* in sacrifice,
51:19 whole burnt offerings to *d* you;
62:4 they take *d* in lies.
68:30 Scatter the nations who *d* in war.
111:2 by all who *d* in them.
112:1 who finds great *d* in his commands.
119:16 I *d* in your decrees;
119:24 Your statutes are my *d*;
119:35 for there I find *d*.
119:47 for I *d* in your commands
119:70 but I *d* in your law.
119:77 for your law is my *d*.
119:92 If your law had not been my *d*,
119:143 but your commands are my *d*.
119:174 and your law is my *d*.
147:10 nor his *d* in the legs of a man;
149:4 For the LORD takes *d*
Pr 1:22 How long will mockers *d*
2:14 who *d* in doing wrong
8:30 I was filled with *d* day after day,
11:1 but accurate weights are his *d*.
29:17 he will bring *d* to your soul.
Ecc 2:10 My heart took *d* in all my work,
SS 1:4 We rejoice and *d* in you;
2:3 I *d* to sit in his shade,
Isa 5:7 are the garden of his *d*.
11:3 he will *d* in the fear of the LORD.
13:17 and have no *d* in gold.
32:14 the *d* of donkeys, a pasture
42:1 my chosen one in whom I *d*;
55:2 and your soul will *d* in the richest
58:13 if you call the Sabbath a *d*
61:10 I *d* greatly in the LORD;
62:4 for the LORD will take *d* in you,
65:18 for I will create Jerusalem to be a *d*
65:19 and take *d* in my people;
66:3 their souls *d* in their abominations;
66:11 *d* in her overflowing abundance."
Jer 9:24 for in these I *d*,"
15:16 they were my joy and my heart's *d*,
31:20 the child in whom I *d*?
49:25 the town in which I *d*?
Eze 24:16 away from you the *d* of your eyes.
24:21 in which you take pride, the *d*
24:25 and glory, the *d* of their eyes,
Hos 7:3 *d* the king with their wickedness,
Mic 1:16 for the children in whom you *d*;
7:18 but *d* to show mercy.
Zep 3:17 He will take great *d* in you,
Mt 12:18 the one I love, in whom I *d*;
Mk 12:37 large crowd listened to him with *d*.
Lk 1:14 He will be a joy and *d* to you,
Ro 7:22 in my inner being I *d* in God's law;
1Co 13:6 Love does not *d* in evil
2Co 12:10 for Christ's sake, I *d* in weaknesses,
Col 2:5 and *d* to see how orderly you are

DELIGHTED (DELIGHT)

2Sa 22:20 he rescued me because he *d* in me.
1Ki 10:9 who has *d* in you and placed you
2Ch 9:8 who has *d* in you and placed you
Ps 18:19 he rescued me because he *d* in me.
Lk 13:17 but the people were *d* with all

DELIGHTFUL* (DELIGHT)

Ps 16:6 surely I have a *d* inheritance.
SS 1:2 for your love is more *d* than wine.
4:10 How *d* is your love, my sister,
Mal 3:12 for yours will be a *d* land,"

DELIGHTING* (DELIGHT)

Pr 8:31 and *d* in mankind.

DELIGHTS (DELIGHT)

Est 6:6 for the man the king *d* to honor?"
Ps 22:8 since he *d* in him."
35:27 who *d* in the well-being
36:8 from your river of *d*.
37:23 if the LORD *d* in a man's way
147:11 the LORD *d* in those who fear him,
Pr 3:12 as a father the son he *d* in.
10:23 of understanding *d* in wisdom.
11:20 he *d* in those whose ways are
12:22 but he *d* in men who are truthful.
14:35 A king *d* in a wise servant,
18:2 but *d* in airing his own opinions.
23:24 he who has a wise son *d* in him.
Col 2:18 Do not let anyone who *d*

DELILAH*

Woman who betrayed Samson (Jdg 16:4-22).

DELIVER (DELIVERANCE DELIVERED DELIVERER DELIVERS)

Dt 32:39 and no one can *d* out of my hand.
Ps 22:8 Let him *d* him,
72:12 For he will *d* the needy who cry out
79:9 *d* us and forgive our sins
109:21 of the goodness of your love, *d* me.
119:170 *d* me according to your promise.
Mt 6:13 but *d* us from the evil one.'
2Co 1:10 hope that he will continue to *d* us,

DELIVERANCE (DELIVER)

1Sa 2:1 for I delight in your *d*.
Ps 3:8 From the LORD comes *d*.
32:7 and surround me with songs of *d*.
33:17 A horse is a vain hope for *d*;
Ob :17 But on Mount Zion will be *d*;

DELIVERED (DELIVER)

Ps 34:4 he *d* me from all my fears.
107:6 and he *d* them from their distress.
116:8 have *d* my soul from death,
Da 12:1 written in the book—will be *d*.
Ro 4:25 He was *d* over to death for our sins

DELIVERER* (DELIVER)

Jdg 3:9 for them a *d*, Othniel son of Kenaz,
3:15 and he gave them a *d*—Ehud,
2Sa 22:2 is my rock, my fortress and my *d*;
2Ki 13:5 The LORD provided a *d* for Israel,
Ps 18:2 is my rock, my fortress and my *d*;
40:17 You are my help and my *d*;
70:5 You are my help and my *d*;
140:7 O Sovereign LORD, my strong *d*,
144:2 my stronghold and my *d*,
Ac 7:35 sent to be their ruler and *d*
Ro 11:26 "The *d* will come from Zion;

DELIVERS (DELIVER)

Ps 34:17 he *d* them from all their troubles.
34:19 but the LORD *d* him from them all
37:40 The LORD helps them and *d* them
37:40 he *d* them from the wicked

DELUSION*

2Th 2:11 God sends them a powerful *d*

DEMAND (DEMANDED)

Lk 6:30 belongs to you, do not *d* it back.

DEMANDED (DEMAND)

Lk 12:20 This very night your life will be *d*
12:48 been given much, much will be *d*;

DEMETRIUS

Ac 19:24 A silversmith named *D*, who made

DEMON* (DEMONS)

Mt 9:33 And when the *d* was driven out,
11:18 and they say, 'He has a *d*.'
17:18 Jesus rebuked the *d*, and it came
Mk 7:26 to drive the *d* out of her daughter.
7:29 the *d* has left your daughter."
7:30 lying on the bed, and the *d* gone.
Lk 4:33 there was a man possessed by a *d*,
4:35 Then the *d* threw the man
7:33 wine, and you say, 'He has a *d*.'
8:29 driven by the *d* into solitary places.
9:42 the *d* threw him to the ground
11:14 When the *d* left, the man who had
11:14 was driving out a *d* that was mute.
Jn 8:49 "I am not possessed by a *d*,"
10:21 Can a *d* open the eyes of the blind
10:21 sayings of a man possessed by a *d*.

DEMON-POSSESSED* (DEMON-POSSESSION)

Mt 4:24 those suffering severe pain, the *d*,
8:16 many who were *d* were brought
8:28 two *d* men coming
8:33 what had happened to the *d* men.
9:32 man who was *d* and could not talk
12:22 they brought him a *d* man who was
Mk 1:32 brought to Jesus all the sick and *d*.
5:16 what had happened to the *d* man—
5:18 the man who had been *d* begged
Lk 8:27 met by a *d* man from the town.
8:36 the people how the *d* man had been
Jn 7:20 "You are *d*," the crowd answered.
8:48 that you are a Samaritan and *d*?"
8:52 "Now we know that you are *d*!
10:20 Many of them said, "He is *d*
Ac 19:13 Jesus over those who were *d*.

DEMON-POSSESSION* (DEMON-POSSESSED)
Mt 15:22 is suffering terribly from *d.*"

DEMONS* (DEMON)
Dt 32:17 to *d,* which are not God—
Ps 106:37 and their daughters to *d.*
Mt 7:22 and in your name drive out *d*
8:31 *d* begged Jesus, "If you drive us
9:34 prince of *d* that he drives out *d.*"
10:8 who have leprosy, drive out *d.*
12:24 of *d,* that this fellow drives out
12:24 that this fellow drives out *d.*"
12:27 And if I drive out *d* by Beelzebub,
12:28 if I drive out *d* by the Spirit of God,
Mk 1:34 He also drove out many *d,*
1:34 but he would not let the *d* speak
1:39 their synagogues and driving out *d.*
3:15 to have authority to drive out *d.*
3:22 the prince of *d* he is driving out *d.*"
5:12 The *d* begged Jesus, "Send us
5:15 possessed by the legion of *d,*
6:13 They drove out many *d*
9:38 "we saw a man driving out *d*
16:9 out of whom he had driven seven *d*
16:17 In my name they will drive out *d;*
Lk 4:41 *d* came out of many people,
8:2 from whom seven *d* had come out;
8:30 because many *d* had gone into him.
8:32 The *d* begged Jesus to let them go
8:33 When the *d* came out of the man,
8:35 from whom the *d* had gone out,
8:38 from whom the *d* had gone out
9:1 and authority to drive out all *d*
9:49 "we saw a man driving out *d*
10:17 the *d* submit to us in your name."
11:15 the prince of *d,* he is driving out *d.*"
11:18 you claim that I drive out *d*
11:19 Now if I drive out *d* by Beelzebub,
11:20 if I drive out *d* by the finger of God,
13:32 'I will drive out *d* and heal people
Ro 8:38 neither angels nor *d,* neither
1Co 10:20 of pagans are offered to *d,*
10:20 you to be participants with *d.*
10:21 of the Lord and the cup of *d* too;
10:21 the Lord's table and the table of *d.*
1Ti 4:1 spirits and things taught by *d.*
Jas 2:19 Good! Even the *d* believe that—
Rev 9:20 they did not stop worshiping *d,*
16:14 of *d* performing miraculous signs,
18:2 She has become a home for *d*

DEMONSTRATE* (DEMONSTRATES DEMONSTRATION)
Ro 3:25 He did this to *d* his justice,
3:26 he did it to *d* his justice

DEMONSTRATES* (DEMONSTRATE)
Ro 5:8 God *d* his own love for us in this:

DEMONSTRATION* (DEMONSTRATE)
1Co 2:4 but with a *d* of the Spirit's power,

DEN
Da 6:16 and threw him into the lions' *d.*
Mt 21:13 you are making it a '*d* of robbers.' "
Mk 11:17 you have made it 'a *d* of robbers.' "
Lk 19:46 but you have made it 'a *d* of robbers

DENARII* (DENARIUS)
Mt 18:28 who owed him a hundred *d.*
Lk 7:41 One owed him five hundred *d,*

DENARIUS (DENARII)
Mt 20:2 agreed to pay them a *d* for the day
Mk 12:15 Bring me a *d* and let me look at it."

DENIED (DENY)
Mt 26:70 But he *d* it before them all.
Mk 14:68 But he *d* it.
Lk 22:57 But he *d* it.
Jn 18:25 He *d* it, saying, "I am not."
1Ti 5:8 he has *d* the faith and is worse
Rev 3:8 my word and have not *d* my name.

DENIES (DENY)
1Jn 2:22 It is the man who *d* that Jesus is
2:23 No one who *d* the Son has

DENY (DENIED DENIES DENYING)
Ex 23:6 "Do not *d* justice to your poor
Job 27:5 till I die, I will not *d* my integrity.
Isa 5:23 but *d* justice to the innocent.
La 3:35 to *d* a man his rights
Am 2:7 and *d* justice to the oppressed.
Mt 16:24 he must *d* himself and take up his
Mk 8:34 he must *d* himself and take up his
Lk 9:23 he must *d* himself and take up his
22:34 you will *d* three times that you
Ac 4:16 miracle, and we cannot *d* it.
Tit 1:16 but by their actions they *d* him.
Jas 3:14 do not boast about it or *d* the truth.
Jude :4 *d* Jesus Christ our only Sovereign

DENYING* (DENY)
Eze 22:29 mistreat the alien, *d* them justice.
2Ti 3:5 a form of godliness but *d* its power.
2Pe 2:1 *d* the sovereign Lord who bought

DEPART (DEPARTED DEPARTS DEPARTURE)
Ge 49:10 The scepter will not *d* from Judah,
Job 1:21 and naked I will *d.*
Mt 25:41 '*D* from me, you who are cursed,
Php 1:23 I desire to *d* and be with Christ,

DEPARTED (DEPART)
1Sa 4:21 "The glory has *d* from Israel"—
Ps 119:102 I have not *d* from your laws,

DEPARTS (DEPART)
Ecc 5:15 and as he comes, so he *d.*

DEPARTURE (DEPART)
Lk 9:31 spoke about his *d,* which he was
2Ti 4:6 and the time has come for my *d.*
2Pe 1:15 after my *d* you will always be able

DEPEND
Ps 62:7 My salvation and my honor *d*

DEPOSES*
Da 2:21 he sets up kings and *d* them.

DEPOSIT
Mt 25:27 money on *d* with the bankers,
Lk 19:23 didn't you put my money on *d,*
2Co 1:22 put his Spirit in our hearts as a *d,*
5:5 and has given us the Spirit as a *d,*
Eph 1:14 who is a *d* guaranteeing our
2Ti 1:14 Guard the good *d* that was

DEPRAVED* (DEPRAVITY)
Eze 16:47 ways you soon became more *d*
23:11 and prostitution she was more *d*
Ro 1:28 he gave them over to a *d* mind,
Php 2:15 fault in a crooked and *d* generation,
2Ti 3:8 oppose the truth—men of *d* minds,

DEPRAVITY* (DEPRAVED)
Ro 1:29 of wickedness, evil, greed and *d.*
2Pe 2:19 they themselves are slaves of *d*—

DEPRIVE
Dt 24:17 Do not *d* the alien or the fatherless
Pr 18:5 or to *d* the innocent of justice.
31:5 *d* all the oppressed of their rights.
Isa 10:2 to *d* the poor of their rights
29:21 with false testimony *d* the innocent
La 3:36 to *d* a man of justice—
1Co 7:5 Do not *d* each other
9:15 die than have anyone *d* me

DEPTH (DEEP)
Ro 8:39 any powers, neither height nor *d,*
11:33 the *d* of the riches of the wisdom

DEPTHS (DEEP)
Ps 130:1 Out of the *d* I cry to you, O LORD;

DERIDES*
Pr 11:12 who lacks judgment *d* his neighbor,

DERIVES*
Eph 3:15 in heaven and on earth *d* its name.

DESCEND (DESCENDED DESCENDING)
Ro 10:7 "or 'Who will *d* into the deep?' "

DESCENDED (DESCEND)
Eph 4:9 except that he also *d* to the lower,
Heb 7:14 For it is clear that our Lord *d*

DESCENDING (DESCEND)
Ge 28:12 of God were ascending and *d* on it.
Mt 3:16 the Spirit of God *d* like a dove
Mk 1:10 and the Spirit *d* on him like a dove.
Jn 1:51 and *d* on the Son of Man."

DESECRATING*
Ne 13:17 you are doing—*d* the Sabbath day?
13:18 against Israel by *d* the Sabbath."
Isa 56:2 who keeps the Sabbath without *d* it
56:6 who keep the Sabbath without *d* it
Eze 44:7 *d* my temple while you offered me

DESERT
Nu 32:13 wander in the *d* forty years,
Dt 8:16 He gave you manna to eat in the *d,*
29:5 years that I led you through the *d,*
Ne 9:19 you did not abandon them in the *d.*
Ps 78:19 "Can God spread a table in the *d?*
78:52 led them like sheep through the *d.*
Pr 21:19 Better to live in a *d*
Isa 32:2 like streams of water in the *d*
32:15 and the *d* becomes a fertile field,
35:6 and streams in the *d.*
43:20 because I provide water in the *d*
Mk 1:3 "a voice of one calling in the *d,*
1:13 and he was in the *d* forty days,
Rev 12:6 fled into the *d* to a place prepared

DESERTED (DESERTS)
Ezr 9:9 our God has not *d* us
Mt 26:56 all the disciples *d* him and fled.
2Ti 1:15 in the province of Asia has *d* me,

DESERTING (DESERTS)
Gal 1:6 are so quickly *d* the one who called

DESERTS (DESERTED DESERTING)
Zec 11:17 who *d* the flock!

DESERVE* (DESERVED DESERVES)
Ge 40:15 to *d* being put in a dungeon."
Lev 26:21 times over, as your sins *d.*
Jdg 20:10 it can give them what they *d*
1Sa 26:16 you and your men *d* to die,
1Ki 2:26 You *d* to die, but I will not put you
Ps 28:4 bring back upon them what they *d.*
94:2 pay back to the proud what they *d.*
103:10 he does not treat us as our sins *d*
Pr 3:27 from those who *d* it,
Ecc 8:14 men who get what the righteous *d,*
8:14 men who get what the wicked *d,*
Isa 66:6 repaying his enemies all they *d.*
Jer 14:16 out on them the calamity they *d.*
17:10 according to what his deeds *d.*"
21:14 I will punish you as your deeds *d,*
32:19 to his conduct and as his deeds *d.*
49:12 "If those who do not *d*
La 3:64 Pay them back what they *d,*
Eze 16:59 I will deal with you as you *d,*
Zec 1:6 to us what our ways and practices *d*
Mt 8:8 I do not *d* to have you come
22:8 those I invited did not *d* to come.
Lk 7:6 for I do not *d* to have you come
23:15 he has done nothing to *d* death.
23:41 for we are getting what our deeds *d*
Ro 1:32 those who do such things *d* death,
1Co 15:9 even *d* to be called an apostle,
16:18 Such men *d* recognition.
2Co 11:15 end will be what their actions *d.*
Rev 16:6 blood to drink as they *d.*"

DESERVED* (DESERVE)
2Sa 19:28 descendants *d* nothing
Ezr 9:13 less than our sins have *d*
Job 33:27 but I did not get what I *d.*
Ac 23:29 charge against him that *d* death
Ro 3:8 Their condemnation is *d.*

DESERVES* (DESERVE)
Nu 35:31 the life of a murderer, who *d* to die.
Dt 25:2 If the guilty man *d* to be beaten,
25:2 the number of lashes his crime *d,*
Jdg 9:16 and if you have treated him as he *d*
2Sa 12:5 the man who did this *d* to die!
Job 34:11 upon him what his conduct *d.*
Jer 51:6 he will pay her what she *d.*
Lk 7:4 "This man *d* to have you do this,
10:7 for the worker *d* his wages.
Ac 26:31 is not doing anything that *d* death
1Ti 1:15 saying that *d* full acceptance:
4:9 saying that *d* full acceptance
5:18 and "The worker *d* his wages."
Heb 10:29 severely do you think a man *d*

DESIGNATED
Lk 6:13 also *d* apostles: Simon (whom he
Heb 5:10 and was *d* by God to be high priest

DESIRABLE* (DESIRE)
Ge 3: 6 and also *d* for gaining wisdom,
Pr 22: 1 A good name is more *d*
Jer 3: 19 and give you a *d* land,

DESIRE* (DESIRABLE DESIRED DESIRES)
Ge 3: 16 Your *d* will be for your husband,
Dt 5: 21 You shall not set your *d*
1Sa 9: 20 to whom is all the *d* of Israel turned
2Sa 19: 38 anything you *d* from me I will do
23: 5 and grant me my every *d?*
1Ch 29: 18 keep this *d* in the hearts
2Ch 1: 11 "Since this is your heart's *d*
9: 8 and his *d* to uphold them forever,
Job 13: 3 But I *d* to speak to the Almighty
21: 14 We have no *d* to know your ways.
Ps 10: 17 O LORD, the *d* of the afflicted;
20: 4 May he give you the *d*
21: 2 You have granted him the *d*
27: 12 me over to the *d* of my foes,
40: 6 Sacrifice and offering you did not *d*
40: 8 I *d* to do your will, O my God;
40: 14 may all who *d* my ruin
41: 2 him to the *d* of his foes.
51: 6 Surely you *d* truth
70: 2 may all who *d* my ruin
73: 25 earth has nothing I *d* besides you
Pr 3: 15 nothing you *d* can compare
8: 11 and nothing you *d* can compare
10: 24 what the righteous *d* will be
11: 23 The *d* of the righteous ends only
12: 12 The wicked *d* the plunder
17: 16 since he has no *d* to get wisdom?
24: 1 do not *d* their company;
Ecc 12: 5 and *d* no longer is stirred.
SS 6: 12 my *d* set me among the royal
7: 10 and his *d* is for me.
Isa 26: 8 are the *d* of our hearts.
53: 2 appearance that we should *d* him.
55: 11 but will accomplish what I *d*
Eze 24: 25 delight of their eyes, their heart's *d*,
Hos 6: 6 For I *d* mercy, not sacrifice,
Mic 7: 3 the powerful dictate what they *d*—
Mal 3: 1 whom you *d*, will come," says
Mt 9: 13 learn what this means: 'I *d* mercy,
12: 7 what these words mean, 'I *d* mercy,
Jn 8: 44 want to carry out your father's *d*.
Ro 7: 8 in me every kind of covetous *d*.
7: 18 For I have the *d* to do what is good,
9: 16 depend on man's *d* or effort,
10: 1 my heart's *d* and prayer to God
1Co 12: 31 But eagerly *d* the greater gifts.
14: 1 and eagerly *d* spiritual gifts,
2Co 8: 10 but also to have the *d* to do so.
8: 13 Our *d* is not that others might be
Php 1: 23 I *d* to depart and be with Christ,
Heb 10: 5 Sacrifice and offering you did not *d*
10: 8 and sin offerings you did not *d*,
13: 18 *d* to live honorably in every way.
Jas 1: 14 by his own evil *d*, he is dragged
1: 15 Then, after *d* has conceived,
2Pe 2: 10 of those who follow the corrupt *d*

DESIRED (DESIRE)
Hag 2: 7 and the *d* of all nations will come,
Lk 22: 15 "I have eagerly *d* to eat this

DESIRES* (DESIRE)
Ge 4: 7 at your door; it *d* to have you,
41: 16 will give Pharaoh the answer he *d*."
2Sa 3: 21 rule over all that your heart *d*."
1Ki 11: 37 rule over all that your heart *d*;
Job 17: 11 and so are the *d* of my heart.
31: 16 "If I have denied the *d* of the poor
Ps 34: 12 and *d* to see many good days,
37: 4 he will give you the *d* of your heart.
103: 5 who satisfies your *d* with good things,
140: 8 do not grant the wicked their *d*,
145: 16 satisfy the *d* of every living thing.
145: 19 He fulfills the *d* of those who fear
Pr 11: 6 the unfaithful are trapped by evil *d*.
13: 4 *d* of the diligent are fully satisfied.
19: 22 What a man *d* is unfailing love;
Ecc 6: 2 so that he lacks nothing his heart *d*,
SS 2: 7 or awaken love / until it so *d*.
3: 5 or awaken love / until it so *d*.
8: 4 or awaken love / until it so *d*.
Hab 2: 4 his *d* are not upright—
Mk 4: 19 and the *d* for other things come in
Ro 1: 24 over in the sinful *d* of their hearts
6: 12 body so that you obey its evil *d*.
8: 5 set on what that nature *d*;
8: 5 set on what the Spirit *d*.
13: 14 to gratify the *d* of the sinful nature.
Gal 5: 16 and you will not gratify the *d*
5: 17 the sinful nature *d* what is contrary
5: 24 nature with its passions and *d*.
Eph 2: 3 and following its *d* and thoughts.
4: 22 being corrupted by its deceitful *d*;
Col 3: 5 impurity, lust, evil *d* and greed,
1Ti 3: 1 an overseer, he *d* a noble task.
5: 11 their sensual *d* overcome their
6: 9 and harmful *d* that plunge men
2Ti 2: 22 Flee the evil *d* of youth,
3: 6 are swayed by all kinds of evil *d*,
4: 3 Instead, to suit their own *d*,
Jas 1: 20 about the righteous life that God *d*.
4: 1 from your *d* that battle within you?
1Pe 1: 14 conform to the evil *d* you had
2: 11 to abstain from sinful *d*, which war
4: 2 of his earthly life for evil human *d*,
2Pe 1: 4 in the world caused by evil *d*.
2: 18 to the lustful *d* of sinful human
3: 3 and following their own evil *d*.
1Jn 2: 17 The world and its *d* pass away,
Jude : 16 they follow their own evil *d*;
: 18 will follow their own ungodly *d*."

DESOLATE (DESOLATION)
Isa 54: 1 are the children of the *d* woman
Gal 4: 27 are the children of the *d* woman

DESOLATION (DESOLATE)
Da 11: 31 up the abomination that causes *d*.
12: 11 abomination that causes *d* is set up,
Mt 24: 15 'the abomination that causes *d*,'

DESPAIR (DESPAIRED)
Isa 61: 3 instead of a spirit of *d*.
2Co 4: 8 perplexed, but not in *d*; persecuted,

DESPAIRED* (DESPAIR)
2Co 1: 8 ability to endure, so that we *d*

DESPERATE*
2Sa 12: 18 He may do something *d*."
Ps 60: 3 have shown your people *d* times;
79: 8 for we are in *d* need.
142: 6 for I am in *d* need;

DESPISE (DESPISED DESPISES)
2Sa 12: 9 Why did you *d* the word
Job 5: 17 so do not *d* the discipline
36: 5 God is mighty, but does not *d* men;
42: 6 Therefore I *d* myself
Ps 51: 17 O God, you will not *d*.
102: 17 he will not *d* their plea.
Pr 1: 7 but fools *d* wisdom and discipline.
3: 11 do not *d* the LORD's discipline
6: 30 Men do not *d* a thief if he steals
23: 22 do not *d* your mother
Jer 14: 21 of your name do not *d* us;
Am 5: 10 and *d* him who tells the truth.
5: 21 "I hate, I *d* your religious feasts;
Mt 6: 24 devoted to the one and *d* the other.
Lk 16: 13 devoted to the one and *d* the other.
1Co 11: 22 Or do you *d* the church of God
Tit 2: 15 Do not let anyone *d* you.
2Pe 2: 10 of the sinful nature and *d* authority.

DESPISED (DESPISE)
Ge 25: 34 So Esau *d* his birthright.
Ps 22: 6 by men and *d* by the people.
Pr 12: 8 but men with warped minds are *d*.
Isa 53: 3 He was *d* and rejected by men,
53: 3 he was *d*, and we esteemed him not
1Co 1: 28 of this world and the *d* things—

DESPISES (DESPISE)
Pr 14: 21 He who *d* his neighbor sins,
15: 20 but a foolish man *d* his mother.
15: 32 who ignores discipline *d* himself,
Zec 4: 10 "Who *d* the day of small things?

DESTINED (DESTINY)
Lk 2: 34 "This child is *d* to cause the falling
1Co 2: 7 and that God *d* for our glory
Col 2: 22 These are all *d* to perish with use,
1Th 3: 3 know quite well that we were *d*
Heb 9: 27 Just as man is *d* to die once,
1Pe 2: 8 which is also what they were *d* for.

DESTINY* (DESTINED PREDESTINED)
Job 8: 13 Such is the *d* of all who forget God;
Ps 73: 17 then I understood their final *d*.
Ecc 7: 2 for death is the *d* of every man;
9: 2 share a common *d*—the righteous
9: 3 the sun: The same *d* overtakes all.
Isa 65: 11 and fill bowls of mixed wine for *D*,
Php 3: 19 Their *d* is destruction, their god is

DESTITUTE
Ps 102: 17 to the prayer of the *d*;
Pr 31: 8 for the rights of all who are *d*.
Heb 11: 37 *d*, persecuted and mistreated—

DESTROY (DESTROYED DESTROYING DESTROYS DESTRUCTION DESTRUCTIVE)
Ge 6: 17 floodwaters on the earth to *d* all life
9: 11 will there be a flood to *d* the earth."
Pr 1: 32 complacency of fools will *d* them;
Mt 10: 28 of the One who can *d* both soul
Mk 14: 58 'I will *d* this man-made temple
Lk 4: 34 to *d* us? I know who you are—
Jn 10: 10 only to steal and kill and *d*;
Ac 8: 3 But Saul began to *d* the church.
Rev 11: 18 destroying those who *d* the earth."

DESTROYED (DESTROY)
Dt 8: 19 you today that you will surely be *d*.
Job 19: 26 And after my skin has been *d*,
Pr 6: 15 he will suddenly be *d*—
11: 3 the unfaithful are *d*
21: 28 listens to him will be *d* forever.
29: 1 will suddenly be *d*—
Isa 55: 13 which will not be *d*."
Da 2: 44 up a kingdom that will never be *d*,
6: 26 his kingdom will not be *d*,
1Co 5: 5 so that the sinful nature may be *d*
8: 11 for whom Christ died, is *d*
15: 24 Father after he has *d* all dominion,
15: 26 The last enemy to be *d* is death.
2Co 4: 9 abandoned; struck down, but not *d*.
5: 1 if the earthly tent we live in is *d*,
Gal 5: 15 or you will be *d* by each other.
Eph 2: 14 the two one and has *d* the barrier,
2Ti 1: 10 who has *d* death and has brought
Heb 10: 39 of those who shrink back and are *d*,
2Pe 2: 12 born only to be caught and *d*,
3: 10 the elements will be *d* by fire,
3: 11 Since everything will be *d*
Jude : 5 later *d* those who did not believe.
: 11 have been *d* in Korah's rebellion.

DESTROYING (DESTROY)
Jer 23: 1 "Woe to the shepherds who are *d*

DESTROYS (DESTROY)
Pr 6: 32 whoever does so *d* himself.
11: 9 mouth the godless *d* his neighbor,
18: 9 is brother to one who *d*.
28: 24 he is partner to him who *d*.
Ecc 9: 18 but one sinner *d* much good.
1Co 3: 17 If anyone *d* God's temple,

DESTRUCTION (DESTROY)
Nu 32: 15 and you will be the cause of their *d*
Pr 16: 18 Pride goes before *d*,
17: 19 he who builds a high gate invites *d*.
24: 22 for those two will send sudden *d*
Hos 13: 14 Where, O grave, is your *d?*
Mt 7: 13 broad is the road that leads to *d*,
Lk 6: 49 it collapsed and its *d* was complete
Jn 17: 12 except the one doomed to *d*
Ro 9: 22 of his wrath—prepared for *d?*
Gal 6: 8 from that nature will reap *d*;
Php 3: 19 Their destiny is *d*, their god is their
1Th 5: 3 *d* will come on them suddenly,
2Th 1: 9 punished with everlasting *d*
2: 3 is revealed, the man doomed to *d*.
1Ti 6: 9 that plunge men into ruin and *d*.
2Pe 2: 1 bringing swift *d* on themselves.
2: 3 and their *d* has not been sleeping.
3: 7 of judgment and *d* of ungodly men.
3: 12 That day will bring about the *d*
3: 16 other Scriptures, to their own *d*.
Rev 17: 8 out of the Abyss and go to his *d*.
17: 11 to the seven and is going to his *d*.

DESTRUCTIVE (DESTROY)
2Pe 2: 1 will secretly introduce *d* heresies,

DETERMINED (DETERMINES)
Job 14: 5 Man's days are *d*;
Isa 14: 26 This is the plan *d* for the whole
Da 11: 36 for what has been *d* must take place
Ac 17: 26 and he *d* the times set for them

DETERMINES* (DETERMINED)
Ps 147: 4 He *d* the number of the stars
Pr 16: 9 but the LORD *d* his steps.
1Co 12: 11 them to each one, just as he *d*.

DETEST (DETESTABLE DETESTED DETESTS)

Lev 11:10 in the water—you are to *d*.
Pr 8:7 for my lips *d* wickedness.
13:19 but fools *d* turning from evil.
16:12 Kings *d* wrongdoing,
24:9 and men *d* a mocker.
29:27 The righteous *d* the dishonest;
29:27 the wicked *d* the upright.

DETESTABLE (DETEST)

Pr 6:16 seven that are *d* to him:
21:27 The sacrifice of the wicked is *d*—
28:9 even his prayers are *d*.
Isa 1:13 Your incense is *d* to me.
41:24 he who chooses you is *d*.
44:19 Shall I make a *d* thing
Jer 44:4 'Do not do this *d* thing that I hate!'
Eze 8:13 doing things that are even more *d*."
Lk 16:15 among men is *d* in God's sight.
Tit 1:16 They are *d*, disobedient
1Pe 4:3 orgies, carousing and *d* idolatry.

DETESTED* (DETEST)

Zec 11:8 The flock *d* me, and I grew weary

DETESTS* (DETEST)

Dt 22:5 LORD your God *d* anyone who
23:18 the LORD your God *d* them both.
25:16 LORD your God *d* anyone who
Pr 3:32 for the LORD *d* a perverse man
11:20 The LORD *d* men
12:22 The LORD *d* lying lips,
15:8 The LORD *d* the sacrifice
15:9 The LORD *d* the way
15:26 The LORD *d* the thoughts
16:5 The LORD *d* all the proud of heart
17:15 the LORD *d* them both.
20:10 the LORD *d* them both.
20:23 The LORD *d* differing weights,

DEVIATE*

2Ch 8:15 They did not *d* from the king's

DEVICES*

Ps 81:12 to follow their own *d*.

DEVIL* (DEVIL'S)

Mt 4:1 the desert to be tempted by the *d*.
4:5 the *d* took him to the holy city
4:8 *d* took him to a very high mountain
4:11 the *d* left him, and angels came
13:39 the enemy who sows them is the *d*.
25:41 the eternal fire prepared for the *d*
Lk 4:2 forty days he was tempted by the *d*.
4:3 *d* said to him, "If you are the Son
4:5 The *d* led him up to a high place
4:9 The *d* led him to Jerusalem
4:13 When the *d* had finished all this
8:12 then the *d* comes and takes away
Jn 6:70 of you is a *d!*" (He meant Judas,
8:44 You belong to your father, the *d*,
13:2 the *d* had already prompted Judas
Ac 10:38 were under the power of the *d*,
13:10 "You are a child of the *d*
Eph 4:27 and do not give the *d* a foothold.
1Ti 3:6 under the same judgment as the *d*.
2Ti 2:26 and escape from the trap of the *d*,
Heb 2:14 the *d*—and free those who all their
Jas 3:15 but is earthly, unspiritual, of the *d*.
4:7 Resist the *d*, and he will flee
1Pe 5:8 Your enemy the *d* prowls
1Jn 3:8 because the *d* has been sinning
3:8 who does what is sinful is of the *d*,
3:10 and who the children of the *d* are:
Jude :9 with the *d* about the body of Moses
Rev 2:10 the *d* will put some of you in prison
12:9 that ancient serpent called the *d*
12:12 the *d* has gone down to you!
20:2 that ancient serpent, who is the *d*,
20:10 And the *d*, who deceived them,

DEVIL'S* (DEVIL)

Eph 6:11 stand against the *d* schemes.
1Ti 3:7 into disgrace and into the *d* trap.
1Jn 3:8 was to destroy the *d* work.

DEVILS see DEMONS

DEVIOUS*

Pr 2:15 and who are *d* in their ways.
14:2 he whose ways are *d* despises him.
21:8 The way of the guilty is *d*,

DEVOTE* (DEVOTED DEVOTING DEVOTION DEVOUT)

1Ch 22:19 Now *d* your heart and soul
2Ch 31:4 Levites so they could *d* themselves
Job 11:13 "Yet if you *d* your heart to him
Jer 30:21 for who is he who will *d* himself
Mic 4:13 You will *d* their ill-gotten gains
1Co 7:5 so that you may *d* yourselves
Col 4:2 *D* yourselves to prayer, being
1Ti 1:4 nor to *d* themselves to myths
4:13 *d* yourself to the public reading
Tit 3:8 may be careful to *d* themselves
3:14 people must learn to *d* themselves

DEVOTED (DEVOTE)

1Ki 11:4 and his heart was not fully *d*
Ezr 7:10 For Ezra had *d* himself to the study
Ps 86:2 Guard my life, for I am *d* to you.
Mt 6:24 or he will be *d* to the one
Mk 7:11 from me is Corban' (that is, a gift *d*
Ac 2:42 They *d* themselves
18:5 Paul *d* himself exclusively
Ro 12:10 Be *d* to one another
1Co 7:34 Her aim is to be *d* to the Lord
16:15 and they have *d* themselves
2Co 7:12 for yourselves how *d* to us you are.

DEVOTING* (DEVOTE)

1Ti 5:10 *d* herself to all kinds of good deeds.

DEVOTION* (DEVOTE)

2Ki 20:3 and with wholehearted *d* and have
1Ch 28:9 and serve him with wholehearted *d*
29:3 in my *d* to the temple
29:19 son Solomon the wholehearted *d*
2Ch 32:32 and his acts of *d* are written
35:26 of Josiah's reign and his acts of *d*,
Job 6:14 despairing man should have the *d*
15:4 and hinder *d* to God.
Isa 38:3 and with wholehearted *d* and have
Jer 2:2 " 'I remember the *d* of your youth,
Eze 33:31 With their mouths they express *d*,
1Co 7:35 way in undivided *d* to the Lord.
2Co 11:3 from your sincere and pure *d*

DEVOUR (DEVOURED DEVOURING DEVOURS)

2Sa 2:26 "Must the sword *d* forever?
Mk 12:40 They *d* widows' houses
1Pe 5:8 lion looking for someone to *d*.

DEVOURED (DEVOUR)

Jer 30:16 But all who devour you will be *d*;

DEVOURING (DEVOUR)

Gal 5:15 keep on biting and *d* each other,

DEVOURS (DEVOUR)

2Sa 11:25 the sword *d* one as well as another.
Pr 21:20 but a foolish man *d* all he has.

DEVOUT* (DEVOTE)

1Ki 18:3 (Obadiah was a *d* believer
Isa 57:1 *d* men are taken away,
Lk 2:25 Simeon, who was righteous and *d*.
Ac 10:2 his family were *d* and God-fearing;
10:7 a *d* soldier who was one of his attendants
13:43 and *d* converts to Judaism followed
22:12 He was a *d* observer of the law

DEW

Jdg 6:37 If there is *d* only on the fleece

DICTATED

Jer 36:4 and while Jeremiah *d* all the words

DIE (DEAD DEADENED DEATH DIED DIES DYING)

Ge 2:17 when you eat of it you will surely *d*
3:3 you must not touch it, or you will *d*
3:4 will not surely *d*," the serpent said
Ex 11:5 Every firstborn son in Egypt will *d*,
Ru 1:17 Where you *d* I will *d*, and there I
2Ki 14:6 each is to *d* for his own sins."
Job 2:9 Curse God and *d!*" He replied,
Pr 5:23 He will *d* for lack of discipline,
10:21 but fools *d* for lack of judgment.
15:10 he who hates correction will *d*.
23:13 with the rod, he will not *d*.
Ecc 3:2 a time to be born and a time to *d*,
Isa 22:13 "for tomorrow we *d!*"
66:24 their worm will not *d*, nor will their
Jer 31:30 everyone will *d* for his own sin;
Eze 3:18 that wicked man will *d* for his sin,
3:19 he will *d* for his sin; but you will
3:20 block before him, he will *d*.
18:4 soul who sins is the one who will *d*.
18:20 soul who sins is the one who will *d*.
18:31 Why will you *d*, O house of Israel?
33:8 'O wicked man, you will surely *d*,'
Mt 26:52 "for all who draw the sword will *d*
Mk 9:48 " 'their worm does not *d*,
Jn 8:21 and you will *d* in your sin.
11:26 and believes in me will never *d*.
Ro 5:7 Very rarely will anyone *d*
14:8 and if we *d*, we *d* to the Lord.
1Co 15:22 in Adam all *d*, so in Christ all will
15:31 I *d* every day—I mean that,
15:32 for tomorrow we *d*."
Php 1:21 to live is Christ and to *d* is gain.
Heb 9:27 Just as man is destined to *d* once,
1Pe 2:24 so that we might *d* to sins
Rev 14:13 Blessed are the dead who *d*

DIED (DIE)

1Ki 16:18 So he *d*, because of the sins he had
1Ch 1:51 Hadad also *d*.
10:13 Saul *d* because he was unfaithful
Lk 16:22 "The time came when the beggar *d*
Ro 5:6 we were still powerless, Christ *d*
5:8 we were still sinners, Christ *d*
6:2 By no means! We *d* to sin;
6:7 anyone who has *d* has been freed
6:8 if we *d* with Christ, we believe that
6:10 The death he *d*, he *d* to sin once
14:9 Christ *d* and returned to life
14:15 brother for whom Christ *d*.
1Co 8:11 for whom Christ *d*, is destroyed
15:3 that Christ *d* for our sins according
2Co 5:14 *d* for all, and therefore all *d*.
5:15 he *d* for all, that those who live
Col 2:20 Since you *d* with Christ
3:3 For you *d*, and your life is now
1Th 4:14 We believe that Jesus *d*
5:10 He *d* for us so that, whether we are
2Ti 2:11 If we *d* with him,
Heb 9:15 now that he has *d* as a ransom
9:17 in force only when somebody has *d*
1Pe 3:18 For Christ *d* for sins once for all,
Rev 2:8 who *d* and came to life again.

DIES (DIE)

Job 14:14 If a man *d*, will he live again?
Pr 11:7 a wicked man *d*, his hope perishes;
26:20 without gossip a quarrel *d* down.
Jn 11:25 in me will live, even though he *d*;
12:24 But if it *d*, it produces many seeds.
Ro 7:2 but if her husband *d*, she is released
14:7 and none of us *d* to himself alone.
1Co 7:39 But if her husband *d*, she is free
15:36 does not come to life unless it *d*.

DIFFERENCE* (DIFFERENT)

2Sa 19:35 Can I tell the *d* between what is
2Ch 12:8 so that they may learn the *d*
Eze 22:26 they teach that there is no *d*
44:23 are to teach my people the *d*
Ro 3:22 There is no *d*, for all have sinned
10:12 For there is no *d* between Jew
Gal 2:6 whatever they were makes no *d*

DIFFERENCES* (DIFFERENT)

1Co 11:19 to be *d* among you to show which

DIFFERENT* (DIFFERENCE DIFFERENCES DIFFERING DIFFERS)

Lev 19:19 " 'Do not mate *d* kinds of animals.
Nu 14:24 my servant Caleb has a *d* spirit
1Sa 10:6 you will be changed into a *d* person
Est 1:7 each one *d* from the other,
3:8 whose customs are *d* from those
Da 7:3 Four great beasts, each *d*
7:7 It was *d* from all the former beasts,
7:19 which was *d* from all the others
7:23 It will be *d* from all the other
7:24 them another king will arise, *d*
11:29 but this time the outcome will be *d*
Mk 16:12 Jesus appeared in a *d* form
Ro 12:6 We have *d* gifts, according
1Co 4:7 For who makes you *d*
12:4 There are *d* kinds of gifts,
12:5 There are *d* kinds of service,
12:6 There are *d* kinds of working,
12:10 speaking in *d* kinds of tongues,
12:28 and those speaking in *d* kinds
2Co 11:4 or a *d* gospel from the one you
11:4 or if you receive a *d* spirit
Gal 1:6 and are turning to a *d* gospel—

Gal 4: 1 he is no *d* from a slave,
Heb 7: 13 are said belonged to a *d* tribe,
Jas 2: 25 and sent them off in a *d* direction?

DIFFERING* (DIFFERENT)

Dt 25: 13 Do not have two *d* weights
25: 14 Do not have two *d* measures
Pr 20: 10 Differing weights and *d* measures
20: 10 *D* weights and differing measures
20: 23 The LORD detests *d* weights,

DIFFERS* (DIFFERENT)

1Co 15: 41 and star *d* from star in splendor.

DIFFICULT (DIFFICULTIES)

Ex 18: 22 but have them bring every *d* case
Dt 30: 11 commanding you today is not too *d*
2Ki 2: 10 "You have asked a *d* thing,"
Eze 3: 5 of obscure speech and *d* language,
Ac 15: 19 that we should not make it *d*

DIFFICULTIES* (DIFFICULT)

Dt 31: 17 and *d* will come upon them,
31: 21 when many disasters and *d* come
2Co 12: 10 in hardships, in persecutions, in *d.*

DIGNITY

Pr 31: 25 She is clothed with strength and *d;*

DIGS

Pr 26: 27 If a man *d* a pit, he will fall into it;

DILIGENCE (DILIGENT)

Ezr 5: 8 The work is being carried on with *d*
Heb 6: 11 to show this same *d* to the very end

DILIGENT (DILIGENCE)

Pr 10: 4 but *d* hands bring wealth.
12: 24 *D* hands will rule,
12: 27 the *d* man prizes his possessions.
13: 4 of the *d* are fully satisfied.
21: 5 The plans of the *d* lead to profit
1Ti 4: 15 Be *d* in these matters; give yourself

DINAH*

Only daughter of Jacob, by Leah (Ge 30:21; 46:15). Raped by Shechem; avenged by Simeon and Levi (Ge 34).

DINE

Pr 23: 1 When you sit to *d* with a ruler,

DIOTREPHES*

3Jn : 9 but *D,* who loves to be first,

DIRECT (DIRECTED DIRECTIVES DIRECTS)

Ge 18: 19 so that he will *d* his children
Dt 17: 10 to do everything they *d* you to do.
Ps 119: 35 *D* me in the path of your
119:133 *D* my footsteps according
Jer 10: 23 it is not for man to *d* his steps.
2Th 3: 5 May the Lord *d* your hearts
1Ti 5: 17 The elders who *d* the affairs

DIRECTED (DIRECT)

Ge 24: 51 master's son, as the LORD has *d.*"
Nu 16: 40 as the LORD *d* him through Moses
Dt 2: 1 Sea, as the LORD had *d* me.
6: 1 laws the LORD your God *d* me
Jos 11: 9 did to them as the LORD had *d:*
11: 23 just as the LORD had *d* Moses,
Pr 20: 24 A man's steps are *d* by the LORD.
Jer 13: 2 as the LORD *d,* and put it
Ac 7: 44 It had been made as God *d* Moses,
Tit 1: 5 elders in every town, as I *d* you.

DIRECTIVES* (DIRECT)

1Co 11: 17 In the following *d* I have no praise

DIRECTS (DIRECT)

Ps 42: 8 By day the LORD *d* his love,
Isa 48: 17 who *d* you in the way you should

DIRGE*

Mt 11: 17 we sang a *d,*
Lk 7: 32 we sang a *d,*

DISABLED*

Jn 5: 3 number of *d* people used to lie—
Heb 12: 13 so that the lame may not be *d,*

DISAGREEMENT*

Ac 15: 39 had such a sharp *d* that they parted

DISAPPEAR (DISAPPEARED DISAPPEARS)

Mt 5: 18 will by any means *d* from the Law
Lk 16: 17 earth to *d* than for the least stroke
Heb 8: 13 is obsolete and aging will soon *d.*
2Pe 3: 10 The heavens will *d* with a roar;

DISAPPEARED (DISAPPEAR)

1Ki 20: 40 busy here and there, the man *d.*"

DISAPPEARS (DISAPPEAR)

1Co 13: 10 perfection comes, the imperfect *d.*

DISAPPOINT* (DISAPPOINTED)

Ro 5: 5 And hope does not *d* us,

DISAPPOINTED (DISAPPOINT)

Ps 22: 5 in you they trusted and were not *d.*

DISAPPROVE*

Pr 24: 18 or the LORD will see and *d*

DISARMED*

Col 2: 15 And having *d* the powers

DISASTER

Ex 32: 12 and do not bring *d* on your people.
Ps 57: 1 wings until the *d* has passed.
Pr 1: 26 I in turn will laugh at your *d;*
3: 25 Have no fear of sudden *d*
6: 15 Therefore *d* will overtake him
16: 4 even the wicked for a day of *d.*
17: 5 over *d* will not go unpunished.
27: 10 house when *d* strikes you—
Isa 45: 7 I bring prosperity and create *d;*
Jer 17: 17 you are my refuge in the day of *d.*
Eze 7: 5 An unheard-of *d* is coming.

DISCERN (DISCERNED DISCERNING DISCERNMENT)

Ps 19: 12 Who can *d* his errors?
139: 3 You *d* my going out and my lying
Php 1: 10 you may be able to *d* what is best

DISCERNED (DISCERN)

1Co 2: 14 because they are spiritually *d.*

DISCERNING (DISCERN)

1Ki 3: 9 So give your servant a *d* heart
3: 12 I will give you a wise and *d* heart,
Pr 1: 5 and let the *d* get guidance—
8: 9 To the *d* all of them are right;
10: 13 on the lips of the *d,*
14: 6 knowledge comes easily to the *d.*
14: 33 in the heart of the *d*
15: 14 The *d* heart seeks knowledge,
16: 21 The wise in heart are called *d,*
17: 24 A *d* man keeps wisdom in view,
17: 28 and *d* if he holds his tongue.
18: 15 heart of the *d* acquires knowledge;
19: 25 rebuke a *d* man, and he will gain
28: 7 He who keeps the law is a *d* son,

DISCERNMENT (DISCERN)

Ps 119:125 I am your servant; give me *d*
Pr 3: 21 preserve sound judgment and *d,*
17: 10 A rebuke impresses a man of *d*
28: 11 a poor man who has *d* sees

DISCHARGED* (DISCHARGING)

Ecc 8: 8 As no one is *d* in time of war,

DISCHARGING* (DISCHARGED)

1Co 9: 17 I am simply *d* the trust committed

DISCIPLE (DISCIPLES DISCIPLES')

Mt 10: 42 these little ones because he is my *d,*
Lk 14: 26 his own life—he cannot be my *d.*
14: 27 and follow me cannot be my *d.*
14: 33 everything he has cannot be my *d.*
Jn 13: 23 of them, the *d* whom Jesus loved,
19: 26 and the *d* whom he loved standing
21: 7 Then the *d* whom Jesus loved said
21: 20 saw that the *d* whom Jesus loved

DISCIPLES (DISCIPLE)

Mt 10: 1 He called his twelve *d* to him
26: 56 Then all the *d* deserted him
28: 19 Therefore go and make *d*
Mk 3: 7 withdrew with his *d* to the lake,
16: 20 Then the *d* went out and preached
Lk 6: 13 he called his *d* to him and chose
Jn 2: 11 and his *d* put their faith in him.
6: 66 many of his *d* turned back
8: 31 to my teaching, you are really my *d*
12: 16 At first his *d* did not understand all
13: 35 men will know that you are my *d*
15: 8 showing yourselves to be my *d.*
20: 20 The *d* were overjoyed
Ac 6: 1 the number of *d* was increasing,
11: 26 The *d* were called Christians first
14: 22 strengthening the *d*
18: 23 Phrygia, strengthening all the *d.*

DISCIPLES' (DISCIPLE)

Jn 13: 5 and began to wash his *d* feet,

DISCIPLINE* (DISCIPLINED DISCIPLINES SELF-DISCIPLINE)

Dt 4: 36 made you hear his voice to *d* you.
11: 2 and experienced the *d*
21: 18 listen to them when they *d* him,
Job 5: 17 so do not despise the *d*
Ps 6: 1 or *d* me in your wrath.
38: 1 or *d* me in your wrath.
39: 11 You rebuke and *d* men for their sin;
94: 12 Blessed is the man you *d,* O LORD
Pr 1: 2 for attaining wisdom and *d;*
1: 7 but fools despise wisdom and *d.*
3: 11 do not despise the LORD's *d*
5: 12 You will say, "How I hated *d!*
5: 23 He will die for lack of *d,*
6: 23 and the corrections of *d*
10: 17 He who heeds *d* shows the way
12: 1 Whoever loves *d* loves knowledge,
13: 18 He who ignores *d* comes to poverty
13: 24 who loves him is careful to *d* him.
15: 5 A fool spurns his father's *d,*
15: 10 Stern *d* awaits him who leaves
15: 32 He who ignores *d* despises himself,
19: 18 *D* your son, for in that there is hope
22: 15 the rod of *d* will drive it far
23: 13 Do not withhold *d* from a child;
23: 23 get wisdom, *d* and understanding.
29: 17 *D* your son, and he will give you
Jer 17: 23 would not listen or respond to *d.*
30: 11 I will *d* you but only with justice;
32: 33 would not listen or respond to *d.*
46: 28 I will *d* you but only with justice;
Hos 5: 2 I will *d* all of them.
Heb 12: 5 do not make light of the Lord's *d,*
12: 7 as *d;* God is treating you
12: 8 (and everyone undergoes *d*),
12: 11 No *d* seems pleasant at the time,
Rev 3: 19 Those whom I love I rebuke and *d.*

DISCIPLINED* (DISCIPLINE)

Pr 1: 3 for acquiring a *d* and prudent life,
Isa 26: 16 when you *d* them,
Jer 31: 18 and I have been *d.*
31: 18 'You *d* me like an unruly calf,
1Co 11: 32 we are being *d* so that we will not
Tit 1: 8 upright, holy and *d.*
Heb 12: 7 For what son is not *d* by his father?
12: 8 you are not *d* (and everyone
12: 9 all had human fathers who *d* us
12: 10 Our fathers *d* us for a little while

DISCIPLINES* (DISCIPLINE)

Dt 8: 5 so the LORD your God *d* you.
8: 5 your heart that as a man *d* his son,
Ps 94: 10 Does he who *d* nations not punish?
Pr 3: 12 the LORD *d* those he loves,
Heb 12: 6 because the Lord *d* those he loves,
12: 10 but God *d* us for our good,

DISCLOSED

Lk 8: 17 is nothing hidden that will not be *d,*
Col 1: 26 and generations, but is now *d*
Heb 9: 8 Holy Place had not yet been *d*

DISCORD

Gal 5: 20 idolatry and witchcraft; hatred, *d,*

DISCOURAGED* (DISCOURAGEMENT)

Nu 32: 9 they *d* the Israelites
Dt 1: 21 Do not be afraid; do not be *d.*"
31: 8 Do not be afraid; do not be *d.*"
Jos 1: 9 Do not be terrified; do not be *d,*
8: 1 "Do not be afraid; do not be *d.*
10: 25 "Do not be afraid; do not be *d.*
1Ch 22: 13 Do not be afraid or *d.*
28: 20 or *d,* for the LORD God,
2Ch 20: 15 or *d* because of this vast army.
20: 17 Do not be afraid; do not be *d.*
32: 7 or *d* because of the king of Assyria
Job 4: 5 to you, and you are *d;*
Isa 42: 4 he will not falter or be *d*
Eph 3: 13 to be *d* because of my sufferings
Col 3: 21 children, or they will become *d.*

DISCOURAGEMENT* (DISCOURAGED)
Ex 6: 9 of their *d* and cruel bondage.

DISCOVERED
2Ki 23:24 book that Hilkiah the priest had *d*

DISCREDIT* (DISCREDITED)
Ne 6:13 would give me a bad name to *d* me.
Job 40: 8 "Would you *d* my justice?

DISCREDITED (DISCREDIT)
2Co 6: 3 so that our ministry will not be *d.*

DISCRETION*
1Ch 22:12 May the LORD give you *d*
Pr 1: 4 knowledge and *d* to the young—
2:11 *D* will protect you,
5: 2 that you may maintain *d*
8:12 I possess knowledge and *d.*
11:22 a beautiful woman who shows no *d.*

DISCRIMINATED*
Jas 2: 4 have you not *d* among yourselves

DISEASE (DISEASES)
Mt 4:23 and healing every *d* and sickness
9:35 and healing every *d* and sickness.
10: 1 and to heal every *d* and sickness.

DISEASES (DISEASE)
Ps 103: 3 and heals all my *d;*
Mt 8:17 and carried our *d.*"
Mk 3:10 those with *d* were pushing forward
Lk 9: 1 drive out all demons and to cure *d,*

DISFIGURE* (DISFIGURED)
Mt 6:16 for they *d* their faces

DISFIGURED (DISFIGURE)
Isa 52:14 his appearance was so *d*

DISGRACE (DISGRACEFUL DISGRACES)
Ps 44:15 My *d* is before me all day long,
52: 1 you who are a *d* in the eyes of God?
74:21 not let the oppressed retreat in *d;*
Pr 6:33 Blows and *d* are his lot,
11: 2 When pride comes, then comes *d,*
14:34 but sin is a *d* to any people.
19:26 is a son who brings shame and *d.*
Mt 1:19 want to expose her to public *d,*
Ac 5:41 of suffering *d* for the Name.
1Co 11: 6 and if it is a *d* for a woman
11:14 it is a *d* to him, but that
1Ti 3: 7 so that he will not fall into *d*
Heb 6: 6 and subjecting him to public *d.*
11:26 He regarded *d* for the sake
13:13 the camp, bearing the *d* he bore.

DISGRACEFUL (DISGRACE)
Pr 10: 5 during harvest is a *d* son.
12: 4 a *d* wife is like decay in his bones.
17: 2 wise servant will rule over a *d* son,
1Co 14:35 for it is *d* for a woman to speak

DISGRACES (DISGRACE)
Pr 28: 7 of gluttons *d* his father.
29:15 but a child left to himself *d* his mother

DISGUISES*
Pr 26:24 A malicious man *d* himself

DISH
Pr 19:24 sluggard buries his hand in the *d;*
Mt 23:25 the outside of the cup and *d,*

DISHONEST*
Ex 18:21 trustworthy men who hate *d* gain
Lev 19:35 " 'Do not use *d* standards
1Sa 8: 3 They turned aside after *d* gain
Pr 11: 1 The LORD abhors *d* scales,
13:11 *D* money dwindles away,
20:23 and *d* scales do not please him.
29:27 The righteous detest the *d;*
Jer 22:17 are set only on *d* gain,
Eze 28:18 By your many sins and *d* trade
Hos 12: 7 The merchant uses *d* scales;
Am 8: 5 and cheating with *d* scales,
Mic 6:11 Shall I acquit a man with *d* scales,
Lk 16: 8 master commended the *d* manager
16:10 whoever is *d* with very little will
16:10 with very little will also be *d*
1Ti 3: 8 wine, and not pursuing *d* gain.
Tit 1: 7 not violent, not pursuing *d* gain.
1:11 and that for the sake of *d* gain.

DISHONOR* (DISHONORED DISHONORS)
Lev 18: 7 " 'Do not *d* your father
18: 8 wife; that would *d* your father.
18:10 daughter; that would *d* you.
18:14 " 'Do not *d* your father's brother
18:16 that would *d* your brother.
20:19 for that would *d* a close relative;
Dt 22:30 he must not *d* his father's bed.
Pr 30: 9 and so *d* the name of my God.
Jer 14:21 do not *d* your glorious throne.
20:11 their *d* will never be forgotten.
La 2: 2 princes down to the ground in *d.*
Eze 22:10 are those who *d* their fathers' bed;
Jn 8:49 I honor my Father and you *d* me.
Ro 2:23 do you *d* God by breaking the law?
1Co 15:43 it is sown in *d,* it is raised in glory;
2Co 6: 8 through glory and *d,* bad report

DISHONORED* (DISHONOR)
Lev 20:11 father's wife, he has *d* his father.
20:17 He has *d* his sister and will be held
20:20 with his aunt, he has *d* his uncle.
20:21 of impurity; he has *d* his brother.
Dt 21:14 as a slave, since you have *d* her.
Ezr 4:14 proper for us to see the king *d,*
1Co 4:10 You are honored, we are *d!*

DISHONORS* (DISHONOR)
Dt 27:16 Cursed is the man who *d* his father
27:20 for he *d* his father's bed."
Job 20: 3 I hear a rebuke that *d* me,
Mic 7: 6 For a son *d* his father,
1Co 11: 4 with his head covered *d* his head.
11: 5 her head uncovered *d* her head—

DISILLUSIONMENT*
Ps 7:14 conceives trouble gives birth to *d.*

DISMAYED
Isa 28:16 the one who trusts will never be *d.*
41:10 do not be *d,* for I am your God.

DISOBEDIENCE* (DISOBEY)
Jos 22:22 in rebellion or *d* to the LORD,
Jer 43: 7 So they entered Egypt in *d*
Ro 5:19 as through the *d* of the one man
11:30 mercy as a result of their *d,*
11:32 to *d* so that he may have mercy
2Co 10: 6 ready to punish every act of *d,*
Heb 2: 2 and *d* received its just punishment,
4: 6 go in, because of their *d.*
4:11 fall by following their example of *d.*

DISOBEDIENT* (DISOBEY)
Ne 9:26 "But they were *d* and rebelled
Lk 1:17 and the *d* to the wisdom
Ac 26:19 I was not *d* to the vision
Ro 10:21 hands to a *d* and obstinate people."
11:30 as you who were at one time *d*
11:31 so they too have now become *d*
Eph 2: 2 now at work in those who are *d.*
5: 6 comes on those who are *d.*
5:12 to mention what the *d* do in secret.
2Ti 3: 2 proud, abusive, *d* to their parents,
Tit 1: 6 to the charge of being wild and *d.*
1:16 *d* and unfit for doing anything
3: 3 At one time we too were foolish, *d,*
Heb 11:31 killed with those who were *d.*

DISOBEY* (DISOBEDIENCE DISOBEDIENT DISOBEYED DISOBEYING DISOBEYS)
Dt 11:28 the curse if you *d* the commands
2Ch 24:20 'Why do you *d* the LORD's
Est 3: 3 Why do you *d* the king's command
Jer 42:13 and so *d* the LORD your God,
Ro 1:30 they *d* their parents; they are
1Pe 2: 8 because they *d* the message—

DISOBEYED* (DISOBEY)
Nu 14:22 and in the desert but who *d* me
27:14 both of you *d* my command
Jdg 2: 2 Yet you have *d* me.
Ne 9:29 arrogant and *d* your commands.
Isa 24: 5 they have *d* the laws,
Jer 43: 4 and all the people *d* the LORD's
Lk 15:29 for you and never *d* your orders.
Heb 3:18 rest if not to those who *d?*
1Pe 3:20 the spirits in prison who *d* long ago

DISOBEYING* (DISOBEY)
Nu 14:41 "Why are you *d* the LORD's

DISOBEYS* (DISOBEY)
Eze 33:12 man will not save him when he *d,*

DISORDER
1Co 14:33 For God is not a God of *d*
2Co 12:20 slander, gossip, arrogance and *d.*
Jas 3:16 there you find *d* and every evil

DISOWN (DISOWNS)
Pr 30: 9 I may have too much and *d* you
Mt 10:33 I will *d* him before my Father
26:35 to die with you, I will never *d* you."
2Ti 2:12 If we *d* him,

DISOWNS (DISOWN)
Lk 12: 9 he who *d* me before men will be

DISPENSATION see ADMINISTRATION, TRUST

DISPLACES
Pr 30:23 a maidservant who *d* her mistress.

DISPLAY (DISPLAYED DISPLAYS)
Ps 45: 4 your right hand *d* awesome deeds.
Eze 39:21 I will *d* my glory among the nations
Ro 9:17 that I might *d* my power in you
1Co 4: 9 on *d* at the end of the procession,
1Ti 1:16 Christ Jesus might *d* his unlimited

DISPLAYED (DISPLAY)
Jn 9: 3 work of God might be *d* in his life.
2Th 2: 9 the work of Satan *d* in all kinds

DISPLAYS (DISPLAY)
Isa 44:23 he *d* his glory in Israel.

DISPLEASE (DISPLEASED)
1Th 2:15 They *d* God and are hostile

DISPLEASED (DISPLEASE)
2Sa 11:27 David had done *d* the LORD.

DISPUTABLE* (DISPUTE)
Ro 14: 1 passing judgment on *d* matters.

DISPUTE (DISPUTABLE DISPUTES DISPUTING)
Pr 17:14 before a *d* breaks out.
1Co 6: 1 If any of you has a *d* with another,

DISPUTES (DISPUTE)
Pr 18:18 Casting the lot settles *d*

DISPUTING (DISPUTE)
1Ti 2: 8 in prayer, without anger or *d.*

DISQUALIFIED*
1Co 9:27 I myself will not be *d* for the prize.

DISREPUTE*
2Pe 2: 2 will bring the way of truth into *d.*

DISSENSION* (DISSENSIONS)
Pr 6:14 he always stirs up *d.*
6:19 and a man who stirs up *d*
10:12 Hatred stirs up *d,*
15:18 A hot-tempered man stirs up *d,*
16:28 A perverse man stirs up *d,*
28:25 A greedy man stirs up *d,*
29:22 An angry man stirs up *d,*
Ro 13:13 debauchery, not in *d* and jealousy.

DISSENSIONS* (DISSENSION)
Gal 5:20 selfish ambition, *d,* factions

DISSIPATION*
Lk 21:34 will be weighed down with *d,*
1Pe 4: 4 with them into the same flood of *d,*

DISTINCTION
Ac 15: 9 He made no *d* between us

DISTINGUISH (DISTINGUISHING)
1Ki 3: 9 and to *d* between right and wrong.
Heb 5:14 themselves to *d* good from evil.

DISTINGUISHING
1Co 12:10 the *d* between spirits,

DISTORT
Ac 20:30 and *d* the truth in order
2Co 4: 2 nor do we *d* the word of God.
2Pe 3:16 ignorant and unstable people *d,*

DISTRACTED*
Lk 10:40 But Martha was *d* by all

DISTRESS (DISTRESSED)
2Ch 15: 4 in their *d* they turned to the LORD
Ps 18: 6 In my *d* I called to the LORD;
81: 7 In your *d* you called and I rescued
120: 1 I call on the LORD in my *d,*
Jnh 2: 2 "In my *d* I called to the LORD,
Mt 24:21 For then there will be great *d,*
Jas 1:27 after orphans and widows in their *d*

DISTRESSED (DISTRESS)
Lk 12:50 how *d* I am until it is completed!
Ro 14:15 If your brother is *d*

DIVIDE (DIVIDED DIVIDING DIVISION DIVISIONS DIVISIVE)
Ps 22:18 They *d* my garments among them

DIVIDED (DIVIDE)
Mt 12:25 household *d* against itself will not
Lk 23:34 they *d* up his clothes by casting lots
1Co 1:13 Is Christ *d?* Was Paul crucified

DIVIDING (DIVIDE)
Eph 2:14 destroyed the barrier, the *d* wall
Heb 4:12 it penetrates even to *d* soul

DIVINATION
Lev 19:26 " 'Do not practice *d* or sorcery.

DIVINE
Ro 1:20 his eternal power and *d* nature—
2Co 10: 4 they have *d* power
2Pe 1: 4 you may participate in the *d* nature

DIVISION (DIVIDE)
Lk 12:51 on earth? No, I tell you, but *d.*
1Co 12:25 so that there should be no *d*

DIVISIONS (DIVIDE)
Ro 16:17 to watch out for those who cause *d*
1Co 1:10 another so that there may be no *d*
11:18 there are *d* among you,

DIVISIVE* (DIVIDE)
Tit 3:10 Warn a *d* person once,

DIVORCE* (DIVORCED DIVORCES)
Dt 22:19 he must not *d* her as long as he lives
22:29 He can never *d* her as long
24: 1 and he writes her a certificate of *d,*
24: 3 and writes her a certificate of *d,*
Isa 50: 1 is your mother's certificate of *d*
Jer 3: 8 faithless Israel her certificate of *d*
Mal 2:16 "I hate *d,*" says the LORD God
Mt 1:19 he had in mind to *d* her quietly.
5:31 must give her a certificate of *d.'*
19: 3 for a man to *d* his wife for any
19: 7 man give his wife a certificate of *d*
19: 8 permitted you to *d* your wives
Mk 10: 2 Is it lawful for a man to *d* his wife?"
10: 4 a man to write a certificate of *d*
1Co 7:11 And a husband must not *d* his wife.
7:12 to live with him, he must not *d* her.
7:13 to live with her, she must not *d* him
7:27 Are you married? Do not seek a *d.*

DIVORCED* (DIVORCE)
Lev 21: 7 or *d* from their husbands,
21:14 not marry a widow, a *d* woman,
22:13 daughter becomes a widow or is *d,*
Nu 30: 9 or *d* woman will be binding on her.
Dt 24: 4 then her first husband, who *d* her,
1Ch 8: 8 after he had *d* his wives Hushim
Eze 44:22 not marry widows or *d* women;
Mt 5:32 marries the *d* woman commits adultery.
Lk 16:18 who marries a *d* woman commits

DIVORCES* (DIVORCE)
Jer 3: 1 "If a man *d* his wife
Mt 5:31 'Anyone who *d* his wife must give
5:32 tell you that anyone who *d* his wife,
19: 9 tell you that anyone who *d* his wife,
Mk 10:11 "Anyone who *d* his wife
10:12 And if she *d* her husband
Lk 16:18 "Anyone who *d* his wife

DOCTOR
Mt 9:12 "It is not the healthy who need a *d,*

DOCTRINE* (DOCTRINES)
1Ti 1:10 to the sound *d* that conforms
4:16 Watch your life and *d* closely.
2Ti 4: 3 men will not put up with sound *d.*
Tit 1: 9 can encourage others by sound *d*
2: 1 is in accord with sound *d.*

DOCTRINES* (DOCTRINE)
1Ti 1: 3 not to teach false *d* any longer
6: 3 If anyone teaches false *d*

DOEG*
Edomite; Saul's head shepherd; responsible for murder of priests at Nob (1Sa 21:7; 22:6-23; Ps 52).

DOG (DOGS)
Pr 26:11 As a *d* returns to its vomit,
Ecc 9: 4 a live *d* is better off than a dead lion
2Pe 2:22 "A *d* returns to its vomit," and,

DOGS (DOG)
Mt 7: 6 "Do not give *d* what is sacred;
15:26 bread and toss it to their *d.*"

DOMINION
Job 25: 2 "*D* and awe belong to God;
Ps 22:28 for *d* belongs to the LORD

DONKEY
Nu 22:30 *d* said to Balaam, "Am I not your
Zec 9: 9 gentle and riding on a *d,*
Mt 21: 5 gentle and riding on a *d,*
2Pe 2:16 for his wrongdoing by a *d*—

DOOR (DOORS)
Job 31:32 for my *d* was always open
Ps 141: 3 keep watch over the *d* of my lips.
Mt 6: 6 close the *d* and pray to your Father
7: 7 and the *d* will be opened to you.
Ac 14:27 how he had opened the *d* of faith
1Co 16: 9 a great *d* for effective work has
2Co 2:12 found that the Lord had opened a *d*
Rev 3:20 I stand at the *d* and knock.

DOORFRAMES
Dt 6: 9 Write them on the *d* of your houses

DOORKEEPER
Ps 84:10 I would rather be a *d* in the house

DOORS (DOOR)
Ps 24: 7 be lifted up, you ancient *d,*

DORCAS
Ac 9:36 is *D*), who was always doing good

DOUBLE
2Ki 2: 9 "Let me inherit a *d* portion
1Ti 5:17 church well are worthy of *d* honor,

DOUBLE-EDGED (EDGE)
Heb 4:12 Sharper than any *d* sword,
Rev 1:16 of his mouth came a sharp *d* sword.
2:12 of him who has the sharp, *d* sword.

DOUBLE-MINDED* (MIND)
Ps 119:113 I hate *d* men,
Jas 1: 8 he is a *d* man, unstable
4: 8 and purify your hearts, you *d.*

DOUBT (DOUBTING DOUBTS)
Mt 14:31 he said, "why did you *d?*"
21:21 if you have faith and do not *d,*
Mk 11:23 and does not *d* in his heart
Jas 1: 6 he must believe and not *d,*
Jude :22 Be merciful to those who *d;*

DOUBTING* (DOUBT)
Jn 20:27 Stop *d* and believe."

DOUBTS* (DOUBT)
Lk 24:38 and why do *d* rise in your minds?
Ro 14:23 the man who has *d* is condemned
Jas 1: 6 he who *d* is like a wave of the sea,

DOVE (DOVES)
Ge 8: 8 Then he sent out a *d* to see
Mt 3:16 Spirit of God descending like a *d*

DOVES (DOVE)
Lev 12: 8 is to bring two *d* or two young
Mt 10:16 as snakes and as innocent as *d.*
Lk 2:24 "a pair of *d* or two young pigeons."

DOWNCAST
Ps 42: 5 Why are you *d,* O my soul?
2Co 7: 6 But God, who comforts the *d,*

DOWNFALL
Hos 14: 1 Your sins have been your *d!*

DRAGON
Rev 12: 7 and his angels fought against the *d,*
13: 2 The *d* gave the beast his power
20: 2 He seized the *d,* that ancient

DRAW (DRAWING DRAWS)
Mt 26:52 "for all who *d* the sword will die
Jn 12:32 up from the earth, will *d* all men
Heb 10:22 let us *d* near to God

DRAWING (DRAW)
Lk 21:28 because your redemption is *d* near

DRAWS (DRAW)
Jn 6:44 the Father who sent me *d* him,

DREAD (DREADFUL)
Ps 53: 5 they were, overwhelmed with *d,*

DREADFUL (DREAD)
Mt 24:19 How *d* it will be in those days
Heb 10:31 It is a *d* thing to fall into the hands

DREAM
Joel 2:28 your old men will *d* dreams,
Ac 2:17 your old men will *d* dreams.

DRESS
1Ti 2: 9 I also want women to *d* modestly,

DRIFT*
Heb 2: 1 so that we do not *d* away.

DRINK (DRINKING DRINKS DRUNK DRUNKARD DRUNKARD'S DRUNKARDS DRUNKENNESS)
Ex 29:40 of a hin of wine as a *d* offering.
Nu 6: 3 He must not *d* grape juice
Jdg 7: 5 from those who kneel down to *d.*"
2Sa 23:15 that someone would get me a *d*
Pr 5:15 *D* water from your own cistern,
Mt 20:22 "Can you *d* the cup I am going to *d*
26:27 saying, "*D* from it, all of you.
Mk 16:18 and when they *d* deadly poison,
Lk 12:19 Take life easy; eat, *d* and be merry
Jn 7:37 let him come to me and *d.*
18:11 Shall I not *d* the cup the Father has
1Co 10: 4 and drank the same spiritual *d;*
12:13 were all given the one Spirit to *d.*
Php 2:17 being poured out like a *d* offering
2Ti 4: 6 being poured out like a *d* offering,
Rev 14:10 too, will *d* of the wine of God's fury
21: 6 to *d* without cost from the spring

DRINKING (DRINK)
Ro 14:17 God is not a matter of eating and *d,*

DRINKS (DRINK)
Isa 5:22 and champions at mixing *d,*
Jn 4:13 "Everyone who *d* this water will be
6:54 and *d* my blood has eternal life,
1Co 11:27 or *d* the cup of the Lord

DRIPPING
Pr 19:13 wife is like a constant *d.*
27:15 a constant *d* on a rainy day;

DRIVE (DRIVES)
Ex 23:30 Little by little I will *d* them out
Nu 33:52 *d* out all the inhabitants of the land
Jos 13:13 Israelites did not *d* out the people
23:13 will no longer *d* out these nations
Pr 22:10 *D* out the mocker, and out goes
Mt 10: 1 authority to *d* out evil spirits
Jn 6:37 comes to me I will never *d* away.

DRIVES (DRIVE)
Mt 12:26 If Satan *d* out Satan, he is divided
1Jn 4:18 But perfect love *d* out fear,

DROP (DROPS)
Pr 17:14 so *d* the matter before a dispute
Isa 40:15 Surely the nations are like a *d*

DROPS (DROP)
Lk 22:44 his sweat was like *d* of blood falling

DROSS
Ps 119:119 of the earth you discard like *d;*
Pr 25: 4 Remove the *d* from the silver,

DROUGHT

Jer 17: 8 It has no worries in a year of *d*

DROWNED

Ex 15: 4 are *d* in the Red Sea.
Mt 18: 6 and to be *d* in the depths of the sea.
Heb 11:29 tried to do so, they were *d*.

DROWSINESS*

Pr 23:21 and *d* clothes them in rags.

DRUNK (DRINK)

1Sa 1:13 Eli thought she was *d* and said
Ac 2:15 men are not *d*, as you suppose.
Eph 5:18 Do not get *d* on wine, which leads

DRUNKARD (DRINK)

Mt 11:19 and a *d*, a friend of tax collectors
1Co 5:11 or a slanderer, a *d* or a swindler.

DRUNKARD'S* (DRINK)

Pr 26: 9 Like a thornbush in a *d* hand

DRUNKARDS (DRINK)

Pr 23:21 for *d* and gluttons become poor,
1Co 6:10 nor the greedy nor *d* nor slanderers

DRUNKENNESS (DRINK)

Lk 21:34 weighed down with dissipation, *d*
Ro 13:13 and *d*, not in sexual immorality
Gal 5:21 factions and envy; *d*, orgies,
1Ti 3: 3 not given to *d*, not violent
1Pe 4: 3 living in debauchery, lust, *d*, orgies,

DRY

Ge 1: 9 place, and let *d* ground appear."
Ex 14:16 go through the sea on *d* ground.
Jos 3:17 the crossing on *d* ground.
Isa 53: 2 and like a root out of *d* ground.
Eze 37: 4 '*D* bones, hear the word

DULL

Isa 6:10 make their ears *d*
2Co 3:14 But their minds were made *d*,

DUST

Ge 2: 7 man from the *d* of the ground
3:19 for *d* you are
Job 42: 6 and repent in *d* and ashes."
Ps 22:15 you lay me in the *d* of death.
103:14 he remembers that we are *d*.
Ecc 3:20 all come from *d*, and to *d* all return.
Mt 10:14 shake the *d* off your feet
1Co 15:47 was of the *d* of the earth,

DUTIES (DUTY)

2Ti 4: 5 discharge all the *d* of your ministry

DUTY (DUTIES)

Ecc 12:13 for this is the whole *d* of man.
Ac 23: 1 I have fulfilled my *d* to God
1Co 7: 3 husband should fulfill his marital *d*

DWELL (DWELLING DWELLINGS DWELLS DWELT)

Ex 25: 8 for me, and I will *d* among them.
2Sa 7: 5 the one to build me a house to *d* in?
1Ki 8:27 "But will God really *d* on earth?
Ps 23: 6 I will *d* in the house of the LORD
37: 3 *d* in the land and enjoy safe pasture
61: 4 I long to *d* in your tent forever
Pr 8:12 wisdom, *d* together with prudence;
Isa 33:14 of us can *d* with the consuming fire
43:18 do not *d* on the past.
Jn 5:38 nor does his word *d* in you,
Eph 3:17 so that Christ may *d* in your hearts
Col 1:19 to have all his fullness *d* in him,
3:16 the word of Christ *d* in you richly

DWELLING (DWELL)

Lev 26:11 I will put my *d* place among you,
Dt 26:15 from heaven, your holy *d* place,
Ps 90: 1 Lord, you have been our *d* place
2Co 5: 2 to be clothed with our heavenly *d*,
Eph 2:22 to become a *d* in which God lives

DWELLINGS (DWELL)

Lk 16: 9 will be welcomed into eternal *d*.

DWELLS (DWELL)

Ps 46: 4 holy place where the Most High *d*.
91: 1 He who *d* in the shelter

DWELT (DWELL)

Dt 33:16 of him who *d* in the burning bush.

DYING (DIE)

Ro 7: 6 by *d* to what once bound us,
2Co 6: 9 yet regarded as unknown; *d*,

EAGER

Pr 31:13 and works with *e* hands.
Ro 8:19 The creation waits in *e* expectation
1Co 14:12 Since you are *e* to have spiritual
14:39 my brothers, be *e* to prophesy,
Tit 2:14 a people that are his very own, *e*
1Pe 5: 2 greedy for money, but *e* to serve;

EAGLE (EAGLE'S EAGLES)

Dt 32:11 like an *e* that stirs up its nest
Eze 1:10 each also had the face of an *e*.
Rev 4: 7 the fourth was like a flying *e*.
12:14 given the two wings of a great *e*,

EAGLE'S (EAGLE)

Ps 103: 5 your youth is renewed like the *e*.

EAGLES (EAGLE)

Isa 40:31 They will soar on wings like *e*;

EAR (EARS)

Ex 21: 6 and pierce his *e* with an awl.
Ps 5: 1 Give *e* to my words, O LORD,
Pr 2: 2 turning your *e* to wisdom
1Co 2: 9 no *e* has heard,
12:16 if the *e* should say, "Because I am
Rev 2: 7 He who has an *e*, let him hear what

EARN (EARNED EARNINGS)

2Th 3:12 down and *e* the bread they eat.

EARNED (EARN)

Pr 31:31 Give her the reward she has *e*,

EARNEST see DEPOSIT

EARNESTNESS

2Co 7:11 what *e*, what eagerness
8: 7 in complete *e* and in your love

EARNINGS (EARN)

Pr 31:16 out of her *e* she plants a vineyard.

EARRING (EARRINGS)

Pr 25:12 Like an *e* of gold or an ornament

EARRINGS (EARRING)

Ex 32: 2 Take off the gold *e* that your wives,

EARS (EAR)

Job 42: 5 My *e* had heard of you
Ps 34:15 and his *e* are attentive to their cry;
Pr 21:13 If a man shuts his *e* to the cry
26:17 Like one who seizes a dog by the *e*
Isa 6:10 hear with their *e*,
Mt 11:15 He who has *e*, let him hear.
2Ti 4: 3 to say what their itching *e* want
1Pe 3:12 his *e* are attentive to their prayer,

EARTH (EARTH'S EARTHLY)

Ge 1: 1 God created the heavens and the *e*.
1: 2 Now the *e* was formless and empty,
7:24 The waters flooded the *e*
14:19 Creator of heaven and *e*.
1Ki 8:27 "But will God really dwell on *e*?
Job 26: 7 he suspends the *e* over nothing.
Ps 24: 1 *e* is the LORD's, and everything
46: 6 he lifts his voice, the *e* melts.
90: 2 or you brought forth the *e*
97: 5 before the Lord of all the *e*.
102:25 you laid the foundations of the *e*,
108: 5 and let your glory be over all the *e*.
Pr 8:26 before he made the *e* or its fields
Isa 6: 3 the whole *e* is full of his glory."
24:20 The *e* reels like a drunkard,
37:16 You have made heaven and *e*.
40:22 enthroned above the circle of the *e*,
51: 6 the *e* will wear out like a garment
54: 5 he is called the God of all the *e*.
55: 9 the heavens are higher than the *e*,
65:17 new heavens and a new *e*.
66: 1 and the *e* is my footstool.
Jer 10:10 When he is angry, the *e* trembles;
23:24 "Do not I fill heaven and *e*?"
33:25 and the fixed laws of heaven and *e*,
Hab 2:20 let all the *e* be silent before him."
Mt 5: 5 for they will inherit the *e*.
5:35 or by the *e*, for it is his footstool;
6:10 done on *e* as it is in heaven.
16:19 bind on *e* will be bound
24:35 Heaven and *e* will pass away,
28:18 and on *e* has been given to me.
Lk 2:14 on *e* peace to men
Jn 12:32 when I am lifted up from the *e*,
Ac 4:24 "you made the heaven and the *e*
7:49 and the *e* is my footstool.
1Co 10:26 The *e* is the Lord's, and everything
Eph 3:15 in heaven and on *e* derives its name
Php 2:10 in heaven and on *e* and under the *e*,
Heb 1:10 you laid the foundations of the *e*,
2Pe 3:13 to a new heaven and a new *e*,
Rev 8: 7 A third of the *e* was burned up,
12:12 But woe to the *e* and the sea,
20:11 *E* and sky fled from his presence,
21: 1 I saw a new heaven and a new *e*,
21: 1 and the first *e* had passed away,

EARTH'S (EARTH)

Job 38: 4 when I laid the *e* foundation?

EARTHENWARE

Pr 26:23 Like a coating of glaze over *e*

EARTHLY (EARTH)

Eph 4: 9 descended to the lower, *e* regions?
Php 3:19 Their mind is on *e* things.
Col 3: 2 on things above, not on *e* things.
3: 5 whatever belongs to your *e* nature:

EARTHQUAKE (EARTHQUAKES)

Eze 38:19 at that time there shall be a great *e*
Mt 28: 2 There was a violent *e*, for an angel
Rev 6:12 There was a great *e*.

EARTHQUAKES (EARTHQUAKE)

Mt 24: 7 There will be famines and *e*

EASE

Pr 1:33 and be at *e*, without fear of harm."

EASIER (EASY)

Lk 16:17 It is *e* for heaven and earth
18:25 it is *e* for a camel to go

EAST

Ge 2: 8 God had planted a garden in the *e*,
Ps 103:12 as far as the *e* is from the west,
Eze 43: 2 God of Israel coming from the *e*.
Mt 2: 1 Magi from the *e* came to Jerusalem
2: 2 We saw his star in the *e*

EASY (EASIER)

Mt 11:30 For my yoke is *e* and my burden is

EAT (ATE EATEN EATER EATING EATS)

Ge 2:16 "You are free to *e* from any tree
2:17 but you must not *e* from the tree
3:19 you will *e* your food
Ex 12:11 *E* it in haste; it is the LORD's
Lev 11: 2 these are the ones you may *e*:
17:12 "None of you may *e* blood,
Dt 8:16 He gave you manna to *e*
14: 4 These are the animals you may *e*:
Jdg 14:14 "Out of the eater, something to *e*;
2Sa 9: 7 and you will always *e* at my table."
Pr 31:27 and does not *e* the bread of idleness
Isa 55: 1 come, buy and *e*!
65:25 and the lion will *e* straw like the ox,
Eze 3: 1 *e* what is before you, *e* this scroll;
Mt 14:16 You give them something to *e*."
15: 2 wash their hands before they *e*!"
26:26 "Take and *e*; this is my body."
Mk 14:14 where I may *e* the Passover
Lk 10: 8 and are welcomed, *e* what is set
12:19 Take life easy; *e*, drink
12:22 what you will *e*; or about your body
Jn 4:32 to *e* that you know nothing about."
6:31 bread from heaven to *e*.' "
6:52 can this man give us his flesh to *e*?"
Ac 10:13 Kill and *e*."
Ro 14: 2 faith allows him to *e* everything,
14:15 is distressed because of what you *e*,
14:20 to *e* anything that causes someone
14:21 It is better not to *e* meat
1Co 5:11 With such a man do not even *e*.
8:13 if what I *e* causes my brother to fall
10:25 *E* anything sold in the meat market
10:27 *e* whatever is put before you
10:31 So whether you *e* or drink
11:26 For whenever you *e* this bread
2Th 3:10 man will not work, he shall not *e*."
Rev 2: 7 the right to *e* from the tree of life,
3:20 I will come in and *e* with him,

EATEN (EAT)

Ge 3: 11 Have you *e* from the tree that I
Ac 10: 14 "I have never *e* anything impure
Rev 10: 10 when I had *e* it, my stomach turned

EATER (EAT)

Isa 55: 10 for the sower and bread for the *e*,

EATING (EAT)

Ex 34: 28 and forty nights without *e* bread
Ro 14: 15 not by your *e* destroy your brother
14: 17 kingdom of God is not a matter of *e*
14: 23 because his *e* is not from faith;
1Co 8: 4 about *e* food sacrificed to idols:
8: 10 you who have this knowledge *e*
Jude : 12 *e* with you without the slightest

EATS (EAT)

1Sa 14: 24 "Cursed be any man who *e* food
Lk 15: 2 "This man welcomes sinners and *e*
Jn 6: 51 If anyone *e* of this bread, he will live
6: 54 Whoever *e* my flesh and drinks my
Ro 14: 2 faith is weak, *e* only vegetables.
14: 3 man who *e* everything must not
14: 6 He who *e* meat, *e* to the Lord,
14: 23 has doubts is condemned if he *e*,
1Co 11: 27 whoever *e* the bread or drinks

EBAL

Dt 11: 29 and on Mount *E* the curses.
Jos 8: 30 Joshua built on Mount *E* an altar

EBENEZER

1Sa 7: 12 He named it *E*, saying, "Thus far

EDEN

Ge 2: 8 in *E*; and there he put the man
Eze 28: 13 You were in *E*,

EDGE (DOUBLE-EDGED)

Mt 9: 20 and touched the *e* of his cloak.

EDICT

Heb 11: 23 they were not afraid of the king's *e*.

EDIFICATION (EDIFIED EDIFIES)

Ro 14: 19 leads to peace and to mutual *e*.

EDIFIED* (EDIFICATION)

1Co 14: 5 so that the church may be *e*.
14: 17 but the other man is not *e*.

EDIFIES* (EDIFICATION)

1Co 14: 4 but he who prophesies *e* the church
14: 4 speaks in a tongue *e* himself,

EDOM

Ge 36: 1 the account of Esau (that is, *E*).
36: 8 *E*) settled in the hill country of Seir
Isa 63: 1 Who is this coming from *E*,
Ob : 1 Sovereign LORD says about *E*—

EDUCATED*

Ac 7: 22 Moses was *e* in all the wisdom

EFFECT* (EFFECTIVE)

Job 41: 26 sword that reaches him has no *e*,
Isa 32: 17 *e* of righteousness will be quietness
Ac 7: 53 put into *e* through angels
1Co 15: 10 his grace to me was not without *e*.
Gal 3: 19 put into *e* through angels
Eph 1: 10 put into *e* when the times will have
Heb 9: 17 it never takes *e* while the one who
9: 18 put into *e* without blood.

EFFECTIVE* (EFFECT)

1Co 16: 9 a great door for *e* work has opened
Jas 5: 16 a righteous man is powerful and *e*.

EFFORT*

Ecc 2: 19 into which I have poured my *e*
Da 6: 14 and made every *e* until sundown
Lk 13: 24 "Make every *e* to enter
Jn 5: 44 yet make no *e* to obtain the praise
Ro 9: 16 depend on man's desire or *e*,
14: 19 make every *e* to do what leads
Gal 3: 3 to attain your goal by human *e*?
Eph 4: 3 Make every *e* to keep the unity
1Th 2: 16 to all men in their *e* to keep us
2: 17 intense longing we made every *e*
Heb 4: 11 make every *e* to enter that rest,
12: 14 Make every *e* to live in peace
2Pe 1: 5 make every *e* to add
1: 15 And I will make every *e* to see that
3: 14 make every *e* to be found spotless,

EGG

Lk 11: 12 for an *e*, will give him a scorpion?

EGLON

1. Fat king of Moab killed by Ehud (Jdg 3: 12-30).
2. City in Canaan (Jos 10).

EGYPT (EGYPTIANS)

Ge 12: 10 went down to *E* to live there
37: 28 Ishmaelites, who took him to *E*.
42: 3 went down to buy grain from *E*.
45: 20 the best of all *E* will be yours.' "
46: 6 and all his offspring went to *E*.
47: 27 Now the Israelites settled in *E*
Ex 3: 11 and bring the Israelites out of *E*?"
12: 40 lived in *E* was 430 years.
12: 41 all the LORD's divisions left *E*.
32: 1 Moses who brought us up out of *E*,
Nu 11: 18 We were better off in *E*!"
14: 4 choose a leader and go back to *E*."
24: 8 "God brought them out of *E*;
Dt 6: 21 "We were slaves of Pharaoh in *E*,
1Ki 4: 30 greater than all the wisdom of *E*.
10: 28 horses were imported from *E*
11: 40 but Jeroboam fled to *E*,
14: 25 king of *E* attacked Jerusalem.
2Ch 35: 20 Neco king of *E* went up to fight
36: 3 The king of *E* dethroned him
Isa 19: 23 a highway from *E* to Assyria.
Hos 11: 1 and out of *E* I called my son.
Mt 2: 15 "Out of *E* I called my son."
Heb 11: 27 By faith he left *E*, not fearing
Rev 11: 8 is figuratively called Sodom and *E*,

EGYPTIANS (EGYPT)

Nu 14: 13 "Then the *E* will hear about it!

EHUD

Left-handed judge who delivered Israel from Moabite king, Eglon (Jdg 3:12-30).

EKRON

1Sa 5: 10 So they sent the ark of God to *E*.

ELAH

Son of Baasha; king of Israel (1Ki 16:6-14).

ELATION

Pr 28: 12 righteous triumph, there is great *e*;

ELDER* (ELDERLY ELDERS)

Isa 3: 2 the soothsayer and *e*,
1Ti 5: 19 an accusation against an *e*
Tit 1: 6 *e* must be blameless, the husband
1Pe 5: 1 among you, I appeal as a fellow *e*,
2Jn : 1 The *e*, To the chosen lady
3Jn : 1 The *e*, To my dear friend Gaius,

ELDERLY* (ELDER)

Lev 19: 32 show respect for the *e*

ELDERS (ELDER)

1Ki 12: 8 rejected the advice the *e* gave him
Mt 15: 2 break the tradition of the *e*?
Mk 7: 3 holding to the tradition of the *e*.
7: 5 to the tradition of the *e* instead
Ac 11: 30 gift to the *e* by Barnabas
14: 23 and Barnabas appointed *e* for them
15: 2 the apostles and *e* about this
15: 4 the church and the apostles and *e*,
15: 6 and *e* met to consider this question.
15: 22 and *e*, with the whole church,
15: 23 The apostles and *e*, your brothers,
16: 4 and *e* in Jerusalem for the people
20: 17 to Ephesus for the *e* of the church.
21: 18 and all the *e* were present.
23: 14 They went to the chief priests and *e*
24: 1 to Caesarea with some of the *e*
1Ti 4: 14 when the body of *e* laid their hands
5: 17 The *e* who direct the affairs
Tit 1: 5 and appoint *e* in every town,
Jas 5: 14 He should call the *e* of the church
1Pe 5: 1 To the *e* among you, I appeal
Rev 4: 4 seated on them were twenty-four *e*.
4: 10 the twenty-four *e* fall

ELEAZAR

Third son of Aaron (Ex 6:23-25). Succeeded Aaron as high priest (Nu 20:26; Dt 10:6). Allotted land to tribes (Jos 14:1). Death (Jos 24:33).

ELECT* (ELECTION)

Mt 24: 22 the sake of the *e* those days will be
24: 24 miracles to deceive even the *e*—
24: 31 and they will gather his *e*
Mk 13: 20 sake of the *e*, whom he has chosen,
13: 22 and miracles to deceive the *e*—
13: 27 gather his *e* from the four winds,
Ro 11: 7 it did not obtain, but the *e* did.
1Ti 5: 21 and Christ Jesus and the *e* angels,
2Ti 2: 10 everything for the sake of the *e*,
Tit 1: 1 Christ for the faith of God's *e*
1Pe 1: 1 To God's *e*, strangers in the world,

ELECTION* (ELECT)

Ro 9: 11 God's purpose in *e* might stand:
11: 28 but as far as *e* is concerned,
2Pe 1: 10 to make your calling and *e* sure.

ELEMENTARY* (ELEMENTS)

Heb 5: 12 someone to teach you the *e* truths
6: 1 us leave the *e* teachings about

ELEMENTS* (ELEMENTARY)

2Pe 3: 10 the *e* will be destroyed by fire,
3: 12 and the *e* will melt in the heat.

ELEVATE*

2Co 11: 7 to *e* you by preaching the gospel

ELI

High priest in youth of Samuel (1Sa 1-4). Blessed Hannah (1Sa 1:12-18); raised Samuel (1Sa 2:11-26). Prophesied against because of wicked sons (1Sa 2:27-36). Death of Eli and sons (1Sa 4:11-22).

ELIHU

One of Job's friends (Job 32-37).

ELIJAH

Prophet; predicted famine in Israel (1Ki 17:1; Jas 5:17). Fed by ravens (1Ki 17:2-6). Raised Sidonian widow's son (1Ki 17:7-24). Defeated prophets of Baal at Carmel (1Ki 18:16-46). Ran from Jezebel (1Ki 19:1-9). Prophesied death of Azariah (2Ki 1). Succeeded by Elishah (1Ki 19: 19-21; 2Ki 2:1-18). Taken to heaven in whirlwind (2Ki 2:11-12).

Return prophesied (Mal 4:5-6); equated with John the Baptist (Mt 17:9-13; Mk 9:9-13; Lk 1: 17). Appeared with Moses in transfiguration of Jesus (Mt 17:1-8; Mk 9:1-8).

ELIMELECH

Ru 1: 3 Now *E*, Naomi's husband, died,

ELIPHAZ

1. Firstborn of Esau (Ge 36).
2. One of Job's friends (Job 4-5; 15; 22).

ELISHA

Prophet; successor of Elijah (1Ki 19:16-21); inherited his cloak (2Ki 2:1-18). Purified bad water (2Ki 2:19-22). Cursed young men (2Ki 2: 23-25). Aided Israel's defeat of Moab (2Ki 3). Provided widow with oil (2Ki 4:1-7). Raised Shunammite woman's son (2Ki 4:8-37). Purified food (2Ki 4:38-41). Fed 100 men (2Ki 4:42-44). Healed Naaman's leprosy (2Ki 5). Made axhead float (2Ki 6:1-7). Captured Arameans (2Ki 6:8-23). Political adviser to Israel (2Ki 6:24-8:6; 9: 1-3; 13:14-19), Damascus (2Ki 8:7-15). Death (2Ki 13:20).

ELIZABETH*

Mother of John the Baptist, relative of Mary (Lk 1:5-58).

ELKANAH

Husband of Hannah, father of Samuel (1Sa 1-2).

ELOI*

Mt 27: 46 "*E, E, lama sabachthani?*"—
Mk 15: 34 "*E, E, lama sabachthani?*"—

ELOQUENCE* (ELOQUENT)

1Co 2: 1 come with *e* or superior wisdom

ELOQUENT* (ELOQUENCE)

Ex 4: 10 "O Lord, I have never been *e*,

ELYMAS

Ac 13: 8 *E* the sorcerer (for that is what his

EMBEDDED*
Ecc 12:11 sayings like firmly *e* nails—

EMBERS
Pr 26:21 As charcoal to *e* and as wood to fire

EMBITTER* (BITTER)
Col 3:21 Fathers, do not *e* your children,

EMBODIMENT* (BODY)
Ro 2:20 have in the law the *e* of knowledge

EMPTIED (EMPTY)
1Co 1:17 the cross of Christ be *e* of its power.

EMPTY (EMPTIED)
Ge 1: 2 Now the earth was formless and *e*,
Job 26: 7 the northern skies over *e* space;
Isa 45:18 he did not create it to be *e*,
55:11 It will not return to me *e*,
Jer 4:23 and it was formless and *e*;
Lk 1:53 but has sent the rich away *e*.
Eph 5: 6 no one deceive you with *e* words,
1Pe 1:18 from the *e* way of life handed
2Pe 2:18 For they mouth *e*, boastful words

ENABLE (ABLE)
Lk 1:74 to *e* us to serve him without fear
Ac 4:29 *e* your servants to speak your word

ENABLED* (ABLE)
Lev 26:13 *e* you to walk with heads held high.
Ru 4:13 And the LORD *e* her to conceive,
Jn 6:65 unless the Father has *e* him."
Ac 2: 4 other tongues as the Spirit *e* them.
7:10 and *e* him to gain the goodwill
Heb 11:11 was *e* to become a father

ENABLES (ABLE)
Php 3:21 by the power that *e* him

ENABLING* (ABLE)
Ac 14: 3 the message of his grace by *e* them

ENCAMPS* (CAMP)
Ps 34: 7 The angel of the LORD *e*

ENCOURAGE* (ENCOURAGED ENCOURAGEMENT ENCOURAGES ENCOURAGING)
Dt 1:38 *E* him, because he will lead Israel
3:28 and *e* and strengthen him,
2Sa 11:25 Say this to *e* Joab."
19: 7 Now go out and *e* your men.
Job 16: 5 But my mouth would *e* you;
Ps 10:17 you *e* them, and you listen
64: 5 They *e* each other in evil plans,
Isa 1:17 *e* the oppressed.
Jer 29: 8 to the dreams you *e* them to have.
Ac 15:32 to *e* and strengthen the brothers.
Ro 12: 8 if it is encouraging, let him *e*;
Eph 6:22 how we are, and that he may *e* you.
Col 4: 8 and that he may *e* your hearts.
1Th 3: 2 to strengthen and *e* you
4:18 Therefore *e* each other
5:11 Therefore *e* one another
5:14 those who are idle, *e* the timid,
2Th 2:17 *e* your hearts and strengthen you
2Ti 4: 2 rebuke and *e*—with great patience
Tit 1: 9 so that he can *e* others
2: 6 *e* the young men to be
2:15 *E* and rebuke with all authority.
Heb 3:13 But *e* one another daily, as long
10:25 but let us *e* one another—

ENCOURAGED* (ENCOURAGE)
Jdg 7:11 you will be *e* to attack the camp."
20:22 But the men of Israel *e* one another
2Ch 22: 3 for his mother *e* him
32: 6 and *e* them with these words:
35: 2 and *e* them in the service
Eze 13:22 you *e* the wicked not to turn
Ac 9:31 It was strengthened; and *e*
11:23 and *e* them all to remain true
16:40 met with the brothers and *e* them.
18:27 the brothers *e* him and wrote
27:36 They were all *e* and ate some food
28:15 men Paul thanked God and was *e*.
Ro 1:12 and I may be mutually *e*
1Co 14:31 everyone may be instructed and *e*.
2Co 7: 4 I am greatly *e*; in all our troubles
7:13 By all this we are *e*.
Php 1:14 brothers in the Lord have been *e*
Col 2: 2 My purpose is that they may be *e*
1Th 3: 7 persecution we were *e* about you
Heb 6:18 offered to us may be greatly *e*.

ENCOURAGEMENT* (ENCOURAGE)
Ac 4:36 Barnabas (which means Son of *E*),
13:15 a message of *e* for the people,
20: 2 speaking many words of *e*
Ro 15: 4 *e* of the Scriptures we might have
15: 5 and *e* give you a spirit of unity
1Co 14: 3 to men for their strengthening, *e*
2Co 7:13 to our own *e*, we were especially
Php 2: 1 If you have any *e* from being united
2Th 2:16 and by his grace gave us eternal *e*
Phm : 7 love has given me great joy and *e*,
Heb 12: 5 word of *e* that addresses you

ENCOURAGES* (ENCOURAGE)
Isa 41: 7 The craftsman *e* the goldsmith,

ENCOURAGING* (ENCOURAGE)
Ac 14:22 *e* them to remain true to the faith.
15:31 and were glad for its *e* message.
20: 1 for the disciples and, after *e* them,
Ro 12: 8 if it is *e*, let him encourage;
1Th 2:12 *e*, comforting and urging you
1Pe 5:12 *e* you and testifying that this is

ENCROACH
Pr 23:10 or *e* on the fields of the fatherless,

END (ENDS)
Ps 119:33 then I will keep them to the *e*.
119:112 to the very *e*.
Pr 1:19 Such is the *e* of all who go
5: 4 but in the *e* she is bitter as gall,
5:11 At the *e* of your life you will groan,
14:12 but in the *e* it leads to death.
14:13 and joy may *e* in grief.
16:25 but in the *e* it leads to death.
19:20 and in the *e* you will be wise.
20:21 will not be blessed at the *e*.
23:32 In the *e* it bites like a snake
25: 8 for what will you do in the *e*
28:23 in the *e* gain more favor
29:21 he will bring grief in the *e*.
Ecc 3:11 done from beginning to *e*.
7: 8 The *e* of a matter is better
12:12 making many books there is no *e*,
Eze 7: 2 The *e*! The *e* has come
Mt 10:22 firm to the *e* will be saved.
24:13 firm to the *e* will be saved.
24:14 nations, and then the *e* will come.
Lk 21: 9 but the *e* will not come right away
Ro 10: 4 Christ is the *e* of the law
1Co 15:24 the *e* will come, when he hands
Rev 21: 6 Omega, the Beginning and the *E*.
22:13 the Last, the Beginning and the *E*.

ENDS (END)
Ps 19: 4 their words to the *e* of the world.
Pr 20:17 he *e* up with a mouth full of gravel.
Isa 49: 6 salvation to the *e* of the earth."
62:11 proclamation to the *e* of the earth:
Ac 13:47 salvation to the *e* of the earth.' "
Ro 10:18 their words to the *e* of the world."

ENDURANCE* (ENDURE)
Ro 15: 4 through *e* and the encouragement
15: 5 May the God who gives *e*
2Co 1: 6 which produces in you patient *e*
6: 4 in great *e*; in troubles, hardships
Col 1:11 might so that you may have great *e*
1Th 1: 3 and your *e* inspired by hope
1Ti 6:11 faith, love, *e* and gentleness.
2Ti 3:10 patience, love, *e*, persecutions,
Tit 2: 2 and sound in faith, in love and in *e*.
Rev 1: 9 and patient *e* that are ours in Jesus,
13:10 This calls for patient *e*
14:12 This calls for patient *e* on the part

ENDURE (ENDURANCE ENDURED ENDURES ENDURING)
Ps 72:17 May his name *e* forever;
Pr 12:19 Truthful lips *e* forever,
27:24 for riches do not *e* forever,
Ecc 3:14 everything God does will *e* forever;
Da 2:44 to an end, but it will itself *e* forever.
Mal 3: 2 who can *e* the day of his coming?
1Co 4:12 when we are persecuted, we *e* it;
2Co 1: 8 far beyond our ability to *e*,
2Ti 2: 3 *E* hardship with us like a good
2:10 Therefore I *e* everything
2:12 if we *e*, / we will also reign
4: 5 head in all situations, *e* hardship,
Heb 12: 7 *E* hardship as discipline; God is
1Pe 2:20 a beating for doing wrong and *e* it?
2:20 suffer for doing good and you *e* it,
Rev 3:10 kept my command to *e* patiently,

ENDURED* (ENDURE)
Ps 123: 3 for we have *e* much contempt.
123: 4 We have *e* much ridicule
132: 1 and all the hardships he *e*.
Ac 13:18 and *e* their conduct forty years
2Ti 3:11 and Lystra, the persecutions I *e*.
Heb 12: 2 set before him *e* the cross,
12: 3 him who *e* such opposition
Rev 2: 3 and have *e* hardships for my name,

ENDURES (ENDURE)
Ps 102:12 renown *e* through all generations.
112: 9 his righteousness *e* forever;
136: 1 *His love e forever.*
Da 9:15 made for yourself a name that *e*
2Co 9: 9 his righteousness *e* forever."

ENDURING (ENDURE)
2Th 1: 4 persecutions and trials you are *e*.
1Pe 1:23 through the living and *e* word

ENEMIES (ENEMY)
Ps 23: 5 in the presence of my *e*.
110: 1 hand until I make your *e*
Pr 16: 7 his *e* live at peace with him.
Isa 59:18 wrath to his *e*
Mic 7: 6 a man's *e* are the members
Mt 5:44 Love your *e* and pray
10:36 a man's *e* will be the members
Lk 6:27 Love your *e*, do good
6:35 But love your *e*, do good to them,
20:43 hand until I make your *e*
Ro 5:10 For if, when we were God's *e*,
1Co 15:25 reign until he has put all his *e*
Php 3:18 many live as *e* of the cross of Christ
Heb 1:13 hand until I make your *e*
10:13 for his *e* to be made his footstool,

ENEMY (ENEMIES ENMITY)
Pr 24:17 Do not gloat when your *e* falls;
25:21 If your *e* is hungry, give him food
27: 6 but an *e* multiplies kisses.
29:24 of a thief is his own *e*;
Lk 10:19 to overcome all the power of the *e*;
Ro 12:20 "If your *e* is hungry, feed him;
1Co 15:26 The last *e* to be destroyed is death.
1Ti 5:14 and to give the *e* no opportunity
1Pe 5: 8 Your *e* the devil prowls

ENERGY*
Col 1:29 struggling with all his *e*, which

ENGRAVED
Isa 49:16 I have *e* you on the palms
2Co 3: 7 which was *e* in letters on stone,

ENHANCES*
Ro 3: 7 my falsehood *e* God's truthfulness

ENJOY (JOY)
Dt 6: 2 and so that you may *e* long life.
Ps 37: 3 dwell in the land and *e* safe pasture.
Pr 28:16 ill-gotten gain will *e* a long life.
Ecc 3:22 better for a man than to *e* his work,
Eph 6: 3 and that you may *e* long life
Heb 11:25 rather than to *e* the pleasures of sin
3Jn : 2 I pray that you may *e* good health

ENJOYMENT (JOY)
Ecc 4: 8 and why am I depriving myself of *e*
1Ti 6:17 us with everything for our *e*.

ENLARGE (ENLARGES)
2Co 9:10 *e* the harvest of your righteousness.

ENLARGES (ENLARGE)
Dt 33:20 Blessed is he who *e* God's domain!

ENLIGHTENED* (LIGHT)
Eph 1:18 that the eyes of your heart may be *e*
Heb 6: 4 for those who have once been *e*,

ENMITY* (ENEMY)
Ge 3:15 And I will put *e*

ENOCH
1. Son of Cain (Ge 4:17-18).
2. Descendant of Seth; walked with God and taken by him (Ge 5:18-24; Heb 11:5). Prophet (Jude 14).

ENSLAVED (SLAVE)
Gal 4: 9 Do you wish to be *e* by them all
Tit 3: 3 and *e* by all kinds of passions

ENSNARE (SNARE)
Pr 5:22 of a wicked man *e* him;
Ecc 7:26 but the sinner she will *e*.

ENSNARED* (SNARE)
Dt 7:25 for yourselves, or you will be *e* by it
12:30 be careful not to be *e*
Ps 9:16 the wicked are *e* by the work
Pr 6: 2 *e* by the words of your mouth,
22:25 and get yourself *e*.

ENTANGLED (ENTANGLES)
2Pe 2:20 and are again *e* in it and overcome,

ENTANGLES* (ENTANGLED)
Heb 12: 1 and the sin that so easily *e*,

ENTER (ENTERED ENTERING ENTERS ENTRANCE)
Ps 95:11 "They shall never *e* my rest."
100: 4 *E* his gates with thanksgiving
Pr 2:10 For wisdom will *e* your heart,
Mt 5:20 will certainly not *e* the kingdom
7:13 "*E* through the narrow gate.
7:21 Lord,' will *e* the kingdom of heaven
18: 3 you will never *e* the kingdom
18: 8 It is better for you to *e* life maimed
19:17 to *e* life, obey the commandments
19:23 man to *e* the kingdom of heaven.
Mk 9:43 It is better for you to *e* life maimed
9:45 It is better for you to *e* life crippled
9:47 for you to *e* the kingdom of God
10:15 like a little child will never *e* it."
10:23 is for the rich to *e* the kingdom
Lk 13:24 will try to *e* and will not be able to.
13:24 "Make every effort to *e*
18:17 like a little child will never *e* it."
18:24 is for the rich to *e* the kingdom
Jn 3: 5 no one can *e* the kingdom of God.
Heb 3:11 'They shall never *e* my rest.'"
4:11 make every effort to *e* that rest,

ENTERED (ENTER)
Ps 73:17 me till I *e* the sanctuary of God;
Eze 4:14 meat has ever *e* my mouth."
Ac 11: 8 or unclean has ever *e* my mouth.'
Ro 5:12 as sin *e* the world through one man,
Heb 9:12 but he *e* the Most Holy Place once

ENTERING (ENTER)
Mt 21:31 the prostitutes are *e* the kingdom
Lk 11:52 have hindered those who were *e*."
Heb 4: 1 the promise of *e* his rest still stands,

ENTERS (ENTER)
Mk 7:18 you see that nothing that *e* a man
Jn 10: 2 The man who *e* by the gate is

ENTERTAIN* (ENTERTAINED ENTERTAINMENT)
Jdg 16:25 "Bring out Samson to *e* us."
Mt 9: 4 "Why do you *e* evil thoughts
1Ti 5:19 Do not *e* an accusation
Heb 13: 2 Do not forget to *e* strangers,

ENTERTAINED* (ENTERTAIN)
Ac 28: 7 and for three days *e* us hospitably.
Heb 13: 2 so doing some people have *e* angels

ENTERTAINMENT* (ENTERTAIN)
Da 6:18 without any *e* being brought to him

ENTHRALLED*
Ps 45:11 The king is *e* by your beauty;

ENTHRONED* (THRONE)
1Sa 4: 4 who is *e* between the cherubim.
2Sa 6: 2 who is *e* between the cherubim that
2Ki 19:15 of Israel, *e* between the cherubim,
1Ch 13: 6 who is *e* between the cherubim—
Ps 2: 4 The One *e* in heaven laughs;
9:11 to the LORD, *e* in Zion;
22: 3 Yet you are *e* as the Holy One;
29:10 The LORD sits *e* over the flood;
29:10 the LORD is *e* as King forever.
55:19 God, who is *e* forever,
61: 7 May he be *e* in God's presence
80: 1 who sit *e* between the cherubim,
99: 1 he sits *e* between the cherubim,
102:12 But you, O LORD, sit *e* forever;
113: 5 the One who sits *e* on high,
132:14 here I will sit *e*, for I have desired it
Isa 14:13 I will sit *e* on the mount
37:16 of Israel, *e* between the cherubim,
40:22 He sits *e* above the circle
52: 2 rise up, sit *e*, O Jerusalem.

ENTHRONES* (THRONE)
Job 36: 7 he *e* them with kings

ENTHUSIASM*
2Co 8:17 he is coming to you with much *e*
9: 2 and your *e* has stirred most of them

ENTICE* (ENTICED ENTICES)
Pr 1:10 My son, if sinners *e* you,
2Pe 2:18 they *e* people who are just escaping
Rev 2:14 who taught Balak to *e* the Israelites

ENTICED* (ENTICE)
Dt 4:19 do not be *e* into bowing
11:16 or you will be *e* to turn away
2Ki 17:21 Jeroboam *e* Israel away
Job 31: 9 If my heart has been *e* by a woman,
31:27 so that my heart was secretly *e*
Jas 1:14 desire, he is dragged away and *e*.

ENTICES* (ENTICE)
Dt 13: 6 your closest friend secretly *e* you,
Job 36:18 Be careful that no one *e* you
Pr 16:29 A violent man *e* his neighbor

ENTIRE
Gal 5:14 The *e* law is summed up

ENTRANCE (ENTER)
Mt 27:60 stone in front of the *e* to the tomb
Mk 15:46 a stone against the *e* of the tomb.
16: 3 away from the *e* of the tomb?"
Jn 11:38 cave with a stone laid across the *e*.
20: 1 had been removed from the *e*.

ENTRUST (TRUST)
Jn 2:24 Jesus would not *e* himself to them,
2Ti 2: 2 the presence of many witnesses *e*

ENTRUSTED (TRUST)
Jer 13:20 Where is the flock that was *e* to you
Jn 5:22 but has *e* all judgment to the Son,
Ro 3: 2 they have been *e* with the very
6:17 of teaching to which you were *e*.
1Co 4: 1 as those *e* with the secret things
1Th 2: 4 by God to be *e* with the gospel.
1Ti 1:11 of the blessed God, which he *e*
6:20 guard what has been *e* to your care.
2Ti 1:12 able to guard what I have *e* to him
1:14 Guard the good deposit that was *e*
Tit 1: 3 light through the preaching *e* to me
1: 7 Since an overseer is *e*
1Pe 2:23 he *e* himself to him who judges
5: 3 not lording it over those *e* to you,
Jude : 3 once for all *e* to the saints.

ENVIES
Jas 4: 5 spirit he caused to live in us *e*

ENVIOUS (ENVY)
Dt 32:21 I will make them *e*
Pr 24:19 or be *e* of the wicked,
Ro 10:19 "I will make you *e*

ENVOY
Pr 13:17 but a trustworthy *e* brings healing.

ENVY (ENVIOUS ENVYING)
Pr 3:31 Do not *e* a violent man
14:30 but *e* rots the bones.
23:17 Do not let your heart *e* sinners,
24: 1 Do not *e* wicked men,
Mk 7:22 malice, deceit, lewdness, *e*, slander
Ro 1:29 They are full of *e*, murder, strife,
11:14 arouse my own people to *e*
1Co 13: 4 It does not *e*, it does not boast,
Gal 5:21 factions and *e*; drunkenness, orgies
Php 1:15 that some preach Christ out of *e*
1Ti 6: 4 and quarrels about words that result in *e*,
Tit 3: 3 lived in malice and *e*, being hated
Jas 3:14 But if you harbor bitter *e*
3:16 where you have *e* and selfish
1Pe 2: 1 *e*, and slander of every kind.

ENVYING* (ENVY)
Gal 5:26 provoking and *e* each other.

EPHAH
Eze 45:11 The *e* and the bath are

EPHESUS
Ac 18:19 at *E*, where Paul left Priscilla
19: 1 the interior and arrived at *E*.
Eph 1: 1 To the saints in *E*, the faithful
Rev 2: 1 the angel of the church in *E* write:

EPHRAIM

1. Second son of Joseph (Ge 41:52; 46:20). Blessed as firstborn by Jacob (Ge 48). Tribe of numbered (Nu 1:33; 26:37), blessed (Dt 33:17), allotted land (Jos 16:4-9; Eze 48:5), failed to fully possess (Jos 16:10; Jdg 1:29).

2. Synonymous with Northern Kingdom (Isa 7:17; Hos 5).

EQUAL (EQUALITY EQUITY)
Dt 33:25 and your strength will *e* your days.
1Sa 9: 2 without *e* among the Israelites—
Isa 40:25 who is my *e*?" says the Holy One.
46: 5 you compare me or count me *e*?
Da 1:19 and he found none *e* to Daniel,
Jn 5:18 making himself *e* with God.
1Co 12:25 that its parts should have *e* concern
2Co 2:16 And who is *e* to such a task?

EQUALITY* (EQUAL)
2Co 8:13 pressed, but that there might be *e*.
8:14 Then there will be *e*, as it is written:
Php 2: 6 did not consider *e*

EQUIP* (EQUIPPED)
Heb 13:21 *e* you with everything good

EQUIPPED (EQUIP)
2Ti 3:17 man of God may be thoroughly *e*

EQUITY* (EQUAL)
Ps 96:10 he will judge the peoples with *e*.
98: 9 and the peoples with *e*.
99: 4 you have established *e*;

ERODES*
Job 14:18 "But as a mountain *e* and crumbles

ERROR (ERRORS)
Jas 5:20 Whoever turns a sinner from the *e*
2Pe 2:18 escaping from those who live in *e*.

ERRORS* (ERROR)
Ps 19:12 Who can discern his *e*?
Ecc 10: 4 calmness can lay great *e* to rest.

ESAU

Firstborn of Isaac, twin of Jacob (Ge 25:21-26). Also called Edom (Ge 25:30). Sold Jacob his birthright (Ge 25:29-34); lost blessing (Gen 27). Married Hittites (Ge 26:34), Ishmaelites (Ge 28:6-9). Reconciled to Jacob (Gen 33). Genealogy (Ge 36). The LORD chose Jacob over Esau (Mal 1:2-3), but gave Esau land (Dt 2:2-12). Descendants eventually obliterated (Ob 1-21; Jer 49:7-22).

ESCAPE (ESCAPED ESCAPES ESCAPING)
Ps 68:20 from the Sovereign LORD comes *e*
Pr 11: 9 through knowledge the righteous *e*.
Ro 2: 3 think you will *e* God's judgment?
1Th 5: 3 woman, and they will not *e*.
2Ti 2:26 and *e* from the trap of the devil,
Heb 2: 3 how shall we *e* if we ignore such
12:25 If they did not *e* when they refused
2Pe 1: 4 and *e* the corruption in the world

ESCAPED (ESCAPE)
2Pe 2:20 If they have *e* the corruption

ESCAPES (ESCAPE)
Pr 12:13 but a righteous man *e* trouble.

ESCAPING (ESCAPE)
1Co 3:15 only as one *e* through the flames.
2Pe 2:18 they entice people who are just *e*

ESTABLISH (ESTABLISHED ESTABLISHES)
Ge 6:18 But I will *e* my covenant with you,
17:21 But my covenant I will *e* with Isaac
2Sa 7:11 the LORD himself will *e* a house
1Ki 9: 5 I will *e* your royal throne
1Ch 28: 7 I will *e* his kingdom forever
Ps 90:17 *e* the work of our hands for us—

Isa 26:12 LORD, you *e* peace for us;
Ro 10:3 God and sought to *e* their own,
16:25 able to *e* you by my gospel
Heb 10:9 sets aside the first to *e* the second.

ESTABLISHED (ESTABLISH)

Ge 9:17 the sign of the covenant I have *e*
Ex 6:4 also *e* my covenant with them
Pr 16:12 a throne is *e* through righteousness.

ESTABLISHES (ESTABLISH)

Job 25:2 he *e* order in the heights of heaven.
Isa 42:4 till he *e* justice on earth.

ESTATE

Ps 136:23 who remembered us in our low *e*

ESTEEMED

Pr 22:1 to be *e* is better than silver or gold.
Isa 53:3 he was despised, and we *e* him not.

ESTHER

Jewess, originally named Hadassah, who lived in Persia; cousin of Mordecai (Est 2:7). Chosen queen of Xerxes (Est 2:8-18). Persuaded by Mordecai to foil Haman's plan to exterminate the Jews (Est 3-4). Revealed Haman's plans to Xerxes, resulting in Haman's death (Est 7), the Jews' preservation (Est 8-9), Mordecai's exaltation (Est 8:15; 9:4; 10). Decreed celebration of Purim (Est 9:18-32).

ETERNAL* (ETERNALLY ETERNITY)

Ge 21:33 the name of the LORD, the *E* God.
Dt 33:27 The *e* God is your refuge,
1Ki 10:9 of the LORD's *e* love for Israel,
Ps 16:11 with *e* pleasures at your right hand.
21:6 you have granted him *e* blessings
111:10 To him belongs *e* praise.
119:89 Your word, O LORD, is *e*;
119:160 all your righteous laws are *e*.
Ecc 12:5 Then man goes to his *e* home
Isa 26:4 LORD, the LORD, is the Rock *e*.
47:7 the *e* queen!'
Jer 10:10 he is the living God, the *e* King.
Da 4:3 His kingdom is an *e* kingdom;
4:34 His dominion is an *e* dominion;
Hab 3:6 His ways are *e*.
Mt 18:8 two feet and be thrown into *e* fire.
19:16 good thing must I do to get *e* life?"
19:29 as much and will inherit *e* life.
25:41 into the *e* fire prepared for the devil
25:46 but the righteous to *e* life."
25:46 they will go away to *e* punishment,
Mk 3:29 be forgiven; he is guilty of an *e* sin."
10:17 "what must I do to inherit *e* life?"
10:30 and in the age to come, *e* life.
Lk 10:25 "what must I do to inherit *e* life?"
16:9 will be welcomed into *e* dwellings.
18:18 what must I do to inherit *e* life?"
18:30 and, in the age to come, *e* life."
Jn 3:15 believes in him may have *e* life.
3:16 him shall not perish but have *e* life.
3:36 believes in the Son has *e* life,
4:14 spring of water welling up to *e* life."
4:36 now he harvests the crop for *e* life,
5:24 believes him who sent me has *e* life
5:39 that by them you possess *e* life.
6:27 but for food that endures to *e* life,
6:40 believes in him shall have *e* life,
6:54 and drinks my blood has *e* life,
6:68 You have the words of *e* life.
10:28 I give them *e* life, and they shall
12:25 in this world will keep it for *e* life.
12:50 that his command leads to *e* life.
17:2 all people that he might give *e* life
17:3 this is *e* life: that they may know
Ac 13:46 yourselves worthy of *e* life,
13:48 were appointed for *e* life believed.
Ro 1:20 his *e* power and divine nature—
2:7 and immortality, he will give *e* life.
5:21 righteousness to bring *e* life
6:22 to holiness, and the result is *e* life.
6:23 but the gift of God is *e* life
16:26 by the command of the *e* God,
2Co 4:17 for us an *e* glory that far outweighs
4:18 temporary, but what is unseen is *e*.
5:1 from God, an *e* house in heaven,
Gal 6:8 from the Spirit will reap *e* life.
Eph 3:11 to his *e* purpose which he
2Th 2:16 his grace gave us *e* encouragement
1Ti 1:16 believe on him and receive *e* life.
1:17 Now to the King *e*, immortal,
6:12 Take hold of the *e* life
2Ti 2:10 is in Christ Jesus, with *e* glory.
Tit 1:2 resting on the hope of *e* life,
3:7 heirs having the hope of *e* life.
Heb 5:9 he became the source of *e* salvation
6:2 of the dead, and *e* judgment.
9:12 having obtained *e* redemption.
9:14 through the *e* Spirit offered himself
9:15 the promised *e* inheritance—
13:20 of the *e* covenant brought back
1Pe 5:10 you to his *e* glory in Christ,
2Pe 1:11 into the *e* kingdom of our Lord
1Jn 1:2 and we proclaim to you the *e* life,
2:25 what he promised us—even *e* life.
3:15 know that no murderer has *e* life
5:11 God has given us *e* life,
5:13 you may know that you have *e* life.
5:20 He is the true God and *e* life.
Jude :7 who suffer the punishment of *e* fire.
:21 Christ to bring you to *e* life.
Rev 14:6 and he had the *e* gospel to proclaim

ETERNALLY* (ETERNAL)

Gal 1:8 let him be *e* condemned! As we
1:9 let him be *e* condemned! Am I now

ETERNITY* (ETERNAL)

Ps 93:2 you are from all *e*.
Pr 8:23 I was appointed from *e*,
Ecc 3:11 also set *e* in the hearts of men;

ETHIOPIAN*

Jer 13:23 Can the *E* change his skin
Ac 8:27 and on his way he met an *E* eunuch

EUNUCH (EUNUCHS)

Ac 8:27 on his way he met an Ethiopian *e*,

EUNUCHS (EUNUCH)

Isa 56:4 "To the *e* who keep my Sabbaths,
Mt 19:12 For some are *e* because they were

EUTYCHUS*

Ac 20:9 was a young man named *E*,

EVANGELIST* (EVANGELISTS)

Ac 21:8 stayed at the house of Philip the *e*,
2Ti 4:5 hardship, do the work of an *e*,

EVANGELISTS* (EVANGELIST)

Eph 4:11 some to be prophets, some to be *e*,

EVE*

Ge 3:20 Adam named his wife *E*,
4:1 Adam lay with his wife *E*,
2Co 11:3 as *E* was deceived by the serpent's
1Ti 2:13 For Adam was formed first, then *E*

EVEN-TEMPERED* (TEMPER)

Pr 17:27 and a man of understanding is *e*.

EVENING

Ge 1:5 there was *e*, and there was morning

EVER (EVERLASTING FOREVER FOREVERMORE)

Ex 15:18 LORD will reign for *e* and *e*."
Dt 8:19 If you *e* forget the LORD your
1Ki 3:12 anyone like you, nor will there *e* be.
Job 4:7 were the upright *e* destroyed?
Ps 5:11 let them *e* sing for joy.
10:16 The LORD is King for *e* and *e*;
21:4 length of days, for *e* and *e*.
25:3 will *e* be put to shame,
25:15 My eyes are *e* on the LORD,
26:3 for your love is *e* before me,
45:6 O God, will last for *e* and *e*;
45:17 nations will praise you for *e* and *e*.
48:14 For this God is our God for *e* and *e*;
52:8 God's unfailing love for *e* and *e*.
61:8 will I *e* sing praise to your name
71:6 I will *e* praise you.
84:4 they are *e* praising you.
89:33 nor will I *e* betray my faithfulness.
111:8 They are steadfast for *e* and *e*,
119:44 your law, for *e* and *e*.
119:98 for they are *e* with me.
132:12 sit on your throne for *e* and *e*."
145:1 I will praise your name for *e* and *e*.
145:2 and extol your name for *e* and *e*.
145:21 his holy name for *e* and *e*.
Pr 4:18 shining *e* brighter till the full light
5:19 may you *e* be captivated
Isa 66:8 Who has *e* heard of such a thing?
66:8 Who has *e* seen such things?
Jer 7:7 I gave your forefathers for *e* and *e*.
25:5 and your fathers for *e* and *e*.
Jer 31:36 the descendants of Israel *e* cease
Da 2:20 be to the name of God for *e* and *e*;
7:18 it forever—yes, for *e* and *e*.'
12:3 like the stars for *e* and *e*.
Mic 4:5 our God for *e* and *e*.
Mt 13:14 you will be *e* seeing but never
13:14 " 'You will be *e* hearing
Mk 4:12 *e* hearing but never understanding;
Jn 1:18 No one has *e* seen God,
Gal 1:5 to whom be glory for *e* and *e*.
Eph 3:21 all generations, for *e* and *e*!
Php 4:20 and Father be glory for *e* and *e*.
1Ti 1:17 be honor and glory for *e* and *e*.
2Ti 4:18 To him be glory for *e* and *e*.
Heb 1:8 O God, will last for *e* and *e*,
13:21 to whom be glory for *e* and *e*.
1Pe 4:11 the glory and the power for *e* and *e*.
5:11 To him be the power for *e* and *e*.
1Jn 4:12 No one has *e* seen God;
Rev 1:6 him be glory and power for *e* and *e*!
1:18 and behold I am alive for *e* and *e*!
21:27 Nothing impure will *e* enter it,
22:5 And they will reign for *e* and *e*.

EVER-INCREASING* (INCREASE)

Ro 6:19 to impurity and to *e* wickedness,
2Co 3:18 into his likeness with *e* glory,

EVERLASTING* (EVER)

Ge 9:16 and remember the *e* covenant
17:7 an *e* covenant between me and you
17:8 I will give as an *e* possession to you
17:13 in your flesh is to be an *e* covenant.
17:19 an *e* covenant for his descendants
48:4 *e* possession to your descendants
Nu 18:19 It is an *e* covenant of salt
Dt 33:15 and the fruitfulness of the *e* hills;
33:27 and underneath are the *e* arms.
2Sa 23:5 made with me an *e* covenant,
1Ch 16:17 to Israel as an *e* covenant:
16:36 from *e* to *e*.
29:10 from *e* to *e*.
Ezr 9:12 to your children as an *e* inheritance
Ne 9:5 your God, who is from *e* to *e*."
Ps 41:13 from *e* to *e*.
52:5 God will bring you down to *e* ruin:
74:3 toward these *e* ruins,
78:66 he put them to *e* shame.
90:2 from *e* to *e* you are God.
103:17 But from *e* to *e*
105:10 to Israel as an *e* covenant:
106:48 from *e* to *e*.
119:142 Your righteousness is *e*
139:24 and lead me in the way *e*.
145:13 Your kingdom is an *e* kingdom,
Isa 9:6 *E* Father, Prince of Peace.
24:5 and broken the *e* covenant.
30:8 it may be an *e* witness.
33:14 Who of us can dwell with *e* burning
35:10 *e* joy will crown their heads.
40:28 The LORD is the *e* God,
45:17 the LORD with an *e* salvation;
45:17 to ages *e*.
51:11 *e* joy will crown their heads.
54:8 but with *e* kindness
55:3 I will make an *e* covenant with you,
55:13 for an *e* sign,
56:5 I will give them an *e* name
60:15 I will make you the *e* pride
60:19 for the LORD will be your *e* light,
60:20 the LORD will be your *e* light,
61:7 and *e* joy will be theirs.
61:8 and make an *e* covenant with them.
63:12 to gain for himself *e* renown,
Jer 5:22 an *e* barrier it cannot cross.
23:40 I will bring upon you *e* disgrace—
23:40 *e* shame that will not be forgotten."
25:9 of horror and scorn, and an *e* ruin.
31:3 "I have loved you with an *e* love;
32:40 I will make an *e* covenant
50:5 the LORD in an *e* covenant
Eze 16:60 and I will establish an *e* covenant
37:26 with them; it will be an *e* covenant.
Da 7:14 dominion is an *e* dominion that will
7:27 His kingdom will be an *e* kingdom,
9:24 to bring in *e* righteousness,
12:2 others to shame and *e* contempt.
12:2 some to *e* life, others to shame
Mic 6:2 you *e* foundations of the earth.
Hab 1:12 O LORD, are you not from *e*?
Jn 6:47 the truth, he who believes has *e* life.
2Th 1:9 punished with *e* destruction
Jude :6 bound with *e* chains for judgment

EVER-PRESENT*
Ps 46: 1 an *e* help in trouble

EVIDENCE (EVIDENT)
Jn 14: 11 on the *e* of the miracles themselves.
Ac 11: 23 and saw the *e* of the grace of God,
2Th 1: 5 All this is *e* that God's judgment is
Jas 2: 20 do you want *e* that faith

EVIDENT (EVIDENCE)
Php 4: 5 Let your gentleness be *e* to all.

EVIL (EVILDOER EVILDOERS EVILS)
Ge 2: 9 of the knowledge of good and *e.*
3: 5 be like God, knowing good and *e.*"
6: 5 of his heart was only *e* all the time.
Ex 32: 22 how prone these people are to *e.*
Jdg 2: 11 Then the Israelites did *e* in the eyes
3: 7 The Israelites did *e* in the eyes
3: 12 Once again the Israelites did *e*
4: 1 the Israelites once again did *e*
6: 1 Again the Israelites did *e*
10: 6 Again the Israelites did *e*
13: 1 Again the Israelites did *e*
1Ki 11: 6 So Solomon did *e* in the eyes
16: 25 But Omri did *e* in the eyes
2Ki 15: 24 Pekahiah did *e* in the eyes
Job 1: 1 he feared God and shunned *e.*
1: 8 a man who fears God and shuns *e.*"
34: 10 Far be it from God to do *e,*
36: 21 Beware of turning to *e,*
Ps 5: 4 not a God who takes pleasure in *e;*
23: 4 I will fear no *e,*
34: 13 keep your tongue from *e*
34: 14 Turn from *e* and do good;
34: 16 is against those who do *e,*
37: 1 Do not fret because of *e* men
37: 8 do not fret—it leads only to *e.*
37: 27 Turn from *e* and do good;
49: 5 fear when *e* days come,
51: 4 and done what is *e* in your sight,
97: 10 those who love the LORD hate *e,*
101: 4 I will have nothing to do with *e.*
141: 4 not my heart be drawn to what is *e,*
Pr 4: 27 keep your foot from *e.*
8: 13 To fear the LORD is to hate *e;*
10: 23 A fool finds pleasure in *e* conduct,
11: 19 he who pursues *e* goes to his death.
11: 27 *e* comes to him who searches for it.
14: 16 man fears the LORD and shuns *e,*
17: 13 If a man pays back *e* for good,
20: 30 Blows and wounds cleanse away *e,*
24: 19 Do not fret because of *e* men
24: 20 for the *e* man has no future hope,
26: 23 are fervent lips with an *e* heart.
28: 5 *E* men do not understand justice,
29: 6 An *e* man is snared by his own sin,
Ecc 12: 14 whether it is good or *e.*
Isa 5: 20 Woe to those who call *e* good
13: 11 I will punish the world for its *e,*
55: 7 and the *e* man his thoughts.
Jer 4: 14 wash the *e* from your heart
18: 8 nation I warned repents of its *e,*
18: 11 So turn from your *e* ways,
Eze 33: 11 Turn! Turn from your *e* ways!
33: 13 he will die for the *e* he has done.
33: 15 and does no *e,* he will surely live;
Am 5: 13 for the times are *e.*
Hab 1: 13 Your eyes are too pure to look on *e;*
Zec 8: 17 do not plot *e* against your neighbor,
Mt 5: 45 He causes his sun to rise on the *e*
6: 13 but deliver us from the *e* one.'
7: 11 If you, then, though you are *e,*
12: 34 you who are *e* say anything good?
12: 35 and the *e* man brings *e* things out
12: 35 out of the *e* stored up in him.
12: 43 "When an *e* spirit comes out
15: 19 out of the heart come *e* thoughts,
Mk 7: 21 come *e* thoughts, sexual
Lk 6: 45 and the *e* man brings *e* things out
11: 13 If you then, though you are *e,*
Jn 3: 19 of light because their deeds were *e.*
3: 20 Everyone who does *e* hates
17: 15 you protect them from the *e* one.
Ro 1: 30 they invent ways of doing *e;*
2: 8 who reject the truth and follow *e,*
2: 9 for every human being who does *e:*
3: 8 "Let us do *e* that good may result"?
6: 12 body so that you obey its *e* desires.
7: 19 no, the *e* I do not want to do—
7: 21 to do good, *e* is right there with me.
12: 9 Hate what is *e;* cling
12: 17 Do not repay anyone *e* for *e.*
12: 21 Do not be overcome by *e,*
Ro 14: 16 good to be spoken of as *e.*
16: 19 and innocent about what is *e.*
1Co 13: 6 Love does not delight in *e*
14: 20 In regard to *e* be infants,
Eph 5: 16 because the days are *e.*
6: 12 forces of *e* in the heavenly realms.
6: 16 all the flaming arrows of the *e* one.
Col 3: 5 impurity, lust, *e* desires and greed,
1Th 5: 22 Avoid every kind of *e.*
2Th 3: 3 and protect you from the *e* one.
1Ti 6: 10 of money is a root of all kinds of *e.*
2Ti 2: 22 Flee the *e* desires of youth,
3: 6 are swayed by all kinds of *e* desires,
3: 13 while *e* men and impostors will go
Heb 5: 14 to distinguish good from *e.*
Jas 1: 13 For God cannot be tempted by *e,*
1: 21 and the *e* that is so prevalent,
3: 6 a world of *e* among the parts
3: 8 It is a restless *e,* full
1Pe 2: 16 your freedom as a cover-up for *e;*
3: 9 Do not repay *e* with *e* or insult
3: 10 must keep his tongue from *e*
3: 17 for doing good than for doing *e.*
1Jn 2: 13 you have overcome the *e* one.
2: 14 and you have overcome the *e* one.
3: 12 who belonged to the *e* one
5: 18 and the *e* one cannot harm him.
5: 19 is under the control of the *e* one.
3Jn : 11 do not imitate what is *e*

EVILDOER* (EVIL)
2Sa 3: 39 the LORD repay the *e* according
Ps 101: 8 I will cut off every *e*
Mal 4: 1 and every *e* will be stubble,

EVILDOERS* (EVIL)
1Sa 24: 13 saying goes, 'From *e* come evil
Job 8: 20 or strengthen the hands of *e.*
34: 8 He keeps company with *e;*
34: 22 where *e* can hide.
Ps 14: 4 Will *e* never learn—
14: 6 You *e* frustrate the plans
26: 5 I abhor the assembly of *e*
36: 12 See how the *e* lie fallen—
53: 4 Will the *e* never learn—
59: 2 Deliver me from *e*
64: 2 from that noisy crowd of *e.*
92: 7 and all *e* flourish,
92: 9 all *e* will be scattered.
94: 4 all the *e* are full of boasting.
94: 16 will take a stand for me against *e?*
119: 115 Away from me, you *e,*
125: 5 the LORD will banish with the *e.*
141: 4 deeds with men who are *e;*
141: 5 ever against the deeds of *e;*
141: 9 from the traps set by *e.*
Pr 21: 15 but terror to *e.*
Isa 1: 4 a brood of *e,*
31: 2 against those who help *e.*
Jer 23: 14 They strengthen the hands of *e,*
Hos 10: 9 the *e* in Gibeah?
Mal 3: 15 Certainly the *e* prosper, and
Mt 7: 23 you *e!*' "Therefore everyone who
Lk 13: 27 Away from me, all you *e!*'
18: 11 *e,* adulterers—or even like this tax

EVILS* (EVIL)
Mk 7: 23 All these *e* come from inside

EWE
2Sa 12: 3 one little *e* lamb he had bought.

EXACT*
Ge 43: 21 the *e* weight—in the mouth
Est 4: 7 including the *e* amount
Mt 2: 7 from them the *e* time the star had
Jn 4: 53 realized that this was the *e* time
Ac 17: 26 the *e* places where they should live.
Heb 1: 3 the *e* representation of his being,

EXALT* (EXALTED EXALTS)
Ex 15: 2 my father's God, and I will *e* him.
Jos 3: 7 begin to *e* you in the eyes
1Sa 2: 10 and *e* the horn of his anointed."
1Ch 25: 5 the promises of God to *e* him.
29: 12 power to *e* and give strength to all.
Job 19: 5 If indeed you would *e* yourselves
Ps 30: 1 I will *e* you, O LORD,
34: 3 let us *e* his name together.
35: 26 may all who *e* themselves over me
37: 34 He will *e* you to inherit the land;
38: 16 *e* themselves over me
75: 6 or from the desert can *e* a man.
89: 17 and by your favor you *e* our horn.
99: 5 *E* the LORD our God
Ps 99: 9 *E* the LORD our God
107: 32 Let them *e* him in the assembly
118: 28 you are my God, and I will *e* you.
145: 1 I will *e* you, my God the King;
Pr 4: 8 Esteem her, and she will *e* you;
25: 6 Do not *e* yourself in the king's
Isa 24: 15 *e* the name of the LORD, the God
25: 1 I will *e* you and praise your name,
Eze 29: 15 and will never again *e* itself
Da 4: 37 *e* and glorify the King of heaven,
11: 36 He will *e* and magnify himself
11: 37 but will *e* himself above them all.
Hos 11: 7 he will by no means *e* them.
2Th 2: 4 will *e* himself over everything that is

EXALTED* (EXALT)
Ex 15: 1 for he is highly *e.*
15: 21 for he is highly *e.*
Nu 24: 7 their kingdom will be *e.*
Jos 4: 14 That day the LORD *e* Joshua
2Sa 5: 12 and had *e* his kingdom for the sake
22: 47 *E* be God, the Rock, my Savior!
22: 49 You *e* me above my foes;
23: 1 of the man *e* by the Most High,
1Ch 14: 2 that his kingdom had been highly *e*
17: 17 as though I were the most *e* of men,
29: 11 you are *e* as head over all.
29: 25 The LORD highly *e* Solomon
Ne 9: 5 and may it be *e* above all blessing
Job 24: 24 For a little while they are *e,*
36: 22 "God is *e* in his power.
37: 23 beyond our reach and *e* in power;
Ps 18: 46 *E* be God my Savior!
18: 48 You *e* me above my foes;
21: 13 Be *e,* O LORD, in your strength;
27: 6 Then my head will be *e*
35: 27 they always say, "The LORD be *e,*
40: 16 "The LORD be *e!*"
46: 10 I will be *e* among the nations,
46: 10 I will be *e* in the earth."
47: 9 he is greatly *e.*
57: 5 Be *e,* O God, above the heavens;
57: 11 Be *e,* O God, above the heavens;
70: 4 "Let God be *e!*"
89: 13 hand is strong, your right hand *e.*
89: 19 I have *e* a young man
89: 24 through my name his horn will be *e*
89: 27 the most *e* of the kings of the earth.
89: 42 You have *e* the right hand
92: 8 But you, O LORD, are *e* forever.
92: 10 You have *e* my horn like that
97: 9 you are *e* far above all gods.
99: 2 he is *e* over all the nations.
108: 5 Be *e,* O God, above the heavens,
113: 4 The LORD is *e* over all the nations
138: 2 for you have *e* above all things
148: 13 for his name alone is *e;*
Pr 11: 11 of the upright a city is *e,*
30: 32 have played the fool and *e* yourself,
Isa 2: 11 the LORD alone will be *e*
2: 12 for all that is *e*
2: 17 the LORD alone will be *e*
5: 16 the LORD Almighty will be *e*
6: 1 *e,* and the train of his robe filled
12: 4 and proclaim that his name is *e.*
24: 4 the *e* of the earth languish.
33: 5 The LORD is *e,* for he dwells
33: 10 "Now will I be *e;*
52: 13 be raised and lifted up and highly *e.*
Jer 17: 12 A glorious throne, *e*
La 2: 17 he has *e* the horn of your foes.
Eze 21: 26 The lowly will be *e* and the *e* will be
Hos 13: 1 he was *e* in Israel.
Mic 6: 6 and bow down before the *e* God?
Mt 23: 12 whoever humbles himself will be *e.*
Lk 14: 11 he who humbles himself will be *e.*"
18: 14 he who humbles himself will be *e.*"
Ac 2: 33 *E* to the right hand of God,
5: 31 God *e* him to his own right hand
Php 1: 20 always Christ will be *e* in my body,
2: 9 Therefore God *e* him
Heb 7: 26 from sinners, *e* above the heavens.

EXALTS* (EXALT)
1Sa 2: 7 he humbles and he *e.*
Job 36: 7 and *e* them forever.
Ps 75: 7 He brings one down, he *e* another.
Pr 14: 34 Righteousness *e* a nation,
Mt 23: 12 For whoever *e* himself will be
Lk 14: 11 For everyone who *e* himself will be
18: 14 For everyone who *e* himself will be

EXAMINE (EXAMINED EXAMINES)
Ps 11: 4 his eyes *e* them.
17: 3 you probe my heart and *e* me

Ps 26: 2 *e* my heart and my mind;
Jer 17: 10 and *e* the mind,
20: 12 Almighty, you who *e* the righteous
La 3: 40 Let us *e* our ways and test them,
1Co 11: 28 A man ought to *e* himself
2Co 13: 5 *E* yourselves to see whether you

EXAMINED (EXAMINE)

Job 13: 9 Would it turn out well if he *e* you?
Ac 17: 11 *e* the Scriptures every day to see

EXAMINES (EXAMINE)

Ps 11: 5 The LORD *e* the righteous,
Pr 5: 21 and he *e* all his paths.

EXAMPLE* (EXAMPLES)

2Ki 14: 3 In everything he followed the *e*
Ecc 9: 13 also saw under the sun this *e*
Eze 14: 8 and make him an *e* and a byword.
Jn 13: 15 have set you an *e* that you should
Ro 7: 2 as long as he lives? For *e*,
1Co 11: 1 Follow my *e*, as I follow
11: 1 as I follow the *e* of Christ.
Gal 3: 15 let me take an *e* from everyday life.
Php 3: 17 Join with others in following my *e*,
2Th 3: 7 how you ought to follow our *e*.
1Ti 1: 16 as an *e* for those who would believe
4: 12 set an *e* for the believers in speech,
Tit 2: 7 In everything set them an *e*
Heb 4: 11 fall by following their *e*
Jas 3: 4 Or take ships as an *e*.
5: 10 as an *e* of patience in the face
1Pe 2: 21 leaving you an *e*, that you should
2Pe 2: 6 made them an *e* of what is going
Jude : 7 as an *e* of those who suffer

EXAMPLES* (EXAMPLE)

1Co 10: 6 Now these things occurred as *e*
10: 11 as *e* and were written down
1Pe 5: 3 to you, but being *e* to the flock.

EXASPERATE*

Eph 6: 4 Fathers, do not *e* your children;

EXCEL* (EXCELLENT)

Ge 49: 4 as the waters, you will no longer *e*,
1Co 14: 12 to *e* in gifts that build up the church
2Co 8: 7 But just as you *e* in everything—
8: 7 also *e* in this grace of giving.

EXCELLENT (EXCEL)

1Co 12: 31 now I will show you the most *e* way
Php 4: 8 if anything is *e* or praiseworthy—
1Ti 3: 13 have served well gain an *e* standing
Tit 3: 8 These things are *e* and profitable

EXCESSIVE

Eze 18: 8 or take *e* interest.
2Co 2: 7 not be overwhelmed by *e* sorrow.

EXCHANGE (EXCHANGED)

Mt 16: 26 Or what can a man give in *e*
Mk 8: 37 Or what can a man give in *e*
2Co 6: 13 As a fair *e*—I speak

EXCHANGED (EXCHANGE)

Ps 106: 20 They *e* their Glory
Jer 2: 11 But my people have *e* their Glory
Hos 4: 7 they *e* their Glory
Ro 1: 23 *e* the glory of the immortal God
1: 25 They *e* the truth of God for a lie,
1: 26 their women *e* natural relations

EXCLAIM

Ps 35: 10 My whole being will *e*,

EXCUSE* (EXCUSES)

Ps 25: 3 who are treacherous without *e*.
Lk 14: 18 Please *e* me.'
14: 19 Please *e* me.'
Jn 15: 22 they have no *e* for their sin.
Ro 1: 20 so that men are without *e*.
2: 1 You, therefore, have no *e*,

EXCUSES* (EXCUSE)

Lk 14: 18 "But they all alike began to make *e*.

EXERTED*

Eph 1: 20 which he *e* in Christ

EXHORT*

1Ti 5: 1 but *e* him as if he were your father.

EXILE

2Ki 17: 23 taken from their homeland into *e*
2Ki 25: 11 into *e* the people who remained

EXISTED* (EXISTS)

2Pe 3: 5 ago by God's word the heavens *e*

EXISTS (EXISTED)

Heb 2: 10 and through whom everything *e*,
11: 6 to him must believe that he *e*

EXPANSE

Ge 1: 7 So God made the *e* and separated
1: 8 God called the *e* "sky."

EXPECT (EXPECTATION EXPECTED EXPECTING)

Mt 24: 44 at an hour when you do not *e* him.
Lk 12: 40 at an hour when you do not *e* him."
Php 1: 20 I eagerly *e* and hope that I will

EXPECTATION (EXPECT)

Ro 8: 19 waits in eager *e* for the sons
Heb 10: 27 but only a fearful *e* of judgment

EXPECTED (EXPECT)

Pr 11: 7 all he *e* from his power comes
Hag 1: 9 "You *e* much, but see, it turned out

EXPECTING (EXPECT)

Lk 6: 35 and lend to them without *e*

EXPEL* (EXPELLED)

1Co 5: 13 *E* the wicked man from among you

EXPELLED (EXPEL)

Eze 28: 16 and I *e* you, O guardian cherub,

EXPENSE (EXPENSIVE)

1Co 9: 7 Who serves as a soldier at his own *e*

EXPENSIVE* (EXPENSE)

Mt 26: 7 jar of very *e* perfume,
Mk 14: 3 jar of very *e* perfume,
Lk 7: 25 those who wear *e* clothes
Jn 12: 3 a pint of pure nard, an *e* perfume;
1Ti 2: 9 or gold or pearls or *e* clothes,

EXPERT

1Co 3: 10 I laid a foundation as an *e* builder,

EXPLAINING (EXPLAINS)

Ac 17: 3 *e* and proving that the Christ had

EXPLAINS* (EXPLAINING)

Ac 8: 31 he said, "unless someone *e* it to me

EXPLOIT* (EXPLOITED EXPLOITING EXPLOITS)

Pr 22: 22 Do not *e* the poor because they are
Isa 58: 3 and *e* all your workers.
2Co 12: 17 Did I *e* you through any
12: 18 Titus did not *e* you, did he?
2Pe 2: 3 greed these teachers will *e* you

EXPLOITED* (EXPLOIT)

2Co 7: 2 no one, we have *e* no one.

EXPLOITING* (EXPLOIT)

Jas 2: 6 Is it not the rich who are *e* you?

EXPLOITS (EXPLOIT)

2Co 11: 20 or *e* you or takes advantage of you

EXPLORE

Nu 13: 2 "Send some men to *e* the land

EXPOSE (EXPOSED)

1Co 4: 5 will *e* the motives of men's hearts.
Eph 5: 11 of darkness, but rather *e* them.

EXPOSED (EXPOSE)

Jn 3: 20 for fear that his deeds will be *e*.
Eph 5: 13 everything *e* by the light becomes

EXPRESS (EXPRESSING)

Ro 8: 26 us with groans that words cannot *e*.

EXPRESSING* (EXPRESS)

1Co 2: 13 *e* spiritual truths in spiritual words.
Gal 5: 6 thing that counts is faith *e* itself

EXTENDS (EXTENT)

Pr 31: 20 and *e* her hands to the needy.
Lk 1: 50 His mercy *e* to those who fear him,

EXTENT (EXTENDS)

Jn 13: 1 he now showed them the full *e*

EXTERNAL

Gal 2: 6 judge by *e* appearance—

EXTINGUISH (EXTINGUISHED)

Eph 6: 16 which you can *e* all the flaming

EXTINGUISHED (EXTINGUISH)

2Sa 21: 17 the lamp of Israel will not be *e*."

EXTOL*

Job 36: 24 Remember to *e* his work,
Ps 34: 1 I will *e* the LORD at all times;
68: 4 *e* him who rides on the clouds—
95: 2 and *e* him with music and song.
109: 30 mouth I will greatly *e* the LORD;
111: 1 I will *e* the LORD with all my heart
115: 18 it is we who *e* the LORD,
117: 1 *e* him, all you peoples.
145: 2 and *e* your name for ever and ever.
145: 10 your saints will *e* you.
147: 12 *E* the LORD, O Jerusalem;

EXTORT*

Lk 3: 14 "Don't *e* money and don't accuse

EXTRAORDINARY*

Ac 19: 11 God did *e* miracles through Paul,

EXTREME (EXTREMES)

2Co 8: 2 and their *e* poverty welled up

EXTREMES* (EXTREME)

Ecc 7: 18 who fears God will avoid all *e*.

EXULT

Ps 89: 16 they *e* in your righteousness.
Isa 45: 25 will be found righteous and will *e*.

EYE (EYES)

Ge 3: 6 good for food and pleasing to the *e*,
Ex 21: 24 you are to take life for life, *e* for *e*,
Dt 19: 21 life for life, *e* for *e*, tooth for tooth,
Ps 94: 9 Does he who formed the *e* not see?
Mt 5: 29 If your right *e* causes you to sin,
5: 38 '*E* for *e*, and tooth for tooth.'
6: 22 "The *e* is the lamp of the body.
7: 3 of sawdust in your brother's *e*
1Co 2: 9 "No *e* has seen,
12: 16 I am not an *e*, I do not belong
15: 52 of an *e*, at the last trumpet.
Eph 6: 6 favor when their *e* is on you,
Col 3: 22 not only when their *e* is on you
Rev 1: 7 and every *e* will see him,

EYES (EYE)

Nu 15: 39 the lusts of your own hearts and *e*.
33: 55 remain will become barbs in your *e*
Dt 11: 12 the *e* of the LORD your God are
12: 25 right in the *e* of the LORD.
16: 19 for a bribe blinds the *e* of the wise
Jos 23: 13 on your backs and thorns in your *e*,
1Sa 15: 17 you were once small in your own *e*,
1Ki 10: 7 I came and saw with my own *e*.
2Ki 9: 30 heard about it, she painted her *e*,
2Ch 16: 9 For the *e* of the LORD range
Job 31: 1 "I made a covenant with my *e*
36: 7 He does not take his *e*
Ps 25: 15 My *e* are ever on the LORD,
36: 1 God before his *e*.
101: 6 My *e* will be on the faithful
118: 23 and it is marvelous in our *e*.
119: 18 Open my *e* that I may see
119: 37 my *e* away from worthless things;
121: 1 I lift up my *e* to the hills—
123: 1 I lift up my *e* to you,
139: 16 your *e* saw my unformed body.
141: 8 But my *e* are fixed on you,
Pr 3: 7 Do not be wise in your own *e*;
4: 25 Let your *e* look straight ahead,
15: 3 The *e* of the LORD are everywhere
17: 24 a fool's *e* wander to the ends
Isa 6: 5 and my *e* have seen the King,
33: 17 Your *e* will see the king
42: 7 to open *e* that are blind,
Jer 24: 6 My *e* will watch over them
Hab 1: 13 Your *e* are too pure to look on evil;
Mt 6: 22 If your *e* are good, your whole
21: 42 and it is marvelous in our *e*'?
Lk 16: 15 ones who justify yourselves in the *e*
24: 31 Then their *e* were opened
Jn 4: 35 open your *e* and look at the fields!

Ac 1: 9 he was taken up before their very e,
2Co 4: 18 So we fix our e not on what is seen,
8: 21 not only in the e of the Lord but
Eph 1: 18 also that the e of your heart may be
Heb 12: 2 Let us fix our e on Jesus, the author
Jas 2: 5 poor in the e of the world to be rich
1Pe 3: 12 For the e of the Lord are
Rev 7: 17 wipe away every tear from their e."
21: 4 He will wipe every tear from their e

EYEWITNESSES* (WITNESS)

Lk 1: 2 by those who from the first were e
2Pe 1: 16 but we were e of his majesty.

EZEKIEL*

Priest called to be prophet to the exiles (Eze 1-3). Symbolically acted out destruction of Jerusalem (Eze 4-5; 12; 24).

EZRA*

Priest and teacher of the Law who led a return of exiles to Israel to reestablish temple and worship (Ezr 7-8). Corrected intermarriage of priests (Ezr 9-10). Read Law at celebration of Feast of Tabernacles (Ne 8). Participated in dedication of Jerusalem's walls (Ne 12).

FACE (FACES)

Ge 32: 30 "It is because I saw God f to f,
Ex 3: 6 Moses hid his f, because he was
33: 11 would speak to Moses f to f,
33: 20 But," he said, "you cannot see my f
34: 29 was not aware that his f was radiant
Nu 6: 25 the LORD make his f shine
12: 8 With him I speak f to f,
14: 14 O LORD, have been seen f to f,
Dt 5: 4 The LORD spoke to you f to f out
31: 17 I will hide my f from them,
34: 10 whom the LORD knew f to f,
Jdg 6: 22 the angel of the LORD f to f!"
2Ki 14: 8 challenge: "Come, meet me f to f."
1Ch 16: 11 seek his f always.
2Ch 7: 14 and seek my f and turn
25: 17 of Israel: "Come, meet me f to f."
Ezr 9: 6 and disgraced to lift up my f to you,
Ps 4: 6 Let the light of your f shine upon us
27: 8 Your f, LORD, I will seek.
31: 16 Let your f shine on your servant;
44: 3 and the light of your f,
44: 22 Yet for your sake we f death all day
51: 9 Hide your f from my sins
67: 1 and make his f shine upon us; Selah
80: 3 make your f shine upon us,
105: 4 seek his f always.
119: 135 Make your f shine
SS 2: 14 and your f is lovely.
Isa 50: 7 Therefore have I set my f like flint,
50: 8 Let us f each other!
54: 8 I hid my f from you for a moment,
Jer 32: 4 and will speak with him f to f
34: 3 and he will speak with you f to f.
Eze 1: 10 Each of the four had the f of a man,
20: 35 f to f, I will execute judgment
Mt 17: 2 His f shone like the sun,
18: 10 angels in heaven always see the f
Lk 9: 29 the appearance of his f changed,
Ro 8: 36 "For your sake we f death all day
1Co 13: 12 mirror; then we shall see f to f.
2Co 3: 7 could not look steadily at the f
4: 6 the glory of God in the f of Christ.
10: 1 who am "timid" when f to f
1Pe 3: 12 but the f of the Lord is
2Jn : 12 to visit you and talk with you f to f,
3Jn : 14 see you soon, and we will talk f to f.
Rev 1: 16 His f was like the sun shining
22: 4 They will see his f, and his name

FACES (FACE)

2Co 3: 18 who with unveiled f all reflect

FACTIONS

2Co 12: 20 outbursts of anger, f, slander,
Gal 5: 20 selfish ambition, dissensions, f

FADE (FADING)

Jas 1: 11 the rich man will f away
1Pe 5: 4 of glory that will never f away.

FADING (FADE)

2Co 3: 7 f though it was, will not
3: 11 if what was f away came with glory,
3: 13 at it while the radiance was f away.

FAIL (FAILED FAILING FAILINGS FAILS FAILURE)

Lev 26: 15 and f to carry out all my commands
1Ki 2: 4 you will never f to have a man
1Ch 28: 20 He will not f you or forsake you
2Ch 34: 33 they did not f to follow the LORD,
Ps 89: 28 my covenant with him will never f.
Pr 15: 22 Plans f for lack of counsel,
Isa 51: 6 my righteousness will never f.
La 3: 22 for his compassions never f.
Lk 22: 32 Simon, that your faith may not f.
2Co 13: 5 unless, of course, you f the test?

FAILED (FAIL)

Jos 23: 14 has been fulfilled; not one has f.
1Ki 8: 56 Not one word has f
Ps 77: 8 Has his promise f for all time?
Ro 9: 6 as though God's word had f.
2Co 13: 6 discover that we have not f the test.

FAILING (FAIL)

1Sa 12: 23 sin against the LORD by f to pray

FAILINGS (FAIL)

Ro 15: 1 ought to bear with the f of the weak

FAILS (FAIL)

Jer 14: 6 their eyesight f
Joel 1: 10 the oil f.
1Co 13: 8 Love never f.

FAILURE* (FAIL)

1Th 2: 1 that our visit to you was not a f.

FAINT

Isa 40: 31 they will walk and not be f.

FAINTHEARTED* (HEART)

Dt 20: 3 Do not be f or afraid; do not be
20: 8 shall add, "Is any man afraid or f?

FAIR (FAIRNESS)

Pr 1: 3 doing what is right and just and f;
Col 4: 1 slaves with what is right and f,

FAIRNESS* (FAIR)

Pr 29: 14 If a king judges the poor with f,

FAITH* (FAITHFUL FAITHFULLY FAITHFULNESS FAITHLESS)

Ex 21: 8 because he has broken f with her.
Dt 32: 51 both of you broke f with me
Jos 22: 16 'How could you break f
Jdg 9: 16 and in good f when you made
9: 19 and in good f toward Jerub-Baal
1Sa 14: 33 "You have broken f," he said.
2Ch 20: 20 Have f in the LORD your God
20: 20 have f in his prophets and you will
Isa 7: 9 If you do not stand firm in your f,
26: 2 the nation that keeps f.
Hab 2: 4 but the righteous will live by his f—
Mal 2: 10 by breaking f with one another?
2: 11 one another? Judah has broken f.
2: 14 because you have broken f with her
2: 15 and do not break f with the wife
2: 16 in your spirit, and do not break f.
Mt 6: 30 O you of little f? So do not worry,
8: 10 anyone in Israel with such great f.
8: 26 He replied, "You of little f,
9: 2 When Jesus saw their f, he said
9: 22 he said, "your f has healed you."
9: 29 According to your f will it be done
13: 58 there because of their lack of f.
14: 31 of little f," he said, "why did you
15: 28 "Woman, you have great f!
16: 8 Jesus asked, "You of little f,
17: 20 if you have f as small as a mustard
17: 20 "Because you have so little f.
21: 21 if you have f and do not doubt,
24: 10 many will turn away from the f
Mk 2: 5 When Jesus saw their f, he said
4: 40 still have no f?" They were
5: 34 "Daughter, your f has healed you.
6: 6 he was amazed at their lack of f.
10: 52 said Jesus, "your f has healed you."
11: 22 "Have f in God," Jesus answered.
16: 14 he rebuked them for their lack of f
Lk 5: 20 When Jesus saw their f, he said,
7: 9 I have not found such great f
7: 50 the woman, "Your f has saved you;
8: 25 "Where is your f?" he asked his
8: 48 "Daughter, your f has healed you.
12: 28 will he clothe you, O you of little f!
17: 5 "Increase our f!" He replied,
Lk 17: 6 "If you have f as small
17: 19 your f has made you well."
18: 8 will he find f on the earth?"
18: 42 your sight; your f has healed you."
22: 32 Simon, that your f may not fail.
Jn 2: 11 and his disciples put their f in him.
7: 31 in the crowd put their f in him.
8: 30 he spoke, many put their f in him.
11: 45 had seen what Jesus did, put their f
12: 11 to Jesus and putting their f in him.
12: 42 they would not confess their f
14: 12 anyone who has f in me will do
Ac 3: 16 By f in the name of Jesus, this man
3: 16 f that comes through him that has
6: 5 full of f and of the Holy Spirit;
6: 7 of priests became obedient to the f.
11: 24 full of the Holy Spirit and f,
13: 8 to turn the proconsul from the f.
14: 9 saw that he had f to be healed
14: 22 them to remain true to the f.
14: 27 the door of f to the Gentiles.
15: 9 for he purified their hearts by f.
16: 5 were strengthened in the f
20: 21 and have f in our Lord Jesus.
24: 24 as he spoke about f in Christ Jesus.
26: 18 those who are sanctified by f
27: 25 for I have f in God that it will
Ro 1: 5 to the obedience that comes from f.
1: 8 because your f is being reported all
1: 12 encouraged by each other's f.
1: 17 is by f from first to last,
1: 17 "The righteous will live by f."
3: 3 What if some did not have f?
3: 3 lack of f nullify God's faithfulness?
3: 22 comes through f in Jesus Christ
3: 25 a sacrifice of atonement, through f
3: 26 one who justifies those who have f
3: 27 the law? No, but on that of f.
3: 28 by f apart from observing the law.
3: 30 through that same f.
3: 30 will justify the circumcised by f
3: 31 nullify the law by this f? Not at all!
4: 5 his f is credited as righteousness.
4: 9 that Abraham's f was credited
4: 11 had by f while he was still
4: 12 of the f that our father Abraham
4: 13 the righteousness that comes by f.
4: 14 f has no value and the promise is
4: 16 Therefore, the promise comes by f,
4: 16 are of the f of Abraham.
4: 19 Without weakening in his f,
4: 20 but was strengthened in his f
5: 1 we have been justified through f,
5: 2 access by f into this grace
9: 30 a righteousness that is by f;
9: 32 Because they pursued it not by f
10: 6 the righteousness that is by f says:
10: 8 the word of f we are proclaiming:
10: 17 f comes from hearing the message,
11: 20 of unbelief, and you stand by f.
12: 3 measure of f God has given you.
12: 6 let him use it in proportion to his f.
14: 1 Accept him whose f is weak,
14: 2 One man's f allows him
14: 2 but another man, whose f is weak,
14: 23 because his eating is not from f;
14: 23 that does not come from f is sin.
1Co 2: 5 so that your f might not rest
12: 9 to another f by the same Spirit,
13: 2 and if I have a f that can move
13: 13 And now these three remain: f,
15: 14 is useless and so is your f.
15: 17 has not been raised, your f is futile;
16: 13 stand firm in the f; be men
2Co 1: 24 Not that we lord it over your f,
1: 24 because it is by f you stand firm.
4: 13 With that same spirit of f we
5: 7 We live by f, not by sight.
8: 7 in f, in speech, in knowledge,
10: 15 as your f continues to grow,
13: 5 to see whether you are in the f;
Gal 1: 23 now preaching the f he once tried
2: 16 Jesus that we may be justified by f
2: 16 but by f in Jesus Christ.
2: 16 have put our f in Christ Jesus that
2: 20 I live by f in the Son of God,
3: 8 would justify the Gentiles by f,
3: 9 So those who have f are blessed
3: 9 along with Abraham, the man of f.
3: 11 "The righteous will live by f."
3: 12 based on f; on the contrary,
3: 14 by f we might receive the promise
3: 22 being given through f
3: 23 Before this f came, we were held
3: 23 up until f should be revealed.

Gal 3:24 that we might be justified by *f.*
3:25 that *f* has come, we are no longer
3:26 of God through *f* in Christ Jesus,
5: 5 But by *f* we eagerly await
5: 6 that counts is *f* expressing itself
Eph 1:15 ever since I heard about your *f*
2: 8 through *f*—and this not
3:12 through *f* in him we may approach
3:17 dwell in your hearts through *f.*
4: 5 one Lord, one *f,* one baptism;
4:13 up until we all reach unity in the *f*
6:16 to all this, take up the shield of *f,*
6:23 love with *f* from God the Father
Php 1:25 for your progress and joy in the *f,*
1:27 as one man for the *f* of the gospel
2:17 and service coming from your *f,*
3: 9 comes from God and is by *f.*
3: 9 that which is through *f* in Christ—
Col 1: 4 heard of your *f* in Christ Jesus
1: 5 the *f* and love that spring
1:23 continue in your *f,* established
2: 5 and how firm your *f* in Christ is.
2: 7 in the *f* as you were taught,
2:12 him through your *f* in the power
1Th 1: 3 Father your work produced by *f,*
1: 8 your *f* in God has become known
3: 2 and encourage you in your *f,*
3: 5 I sent to find out about your *f.*
3: 6 brought good news about your *f*
3: 7 about you because of your *f.*
3:10 supply what is lacking in your *f.*
5: 8 on *f* and love as a breastplate,
2Th 1: 3 because your *f* is growing more
1: 4 and *f* in all the persecutions
1:11 and every act prompted by your *f.*
3: 2 evil men, for not everyone has *f.*
1Ti 1: 2 To Timothy my true son in the *f:*
1: 4 than God's work—which is by *f.*
1: 5 a good conscience and a sincere *f.*
1:14 along with the *f* and love that are
1:19 and so have shipwrecked their *f.*
1:19 on to *f* and a good conscience.
2: 7 of the true *f* to the Gentiles.
2:15 if they continue in *f,* love
3: 9 of the *f* with a clear conscience.
3:13 assurance in their *f* in Christ Jesus.
4: 1 later times some will abandon the *f*
4: 6 brought up in the truths of the *f*
4:12 in life, in love, in *f* and in purity.
5: 8 he has denied the *f* and is worse
6:10 have wandered from the *f*
6:11 pursue righteousness, godliness, *f,*
6:12 Fight the good fight of the *f.*
6:21 so doing have wandered from the *f.*
2Ti 1: 5 been reminded of your sincere *f,*
1:13 with *f* and love in Christ Jesus.
2:18 and they destroy the *f* of some.
2:22 and pursue righteousness, *f,*
3: 8 as far as the *f* is concerned,
3:10 my purpose, *f,* patience, love,
3:15 wise for salvation through *f*
4: 7 finished the race, I have kept the *f.*
Tit 1: 1 Christ for the *f* of God's elect
1: 2 a *f* and knowledge resting
1: 4 my true son in our common *f:*
1:13 so that they will be sound in the *f*
2: 2 self-controlled, and sound in *f,*
3:15 Greet those who love us in the *f.*
Phm : 5 because I hear about your *f*
: 6 may be active in sharing your *f,*
Heb 4: 2 heard did not combine it with *f.*
4:14 firmly to the *f* we profess.
6: 1 and of *f* in God, instruction about
6:12 but to imitate those who through *f*
10:22 heart in full assurance of *f,*
10:38 But my righteous one will live by *f.*
11: 1 *f* is being sure of what we hope for
11: 3 By *f* we understand that
11: 4 And by *f* he still speaks, even
11: 4 By *f* Abel offered God a better
11: 4 By *f* he was commended
11: 5 By *f* Enoch was taken from this life
11: 6 And without *f* it is impossible
11: 7 By his *f* he condemned the world
11: 7 By *f* Noah, when warned about
11: 7 the righteousness that comes by *f.*
11: 8 By *f* Abraham, when called to go
11: 9 By *f* he made his home
11:11 By *f* Abraham, even though he was
11:13 living by *f* when they died.
11:17 By *f* Abraham, when God tested
11:20 By *f* Isaac blessed Jacob
11:21 By *f* Jacob, when he was dying,
11:22 By *f* Joseph, when his end was near
11:23 By *f* Moses' parents hid him
Heb 11:24 By *f* Moses, when he had grown up
11:27 By *f* he left Egypt, not fearing
11:28 By *f* he kept the Passover
11:29 By *f* the people passed
11:30 By *f* the walls of Jericho fell,
11:31 By *f* the prostitute Rahab,
11:33 through *f* conquered kingdoms,
11:39 were all commended for their *f,*
12: 2 the author and perfecter of our *f,*
13: 7 way of life and imitate their *f.*
Jas 1: 3 of your *f* develops perseverance.
2: 5 the eyes of the world to be rich in *f*
2:14 has no deeds? Can such *f* save him?
2:14 if a man claims to have *f*
2:17 In the same way, *f* by itself,
2:18 I will show you my *f* by what I do.
2:18 Show me your *f* without deeds,
2:18 "You have *f;* I have deeds."
2:20 do you want evidence that *f*
2:22 You see that his *f* and his actions
2:22 and his *f* was made complete
2:24 by what he does and not by *f* alone.
2:26 so *f* without deeds is dead.
5:15 in *f* will make the sick person well;
1Pe 1: 5 who through *f* are shielded
1: 7 These have come so that your *f*—
1: 9 you are receiving the goal of your *f,*
1:21 and so your *f* and hope are in God.
5: 9 Resist him, standing firm in the *f,*
2Pe 1: 1 Jesus Christ have received a *f*
1: 5 effort to add to your *f* goodness;
1Jn 5: 4 overcome the world, even our *f.*
Jude : 3 to contend for the *f* that was once
:20 up in your most holy *f*
Rev 2:13 You did not renounce your *f* in me,
2:19 your love and *f,* your service

FAITHFUL* (FAITH)

Nu 12: 7 he is *f* in all my house.
Dt 7: 9 your God is God; he is the *f* God,
32: 4 A *f* God who does no wrong,
1Sa 2:35 I will raise up for myself a *f* priest,
2Sa 20:19 We are the peaceful and *f* in Israel.
22:26 "To the *f* you show yourself *f,*
1Ki 3: 6 because he was *f* to you
2Ch 31:18 were *f* in consecrating themselves.
31:20 and *f* before the LORD his God.
Ne 9: 8 You found his heart *f* to you,
Ps 12: 1 the *f* have vanished
18:25 To the *f* you show yourself *f,*
25:10 of the LORD are loving and *f*
31:23 The LORD preserves the *f,*
33: 4 he is *f* in all he does.
37:28 and will not forsake his *f* ones.
78: 8 whose spirits were not *f* to him.
78:37 they were not *f* to his covenant.
89:19 to your *f* people you said:
89:24 My *f* love will be with him,
89:37 the *f* witness in the sky."
97:10 for he guards the lives of his *f* ones
101: 6 My eyes will be on the *f* in the land,
111: 7 The works of his hands are *f*
145:13 The LORD is *f* to all his promises
146: 6 the LORD, who remains *f* forever.
Pr 2: 8 and protects the way of his *f* ones.
20: 6 but a *f* man who can find?
28:20 A *f* man will be richly blessed,
31:26 and *f* instruction is on her tongue.
Isa 1:21 See how the *f* city has become
1:26 the *F* City."
49: 7 because of the LORD, who is *f,*
55: 3 my *f* love promised to David.
Jer 42: 5 *f* witness against us if we do not act
Eze 43:11 so that they may be *f* to its design
48:11 who were *f* in serving me
Hos 11:12 even against the *f* Holy One.
Zec 8: 8 I will be *f* and righteous to them
Mt 24:45 Who then is the *f* and wise servant,
25:21 'Well done, good and *f* servant!
25:21 You have been *f* with a few things;
25:23 You have been *f* with a few things;
25:23 'Well done, good and *f* servant!
Lk 12:42 then is the *f* and wise manager,
Ro 12:12 patient in affliction, *f* in prayer.
1Co 1: 9 his Son Jesus Christ our Lord, is *f.*
4: 2 been given a trust must prove *f.*
4:17 my son whom I love, who is *f*
10:13 And God is *f;* he will not let you be
2Co 1:18 no"? But as surely as God is *f,*
Eph 1: 1 in Ephesus, the *f* in Christ Jesus:
6:21 the dear brother and *f* servant
Col 1: 2 and *f* brothers in Christ at Colosse:
1: 7 who is a *f* minister of Christ
4: 7 a *f* minister and fellow servant
4: 9 He is coming with Onesimus, our *f*
1Th 5:24 The one who calls you is *f*
2Th 3: 3 the Lord is *f,* and he will strengthen
1Ti 1:12 he considered me *f,* appointing me
5: 9 has been *f* to her husband,
2Ti 2:13 he will remain *f,*
Heb 2:17 and *f* high priest in service to God,
3: 2 He was *f* to the one who appointed
3: 2 as Moses was *f* in all God's house.
3: 5 Moses was *f* as a servant
3: 6 But Christ is *f* as a son
8: 9 because they did not remain *f*
10:23 for he who promised is *f.*
11:11 he considered him *f* who had made
1Pe 4:19 themselves to their *f* Creator
5:12 whom I regard as a *f* brother,
1Jn 1: 9 he is *f* and just and will forgive us
3Jn : 5 you are *f* in what you are doing
Rev 1: 5 who is the *f* witness, the firstborn
2:10 Be *f,* even to the point of death,
2:13 the days of Antipas, my *f* witness,
3:14 the words of the Amen, the *f*
14:12 commandments and remain *f*
17:14 his called, chosen and *f* followers."
19:11 whose rider is called *F* and True.

FAITHFULLY* (FAITH)

Dt 11:13 if you *f* obey the commands I am
Jos 2:14 *f* when the LORD gives us the land
1Sa 12:24 and serve him *f* with all your heart;
1Ki 2: 4 and if they walk *f* before me
2Ki 20: 3 how I have walked before you *f*
22: 7 because they are acting *f."*
2Ch 19: 9 must serve *f* and wholeheartedly
31:12 they *f* brought in the contributions,
31:15 and Shecaniah assisted him *f*
32: 1 all that Hezekiah had so *f* done,
34:12 The men did the work *f.*
Ne 9:33 you have acted *f,* while we did
13:14 so *f* done for the house of my God
Isa 38: 3 how I have walked before you *f*
Jer 23:28 one who has my word speak it *f.*
Eze 18: 9 and *f* keeps my laws.
44:15 and who *f* carried out the duties
1Pe 4:10 *f* administering God's grace

FAITHFULNESS* (FAITH)

Ge 24:27 not abandoned his kindness and *f*
24:49 if you will show kindness and *f*
32:10 and *f* you have shown your servant.
47:29 you will show me kindness and *f.*
Ex 34: 6 *f,* maintaining love to thousands,
Jos 24:14 the LORD and serve him with all *f.*
1Sa 26:23 man for his righteousness and *f.*
2Sa 2: 6 now show you kindness and *f,*
15:20 May kindness and *f* be with you."
Ps 30: 9 Will it proclaim your *f?*
36: 5 your *f* to the skies.
40:10 I speak of your *f* and salvation.
54: 5 in your *f* destroy them.
57: 3 God sends his love and his *f.*
57:10 your *f* reaches to the skies.
61: 7 appoint your love and *f*
71:22 the harp for your *f,* O my God;
85:10 Love and *f* meet together;
85:11 *F* springs forth from the earth,
86:15 to anger, abounding in love and *f.*
88:11 your *f* in Destruction?
89: 1 mouth I will make your *f* known
89: 2 that you established your *f*
89: 5 your *f* too, in the assembly
89: 8 and your *f* surrounds you.
89:14 love and *f* go before you.
89:33 nor will I ever betray my *f.*
89:49 which in your *f* you swore to David
91: 4 his *f* will be your shield
92: 2 and your *f* at night,
98: 3 and his *f* to the house of Israel;
100: 5 *f* continues through all
108: 4 your *f* reaches to the skies.
111: 8 done in *f* and uprightness.
115: 1 because of your love and *f.*
117: 2 the *f* of the LORD endures forever.
119:75 and in *f* you have afflicted me.
119:90 *f* continues through all
138: 2 name for your love and your *f,*
143: 1 in your *f* and righteousness
Pr 3: 3 Let love and *f* never leave you;
14:22 plan what is good find love and *f.*
16: 6 Through love and *f* sin is atoned for
20:28 Love and *f* keep a king safe;
Isa 11: 5 and *f* the sash around his waist.
16: 5 in *f* a man will sit on it—
25: 1 for in perfect *f*
38:18 cannot hope for your *f.*
38:19 about your *f.*

Isa 42: 3 In f he will bring forth justice;
61: 8 In my f I will reward them
La 3:23 great is your f.
Hos 2:20 I will betroth you in f,
4: 1 "There is no f, no love,
Mt 23:23 of the law—justice, mercy and f.
Ro 3: 3 lack of faith nullify God's f?
Gal 5:22 patience, kindness, goodness, f,
3Jn : 3 and tell about your f to the truth
Rev 13:10 and f on the part of the saints.

FAITHLESS* (FAITH)

Ps 78:57 fathers they were disloyal and f,
101: 3 The deeds of f men I hate;
119:158 I look on the f with loathing,
Pr 14:14 The f will be fully repaid
Jer 3: 6 you seen what f Israel has done?
3: 8 I gave f Israel her certificate
3:11 "F Israel is more righteous
3:12 f Israel,' declares the LORD,
3:14 f people," declares the LORD,
3:22 "Return, f people;
12: 1 Why do all the f live at ease?
Ro 1:31 they are senseless, f, heartless,
2Ti 2:13 if we are f,

FALL (FALLEN FALLING FALLS)

Ps 37:24 though he stumble, he will not f,
55:22 he will never let the righteous f.
69: 9 of those who insult you f on me.
145: 14 The LORD upholds all those who f
Pr 11:28 Whoever trusts in his riches will f,
Isa 40: 7 The grass withers and the flowers f,
Mt 7:25 yet it did not f, because it had its
Lk 10:18 "I saw Satan f like lightning
11:17 a house divided against itself will f.
23:30 say to the mountains, "F on us!"
Ro 3:23 and f short of the glory of God,
Heb 6: 6 if they f away, to be brought back

FALLEN (FALL)

2Sa 1:19 How the mighty have f!
Isa 14:12 How you have f from heaven,
1Co 11:30 and a number of you have f asleep.
15: 6 though some have f asleep.
15:18 who have f asleep in Christ are lost.
15:20 of those who have f asleep.
Gal 5: 4 you have f away from grace.
1Th 4:15 precede those who have f asleep.

FALLING (FALL)

Jude :24 able to keep you from f

FALLS (FALL)

Pr 11:14 For lack of guidance a nation f,
24:17 Do not gloat when your enemy f;
28:14 he who hardens his heart f
Mt 13:21 of the word, he quickly f away.
21:44 He who f on this stone will be
Jn 12:24 a kernel of wheat f to the ground
Ro 14: 4 To his own master he stands or f.

FALSE (FALSEHOOD FALSELY)

Ex 20:16 "You shall not give f testimony
23: 1 "Do not spread f reports.
23: 7 Have nothing to do with a f charge
Dt 5:20 "You shall not give f testimony
Pr 12:17 but a f witness tells lies.
13: 5 The righteous hate what is f,
14: 5 but a f witness pours out lies.
14:25 but a f witness is deceitful.
19: 5 A f witness will not go unpunished,
19: 9 A f witness will not go unpunished,
21:28 A f witness will perish,
25:18 is the man who gives f testimony
Isa 44:25 who foils the signs of f prophets
Jer 23:16 they fill you with f hopes.
Mt 7:15 "Watch out for f prophets.
15:19 theft, f testimony, slander.
19:18 not steal, do not give f testimony,
24:11 and many f prophets will appear
24:24 For f Christs and f prophets will
Mk 10:19 do not give f testimony, do not
13:22 For f Christs and f prophets will
Lk 6:26 their fathers treated the f prophets.
18:20 not steal, do not give f testimony,
Jn 1:47 in whom there is nothing f."
1Co 15:15 found to be f witnesses about God,
2Co 11:13 For such men are f apostles,
11:26 and in danger from f brothers.
Gal 2: 4 some f brothers had infiltrated our
Php 1:18 whether from f motives or true,
Col 2:18 anyone who delights in f humility
2:23 their f humility and their harsh
1Ti 1: 3 not to teach f doctrines any longer
1Ti 6: 3 If anyone teaches f doctrines
2Pe 2: 1 also f prophets among the people,
2: 1 there will be f teachers among you.
1Jn 4: 1 many f prophets have gone out
Rev 16:13 out of the mouth of the f prophet.
19:20 with him the f prophet who had
20:10 and the f prophet had been thrown.

FALSEHOOD* (FALSE)

Job 21:34 left of your answers but f!"
31: 5 "If I have walked in f
Ps 52: 3 f rather than speaking the truth.
119:163 I hate and abhor f
Pr 30: 8 Keep f and lies far from me;
Isa 28:15 and f our hiding place."
Ro 3: 7 "If my f enhances God's
Eph 4:25 each of you must put off f
1Jn 4: 6 Spirit of truth and the spirit of f.
Rev 22:15 everyone who loves and practices f

FALSELY (FALSE)

Lev 19:12 " 'Do not swear f by my name
Mt 5:11 f say all kinds of evil against you
Lk 3:14 and don't accuse people f—
1Ti 6:20 ideas of what is f called knowledge,

FALTER*

Pr 24:10 If you f in times of trouble,
Isa 42: 4 he will not f or be discouraged

FAME

Jos 9: 9 of the f of the LORD your God.
Isa 66:19 islands that have not heard of my f
Hab 3: 2 LORD, I have heard of your f;

FAMILIES (FAMILY)

Ps 68: 6 God sets the lonely in f,

FAMILY (FAMILIES)

Pr 15:27 greedy man brings trouble to his f,
31:15 she provides food for her f
Mk 5:19 to your f and tell them how much
Lk 9:61 go back and say good-by to my f."
12:52 in one f divided against each other,
Ac 10: 2 He and all his f were devout
16:33 and all his f were baptized.
16:34 he and his whole f.
1Ti 3: 4 He must manage his own f well
3: 5 how to manage his own f,
5: 4 practice by caring for their own f
5: 8 and especially for his immediate f,

FAMINE

Ge 12:10 Now there was a f in the land,
26: 1 Now there was a f in the land—
41:30 seven years of f will follow them.
Ru 1: 1 the judges ruled, there was a f
1Ki 18: 2 Now the f was severe in Samaria,
Am 8:11 but a f of hearing the words
Ro 8:35 or persecution or f or nakedness

FAN*

2Ti 1: 6 you to f into flame the gift of God,

FANTASIES*

Ps 73:20 you will despise them as f.
Pr 12:11 but he who chases f lacks judgment
28:19 one who chases f will have his fill

FAST (FASTING)

Dt 10:20 Hold f to him and take your oaths
11:22 in all his ways and to hold f to him
13: 4 serve him and hold f to him.
30:20 to his voice, and hold f to him.
Jos 22: 5 to hold f to him and to serve him
23: 8 to hold f to the LORD your God,
2Ki 18: 6 He held f to the LORD
Ps 119: 31 I hold f to your statutes, O LORD;
139: 10 your right hand will hold me f.
Mt 6:16 "When you f, do not look somber
1Pe 5:12 Stand f in it.

FASTING (FAST)

Ps 35:13 and humbled myself with f.
Ac 13: 2 were worshiping the Lord and f,
14:23 and f, committed them to the Lord

FATHER (FATHER'S FATHERED FATHERLESS FATHERS FOREFATHERS)

Ge 2:24 this reason a man will leave his f
17: 4 You will be the f of many nations.
Ex 20:12 "Honor your f and your mother,
21:15 "Anyone who attacks his f
21:17 "Anyone who curses his f
Lev 18: 7 " 'Do not dishonor your f
Lev 19: 3 you must respect his mother and f,
20: 9 " 'If anyone curses his f or mother,
Dt 1:31 carried you, as a f carries his son,
5:16 "Honor your f and your mother,
21:18 son who does not obey his f
32: 6 Is he not your F, your Creator,
2Sa 7:14 I will be his f, and he will be my son
1Ch 17:13 I will be his f, and he will be my son
22:10 will be my son, and I will be his f.
28: 6 to be my son, and I will be his f.
Job 38:28 Does the rain have a f?
Ps 2: 7 today I have become your F.
27:10 Though my f and mother forsake
68: 5 A f to the fatherless, a defender
89:26 to me, 'You are my F,
103: 13 As a f has compassion
Pr 3:12 as a f the son he delights in.
10: 1 A wise son brings joy to his f,
17:21 there is no joy for the f of a fool.
17:25 A foolish son brings grief to his f
23:22 Listen to your f, who gave you life,
23:24 f of a righteous man has great joy;
28: 7 of gluttons disgraces his f.
28:24 He who robs his f or mother
29: 3 loves wisdom brings joy to his f,
Isa 9: 6 Everlasting F, Prince of Peace.
45:10 Woe to him who says to his f,
63:16 But you are our F,
Jer 2:27 They say to wood, 'You are my f,'
3:19 I thought you would call me 'F'
31: 9 because I am Israel's f,
Eze 18:19 the son not share the guilt of his f?'
Mic 7: 6 For a son dishonors his f,
Mal 1: 6 If I am a f, where is the honor due
2:10 we not all one F? Did not one God
Mt 3: 9 'We have Abraham as our f.'
5:16 and praise your F in heaven.
6: 9 " 'Our F in heaven,
6:26 yet your heavenly F feeds them.
10:37 "Anyone who loves his f
11:27 no one knows the F except the Son
15: 4 'Honor your f and mother'
18:10 the face of my F in heaven.
19: 5 this reason a man will leave his f
19:19 honor your f and mother,'
19:29 or brothers or sisters or f or mother
23: 9 And do not call anyone on earth 'f,'
Mk 7:10 'Honor your f and your mother,' and,
Lk 9:59 "Lord, first let me go and bury my f
12:53 f against son and son against f,
14:26 and does not hate his f and mother,
18:20 honor your f and mother.' "
23:34 Jesus said, "F, forgive them,
Jn 3:35 The F loves the Son and has placed
4:21 you will worship the F neither
5:17 "My F is always at his work
5:18 he was even calling God his own F,
5:20 For the F loves the Son
6:44 the F who sent me draws him,
6:46 No one has seen the F
8:19 "You do not know me or my F,"
8:28 speak just what the F has taught me
8:41 The only F we have is God himself
8:42 God were your F, you would love
8:44 You belong to your f, the devil,
10:17 reason my F loves me is that I lay
10:30 I and the F are one."
10:38 and understand that the F is in me,
14: 6 No one comes to the F
14: 9 who has seen me has seen the F.
14:28 for the F is greater than I.
15: 9 "As the F has loved me,
15:23 He who hates me hates my F
20:17 'I am returning to my F and your F,
Ac 13:33 today I have become your F.'
Ro 4:11 he is the f of all who believe
4:16 He is the f of us all.
8:15 And by him we cry, "Abba, F."
1Co 4:15 for in Christ Jesus I became your f
2Co 6:18 "I will be a F to you,
Eph 5:31 this reason a man will leave his f
6: 2 "Honor your f and mother"—
Php 2:11 to the glory of God the F.
Heb 1: 5 today I have become your F"?
12: 7 what son is not disciplined by his f?
1Jn 1: 3 And our fellowship is with the F
2:15 the love of the F is not in him.
2:22 he denies the F and the Son.

FATHER'S (FATHER)

Pr 13: 1 A wise son heeds his f instruction,
15: 5 A fool spurns his f discipline,
19:13 A foolish son is his f ruin,
Mt 16:27 going to come in his F glory
Lk 2:49 had to be in my F house?"

Jn 2:16 How dare you turn my F house
10:29 can snatch them out of my F hand.
14:2 In my F house are many rooms;
15:8 to my F glory, that you bear much

FATHERED (FATHER)

Dt 32:18 You deserted the Rock, who f you;

FATHERLESS (FATHER)

Dt 10:18 He defends the cause of the f
14:29 the f and the widows who live
24:17 Do not deprive the alien or the f
24:19 Leave it for the alien, the f
26:12 the alien, the f and the widow,
Ps 68:5 A father to the f, a defender
82:3 Defend the cause of the weak and f
Pr 23:10 or encroach on the fields of the f,

FATHERS (FATHER)

Ex 20:5 for the sin of the f to the third
Jer 31:29 'The f have eaten sour grapes,
Mal 4:6 the hearts of the children to their f;
Lk 1:17 the hearts of the f to their children
11:11 "Which of you f, if your son asks
Jn 4:20 Our f worshiped on this mountain,
1Co 4:15 you do not have many f,
Eph 6:4 F, do not exasperate your children;
Col 3:21 F, do not embitter your children,
Heb 12:9 all had human f who disciplined us

FATHOM* (FATHOMED)

Job 11:7 "Can you f the mysteries of God?
Ps 145:3 his greatness no one can f.
Ecc 3:11 yet they cannot f what God has
Isa 40:28 and his understanding no one can f
1Co 13:2 and can f all mysteries and all

FATHOMED* (FATHOM)

Job 5:9 performs wonders that cannot be f,
9:10 performs wonders that cannot be f,

FATTENED

Pr 15:17 than a f calf with hatred.
Lk 15:23 Bring the f calf and kill it.

FAULT (FAULTS)

1Sa 29:3 I have found no f in him."
Mt 18:15 and show him his f, just
Php 2:15 of God without f in a crooked
Jas 1:5 generously to all without finding f,
Jude :24 his glorious presence without f

FAULTFINDERS*

Jude :16 These men are grumblers and f;

FAULTLESS*

Pr 8:9 they are f to those who have
Php 3:6 as for legalistic righteousness, f.
Jas 1:27 Father accepts as pure and f is this:

FAULTS* (FAULT)

Job 10:6 that you must search out my f
Ps 19:12 Forgive my hidden f.

FAVOR (FAVORITISM)

Ge 4:4 The LORD looked with f on Abel
6:8 But Noah found f in the eyes
Ex 33:12 and you have found f with me.'
34:9 if I have found f in your eyes,"
Lev 26:9 " 'I will look on you with f
Nu 11:15 if I have found f in your eyes—
Jdg 6:17 "If now I have found f in your eyes,
1Sa 2:26 in f with the LORD and with men.
2Sa 2:6 and I too will show you the same f
2Ki 13:4 Jehoahaz sought the LORD's f,
2Ch 33:12 In his distress he sought the f
Est 7:3 "If I have found f with you, O king,
Ps 90:17 May the f of the Lord our God rest
Pr 8:35 and receives f from the LORD.
18:22 and receives f from the LORD.
19:6 Many curry f with a ruler,
Isa 61:2 proclaim the year of the LORD's f
Zec 11:7 called one F and the other Union,
Lk 1:30 Mary, you have found f with God.
2:14 to men on whom his f rests."
2:52 and in f with God and men.
4:19 to proclaim the year of the Lord's f
2Co 6:2 now is the time of God's f,

FAVORITISM* (FAVOR)

Ex 23:3 and do not show f to a poor man
Lev 19:15 to the poor or f to the great,
Ac 10:34 true it is that God does not show f
Ro 2:11 For God does not show f.
Eph 6:9 and there is no f with him.
Col 3:25 for his wrong, and there is no f.
1Ti 5:21 and to do nothing out of f.
Jas 2:1 Lord Jesus Christ, don't show f.
2:9 But if you show f, you sin

FEAR (AFRAID FEARED FEARS FRIGHTENED GOD-FEARING)

Dt 6:13 F the LORD your God, serve him
10:12 but to f the LORD your God,
31:12 and learn to f the LORD your God
31:13 and learn to f the LORD your God
Jos 4:24 you might always f the LORD
24:14 "Now f the LORD and serve him
1Sa 12:14 If you f the LORD and serve
12:24 But be sure to f the LORD
2Sa 23:3 when he rules in the f of God,
2Ch 19:7 let the f of the LORD be upon you.
26:5 who instructed him in the f of God.
Job 1:9 "Does Job f God for nothing?"
Ps 2:11 Serve the LORD with f
19:9 The f of the LORD is pure,
23:4 I will f no evil,
27:1 whom shall I f?
33:8 Let all the earth f the LORD;
34:7 around those who f him,
34:9 F the LORD, you his saints,
46:2 Therefore we will not f,
86:11 that I may f your name.
90:11 great as the f that is due you.
91:5 You will not f the terror of night,
111:10 f of the LORD is the beginning
118:4 Let those who f the LORD say:
128:1 Blessed are all who f the LORD,
145:19 of those who f him;
147:11 delights in those who f him,
Pr 1:7 f of the LORD is the beginning
1:33 and be at ease, without f of harm."
8:13 To f the LORD is to hate evil;
9:10 f of the LORD is the beginning
10:27 The f of the LORD adds length
14:27 The f of the LORD is a fountain
15:33 f of the LORD teaches a man
16:6 through the f of the LORD a man
19:23 The f of the LORD leads to life:
22:4 Humility and the f of the LORD
29:25 F of man will prove to be a snare,
31:21 she has no f for her household;
Ecc 12:13 F God and keep his
Isa 11:3 delight in the f of the LORD.
33:6 the f of the LORD is the key
35:4 "Be strong, do not f;
41:10 So do not f, for I am with you;
41:13 and says to you, Do not f;
43:1 "F not, for I have redeemed you;
51:7 Do not f the reproach of men
54:14 you will have nothing to f.
Jer 17:8 It does not f when heat comes;
Lk 12:5 I will show you whom you should f:
2Co 5:11 we know what it is to f the Lord,
Php 2:12 to work out your salvation with f
1Jn 4:18 But perfect love drives out f,
Jude :23 to others show mercy, mixed with f
Rev 14:7 "F God and give him glory,

FEARED (FEAR)

Job 1:1 he f God and shunned evil.
Ps 76:7 You alone are to be f.
Mal 3:16 those who f the LORD talked

FEARS (FEAR)

Job 1:8 a man who f God and shuns evil."
2:3 a man who f God and shuns evil.
Ps 34:4 he delivered me from all my f.
112:1 is the man who f the LORD,
Pr 14:16 A wise man f the LORD
14:26 He who f the LORD has a secure
31:30 a woman who f the LORD is
2Co 7:5 conflicts on the outside, f within.
1Jn 4:18 The one who f is not made perfect

FEAST (FEASTING FEASTS)

Pr 15:15 the cheerful heart has a continual f.
2Pe 2:13 pleasures while they f with you.

FEASTING (FEAST)

Pr 17:1 than a house full of f, with strife.

FEASTS (FEAST)

Am 5:21 "I hate, I despise your religious f;
Jude :12 men are blemishes at your love f,

FEATHERS

Ps 91:4 He will cover you with his f,

FEEBLE

Job 4:3 you have strengthened f hands.
Isa 35:3 Strengthen the f hands,
Heb 12:12 strengthen your f arms

FEED (FEEDS)

Jn 21:15 Jesus said, "F my lambs."
21:17 Jesus said, "F my sheep.
Ro 12:20 "If your enemy is hungry, f him;
Jude :12 shepherds who f only themselves.

FEEDS (FEED)

Pr 15:14 but the mouth of a fool f on folly.
Mt 6:26 yet your heavenly Father f them.
Jn 6:57 so the one who f on me will live

FEEL

Jdg 16:26 me where I can f the pillars that
Ps 115:7 they have hands, but cannot f,

FEET (FOOT)

Ru 3:8 discovered a woman lying at his f.
Ps 8:6 you put everything under his f:
22:16 have pierced my hands and my f.
40:2 he set my f on a rock
56:13 and my f from stumbling,
66:9 and kept our f from slipping.
73:2 as for me, my f had almost slipped;
110:1 a footstool for your f."
119:105 Your word is a lamp to my f
Pr 4:26 Make level paths for your f
Isa 52:7 are the f of those who bring good
Da 2:33 its f partly of iron and partly
Na 1:15 the f of one who brings good news,
Mt 10:14 shake the dust off your f
22:44 enemies under your f." '
Lk 1:79 to guide our f into the path of peace
20:43 a footstool for your f." '
24:39 Look at my hands and my f.
Jn 13:5 and began to wash his disciples' f,
13:14 also should wash one another's f.
Ro 3:15 "Their f are swift to shed blood;
10:15 "How beautiful are the f
16:20 will soon crush Satan under your f.
1Co 12:21 And the head cannot say to the f,
15:25 has put all his enemies under his f.
Eph 1:22 God placed all things under his f
1Ti 5:10 washing the f of the saints,
Heb 1:13 a footstool for your f"?
2:8 and put everything under his f."
12:13 "Make level paths for your f,"
Rev 1:15 His f were like bronze glowing

FELIX

Governor before whom Paul was tried (Ac 23:23-24:27).

FELLOWSHIP

Ex 20:24 burnt offerings and f offerings,
Lev 3:1 If someone's offering is a f offering,
1Co 1:9 who has called you into f
5:2 out of your f the man who did this?
2Co 6:14 what f can light have with darkness
13:14 and the f of the Holy Spirit be
Gal 2:9 and Barnabas the right hand of f
Php 2:1 if any f with the Spirit,
3:10 the f of sharing in his sufferings,
1Jn 1:3 And our f is with the Father
1:3 so that you also may have f with us.
1:6 claim to have f with him yet walk
1:7 we have f with one another,

FEMALE

Ge 1:27 male and f he created them.
5:2 He created them male and f
Mt 19:4 Creator 'made them male and f,'
Mk 10:6 God 'made them male and f.'
Gal 3:28 f, for you are all one in Christ Jesus

FEROCIOUS

Mt 7:15 but inwardly they are f wolves.

FERTILE (FERTILIZE)

Isa 32:15 and the desert becomes a f field,
Jer 2:7 I brought you into a f land

FERTILIZE* (FERTILE)

Lk 13:8 and I'll dig around it and f it.

FERVOR*

Ac 18:25 and he spoke with great f
Ro 12:11 but keep your spiritual f, serving

FESTIVAL

1Co 5: 8 Therefore let us keep the F,
Col 2: 16 or with regard to a religious f,

FESTUS

Successor of Felix; sent Paul to Caesar (Ac 25-26).

FEVER

Job 30: 30 my body burns with f.
Mt 8: 14 mother-in-law lying in bed with a f.
Lk 4: 38 was suffering from a high f,
Jn 4: 52 "The f left him yesterday
Ac 28: 8 suffering from f and dysentery.

FIELD (FIELDS)

Ge 4: 8 Abel, "Let's go out to the f."
Lev 19: 9 reap to the very edges of your f
19: 19 Do not plant your f with two kinds
Pr 31: 16 She considers a f and buys it;
Isa 40: 6 glory is like the flowers of the f.
Mt 6: 28 See how the lilies of the f grow.
6: 30 how God clothes the grass of the f,
13: 38 f is the world, and the good seed
13: 44 is like treasure hidden in a f.
Lk 14: 18 I have just bought a f, and I must go
1Co 3: 9 you are God's f, God's building.
1Pe 1: 24 glory is like the flowers of the f;

FIELDS (FIELD)

Ru 2: 2 go to the f and pick up the leftover
Lk 2: 8 were shepherds living out in the f
Jn 4: 35 open your eyes and look at the f!

FIG (FIGS SYCAMORE-FIG)

Ge 3: 7 so they sewed f leaves together
Jdg 9: 10 "Next, the trees said to the f tree,
1Ki 4: 25 man under his own vine and f tree.
Pr 27: 18 He who tends a f tree will eat its
Mic 4: 4 and under his own f tree,
Zec 3: 10 to sit under his vine and f tree,'
Mt 21: 19 Seeing a f tree by the road,
Lk 13: 6 "A man had a f tree, planted
Jas 3: 12 brothers, can a f tree bear olives,
Rev 6: 13 drop from a f tree when shaken

FIGHT (FIGHTING FIGHTS FOUGHT)

Ex 14: 14 The LORD will f for you; you need
Dt 1: 30 going before you, will f for you,
3: 22 the LORD your God himself will f
Ne 4: 20 Our God will f for us!"
Ps 35: 1 f against those who f against me.
Jn 18: 36 my servants would f
1Co 9: 26 I do not f like a man beating the air.
2Co 10: 4 The weapons we f
1Ti 1: 18 them you may f the good f,
6: 12 Fight the good f of the faith.
2Ti 4: 7 fought the good f, I have finished

FIGHTING (FIGHT)

Jos 10: 14 Surely the LORD was f for Israel!

FIGHTS (FIGHT)

Jos 23: 10 the LORD your God f for you,
1Sa 25: 28 because he f the LORD's battles.
Jas 4: 1 What causes f and quarrels

FIGS (FIG)

Lk 6: 44 People do not pick f
Jas 3: 12 grapevine bear f? Neither can a salt

FILL (FILLED FILLING FILLS FULL FULLNESS FULLY)

Ge 1: 28 and increase in number; f the earth
Ps 16: 11 you will f me with joy
81: 10 wide your mouth and I will f it.
Pr 28: 19 who chases fantasies will have his f
Hag 2: 7 and I will f this house with glory,'
Jn 6: 26 you ate the loaves and had your f.
Ac 2: 28 you will f me with joy
Ro 15: 13 the God of hope f you with all joy

FILLED (FILL)

Ex 31: 3 I have f him with the Spirit of God,
35: 31 he has f him with the Spirit of God,
Dt 34: 9 son of Nun was f with the spirit
1Ki 8: 10 the cloud f the temple
8: 11 glory of the LORD f his temple.
2Ch 5: 14 of the LORD f the temple of God.
7: 1 the glory of the LORD f the temple
Ps 72: 19 may the whole earth be f
119: 64 The earth is f with your love,
Isa 6: 4 and the temple was f with smoke.
Eze 10: 3 and a cloud f the inner court.
Eze 10: 4 The cloud f the temple,
43: 5 the glory of the LORD f the temple
Hab 2: 14 For the earth will be f
3: 3 and his praise f the earth.
Mt 5: 6 for they will be f.
Lk 1: 15 and he will be f with the Holy Spirit
1: 41 and Elizabeth was f with the Holy
1: 67 His father Zechariah was f
2: 40 and became strong; he was f
Jn 12: 3 the house was f with the fragrance
Ac 2: 2 f the whole house where they were
2: 4 All of them were f
4: 8 Then Peter, f with the Holy Spirit,
4: 31 they were all f with the Holy Spirit
9: 17 and be f with the Holy Spirit."
13: 9 called Paul, f with the Holy Spirit,
Eph 5: 18 Instead, be f with the Spirit.
Php 1: 11 f with the fruit of righteousness
Rev 15: 8 And the temple was f with smoke

FILLING (FILL)

Eze 44: 4 the glory of the LORD f the temple

FILLS (FILL)

Nu 14: 21 of the LORD f the whole earth,
Ps 107: 9 and f the hungry with good things.
Eph 1: 23 fullness of him who f everything

FILTH (FILTHY)

Isa 4: 4 The Lord will wash away the f
Jas 1: 21 rid of all moral f and the evil that is

FILTHY (FILTH)

Isa 64: 6 all our righteous acts are like f rags;
Col 3: 8 and f language from your lips.
2Pe 2: 7 by the f lives of lawless men

FINAL (FINALITY)

Ps 73: 17 then I understood their f destiny.

FINALITY* (FINAL)

Ro 9: 28 on earth with speed and f."

FINANCIAL*

1Ti 6: 5 that godliness is a means to f gain.

FIND (FINDS FOUND)

Nu 32: 23 be sure that your sin will f you out.
Dt 4: 29 you will f him if you look for him
1Sa 23: 16 and helped him f strength in God.
Job 23: 3 If only I knew where to f him;
Ps 36: 7 f refuge in the shadow
62: 5 F rest, O my soul, in God alone;
91: 4 under his wings you will f refuge;
Pr 8: 17 and those who seek me f me.
14: 22 those who plan what is good f love
20: 6 but a faithful man who can f?
24: 14 if you f it, there is a future hope
31: 10 A wife of noble character who can f
Jer 6: 16 and you will f rest for your souls.
29: 13 and f me when you seek me
Mt 7: 7 seek and you will f; knock
11: 29 and you will f rest for your souls.
16: 25 loses his life for me will f it.
22: 9 invite to the banquet anyone you f.'
Lk 11: 9 seek and you will f; knock
18: 8 will he f faith on the earth?"
Jn 10: 9 come in and go out, and f pasture.

FINDS (FIND)

Ps 62: 1 My soul f rest in God alone;
112: 1 who f great delight
119: 162 like one who f great spoil.
Pr 3: 13 Blessed is the man who f wisdom,
8: 35 For whoever f me f life
11: 27 He who seeks good f good will,
18: 22 He who f a wife f what is good
Mt 7: 8 he who seeks f; and to him who
10: 39 Whoever f his life will lose it,
Lk 11: 10 he who seeks f; and to him who
12: 37 whose master f them watching
12: 43 servant whom the master f doing
15: 4 go after the lost sheep until he f it?
15: 8 and search carefully until she f it?

FINE-SOUNDING* (SOUND)

Col 2: 4 may deceive you by f arguments.

FINGER

Ex 8: 19 to Pharaoh, "This is the f of God."
31: 18 of stone inscribed by the f of God.
Dt 9: 10 two stone tablets inscribed by the f
Lk 11: 20 But if I drive out demons by the f
16: 24 to dip the tip of his f in water
Jn 8: 6 to write on the ground with his f.
Jn 20: 25 and put my f where the nails were,

FINISH (FINISHED)

Jn 4: 34 him who sent me and to f his work.
5: 36 that the Father has given me to f,
Ac 20: 24 if only I may f the race
2Co 8: 11 Now f the work, so that your eager
Jas 1: 4 Perseverance must f its work

FINISHED (FINISH)

Ge 2: 2 seventh day God had f the work he
Jn 19: 30 the drink, Jesus said, "It is f."
2Ti 4: 7 I have f the race, I have kept

FIRE

Ex 3: 2 in flames of f from within a bush.
13: 21 in a pillar of f to give them light,
Lev 6: 12 f on the altar must be kept burning;
9: 24 F came out from the presence
1Ki 18: 38 Then the f of the LORD fell
2Ki 2: 11 suddenly a chariot of f
Isa 5: 24 as tongues of f lick up straw
30: 27 and his tongue is a consuming f.
Jer 23: 29 my word like f," declares
Da 3: 25 four men walking around in the f,
Zec 3: 2 stick snatched from the f?"
Mal 3: 2 For he will be like a refiner's f
Mt 3: 11 you with the Holy Spirit and with f.
3: 12 the chaff with unquenchable f."
5: 22 will be in danger of the f of hell.
18: 8 and be thrown into eternal f.
25: 41 into the eternal f prepared
Mk 9: 43 where the f never goes out.
9: 48 and the f is not quenched.'
9: 49 Everyone will be salted with f.
Lk 3: 16 you with the Holy Spirit and with f.
12: 49 I have come to bring f on the earth,
Ac 2: 3 to be tongues of f that separated
1Co 3: 13 It will be revealed with f,
1Th 5: 19 Do not put out the Spirit's f;
Heb 12: 29 for our "God is a consuming f."
Jas 3: 5 set on f by a small spark.
3: 6 also is a f, a world of evil
2Pe 3: 10 the elements will be destroyed by f,
Jude : 7 suffer the punishment of eternal f.
: 23 snatch others from the f
Rev 1: 14 and his eyes were like blazing f.
20: 14 The lake of f is the second death.

FIRM*

Ex 14: 13 Stand f and you will see
15: 8 surging waters stood f like a wall;
Jos 3: 17 the covenant of the LORD stood f
2Ch 20: 17 stand f and see the deliverance
Ezr 9: 8 giving us a f place in his sanctuary,
Job 11: 15 you will stand f and without fear.
36: 5 he is mighty, and f in his purpose.
41: 23 they are f and immovable.
Ps 20: 8 but we rise up and stand f.
30: 7 you made my mountain stand f;
33: 9 he commanded, and it stood f.
33: 11 of the LORD stand f forever,
37: 23 he makes his steps f;
40: 2 and gave me a f place to stand.
75: 3 it is I who hold its pillars f.
78: 13 made the water stand f like a wall.
89: 2 that your love stands f forever,
89: 4 and make your throne f
93: 5 Your statutes stand f;
119: 89 it stands f in the heavens.
Pr 4: 26 and take only ways that are f.
10: 25 but the righteous stand f forever.
12: 7 the house of the righteous stands f.
Isa 7: 9 If you do not stand f in your faith,
22: 17 about to take f hold of you
22: 23 drive him like a peg into a f place;
22: 25 into the f place will give way;
Eze 13: 5 so that it will stand f in the battle
Zec 8: 23 nations will take f hold of one Jew
Mt 10: 22 he who stands f to the end will be
24: 13 he who stands f to the end will be
Mk 13: 13 he who stands f to the end will be
Lk 21: 19 By standing f you will gain life.
1Co 10: 12 So, if you think you are standing f,
15: 58 my dear brothers, stand f.
16: 13 on your guard; stand f in the faith;
2Co 1: 7 for you is f, because we know that
1: 21 who makes both us and you stand f
1: 24 because it is by faith you stand f.
Gal 5: 1 Stand f, then, and do not let
Eph 6: 14 Stand f then, with the belt
Php 1: 27 I will know that you stand f
4: 1 that is how you should stand f
Col 1: 23 in your faith, established and f,
2: 5 and how f your faith in Christ is.

Col 4: 12 that you may stand *f* in all the will
1Th 3: 8 since you are standing *f* in the Lord
2Th 2: 15 stand *f* and hold to the teachings
1Ti 6: 19 a *f* foundation for the coming age,
2Ti 2: 19 God's solid foundation stands *f*,
Heb 6: 19 an anchor for the soul, *f* and secure
Jas 5: 8 You too, be patient and stand *f*,
1Pe 5: 9 Resist him, standing *f* in the faith,
5: 10 make you strong, *f* and steadfast.

FIRMAMENT see EXPANSE, HEAVENS, SKIES

FIRST

Ge 1: 5 and there was morning—the *f* day.
13: 4 and where he had *f* built an altar.
Ex 34: 19 *f* offspring of every womb belongs
1Ki 22: 5 "*F* seek the counsel of the LORD."
Pr 18: 17 *f* to present his case seems right,
Isa 44: 6 I am the *f* and I am the last;
48: 12 I am the *f* and I am the last.
Mt 5: 24 *F* go and be reconciled
6: 33 But seek *f* his kingdom
7: 5 *f* take the plank out
19: 30 But many who are *f* will be last,
20: 16 last will be *f*, and the *f* will be last."
20: 27 wants to be *f* must be your slave—
22: 38 This is the *f* and greatest
23: 26 *F* clean the inside of the cup
Mk 9: 35 to be *f*, he must be the very last,
10: 31 are *f* will be last, and the last *f*."
10: 44 wants to be *f* must be slave
13: 10 And the gospel must *f* be preached
Lk 13: 30 will be *f*, and *f* who will be last."
Jn 8: 7 let him be the *f* to throw a stone
Ac 11: 26 disciples were called Christians *f*
Ro 1: 16 *f* for the Jew, then for the Gentile.
1: 17 is by faith from *f* to last,
2: 9 *f* for the Jew, then for the Gentile;
2: 10 *f* for the Jew, then for the Gentile.
1Co 12: 28 in the church God has appointed *f*
15: 45 "The *f* man Adam became a living
2Co 8: 5 they gave themselves *f* to the Lord
Eph 6: 2 which is the *f* commandment
1Th 4: 16 and the dead in Christ will rise *f*.
1Ti 2: 13 For Adam was formed *f*, then Eve.
Heb 10: 9 He sets aside the *f*
Jas 3: 17 comes from heaven is *f* of all pure;
1Jn 4: 19 We love because he *f* loved us.
3Jn : 9 but Diotrephes, who loves to be *f*,
Rev 1: 17 I am the *F* and the Last.
2: 4 You have forsaken your *f* love.
22: 13 and the Omega, the *F* and the Last,

FIRSTBORN (BEAR)

Ex 11: 5 Every *f* son in Egypt will die,
34: 20 Redeem all your *f* sons.
Ps 89: 27 I will also appoint him my *f*,
Lk 2: 7 and she gave birth to her *f*, a son.
Ro 8: 29 that he might be the *f*
Col 1: 15 image of the invisible God, the *f*
1: 18 and the *f* from among the dead,
Heb 1: 6 when God brings his *f*
12: 23 of the *f*, whose names are written
Rev 1: 5 who is the faithful witness, the *f*

FIRSTFRUITS

Ex 23: 16 the Feast of Harvest with the *f*
23: 19 "Bring the best of the *f* of your soil
Ro 8: 23 who have the *f* of the Spirit,
1Co 15: 23 Christ, the *f*; then, when he comes,
Rev 14: 4 offered as *f* to God and the Lamb.

FISH (FISHERS)

Ge 1: 26 let them rule over the *f* of the sea
Jnh 1: 17 But the LORD provided a great *f*
Mt 7: 10 asks for a *f*, will give him a snake?
12: 40 three nights in the belly of a huge *f*,
14: 17 loaves of bread and two *f*,"
Mk 6: 38 they said, "Five—and two *f*."
Lk 5: 6 of *f* that their nets began to break.
9: 13 loaves of bread and two *f*—
Jn 6: 9 small barley loaves and two small *f*,
21: 5 haven't you any *f*?" "No,"
21: 11 It was full of large *f*, 153, but

FISHERMEN

Mk 1: 16 a net into the lake, for they were *f*.

FISHERS (FISH)

Mt 4: 19 "and I will make you *f* of men."
Mk 1: 17 "and I will make you *f* of men."

FISHHOOK*

Job 41: 1 pull in the leviathan with a *f*

FISTS

Mt 26: 67 and struck him with their *f*.

FIT (FITTING)

Jdg 17: 6 no king; everyone did as he saw *f*.
21: 25 no king; everyone did as he saw *f*.

FITTING* (FIT)

Ps 33: 1 it is *f* for the upright to praise him.
147: 1 how pleasant and *f* to praise him!
Pr 10: 32 of the righteous know what is *f*,
19: 10 It is not *f* for a fool to live in luxury
26: 1 honor is not *f* for a fool.
1Co 14: 40 everything should be done in a *f*
Col 3: 18 to your husbands, as is *f* in the Lord
Heb 2: 10 sons to glory, it was *f* that God,

FIX* (FIXED)

Dt 11: 18 *F* these words of mine
Job 14: 3 Do you *f* your eye on such a one?
Pr 4: 25 *f* your gaze directly before you.
Isa 46: 8 "Remember this, *f* it in mind,
Am 9: 4 I will *f* my eyes upon them
2Co 4: 18 we *f* our eyes not on what is seen,
Heb 3: 1 heavenly calling, *f* your thoughts
12: 2 Let us *f* our eyes on Jesus,

FIXED* (FIX)

2Ki 8: 11 stared at him with a *f* gaze
Job 38: 10 when I *f* limits for it
Ps 141: 8 my eyes are *f* on you, O Sovereign
Pr 8: 28 *f* securely the fountains of the deep
Jer 33: 25 and night and the *f* laws of heaven
Lk 16: 26 and you a great chasm has been *f*,

FLAME (FLAMES FLAMING)

2Ti 1: 6 you to fan into *f* the gift of God,

FLAMES (FLAME)

1Co 3: 15 only as one escaping through the *f*.
13: 3 and surrender my body to the *f*,

FLAMING (FLAME)

Eph 6: 16 you can extinguish all the *f* arrows

FLANK

Eze 34: 21 Because you shove with *f*

FLASH

1Co 15: 52 in a *f*, in the twinkling of an eye,

FLATTER* (FLATTERING FLATTERS FLATTERY)

Job 32: 21 nor will I *f* any man;
Ps 78: 36 But then they would *f* him
Jude : 16 *f* others for their own advantage.

FLATTERING* (FLATTER)

Ps 12: 2 their *f* lips speak with deception.
12: 3 May the LORD cut off all *f* lips
Pr 26: 28 and a *f* mouth works ruin.
28: 23 than he who has a *f* tongue.
Eze 12: 24 or *f* divinations among the people

FLATTERS* (FLATTER)

Ps 36: 2 For in his own eyes he *f* himself
Pr 29: 5 Whoever *f* his neighbor

FLATTERY* (FLATTER)

Job 32: 22 for if I were skilled in *f*,
Da 11: 32 With *f* he will corrupt those who
Ro 16: 18 and *f* they deceive the minds
1Th 2: 5 You know we never used *f*,

FLAWLESS*

2Sa 22: 31 the word of the LORD is *f*.
Job 11: 4 You say to God, 'My beliefs are *f*
Ps 12: 6 And the words of the LORD are *f*,
18: 30 the word of the LORD is *f*.
Pr 30: 5 "Every word of God is *f*;
SS 5: 2 my dove, my *f* one.

FLEE (FLEES)

Ps 139: 7 Where can I *f* from your presence?
1Co 6: 18 *F* from sexual immorality.
10: 14 my dear friends, *f* from idolatry.
1Ti 6: 11 But you, man of God, *f* from all this
2Ti 2: 22 *F* the evil desires of youth,
Jas 4: 7 Resist the devil, and he will *f*

FLEECE

Jdg 6: 37 I will place a wool *f*

FLEES (FLEE)

Pr 28: 1 The wicked man *f* though no one

FLEETING*

Job 14: 2 like a *f* shadow, he does not endure
Ps 39: 4 let me know how *f* is my life.
89: 47 Remember how *f* is my life.
144: 4 his days are like a *f* shadow.
Pr 21: 6 is a *f* vapor and a deadly snare.
31: 30 Charm is deceptive, and beauty is *f*

FLESH see also BODY, MANKIND, PEOPLE, SINFUL (nature)

Ge 2: 23 and *f* of my *f*;
2: 24 and they will become one *f*.
2Ch 32: 8 With him is only the arm of *f*,
Job 19: 26 yet in my *f* I will see God;
Eze 11: 19 of stone and give them a heart of *f*.
36: 26 of stone and give you a heart of *f*.
Mt 19: 5 and the two will become one *f*?
Mk 10: 8 and the two will become one *f*.'
Jn 1: 14 The Word became *f* and made his
6: 51 This bread is my *f*, which I will give
1Co 6: 16 "The two will become one *f*."
15: 39 All *f* is not the same: Men have one
Eph 5: 31 and the two will become one *f*."
6: 12 For our struggle is not against *f*
Php 3: 2 do evil, those mutilators of the *f*.
1Jn 4: 2 come in the *f* is from God,
Jude : 23 the clothing stained by corrupted *f*.

FLIGHT

Dt 32: 30 or two put ten thousand to *f*,

FLINT

Isa 50: 7 Therefore have I set my face like *f*,
Zec 7: 12 They made their hearts as hard as *f*

FLIRTING*

Isa 3: 16 *f* with their eyes,

FLOCK (FLOCKS)

Ps 77: 20 You led your people like a *f*
78: 52 he brought his people out like a *f*;
95: 7 the *f* under his care.
Isa 40: 11 He tends his *f* like a shepherd:
Jer 10: 21 and all their *f* is scattered.
23: 2 "Because you have scattered my *f*
31: 10 watch over his *f* like a shepherd.'
Eze 34: 2 not shepherds take care of the *f*?
Zec 11: 17 who deserts the *f*!
Mt 26: 31 the sheep of the *f* will be scattered.'
Lk 12: 32 little *f*, for your Father has been
Jn 10: 16 shall be one *f* and one shepherd.
Ac 20: 28 all the *f* of which the Holy Spirit
1Co 9: 7 Who tends a *f* and does not drink
1Pe 5: 2 Be shepherds of God's *f* that is
5: 3 but being examples to the *f*.

FLOCKS (FLOCK)

Lk 2: 8 keeping watch over their *f* at night.

FLOG (FLOGGED FLOGGING)

Pr 19: 25 *F* a mocker, and the simple will
Ac 22: 25 to *f* a Roman citizen who hasn't

FLOGGED (FLOG)

Jn 19: 1 Pilate took Jesus and had him *f*.
Ac 5: 40 the apostles in and had them *f*.
16: 23 After they had been severely *f*,
2Co 11: 23 frequently, been *f* more severely,

FLOGGING (FLOG)

Heb 11: 36 *f*, while still others were chained

FLOOD (FLOODGATES)

Ge 7: 7 ark to escape the waters of the *f*.
Mal 2: 13 You *f* the LORD's altar with tears.
Mt 24: 38 For in the days before the *f*,
2Pe 2: 5 world when he brought the *f*

FLOODGATES (FLOOD)

Ge 7: 11 the *f* of the heavens were opened.
Mal 3: 10 see if I will not throw open the *f*

FLOOR

Jas 2: 3 or "Sit on the *f* by my feet,"

FLOUR

Lev 2: 1 his offering is to be of fine *f*.
Nu 7: 13 filled with fine *f* mixed with oil
28: 9 of an ephah of fine *f* mixed with oil.

FLOURISH (FLOURISHES FLOURISHING)
Ps 72: 7 In his days the righteous will f;
92: 7 and all evildoers f,
92: 12 The righteous will f like a palm tree
Pr 14: 11 but the tent of the upright will f.

FLOURISHES (FLOURISH)
Pr 12: 12 but the root of the righteous f.

FLOURISHING (FLOURISH)
Ps 52: 8 f in the house of God;

FLOW (FLOWING)
Nu 13: 27 and it does f with milk and honey!
Jn 7: 38 streams of living water will f

FLOWER (FLOWERS)
Job 14: 2 up like a f and withers away;
Ps 103: 15 he flourishes like a f of the field;
Jas 1: 10 he will pass away like a wild f.

FLOWERS (FLOWER)
Isa 40: 6 and all their glory is like the f
40: 7 The grass withers and the f fall,
1Pe 1: 24 and all their glory is like the f

FLOWING (FLOW)
Ex 3: 8 a land f with milk and honey—
33: 3 Go up to the land f with milk
Nu 16: 14 us into a land f with milk
Jos 5: 6 a land f with milk and honey.
Ps 107: 33 f springs into thirsty ground,
107: 35 the parched ground into f springs;
Jer 32: 22 a land f with milk and honey.
Eze 20: 6 a land f with milk and honey,
Rev 22: 1 f from the throne of God

FLUTE
Ps 150: 4 praise him with the strings and f,
Mt 11: 17 " 'We played the f for you,
1Co 14: 7 that make sounds, such as the f

FOAL*
Zec 9: 9 on a colt, the f of a donkey.
Mt 21: 5 on a colt, the f of a donkey.' "

FOILS*
Ps 33: 10 The LORD f the plans
Isa 44: 25 who f the signs of false prophets

FOLDING* (FOLDS)
Pr 6: 10 a little f of the hands to rest—
24: 33 a little f of the hands to rest—

FOLDS (FOLDING)
Ecc 4: 5 The fool f his hands

FOLLOW (FOLLOWED FOLLOWING FOLLOWS)
Ex 23: 2 Do not f the crowd in doing wrong.
Lev 18: 4 and be careful to f my decrees.
Dt 5: 1 Learn them and be sure to f them.
17: 19 f carefully all the words of this law
1Ki 11: 6 he did not f the LORD completely,
2Ch 34: 33 they did not fail to f the LORD,
Ps 23: 6 Surely goodness and love will f me
119: 166 and I f your commands.
Mt 4: 19 f me," Jesus said, "and I will make
8: 19 I will f you wherever you go."
8: 22 But Jesus told him, "F me,
16: 24 and take up his cross and f me.
19: 27 "We have left everything to f you!
Lk 9: 23 take up his cross daily and f me.
9: 61 Still another said, "I will f you,
Jn 10: 4 his sheep f him because they know
10: 5 But they will never f a stranger;
10: 27 I know them, and they f me.
12: 26 Whoever serves me must f me;
21: 19 Then he said to him, "F me!"
1Co 1: 12 One of you says, "I f Paul";
11: 1 F my example, as I follow
14: 1 F the way of love and eagerly
2Th 3: 9 ourselves a model for you to f.
1Pe 2: 21 that you should f in his steps.
Rev 14: 4 They f the Lamb wherever he goes.

FOLLOWED (FOLLOW)
Nu 32: 11 they have not f me wholeheartedly,
Dt 1: 36 he f the LORD wholeheartedly."
Jos 14: 14 he f the LORD, the God of Israel,
2Ch 10: 14 he f the advice of the young men
Mt 4: 20 once they left their nets and f him.
9: 9 and Matthew got up and f him.
26: 58 But Peter f him at a distance,
Lk 18: 43 he received his sight and f Jesus,

FOLLOWING (FOLLOW)
Ps 119: 14 I rejoice in f your statutes
Php 3: 17 Join with others in f my example,
1Ti 1: 18 by f them you may fight the good

FOLLOWS (FOLLOW)
Jn 8: 12 Whoever f me will never walk

FOLLY (FOOL)
Pr 14: 29 a quick-tempered man displays f.
19: 3 A man's own f ruins his life,
Ecc 10: 1 so a little f outweighs wisdom
Mk 7: 22 envy, slander, arrogance and f.
2Ti 3: 9 their f will be clear to everyone.

FOOD (FOODS)
Ge 1: 30 I give every green plant for f."
Pr 12: 9 to be somebody and have no f.
12: 11 his land will have abundant f,
20: 13 you will have f to spare.
20: 17 F gained by fraud tastes sweet
21: 20 of the wise are stores of choice f
22: 9 for he shares his f with the poor.
23: 3 for that f is deceptive.
23: 6 Do not eat the f of a stingy man,
25: 21 If your enemy is hungry, give him f
31: 14 bringing her f from afar.
31: 15 she provides f for her family
Isa 58: 7 not to share your f with the hungry
Eze 18: 7 but gives his f to the hungry
Da 1: 8 to defile himself with the royal f
Mt 3: 4 His f was locusts and wild honey.
6: 25 Is not life more important than f,
Jn 4: 32 "I have f to eat that you know
4: 34 have brought him f?" "My f,"
6: 27 Do not work for f that spoils,
6: 55 my flesh is real f and my blood is
Ac 15: 20 to abstain from f polluted by idols,
Ro 14: 14 fully convinced that no f is unclean
1Co 8: 1 Now about f sacrificed to idols:
8: 8 But f does not bring us near to God
2Co 11: 27 and have often gone without f;
1Ti 6: 8 But if we have f and clothing,
Heb 5: 14 But solid f is for the mature,
Jas 2: 15 sister is without clothes and daily f.

FOODS (FOOD)
Mk 7: 19 Jesus declared all f "clean.")

FOOL (FOLLY FOOL'S FOOLISH FOOLISHNESS FOOLS)
1Sa 25: 25 his name is F, and folly goes
Ps 14: 1 The f says in his heart,
Pr 10: 10 and a chattering f comes to ruin.
10: 18 and whoever spreads slander is a f.
12: 15 The way of a f seems right to him,
12: 16 A f shows his annoyance at once,
14: 16 but a f is hotheaded and reckless.
15: 5 A f spurns his father's discipline,
17: 12 than a f in his folly.
17: 16 use is money in the hand of a f,
17: 21 To have a f for a son brings grief;
17: 28 Even a f is thought wise
18: 2 A f finds no pleasure
20: 3 but every f is quick to quarrel.
23: 9 Do not speak to a f,
24: 7 Wisdom is too high for a f;
26: 4 Do not answer a f according
26: 5 Answer a f according to his folly,
26: 7 is a proverb in the mouth of a f.
26: 11 so a f repeats his folly.
26: 12 for a f than for him.
27: 22 Though you grind a f in a mortar,
28: 26 He who trusts in himself is a f,
29: 11 A f gives full vent to his anger,
29: 20 for a f than for him.
Mt 5: 22 But anyone who says, 'You f!'
Lk 12: 20 "But God said to him, 'You f!
1Co 3: 18 he should become a "f"
2Co 11: 21 I am speaking as a f—I

FOOL'S (FOOL)
Pr 14: 3 A f talk brings a rod to his back,
18: 7 A f mouth is his undoing,

FOOLISH (FOOL)
Pr 10: 1 but a f son grief to his mother.
14: 1 her own hands the f one tears hers
15: 20 but a f man despises his mother.
17: 25 A f son brings grief to his father
19: 13 A f son is his father's ruin,
Mt 7: 26 practice is like a f man who built
25: 2 of them were f and five were wise.
Lk 11: 40 You f people! Did not the one who
24: 25 He said to them, "How f you are,
1Co 1: 20 Has not God made f the wisdom
1: 27 God chose the f things of the world
Gal 3: 1 died for nothing!" You f Galatians!
Eph 5: 4 should there be obscenity, f talk
5: 17 Therefore do not be f,
Tit 3: 9 But avoid f controversies

FOOLISHNESS (FOOL)
1Co 1: 18 of the cross is f to those who are
1: 21 through the f of what was preached
1: 23 block to Jews and f to Gentiles,
1: 25 For the f of God is wiser
2: 14 for they are f to him, and he cannot
3: 19 of this world is f in God's sight.

FOOLS (FOOL)
Pr 1: 7 but f despise wisdom and discipline
3: 35 but f he holds up to shame.
12: 23 but the heart of f blurts out folly.
13: 19 but f detest turning from evil.
13: 20 but a companion of f suffers harm.
14: 9 F mock at making amends for sin,
14: 24 but the folly of f yields folly.
Ecc 7: 5 than to listen to the song of f.
7: 6 so is the laughter of f.
10: 6 F are put in many high positions,
Mt 23: 17 You blind f! Which is greater:
Ro 1: 22 they became f and exchanged
1Co 4: 10 We are f for Christ, but you are

FOOT (FEET FOOTHOLD)
Jos 1: 3 every place where you set your f,
Ps 121: 3 He will not let your f slip—
Pr 3: 23 and your f will not stumble;
4: 27 keep your f from evil.
25: 17 Seldom set f in your neighbor's
Isa 1: 6 From the sole of your f to the top
Mt 18: 8 or your f causes you to sin,
Lk 4: 11 so that you will not strike your f
1Co 12: 15 If the f should say, "Because I am
Rev 10: 2 He planted his right f on the sea

FOOTHOLD* (FOOT)
Ps 69: 2 where there is no f.
73: 2 I had nearly lost my f.
Eph 4: 27 and do not give the devil a f.

FOOTSTEPS (STEP)
Ps 119: 133 Direct my f according

FOOTSTOOL
Ps 99: 5 and worship at his f;
110: 1 a f for your feet."
Isa 66: 1 and the earth is my f.
Mt 5: 35 for it is his f; or by Jerusalem,
Ac 7: 49 and the earth is my f.
Heb 1: 13 a f for your feet"?
10: 13 for his enemies to be made his f,

FORBEARANCE*
Ro 3: 25 because in his f he had left the sins

FORBID
1Co 14: 39 and do not f speaking in tongues.
1Ti 4: 3 They f people to marry

FORCE (FORCED FORCEFUL FORCES FORCING)
Jn 6: 15 to come and make him king by f,
Ac 26: 11 and I tried to f them to blaspheme.
Gal 2: 14 that you f Gentiles

FORCED (FORCE)
Mt 27: 32 and they f him to carry the cross.
Phm : 14 do will be spontaneous and not f.

FORCEFUL* (FORCE)
Mt 11: 12 forcefully advancing, and f men lay
2Co 10: 10 "His letters are weighty and f,

FORCES (FORCE)
Mt 5: 41 If someone f you to go one mile,
Eph 6: 12 and against the spiritual f of evil

FORCING (FORCE)
Lk 16: 16 and everyone is f his way into it.

FOREFATHERS (FATHER)
Heb 1: 1 spoke to our f through the prophets
1Pe 1: 18 handed down to you from your f,

FOREHEAD (FOREHEADS)
Ex 13: 9 a reminder on your f that the law

Ex 13:16 on your f that the LORD brought
1Sa 17:49 and struck the Philistine on the f.
Rev 13:16 a mark on his right hand or on his f,

FOREHEADS (FOREHEAD)

Dt 6: 8 hands and bind them on your f.
Rev 9: 4 not have the seal of God on their f.
14: 1 his Father's name written on their f

FOREIGN (FOREIGNER FOREIGNERS)

Ge 35: 2 "Get rid of the f gods you have
2Ch 14: 3 He removed the f altars
33:15 He got rid of the f gods
Isa 28:11 with f lips and strange tongues

FOREIGNER (FOREIGN)

Lk 17:18 give praise to God except this f?"
1Co 14:11 I am a f to the speaker,

FOREIGNERS (FOREIGN)

Eph 2:12 f to the covenants of the promise,
2:19 you are no longer f and aliens,

FOREKNEW* (KNOW)

Ro 8:29 For those God f he
11: 2 not reject his people, whom he f.

FOREKNOWLEDGE* (KNOW)

Ac 2:23 to you by God's set purpose and f;
1Pe 1: 2 to the f of God the Father,

FORESAW*

Gal 3: 8 Scripture f that God would justify

FOREST

Jas 3: 5 Consider what a great f is set

FOREVER (EVER)

Ge 3:22 the tree of life and eat, and live f."
6: 3 Spirit will not contend with man f,
Ex 3:15 This is my name f, the name
2Sa 7:26 so that your name will be great f.
1Ki 2:33 may there be the LORD's peace f."
9: 3 by putting my Name there f.
1Ch 16:15 He remembers his covenant f,
16:34 his love endures f.
16:41 "for his love endures f."
17:24 and that your name will be great f.
2Ch 5:13 his love endures f."
20:21 for his love endures f."
Ps 9: 7 The LORD reigns f;
23: 6 dwell in the house of the LORD f.
28: 9 be their shepherd and carry them f.
29:10 the LORD is enthroned as King f.
33:11 the plans of the LORD stand firm f
37:28 They will be protected f,
44: 8 and we will praise your name f.
61: 4 I long to dwell in your tent f
72:19 Praise be to his glorious name f;
73:26 and my portion f.
77: 8 Has his unfailing love vanished f?
79:13 will praise you f;
81:15 and their punishment would last f.
86:12 I will glorify your name f.
89: 1 of the LORD's great love f;
92: 8 But you, O LORD, are exalted f.
100: 5 is good and his love endures f;
102:12 But you, O LORD, sit enthroned f;
104:31 of the LORD endure f;
107: 1 his love endures f.
110: 4 "You are a priest f,
111: 3 and his righteousness endures f.
112: 6 man will be remembered f.
117: 2 of the LORD endures f.
118: 1 his love endures f.
119:111 Your statutes are my heritage f;
119:152 that you established them to last f.
136: 1 *His love endures f.*
146: 6 the LORD, who remains faithful f.
Pr 10:25 but the righteous stand firm f.
27:24 for riches do not endure f,
Isa 25: 8 he will swallow up death f.
26: 4 Trust in the LORD f,
32:17 will be quietness and confidence f.
40: 8 but the word of our God stands f."
51: 6 But my salvation will last f,
51: 8 But my righteousness will last f,
57:15 he who lives f, whose name is holy:
59:21 from this time on and f,"
Jer 33:11 his love endures f."
Eze 37:26 put my sanctuary among them f.
Da 2:44 to an end, but it will itself endure f.
3: 9 live f! You have issued a decree,
Jn 6:51 eats of this bread, he will live f.
14:16 Counselor to be with you f—
Ro 9: 5 who is God over all, f praised!
16:27 to the only wise God be glory f
1Co 9:25 it to get a crown that will last f.
1Th 4:17 And so we will be with the Lord f.
Heb 5: 6 "You are a priest f,
7:17 "You are a priest f,
7:24 Jesus lives f, he has a permanent
13: 8 same yesterday and today and f.
1Pe 1:25 but the word of the Lord stands f."
1Jn 2:17 who does the will of God lives f.
2Jn : 2 lives in us and will be with us f:

FOREVERMORE (EVER)

Ps 113: 2 both now and f.

FORFEIT

Mk 8:36 the whole world, yet f his soul?
Lk 9:25 and yet lose or f his very self?

FORGAVE (FORGIVE)

Ps 32: 5 and you f
65: 3 you f our transgressions
78:38 you f their iniquities
Eph 4:32 just as in Christ God f you.
Col 2:13 He f us all our sins, having
3:13 Forgive as the Lord f you.

FORGET (FORGETS FORGETTING FORGOT FORGOTTEN)

Dt 4:23 Be careful not to f the covenant
6:12 that you do not f the LORD,
2Ki 17:38 Do not f the covenant I have made
Ps 9:17 all the nations that f God.
10:12 Do not f the helpless.
50:22 "Consider this, you who f God,
78: 7 and would not f his deeds
103: 2 and f not all his benefits.
119:93 I will never f your precepts,
137: 5 may my right hand f its skill.
Pr 3: 1 My son, do not f my teaching,
4: 5 do not f my words or swerve
Isa 49:15 "Can a mother f the baby
51:13 that you f the LORD your Maker,
Jer 2:32 Does a maiden f her jewelry,
23:39 I will surely f you and cast you out
Heb 6:10 he will not f your work
13: 2 Do not f to entertain strangers,
13:16 And do not f to do good
2Pe 3: 8 But do not f this one thing,

FORGETS (FORGET)

Jn 16:21 her baby is born she f the anguish
Jas 1:24 immediately f what he looks like.

FORGETTING* (FORGET)

Php 3:13 F what is behind and straining
Jas 1:25 to do this, not f what he has heard,

FORGIVE* (FORGAVE FORGIVENESS FORGIVES FORGIVING)

Ge 50:17 I ask you to f your brothers the sins
50:17 please f the sins of the servants
Ex 10:17 Now f my sin once more
23:21 he will not f your rebellion,
32:32 But now, please f their sin—
34: 9 f our wickedness and our sin,
Nu 14:19 with your great love, f the sin
Dt 29:20 will never be willing to f him;
Jos 24:19 He will not f your rebellion
1Sa 15:25 f my sin and come back with me,
25:28 Please f your servant's offense,
1Ki 8:30 place, and when you hear, f.
8:34 and f the sin of your people Israel
8:36 and f the sin of your servants,
8:39 F and act; deal with each man
8:50 f all the offenses they have
8:50 f your people, who have sinned
2Ki 5:18 But may the LORD f your servant
5:18 may the LORD f your servant
24: 4 and the LORD was not willing to f.
2Ch 6:21 place; and when you hear, f.
6:25 and f the sin of your people Israel
6:27 and f the sin of your servants,
6:30 F, and deal with each man
6:39 f your people, who have sinned
7:14 will f their sin and will heal their
Job 7:21 and f my sins?
Ps 19:12 F my hidden faults.
25:11 f my iniquity, though it is great.
79: 9 deliver us and f our sins
Isa 2: 9 do not f them.
Jer 5: 1 I will f this city.
5: 7 "Why should I f you?
18:23 Do not f their crimes
31:34 "For I will f their wickedness
Jer 33: 8 and will f all their sins of rebellion
36: 3 then I will f their wickedness
50:20 for I will f the remnant I spare.
Da 9:19 O Lord, listen! O Lord, f! O Lord,
Hos 1: 6 that I should at all f them.
14: 2 "F all our sins
Am 7: 2 f! How can Jacob survive?
Mt 6:12 F us our debts,
6:14 For if you f men when they sin
6:14 heavenly Father will also f you.
6:15 But if you do not f men their sins,
6:15 your Father will not f your sins.
9: 6 authority on earth to f sins..
18:21 many times shall I f my brother
18:35 you f your brother from your heart
Mk 2: 7 Who can f sins but God alone?"
2:10 authority on earth to f sins
11:25 anything against anyone, f him,
11:25 in heaven may f you your sins."
Lk 5:21 Who can f sins but God alone?"
5:24 authority on earth to f sins..
6:37 F, and you will be forgiven.
11: 4 F us our sins,
11: 4 f everyone who sins against us.
17: 3 rebuke him, and if he repents, f him
17: 4 and says, 'I repent,' f him."
23:34 Jesus said, "Father, f them,
Jn 20:23 If you f anyone his sins, they are
20:23 if you do not f them, they are not
Ac 8:22 Perhaps he will f you
2Co 2: 7 you ought to f and comfort him,
2:10 If you f anyone, I also f him.
2:10 if there was anything to f—
12:13 a burden to you? F me this wrong!
Col 3:13 and f whatever grievances you may
3:13 F as the Lord forgave you.
Heb 8:12 For I will f their wickedness
1Jn 1: 9 and just and will f us our sins

FORGIVENESS* (FORGIVE)

Ps 130: 4 But with you there is f;
Mt 26:28 out for many for the f of sins.
Mk 1: 4 of repentance for the f of sins.
Lk 1:77 salvation through the f of their sins,
3: 3 of repentance for the f of sins.
24:47 and f of sins will be preached
Ac 5:31 that he might give repentance and f
10:43 believes in him receives f of sins
13:38 that through Jesus the f
26:18 so that they may receive f of sins
Eph 1: 7 through his blood, the f of sins,
Col 1:14 in whom we have redemption, the f
Heb 9:22 the shedding of blood there is no f.

FORGIVES* (FORGIVE)

Ps 103: 3 He f all my sins
Mic 7:18 pardons sin and f the transgression
Lk 7:49 "Who is this who even f sins?"

FORGIVING* (FORGIVE)

Ex 34: 7 and f wickedness, rebellion and sin.
Nu 14:18 abounding in love and f sin
Ne 9:17 But you are a f God, gracious
Ps 86: 5 You are f and good, O Lord,
99: 8 you were to Israel a f God,
Da 9: 9 The Lord our God is merciful and f
Eph 4:32 to one another, f each other,

FORGOT (FORGET)

Dt 32:18 you f the God who gave you birth.
Ps 78:11 They f what he had done,
106:13 But they soon f what he had done

FORGOTTEN (FORGET)

Job 11: 6 God has even f some of your sin.
Ps 44:20 If we had f the name of our God
Isa 17:10 You have f God your Savior;
Hos 8:14 Israel has f his Maker
Lk 12: 6 Yet not one of them is f by God.
2Pe 1: 9 and has f that he has been cleansed

FORM (FORMED)

Isa 52:14 f marred beyond human likeness—
2Ti 3: 5 having a f of godliness

FORMED (FORM)

Ge 2: 7 —the LORD God f the man
2:19 Now the LORD God had f out
Ps 103: 14 for he knows how we are f,
Ecc 11: 5 or how the body is f in a mother's
Isa 29:16 Shall what is f say to him who f it,
45:18 but f it to be inhabited—
49: 5 he who f me in the womb
Jer 1: 5 "Before I f you in the womb I knew
Ro 9:20 "Shall what is f say to him who f it,

Gal 4:19 of childbirth until Christ is *f* in you,
1Ti 2:13 For Adam was *f* first, then Eve.
Heb 11:3 understand that the universe was *f*
2Pe 3:5 and the earth was *f* out of water

FORMLESS*

Ge 1:2 Now the earth was *f* and empty,
Jer 4:23 and it was *f* and empty;

FORNICATION see IMMORALITY, UNFAITHFULNESS

FORSAKE (FORSAKEN)

Dt 31:6 he will never leave you nor *f* you."
Jos 1:5 I will never leave you nor *f* you.
24:16 "Far be it from us to *f* the LORD
2Ch 15:2 but if you *f* him, he will *f* you.
Ps 27:10 Though my father and mother *f* me
94:14 he will never *f* his inheritance.
Isa 55:7 Let the wicked *f* his way
Heb 13:5 never will I *f* you."

FORSAKEN (FORSAKE)

Ps 22:1 my God, why have you *f* me?
37:25 I have never seen the righteous *f*
Mt 27:46 my God, why have you *f* me?"
Rev 2:4 You have *f* your first love.

FORTRESS

2Sa 22:2 "The LORD is my rock, my *f*
Ps 18:2 The LORD is my rock, my *f*
31:2 a strong *f* to save me.
59:16 for you are my *f*,
71:3 for you are my rock and my *f*.
Pr 14:26 who fears the LORD has a secure *f*,

FORTUNE-TELLING*

Ac 16:16 deal of money for her owners by *f*.

FORTY

Ge 7:4 on the earth for *f* days and *f* nights,
18:29 "What if only *f* are found there?"
Ex 16:35 The Israelites ate manna *f* years,
24:18 on the mountain *f* days and *f* nights
Nu 14:34 For *f* years—one year for each
Jos 14:7 I was *f* years old when Moses
1Sa 4:18 He had led Israel *f* years.
2Sa 5:4 king, and he reigned *f* years.
1Ki 19:8 he traveled *f* days and *f* nights
2Ki 12:1 and he reigned in Jerusalem *f* years
2Ch 9:30 in Jerusalem over all Israel *f* years.
Eze 29:12 her cities will lie desolate *f* years
Jnh 3:4 "*F* more days and Nineveh will be
Mt 4:2 After fasting *f* days and *f* nights,

FOUGHT (FIGHT)

1Co 15:32 If I *f* wild beasts in Ephesus
2Ti 4:7 I have *f* the good fight, I have

FOUND (FIND)

2Ki 22:8 "I have *f* the Book of the Law
1Ch 28:9 If you seek him, he will be *f* by you;
2Ch 15:15 sought God eagerly, and he was *f*
Isa 55:6 Seek the LORD while he may be *f*;
65:1 I was *f* by those who did not seek
Da 5:27 on the scales and *f* wanting.
Mt 1:18 she was *f* to be with child
Lk 15:6 with me; I have *f* my lost sheep.'
15:9 with me; I have *f* my lost coin.'
15:24 is alive again; he was lost and is *f*.'
Ac 4:12 Salvation is *f* in no one else,
Ro 10:20 "I was *f* by those who did not seek
Jas 2:8 If you really keep the royal law *f*
Rev 5:4 no one was *f* who was worthy

FOUNDATION (FOUNDATIONS FOUNDED)

Isa 28:16 a precious cornerstone for a sure *f*;
Mt 7:25 because it had its *f* on the rock.
Lk 14:29 For if he lays the *f* and is not able
Ro 15:20 building on someone else's *f*.
1Co 3:10 I laid a *f* as an expert builder,
3:11 For no one can lay any *f* other
Eph 2:20 built on the *f* of the apostles
1Ti 3:15 the pillar and *f* of the truth.
2Ti 2:19 God's solid *f* stands firm,
Heb 6:1 not laying again the *f* of repentance

FOUNDATIONS (FOUNDATION)

Ps 102:25 In the beginning you laid the *f*
Heb 1:10 O Lord, you laid the *f* of the earth,

FOUNDED (FOUNDATION)

Jer 10:12 he *f* the world by his wisdom
Heb 8:6 and it is *f* on better promises.

FOUNTAIN

Ps 36:9 For with you is the *f* of life;
Pr 14:27 The fear of the LORD is a *f* of life,
18:4 the *f* of wisdom is a bubbling brook.
Zec 13:1 "On that day a *f* will be opened

FOX (FOXES)

Lk 13:32 He replied, "Go tell that *f*,

FOXES (FOX)

SS 2:15 the little *f*
Mt 8:20 "*F* have holes and birds

FRAGRANCE (FRAGRANT)

Ex 30:38 it to enjoy its *f* must be cut
Jn 12:3 filled with the *f* of the perfume.
2Co 2:14 us spreads everywhere the *f*
2:16 of death; to the other, the *f* of life.

FRAGRANT (FRAGRANCE)

Eph 5:2 as a *f* offering and sacrifice to God.
Php 4:18 They are a *f* offering, an acceptable

FREE (FREED FREEDOM FREELY)

Ge 2:16 "You are *f* to eat from any tree
Ps 118:5 and he answered by setting me *f*.
119:32 for you have set my heart *f*.
146:7 The LORD sets prisoners *f*,
Pr 6:3 then do this, my son, to *f* yourself,
Jn 8:32 and the truth will set you *f*."
8:36 if the Son sets you *f*, you will be *f*
Ro 6:18 You have been set *f* from sin
8:2 of life set me *f* from the law of sin
1Co 12:13 whether Jews or Greeks, slave or *f*
Gal 3:28 slave nor *f*, male nor female,
5:1 for freedom that Christ has set us *f*.
1Pe 2:16 *f* men, but do not use your freedom

FREED (FREE)

Ps 116:16 you have *f* me from my chains.
Ro 6:7 anyone who has died has been *f*
Rev 1:5 has *f* us from our sins by his blood,

FREEDOM (FREE)

Ps 119:45 I will walk about in *f*,
Isa 61:1 to proclaim *f* for the captives
Lk 4:18 me to proclaim *f* for the prisoners
Ro 8:21 into the glorious *f* of the children
1Co 7:21 although if you can gain your *f*,
2Co 3:17 the Spirit of the Lord is, there is *f*.
Gal 2:4 ranks to spy on the *f* we have
5:13 But do not use your *f* to indulge
Jas 1:25 into the perfect law that gives *f*,
1Pe 2:16 but do not use your *f* as a cover-up

FREELY (FREE)

Isa 55:7 and to our God, for he will *f* pardon
Mt 10:8 Freely you have received, *f* give.
Ro 3:24 and are justified *f* by his grace
Eph 1:6 which he has *f* given us

FRESH

Jas 3:11 Can both *f* water and salt water

FRET*

Ps 37:1 Do not *f* because of evil men
37:7 do not *f* when men succeed
37:8 do not *f*—it leads only to evil.
Pr 24:19 Do not *f* because of evil men

FRICTION

1Ti 6:5 and constant *f* between men

FRIEND (FRIENDS FRIENDSHIP)

Ex 33:11 as a man speaks with his *f*.
2Ch 20:7 descendants of Abraham your *f*?
Pr 17:17 A *f* loves at all times,
18:24 there is a *f* who sticks closer
27:6 Wounds from a *f* can be trusted
27:10 Do not forsake your *f* and the *f*
Isa 41:8 you descendants of Abraham my *f*,
Mt 11:19 a *f* of tax collectors and "sinners." '
Lk 11:8 him the bread because he is his *f*,
Jn 19:12 "If you let this man go, you are no *f*
Jas 2:23 and he was called God's *f*.
4:4 Anyone who chooses to be a *f*

FRIENDS (FRIEND)

Pr 16:28 and a gossip separates close *f*.
17:9 the matter separates close *f*.
Zec 13:6 given at the house of my *f*.'
Jn 15:13 that he lay down his life for his *f*.
15:14 You are my *f* if you do what I

FRIENDSHIP (FRIEND)

Jas 4:4 don't you know that *f*

FRIGHTENED (FEAR)

Php 1:28 gospel without being *f* in any way
1Pe 3:14 fear what they fear; do not be *f*."

FROGS

Ex 8:2 plague your whole country with *f*.
Rev 16:13 three evil spirits that looked like *f*;

FRUIT (FRUITFUL)

Jdg 9:11 'Should I give up my *f*, so good
Ps 1:3 which yields its *f* in season
Pr 11:30 The *f* of the righteous is a tree
12:14 From the *f* of his lips a man is filled
27:18 He who tends a fig tree will eat its *f*
Isa 11:1 from his roots a Branch will bear *f*.
27:6 and fill all the world with *f*.
32:17 The *f* of righteousness will be peace
Jer 17:8 and never fails to bear *f*."
Hos 10:12 reap the *f* of unfailing love,
14:2 that we may offer the *f* of our lips.
Am 8:1 showed me: a basket of ripe *f*.
Mt 3:8 Produce *f* in keeping
3:10 does not produce good *f* will be cut
7:16 By their *f* you will recognize them.
7:17 good *f*, but a bad tree bears bad *f*.
7:20 by their *f* you will recognize them.
12:33 a tree good and its *f* will be good,
Lk 3:9 does not produce good *f* will be cut
6:43 nor does a bad tree bear good *f*.
13:6 and he went to look for *f* on it,
Jn 15:2 branch in me that bears no *f*,
15:16 and bear *f*—*f* that will last.
Ro 7:4 in order that we might bear *f*
Gal 5:22 But the *f* of the Spirit is love, joy,
Php 1:11 with the *f* of righteousness that
Col 1:10 bearing *f* in every good work,
Heb 13:15 the *f* of lips that confess his name.
Jas 3:17 and good *f*, impartial and sincere.
Jude :12 autumn trees, without *f*
Rev 22:2 of *f*, yielding its *f* every month.

FRUITFUL (FRUIT)

Ge 1:22 "Be *f* and increase in number
9:1 "Be *f* and increase in number
35:11 be *f* and increase in number.
Ex 1:7 the Israelites were *f* and multiplied
Ps 128:3 Your wife will be like a *f* vine
Jn 15:2 prunes so that it will be even more *f*.
Php 1:22 this will mean *f* labor for me.

FRUITLESS*

Eph 5:11 to do with the *f* deeds of darkness,

FRUSTRATION

Ro 8:20 For the creation was subjected to *f*,

FUEL

Isa 44:19 "Half of it I used for *f*;

FULFILL (FULFILLED FULFILLMENT FULFILLS)

Nu 23:19 Does he promise and not *f*?
Ps 61:8 and *f* my vows day after day.
116:14 I will *f* my vows to the LORD
138:8 The LORD will *f* his purpose,
Ecc 5:5 than to make a vow and not *f* it.
Isa 46:11 far-off land, a man to *f* my purpose.
Jer 33:14 'when I will *f* the gracious promise
Mt 1:22 place to *f* what the Lord had said
3:15 us to do this to *f* all righteousness."
4:14 *f* what was said
5:17 come to abolish them but to *f* them.
8:17 This was to *f* what was spoken
12:17 This was to *f* what was spoken
21:4 place to *f* what was spoken
Jn 12:38 This was to *f* the word
13:18 But this is to *f* the scripture:
15:25 But this is to *f* what is written
1Co 7:3 husband should *f* his marital duty

FULFILLED (FULFILL)

Jos 21:45 of Israel failed; every one was *f*.
23:14 Every promise has been *f*;
Pr 13:12 but a longing *f* is a tree of life.
13:19 A longing *f* is sweet to the soul,
Mt 2:15 so was *f* what the Lord had said
2:17 the prophet Jeremiah was *f*:
2:23 So was *f* what was said
13:14 In them is *f* the prophecy of Isaiah:
13:35 So was *f* what was spoken
26:54 would the Scriptures be *f* that say it

Mt 26:56 of the prophets might be *f.*"
27: 9 by Jeremiah the prophet was *f:*
Mk 13: 4 that they are all about to be *f?*"
14:49 But the Scriptures must be *f.*"
Lk 4:21 "Today this scripture is *f*
18:31 about the Son of Man will be *f.*
24:44 Everything must be *f* that is
Jn 18: 9 words he had spoken would be *f:*
19:24 the Scripture might be *f* which said,
19:28 and so that the Scripture would be *f*
19:36 so that the Scripture would be *f:*
Ac 1:16 to be *f* which the Holy Spirit spoke
Ro 13: 8 loves his fellowman has *f* the law.
Jas 2:23 And the scripture was *f* that says,

FULFILLMENT (FULFILL)

Ro 13:10 Therefore love is the *f* of the law.

FULFILLS (FULFILL)

Ps 57: 2 to God, who *f* ⌊his purpose⌋ for me.
145:19 He *f* the desires of those who fear

FULL (FILL)

2Ch 24:10 them into the chest until it was *f.*
Ps 127: 5 whose quiver is *f* of them.
Pr 27: 7 He who is *f* loathes honey,
31:11 Her husband has *f* confidence
Isa 6: 3 the whole earth is *f* of his glory."
11: 9 for the earth will be *f*
Lk 4: 1 Jesus, *f* of the Holy Spirit,
Jn 10:10 may have life, and have it to the *f.*
Ac 6: 3 known to be *f* of the Spirit
6: 5 a man *f* of faith and of the Holy
7:55 But Stephen, *f* of the Holy Spirit,
11:24 *f* of the Holy Spirit and faith,

FULL-GROWN* (GROW)

Jas 1:15 when it is *f,* gives birth to death.

FULLNESS* (FILL)

Dt 33:16 gifts of the earth and its *f*
Jn 1:16 From the *f* of his grace we have all
Ro 11:12 greater riches will their *f* bring!
Eph 1:23 the *f* of him who fills everything
3:19 to the measure of all the *f* of God.
4:13 to the whole measure of the *f*
Col 1:19 to have all his *f* dwell in him,
1:25 to you the word of God in its *f*—
2: 9 in Christ all the *f* of the Deity lives
2:10 and you have been given *f* in Christ

FULLY (FILL)

1Ki 8:61 your hearts must be *f* committed
2Ch 16: 9 whose hearts are *f* committed
Ps 119: 4 that are to be *f* obeyed.
119:138 they are *f* trustworthy.
Pr 13: 4 of the diligent are *f* satisfied.
Lk 6:40 everyone who is *f* trained will be
Ro 4:21 being *f* persuaded that God had
14: 5 Each one should be *f* convinced
1Co 13:12 shall know *f,* even as I am *f* known.
15:58 Always give yourselves *f*
2Ti 4:17 the message might be *f* proclaimed

FURIOUS (FURY)

Dt 29:28 In *f* anger and in great wrath
Jer 32:37 where I banish them in my *f* anger

FURNACE

Isa 48:10 in the *f* of affliction.
Da 3: 6 be thrown into a blazing *f.*"
Mt 13:42 will throw them into the fiery *f,*

FURY (FURIOUS)

Isa 14: 6 and in *f* subdued nations
Jer 21: 5 and a mighty arm in anger and *f*
Rev 14:10 will drink of the wine of God's *f,*
16:19 with the wine of the *f* of his wrath.
19:15 the winepress of the *f* of the wrath

FUTILE (FUTILITY)

Mal 3:14 You have said, 'It is *f* to serve God.
1Co 3:20 that the thoughts of the wise are *f.*"

FUTILITY (FUTILE)

Eph 4:17 in the *f* of their thinking.

FUTURE

Ps 37:37 there is a *f* for the man of peace.
Pr 23:18 There is surely a *f* hope for you,
Ecc 7:14 anything about his *f.*
8: 7 Since no man knows the *f,*
Jer 29:11 plans to give you hope and a *f.*
31:17 So there is hope for your *f,*"
Ro 8:38 neither the present nor the *f,*
1Co 3:22 life or death or the present or the *f*

GABRIEL*

Angel who interpreted Daniel's visions (Da 8:16-26; 9:20-27); announced births of John (Lk 1:11-20), Jesus (Lk 1:26-38).

GAD

1. Son of Jacob by Zilpah (Ge 30:9-11; 35:26; 1Ch 2:2). Tribe of blessed (Ge 49:19; Dt 33:20-21), numbered (Nu 1:25; 26:18), allotted land east of the Jordan (Nu 32; 34:14; Jos 18:7; 22), west (Eze 48:27-28), 12,000 from (Rev 7:5).

2. Prophet; seer of David (1Sa 22:5; 2Sa 24:11-19; 1Ch 29:29).

GAIN (GAINED GAINS)

Ex 14:17 And I will *g* glory through Pharaoh
Ps 60:12 With God we will *g* the victory,
Pr 4: 1 pay attention and *g* understanding.
8: 5 You who are simple, *g* prudence;
28:16 he who hates ill-gotten *g* will enjoy
28:23 in the end *g* more favor
Isa 63:12 to *g* for himself everlasting renown
Da 2: 8 that you are trying to *g* time,
Mk 8:36 it for a man to *g* the whole world,
Lk 9:25 it for a man to *g* the whole world,
21:19 standing firm you will *g* life.
1Co 13: 3 but have not love, I *g* nothing.
Php 1:21 to live is Christ and to die is *g.*
3: 8 that I may *g* Christ and be found
1Ti 3:13 have served well *g* an excellent
6: 5 godliness is a means to financial *g.*
6: 6 with contentment is great *g.*

GAINED (GAIN)

Jer 32:20 have *g* the renown that is still yours
Ro 5: 2 through whom we have *g* access

GAINS (GAIN)

Pr 3:13 the man who *g* understanding,
11:16 A kindhearted woman *g* respect,
15:32 heeds correction *g* understanding.
29:23 but a man of lowly spirit *g* honor.
Mt 16:26 for a man if he *g* the whole world,

GALILEE

Isa 9: 1 but in the future he will honor *G*
Mt 4:15 *G* of the Gentiles—
26:32 I will go ahead of you into *G.*"
28:10 Go and tell my brothers to go to *G;*

GALL

Mt 27:34 mixed with *g;* but after tasting it,

GALLIO

Ac 18:12 While *G* was proconsul of Achaia,

GALLOWS

Est 7:10 Haman on the *g* he had prepared

GAMALIEL

Ac 5:34 But a Pharisee named *G,* a teacher

GAMES

1Co 9:25 in the *g* goes into strict training.

GAP

Eze 22:30 stand before me in the *g* on behalf

GAPE*

Ps 35:21 They *g* at me and say, "Aha! Aha!

GARDEN (GARDENER)

Ge 2: 8 the LORD God had planted a *g*
2:15 put him in the *G* of Eden to work it
SS 4:12 You are a *g* locked up, my sister,
Isa 58:11 You will be like a well-watered *g,*
Jer 31:12 They will be like a well-watered *g,*
Eze 28:13 the *g* of God;
31: 9 Eden in the *g* of God.

GARDENER (GARDEN)

Jn 15: 1 true vine, and my Father is the *g.*

GARLAND*

Pr 1: 9 They will be a *g* to grace your head
4: 9 She will set a *g* of grace

GARMENT (GARMENTS)

Ps 102:26 they will all wear out like a *g.*
Isa 50: 9 They will all wear out like a *g;*
51: 6 the earth will wear out like a *g*
61: 3 and a *g* of praise
Mt 9:16 of unshrunk cloth on an old *g,*
Jn 19:23 This *g* was seamless, woven
Heb 1:11 they will all wear out like a *g.*

GARMENTS (GARMENT)

Ge 3:21 The LORD God made *g* of skin
Ex 28: 2 Make sacred *g* for your brother
Lev 16:23 and take off the linen *g* he put
16:24 holy place and put on his regular *g.*
Isa 61:10 me with *g* of salvation
63: 1 with his *g* stained crimson?
Joel 2:13 and not your *g.*
Zec 3: 4 and I will put rich *g* on you."
Jn 19:24 "They divided my *g* among them

GATE (GATES)

Ps 118:20 This is the *g* of the LORD
Pr 31:23 husband is respected at the city *g,*
31:31 works bring her praise at the city *g.*
Mt 7:13 For wide is the *g* and broad is
7:13 "Enter through the narrow *g.*
Jn 10: 1 not enter the sheep pen by the *g,*
10: 2 enters by the *g* is the shepherd
10: 7 "I tell you the truth, I am the *g*
10: 9 I am the *g;* whoever enters
Heb 13:12 also suffered outside the city *g*
Rev 21:21 each *g* made of a single pearl.

GATES (GATE)

Ps 24: 7 Lift up your heads, O you *g;*
24: 9 Lift up your heads, O you *g;*
100: 4 Enter his *g* with thanksgiving
118:19 Open for me the *g* of righteousness
Isa 60:11 Your *g* will always stand open,
60:18 and your *g* Praise.
62:10 Pass through, pass through the *g!*
Mt 16:18 the *g* of Hades will not overcome it
Rev 21:12 On the *g* were written the names
21:21 The twelve *g* were twelve pearls,
21:25 On no day will its *g* ever be shut,
22:14 may go through the *g* into the city.

GATH

1Sa 17:23 the Philistine champion from *G,*
2Sa 1:20 "Tell it not in *G,*
Mic 1:10 Tell it not in *G;*

GATHER (GATHERED GATHERS)

Ps 106:47 and *g* us from the nations,
Isa 11:12 and *g* the exiles of Israel;
Jer 3:17 and all nations will *g* in Jerusalem
23: 3 "I myself will *g* the remnant
31:10 who scattered Israel will *g* them
Zep 2: 1 *G* together, *g* together,
3:20 At that time I will *g* you;
Zec 14: 2 I will *g* all the nations to Jerusalem
Mt 12:30 he who does not *g* with me scatters
13:30 then *g* the wheat and bring it
23:37 longed to *g* your children together,
24:31 and they will *g* his elect
25:26 *g* where I have not scattered seed?
Mk 13:27 and *g* his elect from the four winds,
Lk 3:17 and to *g* the wheat into his barn,
11:23 and he who does not *g* with me,
13:34 longed to *g* your children together,

GATHERED (GATHER)

Ex 16:18 and he who *g* little did not have too
Pr 30: 4 Who has *g* up the wind
Mt 25:32 All the nations will be *g* before him
2Co 8:15 and he who *g* little did not have too
2Th 2: 1 Lord Jesus Christ and our being *g*
Rev 16:16 Then they *g* the kings together

GATHERS (GATHER)

Ps 147: 2 he *g* the exiles of Israel.
Pr 10: 5 He who *g* crops in summer is a wise
Isa 40:11 He *g* the lambs in his arms
Mt 23:37 a hen *g* her chicks under her wings,

GAVE (GIVE)

Ge 2:20 man *g* names to all the livestock,
3: 6 She also *g* some to her husband,
14:20 Abram *g* him a tenth of everything.
28: 4 the land God *g* to Abraham."
35:12 The land I *g* to Abraham
39:23 *g* him success in whatever he did.
47:11 *g* them property in the best part
Ex 4:11 to him, "Who *g* man his mouth?
31:18 he *g* him the two tablets
Dt 2:12 did in the land the LORD *g* them
2:36 The LORD our God *g* us all
3:12 I *g* the Reubenites and the Gadites
3:13 I *g* to the half tribe of Manasseh.
3:15 And I *g* Gilead to Makir.
3:16 Gadites I *g* the territory extending

Dt 8:16 He *g* you manna to eat in the desert
26: 9 us to this place and *g* us this land,
32: 8 the Most High *g* the nations their
Jos 11:23 and he *g* it as an inheritance
13:14 tribe of Levi he *g* no inheritance,
14:13 *g* him Hebron as his inheritance.
21:44 The LORD *g* them rest
24:13 I *g* you a land on which you did not
1Sa 27: 6 So on that day Achish *g* him Ziklag
2Sa 12: 8 I *g* you the house of Israel
1Ki 4:29 God *g* Solomon wisdom
5:12 The LORD *g* Solomon wisdom,
Ezr 2:69 According to their ability they *g*
Ne 9:15 In their hunger you *g* them bread
9:20 You *g* your good Spirit
9:22 You *g* them kingdoms and nations,
9:27 compassion you *g* them deliverers,
Job 1:21 LORD *g* and the LORD has taken
42:10 prosperous again and *g* him twice
Ps 69:21 and *g* me vinegar for my thirst.
135:12 he *g* their land as an inheritance,
Ecc 12: 7 the spirit returns to God who *g* it.
Eze 3: 2 and he *g* me the scroll to eat.
Mt 1:25 And he *g* him the name Jesus.
25:35 and you *g* me something to drink,
25:42 and you *g* me nothing to drink,
26:26 Jesus took bread, *g* thanks
27:50 in a loud voice, he *g* up his spirit.
Mk 6: 7 *g* them authority over evil spirits.
Jn 1:12 he *g* the right to become children
3:16 so loved the world that he *g* his one
17: 4 by completing the work you *g* me
17: 6 you *g* them to me and they have
19:30 bowed his head and *g* up his spirit.
Ac 1: 3 *g* many convincing proofs that he
2:45 they *g* to anyone as he had need.
11:17 *g* them the same gift as he *g* us,
Ro 1:24 Therefore God *g* them
1:26 God *g* them over to shameful lusts.
1:28 he *g* them over to a depraved mind,
8:32 not spare his own Son, but *g* him up
2Co 5:18 *g* us the ministry of reconciliation:
8: 3 For I testify that they *g* as much
8: 5 they *g* themselves first to the Lord
Gal 1: 4 who *g* himself for our sins
2:20 who loved me and *g* himself for me
Eph 4: 8 and *g* gifts to men."
5: 2 as Christ loved us and *g* himself up
5:25 and *g* himself up for her
2Th 2:16 and by his grace *g* us eternal
1Ti 2: 6 who *g* himself as a ransom
Tit 2:14 who *g* himself for us to redeem us
1Jn 3:24 We know it by the Spirit he *g* us.

GAZE

Ps 27: 4 to *g* upon the beauty of the LORD
Pr 4:25 fix your *g* directly before you.

GEDALIAH

Governor of Judah appointed by Nebuchadnezzar (2Ki 25:22-26; Jer 39-41).

GEHAZI*

Servant of Elisha (2Ki 4:12-5:27; 8:4-5).

GENEALOGIES

1Ti 1: 4 themselves to myths and endless *g*.
Tit 3: 9 avoid foolish controversies and *g*

GENERATION (GENERATIONS)

Ex 3:15 am to be remembered from *g* to *g*.
Nu 32:13 until the whole *g* of those who had
Dt 1:35 of this evil *g* shall see the good land
Jdg 2:10 After that whole *g* had been
Ps 24: 6 Such is the *g* of those who seek him
48:13 tell of them to the next *g*.
71:18 I declare your power to the next *g*,
78: 4 we will tell the next *g*
102:18 Let this be written for a future *g*,
112: 2 the *g* of the upright will be blessed
145: 4 One *g* will commend your works
La 5:19 your throne endures from *g* to *g*.
Da 4: 3 his dominion endures from *g* to *g*.
4:34 his kingdom endures from *g* to *g*.
Joel 1: 3 and their children to the next *g*.
Mt 12:39 adulterous *g* asks for a miraculous
17:17 "O unbelieving and perverse *g*,"
23:36 all this will come upon this *g*.
24:34 this *g* will certainly not pass away
Mk 9:19 "O unbelieving *g*," Jesus replied,
13:30 this *g* will certainly not pass away
Lk 1:50 who fear him, from *g* to *g*.
11:29 Jesus said, "This is a wicked *g*.
11:30 will the Son of Man be to this *g*.
11:50 Therefore this *g* will be held
Lk 21:32 this *g* will certainly not pass away
Ac 2:40 Save yourselves from this corrupt *g*
Php 2:15 fault in a crooked and depraved *g*,

GENERATIONS (GENERATION)

Ge 9:12 a covenant for all *g* to come:
17: 7 after you for the *g* to come,
17: 9 after you for the *g* to come.
Ex 20: 6 a thousand *g* of those
31:13 and you for the *g* to come,
Dt 7: 9 covenant of love to a thousand *g*
32: 7 consider the *g* long past.
1Ch 16:15 he commanded, for a thousand *g*,
Job 8: 8 "Ask the former *g*
Ps 22:30 future *g* will be told about the Lord
33:11 of his heart through all *g*.
45:17 your memory through all *g*;
89: 1 faithfulness known through all *g*.
90: 1 throughout all *g*.
100: 5 continues through all *g*.
102:12 your renown endures through all *g*.
105: 8 he commanded, for a thousand *g*,
119:90 continues through all *g*;
135:13 renown, O LORD, through all *g*.
145:13 dominion endures through all *g*.
146:10 your God, O Zion, for all *g*.
Pr 27:24 and a crown is not secure for all *g*.
Isa 41: 4 forth the *g* from the beginning?
51: 8 my salvation through all *g*."
Lk 1:48 now on all *g* will call me blessed,
Eph 3: 5 not made known to men in other *g*
3:21 in Christ Jesus throughout all *g*,
Col 1:26 been kept hidden for ages and *g*,

GENEROSITY* (GENEROUS)

2Co 8: 2 poverty welled up in rich *g*.
9:11 and through us your *g* will result
9:13 and for your *g* in sharing with them

GENEROUS* (GENEROSITY)

Ps 37:26 They are always *g* and lend freely;
112: 5 Good will come to him who is *g*
Pr 11:25 A *g* man will prosper;
22: 9 A *g* man will himself be blessed,
Mt 20:15 Or are you envious because I am *g*
2Co 9: 5 Then it will be ready as a *g* gift,
9: 5 for the *g* gift you had promised.
9:11 way so that you can be *g*
1Ti 6:18 and to be *g* and willing to share.

GENTILE (GENTILES)

Ac 21:25 As for the *G* believers, we have
Ro 1:16 first for the Jew, then for the *G*.
2: 9 first for the Jew, then for the *G*;
2:10 first for the Jew, then for the *G*.
10:12 difference between Jew and *G*—

GENTILES (GENTILE)

Isa 42: 6 and a light for the *G*,
49: 6 also make you a light for the *G*,
49:22 "See, I will beckon to the *G*,
Lk 2:32 a light for revelation to the *G*
21:24 on by the *G* until the times
Ac 9:15 to carry my name before the *G*
10:45 been poured out even on the *G*.
11:18 granted even the *G* repentance unto
13:16 and you *G* who worship God,
13:46 of eternal life, we now turn to the *G*
13:47 I have made you a light for the *G*,
14:27 opened the door of faith to the *G*.
15:14 by taking from the *G* a people
18: 6 From now on I will go to the *G*."
22:21 I will send you far away to the *G*.' "
26:20 and in all Judea, and to the *G* also,
28:28 salvation has been sent to the *G*,
Ro 2:14 when *G*, who do not have the law,
3: 9 and *G* alike are all under sin.
3:29 Is he not the God of *G* too? Yes,
9:24 from the Jews but also from the *G*?
11:11 to the *G* to make Israel envious.
11:12 their loss means riches for the *G*,
11:13 as I am the apostle to the *G*,
15: 9 I will praise you among the *G*;
15: 9 so that the *G* may glorify God
1Co 1:23 block to Jews and foolishness to *G*,
Gal 1:16 I might preach him among the *G*,
2: 2 gospel that I preach among the *G*.
2: 8 my ministry as an apostle to the *G*.
2: 9 agreed that we should go to the *G*,
3: 8 that God would justify the *G*
3:14 to the *G* through Christ Jesus,
Eph 3: 6 the gospel the *G* are heirs together
3: 8 to the *G* the unsearchable riches
Col 1:27 among the *G* the glorious riches
1Ti 2: 7 a teacher of the true faith to the *G*.
2Ti 4:17 and all the *G* might hear it.

GENTLE* (GENTLENESS)

Dt 28:54 Even the most *g* and sensitive man
28:56 The most *g* and sensitive woman
28:56 and *g* that she would not venture
2Sa 18: 5 Be *g* with the young man Absalom
1Ki 19:12 And after the fire came a *g* whisper
Job 41: 3 Will he speak to you with *g* words?
Pr 15: 1 A *g* answer turns away wrath,
25:15 and a *g* tongue can break a bone.
Jer 11:19 I had been like a *g* lamb led
Zec 9: 9 *g* and riding on a donkey,
Mt 11:29 for I am *g* and humble in heart,
21: 5 *g* and riding on a donkey,
Ac 27:13 When a *g* south wind began
1Co 4:21 or in love and with a *g* spirit?
Eph 4: 2 Be completely humble and *g*;
1Th 2: 7 but we were *g* among you,
1Ti 3: 3 not violent but *g*, not quarrelsome,
1Pe 3: 4 the unfading beauty of a *g*

GENTLENESS* (GENTLE)

2Co 10: 1 By the meekness and *g* of Christ,
Gal 5:23 faithfulness, *g* and self-control.
Php 4: 5 Let your *g* be evident to all.
Col 3:12 kindness, humility, *g* and patience.
1Ti 6:11 faith, love, endurance and *g*.
1Pe 3:15 But do this with *g* and respect,

GENUINE*

2Co 6: 8 *g*, yet regarded as impostors;
Php 2:20 who takes a *g* interest
1Pe 1: 7 may be proved *g* and may result

GERIZIM

Dt 27:12 on Mount *G* to bless the people:

GERSHOM

Ex 2:22 and Moses named him *G*, saying,

GETHSEMANE*

Mt 26:36 disciples to a place called *G*,
Mk 14:32 They went to a place called *G*,

GHOST see also SPIRIT

Lk 24:39 a *g* does not have flesh and bones,

GIBEON

Jos 10:12 "O sun, stand still over *G*,

GIDEON*

Judge, also called Jerub-Baal; freed Israel from Midianites (Jdg 6-8; Heb 11:32). Given sign of fleece (Jdg 8:36-40).

GIFT (GIFTED GIFTS)

Pr 18:16 A *g* opens the way for the giver
21:14 A *g* given in secret soothes anger,
Ecc 3:13 in all his toil—this is the *g* of God.
Mt 5:23 if you are offering your *g*
Jn 4:10 "If you knew the *g* of God
Ac 1: 4 wait for the *g* my Father promised,
2:38 And you will receive the *g*
11:17 So if God gave them the same *g*
Ro 6:23 but the *g* of God is eternal life
12: 6 If a man's *g* is prophesying,
1Co 7: 7 each man has his own *g* from God;
2Co 8:12 the *g* is acceptable according
9:15 be to God for his indescribable *g*!
Eph 2: 8 it is the *g* of God—not by works,
1Ti 4:14 not neglect your *g*, which was
2Ti 1: 6 you to fan into flame the *g* of God,
Heb 6: 4 who have tasted the heavenly *g*,
Jas 1:17 and perfect *g* is from above,
1Pe 3: 7 with you of the gracious *g* of life,
4:10 should use whatever *g* he has
Rev 22:17 let him take the free *g* of the water

GIFTED* (GIFT)

1Co 14:37 he is a prophet or spiritually *g*,

GIFTS (GIFT)

Ps 76:11 bring *g* to the One to be feared.
112: 9 He has scattered abroad his *g*
Pr 25:14 of *g* he does not give.
Mt 2:11 and presented him with *g* of gold
7:11 Father in heaven give good *g*
7:11 to give good *g* to your children,
Lk 11:13 to give good *g* to your children,
Ac 10: 4 and *g* to the poor have come up
Ro 11:29 for God's *g* and his call are
12: 6 We have different *g*, according
1Co 12: 1 Now about spiritual *g*, brothers,
12: 4 There are different kinds of *g*,

1Co 12:28 those with *g* of administration,
12:30 all work miracles? Do all have *g*
12:31 But eagerly desire the greater *g*.
14: 1 and eagerly desire spiritual *g*,
14:12 eager to have spiritual *g*,
14:12 excel in *g* that build up the church.
2Co 9: 9 "He has scattered abroad his *g*
Eph 4: 8 and gave *g* to men."
Heb 2: 4 and *g* of the Holy Spirit distributed
9: 9 indicating that the *g* and sacrifices

GILEAD

1Ch 27:21 the half-tribe of Manasseh in *G*:
Jer 8:22 Is there no balm in *G*?
46:11 "Go up to *G* and get balm,

GILGAL

Jos 5: 9 So the place has been called *G*

GIRD*

Ps 45: 3 *G* your sword upon your side,

GIRL

Ge 24:16 *g* was very beautiful, a virgin;
2Ki 5: 2 a young *g* from Israel.
Mk 5:41 Little *g*, I say to you, get up!

GIVE (GAVE GIVEN GIVER GIVES GIVING LIFE-GIVING)

Ge 28: 4 you and your descendants the blessing *g* to Abraham
28:22 that you *g* me I will *g* you a tenth."
Ex 20:16 "You shall not *g* false testimony
30:15 The rich are not to *g* more
Nu 6:26 and *g* you peace." '
Dt 5:20 "You shall not *g* false testimony
15:10 *G* generously to him and do
15:14 *G* to him as the LORD your God
1Sa 1:11 then I will *g* him to the LORD
1:28 So now I *g* him to the LORD.
2Ch 15: 7 be strong and do not *g* up,
Pr 21:26 but the righteous *g* without sparing
23:26 My son, *g* me your heart
25:21 if he is thirsty, *g* him water to drink
30: 8 but *g* me only my daily bread.
31:31 *G* her the reward she has earned,
Ecc 3: 6 a time to search and a time to *g* up,
Isa 42: 8 I will not *g* my glory to another
Eze 36:26 I will *g* you a new heart
Mt 6:11 *G* us today our daily bread.
7:11 know how to *g* good gifts
10: 8 Freely you have received, freely *g*.
16:19 I will *g* you the keys
22:21 "*G* to Caesar what is Caesar's,
Mk 8:37 Or what can a man *g* in exchange
10:19 not steal, do not *g* false testimony,
Lk 6:38 *G*, and it will be given to you.
11: 3 *G* us each day our daily bread.
11:13 Father in heaven *g* the Holy Spirit
14:33 who does not *g* up everything he
Jn 10:28 I *g* them eternal life, and they shall
13:34 "A new commandment I *g* you:
14:16 he will *g* you another Counselor
14:27 I do not *g* to you as the world gives.
14:27 leave with you; my peace I *g* you.
17: 2 people that he might *g* eternal life
Ac 20:35 blessed to *g* than to receive.' "
Ro 2: 7 immortality, he will *g* eternal life.
8:32 with him, graciously *g* us all things
12: 8 let him *g* generously;
13: 7 *G* everyone what you owe him:
14:12 each of us will *g* an account
2Co 9: 7 Each man should *g* what he has
Gal 2: 5 We did not *g* in to them
6: 9 reap a harvest if we do not *g* up.
Heb 10:25 Let us not *g* up meeting together,
Rev 14: 7 "Fear God and *g* him glory,

GIVEN (GIVE)

Nu 8:16 are to be *g* wholly to me.
Dt 26:11 things the LORD your God has *g*
Job 3:23 Why is life *g* to a man
Ps 115:16 but the earth he has *g* to man.
Isa 9: 6 to us a son is *g*,
Mt 6:33 and all these things will be *g* to you
7: 7 "Ask and it will be *g* to you;
13:12 Whoever has will be *g* more,
22:30 people will neither marry nor be *g*
25:29 everyone who has will be *g* more,
Lk 6:38 Give, and it will be *g* to you.
8:10 kingdom of God has been *g* to you,
11: 9 Ask and it will be *g* to you;
22:19 saying, "This is my body *g* for you;
Jn 3:27 man can receive only what is *g* him
15: 7 you wish, and it will be *g* you.
17:24 I want those you have *g* me to be
17:24 the glory you have *g* me
18:11 the cup the Father has *g* me?"
Ac 5:32 whom God has *g* to those who
20:24 the task the Lord Jesus has *g* me—
Ro 5: 5 the Holy Spirit, whom he has *g* us.
1Co 4: 2 those who have been *g* a trust must
11:24 and when he had *g* thanks,
12:13 we were all *g* the one Spirit to drink
2Co 5: 5 and has *g* us the Spirit as a deposit,
Eph 1: 6 which he has freely *g* us
4: 7 to each one of us grace has been *g*
1Ti 4:14 was *g* you through a prophetic
1Jn 4:13 because he has *g* us of his Spirit.

GIVER* (GIVE)

Pr 18:16 A gift opens the way for the *g*
2Co 9: 7 for God loves a cheerful *g*.

GIVES (GIVE)

Job 35:10 who *g* songs in the night,
Ps 119:130 The unfolding of your words *g* light;
Pr 3:34 but *g* grace to the humble.
11:24 One man *g* freely, yet gains
14:30 A heart at peace *g* life to the body,
15:30 good news *g* health to the bones.
19: 6 of a man who *g* gifts.
25:26 is a righteous man who *g* way
28:27 He who *g* to the poor will lack
29: 4 justice a king *g* a country stability,
Isa 40:29 He *g* strength to the weary
Hab 2:15 "Woe to him who *g* drink
Mt 10:42 if anyone *g* even a cup of cold water
Jn 5:21 even so the Son *g* life to whom he is
6:63 The Spirit *g* life; the flesh counts
1Co 15:57 He *g* us the victory
2Co 3: 6 the letter kills, but the Spirit *g* life.
1Th 4: 8 who *g* you his Holy Spirit.
Jas 1:25 into the perfect law that *g* freedom,
4: 6 but *g* grace to the humble."
1Pe 5: 5 but *g* grace to the humble."

GIVING (GIVE)

Ne 8: 8 *g* the meaning so that the people
Est 9:19 a day for *g* presents to each other.
Ps 19: 8 *g* joy to the heart.
Pr 15:23 A man finds joy in *g* an apt reply—
Mt 6: 4 so that your *g* may be in secret.
24:38 marrying and *g* in marriage,
Ac 15: 8 them by *g* the Holy Spirit to them,
2Co 8: 7 also excel in this grace of *g*.
Php 4:15 shared with me in the matter of *g*

GLAD* (GLADDENS GLADNESS)

Ex 4:14 his heart will be *g* when he sees you
Jos 22:33 They were *g* to hear the report
Jdg 8:25 "We'll be *g* to give them."
18:20 household?" Then the priest was *g*.
1Sa 19: 5 and you saw it and were *g*.
2Sa 1:20 daughters of the Philistines be *g*,
1Ki 8:66 *g* in heart for all the good things
1Ch 16:31 heavens rejoice, let the earth be *g*;
2Ch 7:10 and *g* in heart for the good things
Ps 5:11 let all who take refuge in you be *g*;
9: 2 I will be *g* and rejoice in you;
14: 7 let Jacob rejoice and Israel be *g*!
16: 9 Therefore my heart is *g*
21: 6 made him *g* with the joy
31: 7 I will be *g* and rejoice in your love,
32:11 Rejoice in the LORD and be *g*,
40:16 rejoice and be *g* in you;
45: 8 music of the strings makes you *g*.
46: 4 whose streams make *g* the city
48:11 the villages of Judah are *g*
53: 6 let Jacob rejoice and Israel be *g*!
58:10 The righteous will be *g*
67: 4 May the nations be *g* and sing
68: 3 But may the righteous be *g*
69:32 The poor will see and be *g*—
70: 4 rejoice and be *g* in you;
90:14 for joy and be *g* all our days.
90:15 Make us *g* for as many days
92: 4 For you make me *g* by your deeds,
96:11 heavens rejoice, let the earth be *g*;
97: 1 LORD reigns, let the earth be *g*;
97: 8 and the villages of Judah are *g*
105:38 Egypt was *g* when they left,
107:30 They were *g* when it grew calm,
118:24 let us rejoice and be *g* in it.
149: 2 of Zion be *g* in their King.
Pr 23:15 then my heart will be *g*;
23:25 May your father and mother be *g*;
29: 6 a righteous one can sing and be *g*.
Ecc 8:15 sun than to eat and drink and be *g*.
Isa 25: 9 let us rejoice and be *g*
35: 1 and the parched land will be *g*;
65:18 But be *g* and rejoice forever
66:10 with Jerusalem and be *g* for her,
Jer 20:15 who made him very *g*, saying,
31:13 Then maidens will dance and be *g*,
41:13 were with him, they were *g*.
50:11 "Because you rejoice and are *g*,
La 4:21 be *g*, O Daughter of Edom,
Joel 2:21 be *g* and rejoice.
2:23 Be *g*, O people of Zion,
Hab 1:15 and so he rejoices and is *g*.
Zep 3:14 Be *g* and rejoice with all your heart
Zec 2:10 and be *g*, O Daughter of Zion.
8:19 will become joyful and *g* occasions
10: 7 their hearts will be *g* as with wine.
Mt 5:12 be *g*, because great is your reward
Lk 15:32 But we had to celebrate and be *g*,
Jn 4:36 and the reaper may be *g* together.
8:56 my day; he saw it and was *g*."
11:15 for your sake I am *g* I was not there
14:28 you would be *g* that I am going
Ac 2:26 Therefore my heart is *g*
2:46 together with *g* and sincere hearts,
11:23 he was *g* and encouraged them all
13:48 they were *g* and honored the word
15: 3 news made all the brothers very *g*.
15:31 were *g* for its encouraging message.
1Co 16:17 was *g* when Stephanas, Fortunatus
2Co 2: 2 who is left to make me *g*
7:16 I am *g* I can have complete
13: 9 We are *g* whenever we are weak
Gal 4:27 "Be *g*, O barren woman,
Php 2:17 I am *g* and rejoice with all of you.
2:18 So you too should be *g* and rejoice
2:28 you see him again you may be *g*
Rev 19: 7 Let us rejoice and be *g*

GLADDENS* (GLAD)

Ps 104:15 wine that *g* the heart of man,

GLADNESS* (GLAD)

2Ch 29:30 So they sang praises with *g*
Est 8:16 a time of happiness and joy, *g*
8:17 there was joy and *g*
Job 3:22 who are filled with *g*
Ps 35:27 shout for joy and *g*;
45:15 They are led in with joy and *g*;
51: 8 Let me hear joy and *g*;
65:12 the hills are clothed with *g*.
100: 2 Worship the LORD with *g*;
Ecc 5:20 God keeps him occupied with *g*
9: 7 Go, eat your food with *g*,
Isa 16:10 *g* are taken away from the orchards
35:10 *G* and joy will overtake them,
51: 3 Joy and *g* will be found in her,
51:11 *G* and joy will overtake them,
61: 3 the oil of *g* instead of mourning,
Jer 7:34 and *g* and to the voices of bride
16: 9 and *g* and to the voices of bride
25:10 from them the sounds of joy and *g*,
31:13 I will turn their mourning into *g*;
33:11 once more the sounds of joy and *g*,
48:33 Joy and *g* are gone
Joel 1:16 joy and *g*

GLAZE*

Pr 26:23 of *g* over earthenware

GLEAM*

Pr 4:18 of the righteous is like the first *g*
Da 10: 6 legs like the *g* of burnished bronze,

GLOAT (GLOATS)

Pr 24:17 Do not *g* when your enemy falls;

GLOATS* (GLOAT)

Pr 17: 5 whoever *g* over disaster will not go

GLORIES* (GLORY)

1Pe 1:11 and the *g* that would follow.

GLORIFIED* (GLORY)

Isa 66: 5 'Let the LORD be *g*,
Eze 39:13 day I am *g* will be a memorable day
Da 4:34 and *g* him who lives forever.
Jn 7:39 since Jesus had not yet been *g*.
11: 4 glory so that God's Son may be *g*
12:16 after Jesus was *g* did they realize
12:23 come for the Son of Man to be *g*.
12:28 "I have *g* it, and will glorify it again
13:31 Son of Man *g* and God is *g* in him.
13:32 If God is *g* in him, God will glorify
Ac 3:13 our fathers, has *g* his servant Jesus.
Ro 1:21 they neither *g* him as God
8:30 those he justified, he also *g*.

2Th 1:10 comes to be *g* in his holy people
1:12 of our Lord Jesus may be *g* in you,
1Pe 1:21 him from the dead and *g* him,

GLORIFIES* (GLORY)

Lk 1:46 My soul *g* the Lord
Jn 8:54 as your God, is the one who *g* me.

GLORIFY* (GLORY)

Ps 34: 3 *G* the LORD with me;
63: 3 my lips will *g* you.
69:30 and *g* him with thanksgiving.
86:12 I will *g* your name forever.
Isa 60:13 and I will *g* the place of my feet.
Da 4:37 and exalt and *g* the King of heaven,
Jn 8:54 Jesus replied, "If I *g* myself,
12:28 glorified it, and will *g* it again."
12:28 *g* your name!" Then a voice came
13:32 God will *g* the Son in himself,
13:32 in himself, and will *g* him at once.
17: 1 *G* your Son, that your Son may
17: 1 your Son, that your Son may *g* you.
17: 5 *g* me in your presence
21:19 death by which Peter would *g* God.
Ro 15: 6 and mouth you may *g* the God
15: 9 so that the Gentiles may *g* God
1Pe 2:12 and *g* God on the day he visits us.
Rev 16: 9 they refused to repent and *g* him.

GLORIFYING* (GLORY)

Lk 2:20 *g* and praising God

GLORIOUS* (GLORY)

Dt 28:58 not revere this *g* and awesome
33:29 and your *g* sword.
1Ch 29:13 and praise your *g* name.
Ne 9: 5 "Blessed be your *g* name,
Ps 16: 3 they are the *g* ones
45:13 All *g* is the princess
66: 2 make his praise *g*.
72:19 Praise be to his *g* name forever;
87: 3 *G* things are said of you,
111: 3 *G* and majestic are his deeds,
145: 5 of the *g* splendor of your majesty,
145:12 the *g* splendor of your kingdom.
Isa 3: 8 defying his *g* presence.
4: 2 the LORD will be beautiful and *g*,
11:10 and his place of rest will be *g*.
12: 5 for he has done *g* things;
28: 1 to the fading flower, his *g* beauty,
28: 4 That fading flower, his *g* beauty,
28: 5 will be a *g* crown,
42:21 to make his law great and *g*.
60: 7 and I will adorn my *g* temple.
63:12 who sent his *g* arm of power
63:14 to make for yourself a *g* name.
63:15 from your lofty throne, holy and *g*.
64:11 *g* temple, where our fathers praised
Jer 13:18 for your *g* crowns
14:21 do not dishonor your *g* throne.
17:12 A *g* throne, exalted
48:17 how broken the *g* staff!'
Mt 19:28 the Son of Man sits on his *g* throne,
Lk 9:31 appeared in *g* splendor, talking
Ac 2:20 of the great and *g* day of the Lord.
Ro 8:21 and brought into the *g* freedom
2Co 3: 8 of the Spirit be even more *g*?
3: 9 how much more *g* is the ministry
3: 9 ministry that condemns men is *g*,
3:10 For what was *g* has no glory now
Eph 1: 6 to the praise of his *g* grace,
1:17 *g* Father, may give you the Spirit
1:18 the riches of his *g* inheritance
3:16 of his *g* riches he may strengthen
Php 3:21 so that they will be like his *g* body.
4:19 to his *g* riches in Christ Jesus.
Col 1:11 all power according to his *g* might
1:27 among the Gentiles the *g* riches
1Ti 1:11 to the *g* gospel of the blessed God,
Tit 2:13 the *g* appearing of our great God
Jas 2: 1 believers in our *g* Lord Jesus Christ
1Pe 1: 8 with an inexpressible and *g* joy,
Jude :24 before his *g* presence without fault

GLORIOUSLY* (GLORY)

Isa 24:23 and before its elders, *g*.

GLORY (GLORIES GLORIFIED GLORIFIES GLORIFY GLORIFYING GLORIOUS GLORIOUSLY)

Ex 14: 4 But I will gain *g* for myself
14:17 And I will gain *g* through Pharaoh
15:11 awesome in *g*,
16:10 and there was the *g* of the LORD
24:16 and the *g* of the LORD settled
33:18 Moses said, "Now show me your *g*
40:34 and the *g* of the LORD filled
Nu 14:21 the *g* of the LORD fills the whole
Dt 5:24 LORD our God has shown us his *g*
Jos 7:19 "My son, give *g* to the LORD,
1Sa 4:21 "The *g* has departed from Israel"—
1Ch 16:10 *G* in his holy name;
16:24 Declare his *g* among the nations,
16:28 ascribe to the LORD *g*
29:11 and the *g* and the majesty
Ps 8: 1 You have set your *g*
8: 5 and crowned him with *g* and honor
19: 1 The heavens declare the *g* of God;
24: 7 that the King of *g* may come in.
26: 8 the place where your *g* dwells.
29: 1 ascribe to the LORD *g*
29: 9 And in his temple all cry, *"G!"*
57: 5 let your *g* be over all the earth.
66: 2 Sing the *g* of his name;
72:19 the whole earth be filled with his *g*.
96: 3 Declare his *g* among the nations,
102:15 of the earth will revere your *g*.
108: 5 and let your *g* be over all the earth.
149: 9 This is the *g* of all his saints.
Pr 19:11 it is to his *g* to overlook an offense.
25: 2 It is the *g* of God to conceal
Isa 4: 5 over all the *g* will be a canopy.
6: 3 the whole earth is full of his *g*."
24:16 *"G* to the Righteous One."
26:15 You have gained *g* for yourself;
35: 2 they will see the *g* of the LORD,
40: 5 the *g* of the LORD will be revealed
42: 8 I will not give my *g* to another
42:12 Let them give *g* to the LORD
43: 7 whom I created for my *g*,
44:23 he displays his *g* in Israel.
48:11 I will not yield my *g* to another.
66:18 and they will come and see my *g*.
66:19 They will proclaim my *g*
Eze 1:28 the likeness of the *g* of the LORD.
10: 4 the radiance of the *g* of the LORD.
43: 2 and the land was radiant with his *g*.
44: 4 and saw the *g* of the LORD filling
Hab 2:14 knowledge of the *g* of the LORD,
3: 3 His *g* covered the heavens
Zec 2: 5 'and I will be its *g* within.'
Mt 16:27 in his Father's *g* with his angels,
24:30 of the sky, with power and great *g*.
25:31 sit on his throne in heavenly *g*.
25:31 the Son of Man comes in his *g*,
Mk 8:38 in his Father's *g* with the holy
13:26 in clouds with great power and *g*.
Lk 2: 9 and the *g* of the Lord shone
2:14 saying, *"G* to God in the highest,
9:26 and in the *g* of the Father
9:26 of him when he comes in his *g*
9:32 they saw his *g* and the two men
19:38 in heaven and *g* in the highest!"
21:27 in a cloud with power and great *g*.
24:26 these things and then enter his *g*?"
Jn 1:14 We have seen his *g*, the *g* of the One
2:11 He thus revealed his *g*,
8:50 I am not seeking *g* for myself;
8:54 myself, my *g* means nothing.
11: 4 for God's *g* so that God's Son may
11:40 you would see the *g* of God?"
12:41 he saw Jesus' *g* and spoke about
14:13 so that the Son may bring *g*
15: 8 is to my Father's *g*, that you bear
16:14 He will bring *g* to me by taking
17: 4 I have brought you *g* on earth
17: 5 presence with the *g* I had with you
17:10 *g* has come to me through them.
17:22 given them the *g* that you gave
17:24 to see my *g*, the *g* you have given
Ac 7: 2 The God of *g* appeared
7:55 up to heaven and saw the *g* of God,
Ro 1:23 exchanged the *g* of the immortal
2: 7 by persistence in doing good seek *g*
2:10 then for the Gentile; but *g*,
3: 7 truthfulness and so increases his *g*,
3:23 and fall short of the *g* of God,
4:20 in his faith and gave *g* to God,
8:17 that we may also share in his *g*.
8:18 with the *g* that will be revealed
9: 4 theirs the divine *g*, the covenants,
9:23 riches of his *g* known to the objects
9:23 whom he prepared in advance for *g*
11:36 To him be the *g* forever! Amen.
15:17 Therefore I *g* in Christ Jesus
16:27 to the only wise God be *g* forever
1Co 2: 7 for our *g* before time began.
10:31 whatever you do, do it all for the *g*
11: 7 but the woman is the *g* of man.
11: 7 since he is the image and *g* of God;
1Co 11:15 it is her *g*? For long hair is given
15:43 it is raised in *g*; it is sown
2Co 1:20 spoken by us to the *g* of God.
3: 7 in letters on stone, came with *g*,
3: 7 the face of Moses because of its *g*,
3:10 comparison with the surpassing *g*.
3:10 what was glorious has no *g* now
3:11 how much greater is the *g*
3:11 what was fading away came with *g*,
3:18 faces all reflect the Lord's *g*,
3:18 likeness with ever-increasing *g*,
4: 4 of the gospel of the *g* of Christ,
4: 6 of the knowledge of the *g* of God
4:15 to overflow to the *g* of God.
4:17 us an eternal *g* that far outweighs
Gal 1: 5 to whom be *g* for ever and ever.
Eph 1:12 might be for the praise of his *g*.
1:14 to the praise of his *g*.
3:13 for you, which are your *g*.
3:21 to him be *g* in the church
Php 1:11 to the *g* and praise of God.
2:11 to the *g* of God the Father.
3: 3 of God, who *g* in Christ Jesus,
4:20 and Father be *g* for ever and ever.
Col 1:27 Christ in you, the hope of *g*.
3: 4 also will appear with him in *g*.
1Th 2:12 you into his kingdom and *g*.
2:19 in which we will *g* in the presence
2:20 Indeed, you are our *g* and joy.
2Th 2:14 in the *g* of our Lord Jesus Christ.
1Ti 1:17 be honor and *g* for ever and ever.
3:16 was taken up in *g*.
2Ti 2:10 is in Christ Jesus, with eternal *g*.
4:18 To him be *g* for ever and ever.
Heb 1: 3 The Son is the radiance of God's *g*
2: 7 you crowned him with *g* and honor
2: 9 now crowned with *g* and honor
2:10 In bringing many sons to *g*,
5: 5 take upon himself the *g*
9: 5 the ark were the cherubim of the *G*,
13:21 to whom be *g* for ever and ever.
1Pe 1: 7 *g* and honor when Jesus Christ is
1:24 and all their *g* is like the flowers
4:11 To him be the *g* and the power
4:13 overjoyed when his *g* is revealed.
4:14 for the Spirit of *g* and of God rests
5: 1 will share in the *g* to be revealed:
5: 4 of *g* that will never fade away.
5:10 you to his eternal *g* in Christ,
2Pe 1: 3 of him who called us by his own *g*
1:17 and *g* from God the Father
1:17 came to him from the Majestic *G*,
3:18 To him be *g* both now and forever!
Jude :25 to the only God our Savior be *g*,
Rev 1: 6 to him be *g* and power for ever
4: 9 the living creatures give *g*,
4:11 to receive *g* and honor and power,
5:12 and honor and *g* and praise!"
5:13 and honor and *g* and power,
7:12 Praise and *g*
11:13 and gave *g* to the God of heaven.
14: 7 "Fear God and give him *g*,
15: 4 and bring *g* to your name?
15: 8 with smoke from the *g* of God
19: 1 *g* and power belong to our God,
19: 7 and give him *g*!
21:11 It shone with the *g* of God,
21:23 for the *g* of God gives it light,
21:26 *g* and honor of the nations will be

GLOWING

Eze 8: 2 was as bright as *g* metal.
Rev 1:15 His feet were like bronze *g*

GLUTTONS* (GLUTTONY)

Pr 23:21 for drunkards and *g* become poor,
28: 7 of *g* disgraces his father.
Tit 1:12 always liars, evil brutes, lazy *g*."

GLUTTONY* (GLUTTONS)

Pr 23: 2 throat if you are given to *g*.

GNASHING

Mt 8:12 where there will be weeping and *g*

GNAT* (GNATS)

Mt 23:24 You strain out a *g* but swallow

GNATS (GNAT)

Ex 8:16 of Egypt the dust will become *g*."

GOADS

Ecc 12:11 The words of the wise are like *g*,
Ac 26:14 hard for you to kick against the *g*.'

GOAL*

Lk 13:32 on the third day I will reach my g.'
2Co 5: 9 So we make it our g to please him,
Gal 3: 3 to attain your g by human effort?
Php 3:14 on toward the g to win the prize
1Ti 1: 5 The g of this command is love,
1Pe 1: 9 for you are receiving the g

GOAT (GOATS SCAPEGOAT)

Ge 15: 9 "Bring me a heifer, a g and a ram,
30:32 and every spotted or speckled g.
37:31 slaughtered a g and dipped
Ex 26: 7 Make curtains of g hair for the tent
Lev 16: 9 shall bring the g whose lot falls
Nu 7:16 one male g for a sin offering;
Isa 11: 6 the leopard will lie down with the g
Da 8: 5 suddenly a g with a prominent

GOATS (GOAT)

Nu 7:17 five male g and five male lambs
Mt 25:32 separates the sheep from the g.
Heb 10: 4 of bulls and g to take away sins.

GOD (GOD'S GODLINESS GODLY GODS)

Ge 1: 1 In the beginning G created
1: 2 and the Spirit of G was hovering
1: 3 And G said, "Let there be light,"
1: 7 So G made the expanse
1: 9 And G said, "Let the water
1:11 Then G said, "Let the land produce
1:20 And G said, "Let the water teem
1:21 So G created the great creatures
1:25 G made the wild animals according
1:26 Then G said, "Let us make man
1:27 So G created man in his own image
1:31 G saw all that he had made,
2: 3 And G blessed the seventh day
2: 7 And the LORD G formed the man
2: 8 the LORD G had planted a garden
2:18 The LORD G said, "It is not good
2:22 Then the LORD G made a woman
3: 1 to the woman, "Did G really say,
3: 5 you will be like G, knowing good
3: 8 from the LORD G among the trees
3: 9 But the LORD G called to the man
3:21 The LORD G made garments
3:22 LORD G said, "The man has now
3:23 So the LORD G banished him
5: 1 When G created man, he made him
5:22 Enoch walked with G 300 years
5:24 because G took him away.
6: 2 sons of G saw that the daughters
6: 9 of his time, and he walked with G.
6:12 G saw how corrupt the earth had
8: 1 But G remembered Noah
9: 1 Then G blessed Noah and his sons,
9: 6 for in the image of G
9:16 everlasting covenant between G
14:18 He was priest of G Most High,
14:19 Blessed be Abram by G Most High,
16:13 "You are the G who sees me,"
17: 1 "I am G Almighty; walk before me
17: 7 to be your G and the G
21: 4 him, as G commanded him.
21: 6 "G has brought me laughter,
21:20 G was with the boy as he grew up.
21:22 G is with you in everything you do.
21:33 name of the LORD, the Eternal G.
22: 1 Some time later G tested Abraham.
22: 8 "G himself will provide the lamb
22:12 Now I know that you fear G,
25:11 Abraham's death, G blessed his
28:12 and the angels of G were ascending
28:17 other than the house of G;
31:42 But G has seen my hardship
31:50 remember that G is a witness
32: 1 and the angels of G met him.
32:28 because you have struggled with G
32:30 "It is because I saw G face to face,
33:11 for G has been gracious to me
35: 1 and build an altar there to G,
35: 5 and the terror of G fell
35:10 G said to him, "Your name is Jacob
35:11 G said to him, "I am G Almighty;
41:51 G has made me forget all my
41:52 G has made me fruitful in the land
50:20 but G intended it for good
50:24 But G will surely come to your aid
Ex 2:24 G heard their groaning
3: 5 "Do not come any closer," G said.
3: 6 because he was afraid to look at G.
3:12 And G said, "I will be with you.
3:14 what shall I tell them?" G said
4:27 he met Moses at the mountain of G
Ex 6: 7 own people, and I will be your G.
8:10 is no one like the LORD our G.
10:16 sinned against the LORD your G
13:18 So G led the people
15: 2 He is my G, and I will praise him,
16:12 that I am the LORD your G.' "
17: 9 with the staff of G in my hands."
18: 5 camped near the mountain of G.
19: 3 Then Moses went up to G,
20: 1 And G spoke all these words:
20: 2 the LORD your G, who brought
20: 5 the LORD your G, am a jealous G,
20: 7 the name of the LORD your G,
20:10 a Sabbath to the LORD your G.
20:12 the LORD your G is giving you.
20:19 But do not have G speak to us
20:20 the fear of G will be with you
22:20 "Whoever sacrifices to any g other
22:28 "Do not blaspheme G
23:19 to the house of the LORD your G.
31:18 inscribed by the finger of G.
34: 6 the compassionate and gracious G,
34:14 name is Jealous, is a jealous G.
Lev 2:13 salt of the covenant of your G out
11:44 the LORD your G; consecrate
18:21 not profane the name of your G.
19: 2 the LORD your G, am holy.
20: 7 because I am the LORD your G.
21: 6 They must be holy to their G
22:33 out of Egypt to be your G.
26:12 walk among you and be your G,
Nu 15:40 and will be consecrated to your G.
22:18 the command of the LORD my G.
22:38 I must speak only what G puts
23:19 G is not a man, that he should lie,
25:13 zealous for the honor of his G
Dt 1:17 for judgment belongs to G.
1:21 the LORD your G has given you
1:30 The LORD your G, who is going
3:22 LORD your G himself will fight
3:24 For what g is there in heaven
4:24 is a consuming fire, a jealous G.
4:29 there you seek the LORD your G,
4:31 the LORD your G is a merciful G;
4:39 heart this day that the LORD is G
5: 9 the LORD your G, am a jealous G,
5:11 the name of the LORD your G,
5:12 the LORD your G has commanded
5:14 a Sabbath to the LORD your G.
5:15 the LORD your G brought you out
5:16 the LORD your G has commanded
5:16 the LORD your G is giving you.
5:24 LORD our G has shown us his
5:26 of the living G speaking out of fire,
6: 2 them may fear the LORD your G
6: 4 LORD our G, the LORD is one.
6: 5 Love the LORD your G
6:13 the LORD your G, serve him only
6:16 Do not test the LORD your G
7: 6 holy to the LORD your G.
7: 9 your G is G; he is the faithful G,
7:12 the LORD your G will keep his
7:19 LORD your G will do the same
7:21 is a great and awesome G.
8: 5 the LORD your G disciplines you.
8:11 do not forget the LORD your G,
8:18 But remember the LORD your G,
9:10 inscribed by the finger of G.
10:12 but to fear the LORD your G,
10:14 the LORD your G belong
10:17 For the LORD your G is G of gods
10:21 He is your praise; he is your G,
11: 1 Love the LORD your G
11:13 to love the LORD your G
12:12 rejoice before the LORD your G,
12:28 in the eyes of the LORD your G.
13: 3 The LORD your G is testing you
13: 4 the LORD your G you must
15: 6 the LORD your G will bless you
15:19 the LORD your G every firstborn
16:11 rejoice before the LORD your G
16:17 the LORD your G has blessed you.
18:13 before the LORD your G.
18:15 The LORD your G will raise up
19: 9 to love the LORD your G
22: 5 the LORD your G detests anyone
23: 5 the LORD your G loves you.
23:14 the LORD your G moves about
23:21 a vow to the LORD your G,
25:16 the LORD your G detests anyone
26: 5 declare before the LORD your G:
29:13 that he may be your G
29:29 belong to the LORD our G,
30: 2 return to the LORD your G
30: 4 the LORD your G will gather you
Dt 30: 6 The LORD your G will circumcise
30:16 today to love the LORD your G,
30:20 you may love the LORD your G,
31: 6 for the LORD your G goes
32: 3 Oh, praise the greatness of our G!
32: 4 A faithful G who does no wrong,
33:27 The eternal G is your refuge,
Jos 1: 9 for the LORD your G will be
14: 8 the LORD my G wholeheartedly.
14: 9 the LORD my G wholeheartedly.'
14:14 the G of Israel, wholeheartedly.
22: 5 to love the LORD your G,
22:22 The Mighty One, G, the LORD!
22:34 Between Us that the LORD is G.
23: 8 to hold fast to the LORD your G,
23:11 careful to love the LORD your G.
23:14 the LORD your G gave you has
23:15 of the LORD your G has come true
24:19 He is a holy G; he is a jealous G.
24:23 to the LORD, the G of Israel."
Jdg 5: 3 to the LORD, the G of Israel.
16:28 O G, please strengthen me just
Ru 1:16 be my people and your G my G.
2:12 by the LORD, the G of Israel,
1Sa 2: 2 there is no Rock like our G.
2: 3 for the LORD is a G who knows,
2:25 another man, G may mediate
10:26 men whose hearts G had touched.
12:12 the LORD your G was your king.
16:15 spirit from G is tormenting you.
17:26 defy the armies of the living G?"
17:36 defied the armies of the living G.
17:45 the G of the armies of Israel,
17:46 world will know that there is a G
23:16 and helped him find strength in G.
28:15 and G has turned away from me.
30: 6 strength in the LORD his G.
2Sa 7:22 and there is no G but you,
7:23 on earth that G went out to redeem
14:14 But G does not take away life;
21:14 G answered prayer in behalf
22: 3 my G is my rock, in whom I take
22:31 "As for G, his way is perfect;
22:32 And who is the Rock except our G
22:33 It is G who arms me with strength
22:47 Exalted be G, the Rock, my Savior!
1Ki 2: 3 what the LORD your G requires:
4:29 G gave Solomon wisdom
5: 5 for the Name of the LORD my G,
8:23 there is no G like you in heaven
8:27 "But will G really dwell on earth?
8:60 may know that the LORD is G
8:61 committed to the LORD our G,
10:24 to hear the wisdom G had put
15:30 he provoked the LORD, the G
18:21 If the LORD is G, follow him;
18:36 it be known today that you are G
18:37 are G, and that you are turning
20:28 a g of the hills and not a g
2Ki 5:15 "Now I know that there is no G
18: 5 in the LORD, the G of Israel.
19:15 G of Israel, enthroned
19:19 Now, O LORD our G, deliver us
1Ch 12:18 for your G will help you."
13: 2 if it is the will of the LORD our G,
16:35 Cry out, "Save us, O G our Savior;
17:20 and there is no G but you,
17:24 the G over Israel, is Israel's G!'
21: 8 said to G, "I have sinned greatly
22: 1 house of the LORD G is to be here,
22:19 soul to seeking the LORD your G.
28: 2 for the footstool of our G,
28: 9 acknowledge the G of your father,
28:20 for the LORD G, my G, is with you
29: 1 not for man but for the LORD G.
29: 2 provided for the temple of my G—
29: 3 of my G I now give my personal
29:10 G of our father Israel,
29:13 Now, our G, we give you thanks,
29:16 O LORD our G, as for all this
29:17 my G, that you test the heart
29:18 G of our fathers Abraham,
2Ch 2: 4 for the Name of the LORD my G
5:14 of the LORD filled the temple of G
6: 4 be to the LORD, the G of Israel,
6:14 there is no G like you in heaven
6:18 "But will G really dwell on earth
10:15 for this turn of events was from G,
13:12 G is with us; he is our leader.
15: 3 was without the true G,
15:12 the G of their fathers,
15:15 They sought G eagerly,
18:13 I can tell him only what my G says
19: 3 have set your heart on seeking G."
19: 7 with the LORD our G there is no

2Ch 20: 6 are you not the G who is in heaven?
20:20 Have faith in the LORD your G
25: 8 for G has the power to help
26: 5 sought the LORD, G gave him
30: 9 for the LORD your G is gracious
30: 19 who sets his heart on seeking G—
31:21 he sought his G and worked
32:31 G left him to test him
33: 12 the favor of the LORD his G
34:33 fail to follow the LORD, the G
Ezr 6:21 to seek the LORD, the G of Israel.
7: 18 accordance with the will of your G.
7:23 Whatever the G of heaven has
8:22 "The gracious hand of our G is
8:31 The hand of our G was on us,
9: 6 "O my G, I am too ashamed
9: 9 our G has not deserted us
9: 13 our G, you have punished us less
9: 15 G of Israel, you are righteous!
Ne 1: 5 the great and awesome G,
5: 9 fear of our G to avoid the reproach
5: 15 for G I did not act like that.
7: 2 feared G more than most men do.
8: 8 from the Book of the Law of G,
8: 18 from the Book of the Law of G.
9: 5 and praise the LORD your G,
9: 17 But you are a forgiving G,
9:31 you are a gracious and merciful G.
9:32 the great, mighty and awesome G,
10:29 oath to follow the Law of G given
10:39 not neglect the house of our G."
12:43 G had given them great joy.
13: 11 Why is the house of G neglected?"
13:26 He was loved by his G,
13:31 Remember me with favor, O my G.
Job 1: 1 he feared G and shunned evil.
1:22 by charging G with wrongdoing.
2: 10 Shall we accept good from G,
4: 17 a mortal be more righteous than G?
5: 17 is the man whom G corrects;
8: 3 Does G pervert justice?
8:20 "Surely G does not reject
9: 2 a mortal be righteous before G?
11: 7 Can you fathom the mysteries of G
12: 13 "To G belong wisdom and power;
16: 7 Surely, O G, you have worn me out
19:26 yet in my flesh I will see G;
21: 19 'G stores up a man's punishment
21:22 Can anyone teach knowledge to G,
22: 12 "Is not G in the heights of heaven?
22: 13 Yet you say, 'What does G know?
22:21 "Submit to G and be at peace
25: 2 "Dominion and awe belong to G;
25: 4 can a man be righteous before G?
26: 6 Death is naked before G;
30:20 O G, but you do not answer;
31: 6 let G weigh me in honest scales
31: 14 do when G confronts me?
32: 13 let G refute him, not man.'
33: 6 I am just like you before G;
33: 14 For G does speak—now one way,
33:26 He prays to G and finds favor
34: 10 Far be it from G to do evil,
34: 12 is unthinkable that G would do
34:23 G has no need to examine men
34:33 Should G then reward you
36: 5 "G is mighty, but does not despise
36:26 is G—beyond our understanding!
37:22 G comes in awesome majesty.
Ps 5: 4 You are not a G who takes pleasure
7: 11 G is a righteous judge,
10: 14 O G, do see trouble and grief;
14: 5 for G is present in the company
18: 2 my G is my rock, in whom I take
18:28 my G turns my darkness into light.
18:30 As for G, his way is perfect;
18:31 And who is the Rock except our G
18:32 It is G who arms me with strength
18:46 Exalted be G my Savior!
19: 1 The heavens declare the glory of G;
22: 1 G, my G, why have you forsaken
22: 10 womb you have been my G.
27: 9 O G my Savior.
29: 3 the G of glory thunders,
31: 5 redeem me, O LORD, the G
31: 14 I say, "You are my G."
33: 12 the nation whose G is the LORD,
35:24 righteousness, O LORD my G;
37:31 The law of his G is in his heart;
40: 3 a hymn of praise to our G.
40: 8 I desire to do your will, O my G;
42: 1 so my soul pants for you, O G.
42: 2 thirsts for G, for the living G.
42: 5 Put your hope in G,
42: 8 a prayer to the G of my life.
Ps 42: 11 Put your hope in G,
43: 4 to G, my joy and my delight.
44: 8 In G we make our boast all day
45: 6 O G, will last for ever and ever;
45: 7 therefore G, your G, has set you
46: 1 G is our refuge and strength,
46: 5 G will help her at break of day.
46: 10 "Be still, and know that I am G;
47: 1 shout to G with cries of joy.
47: 6 Sing praises to G, sing praises;
47: 7 For G is the King of all the earth;
48: 9 Within your temple, O G,
49: 7 or give to G a ransom for him—
50: 2 G shines forth.
50: 3 Our G comes and will not be silent;
51: 1 Have mercy on me, O G,
51: 10 Create in me a pure heart, O G,
51: 17 O G, you will not despise.
53: 2 any who seek G.
54: 4 Surely G is my help;
55: 19 G, who is enthroned forever,
56: 4 In G, whose word I praise,
56: 10 In G, whose word I praise,
56: 13 that I may walk before G
57: 3 G sends his love and his
57: 7 My heart is steadfast, O G,
59: 17 are my fortress, my loving G.
62: 1 My soul finds rest in G alone;
62: 7 my honor depend on G;
62: 8 for G is our refuge.
62: 11 One thing G has spoken,
63: 1 O G, you are my G,
65: 5 O G our Savior,
66: 1 Shout with joy to G, all the earth!
66: 3 Say to G, "How awesome are your
66: 5 Come and see what G has done,
66: 16 listen, all you who fear G;
66:20 Praise be to G,
68: 4 Sing to G, sing praise to his name,
68: 6 G sets the lonely in families,
68:20 Our G is a G who saves;
68:24 has come into view, O G,
68:35 You are awesome, O G,
69: 5 You know my folly, O G;
70: 1 Hasten, O G, to save me;
70: 4 "Let G be exalted!"
70: 5 come quickly to me, O G.
71: 17 my youth, O G, you have taught
71: 18 do not forsake me, O G,
71: 19 reaches to the skies, O G,
71:22 harp for your faithfulness, O my G;
73: 17 me till I entered the sanctuary of G;
73:26 but G is the strength of my heart
76: 11 Make vows to the LORD your G
77: 13 What g is so great as our God?
77: 14 You are the G who performs
78: 19 Can G spread a table in the desert?
79: 9 Help us, O G our Savior,
81: 1 Sing for joy to G our strength;
82: 1 G presides in the great assembly;
84: 2 out for the living G.
84: 10 a doorkeeper in the house of my G
84: 11 For the LORD G is a sun
86: 12 O Lord my G, with all my heart;
86: 15 a compassionate and gracious G,
87: 3 O city of G: Selah
89: 7 of the holy ones G is greatly feared;
90: 2 to everlasting you are G.
91: 2 my G, in whom I trust."
94:22 my G the rock in whom I take
95: 7 for he is our G
99: 8 you were to Israel a forgiving G,
99: 9 Exalt the LORD our G
100: 3 Know that the LORD is G.
108: 1 My heart is steadfast, O G;
113: 5 Who is like the LORD our G,
115: 3 Our G is in heaven;
116: 5 our G is full of compassion.
123: 2 look to the LORD our G,
136: 2 Give thanks to the G of gods.
136: 26 Give thanks to the G of heaven.
139: 17 to me are your thoughts, O G!
139: 23 Search me, O G, and know my
143: 10 for you are my G;
144: 2 He is my loving G and my fortress,
147: 1 is to sing praises to our G,
Pr 3: 4 in the sight of G and man.
14:31 to the needy honors G.
25: 2 of G to conceal a matter;
30: 5 "Every word of G is flawless;
Ecc 2:26 G gives wisdom, knowledge
3: 11 cannot fathom what G has done
3: 13 in all his toil—this is the gift of G.
3: 14 G does it so that men will revere him.
5: 4 When you make a vow to G,
Ecc 5: 19 in his work—this is a gift of G.
8: 12 who are reverent before G.
11: 5 cannot understand the work of G,
12: 7 the spirit returns to G who gave it.
12: 13 Fear G and keep his
Isa 5: 16 the holy G will show himself holy
9: 6 Wonderful Counselor, Mighty G,
12: 2 Surely G is my salvation;
25: 9 "Surely this is our G;
28: 11 G will speak to this people,
29:23 will stand in awe of the G of Israel.
30: 18 For the LORD is a G of justice.
35: 4 your G will come,
37: 16 you alone are G over all
40: 1 says your G.
40: 3 a highway for our G.
40: 8 the word of our G stands forever."
40: 18 then, will you compare G?
40:28 The LORD is the everlasting G,
41: 10 not be dismayed, for I am your G.
41: 13 For I am the LORD, your G,
43: 10 Before me no g was formed,
44: 6 apart from me there is no G.
44: 15 he also fashions a g and worships it;
45: 18 he is G;
48: 17 "I am the LORD your G,
52: 7 "Your G reigns!"
52: 12 G of Israel will be your rear guard.
55: 7 to our G, for he will freely pardon.
57:21 says my G, "for the wicked."
59: 2 you from your G;
60: 19 and your G will be your glory.
61: 2 and the day of vengeance of our G,
61: 10 my soul rejoices in my G.
62: 5 so will your G rejoice over you.
Jer 7:23 I will be your G and you will be my
10: 10 But the LORD is the true G;
10: 12 But G made the earth by his power;
23:23 "Am I only a G nearby,"
23:36 distort the words of the living G,
31:33 I will be their G,
32:27 "I am the LORD, the G
42: 6 for we will obey the LORD our G."
51: 10 what the LORD our G has done.'
51:56 For the LORD is a G of retribution
Eze 28: 13 the garden of G;
34:31 and I am your G, declares
Da 2:28 there is a G in heaven who reveals
3: 17 the G we serve is able to save us
3:29 for no other g can save in this way
6: 16 "May your G, whom you serve
9: 4 O Lord, the great and awesome G,
10: 12 to humble yourself before your G,
11:36 things against the G of gods.
Hos 1: 9 my people, and I am not your G.
1: 10 will be called 'sons of the living G.'
4: 6 you have ignored the law of your G
6: 6 acknowledgment of G rather
9: 8 The prophet, along with my G,
12: 6 and wait for your G always.
Joel 2: 13 Return to the LORD your G,
2:23 rejoice in the LORD your G,
Am 4: 12 prepare to meet your G, O Israel."
4: 13 the LORD G Almighty is his name
Jnh 1: 6 Get up and call on your g!
4: 2 a gracious and compassionate G,
Mic 6: 8 and to walk humbly with your G.
7: 7 I wait for G my Savior;
7: 18 Who is a G like you,
Na 1: 2 LORD is a jealous and avenging G;
Hab 3: 18 I will be joyful in G my Savior.
Zep 3: 17 The LORD your G is with you,
Zec 14: 5 Then the LORD my G will come,
Mal 2: 10 Father? Did not one G create us?
2: 16 says the LORD G of Israel,
3: 8 Will a man rob G? Yet you rob me.
Mt 1:23 which means, "G with us."
4: 4 comes from the mouth of G.'"
4: 7 'Do not put the Lord your G
4: 10 'Worship the Lord your G,
5: 8 for they will see G.
6:24 You cannot serve both G
19: 6 Therefore what G has joined
19:26 but with G all things are possible."
22:21 and to G what is God's."
22:32 He is not the G of the dead
22:37 "'Love the Lord your G
27:46 which means, "My G, my G,
Mk 2: 7 Who can forgive sins but G alone?"
7: 13 Thus you nullify the word of G
10: 6 of creation G 'made them male
10: 9 Therefore what G has joined
10: 18 "No one is good—except G alone.
10:27 all things are possible with G."
11:22 "Have faith in G," Jesus answered.

Mk 12:17 and to G what is God's."
12:29 the Lord our G, the Lord is one.
12:30 Love the Lord your G
15:34 which means, "My G, my G,
16:19 and he sat at the right hand of G.
Lk 1:30 Mary, you have found favor with G
1:37 For nothing is impossible with G."
1:47 my spirit rejoices in G my Savior,
2:14 "Glory to G in the highest,
2:52 and in favor with G and men.
4:8 'Worship the Lord your G
5:21 Who can forgive sins but G alone?"
8:39 tell how much G has done for you."
10:9 'The kingdom of G is near you.'
10:27 " 'Love the Lord your G
13:18 "What is the kingdom of G like?
18:19 "No one is good—except G alone.
18:27 with men is possible with G."
20:25 and to G what is God's."
20:38 He is not the G of the dead,
22:69 at the right hand of the mighty G."
Jn 1:1 was with G, and the Word was G.
1:18 ever seen G, but G the One and Only,
1:29 Lamb of G, who takes away the sin
3:16 "For G so loved the world that he
3:34 the one whom G has sent speaks
4:24 G is spirit, and his worshipers must
5:44 praise that comes from the only G?
6:29 answered, "The work of G is this:
7:17 my teaching comes from G
8:42 to them, "If G were your Father,
8:47 belongs to G hears what G says.
11:40 you would see the glory of G?"
13:3 from G and was returning to G;
13:31 of Man glorified and G is glorified
14:1 Trust in G; trust also in me.
17:3 the only true G, and Jesus Christ,
20:17 your Father, to my G and your G
20:28 "My Lord and my G!"
20:31 the Son of G, and that
Ac 2:11 wonders of G in our own tongues!"
2:24 But G raised him from the dead,
2:33 Exalted to the right hand of G,
2:36 G has made this Jesus, whom you
3:15 but G raised him from the dead.
3:19 Repent, then, and turn to G,
4:31 and spoke the word of G boldly.
5:4 You have not lied to men but to G
5:29 "We must obey G rather than men!
5:31 G exalted him to his own right
5:32 whom G has given
7:55 to heaven and saw the glory of G,
8:21 your heart is not right before G.
11:9 anything impure that G has made
12:24 But the word of G continued
13:32 What G promised our fathers he
15:10 to test G by putting on the necks
17:23 TO AN UNKNOWN G.
17:30 In the past G overlooked such
20:27 to you the whole will of G.
20:32 "Now I commit you to G
24:16 keep my conscience clear before G
Ro 1:16 the power of G for the salvation
1:17 a righteousness from G is revealed,
1:18 The wrath of G is being revealed
1:24 Therefore G gave them
1:26 G gave them over to shameful lusts
2:11 For G does not show favoritism.
2:16 when G will judge men's secrets
3:4 Let G be true, and every man a liar.
3:19 world held accountable to G.
3:23 and fall short of the glory of G,
3:29 Is G the G of Jews only? Is he not
4:3 say? "Abraham believed G,
4:6 to whom G credits righteousness
4:17 the G who gives life to the dead
4:24 to whom G will credit
5:1 we have peace with G
5:5 because G has poured out his love
5:8 G demonstrates his own love for us
6:22 and have become slaves to G,
6:23 but the gift of G is eternal life
8:7 the sinful mind is hostile to G.
8:17 heirs of G and co-heirs with Christ,
8:28 in all things G works for the good
9:14 What then shall we say? Is G unjust
9:18 Therefore G has mercy
10:9 in your heart that G raised him
11:2 G did not reject his people,
11:22 the kindness and sternness of G:
11:32 For G has bound all men
13:1 exist have been established by G.
14:12 give an account of himself to G.
16:20 G of peace will soon crush Satan
1Co 1:18 are being saved it is the power of G.
1Co 1:20 Has not G made foolish
1:25 For the foolishness of G is wiser
1:27 But G chose the foolish things
2:9 what G has prepared
2:11 of G except the Spirit of G.
3:6 watered it, but G made it grow.
3:17 God's temple, G will destroy
6:20 Therefore honor G with your body.
7:7 each man has his own gift from G;
7:15 G has called us to live in peace.
7:20 was in when G called him.
7:24 each man, as responsible to G,
8:3 man who loves G is known by G.
8:8 food does not bring us near to G;
10:13 G is faithful; he will not let you be
10:31 do it all for the glory of G.
12:24 But G has combined the members
14:33 For G is not a G of disorder
15:24 over the kingdom to G the Father
15:28 so that G may be all in all.
15:34 are some who are ignorant of G—
15:57 be to G! He gives us the victory
2Co 1:9 rely on ourselves but on G,
2:14 be to G, who always leads us
2:15 For we are to G the aroma of Christ
2:17 we do not peddle the word of G
3:5 but our competence comes from G.
4:2 nor do we distort the word of G.
4:7 this all-surpassing power is from G
5:5 Now it is G who has made us
5:19 that G was reconciling the world
5:20 though G were making his appeal
5:21 G made him who had no sin
6:16 we are the temple of the living G.
9:7 for G loves a cheerful giver.
9:8 G is able to make all grace abound
10:13 to the field G has assigned to us,
Gal 2:6 G does not judge by external
3:5 Does G give you his Spirit
3:6 Abraham: "He believed G,
3:11 justified before G by the law,
3:26 You are all sons of G through faith
6:7 not be deceived: G cannot be
Eph 1:22 G placed all things under his feet
2:8 it is the gift of G—not by works,
2:10 which G prepared in advance for us
2:22 in which G lives by his Spirit.
4:6 one baptism; one G and Father
4:24 to be like G in true righteousness
5:1 Be imitators of G, therefore,
6:6 doing the will of G from your heart.
Php 2:6 Who, being in very nature G,
2:9 Therefore G exalted him
2:13 for it is G who works in you to will
4:7 peace of G, which transcends all
4:19 And my G will meet all your needs
Col 1:19 For G was pleased
2:13 G made you alive with Christ.
1Th 2:4 trying to please men but G,
2:13 but as it actually is, the word of G,
3:9 How can we thank G enough
4:7 For G did not call us to be impure,
4:9 taught by G to love each other.
5:9 For G did not appoint us
1Ti 2:5 one mediator between G and men,
4:4 For everything G created is good,
5:4 for this is pleasing to G.
2Ti 1:6 you to fan into flame the gift of G,
Tit 1:2 which G, who does not lie,
2:13 glorious appearing of our great G
Heb 1:1 In the past G spoke
3:4 but G is the builder of everything.
4:4 "And on the seventh day G rested
4:12 For the word of G is living
6:10 G is not unjust; he will not forget
6:18 in which it is impossible for G to lie
7:19 by which we draw near to G.
7:25 come to G through him,
10:22 draw near to G with a sincere heart
10:31 to fall into the hands of the living G
11:5 commended as one who pleased G.
11:6 faith it is impossible to please G,
12:7 as discipline; G is treating you
12:10 but G disciplines us for our good,
12:29 for our "G is a consuming fire."
13:15 offer to G a sacrifice of praise—
Jas 1:12 crown of life that G has promised
1:13 For G cannot be tempted by evil,
1:27 Religion that G our Father accepts
2:19 You believe that there is one G.
2:23 "Abraham believed G,
4:4 the world becomes an enemy of G.
4:6 "G opposes the proud
4:8 Come near to G and he will come
1Pe 1:23 the living and enduring word of G.
1Pe 2:20 this is commendable before G.
3:18 the unrighteous, to bring you to G.
4:11 it with the strength G provides,
5:5 because, "G opposes the proud
2Pe 1:21 but men spoke from G
2:4 For if G did not spare angels
1Jn 1:5 G is light; in him there is no
2:17 the will of G lives forever.
3:1 we should be called children of G!
3:9 born of G will continue to sin,
3:10 we know who the children of G are
3:20 For G is greater than our hearts,
4:7 for love comes from G.
4:8 not know G, because G is love.
4:9 This is how G showed his love
4:11 Dear friends, since G so loved us,
4:12 No one has ever seen G;
4:15 G lives in him and he in G.
4:16 G is love.
4:20 "I love G," yet hates his brother,
4:21 Whoever loves G must
5:2 that we love the children of G:
5:3 love for G: to obey his commands.
5:4 born of G overcomes the world.
5:10 does not believe G has made him
5:14 have in approaching G:
5:18 born of G does not continue to sin;
Rev 4:8 holy is the Lord G Almighty,
7:12 be to our G for ever and ever.
7:17 G will wipe away every tear
11:16 fell on their faces and worshiped G,
15:3 Lord G Almighty.
17:17 For G has put it into their hearts
19:6 For our Lord G Almighty reigns.
21:3 Now the dwelling of G is with men,
21:23 for the glory of G gives it light,

GOD-BREATHED* (BREATH)

2Ti 3:16 All Scripture is G and is useful

GOD-FEARING* (FEAR)

Ecc 8:12 that it will go better with G men,
Ac 2:5 staying in Jerusalem G Jews
10:2 all his family were devout and G;
10:22 He is a righteous and G man,
13:26 of Abraham, and you G Gentiles,
13:50 But the Jews incited the G women
17:4 as did a large number of G Greeks
17:17 with the Jews and the G Greeks,

GOD-HATERS* (HATE)

Ro 1:30 They are gossips, slanderers, G,

GOD'S (GOD)

2Ch 20:15 For the battle is not yours, but G.
Job 37:14 stop and consider G wonders.
Ps 52:8 I trust in G unfailing love
69:30 I will praise G name in song
Mk 3:35 Whoever does G will is my brother
Jn 7:17 If anyone chooses to do G will,
10:36 'I am G Son'? Do not believe me
Ro 2:3 think you will escape G judgment?
2:4 not realizing that G kindness leads
3:3 lack of faith nullify G faithfulness?
7:22 in my inner being I delight in G law
9:16 or effort, but on G mercy.
11:29 for G gifts and his call are
12:2 and approve what G will is—
12:13 Share with G people who are
13:6 for the authorities are G servants,
1Co 7:19 Keeping G commands is what
2Co 6:2 now is the time of G favor,
Eph 1:7 riches of G grace that he lavished
1Th 4:3 It is G will that you should be sancti-fied;
5:18 for this is G will for you
1Ti 6:1 so that G name and our teaching
2Ti 2:19 G solid foundation stands firm,
Tit 1:7 overseer is entrusted with G work,
Heb 1:3 The Son is the radiance of G glory
9:24 now to appear for us in G presence.
11:3 was formed at G command,
1Pe 2:15 For it is G will that
3:4 which is of great worth in G sight.
1Jn 2:5 G love is truly made complete

GODLESS

Job 20:5 the joy of the g lasts but a moment.
1Ti 6:20 Turn away from g chatter

GODLINESS (GOD)

1Ti 2:2 and quiet lives in all g and holiness.
4:8 but g has value for all things,
6:5 and who think that g is a means
6:6 g with contentment is great gain.

1Ti 6:11 and pursue righteousness, g, faith,
2Pe 1:6 and to perseverance, g;

GODLY (GOD)

Ps 4:3 that the LORD has set apart the g
2Co 7:10 G sorrow brings repentance that
11:2 jealous for you with a g jealousy.
2Ti 3:12 everyone who wants to live a g life
2Pe 3:11 You ought to live holy and g lives

GODS (GOD)

Ex 20:3 "You shall have no other g
Dt 5:7 "You shall have no other g
1Ch 16:26 For all the g of the nations are idols
Ps 82:6 "I said, 'You are "g";
Jn 10:34 have said you are g'? If he called
Ac 19:26 He says that man-made g are no g

GOG

Eze 38:18 When G attacks the land of Israel,
Rev 20:8 G and Magog—to gather them

GOLD

1Ki 20:3 'Your silver and g are mine,
Job 22:25 then the Almighty will be your g,
23:10 tested me, I will come forth as g.
28:15 cannot be bought with the finest g,
31:24 "If I have put my trust in g
Ps 19:10 They are more precious than g,
119:127 more than g, more than pure g,
Pr 3:14 and yields better returns than g.
22:1 esteemed is better than silver or g.
Hag 2:8 The silver is mine and the g is mine
Mt 2:11 and presented him with gifts of g
Rev 3:18 to buy from me g refined in the fire,

GOLGOTHA*

Mt 27:33 to a place called G (which means
Mk 15:22 to the place called G (which means
Jn 19:17 (which in Aramaic is called G).

GOLIATH

Philistine giant killed by David (1Sa 17; 21:9).

GOMORRAH

Ge 19:24 sulfur on Sodom and G—
Mt 10:15 and G on the day of judgment
2Pe 2:6 and G by burning them to ashes,
Jude :7 G and the surrounding towns gave

GOOD

Ge 1:4 God saw that the light was g,
1:10 And God saw that it was g.
1:12 And God saw that it was g.
1:18 And God saw that it was g.
1:21 And God saw that it was g.
1:25 And God saw that it was g.
1:31 he had made, and it was very g.
2:9 and the tree of the knowledge of g
2:9 pleasing to the eye and g for food.
2:18 "It is not g for the man to be alone.
3:22 become like one of us, knowing g
50:20 but God intended it for g
2Ch 7:3 "He is g; / his love endures
31:20 doing what was g and right
Job 2:10 Shall we accept g from God,
Ps 14:1 there is no one who does g.
34:8 Taste and see that the LORD is g;
34:14 Turn from evil and do g;
37:3 Trust in the LORD and do g;
37:27 Turn from evil and do g;
52:9 for your name is g.
53:3 there is no one who does g,
84:11 no g thing does he withhold
86:5 You are forgiving and g, O Lord
100:5 For the LORD is g and his love
103:5 satisfies your desires with g things,
112:5 G will come to him who is
119:68 You are g, and what you do is g;
133:1 How g and pleasant it is
145:9 The LORD is g to all;
147:1 How g it is to sing praises
Pr 3:4 you will win favor and a g name
3:27 Do not withhold g
11:27 He who seeks g finds g will,
13:22 A g man leaves an inheritance
14:22 those who plan what is g find love
15:3 on the wicked and the g.
15:23 and how g is a timely word!
15:30 g news gives health to the bones.
17:22 A cheerful heart is g medicine,
18:22 He who finds a wife finds what is g
19:2 It is not g to have zeal
22:1 A g name is more desirable
31:12 She brings him g, not harm,
Ecc 12:14 whether it is g or evil.
Isa 5:20 Woe to those who call evil g
40:9 You who bring g tidings
52:7 the feet of those who bring g news,
61:1 me to preach g news to the poor.
Jer 6:16 ask where the g way is,
13:23 Neither can you do g
32:39 the g of their children after them.
Eze 34:14 I will tend them in a g pasture,
Mic 6:8 has showed you, O man, what is g.
Na 1:15 the feet of one who brings g news,
Mt 5:45 sun to rise on the evil and the g,
7:11 Father in heaven give g gifts
7:17 Likewise every g tree bears g fruit,
7:18 A g tree cannot bear bad fruit,
12:35 The g man brings g things out
13:8 Still other seed fell on g soil,
13:24 is like a man who sowed g seed
13:48 and collected the g fish in baskets,
19:17 "There is only One who is g.
22:10 both g and bad, and the wedding
25:21 'Well done, g and faithful servant!
Mk 1:15 Repent and believe the g news!"
3:4 lawful on the Sabbath: to do g
4:8 Still other seed fell on g soil.
8:36 What g is it for a man
10:18 "No one is g—except God alone.
16:15 preach the g news to all creation.
Lk 2:10 I bring you g news
3:9 does not produce g fruit will be
6:27 do g to those who hate you,
6:43 nor does a bad tree bear g fruit.
6:45 The g man brings g things out
8:8 Still other seed fell on g soil.
9:25 What g is it for a man
14:34 "Salt is g, but if it loses its saltiness,
18:19 "No one is g—except God alone.
19:17 " 'Well done, my g servant!'
Jn 10:11 "I am the g shepherd.
Ro 3:12 there is no one who does g,
7:12 is holy, righteous and g.
7:16 want to do, I agree that the law is g.
7:18 I have the desire to do what is g,
8:28 for the g of those who love him,
10:15 feet of those who bring g news!"
12:2 his g, pleasing and perfect will.
12:9 Hate what is evil; cling to what is g.
13:4 For he is God's servant to do you g
16:19 you to be wise about what is g,
1Co 7:1 It is g for a man not to marry.
10:24 should seek his own g, but the g
15:33 Bad company corrupts g character
2Co 9:8 you will abound in every g work.
Gal 4:18 provided the purpose is g,
6:9 us not become weary in doing g,
6:10 as we have opportunity, let us do g
Eph 2:10 in Christ Jesus to do g works,
6:8 everyone for whatever g he does,
Php 1:6 that he who began a g work
Col 1:10 bearing fruit in every g work,
1Th 5:21 Hold on to the g.
1Ti 3:7 have a g reputation with outsiders,
4:4 For everything God created is g,
6:12 Fight the g fight of the faith.
6:18 them to do g, to be rich in g deeds,
2Ti 3:17 equipped for every g work.
4:7 I have fought the g fight, I have
Tit 1:8 loves what is g, who is
2:7 an example by doing what is g.
2:14 his very own, eager to do what is g.
Heb 5:14 to distinguish g from evil.
10:24 on toward love and g deeds.
12:10 but God disciplines us for our g,
13:16 do not forget to do g and to share
Jas 4:17 who knows the g he ought to do
1Pe 2:3 you have tasted that the Lord is g.
2:12 Live such g lives among the pagans
2:18 not only to those who are g
3:17 to suffer for doing g

GOODS

Ecc 5:11 As g increase,

GORGE

Pr 23:20 or g themselves on meat,

GOSHEN

Ge 45:10 You shall live in the region of G
Ex 8:22 differently with the land of G,

GOSPEL

Ro 1:16 I am not ashamed of the g,
15:16 duty of proclaiming the g of God,
15:20 to preach the g where Christ was
1Co 1:17 to preach the g—not with words
9:12 rather than hinder the g of Christ.
9:14 who preach the g should receive
9:16 Woe to me if I do not preach the g!
15:1 you of the g I preached to you,
15:2 By this g you are saved,
2Co 4:4 light of the g of the glory of Christ,
9:13 your confession of the g
Gal 1:7 a different g—which is really no g
Eph 6:15 comes from the g of peace.
Php 1:27 in a manner worthy of the g
Col 1:23 This is the g that you heard
1Th 2:4 by God to be entrusted with the g.
2Th 1:8 do not obey the g of our Lord Jesus
2Ti 1:10 immortality to light through the g.
Rev 14:6 he had the eternal g to proclaim

GOSSIP*

Pr 11:13 A g betrays a confidence,
16:28 and a g separates close friends.
18:8 of a g are like choice morsels;
20:19 A g betrays a confidence;
26:20 without g a quarrel dies down.
26:22 of a g are like choice morsels;
2Co 12:20 slander, g, arrogance and disorder.

GOVERN (GOVERNMENT)

Ge 1:16 the greater light to g the day
Job 34:17 Can he who hates justice g?
Ro 12:8 it is leadership, let him g diligently;

GOVERNMENT (GOVERN)

Isa 9:6 and the g will be on his shoulders.

GRACE* (GRACIOUS)

Ps 45:2 lips have been anointed with g,
Pr 1:9 will be a garland to g your head
3:22 an ornament to g your neck.
3:34 but gives g to the humble.
4:9 She will set a garland of g
Isa 26:10 Though g is shown to the wicked,
Jnh 2:8 forfeit the g that could be theirs.
Zec 12:10 of Jerusalem a spirit of g
Lk 2:40 and the g of God was upon him.
Jn 1:14 who came from the Father, full of g
1:16 of his g we have all received one
1:17 g and truth came through Jesus
Ac 4:33 and much g was upon them all.
6:8 a man full of God's g and power,
11:23 saw the evidence of the g of God,
13:43 them to continue in the g of God.
14:3 message of his g by enabling them
14:26 they had been committed to the g
15:11 We believe it is through the g
15:40 by the brothers to the g of the Lord
18:27 to those who by g had believed.
20:24 testifying to the gospel of God's g.
20:32 to God and to the word of his g,
Ro 1:5 we received g and apostleship
1:7 G and peace to you
3:24 and are justified freely by his g
4:16 be by g and may be guaranteed
5:2 access by faith into this g
5:15 came by the g of the one man,
5:15 how much more did God's g
5:17 God's abundant provision of g
5:20 where sin increased, g increased all
5:21 also g might reign
6:1 on sinning so that g may increase?
6:14 you are not under law, but under g.
6:15 we are not under law but under g?
11:5 there is a remnant chosen by g.
11:6 if by g, then it is no longer by works
11:6 if it were, g would no longer be g.
12:3 For by the g given me I say
12:6 according to the g given us.
15:15 because of the g God gave me
16:20 The g of our Lord Jesus be
1Co 1:3 G and peace to you
1:4 of his g given you in Christ Jesus.
3:10 By the g God has given me,
15:10 But by the g of God I am what I am
15:10 but the g of God that was with me.
15:10 his g to me was not without effect.
16:23 The g of the Lord Jesus be with you
2Co 1:2 G and peace to you
1:12 wisdom but according to God's g.
4:15 so that the g that is reaching more
6:1 not to receive God's g in vain.
8:1 to know about the g that God has
8:6 also to completion this act of g
8:7 also excel in this g of giving.
8:9 For you know the g
9:8 able to make all g abound to you,
9:14 of the surpassing g God has given
12:9 "My g is sufficient for you,

2Co 13:14 May the g of the Lord Jesus Christ,
Gal 1: 3 G and peace to you
1: 6 the one who called you by the g
1:15 from birth and called me by his g,
2: 9 when they recognized the g given
2:21 I do not set aside the g of God,
3:18 God in his g gave it to Abraham
5: 4 you have fallen away from g.
6:18 The g of our Lord Jesus Christ be
Eph 1: 2 G and peace to you
1: 6 to the praise of his glorious g,
1: 7 riches of God's g that he lavished
2: 5 it is by g you have been saved.
2: 7 the incomparable riches of his g,
2: 8 For it is by g you have been saved,
3: 2 of God's g that was given to me
3: 7 by the gift of God's g given me
3: 8 God's people, this g was given me:
4: 7 to each one of us g has been given
6:24 G to all who love our Lord Jesus
Php 1: 2 G and peace to you
1: 7 all of you share in God's g with me.
4:23 The g of the Lord Jesus Christ be
Col 1: 2 G and peace to you
1: 6 understood God's g in all its truth.
4: 6 conversation be always full of g,
4:18 G be with you.
1Th 1: 1 and the Lord Jesus Christ: G
5:28 The g of our Lord Jesus Christ be
2Th 1: 2 G and peace to you
1:12 according to the g of our God
2:16 and by his g gave us eternal
3:18 The g of our Lord Jesus Christ be
1Ti 1: 2 my true son in the faith: G,
1:14 The g of our Lord was poured out
6:21 G be with you.
2Ti 1: 2 To Timothy, my dear son: G,
1: 9 This g was given us in Christ Jesus
1: 9 because of his own purpose and g.
2: 1 be strong in the g that is
4:22 G be with you.
Tit 1: 4 G and peace from God the Father
2:11 For the g of God that brings
3: 7 having been justified by his g,
3:15 G be with you all.
Phm :3 G to you and peace
:25 The g of the Lord Jesus Christ be
Heb 2: 9 that by the g of God he might taste
4:16 find g to help us in our time of need
4:16 the throne of g with confidence,
10:29 and who has insulted the Spirit of g
12:15 See to it that no one misses the g
13: 9 hearts to be strengthened by g,
13:25 G be with you all.
Jas 4: 6 but gives g to the humble."
4: 6 But he gives us more g. That is why
1Pe 1: 2 G and peace be yours in abundance
1:10 who spoke of the g that was
1:13 fully on the g to be given you
4:10 faithfully administering God's g
5: 5 but gives g to the humble."
5:10 the God of all g, who called you
5:12 and testifying that this is the true g
2Pe 1: 2 G and peace be yours in abundance
3:18 But grow in the g and knowledge
2Jn :3 and will be with us forever: G,
Jude :4 who change the g of our God
Rev 1: 4 G and peace to you
22:21 The g of the Lord Jesus be

GRACIOUS (GRACE)

Ex 34: 6 the compassionate and g God,
Nu 6:25 and be g to you;
Ne 9:17 But you are a forgiving God, g
Ps 67: 1 May God be g to us and bless us
Pr 22:11 a pure heart and whose speech is g
Isa 30:18 Yet the LORD longs to be g to you

GRAIN

Lev 2: 1 When someone brings a g offering
Lk 17:35 women will be grinding g together;
1Co 9: 9 ox while it is treading out the g."

GRANDCHILDREN (CHILD)

1Ti 5: 4 But if a widow has children or g,

GRANDMOTHER (MOTHER)

2Ti 1: 5 which first lived in your g Lois

GRANT (GRANTED)

Ps 20: 5 May the LORD g all your requests
51:12 g me a willing spirit, to sustain me.

GRANTED (GRANT)

Pr 10:24 what the righteous desire will be g.
Mt 15:28 great faith! Your request is g."
Php 1:29 For it has been g to you on behalf

GRAPES

Nu 13:23 branch bearing a single cluster of g.
Jer 31:29 'The fathers have eaten sour g,
Eze 18: 2 " 'The fathers eat sour g,
Mt 7:16 Do people pick g from thornbushes
Rev 14:18 and gather the clusters of g

GRASPED

Php 2: 6 with God something to be g,

GRASS

Ps 103:15 As for man, his days are like g,
Isa 40: 6 "All men are like g,
Mt 6:30 If that is how God clothes the g
1Pe 1:24 "All men are like g,

GRASSHOPPERS

Nu 13:33 We seemed like g in our own eyes,

GRATIFY* (GRATITUDE)

Ro 13:14 think about how to g the desires
Gal 5:16 and you will not g the desires

GRATITUDE (GRATIFY)

Col 3:16 and spiritual songs with g

GRAVE (GRAVES)

Nu 19:16 who touches a human bone or a g,
Dt 34: 6 day no one knows where his g is.
Ps 5: 9 Their throat is an open g;
49:15 will redeem my life from the g;
Pr 7:27 Her house is a highway to the g,
Hos 13:14 Where, O g, is your destruction?
Jn 11:44 "Take off the g clothes
Ac 2:27 you will not abandon me to the g,

GRAVES (GRAVE)

Eze 37:12 I am going to open your g
Jn 5:28 are in their g will hear his voice
Ro 3:13 "Their throats are open g;

GRAY

Pr 16:31 G hair is a crown of splendor;
20:29 g hair the splendor of the old.

GREAT (GREATER GREATEST GREATNESS)

Ge 12: 2 I will make your name g,
12: 2 "I will make you into a g nation
Ex 32:11 out of Egypt with g power
Nu 14:19 In accordance with your g love,
Dt 4:32 so g as this ever happened,
10:17 the g God, mighty and awesome,
29:28 in g wrath the LORD uprooted
Jos 7: 9 do for your own g name?"
Jdg 16: 5 you the secret of his g strength
2Sa 7:22 "How g you are, O Sovereign
22:36 you stoop down to make me g.
24:14 for his mercy is g; but do not let me
1Ch 17:19 made known all these g promises.
Ps 18:35 you stoop down to make me g.
19:11 in keeping them there is g reward.
47: 2 the g King over all the earth!
57:10 For g is your love, reaching
68:11 and g was the company
89: 1 of the LORD's g love forever;
103:11 so g is his love for those who fear
107:43 consider the g love of the LORD.
108: 4 For g is your love, higher
117: 2 For g is his love toward us,
119:165 G peace have they who love your
145: 3 G is the LORD and most worthy
Pr 22: 1 is more desirable than g riches;
23:24 of a righteous man has g joy;
Isa 42:21 to make his law g and glorious.
Jer 27: 5 With my g power and outstretched
32:19 g are your purposes and mighty are
La 3:23 g is your faithfulness.
Da 9: 4 "O Lord, the g and awesome God,
Joel 2:11 The day of the LORD is g;
2:20 Surely he has done g things.
Zep 1:14 "The g day of the LORD is near—
Mal 1:11 My name will be g
4: 5 the prophet Elijah before that g
Mt 20:26 whoever wants to become g
Mk 10:43 whoever wants to become g
Lk 6:23 because g is your reward in heaven.
6:35 Then your reward will be g,
21:27 in a cloud with power and g glory.
Eph 1:19 and his incomparably g power
2: 4 But because of his g love for us,
1Ti 6: 6 with contentment is g gain.
Tit 2:13 glorious appearing of our g God
Heb 2: 3 if we ignore such a g salvation?
1Jn 3: 1 How g is the love the Father has
Rev 6:17 For the g day of their wrath has
20:11 Then I saw a g white throne

GREATER (GREAT)

Mt 11:11 there has not risen anyone g
12: 6 I tell you that one g
12:41 and now one g than Jonah is here.
12:42 now one g than Solomon is here.
Mk 12:31 There is no commandment g
Jn 1:50 You shall see g things than that."
3:30 He must become g; I must become
14:12 He will do even g things than these
15:13 G love has no one than this,
1Co 12:31 But eagerly desire the g gifts.
2Co 3:11 how much g is the glory
Heb 3: 3 the builder of a house has g honor
3: 3 worthy of g honor than Moses,
7: 7 lesser person is blessed by the g.
11:26 as of g value than the treasures
1Jn 3:20 For God is g than our hearts,
4: 4 is in you is g than the one who is

GREATEST (GREAT)

Mt 22:38 is the first and g commandment.
23:11 g among you will be your servant.
Lk 9:48 least among you all—he is the g."
1Co 13:13 But the g of these is love.

GREATNESS* (GREAT)

Ex 15: 7 In the g of your majesty
Dt 3:24 to show to your servant your g
32: 3 Oh, praise the g of our God!
1Ch 29:11 O LORD, is the g and the power
2Ch 9: 6 half the g of your wisdom was told
Est 10: 2 account of the g of Mordecai
Ps 145: 3 his g no one can fathom.
150: 2 praise him for his surpassing g.
Isa 63: 1 forward in the g of his strength?
Eze 38:23 I will show my g and my holiness,
Da 4:22 your g has grown until it reaches
5:18 and g and glory and splendor.
7:27 and g of the kingdoms
Mic 5: 4 will live securely, for then his g
Lk 9:43 And they were all amazed at the g
Php 3: 8 compared to the surpassing g

GREED (GREEDY)

Lk 12:15 on your guard against all kinds of g
Ro 1:29 kind of wickedness, evil, g
Eph 5: 3 or of any kind of impurity, or of g,
Col 3: 5 evil desires and g, which is idolatry
2Pe 2:14 experts in g—an accursed brood!

GREEDY (GREED)

Pr 15:27 A g man brings trouble
1Co 6:10 nor thieves nor the g nor drunkards
Eph 5: 5 No immoral, impure or g person—
1Pe 5: 2 not g for money, but eager to serve;

GREEK (GREEKS)

Gal 3:28 There is neither Jew nor G,
Col 3:11 Here there is no G or Jew,

GREEKS (GREEK)

1Co 1:22 miraculous signs and G look

GREEN

Ps 23: 2 makes me lie down in g pastures,

GREW (GROW)

Lk 1:80 And the child g and became strong
2:52 And Jesus g in wisdom and stature,
Ac 9:31 by the Holy Spirit, it g in numbers,
16: 5 in the faith and g daily in numbers.

GRIEF (GRIEFS GRIEVANCES GRIEVE GRIEVED)

Ps 10:14 O God, do see trouble and g;
Pr 10: 1 but a foolish son g to his mother.
14:13 and joy may end in g.
17:21 To have a fool for a son brings g;
Ecc 1:18 the more knowledge, the more g.
La 3:32 Though he brings g, he will show
Jn 16:20 but your g will turn to joy.
1Pe 1: 6 had to suffer g in all kinds of trials.

GRIEFS* (GRIEF)

1Ti 6:10 pierced themselves with many g.

GRIEVANCES* (GRIEF)

Col 3:13 forgive whatever g you may have

GRIEVE (GRIEF)
Eph 4:30 do not g the Holy Spirit of God,
1Th 4:13 or to g like the rest of men,

GRIEVED (GRIEF)
Isa 63:10 and g his Holy Spirit.

GRINDING
Lk 17:35 women will be g grain together;

GROAN (GROANING GROANS)
Ro 8:23 g inwardly as we wait eagerly
2Co 5:4 For while we are in this tent, we g

GROANING (GROAN)
Ex 2:24 God heard their g and he
Eze 21:7 'Why are you g?' you shall say,
Ro 8:22 that the whole creation has been g

GROANS (GROAN)
Ro 8:26 with g that words cannot express.

GROUND
Ge 1:10 God called the dry g "land,"
3:17 "Cursed is the g because of you;
4:10 blood cries out to me from the g.
Ex 3:5 where you are standing is holy g."
15:19 walked through the sea on dry g.
Isa 53:2 and like a root out of dry g.
Mt 10:29 fall to the g apart from the will
25:25 and hid your talent in the g.
Jn 8:6 to write on the g with his finger.
Eph 6:13 you may be able to stand your g,

GROW (FULL-GROWN GREW GROWING GROWS)
Pr 13:11 by little makes it g.
20:13 not love sleep or you will g poor;
Isa 40:31 they will run and not g weary,
Mt 6:28 See how the lilies of the field g.
1Co 3:6 watered it, but God made it g.
2Pe 3:18 But g in the grace and knowledge

GROWING (GROW)
Col 1:6 this gospel is bearing fruit and g,
1:10 g in the knowledge of God,
2Th 1:3 your faith is g more and more,

GROWS (GROW)
Eph 4:16 g and builds itself up in love,
Col 2:19 g as God causes it to grow.

GRUMBLE (GRUMBLED GRUMBLERS GRUMBLING)
1Co 10:10 And do not g, as some of them did
Jas 5:9 Don't g against each other,

GRUMBLED (GRUMBLE)
Ex 15:24 So the people g against Moses,
Nu 14:29 and who has g against me.

GRUMBLERS* (GRUMBLE)
Jude :16 These men are g and faultfinders;

GRUMBLING (GRUMBLE)
Jn 6:43 "Stop g among yourselves,"
1Pe 4:9 to one another without g.

GUARANTEE (GUARANTEEING)
Heb 7:22 Jesus has become the g

GUARANTEEING* (GUARANTEE)
2Co 1:22 as a deposit, g what is to come.
5:5 as a deposit, g what is to come.
Eph 1:14 who is a deposit g our inheritance

GUARD (GUARDS)
1Sa 2:9 He will g the feet of his saints,
Ps 141:3 Set a g over my mouth, O LORD;
Pr 2:11 and understanding will g you.
4:13 g it well, for it is your life.
4:23 Above all else, g your heart,
7:2 g my teachings as the apple
Isa 52:12 the God of Israel will be your rear g
Mk 13:33 Be on g! Be alert! You do not know
Lk 12:1 "Be on your g against the yeast
12:15 Be on your g against all kinds
Ac 20:31 So be on your g! Remember that
1Co 16:13 Be on your g; stand firm in the faith
Php 4:7 will g your hearts and your minds
1Ti 6:20 g what has been entrusted
2Ti 1:14 G the good deposit that was

GUARDS (GUARD)
Pr 13:3 He who g his lips g his life,
19:16 who obeys instructions g his life,
21:23 He who g his mouth and his tongue
22:5 he who g his soul stays far

GUIDANCE (GUIDE)
Pr 1:5 and let the discerning get g—
11:14 For lack of g a nation falls,
24:6 for waging war you need g,

GUIDE (GUIDANCE GUIDED GUIDES)
Ex 13:21 of cloud to g them on their way
15:13 In your strength you will g them
Ne 9:19 cease to g them on their path,
Ps 25:5 g me in your truth and teach me,
43:3 let them g me;
48:14 he will be our g even to the end.
67:4 and g the nations of the earth.
73:24 You g me with your counsel,
139:10 even there your hand will g me,
Pr 4:11 I g you in the way of wisdom
6:22 When you walk, they will g you;
Isa 58:11 The LORD will g you always;
Jn 16:13 comes, he will g you into all truth.

GUIDED (GUIDE)
Ps 107:30 he g them to their desired haven.

GUIDES (GUIDE)
Ps 23:3 He g me in paths of righteousness
25:9 He g the humble in what is right
Pr 11:3 The integrity of the upright g them,
16:23 A wise man's heart g his mouth,
Mt 23:16 "Woe to you, blind g! You say,
23:24 You blind g! You strain out a gnat

GUILT (GUILTY)
Lev 5:15 It is a g offering.
Ps 32:5 the g of my sin.
38:4 My g has overwhelmed me
Isa 6:7 your g is taken away and your sin
Jer 2:22 the stain of your g is still before me
Eze 18:19 'Why does the son not share the g

GUILTY (GUILT)
Ex 34:7 does not leave the g unpunished;
Mk 3:29 Spirit will never be forgiven; he is g
Jn 8:46 Can any of you prove me g of sin?
1Co 11:27 in an unworthy manner will be g
Heb 10:2 and would no longer have felt g
10:22 to cleanse us from a g conscience
Jas 2:10 at just one point is g of breaking all

HABAKKUK*
Prophet to Judah (Hab 1:1; 3:1).

HABIT
1Ti 5:13 they get into the h of being idle
Heb 10:25 as some are in the h of doing,

HADAD
Edomite adversary of Solomon (1Ki 11:14-25).

HADES*
Mt 16:18 the gates of H will not overcome it.
Rev 1:18 And I hold the keys of death and H
6:8 H was following close behind him.
20:13 and H gave up the dead that were
20:14 H were thrown into the lake of fire.

HAGAR
Servant of Sarah, wife of Abraham, mother of Ishmael (Ge 16:1-6; 25:12). Driven away by Sarah while pregnant (Ge 16:5-16); after birth of Isaac (Ge 21:9-21; Gal 4:21-31).

HAGGAI*
Post-exilic prophet who encouraged rebuilding of the temple (Ezr 5:1; 6:14; Hag 1-2).

HAIL
Ex 9:19 the h will fall on every man
Rev 8:7 and there came h and fire mixed

HAIR (HAIRS HAIRY)
Lev 19:27 " 'Do not cut the h at the sides
Nu 6:5 he must let the h of his head grow
Pr 16:31 Gray h is a crown of splendor;
20:29 gray h the splendor of the old.
Lk 7:44 and wiped them with her h.
21:18 But not a h of your head will perish
Jn 11:2 and wiped his feet with her h.
Jn 12:3 and wiped his feet with her h.
1Co 11:6 for a woman to have her h cut
11:6 she should have her h cut off;
11:14 that if a man has long h,
11:15 For long h is given to her
11:15 but that if a woman has long h,
1Ti 2:9 not with braided h or gold or pearls
1Pe 3:3 as braided h and the wearing
Rev 1:14 and h were white like wool,

HAIRS (HAIR)
Mt 10:30 even the very h of your head are all
Lk 12:7 the very h of your head are all

HAIRY (HAIR)
Ge 27:11 "But my brother Esau is a h man,

HALF
Ex 30:13 This h shekel is an offering
Jos 8:33 H of the people stood in front
1Ki 3:25 give h to one and h to the other."
10:7 Indeed, not even h was told me;
Est 5:3 Even up to h the kingdom,
Da 7:25 him for a time, times and h a time.
Mk 6:23 up to h my kingdom."

HALF-TRIBE (TRIBE)
Nu 32:33 and the h of Manasseh son

HALLELUJAH*
Rev 19:1 3, 4, 6.

HALLOWED* (HOLY)
Mt 6:9 h be your name,
Lk 11:2 h be your name,

HALT
Job 38:11 here is where your proud waves h'?

HALTER*
Pr 26:3 for the horse, a h for the donkey,

HAM
Son of Noah (Ge 5:32; 1Ch 1:4), father of Canaan (Ge 9:18; 10:6-20; 1Ch 1:8-16). Saw Noah's nakedness (Ge 9:20-27).

HAMAN
Agagite nobleman honored by Xerxes (Est 3:1-2). Plotted to exterminate the Jews because of Mordecai (Est 3:3-15). Forced to honor Mordecai (Est 5-6). Plot exposed by Esther (Est 5:1-8; 7:1-8). Hanged (Est 7:9-10).

HAMPERED*
Pr 4:12 you walk, your steps will not be h;

HAND (HANDED HANDFUL HANDS OPENHANDED)
Ge 24:2 "Put your h under my thigh.
47:29 put your h under my thigh
Ex 13:3 out of it with a mighty h.
15:6 Your right h, O LORD,
33:22 and cover you with my h
Dt 12:7 in everything you have put your h
1Ki 8:42 and your mighty h and your
13:4 But the h he stretched out
1Ch 29:14 you only what comes from your h.
29:16 it comes from your h, and all
2Ch 6:15 with your h you have fulfilled it—
Ne 4:17 materials did their work with one h
Job 40:4 I put my h over my mouth.
Ps 16:8 Because he is at my right h,
32:4 your h was heavy upon me;
37:24 the LORD upholds him with his h.
44:3 it was your right h, your arm,
45:9 at your right h is the royal bride
63:8 your right h upholds me.
75:8 In the h of the LORD is a cup
91:7 ten thousand at your right h,
98:1 his right h and his holy arm
109:31 at the right h of the needy one,
110:1 "Sit at my right h
137:5 may my right h forget its skill.
139:10 even there your h will guide me,
145:16 You open your h
Pr 27:16 or grasping oil with the h.
Ecc 5:15 that he can carry in his h.
9:10 Whatever your h finds to do,
Isa 11:8 the young child put his h
40:12 the waters in the hollow of his h,
41:13 who takes hold of your right h
44:5 still another will write on his h,
48:13 My own h laid the foundations
64:8 we are all the work of your h.

La 3: 3 he has turned his *h* against me
Da 10: 10 *h* touched me and set me trembling
Jnh 4: 11 people who cannot tell their right *h*
Hab 3: 4 rays flashed from his *h*,
Mt 5: 30 if your right *h* causes you to sin,
6: 3 know what your right *h* is doing,
12: 10 a man with a shriveled *h* was there.
18: 8 If your *h* or your foot causes you
22: 44 "Sit at my right *h*
26: 64 at the right *h* of the Mighty One
Mk 3: 1 a man with a shriveled *h* was there.
9: 43 If your *h* causes you to sin, cut it off
12: 36 "Sit at my right *h*
16: 19 and he sat at the right *h* of God.
Lk 6: 6 there whose right *h* was shriveled.
20: 42 "Sit at my right *h*
22: 69 at the right *h* of the mighty God."
Jn 10: 28 one can snatch them out of my *h*.
20: 27 Reach out your *h* and put it
Ac 7: 55 Jesus standing at the right *h* of God
1Co 12: 15 I am not a *h*, I do not belong
Heb 1: 13 "Sit at my right *h*
Rev 13: 16 to receive a mark on his right *h*

HANDED (HAND)

Da 7: 25 The saints will be *h* over to him
1Ti 1: 20 whom I have *h* over to Satan

HANDFUL (HAND)

Ecc 4: 6 Better one *h* with tranquillity

HANDLE (HANDLES)

Col 2: 21 "Do not *h*! Do not taste! Do not

HANDLES (HANDLE)

2Ti 2: 15 who correctly *h* the word of truth.

HANDS (HAND)

Ge 27: 22 but the *h* are the *h* of Esau."
Ex 17: 11 As long as Moses held up his *h*,
29: 10 his sons shall lay their *h* on its head
Dt 6: 8 Tie them as symbols on your *h*
Jdg 7: 6 lapped with their *h* to their mouths.
2Ki 11: 12 and the people clapped their *h*
2Ch 6: 4 who with his *h* has fulfilled what he
Ps 22: 16 they have pierced my *h*
24: 4 He who has clean *h* and a pure
31: 5 Into your *h* I commit my spirit;
31: 15 My times are in your *h*;
47: 1 Clap your *h*, all you nations;
63: 4 and in your name I will lift up my *h*
Pr 10: 4 Lazy *h* make a man poor,
21: 25 because his *h* refuse to work.
31: 13 and works with eager *h*.
31: 20 and extends her *h* to the needy.
Ecc 10: 18 if his *h* are idle, the house leaks.
Isa 35: 3 Strengthen the feeble *h*,
49: 16 you on the palms of my *h*;
55: 12 will clap their *h*.
65: 2 All day long I have held out my *h*
La 3: 41 Let us lift up our hearts and our *h*
Lk 23: 46 into your *h* I commit my spirit."
Ac 6: 6 who prayed and laid their *h*
8: 18 at the laying on of the apostles' *h*,
13: 3 they placed their *h* on them
19: 6 When Paul placed his *h* on them,
28: 8 placed his *h* on him and healed him
1Th 4: 11 and to work with your *h*,
1Ti 2: 8 to lift up holy *h* in prayer,
4: 14 body of elders laid their *h* on you.
5: 22 hasty in the laying on of *h*,
2Ti 1: 6 you through the laying on of my *h*.
Heb 6: 2 the laying on of *h*, the resurrection

HANDSOME*

Ge 39: 6 Now Joseph was well-built and *h*,
1Sa 16: 12 a fine appearance and *h* features.
17: 42 ruddy and *h*, and he despised him.
2Sa 14: 25 praised for his *h* appearance
1Ki 1: 6 also very *h* and was born next
SS 1: 16 *Beloved* How *h* you are, my lover!
Eze 23: 6 all of them *h* young men,
23: 12 horsemen, all *h* young men.
23: 23 with them, *h* young men,
Da 1: 4 without any physical defect, *h*,
Zec 11: 13 the *h* price at which they priced me

HANG (HANGED HANGING HUNG)

Mt 22: 40 and the Prophets *h* on these two

HANGED (HANG)

Mt 27: 5 Then he went away and *h* himself.

HANGING (HANG)

Ac 10: 39 They killed him by *h* him on a tree,

HANNAH*

Wife of Elkanah, mother of Samuel (1Sa 1). Prayer at dedication of Samuel (1Sa 2:1-10). Blessed (1Sa 2:18-21).

HAPPIER (HAPPY)

Mt 18: 13 he is *h* about that one sheep
1Co 7: 40 she is *h* if she stays as she is—

HAPPINESS* (HAPPY)

Dt 24: 5 bring *h* to the wife he has married.
Est 8: 16 For the Jews it was a time of *h*
Job 7: 7 my eyes will never see *h* again.
Ecc 2: 26 gives wisdom, knowledge and *h*,
Mt 25: 21 Come and share your master's *h*!'
25: 23 Come and share your master's *h*!'

HAPPY* (HAPPIER HAPPINESS)

Ge 30: 13 The women will call me *h*."
30: 13 Then Leah said, "How *h* I am!
1Ki 4: 20 they drank and they were *h*.
10: 8 How *h* your men must be!
10: 8 men must be! How *h* your officials,
2Ch 9: 7 How *h* your men must be!
9: 7 men must be! How *h* your officials,
Est 5: 9 Haman went out that day *h*
5: 14 the king to the dinner and be *h*."
Ps 10: 6 I'll always be *h* and never have
68: 3 may they be *h* and joyful.
113: 9 as a *h* mother of children.
137: 8 *h* is he who repays you
Pr 15: 13 A *h* heart makes the face cheerful,
Ecc 3: 12 better for men than to be *h*
5: 19 to accept his lot and be *h*
7: 14 When times are good, be *h*;
11: 9 Be *h*, young man, while you are
Jnh 4: 6 Jonah was very *h* about the vine.
Zec 8: 19 and glad occasions and *h* festivals
1Co 7: 30 those who are *h*, as if they were not
2Co 7: 9 yet now I am *h*, not because you
7: 13 delighted to see how *h* Titus was,
Jas 5: 13 Is anyone *h*? Let him sing songs

HARD (HARDEN HARDENED HARDENING HARDENS HARDER HARDSHIP HARDSHIPS)

Ge 18: 14 Is anything too *h* for the LORD?
1Ki 10: 1 came to test him with *h* questions.
Pr 14: 23 All *h* work brings a profit,
Jer 32: 17 Nothing is too *h* for you.
Zec 7: 12 They made their hearts as *h* as flint
Mt 19: 23 it is *h* for a rich man
Mk 10: 5 your hearts were *h* that Moses
Jn 6: 60 disciples said, "This is a *h* teaching.
Ac 20: 35 of *h* work we must help the weak,
26: 14 It is *h* for you to kick
Ro 16: 12 woman who has worked very *h*
1Co 4: 12 We work *h* with our own hands.
2Co 6: 5 imprisonments and riots; in *h* work
1Th 5: 12 to respect those who work *h*
Rev 2: 2 your *h* work and your

HARDEN (HARD)

Ex 4: 21 I will *h* his heart so that he will not
Ps 95: 8 do not *h* your hearts as you did
Ro 9: 18 he hardens whom he wants to *h*.
Heb 3: 8 do not *h* your hearts

HARDENED (HARD)

Ex 10: 20 But the LORD *h* Pharaoh's heart,

HARDENING* (HARD)

Ro 11: 25 Israel has experienced a *h* in part
Eph 4: 18 in them due to the *h* of their hearts.

HARDENS* (HARD)

Pr 28: 14 he who *h* his heart falls into trouble
Ro 9: 18 and he *h* whom he wants to harden.

HARDER (HARD)

1Co 15: 10 No, I worked *h* than all of them—
2Co 11: 23 I have worked much *h*, been

HARDHEARTED* (HEART)

Dt 15: 7 do not be *h* or tightfisted

HARDSHIP (HARD)

Ro 8: 35 Shall trouble or *h* or persecution
2Ti 2: 3 Endure *h* with us like a good
4: 5 endure *h*, do the work
Heb 12: 7 Endure *h* as discipline; God is

HARDSHIPS (HARD)

Ac 14: 22 go through many *h* to enter

2Co 6: 4 in troubles, *h* and distresses;
12: 10 in insults, in *h*, in persecutions,
Rev 2: 3 and have endured *h* for my name,

HARLOT see PROSTITUTE

HARM (HARMS)

1Ch 16: 22 do my prophets no *h*."
Ps 105: 15 do my prophets no *h*."
121: 6 the sun will not *h* you by day,
Pr 3: 29 not plot *h* against your neighbor,
12: 21 No *h* befalls the righteous,
31: 12 She brings him good, not *h*,
Jer 10: 5 they can do no *h*
29: 11 to prosper you and not to *h* you,
Ro 13: 10 Love does no *h* to its neighbor.
1Co 11: 17 for your meetings do more *h*
1Jn 5: 18 the evil one cannot *h* him.

HARMONY*

Zec 6: 13 there will be *h* between the two.'
Ro 12: 16 Live in *h* with one another.
2Co 6: 15 What *h* is there between Christ
1Pe 3: 8 live in *h* with one another;

HARMS* (HARM)

Pr 8: 36 whoever fails to find me *h* himself;

HARP (HARPS)

Ge 4: 21 the father of all who play the *h*
1Sa 16: 23 David would take his *h* and play.
Ps 33: 2 Praise the LORD with the *h*;
98: 5 with the *h* and the sound of singing
150: 3 praise him with the *h* and lyre,
Rev 5: 8 Each one had a *h* and they were

HARPS (HARP)

Ps 137: 2 we hung our *h*,

HARSH

Pr 15: 1 but a *h* word stirs up anger.
Col 2: 23 and their *h* treatment of the body,
3: 19 and do not be *h* with them.
1Pe 2: 18 but also to those who are *h*.
Jude : 15 of all the *h* words ungodly sinners

HARVEST (HARVESTERS)

Ge 8: 22 seedtime and *h*,
Ex 23: 16 the Feast of *H* with the firstfruits
Dt 16: 15 God will bless you in all your *h*
Pr 10: 5 during *h* is a disgraceful son.
Jer 8: 20 "The *h* is past,
Joel 3: 13 for the *h* is ripe.
Mt 9: 37 *h* is plentiful but the workers are
Lk 10: 2 He told them, "The *h* is plentiful,
Jn 4: 35 at the fields! They are ripe for *h*.
1Co 9: 11 if we reap a material *h* from you?
2Co 9: 10 the *h* of your righteousness.
Gal 6: 9 at the proper time we will reap a *h*
Heb 12: 11 it produces a *h* of righteousness
Jas 3: 18 in peace raise a *h* of righteousness.
Rev 14: 15 for the *h* of the earth is ripe."

HARVESTERS (HARVEST)

Ru 2: 3 to glean in the fields behind the *h*.

HASTE (HASTEN HASTY)

Ex 12: 11 it in *h*; it is the LORD's Passover.
Pr 21: 5 as surely as *h* leads to poverty.
29: 20 Do you see a man who speaks in *h*?

HASTEN (HASTE)

Ps 70: 1 *H*, O God, to save me;
119: 60 I will *h* and not delay

HASTY* (HASTE)

Pr 19: 2 nor to be *h* and miss the way.
Ecc 5: 2 do not be *h* in your heart
1Ti 5: 22 Do not be *h* in the laying

HATE (GOD-HATERS HATED HATES HATING HATRED)

Lev 19: 17 " 'Do not *h* your brother
Ps 5: 5 you *h* all who do wrong.
36: 2 too much to detect or *h* his sin.
45: 7 righteousness and *h* wickedness;
97: 10 those who love the LORD *h* evil,
119: 104 therefore I *h* every wrong path.
119: 163 I *h* and abhor falsehood
139: 21 Do I not *h* those who *h* you,
Pr 8: 13 To fear the LORD is to *h* evil;
9: 8 rebuke a mocker or he will *h* you;
13: 5 The righteous *h* what is false,
25: 17 too much of you, and he will *h* you.
29: 10 Bloodthirsty men *h* a man

Ecc 3: 8 a time to love and a time to *h*,
Isa 61: 8 I *h* robbery and iniquity.
Eze 35: 6 Since you did not *h* bloodshed,
Am 5: 15 *H* evil, love good;
Mal 2: 16 "I *h* divorce," says the LORD God
Mt 5: 43 your neighbor and *h* your enemy.'
10: 22 All men will *h* you because of me,
Lk 6: 22 Blessed are you when men *h* you,
6: 27 do good to those who *h* you,
14: 26 does not *h* his father and mother,
Ro 12: 9 *H* what is evil; cling to what is good

HATED (HATE)

Mal 1: 3 loved Jacob, but Esau I have *h*,
Jn 15: 18 keep in mind that it *h* me first.
Ro 9: 13 "Jacob I loved, but Esau I *h*."
Eph 5: 29 no one ever *h* his own body,
Heb 1: 9 righteousness and *h* wickedness;

HATES (HATE)

Pr 6: 16 There are six things the LORD *h*,
13: 24 He who spares the rod *h* his son,
15: 27 but he who *h* bribes will live.
26: 28 A lying tongue *h* those it hurts,
Jn 3: 20 Everyone who does evil *h* the light,
12: 25 while the man who *h* his life
1Jn 2: 9 *h* his brother is still in the darkness.
4: 20 "I love God," yet *h* his brother,

HATING (HATE)

Jude :23 *h* even the clothing stained

HATRED (HATE)

Pr 10: 12 *H* stirs up dissension,
15: 17 than a fattened calf with *h*.
Jas 4: 4 with the world is *h* toward God?

HAUGHTY

Pr 6: 17 detestable to him: / *h* eyes,
16: 18 a *h* spirit before a fall.

HAVEN

Ps 107: 30 he guided them to their desired *h*.

HAY

1Co 3: 12 costly stones, wood, *h* or straw,

HEAD (HEADS HOTHEADED)

Ge 3: 15 he will crush your *h*,
Nu 6: 5 no razor may be used on his *h*.
Jdg 16: 17 If my *h* were shaved, my strength
1Sa 9: 2 a *h* taller than any of the others.
2Sa 18: 9 Absalom's *h* got caught in the tree.
Ps 23: 5 You anoint my *h* with oil;
133: 2 is like precious oil poured on the *h*,
Pr 10: 6 Blessings crown the *h*
25: 22 will heap burning coals on his *h*,
Isa 59: 17 and the helmet of salvation on his *h*
Eze 33: 4 his blood will be on his own *h*.
Mt 8: 20 of Man has no place to lay his *h*."
Jn 19: 2 crown of thorns and put it on his *h*.
Ro 12: 20 will heap burning coals on his *h*."
1Co 11: 3 and the *h* of Christ is God.
11: 5 her *h* uncovered dishonors her *h*—
12: 21 And the *h* cannot say to the feet,
Eph 1: 22 him to be *h* over everything
5: 23 For the husband is the *h* of the wife
Col 1: 18 And he is the *h* of the body,
2Ti 4: 5 keep your *h* in all situations,
Rev 14: 14 with a crown of gold on his *h*
19: 12 and on his *h* are many crowns.

HEADS (HEAD)

Lev 26: 13 you to walk with *h* held high.
Ps 22: 7 they hurl insults, shaking their *h*:
24: 7 Lift up your *h*, O you gates;
Isa 35: 10 everlasting joy will crown their *h*.
51: 11 everlasting joy will crown their *h*.
Mt 27: 39 shaking their *h* and saying,
Lk 21: 28 stand up and lift up your *h*,
Ac 18: 6 "Your blood be on your own *h*!
Rev 4: 4 and had crowns of gold on their *h*.

HEAL* (HEALED HEALING HEALS)

Nu 12: 13 please *h* her!" The LORD replied
Dt 32: 39 I have wounded and I will *h*,
2Ki 20: 5 and seen your tears; I will *h* you.
20: 8 the sign that the LORD will *h* me
2Ch 7: 14 their sin and will *h* their land.
Job 5: 18 he injures, but his hands also *h*.
Ps 6: 2 *h* me, for my bones are in agony.
41: 4 *h* me, for I have sinned against you
Ecc 3: 3 a time to kill and a time to *h*,
Isa 19: 22 he will strike them and *h* them.
19: 22 respond to their pleas and *h* them.
Isa 57: 18 seen his ways, but I will *h* him;
57: 19 "And I will *h* them."
Jer 17: 14 *H* me, O LORD, and I will be
30: 17 and *h* your wounds,'
33: 6 I will *h* my people and will let them
La 2: 13 Who can *h* you?
Hos 5: 13 not able to *h* your sores,
6: 1 but he will *h* us;
7: 1 whenever I would *h* Israel,
14: 4 "I will *h* their waywardness
Na 3: 19 Nothing can *h* your wound;
Zec 11: 16 or seek the young, or *h* the injured,
Mt 8: 7 said to him, "I will go and *h* him."
10: 1 to *h* every disease and sickness.
10: 8 *H* the sick, raise the dead,
12: 10 "Is it lawful to *h* on the Sabbath?"
13: 15 and turn, and I would *h* them.'
17: 16 but they could not *h* him."
Mk 3: 2 if he would *h* him on the Sabbath.
6: 5 on a few sick people and *h* them.
Lk 4: 23 to me: 'Physician, *h* yourself!
5: 17 present for him to *h* the sick.
6: 7 to see if he would *h* on the Sabbath.
7: 3 him to come and *h* his servant.
8: 43 years, but no one could *h* her.
9: 2 kingdom of God and to *h* the sick.
10: 9 *H* the sick who are there
13: 32 and *h* people today and tomorrow,
14: 3 "Is it lawful to *h* on the Sabbath
Jn 4: 47 begged him to come and *h* his son,
12: 40 nor turn—and I would *h* them."
Ac 4: 30 Stretch out your hand to *h*
28: 27 and turn, and I would *h* them.'

HEALED* (HEAL)

Ge 20: 17 to God, and God *h* Abimelech,
Ex 21: 19 and see that he is completely *h*.
Lev 13: 37 hair has grown in it, the itch is *h*.
14: 3 If the person has been *h*
Jos 5: 8 were in camp until they were *h*.
1Sa 6: 3 you will be *h*, and you will know
2Ki 2: 21 LORD says: 'I have *h* this water.
2Ch 30: 20 heard Hezekiah and *h* the people.
Ps 30: 2 and you *h* me.
107: 20 He sent forth his word and *h* them;
Isa 6: 10 and turn and be *h*."
53: 5 and by his wounds we are *h*.
Jer 14: 19 us so that we cannot be *h*?
17: 14 Heal me, O LORD, and I will be *h*;
51: 8 perhaps she can be *h*.
51: 9 but she cannot be *h*;
51: 9 " 'We would have *h* Babylon,
Eze 34: 4 the weak or *h* the sick
Hos 11: 3 it was I who *h* them.
Mt 4: 24 and the paralyzed, and he *h* them.
8: 8 the word, and my servant will be *h*.
8: 13 his servant was *h* at that very hour.
8: 16 with a word and *h* all the sick.
9: 21 If I only touch his cloak, I will be *h*
9: 22 he said, "your faith has *h* you."
9: 22 woman was *h* from that moment.
12: 15 him, and he *h* all their sick,
12: 22 Jesus *h* him, so that he could both
14: 14 on them and *h* their sick.
14: 36 and all who touched him were *h*.
15: 28 And her daughter was *h*
15: 30 laid them at his feet; and he *h* them
17: 18 and he was *h* from that moment.
19: 2 followed him, and he *h* them there.
21: 14 to him at the temple, and he *h* them
Mk 1: 34 and Jesus *h* many who had various
3: 10 For he had *h* many, so that those
5: 23 hands on her so that she will be *h*
5: 28 If I just touch his clothes, I will be *h*
5: 34 "Daughter, your faith has *h* you.
6: 13 people with oil and *h* them.
6: 56 and all who touched him were *h*.
10: 52 said Jesus, "your faith has *h* you."
Lk 4: 40 hands on each one, he *h* them.
5: 15 and to be *h* of their sicknesses.
6: 18 and to be *h* of their diseases.
7: 7 the word, and my servant will be *h*.
8: 47 and how she had been instantly *h*.
8: 48 "Daughter, your faith has *h* you.
8: 50 just believe, and she will be *h*."
9: 11 and *h* those who needed healing.
9: 42 *h* the boy and gave him back
13: 14 Jesus had *h* on the Sabbath,
13: 14 So come and be *h* on those days,
14: 4 he *h* him and sent him away.
17: 15 when he saw he was *h*, came back,
18: 42 your sight; your faith has *h* you."
22: 51 touched the man's ear and *h* him.
Jn 5: 10 said to the man who had been *h*,
5: 13 man who was *h* had no idea who it
Ac 4: 9 and are asked how he was *h*,
4: 10 stands before you *h*.
4: 14 who had been *h* standing there
4: 22 man who was miraculously *h* was
5: 16 evil spirits, and all of them were *h*.
8: 7 paralytics and cripples were *h*.
14: 9 saw that he had faith to be *h*
28: 8 placed his hands on him and *h* him.
Heb 12: 13 may not be disabled, but rather *h*.
Jas 5: 16 for each other so that you may be *h*
1Pe 2: 24 by his wounds you have been *h*.
Rev 13: 3 but the fatal wound had been *h*.
13: 12 whose fatal wound had been *h*.

HEALING* (HEAL)

2Ch 28: 15 food and drink, and *h* balm.
Pr 12: 18 but the tongue of the wise brings *h*.
13: 17 but a trustworthy envoy brings *h*.
15: 4 The tongue that brings *h* is a tree
16: 24 sweet to the soul and *h* to the bones
Isa 58: 8 and your *h* will quickly appear;
Jer 8: 15 for a time of *h*
8: 22 Why then is there no *h*
14: 19 for a time of *h*
30: 12 your injury beyond *h*.
30: 13 no *h* for you.
33: 6 I will bring health and *h* to it;
46: 11 there is no *h* for you.
Eze 30: 21 It has not been bound up for *h*
47: 12 for food and their leaves for *h*."
Mal 4: 2 rise with *h* in its wings.
Mt 4: 23 and *h* every disease and sickness
9: 35 and *h* every disease and sickness.
Lk 6: 19 coming from him and *h* them all.
9: 6 gospel and *h* people everywhere.
9: 11 and healed those who needed *h*.
Jn 7: 23 angry with me for *h* the whole man
Ac 3: 16 him that has given this complete *h*
10: 38 *h* all who were under the power
1Co 12: 9 to another gifts of *h*
12: 28 also those having gifts of *h*,
12: 30 Do all have gifts of *h*? Do all speak
Rev 22: 2 are for the *h* of the nations.

HEALS* (HEAL)

Ex 15: 26 for I am the LORD, who *h* you."
Lev 13: 18 a boil on his skin and it *h*,
Ps 103: 3 and *h* all your diseases;
147: 3 He *h* the brokenhearted
Isa 30: 26 and *h* the wounds he inflicted.
Ac 9: 34 said to him, "Jesus Christ *h* you.

HEALTH* (HEALTHIER HEALTHY)

1Sa 25: 6 And good *h* to all that is yours!
25: 6 Good *h* to you and your household
Ps 38: 3 of your wrath there is no *h*
38: 7 there is no *h* in my body.
Pr 3: 8 This will bring *h* to your body
4: 22 and *h* to a man's whole body.
15: 30 and good news gives *h* to the bones
Isa 38: 16 You restored me to *h*
Jer 30: 17 But I will restore you to *h*
33: 6 I will bring *h* and healing to it;
3Jn : 2 I pray that you may enjoy good *h*

HEALTHIER* (HEALTH)

Da 1: 15 end of the ten days they looked *h*

HEALTHY* (HEALTH)

Ge 41: 5 Seven heads of grain, *h* and good,
41: 7 of grain swallowed up the seven *h*,
Ps 73: 4 their bodies are *h* and strong.
Zec 11: 16 or heal the injured, or feed the *h*,
Mt 9: 12 "It is not the *h* who need a doctor,
Mk 2: 17 "It is not the *h* who need a doctor,
Lk 5: 31 "It is not the *h* who need a doctor,

HEAP

Pr 25: 22 you will *h* burning coals
Ro 12: 20 you will *h* burning coals

HEAR (HEARD HEARING HEARS)

Ex 15: 14 The nations will *h* and tremble;
22: 27 I will *h*, for I am compassionate.
Nu 14: 13 Then the Egyptians will *h* about it!
Dt 1: 16 *H* the disputes between your
4: 36 heaven he made you *h* his voice
6: 4 *H*, O Israel: The LORD our God,
19: 20 The rest of the people will *h* of this
31: 13 must *h* it and learn
Jos 7: 9 of the country will *h* about this
1Ki 8: 30 *H* the supplication of your servant
2Ki 19: 16 O LORD, and *h*; open your eyes,
2Ch 7: 14 then will I *h* from heaven
Job 31: 35 ("Oh, that I had someone to *h* me!

Ps 94: 9 he who implanted the ear not *h?*
95: 7 Today, if you *h* his voice,
Ecc 7:21 or you may *h* your servant cursing
Isa 21: 3 I am staggered by what I *h,*
29:18 that day the deaf will *h* the words
30:21 your ears will *h* a voice behind you,
51: 7 *H* me, you who know what is right,
59: 1 nor his ear too dull to *h.*
65:24 while they are still speaking I will *h*
Jer 5:21 who have ears but do not *h:*
Eze 33: 7 so *h* the word I speak and give
37: 4 'Dry bones, *h* the word
Mt 11: 5 the deaf *h,* the dead are raised,
11:15 He who has ears, let him *h.*
13:17 and to *h* what you *h* but did not *h* it
Mk 12:29 answered Jesus, "is this: *'H,*
Lk 7:22 the deaf *h,* the dead are raised,
Jn 8:47 reason you do not *h* is that you do
Ac 13: 7 he wanted to *h* the word of God.
13:44 gathered to *h* the word of the Lord.
17:32 "We want to *h* you again
Ro 2:13 is not those who *h* the law who are
10:14 they *h* without someone preaching
2Ti 4: 3 what their itching ears want to *h.*
Heb 3: 7 "Today, if you *h* his voice,
Rev 1: 3 and blessed are those who *h* it

HEARD (HEAR)

Ex 2:24 God *h* their groaning and he
Dt 4:32 has anything like it ever been *h* of?
2Sa 7:22 as we have *h* with our own ears.
Job 42: 5 My ears had *h* of you
Isa 40:21 Have you not *h?*
40:28 Have you not *h?*
66: 8 Who has ever *h* of such a thing?
Jer 18:13 Who has ever *h* anything like this?
Da 10:12 your words were *h,* and I have
12: 8 I *h,* but I did not understand.
Hab 3:16 I *h* and my heart pounded,
Mt 5:21 "You have *h* that it was said
5:27 "You have *h* that it was said,
5:33 you have *h* that it was said
5:38 "You have *h* that it was said,
5:43 "You have *h* that it was said,
Lk 12: 3 in the dark will be *h* in the daylight,
Jn 8:26 and what I have *h* from him I tell
Ac 2: 6 because each one *h* them speaking
1Co 2: 9 no ear has *h,*
2Co 12: 4 He *h* inexpressible things,
1Th 2:13 word of God, which you *h* from us,
2Ti 1:13 What you *h* from me, keep
Jas 1:25 not forgetting what he has *h,*
Rev 22: 8 am the one who *h* and saw these

HEARING (HEAR)

Isa 6: 9 Be ever *h,* but never understanding
Mt 13:14 will be ever *h* but never
Mk 4:12 ever *h* but never understanding;
Ac 28:26 will be ever *h* but never
Ro 10:17 faith comes from *h* the message,
1Co 12:17 where would the sense of *h* be?

HEARS (HEAR)

Jn 5:24 whoever *h* my word and believes
1Jn 5:14 according to his will, he *h* us.
Rev 3:20 If anyone *h* my voice and opens

HEART (BROKENHEARTED FAINT-HEARTED HARDHEARTED HEART'S HEARTACHE HEARTS KINDHEARTED SIMPLEHEARTED STOUTHEARTED WHOLEHEARTED WHOLEHEARTEDLY)

Ge 6: 5 of his *h* was only evil all the time.
Ex 4:21 But I will harden his *h*
25: 2 each man whose *h* prompts him
35:21 and whose *h* moved him came
Lev 19:17 Do not hate your brother in your *h.*
Dt 4: 9 or let them slip from your *h* as long
4:29 if you look for him with all your *h*
6: 5 LORD your God with all your *h*
10:12 LORD your God with all your *h*
11:13 and to serve him with all your *h*
13: 3 you love him with all your *h*
15:10 and do so without a grudging *h;*
26:16 observe them with all your *h*
29:18 you today whose *h* turns away
30: 2 and obey him with all your *h*
30: 6 you may love him with all your *h*
30:10 LORD your God with all your *h*
Jos 22: 5 and to serve him with all your *h*
23:14 You know with all your *h*
1Sa 10: 9 God changed Saul's *h,*
12:20 serve the LORD with all your *h.*
12:24 serve him faithfully with all your *h;*
13:14 sought out a man after his own *h*
1Sa 14: 7 I am with you *h* and soul."
16: 7 but the LORD looks at the *h."*
17:32 "Let no one lose *h* on account
1Ki 2: 4 faithfully before me with all their *h*
3: 9 So give your servant a discerning *h*
3:12 give you a wise and discerning *h,*
8:48 back to you with all their *h*
9: 3 and my *h* will always be there.
9: 4 walk before me in integrity of *h*
10:24 the wisdom God had put in his *h.*
11: 4 and his *h* was not fully devoted
14: 8 and followed me with all his *h,*
15:14 Asa's *h* was fully committed
2Ki 22:19 Because your *h* was responsive
23: 3 with all his *h* and all his soul,
1Ch 28: 9 for the LORD searches every *h*
2Ch 6:38 back to you with all their *h*
7:16 and my *h* will always be there.
15:12 of their fathers, with all their *h*
15:17 Asa's *h* was fully committed
17: 6 His *h* was devoted to the ways
22: 9 sought the LORD with all his *h."*
34:31 with all his *h* and all his soul,
36:13 stiff-necked and hardened his *h*
Ezr 1: 5 everyone whose *h* God had moved
Ne 4: 6 the people worked with all their *h.*
Job 19:27 How my *h* yearns within me!
22:22 and lay up his words in your *h.*
37: 1 "At this my *h* pounds
Ps 9: 1 you, O LORD, with all my *h;*
14: 1 The fool says in his *h,*
16: 9 Therefore my *h* is glad
19:14 and the meditation of my *h*
20: 4 he give you the desire of your *h*
24: 4 who has clean hands and a pure *h,*
26: 2 examine my *h* and my mind;
37: 4 will give you the desires of your *h.*
37:31 The law of his God is in his *h;*
44:21 since he knows the secrets of the *h*
45: 1 My *h* is stirred by a noble theme
51:10 Create in me a pure *h,* O God,
51:17 a broken and contrite *h,*
53: 1 The fool says in his *h,*
66:18 If I had cherished sin in my *h,*
73: 1 to those who are pure in *h.*
73:26 My flesh and my *h* may fail,
86:11 give me an undivided *h,*
90:12 that we may gain a *h* of wisdom.
97:11 and joy on the upright in *h.*
108: 1 My *h* is steadfast, O God;
109:22 and my *h* is wounded within me.
111: 1 will extol the LORD with all my *h*
112: 7 his *h* is steadfast, trusting
112: 8 His *h* is secure, he will have no fear
119: 2 and seek him with all their *h.*
119:10 I seek you with all my *h;*
119:11 I have hidden your word in my *h*
119:30 I have set my *h* on your laws.
119:32 for you have set my *h* free.
119:34 and obey it with all my *h.*
119:36 Turn my *h* toward your statutes
119:58 sought your face with all my *h;*
119:69 I keep your precepts with all my *h.*
119:111 they are the joy of my *h.*
119:112 My *h* is set on keeping your
119:145 I call with all my *h;* answer me,
125: 4 to those who are upright in *h.*
138: 1 you, O LORD, with all my *h;*
139:23 Search me, O God, and know my *h*
Pr 2: 2 applying your *h* to understanding,
3: 1 but keep my commands in your *h,*
3: 3 write them on the tablet of your *h.*
3: 5 Trust in the LORD with all your *h*
4: 4 hold of my words with all your *h;*
4:21 keep them within your *h;*
4:23 Above all else, guard your *h,*
6:21 Bind them upon your *h* forever;
7: 3 write them on the tablet of your *h.*
10: 8 The wise in *h* accept commands,
13:12 Hope deferred makes the *h* sick,
14:13 Even in laughter the *h* may ache,
14:30 A *h* at peace gives life to the body,
15:13 A happy *h* makes the face cheerful,
15:15 the cheerful *h* has a continual feast.
15:28 *h* of the righteous weighs its
15:30 A cheerful look brings joy to the *h,*
16:23 A wise man's *h* guides his mouth,
17:22 A cheerful *h* is good medicine,
20: 9 can say, "I have kept my *h* pure;
22:11 He who loves a pure *h*
22:17 apply your *h* to what I teach,
22:18 when you keep them in your *h*
23:15 My son, if your *h* is wise,
23:19 and keep your *h* on the right path.
23:26 My son, give me your *h*
Pr 24:17 stumbles, do not let your *h* rejoice,
27:19 so a man's *h* reflects the man.
Ecc 5: 2 do not be hasty in your *h*
8: 5 wise *h* will know the proper time
11:10 banish anxiety from your *h*
SS 3: 1 I looked for the one my *h* loves;
4: 9 You have stolen my *h,* my sister,
5: 2 *Beloved* I slept but my *h* was awake
5: 4 my *h* began to pound for him.
8: 6 Place me like a seal over your *h,*
Isa 6:10 Make the *h* of this people calloused
40:11 and carries them close to his *h;*
57:15 and to revive the *h* of the contrite.
66:14 you see this, your *h* will rejoice
Jer 3:15 give you shepherds after my own *h,*
4:14 wash the evil from your *h*
9:26 of Israel is uncircumcised in *h."*
17: 9 The *h* is deceitful above all things
20: 9 is in my *h* like a fire,
24: 7 I will give them a *h* to know me,
29:13 when you seek me with all your *h.*
32:39 I will give them singleness of *h*
32:41 them in this land with all my *h*
51:46 Do not lose *h* or be afraid
Eze 11:19 I will give them an undivided *h*
18:31 and get a new *h* and a new spirit.
36:26 I will give you a new *h*
44: 7 foreigners uncircumcised in *h*
Da 7: 4 and the *h* of a man was given to it.
Joel 2:12 "return to me with all your *h,*
2:13 Rend your *h*
Zep 3:14 Be glad and rejoice with all your *h,*
Mt 5: 8 Blessed are the pure in his *h.*
5:28 adultery with her in his *h.*
6:21 treasure is, there your *h* will be
11:29 for I am gentle and humble in *h,*
12:34 of the *h* the mouth speaks.
13:15 For this people's *h* has become
15:18 out of the mouth come from the *h,*
15:19 For out of the *h* come evil thoughts
18:35 forgive your brother from your *h."*
22:37 the Lord your God with all your *h*
Mk 11:23 and does not doubt in his *h*
12:30 the Lord your God with all your *h*
12:33 To love him with all your *h,*
Lk 2:19 and pondered them in her *h.*
2:51 treasured all these things in her *h.*
6:45 out of the good stored up in his *h,*
6:45 overflow of his *h* his mouth speaks.
8:15 for those with a noble and good *h,*
10:27 the Lord your God with all your *h*
12:34 treasure is, there your *h* will be
Jn 12:27 "Now my *h* is troubled,
Ac 1:24 "Lord, you know everyone's *h.*
2:37 they were cut to the *h*
4:32 All the believers were one in *h*
8:21 your *h* is not right before God.
15: 8 who knows the *h,* showed that he
16:14 The Lord opened her *h* to respond
28:27 For this people's *h* has become
Ro 1: 9 with my whole *h* in preaching
2:29 is circumcision of the *h,*
10: 9 in your *h* that God raised him
10:10 is with your *h* that you believe
15: 6 with one *h* and mouth you may
1Co 14:25 the secrets of his *h* will be laid bare.
2Co 2: 4 anguish of *h* and with many tears,
4: 1 this ministry, we do not lose *h.*
4:16 Therefore we do not lose *h.*
9: 7 give what he has decided in his *h*
Eph 1:18 eyes of your *h* may be enlightened
5:19 make music in your *h* to the Lord,
6: 5 and with sincerity of *h,* just
6: 6 doing the will of God from your *h.*
Php 1: 7 since I have you in my *h;* for
Col 2: 2 is that they may be encouraged in *h*
3:22 but with sincerity of *h*
3:23 work at it with all your *h,*
1Ti 1: 5 which comes from a pure *h*
3: 1 If anyone sets his *h*
2Ti 2:22 call on the Lord out of a pure *h.*
Phm :12 who is my very *h*—back to you.
:20 in the Lord; refresh my *h* in Christ.
Heb 4:12 the thoughts and attitudes of the *h.*
1Pe 1:22 one another deeply, from the *h.*

HEART'S* (HEART)

2Ch 1:11 "Since this is your *h* desire
Jer 15:16 they were my joy and my *h* delight,
Eze 24:25 delight of their eyes, their *h* desire,
Ro 10: 1 my *h* desire and prayer to God

HEARTACHE* (HEART)

Pr 15:13 but *h* crushes the spirit.

HEARTLESS*
La 4: 3 but my people have become *h*
Ro 1:31 they are senseless, faithless, *h,*

HEARTS (HEART)
Lev 26:41 their uncircumcised *h* are humbled
Dt 6: 6 are to be upon your *h.*
10:16 Circumcise your *h,* therefore,
11:18 Fix these words of mine in your *h*
30: 6 your God will circumcise your *h*
Jos 11:20 himself who hardened their *h*
24:23 and yield your *h* to the LORD,
1Sa 7: 3 to the LORD with all your *h,*
10:26 valiant men whose *h* God had
2Sa 15: 6 and so he stole the *h* of the men
1Ki 8:39 for you alone know the *h* of all men
8:61 your *h* must be fully committed
18:37 are turning their *h* back again."
1Ch 29:18 and keep their *h* loyal to you.
2Ch 6:30 (for you alone know the *h* of men),
11:16 tribe of Israel who set their *h*
29:31 all whose *h* were willing brought
Ps 7: 9 who searches minds and *h,*
33:21 In him our *h* rejoice,
62: 8 pour out your *h* to him,
95: 8 do not harden your *h* as you did
Ecc 3:11 also set eternity in the *h* of men;
Isa 26: 8 are the desire of our *h.*
29:13 but their *h* are far from me.
35: 4 say to those with fearful *h,*
51: 7 people who have my law in your *h:*
63:17 harden our *h* so we do not revere
65:14 out of the joy of their *h,*
Jer 4: 4 circumcise your *h,*
12: 2 but far from their *h.*
17: 1 on the tablets of their *h*
31:33 and write it on their *h.*
Mal 4: 6 He will turn the *h* of the fathers
Mt 15: 8 but their *h* are far from me.
Mk 6:52 the loaves; their *h* were hardened.
7: 6 but their *h* are far from me.
7:21 out of men's *h,* come evil thoughts,
Lk 1:17 to turn the *h* of the fathers
16:15 of men, but God knows your *h.*
24:32 "Were not our *h* burning within us
Jn 5:42 not have the love of God in your *h.*
14: 1 "Do not let your *h* be troubled.
14:27 Do not let your *h* be troubled
Ac 7:51 with uncircumcised *h* and ears!
11:23 true to the Lord with all their *h.*
15: 9 for he purified their *h* by faith.
28:27 understand with their *h*
Ro 1:21 and their foolish *h* were darkened.
2:15 of the law are written on their *h,*
5: 5 love into our *h* by the Holy Spirit,
8:27 who searches our *h* knows
1Co 4: 5 will expose the motives of men's *h.*
2Co 1:22 put his Spirit in our *h* as a deposit,
3: 2 written on our *h,* known
3: 3 but on tablets of human *h.*
4: 6 shine in our *h* to give us the light
6:11 and opened wide our *h* to you.
6:13 to my children—open wide your *h*
7: 2 Make room for us in your *h.*
Gal 4: 6 the Spirit of his Son into our *h,*
Eph 3:17 dwell in your *h* through faith.
Php 4: 7 will guard your *h* and your minds
Col 3: 1 set your *h* on things above,
3:15 the peace of Christ rule in your *h,*
3:16 with gratitude in your *h* to God.
1Th 2: 4 men but God, who tests our *h.*
3:13 May he strengthen your *h*
2Th 2:17 encourage your *h* and strengthen
Phm : 7 have refreshed the *h* of the saints.
Heb 3: 8 do not harden your *h*
8:10 and write them on their *h.*
10:16 I will put my laws in their *h,*
10:22 having our *h* sprinkled
Jas 4: 8 purify your *h,* you double-minded.
2Pe 1:19 the morning star rises in your *h.*
1Jn 3:20 For God is greater than our *h,*

HEAT
Ps 19: 6 nothing is hidden from its *h.*
2Pe 3:12 and the elements will melt in the *h.*

HEATHEN see GENTILES, NATIONS

HEAVEN (HEAVENLY HEAVENS HEAVENWARD)
Ge 14:19 Creator of *h* and earth.
28:12 with its top reaching to *h,*
Ex 16: 4 rain down bread from *h* for you.
20:22 that I have spoken to you from *h:*
Dt 26:15 from *h,* your holy dwelling place,
30:12 "Who will ascend into *h* to get it
1Ki 8:27 the highest *h,* cannot contain you.
8:30 Hear from *h,* your dwelling place,
22:19 the host of *h* standing around him
2Ki 2: 1 up to *h* in a whirlwind,
19:15 You have made *h* and earth.
2Ch 7:14 then will I hear from *h*
Isa 14:12 How you have fallen from *h,*
66: 1 "*H* is my throne,
Da 7:13 coming with the clouds of *h.*
Mt 3: 2 for the kingdom of *h* is near."
3:16 At that moment *h* was opened,
4:17 for the kingdom of *h* is near."
5:12 because great is your reward in *h,*
5:19 great in the kingdom of *h.*
6: 9 " 'Our Father in *h,*
6:10 done on earth as it is in *h.*
6:20 up for yourselves treasures in *h,*
7:21 Lord,' will enter the kingdom of *h,*
16:19 bind on earth will be bound in *h,*
18: 3 will never enter the kingdom of *h.*
18:18 bind on earth will be bound in *h,*
19:14 the kingdom of *h* belongs to such
19:21 and you will have treasure in *h.*
19:23 man to enter the kingdom of *h.*
23:13 the kingdom of *h* in men's faces.
24:35 *H* and earth will pass away,
26:64 and coming on the clouds of *h.*"
28:18 "All authority in *h*
Mk 1:10 he saw *h* being torn open
10:21 and you will have treasure in *h.*
13:31 *H* and earth will pass away,
14:62 and coming on the clouds of *h.*"
16:19 he was taken up into *h*
Lk 3:21 *h* was opened and the Holy Spirit
10:18 saw Satan fall like lightning from *h.*
10:20 that your names are written in *h.*"
12:33 in *h* that will not be exhausted,
15: 7 in *h* over one sinner who repents
18:22 and you will have treasure in *h.*
21:33 *H* and earth will pass away,
24:51 left them and was taken up into *h.*
Jn 3:13 No one has ever gone into *h*
6:38 down from *h* not to do my will
12:28 Then a voice came from *h,*
Ac 1:11 has been taken from you into *h,*
7:49 the prophet says: " '*H* is my
7:55 looked up to *h* and saw the glory
9: 3 a light from *h* flashed around him.
26:19 disobedient to the vision from *h.*
Ro 10: 6 'Who will ascend into *h?*' " (that is,
1Co 15:47 the earth, the second man from *h.*
2Co 5: 1 an eternal house in *h,* not built
12: 2 ago was caught up to the third *h.*
Eph 1:10 to bring all things in *h*
Php 2:10 *h* and on earth and under the earth,
3:20 But our citizenship is in *h.*
Col 1:16 things in *h* and on earth, visible
4: 1 that you also have a Master in *h.*
1Th 1:10 and to wait for his Son from *h,*
4:16 himself will come down from *h,*
Heb 1: 3 hand of the Majesty in *h.*
8: 5 and shadow of what is in *h.*
9:24 he entered *h* itself, now to appear
12:23 whose names are written in *h.*
1Pe 1: 4 spoil or fade—kept in *h* for you,
3:22 who has gone into *h* and is
2Pe 3:13 we are looking forward to a new *h*
Rev 5:13 Then I heard every creature in *h*
11:19 God's temple in *h* was opened,
12: 7 And there was war in *h.*
15: 5 this I looked and in *h* the temple,
19: 1 of a great multitude in *h* shouting:
19:11 I saw *h* standing open and there
21: 1 Then I saw a new *h* and a new earth
21:10 coming down out of *h* from God.

HEAVENLY (HEAVEN)
Ps 8: 5 him a little lower than the *h* beings
2Co 5: 2 to be clothed with our *h* dwelling,
Eph 1: 3 in the *h* realms with every spiritual
1:20 at his right hand in the *h* realms,
2Ti 4:18 bring me safely to his *h* kingdom.
Heb 12:22 to the *h* Jerusalem, the city

HEAVENS (HEAVEN)
Ge 1: 1 In the beginning God created the *h*
11: 4 with a tower that reaches to the *h,*
Dt 33:26 who rides on the *h* to help you
1Ki 8:27 The *h,* even the highest heaven,
2Ch 2: 6 since the *h,* even the highest
Ezr 9: 6 and our guilt has reached to the *h.*
Ne 9: 6 You made the *h,* even the highest
Job 11: 8 They are higher than the *h*—
38:33 Do you know the laws of the *h?*
Ps 8: 3 When I consider your *h,*
19: 1 The *h* declare the glory of God;
33: 6 of the LORD were the *h* made,
57: 5 Be exalted, O God, above the *h;*
102:25 the *h* are the work of your hands.
103:11 as high as the *h* are above the earth,
108: 4 is your love, higher than the *h;*
115:16 The highest *h* belong to the LORD
119:89 it stands firm in the *h.*
135: 6 in the *h* and on the earth,
139: 8 If I go up to the *h,* you are there;
148: 1 Praise the LORD from the *h,*
Isa 40:26 Lift your eyes and look to the *h:*
45: 8 "You *h* above, rain
51: 6 Lift up your eyes to the *h,*
55: 9 "As the *h* are higher than the earth,
65:17 new *h* and a new earth.
Jer 31:37 if the *h* above can be measured
32:17 you have made the *h* and the earth
Eze 1: 1 *h* were opened and I saw visions
Da 12: 3 shine like the brightness of the *h,*
Joel 2:30 I will show wonders in the *h*
Mt 24:31 from one end of the *h* to the other.
Mk 13:27 of the earth to the ends of the *h.*
Eph 4:10 who ascended higher than all the *h,*
Heb 4:14 priest who has gone through the *h,*
7:26 from sinners, exalted above the *h.*
2Pe 3: 5 ago by God's word the *h* existed
3:10 The *h* will disappear with a roar;

HEAVENWARD (HEAVEN)
Php 3:14 for which God has called me *h*

HEAVIER (HEAVY)
Pr 27: 3 provocation by a fool is *h* than both

HEAVY (HEAVIER)
1Ki 12: 4 and the *h* yoke he put on us,
Ecc 1:13 What a *h* burden God has laid
Isa 47: 6 you laid a very *h* yoke.
Mt 23: 4 They tie up *h* loads and put them

HEBREW (HEBREWS)
Ge 14:13 and reported this to Abram the *H.*
2Ki 18:26 speak to us in *H* in the hearing
Php 3: 5 tribe of Benjamin, a *H* of Hebrews;

HEBREWS (HEBREW)
Ex 9: 1 of the *H,* says: "Let my people go,
2Co 11:22 Are they *H?* So am I.

HEBRON
Ge 13:18 near the great trees of Mamre at *H,*
23: 2 died at Kiriath Arba (that is, *H)*
Jos 14:13 and gave him *H* as his inheritance.
20: 7 *H)* in the hill country of Judah.
21:13 the priest they gave *H* (a city
2Sa 2:11 king in *H* over the house

HEDGE
Job 1:10 "Have you not put a *h* around him

HEED (HEEDS)
Ecc 7: 5 It is better to *h* a wise man's rebuke

HEEDS (HEED)
Pr 13: 1 wise son *h* his father's instruction,
13:18 whoever *h* correction is honored.
15: 5 whoever *h* correction shows
15:32 whoever *h* correction gains

HEEL
Ge 3:15 and you will strike his *h.*"

HEIR (INHERIT)
Gal 4: 7 God has made you also an *h.*
Heb 1: 2 whom he appointed *h* of all things,

HEIRS (INHERIT)
Ro 8:17 then we are *h*— *h* of God
Gal 3:29 and *h* according to the promise.
Eph 3: 6 gospel the Gentiles are *h* together
1Pe 3: 7 as *h* with you of the gracious gift

HELD (HOLD)
Ex 17:11 As long as Moses *h* up his hands,
Dt 4: 4 but all of you who *h* fast
2Ki 18: 6 He *h* fast to the LORD
SS 3: 4 I *h* him and would not let him go
Isa 65: 2 All day long I have *h* out my hands
Ro 10:21 day long I have *h* out my hands
Col 2:19 and *h* together by its ligaments

HELL*
Mt 5:22 will be in danger of the fire of *h.*

Mt 5:29 body to be thrown into *h.*
5:30 for your whole body to go into *h.*
10:28 destroy both soul and body in *h.*
18: 9 and be thrown into the fire of *h.*
23:15 as much a son of *h* as you are.
23:33 you escape being condemned to *h?*
Mk 9:43 than with two hands to go into *h,*
9:45 have two feet and be thrown into *h.*
9:47 two eyes and be thrown into *h,*
Lk 12: 5 has power to throw you into *h.*
16:23 In *h,* where he was in torment,
Jas 3: 6 and is itself set on fire by *h.*
2Pe 2: 4 but sent them to *h,* putting them

HELMET

Isa 59:17 and the *h* of salvation on his head;
Eph 6:17 Take the *h* of salvation
1Th 5: 8 and the hope of salvation as a *h.*

HELP (HELPED HELPER HELPFUL HELPING HELPLESS HELPS)

Ex 23: 5 leave it there; be sure you *h* him
Lev 25:35 *h* him as you would an alien
Dt 33:26 who rides on the heavens to *h* you
2Ch 16:12 even in his illness he did not seek *h*
Ps 18: 6 I cried to my God for *h.*
30: 2 my God, I called to you for *h*
33:20 he is our *h* and our shield.
46: 1 an ever-present *h* in trouble.
72:12 the afflicted who have no one to *h.*
79: 9 *H* us, O God our Savior,
108:12 for the *h* of man is worthless.
115: 9 he is their *h* and shield.
121: 1 where does my *h* come from?
Ecc 4:10 his friend can *h* him up.
Isa 41:10 I will strengthen you and *h* you;
Jnh 2: 2 depths of the grave I called for *h,*
Mk 9:24 *h* me overcome my unbelief!"
Lk 11:46 will not lift one finger to *h* them.
Ac 16: 9 Come over to Macedonia and *h* us
18:27 he was a great *h* to those who
20:35 of hard work we must *h* the weak,
26:22 I have had God's *h* to this very day,
1Co 12:28 those able to *h* others, those
2Co 9: 2 For I know your eagerness to *h,*
1Ti 5:16 she should *h* them and not let

HELPED (HELP)

1Sa 7:12 "Thus far has the LORD *h* us."

HELPER (HELP)

Ge 2:18 I will make a *h* suitable for him."
Ps 10:14 you are the *h* of the fatherless.
Heb 13: 6 Lord is my *h;* I will not be afraid.

HELPFUL (HELP)

Eph 4:29 only what is *h* for building others

HELPING (HELP)

Ac 9:36 always doing good and *h* the poor.
1Ti 5:10 *h* those in trouble and devoting

HELPLESS (HELP)

Ps 10:12 Do not forget the *h.*
Mt 9:36 because they were harassed and *h,*

HELPS (HELP)

Ro 8:26 the Spirit *h* us in our weakness.

HEN

Mt 23:37 as a *h* gathers her chicks
Lk 13:34 as a *h* gathers her chicks

HERALD

1Ti 2: 7 for this purpose I was appointed a *h*
2Ti 1:11 of this gospel I was appointed a *h*

HERBS

Ex 12: 8 with bitter *h,* and bread made

HERITAGE (INHERIT)

Ps 61: 5 you have given me the *h*
119:111 Your statutes are my *h* forever;
127: 3 Sons are a *h* from the LORD,

HEROD

1. King of Judea who tried to kill Jesus (Mt 2; Lk 1:5).

2. Son of 1. Tetrarch of Galilee who arrested and beheaded John the Baptist (Mt 14:1-12; Mk 6:14-29; Lk 3:1, 19-20; 9:7-9); tried Jesus (Lk 23:6-15).

3. Grandson of 1. King of Judea who killed James (Ac 12:2); arrested Peter (Ac 12:3-19). Death (Ac 12:19-23).

HERODIAS

Wife of Herod the Tetrarch who persuaded her daughter to ask for John the Baptist's head (Mt 14:1-12; Mk 6:14-29).

HEWN

Isa 51: 1 the quarry from which you were *h;*

HEZEKIAH

King of Judah. Restored the temple and worship (2Ch 29-31). Sought the LORD for help against Assyria (2Ki 18-19; 2Ch 32:1-23; Isa 36-37). Illness healed (2Ki 20:1-11; 2Ch 32:24-26; Isa 38). Judged for showing Babylonians his treasures (2Ki 20:12-21; 2Ch 32:31; Isa 39).

HID (HIDE)

Ge 3: 8 and they *h* from the LORD God
Ex 2: 2 she *h* him for three months.
Jos 6:17 because she *h* the spies we sent.
1Ki 18:13 I *h* a hundred of the LORD's
2Ch 22:11 she *h* the child from Athaliah
Isa 54: 8 I *h* my face from you for a moment,
Mt 13:44 When a man found it, he *h* it again,
25:25 and *h* your talent in the ground.
Heb 11:23 By faith Moses' parents *h* him

HIDDEN (HIDE)

1Sa 10:22 has *h* himself among the baggage."
Job 28:11 and brings *h* things to light.
Ps 19:12 Forgive my *h* faults.
78: 2 I will utter *h* things, things from of old—
119:11 I have *h* your word in my heart
Pr 2: 4 and search for it as for *h* treasure,
27: 5 rebuke than *h* love.
Isa 59: 2 your sins have *h* his face from you,
Da 2:22 He reveals deep and *h* things;
Mt 5:14 A city on a hill cannot be *h.*
10:26 or *h* that will not be made known.
11:25 because you have *h* these things
13:35 I will utter things *h*
13:44 of heaven is like treasure *h*
Mk 4:22 For whatever is *h* is meant
Ro 16:25 of the mystery *h* for long ages past,
1Co 2: 7 a wisdom that has been *h*
Eph 3: 9 for ages past was kept *h* in God,
Col 1:26 the mystery that has been kept *h*
2: 3 in whom are *h* all the treasures
3: 3 and your life is now *h* with Christ

HIDE (HID HIDDEN HIDING)

Dt 31:17 I will *h* my face from them,
Ps 17: 8 *h* me in the shadow of your wings
27: 5 he will *h* me in the shelter
143: 9 for I *h* myself in you.
Isa 53: 3 one from whom men *h* their faces

HIDING (HIDE)

Ps 32: 7 You are my *h* place;
Pr 28:12 to power, men go into *h.*

HIGH

Ge 14:18 He was priest of God Most *H,*
14:22 God Most *H,* Creator of heaven
Ps 21: 7 the unfailing love of the Most *H*
82: 6 you are all sons of the Most *H.'*
Isa 14:14 I will make myself like the Most *H*
Da 4:17 know that the Most *H* is sovereign
Mk 5: 7 Jesus, Son of the Most *H* God?
Heb 7: 1 and priest of God Most *H.*

HIGHWAY

Isa 40: 3 a *h* for our God.

HILL (HILLS)

Ps 24: 3 ascend the *h* of the LORD?
Isa 40: 4 every mountain and *h* made low;
Mt 5:14 A city on a *h* cannot be hidden.
Lk 3: 5 every mountain and *h* made low.

HILLS (HILL)

1Ki 20:23 "Their gods are gods of the *h.*
Ps 50:10 and the cattle on a thousand *h.*
121: 1 I lift up my eyes to the *h*—
Hos 10: 8 and to the *h,* "Fall on us!"
Lk 23:30 and to the *h,* "Cover us!" '
Rev 17: 9 The seven heads are seven *h*

HINDER (HINDERED HINDERS)

1Sa 14: 6 Nothing can *h* the LORD
Mt 19:14 come to me, and do not *h* them,
1Co 9:12 anything rather than *h* the gospel
1Pe 3: 7 so that nothing will *h* your prayers.

HINDERED (HINDER)

Lk 11:52 and you have *h* those who were

HINDERS (HINDER)

Heb 12: 1 let us throw off everything that *h*

HINT*

Eph 5: 3 even a *h* of sexual immorality,

HIP

Ge 32:32 socket of Jacob's *h* was touched

HIRAM

King of Tyre; helped David build his palace (2Sa 5:11-12; 1Ch 14:1); helped Solomon build the temple (1Ki 5; 2Ch 2) and his navy (1Ki 9:10-27; 2Ch 8).

HIRED

Lk 15:15 and *h* himself out to a citizen
Jn 10:12 *h* hand is not the shepherd who

HOARDED (HOARDS)

Ecc 5:13 wealth *h* to the harm of its owner,
Jas 5: 3 You have *h* wealth in the last days.

HOARDS (HOARDED)

Pr 11:26 People curse the man who *h* grain,

HOLD (HELD HOLDS)

Ex 20: 7 LORD will not *h* anyone guiltless
Lev 19:13 " 'Do not *h* back the wages
Dt 5:11 LORD will not *h* anyone guiltless
11:22 in all his ways and to *h* fast to him
13: 4 serve him and *h* fast to him.
30:20 listen to his voice, and *h* fast to him
Jos 22: 5 to *h* fast to him and to serve him
2Ki 4:16 "you will *h* a son in your arms."
Ps 18:16 from on high and took *h* of me;
73:23 you *h* me by my right hand.
Pr 4: 4 "Lay *h* of my words
Isa 41:13 who takes *h* of your right hand
54: 2 do not *h* back;
Eze 3:18 and I will *h* you accountable
3:20 and I will *h* you accountable
33: 6 I will *h* the watchman accountable
Zec 8:23 nations will take firm *h* of one Jew
Mk 11:25 if you *h* anything against anyone,
Jn 20:17 Jesus said, "Do not *h* on to me,
Php 2:16 as you *h* out the word of life—
3:12 but I press on to take *h* of that
Col 1:17 and in him all things *h* together.
1Th 5:21 *H* on to the good.
1Ti 6:12 Take *h* of the eternal life
Heb 10:23 Let us *h* unswervingly

HOLDS (HOLD)

Pr 10:19 but he who *h* his tongue is wise.
17:28 and discerning if he *h* his tongue.

HOLES

Hag 1: 6 to put them in a purse with *h* in it."
Mt 8:20 "Foxes have *h* and birds

HOLINESS* (HOLY)

Ex 15:11 majestic in *h,*
Dt 32:51 because you did not uphold my *h*
1Ch 16:29 the LORD in the splendor of his *h.*
2Ch 20:21 him for the splendor of his *h*
Ps 29: 2 in the splendor of his *h.*
89:35 Once for all, I have sworn by my *h*
93: 5 *h* adorns your house
96: 9 in the splendor of his *h;*
Isa 29:23 they will acknowledge the *h*
35: 8 it will be called the Way of *H.*
Eze 36:23 I will show the *h* of my great name,
38:23 I will show my greatness and my *h,*
Am 4: 2 LORD has sworn by his *h:*
Lk 1:75 fear in *h* and righteousness
Ro 1: 4 the Spirit of *h* was declared
6:19 to righteousness leading to *h.*
6:22 the benefit you reap leads to *h,*
1Co 1:30 our righteousness, *h*
2Co 1:12 in the *h* and sincerity that are
7: 1 perfecting *h* out of reverence
Eph 4:24 God in true righteousness and *h.*
1Ti 2: 2 quiet lives in all godliness and *h.*
2:15 love and *h* with propriety.
Heb 12:10 that we may share in his *h.*
12:14 without *h* no one will see the Lord.

HOLY (HALLOWED HOLINESS)

Ge 2: 3 the seventh day and made it *h,*
Ex 3: 5 you are standing is *h* ground."

Ex 16:23 a *h* Sabbath to the LORD.
19: 6 kingdom of priests and a *h* nation.'
20: 8 the Sabbath day by keeping it *h*.
26:33 Place from the Most *H* Place.
26:33 curtain will separate the *H* Place
28:36 seal: *H* TO THE LORD.
29:37 Then the altar will be most *h*,
30:10 It is most *h* to the LORD."
30:29 them so they will be most *h*,
31:13 I am the LORD, who makes you *h*.
40: 9 all its furnishings, and it will be *h*.
Lev 10: 3 I will show myself *h*;
10:10 must distinguish between the *h*
10:13 in a *h* place, because it is your share
11:44 and be *h*, because I am *h*.
11:45 therefore be *h*, because I am *h*.
19: 2 'Be *h* because I, the LORD your
19: 8 he has desecrated what is *h*
19:24 the fourth year all its fruit will be *h*,
20: 3 and profaned my *h* name.
20: 7 " 'Consecrate yourselves and be *h*,
20: 8 I am the LORD, who makes you *h*.
20:26 You are to be *h* to me because I,
21: 6 They must be *h* to their God
21: 8 Consider them *h*, because I
22: 9 am the LORD, who makes them *h*.
22:32 Do not profane my *h* name.
25:12 For it is a jubilee and is to be *h*
27: 9 given to the LORD becomes *h*.
Nu 4:15 they must not touch the *h* things
6: 5 He must be *h* until the period
20:12 as *h* in the sight of the Israelites,
20:13 and where he showed himself *h*
Dt 5:12 the Sabbath day by keeping it *h*,
23:14 Your camp must be *h*,
26:15 from heaven, your *h* dwelling place
33: 2 He came with myriads of *h* ones
Jos 5:15 place where you are standing is *h*."
24:19 He is a *h* God; he is a jealous God.
1Sa 2: 2 "There is no one *h* like the LORD;
6:20 of the LORD, this *h* God?
21: 5 even on missions that are not *h*.
2Ki 4: 9 often comes our way is a *h* man
1Ch 16:10 Glory in his *h* name;
16:35 may give thanks to your *h* name,
29: 3 I have provided for this *h* temple:
2Ch 30:27 heaven, his *h* dwelling place.
Ezr 9: 2 and have mingled the *h* race
Ne 11: 1 the *h* city, while the remaining nine
Job 6:10 not denied the words of the *H* One.
Ps 2: 6 King on Zion, my *h* hill."
11: 4 The LORD is in his *h* temple;
16:10 will you let your *H* One see decay.
22: 3 you are enthroned as the *H* One;
24: 3 Who may stand in his *h* place?
30: 4 praise his *h* name.
77:13 Your ways, O God, are *h*.
78:54 to the border of his *h* land,
99: 3 he is *h*.
99: 5 he is *h*.
99: 9 for the LORD our God is *h*.
105: 3 Glory in his *h* name;
111: 9 *h* and awesome is his name.
Pr 9:10 of the *H* One is understanding.
Isa 5:16 the *h* God will show himself *h*
6: 3 *H*, *h*, *h* is the LORD Almighty;
8:13 is the one you are to regard as *h*,
29:23 they will keep my name *h*;
40:25 who is my equal?" says the *H* One.
43: 3 the *H* One of Israel, your Savior;
54: 5 *H* One of Israel is your Redeemer;
57:15 who lives forever, whose name is *h*:
58:13 and the LORD's *h* day honorable,
Jer 17:22 but keep the Sabbath day *h*,
Eze 20:41 I will show myself *h* among you
22:26 to my law and profane my *h* things;
28:22 and show myself *h* within her.
28:25 I will show myself *h* among them
36:20 nations they profaned my *h* name,
38:16 when I show myself *h* through you
44:23 the difference between the *h*
Da 9:24 prophecy and to anoint the most *h*.
Hab 2:20 But the LORD is in his *h* temple;
Zec 14: 5 and all the *h* ones with him.
14:20 On that day *H* TO THE LORD
Mt 24:15 in the *h* place 'the abomination
Mk 1:24 the *H* One of God!" "Be quiet!"
Lk 1:35 the *h* one to be born will be called
1:49 *h* is his name.
4:34 the *H* One of God!" "Be quiet!"
Jn 6:69 and know that you are the *H* One
Ac 2:27 will you let your *H* One see decay.
13:35 will not let your *H* One see decay.'
Ro 1: 2 prophets in the *H* Scriptures
7:12 and the commandment is *h*,
Ro 11:16 if the root is *h*, so are the branches.
12: 1 as living sacrifices, *h* and pleasing
1Co 1: 2 in Christ Jesus and called to be *h*,
7:14 be unclean, but as it is, they are *h*.
Eph 1: 4 the creation of the world to be *h*
2:21 and rises to become a *h* temple
3: 5 by the Spirit to God's *h* apostles
5: 3 improper for God's *h* people.
5:26 up for her to make her *h*,
Col 1:22 death to present you *h* in his sight,
1Th 2:10 and so is God, of how *h*,
3:13 and *h* in the presence of our God
3:13 comes with all his *h* ones.
4: 7 us to be impure, but to live a *h* life.
2Th 1:10 to be glorified in his *h* people
1Ti 2: 8 to lift up *h* hands in prayer,
2Ti 1: 9 saved us and called us to a *h* life—
2:21 for noble purposes, made *h*,
3:15 you have known the *h* Scriptures,
Tit 1: 8 upright, *h* and disciplined.
Heb 2:11 Both the one who makes men *h*
7:26 one who is *h*, blameless, pure,
10:10 we have been made *h*
10:14 those who are being made *h*.
10:19 to enter the Most *H* Place
12:14 in peace with all men and to be *h*;
13:12 gate to make the people *h*
1Pe 1:15 But just as he who called you is *h*,
1:16 is written: "Be *h*, because I am *h*."
2: 5 house to be a *h* priesthood,
2: 9 a royal priesthood, a *h* nation,
3: 5 For this is the way the *h* women
2Pe 3:11 You ought to live *h* and godly lives
Jude :14 upon thousands of his *h* ones
Rev 3: 7 are the words of him who is *h*
4: 8 "*H*, *h*, *h* is the Lord God
15: 4 For you alone are *h*.
20: 6 and *h* are those who have part
22:11 let him who is *h* continue to be *h*."

HOME (HOMES)

Dt 6: 7 Talk about them when you sit at *h*
11:19 about them when you sit at *h*
20: 5 Let him go *h*, or he may die
24: 5 is to be free to stay at *h*
Ru 1:11 "Return *h*, my daughters.
2Sa 7:10 them so that they can have a *h*
1Ch 16:43 and David returned *h* to bless his
Ps 84: 3 Even the sparrow has found a *h*,
113: 9 settles the barren woman in her *h*
Pr 3:33 but he blesses the *h* of the righteous
27: 8 is a man who strays from his *h*.
Ecc 12: 5 Then man goes to his eternal *h*
Eze 36: 8 for they will soon come *h*.
Mic 2: 2 They defraud a man of his *h*,
Mt 1:24 and took Mary *h* as his wife.
Mk 10:29 "no one who has left *h* or brothers
Lk 10:38 named Martha opened her *h*
Jn 14:23 to him and make our *h* with him.
19:27 this disciple took her into his *h*.
Ac 16:15 baptized, she invited us to her *h*.
Tit 2: 5 to be busy at *h*, to be kind,

HOMELESS*

1Co 4:11 we are brutally treated, we are *h*.

HOMES (HOME)

Ne 4:14 daughters, your wives and your *h*."
Isa 32:18 in secure *h*,
Mk 10:30 as much in this present age (*h*,
1Ti 5:14 to manage their *h* and to give

HOMETOWN

Mt 13:57 "Only in his *h*
Lk 4:24 "no prophet is accepted in his *h*.

HOMOSEXUAL*

1Co 6: 9 male prostitutes nor *h* offenders

HONEST (HONESTY)

Lev 19:36 Use *h* scales and *h* weights,
Dt 25:15 and *h* weights and measures,
Job 31: 6 let God weigh me in *h* scales
Pr 12:17 truthful witness gives *h* testimony,

HONESTY (HONEST)

2Ki 12:15 they acted with complete *h*.

HONEY (HONEYCOMB)

Ex 3: 8 a land flowing with milk and *h*—
Jdg 14: 8 a swarm of bees and some *h*,
1Sa 14:26 they saw the *h* oozing out,
Ps 19:10 than *h* from the comb.
119:103 sweeter than *h* to my mouth!
Pr 25:16 If you find *h*, eat just enough—
SS 4:11 milk and *h* are under your tongue.
Isa 7:15 and *h* when he knows enough
Eze 3: 3 it tasted as sweet as *h* in my mouth.
Mt 3: 4 His food was locusts and wild *h*.
Rev 10: 9 mouth it will be as sweet as *h*."

HONEYCOMB (HONEY)

SS 4:11 Your lips drop sweetness as the *h*,
5: 1 I have eaten my *h* and my honey;

HONOR (HONORABLE HONORABLY HONORED HONORS)

Ex 20:12 "*H* your father and your mother,
Nu 20:12 trust in me enough to *h* me
25:13 he was zealous for the *h* of his God
Dt 5:16 "*H* your father and your mother,
Jdg 4: 9 going about this, the *h* will not be
1Sa 2: 8 and has them inherit a throne of *h*.
2:30 Those who *h* me I will *h*,
1Ch 29:12 Wealth and *h* come from you;
2Ch 1:11 or *h*, nor for the death
18: 1 had great wealth and *h*,
Est 6: 6 for the man the king delights to *h*
Ps 8: 5 and crowned him with glory and *h*.
45:11 *h* him, for he is your lord.
84:11 the LORD bestows favor and *h*;
Pr 3: 9 *H* the LORD with your wealth,
3:35 The wise inherit *h*,
15:33 and humility comes before *h*.
18:12 but humility comes before *h*.
20: 3 It is to a man's *h* to avoid strife,
25:27 is it honorable to seek one's own *h*.
Isa 29:13 and *h* me with their lips,
Jer 33: 9 and *h* before all nations
Mt 13:57 own house is a prophet without *h*."
15: 4 '*H* your father and mother'
15: 8 These people *h* me with their lips,
19:19 *h* your father and mother,'
23: 6 they love the place of *h* at banquets
Mk 6: 4 own house is a prophet without *h*."
Lk 14: 8 do not take the place of *h*,
Jn 5:23 that all may *h* the Son just
7:18 does so to gain *h* for himself,
12:26 My Father will *h* the one who
Ro 12:10 *H* one another above yourselves.
1Co 6:20 Therefore *h* God with your body.
Eph 6: 2 "*H* your father and mother"—
1Ti 5:17 well are worthy of double *h*,
Heb 2: 7 you crowned him with glory and *h*
Rev 4: 9 *h* and thanks to him who sits

HONORABLE (HONOR)

1Th 4: 4 body in a way that is holy and *h*,

HONORABLY (HONOR)

Heb 13:18 and desire to live *h* in every way.

HONORED (HONOR)

Ps 12: 8 when what is vile is *h* among men.
Pr 13:18 but whoever heeds correction is *h*.
Da 4:34 I *h* and glorified him who lives
1Co 12:26 if one part is *h*, every part rejoices
Heb 13: 4 Marriage should be *h* by all,

HONORS (HONOR)

Ps 15: 4 but *h* those who fear the LORD,
Pr 14:31 to the needy *h* God.

HOOF

Ex 10:26 not a *h* is to be left behind.

HOOKS

Isa 2: 4 and their spears into pruning *h*.
Joel 3:10 and your pruning *h* into spears.
Mic 4: 3 and their spears into pruning *h*.

HOPE (HOPES)

Job 13:15 Though he slay me, yet will I *h*
Ps 25: 3 No one whose *h* is in you
33:17 A horse is a vain *h* for deliverance;
33:18 on those whose *h* is
42: 5 Put your *h* in God,
62: 5 my *h* comes from him.
119: 74 for I have put my *h* in your word.
130: 5 and in his word I put my *h*.
130: 7 O Israel, put your *h* in the LORD,
146: 5 whose *h* is in the LORD his God,
147: 11 who put their *h* in his unfailing love
Pr 13:12 *H* deferred makes the heart sick,
23:18 There is surely a future *h* for you,
Isa 40:31 but those who *h* in the LORD
Jer 29:11 plans to give you *h* and a future.
La 3:21 and therefore I have *h*:
Zec 9:12 to your fortress, O prisoners of *h*;
Ro 5: 4 character; and character, *h*.

Ro 8:20 in h that the creation itself will be
8:24 But h that is seen is no h at all.
8:25 if we h for what we do not yet have,
12:12 Be joyful in h, patient in affliction,
15:4 of the Scriptures we might have h.
15:13 May the God of h fill you
1Co 13:13 now these three remain: faith, h
15:19 for this life we have h in Christ,
Eph 2:12 without h and without God
Col 1:27 Christ in you, the h of glory.
1Th 1:3 and your endurance inspired by h
5:8 and the h of salvation as a helmet.
1Ti 4:10 that we have put our h
6:17 but to put their h in God,
Tit 1:2 resting on the h of eternal life,
2:13 while we wait for the blessed h—
Heb 6:19 We have this h as an anchor
10:23 unswervingly to the h we profess,
11:1 faith is being sure of what we h for
1Jn 3:3 Everyone who has this h

HOPES (HOPE)

1Co 13:7 always h, always perseveres.

HORN (HORNS)

Ex 19:13 when the ram's h sounds a long
27:2 Make a h at each of the four
Da 7:8 This h had eyes like the eyes

HORNS (HORN)

Da 7:24 ten h are ten kings who will come
Rev 5:6 He had seven h and seven eyes,
12:3 and ten h and seven crowns
13:1 He had ten h and seven heads,
17:3 and had seven heads and ten h.

HORRIBLE (HORROR)

Jer 5:30 "A h and shocking thing

HORROR (HORRIBLE)

Jer 2:12 and shudder with great h,"

HORSE

Ps 147:10 not in the strength of the h,
Pr 26:3 A whip for the h, a halter
Zec 1:8 before me was a man riding a red h
Rev 6:2 and there before me was a white h!
6:4 Come!" Then another h came out,
6:5 and there before me was a black h!
6:8 and there before me was a pale h!
19:11 and there before me was a white h,

HOSANNA

Mt 21:9 "H in the highest!"
Mk 11:9 "H!"
Jn 12:13 "H!"

HOSEA

Prophet whose wife and family pictured the unfaithfulness of Israel (Hos 1-3).

HOSHEA (JOSHUA)

1. Original name of Joshua (Nu 13:16).
2. Last king of Israel (2Ki 15:30; 17:1-6).

HOSPITABLE* (HOSPITALITY)

1Ti 3:2 self-controlled, respectable, h,
Tit 1:8 Rather he must be h, one who loves

HOSPITABLY* (HOSPITALITY)

Ac 28:7 and for three days entertained us h.

HOSPITALITY* (HOSPITABLE HOSPITABLY)

Ro 12:13 Practice h.
16:23 whose h I and the whole church
1Ti 5:10 as bringing up children, showing h,
1Pe 4:9 Offer h to one another
3Jn :8 therefore to show h to such men

HOSTILE (HOSTILITY)

Ro 8:7 the sinful mind is h to God.

HOSTILITY (HOSTILE)

Eph 2:14 wall of h, by abolishing
2:16 by which he put to death their h.

HOT

1Ti 4:2 have been seared as with a h iron.
Rev 3:15 that you are neither cold nor h.

HOT-TEMPERED (TEMPER)

Pr 15:18 A h man stirs up dissension,
19:19 A h man must pay the penalty;
22:24 Do not make friends with a h man,
29:22 and a h one commits many sins.

HOTHEADED (HEAD)

Pr 14:16 but a fool is h and reckless.

HOUR

Ecc 9:12 knows when his h will come:
Mt 6:27 you by worrying can add a single h
Lk 12:40 the Son of Man will come at an h
Jn 12:23 The h has come for the Son of Man
12:27 for this very reason I came to this h

HOUSE (HOUSEHOLD HOUSEHOLDS HOUSES STOREHOUSE)

Ex 12:22 the door of his h until morning.
20:17 shall not covet your neighbor's h.
Nu 12:7 he is faithful in all my h.
Dt 5:21 desire on your neighbor's h
2Sa 7:11 LORD himself will establish a h
1Ch 17:23 and his h be established forever.
Ne 10:39 "We will not neglect the h
Ps 23:6 I will dwell in the h of the LORD
27:4 dwell in the h of the LORD
69:9 for zeal for your h consumes me,
84:10 a doorkeeper in the h of my God
122:1 "Let us go to the h of the LORD."
127:1 Unless the LORD builds the h,
Pr 7:27 Her h is a highway to the grave,
21:9 than share a h with a quarrelsome
Isa 56:7 a h of prayer for all nations."
Jer 7:11 Has this h, which bears my Name,
18:2 "Go down to the potter's h,
Eze 33:7 made you a watchman for the h
Joel 3:18 will flow out of the LORD's h
Zec 13:6 given at the h of my friends.'
Mt 7:24 is like a wise man who built his h
10:11 and stay at his h until you leave.
12:29 can anyone enter a strong man's h
21:13 My h will be called a h of prayer,'
Mk 3:25 If a h is divided against itself,
11:17 " 'My h will be called
Lk 6:48 He is like a man building a h,
10:7 Do not move around from h to h.
11:17 a h divided against itself will fall.
11:24 'I will return to the h I left.'
15:8 sweep the h and search carefully
19:9 Today salvation has come to this h,
Jn 2:16 How dare you turn my Father's h
2:17 "Zeal for your h will consume me."
12:3 the h was filled with the fragrance
14:2 In my Father's h are many rooms;
Ac 20:20 you publicly and from h to h.
Ro 16:5 the church that meets at their h.
Heb 3:3 the builder of a h has greater honor
1Pe 2:5 built into a spiritual h to be a holy

HOUSEHOLD (HOUSE)

Ex 12:3 lamb for his family, one for each h.
Jos 24:15 my h, we will serve the LORD."
Pr 31:21 it snows, she has no fear for her h;
31:27 over the affairs of her h
Mic 7:6 are the members of his own h.
Mt 10:36 will be the members of his own h.'
12:25 or h divided against itself will not
Ac 16:31 you will be saved—you and your h
Eph 2:19 people and members of God's h,
1Ti 3:12 manage his children and his h well.
3:15 to conduct themselves in God's h,

HOUSEHOLDS (HOUSE)

Tit 1:11 because they are ruining whole h

HOUSES (HOUSE)

Ex 12:27 passed over the h of the Israelites
Mt 19:29 everyone who has left h or brothers

HOVERING* (HOVERS)

Ge 1:2 of God was h over the waters.
Isa 31:5 Like birds h overhead,

HOVERS* (HOVERING)

Dt 32:11 and h over its young,

HULDAH*

Prophetess inquired by Hilkiah for Josiah (2Ki 22; 2Ch 34:14-28).

HUMAN (HUMANITY)

Lev 24:17 If anyone takes the life of a h being,
Isa 52:14 his form marred beyond h likeness
Jn 8:15 You judge by h standards;
Ro 1:3 as to his h nature was a descendant
9:5 from them is traced the h ancestry
1Co 1:17 not with words of h wisdom,
1:26 of you were wise by h standards;
2:13 not in words taught us by h wisdom
2Co 3:3 of stone but on tablets of h hearts.
Gal 3:3 to attain your goal by h effort?
2Pe 2:18 lustful desires of sinful h nature,

HUMANITY* (HUMAN)

Heb 2:14 he too shared in their h so that

HUMBLE (HUMBLED HUMBLES HUMILIATE HUMILIATED HUMILITY)

Nu 12:3 (Now Moses was a very h man,
2Ch 7:14 will h themselves and pray
Ps 18:27 You save the h
25:9 He guides the h in what is right
149:4 he crowns the h with salvation.
Pr 3:34 but gives grace to the h.
Isa 66:2 he who is h and contrite in spirit,
Mt 11:29 for I am gentle and h in heart,
Eph 4:2 Be completely h and gentle;
Jas 4:6 but gives grace to the h."
4:10 H yourselves before the Lord,
1Pe 5:5 but gives grace to the h."
5:6 H yourselves,

HUMBLED (HUMBLE)

Mt 23:12 whoever exalts himself will be h,
Lk 14:11 who exalts himself will be h,
Php 2:8 he h himself

HUMBLES* (HUMBLE)

1Sa 2:7 he h and he exalts.
Isa 26:5 He h those who dwell on high,
Mt 18:4 whoever h himself like this child is
23:12 whoever h himself will be exalted.
Lk 14:11 he who h himself will be exalted."
18:14 he who h himself will be exalted."

HUMILIATE* (HUMBLE)

Pr 25:7 than for him to h you
1Co 11:22 and h those who have nothing?

HUMILIATED (HUMBLE)

Jer 31:19 I was ashamed and h
Lk 14:9 h, you will have to take the least

HUMILITY* (HUMBLE)

Ps 45:4 of truth, h and righteousness;
Pr 11:2 but with h comes wisdom.
15:33 and h comes before honor.
18:12 but h comes before honor.
22:4 H and the fear of the LORD
Zep 2:3 Seek righteousness, seek h;
Ac 20:19 I served the Lord with great h
Php 2:3 but in h consider others better
Col 2:18 let anyone who delights in false h
2:23 their false h and their harsh
3:12 h, gentleness and patience.
Tit 3:2 and to show true h toward all men.
Jas 3:13 in the h that comes from wisdom.
1Pe 5:5 clothe yourselves with h

HUNG (HANG)

Dt 21:23 anyone who is h on a tree is
Mt 18:6 him to have a large millstone h
Lk 19:48 all the people h on his words.
Gal 3:13 "Cursed is everyone who is h

HUNGER (HUNGRY)

Ne 9:15 In their h you gave them bread
Pr 6:30 to satisfy his h when he is starving.
Mt 5:6 Blessed are those who h
Lk 6:21 Blessed are you who h now,
2Co 6:5 sleepless nights and h; in purity,
11:27 I have known h and thirst
Rev 7:16 Never again will they h;

HUNGRY (HUNGER)

Job 24:10 carry the sheaves, but still go h.
Ps 107:9 and fills the h with good things.
146:7 and gives food to the h.
Pr 19:15 and the shiftless man goes h.
25:21 If your enemy is h, give him food
27:7 to the h even what is bitter tastes
Isa 58:7 not to share your food with the h
58:10 spend yourselves in behalf of the h
Eze 18:7 but gives his food to the h
18:16 but gives his food to the h
Mt 15:32 I do not want to send them away h,
25:35 For I was h and you gave me
25:42 For I was h and you gave me
Lk 1:53 He has filled the h with good things
Jn 6:35 comes to me will never go h,
Ro 12:20 "If your enemy is h, feed him;
1Co 4:11 To this very hour we go h
Php 4:12 whether well fed or h,

HUR

Ex 17:12 Aaron and *H* held his hands up—

HURL

Mic 7:19 *h* all our iniquities into the depths

HURT (HURTS)

Ecc 8: 9 it over others to his own *h.*
Mk 16:18 deadly poison, it will not *h* them
Rev 2:11 He who overcomes will not be *h*

HURTS* (HURT)

Ps 15: 4 even when it *h,*
Pr 26:28 A lying tongue hates those it *h,*

HUSBAND (HUSBAND'S HUSBANDS)

Pr 31:11 Her *h* has full confidence in her
31:23 Her *h* is respected at the city gate,
31:28 her *h* also, and he praises her:
Isa 54: 5 For your Maker is your *h*—
Jer 3:14 the LORD, "for I am your *h.*
3:20 like a woman unfaithful to her *h,*
Jn 4:17 "I have no *h,*" she replied.
Ro 7: 2 a married woman is bound to her *h*
1Co 7: 2 and each woman her own *h.*
7: 3 The *h* should fulfill his marital duty
7:10 wife must not separate from her *h.*
7:11 And a *h* must not divorce his wife.
7:13 And if a woman has a *h* who is not
7:14 For the unbelieving *h* has been
7:39 A woman is bound to her *h* as long
7:39 But if her *h* dies, she is free
2Co 11: 2 I promised you to one *h,* to Christ,
Gal 4:27 woman than of her who has a *h.*"
Eph 5:23 For the *h* is the head of the wife
5:33 and the wife must respect her *h.*
1Ti 3: 2 the *h* of but one wife, temperate,
3:12 A deacon must be the *h* of
5: 9 has been faithful to her *h,*
Tit 1: 6 An elder must be blameless, the *h*

HUSBANDMAN see GARDENER

HUSBAND'S (HUSBAND)

Dt 25: 5 Her *h* brother shall take her
Pr 12: 4 of noble character is her *h* crown,
1Co 7: 4 the *h* body does not belong

HUSBANDS (HUSBAND)

Eph 5:22 submit to your *h* as to the Lord.
5:25 *H,* love your wives, just
5:28 *h* ought to love their wives
Col 3:18 submit to your *h,* as is fitting
3:19 *H,* love your wives and do not be
Tit 2: 4 the younger women to love their *h*
2: 5 and to be subject to their *h,*
1Pe 3: 1 same way be submissive to your *h*
3: 7 *H,* in the same way be considerate

HUSHAI

Wise man of David who frustrated Ahithophel's advice and foiled Absalom's revolt (2Sa 15:32-37; 16:15-17:16; 1Ch 27:33).

HYMN* (HYMNS)

Ps 40: 3 a *h* of praise to our God.
Mt 26:30 they had sung a *h,* they went out
Mk 14:26 they had sung a *h,* they went out
1Co 14:26 everyone has a *h,* or a word

HYMNS* (HYMN)

Ac 16:25 Silas were praying and singing *h*
Ro 15: 9 I will sing *h* to your name."
Eph 5:19 to one another with psalms, *h*
Col 3:16 *h* and spiritual songs with gratitude

HYPOCRISY* (HYPOCRITE HYPOCRITES HYPOCRITICAL)

Mt 23:28 but on the inside you are full of *h*
Mk 12:15 we?" But Jesus knew their *h.*
Lk 12: 1 yeast of the Pharisees, which is *h.*
Gal 2:13 The other Jews joined him in his *h,*
2:13 by their *h* even Barnabas was led
1Pe 2: 1 *h,* envy, and slander of every kind.

HYPOCRITE* (HYPOCRISY)

Mt 7: 5 You *h,* first take the plank out
Lk 6:42 You *h,* first take the plank out

HYPOCRITES* (HYPOCRISY)

Ps 26: 4 nor do I consort with *h;*
Mt 6: 2 as the *h* do in the synagogues
6: 5 when you pray, do not be like the *h*
6:16 do not look somber as the *h* do,
15: 7 You *h!* Isaiah was right
22:18 their evil intent, said, "You *h,*
23:13 of the law and Pharisees, you *h!*
23:15 of the law and Pharisees, you *h!*
23:23 of the law and Pharisees, you *h!*
23:25 of the law and Pharisees, you *h!*
23:27 you *h!* You are like whitewashed
23:29 of the law and Pharisees, you *h!*
24:51 and assign him a place with the *h,*
Mk 7: 6 when he prophesied about you *h;*
Lk 12:56 *H!* You know how
13:15 The Lord answered him, "You *h!*

HYPOCRITICAL* (HYPOCRISY)

1Ti 4: 2 teachings come through *h* liars,

HYSSOP

Ex 12:22 Take a bunch of *h,* dip it
Ps 51: 7 with *h,* and I will be clean;
Jn 19:29 the sponge on a stalk of the *h* plant,

ICHABOD

1Sa 4:21 She named the boy *I,* saying,

IDLE* (IDLENESS IDLERS)

Dt 32:47 They are not just *i* words for you—
Job 11: 3 Will your *i* talk reduce men
Ecc 10:18 if his hands are *i,* the house leaks.
11: 6 at evening let not your hands be *i,*
Isa 58:13 as you please or speaking *i* words,
Col 2:18 mind puffs him up with *i* notions.
1Th 5:14 those who are *i,* encourage
2Th 3: 6 away from every brother who is *i*
3: 7 We were not *i* when we were
3:11 We hear that some among you are *i*
1Ti 5:13 they get into the habit of being *i*

IDLENESS* (IDLE)

Pr 31:27 and does not eat the bread of *i.*

IDLERS* (IDLE)

1Ti 5:13 And not only do they become *i,*

IDOL (IDOLATER IDOLATERS IDOLATRY IDOLS)

Ex 20: 4 make for yourself an *i* in the form
32: 4 made it into an *i* cast in the shape
Isa 40:19 As for an *i,* a craftsman casts it,
41: 7 He nails down the *i*
44:15 he makes an *i* and bows down to it.
44:17 From the rest he makes a god, his *i;*
Hab 2:18 "Of what value is an *i,*
1Co 8: 4 We know that an *i* is nothing at all

IDOLATER* (IDOL)

1Co 5:11 an *i* or a slanderer, a drunkard
Eph 5: 5 greedy person—such a man is an *i*

IDOLATERS (IDOL)

1Co 5:10 or the greedy and swindlers, or *i.*
6: 9 Neither the sexually immoral nor *i*

IDOLATRY (IDOL)

1Sa 15:23 and arrogance like the evil of *i.*
1Co 10:14 my dear friends, flee from *i.*
Gal 5:20 and debauchery; *i* and witchcraft;
Col 3: 5 evil desires and greed, which is *i.*
1Pe 4: 3 orgies, carousing and detestable *i.*

IDOLS (IDOL)

Dt 32:16 angered him with their detestable *i.*
Ps 78:58 aroused his jealousy with their *i.*
Isa 44: 9 All who make *i* are nothing,
Eze 23:39 sacrificed their children to their *i,*
Ac 15:20 to abstain from food polluted by *i,*
21:25 abstain from food sacrificed to *i,*
1Co 8: 1 Now about food sacrificed to *i:*
1Jn 5:21 children, keep yourselves from *i.*
Rev 2:14 to sin by eating food sacrificed to *i*

IGNORANT (IGNORE)

1Co 15:34 for there are some who are *i* of God
Heb 5: 2 to deal gently with those who are *i*
1Pe 2:15 good you should silence the *i* talk
2Pe 3:16 which *i* and unstable people distort

IGNORE (IGNORANT IGNORED IGNORES)

Dt 22: 1 do not *i* it but be sure
Ps 9:12 he does not *i* the cry of the afflicted
Heb 2: 3 if we *i* such a great salvation?

IGNORED (IGNORE)

Hos 4: 6 you have *i* the law of your God,
1Co 14:38 he ignores this, he himself will be *i.*

IGNORES* (IGNORE)

Pr 10:17 whoever *i* correction leads others
13:18 He who *i* discipline comes
15:32 He who *i* discipline despises
1Co 14:38 If he *i* this, he himself will be

ILL (ILLNESS)

Mt 4:24 brought to him all who were *i*

ILL-GOTTEN

Pr 1:19 the end of all who go after *i* gain;
10: 2 *I* treasures are of no value,

ILL-TEMPERED* (TEMPER)

Pr 21:19 than with a quarrelsome and *i* wife.

ILLEGITIMATE

Heb 12: 8 then you are *i* children

ILLNESS (ILL)

2Ki 8: 9 'Will I recover from this *i?*' "
2Ch 16:12 even in his *i* he did not seek help
Ps 41: 3 and restore him from his bed of *i.*
Isa 38: 9 king of Judah after his *i*

ILLUMINATED*

Rev 18: 1 and the earth was *i* by his splendor.

IMAGE (IMAGES)

Ge 1:26 "Let us make man in our *i,*
1:27 So God created man in his own *i,*
9: 6 for in the *i* of God
Dt 27:15 "Cursed is the man who carves an *i*
Isa 40:18 What *i* will you compare him to?
Da 3: 1 King Nebuchadnezzar made an *i*
1Co 11: 7 since he is the *i* and glory of God;
2Co 4: 4 glory of Christ, who is the *i* of God.
Col 1:15 He is the *i* of the invisible God,
3:10 in knowledge in the *i* of its Creator.
Rev 13:14 them to set up an *i* in honor

IMAGES (IMAGE)

Ps 97: 7 All who worship *i* are put to shame,
Jer 10:14 His *i* are a fraud;
Ro 1:23 of the immortal God for *i* made

IMAGINATION (IMAGINE)

Eze 13: 2 who prophesy out of their own *i:*

IMAGINE (IMAGINATION)

Eph 3:20 more than all we ask or *i,*

IMITATE (IMITATORS)

1Co 4:16 Therefore I urge you to *i* me.
Heb 6:12 but to *i* those who through faith
13: 7 of their way of life and *i* their faith.
3Jn :11 do not *i* what is evil but what is

IMITATORS* (IMITATE)

Eph 5: 1 Be *i* of God, therefore,
1Th 1: 6 You became *i* of us and of the Lord
2:14 became *i* of God's churches

IMMANUEL*

Isa 7:14 birth to a son, and will call him *I.*
8: 8 O *I!*"
Mt 1:23 and they will call him *I*"—

IMMORAL* (IMMORALITY)

Pr 6:24 keeping you from the *i* woman,
1Co 5: 9 to associate with sexually *i* people
5:10 the people of this world who are *i,*
5:11 but is sexually *i* or greedy,
6: 9 Neither the sexually *i* nor idolaters
Eph 5: 5 No *i,* impure or greedy person—
Heb 12:16 See that no one is sexually *i,*
13: 4 the adulterer and all the sexually *i.*
Rev 21: 8 the murderers, the sexually *i,*
22:15 the sexually *i,* the murderers,

IMMORALITY* (IMMORAL)

Nu 25: 1 in sexual *i* with Moabite women,
Jer 3: 9 Because Israel's *i* mattered so little
Mt 15:19 murder, adultery, sexual *i,* theft,
Mk 7:21 sexual *i,* theft, murder, adultery,
Ac 15:20 from sexual *i,* from the meat
15:29 animals and from sexual *i.*
21:25 animals and from sexual *i.*"
Ro 13:13 not in sexual *i* and debauchery,
1Co 5: 1 reported that there is sexual *i*
6:13 The body is not meant for sexual *i,*
6:18 Flee from sexual *i.*
7: 2 But since there is so much *i,*
10: 8 We should not commit sexual *i,*

Gal 5: 19 sexual *i*, impurity and debauchery;
Eph 5: 3 must not be even a hint of sexual *i*,
Col 3: 5 sexual *i*, impurity, lust, evil desires
1Th 4: 3 that you should avoid sexual *i*;
Jude : 4 grace of our God into a license for *i*
: 7 gave themselves up to sexual *i*
Rev 2: 14 and by committing sexual *i*.
2: 20 misleads my servants into sexual *i*
2: 21 given her time to repent of her *i*,
9: 21 their sexual *i* or their thefts.

IMMORTAL* (IMMORTALITY)

Ro 1: 23 glory of the *i* God for images made
1Ti 1: 17 Now to the King eternal, *i*,
6: 16 who alone is *i* and who lives

IMMORTALITY* (IMMORTAL)

Pr 12: 28 along that path is *i*.
Ro 2: 7 honor and *i*, he will give eternal life
1Co 15: 53 and the mortal with *i*.
15: 54 with *i*, then the saying that is
2Ti 1: 10 and *i* to light through the gospel.

IMPARTIAL*

Jas 3: 17 and good fruit, *i* and sincere.

IMPARTS*

Pr 29: 15 The rod of correction *i* wisdom,

IMPERFECT*

1Co 13: 10 perfection comes, the *i* disappears.

IMPERISHABLE

1Co 15: 42 it is raised *i*; it is sown in dishonor,
15: 50 nor does the perishable inherit the *i*
1Pe 1: 23 not of perishable seed, but of *i*,

IMPLANTED*

Ps 94: 9 Does he who *i* the ear not hear?

IMPLORE*

Mal 1: 9 "Now *i* God to be gracious to us.
2Co 5: 20 We *i* you on Christ's behalf:

IMPORTANCE* (IMPORTANT)

1Co 15: 3 passed on to you as of first *i*:

IMPORTANT (IMPORTANCE)

Mt 6: 25 Is not life more *i* than food,
23: 23 have neglected the more *i* matters
Mk 12: 29 "The most *i* one," answered Jesus,
12: 33 as yourself is more *i* than all burnt
Php 1: 18 The *i* thing is that in every way,

IMPOSSIBLE

Mt 17: 20 Nothing will be *i* for you."
19: 26 "With man this is *i*,
Mk 10: 27 "With man this is *i*, but not
Lk 1: 37 For nothing is *i* with God."
18: 27 "What is *i* with men is possible
Ac 2: 24 it was *i* for death to keep its hold
Heb 6: 4 It is *i* for those who have once been
6: 18 things in which it is *i* for God to lie,
10: 4 because it is *i* for the blood of bulls
11: 6 without faith it is *i* to please God,

IMPOSTORS

2Ti 3: 13 and *i* will go from bad to worse,

IMPRESS* (IMPRESSES)

Dt 6: 7 *I* them on your children.

IMPRESSES* (IMPRESS)

Pr 17: 10 A rebuke *i* a man of discernment

IMPROPER*

Eph 5: 3 these are *i* for God's holy people.

IMPURE (IMPURITY)

Ac 10: 15 not call anything *i* that God has
Eph 5: 5 No immoral, *i* or greedy person—
1Th 2: 3 spring from error or *i* motives,
4: 7 For God did not call us to be *i*,
Rev 21: 27 Nothing *i* will ever enter it,

IMPURITY (IMPURE)

Ro 1: 24 hearts to sexual *i* for the degrading
Gal 5: 19 sexual immorality, *i*
Eph 4: 19 as to indulge in every kind of *i*,
5: 3 or of any kind of *i*, or of greed,
Col 3: 5 *i*, lust, evil desires and greed,

INCENSE

Ex 30: 1 altar of acacia wood for burning *i*.
40: 5 Place the gold altar of *i* in front
Ps 141: 2 my prayer be set before you like *i*;
Mt 2: 11 him with gifts of gold and of *i*
Heb 9: 4 which had the golden altar of *i*
Rev 5: 8 were holding golden bowls full of *i*,
8: 4 The smoke of the *i*, together

INCLINATION (INCLINES)

Ge 6: 5 and that every *i* of the thoughts

INCLINES* (INCLINATION)

Ecc 10: 2 The heart of the wise *i* to the right,

INCOME

Ecc 5: 10 wealth is never satisfied with his *i*.
1Co 16: 2 sum of money in keeping with his *i*,

INCOMPARABLE*

Eph 2: 7 ages he might show the *i* riches

INCREASE (EVER-INCREASING INCREASED INCREASES INCREASING)

Ge 1: 22 "Be fruitful and *i* in number
3: 16 "I will greatly *i* your pains
8: 17 be fruitful and *i* in number upon it
Ps 62: 10 though your riches *i*,
Pr 22: 16 oppresses the poor to *i* his wealth
Isa 9: 7 Of the *i* of his government
Mt 24: 12 Because of the *i* of wickedness,
Lk 17: 5 said to the Lord, "*I* our faith!"
Ac 12: 24 But the word of God continued to *i*
Ro 5: 20 added so that the trespass might *i*.
1Th 3: 12 May the Lord make your love *i*

INCREASED (INCREASE)

Ac 6: 7 of disciples in Jerusalem *i* rapidly,
Ro 5: 20 But where sin *i*, grace *i* all the more

INCREASES (INCREASE)

Pr 24: 5 and a man of knowledge *i* strength;

INCREASING (INCREASE)

Ac 6: 1 when the number of disciples was *i*,
2Th 1: 3 one of you has for each other is *i*.
2Pe 1: 8 these qualities in *i* measure,

INCREDIBLE*

Ac 26: 8 of you consider it *i* that God raises

INDECENT

Ro 1: 27 Men committed *i* acts

INDEPENDENT*

1Co 11: 11 however, woman is not *i* of man,
11: 11 of man, nor is man *i* of woman.

INDESCRIBABLE*

2Co 9: 15 Thanks be to God for his *i* gift!

INDESTRUCTIBLE*

Heb 7: 16 on the basis of the power of an *i* life

INDIGNANT

Mk 10: 14 When Jesus saw this, he was *i*.

INDISPENSABLE*

1Co 12: 22 seem to be weaker are *i*,

INEFFECTIVE*

2Pe 1: 8 they will keep you from being *i*

INEXPRESSIBLE*

2Co 12: 4 He heard *i* things, things that man
1Pe 1: 8 are filled with an *i* and glorious joy,

INFANCY* (INFANTS)

2Ti 3: 15 from *i* you have known the holy

INFANTS (INFANCY)

Ps 8: 2 From the lips of children and *i*
Mt 21: 16 " 'From the lips of children and *i*
1Co 3: 1 but as worldly—mere *i* in Christ.
14: 20 In regard to evil be *i*,
Eph 4: 14 Then we will no longer be *i*,

INFIRMITIES*

Isa 53: 4 Surely he took up our *i*
Mt 8: 17 "He took up our *i*

INFLAMED

Ro 1: 27 were *i* with lust for one another.

INFLUENTIAL*

1Co 1: 26 not many were *i*; not many were

INHABITANTS (INHABITED)

Nu 33: 55 " 'But if you do not drive out the *i*
Rev 8: 13 Woe! Woe to the *i* of the earth,

INHABITED (INHABITANTS)

Isa 45: 18 but formed it to be *i*—

INHERIT (CO-HEIRS HEIR HEIRS HERITAGE INHERITANCE)

Dt 1: 38 because he will lead Israel to *i* it.
Jos 1: 6 people to *i* the land I swore
Ps 37: 11 But the meek will *i* the land
37: 29 the righteous will *i* the land
Zec 2: 12 The LORD will *i* Judah
Mt 5: 5 for they will *i* the earth.
19: 29 as much and will *i* eternal life.
Mk 10: 17 "what must I do to *i* eternal life?"
Lk 10: 25 "what must I do to *i* eternal life?"
18: 18 what must I do to *i* eternal life?"
1Co 6: 9 the wicked will not *i* the kingdom
15: 50 blood cannot *i* the kingdom of God
Rev 21: 7 He who overcomes will *i* all this,

INHERITANCE (INHERIT)

Lev 20: 24 I will give it to you as an *i*,
Dt 4: 20 to be the people of his *i*,
10: 9 the LORD is their *i*, as the LORD
Jos 14: 3 two-and-a-half tribes their *i* east
Ps 16: 6 surely I have a delightful *i*.
33: 12 the people he chose for his *i*.
136: 21 and gave their land as an *i*,
Pr 13: 22 A good man leaves an *i*
Mt 25: 34 blessed by my Father; take your *i*,
Eph 1: 14 who is a deposit guaranteeing our *i*
5: 5 has any *i* in the kingdom of Christ
Col 1: 12 you to share in the *i* of the saints
3: 24 you know that you will receive an *i*
Heb 9: 15 receive the promised eternal *i*—
1Pe 1: 4 and into an *i* that can never perish,

INIQUITIES (INIQUITY)

Ps 78: 38 he forgave their *i*
103: 10 or repay us according to our *i*.
Isa 53: 5 he was crushed for our *i*;
53: 11 and he will bear their *i*.
59: 2 But your *i* have separated
Mic 7: 19 and hurl all our *i* into the depths

INIQUITY (INIQUITIES)

Ps 25: 11 forgive my *i*, though it is great.
32: 5 and did not cover up my *i*.
51: 2 Wash away all my *i*
51: 9 and blot out all my *i*.
Isa 53: 6 the *i* of us all.

INJURED

Eze 34: 16 will bind up the *i* and strengthen
Zec 11: 16 or heal the *i*, or feed the healthy,

INJUSTICE

2Ch 19: 7 the LORD our God there is no *i*

INK

2Co 3: 3 not with *i* but with the Spirit

INN*

Lk 2: 7 there was no room for them in the *i*
10: 34 took him to an *i* and took care

INNOCENT

Ex 23: 7 do not put an *i* or honest person
Dt 25: 1 acquitting the *i* and condemning
Pr 6: 17 hands that shed *i* blood,
17: 26 It is not good to punish an *i* man,
Mt 10: 16 shrewd as snakes and as *i* as doves.
27: 4 "for I have betrayed *i* blood."
27: 24 I am *i* of this man's blood," he said.
Ac 20: 26 declare to you today that I am *i*
Ro 16: 19 what is good, and *i* about what is
1Co 4: 4 but that does not make me *i*.

INQUIRE

Isa 8: 19 should not a people *i* of their God?

INSCRIPTION

Mt 22: 20 And whose *i*?" "Caesar's,"
2Ti 2: 19 with this *i*: "The Lord knows those

INSIGHT

1Ki 4: 29 Solomon wisdom and very great *i*,
Ps 119: 99 I have more *i* than all my teachers,
Pr 5: 1 listen well to my words of *i*,
21: 30 There is no wisdom, no *i*, no plan
Php 1: 9 more in knowledge and depth of *i*,

2Ti 2: 7 for the Lord will give you *i*

INSOLENT

Ro 1:30 God-haters, *i*, arrogant

INSPIRED*

Hos 9: 7 the *i* man a maniac.
1Th 1: 3 and your endurance *i* by hope

INSTALLED

Ps 2: 6 "I have *i* my King

INSTINCT* (INSTINCTS)

2Pe 2:12 are like brute beasts, creatures of *i*,
Jude :10 things they do understand by *i*,

INSTINCTS* (INSTINCT)

Jude :19 who follow mere natural *i*

INSTITUTED

Ro 13: 2 rebelling against what God has *i*,
1Pe 2:13 to every authority *i* among men:

INSTRUCT (INSTRUCTED INSTRUCTION INSTRUCTIONS INSTRUCTOR)

Ps 32: 8 I will *i* you and teach you
105:22 to *i* his princes as he pleased
Pr 9: 9 *I* a wise man and he will be wiser
Ro 15:14 and competent to *i* one another.
1Co 2:16 that he may *i* him?"
14:19 to *i* others than ten thousand words
2Ti 2:25 who oppose him he must gently *i*,

INSTRUCTED (INSTRUCT)

2Ch 26: 5 who *i* him in the fear of God.
Pr 21:11 a wise man is *i*, he gets knowledge.
Isa 50: 4 LORD has given me an *i* tongue,
Mt 13:52 who has been *i* about the kingdom
1Co 14:31 in turn so that everyone may be *i*

INSTRUCTION (INSTRUCT)

Pr 1: 8 Listen, my son, to your father's *i*
4: 1 Listen, my sons, to a father's *i*;
4:13 Hold on to *i*, do not let it go;
8:10 Choose my *i* instead of silver,
8:33 Listen to my *i* and be wise;
13: 1 A wise son heeds his father's *i*,
13:13 He who scorns *i* will pay for it,
16:20 Whoever gives heed to *i* prospers,
16:21 and pleasant words promote *i*.
19:20 Listen to advice and accept *i*,
23:12 Apply your heart to *i*
1Co 14: 6 or prophecy or word of *i*?
14:26 or a word of *i*, a revelation,
Eph 6: 4 up in the training and *i* of the Lord.
1Th 4: 8 he who rejects this *i* does not reject
2Th 3:14 If anyone does not obey our *i*
1Ti 1:18 I give you this *i* in keeping
6: 3 to the sound *i* of our Lord Jesus
2Ti 4: 2 with great patience and careful *i*.

INSTRUCTIONS (INSTRUCT)

1Ti 3:14 I am writing you these *i* so that,

INSTRUCTOR (INSTRUCT)

Gal 6: 6 share all good things with his *i*.

INSTRUMENT* (INSTRUMENTS)

Eze 33:32 beautiful voice and plays an *i* well,
Ac 9:15 This man is my chosen *i*
2Ti 2:21 he will be an *i* for noble purposes,

INSTRUMENTS (INSTRUMENT)

Ro 6:13 as *i* of wickedness, but rather offer

INSULT (INSULTED INSULTS)

Pr 9: 7 corrects a mocker invites *i*;
12:16 but a prudent man overlooks an *i*.
Mt 5:11 Blessed are you when people *i* you,
Lk 6:22 when they exclude you and *i* you
1Pe 3: 9 evil with evil or *i* with *i*,

INSULTED (INSULT)

Heb 10:29 and who has *i* the Spirit of grace?
Jas 2: 6 love him? But you have *i* the poor.
1Pe 4:14 If you are *i* because of the name

INSULTS (INSULT)

Ps 22: 7 they hurl *i*, shaking their heads:
69: 9 the *i* of those who insult you fall
Pr 22:10 quarrels and *i* are ended.
Mk 15:29 passed by hurled *i* at him,
Jn 9:28 Then they hurled *i* at him and said,
Ro 15: 3 "The *i* of those who insult you have
2Co 12:10 in *i*, in hardships, in persecutions,
1Pe 2:23 When they hurled their *i* at him,

INTEGRITY*

Dt 9: 5 or your *i* that you are going
1Ki 9: 4 if you walk before me in *i* of heart
1Ch 29:17 the heart and are pleased with *i*.
Ne 7: 2 because he was a man of *i*
Job 2: 3 And he still maintains his *i*,
2: 9 "Are you still holding on to your *i*?
6:29 reconsider, for my *i* is at stake.
27: 5 till I die, I will not deny my *i*.
Ps 7: 8 according to my *i*, O Most High.
25:21 May *i* and uprightness protect me,
41:12 In my *i* you uphold me
78:72 David shepherded them with *i*
Pr 10: 9 The man of *i* walks securely,
11: 3 The *i* of the upright guides them,
13: 6 Righteousness guards the man of *i*,
17:26 or to flog officials for their *i*.
29:10 Bloodthirsty men hate a man of *i*
Isa 45:23 my mouth has uttered in all *i*
59: 4 no one pleads his case with *i*.
Mt 22:16 "we know you are a man of *i*
Mk 12:14 we know you are a man of *i*.
Tit 2: 7 your teaching show *i*, seriousness

INTELLIGENCE (INTELLIGENT)

Isa 29:14 the *i* of the intelligent will vanish."
1Co 1:19 *i* of the intelligent I will frustrate."

INTELLIGENT (INTELLIGENCE)

Isa 29:14 the intelligence of the *i* will vanish

INTELLIGIBLE

1Co 14:19 I would rather speak five *i* words

INTENDED

Ge 50:20 place of God? You *i* to harm me,

INTENSE

1Th 2:17 out of our *i* longing we made every
Rev 16: 9 They were seared by the *i* heat

INTERCEDE (INTERCEDES INTERCEDING INTERCESSION INTERCESSOR)

Heb 7:25 he always lives to *i* for them.

INTERCEDES* (INTERCEDE)

Ro 8:26 but the Spirit himself *i* for us
8:27 because the Spirit *i* for the saints

INTERCEDING* (INTERCEDE)

Ro 8:34 hand of God and is also *i* for us.

INTERCESSION* (INTERCEDE)

Isa 53:12 and made *i* for the transgressors.
1Ti 2: 1 *i* and thanksgiving be made

INTERCESSOR* (INTERCEDE)

Job 16:20 My *i* is my friend

INTEREST (INTERESTS)

Lev 25:36 Do not take *i* of any kind from him,
Dt 23:20 You may charge a foreigner *i*,
Mt 25:27 would have received it back with *i*.
Php 2:20 who takes a genuine *i*

INTERESTS (INTEREST)

1Co 7:34 his wife—and his *i* are divided.
Php 2: 4 only to your own *i*, but also to the *i*
2:21 everyone looks out for his own *i*,

INTERFERE*

Ezr 6: 7 Do not *i* with the work

INTERMARRY (MARRY)

Dt 7: 3 Do not *i* with them.
Ezr 9:14 and *i* with the peoples who commit

INTERPRET (INTERPRETATION INTERPRETER INTERPRETS)

Ge 41:15 "I had a dream, and no one can *i* it.
Mt 16: 3 you cannot *i* the signs of the times.
1Co 12:30 Do all *i*? But eagerly desire
14:13 pray that he may *i* what he says.
14:27 one at a time, and someone must *i*.

INTERPRETATION (INTERPRET)

1Co 12:10 and to still another the *i* of tongues.
14:26 a revelation, a tongue or an *i*.
2Pe 1:20 about by the prophet's own *i*.

INTERPRETER (INTERPRET)

1Co 14:28 If there is no *i*, the speaker should

INTERPRETS (INTERPRET)

1Co 14: 5 he *i*, so that the church may be

INVADED

2Ki 17: 5 king of Assyria *i* the entire land,
24: 1 king of Babylon *i* the land,

INVENT* (INVENTED)

Ro 1:30 boastful; they *i* ways of doing evil;

INVENTED* (INVENT)

2Pe 1:16 We did not follow cleverly *i* stories

INVESTIGATED

Lk 1: 3 I myself have carefully *i* everything

INVISIBLE*

Ro 1:20 of the world God's *i* qualities—
Col 1:15 He is the image of the *i* God,
1:16 and on earth, visible and *i*,
1Ti 1:17 immortal, *i*, the only God,
Heb 11:27 because he saw him who is *i*.

INVITE (INVITED INVITES)

Mt 22: 9 *i* to the banquet anyone you find.'
25:38 did we see you a stranger and *i* you
Lk 14:12 do not *i* your friends, your brothers
14:13 you give a banquet, *i* the poor,

INVITED (INVITE)

Zep 1: 7 he has consecrated those he has *i*.
Mt 22:14 For many are *i*, but few are chosen
25:35 I was a stranger and you *i* me in,
Lk 14:10 But when you are *i*, take the lowest
Rev 19: 9 'Blessed are those who are *i*

INVITES (INVITE)

Pr 18: 6 and his mouth *i* a beating.
1Co 10:27 If some unbeliever *i* you to a meal

INVOLVED

2Ti 2: 4 a soldier gets *i* in civilian affairs—

IRON

2Ki 6: 6 threw it there, and made the *i* float.
Ps 2: 9 will rule them with an *i* scepter;
Pr 27:17 As *i* sharpens *i*,
Da 2:33 and thighs of bronze, its legs of *i*,
1Ti 4: 2 have been seared as with a hot *i*.
Rev 2:27 He will rule them with an *i* scepter;
12: 5 all the nations with an *i* scepter.
19:15 He will rule them with an *i* scepter

IRRELIGIOUS*

1Ti 1: 9 and sinful, the unholy and *i*;

IRREVOCABLE*

Ro 11:29 for God's gifts and his call are *i*.

ISAAC

Son of Abraham by Sarah (Ge 17:19; 21:1-7; 1Ch 1:28). Abrahamic covenant perpetuated through (Ge 17:21; 26:2-5). Offered up by Abraham (Ge 22; Heb 11:17-19). Rebekah taken as wife (Ge 24). Inherited Abraham's estate (Ge 25:5). Fathered Esau and Jacob (Ge 25:19-26; 1Ch 1:34). Nearly lost Rebekah to Abimelech (Ge 26:1-11). Covenant with Abimelech (Ge 26:12-31). Tricked into blessing Jacob (Ge 27). Death (Ge 35:27-29). Father of Israel (Ex 3:6; Dt 29:13; Ro 9:10).

ISAIAH

Prophet to Judah (Isa 1:1). Called by the LORD (Isa 6). Announced judgment to Ahaz (Isa 7), deliverance from Assyria to Hezekiah (2Ki 19; Isa 36-37), deliverance from death to Hezekiah (2Ki 20:1-11; Isa 38). Chronicler of Judah's history (2Ch 26:22; 32:32).

ISCARIOT see JUDAS

ISH-BOSHETH*

Son of Saul who attempted to succeed him as king (2Sa 2:8-4:12; 1Ch 8:33).

ISHMAEL

Son of Abraham by Hagar (Ge 16; 1Ch 1:28). Blessed, but not son of covenant (Ge 17:18-21; Gal 4:21-31). Sent away by Sarah (Ge 21:8-21). Children (Ge 25:12-18; 1Ch 1:29-31). Death (Ge 25:17).

ISLAND

Rev 1: 9 was on the *i* of Patmos

Rev 16:20 Every i fled away

ISRAEL (ISRAEL'S ISRAELITE ISRAELITES)

1. Name given to Jacob (see JACOB).
2. Corporate name of Jacob's descendants; often specifically Northern Kingdom.

Ex 28:11 Engrave the names of the sons of I
28:29 of the sons of I over his heart
Nu 24:17 a scepter will rise out of I.
Dt 6:4 Hear, O I: The LORD our God,
10:12 O I, what does the LORD your
Jos 4:22 I crossed the Jordan on dry ground
Jdg 17:6 In those days I had no king;
Ru 2:12 of I, under whose wings you have
1Sa 3:20 I from Dan to Beersheba
4:21 "The glory has departed from I"—
14:23 So the LORD rescued I that day,
15:26 has rejected you as king over I!"
17:46 will know that there is a God in I.
18:16 But all I and Judah loved David,
2Sa 5:2 'You will shepherd my people I,
5:3 they anointed David king over I.
14:25 In all I there was not a man
1Ki 1:35 I have appointed him ruler over I
10:9 of the LORD's eternal love for I,
18:17 "Is that you, you troubler of I?"
19:18 Yet I reserve seven thousand in I—
2Ki 5:8 know that there is a prophet in I."
1Ch 17:22 made your people I your very own
21:1 incited David to take a census of I.
29:25 Solomon in the sight of all I
2Ch 9:8 of the love of your God for I
Ps 73:1 Surely God is good to I,
81:8 if you would but listen to me, O I!
98:3 his faithfulness to the house of I;
99:8 you were to I a forgiving God,
Isa 11:12 and gather the exiles of I;
27:6 I will bud and blossom
44:21 O I, I will not forget you.
46:13 my splendor to I.
Jer 2:3 I was holy to the LORD,
23:6 and I will live in safety.
31:2 I will come to give rest to I."
31:10 'He who scattered I will gather
31:31 covenant with the house of I
33:17 sit on the throne of the house of I,
Eze 3:17 you a watchman for the house of I;
33:7 you a watchman for the house of I;
34:2 prophesy against the shepherds of I
37:28 that I the LORD make I holy,
39:23 of I went into exile for their sin,
Da 9:20 my sin and the sin of my people I
Hos 11:1 "When I was a child, I loved him,
Am 4:12 prepare to meet your God, O I."
7:11 and I will surely go into exile,
8:2 "The time is ripe for my people I;
9:14 I will bring back my exiled people I
Mic 5:2 one who will be ruler over I,
Zep 3:13 The remnant of I will do no wrong;
Zec 11:14 brotherhood between Judah and I.
Mal 1:5 even beyond the borders of I!'
Mt 2:6 be the shepherd of my people I.'"
10:6 Go rather to the lost sheep of I.
15:24 only to the lost sheep of I."
Mk 12:29 'Hear, O I, the Lord our God,
Lk 22:30 judging the twelve tribes of I.
Ac 1:6 going to restore the kingdom to I?"
9:15 and before the people of I.
Ro 9:4 of my own race, the people of I.
9:6 all who are descended from I are I.
9:31 but I, who pursued a law
11:7 What I sought so earnestly it did
11:26 And so all I will be saved,
Gal 6:16 who follow this rule, even to the I
Eph 2:12 excluded from citizenship in I
3:6 Gentiles are heirs together with I,
Heb 8:8 covenant with the house of I
Rev 7:4 144,000 from all the tribes of I.
21:12 the names of the twelve tribes of I.

ISRAEL'S (ISRAEL)

Jdg 10:16 he could bear I misery no longer.
2Sa 23:1 I singer of songs:
Isa 44:6 I King and Redeemer, the LORD
Jer 3:9 Because I immorality mattered
31:9 because I am I father,
Jn 3:10 "You are I teacher," said Jesus,

ISRAELITE (ISRAEL)

Ex 16:1 The whole I community set out
35:29 All the I men and women who
Nu 8:16 offspring from every I woman.
20:1 the whole I community arrived
20:22 The whole I community set out
Jn 1:47 "Here is a true I, in whom there is
Ro 11:1 I am an I myself, a descendant

ISRAELITES (ISRAEL)

Ex 1:7 the I were fruitful and multiplied
2:23 The I groaned in their slavery
3:9 the cry of the I has reached me,
12:35 The I did as Moses instructed
12:37 The I journeyed from Rameses
14:22 and the I went through the sea
16:12 I have heard the grumbling of the I.
16:35 The I ate manna forty years,
24:17 To the I the glory of the LORD
28:30 decisions for the I over his heart
29:45 Then I will dwell among the I
31:16 The I are to observe the Sabbath,
33:5 "Tell the I, 'You are a stiff-necked
39:42 The I had done all the work just
Lev 22:32 be acknowledged as holy by the I.
25:46 rule over your fellow I ruthlessly.
25:55 for the I belong to me as servants.
Nu 2:32 These are the I, counted according
6:23 'This is how you are to bless the I.
9:2 "Have the I celebrate the Passover
9:17 the I set out; wherever the cloud
10:12 Then the I set out from the Desert
14:2 All the I grumbled against Moses
20:12 as holy in the sight of the I,
21:6 they bit the people and many I died
26:65 had told those I they would surely
27:12 and see the land I have given the I.
33:3 The I set out from Rameses
35:10 "Speak to the I and say to them:
Dt 33:1 on the I before his death.
Jos 1:2 about to give to them—to the I.
5:6 The I had moved about
7:1 the I acted unfaithfully in regard
8:32 There in the presence of the I,
18:1 of the I gathered at Shiloh
21:3 the I gave the Levites the following
22:9 of Manasseh left the I at Shiloh
Jdg 2:11 Then the I did evil in the eyes
3:12 Once again the I did evil
4:1 the I once again did evil in the eyes
6:1 Again the I did evil in the eyes
10:6 Again the I did evil in the eyes
13:1 Again the I did evil in the eyes
1Sa 17:2 Saul and the I assembled
1Ki 8:63 and all the I dedicated the temple
9:22 did not make slaves of any of the I;
12:1 for all the I had gone there
12:17 But as for the I who were living
2Ki 17:24 towns of Samaria to replace the I.
1Ch 9:2 in their own towns were some I,
10:1 fought against Israel; the I fled
11:4 and all the I marched to Jerusalem,
2Ch 7:6 and all the I were standing.
Ne 1:6 the sins we I, including myself
Jer 16:14 who brought the I up out of Egypt,'
Hos 1:10 "Yet the I will be like the sand
3:1 Love her as the LORD loves the I,
Am 4:5 boast about them, you I,
Mic 5:3 return to join the I.
Ro 9:27 the number of the I be like the sand
10:1 for the I is that they may be saved.
10:16 But not all the I accepted the good
2Co 11:22 Are they I? So am I.

ISSACHAR

Son of Jacob by Leah (Ge 30:18; 35:23; 1Ch 2:1). Tribe of blessed (Ge 49:14-15; Dt 33:18-19), numbered (Nu 1:29; 26:25), allotted land (Jos 19:17-23; Eze 48:25), assisted Deborah (Jdg 5:15), 12,000 from (Rev 7:7).

ISSUING*

Da 9:25 From the i of the decree to restore

ITALY

Ac 27:1 decided that we would sail for I,
Heb 13:24 from I send you their greetings.

ITCHING*

2Ti 4:3 to say what their i ears want to hear

ITHAMAR

Son of Aaron (Ex 6:23; 1Ch 6:3). Duties at tabernacle (Ex 38:21; Nu 4:21-33; 7:8).

ITTAI

2Sa 15:19 The king said to I the Gittite,

IVORY

1Ki 10:22 silver and i, and apes and baboons.
22:39 the palace he built and inlaid with i

JABBOK

Ge 32:22 and crossed the ford of the J.
Dt 3:16 and out to the J River,

JABESH

1Sa 11:1 And all the men of J said to him,
31:12 wall of Beth Shan and went to J,
1Ch 10:12 and his sons and brought them to J.

JABESH GILEAD

Jdg 21:8 that no one from J had come to
2Sa 2:4 the men of J who had buried Saul,
1Ch 10:11 the inhabitants of J heard

JACOB

Second son of Isaac, twin of Esau (Ge 26:21-26; 1Ch 1:34). Bought Esau's birthright (Ge 26:29-34); tricked Isaac into blessing him (Ge 27:1-37). Fled to Haran (Ge 28:1-5). Abrahamic covenant perpetuated through (Ge 28:13-15; Mal 1:2). Vision at Bethel (Ge 28:10-22). Served Laban for Rachel and Leah (Ge 29:1-30). Children (Ge 29:31-30:24; 35:16-26; 1Ch 2-9). Flocks increased (Ge 30:25-43). Returned to Canaan (Ge 31). Wrestled with God; name changed to Israel (Ge 32:22-32). Reconciled to Esau (Ge 33). Returned to Bethel (Ge 35:1-15). Favored Joseph (Ge 37:3). Sent sons to Egypt during famine (Ge 42-43). Settled in Egypt (Ge 46). Blessed Ephraim and Manasseh (Ge 48). Blessed sons (Ge 49:1-28; Heb 11:21). Death (Ge 49:29-33). Burial (Ge 50:1-14).

JAEL*

Woman who killed Canaanite general, Sisera (Jdg 4:17-22; 5:24-27).

JAIR

Judge from Gilead (Jdg 10:3-5).

JAIRUS*

Synagogue ruler whose daughter Jesus raised (Mk 5:22-43; Lk 8:41-56).

JAMES

1. Apostle; brother of John (Mt 4:21-22; 10:2; Mk 3:17; Lk 5:1-10). At transfiguration (Mt 17:1-13; Mk 9:1-13; Lk 9:28-36). Killed by Herod (Ac 12:2).

2. Apostle; son of Alphaeus (Mt 10:3; Mk 3:18; Lk 6:15).

3. Brother of Jesus (Mt 13:55; Mk 6:3; Lk 24:10; Gal 1:19) and Judas (Jude 1). With believers before Pentecost (Ac 1:13). Leader of church at Jerusalem (Ac 12:17; 15; 21:18; Gal 2:9, 12). Author of epistle (Jas 1:1).

JAPHETH

Son of Noah (Ge 5:32; 1Ch 1:4-5). Blessed (Ge 9:18-28). Sons of (Ge 10:2-5).

JAR (JARS)

Ge 24:14 let down your j that I may have
1Ki 17:14 'The j of flour will not be used up
Jer 19:1 "Go and buy a clay j from a potter.
Lk 8:16 hides it in a j or puts it under a bed.

JARS (JAR)

Jn 2:6 Nearby stood six stone water j,
2Co 4:7 we have this treasure in j of clay

JASPER

Ex 28:20 row a chrysolite, an onyx and a j.
Eze 28:13 chrysolite, onyx and j,
Rev 4:3 sat there had the appearance of j
21:19 The first foundation was j,

JAVELIN

1Sa 17:45 me with sword and spear and j,

JAWBONE

Jdg 15:15 Finding a fresh j of a donkey,

JEALOUS (JEALOUSY)

Ex 20:5 the LORD your God, am a j God,
34:14 whose name is Jealous, is a j God.
Dt 4:24 God is a consuming fire, a j God.
6:15 is a j God and his anger will burn
32:21 They made me j by what is no god
Jos 24:19 He is a holy God; he is a j God.
Eze 16:38 of my wrath and j anger.
16:42 my j anger will turn away from you
23:25 I will direct my j anger against you,
36:6 in my j wrath because you have

Joel 2:18 the LORD will be *j* for his land
Na 1:2 LORD is a *j* and avenging God;
Zep 3:8 consumed by the fire of my *j* anger.
Zec 1:14 I am very *j* for Jerusalem and Zion,
8:2 "I am very *j* for Zion; I am burning
2Co 11:2 I am *j* for you with a godly jealousy

JEALOUSY (JEALOUS)

Ps 79:5 How long will your *j* burn like fire?
Pr 6:34 for *j* arouses a husband's fury,
27:4 but who can stand before *j*?
SS 8:6 its *j* unyielding as the grave.
Zep 1:18 In the fire of his *j*
Zec 8:2 I am burning with *j* for her."
Ro 13:13 debauchery, not in dissension and *j*
1Co 3:3 For since there is *j* and quarreling
10:22 trying to arouse the Lord's *j*?
2Co 11:2 I am jealous for you with a godly *j*.
12:20 *j*, outbursts of anger, factions,
Gal 5:20 hatred, discord, *j*, fits of rage,

JECONIAH see JEHOIACHIN

JEERS*

Heb 11:36 Some faced *j* and flogging,

JEHOAHAZ

1. Son of Jehu; king of Israel (2Ki 13:1-9).
2. Son of Josiah; king of Judah (2Ki 23:31-34; 2Ch 36:1-4).

JEHOASH

1. See JOASH.
2. Son of Jehoahaz; king of Israel. Defeat of Aram prophesied by Elisha (2Ki 13:10-25). Defeated Amaziah in Jerusalem (2Ki 14:1-16; 2Ch 25:17-24).

JEHOIACHIN

Son of Jehoiakim; king of Judah exiled by Nebuchadnezzar (2Ki 24:8-17; 2Ch 36:8-10; Jer 22:24-30; 24:1). Raised from prisoner status (2Ki 25:27-30; Jer 52:31-34).

JEHOIADA

Priest who sheltered Joash from Athaliah (2Ki 11-12; 2Ch 22:11-24:16).

JEHOIAKIM

Son of Jehoahaz; made king of Judah by Pharaoh Neco (2Ki 23:34-24:6; 2Ch 36:4-8; Jer 22:18-23). Burned scroll of Jeremiah's prophecies (Jer 36).

JEHORAM

1. Son of Jehoshaphat; king of Judah (2Ki 8:16-24). Prophesied against by Elijah; killed by the LORD (2Ch 21).
2. See JORAM.

JEHOSHAPHAT

Son of Asa; king of Judah. Strengthened his kingdom (2Ch 17). Joined with Ahab against Aram (2Ki 22; 2Ch 18). Established judges (2Ch 19). Joined with Joram against Moab (2Ki 3; 2Ch 20).

JEHOVAH see LORD‡

JEHU

1. Prophet against Baasha (2Ki 16:1-7).
2. King of Israel. Anointed by Elijah to obliterate house of Ahab (1Ki 19:16-17); anointed by servant of Elisha (2Ki 9:1-13). Killed Joram and Ahaziah (2Ki 9:14-29; 2Ch 22:7-9), Jezebel (2Ki 9:30-37), relatives of Ahab (2Ki 10:1-17), ministers of Baal (2Ki 10:18-29). Death (2Ki 10:30-36).

JEPHTHAH

Judge from Gilead who delivered Israel from Ammon (Jdg 10:6-12:7). Made rash vow concerning his daughter (Jdg 11:30-40).

JEREMIAH

Prophet to Judah (Jer 1:1-3). Called by the LORD (Jer 1). Put in stocks (Jer 20:1-3). Threatened for prophesying (Jer 11:18-23; 26). Opposed by Hananiah (Jer 28). Scroll burned (Jer 36). Imprisoned (Jer 37). Thrown into cistern (Jer 38). Forced to Egypt with those fleeing Babylonians (Jer 43).

JERICHO

Nu 22:1 along the Jordan across from *J*.
Jos 3:16 the people crossed over opposite *J*.
5:10 camped at Gilgal on the plains of *J*,
Lk 10:30 going down from Jerusalem to *J*,
Heb 11:30 By faith the walls of *J* fell,

JEROBOAM

1. Official of Solomon; rebelled to become first king of Israel (1Ki 11:26-40; 12:1-20; 2Ch 10). Idolatry (1Ki 12:25-33); judgment for (1Ki 13-14; 2Ch 13).
2. Son of Jehoash; king of Israel (1Ki 14:23-29).

JERUB-BAAL see GIDEON

JERUSALEM

Jos 10:1 of *J* heard that Joshua had taken Ai
15:8 of the Jebusite city (that is, *J*).
Jdg 1:8 The men of Judah attacked *J* also
1Sa 17:54 head and brought it to *J*,
2Sa 5:5 and in *J* he reigned over all Israel
5:6 and his men marched to *J*
9:13 And Mephibosheth lived in *J*,
11:1 But David remained in *J*.
15:29 took the ark of God back to *J*
24:16 stretched out his hand to destroy *J*,
1Ki 3:1 the LORD, and the wall around *J*.
9:15 the wall of *J*, and Hazor, Megiddo
9:19 whatever he desired to build in *J*,
10:26 cities and also with him in *J*.
10:27 as common in *J* as stones,
11:7 of *J*, Solomon built a high place
11:13 my servant and for the sake of *J*,
11:36 always have a lamp before me in *J*,
11:42 Solomon reigned in *J*
12:27 at the temple of the LORD in *J*,
14:21 and he reigned seventeen years in *J*
14:25 Shishak king of Egypt attacked *J*.
15:2 and he reigned in *J* three years.
15:10 and he reigned in *J* forty-one years.
22:42 he reigned in *J* twenty-five years.
2Ki 8:17 and he reigned in *J* eight years.
8:26 and he reigned in *J* one year.
12:1 and he reigned in *J* forty years.
12:17 Then he turned to attack *J*.
14:2 he reigned in *J* twenty-nine years.
14:13 Then Jehoash went to *J*
15:2 and he reigned in *J* fifty-two years.
15:33 and he reigned in *J* sixteen years.
16:2 and he reigned in *J* sixteen years.
16:5 Israel marched up to fight against *J*
18:2 he reigned in *J* twenty-nine years.
18:17 Lachish to King Hezekiah at *J*.
19:31 For out of *J* will come a remnant,
21:1 and he reigned in *J* fifty-five years.
21:12 going to bring such disaster on *J*
21:19 and he reigned in *J* two years.
22:1 he reigned in *J* thirty-one years.
23:27 and I will reject *J*, the city I chose,
23:31 and he reigned in *J* three months.
23:36 and he reigned in *J* eleven years.
24:8 and he reigned in *J* three months.
24:10 king of Babylon advanced on *J*
24:14 He carried into exile all *J*:
24:18 and he reigned in *J* eleven years.
24:20 anger that all this happened to *J*
25:1 king of Babylon marched against *J*
25:9 royal palace and all the houses of *J*.
1Ch 11:4 and all the Israelites marched to *J*,
21:16 sword in his hand extended over *J*.
2Ch 1:4 he had pitched a tent for it in *J*.
3:1 the LORD in *J* on Mount Moriah,
6:6 now I have chosen *J* for my Name
9:1 she came to *J* to test him
20:15 and all who live in Judah and *J*!
20:27 and *J* returned joyfully to *J*,
29:8 LORD has fallen on Judah and *J*;
36:19 and broke down the wall of *J*;
Ezr 1:2 a temple for him at *J* in Judah.
2:1 to Babylon (they returned to *J*
3:1 people assembled as one man in *J*.
4:12 up to us from you have gone to *J*
4:24 of God in *J* came to a standstill
6:12 or to destroy this temple in *J*.
7:8 Ezra arrived in *J* in the fifth month
9:9 a wall of protection in Judah and *J*.
10:7 for all the exiles to assemble in *J*.
Ne 1:2 the exile, and also about *J*.
1:3 The wall of *J* is broken down,
2:11 to *J*, and after staying there three
2:17 Come, let us rebuild the wall of *J*,
2:20 you have no share in *J* or any claim
3:8 They restored *J* as far as the Broad
4:8 fight against *J* and stir up trouble
11:1 leaders of the people settled in *J*,
12:27 At the dedication of the wall of *J*,
12:43 in *J* could be heard far away.
Ps 51:18 build up the walls of *J*.
79:1 they have reduced *J* to rubble.
122:2 in your gates, O *J*.
122:3 *J* is built like a city
122:6 Pray for the peace of *J*:
125:2 As the mountains surround *J*,
128:5 may you see the prosperity of *J*,
137:5 If I forget you, O *J*,
147:2 The LORD builds up *J*;
147:12 Extol the LORD, O *J*;
SS 6:4 lovely as *J*,
Isa 1:1 and *J* that Isaiah son of Amoz saw
2:1 saw concerning Judah and *J*:
3:1 is about to take from *J* and Judah
3:8 *J* staggers,
4:3 recorded among the living in *J*.
8:14 And for the people of *J* he will be
27:13 LORD on the holy mountain in *J*.
31:5 the LORD Almighty will shield *J*;
33:20 your eyes will see *J*,
40:2 Speak tenderly to *J*,
40:9 You who bring good tidings to *J*,
52:1 O *J*, the holy city.
52:2 rise up, sit enthroned, O *J*.
62:6 on your walls, O *J*;
62:7 give him no rest till he establishes *J*
65:18 for I will create *J* to be a delight
Jer 2:2 and proclaim in the hearing of *J*:
3:17 time they will call *J* The Throne
4:5 and proclaim in *J* and say:
4:14 O *J*, wash the evil from your heart
5:1 "Go up and down the streets of *J*,
6:6 and build siege ramps against *J*.
8:5 Why does *J* always turn away?
9:11 "I will make *J* a heap of ruins,
13:27 Woe to you, O *J*!
23:14 And among the prophets of *J*
24:1 into exile from *J* to Babylon
26:18 *J* will become a heap of rubble,
32:2 of Babylon was then besieging *J*,
33:10 the streets of *J* that are deserted,
39:1 This is how *J* was taken: In
51:50 and think on *J*."
52:14 broke down all the walls around *J*.
La 1:7 *J* remembers all the treasures
Eze 14:21 send against *J* my four dreadful
16:2 confront *J* with her detestable
Da 6:10 the windows opened toward *J*.
9:2 of *J* would last seventy years.
9:12 done like what has been done to *J*.
9:25 and rebuild *J* until the Anointed
Joel 3:1 restore the fortunes of Judah and *J*,
3:16 and thunder from *J*;
3:17 *J* will be holy;
Am 2:5 will consume the fortresses of *J*."
Ob :11 and cast lots for *J*,
Mic 1:5 Is it not *J*?
4:2 the word of the LORD from *J*.
Zep 3:16 On that day they will say to *J*,
Zec 1:14 'I am very jealous for *J* and Zion,
1:17 comfort Zion and choose *J*.'"
2:2 He answered me, "To measure *J*,
2:4 '*J* will be a city without walls
8:3 I will return to Zion and dwell in *J*.
8:8 I will bring them back to live in *J*;
8:15 determined to do good again to *J*
8:22 powerful nations will come to *J*
9:9 Shout, Daughter of *J*!
9:10 and the war-horses from *J*,
12:3 I will make *J* an immovable rock
12:10 the inhabitants of *J* a spirit of grace
14:2 the nations to *J* to fight against it;
14:8 living water will flow out from *J*,
14:16 that have attacked *J* will go up
Mt 16:21 to his disciples that he must go to *J*
20:18 said to them, "We are going up to *J*
21:10 When Jesus entered *J*, the whole
23:37 "O *J*, *J*, you who kill the prophets
Mk 10:33 "We are going up to *J*," he said,
Lk 2:22 Mary took him to *J* to present him
2:41 Every year his parents went to *J*
2:43 the boy Jesus stayed behind in *J*,
4:9 The devil led him to *J*
9:31 about to bring to fulfillment at *J*.
9:51 Jesus resolutely set out for *J*,
13:34 die outside *J*!"O *J*, *J*,
18:31 told them, "We are going up to *J*,
19:41 As he approached *J* and saw
21:20 "When you see *J* being surrounded
21:24 *J* will be trampled
24:47 name to all nations, beginning at *J*.
Jn 4:20 where we must worship is in *J*."
Ac 1:4 this command: "Do not leave *J*,

Ac 1: 8 and you will be my witnesses in *J*,
6: 7 of disciples in *J* increased rapidly,
20: 22 by the Spirit, I am going to *J*,
23: 11 As you have testified about me in *J*
Ro 15: 19 So from *J* all the way
Gal 4: 25 corresponds to the present city of *J*
4: 26 But the *J* that is above is free,
Heb 12: 22 to the heavenly *J*, the city
Rev 3: 12 the new *J*, which is coming
21: 2 I saw the Holy City, the new *J*,
21: 10 and showed me the Holy City, *J*,

JESSE

Father of David (Ru 4:17-22; 1Sa 16; 1Ch 2: 12-17).

JESUS

LIFE: Genealogy (Mt 1:1-17; Lk 3:21-37). Birth announced (Mt 1:18-25; Lk 1:26-45). Birth (Mt 2:1-12; Lk 2:1-40). Escape to Egypt (Mt 2: 13-23). As a boy in the temple (Lk 2:41-52). Baptism (Mt 3:13-17; Mk 1:9-11; Lk 3:21-22; Jn 1:32-34). Temptation (Mt 4:1-11; Mk 1:12-13; Lk 4:1-13). Ministry in Galilee (Mt 4:12-18:35; Mk 1: 14-9:50; Lk 4:14-13:9; Jn 1:35-2:11; 4; 6), Transfiguration (Mt 17:1-8; Mk 9:2-8; Lk 9:28-36), on the way to Jerusalem (Mt 19-20; Mk 10; Lk 13: 10-19:27), in Jerusalem (Mt 21-25; Mk 11-13; Lk 19:28-21:38; Jn 2:12-3:36; 5; 7-12). Last supper (Mt 26:17-35; Mk 14:12-31; Lk 22:1-38; Jn 13-17). Arrest and trial (Mt 26:36-27:31; Mk 14:43-15:20; Lk 22:39-23:25; Jn 18:1-19:16). Crucifixion (Mt 27:32-66; Mk 15:21-47; Lk 23:26-55; Jn 19:28-42). Resurrection and appearances (Mt 28; Mk 16; Lk 24; Jn 20-21; Ac 1:1-11; 7:56; 9: 3-6; 1Co 15:1-8; Rev 1:1-20).

MIRACLES. Healings: official's son (Jn 4:43-54), demoniac in Capernaum (Mk 1:23-26; Lk 4: 33-35), Peter's mother-in-law (Mt 8:14-17; Mk 1: 29-31; Lk 4:38-39), leper (Mt 8:2-4; Mk 1:40-45; Lk 5:12-16), paralytic (Mt 9:1-8; Mk 2:1-12; Lk 5: 17-26), cripple (Jn 5:1-9), shriveled hand (Mt 12: 10-13; Mk 3:1-5; Lk 6:6-11), centurion's servant (Mt 8:5-13; Lk 7:1-10), widow's son raised (Lk 7: 11-17), demoniac (Mt 12:22-23; Lk 11:14), Gadarene demoniacs (Mt 8:28-34; Mk 5:1-20; Lk 8:26-39), woman's bleeding and Jairus' daughter (Mt 9:18-26; Mk 5:21-43; Lk 8:40-56), blind man (Mt 9:27-31), mute man (Mt 9:32-33), Canaanite woman's daughter (Mt 15:21-28; Mk 7: 24-30), deaf man (Mk 7:31-37), blind man (Mk 8: 22-26), demoniac boy (Mt 17:14-18; Mk 9:14-29; Lk 9:37-43), ten lepers (Lk 17:11-19), man born blind (Jn 9:1-7), Lazarus raised (Jn 11), crippled woman (Lk 13:11-17), man with dropsy (Lk 14: 1-6), two blind men (Mt 20:29-34; Mk 10:46-52; Lk 18:35-43), Malchus' ear (Lk 22:50-51). Other Miracles: water to wine (Jn 2:1-11), catch of fish (Lk 5:1-11), storm stilled (Mt 8:23-27; Mk 4:37-41; Lk 8:22-25), 5,000 fed (Mt 14:15-21; Mk 6: 35-44; Lk 9:10-17; Jn 6:1-14), walking on water (Mt 14:25-33; Mk 6:48-52; Jn 6:15-21), 4,000 fed (Mt 15:32-39; Mk 8:1-9), money from fish (Mt 17: 24-27), fig tree cursed (Mt 21:18-22; Mk 11:12-14), catch of fish (Jn 21:1-14).

MAJOR TEACHING: Sermon on the Mount (Mt 5-7; Lk 6:17-49), to Nicodemus (Jn 3), to Samaritan woman (Jn 4), Bread of Life (Jn 6: 22-59), at Feast of Tabernacles (Jn 7-8), woes to Pharisees (Mt 23; Lk 11:37-54), Good Shepherd (Jn 10:1-18), Olivet Discourse (Mt 24-25; Mk 13; Lk 21:5-36), Upper Room Discourse (Jn 13-16).

PARABLES: Sower (Mt 13:3-23; Mk 4:3-25; Lk 8:5-18), seed's growth (Mk 4:26-29), wheat and weeds (Mt 13:24-30, 36-43), mustard seed (Mt 13:31-32; Mk 4:30-32), yeast (Mt 13:33-35; Mk 4:33-34), hidden treasure (Mt 13:44), valuable pearl (Mt 13:45-46), net (Mt 13:47-51), house owner (Mt 13:52), good Samaritan (Lk 10: 25-37), unmerciful servant (Mt 18:15-35), lost sheep (Mt 18:10-14; Lk 15:4-7), lost coin (Lk 15: 8-10), prodigal son (Lk 15:11-32), dishonest manager (Lk 16:1-13), rich man and Lazarus (Lk 16:19-31), persistent widow (Lk 18:1-8), Pharisee and tax collector (Lk 18:9-14), payment of workers (Mt 20:1-16), tenants and the vineyard (Mt 21:28-46; Mt 12:1-12; Lk 20:9-19), wedding banquet (Mt 22:1-14), faithful servant (Mt 24: 45-51), ten virgins (Mt 25:1-13), talents (Mt 25: 1-30; Lk 19:12-27).

DISCIPLES see APOSTLES. Call of (Jn 1: 35-51; Mt 4:18-22; 9:9; Mk 1:16-20; 2:13-14; Lk 5:1-11, 27-28). Named Apostles (Mk 3:13-19; Lk 6:12-16). Twelve sent out (Mt 10; Mk 6:7-11; Lk 9:1-5). Seventy sent out (Lk 10:1-24). Defection of (Jn 6:60-71; Mt 26:56; Mk 14:50-52). Final commission (Mt 28:16-20; Jn 21:15-23; Ac 1: 3-8).

Ac 2: 32 God has raised this *J* to life,
9: 5 "I am *J*, whom you are persecuting
9: 34 said to him, "*J* Christ heals you.
15: 11 of our Lord *J* that we are saved,
16: 31 "Believe in the Lord *J*,
20: 24 the task the Lord *J* has given me—
Ro 3: 24 redemption that came by Christ *J*.
5: 17 life through the one man, *J* Christ.
8: 1 for those who are in Christ *J*,
1Co 1: 7 for our Lord *J* Christ to be revealed
2: 2 except *J* Christ and him crucified.
6: 11 in the name of the Lord *J* Christ
8: 6 and there is but one Lord, *J* Christ,
12: 3 and no one can say, "*J* is Lord,"
2Co 4: 5 not preach ourselves, but *J* Christ
13: 5 Do you not realize that Christ *J* is
Gal 2: 16 but by faith in *J* Christ.
3: 28 for you are all one in Christ *J*.
5: 6 in Christ *J* neither circumcision
6: 17 bear on my body the marks of *J*.
Eph 1: 5 as his sons through *J* Christ,
2: 10 created in Christ *J*
2: 20 with Christ *J* himself as the chief
Php 1: 6 until the day of Christ *J*.
2: 5 be the same as that of Christ *J*:
2: 10 name of *J* every knee should bow,
Col 3: 17 do it all in the name of the Lord *J*,
1Th 1: 10 whom he raised from the dead—*J*,
4: 14 We believe that *J* died
5: 23 at the coming of our Lord *J* Christ.
2Th 1: 7 when the Lord *J* is revealed
2: 1 the coming of our Lord *J* Christ
1Ti 1: 15 Christ *J* came into the world
2Ti 1: 10 appearing of our Savior, Christ *J*,
2: 3 us like a good soldier of Christ *J*.
3: 12 life in Christ *J* will be persecuted,
Tit 2: 13 our great God and Savior, *J* Christ,
Heb 2: 9 But we see *J*, who was made a little
2: 11 So *J* is not ashamed to call them
3: 1 fix your thoughts on *J*, the apostle
3: 3 *J* has been found worthy
4: 14 through the heavens, *J* the Son
6: 20 where *J*, who went before us,
7: 22 *J* has become the guarantee
7: 24 but because *J* lives forever,
8: 6 But the ministry *J* has received is
12: 2 Let us fix our eyes on *J*, the author
12: 24 to *J* the mediator of a new
1Pe 1: 3 the resurrection of *J* Christ
2Pe 1: 16 and coming of our Lord *J* Christ,
1Jn 1: 7 and the blood of *J*, his Son,
2: 1 *J* Christ, the Righteous One.
2: 6 to live in him must walk as *J* did.
4: 15 anyone acknowledges that *J* is
Rev 1: 1 The revelation of *J* Christ,
22: 16 *J*, have sent my angel
22: 20 Come, Lord *J*.

JETHRO

Father-in-law and adviser of Moses (Ex 3:1; 18). Also known as Reuel (Ex 2:18).

JEW (JEWS JEWS' JUDAISM)

Est 2: 5 of Susa a *J* of the tribe of Benjamin,
Zec 8: 23 of one *J* by the hem of his robe
Ac 21: 39 "I am a *J*, from Tarsus in Cilicia,
Ro 1: 16 first for the *J*, then for the Gentile.
2: 28 A man is not a *J* if he is only one
10: 12 there is no difference between *J*
1Co 9: 20 To the Jews I became like a *J*,
Gal 2: 14 "You are a *J*, yet you live like
3: 28 There is neither *J* nor Greek,
Col 3: 11 Here there is no Greek or *J*,

JEWEL (JEWELRY JEWELS)

Pr 20: 15 that speak knowledge are a rare *j*.
SS 4: 9 with one *j* of your necklace.
Rev 21: 11 that of a very precious *j*,

JEWELRY (JEWEL)

Ex 35: 22 and brought gold *j* of all kinds:
Jer 2: 32 Does a maiden forget her *j*,
Eze 16: 11 you with *j*: I put bracelets
1Pe 3: 3 wearing of gold *j* and fine clothes.

JEWELS (JEWEL)

Isa 54: 12 your gates of sparkling *j*,
61: 10 as a bride adorns herself with her *j*.
Zec 9: 16 like *j* in a crown.

JEWS (JEW)

Ne 4: 1 He ridiculed the *J*,
Est 3: 13 kill and annihilate all the *J*—
4: 14 and deliverance for the *J* will arise
Mt 2: 2 who has been born king of the *J*?
27: 11 "Are you the king of the *J*?" "Yes,
Jn 4: 9 (For *J* do not associate
4: 22 for salvation is from the *J*.
19: 3 saying, "Hail, king of the *J*!"
Ac 20: 21 I have declared to both *J*
Ro 3: 29 Is God the God of *J* only?
9: 24 not only from the *J* but
15: 27 they owe it to the *J* to share
1Co 1: 22 *J* demand miraculous signs
9: 20 To the *J* I became like a Jew,
12: 13 whether *J* or Greeks, slave or free
Gal 2: 8 of Peter as an apostle to the *J*,
Rev 2: 9 slander of those who say they are *J*
3: 9 claim to be *J* though they are not,

JEWS' (JEW)

Ro 15: 27 shared in the *J* spiritual blessings,

JEZEBEL

Sidonian wife of Ahab (1Ki 16:31). Promoted Baal worship (1Ki 16:32-33). Killed prophets of the LORD (1Ki 18:4, 13). Opposed Elijah (1Ki 19: 1-2). Had Naboth killed (1Ki 21). Death prophesied (1Ki 21:17-24). Killed by Jehu (2Ki 9:30-37).

JEZREEL

2Ki 9: 36 at *J* dogs will devour Jezebel's flesh
10: 7 and sent them to Jehu in *J*.
Hos 1: 4 house of Jehu for the massacre at *J*,

JOAB

Nephew of David (1Ch 2:16). Commander of his army (2Sa 8:16). Victorious over Ammon (2Sa 10; 1Ch 19), Rabbah (2Sa 11; 1Ch 20), Jerusalem (1Ch 11:6), Absalom (2Sa 18), Sheba (2Sa 20). Killed Abner (2Sa 3:22-39), Amasa (2Sa 20:1-13). Numbered David's army (2Sa 24; 1Ch 21). Sided with Adonijah (1Ki 1:17, 19). Killed by Benaiah (1Ki 2:5-6, 28-35).

JOASH

Son of Ahaziah; king of Judah. Sheltered from Athaliah by Jehoiada (2Ki 11; 2Ch 22:10-23:21). Repaired temple (2Ki 12; 2Ch 24).

JOB

Wealthy man from Uz; feared God (Job 1: 1-5). Righteousness tested by disaster (Job 1: 6-22), personal affliction (Job 2). Maintained innocence in debate with three friends (Job 3-31), Elihu (Job 32-37). Rebuked by the LORD (Job 38-41). Vindicated and restored to greater stature by the LORD (Job 42). Example of righteousness (Eze 14:14, 20).

JOCHEBED*

Mother of Moses and Aaron (Ex 6:20; Nu 26: 59).

JOEL

Prophet (Joel 1:1; Ac 2:16).

JOHN

1. Son of Zechariah and Elizabeth (Lk 1). Called the Baptist (Mt 3:1-12; Mk 1:2-8). Witness to Jesus (Mt 3:11-12; Mk 1:7-8; Lk 3:15-18; Jn 1: 6-35; 3:27-30; 5:33-36). Doubts about Jesus (Mt 11:2-6; Lk 7:18-23). Arrest (Mt 4:12; Mk 1:14). Execution (Mt 14:1-12; Mk 6:14-29; Lk 9:7-9). Ministry compared to Elijah (Mt 11:7-19; Mk 9: 11-13; Lk 7:24-35).

2. Apostle; brother of James (Mt 4:21-22; 10: 2; Mk 3:17; Lk 5:1-10). At transfiguration (Mt 17: 1-13; Mk 9:1-13; Lk 9:28-36). Desire to be greatest (Mk 10:35-45). Leader of church at Jerusalem (Ac 4:1-3; Gal 2:9). Elder who wrote epistles (2Jn 1; 3Jn 1). Prophet who wrote Revelation (Rev 1:1; 22:8).

3. Cousin of Barnabas, co-worker with Paul, (Ac 12:12-13:13; 15:37), see MARK.

JOIN (JOINED JOINS)

Ne 10: 29 all these now *j* their brothers
Pr 23: 20 Do not *j* those who drink too much
24: 21 and do not *j* with the rebellious,
Jer 3: 18 of Judah will *j* the house of Israel,
Eze 37: 17 *J* them together into one stick
Da 11: 34 who are not sincere will *j* them.
Ro 15: 30 to *j* me in my struggle by praying
2Ti 1: 8 *j* with me in suffering for the gospel

JOINED (JOIN)
Zec 2:11 "Many nations will be j
Mt 19: 6 Therefore what God has j together,
Mk 10: 9 Therefore what God has j together,
Ac 1:14 They all j together constantly
Eph 2:21 him the whole building is j together
4:16 j and held together

JOINS (JOIN)
1Co 16:16 and to everyone who j in the work,

JOINT (JOINTS)
Ps 22:14 and all my bones are out of j.

JOINTS (JOINT)
Heb 4:12 even to dividing soul and spirit, j

JOKING*
Ge 19:14 his sons-in-law thought he was j.
Pr 26:19 and says, "I was only j!"
Eph 5: 4 or coarse j, which are out of place,

JONAH
Prophet in days of Jeroboam II (2Ki 14:25). Called to Nineveh; fled to Tarshish (Jnh 1:1-3). Cause of storm; thrown into sea (Jnh 1:4-16). Swallowed by fish (Jnh 1:17). Prayer (Jnh 2). Preached to Nineveh (Jnh 3). Attitude reproved by the LORD (Jnh 4). Sign of (Mt 12:39-41; Lk 11:29-32).

JONATHAN
Son of Saul (1Sa 13:16; 1Ch 8:33). Valiant warrior (1Sa 13-14). Relation to David (1Sa 18:1-4; 19:1-20; 23:16-18). Killed at Gilboa (1Sa 31). Mourned by David (2Sa 1).

JOPPA
Ezr 3: 7 logs by sea from Lebanon to J,
Jnh 1: 3 to J, where he found a ship bound
Ac 9:43 Peter stayed in J for some time

JORAM
1. Son of Ahab; king of Israel. Fought with Jehoshaphat against Moab (2Ki 3). Killed with Ahaziah by Jehu (2Ki 8:25-29; 9:14-26; 2Ch 22:5-9).
2. See JEHORAM.

JORDAN
Ge 13:10 plain of the J was well watered,
Nu 22: 1 and camped along the J
34:12 boundary will go down along the J
Dt 3:27 you are not going to cross this J.
Jos 1: 2 get ready to cross the J River
3:11 go into the J ahead of you.
3:17 ground in the middle of the J,
4:22 Israel crossed the J on dry ground.'
2Ki 2: 7 and Elisha had stopped at the J.
2:13 and stood on the bank of the J.
5:10 wash yourself seven times in the J,
6: 4 They went to the J and began
Ps 114: 3 the J turned back;
Isa 9: 1 along the J— The people walking
Jer 12: 5 manage in the thickets by the J?
Mt 3: 6 baptized by him in the J River.
4:15 the way to the sea, along the J,
Mk 1: 9 and was baptized by John in the J.

JOSEPH
1. Son of Jacob by Rachel (Ge 30:24; 1Ch 2:2). Favored by Jacob, hated by brothers (Ge 37:3-4). Dreams (Ge 37:5-11). Sold by brothers (Ge 37:12-36). Served Potiphar; imprisoned by false accusation (Ge 39). Interpreted dreams of Pharaoh's servants (Ge 40), of Pharaoh (Ge 41:4-40). Made greatest in Egypt (Ge 41:41-57). Sold grain to brothers (Ge 42-45). Brought Jacob and sons to Egypt (Ge 46-47). Sons Ephraim and Manasseh blessed (Ge 48). Blessed (Ge 49:22-26; Dt 33:13-17). Death (Ge 50:22-26; Ex 13:19; Heb 11:22). 12,000 from (Rev 7:8).
2. Husband of Mary, mother of Jesus (Mt 1:16-24; 2:13-19; Lk 1:27; 2; Jn 1:45).
3. Disciple from Arimathea, who gave his tomb for Jesus' burial (Mt 27:57-61; Mk 15:43-47; Lk 24:50-52).
4. Original name of Barnabas (Ac 4:36).

JOSHUA (HOSHEA)
1. Son of Nun; name changed from Hoshea (Nu 13:8, 16; 1Ch 7:27). Fought Amalekites under Moses (Ex 17:9-14). Servant of Moses on Sinai (Ex 24:13; 32:17). Spied Canaan (Nu 13). With Caleb, allowed to enter land (Nu 14:6, 30). Succeeded Moses (Dt 1:38; 31:1-18; 33:9).
Charged Israel to conquer Canaan (Jos 1). Crossed Jordan (Jos 3-4). Circumcised sons of wilderness wanderings (Jos 5). Conquered Jericho (Jos 6), Ai (Jos 7-8), five kings at Gibeon (Jos 10:1-28), southern Canaan (Jos 10:29-43), northern Canaan (Jos 11-12). Defeated at Ai (Jos 7). Deceived by Gibeonites (Jos 9). Renewed covenant (Jos 8:30-35; 24:1-27). Divided land among tribes (Jos 13-22). Last words (Jos 23). Death (Jos 24:28-31).
2. High priest during rebuilding of temple (Hag 1-2; Zec 3:1-9; 6:11).

JOSIAH
Son of Amon; king of Judah (2Ki 21:26; 1Ch 3:14). Prophesied (1Ki 13:2). Book of Law discovered during his reign (2Ki 22; 2Ch 34:14-31). Reforms (2Ki 23:1-25; 2Ch 34:1-13; 35:1-19). Killed by Pharaoh Neco (2Ki 23:29-30; 2Ch 35:20-27).

JOTHAM
1. Son of Gideon (Jdg 9).
2. Son of Azariah (Uzziah); king of Judah (2Ki 15:32-38; 2Ch 26:21-27:9).

JOURNEY
Dt 1:33 who went ahead of you on your j,
2: 7 over your j through this vast desert
Jdg 18: 6 Your j has the LORD's approval."
Ezr 8:21 and ask him for a safe j for us
Job 16:22 before I go on the j of no return.
Isa 35: 8 The unclean will not j on it;
Mt 25:14 it will be like a man going on a j,
Ro 15:24 to have you assist me on my j there

JOY* (ENJOY ENJOYMENT JOYFUL JOYOUS OVERJOYED REJOICE REJOICES REJOICING)
Ge 31:27 so I could send you away with j
Lev 9:24 shouted for j and fell facedown.
Dt 16:15 and your j will be complete.
Jdg 9:19 may Abimelech be your j,
1Ch 12:40 and sheep, for there was j in Israel.
16:27 strength and j in his dwelling place.
16:33 sing for j before the LORD,
29:17 with j how willingly your people
29:22 drank with great j in the presence
2Ch 30:26 There was great j in Jerusalem,
Ezr 3:12 while many others shouted for j.
3:13 of the shouts of j from the sound
6:16 of the house of God with j.
6:22 with j by changing the attitude
6:22 j the Feast of Unleavened Bread,
Ne 8:10 for the j of the LORD is your
8:12 and to celebrate with great j,
8:17 And their j was very great.
12:43 God had given them great j.
Est 8:16 a time of happiness and j,
8:17 there was j and gladness
9:17 and made it a day of feasting and j.
9:18 and made it a day of feasting and j.
9:19 as a day of j and feasting,
9:22 and j and giving presents of food
9:22 their sorrow was turned into j
Job 3: 7 may no shout of j be heard in it.
6:10 my j in unrelenting pain—
8:21 and your lips with shouts of j.
9:25 they fly away without a glimpse of j
10:20 from me so I can have a moment's j
20: 5 the j of the godless lasts
33:26 he sees God's face and shouts for j;
38: 7 and all the angels shouted for j?
Ps 4: 7 have filled my heart with greater j
5:11 let them ever sing for j.
16:11 me with j in your presence,
19: 8 giving j to the heart.
20: 5 We will shout for j
21: 1 How great is his j in the victories
21: 6 with the j of your presence.
27: 6 will I sacrifice with shouts of j;
28: 7 My heart leaps for j
30:11 sackcloth and clothed me with j,
33: 3 play skillfully, and shout for j.
35:27 shout for j and gladness;
42: 4 with shouts of j and thanksgiving
43: 4 to God, my j and my delight.
45: 7 by anointing you with the oil of j.
45:15 They are led in with j and gladness;
47: 1 shout to God with cries of j.
47: 5 God has ascended amid shouts of j,
48: 2 the j of the whole earth.
51: 8 Let me hear j and gladness;
51:12 to me the j of your salvation
65: 8 you call forth songs of j.
65:13 they shout for j and sing.
66: 1 Shout with j to God, all the earth!
67: 4 the nations be glad and sing for j,
71:23 My lips will shout for j
81: 1 Sing for j to God our strength;
86: 4 Bring j to your servant,
89:12 Hermon sing for j at your name.
90:14 for j and be glad all our days.
92: 4 I sing for j at the works
94:19 your consolation brought j
95: 1 let us sing for j to the LORD;
96:12 the trees of the forest will sing for j;
97:11 and j on the upright in heart.
98: 4 for j to the LORD, all the earth,
98: 6 shout for j before the LORD,
98: 8 the mountains sing together for j;
100: 1 for j to the LORD, all the earth.
105:43 his chosen ones with shouts of j;
106: 5 share in the j of your nation
107:22 and tell of his works with songs of j
118:15 Shouts of j and victory
119:111 they are the j of my heart.
126: 2 our tongues with songs of j.
126: 3 and we are filled with j.
126: 5 will reap with songs of j.
126: 6 will return with songs of j,
132: 9 may your saints sing for j."
132:16 and her saints will ever sing for j.
137: 3 tormentors demanded songs of j;
137: 6 my highest j.
149: 5 and sing for j on their beds.
Pr 10: 1 A wise son brings j to his father,
10:28 The prospect of the righteous is j,
11:10 wicked perish, there are shouts of j.
12:20 but j for those who promote peace.
14:10 and no one else can share its j.
14:13 and j may end in grief.
15:20 A wise son brings j to his father,
15:23 A man finds j in giving an apt reply
15:30 A cheerful look brings j
17:21 there is no j for the father of a fool.
21:15 it brings j to the righteous
23:24 of a righteous man has great j;
27: 9 incense bring j to the heart,
27:11 my son, and bring j to my heart;
29: 3 A man who loves wisdom brings j
Ecc 8:15 Then j will accompany him
11: 9 let your heart give you j in the days
Isa 9: 3 and increased their j;
12: 3 With j you will draw water
12: 6 Shout aloud and sing for j,
16: 9 shouts of j over your ripened fruit
16:10 J and gladness are taken away
22:13 But see, there is j and revelry,
24:11 all j turns to gloom,
24:14 raise their voices, they shout for j;
26:19 wake up and shout for j.
35: 2 will rejoice greatly and shout for j.
35: 6 the mute tongue shout for j.
35:10 Gladness and j will overtake them,
35:10 everlasting j will crown their heads
42:11 Let the people of Sela sing for j;
44:23 Sing for j, O heavens,
48:20 Announce this with shouts of j
49:13 Shout for j, O heavens;
51: 3 J and gladness will be found in her,
51:11 Gladness and j will overtake them,
51:11 everlasting j will crown their heads
52: 8 together they shout for j.
52: 9 Burst into songs of j together,
54: 1 burst into song, shout for j,
55:12 You will go out in j
56: 7 give them j in my house of prayer.
58:14 then you will find your j
60: 5 heart will throb and swell with j;
60:15 and the j of all generations.
61: 7 and everlasting j will be theirs.
65:14 out of the j of their hearts,
65:18 and its people a j.
66: 5 that we may see your j!'
Jer 7:34 will bring an end to the sounds of j
15:16 they were my j and my heart's
16: 9 will bring an end to the sounds of j
25:10 banish from them the sounds of j
31: 7 "Sing with j for Jacob;
31:12 shout for j on the heights of Zion;
31:13 give them comfort and j instead
33: 9 this city will bring me renown, j,
33:11 be heard once more the sounds of j
48:33 J and gladness are gone
48:33 no one treads them with shouts of j
48:33 they are not shouts of j.
51:48 will shout for j over Babylon,

La 2:15 the j of the whole earth?"
5:15 J is gone from our hearts;
Eze 7: 7 not j, upon the mountains.
24:25 their j and glory, the delight
Joel 1:12 Surely the j of mankind
1:16 j and gladness
Mt 13:20 and at once receives it with j.
13:44 in his j went and sold all he had
28: 8 afraid yet filled with j,
Mk 4:16 and at once receive it with j.
Lk 1:14 He will be a j and delight to you,
1:44 the baby in my womb leaped for j.
1:58 great mercy, and they shared her j.
2:10 news of great j that will be
6:23 "Rejoice in that day and leap for j,
8:13 the word with j when they hear it,
10:17 The seventy-two returned with j
10:21 full of j through the Holy Spirit,
24:41 still did not believe it because of j
24:52 returned to Jerusalem with great j.
Jn 3:29 That j is mine, and it is now
3:29 full of j when he hears
15:11 and that your j may be complete.
15:11 this so that my j may be in you
16:20 but your grief will turn to j.
16:21 because of her j that a child is born
16:22 and no one will take away your j.
16:24 and your j will be complete.
17:13 measure of my j within them.
Ac 2:28 with j in your presence.'
8: 8 So there was great j in that city.
13:52 And the disciples were filled with j
14:17 and fills your hearts with j."
16:34 he was filled with j because he had come
Ro 14:17 peace and j in the Holy Spirit,
15:13 the God of hope fill you with all j
15:32 will I may come to you with j
16:19 so I am full of j over you;
2Co 1:24 but we work with you for your j,
2: 3 that you would all share my j.
7: 4 our troubles my j knows no
7: 7 so that my j was greater than ever.
8: 2 their overflowing j and their
Gal 4:15 What has happened to all your j?
5:22 j, peace, patience, kindness,
Php 1: 4 I always pray with j
1:25 for your progress and j in the faith,
1:26 being with you again your j
2: 2 then make my j complete
2:29 him in the Lord with great j,
4: 1 and long for, my j and crown,
1Th 1: 6 with the j given by the Holy Spirit.
2:19 For what is our hope, our j,
2:20 Indeed, you are our glory and j.
3: 9 you in return for all the j we have
2Ti 1: 4 so that I may be filled with j.
Phm : 7 Your love has given me great j
Heb 1: 9 by anointing you with the oil of j."
12: 2 for the j set before him endured
13:17 them so that their work will be a j,
Jas 1: 2 Consider it pure j, my brothers,
4: 9 to mourning and your j to gloom.
1Pe 1: 8 with an inexpressible and glorious j
1Jn 1: 4 this to make our j complete.
2Jn : 4 It has given me great j to find some
:12 so that our j may be complete.
3Jn : 3 It gave me great j to have some
: 4 I have no greater j
Jude :24 without fault and with great j—

JOYFUL* (JOY)

Dt 16:14 Be j at your Feast—you, your sons
1Sa 18: 6 with j songs and with tambourines
1Ki 8:66 j and glad in heart
1Ch 15:16 as singers to sing j songs,
2Ch 7:10 j and glad in heart
Ps 68: 3 may they be happy and j.
100: 2 come before him with j songs.
Ecc 9: 7 and drink your wine with a j heart,
Isa 24: 8 the j harp is silent.
Jer 31: 4 and go out to dance with the j.
Hab 3:18 I will be j in God my Savior.
Zec 8:19 and tenth months will become j
10: 7 Their children will see it and be j;
Ro 12:12 Be j in hope, patient in affliction,
1Th 5:16 Be j always; pray continually;
Heb 12:22 thousands of angels in j assembly,

JOYOUS* (JOY)

Est 8:15 the city of Susa held a j celebration.

JUBILANT

Ps 96:12 let the fields be j, and everything
98: 4 burst into j song with music;

JUBILEE

Lev 25:11 The fiftieth year shall be a j for you;

JUDAH (JUDEA)

1. Son of Jacob by Leah (Ge 29:35; 35:23; 1Ch 2:1). Did not want to kill Joseph (Ge 37:26-27). Among Canaanites, fathered Perez by Tamar (Ge 38). Tribe of blessed as ruling tribe (Ge 49:8-12; Dt 33:7), numbered (Nu 1:27; 26:22), allotted land (Jos 15; Eze 48:7), failed to fully possess (Jos 15:63; Jdg 1:1-20).

2. Name used for people and land of Southern Kingdom.

Ru 1: 7 take them back to the land of J.
2Sa 2: 4 king over the house of J.
Isa 1: 1 The vision concerning J
3: 8 J is falling;
Jer 13:19 All J will be carried into exile,
30: 3 bring my people Israel and J back
Hos 1: 7 I will show love to the house of J;
Zec 10: 4 From J will come the cornerstone,
Mt 2: 6 least among the rulers of J;
Heb 7:14 that our Lord descended from J,
8: 8 and with the house of J.
Rev 5: 5 of the tribe of J, the Root of David,

JUDAISM (JEW)

Ac 13:43 devout converts to J followed Paul
Gal 1:13 of my previous way of life in J,
1:14 advancing in J beyond many Jews

JUDAS

1. Apostle; son of James (Lk 6:16; Jn 14:22; Ac 1:13). Probably also called Thaddaeus (Mt 10:3; Mk 3:18).

2. Brother of James and Jesus (Mt 13:55; Mk 6:3), also called Jude (Jude 1).

3. Christian prophet (Ac 15:22-32).

4. Apostle, also called Iscariot, who betrayed Jesus (Mt 10:4; 26:14-56; Mk 3:19; 14:10-50; Lk 6:16; 22:3-53; Jn 6:71; 12:4; 13:2-30; 18:2-11). Suicide of (Mt 27:3-5; Ac 1:16-25).

JUDE see JUDAS

JUDEA (JUDAH)

Mt 2: 1 born in Bethlehem in J,
24:16 are in J flee to the mountains.
Lk 3: 1 Pontius Pilate was governor of J,
Ac 1: 8 and in all J and Samaria,
9:31 Then the church throughout J,
1Th 2:14 imitators of God's churches in J,

JUDGE (JUDGED JUDGES JUDGING JUDGMENT JUDGMENTS)

Ge 16: 5 May the LORD j between you
18:25 Will not the J of all the earth do
Lev 19:15 but j your neighbor fairly.
Dt 1:16 between your brothers and j fairly,
17:12 man who shows contempt for the j
32:36 The LORD will j his people
Jdg 2:18 Whenever the LORD raised up a j
1Sa 2:10 the LORD will j the ends
3:13 that I would j his family forever
7:15 j over Israel all the days of his life.
24:12 May the LORD j between you
1Ki 8:32 J between your servants,
1Ch 16:33 for he comes to j the earth.
2Ch 6:23 J between your servants, repaying
19: 7 J carefully, for with the LORD our
Job 9:15 plead with my J for mercy.
Ps 7: 8 J me, O LORD, according
7: 8 let the LORD j the peoples.
7:11 God is a righteous j,
9: 8 He will j the world in righteousness
50: 6 for God himself is j.
51: 4 and justified when you j.
75: 2 it is I who j uprightly.
76: 9 when you, O God, rose up to j,
82: 8 Rise up, O God, j the earth,
94: 2 Rise up, O J of the earth;
96:10 he will j the peoples with equity.
96:13 He will j the world in righteousness
98: 9 He will j the world in righteousness
110: 6 He will j the nations, heaping up
Pr 31: 9 Speak up and j fairly;
Isa 2: 4 He will j between the nations
3:13 he rises to j the people.
11: 3 He will not j by what he sees
33:22 For the LORD is our j,
Jer 11:20 Almighty, you who j righteously
Eze 7: 3 I will j you according
7:27 by their own standards I will j them
18:30 O house of Israel, I will j you,
20:36 so I will j you, declares
Eze 22: 2 "Son of man, will you j her?
34:17 I will j between one sheep
Joel 3:12 sit to j all the nations on every side.
Mic 3:11 Her leaders j for a bribe,
4: 3 He will j between many peoples
Mt 7: 1 Do not j, or you too will be judged.
Lk 6:37 "Do not j, and you will not be
18: 2 there was a j who neither feared
Jn 5:27 And he has given him authority to j
5:30 By myself I can do nothing; I j only
8:16 But if I do j, my decisions are right,
12:47 For I did not come to j the world,
12:48 There is a j for the one who rejects
Ac 10:42 as j of the living and the dead.
17:31 a day when he will j the world
Ro 2:16 day when God will j men's secrets
3: 6 how could God j the world?
14:10 then, why do you j your brother?
1Co 4: 3 indeed, I do not even j myself.
4: 5 Therefore j nothing
6: 2 And if you are to j the world,
6: 2 that the saints will j the world?
Gal 2: 6 not j by external appearance—
Col 2:16 Therefore do not let anyone j you
2Ti 4: 1 who will j the living and the dead,
4: 8 which the Lord, the righteous J,
Heb 10:30 "The Lord will j his people."
12:23 come to God, the j of all men,
13: 4 for God will j the adulterer
Jas 4:12 There is only one Lawgiver and J,
4:12 who are you to j your neighbor?
1Pe 4: 5 to him who is ready to j the living
Rev 20: 4 who had been given authority to j.

JUDGED (JUDGE)

Mt 7: 1 "Do not judge, or you too will be j.
1Co 4: 3 I care very little if I am j by you
10:29 For why should my freedom be j
11:31 But if we j ourselves, we would not
14:24 all that he is a sinner and will be j
Jas 3: 1 who teach will be j more strictly.
Rev 20:12 The dead were j according

JUDGES (JUDGE)

Jdg 2:16 Then the LORD raised up j,
Job 9:24 he blindfolds its j.
Ps 58:11 there is a God who j the earth."
75: 7 But it is God who j:
Pr 29:14 If a king j the poor with fairness,
Jn 5:22 Moreover, the Father j no one,
1Co 4: 4 It is the Lord who j me.
Heb 4:12 it j the thoughts and attitudes
1Pe 1:17 on a Father who j each man's work
2:23 himself to him who j justly.
Rev 19:11 With justice he j and makes war.

JUDGING (JUDGE)

Ps 9: 4 on your throne, j righteously.
Pr 24:23 To show partiality in j is not good:
Isa 16: 5 one who in j seeks justice
Mt 19:28 j the twelve tribes of Israel.
Jn 7:24 Stop j by mere appearances,

JUDGMENT (JUDGE)

Nu 33: 4 for the LORD had brought j
Dt 1:17 of any man, for j belongs to God.
32:41 and my hand grasps it in j,
1Sa 25:33 May you be blessed for your good j
Ps 1: 5 the wicked will not stand in the j,
9: 7 he has established his throne for j.
76: 8 From heaven you pronounced j,
82: 1 he gives j among the "gods":
119:66 Teach me knowledge and good j,
143: 2 Do not bring your servant into j,
Pr 3:21 preserve sound j and discernment,
6:32 man who commits adultery lacks j;
8:14 Counsel and sound j are mine;
10:21 but fools die for lack of j.
11:12 man who lacks j derides his
12:11 but he who chases fantasies lacks j.
17:18 A man lacking in j strikes hands
18: 1 he defies all sound j.
28:16 A tyrannical ruler lacks j,
Ecc 12:14 God will bring every deed into j,
Isa 3:14 The LORD enters into j
28: 6 justice to him who sits in j,
53: 8 By oppression and j he was taken
66:16 the LORD will execute j
Jer 2:35 But I will pass j on you
25:31 he will bring j on all mankind
51:18 when their j comes, they will
Eze 11:10 and I will execute j on you
Da 7:22 pronounced j in favor of the saints
Am 7: 4 Sovereign LORD was calling for j
Zec 8:16 and sound j in your courts;

Mal 3: 5 "So I will come near to you for *j*.
Mt 5:21 who murders will be subject to *j*.'
5:22 with his brother will be subject to *j*.
10:15 on the day of *j* than for that town.
11:24 on the day of *j* than for you."
12:36 have to give account on the day of *j*
12:41 up at the *j* with this generation
Jn 5:22 but has entrusted all *j* to the Son,
5:30 as I hear, and my *j* is just,
7:24 appearances, and make a right *j*."
8:26 "I have much to say in *j* of you.
9:39 "For *j* I have come into this world,
12:31 Now is the time for *j* on this world;
16: 8 to sin and righteousness and *j*:
16:11 in regard to *j*, because the prince
Ac 24:25 self-control and the *j* to come,
Ro 2: 1 you who pass *j* on someone else,
2: 2 Now we know that God's *j*
5:16 The *j* followed one sin
12: 3 rather think of yourself with sober *j*
14:10 stand before God's *j* seat.
14:13 Therefore let us stop passing *j*
1Co 7:40 In my *j*, she is happier if she stays
11:29 body of the Lord eats and drinks *j*
2Co 5:10 appear before the *j* seat of Christ,
2Th 1: 5 is evidence that God's *j* is right,
1Ti 3: 6 fall under the same *j* as the devil.
5:12 Thus they bring *j* on themselves,
Heb 6: 2 of the dead, and eternal *j*.
9:27 to die once, and after that to face *j*,
10:27 but only a fearful expectation of *j*
Jas 2:13 *j* without mercy will be shown
4:11 are not keeping it, but sitting in *j*
1Pe 4:17 For it is time for *j* to begin
2Pe 2: 9 the unrighteous for the day of *j*,
3: 7 being kept for the day of *j*
1Jn 4:17 have confidence on the day of *j*,
Jude : 6 bound with everlasting chains for *j*
Rev 14: 7 because the hour of his *j* has come.

JUDGMENTS (JUDGE)

Jer 1:16 I will pronounce my *j* on my people
Da 9:11 and sworn *j* written in the Law
Hos 6: 5 my *j* flashed like lightning
Ro 11:33 How unsearchable his *j*,
1Co 2:15 spiritual man makes *j* about all
Rev 16: 7 true and just are your *j*."

JUG

1Sa 26:12 and water *j* near Saul's head,
1Ki 17:12 of flour in a jar and a little oil in a *j*.

JUST* (JUSTICE JUSTIFICATION JUSTIFIED JUSTIFIES JUSTIFY JUSTIFYING JUSTLY)

Ge 18:19 LORD by doing what is right and *j*,
Dt 2:12 *j* as Israel did in the land
6: 3 *j* as the LORD, the God
27: 3 and honey, *j* as the LORD,
30: 9 *j* as he delighted in your fathers,
32: 4 and all his ways are *j*.
32: 4 upright and *j* is he.
32:47 They are not *j* idle words for you—
32:50 *j* as your brother Aaron died
2Sa 8:15 doing what was *j* and right
1Ch 18:14 doing what was *j* and right
2Ch 12: 6 and said, "The LORD is *j*."
Ne 9:13 and laws that are *j* and right,
9:33 you have been *j*; you have acted
Job 34:17 Will you condemn the *j*
35: 2 Elihu said: "Do you think this is *j*?
Ps 37:28 For the LORD loves the *j*
37:30 and his tongue speaks what is *j*.
99: 4 what is *j* and right.
111: 7 of his hands are faithful and *j*;
119:121 I have done what is righteous and *j*;
Pr 1: 3 doing what is right and *j* and fair;
2: 8 for he guards the course of the *j*
2: 9 will understand what is right and *j*
8: 8 All the words of my mouth are *j*;
8:15 and rulers make laws that are *j*;
12: 5 The plans of the righteous are *j*,
21: 3 To do what is right and *j*
Isa 32: 7 even when the plea of the needy is *j*
58: 2 They ask me for *j* decisions
Jer 4: 2 if in a truthful, *j* and righteous way
22: 3 what the LORD says: Do what is *j*
22:15 He did what was right and *j*,
23: 5 do what is *j* and right in the land.
33:15 he will do what is *j* and right
Eze 18: 5 who does what is *j* and right.
18:19 Since the son has done what is *j*
18:21 and does what is *j* and right,
18:25 'The way of the Lord is not *j*.'
18:27 and does what is *j* and right,
18:29 'The way of the Lord is not *j*.'
33:14 and does what is *j* and right—
33:16 He has done what is *j* and right;
33:17 But it is their way that is not *j*.
33:17 'The way of the Lord is not *j*.'
33:19 and does what is *j* and right,
33:20 'The way of the Lord is not *j*.'
45: 9 and oppression and do what is *j*
Da 4:37 does is right and all his ways are *j*.
Jn 5:30 as I hear, and my judgment is *j*,
Ro 3:26 as to be *j* and the one who justifies
2Th 1: 6 God is *j*: He will pay back trouble
Heb 2: 2 received its *j* punishment,
1Jn 1: 9 and *j* and will forgive us our sins
Rev 15: 3 *J* and true are your ways,
16: 5 "You are *j* in these judgments,
16: 7 true and *j* are your judgments."
19: 2 for true and *j* are his judgments.

JUSTICE* (JUST)

Ge 49:16 "Dan will provide *j* for his people
Ex 23: 2 do not pervert *j* by siding
23: 6 "Do not deny *j* to your poor people
Lev 19:15 " 'Do not pervert *j*; do not show
Dt 16:19 Do not pervert *j* or show partiality.
16:20 Follow *j* and *j* alone,
24:17 the alien or the fatherless of *j*,
27:19 Cursed is the man who withholds *j*
1Sa 8: 3 accepted bribes and perverted *j*.
2Sa 15: 4 and I would see that he gets *j*."
15: 6 came to the king asking for *j*,
1Ki 3:11 for discernment in administering *j*,
3:28 wisdom from God to administer *j*.
7: 7 the Hall of *J*, where he was to judge
10: 9 to maintain *j* and righteousness."
2Ch 9: 8 to maintain *j* and righteousness."
Ezr 7:25 and judges to administer *j*
Est 1:13 experts in matters of law and *j*,
Job 8: 3 Does God pervert *j*?
9:19 matter of *j*, who will summon him?
19: 7 though I call for help, there is no *j*.
27: 2 as God lives, who has denied me *j*,
29:14 *j* was my robe and my turban.
31:13 "If I have denied *j*
34: 5 but God denies me *j*.
34:12 that the Almighty would pervert *j*.
34:17 Can he who hates *j* govern?
36: 3 I will ascribe *j* to my Maker.
36:17 *j* have taken hold of you.
37:23 in his *j* and great righteousness,
40: 8 "Would you discredit my *j*?
Ps 7: 6 Awake, my God; decree *j*.
9: 8 he will govern the peoples with *j*.
9:16 The LORD is known by his *j*;
11: 7 he loves *j*;
33: 5 LORD loves righteousness and *j*;
36: 6 your *j* like the great deep.
37: 6 *j* of your cause like the noonday
45: 6 a scepter of *j* will be the scepter
72: 1 Endow the king with your *j*, O God
72: 2 your afflicted ones with *j*.
89:14 *j* are the foundation of your throne;
97: 2 *j* are the foundation of his throne.
99: 4 The King is mighty, he loves *j*—
101: 1 I will sing of your love and *j*;
103: 6 and *j* for all the oppressed.
106: 3 Blessed are they who maintain *j*,
112: 5 who conducts his affairs with *j*.
140:12 I know that the LORD secures *j*
Pr 8:20 along the paths of *j*,
16:10 and his mouth should not betray *j*.
17:23 to pervert the course of *j*.
18: 5 or to deprive the innocent of *j*.
19:28 A corrupt witness mocks at *j*,
21:15 When *j* is done, it brings joy
28: 5 Evil men do not understand *j*,
29: 4 By *j* a king gives a country stability
29: 7 The righteous care about *j*
29:26 from the LORD that man gets *j*.
Ecc 3:16 place of *j*—wickedness was there.
5: 8 poor oppressed in a district, and *j*
Isa 1:17 Seek *j*,
1:21 She once was full of *j*;
1:27 Zion will be redeemed with *j*,
5: 7 he looked for *j*, but saw bloodshed;
5:16 Almighty will be exalted by his *j*,
5:23 but deny *j* to the innocent.
9: 7 it with *j* and righteousness
10: 2 and withhold *j* from the oppressed of my people
11: 4 with *j* he will give decisions
16: 5 one who in judging seeks *j*
28: 6 He will be a spirit of *j*
28:17 I will make *j* the measuring line
29:21 deprive the innocent of *j*.
Isa 30:18 For the LORD is a God of *j*.
32: 1 and rulers will rule with *j*.
32:16 *J* will dwell in the desert
33: 5 with *j* and righteousness.
42: 1 and he will bring *j* to the nations.
42: 3 In faithfulness he will bring forth *j*;
42: 4 till he establishes *j* on earth.
51: 4 my *j* will become a light
51: 5 my arm will bring *j* to the nations.
56: 1 "Maintain *j*
59: 4 No one calls for *j*;
59: 8 there is no *j* in their paths.
59: 9 So *j* is far from us,
59:11 We look for *j*, but find none;
59:14 So *j* is driven back,
59:15 that there was no *j*.
61: 8 "For I, the LORD, love *j*;
Jer 9:24 *j* and righteousness on earth,
10:24 Correct me, LORD, but only with *j*
12: 1 speak with you about your *j*:
21:12 " 'Administer *j* every morning;
30:11 I will discipline you but only with *j*;
46:28 I will discipline you but only with *j*;
La 3:36 to deprive a man of *j*—
Eze 22:29 mistreat the alien, denying them *j*.
34:16 I will shepherd the flock with *j*.
Hos 2:19 you in righteousness and *j*,
12: 6 maintain love and *j*,
Am 2: 7 and deny *j* to the oppressed.
5: 7 You who turn *j* into bitterness
5:12 and you deprive the poor of *j*
5:15 maintain *j* in the courts.
5:24 But let *j* roll on like a river,
6:12 But you have turned *j* into poison
Mic 3: 1 Should you not know *j*,
3: 8 and with *j* and might,
3: 9 who despise *j*
Hab 1: 4 and *j* never prevails.
1: 4 so that *j* is perverted.
Zep 3: 5 by morning he dispenses his *j*,
Zec 7: 9 'Administer true *j*; show mercy
Mal 2:17 or "Where is the God of *j*?"
3: 5 and deprive aliens of *j*,
Mt 12:18 he will proclaim *j* to the nations.
12:20 till he leads *j* to victory.
23:23 important matters of the law—*j*,
Lk 11:42 you neglect *j* and the love of God.
18: 3 'Grant me *j* against my adversary.'
18: 5 I will see that she gets *j*,
18: 7 And will not God bring about *j*
18: 8 he will see that they get *j*,
Ac 8:33 humiliation he was deprived of *j*.
17:31 with *j* by the man he has appointed.
28: 4 *J* has not allowed him to live."
Ro 3:25 He did this to demonstrate his *j*,
3:26 it to demonstrate his *j*
2Co 7:11 what readiness to see *j* done.
Heb 11:33 administered *j*, and gained what
Rev 19:11 With *j* he judges and makes war.

JUSTIFICATION* (JUST)

Eze 16:52 for you have furnished some *j*
Ro 4:25 and was raised to life for our *j*.
5:16 many trespasses and brought *j*.
5:18 of righteousness was *j* that brings

JUSTIFIED* (JUST)

Ps 51: 4 and *j* when you judge.
Lk 18:14 rather than the other, went home *j*
Ac 13:39 from everything you could not be *j*
13:39 him everyone who believes is *j*
Ro 3:24 and are *j* freely by his grace
3:28 For we maintain that a man is *j*
4: 2 If, in fact, Abraham was *j* by works,
5: 1 since we have been *j* through faith,
5: 9 Since we have now been *j*
8:30 those he called, he also *j*; those he *j*,
10:10 heart that you believe and are *j*,
1Co 6:11 you were *j* in the name
Gal 2:16 in Christ Jesus that we may be *j*
2:16 observing the law no one will be *j*.
2:16 sinners' know that a man is not *j*
2:17 "If, while we seek to be *j* in Christ,
3:11 Clearly no one is *j* before God
3:24 to Christ that we might be *j* by faith
5: 4 to be *j* by law have been alienated
Tit 3: 7 so that, having been *j* by his grace,
Jas 2:24 You see that a person is *j*

JUSTIFIES* (JUST)

Ro 3:26 one who *j* those who have faith
4: 5 but trusts God who *j* the wicked,
8:33 God has chosen? It is God who *j*.

JUSTIFY* (JUST)

Est 7: 4 such distress would *j* disturbing
Job 40: 8 you condemn me to *j* yourself?
Isa 53: 11 my righteous servant will *j* many,
Lk 10: 29 But he wanted to *j* himself,
16: 15 "You are the ones who *j* yourselves
Ro 3: 30 who will *j* the circumcised by faith
Gal 3: 8 that God would *j* the Gentiles

JUSTIFYING* (JUST)

Job 32: 2 angry with Job for *j* himself rather

JUSTLY* (JUST)

Ps 58: 1 Do you rulers indeed speak *j*?
67: 4 for you rule the peoples *j*
Jer 7: 5 and deal with each other *j*,
Mic 6: 8 To act *j* and to love mercy
Lk 23: 41 We are punished *j*,
1Pe 2: 23 himself to him who judges *j*.

KADESH

Nu 20: 1 of Zin, and they stayed at *K*.
Dt 1: 46 And so you stayed in *K* many days

KADESH BARNEA

Nu 32: 8 I sent them from *K* to look over

KEBAR

Eze 1: 1 among the exiles by the *K* River,

KEDORLAOMER

Ge 14: 17 Abram returned from defeating *K*

KEEP (KEEPER KEEPING KEEPS KEPT)

Ge 31: 49 "May the LORD *k* watch
Ex 15: 26 his commands and *k* all his
20: 6 and *k* my commandments.
Lev 15: 31 You must *k* the Israelites separate
Nu 6: 24 and *k* you;
Dt 4: 2 but *k* the commands of the LORD
6: 17 Be sure to *k* the commands
7: 9 who love him and *k* his commands.
7: 12 your God will *k* his covenant
11: 1 your God and *k* his requirements,
13: 4 *K* his commands and obey him;
30: 10 your God and *k* his commands
30: 16 and to *k* his commands, decrees
Jos 22: 5 careful to *k* the commandment
1Ki 8: 58 and to *k* the commands,
2Ki 17: 19 Judah did not *k* the commands
23: 3 the LORD and *k* his commands,
1Ch 29: 18 and *k* their hearts loyal to you.
2Ch 6: 14 you who *k* your covenant of love
34: 31 the LORD and *k* his commands,
Job 14: 16 but not *k* track of my sin.
Ps 18: 28 You, O LORD, *k* my lamp burning
19: 13 *K* your servant also from willful
78: 10 they did not *k* God's covenant
119: 2 Blessed are they who *k* his statutes
119: 9 can a young man *k* his way pure?
121: 7 The LORD will *k* you
141: 3 *k* watch over the door of my lips.
Pr 4: 21 *k* them within your heart;
4: 24 *k* corrupt talk far from your lips.
30: 8 *K* falsehood and lies far from me;
Ecc 3: 6 a time to *k* and a time
12: 13 and *k* his commandments,
Isa 26: 3 You will *k* in perfect peace
42: 6 I will *k* you and will make you
58: 13 "If you *k* your feet
Jer 16: 11 forsook me and did not *k* my law.
Eze 20: 19 and be careful to *k* my laws.
Mt 10: 10 for the worker is worth his *k*.
Lk 12: 35 and *k* your lamps burning,
17: 33 tries to *k* his life will lose it,
Jn 10: 24 How long will you *k* us in suspense
12: 25 in this world will *k* it for eternal life
Ac 2: 24 for death to *k* its hold on him.
18: 9 "Do not be afraid; *k* on speaking,
Ro 7: 19 want to do—this I *k* on doing.
12: 11 but *k* your spiritual fervor,
14: 22 you believe about these things *k*
16: 17 *K* away from them.
1Co 1: 8 He will *k* you strong to the end,
2Co 12: 7 To *k* me from becoming conceited
Gal 5: 25 let us *k* in step with the Spirit.
Eph 4: 3 Make every effort to *k* the unity
2Th 3: 6 to *k* away from every brother who
1Ti 5: 22 *K* yourself pure.
2Ti 4: 5 *k* your head in all situations,
Heb 9: 20 God has commanded you to *k*."
13: 5 *K* your lives free from the love
Jas 1: 26 and yet does not *k* a tight rein
2: 8 If you really *k* the royal law found
Jas 3: 2 able to *k* his whole body in check.
2Pe 1: 8 will *k* you from being ineffective
Jude :21 *K* yourselves in God's love
:24 able to *k* you from falling
Rev 3: 10 also *k* you from the hour
22: 9 of all who *k* the words of this book.

KEEPER (KEEP)

Ge 4: 9 I my brother's *k*?" The LORD

KEEPING (KEEP)

Ex 20: 8 the Sabbath day by *k* it holy.
Dt 5: 12 the Sabbath day by *k* it holy,
13: 18 *k* all his commands that I am
Ps 19: 11 in *k* them there is great reward.
119: 112 My heart is set on *k* your decrees
Pr 15: 3 *k* watch on the wicked
Mt 3: 8 Produce fruit in *k* with repentance.
Lk 2: 8 *k* watch over their flocks at night.
1Co 7: 19 *K* God's commands is what counts.
2Co 8: 5 and then to us in *k* with God's will.
Jas 4: 11 you are not *k* it, but sitting
1Pe 3: 16 and respect, *k* a clear conscience,
2Pe 3: 9 Lord is not slow in *k* his promise,

KEEPS (KEEP)

Ne 1: 5 who *k* his covenant of love
Ps 15: 4 who *k* his oath
Pr 12: 23 A prudent man *k* his knowledge
15: 21 of understanding *k* a straight
17: 28 a fool is thought wise if he *k* silent,
29: 11 a wise man *k* himself under control
Isa 56: 2 who *k* the Sabbath
Da 9: 4 who *k* his covenant of love
Am 5: 13 Therefore the prudent man *k* quiet
Jn 7: 19 Yet not one of you *k* the law.
8: 51 if anyone *k* my word, he will never
1Co 13: 5 is not easily angered, it *k* no record
Jas 2: 10 For whoever *k* the whole law
Rev 22: 7 Blessed is he who *k* the words

KEILAH

1Sa 23: 13 that David had escaped from *K*,

KEPT (KEEP)

Ex 12: 42 Because the LORD *k* vigil that
Dt 7: 8 and *k* the oath he swore
2Ki 18: 6 he *k* the commands the LORD had
Ne 9: 8 You have *k* your promise
Ps 130: 3 If you, O LORD, *k* a record of sins,
Isa 38: 17 In your love you *k* me
Mt 19: 20 these I have *k*," the young man
2Co 11: 9 I have *k* myself from being
2Ti 4: 7 finished the race, I have *k* the faith.
1Pe 1: 4 spoil or fade—*k* in heaven for you,

KERNEL

Mk 4: 28 then the full *k* in the head.
Jn 12: 24 a *k* of wheat falls to the ground

KEY (KEYS)

Isa 33: 6 the fear of the LORD is the *k*
Rev 20: 1 having the *k* to the Abyss

KEYS* (KEY)

Mt 16: 19 I will give you the *k* of the kingdom
Rev 1: 18 And I hold the *k* of death

KICK*

Ac 26: 14 for you to *k* against the goads.'

KILL (KILLED KILLS)

Ecc 3: 3 a time to *k* and a time to heal,
Mt 10: 28 *k* the body but cannot *k* the soul.
17: 23 They will *k* him, and on the third
Mk 9: 31 will *k* him, and after three days
10: 34 spit on him, flog him and *k* him.

KILLED (KILL)

Ge 4: 8 his brother Abel and *k* him.
Ex 2: 12 he *k* the Egyptian and hid him
13: 15 the LORD *k* every firstborn
Nu 35: 11 who has *k* someone accidentally
1Sa 17: 50 down the Philistine and *k* him.
Ne 9: 26 They *k* your prophets, who had
Hos 6: 5 I *k* you with the words
Lk 11: 48 they *k* the prophets, and you build
Ac 3: 15 You *k* the author of life,

KILLS (KILL)

Ex 21: 12 *k* him shall surely be put to death.
Lev 24: 21 but whoever *k* a man must be put
2Co 3: 6 for the letter *k*, but the Spirit gives

KIND (KINDNESS KINDNESSES KINDS)

Ge 1: 24 animals, each according to its *k*."
2Ch 10: 7 "If you will be *k* to these people
Pr 11: 17 A *k* man benefits himself,
12: 25 but a *k* word cheers him up.
14: 21 blessed is he who is *k* to the needy.
14: 31 whoever is *k* to the needy honors
19: 17 He who is *k* to the poor lends
Da 4: 27 by being *k* to the oppressed.
Lk 6: 35 because he is *k* to the ungrateful
1Co 13: 4 Love is patient, love is *k*.
15: 35 With what *k* of body will they
Eph 4: 32 Be *k* and compassionate
1Th 5: 15 but always try to be *k* to each other
2Ti 2: 24 instead, he must be *k* to everyone,
Tit 2: 5 to be busy at home, to be *k*,

KINDHEARTED* (HEART)

Pr 11: 16 A *k* woman gains respect,

KINDNESS (KIND)

Ge 24: 12 and show *k* to my master Abraham
32: 10 I am unworthy of all the *k*
39: 21 he showed him *k* and granted him
Jdg 8: 35 failed to show *k* to the family
Ru 2: 20 has not stopped showing his *k*
2Sa 9: 3 to whom I can show God's *k*?"
22: 51 he shows unfailing *k*
Ps 18: 50 he shows unfailing *k*
141: 5 righteous man strike me—it is a *k*;
Isa 54: 8 but with everlasting *k*
Jer 9: 24 I am the LORD, who exercises *k*,
Hos 11: 4 I led them with cords of human *k*,
Ac 14: 17 He has shown *k* by giving you rain
Ro 11: 22 Consider therefore the *k*
2Co 6: 6 understanding, patience and *k*;
Gal 5: 22 peace, patience, *k*, goodness,
Eph 2: 7 expressed in his *k* to us
Col 3: 12 yourselves with compassion, *k*,
Tit 3: 4 But when the *k* and love
2Pe 1: 7 brotherly *k*; and to brotherly *k*,

KINDNESSES* (KIND)

Ps 106: 7 did not remember your many *k*,
Isa 63: 7 I will tell of the *k* of the LORD,
63: 7 to his compassion and many *k*.

KINDS (KIND)

Ge 1: 12 bearing seed according to their *k*
1Co 12: 4 There are different *k* of gifts,
1Ti 6: 10 of money is a root of all *k* of evil.
1Pe 1: 6 had to suffer grief in all *k* of trials.

KING (KING'S KINGDOM KINGDOMS KINGS)

1. Kings of Judah and Israel: see Saul, David, Solomon.

2. Kings of Judah: see Rehoboam, Abijah, Asa, Jehoshaphat, Jehoram, Ahaziah, Athaliah (Queen), Joash, Amaziah, Azariah (Uzziah), Jotham, Ahaz, Hezekiah, Manasseh, Amon, Josiah, Jehoahaz, Jehoiakim, Jehoiachin, Zedekiah.

3. Kings of Israel: see Jeroboam I, Nadab, Baasha, Elah, Zimri, Tibni, Omri, Ahab, Ahaziah, Joram, Jehu, Jehoahaz, Jehoash, Jeroboam II, Zechariah, Shallum, Menahem, Pekah, Pekahiah, Hoshea.

Ex 1: 8 a new *k*, who did not know about
Dt 17: 14 "Let us set a *k* over us like all
Jdg 17: 6 In those days Israel had no *k*;
1Sa 8: 5 now appoint a *k* to lead us,
11: 15 as *k* in the presence of the LORD.
12: 12 the LORD your God was your *k*.
2Sa 2: 4 and there they anointed David *k*
1Ki 1: 30 Solomon your son shall be *k*
Ps 2: 6 "I have installed my *K*
24: 7 that the *K* of glory may come in.
44: 4 You are my *K* and my God,
47: 7 For God is the *K* of all the earth;
Isa 32: 1 See, a *k* will reign in righteousness
Jer 30: 9 and David their *k*,
Hos 3: 5 their God and David their *k*.
Mic 2: 13 *k* will pass through before them,
Zec 9: 9 See, your *k* comes to you,
Mt 2: 2 is the one who has been born *k*
27: 11 "Are you the *k* of the Jews?" "Yes,
Lk 19: 38 "Blessed is the *k* who comes
23: 3 "Are you the *k* of the Jews?" "Yes,
23: 38 THE *K* OF THE JEWS.
Jn 1: 49 of God; you are the *K* of Israel."
12: 13 "Blessed is the *K* of Israel!"
Ac 17: 7 saying that there is another *k*,
1Ti 1: 17 Now to the *K* eternal, immortal,

1Ti 6:15 the *K* of kings and Lord of lords,
Heb 7:1 This Melchizedek was *k* of Salem
1Pe 2:13 to the *k*, as the supreme authority,
2:17 of believers, fear God, honor the *k*.
Rev 15:3 *K* of the ages.
17:14 he is Lord of lords and *K* of kings—
19:16 *K* OF KINGS AND LORD

KING'S (KING)

Pr 21:1 The *k* heart is in the hand
Ecc 8:3 in a hurry to leave the *k* presence.

KINGDOM (KING)

Ex 19:6 you will be for me a *k* of priests
Dt 17:18 When he takes the throne of his *k*,
2Sa 7:12 body, and I will establish his *k*.
1Ki 11:31 to tear the *k* out of Solomon's hand
1Ch 17:11 own sons, and I will establish his *k*.
29:11 Yours, O LORD, is the *k*;
Ps 45:6 justice will be the scepter of your *k*.
103:19 and his *k* rules over all.
145:11 They will tell of the glory of your *k*
Eze 29:14 There they will be a lowly *k*.
Da 2:39 "After you, another *k* will rise,
4:3 His *k* is an eternal *k*;
7:27 His *k* will be an everlasting *k*,
Ob :21 And the *k* will be the LORD's.
Mt 3:2 Repent, for the *k* of heaven is near
4:17 Repent, for the *k* of heaven is near
4:23 preaching the good news of the *k*,
5:3 for theirs is the *k* of heaven.
5:10 for theirs is the *k* of heaven.
5:19 great in the *k* of heaven.
5:19 least in the *k* of heaven,
5:20 you will certainly not enter the *k*
6:10 your *k* come,
6:33 But seek first his *k* and his
7:21 Lord,' will enter the *k* of heaven,
8:11 Isaac and Jacob in the *k* of heaven.
8:12 the subjects of the *k* will be thrown
9:35 preaching the good news of the *k*
10:7 preach this message: 'The *k*
11:11 least in the *k* of heaven is greater
11:12 the *k* of heaven has been forcefully
12:25 "Every *k* divided against itself will
12:26 How then can his *k* stand?
12:28 then the *k* of God has come
13:11 knowledge of the secrets of the *k*
13:19 hears the message about the *k*
13:24 "The *k* of heaven is like a man who
13:31 *k* of heaven is like a mustard seed,
13:33 "The *k* of heaven is like yeast that
13:38 stands for the sons of the *k*.
13:41 of his *k* everything that causes sin
13:43 the sun in the *k* of their Father.
13:44 *k* of heaven is like treasure hidden
13:45 the *k* of heaven is like a merchant
13:47 *k* of heaven is like a net that was let
13:52 has been instructed about the *k*
16:19 the keys of the *k* of heaven;
16:28 the Son of Man coming in his *k*."
18:1 the greatest in the *k* of heaven?"
18:3 you will never enter the *k*
18:4 the greatest in the *k* of heaven.
18:23 the *k* of heaven is like a king who
19:12 because of the *k* of heaven.
19:14 for the *k* of heaven belongs to such
19:23 man to enter the *k* of heaven.
19:24 for a rich man to enter the *k* of God
20:1 "For the *k* of heaven is like
20:21 the other at your left in your *k*."
21:31 the prostitutes are entering the *k*
21:43 "Therefore I tell you that the *k*
22:2 "The *k* of heaven is like a king who
23:13 You shut the *k* of heaven
24:7 rise against nation, and *k* against *k*.
24:14 gospel of the *k* will be preached
25:1 "At that time the *k*
25:34 the *k* prepared for you
26:29 anew with you in my Father's *k*."
Mk 1:15 "The *k* of God is near.
3:24 If a *k* is divided against itself,
3:24 against itself, that *k* cannot stand.
4:11 "The secret of the *k*
4:26 "This is what the *k* of God is like.
4:30 "What shall we say the *k*
6:23 I will give you, up to half my *k*."
9:1 before they see the *k* of God come
9:47 better for you to enter the *k* of God
10:14 for the *k* of God belongs to such
10:15 anyone who will not receive the *k*
10:23 for the rich to enter the *k* of God!"
10:24 how hard it is to enter the *k* of God
10:25 for a rich man to enter the *k* of God
11:10 "Blessed is the coming *k*
Mk 12:34 "You are not far from the *k* of God
13:8 rise against nation, and *k* against *k*.
14:25 day when I drink it anew in the *k*
15:43 who was himself waiting for the *k*
Lk 1:33 Jacob forever; his *k* will never
4:43 of the *k* of God to the other towns
6:20 for yours is the *k* of God.
7:28 in the *k* of God is greater than he."
8:1 proclaiming the good news of the *k*
8:10 knowledge of the secrets of the *k*
9:2 out to preach the *k* of God
9:11 spoke to them about the *k* of God,
9:27 before they see the *k* of God."
9:60 you go and proclaim the *k* of God
9:62 fit for service in the *k* of God."
10:9 'The *k* of God is near you.'
10:11 sure of this: The *k* of God is near.'
11:2 your *k* come.
11:17 "Any *k* divided against itself will
11:18 himself, how can his *k* stand?
11:20 then the *k* of God has come to you.
12:31 seek his *k*, and these things will be
12:32 has been pleased to give you the *k*.
13:18 "What is the *k* of God like?
13:20 What shall I compare the *k* of God
13:28 all the prophets in the *k* of God,
13:29 places at the feast in the *k* of God.
14:15 eat at the feast in the *k* of God."
16:16 the good news of the *k*
17:20 when the *k* of God would come,
17:20 *k* of God does not come with careful observation,
17:21 because the *k* of God is within you
18:16 for the *k* of God belongs to such
18:17 anyone who will not receive the *k*
18:24 for the rich to enter the *k* of God!
18:25 for a rich man to enter the *k* of God
18:29 for the sake of the *k* of God will fail
19:11 and the people thought that the *k*
21:10 rise against nation, and *k* against *k*.
21:31 you know that the *k* of God is near.
22:16 until it finds fulfillment in the *k*
22:18 the vine until the *k* of God comes."
22:29 And I confer on you a *k*, just
22:30 and drink at my table in my *k*
23:42 me when you come into your *k*."
23:51 he was waiting for the *k* of God.
Jn 3:3 no one can see the *k* of God.
3:5 no one can enter the *k* of God.
18:36 now my *k* is from another place."
18:36 "My *k* is not of this world.
Ac 1:3 and spoke about the *k* of God.
1:6 going to restore the *k* to Israel?"
8:12 he preached the good news of the *k*
14:22 hardships to enter the *k* of God,"
19:8 arguing persuasively about the *k*
20:25 about preaching the *k* will ever see
28:23 and declared to them the *k* of God
28:31 hindrance he preached the *k*
Ro 14:17 For the *k* of God is not a matter
1Co 4:20 For the *k* of God is not a matter
6:9 the wicked will not inherit the *k*
6:10 swindlers will inherit the *k* of God.
15:24 hands over the *k* to God the Father
15:50 blood cannot inherit the *k* of God,
Gal 5:21 live like this will not inherit the *k*
Eph 2:2 and of the ruler of the *k* of the air,
5:5 has any inheritance in the *k*
Col 1:12 of the saints in the *k* of light.
1:13 and brought us into the *k*
4:11 among my fellow workers for the *k*
1Th 2:12 who calls you into his *k* and glory.
2Th 1:5 will be counted worthy of the *k*
2Ti 4:1 in view of his appearing and his *k*,
4:18 bring me safely to his heavenly *k*.
Heb 1:8 will be the scepter of your *k*.
12:28 we are receiving a *k* that cannot be
Jas 2:5 to inherit the *k* he promised those
2Pe 1:11 into the eternal *k* of our Lord
Rev 1:6 has made us to be a *k* and priests
1:9 companion in the suffering and *k*
5:10 You have made them to be a *k*
11:15 of the world has become the *k*
11:15 "The *k* of the world has become
12:10 the power and the *k* of our God,
16:10 his *k* was plunged into darkness.
17:12 who have not yet received a *k*,

KINGDOMS (KING)

2Ki 19:15 God over all the *k* of the earth.
19:19 so that all *k* on earth may know
2Ch 20:6 rule over all the *k* of the nations.
Ps 68:32 Sing to God, O *k* of the earth,
Isa 37:16 God over all the *k* of the earth.
37:20 so that all *k* on earth may know
Eze 29:15 It will be the lowliest of *k*
37:22 or be divided into two *k*.
Da 4:17 Most High is sovereign over the *k*
7:17 great beasts are four *k* that will rise
Zep 3:8 to gather the *k*

KINGS (KING)

Ps 2:2 The *k* of the earth take their stand
47:9 for the *k* of the earth belong to God
68:29 *k* will bring you gifts.
72:11 All *k* will bow down to him
110:5 he will crush *k* on the day
149:8 to bind their *k* with fetters,
Pr 16:12 *K* detest wrongdoing,
Isa 24:21 and the *k* on the earth below.
52:15 and *k* will shut their mouths
60:11 their *k* led in triumphal procession.
Da 2:21 he sets up *k* and deposes them.
7:24 ten horns are ten *k* who will come
Lk 21:12 and you will be brought before *k*
1Co 4:8 You have become *k*—
1Ti 2:2 for *k* and all those in authority,
6:15 the King of *k* and Lord of lords,
Rev 1:5 and the ruler of the *k* of the earth.
17:14 he is Lord of lords and King of *k*—
19:16 KING OF *K* AND LORD

KINSMAN-REDEEMER (REDEEM)

Ru 3:9 over me, since you are a *k*."
4:14 day has not left you without a *k*.

KISS (KISSED KISSES)

Ps 2:12 *K* the Son, lest he be angry
Pr 24:26 is like a *k* on the lips.
SS 1:2 *Beloved* Let him *k* me
8:1 I would *k* you,
Lk 22:48 the Son of Man with a *k*?"
Ro 16:16 Greet one another with a holy *k*.
1Co 16:20 Greet one another with a holy *k*.
2Co 13:12 Greet one another with a holy *k*.
1Th 5:26 Greet all the brothers with a holy *k*
1Pe 5:14 Greet one another with a *k* of love.

KISSED (KISS)

Mk 14:45 Judas said, "Rabbi!" and *k* him.
Lk 7:38 *k* them and poured perfume

KISSES* (KISS)

Pr 27:6 but an enemy multiplies *k*.
SS 1:2 with the *k* of his mouth—

KNEE (KNEES)

Isa 45:23 Before me every *k* will bow;
Ro 14:11 'every *k* will bow before me;
Php 2:10 name of Jesus every *k* should bow,

KNEEL (KNELT)

Est 3:2 But Mordecai would not *k* down
Ps 95:6 let us *k* before the LORD our
Eph 3:14 For this reason I *k*

KNEES (KNEE)

1Ki 19:18 all whose *k* have not bowed
Isa 35:3 steady the *k* that give way;
Da 6:10 times a day he got down on his *k*
Lk 5:8 he fell at Jesus' *k* and said,
Heb 12:12 your feeble arms and weak *k*.

KNELT* (KNEEL)

1Ki 1:16 Bathsheba bowed low and *k*
2Ch 6:13 and then *k* down before the whole
7:3 they *k* on the pavement
29:29 everyone present with him *k* down
Est 3:2 officials at the king's gate *k* down
Mt 8:2 and *k* before him and said,
9:18 a ruler came and *k* before him
15:25 The woman came and *k* before him
17:14 a man approached Jesus and *k*
27:29 *k* in front of him and mocked him.
Lk 22:41 *k* down and prayed, "Father,
Ac 20:36 he *k* down with all of them
21:5 there on the beach we *k* to pray.

KNEW (KNOW)

2Ch 33:13 Manasseh *k* that the LORD is God
Job 23:3 If only I *k* where to find him;
Pr 24:12 "But we *k* nothing about this,"
Jer 1:5 you in the womb I *k* you,
Jnh 4:2 I *k* that you are a gracious
Mt 7:23 tell them plainly, 'I never *k* you.
12:25 Jesus *k* their thoughts
Jn 2:24 himself to them, for he *k* all men.
14:7 If you really *k* me, you would know

KNIFE

Ge 22:10 and took the k to slay his son.
Pr 23: 2 and put a k to your throat

KNOCK* (KNOCKS)

Mt 7: 7 k and the door will be opened
Lk 11: 9 k and the door will be opened
Rev 3:20 I am! I stand at the door and k.

KNOCKS (KNOCK)

Mt 7: 8 and to him who k, the door will be

KNOW (FOREKNEW FOREKNOWLEDGE KNEW KNOWING KNOWLEDGE KNOWN KNOWS)

Ge 22:12 Now I k that you fear God,
Ex 6: 7 you will k that I am the LORD
14: 4 and the Egyptians will k that I am
33:13 teach me your ways so I may k you
Dt 7: 9 K therefore that the LORD your
18:21 "How can we k when a message
Jos 4:24 of the earth might k that the hand
23:14 You k with all your heart
1Sa 17:46 the whole world will k that there is
1Ki 8:39 heart (for you alone k the hearts
Job 11: 6 K this: God has even forgotten
19:25 I k that my Redeemer lives,
42: 3 things too wonderful for me to k.
Ps 9:10 Those who k your name will trust
46:10 "Be still, and k that I am God;
100: 3 K that the LORD is God.
139: 1 and you k me.
139: 23 Search me, O God, and k my heart;
145: 12 so that all men may k
Pr 27: 1 for you do not k what a day may
30: 4 Tell me if you k!
Ecc 8: 5 wise heart will k the proper time
Isa 29:15 "Who sees us? Who will k?"
40:21 Do you not k?
Jer 6:15 they do not even k how to blush.
22:16 Is that not what it means to k me?"
24: 7 I will give them a heart to k me,
31:34 his brother, saying, 'K the LORD,'
33: 3 unsearchable things you do not k.'
Eze 2: 5 they will k that a prophet has been
6:10 they will k that I am the LORD;
Da 11:32 people who k their God will firmly
Mt 6: 3 let your left hand k what your right
7:11 k how to give good gifts
9: 6 But so that you may k that the Son
22:29 you do not k the Scriptures
24:42 you do not k on what day your
26:74 "I don't k the man!" Immediately
Mk 12:24 you do not k the Scriptures
Lk 1: 4 so that you may k the certainty
11:13 k how to give good gifts
12:48 But the one who does not k
13:25 'I don't k you or where you come
21:31 you k that the kingdom of God is
23:34 for they do not k what they are
Jn 1:26 among you stands one you do not k
3:11 we speak of what we k,
4:22 we worship what we do k,
4:42 and we k that this man really is
6:69 and k that you are the Holy One
7:28 You do not k him, but I k him
8:14 for I k where I came from
8:19 "You do not k me or my Father,"
8:32 Then you will k the truth,
8:55 Though you do not k him, I k him.
9:25 One thing I do k.
10: 4 him because they k his voice.
10:14 I k my sheep and my sheep k me—
10:27 I k them, and they follow me.
12:35 the dark does not k where he is
13:17 Now that you k these things,
13:35 all men will k that you are my
14:17 you k him, for he lives with you
15:21 for they do not k the One who sent
16:30 we can see that you k all things
17: 3 that they may k you, the only true
17:23 to let the world k that you sent me
21:15 he said, "you k that I love you."
21:24 We k that his testimony is true.
Ac 1: 7 "It is not for you to k the times
1:24 "Lord, you k everyone's heart.
Ro 3:17 and the way of peace they do not k
6: 3 Or don't you k that all
6: 6 For we k that our old self was
6:16 Don't you k that when you offer
7:14 We k that the law is spiritual;
7:18 I k that nothing good lives in me,
8:22 We k that the whole creation has
8:26 We do not k what we ought to pray
Ro 8:28 we k that in all things God works
1Co 1:21 through its wisdom did not k him,
2: 2 For I resolved to k nothing
3:16 Don't you k that you yourselves
5: 6 Don't you k that a little yeast
6: 2 Do you not k that the saints will
6:15 Do you not k that your bodies are
6:16 Do you not k that he who unites
6:19 Do you not k that your body is
7:16 How do you k, wife, whether you
8: 2 does not yet k as he ought to k.
9:13 Don't you k that those who work
9:24 Do you not k that
13: 9 For we k in part and we prophesy
13:12 Now I k in part; then I shall k fully,
15:58 because you k that your labor
2Co 5: 1 we k that if the earthly tent we live
5:11 we k what it is to fear the Lord,
8: 9 For you k the grace
Gal 1:11 you to k, brothers, that the gospel I
2:16 not 'Gentile sinners' k that a man
Eph 1:17 so that you may k him better.
1:18 in order that you may k the hope
6: 8 you k that the Lord will reward
6: 9 since you k that he who is both
Php 3:10 I want to k Christ and the power
4:12 I k what it is to be in need,
Col 2: 2 order that they may k the mystery
4: 1 because you k that you
4: 6 so that you may k how
1Th 3: 3 You k quite well that we were
5: 2 for you k very well that the day
2Th 1: 8 punish those who do not k God
1Ti 1: 7 they do not k what they are talking
3: 5 (If anyone does not k how
3:15 you will k how people ought
2Ti 1:12 because I k whom I have believed,
2:23 you k they produce quarrels.
3:14 you k those from whom you
Heb 8:11 because they will all k me,
11: 8 he did not k where he was going.
Jas 1: 3 because you k that the testing
3: 1 you k that we who teach will be
4: 4 don't you k that friendship
4:14 k what will happen tomorrow.
1Pe 1:18 For you k that it was not
2Pe 1:12 even though you k them
1Jn 2: 3 We k that we have come
2: 4 The man who says, "I k him,"
2: 5 This is how we k we are in him:
2:11 he does not k where he is going,
2:20 and all of you k the truth.
2:29 you k that everyone who does
3: 1 not k us is that it did not k him.
3: 2 But we k that when he appears,
3:10 This is how we k who the children
3:14 We k that we have passed
3:16 This is how we k what love is:
3:19 then is how we k that we belong
3:24 We k it by the Spirit he gave us.
4: 8 does not love does not k God,
4:13 We k that we live in him
4:16 so we k and rely on the love God
5: 2 This is how we k that we love
5:13 so that you may k that you have
5:15 And if we k that he hears us—
5:18 We k that anyone born
5:20 We k also that the Son
Rev 2: 2 I k your deeds, your hard work
2: 9 I k your afflictions and your
2:19 I k your deeds, your love and faith,
3: 3 you will not k at what time I will
3:15 I k your deeds, that you are neither

KNOWING (KNOW)

Ge 3: 5 and you will be like God, k good
3:22 now become like one of us, k good
Jn 19:28 k that all was now completed,
Php 3: 8 of k Christ Jesus my Lord,
Phm :21 k that you will do even more
Heb 13: 2 entertained angels without k it.

KNOWLEDGE (KNOW)

Ge 2: 9 the tree of the k of good and evil.
2:17 eat from the tree of the k of good
2Ch 1:10 and k, that I may lead this people,
Job 21:22 "Can anyone teach k to God,
38: 2 counsel with words without k?
42: 3 obscures my counsel without k?'
Ps 19: 2 night after night they display k.
73:11 Does the Most High have k?"
94:10 Does he who teaches man lack k?
119: 66 Teach me k and good judgment,
139: 6 Such k is too wonderful for me,
Pr 1: 4 k and discretion to the young—
Pr 1: 7 of the LORD is the beginning of k,
2: 5 and find the k of God.
2: 6 from his mouth come k
2:10 and k will be pleasant to your soul.
3:20 by his k the deeps were divided,
8:10 k rather than choice gold,
8:12 I possess k and discretion.
9:10 k of the Holy One is understanding
10:14 Wise men store up k,
12: 1 Whoever loves discipline loves k,
12:23 A prudent man keeps his k
13:16 Every prudent man acts out of k,
14: 6 k comes easily to the discerning.
15: 7 The lips of the wise spread k;
15:14 The discerning heart seeks k,
17:27 A man of k uses words
18:15 heart of the discerning acquires k;
19: 2 to have zeal without k,
19:25 discerning man, and he will gain k.
20:15 lips that speak k are a rare jewel.
23:12 and your ears to words of k.
24: 4 through k its rooms are filled
Ecc 7:12 but the advantage of k is this:
Isa 11: 2 the Spirit of k and of the fear
11: 9 full of the k of the LORD
40:14 Who was it that taught him k
Jer 3:15 who will lead you with k
Hos 4: 6 are destroyed from lack of k.
Hab 2:14 filled with the k of the glory
Mal 2: 7 lips of a priest ought to preserve k,
Mt 13:11 The k of the secrets of the kingdom
Lk 8:10 The k of the secrets of the kingdom
11:52 you have taken away the key to k.
Ac 18:24 with a thorough k of the Scriptures
Ro 1:28 worthwhile to retain the k of God,
10: 2 but their zeal is not based on k.
11:33 riches of the wisdom and k of God!
1Co 8: 1 K puffs up, but love builds up.
8:11 Christ died, is destroyed by your k.
12: 8 to another the message of k
13: 2 can fathom all mysteries and all k,
13: 8 where there is k, it will pass away.
2Co 2:14 everywhere the fragrance of the k
4: 6 light of the k of the glory of God
8: 7 in k, in complete earnestness
11: 6 a trained speaker, but I do have k.
Eph 3:19 to know this love that surpasses k
4:13 and in the k of the Son of God
Php 1: 9 and more in k and depth of insight,
Col 1: 9 God to fill you with the k of his will
1:10 every good work, growing in the k
2: 3 all the treasures of wisdom and k.
3:10 which is being renewed in k
1Ti 2: 4 and to come to a k of the truth.
6:20 ideas of what is falsely called k,
Tit 1: 1 and the k of the truth that leads
Heb 10:26 after we have received the k
2Pe 1: 5 and to goodness, k; and to k,
3:18 grow in the grace and k of our Lord

KNOWN (KNOW)

Ex 6: 3 the LORD I did not make myself k
Ps 16:11 You have made k to me the path
89: 1 I will make your faithfulness k
98: 2 LORD has made his salvation k
105: 1 make k among the nations what he
119:168 for all my ways are k to you.
Pr 20:11 Even a child is k by his actions,
Isa 12: 4 make k among the nations what he
46:10 k the end from the beginning,
61: 9 Their descendants will be k
Eze 38:23 I will make myself k in the sight
39: 7 " 'I will make k my holy name
Mt 10:26 or hidden that will not be made k.
24:43 of the house had k at what time
Lk 19:42 had only k on this day what would
Jn 15:15 from my Father I have made k
16:14 from what is mine and making it k
17:26 I have made you k to them,
Ac 2:28 You have made k to me the paths
Ro 1:19 since what may be k about God is
3:21 apart from law, has been made k,
9:22 his wrath and make his power k,
11:34 "Who has k the mind of the Lord?
15:20 the gospel where Christ was not k,
16:26 and made k through the prophetic
1Co 2:16 "For who has k the mind
8: 3 But the man who loves God is k
13:12 know fully, even as I am fully k.
2Co 3: 2 written on our hearts, k
Gal 4: 9 or rather are k by God—
Eph 3: 5 which was not made k to men
6:19 will fearlessly make k the mystery
2Ti 3:15 infancy you have k the holy
2Pe 2:21 than to have k it and then

KNOWS (KNOW)

1Sa 2: 3 for the LORD is a God who *k,*
Est 4: 14 And who *k* but that you have come
Job 23: 10 But he *k* the way that I take;
Ps 44: 21 since he *k* the secrets of the heart?
94: 11 The LORD *k* the thoughts of man;
103: 14 for he *k* how we are formed,
Ecc 8: 7 Since no man *k* the future,
8: 17 Even if a wise man claims he *k,*
9: 12 no man *k* when his hour will come:
Isa 29: 16 "He *k* nothing"?
Jer 9: 24 that he understands and *k* me,
Mt 6: 8 for your Father *k* what you need
11: 27 No one *k* the Son
24: 36 "No one *k* about that day or hour,
Lk 12: 47 "That servant who *k* his master's
16: 15 of men, but God *k* your hearts.
Ac 15: 8 who *k* the heart, showed that he
Ro 8: 27 who searches our hearts *k* the mind
1Co 2: 11 who among men *k* the thoughts
8: 2 who thinks he *k* something does
2Ti 2: 19 The Lord *k* those who are his," and
Jas 4: 17 who *k* the good he ought to do
1Jn 4: 6 and whoever *k* God listens to us;
4: 7 born of God and *k* God.

KOHATHITE (KOHATHITES)

Nu 3: 29 The *K* clans were to camp

KOHATHITES (KOHATHITE)

Nu 3: 28 The *K* were responsible
4: 15 *K* are to carry those things that are

KORAH

Levite who led rebellion against Moses and Aaron (Nu 16; Jude 11).

KORAZIN

Mt 11: 21 "Woe to you, *K!* Woe to you,

LABAN

Brother of Rebekah (Ge 24:29), father of Rachel and Leah (Ge 29:16). Received Abraham's servant (Ge 24:29-51). Provided daughters as wives for Jacob in exchange for Jacob's service (Ge 29:1-30). Provided flocks for Jacob's service (Ge 30:25-43). After Jacob's departure, pursued and covenanted with him (Ge 31).

LABOR (LABORING)

Ex 1: 11 to oppress them with forced *l,*
20: 9 Six days you shall *l* and do all your
Dt 5: 13 Six days you shall *l* and do all your
Ps 127: 1 its builders *l* in vain.
128: 2 You will eat the fruit of your *l;*
Pr 12: 24 but laziness ends in slave *l.*
Isa 54: 1 you who were never in *l;*
55: 2 and your *l* on what does not satisfy
Mt 6: 28 They do not *l* or spin.
Jn 4: 38 have reaped the benefits of their *l.*"
1Co 3: 8 rewarded according to his own *l.*
15: 58 because you know that your *l*
Gal 4: 27 you who have no *l* pains;
Php 2: 16 day of Christ that I did not run or *l*
Rev 14: 13 "they will rest from their *l,*

LABORING* (LABOR)

2Th 3: 8 *l* and toiling so that we would not

LACK (LACKED LACKING LACKS)

Ps 34: 9 for those who fear him *l* nothing.
Pr 5: 23 He will die for *l* of discipline,
10: 21 but fools die for *l* of judgment.
11: 14 For *l* of guidance a nation falls,
15: 22 Plans fail for *l* of counsel,
28: 27 to the poor will *l* nothing,
Mk 6: 6 he was amazed at their *l* of faith.
16: 14 he rebuked them for their *l* of faith
Ro 3: 3 Will their *l* of faith nullify God's
1Co 1: 7 you do not *l* any spiritual gift
7: 5 because of your *l* of self-control.
Col 2: 23 *l* any value in restraining sensual

LACKED (LACK)

Dt 2: 7 and you have not *l* anything.
Ne 9: 21 them in the desert; they *l* nothing,
1Co 12: 24 honor to the parts that *l* it,

LACKING (LACK)

Pr 17: 18 A man *l* in judgment strikes hands
Ro 12: 11 Never be *l* in zeal, but keep your
Jas 1: 4 and complete, not *l* anything.

LACKS (LACK)

Pr 6: 32 who commits adultery *l* judgment;
11: 12 man who *l* judgment derides his
12: 11 he who chases fantasies *l* judgment
15: 21 delights a man who *l* judgment,
24: 30 of the man who *l* judgment;
25: 28 is a man who *l* self-control.
28: 16 A tyrannical ruler *l* judgment,
31: 11 and *l* nothing of value.
Eze 34: 8 because my flock *l* a shepherd
Jas 1: 5 any of you *l* wisdom, he should ask

LAID (LAY)

Isa 53: 6 and the LORD has *l* on him
Mk 6: 29 took his body and *l* it in a tomb.
Lk 6: 48 and *l* the foundation on rock.
Ac 6: 6 and *l* their hands on them.
1Co 3: 11 other than the one already *l,*
1Ti 4: 14 body of elders *l* their hands on you.
1Jn 3: 16 Jesus Christ *l* down his life for us.

LAKE

Mt 8: 24 a furious storm came up on the *l,*
14: 25 out to them, walking on the *l.*
Mk 4: 1 into a boat and sat in it out on the *l,*
Lk 8: 33 down the steep bank into the *l*
Jn 6: 25 him on the other side of the *l,*
Rev 19: 20 into the fiery *l* of burning sulfur.
20: 14 The *l* of fire is the second death.

LAMB (LAMB'S LAMBS)

Ge 22: 8 "God himself will provide the *l*
Ex 12: 21 and slaughter the Passover *l.*
Nu 9: 11 are to eat the *l,* together
2Sa 12: 4 he took the ewe *l* that belonged
Isa 11: 6 The wolf will live with the *l,*
53: 7 he was led like a *l* to the slaughter,
Mk 14: 12 to sacrifice the Passover *l,*
Jn 1: 29 *L* of God, who takes away the sin
Ac 8: 32 as a *l* before the shearer is silent,
1Co 5: 7 our Passover *l,* has been sacrificed.
1Pe 1: 19 a *l* without blemish or defect.
Rev 5: 6 Then I saw a *L,* looking
5: 12 "Worthy is the *L,* who was slain,
7: 14 white in the blood of the *L.*
14: 4 They follow the *L* wherever he
15: 3 of God and the song of the *L:*
17: 14 but the *L* will overcome them
19: 9 to the wedding supper of the *L!*' "
21: 23 gives it light, and the *L* is its lamp.

LAMB'S (LAMB)

Rev 21: 27 written in the *L* book of life.

LAMBS (LAMB)

Lk 10: 3 I am sending you out like *l*
Jn 21: 15 Jesus said, "Feed my *l.*"

LAME

Isa 33: 23 even the *l* will carry off plunder.
35: 6 Then will the *l* leap like a deer,
Mt 11: 5 The blind receive sight, the *l* walk,
15: 31 the *l* walking and the blind seeing.
Lk 14: 21 the crippled, the blind and the *l.*'

LAMENT

2Sa 1: 17 took up this *l* concerning Saul
Eze 19: 1 Take up a *l* concerning the princes

LAMP (LAMPS LAMPSTAND LAMPSTANDS)

2Sa 22: 29 You are my *l,* O LORD;
Ps 18: 28 You, O LORD, keep my *l* burning;
119: 105 Your word is a *l* to my feet
132: 17 and set up a *l* for my anointed one.
Pr 6: 23 For these commands are a *l,*
20: 27 *l* of the LORD searches the spirit
31: 18 and her *l* does not go out at night.
Mt 6: 22 "The eye is the *l* of the body.
Lk 8: 16 "No one lights a *l* and hides it
Rev 21: 23 gives it light, and the Lamb is its *l.*
22: 5 They will not need the light of a *l*

LAMPS (LAMP)

Mt 25: 1 be like ten virgins who took their *l*
Lk 12: 35 for service and keep your *l* burning,
Rev 4: 5 the throne, seven *l* were blazing.

LAMPSTAND (LAMP)

Ex 25: 31 "Make a *l* of pure gold
Zec 4: 2 "I see a solid gold *l* with a bowl
4: 11 on the right and the left of the *l?*"
Heb 9: 2 In its first room were the *l,*
Rev 2: 5 and remove your *l* from its place.

LAMPSTANDS (LAMP)

2Ch 4: 7 He made ten gold *l* according
Rev 1: 12 when I turned I saw seven golden *l,*
1: 20 and of the seven golden *l* is this:

LAND (LANDS)

Ge 1: 10 God called the dry ground "*l,*"
1: 11 "Let the *l* produce vegetation:
1: 24 "Let the *l* produce living creatures
12: 1 and go to the *l* I will show you.
12: 7 To your offspring I will give this *l.*"
13: 15 All the *l* that you see I will give
15: 18 "To your descendants I give this *l,*
50: 24 out of this *l* to the *l* he promised
Ex 3: 8 a *l* flowing with milk and honey—
6: 8 to the *l* I swore with uplifted hand
33: 3 Go up to the *l* flowing with milk
Lev 25: 23 *l* must not be sold permanently,
Nu 14: 8 us into that *l,* a *l* flowing with milk
35: 33 Do not pollute the *l* where you are.
Dt 1: 8 See, I have given you this *l.*
8: 7 God is bringing you into a good *l*—
11: 10 The *l* you are entering to take
28: 21 you from the *l* you are entering
29: 19 will bring disaster on the watered *l*
34: 1 LORD showed him the whole *l*—
Jos 13: 2 "This is the *l* that remains:
14: 4 Levites received no share of the *l*
14: 9 *l* on which your feet have walked
2Sa 21: 14 answered prayer in behalf of the *l.*
2Ki 17: 5 of Assyria invaded the entire *l,*
24: 1 king of Babylon invaded the *l,*
25: 21 into captivity, away from her *l.*
2Ch 7: 14 their sin and will heal their *l.*
7: 20 then I will uproot Israel from my *l,*
36: 21 The *l* enjoyed its sabbath rests;
Ezr 9: 11 entering to possess is a *l* polluted
Ne 9: 36 in the *l* you gave our forefathers
Ps 37: 11 But the meek will inherit the *l*
37: 29 the righteous will inherit the *l*
136: 21 and gave their *l* as an inheritance,
142: 5 my portion in the *l* of the living."
Pr 2: 21 For the upright will live in the *l,*
12: 11 who works his *l* will have abundant
Isa 6: 13 though a tenth remains in the *l,*
53: 8 cut off from the *l* of the living;
Jer 2: 7 But you came and defiled my *l*
Eze 36: 24 and bring you back into your own *l.*

LANDS (LAND)

Ps 111: 6 giving them the *l* of other nations.
Eze 20: 6 honey, the most beautiful of all *l.*
Zec 10: 9 in distant *l* they will remember me.

LANGUAGE (LANGUAGES)

Ge 11: 1 Now the whole world had one *l*
11: 9 there the LORD confused the *l*
Ps 19: 3 There is no speech or *l*
Jn 8: 44 When he lies, he speaks his native *l*
Ac 2: 6 heard them speaking in his own *l.*
Col 3: 8 slander, and filthy *l* from your lips.
Rev 5: 9 from every tribe and *l* and people
7: 9 every nation, tribe, people and *l,*
14: 6 to every nation, tribe, *l* and people.

LANGUAGES (LANGUAGE)

Zec 8: 23 "In those days ten men from all *l*

LAODICEA

Rev 3: 14 the angel of the church in *L* write:

LAP

Jdg 7: 5 "Separate those who *l* the water

LASHES

Pr 17: 10 more than a hundred *l* a fool.
2Co 11: 24 from the Jews the forty *l* minus one

LAST (LASTING LASTS LATTER)

Ex 14: 24 During the *l* watch of the night
2Sa 23: 1 These are the *l* words of David:
Isa 2: 2 and Jerusalem: In the *l* days
41: 4 and with the *l*—I am he."
44: 6 I am the first and I am the *l;*
48: 12 I am the first and I am the *l.*
Hos 3: 5 and to his blessings in the *l* days.
Mic 4: 1 In the *l* days
Mt 19: 30 But many who are first will be *l,*
20: 8 beginning with the *l* ones hired
21: 37 *L* of all, he sent his son to them.
Mk 9: 35 must be the very *l,* and the servant
10: 31 are first will be *l,* and the *l* first."
15: 37 a loud cry, Jesus breathed his *l.*
Jn 6: 40 and I will raise him up at the *l* day."

Jn 15:16 and bear fruit—fruit that will *l*.
Ac 2:17 " 'In the *l* days, God says,
Ro 1:17 is by faith from first to *l*,
1Co 15:26 *l* enemy to be destroyed is death.
15:52 of an eye, at the *l* trumpet.
2Ti 3: 1 will be terrible times in the *l* days.
2Pe 3: 3 in the *l* days scoffers will come,
Jude :18 "In the *l* times there will be
Rev 1:17 I am the First and the *L*.
22:13 the First and the *L*, the Beginning

LASTING (LAST)

Ex 12:14 to the LORD—a *l* ordinance.
Lev 24: 8 of the Israelites, as a *l* covenant.
Nu 25:13 have a covenant of a *l* priesthood,
Heb 10:34 had better and *l* possessions.

LASTS (LAST)

Ps 30: 5 For his anger *l* only a moment,
2Co 3:11 greater is the glory of that which *l*!

LATTER (LAST)

Job 42:12 The LORD blessed the *l* part
Mt 23:23 You should have practiced the *l*,
Php 1:16 *l* do so in love, knowing that I am

LAUGH (LAUGHED LAUGHS LAUGHTER)

Ps 59: 8 But you, O LORD, *l* at them;
Pr 31:25 she can *l* at the days to come.
Ecc 3: 4 a time to weep and a time to *l*,
Lk 6:21 for you will *l*.
6:25 Woe to you who *l* now,

LAUGHED (LAUGH)

Ge 17:17 Abraham fell facedown; he *l*
18:12 So Sarah *l* to herself as she thought,

LAUGHS (LAUGH)

Ps 2: 4 The One enthroned in heaven *l*;
37:13 but the Lord *l* at the wicked,

LAUGHTER (LAUGH)

Ge 21: 6 Sarah said, "God has brought me *l*,
Ps 126: 2 Our mouths were filled with *l*,
Pr 14:13 Even in *l* the heart may ache,
Jas 4: 9 Change your *l* to mourning

LAVISHED

Eph 1: 8 of God's grace that he *l* on us
1Jn 3: 1 great is the love the Father has *l*

LAW (LAWFUL LAWGIVER LAWS)

Lev 24:22 are to have the same *l* for the alien
Nu 6:13 " 'Now this is the *l* for the Nazirite
Dt 1: 5 Moses began to expound this *l*,
6:25 to obey all this *l* before the LORD
27:26 of this *l* by carrying them out."
31:11 you shall read this *l* before them
31:26 "Take this Book of the *L*
Jos 1: 7 to obey all the *l* my servant Moses
1: 8 of the *L* depart from your mouth;
22: 5 and the *l* that Moses the servant
2Ki 22: 8 of the *L* in the temple of the LORD
2Ch 6:16 walk before me according to my *l*,
17: 9 the Book of the *L* of the LORD;
34:14 of the *L* of the LORD that had
Ezr 7: 6 versed in the *L* of Moses,
Ne 8: 2 Ezra the priest brought the *L*
8: 8 from the Book of the *L* of God,
Ps 1: 2 and on his *l* he meditates day
19: 7 The *l* of the LORD is perfect,
37:31 The *l* of his God is in his heart;
40: 8 your *l* is within my heart."
119: 18 wonderful things in your *l*.
119: 70 but I delight in your *l*.
119: 72 *l* from your mouth is more precious
119: 77 for your *l* is my delight.
119: 97 Oh, how I love your *l*!
119:163 but I love your *l*.
119:165 peace have they who love your *l*,
Pr 28: 9 If anyone turns a deaf ear to the *l*,
29:18 but blessed is he who keeps the *l*.
Isa 2: 3 The *l* will go out from Zion,
8:20 To the *l* and to the testimony!
42:21 to make his *l* great and glorious.
Jer 2: 8 deal with the *l* did not know me;
8: 8 for we have the *l* of the LORD,"
31:33 "I will put my *l* in their minds
Mic 4: 2 The *l* will go out from Zion,
Hab 1: 7 they are a *l* to themselves
Zec 7:12 as flint and would not listen to the *l*
Mt 5:17 that I have come to abolish the *L*
7:12 sums up the *L* and the Prophets.
22:36 greatest commandment in the *L*?"
22:40 All the *L* and the Prophets hang
Mt 23:23 more important matters of the *l*—
Lk 11:52 "Woe to you experts in the *l*,
16:17 stroke of a pen to drop out of the *L*.
24:44 me in the *L* of Moses,
Jn 1:17 For the *l* was given through Moses;
Ac 13:39 justified from by the *l* of Moses.
Ro 2:12 All who sin apart from the *l* will
2:15 of the *l* are written on their hearts,
2:20 you have in the *l* the embodiment
2:25 value if you observe the *l*,
3:19 we know that whatever the *l* says,
3:20 in his sight by observing the *l*;
3:21 apart from *l*, has been made known
3:28 by faith apart from observing the *l*.
3:31 Not at all! Rather, we uphold the *l*.
4:13 It was not through *l* that Abraham
4:15 worthless, because *l* brings wrath.
4:16 not only to those who are of the *l*
5:13 for before the *l* was given,
5:20 *l* was added so that the trespass
6:14 because you are not under *l*,
6:15 we are not under *l* but under grace?
7: 1 that the *l* has authority
7: 4 also died to the *l* through the body
7: 5 aroused by the *l* were at work
7: 6 released from the *l* so that we serve
7: 7 then? Is the *l* sin? Certainly not!
7: 8 For apart from *l*, sin is dead.
7:12 *l* is holy, and the commandment is
7:14 We know that the *l* is spiritual;
7:22 my inner being I delight in God's *l*;
7:25 in my mind am a slave to God's *l*,
8: 2 because through Christ Jesus the *l*
8: 3 For what the *l* was powerless to do
8: 4 of the *l* might be fully met in us,
8: 7 It does not submit to God's *l*,
9: 4 covenants, the receiving of the *l*,
9:31 who pursued a *l* of righteousness,
10: 4 Christ is the end of the *l*
13: 8 his fellowman has fulfilled the *l*.
13:10 love is the fulfillment of the *l*.
1Co 6: 6 goes to *l* against another—
9: 9 For it is written in the *L* of Moses:
9:20 the *l* I became like one under the *l*
9:21 I became like one not having the *l*
15:56 and the power of sin is the *l*.
Gal 2:16 justified by observing the *l*,
2:19 For through the *l* I died to the *l*
3: 2 the Spirit by observing the *l*,
3: 5 you because you observe the *l*,
3:10 on observing the *l* are under a curse
3:11 justified before God by the *l*,
3:13 curse of the *l* by becoming a curse
3:17 The *l*, introduced 430 years later,
3:19 then, was the purpose of the *l*?
3:21 Is the *l*, therefore, opposed
3:23 we were held prisoners by the *l*,
3:24 So the *l* was put in charge to lead us
4:21 you who want to be under the *l*,
5: 3 obligated to obey the whole *l*.
5: 4 justified by *l* have been alienated
5:14 The entire *l* is summed up
5:18 by the Spirit, you are not under *l*.
6: 2 and in this way you will fulfill the *l*
Eph 2:15 flesh the *l* with its commandments
Php 3: 9 of my own that comes from the *l*,
1Ti 1: 8 We know that the *l* is good
Heb 7:12 there must also be a change of the *l*.
7:19 (for the *l* made nothing perfect),
10: 1 The *l* is only a shadow
Jas 1:25 intently into the perfect *l* that gives
2: 8 If you really keep the royal *l* found
2:10 For whoever keeps the whole *l*
4:11 or judges him speaks against the *l*
1Jn 3: 4 Everyone who sins breaks the *l*;

LAWFUL (LAW)

Mt 12:12 Therefore it is *l* to do good

LAWGIVER* (LAW)

Isa 33:22 the LORD is our *l*,
Jas 4:12 There is only one *L* and Judge,

LAWLESS (LAWLESSNESS)

2Th 2: 8 And then the *l* one will be revealed
Heb 10:17 "Their sins and *l* acts

LAWLESSNESS* (LAWLESS)

2Th 2: 3 and the man of *l* is revealed,
2: 7 power of *l* is already at work;
1Jn 3: 4 sins breaks the law; in fact, sin is *l*.

LAWS (LAW)

Ex 21: 1 "These are the *l* you are to set
Lev 25:18 and be careful to obey my *l*,
Dt 4: 1 and *l* I am about to teach you.
30:16 decrees and *l*; then you will live
Ps 119: 30 I have set my heart on your *l*.
119: 43 for I have put my hope in your *l*.
119:120 I stand in awe of your *l*.
119:164 for your righteous *l*.
119:175 and may your *l* sustain me.
Eze 36:27 and be careful to keep my *l*.
Heb 8:10 I will put my *l* in their minds
10:16 I will put my *l* in their hearts,

LAWSUITS

Hos 10: 4 therefore *l* spring up
1Co 6: 7 The very fact that you have *l*

LAY (LAID LAYING LAYS)

Ex 29:10 and his sons shall *l* their hands
Lev 1: 4 He is to *l* his hand on the head
4:15 the community are to *l* their hands
Nu 8:10 the Israelites are to *l* their hands
27:18 whom is the spirit, and *l* your hand
1Sa 26: 9 Who can *l* a hand on the LORD's
Job 1:12 on the man himself do not *l* a finger
22:22 and *l* up his words in your heart.
Ecc 10: 4 calmness can *l* great errors to rest.
Isa 28:16 "See, I *l* a stone in Zion,
Mt 8:20 of Man has no place to *l* his head."
28: 6 Come and see the place where he *l*.
Mk 6: 5 *l* his hands on a few sick people
Lk 9:58 of Man has no place to *l* his head."
Jn 10:15 and I *l* down my life for the sheep.
10:18 but I *l* it down of my own accord.
15:13 that he *l* down his life
Ac 8:19 on whom I *l* my hands may receive
Ro 9:33 I *l* in Zion a stone that causes men
1Co 3:11 no one can *l* any foundation other
1Pe 2: 6 "See, I *l* a stone in Zion,
1Jn 3:16 And we ought to *l* down our lives
Rev 4:10 They *l* their crowns

LAYING (LAY)

Lk 4:40 and *l* his hands on each one,
Ac 8:18 at the *l* on of the apostles' hands,
1Ti 5:22 Do not be hasty in the *l* on of hands
2Ti 1: 6 is in you through the *l*
Heb 6: 1 not *l* again the foundation
6: 2 instruction about baptisms, the *l*

LAYS (LAY)

Jn 10:11 The good shepherd *l* down his life

LAZARUS

1. Poor man in Jesus' parable (Lk 16:19-31).
2. Brother of Mary and Martha whom Jesus raised from the dead (Jn 11:1-12:19).

LAZINESS* (LAZY)

Pr 12:24 but *l* ends in slave labor.
19:15 *L* brings on deep sleep,

LAZY* (LAZINESS)

Ex 5: 8 They are *l*; that is why they are
5:17 Pharaoh said, "*L*, that's what you
5:17 "Lazy, that's what you are—*l*!
Pr 10: 4 *L* hands make a man poor,
12:27 The *l* man does not roast his game,
26:15 he is too *l* to bring it back
Ecc 10:18 If a man is *l*, the rafters sag;
Mt 25:26 replied, 'You wicked, *l* servant!
Tit 1:12 liars, evil brutes, *l* gluttons."
Heb 6:12 We do not want you to become *l*,

LEAD (LEADER LEADERS LEADERSHIP LEADS LED)

Ex 15:13 "In your unfailing love you will *l*
Nu 14: 8 with us, he will *l* us into that land,
Dt 31: 2 and I am no longer able to *l* you.
Jos 1: 6 because you will *l* these people
1Sa 8: 5 now appoint a king to *l* us,
2Ch 1:10 knowledge, that I may *l* this people
Ps 27:11 *l* me in a straight path
61: 2 *l* me to the rock that is higher
139: 24 and *l* me in the way everlasting.
143: 10 *l* me on level ground.
Pr 4:11 and *l* you along straight paths.
Ecc 5: 6 Do not let your mouth *l* you
Isa 11: 6 and a little child will *l* them.
49:10 and *l* them beside springs of water.
Da 12: 3 those who *l* many to righteousness,
Mt 6:13 And *l* us not into temptation,
Lk 11: 4 And *l* us not into temptation.' "
Gal 3:24 So the law was put in charge to *l* us
1Th 4:11 it your ambition to *l* a quiet life,
1Jn 3: 7 do not let anyone *l* you astray.
Rev 7:17 he will *l* them to springs

LEADER (LEAD)
1Sa 7: 6 Samuel was *l* of Israel at Mizpah.
10: 1 Has not the LORD anointed you *l*
12: 2 I have been your *l* from my youth
13: 14 and appointed him *l* of his people,

LEADERS (LEAD)
Heb 13: 7 Remember your *l*, who spoke
13: 17 Obey your *l* and submit

LEADERSHIP* (LEAD)
Nu 33: 1 by divisions under the *l* of Moses
Ps 109: 8 may another take his place of *l*.
Ac 1: 20 " 'May another take his place of *l*.'
Ro 12: 8 if it is *l*, let him govern diligently;

LEADS (LEAD)
Dt 27: 18 is the man who *l* the blind astray
Ps 23: 2 he *l* me beside quiet waters,
37: 8 do not fret—it *l* only to evil.
68: 6 he *l* forth the prisoners
Pr 2: 18 For her house *l* down to death
10: 17 ignores correction *l* others astray.
14: 23 but mere talk *l* only to poverty.
16: 25 but in the end it *l* to death.
19: 23 The fear of the LORD *l* to life:
20: 7 righteous man *l* a blameless life;
21: 5 as surely as haste *l* to poverty.
Isa 40: 11 he gently *l* those that have young.
Mt 7: 13 and broad is the road that *l*
12: 20 till he *l* justice to victory.
15: 14 If a blind man *l* a blind man,
Jn 10: 3 sheep by name and *l* them out.
Ro 6: 16 which *l* to death, or to obedience,
6: 22 the benefit you reap *l* to holiness,
14: 19 effort to do what *l* to peace
2Co 2: 14 always *l* us in triumphal procession
7: 10 sorrow brings repentance that *l*
Tit 1: 1 of the truth that *l* to godliness—

LEAH
Wife of Jacob (Ge 29:16-30); bore six sons and one daughter (Ge 29:31-30:21; 34:1; 35:23).

LEAN (LEANED)
Pr 3: 5 *l* not on your own understanding;

LEANED (LEAN)
Ge 47: 31 as he *l* on the top of his staff.
Jn 21: 20 (This was the one who had *l* back
Heb 11: 21 as he *l* on the top of his staff.

LEAP (LEAPED LEAPS)
Isa 35: 6 Then will the lame *l* like a deer,
Mal 4: 2 *l* like calves released from the stall.
Lk 6: 23 "Rejoice in that day and *l* for joy,

LEAPED (LEAP)
Lk 1: 41 heard Mary's greeting, the baby *l*

LEAPS (LEAP)
Ps 28: 7 My heart *l* for joy

LEARN (LEARNED LEARNING LEARNS)
Dt 4: 10 so that they may *l* to revere me
5: 1 *L* them and be sure to follow them.
31: 12 and *l* to fear the LORD your God
Ps 119: 7 as I *l* your righteous laws.
Isa 1: 17 *l* to do right!
26: 9 of the world *l* righteousness.
Mt 11: 29 yoke upon you and *l* from me,
Jn 14: 31 world must *l* that I love the Father
1Th 4: 4 that each of you should *l*
1Ti 2: 11 A woman should *l* in quietness
5: 4 these should *l* first of all

LEARNED (LEARN)
Ps 119: 152 Long ago I *l* from your statutes
Mt 11: 25 things from the wise and *l*,
Php 4: 9 Whatever you have *l* or received
4: 11 for I have *l* to be content whatever
2Ti 3: 14 continue in what you have *l*
Heb 5: 8 he *l* obedience from what he

LEARNING (LEARN)
Pr 1: 5 let the wise listen and add to their *l*,
9: 9 man and he will add to his *l*.
Isa 44: 25 who overthrows the *l* of the wise
Jn 7: 15 "How did this man get such *l*
2Ti 3: 7 always *l* but never able

LEARNS (LEARN)
Jn 6: 45 and *l* from him comes to me.

LEATHER
2Ki 1: 8 and with a *l* belt around his waist."
Mt 3: 4 and he had a *l* belt around his waist

LEAVES
Ge 3: 7 so they sewed fig *l* together
Eze 47: 12 for food and their *l* for healing."
Rev 22: 2 the *l* of the tree are for the healing

LEBANON
Dt 11: 24 from the desert to *L*,
1Ki 4: 33 from the cedar of *L*

LED (LEAD)
Ex 3: 1 and he *l* the flock to the far side
Dt 8: 2 the LORD your God *l* you all
1Ki 11: 3 and his wives *l* him astray.
2Ch 26: 16 his pride *l* to his downfall.
Ne 13: 26 he was *l* into sin by foreign women.
Ps 68: 18 you *l* captives in your train;
78: 52 he *l* them like sheep
Pr 7: 21 persuasive words she *l* him astray;
20: 1 whoever is *l* astray
Isa 53: 7 he was *l* like a lamb to the slaughter
Jer 11: 19 I had been like a gentle lamb *l*
Am 2: 10 and I *l* you forty years in the desert
Mt 4: 1 Then Jesus was *l* by the Spirit
27: 31 they *l* him away to crucify him.
Lk 4: 1 was *l* by the Spirit in the desert,
Ac 8: 32 "He was *l* like a sheep
Ro 8: 14 those who are *l* by the Spirit
2Co 7: 9 your sorrow *l* you to repentance.
Gal 5: 18 But if you are *l* by the Spirit,
Eph 4: 8 he *l* captives in his train

LEEKS*
Nu 11: 5 melons, *l*, onions and garlic.

LEFT
Dt 28: 14 or to the *l*, following other gods
Jos 1: 7 turn from it to the right or to the *l*,
23: 6 aside to the right or to the *l*.
2Ki 22: 2 aside to the right or to the *l*.
Pr 4: 27 Do not swerve to the right or the *l*;
Isa 30: 21 turn to the right or to the *l*,
Mt 6: 3 do not let your *l* hand know what
25: 33 on his right and the goats on his *l*.

LEGALISTIC*
Php 3: 6 as for *l* righteousness, faultless.

LEGION
Mk 5: 9 "My name is *L*," he replied,

LEND (LENDER LENDS MONEYLENDER)
Lev 25: 37 You must not *l* him money
Dt 15: 8 freely *l* him whatever he needs.
Ps 37: 26 are always generous and *l* freely;
Eze 18: 8 He does not *l* at usury
Lk 6: 34 if you *l* to those from whom you

LENDER (LEND)
Pr 22: 7 and the borrower is servant to the *l*.
Isa 24: 2 for borrower as for *l*,

LENDS (LEND)
Ps 15: 5 who *l* his money without usury
112: 5 to him who is generous and *l* freely,
Pr 19: 17 to the poor *l* to the LORD,

LENGTH (LONG)
Ps 90: 10 The *l* of our days is seventy years—
Pr 10: 27 The fear of the LORD adds *l* to life

LENGTHY* (LONG)
Mk 12: 40 and for a show make *l* prayers.
Lk 20: 47 and for a show make *l* prayers.

LEOPARD
Isa 11: 6 the *l* will lie down with the goat,
Da 7: 6 beast, one that looked like a *l*.
Rev 13: 2 The beast I saw resembled a *l*,

LEPROSY (LEPROUS)
Nu 12: 10 toward her and saw that she had *l*;
2Ki 5: 1 was a valiant soldier, but he had *l*.
7: 3 men with *l* at the entrance
2Ch 26: 21 King Uzziah had *l*
Mt 11: 5 those who have *l* are cured,
Lk 17: 12 ten men who had *l* met him.

LEPROUS (LEPROSY)
Ex 4: 6 and when he took it out, it was *l*,

LETTER (LETTERS)
Mt 5: 18 not the smallest *l*, not the least
2Co 3: 2 You yourselves are our *l*, written
3: 6 for the *l* kills, but the Spirit gives
2Th 3: 14 not obey our instruction in this *l*,

LETTERS (LETTER)
2Co 3: 7 which was engraved in *l* on stone,
10: 10 "His *l* are weighty and forceful,
2Pe 3: 16 His *l* contain some things that are

LEVEL
Ps 143: 10 lead me on *l* ground.
Pr 4: 26 Make *l* paths for your feet
Isa 26: 7 The path of the righteous is *l*;
40: 4 the rough ground shall become *l*,
Jer 31: 9 on a *l* path where they will not
Heb 12: 13 "Make *l* paths for your feet,"

LEVI (LEVITE LEVITES LEVITICAL)
1. Son of Jacob by Leah (Ge 29:34; 46:11; 1Ch 2:1). With Simeon avenged rape of Dinah (Ge 34). Tribe of blessed (Ge 49:5-7; Dt 33:8-11), chosen as priests (Nu 3-4), numbered (Nu 3:39; 26:62), allotted cities, but not land (Nu 18; 35; Dt 10:9; Jos 13:14; 21), land (Eze 48:8-22), 12,000 from (Rev 7:7).
2. See MATTHEW.

LEVIATHAN
Job 41: 1 pull in the *l* with a fishhook
Ps 74: 14 you who crushed the heads of *L*
Isa 27: 1 *L* the gliding serpent,

LEVITE (LEVI)
Dt 26: 12 you shall give it to the *L*, the alien,
Jdg 19: 1 a *L* who lived in a remote area

LEVITES (LEVI)
Nu 1: 53 The *L* are to be responsible
3: 12 "I have taken the *L*
8: 6 "Take the *L* from among the other
18: 21 I give to the *L* all the tithes in Israel
35: 7 must give the *L* forty-eight towns,
2Ch 31: 2 assigned the priests and *L*
Mal 3: 3 he will purify the *L* and refine them

LEVITICAL (LEVI)
Heb 7: 11 attained through the *L* priesthood

LEWDNESS
Mk 7: 22 malice, deceit, *l*, envy, slander,

LIAR* (LIE)
Dt 19: 18 and if the witness proves to be a *l*,
Job 34: 6 I am considered a *l*;
Pr 17: 4 *l* pays attention to a malicious
19: 22 better to be poor than a *l*.
30: 6 will rebuke you and prove you a *l*.
Mic 2: 11 If a *l* and deceiver comes and says,
Jn 8: 44 for he is a *l* and the father of lies.
8: 55 I did not, I would be a *l* like you,
Ro 3: 4 Let God be true, and every man a *l*.
1Jn 1: 10 we make him out to be a *l*
2: 4 not do what he commands is a *l*,
2: 22 Who is the *l*? It is the man who
4: 20 yet hates his brother, he is a *l*.
5: 10 God has made him out to be a *l*,

LIARS* (LIE)
Ps 63: 11 the mouths of *l* will be silenced.
116: 11 "All men are *l*."
Isa 57: 4 the offspring of *l*?
Mic 6: 12 her people are *l*
1Ti 1: 10 for slave traders and *l* and perjurers
4: 2 come through hypocritical *l*,
Tit 1: 12 "Cretans are always *l*, evil brutes,
Rev 3: 9 though they are not, but are *l*—
21: 8 magic arts, the idolaters and all *l*—

LIBERATED*
Ro 8: 21 that the creation itself will be *l*

LICENSE
Jude : 4 of our God into a *l* for immorality

LICK
Ps 72: 9 and his enemies will *l* the dust.
Isa 49: 23 they will *l* the dust at your feet.
Mic 7: 17 They will *l* dust like a snake,

LIE (LIAR LIARS LIED LIES LYING)
Lev 18: 22 " 'Do not *l* with a man
19: 11 " 'Do not *l*.

Nu 23:19 God is not a man, that he should *l*,
Dt 6: 7 when you *l* down and when you get
25: 2 the judge shall make him *l* down
1Sa 15:29 the Glory of Israel does not *l*
Ps 4: 8 I will *l* down and sleep in peace,
23: 2 me *l* down in green pastures,
89:35 and I will not *l* to David—
Pr 3:24 when you *l* down, you will not be
Isa 11: 6 leopard will *l* down with the goat,
28:15 for we have made a *l* our refuge
Jer 9: 5 They have taught their tongues to *l*
23:14 They commit adultery and live a *l*.
Eze 13: 6 are false and their divinations a *l*.
34:14 they will *l* down in good grazing
Ro 1:25 exchanged the truth of God for a *l*,
Col 3: 9 Do not *l* to each other,
2Th 2:11 so that they will believe the *l*
Tit 1: 2 which God, who does not *l*,
Heb 6:18 which it is impossible for God to *l*,
1Jn 2:21 because no *l* comes from the truth.
Rev 14: 5 No *l* was found in their mouths;

LIED (LIE)

Ac 5: 4 You have not *l* to men but to God."

LIES (LIE)

Lev 6: 3 finds lost property and *l* about it,
Ps 5: 6 You destroy those who tell *l*;
10: 7 His mouth is full of curses and *l*
12: 2 Everyone *l* to his neighbor;
34:13 and your lips from speaking *l*.
58: 3 they are wayward and speak *l*.
144: 8 whose mouths are full of *l*,
Pr 6:19 a false witness who pours out *l*
12:17 but a false witness tells *l*.
19: 5 he who pours out *l* will not go free.
19: 9 and he who pours out *l* will perish.
29:12 If a ruler listens to *l*,
30: 8 Keep falsehood and *l* far from me;
Isa 59: 3 Your lips have spoken *l*,
Jer 5:31 The prophets prophesy *l*,
9: 3 like a bow, to shoot *l*;
14:14 "The prophets are prophesying *l*
Hos 11:12 Ephraim has surrounded me with *l*,
Jn 8:44 for he is a liar and the father of *l*.

LIFE (LIVE)

Ge 1:30 everything that has the breath of *l*
2: 7 into his nostrils the breath of *l*,
2: 9 of the garden were the tree of *l*
6:17 to destroy all *l* under the heavens,
9: 5 for the *l* of his fellow man.
9:11 Never again will all *l* be cut
Ex 21: 6 Then he will be his servant for *l*.
21:23 you are to take *l* for *l*, eye for eye,
23:26 I will give you a full *l* span.
Lev 17:14 the *l* of every creature is its blood.
24:17 " 'If anyone takes the *l*
24:18 must make restitution—*l* for *l*.
Nu 35:31 a ransom for the *l* of a murderer,
Dt 4:42 one of these cities and save his *l*.
12:23 because the blood is the *l*,
19:21 Show no pity: *l* for *l*, eye for eye,
30:15 I set before you today *l*
30:19 Now choose *l*, so that you
30:20 For the LORD is your *l*,
32:39 I put to death and I bring to *l*,
32:47 words for you—they are your *l*.
1Sa 19: 5 He took his *l* in his hands
Job 2: 6 hands; but you must spare his *l*."
33: 4 of the Almighty gives me *l*.
33:30 that the light of *l* may shine on him.
Ps 16:11 known to me the path of *l*;
17:14 this world whose reward is in this *l*.
23: 6 all the days of my *l*,
27: 1 LORD is the stronghold of my *l*—
34:12 Whoever of you loves *l*
36: 9 For with you is the fountain of *l*;
39: 4 let me know how fleeting is my *l*.
41: 2 will protect him and preserve his *l*;
49: 7 No man can redeem the *l*
49: 8 the ransom for a *l* is costly,
63: 3 Because your love is better than *l*,
69:28 they be blotted out of the book of *l*
91:16 With long *l* will I satisfy him
104:33 I will sing to the LORD all my *l*;
119:25 preserve my *l* according to your word
Pr 1: 3 a disciplined and prudent *l*,
3: 2 will prolong your *l* many years
3:18 of *l* to those who embrace her;
4:23 for it is the wellspring of *l*.
6:23 are the way to *l*,
6:26 adulteress preys upon your very *l*.
7:23 little knowing it will cost him his *l*.
8:35 For whoever finds me finds *l*
Pr 10:11 of the righteous is a fountain of *l*,
10:27 of the LORD adds length to *l*,
11:30 of the righteous is a tree of *l*,
13: 3 He who guards his lips guards his *l*,
13:12 but a longing fulfilled is a tree of *l*.
13:14 of the wise is a fountain of *l*,
14:27 of the LORD is a fountain of *l*,
15: 4 that brings healing is a tree of *l*,
16:22 Understanding is a fountain of *l*
19: 3 A man's own folly ruins his *l*,
19:23 The fear of the LORD leads to *l*:
21:21 finds *l*, prosperity and honor.
Isa 53:10 LORD makes his *l* a guilt offering,
53:11 he will see the light of *l*
53:12 he poured out his *l* unto death,
Jer 10:23 that a man's *l* is not his own;
La 3:58 you redeemed my *l*.
Eze 18:27 and right, he will save his *l*.
37: 5 enter you, and you will come to *l*.
Da 12: 2 some to everlasting *l*, others
Jnh 2: 6 you brought my *l* up from the pit,
Mal 2: 5 a covenant of *l* and peace,
Mt 6:25 Is not *l* more important than food,
7:14 and narrow the road that leads to *l*,
10:39 Whoever finds his *l* will lose it,
16:21 and on the third day be raised to *l*.
16:25 wants to save his *l* will lose it,
18: 8 better for you to enter *l* maimed
19:16 thing must I do to get eternal *l*?"
19:29 as much and will inherit eternal *l*.
20:28 to give his *l* as a ransom for many."
25:46 but the righteous to eternal *l*."
Mk 8:35 but whoever loses his *l* for me
9:43 better for you to enter *l* maimed
10:17 "what must I do to inherit eternal *l*
10:30 and in the age to come, eternal *l*.
10:45 to give his *l* as a ransom for many."
Lk 6: 9 to save *l* or to destroy it?"
9:22 and on the third day be raised to *l*."
9:24 wants to save his *l* will lose it,
12:15 a man's *l* does not consist
12:22 do not worry about your *l*,
12:25 can add a single hour to his *l*?
14:26 even his own *l*—he cannot be my
17:33 tries to keep his *l* will lose it,
21:19 standing firm you will gain *l*.
Jn 1: 4 In him was *l*, and that *l* was
3:15 believes in him may have eternal *l*.
3:36 believes in the Son has eternal *l*,
4:14 of water welling up to eternal *l*."
5:21 raises the dead and gives them *l*,
5:24 him who sent me has eternal *l*
5:26 For as the Father has *l* in himself,
5:39 that by them you possess eternal *l*.
5:40 refuse to come to me to have *l*.
6:27 for food that endures to eternal *l*,
6:33 down from heaven and gives *l*
6:35 Jesus declared, "I am the bread of *l*
6:40 believes in him shall have eternal *l*,
6:47 he who believes has everlasting *l*.
6:48 I am the bread of *l*.
6:51 give for the *l* of the world."
6:53 and drink his blood, you have no *l*
6:63 The Spirit gives *l*; the flesh counts
6:68 You have the words of eternal *l*.
8:12 but will have the light of *l*."
10:10 I have come that they may have *l*,
10:15 and I lay down my *l* for the sheep.
10:17 loves me is that I lay down my *l*—
10:28 I give them eternal *l*, and they shall
11:25 "I am the resurrection and the *l*.
12:25 The man who loves his *l* will lose it,
12:50 his command leads to eternal *l*.
13:37 I will lay down my *l* for you."
14: 6 am the way and the truth and the *l*.
15:13 lay down his *l* for his friends.
17: 2 people that he might give eternal *l*
17: 3 Now this is eternal *l*: that they may
20:31 that by believing you may have *l*
Ac 2:32 God has raised this Jesus to *l*,
3:15 You killed the author of *l*,
11:18 the Gentiles repentance unto *l*."
13:48 appointed for eternal *l* believed.
Ro 2: 7 immortality, he will give eternal *l*.
4:25 was raised to *l* for our justification.
5:10 shall we be saved through his *l*!
5:18 was justification that brings *l*
5:21 righteousness to bring eternal *l*
6: 4 the Father, we too may live a new *l*.
6:13 have been brought from death to *l*;
6:22 holiness, and the result is eternal *l*.
6:23 but the gift of God is eternal *l*
8: 6 mind controlled by the Spirit is *l*
8:11 also give *l* to your mortal bodies
8:38 convinced that neither death nor *l*,
1Co 15:19 If only for this *l* we have hope
15:36 What you sow does not come to *l*
2Co 2:16 to the other, the fragrance of *l*.
3: 6 letter kills, but the Spirit gives *l*.
4:10 so that the *l* of Jesus may
5: 4 is mortal may be swallowed up by *l*.
Gal 2:20 The *l* I live in the body, I live
3:21 had been given that could impart *l*,
6: 8 from the Spirit will reap eternal *l*.
Eph 4: 1 I urge you to live a *l* worthy
Php 2:16 as you hold out the word of *l*—
4: 3 whose names are in the book of *l*.
Col 1:10 order that you may live a *l* worthy
3: 3 your *l* is now hidden with Christ
1Th 4:12 so that your daily *l* may win
1Ti 1:16 on him and receive eternal *l*.
4: 8 for both the present *l* and the *l*
4:12 in *l*, in love, in faith and in purity.
4:16 Watch your *l* and doctrine closely.
6:12 Take hold of the eternal *l*
6:19 hold of the *l* that is truly *l*.
2Ti 1: 9 saved us and called us to a holy *l*—
1:10 destroyed death and has brought *l*
3:12 to live a godly *l* in Christ Jesus will
Tit 1: 2 resting on the hope of eternal *l*,
3: 7 heirs having the hope of eternal *l*.
Heb 7:16 of the power of an indestructible *l*.
Jas 1:12 crown of *l* that God has promised
3:13 Let him show it by his good *l*,
1Pe 3: 7 with you of the gracious gift of *l*,
3:10 "Whoever would love *l*
4: 2 rest of his earthly *l* for evil human
2Pe 1: 3 given us everything we need for *l*
1Jn 1: 1 proclaim concerning the Word of *l*.
2:25 he promised us—even eternal *l*.
3:14 we have passed from death to *l*,
3:16 Jesus Christ laid down his *l* for us.
5:11 has given us eternal *l*, and this *l* is
5:20 He is the true God and eternal *l*.
Jude :21 Christ to bring you to eternal *l*.
Rev 2: 7 the right to eat from the tree of *l*,
2: 8 who died and came to *l* again.
2:10 and I will give you the crown of *l*.
3: 5 name from the book of *l*,
13: 8 written in the book of *l* belonging
17: 8 in the book of *l* from the creation
20:12 was opened, which is the book of *l*.
20:15 not found written in the book of *l*,
21: 6 from the spring of the water of *l*.
21:27 written in the Lamb's book of *l*.
22: 1 me the river of the water of *l*,
22: 2 side of the river stood the tree of *l*,
22:14 may have the right to the tree of *l*
22:17 take the free gift of the water of *l*.
22:19 from him his share in the tree of *l*

LIFE-GIVING (GIVE)

Pr 15:31 He who listens to a *l* rebuke
1Co 15:45 being"; the last Adam, a *l* spirit.

LIFETIME (LIVE)

Ps 30: 5 but his favor lasts a *l*;
Lk 16:25 in your *l* you received your good

LIFT (LIFTED LIFTING LIFTS)

Ps 3: 3 you bestow glory on me and *l*
28: 2 as I *l* up my hands
63: 4 in your name I will *l* up my hands.
91:12 they will *l* you up in their hands,
121: 1 I *l* up my eyes to the hills—
123: 1 I *l* up my eyes to you,
134: 2 *L* up your hands in the sanctuary
143: 8 for to you I *l* up my soul.
Isa 40: 9 *l* up your voice with a shout,
La 2:19 *L* up your hands to him
3:41 Let us *l* up our hearts and our
Mt 4: 6 they will *l* you up in their hands,
Lk 21:28 stand up and *l* up your heads,
1Ti 2: 8 everywhere to *l* up holy hands
Jas 4:10 the Lord, and he will *l* you up.
1Pe 5: 6 that he may *l* you up in due time.

LIFTED (LIFT)

Ne 8: 6 and all the people *l* their hands
Ps 24: 7 be *l* up, you ancient doors,
40: 2 He *l* me out of the slimy pit,
41: 9 has *l* up his heel against me.
Isa 52:13 *l* up and highly exalted.
63: 9 he *l* them up and carried them
Jn 3:14 Moses *l* up the snake in the desert,
8:28 "When you have *l* up the Son
12:32 when I am *l* up from the earth,
12:34 'The Son of Man must be *l* up'?
13:18 shares my bread has *l* up his heel

LIFTING (LIFT)

Ps 141: 2 may the *l* up of my hands be like

LIFTS (LIFT)

Ps 113: 7 and *l* the needy from the ash heap;

LIGAMENT* (LIGAMENTS)

Eph 4: 16 held together by every supporting *l*

LIGAMENTS* (LIGAMENT)

Col 2: 19 held together by its *l* and sinews,

LIGHT (ENLIGHTENED LIGHTS)

Ge 1: 3 "Let there be *l*," and there was *l*.
Ex 13: 21 in a pillar of fire to give them *l*,
25: 37 it so that they *l* the space in front
2Sa 22: 29 LORD turns my darkness into *l*.
Job 38: 19 "What is the way to the abode of *l*?
Ps 4: 6 Let the *l* of your face shine upon us
18: 28 my God turns my darkness into *l*.
19: 8 giving *l* to the eyes.
27: 1 LORD is my *l* and my salvation—
36: 9 in your *l* we see *l*.
56: 13 God in the *l* of life.
76: 4 You are resplendent with *l*,
89: 15 who walk in the *l* of your presence,
104: 2 He wraps himself in *l*
119:105 and a *l* for my path.
119:130 The unfolding of your words gives *l*;
139: 12 for darkness is as *l* to you.
Pr 4: 18 till the full *l* of day.
Isa 2: 5 let us walk in the *l* of the LORD.
9: 2 have seen a great *l*;
42: 6 and a *l* for the Gentiles,
45: 7 I form the *l* and create darkness,
49: 6 also make you a *l* for the Gentiles,
53: 11 he will see the *l* of life
60: 1 "Arise, shine, for your *l* has come,
60: 19 LORD will be your everlasting *l*,
Eze 1: 27 and brilliant *l* surrounded him.
Mic 7: 8 the LORD will be my *l*.
Mt 4: 16 have seen a great *l*;
5: 14 "You are the *l* of the world.
5: 15 it gives *l* to everyone in the house.
5: 16 let your *l* shine before men,
6: 22 your whole body will be full of *l*.
11: 30 yoke is easy and my burden is *l*."
17: 2 his clothes became as white as the *l*
24: 29 and the moon will not give its *l*;
Mk 13: 24 and the moon will not give its *l*;
Lk 2: 32 a *l* for revelation to the Gentiles
8: 16 those who come in can see the *l*.
11: 33 those who come in may see the *l*.
Jn 1: 4 and that life was the *l* of men.
1: 5 The *l* shines in the darkness,
1: 7 witness to testify concerning that *l*,
1: 9 The true *l* that gives *l*
3: 19 but men loved darkness instead of *l*
3: 20 Everyone who does evil hates the *l*,
8: 12 he said, "I am the *l* of the world.
9: 5 in the world, I am the *l* of the world
12: 35 Walk while you have the *l*,
12: 46 I have come into the world as a *l*,
Ac 13: 47 " 'I have made you a *l*
Ro 13: 12 darkness and put on the armor of *l*.
2Co 4: 6 made his *l* shine in our hearts
6: 14 Or what fellowship can *l* have
11: 14 masquerades as an angel of *l*.
Eph 5: 8 but now you are *l* in the Lord.
1Th 5: 5 You are all sons of the *l*
1Ti 6: 16 and who lives in unapproachable *l*,
1Pe 2: 9 of darkness into his wonderful *l*.
2Pe 1: 19 as to a *l* shining in a dark place,
1Jn 1: 5 God is *l*; in him there is no
1: 7 But if we walk in the *l*,
2: 9 Anyone who claims to be in the *l*
Rev 21: 23 for the glory of God gives it *l*,
22: 5 for the Lord God will give them *l*.

LIGHTNING

Ex 9: 23 and *l* flashed down to the ground.
20: 18 and *l* and heard the trumpet
Ps 18: 12 with hailstones and bolts of *l*.
Eze 1: 13 it was bright, and *l* flashed out of it.
Da 10: 6 his face like *l*, his eyes like flaming
Mt 24: 27 For as the *l* that comes from the east
28: 3 His appearance was like *l*,
Lk 10: 18 "I saw Satan fall like *l* from heaven.
Rev 4: 5 From the throne came flashes of *l*,

LIGHTS (LIGHT)

Ge 1: 14 "Let there be *l* in the expanse
Lk 8: 16 No one *l* a lamp and hides it in a jar

LIKE-MINDED* (MIND)

Php 2: 2 make my joy complete by being *l*,

LIKENESS

Ge 1: 26 man in our image, in our *l*,
Ps 17: 15 I will be satisfied with seeing your *l*
Isa 52: 14 his form marred beyond human *l*—
Ro 8: 3 Son in the *l* of sinful man
8: 29 to be conformed to the *l* of his Son,
2Co 3: 18 his *l* with ever-increasing glory,
Php 2: 7 being made in human *l*.
Jas 3: 9 who have been made in God's *l*.

LILIES (LILY)

Lk 12: 27 "Consider how the *l* grow.

LILY (LILIES)

SS 2: 1 a *l* of the valleys.
2: 2 *Lover* Like a *l* among thorns

LIMIT

Ps 147: 5 his understanding has no *l*.
Jn 3: 34 for God gives the Spirit without *l*.

LINEN

Lev 16: 4 He is to put on the sacred *l* tunic,
Pr 31: 22 she is clothed in fine *l* and purple.
31: 24 She makes *l* garments
Mk 15: 46 So Joseph bought some *l* cloth,
Jn 20: 6 He saw the strips of *l* lying there,
Rev 15: 6 shining *l* and wore golden sashes
19: 8 Fine *l*, bright and clean,

LINGER

Hab 2: 3 Though it *l*, wait for it;

LION (LION'S LIONS')

Jdg 14: 6 power so that he tore the *l* apart
1Sa 17: 34 When a *l* or a bear came
Isa 11: 7 and the *l* will eat straw like the ox.
65: 25 and the *l* will eat straw like the ox.
Eze 1: 10 right side each had the face of a *l*,
10: 14 the third the face of a *l*,
Da 7: 4 "The first was like a *l*,
1Pe 5: 8 around like a roaring *l* looking
Rev 4: 7 The first living creature was like a *l*
5: 5 See, the *L* of the tribe of Judah,

LION'S (LION)

Ge 49: 9 You are a *l* cub, O Judah;

LIONS' (LION)

Da 6: 7 shall be thrown into the *l* den.

LIPS

Ps 8: 2 From the *l* of children and infants
34: 1 his praise will always be on my *l*.
40: 9 I do not seal my *l*,
63: 3 my *l* will glorify you.
119:171 May my *l* overflow with praise,
140: 3 the poison of vipers is on their *l*.
141: 3 keep watch over the door of my *l*.
Pr 10: 13 on the *l* of the discerning,
10: 18 who conceals his hatred has lying *l*,
10: 32 *l* of the righteous know what is
12: 22 The LORD detests lying *l*,
13: 3 He who guards his *l* guards his life,
14: 7 will not find knowledge on his *l*.
24: 26 is like a kiss on the *l*.
26: 23 are fervent *l* with an evil heart.
27: 2 someone else, and not your own *l*.
Isa 6: 5 For I am a man of unclean *l*,
28: 11 with foreign *l* and strange tongues
29: 13 and honor me with their *l*,
Mal 2: 7 "For the *l* of a priest ought
Mt 15: 8 These people honor me with their *l*
21: 16 " 'From the *l* of children
Lk 4: 22 words that came from his *l*.
Ro 3: 13 "The poison of vipers is on their *l*."
Col 3: 8 and filthy language from your *l*.
Heb 13: 15 the fruit of *l* that confess his name.
1Pe 3: 10 and his *l* from deceitful speech.

LISTEN (LISTENED LISTENING LISTENS)

Dt 18: 15 You must *l* to him.
30: 20 *l* to his voice, and hold fast to him.
1Ki 4: 34 came to *l* to Solomon's wisdom,
2Ki 21: 9 But the people did not *l*.
Pr 1: 5 let the wise *l* and add
Ecc 5: 1 Go near to *l* rather
Eze 2: 5 And whether they *l* or fail to *l*—
Mt 12: 42 earth to *l* to Solomon's wisdom,
Mk 9: 7 *L* to him!" Suddenly,
Jn 10: 27 My sheep *l* to my voice; I know
Ac 3: 22 you must *l* to everything he tells
Jas 1: 19 Everyone should be quick to *l*,
1: 22 Do not merely *l* to the word,
1Jn 4: 6 not from God does not *l* to us.

LISTENED (LISTEN)

Ne 8: 3 And all the people *l* attentively
Isa 66: 4 when I spoke, no one *l*.
Da 9: 6 We have not *l* to your servants

LISTENING (LISTEN)

1Sa 3: 9 Speak, LORD, for your servant is *l*
Pr 18: 13 He who answers before *l*—
Lk 10: 39 at the Lord's feet *l* to what he said.

LISTENS (LISTEN)

Pr 12: 15 but a wise man *l* to advice.
Lk 10: 16 "He who *l* to you *l*
1Jn 4: 6 and whoever knows God *l* to us;

LIVE (ALIVE LIFE LIFETIME LIVES LIVING)

Ge 3: 22 tree of life and eat, and *l* forever."
Ex 20: 12 so that you may *l* long
33: 20 for no one may see me and *l*."
Nu 21: 8 who is bitten can look at it and *l*."
Dt 5: 24 we have seen that a man can *l*
6: 2 as you *l* by keeping all his decrees
8: 3 to teach you that man does not *l*
Job 14: 14 If a man dies, will he *l* again?
Ps 15: 1 Who may *l* on your holy hill?
24: 1 the world, and all who *l* in it;
26: 8 I love the house where you *l*,
119:175 Let me *l* that I may praise you,
Pr 21: 9 Better to *l* on a corner of the roof
21: 19 Better to *l* in a desert
Ecc 9: 4 a *l* dog is better off than a dead lion
Isa 26: 19 But your dead will *l*;
55: 3 hear me, that your soul may *l*.
Eze 17: 19 LORD says: As surely as I *l*,
20: 11 for the man who obeys them will *l*
37: 3 can these bones *l*?" I said,
Am 5: 6 Seek the LORD and *l*,
Hab 2: 4 but the righteous will *l* by his faith
Zec 2: 11 I will *l* among you and you will
Mt 4: 4 'Man does not *l* on bread alone,
Lk 4: 4 'Man does not *l* on bread alone.' "
Jn 14: 19 Because I *l*, you also will *l*.
Ac 17: 24 does not *l* in temples built by hands
17: 28 'For in him we *l* and move
Ro 1: 17 "The righteous will *l* by faith."
2Co 5: 7 We *l* by faith, not by sight.
6: 16 "I will *l* with them and walk
Gal 2: 20 The life I *l* in the body, I *l* by faith
3: 11 "The righteous will *l* by faith."
5: 25 Since we *l* by the Spirit, let us keep
Eph 4: 17 that you must no longer *l*
Php 1: 21 to *l* is Christ and to die is gain.
Col 1: 10 order that you may *l* a life worthy
1Th 4: 1 we instructed you how to *l* in order
5: 13 *L* in peace with each other.
1Ti 2: 2 that we may *l* peaceful
2Ti 3: 12 who wants to *l* a godly life
Tit 2: 12 and to *l* self-controlled, upright
Heb 10: 38 But my righteous one will *l* by faith
12: 14 Make every effort to *l* in peace
1Pe 1: 17 *l* your lives as strangers here
3: 8 *l* in harmony with one another;

LIVES (LIVE)

Ge 45: 7 and to save your *l* by a great
Job 19: 25 I know that my Redeemer *l*,
Pr 1: 19 it takes away the *l*
Isa 57: 15 he who *l* forever, whose name is
Da 3: 28 to give up their *l* rather than serve
Jn 14: 17 for he *l* with you and will be in you.
Ro 6: 10 but the life he *l*, he *l* to God.
7: 18 I know that nothing good *l* in me,
8: 9 if the Spirit of God *l* in you.
14: 7 For none of us *l* to himself alone
1Co 3: 16 and that God's Spirit *l* in you?
Gal 2: 20 I no longer live, but Christ *l* in me.
1Th 2: 8 only the gospel of God but our *l*
1Ti 2: 2 quiet *l* in all godliness and holiness.
Tit 2: 12 and godly *l* in this present age,
Heb 7: 24 but because Jesus *l* forever,
13: 5 Keep your *l* free from the love
1Pe 3: 2 the purity and reverence of your *l*.
2Pe 3: 11 You ought to live holy and godly *l*
1Jn 3: 16 to lay down our *l* for our brothers.
4: 16 Whoever *l* in love *l* in God,

LIVING (LIVE)

Ge 2: 7 and the man became a *l* being.
1Sa 17: 26 defy the armies of the *l* God?"
Isa 53: 8 cut off from the land of the *l*;

Jer 2:13 the spring of *l* water,
Eze 1: 5 what looked like four *l* creatures.
Zec 14: 8 On that day *l* water will flow out
Mt 22:32 the God of the dead but of the *l*."
Jn 4:10 he would have given you *l* water."
6:51 I am the *l* bread that came
7:38 streams of *l* water will flow
Ro 8:11 Jesus from the dead is *l* in you,
12: 1 to offer your bodies as *l* sacrifices,
1Co 9:14 the gospel should receive their *l*
Heb 4:12 For the word of God is *l* and active.
10:20 and *l* way opened for us
10:31 to fall into the hands of the *l* God.
1Pe 1:23 through the *l* and enduring word
Rev 1:18 I am the *L* One; I was dead,
4: 6 the throne, were four *l* creatures,
7:17 to springs of *l* water.

LOAD (LOADS)

Gal 6: 5 for each one should carry his own *l*.

LOADS (LOAD)

Mt 23: 4 They tie up heavy *l* and put them

LOAF (LOAVES)

1Co 10:17 for we all partake of the one *l*.

LOAVES (LOAF)

Mk 6:41 Taking the five *l* and the two fish
8: 6 When he had taken the seven *l*
Lk 11: 5 'Friend, lend me three *l* of bread,

LOCKED

Jn 20:26 the doors were *l*, Jesus came
Gal 3:23 *l* up until faith should be revealed.

LOCUSTS

Ex 10: 4 I will bring *l* into your country
Joel 2:25 you for the years the *l* have eaten—
Mt 3: 4 His food was *l* and wild honey.
Rev 9: 3 And out of the smoke *l* came

LOFTY

Ps 139: 6 too *l* for me to attain.
Isa 57:15 is what the high and *l* One says—

LONELY

Ps 68: 6 God sets the *l* in families,
Lk 5:16 Jesus often withdrew to *l* places

LONG (LENGTH LENGTHY LONGED LONGING LONGINGS LONGS)

Ex 17:11 As *l* as Moses held up his hands,
Nu 6: 5 the hair of his head grow *l*.
1Ki 18:21 "How *l* will you waver
Ps 119: 97 I meditate on it all day *l*.
119:174 I *l* for your salvation, O LORD,
Hos 7:13 I *l* to redeem them
Am 5:18 Why do you *l* for the day
Mt 25: 5 The bridegroom was a *l* time
Jn 9: 4 As *l* as it is day, we must do
1Co 11:14 that if a man has *l* hair,
Eph 3:18 to grasp how wide and *l* and high
Php 1: 8 God can testify how I *l* for all
1Pe 1:12 Even angels *l* to look

LONGED (LONG)

Mt 13:17 righteous men *l* to see what you see
23:37 how often I have *l*
Lk 13:34 how often I have *l*
2Ti 4: 8 to all who have *l* for his appearing.

LONGING* (LONG)

Dt 28:65 with *l*, and a despairing heart.
Job 7: 2 Like a slave *l* for the evening
Ps 119: 20 My soul is consumed with *l*
119: 81 with *l* for your salvation,
119:131 *l* for your commands.
143: 7 my spirit faints with *l*.
Pr 13:12 but a *l* fulfilled is a tree of life.
13:19 A *l* fulfilled is sweet to the soul,
Eze 23:27 look on these things with *l*
Lk 16:21 and *l* to eat what fell from the rich
Ro 15:23 since I have been *l* for many years
2Co 5: 2 *l* to be clothed with our heavenly
7: 7 He told us about your *l* for me,
7:11 what alarm, what *l*, what concern,
1Th 2:17 out of our intense *l* we made every
Heb 11:16 they were *l* for a better country—

LONGINGS* (LONG)

Ps 38: 9 All my *l* lie open before you,
112: 10 the *l* of the wicked will come

LONGS* (LONG)

Ps 63: 1 my body *l* for you,
Isa 26: 9 in the morning my spirit *l* for you.
30:18 Yet the LORD *l* to be gracious
Php 2:26 For he *l* for all of you and is

LOOK (LOOKED LOOKING LOOKS)

Ge 19:17 "Flee for your lives! Don't *l* back,
Ex 3: 6 because he was afraid to *l* at God.
Nu 21: 8 anyone who is bitten can *l* at it
32: 8 Kadesh Barnea to *l* over the land.
Dt 4:29 you will find him if you *l* for him
1Sa 16: 7 The LORD does not *l*
Job 31: 1 not to *l* lustfully at a girl.
Ps 34: 5 Those who *l* to him are radiant;
105: 4 *L* to the LORD and his strength;
113: 6 who stoops down to *l*
123: 2 As the eyes of slaves *l* to the hand
Pr 1:28 they will *l* for me but will not find
4:25 Let your eyes *l* straight ahead,
15:30 A cheerful *l* brings joy to the heart,
Isa 17: 7 In that day men will *l*
31: 1 do not *l* to the Holy One of Israel,
40:26 Lift your eyes and *l* to the heavens:
60: 5 Then you will *l* and be radiant,
Jer 3: 3 Yet you have the brazen *l*
6:16 "Stand at the crossroads and *l*;
Eze 34:11 for my sheep and *l* after them.
Hab 1:13 Your eyes are too pure to *l* on evil;
Zec 12:10 They will *l* on me, the one they
Mt 18:10 "See that you do not *l* down on one
18:12 go to *l* for the one that wandered
23:27 which *l* beautiful on the outside
Mk 13:21 '*L*, here is the Christ!' or, '*L*,
Lk 6:41 "Why do you *l* at the speck
24:39 *L* at my hands and my feet.
Jn 1:36 he said, "*L*, the Lamb of God!"
4:35 open your eyes and *l* at the fields!
19:37 "They will *l* on the one they have
Ro 14:10 why do you *l* down on your brother
Php 2: 4 Each of you should *l* not only
1Ti 4:12 Don't let anyone *l* down on you
Jas 1:27 to *l* after orphans and widows
1Pe 1:12 long to *l* into these things.
2Pe 3:12 as you *l* forward to the day of God

LOOKED (LOOK)

Ge 19:26 Lot's wife *l* back, and she became
Ex 2:25 So God *l* on the Israelites
1Sa 6:19 because they had *l* into the ark
SS 3: 1 I *l* for the one my heart loves;
Eze 22:30 "I *l* for a man among them who
34: 6 and no one searched or *l* for them.
44: 4 I *l* and saw the glory
Da 7: 9 "As I *l*,
10: 5 I *l* up and there before me was
Hab 3: 6 he *l*, and made the nations tremble.
Mt 25:36 I was sick and you *l* after me,
Lk 18: 9 and *l* down on everybody else,
22:61 The Lord turned and *l* straight
1Jn 1: 1 which we have *l* at and our hands

LOOKING (LOOK)

Ps 69: 3 *l* for my God.
119: 82 My eyes fail, *l* for your promise;
119:123 My eyes fail, *l* for your salvation,
Mk 16: 6 "You are *l* for Jesus the Nazarene,
2Co 10: 7 You are *l* only on the surface
Php 4:17 Not that I am *l* for a gift,
1Th 2: 6 We were not *l* for praise from men,
2Pe 3:13 with his promise we are *l* forward
Rev 5: 6 I saw a Lamb, *l* as if it had been

LOOKS (LOOK)

1Sa 16: 7 Man *l* at the outward appearance,
Ezr 8:22 is on everyone who *l* to him,
Ps 104: 32 who *l* at the earth, and it trembles;
138: 6 on high, he *l* upon the lowly,
Pr 27:18 he who *l* after his master will be
Eze 34:12 As a shepherd *l* after his scattered
Mt 5:28 But I tell you that anyone who *l*
16: 4 and adulterous generation *l*
Lk 9:62 and *l* back is fit for service
Jn 6:40 Father's will is that everyone who *l*
12:45 When he *l* at me, he sees the one
Php 2:21 For everyone *l* out
Jas 1:25 But the man who *l* intently

LOOSE

Isa 33:23 Your rigging hangs *l*:
Mt 16:19 and whatever you *l* on earth will be
18:18 and whatever you *l* on earth will be

LORD† (LORD'S† LORDED LORDING)

Ge 18:27 been so bold as to speak to the *L*,
Ex 15:17 O *L*, your hands established.
Nu 16:13 now you also want to *l* it over us?
Dt 10:17 God of gods and *L* of lords,
Jos 3:13 the *L* of all the earth—set foot
1Ki 3:10 *L* was pleased that Solomon had
Ne 4:14 Remember the *L*, who is great
Job 28:28 'The fear of the *L*—that is wisdom,
Ps 37:13 but the *L* laughs at the wicked,
38:22 O *L* my Savior.
54: 4 the *L* is the one who sustains me.
62:12 and that you, O *L*, are loving.
69: 6 O *L*, the LORD Almighty;
86: 5 You are forgiving and good, O *L*,
86: 8 gods there is none like you, O *L*;
89:49 O *L*, where is your former great
110: 1 The LORD says to my *L*:
110: 5 The *L* is at your right hand;
130: 3 O *L*, who could stand?
135: 5 that our *L* is greater than all gods.
136: 3 Give thanks to the *L* of lords:
147: 5 Great is our *L* and mighty in power
Isa 6: 1 I saw the *L* seated on a throne,
Da 2:47 and the *L* of kings and a revealer
9: 4 "O *L*, the great and awesome God,
9: 7 "*L*, you are righteous,
9: 9 The *L* our God is merciful
9:19 O *L*, listen! O *L*, forgive! O *L*,
Mt 3: 3 'Prepare the way for the *L*,
4: 7 'Do not put the *L* your God
4:10 'Worship the *L* your God,
7:21 "Not everyone who says to me, '*L*,
9:38 Ask the *L* of the harvest, therefore,
12: 8 Son of Man is *L* of the Sabbath."
20:25 of the Gentiles *l* it over them,
21: 9 comes in the name of the *L*!"
22:37 " 'Love the *L* your God
22:44 For he says, " 'The *L* said to my *L*:
23:39 comes in the name of the *L*.' "
Mk 1: 3 'Prepare the way for the *L*,
12:11 the *L* has done this,
12:29 the *L* our God, the *L* is one.
12:30 Love the *L* your God
Lk 2: 9 glory of the *L* shone around them,
6: 5 The Son of Man is *L* of the Sabbath
6:46 "Why do you call me, '*L*, *L*,'
10:27 " 'Love the *L* your God
11: 1 one of his disciples said to him, "*L*,
24:34 The *L* has risen and has appeared
Jn 1:23 'Make straight the way for the *L*.' "
Ac 2:21 on the name of the *L* will be saved.'
2:25 " 'I saw the *L* always before me.
2:34 " 'The *L* said to my *L*:
8:16 into the name of the *L* Jesus.
9: 5 "Who are you, *L*?" Saul asked.
10:36 through Jesus Christ, who is *L*
11:23 true to the *L* with all their hearts.
16:31 replied, "Believe in the *L* Jesus,
Ro 4:24 in him who raised Jesus our *L*
5:11 in God through our *L* Jesus Christ,
6:23 life in Christ Jesus our *L*.
8:39 of God that is in Christ Jesus our *L*.
10: 9 with your mouth, "Jesus is *L*,"
10:13 on the name of the *L* will be saved
10:16 *L*, who has believed our message?"
11:34 Who has known the mind of the *L*?
12:11 your spiritual fervor, serving the *L*.
13:14 yourselves with the *L* Jesus Christ,
14: 4 for the *L* is able to make him stand.
14: 8 we live to the *L*; and if we die,
1Co 1:31 Let him who boasts boast in the *L*."
3: 5 the *L* has assigned to each his task.
4: 5 time; wait till the *L* comes.
6:13 for the *L*, and the *L* for the body.
6:14 By his power God raised the *L*
7:32 affairs—how he can please the *L*.
7:34 to be devoted to the *L* in both body
7:35 in undivided devotion to the *L*.
7:39 but he must belong to the *L*.
8: 6 and there is but one *L*, Jesus Christ,
10: 9 We should not test the *L*,
11:23 For I received from the *L* what I
12: 3 "Jesus is *L*," except by the Holy
15:57 victory through our *L* Jesus Christ.
15:58 fully to the work of the *L*,
16:22 If anyone does not love the *L*—
2Co 1:24 Not that we *l* it over your faith,
2:12 found that the *L* had opened a door
3:17 Now the *L* is the Spirit,
4: 5 but Jesus Christ as *L*, and ourselves
5: 6 in the body we are away from the *L*
8: 5 they gave themselves first to the *L*
8:21 not only in the eyes of the *L* but

2Co 10:17 Let him who boasts boast in the *L*."
10:18 but the one whom the *L* commends
13:10 the authority the *L* gave me
Gal 6:14 in the cross of our *L* Jesus Christ,
Eph 4:5 one *L*, one faith, one baptism;
5:8 but now you are light in the *L*.
5:10 and find out what pleases the *L*.
5:19 make music in your heart to the *L*,
5:22 submit to your husbands as to the *L*
6:1 obey your parents in the *L*,
6:7 as if you were serving the *L*,
6:8 know that the *L* will reward
6:10 in the *L* and in his mighty power.
Php 2:11 confess that Jesus Christ is *L*,
3:1 my brothers, rejoice in the *L*!
3:8 of knowing Christ Jesus my *L*,
4:1 you should stand firm in the *L*,
4:4 Rejoice in the *L* always.
4:5 The *L* is near.
Col 1:10 you may live a life worthy of the *L*
2:6 as you received Christ Jesus as *L*,
3:13 Forgive as the *L* forgave you.
3:17 do it all in the name of the *L* Jesus,
3:18 your husbands, as is fitting in the *L*.
3:20 in everything, for this pleases the *L*
3:23 as working for the *L*, not for men,
3:24 It is the *L* Christ you are serving.
3:24 receive an inheritance from the *L*
4:17 work you have received in the *L*."
1Th 3:8 since you are standing firm in the *L*
3:12 May the *L* make your love increase
4:1 and urge you in the *L* Jesus
4:6 The *L* will punish men
4:15 who are left till the coming of the *L*
5:2 day of the *L* will come like a thief
5:23 at the coming of our *L* Jesus Christ.
2Th 1:7 when the *L* Jesus is revealed
1:12 of our *L* Jesus may be glorified
2:1 the coming of our *L* Jesus Christ
2:8 whom the *L* Jesus will overthrow
3:3 *L* is faithful, and he will strengthen
3:5 May the *L* direct your hearts
1Ti 6:15 the King of kings and *L* of lords,
2Ti 1:8 ashamed to testify about our *L*,
2:19 "The *L* knows those who are his,"
4:8 which the *L*, the righteous Judge,
4:17 But the *L* stood at my side
Heb 1:10 O *L*, you laid the foundations
10:30 "The *L* will judge his people."
12:14 holiness no one will see the *L*.
13:6 *L* is my helper; I will not be afraid.
Jas 3:9 With the tongue we praise our *L*
4:10 Humble yourselves before the *L*,
5:11 The *L* is full of compassion
1Pe 1:25 the word of the *L* stands forever."
2:3 you have tasted that the *L* is good.
3:12 eyes of the *L* are on the righteous
3:15 in your hearts set apart Christ as *L*.
2Pe 1:11 into the eternal kingdom of our *L*
1:16 and coming of our *L* Jesus Christ,
2:1 the sovereign *L* who bought
2:9 then the *L* knows how
3:9 The *L* is not slow in keeping his
3:18 and knowledge of our *L* and Savior
Jude :14 the *L* is coming with thousands
Rev 4:8 holy, holy is the *L* God Almighty,
4:11 "You are worthy, our *L* and God,
11:15 has become the kingdom of our *L*
17:14 he is *L* of lords and King of kings—
19:16 KINGS AND *L* OF LORDS.
22:5 for the *L* God will give them light.
22:20 Come, *L* Jesus.

LORD'S† (LORD†)

Lk 1:38 "I am the *L* servant," Mary
Ac 11:21 The *L* hand was with them,
21:14 and said, "The *L* will be done."
1Co 7:32 is concerned about the *L* affairs—
10:26 "The earth is the *L*, and everything
11:26 you proclaim the *L* death
2Co 3:18 faces all reflect the *L* glory,
Eph 5:17 but understand what the *L* will is.
2Ti 2:24 And the *L* servant must not quarrel
Heb 12:5 light of the *L* discipline,
Jas 4:15 you ought to say, "If it is the *L* will,
5:8 because the *L* coming is near.
1Pe 2:13 Submit yourselves for the *L* sake

LORDED* (LORD†)

Ne 5:15 Their assistants also *l* it

LORDING* (LORD†)

1Pe 5:3 not *l* it over those entrusted to you,

LORD‡ (LORD'S‡)

Ge 2:4 When the *L* God made the earth
2:7 the *L* God formed the man
2:22 Then the *L* God made a woman
3:21 The *L* God made garments of skin
3:23 So the *L* God banished him
4:4 The *L* looked with favor on Abel
4:26 began to call on the name of the *L*.
6:7 So the *L* said, "I will wipe mankind
7:16 Then the *L* shut him in.
9:26 Blessed be the *L*, the God of Shem!
11:9 there the *L* confused the language
12:1 *L* had said to Abram, "Leave your
15:6 Abram believed the *L*,
15:18 On that day the *L* made a covenant
17:1 the *L* appeared to him and said,
18:1 The *L* appeared to Abraham
18:14 Is anything too hard for the *L*?
18:19 way of the *L* by doing what is right
21:1 Now the *L* was gracious to Sarah
22:14 that place The *L* Will Provide.
24:1 the *L* had blessed him in every way
26:2 The *L* appeared to Isaac and said,
28:13 There above it stood the *L*,
31:49 "May the *L* keep watch
39:2 The *L* was with Joseph
39:21 in the prison, the *L* was with him;
Ex 3:2 the angel of the *L* appeared to him
4:11 Is it not I, the *L*? Now go;
4:31 heard that the *L* was concerned
6:2 also said to Moses, "I am the *L*.
9:12 the *L* hardened Pharaoh's heart
12:27 'It is the Passover sacrifice to the *L*,
12:43 The *L* said to Moses and Aaron,
13:9 For the *L* brought you out of Egypt
13:21 By day the *L* went ahead of them
14:13 the deliverance the *L* will bring
14:30 That day the *L* saved Israel
15:3 The *L* is a warrior;
15:11 among the gods is like you, O *L*?
15:26 for I am the *L*, who heals you."
16:12 know that I am the *L* your God.' "
16:23 day of rest, a holy Sabbath to the *L*.
17:15 and called it The *L* is my Banner.
19:8 will do everything the *L* has said."
19:20 The *L* descended to the top
20:2 "I am the *L* your God, who
20:5 the *L* your God, am a jealous God,
20:7 for the *L* will not hold anyone
20:10 a Sabbath to the *L* your God.
20:11 in six days the *L* made the heavens
20:12 in the land the *L* your God is giving
23:25 Worship the *L* your God,
24:3 "Everything the *L* has said we will
24:12 The *L* said to Moses, "Come up
24:16 and the glory of the *L* settled
25:1 The *L* said to Moses, "Tell
28:36 HOLY TO THE *L*.
30:11 Then the *L* said to Moses,
31:13 so you may know that I am the *L*,
31:18 When the *L* finished speaking
33:11 The *L* would speak to Moses face
33:19 And the *L* said, "I will cause all my
34:1 *L* said to Moses, "Chisel out two
34:6 proclaiming, "The *L*, the *L*,
34:10 awesome is the work that I, the *L*,
34:29 because he had spoken with the *L*.
40:34 glory of the *L* filled the tabernacle.
40:38 So the cloud of the *L* was
Lev 8:36 did everything the *L* commanded
9:23 and the glory of the *L* appeared
10:2 and they died before the *L*.
19:2 'Be holy because I, the *L* your God,
20:8 I am the *L*, who makes you holy.
20:26 to be holy to me because I, the *L*,
23:40 and rejoice before the *L* your God
Nu 6:24 Say to them: " ' "The *L* bless you
8:5 *L* said to Moses: "Take the Levites
11:1 hardships in the hearing of the *L*,
14:14 O *L*, have been seen face to face,
14:18 you have declared: 'The *L* is slow
14:21 glory of the *L* fills the whole earth,
21:6 Then the *L* sent venomous snakes
22:31 Then the *L* opened Balaam's eyes,
23:12 "Must I not speak what the *L* puts
30:2 When a man makes a vow to the *L*
32:12 followed the *L* wholeheartedly.'
Dt 1:21 and take possession of it as the *L*,
2:7 forty years the *L* your God has
4:29 there you seek the *L* your God,
5:6 And he said: "I am the *L* your God,
5:9 the *L* your God, am a jealous God,
6:4 The *L* our God, the *L* is one.
6:5 Love the *L* your God
6:16 Do not test the *L* your God
6:25 law before the *L* our God,
7:1 When the *L* your God brings you
7:6 holy to the *L* your God.
7:8 But it was because the *L* loved you
7:9 that the *L* your God is God;
7:12 then the *L* your God will keep his
8:5 so the *L* your God disciplines you.
9:10 The *L* gave me two stone tablets
10:12 but to fear the *L* your God,
10:14 To the *L* your God belong
10:17 For the *L* your God is God of gods
10:20 Fear the *L* your God and serve him
10:22 now the *L* your God has made you
11:1 Love the *L* your God and keep his
11:13 to love the *L* your God
16:1 the Passover of the *L* your God,
17:15 the king the *L* your God chooses.
28:1 If you fully obey the *L* your God
28:15 if you do not obey the *L* your God
29:1 covenant the *L* commanded Moses
29:29 things belong to the *L* our God,
30:4 from there the *L* your God will
30:6 *L* your God will circumcise your
30:10 if you obey the *L* your God
30:16 today to love the *L* your God,
30:20 For the *L* is your life, and he will
31:6 for the *L* your God goes with you;
34:5 of the *L* died there in Moab,
Jos 10:14 a day when the *L* listened to a man.
22:5 to love the *L* your God, to walk
23:11 careful to love the *L* your God.
24:15 my household, we will serve the *L*
24:18 We too will serve the *L*,
Jdg 2:12 They forsook the *L*, the God
Ru 1:8 May the *L* show kindness to you,
4:13 And the *L* enabled her to conceive,
1Sa 1:11 him to the *L* for all the days
1:15 I was pouring out my soul to the *L*.
1:28 So now I give him to the *L*.
2:2 "There is no one holy like the *L*;
2:25 but if a man sins against the *L*,
2:26 in favor with the *L* and with men.
3:9 *L*, for your servant is listening.' "
3:19 The *L* was with Samuel
7:12 "Thus far has the *L* helped us."
9:17 sight of Saul, the *L* said to him,
11:15 as king in the presence of the *L*.
12:18 all the people stood in awe of the *L*
12:22 his great name the *L* will not reject
12:24 But be sure to fear the *L*
13:14 the *L* has sought out a man
14:6 Nothing can hinder the *L*
15:22 "Does the *L* delight
16:13 Spirit of the *L* came upon David
17:45 you in the name of the *L* Almighty,
2Sa 6:14 danced before the *L*
7:22 How great you are, O Sovereign *L*!
8:6 *L* gave David victory everywhere
12:7 This is what the *L*, the God
22:2 "The *L* is my rock, my fortress
22:29 You are my lamp, O *L*;
22:31 the word of the *L* is flawless.
1Ki 1:30 today what I swore to you by the *L*,
2:3 and observe what the *L* your God
3:7 O *L* my God, you have made your
5:5 for the Name of the *L* my God,
5:12 The *L* gave Solomon wisdom,
8:11 the glory of the *L* filled his temple.
8:23 toward heaven and said: "O *L*,
8:61 fully committed to the *L* our God,
9:3 The *L* said to him: "I have heard
10:9 Praise be to the *L* your God,
15:14 committed to the *L* all his life.
18:21 If the *L* is God, follow him;
18:36 "O *L*, God of Abraham, Isaac
18:39 "The *L*—he is God! The *L*—
21:23 also concerning Jezebel the *L* says:
2Ki 13:23 But the *L* was gracious to them
17:18 So the *L* was very angry with Israel
18:5 Hezekiah trusted in the *L*,
19:1 and went into the temple of the *L*.
20:11 *L* made the shadow go back the ten
21:12 Therefore this is what the *L*,
22:2 right in the eyes of the *L*
22:8 of the Law in the temple of the *L*."

‡This entry represents the translation of the Hebrew name for God, *Yahweh*, always indicated in the NIV by LORD. For Lord, see the concordance entries **LORD†** and **LORD'S†**.

2Ki 23: 3 to follow the *L* and keep his
23:21 the Passover to the *L* your God,
23:25 a king like him who turned to the *L*
24: 2 The *L* sent Babylonian, Aramean,
24: 4 and the *L* was not willing to forgive
1Ch 10:13 because he was unfaithful to the *L*;
11: 3 with them at Hebron before the *L*,
11: 9 the *L* Almighty was with him.
13: 6 from there the ark of God the *L*, who
16: 8 Give thanks to the *L*, call
16:11 Look to the *L* and his strength;
16:14 He is the *L* our God;
16:23 Sing to the *L*, all the earth;
17: 1 covenant of the *L* is under a tent."
21:24 take for the *L* what is yours,
22: 5 to be built for the *L* should be
22:11 build the house of the *L* your God,
22:13 and laws that the *L* gave Moses
22:16 Now begin the work, and the *L* be
22:19 soul to seeking the *L* your God.
25: 7 and skilled in music for the *L*—
28: 9 for the *L* searches every heart
28:20 for the *L* God, my God, is with you
29: 1 not for man but for the *L* God.
29:11 O *L*, is the greatness and the power
29:18 O *L*, God of our fathers Abraham,
29:25 The *L* highly exalted Solomon
2Ch 1: 1 for the *L* his God was with him
5:13 to give praise and thanks to the *L*.
5:14 the glory of the *L* filled the temple
6:16 "Now *L*, God of Israel, keep
6:41 O *L* God, and come
6:42 O *L* God, do not reject your
7: 1 the glory of the *L* filled the temple.
7:12 the *L* appeared to him at night
7:21 'Why has the *L* done such a thing
9: 8 as king to rule for the *L* your God.
13:12 do not fight against the *L*,
14: 2 right in the eyes of the *L* his God.
15:14 to the *L* with loud acclamation,
16: 9 of the *L* range throughout the earth
17: 9 the Book of the Law of the *L*;
18:13 said, "As surely as the *L* lives,
19: 6 judging for man but for the *L*,
19: 9 wholeheartedly in the fear of the *L*.
20:15 This is what the *L* says to you:
20:20 Have faith in the *L* your God
20:21 appointed men to sing to the *L*
26: 5 As long as he sought the *L*,
26:16 He was unfaithful to the *L* his God,
29:30 to praise the *L* with the words
30: 9 for the *L* your God is gracious
31:20 and faithful before the *L* his God.
32: 8 with us is the *L* our God to help us
34:14 Law of the *L* that had been given
34:31 to follow the *L* and keep his
Ezr 3:10 foundation of the temple of the *L*,
7: 6 for the hand of the *L* his God was
7:10 observance of the Law of the *L*,
9: 5 hands spread out to the *L* my God
9: 8 the *L* our God has been gracious
9:15 O *L*, God of Israel, you are
Ne 1: 5 Then I said: "O *L*, God of heaven,
8: 1 which the *L* had commanded
9: 6 You alone are the *L*.
Job 1: 6 to present themselves before the *L*,
1:21 *L* gave and the *L* has taken away;
38: 1 the *L* answered Job out
42: 9 and the *L* accepted Job's prayer.
42:12 The *L* blessed the latter part
Ps 1: 2 But his delight is in the law of the *L*
1: 6 For the *L* watches over the way
4: 6 of your face shine upon us, O *L*.
4: 8 for you alone, O *L*,
5: 3 In the morning, O *L*,
6: 1 O *L*, do not rebuke me
8: 1 O *L*, our Lord,
9: 9 The *L* is a refuge for the oppressed,
9:19 Arise, O *L*, let not man triumph;
10:16 The *L* is King for ever and ever;
12: 6 And the words of the *L* are flawless
16: 5 *L*, you have assigned me my
16: 8 I have set the *L* always before me.
18: 1 I love you, O *L*, my strength.
18: 6 In my distress I called to the *L*;
18:30 the word of the *L* is flawless.
19: 7 The law of the *L* is perfect,
19:14 O *L*, my Rock and my Redeemer.
20: 5 May the *L* grant all your requests.
20: 7 in the name of the *L* our God.
22: 8 let the *L* rescue him.
23: 1 The *L* is my shepherd, I shall
23: 6 I will dwell in the house of the *L*
24: 3 Who may ascend the hill of the *L*?
24: 8 The *L* strong and mighty,

Ps 25:10 All the ways of the *L* are loving
27: 1 The *L* is my light and my salvation
27: 4 to gaze upon the beauty of the *L*
27: 6 I will sing and make music to the *L*.
29: 1 Ascribe to the *L*, O mighty ones,
29: 4 The voice of the *L* is powerful;
30: 4 Sing to the *L*, you saints of his;
31: 5 redeem me, O *L*, the God of truth.
32: 2 whose sin the *L* does not count
33: 1 joyfully to the *L*, you righteous;
33: 6 of the *L* were the heavens made,
33:12 is the nation whose God is the *L*,
33:18 But the eyes of the *L* are
34: 1 I will extol the *L* at all times;
34: 3 Glorify the *L* with me;
34: 4 I sought the *L*, and he answered me
34: 7 The angel of the *L* encamps
34: 8 Taste and see that the *L* is good;
34: 9 Fear the *L*, you his saints,
34:15 The eyes of the *L* are
34:18 The *L* is close to the brokenhearted
37: 4 Delight yourself in the *L*
37: 5 Commit your way to the *L*;
39: 4 "Show me, O *L*, my life's end
40: 1 I waited patiently for the *L*;
40: 5 Many, O *L* my God,
46: 8 Come and see the works of the *L*,
47: 2 How awesome is the *L* Most High,
48: 1 Great is the *L*, and most worthy
50: 1 The Mighty One, God, the *L*,
55:22 Cast your cares on the *L*
59: 8 But you, O *L*, laugh at them;
68: 4 his name is the *L*—
68:18 O *L* God, might dwell there.
68:20 from the Sovereign *L* comes escape
69:31 This will please the *L* more
72:18 Praise be to the *L* God, the God
75: 8 In the hand of the *L* is a cup
78: 4 the praiseworthy deeds of the *L*,
84: 8 my prayer, O *L* God Almighty;
84:11 For the *L* God is a sun and shield;
85: 7 Show us your unfailing love, O *L*,
86:11 Teach me your way, O *L*,
87: 2 the *L* loves the gates of Zion
89: 5 heavens praise your wonders, O *L*,
89: 8 O *L* God Almighty, who is like you
91: 2 I will say of the *L*, "He is my refuge
92: 1 It is good to praise the *L*
92: 4 by your deeds, O *L*;
92:13 planted in the house of the *L*,
93: 1 The *L* reigns, he is robed in majesty
93: 5 house for endless days, O *L*.
94: 1 O *L*, the God who avenges,
94:12 is the man you discipline, O *L*,
94:18 your love, O *L*, supported me.
95: 1 Come, let us sing for joy to the *L*;
95: 3 For the *L* is the great God,
95: 6 let us kneel before the *L* our Maker
96: 1 Sing to the *L* a new song;
96: 5 but the *L* made the heavens.
96: 8 to the *L* the glory due his name;
96: 9 Worship the *L* in the splendor
96:13 they will sing before the *L*,
97: 1 The *L* reigns, let the earth be glad;
97: 9 O *L*, are the Most High
98: 1 Sing to the *L* a new song,
98: 2 *L* has made his salvation known
98: 4 Shout for joy to the *L*, all the earth,
99: 1 The *L* reigns,
99: 2 Great is the *L* in Zion;
99: 5 Exalt the *L* our God
99: 9 Exalt the *L* our God
100: 1 Shout for joy to the *L*, all the earth.
100: 2 Worship the *L* with gladness;
100: 3 Know that the *L* is God.
100: 5 For the *L* is good and his love
101: 1 to you, O *L*, I will sing praise.
102:12 But you, O *L*, sit enthroned forever
103: 1 Praise the *L*, O my soul;
103: 8 The *L* is compassionate
103:19 The *L* has established his throne
104: 1 O *L* my God, you are very great;
104:24 How many are your works, O *L*!
104:33 I will sing to the *L* all my life;
105: 4 Look to the *L* and his strength;
105: 7 He is the *L* our God;
106: 2 proclaim the mighty acts of the *L*
107: 1 Give thanks to the *L*, for he is good
107: 8 to the *L* for his unfailing love
107:21 to the *L* for his unfailing love
107:43 and consider the great love of the *L*
108: 3 I will praise you, O *L*,
109:26 Help me, O *L* my God;
110: 1 The *L* says to my Lord:
110: 4 The *L* has sworn

Ps 111: 2 Great are the works of the *L*;
111: 4 *L* is gracious and compassionate.
111:10 The fear of the *L* is the beginning
112: 1 Blessed is the man who fears the *L*,
113: 1 Praise, O servants of the *L*,
113: 2 Let the name of the *L* be praised,
113: 4 *L* is exalted over all the nations,
113: 5 Who is like the *L* our God,
115: 1 Not to us, O *L*, not to us
115:18 it is we who extol the *L*,
116:12 How can I repay the *L*
116:15 Precious in the sight of the *L*
117: 1 Praise the *L*, all you nations;
118: 1 Give thanks to the *L*, for he is good
118: 5 In my anguish I cried to the *L*,
118: 8 It is better to take refuge in the *L*
118:18 The *L* has chastened me severely,
118:23 the *L* has done this,
118:24 This is the day the *L* has made;
118:26 comes in the name of the *L*.
119: 1 to the law of the *L*.
119:64 with your love, O *L*;
119:89 Your word, O *L*, is eternal;
119:126 It is time for you to act, O *L*;
119:159 O *L*, according to your love.
120: 1 I call on the *L* in my distress,
121: 2 My help comes from the *L*,
121: 5 The *L* watches over you—
121: 8 the *L* will watch over your coming
122: 1 "Let us go to the house of the *L*."
123: 2 so our eyes look to the *L* our God,
124: 1 If the *L* had not been on our side—
124: 8 Our help is in the name of the *L*,
125: 2 so the *L* surrounds his people
126: 3 The *L* has done great things for us,
126: 4 Restore our fortunes, O *L*,
127: 1 Unless the *L* builds the house,
127: 3 Sons are a heritage from the *L*,
128: 1 Blessed are all who fear the *L*,
130: 1 O *L*; O Lord, hear my voice.
130: 3 If you, O *L*, kept a record of sins,
130: 5 I wait for the *L*, my soul waits,
131: 3 O Israel, put your hope in the *L*
132: 1 O *L*, remember David
132:13 For the *L* has chosen Zion,
133: 3 For there the *L* bestows his
134: 3 May the *L*, the Maker of heaven
135: 4 For the *L* has chosen Jacob
135: 6 The *L* does whatever pleases him,
136: 1 Give thanks to the *L*, for he is good
137: 4 How can we sing the songs of the *L*
138: 1 I will praise you, O *L*,
138: 8 The *L* will fulfill ⌊his purpose⌋
139: 1 O *L*, you have searched me
140: 1 Rescue me, O *L*, from evil men;
141: 1 O *L*, I call to you; come quickly
141: 3 Set a guard over my mouth, O *L*;
142: 5 I cry to you, O *L*;
143: 9 Rescue me from my enemies, O *L*,
144: 3 O *L*, what is man that you care
145: 3 Great is the *L* and most worthy
145: 8 *L* is gracious and compassionate,
145: 9 The *L* is good to all;
145:17 The *L* is righteous in all his ways
145:18 The *L* is near to all who call on him
146: 5 whose hope is in the *L* his God,
146: 7 The *L* sets prisoners free,
147: 2 The *L* builds up Jerusalem;
147: 7 Sing to the *L* with thanksgiving;
147:11 *L* delights in those who fear him,
147:12 Extol the *L*, O Jerusalem;
148: 1 Praise the *L* from the heavens,
148: 7 Praise the *L* from the earth,
149: 4 For the *L* takes delight
150: 1 Praise the *L*.
150: 6 that has breath praise the *L*.
Pr 1: 7 The fear of the *L* is the beginning
1:29 and did not choose to fear the *L*,
2: 5 will understand the fear of the *L*
2: 6 For the *L* gives wisdom,
3: 5 Trust in the *L* with all your heart
3: 7 fear the *L* and shun evil.
3: 9 Honor the *L* with your wealth,
3:12 the *L* disciplines those he loves,
3:19 By wisdom the *L* laid the earth's
5:21 are in full view of the *L*,
6:16 There are six things the *L* hates,
8:13 To fear the *L* is to hate evil;
9:10 "The fear of the *L* is the beginning
10:27 The fear of the *L* adds length to life
11: 1 The *L* abhors dishonest scales,
12:22 The *L* detests lying lips,
14: 2 whose walk is upright fears the *L*,
14:26 He who fears the *L* has a secure
14:27 The fear of the *L* is a fountain

Pr 15: 3 The eyes of the *L* are everywhere,
15: 16 Better a little with the fear of the *L*
15: 33 of the *L* teaches a man wisdom,
16: 2 but motives are weighed by the *L*.
16: 3 Commit to the *L* whatever you do,
16: 4 The *L* works out everything
16: 5 The *L* detests all the proud of heart
16: 9 but the *L* determines his steps.
16: 33 but its every decision is from the *L*.
18: 10 The name of the *L* is a strong tower
18: 22 and receives favor from the *L*.
19: 14 but a prudent wife is from the *L*.
19: 17 to the poor lends to the *L*,
19: 23 The fear of the *L* leads to life:
20: 10 the *L* detests them both.
21: 2 but the *L* weighs the heart.
21: 3 to the *L* than sacrifice.
21: 30 that can succeed against the *L*.
21: 31 but victory rests with the *L*.
22: 2 The *L* is the Maker of them all.
22: 23 for the *L* will take up their case
23: 17 for the fear of the *L*.
24: 18 or the *L* will see and disapprove
24: 21 Fear the *L* and the king, my son,
25: 22 and the *L* will reward you.
28: 14 is the man who always fears the *L*,
29: 26 from the *L* that man gets justice.
30: 7 "Two things I ask of you, O *L*;
31: 30 a woman who fears the *L* is
Isa 2: 3 up to the mountain of the *L*,
2: 10 the ground from dread of the *L*
3: 17 the *L* will make their scalps bald."
4: 2 of the *L* will be beautiful
5: 16 the *L* Almighty will be exalted
6: 3 holy, holy is the *L* Almighty;
9: 7 The zeal of the *L* Almighty
11: 2 The Spirit of the *L* will rest on him
11: 9 full of the knowledge of the *L*
12: 2 The *L*, the *L*, is my strength
18: 7 of the Name of the *L* Almighty.
24: 1 the *L* is going to lay waste the earth
25: 1 O *L*, you are my God;
25: 6 this mountain the *L* Almighty will
25: 8 The Sovereign *L* will wipe away
26: 4 Trust in the *L* forever,
26: 8 *L*, walking in the way of your laws,
26: 13 O *L*, our God, other lords
26: 21 the *L* is coming out of his dwelling
27: 1 the *L* will punish with his sword,
27: 12 In that day the *L* will thresh
28: 5 In that day the *L* Almighty
29: 6 the *L* Almighty will come
29: 15 to hide their plans from the *L*,
30: 18 For the *L* is a God of justice.
30: 26 when the *L* binds up the bruises
30: 27 the Name of the *L* comes from afar
30: 30 The *L* will cause men
33: 2 O *L*, be gracious to us;
33: 6 the fear of the *L* is the key
33: 22 For the *L* is our judge,
34: 2 The *L* is angry with all nations;
35: 2 they will see the glory of the *L*,
35: 10 the ransomed of the *L* will return.
38: 7 to you that the *L* will do what he
40: 3 the way for the *L*;
40: 5 the glory of the *L* will be revealed,
40: 7 the breath of the *L* blows on them.
40: 10 the Sovereign *L* comes with power,
40: 14 Whom did the *L* consult
40: 28 The *L* is the everlasting God,
40: 31 but those who hope in the *L*
41: 14 will help you," declares the *L*,
41: 20 that the hand of the *L* has done this
42: 6 the *L*, have called you
42: 8 "I am the *L*; that is my name!
42: 13 The *L* will march out like a mighty
42: 21 It pleased the *L*
43: 3 For I am the *L*, your God,
43: 11 I, even I, am the *L*,
44: 6 "This is what the *L* says—
44: 24 I am the *L*,
45: 5 I am the *L*, and there is no other;
45: 7 I, the *L*, do all these things.
45: 21 Was it not I, the *L*?
48: 17 "I am the *L* your God,
50: 4 Sovereign *L* has given me
50: 10 Who among you fears the *L*
51: 1 and who seek the *L*:
51: 11 The ransomed of the *L* will return.
51: 15 the *L* Almighty is his name.
53: 1 the arm of the *L* been revealed?
53: 6 and the *L* has laid on him
53: 10 and the will of the *L* will prosper
54: 5 the *L* Almighty is his name—
55: 6 Seek the *L* while he may be found;
Isa 55: 7 to the *L*, and he will have mercy
56: 6 who bind themselves to the *L*
58: 8 of the *L* will be your rear guard.
58: 11 The *L* will guide you always;
59: 1 the arm of the *L* is not too short
60: 1 the glory of the *L* rises upon you.
60: 16 Then you will know that I, the *L*,
60: 20 the *L* will be your everlasting light,
61: 1 Spirit of the Sovereign *L* is on me,
61: 3 a planting of the *L*
61: 10 I delight greatly in the *L*;
61: 11 so the Sovereign *L* will make
62: 4 for the *L* will take delight in you,
63: 7 I will tell of the kindnesses of the *L*,
64: 8 Yet, O *L*, you are our Father.
66: 15 See, the *L* is coming with fire,
Jer 1: 9 Then the *L* reached out his hand
2: 19 when you forsake the *L* your God
3: 25 sinned against the *L* our God,
4: 4 Circumcise yourselves to the *L*,
8: 7 the requirements of the *L*.
9: 24 I am the *L*, who exercises kindness,
10: 6 No one is like you, O *L*;
10: 10 But the *L* is the true God;
12: 1 You are always righteous, O *L*,
14: 7 O *L*, do something for the sake
14: 20 O *L*, we acknowledge our
16: 15 will say, 'As surely as the *L* lives,
16: 19 O *L*, my strength and my fortress,
17: 7 is the man who trusts in the *L*,
17: 10 "I the *L* search the heart
20: 11 *L* is with me like a mighty warrior;
23: 6 The *L* Our Righteousness.
24: 7 heart to know me, that I am the *L*.
28: 9 as one truly sent by the *L* only
31: 11 For the *L* will ransom Jacob
31: 22 The *L* will create a new thing
31: 34 his brother, saying, 'Know the *L*,'
32: 27 I am the *L*, the God of all mankind.
33: 16 The *L* Our Righteousness.'
36: 6 the words of the *L* that you wrote
40: 3 now the *L* has brought it about;
42: 3 Pray that the *L* your God will tell
42: 4 I will tell you everything the *L* says
42: 6 we will obey the *L* our God,
50: 4 go in tears to seek the *L* their God.
51: 10 " 'The *L* has vindicated us;
51: 56 For the *L* is a God of retribution;
La 3: 24 to myself, "The *L* is my portion;
3: 25 *L* is good to those whose hope is
3: 40 and let us return to the *L*.
Eze 1: 3 the word of the *L* came
1: 28 of the likeness of the glory of the *L*.
4: 14 Sovereign *L*! I have never defiled
10: 4 Then the glory of the *L* rose
15: 7 you will know that I am the *L*.
30: 3 the day of the *L* is near—
36: 23 nations will know that I am the *L*,
37: 4 'Dry bones, hear the word of the *L*!
43: 4 glory of the *L* entered the temple
44: 4 LORD filling the temple of the *L*,
Da 9: 2 to the word of the *L* given
Hos 1: 7 horsemen, but by the *L* their God."
2: 20 and you will acknowledge the *L*.
3: 1 as the *L* loves the Israelites,
3: 5 They will come trembling to the *L*
6: 1 "Come, let us return to the *L*.
6: 3 Let us acknowledge the *L*;
10: 12 for it is time to seek the *L*,
12: 5 the *L* is his name of renown!
14: 1 O Israel, to the *L* your God.
Joel 1: 1 The word of the *L* that came
1: 15 For the day of the *L* is near;
2: 1 for the day of the *L* is coming.
2: 11 The day of the *L* is great;
2: 13 Return to the *L* your God,
2: 23 rejoice in the *L* your God,
2: 31 the great and dreadful day of the *L*.
2: 32 on the name of the *L* will be saved;
3: 14 For the day of the *L* is near
3: 16 the *L* will be a refuge for his people,
Am 4: 13 the *L* God Almighty is his name.
5: 6 Seek the *L* and live,
5: 15 Perhaps the *L* God Almighty will
5: 18 long for the day of the *L*?
7: 15 *L* took me from tending the flock
8: 12 searching for the word of the *L*,
9: 5 The Lord, the *L* Almighty,
Ob :15 "The day of the *L* is near
Jnh 1: 3 But Jonah ran away from the *L*
1: 4 the *L* sent a great wind on the sea,
1: 17 But the *L* provided a great fish
2: 9 Salvation comes from the *L*."
4: 2 He prayed to the *L*, "O *L*,
4: 6 Then the *L* God provided a vine
Mic 1: 1 The word of the *L* that came to Micah
4: 2 up to the mountain of the *L*,
5: 4 flock in the strength of the *L*,
6: 2 For the *L* has a case
6: 8 And what does the *L* require of you
7: 7 as for me, I watch in hope for the *L*,
Na 1: 2 The *L* takes vengeance on his foes
1: 3 The *L* is slow to anger
Hab 2: 14 knowledge of the glory of the *L*,
2: 20 But the *L* is in his holy temple;
3: 2 I stand in awe of your deeds, O *L*.
Zep 1: 1 The word of the *L* that came
1: 7 for the day of the *L* is near.
3: 17 The *L* your God is with you,
Hag 1: 1 the word of the *L* came
1: 8 and be honored," says the *L*.
2: 23 that day,' declares the *L* Almighty,
Zec 1: 1 the word of the *L* came
1: 17 and the *L* will again comfort Zion
3: 1 standing before the angel of the *L*,
4: 6 by my Spirit,' says the *L* Almighty.
6: 12 and build the temple of the *L*.
8: 21 the *L* and seek the *L* Almighty.
9: 16 The *L* their God will save them
14: 5 Then the *L* my God will come,
14: 9 The *L* will be king
14: 16 the *L* Almighty, and to celebrate
Mal 1: 1 The word of the *L* to Israel
3: 6 "I the *L* do not change.
4: 5 and dreadful day of the *L* comes.

LORD'S‡ (LORD‡)

Ex 4: 14 the *L* anger burned against Moses
12: 11 Eat it in haste; it is the *L* Passover.
34: 34 he entered the *L* presence
Lev 23: 4 " 'These are the *L* appointed feasts,
Nu 9: 23 At the *L* command they encamped
14: 41 you disobeying the *L* command?
32: 13 The *L* anger burned against Israel
Dt 6: 18 is right and good in the *L* sight,
10: 13 and to observe the *L* commands
32: 9 For the *L* portion is his people,
Jos 21: 45 Not one of all the *L* good promises
1Sa 24: 10 because he is the *L* anointed.'
1Ki 10: 9 Because of the *L* eternal love
Ps 24: 1 The earth is the *L*, and everything
32: 10 but the *L* unfailing love
89: 1 of the *L* great love forever;
103: 17 *L* love is with those who fear him,
118: 15 "The *L* right hand has done mighty
Pr 3: 11 do not despise the *L* discipline
19: 21 but it is the *L* purpose that prevails.
Isa 24: 14 west they acclaim the *L* majesty.
30: 9 to listen to the *L* instruction.
49: 4 Yet what is due me is in the *L* hand
53: 10 Yet it was the *L* will to crush him
55: 13 This will be for the *L* renown,
61: 2 to proclaim the year of the *L* favor
62: 3 of splendor in the *L* hand,
Jer 25: 17 So I took the cup from the *L* hand
48: 10 lax in doing the *L* work!
51: 7 was a gold cup in the *L* hand;
La 3: 22 of the *L* great love we are not
Eze 7: 19 them in the day of the *L* wrath.
Joel 3: 18 will flow out of the *L* house
Ob :21 And the kingdom will be the *L*.
Mic 4: 1 of the *L* temple will be established
6: 2 O mountains, the *L* accusation;
Hab 2: 16 from the *L* right hand is coming
Zep 2: 3 sheltered on the day of the *L* anger.

LOSE (LOSES LOSS LOST)

Dt 1: 28 Our brothers have made us *l* heart.
1Sa 17: 32 "Let no one *l* heart on account
Isa 7: 4 Do not *l* heart because of these two
Mt 10: 39 Whoever finds his life will *l* it,
Lk 9: 25 and yet *l* or forfeit his very self?
Jn 6: 39 that I shall *l* none of all that he has
2Co 4: 1 this ministry, we do not *l* heart.
4: 16 Therefore we do not *l* heart.
Heb 12: 3 will not grow weary and *l* heart.
12: 5 do not *l* heart when he rebukes you
2Jn : 8 that you do not *l* what you have

LOSES (LOSE)

Mt 5: 13 But if the salt *l* its saltiness,
Lk 15: 4 you has a hundred sheep and *l* one
15: 8 has ten silver coins and *l* one.

LOSS (LOSE)

Ro 11: 12 and their *l* means riches
1Co 3: 15 he will suffer *l*; he himself will be
Php 3: 8 I consider everything a *l* compared

LOST (LOSE)

Ps 73: 2 I had nearly *l* my foothold.
Jer 50: 6 "My people have been *l* sheep;
Eze 34: 4 the strays or searched for the *l*.
34:16 for the *l* and bring back the strays.
Mt 18:14 any of these little ones should be *l*.
Lk 15: 4 go after the *l* sheep until he finds it?
15: 6 with me; I have found my *l* sheep.'
15: 9 with me; I have found my *l* coin.'
15:24 is alive again; he was *l* and is found
19:10 to seek and to save what was *l*."
Php 3: 8 for whose sake I have *l* all things.

LOT (LOTS)

Nephew of Abraham (Ge 11:27; 12:5). Chose to live in Sodom (Ge 13). Rescued from four kings (Ge 14). Rescued from Sodom (Ge 19:1-29; 2Pe 2:7). Fathered Moab and Ammon by his daughters (Ge 19:30-38).

Est 3: 7 the *l*) in the presence of Haman
9:24 the *l*) for their ruin and destruction.
Pr 16:33 The *l* is cast into the lap,
18:18 Casting the *l* settles disputes
Ecc 3:22 his work, because that is his *l*.
Ac 1:26 Then they cast lots, and the *l* fell

LOTS (LOT)

Jos 18:10 Joshua then cast *l* for them
Ps 22:18 and cast *l* for my clothing.
Joel 3: 3 They cast *l* for my people
Ob :11 and cast *l* for Jerusalem,
Mt 27:35 divided up his clothes by casting *l*.
Ac 1:26 Then they cast *l*, and the lot fell

LOVE* (BELOVED LOVED LOVELY LOVER LOVER'S LOVERS LOVES LOVING LOVING-KINDNESS)

Ge 20:13 'This is how you can show your *l*
22: 2 your only son, Isaac, whom you *l*,
29:18 Jacob was in *l* with Rachel and said
29:20 days to him because of his *l* for her.
29:32 Surely my husband will *l* me now."
Ex 15:13 "In your unfailing *l* you will lead
20: 6 showing *l* to a thousand generations
20: 6 of those who *l* me
21: 5 'I *l* my master and my wife
34: 6 abounding in *l* and faithfulness,
34: 7 maintaining *l* to thousands,
Lev 19:18 but *l* your neighbor as yourself.
19:34 *L* him as yourself,
Nu 14:18 abounding in *l* and forgiving sin
14:19 In accordance with your great *l*,
Dt 5:10 showing *l* to a thousand generations
5:10 of those who *l* me
6: 5 *L* the LORD your God
7: 9 generations of those who *l* him
7: 9 keeping his covenant of *l*
7:12 God will keep his covenant of *l*
7:13 He will *l* you and bless you
10:12 to walk in all his ways, to *l* him,
10:19 you are to *l* those who are aliens,
11: 1 *L* the LORD your God
11:13 to *l* the LORD your God
11:22 to *l* the LORD your God,
13: 3 you *l* him with all your heart
13: 6 wife you *l*, or your closest friend
19: 9 to *l* the LORD your God
21:15 the son of the wife he does not *l*,
21:16 the son of the wife he does not *l*.
30: 6 so that you may *l* him
30:16 today to *l* the LORD your God,
30:20 and that you may *l* the LORD your
33: 3 Surely it is you who *l* the people;
Jos 22: 5 to *l* the LORD your God, to walk
23:11 careful to *l* the LORD your God.
Jdg 5:31 may they who *l* you be like the sun
14:16 You hate me! You don't really *l* me
16: 4 he fell in *l* with a woman
16:15 "How can you say, 'I *l* you,'
1Sa 18:20 Saul's daughter Michal was in *l*
20:17 had David reaffirm his oath out of *l*
2Sa 1:26 Your *l* for me was wonderful,
7:15 But my *l* will never be taken away
13: 1 son of David fell in *l* with Tamar,
13: 4 said to him, "I'm in *l* with Tamar,
16:17 "Is this the *l* you show your friend?
19: 6 You *l* those who hate you
19: 6 hate you and hate those who *l* you.
1Ki 3: 3 Solomon showed his *l*
8:23 you who keep your covenant of *l*
10: 9 of the LORD's eternal *l* for Israel,
11: 2 Solomon held fast to them in *l*.
1Ch 16:34 his *l* endures forever.
16:41 "for his *l* endures forever."
1Ch 17:13 I will never take my *l* away
2Ch 5:13 his *l* endures forever."
6:14 you who keep your covenant of *l*
6:42 Remember the great *l* promised
7: 3 his *l* endures forever."
7: 6 saying, "His *l* endures forever."
9: 8 Because of the *l* of your God
19: 2 and *l* those who hate the LORD?
20:21 for his *l* endures forever."
Ezr 3:11 his *l* to Israel endures forever."
Ne 1: 5 covenant of *l* with those who *l* him
9:17 slow to anger and abounding in *l*.
9:32 who keeps his covenant of *l*,
13:22 to me according to your great *l*.
Job 15:34 of those who *l* bribes.
19:19 those I *l* have turned against me.
37:13 or to water his earth and show his *l*.
Ps 4: 2 How long will you *l* delusions
5:11 that those who *l* your name may
6: 4 save me because of your unfailing *l*.
11: 5 wicked and those who *l* violence
13: 5 But I trust in your unfailing *l*;
17: 7 Show the wonder of your great *l*,
18: 1 I *l* you, O LORD, my strength.
21: 7 through the unfailing *l*
23: 6 Surely goodness and *l* will follow
25: 6 O LORD, your great mercy and *l*,
25: 7 according to your *l* remember me,
26: 3 for your *l* is ever before me,
26: 8 I *l* the house where you live,
31: 7 I will be glad and rejoice in your *l*,
31:16 save me in your unfailing *l*.
31:21 for he showed his wonderful *l*
31:23 *L* the LORD, all his saints!
32:10 but the LORD's unfailing *l*
33: 5 the earth is full of his unfailing *l*.
33:18 whose hope is in his unfailing *l*,
33:22 May your unfailing *l* rest upon us,
36: 5 Your *l*, O LORD, reaches
36: 7 How priceless is your unfailing *l*!
36:10 Continue your *l* to those who know
40:10 I do not conceal your *l*
40:11 may your *l* and your truth always
40:16 may those who *l* your salvation
42: 8 By day the LORD directs his *l*,
44:26 of your unfailing *l*.
45: 7 You *l* righteousness and hate
48: 9 we meditate on your unfailing *l*.
51: 1 according to your unfailing *l*;
52: 3 You *l* evil rather than good,
52: 4 You *l* every harmful word,
52: 8 I trust in God's unfailing *l*
57: 3 God sends his *l* and his faithfulness
57:10 For great is your *l*, reaching
59:16 in the morning I will sing of your *l*;
60: 5 that those you *l* may be delivered.
61: 7 appoint your *l* and faithfulness
63: 3 Because your *l* is better than life,
66:20 or withheld his *l* from me!
69:13 in your great *l*, O God,
69:16 out of the goodness of your *l*;
69:36 and those who *l* his name will dwell
70: 4 may those who *l* your salvation
77: 8 Has his unfailing *l* vanished forever
85: 7 Show us your unfailing *l*, O LORD
85:10 *L* and faithfulness meet together;
86: 5 abounding in *l* to all who call
86:13 For great is your *l* toward me;
86:15 abounding in *l* and faithfulness.
88:11 Is your *l* declared in the grave,
89: 1 of the LORD's great *l* forever;
89: 2 declare that your *l* stands firm
89:14 *l* and faithfulness go before you.
89:24 My faithful *l* will be with him,
89:28 I will maintain my *l* to him forever,
89:33 but I will not take my *l* from him,
89:49 where is your former great *l*,
90:14 with your unfailing *l*,
92: 2 to proclaim your *l* in the morning
94:18 your *l*, O LORD, supported me.
97:10 Let those who *l* the LORD hate
98: 3 He has remembered his *l*
100: 5 is good and his *l* endures forever;
101: 1 I will sing of your *l* and justice;
103: 4 crowns you with *l* and compassion.
103: 8 slow to anger, abounding in *l*.
103:11 so great is his *l* for those who fear
103:17 LORD's *l* is with those who fear
106: 1 his *l* endures forever.
106:45 and out of his great *l* he relented.
107: 1 his *l* endures forever.
107: 8 to the LORD for his unfailing *l*
107:15 to the LORD for his unfailing *l*
107:21 to the LORD for his unfailing *l*
107:31 to the LORD for his unfailing *l*
Ps 107:43 consider the great *l* of the LORD.
108: 4 For great is your *l*, higher
108: 6 that those you *l* may be delivered.
109:21 out of the goodness of your *l*,
109:26 save me in accordance with your *l*.
115: 1 because of your *l* and faithfulness.
116: 1 I *l* the LORD, for he heard my
117: 2 For great is his *l* toward us,
118: 1 his *l* endures forever.
118: 2 "His *l* endures forever."
118: 3 "His *l* endures forever."
118: 4 "His *l* endures forever."
118:29 his *l* endures forever.
119:41 May your unfailing *l* come to me,
119:47 because I *l* them.
119:48 to your commands, which I *l*,
119:64 The earth is filled with your *l*,
119:76 May your unfailing *l* be my
119:88 my life according to your *l*,
119:97 Oh, how I *l* your law!
119:113 but I *l* your law.
119:119 therefore I *l* your statutes.
119:124 your servant according to your *l*
119:127 Because I *l* your commands
119:132 to those who *l* your name.
119:149 in accordance with your *l*;
119:159 O LORD, according to your *l*.
119:159 See how I *l* your precepts;
119:163 but I *l* your law.
119:165 peace have they who *l* your law,
119:167 for I *l* them greatly.
122: 6 "May those who *l* you be secure.
130: 7 for with the LORD is unfailing *l*
136: 1-26 *His l endures forever.*
138: 2 for your *l* and your faithfulness,
138: 8 your *l*, O LORD, endures forever
143: 8 of your unfailing *l*,
143:12 In your unfailing *l*, silence my
145: 8 slow to anger and rich in *l*.
145:20 over all who *l* him,
147:11 who put their hope in his unfailing *l*
Pr 1:22 you simple ones *l* your simple
3: 3 Let *l* and faithfulness never leave
4: 6 *l* her, and she will watch over you.
5:19 you ever be captivated by her *l*.
7:18 let's drink deep of *l* till morning;
7:18 let's enjoy ourselves with *l*!
8:17 I *l* those who *l* me,
8:21 wealth on those who *l* me
8:36 all who hate me *l* death."
9: 8 rebuke a wise man and he will *l* you
10:12 but *l* covers over all wrongs.
14:22 those who plan what is good find *l*
15:17 of vegetables where there is *l*
16: 6 Through *l* and faithfulness sin is
17: 9 over an offense promotes *l*,
18:21 and those who *l* it will eat its fruit.
19:22 What a man desires is unfailing *l*;
20: 6 claims to have unfailing *l*,
20:13 Do not *l* sleep or you will grow
20:28 *L* and faithfulness keep a king safe;
20:28 through *l* his throne is made secure
21:21 who pursues righteousness and *l*
27: 5 rebuke than hidden *l*.
Ecc 3: 8 a time to *l* and a time to hate,
9: 1 but no man knows whether *l*
9: 6 Their *l*, their hate
9: 9 life with your wife, whom you *l*,
SS 1: 2 for your *l* is more delightful
1: 3 No wonder the maidens *l* you!
1: 4 we will praise your *l* more
1: 7 you whom I *l*, where you graze
2: 4 and his banner over me is *l*.
2: 5 for I am faint with *l*.
2: 7 Do not arouse or awaken *l*
3: 5 Do not arouse or awaken *l*
4:10 How delightful is your *l*, my sister,
4:10 How much more pleasing is your *l*
5: 8 Tell him I am faint with *l*.
7: 6 O *l*, with your delights!
7:12 there I will give you my *l*.
8: 4 Do not arouse or awaken *l*
8: 6 for *l* is as strong as death,
8: 7 Many waters cannot quench *l*;
8: 7 all the wealth of his house for *l*,
Isa 1:23 they all *l* bribes
5: 1 I will sing for the one I *l*
16: 5 In *l* a throne will be established;
38:17 In your *l* you kept me
43: 4 and because I *l* you,
54:10 yet my unfailing *l* for you will not
55: 3 my faithful *l* promised to David.
56: 6 to *l* the name of the LORD,
56:10 they *l* to sleep.
57: 8 a pact with those whose beds you *l*

Isa 61: 8 "For I, the LORD, l justice;
63: 9 In his l and mercy he redeemed
66: 10 all you who l her;
Jer 2: 25 I l foreign gods,
2: 33 How skilled you are at pursuing l!
5: 31 and my people l it this way.
12: 7 I will give the one I l
14: 10 "They greatly l to wander;
16: 5 my l and my pity from this people
31: 3 you with an everlasting l;
32: 18 You show l to thousands
33: 11 his l endures forever."
La 3: 22 of the LORD's great l we are not
3: 32 so great is his unfailing l.
Eze 16: 8 saw that you were old enough for l,
23: 17 of l, and in their lust they defiled
33: 32 more than one who sings l songs
Da 9: 4 covenant of l with all who l him
Hos 1: 6 for I will no longer show l
1: 7 Yet I will show l to the house
2: 4 I will not show my l to her children
2: 19 in l and compassion.
2: 23 I will show my l to the one I called
3: 1 Go, show your l to your wife again,
3: 1 and l the sacred raisin cakes."
3: 1 L her as the LORD loves
4: 1 "There is no faithfulness, no l,
4: 18 their rulers dearly l shameful ways.
6: 4 Your l is like the morning mist,
9: 1 you l the wages of a prostitute
9: 15 I will no longer l them;
10: 12 reap the fruit of unfailing l,
11: 4 with ties of l;
12: 6 maintain l and justice,
14: 4 and l them freely,
Joel 2: 13 slow to anger and abounding in l,
Am 4: 5 for this is what you l to do,"
5: 15 Hate evil, l good;
Jnh 4: 2 slow to anger and abounding in l,
Mic 3: 2 you who hate good and l evil;
6: 8 To act justly and to l mercy
Zep 3: 17 he will quiet you with his l,
Zec 8: 17 and do not l to swear falsely.
8: 19 Therefore l truth and peace."
Mt 3: 17 "This is my Son, whom I l;
5: 43 'L your neighbor and hate your
5: 44 L your enemies and pray
5: 46 you l those who l you, what reward
6: 5 for they l to pray standing
6: 24 he will hate the one and l the other,
12: 18 the one I l, in whom I delight;
17: 5 "This is my Son, whom I l;
19: 19 and 'l your neighbor as yourself.' "
22: 37 " 'L the Lord your God
22: 39 'L your neighbor as yourself.'
23: 6 they l the place of honor
23: 7 they l to be greeted
24: 12 the l of most will grow cold,
Mk 1: 11 "You are my Son, whom I l;
9: 7 "This is my Son, whom I l.
12: 30 L the Lord your God
12: 31 'L your neighbor as yourself.'
12: 33 To l him with all your heart,
12: 33 and to l your neighbor
Lk 3: 22 "You are my Son, whom I l;
6: 27 you who hear me: L your enemies,
6: 32 Even 'sinners' l those who l them.
6: 32 you l those who l you, what credit
6: 35 l your enemies, do good to them,
7: 42 which of them will l him more?"
10: 27 and, 'L your neighbor as yourself
10: 27 " 'L the Lord your God
11: 42 you neglect justice and the l of God
11: 43 you l the most important seats
16: 13 he will hate the one and l the other,
20: 13 whom I l; perhaps they will respect
20: 46 l to be greeted in the marketplaces
Jn 5: 42 I know that you do not have the l
8: 42 were your Father, you would l me,
11: 3 "Lord, the one you l is sick."
13: 1 them the full extent of his l.
13: 34 I give you: L one another.
13: 34 so you must l one another.
13: 35 disciples, if you l one another."
14: 15 "If you l me, you will obey what I
14: 21 I too will l him and show myself
14: 23 My Father will l him, and we will
14: 24 He who does not l me will not obey
14: 31 world must learn that I l the Father
15: 9 Now remain in my l.
15: 10 commands and remain in his l.
15: 10 you will remain in my l,
15: 12 L each other as I have loved you.
15: 13 Greater l has no one than this,
15: 17 This is my command: L each other.
Jn 15: 19 to the world, it would l you
17: 26 known in order that the l you have
21: 15 do you truly l me more than these
21: 15 he said, "you know that I l you."
21: 16 Yes, Lord, you know that I l you."
21: 16 do you truly l me?" He answered,
21: 17 all things; you know that I l you."
21: 17 "Do you l me?" He said, "Lord,
21: 17 "Simon son of John, do you l me?"
Ro 5: 5 because God has poured out his l
5: 8 God demonstrates his own l for us
8: 28 for the good of those who l him,
8: 35 us from the l of Christ?
8: 39 us from the l of God that is
12: 9 L must be sincere.
12: 10 to one another in brotherly l.
13: 8 continuing debt to l one another,
13: 9 "L your neighbor as yourself."
13: 10 Therefore l is the fulfillment
13: 10 L does no harm to its neighbor.
14: 15 you are no longer acting in l.
15: 30 and by the l of the Spirit,
16: 8 Greet Ampliatus, whom I l
1Co 2: 9 prepared for those who l him"—
4: 17 my son whom I l, who is faithful
4: 21 or in l and with a gentle spirit?
8: 1 Knowledge puffs up, but l builds up
13: 1 have not l, I am only a resounding
13: 2 but have not l, I am nothing.
13: 3 but have not l, I gain nothing.
13: 4 Love is patient, l is kind.
13: 4 L is patient, love is kind.
13: 6 L does not delight in evil
13: 8 L never fails.
13: 13 But the greatest of these is l.
13: 13 three remain: faith, hope and l.
14: 1 way of l and eagerly desire spiritual
16: 14 Do everything in l.
16: 22 If anyone does not l the Lord—
16: 24 My l to all of you in Christ Jesus.
2Co 2: 4 to let you know the depth of my l
2: 8 therefore, to reaffirm your l for him
5: 14 For Christ's l compels us,
6: 6 in the Holy Spirit and in sincere l;
8: 7 complete earnestness and in your l
8: 8 sincerity of your l by comparing it
8: 24 show these men the proof of your l
11: 11 Why? Because I do not l you?
12: 15 If I l you more, will you l me less?
13: 11 And the God of l and peace will be
13: 14 of the Lord Jesus Christ, and the l
Gal 5: 6 is faith expressing itself through l.
5: 13 rather, serve one another in l.
5: 14 "L your neighbor as yourself."
5: 22 But the fruit of the Spirit is l, joy,
Eph 1: 4 In l he predestined us
1: 15 and your l for all the saints,
2: 4 But because of his great l for us,
3: 17 being rooted and established in l,
3: 18 and high and deep is the l of Christ,
3: 19 and to know this l that surpasses
4: 2 bearing with one another in l.
4: 15 Instead, speaking the truth in l,
4: 16 grows and builds itself up in l,
5: 2 loved children and live a life of l,
5: 25 l your wives, just as Christ loved
5: 28 husbands ought to l their wives
5: 33 each one of you also must l his wife
6: 23 l with faith from God the Father
6: 24 Christ with an undying l.
6: 24 to all who l our Lord Jesus Christ
Php 1: 9 that your l may abound more
1: 16 so in l, knowing that I am put here
2: 1 from his l, if any fellowship
2: 2 having the same l, being one
4: 1 you whom I l and long for,
Col 1: 4 of the l you have for all the saints—
1: 5 l that spring from the hope that is
1: 8 also told us of your l in the Spirit.
2: 2 in heart and united in l,
3: 14 And over all these virtues put on l,
3: 19 l your wives and do not be harsh
1Th 1: 3 your labor prompted by l,
3: 6 good news about your faith and l.
3: 12 May the Lord make your l increase
4: 9 about brotherly l we do not need
4: 9 taught by God to l each other.
4: 10 you do l all the brothers
5: 8 on faith and l as a breastplate,
5: 13 them in the highest regard in l
2Th 1: 3 and the l every one of you has
2: 10 because they refused to l the truth
3: 5 direct your hearts into God's l
1Ti 1: 5 The goal of this command is l,
1: 14 and l that are in Christ Jesus.
1Ti 2: 15 l and holiness with propriety.
4: 12 in life, in l, in faith and in purity.
6: 10 For the l of money is a root
6: 11 faith, l, endurance and gentleness.
2Ti 1: 7 of power, of l and of self-discipline.
1: 13 with faith and l in Christ Jesus.
2: 22 and pursue righteousness, faith, l
3: 3 unholy, without l, unforgiving,
3: 10 faith, patience, l, endurance,
Tit 2: 2 in faith, in l and in endurance.
2: 4 women to l their husbands
3: 4 and l of God our Savior appeared,
3: 15 Greet those who l us in the faith.
Phm : 5 and your l for all the saints.
: 7 Your l has given me great joy
: 9 yet I appeal to you on the basis of l.
Heb 6: 10 and the l you have shown him
10: 24 may spur one another on toward l
13: 5 free from the l of money
Jas 1: 12 promised to those who l him.
2: 5 he promised those who l him?
2: 8 "L your neighbor as yourself,"
1Pe 1: 8 you have not seen him, you l him;
1: 22 the truth so that you have sincere l
1: 22 l one another deeply,
2: 17 L the brotherhood of believers,
3: 8 be sympathetic, l as brothers,
3: 10 "Whoever would l life
4: 8 Above all, l each other deeply,
4: 8 l covers over a multitude of sins.
5: 14 Greet one another with a kiss of l.
2Pe 1: 7 and to brotherly kindness, l.
1: 17 "This is my Son, whom I l;
1Jn 2: 5 God's l is truly made complete
2: 15 Do not l the world or anything
2: 15 the l of the Father is not in him.
3: 1 How great is the l the Father has
3: 10 anyone who does not l his brother.
3: 11 We should l one another.
3: 14 Anyone who does not l remains
3: 14 because we l our brothers.
3: 16 This is how we know what l is:
3: 17 how can the l of God be in him?
3: 18 let us not l with words or tongue
3: 23 to l one another as he commanded
4: 7 Dear friends, let us l one another,
4: 7 for l comes from God.
4: 8 Whoever does not l does not know
4: 8 not know God, because God is l.
4: 9 This is how God showed his l
4: 10 This is l: not that we loved God,
4: 11 we also ought to l one another.
4: 12 seen God; but if we l one another,
4: 12 and his l is made complete in us.
4: 16 God is l.
4: 16 Whoever lives in l lives in God,
4: 16 and rely on the l God has for us.
4: 17 l is made complete among us
4: 18 But perfect l drives out fear,
4: 18 There is no fear in l.
4: 18 who fears is not made perfect in l.
4: 19 We l because he first loved us.
4: 20 If anyone says, "I l God,"
4: 20 anyone who does not l his brother,
4: 20 whom he has seen, cannot l God,
4: 21 loves God must also l his brother.
5: 2 we know that we l the children
5: 3 This is l for God: to obey his
2Jn : 1 whom I l in the truth—
: 3 will be with us in truth and l.
: 5 I ask that we l one another.
: 6 his command is that you walk in l.
: 6 this is l: that we walk in obedience
3Jn : 1 To my dear friend Gaius, whom I l
: 6 have told the church about your l.
Jude : 2 peace and l be yours in abundance.
: 12 men are blemishes at your l feasts,
: 21 Keep yourselves in God's l
Rev 2: 4 You have forsaken your first l.
2: 19 I know your deeds, your l and faith
3: 19 Those whom I l I rebuke
12: 11 they did not l their lives so much

LOVED* (LOVE)

Ge 24: 67 she became his wife, and he l her;
25: 28 l Esau, but Rebekah l Jacob.
29: 30 and he l Rachel more than Leah.
29: 31 the LORD saw that Leah was not l,
29: 33 the LORD heard that I am not l,
34: 3 and he l the girl and spoke tenderly
37: 3 Now Israel l Joseph more than any
37: 4 saw that their father l him more
Dt 4: 37 Because he l your forefathers
7: 8 But it was because the LORD l you
10: 15 on your forefathers and l them,

1Sa 1: 5 a double portion because he l her,
18: 1 in spirit with David, and he l him
18: 3 with David because he l him
18: 16 But all Israel and Judah l David,
18: 28 that his daughter Michal l David,
20: 17 because he l him as he l himself.
2Sa 1: 23 in life they were l and gracious,
12: 24 The LORD l him; and
12: 25 and because the LORD l him,
13: 15 hated her more than he had l her.
1Ki 11: 1 l many foreign women
2Ch 11: 21 Rehoboam l Maacah daughter
26: 10 in the fertile lands, for he l the soil.
Ne 13: 26 He was l by his God, and God
Ps 44: 3 light of your face, for you l them.
47: 4 the pride of Jacob, whom he l.
78: 68 Mount Zion, which he l.
88: 18 taken my companions and l ones
109: 17 He l to pronounce a curse—
Isa 5: 1 My l one had a vineyard
Jer 2: 2 how as a bride you l me
8: 2 which they have l and served
31: 3 "I have l you with an everlasting
Eze 16: 37 those you l as well as those you
Hos 2: 1 and of your sisters, 'My l one.'
2: 23 to the one I called 'Not my l one.'
3: 1 though she is l by another
9: 10 became as vile as the thing they l.
11: 1 "When Israel was a child, I l him,
Mal 1: 2 "But you ask, 'How have you l us?'
1: 2 "I have l you," says the LORD.
1: 2 "Yet I have l Jacob, but Esau I
Mk 10: 21 Jesus looked at him and l him.
12: 6 left to send, a son, whom he l.
Lk 7: 47 been forgiven—for she l much.
16: 14 The Pharisees, who l money,
Jn 3: 16 so l the world that he gave his one
3: 19 but men l darkness instead of light
11: 5 Jesus l Martha and her sister
11: 36 "See how he l him!" But some
12: 43 for they l praise from men more
13: 1 Having l his own who were
13: 23 the disciple whom Jesus l,
13: 34 As I have l you, so you must love
14: 21 He who loves me will be l
14: 28 If you l me, you would be glad that
15: 9 the Father has l me, so have I l you.
15: 12 Love each other as I have l you.
16: 27 loves you because you have l me
17: 23 have l them even as you have l me.
17: 24 you l me before the creation
19: 26 the disciple whom he l standing
20: 2 one Jesus l, and said, "They have
21: 7 the disciple whom Jesus l said
21: 20 whom Jesus l was following
Ro 1: 7 To all in Rome who are l by God
8: 37 conquerors through him who l us.
9: 13 "Jacob I l, but Esau I hated."
9: 25 her 'my l one' who is not my l one,"
11: 28 they are l on account
Gal 2: 20 who l me and gave himself for me.
Eph 5: 1 as dearly l children and live a life
5: 2 as Christ l us and gave himself up
5: 25 just as Christ l the church
Col 3: 12 and dearly l, clothe yourselves
1Th 1: 4 For we know, brothers l by God,
2: 8 We l you so much that we were
2Th 2: 13 for you, brothers l by the Lord,
2: 16 who l us and by his grace gave us
2Ti 4: 10 for Demas, because he l this world,
Heb 1: 9 You have l righteousness
2Pe 2: 15 who l the wages of wickedness.
1Jn 4: 10 This is love: not that we l God,
4: 10 but that he l us and sent his Son
4: 11 Dear friends, since God so l us,
4: 19 We love because he first l us.
Jude : 1 who are l by God the Father
Rev 3: 9 and acknowledge that I have l you.

LOVELY* (LOVE)

Ge 29: 17 but Rachel was l in form,
Est 1: 11 and nobles, for she was l to look at.
2: 7 was l in form and features,
Ps 84: 1 How l is your dwelling place,
SS 1: 5 Dark am I, yet l,
2: 14 and your face is l.
4: 3 your mouth is l.
5: 16 he is altogether l.
6: 4 l as Jerusalem,
Am 8: 13 l young women and strong young
Php 4: 8 whatever is l, whatever is

LOVER* (LOVE)

SS 1: 13 My l is to me a sachet of myrrh
1: 14 My l is to me a cluster
1: 16 How handsome you are, my l!
2: 3 is my l among the young men.
2: 8 Listen! My l!
2: 9 My l is like a gazelle or a young
2: 10 My l spoke and said to me,
2: 16 *Beloved* My l is mine and I am his;
2: 17 turn, my l,
4: 16 Let my l come into his garden
5: 2 Listen! My l is knocking:
5: 4 My l thrust his hand
5: 5 I arose to open for my l,
5: 6 I opened for my l,
5: 6 but my l had left; he was gone.
5: 8 if you find my l,
5: 10 *Beloved* My l is radiant and ruddy,
5: 16 This is my l, this my friend,
6: 1 Where has your l gone,
6: 1 Which way did your l turn,
6: 2 *Beloved* My l has gone
6: 3 I am my lover's and my l is mine;
7: 9 May the wine go straight to my l,
7: 10 I belong to my l,
7: 11 my l, let us go to the countryside,
7: 13 that I have stored up for you, my l.
8: 5 leaning on her l?
8: 14 *Beloved* Come away, my l,
1Ti 3: 3 not quarrelsome, not a l of money.

LOVER'S* (LOVE)

SS 6: 3 I am my l and my lover is mine;

LOVERS* (LOVE)

SS 5: 1 drink your fill, O l.
Jer 3: 1 as a prostitute with many l—
3: 2 the roadside you sat waiting for l,
4: 30 Your l despise you;
La 1: 2 Among all her l
Eze 16: 33 but you give gifts to all your l,
16: 36 in your promiscuity with your l,
16: 37 I am going to gather all your l,
16: 39 Then I will hand you over to your l,
16: 41 and you will no longer pay your l.
23: 5 she lusted after her l, the Assyrians
23: 9 I handed her over to her l,
23: 20 There she lusted after her l,
23: 22 I will stir up your l against you,
Hos 2: 5 She said, 'I will go after my l,
2: 7 She will chase after her l
2: 10 lewdness before the eyes of her l;
2: 12 she said were her pay from her l;
2: 13 and went after her l,
8: 9 Ephraim has sold herself to l.
2Ti 3: 2 People will be l of themselves,
3: 2 l of money, boastful, proud,
3: 3 without self-control, brutal, not l
3: 4 l of pleasure rather than l of God—

LOVES* (LOVE)

Ge 44: 20 sons left, and his father l him.'
Dt 10: 18 and l the alien, giving him food
15: 16 because he l you and your family
21: 15 and he l one but not the other,
21: 16 son of the wife he l in preference
23: 5 because the LORD your God l you
28: 54 wife he l or his surviving children,
28: 56 will begrudge the husband she l
33: 12 and the one the LORD l rests
Ru 4: 15 who l you and who is better to you
2Ch 2: 11 "Because the LORD l his people,
Ps 11: 7 he l justice;
33: 5 The LORD l righteousness
34: 12 Whoever of you l life
37: 28 For the LORD l the just
87: 2 the LORD l the gates of Zion
91: 14 Because he l me," says the LORD,
99: 4 The King is mighty, he l justice—
119: 140 and your servant l them.
127: 2 for he grants sleep to those he l.
146: 8 the LORD l the righteous.
Pr 3: 12 the LORD disciplines those he l,
12: 1 Whoever l discipline l knowledge,
13: 24 he who l him is careful
15: 9 he l those who pursue
17: 17 A friend l at all times,
17: 19 He who l a quarrel l sin;
19: 8 He who gets wisdom l his own soul
21: 17 He who l pleasure will become
21: 17 whoever l wine and oil will never
22: 11 He who l a pure heart and whose
29: 3 A man who l wisdom brings joy
Ecc 5: 10 Whoever l money never has
5: 10 whoever l wealth is never satisfied
SS 3: 1 I looked for the one my heart l;
3: 2 I will search for the one my heart l.
3: 3 "Have you seen the one my heart l
3: 4 when I found the one my heart l.
Hos 3: 1 as the LORD l the Israelites,
10: 11 that l to thresh;
12: 7 he l to defraud.
Mal 2: 11 the sanctuary the LORD l,
Mt 10: 37 anyone who l his son or daughter
10: 37 "Anyone who l his father
Lk 7: 5 because he l our nation
7: 47 has been forgiven little l little."
Jn 3: 35 Father l the Son and has placed
5: 20 For the Father l the Son
10: 17 reason my Father l me is that I lay
12: 25 The man who l his life will lose it,
14: 21 He who l me will be loved
14: 21 obeys them, he is the one who l me.
14: 23 Jesus replied, "If anyone l me,
16: 27 the Father himself l you
Ro 13: 8 for he who l his fellowman has
1Co 8: 3 But the man who l God is known
2Co 9: 7 for God l a cheerful giver.
Eph 1: 6 has freely given us in the One he l.
5: 28 He who l his wife l himself.
5: 33 must love his wife as he l himself,
Col 1: 13 us into the kingdom of the Son he l,
Tit 1: 8 one who l what is good, who is
Heb 12: 6 the Lord disciplines those he l,
1Jn 2: 10 Whoever l his brother lives
2: 15 If anyone l the world, the love
4: 7 Everyone who l has been born
4: 21 Whoever l God must also love his
5: 1 who l the father l his child
3Jn : 9 but Diotrephes, who l to be first,
Rev 1: 5 To him who l us and has freed us
20: 9 camp of God's people, the city he l.
22: 15 and everyone who l and practices

LOVING* (LOVE)

Ps 25: 10 All the ways of the LORD are l
59: 10 my l God.
59: 17 O God, are my fortress, my l God.
62: 12 and that you, O Lord, are l.
144: 2 He is my l God and my fortress,
145: 13 and l toward all he has made.
145: 17 and l toward all he has made.
Pr 5: 19 A l doe, a graceful deer—
Heb 13: 1 Keep on l each other as brothers.
1Jn 5: 2 by l God and carrying out his

LOVING-KINDNESS* (LOVE)

Jer 31: 3 I have drawn you with l.

LOWER

Ps 8: 5 You made him a little l
2Co 11: 7 a sin for me to l myself in order
Heb 2: 7 You made him a little l

LOWING

1Sa 15: 14 What is this l of cattle that I hear?"

LOWLY

Job 5: 11 The l he sets on high,
Ps 138: 6 on high, he looks upon the l,
Pr 29: 23 but a man of l spirit gains honor.
Isa 57: 15 also with him who is contrite and l
Eze 21: 26 l will be exalted and the exalted
1Co 1: 28 He chose the l things of this world

LOYAL

1Ch 29: 18 and keep their hearts l to you.
Ps 78: 8 whose hearts were not l to God,

LUKE*

Co-worker with Paul (Col 4:14; 2Ti 4:11; Phm 24).

LUKEWARM*

Rev 3: 16 So, because you are l—neither hot

LUST (LUSTED LUSTS)

Pr 6: 25 Do not l in your heart
Eze 20: 30 and l after their vile images?
Col 3: 5 sexual immorality, impurity, l,
1Th 4: 5 not in passionate l like the heathen,
1Pe 4: 3 in debauchery, l, drunkenness,
1Jn 2: 16 the l of his eyes and the boasting

LUSTED (LUST)

Eze 23: 5 she l after her lovers, the Assyrians

LUSTS* (LUST)

Nu 15: 39 yourselves by going after the l
Ro 1: 26 God gave them over to shameful l.

LUXURY

Jas 5: 5 You have lived on earth in l

LYDIA'S*

Ac 16:40 went to *L* house, where they met

LYING (LIE)

Pr 6:17 a *l* tongue,
12:22 The LORD detests *l* lips,
21:6 A fortune made by a *l* tongue
26:28 A *l* tongue hates those it hurts,

MACEDONIA

Ac 16:9 "Come over to *M* and help us."

MAD

Dt 28:34 The sights you see will drive you *m*

MADE (MAKE)

Ge 1:7 So God *m* the expanse
1:16 God *m* two great lights—
1:16 He also *m* the stars.
1:25 God *m* the wild animals according
1:31 God saw all that he had *m*,
2:22 Then the LORD God *m* a woman
6:6 was grieved that he had *m* man
9:6 has God *m* man.
15:18 that day the LORD *m* a covenant
Ex 20:11 six days the LORD *m* the heavens
20:11 the Sabbath day and *m* it holy.
24:8 the covenant that the LORD has *m*
32:4 *m* it into an idol cast in the shape
Lev 16:34 Atonement is to be *m* once a year
Dt 32:6 who *m* you and formed you?
Jos 24:25 On that day Joshua *m* a covenant
2Ki 19:15 You have *m* heaven and earth.
2Ch 2:12 the God of Israel, who *m* heaven
Ne 9:6 You *m* the heavens,
9:10 You *m* a name for yourself,
Ps 33:6 of the LORD were the heavens *m*,
95:5 The sea is his, for he *m* it,
96:5 but the LORD *m* the heavens.
100:3 It is he who *m* us, and we are his;
118:24 This is the day the LORD has *m*;
136:7 who *m* the great lights—
139:14 I am fearfully and wonderfully *m*;
Ecc 3:11 He has *m* everything beautiful
Isa 43:7 whom I formed and *m*."
45:12 It is I who *m* the earth
45:18 he who fashioned and *m* the earth,
66:2 Has not my hand *m* all these things
Jer 10:12 But God *m* the earth by his power;
27:5 and outstretched arm I *m* the earth
32:17 you have *m* the heavens
33:2 LORD says, he who *m* the earth,
51:15 "He *m* the earth by his power;
Eze 3:17 I have *m* you a watchman
33:7 I have *m* you a watchman
Am 5:8 (he who *m* the Pleiades and Orion,
Jnh 1:9 who *m* the sea and the land."
Mk 2:27 "The Sabbath was *m* for man,
Jn 1:3 Through him all things were *m*;
Ac 17:24 "The God who *m* the world
1Co 3:6 watered it, but God *m* it grow.
Heb 1:2 through whom he *m* the universe.
Jas 3:9 who have been *m* in God's likeness
Rev 14:7 Worship him who *m* the heavens,

MAGDALENE

Lk 8:2 Mary (called *M*) from whom seven

MAGI

Mt 2:1 *M* from the east came to Jerusalem

MAGIC (MAGICIANS)

Eze 13:20 I am against your *m* charms
Rev 21:8 those who practice *m* arts,
22:15 those who practice *m* arts,

MAGICIANS (MAGIC)

Ex 7:11 the Egyptian *m* also did the same
Da 2:2 So the king summoned the *m*,

MAGNIFICENCE* (MAGNIFICENT)

1Ch 22:5 for the LORD should be of great *m*

MAGNIFICENT (MAGNIFICENCE)

1Ki 8:13 I have indeed built a *m* temple
Isa 28:29 in counsel and *m* in wisdom.
Mk 13:1 stones! What *m* buildings!"

MAGOG

Eze 38:2 of the land of *M*, the chief prince
39:6 I will send fire on *M*
Rev 20:8 and *M*—to gather them for battle.

MAIDEN (MAIDENS)

Pr 30:19 and the way of a man with a *m*.
Isa 62:5 As a young man marries a *m*,
Jer 2:32 Does a *m* forget her jewelry,

MAIDENS (MAIDEN)

SS 1:3 No wonder the *m* love you!

MAIMED

Mt 18:8 It is better for you to enter life *m*

MAINTAIN (MAINTAINING)

Ps 82:3 *m* the rights of the poor
106:3 Blessed are they who *m* justice,
Hos 12:6 *m* love and justice,
Am 5:15 *m* justice in the courts.
Ro 3:28 For we *m* that a man is justified

MAINTAINING* (MAINTAIN)

Ex 34:7 faithfulness, *m* love to thousands,

MAJESTIC* (MAJESTY)

Ex 15:6 was *m* in power.
15:11 *m* in holiness,
Job 37:4 he thunders with his *m* voice.
Ps 8:1 how *m* is your name in all the earth
8:9 how *m* is your name in all the earth
29:4 the voice of the LORD is *m*.
68:15 of Bashan are *m* mountains;
76:4 more *m* than mountains rich
111:3 Glorious and *m* are his deeds,
SS 6:4 *m* as troops with banners.
6:10 *m* as the stars in procession?
Isa 30:30 men to hear his *m* voice
Eze 31:7 It was *m* in beauty,
2Pe 1:17 came to him from the *M* Glory,

MAJESTY* (MAJESTIC)

Ex 15:7 In the greatness of your *m*
Dt 5:24 has shown us his glory and his *m*,
11:2 his *m*, his mighty hand, his
33:17 In *m* he is like a firstborn bull;
33:26 and on the clouds in his *m*.
1Ch 16:27 Splendor and *m* are before him;
29:11 and the *m* and the splendor,
Est 1:4 the splendor and glory of his *m*.
7:3 if it pleases your *m*, grant me my
Job 37:22 God comes in awesome *m*.
40:10 and clothe yourself in honor and *m*
Ps 21:5 on him splendor and *m*.
45:3 with splendor and *m*.
45:4 In your *m* ride forth victoriously
68:34 whose *m* is over Israel,
93:1 The LORD reigns, he is robed in *m*
93:1 the LORD is robed in *m*
96:6 Splendor and *m* are before him;
104:1 clothed with splendor and *m*.
110:3 Arrayed in holy *m*,
145:5 of the glorious splendor of your *m*,
Isa 2:10 and the splendor of his *m*!
2:19 and the splendor of his *m*,
2:21 and the splendor of his *m*,
24:14 west they acclaim the LORD's *m*.
26:10 and regard not the *m* of the LORD.
53:2 or *m* to attract us to him,
Eze 31:2 can be compared with you in *m*?
31:18 with you in splendor and *m*?
Da 4:30 and for the glory of my *m*?"
Mic 5:4 in the *m* of the name
Zec 6:13 and he will be clothed with *m*
Ac 19:27 will be robbed of her divine *m*."
25:26 to write to His *M* about him.
2Th 1:9 and from the *m* of his power
Heb 1:3 hand of the *M* in heaven.
8:1 of the throne of the *M* in heaven,
2Pe 1:16 but we were eyewitnesses of his *m*.
Jude :25 only God our Savior be glory, *m*,

MAKE (MADE MAKER MAKERS MAKES MAKING MAN-MADE)

Ge 1:26 "Let us *m* man in our image,
2:18 I will *m* a helper suitable for him."
6:14 *m* yourself an ark of cypress wood;
12:2 "I will *m* you into a great nation
Ex 22:3 thief must certainly *m* restitution,
25:9 *M* this tabernacle and all its
25:40 See that you *m* them according
Nu 6:25 the LORD *m* his face shine
2Sa 7:9 Now I will *m* your name great,
Job 7:17 "What is man that you *m* so much
Ps 4:8 *m* me dwell in safety.
20:4 and *m* all your plans succeed.
108:1 *m* music with all my soul.
110:1 hand until I *m* your enemies
Ps 119:165 and nothing can *m* them stumble.
Pr 3:6 and he will *m* your paths straight.
4:26 *M* level paths for your feet
20:18 *M* plans by seeking advice;
Isa 14:14 I will *m* myself like the Most High
29:16 "He did not *m* me"?
55:3 I will *m* an everlasting covenant
61:8 and *m* an everlasting covenant
Jer 31:31 "when I will *m* a new covenant
Eze 37:26 I will *m* a covenant of peace
Mt 3:3 *m* straight paths for him.'"
28:19 and *m* disciples of all nations,
Mk 1:17 "and I will *m* you fishers of men."
Lk 13:24 "*M* every effort to enter
14:23 country lanes and *m* them come in,
Ro 14:19 *m* every effort to do what leads
2Co 5:9 So we *m* it our goal to please him,
Eph 4:3 *M* every effort to keep the unity
Col 4:5 *m* the most of every opportunity.
1Th 4:11 *M* it your ambition
Heb 4:11 *m* every effort to enter that rest,
8:5 it that you *m* everything according
12:14 *M* every effort to live in peace
2Pe 1:5 *m* every effort to add
3:14 *m* every effort to be found spotless,

MAKER* (MAKE)

Job 4:17 Can a man be more pure than his *M*
9:9 He is the *M* of the Bear and Orion,
32:22 my *M* would soon take me away.
35:10 no one says, 'Where is God my *M*,
36:3 I will ascribe justice to my *M*.
40:19 yet his *M* can approach him
Ps 95:6 kneel before the LORD our *M*;
115:15 the *M* of heaven and earth.
121:2 the *M* of heaven and earth.
124:8 the *M* of heaven and earth.
134:3 the *M* of heaven and earth,
146:6 the *M* of heaven and earth,
149:2 Let Israel rejoice in their *M*;
Pr 14:31 poor shows contempt for their *M*,
17:5 poor shows contempt for their *M*;
22:2 The LORD is the *M* of them all.
Ecc 11:5 the *M* of all things.
Isa 17:7 that day men will look to their *M*
27:11 so their *M* has no compassion
45:9 to him who quarrels with his *M*,
45:11 the Holy One of Israel, and its *M*:
51:13 that you forget the LORD your *M*,
54:5 For your *M* is your husband—
Jer 10:16 for he is the *M* of all things,
51:19 for he is the *M* of all things,
Hos 8:14 Israel has forgotten his *M*

MAKERS* (MAKE)

Isa 45:16 All the *m* of idols will be put

MAKES (MAKE)

Ps 23:2 *m* me lie down in green pastures,
Pr 13:12 Hope deferred *m* the heart sick,
1Co 3:7 but only God, who *m* things grow.

MAKING (MAKE)

Ps 19:7 *m* wise the simple.
Ecc 12:12 Of *m* many books there is no end,
Jn 5:18 *m* himself equal with God.
Eph 5:16 *m* the most of every opportunity,

MALACHI*

Mal 1:1 of the LORD to Israel through *M*.

MALE

Ge 1:27 *m* and female he created them.
Ex 13:2 to me every firstborn *m*.
Nu 8:16 the first *m* offspring
Mt 19:4 the Creator 'made them *m*
Gal 3:28 slave nor free, *m* nor female,

MALICE (MALICIOUS)

Mk 7:22 adultery, greed, *m*, deceit,
Ro 1:29 murder, strife, deceit and *m*.
1Co 5:8 the yeast of *m* and wickedness,
Eph 4:31 along with every form of *m*.
Col 3:8 *m*, slander, and filthy language
1Pe 2:1 rid yourselves of all *m*

MALICIOUS (MALICE)

Pr 26:24 A *m* man disguises himself
1Ti 3:11 not *m* talkers but temperate
6:4 *m* talk, evil suspicions

MALIGN

Tit 2:5 so that no one will *m* the word

MAMMON see MONEY, WEALTH

MAN (MAN'S MANKIND MEN MEN'S WOMAN WOMEN)

Ge 1:26 "Let us make m in our image,
2: 7 God formed the m from the dust
2: 8 m became a living being
2:15 God took the m and put
2:18 for the m to be alone
2:20 m gave names to all the
2:23 she was taken out of m.
2:25 m and his wife were both
3: 9 God called to the m,
3:22 m has now become like
4: 1 I have brought forth a m.
6: 3 not contend with m forever,
6: 6 grieved that he had made m
9: 6 Whoever sheds the blood of m,
Dt 8: 3 m does not live on bread
1Sa 13:14 a m after his own heart
15:29 he is not a m that he
16: 7 at the things m looks at.
Job 14: 1 M born of woman is of few
14:14 If a m dies, will he live
Ps 1: 1 Blessed is the m who does
8: 4 what is m that you are
32: 2 Blessed is the m whose sin
40: 4 Blessed is the m who makes
84:12 blessed is the m who trusts
103: 15 As for m, his days are
112: 1 Blessed is the m who fears
119: 9 can a young m keep his
127: 5 Blessed is the m whose quiver
144: 3 what is m that you care
Pr 3:13 Blessed is the m who finds
9: 9 Instruct a wise m
14:12 that seems right to a m,
30:19 way of a m with a maiden.
Isa 53: 3 a m of sorrows,
Jer 17: 5 the one who trusts in m,
17: 7 blessed is the m who trusts
Eze 22:30 I looked for a m
Mt 4: 4 M does not live on bread
19: 5 a m will leave his father
Mk 8:36 What good is it for a m
Lk 4: 4 'M does not live on bread
Ro 5:12 entered the world through one m
1Co 2:15 spiritual m makes judgments
3:12 If any m builds on this
7: 1 good for a m not to marry.
7: 2 each m should have his own
11: 3 head of every m is Christ,
11: 3 head of woman is m
13:11 When I became a m,
15:21 death came through a m,
15:45 first m Adam became a
15:47 the second m from heaven
2Co 12: 2 I know a m in Christ
Eph 2:15 create in himself one new m
5:31 a m will leave his father
Php 2: 8 found in appearance as a m,
1Ti 2: 5 the m Christ Jesus,
2:11 have authority over a m;
2Ti 3:17 that the m of God may be
Heb 2: 6 what is m that you are
9:27 as m is destined to die

MAN'S (MAN)

Pr 20:24 A m steps are directed by
Jer 10:23 a m life is not his own;
1Co 1:25 is wiser than m wisdom,

MAN-MADE (MAKE)

Heb 9:11 perfect tabernacle that is not m,
9:24 not enter a m sanctuary that was

MANAGE (MANAGER)

Jer 12: 5 how will you m in the thickets
1Ti 3: 4 He must m his own family well
3:12 one wife and must m his children
5:14 to m their homes and to give

MANAGER (MANAGE)

Lk 12:42 Who then is the faithful and wise m
16: 1 a rich man whose m was accused

MANASSEH

1. Firstborn of Joseph (Ge 41:51; 46:20). Blessed by Jacob but not firstborn (Ge 48). Tribe of blessed (Dt 33:17), numbered (Nu 1:35; 26:34), half allotted land east of Jordan (Nu 32; Jos 13:8-33), half west (Jos 16; Eze 48:4), failed to fully possess (Jos 16:10; Jdg 1:27), 12,000 from (Rev 7:6).

2. Son of Hezekiah; king of Judah (2Ki 21:1-18; 2Ch 33:1-20). Judah exiled for his detestable sins (2Ki 21:10-15). Repentance (2Ch 33:12-19).

MANDRAKES

Ge 30:14 give me some of your son's m."

MANGER

Lk 2:12 in strips of cloth and lying in a m."

MANIFESTATION*

1Co 12: 7 to each one the m of the Spirit is

MANKIND (MAN)

Ge 6: 7 I will wipe m, whom I have created
Ps 33:13 and sees all m;
Pr 8:31 and delighting in m.
Ecc 7:29 God made m upright,
Isa 40: 5 and all m together will see it.
45:12 and created m upon it.
Jer 32:27 "I am the LORD, the God of all m.
Zec 2:13 Be still before the LORD, all m,
Lk 3: 6 And all m will see God's salvation

MANNA

Ex 16:31 people of Israel called the bread m.
Dt 8:16 He gave you m to eat in the desert,
Jn 6:49 Your forefathers ate the m
Rev 2:17 I will give some of the hidden m.

MANNER

1Co 11:27 in an unworthy m will be guilty
Php 1:27 conduct yourselves in a m worthy

MANSIONS*

Ps 49:14 far from their princely m.
Isa 5: 9 the fine m left without occupants.
Am 3:15 and the m will be demolished,"
5:11 though you have built stone m,

MARCH

Jos 6: 4 m around the city seven times,
Isa 42:13 LORD will m out like a mighty

MARITAL* (MARRY)

Ex 21:10 of her food, clothing and m rights.
Mt 5:32 except for m unfaithfulness,
19: 9 except for m unfaithfulness,
1Co 7: 3 husband should fulfill his m duty

MARK (MARKS)

Cousin of Barnabas (Col 4:10; 2Ti 4:11; Phm 24; 1Pe 5:13), see JOHN.
Ge 4:15 Then the LORD put a m on Cain
Rev 13:16 to receive a m on his right hand

MARKET (MARKETPLACE MARKETPLACES)

Jn 2:16 turn my Father's house into a m!"

MARKETPLACE (MARKET)

Lk 7:32 are like children sitting in the m

MARKETPLACES (MARKET)

Mt 23: 7 they love to be greeted in the m

MARKS (MARK)

Jn 20:25 Unless I see the nail m in his hands
Gal 6:17 bear on my body the m of Jesus.

MARRED

Isa 52:14 his form m beyond human likeness

MARRIAGE (MARRY)

Mt 22:30 neither marry nor be given in m;
24:38 marrying and giving in m,
Ro 7: 2 she is released from the law of m.
Heb 13: 4 by all, and the m bed kept pure,

MARRIED (MARRY)

Dt 24: 5 happiness to the wife he has m.
Ezr 10:10 you have m foreign women,
Pr 30:23 an unloved woman who is m,
Mt 1:18 pledged to be m to Joseph,
Mk 12:23 since the seven were m to her?"
Ro 7: 2 by law a m woman is bound
1Co 7:27 Are you m? Do not seek a divorce.
7:33 But a m man is concerned about
7:36 They should get m.

MARRIES (MARRY)

Mt 5:32 anyone who m the divorced woman
19: 9 and m another woman commits
Lk 16:18 the man who m a divorced woman

MARROW

Heb 4:12 joints and m; it judges the thoughts

MARRY (INTERMARRY MARITAL MARRIAGE MARRIED MARRIES)

Dt 25: 5 brother shall take her and m her
Mt 22:30 resurrection people will neither m
1Co 7: 1 It is good for a man not to m.
7: 9 control themselves, they should m,
7:28 if you do m, you have not sinned;
1Ti 4: 3 They forbid people to m
5:14 So I counsel younger widows to m,

MARTHA*

Sister of Mary and Lazarus (Lk 10:38-42; Jn 11; 12:2).

MARVELED* (MARVELOUS)

Lk 2:33 mother m at what was said about
2Th 1:10 and to be m at among all those who

MARVELING* (MARVELOUS)

Lk 9:43 While everyone was m

MARVELOUS* (MARVELED MARVELING)

1Ch 16:24 his m deeds among all peoples.
Job 37: 5 God's voice thunders in m ways;
Ps 71:17 to this day I declare your m deeds.
72:18 who alone does m deeds.
86:10 For you are great and do m deeds;
96: 3 his m deeds among all peoples.
98: 1 for he has done m things;
118: 23 and it is m in our eyes.
Isa 25: 1 you have done m things,
Zec 8: 6 but will it seem m to me?"
8: 6 "It may seem m to the remnant
Mt 21:42 and it is m in our eyes'?
Mk 12:11 and it is m in our eyes'?"
Rev 15: 1 in heaven another great and m sign
15: 3 "Great and m are your deeds,

MARY

1. Mother of Jesus (Mt 1:16-25; Lk 1:27-56; 2:1-40). With Jesus at temple (Lk 2:41-52), at the wedding in Cana (Jn 2:1-5), questioning his sanity (Mk 3:21), at the cross (Jn 19:25-27). Among disciples after Ascension (Ac 1:14).

2. Magdalene; former demoniac (Lk 8:2). Helped support Jesus' ministry (Lk 8:1-3). At the cross (Mt 27:56; Mk 15:40; Jn 19:25), burial (Mt 27:61; Mk 15:47). Saw angel after resurrection (Mt 28:1-10; Mk 16:1-9; Lk 24:1-12); also Jesus (Jn 20:1-18).

3. Sister of Martha and Lazarus (Jn 11). Washed Jesus' feet (Jn 12:1-8).

MASQUERADES*

2Co 11:14 for Satan himself m as an angel

MASTER (MASTER'S MASTERED MASTERS MASTERY)

Ge 4: 7 to have you, but you must m it."
Hos 2:16 you will no longer call me 'my m.'
Mal 1: 6 If I am a m, where is the respect
Mt 10:24 nor a servant above his m.
23: 8 for you have only one M
24:46 that servant whose m finds him
25:21 "His m replied, 'Well done,
25:23 "His m replied, 'Well done,
Ro 6:14 For sin shall not be your m,
14: 4 To his own m he stands or falls.
Col 4: 1 you know that you also have a M
2Ti 2:21 useful to the M and prepared

MASTER'S (MASTER)

Mt 25:21 Come and share your m happiness

MASTERED* (MASTER)

1Co 6:12 but I will not be m by anything.
2Pe 2:19 a slave to whatever has m him.

MASTERS (MASTER)

Pr 25:13 he refreshes the spirit of his m.
Mt 6:24 "No one can serve two m.
Lk 16:13 "No servant can serve two m.
Eph 6: 5 obey your earthly m with respect
6: 9 And m, treat your slaves
Col 3:22 obey your earthly m in everything;
4: 1 M, provide your slaves
1Ti 6: 1 should consider their m worthy
6: 2 who have believing m are not
Tit 2: 9 subject to their m in everything,
1Pe 2:18 to your m with all respect,

MASTERY* (MASTER)
Ro 6: 9 death no longer has *m* over him.

MAT
Mk 2: 9 'Get up, take your *m* and walk'?
Ac 9:34 Get up and take care of your *m*."

MATCHED*
2Co 8:11 do it may be *m* by your completion

MATTHEW*
Apostle; former tax collector (Mt 9:9-13; 10:3; Mk 3:18; Lk 6:15; Ac 1:13). Also called Levi (Mk 2:14-17; Lk 5:27-32).

MATTHIAS
Ac 1:26 the lot fell to *M*; so he was added

MATURE* (MATURITY)
Lk 8:14 and pleasures, and they do not *m*.
1Co 2: 6 a message of wisdom among the *m*,
Eph 4:13 of the Son of God and become *m*,
Php 3:15 of us who are *m* should take such
Col 4:12 firm in all the will of God, *m*
Heb 5:14 But solid food is for the *m*,
Jas 1: 4 work so that you may be *m*

MATURITY* (MATURE)
Heb 6: 1 about Christ and go on to *m*,

MEAL
Pr 15:17 Better a *m* of vegetables where
1Co 10:27 some unbeliever invites you to a *m*
Heb 12:16 for a single *m* sold his inheritance

MEANING
Ne 8: 8 and giving the *m* so that the people

MEANINGLESS
Ecc 1: 2 *"M! M!"* says the Teacher.
1Ti 1: 6 from these and turned to *m* talk.

MEANS
1Co 9:22 by all possible *m* I might save some

MEASURE (MEASURED MEASURES)
Ps 71:15 though I know not its *m*.
Eze 45: 3 In the sacred district, *m*
Zec 2: 2 He answered me, "To *m* Jerusalem
Lk 6:38 A good *m*, pressed
Eph 3:19 to the *m* of all the fullness of God.
4:13 to the whole *m* of the fullness
Rev 11: 1 "Go and *m* the temple of God

MEASURED (MEASURE)
Isa 40:12 Who has *m* the waters
Jer 31:37 if the heavens above can be *m*

MEASURES (MEASURE)
Dt 25:14 Do not have two differing *m*
Pr 20:10 Differing weights and differing *m*

MEAT
Pr 23:20 or gorge themselves on *m*,
Ro 14: 6 He who eats *m*, eats to the Lord,
14:21 It is better not to eat *m*
1Co 8:13 I will never eat *m* again,
10:25 *m* market without raising questions

MEDDLER* (MEDDLES)
1Pe 4:15 kind of criminal, or even as a *m*.

MEDDLES* (MEDDLER)
Pr 26:17 is a passer-by who *m*

MEDIATOR
1Ti 2: 5 and one *m* between God and men,
Heb 8: 6 of which he is *m* is superior
9:15 For this reason Christ is the *m*
12:24 to Jesus the *m* of a new covenant,

MEDICINE*
Pr 17:22 A cheerful heart is good *m*,

MEDITATE* (MEDITATED MEDITATES MEDITATION)
Ge 24:63 out to the field one evening to *m*,
Jos 1: 8 from your mouth; *m* on it day
Ps 48: 9 we *m* on your unfailing love.
77:12 I will *m* on all your works
119: 15 I *m* on your precepts
119: 23 your servant will *m*
119: 27 then I will *m* on your wonders.
119: 48 and I *m* on your decrees.
Ps 119: 78 but I will *m* on your precepts.
119: 97 I *m* on it all day long.
119: 99 for I *m* on your statutes.
119:148 that I may *m* on your promises.
143: 5 I *m* on all your works
145: 5 I will *m* on your wonderful works.

MEDITATED* (MEDITATE)
Ps 39: 3 and as I *m*, the fire burned;

MEDITATES* (MEDITATE)
Ps 1: 2 and on his law he *m* day and night.

MEDITATION* (MEDITATE)
Ps 19:14 of my mouth and the *m* of my heart
104: 34 May my *m* be pleasing to him,

MEDIUM
Lev 20:27 " 'A man or woman who is a *m*

MEEK* (MEEKNESS)
Ps 37:11 But the *m* will inherit the land
Zep 3:12 the *m* and humble,
Mt 5: 5 Blessed are the *m*,

MEEKNESS* (MEEK)
2Co 10: 1 By the *m* and gentleness of Christ,

MEET (MEETING MEETINGS MEETS)
Ps 42: 2 When can I go and *m* with God?
85:10 Love and faithfulness *m* together;
Am 4:12 prepare to *m* your God, O Israel."
1Co 11:34 when you *m* together it may not
1Th 4:17 them in the clouds to *m* the Lord

MEETING (MEET)
Ex 40:34 the cloud covered the Tent of *M*,
Heb 10:25 Let us not give up *m* together,

MEETINGS* (MEET)
1Co 11:17 for your *m* do more harm

MEETS (MEET)
Heb 7:26 Such a high priest *m* our need—

MELCHIZEDEK
Ge 14:18 *M* king of Salem brought out bread
Ps 110: 4 in the order of *M*."
Heb 7:11 in the order of *M*, not in the order

MELT (MELTS)
2Pe 3:12 and the elements will *m* in the heat.

MELTS (MELT)
Am 9: 5 he who touches the earth and it *m*,

MEMBER (MEMBERS)
Ro 12: 5 each *m* belongs to all the others.

MEMBERS (MEMBER)
Mic 7: 6 a man's enemies are the *m*
Mt 10:36 a man's enemies will be the *m*
Ro 7:23 law at work in the *m* of my body,
12: 4 of us has one body with many *m*,
1Co 6:15 not know that your bodies are *m*
12:24 But God has combined the *m*
Eph 3: 6 *m* together of one body,
4:25 for we are all *m* of one body.
5:30 for we are *m* of his body.
Col 3:15 as *m* of one body you were called

MEMORABLE* (MEMORY)
Eze 39:13 day I am glorified will be a *m* day

MEMORIES* (MEMORY)
1Th 3: 6 us that you always have pleasant *m*

MEMORY (MEMORABLE MEMORIES)
Pr 10: 7 *m* of the righteous will be
Mt 26:13 she has done will also be told, in *m*

MEN (MAN)
Ge 6: 2 daughter of *m* were beautiful,
6: 4 heroes of old, *m* of renown
Ps 9:20 nations know they are but *m*.
11: 4 He observes the sons of *m*;
Mt 4:19 will make you fishers of *m*
5:16 your light shine before *m*
6:14 if you forgive *m* when
10:32 acknowledges me before *m*
12:31 blasphemy will be forgiven *m*,
12:36 *m* will have to give account
23: 5 is done for *m* to see:
Mk 7: 7 are but rules taught by *m*.
Lk 6:22 Blessed are you when *m*
Lk 6:26 Woe to you when all *m*
Jn 1: 4 life was the light of *m*.
2:24 for he knew all *m*.
3:19 *m* loved darkness instead
12:32 will draw all *m* to myself
13:35 all *m* will know that you
Ac 5:29 obey God rather than *m*!
Ro 1:18 wickedness of *m*
1:27 indecent acts with other *m*,
5:12 death came to all *m*,
1Co 2:11 among *m* knows the thoughts
3: 3 acting like mere *m*?
3:21 no more boasting about *m*!
9:22 all things to all *m*
13: 1 tongues of *m* and of angels
16:13 be *m* of courage;
16:18 Such *m* deserve recognition.
2Co 5:11 we try to persuade *m*.
8:21 but also in the eyes of *m*.
Gal 1: 1 sent not from *m* nor
1:10 to win approval of *m*, or
Eph 4: 8 and gave gifts to *m*.
1Th 2: 4 as *m* approved by God
2:13 not as the word of *m*,
1Ti 2: 4 wants all *m* to be saved
2: 6 as a ransom for all *m*—
4:10 the Savior of all *m*
5: 2 younger *m* as brothers
2Ti 2: 2 entrust to reliable *m*
Tit 2:11 has appeared to all *m*.
Heb 5: 1 is selected from among *m*
7:28 high priests *m* who are weak;
2Pe 1:21 but *m* spoke from God
Rev 21: 3 dwelling of God is with *m*,

MEN'S (MAN)
2Ki 19:18 fashioned by *m* hands.
2Ch 32:19 the work of *m* hands.
1Co 2: 5 not rest on *m* wisdom,

MENAHEM*
King of Israel (2Ki 15:17-22).

MENE
Da 5:25 that was written: *M, M,*

MEPHIBOSHETH
Son of Jonathan shown kindness by David (2Sa 4:4; 9; 21:7). Accused of siding with Absalom (2Sa 16:1-4; 19:24-30).

MERCHANT
Pr 31:14 She is like the *m* ships,
Mt 13:45 of heaven is like a *m* looking

MERCIFUL (MERCY)
Dt 4:31 the LORD your God is a *m* God;
Ne 9:31 for you are a gracious and *m* God.
Ps 77: 9 Has God forgotten to be *m*?
78:38 Yet he was *m*;
Jer 3:12 for I am *m*,' declares the LORD,
Da 9: 9 The Lord our God is *m*
Mt 5: 7 Blessed are the *m*,
Lk 1:54 remembering to be *m*
6:36 Be *m*, just as your Father is *m*.
Heb 2:17 in order that he might become a *m*
Jas 2:13 to anyone who has not been *m*.
Jude :22 Be *m* to those who doubt; snatch

MERCY (MERCIFUL)
Ex 33:19 *m* on whom I will have *m*,
2Sa 24:14 of the LORD, for his *m* is great;
1Ch 21:13 for his *m* is very great;
Ne 9:31 But in your great *m* you did not put
Ps 25: 6 O LORD, your great *m* and love,
28: 6 for he has heard my cry for *m*.
57: 1 Have *m* on me, O God, have *m*
Pr 28:13 renounces them finds *m*.
Isa 63: 9 and *m* he redeemed them;
Da 9:18 but because of your great *m*.
Hos 6: 6 For I desire *m*, not sacrifice,
Am 5:15 LORD God Almighty will have *m*
Mic 6: 8 To act justly and to love *m*
7:18 but delight to show *m*.
Hab 3: 2 in wrath remember *m*.
Zec 7: 9 show *m* and compassion
Mt 5: 7 for they will be shown *m*.
9:13 learn what this means: 'I desire *m*,
12: 7 'I desire *m*, not sacrifice,' you
18:33 Shouldn't you have had *m*
23:23 justice, *m* and faithfulness.
Lk 1:50 His *m* extends to those who fear
Ro 9:15 "I will have *m* on whom I have *m*,
9:18 Therefore God has *m*
11:32 so that he may have *m* on them all.

Ro 12: 1 brothers, in view of God's *m,*
12: 8 if it is showing *m,* let him do it
Eph 2: 4 who is rich in *m,* made us alive
1Ti 1: 13 I was shown *m* because I acted
1: 16 for that very reason I was shown *m*
Tit 3: 5 we had done, but because of his *m.*
Heb 4: 16 so that we may receive *m*
Jas 2: 13 judgment without *m* will be shown
2: 13 *M* triumphs over judgment!
3: 17 submissive, full of *m* and good fruit
5: 11 full of compassion and *m.*
1Pe 1: 3 In his great *m* he has given us new
2: 10 once you had not received *m,*
Jude :23 to others show *m,* mixed with fear

MERRY

Lk 12: 19 Take life easy; eat, drink and be *m*

MESHACH

Hebrew exiled to Babylon; name changed from Mishael (Da 1:6-7). Refused defilement by food (Da 1:8-20). Refused to worship idol (Da 3: 1-18); saved from furnace (Da 3:19-30).

MESSAGE (MESSENGER)

Isa 53: 1 Who has believed our *m*
Jn 12: 38 "Lord, who has believed our *m*
Ac 5: 20 "and tell the people the full *m*
10: 36 You know the *m* God sent
17: 11 for they received the *m*
Ro 10: 16 who has believed our *m?"*
10: 17 faith comes from hearing the *m,*
1Co 1: 18 For the *m* of the cross is
2: 4 My *m* and my preaching were not
2Co 5: 19 to us the *m* of reconciliation.
2Th 3: 1 pray for us that the *m*
Tit 1: 9 firmly to the trustworthy *m*
Heb 4: 2 the *m* they heard was of no value
1Pe 2: 8 because they disobey the *m—*

MESSENGER (MESSAGE)

Pr 25: 13 is a trustworthy *m*
Mal 3: 1 I will send my *m,* who will prepare
Mt 11: 10 " 'I will send my *m* ahead of you,
2Co 12: 7 a *m* of Satan, to torment me.

MESSIAH*

Jn 1: 41 "We have found the *M"* (that is,
4: 25 "I know that *M"* (called Christ) "is

METHUSELAH

Ge 5: 27 Altogether, *M* lived 969 years,

MICAH

1. Idolater from Ephraim (Jdg 17-18).
2. Prophet from Moresheth (Jer 26:18-19; Mic 1:1).

MICAIAH

Prophet of the LORD who spoke against Ahab (1Ki 22:1-28; 2Ch 18:1-27).

MICHAEL

Archangel (Jude 9); warrior in angelic realm, protector of Israel (Da 10:13, 21; 12:1; Rev 12:7).

MICHAL

Daughter of Saul, wife of David (1Sa 14:49; 18:20-28). Warned David of Saul's plot (1Sa 19). Saul gave her to Paltiel (1Sa 25:44); David retrieved her (2Sa 3:13-16). Criticized David for dancing before the ark (2Sa 6:16-23); 1Ch 15: 29).

MIDIAN

Ex 2: 15 Pharaoh and went to live in *M,*
Jdg 7: 2 me to deliver *M* into their hands.

MIDWIVES

Ex 1: 17 The *m,* however, feared God

MIGHT (ALMIGHTY MIGHTIER MIGHTY)

Jdg 16: 30 Then he pushed with all his *m,*
2Sa 6: 5 with all their *m* before the LORD,
6: 14 before the LORD with all his *m,*
2Ch 20: 6 Power and *m* are in your hand,
Ps 21: 13 we will sing and praise your *m.*
54: 1 vindicate me by your *m.*
Isa 63: 15 Where are your zeal and your *m?*
Mic 3: 8 and with justice and *m,*
Zec 4: 6 'Not by *m* nor by power,
Col 1: 11 power according to his glorious *m*
1Ti 6: 16 To him be honor and *m* forever.

MIGHTIER (MIGHT)

Ps 93: 4 *M* than the thunder

MIGHTY (MIGHT)

Ge 49: 24 of the hand of the *M* One of Jacob,
Ex 6: 1 of my *m* hand he will drive them
13: 3 out of it with a *m* hand.
Dt 5: 15 out of there with a *m* hand
7: 8 he brought you out with a *m* hand
10: 17 the great God, *m* and awesome,
34: 12 one has ever shown the *m* power
2Sa 1: 19 How the *m* have fallen!
23: 8 the names of David's *m* men:
Ne 9: 32 the great, *m* and awesome God,
Job 36: 5 God is *m,* but does not despise men
Ps 24: 8 The LORD strong and *m,*
45: 3 upon your side, O *m* one;
50: 1 The *M* One, God, the LORD,
62: 7 he is my *m* rock, my refuge.
68: 33 who thunders with *m* voice.
71: 16 proclaim your *m* acts,
77: 12 and consider all your *m* deeds.
77: 15 With your *m* arm you redeemed
89: 8 You are *m,* O LORD,
93: 4 the LORD on high is *m.*
99: 4 The King is *m,* he loves justice—
110: 2 LORD will extend your *m* scepter
118: 15 right hand has done *m* things!
136: 12 with a *m* hand and outstretched
145: 4 they will tell of your *m* acts.
145: 12 all men may know of your *m* acts
147: 5 Great is our Lord and *m* in power;
SS 8: 6 like a *m* flame.
Isa 9: 6 Wonderful Counselor, *M* God,
60: 16 your Redeemer, the *M* One
63: 1 *m* to save."
Jer 10: 6 and your name is *m* in power.
20: 11 with me like a *m* warrior;
32: 19 your purposes and *m* are your
Eze 20: 33 I will rule over you with a *m* hand
Zep 3: 17 he is *m* to save.
Mt 26: 64 at the right hand of the *M* One
Eph 1: 19 like the working of his *m* strength,
6: 10 in the Lord and in his *m* power.
1Pe 5: 6 therefore, under God's *m* hand,

MILE*

Mt 5: 41 If someone forces you to go one *m,*

MILK

Ex 3: 8 a land flowing with *m* and honey—
23: 19 a young goat in its mother's *m.*
Pr 30: 33 as churning the *m* produces butter,
Isa 55: 1 Come, buy wine and *m*
1Co 3: 2 I gave you *m,* not solid food,
Heb 5: 12 You need *m,* not solid food!
1Pe 2: 2 babies, crave pure spiritual *m,*

MILLSTONE (STONE)

Lk 17: 2 sea with a *m* tied around his neck

MIND (DOUBLE-MINDED LIKE-MINDED MINDED MINDFUL MINDS)

Nu 23: 19 that he should change his *m.*
Dt 28: 65 LORD will give you an anxious *m,*
1Sa 15: 29 Israel does not lie or change his *m;*
1Ch 28: 9 devotion and with a willing *m,*
2Ch 30: 12 the people to give them unity of *m*
Ps 26: 2 examine my heart and my *m;*
110: 4 and will not change his *m:*
Isa 26: 3 him whose *m* is steadfast,
Jer 17: 10 and examine the *m,*
Mt 22: 37 all your soul and with all your *m.'*
Mk 12: 30 with all your *m* and with all your
Lk 10: 27 your strength and with all your *m';*
Ac 4: 32 believers were one in heart and *m.*
Ro 1: 28 he gave them over to a depraved *m*
7: 25 I myself in my *m* am a slave
8: 6 The *m* of sinful man is death,
8: 7 the sinful *m* is hostile to God.
12: 2 by the renewing of your *m.*
14: 13 make up your *m* not
1Co 1: 10 you may be perfectly united in *m*
2: 9 no *m* has conceived
14: 14 spirit prays, but my *m* is unfruitful.
2Co 13: 11 be of one *m,* live in peace.
Php 3: 19 Their *m* is on earthly things.
Col 2: 18 and his unspiritual *m* puffs him up
1Th 4: 11 to *m* your own business
Heb 7: 21 and will not change his *m:*

MINDED* (MIND)

1Pe 4: 7 be clear *m* and self-controlled

MINDFUL* (MIND)

Ps 8: 4 what is man that you are *m* of him,
Lk 1: 48 God my Savior, for he has been *m*
Heb 2: 6 What is man that you are *m* of him,

MINDS (MIND)

Dt 11: 18 of mine in your hearts and *m;*
Ps 7: 9 who searches *m* and hearts,
Jer 31: 33 "I will put my law in their *m*
Lk 24: 38 and why do doubts rise in your *m?*
24: 45 Then he opened their *m*
Ro 8: 5 to the sinful nature have their *m* set
2Co 4: 4 god of this age has blinded the *m*
Eph 4: 23 new in the attitude of your *m;*
Col 3: 2 Set your *m* on things above,
Heb 8: 10 I will put my laws in their *m*
10: 16 and I will write them on their *m."*
1Pe 1: 13 prepare your *m* for action;
Rev 2: 23 I am he who searches hearts and *m,*

MINISTER (MINISTERING MINISTERS MINISTRY)

Ps 101: 6 will *m* to me.
1Ti 4: 6 you will be a good *m*

MINISTERING (MINISTER)

Heb 1: 14 Are not all angels *m* spirits sent

MINISTERS (MINISTER)

2Co 3: 6 as *m* of a new covenant—

MINISTRY (MINISTER)

Ac 6: 4 to prayer and the *m* of the word."
Ro 11: 13 I make much of my *m*
2Co 4: 1 God's mercy we have this *m,*
5: 18 gave us the *m* of reconciliation:
6: 3 so that our *m* will not be
Gal 2: 8 who was at work in the *m* of Peter
2Ti 4: 5 discharge all the duties of your *m.*
Heb 8: 6 But the *m* Jesus has received is

MIRACLE* (MIRACLES MIRACULOUS)

Ex 7: 9 'Perform a *m,'* then say to Aaron,
Mk 9: 39 "No one who does a *m*
Lk 23: 8 hoped to see him perform some *m.*
Jn 7: 21 "I did one *m,* and you are all
Ac 4: 16 they have done an outstanding *m,*

MIRACLES* (MIRACLE)

1Ch 16: 12 his *m,* and the judgments he
Ne 9: 17 to remember the *m* you performed
Job 5: 9 *m* that cannot be counted.
9: 10 *m* that cannot be counted.
Ps 77: 11 I will remember your *m* of long ago
77: 14 You are the God who performs *m;*
78: 12 He did *m* in the sight
105: 5 his *m,* and the judgments he
106: 7 they gave no thought to your *m;*
106: 22 *m* in the land of Ham
Mt 7: 22 out demons and perform many *m?'*
11: 20 most of his *m* had been performed,
11: 21 If the *m* that were performed
11: 23 If the *m* that were performed
13: 58 And he did not do many *m* there
24: 24 and perform great signs and *m*
Mk 6: 2 does *m!* Isn't this the carpenter?
6: 5 He could not do any *m* there,
13: 22 and *m* to deceive the elect—
Lk 10: 13 For if the *m* that were performed
19: 37 for all the *m* they had seen:
Jn 7: 3 disciples may see the *m* you do.
10: 25 *m* I do in my Father's name speak
10: 32 "I have shown you many great *m*
10: 38 do not believe me, believe the *m,*
14: 11 the evidence of the *m* themselves.
15: 24 But now they have seen these *m,*
Ac 2: 22 accredited by God to you by *m,*
8: 13 by the great signs and *m* he saw.
19: 11 God did extraordinary *m*
Ro 15: 19 by the power of signs and *m,*
1Co 12: 28 third teachers, then workers of *m,*
12: 29 Are all teachers? Do all work *m?*
2Co 12: 12 and *m*—were done among you
Gal 3: 5 work *m* among you because you
2Th 2: 9 in all kinds of counterfeit *m,*
Heb 2: 4 it by signs, wonders and various *m,*

MIRACULOUS (MIRACLE)

Dt 13: 1 and announces to you a *m* sign
Mt 12: 39 generation asks for a *m* sign!
13: 54 this wisdom and these *m* powers?"
Jn 2: 11 This, the first of his *m* signs,
2: 23 people saw the *m* signs he was
3: 2 could perform the *m* signs you are

Jn 4:48 "Unless you people see *m* signs
7:31 will he do more *m* signs
9:16 "How can a sinner do such *m* signs
12:37 Jesus had done all these *m* signs
20:30 Jesus did many other *m* signs
Ac 2:43 *m* signs were done by the apostles.
5:12 apostles performed many *m* signs
1Co 1:22 Jews demand *m* signs and Greeks
12:10 to another *m* powers,

MIRE

Ps 40: 2 out of the mud and *m;*
Isa 57:20 whose waves cast up *m* and mud.

MIRIAM

Sister of Moses and Aaron (Nu 26:59). Led dancing at Red Sea (Ex 15:20-21). Struck with leprosy for criticizing Moses (Nu 12). Death (Nu 20:1).

MIRROR

1Co 13:12 but a poor reflection as in a *m;*
Jas 1:23 a man who looks at his face in a *m*

MISDEEDS*

Ps 99: 8 though you punished their *m.*
Ro 8:13 put to death the *m* of the body,

MISERY

Ex 3: 7 "I have indeed seen the *m*
Jdg 10:16 he could bear Israel's *m* no longer.
Hos 5:15 in their *m* they will earnestly seek
Ro 3:16 ruin and *m* mark their ways,
Jas 5: 1 of the *m* that is coming upon you.

MISFORTUNE

Ob :12 brother in the day of his *m,*

MISLEAD (MISLED)

Isa 47:10 wisdom and knowledge *m* you

MISLED (MISLEAD)

1Co 15:33 Do not be *m:* "Bad company

MISS (MISSES)

Pr 19: 2 nor to be hasty and *m* the way.

MISSES (MISS)

Heb 12:15 See to it that no one *m* the grace

MIST

Hos 6: 4 Your love is like the morning *m,*
Jas 4:14 You are a *m* that appears for a little

MISTREAT (MISTREATED)

Ex 22:21 "Do not *m* an alien or oppress him,
Eze 22:29 and needy and *m* the alien,
Lk 6:28 pray for those who *m* you.

MISTREATED (MISTREAT)

Eze 22: 7 *m* the fatherless and the widow.
Heb 11:25 to be *m* along with the people
11:37 destitute, persecuted and *m*—
13: 3 who are *m* as if you yourselves

MISUSE* (MISUSES)

Ex 20: 7 "You shall not *m* the name
Dt 5:11 "You shall not *m* the name
Ps 139:20 your adversaries *m* your name.

MISUSES* (MISUSE)

Ex 20: 7 anyone guiltless who *m* his name.
Dt 5:11 anyone guiltless who *m* his name.

MIXED (MIXING)

Da 2:41 even as you saw iron *m* with clay.

MIXING (MIXED)

Isa 5:22 and champions at *m* drinks,

MOAB (MOABITESS)

Ge 19:37 she named him *M;* he is the father
Dt 34: 6 He buried him in *M,* in the valley
Ru 1: 1 live for a while in the country of *M.*
Isa 15: 1 An oracle concerning *M:*
Jer 48:16 "The fall of *M* is at hand;
Am 2: 1 "For three sins of *M,*

MOABITESS (MOAB)

Ru 1:22 accompanied by Ruth the *M,*

MOAN

Ps 90: 9 we finish our years with a *m.*

MOCK (MOCKED MOCKER MOCKERS MOCKING MOCKS)

Ps 22: 7 All who see me *m* me;
119:51 The arrogant *m* me
Pr 1:26 I will *m* when calamity overtakes
14: 9 Fools *m* at making amends for sin,
Mk 10:34 who will *m* him and spit on him,

MOCKED (MOCK)

Ps 89:51 with which they have *m* every step
Mt 27:29 knelt in front of him and *m* him.
27:41 of the law and the elders *m* him.
Gal 6: 7 not be deceived: God cannot be *m.*

MOCKER (MOCK)

Pr 9: 7 corrects a *m* invites insult;
9:12 if you are a *m,* you alone will suffer
20: 1 Wine is a *m* and beer a brawler;
22:10 Drive out the *m,* and out goes strife

MOCKERS (MOCK)

Ps 1: 1 or sit in the seat of *m.*
Pr 29: 8 *M* stir up a city,

MOCKING (MOCK)

Isa 50: 6 face from *m* and spitting.

MOCKS (MOCK)

Pr 17: 5 He who *m* the poor shows
30:17 "The eye that *m* a father,

MODEL*

Eze 28:12 " 'You were the *m* of perfection,
1Th 1: 7 And so you became a *m*
2Th 3: 9 to make ourselves a *m* for you

MODESTY*

1Co 12:23 are treated with special *m,*

MOLDED*

Job 10: 9 Remember that you *m* me like clay

MOLDY

Jos 9: 5 of their food supply was dry and *m.*

MOLECH

Lev 20: 2 of his children to *M* must be put
1Ki 11:33 and *M* the god of the Ammonites,

MOMENT (MOMENTARY)

Job 20: 5 the joy of the godless lasts but a *m.*
Ps 2:12 for his wrath can flare up in a *m.*
30: 5 For his anger lasts only a *m,*
Pr 12:19 but a lying tongue lasts only a *m.*
Isa 54: 7 "For a brief *m* I abandoned you,
66: 8 or a nation be brought forth in a *m?*
Gal 2: 5 We did not give in to them for a *m,*

MOMENTARY* (MOMENT)

2Co 4:17 and *m* troubles are achieving

MONEY

Pr 13:11 Dishonest *m* dwindles away,
Ecc 5:10 Whoever loves *m* never has *m*
Isa 55: 1 and you who have no *m,*
Mt 6:24 You cannot serve both God and *M.*
27: 5 Judas threw the *m* into the temple
Lk 3:14 "Don't extort *m* and don't accuse
9: 3 no bread, no *m,* no extra tunic.
16:13 You cannot serve both God and *M*
Ac 5: 2 part of the *m* for himself,
1Co 16: 2 set aside a sum of *m* in keeping
1Ti 3: 3 not quarrelsome, not a lover of *m.*
6:10 For the love of *m* is a root
2Ti 3: 2 lovers of *m,* boastful, proud,
Heb 13: 5 free from the love of *m*
1Pe 5: 2 not greedy for *m,* but eager to serve

MONEYLENDER* (LEND)

Ex 22:25 not be like a *m;* charge him no
Lk 7:41 men owed money to a certain *m.*

MONTH (MONTHS)

Ex 12: 2 "This *m* is to be for you the first
Eze 47:12 Every *m* they will bear,
Rev 22: 2 of fruit, yielding its fruit every *m.*

MONTHS (MONTH)

Gal 4:10 and *m* and seasons and years!
Rev 11: 2 trample on the holy city for 42 *m.*
13: 5 his authority for forty-two *m.*

MOON

Jos 10:13 and the *m* stopped,
Ps 8: 3 the *m* and the stars,
74:16 you established the sun and *m.*
89:37 be established forever like the *m,*
104:19 The *m* marks off the seasons,
121: 6 nor the *m* by night.
136: 9 the *m* and stars to govern the night;
148: 3 Praise him, sun and *m,*
SS 6:10 fair as the *m,* bright as the sun,
Joel 2:31 and the *m* to blood
Hab 3:11 and *m* stood still in the heavens
Mt 24:29 and the *m* will not give its light;
Ac 2:20 and the *m* to blood
1Co 15:41 *m* another and the stars another;
Col 2:16 a New *M* celebration or a Sabbath
Rev 6:12 the whole *m* turned blood red,
21:23 city does not need the sun or the *m*

MORAL*

Jas 1:21 rid of all *m* filth and the evil that is

MORDECAI

Benjamite exile who raised Esther (Est 2:5-15). Exposed plot to kill Xerxes (Est 2:19-23). Refused to honor Haman (Est 3:1-6; 5:9-14). Charged Esther to foil Haman's plot against the Jews (Est 4). Xerxes forced Haman to honor Mordecai (Est 6). Mordecai exalted (Est 8-10). Established Purim (Est 9:18-32).

MORIAH*

Ge 22: 2 and go to the region of *M.*
2Ch 3: 1 LORD in Jerusalem on Mount *M,*

MORNING

Ge 1: 5 and there was *m*—the first day.
Dt 28:67 In the *m* you will say, "If only it
2Sa 23: 4 he is like the light of *m* at sunrise
Ps 5: 3 In the *m,* O LORD,
Pr 27:14 blesses his neighbor early in the *m,*
Isa 14:12 O *m* star, son of the dawn!
La 3:23 They are new every *m;*
2Pe 1:19 and the *m* star rises in your hearts.
Rev 2:28 I will also give him the *m* star.
22:16 of David, and the bright *M* Star."

MORTAL

Ge 6: 3 for he is *m;* his days will be
Job 10: 4 Do you see as a *m* sees?
Ro 8:11 also give life to your *m* bodies
1Co 15:53 and the *m* with immortality.
2Co 5: 4 that what is *m* may be swallowed

MOSES

Levite; brother of Aaron (Ex 6:20; 1Ch 6:3). Put in basket into Nile; discovered and raised by Pharaoh's daughter (Ex 2:1-10). Fled to Midian after killing Egyptian (Ex 2:11-15). Married to Zipporah, fathered Gershom (Ex 2:16-22).

Called by the LORD to deliver Israel (Ex 3-4). Pharaoh's resistance (Ex 5). Ten plagues (Ex 7-11). Passover and Exodus (Ex 12-13). Led Israel through Red Sea (Ex 14). Song of deliverance (Ex 15:1-21). Brought water from rock (Ex 17:1-7). Raised hands to defeat Amalekites (Ex 17:8-16). Delegated judges (Ex 18; Dt 1:9-18).

Received Law at Sinai (Ex 19-23; 25-31; Jn 1:17). Announced Law to Israel (Ex 19:7-8; 24; 35). Broke tablets because of golden calf (Ex 32; Dt 9). Saw glory of the LORD (Ex 33-34). Supervised building of tabernacle (Ex 36-40). Set apart Aaron and priests (Lev 8-9). Numbered tribes (Nu 1-4; 26). Opposed by Aaron and Miriam (Nu 12). Sent spies into Canaan (Nu 13). Announced forty years of wandering for failure to enter land (Nu 14). Opposed by Korah (Nu 16). Forbidden to enter land for striking rock (Nu 20:1-13; Dt 1:37). Lifted bronze snake for healing (Nu 21:4-9; Jn 3:14). Final address to Israel (Dt 1-33). Succeeded by Joshua (Nu 27:12-23; Dt 34). Death (Dt 34:5-12).

"Law of Moses" (1Ki 2:3; Ezr 3:2; Mk 12:26; Lk 24:44). "Book of Moses" (2Ch 25:12; Ne 13:1). "Song of Moses" (Ex 15:1-21; Rev 15:3). "Prayer of Moses" (Ps 90).

MOTH

Mt 6:19 where *m* and rust destroy,

MOTHER (GRANDMOTHER MOTHER-IN-LAW MOTHER'S)

Ge 2:24 and *m* and be united to his wife,
3:20 because she would become the *m*
Ex 20:12 "Honor your father and your *m,*
Lev 20: 9 " 'If anyone curses his father or *m,*
Dt 5:16 "Honor your father and your *m,*

Dt 21:18 who does not obey his father and *m*
27:16 who dishonors his father or his *m*."
Jdg 5: 7 arose a *m* in Israel.
1Sa 2:19 Each year his *m* made him a little
Ps 113: 9 as a happy *m* of children.
Pr 10: 1 but a foolish son grief to his *m*.
23:22 do not despise your *m*
23:25 May your father and *m* be glad;
29:15 a child left to himself disgraces his *m*.
30:17 that scorns obedience to a *m*,
31: 1 an oracle his *m* taught him:
Isa 49:15 "Can a *m* forget the baby
66:13 As a *m* comforts her child,
Jer 20:17 with my *m* as my grave,
Mic 7: 6 a daughter rises up against her *m*,
Mt 10:35 a daughter against her *m*,
10:37 or *m* more than me is not worthy
12:48 He replied to him, "Who is my *m*,
15: 4 'Honor your father and *m*'
19: 5 and *m* and be united to his wife,
19:19 honor your father and *m*,'
Mk 7:10 'Honor your father and your *m*,' and,
10:19 honor your father and *m*.'"
Lk 11:27 "Blessed is the *m* who gave you
12:53 daughter and daughter against *m*,
18:20 honor your father and *m*.'"
Jn 19:27 to the disciple, "Here is your *m*."
Gal 4:26 is above is free, and she is our *m*.
Eph 5:31 and *m* and be united to his wife,
6: 2 "Honor your father and *m*"—
1Th 2: 7 like a *m* caring for her little
2Ti 1: 5 and in your *m* Eunice and,

MOTHER-IN-LAW (MOTHER)

Ru 2:19 Ruth told her *m* about the one
Mt 10:35 a daughter-in-law against her *m*—

MOTHER'S (MOTHER)

Job 1:21 "Naked I came from my *m* womb,
Pr 1: 8 and do not forsake your *m* teaching
Ecc 5:15 from his *m* womb,
11: 5 the body is formed in a *m* womb,
Jn 3: 4 time into his *m* womb to be born!"

MOTIVE* (MOTIVES)

1Ch 28: 9 and understands every *m*

MOTIVES* (MOTIVE)

Pr 16: 2 but *m* are weighed by the LORD.
1Co 4: 5 will expose the *m* of men's hearts.
Php 1:18 whether from false *m* or true,
1Th 2: 3 spring from error or impure *m*,
Jas 4: 3 because you ask with wrong *m*,

MOUNT (MOUNTAIN MOUNTAINS MOUNTAINTOPS)

Ps 89: 9 when its waves *m* up, you still them
Isa 14:13 enthroned on the *m* of assembly,
Eze 28:14 You were on the holy *m* of God;
Zec 14: 4 stand on the *M* of Olives,

MOUNTAIN (MOUNT)

Ge 22:14 "On the *m* of the LORD it will be
Ex 24:18 And he stayed on the *m* forty days
Dt 5: 4 face to face out of the fire on the *m*.
Job 14:18 "But as a *m* erodes and crumbles
Ps 48: 1 in the city of our God, his holy *m*.
Isa 40: 4 every *m* and hill made low;
Mic 4: 2 let us go up to the *m* of the LORD,
Mt 4: 8 the devil took him to a very high *m*
17:20 say to this *m*, 'Move from here
Mk 9: 2 with him and led them up a high *m*,
Lk 3: 5 every *m* and hill made low.
Jn 4:21 the Father neither on this *m*
2Pe 1:18 were with him on the sacred *m*.

MOUNTAINS (MOUNT)

Ps 36: 6 righteousness is like the mighty *m*,
46: 2 the *m* fall into the heart of the sea,
90: 2 Before the *m* were born
Isa 52: 7 How beautiful on the *m*
54:10 Though the *m* be shaken
55:12 the *m* and hills
Eze 34: 6 My sheep wandered over all the *m*
Mt 24:16 are in Judea flee to the *m*.
Lk 23:30 they will say to the *m*, "Fall on us!"
1Co 13: 2 if I have a faith that can move *m*,
Rev 6:16 They called to the *m* and the rocks,

MOUNTAINTOPS (MOUNT)

Isa 42:11 let them shout from the *m*.

MOURN (MOURNING MOURNS)

Ecc 3: 4 a time to *m* and a time to dance,
Isa 61: 2 to comfort all who *m*,
Mt 5: 4 Blessed are those who *m*,
Ro 12:15 *m* with those who *m*.

MOURNING (MOURN)

Isa 61: 3 instead of *m*,
Jer 31:13 I will turn their *m* into gladness;
Rev 21: 4 There will be no more death or *m*

MOURNS (MOURN)

Zec 12:10 as one *m* for an only child,

MOUTH (MOUTHS)

Nu 22:38 only what God puts in my *m*."
Dt 8: 3 comes from the *m* of the LORD.
18:18 I will put my words in his *m*,
30:14 it is in your *m* and in your heart
Jos 1: 8 of the Law depart from your *m*;
2Ki 4:34 *m* to *m*, eyes to eyes, hands
Ps 10: 7 His *m* is full of curses and lies
17: 3 resolved that my *m* will not sin.
19:14 May the words of my *m*
37:30 *m* of the righteous man utters
40: 3 He put a new song in my *m*,
71: 8 My *m* is filled with your praise,
119:103 sweeter than honey to my *m*!
141: 3 Set a guard over my *m*, O LORD;
Pr 2: 6 and from his *m* come knowledge
4:24 Put away perversity from your *m*;
10:11 The *m* of the righteous is a fountain
10:31 *m* of the righteous brings forth
16:23 A wise man's heart guides his *m*,
26:28 and a flattering *m* works ruin.
27: 2 praise you, and not your own *m*;
Ecc 5: 2 Do not be quick with your *m*,
SS 1: 2 with the kisses of his *m*—
5:16 His *m* is sweetness itself;
Isa 29:13 come near to me with their *m*
40: 5 For the *m* of the LORD has spoken
45:23 my *m* has uttered in all integrity
51:16 I have put my words in your *m*
53: 7 so he did not open his *m*.
55:11 my word that goes out from my *m*:
59:21 *m* will not depart from your *m*,
Eze 3: 2 So I opened my *m*, and he gave me
Mal 2: 7 and from his *m* men should seek
Mt 4: 4 comes from the *m* of God.'"
12:34 overflow of the heart the *m* speaks.
15:11 into a man's *m* does not make him
15:18 out of the *m* come from the heart,
Lk 6:45 overflow of his heart his *m* speaks.
Ro 10: 9 That if you confess with your *m*,
15: 6 and *m* you may glorify the God
1Pe 2:22 and no deceit was found in his *m*."
Rev 1:16 and out of his *m* came a sharp
2:16 them with the sword of my *m*.
3:16 I am about to spit you out of my *m*.
19:15 Out of his *m* comes a sharp sword

MOUTHS (MOUTH)

Ps 78:36 would flatter him with their *m*,
Eze 33:31 With their *m* they express devotion
Ro 3:14 "Their *m* are full of cursing
Eph 4:29 talk come out of your *m*,
Jas 3: 3 bits into the *m* of horses

MOVE (MOVED MOVES)

Dt 19:14 Do not *m* your neighbor's
Pr 23:10 Do not *m* an ancient boundary
Ac 17:28 and *m* and have our being.'
1Co 13: 2 have a faith that can *m* mountains,
15:58 Let nothing *m* you.

MOVED (MOVE)

Ex 35:21 and whose heart *m* him came
2Ch 36:22 the LORD *m* the heart
Ezr 1: 5 everyone whose heart God had *m*
Ps 93: 1 it cannot be *m*.
Jn 11:33 he was deeply *m* in spirit
Col 1:23 not *m* from the hope held out

MOVES (MOVE)

Dt 23:14 For the LORD your God *m* about

MUD (MUDDIED)

Ps 40: 2 out of the *m* and mire;
Isa 57:20 whose waves cast up mire and *m*.
Jn 9: 6 made some *m* with the saliva,
2Pe 2:22 back to her wallowing in the *m*."

MUDDIED (MUD)

Pr 25:26 Like a *m* spring or a polluted well
Eze 32:13 or *m* by the hoofs of cattle.

MULBERRY*

Lk 17: 6 you can say to this *m* tree,

MULTITUDE (MULTITUDES)

Isa 31: 1 who trust in the *m* of their chariots
Jas 5:20 and cover over a *m* of sins.
1Pe 4: 8 love covers over a *m* of sins.
Rev 7: 9 me was a great *m* that no one could
19: 1 of a great *m* in heaven shouting:

MULTITUDES (MULTITUDE)

Ne 9: 6 and the *m* of heaven worship you.
Da 12: 2 *M* who sleep in the dust
Joel 3:14 *M*, *m* in the valley of decision!

MURDER (MURDERED MURDERER MURDERERS)

Ex 20:13 "You shall not *m*.
Dt 5:17 "You shall not *m*.
Pr 28:17 A man tormented by the guilt of *m*
Mt 5:21 'Do not *m*, and anyone who
15:19 *m*, adultery, sexual immorality,
Ro 1:29 *m*, strife, deceit and malice.
13: 9 "Do not *m*," "Do not steal,"
Jas 2:11 adultery," also said, "Do not *m*."

MURDERED (MURDER)

Mt 23:31 of those who *m* the prophets.
Ac 7:52 now you have betrayed and *m* him
1Jn 3:12 to the evil one and *m* his brother.

MURDERER (MURDER)

Nu 35:16 he is a *m*; the *m* shall be put
Jn 8:44 He was a *m* from the beginning,
1Jn 3:15 who hates his brother is a *m*,

MURDERERS (MURDER)

1Ti 1: 9 for *m*, for adulterers and perverts,
Rev 21: 8 the *m*, the sexually immoral,
22:15 the sexually immoral, the *m*,

MUSIC* (MUSICAL MUSICIAN MUSICIANS)

Ge 31:27 singing to the *m* of tambourines
Jdg 5: 3 I will make *m* to the LORD,
1Ch 6:31 put in charge of the *m* in the house
6:32 They ministered with *m*
25: 6 fathers for the *m* of the temple
25: 7 and skilled in *m* for the LORD—
Ne 12:27 and with the *m* of cymbals,
Job 21:12 They sing to the *m* of tambourine
Ps 27: 6 and make *m* to the LORD.
33: 2 make *m* to him on the ten-stringed
45: 8 the *m* of the strings makes you glad
57: 7 I will sing and make *m*.
81: 2 Begin the *m*, strike the tambourine,
87: 7 As they make *m* they will sing,
92: 1 and make *m* to your name,
92: 3 to the *m* of the ten-stringed lyre
95: 2 and extol him with *m* and song.
98: 4 burst into jubilant song with *m*;
98: 5 make *m* to the LORD
108: 1 make *m* with all my soul.
144: 9 the ten-stringed lyre I will make *m*
147: 7 make *m* to our God on the harp.
149: 3 make *m* to him with tambourine
Isa 30:32 will be to the *m* of tambourines
La 5:14 young men have stopped their *m*.
Eze 26:13 *m* of your harps will be heard no
Da 3: 5 lyre, harp, pipes and all kinds of *m*,
3: 7 and all kinds of *m*, all the peoples,
3:10 and all kinds of *m* must fall down
3:15 lyre, harp, pipes and all kinds of *m*,
Am 5:23 to the *m* of your harps.
Hab 3:19 For the director of *m*.
Lk 15:25 came near the house, he heard *m*
Eph 5:19 make *m* in your heart to the Lord,
Rev 18:22 The *m* of harpists and musicians,

MUSICAL* (MUSIC)

1Ch 15:16 accompanied by *m* instruments:
23: 5 with the *m* instruments I have
2Ch 7: 6 with the LORD's *m* instruments,
23:13 with *m* instruments were leading
34:12 skilled in playing *m* instruments—
Ne 12:36 with *m* instruments prescribed
Am 6: 5 and improvise on *m* instruments.

MUSICIAN* (MUSIC)

1Ch 6:33 Heman, the *m*, the son of Joel,

MUSICIANS* (MUSIC)

1Ki 10:12 to make harps and lyres for the *m*.
1Ch 9:33 Those who were *m*, heads
15:19 The *m* Heman, Asaph
2Ch 5:12 All the Levites who were *m*—
9:11 to make harps and lyres for the *m*.
35:15 The *m*, the descendants of Asaph,

Ps 68:25 are the singers, after them the *m;*
Rev 18:22 The music of harpists and *m,*

MUSTARD

Mt 13:31 kingdom of heaven is like a *m* seed,
17:20 you have faith as small as a *m* seed,
Mk 4:31 It is like a *m* seed, which is

MUTILATORS*

Php 3: 2 those men who do evil, those *m*

MUTUAL* (MUTUALLY)

Ro 14:19 leads to peace and to *m* edification.
1Co 7: 5 by *m* consent and for a time,

MUTUALLY* (MUTUAL)

Ro 1:12 and I may be *m* encouraged

MUZZLE*

Dt 25: 4 Do not *m* an ox while it is treading
Ps 39: 1 I will put a *m* on my mouth
1Co 9: 9 "Do not *m* an ox while it is
1Ti 5:18 "Do not *m* the ox while it is

MYRRH

Ps 45: 8 All your robes are fragrant with *m*
SS 1:13 My lover is to me a sachet of *m*
Mt 2:11 of gold and of incense and of *m.*
Mk 15:23 offered him wine mixed with *m,*
Jn 19:39 Nicodemus brought a mixture of *m*
Rev 18:13 of incense, *m* and frankincense,

MYSTERIES* (MYSTERY)

Job 11: 7 "Can you fathom the *m* of God?
Da 2:28 a God in heaven who reveals *m.*
2:29 of *m* showed you what is going
2:47 Lord of kings and a revealer of *m,*
1Co 13: 2 can fathom all *m* and all knowledge
14: 2 he utters *m* with his spirit.

MYSTERY* (MYSTERIES)

Da 2:18 God of heaven concerning this *m,*
2:19 the night the *m* was revealed
2:27 to the king the *m* he has asked
2:30 this *m* has been revealed to me,
2:47 for you were able to reveal this *m."*
4: 9 and no *m* is too difficult for you.
Ro 11:25 you to be ignorant of this *m,*
16:25 to the revelation of the *m* hidden
1Co 15:51 I tell you a *m:* We will not all sleep,
Eph 1: 9 to us the *m* of his will according
3: 3 the *m* made known to me
3: 4 insight into the *m* of Christ,
3: 6 This *m* is that through the gospel
3: 9 the administration of this *m,*
5:32 This is a profound *m*—
6:19 I will fearlessly make known the *m*
Col 1:26 the *m* that has been kept hidden
1:27 the glorious riches of this *m,*
2: 2 in order that they may know the *m*
4: 3 so that we may proclaim the *m*
1Ti 3:16 the *m* of godliness is great:
Rev 1:20 *m* of the seven stars that you saw
10: 7 the *m* of God will be accomplished,
17: 5 written on her forehead: *M*
17: 7 explain to you the *m* of the woman

MYTHS*

1Ti 1: 4 nor to devote themselves to *m*
4: 7 Have nothing to do with godless *m*
2Ti 4: 4 from the truth and turn aside to *m.*
Tit 1:14 will pay no attention to Jewish *m*

NAAMAN

Aramean general whose leprosy was cleansed by Elisha (2Ki 5).

NABAL

Wealthy Carmelite the LORD killed for refusing to help David (1Sa 25). David married Abigail, his widow (1Sa 25:39-42).

NABOTH*

Jezreelite killed by Jezebel for his vineyard (1Ki 21). Ahab's family destroyed for this (1Ki 21:17-24; 2Ki 9:21-37).

NADAB

1. Firstborn of Aaron (Ex 6:23); killed with Abihu for offering unauthorized fire (Lev 10; Nu 3:4).
2. Son of Jeroboam I; king of Israel (1Ki 15:25-32).

NAHUM

Prophet against Nineveh (Na 1:1).

NAIL* (NAILING)

Jn 20:25 "Unless I see the *n* marks

NAILING* (NAIL)

Ac 2:23 him to death by *n* him to the cross.
Col 2:14 he took it away, *n* it to the cross.

NAIVE

Ro 16:18 they deceive the minds of *n* people.

NAKED

Ge 2:25 The man and his wife were both *n,*
Job 1:21 *N* I came from my mother's womb,
Isa 58: 7 when you see the *n,* to clothe him,
2Co 5: 3 are clothed, we will not be found *n.*

NAME (NAMES)

Ge 2:19 man to see what he would *n* them;
4:26 to call on the *n* of the LORD.
11: 4 so that we may make a *n*
12: 2 I will make your *n* great,
32:29 Jacob said, "Please tell me your *n."*
Ex 3:15 This is my *n* forever, the *n*
20: 7 "You shall not misuse the *n*
34:14 for the LORD, whose *n* is Jealous,
Lev 24:11 Israelite woman blasphemed the *N*
Dt 5:11 "You shall not misuse the *n*
12:11 choose as a dwelling for his *N*—
18: 5 minister in the LORD's *n* always.
25: 6 carry on the *n* of the dead brother
28:58 this glorious and awesome *n*—
Jos 7: 9 do for your own great *n?"*
Jdg 13:17 "What is your *n,* so that we may
1Sa 12:22 of his great *n* the LORD will not
2Sa 6: 2 which is called by the *N,* the name
7: 9 Now I will make your *n* great,
1Ki 5: 5 will build the temple for my *N.'*
8:29 you said, 'My *N* shall be there,'
1Ch 17: 8 I will make your *n* like the names
2Ch 7:14 my people, who are called by my *n,*
Ne 9:10 You made a *n* for yourself,
Ps 8: 1 how majestic is your *n*
9:10 Those who know your *n* will trust
20: 7 in the *n* of the LORD our God.
29: 2 to the LORD the glory due his *n;*
34: 3 let us exalt his *n* together.
44:20 If we had forgotten the *n*
66: 2 Sing the glory of his *n;*
68: 4 Sing to God, sing praise to his *n,*
79: 9 for the glory of your *n;*
96: 8 to the LORD the glory due his *n;*
103: 1 my inmost being, praise his holy *n.*
115: 1 but to your *n* be the glory,
138: 2 your *n* and your word.
145: 1 I will praise your *n* for ever
147: 4 and calls them each by *n.*
Pr 3: 4 you will win favor and a good *n*
18:10 *n* of the LORD is a strong tower;
22: 1 A good *n* is more desirable
30: 4 What is his *n,* and the *n* of his son?
Ecc 7: 1 A good *n* is better
SS 1: 3 your *n* is like perfume poured out.
Isa 12: 4 thanks to the LORD, call on his *n;*
26: 8 your *n* and renown
40:26 and calls them each by *n.*
42: 8 "I am the LORD; that is my *n!*
56: 5 I will give them an everlasting *n*
57:15 who lives forever, whose *n* is holy:
63:14 to make for yourself a glorious *n.*
Jer 14: 7 do something for the sake of your *n*
15:16 for I bear your *n,*
Eze 20: 9 of my *n* I did what would keep it
20:14 of my *n* I did what would keep it
20:22 of my *n* I did what would keep it
Da 12: 1 everyone whose *n* is found written
Hos 12: 5 the LORD is his *n* of renown!
Joel 2:32 on the *n* of the LORD will be saved
Mic 5: 4 in the majesty of the *n*
Zep 3: 9 call on the *n* of the LORD
Zec 6:12 is the man whose *n* is the Branch,
14: 9 one LORD, and his *n* the only *n.*
Mal 1: 6 O priests, who show contempt for my *n.*
Mt 1:21 and you are to give him the *n* Jesus,
6: 9 hallowed be your *n,*
18:20 or three come together in my *n,*
24: 5 For many will come in my *n,*
28:19 them in the *n* of the Father
Mk 9:41 gives you a cup of water in my *n*
Lk 11: 2 hallowed be your *n,*
Jn 10: 3 He calls his own sheep by *n*
14:13 I will do whatever you ask in my *n,*
16:24 asked for anything in my *n.*
Ac 2:21 on the *n* of the Lord will be saved.'
4:12 for there is no other *n*
Ro 10:13 "Everyone who calls on the *n*
Php 2: 9 him the *n* that is above every *n,*
2:10 at the *n* of Jesus every knee should
Col 3:17 do it all in the *n* of the Lord Jesus,
Heb 1: 4 as the *n* he has inherited is superior
Jas 5:14 him with oil in the *n* of the Lord.
1Jn 5:13 believe in the *n* of the Son of God
Rev 2:17 stone with a new *n* written on it,
3: 5 I will never blot out his *n*
3:12 I will also write on him my new *n.*
19:13 and his *n* is the Word of God.
20:15 If anyone's *n* was not found written

NAMES (NAME)

Ex 28: 9 engrave on them the *n* of the sons
Lk 10:20 but rejoice that your *n* are written
Php 4: 3 whose *n* are in the book of life.
Heb 12:23 whose *n* are written in heaven.
Rev 21:27 but only those whose *n* are written

NAOMI

Wife of Elimelech, mother-in-law of Ruth (Ru 1:2, 4). Left Bethlehem for Moab during famine (Ru 1:1). Returned a widow, with Ruth (Ru 1:6-22). Advised Ruth to seek marriage with Boaz (Ru 2:17-3:4). Cared for Ruth's son Obed (Ru 4:13-17).

NAPHTALI

Son of Jacob by Bilhah (Ge 30:8; 35:25; 1Ch 2:2). Tribe of blessed (Ge 49:21; Dt 33:23), numbered (Nu 1:43; 26:50), allotted land (Jos 19:32-39; Eze 48:3), failed to fully possess (Jdg 1:33), supported Deborah (Jdg 4:10; 5:18), David (1Ch 12:34), 12,000 from (Rev 7:6).

NARROW

Mt 7:13 "Enter through the *n* gate.
7:14 and *n* the road that leads to life,

NATHAN

Prophet and chronicler of Israel's history (1Ch 29:29; 2Ch 9:29). Announced the Davidic covenant (2Sa 7; 1Ch 17). Denounced David's sin with Bathsheba (2Sa 12). Supported Solomon (1Ki 1).

NATHANAEL*

Apostle (Jn 1:45-49; 21:2). Probably also called Bartholomew (Mt 10:3).

NATION (NATIONS)

Ge 12: 2 "I will make you into a great *n*
Ex 19: 6 a kingdom of priests and a holy *n.'*
Dt 4: 7 What other *n* is so great
Jos 5: 8 And after the whole *n* had been
2Sa 7:23 one *n* on earth that God went out
Ps 33:12 Blessed is the *n* whose God is
Pr 11:14 For lack of guidance a *n* falls,
14:34 Righteousness exalts a *n,*
Isa 2: 4 *N* will not take up sword
26: 2 that the righteous *n* may enter,
60:12 For the *n* or kingdom that will not
65: 1 To a *n* that did not call on my name
66: 8 a *n* be brought forth in a moment?
Mic 4: 3 *N* will not take up sword
Mt 24: 7 *N* will rise against *n,*
Mk 13: 8 *N* will rise against *n,*
1Pe 2: 9 a royal priesthood, a holy *n,*
Rev 5: 9 and language and people and *n.*
7: 9 from every *n,* tribe, people
14: 6 to every *n,* tribe, language

NATIONS (NATION)

Ge 17: 4 You will be the father of many *n.*
18:18 and all *n* on earth will be blessed
Ex 19: 5 of all *n* you will be my treasured
Lev 20:26 apart from the *n* to be my own.
Dt 7: 1 drives out before you many *n*—
15: 6 You will rule over many *n*
Jdg 3: 1 These are the *n* the LORD left
2Ch 20: 6 rule over all the kingdoms of the *n.*
Ne 1: 8 I will scatter you among the *n,*
Ps 2: 1 Why do the *n* conspire
2: 8 I will make the *n* your inheritance,
9: 5 You have rebuked the *n*
22:28 and he rules over the *n.*
46:10 I will be exalted among the *n,*
47: 8 God reigns over the *n;*
66: 7 his eyes watch the *n*—
67: 2 your salvation among all *n.*

Ps 68:30 Scatter the *n* who delight in war.
72:17 All *n* will be blessed through him,
96:3 Declare his glory among the *n*,
99:2 he is exalted over all the *n*.
106:35 but they mingled with the *n*
110:6 He will judge the *n*, heaping up
113:4 The LORD is exalted over all the *n*
Isa 2:2 and all *n* will stream to it.
11:10 the *n* will rally to him,
12:4 among the *n* what he has done,
40:15 Surely the *n* are like a drop
42:1 and he will bring justice to the *n*.
51:4 justice will become a light to the *n*.
52:15 so will he sprinkle many *n*,
56:7 a house of prayer for all *n*."
60:3 *N* will come to your light,
66:18 and gather all *n* and tongues,
Jer 1:5 you as a prophet to the *n*."
3:17 and all *n* will gather in Jerusalem
31:10 "Hear the word of the LORD, O *n*;
33:9 and honor before all *n*
46:28 I completely destroy all the *n*
Eze 22:4 you an object of scorn to the *n*
34:13 I will bring them out from the *n*
36:23 *n* will know that I am the LORD,
37:22 and they will never again be two *n*
39:21 I will display my glory among the *n*
Hos 7:8 "Ephraim mixes with the *n*;
Joel 2:17 a byword among the *n*.
3:2 I will gather all *n*
Am 9:12 and all the *n* that bear my name,"
Zep 3:8 I have decided to assemble the *n*,
Hag 2:7 and the desired of all *n* will come,
Zec 8:13 an object of cursing among the *n*,
8:23 *n* will take firm hold of one Jew
9:10 He will proclaim peace to the *n*.
14:2 I will gather all the *n* to Jerusalem
Mt 12:18 he will proclaim justice to the *n*.
24:9 and you will be hated by all *n*
24:14 whole world as a testimony to all *n*,
25:32 All the *n* will be gathered
28:19 and make disciples of all *n*,
Mk 11:17 a house of prayer for all *n*'?
Ac 4:25 "'Why do the *n* rage
Ro 15:12 who will arise to rule over the *n*;
Gal 3:8 All *n* will be blessed through you."
1Ti 3:16 was preached among the *n*,
Rev 15:4 All *n* will come
21:24 The *n* will walk by its light,
22:2 are for the healing of the *n*.

NATURAL (NATURE)

Ro 6:19 you are weak in your *n* selves.
1Co 15:44 If there is a *n* body, there is

NATURE (NATURAL)

Ro 1:20 his eternal power and divine *n*—
7:18 lives in me, that is, in my sinful *n*.
8:4 do not live according to the sinful *n*
8:5 to the sinful *n* have their minds set
8:8 by the sinful *n* cannot please God.
13:14 to gratify the desires of the sinful *n*.
Gal 5:13 freedom to indulge the sinful *n*;
5:19 The acts of the sinful *n* are obvious:
5:24 Jesus have crucified the sinful *n*
Php 2:6 Who, being in very *n* God,
Col 3:5 whatever belongs to your earthly *n*
2Pe 1:4 you may participate in the divine *n*

NAZARENE* (NAZARETH)

Mt 2:23 prophets: "He will be called a *N*."
Mk 14:67 "You also were with that *N*, Jesus,"
16:6 "You are looking for Jesus the *N*,
Ac 24:5 He is a ringleader of the *N* sect and

NAZARETH (NAZARENE)

Mt 4:13 Leaving *N*, he went and lived
Lk 4:16 to *N*, where he had been brought
Jn 1:46 "*N*! Can anything good come

NAZIRITE

Nu 6:2 of separation to the LORD as a *N*,
Jdg 13:7 because the boy will be a *N* of God

NEBO

Dt 34:1 Then Moses climbed Mount *N*

NEBUCHADNEZZAR

Babylonian king. Subdued and exiled Judah (2Ki 24-25; 2Ch 36; Jer 39). Dreams interpreted by Daniel (Da 2; 4). Worshiped God (Da 3:28-29; 4:34-37).

NECESSARY*

Ac 1:21 Therefore it is *n* to choose one
Ro 13:5 it is *n* to submit to the authorities,
2Co 9:5 I thought it *n* to urge the brothers
Php 1:24 it is more *n* for you that I remain
2:25 But I think it is *n* to send back
Heb 8:3 and so it was *n* for this one
9:16 it is *n* to prove the death
9:23 It was *n*, then, for the copies

NECK (STIFF-NECKED)

Pr 3:22 an ornament to grace your *n*.
6:21 fasten them around your *n*.
Mt 18:6 a large millstone hung around his *n*

NECO

Pharaoh who killed Josiah (2Ki 23:29-30; 2Ch 35:20-22), deposed Jehoahaz (2Ki 23:33-35; 2Ch 36:3-4).

NEED (NEEDS NEEDY)

1Ki 8:59 Israel according to each day's *n*,
Ps 79:8 for we are in desperate *n*.
116:6 when I was in great *n*, he saved me.
142:6 for I am in desperate *n*;
Mt 6:8 for your Father knows what you *n*
Lk 15:14 country, and he began to be in *n*.
Ac 2:45 they gave to anyone as he had *n*.
Ro 12:13 with God's people who are in *n*.
1Co 12:21 say to the hand, "I don't *n* you!"
Eph 4:28 something to share with those in *n*.
1Ti 5:3 to those widows who are really in *n*
Heb 4:16 grace to help us in our time of *n*.
1Jn 3:17 sees his brother in *n* but has no pity

NEEDLE

Mt 19:24 go through the eye of a *n*

NEEDS (NEED)

Isa 58:11 he will satisfy your *n*
Php 2:25 sent to take care of my *n*.
4:19 God will meet all your *n* according
Jas 2:16 does nothing about his physical *n*,

NEEDY (NEED)

Dt 15:11 toward the poor and *n* in your land.
1Sa 2:8 and lifts the *n* from the ash heap;
Ps 35:10 and *n* from those who rob them."
69:33 The LORD hears the *n*
72:12 he will deliver the *n* who cry out,
140:12 and upholds the cause of the *n*.
Pr 14:21 blessed is he who is kind to the *n*.
14:31 to the *n* honors God.
22:22 and do not crush the *n* in court,
31:9 defend the rights of the poor and *n*
31:20 and extends her hands to the *n*.
Mt 6:2 "So when you give to the *n*,

NEGLECT* (NEGLECTED)

Dt 12:19 Be careful not to *n* the Levites
14:27 And do not *n* the Levites living
Ezr 4:22 Be careful not to *n* this matter.
Ne 10:39 We will not *n* the house of our God
Est 6:10 Do not *n* anything you have
Ps 119:16 I will not *n* your word.
Lk 11:42 you *n* justice and the love of God.
Ac 6:2 for us to *n* the ministry of the word
1Ti 4:14 Do not *n* your gift, which was

NEGLECTED (NEGLECT)

Mt 23:23 But you have *n* the more important

NEHEMIAH

Cupbearer of Artaxerxes (Ne 2:1); governor of Israel (Ne 8:9). Returned to Jerusalem to rebuild walls (Ne 2-6). With Ezra, reestablished worship (Ne 8). Prayer confessing nation's sin (Ne 9). Dedicated wall (Ne 12).

NEIGHBOR (NEIGHBOR'S)

Ex 20:16 give false testimony against your *n*.
20:17 or anything that belongs to your *n*
Lev 19:13 Do not defraud your *n* or rob him.
19:17 Rebuke your *n* frankly
19:18 but love your *n* as yourself.
Ps 15:3 who does his *n* no wrong
Pr 3:29 Do not plot harm against your *n*,
11:12 who lacks judgment derides his *n*,
14:21 He who despises his *n* sins,
16:29 A violent man entices his *n*
24:28 against your *n* without cause,
25:18 gives false testimony against his *n*.
27:10 better a *n* nearby than a brother far
27:14 If a man loudly blesses his *n*
29:5 Whoever flatters his *n*
Jer 31:34 No longer will a man teach his *n*,
Zec 8:17 do not plot evil against your *n*,
Mt 5:43 Love your *n* and hate your enemy.'
19:19 and 'love your *n* as yourself.'"
Mk 12:31 The second is this: 'Love your *n*
Lk 10:27 and, 'Love your *n* as yourself.'"
10:29 who is my *n*?" In reply Jesus said:
Ro 13:9 "Love your *n* as yourself."
13:10 Love does no harm to its *n*.
15:2 Each of us should please his *n*
Gal 5:14 "Love your *n* as yourself."
Eph 4:25 and speak truthfully to his *n*,
Heb 8:11 No longer will a man teach his *n*,
Jas 2:8 "Love your *n* as yourself,"

NEIGHBOR'S (NEIGHBOR)

Ex 20:17 You shall not covet your *n* wife,
Dt 5:21 not set your desire on your *n* house
19:14 not move your *n* boundary stone
27:17 who moves his *n* boundary stone."
Pr 25:17 Seldom set foot in your *n* house—

NESTS

Mt 8:20 and birds of the air have *n*,

NET (NETS)

Pr 1:17 How useless to spread a *n*
Hab 1:15 he catches them in his *n*,
Mt 13:47 of heaven is like a *n* that was let
Jn 21:6 "Throw your *n* on the right side

NETS (NET)

Ps 141:10 Let the wicked fall into their own *n*
Mt 4:20 At once they left their *n*
Lk 5:4 and let down the *n* for a catch."

NEVER-FAILING*

Am 5:24 righteousness like a *n* stream!

NEW

Ps 40:3 He put a *n* song in my mouth,
98:1 Sing to the LORD a *n* song,
Ecc 1:9 there is nothing *n* under the sun.
Isa 42:9 and *n* things I declare;
62:2 you will be called by a *n* name
65:17 *n* heavens and a *n* earth.
66:22 "As the *n* heavens and the *n* earth
Jer 31:31 "when I will make a *n* covenant
La 3:23 They are *n* every morning;
Eze 11:19 undivided heart and put a *n* spirit
18:31 and get a *n* heart and a *n* spirit.
36:26 give you a *n* heart and put a *n* spirit
Zep 3:5 and every *n* day he does not fail,
Mt 9:17 Neither do men pour *n* wine
Mk 16:17 they will speak in *n* tongues;
Lk 5:39 after drinking old wine wants the *n*
22:20 "This cup is the *n* covenant
Jn 13:34 "A *n* commandment I give you:
Ac 5:20 the full message of this *n* life."
Ro 6:4 the Father, we too may live a *n* life.
1Co 5:7 old yeast that you may be a *n* batch
11:25 "This cup is the *n* covenant
2Co 3:6 as ministers of a *n* covenant—
5:17 he is a *n* creation; the old has gone,
Gal 6:15 what counts is a *n* creation.
Eph 4:23 to be made *n* in the attitude
4:24 and to put on the *n* self, created
Col 3:10 and have put on the *n* self,
Heb 8:8 when I will make a *n* covenant
9:15 is the mediator of a *n* covenant,
10:20 by a *n* and living way opened for us
12:24 Jesus the mediator of a *n* covenant,
1Pe 1:3 great mercy he has given us *n* birth
2Pe 3:13 to a *n* heaven and a *n* earth,
1Jn 2:8 Yet I am writing you a *n* command;
Rev 2:17 stone with a *n* name written on it,
3:12 the *n* Jerusalem, which is coming
21:1 I saw a *n* heaven and a *n* earth,

NEWBORN (BEAR)

1Pe 2:2 Like *n* babies, crave pure spiritual

NEWS

2Ki 7:9 This is a day of good *n*
Ps 112:7 He will have no fear of bad *n*;
Pr 15:30 good *n* gives health to the bones.
25:25 is good *n* from a distant land.
Isa 52:7 the feet of those who bring good *n*,
61:1 me to preach good *n* to the poor.
Na 1:15 the feet of one who brings good *n*,
Mt 4:23 preaching the good *n*
9:35 preaching the good *n*
11:5 the good *n* is preached to the poor.
Mk 1:15 Repent and believe the good *n*!"
16:15 preach the good *n* to all creation.
Lk 1:19 and to tell you this good *n*.
2:10 I bring you good *n*

Lk 3:18 and preached the good n to them.
4:43 "I must preach the good n
8: 1 proclaiming the good n
16:16 the good n of the kingdom
Ac 5:42 proclaiming the good n that Jesus
10:36 telling the good n of peace
14: 7 continued to preach the good n.
14:21 They preached the good n
17:18 preaching the good n about Jesus
Ro 10:15 feet of those who bring good n!"

NICODEMUS*

Pharisee who visted Jesus at night (Jn 3). Argued fair treatment of Jesus (Jn 7:50-52). With Joseph, prepared Jesus for burial (Jn 19:38-42).

NIGHT (NIGHTS NIGHTTIME)

Ge 1: 5 and the darkness he called "n."
1:16 and the lesser light to govern the n.
Ex 13:21 and by n in a pillar of fire
14:24 During the last watch of the n.
Dt 28:66 filled with dread both n and day,
Jos 1: 8 and n, so that you may be careful
Job 35:10 who gives songs in the n,
Ps 1: 2 on his law he meditates day and n.
19: 2 n after n they display knowledge.
42: 8 at n his song is with me—
63: 6 of you through the watches of the n
77: 6 I remembered my songs in the n.
90: 4 or like a watch in the n.
91: 5 You will not fear the terror of n,
119:148 through the watches of the n,
121: 6 nor the moon by n.
136: 9 the moon and stars to govern the n;
Pr 31:18 and her lamp does not go out at n.
Isa 21:11 Watchman, what is left of the n?"
58:10 and your n will become like
Jer 33:20 and my covenant with the n,
Lk 2: 8 watch over their flocks at n.
6:12 and spent the n praying to God.
Jn 3: 2 He came to Jesus at n and said,
9: 4 N is coming, when no one can work
1Th 5: 2 Lord will come like a thief in the n.
5: 5 We do not belong to the n
Rev 21:25 for there will be no n there.

NIGHTS (NIGHT)

Jnh 1:17 the fish three days and three n.
Mt 4: 2 After fasting forty days and forty n
12:40 three n in the belly of a huge fish,
2Co 6: 5 in hard work, sleepless n

NIGHTTIME* (NIGHT)

Zec 14: 7 or n—a day known to the LORD.

NIMROD

Ge 10: 9 "Like N, a mighty hunter

NINEVEH

Jnh 1: 2 "Go to the great city of N
Na 1: 1 An oracle concerning N.
Mt 12:41 The men of N will stand up

NOAH

Righteous man (Eze 14:14, 20) called to build ark (Ge 6-8; Heb 11:7; 1Pe 3:20; 2Pe 2:5). God's covenant with (Ge 9:1-17). Drunkenness of (Ge 9:18-23). Blessed sons, cursed Canaan (Ge 9:24-27).

NOBLE

Ru 3:11 you are a woman of n character.
Ps 45: 1 My heart is stirred by a n theme
Pr 12: 4 of n character is her husband's
31:10 A wife of n character who can find?
31:29 "Many women do n things,
Isa 32: 8 But the n man makes n plans,
Lk 8:15 good soil stands for those with a n
Ro 9:21 of clay some pottery for n purposes
Php 4: 8 whatever is n, whatever is right,
2Ti 2:20 some are for n purposes

NOSTRILS

Ge 2: 7 and breathed into his n the breath
Ex 15: 8 By the blast of your n
Ps 18:15 at the blast of breath from your n.

NOTE

Ac 4:13 and they took n that these men had
Php 3:17 take n of those who live according

NOTHING

2Sa 24:24 offerings that cost me n."
Ne 9:21 in the desert; they lacked n,
Ps 73:25 earth has n I desire besides you
Jer 32:17 N is too hard for you
Jn 15: 5 apart from me you can do n.

NOURISH

Pr 10:21 The lips of the righteous n many,

NULLIFY

Mt 15: 6 Thus you n the word of God
Ro 3:31 Do we, then, n the law by this faith

OATH

Ex 33: 1 up to the land I promised on o
Nu 30: 2 or takes an o to obligate himself
Dt 6:18 promised on o to your forefathers,
7: 8 and kept the o he swore
29:12 you this day and sealing with an o,
Ps 95:11 So I declared on o in my anger,
119:106 I have taken an o and confirmed it,
132:11 The LORD swore an o to David,
Ecc 8: 2 because you took an o before God.
Mt 5:33 'Do not break your o, but keep
Heb 7:20 And it was not without an o!

OBADIAH

1. Believer who sheltered 100 prophets from Jezebel (1Ki 18:1-16).
2. Prophet against Edom (Ob 1).

OBEDIENCE* (OBEY)

Ge 49:10 and the o of the nations is his.
Jdg 2:17 of o to the LORD's commands.
1Ch 21:19 So David went up in o
2Ch 31:21 in o to the law and the commands,
Pr 30:17 that scorns o to a mother,
Lk 23:56 Sabbath in o to the commandment.
Ac 21:24 but that you yourself are living in o
Ro 1: 5 to the o that comes from faith.
5:19 also through the o of the one man
6:16 to o, which leads to righteousness?
16:19 Everyone has heard about your o,
2Co 9:13 for the o that accompanies your
10: 6 once your o is complete.
Phm :21 Confident of your o, I write to you,
Heb 5: 8 he learned o from what he suffered
1Pe 1: 2 for o to Jesus Christ and sprinkling
2Jn : 6 that we walk in o to his commands.

OBEDIENT* (OBEY)

Dt 30:17 heart turns away and you are not o,
Isa 1:19 If you are willing and o,
Lk 2:51 with them and was o to them.
Ac 6: 7 of priests became o to the faith.
2Co 2: 9 if you would stand the test and be o
7:15 he remembers that you were all o,
10: 5 thought to make it o to Christ.
Php 2: 8 and became o to death—
Tit 3: 1 to be o, to be ready
1Pe 1:14 As o children, do not conform

OBEY (OBEDIENCE OBEDIENT OBEYED OBEYING OBEYS)

Ex 12:24 "O these instructions as a lasting
19: 5 Now if you o me fully and keep my
24: 7 the LORD has said; we will o."
Lev 18: 4 You must o my laws and be careful
25:18 and be careful to o my laws,
Nu 15:40 remember to o all my commands
Dt 5:27 We will listen and o."
6: 3 careful to o so that it may go well
6:24 us to o all these decrees
11:13 if you faithfully o the commands I
12:28 to o all these regulations I am
13: 4 Keep his commands and o him;
21:18 son who does not o his father
28: 1 If you fully o the LORD your God
28:15 if you do not o the LORD your
30: 2 and o him with all your heart
30:10 if you o the LORD your God
30:14 and in your heart so you may o it.
32:46 children to o carefully all the words
Jos 1: 7 to o all the law my servant Moses
22: 5 in all his ways, to o his commands,
24:24 the LORD our God and o him."
1Sa 15:22 To o is better than sacrifice,
1Ki 8:61 by his decrees and o his commands
2Ki 17:13 that I commanded your fathers to o
2Ch 34:31 and to o the words of the covenant
Ne 1: 5 who love him and o his commands,
Ps 103: 18 and remember to o his precepts.
103: 20 who o his word.
119: 17 I will o your word.
119: 34 and o it with all my heart.
119: 57 I have promised to o your words.
119: 67 but now I o your word.
119:100 for I o your precepts.
Ps 119:129 therefore I o them.
119:167 I o your statutes,
Pr 5:13 I would not o my teachers
Jer 7:23 I gave them this command: O me,
11: 4 'O me and do everything I
11: 7 and again, saying, "O me."
42: 6 we will o the LORD our God,
Da 9: 4 who love him and o his commands,
Mt 8:27 the winds and the waves o him!"
19:17 to enter life, o the commandments
28:20 to o everything I have commanded
Lk 11:28 hear the word of God and o it."
Jn 14:15 you will o what I command.
14:23 loves me, he will o my teaching.
14:24 not love me will not o my teaching.
15:10 If you o my commands, you will
Ac 5:29 "We must o God rather than men!
5:32 given to those who o him."
Ro 2:13 it is those who o the law who will
6:12 body so that you o its evil desires.
6:16 slaves to the one whom you o—
6:16 yourselves to someone to o him
15:18 in leading the Gentiles to o God
16:26 nations might believe and o him—
Gal 5: 3 obligated to o the whole law.
Eph 6: 1 o your parents in the Lord,
6: 5 o your earthly masters with respect
Col 3:20 o your parents in everything,
3:22 o your earthly masters
2Th 3:14 anyone does not o our instruction
1Ti 3: 4 and see that his children o him
Heb 5: 9 eternal salvation for all who o him
13:17 O your leaders and submit
1Pe 4:17 for those who do not o the gospel
1Jn 3:24 Those who o his commands live
5: 3 love for God: to o his commands.
Rev 12:17 those who o God's commandments
14:12 the saints who o God's

OBEYED (OBEY)

Ge 22:18 blessed, because you have o me."
Jos 1:17 we fully o Moses, so we will obey
Ps 119: 4 that are to be fully o.
Da 9:10 we have not o the LORD our God
Jnh 3: 3 Jonah o the word of the LORD
Mic 5:15 the nations that have not o me."
Jn 15:10 as I have o my Father's commands
15:20 If they o my teaching, they will
17: 6 and they have o your word.
Ac 7:53 through angels but have not o it."
Ro 6:17 you wholeheartedly o the form
Php 2:12 as you have always o—not only
Heb 11: 8 o and went, even though he did not
1Pe 3: 6 who o Abraham and called him her

OBEYING (OBEY)

1Sa 15:22 as in o the voice of the LORD?
Ps 119: 5 steadfast in o your decrees!
Gal 5: 7 and kept you from o the truth?
1Pe 1:22 purified yourselves by o the truth

OBEYS (OBEY)

Lev 18: 5 for the man who o them will live
Pr 19:16 He who o instructions guards his
Eze 20:11 for the man who o them will live
Jn 14:21 has my commands and o them,
Ro 2:27 and yet o the law will condemn you
1Jn 2: 5 if anyone o his word, God's love is

OBLIGATED (OBLIGATION)

Ro 1:14 I am o both to Greeks
Gal 5: 3 himself be circumcised that he is o

OBLIGATION (OBLIGATED)

Ro 8:12 Therefore, brothers, we have an o

OBSCENITY*

Eph 5: 4 Nor should there be o, foolish talk

OBSCURES*

Job 42: 3 'Who is this that o my counsel

OBSERVE (OBSERVING)

Ex 31:13 'You must o my Sabbaths.
Lev 25: 2 the land itself must o a sabbath
Dt 4: 6 O them carefully, for this will show
5:12 "O the Sabbath day
8: 6 O the commands of the LORD
11:22 If you carefully o all these
26:16 carefully o them with all your heart
Ps 37:37 the blameless, o the upright;

OBSERVING (OBSERVE)

Ro 3:27 principle? On that of o the law?
Gal 2:16 a man is not justified by o the law,

Gal 3: 2 you receive the Spirit by o the law,
3: 10 All who rely on o the law are

OBSOLETE

Heb 8: 13 he has made the first one o;

OBSTACLE* (OBSTACLES)

Ro 14: 13 or o in your brother's way.

OBSTACLES (OBSTACLE)

Ro 16: 17 put o in your way that are contrary

OBSTINATE

Isa 65: 2 hands to an o people,
Ro 10: 21 to a disobedient and o people."

OBTAIN (OBTAINED OBTAINS)

Ro 11: 7 sought so earnestly it did not o,
2Ti 2: 10 they too may o the salvation that

OBTAINED (OBTAIN)

Ro 9: 30 not pursue righteousness, have o it,
Php 3: 12 Not that I have already o all this,
Heb 9: 12 having o eternal redemption.

OBTAINS* (OBTAIN)

Pr 12: 2 A good man o favor

OBVIOUS*

Mt 6: 18 so that it will not be o
Gal 5: 19 The acts of the sinful nature are o:
1Ti 5: 24 The sins of some men are o,
5: 25 In the same way, good deeds are o,

OCCASIONS

Eph 6: 18 in the Spirit on all o with all kinds

OFFENDED (OFFENSE)

Pr 18: 19 An o brother is more unyielding

OFFENDERS* (OFFENSE)

1Co 6: 9 nor homosexual o nor thieves

OFFENSE (OFFENDED OFFENDERS OFFENSES OFFENSIVE)

Pr 17: 9 over an o promotes love,
19: 11 it is to his glory to overlook an o.
Gal 5: 11 In that case the o of the cross has

OFFENSES (OFFENSE)

Isa 44: 22 swept away your o like a cloud,
59: 12 For our o are many in your sight,
Eze 18: 30 Repent! Turn away from all your o;
33: 10 "Our o and sins weigh us down,

OFFENSIVE (OFFENSE)

Ps 139: 24 See if there is any o way in me,

OFFER (OFFERED OFFERING OFFERINGS OFFERS)

Ps 4: 5 O right sacrifices
Ro 6: 13 Do not o the parts of your body
12: 1 to o your bodies as living sacrifices,
Heb 9: 25 he enter heaven to o himself again
13: 15 therefore, let us continually o

OFFERED (OFFER)

Isa 50: 6 I o my back to those who beat me,
1Co 9: 13 share in what is o on the altar?
10: 20 of pagans are o to demons,
Heb 7: 27 once for all when he o himself.
9: 14 the eternal Spirit o himself
11: 4 By faith Abel o God a better
11: 17 when God tested him, o Isaac
Jas 5: 15 prayer o in faith will make the sick

OFFERING (OFFER)

Ge 4: 3 of the soil as an o to the LORD.
22: 2 a burnt o on one of the mountains I
22: 8 provide the lamb for the burnt o,
Ex 29: 24 before the LORD as a wave o.
29: 40 quarter of a hin of wine as a drink o.
Lev 1: 3 If the o is a burnt o from the herd,
2: 4 " 'If you bring a grain o baked
3: 1 " 'If someone's o is a fellowship o,
4: 3 a sin o for the sin he has committed
5: 15 It is a guilt o.
7: 37 ordination o and the fellowship o,
9: 24 and consumed the burnt o
22: 18 to fulfill a vow or as a freewill o,
22: 21 a special vow or as a freewill o,
1Sa 13: 9 And Saul offered up the burnt o.
1Ch 21: 26 from heaven on the altar of burnt o.
2Ch 7: 1 and consumed the burnt o
Ps 40: 6 Sacrifice and o you did not desire,
Ps 116: 17 I will sacrifice a thank o to you
Isa 53: 10 the LORD makes his life a guilt o,
Mt 5: 23 if you are o your gift at the altar
Ro 8: 3 likeness of sinful man to be a sin o.
Eph 5: 2 as a fragrant o and sacrifice to God.
Php 2: 17 I am being poured out like a drink o
4: 18 are a fragrant o, an acceptable
2Ti 4: 6 being poured out like a drink o,
Heb 10: 5 "Sacrifice and o you did not desire,
1Pe 2: 5 o spiritual sacrifices acceptable

OFFERINGS (OFFER)

1Sa 15: 22 Does the LORD delight in burnt o
2Ch 35: 7 and goats for the Passover o,
Isa 1: 13 Stop bringing meaningless o!
Hos 6: 6 of God rather than burnt o.
Mal 3: 8 do we rob you?' "In tithes and o.
Mk 12: 33 is more important than all burnt o
Heb 10: 8 First he said, "Sacrifices and o,

OFFERS (OFFER)

Heb 10: 11 and again he o the same sacrifices,

OFFICER (OFFICIALS)

2Ti 2: 4 wants to please his commanding o.

OFFICIALS (OFFICER)

Ex 5: 21 a stench to Pharaoh and his o.
Pr 17: 26 or to flog o for their integrity.
29: 12 all his o become wicked.

OFFSPRING

Ge 3: 15 and between your o and hers;
12: 7 "To your o I will give this land."
13: 16 I will make your o like the dust
26: 4 and through your o all nations
28: 14 blessed through you and your o.
Ex 13: 2 The first o of every womb
Ru 4: 12 Through the o the LORD gives
Isa 44: 3 I will pour out my Spirit on your o,
53: 10 he will see his o and prolong his
Ac 3: 25 'Through your o all peoples
17: 28 own poets have said, 'We are his o.'
17: 29 "Therefore since we are God's o,
Ro 4: 18 said to him, "So shall your o be."
9: 8 who are regarded as Abraham's o.

OG

Nu 21: 33 O king of Bashan and his whole
Ps 136: 20 and O king of Bashan—

OIL

Ex 29: 7 Take the anointing o and anoint
30: 25 It will be the sacred anointing o.
Dt 14: 23 tithe of your grain, new wine and o,
1Sa 10: 1 Then Samuel took a flask of o
16: 13 So Samuel took the horn of o
1Ki 17: 16 and the jug of o did not run dry,
2Ki 4: 6 Then the o stopped flowing.
Ps 23: 5 You anoint my head with o;
45: 7 by anointing you with the o of joy.
104: 15 o to make his face shine,
133: 2 It is like precious o poured
Pr 21: 17 loves wine and o will never be
Isa 1: 6 or soothed with o.
61: 3 the o of gladness
Mt 25: 3 but did not take any o with them.
Heb 1: 9 by anointing you with the o of joy."

OLIVE (OLIVES)

Ge 8: 11 beak was a freshly plucked o leaf!
Jdg 9: 8 said to the o tree, 'Be our king.'
Jer 11: 16 LORD called you a thriving o tree
Zec 4: 3 Also there are two o trees by it,
Ro 11: 17 and you, though a wild o shoot,
11: 24 of an o tree that is wild by nature,
Rev 11: 4 These are the two o trees

OLIVES (OLIVE)

Zec 14: 4 stand on the Mount of O,
Mt 24: 3 sitting on the Mount of O,
Jas 3: 12 a fig tree bear o, or a grapevine bear

OMEGA*

Rev 1: 8 "I am the Alpha and the O,"
21: 6 I am the Alpha and the O,
22: 13 I am the Alpha and the O,

OMIT*

Jer 26: 2 I command you; do not o a word.

OMRI

King of Israel (1Ki 16:21-26).

ONESIMUS*

Col 4: 9 He is coming with O, our faithful
Phm : 10 I appeal to you for my son O,

ONESIPHORUS*

2Ti 1: 16 mercy to the household of O,
4: 19 Aquila and the household of O.

ONIONS*

Nu 11: 5 melons, leeks, o and garlic.

ONYX

Ex 28: 9 "Take two o stones and engrave
28: 20 in the fourth row a chrysolite, an o

OPENHANDED* (HAND)

Dt 15: 8 Rather be o and freely lend him
15: 11 you to be o toward your brothers

OPINIONS*

1Ki 18: 21 will you waver between two o?
Pr 18: 2 but delights in airing his own o.

OPPONENTS (OPPOSE)

Pr 18: 18 and keeps strong o apart.

OPPORTUNE (OPPORTUNITY)

Lk 4: 13 he left him until an o time.

OPPORTUNITY* (OPPORTUNE)

1Sa 18: 21 "Now you have a second o
Jer 46: 17 he has missed his o.'
Mt 26: 16 watched for an o to hand him over.
Mk 14: 11 So he watched for an o to hand him
Lk 22: 6 and watched for an o to hand Jesus
Ac 25: 16 and has had an o to defend himself
Ro 7: 8 seizing the o afforded
7: 11 seizing the o afforded
1Co 16: 12 but he will go when he has the o.
2Co 5: 12 are giving you an o to take pride
11: 12 from under those who want an o
Gal 6: 10 as we have o, let us do good
Eph 5: 16 making the most of every o,
Php 4: 10 but you had no o to show it.
Col 4: 5 make the most of every o.
1Ti 5: 14 to give the enemy no o for slander.
Heb 11: 15 they would have had o to return.

OPPOSE (OPPONENTS OPPOSED OPPOSES OPPOSING OPPOSITION)

Ex 23: 22 and will o those who o you.
1Sa 2: 10 those who o the LORD will be
Job 23: 13 he stands alone, and who can o him
Ac 11: 17 I to think that I could o God?"
2Ti 2: 25 Those who o him he must gently
Tit 1: 9 doctrine and refute those who o it.
2: 8 so that those who o you may be

OPPOSED (OPPOSE)

Gal 2: 11 to Antioch, I o him to his face,
3: 21 therefore, o to the promises of God

OPPOSES (OPPOSE)

Jas 4: 6 "God o the proud
1Pe 5: 5 because, "God o the proud

OPPOSING (OPPOSE)

1Ti 6: 20 the o ideas of what is falsely called

OPPOSITION (OPPOSE)

Heb 12: 3 Consider him who endured such o

OPPRESS (OPPRESSED OPPRESSES OPPRESSION OPPRESSOR)

Ex 1: 11 masters over them to o them
22: 21 "Do not mistreat an alien or o him,
Isa 3: 5 People will o each other—
Eze 22: 29 they o the poor and needy
Da 7: 25 the Most High and o his saints
Am 5: 12 You o the righteous and take bribes
Zec 7: 10 Do not o the widow
Mal 3: 5 who o the widows

OPPRESSED (OPPRESS)

Jdg 2: 18 as they groaned under those who o
Ps 9: 9 The LORD is a refuge for the o,
82: 3 the rights of the poor and o.
146: 7 He upholds the cause of the o
Pr 16: 19 in spirit and among the o
31: 5 and deprive all the o of their rights.
Isa 1: 17 encourage the o.
53: 7 He was o and afflicted,
58: 10 and satisfy the needs of the o,
Zec 10: 2 o for lack of a shepherd.

2Co 2: 1 I would not make another *p* visit
Heb 12: 11 seems pleasant at the time, but *p.*
1Pe 4: 12 at the *p* trial you are suffering,

PAINS (PAIN)
Ge 3: 16 "I will greatly increase your *p*
Mt 24: 8 these are the beginning of birth *p.*
Ro 8: 22 as in the *p* of childbirth right up
Gal 4: 19 again in the *p* of childbirth
1Th 5: 3 as labor *p* on a pregnant woman,

PAIRS
Ge 7: 8 *P* of clean and unclean animals,

PALACE (PALACES)
2Sa 7: 2 "Here I am, living in a *p* of cedar,
Jer 22: 6 is what the LORD says about the *p*
22: 13 "Woe to him who builds his *p*

PALACES (PALACE)
Mt 11: 8 wear fine clothes are in kings' *p.*
Lk 7: 25 and indulge in luxury are in *p.*

PALE
Isa 29: 22 no longer will their faces grow *p.*
Jer 30: 6 every face turned deathly *p?*
Da 10: 8 my face turned deathly *p*
Rev 6: 8 and there before me was a *p* horse!

PALM (PALMS)
Jn 12: 13 They took *p* branches and went out
Rev 7: 9 and were holding *p* branches

PALMS (PALM)
Isa 49: 16 you on the *p* of my hands;

PAMPERS*
Pr 29: 21 If a man *p* his servant from youth,

PANIC
Dt 20: 3 or give way to *p* before them.
1Sa 14: 15 It was a *p* sent by God.
Eze 7: 7 there is *p,* not joy,
Zec 14: 13 by the LORD with great *p.*

PANTS
Ps 42: 1 As the deer *p* for streams of water,

PARABLES
See also JESUS: Parables
Ps 78: 2 I will open my mouth in *p,*
Mt 13: 35 "I will open my mouth in *p,*
Lk 8: 10 but to others I speak in *p,* so that,

PARADISE*
Lk 23: 43 today you will be with me in *p."*
2Co 12: 4 God knows—was caught up to *p.*
Rev 2: 7 of life, which is in the *p* of God.

PARALYTIC
Mt 9: 2 Some men brought to him a *p,*
Mk 2: 3 bringing to him a *p,* carried by four
Ac 9: 33 a *p* who had been bedridden

PARCHED
Ps 143: 6 my soul thirsts for you like a *p* land.

PARCHMENTS*
2Ti 4: 13 and my scrolls, especially the *p.*

PARDON* (PARDONED PARDONS)
2Ch 30: 18 *p* everyone who sets his heart
Job 7: 21 Why do you not *p* my offenses
Isa 55: 7 and to our God, for he will freely *p.*
Joel 3: 21 I will *p."*

PARDONED* (PARDON)
Nu 14: 19 as you have *p* them from the time
Joel 3: 21 bloodguilt, which I have not *p,*

PARDONS* (PARDON)
Mic 7: 18 who *p* sin and forgives

PARENTS
Pr 17: 6 and *p* are the pride of their children
19: 14 wealth are inherited from *p,*
Mt 10: 21 children will rebel against their *p*
Lk 18: 29 left home or wife or brothers or *p*
21: 16 You will be betrayed even by *p,* brothers,
Jn 9: 3 Neither this man nor his *p* sinned,"
Ro 1: 30 they disobey their *p;* they are
2Co 12: 14 for their *p,* but *p* for their children.
Eph 6: 1 Children, obey your *p* in the Lord,
Col 3: 20 obey your *p* in everything,
1Ti 5: 4 repaying their *p* and grandparents,
2Ti 3: 2 disobedient to their *p,* ungrateful,

PARTAKE*
1Co 10: 17 for we all *p* of the one loaf.

PARTIAL* (PARTIALITY)
Pr 18: 5 It is not good to be *p* to the wicked

PARTIALITY (PARTIAL)
Lev 19: 15 do not show *p* to the poor
Dt 1: 17 Do not show *p* in judging;
10: 17 who shows no *p* and accepts no
16: 19 Do not pervert justice or show *p.*
2Ch 19: 7 our God there is no injustice or *p*
Job 32: 21 I will show *p* to no one,
34: 19 who shows no *p* to princes
Pr 24: 23 To show *p* in judging is not good:
Mal 2: 9 have shown *p* in matters of the law
Lk 20: 21 and that you do not show *p*
1Ti 5: 21 keep these instructions without *p,*

PARTICIPANTS (PARTICIPATE)
1Co 10: 20 you to be *p* with demons.

PARTICIPATE (PARTICIPANTS PARTICIPATION)
1Pe 4: 13 rejoice that you *p* in the sufferings
2Pe 1: 4 that through them you may *p*

PARTICIPATION (PARTICIPATE)
1Co 10: 16 is not the bread that we break a *p*

PARTNER (PARTNERS PARTNERSHIP)
Pr 2: 17 who has left the *p* of her youth
Mal 2: 14 though she is your *p,* the wife
1Pe 3: 7 them with respect as the weaker *p*

PARTNERS (PARTNER)
Eph 5: 7 Therefore do not be *p* with them.

PARTNERSHIP* (PARTNER)
Php 1: 5 because of your *p* in the gospel

PASS (PASSED PASSER-BY PASSING)
Ex 12: 13 and when I see the blood, I will *p*
33: 19 goodness to *p* in front of you,
1Ki 9: 8 all who *p* by will be appalled
19: 11 for the LORD is about to *p* by."
Ps 90: 10 for they quickly *p,* and we fly away.
105: 19 till what he foretold came to *p,*
Isa 31: 5 he will *'p* over' it and will rescue it
43: 2 When you *p* through the waters,
62: 10 *P* through, *p* through the gates!
Jer 22: 8 "People from many nations will *p*
La 1: 12 to you, all you who *p* by?
Da 7: 14 dominion that will not *p* away,
Am 5: 17 for I will *p* through your midst,"
Mt 24: 34 will certainly not *p* away
24: 35 Heaven and earth will *p* away,
Mk 13: 31 Heaven and earth will *p* away,
Lk 21: 33 Heaven and earth will *p* away,
1Co 13: 8 there is knowledge, it will *p* away.
Jas 1: 10 he will *p* away like a wild flower.
1Jn 2: 17 The world and its desires *p* away,

PASSED (PASS)
Ge 15: 17 a blazing torch appeared and *p*
Ex 33: 22 you with my hand until I have *p* by.
2Ch 21: 20 He *p* away, to no one's regret,
Ps 57: 1 wings until the disaster has *p.*
Lk 10: 32 saw him, *p* by on the other side.
1Co 15: 3 For what I received I *p* on to you
Heb 11: 29 By faith the people *p*

PASSER-BY* (PASS)
Pr 26: 10 is he who hires a fool or any *p.*
26: 17 is a *p* who meddles

PASSING (PASS)
1Co 7: 31 world in its present form is *p* away.
1Jn 2: 8 because the darkness is *p*

PASSION* (PASSIONATE PASSIONS)
Hos 7: 6 Their *p* smolders all night;
1Co 7: 9 better to marry than to burn with *p.*

PASSIONATE* (PASSION)
1Th 4: 5 not in *p* lust like the heathen,

PASSIONS* (PASSION)
Ro 7: 5 the sinful *p* aroused
Gal 5: 24 crucified the sinful nature with its *p*
Tit 2: 12 to ungodliness and worldly *p,*
3: 3 and enslaved by all kinds of *p*

PASSOVER
Ex 12: 11 Eat it in haste; it is the LORD's *P.*
Nu 9: 2 Have the Israelites celebrate the *P*
Dt 16: 1 celebrate the *P* of the LORD your
Jos 5: 10 the Israelites celebrated the *P.*
2Ki 23: 21 "Celebrate the *P* to the LORD
Ezr 6: 19 the exiles celebrated the *P.*
Mk 14: 12 customary to sacrifice the *P* lamb,
Lk 22: 1 called the *P,* was approaching,
1Co 5: 7 our *P* lamb, has been sacrificed.
Heb 11: 28 he kept the *P* and the sprinkling

PAST
Isa 43: 18 do not dwell on the *p.*
65: 16 For the *p* troubles will be forgotten
Ro 15: 4 in the *p* was written to teach us,
16: 25 the mystery hidden for long ages *p,*
Eph 3: 9 which for ages *p* was kept hidden
Heb 1: 1 In the *p* God spoke

PASTORS*
Eph 4: 11 and some to be *p* and teachers,

PASTURE (PASTURES)
Ps 37: 3 dwell in the land and enjoy safe *p.*
95: 7 and we are the people of his *p,*
100: 3 we are his people, the sheep of his *p*
Jer 50: 7 against the LORD, their true *p,*
Eze 34: 13 I will *p* them on the mountains
Zec 11: 4 "*P* the flock marked for slaughter.
Jn 10: 9 come in and go out, and find *p.*

PASTURES (PASTURE)
Ps 23: 2 He makes me lie down in green *p,*

PATCH
Jer 10: 5 Like a scarecrow in a melon *p,*
Mt 9: 16 No one sews a *p* of unshrunk cloth

PATH (PATHS)
Ps 16: 11 known to me the *p* of life;
27: 11 lead me in a straight *p*
119: 32 I run in the *p* of your commands,
119: 105 and a light for my *p.*
Pr 2: 9 and fair—every good *p.*
12: 28 along that *p* is immortality.
15: 10 awaits him who leaves the *p;*
15: 19 the *p* of the upright is a highway.
15: 24 The *p* of life leads upward
21: 16 from the *p* of understanding
Isa 26: 7 The *p* of the righteous is level;
Jer 31: 9 on a level *p* where they will not
Mt 13: 4 fell along the *p,* and the birds came
Lk 1: 79 to guide our feet into the *p* of peace
2Co 6: 3 no stumbling block in anyone's *p,*

PATHS (PATH)
Ps 23: 3 He guides me in *p* of righteousness
25: 4 teach me your *p;*
Pr 2: 13 who leave the straight *p*
3: 6 and he will make your *p* straight.
4: 11 and lead you along straight *p.*
4: 26 Make level *p* for your feet
5: 21 and he examines all his *p.*
8: 20 along the *p* of justice,
22: 5 In the *p* of the wicked lie thorns
Isa 2: 3 so that we may walk in his *p."*
Jer 6: 16 ask for the ancient *p,*
Mic 4: 2 so that we may walk in his *p."*
Mt 3: 3 make straight *p* for him.' "
Ac 2: 28 to me the *p* of life;
Ro 11: 33 and his *p* beyond tracing out!
Heb 12: 13 "Make level *p* for your feet,"

PATIENCE* (PATIENT)
Pr 19: 11 A man's wisdom gives him *p;*
25: 15 Through *p* a ruler can be persuaded
Ecc 7: 8 and *p* is better than pride.
Isa 7: 13 Is it not enough to try the *p* of men?
7: 13 Will you try the *p* of my God also?
Ro 2: 4 and *p,* not realizing that God's
9: 22 bore with great *p* the objects
2Co 6: 6 understanding, *p* and kindness;
Gal 5: 22 joy, peace, *p,* kindness, goodness,
Col 1: 11 may have great endurance and *p,*
3: 12 humility, gentleness and *p.*
1Ti 1: 16 Jesus might display his unlimited *p*
2Ti 3: 10 my purpose, faith, *p,* love,
4: 2 with great *p* and careful instruction
Heb 6: 12 *p* inherit what has been promised.
Jas 5: 10 as an example of *p* in the face
2Pe 3: 15 that our Lord's *p* means salvation,

PATIENT* (PATIENCE PATIENTLY)
Ne 9:30 For many years you were *p*
Job 6:11 What prospects, that I should be *p?*
Pr 14:29 A *p* man has great understanding,
15:18 but a *p* man calms a quarrel.
16:32 Better a *p* man than a warrior,
Mt 18:26 'Be *p* with me,' he begged,
18:29 'Be *p* with me, and I will pay you
Ro 12:12 Be joyful in hope, *p* in affliction,
1Co 13: 4 Love is *p*, love is kind.
2Co 1: 6 produces in you *p* endurance
Eph 4: 2 humble and gentle; be *p*,
1Th 5:14 help the weak, be *p* with everyone.
Jas 5: 7 Be *p*, then, brothers,
5: 7 and how *p* he is for the autumn
5: 8 You too, be *p* and stand firm,
2Pe 3: 9 He is *p* with you, not wanting
Rev 1: 9 *p* endurance that are ours in Jesus,
13:10 This calls for *p* endurance
14:12 This calls for *p* endurance

PATIENTLY* (PATIENT)
Ps 37: 7 still before the LORD and wait *p*
40: 1 I waited *p* for the LORD;
Isa 38:13 I waited *p* till dawn,
Hab 3:16 Yet I will wait *p* for the day
Ac 26: 3 I beg you to listen to me *p*.
Ro 8:25 we do not yet have, we wait for it *p*.
Heb 6:15 after waiting *p*, Abraham received
1Pe 3:20 ago when God waited *p* in the days
Rev 3:10 kept my command to endure *p*,

PATTERN
Ex 25:40 according to the *p* shown you
Ro 5:14 who was a *p* of the one to come.
12: 2 longer to the *p* of this world,
2Ti 1:13 keep as the *p* of sound teaching,
Heb 8: 5 according to the *p* shown you

PAUL
Also called Saul (Ac 13:9). Pharisee from Tarsus (Ac 9:11; Php 3:5). Apostle (Gal 1). At stoning of Stephen (Ac 8:1). Persecuted Church (Ac 9:1-2; Gal 1:13). Vision of Jesus on road to Damascus (Ac 9:4-9; 26:12-18). In Arabia (Gal 1:17). Preached in Damascus; escaped death through the wall in a basket (Ac 9:19-25). In Jerusalem; sent back to Tarsus (Ac 9:26-30).
Brought to Antioch by Barnabas (Ac 11:22-26). First missionary journey to Cyprus and Galatia (Ac 13-14). Stoned at Lystra (Ac 14:19-20). At Jerusalem council (Ac 15). Split with Barnabas over Mark (Ac 15:36-41).
Second missionary journey with Silas (Ac 16-20). Called to Macedonia (Ac 16:6-10). Freed from prison in Philippi (Ac 16:16-40). In Thessalonica (Ac 17:1-9). Speech in Athens (Ac 17:16-33). In Corinth (Ac 18). In Ephesus (Ac 19). Return to Jerusalem (Ac 20). Farewell to Ephesian elders (Ac 20:13-38). Arrival in Jerusalem (Ac 21:1-26). Arrested (Ac 21:27-36). Addressed crowds (Ac 22), Sanhedrin (Ac 23:1-11). Transferred to Caesarea (Ac 23:12-35). Trial before Felix (Ac 24), Festus (Ac 25:1-12). Before Agrippa (Ac 25:13-26:32). Voyage to Rome; shipwreck (Ac 27). Arrival in Rome (Ac 28).
Epistles: Romans, 1 and 2 Corinthians, Galatians, Ephesians, Philippians, Colossians, 1 and 2 Thessalonians, 1 and 2 Timothy, Titus, Philemon.

PAVEMENT
Jn 19:13 as the Stone *P* (which

PAY (PAID PAYMENT PAYS REPAID REPAY REPAYING)
Lev 26:43 They will *p* for their sins
Dt 7:12 If you *p* attention to these laws
Pr 4: 1 *p* attention and gain understanding
4:20 My son, *p* attention to what I say;
5: 1 My son, *p* attention to my wisdom,
6:31 if he is caught, he must *p* sevenfold,
19:19 man must *p* the penalty;
22:17 *P* attention and listen
24:29 I'll *p* that man back for what he did
Eze 40: 4 and *p* attention to everything I am
Zec 11:12 give me my *p*; but if not, keep it."
Mt 20: 2 He agreed to *p* them a denarius
22:16 you *p* no attention to who they are.
22:17 Is it right to *p* taxes to Caesar
Lk 3:14 falsely—be content with your *p*."
19: 8 I will *p* back four times the amount
Ro 13: 6 This is also why you *p* taxes,
2Pe 1:19 you will do well to *p* attention to it,

PAYMENT (PAY)
Ps 49: 8 no *p* is ever enough—
Php 4:18 I have received full *p* and

PAYS (PAY)
Pr 17:13 If a man *p* back evil for good,
1Th 5:15 sure that nobody *p* back wrong

PEACE (PEACEABLE PEACEFUL PEACEMAKERS)
Lev 26: 6 " 'I will grant *p* in the land,
Nu 6:26 and give you *p*." '
25:12 him I am making my covenant of *p*
Dt 20:10 make its people an offer of *p*.
Jdg 3:11 So the land had *p* for forty years,
3:30 and the land had *p* for eighty years.
5:31 Then the land had *p* forty years.
6:24 and called it The LORD is *P*.
8:28 the land enjoyed *p* forty years.
1Sa 7:14 And there was *p* between Israel
2Sa 10:19 they made *p* with the Israelites
1Ki 2:33 may there be the LORD's *p* forever
22:44 also at *p* with the king of Israel.
2Ki 9:17 come in *p*?' "The horseman rode
1Ch 19:19 they made *p* with David
22: 9 and I will grant Israel *p*
2Ch 14: 1 and in his days the country was at *p*
20:30 kingdom of Jehoshaphat was at *p*,
Job 3:26 I have no *p*, no quietness;
22:21 to God and be at *p* with him;
Ps 29:11 LORD blesses his people with *p*.
34:14 seek *p* and pursue it.
37:11 and enjoy great *p*.
37:37 there is a future for the man of *p*.
85:10 righteousness and *p* kiss each other
119:165 Great *p* have they who love your
120: 7 I am a man of *p*;
122: 6 Pray for the *p* of Jerusalem:
147:14 He grants *p* to your borders
Pr 12:20 but joy for those who promote *p*.
14:30 A heart at *p* gives life to the body,
16: 7 his enemies live at *p* with him.
17: 1 Better a dry crust with *p* and quiet
Ecc 3: 8 a time for war and a time for *p*.
Isa 9: 6 Everlasting Father, Prince of *P*.
14: 7 All the lands are at rest and at *p*;
26: 3 You will keep in perfect *p*
32:17 The fruit of righteousness will be *p*;
48:18 your *p* would have been like a river,
48:22 "There is no *p*," says the LORD,
52: 7 who proclaim *p*,
53: 5 punishment that brought us *p* was
54:10 nor my covenant of *p* be removed,"
55:12 and be led forth in *p*;
57: 2 enter into *p*;
57:19 *P*, *p*, to those far and near,"
57:21 "There is no *p*," says my God,
59: 8 The way of *p* they do not know;
Jer 6:14 '*P*, *p*,' they say,
8:11 "*P*, *p*," . . . there is no *p*.
30:10 Jacob will again have *p*
46:27 Jacob will again have *p*
Eze 13:10 "*P*," when there is no *p*,
34:25 " 'I will make a covenant of *p*
37:26 I will make a covenant of *p*
Mic 5: 5 And he will be their *p*.
Zec 8:19 Therefore love truth and *p*."
9:10 He will proclaim *p* to the nations.
Mal 2: 5 a covenant of life and *p*,
2: 6 He walked with me in *p*
Mt 10:34 I did not come to bring *p*,
Mk 9:50 and be at *p* with each other."
Lk 1:79 to guide our feet into the path of *p*
2:14 on earth *p* to men on whom his
19:38 "*P* in heaven and glory
Jn 14:27 *P* I leave with you; my *p*
16:33 so that in me you may have *p*.
Ro 1: 7 and *p* to you from God our Father
2:10 and *p* for everyone who does good:
5: 1 we have *p* with God
8: 6 by the Spirit is life and *p*;
12:18 on you, live at *p* with everyone.
14:19 effort to do what leads to *p*
1Co 7:15 God has called us to live in *p*.
14:33 a God of disorder but of *p*.
2Co 13:11 be of one mind, live in *p*.
Gal 5:22 joy, *p*, patience, kindness,
Eph 2:14 he himself is our *p*, who has made
2:15 thus making *p*, and in this one body
2:17 and *p* to those who were near.
6:15 comes from the gospel of *p*.
Php 4: 7 the *p* of God, which transcends all
Col 1:20 by making *p* through his blood,
3:15 Let the *p* of Christ rule
Col 3:15 of one body you were called to *p*.
1Th 5: 3 While people are saying, "*P*
5:13 Live in *p* with each other.
5:23 the God of *p*, sanctify you through
2Th 3:16 the Lord of *p* himself give you *p*
2Ti 2:22 righteousness, faith, love and *p*,
Heb 7: 2 "king of Salem" means "king of *p*."
12:11 *p* for those who have been trained
12:14 effort to live in *p* with all men
13:20 May the God of *p*, who
1Pe 3:11 he must seek *p* and pursue it.
2Pe 3:14 blameless and at *p* with him.
Rev 6: 4 power to take *p* from the earth

PEACEABLE* (PEACE)
Tit 3: 2 to slander no one, to be *p*

PEACEFUL (PEACE)
1Ti 2: 2 that we may live *p* and quiet lives

PEACE-LOVING
Jas 3:17 then *p*, considerate

PEACEMAKERS* (PEACE)
Mt 5: 9 Blessed are the *p*,
Jas 3:18 *P* who sow in peace raise a harvest

PEARL* (PEARLS)
Rev 21:21 each gate made of a single *p*.

PEARLS (PEARL)
Mt 7: 6 do not throw your *p* to pigs.
13:45 like a merchant looking for fine *p*.
1Ti 2: 9 or gold or *p* or expensive clothes,
Rev 21:21 The twelve gates were twelve *p*,

PEDDLE*
2Co 2:17 we do not *p* the word of God

PEG
Jdg 4:21 She drove the *p* through his temple

PEKAH
King of Israel (2Ki 16:25-31; Isa 7:1).

PEKAHIAH*
Son of Menahem; king of Israel (2Ki 16:22-26).

PEN
Ps 45: 1 my tongue is the *p*
Mt 5:18 letter, not the least stroke of a *p*,
Jn 10: 1 who does not enter the sheep *p*

PENETRATES*
Heb 4:12 it *p* even to dividing soul and spirit,

PENNIES* (PENNY)
Lk 12: 6 not five sparrows sold for two *p?*

PENNY* (PENNIES)
Mt 5:26 out until you have paid the last *p*.
10:29 Are not two sparrows sold for a *p?*
Mk 12:42 worth only a fraction of a *p*.
Lk 12:59 out until you have paid the last *p*."

PENTECOST*
Ac 2: 1 of *P* came, they were all together
20:16 if possible, by the day of *P*.
1Co 16: 8 I will stay on at Ephesus until *P*,

PEOPLE (PEOPLES)
Ge 11: 6 as one *p* speaking the same
Ex 5: 1 Let my *p* go,
6: 7 take you as my own *p*,
8:23 between my *p* and your *p*.
15:13 the *p* you have redeemed.
19: 8 The *p* all responded together,
24: 3 Moses went and told the *p*
32: 1 When the *p* saw that Moses
32: 9 they are a stiff-necked *p*.
33:13 this nation is your *p*.
Lev 9: 7 for yourself and the *p*;
16:24 the burnt offering for the *p*,
26:12 and you will be my *p*.
Nu 11:11 burden of all these *p* on
14:11 *p* treat me with contempt?
14:19 forgive the sin of these *p*,
22: 5 A *p* has come out of Egypt
Dt 4: 6 a wise and understanding *p*.
4:20 the *p* of his inheritance,
5:28 what this *p* said to you.
7: 6 a *p* holy to the LORD
26:18 that you are his *p*,
31: 7 you must go with this *p*

Dt 31:16 these *p* will soon prostitute
32: 9 the LORD's portion is his *p*,
32:43 atonement for his land and *p*.
33:29 a *p* saved by the LORD?
Jos 1: 6 you will lead this *p*
24:24 the *p* said to Joshua,
Jdg 2: 7 *p* served the LORD throughout
Ru 1:16 Your *p* will be my *p*
1Sa 8: 7 the *p* are saying to you;
12:22 LORD will not reject his *p*,
2Sa 5: 2 will shepherd my *p* Israel
7:10 provide a place for my *p*
1Ki 3: 8 among the *p* you have chosen,
8:30 your *p* Israel when they pray
8:56 has given rest to his *p*
18:39 when all the *p* saw this,
2Ki 23: 3 all the *p* pledged themselves
1Ch 17:21 to redeem *p* for himself
29:17 how willingly your *p* who are
2Ch 2:11 Because the LORD loves his *p*,
7: 5 *p* dedicated the temple
7:14 if my *p*, who are called
30: 6 "*P* of Israel, return to
36:16 was aroused against his *p*
Ezr 2: 1 These are the *p* of the
3: 1 *p* assembled as one man
Ne 1:10 your *p*, whom you redeemed
4: 6 *p* worked with all their heart
8: 1 *p* assembled as one man
Est 3: 6 to destroy all Mordecai's *p*,
Job 12: 2 Doubtless you are the *p*,
Ps 29:11 gives strength to his *p*;
33:12 *p* he chose for his inheritance
50: 4 that he may judge his *p*
53: 6 restores the fortunes of his *p*,
81:13 If my *p* would but listen
94:14 LORD will not reject his *p*;
95: 7 we are the *p* of his pasture,
95:10 a *p* whose hearts go astray,
125: 2 the LORD surrounds his *p*
135: 14 LORD will vindicate his *p*
144: 15 *p* whose God is the LORD.
Pr 14:34 sin is a disgrace to any *p*.
29: 2 righteous thrive, the *p* rejoice
29:18 the *p* cast off restraint
Isa 1: 3 my *p* do not understand.
1: 4 a *p* loaded with guilt,
5:13 my *p* will go into exile
6:10 the heart of this *p* calloused;
9: 2 the *p* walking in darkness
12:12 will assemble the scattered *p*
19:25 Blessed be Egypt my *p*,
25: 8 remove the disgrace of his *p*
29:13 These *p* come near to me
40: 1 Comfort, comfort my *p*
40: 7 Surely the *p* are grass.
42: 6 a covenant for the *p*
49:13 the LORD comforts his *p*
51: 4 "Listen to me, my *p*;
52: 6 my *p* will know my name;
53: 8 for the transgression of my *p*
60:21 will all your *p* be righteous
62:12 will be called the Holy *P*,
65:23 they will be a *p* blessed
Jer 2:11 my *p* have exchanged their
2:13 *p* have committed two sins:
2:32 my *p* have forgotten me,
4:22 My *p* are fools;
5:14 Because the *p* have spoken
5:31 my *p* love it this way
7:16 do not pray for this *p*
18:15 my *p* have forgotten me;
25: 7 They will be my *p*,
30: 3 I will bring my *p* Israel
Eze 13:23 I will save my *p* from
36: 8 fruit for my *p* Israel,
36:28 you will be my *p*,
36:38 be filled with flocks of *p*.
37:13 Then you, my *p*, will know
38:14 *p* Israel are living in safety
39: 7 name among my *p* Israel.
Da 7:27 saints, the *p* of the Most High.
8:24 mighty men and the holy *p*
9:19 your *p* bear your name
9:24 are decreed for your *p*
9:26 *p* of the ruler who will come
10:14 will happen to your *p*
11:32 *p* who know their God will
12: 1 prince who protects your *p*.
Hos 1:10 'You are not my *p*,'
2:23 'You are my *p*';
4:14 a *p* without understanding
Joel 2:18 and take pity on his *p*.
3:16 be a refuge for his *p*,
Am 9:14 back my exiled *p* Israel;
Mic 6: 2 a case against his *p*;
7:14 Shepherd your *p* with
Hag 1:12 remnant of the *p* obeyed
Zec 2:11 and will become my *p*.
8: 7 I will save my *p*
13: 9 will say, 'They are my *p*,'
Mk 7: 6 *p* honor me with their lips
8:27 "Who do *p* say I am?"
Lk 1:17 make ready a *p* prepared
1:68 and has redeemed his *p*.
2:10 joy that will be for all the *p*.
21:23 and wrath against this *p*.
Jn 11:50 one man die for the *p*
18:14 if one man died for the *p*.
Ac 15:14 from the Gentiles a *p*.
18:10 have many *p* in this city.
Ro 9:25 will call them 'my *p*.'
11: 1 Did God reject his *p*?
15:10 O Gentiles, with his *p*."
2Co 6:16 and they will be my *p*."
Tit 2:14 a *p* that are his very own,
Heb 2:17 for the sins of the *p*.
4: 9 a Sabbath-rest for the *p*
5: 3 for the sins of the *p*.
10:30 Lord will judge his *p*.
11:25 mistreated along with the *p*
13:12 to make the *p* holy
1Pe 2: 9 you are a chosen *p*,
2:10 Once you were not a *p*,
2:10 you are the *p* of God;
2Pe 2: 1 false prophets among the *p*,
3:11 kind of *p* ought you to be?
Rev 18: 4 "Come out of her, my *p*,
21: 3 They will be his *p*,

PEOPLES (PEOPLE)

Ge 17:16 kings of *p* will come from her
25:23 two *p* from within you will
27:29 and *p* bow down to you
28: 3 become a community of *p*.
48: 4 you a community of *p*.
Dt 14: 2 of all the *p* on the face of
28:10 Then all the *p* on earth
32: 8 set up boundaries for the *p*
Jos 4:24 all the *p* of the earth might
1Ki 8:43 all the *p* of the earth may
2Ch 7:20 of ridicule among all *p*.
Ps 9: 8 he will govern the *p*
67: 5 may all the *p* praise you.
87: 6 in the register of the *p*:
96:10 he will judge the *p*
Isa 2: 4 settle disputes for many *p*.
17:12 Oh, the uproar of the *p*—
25: 6 of rich food for all *p*,
34: 1 pay attention, you *p*!
55: 4 him a witness to the *p*,
Jer 10: 3 customs of the *p* are worthless
Da 7:14 all *p*, nations and men
Mic 4: 1 and *p* will stream to it.
4: 3 will judge between many *p*
5: 7 in the midst of many *p*
Zep 3: 9 purify the lips of the *p*,
3:20 among all the *p* of the
Zec 8:20 Many *p* and the inhabitants
12: 2 all the surrounding *p* reeling.
Rev 10:11 prophesy again about many *p*,
17:15 the prostitute sits, are *p*,

PEOR

Nu 25: 3 joined in worshiping the Baal of *P*.
Dt 4: 3 who followed the Baal of *P*,

PERCEIVE (PERCEIVING)

Ps 139: 2 you *p* my thoughts from afar.
Pr 24:12 not he who weighs the heart *p* it?

PERCEIVING* (PERCEIVE)

Isa 6: 9 be ever seeing, but never *p*.'
Mt 13:14 you will be ever seeing but never *p*.
Mk 4:12 may be ever seeing but never *p*,
Ac 28:26 you will be ever seeing but never *p*

PERFECT* (PERFECTER PERFECTING PERFECTION)

Dt 32: 4 He is the Rock, his works are *p*,
2Sa 22:31 "As for God, his way is *p*;
22:33 and makes my way *p*.
Job 36: 4 one *p* in knowledge is with you.
37:16 of him who is *p* in knowledge?
Ps 18:30 As for God, his way is *p*;
18:32 and makes my way *p*.
19: 7 The law of the LORD is *p*,
50: 2 From Zion, *p* in beauty,
64: 6 "We have devised a *p* plan!"
SS 6: 9 but my dove, my *p* one, is unique,
Isa 25: 1 for in *p* faithfulness
26: 3 You will keep in *p* peace
Eze 16:14 had given you made your beauty *p*,
27: 3 "I am *p* in beauty."
28:12 full of wisdom and *p* in beauty.
Mt 5:48 Do not even pagans do that? Be *p*,
5:48 as your heavenly Father is *p*.
19:21 answered, "If you want to be *p*,
Ro 12: 2 his good, pleasing and *p* will.
2Co 12: 9 for my power is made *p*
Php 3:12 or have already been made *p*,
Col 1:28 so that we may present everyone *p*
3:14 binds them all together in *p* unity.
Heb 2:10 the author of their salvation *p*
5: 9 what he suffered and, once made *p*,
7:19 useless (for the law made nothing *p*
7:28 who has been made *p* forever.
9:11 and more *p* tabernacle that is not
10: 1 make *p* those who draw
10:14 he has made *p* forever those who
11:40 with us would they be made *p*.
12:23 spirits of righteous men made *p*,
Jas 1:17 Every good and *p* gift is from above
1:25 into the *p* law that gives freedom,
3: 2 he is a *p* man, able
1Jn 4:18 But *p* love drives out fear,
4:18 The one who fears is not made *p*

PERFECTER* (PERFECT)

Heb 12: 2 the author and *p* of our faith,

PERFECTING* (PERFECT)

2Co 7: 1 *p* holiness out of reverence for God

PERFECTION* (PERFECT)

Ps 119: 96 To all *p* I see a limit;
La 2:15 the *p* of beauty,
Eze 27: 4 builders brought your beauty to *p*.
27:11 they brought your beauty to *p*.
28:12 " 'You were the model of *p*,
1Co 13:10 but when *p* comes, the imperfect
2Co 13: 9 and our prayer is for your *p*.
13:11 Aim for *p*, listen to my appeal,
Heb 7:11 If *p* could have been attained

PERFORM (PERFORMED PERFORMS)

Ex 3:20 with all the wonders that I will *p*
2Sa 7:23 to *p* great and awesome wonders
Jn 3: 2 no one could *p* the miraculous

PERFORMED (PERFORM)

Mt 11:21 If the miracles that were *p*
Jn 10:41 John never *p* a miraculous

PERFORMS (PERFORM)

Ps 77:14 You are the God who *p* miracles;

PERFUME

Ecc 7: 1 A good name is better than fine *p*,
SS 1: 3 your name is like *p* poured out.
Mk 14: 3 jar of very expensive *p*,

PERIL

2Co 1:10 us from such a deadly *p*,

PERISH (PERISHABLE PERISHED PERISHES PERISHING)

Ge 6:17 Everything on earth will *p*.
Est 4:16 And if I *p*, I *p*."
Ps 1: 6 but the way of the wicked will *p*.
37:20 But the wicked will *p*:
73:27 Those who are far from you will *p*;
102: 26 They will *p*, but you remain;
Pr 11:10 when the wicked *p*, there are
19: 9 and he who pours out lies will *p*.
21:28 A false witness will *p*,
28:28 when the wicked *p*, the righteous
Isa 1:28 who forsake the LORD will *p*.
29:14 the wisdom of the wise will *p*,
60:12 that will not serve you will *p*;
Zec 11: 9 the dying die, and the perishing *p*.
Lk 13: 3 unless you repent, you too will all *p*.
13: 5 unless you repent, you too will all *p*
21:18 But not a hair of your head will *p*.
Jn 3:16 whoever believes in him shall not *p*
10:28 eternal life, and they shall never *p*;
Ro 2:12 apart from the law will also *p* apart
Col 2:22 These are all destined to *p* with use,
2Th 2:10 They *p* because they refused
Heb 1:11 They will *p*, but you remain;
1Pe 1: 4 into an inheritance that can never *p*
2Pe 3: 9 not wanting anyone to *p*,

PERISHABLE (PERISH)

1Co 15:42 The body that is sown is *p*,

PIGEONS

Lev 5:11 afford two doves or two young *p*,
Lk 2:24 "a pair of doves or two young *p*."

PIGS (PIG'S)

Mt 7:6 do not throw your pearls to *p*.
Mk 5:11 A large herd of *p* was feeding on

PILATE

Governor of Judea. Questioned Jesus (Mt 27:1-26; Mk 15:15; Lk 22:66-23:25; Jn 18:28-19:16); sent him to Herod (Lk 23:6-12); consented to his crucifixion when crowds chose Barabbas (Mt 27:15-26; Mk 15:6-15; Lk 23:13-25; Jn 19:1-10).

PILLAR (PILLARS)

Ge 19:26 and she became a *p* of salt.
Ex 13:21 ahead of them in a *p* of cloud
1Ti 3:15 the *p* and foundation of the truth.
Rev 3:12 who overcomes I will make a *p*

PILLARS (PILLAR)

Gal 2:9 and John, those reputed to be *p*,

PINIONS

Dt 32:11 and carries them on its *p*.

PISGAH

Dt 3:27 Go up to the top of *P* and look west

PIT

Ps 7:15 falls into the *p* he has made.
40:2 He lifted me out of the slimy *p*,
103:4 who redeems your life from the *p*
Pr 23:27 for a prostitute is a deep *p*
26:27 If a man digs a *p*, he will fall into it;
Isa 24:17 Terror and *p* and snare await you,
38:17 me from the *p* of destruction;
Mt 15:14 a blind man, both will fall into a *p*."

PITCH

Ge 6:14 and coat it with *p* inside and out.
Ex 2:3 and coated it with tar and *p*.

PITIED (PITY)

1Co 15:19 we are to be *p* more than all men.

PITY (PITIED)

Ps 72:13 He will take *p* on the weak
Ecc 4:10 But *p* the man who falls
Lk 10:33 when he saw him, he took *p* on him

PLAGUE (PLAGUED PLAGUES)

2Ch 6:28 "When famine or *p* comes
Ps 91:6 nor the *p* that destroys at midday.

PLAGUED* (PLAGUE)

Ps 73:5 they are not *p* by human ills.
73:14 All day long I have been *p*;

PLAGUES (PLAGUE)

Hos 13:14 Where, O death, are your *p*?
Rev 21:9 full of the seven last *p* came
22:18 to him the *p* described in this book.

PLAIN

Isa 40:4 the rugged places a *p*.
Ro 1:19 what may be known about God is *p*

PLAN (PLANNED PLANS)

Ex 26:30 according to the *p* shown you
Job 42:2 no *p* of yours can be thwarted.
Pr 14:22 those who *p* what is good find love
21:30 is no wisdom, no insight, no *p*
Am 3:7 nothing without revealing his *p*
Eph 1:11 predestined according to the *p*

PLANK

Mt 7:3 attention to the *p* in your own eye?
Lk 6:41 attention to the *p* in your own eye?

PLANNED (PLAN)

Ps 40:5 The things you *p* for us
Isa 14:24 "Surely, as I have *p*, so it will be,
23:9 The LORD Almighty *p* it,
46:11 what I have *p*, that will I do.
Heb 11:40 God had *p* something better for us

PLANS (PLAN)

Ps 20:4 and make all your *p* succeed.
33:11 *p* of the LORD stand firm forever,
Pr 15:22 *P* fail for lack of counsel,
16:3 and your *p* will succeed.
19:21 Many are the *p* in a man's heart,
20:18 Make *p* by seeking advice;
Isa 29:15 to hide their *p* from the LORD,
30:1 those who carry out *p* that are not
32:8 But the noble man makes noble *p*,
2Co 1:17 Or do I make my *p* in a worldly

PLANT (PLANTED PLANTING PLANTS)

Am 9:15 I will *p* Israel in their own land,
Mt 15:13 "Every *p* that my heavenly Father

PLANTED (PLANT)

Ge 2:8 the LORD God had *p* a garden
Ps 1:3 He is like a tree *p* by streams
Jer 17:8 He will be like a tree *p* by the water
Mt 15:13 Father has not *p* will be pulled
21:33 was a landowner who *p* a vineyard.
Lk 13:6 "A man had a fig tree, *p*
1Co 3:6 I *p* the seed, Apollos watered it,
Jas 1:21 humbly accept the word *p* in you,

PLANTING (PLANT)

Isa 61:3 a *p* of the LORD

PLANTS (PLANT)

Pr 31:16 out of her earnings she *p* a vineyard
1Co 3:7 So neither he who *p* nor he who
9:7 Who *p* a vineyard and does not eat

PLATTER

Mk 6:25 head of John the Baptist on a *p*."

PLAY (PLAYED)

1Sa 16:23 David would take his harp and *p*.
Isa 11:8 The infant will *p* near the hole

PLAYED (PLAY)

Lk 7:32 " 'We *p* the flute for you,
1Co 14:7 anyone know what tune is being *p*

PLEA (PLEAD PLEADED PLEADS)

1Ki 8:28 to your servant's prayer and his *p*
Ps 102:17 he will not despise their *p*.
La 3:56 You heard my *p*: "Do not close

PLEAD (PLEA)

Isa 1:17 *p* the case of the widow.

PLEADED (PLEA)

2Co 12:8 Three times I *p* with the Lord

PLEADS (PLEA)

Job 16:21 on behalf of a man he *p* with God

PLEASANT (PLEASE)

Ge 49:15 and how *p* is his land,
Ps 16:6 for me in *p* places;
133:1 How good and *p* it is
135:3 sing praise to his name, for that is *p*
147:1 how *p* and fitting to praise him!
Pr 2:10 knowledge will be *p* to your soul.
3:17 Her ways are *p* ways,
16:21 and *p* words promote instruction.
16:24 *P* words are a honeycomb,
Isa 30:10 Tell us *p* things,
1Th 3:6 that you always have *p* memories
Heb 12:11 No discipline seems *p* at the time,

PLEASANTNESS* (PLEASE)

Pr 27:9 the *p* of one's friend springs

PLEASE (PLEASANT PLEASANTNESS PLEASED PLEASES PLEASING PLEASURE PLEASURES)

Ps 69:31 This will *p* the LORD more
Pr 20:23 and dishonest scales do not *p* him.
Isa 46:10 and I will do all that I *p*.
Jer 6:20 your sacrifices do not *p* me."
27:5 and I give it to anyone I *p*.
Jn 5:30 for I seek not to *p* myself
Ro 8:8 by the sinful nature cannot *p* God.
15:1 of the weak and not to *p* ourselves.
15:2 Each of us should *p* his neighbor
1Co 7:32 affairs—how he can *p* the Lord.
10:33 I try to *p* everybody in every way.
2Co 5:9 So we make it our goal to *p* him,
Gal 1:10 or of God? Or am I trying to *p* men
6:8 the one who sows to *p* the Spirit,
Col 1:10 and may *p* him in every way:
1Th 2:4 We are not trying to *p* men
4:1 how to live in order to *p* God,
2Ti 2:4 wants to *p* his commanding officer.
Tit 2:9 to try to *p* them, not to talk back
Heb 11:6 faith it is impossible to *p* God,

PLEASED (PLEASE)

Dt 28:63 as it *p* the LORD to make you
1Sa 12:22 LORD was *p* to make you his own.
1Ki 3:10 The Lord was *p* that Solomon had
1Ch 29:17 that you test the heart and are *p*
Mic 6:7 Will the LORD be *p*
Mal 1:10 I am not *p* with you," says
Mt 3:17 whom I love; with him I am well *p*
17:5 whom I love; with him I am well *p*.
Mk 1:11 whom I love; with you I am well *p*
Lk 3:22 whom I love; with you I am well *p*
1Co 1:21 God was *p* through the foolishness
Col 1:19 For God was *p* to have all his
Heb 10:6 you were not *p*.
10:8 nor were you *p* with them"
10:38 I will not be *p* with him."
11:5 commended as one who *p* God.
13:16 for with such sacrifices God is *p*.
2Pe 1:17 whom I love; with him I am well *p*

PLEASES (PLEASE)

Job 23:13 He does whatever he *p*.
Ps 115:3 he does whatever *p* him.
135:6 The LORD does whatever *p* him,
Pr 15:8 but the prayer of the upright *p* him.
21:1 it like a watercourse wherever he *p*.
Ecc 2:26 To the man who *p* him, God gives
7:26 man who *p* God will escape her,
Da 4:35 He does as he *p*
Jn 3:8 The wind blows wherever it *p*.
8:29 for I always do what *p* him."
Eph 5:10 truth) and find out what *p* the Lord
Col 3:20 in everything, for this *p* the Lord.
1Ti 2:3 This is good, and *p* God our Savior,
1Jn 3:22 his commands and do what *p* him.

PLEASING (PLEASE)

Ge 2:9 trees that were *p* to the eye
Lev 1:9 an aroma *p* to the LORD.
Ps 19:14 be *p* in your sight,
104:34 May my meditation be *p* to him,
Pr 15:26 but those of the pure are *p* to him.
16:7 When a man's ways are *p*
SS 1:3 *P* is the fragrance of your perfumes
4:10 How much more *p* is your love
7:6 How beautiful you are and how *p*,
Ro 12:1 *p* to God—this is your spiritual
14:18 Christ in this way is *p* to God
Php 4:18 an acceptable sacrifice, *p* to God.
1Ti 5:4 grandparents, for this is *p* to God.
Heb 13:21 may he work in us what is *p* to him,

PLEASURE (PLEASE)

Ps 5:4 You are not a God who takes *p*
51:16 you do not take *p* in burnt offerings
147:10 His *p* is not in the strength
Pr 10:23 A fool finds *p* in evil conduct,
18:2 A fool finds no *p* in understanding
21:17 He who loves *p* will become poor;
Isa 1:11 I have no *p*
Jer 6:10 they find no *p* in it.
Eze 18:23 Do I take any *p* in the death
18:32 For I take no *p* in the death
33:11 I take no *p* in the death
Lk 10:21 Father, for this was your good *p*.
Eph 1:5 in accordance with his *p* and will—
1:9 of his will according to his good *p*,
1Ti 5:6 the widow who lives for *p* is dead
2Ti 3:4 lovers of *p* rather than lovers
2Pe 2:13 Their idea of *p* is to carouse

PLEASURES* (PLEASE)

Ps 16:11 with eternal *p* at your right hand,
Lk 8:14 and *p*, and they do not mature.
Tit 3:3 by all kinds of passions and *p*.
Heb 11:25 rather than to enjoy the *p* of sin
Jas 4:3 may spend what you get on your *p*.
2Pe 2:13 reveling in their *p* while they feast

PLEDGE

Dt 24:17 take the cloak of the widow as a *p*.
1Pe 3:21 but the *p* of a good conscience

PLEIADES

Job 38:31 "Can you bind the beautiful *P*?
Am 5:8 (he who made the *P* and Orion,

PLENTIFUL (PLENTY)

Mt 9:37 harvest is *p* but the workers are
Lk 10:2 harvest is *p*, but the workers are

PLENTY (PLENTIFUL)

2Co 8:14 the present time your *p* will supply
Php 4:12 whether living in *p* or in want.

PLOT (PLOTS)

Est 2:22 Mordecai found out about the p
Ps 2: 1 and the peoples p in vain?
Pr 3:29 not p harm against your neighbor,
Zec 8:17 do not p evil against your neighbor,
Ac 4:25 and the peoples p in vain?

PLOTS (PLOT)

Pr 6:14 who p evil with deceit in his heart

PLOW (PLOWMAN PLOWSHARES)

Lk 9:62 "No one who puts his hand to the p

PLOWMAN (PLOW)

1Co 9:10 because when the p plows

PLOWSHARES (PLOW)

1Sa 13:20 to the Philistines to have their p,
Isa 2: 4 They will beat their swords into p
Joel 3:10 Beat your p into swords
Mic 4: 3 They will beat their swords into p

PLUCK

Mk 9:47 your eye causes you to sin, p it out.

PLUNDER (PLUNDERED)

Ex 3:22 And so you will p the Egyptians."
Est 3:13 of Adar, and to p their goods.
8:11 to p the property of their enemies.
9:10 did not lay their hands on the p.
Pr 22:23 and will p those who p them.
Isa 3:14 the p from the poor is

PLUNDERED (PLUNDER)

Eze 34: 8 lacks a shepherd and so has been p

PLUNGE

1Ti 6: 9 and harmful desires that p men
1Pe 4: 4 think it strange that you do not p

PODS

Lk 15:16 with the p that the pigs were eating,

POINT

Mt 4: 5 on the highest p of the temple.
26:38 with sorrow to the p of death.
Jas 2:10 yet stumbles at just one p is guilty
Rev 2:10 Be faithful, even to the p of death,

POISON

Ps 140: 3 the p of vipers is on their lips.
Mk 16:18 and when they drink deadly p,
Ro 3:13 "The p of vipers is on their lips."
Jas 3: 8 It is a restless evil, full of deadly p.

POLE (POLES)

Nu 21: 8 "Make a snake and put it up on a p;
Dt 16:21 not set up any wooden Asherah p

POLES (POLE)

Ex 25:13 Then make p of acacia wood

POLISHED

Isa 49: 2 he made me into a p arrow

POLLUTE* (POLLUTED POLLUTES)

Nu 35:33 " 'Do not p the land where you are.
Jude : 8 these dreamers p their own bodies,

POLLUTED* (POLLUTE)

Ezr 9:11 entering to possess is a land p
Pr 25:26 Like a muddied spring or a p well
Ac 15:20 to abstain from food p by idols,
Jas 1:27 oneself from being p by the world.

POLLUTES* (POLLUTE)

Nu 35:33 Bloodshed p the land,

PONDER (PONDERED)

Ps 64: 9 and p what he has done.
119:95 but I will p your statutes.

PONDERED (PONDER)

Ps 111: 2 they are p by all who delight
Lk 2:19 up all these things and p them

POOR (POVERTY)

Lev 19:10 Leave them for the p and the alien.
23:22 Leave them for the p and the alien.
27: 8 If anyone making the vow is too p
Dt 15: 4 there should be no p among you,
15: 7 is a p man among your brothers
15:11 There will always be p people
24:12 If the man is p, do not go to sleep
Dt 24:14 advantage of a hired man who is p
Job 5:16 So the p have hope,
24: 4 force all the p of the land
Ps 14: 6 frustrate the plans of the p,
34: 6 This p man called, and the LORD
35:10 You rescue the p from those too
40:17 Yet I am p and needy;
68:10 O God, you provided for the p.
82: 3 maintain the rights of the p
112: 9 scattered abroad his gifts to the p,
113: 7 He raises the p from the dust
140:12 the LORD secures justice for the p
Pr 10: 4 Lazy hands make a man p,
13: 7 to be p, yet has great wealth.
14:20 The p are shunned
14:31 oppresses the p shows contempt
17: 5 who mocks the p shows contempt
19: 1 Better a p man whose walk is
19:17 to the p lends to the LORD,
19:22 better to be p than a liar.
20:13 not love sleep or you will grow p;
21:13 to the cry of the p,
21:17 who loves pleasure will become p;
22: 2 Rich and p have this in common:
22: 9 for he shares his food with the p.
22:22 not exploit the p because they are p
28: 6 Better a p man whose walk is
28:27 to the p will lack nothing,
29: 7 care about justice for the p,
31: 9 defend the rights of the p
31:20 She opens her arms to the p
Ecc 4:13 Better a p but wise youth
Isa 3:14 the plunder from the p is
10: 2 to deprive the p of their rights
14:30 of the p will find pasture,
25: 4 You have been a refuge for the p,
32: 7 schemes to destroy the p with lies,
61: 1 me to preach good news to the p.
Jer 22:16 He defended the cause of the p
Eze 18:12 He oppresses the p and needy.
Am 2: 7 They trample on the heads of the p
4: 1 you women who oppress the p
5:11 You trample on the p
Zec 7:10 or the fatherless, the alien or the p.
Mt 5: 3 saying: "Blessed are the p in spirit,
11: 5 the good news is preached to the p.
19:21 your possessions and give to the p,
26:11 The p you will always have
Mk 12:42 But a p widow came and put
14: 7 The p you will always have
Lk 4:18 me to preach good news to the p.
6:20 "Blessed are you who are p,
11:41 is inside the dish, to the p,
14:13 invite the p, the crippled, the lame,
21: 2 also saw a p widow put
Jn 12: 8 You will always have the p
Ac 9:36 doing good and helping the p.
10: 4 and gifts to the p have come up
24:17 to bring my people gifts for the p
Ro 15:26 for the p among the saints
1Co 13: 3 If I give all I possess to the p
2Co 6:10 sorrowful, yet always rejoicing; p,
8: 9 yet for your sakes he became p,
Gal 2:10 continue to remember the p,
Jas 2: 2 and a p man in shabby clothes
2: 5 not God chosen those who are p
2: 6 But you have insulted the p.

POPULATION*

Pr 14:28 A large p is a king's glory,

PORTION

Nu 18:29 as the LORD's p the best
Dt 32: 9 For the LORD's p is his people,
1Sa 1: 5 But to Hannah he gave a double p
2Ki 2: 9 "Let me inherit a double p
Ps 73:26 and my p forever.
119:57 You are my p, O LORD;
Isa 53:12 Therefore I will give him a p
Jer 10:16 He who is the P of Jacob is not like
La 3:24 to myself, "The LORD is my p;
Zec 2:12 LORD will inherit Judah as his p

PORTRAIT

Lk 20:24 Whose p and inscription are on it?"

PORTRAYED

Gal 3: 1 very eyes Jesus Christ was clearly p

POSITION (POSITIONS)

Ro 12:16 to associate with people of low p.
Jas 1: 9 ought to take pride in his high p.
2Pe 3:17 and fall from your secure p.

POSITIONS (POSITION)

2Ch 20:17 Take up your p; stand firm
Jude : 6 the angels who did not keep their p

POSSESS (POSSESSED POSSESSING POSSESSION POSSESSIONS)

Nu 33:53 for I have given you the land to p.
Dt 4:14 you are crossing the Jordan to p.
Pr 8:12 I p knowledge and discretion.
Jn 5:39 that by them you p eternal life.

POSSESSED (POSSESS)

Jn 10:21 the sayings of a man p by a demon.

POSSESSING* (POSSESS)

2Co 6:10 nothing, and yet p everything.

POSSESSION (POSSESS)

Ge 15: 7 to give you this land to take p of it
Ex 6: 8 I will give it to you as a p.
19: 5 nations you will be my treasured p.
Nu 13:30 "We should go up and take p
Dt 7: 6 to be his people, his treasured p.
Jos 1:11 take p of the land the LORD your
Ps 2: 8 the ends of the earth your p.
135: 4 Israel to be his treasured p.
Eph 1:14 of those who are God's p—

POSSESSIONS (POSSESS)

Mt 19:21 go, sell your p and give to the poor,
Lk 11:21 guards his own house, his p are safe
12:15 consist in the abundance of his p."
19: 8 now I give half of my p to the poor,
Ac 4:32 any of his p was his own,
2Co 12:14 what I want is not your p but you.
Heb 10:34 yourselves had better and lasting p.
1Jn 3:17 If anyone has material p

POSSIBLE

Mt 19:26 but with God all things are p."
26:39 if it is p, may this cup be taken
Mk 9:23 "Everything is p for him who
10:27 all things are p with God."
14:35 prayed that if p the hour might pass
Ro 12:18 If it is p, as far as it depends on you,
1Co 6: 5 Is it p that there is nobody
9:19 to everyone, to win as many as p.
9:22 by all p means I might save some.

POT (POTSHERD POTTER POTTER'S POTTERY)

2Ki 4:40 there is death in the p!"
Jer 18: 4 But the p he was shaping

POTIPHAR*

Egyptian who bought Joseph (Ge 37:36), set him over his house (Ge 39:1-6), sent him to prison (Ge 39:7-30).

POTSHERD (POT)

Isa 45: 9 a p among the potsherds

POTTER (POT)

Isa 29:16 Can the pot say of the p,
45: 9 Does the clay say to the p,
64: 8 We are the clay, you are the p;
Jer 18: 6 "Like clay in the hand of the p,
Zec 11:13 it to the p"—the handsome price
Ro 9:21 Does not the p have the right

POTTER'S (POT)

Mt 27: 7 to use the money to buy the p field

POTTERY (POT)

Ro 9:21 of clay some p for noble purposes

POUR (POURED POURS)

Ps 62: 8 p out your hearts to him,
Isa 44: 3 I will p out my Spirit
Eze 20: 8 So I said I would p out my wrath
39:29 for I will p out my Spirit
Joel 2:28 I will p out my Spirit on all people.
Zec 12:10 I will p out on the house of David
Mal 3:10 p out so much blessing that you
Ac 2:17 I will p out my Spirit on all people.

POURED (POUR)

Ps 22:14 I am p out like water,
Isa 32:15 till the Spirit is p upon us
Mt 26:28 which is p out for many
Lk 22:20 in my blood, which is p out for you.
Ac 2:33 and has p out what you now see
10:45 of the Holy Spirit had been p out
Ro 5: 5 because God has p out his love

Php 2:17 even if I am being p out like a drink
2Ti 4: 6 I am already being p out like
Tit 3: 6 whom he p out on us generously
Rev 16: 2 and p out his bowl on the land,

POURS (POUR)

Lk 5:37 And no one p new wine

POVERTY* (POOR)

Dt 28:48 and thirst, in nakedness and dire p,
1Sa 2: 7 The LORD sends p and wealth;
Pr 6:11 p will come on you like a bandit
10:15 but p is the ruin of the poor.
11:24 withholds unduly, but comes to p.
13:18 who ignores discipline comes to p
14:23 but mere talk leads only to p.
21: 5 as surely as haste leads to p.
22:16 to the rich—both come to p.
24:34 p will come on you like a bandit
28:19 fantasies will have his fill of p.
28:22 and is unaware that p awaits him.
30: 8 give me neither p nor riches,
31: 7 let them drink and forget their p
Ecc 4:14 born in p within his kingdom.
Mk 12:44 out of her p, put in everything—
Lk 21: 4 she out of her p put in all she had
2Co 8: 2 and their extreme p welled up
8: 9 through his p might become rich.
Rev 2: 9 I know your afflictions and your p

POWER (POWERFUL POWERS)

Ex 15: 6 was majestic in p.
32:11 out of Egypt with great p
Dt 8:17 "My p and the strength
34:12 one has ever shown the mighty p
1Sa 10: 6 LORD will come upon you in p,
10:10 Spirit of God came upon him in p,
11: 6 Spirit of God came upon him in p,
16:13 the LORD came upon David in p.
1Ch 29:11 LORD, is the greatness and the p
2Ch 20: 6 P and might are in your hand,
32: 7 for there is a greater p with us
Job 9: 4 wisdom is profound, his p is vast.
36:22 "God is exalted in his p.
37:23 beyond our reach and exalted in p;
Ps 20: 6 with the saving p of his right hand.
63: 2 and beheld your p and your glory.
66: 3 So great is your p
68:34 Proclaim the p of God,
77:14 you display your p
89:13 Your arm is endued with p;
145: 6 of the p of your awesome works,
147: 5 Great is our Lord and mighty in p;
150: 2 Praise him for his acts of p;
Pr 3:27 when it is in your p to act.
18:21 The tongue has the p of life
24: 5 A wise man has great p,
Isa 11: 2 the Spirit of counsel and of p,
40:10 the Sovereign LORD comes with p
40:26 of his great p and mighty strength,
63:12 who sent his glorious arm of p
Jer 10: 6 and your name is mighty in p.
10:12 But God made the earth by his p;
27: 5 With my great p and outstretched
32:17 and the earth by your great p
Hos 13:14 from the p of the grave;
Na 1: 3 to anger and great in p;
Zec 4: 6 nor by p, but by my Spirit,'
Mt 22:29 do not know the Scriptures or the p
24:30 on the clouds of the sky, with p
Lk 1:35 and the p of the Most High will
4:14 to Galilee in the p of the Spirit,
9: 1 he gave them p and authority
10:19 to overcome all the p of the enemy;
24:49 clothed with p from on high."
Ac 1: 8 you will receive p when the Holy
4:28 They did what your p and will had
4:33 With great p the apostles
10:38 with the Holy Spirit and p,
26:18 and from the p of Satan to God,
Ro 1:16 it is the p of God for the salvation
1:20 his eternal p and divine nature—
4:21 fully persuaded that God had p
9:17 that I might display my p in you
15:13 overflow with hope by the p
15:19 through the p of the Spirit.
1Co 1:17 cross of Christ be emptied of its p.
1:18 to us who are being saved it is the p
2: 4 a demonstration of the Spirit's p,
6:14 By his p God raised the Lord
15:24 all dominion, authority and p.
15:56 of death is sin, and the p
2Co 4: 7 to show that this all-surpassing p is
6: 7 in truthful speech and in the p
10: 4 they have divine p
12: 9 for my p is made perfect
13: 4 weakness, yet he lives by God's p.
Eph 1:19 and his incomparably great p
3:16 you with p through his Spirit
3:20 according to his p that is at work
6:10 in the Lord and in his mighty p.
Php 3:10 and the p of his resurrection
3:21 by the p that enables him
Col 1:11 strengthened with all p according
2:10 who is the head over every p
1Th 1: 5 also with p, with the Holy Spirit
2Ti 1: 7 but a spirit of p, of love
3: 5 form of godliness but denying its p.
Heb 2:14 might destroy him who holds the p
7:16 of the p of an indestructible life.
1Pe 1: 5 by God's p until the coming
2Pe 1: 3 His divine p has given us
Jude :25 p and authority, through Jesus
Rev 4:11 to receive glory and honor and p,
5:12 to receive p and wealth
11:17 you have taken your great p
19: 1 and glory and p belong to our God,
20: 6 The second death has no p

POWERFUL (POWER)

2Ch 27: 6 Jotham grew p because he walked
Est 9: 4 and he became more and more p.
Ps 29: 4 The voice of the LORD is p;
Jer 32:18 p God, whose name is the LORD
Zec 8:22 p nations will come to Jerusalem
Mk 1: 7 "After me will come one more p
Lk 24:19 p in word and deed before God
2Th 1: 7 in blazing fire with his p angels.
Heb 1: 3 sustaining all things by his p word.
Jas 5:16 The prayer of a righteous man is p

POWERLESS

Ro 5: 6 when we were still p, Christ died
8: 3 For what the law was p to do

POWERS (POWER)

Da 4:35 pleases with the p of heaven
Ro 8:38 nor any p, neither height nor depth
1Co 12:10 to another miraculous p,
Eph 6:12 against the p of this dark world
Col 1:16 whether thrones or p or rulers
2:15 And having disarmed the p
Heb 6: 5 and the p of the coming age,
1Pe 3:22 and p in submission to him.

PRACTICE (PRACTICED PRACTICES)

Lev 19:26 " 'Do not p divination or sorcery.
Ps 119:56 This has been my p:
Eze 33:31 but they do not put them into p.
Mt 7:24 into p is like a wise man who built
23: 3 for they do not p what they preach.
Lk 8:21 hear God's word and put it into p."
Ro 12:13 P hospitality.
Php 4: 9 or seen in me—put it into p.
1Ti 5: 4 to put their religion into p by caring

PRACTICED (PRACTICE)

Mt 23:23 You should have p the latter,

PRACTICES (PRACTICE)

Ps 101: 7 No one who p deceit
Mt 5:19 but whoever p and teaches these
Col 3: 9 taken off your old self with its p

PRAISE (PRAISED PRAISES PRAISEWORTHY PRAISING)

Ex 15: 2 He is my God, and I will p him,
Dt 10:21 He is your p; he is your God,
26:19 declared that he will set you in p,
32: 3 Oh, p the greatness of our God!
Ru 4:14 said to Naomi: "P be to the LORD,
2Sa 22: 4 to the LORD, who is worthy of p,
22:47 The LORD lives! P be to my Rock
1Ch 16:25 is the LORD and most worthy of p;
16:35 that we may glory in your p."
23: 5 four thousand are to p the LORD
29:10 "P be to you, O LORD,
2Ch 5:13 they raised their voices in p
20:21 and to p him for the splendor
29:30 to p the LORD with the words
Ezr 3:10 took their places to p the LORD,
Ne 9: 5 and p the LORD your God,
Ps 8: 2 you have ordained p
9: 1 I will p you, O LORD,
16: 7 I will p the LORD, who counsels
26: 7 proclaiming aloud your p
30: 4 p his holy name.
33: 1 it is fitting for the upright to p him.
34: 1 his p will always be on my lips.
40: 3 a hymn of p to our God.
42: 5 for I will yet p him,
43: 5 for I will yet p him,
45:17 the nations will p you for ever
47: 7 sing to him a psalm of p.
48: 1 the LORD, and most worthy of p,
51:15 and my mouth will declare your p.
56: 4 In God, whose word I p,
57: 9 I will p you, O Lord,
63: 4 I will p you as long as I live,
65: 1 P awaits you, O God, in Zion;
66: 2 make his p glorious.
66: 8 P our God, O peoples,
68:19 P be to the Lord, to God our Savior
68:26 p the LORD in the assembly
69:30 I will p God's name in song
69:34 Let heaven and earth p him,
71: 8 My mouth is filled with your p,
71:14 I will p you more and more.
71:22 I will p you with the harp
74:21 the poor and needy p your name.
86:12 I will p you, O Lord my God,
89: 5 The heavens p your wonders,
92: 1 It is good to p the LORD
96: 2 Sing to the LORD, p his name;
100: 4 and his courts with p;
101: 1 to you, O LORD, I will sing p.
102:18 not yet created may p the LORD:
103: 1 P the LORD, O my soul;
103:20 P the LORD, you his angels,
104: 1 P the LORD, O my soul.
105: 2 Sing to him, sing p to him;
106: 1 P the LORD.
108: 3 I will p you, O LORD,
111: 1 P the LORD.
113: 1 P the LORD.
117: 1 P the LORD, all you nations;
119:175 Let me live that I may p you,
135: 1 P the LORD.
135:20 you who fear him, p the LORD.
138: 1 I will p you, O LORD,
139:14 I p you because I am fearfully
144: 1 P be to the LORD my Rock,
145: 3 is the LORD and most worthy of p;
145:10 All you have made will p you,
145:21 Let every creature p his holy name
146: 1 P the LORD, O my soul.
147: 1 how pleasant and fitting to p him!
148: 1 P the LORD from the heavens,
148:13 Let them p the name of the LORD,
149: 1 his p in the assembly of the saints.
149: 6 May the p of God be
149: 9 P the LORD.
150: 2 p him for his surpassing greatness.
150: 6 that has breath p the LORD.
Pr 27: 2 Let another p you, and not your
27:21 man is tested by the p he receives.
31:31 let her works bring her p
SS 1: 4 we will p your love more than wine
Isa 12: 1 "I will p you, O LORD.
42:10 his p from the ends of the earth,
61: 3 and a garment of p
Jer 33: 9 p and honor before all nations
Da 2:20 "P be to the name of God for ever
4:37 p and exalt and glorify the King
Mt 5:16 and p your Father in heaven.
21:16 you have ordained p'?"
Lk 19:37 to p God in loud voices
Jn 5:44 effort to obtain the p that comes
12:43 for they loved p from men more
Ro 2:29 Such a man's p is not from men,
15: 7 in order to bring p to God.
2Co 1: 3 P be to the God and Father
Eph 1: 3 P be to the God and Father
1: 6 to the p of his glorious grace,
1:12 might be for the p of his glory.
1:14 to the p of his glory.
1Th 2: 6 We were not looking for p
Heb 13:15 offer to God a sacrifice of p—
Jas 3: 9 With the tongue we p our Lord
5:13 happy? Let him sing songs of p.
Rev 5:13 be p and honor and glory
7:12 P and glory

PRAISED (PRAISE)

1Ch 29:10 David p the LORD in the presence
Ne 8: 6 Ezra p the LORD, the great God;
Job 1:21 may the name of the LORD be p."
Ps 113: 2 Let the name of the LORD be p,
Pr 31:30 who fears the LORD is to be p.
Isa 63: 7 the deeds for which he is to be p,
Da 2:19 Then Daniel p the God of heaven
4:34 Then I p the Most High; I honored
Lk 18:43 the people saw it, they also p God.
23:47 seeing what had happened, p God
Ro 9: 5 who is God over all, forever p!

Gal 1:24 And they *p* God because of me.
1Pe 4:11 that in all things God may be *p*

PRAISES (PRAISE)

2Sa 22:50 I will sing *p* to your name.
Ps 18:49 I will sing *p* to your name.
47: 6 Sing *p* to God, sing *p*;
147: 1 How good it is to sing *p* to our God,
Pr 31:28 her husband also, and he *p* her:
1Pe 2: 9 that you may declare the *p*

PRAISEWORTHY* (PRAISE)

Ps 78: 4 the *p* deeds of the LORD,
Php 4: 8 if anything is excellent or *p*—

PRAISING (PRAISE)

Lk 2:13 *p* God and saying, "Glory to God
2:20 *p* God for all the things they had
Ac 2:47 *p* God and enjoying the favor
10:46 speaking in tongues and *p* God.
1Co 14:16 If you are *p* God with your spirit,

PRAY (PRAYED PRAYER PRAYERS PRAYING PRAYS)

Dt 4: 7 is near us whenever we *p* to him?
1Sa 12:23 the LORD by failing to *p* for you.
1Ki 8:30 when they *p* toward this place.
2Ch 7:14 will humble themselves and *p*
Ezr 6:10 and *p* for the well-being of the king
Job 42: 8 My servant Job will *p* for you,
Ps 5: 2 for to you I *p*.
32: 6 let everyone who is godly *p*
122: 6 *P* for the peace of Jerusalem:
Jer 29: 7 *P* to the LORD for it,
29:12 upon me and come and *p* to me,
42: 3 *P* that the LORD your God will
Mt 5:44 and *p* for those who persecute you,
6: 5 "And when you *p*, do not be like
6: 9 "This, then, is how you should *p*:
14:23 up on a mountainside by himself to *p*.
19:13 hands on them and *p* for them.
26:36 Sit here while I go over there and *p*
Lk 6:28 *p* for those who mistreat you.
11: 1 us to *p*, just as John taught his
18: 1 them that they should always *p*
22:40 "*P* that you will not fall
Jn 17:20 I *p* also for those who will believe
Ro 8:26 do not know what we ought to *p* for,
1Co 14:13 in a tongue should *p* that he may
Eph 1:18 I *p* also that the eyes
3:16 I *p* that out of his glorious riches he
6:18 And *p* in the Spirit on all occasions
Col 1:10 we *p* this in order that you may live
4: 3 *p* for us, too, that God may open
1Th 5:17 Be joyful always; *p* continually;
2Th 1:11 in mind, we constantly *p* for you,
Jas 5:13 one of you in trouble? He should *p*.
5:16 *p* for each other so that you may be
1Pe 4: 7 self-controlled so that you can *p*.
Jude :20 up in your most holy faith and *p*

PRAYED (PRAY)

1Sa 1:27 I *p* for this child, and the LORD
1Ki 18:36 Elijah stepped forward and *p*:
19: 4 under it and *p* that he might die.
2Ki 6:17 And Elisha *p*, "O LORD,
2Ch 30:18 But Hezekiah *p* for them, saying,
Ne 4: 9 we *p* to our God and posted a guard
Job 42:10 After Job had *p* for his friends,
Da 6:10 got down on his knees and *p*,
9: 4 I *p* to the LORD my God
Jnh 2: 1 From inside the fish Jonah *p*
Mt 26:39 with his face to the ground and *p*,
Mk 1:35 off to a solitary place, where he *p*.
14:35 *p* that if possible the hour might
Lk 22:41 knelt down and *p*, "Father,
Jn 17: 1 he looked toward heaven and *p*:
Ac 4:31 After they *p*, the place where they
6: 6 who *p* and laid their hands on them
8:15 they *p* for them that they might
13: 3 So after they had fasted and *p*,

PRAYER (PRAY)

2Ch 30:27 for their *p* reached heaven,
Ezr 8:23 about this, and he answered our *p*.
Ps 4: 1 be merciful to me and hear my *p*.
6: 9 the LORD accepts my *p*.
17: 1 Give ear to my *p*—
17: 6 give ear to me and hear my *p*.
65: 2 O you who hear *p*,
66:20 who has not rejected my *p*
86: 6 Hear my *p*, O LORD;
Pr 15: 8 but the *p* of the upright pleases him
15:29 but he hears the *p* of the righteous.
Isa 56: 7 a house of *p* for all nations."
Mt 21:13 house will be called a house of *p*,'
21:22 receive whatever you ask for in *p*."
Mk 9:29 This kind can come out only by *p*."
11:24 whatever you ask for in *p*,
Jn 17:15 My *p* is not that you take them out
Ac 1:14 all joined together constantly in *p*,
2:42 to the breaking of bread and to *p*.
6: 4 and will give our attention to *p*
10:31 has heard your *p* and remembered
16:13 expected to find a place of *p*.
Ro 12:12 patient in affliction, faithful in *p*.
1Co 7: 5 you may devote yourselves to *p*.
2Co 13: 9 and our *p* is for your perfection.
Php 1: 9 this is my *p*: that your love may
4: 6 but in everything, by *p* and petition
Col 4: 2 yourselves to *p*, being watchful
1Ti 2: 8 to lift up holy hands in *p*,
4: 5 by the word of God and *p*.
Jas 5:15 *p* offered in faith will make the sick
1Pe 3:12 and his ears are attentive to their *p*,

PRAYERS (PRAY)

1Ch 5:20 He answered their *p*, because they
Isa 1:15 even if you offer many *p*,
Mk 12:40 and for a show make lengthy *p*.
2Co 1:11 as you help us by your *p*.
Eph 6:18 on all occasions with all kinds of *p*
1Ti 2: 1 then, first of all, that requests, *p*,
1Pe 3: 7 so that nothing will hinder your *p*.
Rev 5: 8 which are the *p* of the saints.
8: 3 with the *p* of all the saints,

PRAYING (PRAY)

Ge 24:45 "Before I finished *p* in my heart,
1Sa 1:12 As she kept on *p* to the LORD,
Mk 11:25 And when you stand *p*,
Lk 3:21 as he was *p*, heaven was opened
6:12 and spent the night *p* to God.
9:29 As he was *p*, the appearance
Jn 17: 9 I am not *p* for the world,
Ac 9:11 from Tarsus named Saul, for he is *p*
16:25 and Silas were *p* and singing hymns
Ro 15:30 in my struggle by *p* to God for me.
Eph 6:18 always keep on *p* for all the saints.

PRAYS (PRAY)

1Co 14:14 my spirit *p*, but my mind is

PREACH (PREACHED PREACHING)

Isa 61: 1 me to *p* good news to the poor.
Mt 10: 7 As you go, *p* this message:
23: 3 they do not practice what they *p*.
Mk 16:15 and *p* the good news to all creation.
Lk 4:18 me to *p* good news to the poor.
Ac 9:20 At once he began to *p*
16:10 us to *p* the gospel to them.
Ro 1:15 am so eager to *p* the gospel
10:15 how can they *p* unless they are sent
15:20 to *p* the gospel where Christ was
1Co 1:17 to *p* the gospel—not with words
1:23 wisdom, but we *p* Christ crucified:
9:14 that those who *p* the gospel should
9:16 Woe to me if I do not *p* the gospel!
2Co 4: 5 For we do not *p* ourselves,
10:16 so that we can *p* the gospel
Gal 1: 8 from heaven should *p* a gospel
2Ti 4: 2 I give you this charge: *P* the Word;

PREACHED (PREACH)

Mt 24:14 gospel of the kingdom will be *p*
Mk 6:12 and *p* that people should repent.
13:10 And the gospel must first be *p*
14: 9 wherever the gospel is *p*
Ac 8: 4 had been scattered *p* the word
28:31 hindrance he *p* the kingdom
1Co 9:27 so that after I have *p* to others,
15: 1 you of the gospel I *p* to you,
2Co 11: 4 other than the Jesus we *p*,
Gal 1: 8 other than the one we *p* to you,
Eph 2:17 *p* peace to you who were far away
Php 1:18 false motives or true, Christ is *p*.
1Ti 3:16 was *p* among the nations,
1Pe 1:25 this is the word that was *p* to you.
3:19 and *p* to the spirits in prison who

PREACHING (PREACH)

Lk 9: 6 *p* the gospel and healing people
Ac 18: 5 devoted himself exclusively to *p*,
Ro 10:14 hear without someone *p* to them?
1Co 2: 4 and my *p* were not with wise
9:18 in *p* the gospel I may offer it free
Gal 1: 9 If anybody is *p* to you a gospel
1Ti 4:13 the public reading of Scripture, to *p*
5:17 especially those whose work is *p*

PRECEDE*

1Th 4:15 will certainly not *p* those who have

PRECEPTS*

Dt 33:10 He teaches your *p* to Jacob
Ps 19: 8 The *p* of the LORD are right,
103:18 and remember to obey his *p*.
105:45 that they might keep his *p*
111: 7 all his *p* are trustworthy.
111:10 who follow his *p* have good
119: 4 You have laid down *p*
119:15 I meditate on your *p*
119:27 understand the teaching of your *p*;
119:40 How I long for your *p*!
119:45 for I have sought out your *p*.
119:56 I obey your *p*.
119:63 to all who follow your *p*.
119:69 I keep your *p* with all my heart.
119:78 but I will meditate on your *p*.
119:87 but I have not forsaken your *p*.
119:93 I will never forget your *p*,
119:94 I have sought out your *p*.
119:100 for I obey your *p*.
119:104 I gain understanding from your *p*;
119:110 but I have not strayed from your *p*.
119:128 because I consider all your *p* right,
119:134 that I may obey your *p*.
119:141 I do not forget your *p*.
119:159 See how I love your *p*;
119:168 I obey your *p* and your statutes,
119:173 for I have chosen your *p*.

PRECIOUS

Ps 19:10 They are more *p* than gold,
72:14 for *p* is their blood in his sight.
116:15 *P* in the sight of the LORD
119:72 from your mouth is more *p* to me
139:17 How *p* to me are your thoughts,
Pr 8:11 for wisdom is more *p* than rubies,
Isa 28:16 a *p* cornerstone for a sure
1Pe 1:19 but with the *p* blood of Christ,
2: 4 but chosen by God and *p* to him—
2: 6 a chosen and *p* cornerstone,
2Pe 1: 1 Christ have received a faith as *p*
1: 4 us his very great and *p* promises,

PREDESTINED* (DESTINY)

Ro 8:29 *p* to be conformed to the likeness
8:30 And those he *p*, he also called;
Eph 1: 5 In love he *p* us to be adopted
1:11 having been *p* according

PREDICTED (PREDICTION)

1Sa 28:17 The LORD has done what he *p*
Ac 7:52 killed those who *p* the coming
1Pe 1:11 when he *p* the sufferings of Christ

PREDICTION* (PREDICTED PREDICTIONS)

Jer 28: 9 only if his *p* comes true."

PREDICTIONS (PREDICTION)

Isa 44:26 and fulfills the *p* of his messengers,

PREGNANT

Ex 21:22 who are fighting hit a *p* woman
Mt 24:19 be in those days for *p* women
1Th 5: 3 as labor pains on a *p* woman,

PREPARE (PREPARED)

Ps 23: 5 You *p* a table before me
Isa 25: 6 the LORD Almighty will *p*
40: 3 "In the desert *p*
Am 4:12 *p* to meet your God, O Israel."
Mal 3: 1 who will *p* the way before me.
Mt 3: 3 '*P* the way for the Lord,
Jn 14: 2 there to *p* a place for you.
Eph 4:12 to *p* God's people for works
1Pe 1:13 Therefore, *p* your minds for action;

PREPARED (PREPARE)

Ex 23:20 to bring you to the place I have *p*.
Mt 25:34 the kingdom *p* for you
Ro 9:22 of his wrath—*p* for destruction?
1Co 2: 9 what God has *p* for those who love
Eph 2:10 which God *p* in advance for us
2Ti 2:21 and *p* to do any good work.
4: 2 be *p* in season and out of season;
1Pe 3:15 Always be *p* to give an answer

PRESCRIBED

Ezr 7:23 Whatever the God of heaven has *p*,

PRESENCE (PRESENT)

Ex 25:30 Put the bread of the *P* on this table

Ex 33:14 The LORD replied, "My *P* will go
Nu 4:7 "Over the table of the *P* they are
1Sa 6:20 in the *p* of the LORD, this
21:6 of the *P* that had been removed
2Sa 22:13 Out of the brightness of his *p*
2Ki 17:23 LORD removed them from his *p*,
23:27 also from my *p* as I removed Israel,
Ezr 9:15 one of us can stand in your *p*."
Ps 16:11 you will fill me with joy in your *p*,
21:6 with the joy of your *p*.
23:5 in the *p* of my enemies.
31:20 the shelter of your *p* you hide them
41:12 and set me in your *p* forever.
51:11 Do not cast me from your *p*
52:9 in the *p* of your saints.
89:15 who walk in the light of your *p*,
90:8 our secret sins in the light of your *p*
114:7 O earth, at the *p* of the Lord,
139:7 Where can I flee from your *p*?
Isa 26:17 so were we in your *p*, O LORD.
Jer 5:22 "Should you not tremble in my *p*?
Eze 38:20 of the earth will tremble at my *p*.
Hos 6:2 that we may live in his *p*.
Na 1:5 The earth trembles at his *p*,
Mal 3:16 in his *p* concerning those who
Ac 2:28 you will fill me with joy in your *p*.'
1Th 3:9 have in the *p* of our God
3:13 and holy in the *p* of our God
2Th 1:9 and shut out from the *p* of the Lord
Heb 9:24 now to appear for us in God's *p*.
1Jn 3:19 rest in his *p* whenever our hearts
Jude :24 before his glorious *p* without fault

PRESENT (PRESENCE)

1Co 3:22 life or death or the *p* or the future—
7:26 of the *p* crisis, I think that it is good
2Co 11:2 so that I might *p* you as a pure
Eph 5:27 and to *p* her to himself
1Ti 4:8 holding promise for both the *p* life
2Ti 2:15 Do your best to *p* yourself to God
Jude :24 and to *p* you before his glorious

PRESERVE

Lk 17:33 and whoever loses his life will *p* it.

PRESERVES

Ps 119:50 Your promise *p* my life.

PRESS (PRESSED PRESSURE)

Php 3:12 but I *p* on to take hold of that
3:14 I *p* on toward the goal

PRESSED (PRESS)

Lk 6:38 *p* down, shaken together

PRESSURE (PRESS)

2Co 1:8 We were under great *p*, far
11:28 I face daily the *p* of my concern

PRETENDED

1Sa 21:13 So he *p* to be insane

PREVAILS

1Sa 2:9 "It is not by strength that one *p*;
Pr 19:21 but it is the LORD's purpose that *p*

PRICE (PRICELESS)

Job 28:18 the *p* of wisdom is beyond rubies.
1Co 6:20 your own; you were bought at a *p*.
7:23 bought at a *p*; do not become slaves

PRICELESS* (PRICE)

Ps 36:7 How *p* is your unfailing love!

PRIDE (PROUD)

Pr 8:13 I hate *p* and arrogance,
11:2 When *p* comes, then comes
13:10 *P* only breeds quarrels,
16:18 *P* goes before destruction,
29:23 A man's *p* brings him low,
Isa 25:11 God will bring down their *p*
Da 4:37 And those who walk in *p* he is able
Am 8:7 The LORD has sworn by the *P*
2Co 5:12 giving you an opportunity to take *p*
7:4 in you; I take great *p* in you.
8:24 and the reason for our *p* in you,
Gal 6:4 Then he can take *p* in himself,
Jas 1:9 ought to take *p* in his high position.

PRIEST (PRIESTHOOD PRIESTLY PRIESTS)

Ge 14:18 He was *p* of God Most High,
Nu 5:10 to the *p* will belong to the *p*.'"
2Ch 13:9 and seven rams may become a *p*
Ps 110:4 "You are a *p* forever,
Heb 2:17 faithful high *p* in service to God,
3:1 and high *p* whom we confess.
4:14 have a great high *p* who has gone
4:15 do not have a high *p* who is unable
5:6 "You are a *p* forever,
6:20 He has become a high *p* forever,
7:3 Son of God he remains a *p* forever.
7:15 clear if another *p* like Melchizedek
7:26 Such a high *p* meets our need—
8:1 We do have such a high *p*,
10:11 Day after day every *p* stands
13:11 The high *p* carries the blood

PRIESTHOOD (PRIEST)

Heb 7:24 lives forever, he has a permanent *p*.
1Pe 2:5 into a spiritual house to be a holy *p*,
2:9 you are a chosen people, a royal *p*,

PRIESTLY (PRIEST)

Ro 15:16 to the Gentiles with the *p* duty

PRIESTS (PRIEST)

Ex 19:6 you will be for me a kingdom of *p*
Lev 21:1 "Speak to the *p*, the sons of Aaron,
Eze 42:13 where the *p* who approach
46:2 *p* are to sacrifice his burnt offering
Mal 1:6 O *p*, who show contempt for my name.
Rev 5:10 to be a kingdom and *p*
20:6 but they will be *p* of God

PRIME

Isa 38:10 recovery: I said, "In the *p* of my life

PRINCE (PRINCES PRINCESS)

Isa 9:6 Everlasting Father, *P* of Peace.
Eze 34:24 and my servant David will be *p*
37:25 my servant will be their *p* forever.
Da 8:25 stand against the *P* of princes.
Jn 12:31 now the *p* of this world will be
Ac 5:31 as *P* and Savior that he might give

PRINCES (PRINCE)

Ps 118:9 than to trust in *p*.
148:11 you *p* and all rulers on earth,
Isa 40:23 He brings *p* to naught

PRINCESS* (PRINCE)

Ps 45:13 All glorious is the *p*

PRISCILLA*

Wife of Aquila; co-worker with Paul (Ac 18; Ro 16:3; 1Co 16:19; 2Ti 4:19); instructor of Apollos (Ac 18:24-28).

PRISON (PRISONER PRISONERS)

Ps 66:11 You brought us into *p*
142:7 Set me free from my *p*,
Isa 42:7 to free captives from *p*
Mt 25:36 I was in *p* and you came to visit me
2Co 11:23 been in *p* more frequently,
Heb 11:36 others were chained and put in *p*.
13:3 Remember those in *p*
1Pe 3:19 spirits in *p* who disobeyed long ago
Rev 20:7 Satan will be released from his *p*

PRISONER (PRISON)

Ro 7:23 and making me a *p* of the law of sin
Gal 3:22 declares that the whole world is a *p*
Eph 3:1 the *p* of Christ Jesus for the sake

PRISONERS (PRISON)

Ps 68:6 he leads forth the *p* with singing;
79:11 groans of the *p* come before you;
107:10 *p* suffering in iron chains,
146:7 The LORD sets *p* free,
Zec 9:12 to your fortress, O *p* of hope;
Lk 4:18 me to proclaim freedom for the *p*
Gal 3:23 we were held *p* by the law,

PRIVILEGE*

2Co 8:4 pleaded with us for the *p* of sharing

PRIZE*

1Co 9:24 Run in such a way as to get the *p*.
9:24 but only one gets the *p*? Run
9:27 will not be disqualified for the *p*.
Php 3:14 on toward the goal to win the *p*
Col 2:18 of angels disqualify you for the *p*.

PROBE

Job 11:7 Can you *p* the limits
Ps 17:3 Though you *p* my heart

PROCEDURE

Ecc 8:6 For there is a proper time and *p*

PROCESSION

Ps 68:24 Your *p* has come into view, O God,
118:27 boughs in hand, join in the festal *p*
1Co 4:9 on display at the end of the *p*,
2Co 2:14 us in triumphal *p* in Christ

PROCLAIM (PROCLAIMED PROCLAIMING PROCLAIMS PROCLAMATION)

Ex 33:19 and I will *p* my name, the LORD,
Lev 25:10 and *p* liberty throughout the land
Dt 30:12 and *p* it to us so we may obey it?"
2Sa 1:20 *p* it not in the streets of Ashkelon,
1Ch 16:23 *p* his salvation day after day.
Ne 8:15 and that they should *p* this word
Ps 2:7 I will *p* the decree of the LORD:
9:11 *p* among the nations what he has
19:1 the skies *p* the work of his hands.
22:31 They will *p* his righteousness
40:9 I *p* righteousness in the great
50:6 the heavens *p* his righteousness,
64:9 they will *p* the works of God
68:34 *P* the power of God,
71:16 I will come and *p* your mighty acts,
92:2 to *p* your love in the morning
96:2 *p* his salvation day after day.
97:6 The heavens *p* his righteousness,
106:2 Who can *p* the mighty acts
118:17 will *p* what the LORD has done.
145:6 and I will *p* your great deeds.
Isa 12:4 and *p* that his name is exalted.
42:12 and *p* his praise in the islands.
52:7 who *p* salvation,
61:1 to *p* freedom for the captives
66:19 They will *p* my glory
Jer 7:2 house and there *p* this message:
50:2 lift up a banner and *p* it;
Hos 5:9 I *p* what is certain.
Zec 9:10 He will *p* peace to the nations.
Mt 10:27 in your ear, *p* from the roofs.
12:18 and he will *p* justice to the nations.
Lk 4:18 me to *p* freedom for the prisoners
9:60 you go and *p* the kingdom of God."
Ac 17:23 unknown I am going to *p*
20:27 hesitated to *p* to you the whole will
1Co 11:26 you *p* the Lord's death
Col 1:28 We *p* him, admonishing
4:4 Pray that I may *p* it clearly,
1Jn 1:1 this we *p* concerning the Word

PROCLAIMED (PROCLAIM)

Ex 9:16 and that my name might be *p*
34:5 there with him and *p* his name,
Ps 68:11 was the company of those who *p* it:
Ro 15:19 I have fully *p* the gospel of Christ.
Col 1:23 that has been *p* to every creature
2Ti 4:17 me the message might be fully *p*

PROCLAIMING (PROCLAIM)

Ps 26:7 *p* aloud your praise
92:15 *p*, "The LORD is upright;
Ac 5:42 and *p* the good news that Jesus is
Ro 10:8 the word of faith we are *p*:

PROCLAIMS (PROCLAIM)

Dt 18:22 If what a prophet *p* in the name

PROCLAMATION (PROCLAIM)

Isa 62:11 The LORD has made *p*

PRODUCE (PRODUCES)

Mt 3:8 *P* fruit in keeping with repentance.
3:10 tree that does not *p* good fruit will

PRODUCES (PRODUCE)

Pr 30:33 so stirring up anger *p* strife."
Ro 5:3 that suffering *p* perseverance;
Heb 12:11 it *p* a harvest of righteousness

PROFANE (PROFANED)

Lev 19:12 and so *p* the name of your God.
22:32 Do not *p* my holy name.
Mal 2:10 Why do we *p* the covenant

PROFANED (PROFANE)

Eze 36:20 the nations they *p* my holy name,

PROFESS*

1Ti 2:10 for women who *p* to worship God.
Heb 4:14 let us hold firmly to the faith we *p*.
10:23 unswervingly to the hope we *p*,

PROFIT (PROFITABLE)

Pr 14:23 All hard work brings a p,
21: 5 The plans of the diligent lead to p
Isa 44:10 which can p him nothing?
2Co 2:17 not peddle the word of God for p.
Php 3: 7 was to my p I now consider loss

PROFITABLE* (PROFIT)

Pr 3:14 for she is more p than silver
31:18 She sees that her trading is p,
Tit 3: 8 These things are excellent and p

PROFOUND

Job 9: 4 His wisdom is p, his power is vast.
Ps 92: 5 how p your thoughts!
Eph 5:32 This is a p mystery—but I am

PROGRESS

Php 1:25 continue with all of you for your p
1Ti 4:15 so that everyone may see your p.

PROLONG*

Dt 5:33 p your days in the land that you
Ps 85: 5 Will you p your anger
Pr 3: 2 for they will p your life many years
Isa 53:10 will see his offspring and p his days,
La 4:22 he will not p your exile.

PROMISE (PROMISED PROMISES)

Nu 23:19 Does he p and not fulfill?
Jos 23:14 Every p has been fulfilled;
2Sa 7:25 keep forever the p you have made
1Ki 8:20 The LORD has kept the p he made
8:24 You have kept your p
Ne 5:13 man who does not keep this p.
9: 8 have kept your p because you are
Ps 77: 8 Has his p failed for all time?
119: 41 your salvation according to your p;
119: 50 Your p preserves my life.
119: 58 to me according to your p.
119:162 I rejoice in your p
Ac 2:39 The p is for you and your children
Ro 4:13 offspring received the p that he
4:20 unbelief regarding the p of God,
Gal 3:14 that by faith we might receive the p
Eph 2:12 foreigners to the covenants of the p
1Ti 4: 8 holding p for both the present life
Heb 6:13 When God made his p to Abraham
11:11 him faithful who had made the p.
2Pe 3: 9 Lord is not slow in keeping his p,
3:13 with his p we are looking forward

PROMISED (PROMISE)

Ge 21: 1 did for Sarah what he had p.
24: 7 who spoke to me and p me on oath,
Ex 3:17 And I have p to bring you up out
Nu 10:29 for the LORD has p good things
Dt 15: 6 your God will bless you as he has p,
26:18 his treasured possession as he p,
2Sa 7:28 and you have p these good things
1Ki 9: 5 I p David your father when I said,
2Ch 6:15 with your mouth you have p
Ps 119: 57 I have p to obey your words.
Lk 24:49 to send you what my Father has p;
Ac 1: 4 but wait for the gift my Father p,
13:32 What God p our fathers he has
Ro 4:21 power to do what he had p.
Tit 1: 2 p before the beginning of time,
Heb 10:23 for he who p is faithful.
10:36 you will receive what he has p.
Jas 1:12 the crown of life that God has p
2: 5 the kingdom he p those who love
2Pe 3: 4 "Where is this 'coming' he p?
1Jn 2:25 And this is what he p us—

PROMISES (PROMISE)

Jos 21:45 one of all the LORD's good p
23:14 of all the good p the LORD your
1Ki 8:56 failed of all the good p he gave
1Ch 17:19 and made known all these great p.
Ps 85: 8 he p peace to his people, his saints
106: 12 Then they believed his p
119:140 Your p have been thoroughly
119:148 that I may meditate on your p.
145: 13 The LORD is faithful to all his p
Ro 9: 4 the temple worship and the p.
2Co 1:20 matter how many p God has made,
7: 1 Since we have these p, dear friends,
Heb 8: 6 and it is founded on better p.
2Pe 1: 4 us his very great and precious p,

PROMOTE (PROMOTES)

Pr 12:20 but joy for those who p peace.
16:21 and pleasant words p instruction.

1Ti 1: 4 These p controversies rather

PROMOTES (PROMOTE)

Pr 17: 9 over an offense p love,

PROMPTED

1Th 1: 3 your labor p by love, and your
2Th 1:11 and every act p by your faith.

PRONOUNCE (PRONOUNCED)

1Ch 23:13 to p blessings in his name forever.

PRONOUNCED (PRONOUNCE)

1Ch 16:12 miracles, and the judgments he p,

PROOF (PROVE)

Ac 17:31 He has given p of this to all men
2Co 8:24 Therefore show these men the p

PROPER

Ps 104: 27 give them their food at the p time.
145: 15 give them their food at the p time.
Ecc 5:18 Then I realized that it is good and p
8: 5 the wise heart will know the p time
Mt 24:45 give them their food at the p time?
Lk 1:20 which will come true at their p time
1Co 11:13 Is it p for a woman to pray to God
Gal 6: 9 at the p time we will reap a harvest
1Ti 2: 6 the testimony given in its p time.
1Pe 2:17 Show p respect to everyone:

PROPERTY

Heb 10:34 the confiscation of your p,

PROPHECIES (PROPHESY)

1Co 13: 8 where there are p, they will cease;
1Th 5:20 do not treat p with contempt.

PROPHECY (PROPHESY)

Da 9:24 to seal up vision and p
1Co 12:10 miraculous powers, to another p,
13: 2 of p and can fathom all mysteries
14: 1 gifts, especially the gift of p.
14: 6 or p or word of instruction?
14:22 p, however, is for believers,
2Pe 1:20 you must understand that no p
Rev 22:18 the words of the p of this book:

PROPHESIED (PROPHESY)

Nu 11:25 the Spirit rested on them, they p,
1Sa 19:24 and also p in Samuel's presence.
Jn 11:51 that year he p that Jesus would
Ac 19: 6 and they spoke in tongues and p.
21: 9 four unmarried daughters who p.

PROPHESIES (PROPHESY)

Jer 28: 9 the prophet who p peace will be
Eze 12:27 and he p about the distant future.'
1Co 11: 4 p with his head covered dishonors
14: 3 But everyone who p speaks to men

PROPHESY (PROPHECIES PROPHECY PROPHESIED PROPHESIES PROPHESYING PROPHET PROPHET'S PROPHETESS PROPHETS)

1Sa 10: 6 and you will p with them;
Eze 13: 2 Say to those who p out
13:17 daughters of your people who p out
34: 2 p against the shepherds of Israel;
37: 4 "P to these bones and say to them,
Joel 2:28 Your sons and daughters will p,
Mt 7:22 Lord, did we not p in your name,
Ac 2:17 Your sons and daughters will p,
1Co 13: 9 know in part and we p in part,
14:39 my brothers, be eager to p,
Rev 11: 3 and they will p for 1,260 days,

PROPHESYING (PROPHESY)

1Ch 25: 1 and Jeduthun for the ministry of p,
Ro 12: 6 If a man's gift is p, let him use it

PROPHET (PROPHESY)

Ex 7: 1 your brother Aaron will be your p.
Nu 12: 6 "When a p of the LORD is
Dt 13: 1 If a p, or one who foretells
18:18 up for them a p like you
18:22 If what a p proclaims in the name
1Sa 3:20 that Samuel was attested as a p
9: 9 because the p of today used
1Ki 1: 8 son of Jehoiada, Nathan the p,
18:36 the p Elijah stepped forward
2Ki 5: 8 and he will know that there is a p
6:12 "but Elisha, the p who is in Israel,
20: 1 The p Isaiah son of Amoz went
2Ch 35:18 since the days of the p Samuel;
36:12 himself before Jeremiah the p,
Ezr 5: 1 Haggai the p and Zechariah the p,
Eze 2: 5 they will know that a p has been
33:33 they will know that a p has been
Hos 9: 7 the p is considered a fool,
Am 7:14 "I was neither a p nor a prophet's
Hab 1: 1 that Habakkuk the p received.
Hag 1: 1 came through the p Haggai
Zec 1: 1 to the p Zechariah son of Berekiah,
13: 4 that day every p will be ashamed
Mal 4: 5 I will send you the p Elijah
Mt 10:41 Anyone who receives a p
11: 9 what did you go out to see? A p?
12:39 except the sign of the p Jonah.
Lk 1:76 will be called a p of the Most High;
4:24 "no p is accepted in his hometown.
7:16 A great p has appeared among us,"
24:19 "He was a p, powerful in word
Jn 1:21 "Are you the P?" He answered,
Ac 7:37 'God will send you a p like me
21:10 a p named Agabus came
1Co 14:37 If anybody thinks he is a p
Rev 16:13 and out of the mouth of the false p.

PROPHET'S (PROPHESY)

2Pe 1:20 about by the p own interpretation.

PROPHETESS (PROPHESY)

Ex 15:20 Then Miriam the p, Aaron's sister,
Jdg 4: 4 a p, the wife of Lappidoth,
Isa 8: 3 I went to the p, and she conceived
Lk 2:36 a p, Anna, the daughter of Phanuel,

PROPHETS (PROPHESY)

Nu 11:29 that all the LORD's people were p
1Sa 10:11 Is Saul also among the p?"
28: 6 him by dreams or Urim or p.
1Ki 19:10 put your p to death with the sword.
1Ch 16:22 do my p no harm."
Ps 105: 15 do my p no harm."
Jer 23: 9 Concerning the p:
23:30 "I am against the p who steal
Eze 13: 2 prophesy against the p
Mt 5:17 come to abolish the Law or the P;
7:12 for this sums up the Law and the P.
7:15 "Watch out for false p.
22:40 and the P hang on these two
23:37 you who kill the p and stone those
24:24 false Christs and false p will appear
26:56 of the p might be fulfilled."
Lk 10:24 For I tell you that many p
11:49 'I will send them p and apostles,
24:25 believe all that the p have spoken!
24:44 me in the Law of Moses, the P
Ac 3:24 "Indeed, all the p from Samuel on,
10:43 All the p testify about him that
13: 1 the church at Antioch there were p
26:22 nothing beyond what the p
28:23 the Law of Moses and from the P.
Ro 1: 2 through his p in the Holy
3:21 to which the Law and the P testify.
11: 3 they have killed your p
1Co 12:28 second p, third teachers, then
12:29 Are all p? Are all teachers?
14:32 The spirits of p are subject
Eph 2:20 foundation of the apostles and p,
3: 5 Spirit to God's holy apostles and p.
4:11 some to be p, some
Heb 1: 1 through the p at many times
1Pe 1:10 Concerning this salvation, the p,
2Pe 1:19 word of the p made more certain,
3: 2 spoken in the past by the holy p
1Jn 4: 1 because many false p have gone out
Rev 11:10 these two p had tormented those
18:20 Rejoice, saints and apostles and p!

PROPITIATION see (atoning) SACRIFICE

PROPORTION

Dt 16:10 by giving a freewill offering in p
16:17 Each of you must bring a gift in p

PROPRIETY*

1Ti 2: 9 with decency and p,
2:15 in faith, love and holiness with p.

PROSPECT*

Pr 10:28 The p of the righteous is joy,

PROSPER (PROSPERED PROSPERITY PROSPEROUS PROSPERS)

Dt 5:33 so that you may live and p
28:63 pleased the LORD to make you p
29: 9 that you may p in everything you
1Ki 2: 3 so that you may p in all you do

Ezr 6:14 and *p* under the preaching
Pr 11:10 When the righteous *p*, the city
11:25 A generous man will *p*;
17:20 A man of perverse heart does not *p*
28:13 who conceals his sins does not *p*,
28:25 he who trusts in the LORD will *p*.
Isa 53:10 of the LORD will *p* in his hand.
Jer 12:1 Why does the way of the wicked *p*?

PROSPERED (PROSPER)

Ge 39:2 was with Joseph and he *p*,
2Ch 14:7 So they built and *p*.
31:21 And so he *p*.

PROSPERITY (PROSPER)

Dt 28:11 will grant you abundant *p*—
30:15 I set before you today life and *p*,
Job 36:11 will spend the rest of their days in *p*
Ps 73:3 when I saw the *p* of the wicked.
122:9 I will seek your *p*.
128:2 blessings and *p* will be yours.
Pr 3:2 and bring you *p*.
13:21 but *p* is the reward of the righteous.
21:21 finds life, *p* and honor.
Isa 45:7 I bring *p* and create disaster;

PROSPEROUS (PROSPER)

Dt 30:9 your God will make you most *p*
Jos 1:8 Then you will be *p* and successful.
Job 42:10 the LORD made him *p* again

PROSPERS (PROSPER)

Ps 1:3 Whatever he does *p*.
Pr 16:20 gives heed to instruction *p*,
19:8 he who cherishes understanding *p*.

PROSTITUTE (PROSTITUTES PROSTITUTION)

Lev 20:6 and spiritists to *p* himself
Nu 15:39 and not *p* yourselves by going
Jos 2:1 the house of a *p* named Rahab
Pr 6:26 for the *p* reduces you to a loaf
7:10 like a *p* and with crafty intent.
23:27 for a *p* is a deep pit
Eze 16:15 and used your fame to become a *p*.
23:7 a *p* to all the elite of the Assyrians
Hos 3:3 you must not be a *p* or be intimate
1Co 6:15 of Christ and unite them with a *p*?
6:16 with a *p* is one with her in body?
Rev 17:1 you the punishment of the great *p*,

PROSTITUTES (PROSTITUTE)

Pr 29:3 of *p* squanders his wealth.
Mt 21:31 and the *p* are entering the kingdom
Lk 15:30 property with *p* comes home,
1Co 6:9 male *p* nor homosexual offenders

PROSTITUTION (PROSTITUTE)

Eze 16:16 where you carried on your *p*.
23:3 engaging in *p* from their youth.
Hos 4:10 engage in *p* but not increase,

PROSTRATE

Dt 9:18 again I fell *p* before the LORD
1Ki 18:39 they fell *p* and cried, "The LORD

PROTECT (PROTECTED PROTECTION PROTECTS)

Dt 23:14 about in your camp to *p* you
Ps 25:21 integrity and uprightness *p* me,
32:7 you will *p* me from trouble
40:11 your truth always *p* me.
41:2 The LORD will *p* him
91:14 I will *p* him, for he acknowledges
140:1 *p* me from men of violence,
Pr 2:11 Discretion will *p* you,
4:6 forsake wisdom, and she will *p* you;
Jn 17:11 *p* them by the power of your name
17:15 that you *p* them from the evil one.
2Th 3:3 and *p* you from the evil one.

PROTECTED (PROTECT)

Jos 24:17 He *p* us on our entire journey
1Sa 30:23 He has *p* us and handed
Ps 37:28 They will be *p* forever,
Jn 17:12 I *p* them and kept them safe

PROTECTION (PROTECT)

Ezr 9:9 he has given us a wall of *p* in Judah
Ps 5:11 Spread your *p* over them,

PROTECTS (PROTECT)

Ps 116:6 The LORD *p* the simplehearted;
Pr 2:8 and *p* the way of his faithful ones.
1Co 13:7 It always *p*, always trusts,

PROUD (PRIDE)

Ps 31:23 but the *p* he pays back in full.
101:5 has haughty eyes and a *p* heart,
138:6 but the *p* he knows from afar.
Pr 3:34 He mocks *p* mockers
16:5 The LORD detests all the *p*
16:19 than to share plunder with the *p*.
18:12 his downfall a man's heart is *p*,
21:4 Haughty eyes and a *p* heart,
Isa 2:12 store for all the *p* and lofty,
Ro 12:16 Do not be *p*, but be willing
1Co 13:4 it does not boast, it is not *p*.
2Ti 3:2 lovers of money, boastful, *p*,
Jas 4:6 "God opposes the *p*
1Pe 5:5 because, "God opposes the *p*

PROVE (PROOF PROVED PROVING)

Pr 29:25 Fear of man will *p* to be a snare,
Jn 8:46 Can any of you *p* me guilty of sin?
Ac 26:20 *p* their repentance by their deeds.
1Co 4:2 been given a trust must *p* faithful.

PROVED (PROVE)

Ps 51:4 so that you are *p* right
Mt 11:19 wisdom is *p* right by her actions."
Ro 3:4 "So that you may be *p* right
1Pe 1:7 may be *p* genuine and may result

PROVIDE (PROVIDED PROVIDES PROVISION)

Ge 22:8 "God himself will *p* the lamb
22:14 that place "The LORD will *P*."
Isa 43:20 because I *p* water in the desert
61:3 and *p* for those who grieve in Zion
1Co 10:13 *p* a way out so that you can stand
1Ti 5:8 If anyone does not *p*
Tit 3:14 in order that they may *p*

PROVIDED (PROVIDE)

Ps 68:10 O God, you *p* for the poor.
111:9 He *p* redemption for his people;
Jnh 1:17 But the LORD *p* a great fish
4:6 Then the LORD God *p* a vine
4:7 dawn the next day God *p* a worm,
4:8 God *p* a scorching east wind,
Gal 4:18 to be zealous, *p* the purpose is good
Heb 1:3 After he had *p* purification for sins,

PROVIDES (PROVIDE)

Ps 111:5 He *p* food for those who fear him;
Pr 31:15 she *p* food for her family
Eze 18:7 and *p* clothing for the naked.
1Ti 6:17 who richly *p* us with everything
1Pe 4:11 it with the strength God *p*,

PROVING* (PROVE)

Ac 9:22 by *p* that Jesus is the Christ.
17:3 and *p* that the Christ had to suffer
18:28 *p* from the Scriptures that Jesus

PROVISION (PROVIDE)

Ro 5:17 who receive God's abundant *p*

PROVOKED

Ecc 7:9 Do not be quickly *p* in your spirit,
Jer 32:32 Judah have *p* me by all the evil they

PROWLS

1Pe 5:8 Your enemy the devil *p*

PRUDENCE* (PRUDENT)

Pr 1:4 for giving *p* to the simple,
8:5 You who are simple, gain *p*;
8:12 "I, wisdom, dwell together with *p*;
15:5 whoever heeds correction shows *p*.
19:25 and the simple will learn *p*;

PRUDENT* (PRUDENCE)

Pr 1:3 acquiring a disciplined and *p* life,
12:16 but a *p* man overlooks an insult.
12:23 A *p* man keeps his knowledge
13:16 Every *p* man acts out of knowledge
14:8 The wisdom of the *p* is
14:15 a *p* man gives thought to his steps.
14:18 the *p* are crowned with knowledge.
19:14 but a *p* wife is from the LORD.
22:3 *p* man sees danger and takes
27:12 The *p* see danger and take refuge,
Jer 49:7 Has counsel perished from the *p*?
Am 5:13 Therefore the *p* man keeps quiet

PRUNES (PRUNING)

Jn 15:2 that does bear fruit he *p*

PRUNING (PRUNES)

Isa 2:4 and their spears into *p* hooks.
Joel 3:10 and your *p* hooks into spears.

PSALMS

Eph 5:19 Speak to one another with *p*,
Col 3:16 and as you sing *p*, hymns

PUBLICLY

Ac 20:20 have taught you *p* and from house
1Ti 5:20 Those who sin are to be rebuked *p*,

PUFFS

1Co 8:1 Knowledge *p* up, but love builds up

PULLING

2Co 10:8 building you up rather than *p* you

PUNISH (PUNISHED PUNISHES PUNISHMENT)

Ge 15:14 But I will *p* the nation they serve
Ex 32:34 I will *p* them for their sin."
Pr 17:26 It is not good to *p* an innocent man,
23:13 if you *p* him with the rod, he will
Isa 13:11 I will *p* the world for its evil,
Jer 2:19 Your wickedness will *p* you;
21:14 I will *p* you as your deeds deserve,
Zep 1:12 and *p* those who are complacent,
Ac 7:7 But I will *p* the nation they serve
2Th 1:8 He will *p* those who do not know
1Pe 2:14 by him to *p* those who do wrong

PUNISHED (PUNISH)

Ezr 9:13 you have *p* us less than our sins
Ps 99:8 though you *p* their misdeeds.
La 3:39 complain when *p* for his sins?
Mk 12:40 Such men will be *p* most severely."
Lk 23:41 the same sentence? We are *p* justly,
2Th 1:9 be *p* with everlasting destruction
Heb 10:29 to be *p* who has trampled the Son

PUNISHES (PUNISH)

Heb 12:6 and he *p* everyone he accepts

PUNISHMENT (PUNISH)

Isa 53:5 the *p* that brought us peace was
Jer 4:18 This is your *p*.
Mt 25:46 Then they will go away to eternal *p*
Lk 12:48 and does things deserving *p* will be
21:22 For this is the time of *p*
Ro 13:4 wrath to bring *p* on the wrongdoer.
Heb 2:2 disobedience received its just *p*,
2Pe 2:9 while continuing their *p*.

PURCHASED

Ps 74:2 Remember the people you *p* of old,
Rev 5:9 with your blood you *p* men for God

PURE (PURIFICATION PURIFIED PURIFIES PURIFY PURITY)

2Sa 22:27 to the *p* you show yourself *p*,
Job 14:4 Who can bring what is *p*
Ps 19:9 The fear of the LORD is *p*,
24:4 who has clean hands and a *p* heart,
51:10 Create in me a *p* heart, O God,
119:9 can a young man keep his way *p*?
Pr 15:26 those of the *p* are pleasing to him.
20:9 can say, "I have kept my heart *p*;
Isa 52:11 Come out from it and be *p*,
Hab 1:13 Your eyes are too *p* to look on evil;
Mt 5:8 Blessed are the *p* in heart,
2Co 11:2 I might present you as a *p* virgin
Php 4:8 whatever is *p*, whatever is lovely,
1Ti 1:5 which comes from a *p* heart
5:22 Keep yourself *p*.
2Ti 2:22 call on the Lord out of a *p* heart.
Tit 1:15 To the *p*, all things are *p*,
2:5 to be self-controlled and *p*,
Heb 7:26 blameless, *p*, set apart from sinners
13:4 and the marriage bed kept *p*,
Jas 1:27 that God our Father accepts as *p*
3:17 comes from heaven is first of all *p*;
1Jn 3:3 him purifies himself, just as he is *p*.

PURGE

Pr 20:30 and beatings *p* the inmost being.

PURIFICATION (PURE)

Heb 1:3 After he had provided *p* for sins,

PURIFIED (PURE)

Ac 15:9 for he *p* their hearts by faith.
1Pe 1:22 Now that you have *p* yourselves

PURIFIES* (PURE)
1Jn 1: 7 of Jesus, his Son, p us from all sin.
3: 3 who has this hope in him p himself,

PURIFY (PURE)
Nu 19: 12 He must p himself with the water
2Co 7: 1 us p ourselves from everything that
Tit 2: 14 to p for himself a people that are
Jas 4: 8 you sinners, and p your hearts,
1Jn 1: 9 and p us from all unrighteousness.

PURIM
Est 9: 26 Therefore these days were called P

PURITY* (PURE)
Hos 8: 5 long will they be incapable of p?
2Co 6: 6 in p, understanding, patience
1Ti 4: 12 in life, in love, in faith and in p.
5: 2 as sisters, with absolute p.
1Pe 3: 2 when they see the p and reverence

PURPLE
Pr 31: 22 she is clothed in fine linen and p.
Mk 15: 17 They put a p robe on him, then

PURPOSE (PURPOSED PURPOSES)
Ex 9: 16 I have raised you up for this very p,
Job 36: 5 he is mighty, and firm in his p.
Pr 19: 21 but it is the LORD's p that prevails
Isa 46: 10 I say: My p will stand,
55: 11 and achieve the p for which I sent it
Ac 2: 23 handed over to you by God's set p
Ro 8: 28 have been called according to his p.
9: 11 in order that God's p
9: 17 "I raised you up for this very p,
1Co 3: 8 the man who waters have one p,
2Co 5: 5 who has made us for this very p
Gal 4: 18 be zealous, provided the p is good,
Eph 1: 11 in conformity with the p of his will,
3: 11 according to his eternal p which he
Php 2: 2 love, being one in spirit and p.
2: 13 and to act according to his good p.
2Ti 1: 9 but because of his own p and grace.

PURPOSED (PURPOSE)
Isa 14: 24 and as I have p, so it will stand.
14: 27 For the LORD Almighty has p,
Eph 1: 9 which he p in Christ, to be put

PURPOSES (PURPOSE)
Ps 33: 10 he thwarts the p of the peoples.
Jer 23: 20 the p of his heart.
32: 19 great are your p and mighty are

PURSE (PURSES)
Hag 1: 6 to put them in a p with holes in it."
Lk 10: 4 Do not take a p or bag or sandals;
22: 36 "But now if you have a p, take it,

PURSES (PURSE)
Lk 12: 33 Provide p for yourselves that will

PURSUE (PURSUES)
Ps 34: 14 seek peace and p it.
Pr 15: 9 he loves those who p righteousness
Ro 9: 30 who did not p righteousness,
1Ti 6: 11 and p righteousness, godliness,
2Ti 2: 22 and p righteousness, faith,
1Pe 3: 11 he must seek peace and p it.

PURSUES (PURSUE)
Pr 21: 21 He who p righteousness and love
28: 1 wicked man flees though no one p,

QUAIL
Ex 16: 13 That evening q came and covered
Nu 11: 31 and drove q in from the sea.

QUALITIES* (QUALITY)
Da 6: 3 by his exceptional q that the king
Ro 1: 20 of the world God's invisible q—
2Pe 1: 8 For if you possess these q

QUALITY (QUALITIES)
1Co 3: 13 and the fire will test the q

QUARREL (QUARRELING QUARRELS QUARRELSOME)
Pr 15: 18 but a patient man calms a q.
17: 14 Starting a q is like breaching a dam;
17: 19 He who loves a q loves sin;
20: 3 but every fool is quick to q.
26: 17 in a q not his own.
26: 20 without gossip a q dies down.
2Ti 2: 24 And the Lord's servant must not q;
Jas 4: 2 You q and fight.

QUARRELING (QUARREL)
1Co 3: 3 For since there is jealousy and q
2Ti 2: 14 before God against q about words;

QUARRELS (QUARREL)
Pr 13: 10 Pride only breeds q,
Isa 45: 9 Woe to him who q with his Maker,
2Ti 2: 23 because you know they produce q.
Jas 4: 1 What causes fights and q

QUARRELSOME (QUARREL)
Pr 19: 13 a q wife is like a constant dripping.
21: 9 than share a house with a q wife.
26: 21 so is a q man for kindling strife.
1Ti 3: 3 not violent but gentle, not q,

QUEEN
1Ki 10: 1 When the q of Sheba heard about
2Ch 9: 1 When the q of Sheba heard
Mt 12: 42 The Q of the South will rise

QUENCH (QUENCHED)
SS 8: 7 Many waters cannot q love;

QUENCHED (QUENCH)
Isa 66: 24 nor will their fire be q,
Mk 9: 48 and the fire is not q.'

QUICKEN see (make) ALIVE, (give) LIFE, RESTORE, REVIVE

QUICK-TEMPERED* (TEMPER)
Pr 14: 17 A q man does foolish things,
14: 29 but a q man displays folly.
Tit 1: 7 not q, not given to drunkenness,

QUIET (QUIETNESS)
Ps 23: 2 he leads me beside q waters,
Pr 17: 1 Better a dry crust with peace and q
Ecc 9: 17 The q words of the wise are more
Am 5: 13 Therefore the prudent man keeps q
Zep 3: 17 he will q you with his love,
Lk 19: 40 he replied, "if they keep q,
1Th 4: 11 it your ambition to lead a q life,
1Ti 2: 2 we may live peaceful and q lives
1Pe 3: 4 beauty of a gentle and q spirit,

QUIETNESS (QUIET)
Isa 30: 15 in q and trust is your strength,
32: 17 the effect of righteousness will be q
1Ti 2: 11 A woman should learn in q

QUIVER
Ps 127: 5 whose q is full of them.

RACE
Ecc 9: 11 The r is not to the swift
Ac 20: 24 if only I may finish the r
1Co 9: 24 that in a r all the runners run,
Gal 2: 2 that I was running or had run my r
5: 7 You were running a good r.
2Ti 4: 7 I have finished the r, I have kept
Heb 12: 1 perseverance the r marked out

RACHEL
Daughter of Laban (Ge 29:16); wife of Jacob (Ge 29:28); bore two sons (Ge 30:22-24; 35:16-24; 46:19). Stole Laban's gods (Ge 31:19, 32-35). Death (Ge 35:19-20).

RADIANCE (RADIANT)
Eze 1: 28 so was the r around him.
Heb 1: 3 The Son is the r of God's glory

RADIANT (RADIANCE)
Ex 34: 29 he was not aware that his face was r
Ps 34: 5 Those who look to him are r;
SS 5: 10 *Beloved* My lover is r and ruddy,
Isa 60: 5 Then you will look and be r,
Eph 5: 27 her to himself as a r church,

RAGE
Ac 4: 25 " 'Why do the nations r
Col 3: 8 r, malice, slander, and filthy

RAGS
Isa 64: 6 our righteous acts are like filthy r;

RAHAB
Prostitute of Jericho who hid Israelite spies (Jos 2; 6:22-25; Heb 11:31; Jas 2:25). Mother of Boaz (Mt 1:5).

RAIN (RAINBOW)
Ge 7: 4 from now I will send r on the earth
1Ki 17: 1 nor r in the next few years
18: 1 and I will send r on the land."
Mt 5: 45 and sends r on the righteous
Jas 5: 17 it did not r on the land for three
Jude : 12 They are clouds without r,

RAINBOW (RAIN)
Ge 9: 13 I have set my r in the clouds,

RAISE (RISE)
Jn 6: 39 but r them up at the last day.
1Co 15: 15 he did not r him if in fact the dead

RAISED (RISE)
Isa 52: 13 he will be r and lifted up
Mt 17: 23 on the third day he will be r to life
Lk 7: 22 the deaf hear, the dead are r,
Ac 2: 24 But God r him from the dead,
Ro 4: 25 was r to life for our justification.
6: 4 as Christ was r from the dead
8: 11 And if the Spirit of him who r Jesus
10: 9 in your heart that God r him
1Co 15: 4 that he was r on the third day
15: 20 But Christ has indeed been r

RALLY*
Isa 11: 10 the nations will r to him,

RAM (RAMS)
Ge 22: 13 there in a thicket he saw a r caught
Da 8: 3 before me was a r with two horns,

RAMPART*
Ps 91: 4 will be your shield and r.

RAMS (RAM)
1Sa 15: 22 to heed is better than the fat of r.
Mic 6: 7 pleased with thousands of r,

RAN (RUN)
Jnh 1: 3 But Jonah r away from the LORD

RANSOM (RANSOMED)
Isa 50: 2 Was my arm too short to r you?
Hos 13: 14 "I will r them from the power
Mt 20: 28 and to give his life as a r for many."
Mk 10: 45 and to give his life as a r for many."
1Ti 2: 6 who gave himself as a r for all men
Heb 9: 15 as a r to set them free

RANSOMED (RANSOM)
Isa 35: 10 and the r of the LORD will return.

RARE
Pr 20: 15 that speak knowledge are a r jewel.

RAVEN (RAVENS)
Ge 8: 7 made in the ark and sent out a r,
Job 38: 41 Who provides food for the r

RAVENS (RAVEN)
1Ki 17: 6 The r brought him bread
Ps 147: 9 and for the young r when they call.
Lk 12: 24 Consider the r: They do not sow

READ (READING READS)
Dt 17: 19 he is to r it all the days of his life
Jos 8: 34 Joshua r all the words of the law—
2Ki 23: 2 He r in their hearing all the words
Ne 8: 8 They r from the Book of the Law
Jer 36: 6 and r to the people from the scroll
2Co 3: 2 known and r by everybody.

READING (READ)
1Ti 4: 13 to the public r of Scripture,

READS (READ)
Rev 1: 3 Blessed is the one who r the words

REAFFIRM
2Co 2: 8 therefore, to r your love for him.

REAL* (REALITIES REALITY)
Jn 6: 55 is r food and my blood is r drink.
1Jn 2: 27 all things and as that anointing is r,

REALITIES* (REAL)
Heb 10: 1 are coming—not the r themselves.

REALITY* (REAL)
Col 2: 17 the r, however, is found in Christ.

REALM (REALMS)
Hab 2: 9 "Woe to him who builds his *r*

REALMS (REALM)
Eph 1: 3 the heavenly *r* with every spiritual
2: 6 in the heavenly *r* in Christ Jesus,

REAP (REAPER REAPS)
Job 4: 8 and those who sow trouble *r* it.
Ps 126: 5 will *r* with songs of joy.
Hos 8: 7 and *r* the whirlwind.
10: 12 *r* the fruit of unfailing love,
Jn 4: 38 you to *r* what you have not worked
Ro 6: 22 the benefit you *r* leads to holiness,
2Co 9: 6 generously will also *r* generously.
Gal 6: 8 from that nature will *r* destruction;

REAPER (REAP)
Jn 4: 36 and the *r* may be glad together.

REAPS (REAP)
Pr 11: 18 who sows righteousness *r* a sure
22: 8 He who sows wickedness *r* trouble,
Gal 6: 7 A man *r* what he sows.

REASON (REASONED)
Ge 2: 24 For this *r* a man will leave his
Isa 1: 18 "Come now, let us *r* together,"
Mt 19: 5 'For this *r* a man will leave his
Jn 12: 27 it was for this very *r* I came
15: 25 'They hated me without *r*.'
1Pe 3: 15 to give the *r* for the hope that you
2Pe 1: 5 For this very *r*, make every effort

REASONED (REASON)
1Co 13: 11 thought like a child, I *r* like a child.

REBEKAH

Sister of Laban, secured as bride for Isaac (Ge 24). Mother of Esau and Jacob (Ge 25:19-26). Taken by Abimelech as sister of Isaac; returned (Ge 26:1-11). Encouraged Jacob to trick Isaac out of blessing (Ge 27:1-17).

REBEL (REBELLED REBELLION REBELS)
Nu 14: 9 Only do not *r* against the LORD.
1Sa 12: 14 and do not *r* against his commands,
Mt 10: 21 children will *r* against their parents

REBELLED (REBEL)
Ps 78: 56 and *r* against the Most High;
Isa 63: 10 Yet they *r*

REBELLION (REBEL)
Ex 34: 7 and forgiving wickedness, *r* and sin
Nu 14: 18 in love and forgiving sin and *r*.
1Sa 15: 23 For *r* is like the sin of divination,
2Th 2: 3 will not come, until the *r* occurs

REBELS (REBEL)
Ro 13: 2 he who *r* against the authority is
1Ti 1: 9 but for lawbreakers and *r*,

REBIRTH* (BEAR)
Tit 3: 5 us through the washing of *r*

REBUILD (BUILD)
Ezr 5: 2 set to work to *r* the house of God
Ne 2: 17 let us *r* the wall of Jerusalem,
Ps 102: 16 For the LORD will *r* Zion
Da 9: 25 and *r* Jerusalem until the Anointed
Am 9: 14 they will *r* the ruined cities
Ac 15: 16 Its ruins I will *r*,

REBUILT (BUILD)
Zec 1: 16 and there my house will be *r*.

REBUKE (REBUKED REBUKES REBUKING)
Lev 19: 17 *R* your neighbor frankly
Ps 141: 5 let him *r* me—it is oil on my head.
Pr 3: 11 and do not resent his *r*,
9: 8 *r* a wise man and he will love you.
15: 31 He who listens to a life-giving *r*
17: 10 A *r* impresses a man
19: 25 *r* a discerning man, and he will gain
25: 12 is a wise man's *r* to a listening ear.
27: 5 Better is open *r*
30: 6 or he will *r* you and prove you a liar.
Ecc 7: 5 It is better to heed a wise man's *r*
Isa 54: 9 never to *r* you again.
Jer 2: 19 your backsliding will *r* you.
Lk 17: 3 "If your brother sins, *r* him,
1Ti 5: 1 Do not *r* an older man harshly,
2Ti 4: 2 correct, *r* and encourage—
Tit 1: 13 Therefore, *r* them sharply,
2: 15 Encourage and *r* with all authority.
Rev 3: 19 Those whom I love I *r*

REBUKED (REBUKE)
Mk 16: 14 he *r* them for their lack of faith
1Ti 5: 20 Those who sin are to be *r* publicly,

REBUKES (REBUKE)
Job 22: 4 "Is it for your piety that he *r* you
Pr 28: 23 He who *r* a man will
29: 1 remains stiff-necked after many *r*
Heb 12: 5 do not lose heart when he *r* you,

REBUKING (REBUKE)
2Ti 3: 16 *r*, correcting and training

RECEIVE (RECEIVED RECEIVES)
Mt 10: 41 a righteous man will *r* a righteous
Mk 10: 15 anyone who will not *r* the kingdom
Jn 20: 22 and said, "*R* the Holy Spirit.
Ac 1: 8 you will *r* power when the Holy
2: 38 you will *r* the gift of the Holy Spirit
19: 2 "Did you *r* the Holy Spirit
20: 35 'It is more blessed to give than to *r*
1Co 9: 14 the gospel should *r* their living
2Co 6: 17 and I will *r* you."
1Ti 1: 16 believe on him and *r* eternal life.
Jas 1: 7 should not think he will *r* anything
2Pe 1: 11 and you will *r* a rich welcome
1Jn 3: 22 and *r* from him anything we ask,
Rev 4: 11 to *r* glory and honor and power,
5: 12 to *r* power and wealth and wisdom

RECEIVED (RECEIVE)
Mt 6: 2 they have *r* their reward in full.
10: 8 Freely you have *r*, freely give.
Mk 11: 24 believe that you have *r* it,
Jn 1: 12 Yet to all who *r* him,
1: 16 his grace we have all *r* one blessing
Ac 8: 17 and they *r* the Holy Spirit.
10: 47 They have *r* the Holy Spirit just
Ro 8: 15 but you *r* the Spirit of sonship.
1Co 11: 23 For I *r* from the Lord what I
2Co 1: 4 the comfort we ourselves have *r*
Col 2: 6 just as you *r* Christ Jesus as Lord,
1Pe 4: 10 should use whatever gift he has *r*

RECEIVES (RECEIVE)
Pr 18: 22 and *r* favor from the LORD.
27: 21 but man is tested by the praise he *r*.
Mt 7: 8 everyone who asks *r*; he who seeks
10: 40 he who *r* me *r* the one who sent me.
10: 40 "He who *r* you *r* me, and he who
Ac 10: 43 believes in him *r* forgiveness of sins

RECITE
Ps 45: 1 as I *r* my verses for the king;

RECKLESS
Pr 12: 18 *R* words pierce like a sword,
14: 16 but a fool is hotheaded and *r*.

RECKONING
Isa 10: 3 What will you do on the day of *r*,
Hos 9: 7 the days of *r* are at hand.

RECLAIM* (CLAIM)
Isa 11: 11 time to *r* the remnant that is left

RECOGNITION (RECOGNIZE)
1Co 16: 18 Such men deserve *r*.
1Ti 5: 3 Give proper *r* to those widows who

RECOGNIZE (RECOGNITION RECOGNIZED)
Mt 7: 16 By their fruit you will *r* them.
1Jn 4: 2 This is how you can *r* the Spirit
4: 6 This is how we *r* the Spirit of truth

RECOGNIZED (RECOGNIZE)
Mt 12: 33 for a tree is *r* by its fruit.
Ro 7: 13 in order that sin might be *r* as sin,

RECOMPENSE*
Isa 40: 10 and his *r* accompanies him.
62: 11 and his *r* accompanies him.'"

RECONCILE* (RECONCILED RECONCILIATION RECONCILING)
Ac 7: 26 He tried to *r* them by saying, 'Men,
Eph 2: 16 in this one body to *r* both of them
Col 1: 20 him to *r* to himself all things,

RECONCILED* (RECONCILE)
Mt 5: 24 First go and be *r* to your brother;
Lk 12: 58 try hard to be *r* to him on the way,
Ro 5: 10 how much more, having been *r*,
5: 10 we were *r* to him through the death
1Co 7: 11 or else be *r* to her husband.
2Co 5: 18 who *r* us to himself through Christ
5: 20 you on Christ's behalf: Be *r* to God.
Col 1: 22 he has *r* you by Christ's physical

RECONCILIATION* (RECONCILE)
Ro 5: 11 whom we have now received *r*.
11: 15 For if their rejection is the *r*
2Co 5: 18 and gave us the ministry of *r*:
5: 19 committed to us the message of *r*.

RECONCILING* (RECONCILE)
2Co 5: 19 that God was *r* the world to himself

RECORD (RECORDED)
Ps 130: 3 If you, O LORD, kept a *r* of sins,
Hos 13: 12 his sins are kept on *r*.
1Co 13: 5 is not easily angered, it keeps no *r*

RECORDED (RECORD)
Job 19: 23 "Oh, that my words were *r*,
Jn 20: 30 which are not *r* in this book.

RECOUNT*
Ps 40: 5 no one can *r* to you;
79: 13 we will *r* your praise.
119: 13 With my lips I *r*

RED
Ex 15: 4 are drowned in the *R* Sea.
Ps 106: 9 He rebuked the *R* Sea,
Pr 23: 31 Do not gaze at wine when it is *r*,
Isa 1: 18 though they are *r* as crimson,

REDEEM (KINSMAN-REDEEMER REDEEMED REDEEMER REDEEMS REDEMPTION)
Ex 6: 6 will *r* you with an outstretched arm
2Sa 7: 23 on earth that God went out to *r*
Ps 44: 26 *r* us because of your unfailing love.
49: 7 No man can *r* the life of another
49: 15 God will *r* my life from the grave;
130: 8 He himself will *r* Israel
Hos 13: 14 I will *r* them from death.
Gal 4: 5 under law, to *r* those under law,
Tit 2: 14 for us to *r* us from all wickedness

REDEEMED (REDEEM)
Job 33: 28 He *r* my soul from going
Ps 71: 23 I, whom you have *r*.
107: 2 Let the *r* of the LORD say this—
Isa 35: 9 But only the *r* will walk there,
63: 9 In his love and mercy he *r* them;
Gal 3: 13 Christ *r* us from the curse
1Pe 1: 18 or gold that you were *r*

REDEEMER (REDEEM)
Job 19: 25 I know that my *R* lives,
Ps 19: 14 O LORD, my Rock and my *R*.
Isa 44: 6 and *R*, the LORD Almighty:
48: 17 your *R*, the Holy One of Israel:
59: 20 "The *R* will come to Zion,

REDEEMS (REDEEM)
Ps 34: 22 The LORD *r* his servants;
103: 4 he *r* my life from the pit

REDEMPTION (REDEEM)
Ps 130: 7 and with him is full *r*.
Lk 21: 28 because your *r* is drawing near."
Ro 3: 24 grace through the *r* that came
8: 23 as sons, the *r* of our bodies.
1Co 1: 30 our righteousness, holiness and *r*.
Eph 1: 7 In him we have *r* through his blood
1: 14 until the *r* of those who are God's
4: 30 you were sealed for the day of *r*.
Col 1: 14 in whom we have *r*, the forgiveness
Heb 9: 12 having obtained eternal *r*.

REED
Isa 42: 3 A bruised *r* he will not break,
Mt 12: 20 A bruised *r* he will not break,

REFINE*
Jer 9: 7 "See, I will *r* and test them,
Zec 13: 9 I will *r* them like silver
Mal 3: 3 and *r* them like gold and silver.

REFLECT (REFLECTS)
2Co 3:18 unveiled faces all *r* the Lord's

REFLECTS (REFLECT)
Pr 27:19 As water *r* a face,

REFRESH (REFRESHED REFRESHING)
Phm .20 in the Lord, *r* my heart in Christ.

REFRESHED (REFRESH)
Pr 11:25 refreshes others will himself be *r*.

REFRESHING* (REFRESH)
Ac 3:19 that times of *r* may come

REFUGE
Nu 35:11 towns to be your cities of *r*,
Dt 33:27 The eternal God is your *r*,
Jos 20: 2 to designate the cities of *r*,
Ru 2:12 wings you have come to take *r*."
2Sa 22: 3 God is my rock, in whom I take *r*,
22:31 a shield for all who take *r* in him.
Ps 2:12 Blessed are all who take *r* in him.
5:11 But let all who take *r* in you be glad
9: 9 The LORD is a *r* for the oppressed,
16: 1 for in you I take *r*.
17: 7 those who take *r* in you
18: 2 God is my rock, in whom I take *r*.
31: 2 be my rock of *r*,
34: 8 blessed is the man who takes *r*
36: 7 find *r* in the shadow of your wings.
46: 1 God is our *r* and strength,
62: 8 for God is our *r*.
71: 1 In you, O LORD, I have taken *r*;
91: 2 "He is my *r* and my fortress,
144: 2 my shield, in whom I take *r*,
Pr 14:26 and for his children it will be a *r*.
30: 5 a shield to those who take *r* in him.
Na 1: 7 a *r* in times of trouble.

REFUSE (REFUSED)
Jn 5:40 yet you *r* to come to me to have life

REFUSED (REFUSE)
2Th 2:10 because they *r* to love the truth
Rev 16: 9 but they *r* to repent and glorify him

REGARD (REGARDS)
1Th 5:13 Hold them in the highest *r* in love

REGARDS (REGARD)
Ro 14:14 But if anyone *r* something

REGRET
2Co 7:10 leads to salvation and leaves no *r*,

REHOBOAM
Son of Solomon (1Ki 11:43; 1Ch 3:10). Harsh treatment of subjects caused divided kingdom (1Ki 12:1-24; 14:21-31; 2Ch 10-12).

REIGN (REIGNED REIGNS)
Ex 15:18 The LORD will *r*
Ps 68:16 mountain where God chooses to *r*,
Isa 9: 7 He will *r* on David's throne
24:23 for the LORD Almighty will *r*
32: 1 See, a king will *r* in righteousness
Jer 23: 5 a King who will *r* wisely
Lk 1:33 and he will *r* over the house
Ro 6:12 Therefore do not let sin *r*
1Co 15:25 For he must *r* until he has put all
2Ti 2:12 we will also *r* with him.
Rev 11:15 and he will *r* for ever and ever."
20: 6 will *r* with him for a thousand years
22: 5 And they will *r* for ever and ever.

REIGNED (REIGN)
Ro 5:21 so that, just as sin *r* in death,
Rev 20: 4 and *r* with Christ a thousand years.

REIGNS (REIGN)
Ps 9: 7 The LORD *r* forever;
47: 8 God *r* over the nations;
93: 1 The LORD *r*, he is robed
96:10 among the nations, "The LORD *r*
97: 1 The LORD *r*, let the earth be glad;
99: 1 The LORD *r*, / let the nations tremble;
146:10 The LORD *r* forever,
Isa 52: 7 "Your God *r*!"
Rev 19: 6 For our Lord God Almighty *r*.

REIN
Jas 1:26 and yet does not keep a tight *r*

REJECT (REJECTED REJECTION REJECTS)
Ps 94:14 For the LORD will not *r* his people
Ro 11: 1 I ask then: Did God *r* his people?

REJECTED (REJECT)
1Sa 8: 7 it is not you they have *r*,
1Ki 19:10 The Israelites have *r* your covenant
2Ki 17:15 They *r* his decrees
Ps 66:20 who has not *r* my prayer
118:22 The stone the builders *r*
Isa 5:24 for they have *r* the law
41: 9 chosen you and have not *r* you.
53: 3 He was despised and *r* by men,
Jer 8: 9 Since they have *r* the word
Mt 21:42 " 'The stone the builders *r*
1Ti 4: 4 nothing is to be *r* if it is received
1Pe 2: 4 *r* by men but chosen by God
2: 7 "The stone the builders *r*

REJECTION* (REJECT)
Ro 11:15 For if their *r* is the reconciliation

REJECTS (REJECT)
Lk 10:16 but he who *r* me *r* him who sent me
Jn 3:36 whoever *r* the Son will not see life,
1Th 4: 8 he who *r* this instruction does not

REJOICE (JOY)
Dt 12: 7 shall *r* in everything you have put
1Ch 16:10 of those who seek the LORD *r*.
16:31 Let the heavens *r*, let the earth be
Ps 2:11 and *r* with trembling.
5:11 those who love your name may *r*
9:14 and there *r* in your salvation.
34: 2 let the afflicted hear and *r*.
63:11 But the king will *r* in God;
66: 6 come, let us *r* in him.
68: 3 and *r* before God;
105: 3 of those who seek the LORD *r*.
118:24 let us *r* and be glad in it.
119: 14 I *r* in following your statutes
119:162 I *r* in your promise
149: 2 Let Israel *r* in their Maker;
Pr 5:18 may you *r* in the wife of your youth
23:25 may she who gave you birth *r*!
24:17 stumbles, do not let your heart *r*,
Isa 9: 3 as men *r*
35: 1 the wilderness will *r* and blossom.
61: 7 they will *r* in their inheritance;
62: 5 so will your God *r* over you.
Jer 31:12 they will *r* in the bounty
Zep 3:17 he will *r* over you with singing."
Zec 9: 9 *R* greatly, O Daughter of Zion!
Lk 6:23 "*R* in that day and leap for joy,
10:20 but *r* that your names are written
15: 6 '*R* with me; I have found my lost
15: 9 '*R* with me; I have found my lost
Ro 5: 2 And we *r* in the hope of the glory
12:15 Rejoice with those who *r*; mourn
Php 2:17 I am glad and *r* with all of you.
3: 1 Finally, my brothers, *r* in the Lord!
4: 4 *R* in the Lord always.
1Pe 4:13 But *r* that you participate
Rev 19: 7 Let us *r* and be glad

REJOICES (JOY)
Ps 13: 5 my heart *r* in your salvation.
16: 9 my heart is glad and my tongue *r*;
Isa 61:10 my soul *r* in my God.
62: 5 as a bridegroom *r* over his bride,
Lk 1:47 and my spirit *r* in God my Savior,
Ac 2:26 my heart is glad and my tongue *r*;
1Co 12:26 if one part is honored, every part *r*
13: 6 delight in evil but *r* with the truth.

REJOICING (JOY)
2Sa 6:12 to the City of David with *r*.
Ne 12:43 *r* because God had given them
Ps 30: 5 but *r* comes in the morning.
Lk 15: 7 in the same way there will be more *r*
Ac 5:41 *r* because they had been counted
2Co 6:10 sorrowful, yet always *r*; poor,

RELATIVES
Pr 19: 7 A poor man is shunned by all his *r*
Mk 6: 4 among his *r* and in his own house is
Lk 21:16 betrayed even by parents, brothers, *r*
1Ti 5: 8 If anyone does not provide for his *r*

RELEASE (RELEASED)
Isa 61: 1 and *r* from darkness,
Lk 4:18 to *r* the oppressed,

RELEASED (RELEASE)
Ro 7: 6 we have been *r* from the law
Rev 20: 7 Satan will be *r* from his prison

RELENTED (RELENTS)
Ex 32:14 the LORD *r* and did not bring
Ps 106:45 and out of his great love he *r*.

RELENTS* (RELENTED)
Joel 2:13 and he *r* from sending calamity.
Jnh 4: 2 a God who *r* from sending calamity

RELIABLE (RELY)
Pr 22:21 teaching you true and *r* words,
Jn 8:26 But he who sent me is *r*,
2Ti 2: 2 witnesses entrust to *r* men who will

RELIANCE* (RELY)
Pr 25:19 is *r* on the unfaithful in times

RELIED (RELY)
2Ch 13:18 were victorious because they *r*
16: 8 Yet when you *r* on the LORD,
Ps 71: 6 From birth I have *r* on you;

RELIEF
Job 35: 9 they plead for *r* from the arm
Ps 94:13 you grant him *r* from days
143: 1 come to my *r*.
La 3:49 without *r*,
3:56 to my cry for *r*."
2Th 1: 7 and give *r* to you who are troubled,

RELIGION* (RELIGIOUS)
Ac 25:19 dispute with him about their own *r*
26: 5 to the strictest sect of our *r*,
1Ti 5: 4 all to put their *r* into practice
Jas 1:26 himself and his *r* is worthless.
1:27 *R* that God our Father accepts

RELIGIOUS (RELIGION)
Jas 1:26 If anyone considers himself *r*

RELY (RELIABLE RELIANCE RELIED)
Isa 50:10 and *r* on his God.
Eze 33:26 you then possess the land? You *r*
2Co 1: 9 this happened that we might not *r*
Gal 3:10 All who *r* on observing the law are
1Jn 4:16 and *r* on the love God has for us.

REMAIN (REMAINS)
Nu 33:55 allow to *r* will become barbs
Ps 102:27 But you *r* the same,
Jn 1:32 from heaven as a dove and *r* on him
15: 4 *R* in me, and I will *r* in you.
15: 7 If you *r* in me and my words
15: 9 Now *r* in my love.
Ro 13: 8 Let no debt *r* outstanding,
1Co 13:13 And now these three *r*: faith,
2Ti 2:13 he will *r* faithful,
Heb 1:11 They will perish, but you *r*;
1Jn 2:27 just as it has taught you, *r* in him.

REMAINS (REMAIN)
Ps 146: 6 the LORD, who *r* faithful forever.
Heb 7: 3 Son of God he *r* a priest forever.

REMEDY
Isa 3: 7 "I have no *r*.

REMEMBER (REMEMBERED REMEMBERS REMEMBRANCE)
Ge 9:15 I will *r* my covenant between me
Ex 20: 8 "*R* the Sabbath day
33:13 *R* that this nation is your people."
Dt 5:15 *R* that you were slaves in Egypt
1Ch 16:12 *R* the wonders he has done,
Job 36:24 *R* to extol his work,
Ps 25: 6 *R*, O LORD, your great mercy
63: 6 On my bed I *r* you;
74: 2 *R* the people you purchased of old,
77:11 I will *r* the deeds of the LORD;
Ecc 12: 1 *R* your Creator
Isa 46: 8 "*R* this, fix it in mind,
Jer 31:34 and will *r* their sins no more."
Hab 3: 2 in wrath *r* mercy.
Lk 1:72 and to *r* his holy covenant,
Gal 2:10 we should continue to *r* the poor,
Php 1: 3 I thank my God every time I *r* you.
2Ti 2: 8 *R* Jesus Christ, raised
Heb 8:12 and will *r* their sins no more."

REMEMBERED (REMEMBER)
Ex 2:24 he r his covenant with Abraham,
3:15 am to be r from generation
Ps 98: 3 He has r his love
106:45 for their sake he r his covenant
111: 4 He has caused his wonders to be r;
136:23 to the One who r us
Isa 65:17 The former things will not be r,
Eze 18:22 offenses he has committed will be r
33:13 things he has done will be r;

REMEMBERS (REMEMBER)
Ps 103:14 he r that we are dust.
111: 5 he r his covenant forever.
Isa 43:25 and r your sins no more.

REMEMBRANCE (REMEMBER)
Lk 22:19 given for you; do this in r of me."
1Co 11:24 which is for you; do this in r of me
11:25 whenever you drink it, in r of me."

REMIND
Jn 14:26 will r you of everything I have said
2Pe 1:12 I will always r you of these things,

REMNANT
Ezr 9: 8 has been gracious in leaving us a r
Isa 11:11 time to reclaim the r that is left
Jer 23: 3 "I myself will gather the r
Zec 8:12 inheritance to the r of this people.
Ro 11: 5 the present time there is a r chosen

REMOVED
Ps 30:11 you r my sackcloth and clothed me
103:12 so far has he r our transgressions
Jn 20: 1 and saw that the stone had been r

REND
Joel 2:13 R your heart

RENEW (RENEWAL RENEWED RENEWING)
Ps 51:10 and r a steadfast spirit within me.
Isa 40:31 will r their strength.

RENEWAL (RENEW)
Isa 57:10 You found r of your strength,
Tit 3: 5 of rebirth and r by the Holy Spirit,

RENEWED (RENEW)
Ps 103: 5 that your youth is r like the eagle's.
2Co 4:16 yet inwardly we are being r day

RENEWING* (RENEW)
Ro 12: 2 transformed by the r of your mind.

RENOUNCE (RENOUNCED RENOUNCES)
Da 4:27 R your sins by doing what is right,

RENOUNCED (RENOUNCE)
2Co 4: 2 we have r secret and shameful

RENOUNCES (RENOUNCE)
Pr 28:13 confesses and r them finds

RENOWN*
Ge 6: 4 were the heroes of old, men of r.
Ps 102:12 r endures through all generations.
135:13 r, O LORD, through all
Isa 26: 8 your name and r
55:13 This will be for the LORD's r,
63:12 to gain for himself everlasting r,
Jer 13:11 to be my people for my r and praise
32:20 have gained the r that is still yours.
33: 9 Then this city will bring me r, joy,
49:25 the city of r not been abandoned,
Eze 26:17 How you are destroyed, O city of r,
Hos 12: 5 the LORD is his name of r!

REPAID (PAY)
Lk 6:34 to 'sinners,' expecting to be r in full
14:14 you will be r at the resurrection
Col 3:25 Anyone who does wrong will be r

REPAY (PAY)
Dt 7:10 But those who hate him he will r
32:35 It is mine to avenge; I will r.
Ru 2:12 May the LORD r you
Ps 103:10 or r us according to our iniquities.
116:12 How can I r the LORD
Jer 25:14 I will r them according
Ro 12:17 Do not r anyone evil for evil.
12:19 "It is mine to avenge; I will r,"
1Pe 3: 9 Do not r evil with evil

REPAYING (PAY)
2Ch 6:23 r the guilty by bringing
1Ti 5: 4 so r their parents and grandparents

REPEATED
Heb 10: 1 the same sacrifices r endlessly year

REPENT (REPENTANCE REPENTED REPENTS)
1Ki 8:47 r and plead with you in the land
Job 36:10 commands them to r of their evil.
42: 6 and r in dust and ashes."
Jer 15:19 "If you r, I will restore you
Eze 18:30 R! Turn away from all your
18:32 R and live! "Take up a lament
Mt 3: 2 "R, for the kingdom of heaven is
4:17 "R, for the kingdom of heaven is
Mk 6:12 and preached that people should r.
Lk 13: 3 unless you r, you too will all perish.
Ac 2:38 Peter replied, "R and be baptized,
3:19 R, then, and turn to God,
17:30 all people everywhere to r.
26:20 also, I preached that they should r
Rev 2: 5 R and do the things you did at first.

REPENTANCE (REPENT)
Isa 30:15 "In r and rest is your salvation,
Mt 3: 8 Produce fruit in keeping with r.
Mk 1: 4 a baptism of r for the forgiveness
Lk 3: 8 Produce fruit in keeping with r.
5:32 call the righteous, but sinners to r."
24:47 and r and forgiveness of sins will be
Ac 20:21 that they must turn to God in r
26:20 and prove their r by their deeds.
Ro 2: 4 kindness leads you toward r?
2Co 7:10 Godly sorrow brings r that leads
2Pe 3: 9 but everyone to come to r.

REPENTED (REPENT)
Mt 11:21 they would have r long ago

REPENTS (REPENT)
Lk 15: 7 in heaven over one sinner who r
15:10 of God over one sinner who r."
17: 3 rebuke him, and if he r, forgive him

REPORTS
Ex 23: 1 "Do not spread false r.

REPOSES*
Pr 14:33 Wisdom r in the heart

REPRESENTATION*
Heb 1: 3 and the exact r of his being,

REPROACH
Job 27: 6 my conscience will not r me
Isa 51: 7 Do not fear the r of men
1Ti 3: 2 Now the overseer must be above r,

REPUTATION
1Ti 3: 7 also have a good r with outsiders,

REQUESTS
Ps 20: 5 May the LORD grant all your r.
Php 4: 6 with thanksgiving, present your r

REQUIRE (REQUIRED REQUIRES)
Mic 6: 8 And what does the LORD r of you

REQUIRED (REQUIRE)
1Co 4: 2 it is r that those who have been

REQUIRES (REQUIRE)
1Ki 2: 3 what the LORD your God r:
Heb 9:22 the law r that nearly everything be

RESCUE (RESCUED RESCUES)
Ps 22: 8 let the LORD r him.
31: 2 come quickly to my r;
69:14 R me from the mire,
91:14 says the LORD, "I will r him;
143: 9 R me from my enemies, O LORD,
Da 6:20 been able to r you from the lions?"
Ro 7:24 Who will r me from this body
Gal 1: 4 himself for our sins to r us
2Pe 2: 9 how to r godly men from trials

RESCUED (RESCUE)
Ps 18:17 He r me from my powerful enemy,
Pr 11: 8 The righteous man is r
Col 1:13 For he has r us from the dominion

RESCUES (RESCUE)
Da 6:27 He r and he saves;
1Th 1:10 who r us from the coming wrath.

RESENT* (RESENTFUL RESENTS)
Pr 3:11 and do not r his rebuke,

RESENTFUL* (RESENT)
2Ti 2:24 to everyone, able to teach, not r.

RESENTS* (RESENT)
Pr 15:12 A mocker r correction;

RESERVE (RESERVED)
1Ki 19:18 Yet I r seven thousand in Israel—

RESERVED (RESERVE)
Ro 11: 4 "I have r for myself seven

RESIST (RESISTED RESISTS)
Da 11:32 know their God will firmly r him.
Mt 5:39 I tell you, Do not r an evil person.
Lk 21:15 of your adversaries will be able to r
Jas 4: 7 R the devil, and he will flee
1Pe 5: 9 R him, standing firm in the faith,

RESISTED (RESIST)
Job 9: 4 Who has r him and come out

RESISTS* (RESIST)
Ro 9:19 For who r his will?" But who are

RESOLVED
Ps 17: 3 I have r that my mouth will not sin.
Da 1: 8 But Daniel r not to defile himself
1Co 2: 2 For I r to know nothing while I was

RESOUNDING*
Ps 150: 5 praise him with r cymbals.
1Co 13: 1 I am only a r gong or a clanging

RESPECT (RESPECTABLE RESPECTED RESPECTS)
Lev 19: 3 " 'Each of you must r his mother
19:32 show r for the elderly and revere
Pr 11:16 A kindhearted woman gains r,
Mal 1: 6 where is the r due me?" says
Eph 5:33 and the wife must r her husband.
6: 5 obey your earthly masters with r
1Th 4:12 so that your daily life may win the r
5:12 to r those who work hard
1Ti 3: 4 children obey him with proper r.
3: 8 are to be men worthy of r, sincere,
3:11 are to be women worthy of r,
6: 1 their masters worthy of full r,
Tit 2: 2 worthy of r, self-controlled,
1Pe 2:17 Show proper r to everyone:
3: 7 them with r as the weaker partner
3:16 But do this with gentleness and r,

RESPECTABLE* (RESPECT)
1Ti 3: 2 self-controlled, r, hospitable,

RESPECTED (RESPECT)
Pr 31:23 Her husband is r at the city gate,

RESPECTS (RESPECT)
Pr 13:13 he who r a command is rewarded.

RESPLENDENT*
Ps 76: 4 You are r with light,
132:18 but the crown on his head will be r

RESPOND
Ps 102:17 He will r to the prayer
Hos 2:21 "I will r to the skies,

RESPONSIBILITY (RESPONSIBLE)
Ac 18: 6 your own heads! I am clear of my r.

RESPONSIBLE (RESPONSIBILITY)
Nu 1:53 The Levites are to be r for the care
1Co 7:24 Brothers, each man, as r to God,

REST (RESTED RESTS SABBATH-REST)
Ex 31:15 the seventh day is a Sabbath of r,
33:14 go with you, and I will give you r."
Lev 25: 5 The land is to have a year of r.
Dt 31:16 going to r with your fathers,
Jos 14:15 Then the land had r from war.
21:44 The LORD gave them r
1Ki 5: 4 The LORD my god has given me r
1Ch 22: 9 who will be a man of peace and r,
Job 3:17 and there the weary are at r.

Ps 16: 9 my body also will r secure,
33: 22 May your unfailing love r upon us,
62: 1 My soul finds r in God alone;
62: 5 Find r, O my soul, in God alone;
90: 17 of the Lord our God r upon us;
91: 1 will r in the shadow
95: 11 "They shall never enter my r."
Pr 6: 10 a little folding of the hands to r—
Isa 11: 2 Spirit of the LORD will r on him—
11: 10 and his place of r will be glorious.
30: 15 "In repentance and r is your
32: 18 in undisturbed places of r.
57: 20 which cannot r,
Jer 6: 16 and you will find r for your souls.
47: 6 'how long till you r?
Mt 11: 28 and burdened, and I will give you r.
2Co 12: 9 so that Christ's power may r on me
Heb 3: 11 'They shall never enter my r.' "
4: 3 'They shall never enter my r.' "
4: 10 for anyone who enters God's r
Rev 14: 13 "they will r from their labor,

RESTED (REST)

Ge 2: 2 so on the seventh day he r
Heb 4: 4 "And on the seventh day God r

RESTITUTION

Ex 22: 3 "A thief must certainly make r,
Lev 6: 5 He must make r in full, add a fifth
Nu 5: 8 the r belongs to the LORD

RESTORE (RESTORES)

Ps 51: 12 R to me the joy of your salvation
80: 3 R us, O God;
126: 4 R our fortunes, O LORD,
Jer 31: 18 R me, and I will return,
La 5: 21 R us to yourself, O LORD,
Da 9: 25 From the issuing of the decree to r
Na 2: 2 The LORD will r the splendor
Gal 6: 1 are spiritual should r him gently.
1Pe 5: 10 will himself r you and make you

RESTORES (RESTORE)

Ps 23: 3 he r my soul.

RESTRAINED (RESTRAINT)

Ps 78: 38 Time after time he r his anger

RESTRAINING (RESTRAINT)

Pr 27: 16 r her is like r the wind
Col 2: 23 value in r sensual indulgence.

RESTRAINT (RESTRAINED RESTRAINING)

Pr 17: 27 of knowledge uses words with r,
23: 4 have the wisdom to show r.
29: 18 no revelation, the people cast off r;

RESTS (REST)

Dt 33: 12 and the one the LORD loves r
Pr 19: 23 one r content, untouched
Lk 2: 14 to men on whom his favor r."

RESULT

Lk 21: 13 This will r in your being witnesses
Ro 6: 22 to holiness, and the r is eternal life.
11: 31 as a r of God's mercy to you.
2Co 3: 3 from Christ, the r of our ministry,
2Th 1: 5 as a r you will be counted worthy
1Pe 1: 7 may be proved genuine and may r

RESURRECTION*

Mt 22: 23 who say there is no r, came to him
22: 28 at the r, whose wife will she be
22: 30 At the r people will neither marry
22: 31 But about the r of the dead—
27: 53 and after Jesus' r they went
Mk 12: 18 who say there is no r, came to him
12: 23 At the r whose wife will she be,
Lk 14: 14 repaid at the r of the righteous."
20: 27 who say there is no r, came to Jesus
20: 33 at the r whose wife will she be,
20: 35 in the r from the dead will neither
20: 36 since they are children of the r.
Jn 11: 24 again in the r at the last day."
11: 25 Jesus said to her, "I am the r
Ac 1: 22 become a witness with us of his r."
2: 31 he spoke of the r of the Christ,
4: 2 in Jesus the r of the dead.
4: 33 to testify to the r of the Lord Jesus,
17: 18 good news about Jesus and the r.
17: 32 When they heard about the r
23: 6 of my hope in the r of the dead."
23: 8 Sadducees say that there is no r,
24: 15 that there will be a r
24: 21 'It is concerning the r
Ro 1: 4 Son of God by his r from the dead:
6: 5 also be united with him in his r.
1Co 15: 12 some of you say that there is no r
15: 13 If there is no r of the dead,
15: 21 the r of the dead comes
15: 29 if there is no r, what will those do
15: 42 So will it be with the r of the dead.
Php 3: 10 power of his r and the fellowship
3: 11 to attain to the r from the dead.
2Ti 2: 18 say that the r has already taken
Heb 6: 2 on of hands, the r of the dead,
11: 35 so that they might gain a better r.
1Pe 1: 3 hope through the r of Jesus Christ
3: 21 It saves you by the r of Jesus Christ
Rev 20: 5 This is the first r.
20: 6 those who have part in the first r.

RETALIATE*

1Pe 2: 23 he did not r; when he suffered,

RETRIBUTION

Ps 69: 22 may it become r and a trap.
Jer 51: 56 For the LORD is a God of r;
Ro 11: 9 a stumbling block and a r for them.

RETURN (RETURNED RETURNS)

Ge 3: 19 and to dust you will r."
2Sa 12: 23 go to him, but he will not r to me."
2Ch 30: 9 If you r to the LORD, then your
Ne 1: 9 but if you r to me and obey my
Job 10: 21 joy before I go to the place of no r,
16: 22 before I go on the journey of no r.
22: 23 If you r to the Almighty, you will
Ps 80: 14 R to us, O God Almighty!
126: 6 will r with songs of joy,
Isa 10: 21 A remnant will r, a remnant
35: 10 the ransomed of the LORD will r.
55: 11 It will not r to me empty,
Jer 24: 7 for they will r to me
31: 8 a great throng will r.
La 3: 40 and let us r to the LORD.
Hos 6: 1 "Come, let us r to the LORD.
12: 6 But you must r to your God;
14: 1 R, O Israel, to the LORD your
Joel 2: 12 "r to me with all your heart,
Zec 1: 3 'R to me,' declares the LORD
10: 9 and they will r.

RETURNED (RETURN)

Ps 35: 13 When my prayers r
Am 4: 6 yet you have not r to me,"
1Pe 2: 25 now you have r to the Shepherd

RETURNS (RETURN)

Pr 3: 14 and yields better r than gold.
Isa 52: 8 When the LORD r to Zion,
Mt 24: 46 finds him doing so when he r.

REUBEN

Firstborn of Jacob by Leah (Ge 29:32; 46:8; 1Ch 2:1). Attempted to rescue Joseph (Ge 37:21-30). Lost birthright for sleeping with Bilhah (Ge 35:22; 49:4). Tribe of blessed (Ge 49:3-4; Dt 33:6), numbered (Nu 1:21; 26:7), allotted land east of Jordan (Nu 32; 34:14; Jos 13:15), west (Eze 48:6), failed to help Deborah (Jdg 5:15-16), supported David (1Ch 12:37), 12,000 from (Rev 7:5).

REVEAL (REVEALED REVEALS REVELATION REVELATIONS)

Mt 11: 27 to whom the Son chooses to r him.
Gal 1: 16 was pleased to r his Son in me

REVEALED (REVEAL)

Dt 29: 29 but the things r belong to us
Isa 40: 5 the glory of the LORD will be r,
43: 12 I have r and saved and proclaimed
53: 1 the arm of the LORD been r?
65: 1 I r myself to those who did not ask
Mt 11: 25 and r them to little children.
Jn 12: 38 the arm of the Lord been r?"
17: 6 "I have r you to those whom you
Ro 1: 17 a righteousness from God is r,
8: 18 with the glory that will be r in us.
10: 20 I r myself to those who did not ask
16: 26 but now r and made known
1Co 2: 10 but God has r it to us by his Spirit.
2Th 1: 7 happen when the Lord Jesus is r
2: 3 and the man of lawlessness is r,
1Pe 1: 7 and honor when Jesus Christ is r.
1: 20 but was r in these last times
4: 13 overjoyed when his glory is r.

REVEALS* (REVEAL)

Nu 23: 3 Whatever he r to me I will tell you
Job 12: 22 He r the deep things of darkness
Da 2: 22 He r deep and hidden things;
2: 28 a God in heaven who r mysteries.
Am 4: 13 and r his thoughts to man,

REVELATION* (REVEAL)

2Sa 7: 17 David all the words of this entire r.
1Ch 17: 15 David all the words of this entire r.
Pr 29: 18 Where there is no r, the people cast
Da 10: 1 a r was given to Daniel (who was
Hab 2: 2 "Write down the r
2: 3 For the r awaits an appointed time;
Lk 2: 32 a light for r to the Gentiles
Ro 16: 25 according to the r
1Co 14: 6 I bring you some r or knowledge
14: 26 a r, a tongue or an interpretation.
14: 30 And if a r comes to someone who is
Gal 1: 12 I received it by r from Jesus Christ.
2: 2 I went in response to a r
Eph 1: 17 you the Spirit of wisdom and r,
3: 3 mystery made known to me by r,
Rev 1: 1 r of Jesus Christ, which God gave

REVELATIONS* (REVEAL)

2Co 12: 1 on to visions and r from the Lord.
12: 7 of these surpassingly great r,

REVELED* (REVELRY)

Ne 9: 25 they r in your great goodness.

REVELRY (REVELED)

Ex 32: 6 drink and got up to indulge in r.
1Co 10: 7 and got up to indulge in pagan r."

REVENGE (VENGEANCE)

Lev 19: 18 " 'Do not seek r or bear a grudge
Ro 12: 19 Do not take r, my friends,

REVERE* (REVERENCE REVERENT REVERING)

Lev 19: 32 for the elderly and r your God.
Dt 4: 10 so that they may learn to r me
13: 4 must follow, and him you must r.
14: 23 to r the LORD your God always.
17: 19 learn to r the LORD his God
28: 58 and do not r this glorious
Job 37: 24 Therefore, men r him,
Ps 22: 23 R him, all you descendants
33: 8 let all the people of the world r him
102: 15 of the earth will r your glory.
Ecc 3: 14 God does it so that men will r him.
Isa 25: 3 cities of ruthless nations will r you.
59: 19 of the sun, they will r his glory.
63: 17 hearts so we do not r you?
Jer 10: 7 Who should not r you,
Hos 10: 3 because we did not r the LORD.
Mal 4: 2 But for you who r my name,

REVERENCE (REVERE)

Lev 19: 30 and have r for my sanctuary.
Ne 5: 15 of r for God I did not act like that.
Ps 5: 7 in r will I bow down
Da 6: 26 people must fear and r the God
2Co 7: 1 perfecting holiness out of r for God
Eph 5: 21 to one another out of r for Christ.
Col 3: 22 of heart and r for the Lord.
1Pe 3: 2 when they see the purity and r
Rev 11: 18 and those who r your name,

REVERENT* (REVERE)

Ecc 8: 12 with God-fearing men, who are r
Tit 2: 3 women to be r in the way they live,
Heb 5: 7 because of his r submission.
1Pe 1: 17 as strangers here in r fear.

REVERING* (REVERE)

Dt 8: 6 walking in his ways and r him.
Ne 1: 11 who delight in r your name.

REVERSE*

Isa 43: 13 When I act, who can r it?"

REVIVE* (REVIVING)

Ps 80: 18 r us, and we will call on your name.
85: 6 Will you not r us again,
Isa 57: 15 and to r the heart of the contrite.
57: 15 to r the spirit of the lowly
Hos 6: 2 After two days he will r us;

REVIVING* (REVIVE)

Ps 19: 7 r the soul.

REVOKED
Isa 45:23 a word that will not be *r:*

REWARD (REWARDED REWARDING REWARDS)
Ge 15: 1 your very great *r.*"
1Sa 24:19 May the LORD *r* you well
Ps 19:11 in keeping them there is great *r.*
62:12 Surely you will *r* each person
127: 3 children a *r* from him.
Pr 9:12 are wise, your wisdom will *r* you;
11:18 sows righteousness reaps a sure *r.*
13:21 prosperity is the *r* of the righteous.
19:17 he will *r* him for what he has done.
25:22 and the LORD will *r* you.
31:31 Give her the *r* she has earned,
Isa 40:10 See, his *r* is with him,
49: 4 and my *r* is with my God."
61: 8 In my faithfulness I will *r* them
62:11 See, his *r* is with him,
Jer 17:10 to *r* a man according to his conduct
32:19 you *r* everyone according
Mt 5:12 because great is your *r* in heaven,
6: 1 you will have no *r*
6: 5 they have received their *r* in full.
10:41 a prophet will receive a prophet's *r,*
16:27 and then he will *r* each person
Lk 6:23 because great is your *r* in heaven.
6:35 Then your *r* will be great,
1Co 3:14 built survives, he will receive his *r.*
Eph 6: 8 know that the Lord will *r* everyone
Col 3:24 an inheritance from the Lord as a *r.*
Heb 11:26 he was looking ahead to his *r.*
Rev 22:12 I am coming soon! My *r* is with me

REWARDED (REWARD)
Ru 2:12 May you be richly *r* by the LORD,
2Sa 22:21 of my hands he has *r* me.
2Ch 15: 7 for your work will be *r.*"
Ps 18:24 The LORD has *r* me according
Pr 13:13 he who respects a command is *r.*
14:14 and the good man *r* for his.
Jer 31:16 for your work will be *r,*"
1Co 3: 8 and each will be *r* according
Heb 10:35 your confidence; it will be richly *r.*
2Jn : 8 but that you may be *r* fully.

REWARDING* (REWARD)
Rev 11:18 for *r* your servants the prophets

REWARDS (REWARD)
1Sa 26:23 The LORD *r* every man
Pr 12:14 the work of his hands *r* him.
Heb 11: 6 that he *r* those who earnestly seek

RIBS
Ge 2:21 he took one of the man's *r*

RICH (RICHES RICHEST)
Job 34:19 does not favor the *r* over the poor,
Ps 49:16 overawed when a man grows *r,*
145: 8 slow to anger and *r* in love.
Pr 21:17 loves wine and oil will never be *r.*
22: 2 *R* and poor have this in common:
23: 4 Do not wear yourself out to get *r;*
28: 6 than a *r* man whose ways are
28:20 to get *r* will not go unpunished.
28:22 A stingy man is eager to get *r*
Ecc 5:12 but the abundance of a *r* man
Isa 33: 6 a *r* store of salvation and wisdom
53: 9 and with the *r* in his death,
Jer 9:23 or the *r* man boast of his riches,
Zec 3: 4 and I will put *r* garments on you."
Mt 19:23 it is hard for a *r* man
Lk 1:53 but has sent the *r* away empty.
6:24 "But woe to you who are *r,*
12:21 for himself but is not *r* toward God
16: 1 "There was a *r* man whose
21: 1 Jesus saw the *r* putting their gifts
2Co 6:10 yet making many *r;* having nothing
8: 2 poverty welled up in *r* generosity.
8: 9 he was *r,* yet for your sakes he
9:11 You will be made *r* in every way
Eph 2: 4 love for us, God, who is *r* in mercy,
1Ti 6: 9 want to get *r* fall into temptation
6:17 Command those who are *r*
6:18 to do good, to be *r* in good deeds,
Jas 1:10 the one who is *r* should take pride
2: 5 the eyes of the world to be *r* in faith
5: 1 you *r* people, weep and wail
Rev 2: 9 and your poverty—yet you are *r!*
3:18 you can become *r;* and white

RICHES (RICH)
Job 36:18 that no one entices you by *r;*
Ps 49: 6 and boast of their great *r?*
49:12 despite his *r,* does not endure;
62:10 though your *r* increase,
119:14 as one rejoices in great *r.*
Pr 3:16 in her left hand are *r* and honor.
11:28 Whoever trusts in his *r* will fall,
22: 1 is more desirable than great *r;*
27:24 for *r* do not endure forever,
30: 8 give me neither poverty nor *r,*
Isa 10: 3 Where will you leave your *r?*
60: 5 to you the *r* of the nations will
Jer 9:23 or the rich man boast of his *r,*
Lk 8:14 *r* and pleasures, and they do not
Ro 9:23 to make the *r* of his glory known
11:33 the depth of the *r* of the wisdom
Eph 2: 7 he might show the incomparable *r*
3: 8 to the Gentiles the unsearchable *r*
Col 1:27 among the Gentiles the glorious *r*
2: 2 so that they may have the full *r*

RICHEST (RICH)
Isa 55: 2 and your soul will delight in the *r*

RID
Ge 21:10 "Get *r* of that slave woman
1Co 5: 7 Get *r* of the old yeast that you may
Gal 4:30 "Get *r* of the slave woman

RIDE (RIDER RIDING)
Ps 45: 4 In your majesty *r* forth victoriously

RIDER (RIDE)
Rev 6: 2 was a white horse! Its *r* held a bow,
19:11 whose *r* is called Faithful and True.

RIDING (RIDE)
Zec 9: 9 gentle and *r* on a donkey,
Mt 21: 5 gentle and *r* on a donkey,

RIGGING
Isa 33:23 Your *r* hangs loose:

RIGHT (RIGHTS)
Ge 4: 7 But if you do not do what is *r,*
18:19 of the LORD by doing what is *r*
18:25 the Judge of all the earth do *r?*"
48:13 on his left toward Israel's *r* hand,
Ex 15: 6 Your *r* hand, O LORD,
15:26 and do what is *r* in his eyes,
Dt 5:32 do not turn aside to the *r*
6:18 Do what is *r* and good
13:18 and doing what is *r* in his eyes.
Jos 1: 7 do not turn from it to the *r*
1Sa 12:23 you the way that is good and *r.*
1Ki 3: 9 to distinguish between *r* and wrong
15: 5 For David had done what was *r*
2Ki 7: 9 to each other, "We're not doing *r.*
Ne 9:13 and laws that are just and *r,*
Ps 16: 8 Because he is at my *r* hand,
16:11 eternal pleasures at your *r* hand.
17: 7 you who save by your *r* hand
18:35 and your *r* hand sustains me;
19: 8 The precepts of the LORD are *r,*
25: 9 He guides the humble in what is *r*
33: 4 For the word of the LORD is *r*
44: 3 it was your *r* hand, your arm,
45: 4 let your *r* hand display awesome
51: 4 so that you are proved *r*
63: 8 your *r* hand upholds me.
73:23 you hold me by my *r* hand.
91: 7 ten thousand at your *r* hand,
98: 1 his *r* hand and his holy arm
106: 3 who constantly do what is *r.*
110: 1 "Sit at my *r* hand
118:15 LORD's *r* hand has done mighty
119:144 Your statutes are forever *r;*
137: 5 may my *r* hand forget its skill.
139:10 your *r* hand will hold me fast.
Pr 1: 3 doing what is *r* and just and fair;
4:27 Do not swerve to the *r* or the left;
14:12 There is a way that seems *r*
18:17 The first to present his case seems *r*
Ecc 7:20 who does what is *r* and never sins.
SS 1: 4 How *r* they are to adore you!
Isa 1:17 learn to do *r!*
7:15 reject the wrong and choose the *r.*
30:10 us no more visions of what is *r!*
30:21 Whether you turn to the *r*
41:10 you with my righteous *r* hand.
41:13 who takes hold of your *r* hand
48:13 my *r* hand spread out the heavens;
64: 5 to the help of those who gladly do *r*
Jer 23: 5 and do what is just and *r* in the land
Eze 18: 5 who does what is just and *r.*
18:21 and does what is just and *r,*
33:14 and does what is just and *r*—
Hos 14: 9 The ways of the LORD are *r;*
Mt 5:29 If your *r* eye causes you to sin,
6: 3 know what your *r* hand is doing,
22:44 "Sit at my *r* hand
25:33 He will put the sheep on his *r*
Jn 1:12 he gave the *r* to become children
Ac 2:34 "Sit at my *r* hand
7:55 Jesus standing at the *r* hand of God
Ro 3: 4 "So that you may be proved *r*
8:34 is at the *r* hand of God and is
9:21 Does not the potter have the *r*
12:17 careful to do what is *r* in the eyes
1Co 9: 4 Don't we have the *r* to food
2Co 8:21 we are taking pains to do what is *r,*
Eph 1:20 and seated him at his *r* hand
6: 1 parents in the Lord, for this is *r.*
Php 4: 8 whatever is *r,* whatever is pure,
2Th 3:13 never tire of doing what is *r.*
Heb 1: 3 down at the *r* hand of the Majesty
Jas 2: 8 as yourself," you are doing *r.*
1Pe 3:14 if you should suffer for what is *r,*
1Jn 2:29 who does what is *r* has been born
Rev 2: 7 I will give the *r* to eat from the tree
3:21 I will give the *r* to sit with me
22:11 let him who does *r* continue to do *r*

RIGHTEOUS (RIGHTEOUSLY RIGHTEOUSNESS)
Ge 6: 9 Noah was a *r* man, blameless
18:23 "Will you sweep away the *r*
Nu 23:10 Let me die the death of the *r,*
Ne 9: 8 your promise because you are *r.*
Job 36: 7 He does not take his eyes off the *r;*
Ps 1: 5 nor sinners in the assembly of the *r.*
5:12 O LORD, you bless the *r;*
11: 7 For the LORD is *r,*
15: 2 and who does what is *r,*
34:15 The eyes of the LORD are on the *r*
37:16 Better the little that the *r* have
37:21 but the *r* give generously;
37:25 yet I have never seen the *r* forsaken
37:30 of the *r* man utters wisdom,
55:22 he will never let the *r* fall.
64:10 Let the *r* rejoice in the LORD
68: 3 But may the *r* be glad
112: 4 compassionate and *r* man.
118:20 through which the *r* may enter.
119: 7 as I learn your *r* laws.
119:137 *R* are you, O LORD,
140:13 Surely the *r* will praise your name
143: 2 for no one living is *r* before you.
145:17 The LORD is *r* in all his ways
Pr 3:33 but he blesses the home of the *r.*
4:18 of the *r* is like the first gleam
10: 7 of the *r* will be a blessing,
10:11 The mouth of the *r* is a fountain
10:16 The wages of the *r* bring them life,
10:20 The tongue of the *r* is choice silver,
10:24 what the *r* desire will be granted.
10:28 The prospect of the *r* is joy,
10:32 of the *r* know what is fitting,
11:23 The desire of the *r* ends only
11:30 The fruit of the *r* is a tree of life,
12:10 A *r* man cares for the needs
12:21 No harm befalls the *r,*
13: 9 The light of the *r* shines brightly,
15:28 of the *r* weighs its answers,
15:29 but he hears the prayer of the *r.*
16:31 it is attained by a *r* life.
18:10 the *r* run to it and are safe.
20: 7 The *r* man leads a blameless life;
21:15 justice is done, it brings joy to the *r*
23:24 The father of a *r* man has great joy;
28: 1 but the *r* are as bold as a lion.
29: 6 but a *r* one can sing and be glad.
29: 7 The *r* care about justice
29:27 The *r* detest the dishonest;
Ecc 7:20 There is not a *r* man on earth
Isa 26: 7 The path of the *r* is level;
41:10 you with my *r* right hand.
45:21 a *r* God and a Savior;
53:11 his knowledge my *r* servant will
64: 6 and all our *r* acts are like filthy rags
Jer 23: 5 up to David a *r* Branch,
Eze 3:20 when a *r* man turns
18: 5 "Suppose there is a *r* man
18:20 of the *r* man will be credited
33:12 The *r* man, if he sins, will not be
Da 9:18 requests of you because we are *r,*
Hab 2: 4 but the *r* will live by his faith—
Zec 9: 9 *r* and having salvation,

Mal 3:18 see the distinction between the *r*
Mt 5:45 rain on the *r* and the unrighteous.
9:13 For I have not come to call the *r*,
10:41 and anyone who receives a *r* man
13:43 Then the *r* will shine like the sun
13:49 and separate the wicked from the *r*
25:37 "Then the *r* will answer him, 'Lord,
25:46 to eternal punishment, but the *r*
Ac 24:15 will be a resurrection of both the *r*
Ro 1:17 as it is written: "The *r* will live
2:5 when his *r* judgment will be
2:13 the law who will be declared *r*.
3:10 "There is no one *r*, not even one;
3:20 Therefore no one will be declared *r*
5:19 one man the many will be made *r*.
Gal 3:11 because, "The *r* will live by faith."
1Ti 1:9 that law is made not for the *r*
2Ti 4:8 which the Lord, the *r* Judge,
Tit 3:5 because of *r* things we had done,
Heb 10:38 But my *r* one will live by faith.
Jas 5:16 The prayer of a *r* man is powerful
1Pe 3:12 the eyes of the Lord are on the *r*
3:18 the *r* for the unrighteous,
4:18 "If it is hard for the *r* to be saved,
1Jn 2:1 defense—Jesus Christ, the *R* One.
3:7 does what is right is *r*, just as he is *r*.
Rev 19:8 stands for the *r* acts of the saints.)

RIGHTEOUSLY* (RIGHTEOUS)

Ps 9:4 on your throne, judging *r*.
Isa 33:15 He who walks *r*
Jer 11:20 LORD Almighty, you who judge *r*

RIGHTEOUSNESS (RIGHTEOUS)

Ge 15:6 and he credited it to him as *r*.
Dt 9:4 of this land because of my *r*."
1Sa 26:23 LORD rewards every man for his *r*
1Ki 10:9 to maintain justice and *r*."
Job 37:23 great *r*, he does not oppress.
Ps 7:17 to the LORD because of his *r*
9:8 He will judge the world in *r*;
17:15 And I—in *r* I will see your face;
23:3 He guides me in paths of *r*
33:5 The LORD loves *r* and justice;
35:28 My tongue will speak of your *r*
36:6 Your *r* is like the mighty
37:6 He will make your *r* shine like
40:9 I proclaim *r* in the great assembly;
45:4 in behalf of truth, humility and *r*;
45:7 You love *r* and hate wickedness;
48:10 your right hand is filled with *r*.
65:5 us with awesome deeds of *r*,
71:2 Rescue me and deliver me in your *r*
71:15 My mouth will tell of your *r*,
71:19 Your *r* reaches to the skies, O God,
85:10 *r* and peace kiss each other.
89:14 *R* and justice are the foundation
96:13 He will judge the world in *r*
98:9 He will judge the world in *r*
103:6 The LORD works *r*
103:17 his *r* with their children's children
106:31 This was credited to him as *r*
111:3 and his *r* endures forever.
118:19 Open for me the gates of *r*;
132:9 May your priests be clothed with *r*;
145:7 and joyfully sing of your *r*.
Pr 11:5 *r* of the blameless makes a straight
11:18 he who sows *r* reaps a sure reward.
13:6 *R* guards the man of integrity,
14:34 *R* exalts a nation,
16:8 Better a little with *r*
16:12 a throne is established through *r*.
21:21 He who pursues *r* and love
Isa 5:16 will show himself holy by his *r*.
9:7 it with justice and *r*
11:4 but with *r* he will judge the needy,
16:5 and speeds the cause of *r*.
26:9 the people of the world learn *r*.
32:17 The fruit of *r* will be peace;
42:6 "I, the LORD, have called you in *r*;
42:21 the LORD for the sake of his *r*
45:8 "You heavens above, rain down *r*;
51:1 "Listen to me, you who pursue *r*
51:6 my *r* will never fail.
51:8 But my *r* will last forever,
58:8 then your *r* will go before you,
59:17 He put on *r* as his breastplate,
61:10 and arrayed me in a robe of *r*,
63:1 "It is I, speaking in *r*,
Jer 9:24 justice and *r* on earth,
23:6 The LORD Our *R*.
Eze 3:20 a righteous man turns from his *r*
14:20 save only themselves by their *r*.
18:20 The *r* of the righteous man will be
33:12 *r* of the righteous man will not save
Da 9:24 to bring in everlasting *r*,
12:3 and those who lead many to *r*,
Hos 10:12 Sow for yourselves *r*,
Am 5:24 *r* like a never-failing stream!
Mic 7:9 I will see his *r*.
Zep 2:3 Seek *r*, seek humility;
Mal 4:2 the sun of *r* will rise with healing
Mt 5:6 those who hunger and thirst for *r*,
5:10 who are persecuted because of *r*,
5:20 unless your *r* surpasses that
6:1 to do your 'acts of *r*' before men,
6:33 But seek first his kingdom and his *r*
Jn 16:8 world of guilt in regard to sin and *r*
Ac 24:25 Paul discoursed on *r*, self-control
Ro 1:17 For in the gospel a *r* from God is
3:5 brings out God's *r* more clearly,
3:22 This *r* from God comes
4:3 and it was credited to him as *r*."
4:5 wicked, his faith is credited as *r*.
4:6 man to whom God credits *r* apart
4:9 faith was credited to him as *r*.
4:13 through the *r* that comes by faith.
4:22 why "it was credited to him as *r*."
5:18 of *r* was justification that brings life
6:13 body to him as instruments of *r*.
6:16 or to obedience, which leads to *r*?
6:18 and have become slaves to *r*.
6:19 in slavery to *r* leading to holiness.
8:10 yet your spirit is alive because of *r*.
9:30 did not pursue *r*, have obtained it,
10:3 they did not know the *r* that comes
14:17 but of *r*, peace and joy
1Co 1:30 our *r*, holiness and redemption.
2Co 3:9 is the ministry that brings *r*!
5:21 that in him we might become the *r*
6:7 with weapons of *r* in the right hand
6:14 For what do *r* and wickedness have
9:9 his *r* endures forever."
Gal 2:21 for if *r* could be gained
3:6 and it was credited to him as *r*."
3:21 then *r* would certainly have come
Eph 4:24 created to be like God in true *r*
5:9 *r* and truth) and find out what
6:14 with the breastplate of *r* in place,
Php 1:11 filled with the fruit of *r* that comes
3:6 as for legalistic *r*, faultless.
3:9 not having a *r* of my own that
1Ti 6:11 and pursue *r*, godliness, faith, love,
2Ti 2:22 and pursue *r*, faith, love and peace,
3:16 correcting and training in *r*,
4:8 is in store for me the crown of *r*,
Heb 1:8 and *r* will be the scepter
5:13 with the teaching about *r*.
7:2 his name means "king of *r*";
11:7 became heir of the *r* that comes
12:11 it produces a harvest of *r*
Jas 2:23 and it was credited to him as *r*,"
3:18 sow in peace raise a harvest of *r*.
1Pe 2:24 die to sins and live for *r*;
2Pe 2:21 not to have known the way of *r*,
3:13 and a new earth, the home of *r*.

RIGHTS (RIGHT)

Ps 82:3 maintain the *r* of the poor
Pr 31:8 for the *r* of all who are destitute.
Isa 10:2 to deprive the poor of their *r*
La 3:35 to deny a man his *r*
Gal 4:5 that we might receive the full *r*

RING

Pr 11:22 Like a gold *r* in a pig's snout
Lk 15:22 Put a *r* on his finger and sandals

RIOTS

2Co 6:5 imprisonments and *r*; in hard work,

RIPE

Joel 3:13 for the harvest is *r*.
Am 8:1 showed me: a basket of *r* fruit.
Jn 4:35 at the fields! They are *r* for harvest.
Rev 14:15 for the harvest of the earth is *r*."

RISE (RAISE RAISED RISEN ROSE)

Lev 19:32 " '*R* in the presence of the aged,
Nu 24:17 a scepter will *r* out of Israel.
Isa 26:19 their bodies will *r*.
Mal 4:2 of righteousness will *r* with healing
Mt 27:63 'After three days I will *r* again.'
Mk 8:31 and after three days *r* again.
Lk 18:33 On the third day he will *r* again."
Jn 5:29 those who have done good will *r*
20:9 had to *r* from the dead.)
Ac 17:3 had to suffer and *r* from the dead.
1Th 4:16 and the dead in Christ will *r* first.

RISEN (RISE)

Mt 28:6 He is not here; he has *r*, just
Mk 16:6 He has *r*! He is not here.
Lk 24:34 The Lord has *r* and has appeared

RIVER (RIVERS)

Ps 46:4 There is a *r* whose streams make
Isa 66:12 "I will extend peace to her like a *r*,
Eze 47:12 grow on both banks of the *r*.
Rev 22:1 Then the angel showed me the *r*

RIVERS (RIVER)

Ps 137:1 By the *r* of Babylon we sat

ROAD (CROSSROADS ROADS)

Mt 7:13 and broad is the *r* that leads

ROADS (ROAD)

Lk 3:5 crooked *r* shall become straight,

ROARING

1Pe 5:8 prowls around like a *r* lion looking

ROB (ROBBERS ROBBERY ROBS)

Mal 3:8 "Will a man *r* God? Yet you *r* me.

ROBBERS (ROB)

Jer 7:11 become a den of *r* to you?
Mk 15:27 They crucified two *r* with him,
Lk 19:46 but you have made it 'a den of *r*.' "
Jn 10:8 came before me were thieves and *r*,

ROBBERY (ROB)

Isa 61:8 I hate *r* and iniquity.

ROBE (ROBED ROBES)

Ge 37:3 and he made a richly ornamented *r*
Isa 6:1 the train of his *r* filled the temple.
61:10 arrayed me in a *r* of righteousness,
Rev 6:11 each of them was given a white *r*,

ROBED (ROBE)

Ps 93:1 the LORD is *r* in majesty
Isa 63:1 Who is this, *r* in splendor,

ROBES (ROBE)

Ps 45:8 All your *r* are fragrant with myrrh
Rev 7:13 "These in white *r*—who are they,

ROBS* (ROB)

Pr 19:26 He who *r* his father and drives out
28:24 He who *r* his father or mother

ROCK

Ge 49:24 of the Shepherd, the *R* of Israel,
Ex 17:6 Strike the *r*, and water will come
Nu 20:8 Speak to that *r* before their eyes
Dt 32:4 He is the *R*, his works are perfect,
32:13 him with honey from the *r*,
2Sa 22:2 "The LORD is my *r*, my fortress
Ps 18:2 The LORD is my *r*, my fortress
19:14 O LORD, my *R* and my Redeemer
40:2 he set my feet on a *r*
61:2 lead me to the *r* that is higher
92:15 he is my *R*, and there is no
Isa 26:4 the LORD, is the *R* eternal.
51:1 to the *r* from which you were cut
Da 2:34 you were watching, a *r* was cut out,
Mt 7:24 man who built his house on the *r*.
16:18 and on this *r* I will build my church
Ro 9:33 and a *r* that makes them fall,
1Co 10:4 the spiritual *r* that accompanied
1Pe 2:8 and a *r* that makes them fall."

ROD (RODS)

2Sa 7:14 I will punish him with the *r* of men,
Ps 23:4 your *r* and your staff,
Pr 13:24 He who spares the *r* hates his son,
22:15 the *r* of discipline will drive it far
23:13 if you punish him with the *r*,
29:15 *r* of correction imparts wisdom,
Isa 11:4 the earth with the *r* of his mouth;

RODS (ROD)

2Co 11:25 Three times I was beaten with *r*,

ROLL (ROLLED)

Mk 16:3 "Who will *r* the stone away

ROLLED (ROLL)

Lk 24:2 They found the stone *r* away

ROMAN

Ac 16:37 even though we are *R* citizens,

Ac 22:25 you to flog a *R* citizen who hasn't

ROOF (ROOFS)

Pr 21: 9 Better to live on a corner of the *r*

ROOFS

Mt 10:27 in your ear, proclaim from the *r*.

ROOM (ROOMS)

Mt 6: 6 But when you pray, go into your *r*,
Mk 14:15 He will show you a large upper *r*,
Lk 2: 7 there was no *r* for them in the inn.
Jn 8:37 because you have no *r* for my word
21:25 the whole world would not have *r*
2Co 7: 2 Make *r* for us in your hearts.

ROOMS (ROOM)

Jn 14: 2 In my Father's house are many *r*;

ROOSTER

Mt 26:34 this very night, before the *r* crows,

ROOT (ROOTED ROOTS)

Isa 11:10 In that day the *R* of Jesse will stand
53: 2 and like a *r* out of dry ground.
Mt 3:10 already at the *r* of the trees,
13:21 But since he has no *r*, he lasts only
Ro 11:16 if the *r* is holy, so are the branches.
15:12 "The *R* of Jesse will spring up,
1Ti 6:10 of money is a *r* of all kinds of evil.
Rev 5: 5 the *R* of David, has triumphed.
22:16 I am the *R* and the Offspring

ROOTED (ROOT)

Eph 3:17 being *r* and established in love,

ROOTS (ROOT)

Isa 11: 1 from his *r* a Branch will bear fruit.

ROSE (RISE)

SS 2: 1 I am a *r* of Sharon,
1Th 4:14 believe that Jesus died and *r* again

ROTS

Pr 14:30 but envy *r* the bones.

ROUGH

Isa 42:16 and make the *r* places smooth.
Lk 3: 5 the *r* ways smooth.

ROUND

Ecc 1: 6 *r* and *r* it goes,

ROYAL

Ps 45: 9 at your right hand is the *r* bride
Da 1: 8 not to defile himself with the *r* food
Jas 2: 8 If you really keep the *r* law found
1Pe 2: 9 a *r* priesthood, a holy nation,

RUBBISH*

Php 3: 8 I consider them *r*, that I may gain

RUBIES

Job 28:18 the price of wisdom is beyond *r*.
Pr 3:15 She is more precious than *r*;
8:11 for wisdom is more precious than *r*,
31:10 She is worth far more than *r*.

RUDDER*

Jas 3: 4 by a very small *r* wherever the pilot

RUDDY

1Sa 16:12 He was *r*, with a fine appearance
SS 5:10 *Beloved* My lover is radiant and *r*,

RUDE*

1Co 13: 5 It is not *r*, it is not self-seeking,

RUIN (RUINED RUINING RUINS)

Pr 10: 8 but a chattering fool comes to *r*.
10:10 and a chattering fool comes to *r*.
10:14 but the mouth of a fool invites *r*.
10:29 but it is the *r* of those who do evil.
18:24 many companions may come to *r*,
19:13 A foolish son is his father's *r*,
26:28 and a flattering mouth works *r*.
SS 2:15 that *r* the vineyards,
Eze 21:27 A *r*! A *r*! I will make it a *r*!
1Ti 6: 9 desires that plunge men into *r*

RUINED (RUIN)

Isa 6: 5 "I am *r*! For I am a man
Mt 9:17 and the wineskins will be *r*.
12:25 divided against itself will be *r*,

RUINING* (RUIN)

Tit 1:11 they are *r* whole households

RUINS (RUIN)

Pr 19: 3 A man's own folly *r* his life,
Ecc 4: 5 and *r* himself.
2Ti 2:14 and only *r* those who listen.

RULE (RULER RULERS RULES)

Ge 1:26 let them *r* over the fish of the sea
3:16 and he will *r* over you."
Jdg 8:22 said to Gideon, "*R* over us—
1Sa 12:12 'No, we want a king to *r* over us'—
Ps 2: 9 You will *r* them with an iron
67: 4 for you *r* the peoples justly
119:133 let no sin *r* over me.
Pr 17: 2 A wise servant will *r*
Isa 28:10 *r* on *r*, *r* on *r*;
Eze 20:33 I will *r* over you with a mighty
Zec 6:13 and will sit and *r* on his throne.
9:10 His *r* will extend from sea to sea
Ro 13: 9 are summed up in this one *r*:
15:12 arise to *r* over the nations;
1Co 7:17 This is the *r* I lay down in all
Gal 6:16 and mercy to all who follow this *r*,
Eph 1:21 far above all *r* and authority,
Col 3:15 the peace of Christ *r* in your hearts,
2Th 3:10 we gave you this *r*: "If a man will
Rev 2:27 He will *r* them with an iron scepter;
12: 5 who will *r* all the nations
19:15 He will *r* them with an iron scepter

RULER (RULE)

Ps 8: 6 You made him *r* over the works
Pr 19: 6 Many curry favor with a *r*,
23: 1 When you sit to dine with a *r*,
25:15 Through patience a *r* can be
29:26 Many seek an audience with a *r*,
Isa 60:17 and righteousness your *r*.
Da 9:25 the *r*, comes, there will be seven
Mic 5: 2 one who will be *r* over Israel,
Mt 2: 6 for out of you will come a *r*
Eph 2: 2 of the *r* of the kingdom of the air,
1Ti 6:15 God, the blessed and only *R*,
Rev 1: 5 and the *r* of the kings of the earth.

RULERS (RULE)

Ps 2: 2 and the *r* gather together
119:161 *R* persecute me without cause,
Isa 40:23 reduces the *r* of this world
Da 7:27 and all *r* will worship and obey him
Mt 20:25 "You know that the *r*
Ac 13:27 and their *r* did not recognize Jesus,
Ro 13: 3 For *r* hold no terror
1Co 2: 6 of this age or of the *r* of this age,
Eph 3:10 should be made known to the *r*
6:12 the *r*, against the authorities,
Col 1:16 or powers or *r* or authorities;

RULES (RULE)

Nu 15:15 is to have the same *r* for you
2Sa 23: 3 when he *r* in the fear of God,
Ps 22:28 and he *r* over the nations.
66: 7 He *r* forever by his power,
103: 19 and his kingdom *r* over all.
Isa 29:13 is made up only of *r* taught by men.
40:10 and his arm *r* for him.
Mt 15: 9 their teachings are but *r* taught
Lk 22:26 one who *r* like the one who serves.
2Ti 2: 5 he competes according to the *r*.

RUMORS

Jer 51:46 afraid when *r* are heard in the land;
Mt 24: 6 You will hear of wars and *r* of wars,

RUN (RAN RUNNERS RUNNING RUNS)

Ps 19: 5 champion rejoicing to *r* his course.
Pr 4:12 when you *r*, you will not stumble.
18:10 the righteous *r* to it and are safe.
Isa 10: 3 To whom will you *r* for help?
40:31 they will *r* and not grow weary,
Joel 3:18 ravines of Judah will *r* with water.
Hab 2: 2 so that a herald may *r* with it.
1Co 9:24 *R* in such a way as to get the prize.
Gal 2: 2 that I was running or had *r* my race
Php 2:16 on the day of Christ that I did not *r*
Heb 12: 1 let us *r* with perseverance the race

RUNNERS* (RUN)

1Co 9:24 that in a race all the *r* run,

RUNNING (RUN)

Ps 133: 2 *r* down on Aaron's beard,
Lk 17:23 Do not go *r* off after them.

1Co 9:26 I do not run like a man *r* aimlessly;
Gal 5: 7 You were *r* a good race.

RUNS (RUN)

Jn 10:12 he abandons the sheep and *r* away.

RUSH

Pr 1:16 for their feet *r* into sin,
6:18 feet that are quick to *r* into evil,
Isa 59: 7 Their feet *r* into sin;

RUST

Mt 6:19 where moth and *r* destroy,

RUTH*

Moabitess; widow who went to Bethlehem with mother-in-law Naomi (Ru 1). Gleaned in field of Boaz; shown favor (Ru 2). Proposed marriage to Boaz (Ru 3). Married (Ru 4:1-12); bore Obed, ancestor of David (Ru 4:13-22), Jesus (Mt 1:5).

RUTHLESS

Pr 11:16 but *r* men gain only wealth.
Ro 1:31 are senseless, faithless, heartless, *r*.

SABBATH (SABBATHS)

Ex 20: 8 "Remember the *S* day
31:14 " 'Observe the *S*, because it is holy
Lev 25: 2 the land itself must observe a *s*
Dt 5:12 "Observe the *S* day
Isa 56: 2 keeps the *S* without desecrating it,
56: 6 all who keep the *S*
58:13 if you call the *S* a delight
Jer 17:21 not to carry a load on the *S* day
Mt 12: 1 through the grainfields on the *S*.
Lk 13:10 On a *S* Jesus was teaching in one
Col 2:16 a New Moon celebration or a *S* day

SABBATH-REST* (REST)

Heb 4: 9 then, a *S* for the people of God;

SABBATHS (SABBATH)

2Ch 2: 4 evening and on *S* and New Moons
Eze 20:12 Also I gave them my *S*

SACKCLOTH

Ps 30:11 you removed my *s* and clothed me
Da 9: 3 in fasting, and in *s* and ashes.
Mt 11:21 would have repented long ago in *s*

SACRED

Lev 23: 2 are to proclaim as *s* assemblies.
Mt 7: 6 "Do not give dogs what is *s*;
Ro 14: 5 One man considers one day more *s*
1Co 3:17 for God's temple is *s*, and you are
2Pe 1:18 were with him on the *s* mountain.
2:21 on the *s* command that was

SACRIFICE (SACRIFICED SACRIFICES)

Ge 22: 2 *S* him there as a burnt offering
Ex 12:27 'It is the Passover *s* to the LORD,
1Sa 15:22 To obey is better than *s*,
1Ki 18:38 the LORD fell and burned up the *s*,
1Ch 21:24 or *s* a burnt offering that costs me
Ps 40: 6 *S* and offering you did not desire,
50:14 *S* thank offerings to God,
51:16 You do not delight in *s*,
54: 6 I will *s* a freewill offering to you;
107: 22 Let them *s* thank offerings
141: 2 of my hands be like the evening *s*.
Pr 15: 8 The LORD detests the *s*
21: 3 to the LORD than *s*.
Da 9:27 the 'seven' he will put an end to *s*
12:11 time that the daily *s* is abolished
Hos 6: 6 For I desire mercy, not *s*,
Mt 9:13 this means: 'I desire mercy, not *s*.'
Ro 3:25 God presented him as a *s*
Eph 5: 2 as a fragrant offering and *s* to God.
Php 4:18 an acceptable *s*, pleasing to God.
Heb 9:26 away with sin by the *s* of himself.
10: 5 "*S* and offering you did not desire,
10:10 holy through the *s* of the body
10:14 by one *s* he has made perfect
10:18 there is no longer any *s* for sin.
11: 4 faith Abel offered God a better *s*
13:15 offer to God a *s* of praise—
1Jn 2: 2 He is the atoning *s* for our sins,
4:10 as an atoning *s* for our sins.

SACRIFICED (SACRIFICE)

Ac 15:29 are to abstain from food *s* to idols,
1Co 5: 7 our Passover lamb, has been *s*.
8: 1 Now about food *s* to idols:
Heb 7:27 He *s* for their sins once for all

Heb 9:28 so Christ was s once

SACRIFICES (SACRIFICE)

Ps 51:17 The s of God are a broken spirit;
Mk 12:33 than all burnt offerings and s."
Ro 12:1 to offer your bodies as living s,
Heb 9:23 with better s than these.
13:16 for with such s God is pleased.
1Pe 2:5 offering spiritual s acceptable

SAD

Lk 18:23 he heard this, he became very s,

SADDUCEES

Mt 16:6 the yeast of the Pharisees and S."
Mk 12:18 S, who say there is no resurrection,
Ac 23:8 S say that there is no resurrection,

SAFE (SAVE)

Ps 27:5 he will keep me s in his dwelling;
37:3 in the land and enjoy s pasture.
Pr 18:10 the righteous run to it and are s.
28:26 he who walks in wisdom is kept s.
29:25 in the LORD is kept s.
Jer 12:5 If you stumble in s country,
Jn 17:12 kept them s by that name you gave
1Jn 5:18 born of God keeps him s,

SAFETY (SAVE)

Ps 4:8 make me dwell in s.
Hos 2:18 so that all may lie down in s.
1Th 5:3 people are saying, "Peace and s,"

SAINTS

1Sa 2:9 He will guard the feet of his s,
Ps 16:3 As for the s who are in the land,
30:4 Sing to the LORD, you s of his;
31:23 Love the LORD, all his s!
34:9 Fear the LORD, you his s,
116:15 is the death of his s.
149:1 his praise in the assembly of the s.
149:5 Let the s rejoice in this honor
Da 7:18 the s of the Most High will receive
Ro 8:27 intercedes for the s in accordance
1Co 6:2 not know that the s will judge
Eph 1:15 Jesus and your love for all the s,
1:18 of his glorious inheritance in the s,
6:18 always keep on praying for all the s
Phm :7 have refreshed the hearts of the s.
Rev 5:8 which are the prayers of the s.
19:8 for the righteous acts of the s.)

SAKE (SAKES)

1Sa 12:22 For the s of his great name
Ps 23:3 righteousness for his name's s.
44:22 Yet for your s we face death all day
106:8 Yet he saved them for his name's s,
Isa 42:21 for the s of his righteousness
43:25 your transgressions, for my own s,
48:9 For my own name's s I delay my
48:11 For my own s, for my own s,
Jer 14:7 for the s of your name.
14:21 For the s of your name do not
Eze 20:9 But for the s of my name I did what
20:14 But for the s of my name I did what
20:22 and for the s of my name I did what
36:22 but for the s of my holy name,
Da 9:17 For your s, O Lord, look with favor
Mt 10:39 life for my s will find it.
19:29 for my s will receive a hundred
1Co 9:23 I do all this for the s of the gospel,
2Co 12:10 for Christ's s, I delight
Php 3:7 loss for the s of Christ.
Heb 11:26 He regarded disgrace for the s
1Pe 2:13 for the Lord's s to every authority
3Jn :7 was for the s of the Name that they

SAKES* (SAKE)

2Co 8:9 yet for your s he became poor,

SALEM

Ge 14:18 king of S brought out bread
Heb 7:2 "king of S" means "king of peace."

SALT

Ge 19:26 and she became a pillar of s.
Nu 18:19 covenant of s before the LORD
Mt 5:13 "You are the s of the earth.
Col 4:6 with s, so that you may know how
Jas 3:11 s water flow from the same spring?

SALVATION* (SAVE)

Ex 15:2 he has become my s.
2Sa 22:3 my shield and the horn of my s.
23:5 Will he not bring to fruition my s
1Ch 16:23 proclaim his s day after day.
2Ch 6:41 O LORD God, be clothed with s,
Ps 9:14 and there rejoice in your s.
13:5 my heart rejoices in your s.
14:7 that s for Israel would come out
18:2 is my shield and the horn of my s,
27:1 The LORD is my light and my s—
28:8 a fortress of s for his anointed one.
35:3 "I am your s."
35:9 and delight in his s.
37:39 The s of the righteous comes
40:10 I speak of your faithfulness and s.
40:16 those who love your s always say,
50:23 way so that I may show him the s
51:12 Restore to me the joy of your s
53:6 that s for Israel would come out
62:1 my s comes from him.
62:2 He alone is my rock and my s;
62:6 He alone is my rock and my s;
62:7 My s and my honor depend
67:2 your s among all nations.
69:13 answer me with your sure s.
69:27 do not let them share in your s.
69:29 may your s, O God, protect me.
70:4 those who love your s always say,
71:15 of your s all day long,
74:12 you bring s upon the earth.
85:7 and grant us your s.
85:9 Surely his s is near those who fear
91:16 and show him my s."
95:1 to the Rock of our s.
96:2 proclaim his s day after day.
98:1 have worked s for him.
98:2 The LORD has made his s known
98:3 the s of our God.
116:13 I will lift up the cup of s
118:14 he has become my s.
118:21 you have become my s.
119:41 your s according to your promise;
119:81 with longing for your s,
119:123 My eyes fail, looking for your s,
119:155 S is far from the wicked,
119:166 I wait for your s, O LORD,
119:174 I long for your s, O LORD,
132:16 I will clothe her priests with s,
149:4 he crowns the humble with s.
Isa 12:2 Surely God is my s;
12:2 he has become my s."
12:3 from the wells of s.
25:9 let us rejoice and be glad in his s."
26:1 God makes s
26:18 We have not brought s to the earth;
30:15 "In repentance and rest is your s,
33:2 our s in time of distress.
33:6 a rich store of s and wisdom
45:8 let s spring up,
45:17 the LORD with an everlasting s;
46:13 I will grant s to Zion,
46:13 and my s will not be delayed.
49:6 that you may bring my s
49:8 and in the day of s I will help you;
51:5 my s is on the way,
51:6 But my s will last forever,
51:8 my s through all generations."
52:7 who proclaim s,
52:10 the s of our God.
56:1 for my s is close at hand
59:16 so his own arm worked s for him,
59:17 and the helmet of s on his head;
60:18 but you will call your walls S
61:10 me with garments of s
62:1 her s like a blazing torch.
63:5 so my own arm worked s for me,
Jer 3:23 is the s of Israel.
La 3:26 quietly for the s of the LORD.
Jnh 2:9 S comes from the LORD."
Zec 9:9 righteous and having s,
Lk 1:69 He has raised up a horn of s for us
1:71 of long ago), s from our enemies
1:77 give his people the knowledge of s
2:30 For my eyes have seen your s,
3:6 And all mankind will see God's s
19:9 "Today s has come to this house,
Jn 4:22 for s is from the Jews.
Ac 4:12 S is found in no one else,
13:26 message of s has been sent.
13:47 that you may bring s to the ends
28:28 to know that God's s has been sent
Ro 1:16 for the s of everyone who believes:
11:11 s has come to the Gentiles
13:11 because our s is nearer now
2Co 1:6 it is for your comfort and s;
6:2 and in the day of s I helped you."
6:2 of God's favor, now is the day of s.
7:10 brings repentance that leads to s
Eph 1:13 word of truth, the gospel of your s.
6:17 Take the helmet of s and the sword
Php 2:12 to work out your s with fear
1Th 5:8 and the hope of s as a helmet.
5:9 to receive s through our Lord Jesus
2Ti 2:10 they too may obtain the s that is
3:15 wise for s through faith
Tit 2:11 of God that brings s has appeared
Heb 1:14 to serve those who will inherit s?
2:3 This s, which was first announced
2:3 escape if we ignore such a great s?
2:10 of their s perfect through suffering.
5:9 of eternal s for all who obey him
6:9 case—things that accompany s.
9:28 to bring s to those who are waiting
1Pe 1:5 the coming of the s that is ready
1:9 of your faith, the s of your souls.
1:10 Concerning this s, the prophets,
2:2 by it you may grow up in your s,
2Pe 3:15 that our Lord's patience means s,
Jude :3 to write to you about the s we share
Rev 7:10 "S belongs to our God,
12:10 have come the s and the power
19:1 S and glory and power belong

SAMARIA (SAMARITAN)

1Ki 16:24 He bought the hill of S
2Ki 17:6 the king of Assyria captured S
Jn 4:4 Now he had to go through S.
4:5 came to a town in S called Sychar,

SAMARITAN (SAMARIA)

Lk 10:33 But a S, as he traveled, came where
17:16 and thanked him—and he was a S.
Jn 4:7 When a S woman came

SAMSON

Danite judge. Birth promised (Jdg 13). Married to Philistine, but wife given away (Jdg 14). Vengeance on Philistines (Jdg 15). Betrayed by Delilah (Jdg 16:1-22). Death (Jdg 16:23-31). Feats of strength: killed lion (Jdg 14:6), 30 Philistines (Jdg 14:19), 1,000 Philistines with jawbone (Jdg 15:13-17), carried off gates of Gaza (Jdg 16:3), pushed down temple of Dagon (Jdg 16:25-30).

SAMUEL

Ephraimite judge and prophet (Heb 11:32). Birth prayed for (1Sa 1:10-18). Dedicated to temple by Hannah (1Sa 1:21-28). Raised by Eli (1Sa 2:11, 18-26). Called as prophet (1Sa 3). Led Israel to victory over Philistines (1Sa 7). Asked by Israel for a king (1Sa 8). Anointed Saul as king (1Sa 9-10). Farewell speech (1Sa 12). Rebuked Saul for sacrifice (1Sa 13). Announced rejection of Saul (1Sa 15). Anointed David as king (1Sa 16). Protected David from Saul (1Sa 19:18-24). Death (1Sa 25:1). Returned from dead to condemn Saul (1Sa 28).

SANBALLAT

Led opposition to Nehemiah's rebuilding of Jerusalem (Ne 2:10, 19; 4; 6).

SANCTIFIED* (SANCTIFY)

Jn 17:19 that they too may be truly s.
Ac 20:32 among all those who are s.
26:18 among those who are s by faith
Ro 15:16 to God, s by the Holy Spirit.
1Co 1:2 to those s in Christ Jesus
6:11 But you were washed, you were s,
7:14 and the unbelieving wife has been s
7:14 the unbelieving husband has been s
1Th 4:3 It is God's will that you should be s
Heb 10:29 blood of the covenant that s him,

SANCTIFY* (SANCTIFIED SANCTIFYING)

Jn 17:17 S them by the truth; your word is
17:19 For them I s myself, that they too
1Th 5:23 s you through and through.
Heb 9:13 are ceremonially unclean s them

SANCTIFYING* (SANCTIFY)

2Th 2:13 through the s work of the Spirit
1Pe 1:2 through the s work of the Spirit,

SANCTUARY

Ex 25:8 "Then have them make a s for me,
Lev 19:30 and have reverence for my s,
Ps 15:1 LORD, who may dwell in your s?
63:2 I have seen you in the s
68:24 of my God and King into the s.
68:35 are awesome, O God, in your s;
73:17 me till I entered the s of God;

Ps 102: 19 looked down from his *s* on high,
134: 2 Lift up your hands in the *s*
150: 1 Praise God in his *s*;
Eze 37: 26 I will put my *s* among them forever
41: 1 the man brought me to the outer *s*
Da 9: 26 will destroy the city and the *s*.
Heb 6: 19 It enters the inner *s*
8: 2 in the *s*, the true tabernacle set up
8: 5 They serve at a *s* that is a copy
9: 24 enter a man-made *s* that was only

SAND

Ge 22: 17 and as the *s* on the seashore.
Mt 7: 26 man who built his house on *s*.

SANDAL (SANDALS)

Ru 4: 7 one party took off his *s*

SANDALS (SANDAL)

Ex 3: 5 off your *s*, for the place where you
Dt 25: 9 take off one of his *s*, spit in his face
Jos 5: 15 off your *s*, for the place where you
Mt 3: 11 whose *s* I am not fit to carry.

SANG (SING)

Ex 15: 1 and the Israelites *s* this song
15: 21 Miriam *s* to them:
Nu 21: 17 Then Israel *s* this song:
Jdg 5: 1 Barak son of Abinoam *s* this song:
1Sa 18: 7 As they danced, they *s*:
2Sa 22: 1 David *s* to the LORD the words
2Ch 5: 13 in praise to the LORD and *s*:
29: 30 So they *s* praises with gladness
Ezr 3: 11 thanksgiving they *s* to the LORD:
Job 38: 7 while the morning stars *s* together
Ps 106: 12 and *s* his praise.
Rev 5: 9 And they *s* a new song:
5: 12 In a loud voice they *s*:
14: 3 they *s* a new song before the throne
15: 3 and *s* the song of Moses the servant

SAP

Ro 11: 17 share in the nourishing *s*

SAPPHIRA*

Ac 5: 1 together with his wife *S*,

SARAH

Wife of Abraham, originally named Sarai; barren (Ge 11:29-31; 1Pe 3:6). Taken by Pharaoh as Abraham's sister; returned (Ge 12:10-20). Gave Hagar to Abraham; sent her away in pregnancy (Ge 16). Name changed; Isaac promised (Ge 17:15-21; 18:10-15; Heb 11:11). Taken by Abimelech as Abraham's sister; returned (Ge 20). Isaac born; Hagar and Ishmael sent away (Ge 21:1-21; Gal 4:21-31). Death (Ge 23).

SARDIS

Rev 3: 1 the angel of the church in *S* write:

SASH (SASHES)

Rev 1: 13 with a golden *s* around his chest.

SASHES (SASH)

Rev 15: 6 wore golden *s* around their chests.

SAT (SIT)

Ps 137: 1 By the rivers of Babylon we *s*
Mk 16: 19 and he *s* at the right hand of God.
Lk 10: 39 who *s* at the Lord's feet listening
Heb 1: 3 he *s* down at the right hand
8: 1 who *s* down at the right hand
10: 12 he *s* down at the right hand of God.
12: 2 and *s* down at the right hand

SATAN

Job 1: 6 and *S* also came with them.
Zec 3: 2 said to *S*, "The LORD rebuke you,
Mt 12: 26 If *S* drives out *S*, he is divided
16: 23 *S*! You are a stumbling block to me;
Mk 4: 15 *S* comes and takes away the word
Lk 10: 18 "I saw *S* fall like lightning
22: 3 *S* entered Judas, called Iscariot,
Ro 16: 20 The God of peace will soon crush *S*
1Co 5: 5 is present, hand this man over to *S*,
2Co 11: 14 for *S* himself masquerades
12: 7 a messenger of *S*, to torment me.
1Ti 1: 20 handed over to *S* to be taught not
Rev 12: 9 serpent called the devil, or *S*,
20: 2 or *S*, and bound him for a thousand
20: 7 *S* will be released from his prison

SATISFIED (SATISFY)

Ps 17: 15 I will be *s* with seeing your likeness
22: 26 The poor will eat and be *s*;
63: 5 My soul will be *s* as with the richest
104: 28 they are *s* with good things.
105: 40 *s* them with the bread of heaven.
Pr 13: 4 the desires of the diligent are fully *s*
30: 15 are three things that are never *s*,
Ecc 5: 10 whoever loves wealth is never *s*
Isa 53: 11 he will see the light ⌊of life⌋ and be *s*
Mt 14: 20 They all ate and were *s*,
Lk 6: 21 for you will be *s*.

SATISFIES* (SATISFY)

Ps 103: 5 who *s* your desires with good things,
107: 9 for he *s* the thirsty
147: 14 and *s* you with the finest of wheat.

SATISFY (SATISFIED SATISFIES)

Ps 90: 14 *S* us in the morning
145: 16 *s* the desires of every living thing.
Pr 5: 19 may her breasts *s* you always,
Isa 55: 2 and your labor on what does not *s*?
58: 10 and *s* the needs of the oppressed,

SAUL

1. Benjamite; anointed by Samuel as first king of Israel (1Sa 9-10). Defeated Ammonites (1Sa 11). Rebuked for offering sacrifice (1Sa 13:1-15). Defeated Philistines (1Sa 14). Rejected as king for failing to annihilate Amalekites (1Sa 15). Soothed from evil spirit by David (1Sa 16:14-23). Sent David against Goliath (1Sa 17). Jealousy and attempted murder of David (1Sa 18:1-11). Gave David Michal as wife (1Sa 18:12-30). Second attempt to kill David (1Sa 19). Anger at Jonathan (1Sa 20:26-34). Pursued David: killed priests at Nob (1Sa 22), went to Keilah and Ziph (1Sa 23), life spared by David at En Gedi (1Sa 24) and in his tent (1Sa 26). Rebuked by Samuel's spirit for consulting witch at Endor (1Sa 28). Wounded by Philistines; took his own life (1Sa 31; 1Ch 10). Lamented by David (2Sa 1:17-27). Children (1Sa 14:49-51; 1Ch 8).

2. See PAUL

SAVAGE

Ac 20: 29 *s* wolves will come in among you

SAVE (SAFE SAFETY SALVATION SAVED SAVES SAVIOR)

Ge 45: 5 to *s* lives that God sent me ahead
1Ch 16: 35 Cry out, "*S* us, O God our Savior;
Job 40: 14 that your own right hand can *s* you.
Ps 17: 7 you who *s* by your right hand
18: 27 You *s* the humble
28: 9 *S* your people and bless your
31: 16 *s* me in your unfailing love.
69: 35 for God will *s* Zion
71: 2 turn your ear to me and *s* me.
72: 13 and *s* the needy from death.
89: 48 or *s* himself from the power
91: 3 Surely he will *s* you
109: 31 to *s* his life from those who
146: 3 in mortal men, who cannot *s*.
Pr 2: 16 will *s* you also from the adulteress,
Isa 35: 4 he will come to *s* you."
38: 20 The LORD will *s* me,
46: 7 it cannot *s* him from his troubles.
59: 1 of the LORD is not too short to *s*,
63: 1 mighty to *s*."
Jer 17: 14 *s* me and I will be saved,
Eze 3: 18 ways in order to *s* his life,
7: 19 able to *s* them in the day
14: 14 they could *s* only themselves
33: 12 of the righteous man will not *s* him
34: 22 I will *s* my flock, and they will no
Da 3: 17 the God we serve is able to *s* us
Hos 1: 7 and I will *s* them—not by bow,
Zep 1: 18 will be able to *s* them
3: 17 he is mighty to *s*.
Zec 8: 7 "I will *s* my people
Mt 1: 21 he will *s* his people from their sins
16: 25 wants to *s* his life will lose it,
Lk 19: 10 to seek and to *s* what was lost."
Jn 3: 17 but to *s* the world through him.
12: 47 come to judge the world, but to *s* it.
Ro 11: 14 people to envy and *s* some of them.
1Co 7: 16 whether you will *s* your husband?
1Ti 1: 15 came into the world to *s* sinners—
Heb 7: 25 to *s* completely those who come
Jas 5: 20 of his way will *s* him from death
Jude :23 others from the fire and *s* them;

SAVED (SAVE)

Ps 22: 5 They cried to you and were *s*;
33: 16 No king is *s* by the size of his army;
34: 6 he *s* him out of all his troubles.
106: 21 They forgot the God who *s* them,
116: 6 when I was in great need, he *s* me.
Isa 25: 9 we trusted in him, and he *s* us.
45: 22 "Turn to me and be *s*,
64: 5 How then can we be *s*?
Jer 4: 14 from your heart and be *s*.
8: 20 and we are not *s*."
Eze 3: 19 but you will have *s* yourself.
33: 5 warning, he would have *s* himself.
Joel 2: 32 on the name of the LORD will be *s*;
Mt 10: 22 firm to the end will be *s*.
24: 13 firm to the end will be *s*.
Mk 13: 13 firm to the end will be *s*.
16: 16 believes and is baptized will be *s*,
Jn 10: 9 enters through me will be *s*.
Ac 2: 21 on the name of the Lord will be *s*.'
2: 47 daily those who were being *s*.
4: 12 to men by which we must be *s*."
15: 11 of our Lord Jesus that we are *s*,
16: 30 do to be *s*?" They replied,
Ro 5: 9 how much more shall we be *s*
9: 27 only the remnant will be *s*.
10: 1 the Israelites is that they may be *s*.
10: 9 him from the dead, you will be *s*.
10: 13 on the name of the Lord will be *s*."
11: 26 so all Israel will be *s*, as it is written:
1Co 1: 18 to us who are being *s* it is the power
3: 15 will suffer loss; he himself will be *s*,
5: 5 his spirit *s* on the day of the Lord.
10: 33 of many, so that they may be *s*.
15: 2 By this gospel you are *s*,
Eph 2: 5 it is by grace you have been *s*.
2: 8 For it is by grace you have been *s*,
2Th 2: 13 you to be *s* through the sanctifying
1Ti 2: 4 who wants all men to be *s*
2: 15 But women will be *s*
2Ti 1: 9 who has *s* us and called us
Tit 3: 5 He *s* us through the washing
Heb 10: 39 but of those who believe and are *s*.

SAVES (SAVE)

Ps 7: 10 who *s* the upright in heart.
68: 20 Our God is a God who *s*;
145: 19 he hears their cry and *s* them.
1Pe 3: 21 It *s* you by the resurrection

SAVIOR* (SAVE)

Dt 32: 15 and rejected the Rock his *S*.
2Sa 22: 3 stronghold, my refuge and my *s*—
22: 47 Exalted be God, the Rock, my *S*!
1Ch 16: 35 Cry out, "Save us, O God our *S*;
Ps 18: 46 Exalted be God my *S*!
24: 5 and vindication from God his *S*.
25: 5 for you are God my *S*,
27: 9 O God my *S*.
38: 22 O Lord my *S*.
42: 5 my *S* and
42: 11 my *S* and my God.
43: 5 my *S* and my God.
65: 5 O God our *S*,
68: 19 Praise be to the Lord, to God our *S*,
79: 9 Help us, O God our *S*,
85: 4 Restore us again, O God our *S*,
89: 26 my God, the Rock my *S*.'
Isa 17: 10 You have forgotten God your *S*;
19: 20 he will send them a *s* and defender,
43: 3 the Holy One of Israel, your *S*;
43: 11 and apart from me there is no *s*.
45: 15 O God and *S* of Israel.
45: 21 a righteous God and a *S*;
49: 26 that I, the LORD, am your *S*,
60: 16 know that I, the LORD, am your *S*,
62: 11 'See, your *S* comes!
63: 8 and so he became their *S*.
Jer 14: 8 its *S* in times of distress,
Hos 13: 4 no *S* except me.
Mic 7: 7 I wait for God my *S*;
Hab 3: 18 I will be joyful in God my *S*.
Lk 1: 47 and my spirit rejoices in God my *S*,
2: 11 of David a *S* has been born to you;
Jn 4: 42 know that this man really is the *S*
Ac 5: 31 *S* that he might give repentance
13: 23 God has brought to Israel the *S*
Eph 5: 23 his body, of which he is the *S*.
Php 3: 20 we eagerly await a *S* from there,
1Ti 1: 1 by the command of God our *S*
2: 3 This is good, and pleases God our *S*
4: 10 who is the *S* of all men,
2Ti 1: 10 through the appearing of our *S*,
Tit 1: 3 me by the command of God our *S*,
1: 4 the Father and Christ Jesus our *S*.
2: 10 about God our *S* attractive.
2: 13 appearing of our great God and *S*,
3: 4 and love of God our *S* appeared,

Tit 3: 6 through Jesus Christ our *S*,
2Pe 1: 1 *S* Jesus Christ have received a faith
1: 11 eternal kingdom of our Lord and *S*
2: 20 and *S* Jesus Christ and are again
3: 2 and *S* through your apostles.
3: 18 and knowledge of our Lord and *S*
1Jn 4: 14 Son to be the *S* of the world.
Jude :25 to the only God our *S* be glory,

SCALE (SCALES)
Ps 18: 29 with my God I can *s* a wall.

SCALES (SCALE)
Lev 11: 9 may eat any that have fins and *s*.
19: 36 Use honest *s* and honest weights,
Pr 11: 1 The LORD abhors dishonest *s*,
Da 5: 27 You have been weighed on the *s*
Rev 6: 5 Its rider was holding a pair of *s*

SCAPEGOAT (GOAT)
Lev 16: 10 by sending it into the desert as a *s*.

SCARECROW*
Jer 10: 5 Like a *s* in a melon patch,

SCARLET
Jos 2: 21 she tied the *s* cord in the window.
Isa 1: 18 "Though your sins are like *s*,
Mt 27: 28 They stripped him and put a *s* robe

SCATTER (SCATTERED SCATTERS)
Dt 4: 27 The LORD will *s* you
Ne 1: 8 I will *s* you among the nations,
Jer 9: 16 I will *s* them among nations that
30: 11 the nations among which I *s* you,
Zec 10: 9 I *s* them among the peoples,

SCATTERED (SCATTER)
Isa 11: 12 he will assemble the *s* people
Jer 31: 10 'He who *s* Israel will gather them
Zec 2: 6 "for I have *s* you to the four winds
13: 7 and the sheep will be *s*,
Mt 26: 31 and the sheep of the flock will be *s*.'
Jn 11: 52 but also for the *s* children of God,
Ac 8: 4 who had been *s* preached the word
Jas 1: 1 To the twelve tribes *s*
1Pe 1: 1 *s* throughout Pontus, Galatia,

SCATTERS (SCATTER)
Mt 12: 30 he who does not gather with me *s*.

SCEPTER
Ge 49: 10 The *s* will not depart from Judah,
Nu 24: 17 a *s* will rise out of Israel.
Ps 2: 9 You will rule them with an iron *s*;
45: 6 a *s* of justice will be the *s*
Heb 1: 8 and righteousness will be the *s*
Rev 2: 27 'He will rule them with an iron *s*;
12: 5 rule all the nations with an iron *s*.
19: 15 "He will rule them with an iron *s*."

SCHEMES
Pr 6: 18 a heart that devises wicked *s*,
24: 9 The *s* of folly are sin,
2Co 2: 11 For we are not unaware of his *s*.
Eph 6: 11 stand against the devil's *s*.

SCHOLAR*
1Co 1: 20 Where is the *s*? Where is

SCOFFERS
2Pe 3: 3 that in the last days *s* will come,

SCORN (SCORNED SCORNING SCORNS)
Ps 69: 7 For I endure *s* for your sake,
69: 20 *S* has broken my heart
89: 41 he has become the *s*
109: 25 I am an object of *s* to my accusers;
119: 22 Remove from me *s* and contempt,
Mic 6: 16 you will bear the *s* of the nations."

SCORNED (SCORN)
Ps 22: 6 *s* by men and despised

SCORNING (SCORN)
Heb 12: 2 him endured the cross, *s* its shame,

SCORNS (SCORN)
Pr 13: 13 He who *s* instruction will pay for it,
30: 17 that *s* obedience to a mother,

SCORPION
Lk 11: 12 will give him a *s*? If you then,
Rev 9: 5 sting of a *s* when it strikes a man.

SCOUNDREL
Pr 6: 12 A *s* and villain,

SCRIPTURE (SCRIPTURES)
Jn 2: 22 Then they believed the *S*
7: 42 Does not the *S* say that the Christ
10: 35 and the *S* cannot be broken—
Ac 8: 32 was reading this passage of *S*:
1Ti 4: 13 yourself to the public reading of *S*,
2Ti 3: 16 All *S* is God-breathed
2Pe 1: 20 that no prophecy of *S* came about

SCRIPTURES (SCRIPTURE)
Mt 22: 29 because you do not know the *S*
Lk 24: 27 said in all the *S* concerning himself.
24: 45 so they could understand the *S*.
Jn 5: 39 These are the *S* that testify about
Ac 17: 11 examined the *S* every day to see
2Ti 3: 15 you have known the holy *S*,
2Pe 3: 16 as they do the other *S*,

SCROLL
Ps 40: 7 it is written about me in the *s*.
Isa 34: 4 and the sky rolled up like a *s*;
Eze 3: 1 eat what is before you, eat this *s*;
Heb 10: 7 it is written about me in the *s*—
Rev 6: 14 The sky receded like a *s*, rolling up,
10: 8 take the *s* that lies open in the hand

SCUM
1Co 4: 13 this moment we have become the *s*

SEA (SEASHORE)
Ex 14: 16 go through the *s* on dry ground.
Dt 30: 13 "Who will cross the *s* to get it
1Ki 7: 23 He made the *S* of cast metal,
Job 11: 9 and wider than the *s*.
Ps 93: 4 mightier than the breakers of the *s*
95: 5 The *s* is his, for he made it,
Ecc 1: 7 All streams flow into the *s*,
Isa 57: 20 the wicked are like the tossing *s*,
Jnh 1: 4 LORD sent a great wind on the *s*,
Mic 7: 19 iniquities into the depths of the *s*.
Hab 2: 14 as the waters cover the *s*.
Zec 9: 10 His rule will extend from *s* to *s*
Mt 18: 6 drowned in the depths of the *s*.
1Co 10: 1 that they all passed through the *s*.
Jas 1: 6 who doubts is like a wave of the *s*,
Jude :13 They are wild waves of the *s*,
Rev 10: 2 He planted his right foot on the *s*
13: 1 I saw a beast coming out of the *s*.
20: 13 The *s* gave up the dead that were
21: 1 and there was no longer any *s*.

SEAL (SEALED SEALS)
Ps 40: 9 I do not *s* my lips,
SS 8: 6 Place me like a *s* over your heart,
Da 12: 4 and *s* the words of the scroll
Jn 6: 27 God the Father has placed his *s*
1Co 9: 2 For you are the *s* of my apostleship
2Co 1: 22 set his *s* of ownership on us,
Eph 1: 13 you were marked in him with a *s*,
Rev 6: 3 the Lamb opened the second *s*,
6: 5 When the Lamb opened the third *s*,
6: 7 the Lamb opened the fourth *s*,
6: 9 When he opened the fifth *s*,
6: 12 I watched as he opened the sixth *s*.
8: 1 When he opened the seventh *s*,
9: 4 people who did not have the *s*
22: 10 "Do not *s* up the words

SEALED (SEAL)
Eph 4: 30 with whom you were *s* for the day
2Ti 2: 19 solid foundation stands firm, *s*
Rev 5: 1 on both sides and *s* with seven seals

SEALS (SEAL)
Rev 5: 2 "Who is worthy to break the *s*
6: 1 opened the first of the seven *s*.

SEAMLESS*
Jn 19: 23 This garment was *s*, woven

SEARCH (SEARCHED SEARCHES SEARCHING)
Ps 4: 4 *s* your hearts and be silent.
139: 23 *S* me, O God, and know my heart;
Pr 2: 4 and *s* for it as for hidden treasure,
25: 2 to *s* out a matter is the glory
SS 3: 2 I will *s* for the one my heart loves.
Jer 17: 10 "I the LORD *s* the heart
Eze 34: 11 I myself will *s* for my sheep
34: 16 I will *s* for the lost and bring back
Lk 15: 8 and *s* carefully until she finds it?

SEARCHED (SEARCH)
Ps 139: 1 O LORD, you have *s* me
Ecc 12: 10 The Teacher *s* to find just the right
1Pe 1: 10 *s* intently and with the greatest

SEARCHES (SEARCH)
1Ch 28: 9 for the LORD *s* every heart
Ps 7: 9 who *s* minds and hearts,
Pr 11: 27 but evil comes to him who *s* for it.
20: 27 The lamp of the LORD *s* the spirit
Ro 8: 27 And he who *s* our hearts knows
1Co 2: 10 The Spirit *s* all things,
Rev 2: 23 will know that I am he who *s* hearts

SEARCHING (SEARCH)
Jdg 5: 15 there was much *s* of heart.
Am 8: 12 *s* for the word of the LORD,

SEARED
1Ti 4: 2 whose consciences have been *s*

SEASHORE (SEA)
Jos 11: 4 as numerous as the sand on the *s*.
1Ki 4: 29 as measureless as the sand on the *s*.

SEASON (SEASONED SEASONS)
Lev 26: 4 I will send you rain in its *s*,
Ps 1: 3 which yields its fruit in *s*
2Ti 4: 2 be prepared in *s* and out of *s*;

SEASONED* (SEASON)
Col 4: 6 full of grace, *s* with salt,

SEASONS (SEASON)
Ge 1: 14 signs to mark *s* and days and years,
Gal 4: 10 and months and *s* and years!

SEAT (SEATED SEATS)
Ps 1: 1 or sit in the *s* of mockers.
Pr 31: 23 where he takes his *s*
Da 7: 9 and the Ancient of Days took his *s*.
Lk 14: 9 say to you, 'Give this man your *s*.'
2Co 5: 10 before the judgment *s* of Christ,

SEATED (SEAT)
Ps 47: 8 God is *s* on his holy throne.
Isa 6: 1 I saw the Lord *s* on a throne,
Lk 22: 69 of Man will be *s* at the right hand
Eph 1: 20 and *s* him at his right hand
2: 6 and *s* us with him in the heavenly
Col 3: 1 where Christ is *s* at the right hand
Rev 14: 14 *s* on the cloud was one "like a son
20: 11 white throne and him who was *s*

SEATS (SEAT)
Lk 11: 43 you love the most important *s*

SECLUSION*
Lk 1: 24 and for five months remained in *s*.

SECRET (SECRETLY SECRETS)
Dt 29: 29 The *s* things belong
Jdg 16: 6 Tell me the *s* of your great strength
Ps 90: 8 our *s* sins in the light
139: 15 when I was made in the *s* place.
Pr 11: 13 but a trustworthy man keeps a *s*.
21: 14 A gift given in *s* soothes anger,
Jer 23: 24 Can anyone hide in *s* places
Mt 6: 4 so that your giving may be in *s*.
6: 18 who sees what is done in *s*,
Mk 4: 11 "The *s* of the kingdom
1Co 2: 7 No, we speak of God's *s* wisdom,
4: 1 entrusted with the *s* things of God.
2Co 4: 2 we have renounced *s* and shameful
Eph 5: 12 what the disobedient do in *s*.
Php 4: 12 I have learned the *s*

SECRETLY (SECRET)
2Pe 2: 1 They will *s* introduce destructive
Jude :4 about long ago have *s* slipped

SECRETS (SECRET)
Ps 44: 21 since he knows the *s* of the heart?
Ro 2: 16 day when God will judge men's *s*
1Co 14: 25 the *s* of his heart will be laid bare.
Rev 2: 24 Satan's so-called deep *s* (I will not

SECURE (SECURITY)
Dt 33: 12 beloved of the LORD rest *s* in him,
Ps 16: 5 you have made my lot *s*.
16: 9 my body also will rest *s*,
112: 8 His heart is *s*, he will have no fear;
Pr 14: 26 fears the LORD has a *s* fortress,
Heb 6: 19 an anchor for the soul, firm and *s*.

2Pe 3:17 and fall from your *s* position.

SECURITY (SECURE)

Job 31:24 or said to pure gold, 'You are my *s*,'

SEED (SEEDS SEEDTIME)

Ge 1:11 on the land that bear fruit with *s*
Isa 55:10 so that it yields *s* for the sower
Mt 13:3 "A farmer went out to sow his *s*.
13:31 of heaven is like a mustard *s*,
17:20 have faith as small as a mustard *s*,
Lk 8:11 of the parable: The *s* is the word
1Co 3:6 I planted the *s*, Apollos watered it,
2Co 9:10 he who supplies *s* to the sower
Gal 3:29 then you are Abraham's *s*,
1Pe 1:23 not of perishable *s*,
1Jn 3:9 because God's *s* remains in him;

SEEDS (SEED)

Jn 12:24 But if it dies, it produces many *s*.
Gal 3:16 Scripture does not say "and to *s*,"

SEEDTIME* (SEED)

Ge 8:22 *s* and harvest,

SEEK (SEEKING SEEKS SELF-SEEKING SOUGHT)

Lev 19:18 Do not *s* revenge or bear a grudge
Dt 4:29 if from there you *s* the LORD your
1Ki 22:5 "First *s* the counsel of the LORD."
1Ch 28:9 If you *s* him, he will be found
2Ch 7:14 themselves and pray and *s* my face
15:2 If you *s* him, he will be found
Ps 34:10 those who *s* the LORD lack no
105:3 of those who *s* the LORD rejoice.
105:4 *s* his face always.
119:2 and *s* him with all their heart.
119:10 I *s* you with all my heart;
119:176 *S* your servant,
Pr 8:17 and those who *s* me find me.
18:15 the ears of the wise *s* it out.
25:27 is it honorable to *s* one's own honor
28:5 those who *s* the LORD understand
Isa 55:6 *S* the LORD while he may be
65:1 found by those who did not *s* me.
Jer 29:13 You will *s* me and find me
Hos 10:12 for it is time to *s* the LORD,
Am 5:4 "*S* me and live;
Zep 2:3 *S* the LORD, all you humble
Mt 6:33 But *s* first his kingdom
7:7 and it will be given to you; *s*
Lk 12:31 *s* his kingdom, and these things will
19:10 For the Son of Man came to *s*
Jn 5:30 for I *s* not to please myself
Ro 10:20 found by those who did not *s* me;
1Co 7:27 you married? Do not *s* a divorce.
10:24 Nobody should *s* his own good,
Heb 11:6 rewards those who earnestly *s* him.
1Pe 3:11 he must *s* peace and pursue it.

SEEKING (SEEK)

2Ch 30:19 who sets his heart on *s* God—
Pr 20:18 Make plans by *s* advice;
Mal 3:1 the Lord you are *s* will come
Jn 8:50 I am not *s* glory for myself;
1Co 10:33 For I am not *s* my own good

SEEKS (SEEK)

Pr 11:27 He who *s* good finds good will,
Mt 7:8 he who *s* finds; and to him who
Jn 4:23 the kind of worshipers the Father *s*.
Ro 3:11 no one who *s* God.

SEER

1Sa 9:9 of today used to be called a *s*.)

SELF-CONTROL* (CONTROL)

Pr 25:28 is a man who lacks *s*.
Ac 24:25 *s* and the judgment to come,
1Co 7:5 you because of your lack of *s*.
Gal 5:23 faithfulness, gentleness and *s*.
2Ti 3:3 slanderous, without *s*, brutal,
2Pe 1:6 and to knowledge, *s*; and to *s*,

SELF-CONTROLLED* (CONTROL)

1Th 5:6 are asleep, but let us be alert and *s*.
5:8 let us be *s*, putting on faith and love
1Ti 3:2 *s*, respectable, hospitable,
Tit 1:8 who is *s*, upright, holy
2:2 worthy of respect, *s*, and sound
2:5 to be *s* and pure, to be busy at home
2:6 encourage the young men to be *s*.
2:12 to live *s*, upright and godly lives
1Pe 1:13 prepare your minds for action; be *s*;
4:7 and *s* so that you can pray.
1Pe 5:8 Be *s* and alert.

SELF-DISCIPLINE* (DISCIPLINE)

2Ti 1:7 a spirit of power, of love and of *s*.

SELF-INDULGENCE*

Mt 23:25 inside they are full of greed and *s*.
Jas 5:5 lived on earth in luxury and *s*.

SELF-SEEKING* (SEEK)

Ro 2:8 But for those who are *s*
1Co 13:5 it is not *s*, it is not easily angered,

SELFISH*

Ps 119:36 and not toward *s* gain.
Pr 18:1 An unfriendly man pursues *s* ends;
Gal 5:20 fits of rage, *s* ambition, dissensions,
Php 1:17 preach Christ out of *s* ambition,
2:3 Do nothing out of *s* ambition
Jas 3:14 and *s* ambition in your hearts,
3:16 you have envy and *s* ambition,

SELL (SELLING SELLS SOLD)

Ge 25:31 "First *s* me your birthright."
Mk 10:21 *s* everything you have
Rev 13:17 or *s* unless he had the mark,

SELLING (SELL)

Lk 17:28 buying and *s*, planting and building

SELLS (SELL)

Pr 31:24 makes linen garments and *s* them,

SEND (SENDING SENDS SENT)

Ps 43:3 *S* forth your light and your truth,
Isa 6:8 *S* me!" He said, "Go and tell this
Mal 3:1 "See, I will *s* my messenger,
Mt 9:38 to *s* out workers into his harvest
24:31 And he will *s* his angels
Mk 1:2 I will *s* my messenger ahead of you,
Lk 20:13 I will *s* my son, whom I love;
Jn 3:17 For God did not *s* his Son
16:7 but if I go, I will *s* him to you.
1Co 1:17 For Christ did not *s* me to baptize,

SENDING (SEND)

Mt 10:16 I am *s* you out like sheep
Jn 20:21 Father has sent me, I am *s* you."
Ro 8:3 God did by *s* his own Son

SENDS (SEND)

Ps 57:3 God *s* his love and his faithfulness.

SENNACHERIB

Assyrian king whose siege of Jerusalem was overthrown by the LORD following prayer of Hezekiah and Isaiah (2Ki 18:13-19:37; 2Ch 32:1-21; Isa 36-37).

SENSES*

Lk 15:17 "When he came to his *s*, he said,
1Co 15:34 Come back to your *s* as you ought,
2Ti 2:26 and that they will come to their *s*

SENSITIVITY*

Eph 4:19 Having lost all *s*, they have given

SENSUAL* (SENSUALITY)

Col 2:23 value in restraining *s* indulgence.
1Ti 5:11 For when their *s* desires overcome

SENSUALITY* (SENSUAL)

Eph 4:19 have given themselves over to *s*

SENT (SEND)

Ex 3:14 to the Israelites: 'I AM has *s* me
Isa 55:11 achieve the purpose for which I *s* it.
61:1 He has *s* me to bind up
Jer 28:9 as one truly *s* by the LORD only
Mt 10:40 me receives the one who *s* me.
Mk 6:7 he *s* them out two by two
Lk 4:18 He has *s* me to proclaim freedom
9:2 and he *s* them out to preach
10:16 rejects me rejects him who *s* me."
Jn 1:6 There came a man who was *s*
4:34 "is to do the will of him who *s* me
5:24 believes him who *s* me has eternal
8:16 I stand with the Father, who *s* me.
9:4 must do the work of him who *s* me.
16:5 "Now I am going to him who *s* me,
17:3 and Jesus Christ, whom you have *s*.
17:18 As you *s* me into the world,
20:21 As the Father has *s* me, I am
Ro 10:15 can they preach unless they are *s*?
Gal 4:4 God *s* his Son, born of a woman,
1Jn 4:10 but that he loved us and *s* his Son

SENTENCE

2Co 1:9 in our hearts we felt the *s* of death.

SEPARATE (SEPARATED SEPARATES SEPARATION)

Mt 19:6 has joined together, let man not *s*."
Ro 8:35 Who shall *s* us from the love
1Co 7:10 wife must not *s* from her husband.
2Co 6:17 and be *s*, says the Lord.
Eph 2:12 at that time you were *s* from Christ,

SEPARATED (SEPARATE)

Isa 59:2 But your iniquities have *s*
Eph 4:18 in their understanding and *s*

SEPARATES (SEPARATE)

Pr 16:28 and a gossip *s* close friends.
17:9 repeats the matter *s* close friends.
Mt 25:32 as a shepherd *s* the sheep

SEPARATION (SEPARATE)

Nu 6:2 a vow of *s* to the LORD

SERAPHS*

Isa 6:2 Above him were *s*, each
6:6 Then one of the *s* flew to me

SERIOUSNESS*

Tit 2:7 *s* and soundness of speech that

SERPENT (SERPENT'S)

Ge 3:1 the *s* was more crafty than any
Isa 27:1 Leviathan the coiling *s*;
Rev 12:9 that ancient *s* called the devil
20:2 that ancient *s*, who is the devil,

SERPENT'S (SERPENT)

2Co 11:3 Eve was deceived by the *s* cunning,

SERVANT (SERVANTS)

Ex 14:31 trust in him and in Moses his *s*.
21:2 "If you buy a Hebrew *s*, he is
1Sa 3:10 "Speak, for your *s* is listening."
2Sa 7:19 the future of the house of your *s*.
1Ki 20:40 While your *s* was busy here
Job 1:8 "Have you considered my *s* Job?
Ps 19:11 By them is your *s* warned;
19:13 Keep your *s* also from willful sins;
31:16 Let your face shine on your *s*;
89:3 I have sworn to David my *s*,
Pr 14:35 A king delights in a wise *s*,
17:2 wise *s* will rule over a disgraceful
22:7 and the borrower is *s* to the lender.
31:15 and portions for her *s* girls.
Isa 41:8 "But you, O Israel, my *s*,
49:3 He said to me, "You are my *s*,
53:11 my righteous *s* will justify
Zec 3:8 going to bring my *s*, the Branch.
Mal 1:6 his father, and a *s* his master.
Mt 8:13 his *s* was healed at that very hour.
20:26 great among you must be your *s*,
24:45 Who then is the faithful and wise *s*,
25:21 'Well done, good and faithful *s*!
Lk 1:38 I am the Lord's *s*," Mary answered.
16:13 "No *s* can serve two masters.
Jn 12:26 and where I am, my *s* also will be.
Ro 1:1 a *s* of Christ Jesus, called
13:4 For he is God's *s* to do you good.
Php 2:7 taking the very nature of a *s*,
Col 1:23 of which I, Paul, have become a *s*.
2Ti 2:24 And the Lord's *s* must not quarrel;

SERVANTS (SERVANT)

Lev 25:55 for the Israelites belong to me as *s*.
2Ki 17:13 to you through my *s* the prophets."
Ezr 5:11 "We are the *s* of the God of heaven
Ps 34:22 The LORD redeems his *s*;
103:21 you his *s* who do his will.
104:4 flames of fire his *s*.
Isa 44:26 who carries out the words of his *s*
65:8 so will I do in behalf of my *s*;
65:13 my *s* will drink,
Lk 17:10 should say, 'We are unworthy *s*;
Jn 15:15 longer call you *s*, because a servant
Ro 13:6 for the authorities are God's *s*,
1Co 3:5 And what is Paul? Only *s*,
Heb 1:7 his *s* flames of fire."

SERVE (SERVED SERVES SERVICE SERVING)

Dt 10:12 to *s* the LORD your God
11:13 and to *s* him with all your heart
13:4 *s* him and hold fast to him.

Dt 28:47 you did not *s* the LORD your
Jos 22: 5 and to *s* him with all your heart
24:15 this day whom you will *s*,
24:18 We too will *s* the LORD,
1Sa 7: 3 to the LORD and *s* him only,
12:20 but *s* the LORD with all your heart
12:24 *s* him faithfully with all your heart;
2Ch 19: 9 "You must *s* faithfully
Job 36:11 If they obey and *s* him,
Ps 2:11 *S* the LORD with fear
Da 3:17 the God we *s* is able to save us
Mt 4:10 Lord your God, and *s* him only.'"
6:24 "No one can *s* two masters.
20:28 but to *s*, and to give his life
Ro 12: 7 If it is serving, let him *s*;
Gal 5:13 rather, *s* one another in love.
Eph 6: 7 *S* wholeheartedly,
1Ti 6: 2 they are to *s* them even better,
Heb 9:14 so that we may *s* the living God!
1Pe 4:10 gift he has received to *s* others,
5: 2 greedy for money, but eager to *s*;
Rev 5:10 kingdom and priests to *s* our God,

SERVED (SERVE)

Mt 20:28 Son of Man did not come to be *s*,
Jn 12: 2 Martha *s*, while Lazarus was
Ac 17:25 And he is not *s* by human hands,
Ro 1:25 and *s* created things rather
1Ti 3:13 Those who have *s* well gain

SERVES (SERVE)

Lk 22:26 one who rules like the one who *s*.
22:27 But I am among you as one who *s*.
Jn 12:26 Whoever *s* me must follow me;
Ro 14:18 because anyone who *s* Christ
1Pe 4:11 If anyone *s*, he should do it

SERVICE (SERVE)

Lk 9:62 fit for *s* in the kingdom
12:35 "Be dressed ready for *s*
Ro 15:17 in Christ Jesus in my *s* to God.
1Co 12: 5 There are different kinds of *s*,
16:15 themselves to the *s* of the saints.
2Co 9:12 This *s* that you perform is not only
Eph 4:12 God's people for works of *s*,
Rev 2:19 and faith, your *s* and perseverance,

SERVING (SERVE)

Jos 24:15 if *s* the LORD seems undesirable
2Ch 12: 8 learn the difference between *s* me
Ro 12: 7 If it is *s*, let him serve;
12:11 your spiritual fervor, *s* the Lord.
16:18 people are not *s* our Lord Christ,
Eph 6: 7 as if you were *s* the Lord, not men,
Col 3:24 It is the Lord Christ you are *s*.
2Ti 2: 4 No one *s* as a soldier gets involved

SETH

Ge 4:25 birth to a son and named him *S*,

SETTLE

Mt 5:25 "*S* matters quickly
2Th 3:12 in the Lord Jesus Christ to *s* down

SEVEN (SEVENS SEVENTH)

Ge 7: 2 Take with you *s* of every kind
Jos 6: 4 march around the city *s* times,
1Ki 19:18 Yet I reserve *s* thousand in Israel—
Pr 6:16 *s* that are detestable to him:
24:16 a righteous man falls *s* times,
Isa 4: 1 In that day *s* women
Da 9:25 comes, there will be *s* 'sevens,'
Mt 18:21 Up to *s* times?" Jesus answered,
Lk 11:26 takes *s* other spirits more wicked
Ro 11: 4 for myself *s* thousand who have not
Rev 1: 4 To the *s* churches in the province
6: 1 opened the first of the *s* seals.
8: 2 and to them were given *s* trumpets.
10: 4 And when the *s* thunders spoke,
15: 7 to the *s* angels *s* golden bowls filled

SEVENS* (SEVEN)

Da 9:24 "Seventy *'s'* are decreed
9:25 will be seven *'s,'* and sixty-two *'s.'*
9:26 the sixty-two *'s,'* the Anointed

SEVENTH (SEVEN)

Ge 2: 2 By the *s* day God had finished
Ex 20:10 but the *s* day is a Sabbath
23:11 but during the *s* year let the land lie
23:12 but on the *s* day do not work,
Heb 4: 4 "And on the *s* day God rested

SEVERE

2Co 8: 2 Out of the most *s* trial, their

1Th 1: 6 of the Lord; in spite of *s* suffering,

SEWED (SEWS)

Ge 3: 7 so they *s* fig leaves together

SEWS (SEWED)

Mt 9:16 No one *s* a patch of unshrunk cloth

SEXUAL (SEXUALLY)

Ex 22:19 "Anyone who has *s* relations
Lev 18: 6 relative to have *s* relations.
18: 7 father by having *s* relations
18:20 Do not have *s* relations with
Mt 15:19 murder, adultery, *s* immorality,
Ac 15:20 by idols, from *s* immorality,
1Co 5: 1 reported that there is *s* immorality
6:13 body is not meant for *s* immorality,
6:18 Flee from *s* immorality.
10: 8 should not commit *s* immorality,
2Co 12:21 *s* sin and debauchery
Gal 5:19 *s* immorality, impurity
Eph 5: 3 even a hint of *s* immorality,
Col 3: 5 *s* immorality, impurity, lust,
1Th 4: 3 that you should avoid *s* immorality

SEXUALLY (SEXUAL)

1Co 5: 9 to associate with *s* immoral people
6: 9 Neither the *s* immoral nor idolaters
6:18 he who sins *s* sins against his own
Heb 12:16 See that no one is *s* immoral,
13: 4 the adulterer and all the *s* immoral.
Rev 21: 8 the murderers, the *s* immoral,

SHADE

Ps 121: 5 the LORD is your *s*
Isa 25: 4 and a *s* from the heat.

SHADOW

Ps 17: 8 hide me in the *s* of your wings
23: 4 through the valley of the *s* of death,
36: 7 find refuge in the *s* of your wings.
91: 1 will rest in the *s* of the Almighty.
Isa 51:16 covered you with the *s* of my hand
Col 2:17 These are a *s* of the things that
Heb 8: 5 and *s* of what is in heaven.
10: 1 The law is only a *s*

SHADRACH

Hebrew exiled to Babylon; name changed from Hananiah (Da 1:6-7). Refused defilement by food (Da 1:8-20). Refused to worship idol (Da 3:1-18); saved from furnace (Da 3:19-30).

SHAKE (SHAKEN SHAKING)

Ps 64: 8 all who see them will *s* their heads
99: 1 let the earth *s*.
Hag 2: 6 I will once more *s* the heavens
Heb 12:26 "Once more I will *s* not only

SHAKEN (SHAKE)

Ps 16: 8 I will not be *s*.
30: 6 "I will never be *s*."
62: 2 he is my fortress, I will never be *s*.
112: 6 Surely he will never be *s*;
Isa 54:10 Though the mountains be *s*
Mt 24:29 and the heavenly bodies will be *s*.'
Lk 6:38 *s* together and running over,
Ac 2:25 I will not be *s*.
Heb 12:27 that what cannot be *s* may remain.

SHAKING* (SHAKE)

Ps 22: 7 they hurl insults, *s* their heads:
Mt 27:39 insults at him, *s* their heads
Mk 15:29 *s* their heads and saying, "So!

SHALLUM

King of Israel (2Ki 15:10-16).

SHAME (ASHAMED SHAMED SHAMEFUL)

Ps 25: 3 will ever be put to *s*,
34: 5 their faces are never covered with *s*
69: 6 not be put to *s* because of me,
Pr 13:18 discipline comes to poverty and *s*,
18:13 that is his folly and his *s*.
Jer 8: 9 The wise will be put to *s*;
8:12 No, they have no *s* at all;
Ro 9:33 trusts in him will never be put to *s*."
10:11 trusts in him will never be put to *s*."
1Co 1:27 things of the world to *s* the wise;
Heb 12: 2 endured the cross, scorning its *s*,

SHAMED (SHAME)

Jer 10:14 every goldsmith is *s* by his idols.
Joel 2:26 never again will my people be *s*.

SHAMEFUL (SHAME)

2Co 4: 2 have renounced secret and *s* ways;
2Pe 2: 2 Many will follow their *s* ways
Rev 21:27 nor will anyone who does what is *s*

SHAMGAR

Judge; killed 600 Philistines (Jdg 3:31).

SHAPE (SHAPES SHAPING)

Job 38:14 The earth takes *s* like clay

SHAPES (SHAPE)

Isa 44:10 Who *s* a god and casts an idol,

SHAPING (SHAPE)

Jer 18: 4 the pot he was *s* from the clay was

SHARE (SHARED SHARERS SHARES SHARING)

Ge 21:10 that slave woman's son will never *s*
Lev 19:17 frankly so you will not *s* in his guilt.
Dt 10: 9 That is why the Levites have no *s*
1Sa 30:24 All will *s* alike."
Eze 18:20 The son will not *s* the guilt
Mt 25:21 and *s* your master's happiness!'
Lk 3:11 "The man with two tunics should *s*
Ro 8:17 if indeed we *s* in his sufferings
12:13 *S* with God's people who are
2Co 1: 7 as you *s* in our sufferings,
Gal 4:30 the slave woman's son will never *s*
6: 6 in the word must *s* all good things
Eph 4:28 something to *s* with those in need.
Col 1:12 you to *s* in the inheritance
2Th 2:14 that you might *s* in the glory
1Ti 5:22 and do not *s* in the sins of others.
6:18 and to be generous and willing to *s*.
2Ti 2: 6 the first to receive a *s* of the crops.
Heb 12:10 that we may *s* in his holiness.
13:16 to do good and to *s* with others,
Rev 22:19 from him his *s* in the tree of life

SHARED (SHARE)

Ps 41: 9 he who *s* my bread,
Ac 4:32 but they *s* everything they had.
Heb 2:14 he too *s* in their humanity so that

SHARERS* (SHARE)

Eph 3: 6 and *s* together in the promise

SHARES (SHARE)

Pr 22: 9 for he *s* his food with the poor.
Jn 13:18 'He who *s* my bread has lifted up

SHARING (SHARE)

1Co 9:10 so in the hope of *s* in the harvest.
2Co 9:13 for your generosity in *s* with them
Php 3:10 the fellowship of *s* in his sufferings,
Phm :6 you may be active in *s* your faith,

SHARON

SS 2: 1 I am a rose of *S*,

SHARP (SHARPENED SHARPENS SHARPER)

Pr 5: 4 *s* as a double-edged sword.
Isa 5:28 Their arrows are *s*,
Rev 1:16 came a *s* double-edged sword.
19:15 Out of his mouth comes a *s* sword

SHARPENED (SHARP)

Eze 21: 9 *s* and polished—

SHARPENS* (SHARP)

Pr 27:17 As iron *s* iron,
27:17 so one man *s* another.

SHARPER* (SHARP)

Heb 4:12 *S* than any double-edged sword,

SHATTER (SHATTERED SHATTERS)

Jer 51:20 with you I *s* nations,

SHATTERED (SHATTER)

1Sa 2:10 who oppose the LORD will be *s*.
Job 16:12 All was well with me, but he *s* me;
17:11 days have passed, my plans are *s*,
Ecc 12: 6 before the pitcher is *s* at the spring,

SHATTERS (SHATTER)

Ps 46: 9 he breaks the bow and *s* the spear,

SHAVED

Jdg 16:17 my head were *s*, my strength would
1Co 11: 5 it is just as though her head were *s*.

SHEAF (SHEAVES)
Lev 23:11 is to wave the s before the LORD

SHEARER* (SHEARERS)
Ac 8:32 and as a lamb before the s is silent,

SHEARERS (SHEARER)
Isa 53: 7 and as a sheep before her s is silent,

SHEAVES (SHEAF)
Ge 37: 7 while your s gathered around mine
Ps 126: 6 carrying s with him.

SHEBA
1. Benjamite who rebelled against David (2Sa 20).
2. See QUEEN.

SHECHEM
1. Raped Jacob's daughter Dinah; killed by Simeon and Levi (Ge 34).
2. City where Joshua renewed the covenant (Jos 24).

SHED (SHEDDING SHEDS)
Ge 9: 6 by man shall his blood be s;
Pr 6:17 hands that s innocent blood,
Ro 3:15 "Their feet are swift to s blood;
Col 1:20 through his blood, s on the cross.

SHEDDING (SHED)
Heb 9:22 without the s of blood there is no

SHEDS (SHED)
Ge 9: 6 "Whoever s the blood of man,

SHEEP (SHEEP'S SHEEPSKINS)
Nu 27:17 LORD's people will not be like s
Dt 17: 1 a s that has any defect or flaw in it,
1Sa 15:14 "What then is this bleating of s
Ps 44:22 we are considered as s
78:52 led them like s through the desert.
100: 3 we are his people, the s
119:176 I have strayed like a lost s.
SS 4: 2 teeth are like a flock of s just shorn,
Isa 53: 6 We all, like s, have gone astray,
53: 7 as a s before her shearers is silent,
Jer 50: 6 "My people have been lost s;
Eze 34:11 I myself will search for my s
Zec 13: 7 and the s will be scattered,
Mt 9:36 helpless, like s without a shepherd.
10:16 I am sending you out like s
12:11 "If any of you has a s and it falls
18:13 he is happier about that one s
25:32 as a shepherd separates the s
Jn 10: 1 man who does not enter the s pen
10: 3 He calls his own s by name
10: 7 the truth, I am the gate for the s.
10:15 and I lay down my life for the s.
10:27 My s listen to my voice; I know
21:17 Jesus said, "Feed my s.
1Pe 2:25 For you were like s going astray,

SHEEP'S* (SHEEP)
Mt 7:15 They come to you in s clothing,

SHEEPSKINS* (SHEEP)
Heb 11:37 They went about in s and goatskins

SHEKEL
Ex 30:13 This half s is an offering

SHELTER
Ps 27: 5 me in the s of his tabernacle
31:20 In the s of your presence you hide
55: 8 I would hurry to my place of s,
61: 4 take refuge in the s of your wings.
91: 1 in the s of the Most High
Ecc 7:12 Wisdom is a s
Isa 4: 6 It will be a s and shade
25: 4 a s from the storm
32: 2 Each man will be like a s
58: 7 the poor wanderer with s—

SHEM
Son of Noah (Ge 5:32; 6:10). Blessed (Ge 9:26). Descendants (Ge 10:21-31; 11:10-32).

SHEPHERD (SHEPHERDS)
Ge 48:15 the God who has been my s
49:24 because of the S, the Rock of Israel
Nu 27:17 will not be like sheep without a s."
2Sa 7: 7 commanded to s my people Israel,
1Ki 22:17 on the hills like sheep without a s,
Ps 23: 1 LORD is my s, I shall not be in want.
28: 9 be their s and carry them forever.
80: 1 Hear us, O S of Israel,
Isa 40:11 He tends his flock like a s:
Jer 31:10 will watch over his flock like a s.'
Eze 34: 5 scattered because there was no s,
34:12 As a s looks after his scattered
Zec 11: 9 and said, "I will not be your s.
11:17 "Woe to the worthless s,
13: 7 "Strike the s,
Mt 2: 6 who will be the s of my people
9:36 and helpless, like sheep without a s.
26:31 " 'I will strike the s,
Jn 10:11 The good s lays down his life
10:14 "I am the good s; I know my sheep
10:16 there shall be one flock and one s.
Heb 13:20 that great S of the sheep, equip you
1Pe 5: 4 And when the Chief S appears,
Rev 7:17 of the throne will be their s;

SHEPHERDS (SHEPHERD)
Jer 23: 1 "Woe to the s who are destroying
50: 6 their s have led them astray
Eze 34: 2 prophesy against the s of Israel;
Lk 2: 8 there were s living out in the fields
Ac 20:28 Be s of the church of God,
1Pe 5: 2 Be s of God's flock that is
Jude :12 s who feed only themselves.

SHIBBOLETH*
Jdg 12: 6 No," they said, "All right, say 'S.' "

SHIELD (SHIELDED SHIELDS)
Ge 15: 1 I am your s,
2Sa 22: 3 my s and the horn of my salvation.
22:36 You give me your s of victory;
Ps 3: 3 But you are a s around me,
5:12 with your favor as with a s.
7:10 My s is God Most High,
18: 2 He is my s and the horn
28: 7 LORD is my strength and my s;
33:20 he is our help and our s.
84:11 For the LORD God is a sun and s;
91: 4 his faithfulness will be your s
115: 9 he is their help and s.
119:114 You are my refuge and my s;
144: 2 my s, in whom I take refuge,
Pr 2: 7 he is a s to those whose walk is
30: 5 he is a s to those who take refuge
Eph 6:16 to all this, take up the s of faith,

SHIELDED (SHIELD)
1Pe 1: 5 through faith are s by God's power

SHIELDS (SHIELD)
Dt 33:12 for he s him all day long,

SHIFTLESS*
Pr 19:15 and the s man goes hungry.

SHIMEI
Cursed David (2Sa 16:5-14); spared (2Sa 19:16-23). Killed by Solomon (1Ki 2:8-9, 36-46).

SHINE (SHINES SHINING SHONE)
Nu 6:25 the LORD make his face s
Job 33:30 that the light of life may s on him.
Ps 4: 6 Let the light of your face s upon us,
37: 6 make your righteousness s like
67: 1 and make his face s upon us; *Selah*
80: 1 between the cherubim, s forth
118:27 and he has made his light s upon us.
Isa 60: 1 "Arise, s, for your light has come,
Da 12: 3 are wise will s like the brightness
Mt 5:16 let your light s before men,
13:43 the righteous will s like the sun
2Co 4: 6 made his light s in our hearts
Eph 5:14 and Christ will s on you."
Php 2:15 in which you s like stars

SHINES (SHINE)
Ps 50: 2 God s forth.
Pr 13: 9 The light of the righteous s brightly
Jn 1: 5 The light s in the darkness,

SHINING (SHINE)
Pr 4:18 s ever brighter till the full light
2Pe 1:19 as to a light s in a dark place,
Rev 1:16 His face was like the sun s

SHIPS
Pr 31:14 She is like the merchant s,

SHIPWRECKED*
2Co 11:25 I was stoned, three times I was s,
1Ti 1:19 and so have s their faith.

SHISHAK
1Ki 14:25 S king of Egypt attacked Jerusalem
2Ch 12: 2 S king of Egypt attacked Jerusalem

SHOCKING*
Jer 5:30 "A horrible and s thing

SHONE (SHINE)
Mt 17: 2 His face s like the sun,
Lk 2: 9 glory of the Lord s around them,
Rev 21:11 It s with the glory of God,

SHOOT
Isa 53: 2 up before him like a tender s,
Ro 11:17 and you, though a wild olive s,

SHORE
Lk 5: 3 asked him to put out a little from s.

SHORT (SHORTENED)
Nu 11:23 "Is the LORD's arm too s?
Isa 50: 2 Was my arm too s to ransom you?
59: 1 of the LORD is not too s to save,
Mt 24:22 If those days had not been cut s,
Ro 3:23 and fall s of the glory of God,
1Co 7:29 brothers, is that the time is s.
Heb 4: 1 of you be found to have fallen s of it
Rev 20: 3 he must be set free for a s time.

SHORTENED (SHORT)
Mt 24:22 of the elect those days will be s.

SHOULDER (SHOULDERS)
Zep 3: 9 and serve him s to s.

SHOULDERS (SHOULDER)
Dt 33:12 LORD loves rests between his s."
Isa 9: 6 and the government will be on his s
Lk 15: 5 he joyfully puts it on his s

SHOUT (SHOUTED)
Ps 47: 1 s to God with cries of joy.
66: 1 S with joy to God, all the earth!
95: 1 let us s aloud to the Rock
98: 4 S for joy to the LORD, all the earth
100: 1 S for joy to the LORD, all the earth
Isa 12: 6 S aloud and sing for joy, people
26:19 wake up and s for joy.
35: 6 the mute tongue s for joy.
40: 9 lift up your voice with a s,
42: 2 He will not s or cry out,
44:23 s aloud, O earth beneath.
54: 1 burst into song, s for joy,
Zec 9: 9 S, Daughter of Jerusalem!

SHOUTED (SHOUT)
Job 38: 7 and all the angels s for joy?

SHOW (SHOWED)
Ex 18:20 and s them the way to live
33:18 Moses said, "Now s me your glory
2Sa 22:26 the faithful you s yourself faithful,
1Ki 2: 2 "So be strong, s yourself a man,
Ps 17: 7 S the wonder of your great love,
25: 4 S me your ways, O LORD,
39: 4 "S me, O LORD, my life's end
85: 7 S us your unfailing love, O LORD,
143: 8 S me the way I should go,
Pr 23: 4 have the wisdom to s restraint.
SS 2:14 s me your face,
Isa 5:16 the holy God will s himself holy
30:18 he rises to s you compassion.
Eze 28:25 I will s myself holy among them
Joel 2:30 I will s wonders in the heavens
Zec 7: 9 s mercy and compassion
Ac 2:19 I will s wonders in the heaven
10:34 it is that God does not s favoritism
1Co 12:31 now I will s you the most excellent
Eph 2: 7 ages he might s the incomparable
Tit 2: 7 In your teaching s integrity,
Jas 2:18 I will s you my faith by what I do.
Jude :23 to others s mercy, mixed with fear

SHOWED (SHOW)
1Ki 3: 3 Solomon s his love for the LORD
Lk 24:40 he s them his hands and feet.
1Jn 4: 9 This is how God s his love

SHOWERS
Eze 34:26 in season; there will be s of blessing
Hos 10:12 and s righteousness on you.

SHREWD

2Sa 22:27 to the crooked you show yourself *s.*
Mt 10:16 Therefore be as *s* as snakes and

SHRINK (SHRINKS)

Heb 10:39 But we are not of those who *s* back

SHRINKS* (SHRINK)

Heb 10:38 And if he *s* back,

SHRIVEL

Isa 64: 6 we all *s* up like a leaf,

SHUDDER

Eze 32:10 and their kings will *s* with horror

SHUHITE

Job 2:11 Bildad the *S* and Zophar

SHUN* (SHUNS)

Job 28:28 and to *s* evil is understanding.' "
Pr 3: 7 fear the LORD and *s* evil.

SHUNS (SHUN)

Job 1: 8 a man who fears God and *s* evil."
Pr 14:16 man fears the LORD and *s* evil,

SHUT

Ge 7:16 Then the LORD *s* him in.
Isa 22:22 what he opens no one can *s,*
60:11 they will never be *s,* day or night,
Da 6:22 and he *s* the mouths of the lions.
Heb 11:33 who *s* the mouths of lions,
Rev 3: 7 no one can *s,* and what he shuts
21:25 On no day will its gates ever be *s,*

SICK (SICKNESS)

Pr 13:12 Hope deferred makes the heart *s,*
Eze 34: 4 or healed the *s* or bound up
Mt 9:12 who need a doctor, but the *s.*
10: 8 Heal the *s,* raise the dead, cleanse
25:36 I was *s* and you looked after me,
1Co 11:30 many among you are weak and *s,*
Jas 5:14 of you *s?* He should call the elders

SICKBED* (BED)

Ps 41: 3 LORD will sustain him on his *s*

SICKLE

Joel 3:13 Swing the *s,*
Rev 14:14 gold on his head and a sharp *s*

SICKNESS (SICK)

Mt 4:23 and healing every disease and *s*

SIDE (SIDES)

Ps 91: 7 A thousand may fall at your *s,*
124: 1 If the LORD had not been on our *s*
Jn 18:37 Everyone on the *s* of truth listens
20:20 he showed them his hands and *s.*
2Ti 4:17 But the Lord stood at my *s*
Heb 10:33 at other times you stood *s* by *s*

SIDES (SIDE)

Nu 33:55 in your eyes and thorns in your *s.*

SIFT

Lk 22:31 Satan has asked to *s* you as wheat.

SIGHING

Isa 35:10 and sorrow and *s* will flee away.

SIGHT

Ps 51: 4 and done what is evil in your *s,*
90: 4 For a thousand years in your *s*
116:15 Precious in the *s* of the LORD
Pr 3: 4 in the *s* of God and man.
Mt 11: 5 The blind receive *s,* the lame walk,
Ac 4:19 right in God's *s* to obey you rather
1Co 3:19 this world is foolishness in God's *s.*
2Co 5: 7 We live by faith, not by *s.*
1Pe 3: 4 which is of great worth in God's *s.*

SIGN (SIGNS)

Ge 9:12 "This is the *s* of the covenant I am
17:11 and it will be the *s* of the covenant
Isa 7:14 the Lord himself will give you a *s:*
55:13 for an everlasting *s,*
Eze 20:12 I gave them my Sabbaths as a *s*
Mt 12:38 to see a miraculous *s* from you."
24: 3 what will be the *s* of your coming
24:30 "At that time the *s* of the Son
Lk 2:12 This will be a *s* to you: You will
11:29 It asks for a miraculous *s,*
Ro 4:11 he received the *s* of circumcision,
1Co 11:10 to have a *s* of authority on her head
14:22 are a *s,* not for believers

SIGNS (SIGN)

Ge 1:14 let them serve as *s* to mark seasons
Ps 78:43 day he displayed his miraculous *s*
105:27 They performed his miraculous *s*
Da 6:27 he performs *s* and wonders
Mt 24:24 and perform great *s* and miracles
Mk 16:17 these *s* will accompany those who
Jn 3: 2 perform the miraculous *s* you are
20:30 Jesus did many other miraculous *s*
Ac 2:19 and *s* on the earth below,
1Co 1:22 Jews demand miraculous *s*
2Co 12:12 *s,* wonders and miracles—
2Th 2: 9 *s* and wonders, and in every sort

SIHON

Nu 21:21 to say to *S* king of the Amorites:
Ps 136:19 *S* king of the Amorites

SILAS*

Prophet (Ac 15:22-32); co-worker with Paul on second missionary journey (Ac 16-18; 2Co 1:19). Co-writer with Paul (1Th 1:1; 2Th 1:1); Peter (1Pe 5:12).

SILENCE (SILENCED SILENT)

1Pe 2:15 good you should *s* the ignorant talk
Rev 8: 1 there was *s* in heaven

SILENCED (SILENCE)

Ro 3:19 so that every mouth may be *s*
Tit 1:11 They must be *s,* because they are

SILENT (SILENCE)

Est 4:14 For if you remain *s* at this time,
Ps 30:12 to you and not be *s.*
32: 3 When I kept *s,*
39: 2 But when I was *s* and still,
Pr 17:28 a fool is thought wise if he keeps *s,*
Ecc 3: 7 a time to be *s* and a time to speak,
Isa 53: 7 as a sheep before her shearers is *s,*
62: 1 For Zion's sake I will not keep *s,*
Hab 2:20 let all the earth be *s* before him."
Ac 8:32 and as a lamb before the shearer is *s*
1Co 14:34 women should remain *s*
1Ti 2:12 over a man; she must be *s.*

SILVER

Ps 12: 6 like *s* refined in a furnace of clay,
66:10 you refined us like *s.*
Pr 2: 4 and if you look for it as for *s*
3:14 for she is more profitable than *s*
8:10 Choose my instruction instead of *s,*
22: 1 to be esteemed is better than *s*
25: 4 Remove the dross from the *s,*
25:11 is like apples of gold in settings of *s.*
Isa 48:10 I have refined you, though not as *s;*
Eze 22:18 They are but the dross of *s.*
Da 2:32 its chest and arms of *s,* its belly
Hag 2: 8 'The *s* is mine and the gold is mine,'
Zec 13: 9 I will refine them like *s*
Ac 3: 6 Peter said, "*S* or gold I do not have,
1Co 3:12 *s,* costly stones, wood, hay or straw
1Pe 1:18 not with perishable things such as *s*

SILVERSMITH

Ac 19:24 A *s* named Demetrius, who made

SIMEON

Son of Jacob by Leah (Ge 29:33; 35:23; 1Ch 2:1). With Levi killed Shechem for rape of Dinah (Ge 34:25-29). Held hostage by Joseph in Egypt (Ge 42:24-43:23). Tribe of blessed (Ge 49:5-7), numbered (Nu 1:23; 26:14), allotted land (Jos 19:1-9; Eze 48:24), 12,000 from (Rev 7:7).

SIMON

1. See PETER.
2. Apostle, called the Zealot (Mt 10:4; Mk 3:18; Lk 6:15; Ac 1:13).
3. Samaritan sorcerer (Ac 8:9-24).

SIMPLE

Ps 19: 7 making wise the *s.*
119:130 it gives understanding to the *s.*
Pr 8: 5 You who are *s,* gain prudence;
14:15 A *s* man believes anything,

SIMPLEHEARTED* (HEART)

Ps 116: 6 The LORD protects the *s;*

SIN (SINFUL SINNED SINNER SINNERS SINNING SINS)

Ge 4: 7 *s* is crouching at your door;
Ex 32:32 please forgive their *s*—but if not,
Nu 5: 7 and must confess the *s* he has
32:23 be sure that your *s* will find you
Dt 24:16 each is to die for his own *s.*
1Sa 12:23 it from me that I should *s*
15:23 For rebellion is like the *s*
1Ki 8:46 for there is no one who does not *s*
2Ch 7:14 and will forgive their *s* and will heal
Job 1:22 Job did not *s* by charging God
Ps 4: 4 In your anger do not *s;*
17: 3 resolved that my mouth will not *s.*
32: 2 whose *s* the LORD does not count
32: 5 Then I acknowledged my *s* to you
36: 2 too much to detect or hate his *s.*
38:18 I am troubled by my *s.*
39: 1 and keep my tongue from *s;*
51: 2 and cleanse me from my *s.*
66:18 If I had cherished *s* in my heart,
119:11 that I might not *s* against you.
119:133 let no *s* rule over me.
Pr 5:22 the cords of his *s* hold him fast.
10:19 words are many, *s* is not absent,
14: 9 Fools mock at making amends for *s*
16: 6 faithfulness *s* is atoned for;
17:19 He who loves a quarrel loves *s;*
20: 9 I am clean and without *s*"?
Isa 3: 9 they parade their *s* like Sodom;
6: 7 is taken away and your *s* atoned
64: 5 But when we continued to *s*
Jer 31:30 everyone will die for his own *s;*
Eze 3:18 that wicked man will die for his *s,*
18:26 his righteousness and commits *s,*
33: 8 that wicked man will die for his *s,*
Am 4: 4 "Go to Bethel and *s;*
Mic 6: 7 of my body for the *s* of my soul?
7:18 who pardons *s* and forgives
Zec 3: 4 "See, I have taken away your *s,*
Mt 18: 6 little ones who believe in me to *s,*
Mk 3:29 he is guilty of an eternal *s.*"
9:43 If your hand causes you to *s,*
Lk 17: 1 people to *s* are bound to come,
Jn 1:29 who takes away the *s* of the world!
8: 7 "If any one of you is without *s,*
8:34 everyone who sins is a slave to *s.*
8:46 Can any of you prove me guilty of *s*
Ro 2:12 All who *s* apart from the law will
5:12 as *s* entered the world
5:20 where *s* increased, grace increased
6: 2 By no means! We died to *s;*
6:11 count yourselves dead to *s*
6:14 For *s* shall not be your master,
6:23 For the wages of *s* is death,
7: 7 I would not have known what *s* was
7:25 sinful nature a slave to the law of *s.*
14:23 that does not come from faith is *s.*
1Co 8:12 When you *s* against your brothers
15:56 The sting of death is *s,*
2Co 5:21 God made him who had no *s* to be *s*
Gal 6: 1 if someone is caught in a *s,*
1Ti 5:20 Those who *s* are to be rebuked
Heb 4:15 just as we are—yet was without *s.*
9:26 to do away with *s* by the sacrifice
11:25 the pleasures of *s* for a short time.
12: 1 and the *s* that so easily entangles,
Jas 1:15 it gives birth to *s;* and *s,*
1Pe 2:22 "He committed no *s,*
1Jn 1: 7 his Son, purifies us from all *s.*
1: 8 If we claim to be without *s,*
2: 1 But if anybody does *s,* we have one
3: 4 in fact, *s* is lawlessness.
3: 5 And in him is no *s.*
3: 6 No one who continues to *s* has
3: 9 born of God will continue to *s,*
5:16 There is a *s* that leads to death.
5:17 All wrongdoing is *s,* and there is *s*
5:18 born of God does not continue to *s;*

SINAI

Ex 19:20 descended to the top of Mount *S*
31:18 speaking to Moses on Mount *S,*
Ps 68:17 from *S* into his sanctuary.

SINCERE* (SINCERITY)

Da 11:34 many who are not *s* will join them.
Ac 2:46 ate together with glad and *s* hearts,
Ro 12: 9 Love must be *s.*
2Co 6: 6 in the Holy Spirit and in *s* love;
11: 3 somehow be led astray from your *s*
1Ti 1: 5 a good conscience and a *s* faith.
3: 8 *s,* not indulging in much wine,
2Ti 1: 5 have been reminded of your *s* faith,

Heb 10:22 near to God with a *s* heart
Jas 3:17 and good fruit, impartial and *s.*
1Pe 1:22 the truth so that you have *s* love

SINCERITY* (SINCERE)

1Co 5: 8 bread without yeast, the bread of *s*
2Co 1:12 in the holiness and *s* that are
2:17 speak before God with *s,*
8: 8 but I want to test the *s* of your love
Eph 6: 5 and with *s* of heart, just
Col 3:22 but with *s* of heart and reverence

SINFUL (SIN)

Ps 51: 5 Surely I was *s* at birth,
51: 5 *s* from the time my mother
Lk 5: 8 from me, Lord; I am a *s* man!"
Ro 7: 5 we were controlled by the *s* nature,
7:18 lives in me, that is, in my *s* nature.
7:25 but in the *s* nature a slave to the law
8: 3 Son in the likeness of *s* man
8: 4 not live according to the *s* nature
8: 7 the *s* mind is hostile to God.
8: 8 by the *s* nature cannot please God.
8: 9 are controlled not by the *s* nature
8:13 if you live according to the *s* nature
13:14 to gratify the desires of the *s* nature
1Co 5: 5 so that the *s* nature may be
Gal 5:13 freedom to indulge the *s* nature;
5:16 gratify the desires of the *s* nature.
5:19 The acts of the *s* nature are obvious
5:24 Jesus have crucified the *s* nature
6: 8 sows to please his *s* nature,
Col 2:11 in the putting off of the *s* nature,
Heb 3:12 brothers, that none of you has a *s,*
1Pe 2:11 abstain from *s* desires, which war
1Jn 3: 8 He who does what is *s* is

SING (SANG SINGER SINGING SINGS SONG SONGS SUNG)

Ex 15: 1 "I will *s* to the LORD,
Ps 5:11 let them ever *s* for joy.
13: 6 I will *s* to the LORD,
30: 4 *S* to the LORD, you saints of his;
33: 1 *S* joyfully to the LORD, you
47: 6 *S* praises to God, *s* praises;
57: 7 I will *s* and make music.
59:16 But I will *s* of your strength,
63: 7 I *s* in the shadow of your wings.
66: 2 *S* to the glory of his name;
89: 1 I will *s* of the LORD's great love
95: 1 Come, let us *s* for joy to the LORD
96: 1 *S* to the LORD a new song;
98: 1 *S* to the LORD a new song,
101: 1 I will *s* of your love and justice;
108: 1 I will *s* and make music
137: 3 "*S* us one of the songs of Zion!"
147: 1 is to *s* praises to our God,
149: 1 *S* to the LORD a new song,
Isa 54: 1 "*S,* O barren woman,
1Co 14:15 also pray with my mind; I will *s*
Eph 5:19 *S* and make music in your heart
Col 3:16 and as you *s* psalms, hymns
Jas 5:13 Is anyone happy? Let him *s* songs

SINGER* (SING)

2Sa 23: 1 Israel's *s* of songs:

SINGING (SING)

Ps 63: 5 with *s* lips my mouth will praise
68: 6 he leads forth the prisoners with *s;*
98: 5 with the harp and the sound of *s,*
Isa 35:10 They will enter Zion with *s;*
Zep 3:17 he will rejoice over you with *s."*
Ac 16:25 Silas were praying and *s* hymns
Rev 5:13 on the sea, and all that is in them, *s:*

SINGLE

Ex 23:29 I will not drive them out in a *s* year,
Mt 6:27 you by worrying can add a *s* hour
Gal 5:14 law is summed up in a *s* command:

SINGS (SING)

Eze 33:32 more than one who *s* love songs

SINNED (SIN)

Lev 5: 5 confess in what way he has *s*
1Sa 15:24 Then Saul said to Samuel, "I have *s*
2Sa 12:13 "I have *s* against the LORD."
24:10 I have *s* greatly in what I have done
2Ch 6:37 'We have *s,* we have done wrong
Job 1: 5 "Perhaps my children have *s*
33:27 'I *s,* and perverted what was right,
Ps 51: 4 Against you, you only, have I *s*
Jer 2:35 because you say, 'I have not *s.*'
14:20 we have indeed *s* against you.
Da 9: 5 we have *s* and done wrong.
Mic 7: 9 Because I have *s* against him,
Mt 27: 4 "I have *s,"* he said,
Lk 15:18 I have *s* against heaven
Ro 3:23 for all have *s* and fall short
5:12 all *s*—for before the law was given,
2Pe 2: 4 did not spare angels when they *s,*
1Jn 1:10 claim we have not *s,* we make him

SINNER (SIN)

Ecc 9:18 but one *s* destroys much good.
Lk 15: 7 in heaven over one *s* who repents
18:13 'God, have mercy on me, a *s.*'
1Co 14:24 convinced by all that he is a *s*
Jas 5:20 Whoever turns a *s* from the error
1Pe 4:18 become of the ungodly and the *s?"*

SINNERS (SIN)

Ps 1: 1 or stand in the way of *s*
37:38 But all *s* will be destroyed;
Pr 1:10 My son, if *s* entice you,
23:17 Do not let your heart envy *s,*
Mt 9:13 come to call the righteous, but *s."*
Ro 5: 8 While we were still *s,* Christ died
Gal 2:17 evident that we ourselves are *s,*
1Ti 1:15 came into the world to save *s*—
Heb 7:26 set apart from *s,* exalted

SINNING (SIN)

Ex 20:20 be with you to keep you from *s."*
1Co 15:34 stop *s;* for there are some who are
Heb 10:26 If we deliberately keep on *s*
1Jn 3: 6 No one who lives in him keeps on *s*
3: 9 go on *s,* because he has been born

SINS (SIN)

Lev 5: 1 " 'If a person *s* because he does not
16:30 you will be clean from all your *s.*
26:40 " 'But if they will confess their *s*
Nu 15:30 " 'But anyone who *s* defiantly,
1Sa 2:25 If a man *s* against another man,
2Ki 14: 6 each is to die for his own *s."*
Ezr 9: 6 our *s* are higher than our heads
9:13 less than our *s* have deserved
Ps 19:13 your servant also from willful *s;*
32: 1 whose *s* are covered.
51: 9 Hide your face from my *s*
79: 9 deliver us and forgive our *s*
85: 2 and covered all their *s.*
103: 3 who forgives all your *s*
103: 10 does not treat us as our *s* deserve
130: 3 O LORD, kept a record of *s,*
Pr 14:21 He who despises his neighbor *s,*
28:13 who conceals his *s* does not
29:22 one commits many *s.*
Ecc 7:20 who does what is right and never *s.*
Isa 1:18 "Though your *s* are like scarlet,
38:17 you have put all my *s*
43:25 and remembers your *s* no more.
59: 2 your *s* have hidden his face
64: 6 like the wind our *s* sweep us away.
Jer 31:34 and will remember their *s* no more
La 3:39 complain when punished for his *s?*
Eze 18: 4 soul who *s* is the one who will die.
33:10 Our offenses and *s* weigh us down,
36:33 day I cleanse you from all your *s,*
Hos 14: 1 Your *s* have been your downfall!
Mt 1:21 he will save his people from their *s*
6:15 if you do not forgive men their *s,*
9: 6 authority on earth to forgive *s* . . . . ."
18:15 "If your brother *s* against you,
26:28 for many for the forgiveness of *s.*
Lk 5:24 authority on earth to forgive *s* . . . . ."
11: 4 Forgive us our *s,*
17: 3 "If your brother *s,* rebuke him,
Jn 8:24 you will indeed die in your *s."*
20:23 If you forgive anyone his *s,*
Ac 2:38 for the forgiveness of your *s.*
3:19 so that your *s* may be wiped out,
10:43 forgiveness of *s* through his name."
22:16 be baptized and wash your *s* away,
26:18 they may receive forgiveness of *s*
Ro 4: 7 whose *s* are covered.
4:25 delivered over to death for our *s*
1Co 15: 3 died for our *s* according
2Co 5:19 not counting men's *s* against them.
Gal 1: 4 himself for our *s* to rescue us
Eph 2: 1 dead in your transgressions and *s,*
Col 2:13 us all our *s,* having canceled
1Ti 5:22 and do not share in the *s* of others.
Heb 1: 3 he had provided purification for *s,*
2:17 atonement for the *s* of the people.
7:27 He sacrificed for their *s* once for all
8:12 and will remember their *s* no more
9:28 to take away the *s* of many people;
Heb 10: 4 of bulls and goats to take away *s.*
10:12 for all time one sacrifice for *s,*
10:26 of the truth, no sacrifice for *s* is left,
Jas 4:17 ought to do and doesn't do it, *s.*
5:16 Therefore confess your *s*
5:20 and cover over a multitude of *s.*
1Pe 2:24 He himself bore our *s* in his body
3:18 For Christ died for *s* once for all,
4: 8 love covers over a multitude of *s.*
1Jn 1: 9 If we confess our *s,* he is faithful
2: 2 He is the atoning sacrifice for our *s,*
3: 5 so that he might take away our *s.*
4:10 as an atoning sacrifice for our *s.*
Rev 1: 5 has freed us from our *s* by his blood

SISERA

Jdg 4: 2 The commander of his army was *S,*
5:26 She struck *S,* she crushed his head,

SISTER (SISTERS)

Lev 18: 9 have sexual relations with your *s,*
Mk 3:35 does God's will is my brother and *s*

SISTERS (SISTER)

Mt 19:29 or brothers or *s* or father or mother
1Ti 5: 2 as *s,* with absolute purity.

SIT (SAT SITS SITTING)

Dt 6: 7 them when you *s* at home
1Ki 8:25 fail to have a man to *s* before me
Ps 1: 1 or *s* in the seat of mockers.
26: 5 and refuse to *s* with the wicked.
80: 1 you who *s* enthroned
110: 1 "*S* at my right hand
139: 2 You know when I *s* and when I rise
SS 2: 3 I delight to *s* in his shade,
Isa 16: 5 in faithfulness a man will *s* on it—
Mic 4: 4 Every man will *s* under his own
Mt 20:23 to *s* at my right or left is not for me
22:44 "*S* at my right hand
Lk 22:30 in my kingdom and *s* on thrones,
Heb 1:13 "*S* at my right hand
Rev 3:21 right to *s* with me on my throne,

SITS (SIT)

Ps 99: 1 *s* enthroned between the cherubim,
Isa 40:22 He *s* enthroned above the circle
Mt 19:28 of Man *s* on his glorious throne,
Rev 4: 9 thanks to him who *s* on the throne

SITTING (SIT)

Est 2:19 Mordecai was *s* at the king's gate.
Mt 26:64 the Son of Man *s* at the right hand
Rev 4: 2 in heaven with someone *s* on it.

SITUATION (SITUATIONS)

1Co 7:24 remain in the *s* God called him
Php 4:12 of being content in any and every *s,*

SITUATIONS* (SITUATION)

2Ti 4: 5 head in all *s,* endure hardship,

SKIES (SKY)

Ps 19: 1 the *s* proclaim the work
71:19 Your righteousness reaches to the *s*
108: 4 your faithfulness reaches to the *s.*

SKILL (SKILLED SKILLFUL)

Ps 137: 5 may my right hand forget its *s*.
Ecc 10:10 but *s* will bring success.

SKILLED (SKILL)

Pr 22:29 Do you see a man *s* in his work?

SKILLFUL (SKILL)

Ps 45: 1 my tongue is the pen of a *s* writer.
78:72 with *s* hands he led them.

SKIN (SKINS)

Job 19:20 with only the *s* of my teeth.
19:26 And after my *s* has been destroyed,
Jer 13:23 Can the Ethiopian change his *s*

SKINS (SKIN)

Ex 25: 5 ram *s* dyed red and hides
Lk 5:37 the new wine will burst the *s,*

SKULL

Mt 27:33 (which means The Place of the *S*).

SKY (SKIES)

Ge 1: 8 God called the expanse "*s.*"
Pr 30:19 the way of an eagle in the *s,*
Isa 34: 4 and the *s* rolled up like a scroll;
Jer 33:22 stars of the *s* and as measureless

Mt 24:29 the stars will fall from the *s*,
24:30 coming on the clouds of the *s*,
Rev 20:11 Earth and *s* fled from his presence,

SLACK*

Pr 18: 9 One who is *s* in his work

SLAIN (SLAY)

1Sa 18: 7 "Saul has *s* his thousands,
Eze 37: 9 into these *s*, that they may live.' "
Rev 5: 6 as if it had been *s*, standing
5:12 "Worthy is the Lamb, who was *s*,
6: 9 the souls of those who had been *s*

SLANDER (SLANDERED SLANDERER SLANDERERS SLANDEROUS)

Lev 19:16 " 'Do not go about spreading *s*
Ps 15: 3 and has no *s* on his tongue,
Pr 10:18 and whoever spreads *s* is a fool.
2Co 12:20 outbursts of anger, factions, *s*,
Eph 4:31 rage and anger, brawling and *s*,
1Ti 5:14 the enemy no opportunity for *s*.
Tit 3: 2 to *s* no one, to be peaceable
1Pe 3:16 in Christ may be ashamed of their *s*
2Pe 2:10 afraid to *s* celestial beings;

SLANDERED (SLANDER)

1Co 4:13 when we are *s*, we answer kindly.

SLANDERER (SLANDER)

1Co 5:11 an idolater or a *s*, a drunkard

SLANDERERS (SLANDER)

Ro 1:30 They are gossips, *s*, God-haters,
1Co 6:10 nor the greedy nor drunkards nor *s*
Tit 2: 3 not to be *s* or addicted

SLANDEROUS (SLANDER)

2Ti 3: 3 unforgiving, *s*, without self-control
2Pe 2:11 do not bring *s* accusations

SLAUGHTER (SLAUGHTERED)

Isa 53: 7 he was led like a lamb to the *s*,
Jer 11:19 been like a gentle lamb led to the *s*;
Ac 8:32 "He was led like a sheep to the *s*,

SLAUGHTERED (SLAUGHTER)

Ps 44:22 we are considered as sheep to be *s*.
Ro 8:36 we are considered as sheep to be *s*

SLAVE (ENSLAVED SLAVERY SLAVES)

Ge 21:10 "Get rid of that *s* woman
Mt 20:27 wants to be first must be your *s*—
Jn 8:34 everyone who sins is a *s* to sin.
Ro 7:14 I am unspiritual, sold as a *s* to sin.
1Co 7:21 Were you a *s* when you were called
12:13 whether Jews or Greeks, *s* or free
Gal 3:28 *s* nor free, male nor female,
4: 7 So you are no longer a *s*, but a son;
4:30 Get rid of the *s* woman and her son
Col 3:11 barbarian, Scythian, *s* or free,
1Ti 1:10 for *s* traders and liars and perjurers
Phm :16 no longer as a *s*, but better than a *s*,
2Pe 2:19 a man is a *s* to whatever has

SLAVERY (SLAVE)

Ex 2:23 The Israelites groaned in their *s*
Ro 6:19 parts of your body in *s* to impurity
Gal 4: 3 were in *s* under the basic principles
1Ti 6: 1 of *s* should consider their masters

SLAVES (SLAVE)

Ps 123: 2 As the eyes of *s* look to the hand
Ecc 10: 7 I have seen *s* on horseback,
Ro 6: 6 that we should no longer be *s* to sin
6:16 you are *s* to sin, which leads
6:22 and have become *s* to God,
Gal 2: 4 in Christ Jesus and to make us *s*.
4: 8 you were *s* to those who
Eph 6: 5 *S*, obey your earthly masters
Col 3:22 *S*, obey your earthly masters
4: 1 provide your *s* with what is right
Tit 2: 9 Teach *s* to be subject

SLAY (SLAIN)

Job 13:15 Though he *s* me, yet will I hope

SLEEP (ASLEEP SLEEPER SLEEPING SLEEPS)

Ge 2:21 the man to fall into a deep *s*;
15:12 Abram fell into a deep *s*,
28:11 it under his head and lay down to *s*.
Ps 4: 8 I will lie down and *s* in peace,
121: 4 will neither slumber nor *s*.
127: 2 for he grants *s* to those he loves.
Pr 6: 9 When will you get up from your *s*?
Ecc 5:12 The *s* of a laborer is sweet,
1Co 15:51 We will not all *s*, but we will all be
1Th 5: 7 For those who *s*, *s* at night,

SLEEPER (SLEEP)

Eph 5:14 "Wake up, O *s*,

SLEEPING (SLEEP)

Mk 13:36 suddenly, do not let him find you *s*.

SLEEPLESS*

2Co 6: 5 in hard work, *s* nights and hunger;

SLEEPS (SLEEP)

Pr 10: 5 he who *s* during harvest is

SLIMY

Ps 40: 2 He lifted me out of the *s* pit,

SLING

1Sa 17:50 over the Philistine with a *s*

SLIP (SLIPPING)

Dt 4: 9 let them *s* from your heart as long
Ps 121: 3 He will not let your foot *s*—

SLIPPING (SLIP)

Ps 66: 9 and kept our feet from *s*.

SLOW

Ex 34: 6 and gracious God, *s* to anger,
Jas 1:19 *s* to speak and *s* to become angry,
2Pe 3: 9 The Lord is not *s* in keeping his

SLUGGARD

Pr 6: 6 Go to the ant, you *s*;
13: 4 The *s* craves and gets nothing,
20: 4 A *s* does not plow in season;
26:15 The *s* buries his hand in the dish;

SLUMBER

Ps 121: 3 he who watches over you will not *s*;
Pr 6:10 A little sleep, a little *s*,
Ro 13:11 for you to wake up from your *s*,

SLUR

Ps 15: 3 and casts no *s* on his fellow man,

SMELL

Ecc 10: 1 As dead flies give perfume a bad *s*,
2Co 2:16 To the one we are the *s* of death;

SMITTEN

Isa 53: 4 *s* by him, and afflicted.

SMOKE

Ex 19:18 Mount Sinai was covered with *s*,
Ps 104: 32 touches the mountains, and they *s*.
Isa 6: 4 and the temple was filled with *s*.
Joel 2:30 blood and fire and billows of *s*.
Ac 2:19 blood and fire and billows of *s*.
Rev 15: 8 filled with *s* from the glory

SMYRNA

Rev 2: 8 the angel of the church in *S* write:

SNAKE (SNAKES)

Nu 21: 8 "Make a *s* and put it up on a pole;
Pr 23:32 In the end it bites like a *s*
Jn 3:14 Moses lifted up the *s* in the desert,

SNAKES (SNAKE)

Mt 10:16 as shrewd as *s* and as innocent
Mk 16:18 they will pick up *s* with their hands;

SNARE (ENSNARE ENSNARED SNARED)

Dt 7:16 for that will be a *s* to you.
Ps 69:22 before them become a *s*;
91: 3 from the fowler's *s*
Pr 29:25 Fear of man will prove to be a *s*,
Ro 11: 9 "May their table become a *s*

SNARED (SNARE)

Pr 3:26 will keep your foot from being *s*.

SNATCH

Jn 10:28 no one can *s* them out of my hand.
Jude :23 *s* others from the fire and save

SNOUT

Pr 11:22 Like a gold ring in a pig's *s*

SNOW

Ps 51: 7 and I will be whiter than *s*.
Isa 1:18 they shall be as white as *s*;

SNUFF (SNUFFED)

Isa 42: 3 a smoldering wick he will not *s* out.
Mt 12:20 a smoldering wick he will not *s* out,

SNUFFED (SNUFF)

Pr 13: 9 but the lamp of the wicked is *s* out.

SOAP

Mal 3: 2 a refiner's fire or a launderer's *s*.

SOAR (SOARED)

Isa 40:31 They will *s* on wings like eagles;

SOARED (SOAR)

2Sa 22:11 he *s* on the wings of the wind.

SOBER

Ro 12: 3 think of yourself with *s* judgment,

SODOM

Ge 13:12 and pitched his tents near *S*.
19:24 rained down burning sulfur on *S*
Isa 1: 9 we would have become like *S*,
Lk 10:12 on that day for *S* than for that town
Ro 9:29 we would have become like *S*,
Rev 11: 8 which is figuratively called *S*

SOIL

Ge 4: 2 kept flocks, and Cain worked the *s*.
Mt 13:23 on good *s* is the man who hears

SOLD (SELL)

1Ki 21:25 who *s* himself to do evil in the eyes
Mt 10:29 Are not two sparrows *s* for a penny
13:44 then in his joy went and *s* all he had
Ro 7:14 I am unspiritual, *s* as a slave to sin.

SOLDIER

1Co 9: 7 as a *s* at his own expense?
2Ti 2: 3 with us like a good *s* of Christ Jesus

SOLE

Dt 28:65 place for the *s* of your foot.
Isa 1: 6 From the *s* of your foot to the top

SOLID

2Ti 2:19 God's *s* foundation stands firm,
Heb 5:12 You need milk, not *s* food!

SOLOMON

Son of David by Bathsheba; king of Judah (2Sa 12:24; 1Ch 3:5, 10). Appointed king by David (1Ki 1); adversaries Adonijah, Joab, Shimei killed by Benaiah (1Ki 2). Asked for wisdom (1Ki 3; 2Ch 1). Judged between two prostitutes (1Ki 3:16-28). Built temple (1Ki 5-7; 2Ch 2-5); prayer of dedication (1Ki 8; 2Ch 6). Visited by Queen of Sheba (1Ki 9; 2Ch 9). Wives turned his heart from God (1Ki 11:1-13). Jeroboam rebelled against (1Ki 11:26-40). Death (1Ki 11:41-43; 2Ch 9:29-31).

Proverbs of (1Ki 4:32; Pr 1:1; 10:1; 25:1); psalms of (Ps 72; 127); song of (SS 1:1).

SON (SONS SONSHIP)

Ge 17:19 your wife Sarah will bear you a *s*,
21:10 rid of that slave woman and her *s*,
22: 2 "Take your *s*, your only *s*, Isaac,
Ex 11: 5 Every firstborn *s* in Egypt will die,
Dt 1:31 father carries his *s*, all the way you
6:20 In the future, when your *s* asks you,
8: 5 as a man disciplines his *s*,
21:18 rebellious *s* who does not obey his
2Sa 7:14 be his father, and he will be my *s*.
1Ki 3:20 and put her dead *s* by my breast.
Ps 2: 7 He said to me, "You are my *S*;
2:12 Kiss the *S*, lest he be angry
8: 4 the *s* of man that you care for him?
Pr 3:12 as a father the *s* he delights in.
6:20 My *s*, keep your father's
10: 1 A wise *s* brings joy to his father,
13:24 He who spares the rod hates his *s*,
29:17 Discipline your *s*, and he will give
Isa 7:14 with child and will give birth to a *s*,
Eze 18:20 The *s* will not share the guilt
Da 3:25 the fourth looks like a *s* of the gods
7:13 before me was one like a *s* of man,
Hos 11: 1 and out of Egypt I called my *s*.
Am 7:14 neither a prophet nor a prophet's *s*,
Mt 1: 1 of Jesus Christ the *s* of David,
1:21 She will give birth to a *s*,
2:15 "Out of Egypt I called my *s*."
3:17 "This is my *S*, whom I love;

Mt 4: 3 "If you are the *S* of God, tell these
8: 20 but the *S* of Man has no place
11: 27 one knows the *S* except the Father,
12: 8 For the *S* of Man is Lord
12: 32 a word against the *S* of Man will be
12: 40 so the *S* of Man will be three days
13: 41 *S* of Man will send out his angels,
13: 55 "Isn't this the carpenter's *s?*
14: 33 "Truly you are the *S* of God."
16: 16 "You are the Christ, the *S*
16: 27 For the *S* of Man is going to come
17: 5 "This is my *S*, whom I love;
19: 28 when the *S* of Man sits
20: 18 and the *S* of Man will be betrayed
20: 28 as the *S* of Man did not come
21: 9 "Hosanna to the *S* of David!"
22: 42 Whose *s* is he?" "The *s* of David,"
24: 27 so will be the coming of the *S*
24: 30 They will see the *S* of Man coming
24: 44 the *S* of Man will come at an hour
25: 31 "When the *S* of Man comes
26: 63 if you are the Christ, the *S* of God."
27: 54 "Surely he was the *S* of God!"
28: 19 and of the *S* and of the Holy Spirit,
Mk 1: 11 "You are my *S*, whom I love;
2: 28 So the *S* of Man is Lord
8: 38 the *S* of Man will be ashamed
9: 7 "This is my *S*, whom I love.
10: 45 even the *S* of Man did not come
13: 32 nor the *S*, but only the Father.
14: 62 you will see the *S* of Man sitting
Lk 1: 32 and will be called the *S*
2: 7 she gave birth to her firstborn, a *s*.
3: 22 "You are my *S*, whom I love;
9: 35 This is my *S*, whom I have chosen;
9: 58 but the *S* of Man has no place
12: 8 the *S* of Man will also acknowledge
15: 20 he ran to his *s*, threw his arms
18: 8 when the *S* of Man comes,
18: 31 written by the prophets about the *S*
19: 10 For the *S* of Man came to seek
Jn 1: 34 I testify that this is the *S* of God."
3: 14 so the *S* of Man must be lifted up,
3: 16 that he gave his one and only *S*,
3: 36 believes in the *S* has eternal life,
5: 19 the *S* can do nothing by himself;
6: 40 is that everyone who looks to the *S*
11: 4 so that God's *S* may be glorified
17: 1 Glorify your *S*, that your *S* may
Ac 7: 56 and the *S* of Man standing
13: 33 " 'You are my *S*;
Ro 1: 4 with power to be the *S* of God
5: 10 to him through the death of his *S*,
8: 3 did by sending his own *S*
8: 29 conformed to the likeness of his *S*,
8: 32 He who did not spare his own *S*,
1Co 15: 28 then the *S* himself will be made
Gal 2: 20 I live by faith in the *S* of God,
4: 4 God sent his *S*, born of a woman,
4: 30 rid of the slave woman and her *s*,
1Th 1: 10 and to wait for his *S* from heaven,
Heb 1: 2 days he has spoken to us by his *S*,
1: 5 "You are my *S*;
2: 6 the *s* of man that you care for him?
4: 14 Jesus the *S* of God, let us hold
5: 5 "You are my *S*;
7: 28 appointed the *S*, who has been
10: 29 punished who has trampled the *S*
12: 6 everyone he accepts as a *s*."
2Pe 1: 17 saying, "This is my *S*, whom I love;
1Jn 1: 3 is with the Father and with his *S*,
1: 7 his *S*, purifies us from all sin.
2: 23 whoever acknowledges the *S* has
3: 8 reason the *S* of God appeared was
4: 9 only *S* into the world that we might
4: 14 that the Father has sent his *S*
5: 5 he who believes that Jesus is the *S*
5: 11 eternal life, and this life is in his *S*.
Rev 1: 13 lampstands was someone "like a *s*
14: 14 on the cloud was one "like a *s*

SONG (SING)

Ex 15: 2 LORD is my strength and my *s*;
Ps 40: 3 He put a new *s* in my mouth,
69: 30 I will praise God's name in *s*
96: 1 Sing to the LORD a new *s*;
98: 4 burst into jubilant *s* with music;
119: 54 Your decrees are the theme of my *s*
149: 1 Sing to the LORD a new *s*,
Isa 49: 13 burst into *s*, O mountains!
55: 12 will burst into *s* before you,
Rev 5: 9 And they sang a new *s*:
15: 3 and sang the *s* of Moses the servant

SONGS (SING)

2Sa 23: 1 Israel's singer of *s*:
Job 35: 10 who gives *s* in the night,
Ps 100: 2 come before him with joyful *s*.
126: 6 will return with *s* of joy,
137: 3 "Sing us one of the *s* of Zion!"
Eph 5: 19 with psalms, hymns and spiritual *s*.
Jas 5: 13 Is anyone happy? Let him sing *s*

SONS (SON)

Ge 6: 2 the *s* of God saw that the daughters
10: 20 These are the *s* of Ham
Ru 4: 15 who is better to you than seven *s*,
Ps 127: 3 *S* are a heritage from the LORD,
132: 12 if your *s* keep my covenant
Hos 1: 10 they will be called '*s*
Joel 2: 28 Your *s* and daughters will prophesy
Mt 5: 9 for they will be called *s* of God.
Lk 6: 35 and you will be *s* of the Most High,
Jn 12: 36 so that you may become *s* of light."
Ro 8: 14 by the Spirit of God are *s* of God.
9: 26 they will be called '*s*
2Co 6: 18 and you will be my *s* and daughters
Gal 3: 26 You are all *s* of God through faith
4: 5 we might receive the full rights of *s*.
4: 6 Because you are *s*, God sent
Heb 12: 7 discipline; God is treating you as *s*.

SONSHIP* (SON)

Ro 8: 15 but you received the Spirit of *s*.

SORCERY

Lev 19: 26 " 'Do not practice divination or *s*.

SORROW (SORROWS)

Ps 6: 7 My eyes grow weak with *s*;
116: 3 I was overcome by trouble and *s*.
Isa 60: 20 and your days of *s* will end.
Jer 31: 12 and they will *s* no more.
Ro 9: 2 I have great *s* and unceasing
2Co 7: 10 Godly *s* brings repentance that

SORROWS (SORROW)

Isa 53: 3 a man of *s*, and familiar

SOUGHT (SEEK)

2Ch 26: 5 As long as he *s* the LORD,
31: 21 he *s* his God and worked
Ps 34: 4 I *s* the LORD, and he answered me
119: 58 I have *s* your face with all my heart;

SOUL (SOULS)

Dt 6: 5 with all your *s* and with all your
10: 12 all your heart and with all your *s*,
30: 6 all your heart and with all your *s*,
Jos 22: 5 with all your heart and all your *s*."
2Ki 23: 25 and with all his *s* and with all his
Ps 23: 3 he restores my *s*.
34: 2 My *s* will boast in the LORD;
42: 1 so my *s* pants for you, O God.
42: 11 Why are you downcast, O my *s?*
62: 5 Find rest, O my *s*, in God alone;
63: 8 My *s* clings to you;
94: 19 consolation brought joy to my *s*.
103: 1 Praise the LORD, O my *s*;
Pr 13: 19 A longing fulfilled is sweet to the *s*,
16: 24 sweet to the *s* and healing
22: 5 he who guards his *s* stays far
Isa 55: 2 your *s* will delight in the richest
La 3: 20 and my *s* is downcast within me.
Eze 18: 4 For every living *s* belongs to me,
Mt 10: 28 kill the body but cannot kill the *s*.
16: 26 yet forfeits his *s?* Or what can
22: 37 with all your *s* and with all your
Heb 4: 12 even to dividing *s* and spirit,
3Jn : 2 even as your *s* is getting along well.

SOULS (SOUL)

Pr 11: 30 and he who wins *s* is wise.
Jer 6: 16 and you will find rest for your *s*.
Mt 11: 29 and you will find rest for your *s*.

SOUND (FINE-SOUNDING)

Ge 3: 8 and his wife heard the *s*
Pr 3: 21 preserve *s* judgment
Eze 3: 12 I heard behind me a loud rumbling *s*
Jn 3: 8 You hear its *s*, but you cannot tell
Ac 2: 2 Suddenly a *s* like the blowing
1Co 14: 8 if the trumpet does not *s* a clear call
15: 52 the trumpet will *s*, the dead will
1Ti 1: 10 to the *s* doctrine that conforms
2Ti 4: 3 men will not put up with *s* doctrine.
Tit 1: 9 can encourage others by *s* doctrine
2: 1 is in accord with *s* doctrine.

SOUR

Eze 18: 2 " 'The fathers eat *s* grapes,

SOURCE

Heb 5: 9 became the *s* of eternal salvation

SOVEREIGN (SOVEREIGNTY)

Ge 15: 2 But Abram said, "O *S* LORD,
2Sa 7: 18 O *S* LORD, and what is my family,
Ps 71: 16 your mighty acts, O *S* LORD;
Isa 25: 8 *S* LORD will wipe away the tears
40: 10 the *S* LORD comes with power,
50: 4 *S* LORD has given me
61: 1 The Spirit of the *S* LORD is on me,
61: 11 so the *S* LORD will make
Jer 32: 17 to the LORD: "Ah, *S* LORD,
Eze 12: 28 fulfilled, declares the *S* LORD.' "
Da 4: 25 that the Most High is *s*
2Pe 2: 1 denying the *s* Lord who bought
Jude : 4 and deny Jesus Christ our only *S*

SOVEREIGNTY (SOVEREIGN)

Da 7: 27 Then the *s*, power and greatness

SOW (SOWER SOWN SOWS)

Job 4: 8 and those who *s* trouble reap it.
Ps 126: 5 Those who *s* in tears
Hos 8: 7 "They *s* the wind
10: 12 *S* for yourselves righteousness,
Mt 6: 26 they do not *s* or reap or store away
13: 3 "A farmer went out to *s* his seed.
1Co 15: 36 What you *s* does not come to life
Jas 3: 18 Peacemakers who *s*
2Pe 2: 22 and, "A *s* that is washed goes back

SOWER (SOW)

Isa 55: 10 so that it yields seed for the *s*
Mt 13: 18 to what the parable of the *s* means:
Jn 4: 36 so that the *s* and the reaper may be
2Co 9: 10 Now he who supplies seed to the *s*

SOWN (SOW)

Mt 13: 8 sixty or thirty times what was *s*.
Mk 4: 15 along the path, where the word is *s*.
1Co 15: 42 The body that is *s* is perishable,

SOWS (SOW)

Pr 11: 18 he who *s* righteousness reaps a sure
22: 8 He who *s* wickedness reaps trouble
2Co 9: 6 Whoever *s* sparingly will
Gal 6: 7 A man reaps what he *s*.

SPARE (SPARES SPARING)

Est 7: 3 *s* my people—this is my request.
Ro 8: 32 He who did not *s* his own Son,
11: 21 natural branches, he will not *s* you
2Pe 2: 4 For if God did not *s* angels
2: 5 if he did not *s* the ancient world

SPARES (SPARE)

Pr 13: 24 He who *s* the rod hates his son,

SPARING (SPARE)

Pr 21: 26 but the righteous give without *s*.

SPARKLE

Zec 9: 16 They will *s* in his land

SPARROW (SPARROWS)

Ps 84: 3 Even the *s* has found a home,

SPARROWS (SPARROW)

Mt 10: 29 Are not two *s* sold for a penny?

SPEAR (SPEARS)

1Sa 19: 10 as Saul drove the *s* into the wall.
Ps 46: 9 breaks the bow and shatters the *s*,

SPEARS (SPEAR)

Isa 2: 4 and their *s* into pruning hooks.
Joel 3: 10 and your pruning hooks into *s*.
Mic 4: 3 and their *s* into pruning hooks.

SPECIAL

Jas 2: 3 If you show *s* attention

SPECK

Mt 7: 3 look at the *s* of sawdust

SPECTACLE

1Co 4: 9 We have been made a *s*
Col 2: 15 he made a public *s* of them,

SPEECH
Ps 19: 3 There is no *s* or language
Pr 22: 11 pure heart and whose *s* is gracious
2Co 8: 7 in faith, in *s*, in knowledge,
1Ti 4: 12 set an example for the believers in *s*

SPEND (SPENT)
Pr 31: 3 do not *s* your strength on women,
Isa 55: 2 Why *s* money on what is not bread,
2Co 12: 15 So I will very gladly *s*

SPENT (SPEND)
Mk 5: 26 many doctors and had *s* all she had,
Lk 6: 12 and *s* the night praying to God.
15: 14 After he had *s* everything,

SPIN
Mt 6: 28 They do not labor or *s*.

SPIRIT (SPIRIT'S SPIRITS SPIRITUAL SPIRITUALLY)
Ge 1: 2 and the *S* of God was hovering
6: 3 "My *S* will not contend
Ex 31: 3 I have filled him with the *S* of God,
Nu 11: 25 and put the *S* on the seventy elders.
Dt 34: 9 filled with the *s* of wisdom
Jdg 6: 34 Then the *S* of the LORD came
11: 29 Then the *S* of the LORD came
13: 25 and the *S* of the LORD began
1Sa 10: 10 the *S* of God came upon him
16: 13 day on the *S* of the LORD came
16: 14 the *S* of the LORD had departed
2Sa 23: 2 "The *S* of the LORD spoke
2Ki 2: 9 inherit a double portion of your *s*,"
Ne 9: 20 You gave your good *S*
9: 30 By your *S* you admonished them
Job 33: 4 The *S* of God has made me;
Ps 31: 5 Into your hands I commit my *s*;
34: 18 saves those who are crushed in *s*.
51: 10 and renew a steadfast *s* within me.
51: 11 or take your Holy *S* from me.
51: 17 sacrifices of God are a broken *s*;
106: 33 rebelled against the *S* of God,
139: 7 Where can I go from your *S*?
143: 10 may your good *S*
Isa 11: 2 The *S* of the LORD will rest
30: 1 an alliance, but not by my *S*,
32: 15 till the *S* is poured upon us
44: 3 I will pour out my *S*
57: 15 him who is contrite and lowly in *s*,
61: 1 The *S* of the Sovereign LORD is
63: 10 and grieved his Holy *S*.
Eze 11: 19 an undivided heart and put a new *s*
13: 3 prophets who follow their own *s*
36: 26 you a new heart and put a new *s*
Da 4: 8 and the *s* of the holy gods is in him
Joel 2: 28 I will pour out my *S* on all people.
Zec 4: 6 but by my *S*,' says the LORD
Mt 1: 18 to be with child through the Holy *S*
3: 11 will baptize you with the Holy *S*
3: 16 he saw the *S* of God descending
4: 1 led by the *S* into the desert
5: 3 saying: "Blessed are the poor in *s*,
10: 20 but the *S* of your Father speaking
12: 31 against the *S* will not be forgiven.
26: 41 *s* is willing, but the body is weak."
28: 19 and of the Son and of the Holy *S*,
Mk 1: 8 he will baptize you with the Holy *S*
Lk 1: 35 "The Holy *S* will come upon you,
1: 80 child grew and became strong in *s*;
3: 16 will baptize you with the Holy *S*
4: 18 "The *S* of the Lord is on me,
11: 13 Father in heaven give the Holy *S*
23: 46 into your hands I commit my *s*."
Jn 1: 33 who will baptize with the Holy *S*.'
3: 5 a man is born of water and the *S*,
4: 24 God is *s*, and his worshipers must
6: 63 The *S* gives life; the flesh counts
7: 39 Up to that time the *S* had not been
14: 26 But the Counselor, the Holy *S*,
16: 13 But when he, the *S* of truth, comes,
20: 22 and said, "Receive the Holy *S*.
Ac 1: 5 will be baptized with the Holy *S*."
1: 8 when the Holy *S* comes on you;
2: 4 of them were filled with the Holy *S*
2: 17 I will pour out my *S* on all people.
2: 38 will receive the gift of the Holy *S*.
4: 31 they were all filled with the Holy *S*
5: 3 that you have lied to the Holy *S*
6: 3 who are known to be full of the *S*
8: 15 that they might receive the Holy *S*,
9: 17 and be filled with the Holy *S*."
11: 16 will be baptized with the Holy *S*.'
13: 2 and fasting, the Holy *S* said,
Ac 19: 2 "Did you receive the Holy *S*
Ro 8: 4 nature but according to the *S*.
8: 5 set on what the *S* desires.
8: 9 And if anyone does not have the *S*
8: 13 but if by the *S* you put
8: 16 The *S* himself testifies
8: 23 who have the firstfruits of the *S*,
8: 26 the *S* helps us in our weakness.
1Co 2: 10 God has revealed it to us by his *S*.
2: 14 man without the *S* does not accept
5: 3 present, I am with you in *s*.
6: 19 body is a temple of the Holy *S*,
12: 13 baptized by one *S* into one body—
2Co 1: 22 and put his *S* in our hearts
3: 3 but with the *S* of the living God,
3: 6 the letter kills, but the *S* gives life.
3: 17 Now the Lord is the *S*,
5: 5 and has given us the *S* as a deposit,
7: 1 that contaminates body and *s*,
Gal 3: 2 Did you receive the *S*
5: 16 by the *S*, and you will not gratify
5: 22 But the fruit of the *S* is love, joy,
5: 25 let us keep in step with the *S*.
6: 8 from the *S* will reap eternal life.
Eph 1: 13 with a seal, the promised Holy *S*,
2: 22 in which God lives by his *S*.
4: 4 There is one body and one *S*—
4: 30 do not grieve the Holy *S* of God,
5: 18 Instead, be filled with the *S*.
6: 17 of salvation and the sword of the *S*,
Php 2: 2 being one in *s* and purpose.
1Th 5: 23 May your whole *s*, soul
2Th 2: 13 the sanctifying work of the *S*
1Ti 3: 16 was vindicated by the *S*,
2Ti 1: 7 For God did not give us a *s*
Heb 2: 4 of the Holy *S* distributed according
4: 12 even to dividing soul and *s*,
10: 29 and who has insulted the *S* of grace
1Pe 3: 4 beauty of a gentle and quiet *s*,
2Pe 1: 21 carried along by the Holy *S*.
1Jn 3: 24 We know it by the *S* he gave us.
4: 1 Dear friends, do not believe every *s*
4: 13 because he has given us of his *S*.
Jude : 20 holy faith and pray in the Holy *S*.
Rev 2: 7 let him hear what the *S* says

SPIRIT'S* (SPIRIT)
1Co 2: 4 a demonstration of the *S* power,
1Th 5: 19 not put out the *S* fire; do not treat

SPIRITS (SPIRIT)
1Co 12: 10 to another distinguishing between *s*,
14: 32 The *s* of prophets are subject
1Jn 4: 1 test the *s* to see whether they are

SPIRITUAL (SPIRIT)
Ro 12: 1 to God—this is your *s* act of worship.
12: 11 but keep your *s* fervor, serving
1Co 2: 13 expressing *s* truths in *s* words.
3: 1 I could not address you as *s* but
12: 1 Now about *s* gifts, brothers,
14: 1 of love and eagerly desire *s* gifts,
15: 44 a natural body, it is raised a *s* body.
Gal 6: 1 you who are *s* should restore him
Eph 1: 3 with every *s* blessing in Christ.
5: 19 with psalms, hymns and *s* songs.
6: 12 and against the *s* forces of evil
1Pe 2: 2 newborn babies, crave pure *s* milk,
2: 5 are being built into a *s* house

SPIRITUALLY (SPIRIT)
1Co 2: 14 because they are *s* discerned.

SPIT
Mt 27: 30 They *s* on him, and took the staff
Rev 3: 16 I am about to *s* you out

SPLENDOR
1Ch 16: 29 the LORD in the *s* of his holiness.
29: 11 the glory and the majesty and the *s*,
Job 37: 22 of the north he comes in golden *s*;
Ps 29: 2 in the *s* of his holiness.
45: 3 clothe yourself with *s* and majesty.
96: 6 *S* and majesty are before him;
96: 9 in the *s* of his holiness;
104: 1 you are clothed with *s* and majesty.
145: 5 of the glorious *s* of your majesty,
145: 12 and the glorious *s* of your kingdom.
148: 13 his *s* is above the earth
Pr 4: 9 and present you with a crown of *s*."
16: 31 Gray hair is a crown of *s*;
20: 29 gray hair the *s* of the old.
Isa 55: 5 for he has endowed you with *s*."
60: 21 for the display of my *s*.
61: 3 the LORD for the display of his *s*.
Isa 63: 1 Who is this, robed in *s*,
Hab 3: 4 His *s* was like the sunrise;
Mt 6: 29 in all his *s* was dressed like one
Lk 9: 31 appeared in glorious *s*, talking
2Th 2: 8 and destroy by the *s* of his coming.

SPOIL (SPOILS)
Ps 119: 162 like one who finds great *s*

SPOILS (SPOIL)
Isa 53: 12 he will divide the *s* with the strong,
Jn 6: 27 Do not work for food that *s*,

SPONTANEOUS*
Phm : 14 so that any favor you do will be *s*

SPOTLESS
2Pe 3: 14 make every effort to be found *s*,

SPOTS (SPOTTED)
Jer 13: 23 or the leopard its *s*?

SPOTTED (SPOTS)
Ge 30: 32 and every *s* or speckled goat.

SPREAD (SPREADING SPREADS)
Ps 78: 19 "Can God *s* a table in the desert?
Ac 6: 7 So the word of God *s*.
12: 24 of God continued to increase and *s*.
13: 49 of the Lord *s* through the whole
19: 20 the word of the Lord *s* widely
2Th 3: 1 message of the Lord may *s* rapidly

SPREADING (SPREAD)
Pr 29: 5 is *s* a net for his feet.
1Th 3: 2 God's fellow worker in *s* the gospel

SPREADS (SPREAD)
Pr 10: 18 and whoever *s* slander is a fool.

SPRING (SPRINGS WELLSPRING)
Jer 2: 13 the *s* of living water,
Jn 4: 14 in him a *s* of water welling up
Jas 3: 12 can a salt *s* produce fresh water.

SPRINGS (SPRING)
2Pe 2: 17 These men are *s* without water

SPRINKLE (SPRINKLED SPRINKLING)
Lev 16: 14 and with his finger *s* it on the front

SPRINKLED (SPRINKLE)
Heb 10: 22 having our hearts *s* to cleanse us

SPRINKLING (SPRINKLE)
1Pe 1: 2 to Jesus Christ and *s* by his blood:

SPROUT
Pr 23: 5 for they will surely *s* wings
Jer 33: 15 I will make a righteous Branch *s*

SPUR*
Heb 10: 24 how we may *s* one another

SPURNS*
Pr 15: 5 A fool *s* his father's discipline,

SPY
Gal 2: 4 ranks to *s* on the freedom we have

SQUANDERED (SQUANDERS)
Lk 15: 13 there *s* his wealth in wild living.

SQUANDERS* (SQUANDERED)
Pr 29: 3 of prostitutes *s* his wealth.

SQUARE
Rev 21: 16 The city was laid out like a *s*,

STABILITY*
Pr 29: 4 By justice a king gives a country *s*,

STAFF
Ge 49: 10 the ruler's *s* from between his feet,
Ex 7: 12 Aaron's *s* swallowed up their staffs.
Nu 17: 6 and Aaron's *s* was among them.
Ps 23: 4 your rod and your *s*,

STAIN (STAINED)
Eph 5: 27 without *s* or wrinkle or any other

STAINED (STAIN)
Isa 63: 1 with his garments *s* crimson?

STAKES
Isa 54: 2 strengthen your *s*.

STAND (STANDING STANDS STOOD)
Ex 14: 13 *S* firm and you will see
Jos 10: 12 "O sun, *s* still over Gibeon,
2Ch 20: 17 *s* firm and see the deliverance
Job 19: 25 in the end he will *s* upon the earth.
Ps 1: 1 or *s* in the way of sinners
1: 5 Therefore the wicked will not *s*
24: 3 Who may *s* in his holy place?
33: 11 of the LORD *s* firm forever,
40: 2 and gave me a firm place to *s*.
76: 7 Who can *s* before you
93: 5 Your statutes *s* firm;
119:120 I *s* in awe of your laws.
130: 3 O Lord, who could *s*?
Ecc 5: 7 Therefore *s* in awe of God.
Isa 7: 9 If you do not *s* firm in your faith,
29: 23 will *s* in awe of the God of Israel.
Eze 22: 30 *s* before me in the gap on behalf
Hab 3: 2 I *s* in awe of your deeds, O LORD.
Zec 14: 4 On that day his feet will *s*
Mal 3: 2 Who can *s* when he appears?
Mt 12: 25 divided against itself will not *s*.
Ro 14: 4 for the Lord is able to make him *s*.
14: 10 we will all *s* before God's judgment
1Co 10: 13 out so that you can *s* up under it.
15: 58 Therefore, my dear brothers, *s* firm
16: 13 Be on your guard; *s* firm in the faith
Gal 5: 1 *S* firm, then, and do not let
Eph 6: 14 *S* firm then, with the belt
2Th 2: 15 *s* firm and hold to the teachings we
Jas 5: 8 You too, be patient and *s* firm,
Rev 3: 20 Here I am! I *s* at the door

STANDING (STAND)
Ex 3: 5 where you are *s* is holy ground."
Jos 5: 15 the place where you are *s* is holy."
Ru 2: 1 a man of *s*, whose name was Boaz.
4: 11 May you have *s* in Ephrathah
Lk 21: 19 By *s* firm you will gain life.
1Ti 3: 13 have served well gain an excellent *s*
1Pe 5: 9 Resist him, *s* firm in the faith,

STANDS (STAND)
Ps 89: 2 that your love *s* firm forever,
119: 89 it *s* firm in the heavens.
Pr 12: 7 the house of the righteous *s* firm.
Isa 40: 8 but the word of our God *s* forever."
Mt 10: 22 but he who *s* firm to the end will be
2Ti 2: 19 God's solid foundation *s* firm,
1Pe 1: 25 but the word of the Lord *s* forever

STAR (STARS)
Nu 24: 17 A *s* will come out of Jacob;
Isa 14: 12 O morning *s*, son of the dawn!
Mt 2: 2 We saw his *s* in the east
2Pe 1: 19 the morning *s* rises in your hearts.
Rev 2: 28 I will also give him the morning *s*.
22: 16 and the bright Morning *S*."

STARS (STAR)
Ge 1: 16 He also made the *s*.
Job 38: 7 while the morning *s* sang together
Da 12: 3 like the *s* for ever and ever.
Php 2: 15 in which you shine like *s*

STATURE
1Sa 2: 26 boy Samuel continued to grow in *s*
Lk 2: 52 And Jesus grew in wisdom and *s*,

STATUTES
Ps 19: 7 *s* of the LORD are trustworthy,
93: 5 Your *s* stand firm;
119: 2 Blessed are they who keep his *s*
119: 14 I rejoice in following your *s*
119: 24 Your *s* are my delight;
119: 36 Turn my heart toward your *s*
119: 99 for I meditate on your *s*.
119:111 Your *s* are my heritage forever;
119:125 that I may understand your *s*.
119:129 Your *s* are wonderful;
119:138 The *s* you have laid
119:152 Long ago I learned from your *s*
119:167 I obey your *s*,

STEADFAST*
Ps 51: 10 and renew a *s* spirit within me.
57: 7 My heart is *s*, O God,
57: 7 my heart is *s*;
108: 1 My heart is *s*, O God;
111: 8 They are *s* for ever and ever,
112: 7 his heart is *s*, trusting in the LORD
Ps 119: 5 Oh, that my ways were *s*
Isa 26: 3 him whose mind is *s*,
1Pe 5: 10 and make you strong, firm and *s*.

STEADY
Isa 35: 3 *s* the knees that give way;

STEAL (STOLEN)
Ex 20: 15 "You shall not *s*.
Lev 19: 11 " 'Do not *s*.
Dt 5: 19 "You shall not *s*.
Mt 19: 18 do not *s*, do not give false
Ro 13: 9 "Do not *s*," "Do not covet,"
Eph 4: 28 has been stealing must *s* no longer,

STEP (FOOTSTEPS STEPS)
Job 34: 21 he sees their every *s*.
Gal 5: 25 let us keep in *s* with the Spirit.

STEPHEN
Deacon (Ac 6:5). Arrested (Ac 6:8-15). Speech to Sanhedrin (Ac 7). Stoned (Ac 7:54-60; 22:20).

STEPS (STEP)
Ps 37: 23 he makes his *s* firm;
Pr 14: 15 prudent man gives thought to his *s*.
16: 9 but the LORD determines his *s*.
20: 24 A man's *s* are directed
Jer 10: 23 it is not for man to direct his *s*.
1Pe 2: 21 that you should follow in his *s*.

STERN (STERNNESS)
Pr 15: 10 *S* discipline awaits him who leaves

STERNNESS* (STERN)
Ro 11: 22 and *s* of God: *s* to those who fell,

STICKS
Pr 18: 24 there is a friend who *s* closer

STIFF-NECKED (NECK)
Ex 34: 9 Although this is a *s* people,
Pr 29: 1 A man who remains *s*

STILL
Jos 10: 13 So the sun stood *s*,
Ps 37: 7 Be *s* before the LORD
46: 10 "Be *s*, and know that I am God;
89: 9 its waves mount up, you *s* them.
Zec 2: 13 Be *s* before the LORD, all mankind
Mk 4: 39 said to the waves, "Quiet! Be *s*!"

STIMULATE*
2Pe 3: 1 as reminders to *s* you

STING
1Co 15: 55 Where, O death, is your *s*?"

STINGY
Pr 28: 22 A *s* man is eager to get rich

STIRRED (STIRS)
Ps 45: 1 My heart is *s* by a noble theme

STIRS (STIRRED)
Pr 6: 19 and a man who *s* up dissension
10: 12 Hatred *s* up dissension,
15: 1 but a harsh word *s* up anger.
15: 18 hot-tempered man *s* up dissension,
16: 28 A perverse man *s* up dissension,
28: 25 A greedy man *s* up dissension,
29: 22 An angry man *s* up dissension,

STOLEN (STEAL)
Lev 6: 4 he must return what he has *s*
SS 4: 9 You have *s* my heart, my sister,

STOMACH
1Co 6: 13 Food for the *s* and the *s* for food"—
Php 3: 19 their god is their *s*, and their glory

STONE (CAPSTONE CORNERSTONE MILLSTONE STONED STONES)
Ex 24: 4 set up twelve *s* pillars representing
28: 10 on one *s* and the remaining six
34: 1 "Chisel out two *s* tablets like
Dt 4: 13 then wrote them on two *s* tablets.
19: 14 your neighbor's boundary *s* set up
1Sa 17: 50 the Philistine with a sling and a *s*;
Ps 91: 12 will not strike your foot against a *s*.
118: 22 The *s* the builders rejected
Pr 22: 28 not move an ancient boundary *s*
Isa 8: 14 a *s* that causes men to stumble
28: 16 "See, I lay a *s* in Zion,
Eze 11: 19 remove from them their heart of *s*
36: 26 remove from you your heart of *s*
Mt 7: 9 will give him a *s*? Or if he asks
21: 42 " 'The *s* the builders rejected
24: 2 not one *s* here will be left
Mk 16: 3 "Who will roll the *s* away
Lk 4: 3 tell this *s* to become bread."
Jn 8: 7 the first to throw a *s* at her."
Ac 4: 11 " 'the *s* you builders rejected,
Ro 9: 32 stumbled over the "stumbling *s*."
2Co 3: 3 not on tablets of *s* but on tablets
1Pe 2: 6 "See, I lay a *s* in Zion,
Rev 2: 17 also give him a white *s*

STONED (STONE)
2Co 11: 25 once I was *s*, three times I was
Heb 11: 37 They were *s*; they were sawed

STONES (STONE)
Ex 28: 21 are to be twelve *s*, one for each
Jos 4: 3 to take up twelve *s* from the middle
1Sa 17: 40 chose five smooth *s*
Mt 3: 9 out of these *s* God can raise up
1Co 3: 12 silver, costly *s*, wood, hay or straw,
1Pe 2: 5 also, like living *s*, are being built

STOOD (STAND)
Jos 10: 13 So the sun *s* still,
Lk 22: 28 You are those who have *s* by me
2Ti 4: 17 But the Lord *s* at my side
Jas 1: 12 because when he has *s* the test,

STOOP (STOOPS)
2Sa 22: 36 you *s* down to make me great.

STOOPS (STOOP)
Ps 113: 6 who *s* down to look

STOP
Job 37: 14 *s* and consider God's wonders.
Isa 1: 13 *S* bringing meaningless offerings!
1: 16 *S* doing wrong,
2: 22 *S* trusting in man,
Jer 32: 40 I will never *s* doing good to them,
Mk 9: 39 "Do not *s* him," Jesus said.
Jn 6: 43 "*S* grumbling among yourselves,"
7: 24 *S* judging by mere appearances,
20: 27 *S* doubting and believe."
Ro 14: 13 Therefore let us *s* passing judgment
1Co 14: 20 Brothers, *s* thinking like children.

STORE (STORED)
Pr 2: 1 and *s* up my commands within you,
7: 1 and *s* up my commands within you.
10: 14 Wise men *s* up knowledge,
Isa 33: 6 a rich *s* of salvation and wisdom
Mt 6: 19 not *s* up for yourselves treasures
6: 26 or reap or *s* away in barns,
2Ti 4: 8 Now there is in *s* for me the crown

STORED (STORE)
Lk 6: 45 out of the good *s* up in his heart,
Col 1: 5 from the hope that is *s* up for you

STOREHOUSE (HOUSE)
Mal 3: 10 Bring the whole tithe into the *s*,

STORIES*
2Pe 1: 16 did not follow cleverly invented *s*
2: 3 you with *s* they have made up.

STORM
Job 38: 1 LORD answered Job out of the *s*.
Ps 107: 29 He stilled the *s* to a whisper;
Lk 8: 24 the *s* subsided, and all was calm.

STOUTHEARTED* (HEART)
Ps 138: 3 you made me bold and *s*.

STRAIGHT
Ps 27: 11 lead me in a *s* path
107: 7 He led them by a *s* way
Pr 2: 13 who leave the *s* paths
3: 6 and he will make your paths *s*.
4: 11 and lead you along *s* paths.
4: 25 Let your eyes look *s* ahead,
11: 5 of the blameless makes a *s* way
15: 21 of understanding keeps a *s* course.
Isa 40: 3 make *s* in the wilderness
Mt 3: 3 make *s* paths for him.' "
Jn 1: 23 'Make *s* the way for the Lord.' "
2Pe 2: 15 They have left the *s* way

STRAIN (STRAINING)
Mt 23: 24 You *s* out a gnat but swallow

STRAINING (STRAIN)
Php 3:13 and *s* toward what is ahead,

STRANGE (STRANGER STRANGERS)
Isa 28:11 with foreign lips and *s* tongues
1Co 14:21 "Through men of *s* tongues
1Pe 4:4 They think it *s* that you do not

STRANGER (STRANGE)
Ps 119:19 I am a *s* on earth;
Mt 25:35 I was a *s* and you invited me in,
Jn 10:5 But they will never follow a *s;*

STRANGERS (STRANGE)
Heb 13:2 Do not forget to entertain *s,*
1Pe 2:11 as aliens and *s* in the world,

STRAW
Isa 11:7 and the lion will eat *s* like the ox.
1Co 3:12 silver, costly stones, wood, hay or *s*

STRAYED (STRAYS)
Ps 119:176 I have *s* like a lost sheep.
Jer 31:19 After I *s,*

STRAYS (STRAYED)
Pr 21:16 A man who *s* from the path
Eze 34:16 for the lost and bring back the *s.*

STREAM (STREAMS)
Am 5:24 righteousness like a never-failing *s!*

STREAMS (STREAM)
Ps 1:3 He is like a tree planted by *s*
46:4 is a river whose *s* make glad
Ecc 1:7 All *s* flow into the sea,
Jn 7:38 *s* of living water will flow

STREET
Mt 6:5 on the *s* corners to be seen by men.
22:9 Go to the *s* corners and invite
Rev 21:21 The great *s* of the city was of pure gold,

STRENGTH (STRONG)
Ex 15:2 The LORD is my *s* and my song;
Dt 4:37 by his Presence and his great *s,*
6:5 all your soul and with all your *s.*
Jdg 16:15 told me the secret of your great *s."*
2Sa 22:33 It is God who arms me with *s*
2Ki 23:25 with all his soul and with all his *s,*
1Ch 16:11 Look to the LORD and his *s;*
16:28 ascribe to the LORD glory and *s,*
29:12 In your hands are *s* and power
Ne 8:10 for the joy of the LORD is your *s."*
Ps 18:1 I love you, O LORD, my *s.*
21:13 Be exalted, O LORD, in your *s;*
28:7 The LORD is my *s* and my shield;
29:11 The LORD gives *s* to his people;
33:16 no warrior escapes by his great *s.*
46:1 God is our refuge and *s,*
59:17 O my *S,* I sing praise to you;
65:6 having armed yourself with *s,*
73:26 but God is the *s* of my heart
84:5 Blessed are those whose *s* is in you,
96:7 ascribe to the LORD glory and *s.*
105:4 Look to the LORD and his *s;*
118:14 The LORD is my *s* and my song;
147:10 not in the *s* of the horse,
Pr 24:5 a man of knowledge increases *s;*
30:25 Ants are creatures of little *s,*
Isa 12:2 the LORD, is my *s* and my song;
31:1 and in the great *s* of their horsemen
40:26 of his great power and mighty *s,*
40:31 will renew their *s.*
63:1 forward in the greatness of his *s?*
Jer 9:23 or the strong man boast of his *s*
Mic 5:4 flock in the *s* of the LORD,
Hab 3:19 The Sovereign LORD is my *s;*
Mk 12:30 all your mind and with all your *s.'*
1Co 1:25 of God is stronger than man's *s.*
Eph 1:19 is like the working of his mighty *s,*
Php 4:13 through him who gives me *s.*
Heb 11:34 whose weakness was turned to *s;*
1Pe 4:11 it with the *s* God provides,

STRENGTHEN (STRONG)
2Ch 16:9 to *s* those whose hearts are fully
Ps 119:28 *s* me according to your word.
Isa 35:3 *S* the feeble hands,
41:10 I will *s* you and help you;
Lk 22:32 have turned back, *s* your brothers."
Eph 3:16 of his glorious riches he may *s* you
1Th 3:13 May he *s* your hearts
2Th 2:17 and *s* you in every good deed
Heb 12:12 *s* your feeble arms and weak knees.

STRENGTHENED (STRONG)
Col 1:11 being *s* with all power according
Heb 13:9 good for our hearts to be *s* by grace,

STRENGTHENING (STRONG)
1Co 14:26 done for the *s* of the church.

STRETCHES
Ps 104:2 he *s* out the heavens like a tent

STRICKEN (STRIKE)
Isa 53:8 of my people he was *s.*

STRICT
1Co 9:25 in the games goes into *s* training.

STRIFE (STRIVE)
Pr 17:1 than a house full of feasting, with *s.*
20:3 It is to a man's honor to avoid *s,*
22:10 out the mocker, and out goes *s;*
30:33 so stirring up anger produces *s."*
1Ti 6:4 *s,* malicious talk, evil suspicions

STRIKE (STRIKES STROKE)
Ge 3:15 and you will *s* his heel."
Zec 13:7 "*S* the shepherd,
Mt 4:6 so that you will not *s* your foot
26:31 " 'I will *s* the shepherd,

STRIKES (STRIKE)
Mt 5:39 If someone *s* you on the right

STRIPS
Lk 2:12 You will find a baby wrapped in *s*
Jn 20:5 in at the *s* of linen lying there

STRIVE* (STRIFE)
Ac 24:16 I *s* always to keep my conscience
1Ti 4:10 (and for this we labor and *s*),

STROKE (STRIKE)
Mt 5:18 the smallest letter, not the least *s*

STRONG (STRENGTH STRENGTHEN STRENGTHENED STRENGTHENING STRONGER)
Dt 3:24 your greatness and your *s* hand.
31:6 Be *s* and courageous.
Jos 1:6 "Be *s* and courageous,
Jdg 5:21 March on, my soul; be *s!*
2Sa 10:12 Be *s* and let us fight bravely
1Ki 2:2 "So be *s,* show yourself a man,
1Ch 28:20 "Be *s* and courageous,
2Ch 32:7 them with these words: "Be *s*
Ps 24:8 The LORD *s* and mighty,
31:2 a *s* fortress to save me.
62:11 that you, O God, are *s,*
Pr 18:10 The name of the LORD is a *s* tower
31:17 her arms are *s* for her tasks.
Ecc 9:11 or the battle to the *s,*
SS 8:6 for love is as *s* as death,
Isa 35:4 "Be *s,* do not fear;
53:12 he will divide the spoils with the *s,*
Jer 9:23 or the *s* man boast of his strength
50:34 Yet their Redeemer is *s;*
Hag 2:4 Be *s,* all you people of the land,'
Mt 12:29 can anyone enter a *s* man's house
Lk 2:40 And the child grew and became *s;*
Ro 15:1 We who are *s* ought to bear
1Co 1:8 He will keep you *s* to the end,
1:27 things of the world to shame the *s.*
16:13 in the faith; be men of courage; be *s*
2Co 12:10 For when I am weak, then I am *s.*
Eph 6:10 be *s* in the Lord and in his mighty
2Ti 2:1 be *s* in the grace that is
1Pe 5:10 restore you and make you *s,*

STRONGER (STRONG)
Dt 4:38 before you nations greater and *s*
1Co 1:25 of God is *s* than man's strength.

STRONGHOLD (STRONGHOLDS)
2Sa 22:3 He is my *s,* my refuge and my
Ps 9:9 a *s* in times of trouble.
18:2 the horn of my salvation, my *s.*
27:1 The LORD is the *s* of my life—
144:2 my *s* and my deliverer,

STRONGHOLDS (STRONGHOLD)
Zep 3:6 their *s* are demolished.
2Co 10:4 have divine power to demolish *s.*

STRUGGLE (STRUGGLED STRUGGLING)
Ro 15:30 me in my *s* by praying to God
Eph 6:12 For our *s* is not against flesh
Heb 12:4 In your *s* against sin, you have not

STRUGGLED (STRUGGLE)
Ge 32:28 because you have *s* with God

STRUGGLING* (STRUGGLE)
Col 1:29 To this end I labor, *s*
2:1 to know how much I am *s* for you

STUDENT (STUDY)
Mt 10:24 "A *s* is not above his teacher,

STUDY (STUDENT)
Ezr 7:10 Ezra had devoted himself to the *s*
Ecc 12:12 and much *s* wearies the body.
Jn 5:39 You diligently *s* the Scriptures

STUMBLE (STUMBLES STUMBLING)
Ps 37:24 though he *s,* he will not fall,
119:165 and nothing can make them *s.*
Pr 3:23 and your foot will not *s;*
Isa 8:14 a stone that causes men to *s*
Jer 13:16 before your feet *s*
31:9 a level path where they will not *s,*
Eze 7:19 for it has made them *s* into sin.
Hos 14:9 but the rebellious *s* in them.
Mal 2:8 teaching have caused many to *s;*
Jn 11:9 A man who walks by day will not *s,*
Ro 9:33 in Zion a stone that causes men to *s*
14:20 that causes someone else to *s.*
1Co 10:32 Do not cause anyone to *s,*
Jas 3:2 We all *s* in many ways.
1Pe 2:8 and, "A stone that causes men to *s*
1Jn 2:10 nothing in him to make him *s.*

STUMBLES (STUMBLE)
Pr 24:17 when he *s,* do not let your heart
Jn 11:10 is when he walks by night that he *s,*
Jas 2:10 and yet *s* at just one point is guilty

STUMBLING (STUMBLE)
Lev 19:14 put a *s* block in front of the blind,
Ps 56:13 and my feet from *s,*
Mt 16:23 Satan! You are a *s* block to me;
Ro 9:32 They stumbled over the "*s* stone."
11:9 a *s* block and a retribution for them
14:13 up your mind not to put any *s* block
1Co 1:23 a *s* block to Jews and foolishness
8:9 freedom does not become a *s* block
2Co 6:3 We put no *s* block in anyone's path,

STUMP
Isa 6:13 so the holy seed will be the *s*
11:1 up from the *s* of Jesse;

STUPID
Pr 12:1 but he who hates correction is *s.*
2Ti 2:23 to do with foolish and *s* arguments,

STUPOR
Ro 11:8 "God gave them a spirit of *s,*

SUBDUE (SUBDUED)
Ge 1:28 in number; fill the earth and *s* it.

SUBDUED (SUBDUE)
Jos 10:40 So Joshua *s* the whole region,
Ps 47:3 He *s* nations under us,

SUBJECT (SUBJECTED)
Mt 5:22 angry with his brother will be *s*
1Co 14:32 of prophets are *s* to the control
15:28 then the Son himself will be made *s*
Tit 2:5 and to be *s* to their husbands,
2:9 slaves to be *s* to their masters
3:1 Remind the people to be *s* to rulers

SUBJECTED (SUBJECT)
Ro 8:20 For the creation was *s*

SUBMISSION (SUBMIT)
1Co 14:34 but must be in *s,* as the Law says.
1Ti 2:11 learn in quietness and full *s.*

SUBMISSIVE (SUBMIT)
Jas 3:17 then peace-loving, considerate, *s,*
1Pe 3:1 in the same way be *s*
5:5 in the same way be *s*

SUBMIT (SUBMISSION SUBMISSIVE SUBMITS)
Ro 13: 1 Everyone must *s* himself
13: 5 necessary to *s* to the authorities,
1Co 16: 16 to *s* to such as these
Eph 5: 21 *S* to one another out of reverence
Col 3: 18 Wives, *s* to your husbands,
Heb 12: 9 How much more should we *s*
13: 17 Obey your leaders and *s*
Jas 4: 7 *S* yourselves, then, to God.
1Pe 2: 18 *s* yourselves to your masters

SUBMITS* (SUBMIT)
Eph 5: 24 Now as the church *s* to Christ,

SUBTRACT*
Dt 4: 2 what I command you and do not *s*

SUCCEED (SUCCESS SUCCESSFUL)
Ps 20: 4 and make all your plans *s*.
Pr 15: 22 but with many advisers they *s*.
16: 3 and your plans will *s*.
21: 30 that can *s* against the LORD.

SUCCESS (SUCCEED)
Ge 39: 23 and gave him *s* in whatever he did.
1Sa 18: 14 In everything he did he had great *s*,
1Ch 12: 18 *S*, *s* to you, and *s*
22: 13 you will have *s* if you are careful
2Ch 26: 5 the LORD, God gave him *s*.
Ecc 10: 10 but skill will bring *s*.

SUCCESSFUL (SUCCEED)
Jos 1: 7 that you may be *s* wherever you go.
2Ki 18: 7 he was *s* in whatever he undertook.
2Ch 20: 20 in his prophets and you will be *s*."

SUFFER (SUFFERED SUFFERING SUFFERINGS SUFFERS)
Job 36: 15 those who *s* he delivers
Isa 53: 10 to crush him and cause him to *s*,
Mk 8: 31 the Son of Man must *s* many things
Lk 24: 26 the Christ have to *s* these things
24: 46 The Christ will *s* and rise
2Co 1: 6 of the same sufferings we *s*.
Php 1: 29 to *s* for him, since you are going
Heb 9: 26 would have had to *s* many times
1Pe 3: 17 to *s* for doing good
4: 16 However, if you *s* as a Christian,

SUFFERED (SUFFER)
Heb 2: 9 and honor because he *s* death,
2: 18 Because he himself *s*
1Pe 2: 21 Christ *s* for you, leaving you
4: 1 he who has *s* in his body is done

SUFFERING (SUFFER)
Job 36: 15 who suffer he delivers in their *s*;
Ps 22: 24 the *s* of the afflicted one;
Isa 53: 3 of sorrows, and familiar with *s*.
53: 11 After the *s* of his soul,
La 1: 12 Is any *s* like my *s*
Ac 5: 41 worthy of *s* disgrace for the Name.
Ro 5: 3 know that *s* produces
2Ti 1: 8 But join with me in *s* for the gospel,
Heb 2: 10 of their salvation perfect through *s*.
13: 3 as if you yourselves were *s*.
1Pe 4: 12 at the painful trial you are *s*,

SUFFERINGS (SUFFER)
Ro 5: 3 but we also rejoice in our *s*,
8: 17 share in his *s* in order that we may
8: 18 that our present *s* are not worth
2Co 1: 5 as the *s* of Christ flow
Php 3: 10 the fellowship of sharing in his *s*,
1Pe 4: 13 rejoice that you participate in the *s*
5: 9 are undergoing the same kind of *s*.

SUFFERS (SUFFER)
Pr 13: 20 but a companion of fools *s* harm.
1Co 12: 26 If one part *s*, every part *s* with it;

SUFFICIENT
2Co 12: 9 said to me, "My grace is *s* for you,

SUITABLE
Ge 2: 18 I will make a helper *s* for him."

SUMMED* (SUMS)
Ro 13: 9 there may be, are *s* up
Gal 5: 14 The entire law is *s* up

SUMMONS
Ps 50: 1 speaks and *s* the earth
Isa 45: 3 God of Israel, who *s* you by name.

SUMS* (SUMMED)
Mt 7: 12 for this *s* up the Law

SUN (SUNRISE)
Jos 10: 13 So the *s* stood still,
Jdg 5: 31 may they who love you be like the *s*
Ps 84: 11 For the LORD God is a *s*
121: 6 the *s* will not harm you by day,
136: 8 the *s* to govern the day,
Ecc 1: 9 there is nothing new under the *s*.
Isa 60: 19 The *s* will no more be your light
Mal 4: 2 the *s* of righteousness will rise
Mt 5: 45 He causes his *s* to rise on the evil
13: 43 the righteous will shine like the *s*
17: 2 His face shone like the *s*,
Lk 23: 45 for the *s* stopped shining.
Eph 4: 26 Do not let the *s* go
Rev 1: 16 His face was like the *s* shining
21: 23 The city does not need the *s*

SUNG (SING)
Mt 26: 30 When they had *s* a hymn, they

SUNRISE (SUN)
2Sa 23: 4 he is like the light of morning at *s*
Hab 3: 4 His splendor was like the *s*;

SUPERIOR
Heb 1: 4 he became as much *s* to the angels
8: 6 ministry Jesus has received is as *s*

SUPERVISION
Gal 3: 25 longer under the *s* of the law.

SUPPER
Lk 22: 20 after the *s* he took the cup, saying,
1Co 11: 25 after *s* he took the cup,
Rev 19: 9 to the wedding *s* of the Lamb!' "

SUPPLIED (SUPPLY)
Ac 20: 34 of mine have *s* my own needs
Php 4: 18 and even more; I am amply *s*,

SUPPLY (SUPPLIED SUPPLYING)
2Co 8: 14 your plenty will *s* what they need,
1Th 3: 10 and *s* what is lacking in your faith.

SUPPLYING* (SUPPLY)
2Co 9: 12 you perform is not only *s* the needs

SUPPORT (SUPPORTED SUPPORTING)
Ps 18: 18 but the LORD was my *s*.
Ro 11: 18 consider this: You do not *s* the root
1Co 9: 12 If others have this right of *s*

SUPPORTED (SUPPORT)
Ps 94: 18 your love, O LORD, *s* me.
Col 2: 19 *s* and held together by its ligaments

SUPPORTING (SUPPORT)
Eph 4: 16 held together by every *s* ligament,

SUPPRESS*
Ro 1: 18 wickedness of men who *s* the truth

SUPREMACY* (SUPREME)
Col 1: 18 in everything he might have the *s*.

SUPREME (SUPREMACY)
Pr 4: 7 Wisdom is *s*; therefore get wisdom.

SURE
Nu 28: 31 Be *s* the animals are without defect
32: 23 you may be *s* that your sin will find
Dt 6: 17 Be *s* to keep the commands
14: 22 Be *s* to set aside a tenth
29: 18 make *s* there is no root
Jos 23: 13 then you may be *s* that the LORD
1Sa 12: 24 But be *s* to fear the LORD
Ps 19: 9 The ordinances of the LORD are *s*
132: 11 a *s* oath that he will not revoke:
Pr 27: 23 Be *s* you know the condition
Isa 28: 16 cornerstone for a *s* foundation;
Eph 5: 5 of this you can be *s*: No immoral,
Heb 11: 1 faith is being *s* of what we hope for
2Pe 1: 10 to make your calling and election *s*.

SURFACE
2Co 10: 7 You are looking only on the *s*

SURPASS* (SURPASSED SURPASSES SURPASSING)
Pr 31: 29 but you *s* them all."

SURPASSED* (SURPASS)
Jn 1: 15 'He who comes after me has *s* me
1: 30 man who comes after me has *s* me

SURPASSES* (SURPASS)
Pr 8: 19 what I yield *s* choice silver.
Mt 5: 20 unless your righteousness *s* that
Eph 3: 19 to know this love that *s* knowledge

SURPASSING* (SURPASS)
Ps 150: 2 praise him for his *s* greatness.
2Co 3: 10 in comparison with the *s* glory.
9: 14 of the *s* grace God has given you.
Php 3: 8 the *s* greatness of knowing Christ

SURPRISE (SURPRISED)
1Th 5: 4 that this day should *s* you like

SURPRISED (SURPRISE)
1Pe 4: 12 do not be *s* at the painful trial you
1Jn 3: 13 Do not be *s*, my brothers,

SURRENDER
1Co 13: 3 and *s* my body to the flames,

SURROUND (SURROUNDED SURROUNDS)
Ps 5: 12 you *s* them with your favor
32: 7 and *s* me with songs of deliverance.
89: 7 awesome than all who *s* him.
125: 2 As the mountains *s* Jerusalem,
Jer 31: 22 a woman will *s* a man."

SURROUNDED (SURROUND)
Heb 12: 1 since we are *s* by such a great cloud

SURROUNDS* (SURROUND)
Ps 32: 10 *s* the man who trusts in him.
89: 8 and your faithfulness *s* you.
125: 2 so the LORD *s* his people

SUSA
Ezr 4: 9 and Babylon, the Elamites of *S*,
Ne 1: 1 while I was in the citadel of *S*,

SUSPENDS*
Job 26: 7 he *s* the earth over nothing.

SUSPICIONS*
1Ti 6: 4 evil *s* and constant friction

SUSTAIN (SUSTAINING SUSTAINS)
Ps 55: 22 and he will *s* you;
Isa 46: 4 I am he, I am he who will *s* you.

SUSTAINING* (SUSTAIN)
Heb 1: 3 *s* all things by his powerful word.

SUSTAINS (SUSTAIN)
Ps 18: 35 and your right hand *s* me;
146: 9 and *s* the fatherless and the widow,
147: 6 The LORD *s* the humble
Isa 50: 4 to know the word that *s* the weary.

SWALLOW (SWALLOWED)
Isa 25: 8 he will *s* up death forever.
Jnh 1: 17 provided a great fish to *s* Jonah,
Mt 23: 24 You strain out a gnat but *s* a camel.

SWALLOWED (SWALLOW)
1Co 15: 54 "Death has been *s* up in victory."
2Co 5: 4 so that what is mortal may be *s* up

SWAYED
Mt 11: 7 A reed *s* by the wind? If not,
22: 16 You aren't *s* by men, because you
2Ti 3: 6 are *s* by all kinds of evil desires,

SWEAR (SWORE SWORN)
Lev 19: 12 " 'Do not *s* falsely by my name
Ps 24: 4 or *s* by what is false.
Isa 45: 23 by me every tongue will *s*.
Mt 5: 34 Do not *s* at all: either by heaven,
Jas 5: 12 Above all, my brothers, do not *s*—

SWEAT*
Ge 3: 19 By the *s* of your brow
Lk 22: 44 his *s* was like drops of blood falling

SWEET (SWEETER SWEETNESS)
Job 20:12 "Though evil is s in his mouth
Ps 119:103 How s are your words
Pr 9:17 "Stolen water is s;
13:19 A longing fulfilled is s to the soul,
16:24 s to the soul and healing
20:17 by fraud tastes s to a man,
24:14 also that wisdom is s to your soul;
Ecc 5:12 The sleep of a laborer is s,
Isa 5:20 and s for bitter.
Eze 3:3 it tasted as s as honey in my mouth.
Rev 10:10 It tasted as s as honey in my mouth

SWEETER (SWEET)
Ps 19:10 they are s than honey,
119:103 s than honey to my mouth!

SWEETNESS* (SWEET)
SS 4:11 Your lips drop s as the honeycomb,
5:16 His mouth is s itself;

SWEPT
Mt 12:44 finds the house unoccupied, s clean

SWERVE*
Pr 4:5 do not forget my words or s
4:27 Do not s to the right or the left;

SWIFT
Pr 1:16 they are s to shed blood.
Ecc 9:11 The race is not to the s
Isa 59:7 they are s to shed innocent blood.
Ro 3:15 "Their feet are s to shed blood;
2Pe 2:1 bringing s destruction

SWINDLER* (SWINDLERS)
1Co 5:11 or a slanderer, a drunkard or a s.

SWINDLERS* (SWINDLER)
1Co 5:10 or the greedy and s, or idolaters.
6:10 s will inherit the kingdom of God.

SWORD (SWORDS)
Ge 3:24 and a flaming s flashing back
Dt 32:41 when I sharpen my flashing s
Jos 5:13 of him with a drawn s in his hand.
1Sa 17:45 "You come against me with s
17:47 here will know that it is not by s
31:4 so Saul took his own s and fell on it.
2Sa 12:10 therefore, the s will never depart
Ps 44:6 my s does not bring me victory;
45:3 Gird your s upon your side,
Pr 12:18 Reckless words pierce like a s,
Isa 2:4 Nation will not take up s
Mic 4:3 Nation will not take up s
Mt 10:34 come to bring peace, but a s.
26:52 all who draw the s will die by the s.
Lk 2:35 a s will pierce your own soul too."
Ro 13:4 for he does not bear the s
Eph 6:17 of salvation and the s of the Spirit,
Heb 4:12 Sharper than any double-edged s,
Rev 1:16 came a sharp double-edged s.
19:15 Out of his mouth comes a sharp s

SWORDS (SWORD)
Ps 64:3 who sharpen their tongues like s
Isa 2:4 They will beat their s
Joel 3:10 Beat your plowshares into s

SWORE (SWEAR)
Heb 6:13 for him to swear by, he s by himself

SWORN (SWEAR)
Ps 110:4 The LORD has s
Eze 20:42 the land I had s with uplifted hand
Heb 7:21 "The Lord has s

SYCAMORE-FIG (FIG)
Am 7:14 and I also took care of s trees.
Lk 19:4 and climbed a s tree to see him,

SYMBOLIZES*
1Pe 3:21 this water s baptism that now saves

SYMPATHETIC* (SYMPATHY)
1Pe 3:8 in harmony with one another; be s,

SYMPATHIZED* (SYMPATHY)
Heb 10:34 You s with those in prison

SYMPATHY (SYMPATHETIC SYMPATHIZED)
Ps 69:20 I looked for s, but there was none,

SYNAGOGUE
Lk 4:16 the Sabbath day he went into the s,
Ac 17:2 custom was, Paul went into the s,

TABERNACLE (TABERNACLES)
Ex 40:34 the glory of the LORD filled the t.
Heb 8:2 the true t set up by the Lord,
9:11 and more perfect t that is not
9:21 sprinkled with the blood both the t
Rev 15:5 that is, the t of the Testimony,

TABERNACLES (TABERNACLE)
Lev 23:34 the LORD's Feast of T begins,
Dt 16:16 Feast of Weeks and the Feast of T.
Zec 14:16 and to celebrate the Feast of T.

TABLE (TABLES)
Ex 25:23 "Make a t of acacia wood—
Ps 23:5 You prepare a t before me

TABLES (TABLE)
Jn 2:15 changers and overturned their t.
Ac 6:2 word of God in order to wait on t.

TABLET (TABLETS)
Pr 3:3 write them on the t of your heart.
7:3 write them on the t of your heart.

TABLETS (TABLET)
Ex 31:18 he gave him the two t
Dt 10:5 and put the t in the ark I had made,
2Co 3:3 not on t of stone but on t

TAKE (TAKEN TAKES TAKING TOOK)
Ge 15:7 land to t possession of it."
22:17 Your descendants will t possession
Ex 3:5 "T off your sandals,
21:23 you are to t life for life, eye for eye,
22:22 "Do not t advantage of a widow
Lev 10:17 given to you to t away the guilt
25:14 do not t advantage of each other.
Nu 13:30 and t possession of the land,
Dt 1:8 and t possession of the land that
12:32 do not add to it or t away from it.
31:26 "T this Book of the Law
1Sa 8:11 He will t your sons and make them
1Ch 17:13 I will never t my love away
Job 23:10 But he knows the way that I t;
Ps 2:12 Blessed are all who t refuge in him.
25:18 and t away all my sins.
27:14 be strong and t heart
31:24 Be strong and t heart,
49:17 for he will t nothing with him
51:11 or t your Holy Spirit from me.
73:24 afterward you will t me into glory.
118:8 It is better to t refuge in the LORD
Pr 22:23 for the LORD will t up their case
Isa 62:4 for the LORD will t delight in you,
Eze 3:10 and t to heart all the words I speak
33:11 I t no pleasure in the death
Mt 10:38 anyone who does not t his cross
11:29 T my yoke upon you and learn
16:24 deny himself and t up his cross
26:26 saying, "T and eat; this is my body
Mk 14:36 T this cup from me.
1Ti 6:12 T hold of the eternal life

TAKEN (TAKE)
Ge 2:23 for she was t out of man."
Lev 6:4 must return what he has stolen or t
Nu 8:16 I have t them as my own in place
19:3 it is to be t outside the camp
Ecc 3:14 added to it and nothing t from it.
Isa 6:7 your guilt is t away and your sin
Zec 3:4 "See, I have t away your sin,
Mt 13:12 even what he has will be t from him
24:40 one will be t and the other left.
26:39 may this cup be t from me.
Mk 16:19 he was t up into heaven
Ac 1:9 he was t up before their very eyes,
Ro 5:13 But sin is not t into account
1Ti 3:16 was t up in glory.

TAKES (TAKE)
1Ki 20:11 should not boast like one who t it
Ps 5:4 You are not a God who t pleasure
34:8 blessed is the man who t refuge
Lk 6:30 and if anyone t what belongs to you
Jn 1:29 who t away the sin of the world!
10:18 No one t it from me, but I lay it
Rev 22:19 And if anyone t words away

TAKING (TAKE)
Ac 15:14 by t from the Gentiles a people

Php 2:7 t the very nature of a servant,

TALENT
Mt 25:15 to another one t, each according

TALES*
1Ti 4:7 with godless myths and old wives' t

TALL
1Sa 17:4 He was over nine feet t.
1Ch 11:23 who was seven and a half feet t.

TAMAR
1. Wife of Judah's sons Er and Onan (Ge 38:1-10). Tricked Judah into fathering children when he refused her his third son (Ge 38:11-30).
2. Daughter of David, raped by Amnon (2Sa 13).

TAMBOURINE
Ps 150:4 praise him with t and dancing,

TAME* (TAMED)
Jas 3:8 but no man can t the tongue.

TAMED* (TAME)
Jas 3:7 the sea are being t and have been t

TARSHISH
Jnh 1:3 from the LORD and headed for T.

TARSUS
Ac 9:11 ask for a man from T named Saul,

TASK (TASKS)
1Ch 29:1 The t is great, because this palatial
Mk 13:34 each with his assigned t,
Ac 20:24 complete the t the Lord Jesus has
1Co 3:5 the Lord has assigned to each his t.
2Co 2:16 And who is equal to such a t?
1Ti 3:1 an overseer, he desires a noble t.

TASKS (TASK)
Pr 31:17 her arms are strong for her t.

TASTE (TASTED TASTY)
Ps 34:8 T and see that the LORD is good;
119:103 sweet are your words to my t,
Pr 24:13 from the comb is sweet to your t.
SS 2:3 and his fruit is sweet to my t.
Col 2:21 Do not t! Do not touch!"?
Heb 2:9 the grace of God he might t death

TASTED (TASTE)
Eze 3:3 it t as sweet as honey in my mouth.
1Pe 2:3 now that you have t that the Lord
Rev 10:10 It t as sweet as honey in my mouth,

TASTY (TASTE)
Ge 27:4 Prepare me the kind of t food I like

TATTOO*
Lev 19:28 or put t marks on yourselves.

TAUGHT (TEACH)
1Ki 4:33 He also t about animals and birds,
2Ki 17:28 t them how to worship the LORD.
2Ch 17:9 They t throughout Judah,
Ps 119:102 for you yourself have t me.
Pr 4:4 he t me and said,
31:1 an oracle his mother t him:
Isa 29:13 is made up only of rules t by men.
50:4 ear to listen like one being t.
Mt 7:29 he t as one who had authority,
15:9 their teachings are but rules t
Lk 4:15 He t in their synagogues,
Ac 20:20 have t you publicly and from house
1Co 2:13 but in words t by the Spirit,
Gal 1:12 nor was I t it; rather, I received it
1Ti 1:20 to Satan to be t not to blaspheme.
1Jn 2:27 just as it has t you, remain in him.

TAX (TAXES)
Mt 11:19 a friend of t collectors and "sinners
17:24 of the two-drachma t came to Peter

TAXES (TAX)
Mt 22:17 Is it right to pay t to Caesar or not
Ro 13:7 If you owe t, pay t; if revenue,

TEACH (TAUGHT TEACHER TEACHERS TEACHES TEACHING TEACHINGS)
Ex 4:12 and will t you what to say."
18:20 T them the decrees and laws,
33:13 t me your ways so I may know you

Lev 10: 11 and you must *t* the Israelites all
Dt 4: 9 *T* them to your children
6: 1 me to *t* you to observe
8: 3 to *t* you that man does not live
11: 19 *T* them to your children, talking
1Sa 12: 23 I will *t* you the way that is good
1Ki 8: 36 *T* them the right way to live,
Job 12: 7 ask the animals, and they will *t* you
Ps 32: 8 *t* you in the way you should go;
34: 11 I will *t* you the fear of the LORD.
51: 13 I will *t* transgressors your ways,
78: 5 forefathers to *t* their children,
90: 12 *T* us to number our days aright,
119: 33 *T* me, O LORD, to follow your
143: 10 *T* me to do your will,
Pr 9: 9 *t* a righteous man and he will add
Jer 31: 34 No longer will a man *t* his neighbor
Mic 4: 2 He will *t* us his ways,
Lk 11: 1 said to him, "Lord, *t* us to pray,
12: 12 for the Holy Spirit will *t* you
Jn 14: 26 will *t* you all things and will remind
Ro 2: 21 who *t* others, do you not *t* yourself?
15: 4 in the past was written to *t* us,
1Ti 2: 12 I do not permit a woman to *t*
3: 2 respectable, hospitable, able to *t*,
2Ti 2: 2 also be qualified to *t* others.
2: 24 kind to everyone, able to *t*,
Tit 2: 1 You must *t* what is in accord
2: 15 then, are the things you should *t*.
Heb 8: 11 No longer will a man *t* his neighbor
Jas 3: 1 know that we who *t* will be judged
1Jn 2: 27 you do not need anyone to *t* you.

TEACHER (TEACH)

Ecc 1: 1 The words of the *T*, son of David,
Mt 10: 24 "A student is not above his *t*,
13: 52 "Therefore every *t*
23: 10 Nor are you to be called '*t*,'
Lk 6: 40 A student is not above his *t*,
Jn 3: 2 we know you are a *t* who has come
13: 14 and *T*, have washed your feet,

TEACHERS (TEACH)

Ps 119: 99 I have more insight than all my *t*,
Pr 5: 13 I would not obey my *t*
Lk 20: 46 "Beware of the *t* of the law.
1Co 12: 28 third *t*, then workers of miracles,
Eph 4: 11 and some to be pastors and *t*,
2Ti 4: 3 around them a great number of *t*
Heb 5: 12 by this time you ought to be *t*,
Jas 3: 1 of you should presume to be *t*,
2Pe 2: 1 as there will be false *t* among you.

TEACHES (TEACH)

Ps 25: 9 and *t* them his way.
94: 10 Does he who *t* man lack
Pr 15: 33 of the LORD *t* a man wisdom,
Isa 48: 17 who *t* you what is best for you,
Mt 5: 19 *t* these commands will be called
1Ti 6: 3 If anyone *t* false doctrines
Tit 2: 12 It *t* us to say "No" to ungodliness
1Jn 2: 27 his anointing *t* you about all things

TEACHING (TEACH)

Ezr 7: 10 to *t* its decrees and laws in Israel.
Pr 1: 8 and do not forsake your mother's *t*.
3: 1 My son, do not forget my *t*,
6: 23 this *t* is a light,
Mt 28: 20 *t* them to obey everything I have
Jn 7: 17 whether my *t* comes from God or
8: 31 to my *t*, you are really my disciples.
14: 23 loves me, he will obey my *t*.
Ac 2: 42 themselves to the apostles' *t*
Ro 12: 7 let him serve; if it is *t*, let him teach;
Eph 4: 14 and there by every wind of *t*
2Th 3: 6 to the *t* you received from us.
1Ti 4: 13 of Scripture, to preaching and to *t*.
5: 17 whose work is preaching and *t*.
6: 3 Lord Jesus Christ and to godly *t*,
2Ti 3: 16 is God-breathed and is useful for *t*,
Tit 1: 11 by *t* things they ought not
2: 7 In your *t* show integrity,
Heb 5: 13 with the *t* about righteousness.
2Jn : 9 and does not continue in the *t*

TEACHINGS (TEACH)

Pr 7: 2 guard my *t* as the apple of your eye.
2Th 2: 15 hold to the *t* we passed on to you,
Heb 6: 1 leave the elementary *t* about Christ

TEAR (TEARS)

Rev 7: 17 God will wipe away every *t*
21: 4 He will wipe every *t*

TEARS (TEAR)

Ps 126: 5 Those who sow in *t*
Isa 25: 8 LORD will wipe away the *t*
Jer 31: 16 and your eyes from *t*,
50: 4 in *t* to seek the LORD their God.
Lk 7: 38 she began to wet his feet with her *t*.
2Co 2: 4 anguish of heart and with many *t*,
Php 3: 18 and now say again even with *t*,

TEETH (TOOTH)

Job 19: 20 with only the skin of my *t*.
Ps 35: 16 they gnashed their *t* at me.
Jer 31: 29 and the children's *t* are set on edge
Mt 8: 12 will be weeping and gnashing of *t*."

TEMPER (EVEN-TEMPERED HOT-TEMPERED ILL-TEMPERED QUICK-TEMPERED)

Pr 16: 32 a man who controls his *t*

TEMPERANCE see SELF-CONTROL

TEMPERATE*

1Ti 3: 2 *t*, self-controlled, respectable,
3: 11 not malicious talkers but *t*
Tit 2: 2 Teach the older men to be *t*,

TEMPEST

Ps 50: 3 and around him a *t* rages.
55: 8 far from the *t* and storm."

TEMPLE (TEMPLES)

1Ki 6: 1 began to build the *t* of the LORD.
6: 38 the *t* was finished in all its details
8: 10 the cloud filled the *t* of the LORD.
8: 27 How much less this *t* I have built!
2Ch 36: 19 They set fire to God's *t*
36: 23 me to build a *t* for him at Jerusalem
Ezr 6: 14 finished building the *t* according
Ps 27: 4 and to seek him in his *t*.
Isa 6: 1 and the train of his robe filled the *t*.
Eze 10: 4 cloud filled the *t*, and the court was
43: 4 glory of the LORD entered the *t*
Hab 2: 20 But the LORD is in his holy *t*;
Mt 12: 6 that one greater than the *t* is here.
26: 61 'I am able to destroy the *t* of God
27: 51 of the *t* was torn in two from top
Lk 21: 5 about how the *t* was adorned
Jn 2: 14 In the *t* courts he found men selling
1Co 3: 16 that you yourselves are God's *t*
6: 19 you not know that your body is a *t*
2Co 6: 16 For we are the *t* of the living God.
Rev 21: 22 I did not see a *t* in the city,

TEMPLES (TEMPLE)

Ac 17: 24 does not live in *t* built by hands.

TEMPORARY

2Co 4: 18 what is seen is *t*, but what is unseen

TEMPT* (TEMPTATION TEMPTED TEMPTER TEMPTING)

1Co 7: 5 again so that Satan will not *t* you
Jas 1: 13 does he *t* anyone; but each one is

TEMPTATION* (TEMPT)

Mt 6: 13 And lead us not into *t*,
26: 41 pray so that you will not fall into *t*.
Mk 14: 38 pray so that you will not fall into *t*.
Lk 11: 4 And lead us not into *t*.'"
22: 40 "Pray that you will not fall into *t*."
22: 46 pray so that you will not fall into *t*
1Co 10: 13 No *t* has seized you except what is
1Ti 6: 9 want to get rich fall into *t*

TEMPTED* (TEMPT)

Mt 4: 1 into the desert to be *t* by the devil.
Mk 1: 13 was in the desert forty days, being *t*
Lk 4: 2 for forty days he was *t* by the devil.
1Co 10: 13 But when you are *t*, he will
10: 13 he will not let you be *t*
Gal 6: 1 yourself, or you also may be *t*.
1Th 3: 5 way the tempter might have *t* you
Heb 2: 18 able to help those who are being *t*.
2: 18 he himself suffered when he was *t*,
4: 15 but we have one who has been *t*
Jas 1: 13 For God cannot be *t* by evil,
1: 13 When *t*, no one should say,
1: 14 each one is *t* when, by his own evil

TEMPTER* (TEMPT)

Mt 4: 3 The *t* came to him and said,
1Th 3: 5 some way the *t* might have

TEMPTING* (TEMPT)

Lk 4: 13 the devil had finished all this *t*,
Jas 1: 13 no one should say, "God is *t* me."

TEN (TENTH TITHE TITHES)

Ex 34: 28 covenant—the *T* Commandments.
Lev 26: 8 of you will chase *t* thousand,
Dt 4: 13 covenant, the *T* Commandments,
10: 4 The *T* Commandments he had
Ps 91: 7 *t* thousand at your right hand,
Da 7: 24 *t* horns are *t* kings who will come
Mt 25: 1 will be like *t* virgins who took
25: 28 it to the one who has the *t* talents.
Lk 15: 8 suppose a woman has *t* silver coins
Rev 12: 3 and *t* horns and seven crowns

TENANTS

Mt 21: 34 servants to the *t* to collect his fruit.

TEND

Jer 23: 2 to the shepherds who *t* my people:
Eze 34: 14 I will *t* them in a good pasture,

TENDERNESS*

Isa 63: 15 Your *t* and compassion are
Php 2: 1 fellowship with the Spirit, if any *t*

TENT (TENTMAKER TENTS)

Ex 27: 21 In the *T* of Meeting,
40: 2 "Set up the tabernacle, the *T*
Isa 54: 2 "Enlarge the place of your *t*,
2Co 5: 1 that if the earthly *t* we live
2Pe 1: 13 as long as I live in the *t* of this body,

TENTH (TEN)

Ge 14: 20 Abram gave him a *t* of everything.
Nu 18: 26 you must present a *t* of that tithe
Dt 14: 22 Be sure to set aside a *t*
1Sa 8: 15 He will take a *t* of your grain
Lk 11: 42 you give God a *t* of your mint,
18: 12 I fast twice a week and give a *t*
Heb 7: 4 patriarch Abraham gave him a *t*

TENTMAKER* (TENT)

Ac 18: 3 and because he was a *t* as they were

TENTS (TENT)

Ge 13: 12 and pitched his *t* near Sodom.
Ps 84: 10 than dwell in the *t* of the wicked.

TERAH

Ge 11: 31 *T* took his son Abram, his

TERRIBLE (TERROR)

2Ti 3: 1 There will be *t* times

TERRIFIED (TERROR)

Dt 7: 21 Do not be *t* by them,
20: 3 do not be *t* or give way to panic
Ps 90: 7 and *t* by your indignation.
Mt 14: 26 walking on the lake, they were *t*.
17: 6 they fell facedown to the ground, *t*.
27: 54 they were *t*, and exclaimed,
Mk 4: 41 They were *t* and asked each other,

TERRIFYING (TERROR)

Heb 12: 21 The sight was so *t* that Moses said,

TERRITORY

2Co 10: 16 done in another man's *t*.

TERROR (TERRIBLE TERRIFIED TERRIFYING)

Dt 2: 25 very day I will begin to put the *t*
28: 67 of the *t* that will fill your hearts
Job 9: 34 so that his *t* would frighten me no
Ps 91: 5 You will not fear the *t* of night,
Pr 21: 15 but *t* to evildoers.
Isa 13: 8 *T* will seize them,
24: 17 *T* and pit and snare await you,
51: 13 live in constant *t* every day
54: 14 *T* will be far removed;
Lk 21: 26 Men will faint from *t*, apprehensive
Ro 13: 3 For rulers hold no *t*

TEST (TESTED TESTING TESTS)

Dt 6: 16 Do not *t* the LORD your God
Jdg 3: 1 to *t* all those Israelites who had not
1Ki 10: 1 came to *t* him with hard questions.
1Ch 29: 17 that you *t* the heart and are pleased
Ps 26: 2 *T* me, O LORD, and try me,
78: 18 They willfully put God to the *t*
106: 14 wasteland they put God to the *t*.
139: 23 *t* me and know my anxious

Jer 11:20 and t the heart and mind,
Lk 4:12 put the Lord your God to the t.' "
Ac 5:9 How could you agree to t the Spirit
Ro 12:2 Then you will be able to t
1Co 3:13 and the fire will t the quality
10:9 We should not t the Lord,
2Co 13:5 unless, of course, you fail the t?
1Th 5:21 T everything.
Jas 1:12 because when he has stood the t,
1Jn 4:1 t the spirits to see whether they are

TESTAMENT see COVENANT

TESTED (TEST)

Ge 22:1 Some time later God t Abraham.
Job 23:10 when he has t me, I will come forth
34:36 that Job might be t to the utmost
Ps 66:10 For you, O God, t us;
Pr 27:21 man is t by the praise he receives.
Isa 28:16 a t stone,
48:10 I have t you in the furnace
1Ti 3:10 They must first be t; and then
Heb 11:17 By faith Abraham, when God t him

TESTIFIES (TESTIFY)

Jn 5:32 There is another who t in my favor,
Ro 8:16 The Spirit himself t

TESTIFY (TESTIFIES TESTIMONY)

Pr 24:28 Do not t against your neighbor
Jn 1:7 a witness to t concerning that light,
1:34 and I t that this is the Son of God."
5:39 are the Scriptures that t about me,
7:7 because I t that what it does is evil.
15:26 he will t about me. And you
Ac 4:33 continued to t to the resurrection
10:43 All the prophets t about him that
2Ti 1:8 ashamed to t about our Lord,
1Jn 4:14 t that the Father has sent his Son
5:7 For there are three that t: the Spirit

TESTIMONY (TESTIFY)

Ex 20:16 "You shall not give false t
31:18 gave him the two tablets of the T,
Nu 35:30 only on the t of witnesses.
Dt 19:18 giving false t against his brother,
Pr 12:17 A truthful witness gives honest t,
Isa 8:20 and to the t! If they do not speak
Mt 15:19 sexual immorality, theft, false t,
24:14 preached in the whole world as a t
Lk 18:20 not give false t, honor your father
Jn 2:25 He did not need man's t about man
21:24 We know that his t is true.
1Jn 5:9 but God's t is greater because it is
Rev 12:11 and by the word of their t;

TESTING (TEST)

Lk 8:13 but in the time of t they fall away.
Heb 3:8 during the time of t in the desert,
Jas 1:3 because you know that the t

TESTS (TEST)

Pr 17:3 but the LORD t the heart.
1Th 2:4 but God, who t our hearts.

THADDAEUS

Apostle (Mt 10:3; Mk 3:18); probably also known as Judas son of James (Lk 6:16; Ac 1:13).

THANK (THANKFUL THANKFULNESS THANKS THANKSGIVING)

Php 1:3 I t my God every time I remember
1Th 3:9 How can we t God enough for you

THANKFUL (THANK)

Col 3:15 And be t.
Heb 12:28 let us be t, and so worship God

THANKFULNESS (THANK)

1Co 10:30 If I take part in the meal with t,
Col 2:7 taught, and overflowing with t.

THANKS (THANK)

1Ch 16:8 Give t to the LORD, call
Ne 12:31 assigned two large choirs to give t.
Ps 7:17 I will give t to the LORD
28:7 and I will give t to him in song.
30:12 my God, I will give you t forever.
35:18 I will give you t in the great
75:1 we give t, for your Name is near;
100:4 give t to him and praise his name.
107:1 Give t to the LORD, for he is good;
118:28 are my God, and I will give you t;
136:1 Give t to the LORD, for he is good.
Ro 1:21 as God nor gave t to him,
1Co 11:24 when he had given t, he broke it
15:57 t be to God! He gives us the victory
2Co 2:14 t be to God, who always leads us
9:15 T be to God for his indescribable
1Th 5:18 give t in all circumstances,
Rev 4:9 and t to him who sits on the throne

THANKSGIVING (THANK)

Ps 95:2 Let us come before him with t
100:4 Enter his gates with t
1Co 10:16 cup of t for which we give thanks
Php 4:6 by prayer and petition, with t,
1Ti 4:3 created to be received with t

THEFT (THIEF)

Mt 15:19 sexual immorality, t, false

THEFTS* (THIEF)

Rev 9:21 their sexual immorality or their t.

THEME*

Ps 45:1 My heart is stirred by a noble t
119:54 Your decrees are the t of my song

THIEF (THEFT THEFTS THIEVES)

Ex 22:3 A t must certainly make restitution
Pr 6:30 Men do not despise a t if he steals
Lk 12:39 at what hour the t was coming,
1Th 5:2 day of the Lord will come like a t
1Pe 4:15 or t or any other kind of criminal,
Rev 16:15 I come like a t! Blessed is he who

THIEVES (THIEF)

Mt 6:19 and where t break in and steal.
Jn 10:8 who ever came before me were t
1Co 6:10 nor homosexual offenders nor t

THINK (THINKING THOUGHT THOUGHTS)

Ps 63:6 I t of you through the watches
Isa 44:19 No one stops to t,
Mt 22:42 "What do you t about the Christ?
Ro 12:3 Do not t of yourself more highly
Php 4:8 praiseworthy—t about such things

THINKING (THINK)

Pr 23:7 who is always t about the cost.
1Co 14:20 Brothers, stop t like children.
2Pe 3:1 to stimulate you to wholesome t.

THIRST (THIRSTS THIRSTY)

Ps 69:21 and gave me vinegar for my t.
Mt 5:6 Blessed are those who hunger and t
Jn 4:14 the water I give him will never t.
2Co 11:27 I have known hunger and t
Rev 7:16 never again will they t.

THIRSTS (THIRST)

Ps 42:2 My soul t for God,

THIRSTY (THIRST)

Ps 107:9 for he satisfies the t
Pr 25:21 if he is t, give him water to drink.
Isa 55:1 "Come, all you who are t,
Mt 25:35 I was t and you gave me something
Jn 7:37 "If anyone is t, let him come to me
Ro 12:20 if he is t, give him something
Rev 21:6 To him who is t I will give to drink
22:17 Whoever is t, let him come;

THOMAS

Apostle (Mt 10:3; Mk 3:18; Lk 6:15; Jn 11:16; 14:5; 21:2; Ac 1:13). Doubted resurrection (Jn 20:24-28).

THONGS

Mk 1:7 t of whose sandals I am not worthy

THORN (THORNBUSHES THORNS)

2Co 12:7 there was given me a t in my flesh,

THORNBUSHES (THORN)

Lk 6:44 People do not pick figs from t,

THORNS (THORN)

Ge 3:18 It will produce t and thistles
Nu 33:55 in your eyes and t in your sides.
Mt 13:7 fell among t, which grew up
27:29 and then twisted together a crown of t
Heb 6:8 But land that produces t

THOUGHT (THINK)

Pr 14:15 a prudent man gives t to his steps.
21:29 an upright man gives t to his ways.
1Co 13:11 I talked like a child, I t like a child,

THOUGHTS (THINK)

1Ch 28:9 every motive behind the t.
Ps 94:11 The LORD knows the t of man;
139:23 test me and know my anxious t.
Isa 55:8 "For my t are not your t,
Mt 15:19 For out of the heart come evil t,
1Co 2:11 among men knows the t of a man
Heb 4:12 it judges the t and attitudes

THREE

Ge 6:10 Noah had t sons: Shem, Ham
Ex 23:14 "T times a year you are
Dt 19:15 the testimony of two or t witnesses.
2Sa 23:8 a Tahkemonite, was chief of the T;
Pr 30:15 "There are t things that are never
30:18 "There are t things that are too
30:21 "Under t things the earth trembles,
30:29 "There are t things that are stately
Ecc 4:12 of t strands is not quickly broken.
Da 3:24 "Weren't there t men that we tied up
Am 1:3 "For t sins of Damascus,
Jnh 1:17 inside the fish t days and t nights.
Mt 12:40 so the Son of Man will be t days
12:40 t nights in the belly of a huge fish,
12:40 t nights in the heart of the earth.
17:4 I will put up t shelters—one
18:20 or t come together in my name,
26:34 you will disown me t times."
26:75 you will disown me t times."
27:63 'After t days I will rise again.'
Mk 8:31 and after t days rise again.
9:5 Let us put up t shelters—one
14:30 yourself will disown me t times."
Jn 2:19 and I will raise it again in t days."
1Co 13:13 And now these t remain: faith,
14:27 or at the most t—should speak,
2Co 13:1 testimony of two or t witnesses."
1Jn 5:7 For there are t that testify:

THRESHER* (THRESHING)

1Co 9:10 plowman plows and the t threshes,

THRESHING (THRESHER)

Ru 3:6 So she went down to the t floor
2Sa 24:18 an altar to the LORD on the t floor
Lk 3:17 is in his hand to clear his t floor

THREW (THROW)

Da 6:16 and t him into the lions' den.
Jnh 1:15 took Jonah and t him overboard,

THRIVE

Pr 29:2 When the righteous t, the people

THROAT (THROATS)

Ps 5:9 Their t is an open grave;
Pr 23:2 and put a knife to your t

THROATS (THROAT)

Ro 3:13 "Their t are open graves;

THROB*

Isa 60:5 your heart will t and swell with joy;

THRONE (ENTHRONED ENTHRONES THRONES)

2Sa 7:16 your t will be established forever
1Ch 17:12 and I will establish his t forever.
Ps 11:4 the LORD is on his heavenly t.
45:6 Your t, O God, will last for ever
47:8 God is seated on his holy t.
89:14 justice are the foundation of your t;
Isa 6:1 I saw the Lord seated on a t,
66:1 "Heaven is my t,
Eze 28:2 I sit on the t of a god
Da 7:9 His t was flaming with fire,
Mt 19:28 Son of Man sits on his glorious t,
Ac 7:49 prophet says: " 'Heaven is my t,
Heb 1:8 "Your t, O God, will last for ever
4:16 Let us then approach the t of grace
12:2 at the right hand of the t of God.
Rev 3:21 sat down with my Father on his t.
3:21 the right to sit with me on my t,
4:2 there before me was a t in heaven
4:10 They lay their crowns before the t
20:11 Then I saw a great white t
22:3 t of God and of the Lamb will be

THRONES (THRONE)

Mt 19:28 me will also sit on twelve t,
Rev 4:4 throne were twenty-four other t,

THROW (THREW)

Jn 8:7 the first to t a stone at her."

Heb 10:35 So do not *t* away your confidence;
12: 1 let us *t* off everything that hinders

THUNDER (THUNDERS)

Ps 93: 4 Mightier than the *t*
Mk 3:17 which means Sons of *T*); Andrew,

THUNDERS (THUNDER)

Job 37: 5 God's voice *t* in marvelous ways;
Ps 29: 3 the God of glory *t*,
Rev 10: 3 the voices of the seven *t* spoke.

THWART* (THWARTED)

Isa 14:27 has purposed, and who can *t* him?

THWARTED (THWART)

Job 42: 2 no plan of yours can be *t*.

THYATIRA

Rev 2:18 the angel of the church in *T* write:

TIBNI

King of Israel (1Ki 16:21-22).

TIDINGS

Isa 40: 9 You who bring good *t* to Jerusalem
52: 7 who bring good *t*,

TIES

Hos 11: 4 with *t* of love;
Mt 12:29 unless he first *t* up the strong man?

TIGHT*

Jas 1:26 and yet does not keep a *t* rein

TIGHTFISTED*

Dt 15: 7 or *t* toward your poor brother.

TIME (TIMES)

Est 4:14 come to royal position for such a *t*
Ecc 3: 1 There is a *t* for everything,
8: 5 wise heart will know the proper *t*
Da 7:25 to him for a *t*, times and half a *t*.
12: 7 "It will be for a *t*, times and half a *t*.
Hos 10:12 for it is *t* to seek the LORD,
Jn 2: 4 Jesus replied, "My *t* has not yet
17: 1 prayed: "Father, the *t* has come.
Ro 9: 9 "At the appointed *t* I will return,
13:11 understanding the present *t*.
1Co 7:29 brothers, is that the *t* is short.
2Co 6: 2 now is the *t* of God's favor,
2Ti 1: 9 Jesus before the beginning of *t*,
Tit 1: 2 promised before the beginning of *t*,
Heb 9:28 and he will appear a second *t*,
10:12 for all *t* one sacrifice for sins,
1Pe 4:17 For it is *t* for judgment to begin

TIMES (TIME)

Ps 9: 9 a stronghold in *t* of trouble.
31:15 My *t* are in your hands;
62: 8 Trust in him at all *t*, O people;
Pr 17:17 A friend loves at all *t*,
Isa 46:10 from ancient *t*, what is still to come
Am 5:13 for the *t* are evil.
Mt 16: 3 cannot interpret the signs of the *t*.
18:21 how many *t* shall I forgive my
Ac 1: 7 "It is not for you to know the *t*
Rev 12:14 *t* and half a time, out

TIMID (TIMIDITY)

1Th 5:14 encourage the *t*, help the weak,

TIMIDITY* (TIMID)

2Ti 1: 7 For God did not give us a spirit of *t*

TIMOTHY

Believer from Lystra (Ac 16:1). Joined Paul on second missionary journey (Ac 16-20). Sent to settle problems at Corinth (1Co 4:17; 16:10). Led church at Ephesus (1Ti 1:3). Co-writer with Paul (1Th 1:1; 2Th 1:1; Phm 1).

TIP

Job 33: 2 my words are on the *t* of my tongue

TIRE (TIRED)

2Th 3:13 never *t* of doing what is right.

TIRED (TIRE)

Ex 17:12 When Moses' hands grew *t*,
Isa 40:28 He will not grow *t* or weary,

TITHE (TEN)

Lev 27:30 " 'A *t* of everything from the land,
Dt 12:17 eat in your own towns the *t*
Mal 3:10 the whole *t* into the storehouse,

TITHES (TEN)

Nu 18:21 give to the Levites all the *t* in Israel
Mal 3: 8 'How do we rob you?' "In *t*

TITUS*

Gentile co-worker of Paul (Gal 2:1-3; 2Ti 4:10); sent to Corinth (2Co 2:13; 7-8; 12:18), Crete (Tit 1:4-5).

TODAY

Ps 2: 7 *t* I have become your Father.
95: 7 *T*, if you hear his voice,
Mt 6:11 Give us *t* our daily bread.
Lk 2:11 *T* in the town of David a Savior has
23:43 *t* you will be with me in paradise."
Ac 13:33 *t* I have become your Father.'
Heb 1: 5 *t* I have become your Father"?
3: 7 "*T*, if you hear his voice,
3:13 daily, as long as it is called *T*,
5: 5 *t* I have become your Father."
13: 8 Christ is the same yesterday and *t*

TOIL (TOILED TOILING)

Ge 3:17 through painful *t* you will eat of it

TOILED (TOIL)

2Co 11:27 and *t* and have often gone

TOILING (TOIL)

2Th 3: 8 *t* so that we would not be a burden

TOLERANCE* (TOLERATE)

Ro 2: 4 for the riches of his kindness, *t*

TOLERATE (TOLERANCE)

Hab 1:13 you cannot *t* wrong.
Rev 2: 2 that you cannot *t* wicked men,

TOMB

Mt 27:65 make the *t* as secure as you know
Lk 24: 2 the stone rolled away from the *t*,

TOMORROW

Pr 27: 1 Do not boast about *t*,
Isa 22:13 "for *t* we die!"
Mt 6:34 Therefore do not worry about *t*,
1Co 15:32 for *t* we die."
Jas 4:13 "Today or *t* we will go to this

TONGUE (TONGUES)

Ex 4:10 I am slow of speech and *t*."
Job 33: 2 my words are on the tip of my *t*.
Ps 5: 9 with their *t* they speak deceit.
34:13 keep your *t* from evil
37:30 and his *t* speaks what is just.
39: 1 and keep my *t* from sin;
51:14 my *t* will sing of your righteousness
52: 4 O you deceitful *t*!
71:24 My *t* will tell of your righteous acts
119:172 May my *t* sing of your word,
137: 6 May my *t* cling to the roof
139: 4 Before a word is on my *t*
Pr 6:17 a lying *t*,
10:19 but he who holds his *t* is wise.
12:18 but the *t* of the wise brings healing.
15: 4 The *t* that brings healing is a tree
17:20 he whose *t* is deceitful falls
21:23 He who guards his mouth and his *t*
25:15 and a gentle *t* can break a bone.
26:28 A lying *t* hates those it hurts,
28:23 than he who has a flattering *t*.
31:26 and faithful instruction is on her *t*.
SS 4:11 milk and honey are under your *t*.
Isa 32: 4 and the stammering *t* will be fluent
45:23 by me every *t* will swear.
50: 4 has given me an instructed *t*,
59: 3 and your *t* mutters wicked things.
Lk 16:24 of his finger in water and cool my *t*,
Ro 14:11 every *t* will confess to God.' "
1Co 14: 2 speaks in a *t* does not speak to men
14: 4 He who speaks in a *t* edifies himself
14: 9 intelligible words with your *t*,
14:13 in a *t* should pray that he may
14:19 than ten thousand words in a *t*.
14:26 revelation, a *t* or an interpretation.
14:27 If anyone speaks in a *t*, two—
Php 2:11 every *t* confess that Jesus Christ is
Jas 1:26 does not keep a tight rein on his *t*,
3: 5 Likewise the *t* is a small part
3: 8 but no man can tame the *t*.
1Jn 3:18 or *t* but with actions and in truth.

TONGUES (TONGUE)

Ps 12: 4 "We will triumph with our *t*;
126: 2 our *t* with songs of joy.
Isa 28:11 with foreign lips and strange *t*
66:18 and gather all nations and *t*,
Jer 23:31 the prophets who wag their own *t*
Mk 16:17 in new *t*; they will pick up snakes
Ac 2: 3 to be *t* of fire that separated
2: 4 and began to speak in other *t*
10:46 For they heard them speaking in *t*
19: 6 and they spoke in *t* and prophesied
Ro 3:13 their *t* practice deceit."
1Co 12:10 still another the interpretation of *t*.
12:28 speaking in different kinds of *t*.
12:30 Do all speak in *t*? Do all interpret?
13: 1 If I speak in the *t* of men
13: 8 where there are *t*, they will be
14: 5 greater than one who speaks in *t*,
14:18 speak in *t* more than all of you.
14:21 "Through men of strange *t*
14:39 and do not forbid speaking in *t*.

TOOK (TAKE)

Isa 53: 4 Surely he *t* up our infirmities
Mt 8:17 "He *t* up our infirmities
26:26 they were eating, Jesus *t* bread,
26:27 Then he *t* the cup, gave thanks
1Co 11:23 the night he was betrayed, *t* bread,
11:25 after supper he *t* the cup, saying,
Php 3:12 for which Christ Jesus *t* hold of me.

TOOTH (TEETH)

Ex 21:24 eye for eye, *t* for *t*, hand for hand,
Mt 5:38 'Eye for eye, and *t* for *t*.'

TOP

Dt 28:13 you will always be at the *t*,
Isa 1: 6 of your foot to the *t* of your head
Mt 27:51 torn in two from *t* to bottom.

TORMENT (TORMENTED TORMENTORS)

Lk 16:28 also come to this place of *t*.'
2Co 12: 7 a messenger of Satan, to *t* me.

TORMENTED (TORMENT)

Rev 20:10 They will be *t* day and night

TORMENTORS (TORMENT)

Ps 137: 3 our *t* demanded songs of joy;

TORN

Gal 4:15 you would have *t* out your eyes
Php 1:23 I do not know! I am *t*

TORTURED*

Mt 18:34 turned him over to the jailers to be *t*,
Heb 11:35 Others were *t* and refused

TOSSED (TOSSING)

Eph 4:14 *t* back and forth by the waves,
Jas 1: 6 of the sea, blown and *t* by the wind.

TOSSING (TOSSED)

Isa 57:20 But the wicked are like the *t* sea,

TOUCH (TOUCHED TOUCHES)

Ge 3: 3 you must not *t* it, or you will die.' "
Ex 19:12 go up the mountain or *t* the foot
Ps 105: 15 "Do not *t* my anointed ones;
Mt 9:21 If I only *t* his cloak, I will be healed
Lk 18:15 babies to Jesus to have him *t* them.
24:39 It is I myself! *T* me and see;
2Co 6:17 *T* no unclean thing,
Col 2:21 Do not taste! Do not *t*!"?

TOUCHED (TOUCH)

1Sa 10:26 men whose hearts God had *t*.
Isa 6: 7 With it he *t* my mouth and said,
Mt 14:36 and all who *t* him were healed.
Lk 8:45 "Who *t* me?" Jesus asked.
1Jn 1: 1 looked at and our hands have *t*—

TOUCHES (TOUCH)

Ex 19:12 Whoever *t* the mountain shall
Zec 2: 8 for whoever *t* you *t* the apple

TOWER

Ge 11: 4 with a *t* that reaches to the heavens
Pr 18:10 of the LORD is a strong *t*;

TOWN (TOWNS)

Mt 2:23 and lived in a *t* called Nazareth.

TOWNS (TOWN)
Nu 35: 2 to give the Levites *t* to live
35: 15 These six *t* will be a place of refuge
Jer 11: 13 as many gods as you have *t*,
Mt 9: 35 Jesus went through all the *t*

TRACING*
Ro 11: 33 and his paths beyond *t* out!

TRACK
Job 14: 16 but not keep *t* of my sin.

TRADERS (TRADING)
1Ti 1: 10 for slave *t* and liars and perjurers—

TRADING (TRADERS)
1Ki 10: 22 The king had a fleet of *t* ships at sea
Pr 31: 18 She sees that her *t* is profitable,

TRADITION (TRADITIONS)
Mt 15: 2 "Why do your disciples break the *t*
15: 6 word of God for the sake of your *t*.
Mk 7: 13 by your *t* that you have handed
Col 2: 8 which depends on human *t*

TRADITIONS (TRADITION)
Mk 7: 8 are holding on to the *t* of men."
Gal 1: 14 zealous for the *t* of my fathers.

TRAIL
1Ti 5: 24 the sins of others *t* behind them.

TRAIN* (TRAINED TRAINING)
Ps 68: 18 you led captives in your *t*;
Pr 22: 6 *T* a child in the way he should go,
Isa 2: 4 nor will they *t* for war anymore.
6: 1 the *t* of his robe filled the temple.
Mic 4: 3 nor will they *t* for war anymore.
Eph 4: 8 he led captives in his *t*
1Ti 4: 7 rather, *t* yourself to be godly.
Tit 2: 4 they can *t* the younger women

TRAINED (TRAIN)
Lk 6: 40 everyone who is fully *t* will be like
Ac 22: 3 Under Gamaliel I was thoroughly *t*
2Co 11: 6 I may not be a *t* speaker,
Heb 5: 14 by constant use have *t* themselves
12: 11 for those who have been *t* by it.

TRAINING* (TRAIN)
1Co 9: 25 in the games goes into strict *t*.
Eph 6: 4 up in the *t* and instruction
1Ti 4: 8 For physical *t* is of some value,
2Ti 3: 16 correcting and *t* in righteousness,

TRAITOR (TRAITORS)
Lk 6: 16 and Judas Iscariot, who became a *t*.
Jn 18: 5 Judas the *t* was standing there

TRAITORS (TRAITOR)
Ps 59: 5 show no mercy to wicked *t*.

TRAMPLE (TRAMPLED)
Joel 3: 13 Come, *t* the grapes,
Am 2: 7 They *t* on the heads of the poor
5: 11 You *t* on the poor
8: 4 Hear this, you who *t* the needy
Mt 7: 6 they may *t* them under their feet,
Lk 10: 19 I have given you authority to *t*

TRAMPLED (TRAMPLE)
Isa 63: 6 I *t* the nations in my anger;
Lk 21: 24 Jerusalem will be *t*
Heb 10: 29 to be punished who has *t* the Son
Rev 14: 20 They were *t* in the winepress

TRANCE*
Ac 10: 10 was being prepared, he fell into a *t*.
11: 5 and in a *t* I saw a vision.
22: 17 into a *t* and saw the Lord speaking.

TRANQUILLITY*
Ecc 4: 6 Better one handful with *t*

TRANSACTIONS*
Ru 4: 7 method of legalizing *t* in Israel.)

TRANSCENDS*
Php 4: 7 which *t* all understanding,

TRANSFIGURED*
Mt 17: 2 There he was *t* before them.
Mk 9: 2 There he was *t* before them.

TRANSFORM* (TRANSFORMED)
Php 3: 21 will *t* our lowly bodies

TRANSFORMED (TRANSFORM)
Ro 12: 2 be *t* by the renewing of your mind.
2Co 3: 18 are being *t* into his likeness

TRANSGRESSED* (TRANSGRESSION)
Da 9: 11 All Israel has *t* your law

TRANSGRESSION* (TRANSGRESSED TRANSGRESSIONS TRANSGRESSORS)
Ps 19: 13 innocent of great *t*.
Isa 53: 8 for the *t* of my people he was
Da 9: 24 and your holy city to finish *t*,
Mic 1: 5 All this is because of Jacob's *t*,
1: 5 What is Jacob's *t*?
3: 8 to declare to Jacob his *t*,
6: 7 Shall I offer my firstborn for my *t*,
7: 18 who pardons sin and forgives the *t*
Ro 4: 15 where there is no law there is no *t*.
11: 11 Rather, because of their *t*,
11: 12 if their *t* means riches for the world

TRANSGRESSIONS* (TRANSGRESSION)
Ps 32: 1 whose *t* are forgiven,
32: 5 my *t* to the LORD"—
39: 8 Save me from all my *t*;
51: 1 blot out my *t*.
51: 3 For I know my *t*,
65: 3 you forgave our *t*.
103: 12 so far has he removed our *t* from us
Isa 43: 25 your *t*, for my own sake,
50: 1 of your *t* your mother was sent
53: 5 But he was pierced for our *t*,
Mic 1: 13 for the *t* of Israel
Ro 4: 7 whose *t* are forgiven,
Gal 3: 19 because of *t* until the Seed to whom
Eph 2: 1 you were dead in your *t* and sins,
2: 5 even when we were dead in *t*—

TRANSGRESSORS* (TRANSGRESSION)
Ps 51: 13 Then I will teach *t* your ways,
Isa 53: 12 and made intercession for the *t*.
53: 12 and was numbered with the *t*.
Lk 22: 37 'And he was numbered with the *t*';

TRAP (TRAPPED TRAPS)
Ps 69: 22 may it become retribution and a *t*.
Pr 20: 25 a *t* for a man to dedicate something
28: 10 will fall into his own *t*,
Isa 8: 14 a *t* and a snare.
Mt 22: 15 and laid plans to *t* him in his words.
Lk 21: 34 close on you unexpectedly like a *t*.
Ro 11: 9 their table become a snare and a *t*,
1Ti 3: 7 into disgrace and into the devil's *t*.
6: 9 and a *t* and into many foolish
2Ti 2: 26 and escape from the *t* of the devil,

TRAPPED (TRAP)
Pr 6: 2 if you have been *t* by what you said
12: 13 An evil man is *t* by his sinful talk,

TRAPS (TRAP)
Jos 23: 13 they will become snares and *t*
La 4: 20 was caught in their *t*.

TRAVEL (TRAVELER)
Pr 4: 15 Avoid it, do not *t* on it;
Mt 23: 15 You *t* over land and sea

TRAVELER (TRAVEL)
Job 31: 32 door was always open to the *t*—
Jer 14: 8 like a *t* who stays only a night?

TREACHEROUS (TREACHERY)
Ps 25: 3 who are *t* without excuse.
2Ti 3: 4 not lovers of the good, *t*, rash,

TREACHERY (TREACHEROUS)
Isa 59: 13 rebellion and *t* against the LORD,

TREAD (TREADING TREADS)
Ps 91: 13 You will *t* upon the lion

TREADING (TREAD)
Dt 25: 4 an ox while it is *t* out the grain.
1Co 9: 9 an ox while it is *t* out the grain."
1Ti 5: 18 the ox while it is *t* out the grain,"

TREADS (TREAD)
Rev 19: 15 He *t* the winepress of the fury

TREASURE (TREASURED TREASURES TREASURY)
Pr 2: 4 and search for it as for hidden *t*,
Isa 33: 6 of the LORD is the key to this *t*.
Mt 6: 21 For where your *t* is, there your
13: 44 of heaven is like *t* hidden in a field.
Lk 12: 33 a *t* in heaven that will not be
2Co 4: 7 But we have this *t* in jars of clay
1Ti 6: 19 In this way they will lay up *t*

TREASURED (TREASURE)
Ex 19: 5 you will be my *t* possession.
Dt 7: 6 to be his people, his *t* possession.
26: 18 his *t* possession as he promised,
Job 23: 12 I have *t* the words
Mal 3: 17 when I make up my *t* possession.
Lk 2: 19 But Mary *t* up all these things
2: 51 But his mother *t* all these things

TREASURES (TREASURE)
1Ch 29: 3 my God I now give my personal *t*
Pr 10: 2 Ill-gotten *t* are of no value,
Mt 6: 19 up for yourselves *t* on earth,
13: 52 out of his storeroom new *t*
Col 2: 3 in whom are hidden all the *t*
Heb 11: 26 of greater value than the *t* of Egypt,

TREASURY (TREASURE)
Mk 12: 43 more into the *t* than all the others.

TREAT (TREATED TREATING TREATMENT)
Lev 22: 2 sons to *t* with respect the sacred
Ps 103: 10 he does not *t* us as our sins deserve
Mt 18: 17 *t* him as you would a pagan
18: 35 my heavenly Father will *t* each
Eph 6: 9 *t* your slaves in the same way.
1Th 5: 20 do not *t* prophecies with contempt.
1Ti 5: 1 *T* younger men as brothers,
1Pe 3: 7 and *t* them with respect

TREATED (TREAT)
Lev 19: 34 The alien living with you must be *t*
25: 40 He is to be *t* as a hired worker
1Sa 24: 17 "You have *t* me well, but I have
Heb 10: 29 who has *t* as an unholy thing

TREATING (TREAT)
Ge 18: 25 *t* the righteous and the wicked
Heb 12: 7 as discipline; God is *t* you as sons.

TREATMENT (TREAT)
Col 2: 23 and their harsh *t* of the body,

TREATY
Ex 34: 12 not to make a *t* with those who live
Dt 7: 2 Make no *t* with them, and show
23: 6 Do not seek a *t* of friendship with them

TREE (TREES)
Ge 2: 9 and the *t* of the knowledge of good
2: 9 of the garden were the *t* of life
Dt 21: 23 hung on a *t* is under God's curse.
2Sa 18: 9 Absalom's head got caught in the *t*.
1Ki 14: 23 and under every spreading *t*.
Ps 1: 3 He is like a *t* planted by streams
52: 8 But I am like an olive *t*
92: 12 righteous will flourish like a palm *t*,
Pr 3: 18 She is a *t* of life to those who
11: 30 of the righteous is a *t* of life,
27: 18 He who tends a fig *t* will eat its fruit
Isa 65: 22 For as the days of a *t*,
Jer 17: 8 He will be like a *t* planted
Eze 17: 24 I the LORD bring down the tall *t*
Da 4: 10 before me stood a *t* in the middle
Mic 4: 4 and under his own fig *t*,
Zec 3: 10 to sit under his vine and fig *t*,'
Mt 3: 10 every *t* that does not produce good
12: 33 for a *t* is recognized by its fruit.
Lk 19: 4 climbed a sycamore-fig *t* to see him
Ac 5: 30 killed by hanging him on a *t*.
Ro 11: 24 be grafted into their own olive *t*!
Gal 3: 13 is everyone who is hung on a *t*."
Jas 3: 12 My brothers, can a fig *t* bear olives,
1Pe 2: 24 sins in his body on the *t*,
Rev 2: 7 the right to eat from the *t* of life,
22: 2 side of the river stood the *t* of life,
22: 14 they may have the right to the *t*
22: 19 from him his share in the *t* of life

TREES (TREE)
Jdg 9: 8 One day the *t* went out
Ps 96: 12 Then all the *t* of the forest will sing
Isa 55: 12 and all the *t* of the field
Mt 3: 10 The ax is already at the root of the *t*

Mk 8:24 they look like *t* walking around."
Jude :12 autumn *t*, without fruit

TREMBLE (TREMBLED TREMBLES TREMBLING)

Ex 15:14 The nations will hear and *t*;
1Ch 16:30 *T* before him, all the earth!
Ps 114: 7 *T*, O earth, at the presence
Jer 5:22 "Should you not *t* in my presence?
Eze 38:20 of the earth will *t* at my presence.
Joel 2: 1 Let all who live in the land *t*,
Hab 3: 6 he looked, and made the nations *t*.

TREMBLED (TREMBLE)

Ex 19:16 Everyone in the camp *t*.
20:18 in smoke, they *t* with fear.
2Sa 22: 8 "The earth *t* and quaked,
Ac 7:32 Moses *t* with fear and did not dare

TREMBLES (TREMBLE)

Ps 97: 4 the earth sees and *t*.
104:32 he who looks at the earth, and it *t*,
Isa 66: 2 and *t* at my word.
Jer 10:10 When he is angry, the earth *t*;
Na 1: 5 The earth *t* at his presence,

TREMBLING (TREMBLE)

Ps 2:11 and rejoice with *t*.
Da 10:10 set me *t* on my hands and knees.
Php 2:12 out your salvation with fear and *t*,
Heb 12:21 terrifying that Moses said, "I am *t*

TRESPASS* (TRESPASSES)

Ro 5:15 But the gift is not like the *t*.
5:15 died by the *t* of the one man,
5:17 For if, by the *t* of the one man,
5:18 result of one *t* was condemnation
5:20 added so that the *t* might increase.

TRESPASSES* (TRESPASS)

Ro 5:16 but the gift followed many *t*

TRIAL (TRIALS)

Ps 37:33 condemned when brought to *t*.
Mk 13:11 you are arrested and brought to *t*,
2Co 8: 2 most severe *t*, their overflowing
Jas 1:12 is the man who perseveres under *t*,
1Pe 4:12 at the painful *t* you are suffering,
Rev 3:10 you from the hour of *t* that is going

TRIALS* (TRIAL)

Dt 7:19 saw with your own eyes the great *t*,
29: 3 own eyes you saw those great *t*,
Lk 22:28 who have stood by me in my *t*.
1Th 3: 3 one would be unsettled by these *t*.
2Th 1: 4 the persecutions and *t* you are
Jas 1: 2 whenever you face *t* of many kinds,
1Pe 1: 6 had to suffer grief in all kinds of *t*.
2Pe 2: 9 how to rescue godly men from *t*

TRIBE (HALF-TRIBE TRIBES)

Heb 7:13 no one from that *t* has ever served
Rev 5: 5 See, the Lion of the *t* of Judah,
5: 9 God from every *t* and language
11: 9 men from every people, *t*,
14: 6 to every nation, *t*, language

TRIBES (TRIBE)

Ge 49:28 All these are the twelve *t* of Israel,
Mt 19:28 judging the twelve *t* of Israel.

TRIBULATION*

Rev 7:14 who have come out of the great *t*;

TRICKERY*

Ac 13:10 full of all kinds of deceit and *t*.
2Co 12:16 fellow that I am, I caught you by *t*!

TRIED (TRY)

Ps 73:16 When I *t* to understand all this,
95: 9 where your fathers tested and *t* me,
Heb 3: 9 where your fathers tested and *t* me

TRIES (TRY)

Lk 17:33 Whoever *t* to keep his life will lose

TRIMMED

Mt 25: 7 virgins woke up and *t* their lamps.

TRIUMPH (TRIUMPHAL TRIUMPHED TRIUMPHING TRIUMPHS)

Ps 25: 2 nor let my enemies *t* over me.
54: 7 my eyes have looked in *t*
112: 8 in the end he will look in *t*
118: 7 I will look in *t* on my enemies.
Pr 28:12 When the righteous *t*, there is great
Isa 42:13 and will *t* over his enemies.

TRIUMPHAL* (TRIUMPH)

Isa 60:11 their kings led in *t* procession.
2Co 2:14 us in *t* procession in Christ

TRIUMPHED (TRIUMPH)

Rev 5: 5 of Judah, the Root of David, has *t*.

TRIUMPHING* (TRIUMPH)

Col 2:15 of them, *t* over them by the cross.

TRIUMPHS* (TRIUMPH)

Jas 2:13 Mercy *t* over judgment! What

TROUBLE (TROUBLED TROUBLES)

Ge 41:51 God has made me forget all my *t*
Jos 7:25 Why have you brought this *t* on us?
Job 2:10 good from God, and not *t*?"
5: 7 Yet man is born to *t*
14: 1 is of few days and full of *t*.
42:11 him over all the *t* the LORD had
Ps 7:14 conceives *t* gives birth
7:16 The *t* he causes recoils on himself;
9: 9 a stronghold in times of *t*.
10:14 But you, O God, do see *t* and grief;
22:11 for *t* is near
27: 5 For in the day of *t*
32: 7 you will protect me from *t*
37:39 he is their stronghold in time of *t*.
41: 1 LORD delivers him in times of *t*.
46: 1 an ever-present help in *t*.
50:15 and call upon me in the day of *t*;
59:16 my refuge in times of *t*.
66:14 spoke when I was in *t*.
86: 7 In the day of my *t* I will call to you,
91:15 I will be with him in *t*,
107: 6 to the LORD in their *t*,
107:13 they cried to the LORD in their *t*,
116: 3 I was overcome by *t* and sorrow.
119:143 *T* and distress have come upon me,
138: 7 Though I walk in the midst of *t*,
143:11 righteousness, bring me out of *t*.
Pr 11: 8 righteous man is rescued from *t*,
11:17 a cruel man brings *t* on himself
11:29 He who brings *t* on his family will
12:13 but a righteous man escapes *t*.
12:21 but the wicked have their fill of *t*.
15:27 A greedy man brings *t* to his family
19:23 one rests content, untouched by *t*.
22: 8 He who sows wickedness reaps *t*,
24:10 If you falter in times of *t*,
25:19 on the unfaithful in times of *t*.
28:14 he who hardens his heart falls into *t*
Jer 30: 7 It will be a time of *t* for Jacob,
Na 1: 7 a refuge in times of *t*.
Zep 1:15 a day of *t* and ruin,
Mt 6:34 Each day has enough *t* of its own.
13:21 When *t* or persecution comes
Jn 16:33 In this world you will have *t*.
Ro 8:35 Shall *t* or hardship or persecution
2Co 1: 4 those in any *t* with the comfort we
2Th 1: 6 *t* to those who *t* you
Jas 5:13 one of you in *t*? He should pray.

TROUBLED (TROUBLE)

Ps 38:18 I am *t* by my sin.
Isa 38:14 I am *t*; O Lord, come to my aid!"
Mk 14:33 began to be deeply distressed and *t*.
Jn 14: 1 "Do not let your hearts be *t*.
14:27 Do not let your hearts be *t*
2Th 1: 7 and give relief to you who are *t*,

TROUBLES (TROUBLE)

Ps 34: 6 he saved him out of all his *t*.
34:17 he delivers them from all their *t*.
34:19 A righteous man may have many *t*,
40:12 For *t* without number surround me
54: 7 he has delivered me from all my *t*,
1Co 7:28 those who marry will face many *t*
2Co 1: 4 who comforts us in all our *t*,
4:17 and momentary *t* are achieving
6: 4 in *t*, hardships and distresses;
7: 4 in all our *t* my joy knows no bounds
Php 4:14 good of you to share in my *t*.

TRUE (TRUTH)

Nu 11:23 not what I say will come *t* for you."
12: 7 this is not *t* of my servant Moses;
Dt 18:22 does not take place or come *t*,
Jos 23:15 of the LORD your God has come *t*
1Sa 9: 6 and everything he says comes *t*.
1Ki 10: 6 and your wisdom is *t*.
2Ch 6:17 your servant David come *t*.
2Ch 15: 3 was without the *t* God,
Ps 33: 4 of the LORD is right and *t*;
119:142 and your law is *t*.
119:151 and all your commands are *t*.
119:160 All your words are *t*;
Pr 8: 7 My mouth speaks what is *t*,
22:21 teaching you *t* and reliable words,
Jer 10:10 But the LORD is the *t* God;
28: 9 only if his prediction comes *t*."
Eze 33:33 "When all this comes *t*—
Lk 16:11 who will trust you with *t* riches?
Jn 1: 9 The *t* light that gives light
4:23 when the *t* worshipers will worship
6:32 Father who gives you the *t* bread
7:28 on my own, but he who sent me is *t*
15: 1 "I am the *t* vine, and my Father is
17: 3 the only *t* God, and Jesus Christ,
19:35 testimony, and his testimony is *t*.
21:24 We know that his testimony is *t*.
Ac 10:34 "I now realize how *t* it is that God
11:23 all to remain *t* to the Lord
14:22 them to remain *t* to the faith.
17:11 day to see if what Paul said was *t*.
Ro 3: 4 Let God be *t*, and every man a liar.
Php 4: 8 whatever is *t*, whatever is noble,
1Jn 2: 8 and the *t* light is already shining.
5:20 He is the *t* God and eternal life.
Rev 19: 9 "These are the *t* words of God."
22: 6 These words are trustworthy and *t*.

TRUMPET (TRUMPETS)

Isa 27:13 And in that day a great *t* will sound
Eze 33: 5 Since he heard the sound of the *t*
Zec 9:14 Sovereign LORD will sound the *t*;
Mt 24:31 send his angels with a loud *t* call,
1Co 14: 8 if the *t* does not sound a clear call,
15:52 For the *t* will sound, the dead will
1Th 4:16 and with the *t* call of God,
Rev 8: 7 The first angel sounded his *t*,

TRUMPETS (TRUMPET)

Jdg 7:19 They blew their *t* and broke the jars
Rev 8: 2 and to them were given seven *t*.

TRUST* (ENTRUST ENTRUSTED TRUSTED TRUSTFULLY TRUSTING TRUSTS TRUSTWORTHY)

Ex 14:31 put their *t* in him and in Moses his
19: 9 and will always put their *t* in you."
Nu 20:12 "Because you did not *t*
Dt 1:32 you did not *t* in the LORD your
9:23 You did not *t* him or obey him.
28:52 walls in which you *t* fall down.
Jdg 11:20 did not *t* Israel to pass
2Ki 17:14 who did not *t* in the LORD their
18:30 to *t* in the LORD when he says,
1Ch 9:22 to their positions of *t* by David
Job 4:18 If God places no *t* in his servants,
15:15 If God places no *t* in his holy ones,
31:24 "If I have put my *t* in gold
39:12 Can you *t* him to bring
Ps 4: 5 and *t* in the LORD.
9:10 Those who know your name will *t*
13: 5 But I *t* in your unfailing love;
20: 7 Some *t* in chariots and some
20: 7 we *t* in the name of the LORD our
22: 4 In you our fathers put their *t*;
22: 9 you made me *t* in you
25: 2 I lift up my soul; in you I *t*,
31: 6 I *t* in the LORD.
31:14 But I *t* in you, O LORD;
33:21 for we *t* in his holy name.
37: 3 *T* in the LORD and do good;
37: 5 *t* in him and he will do this:
40: 3 and put their *t* in the LORD.
40: 4 who makes the LORD his *t*,
44: 6 I do not *t* in my bow,
49: 6 those who *t* in their wealth
49:13 of those who *t* in themselves,
52: 8 I *t* in God's unfailing love
55:23 But as for me, I *t* in you.
56: 3 I will *t* in you.
56: 4 in God I *t*; I will not be afraid.
56:11 in God I *t*; I will not be afraid.
62: 8 *T* in him at all times, O people;
62:10 Do not *t* in extortion
78: 7 Then they would put their *t* in God
78:22 or *t* in his deliverance.
91: 2 my God, in whom I *t*."
115: 8 and so will all who *t* in them.
115: 9 O house of Israel, *t* in the LORD—
115:10 O house of Aaron, *t* in the LORD
115:11 You who fear him, *t* in the LORD
118: 8 than to *t* in man.
118: 9 than to *t* in princes.

Ps 119: 42 for I *t* in your word.
125: 1 Those who *t* in the LORD are like
135: 18 and so will all who *t* in them.
143: 8 for I have put my *t* in you.
146: 3 Do not put your *t* in princes,
Pr 3: 5 *T* in the LORD with all your heart
21:22 the stronghold in which they *t*.
22:19 So that your *t* may be in the LORD
Isa 8:17 I will put my *t* in him.
12: 2 I will *t* and not be afraid.
26: 4 *T* in the LORD forever,
30:15 in quietness and *t* is your strength,
31: 1 who *t* in the multitude
36:15 to *t* in the LORD when he says,
42:17 But those who *t* in idols,
50:10 *t* in the name of the LORD
Jer 2:37 LORD has rejected those you *t*;
5:17 the fortified cities in which you *t*.
7: 4 Do not *t* in deceptive words
7:14 the temple you *t* in, the place I gave
9: 4 do not *t* your brothers.
12: 6 Do not *t* them,
28:15 you have persuaded this nation to *t*
39:18 you *t* in me, declares the LORD.' "
48: 7 Since you *t* in your deeds
49: 4 you *t* in your riches and say,
49:11 Your widows too can *t* in me."
Mic 7: 5 Do not *t* a neighbor;
Na 1: 7 He cares for those who *t* in him,
Zep 3: 2 She does not *t* in the LORD,
3:12 who *t* in the name of the LORD.
Lk 16:11 who will *t* you with true riches?
Jn 12:36 Put your *t* in the light
14: 1 *T* in God; *t* also in me.
Ac 14:23 Lord, in whom they had put their *t*.
Ro 15:13 you with all joy and peace as you *t*
1Co 4: 2 been given a *t* must prove faithful.
9:17 discharging the *t* committed
2Co 13: 6 I *t* that you will discover that we
Heb 2:13 "I will put my *t* in him."

TRUSTED* (TRUST)

1Sa 27:12 Achish *t* David and said to himself,
2Ki 18: 5 Hezekiah *t* in the LORD, the God
1Ch 5:20 their prayers, because they *t*
Job 12:20 He silences the lips of *t* advisers
Ps 5: 9 from their mouth can be *t*;
22: 4 they *t* and you delivered them.
22: 5 in you they *t* and were not
26: 1 I have *t* in the LORD
41: 9 Even my close friend, whom I *t*,
52: 7 but *t* in his great wealth
Isa 20: 5 Those who *t* in Cush and boasted
25: 9 This is the LORD, we *t* in him;
25: 9 we *t* in him, and he saved us.
47:10 You have *t* in your wickedness
Jer 13:25 and *t* in false gods.
38:22 those *t* friends of yours.
48:13 ashamed when they *t* in Bethel.
Eze 16:15 " 'But you *t* in your beauty
Da 3:28 They *t* in him and defied the king's
6:23 because he had *t* in his God.
Lk 11:22 the armor in which the man *t*
16:10 *t* with very little can also be *t*
Ac 12:20 a *t* personal servant of the king,
Tit 2:10 but to show that they can be fully *t*,
3: 8 so that those who have *t*

TRUSTFULLY* (TRUST)

Pr 3:29 who lives *t* near you.

TRUSTING* (TRUST)

Job 15:31 by *t* what is worthless,
Ps 112: 7 his heart is steadfast, *t*
Isa 2:22 Stop *t* in man,
Jer 7: 8 you are *t* in deceptive words that

TRUSTS* (TRUST)

Job 8:14 What he *t* in is fragile;
Ps 21: 7 For the king *t* in the LORD;
22: 8 "He *t* in the LORD;
28: 7 my heart *t* in him, and I am helped.
32:10 surrounds the man who *t* in him.
84:12 blessed is the man who *t* in you.
86: 2 who *t* in you.
Pr 11:28 Whoever *t* in his riches will fall,
16:20 blessed is he who *t* in the LORD.
28:25 he who *t* in the LORD will prosper.
28:26 He who *t* in himself is a fool,
29:25 whoever *t* in the LORD is kept safe
Isa 26: 3 because he *t* in you.
28:16 one who *t* will never be dismayed.
Jer 17: 5 "Cursed is the one who *t* in man,
17: 7 blessed is the man who *t*
Eze 33:13 but then he *t* in his righteousness
Hab 2:18 For he who makes it *t*
Mt 27:43 He *t* in God.
Ro 4: 5 but *t* God who justifies the wicked,
9:33 one who *t* in him will never be put
10:11 "Anyone who *t* in him will never
1Co 13: 7 always protects, always *t*,
1Pe 2: 6 and the one who *t* in him

TRUSTWORTHY* (TRUST)

Ex 18:21 *t* men who hate dishonest gain—
2Sa 7:28 you are God! Your words are *t*,
Ne 13:13 these men were considered *t*.
Ps 19: 7 The statutes of the LORD are *t*,
111: 7 all his precepts are *t*.
119: 86 All your commands are *t*;
119:138 they are fully *t*.
Pr 11:13 but a *t* man keeps a secret.
13:17 but a *t* envoy brings healing.
25:13 is a *t* messenger to those who send
Da 2:45 and the interpretation is *t*."
6: 4 he was *t* and neither corrupt
Lk 16:11 So if you have not been *t*
16:12 And if you have not been *t*
19:17 'Because you have been *t*
1Co 7:25 one who by the Lord's mercy is *t*.
1Ti 1:15 Here is a *t* saying that deserves full
3: 1 Here is a *t* saying: If anyone sets his
3:11 but temperate and *t* in everything.
4: 9 This is a *t* saying that deserves full
2Ti 2:11 Here is a *t* saying:
Tit 1: 9 must hold firmly to the *t* message
3: 8 This is a *t* saying.
Rev 21: 5 for these words are *t* and true."
22: 6 "These words are *t* and true.

TRUTH* (TRUE TRUTHFUL TRUTHFULNESS TRUTHS)

Ge 42:16 tested to see if you are telling the *t*.
1Ki 17:24 LORD from your mouth is the *t*."
22:16 the *t* in the name of the LORD?"
2Ch 18:15 the *t* in the name of the LORD?"
Ps 15: 2 who speaks the *t* from his heart
25: 5 guide me in your *t* and teach me,
26: 3 and I walk continually in your *t*.
31: 5 redeem me, O LORD, the God of *t*
40:10 do not conceal your love and your *t*
40:11 your *t* always protect me.
43: 3 Send forth your light and your *t*,
45: 4 victoriously in behalf of *t*, humility
51: 6 Surely you desire *t*
52: 3 than speaking the *t*.
86:11 and I will walk in your *t*;
96:13 and the peoples in his *t*.
119: 30 I have chosen the way of *t*;
119: 43 of *t* from my mouth,
145: 18 to all who call on him in *t*.
Pr 16:13 they value a man who speaks the *t*.
23:23 Buy the *t* and do not sell it;
Isa 45:19 I, the LORD, speak the *t*;
48: 1 but not in *t* or righteousness—
59:14 *t* has stumbled in the streets,
59:15 *T* is nowhere to be found,
65:16 will do so by the God of *t*;
65:16 will swear by the God of *t*.
Jer 5: 1 who deals honestly and seeks the *t*,
5: 3 do not your eyes look for *t*?
7:28 *T* has perished; it has vanished
9: 3 it is not by *t*
9: 5 and no one speaks the *t*.
26:15 for in *t* the LORD has sent me
Da 8:12 and *t* was thrown to the ground.
9:13 and giving attention to your *t*.
10:21 what is written in the Book of *T*.
11: 2 "Now then, I tell you the *t*:
Am 5:10 and despise him who tells the *t*.
Zec 8: 3 will be called the City of *T*,
8:16 are to do: Speak the *t* to each other,
8:19 Therefore love *t* and peace."
Mt 5:18 I tell you the *t*, until heaven
5:26 I tell you the *t*, you will not get out
6: 2 I tell you the *t*, they have received
6: 5 I tell you the *t*, they have received
6:16 I tell you the *t*, they have received
8:10 "I tell you the *t*, I have not found
10:15 I tell you the *t*, it will be more
10:23 I tell you the *t*, you will not finish
10:42 I tell you the *t*, he will certainly not
11:11 I tell you the *t*: Among those born
13:17 For I tell you the *t*, many prophets
16:28 I tell you the *t*, some who are
17:20 I tell you the *t*, if you have faith
18: 3 And he said: "I tell you the *t*,
18:13 And if he finds it, I tell you the *t*,
18:18 "I tell you the *t*, whatever you bind
19:23 to his disciples, "I tell you the *t*,
Mt 19:28 "I tell you the *t*, at the renewal
21:21 Jesus replied, "I tell you the *t*,
21:31 Jesus said to them, "I tell you the *t*,
22:16 of God in accordance with the *t*.
23:36 I tell you the *t*, all this will come
24: 2 "I tell you the *t*, not one stone here
24:34 I tell you the *t*, this generation will
24:47 I tell you the *t*, he will put him
25:12 'I tell you the *t*, I don't know you.'
25:40 The King will reply, 'I tell you the *t*
25:45 "He will reply, 'I tell you the *t*,
26:13 tell you the *t*, wherever this gospel
26:21 "I tell you the *t*, one
26:34 "I tell you the *t*," Jesus answered,
Mk 3:28 I tell you the *t*, all the sins
5:33 with fear, told him the whole *t*.
8:12 I tell you the *t*, no sign will be given
9: 1 he said to them, "I tell you the *t*,
9:41 I tell you the *t*, anyone who gives
10:15 I tell you the *t*, anyone who will not
10:29 "I tell you the *t*," Jesus replied,
11:23 "I tell you the *t*, if anyone says
12:14 of God in accordance with the *t*.
12:43 Jesus said, "I tell you the *t*,
13:30 I tell you the *t*, this generation will
14: 9 I tell you the *t*, wherever the gospel
14:18 "I tell you the *t*, one
14:25 "I tell you the *t*, I will not drink
14:30 "I tell you the *t*," Jesus answered,
Lk 4:24 "I tell you the *t*," he continued,
9:27 I tell you the *t*, some who are
12:37 I tell you the *t*, he will dress himself
12:44 I tell you the *t*, he will put him
18:17 I tell you the *t*, anyone who will not
18:29 I tell you the *t*," Jesus said to them,
20:21 of God in accordance with the *t*.
21: 3 "I tell you the *t*," he said, "this
21:32 tell you the *t*, this generation will
23:43 answered him, "I tell you the *t*,
Jn 1:14 from the Father, full of grace and *t*.
1:17 and *t* came through Jesus Christ.
1:51 "I tell you the *t*, you shall see
3: 3 "I tell you the *t*, no one can see
3: 5 Jesus answered, "I tell you the *t*,
3:11 I tell you the *t*, we speak
3:21 But whoever lives by the *t* comes
4:23 worship the Father in spirit and *t*,
4:24 must worship in spirit and in *t*."
5:19 "I tell you the *t*, the Son can do
5:24 "I tell you the *t*, whoever hears my
5:25 I tell you the *t*, a time is coming
5:33 and he has testified to the *t*.
6:26 "I tell you the *t*, you are looking
6:32 Jesus said to them, "I tell you the *t*,
6:47 I tell you the *t*, he who believes has
6:53 Jesus said to them, "I tell you the *t*,
7:18 the one who sent him is a man of *t*;
8:32 Then you will know the *t*,
8:32 and the *t* will set you free."
8:34 Jesus replied, "I tell you the *t*,
8:40 who has told you the *t* that I heard
8:44 to the *t*, for there is no *t* in him.
8:45 I tell the *t*, you do not believe me!
8:46 I am telling the *t*, why don't you
8:51 I tell you the *t*, if anyone keeps my
8:58 "I tell you the *t*," Jesus answered,
10: 1 "I tell you the *t*, the man who does
10: 7 "I tell you the *t*, I am the gate
12:24 I tell you the *t*, unless a kernel
13:16 I tell you the *t*, no servant is greater
13:20 I tell you the *t*, whoever accepts
13:21 "I tell you the *t*, one of you is going
13:38 I tell you the *t*, before the rooster
14: 6 I am the way and the *t* and the life.
14:12 I tell you the *t*, anyone who has
14:17 with you forever—the Spirit of *t*.
15:26 the Spirit of *t* who goes out
16: 7 But I tell you the *t*: It is
16:13 But when he, the Spirit of *t*, comes,
16:13 comes, he will guide you into all *t*.
16:20 I tell you the *t*, you will weep
16:23 I tell you the *t*, my Father will give
17:17 them by the *t*; your word is *t*.
18:23 if I spoke the *t*, why did you strike
18:37 into the world, to testify to the *t*.
18:37 on the side of *t* listens to me."
18:38 "What is *t*?" Pilate asked.
19:35 He knows that he tells the *t*,
21:18 I tell you the *t*, when you were
Ac 20:30 and distort the *t* in order
21:24 everybody will know there is no *t*
21:34 commander could not get at the *t*
24: 8 able to learn the *t* about all these
28:25 "The Holy Spirit spoke the *t*
Ro 1:18 of men who suppress the *t*

UNCIRCUMCISION

1Co 7:19 is nothing and *u* is nothing.
Gal 5: 6 neither circumcision nor *u* has any

UNCLEAN

Ge 7: 2 and two of every kind of *u* animal,
Lev 10:10 between the *u* and the clean,
11: 4 it is ceremonially *u* for you.
17:15 he will be ceremonially *u* till evening.
Isa 6: 5 ruined! For I am a man of *u* lips,
52:11 Touch no *u* thing!
Mt 15:11 mouth does not make him '*u*,'
Ac 10:14 never eaten anything impure or *u*."
Ro 14:14 fully convinced that no food is *u*
2Co 6:17 Touch no *u* thing,

UNCLOTHED*

2Co 5: 4 because we do not wish to be *u*

UNCONCERNED*

Eze 16:49 were arrogant, overfed and *u*;

UNCOVERED

Ru 3: 7 Ruth approached quietly, *u* his feet
1Co 11: 5 with her head *u* dishonors her head
11:13 to pray to God with her head *u*?
Heb 4:13 Everything is *u* and laid bare

UNDERGOES* (UNDERGOING)

Heb 12: 8 (and everyone *u* discipline),

UNDERGOING* (UNDERGOES)

1Pe 5: 9 the world are *u* the same kind

UNDERSTAND (UNDERSTANDING UNDERSTANDS UNDERSTOOD)

Ne 8: 8 the people could *u* what was being
Job 38: 4 Tell me, if you *u*.
42: 3 Surely I spoke of things I did not *u*,
Ps 14: 2 men to see if there are any who *u*,
73:16 When I tried to *u* all this,
119: 27 Let me *u* the teaching
119:125 that I may *u* your statutes.
Pr 2: 5 then you will *u* the fear
2: 9 Then you will *u* what is right
30:18 four that I do not *u*:
Ecc 7:25 to *u* the stupidity of wickedness
11: 5 so you cannot *u* the work of God,
Isa 6:10 *u* with their hearts,
44:18 know nothing, they *u* nothing;
52:15 they have not heard, they will *u*.
Jer 17: 9 Who can *u* it?
31:19 after I came to *u*,
Da 9:25 and *u* this: From the issuing
Hos 14: 9 Who is discerning? He will *u* them.
Mt 13:15 *u* with their hearts
24:15 Daniel—let the reader *u*—
Lk 24:45 so they could *u* the Scriptures.
Ac 8:30 "Do you *u* what you are reading?"
Ro 7:15 I do not *u* what I do.
15:21 those who have not heard will *u*."
1Co 2:12 that we may *u* what God has freely
2:14 and he cannot *u* them,
14:16 those who do not *u* say "Amen"
Eph 5:17 but *u* what the Lord's will is.
Heb 11: 3 By faith we *u* that the universe was
2Pe 1:20 you must *u* that no prophecy
3: 3 you must *u* that in the last days
3:16 some things that are hard to *u*,

UNDERSTANDING (UNDERSTAND)

1Ki 4:29 and a breadth of *u* as measureless
Job 12:12 Does not long life bring *u*?
28:12 Where does *u* dwell?
28:28 and to shun evil is *u*.' "
32: 8 of the Almighty, that gives him *u*.
36:26 How great is God—beyond our *u*!
37: 5 he does great things beyond our *u*.
Ps 111: 10 follow his precepts have good *u*.
119: 34 Give me *u*, and I will keep your law
119:100 I have more *u* than the elders,
119:104 I gain *u* from your precepts;
119:130 it gives *u* to the simple.
136: 5 who by his *u* made the heavens,
147: 5 his *u* has no limit.
Pr 2: 2 and applying your heart to *u*,
2: 6 his mouth come knowledge and *u*.
3: 5 and lean not on your own *u*;
3:13 the man who gains *u*,
4: 5 Get wisdom, get *u*;
4: 7 Though it cost all you have, get *u*.
7: 4 and call *u* your kinsman;
9:10 knowledge of the Holy One is *u*.
10:23 but a man of *u* delights in wisdom.
Pr 11:12 but a man of *u* holds his tongue.
14:29 A patient man has great *u*,
15:21 a man of *u* keeps a straight course.
15:32 whoever heeds correction gains *u*.
16:16 to choose *u* rather than silver!
16:22 *U* is a fountain of life
17:27 and a man of *u* is even-tempered.
18: 2 A fool finds no pleasure in *u*
19: 8 he who cherishes *u* prospers.
20: 5 but a man of *u* draws them out.
23:23 get wisdom, discipline and *u*.
Isa 11: 2 the Spirit of wisdom and of *u*,
40:28 and his *u* no one can fathom.
56:11 They are shepherds who lack *u*;
Jer 3:15 you with knowledge and *u*.
10:12 stretched out the heavens by his *u*.
Da 5:12 a keen mind and knowledge and *u*,
10:12 that you set your mind to gain *u*
Hos 4:11 which take away the *u*
Mk 4:12 and ever hearing but never *u*;
12:33 with all your *u* and with all your
Lk 2:47 who heard him was amazed at his *u*
2Co 6: 6 in purity, *u*, patience and kindness;
Eph 1: 8 on us with all wisdom and *u*.
Php 4: 7 of God, which transcends all *u*,
Col 1: 9 through all spiritual wisdom and *u*.
2: 2 have the full riches of complete *u*,
1Jn 5:20 God has come and has given us *u*,

UNDERSTANDS (UNDERSTAND)

1Ch 28: 9 and *u* every motive
Jer 9:24 that he *u* and knows me,
Mt 13:23 man who hears the word and *u* it.
Ro 3:11 there is no one who *u*,
1Ti 6: 4 he is conceited and *u* nothing.

UNDERSTOOD (UNDERSTAND)

Ne 8:12 they now *u* the words that had
Ps 73:17 then I *u* their final destiny.
Isa 40:13 Who has *u* the mind of the LORD,
40:21 Have you not *u* since the earth was
Jn 1: 5 but the darkness has not *u* it.
Ro 1:20 being *u* from what has been made,

UNDESIRABLE*

Jos 24:15 But if serving the LORD seems *u*

UNDIVIDED*

1Ch 12:33 to help David with *u* loyalty—
Ps 86:11 give me an *u* heart,
Eze 11:19 I will give them an *u* heart
1Co 7:35 way in *u* devotion to the Lord.

UNDOING

Pr 18: 7 A fool's mouth is his *u*,

UNDYING*

Eph 6:24 Lord Jesus Christ with an *u* love.

UNEQUALED*

Mt 24:21 *u* from the beginning of the world
Mk 13:19 of distress *u* from the beginning,

UNFADING*

1Pe 3: 4 the *u* beauty of a gentle

UNFAILING*

Ex 15:13 "In your *u* love you will lead
1Sa 20:14 But show me *u* kindness like that
2Sa 22:51 he shows *u* kindness
Ps 6: 4 save me because of your *u* love.
13: 5 But I trust in your *u* love;
18:50 he shows *u* kindness
21: 7 through the *u* love
31:16 save me in your *u* love.
32:10 but the LORD's *u* love
33: 5 the earth is full of his *u* love.
33:18 those whose hope is in his *u* love,
33:22 May your *u* love rest upon us,
36: 7 How priceless is your *u* love!
44:26 redeem us because of your *u* love.
48: 9 we meditate on your *u* love.
51: 1 according to your *u* love;
52: 8 I trust in God's *u* love
77: 8 Has his *u* love vanished forever?
85: 7 Show us your *u* love, O LORD,
90:14 in the morning with your *u* love,
107: 8 thanks to the LORD for his *u* love
107: 15 thanks to the LORD for his *u* love
107: 21 to the LORD for his *u* love
107: 31 to the LORD for his *u* love
119: 41 May your *u* love come to me,
119: 76 May your *u* love be my comfort,
130: 7 for with the LORD is *u* love
143: 8 bring me word of your *u* love,
Ps 143: 12 In your *u* love, silence my enemies;
147: 11 who put their hope in his *u* love.
Pr 19:22 What a man desires is *u* love;
20: 6 Many a man claims to have *u* love,
Isa 54:10 yet my *u* love for you will not be
La 3:32 so great is his *u* love.
Hos 10:12 reap the fruit of *u* love,

UNFAITHFUL (UNFAITHFULNESS)

Lev 6: 2 is *u* to the LORD by deceiving his
Nu 5: 6 and so is *u* to the LORD,
1Ch 10:13 because he was *u* to the LORD;
Pr 11: 6 the *u* are trapped by evil desires.
13: 2 the *u* have a craving for violence.
13:15 but the way of the *u* is hard.
22:12 but he frustrates the words of the *u*.
23:28 and multiplies the *u* among men.
25:19 is reliance on the *u* in times
Jer 3:20 But like a woman *u* to her husband,

UNFAITHFULNESS (UNFAITHFUL)

1Ch 9: 1 to Babylon because of their *u*.
Mt 5:32 except for marital *u*, causes her
19: 9 for marital *u*, and marries another

UNFIT*

Tit 1:16 and *u* for doing anything good.

UNFOLDING

Ps 119:130 the *u* of your words gives light;

UNFORGIVING*

2Ti 3: 3 unholy, without love, *u*, slanderous

UNFRIENDLY*

Pr 18: 1 An *u* man pursues selfish ends;

UNFRUITFUL

1Co 14:14 my spirit prays, but my mind is *u*.

UNGODLINESS (UNGODLY)

Tit 2:12 It teaches us to say "No" to *u*

UNGODLY (UNGODLINESS)

Ro 5: 6 powerless, Christ died for the *u*.
1Ti 1: 9 the *u* and sinful, the unholy
2Ti 2:16 in it will become more and more *u*.
2Pe 2: 6 of what is going to happen to the *u*;
Jude :15 and to convict all the *u*

UNGRATEFUL*

Lk 6:35 he is kind to the *u* and wicked.
2Ti 3: 2 disobedient to their parents, *u*,

UNHOLY*

1Ti 1: 9 and sinful, the *u* and irreligious;
2Ti 3: 2 ungrateful, *u*, without love,
Heb 10:29 as an *u* thing the blood

UNINTENTIONALLY

Lev 4: 2 'When anyone sins *u* and does
Nu 15:22 " 'Now if you *u* fail to keep any
Dt 4:42 flee if he had *u* killed his neighbor

UNIT

1Co 12:12 body is a *u*, though it is made up

UNITE (UNITED UNITY)

1Co 6:15 and *u* them with a prostitute?

UNITED (UNITE)

Ge 2:24 and mother and be *u* to his wife,
Mt 19: 5 and mother and be *u* to his wife,
Ro 6: 5 If we have been *u* with him like this
Eph 5:31 and mother and be *u* to his wife,
Php 2: 1 from being *u* with Christ,
Col 2: 2 encouraged in heart and *u* in love,

UNITY* (UNITE)

2Ch 30:12 the people to give them *u* of mind
Ps 133: 1 is when brothers live together in *u*!
Jn 17:23 May they be brought to complete *u*
Ro 15: 5 a spirit of *u* among yourselves
Eph 4: 3 effort to keep the *u* of the Spirit
4:13 up until we all reach *u* in the faith
Col 3:14 them all together in perfect *u*.

UNIVERSE*

1Co 4: 9 made a spectacle to the whole *u*,
Eph 4:10 in order to fill the whole *u*.)
Php 2:15 which you shine like stars in the *u*
Heb 1: 2 and through whom he made the *u*.
11: 3 understand that the *u* was formed

UNJUST
Ro 3: 5 That God is *u* in bringing his wrath
9: 14 What then shall we say? Is God *u*?
1Pe 2: 19 up under the pain of *u* suffering

UNKNOWN
Ac 17:23 TO AN *U* GOD.

UNLEAVENED
Ex 12: 17 "Celebrate the Feast of *U* Bread,
Dt 16: 16 at the Feast of *U* Bread, the Feast

UNLIMITED*
1Ti 1: 16 Jesus might display his *u* patience

UNLOVED
Pr 30: 23 an *u* woman who is married,

UNMARRIED
1Co 7: 8 It is good for them to stay *u*,
7: 27 Are you *u*? Do not look for a wife.
7: 32 An *u* man is concerned about

UNPLOWED
Ex 23: 11 the seventh year let the land lie *u*
Hos 10: 12 and break up your *u* ground;

UNPRODUCTIVE
Tit 3: 14 necessities and not live *u* lives.
2Pe 1: 8 and *u* in your knowledge

UNPROFITABLE
Tit 3: 9 because these are *u* and useless.

UNPUNISHED
Ex 34: 7 Yet he does not leave the guilty *u*;
Pr 6: 29 no one who touches her will go *u*.
11: 21 of this: The wicked will not go *u*,
19: 5 A false witness will not go *u*,

UNQUENCHABLE
Lk 3: 17 he will burn up the chaff with *u* fire

UNREPENTANT*
Ro 2: 5 stubbornness and your *u* heart,

UNRIGHTEOUS*
Zep 3: 5 yet the *u* know no shame.
Mt 5: 45 rain on the righteous and the *u*.
1Pe 3: 18 the righteous for the *u*, to bring you
2Pe 2: 9 and to hold the *u* for the day

UNSEARCHABLE
Ro 11: 33 How *u* his judgments,
Eph 3: 8 preach to the Gentiles the *u* riches

UNSEEN*
Mt 6: 6 and pray to your Father, who is *u*.
6: 18 who is *u*; and your Father,
2Co 4: 18 on what is seen, but on what is *u*.
4: 18 temporary, but what is *u* is eternal.

UNSETTLED*
1Th 3: 3 so that no one would be *u*
2Th 2: 2 not to become easily *u*

UNSHRUNK
Mt 9: 16 patch of *u* cloth on an old garment,

UNSPIRITUAL*
Ro 7: 14 but I am *u*, sold as a slave to sin.
Col 2: 18 and his *u* mind puffs him up
Jas 3: 15 down from heaven but is earthly, *u*,

UNSTABLE*
Jas 1: 8 he is a double-minded man, *u*
2Pe 2: 14 they seduce the *u*; they are experts
3: 16 ignorant and *u* people distort,

UNTHINKABLE*
Job 34: 12 It is *u* that God would do wrong,

UNTIE
Mk 1: 7 worthy to stoop down and *u*.
Lk 13: 15 each of you on the Sabbath *u* his ox

UNVEILED*
2Co 3: 18 with *u* faces all reflect the Lord's

UNWHOLESOME*
Eph 4: 29 Do not let any *u* talk come out

UNWISE
Eph 5: 15 how you live—not as *u* but as wise,

UNWORTHY*
Ge 32: 10 I am *u* of all the kindness
Job 40: 4 "I am *u*—how can I reply to you?
Lk 17: 10 should say, 'We are *u* servants;
1Co 11: 27 Lord in an *u* manner will be guilty

UPHOLD (UPHOLDS)
Isa 41: 10 I will *u* you with my righteous right
Ro 3: 31 Not at all! Rather, we *u* the law.

UPHOLDS* (UPHOLD)
Ps 37: 17 but the LORD *u* the righteous.
37: 24 for the LORD *u* him with his hand.
63: 8 your right hand *u* me.
140: 12 and *u* the cause of the needy.
145: 14 The LORD *u* all those who fall
146: 7 He *u* the cause of the oppressed

UPRIGHT
Dt 32: 4 *u* and just is he.
Job 1: 1 This man was blameless and *u*;
Ps 7: 10 who saves the *u* in heart.
11: 7 *u* men will see his face.
25: 8 Good and *u* is the LORD;
33: 1 it is fitting for the *u* to praise him.
64: 10 let all the *u* in heart praise him!
92: 15 proclaiming, "The LORD is *u*;
97: 11 and joy on the *u* in heart.
119: 7 I will praise you with an *u* heart
Pr 2: 7 He holds victory in store for the *u*,
3: 32 but takes the *u* into his confidence.
14: 2 whose walk is *u* fears the LORD,
15: 8 but the prayer of the *u* pleases him.
21: 29 an *u* man gives thought to his ways.
Isa 26: 7 O *u* One, you make the way
Tit 1: 8 who is self-controlled, *u*, holy
2: 12 *u* and godly lives in this present

UPROOTED
Dt 28: 63 You will be *u* from the land you are
Jer 31: 40 The city will never again be *u*
Jude : 12 without fruit and *u*—twice dead.

UPSET
Lk 10: 41 are worried and *u* about many

URIAH
Hittite husband of Bathsheba, killed by David's order (2Sa 11).

USEFUL
Eph 4: 28 doing something *u*
2Ti 2: 21 *u* to the Master and prepared
3: 16 Scripture is God-breathed and is *u*
Phm : 11 now he has become *u* both to you

USELESS
1Co 15: 14 our preaching is *u*
Tit 3: 9 these are unprofitable and *u*.
Phm : 11 Formerly he was *u* to you,
Heb 7: 18 *u* (for the law made nothing perfect
Jas 2: 20 faith without deeds is *u*?

USURY
Ne 5: 10 But let the exacting of *u* stop!
Ps 15: 5 who lends his money without *u*

UTMOST
Job 34: 36 that Job might be tested to the *u*

UTTER (UTTERS)
Ps 78: 2 I will *u* hidden things, things from of old—
Mt 13: 35 I will *u* things hidden

UTTERS (UTTER)
1Co 14: 2 he *u* mysteries with his spirit.

UZZIAH
Son of Amaziah; king of Judah also known as Azariah (2Ki 15:1-7; 1Ch 6:24; 2Ch 26). Struck with leprosy because of pride (2Ch 26:16-23).

VAIN
Ps 33: 17 A horse is a *v* hope for deliverance;
73: 13 in *v* have I kept my heart pure;
127: 1 its builders labor in *v*.
Isa 65: 23 They will not toil in *v*
1Co 15: 2 Otherwise, you have believed in *v*.
15: 58 labor in the Lord is not in *v*.
2Co 6: 1 not to receive God's grace in *v*.
Gal 2: 2 running or had run my race in *v*.

VALIANT
1Sa 10: 26 by *v* men whose hearts God had

VALID
Jn 8: 14 my own behalf, my testimony is *v*,

VALLEY (VALLEYS)
Ps 23: 4 walk through the *v* of the shadow
Isa 40: 4 Every *v* shall be raised up,
Joel 3: 14 multitudes in the *v* of decision!

VALLEYS (VALLEY)
SS 2: 1 a lily of the *v*.

VALUABLE (VALUE)
Lk 12: 24 And how much more *v* you are

VALUE (VALUABLE VALUED)
Lev 27: 3 set the *v* of a male between the ages
Pr 16: 13 they *v* a man who speaks the truth.
31: 11 and lacks nothing of *v*.
Mt 13: 46 When he found one of great *v*,
1Ti 4: 8 For physical training is of some *v*,
Heb 11: 26 as of greater *v* than the treasures

VALUED (VALUE)
Lk 16: 15 What is highly *v* among men is

VANISHES
Jas 4: 14 appears for a little while and then *v*.

VASHTI*
Queen of Persia replaced by Esther (Est 1-2).

VAST
Ge 2: 1 completed in all their *v* array.
Dt 1: 19 of the Amorites through all that *v*
8: 15 He led you through the *v*
Ps 139: 17 How *v* is the sum of them!

VEGETABLES
Pr 15: 17 of *v* where there is love
Ro 14: 2 whose faith is weak, eats only *v*.

VEIL
Ex 34: 33 to them, he put a *v* over his face.
2Co 3: 14 for to this day the same *v* remains

VENGEANCE (AVENGE AVENGER AVENGES AVENGING REVENGE)
Nu 31: 3 to carry out the LORD's *v* on them
Isa 34: 8 For the LORD has a day of *v*,
Na 1: 2 The LORD takes *v* on his foes

VERDICT
Jn 3: 19 This is the *v*: Light has come

VICTOR'S* (VICTORY)
2Ti 2: 5 he does not receive the *v* crown

VICTORIES* (VICTORY)
2Sa 22: 51 He gives his king great *v*;
Ps 18: 50 He gives his king great *v*;
21: 1 great is his joy in the *v* you give!
21: 5 Through the *v* you gave, his glory is
44: 4 who decrees *v* for Jacob.

VICTORIOUS (VICTORY)
Ps 20: 5 for joy when you are *v*

VICTORIOUSLY* (VICTORY)
Ps 45: 4 In your majesty ride forth *v*

VICTORY (VICTOR'S VICTORIES VICTORIOUS VICTORIOUSLY)
2Sa 8: 6 gave David *v* wherever he
Ps 44: 6 my sword does not bring me *v*;
60: 12 With God we will gain the *v*,
129: 2 they have not gained the *v* over me.
Pr 11: 14 but many advisers make *v* sure.
1Co 15: 54 "Death has been swallowed up in *v*
15: 57 He gives us the *v* through our Lord
1Jn 5: 4 This is the *v* that has overcome

VIEW
Pr 5: 21 are in full *v* of the LORD,
2Ti 4: 1 and in *v* of his appearing

VILLAGE
Mk 6: 6 went around teaching from *v* to *v*.

VINDICATED (VINDICATION)
Job 13: 18 I know I will be *v*.
1Ti 3: 16 was *v* by the Spirit,

VINDICATION (VINDICATED)
Ps 24: 5 and *v* from God his Savior.

VINE (VINEYARD)
Ps 128: 3 Your wife will be like a fruitful *v*
Isa 36: 16 one of you will eat from his own *v*
Jnh 4: 6 Jonah was very happy about the *v*.
Jn 15: 1 "I am the true *v*, and my Father is

VINEGAR
Pr 10: 26 As *v* to the teeth and smoke
Mk 15: 36 filled a sponge with wine *v*,

VINEYARD (VINE)
1Ki 21: 1 an incident involving a *v* belonging
Pr 31: 16 out of her earnings she plants a *v*.
SS 1: 6 my own *v* I have neglected.
Isa 5: 1 My loved one had a *v*
1Co 9: 7 Who plants a *v* and does not eat

VIOLATION
Heb 2: 2 every *v* and disobedience received

VIOLENCE (VIOLENT)
Ge 6: 11 in God's sight and was full of *v*.
Isa 53: 9 though he had done no *v*,
60: 18 No longer will *v* be heard
Eze 45: 9 Give up your *v* and oppression
Joel 3: 19 of *v* done to the people of Judah,
Jnh 3: 8 give up their evil ways and their *v*.

VIOLENT (VIOLENCE)
Eze 18: 10 "Suppose he has a *v* son, who sheds
1Ti 1: 13 and a persecutor and a *v* man,
3: 3 not *v* but gentle, not quarrelsome,
Tit 1: 7 not *v*, not pursuing dishonest gain.

VIPERS
Ps 140: 3 the poison of *v* is on their lips.
Lk 3: 7 "You brood of *v*! Who warned you
Ro 3: 13 "The poison of *v* is on their lips."

VIRGIN (VIRGINS)
Dt 22: 15 shall bring proof that she was a *v*
Isa 7: 14 The *v* will be with child
Mt 1: 23 "The *v* will be with child
Lk 1: 34 I am a *v*?" The angel answered,
2Co 11: 2 that I might present you as a pure *v*

VIRGINS (VIRGIN)
Mt 25: 1 will be like ten *v* who took their
1Co 7: 25 Now about *v*: I have no command

VIRTUES*
Col 3: 14 And over all these *v* put on love,

VISIBLE
Eph 5: 13 exposed by the light becomes *v*,
Col 1: 16 and on earth, *v* and invisible,

VISION (VISIONS)
Da 9: 24 to seal up *v* and prophecy
Ac 26: 19 disobedient to the *v* from heaven.

VISIONS (VISION)
Nu 12: 6 I reveal myself to him in *v*,
Joel 2: 28 your young men will see *v*.
Ac 2: 17 your young men will see *v*,

VOICE
Dt 30: 20 listen to his *v*, and hold fast to him.
1Sa 15: 22 as in obeying the *v* of the LORD?
Job 40: 9 and can your *v* thunder like his?
Ps 19: 4 Their *v* goes out into all the earth,
29: 3 The *v* of the LORD is
66: 19 and heard my *v* in prayer.
95: 7 Today, if you hear his *v*,
Pr 8: 1 Does not understanding raise her *v*
Isa 30: 21 your ears will hear a *v* behind you,
40: 3 A *v* of one calling:
Mk 1: 3 "a *v* of one calling in the desert,
Jn 5: 28 are in their graves will hear his *v*
10: 3 and the sheep listen to his *v*.
Ro 10: 18 "Their *v* has gone out
Heb 3: 7 "Today, if you hear his *v*,
Rev 3: 20 If anyone hears my *v* and opens

VOMIT
Lev 18: 28 it will *v* you out as it vomited out
Pr 26: 11 As a dog returns to its *v*,
2Pe 2: 22 "A dog returns to its *v*," and,

VOW (VOWS)
Nu 6: 2 a *v* of separation to the LORD
Nu 30: 2 When a man makes a *v*
Jdg 11: 30 Jephthah made a *v* to the LORD:

VOWS (VOW)
Ps 116: 14 I will fulfill my *v* to the LORD
Pr 20: 25 and only later to consider his *v*.

VULTURES
Mt 24: 28 is a carcass, there the *v* will gather.

WAGE (WAGES WAGING)
2Co 10: 3 we do not *w* war as the world does.

WAGES (WAGE)
Mal 3: 5 who defraud laborers of their *w*,
Lk 10: 7 for the worker deserves his *w*.
Ro 4: 4 his *w* are not credited to him
6: 23 For the *w* of sin is death,
1Ti 5: 18 and "The worker deserves his *w*."

WAGING (WAGE)
Ro 7: 23 *w* war against the law of my mind

WAILING
Ps 30: 11 You turned my *w* into dancing;

WAIST
2Ki 1: 8 and with a leather belt around his *w*."
Mt 3: 4 he had a leather belt around his *w*.

WAIT (AWAITS WAITED WAITING WAITS)
Ps 27: 14 *W* for the LORD;
130: 5 I *w* for the LORD, my soul waits,
Isa 30: 18 Blessed are all who *w* for him!
Ac 1: 4 *w* for the gift my Father promised,
Ro 8: 23 as we *w* eagerly for our adoption
1Th 1: 10 and to *w* for his Son from heaven,
Tit 2: 13 while we *w* for the blessed hope—

WAITED (WAIT)
Ps 40: 1 I *w* patiently for the LORD;

WAITING (WAIT)
Heb 9: 28 to those who are *w* for him.

WAITS (WAIT)
Ro 8: 19 creation *w* in eager expectation

WAKE (AWAKE WAKENS)
Eph 5: 14 "*W* up, O sleeper,

WAKENS* (WAKE)
Isa 50: 4 He *w* me morning by morning,
50: 4 *w* my ear to listen like one being

WALK (WALKED WALKING WALKS)
Lev 26: 12 I will *w* among you and be your
Dt 5: 33 *W* in all the way that the LORD
6: 7 and when you *w* along the road,
10: 12 to *w* in all his ways, to love him,
11: 19 and when you *w* along the road,
11: 22 to *w* in all his ways and to hold fast
26: 17 and that you will *w* in his ways,
Jos 22: 5 to *w* in all his ways,
Ps 1: 1 who does not *w* in the counsel
15: 2 He whose *w* is blameless
23: 4 Even though I *w*
84: 11 from those whose *w* is blameless.
89: 15 who *w* in the light of your presence
119: 45 I will *w* about in freedom,
Pr 4: 12 When you *w*, your steps will not be
6: 22 When you *w*, they will guide you;
Isa 2: 3 so that we may *w* in his paths."
2: 5 let us *w* in the light of the LORD.
30: 21 saying, "This is the way; *w* in it."
40: 31 they will *w* and not be faint.
57: 2 Those who *w* uprightly
Jer 6: 16 ask where the good way is, and *w*
Da 4: 37 And those who *w* in pride he is able
Am 3: 3 Do two *w* together
Mic 4: 5 All the nations may *w*
6: 8 and to *w* humbly with your God.
Mk 2: 9 'Get up, take your mat and *w*'?
Jn 8: 12 Whoever follows me will never *w*
1Jn 1: 6 with him yet *w* in the darkness,
1: 7 But if we *w* in the light,
2Jn : 6 his command is that you *w* in love.

WALKED (WALK)
Ge 5: 24 Enoch *w* with God; then he was no
Jos 14: 9 which your feet have *w* will be your
Mt 14: 29 *w* on the water and came toward Jesus.

WALKING (WALK)
1Ki 3: 3 love for the LORD by *w* according
Da 3: 25 I see four men *w* around in the fire,
2Jn : 4 of your children *w* in the truth,

WALKS (WALK)
Pr 10: 9 The man of integrity *w* securely,
13: 20 He who *w* with the wise grows wise
Isa 33: 15 He who *w* righteously
Jn 11: 9 A man who *w* by day will not

WALL (WALLS)
Jos 6: 20 *w* collapsed; so every man charged
Ne 2: 17 let us rebuild the *w* of Jerusalem,
Eph 2: 14 the dividing *w* of hostility,
Rev 21: 12 It had a great, high *w*

WALLOWING
2Pe 2: 22 back to her *w* in the mud."

WALLS (WALL)
Isa 58: 12 be called Repairer of Broken *W*,
60: 18 but you will call your *w* Salvation
Heb 11: 30 By faith the *w* of Jericho fell,

WANDER (WANDERED)
Nu 32: 13 he made them *w* in the desert forty
Jas 5: 19 one of you should *w* from the truth

WANDERED (WANDER)
Eze 34: 6 My sheep *w* over all the mountains
Mt 18: 12 go to look for the one that *w* off?
1Ti 6: 10 have *w* from the faith and pierced
2Ti 2: 18 who have *w* away from the truth.

WANT (WANTED WANTING WANTS)
1Sa 8: 19 "We *w* a king over us.
Mt 19: 21 Jesus answered, "If you *w*
Lk 19: 14 'We don't *w* this man to be our king'
Ro 7: 15 For what I *w* to do I do not do,
13: 3 Do you *w* to be free from fear
2Co 12: 14 what I *w* is not your possessions
Php 3: 10 I *w* to know Christ and the power

WANTED (WANT)
1Co 12: 18 of them, just as he *w* them to be.
Heb 6: 17 Because God *w* to make

WANTING (WANT)
Da 5: 27 weighed on the scales and found *w*.
2Pe 3: 9 with you, not *w* anyone to perish,

WANTS (WANT)
Mt 5: 42 from the one who *w* to borrow
20: 26 whoever *w* to become great
Mk 8: 35 For whoever *w* to save his life will
10: 43 whoever *w* to become great
Ro 9: 18 he hardens whom he *w* to harden.
1Ti 2: 4 who *w* all men to be saved
1Pe 5: 2 you are willing, as God *w* you to be;

WAR (WARRIOR WARS)
Jos 11: 23 Then the land had rest from *w*.
1Sa 15: 18 make *w* on them until you have
Ps 68: 30 the nations who delight in *w*.
120: 7 but when I speak, they are for *w*.
144: 1 who trains my hands for *w*,
Isa 2: 4 nor will they train for *w* anymore.
Da 9: 26 *W* will continue until the end,
Ro 7: 23 waging *w* against the law
2Co 10: 3 we do not wage *w* as the world does
1Pe 2: 11 which *w* against your soul.
Rev 12: 7 And there was *w* in heaven.
19: 11 With justice he judges and makes *w*

WARN* (WARNED WARNING WARNINGS)
Ex 19: 21 *w* the people so they do not force
Nu 24: 14 let me *w* you of what this people
1Sa 8: 9 but *w* them solemnly and let them
1Ki 2: 42 swear by the LORD and *w* you,
2Ch 19: 10 you are to *w* them not to sin
Ps 81: 8 O my people, and I will *w* you—
Jer 42: 19 I *w* you today that you made a fatal
Eze 3: 18 and you do not *w* him or speak out
3: 19 But if you do *w* the wicked man
3: 20 Since you did not *w* him, he will die
3: 21 if you do *w* the righteous man not
33: 3 blows the trumpet to *w* the people,
33: 6 blow the trumpet to *w* the people
33: 9 if you do *w* the wicked man to turn
Lk 16: 28 Let him *w* them, so that they will
Ac 4: 17 we must *w* these men
1Co 4: 14 but to *w* you, as my dear children.
Gal 5: 21 I *w* you, as I did before, that those

2Co 12: 9 all the more gladly about my *w*,
12: 10 I delight in *w*, in insults,
Heb 4: 15 unable to sympathize with our *w*,

WEALTH

Dt 8: 18 gives you the ability to produce *w*,
2Ch 1: 11 and you have not asked for *w*,
Ps 39: 6 he heaps up *w*, not knowing who
Pr 3: 9 Honor the LORD with your *w*,
10: 4 but diligent hands bring *w*.
11: 4 *W* is worthless in the day of wrath,
13: 7 to be poor, yet has great *w*.
15: 16 than great *w* with turmoil.
22: 4 bring *w* and honor and life.
Ecc 5: 10 whoever loves *w* is never satisfied
5: 13 *w* hoarded to the harm of its owner,
SS 8: 7 all the *w* of his house for love,
Mt 13: 22 and the deceitfulness of *w* choke it,
Mk 10: 22 away sad, because he had great *w*.
12: 44 They all gave out of their *w*; but she
Lk 15: 13 and there squandered his *w*
1Ti 6: 17 nor to put their hope in *w*,
Jas 5: 2 Your *w* has rotted, and moths have
5: 3 You have hoarded *w*

WEAPON (WEAPONS)

Ne 4: 17 work with one hand and held a *w*

WEAPONS (WEAPON)

Ecc 9: 18 Wisdom is better than *w* of war,
2Co 6: 7 with *w* of righteousness
10: 4 The *w* we fight with are not

WEAR (WEARING)

Dt 8: 4 Your clothes did not *w* out
22: 5 nor a man *w* women's clothing,
Ps 102: 26 they will all *w* out like a garment.
Pr 23: 4 Do not *w* yourself out to get rich;
Isa 51: 6 the earth will *w* out like a garment
Heb 1: 11 they will all *w* out like a garment.
Rev 3: 18 and white clothes to *w*,

WEARIES (WEARY)

Ecc 12: 12 and much study *w* the body.

WEARING (WEAR)

Jn 19: 5 When Jesus came out *w* the crown
Jas 2: 3 attention to the man *w* fine clothes
1Pe 3: 3 as braided hair and the *w*
Rev 7: 9 They were *w* white robes

WEARY (WEARIES)

Isa 40: 28 He will not grow tired or *w*,
40: 31 they will run and not grow *w*,
50: 4 know the word that sustains the *w*.
Mt 11: 28 all you who are *w* and burdened,
Gal 6: 9 Let us not become *w* in doing good,
Heb 12: 3 so that you will not grow *w*
Rev 2: 3 my name, and have not grown *w*.

WEDDING

Mt 22: 11 who was not wearing *w* clothes.
Rev 19: 7 For the *w* of the Lamb has come,

WEEDS

Mt 13: 25 and sowed *w* among the wheat,

WEEK

Mt 28: 1 at dawn on the first day of the *w*,
1Co 16: 2 On the first day of every *w*,

WEEP (WEEPING WEPT)

Ecc 3: 4 a time to *w* and a time to laugh,
Lk 6: 21 Blessed are you who *w* now,
23: 28 *w* for yourselves and for your

WEEPING (WEEP)

Ps 30: 5 *w* may remain for a night,
126: 6 He who goes out *w*,
Jer 31: 15 Rachel *w* for her children
Mt 2: 18 Rachel *w* for her children
8: 12 where there will be *w* and gnashing

WEIGH (OUTWEIGHS WEIGHED WEIGHS WEIGHTIER WEIGHTS)

1Co 14: 29 others should *w* carefully what is

WEIGHED (WEIGH)

Job 28: 15 nor can its price be *w* in silver.
Da 5: 27 You have been *w* on the scales
Lk 21: 34 or your hearts will be *w*

WEIGHS (WEIGH)

Pr 12: 25 An anxious heart *w* a man down,
15: 28 of the righteous *w* its answers,
21: 2 but the LORD *w* the heart.
24: 12 not he who *w* the heart perceive

WEIGHTIER* (WEIGH)

Jn 5: 36 "I have testimony *w* than that

WEIGHTS (WEIGH)

Lev 19: 36 Use honest scales and honest *w*,
Dt 25: 13 Do not have two differing *w*
Pr 11: 1 but accurate *w* are his delight.

WELCOME (WELCOMES)

Mk 9: 37 welcomes me does not *w* me
2Pe 1: 11 and you will receive a rich *w*

WELCOMES (WELCOME)

Mt 18: 5 whoever *w* a little child like this
2Jn : 11 Anyone who *w* him shares

WELL (WELLED WELLING WELLS)

Mt 15: 31 crippled made *w*, the lame walking
Lk 14: 5 falls into a *w* on the Sabbath day,
17: 19 your faith has made you *w*."
Jas 5: 15 in faith will make the sick person *w*

WELL-WATERED (WATER)

Isa 58: 11 You will be like a *w* garden,

WELLED* (WELL)

2Co 8: 2 and their extreme poverty *w* up

WELLING* (WELL)

Jn 4: 14 of water *w* up to eternal life."

WELLS (WELL)

Isa 12: 3 from the *w* of salvation.

WELLSPRING* (SPRING)

Pr 4: 23 for it is the *w* of life.

WEPT (WEEP)

Ps 137: 1 of Babylon we sat and *w*
Lk 22: 62 And he went outside and *w* bitterly
Jn 11: 35 Jesus *w*.

WEST

Ps 103: 12 as far as the east is from the *w*,
107: 3 from east and *w*, from north

WHEAT

Mt 3: 12 gathering his *w* into the barn
13: 25 and sowed weeds among the *w*,
Lk 22: 31 Satan has asked to sift you as *w*.
Jn 12: 24 a kernel of *w* falls to the ground

WHEELS

Eze 1: 16 appearance and structure of the *w*:

WHIRLWIND (WIND)

2Ki 2: 1 to take Elijah up to heaven in a *w*,
Hos 8: 7 and reap the *w*.
Na 1: 3 His way is in the *w* and the storm,

WHISPER (WHISPERED)

1Ki 19: 12 And after the fire came a gentle *w*.
Job 26: 14 how faint the *w* we hear of him!
Ps 107: 29 He stilled the storm to a *w*;

WHISPERED (WHISPER)

Mt 10: 27 speak in the daylight; what is *w*

WHITE (WHITER)

Isa 1: 18 they shall be as *w* as snow;
Da 7: 9 His clothing was as *w* as snow;
7: 9 the hair of his head was *w* like wool
Mt 28: 3 and his clothes were *w* as snow.
Rev 1: 14 hair were *w* like wool, as *w* as snow,
3: 4 dressed in *w*, for they are worthy.
6: 2 and there before me was a *w* horse!
7: 13 "These in *w* robes—who are they,
19: 11 and there before me was a *w* horse,
20: 11 Then I saw a great *w* throne

WHITER (WHITE)

Ps 51: 7 and I will be *w* than snow.

WHOLE

Ge 1: 29 plant on the face of the *w* earth
2: 6 and watered the *w* surface
11: 1 Now the *w* world had one language
Ex 12: 47 The *w* community
19: 5 Although the *w* earth is mine,
Lev 16: 17 and the *w* community of Israel.
Nu 14: 21 of the LORD fills the *w* earth,
32: 13 until the *w* generation
Dt 13: 16 *w* burnt offering to the LORD your
19: 8 gives you the *w* land he promised
Jos 2: 3 come to spy out the *w* land."
1Sa 1: 28 For his *w* life he will be given
17: 46 the *w* world will know that there is
1Ki 10: 24 The *w* world sought audience
2Ki 21: 8 and will keep the *w* Law that my
Ps 72: 19 may the *w* earth be filled
Pr 4: 22 and health to a man's *w* body.
8: 31 rejoicing in his *w* world
Ecc 12: 13 for this is the *w* duty of man.
Isa 1: 5 Your *w* head is injured,
6: 3 the *w* earth is full of his glory."
14: 26 plan determined for the *w* world;
Eze 34: 6 were scattered over the *w* earth,
37: 11 these bones are the *w* house
Da 2: 35 mountain and filled the *w* earth.
Zep 1: 18 the *w* world will be consumed,
Zec 14: 9 will be king over the *w* earth.
Mal 3: 10 the *w* tithe into the storehouse,
Mt 5: 29 than for your *w* body to be thrown
6: 22 your *w* body will be full of light.
16: 26 for a man if he gains the *w* world,
24: 14 will be preached in the *w* world
Lk 21: 35 live on the face of the *w* earth.
Jn 12: 19 Look how the *w* world has gone
13: 10 to wash his feet; his *w* body is clean
21: 25 the *w* world would not have room
Ac 17: 26 they should inhabit the *w* earth;
20: 27 proclaim to you the *w* will of God.
Ro 1: 9 whom I serve with my *w* heart
3: 19 and the *w* world held accountable
8: 22 know that the *w* creation has been
1Co 4: 9 made a spectacle to the *w* universe,
12: 17 If the *w* body were an ear,
Gal 3: 22 declares that the *w* world is
5: 3 obligated to obey the *w* law.
Eph 4: 10 in order to fill the *w* universe.)
4: 13 attaining to the *w* measure
1Th 5: 23 May your *w* spirit, soul
Jas 2: 10 For whoever keeps the *w* law
1Jn 2: 2 but also for the sins of the *w* world.
Rev 3: 10 going to come upon the *w* world

WHOLEHEARTED* (HEART)

2Ki 20: 3 you faithfully and with *w* devotion
1Ch 28: 9 and serve him with *w* devotion
29: 19 my son Solomon the *w* devotion
Isa 38: 3 you faithfully and with *w* devotion

WHOLEHEARTEDLY* (HEART)

Nu 14: 24 a different spirit and follows me *w*,
32: 11 they have not followed me *w*,
32: 12 for they followed the LORD *w*.'
Dt 1: 36 because he followed the LORD *w*
Jos 14: 8 followed the LORD my God *w*.
14: 9 followed the LORD my God *w*.'
14: 14 the LORD, the God of Israel, *w*.
1Ki 8: 23 with your servants who continue *w*
1Ch 29: 9 for they had given freely and *w*
2Ch 6: 14 with your servants who continue *w*
15: 15 oath because they had sworn it *w*.
19: 9 and *w* in the fear of the LORD.
25: 2 in the eyes of the LORD, but not *w*
31: 21 he sought his God and worked *w*.
Ro 6: 17 you *w* obeyed the form of teaching
Eph 6: 7 Serve *w*, as if you were serving

WHOLESOME*

2Ki 2: 22 And the water has remained *w*
2Pe 3: 1 to stimulate you to *w* thinking.

WICK

Isa 42: 3 a smoldering *w* he will not snuff out
Mt 12: 20 a smoldering *w* he will not snuff out

WICKED (WICKEDNESS)

Ge 13: 13 Now the men of Sodom were *w*
39: 9 How then could I do such a *w* thing
Ex 23: 1 Do not help a *w* man
Nu 14: 35 things to this whole *w* community,
Dt 15: 9 not to harbor this *w* thought:
Jdg 19: 22 some of the *w* men
1Sa 2: 12 Eli's sons were *w* men; they had no
15: 18 completely destroy those *w* people,
25: 17 He is such a *w* man that no one can
2Sa 13: 12 in Israel! Don't do this *w* thing.
2Ki 17: 11 They did *w* things that provoked
2Ch 7: 14 and turn from their *w* ways,
19: 2 "Should you help the *w*
Ne 13: 17 "What is this *w* thing you are doing
Ps 1: 1 walk in the counsel of the *w*
1: 5 Therefore the *w* will not stand
7: 9 to an end the violence of the *w*
10: 13 Why does the *w* man revile God?

Ps 11: 5 the w and those who love violence
12: 8 The w freely strut about
26: 5 and refuse to sit with the w.
32: 10 Many are the woes of the w,
36: 1 concerning the sinfulness of the w:
37: 13 but the Lord laughs at the w,
49: 5 when w deceivers surround me—
50: 16 But to the w, God says:
58: 3 Even from birth the w go astray;
73: 3 when I saw the prosperity of the w.
82: 2 and show partiality to the w? Selah
112: 10 the longings of the w will come
119: 61 Though the w bind me with ropes,
119:155 Salvation is far from the w,
140: 8 do not grant the w their desires,
141: 10 Let the w fall into their own nets,
146: 9 but he frustrates the ways of the w.
Pr 2: 12 you from the ways of w men,
4: 14 Do not set foot on the path of the w
6: 18 a heart that devises w schemes,
9: 7 whoever rebukes a w man incurs
10: 20 the heart of the w is of little value.
10: 28 the hopes of the w come to nothing
11: 5 w are brought down by their own
11: 10 when the w perish, there are shouts
11: 21 The w will not go unpunished,
12: 5 but the advice of the w is deceitful.
12: 10 the kindest acts of the w are cruel.
14: 19 the w at the gates of the righteous.
15: 3 keeping watch on the w
15: 26 detests the thoughts of the w,
21: 10 The w man craves evil;
21: 29 A w man puts up a bold front,
28: 1 w man flees though no one pursues,
28: 4 who forsake the law praise the w,
29: 7 but the w have no such concern.
29: 16 When the w thrive, so does sin,
29: 27 the w detest the upright.
Isa 11: 4 breath of his lips he will slay the w.
13: 11 the w for their sins.
26: 10 Though grace is shown to the w,
48: 22 says the LORD, "for the w."
53: 9 He was assigned a grave with the w
55: 7 Let the w forsake his way
57: 20 But the w are like the tossing sea,
Jer 35: 15 of you must turn from your w ways
Eze 3: 18 that w man will die for his sin,
13: 22 you encouraged the w not to turn
14: 7 and puts a w stumbling block
18: 21 "But if a w man turns away
18: 23 pleasure in the death of the w?
21: 25 " 'O profane and w prince of Israel,
33: 8 When I say to the w, 'O w man,
33: 11 pleasure in the death of the w,
33: 14 to the w man, 'You will surely die,'
33: 19 And if a w man turns away
Da 12: 10 but the w will continue to be w.
Mt 12: 39 w and adulterous generation asks
12: 45 be with this w generation."
12: 45 with it seven other spirits more w
Lk 6: 35 he is kind to the ungrateful and w.
Ac 2: 23 and you, with the help of w men,
Ro 4: 5 but trusts God who justifies the w,
1Co 5: 13 "Expel the w man from among you
6: 9 not know that the w will not inherit
Rev 2: 2 that you cannot tolerate w men,

WICKEDNESS (WICKED)

Ge 6: 5 The LORD saw how great man's w
Ex 34: 7 and forgiving w, rebellion and sin.
Lev 16: 21 and confess over it all the w
19: 29 to prostitution and be filled with w.
Dt 9: 4 it is on account of the w
Ne 9: 2 and confessed their sins and the w
Ps 45: 7 You love righteousness and hate w;
92: 15 he is my Rock, and there is no w
Pr 13: 6 but w overthrows the sinner.
Jer 3: 2 land with your prostitution and w.
8: 6 No one repents of his w,
14: 20 O LORD, we acknowledge our w
Eze 18: 20 the w of the wicked will be charged
28: 15 created till w was found in you.
33: 19 wicked man turns away from his w
Da 4: 27 and your w by being kind
9: 24 to atone for w, to bring
Jnh 1: 2 its w has come up before me."
Mt 24: 12 Because of the increase of w,
Lk 11: 39 inside you are full of greed and w.
Ac 1: 18 (With the reward he got for his w,
Ro 1: 18 who suppress the truth by their w,
1Co 5: 8 the yeast of malice and w,
2Co 6: 14 what do righteousness and w have
2Ti 2: 19 of the Lord must turn away from w
Tit 2: 14 for us to redeem us from all w
Heb 1: 9 loved righteousness and hated w;
8: 12 For I will forgive their w
2Pe 2: 15 who loved the wages of w.

WIDE

Ps 81: 10 Open w your mouth and I will fill it
Isa 54: 2 stretch your tent curtains w,
Mt 7: 13 For w is the gate and broad is
2Co 6: 13 my children—open w your hearts
Eph 3: 18 to grasp how w and long and high

WIDOW (WIDOWS)

Ex 22: 22 "Do not take advantage of a w
Dt 10: 18 cause of the fatherless and the w,
Ps 146: 9 sustains the fatherless and the w,
Isa 1: 17 plead the case of the w.
Lk 21: 2 saw a poor w put in two very small
1Ti 5: 4 But if a w has children

WIDOWS (WIDOW)

Ps 68: 5 to the fatherless, a defender of w,
Ac 6: 1 their w were being overlooked
1Co 7: 8 to the unmarried and the w I say:
1Ti 5: 3 to those w who are really
Jas 1: 27 look after orphans and w

WIFE (WIVES WIVES')

Ge 2: 24 and mother and be united to his w,
19: 26 But Lot's w looked back,
24: 67 she became his w, and he loved her;
Ex 20: 17 shall not covet your neighbor's w,
Lev 20: 10 adultery with another man's w—
Dt 5: 21 shall not covet your neighbor's w.
24: 5 happiness to the w he has married.
Ru 4: 13 took Ruth and she became his w.
Pr 5: 18 in the w of your youth.
12: 4 w of noble character is her
18: 22 He who finds a w finds what is
19: 13 quarrelsome w is like a constant
31: 10 w of noble character who can find?
Hos 1: 2 take to yourself an adulterous w
Mal 2: 14 the witness between you and the w
Mt 1: 20 to take Mary home as your w,
19: 3 for a man to divorce his w for any
Lk 17: 32 Remember Lot's w! Whoever tries
18: 29 or w or brothers or parents
1Co 7: 2 each man should have his own w,
7: 33 how he can please his w—
Eph 5: 23 the husband is the head of the w
5: 33 must love his w as he loves himself,
1Ti 3: 2 husband of but one w, temperate,
Rev 21: 9 I will show you the bride, the w

WILD

Ge 1: 25 God made the w animals according
8: 1 Noah and all the w animals
Lk 15: 13 squandered his wealth in w living.
Ro 11: 17 and you, though a w olive shoot,

WILL (WEAK-WILLED WILLFUL WILLING WILLINGNESS)

Ps 40: 8 I desire to do your w, O my God;
143: 10 Teach me to do your w,
Isa 53: 10 Yet it was the LORD's w
Mt 6: 10 your w be done
7: 21 who does the w of my Father
10: 29 apart from the w of your Father.
12: 50 does the w of my Father
26: 39 Yet not as I w, but as you w."
26: 42 I drink it, may your w be done."
Jn 6: 38 but to do the w of him who sent me.
7: 17 If anyone chooses to do God's w,
Ac 20: 27 to you the whole w of God.
Ro 12: 2 and approve what God's w is—
1Co 7: 37 but has control over his own w,
Eph 5: 17 understand what the Lord's w is.
Php 2: 13 for it is God who works in you to w
1Th 4: 3 God's w that you should be sanctified:
5: 18 for this is God's w for you
2Ti 2: 26 has taken them captive to do his w.
Heb 2: 4 distributed according to his w.
9: 16 In the case of a w, it is necessary
10: 7 I have come to do your w, O God
13: 21 everything good for doing his w,
Jas 4: 15 "If it is the Lord's w,
1Pe 3: 17 It is better, if it is God's w,
4: 2 but rather for the w of God.
2Pe 1: 21 never had its origin in the w
1Jn 5: 14 we ask anything according to his w,
Rev 4: 11 and by your w they were created

WILLFUL (WILL)

Ps 19: 13 Keep your servant also from w sins;

WILLING (WILL)

1Ch 28: 9 devotion and with a w mind,
29: 5 who is w to consecrate himself
Ps 51: 12 grant me a w spirit, to sustain me.
Da 3: 28 were w to give up their lives rather
Mt 18: 14 Father in heaven is not w that any
23: 37 her wings, but you were not w.
26: 41 The spirit is w, but the body is weak
1Ti 6: 18 and to be generous and w to share.
1Pe 5: 2 but because you are w,

WILLINGNESS* (WILL)

2Co 8: 11 so that your eager w
8: 12 For if the w is there, the gift is

WIN (WINS WON)

1Co 9: 19 myself a slave to everyone, to w
Php 3: 14 on toward the goal to w the prize
1Th 4: 12 your daily life may w the respect

WIND (WHIRLWIND WINDS)

Ps 1: 4 that the w blows away.
Ecc 2: 11 meaningless, a chasing after the w;
Hos 8: 7 "They sow the w
Mk 4: 41 Even the w and the waves obey
Jn 3: 8 The w blows wherever it pleases.
Eph 4: 14 and there by every w of teaching
Jas 1: 6 blown and tossed by the w.

WINDOW

Jos 2: 21 she tied the scarlet cord in the w.
Ac 20: 9 in a w was a young man named
2Co 11: 33 in a basket from a w in the wall

WINDS (WIND)

Ps 104: 4 He makes w his messengers,
Mt 24: 31 gather his elect from the four w,
Heb 1: 7 "He makes his angels w,

WINE

Ps 104: 15 w that gladdens the heart of man,
Pr 20: 1 W is a mocker and beer a brawler;
23: 20 join those who drink too much w
23: 31 Do not gaze at w when it is red,
31: 6 w to those who are in anguish;
SS 1: 2 your love is more delightful than w.
Isa 28: 7 And these also stagger from w
55: 1 Come, buy w and milk
Mt 9: 17 Neither do men pour new w
Lk 23: 36 They offered him w vinegar
Jn 2: 3 When the w was gone, Jesus'
Ro 14: 21 not to eat meat or drink w
Eph 5: 18 on w, which leads to debauchery.
1Ti 5: 23 a little w because of your stomach
Rev 16: 19 with the w of the fury of his wrath.

WINEPRESS

Isa 63: 2 like those of one treading the w?
Rev 19: 15 He treads the w of the fury

WINESKINS

Mt 9: 17 do men pour new wine into old w.

WINGS

Ex 19: 4 and how I carried you on eagles' w
Ru 2: 12 under whose w you have come
Ps 17: 8 hide me in the shadow of your w
91: 4 under his w you will find refuge;
Isa 6: 2 him were seraphs, each with six w:
40: 31 They will soar on w like eagles;
Eze 1: 6 of them had four faces and four w.
Zec 5: 9 in their w! They had w like those
Mal 4: 2 rise with healing in its w.
Lk 13: 34 hen gathers her chicks under her w,
Rev 4: 8 the four living creatures had six w

WINS (WIN)

Pr 11: 30 and he who w souls is wise.

WINTER

Mk 13: 18 that this will not take place in w,

WIPE (WIPED)

Isa 25: 8 The Sovereign LORD will w away
Rev 7: 17 God will w away every tear
21: 4 He will w every tear

WIPED (WIPE)

Lk 7: 38 Then she w them with her hair,
Ac 3: 19 so that your sins may be w out,

WISDOM (WISE)

Ge 3: 6 and also desirable for gaining w,
1Ki 4: 29 God gave Solomon w and very
2Ch 1: 10 Give me w and knowledge,
Ps 51: 6 you teach me w in the inmost place
111: 10 of the LORD is the beginning of w;

Pr 2: 6 For the LORD gives *w*,
3: 13 Blessed is the man who finds *w*,
4: 7 *W* is supreme; therefore get
8: 11 for *w* is more precious than rubies,
11: 2 but with humility comes *w*.
13: 10 *w* is found in those who take advice
23: 23 get *w*, discipline and understanding
29: 3 A man who loves *w* brings joy
29: 15 The rod of correction imparts *w*,
31: 26 She speaks with *w*,
Isa 11: 2 Spirit of *w* and of understanding,
28: 29 in counsel and magnificent in *w*.
Jer 10: 12 he founded the world by his *w*
Mic 6: 9 and to fear your name is *w*—
Mt 11: 19 But *w* is proved right by her actions
Lk 2: 52 And Jesus grew in *w* and stature,
Ac 6: 3 known to be full of the Spirit and *w*.
Ro 11: 33 the depth of the riches of the *w*
1Co 1: 17 not with words of human *w*,
1: 30 who has become for us *w* from God
12: 8 through the Spirit the message of *w*
Eph 1: 17 may give you the Spirit of *w*
Col 2: 3 are hidden all the treasures of *w*
2: 23 indeed have an appearance of *w*,
Jas 1: 5 of you lacks *w*, he should ask God,
3: 13 in the humility that comes from *w*.
Rev 5: 12 and wealth and *w* and strength

WISE (WISDOM WISER)
1Ki 3: 12 give you a *w* and discerning heart,
Job 5: 13 He catches the *w* in their craftiness
Ps 19: 7 making *w* the simple.
Pr 3: 7 Do not be *w* in your own eyes;
9: 8 rebuke a *w* man and he will love
10: 1 A *w* son brings joy to his father,
11: 30 and he who wins souls is *w*.
13: 1 A *w* son heeds his father's
13: 20 He who walks with the *w* grows *w*,
16: 23 A *w* man's heart guides his mouth,
17: 28 Even a fool is thought *w*
Ecc 9: 17 The quiet words of the *w* are more
Jer 9: 23 "Let not the *w* man boast
Eze 28: 6 " 'Because you think you are *w*,
Da 2: 21 He gives wisdom to the *w*
12: 3 Those who are *w* will shine like
Mt 11: 25 hidden these things from the *w*
25: 2 them were foolish and five were *w*.
1Co 1: 19 I will destroy the wisdom of the *w*;
1: 27 things of the world to shame the *w*;
3: 19 He catches the *w* in their craftiness
Eph 5: 15 but as *w*, making the most
2Ti 3: 15 able to make you *w* for salvation
Jas 3: 13 Who is *w* and understanding

WISER (WISE)
Pr 9: 9 a wise man and he will be *w* still;
1Co 1: 25 of God is *w* than man's wisdom,

WISH (WISHES)
Jn 15: 7 ask whatever you *w*, and it will be
Ro 9: 3 For I could *w* that I myself were
Rev 3: 15 I *w* you were either one

WISHES (WISH)
Rev 22: 17 let him come; and whoever *w*,

WITCHCRAFT
Dt 18: 10 engages in *w*, or casts spells,
Gal 5: 20 idolatry and *w*; hatred, discord,

WITHDREW
Lk 5: 16 But Jesus often *w* to lonely places

WITHER (WITHERS)
Ps 1: 3 and whose leaf does not *w*.
37: 19 In times of disaster they will not *w*;

WITHERS (WITHER)
Isa 40: 7 The grass *w* and the flowers fall,
1Pe 1: 24 the grass *w* and the flowers fall,

WITHHELD (WITHHOLD)
Ge 22: 12 you have not *w* from me your son,

WITHHOLD (WITHHELD WITHHOLDS)
Ps 84: 11 no good thing does he *w*
Pr 23: 13 Do not *w* discipline from a child;

WITHHOLDS (WITHHOLD)
Dt 27: 19 "Cursed is the man who *w* justice

WITNESS (EYEWITNESSES WITNESSES)
Pr 12: 17 truthful *w* gives honest testimony,
19: 9 A false *w* will not go unpunished,
Jn 1: 8 he came only as a *w* to the light.

WITNESSES (WITNESS)
Dt 19: 15 by the testimony of two or three *w*.
Mt 18: 16 by the testimony of two or three *w*.'
Ac 1: 8 and you will be my *w* in Jerusalem,

WIVES (WIFE)
Eph 5: 22 *W*, submit to your husbands
5: 25 love your *w*, just as Christ loved
1Pe 3: 1 words by the behavior of their *w*,

WIVES' (WIFE)
1Ti 4: 7 with godless myths and old *w* tales

WOE
Isa 6: 5 "*W* to me!" I cried.
Eze 34: 2 *W* to the shepherds
Mt 18: 7 "*W* to the world
23: 13 "*W* to you, teachers of the law
Jude : 11 *W* to them! They have taken

WOLF (WOLVES)
Isa 65: 25 *w* and the lamb will feed together,

WOLVES (WOLF)
Mt 10: 16 you out like sheep among *w*.

WOMAN (MAN)
Ge 2: 22 God made a *w* from
2: 23 she shall be called '*w*,'
3: 6 *w* saw that the fruit
3: 12 The *w* you put here with
3: 15 between you and the *w*,
3: 16 To the *w* he said,
12: 11 a beautiful *w* you are.
20: 3 because of the *w* you have
24: 5 if the *w* is unwilling
Ex 2: 1 married a Levite *w*
3: 22 Every *w* is to ask her
21: 10 If he marries another *w*
21: 22 hit a pregnant *w*
Lev 12: 2 *w* who becomes pregnant
15: 19 *w* has her regular flow
15: 25 a *w* has a discharge
18: 17 sexual relations with both a *w*
20: 13 as one lies with a *w*,
Nu 5: 29 when a *w* goes astray
30: 3 young *w* still living in
30: 9 by a widow or divorced *w*
30: 10 *w* living with her husband
Dt 20: 7 become pledged to a *w*
21: 11 the captives a beautiful *w*
22: 5 *w* must not wear men's
22: 13 married this *w* but when
Jdg 4: 9 hand Sisera over to a *w*.
13: 6 the *w* went to her husband
14: 2 have seen a Philistine *w*
16: 4 he fell in love with a *w*
20: 4 husband of the murdered *w*
Ru 3: 11 a *w* of noble character
1Sa 1: 15 a *w* who is deeply troubled
25: 3 intelligent and beautiful *w*,
28: 7 a *w* who is a medium,
2Sa 11: 2 he saw a *w* bathing
13: 17 "Get this *w* out of here
14: 2 had a wise *w* brought
20: 16 a wise *w* called from
1Ki 3: 18 this *w* also had a baby.
17: 24 the *w* said to Elijah,
2Ki 4: 8 a well-to-do *w* was there,
8: 1 Elisha had said to the *w*
9: 34 "Take care of that cursed *w*,"
Job 14: 1 Man born of *w* is of few
Pr 11: 16 A kindhearted *w* gains respect,
11: 22 a beautiful *w* who shows no
14: 1 a wise *w* builds her house,
30: 23 unloved *w* who is married,
31: 30 a *w* who fears the LORD
Isa 54: 1 O barren *w*, you who never
Mt 5: 28 looks at a *w* lustfully
9: 20 a *w* who had been subject
15: 28 *W* you have great faith!
26: 7 a *w* came to him with
Mk 5: 25 a *w* was there who had
7: 25 a *w* whose little daughter
Lk 7: 39 what kind of a *w* she is
10: 38 a *w* named Martha opened
13: 12 "*W*, you are set free
15: 8 suppose a *w* has ten silver
Jn 2: 4 *w*, why do you involve
4: 7 a Samaritan *w* came
8: 3 a *w* caught in adultery.
19: 26 *w*, here is your son,"
20: 15 *W*,' he said, "Why are you crying?
Ac 9: 40 Turning toward the dead *w*,
16: 14 was a *w* named Lydia,
Ro 7: 2 a married *w* is bound to
1Co 7: 2 each *w* her own husband
7: 15 a believing man or *w* is
7: 34 an unmarried *w* or virgin
7: 39 *w* is bound to her husband
11: 3 the head of the *w* is man,
11: 7 the *w* is the glory of man
11: 13 a *w* to pray to God with
Gal 4: 4 his Son, born of a *w*,
4: 31 not children of the slave *w*,
1Ti 2: 11 A *w* should learn in
5: 16 any *w* who is a believer
Rev 2: 20 You tolerate that *w* Jezebel,
12: 1 a *w* clothed with the sun
12: 13 he pursued the *w* who had
17: 3 a *w* sitting on a scarlet

WOMEN (MAN)
Mt 11: 11 among those born of *w*,
28: 5 The angel said to the *w*,
Mk 15: 41 Many other *w* who had come
Lk 1: 42 Blessed are you among *w*,
8: 2 also some *w* who had been
23: 27 *w* who mourned and wailed
24: 11 they did not believe the *w*,
Ac 1: 14 along with the *w* and Mary
16: 13 speak to the *w* who had
17: 4 not a few prominent *w*.
Ro 1: 26 *w* exchanged natural relations
1Co 14: 34 *w* should remain silent in
Php 4: 3 help these *w* who have
1Ti 2: 9 want *w* to dress modestly
5: 2 older *w* as mothers,
Tit 2: 3 teach the older *w* to be
2: 4 train the younger *w* to love
Heb 11: 35 *W* received back their dead
1Pe 3: 5 the holy *w* of the past

WOMB
Job 1: 21 Naked I came from my mother's *w*,
Ps 139: 13 in my mother's *w*.
Pr 31: 2 "O my son, O son of my *w*,
Jer 1: 5 you in the *w* I knew you,
Lk 1: 44 the baby in my *w* leaped for joy.
Jn 3: 4 into his mother's *w* to be born!"

WON (WIN)
1Pe 3: 1 they may be *w* over without words

WONDER (WONDERFUL WONDERS)
Ps 17: 7 Show the *w* of your great love,
SS 1: 3 No *w* the maidens love you!

WONDERFUL* (WONDER)
2Sa 1: 26 Your love for me was *w*,
1: 26 more *w* than that of women.
1Ch 16: 9 tell of all his *w* acts.
Job 42: 3 things too *w* for me to know.
Ps 26: 7 and telling of all your *w* deeds.
31: 21 for he showed his *w* love to me
75: 1 men tell of your *w* deeds.
105: 2 tell of all his *w* acts.
107: 8 and his *w* deeds for men,
107: 15 and his *w* deeds for men,
107: 21 and his *w* deeds for men.
107: 24 his *w* deeds in the deep.
107: 31 and his *w* deeds for men.
119: 18 *w* things in your law.
119: 129 Your statutes are *w*;
131: 1 or things too *w* for me.
139: 6 Such knowledge is too *w* for me,
139: 14 your works are *w*,
145: 5 I will meditate on your *w* works.
Isa 9: 6 *W* Counselor, Mighty God,
28: 29 *w* in counsel and magnificent
Mt 21: 15 of the law saw the *w* things he did
Lk 13: 17 with all the *w* things he was doing.
1Pe 2: 9 out of darkness into his *w* light.

WONDERS (WONDER)
Ex 3: 20 with all the *w* that I will perform
Dt 10: 21 and awesome *w* you saw
2Sa 7: 23 awesome *w* by driving out nations
Job 37: 14 stop and consider God's *w*.
Ps 9: 1 I will tell of all your *w*.
89: 5 The heavens praise your *w*,
119: 27 then I will meditate on your *w*.
Joel 2: 30 I will show *w* in the heavens
Ac 2: 11 we hear them declaring the *w*
2: 19 I will show *w* in the heaven above
5: 12 many miraculous signs and *w*
2Co 12: 12 that mark an apostle—signs, *w*
2Th 2: 9 and *w*, and in every sort
Heb 2: 4 also testified to it by signs, *w*

WOOD
Isa 44:19 Shall I bow down to a block of *w*?"
1Co 3:12 costly stones, *w*, hay or straw,

WOOL
Pr 31:13 She selects *w* and flax
Isa 1:18 they shall be like *w*.
Da 7:9 hair of his head was white like *w*.
Rev 1:14 and hair were white like *w*,

WORD (BYWORD WORDS)
Nu 30:2 he must not break his *w*
Dt 8:3 but on every *w* that comes
2Sa 22:31 the *w* of the LORD is flawless.
Ps 56:4 In God, whose *w* I praise,
119:9 By living according to your *w*.
119:11 I have hidden your *w* in my heart
119:105 Your *w* is a lamp to my feet
Pr 12:25 but a kind *w* cheers him up.
15:1 but a harsh *w* stirs up anger.
25:11 A *w* aptly spoken
30:5 "Every *w* of God is flawless;
Isa 55:11 so is my *w* that goes out
Jer 23:29 "Is not my *w* like fire," declares
Mt 4:4 but on every *w* that comes
12:36 for every careless *w* they have
15:6 Thus you nullify the *w* of God
Mk 4:14 parable? The farmer sows the *w*.
Jn 1:1 was the *W*, and the *W* was
1:14 The *W* became flesh and made his
17:17 them by the truth; your *w* is truth.
Ac 6:4 and the ministry of the *w*."
2Co 2:17 we do not peddle the *w* of God
4:2 nor do we distort the *w* of God.
Eph 6:17 of the Spirit, which is the *w* of God.
Php 2:16 as you hold out the *w* of life—
Col 3:16 Let the *w* of Christ dwell
2Ti 2:15 and who correctly handles the *w*
Heb 4:12 For the *w* of God is living
Jas 1:22 Do not merely listen to the *w*,
2Pe 1:19 And we have the *w* of the prophets

WORDS (WORD)
Dt 11:18 Fix these *w* of mine in your hearts
Ps 12:6 the *w* of the LORD are flawless,
119:103 How sweet are your *w* to my taste,
119:130 The unfolding of your *w* gives light;
119:160 All your *w* are true;
Pr 2:1 My son, if you accept my *w*
10:19 When *w* are many, sin is not absent
16:24 Pleasant *w* are a honeycomb,
30:6 Do not add to his *w*,
Ecc 12:11 The *w* of the wise are like goads,
Jer 15:16 When your *w* came, I ate them;
Mt 24:35 but my *w* will never pass away.
Lk 6:47 and hears my *w* and puts them
Jn 6:68 You have the *w* of eternal life.
15:7 in me and my *w* remain in you,
1Co 2:13 but in *w* taught by the Spirit,
14:19 rather speak five intelligible *w*
Rev 22:19 And if anyone takes *w* away

WORK (WORKED WORKER WORKERS WORKING WORKMAN WORKMANSHIP WORKS)
Ge 2:2 day he rested from all his *w*.
Ex 23:12 "Six days do your *w*,
Nu 8:11 ready to do the *w* of the LORD.
Dt 5:14 On it you shall not do any *w*,
Ps 19:1 the skies proclaim the *w*
Ecc 5:19 his lot and be happy in his *w*—
Jer 48:10 lax in doing the LORD's *w*!
Mt 20:1 to hire men to *w* in his vineyard.
Jn 6:27 Do not *w* for food that spoils,
9:4 we must do the *w* of him who sent
Ac 13:2 for the *w* to which I have called
1Co 3:13 test the quality of each man's *w*.
4:12 We *w* hard with our own hands.
Eph 4:16 up in love, as each part does its *w*.
Php 1:6 that he who began a good *w*
2:12 continue to *w* out your salvation
Col 3:23 Whatever you do, *w* at it
1Th 4:11 and to *w* with your hands,
5:12 to respect those who *w* hard
2Th 3:10 If a man will not *w*, he shall not eat
2Ti 3:17 equipped for every good *w*.
Heb 6:10 he will not forget your *w*
2Jn :11 him shares in his wicked *w*.
3Jn :8 men so that we may *w* together

WORKED (WORK)
1Co 15:10 No, I *w* harder than all of them—
2Th 3:8 On the contrary, we *w* night

WORKER (WORK)
Lk 10:7 for the *w* deserves his wages.
1Ti 5:18 and "The *w* deserves his wages."

WORKERS (WORK)
Mt 9:37 is plentiful but the *w* are few.
1Co 3:9 For we are God's fellow *w*;

WORKING (WORK)
Col 3:23 as *w* for the Lord, not for men,

WORKMAN (WORK)
2Ti 2:15 a *w* who does not need

WORKMANSHIP* (WORK)
Eph 2:10 For we are God's *w*, created

WORKS (WORK)
Ps 66:5 how awesome his *w* in man's behalf
145:6 of the power of your awesome *w*,
Pr 8:22 As the first of his *w*,
31:31 let her *w* bring her praise
Ro 4:2 in fact, Abraham was justified by *w*
8:28 in all things God *w* for the good
Eph 2:9 not by *w*, so that no one can boast.
4:12 to prepare God's people for *w*

WORLD (WORLDLY)
Ps 9:8 He will judge the *w*
50:12 for the *w* is mine, and all that is in it
96:13 He will judge the *w*
Pr 8:23 before the *w* began.
Isa 13:11 I will punish the *w* for its evil,
Zep 1:18 the whole *w* will be consumed,
Mt 5:14 "You are the light of the *w*.
16:26 for a man if he gains the whole *w*,
Mk 16:15 into all the *w* and preach the good
Jn 1:29 who takes away the sin of the *w*!
3:16 so loved the *w* that he gave his one
8:12 he said, "I am the light of the *w*.
15:19 As it is, you do not belong to the *w*,
16:33 In this *w* you will have trouble.
17:5 had with you before the *w* began.
17:14 not of the *w* any more than I am
18:36 "My kingdom is not of this *w*.
Ac 17:24 "The God who made the *w*
Ro 3:19 and the whole *w* held accountable
10:18 their words to the ends of the *w*."
1Co 1:27 things of the *w* to shame the strong.
3:19 the wisdom of this *w* is foolishness
6:2 that the saints will judge the *w*?
2Co 5:19 that God was reconciling the *w*
10:3 For though we live in the *w*,
1Ti 6:7 For we brought nothing into the *w*,
Heb 11:38 the *w* was not worthy of them.
Jas 2:5 poor in the eyes of the *w* to be rich
4:4 with the *w* is hatred toward God?
1Pe 1:20 before the creation of the *w*,
1Jn 2:2 but also for the sins of the whole *w*.
2:15 not love the *w* or anything in the *w*.
5:4 born of God overcomes the *w*.
Rev 13:8 slain from the creation of the *w*.

WORLDLY (WORLD)
1Co 3:1 address you as spiritual but as *w*—
Tit 2:12 to ungodliness and *w* passions,

WORM
Mk 9:48 " 'their *w* does not die,

WORRY (WORRYING)
Mt 6:25 I tell you, do not *w* about your life,
10:19 do not *w* about what to say

WORRYING (WORRY)
Mt 6:27 of you by *w* can add a single hour

WORSHIP (WORSHIPED WORSHIPS)
Jos 22:27 that we will *w* the LORD
2Ki 17:36 arm, is the one you must *w*.
1Ch 16:29 *w* the LORD in the splendor
Ps 95:6 Come, let us bow down in *w*,
100:2 *w* the LORD with gladness;
Zec 14:17 up to Jerusalem to *w* the King,
Mt 2:2 and have come to *w* him."
4:9 "if you will bow down and *w* me."
Jn 4:24 and his worshipers must *w* in spirit
Ro 12:1 to God—this is your spiritual act of *w*.
Heb 10:1 perfect those who draw near to *w*.

WORSHIPED (WORSHIP)
2Ch 29:30 and bowed their heads and *w*.
Mt 28:9 clasped his feet and *w* him.

WORSHIPS (WORSHIP)
Isa 44:15 But he also fashions a god and *w* it;

WORTH (WORTHY)
Job 28:13 Man does not comprehend its *w*;
Pr 31:10 She is *w* far more than rubies.
Mt 10:31 are *w* more than many sparrows.
Ro 8:18 sufferings are not *w* comparing
1Pe 1:7 of greater *w* than gold,
3:4 which is of great *w* in God's sight.

WORTHLESS
Pr 11:4 Wealth is *w* in the day of wrath,
Jas 1:26 himself and his religion is *w*.

WORTHY (WORTH)
1Ch 16:25 For great is the LORD and most *w*
Mt 10:37 more than me is not *w* of me;
Lk 15:19 I am no longer *w* to be called your
Eph 4:1 to live a life *w* of the calling you
Php 1:27 in a manner *w* of the gospel
Col 1:10 in order that you may live a life *w*
1Ti 3:8 are to be men *w* of respect, sincere,
Heb 3:3 Jesus has been found *w*
3Jn :6 on their way in a manner *w* of God.
Rev 5:2 "Who is *w* to break the seals

WOUND (WOUNDS)
1Co 8:12 and *w* their weak conscience,

WOUNDS (WOUND)
Pr 27:6 *w* from a friend can be trusted
Isa 53:5 and by his *w* we are healed.
Zec 13:6 'What are these *w* on your body?'
1Pe 2:24 by his *w* you have been healed.

WRAPS
Ps 104:2 He *w* himself in light

WRATH
2Ch 36:16 scoffed at his prophets until the *w*
Ps 2:5 and terrifies them in his *w*, saying,
76:10 Surely your *w* against men brings
Pr 15:1 A gentle answer turns away *w*,
Isa 13:13 at the *w* of the LORD Almighty,
51:17 the cup of his *w*,
Jer 25:15 filled with the wine of my *w*
Eze 5:13 my *w* against them will subside,
20:8 So I said I would pour out my *w*
Am 1:3 I will not turn back my *w*.
Na 1:2 maintains his *w* against his enemies
Zep 1:15 That day will be a day of *w*,
Jn 3:36 for God's *w* remains on him."
Ro 1:18 The *w* of God is being revealed
2:5 you are storing up *w*
5:9 saved from God's *w* through him!
9:22 choosing to show his *w*
1Th 5:9 God did not appoint us to suffer *w*
Rev 6:16 and from the *w* of the Lamb!
19:15 the fury of the *w* of God Almighty.

WRESTLED
Ge 32:24 and a man *w* with him till daybreak

WRITE (WRITER WRITING WRITTEN WROTE)
Dt 6:9 *W* them on the doorframes
10:2 I will *w* on the tablets the words
Pr 7:3 *w* them on the tablet of your heart.
Jer 31:33 and *w* it on their hearts.
Heb 8:10 and *w* them on their hearts.
Rev 3:12 I will also *w* on him my new name.

WRITER* (WRITE)
Ps 45:1 my tongue is the pen of a skillful *w*.

WRITING (WRITE)
1Co 14:37 him acknowledge that what I am *w*

WRITTEN (WRITE)
Dt 28:58 which are *w* in this book,
Jos 1:8 careful to do everything *w* in it.
23:6 to obey all that is *w* in the Book
Ps 40:7 it is *w* about me in the scroll.
Da 12:1 everyone whose name is found *w*
Mal 3:16 A scroll of remembrance was *w*
Lk 10:20 but rejoice that your names are *w*
24:44 must be fulfilled that is *w* about me
Jn 20:31 these are *w* that you may believe
21:25 for the books that would be *w*.
Ro 2:15 of the law are *w* on their hearts,
1Co 4:6 "Do not go beyond what is *w*."
10:11 as examples and were *w* down
2Co 3:3 *w* not with ink but with the Spirit

Col 2:14 having canceled the *w* code,
Heb 10: 7 it is *w* about me in the scroll—
12:23 whose names are *w* in heaven.
Rev 21:27 but only those whose names are *w*

WRONG (WRONGDOING WRONGED WRONGS)

Ex 23: 2 Do not follow the crowd in doing *w*
Nu 5: 7 must make full restitution for his *w*,
Dt 32: 4 A faithful God who does no *w*,
Job 34:12 unthinkable that God would do *w*,
Ps 5: 5 you hate all who do *w*.
Gal 2:11 to his face, because he was clearly in the *w*.
1Th 5:15 that nobody pays back *w* for *w*,

WRONGDOING (WRONG)

Job 1:22 sin by charging God with *w*.
1Jn 5:17 All *w* is sin, and there is sin that

WRONGED (WRONG)

1Co 6: 7 not rather be *w*? Why not rather

WRONGS (WRONG)

Pr 10:12 but love covers over all *w*.
1Co 13: 5 angered, it keeps no record of *w*.

WROTE (WRITE)

Ex 34:28 And he *w* on the tablets the words
Jn 5:46 for he *w* about me.
8: 8 down and *w* on the ground.

XERXES

King of Persia, husband of Esther. Deposed Vashti; replaced her with Esther (Est 1-2). Sealed Haman's edict to annihilate the Jews (Est 3). Received Esther without having called her (Est 5:1-8). Honored Mordecai (Est 6). Hanged Haman (Est 7). Issued edict allowing Jews to defend themselves (Est 8). Exalted Mordecai (Est 8:1-2, 15; 9:4; 10).

YEAR (YEARS)

Ex 34:23 Three times a *y* all your men are
Lev 16:34 to be made once a *y* for all the sins
25: 4 But in the seventh *y* the land is
25:11 The fiftieth *y* shall be a jubilee
Heb 10: 1 repeated endlessly *y* after *y*,

YEARS (YEAR)

Ge 1:14 to mark seasons and days and *y*,
Ex 12:40 lived in Egypt was 430 *y*.
16:35 The Israelites ate manna forty *y*,
Job 36:26 of his *y* is past finding out.
Ps 90: 4 For a thousand *y* in your sight
90:10 The length of our days is seventy *y*
Pr 3: 2 they will prolong your life many *y*
Lk 3:23 Jesus himself was about thirty *y* old
2Pe 3: 8 the Lord a day is like a thousand *y*,
Rev 20: 2 and bound him for a thousand *y*.

YEAST

Ex 12:15 are to eat bread made without *y*.
Mt 16: 6 guard against the *y* of the Pharisees
1Co 5: 6 you know that a little *y* works

YESTERDAY

Heb 13: 8 Jesus Christ is the same *y*

YOKE (YOKED)

1Ki 12: 4 and the heavy *y* he put on us,
Mt 11:29 Take my *y* upon you and learn
Gal 5: 1 be burdened again by a *y*

YOKED (YOKE)

2Co 6:14 Do not be *y* together

YOUNG (YOUNGER YOUTH)

2Ch 10:14 he followed the advice of the *y* men
Ps 37:25 I was *y* and now I am old,
119: 9 How can a *y* man keep his way
Pr 20:29 The glory of *y* men is their strength
Isa 40:11 he gently leads those that have *y*.
Joel 2:28 your *y* men will see visions,
Ac 2:17 your *y* men will see visions,
7:58 at the feet of a *y* man named Saul.
1Ti 4:12 down on you because you are *y*,
Tit 2: 6 encourage the *y* men
1Pe 5: 5 *Y* men, in the same way be
1Jn 2:13 I write to you, *y* men,

YOUNGER (YOUNG)

1Ti 5: 1 Treat *y* men as brothers, older
Tit 2: 4 Then they can train the *y* women

YOUTH (YOUNG)

Ps 103: 5 so that your *y* is renewed like
Ecc 12: 1 Creator in the days of your *y*,
2Ti 2:22 Flee the evil desires of *y*,

ZACCHAEUS

Lk 19: 2 A man was there by the name of *Z*;

ZEAL (ZEALOUS)

Ps 69: 9 for *z* for your house consumes me,
Pr 19: 2 to have *z* without knowledge,
Isa 59:17 and wrapped himself in *z*
Jn 2:17 "*Z* for your house will consume me
Ro 10: 2 their *z* is not based on knowledge.
12:11 Never be lacking in *z*,

ZEALOUS (ZEAL)

Nu 25:13 he was *z* for the honor of his God
Pr 23:17 always be *z* for the fear
Eze 39:25 and I will be *z* for my holy name.
Gal 4:18 fine to be *z*, provided the purpose is

ZEBULUN

Son of Jacob by Leah (Ge 30:20; 35:23; 1Ch 2:1). Tribe of blessed (Ge 49:13; Dt 33:18-19), numbered (Nu 1:31; 26:27), allotted land (Jos 19:10-16; Eze 48:26), failed to fully possess (Jdg 1:30), supported Deborah (Jdg 4:6-10; 5:14, 18), David (1Ch 12:33), 12,000 from (Rev 7:8).

ZECHARIAH

1. Son of Jeroboam II; king of Israel (2Ki 15:8-12).

2. Post-exilic prophet who encouraged rebuilding of temple (Ezr 5:1; 6:14; Zec 1:1).

ZEDEKIAH

1. False prophet (1Ki 22:11-24; 2Ch 18:10-23).

2. Mattaniah, son of Josiah (1Ch 3:15), made king of Judah by Nebuchadnezzar (2Ki 24:17-25:7, 2Ch 36:10-14; Jer 37-39; 52:1-11).

ZEPHANIAH

Prophet; descendant of Hezekiah (Zep 1:1).

ZERUBBABEL

Descendant of David (1Ch 3:19; Mt 1:3). Led return from exile (Ezr 2:2; Ne 7:7). Governor of Israel; helped rebuild altar and temple (Ezr 3; Hag 1-2; Zec 4).

ZILPAH

Servant of Leah, mother of Jacob's sons Gad and Asher (Ge 30:9-12; 35:26, 46:16-18).

ZIMRI

King of Israel (1Ki 16:9-20).

ZION

2Sa 5: 7 David captured the fortress of *Z*,
Ps 2: 6 King on *Z*, my holy hill."
9:11 to the LORD, enthroned in *Z*;
74: 2 Mount *Z*, where you dwelt.
87: 2 the LORD loves the gates of *Z*
102: 13 and have compassion on *Z*,
137: 3 "Sing us one of the songs of *Z*!"
Isa 2: 3 The law will go out from *Z*,
28:16 "See, I lay a stone in *Z*,
51:11 They will enter *Z* with singing;
52: 8 When the LORD returns to *Z*,
Jer 50: 5 They will ask the way to *Z*
Joel 3:21 The LORD dwells in *Z*!
Am 6: 1 to you who are complacent in *Z*,
Mic 4: 2 The law will go out from *Z*,
Zec 9: 9 Rejoice greatly, O Daughter of *Z*!
Ro 9:33 I lay in *Z* a stone that causes men
11:26 "The deliverer will come from *Z*;
Heb 12:22 But you have come to Mount *Z*,
Rev 14: 1 standing on Mount *Z*,

ZIPPORAH*

Daughter of Reuel; wife of Moses (Ex 2:21-22; 4:20-26; 18:1-6).

ZOPHAR

One of Job's friends (Job 11; 20).

Map Index

Map Index

A

B

C

D

E

F

G

H

I

J

K

L

M

N

O

P

Q

R

S

Map 1: **WORLD OF THE PATRIARCHS**

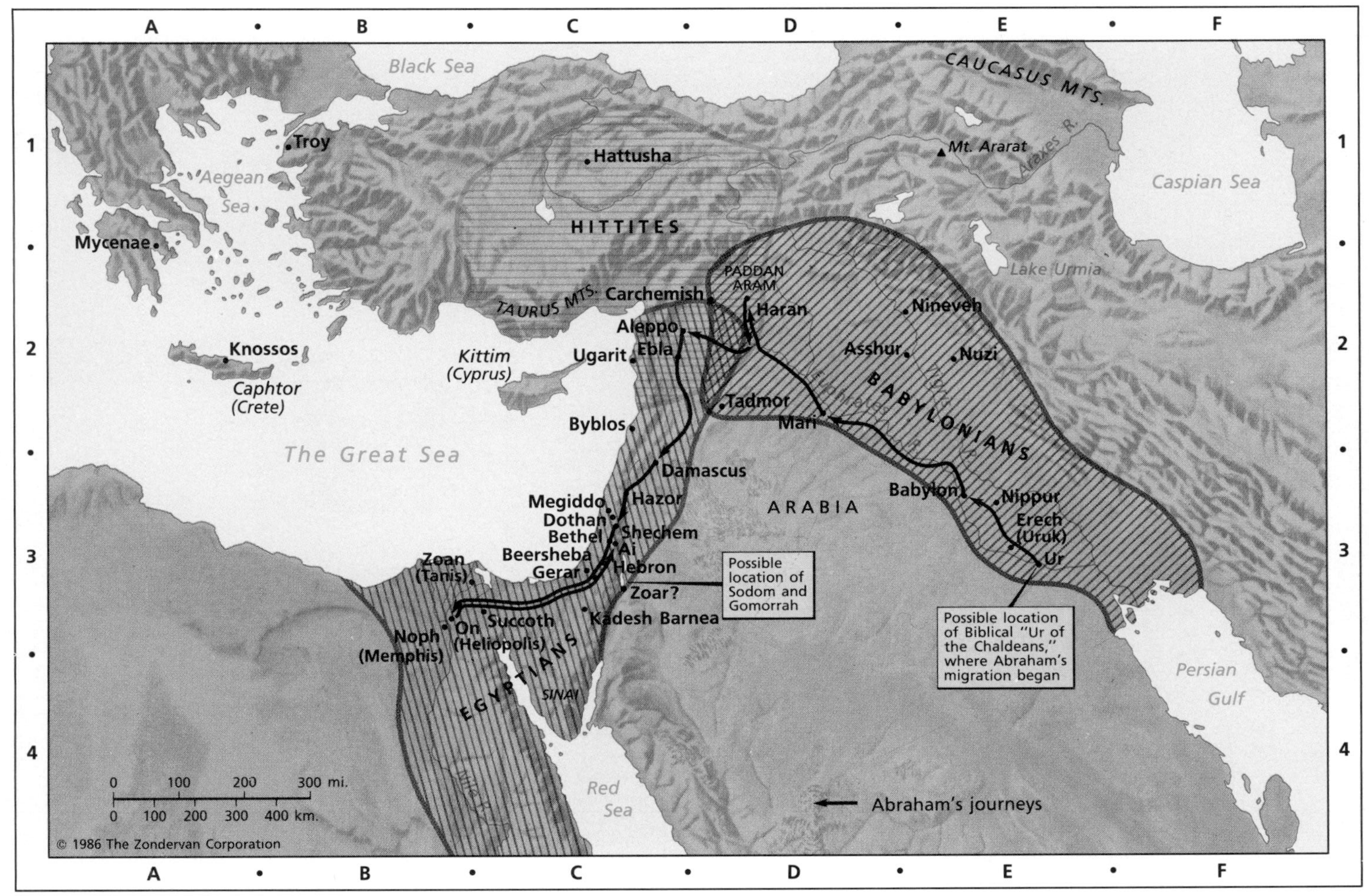

Map 2: **PALESTINE AND SINAI**

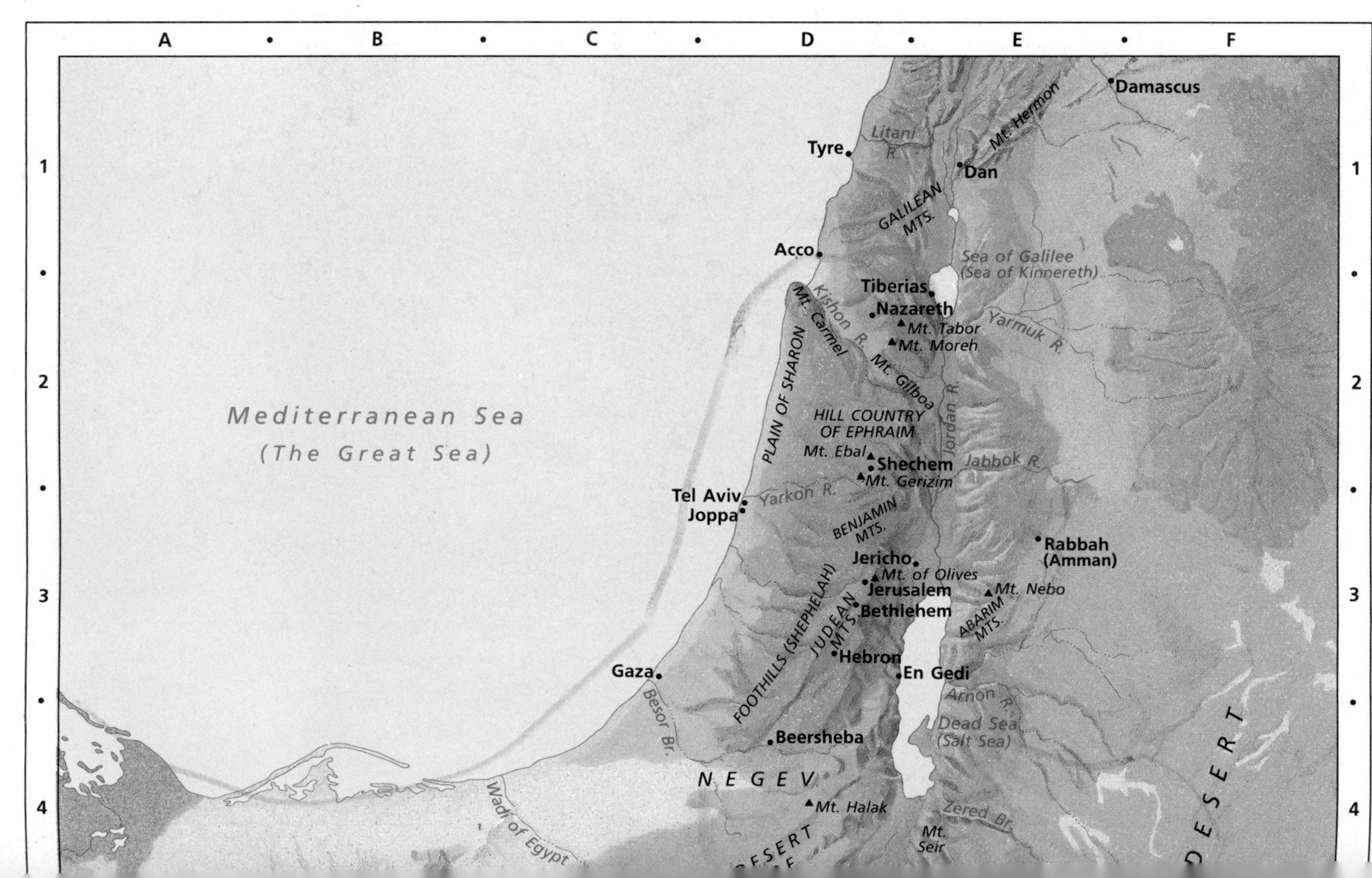

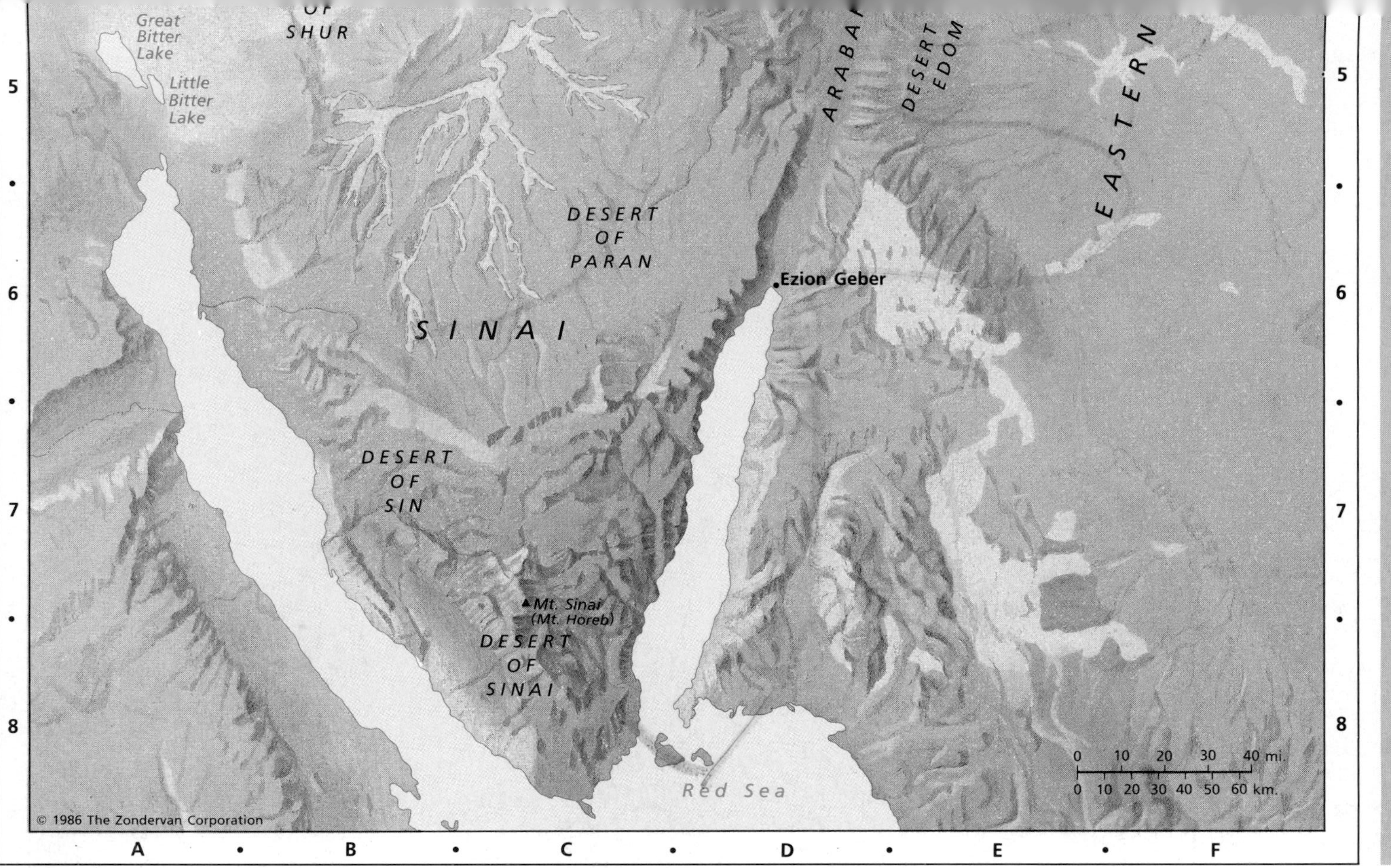

Great Bitter Lake
Little Bitter Lake
SHUR
DESERT OF PARAN
SINAI
Ezion Geber
DESERT EDOM
EASTERN
DESERT OF SIN
Mt. Sinai (Mt. Horeb)
DESERT OF SINAI
Red Sea
0 10 20 30 40 mi.
0 10 20 30 40 50 60 km.
A B C D E F
5 6 7 8

Map 3: **EXODUS AND CONQUEST OF CANAAN**

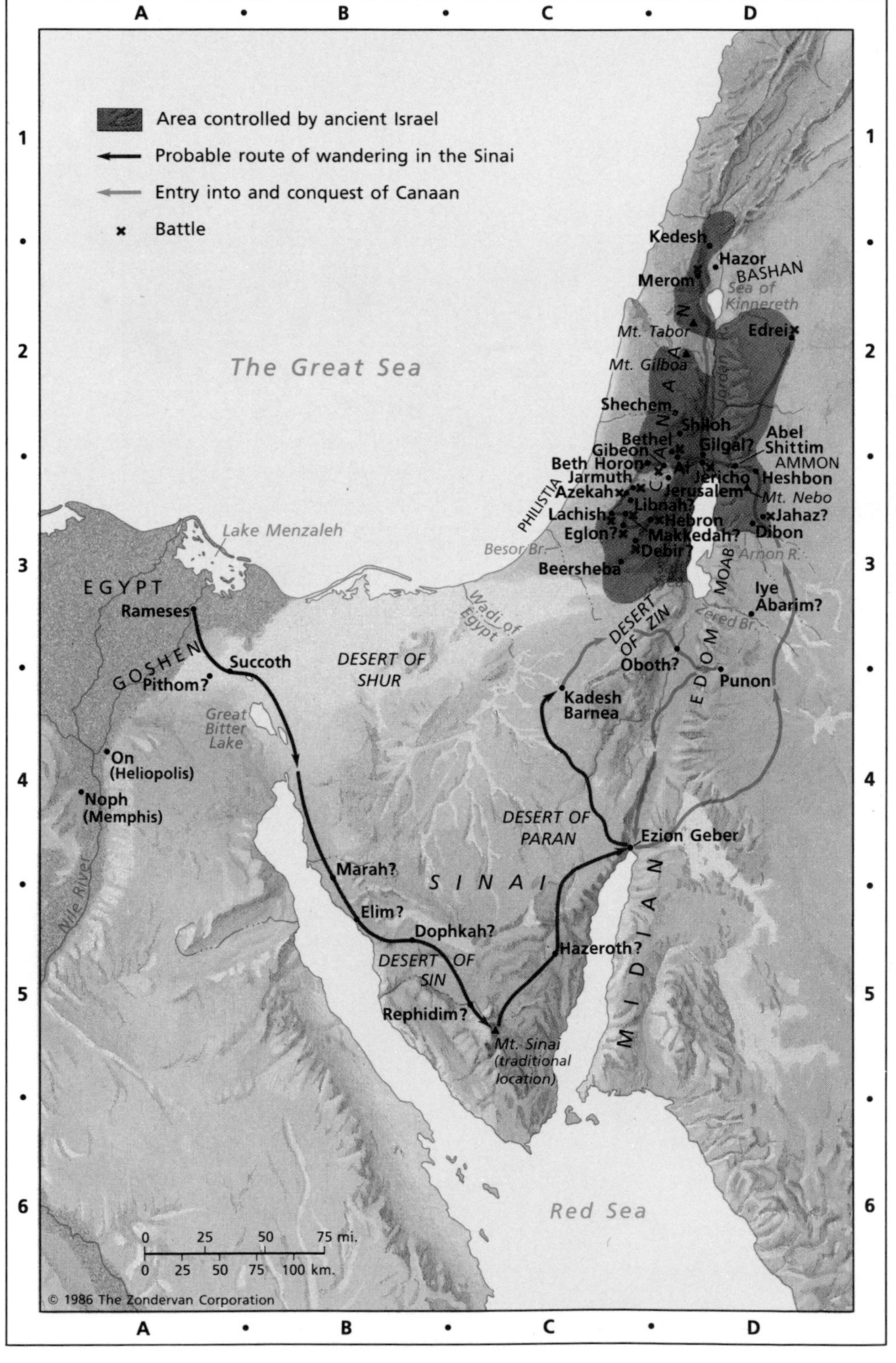

Map 4: LAND OF THE TWELVE TRIBES

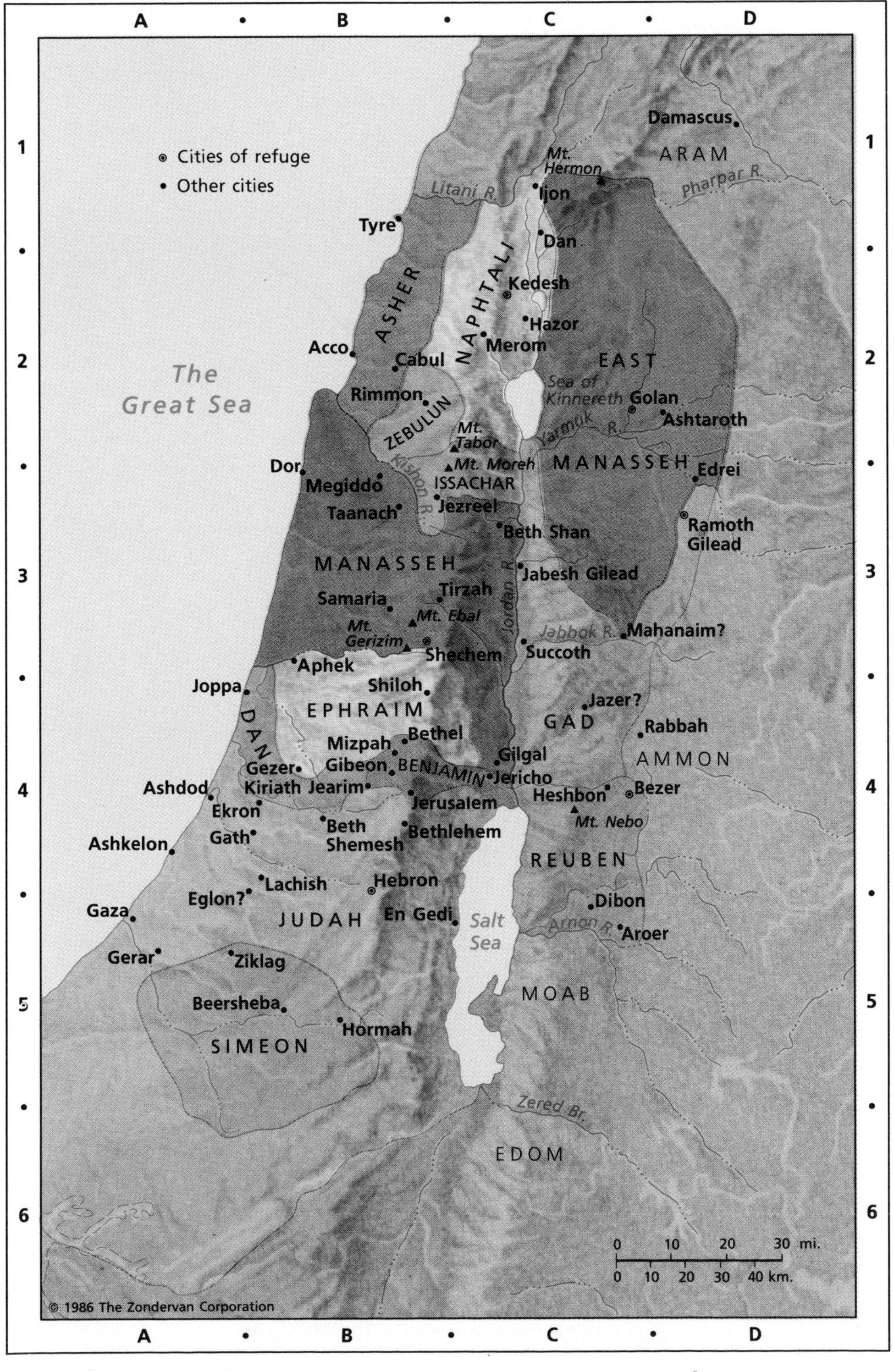

Map 5: **KINGDOM OF DAVID AND SOLOMON**

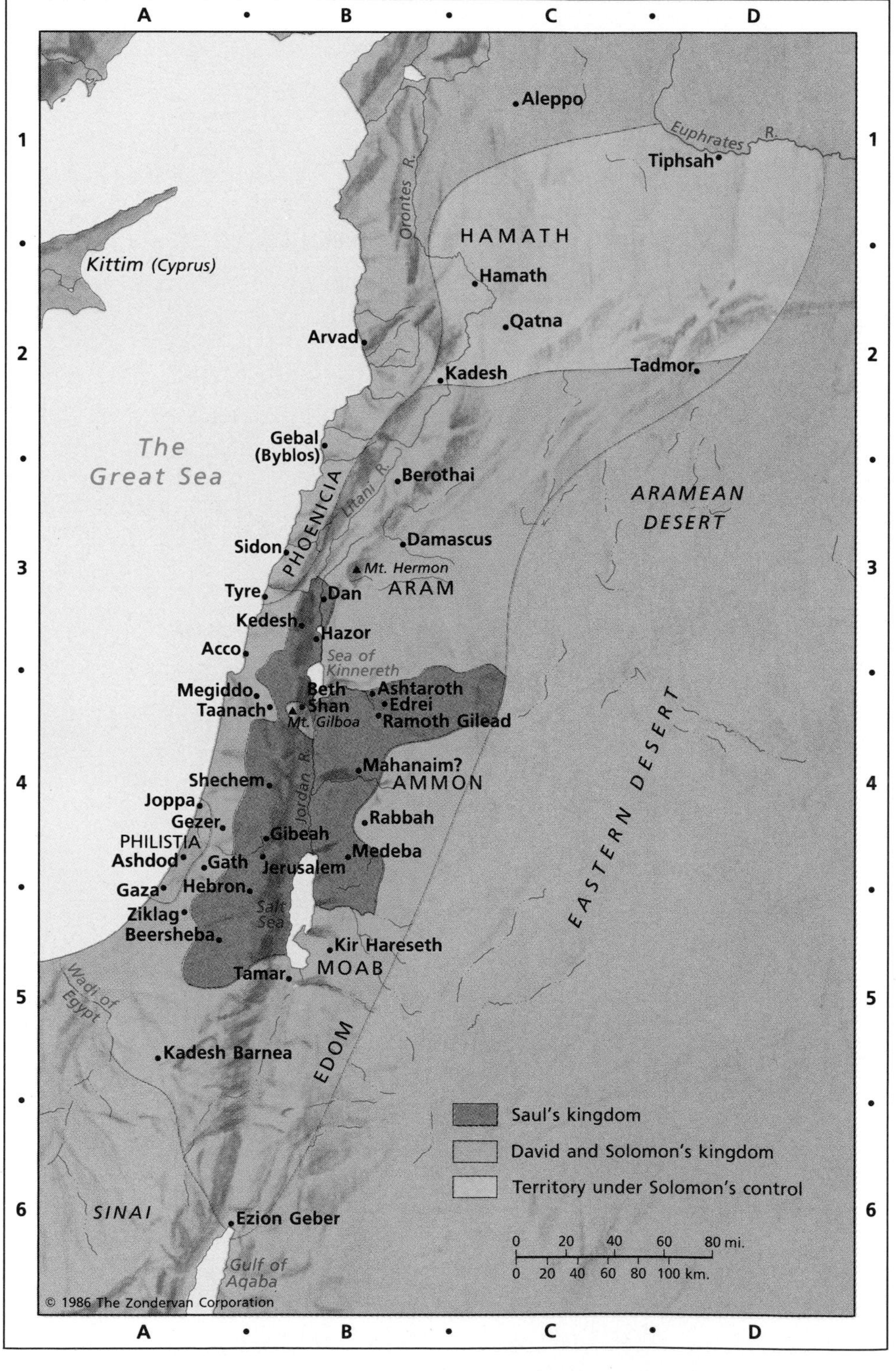

A
B
C
D
1
2
3
4
5
6
Aleppo
Euphrates R.
Tiphsah
Orontes R.
HAMATH
Hamath
Qatna
Kittim (Cyprus)
Arvad
Kadesh
Tadmor
The Great Sea
Gebal (Byblos)
PHOENICIA
Litani R.
Berothai
ARAMEAN DESERT
Sidon
Damascus
Mt. Hermon
ARAM
Tyre
Dan
Kedesh
Hazor
Acco
Sea of Kinnereth
Megiddo
Beth Shan
Ashtaroth
Edrei
Taanach
Mt. Gilboa
Ramoth Gilead
EASTERN DESERT
Mahanaim?
Shechem
AMMON
Joppa
Jordan R.
Gezer
Rabbah
PHILISTIA
Gibeah
Ashdod
Gath
Jerusalem
Medeba
Gaza
Hebron
Ziklag
Salt Sea
Beersheba
Kir Hareseth
MOAB
Tamar
Wadi of Egypt
Kadesh Barnea
EDOM
Saul's kingdom
David and Solomon's kingdom
Territory under Solomon's control
SINAI
Ezion Geber
0 20 40 60 80 mi.
0 20 40 60 80 100 km.
Gulf of Aqaba

Map 6: PROPHETS IN ISRAEL AND JUDAH

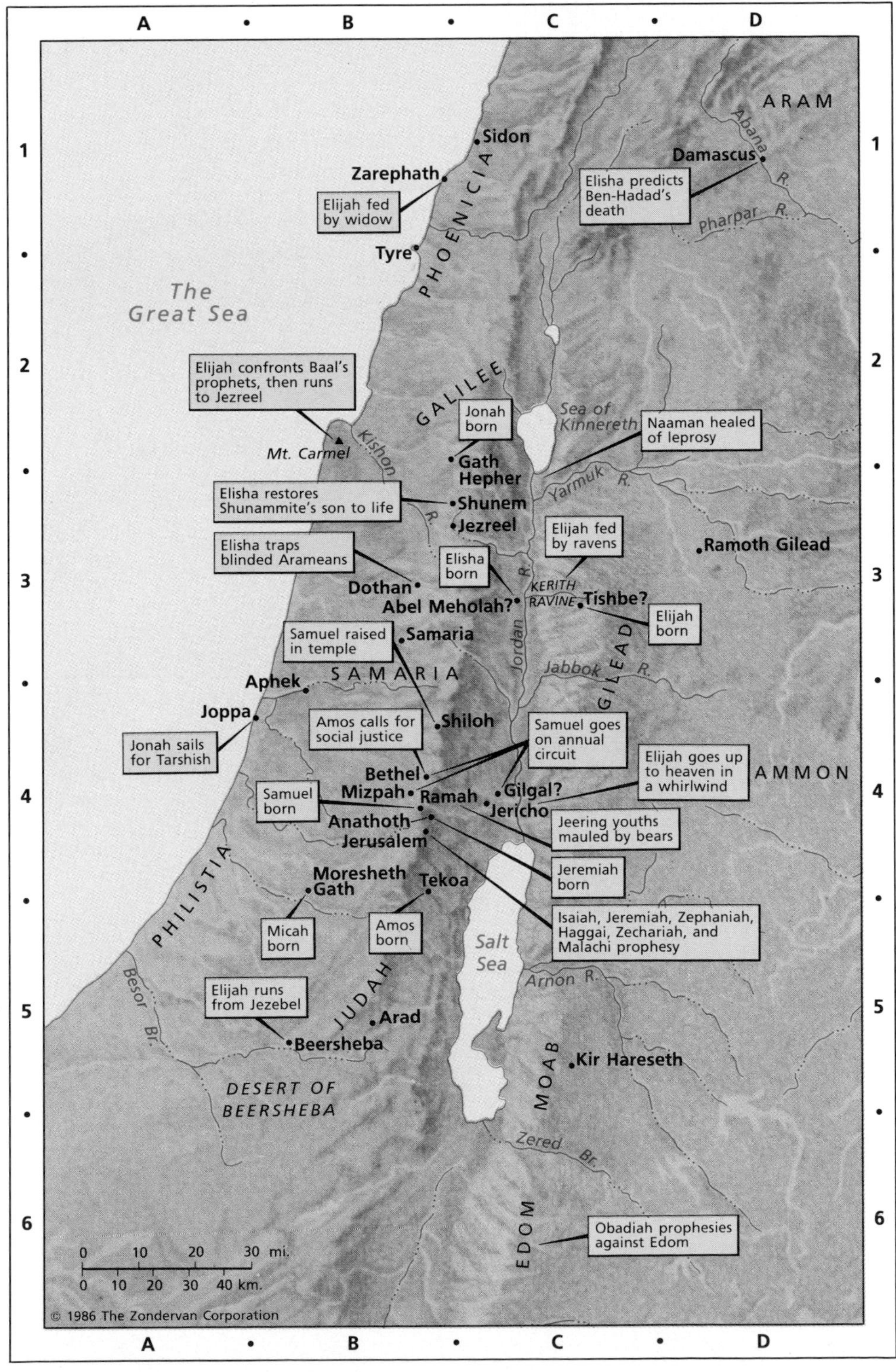
A
B
C
D
1
2
3
4
5
6
ARAM
Abana R.
Pharpar R.
Damascus
Elisha predicts Ben-Hadad's death
Sidon
Zarephath
Elijah fed by widow
PHOENICIA
Tyre
The Great Sea
Elijah confronts Baal's prophets, then runs to Jezreel
Mt. Carmel
Kishon R.
GALILEE
Jonah born
Sea of Kinnereth
Naaman healed of leprosy
Gath Hepher
Yarmuk R.
Elisha restores Shunammite's son to life
Shunem
Jezreel
Elijah fed by ravens
Elisha traps blinded Arameans
Elisha born
Ramoth Gilead
Dothan
KERITH RAVINE
Abel Meholah?
Tishbe?
Elijah born
Samuel raised in temple
Samaria
Jordan R.
Jabbok R.
GILEAD
SAMARIA
Aphek
Joppa
Jonah sails for Tarshish
Amos calls for social justice
Shiloh
Samuel goes on annual circuit
Elijah goes up to heaven in a whirlwind
AMMON
Bethel
Samuel born
Mizpah
Ramah
Gilgal?
Jericho
Anathoth
Jeering youths mauled by bears
Jerusalem
Jeremiah born
PHILISTIA
Moresheth Gath
Tekoa
Isaiah, Jeremiah, Zephaniah, Haggai, Zechariah, and Malachi prophesy
Micah born
Amos born
Salt Sea
Arnon R.
Besor Br.
Elijah runs from Jezebel
JUDAH
Arad
Beersheba
MOAB
Kir Hareseth
DESERT OF BEERSHEBA
Zered Br.
EDOM
Obadiah prophesies against Edom
0 10 20 30 mi.
0 10 20 30 40 km.

Map 7: ASSYRIAN AND BABYLONIAN EMPIRES

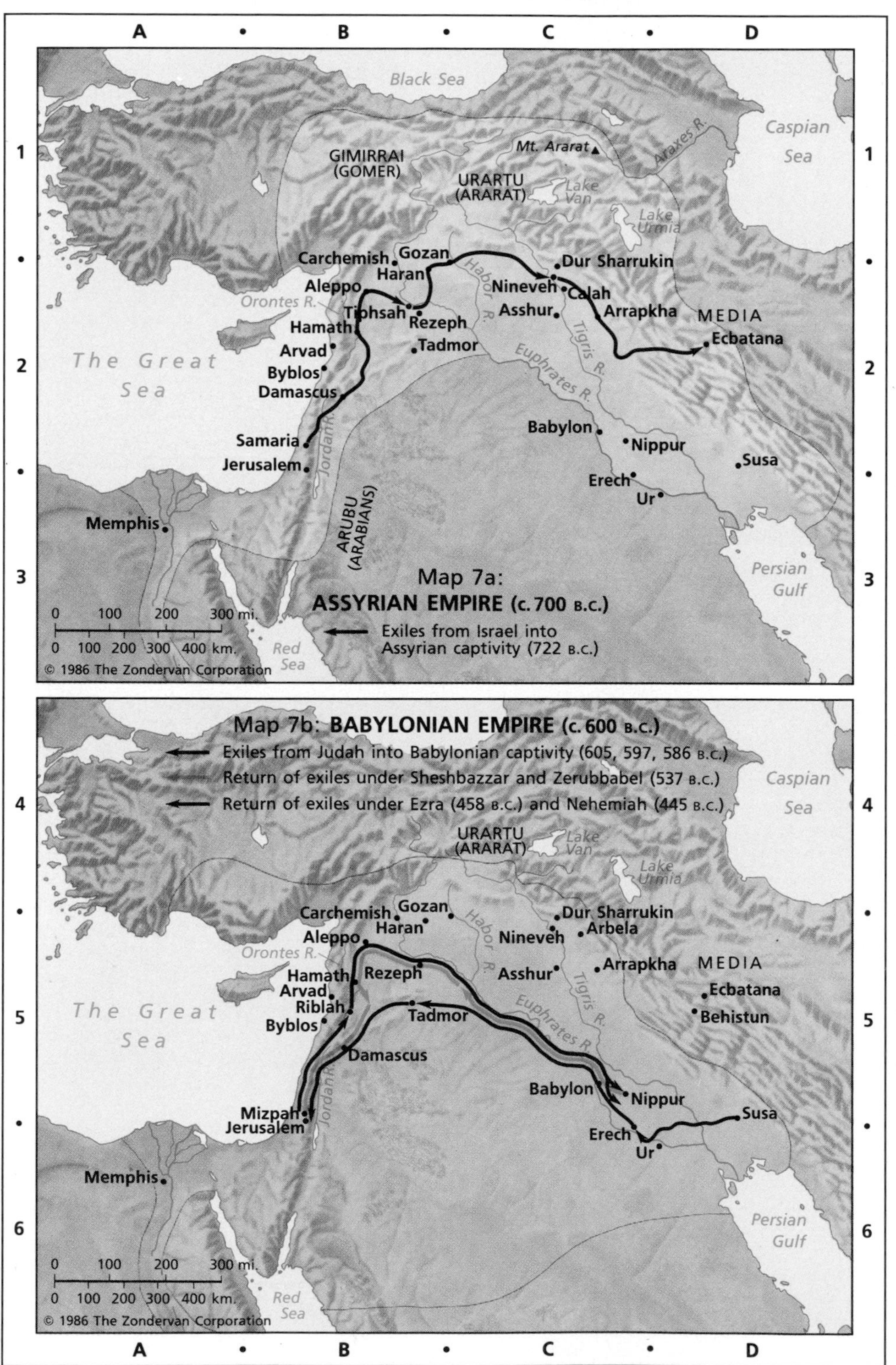

Map 8: **JERUSALEM IN JESUS' TIME**

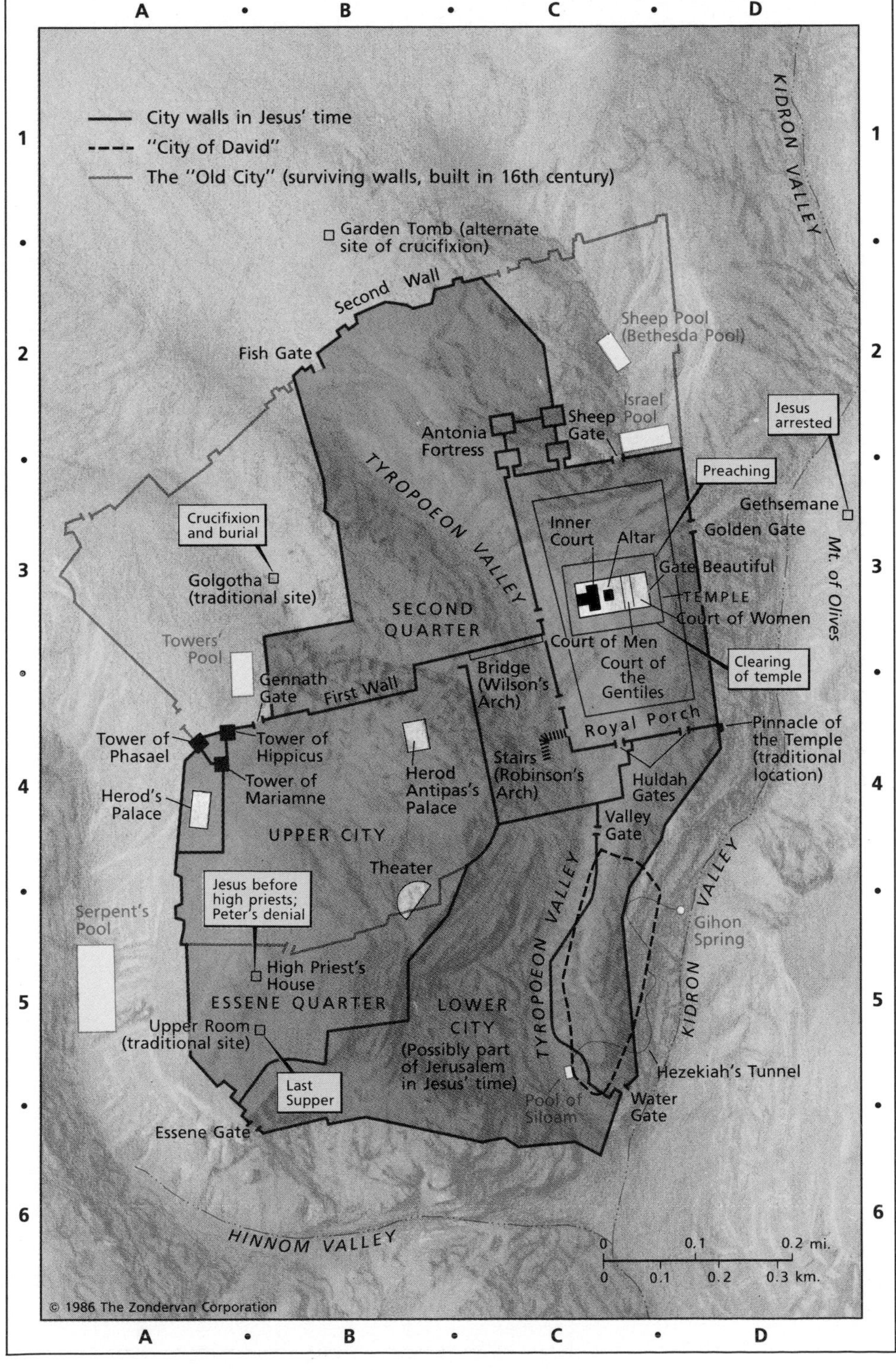
A • B • C • D
1 • 2 • 3 • 4 • 5 • 6
City walls in Jesus' time
"City of David"
The "Old City" (surviving walls, built in 16th century)
KIDRON VALLEY
Garden Tomb (alternate site of crucifixion)
Second Wall
Sheep Pool (Bethesda Pool)
Fish Gate
Israel Pool
Jesus arrested
Antonia Fortress
Sheep Gate
Preaching
TYROPOEON VALLEY
Gethsemane
Golden Gate
Crucifixion and burial
Inner Court
Altar
Mt. of Olives
Gate Beautiful
Golgotha (traditional site)
TEMPLE
SECOND QUARTER
Court of Women
Towers' Pool
Court of Men
Clearing of temple
Gennath Gate
First Wall
Bridge (Wilson's Arch)
Court of the Gentiles
Royal Porch
Tower of Phasael
Tower of Hippicus
Pinnacle of the Temple (traditional location)
Stairs (Robinson's Arch)
Herod Antipas's Palace
Tower of Mariamne
Huldah Gates
Herod's Palace
UPPER CITY
Valley Gate
Theater
Jesus before high priests; Peter's denial
Serpent's Pool
Gihon Spring
KIDRON VALLEY
TYROPOEON VALLEY
High Priest's House
ESSENE QUARTER
LOWER CITY (Possibly part of Jerusalem in Jesus' time)
Upper Room (traditional site)
Hezekiah's Tunnel
Last Supper
Pool of Siloam
Water Gate
Essene Gate
HINNOM VALLEY
0 0.1 0.2 mi.
0 0.1 0.2 0.3 km.
© 1986 The Zondervan Corporation

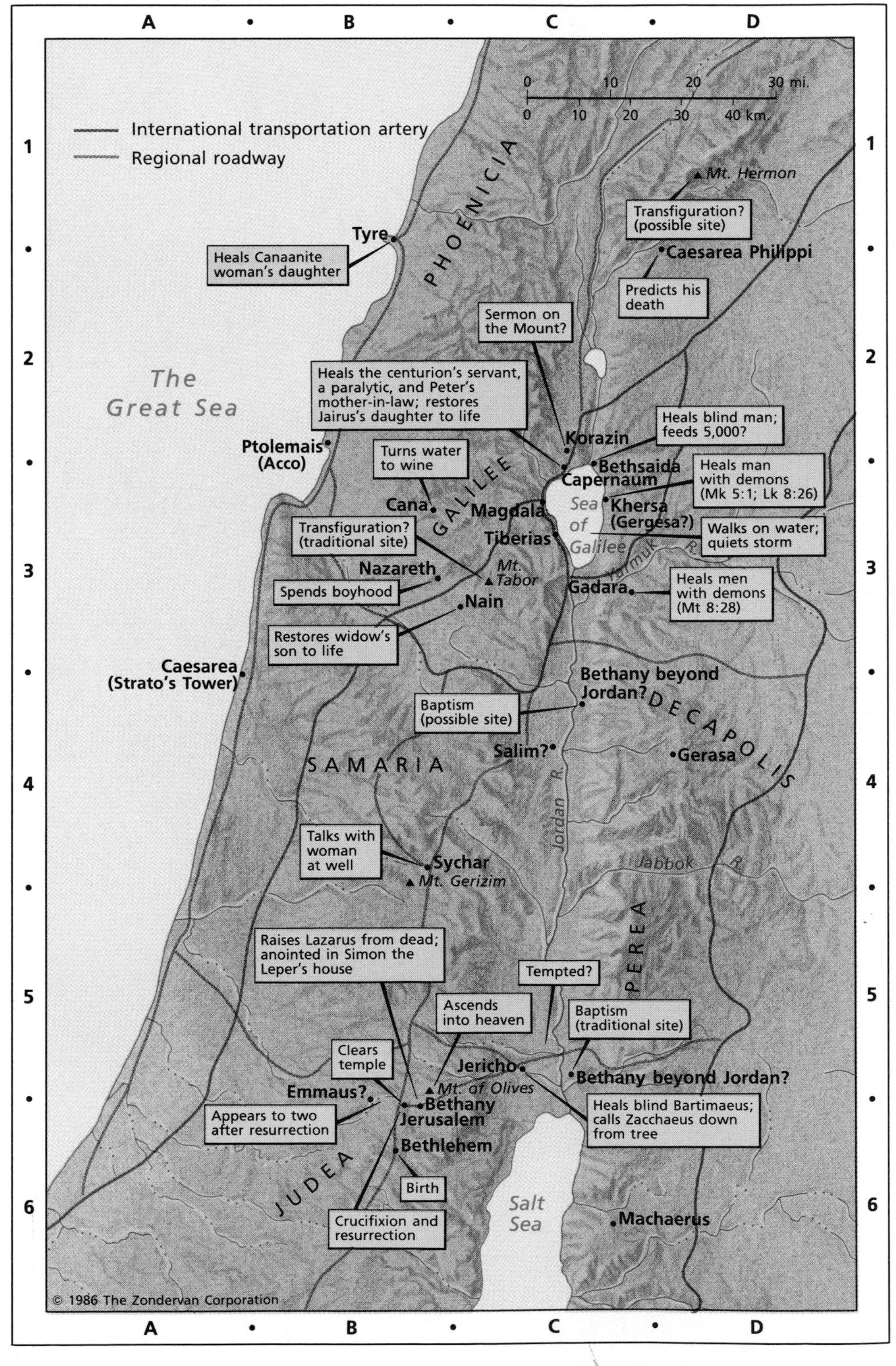

A • B • C • D
1
2
3
4
5
6
0 10 20 30 mi.
0 10 20 30 40 km.
International transportation artery
Regional roadway
PHOENICIA
Mt. Hermon
Transfiguration? (possible site)
Tyre
Heals Canaanite woman's daughter
Caesarea Philippi
Predicts his death
Sermon on the Mount?
The Great Sea
Heals the centurion's servant, a paralytic, and Peter's mother-in-law; restores Jairus's daughter to life
Heals blind man; feeds 5,000?
Korazin
Ptolemais (Acco)
Turns water to wine
Bethsaida
Capernaum
Heals man with demons (Mk 5:1; Lk 8:26)
GALILEE
Cana
Magdala
Sea of Galilee
Khersa (Gergesa?)
Transfiguration? (traditional site)
Tiberias
Walks on water; quiets storm
Yarmuk R.
Nazareth
Mt. Tabor
Spends boyhood
Gadara
Heals men with demons (Mt 8:28)
Nain
Restores widow's son to life
Caesarea (Strato's Tower)
Bethany beyond Jordan?
Baptism (possible site)
DECAPOLIS
Salim?
Gerasa
SAMARIA
Jordan R.
Talks with woman at well
Sychar
Mt. Gerizim
Jabbok R.
PEREA
Raises Lazarus from dead; anointed in Simon the Leper's house
Tempted?
Ascends into heaven
Baptism (traditional site)
Clears temple
Jericho
Bethany beyond Jordan?
Mt. of Olives
Emmaus?
Bethany
Jerusalem
Appears to two after resurrection
Heals blind Bartimaeus; calls Zacchaeus down from tree
Bethlehem
JUDEA
Birth
Salt Sea
Machaerus
Crucifixion and resurrection
© 1986 The Zondervan Corporation

Map 10: **APOSTLES' EARLY TRAVELS**

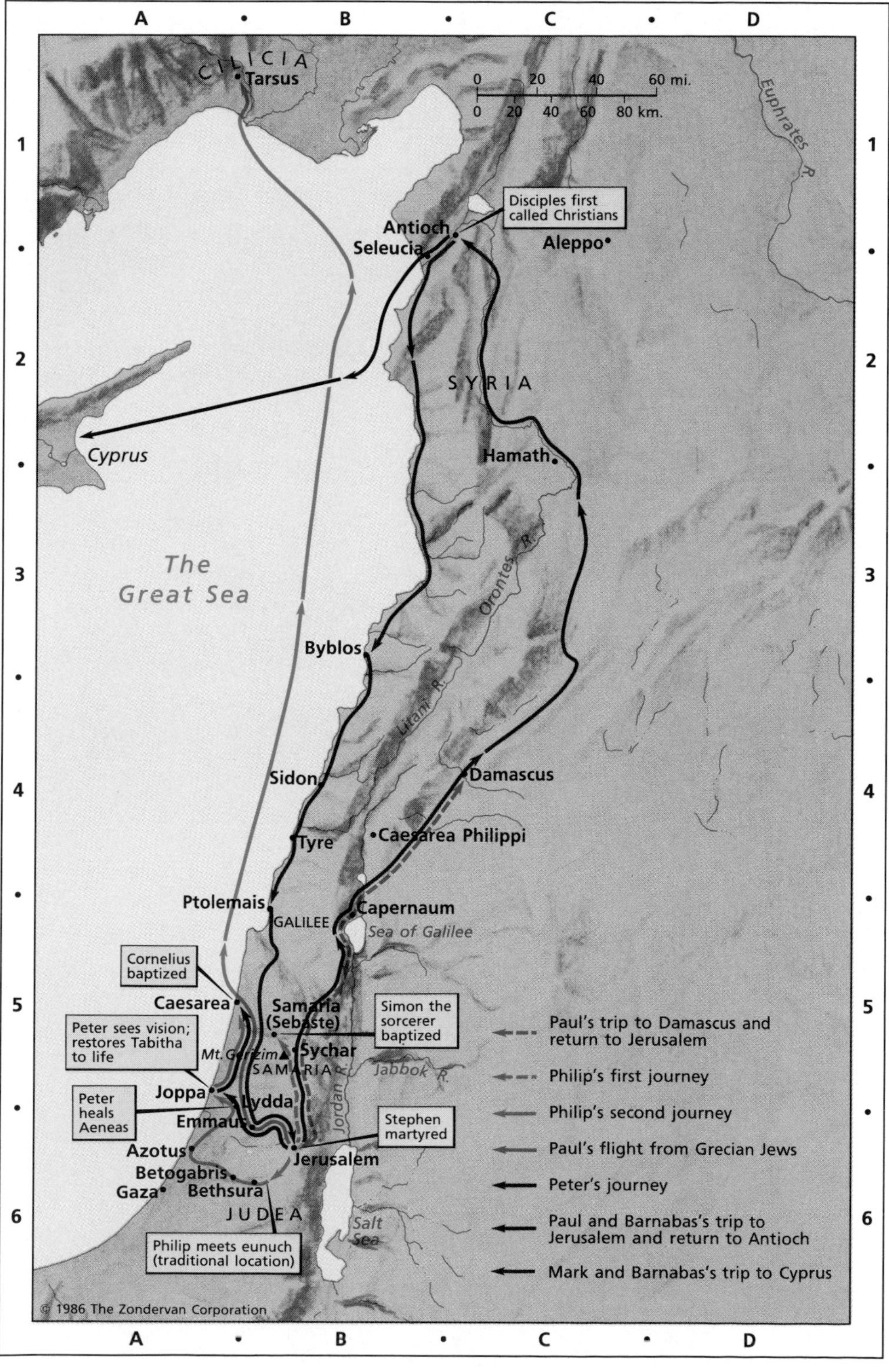

A
B
C
D
1
2
3
4
5
6
CILICIA
Tarsus
0 20 40 60 mi.
0 20 40 60 80 km.
Euphrates R.
Disciples first called Christians
Antioch
Seleucia
Aleppo
SYRIA
Cyprus
Hamath
The Great Sea
Orontes R.
Byblos
Litani R.
Sidon
Damascus
Tyre
Caesarea Philippi
Ptolemais
GALILEE
Capernaum
Sea of Galilee
Cornelius baptized
Caesarea
Samaria (Sebaste)
Simon the sorcerer baptized
Peter sees vision; restores Tabitha to life
Mt. Gerizim
Sychar
SAMARIA
Jabbok R.
Jordan
Joppa
Lydda
Peter heals Aeneas
Emmaus
Stephen martyred
Azotus
Jerusalem
Betogabris
Gaza
Bethsura
JUDEA
Salt Sea
Philip meets eunuch (traditional location)
Paul's trip to Damascus and return to Jerusalem
Philip's first journey
Philip's second journey
Paul's flight from Grecian Jews
Peter's journey
Paul and Barnabas's trip to Jerusalem and return to Antioch
Mark and Barnabas's trip to Cyprus

Map 11: PAUL'S MISSIONARY JOURNEYS

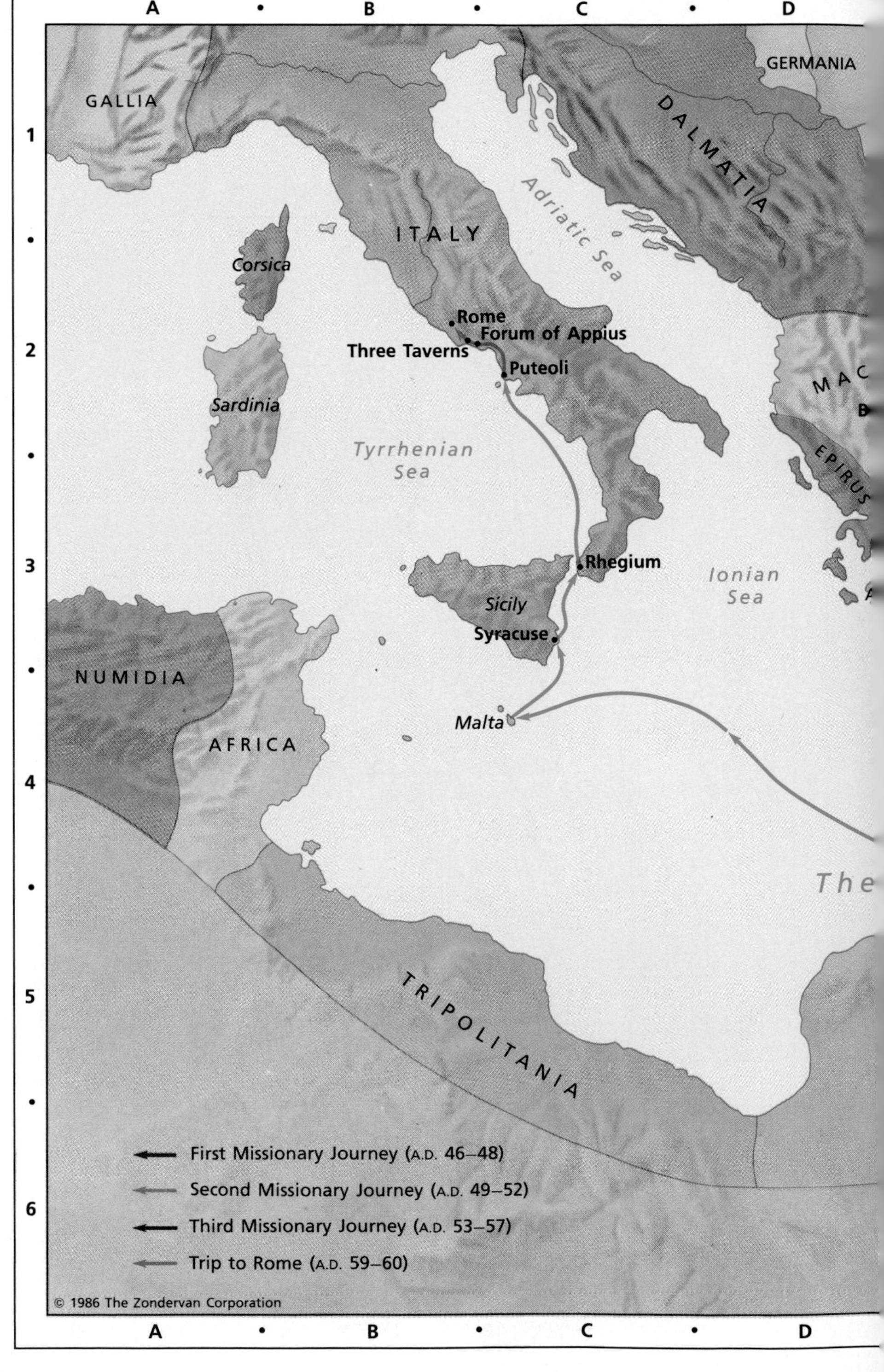

E
F
G
H
1
2
3
4
5
6
DACIA
MOESIA
THRACE
Black Sea
BITHYNIA AND PONTUS
GALATIA
CAPPADOCIA
COMMAGENE
MYSIA
ASIA
LYDIA
PHRYGIA
PISIDIA
LYCAONIA
PAMPHYLIA
LYCIA
CILICIA
SYRIA
PHOENICIA
ABILENE
JUDEA
ARABIA
EGYPT
CYRENAICA
Philippi
Neapolis
Apollonia
Samothrace
Thessalonica
Troas
Assos
Mitylene
Aegean Sea
Pergamum
Thyatira
Sardis
Philadelphia
Smyrna
Kios
Samos
Ephesus
Laodicea
Colosse
Athens
Miletus
Patmos
Cos
Cnidus
Rhodes
Pisidian Antioch
Iconium
Lystra
Derbe
Tarsus
Issus
Antioch
Aleppo
Attalia
Perga
Patara
Myra
Seleucia
Cyprus
Salamis
Paphos
Crete
Lasea
Salmone
Fair Havens
Sidon
Damascus
Tyre
Ptolemais
Caesarea
Jerusalem
Jordan R.
Salt Sea
Euphrates R.
Great Sea
Nile R.
Red Sea
0
100
200 mi.
0
100
200
300 km.

Map 12: CHRISTIANITY IN THE WORLD TODAY

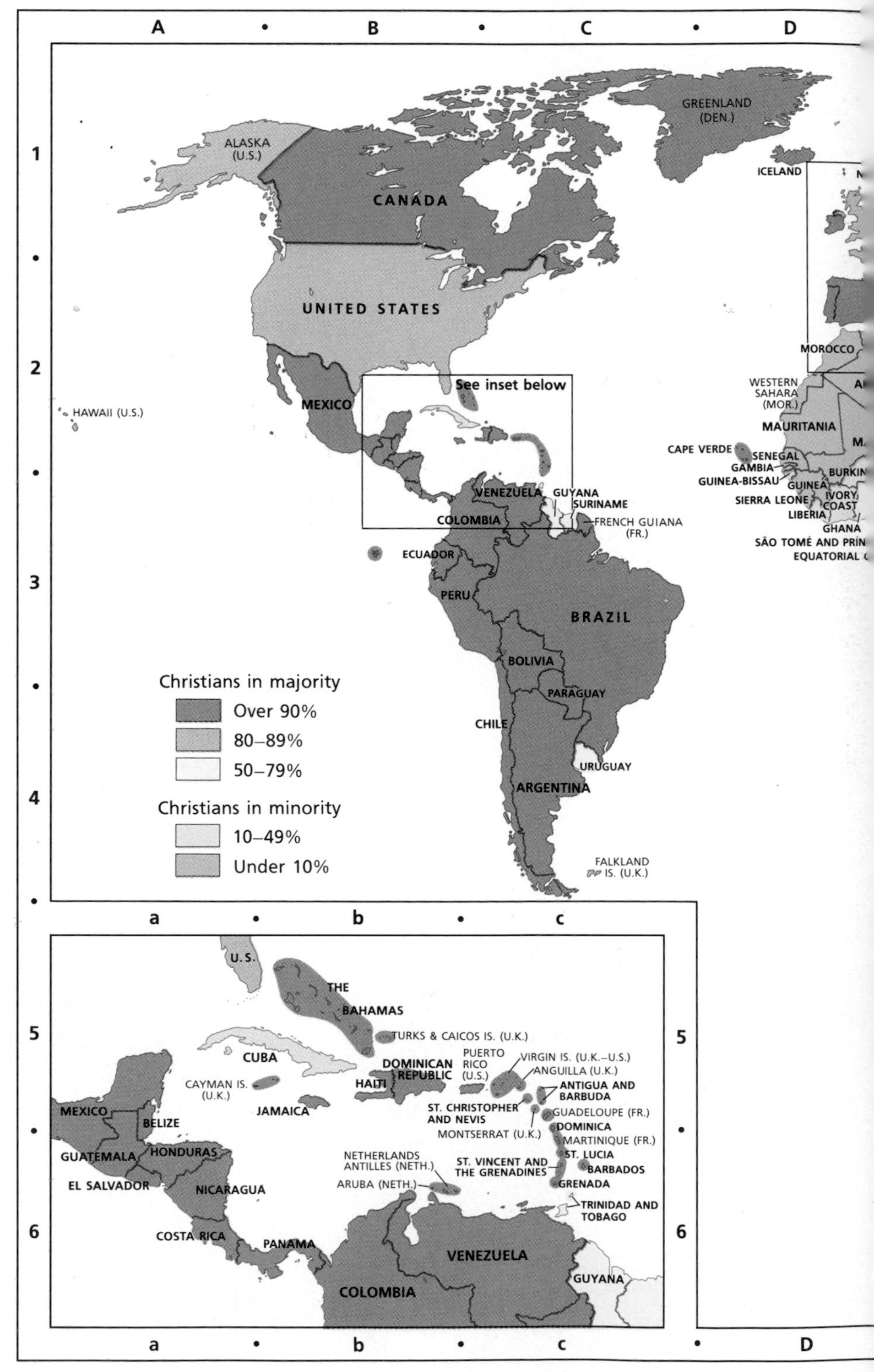

A
B
C
D
1
2
3
4
5
6
ALASKA (U.S.)
CANADA
GREENLAND (DEN.)
ICELAND
UNITED STATES
MEXICO
HAWAII (U.S.)
See inset below
MOROCCO
WESTERN SAHARA (MOR.)
MAURITANIA
CAPE VERDE
SENEGAL
GAMBIA
GUINEA-BISSAU
GUINEA
SIERRA LEONE
LIBERIA
IVORY COAST
GHANA
VENEZUELA
GUYANA
SURINAME
FRENCH GUIANA (FR.)
COLOMBIA
ECUADOR
PERU
BRAZIL
BOLIVIA
PARAGUAY
CHILE
URUGUAY
ARGENTINA
FALKLAND IS. (U.K.)
Christians in majority
Over 90%
80–89%
50–79%
Christians in minority
10–49%
Under 10%
a
b
c
U.S.
THE BAHAMAS
TURKS & CAICOS IS. (U.K.)
CUBA
CAYMAN IS. (U.K.)
JAMAICA
HAITI
DOMINICAN REPUBLIC
PUERTO RICO (U.S.)
VIRGIN IS. (U.K.–U.S.)
ANGUILLA (U.K.)
ANTIGUA AND BARBUDA
ST. CHRISTOPHER AND NEVIS
GUADELOUPE (FR.)
MONTSERRAT (U.K.)
DOMINICA
MARTINIQUE (FR.)
ST. LUCIA
BARBADOS
ST. VINCENT AND THE GRENADINES
GRENADA
NETHERLANDS ANTILLES (NETH.)
ARUBA (NETH.)
TRINIDAD AND TOBAGO
MEXICO
BELIZE
GUATEMALA
HONDURAS
EL SALVADOR
NICARAGUA
COSTA RICA
PANAMA
VENEZUELA
COLOMBIA
GUYANA

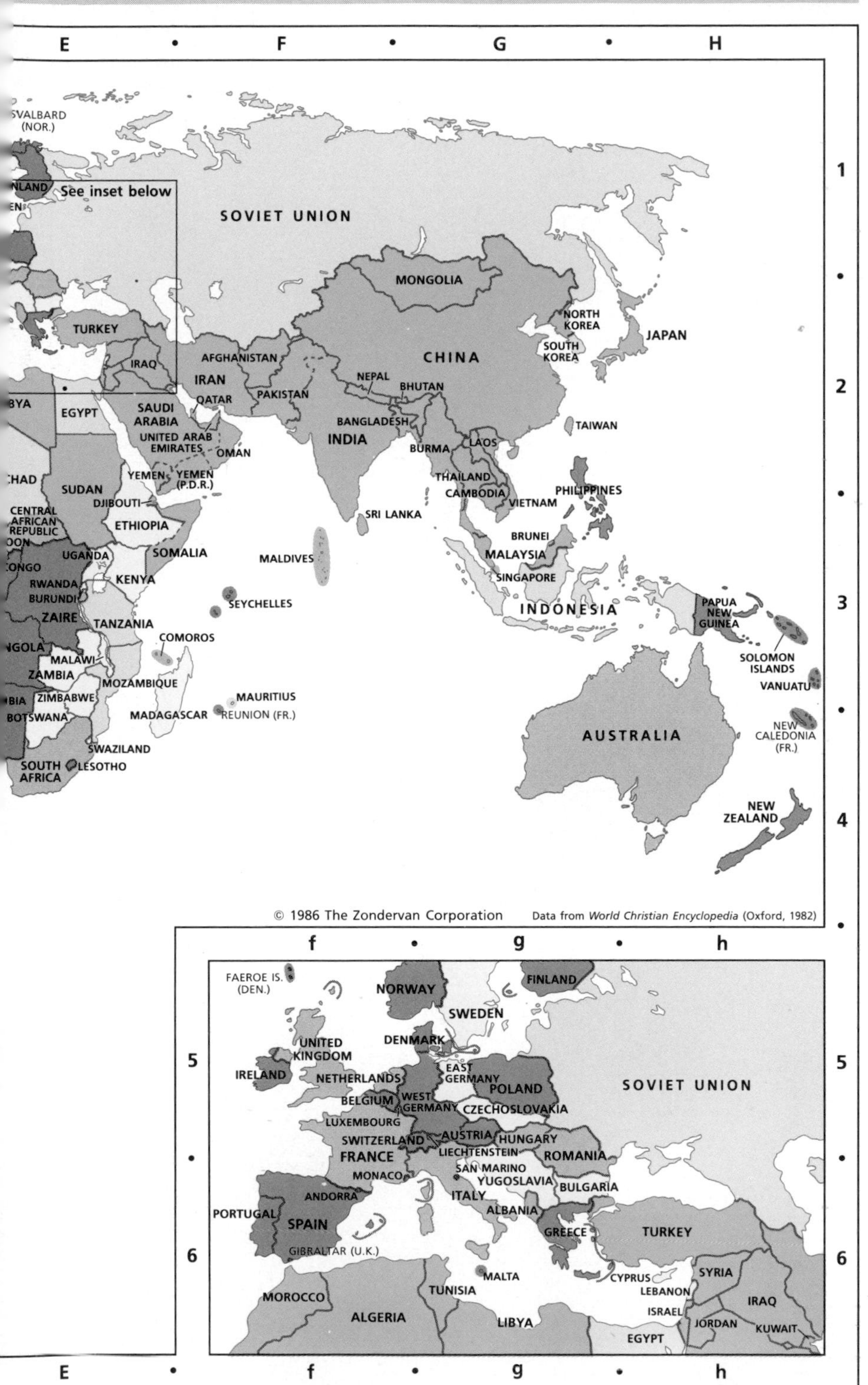

E
F
G
H
SVALBARD
(NOR.)
See inset below
SOVIET UNION
MONGOLIA
NORTH
KOREA
JAPAN
SOUTH
KOREA
CHINA
TURKEY
IRAQ
AFGHANISTAN
IRAN
NEPAL
BHUTAN
QATAR
PAKISTAN
EGYPT
SAUDI
ARABIA
BANGLADESH
TAIWAN
UNITED ARAB
EMIRATES
OMAN
INDIA
BURMA
LAOS
CHAD
SUDAN
YEMEN
YEMEN
(P.D.R.)
THAILAND
CAMBODIA
VIETNAM
PHILIPPINES
CENTRAL
AFRICAN
REPUBLIC
DJIBOUTI
ETHIOPIA
SRI LANKA
BRUNEI
UGANDA
SOMALIA
MALDIVES
MALAYSIA
CONGO
RWANDA
KENYA
SINGAPORE
BURUNDI
SEYCHELLES
PAPUA
NEW
GUINEA
ZAIRE
TANZANIA
INDONESIA
COMOROS
SOLOMON
ISLANDS
MALAWI
ZAMBIA
MOZAMBIQUE
VANUATU
ZIMBABWE
MAURITIUS
BOTSWANA
MADAGASCAR
REUNION (FR.)
NEW
CALEDONIA
(FR.)
AUSTRALIA
SWAZILAND
SOUTH
AFRICA
LESOTHO
NEW
ZEALAND
1
2
3
4
5
6
f
g
h
FAEROE IS.
(DEN.)
NORWAY
FINLAND
SWEDEN
UNITED
KINGDOM
DENMARK
IRELAND
NETHERLANDS
EAST
GERMANY
POLAND
SOVIET UNION
BELGIUM
WEST
GERMANY
CZECHOSLOVAKIA
LUXEMBOURG
SWITZERLAND
AUSTRIA
HUNGARY
FRANCE
LIECHTENSTEIN
ROMANIA
MONACO
SAN MARINO
YUGOSLAVIA
BULGARIA
ANDORRA
ITALY
PORTUGAL
ALBANIA
SPAIN
GREECE
TURKEY
GIBRALTAR (U.K.)
MALTA
CYPRUS
SYRIA
TUNISIA
LEBANON
MOROCCO
IRAQ
ISRAEL
ALGERIA
LIBYA
JORDAN
KUWAIT
EGYPT

Data from *World Christian Encyclopedia* (Oxford, 1982)

Map 13: **ROMAN EMPIRE**

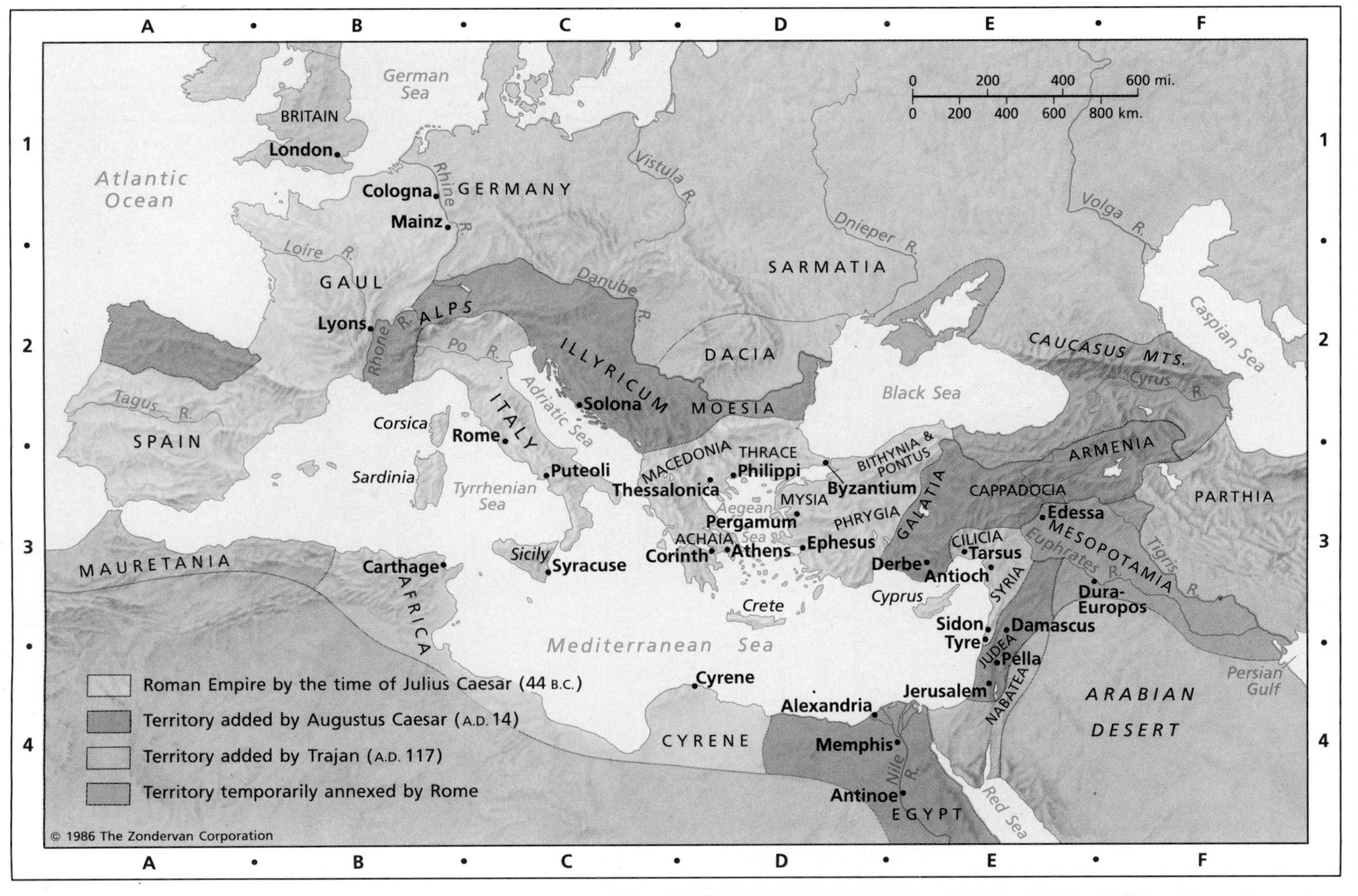

My